THE COLLECTED PLAYS OF EUGENE O'NEILL

THE COLLECTED PLAYS OF EUGENE O'NEILL

With an Introduction by John Lahr

JONATHAN CAPE
THIRTY-TWO BEDFORD SQUARE LONDON

Collected Edition first published in Great Britain 1988
Jonathan Cape Ltd, 32 Bedford Square, London WC1B 3EL

The plays were first published in Great Britain by Jonathan Cape as follows:
The Straw, *The Emperor Jones*, and *Diff'rent*, 1922; *The Moon of the Caribbees*, *Bound East For Cardiff*, *The Long Voyage Home*, *In The Zone*, *Ile*, *Where The Cross Is Made*, *The Rope*, *Anna Christie*, *The First Man*, *The Hairy Ape*, 1923; *Beyond The Horizon*, *Gold*, 1924; *All God's Chillun Got Wings*, *Desire Under The Elms*, *Welded*, 1925; *Before Breakfast*, *The Dreamy Kid*, *The Fountain*, *The Great God Brown*, 1926; *Marco Millions*, 1927; *Strange Interlude*, 1928; *Dynamo*, *Lazarus Laughed*, 1929; *Mourning Becomes Electra*, 1932; *Ah! Wilderness*, *Days Without End*, 1934; *The Iceman Cometh*, 1947; *A Moon For The Misbegotten*, 1953; *Long Day's Journey Into Night*, 1956; *A Touch Of The Poet*, 1957; *Hughie*, 1962; *Thirst*, *The Web*, *Warnings*, *Fog*, *Recklessness*, *Abortion*, *The Movie Man*, *The Sniper*, *A Wife For A Life*, *Servitude*, (Ten 'Lost' Plays), *More Stately Mansions*, 1965.

A CIP catalogue record for this book is available from the British Library

ISBN 0-224-02535-X

Printed in Great Britain by St Edmundsbury Press Ltd, Bury St Edmunds, Suffolk

Contents

Publisher's Note: *The plays in this volume have been offset from Jonathan Cape's individual first editions (thus preserving the typographical idiosyncrasies of the original settings), though the play titles, cast lists and scene settings have been reset for ease of reference.*

Introduction by John Lahr

When Eugene O'Neill's first play was produced, the twentieth century was sixteen years old. Before O'Neill, America had entertainment; after him, it had drama. In O'Neill's plays the crude power and terrible isolation of the new age coalesced.

O'Neill (who lived from 1888 to 1953) was twenty-four when he began writing plays after a bout of tuberculosis. And by then, as the second son of the rich and celebrated James O'Neill, one of America's leading romantic actors, he had lived through both the blessings and the punishment of the American Dream: 'One-night stands, cheap hotels, dirty trains, never having a home.' In his autobiographical masterpiece *Long Day's Journey into Night* (written in 1941, produced in 1956), O'Neill lets his mother articulate the accumulated sense of loss that was the inheritance of James O'Neill's success. The doom and disjointedness that haunt O'Neill's plays have their origin in the restless cupidity and driving ambition of his theatrical family's early years.

As a child, O'Neill was no stranger to luxury. But as a merchant seaman, derelict, and barfly in the rebellion of his early twenties, he also experienced the other side of America's obsession with achievement: exhaustion. 'Be drunken continually,' says O'Neill's spokesman, Edmund Tyrone, in *Long Day's Journey into Night*, quoting Baudelaire. 'With wine, with virtue, as you will. But be drunken.' At first, O'Neill tried to find oblivion in a bottle; later, he found it in work. Both excesses were his way of killing time and pain, his means of rebuking himself and the world for not living up to expectations.

O'Neill's plays made his wound a public event. In revolt against the old orthodoxies, O'Neill bought and finally sold the newest romantic delirium: art. A lapsed Catholic, O'Neill made a myth of his faith in art and its power to renovate life. He began his adulthood trying to wreck himself and ended up glorifying the wreckage. Caught between the century's false gods of art and ego, O'Neill was stamped early in his career as definitively modern.

O'Neill spoke of 'the ache in the heart for the things we can't forget'. Foremost in the sum of agonies was his family. O'Neill's mother and father were, for different reasons, essentially absentee parents. Ella Quinlan O'Neill became addicted to morphine soon after Eugene's birth and never completely focused on her boy, or forgave him. James O'Neill, touring the country in *The Count of Monte Cristo*, the money-spinner to which he sacrificed his considerable talent, hived his son away in boarding school from the age of seven. And O'Neill's older brother, James Jr., was a failed actor and debauched drunk. The family history of betrayal and neglect left the young O'Neill isolated, depressed, and nervous. O'Neill brooded over his childhood and the apparent curse that hung over the O'Neill clan. He even charted the childhood traumas that led to such a remorselessly bleak view of life that he could look kindly on the atom bomb as 'a wonderful invention because it might annihilate the whole human race'.

O'Neill's 'nervousness' was a family talking point before it became public legend. Writing to Eugene after the birth of his second son in 1919, Ella O'Neill said: 'I have such a wonderful grandson but no more wonderful than you were when you were born and weighed *eleven pounds*

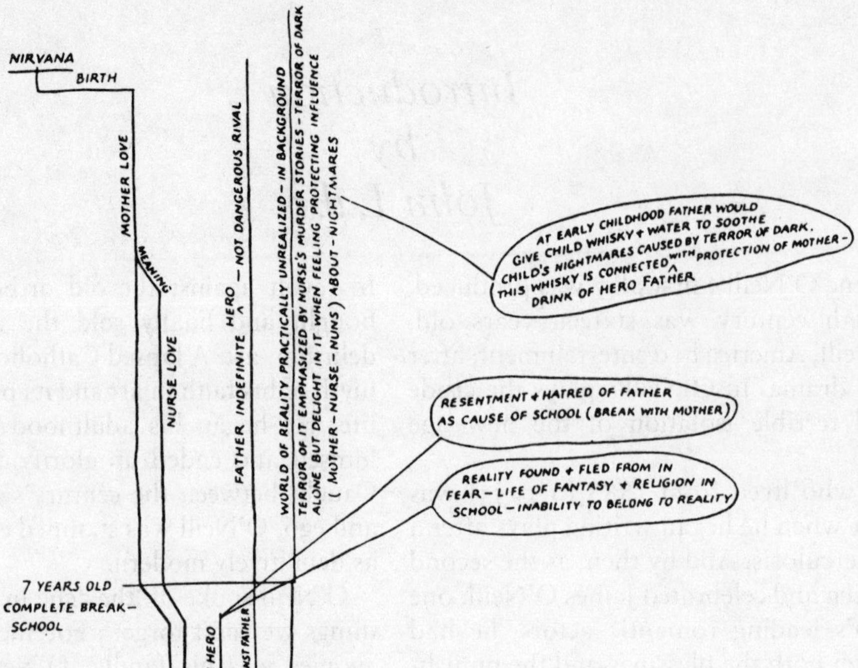

and no *nerves* at that time' (her italics). She signed off with love to 'the biggest baby of all the three, *You*.' In *Long Day's Journey into Night*, Edmund's mother frequently refers to him as a big baby; and there was some truth as well as hostility in Ella O'Neill's attempt at a joke.

The need for total attention (an indulgence his compulsively long plays insist on) was apparent in O'Neill's relationship to the two wives who shared his adult writing life: the writer Agnes Boulton and the actress Carlotta Monterey. 'You are the only one who can make me sure of myself,' O'Neill wrote to Boulton in 1917. 'I want it to be not you and me, but *us* . . . I want you alone—in an aloneness broken by nothing. Not even children. I don't understand children. They make me uneasy, and I don't know how to act with them.' Boulton sent away her child by a previous marriage to live with grandparents and kept the proximity of her relatives to their Rhode Island home a secret from O'Neill. No wonder O'Neill was threatened by children: he wanted to be the child. Once Boulton had borne him two children, Shane and Oona, he soon became discontented and abandoned them all in 1928 for Carlotta Monterey.

As Carlotta remembers O'Neill's first avowal of passion, it was his needs as a son, not as a lover, that drew him to her. 'He never said to me, "I love you, I think you're wonderful." He kept saying, "I need you. I need you." And he did need me, I discovered. He was never in good health. He talked about his early life—that he had no real home, no mother in the real sense, or father, no one to treat him as a child should be treated—and his face became sadder and sadder.' Treating O'Neill as a genius and a child, Carlotta protected him and organized his life, even to the extent of corresponding with his children for him. At the end of his life, bedridden in a Boston hotel with Parkinson's disease, which made it impossible even to hold a pen, O'Neill said to Carlotta: 'You're my Mama now.'

O'Neill's plays make a myth of the sense of service his genius conventionally demanded. In *A Touch of the Poet* (written in 1940, produced in 1958), Nora Melody, who is much abused by her vain and high-falutin' husband, Con, won't let his pretensions dampen her love. The pride of Nora's devotion is somehow rewarded at the finale when Con Melody abandons his patrician airs and shows her some husbandly affection. Nora explains her all-embracing love to her daughter

> . . . It's when you don't give a thought for all the if's and want-to's in the world! It's when, if all the fires of hell was between you, you'd walk in them gladly to be with him, and sing with joy at your own burnin', if only his kiss was on your mouth! That's love, and I'm proud I've known the great sorrow and joy of it!

But the injustice in such unswerving and one-sided loyalty takes its toll in bitterness, which O'Neill's life, if not the wish fulfilments of his plays, dramatized. O'Neill inscribed the manuscript of *Mourning Becomes Electra* (1931) to Carlotta; his fine words cannot make his tyrannical will or her living hell more acceptable

> In memory of the interminable days of rain in which you bravely suffered in silence that this trilogy might be born. Days when I had my work and you had nothing . . . when you had self-forgetting love to greet me at lunchtime, depressing such preoccupations with a courageous, charming banter on days which for you were bitterly lonely, when I seemed far away and lost in a grim savage gloomy country of my own, days which were for you like hateful, boring inseparable enemies. . .

During their stormy relationship, O'Neill and Carlotta separated twice, in 1948 and 1951. On the second occasion, Carlotta charged O'Neill with 'cruel and abusive treatment' on 'diverse occasions'. And O'Neill, for his part, contended that Carlotta was 'incapable of taking care of herself' and threatened to dispatch her to a mental home. Finally, however, the couple reunited, both falling back on the ruling credos of their lives. For Carlotta, it was service. She told the press O'Neill 'needed her more than anything else'. And O'Neill, always prepared to assign to fate what he would not concede to self-awareness, said: 'It's my destiny to go back.'

Because of the maternal deprivation in his own life, O'Neill's attitude toward women was as strident and ambivalent as Anna Christie's (1921) towards men. 'Men, I hate 'em—all of 'em,' says Anna, a whore and, like O'Neill, an abandoned child. Despite the brooding lean good looks that made him catnip to women, O'Neill frequently referred to women as 'pigs'. Anna is one of the early versions of the whore/mother figure that is O'Neill's theatrical erotic ideal. Anna is purified by life on the sea. 'Being on the sea has changed me and made me feel differently about things,' she tells the once-spurned Burke, who is hurt and bewildered by her confession of her 'bad past'. Before they finally agree to marry, Burke makes Anna take an oath of loyalty and purity. She gladly accedes, saying: 'May the blackest curse of God strike me dead if I'm lying.' The obsession never left O'Neill. The virgin whore is personified in Josie Hogan in *A Moon for the Misbegotten* (1947), a character conceived from the first stage direction as an archetypal earth mother. '*She is so oversized for a woman that she is almost a freak—five feet eleven in her stocking feet and weighs around a hundred and eighty.*' Josie broadcasts her sluttishness, but she is really a virgin. She's in love with James Tyrone—O'Neill's stage embodiment of his wayward brother—and schemes to seduce him. When Tyrone comes around for a night of love, what he wants is not a chippie but a mother

> JOSIE *(Watches him for a second, fighting the love that, in spite of her, responds to his appeal—then she springs up and runs to him—with a fierce, possessive, maternal tenderness):* Come here to me, you great fool, and stop your silly blather. There's nothing to hate you for. There's nothing to forgive. Sure I was only trying to give you happiness, because I love you. I'm sorry I was so stupid and didn't see— But I see now, and you'll find I have all the love you need. *(She gives him a hug and kisses him. There is passion in her kiss but it is a tender, protective maternal passion, which he responds to with an instant grateful yielding.)*

All-embracing, all-forgiving, all-constant, Josie brings succour to the drunken and tormented James. He sleeps like a baby with his head in Josie's lap, a consummation in friendship, not lust. In O'Neill's bittersweet daydream, mother love brings a momentary peace. Josie's last elegiac words invoke peace as she speaks of James from the porch of the farm that is destined to be her lonely home. 'May you have your wish and die in your sleep soon, Jim darling,' she says, generous to the end. 'May you rest forever in forgiveness and peace.'

Forgiveness and peace were two things O'Neill never managed in life. His plays brood over the power of the female to bestow this security or destroy it. To O'Neill, women are figures to be at once prized and hated for their power. The duality in O'Neill's temperament is brilliantly captured in the mother-haunted Cabot farm in *Desire Under the Elms* (1924) whose trees, the stage directions read, '*are like exhausted women resting their sagging breasts and hands and hair on its roof . . . a sinister maternity in their aspect.*'

The wife that old Ephraim Cabot brings home to his farm is a young widow with all the calculating, sexual rapacity of a whore. She had married Cabot for his property and finds herself soon coveting his son, Eben. 'I got t' fight fur what's due me out o' life, if I ever 'spect t' git it,' Abbie tells Eben, holding out her hand in a seductive gesture of friendship. But at first Eben doesn't want to be friends. His hostility stems from both reverence for his dead mother and fear of his own sexual longing for his stepmother. 'Nature'll beat ye, Eben,' Abbie shrewdly tells him. And it does. He mourns his mother, 'She was soft an' easy. He couldn't 'preciate her. . . He murdered her with his hardness,' and finally sobs: 'She died. Sometimes she used to sing fur me.' In this moment, O'Neill brings the longing for mother love into violent and losing battle with adult passion, a contest that leads Eben and Abbie into tragedy and ruination. Abbie, '*her arms around him with wild passion*', says: 'I'll sing for you.' The whore mother incarnate, Abbie is irresistible as a source of solace and sexual temptation. '*In spite of her overwhelming desire for him,*' reads the stage direction, '*there is a sincere maternal love in her manner and voice—a horribly frank mixture of lust and mother love.*' Abbie continues

> Don't cry, Eben! I'll take yer Maw's place! I'll be everythin' she was t' ye! Let me kiss ye, Eben . . . same's if I was a Maw t' ye—an' ye kin kiss me back 's if yew was my son—my boy—sayin' good-night t' me! Kiss me, Eben.
>
> *(They kiss in restrained fashion. Then suddenly wild passion overcomes her. She kisses him lustfully again and again and he flings his arms around her and returns her kisses. Suddenly, as in the bedroom, he frees himself from her violently and springs to his feet. He is trembling all over, in a strange state of terror . . .)*
>
> Don't ye leave me, Eben! Can't ye see it hain't enuf—lovin' ye like a Maw—can't ye see it's got t' be that an' more—much more—a hundred times more—fur me t' be happy—fur yew t' be happy?

Caught between the forces of life and death, Abbie and Eben exist in a perpetual restless intensity that typifies O'Neill's alienation. In his plays there is great show of passion but little romance. O'Neill saves romance not for love, but for death. He makes this romantic agony clear in *Long Day's Journey into Night*. 'I will always be a stranger who never feels at home, who does not really want and is not really wanted, who can never belong,' Edmund Tyrone says. 'Who must always be a little in love with death.'

O'Neill's courtship of oblivion began early. Kicked out of Princeton after his freshman year, and at twenty-one the father of a child in a short, hapless first marriage, O'Neill turned these small failures into a destiny of self-destruction. He wandered the globe searching for meanings in the romantic isolation he cultivated. The young man prospected for gold in Spanish Honduras, shipped out to sea, bummed around the waterfront dives of Buenos Aires and New York, where, at the age of twenty-three, he attempted suicide with an overdose of Veronal. In later years, O'Neill came to understand his self-destructive guilt. In *The Iceman Cometh* (written in 1939 and produced in 1946), Hickey explains that Parritt 'has to be pardoned so he can forgive himself'. O'Neill finally sought this forgiveness in the absolution of Art.

'Romantic imagination,' says a character in *Strange Interlude* (1928). 'It has ruined more lives than all diseases. A form of insanity.' O'Neill had been infected early by romanticism. Instead of practising self-destruction in his flophouse benders, he turned in adulthood to idealizing it. In one of his early plays, *Fog* (1916), a character speaks of being so sick of disappointment and weary of life 'that death seems the only way out.' Fog itself is a crucial symbol for O'Neill's romance of death—the twilight zone that typifies his separation from life. 'The fog is where I wanted to be,' says Edmund Tyrone in *Long Day's Journey into Night*. 'I was a ghost belonging to the fog, and the fog was the ghost of the sea.' Besides exemplifying O'Neill's hauntedness, the fog is also a refuge: the impermeable haze behind which he could dream his romantic dreams.

In the poem 'Submarine' (1917), he already had begun to turn his subterranean life into a heroic project

> My soul is a submarine.
> My aspirations are torpedoes.
> I will hide unseen
> Beneath the surface of life
> Watching for ships . . .
>
> I will destroy them
> Because the sea is beautiful.
>
> That is why I lurk
> Menacingly
> In green depths.

Through writing, O'Neill found an anodyne for his anxiety. Writing became a defence. 'Keep writing, no matter what!' he told a discouraged author. 'As long as you have a job on hand that absorbs all your mental energy, you haven't much worry to spare over other things. It serves as a suit of armour.' Art engineered and excused O'Neill's detachment from life. In his notebooks, he copied out Nietzsche's dictum: 'Do I strive after happiness? I strive after my own work.' Both victim and perpetrator of the romance of Art, O'Neill gave everything to his work and little to the real life around him. 'When I am writing, I am alive,' he said. 'Writing is a vacation from living.'

O'Neill glorified his despair. 'My vultures are screaming,' he wrote to a friend. His self-dramatizing anguish was part of his personality as well as his plays. Like Con Melody in *A Touch of the Poet*, O'Neill enjoyed declaiming gloomy portions of Byron's *Childe Harold*. 'He quoted it with a touch of irony,' Agnes Boulton recalled, 'while at the same time it was also clear that he accepted it on its face value.' O'Neill treated himself as the answer to his own prayers. As Boulton remembers, O'Neill's apocalyptic pronouncements were made, where possible, near a mirror. 'If there had been a mirror Gene would have been observing himself in it as he talked,' she says in her account of their courtship and early marriage, *Part of a Long Story*, 'as he always did where there was a mirror around.' O'Neill, who wrote of wanting 'to give pain a voice', needed his 'vultures' and encouraged them. He thought they kept him 'pure'. The 'vultures,' he said, came from the 'great dark behind and inside and not from the bright lights without'; without them, he told the press, he would be 'at a complete loss'. To heal his life might jeopardize his art. And therefore desolation became a self-fulfilling romantic prophecy. 'He saw life as a tragedy and had neither the desire nor the curiosity to go beyond the limits of his own vision,' Boulton explained, implying O'Neill's secondary gain in keeping his wound open. 'He loved his tragic conception of the world and would not have given it up for the world.' In typical romantic fashion, O'Neill saw anguish as the only valid credential for truth. 'Before the soul can fly,' he wrote on his studio wall, 'it must be washed in the blood of the heart.' O'Neill put himself in the avant-garde of suffering and quickly set about making a future of regrets.

O'Neill did for pessimism what the American musical did for 'pep': made it sensational. One pundit counted twelve murders, eight suicides, and seven cases of insanity in his plays.

> Oh, I have tried to scream!
> Give pain a voice!
> Make it a street singer
> Acting a pantomime of tragic song,
> To beg the common copper
> Of response:
> An ear
> To hear.
>
> ('Fragments')

With all the optimism of the plague-stricken, O'Neill contended that in his tragedies, 'we should feel exalted to think that there is something—some vital, unquenchable flame which makes him [man] triumph over his miseries. Dying, he is still victorious.' In life as in his theatre, O'Neill held fast to the idea of psychological fate. The 'O'Neill curse', like the curse on the lives of so many of his characters (Mary Tyrone, Nina Leeds, Lavinia Mannon), is at once awful and comforting. Fate takes the issue of responsibility out of one's hands. However terrible, fate still provides a motive, a symmetry to the chaos the characters find and create about them. O'Neill needed to believe in fate. Like his bar-room daydreamers in *The Iceman Cometh*, it was the saving lie that kept the playwright from facing the brutalities of his own life.

'One's outer life,' O'Neill said, 'passes in a solitude haunted by the ghosts of others. One's inner life passes in a solitude haunted by the masks of oneself.' In *Long Day's Journey into Night*, O'Neill describes himself as a ghost, and shows the sins of the past haunting the present. The ghosts of murdered selves abound in O'Neill's plays. *Strange Interlude* is lover- and child-haunted, as is *Mourning Becomes Electra*. *Emperor Jones* (1920) fires gunshots at the ghosts that oppress him; in *Hughie* (completed in 1942, produced in 1958), the small-time hustler yammering to the night clerk is friend-haunted, his name, 'Erie' Smith, implying his ghostly, threadbare life. And in *Long Day's Journey into Night*, Mary Tyrone's appearance at the finale, 'paler than ever' and 'in her sky blue wedding dress', is preceded by the ghostly effect of lights going out and strange, unexplained music coming from another room. In this moment, Mary Tyrone is the ghost of her marriage and her early hope. 'I fell in love with James Tyrone and was so happy for a time,' she says vaguely in the play's final beat.

These hauntings are manifestations of O'Neill's guilt, a guilt, as Harold Clurman observes in *Lies Like Truth*, 'in relation to love'. Clurman goes on

> From this sense of guilt—all his characters suffer it in one form or another . . . comes a constant alteration of mood. Every character speaks in two voices, two moods—one of rage, the other of apology. This produces a kind of moral schizo-

> phrenia which in some of O'Neill's other plays has necessitated an interior monologue and a speech for social use (*Strange Interlude*) or, as in *The Great God Brown* (1926) and *Days Without End* (1934), two sets of masks. In this everlasting duality, with its equal pressures in several directions, lies the brooding power, the emotional grip of O'Neill's work.

In art, O'Neill tried to admit the pain he would continue to inflict on his own family

> So am I isolate,
> Inviolate
> Untouchable,
> Bitterest of all, ungiveable,
> Unable to bestow,
> Break from my solitude
> A lonely gift,
> Myself.

Having been punished by abandonment as a child, he abandoned his own children, with equally disastrous results. O'Neill's first son, Eugene Jr. (who'd never seen or known his real father until the age of twelve), committed suicide at forty. Shane O'Neill became a drug addict. And Oona O'Neill at seventeen broke off all communication with her father to marry the puckish, flamboyant, comic genius of the twentieth century, the poet of grace, not gravity, whose influence on theatre was greater than her father's: Charlie Chaplin. O'Neill's tragedy was that he could not give to life the dedication and concentration he gave to his work. His predicament, like his plays, was emblematic of his era. Mourning the death of God, O'Neill made a god of the self. Unable to sacrifice himself to God, he ended up sacrificing others to himself.

II

O'Neill means 'champion' in Gaelic. From the outset of his playwrighting career, O'Neill was hellbent on greatness. 'It's because I want to be an artist or nothing', he said, applying to George Pierce Baker's famous Harvard course in playwrighting in 1914, 'that I am writing to you.' Having worked hard at destroying himself, he turned to building an oeuvre of serious drama with a passionate, big-hearted, obsessive energy. 'At first', Lionel Trilling said, 'it was the mere technical inventiveness of Eugene O'Neill, his daring subjects and language which caught the public imagination.' A pathfinder, O'Neill, with fierce single-mindedness, blazed the theatrical trail generations of playwrights would follow. He was the first to stage the life and vernacular of the American lower classes; the first to put the American black man on stage as a figure of substance and complexity; the first to face the soullessness of America's material progress; and the first to adapt the innovations of European drama to the American experience. A man of industry and output, O'Neill was manifest destiny with pen and paper. 'Instantly, or so it seemed, the stage began to breathe again,' George Jean Nathan wrote of O'Neill's emergence on the theatre scene. O'Neill also assumed his stature, and nurtured it. 'Life is growth or a joke one plays on oneself,' he said. 'One has to choose.' O'Neill chose growth—going so far as to withdraw from Broadway and cease the production of his plays from 1933 to 1946 so he could concentrate on his writing. O'Neill disdained Broadway as a 'show shop', and with the example of his father, who had compromised his talent to popular success, O'Neill swore 'that they would never get me. I determined I would never sell out.'

From his earliest production (*Bound East for Cardiff*, 1916, mounted by the Provincetown Players on a Cape Cod wharf with fog in the harbour and the sound of the sea under the floorboards), O'Neill aimed for bold narrative experiment. Although many of these early sea plays now seem creaky, then, in 1916, life at sea had never been shown with such compassion and command of the vernacular. O'Neill's sea tales were autobiographical, and in rebellion against the old, ranting, artificial 'romantic stuff' he associated with his father's performing and that then dominated the American stage. By 1920, with the Broadway production of *Beyond the*

Horizon—a bad play that won him the first of his four Pulitzer prizes—O'Neill was the darling of the Smart Set, and the Roaring Twenties had found its Jeremiah.

Ravished at once by a revolt against the old and the ideas of new 'big work', O'Neill whipped himself up for bigger and more onerous theatrical challenges. 'It seems to me most emphatically a case of shooting at a star or being a dud,' he wrote to his cohort Kenneth Macgowan, who spoke O'Neill's language of aspiration and said that O'Neill got to the 'big emotional heart of things'. 'I want to howl: Imagination, Beauty, Daring, or bust.' O'Neill didn't shy from bold, risky effects: the masks in *The Great God Brown*, the asides in *Strange Interlude*, the gorilla cage in *The Hairy Ape* (1922). The habit of thinking big never left him. Even when he considered writing a comedy, as he did in 1939, projecting *The Iceman Cometh*, it was to be 'a big kind of comedy that doesn't stay funny for very long.' O'Neill was both a hero and a victim of the society's overreaching sense of monumentality. While he didn't fall prey to Broadway, he was trapped early by America's High Culture vultures. O'Neill grumbled that there were no 'Big Men' in experimental theatre, and that 'big work' had to face up to the hard facts of the new century. And what were they?

> . . . the death of an old God and the failures of science and materialism to give any satisfying new one for the surviving primitive religious instinct to find meaning for life in, and to comfort its fears of death with. It seems to me anyone trying to do big work nowadays must have this subject behind all the little subjects of his plays or novels.

The only play in which O'Neill tackled this theme directly was *Dynamo* (1929), a disaster by any standard. But treated early by the public as a colossus, O'Neill was eager to test his power. 'A man wills his own defeat when he pursues the unattainable. But the *struggle* is his success,' he said. 'Such a figure is necessarily tragic. But to me he is not depressing, he is exhilarating.' Often both O'Neill's plays and his pronouncements about them teetered under the weight of the meanings he tried to shoulder. In 1925, like a champion announcing the next contender, O'Neill explained in a letter to Thomas Hobson Quinn that he was about to take on classical tragedy

> . . . the one eternal tragedy of Man in his glorious, self-destructive struggle *to make the Force express him instead of being, as an animal is, an infinitesimal incident in its expression*. And my profound conviction is that this is the only subject worth writing about and that it is possible—or can be—to develop a tragic expression in terms of transfigured modern values and symbols in the theater which may to some degree bring home to members of a modern audience their ennobling identity with the tragic figures on the stage. Of course, this is very much of a dream, but where theater is concerned, one must have a dream and the Greek dream in tragedy is the noblest ever!

Out of O'Neill's dream of himself as a poet on a grand scale came some second-rate experiments with tragic form (*The Great God Brown; Lazarus Laughed*, 1927) and a couple of windy High Art 'victories' in the five-hour *Strange Interlude* and the six-hour trilogy *Mourning Becomes Electra*, which don't so much strip life down as wear it down. They excite pity without admiration, and therefore without terror. O'Neill, as Eric Bentley has said, 'had tragedy in the head . . . the more he attempts, the less he achieves.'

When O'Neill forgoes his big bow-wow ideas, as he does in *Desire Under the Elms*, he can be riveting. In this peasant tragedy, the themes of greed, rootlessness, and psychological fate combine in an obsessive personal way that transcends the play's schematic structure. In Ephraim Cabot's ruthless control of his farm, critics have seen the low peasant cunning of O'Neill's father. But more than his father, O'Neill is writing about his obsession with his own creation. The stone wall in the foreground of the Cabot house is the visual reminder of Cabot's labour, which has turned the unpromising land into profit. Built stone by stone, the wall is a metaphor of the life's work which keeps Cabot tied to his farm in the same dogged, possessive, crazed way that kept O'Neill allied to his writing and not to life. O'Neill finds something of himself in Cabot and his writing takes on a special passion. The old man's myopic egotism eerily foreshadows O'Neill's own story. In the same way, *Mourning Becomes Electra*, which lays an ambush for the imagination by invoking the high shadows of classical associations, actually produces moments of genuine power when the story coalesces with O'Neill's private terror: '. . . there's no one left to punish me. I'm the last Mannon. I've got to punish myself!' says Lavinia at the finale. 'Living alone here with the dead is a worse act of justice than death or prison!' When the shutters close 'with a decisive bang' and Lavinia turns to immure herself in the family home, both her isolation and O'Neill's combine in a chilling, concise stage picture.

After 1933, O'Neill intentionally cut himself off from public life to get on with a projected historical cycle of nine plays with the general title *A Tale of Possessors, Self-Dispossessed. A Touch of the Poet* and *More Stately Mansions* (completed in 1939, produced in 1958) were the only plays to emerge from the project, an undertaking as pretentious and impossible as the general title itself. But in isolating himself from society, O'Neill also set himself apart from the currency of American speech. This deficiency is alibied in his historical plays by the skilful use of Irish dialect, which makes up in rhythm for the freshness he could no longer convey in the American vernacular. 'Musha, but it's you have the blarneyin' tongue. God forgive you,' says Sara Melody, teasing her father's genteel pretensions with her brogue. The issue of dialect is part of the immigrant dilemma O'Neill is dramatizing in *A Touch of the Poet*, and Con Melody sheds his role of aristocrat at the finale, only to adopt the 'begorah' and 'bejaysus' locutions of the shanty Irish bar-keep.

In the final, ambitious burst of energy that created *The Iceman Cometh* and *Long Day's Journey into Night* (O'Neill is the only American playwright to improve with age), the stiltedness of O'Neill's language is hidden by the plays being set just far enough in the past (1912) to make his idiom seem accurate rather than antique. But for a major playwright (he won the Nobel Prize for Literature in 1936), O'Neill always exhibited a tin ear for the spoken word. He was, as George Steiner bitchily observes, 'committed in a sombre, rather moving way, to bad writing.' In *Welded* (1924), an extraordinarily inept account of his second marriage, the playwright hero returns home with a finished manuscript to show his wife: 'It's *real*, Nelly! You'll see when I read you—the whole play has power and truth. I know it.' When O'Neill writes conventional American speech, there is no pulse behind the words. Early in his career O'Neill had complained: 'Oh for a language to write in—I'm so strait-jacketed in terms of talk.'

This creative pressure led him to many evocative aural discoveries (the Creole lament in *The Moon of the Caribbees* (1918); the tom-tom in *Emperor Jones*; the generator in *Dynamo*) and the idiomatic sludge of lower-class talk, which he made poetic. 'Where I feel myself most neglected is just where I set most store by myself—as a bit of a poet, who had laboured with the spoken word to evolve original rhythms of beauty where beauty apparently isn't—*Jones*, *Ape*, *God's Chillun*, *Desire*.' But in his late plays, the poetry in O'Neill's slang is strained rather than achieved. In *Hughie*, an anecdote that has been ballyhooed by critics into a minor O'Neill classic, 'Erie' Smith explains the gambling he used to do with the night clerk to pass the early-morning hours. 'I'd always take him to the cleaners in the end. But he never suspicioned nothing . . .' The archness of the poetic turn of phrase in *Hughie* is as heavy-handed as O'Neill straining for verisimilitude in the bar-room badinage of *The Iceman Cometh*. At one point, after a fight, the bartender Rocky says: 'Aw right, you. Leggo dat shiv and I'll put dis gat away.' In giving 'pain a voice,' O'Neill privately admitted as late as 1942 that his problem was in language

> But something was born wrong.
> The voice
> Strains towards a sob.
> Begins and ends in silence.

Stammering—what O'Neill called 'the native eloquence of us fog people'—was a term he frequently used to describe his attempts to make American speech bend to his dramatic needs. Having explored realistic vernacular in his early period, he turned to eloquence in his middle period. The stop-start staging of *Strange Interlude* is a kind of stammering in action. Both the style of the language and its delivery proclaim its Significance. Theatre, O'Neill said, 'should give us what the church no longer gives us—a meaning. In brief, we should return to the spirit of Greek grandeur. And if we have no Gods, or heroes to portray, we have the subconscious, the mother of all gods and heroes.'

Strange Interlude tries to stage the subconscious; but instead of finding grandeur, it achieves merely affection. 'Little subconscious mind, says I', O'Neill said, describing the gestation of a new play, 'bring home the bacon.' In the case of *Strange Interlude*, the bacon is hard to swallow. 'How we poor monkeys hide from ourselves behind the sounds called words,' says Nina Leeds, who, haunted by the death of her lover, decides on marriage as a cure for her morbidity. Typically, searching for a language that shows this psychological evasion, O'Neill settles for an idiom that describes every feeling. Fine words spew out of the characters, words chiselled in hard work and high seriousness. 'Strange interlude!' says one character. 'Yes, our lives are merely strange dark interludes in the electrical display of God the Father.' O'Neill uses the word 'strange' more than fifty times in the play, but there is nothing strange about it. Every mystery of personality is explained. The cumulative effect of this language is inundation, not illumination. As an act of will, O'Neill's elaborate tale is 'an achievement'; as a piece of writing, it verges on parody

> NINA (*thinking*): Talking . . . his voice like a fatiguing dying tune droned on a beggar's organ . . . his words arising from the tomb of a soul in puffs of ashes . . .
> (*Torturedly*)
> Ashes! . . . oh, Gordon, my dear one! . . . oh, lips on my lips, oh, strong arms around me, oh, spirit so brave and generous and gay! . . . ashes dissolving into mud! . . . mud and ashes! . . . that's all! . . . gone! . . . and gone forever from me . . .

Strange Interlude was a huge commercial success on Broadway. The reason lies not with the success of O'Neill's language but with its failure. Having disdained his father's penchant for melodrama, O'Neill nonetheless couldn't resist it. His language inflates with melodramatic flourishes, confusing impact with thought, oratory with authentic dramatic dialogue. Drama is a game of show and tell; and O'Neill simply tells. The play shoves every emotion right up under the chin of its audience. Through speechifying, O'Neill puts passion on a plate, where it can be easily consumed.

As he seeks forms to give size and grandeur to his own sense of suffering, O'Neill's plays inflate with 'cultural gas' (Eric Bentley's term for the showy articulateness of the playwright's middle period): the masks of *Lazarus Laughed*, the choric chants of *The Great God Brown*, the retelling of the history of the House of Atreus in *Mourning Becomes Electra*. In *Mourning Becomes Electra*, O'Neill corseted the Civil War characters with the Greek story and fleshed it out with sex talk, 'not sex lived and embodied but sex talked. The sex talk of the subintelligentsia', according to Bentley. In this play, like so many others, concept overwhelms character, and eloquence passes for authentic dramatic language. 'O'Neill commits inner vandalism by sheer inadequacy of style,' George Steiner observes of the play O'Neill thought his magnum opus. 'In the morass of his language, the high griefs of the House of Atreus dwindle to a case of adultery and murder in a provincial rathole.' O'Neill himself had to admit that language had yet again defeated him. 'It needed great language to lift it beyond itself. I haven't got that,' he wrote. 'By way of self-consolation . . . I don't think that great language is possible for anyone living in the discordant, broken, faithless rhythm of our time. The best one can do is be pathetically eloquent by one's moving dramatic articulations.' In *Mourning Becomes Electra*, the tedium is the message.

By trying unsuccessfully to force himself into the mould of tragedian, O'Neill played down his more mundane but substantial talent as reporter. Like Theodore Dreiser in the novel and Jacob Riis in photo-journalism, O'Neill called attention to his vision not by the elegance of his style, but by the weight of detail that recorded the split personality of American life. The sounds and cramped space of a ship's engine room (*The Hairy Ape*), the moonlit deck of a freighter (*The Moon of the Caribbees*), the subterranean calm of a derelict saloon (*The Iceman Cometh*), these realistic atmospheres convey the outcast's suffering more eloquently than O'Neill's words often do. O'Neill had a passion for the detritus of American life long before the public saw their own image in his pictures of waste. But striving for the big statement, O'Neill would not let his stage pictures speak for themselves. He is compelled to underline, to decorate, to pin down the mysterious truth of these atmospheres with fine words and big themes. Instead of calling attention to the reality of the experience, the talk calls attention to the playwright's literary gift of gab. Harry Hope's Saloon, for instance, a crucial landmark in O'Neill's personal geography, is explained poetically to the audience by the pessimist Larry Slade in the first moments of *The Iceman Cometh* before the poetry of the place can be made dramatic. The audience knows the experience before it has it. Says Slade

> What is it? It's the No Chance Saloon. It's Bedrock Bar, The End of the Line Café, The Bottom of the Sea Rathskeller! Don't you notice the beautiful calm in the atmosphere? That's because it's the last harbour. No one here has to worry about where they're going next, because there is no farther they can go. It's a great comfort to them. Although even here they keep up the appearances of life with a few harmless pipe dreams about their yesterdays and tomorrows, as you'll see for yourself if you're here long.

In *The Iceman Cometh* and *Long Day's Journey into Night*, O'Neill's lifelong artistic struggle to find a significant form for his intimations about America yielded its most powerful results. 'I'm going on the theory that the United States, instead of being the most successful country in the world, is the greatest failure,' O'Neill told *Time* in 1946, the year *Iceman* was produced.

> It's the greatest failure because it was given everything, more than any other country. Through moving as rapidly as it has, it hasn't acquired any real roots. Its main idea is the everlasting game of trying to possess your own soul by the possession of something outside it, thereby losing your own soul and the thing outside it, too. America is the prime example of this because it happened so quickly and with such immense resources. . . . We are the greatest example of 'For what shall it profit a man, if he shall gain the whole world and lose his own soul.'

The sin O'Neill saw in the land was also the sin he could not face in himself. He was projecting on to society his own personal dilemma. In trying to possess his craft, O'Neill too had lost his soul.

> . . . I,
> A quiet man,
> In love with quiet,
> Live quietly
> Among the visions of my drowned,
> Deep in my silent sea.

Cut off from community, from family, from ordinary life, he floundered. The last plays, so passionate and so nostalgic, brood over the time when his course into adulthood was being set. They are reports from his hellish interior. 'I know 'em all, I've known 'em for years,' O'Neill said in a press conference about *The Iceman Cometh*. 'I've tried to show the inmates of Harry Hope's saloon with their dreams . . . there is always one dream left, one final dream, no matter how low you've fallen. I know because I saw it.' O'Neill also witnessed the punishing scenes played out in *Long Day's Journey into Night*. In *Iceman*, O'Neill's new autobiographical backward glance is mixed with the old impulse to be definitive. O'Neill creates an epic out of the histories of seventeen daydreamers, making up in scope what he can't find in depth. For all its effective bawdy moments and fascinating cameos, the play finally fails to transmute fact into metaphor. But *Long Day's Journey into Night*, a play 'of old sorrows written in tears and blood', which O'Neill never intended to be produced in his lifetime, has no aspirations to big intentions, only authenticity. Written to reveal himself to himself, *Long Day's Journey into Night* is a spiritual necessity; not a theatrical project intended to show off his thought to others. Forcing nothing, O'Neill, astonishingly, finds everything. His writing is direct, unpretentious, poetic. Through the Tyrones, the themes and symbols of his early plays are not imposed but embodied in great drama.

III

The Iceman Cometh, itself a tall tale, serves O'Neill in the same magical way that the tall tales serve the denizens of Harry Hope's Saloon: both as a mask and an admission 'that they cannot forgive themselves for what they're not.' In the case of the play's central drama, the high-rolling salesman Hickey turns out to be a maniac who has killed his 'beloved' wife; and the outsider Don Parritt finally gets the death he seeks after admitting that he informed on his hated activist mother. In O'Neill's case, the play's ungainliness shows him to be not the stage poet he had ruined his life to become. *Iceman* stalls on this failure of imagination. In the play, O'Neill depicts human character as a vital lie, an exercise in heroics in which man's litany of self-revelations hides his own panic and impoverishment. Each character lives a lie to protect himself from a fear of life and of death. The point is made early in the play by Larry Slade, and then restated ad nauseam as each character factors out of O'Neill's dramatic equation. 'To hell with the truth!' says Slade. 'As the history of the world proves, the truth has no bearing on anything . . . The lie of a pipe dream is what gives life to the whole misbegotten mad lot of us, drunk or sober.' O'Neill can face the lie in others, but not the lie in his romance of art.

O'Neill repeats the phrase 'pipe dream' fifteen times in the play, and refused to cut even one mention. But the reiteration of an idea on stage doesn't clinch it. In fact, it's proof positive that the idea has not been successfully dramatized. Besides the repetitiveness of each character's dream and the ineluctable hunger of the spellbound for his spell, O'Neill is at a loss in *Iceman* to analyse the brilliant atmosphere he describes. A dream is something you wake up from; but O'Neill believed in dreaming, and sacrificed not only his life but the lives of his family to the fantasy of literary perfection. 'You can't keep a hophead off his dope,' he said about his own writing, starting *Long Day's Journey into Night* soon after finishing *The Iceman Cometh*. O'Neill was too much part of the problem to offer solutions. The play's sprawling lack of focus reflects the playwright's own moral vacuum. 'O'Neill's eye', writes Eric Bentley of *Iceman* in *In Search of Theater*, 'was off the object and on Dramatic and Poetic Effects . . .' O'Neill insisted on size. 'You would find if I did not build up the complete picture of the group as it is in the first part,' he wrote to Kenneth Macgowan, 'the atmosphere of the place, the humanity and friendship and human warmth, *the deep inner contentment of the bottom*, you would find the impact of what follows a lot less profoundly disturbing.' Size allows O'Neill to show off technique, which he mistakes for content, the inevitable confusion of any writer whose sense of life has been reduced to the puny goal of self-expression.

'Gene came in and talked to me all night which he frequently did when he couldn't sleep. He was thinking about this play, you see, in his youth,' Carlotta O'Neill recalled about the beginnings of *Long Day's Journey into Night*. 'He explained to me then that he had to write this play. He had to write it because it was a thing that haunted him and he had to forgive whatever caused this in them (in his mother and father and brother) and in himself.' In his previous plays, O'Neill had cannibalized aspects of his family history and served them up piecemeal in various theatrical disguises. (His brother James is James Tyrone in *A Moon for the Misbegotten*; parts of his father are in Ephraim Cabot in *Desire Under the Elms*, Con Melody in *A Touch of the Poet*, Chris Christopherson in *Anna Christie*; and his mother's isolation and mistreatment by his father are in *Desire Under the Elms* and *A Touch of the Poet*.) *Long Day's Journey into Night* focuses on a day at the Tyrone's sea-front Connecticut house—a day in which the youngest Tyrone, Edmund, learns that he has tuberculosis and his mother, Mary Tyrone, lapses back into her morphine addiction. Within the melodrama of this painful realistic situation, the family's hopes and past grievances are played out.

In Mary Tyrone's awful isolation, an isolation first enforced by years of touring with her husband and later by the odium of her addiction, O'Neill faces the spiritual malaise which he began by decrying and by which he was finally claimed. 'None of us can help the things life has done to us,' she says, spelling out her fatalism. 'They're done before you realize it, and once they're done they make you do other things until at last everything comes between you and what you'd like to be, and you've lost your true self for ever.' As with O'Neill, Mary Tyrone has lost her soul and says so. '. . . One day long ago I found I could no longer call my soul my own.' And later: 'If I could only find the faith I lost, so I could pray again!' Mary Tyrone's faith and her life have been sacrificed to James Tyrone's work. Irish peasant turned immigrant actor and star, Tyrone's glory and wealth have meant his family's fall and impoverishment. His dream of mobility has condemned his family to a lifetime of restlessness.

Stardom is the heroic face the culture puts on emotional greed—a greed manifested in James Tyrone's case in his property speculation, his tight-fistedness with money, and his obsession with the box-office success of *The Count of Monte Cristo*. '. . . From thirty-five to forty thousand net profit a season! A fortune in those days,' Tyrone tells his son, who would rebel against his father's hunger for money, only to be victimized by the more insidious hunger for greatness. Tyrone continues bitterly: 'What the hell was it I wanted to buy, I wonder, that was worth . . . Well, no matter . . .' The characters see their dilemma but, in their fatalism, won't risk change. The heart-rending poignance of their lives—and O'Neill's—is the moral myopia that prevents them from forestalling the inevitable clash between ego and personal salvation. The tears O'Neill shed in writing *Long Day's Journey into Night* were not only for his past, but for his present.

In the riveting tension of the play, O'Neill's familiar metaphors emerge not as symbols but as active characters in the drama. The fog that sweeps in from the sea surrounds and isolates the Tyrone house. Out of the pain and confusion in the Tyrone family relationships, the fog assumes the impenetrability and protection of the past itself. 'It hides you from the world and the world from you,' says Mary Tyrone, welcoming it. 'You feel that everything has changed and nothing is what it seemed. No one can find or touch you any more.' And Edmund, too, admits his craving for the invisibility of fog. 'The fog was where I wanted to be. Halfway down the path you can't see this house. You'd never know it was here . . . I couldn't see but a few feet ahead,' he says, his words unwittingly heavy with deeper insinuations. 'I didn't meet a soul. . .'

The doom of the foghorn compounds the soulless, lost world the Tyrones inhabit. The fog is a fact of the stage world before the play's passion elevates it, by degrees, to symbol. Likewise, the hauntedness O'Neill so frequently speechified about is here incarnated in Mary Tyrone's punishing spectral presence. As the morphine takes hold, Mary Tyrone starts to withdraw from the life around her, and her 'detached affection' becomes apparent to both the audience and her family. 'You can't talk to her now,' Jamie tells Edmund. 'She'll listen but she won't listen. She'll be here and she won't be here.' In *Long Day's Journey into Night*, O'Neill produces the ghost-in-life his other plays merely talk about. 'You'll be like a mad ghost before the night's over,' James Tyrone sadly warns his wife. And by the end of the play, she is. Haunted and haunting them, she moves dreamily amid her men, recalling an innocence forever lost. And the other Tyrones, who watch this ghostly performance, know that they, too, are among the living dead. James Tyrone's life is a tortured half-life, his accomplishments denied by the destruction they have wreaked on his family. Edmund confesses to 'living as a ghost'. And Jamie, the most self-destructive of the men, admits the dead heart that all can see. 'The dead part of me hopes you won't get well,' he tells Edmund, articulating the revenge that eats away at him. 'Maybe he's even glad the game has got Mama again! He wants company, he doesn't want to be the only corpse in the house!'

Beneath the scars of their family life, the story of the O'Neills contains the deeper brutalizing national themes of immigration and assimilation, mobility and identity, success and failure, well-being and salvation. The Tyrones' house is never a home. The material dream come true does not open the Tyrones up to life, but cuts them off from it. Isolation dominates their life just as it dominates the land. O'Neill's masterpiece puts into dramatic terms a paradox of democracy De Tocqueville had observed as early as 1835: 'Not only does democracy make every man forget his ancestors; but it hides his descendants and separates his contemporaries from him: it throws him back forever upon himself alone and threatens in the end to confine him entirely within the solitude of his own heart.'

Within O'Neill's spectacular solitude, *Long Day's Journey into Night* emerges almost as a freak of his imagination. It is not merely O'Neill's best story; it is, really, his *only* story. The intensely personal mission of the play divests it of O'Neill's familiar artistic swagger. Pursuing the truth of his past with ruthless candour, he confesses his own theatrical limitations. When James Tyrone tells Edmund he has the makings of a poet, Edmund counters: 'The *makings* of a poet. No, I'm afraid I'm like the guy who is always panhandling for a smoke. He hasn't even got the makings. He's only got the habit. I couldn't touch what I tried to tell you just now. I just stammered. That's the best I'll ever do . . .' *Long Day's Journey into Night* was, indeed, the best O'Neill ever did, where his voice found words to elevate his vision beyond a stammer.

'There is something moving, even great, in the impulse of the play.' Harold Clurman said of *Long Day's Journey into Night*. 'And no one can witness it without reverence for the *selflessness* of this extremely personal act.' But there is nothing selfless about the play. It is O'Neill's attempt to redeem the sins of the present by confessing the sins of the past. As a literary gesture, it is bold and big-hearted. Yet the real act of bravery would have been to break the O'Neill neurotic pattern for the living, not chronicle its self-destruction in the dead. O'Neill could make peace with his past but not his present. At the end of his life, he disinherited his children, quarrelled miserably with his wife, and retreated into the kind of barbarous isolation his plays dramatized. Art, O'Neill and his family discovered too late, is no substitute for life.

A WIFE FOR A LIFE

A Play in One Act

Characters

THE OLDER MAN
JACK, *the Younger Man*

OLD PETE, *a miner*

SCENE—*The edge of the Arizona desert; a plain dotted in the foreground with clumps of sagebrush. On the horizon a lonely butte is outlined, black and sinister against the lighter darkness of a sky with stars. The time is in the early hours of the night. In the foreground stands a ragged tent, the flap of which is open. Leaning against it are some shovels and a pick or two. Two saddles are on the ground nearby. Before the tent is a smoldering campfire at which an elderly man of about fifty is seated. He is dressed in miner's costume: flannel shirt, khaki trousers, high boots, etc.—all patched and showing evidence of long wear and tear. His wide-brimmed Stetson hat lies on the ground beside him. His hair is turning gray and his face is the face of one who has wandered far, lived hard, seen life in the rough and is a little weary of it all. Withal, his air and speech are those of an educated man whose native refinement has clung to him in spite of many hard knocks.*

On one side of the tent stands a rough stool and a gold-miner's panning tub—a square box half filled with water.

OLDER MAN (*Stirring the fire in a futile attempt to start it into flame*) I wonder what can be keeping him so long? (*He hears a noise of someone approaching*) Hello, Jack, I was just beginning to think you were lost.

(OLD PETE *enters. He is an old man dressed in rough miner's costume but he wears spurs and carries a quirt in his hand. He is covered with dust and has evidently been riding hard*)

OLD PETE It ain't Jack. It's me.

OLDER MAN (*Disappointed*) Hello, Pete. What brings you around at this time of the night?

OLD PETE (*Taking a telegram from his pocket*) I was just leaving Lawson when the operator stopped me and give me this for Jack. I seen your campfire burning and reckoned I'd bring it right over.

OLDER MAN (*Taking the telegram*) Many thanks, Pete. Won't you sit down and rest a bit?

OLD PETE Much obliged but I reckon I'll travel along. I ain't slept none to speak of in the past few nights and I got to be up at sunrise. (*Grinning sheepishly*) That fool town of Lawson sure does keep you up nights. (*He starts to go, then stops*) Claim panning out as good as ever?

OLDER MAN Better every day. This morning we took a sample from the upper end which we haven't touched so far. It looks good but we haven't panned it yet.

OLD PETE You-alls ought to get rich. You know how to keep money. Now me and money never could get on noway. (*He pulls out pockets ruefully*) They cleaned me out in Lawson this time and I reckon they'll clean me again the next time. (*Shaking his head*) Cities is sure hell that-a-way. Adios. (*He exits*)

OLDER MAN Good night. Poor Pete. Same old story.

Been bucking the faro bank again, I suppose. (*He looks at the telegram*) Hmm. Wonder what this is? Jack has had no correspondence in the five years I've been with him. May be something important in connection with the mine. I guess I'd better open it. He won't mind anyway. (*He opens the telegram and reads aloud*) "I am waiting. Come." No name signed. It comes from New York too. Well, it's too many for me. I give it up. (*He puts the telegram in his pocket*) Must be that fool operator got mixed up in his names. I wouldn't like to see Jack obey any summons like that. He's about all I've got now and I'd hate to see him leave just when we've struck it rich. (*Dismissing the subject*) I guess this wire is all a mistake anyway. (*He looks around yawning and his eye lights on the panning tub*) Now if only the upper part of the claim is as rich as that we've been working—(*The noise of someone approaching is heard*) Here he comes now. Welcome, wanderer! Where have you been all this time?

(JACK *enters. He is dressed about the same as the* OLDER MAN *but is much younger—in the early thirties*)

JACK One of the horses slipped his hobbles and I had quite a hunt for him. I finally found him down by the spring wallowing around as if water was the commonest thing in this section of Arizona. Fool beast!

OLDER MAN (*Forgetting all about the telegram*) It's a strange thing we should run into water out here where the maps say there isn't any. It's the one blessing we've found in this land God forgot. We're fools for luck for once.

JACK (*Nodding*) Yes. (*Then, rather exultantly*) But we have small cause to kick about this lonely hole after all. Any place is God's country to a man if there's gold in it and he finds it. There's gold here and (*Taking a small bag from his pocket and shaking it*) we've found it. So long live the desert say I.

OLDER MAN Those are my sentiments. (*He rolls a cigarette paper and, setting it afire in the flame, lights his pipe*) It sure looks as if our ship has come in at last here on the rim of the world. The luck was due to change. We've had our share of the bad variety; just missing a strike in every jumping-off place from South Africa to Alaska. We've taken our hard knocks with the imitation of a laugh at any rate and (*Stretching out his hand to younger man, who grasps it heartily*) we've been good pals ever since that day in the Transvaal five years ago when you hauled me out of the river, saved my life, and our friendship began. (*As the younger man starts to speak*) No, you needn't try to stop me expressing my gratitude. I haven't forgotten that day and I never will.

JACK (*To change the subject*) I'm going to see what that prospect we took at the other end of the claim looks like. (*He goes into the tent and returns with a gold pan heaped with dirt under his arm, and sitting down in front of the panning tub, proceeds to test the prospect. He washes the heap of dirt down until there is but a handful of gravel left. The* OLDER MAN *comes over and stands behind him looking over his shoulder. Finally, after one quick flip of the pan,* JACK *points to the sediment left in the bottom in which a small heap of bright yellow particles can be seen*) What do you think of that?

OLDER MAN (*Reaching over and feeling them with his fingers*) O' course gold; just as I expected. The upper end of the claim is just as rich as it is down here.

JACK (*With growing excitement*) There's over a quarter of an ounce here at least. That's five dollars a pan—better than we've ever panned down here at any time since we made the strike four months ago. (*He lays the pan aside*) I tell you, this claim is too much for us to handle alone. One of us ought to go East and organize a company.

OLDER MAN Then it will have to be you. I'm too old. (JACK *smiles and makes a deprecating gesture*) Anyway I never could get along with civilization and (*Laughing*) civilization never cared overmuch for me. (*He goes over and sits down by the fire. After a pause*) You've seemed to be hankering after the East quite a lot in the last month or so. (*Smiling*) Getting tired of the company here, eh?

JACK (*Quickly*) No, you know that isn't so, after all the years we've been pals and all we've been through together.

OLDER MAN (*Jokingly*) Then what is the attraction the effete East has to offer? (*Mockingly*) It's a woman I suppose?

JACK (*With dignity*) An angel, rather.

OLDER MAN (*Cynically*) They're all angels—at first.

The only trouble is their angelic attributes lack staying qualities. (*Then, half bitterly*) At any rate, you'd find them hard to prove by my experiences.

JACK (*Shrugging his shoulders a little impatiently*) You're a disgusting cynic and I refuse to argue. You know we've never been able to agree on that subject. I'm going to hunt out that bottle we've carried about so long and we'll drink to the mine and future prosperity. (*He goes into the tent*) Here it is. (*He returns with a quart of whiskey, opens it with a knife and pours out two drinks in the tin cups. Laughing*) I think this is a proper occasion for celebration—the two prodigals welcome the fatted calf. Let's make it a christening also. Here's to the Yvette Mine!

OLDER MAN (*He has been laughing, but turns suddenly grim. His hand trembles as he clinks cups and he almost spills some of the whiskey. He speaks in harsh, jerky tones*) Why the Yvette?

JACK (*Not noticing his agitation*) I know it sounds like rather a frivolous name for a mine but I have a hunch. There's a romance back of it—my romance. That was her name. One rarely speaks of such things. I've never told you but I will now if you care to hear it. It was over a year before I met you. I had just been out of mining school a short time and was prospecting around in the mountains of Peru hoping to hit a bonanza there. At the time I speak of I had returned to re-outfit at a small mining camp near the frontier of Ecuador. It was there I met her. She was the wife of a broken-down mining engineer from the States, over twenty years her senior. (*The* OLDER MAN, *who has been listening intently, is poking the fire nervously and his face becomes harsher and harsher*) According to all accounts he was a drunken brute who left her alone most of the time and only lived from one drunk to another. Personally I never saw him. It was probably better that I did not. You see, I fell in love with her on the spot and the thought of how he treated her made my blood boil.

OLDER MAN (*In stifled tones*) What was the name of the mining town you mention? I've been in that country myself—many years ago.

JACK San Sebastien. Do you know it?

(*At the words "San Sebastien" the* OLDER MAN *seems to crumple up. Nothing seems alive about him but his eyes, staring horribly, and his right hand, which nervously fingers the gun in the belt around his waist*)

OLDER MAN (*In a hoarse whisper*) Yes. I know it. Go on.

JACK (*Dreamily, absorbed in his own thoughts*) I loved her. In the corrupt environment of a mining camp she seemed like a lily growing in a field of rank weeds. I longed to take her away from all that atmosphere of sordid sin and suffering; away from her beast of a husband who was steadily ruining that beautiful young life and driving her to desperation. I overstayed my time. I should have been back in the mountains. I went to see her often. He was always away it seemed. Finally people began to talk. Then I realized that the time had come and told her that I loved her. I shall never forget her face. She looked at me with great calm eyes but her lips trembled as she said: "I know you love me and I—I love you; but you must go away and we must never see each other again. I am his wife and I must keep my pledge."

OLDER MAN (*Starting to his feet and half drawing the pistol from the holster*) You lie!

JACK (*Rudely awakened from his dream, he springs to his feet, his face angry and perplexed*) Why, what do you mean? What is it?

OLDER MAN (*Controlling his rage with a mighty effort and sitting down again*) Nothing. Nerves, I guess. It's my sore spot—the virtue of women. I've seen but little of it in my mining-camp experience and your heroine seems to me too impossible.

(*Wonderingly* JACK *sits down beside him again*)

JACK (*Eagerly*) You wouldn't think so if you could have seen her. (*The* OLDER MAN *covers his face with his hands and groans*) Here's a picture of her she sent me a year ago. (*He takes a small photo out of the pocket of his shirt*) Look at it. (*Handing him the photo*) Do you think a woman with a face like that could be the regular mining-camp kind?

(*He feels in his pocket again and goes into the tent as if searching for something*)

OLDER MAN (*He looks at the photo with haggard eyes for a moment, then whispers in a half sob*) My wife! (*Then, staring into vacancy, he speaks to himself, unconsciously aloud*) She has not changed.

JACK (*Coming back from the tent with a soiled envelope in his hand in time to hear the last sentence.*

Astonished) Changed? Who? Do you know her?

OLDER MAN (*Quickly mastering his emotion and lying bravely*) No. Of course not. But she reminds me of a girl I knew here in the States a long time ago. But the girl I speak of must be an old woman by this time. I forget my gray hairs.

JACK Yvette is only twenty-five. Her parents were poor French people. In a fit of mistaken zeal for her welfare they forced her to marry this man when she was too young to know her own mind. They thought they were making an excellent match. Immediately after the marriage he dragged her off to San Sebastien, where he was half-owner of a small mine. It seems the devil broke out in him before they were hardly settled there. (*After a pause*) I'd like to be fair to him. Maybe he realized that she could never love him and was trying to drown the memory of the mistake he had made. He certainly loved her—in his fashion.

OLDER MAN (*In a pathetic whisper*) Yes. He must have loved her—in his fashion.

JACK (*Looking at the letter in his hand, which he had forgotten*) Ah, I forgot. I have proof positive of her innocence and noble-mindedness. Here is a letter which she wrote and sent to me the morning I was leaving. It's only a few words. Read it, Mr. Doubting Thomas.

(*He hands the letter to the* OLDER MAN)

OLDER MAN (*His hands tremble. Aside*) Her writing. (*Reading aloud*) "I must keep my oath. He needs me and I must stay. To be true to myself I must be true to him." (*Aside: "My God, I was wrong after all"*) "Sometime I may send for you. Goodbye." Signed Yvette. (*He folds the letter up slowly, puts it back in the envelope and hands it to* JACK. *Suddenly he turns to him with quick suspicion*) What does she mean by that last sentence?

JACK When I left I gave her my address in the States and she promised to let me know if she changed her mind or if conditions changed.

OLDER MAN (*With grim irony*) You mean if the drunken husband died.

JACK (*His face growing hard*) Yes. That's what I mean.

OLDER MAN Well, how do you know he hasn't? Have you ever heard from her since?

JACK Only the one time when she sent the picture I showed you. I received the letter from her in Cape Town a year ago. It had been forwarded from the States. She said her husband had disappeared soon after I left. No one knew where he had gone but the rumor was that he had set out on my trail for vengeance, refusing to believe in her innocence. (*Grimly patting his gun*) I'm sorry he didn't find me.

OLDER MAN (*He has by this time regained control of himself and speaks quite calmly*) Where is she now?

JACK Living with her parents in New York. She wrote to say that she would wait a year longer. If he did not return to her by then she would become legally free of him and would send for me. The year is up today but (*Hopelessly*) I have received no word.

(*He walks back and looks into the darkness as if hoping to see someone coming. The* OLDER MAN *suddenly remembers the telegram he has. He takes it from his pocket as if to give it to* JACK; *then hesitates and says in agony, "My God, I cannot!" as he realizes the full significance of what the telegram says. Mastered by a contrary impulse he goes to burn it in the campfire but again hesitates. Finally, as* JACK *returns slowly to the campfire, he turns quickly and hands the telegram to him*)

OLDER MAN Cheer up! Here's a surprise for you. Read this. Old Pete brought it from Lawson before you returned and I forgot all about it. I opened it by mistake thinking it might have something to do with the mine.

(*He turns quickly away as if unable to bear the sight of* JACK'*s elation.* JACK *feverishly opens the yellow envelope. His face lights up and he gives an exclamation of joy and rushes to the* OLDER MAN)

JACK It's too good to be true. Tell me I am not dreaming.

OLDER MAN (*He looks at* JACK *steadily for a moment, then tries hard to smile and mutters*) Congratulations.

(*He is suffering horribly*)

JACK (*Misunderstanding the cause of his emotion*) Never mind, old pal, I won't be gone long and when I come back I'll bring her with me.

OLDER MAN (*Hastily*) No, I'll manage all right. Better stay East for a while. We'll need someone there when the work really starts.

JACK When can I get a train?

OLDER MAN If you ride hard and start right away, you can get to Lawson in time for the Limited at three in the morning.

JACK (*Rushing off with his saddle under his arm*) My horse is hobbled at the mouth of the canyon.

OLDER MAN (*He stands in front of the tent*) So I have found him after all these years and I cannot even hate him. What tricks Fate plays with us. When he told me his name that first day I noticed that it was the same as the man's I was looking for. But he seemed such a boy to me and my heart went out to him so strongly that I never for an instant harbored the idea that he could be the John Sloan I was after. Of course, he never knew my right name. I wonder what he would say if he knew. I've half a mind to tell him. But no, what's the use? Why should I mar his happiness? In this affair I alone am to blame and I must pay. As I listened to his story this evening until no doubt remained that he was the John Sloan I had sworn to kill, my hand reached for my gun and all the old hate flared up in my heart. And then I remembered his face as he looked that day in the Transvaal when he bent over me after saving my life at the risk of his own. I could almost hear his words as he spoke that day when death was so near: "All right, old pal, you're all right." Then my hand left my gun and the old hatred died out forever. I could not do it. (*He pauses and a bitter smile comes over his face as at some new thought*) Oh, what a fool I have been. She was true to me in spite of what I was. God bless him for telling me so. God grant they may both be happy—the only two beings I have ever loved. And I—must keep wandering on. I cannot be the ghost at their feast.

JACK (*Entering hurriedly, putting on spurs, hat, etc.*) Good-bye, old pal. I'm sorry to leave you this way but I have waited so long for this. You understand, don't you?

OLDER MAN (*Slowly*) Yes. (*Grasping his hand and looking deep into his eyes*) Good-bye and God bless you both.

JACK (*Feelingly*) Good-bye.

(*He exits*)

OLDER MAN (*He sits down by the campfire and buries his face in his hands. Finally he rouses himself with an effort, stirs the campfire and, smiling with a whimsical sadness, softly quotes*) "Greater love hath no man than this, that he giveth his wife for his friend."

Curtain

THIRST

A Play in One Act

Characters

A Gentleman
A Dancer
A West Indian Mulatto Sailor

Scene—*A steamer's life raft rising and falling slowly on the long ground swell of a glassy tropic sea. The sky above is pitilessly clear, of a steel-blue color merging into black shadow on the horizon's rim. The sun glares down from straight overhead like a great angry eye of God. The heat is terrific. Writhing, fantastic heat waves rise from the white deck of the raft. Here and there on the still surface of the sea the fins of sharks may be seen slowly cutting the surface of the water in lazy circles.*

Two men and a woman are on the raft. Seated at one end is a West Indian mulatto dressed in the blue uniform of a sailor. Across his jersey may be seen the words "Union Mail Line" in red letters. He has on rough sailor shoes. His head is bare. When he speaks it is in drawling sing-song tones as if he were troubled by some strange impediment of speech. He croons a monotonous Negro song to himself as his round eyes follow the shark fins in their everlasting circles.

At the other end of the raft sits a middle-aged white man in what was once evening dress; but sun and salt water have reduced it to the mere caricature of such a garment. His white shirt is stained and rumpled; his collar a formless pulp about his neck; his black tie a withered ribbon. Evidently he had been a first-class passenger. Just now he cuts a sorry and pitiful figure as he sits staring stupidly at the water with unseeing eyes. His scanty black hair is disheveled, revealing a bald spot burnt crimson by the sun. A mustache droops over his lips, and some of the dye has run off it making a black line down the side of his lean face, blistered with sunburn, haggard with hunger and thirst. From time to time he licks his swollen lips with his blackened tongue.

Between the two men a young woman lies with arms outstretched, face downward on the raft. She is an even more bizarre figure than the man in evening clothes, for she is dressed in a complete short-skirted dancer's costume of black velvet covered with spangles. Her long blond hair streams down over her bare, unprotected shoulders. Her silk stockings are baggy and wrinkled and her dancing shoes swollen and misshapen. When she lifts her head a diamond necklace can be seen glittering coldly on the protruding collarbones of her emaciated shoulders. Continuous weeping has made a blurred smudge of her rouge and the black make-up of her eyes but one can still see that she must have been very beautiful before hunger and thirst had transformed her into a mocking specter of a dancer. She is sobbing endlessly, hopelessly.

In the eyes of all three the light of a dawning madness is shining.

DANCER (*Raising herself to a sitting posture and turning piteously to the* GENTLEMAN) My God! My God! This silence is driving me mad! Why do you not speak to me? Is there no ship in sight yet?

GENTLEMAN (*Dully*) No. I do not think so. At least I cannot see any. (*He tries to rise to his feet but finds himself too weak and sits down again with a groan*) If I could only stand up I could tell better. I cannot see far from this position. I am so near the water. And then my eyes are like two balls of fire. They burn and burn until they feel as if they were boring into my brain.

DANCER I know! I know! Everywhere I look I see great crimson spots. It is as if the sky were raining drops of blood. Do you see them too?

GENTLEMAN Yesterday I did—or some day—I no longer remember days. But today everything is red. The very sea itself seems changed to blood. (*He licks his swollen, cracked lips—then laughs—the shrill cackle of madness*) Perhaps it is the blood of all those who were drowned that night rising to the surface.

DANCER Do not say such things. You are horrible. I do not care to listen to you. (*She turns away from him with a shudder*)

GENTLEMAN (*Sulkily*) Very well. I will not speak. (*He covers his face with his hands*) God! God! How my eyes ache! How my throat burns! (*He sobs heavily —there is a pause—suddenly he turns to the* DANCER *angrily*) Why did you ask me to speak if you do not care to listen to me?

DANCER I did not ask you to speak of blood. I did not ask you to mention that night.

GENTLEMAN Well, I will say no more then. You may talk to him if you wish.

(*He points to the* SAILOR *with a sneer. The Negro does not hear. He is crooning to himself and watching the sharks. There is a long pause. The raft slowly rises and falls on the long swells. The sun blazes down*)

DANCER (*Almost shrieking*) Oh, this silence! I cannot bear this silence. Talk to me about anything you please but, for God's sake, talk to me! I must not think! I must not think!

GENTLEMAN (*Remorsefully*) Your pardon, dear lady! I am afraid I spoke harshly. I am not myself. I think I am a little out of my head. There is so much sun and so much sea. Everything gets vague at times. I am very weak. We have not eaten in so long—we have not even had a drink of water in so long. (*Then in tones of great anguish*) Oh, if we only had some water!

DANCER (*Flinging herself on the raft and beating it with clenched fists*) *Please* do not speak of water!

SAILOR (*Stopping his song abruptly and turning quickly around*) Water? Who's got water?

(*His swollen tongue shows between his dry lips*)

GENTLEMAN (*Turning to the* SAILOR) You know no one here has any water. You stole the last drop we had yourself. (*Irritably*) Why do you ask such questions?

(*The* SAILOR *turns his back again and watches the shark fins. He does not answer nor does he sing any longer. There is a silence, profound and breathless*)

DANCER (*Creeping over to the* GENTLEMAN *and seizing his arm*) Do you not notice how deep the silence is? The world seems emptier than ever. I am afraid. Tell me why it is.

GENTLEMAN I, too, notice it. But I do not know why it is.

DANCER Ah! I know now. He is silent. Do you not remember he was singing? A queer monotonous song it was—more of a dirge than a song. I have heard many songs in many languages in the places I have played, but never a song like that before. Why did he stop, do you think? Maybe something frightened him.

GENTLEMAN I do not know. But I will ask him. (*To the* SAILOR) Why have you stopped singing?

(*The* SAILOR *looks at him with a strange expression in his eyes. He does not answer but turns to the circling fins again and takes up his song, dully, droningly, as if from some place he had left off. The* DANCER *and the* GENTLEMAN *listen in attitudes of strained attention for a long time*)

DANCER (*Laughing hysterically*) What a song! There is no tune to it and I can understand no words. I wonder what it means.

GENTLEMAN Who knows? It is doubtless some folk song of his people which he is singing.

DANCER But I wish to find out. Sailor! Will you tell me what it means—that song you are singing?

(*The Negro stares at her uneasily for a moment*)

SAILOR (*Drawlingly*) It is a song of my people.

DANCER Yes. But what do the words mean?

SAILOR (*Pointing to the shark fins*) I am singing to them. It is a charm. I have been told it is very strong. If I sing long enough they will not eat us.

DANCER (*Terrified*) Eat us? What will eat us?

GENTLEMAN (*Pointing to the moving fins in the still water*) He means the sharks. Those pointed black things you see moving through the water are their fins. Have you not noticed them before?

DANCER Yes, yes. I have seen them. But I did not know they were sharks. (*Sobbing*) Oh, it is horrible, all this!

GENTLEMAN (*To the Negro harshly*) Why do you tell her such things? Do you not know you will frighten her?

SAILOR (*Dully*) She asked me what I was singing.

GENTLEMAN (*Trying to comfort the* DANCER, *who is still sobbing*) At least tell her the truth about the sharks. That is all a children's tale about them eating people. (*Raising his voice*) You know they never eat anyone. And I know it.

(*The Negro looks at him and his lips contract grotesquely. Perhaps he is trying to smile*)

DANCER (*Raising her head and drying her eyes*) You are sure of what you say?

GENTLEMAN (*Confused by the Negro's stare*) Of course I am sure. Everyone knows that sharks are afraid to touch a person. They are all cowards. (*To the Negro*) You were just trying to frighten the lady, were you not?

(*The Negro turns away from them and stares at the sea. He commences to sing again*)

DANCER I no longer like his song. It makes me dream of horrible things. Tell him to stop.

GENTLEMAN Bah! You are nervous. Anything is better than dead silence.

DANCER Yes. Anything is better than silence—even a song like that.

GENTLEMAN He is strange—that sailor. I do not know what to think of him.

DANCER It is a strange song he sings.

GENTLEMAN He does not seem to want to speak to us.

DANCER I have noticed that, too. When I asked him about the song he did not want to answer at all.

GENTLEMAN Yet he speaks good English. It cannot be that he does not understand us.

DANCER When he does speak, it is as if he had some impediment in his throat.

GENTLEMAN Perhaps he has. If so, he is much to be pitied and we are wrong to speak of him so.

DANCER I do not pity him. I am afraid of him.

GENTLEMAN That is foolish. It is the sun which beats down so fiercely which makes you have such thoughts. I, also, have been afraid of him at times, but I know now that I had been gazing at the sea too long and listening to the great silence. Such things distort your brain.

DANCER Then you no longer fear him?

GENTLEMAN I no longer fear him now that I am quite sane. It clears my brain to talk to you. We must talk to each other all the time.

DANCER Yes, we must talk to each other. I do not dream when I talk to you.

GENTLEMAN I think at one time I was going mad. I dreamed he had a knife in his hand and looked at me. But it was all madness; I can see that now. He is only a poor Negro sailor—our companion in misfortune. God knows we are all in the same pitiful plight. We should not grow suspicious of one another.

DANCER All the same, I am afraid of him. There is something in his eyes when he looks at me which makes me tremble.

GENTLEMAN There is nothing, I tell you. It is all your imagination.

(*There is a long pause*)

DANCER Good God! Is there no ship in sight yet?

GENTLEMAN (*Attempting to rise but falling back weakly*) I can see none. And I cannot stand to get a wider view.

DANCER (*Pointing to the Negro*) Ask him. He is stronger than we are. He may be able to see one.

GENTLEMAN Sailor! (*The Negro ceases his chant and turns to him with expressionless eyes*) You are stronger than we are and can see farther. Stand up and tell me if there is any ship in sight.

SAILOR (*Rising slowly to his feet and looking at all points of the horizon*) No. There is none.

(*He sits down again and croons his dreary melody*)

DANCER (*Weeping hopelessly*) My God, this is horrible. To wait and wait for something that never comes.

GENTLEMAN It is indeed horrible. But it is to be expected.

DANCER Why do you say it is to be expected? Have you no hopes, then, of being rescued?

GENTLEMAN (*Wearily*) I have hoped for many things in my life. Always I have hoped in vain. We are far out of the beaten track of steamers. I know little of navigation, yet I heard those on board say that we were following a course but little used. Why we did so, I do not know. I suppose the Captain wished to make a quicker passage. He alone knows what was in his mind and he will probably never tell.

DANCER No, he will never tell.

GENTLEMAN Why do you speak so decidedly? He might have been among those who escaped in the boats.

DANCER He did not escape. He is dead!

GENTLEMAN Dead?

DANCER Yes. He was on the bridge. I can remember seeing his face as he stood in under a lamp. It was pale and drawn like the face of a dead man. His eyes, too, seemed dead. He shouted some orders in a thin, trembling voice. No one paid any attention to him. And then he shot himself. I saw the flash, and heard the report above all the screams of the drowning. Someone grasped me by the arm and I heard a hoarse voice shouting in my ear. Then I fainted.

GENTLEMAN Poor Captain! It is evident, then, that he felt himself guilty—since he killed himself. It must be terrible to hear the screams of the dying and know oneself to blame. I do not wonder that he killed himself.

DANCER He was so kind and good-natured—the Captain. It was only that afternoon on the promenade deck that he stopped beside my chair. "I hear you are to entertain us this evening," he said. "That will be delightful, and it is very kind of you. I had promised myself the pleasure of seeing you in New York, but you have forestalled me." (*After a pause*) How handsome and broad-shouldered he was—the Captain.

GENTLEMAN I would have liked to have seen his soul.

DANCER You would have found it no better and no worse than the souls of other men. If he was guilty he has paid with his life.

GENTLEMAN No. He has avoided payment by taking his life. The dead do not pay.

DANCER And the dead cannot answer when we speak evil of them. All we can know is that he is dead. Let us talk of other things.

(*There is a pause*)

GENTLEMAN (*Fumbles in the inside pocket of his dress coat and pulls out a black object that looks like a large card case. He opens it and stares at it with perplexed eyes. Then, giving a hollow laugh, he holds it over for the* DANCER *to see*) Oh, the damned irony of it!

DANCER What is it? I cannot read very well. My eyes ache so.

GENTLEMAN (*Still laughing mockingly*) Bend closer! Bend closer! It is worth while understanding—the joke that has been played on me.

DANCER (*Reading slowly, her face almost touching the case*) United States Club of Buenos Aires! I do not understand what the joke is.

GENTLEMAN (*Impatiently snatching the case from her hand*) I will explain the joke to you then. Listen! M-e-n-u—menu. That is the joke. This is a souvenir menu of a banquet given in my honor by this club. (*Reading*) "Martini cocktails, soup, sherry, fish, Burgundy, chicken, champagne"—and here we are dying for a crust of bread, for a drink of water! (*His mad laughter suddenly ceases and in a frenzy of rage he shakes his fist at the sky and screams*) God! God! What a joke to play on us!

(*After this outburst he sinks back dejectedly, his trembling hand still clutching the menu*)

DANCER (*Sobbing*) This is too horrible. What have we done that we should suffer so? It is as if one misfortune after another happened to make our agony more terrible. Throw that thing away! The very sight of it is a mockery. (*The* GENTLEMAN *throws the menu into the sea, where it floats, a black spot on the glassy water*) How do you happen to have that thing with you? It is ghastly for you to torment me by reading it.

GENTLEMAN I am sorry to have hurt you. The jest was so grotesque I could not keep it to myself. You ask how I happen to have it with me? I will tell you. It gives the joke an even bitterer flavor. You remember when the crash came? We were all in the salon. You were singing—a Cockney song I think?

DANCER Yes. It is one I first sang at the Palace in London.

GENTLEMAN It was in the salon. You were singing. You were very beautiful. I remember a woman on my right saying: "How pretty she is! I wonder if she is married?" Strange how some idiotic remark like that will stick in one's brain when all else is vague and confused. A tragedy happens—we are in the midst of it—and one of our clearest remembrances afterwards is a remark that might have been overheard in any subway train.

DANCER It is so with me. There was a fat, bald-headed, little man. It was on deck after the crash. Everywhere they were fighting to get into the boats. This poor little man stood by himself. His moon face was convulsed with rage. He kept repeating in loud angry tones: "I shall be late. I must cable! I can never make it!" He was still bewailing his broken appointment when a rush of the crowd swept him off his feet and into the sea. I can see him now. He is the only person besides the Captain I remember clearly.

GENTLEMAN (*Continuing his story in a dead voice*) You were very beautiful. I was looking at you and wondering what kind of a woman you were. You know I had never met you personally—only seen you in my walks around the deck. Then came the crash—that horrible dull crash. We were all thrown forward on the floor of the salon; then screams, oaths, fainting women, the hollow boom of a bulkhead giving way. I vaguely remember rushing to my stateroom and picking up my wallet. It must have been that menu that I took instead. Then I was on deck fighting in the midst of the crowd. Somehow I got into a boat—but it was overloaded and was swamped immediately. I swam to another boat. They beat me off with the oars. That boat too was swamped a moment later. And then the gurgling, choking cries of the drowning! Something huge rushed by me in the water, leaving a gleaming trail of phosphorescence. A woman near me with a life belt around her gave a cry of agony and disappeared—then I realized—sharks! I became frenzied with terror. I swam. I beat the water with my hands. The ship had gone down. I swam and swam with but one idea—to put all that horror behind me. I saw something white on the water before me. I clutched it—climbed on it. It was this raft. You and he were on it. I fainted. The whole thing is a horrible nightmare in my brain—but I remember clearly that idiotic remark of the woman in the salon. What pitiful creatures we are!

DANCER When the crash came I also rushed to my stateroom. I took this (*Pointing to the diamond necklace*), clasped it round my neck and ran on deck; the rest I have told you.

GENTLEMAN Do you not remember how you came on this raft? It is strange that you and he should be on a raft alone when so many died for lack of a place. Were there ever any others on the raft with you?

DANCER No, I am sure there were not. Everything in my memory is blurred. But I feel sure we were always the only ones—until you came. I was afraid of you—your face was livid with fear. You were moaning to yourself.

GENTLEMAN It was the sharks. Until they came I kept a half-control over myself. But when I saw them even my soul quivered with terror.

DANCER (*Horror-stricken, looking at the circling fins*) Sharks! Why they are all around us now. (*Frenziedly*) You lied to me. You said they would not touch us. Oh, I am afraid, I am afraid!

(*She covers her face with her hands*)

GENTLEMAN If I lied to you it was because I wished to spare you. Be brave! We are safe from them as long as we stay on the raft. These things must be faced. (*Then in tones of utter despondency*) Besides, what does it matter—sharks or no sharks—the end is the same.

DANCER (*Taking her hands away from her eyes and looking dully at the water*) You are right. What does it matter?

GENTLEMAN God! How still the sea is! How still the sky is! One would say the world was dead. I think the accursed humming of that nigger only makes one feel the silence more keenly. There is nothing—that seems to live.

DANCER How the sun burns into me! (*Piteously*) My poor skin that I was once so proud of!

GENTLEMAN (*Rousing himself with an effort*) Come! Let us not think about it. It is madness to think about it so. How do you account for your being on the raft alone with this nigger? You have not yet told me.

DANCER—How can I tell? The last thing I remember was that harsh voice in my ear shouting something—what, I cannot recollect.

GENTLEMAN There was nothing else?

DANCER Nothing. (*Pause*) Stop! Yes, there was something I had forgotten. I think that someone kissed me. Yes, I am sure that someone kissed me. But no, I am not sure. It may have all been a dream I dreamed. I have had so many dreams during these awful days and nights—so many mad, mad dreams.

(*Her eyes begin to glaze, her lips to twitch. She murmurs to herself*) Mad, mad dreams.

GENTLEMAN (*Reaching over and shaking her by the shoulder*) Come! You said someone kissed you. You must be mistaken. I surely did not, and it could hardly have been that sailor.

DANCER Yet I am sure someone did. It was not since I have been on this raft. It was on the deck of the ship just as I was fainting.

GENTLEMAN Who could it have been, do you think?

DANCER I hardly dare to say what I think. I might be wrong. You remember the Second Officer—the young Englishman with the great dark eyes who was so tall and handsome? All the women loved him. I, too, I loved him—a little bit. He loved me —very much—so he said. Yes, I know he loved me very much. I think it was he who kissed me. I am almost sure it was he.

GENTLEMAN Yes, he must have been the one. That would explain it all. He must have sent away the raft when only you and this sailor were on it. He probably did not let the others know of the existence of this raft. Indeed he must have loved you to disregard his duty so. I will ask the sailor about it. Maybe he can clear away our doubts. (*To the Negro*) Sailor! (*The Negro stops singing and looks at them with wide, bloodshot eyes*) Did the Second Officer order you to take this lady from the ship?

SAILOR (*Sullenly*) I do not know.

GENTLEMAN Did he tell you to take no one else with you but this lady—and perhaps himself afterwards?

SAILOR (*Angrily*) I do not know.

(*He turns away again and commences to sing*)

DANCER Do not speak to him any more. He is angry at something. He will not answer.

GENTLEMAN He is going mad, I think. However, it seems certain that it was the Second Officer who kissed you and saved your life.

DANCER He was kind and brave to me. He meant well. Yet I wish now he had let me die. I would have way down in the cold green water. I would have been sleeping, coldly sleeping. While now my brain is scorched with sun-fire and dream-fire. And I am going mad. We are all going mad. Your eyes shine with a wild flame at times—and that sailor's are horrible with strangeness—and mine see great drops of blood that dance upon the sea. Yes, we are all mad. (*Pause*) God! Oh God! Must this be the end of all? I was coming home, home after years of struggling, home to success and fame and money. And I must die out here on a raft like a mad dog.

(*She weeps despairingly*)

GENTLEMAN Be still! You must not despair so. I, too, might whine a prayer of protest: Oh God, God! After twenty years of incessant grind, day after weary day, I started on my first vacation. I was going home. And here I sit dying by slow degrees, desolate and forsaken. Is this the meaning of all my years of labor? Is this the end, oh God? So I might wail with equal justice. But the blind sky will not answer your appeals or mine. Nor will the cruel sea grow merciful for any prayer of ours.

DANCER Have you no hope that one of the ship's boats may have reached land and reported the disaster? They would surely send steamers out to search for the other survivors.

GENTLEMAN We have drifted far, very far, in these long, weary days. I am afraid no steamer would find us.

DANCER We are lost then!

(*She falls face downward on the raft. A great sob shakes her thin bare shoulders*)

GENTLEMAN I have not given up hope. These seas, I have heard, are full of coral islands and we surely ought to drift near one of them soon. It was probably an uncharted coral reef that our steamer hit. I heard someone say "derelict" but I saw no sign of one in the water. With us it is only a question of whether we can hold out until we sight land. (*His voice quivers; he licks his blackened lips. His eyes have grown very mad and he is shaking spasmodically from head to foot.*) Water would save us—just a little water—even a few drops would be enough. (*Intensely*) God, if we only had a little water!

DANCER Perhaps there will be water on the island. Look; look hard! An island or a ship may have come in sight while we were talking. (*There is a pause. Suddenly she rises to her knees and pointing straight in front of her, shouts*) See! An island!

GENTLEMAN (*Shading his eyes with a trembling hand and peering wildly around him*) I see nothing—nothing but a red sea and a red sky.

DANCER (*Still looking at some point far out over the water, speaks in disappointed tones*) It is gone. Yet I am quite sure I saw one. It was right out there quite near to us. It was all green and clean-looking with a clear stream that ran into the sea. I could hear the water running over the stones. You do not believe me. You, Sailor, you must have seen it too, did you not? (*The Negro does not answer*) I cannot see it any more. Yet I must see it. I *will* see it!

GENTLEMAN (*Shaking her by the shoulder*) What you say is nonsense. There is no island there, I tell you. There is nothing but sun and sky and sea around us. There are no green trees. There is no water. (*The* SAILOR *has stopped singing and turns and looks at them*)

DANCER (*Angrily*) Do you mean to tell me I lie? Can I not believe my own eyes, then? I tell you I saw it—cool clear water. I heard it bubbling over the stones. But now I hear nothing, nothing at all. (*Turning suddenly to the* SAILOR) Why have you stopped singing? Is not everything awful enough already that you should make it worse?

SAILOR (*Sticking out his swollen tongue and pointing to it with a long brown finger*) Water! I want water! Give me some water and I will sing.

GENTLEMAN (*Furiously*) We have no water, fool! It is your fault we have none. Why did you drink all that was left in the cask when you thought we were asleep? I would not give you any even if we had some. You deserve to suffer, you pig! If any one of the three of us has any water it is you who have hidden some out of what you stole. (*With a laugh of mad cunning*) But you will get no chance to drink it, I promise you that. I am watching you.

(*The Negro sullenly turns away from them*)

DANCER (*Taking hold of the* GENTLEMAN'*s arm and almost hissing into his ear. She is terribly excited and he is still chuckling crazily to himself*) Do you really think he has some?

GENTLEMAN (*Chuckling*) He may have. He may have.

DANCER Why do you say that?

GENTLEMAN He has been acting strangely. He has looked as if he wished to hide something. I was wondering what it could be. Then suddenly I thought to myself: "What if it should be some water?" Then I knew I had found him out. I will not let him get the best of me. I will watch him. He will not drink while I am watching him. I will watch him as long as I can see.

DANCER What could he have put the water in? He has nothing that I can discover.

(*She is rapidly falling in with this mad fixed idea of his*)

GENTLEMAN Who knows? He may have a flask hidden in under his jersey. But he has something, that I am sure of. Why is it he is so much stronger than we are? He can stand up without effort and we can scarcely move. Why is that, I ask you?

DANCER It is true. He stood up and looked for a ship as easily as if he had never known hunger and thirst. You are right. He must have something hidden—food or water.

GENTLEMAN (*With mad eagerness to prove his fixed idea*) No, he has no food. There has never been any food. But there has been water. There was a whole small cask full of it on the raft when I came. On the second or third night, I do not remember which, I awoke and saw him draining the cask. When I reached it, it was empty. (*Furiously shaking his fist at the Negro's back*) Oh, you pig! You rotten pig!

(*The Negro does not seem to hear*)

DANCER That water would have saved our lives. He is no better than a murderer.

GENTLEMAN (*With insane shrewdness*) Listen. I think he must have poured some of the water into his flask. There was quite a little there. He could not have drunk it all. Oh, he is a cunning one! That song of his—it was only a blind. He drinks when we are not looking. But he will drink no more, for I will watch him. I will watch him!

DANCER You will watch him? And what good will that do either of us? Will we die any the less soon for your watching? No! Let us get the water away from him in some way. That is the only thing to do.

GENTLEMAN He will not give it to us.

DANCER We will steal it while he sleeps.

GENTLEMAN I do not think he sleeps. I have never seen him sleep. Besides, we should wake him.

DANCER (*Violently*) We will kill him then. He deserves to be killed.

GENTLEMAN He is stronger than we are—and he has a knife. No, we cannot do that. I would willingly kill him. As you say, he deserves it. But I cannot even stand. I have no strength left. I have no weapons. He would laugh at me.

DANCER There must be some way. You would think even the most heartless savage would share at a time like this. We must get that water. It is horrible to be dying of thirst with water so near. Think! Think! Is there no way?

GENTLEMAN You might buy it from him with that necklace of yours. I have heard his people are very fond of such things.

DANCER This necklace? It is worth a thousand pounds. An English duke gave it to me. I will not part with it. Do you think I am a fool?

GENTLEMAN Think of a drink of water! (*They both lick their dry lips feverishly*) If we do not drink soon we will die. (*Laughing harshly*) You will take your necklace to the sharks with you? Very well then, I will say no more. For my part, I would sell my soul for a *drop* of water.

DANCER (*Shuddering with horror she glances instinctively at the moving shark fins*) You are horrible. I had almost forgotten those monsters. It is not kind of you to be always bringing them back to my memory.

GENTLEMAN It is well that you should not forget them. You will value your duke's present less when you look at them. (*Impatiently pounding the deck with one bony hand*) Come, come, we shall both die of thirst while you are dreaming. Offer it to him! Offer it to him!

DANCER (*She takes off the necklace and, musing vacantly, turns it over in her hands watching it sparkle in the sun*) It is beautiful, is it not? I hate to part with it. He was very much in love with me—the old duke. I think he would even have married me in the end. I did not like him. He was old, very old. Something came up—I forget what. I never saw him again. This is the only gift of his that I have left.

GENTLEMAN (*In a frenzy of impatience—the vision of the water clear before his glaring eyes*) Damn it, why are you chattering so? Think of the water he has got. Offer it to him!

DANCER Yes, yes, my throat is burning up; my eyes are on fire. I must have the water. (*She drags herself on hands and knees across the raft to where the Negro is sitting. He does not notice her approach. She reaches out a trembling hand and touches him on the back. He turns slowly and looks at her, his round, animal eyes dull and lusterless. She holds the necklace out in her right hand before his face and speaks hurriedly in a husky voice*) Look, you have stolen our water. You deserve to be killed. We will forget all that. Look at this necklace. It was given to me by an English duke—a nobleman. It is worth a thousand pounds —five thousand dollars. It will provide for you for the rest of your life. You need not be a sailor any more. You need never work at all any more. Do you understand what that means? (*The Negro does not answer. The* DANCER *hurries on however, her words pouring out in a sing-song jumble*) That water that you stole—well, I will give you this necklace—they are all real diamonds, you know—five thousand dollars—for that water. You need not give me all of it. I am not unreasonable. You may keep some for yourself. I would not have you die. I want just enough for myself and my friend—to keep us alive until we reach some island. My lips are cracked with heat! My head is bursting! Here, take the necklace. It is yours.

(*She tries to force it into his hand. He pushes her hand away and the necklace falls to the deck of the raft, where it lies glittering among the heat waves*)

DANCER (*Her voice raised stridently*) Give me the water! I have given you the necklace. Give me the water! (*The* GENTLEMAN, *who has been watching her with anxious eyes, also cries: "Yes. Give her the water!"*)

SAILOR (*His voice drawling and without expression*) I have no water.

DANCER Oh, you are cruel! Why do you lie? You see me suffering so and you lie to me. I have given you the necklace. It is worth five thousand dollars, do you understand? Surely for five thousand dollars you will give me a drink of water!

SAILOR I have no water, I tell you.

(*He turns his back to her. She crawls over to the* GENTLEMAN *and lies beside him, sobbing brokenly*)

GENTLEMAN (*His face convulsed with rage, shaking both fists in the air*) The pig! The pig! The black dog!

DANCER (*Sitting up and wiping her eyes*) Well, you

have heard him. He will not give it to us. Maybe he only has a little and is afraid to share it. What shall we do now? What can we do?

GENTLEMAN (*Despondently*) Nothing. He is stronger than we are. There is no wind. We will never reach an island. We can die, that is all.

(*He sinks back and buries his head in his hands. A great dry sob shakes his shoulders*)

DANCER (*Her eyes flaming with a sudden resolution*) Ah, who is the coward now? You have given up hope, it seems. Well, I have not. I have still one chance. It has never failed me yet.

GENTLEMAN (*Raising his head and looking at her in amazement*) You are going to offer him more money?

DANCER (*With a strange smile*) No. Not that. I will offer more than money. We shall get our water.

(*She tears a piece of crumpled lace off the front of her costume and carefully wipes her face with it as if she were using a powder puff*)

GENTLEMAN (*Watching her stupidly*) I do not understand.

DANCER (*She pulls up her stockings—tries to smooth the wrinkles out of her dress—then takes her long hair and, having braided it, winds it into a coil around her head. She pinches her cheeks, already crimson with sunburn. Then turning coquettishly to the* GENTLEMAN, *she says*) There! Do I not look better? How do I look?

GENTLEMAN (*Bursting into a mad guffaw*) You look terrible! You are hideous!

DANCER You lie! I am beautiful. Everyone knows I am beautiful. You yourself have said so. It is you who are hideous. You are jealous of me. I will not give you any water.

GENTLEMAN You will get no water. You are frightful. What is it you would do—dance for him? (*Mockingly*) Dance! Dance, Salome! I will be the orchestra. He will be the gallery. We will both applaud you madly.

(*He leans on one elbow and watches her, chuckling to himself*)

DANCER (*Turning from him furiously and crawling on her knees over to the* SAILOR, *calls in her most seductive voice*) Sailor! Sailor! (*He does not seem to hear—she takes his arm and shakes it gently—he turns around and stares wonderingly at her*) Listen to me, Sailor. What is your name—your first name? (*She smiles enticingly at him. He does not answer*) You will not tell me then? You are angry at me, are you not? I cannot blame you. I have called you bad names. I am sorry, very sorry. (*Indicating the* GENTLEMAN, *who has ceased to notice them and is staring at the horizon with blinking eyes*) It was he who put such ideas into my head. He does not like you. Neither did I, but I see now that you are the better of the two. I hate him! He has said dreadful things which I cannot forgive. (*Putting her hand on his shoulder she bends forward with her golden hair almost in his lap and smiles up into his face*) I like you, Sailor. You are big and strong. We are going to be great friends, are we not? (*The Negro is hardly looking at her. He is watching the sharks*) Surely you will not refuse me a little sip of your water?

SAILOR I have no water.

DANCER Oh, why will you keep up this suberfuge? Am I not offering you price enough? (*Putting her arm around his neck and half whispering in his ear*) Do you not understand? I will love you, Sailor! Noblemen and millionaires and all degrees of gentlemen have loved me, have fought for me. I have never loved any of them as I will love you. Look in my eyes, Sailor, look in my eyes! (*Compelled in spite of himself by something in her voice, the Negro gazes deep into her eyes. For a second his nostrils dilate—he draws in his breath with a hissing sound—his body grows tense and it seems as if he is about to sweep her into his arms. Then his expression grows apathetic again. He turns to the sharks*) Oh, will you never understand? Are you so stupid that you do not know what I mean? Look! I am offering myself to you! I am kneeling before you—I who always had men kneel to me! I am offering my body to you—my body that men have called so beautiful. I have promised to love *you*—a Negro sailor—if you will give me one small drink of water. Is that not humiliation enough that you must keep me waiting so? (*Raising her voice*) Answer me! Answer me! Will you give me that water?

SAILOR (*Without even turning to look at her*) I have no water.

DANCER (*Shaking with fury*) Great God, have I

abased myself for this? Have I humbled myself before this black animal only to be spurned like a wench of the streets? It is too much! You lie, you dirty slave! You have water. You have stolen my share of the water. (*In a frenzy she clutches the* SAILOR *about the throat with both hands*) Give it to me! Give it to me!

SAILOR (*Takes her hands from his neck and pushes her roughly away. She falls face downward in the middle of the raft*) Let me alone! I have no water.

GENTLEMAN (*Aroused from the stupor he has been in*) What is it? I was dreaming I was sitting before great tumblers of ice water. They were just beyond my reach. I tried and tried to get one of them. It was horrible. But what has happened here? What is the matter?

(*No one answers him. The Negro is watching the sharks again. The* DANCER *is lying in a huddled heap, moaning to herself. Suddenly she jumps to her feet. All her former weakness seems quite gone. She stands swaying a little with the roll of the raft. Her eyes have a terrible glare in them. They seem bursting out of her head. She mutters incoherently to herself. The last string has snapped. She is mad*)

DANCER (*Smoothing her dress over her hips and looking before her as if in a mirror*) Quick, Marie! You are so slow tonight. I will be late. Did you not hear the bell? I am the next on. Did he send any flowers tonight, Marie? Good, he will be in a stage box. I will smile at him, the poor old fool. He will marry me some day and I will be a duchess. Think of that, Marie—a real duchess! Yes, yes, I am coming! You need not hold the curtain.

(*She drops her head on her breast and mutters to herself. The* GENTLEMAN *has been watching her, at first in astonishment, then in a sort of crazy appreciation. When she stops talking he claps his hands*)

GENTLEMAN Go on! Go on! It is as good as a play.

(*He bursts into cackling laughter*)

DANCER They are laughing. It cannot be at me. How hot it is! How the footlights glare! I shall be glad to get away tonight. I am very thirsty. (*Passing her hand across her eyes*) There he is in the box—the poor old duke. I will wave to him. (*She waves her hand in the air*) He is kind to me. It is a pity he is so old. What song is it I am to sing? Oh yes. (*She sings the last few lines of some music hall ballad in a harsh cracked voice. The Negro turns and looks at her wonderingly. The* GENTLEMAN *claps his hands*) They are applauding. I must dance for them! (*She commences to dance on the swaying surface of the raft, half-stumbling every now and then. Her hair falls down. She is like some ghastly marionette jerked by invisible wires. She dances faster and faster. He arms and legs fly grotesquely around as if beyond control*) Oh, how hot it is! (*She grasps the front of her bodice in both hands and rips it over her shoulders. It hangs down in back. She is almost naked to the waist. Her breasts are withered and shrunken by starvation. She kicks first one foot and then the other frenziedly in the air*) Oh, it is hot! I am stifling. Bring me a drink of water! I am choking!

(*She falls back on the raft. A shudder runs over her whole body. A little crimson foam appears on her lips. Her eyes glaze. The wild stare leaves them. She is dead*)

GENTLEMAN (*Laughing insanely and clapping his hands*) Bravo! Bravo! Give us some more! (*There is no answer. A great stillness hangs over everything. The heat waves rising from the raft near the woman's body seem like her soul departing into the great unknown. A look of fear appears on the* GENTLEMAN'S *face. The Negro wears a strange expression. One might say he looks relieved, even glad, as if some perplexing problem has been solved for him*) She does not answer me. She must be sick. (*He crawls over to her*) She has fainted. (*He puts his hand on her left breast—then bends and rests his ear over her heart. His face grows livid in spite of the sunburn*) My God! She is dead! Poor girl! Poor girl!

(*He whimpers weakly to himself, mechanically running her long golden hair through his fingers with a caressing gesture. He is startled when he hears the Negro's voice*)

SAILOR Is she dead?

GENTLEMAN Yes. She is dead, poor girl. Her heart no longer beats.

SAILOR She is better off. She does not suffer now. One of us had to die. (*After a pause*) It is lucky for us she is dead.

GENTLEMAN What do you mean? What good can her death do us?

SAILOR We will live now.

(*He takes his* SAILOR'S *knife from its sheath and sharpens it on the sole of his shoe. While he is doing this he sings—a happy Negro melody that mocks the great silence*)

GENTLEMAN (*In hushed, frightened tones*) I do not understand.

SAILOR (*His swollen lips parting in a grin as he points with his knife to the body of the* DANCER) We shall eat. We shall drink.

GENTLEMAN (*For a moment struck dumb with loathing —then in tones of anguished horror*) No! No! No! Good God, not that!

(*With a swift movement he grasps the* DANCER'S *body with both hands and, making a tremendous effort, pushes it into the water. There is a swift rush of waiting fins. The sea near the raft is churned into foam. The* DANCER'S *body disappears in a swirling eddy; then all is quiet again. A black stain appears on the surface of the water.*

The SAILOR, *who has jumped forward to save the body, gives a harsh cry of disappointed rage and, knife in hand, springs on the* GENTLEMAN *and drives the knife in his breast. The* GENTLEMAN *rises to his feet with a shriek of agony. As he falls backward into the sea, one of his clutching hands fastens itself in the neck of the* SAILOR'S *jersey. The* SAILOR *tries to force the hand away, stumbles, loses his balance, and plunges headlong after him. There is a great splash. The waiting fins rush in. The water is lashed into foam. The* SAILOR'S *black head appears for a moment, his features distorted with terror, his lips torn with a howl of despair. Then he is drawn under.*

The black stain on the water widens. The fins circle no longer. The raft floats in the midst of a vast silence. The sun glares down like a great angry eye of God. The eerie heat waves float upward in the still air like the souls of the drowned. On the raft a diamond necklace lies glittering in the blazing sunshine)

Curtain

THE WEB

A Play in One Act

Characters

ROSE THOMAS
STEVE, *a "Cadet"*
TIM MORAN, *a Yeggman*
A POLICEMAN
TWO PLAIN-CLOTHES MEN

SCENE—*A squalid bedroom on the top floor of a rooming house on the Lower East Side, New York. The wallpaper is dirty and torn in places, showing the plaster beneath. There is an open window in back looking out on a fire escape on which a bottle of milk can be seen. On the right is a door leading to the hallway. On the left a washstand with a bowl and pitcher, and some meager articles of a woman's toilet set scattered on it. Above the washstand a cracked mirror hangs from a nail in the wall. In the middle of the room stand a rickety table and a chair. In the left-hand corner near the window is a bed in which a baby is lying asleep. A gas jet near the mirror furnishes the only light.*

ROSE THOMAS, *a dark-haired young woman looking thirty but really only twenty-two, is discovered sitting on the chair smoking a cheap Virginia cigarette. An empty beer bottle and a dirty glass stand on the table beside her. Her hat, a gaudy cheap affair with a scraggy imitation plume, is also on the table.* ROSE *is dressed in the tawdry extreme of fashion. She has earrings in her ears, bracelets on both wrists, and a quantity of rings—none of them genuine. Her face is that of a person in an advanced stage of consumption—deathly pale with hollows under the eyes, which are wild and feverish. Her attitude is one of the deepest dejection. When she glances over at the bed, however, her expression grows tenderly maternal. From time to time she coughs—a harsh, hacking cough that shakes her whole body. After these spells she raises her handkerchief to her lips, then glances at it fearfully.*

The time is in the early hours of a rainy summer night. The monotonous sound of the rain falling on the flags of the court below is heard.

ROSE (*Listening to the rain—throws the cigarette wearily on the table*) Gawd! What a night! (*Laughing bitterly*) What a chance I got! (*She has a sudden fit of coughing; then gets up and goes over to the bed and bending down gently kisses the sleeping child on the forehead. She turns away with a sob and murmurs*) What a life! Poor kid!

(*She goes over to the mirror and makes up her eyes and cheeks. The effect is ghastly. Her blackened eyes look enormous and the dabs of rouge on each cheek serve to heighten her aspect of feverish illness. Just as she has completed her toilet and is putting on her hat in front of the mirror, the door is flung open and* STEVE *lurches in and bolts the door after him. He has very evidently been drinking. In appearance he is a typical "cadet," flashily dressed, rat-eyed, weak of mouth, undersized, and showing on his face the effects of drink and drugs*)

ROSE (*Hurriedly putting her hat down on the washstand—half frightened*) Hello, Steve.

STEVE (*Looking her up and down with a sneer*) Yuh're a fine-lookin' mess! (*He walks over and sits down *in the chair*) Yuh look like a dead one. Put on some paint and cheer up! Yuh give me the willies standin' there like a ghost.

ROSE (*Rushes over to the mirror and plasters on more rouge—then turns around*) Look, Steve! Ain't that better?

STEVE Better? Naw, but it'll do. (*Seeing the empty beer bottle*) Gimme a drink!

ROSE Yuh know there ain't any. That's the bottle yuh brought up last night.

STEVE (*With peevish anger*) Yuh lie! I'll bet yuh got some burried around here some place. Yuh're always holdin' out on me and yuh got to quit it, see?

ROSE I never hold out on yuh and yuh know it. That's all the thanks I get. (*Angrily*) What'ud yuh do if I was like Bessie with your friend Jack? Then yuh might have some chance to kick. She's got enough salted to leave him any time she wants to—and he knows it and sticks to her like glue. Yuh don't notice him runnin' after every doll he sees like some guys I know. He's afraid of losin' her—while *you* don't care.

STEVE (*Flattered—in a conciliating tone*) Aw, shut up! Yuh make me sick with dat line of bull. Who said I was chasin' any dolls? (*Then venomously*) I'm not so sure Jack is wise to Bessie holdin' out on him; but I'll tell him, and if he isn't wise to it, Bessie'll be in for a good beatin'.

ROSE Aw, don't do that! What'cha got against her? She ain't done nothin' to you, has she?

STEVE Naw; but she oughta be learned a lesson, dat's all. She oughta be on the level with him. Us guys has got to stand together. What'ud we do if all youse dolls got holdin' out on the side?

ROSE (*Dejectedly*) Don't ask me. I dunno. It's a bum game all round.

(*She has a fit of horrible coughing*)

STEVE (*His nerves shattered*) Dammit! Stop that barkin'. It goes right trou me. Git some medicine for it, why don't yuh?

ROSE (*Wiping her lips with her handkerchief*) I did but it ain't no good.

STEVE Then git somethin' else. I told yuh months ago to go and see a doctor. Did yuh?

ROSE (*Nervously, after a pause*) No.

STEVE Well den, yuh can't blame me. It's up to you.

ROSE (*Speaking eagerly and beseechingly, almost in tears*) Listen, Steve! Let me stay in tonight and go to the doc's. I'm sick. (*Pointing to her breast*) I got pains here and it seems as if I was on fire inside. Sometimes I git dizzy and everythin' goes round and round. Anyway, it's rainin' and my shoes are full of holes. There won't be no one out tonight, and even if there was they're all afraid of me on account of this cough. Gimme a couple of dollars and let me go to the doc's and git some medicine. Please, Steve, for Gawd's sake! I'll make it up to yuh when I'm well. I'll be makin' lots of coin then and yuh kin have it all. (*Goes off into a paroxysm of coughing*) I'm so sick!

STEVE (*In indignant amazement*) A couple of beans! What'd yuh think I am—the mint?

ROSE But yuh had lots of coin this mornin'. Didn't I give yuh all I had?

STEVE (*Sullenly*) Well, I ain't got it now, see? I got into a game at Tony's place and they cleaned me. I ain't got a nick. (*With sudden anger*) And I wouldn't give it to yuh if I had it. D'yuh think I'm a simp to be gittin' yuh protection and keepin' the bulls from runnin' yuh in when all yuh do is to stick at home and play dead? If yuh want any coin git out and make it. That's all I got to say.

ROSE (*Furiously*) So that's all yuh got to say, is it? Well, I'll hand yuh a tip right here. I'm gittin' sick of givin' yuh my roll and gittin' nothin' but abuse in retoin. Yuh're half drunk now. And yuh been hittin' the pipe too; I kin tell by the way your eyes look. D'yuh think I'm goin' to stand for a guy that's always full of booze and hop? Not so yuh could notice it! There's too many others I kin get.

STEVE (*His eyes narrow and his voice becomes loud and threatening*) Can that chatter, d'yuh hear me? If yuh ever t'row me down—look out! I'll get yuh!

ROSE (*In a frenzy*) Get me? Wha'd I care? D'yuh think I'm so stuck on this life I wanta go on livin'? Kill me! Wha'd I care?

STEVE (*Jumps up from the table and raises his hand as if to strike her. He shouts*) Fur Chris' sake, shut up!

(*The baby, awakened by the loud voices, commences to cry*)

ROSE (*Her anger gone in a flash*) Sssshhh! There, we woke her up. Keep still, Steve. I'll go out, yuh needn't worry. Jest don't make so much noise, that's all.

(*She goes over to the bed and cuddles the child. It*

soon falls asleep again. She begins to cough, and rising to her feet walks away from the bed keeping her face turned away from the baby)

STEVE (*Who has been watching her with a malignant sneer*) Yuh'll have to take that kid out of the bed. I gotta git some sleep.

ROSE But, Steve, where'll I put her? There's no place else.

STEVE On the floor—any place. Wha'd I care where yuh put it?

ROSE (*Supplicatingly*) Aw please, Steve! Be a good guy! She won't bother yuh none. She's fast asleep. Yuh got three-quarters of the bed to lie on. Let her stay there.

STEVE Nix! Yuh heard what I said, didn't yuh? Git busy, then. Git her out of there.

ROSE (*With cold fury*) I won't do it.

STEVE Yuh won't, eh? Den I will.

(*He makes a move toward the bed*)

ROSE (*Standing between him and the bed in a resolute attitude, speaks slowly and threateningly*) I've stood about enough from you. Don't yuh dare touch her or I'll—

STEVE (*Blusteringly, a bit shaken in his coward soul however*) What'll yuh do? Don't try and bluff me. And now we're talkin' about it I wanta tell yuh that kid has got to go. I've stood fur it as long as I kin with its bawlin' and whinin'. Yuh gotta git rid of it, that's all. Give it to some orphan asylum. They'll take good care of it. I know what I'm talkin' about cause I was brung up in one myself. (*With a sneer*) What'd *you* want with a kid? (ROSE *winces*) A fine mother *you* are and dis is a swell dump to bring up a family in.

ROSE Please, Steve, for the love of Gawd lemme keep her! She's all I got to live for. If yuh take her away I'll die. I'll kill myself.

STEVE (*Contemptuously*) Dat's what they all say. But she's got to go. All yuh do now is fuss over dat kid, comin' home every ten minutes to see if it's hungry or somethin'! Dat's why we're broke all the time. I've stood fur it long enough.

ROSE (*On her knees—weeping*) Please, Steve, for Gawd's sake lemme keep her!

STEVE (*Coldly*) Stop dat blubberin'. It won't do no good. I give yuh a week. If yuh don't git dat brat outa here in a week, den I will.

ROSE What'd'yuh mean? What'll yuh do?

STEVE I'll have yuh pinched and sent to the Island. The kid'll be took away from yuh then.

ROSE (*In anguish*) Yuh're jest tryin' to scare me, ain't yuh, Steve? They wouldn't do that, would they?

STEVE Yuh'll soon know whether dey would or not.

ROSE But yuh wouldn't have me pinched, would yuh, Steve? Yuh wouldn't do me dirt like that?

STEVE I wouldn't, wouldn't I? Yuh jest wait and see!

ROSE Aw, Steve, I always been good to *you*.

STEVE Git dat kid outa here or I'll put yuh in the cooler as sure as hell!

ROSE (*Maddened, rushing at him with outstretched hands*) Yuh dirty dog!

(*There is a struggle during which the table is overturned. Finally* STEVE *frees himself and hits her in the face with his fist, knocking her down. At the same instant the door from the hallway is forced open and* TIM MORAN *pushes his way in. He is short and thick-set, with a bullet head, close-cropped black hair, a bull neck, and small blue eyes close together. Although distinctly a criminal type his face is in part redeemed by its look of manliness. He is dressed in dark ill-fitting clothes, and has an automatic revolver in his hand which he keeps pointed at* STEVE)

TIM (*Pointing to the door, speaks to* STEVE *with cold contempt*) Git outa here, yuh lousy skunk, and stay out! (*As* STEVE'*s hand goes to his hip*) Take yer hand away from that gat or I'll fill yuh full of holes. (STEVE *is cowed and obeys*) Now git out and don't come back. If you bother this goil again I'll fix yuh and fix yuh right. D'yuh get me?

STEVE (*Snarling, and slinking toward door*) Yuh think yuh're some smart, dontcha, buttin' in dis way on a guy? It ain't none of your business. She's my goil.

TIM D'yuh think I'm goin' to stand by and let yuh beat her up jest cause she wants to keep her kid? D'yuh think I'm as low as you are, yuh dirty mutt? Git outa here before I croak yuh.

STEVE (*Standing in the doorway and looking back*) Yuh got the drop on me now; but I'll get yuh, yuh wait and see! (*To* ROSE) And *you* too.

(*He goes out and can be heard descending the stairs.* ROSE *hurries over to the door and tries to lock it, but the lock is shattered, so she puts the chair against it to keep it shut. She then goes over to the baby, who has been whimpering unnoticed during the quarrel, and soothes her to sleep again.* TIM, *looking embarrassed, puts the revolver back in his pocket, and picking up the table sets it to rights again and sits on the edge of it.* ROSE *looks up at him from the bed, half bewildered at seeing him still there. Then she breaks into convulsive sobbing*)

TIM (*Making a clumsy attempt at consolation*) There, there, Kid, cut the cryin'. He won't bother yuh no more. I know his kind. He's got a streak of yellow a yard wide, and beatin' up women is all he's game for. But he won't hurt *you* no more—not if I know it.

ROSE Yuh don't know him. When he's full of booze and hop he's liable to do anythin'. I don't care what he does to me. I might as well be dead anyway. But there's the kid. I got to look after her. And (*Looking at him gratefully*) I don't want you to git in no mixups on account of me. I ain't worth it.

TIM (*Quickly*) Nix on that stuff about your not bein' worth it!

ROSE (*Smiling*) Thanks. And I'm mighty glad yuh came in when yuh did. Gawd knows what he'd'a done to the kid and me not able to stop him.

TIM Don't yuh worry about my gettin' into no mix-ups. I c'n take care of myself.

ROSE How did yuh happen to blow in when yuh did? There usually ain't no one around in this dump at this time of the night.

TIM I got the room next to yuh. I heard every word the both of yuh said—tonight and every other night since I come here a week ago. I know the way he's treated yuh. I'd'a butted in sooner only I didn't want to mix in other people's business. But tonight when he started in about the kid there I couldn't stand fur it no longer. I was jest wantin' to hand him a call and I let him have it. Why d'yuh stand fur him anyway? Why don't yuh take the kid and beat it away from him?

ROSE (*Despondently*) It's easy to say: "Why don't I beat it?" I can't.

TIM Wha'd'yuh mean? Why can't yuh?

ROSE I never have enough coin to make a good break and git out of town. He takes it all away from me. And if I went to some other part of this burg he'd find me and kill me. Even if he didn't kill me he'd have me pinched and where'ud the kid be then? (*Grimly*) Oh, he's got me where he wants me all right, all right.

TIM I don't get yuh. How could he have yuh pinched if yuh ain't done nothin'?

ROSE Oh, he's got a drag somewhere. He squares it with the cops so they don't hold me up for walkin' the streets. Yuh ought to be wise enough to know all of his kind stand in. If he tipped them off to do it they'd pinch me before I'd gone a block. Then it'ud be the Island fur mine.

TIM Then why don't yuh cut this life and be on the level? Why don't yuh git a job some place? He couldn't touch yuh then.

ROSE (*Scornfully*) Oh, couldn't he? D'yuh suppose they'd keep me any place if they knew what I was? And d'yuh suppose he wouldn't tell them or have someone else tell them? Yuh don't know the game I'm up against. (*Bitterly*) I've tried that job thing. I've looked fur decent work and I've starved at it. A year after I first hit this town I quit and tried to be on the level. I got a job at housework—workin' twelve hours a day for twenty-five dollars a month. And I worked like a dog, too, and never left the house I was so scared of seein' someone who knew me. But what was the use? One night they have a guy to dinner who's seen me some place when I was on the town. He tells the lady—his duty he said it was—and she fires me right off the reel. I tried the same thing a lot of times. But there was always someone who'd drag me back. And then I quit tryin'. There didn't seem to be no use. They—all the good people—they got me where I am and they're goin' to keep me there. Reform? Take it from me it can't be done. They won't let yuh do it, and that's Gawd's truth.

TIM Give it another trial anyway. Yuh never know your luck. Yuh might be able to stick this time.

ROSE (*Wearily*) Talk is cheap. Yuh don't know what yuh're talkin' about. What job c'n I git? What am I fit fur? Housework is the only thing I know about and I don't know much about that. Where else could I make enough to live on? That's the trouble with all us girls. Most all of us ud like to come back but we jest can't and that's all there's to it. We can't work out of this life because we don't know how to work. We was never taught how. (*She shakes with a horrible fit of coughing, wipes her lips, and smiles pitifully*) Who d'yuh think would take a chance on hiring me the way I look and with this cough? Besides, there's the kid. (*Sarcastically*) Yuh may not know it but people ain't strong for hirin' girls with babies—especially when the girls ain't married.

TIM But yuh could send the kid away some place.

ROSE (*Fiercely*) No. She's all I got. I won't give her up.

(*She coughs again*)

TIM (*Kindly*) That's a bad cough yuh got, Kid. I heard yuh tellin' him tonight yuh hadn't seen a doctor. (*Putting a hand in his pocket*) I'll stake yuh and yuh c'n run around and see one now.

ROSE Thanks jest the same but it ain't no use. I lied to Steve. I went to a doc about a month ago. He told me I had the "con" and had it bad. (*With grim humor*) He said the only hope fur me was to git out in the country, sleep in the open air, and eat a lot of good food. He might jest as well 'uv told me to go to Heaven and I told him so. Then he said I could go out to some dump where yuh don't have to pay nothin', but he said I'd have to leave the kid behind. I told him I'd rather die than do that, and he said I'd have to be careful or the kid 'ud catch it from me. And I have been careful. (*She sobs*) I don't even kiss her on the mouth no more.

TIM Yuh sure are up against it, Kid. (*He appears deeply moved*) Gee, I thought I was in bad, but yuh got me skinned to death.

ROSE (*Interested*) You in bad? Yuh don't look it.

TIM Listen! Yuh talk about tryin' to be good and not bein' able to— Well, I been up against the same thing. When I was a kid I was sent to the reform school fur stealin'; and it wasn't my fault. I was mixed up with a gang older than me and wasn't wise to what I was doin'. They made me the goat; and in the reform school they made a crook outa me. When I come out I tried to be straight and hold down a job, but as soon as anyone got wise I'd been in a reform school they canned me same as they did you. Then I stole again—to keep from starvin'. They got me and this time I went to the coop fur five years. Then I give up. I seen it was no use. When I got out again I got in with a gang of yeggmen and learned how to be a yegg—and I've been one ever since. I've spent most of my life in jail but I'm free now.

ROSE What are yuh goin' to do?

TIM (*Fiercely*) What am I goin' to do? They made a yegg outa me! Let 'em look out!

ROSE When did yuh get out?

TIM (*Suspiciously*) What's it to you? (*Then suddenly*) Nix, I didn't mean that. Yuh're a good kid and maybe yuh c'n help me.

ROSE I'd sure like to.

TIM Then listen! (*Looking at her fixedly*) Yuh swear yuh won't squeal on me?

ROSE I won't, so help me Gawd!

TIM Well, I'm Tim Moran. I jest broke out two weeks ago.

ROSE (*Staring at him with a fascinated wonder*) You! Tim Moran! The guy that robbed that bank a week ago! The guy they're all lookin' fur!

TIM Sssshhh! Yuh never c'n tell who's got an ear glued to the wall in a dump like this.

ROSE (*Lowering her voice*) I read about yuh in the papers.

(*She looks at him as if she were half afraid*)

TIM Yuh're not afraid of me, are yuh? I ain't the kind of crook Steve is, yuh know.

ROSE (*Calmly*) No, I ain't afraid of yuh, Tim; but I'm afraid they may find yuh here and take yuh away again. (*Anxiously*) D'yuh think Steve knew yuh? He'd squeal sure if he did—to git the reward.

TIM No, I could tell by his eyes he didn't know me.

ROSE How long have yuh been here?

TIM A week—ever since I cracked that safe. I wanted to give the noise time to blow over. I ain't left that room except when I had to git a bite to eat, and then I got enough fur a couple of days. But when I come in tonight I seen a guy on the corner give me a long look. He looked bad to me and I wanta git out of here before they git wise.

ROSE Yuh think he was a cop?

TIM Yes, I got a hunch. He looked bad to me.

ROSE (*Wonderingly*) And yuh come in here tonight knowin' he was liable to spot yuh! Yuh took that chance fur me when yuh didn't even know me! (*Impulsively going over to him and taking his hand, which he tries to hold back*) Gee, yuh're a regular guy, all right.

TIM (*In great confusion*) Aw, that's nothin'. Anyone would'a done it.

ROSE No one would'a done it in your place. (*A slight noise is heard from the hallway.* ROSE *looks around startled and speaks hurriedly almost in a whisper*) Supposin' that guy was a cop? Supposin' he had a hunch who you was? How're yuh goin' to make a getaway? Can't I help yuh outa this? Can't I do somethin' fur yuh?

TIM (*Points to the window*) That's a fire escape, ain't it?

ROSE Yes.

TIM Where does it lead to?

ROSE Down to the yard and up to the roof.

TIM To hell with the yard. I'll try the roofs if it comes to a showdown. I'll stick in here with you so's if they come I c'n make a quick getaway. Yuh tell 'em yuh don't know anything about me, see? Give 'em a bum steer if you kin. Try and hold 'em so's I c'n get a good start.

ROSE (*Resolutely*) I'll hold 'em as long as I c'n, don't worry. I'll tell 'em I seen yuh goin' downstairs an hour ago.

TIM Good Kid!

(*They are standing in the middle of the room with their backs to the window.* STEVE'S *face appears peering around the edge of the window frame. He is crouched on the fire escape outside. His eyes glare with hatred as he watches the two persons in the room.* ROSE *starts to cough, is frightened by the noise she makes, and holds her handkerchief over her mouth to stifle the sound*)

TIM Ssssshhh! Poor Kid! (*He turns to her and speaks rapidly in low tones*) Here, Kid. (*He takes a large roll of money out of his pocket and forces it into her hand—as she starts to remonstrate*) Shut up! I ain't got time to listen to your beefin'. Take it. It ain't much but it's all I got with me. I don't need it. There's plenty more waitin' fur me outside. This'll be enough to git you and the kid out of town away from that dirty coward. (STEVE'S *face is convulsed with fury*) Go some place out in the mountains and git rid of that cough.

ROSE (*Sobbing*) I can't take it. Yuh been too good to me already. Yuh don't know how rotten I am.

TIM (*Suddenly taking her in his arms and kissing her roughly*) That's how rotten I think yuh are. Yuh're the whitest kid I've ever met, see?

(*They look into each other's eyes. All the hardness of* ROSE'S *expression has vanished. Her face is soft, transfigured by a new emotion.* STEVE *moves his hand into the room. He holds a revolver which he tries to aim at* TIM *but he is afraid to fire*)

ROSE (*Throwing her arms around his neck*) Tim, Tim, yuh been too good to me.

TIM (*Kissing her again*) Lemme know where yuh are and when it's safe I'll come to yuh. (*He releases her and takes a small folded paper from pocket*) This'll find me. (*She takes it, her eyes full of happy tears*) Maybe after a time we c'n start over again—together! (*A sound like the creaking of a floor board is heard from the hallway*) What's that? (*They both stand looking fixedly at the door.* STEVE *noiselessly disappears from the window*) Gee, Kid, I got a feelin' in my bones they're after me. It's only a hunch but it's never gone wrong yet. (*He pulls a cap out of his pocket and puts it on*) I'm goin' to blow.

ROSE (*Goes over to the door and listens*) Sounds as if somebody was sneakin' up the stairs. (*She tiptoes quickly over to him and kisses him*) Go, go while yuh got a chance. Don't let 'em git yuh? I love yuh, Tim.

TIM Good-bye, Kid. I'll come as soon as I c'n.

(*He kisses her again and goes quickly to the window.* STEVE *stretches his hand around the side of the window and fires, the muzzle of the gun almost on* TIM'S *chest. There is a loud report and a little smoke.* TIM *staggers back and falls on the floor.* STEVE *throws the gun into the room, then quietly pulls down the window and disappears. The child in the bed wakes up and cries feebly*)

ROSE (*Rushes to* TIM *and kneels beside him, holding his head on her breast*) Tim! Tim! Speak to me, Tim!

(*She kisses him frantically*)

TIM (*His eyes glazing*) Good Kid—mountains—git rid of that cough.

(*He dies*)

ROSE (*Letting his head fall back on the floor, she sinks to a sitting position beside him. The money is still clutched in her right hand. She stares straight before her and repeats in tones of horrible monotony*) Dead. Oh Gawd, Gawd, Gawd!

(*The sound of people running up the stairs in the hall is heard. A voice shouts: "Must be in here." The door is pushed open and three men enter. One is a* POLICEMAN *in uniform and the other two are evidently* PLAIN-CLOTHES MEN. *The landlady and several roomers stand in the doorway looking in with frightened faces*)

POLICEMAN (*Goes to* ROSE *and, taking her arm, hauls her to her feet*) Come, get up outa that!

(*The two* PLAIN-CLOTHES MEN *take one look at the dead man and both exclaim together: "Tim Moran!"*)

FIRST PLAIN-CLOTHES MAN I told yuh it was him I seen comin' in here tonight. I never forget a face.

SECOND PLAIN-CLOTHES MAN (*Picking the revolver off the floor and examining it*) I didn't think he'd be fool enough to stick around here. (*Turning suddenly to* ROSE) What did yuh croak him for? (*Ironically*) A little love spat, eh? (*He sees the roll of money in her hand and grabs her quickly by the wrist*) Pipe the roll! Little sister here attends to business, all right. Gave him a frisk before we had a chance to get here. (*To* ROSE *in loud, rough tones*) Why did yuh kill him? It was for this coin, wasn't it?

(*During the detective's remarks* ROSE *gradually realizes the position she is in. Her expression becomes one of amazed pain as she sees they think she is guilty of the murder. She speaks brokenly, trying to hold herself in control*)

ROSE Honest to Gawd, I didn't do it. He gave me this money. Someone shot him from the window. (*Then quite simply, as if that explained it all away*) Why, I loved him.

SECOND PLAIN-CLOTHES MAN Stop that noise! Wha'd'-yuh take us for—boobs? The window ain't even open and the glass ain't broken. He gave yuh the money, eh? And then shot himself, I suppose? Aw say, Kid, wha'd'yuh take us for?

ROSE (*Losing all control, frenziedly breaks from the* POLICEMAN'S *grasp and throws herself beside the body*) Tim! Tim! For the love of Gawd speak to them. Tell 'em I didn't do it, Tim! Tell 'em yuh gave that money to me. Yuh know what yuh said —"Take the kid into the mountains and git rid of that cough." Tell 'em yuh said that, Tim! Speak to 'em! Tell 'em I loved yuh, Tim—that I wanted to help yuh git away. Tell 'em yuh kissed me. They think I shot yuh. They don't know I loved yuh. For the love of Gawd speak to 'em. (*Weeping and sobbing bitterly*) Oh Gawd, why don't yuh speak, why don't yuh speak?

FIRST PLAIN-CLOTHES MAN (*Sneeringly*) That's good stuff but it won't get yuh anything. (*Turning to his two companions*) Looks to me as if this doll was full of coke or something. You two better take her to the station and make a report. I'll stay here and keep cases on the room. I'm sick of listenin' to that sob stuff.

ROSE (*The* POLICEMAN *taps her on the shoulder and she rises to her feet with a spring, wildly protesting*) But I tell yuh I didn't do it! It was from the window. Can't yuh believe me? I swear I—

(*She stops, appalled by the unbelieving sneers of the policemen, by the white faces in the doorway gazing at her with fascinated horror. She reads her own guilt in every eye. She realizes the futility of all protest, the maddening hopelessness of it all. The child is still crying. She notices it for the first time and goes over to the bed to soothe it. The* POLICEMAN *keeps a tight hold of one of her arms. She speaks words of tenderness to the child in dull, mechanical tones. It stops crying. All are looking at her in silence with a trace of compassionate pity on their faces.* ROSE *seems in a trance. Her eyes are like the eyes of a blind woman. She seems to be aware of something in the room which none of the others can see—perhaps the personification of the ironic life force that has crushed her*)

FIRST PLAIN-CLOTHES MAN Your kid?

ROSE (*To the unseen presence in the room*) Yes. I suppose yuh'll take her too?

FIRST PLAIN-CLOTHES MAN (*Misunderstanding her, good-naturedly*) I'll take care of her for the time bein'.

ROSE (*To the air*) That's right. Make a good job of me. (*Suddenly she stretches both arms above her head and cries bitterly, mournfully, out of the depths of her desolation*) Gawd! Gawd! Why d'yuh hate me so?

POLICEMAN (*Shocked*) Here, here, no rough talk like that. Come along now!

(ROSE *leans against him weakly and he supports her to the door, where the group of horrified lodgers silently make way for them. The* SECOND PLAIN-CLOTHES MAN *follows them. A moment later* ROSE'S *hollow cough echoes in the dark hallway. The child wakes up and cries fitfully. The* FIRST PLAIN-CLOTHES MAN *goes over to the bed and cuddles her on his lap with elephantine playfulness*)

CHILD (*Feebly*) Maamaaaa!

FIRST PLAIN-CLOTHES MAN Mama's gone. I'm your mama now.

Curtain

WARNINGS

A Play in One Act

Characters

JAMES KNAPP, *wireless operator of the "S.S. Empress"*
MARY KNAPP, *his wife*
CHARLES, *aged fifteen* — *their children*
DOLLY, *aged fourteen* — *their children*
LIZZIE, *aged eleven* — *their children*
SUE, *aged eight* — *their children*
A BABY, *aged one year* — *their children*
CAPTAIN HARDWICK *of the "Empress"*
MASON, *First Officer of the "Empress"*
DICK WHITNEY, *wireless operator of the "S.S. Duchess" of the same line*

SCENE I

The dining room of JAMES KNAPP'S *flat in the Bronx. To the left is a door opening into the main hall; farther back a chair, and then a heavy green curtain which screens off an alcove probably used as a bedroom. To the right, a doorway leading into the kitchen, another chair, and a window, with some plants in pots on the sill, which opens on a court. Hanging in front of the window is a gilt cage in which a canary chirps sleepily. The walls of the room are papered an impossible green and the floor is covered with a worn carpet of nearly the same color. Several gaudy Sunday-supplement pictures in cheap gilt frames are hung at spaced intervals around the walls. The dining table with its flowered cover is pushed back against the middle wall to allow more space for free passage between the kitchen and the front part of the flat. On the wall above the table is a mantelpiece on the middle of which a black marble clock ticks mournfully. The clock is flanked on both sides by a formidable display of family photographs. Above the mantel hangs a "Home Sweet Home" motto in a black frame. A lamp of the Welsbach type, fixed on the chandelier which hangs from the middle of the ceiling, floods the small room with bright light. It is about half-past eight of an October evening. The time is the present.*

MRS. KNAPP *is discovered sitting at the end of the table near the kitchen. She is a pale, thin, peevish-looking woman of about forty, made prematurely old by the thousand worries of a penny-pinching existence. Her originally fine constitution has been broken down by the bearing of many children in conditions under which every new arrival meant a new mouth crying for its share of the already inadequate supply of life's necessities. Her brown hair, thickly streaked with gray, is drawn back tightly over her ears into a knot at the back of her head. Her thin-lipped mouth droops sorrowfully at the corners, and her faded blue eyes have an expression of fretful weariness. She wears a solid gray wrapper and black carpet slippers. When she speaks, her voice is plaintively querulous and without authority.*

Two of the children, LIZZIE *and* SUE, *are seated on her left facing the family photos. They are both bent over the table with curly blond heads close together. Under* LIZZIE'S *guidance* SUE *is attempting to write something on the pad before her. Both are dressed in clean-looking dark clothes with black shoes and stockings.*

LIZZIE That's not the way to make a "g." Give *me* the pencil and *I'll* show you.

(*She tries to take the pencil away from* SUE)

SUE (*Resisting and commencing to cry*) I don' wanta give you the pencil. Mama-a! Make her stop!

MRS. KNAPP (*Wearily*) For goodness' sake stop that racket, Sue! Give her the pencil, Lizzie! You ought to be ashamed to fight with your little sister—and you so much older than her. I declare, a body can't have a moment's peace in this house with you children all the time wranglin' and fightin'.

SUE (*Bawling louder than ever*) Mama-a! She won't give it to me!

MRS. KNAPP (*With an attempt at firmness*) Lizzie! Did you hear what I said? Give her that pencil this instant!

LIZZIE (*Not impressed*) I wanta show her how to make a "g" and she won't let me. Make her stop, Mama!

SUE (*Screaming*) I did make a "g"! I did make a "g"!

LIZZIE Ooo! Listen to her tellin' lies, Mama. She didn't make a "g" at all. She don't know how.

SUE I do! Gimme that pencil.

LIZZIE You don't. I won't give it to you.

MRS. KNAPP (*Aggravated into action, she gets quickly from her chair and gives* LIZZIE *a ringing box on the ear*) There, you naughty child! That will teach you to do what I say. Give me that pencil. (*She snatches it from* LIZZIE'*s hand and gives it to* SUE) There's the pencil! For goodness sake hush up your cryin'!

(SUE *subsides into sobbing but* LIZZIE *puts her hand over the smarting ear and starts to howl with all her might*)

SUE (*Whimpering again as she discovers the point of the pencil has been broken off*) Look Mama! She broke the pencil!

MRS. KNAPP (*Distracted*) Be still and I'll sharpen it for you. (*Turning to* LIZZIE *and taking her on her lap*) There! There! Stop cryin'! Mama didn't mean to hurt you. (LIZZIE *only cries the harder*) Stop crying and I'll give you a piece of candy. (LIZZIE'*s anguish vanishes in a flash*) Kiss Mama now and promise not to be naughty any more!

LIZZIE (*Kissing her obediently*) I promise. Where's the candy, Mama?

SUE (*No longer interested in pencils*) I wanta piece of candy too.

MRS. KNAPP (*Goes to the kitchen and returns with two sticky chunks of molasses candy*) Here, Lizzie! Here, Sue! (SUE *manages with some effort to cram the candy into her small mouth*) Neither one of you said "thank you" (LIZZIE *dutifully mumbles "Thanks" but* SUE *is beyond speech*) I declare I don't know what I'll do with you children. You never seem to learn manners. It's just as if you were brought up on the streets—the way you act. (*The clock strikes eight-thirty and* MRS. KNAPP *looks at it gratefully*) There, children. It's half-past eight and you must both go to bed right away. Goodness knows I have a hard enough time gettin' you up for school in the morning.

SUE (*Having eaten enough of her candy to allow of her voicing a protest*) I don' wanta go to bed.

LIZZIE (*Sulking*) You said you'd let us stay up to see Papa.

SUE I wanta see Papa.

MRS. KNAPP That will do. I won't listen to any more of your talk. You've seen your father all afternoon. That's only an excuse to stay up late. He went to the doctor's and goodness knows when he'll be back. I promised to let you sit up till half-past eight and it's that now. Come now! Kiss me like two good little girls and go straight to bed.

(*The two good little girls perform their kissing with an ill grace and depart slowly for bed through the alcove*)

MRS. KNAPP Mind you don't wake the baby with your carryings-on or I'll tell your father to spank you good. (*She has an afterthought*) And don't forget your prayers!

(*She sinks back with a deep sigh of relief and, taking up an evening paper from the table, commences to read. She has hardly settled back comfortably when shouts and the noise of running steps are heard from the stairs in the hallway. Then a rattling tattoo of knocks shakes the door and a girl's voice laughingly shouts through the key hole: "Open up, Ma!"*)

MRS. KNAPP (*Going quickly to the door and unlocking*

it) Hush up your noise for goodness sakes! Do you want to wake up the baby? I never saw such children. You haven't any feelin' for your mother at all.

(CHARLES *and* DOLLY *push hurriedly into the room.* MRS. KNAPP *locks the door again and resumes her seat at the table.* CHARLES *is a gawky, skinny youth of fifteen who has outgrown his clothes and whose arms and legs seem to have outgrown him. His features are large and irregular; his eyes small and watery-blue in color. When he takes off his cap a mop of sandy hair falls over his forehead. He is dressed in a shabby gray Norfolk suit.*

Although extremely thin, DOLLY *is rather pretty with her dark eyes and her brown curls hanging over her shoulders. She is dressed neatly in a dark blue frock with black shoes and stockings and a black felt hat. Her ordinarily sallow city complexion is flushed from the run upstairs*)

DOLLY (*Rushing over and kissing her mother—mischievously*) What do you think I saw, Ma?

CHARLIE (*In a loud voice—almost a shout*) What do you think *I* saw, Mom?

MRS. KNAPP For heaven's sake, Charlie, speak lower. Do you want the people in the next block to hear you? If you wake up the baby I shall certainly tell your father on you. Take off your hat when you're in the house! Whatever is the matter with you? Can't you remember anything? I'm really ashamed of you—the way you act.

CHARLIE (*Taking off his cap*) Aw, what's the matter, Mom? Gee, you've got an awful grouch on tonight.

MRS. KNAPP Never mind talkin' back to your mother, young man. Why shouldn't I be cranky with you bellowin' around here like a young bull? I just got the baby to sleep and if you wake her up with your noise heaven knows when I'll get any peace again.

DOLLY (*Interrupting her—with a laughing glance at* CHARLIE) You can't guess what I saw, Ma.

CHARLIE (*Sheepishly*) Aw, all right for you. Go ahead and tell her if you wanta. I don't care. I'll tell her what I saw too.

DOLLY You didn't see anything.

CHARLIE I did too.

DOLLY You didn't.

MRS. KNAPP For goodness sake stop your quarrelin'! First it's Lizzie and Sue and then it's you two. I never get time to even read a paper. What was it you saw, Dolly? Tell me if you're going to.

DOLLY—I saw Charlie and that red-headed Harris girl in the corner drug store. He was buying her ice cream soda with that quarter Pop gave him.

CHARLIE I was no such thing.

DOLLY Oh, what a lie! You know you were.

MRS. KNAPP You ought to be ashamed of yourself, you big gump, you, goin' round with girls at your age and spendin' money on them. I'll tell your father how you spend the money he gives you and it'll be a long time before you get another cent.

CHARLIE (*Sullenly*) Aw, you needn't think I'm the only one. (*Pointing to* DOLLY) I saw her down in the hallway with that Dutch kid whose father runs the saloon in the next block. It was dark down there too. I could hardly see them. And he's cross-eyed!

DOLLY He is not.

CHARLIE Aw, g'wan, of course he is. He can't see straight or he'd never look at you.

DOLLY He's better than you are.

CHARLIE (*Losing control of his voice and shouting again*) I'll hand him a punch in the eye the first time I see him. That's what I'll do to him, the Dutch boob. And I'll slap you in the nose too if you get too fresh.

(DOLLY *starts to cry*)

MRS. KNAPP (*Rising up swiftly and giving him a crack over the ear with her open hand*) That'll teach you, young man! Don't you dare to lay a hand on your sister or your father will whip you good.

CHARLIE (*Backing away with his hand on his ear—in a whimper*) Aw, what are you always pickin' on me for? Why don't you say something to her?

MRS. KNAPP (*Turning to the still tearful* DOLLY) And you, miss! Don't you let me hear of you bein' in any dark hallways with young men again or I'll take you over my knee, so I will. The idea of such a thing! I can't understand you at all. I never was allowed out alone with anyone—not even with your father, before I was engaged to be married to him. I don't know what's come over you young folks nowadays.

DOLLY It—wasn't—dark.

MRS. KNAPP It makes no difference. You heard what I said. Don't let it happen again.

(DOLLY *wipes her eyes and makes a face at* CHARLIE)

CHARLIE (*His tones loud with triumph*) It was awful dark. She's lyin' to you, Mom.

MRS. KNAPP Hold your tongue! I've heard enough from you. And don't yell at the top of your voice. You don't have to shout. I'm not deaf.

CHARLIE (*Lower*) All right, Mom. But I've got into the habit of talking loud since Pop's been home. He don't seem to hear me when I talk low.

DOLLY That's right, Ma. I was talking to him this morning and when I got through he didn't know half that I'd told him.

MRS. KNAPP Your father has a bad cold and his head is all stopped up. *He* says he hasn't got a cold but I know better. I've been that way myself. But he won't believe me. So he's gone to pay five dollars to an ear specialist when all he needs is a dose of quinine—says a wireless operator can't afford to take chances. I told him a wireless operator couldn't afford to pay five dollars for nothin'—specially when he's got a wife and five children. (*Peevishly*) I don't know what's come over your father. He don't seem like the same man since this last trip on the *Empress*. I think it must be that South American climate that's affectin' him.

DOLLY He's awful cross since he's been home this time. He yells at Charlie and me for nothing.

MRS. KNAPP He'd be all right if he could get another job. But he's afraid if he gives up this one he won't be able to get another. Your father ain't as young as he used to be and they all want young men now. He's got to keep on workin' or we'd never be able to even pay the rent. Goodness knows his salary is small enough. If it wasn't for your brother Jim sendin' us a few dollars every month, and Charlie earnin' five a week, and me washin', we'd never be able to get along even *with* your father's salary. But heaven knows what we'd do without it. We'd be put out in the streets.

CHARLIE Is that where Pop's gone tonight—to the doctor's?

MRS. KNAPP Yes, and I don't know what can be keepin' him so long. He left after supper right after you did. You'd think he'd spend his last night at home when we won't see him again for three months.

CHARLIE Shall I go out and see if I can see him?

MRS. KNAPP Don't go makin' excuses to get out on the street. You better go to bed if you wanta be up on time in the morning—you too, Dolly.

DOLLY I still got some of my lessons to finish.

(*There is a sound from the hallway of someone coming up the stairs with slow, heavy steps*)

MRS. KNAPP Here your father comes now! Get into the parlor, Dolly, if you wanta do your lessons. Don't let him see you up so late. Keep the light shaded so you won't wake up the baby. (*The steps stop before the door and a knock is heard*) Charlie, go open that door. My feet are worn out from standin' up all day.

(CHARLIE *opens the door and* JAMES KNAPP *enters. He is a slight, stoop-shouldered, thin-faced man of about fifty. When he takes off his derby hat he reveals a long narrow head almost completely bald, with a thin line of gray hair extending over his large ears around the back of his head. His face has been tanned by the tropic sun—but now it seems a sickly yellow in the white glare of the lamp. His eyes are small, dark, and set close together; his nose stubby and of no particular shape; his mouth large and weak. He is dressed in a faded brown suit and unshined tan shoes. His expression must be unusually depressed as he stands nervously fingering his drooping gray mustache, for* MRS. KNAPP *looks at him sharply for a moment, then gets up quickly and goes over and kisses him*)

MRS. KNAPP (*Pulling out the armchair from the other end of the table for him*) Come! Sit down! You look all worn out. You shouldn't walk so much.

KNAPP (*Sinking into the chair and speaking in a slow, dull voice*) I am a bit tired.

(*He stares at the flowered patterns of the table cover for a moment—then sighs heavily*)

MRS. KNAPP Whatever is the matter with you? You look as if you'd lost your last friend.

KNAPP (*Pulling himself together and smiling feebly*) I guess I've got the blues. I get to thinking about how I've got to sail tomorrow on that long, lonesome trip, and how I won't see any of you for three months, and it sort of makes me feel bad. I wish I could throw up this job. I wish I was young enough to try something else.

CHARLIE (*Who is slouched down in a chair with his hands in his pockets, speaks in his lowest, nicest voice*) Aw, cheer up, Pop! It won't seem long. I should think you'd be glad to get out of the cold weather. Gee, I wish't I had a chance.

KNAPP (*Looking at him blankly*) Eh? What was that, Charlie? I didn't hear what you said.

CHARLIE (*In his best bellow*) I said: Cheer up! It won't seem long.

KNAPP (*Shaking his head sadly*) It's easy for you to say that. You're young.

(*The shrill crying of a baby sounds from behind the green curtain of the alcove.*)

MRS. KNAPP (*Turning on* CHARLIE *furiously*) There! You've gone and done it with your big, loud mouth. I told you to speak lower. (*Turning to her husband*) James. I wish you'd do something to make him behave. He don't mind what I say at all. Look at him—sprawled all over the chair with his long legs stretched out for everybody to trip over. Is that the way to sit on a chair? Anybody'd think you were brought up in a barn. I declare I'm ashamed to have you go anywhere for fear you'd disgrace me.

CHARLIE You needn't worry. There's no place for me to go—and if there was, I wouldn't go there with these clothes on. Why don't you ball out Pop? He couldn't hear me, so I had to speak louder.

KNAPP (*With sudden irritation*) Of course I heard you. But I wasn't paying any attention to what you said. I have other things to think about beside your chatter.

(CHARLIE *sulks back in his chair*)

MRS. KNAPP That's right, James. I knew you'd have to tell him where he belongs. You'd think he owned the house the way he acts. (*A piercing wail comes from behind the curtain and* MRS. KNAPP *hurries there, saying*) Hush! Hush! I'm coming.

(*She can be heard soothing the baby.*)

CHARLIE (*Plucking up his courage now that his mother is out of the room*) Say, Pop!

KNAPP Well, Charlie, what is it?

CHARLIE Please, can I have a new suit of clothes? Gee, I need 'em bad enough. This one is full of patches and holes and all the other kids down at the store laugh at me 'cause I ain't got long pants on and these don't fit me any more. Please, can I have a new suit, Pop?

KNAPP (*A look of pain crossing his features*) I'm afraid not just now, boy. (CHARLIE *descends into the depths of gloom*) You see, I've had to go to this doctor about (*He hesitates*) the —er—trouble I've had with my stomach, and he's very expensive. But when I come back from this trip I'll surely buy you a fine new suit with long pants the very first thing I do. I promise it to you and you know I don't break my promises. Try and get along with that one until I get back.

CHARLIE (*Ruefully*) All right, Pop. I'll try, but I'm afraid it's going to bust if I get any bigger.

KNAPP That's a good boy. We haven't been having much luck lately and we've all got to stand for our share of doing without things. I may have to do without a lot—

(*He turns his face away to hide his emotion from* CHARLIE. *A sob shakes his shoulders.* CHARLIE *notices it and goes over clumsily and pats his father on the back*)

CHARLIE Gee Pop, what's the matter? I can get along without a suit all right. I wouldn't have asked you if I thought you was so blue.

KNAPP Never mind me, boy. I'm just not feeling well, that's all—something I must have eaten—or a touch of fever. (*He glances at the clock*) It's getting pretty late, Charlie, and you've got to be up early in the morning. Better go to bed. Your mother and I have a lot to talk about yet—things which wouldn't interest you.

CHARLIE All right, Pop. Good night. I'll see you in the morning before I go.

KNAPP Good night and—remember I'm trying to do the best I know how.

(CHARLIE *disappears behind the green curtain.* KNAPP *stares at the table, his head between his hands, his face full of suffering.* MRS. KNAPP *comes back into the room. The baby is safely asleep again*)

MRS. KNAPP You sent Charlie to bed, didn't you? (*He nods*) That's right. He stays up altogether too late nights. He's always prowlin' around the streets. I don't know what will become of him I'm sure. Dolly told me tonight she saw him buyin' soda for that red-headed Harris girl with the quarter you gave him. What do you think of that? And he says he saw her talkin' in the dark hallway downstairs with some German bartender's boy. What do you think of that?

KNAPP (*Mildly*) Where's the hurt? They're only kids and they're got to have some fun.

MRS. KNAPP Fun? I'm glad you call it fun. I think it's disgraceful.

KNAPP Come, come, you exaggerate everything so. I see no harm in it. God knows I have enough to worry about without being bothered with children's pranks.

MRS. KNAPP (*Scornfully*) You have worries? And what are they, I'd like to know? You sail away and have a fine time with nothin' to do but eat the best of food and talk to the pretty women in the First Class. Worries? I wish you'd stay home and change places with me—cookin', scrubbin', takin' care of the children, puttin' off the grocer and the butcher, doin' washin' and savin' every penny. You'd soon find out what worry meant then.

KNAPP (*Placatingly*) I know you have to put up with a lot, Mary, and I wish I could do something to make it easier for you. (*Brokenly*) I don't know what's going to become of us—now.

MRS. KNAPP Oh, we'll manage to get along as we have been doin', I expect.

KNAPP But—Mary—something terrible has happened. I'm almost afraid to tell you.

MRS. KNAPP What do you mean? You haven't lost your job, have you?

KNAPP I went to see that ear specialist and—

(*His emotion chokes him; he stops to regain his composure*)

MRS. KNAPP Yes?

KNAPP (*His voice breaking in spite of himself*) He says I'm losing my hearing—that I'm liable to go stone-deaf at any moment.

(*He lets his head fall on his arms with a sob*)

MRS. KNAPP (*Coming over and putting her arm around him*) There, Jim! Don't take on about it so. All those doctors make things worse than they really are. He's just trying to scare you so you'll keep comin' to see him. Why, you can hear just as well as I can.

KNAPP No, I've noticed how hard it's been for me to catch some of the messages lately. And since I've been home I've had a hard time of it now and then to understand the children. The doctor said I would probably be able to hear for a long time yet but I got to be prepared for a sudden shock which'll leave me stone-deaf.

MRS. KNAPP (*Quickly*) Does anyone on the ship know?

KNAPP Of course not. If they knew my hearing was going back on me I wouldn't hold my job a minute. (*His voice trembles*) But I've got to tell them now. I've got to give up.

MRS. KNAPP You didn't tell the specialist what you were, did you?

KNAPP No. I said I was a machinist.

MRS. KNAPP (*Getting up from her chair and speaking in a hard voice*) Then why have you got to tell them? If you don't tell them they'll never know. You say yourself the doctor told you your hearin' would hold out for a long time yet.

KNAPP He said "probably."

MRS. KNAPP (*An angry flush spreading over her face*) Give up your job? Are you a fool? Are you such a coward that a doctor can scare you like that?

KNAPP I'm not afraid for myself. I'm not afraid of being deaf if I have to be. You don't understand. You don't know the responsibility of a man in my job.

MRS. KNAPP Responsibility? You've told me lots of times there was so few messages to send and take you wondered why they had a wireless. What's the matter with you all of a sudden? You're not deaf now and even if that lyin' doctor spoke the truth you'll hear for a long time yet. He only told you about that sudden stroke to keep you comin' to him. I know the way they talk.

KNAPP (*Protesting weakly*) But it ain't right. I ought to tell them and give up the job. Maybe I can get work at something else.

MRS. KNAPP (*Furiously*) Right? And I suppose you think it's right to loaf around here until we all get out in the streets? God knows your salary is small enough but without it we'd starve to death. Can't you think of others besides yourself? How about me and the children? What's goin' to buy them clothes and food? I can't earn enough, and what Charlie gets wouldn't keep *him* alive for a week. Jim sends us a few dollars a month but he don't get much and he ain't workin' regular. We owe the grocer and the butcher now. If they found out you wasn't workin' they wouldn't give us any more credit. And the landlord? How long would he let us stay here? You'll get other work? Remember the last time you tried. We had to pawn everything we had then and we was half-starved when you did land this job. You had to go back to the same old work, didn't you? They didn't want you at any telegraph office, did they? You was too old and slow, wasn't you? Well, you're older and slower than ever now and that's the only other job you're fit for. (*With bitter scorn*) You'll get another job! (*She sits down and covers her face with her hands, weeping bitterly*) And this is all the thanks I get for slavin' and workin' my fingers off! What a father for my poor children! Oh, why did I ever marry such a man? It's been nothin' but worryin' and sufferin' ever since.

KNAPP (*Who has been writhing under the lash of her scorn, is tortured beyond endurance at her last reproaches*) For God's sake let me alone! I'll go! I'll go! But this is going to be my last trip. I got to do the right thing. (*He gets up and pushes aside the green curtain*) Come on! I'm going to bed.

(*He leaves* MRS. KNAPP *alone. She lifts her tear-stained face from her hands and sighs with relief as she turns out the gas*)

Scene II

A section of the boat deck of the S. S. Empress *just abaft of the bridge. The deck slants sharply downward in the direction of the bow. To the left are the officers' cabins with several lighted port holes. Just in back of them and in the middle of the deck is the wireless room with its door wide open revealing* JAMES KNAPP *bent over his instrument on the forward side of the compartment. His face is pale and set, and he is busy sending out calls, pausing every now and then with a strained expression as if he were vainly trying to catch some answer to his messages. Every time he taps on the key the snarl of the wireless sounds above the confused babble of frightened voices that rises from the promenade deck. To the right of the wireless room on the port side is a life raft. Still farther to the right is one of the funnels. The background is a tropic sky blazing with stars. The wires running up from the wireless room to the foremast may be seen dimly lined against the sky. The time is about eleven o'clock.*

CAPTAIN HARDWICK *enters hurriedly from the direction of the bridge and walks across to the door of the wireless room, where he stands looking in at* KNAPP. *He is a stocky man about fifty dressed in a simple blue uniform. His face is reddened by sun and wind—that is, all of it which is not hidden by his gray beard and mustache. He drums nervously on the door.* KNAPP *pretends not to see him and appears absorbed in his instrument.*

CAPTAIN HARDWICK No answer yet? (KNAPP *does not reply and the* CAPTAIN *leans over impatiently and shakes him by the shoulder*) I asked you if there was any answer yet?

KNAPP (*Looking at him furtively*) I haven't heard a thing yet, sir.

CAPTAIN HARDWICK Damnation? What in hell is the matter with them? Are they all asleep?

KNAPP I'll try again, sir.

(*He taps on the key before him and the whine of the wireless shrills out discordantly*)

CAPTAIN HARDWICK (*Turning away with a muttered oath*) Well, I've got to get back on the bridge. Let me know the moment you catch anyone.

KNAPP (*Who has been watching his lips move*) Yes, sir.

(*His tone is vague, as if he were guessing at the answer.*)

CAPTAIN HARDWICK Tell 'em we hit a derelict and are sinking. Make it as strong as you can. We need help and we need it right away.

KNAPP (*More vaguely than ever*) Yes, sir.

CAPTAIN HARDWICK You surely ought to get the *Verdari*. She can't be more than a hundred miles away if my reckoning is correct. (*Turning away again*) I've got to go. Keep sending until you get an answer.

KNAPP Yes, sir.

CAPTAIN HARDWICK (*Under his breath*) Damn your "yes, sirs." I believe you're frightened out of your wits. (*He walks quickly toward the bridge. Halfway across the deck he is met by* MASON, *a tall, clean-shaven, middle-aged man in uniform who hurries in from forward*) Well, Mason, how do things look below?

MASON Very bad, sir. I'm afraid the bulkhead can't hold out much longer. They're doing all they can to strengthen it but it don't look to me as if it would stand the pressure. I wouldn't give it more than half an hour—an hour at most, sir.

CAPTAIN HARDWICK She's listing pretty badly. Guess you're right, Mason. When that bulkhead goes it's only a question of five or ten minutes. Are the crew all ready to man the boats?

MASON Yes, sir.

CAPTAIN HARDWICK Good! Passengers all on deck and ready to leave?

MASON Yes, sir.

CAPTAIN HARDWICK Good! Lucky there's only a few of them or we'd be in a nice mess. Lucky it's a calm night too. There'll be no panic. (*There is a pause broken only by the confused sound of voices from below*) Damned funny we get no reply to our calls for help, eh? Don't you think so?

MASON Very funny, sir. The *Verdari* ought to be right around here about this time. There ought to be four or five vessels we could reach, I should think.

CAPTAIN HARDWICK Just what I told Knapp. The poor devil seems scared to death because he can't get an answer. All he says every time I ask him is (*Mimicking* KNAPP) "Haven't heard a thing yet, sir!"

MASON He's told me the same thing three or four times. I don't like the looks of it, sir. He appears to act queer to me.

CAPTAIN HARDWICK You're right. He has been strange all during the trip—didn't seem to want to speak to anyone. I thought he must be sick. Think it's drink?

MASON No, sir. I never saw him touch a drop—even on shore.

CAPTAIN HARDWICK Let's see what he's got to say now. By God, we've got to get a message in soon or there'll be the devil to pay.

(*They both go over to the wireless room where* KNAPP *is frenziedly sending out call after call. The* CAPTAIN *goes into the compartment and stands beside* KNAPP. MASON *remains outside the door.* KNAPP *looks up and sees them. He glances fearfully from one to the other*) Caught the *Verdari* yet?

KNAPP (*In the uncertain tone he had used before*) I haven't heard a thing yet, sir.

CAPTAIN HARDWICK Are you sure there's nothing wrong with this machine of yours?

KNAPP (*Bewilderedly*) No, sir. Not a single answer, sir. I can't account for it, sir.

CAPTAIN HARDWICK (*Angrily*) I know that. You've told me often enough. Answer my question? (KNAPP *looks at him with puzzled eyes; then turns to the key of his instrument. The* CAPTAIN *grabs him by the shoulder*) Did you hear what I said? Dammit, answer my question.

KNAPP (*His lips trembling*) No, sir.

CAPTAIN HARDWICK (*Furiously*) What?

MASON (*Interposing*) Excuse me, sir, but something's wrong with the man. I don't think he heard what you said.

CAPTAIN HARDWICK The coward is frightened silly—that's what's the matter. (*Bending down he shouts against the receivers which* KNAPP *has over both his ears*) Say something, can't you? Are you deaf?

(KNAPP *shrinks away from him, his face ashy with fear, but does not answer*)

MASON Maybe it's those things on his ears, sir.

CAPTAIN HARDWICK (*Taking hold of the metal loops that go over* KNAPP*'s head and jerking the receivers off his ears*) Now! Answer me! What in hell's the matter with you? (*Then, his voice softening a bit*) If you're sick, why don't you say so?

KNAPP (*Looking at him helplessly for a moment—then hiding his face in his arms and weeping hysterically*) Oh my God! It's come! (*The* CAPTAIN *and* MASON *look at each other in amazement as* KNAPP *blurts out between his sobs*) I wasn't sure. I was hoping against hope. I can't hear a word you say. I can't hear anything. It's happened just as the doctor said it might. (*Looking up at the* CAPTAIN *and clasping and unclasping his hands piteously*) Oh, I should have told you, sir, before we started —but we're so poor and I couldn't get another job. I was just going to make this one more trip. I wanted to give up the job this time but she wouldn't let me. She said I wanted them to starve —and Charlie asked me for a suit. (*His sobs stifle him*) Oh God, who would have dreamt this could have happened—at such a time. I thought it would be all right—just this trip. I'm not a bad man, Captain. And now I'm deaf—stone-deaf. I can't hear what you say. I'm deaf! Oh my God! My God!

(*He flings his arms on the instrument in front of him and hides his face on them, sobbing bitterly*)

CAPTAIN HARDWICK (*Turning to* MASON) Well, I'll be damned! What do you make of this?

MASON I guess what he says is true, sir. He's gone deaf. That's why we've had no answer to our calls.

CAPTAIN HARDWICK (*Fuming helplessly*) What in hell can we do? I must know they're coming for us before I send the boats away. (*He thinks a moment. Suddenly his face lights up and he strikes his fist into his open palm*) By God, I've got it. You know Dick Whitney? (MASON *nods*) Operator of the *Duchess*—been laid up in Bahia with fever—came on board there—going home on vacation—he's in the First Cabin—run and get him. (MASON *runs down the deck toward the bridge*) Hurry, for God's sake! (MASON *is gone.* CAPTAIN HARDWICK *turns to* KNAPP, *and lifting him by the arms helps him out of the cabin and sits him down on the life raft. He pats him roughly on the back*) Brace up! Poor beggar!

(KNAPP *continues to sob brokenly.* MASON *reappears followed by* DICK WHITNEY, *a thin, sallow-faced young fellow of about twenty-five, wearing a light sack suit. He shows the effect of his recent battle with tropical fever but he walks over to the wireless room confidently enough and takes his seat before the instrument*)

CAPTAIN HARDWICK Get someone quick, Whitney. Tell 'em we're just about to launch the boats.

WHITNEY (*Who has put the receivers over his ears*) They're calling us now, sir. (*He sends an answering call—a pause*) It's the *Verdari*.

CAPTAIN HARDWICK Good! I knew she ought to be near us.

WHITNEY Operator says they're coming full speed—ought to reach us before daylight—wants to know if we can't keep up till then.

CAPTAIN HARDWICK No. Tell them the bulkhead is almost gone. We're due to sink within an hour at most. (*To* MASON) Better go down and see how things are below.

(MASON *leaves hurriedly*)

WHITNEY All right, sir.

(*He taps on the key—the wail of the wireless sounds again—then a pause*)

CAPTAIN HARDWICK What do they say now?

WHITNEY (*With a slight smile*) "Hard luck."

CAPTAIN HARDWICK (*Exploding*) Damn their sympathy!

WHITNEY The operator says he's been trying to communicate with us for a long time. He got our message all right but we never seemed to get his. (*The* CAPTAIN *glances at* KNAPP, *who is still sitting on the life raft with his face hidden in his hands*) He says he got a call from one of the Fruit Company's boats. She's rushing to help us too. He wants to know if we've heard anything from her.

CAPTAIN HARDWICK No. (*He looks at* KNAPP *again, then speaks dryly*) Tell him our receiving apparatus has been out of order.

WHITNEY (*Looks up in surprise—then sends the message. There is a pause*) He asks if we're sure it was a derelict we struck—says the *Verdari* sighted one about where we are now yesterday and he sent out warnings to all vessels he could reach—says he tried to get us especially because he knew we passed this way; but if our receiving end was bad that explains it.

CAPTAIN HARDWICK (*Staring at* KNAPP) By God!

WHITNEY Anything more you want to say, sir?

CAPTAIN HARDWICK (*Mechanically*) Tell them to hurry, that's all. (*Suddenly in a burst of rage he strides toward* KNAPP *and raises his fist as if to strike him.* MASON *comes in from astern and steps in between them.* CAPTAIN HARDWICK *glares at him for a moment—then recovers himself*) You're right, Mason. I won't touch him; but that miserable, cowardly shrimp has lost my ship for me. (*His face plainly shows how much this loss means to him.* MASON *does not understand what he means.* CAPTAIN HARDWICK *turns to the wireless room again, where young* WHITNEY *is sitting expectantly awaiting orders*) Say, Whitney! Write out that last message from the *Verdari* about her sending out warnings of that derelict yesterday—warnings which we didn't get. Put down how the operator on the *Verdari* tried especially to warn us because he knew we would pass this way.

(MASON *now understands and turns from* KNAPP *with a glance full of scorn.* WHITNEY *writes rapidly on the report pad near him and hands the sheet to the* CAPTAIN, *who walks over to* KNAPP *and, shaking him, holds the message out.* KNAPP *takes it in a trembling hand*)

MASON I've got all the men up from below, sir. The bulkhead's ready to go any minute. Shall I get some of the boats away, sir?

CAPTAIN HARDWICK Yes. (MASON *starts astern*) Wait a moment. I'm coming with you. Come on, Whitney. You can't do any good there any longer. (*He stops in front of* KNAPP *as he walks toward the stern.* KNAPP *is staring at the paper in his hand with wild eyes and pale, twitching features.* CAPTAIN HARDWICK *motions to him to follow them. They go off to right.* KNAPP *sits still with the sheet of paper in his hand. The creaking of blocks is heard and* MASON*'s voice shouting orders*)

KNAPP (*In a hoarse whisper*) God! It's my fault then! It's my fault! (*He staggers weakly to his feet*) What if the ship is lost! (*He looks astern where they are lowering the boats—his face is convulsed with horror—he gives a bitter cry of despair*) O-o-h! They're lowering the boats! She is lost! She is lost! (*He stumbles across the deck into the wireless room, pulls out a drawer and takes out a revolver, which he presses against his temple*) She is lost!

(*There is a sharp report and* KNAPP *falls forward on his face on the floor before his instrument. His body twitches for a moment, then is still. The operator* WHITNEY *comes running in from the right, calling, "Knapp! They're waiting for you." He gives one horrified glance at the body in the room; says, "Good God!" in a stupefied tone, and then, seized with sudden terror, rushes astern again*)

Curtain

FOG

A Play in One Act

Characters

A Poet
A Man of Business
A Polish Peasant Woman
A Dead Child
The Third Officer of a Steamer
Sailors from the Steamer

Scene—*The lifeboat of a passenger steamer is drifting helplessly off the Grand Banks of Newfoundland. A dense fog lies heavily upon the still sea. There is no wind and the long swells of the ocean are barely perceptible. The surface of the water is shadowy and unreal in its perfect calmness. A menacing silence, like the genius of the fog, broods over everything.*

Three figures in the boat are darkly outlined against the gray background of vapor. Two are seated close together on the thwarts in the middle. The other is huddled stiffly at one end. None of their faces can be distinguished.

Day is just about to break, and as the action progresses, the vague twilight of dawn creeps over the sea. This, in turn, is succeeded by as bright a semblance of daylight as can sift through the thick screen of fog.

man's voice (*Appallingly brisk and breezy under the circumstances*) Brrr! I wish daylight would come. I'm beginning to feel pretty chilly. How about you? (*He receives no answer and raises his voice, the fear of solitude suddenly alive within him*) Hello there! You havn't gone to sleep, have you?

another man's voice (*More refined than the first, clear and unobtrusively melancholy*) No, I'm not asleep.

first voice (*Complacently reassured*) Thought you might have dozed off. I did a while ago—eyes refused to stay open any longer—couldn't imagine where I was when I woke up—had forgotten all about the damned wreck.

second voice You are fortunate to be able to sleep. I wish I could go to sleep and forget—all this—

first voice Oh, come now! You mustn't keep thinking about it. That won't do any good. Brace up! We're sure to get out of this mess all right. I've figured it all out. You know how long a time it was between the time we hit the derelict—it was a derelict we hit, wasn't it?

second voice I believe so.

first voice Well, the wireless was going all the time, if you remember, and one of the officers told me we had lots of answers from ships saying they were on the way to help us. One of them is sure to pick us up.

second voice In this fog?

first voice Oh, this'll all go away as soon as the sun goes up. I've seen plenty like it at my country place on the Connecticut shore, maybe not as thick as this one but nearly as bad, and when the sun came up they always disappeared before the morning was over.

second voice You forget we are now near the Grand Banks, the home of fog.

first voice (*With a laugh that is a bit troubled*) I must say you aren't a very cheerful companion.

Why don't you look at the bright side? (*A pause during which he is evidently thinking over what the other man has told him*) The Grand Banks? Hmm, well, I refuse to be scared.

SECOND VOICE I have no intention of making our situation seem worse than it really is. I have every hope that we will eventually be rescued, but it's better not to expect too much. It only makes disappointment more bitter when it comes.

FIRST VOICE I suppose you're right, but I can't help being optimistic.

SECOND VOICE You remember how downcast you were yesterday when we failed to hear any sound of a ship? Today is liable to be the same unless this fog lifts. So don't hope for too much.

FIRST VOICE You're forgetting the fact that there was no sun yesterday. That kind of weather can't last forever.

SECOND VOICE (*Dryly*) Perhaps we could not see the sun on account of the fog.

FIRST VOICE (*After a pause*) I'll admit I did feel pretty dismal yesterday—after that terrible thing happened.

SECOND VOICE (*Softly*) You mean after the child died?

FIRST VOICE (*Gloomily*) Yes. I thought that woman would never stop crying. Ugh! It was awful—her cries, and the fog, and not another sound anywhere.

SECOND VOICE It was the most horrible thing I have ever seen or even heard of. I never dreamed anything could be so full of tragedy.

FIRST VOICE It was enough to give anyone the blues, that's sure. Besides, my clothes were wet and I was freezing cold and you can imagine how merry I felt. (*Grumbling*) Not that they're any dryer now but somehow I feel warmer.

SECOND VOICE (*After a long pause*) So you think the child's death was a terrible thing?

FIRST VOICE (*In astonishment*) Of course. Why? Don't you?

SECOND VOICE No.

FIRST VOICE But you said just a minute ago that—

SECOND VOICE I was speaking of the grief and despair of the mother. But death was kind to the child. It saved him many a long year of sordid drudgery.

FIRST VOICE I don't know as I agree with you there. Everyone has a chance in this world; but we've all got to work hard, of course. That's the way I figure it out.

SECOND VOICE What chance had that poor child? Naturally sickly and weak from underfeeding, transplanted to the stinking room of a tenement or the filthy hovel of a mining village, what glowing opportunities did life hold out that death should not be regarded as a blessing for him? I mean if he possessed the ordinary amount of ability and intelligence—considering him as the average child of ignorant Polish immigrants. Surely his prospects of ever becoming anything but a beast of burden were not bright, were they?

FIRST VOICE Well, no, of course not, but—

SECOND VOICE If you could bring him back to life would you do so? Could you conscientiously drag him away from that fine sleep of his to face what he would have to face? Leaving the joy you would give his mother out of the question, would you do it for him individually?

FIRST VOICE (*Doubtfully*) Perhaps not, looking at it from that standpoint.

SECOND VOICE There is no other standpoint. The child was diseased at birth, stricken with a hereditary ill that only the most vital men are able to shake off.

FIRST VOICE You mean?

SECOND VOICE I mean poverty—the most deadly and prevalent of all diseases.

FIRST VOICE (*Amused*) Oh, that's it, eh? Well, it seems to be a pretty necessary sickness and you'll hardly find a cure for it. I see you're a bit of a reformer.

SECOND VOICE Oh no. But there are times when the frightful injustice of it all sickens me with life in general.

FIRST VOICE I find life pretty good. I don't know as I'd change it even if I could.

SECOND VOICE Spoken like a successful man. For I'm sure you are a successful man, are you not? I mean in a worldly way.

FIRST VOICE (*Flattered*) Yes, you might call me so, I guess. I've made my little pile but it was no easy time getting it, let me tell you.

SECOND VOICE You had some advantages, did you not? Education and plenty to eat, and a clean home, and so forth?

FIRST VOICE I went to high school and of course had

the other things you mentioned. My people were not exactly what you could call poor but they were certainly not rich. Why do you ask?

SECOND VOICE Do you think you would be as successful and satisfied with life if you had started with handicaps like those which that poor dead child would have had to contend with if he had lived?

FIRST VOICE (*Impatiently*) Oh, I don't know! What's the use of talking about what might have happened? I'm not responsible for the way the world is run.

SECOND VOICE But supposing you are responsible?

FIRST VOICE What!

SECOND VOICE I mean supposing we—the self-satisfied, successful members of society—are responsible for the injustice visited upon the heads of our less fortunate "brothers-in-Christ" because of our shameful indifference to it. We see misery all around us and we do not care. We do nothing to prevent it. Are we not then, in part at least, responsible for it? Have you ever thought of that?

FIRST VOICE (*In tones of annoyance*) No, and I'm not going to start in thinking about it now.

SECOND VOICE (*Quietly*) I see. It's a case of what is Hecuba to you that you should weep for her.

FIRST VOICE (*Blankly*) Hecuba? Oh, you mean the woman. You can't accuse me of any heartlessness there. I never felt so sorry for anyone in my life. Why, I was actually crying myself at one time, I felt so sorry for her. By the way, she hasn't made a sound since it got dark last evening. Is she asleep? Can you see her? You're nearer to her than I am.

(*It is becoming gradually lighter although the fog is as thick as ever. The faces of the two men in the boat can be dimly distinguished—one round, jowly, and clean-shaven; the other oval with big dark eyes and a black mustache and black hair pushed back from his high forehead. The huddled figure at the end of the boat is clearly that of a woman. One arm is flung over her face, concealing it. In the other she clutches something like a bundle of white clothes*)

DARK MAN (*He of the Second Voice, who is seated on the thwart nearer to the woman—turning round and peering in her direction*) She is very still. She must be asleep. I hope so, poor woman!

OTHER MAN Yes, a little sleep will do her a world of good.

DARK MAN She still holds the body of the child close to her breast. (*He returns to his former position facing the* OTHER MAN) I suppose you—

OTHER MAN (*Exultingly*) Excuse my interrupting you, but have you noticed how light it's getting? It didn't strike me until you turned around just now. I can see your face plainly and a few minutes ago I couldn't tell whether you were a blond or brunette.

DARK MAN Now if this fog would only lift—

OTHER MAN It's going to lift. You wait and see. You'll find my optimism is justified. But what was it you started to say?

DARK MAN I was saying that I supposed you had never seen this woman on board.

OTHER MAN No. I was in the smoking room playing bridge most of the time. I'm not much of a sailor—don't care much about the water—just went over to Europe because the wife and the girls insisted. I was bored to death—made an excuse to get away as soon as I could. No, sir, you can't teach an old dog new tricks. I'm a businessman pure and simple and the farther I get away from that business the more dissatisfied I am. I've built that business up from nothing and it's sort of like a child of mine. It gives me pleasure to watch over it and when I'm away I'm uneasy. I don't like to leave it in strange hands. As for traveling, little old New York in the U.S.A. is good enough for me. (*He pauses impressively, waiting for some word of approval for his sterling patriotic principles. The* DARK MAN *is silent and he of the U.S.A. continues, a bit disconcerted*) But you asked me if I had seen the woman. I don't think so, because I never went down into the steerage. I know some of the first-class passengers did but I wasn't curious. It's a filthy sort of hole, isn't it?

DARK MAN It's not so bad. I spent quite a good deal of my time down there.

BUSINESSMAN (*For he of the jowly, fat face and the bald spot is such by his own confession. Chuckling*) In your role of reformer?

DARK MAN No. Simply because I found the people in the steerage more interesting to talk to than the second-class passengers. I am not a reformer—at least not in the professional sense.

BUSINESSMAN Do you mind my asking what particular

line you are in?

DARK MAN I am a writer.

BUSINESSMAN I thought it was something of the kind. I knew you weren't in business when I heard those socialistic ideas of yours. (*Condescendingly*) Beautiful idea—socialism—but too impractical—never come about—just a dream.

DARK MAN I'm not a socialist—especially—just a humanist, that is all.

BUSINESSMAN What particular kind of writing do you do?

DARK MAN I write poetry.

BUSINESSMAN (*In a tone indicating that in his mind poets and harmless lunatics have more than one point in common*) Oh, I see. Well, there's not much money in that, is there?

POET No.

BUSINESSMAN (*After a long pause*) I don't know about you but I'm beginning to feel hungry. Is that box of crackers near you? (*The* POET *reaches in under a thwart and pulls out a box of sea biscuits. The* BUSINESSMAN *takes a handful and munches greedily*) Never thought hardtack could taste so good. Aren't you going to have any?

POET No. I am not hungry. The thought of that poor woman takes all my hunger away. I used to watch her every day down in the steerage playing with her little son who is now dead. I think he must have been the only child she ever had, the look on her face was so wonderfully tender as she bent over him. What will her life be now that death has robbed her of the only recompense for her slavery? It seems such needless cruelty. Why was I not taken instead?—I, who have no family or friends to weep, and am not afraid to die.

BUSINESSMAN (*His mouth full*) You take things to heart too much. That's just like a poet. She'll forget all about it—probably sooner than you will. One forgets everything in time. What a devil of a world it would be if we didn't. (*He takes another handful of sea biscuits and continues his munching. The* POET *turns away from him in disgust*) Funny thing when you come to think of it—I mean how we happened to come together in this boat. It's a mystery to me how she ever got in here. And then, how is it there's no oars in this boat and still there's plenty of food? You remember there was no lack of lifeboats, and after the women and children were taken off I was ordered into one and we were rowed away. The damned thing must have gotten smashed somehow, for it leaked like a sieve and in spite of our bailing we were soon dumped in the water. I heard the noise of voices near us and tried to swim to one of the other boats, but I must have got twisted in the fog, for when I did find a boat—and let me tell you I was pretty nearly "all in" about then—it was this one and you and she were in it. Now what I want to know is—

POET It is easily explained. Did you ever become so sick of disappointment and weary of life in general that death appeared to you the only way out?

BUSINESSMAN Hardly. But what has that to do—

POET Listen and you will see. That is the way I felt—sick and weary of soul and longing for sleep. When the ship struck the derelict it seemed to me providential. Here was the solution I had been looking for. I would go down with the ship, and that small part of the world which knew me would think my death an accident.

BUSINESSMAN (*Forgetting to eat in his amazement*) You mean to say you were going to commit—

POET I was going to die, yes. So I hid in the steerage fearing that some of the ship's officers would insist on saving my life in spite of me. Finally, when everyone had gone, I came out and walked around the main deck. I heard the sound of voices come from a dark corner and discovered that this woman and her child had been left behind. How that happened I don't know. Probably she hid because she was afraid the child would be crushed by the terror-stricken immigrants. At any rate there she was and I decided she was so happy in her love for her child that it would be wrong to let her die. I looked around and found this lifeboat had been lowered down to the main deck and left hanging there. The oars had been taken out—probably for extra rowers in some other boat. I persuaded the woman to climb in and then went up to the boat deck and lowered the boat the rest of the way to the water. This was not much of a task, for the steamer was settling lower in the water every minute. I then slid down one of the ropes to the boat and, cutting both of the lines that held her, pushed off. There was a faint breeze which blew us slowly away from the sinking ship until she was hidden in the fog. The suspense of waiting for her to go down was terrible. Even as it was we were nearly swamped by the waves when the steamer took her final plunge.

BUSINESSMAN (*Edges away from the* POET, *firmly convinced that his convictions regarding the similarity of poets and madmen are based upon fact*) I hope you've abandoned that suicide idea.

POET I have—absolutely. I think all that happened to me is an omen sent by the gods to convince me my past unhappiness is past and my fortune will change for the better.

BUSINESSMAN That's the way to talk! Superstition is a good thing sometimes.

POET But if I had known the sufferings that poor woman was to undergo as a result of my reckless life-saving, I would have let her go down with the ship and gone myself.

BUSINESSMAN Don't think of it any longer. You couldn't help that. I wonder what it was the child died of? I thought it was asleep when I heard it choke and cough—and the next minute *she* commenced to scream. I won't forget those screams for the rest of my life.

POET The child was naturally frail and delicate and I suppose the fright he received and the exposure combined to bring on some kind of convulsion. He was dead when I went over to see what was the matter.

BUSINESSMAN (*Peering upward through the fog*) It's getting considerably lighter. It must be about time for the sun to rise—if we're going to have any sun.

POET (*Sadly*) It was just about this time yesterday morning when the poor little fellow died.

BUSINESSMAN (*Looks apprehensively toward the huddled figure in the end of the boat. Now that it is lighter, what appeared before like a bundle of white clothes can be seen to be a child four or five years old with a thin, sallow face and long black curls. The body is rigid, wrapped in a white shawl, and the eyes are open and glassy*) Let's not talk any more about it. She might wake up and start screaming again—and I can't stand that.

POET She does not understand English.

BUSINESSMAN (*Shaking his head*) She'd know we were talking about the kid just the same. Mothers have an instinct when it comes to that. I've seen that proved in my own family more than once.

POET Have you ever lost any of your children?

BUSINESSMAN No. Thank God!

POET You may well thank God, even if people do, as you claimed a while ago, forget so easily.

BUSINESSMAN You're not married, are you?

POET No.

BUSINESSMAN I didn't think you were. (*Jocularly*) You people with artistic temperaments run more to affinities than to wives. I suppose you've lots of those?

POET (*Does not hear or will not notice this question. He is staring through the fog and speaks in excited tones*) Did you hear that?

BUSINESSMAN Hear what?

POET Just now when you were talking. I thought I heard a sound like a steamer's whistle.

(*They both listen intently. After a second or so the sound comes again, faint and far-off, wailing over the water*)

BUSINESSMAN (*Wildly elated*) By God, it is a steamer!

POET It sounded nearer that time. She must be coming this way.

BUSINESSMAN Oh, if only this rotten fog would lift for a minute!

POET Let's hope it will. We run as much risk of being run down as we do of being saved while this continues. They couldn't see us twenty feet away in this.

BUSINESSMAN (*Nervously*) Can't we yell or make some kind of a noise?

POET They couldn't hear us now. We can try when they get close to us. (*A pause during which they hear the steamer whistle again*) How cold the air is! Or is it my imagination?

BUSINESSMAN No, I notice it too. I've been freezing to death for the last five minutes. I wish we had the oars so we could row and keep warm.

POET Sssh! Do you hear that?

BUSINESSMAN What? The whistle? I heard it a moment ago.

POET No. This is a sound like running water. There! Don't you hear it now?

(*A noise as of water falling over rocks comes clearly through the fog*)

BUSINESSMAN Yes, I hear it. What can it be? There isn't any water out here except what's under us. (*With a shiver*) Brrr, but it's chilly!

POET That poor woman will be frozen when she wakes up.

(*He takes off his ulster, and walking carefully to the end of the boat, covers the form of the sleeping woman with it*)

BUSINESSMAN It sounds louder every minute but I can't see anything. Damn this fog!

(*The noise of the falling water grows more and more distinct. At regular intervals the steamer's whistle blows and that, too, seems to be drawing nearer*)

POET (*Still bent over the sleeping woman*) Perhaps it may be land but I hardly think we could have drifted that far.

BUSINESSMAN (*In terrified tones*) Good God, what's that?

(*The* POET *turns quickly around. Something huge and white is looming up through the fog directly beside the boat. The boat drifts up to it sideways and strikes against it with a slight jar. The* BUSINESSMAN *shrinks away as far along the thwart as he can get, causing the boat to tip a little to one side. The spattering splash of falling water sounds from all around them*)

POET (*Looking at the white mass towering above them*) An iceberg! (*Turning to the* BUSINESSMAN) Steady there! You will be in the water in a minute if you're not careful. There is nothing to be frightened over. Lucky for us it's calm or we would be smashed to pieces.

BUSINESSMAN (*Reassured by finding out that what he took for some horrible phantom of the sea is an ice and water reality, he moves over to the center of his thwart and remarks sarcastically*) As it is we'll only freeze to death. Is that what you mean?

POET (*Thumping his hands against his sides*) It *is* cold. I wonder how big the berg is. Help me try to push the boat away from it.

(*They push against the side of the berg. The boat moves away a little but drifts right back again*)

BUSINESSMAN Ouch! My hands are freezing.

POET No use wasting effort on that. The boat is too heavy and you can get no grip on the ice. (*A blast of the steamer's whistle shrills through the fog. It sounds very close to them*) Oh God, I never thought of that.

(*He sits down dejectedly opposite the* BUSINESSMAN)

BUSINESSMAN Never thought of what?

POET (*Excitedly*) The steamer, man, the steamer! Think of the danger she is in. If she were ever to hit this mass of ice she would sink before they could lower a boat.

BUSINESSMAN Can't we do something? We'll yell to them when they get nearer.

POET Oh my God, man, don't do that. This may be one of the rescue ships come to pick up the survivors from our boat, and if they heard any shouts they would think they were cries for help and come right in this direction. Not a sound if you have any regard for the lives of those on board.

BUSINESSMAN (*Almost whimpering*) But if we don't let them know we're here they are liable to pass by us and never know it.

POET (*Sternly*) We can die but we cannot risk the lives of others to save our own.

(*The* BUSINESSMAN *does not reply to this but a look of sullen stubbornness comes over his face. There is a long pause. The silence is suddenly shattered by a deafening blast from the steamer's whistle*)

POET God! She must be right on top of us.

(*They both start to their feet and stand straining their eyes to catch some glimpse of the approaching vessel through the blinding mist. The stillness is so intense that the throb of the engines can be plainly heard. This sound slowly recedes and the next whistle indicates by its lack of volume that the steamer has passed and is proceeding on her way*)

BUSINESSMAN (*Furiously*) She's going away. I'm not going to be left here to die on account of your damn-fool ideas.

(*He turns in the direction he supposes the steamer to be and raises his hands to his mouth, shaping them like a megaphone*)

POET (*Jumping over and forcing his hand over the* BUSINESSMAN's *mouth in time to stifle his call for help*) You damned coward! I might have known what to expect.

(*The* BUSINESSMAN *struggles to free himself, rocking the boat from side to side with his futile twistings, but he is finally forced down to a sitting position on the thwart. The* POET *then releases him. He opens his mouth as if to shout but the* POET *stands over him with his right fist drawn back threateningly and the* BUSINESSMAN *thinks better of it*)

BUSINESSMAN (*Snarling*) I'll get even with you, you loafer, if we ever get on shore.

(*The* POET *pays no attention to this threat but sits down opposite him. They hear the whistle again, seemingly no farther away than before. The* BUSINESSMAN *stirs uneasily. A rending, tearing crash cracks through the silence, followed a moment later by a tremendous splash. Great drops of water fall in the rocking boat*)

BUSINESSMAN (*Trembling with terror*) She must have hit it after all.

POET No. That can't be it. I don't hear any shouts. (*Suddenly smiling with relief as he guesses what has happened*) I know what it is. The berg is melting and breaking up. That was a piece that fell in the water.

BUSINESSMAN It almost landed on us. (*He becomes panic-stricken at this thought and jumps to his feet*) I'm not going to stand this any longer. We'll be crushed like flies. I'll take a chance and swim for it. You can stay here and be killed if you want to. (*Insane with fear of this new menace he puts one foot on the gunwale of the boat and is about to throw himself into the water when the* POET *grabs him by the arm and pulls him back*) Let me go! This is all right for you. You want to die. Do you want to kill me too, you murderer?

(*He hides his face in his hands and weeps like a fat child in a fit of temper*)

POET You fool! You could not swim for five minutes in this icy water. (*More kindly*) Come! Be sensible! Act like a man!

(*The* BUSINESSMAN *shakes with a combination of sigh and sob. The whistle blows again and seems once more to be in their immediate vicinity. The* BUSINESSMAN *takes a new lease on life at this favorable sign and raises his head*)

BUSINESSMAN She seems to be getting quite near us again.

POET Yes, and a moment ago I heard something like oars creaking in the oarlocks and striking the water.

BUSINESSMAN (*Hopefully*) Maybe they've lowered a boat.

(*Even as he is speaking the curtain of fog suddenly lifts. The sun has just risen over the horizon rim, and the berg behind them, its surface carved and fretted by the streams of water from the melting ice, its whiteness vivid above the blue-gray water, seems like the façade of some huge Viking temple*)

POET (*He and the* BUSINESSMAN, *their backs turned to the berg, are looking at something over the water as if they could hardly believe their good fortune*) There's the steamer now and she can hardly be more than a quarter of a mile away. What luck!

BUSINESSMAN And there's the boat you heard. Look! They were rowing straight toward us.

POET (*Half to himself, with a puzzled expression*) I wonder how they knew we were here.

VOICE FROM OVER THE WATER Hello there!

BUSINESSMAN (*Waving frantically*) Hello!

VOICE (*Nearer—the creak of the oars can be clearly heard*) Are you people off the *Starland?*

BUSINESSMAN Yes.

(*With the return of his courage he has regained all his self-assured urbanity. He tries to pull his clothes into some semblance of their former immaculateness, and his round face with its imposing double chin assumes an expression of importance. The* POET'*s face is drawn and melancholy as if he were uncertain of the outcome of this unexpected return to life*)

BUSINESSMAN (*Turning to the* POET *with a smile*) You see, my optimism was justified after all. (*Growing confused before the* POET'*s steady glance*) I wish you'd—er—forget all about the little unpleasantness between us. I must confess I was a bit—er—rattled and didn't exactly know what I was doing.

(*He holds out his hand uncertainly. The* POET *takes it with a quiet smile*)

POET (*Simply*) I had forgotten all about it.

BUSINESSMAN Thank you.

(*The voice that hailed them is heard giving some orders. The sound of the oars ceases and a moment later a lifeboat similar to the one they are in, but manned by a full crew of sailors, comes alongside of them. A young man in uniform, evidently the Third Officer of the ship, is in the stern steering*)

BUSINESSMAN (*Breezily*) Hello! You certainly are a welcome sight.

OFFICER (*Looking up at the towering side of the berg*) You picked out a funny island to land on. What made you cling so close to this berg? Cold, wasn't it?

POET We drifted into it in the fog and having no oars could not get away. It was about the same time we first heard your whistle.

OFFICER (*Nodding toward the woman's figure*) Woman sick?

POET She has been asleep, poor woman.

OFFICER Where's the kid?

POET In her arms. (*Then, wonderingly*) But how did you know—?

OFFICER We'd never have found you but for that. Why didn't you give us a shout or make some kind of a racket?

BUSINESSMAN (*Eagerly*) We were afraid you would come in our direction and hit this iceberg.

OFFICER But we might have passed you and never had an inkling—

BUSINESSMAN (*Impressively*) In a case of that kind one has to take chances.

(*The* POET *smiles quietly. The* OFFICER *looks surprised*)

OFFICER That was very fine of you, I must say. Most people would only have thought of themselves. As it was, if it hadn't been for the kid crying we would have missed you. I was on the bridge with the First Officer. We had been warned about this berg, and when the fog came up we slowed down until we were barely creeping, and stopped altogether every now and then. It was during one of these stops, when everything was still, we heard the crying, and I said to the First Officer: "Sounds like a kid bawling, doesn't it?" And he thought it did too. It kept getting plainer and plainer until there was no chance for a mistake—weird too it sounded with everything so quiet and the fog so heavy. I said to him again: "It's a kid sure enough, but how in the devil did it get out here?" And then we both remembered we had been ordered to keep a lookout for any of the survivors of the *Starland* who hadn't been picked up yet, and the First Officer said: "It's probably some of the poor devils from the *Starland*," and told me to have a boat lowered. I grabbed a compass and jumped in. We could hear the kid crying all the time, couldn't we, boys? (*He turns to the crew, who all answer: "Yes, sir"*) That's how I was able to shape such a direct course for you. I was steering by the sound. It stopped just as the fog rose.

(*During the* OFFICER'*s story the* BUSINESSMAN *has been looking at him with an expression of annoyed stupefaction on his face. He is unable to decide whether the* OFFICER *is fooling or not and turns to the* POET *for enlightenment. But the latter, after listening to the* OFFICER'*s explanation with intense interest, goes quickly to the side of the woman and, removing his ulster from over her shoulders, attempts to awaken her*)

OFFICER (*Noticing what he is doing*) That's right. Better wake her up. The steamer will be ready to pick us up in a minute, and she must be stiff with the cold. (*He turns to one of his crew*) Make a line fast to this boat and we'll tow her back to the ship.

(*The sailor springs into the* Starland'*s boat with a coil of rope in his hand*)

POET (*Failing to awaken the woman he feels for her pulse and then bends down to listen for a heart beat, his ear against her breast. He straightens up finally and stands looking down at the two bodies and speaks to himself half aloud*) Poor happy woman.

(*The* OFFICER *and the* BUSINESSMAN *are watching him*)

OFFICER (*Sharply*) Well?

POET (*Softly*) The woman is dead.

BUSINESSMAN Dead!

(*He casts a horrified glance at the still figures in the end of the boat—then clambers clumsily into the other boat and stands beside the officer*)

OFFICER Too bad! But the child is all right, of course?

POET The child has been dead for twenty-four hours. He died at dawn yesterday.

(*It is the* OFFICER'*s turn to be bewildered. He stares at the* POET *pityingly and then turns to the* BUSINESSMAN)

OFFICER (*Indicating the* POET *with a nod of his head*) A bit out of his head, isn't he? Exposure affects a lot of them that way.

BUSINESSMAN (*Solemnly*) He told you the exact truth of the matter.

OFFICER (*Concluding he has two madmen to deal with instead of one*) Of course. (*To the sailor who has made fast the towing rope*) All fast? (*The sailor jumps into his own boat with a brisk "Aye, aye, sir." The* OFFICER *turns to the* POET) Coming in here or going to stay where you are?

POET (*Gently*) I think I will stay with the dead.

(*He is sitting opposite the two rigid figures, looking at their still white faces with eyes full of a great longing*)

OFFICER (*Mutters*) Cheerful beggar! (*He faces the crew*) Give way all.

(*The oars take the water and the two boats glide swiftly away from the iceberg.*

The fresh morning breeze ripples over the water bringing back to the attentive ear some words of the MAN OF BUSINESS *spoken argumentatively, but in the decided accents of one who is rarely acknowledged to be wrong*)

BUSINESSMAN —the exact truth. So you see that, if you will pardon my saying so, Officer, what you have just finished telling us is almost unbelievable.

Curtain

RECKLESSNESS

A Play in One Act

Characters

ARTHUR BALDWIN
MILDRED, *his wife*
FRED BURGESS, *their chauffeur*
GENE, *Mrs. Baldwin's maid*
MARY, *a housemaid*

SCENE—*The library of Arthur Baldwin's summer home in the Catskills, New York. On the left a door and two large French windows open on the veranda. A bookcase covers the space of wall between the two windows. In the corner is a square wicker worktable. The far side of the room also looks out on the veranda. Two French windows are on each side of a rolltop desk that stands against the wall. Near the desk there is a small telephone such as is used on estates to connect the house with the outbuildings; on top of the desk a Bell telephone and a small pile of letters. In the right background is a divan, then a door leading to the hallway, and a long bookcase. A heavy oak table stands in the center of the room. On it are several magazines and books, an ash receiver, cigar box, etc., and an electric reading lamp wired from the chandelier above. Two Morris chairs are within reading reach of the lamp, and several light rocking chairs are placed about the room. The walls are of light wainscoting. The floor is of polished hard wood with a large darkish-colored rug covering the greater part. Several pictures of a sporting nature, principally of racing automobiles, are hung on the walls in the spaces between windows and bookcases.*

The room is the typical sitting room of a moderately wealthy man who has but little taste and is but little worried by its absence. On this warm August night, with the door and all the windows thrown open, and only the reading lamp burning, it presents a cool and comfortable appearance.

It's about eight o'clock in the evening. The time is the present.

MRS. BALDWIN *is discovered lying back in one of the Morris chairs with an unopened book in her lap. She is holding her head on one side in an attitude of strained attention as if she were waiting for someone or something. In appearance she is a tall, strikingly voluptuous-looking young woman of about twenty-eight. Her hair is reddish-gold, almost a red, and her large eyes are of that dark grayish-blue color which is called violet. She is very pale—a clear transparent pallor that serves to accentuate the crimson of the full lips of her rather large mouth. She is dressed in a low-cut evening gown of a gray that matches her eyes. Her shoulders, neck and arms are beautiful.*

MRS. BALDWIN (*Rousing herself with a sigh of vexation, goes to the wall on the right and pushes an electric button near the bookcase. After a moment a maid enters*) I won't wait any longer, Mary. He evidently isn't coming. You may clear the table. I won't eat anything now. I'll have something after a while.

MARY Very well, ma'am.

(*She goes out*)

MRS. BALDWIN (*Looks around quickly to make sure she

is alone, then locks the door to the hallway and, going to the door on the left opening on the verandah, calls in a low voice) Fred.

(*She beckons with her hand to someone who is evidently waiting outside. A moment later* FRED BURGESS *comes quickly into the room. He throws a furtive glance around him—then, reassured, takes* MRS. BALDWIN *in his arms and kisses her passionately on the lips. In appearance he is a tall, clean-shaven, dark-complected young fellow of twenty-five or so with clear-cut, regular features, big brown eyes and black curly hair. He is dressed in a gray chauffeur's uniform with black puttees around the calves of his legs*)

MRS. BALDWIN (*Putting her arms about his neck and kissing him again and again*) Oh, Fred! Fred! I love you so much!

FRED Ssh! Someone might hear you.

MRS. BALDWIN There's no one around. They're all in back having dinner. You've had your's? (*He nods*) They won't expect you then. There's nothing to fear. I've locked the door. (*He is reassured*) But you do love me, don't you, Fred? (*He kisses her smilingly*) Oh, I know! I know! But say so! I love to hear it.

FRED (*Stroking her hair caressingly with one hand*) Of course I love you. You know I do, Mildred.

(MRS. BALDWIN*'s maid* GENE *appears noiselessly in the doorway from the veranda. They are looking raptly into each other's eyes, and do not notice her. She glares at them for a moment, vindictive hatred shining in her black eyes. Then she disappears as quietly as she came*)

MRS. BALDWIN (*Brokenly*) I can't stand this life much longer, Fred. These last two weeks while he has been away have been heaven to me, but when I think of his coming back tonight—I—I could kill him!

FRED (*Worried by this sudden outbreak*) You mustn't feel so badly about it. You—we have got to make the best of it, that's all.

MRS. BALDWIN (*Reproachfully*) You take it very easily. Think of me.

FRED (*Releasing her and walking nervously up and down the room*) You know, Mildred, I'd like to do something. But how can I help matters? I haven't any money. We can't go away together yet.

MRS. BALDWIN But I can get money—all the money we need.

FRED (*Scornfully*) His money!

MRS. BALDWIN I have my jewels. I can sell those.

FRED He gave you those jewels.

MRS. BALDWIN Oh, why are you so hard on me? (*She sinks down in one of the Morris chairs. He comes over and stands before her*) Why won't you let me help a little?

FRED I don't want to touch any of his money. (*Kneeling beside her he puts one arm around her—then with sudden passion*) I want you! God, how I want you! But I can't do that! (*He leans over and kisses her bare neck. She gives a long shuddering gasp, her white fingers closing and unclosing in his dark curls. He gets suddenly to his feet*) We'll have to wait and love when we can for a while. I promise you it won't be long. I worked my way this far and I don't intend to stop here. As soon as I've passed those engineering examinations—and I will pass them—we'll go away together. I won't be anybody's servant then.

(*He glances down at his livery in disgust*)

MRS. BALDWIN (*Pleading tearfully*) Fred dearest, please take me away now—tonight—before he comes. What difference does the money make as long as I have you?

FRED (*With a harsh laugh*) You don't know what you're talking about. You'd never stand it. Being poor doesn't mean anything to you. You've never been poor. Well, I have, and I know. It's hell, that's what it is. You've been used to having everything, and when you found out you were tied to a servant who could give you nothing, you'd soon get tired. And I'd be the last one to blame you for it. I'm working out and I don't want to go back and drag you with me.

MRS. BALDWIN You don't realize how much I love you or you wouldn't talk like that. I'd rather die of starvation with you than live the way I'm living now.

FRED (*Shaking his head skeptically*) You don't know what starvation means. Besides, how do you know he'll get a divorce? He might keep you bound to him in name for years—just for spite.

MRS. BALDWIN No. I'm sure he isn't as mean as all that. To do him justice, he's been kind to me—in his way. He has looked upon me as his plaything, the slave of his pleasure, a pretty toy to be exhibited that others might envy him his ownership. But he's given me everything I've ever asked for without a word—more than I ever asked for. He hasn't ever known what the word "husband" ought to mean but he's been a very considerate "owner." Let us give him credit for that. I don't think—(*She hesitates*)

FRED Go on! Go on! I expect to hear you love him next.

MRS. BALDWIN (*Smiling*) Don't misunderstand me. I simply can't think him the devil in human form you would make him out to be. (*Grimly*) I love him? It was my kind parents who loved his money. He is so much older than I am and we have nothing in common. Well, I simply don't love him—there's an end to it. And so—being his wife—I hate him! (*Her voice is like a snarl as she says these last words—there is a pause*) But what is your plan?

FRED When the time comes I shall go to him frankly and tell him we love each other. I shall offer to go quietly away with you without any fuss or scandal. If he's the man you think him—and I don't agree with you on that point—he'll get a divorce so secretly it will never even get into the papers. He'll save his own name and yours. If he tries to be nasty about it I know something that'll bring him around. (MRS. BALDWIN *looks at him in astonishment*) Oh, I haven't been idle. His past is none too spotless.

MRS. BALDWIN What have you found out?

FRED I can't tell you now. It's got nothing to do with you anyway. It was a business deal.

MRS. BALDWIN A business deal?

FRED Yes. It happened a long time ago. (*Abruptly changing the subject*) What can be keeping him? What time did he say he'd be here?

MRS. BALDWIN The telegram said "for dinner." (*Suddenly, with intense feeling*) Oh, if you knew the agony that telegram caused me! I knew it had to come but I kept hoping against hope that something would detain him. After the wire came and I knew he would be here, I kept thinking of how he would claim me—force his loathsome kisses on me. (FRED *groans in impotent rage*) I was filled with horror. That is why I asked you to take me away tonight—to save me that degradation. (*After a pause—her face brightening with hope*) It's getting late. Maybe he won't come after all. Fred, dear, we may have one more night together.

(*He bends over and kisses her. The faint throb of a powerful motor with muffler cut out is heard.* FRED *listens for a moment—then kisses* MRS. BALDWIN *hastily*)

FRED There he is now! I know the sound of the car. (*He rushes to the open door and disappears in the darkness*)

MRS. BALDWIN (*Springing tensely to her feet, runs over and unlocks the door to the hall and opens it*) Oh God! (*The noise of the motor sounds louder, then seems to grow fainter, and suddenly ceases altogether*) He's gone to the garage. They're meeting. Oh God!

(*She shrinks away from the door—then remains standing stiffly with one hand clenched on the table. Quick footsteps are heard on the gravel, then on the steps of the veranda. A moment later* ARTHUR BALDWIN *enters from the hall. He comes quickly over to her, takes both of her hands and kisses her. A shudder of disgust runs over her whole body.*

BALDWIN *is a stocky, undersized man of about fifty. His face is puffy and marked by dissipation, and his thick-lipped mouth seems perpetually curled in a smile of cynical scorn. His eyes are small with heavily drooping lids that hide their expression. He talks in rather a bored drawl and exhibits enthusiasm on but two subjects—his racing car and his wife—in the order named. He has on a motoring cap with goggles on it and a linen duster, which he takes off on entering the room and throws in a chair. He is rather foppishly dressed in a perfectly fitting dark gray suit of extreme cut*)

BALDWIN (*Holding his wife at arm's length and throwing an ardent glance at her bare neck and shoulders*) As beautiful as ever, I see. Why, you're all togged out! (*With a half-sneer*) Is it to welcome the prodigal bridegroom?

MRS. BALDWIN (*Forcing a smile*) Of course!

BALDWIN And how has the fairest of the fair been while her lord has been on the broad highway?

MRS. BALDWIN Very well.

BALDWIN Time hang heavily on your hands in this rural paradise?

MRS. BALDWIN (*Nervously avoiding his eyes*) The limousine has been out of commission—Fred has had to send away for some new part or other. I was rather glad of the opportunity to rest up a bit.

You know when you're here we're always on the go. How's the car?

BALDWIN (*Enthusiastically*) Great! (*He drops her hand and takes a cigar out of the box on the table*) I made eighty-six about a week ago. (*He lights the cigar*) Ran across eight straight miles of level road —let her out the limit. It's some car all right! (*His enthusiasm suddenly vanishing—with a frown*) By the way, where's Fred?

MRS. BALDWIN (*Startled*) Wasn't he at the garage?

BALDWIN No. No one was there.

MRS. BALDWIN He must have gone to dinner. We had all given you up. (*Anxiously*) Why do you want to see him?

BALDWIN Because I was forgetting. The car isn't all right just now. I blew out a tire yesterday and went into a ditch—nothing serious. I backed out all right and everything seemed to be okay after I'd put on a new tire. She ran smoothly today until I hit the road up here about six o'clock. That's why I'm so late—had the devil of a time making this hill—or mountain I should say. Engine worked fine but something wrong with the steering gear. It was all I could do to hold the road—and you know I'm no slouch at driving. I nearly ran into boulders and trees innumerable. All the people at the summer camp down the line were looking at me—thought I was drunk I guess. I had to just creep up here. If I'd have gone fast your hubby would be draped around some pine tree right now. (*With a laugh*) Sorry! You'd look well in black. (MRS. BALDWIN *starts guiltily*) I think I'll have to have this house moved into the valley. It's too much of a climb and the roads are devilish. No car, even if it has ninety horsepower, can stand the gaff long. I've paid enough for tires on account of this road to have it macadamized ten times over. Eaten yet?

MRS. BALDWIN No. I wasn't hungry enough to eat alone. I'll have something light later on. And you?

BALDWIN I had something on the way—knew I'd probably be too late up here.

MRS. BALDWIN Shall I have them get you anything?

BALDWIN No. I'm not hungry.

MRS. BALDWIN Then if you don't mind I think I'll go upstairs and take off this dress. I'm rather tired tonight. I'll be with you again in a short time.

BALDWIN Why the formality of asking? Have I been away as long as that? Make yourself comfortable, of course. (*With his cynical laugh*) I have only to humbly thank you for going to all this trouble. I assure you I appreciate it. You look more than charming.

MRS. BALDWIN (*With a cold smile*) Thank you. (*Moving toward the door*) You will find the letters I did not forward on top of the desk.

(*She goes out*)

BALDWIN (*Going to the desk and glancing over the letters*) Humph! There's nothing much here except bills.

(*He throws them down and walks back to the table again.* GENE *enters from the hall and stands just inside the doorway, looking quickly around the room. Having assured herself that* BALDWIN *is alone, she comes farther into the room and waits nervously for him to speak to her. She is a slight, pretty young woman of twenty-one or so neatly dressed in a black ladies-maid costume. Her hair and eyes are black, her features small and regular, her complexion dark*)

BALDWIN (*Glancing up and seeing her*) Why, hello, Gene! As pretty as ever, I see.

GENE Good evening, sir.

BALDWIN Are you looking for Mrs. Baldwin? She just went upstairs to change her dress.

GENE No sir. I just left Mrs. Baldwin. She said she wished to be alone—that I was to tell you she had a headache but would be down later if she felt better.

(*She pauses and clasps her hands nervously together*)

BALDWIN (*Looking at her curiously*) Anything you wish to see me about?

GENE (*A look of resolution coming into her face*) Yes, sir.

BALDWIN (*Half-bored*) All right; what is it? Oh, by the way, before you begin can you tell me if Fred has gone down to the village tonight or not?

GENE I'm quite sure he's over at the garage, sir.

BALDWIN I must phone to him about fixing the car— if he can. Can't use it the way it is. But what is it that's troubling you?

GENE I hardly dare to tell you, sir.

BALDWIN I love to comfort beauty in distress.

GENE I know you'll be awful angry at me when you hear it.

BALDWIN You are foolish to think so. It's a love affair, of course.

GENE Yes, sir.

BALDWIN Well, who is the fortunate party and what has he done or not done?

GENE Oh no, you're mistaken, sir. It isn't my love affair. It's someone else's.

BALDWIN (*Impatiently*) You're very mysterious. Whose is it then?

GENE It's Fred's, sir.

BALDWIN But—I had rather an idea that you and Fred were not altogether indifferent to each other. (*Sarcastically*) You don't mean to tell me the handsome young devil has jilted you?

GENE (*Her voice harsh with anger*) He does not love me any more.

BALDWIN (*Mockingly*) I shall have to chide him. His morals are really too corrupt for his station in life. My only advice to you is to find another sweetheart. There is nothing that consoles one so much for the loss of a lover as—another lover.

GENE (*Trembling with rage at his banter*) I am well through with him. It's you and not me who ought to be concerned the most this time.

BALDWIN (*Frowning*) I? And pray tell me why I should be interested in the amours of my chauffeur?

GENE (*A bit frightened*) There's lots of things happened since you've been away.

BALDWIN (*Irritably*) I am waiting for you to reveal in what way all this concerns me.

GENE They've been together all the time you've been away—every day and (*Hesitating for a moment at the changed look on his face—then resolutely*) every night too. (*Vindictively*) I've watched them when they thought no one was around. I've heard their "I love yous" and their kisses. Oh, they thought they were so safe! But I'll teach him to throw me over the way he did. I'll pay her for all her looking down on me and stealing him away. She's a bad woman, is what I say! Let her keep to her husband like she ought to and not go meddling with other people—

BALDWIN (*Interrupting her in a cold, hard voice and holding himself in control by a mighty effort*) It isn't one of the servants? (GENE *shakes her head*) No. I forget you said she was married. One of the summer people near here? (GENE *shakes her head*) Someone in this house? (GENE *nods.* BALDWIN'S *body grows tense. His heavy lids droop over his eyes, his mouth twitches. He speaks slowly as if the words came with difficulty*) Be careful! Think what you are saying! There is only one other person in this house. Do—you—mean to—say it is that person? (GENE *is too terrified to reply*) Answer me, do you hear? Answer me! Is that the person you refer to?

GENE (*In a frightened whisper*) Yes.

BALDWIN (*Springing at her and clutching her by the throat with both hands*) You lie! You lie! (*He forces her back over the edge of the table. She frantically tries to tear his hands away*) Tell me you lie, damn you, or I'll choke you to hell!

(*She gasps for breath and her face becomes a dark crimson.* BALDWIN *suddenly realizes what he is doing and takes his hands away.* GENE *falls half across the table, her breath coming in great shuddering sobs.* BALDWIN *stands silently beside her waiting until she can speak again. Finally he leads her to one of the Morris chairs and pushes her into it. He stands directly in front of her*)

BALDWIN You can speak again?

GENE (*Weakly*) Yes—no thanks to you.

BALDWIN You understand, don't you, that what you have said requires more proof than the mere statement of a jealous servant.

(*He pronounces the "servant" with a sneer of contempt*)

GENE I've got proof, don't you worry, but I don't know whether I'll show it to you or not. A man that chokes women deserves to be made a fool of.

BALDWIN (*Stung by her scorn*) You will show me, damn you, or—

(*He leans over as if to grab her by the throat again*)

GENE (*Shrinking back in the chair*) Don't you dare touch me or I'll scream and tell them all about it. I'll prove it to you, but it isn't because I'm afraid of you or your threats but simply because I want to get even with her. (*She reaches in under her belt and pulls out a closely folded piece of paper*) Do you recognize her writing when you see it?

BALDWIN Give it to me.

GENE (*Holding it away from him*) Will you promise

to tell her—them—just how you found out—after I'm gone? I'm leaving tomorrow morning. I'd like them to know it was me who spoiled their fun. Will you promise?

BALDWIN Yes! Yes! Anything. Give it to me!

GENE There! Take it.

BALDWIN (*He reads the letter slowly and a terrible expression comes over his pale, twitching features.* GENE *watches him with a smile of triumph. When he speaks his voice is ominously soft and subdued*) What night was this she speaks of?

GENE The night before last.

BALDWIN She says she would come to him at half-past eleven. Did she mean to the garage?

GENE Yes. When she thought we were all in bed in the back part of the house she would slip down and go out the front door. She kept on the grass and in the shade of the trees so no one would notice her.

BALDWIN You know all this?

GENE I followed her on several different nights.

BALDWIN You *must* hate her.

GENE I loved Fred.

BALDWIN Why was she so careless as to write this note? Couldn't she have telephoned or told him?

GENE The little garage telephone was out of order. It was only fixed this morning. The Lynches were here to dinner and she had no chance to speak to him alone. She sent me to the garage to tell him to come over. When he came she pretended to give him some orders and dropped this at his feet. I suspected something, so I was watching and saw it all.

BALDWIN How did you get hold of this?

GENE Yesterday when he went to the village to see if the new part for the limousine had come, I went to the garage and found this in the inside pocket of his other clothes.

BALDWIN (*His eyes narrowing*) He is very careless.

GENE Oh, they knew you wouldn't be home until today and they felt safe. And I knew you wouldn't believe me without proof.

BALDWIN Do you think he has missed this?

GENE No. (*With a sneer*) As you say, he is very careless in such matters. If he does miss it he'll think he has forgotten where he hid it.

BALDWIN (*After a pause—putting the note in his pocket*) You may go. Be sure you do leave in the morning, otherwise—

GENE You needn't fret. I wouldn't stay another day if you paid me a million. (*She yawns heavily*) Oh, I'm glad that's off my mind. I'll sleep tonight. I haven't slept a bit, it seems, since you've been away. (*She goes slowly to the hall door—then turns around and looks at him curiously*) What are you going to do?

BALDWIN Go! Go!

GENE (*With a mocking laugh*) I wish you luck! (*She goes out*)

BALDWIN (*Stares at the rug for a moment—then takes the note out of his pocket and reads it again. In a burst of rage he crumples it up in his hand and curses beneath his breath. His eyes wander to his auto coat and goggles in the chair, then to the garage telephone near his desk. They seem to suggest an idea to him—a way for vengeance. His face lights up with savage joy and he mutters fiercely to himself*) The dirty cur! By God, I'll do it! (*He ponders for a moment, turning over his plan in his mind, then goes over and shuts the door to the hall and striding quickly to the garage telephone, takes off the receiver. After a pause he speaks, making his voice sound as if he were in a state of great anxiety*) Hello! Fred? You haven't touched the car yet? Good! Take it out immediately! Go to the village and get the doctor—any doctor. Mildred—Mrs. Baldwin has been taken very ill. Hemorrhage, I think—blood running from her mouth. She's unconscious—it's a matter of life and death. Drive like hell, do you hear? Drive like hell! Her life's in your hands. Turn the car loose! Drive like hell! (*He hangs up the receiver and stands listening intently, with one hand on the desk. A minute later the purr of an engine is heard. It grows to a roar as the car rushes by on the driveway near the house—then gradually fades in the distance.* BALDWIN'*s thick lips are narrowed taut in a cruel grin*) Drive to hell, you b—rd!

(*The stage is darkened. Half to three-quarters of an hour are supposed to intervene before the lights go up again.*

BALDWIN *is discovered sitting in one of the Morris chairs. He nervously pulls at the cigar he is smoking and glances at the telephone on his desk. There is a ring and goes quickly over to it. He answers in a very low voice)*

BALDWIN Yes. This is Mr. Baldwin. What? Ran into a boulder you say? He's dead? (*This last question burst out exultingly—then in tones of mocking compassion*) How horrible! They're bringing it up here? That's right. How did you happen to find him?—Quite by accident then?—Yes, come right to the house. It *is* terrible—awful road— Knew something of the kind would happen sometime—ever so much obliged for your trouble.

(*He hangs up the receiver and opens the door into the hallway—then pushes the electric bell button in the wall. A moment later* MARY, *the housemaid, enters*)

MARY Yes, sir?

BALDWIN Where's Gene?

MARY She's gone to bed, sir. Shall I call her?

BALDWIN No. You'll do just as well. Will you run up and tell Mrs. Baldwin I'd like very much to see her for a few minutes. Tell her it's something of importance or else I wouldn't disturb her.

MARY Yes, sir.

(*She goes out.* BALDWIN *walks over and fixes the two Morris chairs and lamp so that the light will fall on the face of the person sitting in one while the other will be in shadow. He then sits down in the shaded chair and waits. A minute or so elapses before* MRS. BALDWIN *appears in the doorway. She walks over to him with an expression of wondering curiosity not unmixed with fear. She wears a light blue kimono and bedroom slippers of the same color. Her beautiful hair hangs down her back in loose braid*)

MRS. BALDWIN I'm sorry not to have come down before but my head aches wretchedly. I sent Gene to tell you. Did she?

BALDWIN (*With curious emphasis*) Yes. She told me. Sit down, my dear.

(*He points to the other Morris chair. She sits in it*)

MRS. BALDWIN (*After a pause in which she waits for him to begin and during which he is studying her closely from his position of vantage in the shadow*) I really thought you had gone out again. That was one reason why I didn't come down. I heard the car go out and supposed of course it was you.

BALDWIN No. It was Fred.

MRS. BALDWIN You sent him to the village for something?

BALDWIN No, I simply told him there was something wrong with the steering gear—something I couldn't discover. I told him to attend to it—if he could—the first thing in the morning. It seems he has gone me one better and is trying to locate the trouble tonight. (*With grim sarcasm*) Really, his zeal in my service is astounding.

MRS. BALDWIN (*Trying to conceal her anxiety*) But isn't it very dangerous to go over these roads at night in a car that is practically disabled?

BALDWIN Fred is very careless—very, very careless in some things. I shall have to teach him a lesson. He is absolutely reckless (MRS. BALDWIN *shudders in spite of herself*), especially with other people's property. You are worrying about Fred; but I am bewailing my car, which he is liable to smash from pure overzealousness. Chauffeurs—even overzealous ones—are to be had for the asking, but cars like mine are out of the ordinary.

MRS. BALDWIN (*Coldly*) Why do you talk like that? You know you do not mean it.

BALDWIN I assure you I do—every word of it.

MRS. BALDWIN You said you wished to see me on something of importance?

BALDWIN (*Dryly*) Exactly, my dear. We are coming to that. (*Then, softly*) I wanted to ask you, Mildred, if you are perfectly happy up here.

MRS. BALDWIN (*Astonished*) Why—of course—what makes you ask such a question?

BALDWIN Well, you know I have left you so much alone this summer I feel rather conscience-stricken. You must be bored to death on this mountain with none of your old friends around. I was thinking it might be a good plan for us to economize a bit by letting Fred go and getting along with just my car. It would be quite possible then for you to go to some more fashionable resort where things would be livelier for you.

MRS. BALDWIN (*Eagerly*) I assure you I am quite contented where I am. Of course I miss you and feel a trifle lonely at times, but then I have the other car, and you know I enjoy motoring so much.

BALDWIN Do you? You never seemed to care very much about touring round with me.

MRS. BALDWIN You drive so dreadfully fast I am frightened to death.

BALDWIN Fred is a careful driver then?

MRS. BALDWIN Very careful.

BALDWIN You have no complaint to make against him?

MRS. BALDWIN None at all. I think he is the best chauffeur we have ever had.

BALDWIN Why, I am delighted to hear that. I had an idea he was reckless.

MRS. BALDWIN He is always very careful when he drives me. As for the rest of the help, they are the average with one exception. I think I shall discharge Gene. (BALDWIN *smiles*) She is getting so bold and insolent I can't put up with it any longer. As soon as I can get a new maid I shall let her go.

BALDWIN You may save yourself the trouble. She is going to leave tomorrow. She gave me notice of her departure when you sent her downstairs.

MRS. BALDWIN (*Flushing angrily*) It's just like her to act that way—another piece of her insolence. I suppose I'll have to make the best of it. It's good riddance at all events.

BALDWIN (*In the same soft, half-mocking voice he has used during the whole conversation with his wife*) Do you suppose Fred will stay with us when he finds out?

MRS. BALDWIN (*Puzzled*) Finds out what? Why shouldn't he stay?

BALDWIN He is Gene's lover—or was.

MRS. BALDWIN (*Growing pale—violently*) That is a lie!

BALDWIN (*As if astonished*) Why, my dear, as if it mattered.

MRS. BALDWIN (*Forcing a laugh*) How silly of me! It is my anger at Gene breaking out. But I am sure you are mistaken. I know Gene was very much in love with him but I do not think he ever noticed her.

BALDWIN Now *you* are mistaken. He may not care for her at present but there was a time when—

MRS. BALDWIN (*Biting her lips*) I do not believe it. That was servant's gossip you heard.

BALDWIN It was not what I heard, my dear Mildred, but what I saw with my own eyes.

MRS. BALDWIN (*In an agony of jealousy*) You—saw—them?

BALDWIN (*Apparently oblivious of her agitation*) In a very compromising position, to say the least. (MRS. BALDWIN *winks back her tears of rage*) But that was long ago. (MRS. BALDWIN *sighs as if relieved*) Besides, what have these servant intrigues to do with us? (MRS. BALDWIN *tries to look indifferent*) I was only joking about Fred leaving. In fact, from what Gene said, Fred already has some other foolish woman in love with him. Only this time it is no maid, if you please, but the lady of the house herself who has lost her heart at the sight of his dark curls. The fellow is ambitious.

MRS. BALDWIN (*Her face terror-stricken—her words faltering on her lips*) Do—you—know—who—this woman—is?

BALDWIN (*Watching her with grim amusement*) I have one of her letters here. Would you care to read it?

(*He takes her note from his pocket and gives it to her*)

MRS. BALDWIN (*Taking it in her trembling hand and smoothing it out. One glance and her face grows crimson with shame. She seems to crumple up in her chair. After a moment she throws her head back defiantly and looks up at him—a pause*) Well?

BALDWIN (*Dryly, his voice softly menacing*) Well? You do not know how to play the game, my sweet Mildred. If ever guilt was stamped on a face it was on yours a moment ago.

MRS. BALDWIN (*Her eyes flashing*) Yes. I love him! I acknowledge it.

BALDWIN You are better at affirming than denying. It takes courage to proclaim oneself the mistress of one's chauffeur—to play second fiddle to one's maid!

MRS. BALDWIN (*In a fury*) You lie! He is a man and not the beast you are.

BALDWIN (*Softly*) Be calm! You will awaken your rival and she will listen and gloat!

MRS. BALDWIN (*Lowering her voice to a shrill whisper*) Oh, it was she who stole that letter?

BALDWIN Exactly. You are a novice at the game, my dear. Take the advice of a hardened old sinner—in the years and loves to come never write any more letters. Kisses come and kisses go, but letters remain forever—and are often brought into court.

MRS. BALDWIN (*Relieved at the easy way he takes it*) I cannot help this. I love him—that's all. (*Pause*) What are you going to do?

BALDWIN It was to tell you that, I sent for you.

MRS. BALDWIN You will get a divorce?

BALDWIN No.

MRS. BALDWIN You will keep me tied to you when you know I do not love you—when you know I love someone else? (*In pleading tones*) You will not be as hard on me as that, will you, Arthur? This is not all my fault. You have never really loved me. We are not the same age. (BALDWIN *winces*) We do not look at things in the same light—we have nothing in common. It would be needless cruelty to both of us to keep up this farce. You will not keep me tied to you for mere spite, will you?

BALDWIN (*In his kindest tone*) No. What I intend to do is to *let you* get a divorce. I will give you all the evidence you need. Could I be fairer than that?

MRS. BALDWIN (*Staring at him as if she could not believe her ears*) You will do that? (*She rushes over and kneels at his feet, kissing his hands and sobbing*) Oh, thank you! Thank you!

BALDWIN (*Looking down at her bowed head with a cruel smile*) There! There! It is no more than just. I realize that youth must have its day. You should have trusted me.

MRS. BALDWIN (*Her voice thrilling with gratitude*) How could I dream that you would be so kind? I did not dare to hope that you would ever forgive me—and he was certain you would think only of revenge. Oh, how unjust we have been to you!

(*She takes one of his hands in hers and kisses it*)

BALDWIN It is true neither of you have given me due credit for being the man I am, or you would never have acted as you did. I have known from the first it must have been for money you married me—(*With a twisted smile*) An old man like me. Tell me the truth. Wasn't it?

MRS. BALDWIN (*Falteringly*) Yes. I would not lie to you now. My family forced me into it. You must have realized that. I hardly knew you, but they were nagging me night and day until I gave in. It was anything to get away from home. Oh, I am sorry, so sorry! Will you forgive me?

BALDWIN (*Evading her question*) I have done my best to make you happy. I have given you everything you desired, have I not?

MRS. BALDWIN You have been very good, very kind to me. I have tried to love you but there has always been a gulf separating us. I could never understand you.

BALDWIN I have trusted you, have I not—always and in everything?

MRS. BALDWIN (*Slowly*) Yes, but you have never loved me. I have been just a plaything with which you amused yourself—or so it has always seemed to me. Perhaps I have been unjust to you—in that too.

BALDWIN If I have regarded you as a plaything I was only accepting the valuation your parents set upon you when they sold you. But these things are over and done and it is useless to discuss them. Let us talk of the present. You love Fred?

MRS. BALDWIN Yes, I do.

BALDWIN I will not stand in your way. You shall have him.

MRS. BALDWIN (*Getting up and putting her arms around his neck*) Oh, I do love you now—you are so good to me.

(*She kisses him on the lips. He does not move or touch her in any way but looks at her coldly with half-closed eyes, his thick lips curled in a sneering smile. In sudden fear* MRS. BALDWIN *moves away from him with a shudder. The noise of an automobile is faintly heard.* BALDWIN *springs to his feet, his face transformed with savage exultation*)

BALDWIN (*With a hard laugh*) Thanks for that Judas kiss. I hear a machine coming. It is Fred, I know. We will have him in and relieve his mind by telling him of our agreement.

(*The machine is heard coming slowly up the drive toward the house*)

MRS. BALDWIN (*Frightened by* BALDWIN'*s change of manner*) It does not sound like your car.

BALDWIN It is Fred, I tell you. I know it is Fred. (*The car stops before the house. The horn sounds.* BALDWIN *hurries to the door leading into the hall. Several persons can be heard coming up the steps to the veranda. A door is opened and shut and the hushed murmur of voices comes from the hallway*) In here if you please—in here! (MRS. BALDWIN *moves closer to the door, her face wan with the terror of an unknown fear. Three men, one a chauffeur, the other two servants of some description, enter carrying the dead man. Two are supporting the shoulders and one the feet. A dark robe is wrapped around the whole body. They hurriedly place it on the divan to which* BALDWIN *points and go out quickly, glad to be rid of their gruesome task.* MRS. BALDWIN *is swaying weakly on her feet, her eyes wildly staring at the figure on the divan. Suddenly she gives a frantic cry, and rushing over, pulls the covering from the dead man's head. The livid countenance of* FRED *is revealed. Several crimson streaks run down his cheek from his clotted, curly hair.* MRS. BALDWIN *shrieks and falls senseless on the floor.* BALDWIN, *who has watched her with the same cruel smile on his lips, goes slowly over and pushes the button of the electric bell* MARY *appears*) Help me to get Mrs. Baldwin to her room.

(*He picks up the prostrate woman in his arms, and with the assistance of the maid, carries her out to the hallway. They can be heard stumbling up the stairs to the floor above. A moment later* BALDWIN *reappears, breathing heavily from his exertion, his pale face emotionless and cold. He stands looking down at the dead body on the divan—finally shrugs his shoulders disdainfully, comes over to the table, takes a cigar out of the box and lights it. The maid rushes in, all out of breath and flustered*)

MARY Please go upstairs, sir. Mrs. Baldwin has come to, and she ordered me out of the room. I think she's gone mad, sir. She's pulling out all the drawers looking for something. (*A dull report sounds from upstairs. The maid gives a terrified gasp.* BALDWIN *is startled for a moment and starts as if to run out to the hallway. Then his face hardens and he speaks to the trembling maid in even tones*) Mrs. Baldwin has just shot herself. You had better phone for the doctor, Mary.

Curtain

BOUND EAST FOR CARDIFF

A Play in One Act

Characters

YANK
DRISCOLL
COCKY
DAVIS
SCOTTY
OLSON
PAUL
SMITTY
IVAN
THE CAPTAIN
THE SECOND MATE

The action of the play takes place in the years preceding the outbreak of World War I

SCENE. *The seamen's forecastle of the British tramp steamer Glencairn on a foggy night midway on the voyage between New York and Cardiff. An irregular-shaped compartment, the sides of which almost meet at the far end to from a triangle. Sleeping bunks about six feet long, ranged three deep with a space of three feet separating the upper from the lower, are built against the sides. On the right above the bunks three or four port holes can be seen. In front of the bunks, rough wooden benches. Over the bunks on the left, a lamp in a bracket. In the left foreground, a doorway. On the floor near it, a pail with a tin dipper. Oilskins are hanging from a hook near the doorway.*

The far side of the forecastle is so narrow that it contains only one series of bunks.

In under the bunks a glimpse can be had of sea-chests, suit-cases, sea-boots, etc., jammed in indiscriminately.

At regular intervals of a minute or so the blast of the steamer's whistle can be heard above all the other sounds.

Five men are sitting on the benches talking. They are dressed in dirty patched suits of dungaree, flannel shirts, and all are in their stocking feet. Four of the men are pulling on pipes and the air is heavy with rancid tobacco smoke. Sitting on the top bunk in the left foreground, a Norwegian, Paul, is softly playing some folk song on a battered accordion. He stops from time to time to listen to the conversation.

In the lower bunk in the rear a dark-haired, hard-featured man is lying apparently asleep. One of his arms is stretched limply over the side of the bunk. His face is very pale, and drops of clammy perspiration glisten on his forehead.

It is nearing the end of the dog-watch—about ten minutes to eight in the evening.

COCKY (*a wizened runt of a man. He is telling a story. The others are listening with amused, incredulous faces, interrupting him at the end of each sentence with loud derisive guffaws*). Makin' love to me, she was ! It's Gawd's truth ! A bloomin' nigger ! Greased all over with cocoanut oil, she was. Gawd blimey, I couldn't stand 'er. Bloody old cow, I says ; and with that I fetched 'er a biff on the ear wot knocked 'er silly, an'—— (*He is interrupted by a roar of laughter from the others.*)

DAVIS (*a middle-aged man with black hair and moustache*). You're a liar, Cocky.

SCOTTY (*a dark young fellow*). Ho-ho! Ye werr neverr in New Guinea in yourr life, I'm thinkin'.

OLSON (*a Swede with a drooping blond moustache—with ponderous sarcasm*). Yust tink of it! You say she wass a cannibal, Cocky?

DRISCOLL (*a brawny Irishman with the battered features of a prizefighter*). How cud ye doubt ut, Ollie? A quane av the naygurs she musta been surely. Who else wud think herself aqual to fallin' in love wid a beauthiful, divil-may-care rake av a man the loike av Cocky? (*A burst of laughter from the crowd.*)

COCKY (*indignantly*). Gawd strike me dead if it ain't true, every bleedin' word of it. 'Appened ten year ago come Christmas.

SCOTTY. 'Twas a Christmas dinner she had her eyes on.

DAVIS. He'd a been a tough old bird.

DRISCOLL. 'Tis lucky for both av ye ye escaped; for the quane av the cannibal isles wad 'a died av the belly ache the day afther Christmas, divil a doubt av ut. (*The laughter at this is long and loud.*)

COCKY (*sullenly*). Blarsted fat 'eads!

(*The sick man in the lower bunk in the rear groans and moves restlessly. There is a hushed silence. All the men turn and stare at him.*)

DRISCOLL. Ssshh! (*In a hushed whisper.*) We'd best not be talkin' so loud and him tryin' to have a bit av a sleep. (*He tiptoes softly to the side of the bunk.*) Yank! You'd be wantin' a drink av wather, maybe? (*Yank does not reply. Driscoll bends over and looks at him.*) It's asleep he is, sure enough. His breath is chokin' in his throat loike wather gurglin' in a poipe. (*He comes back quietly and sits down. All are silent, avoiding each other's eyes.*)

COCKY (*after a pause*). Pore devil! It's over the side for 'im, Gawd 'elp 'im.

DRISCOLL. Stop your croakin'! He's not dead yet, and, praise God, he'll have many a long day yet before him.

SCOTTY (*shaking his head doubtfully*). He's bod, mon, he's verry bod.

DAVIS. Lucky he's alive. Many a man's light woulda gone out after a fall like that.

OLSON. You saw him fall?

DAVIS. Right next to him. He and me was goin' down in number two hold to do some chippin'. He puts his leg over careless-like and misses the ladder and plumps straight down to the bottom. I was scared to look over for a minute, and then I heard him groan and I scuttled down after him. He was hurt bad inside, for the blood was drippin' from the side of his mouth. He was groanin' hard, but he never let a word out of him.

COCKY. An' you blokes remember when we 'auled 'im in 'ere? Oh, 'ell, 'e says, oh, 'ell—like that, and nothink else.

OLSON. Did the captain know where he iss hurted?

COCKY. That silly ol' josser! Wot the 'ell would 'e know abaht anythink?

SCOTTY (*scornfully*). He fiddles in his mouth wi' a bit of glass.

DRISCOLL (*angrily*). The divil's own life ut is to be out on the lonely sea wid nothin' betune you and a grave in the ocean but a spindle-shanked, grey-whiskered auld fool the loike av him. 'Twas enough to make a saint shwear to see him wid his gold watch in his hand, tryin' to look as wise as an owl on a tree, and all the toime he not knowin' whether 'twas cholery or the barber's itch was the matther wid Yank.

SCOTTY (*sardonically*). He gave him a dose of salts, na doot?

DRISCOLL. Divil a thing he gave him at all, but looked in the book he had wid him, and shook his head, and walked out widout sayin' a word, the second mate afther him no wiser than himself, God's curse on the two av him!

COCKY (*after a pause*). Yank was a good shipmate, pore beggar. Lend me four bob in Noo Yark, 'e did.

DRISCOLL (*warmly*). A good shipmate he was and is, none betther. Ye said no more than the truth, Cocky. Five years and more ut is since first I shipped wid him, and we've stuck together iver since through good luck and bad. Fights we've had, God help us, but 'twas only when we'd a bit av drink taken, and we always shook hands the nixt mornin'. Whativer was his was mine, and many's the toime I'd a been on the beach or worse, but for him. And now—— (*His voice trembles as he fights to control his emotion.*) Divil take me if I'm not startin' to blubber loike an auld woman, and he not dead at all, but goin' to live many a long year yet, maybe.

DAVIS. The sleep'll do him good. He seems better now.

OLSON. If he wude eat someting——

DRISCOLL. Wud ye have him be eatin' in his condishun? Sure it's hard enough on the rest av us wid nothin' the matther wid our insides to be stomachin' the skoff on this rusty lime-juicer.

SCOTTY (*indignantly*). It's a starvation ship.

DAVIS. Plenty o' work and no food—and the owners ridin' around in carriages!

OLSON. Hash, hash! Stew, stew! Marmalade, py damn! (*He spits disgustedly.*)

COCKY. Bloody swill! Fit only for swine is wot I say.

DRISCOLL. And the dishwather they disguise wid the name av tea! And the putty they call bread! My belly feels loike I'd swalleyed a dozen rivets at the thought av ut! And sea-biscuit that'd break the teeth av a lion if he had the misfortune to take a bite at one!

(*Unconsciously they have all raised their voices, forgetting the sick man in their sailor's delight at finding something to grumble about.*)

PAUL (*swings his feet over the side of his bunk, stops playing his accordion, and says slowly.*) And rot-ten po-tay-toes! (*He starts in playing again. The sick man gives a groan of pain.*)

DRISCOLL (*holding up his hand*). Shut your mouths, all av you. 'Tis a hell av a thing for us to be complainin' about our guts, and a sick man maybe dyin' listenin' to us. (*Gets up and shakes his fist at the Norwegian.*) God stiffen you, ye square-head scut! Put down that organ av yours or I'll break your ugly face for you. Is that banshee schreechin' fit music for a sick man?

(*The Norwegian puts his accordion in the bunk and lies back and closes his eyes. Driscoll goes over and stands beside Yank. The steamer's whistle sounds particularly loud in the silence.*)

DAVIS. Damn this fog! (*Reaches in under a bunk and yanks out a pair of sea-boots, which he pulls on.*) My look-out next, too. Must be nearly eight bells, boys.

(*With the exception of Olson, all the men sitting up put on oilskins, sou'-westers, sea-boots, etc., in preparation for the watch on deck. Olson crawls into a lower bunk on the right.*)

SCOTTY. My wheel.

OLSON (*disgustedly*). Nothin' but yust dirty weather all dis voyage. I yust can't sleep when weestle blow. (*He turns his back to the light and is soon fast asleep and snoring.*)

SCOTTY. If this fog keeps up, I'm tellin' ye, we'll no be in Carrdiff for a week or more.

DRISCOLL. 'Twas just such a night as this the auld Dover wint down. Just about this toime ut was, too, and we all sittin' round in the fo'c'sle, Yank beside me, whin all av a suddint we heard a great slitherin' crash, and the ship heeled over till we was all in a heap on wan side. What came afther I disremimber exactly, except 'twas a hard shift to get the boats over the side before the auld teakittle sank. Yank was in the same boat wid me, and sivin morthal days we drifted wid scarcely a drop of wather or a bite to chew on. 'Twas Yank here that held me down whin I wanted to jump into the ocean, roarin' mad wid the thirst. Picked up we were on the same day wid only Yank in his senses, and him steerin' the boat.

COCKY (*protestingly*). Blimey, but you're a cheerful blighter, Driscoll! Talkin' abaht shipwrecks in this 'ere blushin' fog. (*Yank groans and stirs uneasily, opening his eyes. Driscoll hurries to his side.*)

DRISCOLL. Are ye feelin' any betther, Yank?

YANK (*in a weak voice*). No.

DRISCOLL. Sure, you must be. You look as sthrong as an ox. (*Appealing to the others.*) Am I tellin' him a lie?

DAVIS. The sleep's done you good.

COCKY. You'll be 'avin' your pint of beer in Cardiff this day week.

SCOTTY. And fish and chips, mon!

YANK (*peevishly*). What're yuh all lyin' fur? D'yuh think I'm scared to—— (*He hesitates as if frightened by the word he is about to say.*)

DRISCOLL. Don't be thinkin' such things!

(*The ship's bell is heard heavily tolling eight times. From the forecastle head above the voice of the look-out rises in a long wail:* Aaall's welll. *The men look uncertainly at Yank as if undecided whether to say good-bye or not.*)

YANK (*in an agony of fear*). Don't leave me, Drisc! I'm dyin', I tell yuh. I won't stay here alone with every one snorin'. I'll go out on deck. (*He makes a feeble attempt to rise, but sinks back with a sharp groan. His breath comes in wheezy gasps.*) Don't leave me, Drisc! (*His face grows white and his head falls back with a jerk.*)

DRISCOLL. Don't be worryin', Yank. I'll not move a step out av here—and let that divil av a bosun curse his black head off. You speak a word to the bosun, Cocky. Tell him that Yank is bad took and I'll be stayin' wid him a while yet.

COCKY. Right-o. (*Cocky, Davis, and Scotty go out quietly.*)

COCKY (*from the alleyway*). Gawd blimey, the fog's thick as soup.

DRISCOLL. Are ye satisfied now, Yank? (*Receiving no answer, he bends over the still form.*) He's fainted, God help him! (*He gets a tin dipper from the bucket and bathes Yank's forehead with the water. Yank shudders and opens his eyes.*)

YANK (*slowly*). I thought I was goin' then. Wha' did yuh wanta wake me up fur?

DRISCOLL (*with forced gaiety*). Is it wishful for heaven ye are?

YANK (*gloomily*). Hell, I guess.

DRISCOLL (*crossing himself involuntarily*). For the love av the saints don't be talkin' loike that! You'd give a man the creeps. It's chippin' rust on deck you'll be in a day or two wid the best av us.

(*Yank does not answer, but closes his eyes wearily. The seaman who has been on look-out, Smitty, a young Englishman, comes in and takes off his dripping oil-skins. While he is doing this the man whose turn at the wheel has been relieved enters. He is a dark, burly fellow with a round stupid face. The Englishman steps softly over to Driscoll. The other crawls into a lower bunk.*)

SMITTY (*whispering*). How's Yank?

DRISCOLL. Betther. Ask him yourself. He's awake.

YANK. I'm all right, Smitty.

SMITTY. Glad to hear it, Yank. (*He crawls to an upper bunk and is soon asleep.*)

IVAN (*The stupid-faced seaman who came in after Smitty twists his head in the direction of the sick man.* You feel gude, Jank?

YANK (*wearily*). Yes, Ivan.

IVAN. Dot's gude. (*He rolls over on his side and falls asleep immediately.*)

YANK (*after a pause broken only by snores—with a bitter laugh*). Good-bye and good luck to the lot of you!

DRISCOLL. Is ut painin' you again?

YANK. It hurts like hell—here. (*He points to the lower part of his chest on the left side.*) I guess my old pump's busted. Ooohh!

(*A spasm of pain contracts his pale features. He presses his hand to his side and writhes on the thin mattress of his bunk. The perspiration stands out in beads on his forehead.*)

DRISCOLL (*terrified*). Yank! Yank! What is ut? (*Jumping to his feet.*) I'll run for the captain. (*He starts for the doorway.*)

YANK (*sitting up in his bunk, frantic with fear*). Don't leave me, Drisc! For God's sake don't leave me alone! (*He leans over the side of his bunk and spits. Driscoll comes back to him.*) Blood! Ugh!

DRISCOLL. Blood again! I'd best be gettin' the captain.

YANK. No, no, don't leave me! If yuh do I'll git up and follow you. I ain't no coward, but

I'm scared to stay here with all of them asleep and snorin'. (*Driscoll, not knowing what to do, sits down on the bench beside him. He grows calmer and sinks back on the mattress.*) The captain can't do me no good, yuh know it yourself. The pain ain't so bad now, but I thought it had me then. It was like a buzz-saw cuttin' into me.

DRISCOLL (*fiercely*). God blarst ut!

(*The Captain and the Second Mate of the steamer enter the forecastle. The captain is an old man with grey moustache and whiskers. The Mate is clean-shaven and middle-aged. Both are dressed in simple blue uniforms.*)

THE CAPTAIN (*taking out his watch and feeling Yank's pulse*). And how is the sick man?

YANK (*feebly*). All right, sir.

THE CAPTAIN. And the pain in the chest?

YANK. It still hurts, sir, worse than ever.

THE CAPTAIN (*taking a thermometer from his pocket and putting it into Yank's mouth*). Here. Be sure and keep this in under your tongue, not over it.

THE MATE (*after a pause*). Isn't this your watch on deck, Driscoll?

DRISCOLL. Yes, sorr, but Yank was fearin' to be alone, and——

THE CAPTAIN. That's all right, Driscoll.

DRISCOLL. Thank ye, sorr.

THE CAPTAIN (*stares at his watch for a moment or so; then takes the thermometer from Yank's mouth and goes to the lamp to read it. His expression grows very grave. He beckons the Mate and Driscoll to the corner near the doorway. Yank watches them furtively. The Captain speaks in a low voice to the Mate.*) Way up, both of them. (*To Driscoll.*) Has he been spitting blood again?

DRISCOLL. Not much for the hour just past, sorr, but before that——

THE CAPTAIN. A great deal?

DRISCOLL. Yes, sorr.

THE CAPTAIN. He hasn't eaten anything?

DRISCOLL. No, sorr.

THE CAPTAIN. Did he drink that medicine I sent him?

DRISCOLL. Yes, sorr, but it didn't stay down.

THE CAPTAIN (*shaking his head*). I'm afraid—he's very weak. I can't do anything else for him. It's too serious for me. If this had only happened a week later we'd be in Cardiff in time to——

DRISCOLL. Plaze help him some way, sorr!

THE CAPTAIN (*impatiently*). But, my good man, I'm not a doctor. (*More kindly as he sees Driscoll's grief.*) You and he have been shipmates a long time?

DRISCOLL. Five years and more, sorr.

THE CAPTAIN. I see. Well, don't let him move. Keep him quiet and we'll hope for the best. I'll read the matter up and send him some medicine, something to ease the pain, anyway. (*Goes over to Yank.*) Keep up your courage! You'll be better to-morrow. (*He breaks down lamely before Yank's steady gaze.*) We'll pull you through all right—and—hm—well—coming, Robinson? Dammit! (*He goes out hurriedly, followed by the Mate.*)

DRISCOLL (*trying to conceal his anxiety*). Didn't I tell you you wasn't half as sick as you thought you was? The Captain'll have you out on deck cursin' and swearin' loike a trooper before the week is out.

YANK. Don't lie, Drisc. I heard what he said, and if I didn't I c'd tell by the way I feel. I know what's goin' to happen. I'm goin' to—— (*He hesitates for a second—then resolutely.*) I'm goin' to die, that's what, and the sooner the better!

DRISCOLL (*wildly*). No, and be damned to you, you're not. I'll not let you.

YANK. It ain't no use, Drisc. I ain't got a chance, but I ain't scared. Gimme a drink of water, will yuh, Drisc? My throat's burnin' up. (*Driscoll brings the dipper full of water and supports his head while he drinks in great gulps.*)

DRISCOLL (*seeking vainly for some word of comfort*). Are ye feelin' more aisy loike now?

YANK. Yes—now—when I know it's all up. (*A pause.*) You mustn't take it so hard, Drisc. I was just thinkin' it ain't as bad as people think—dyin'. I ain't never took much stock in the truck them sky-pilots preach. I ain't never had religion; but I know whatever it is what comes after it can't be no worser'n this. I don't like to leave you,

Drisc, but—that's all.

DRISCOLL (*with a groan*). Lad, lad, don't be talkin'.

YANK. This sailor life ain't much to cry about leavin'—just one ship after another, hard work, small pay, and bum grub ; and when we git into port, just a drunk endin' up in a fight, and all your money gone, and then ship away again. Never meetin' no nice people ; never gittin' outa sailor town, hardly, in any port ; travellin' all over the world and never seein' none of it ; without no one to care whether you're alive or dead. (*With a bitter smile.*) There ain't much in all that that'd make yuh sorry to lose it, Drisc.

DRISCOLL (*gloomily*). It's a hell av a life, the sea.

YANK (*musingly*). It must be great to stay on dry land all your life and have a farm with a house of your own with cows and pigs and chickens, 'way in the middle of the land where yuh'd never smell the sea or see a ship. It must be great to have a wife, and kids to play with at night after supper when your work was done. It must be great to have a home of your own, Drisc.

DRISCOLL (*with a great sigh*). It must, surely ; but what's the use av thinkin' av ut ? Such things are not for the loikes av us.

YANK. Sea-farin' is all right when you're young and don't care, but we ain't chickens no more, and somehow, I dunno, this last year has seemed rotten, and I've had a hunch I'd quit—with you, of course—and we'd save our coin, and go to Canada or Argentine or some place and git a farm, just a small one, just enough to live on. I never told yuh this cause I thought you'd laugh at me.

DRISCOLL (*enthusiastically*). Laugh at you, is ut ? When I'm havin' the same thoughts myself, toime afther toime. It's a grand idea and we'll be doin' ut sure if you'll stop your crazy notions—about—about bein' so sick.

YANK (*sadly*). Too late. We shouldn'ta made this trip, and then—— How'd all the fog git in here ?

DRISCOLL. Fog ?

YANK. Everything looks misty. Must be my eyes gittin' weak, I guess. What was we talkin' of a minute ago ? Oh, yes, a farm. It's too late. (*His mind wandering.*) Argentine, did I say ? D'yuh remember the times we've had in Buenos Aires ? The moving pictures in Barracas ? Some class to them, d'yuh remember ?

DRISCOLL (*with satisfaction*). I do that ; and so does the piany player. He'll not be forgettin' the black eye I gave him in a hurry.

YANK. Remember the time we was there on the beach and had to go to Tommy Moore's boarding house to git shipped ? And he sold us rotten oilskins and sea-boots full of holes, and shipped us on a skysail yarder round the Horn, and took two months' pay for it. And the days we used to sit on the park benches along the Paseo Colon with the vigilantes lookin' hard at us ? And the songs at the Sailor's Opera where the guy played ragtime—d'yuh remember them ?

DRISCOLL. I do, surely.

YANK. And La Plata—phew, the stink of the hides ! I always liked Argentine—all except that booze, caña. How drunk we used to git on that, remember ?

DRISCOLL. Cud I forget ut ? My head pains me at the menshun av that divil's brew.

YANK. Remember the night I went crazy with the heat in Singapore ? And the time you was pinched by the cops in Port Said ? And the time we was both locked up in Sydney for fightin' ?

DRISCOLL. I do so.

YANK. And that fight on the dock at Cape Town—— (*His voice betrays great inward perturbation.*)

DRISCOLL (*hastily*). Don't be thinkin' av that now. 'Tis past and gone.

YANK. D'yuh think He'll hold it up against me ?

DRISCOLL (*mystified*). Who's that ?

YANK. God. They say He sees everything. He must know it was done in fair fight, in self-defence, don't yuh think ?

DRISCOLL. Av course. Ye stabbed him, and be damned to him, for the skulkin' swine he was, afther him tryin' to stick you in the back, and you not suspectin'. Let your conscience be aisy. I wisht I had nothin' blacker than that on my sowl. I'd not be afraid av the angel Gabriel himself.

YANK (*with a shudder*). I c'd see him a minute

ago with the blood spurtin' out of his neck. Ugh!

DRISCOLL. The fever, ut is, that makes you see such things. Give no heed to ut.

YANK (*uncertainly*). You don't think He'll hold it up agin me—God, I mean?

DRISCOLL. If there's justice in hiven, no! (*Yank seems comforted by this assurance.*)

YANK (*after a pause*). We won't reach Cardiff for a week at least. I'll be buried at sea.

DRISCOLL (*putting his hands over his ears*) Ssshh! I won't listen to you.

YANK (*as if he had not heard him*). It's as good a place as any other, I s'pose—only I always wanted to be buried on dry land. But what the hell'll I care—then? (*Fretfully.*) Why should it be a rotten night like this with that damned whistle blowin' and people snorin' all round? I wish the stars was out, and the moon, too; I c'd lie out on deck and look at them, and it'd make it easier to go—somehow.

DRISCOLL. For the love av God don't be talkin' loike that!

YANK. Whatever pay's comin' to me yuh can divvy up with the rest of the boys; and you take my watch. It ain't worth much, but it's all I've got.

DRISCOLL. But have ye no relations at all to call your own?

YANK. No, not as I know of. One thing I forgot: You know Fanny the barmaid at the Red Stork in Cardiff?

DRISCOLL. Sure, and who doesn't?

YANK. She's been good to me. She tried to lend me half a crown when I was broke there last trip. Buy her the biggest box of candy yuh c'n find in Cardiff. (*Breaking down—in a choking voice.*) It's hard to ship on this voyage I'm goin' on—alone! (*Driscoll reaches out and grasps his hand. There is a pause, during which both fight to control themselves.*) My throat's like a furnace. (*He gasps for air.*) Gimme a drink of water, will yuh, Drisc? *Driscoll gets him a dipper of water.*) I wish this was a pint of beer. Oooohh!

(*He chokes, his face convulsed with agony, his hands tearing at his shirt front. The dipper falls from his nerveless fingers.*)

DRISCOLL. For the love av God, what is ut, Yank?

YANK (*speaking with tremendous difficulty*). S'long, Drisc! (*He stares straight in front of him with eyes starting from their sockets.*) Who's that?

DRISCOLL. Who? What?

YANK (*faintly*). A pretty lady dressed in black. (*His face twitches and his body writhes in a final spasm, then straightens out rigidly.*)

DRISCOLL (*pale with horror*). Yank! Yank! Say a word to me for the love av hiven! (*He shrinks away from the bunk, making the sign of the cross. Then comes back and puts a trembling hand on Yank's chest and bends closely over the body.*)

COCKY (*from the alleyway*). Oh, Driscoll! Can you leave Yank for arf a mo' and give me a 'and?

DRISCOLL (*with a great sob*). Yank! (*He sinks down on his knees beside the bunk, his head on his hands. His lips move in some half-remembered prayer.*)

COCKY (*enters, his oilskins and sou'-wester glistening with drops of water*). The fog's lifted. (*Cocky sees Driscoll and stands staring at him with open mouth. Driscoll makes the sign of the cross again.*)

COCKY (*mockingly*). Sayin' 'is prayers!

(*He catches sight of the still figure in the bunk and an expression of awed understanding comes over his face. He takes off his dripping sou'-wester and stands, scratching his head.*)

COCKY (*in a hushed whisper*). Gawd blimey!

CURTAIN

SERVITUDE

A Play in Three Acts

Characters

DAVID ROYLSTON, *playwright and novelist*
ALICE ROYLSTON, *his wife*
DAVIE } *their children*
RUTH }
GEORGE FRAZER, *a broker*
ETHEL FRAZER, *his wife*
BENTON, *a manservant*
WESON, *a gardener*

Act One

SCENE—*The study in the house of* DAVID ROYLSTON *at Tarryville-on-Hudson, New York. In the middle of the far side of the room, a fireplace. To the right of it, a door. The remaining space of the back wall is covered by bookcases which frame the fireplace and door. In the left foreground another door. Next to it, a writing desk. Still farther back, a bookcase. On the right, a leather sofa and armchairs. On either side of the sofa, an open window looking out on the garden. In the center of the room, a table on which are a heap of books and an electric reading lamp with a green shade. A few framed prints of Old Masters are hung on the walls.*

It is about ten o'clock on a sultry night in early May. DAVID ROYLSTON *is seated at the table, writing. He is a tall, slender, dark-haired man of thirty-five with large handsome features, a strong, ironical mouth half-hidden by a black mustache, and keenly intelligent dark eyes. He has taken off his coat, which hangs from the back of his chair. He wears a white shirt with soft collar and black bow tie, gray trousers and low tan shoes with rubber soles.*

BENTON *enters from the door at the rear and stands waiting for* ROYLSTON *to notice his presence. He is fifty-five, clean-shaven, discreetly soft-spoken. One of his eyes is badly crossed, giving him a look of sly villainy quite out of keeping with his placid temperament. He wears livery.*

ROYLSTON (*Looking up from his writing*) Well, Benton?

BENTON Shall I shut the windows, sir? It's started to rain a little.

ROYLSTON No, I will close them myself when I go to bed.

BENTON (*Reproachfully*) They were open when I came down this morning, sir.

ROYLSTON Were they? I must have fogotten all about them last night. Never mind; there's nothing much worth the stealing in this house except ideas, and the thieves of ideas are not usually housebreakers. But if it will ease your anxiety, you may close them. There's a draft in here.

BENTON Yes, sir.

(*He closes the windows*)

ROYLSTON Any telephone calls while I was out?

BENTON Mrs. Roylston called up, sir; wished me to tell you that she and the children had arrived safely in New York; had a very pleasant trip in the motor; roads were fine all the way down. She said the children were very excited to think they were really going to the theatre.

ROYLSTON (*Abstractedly*) Ah, indeed. No one else called up?

BENTON No, sir.

ROYLSTON Not even the young lady who has (*Ironically*) asked my advice so frequently of late?

BENTON No, sir.

ROYLSTON Well, whenever the young lady in question calls up again, you are to tell her I am writing and cannot be disturbed.

BENTON Yes, sir.

ROYLSTON (*Impatiently*) She is becoming a bore; and I am in the midst of a play and have no time for such foolishness.

BENTON Very good, sir. Anything else before I go to bed, sir?

ROYLSTON No, you may go. (BENTON *takes* ROYLSTON'*s light overcoat, hat and stick, wihch are lying on one the armchairs, and starts to go out*) Leave those here. I may take a walk later on to get a breath of the spring and blow the cobwebs out of my brain, and I don't care to be barking my shins in the dark hall. (BENTON *lays them down again. A doorbell is heard ringing somewhere in the house*) Who can that be at this time of the night? (*As* BENTON *hurries out through the door on the left*) Remember, Benton, I'm busy—too busy to be disturbed.

BENTON Yes, sir.

(*He goes out.* ROYLSTON *bites his pen nervously, trying to concentrate on his thoughts. A minute or so later* BENTON *enters. He is visibly embarrassed and is turning over a card in his fingers*)

ROYLSTON Well?

BENTON It's a lady, sir.

ROYLSTON Has she gone?

BENTON No, sir, she—

ROYLSTON (*Frowning*) Did you tell her I was busy?

BENTON Yes, sir, but she said she must see you on a very important matter; said she wouldn't leave till she saw you. This is her card, sir.

ROYLSTON (*Looking at it*) Mrs. George Frazer—hm— Mrs., eh? Never heard of her. An old crank of some kind, I suppose?

BENTON Quite the other way, sir; young and pretty, I should say, if I'm any judge.

ROYLSTON Anyone come with her?

BENTON I don't think so, sir.

ROYLSTON Alone, at this time of night, and (*Sarcastically*) a lady, you say?

BENTON (*Promptly*) No doubt of that, sir; but dressed shabby almost, as if she'd seen better days—you know what I mean, sir.

ROYLSTON (*Cynically*) Ah, then, I had better get my checkbook ready.

BENTON Beg your pardon, sir, but she doesn't seem that kind either; not like one that'd beg, I mean. I couldn't make her out exactly.

ROYLSTON Perhaps she's another aspiring playwright who wants me to write her last act for her. At any rate you have aroused my curiosity; so show her in here.

(*He takes his coat off the back of the chair and puts it on*)

BENTON Very well, sir.

(*He goes out through the door on the left. A moment later he shows in* MRS. FRAZER. *She is a tall, strikingly beautiful woman about twenty-eight years old. Her complexion is pale; her eyes large, expressive, dark; her hair black and wavy; her figure inclining a little toward voluptuousness. There are shadows under her eyes and her face is drawn. Her manner is troubled, nervous, uncertain. She has on a plain black dress such as is worn by the poorer class of working women*)

ROYLSTON (*Getting up and staring at her with open admiration*) Ah! (*Turning to* BENTON) You may go, Benton. I shan't need you again. I will take Mrs.—er (*Looking at the card*) Mrs. Frazer to the door myself.

BENTON Yes, sir.

(*He goes out*)

MRS. FRAZER (*Uncertainly*) I hope you will pardon—

ROYLSTON (*Indicating the armchairs on the left*) Won't you sit down, Mrs. Frazer? (*She sits down in the one nearest to him*) And now, what can I do for you?

MRS. FRAZER I know this intrusion of mine is unpardonable. You must be terribly busy, and I have forced myself on you, interrupted your work—

ROYLSTON You must not feel conscience-stricken about that. I was only puzzling over a problem in construction. I am glad to have my mind taken off it for a time.

MRS. FRAZER But my coming here at this time of the

night and alone? (*Forcing a smile*) What can you think of such a breach of all the conventions!

ROYLSTON (*Dryly*) You are the very first to accuse me of conventionality. I see nothing strange in your coming here when you wanted to, when you were able to. I have lived long enough in this suburb to know the difficulties of getting here at the time one wishes.

MRS. FRAZER (*Looking at him for a moment with a questioning smile*) Can't you remember ever having seen me before?

ROYLSTON No, I must confess—

MRS. FRAZER And yet you have met me. I can, at least, plead that much justification for this encroachment on your time.

ROYLSTON (*Trying to remember*) It's no use. My brain is too full of marionettes to recall flesh-and-blood realities. I confess, to my shame, I will have to ask you where it was.

MRS. FRAZER Oh, I did not dream of your remembering. We only spoke about two words to each other, and it was at least a year ago. You remember the ball Mr. Coleman, the artist, gave at his studio?

ROYLSTON So it was there? It would be too trite for me to say I knew I had seen you before; but I really did have that feeling when you came in. One doesn't forget a face like yours. So it was at Coleman's studio? He and I have been friends for years.

MRS. FRAZER He is a very dear friend of my—of mine, also.

ROYLSTON Do take off your hat now that we know who's who. To see you sitting there with your hat on gives me the uncomfortable impression that this is a lawyer's office and you are consulting your attorney—and I warn you I am far from being a *legal* adviser.

MRS. FRAZER (*She takes off her hat and puts it on the sofa; leans back in her chair*) I knew it. That is why I came.

ROYLSTON For advice?

MRS. FRAZER Advice which I must have or—

ROYLSTON Or?

MRS. FRAZER The crowning disillusion.

ROYLSTON (*Smiling*) I hope it is not about me, the illusion.

MRS. FRAZER (*Emphatically*) It is about you but it is not an illusion.

ROYLSTON Certainty goeth before disappointment.

MRS. FRAZER In this case it must not. I have borne so much already—I could not bear it. I must have something firm to stand on.

ROYLSTON Then it is not a play you come to consult me about? (*Seeing her mystified expression*) I beg your pardon, but you know there are so many playwrights-in-embryo who come to me for suggestions about their work—as if I could help them; as if it were not absolutely necessary for them to work out their own salvation!—and I thought when you mentioned advice—

MRS. FRAZER (*Smiling*) I see. No, I almost wish it were. I would like to be able to write a play even if it were only a very bad one. It would at least prove I was capable of creating something; I'm afraid even that is beyond my power.

ROYLSTON (*Perfunctorily*) One never knows till one tries. The thing to do is to make a start; and then, if necessary, realize one's mistake smilingly.

MRS. FRAZER I intend to try sometime. (*Apologetically*) I'm wasting your time and I will come to the point at once; or rather I will have to go back quite a ways to give you a clear idea of my present situation. (*Nervously*) Won't you smoke or appear occupied with something? I won't feel such an intruder if you do.

ROYLSTON (*Laughing*) I would have done so before if I had known you didn't object.

MRS. FRAZER On the contrary, I like it. My hus— I have always been accustomed to men who smoked. My father was a great smoker.

ROYLSTON (*Who has taken a box of cigarettes from his pocket and lighted one*) There.

(*He leans back in his chair in an attitude of attention*)

MRS. FRAZER To begin at the beginning. My father was a prominent lawyer with a wide practice. He died five years ago leaving a large estate to my mother, who is still alive but in very feeble health. They had only two children, my brother, five years older than I am, and myself. I tell you all this because you lay such stress in all your books and plays on the influence of environment, and I want you to understand thoroughly what mine was. Being the baby and pet of the family you can readily guess how I was brought up—governess, private tutors, and finally a finishing school. Of course, at the end of their elaborate system of education I knew only what a young lady of my position should know—nothing of any value.

ROYLSTON (*Smiling*) Naturally; but you have progressed wonderfully since then.

MRS. FRAZER If I have, I have paid for it; and whatever progress I have made I owe to you.

ROYLSTON (*Wonderingly*) To me?

MRS. FRAZER We haven't come to that part of the story yet. When I returned home from the finishing school, my life became one long round of receptions, parties, balls, and so forth, until, in spite of the fact that at that time I was only interested in the most superficial things, I became surfeited, bored, and felt a longing to break away and experience something of more interest.

ROYLSTON You wished to try your wings.

MRS. FRAZER Yes, that was it. It was about this time I met Mr. Frazer, the man who afterward became my husband. He was then, and still is, a broker on the New York Stock Exchange. He fascinated me. I seemed to see personified in him all I had read about the (*Sarcastically*) financial giants, the daring gamblers who fought their battles to the bitter end of ruin. The house he was connected with is one of the largest on the Exchange and some of the so-called Napoleons of finance, whose names were forever in newspaper headlines, did their business through it. I thought of him doing his part in their gigantic enterprises, laboring to effect ever larger combinations in order that this glorious country might thrive and become ever greater and more productive (*With a short laugh*) You can see what a child I was; but I'm afraid you're not listening.

ROYLSTON (*Eagerly*) I assure you, you are mistaken. I am intensely interested. I was simply trying to recall something. Do you know when I watch you and listen to you talk I am forcibly reminded of some other woman. The likeness is so perfect it's uncanny.

MRS. FRAZER May I ask who it is?

ROYLSTON That's exactly what I cannot recollect. I am sure it's someone I know intimately and yet, for the life of me, I cannot bring the exact person to my mind.

MRS. FRAZER How strange.

ROYLSTON But I'm interrupting you. Please go on with your story.

MRS. FRAZER Well, the inevitable happened. I fell in love with George—Mr. Frazer—and he with me, and after a short engagement we were married. My family approved of him in every way. I believe they cherished the same illusion about his business, in a modified form, perhaps, as I did.

ROYLSTON Do you not think your husband also had the same illusions?

MRS. FRAZER It would be hard to say. In justice to him I must acknowledge he always seemed to idealize it. He never could see his business in all its hideousness as I came to see it, and I don't think he wore a mask just for my benefit; but you never can tell.

ROYLSTON Most of them can't see the unpleasant side. It becomes so much a part of themselves, you know. And after you were married?

MRS. FRAZER Oh, the usual honeymoon trip to Europe with its inevitable visits to Westminster Abbey, the tomb of Napoleon, the Cologne Cathedral, and other points of interest.

ROYLSTON (*Ironically*) How ideal!

MRS. FRAZER And yet I was very happy, or thought I was happy, which is much the same thing. Of course, in the light of what I now know, of what you have taught me, I can see it was merely a stupid happiness, the content of the born blind who have never seen the light.

ROYLSTON And I am to blame for your enlightenment?

MRS. FRAZER To blame?

ROYLSTON Since it has made you unhappy it must be blameworthy.

MRS. FRAZER (*With fine scorn*) What is such sluggish content worth? When you had opened my eyes to the truth I repudiated it. I felt I must win to a higher plane—or remain unhappy.

ROYLSTON (*Bewildered—running his fingers through his hair. With laughing impatience*) How you do remind me of someone! And yet I cannot remember— But tell me how this great change came about. After your return from your honeymoon I suppose your husband laid aside his role of lover and became the businessman once more, leaving you to ornament his home, and brood, and read my novels and plays.

MRS. FRAZER That is what you would naturally think, isn't it? However, you are quite wrong. My husband was as much the lover on the day I left him as he had been when we were married seven years before.

ROYLSTON Then you have left him?

MRS. FRAZER Yes, eight months ago.

ROYLSTON Have you no children?

MRS. FRAZER No. I used to be very sorry we had not; but now I am glad. It would have made it so much harder for me when the time came to free myself.

ROYLSTON You fell in love with someone else?

MRS. FRAZER (*Flushing*) If I had ceased to love my husband it is no reason why—

ROYLSTON (*Smiling*) You must not be offended. It usually happens that way you know.

MRS. FRAZER (*Earnestly*) I was in love with an ideal—the ideal of self-realization, of the duty of the individual to assert its supremacy and demand the freedom necessary for its development. You had taught me that ideal and it was that which came in conflict with my marriage. I saw I could never hope to grow in the stifling environment of married life—so I broke away.

ROYLSTON (*Gravely*) Please tell me in what manner I effected this change in you.

MRS. FRAZER I bought one of your novels one day about two years ago, more out of curiosity than anything else. It was the one about Wall Street.

ROYLSTON You mean *The Street*.

MRS. FRAZER Yes, that's the one.

ROYLSTON Then it was that book of mine which disillusioned you about your husband's business?

MRS. FRAZER Yes. When I first read it I couldn't believe it. I began to ask George questions about his deals, and so forth. He was surprised and happy to find me interested in his work and he finally used to explain all his transactions to me—and then I knew.

ROYLSTON Hm.

MRS. FRAZER I tried to persuade him to go into something else. He acknowledged there was a lot of truth in your book but said there were two ways of looking at everything. When I pleaded with him he laughed and called me his "dear little muckraker."

ROYLSTON (*Smiling*) So you became disillusioned about the broker—but how about the man?

MRS. FRAZER Your book made me long to read what you had to say about other things. I bought all your published works, and went to see all your plays, not once but many times. It dawned upon me gradually that the life he and I were living together was the merest sham; that we were contented because he was too busy and I was too lazy to analyze our position, to stop and think. For a long time I was very unhappy. I knew what I must do but I did not have the courage to do it.

ROYLSTON (*Impatiently*) Why didn't you tell him frankly how you felt?

MRS. FRAZER I couldn't. You see, he was so good and kind to me and it seemed such heartless cruelty to hurt him. All the time I felt myself being ground smaller and smaller day by day. I discovered that he and I had not a thought in common. Everything he was interested in was so shallow. He never concerned himself with what lay beneath the surface and I know my thoughts bored him although he was far too kind to ever show it. He observed the change in me and it worried him but the only remedies he could suggest were (*With a short laugh*) Southern California, a trip to Europe, or some other change of air. When I refused to go away he was at a loss what to do. I think toward the end he suspected I was in love with someone else.

ROYLSTON (*With a cynical smile*) I'll wager he did.

MRS. FRAZER I resolved not to think. I plunged into all sorts of activities to try and forget myself. I learned shorthand and typewriting—

ROYLSTON (*Interrupting her enthusiastically*) Good! That is your salvation.

MRS. FRAZER (*Wearily*) My soul refused to be lulled to sleep and there came a day when I left a note for my husband and left the house. I had been to see your play *Sacrifice* the night before for the tenth time. It seemed to breathe a message to me over the footlights. You remember when Mrs. Harding in the play leaves her husband with the words "I have awakened!"?

ROYLSTON (*His eyes searching hers with keen questioning*) Yes, but Mrs. Harding has a lover to go to.

MRS. FRAZER (*Bearing his scrutiny unflinchingly*) And I have an ideal which I love. When I heard her say those words that night they impressed me as never before. I felt that I, too, had awakened; that the time had come to assert my—

ROYLSTON (*With a sudden exclamation—interrupting her*) The puzzle is solved. What a dolt I am! It is Mrs. Harding in my play you resemble so much.

MRS. FRAZER (*Surprised*) Oh, is it? I saw the play so many times, you see.

ROYLSTON And you left your husband the next day?

MRS. FRAZER Yes. I sold some things which I had a right to call my own and bought a plain black dress. I knew I would have to become a worker, a wage-earner, and I wished to take nothing with me to remind me of the old life.

ROYLSTON (*Sympathetically*) I can imagine the ordeals you have been through since then. When one is beautiful it is doubly hard.

MRS. FRAZER (*Blushing—hurriedly*) At first I missed all the little comforts and luxuries I had been used to. I never knew till I had to do without them how they had grown into my life. I got bravely over that. I found it very hard to get work and harder still to keep it. The men were all such beasts and the women I had to come in contact with were so unintelligent and ordinary.

ROYLSTON (*Dryly*) You'll find most people are—rather ordinary.

MRS. FRAZER In my last position I really thought for a time my employer was a gentleman. I discovered he was only playing a part to throw me off my guard, and he turned out the worst of all. And then the unspeakably long nights in the dingy hall bedroom of a boarding house with no one to speak to, no money, no place to go; not able even to take a walk alone on the streets for fear of the insults, the smirking groups in the doorways and on the corners. Oh, yes, it has been hard! (*Her voice trembling*) It has been almost more than I could endure.

ROYLSTON (*Kindly*) Come; it was your ordeal of fire and you have borne up wonderfully. Have you never received word from your husband?

MRS. FRAZER That is the worst of all. He has haunted me, waited for me at the doors of boarding houses, at the entrance of office buildings where I worked, pleading with me to come back, offering to do anything I wished, trying to force money on me, even pushing it in under the door of my room. He cannot understand what has come over me. I think he really believes I am the victim of a mad infatuation for a married man; and yet he has had me followed continually, to protect me, as he says, not to spy on me, and he knows I have seen no one. (*Putting her hands over her face with a sob*) And he looks so unhappy, so miserable. I feel guilty whenever I see him.

ROYLSTON (*Gently*) Are you sure you no longer love him?

MRS. FRAZER (*Hysterically*) Oh, love, love, what is love? How can I know? I am certain I could no longer live with him. How can you doubt it after all I have told you? I know that I like him very much and do not want to see him suffer on my account.

ROYLSTON (*After a pause—frowning*) Have you stopped to think that you might have been followed here?

MRS. FRAZER I am certain I was not. He has given up hope. I haven't seen him in over a month. Besides, I took special pains to throw anyone off the track. I went down to the office building where I used to work this morning and left by a side entrance. I used the freight elevator to come down in. No one could have seen me.

ROYLSTON Where have you been all day?

MRS. FRAZER Sitting on a bench in Central Park.

ROYLSTON But good heavens, Mrs. Frazer, why didn't you come during the day?

MRS. FRAZER I was afraid you might be out. You see, I had read in the paper that you always worked at night and I felt pretty sure of finding you. I could not afford more than one trip. To be quite frank with you, it was with the last dollar I had in the world that I came out here.

ROYLSTON But if I had not been at home?

MRS. FRAZER (*Firmly*) I should have waited until you came. No matter how, I should have waited.

ROYLSTON (*Plainly embarrassed—getting up and walking nervously about the room*) You have been frank with me, Mrs. Frazer. Will you permit me to be the same?

MRS. FRAZER I wish you to be so.

ROYLSTON You promise to take no offense at what I am going to ask you?

MRS. FRAZER I am not afraid. I know you are trying to help me.

ROYLSTON I am glad of that. What I want to ask is:

Will you let me help you in—er—a pecuniary way?

MRS. FRAZER (*Rather indignantly*) How could you think so?

ROYLSTON I mean as a loan, you know. You really ought to—

MRS. FRAZER You know I could not.

ROYLSTON Then you have not freed yourself from all prejudices after all. You will certainly let me see to it that you get a position where you will be well paid and respected?

MRS. FRAZER Gladly, and be more than grateful for your assistance.

ROYLSTON (*With a sigh of relief*) Then that is settled. (MRS. FRAZER *suddenly breaks down and commences to sob.* ROYLSTON *goes to her and lays his hand on her shoulder*) There, there, Mrs. Frazer. I know it has been hard. It's bound to be, you know, for a woman in your position. The future will be much easier, you'll find. Please don't break down that way. (*A pause*) I feel as if I were responsible for all this and yet—

MRS. FRAZER (*Wiping her tears away and trying to control herself*) You don't understand. You are only looking at the material side. I don't care about that. What I came here to demand—yes, demand, for I have a right to do so—was certainty, the assurance that I am on the right path. These past few weeks with their sleepless nights have been terrible.

ROYLSTON How can I—

MRS. FRAZER Had I the right to do what I did? To cause others so much suffering? Am I realizing the best that is in me or the worst? My will to keep on striving is being broken. I doubt the worth of my action. When I see him so unhappy I say to myself: "Have you the right?" and I find no answer to satisfy me. I can only argue and argue until my brain aches. How can I bear hardship for a cause in which my faith is wavering? That is why I come to you.

ROYLSTON (*In a troubled voice*) I cannot tell you how deeply grieved I am to have been even the indirect means of causing you pain.

MRS. FRAZER (*Excitedly*) I have the right to come to you, haven't I? Mentally I am your creation. That you had no knowledge of my existence when you wrote does not lessen your responsibility in my eyes. I demand that you restore my peace of mind by justifying me to myself.

ROYLSTON (*Deeply moved*) What I have written cannot apply to every case. (*With conviction*) But it is my sincerest belief that you have found yourself, that as things stand between you, it would be folly for you to go back to your husband; that out of your present distress will spring a higher satisfaction than you have ever before known or believed possible. Therefore, I urge you not to give up the battle, for in the end you will achieve a victory well worth the winning.

MRS. FRAZER (*Extending both her hands to him—gratefully*) You have given me new hope, new strength.

ROYLSTON (*Taking her hands and looking into her eyes*) Promise me you will call on me whenever you need help in the future.

MRS. FRAZER (*Withdrawing her hands—simply*) I promise to do so.

ROYLSTON (*Smiling*) You must now, you know. You have charged me with the responsibility. You must let me pay off my debt.

MRS. FRAZER (*Forcing a smile*) Whenever my supply of will power runs low I'll come a-borrowing, never fear.

ROYLSTON By the way, I meant to ask you if your mother and brother know anything of all this?

MRS. FRAZER No. My mother is in Switzerland. Her health is so feeble I have not dared to tell her about it; and I know she would never learn of it through Mr. Frazer. My brother is the manager of a railroad in Brazil and very seldom returns to this country or writes to me. So, of course, he knows nothing.

ROYLSTON But your husband's family?

MRS. FRAZER I believe he has told them something about my being in California for my health.

ROYLSTON You have that in your favor. Family interference always complicates matters. As for the position I promised you, I will see what I can do when I go to the city in the morning. I have many influential friends and I have no doubt a real opportunity will be found for you some place. In the meantime I have lots of work which should be typewritten, and if you care to—

MRS. FRAZER Oh, how good of you! Your encouragement has made me feel so hopeful, so full of energy, I am ready for anything. A new life of wonderful possibilities seems opening up before me.

ROYLSTON It will be full of obstacles, too.

MRS. FRAZER (*Spiritedly*) The harder the better. With your help I know I shall overcome them.

ROYLSTON You are overrating me. Take warning!

MRS. FRAZER (*Picking up her hat from the sofa*) And now I had better be going back to my little hall room.

ROYLSTON (*Looking at his watch—then turning to her with a quizzical smile*) Yes, but how?

MRS. FRAZER What do you mean?

ROYLSTON I mean the little hall room will have to remain empty tonight. You have missed the last train.

MRS. FRAZER (*Apparently greatly astonished*) Surely you don't mean it? And I never looked at the timetable! Why didn't you warn me?

ROYLSTON I had no idea what time it was.

MRS. FRAZER How stupid of me! That comes of living in the city, where you can always get the subway or something. I must get back some way.

ROYLSTON It's impossible, I'm afraid.

MRS. FRAZER Then what can I do?

ROYLSTON You must stay here.

MRS. FRAZER Here—in this house?

ROYLSTON There is no alternative unless you wish to pass the night in the fields.

MRS. FRAZER There must be a hotel.

ROYLSTON There is only a roadhouse, a place of very questionable character, frequented by joy-riders and their—companions. You could not go there; and I know of no other place. You see, there are nothing but summer residences around here and I am hardly acquainted with any of the neighbors. (*Gravely*) Think of the time of night, and the rain, of the conclusions which would be drawn. You are beautiful and people have evil minds. Don't you see the impossibility?

MRS. FRAZER Yes—but, oh—how can I stay here? What will your wife think?

ROYLSTON She will not think. She will never know.

MRS. FRAZER I—I don't understand.

ROYLSTON She is not here. Except for the servants I am all alone.

MRS. FRAZER (*Genuinely alarmed*) Then I must go, even if I do have to spend the night in the fields.

ROYLSTON Listen; there is rather a strange coincidence, or shall I say fatality in all this. My wife went with the children to see the fairy play in New York, and contrary to her usual custom—she doesn't care for motoring—she went down in the machine. Otherwise I could have had the chauffeur drive you home; but they won't return before tomorrow afternoon at the earliest.

MRS. FRAZER (*Frightened*) This is terrible. How can I—(*She hurries to the window and looks out*) It's pouring.

ROYLSTON Fatality.

MRS. FRAZER (*Imploringly*) Please, please suggest something! You know I can't stay.

(*She looks at him pleadingly—her lips tremble*)

ROYLSTON Why not? (*Slowly*) Don't you believe you would be as safe here in my house as in your dingy hall bedroom?

MRS. FRAZER (*Looking at him searchingly*) Yes—I know I would be—but—

ROYLSTON (*Impatiently*) But you are afraid of appearances, of what people might think if they knew. You never learned that fear from me. Is not the knowledge of your own innocence enough to raise you above such considerations? Or are you afraid I may be a Don Juan in disguise?

MRS. FRAZER No, I am not afraid of you.

ROYLSTON And even if you fear appearances? Who is to know?

MRS. FRAZER (*Wavering*) You forget your servant.

ROYLSTON He has been with me for years, was with my father before me, all his life has been in our service. I flatter myself he's a model of discretion.

MRS. FRAZER But what will he think of me? (*Seeing* ROYLSTON'S *scornful smile*) But it doesn't matter. I will stay.

ROYLSTON Bravo! It would be foolish and cowardly of you to get soaked with the rain and be insulted, and perhaps worse, in the railroad station for the sake of a worn-out code of ethics.

MRS. FRAZER (*Smiling feebly*) Your wife might not think the ethics worn out

ROYLSTON (*Carelessly*) Oh, my wife; she would not think anything. If it would ease your conscience, I will tell her the whole thing. I'm sure she'd forget all about it ten minutes later (*Contemptuously*) when the butcher came for his order.

MRS. FRAZER (*Impulsively*) You do not love your wife,

do you? (*As* ROYLSTON *looks at her in astonishment, she grows confused*) What an impertinent question! Forgive me!

ROYLSTON (*Lightly*) So impertinent I never dare ask it of myself. I have always rejected the temptation to analyze my home relations. They are pleasant enough and that is all I care to know.

MRS. FRAZER (*With a sad smile*) If I had looked at it that way—

ROYLSTON The family relationship was the most important thing in the world for you at that time. With me it is purely secondary. My work comes first. As long as my home life gives free scope for my creative faculty I will demand nothing further of it. Life is too meager, too stingy with its favors, for us to ask for perfection. So I accept my domestic bliss at its surface value and save my analytical eye for the creations of my brain. (*Smiling*) I see you are vainly trying to stifle a yawn, and I know you must be terribly tired and sleepy. Won't you let me direct you to your room?

(*He goes to the door on the left*)

MRS. FRAZER (*Forgetting her hat, which she leaves lying on the sofa, she smilingly walks over to him*) I am dismissed, then?

ROYLSTON Far from it. I merely wish to save you the embarrassment of falling asleep in the chair. (*Pointing*) You see the light at the top of the stairway? Well, turn to your left when you reach the top and boldly enter the first room on your left. You will find everything there you need, I imagine. It is the official number-one guest chamber.

MRS. FRAZER I suppose you won't retire for hours yet?

ROYLSTON I have some work to finish up.

MRS. FRAZER (*Catching herself in the act of yawning—with a laugh*) I can't deny I'm sleepy—for the first time in months. (*Giving him her hand*) If you only knew how grateful I am! How can I ever thank you?

ROYLSTON (*With sudden passion*) By looking at me like that. How beautiful you are!

MRS. FRAZER (*Withdrawing her hand—a note of warning in her voice*) Remember the princess in the fairy tales who was as good as—

ROYLSTON She was beautiful. I understand. Pardon me. Good—but emancipated.

MRS. FRAZER (*Smiling*) Free to be good.

(*She turns to go out the door*)

ROYLSTON Good night.

(*He goes toward the table*)

MRS. FRAZER (*Turning to him suddenly, a look of resolution on her face*) I must explain one thing before I go, before I accept your hospitality. I have told you a lie. (ROYLSTON *looks at her in surprise*) I never met you at the studio ball. I was there but I did not meet you. I knew I had missed the last train. That is the reason I came so late. I wanted to miss it. And I knew there was no hotel, for I made inquiries at the station. But I had no idea your wife would be away.

ROYLSTON (*Staring at her in amazement*) But why, why?

MRS. FRAZER I wanted to put you to the test, to see if you would help me and let me stay. I wanted to get a glimpse of your home life, to see if you were a real man with the courage of your convictions or just a theorist. (*Hesitatingly*) You see, in my agony of doubt it seemed necessary for me to get back of dry words to a flesh-and-blood reality. (*With a faint smile*) It all appears such a wild idea now; and the test turned out to be a test of myself after all, didn't it?

ROYLSTON (*Not able to recover from his astonishment*) You tell me this—now—that you purposely missed the last train?

MRS. FRAZER (*Flushing*) I am ashamed to say that is the exact truth. (*Avoiding his ardent gaze*) I wish there to be no deception on my part after all your kindness to me.

ROYLSTON (*Intensely*) Do you realize how beautiful you are? Are you not afraid to make such a confession to me—of the conclusions I might be vain enough to draw from it?

(*He moves a step toward her*)

MRS. FRAZER (*Looking straight into his eyes*) No—because I know now you *are* a real man.

ROYLSTON (*Moving still nearer to her*) Take care! The real men are usually the greatest sinners.

MRS. FRAZER But they protect the helpless. (*With a smile*) So you see how safe I am. Good night.

(*She goes out*)

ROYLSTON (*Going to the door*) Good night (*He watches her ascend the stairway*) Good night. (*He comes back and sits down at the table again; starts *to look over his manuscript, glances upward in the direction of her room, throws his manuscript down with an exclamation of disgust, goes to the door on the left again and looks up at the top of the stairway, finally comes back to the table again and stands beside it for a moment, frowning thoughtfully and evidently weighing something in his mind*) Damnation! (*He takes his hat and light overcoat from the chair, puts them on, grabs his cane and hurries out through the door at the back*)

Curtain

Act Two

SCENE—*The same. It is about nine o'clock on the following morning. Bright sunlight streams in through the two open windows.* BENTON *is arranging the papers and books on the table. Having finished he turns and is going out the door in the rear when he catches sight of* MRS. FRAZER*'s hat, which is lying on the sofa. He gives a low whistle of amazement. A shadow falls across the sunlight at one of the windows and a moment later* WESON*, the gardener, puts his head into the room and peers around near-sightedly. He is an old withered man with a drooping gray mustache stained yellow by tobacco juice.*

BENTON Good morning, Weson.

WESON Oh, it's you, is it?

BENTON Who did you think it was?

WESON I thought maybe Mr. Roylston—

BENTON He isn't up yet. Want to see him about anything?

WESON Nothin' special. When I first come out this mornin' I seen a feller hangin' round the house s'picious like. Soon's he seen me he turned round and walked off s'fast s'he could go. "D'you think this is a park?" I shouts after him, but he didn't pay no attention. Thinks I: I better tell Mr. Roylston about you. With all them burglaries happenin' nearabouts you can't be too careful.

BENTON Hm—you're right about that. (*With an involuntary glance at the hat*) Mr. Roylston ought to be more careful.

WESON Oughter hire a watchman, s'what I say. (*In a whining voice*) T'ain't safe for me sleepin' all alone in that house at the end of the drive. S'me they'd tackle first. I was readin' in the papers t'other day where robbers tortured an old gardener same's me to make him tell them how to git into the house; burned his bare feet with a red-hot poker! (*With rising inflection*) Ain't that turrible?

BENTON Oh, I guess you're safe enough. (*Meaningly*) It isn't burglars his nibs ought to be frightened of.

WESON (*Eagerly, scenting a scandal*) What's he been up to now?

BENTON (*Picking up* MRS. FRAZER*'s hat*) Cast your eye on this.

WESON Wait till I git my specs. (*He reaches into his pocket and pulls out a pair of steel-rimmed spectacles*) I can't see nothin' without 'em no more. (*He puts them on and looks at the hat. In disappointed tones*) What's that? One of the Missus' hats?

BENTON Guess again. She don't wear cheap truck like that.

(*He throws the hat contemptuously on the sofa*)

WESON You don't mean—? (*With an explosive chuckle*) If he don't beat the devil! An' the Missus in Noo York! Makes hay while the sun shines, don't he? Don't the Missus never guess nothin'?

BENTON (*Scornfully*) She doesn't know enough; besides, usually he chucks 'em before the thing gets serious. He likes to have them crazy about him but when they get too mushy—he doesn't like complications—they interfere with his work, he says; and then when they call up I have to say he's too busy to be disturbed.

WESON (*Admiringly*) Foxy, ain't he?

BENTON I don't know what's wrong with him this time. I don't blame him, though; she's a beauty. But he ought to be more careful. Once caught, twice shy, they say; and he was caught once, good and proper. (*With a short laugh*) It'll do the Missus good to get a dose of her own medicine. It broke the old man's heart when the young fellow married her, and—(*Stopping abruptly as he sees how avidly* WESON *is drinking his words in*) A fine man to work for, the old gentleman; not that I'm complaining of the son at all.

WESON What was you sayin' about the marriage?

BENTON Nothing that an old scandalmonger like you ought to hear. There's lots of things I could tell if I had a mind to; but I'll keep my mouth shut. It's the best policy, Weson, especially when you're around. You better get out of here. I think I hear someone coming down the stairs.

(WESON *hurriedly withdraws.* BENTON *goes to the table and pretends to be arranging the things on it.* MRS. FRAZER *appears in the doorway on the left. She stops uncertainly when she sees* BENTON)

BENTON (*Affably*) Good morning, ma'am.

MRS. FRAZER (*Embarrassed*) Good morning. I believe I left my hat in here.

BENTON Yes, ma'am. Here it is.

(*He picks up her hat from the sofa*)

MRS. FRAZER (*Walking over and taking it from him*) Thank you.

(*She goes to the window and stands drinking in the beauty of the spring morning*)

BENTON (*With an admiring glance at her figure framed in the sunlight*) Beautiful morning, ma'am.

MRS. FRAZER Yes, isn't it? And what a lovely garden.

BENTON Yes, ma'am, very fine. It has the gardener busy all the time keeping it in shape.

MRS. FRAZER No doubt; they require a great deal of care. Has Mr. Roylston come down yet?

BENTON Lord no, ma'am; won't be down for an hour yet, I should say. He's not what you'd call an early bird; stays up so late nights he couldn't be. (*Insinuatingly*) But he's been so queer and—hm—different from what he usually does, he might do anything this morning.

MRS. FRAZER (*Crushing him with a look of icy hauteur*) What do you mean?

BENTON (*Confused, fumbling with the books on the table*) Nothing at all, ma'am, only—

MRS. FRAZER (*Her curiosity getting the better of her—more kindly*) Only what?

BENTON (*Accepting her change of manner as a confession which equalizes their position*) Only, begging your pardon, he doesn't usually—he isn't in the habit of—he usually thinks that sort of thing too dangerous. Now, when the others—

MRS. FRAZER (*Horrified*) Others?

BENTON (*Grinning*) Loads of 'em. They're all crazy about him. He likes it, too—phone calls and letters and flowers and all such stuff. He pretends not to care, but it tickles him just the same to have them adoring him, asking for his advice—

MRS. FRAZER Stop! Is this the way you slander the man who trusts you?

BENTON (*Offended*) It's no secret. He laughs and talks about it himself. I've heard him read parts of the letters to the Missus, Mrs. Roylston. I was only saying it to you because it's never—he's never taken any chances for the others. I thought you'd like to know you were the only one—

MRS. FRAZER (*Her face crimson*) How dare you?

BENTON (*Quickly*) Beg your pardon, ma'am, no offense intended. (*Slyly*) Of course I don't mean anything wrong. (*The sound of a door closing is heard from the hallway on the left, then children's voices.* BENTON *turns excitedly to* MRS. FRAZER) Good Gawd, it must be Mrs. Roylston and the kids. Go in there where she won't see you.

(MRS. FRAZER, *too overcome with fear and shame to stop and think, hurries through the door at the rear.* BENTON *closes it after her and is busy with the papers on the table when* MRS. ROYLSTON *enters with the children, who are talking and laughing together.*

MRS. ROYLSTON *is a pretty woman of thirty or so, with a mass of light curly brown hair, big thoughtful eyes, rosy complexion, tiny hands and feet, and a slight girlish figure. She is dressed stylishly but with ostentation.*

DAVIE *and* RUTH, *aged nine and seven respectively, are healthy, noisy, delightful children. Their clothes are simple but of expensive material*)

MRS. ROYLSTON Good morning, Benton. Mr. Roylston's not up yet of course?

BENTON No, ma'am.

MRS. ROYLSTON Telephone for Dr. Morse at once, will you, Benton? Tell him to come up at once.

BENTON Yes, ma'am. Nothing serious, I hope, ma'am.

MRS. ROYLSTON Oh no. Ruth was ill last night when we returned from the theatre. Mrs. Dexter sent for her doctor. He said it was nothing but (*Smiling and shaking an accusing finger at* RUTH) too much candy. However, I wanted to make sure. I have no confidence in strange doctors. So I took the first train out this morning and didn't wait for the machine.

RUTH I didn't eat much, Mother.

DAVIE I ate more'n she did, and I was'n sick.

MRS. ROYLSTON But you're a man, dear.

RUTH I feel puffictly well this morning, Mother.

MRS. ROYLSTON (*Kissing her*) Of course you do, dear. Mother wishes to make sure, that's all. So telephone right away, please, Benton.

BENTON Yes, ma'am.

(*With an apprehensive glance at the door in back he hurries out to the left*)

DAVIE Mother, can we go out and play in the sandpile?

RUTH I'm goin' to play I'm the princess in the play last night.

MRS. ROYLSTON And are you going to be the prince, Davie?

DAVIE Nope, I'm goin' to be the dragon.

MRS. ROYLSTON But the dragon was very, very wicked.

DAVIE Tha's why I wanta be him.

MRS. ROYLSTON (*Laughing and kissing both of them*) Run along then, and be sure and stay in the sun; and come in when you see Dr. Morse drive up. Try and be as quiet as you can. You know your father isn't up yet.

(*The children answer: "Yes, Mother," and skip out through the door on the left*)

BENTON (*Appearing in the doorway on the left*) Dr. Morse will be right up, ma'am.

MRS. ROYLSTON Very well. Thank you, Benton. (BENTON, *unwilling to leave the room, and not knowing any excuse for remaining, stands fidgeting nervously in the doorway*) Anything you wish to see me about, Benton?

BENTON No, ma'am, nothing at all. So glad to hear it's not serious—Miss Ruth, I mean.

MRS. ROYLSTON (*Smiling at him kindly*) Thank you, Benton.

(*She sits down, picks up the manuscript from the table and starts to read.* BENTON *turns reluctantly and leaves.* MRS. ROYLSTON *glances over the pages of the manuscript interestedly. The door in the rear is slowly opened and* MRS. FRAZER *comes into the room. Her face wears an expression of defiant shame. She coughs to attract* MRS. ROYLSTON'S *attention. Startled by the sound,* MRS. ROYLSTON *turns around and sees her. The two women stare at each other in silence for a moment.* MRS. ROYLSTON *grows very pale. Her lips tremble and it seems as if she were shrinking up in her chair, becoming small and pitiful. A flush slowly spreads over* MRS. FRAZER'S *face. She drops her eyes*)

MRS. FRAZER I beg your pardon.

MRS. ROYLSTON How did— Who is it you wish to see?

MRS. FRAZER I am waiting to speak to Mr. Roylston.

MRS. ROYLSTON How did you get in that room?

MRS. FRAZER (*Defiantly*) I hid there when I heard you coming.

MRS. ROYLSTON (*With a sigh that is like a moan*) I knew it! I knew it!

MRS. FRAZER (*Embarrassed*) I lost my head completely for a moment, and I ran away. I was so afraid of what you might think. In there I regained my senses. I had done no wrong. Why should I be afraid of you? So I came back.

MRS. ROYLSTON (*Slowly*) I am the one who should be afraid.

MRS. FRAZER I was sure you would misunderstand my presence here.

MRS. ROYLSTON (*Coldly*) I'm afraid I understand it only too well.

MRS. FRAZER Mr. Roylston was so positive you would ignore appearances. I knew better. I am a woman. I should never have allowed myself to be persuaded into remaining here against my better judgment.

MRS. ROYLSTON (*Trying not to understand*) Mr. Roylston? You have seen him? Is he up already?

MRS. FRAZER (*Unflinchingly*) No; I saw him last night.

MRS. ROYLSTON Last night? Then you— When did you come here—

MRS. FRAZER Last night about ten o'clock.

MRS. ROYLSTON (*Her worst fears realized*) Last night? Ten o'clock? Then you were here in this house—you and he—alone?

MRS. FRAZER Yes; but you must not draw any conclusions from that until I—

MRS. ROYLSTON (*Jumping to her feet, her eyes flashing*) Oh!

MRS. FRAZER You will be sorry if you form a hasty judgment.

MRS. ROYLSTON Hasty? As if I had not always a picture of this before my mind! I have known it was coming, dreaded it, for years. Hasty? Oh no! I have prayed this would never happen, but I have seen it drawing nearer every day in spite of my prayers; and I am prepared for it.

MRS. FRAZER If you will permit me to explain—

MRS. ROYLSTON (*With a mocking laugh*) Explain!

MRS. FRAZER (*Firmly*) I came here to ask your husband's advice.

MRS. ROYLSTON They all want advice—so they say.

MRS. FRAZER (*Flushing angrily but controlling herself*) I was in such desperate straits that only he could help me. I was wild with despair. I formed the mad idea of coming here. I never thought of your being away. And I missed the last train. (*She realizes how improbable this explanation must seem to* MRS. ROYLSTON *and continues uncertainly*) There was no hotel to go to; so your husband kindly—

MRS. ROYLSTON (*Her laughter breaking hysterically*) And you expect me to believe this! Do you think I have no intelligence at all? (*Furiously*) Lies! Lies! All lies!

(*Throwing herself in the chair by the table she sobs convulsively, her face hidden in her hands*)

MRS. FRAZER (*Calmly*) I will excuse your insults because I know how you must feel. (*Earnestly*) You will regret this when the truth comes out, when you know you have been insulting an innocent woman. You are judging by appearances and letting them deceive you.

MRS. ROYLSTON Lies, lies! Haven't I read your letters to him?

MRS. FRAZER (*Astonished*) I never wrote to your husband in my life.

MRS. ROYLSTON (*As if she hadn't heard*) "Will you give me permission to come out and see you sometime?" I suppose you never wrote that? Oh, how well I remember them—those letters!

MRS. FRAZER Mrs. Roylston, you are mistaken. I never—

MRS. ROYLSTON To take advantage of my being away with the children; oh, how could he!

MRS. FRAZER Mrs. Roylston, you must listen to me.

MRS. ROYLSTON I won't listen to you. What is there to say—now? You love him. I don't blame you for that; but what will become of me?

(*She breaks down and sobs unrestrainedly*)

MRS. FRAZER (*Waiting until* MRS. ROYLSTON *has regained control of herself*) Listen to me, Mrs. Roylston! I do not love your husband.

MRS. ROYLSTON The more shame, then, for he must love you.

MRS. FRAZER He never saw me before last night.

MRS. ROYLSTON (*Coldly*) I don't believe you.

MRS. FRAZER (*Angrily*) Ah, there is a limit to everything. Since you persist in insulting me, since you refuse to listen to anything, you may continue to believe whatever you please. I will leave Mr. Roylston to do the explaining.

(*She hurries toward the door on the left but* MRS. ROYLSTON *jumps up and reaches it before her, blocking her passage*)

MRS. ROYLSTON (*Fiercely*) You cannot go now.

MRS. FRAZER Cannot?

MRS. ROYLSTON I don't mean that. Please don't go yet, before he comes. There is so much which must be cleared up. I didn't mean to hurt you. If you knew how I am suffering, you wouldn't blame me. Please sit down, won't you, until he comes?

MRS. FRAZER (*On the verge of tears herself*) After the things you have said to me? No, I will not remain in this house a minute longer. Please let me pass.

MRS. ROYLSTON I am sorry. You are not to blame. No one is to blame. I implore you to stay until he comes. He ought to be down in a few minutes. It won't be long.

MRS. FRAZER (*After a moment's indecision*) Very well, I will stay; not because you ask me to but because I wish to hear my own justification.

(*She sits down in one of the armchairs near the sofa*)

MRS. ROYLSTON Thank you. It will help to clear up matters between the three of us once and for all.

(*She chokes back a sob and sits down in the chair by the table*)

MRS. FRAZER In the meantime, if you please, let us not talk about it. It will only make matters worse—if that were possible.

MRS. ROYLSTON (*Strangely*) How you said that! As if you were giving an order. And why shouldn't you? You have more right in this house than I have. (*She sobs*)

MRS. FRAZER (*Moved in spite of herself—with great kindness*) Please, Mrs. Roylston, don't make yourself unhappy in this way. If you only knew how wrong you are.

MRS. ROYLSTON (*More calmly*) I won't break down again. What must be, must be, I suppose. I have known this was coming for a long time. The day I was married I could foresee it. I should have had the courage to refuse then; but I didn't. It all seemed such a wonderful dream come true, I just couldn't refuse even when I knew I was wronging him. I was a coward then and I still am, I guess. Eleven years of happiness and now I have to pay and—I am afraid. (*A pause during which* MRS. FRAZER *looks at her pityingly*) I've pretended not to see a lot of things in those years. I wanted him to be happy, and I knew he wouldn't be if he thought he had a jealous wife prying into his affairs. All the women who sent him flowers and wrote to him and called him up on the phone—I knew they loved him, and I hated them for it; but I never let him think I suspected anything. Until lately I never thought he considered them seriously.

MRS. FRAZER (*Interrupting her indignantly*) And you think I was one of those fools!

MRS. ROYLSTON He used to read parts of their letters to me. He never guessed how it hurt. For I could see in spite of the way he joked they pleased him just the same. Then all at once he stopped showing them to me—and they kept coming, all in the same handwriting. I had never read a letter of his before but I brooded until I couldn't resist the temptation any longer. Two of them were lying open on this table one day and read them. Then I could see the end coming. He had been writing to her, meeting her in New York, and I knew from the letters it was only a question of time.

MRS. FRAZER And those are the letters you think I wrote?

MRS. ROYLSTON (*Dully*) Yes.

MRS. FRAZER But when I swear to you I never wrote a line to your husband in my life, never spoke a word to him before last night!

MRS. ROYLSTON I'd like to believe you. (*Intensely*) Oh, I wish I could believe you! But how can I?

MRS. FRAZER (*Desperately*) You will have to. He will tell you the same thing.

MRS. ROYLSTON (*Her voice low and shaken with pain*) What does it matter? You or someone else. She said she had left her home to work out her own salvation; and I thought you looked that way. I thought she would be younger. Her letters sounded girlish. What does it matter? *You* were here—last night.

MRS. FRAZER (*Quietly*) Mrs. Roylston, I really cannot stay and listen to such implications.

MRS. ROYLSTON I don't blame you or anyone. It's my own sin coming back on me. Marriages like mine are cursed.

MRS. FRAZER Cursed? It seems to me yours has been a very fortunate one.

MRS. ROYLSTON Yes, cursed. Sooner or later the curse falls. Retribution finds you out in the end. Forbidden love—you'll find out the curse of it like I have, when you least expect it, when you think you're happy and the future is all smiling.

MRS. FRAZER (*Interested*) I fail to see how all this can apply to your case.

MRS. ROYLSTON (*Continuing in a lifeless, monotonous voice as if all the spirit in her had been crushed and broken. Her face wears an expression of dazed, almost stupid, resignation*) Give him up before it's too late, for your own sake. You'll have to pay. I'll be frank with you. You can't throw any stone. He married me because he had to, or thought he had to. I was his father's stenographer, we loved each other—too well. His father found out and discharged me. Then David asked me to marry him and I couldn't refuse. I loved him so.

MRS. FRAZER (*Bewildered*) Please, Mrs. Roylston, don't—

MRS. ROYLSTON I want you to understand—whatever happens to me afterwards—it isn't his fault.

MRS. FRAZER Do you know what you are telling me?

MRS. ROYLSTON (*Hotly*) I wouldn't be ashamed to tell it to the whole world. It shows how good he is. If he no longer loves me it's because I allowed him to make too great a sacrifice. His father cut him off and never spoke to him again. The old gentleman was kind enough generally but he had great plans for his only son, David, and I spoiled them all. He died soon afterward—of grief over our marriage, they say. I've always thought that perhaps in his heart David has never forgiven me for—killing his father.

MRS. FRAZER How can you imagine such a thing?

MRS. ROYLSTON When I married him I resolved that as soon as he was able to take care of himself—

MRS. FRAZER (*Astonished*) Take care of himself?

MRS. ROYLSTON He wasn't famous in those days. He

hadn't even had a book published yet. He used to take positions in offices but he never held them long and I could see how he hated them. He wanted to write, write, write all the time. Every once in a while he sold an article, but not often enough to keep him alive. It must have been terribly hard for him—worrying and fretting how to make two ends meet. He had been accustomed to everything he wanted—and I had dragged him down. He wouldn't have been human if he hadn't had a sort of grudge against me for it.

MRS. FRAZER He is hardly as mean as that.

MRS. ROYLSTON I had to stay with him until he got on his feet. I was considered a fine stenographer in those days and my salary was enough to keep us going. Then, too, he had to have someone to typewrite his manuscripts for him.

MRS. FRAZER (*With wondering admiration*) And you did all that?

MRS. ROYLSTON I had plenty of time at night to typewrite what he had written during the day. Those were the happiest days of my life. How often since then I've wished that he had never been successful, that we could have gone on like that always. It was selfish of me to feel that way but I couldn't help it sometimes. (*Musingly*) We had a small flat all to ourselves.

MRS. FRAZER And you did all the housekeeping, too?

MRS. ROYLSTON (*Simply*) Of course. I had made a resolve to leave him and let him get a divorce as soon as he was successful and could get along without me. I saw clearly at that time, before the children came, what I see now—that he was never meant for me. I knew he would come to regret his sacrifice and I would become a dead weight holding him back. I knew nothing of what he knew. Whatever I have learned since, he has taught me. We had been married a little over a year when his first play was produced and made a sensation—and then—

MRS. FRAZER (*Eagerly*) Yes?

MRS. ROYLSTON (*Softly*) Little Davie came. I couldn't think of going away then. It would have killed me. I wasn't strong enough or brave enough for that. I hoped he would love me more for Davie's sake, and he did for a time. He was so kind to me; and when our little girl was born he was so proud. As he became famous he had less and less time to spend at home, and he hated to be disturbed when he was writing. He met so many people, women, of his own kind outside, who could talk about the things he was interested in, that I guess he commenced to despise me a little because I was so stupid.

MRS. FRAZER (*With a strange smile, half to herself*) No, no, he has never analyzed his home relations.

MRS. ROYLSTON (*As if she had not heard*) Lately he has grown more and more indifferent to me and to the children; so that now I'm afraid he only looks on me as a sort of housekeeper. (*With a pitiful attempt at a smile*) He'll have to acknowledge I'm a good one. I've protected him from all the small worries he detests so much. I don't believe he realizes; he thinks things just run along by themselves.

MRS. FRAZER (*Eagerly*) Why have you never asserted yourself, claimed your right as an individual? Why have you never spoken to him, told him how you felt? You have seen him slipping away and made no attempt to hold him.

MRS. ROYLSTON (*Fiercely*) I have loved him, loved him, loved him with all my heart and soul; loved him more than you or any other woman will ever love him. If that has no power to hold him—then I have lost him.

MRS. FRAZER (*After a pause*) How unhappy you must have been!

MRS. ROYLSTON (*Scornfully*) Unhappy? So that's what you think! How little you know! I have been happy in serving him, happy in the knowledge that I have had my little part in helping him to success, happy to be able to shield and protect him. In spite of all you other women with your letters and flowers, I have been happy. (*With a sad smile*) However, it's all ended now. As long as I could pretend I didn't know about you others, as long as I was sure he didn't suspect I knew about you, I could remain and love him and still preserve my self-respect. It's different now. I can't pretend to be blind any longer. I know, and you know I know, and he knows I know. Besides, I see that his future happiness does not depend on me and (*Intensely*) above all else in the world I want him to be happy.

MRS. FRAZER But he *is* happy—now—with you!

MRS. ROYLSTON (*Shaking her head sadly*) My usefulness is past. I can only thank God for granting the beauty and joy of the past eleven years to a woman who sinned and was too cowardly to pay. The payment was never canceled, only postponed, I see that now—postponed until I had the courage to pay. I have that courage now. I will pay. I will leave him to his happiness. (*Her voice thrilling with pride*) How many of you others love him as much as that? Not many, or one, I think. How many of you would make the sacrifice I will make? How many of you would be willing to give him up to another woman because your love was so great? Not one of you! (*Bitterly*) You the least of all—for him or anyone else! I can see it in your face.

MRS. FRAZER (*Slowly*) It is true. Compared to you I am a weakling.

MRS. ROYLSTON I do not boast of my strength, only of the strength of my love. I thank you just the same. You are the only person who has ever given me credit for being what I must be. Not even he ever saw it in all these eleven years.

MRS. FRAZER But did you ever lay bare your soul to anyone, even to him, as you have to me?

MRS. ROYLSTON Yes, to him, every day, every hour; but he never saw it.

MRS. FRAZER (*After a pause—thoughtfully*) How much you have taught me! Happiness, then, means servitude?

MRS. ROYLSTON Love means servitude; and *my* love is *my* happiness.

MRS. FRAZER I should have come to you for advice, not to him.

MRS. ROYLSTON (*With a scornful smile*) Advice? That word has been my torturer. You women of the flowers and letters have stolen him from me in the name of advice.

MRS. FRAZER (*Hurt*) Even now you have no faith in me.

MRS. ROYLSTON It isn't possible. How can I? How can I?

MRS. FRAZER I can't blame you; things are so mixed up. It must appear incredible. But can't you see that I, too, have suffered? Even if what you think were true, could you not pity me?

MRS. ROYLSTON (*Excitedly*) No, no, no, I can only hate you. How can the vanquished pity the victor? You ask too much.

MRS. FRAZER (*Rising from her chair*) I cannot wait any longer. I must go out into the fresh air and be alone for a while—to think.

MRS. ROYLSTON You are afraid to wait until he comes.

MRS. FRAZER I will wait outside. In this room the weight of your suspicion is crushing me. I begin to feel guilty.

MRS. ROYLSTON (*Savagely*) Ah!

MRS. FRAZER (*Weakly*) I will wait outside in the garden if I may.

(*She starts to go. The sound of a door slamming is heard.* MRS. ROYLSTON *goes to the door on the left and looks out. She gives an exclamation of surprise*)

MRS. ROYLSTON (*Slowly*) He has just come in. He must have been out for his morning walk. What could have got him up so early? (*Turning impetuously to* MRS. FRAZER) You must have known of this; and you wanted to sneak away before he came. Lies! Lies! Lies everywhere!

MRS. FRAZER (*Distractedly*) No, no, I swear to you—

MRS. ROYLSTON Ssshh! Here he comes.

(ROYLSTON *enters from the door on the left. He is dressed exactly the same as the night before*)

ROYLSTON (*Concealing his annoyance*) Hello, Alice, what brings you back at this unearthly hour? Good morning, Mrs. Frazer.

MRS. ROYLSTON (*Falteringly*) Ruth was sick last night and I didn't wait for the machine this morning but hurried out on the first train. She seems to be all right this morning but I've sent for Dr. Morse to make sure.

ROYLSTON (*Indifferently, shrugging his shoulders*) Stuffed full of candy, probably. I see you and Mrs. Frazer have already made each other's acquaintance.

MRS. ROYLSTON (*With a short laugh at what she thinks is his attempt to deceive her in the name*) Oh, yes.

(MRS. FRAZER *does not reply but stares at him as if she were seeing him for the first time*)

ROYLSTON (*Searching through the things on the table*) God be thanked I haven't a jealous wife; for I must acknowledge that even to the most unprejudiced observer the events of last night would appear dubious. (*Irritably*) Where did Benton put—? Oh, here it is. (*He finds the fountain pen he has been *looking for and puts it in his pocket*) You see, Mrs. Frazer missed the last train, and when I explained that you were away it was all I could do to persuade her to occupy guest chamber number one instead of melting to death in the rain. Nice situation, wasn't it? Nothing if not compromising. Married man, married lady—not to each other—lonely country house—stormy night—wife returns home unexpectedly the next morning and—does not believe the worst. (*With a laugh which has a trace of mockery in it*) My dear Alice, you are really the perfect wife. (*He goes over to her and puts his arm around her carelessly and continues in the same bantering tone*) I told you, Mrs. Frazer, that Caesar's wife was above harboring suspicion. I welcome you to the model household, where truth reigns, where conventions are as naught, where we believe in each other implicitly because we have found each other so worthy of belief. And I salute you, my angel of trustfulness.

(*He bends to kiss his wife. She gently pushes him away*)

MRS. ROYLSTON Don't, David, please!

ROYLSTON (*Glancing from one to the other.* MRS. FRAZER *is looking at him with frank disgust*) Hm—I was too hasty in my reliance on mutual confidence, it seems. You two have had a run-in already, I see. (*To his wife, impatiently*) I am sorry you should have jumped at conclusions before you heard my explanation. Mrs. Frazer is going to do some work for me and—

MRS. ROYLSTON (*Her eyes filling*) Ah.

ROYLSTON Which will necessitate her being here for some time, and we must clear away all unpleasantness—

MRS. FRAZER (*Interrupting him coldly*) You are mistaken. I have decided I cannot accept the work you offer me.

ROYLSTON (*Perplexed*) Hm—it's as bad as that, eh?

MRS. ROYLSTON (*Turning to* MRS. FRAZER) But you must!

MRS. FRAZER (*Indignantly*) Must?

MRS. ROYLSTON What good can your refusal do now?

MRS. FRAZER (*To* ROYLSTON) Your wife has plainly told me that she is firmly convinced I am your mistress. She has read letters to you from someone and thinks I am the author. You see how plainly impossible it would be for me to work for you or accept your assistance in any way. Besides, there are other reasons. I have made a mistake, a great mistake, and it only remains for me to go. Before I leave I should like to have you try to convince Mrs. Roylston that her suspicions are groundless—as far as I am concerned.

ROYLSTON (*Turning to his wife*) So you read my letters?

MRS. ROYLSTON Yes; you left them on your table and I—couldn't resist the temptation. (ROYLSTON *turns away from her contemptuously*) I saw I was losing you, that you were becoming indifferent to me and the children—

ROYLSTON And you thought opening my letters would cure that?

MRS. ROYLSTON They were already open.

ROYLSTON Reading them, then.

MRS. ROYLSTON I did not stop to think. I love you.

ROYLSTON (*Coldly*) Indeed? You have strange ways of showing it.

MRS. ROYLSTON I wanted to fight for you. I had to know who my enemy was.

ROYLSTON Well, who was this so-called enemy of yours?

MRS. ROYLSTON The letters were signed Julia Wainright.

MRS. FRAZER (*Eagerly*) You see!

ROYLSTON What has she to do with Mrs. Frazer? Why, in heaven's name, should you connect the two? Your insults to Mrs. Frazer are unpardonable and nonsensical. You are letting a narrow-minded suspicion blot out all that is best in you. Appearances have been against me before and yet you never took this attitude.

MRS. ROYLSTON There is such a thing as the last straw.

ROYLSTON (*Sternly*) Alice, what has come over you? You are not yourself. When I tell you we are both blameless, do you still persist—

MRS. ROYLSTON (*Frenziedly*) I don't believe you or her or anyone. I can't, I can't! You call her Mrs. Frazer and expect me to believe her innocent—and she wears no wedding ring. (MRS. FRAZER *instinctively hides her hand behind her back*) Why are you up and out so early? You never get up before ten —Because she is up!

MRS. FRAZER (*Growing crimson*) Oh!

(*The doorbell is heard ringing*)

ROYLSTON (*Bitingly*) You need not tell your woes to the servants, Alice. Please try to control yourself. Here comes Benton.

(*A moment later* BENTON *appears in the doorway*)

BENTON Dr. Morse is here, ma'am.

MRS. ROYLSTON (*Faintly*) Very well, Benton. Tell him I'll be right out; and call the children in.

ROYLSTON (*Turning to his wife—cuttingly*) Your conduct has been rather a revelation to me.

MRS. ROYLSTON (*Wincing*) Don't, David!

ROYLSTON You have called me a liar and you have insulted Mrs. Frazer, who is my friend. (MRS. FRAZER *makes an angry gesture repudiating this statement*) You will have no cause for any suspicions in the future, for I shall not trouble you with my presence in this house any longer. I will have Benton pack up my things at once. I do not care to live with a wife who is also an evil-minded spy. I could vindicate myself beyond all possibility of doubt, in ten words; but I prefer to have you think whatever your jealous whim dictates. I will explain to Mrs. Frazer and she may tell you if she considers your charges against her worth the trouble of refuting.

MRS. ROYLSTON (*Shrinking from him as if he had struck her*) Don't, don't, David! Please don't speak like that—to me. You are killing me. I love you, you must not go away. This is your home. It is I who have no reason here. I will give you (*Sobbing and walking toward the door on the left*) your freedom. I want you to be happy, and—I know I'm only in your way—now. Please forgive me if I can't believe. (*Stretching out her arms to him supplicatingly*) Please forgive me!

(*He turns away from her coldly*)

MRS. FRAZER (*Indignantly*) For shame, Mr. Roylston!

MRS. ROYLSTON (*Turning to her furiously*) How dare you intercede for me! Don't you know how I hate you?

(*She rushes out the door to the left*)

Curtain

Act Three

SCENE—*The same,* ROYLSTON *and* MRS. FRAZER *are still staring at the door through which* MRS. ROYLSTON *has just gone.*

ROYLSTON (*Shrugging his shoulders he turns to* MRS. FRAZER *with a short laugh*) I have lived with that woman for eleven years, and have never known her until ten minutes ago.

(*Benton appears in the doorway to the left. He stands there irresolutely for a second and is turning to go out again when* ROYLSTON *sees him*)

ROYLSTON (*Sharply*) Well, Benton? What is it?

BENTON (*Confused*) Nothing of any importance, sir—just something the gardener, Weson, asked me to tell you.

(*He hesitates, plainly indicating he does not wish to speak before* MRS. FRAZER)

ROYLSTON (*To* MRS. FRAZER) Excuse me. (*He goes over to* BENTON *in the doorway*) Well?

BENTON Weson says he saw a suspicious character hanging around and looking at the house early this morning. Weson shouted at him to find out what he wanted and he ran away.

ROYLSTON (*With a groan*) Damn Weson! Are you never going to get over your idiotic burglar scares, Benton?

BENTON (*Darkly*) I wasn't thinking of burglars—this time. (*With a meaningful glance in* MRS. FRAZER'*s direction*) Look out for the badger game, sir.

ROYLSTON (*Irritably*) Go to the devil! (BENTON *smiles craftily and goes out.* ROYLSTON *comes back to the table*) When I outgrew a governess they gave me Benton. I thought it was a change for the better but it wasn't. I have never been able to outgrow him. He won't let me. (MRS. FRAZER *remains silent.* ROYLSTON *strides up and down nervously, clasping and unclasping his hands and scowling at his disagreeable thoughts. Suddenly he strikes his fist into the palm of his hand with an impatient exclamation*) What a blind fool I am! If there was anything in the world I would have trusted Alice not to do, it was to read my letters. What a contemptible thing to do—to read my letters! And what a trustful simpleton I was to leave them around!

(*With an ironical smile*) Do you remember what I said last night about not caring to analyze my home relations provided the surface remained smooth? Well, your visit has stirred up the depths with a vengeance—the muddy depths.

MRS. FRAZER (*Sarcastically*) What a crushing blow for you!

ROYLSTON In all seriousness, it really is appalling. I feel as if the world were turned topsy-turvy. When you have taken a thing for granted for years, when a faith in it has been one of the main props of your life, although you might not have realized its importance at the time—and suddenly you make the discovery that you have trusted in a sham, that your prop is worm-eaten! It is rather a rough tumble, isn't it?

MRS. FRAZER (*In the same sarcastic tone*) I have found it so myself.

ROYLSTON That's so; I was forgetting. We're in the same boat, aren't we? (*With a sigh*) Well, I shall get bravely over it, as you have escaped from yours. A few bruises, I suppose, must be expected after such a hard fall.

MRS. FRAZER Yes, bruises on the soul.

ROYLSTON I will have to hunt a new illusion. You remember you said last night that when you came here you feared the crowning disillusionment?

MRS. FRAZER My fears were well grounded.

ROYLSTON Hm—you mean you have seen my illusion go up in smoke, too? It is discouraging—as if everything in life were founded upon false appearances. (*He quotes ironically*) "Yea, faileth now dream the dreamer and the lute the lutanist."

MRS. FRAZER You are deceiving yourself as to the nature of my awakening. I have come to regard the prop, as you call it, which I cast aside with scorn as the sound one. The new one, I find, is worm-eaten.

ROYLSTON The new one? Meaning that I am?

MRS. FRAZER Exactly! I asked you to guide my future because I though you were far-sighted. I have discovered you are only in-sighted—as pitifully in-sighted as I was.

ROYLSTON (*Surprised*) In-sighted?

MRS. FRAZER Yes, you see nothing beyond yourself. You are so preoccupied with the workings of your own brain that your vision of outside things is clouded. You are only a cruel egoist.

ROYLSTON Know thyself, sayeth the law.

MRS. FRAZER You make no allowance for the individual.

ROYLSTON Oh, come now, Mrs. Frazer; you have read what I have written. You know if there is one thing I harp on ad nauseam—

MRS. FRAZER It is the duty of the individual to triumph over environment; but in your life you regard yourself as the only individual in the world. You cannot see beyond that. You have reconstructed the world for yourself—well and good. Why try to force your conception on others? Why judge their thoughts by what you would think in their place? When you do so you deprive them of personality. You make them manikins and yourself the master of the show; and you care not a whit how you hurt their feelings when they fail to answer your pull of the string.

ROYLSTON (*With a bitter smile*) You too? It seems this is my day to be properly humbled in spirit.

MRS. FRAZER I know you will never pardon my effrontery in wounding your vanity so. Such colossal conceit!

ROYLSTON (*Flushing*) Mrs. Frazer!

MRS. FRAZER (*Calmly*) Your cruel vanity has torn off the mask. How could *you* help me? You can only help yourself. Perhaps if I were in love with you—but then you know, Mr. Naricissus, I would only be your reflection. However, I do not love you. Last night I thought—you were on such a high pedestal—I thought of the superman, of the creator, the maker of new values. This morning I saw merely an egotist whose hands are bloody with the human sacrifices he has made—to himself!

ROYLSTON (*Jumping from his chair—excitedly*) You are unjust, Mrs. Frazer.

MRS. FRAZER Now you are beginning to be angry.

ROYLSTON (*Indignantly*) Angry? Why should I be? You have a perfect right to your opinion, preposterous as it may be. Go on, let me hear the tale of my iniquities. It is very interesting.

MRS. FRAZER (*Teasingly*) You are losing your temper, you spoiled child.

ROYLSTON I am not losing my temper. (*Pettishly*) I am growing inured to insults this morning.

MRS. FRAZER Why, so am I! I must beg your forgiveness for one thing I said. It was too cruel of me.

(*She pauses, smiling mischievously at him*)

ROYLSTON (*Sulkily*) To what are you alluding?

MRS. FRAZER (*Mockingly*) I was truthful enough to tell you I did not love you. That was horrible of me. How could you endure hearing a woman say she did not love you? And how bored you must be when you hear them say they do love you! Eternal repetition, you know. The petted favorite of fortune stands between the devil and the deep blue sea.

ROYLSTON (*Angrily*) Mrs. Frazer, these personalities are— (*Looking at her and catching the twinkle in her eyes—with an embarrassed laugh*) I'm beaten; I acknowledge defeat. I surrender to the super-woman—only don't hit me when I'm down.

MRS. FRAZER (*Contritely*) I shouldn't have said all this to you, but I had to cure myself of my attack of hero-worship in some way. Besides, the wounds I received in this morning's interview with your wife cried aloud for vengeance. I had to vent my spleen on someone.

ROYLSTON (*Bitterly*) I shall never forgive myself for subjecting you to such a breach of hospitality. It was shameful of her.

MRS. FRAZER (*Sternly*) No, it is shameful of you to speak of her in that way. She is not to blame for her suspicions. She loves you; how could she help thinking what she did? She is the most wonderful woman I have ever known—worlds above poor blind creatures like you and me.

ROYLSTON I am afraid I cannot see it in that light.

MRS. FRAZER No, because in this case truth offends your pride and you will not see. You never misunderstood her as grossly as you do at the present moment.

ROYLSTON And *I* think I have only just begun to understand her.

MRS. FRAZER Take care! You are doing exactly what you rail against in others—judging by appearances. Is the keen analytical eye obstinately closed by wounded vanity?

ROYLSTON (*Impatiently*) No, no—but my letters?

MRS. FRAZER With such a wife you had no right to receive such letters.

ROYLSTON (*Scornfully*) Right?

MRS. FRAZER You'll admit that needless cruelty is wrong, I hope?

ROYLSTON Yes, but I don't see what—

MRS. FRAZER Do you love this woman of the letters?

ROYLSTON No, of course not!

MRS. FRAZER Yet you persuaded her to leave her home—

ROYLSTON Persuaded? No, certainly not! She came to me for advice. She had been impressed by what I had written about the narrowing influence of the conventional home. She had practically the same environment you described to me as yours before your marriage. She was engaged to be married to some cut-and-dried young simpleton. Her life was unsatisfying, gave her no scope for realizing the best that was in her. I saw she had brains, ability. I advised her to learn some occupation which would make her self-sustaining, and then go out into life and see things for herself.

MRS. FRAZER She is young?

ROYLSTON Twenty-one.

MRS. FRAZER And pretty?

ROYLSTON Yes.

MRS. FRAZER You are sure you are not in love with her?

ROYLSTON (*Irritably*) I am sure, yes! (*With a bored smile*) I have been too busy to love anyone.

MRS. FRAZER But yourself. Then you have not even that justification.

ROYLSTON (*Coldly*) I see no necessity for justifying my actions.

MRS. FRAZER You cannot deny this girl loves you?

ROYLSTON (*Cynically*) She may think she does.

MRS. FRAZER And you think she does! It tickles your vanity to think so.

ROYLSTON You are breaking me on the wheel.

(*He laughs helplessly*)

MRS. FRAZER You are a poor blind bat, not a butterfly; you can stand it. It may open your eyes. Can't you see that you have forever ruined all chance of her being happy with her cut-and-dried simpleton or any of his kind? And where is she to find the superman? Even if she gained your love, what a disappointment! What an awakening when she really came to know you!

ROYLSTON (*Forcing a laugh and looking down at his feet*) Poor clay feet!

MRS. FRAZER There is only one salvation for her. You must write to her at once and say—

(*She hesitates*)

ROYLSTON Say what?

MRS. FRAZER Reveal your true self.

ROYLSTON (*Smiling confidently*) You guarantee that will cure the infatuation?

MRS. FRAZER Absolutely!

ROYLSTON Are you sure she won't read her ideal into my words?

MRS. FRAZER (*Biting her lip*) Perhaps you are right. That won't do. I must go to her and tell her—

ROYLSTON She would think you were jealous. She would not believe you.

MRS. FRAZER Tell her flatly you don't love her.

ROYLSTON How about needless cruelty?

MRS. FRAZER (*Alarmed*) But you see yourself you must end it someway.

ROYLSTON I have a way (*Smiling at her*) tried and proved by experience.

MRS. FRAZER (*Scornfully*) I have no doubt.

ROYLSTON (*In a bantering tone*) Shall I tell you what it is? Don't try to look so indifferent. You know you're dying with curiosity. (MRS. FRAZER *shakes her head indignantly*) Well, I write a letter to this effect: "I love you but we must see each other no more."

MRS. FRAZER (*Contemptuously*) Oh!

ROYLSTON (*Continuing with a great show of affected pathos*) "I cannot make you unhappy. Our love is forbidden by cruel, man-made laws and it is on your frail shoulders their punishment would fall, etc., ad nauseam. So you must forget me—or rather, do not forget. Remember in my heart of hearts, my soul of souls, etc., ad lib, your image will remain, the inspiration of my work; that in spirit all my work will be dedicated to you—" And so on ad infinitum.

MRS. FRAZER That is disgusting drivel.

ROYLSTON Of course it is! But don't you know, haven't you ever been in love?

MRS. FRAZER Why?

ROYLSTON Love is the world upside down. Sense is drivel and drivel is sense.

MRS. FRAZER You mean to tell me she will be ridiculous enough to believe that?

ROYLSTON She will revel in it. She will telephone—I cannot be found. She will write—no answer. She may even try to see me—I am invisible. Then she will say: That wonderful man has the strength to sacrifice himself for my sake. *Voilà!* She goes home, marries the cut-and-dried simpleton, adopts a superior air which holds him in awed servitude, pities him—pity is love without jealousy—and whenever his uncouth matter-of-factness grates on her sensitive nerves she reverently takes my image from the inner shrine and indulges in the sweet happiness of melancholy retrospection. The memory of another's sacrifice for love of oneself— That is the most soothing narcotic a woman can possess. I recommend it to you.

MRS. FRAZER (*Dryly*) Thank you.

ROYLSTON (*Enthusiastically*) Just think of the ecstatic joy of a woman grown old and fat when she remembers that in her younger days a discarded lover committed suicide because she refused him. What a recompense for a double chin the memory of such a corpse must be!

MRS. FRAZER (*Controlling an impulse to laugh—coldly*) I was attempting to consider this matter seriously.

ROYLSTON What! Consider love seriously? Set your mind at rest. I have written the letter and I have ordered Benton to stifle the appeals of the telephone. You see, you need not have warned me.

MRS. FRAZER She had become serious, then?

ROYLSTON Why do you say that?

MRS. FRAZER When they become serious you grow afraid of complications. A little bird told me.

ROYLSTON A little bird?

MRS. FRAZER A man is never a hero to his—

ROYLSTON (*Groaning*) Valet! That scoundrel Benton! The model of discretion. Another illusion gone! My house of cards is tumbling about my ears.

MRS. FRAZER No more than you deserve.

ROYLSTON I admit it, Mrs. Frazer. (*Eagerly*) I may mock but I see it just the same. In the future I will send my tickled vanity a-packing and have done with such foolishness. After all, it was only an amusing flirtation—nothing more.

MRS. FRAZER Go and tell Mrs. Roylston that.

ROYLSTON (*His expression grows hard and cold*) Thank you for reminding me.

(*He goes to the electric bell-button in the wall near the door on left*)

MRS. FRAZER (*Anxiously*) What are you going to do?

ROYLSTON Ring for Benton to pack my things.

MRS. FRAZER Please don't!

ROYLSTON Why not?

MRS. FRAZER (*Pleadingly*) Not yet at any rate. Please sit down again. I have something to say to you.

ROYLSTON (*Sitting down*) Whatever you may say, Mrs. Frazer, will not alter my opinion in the least. I have my own ideas of the way Alice has acted and what I must do. With your permission I will go back to New York on the train with you.

MRS. FRAZER No, no, no! Think of how that would hurt her? Have you no pity? I will not allow it. Furthermore, you will never see me again when I leave this house. I have been the cause of too much unhappiness already.

ROYLSTON Don't accuse yourself. I have only gratitude to you for opening my eyes, and I want to help you in every way, as I promised I would.

MRS. FRAZER (*Vehemently*) No!

ROYLSTON Surely you don't mean you refuse—

MRS. FRAZER Yes, I refuse your assistance in any way, shape or manner. I am not going to take any position and I will not need your help; so let us drop that part of the matter. And as for opening your eyes, you have never been as sightless as you are now, poor blind mole!

ROYLSTON (*With smiling protest*) Odious comparisons! First I am a bat, then a mole!

MRS. FRAZER Would you like to see clearly?

ROYLSTON Granted that I am blind—will sight make me any the less miserable?

MRS. FRAZER (*Enthusiastically*) It will make you happy, truly happy. (ROYLSTON *smiles skeptically*) Have I your permission to teach you the lesson I was given this morning.

ROYLSTON (*Frowning*) Lesson?

MRS. FRAZER Yes, a lesson in life your wife gave me this morning.

ROYLSTON (*Icily*) My wife also gave me a lesson in life, if you will remember. (*Dryly*) Her first lesson was not so pleasing that I crave for a second.

MRS. FRAZER For her sake, for my sake, for your own sake you must.

ROYLSTON (*Indifferently*) Very well. (*He gets up from his chair*) In the meantime Benton can be packing up my things.

MRS. FRAZER No, please, not yet. Hear me out first—then pack away if you still care to. (*He hesitates uncertainly*) Come, I ask it as a favor.

(*He sits down in his chair again*)

ROYLSTON I warn you, Mrs. Frazer, I am not to be cajoled into altering my plans. You are wasting your time and eloquence.

MRS. FRAZER We shall see. Remember you are to hear me from beginning to end—of the lesson. All ready? When I came down this morning I found the irreproachable Benton in this room.

ROYLSTON And he showed you the crack in my armor.

MRS. FRAZER He convinced me, without meaning to do so, that the idol's feet were—well—at least only plated.

ROYLSTON (*Sarcastically*) Of course, he meant well.

MRS. FRAZER He meant to flatter me. He had his own convictions as to my status in this household, and when I saw him growing confidential I did not attempt to show him his mistake.

ROYLSTON (*Accusingly*) You wanted to listen to his gossip?

MRS. FRAZER (*With a frank laugh*) I wanted to play detective and find out if my you was the real you. Benton, having approved of your choice of a mistress, flattered me by revealing the fact that you had never cared enough for any of the others to dare to install them in your household.

ROYLSTON (*Raging*) The evil-minded wretch! Others, indeed! I tell you that there never have been any others in the sense he meant. And you allowed him to talk to you like that?

MRS. FRAZER I was making an ineffectual attempt to put him in his place when we heard Mrs. Roylston coming in with the children. And what do you think I did—I, the bold emancipated woman? I ran and hid in that room like the guiltiest of cravens. When I regained control of myself I was furious, and to prove I was not a coward I came in to face your wife. I went to the other extreme in my display of daring. She was not certain I had been here all night but I immediately told her the truth of the whole affair.

ROYLSTON What else could you have done?

MRS. FRAZER Oh, I could have lied a little for the good of her soul. Just consider how damning the facts are! She returns unexpectedly to find me sneaking out of a darkened room, the picture of guilt. I brazenly acknowledge I have been here all night and tell her an absurd story of missing a train, and so forth. She has read letters and—

ROYLSTON (*Impatiently*) I know how sadly the circumstantial evidence is against the truth. I was relying on the implicit trust she has always seemed to have for me.

MRS. FRAZER Trust? After she had read those letters—letters which seemed all the more guilty because you had never mentioned them to her? Trust! You want an angel for a wife, not a human being.

ROYLSTON She had no business to read those letters. The whole thing rests upon that.

MRS. FRAZER You had no business to receive the letters. The whole thing rests upon that. But to go on with my lesson: I asserted my innocence. Your wife refused to believe me—naturally enough. She spoke despondently of having expected something of the sort for a long time because you had been growing indifferent to her and the children.

ROYLSTON (*Indignantly*) That is not so. It's true I haven't had much time. I have been very busy, but—

MRS. FRAZER (*Looking at him searchingly*) Are you sure what you are saying now is the truth. Come, be frank! Remember your statement to me last night when I asked you if you loved her.

ROYLSTON (*After a pause—grudgingly*) Well, I confess I may have seemed indifferent; but, good heavens—

MRS. FRAZER She said she blamed no one but herself for what had happened. How could it be expected that a brilliant genius like you could continue to love a poor ignorant creature like herself?

ROYLSTON (*A bit shamefaced*) She said that?

MRS. FRAZER Those are almost her exact words. She blamed herself for marrying you in the first place. Marriages like yours were cursed, she thought.

ROYLSTON Marriages like ours?

MRS. FRAZER (*Meaningly—looking steadily into his eyes*) She told me of the events which preceded your marriage—of the discovery of your love affair.

ROYLSTON (*Gripping the arms of his chair tensely, and speaking hoarsely*) Good God, she told you that! Poor Alice! (*Half to himself*) What could have made her do that?

MRS. FRAZER She said she thought that perhaps you blamed her for your father's death.

ROYLSTON What an absurd idea!

MRS. FRAZER She described your early life together—the days of struggle with poverty before your first play was produced; the days when you remained home in the little flat to write while she worked in an office as stenographer. She used to typewrite what you had written during the day when she came home at night—after she had cooked dinner and washed the dishes.

ROYLSTON (*His face slowly flushing crimson*) You are right! I see what you are driving at. Whatever I am she has made me. I have been forgetting those early days for the past few years. They do not chime well with the tickled vanity. (*With sudden ingenuousness*) But I did use to dry the dishes, you know.

MRS. FRAZER (*Laughing*) Bravo! Richard is himself again. You only sold a few articles that first year, she said.

ROYLSTON She flattered me. I never sold one. Every cent came through her.

MRS. FRAZER She said those days were the happiest of her life. She had often been selfish enough to wish, since you became indifferent, that you had never succeeded and it could always have been as it was in the little flat.

ROYLSTON Good heavens, she was nothing but a slave in those days.

MRS. FRAZER She knew how hard it must have been for you, who had been used to having everything, to have her drag you down into privation and—

ROYLSTON (*Deeply moved*) What a horribly mistaken thought! I joyed in losing everything for her. It was like paying off part of my debt.

MRS. FRAZER (*Continuing as if he had not interrupted*) So she resolved that as soon as your first book or play was published or produced, and you did not need her any longer, she would leave you, permit you to regain your freedom.

ROYLSTON (*Stupefied—his voice trembling*) Why, that's what she proposed to do—for me—when she was here a little while ago!

MRS. FRAZER Oh yes, she only desires your happiness and, as she thinks you love me, she is perfectly willing to give you up to me—because she loves you so much.

ROYLSTON How is it possible to lose oneself like that—I cannot grasp it—there is too much clay in my make-up— For me, too! Good heavens! She intended to leave me when my first play was produced, you say? But she didn't.

MRS. FRAZER For a very good reason. It was about that time your son was born, wasn't it?

ROYLSTON (*Getting up from his chair and walking nervously about the room—in great agitation*) I see, I see! Poor Alice! What a woman she is! And I—good heavens! You threatened to open my eyes—I've lived with her all these years and forgotten how much I owed to her. She has protected and shielded me from everything—made my opportunity for me, you might say—and I took it all for granted—the finest thing in my life! Took it all for granted without a thought of gratitude, as my due. Lord, what a cad I've been! What a rotten cad!

(*He throws himself into the chair and stares moodily before him*)

MRS. FRAZER (*With a faint smile*) I'd like to deny your statement but I'm afraid it's only too true.

ROYLSTON What I cannot get through my head is why she should tell you all this. Alice is proud. To reveal all this to you, a stranger—it must have humbled her spirit to the breaking point.

MRS. FRAZER I cannot quite understand, myself. She wished to justify you, of course, to prove you were in no way to blame.

ROYLSTON (*Groaning*) Oh!

MRS. FRAZER You see she persisted in regarding this misfortune as the retribution for her sin in the beginning.

ROYLSTON (*Jumping up—excitedly*) Ah, by heavens, that is going too far! Retribution for *her* sin! What a preposterous idea! As if the blame, the sin if it was one, were not all mine! (*Looking at his hands*) Bloody with sacrifices at my own altar—yes, you were right—and she is the woman whom I tortured with my blind egotism not half an hour ago—the woman who pleaded for forgiveness—and I refused and was going to desert her. I am beginning to hate myself for a monster! Those letters! If any woman ever dares to write to me again I'll have her letters burned by the—no, we haven't one—I'll hand them over to the police. (MRS. FRAZER *bursts out laughing*) And my children— Good God, do you know the horrible thought came to me just now that I do not even know my own children?

MRS. FRAZER (*Protestingly*) Now you are carrying your self-accusation too far.

ROYLSTON (*Vehemently*) I tell you it's the truth. I speak to them, I kiss them sometimes; but I do the same for other people's. For all the loving interest I have taken in them they might just as well be the gardener's—or Benton's.

MRS. FRAZER You have the whole future before you for retribution.

ROYLSTON (*Catching at the word eagerly*) Yes, retribution, joyful retribution every day, every hour! Pay off a part of this enormous debt of love which has accumulated against me! Why, life is going to mean more, be finer and happier than I ever dreamed!

MRS. FRAZER Happiness is servitude.

ROYLSTON (*Enthusiastically*) Of course it is! Servitude in love, love in servitude! Logos in Pan, Pan in Logos! That is the great secret—and I never knew! Thank you, thank you! But how did you guess it?

MRS. FRAZER Mrs. Roylston told me this morning—her lesson in life.

ROYLSTON That, too! Her love is great enough to solve all enigmas.

MRS. FRAZER (*Laughing*) But your work? The sovereign individual? The superman? The great lonely one?

ROYLSTON My love will be a superlove worthy of the superman, and— (*Hesitating*) Besides, this is the exceptional case which proves the contrary rule—what are you laughing at?

MRS. FRAZER At your determination to be exceptional though the heavens fall.

ROYLSTON (*Laughing himself*) I have to be exceptional to be worthy of such an exceptional wife.

MRS. FRAZER (*Rising from her chair*) And now I must go. My mission is accomplished.

ROYLSTON Your mission?

(*The doorbell is heard ringing*)

MRS. FRAZER Remember what you said about fatality? I am convinced I had to accomplish something here. It was not what I thought it was, but no matter. I, too, have learned the secret. It was my mission to open your eyes—and my own.

ROYLSTON You are going back to your husband?

MRS. FRAZER Yes, back to the chains which have suddenly become dear to me. Like you I had grown so accustomed to the best things in life that I scorned it. I, too, have my joyful retribution to make, my debt of love to pay.

ROYLSTON (*Going to her and taking her hand*) And how can I ever thank you for my awakening?

MRS. FRAZER The fact that you have wakened is thanks enough.

ROYLSTON And will you not become—my wife's friend?

MRS. FRAZER With all my heart—if she will allow it.

(BENTON *appears in the doorway on the left. He is greatly excited*)

BENTON Excuse me, sir, but there's a man who insisted on seeing you and—

(GEORGE FRAZER *pushes* BENTON *roughly aside and steps into the room. He is a man of about thirty-five, thick-set, of medium height, black hair gray at the temples, square jaw, irregular features, broad clean-shaven face and shrewd blue eyes. His face is haggard and shows plainly the traces of deep-rooted grief and anxiety with their consequent sleepless nights. He is dressed in a business suit of dark material*)

FRAZER (*He gives a groan of suppressed rage as he sees the two standing together*) Ethel!

MRS. FRAZER George!

(*She makes a movement toward him. He throws himself at* ROYLSTON, *pulling a revolver from his coat pocket.* MRS. FRAZER *springs between them*)

MRS. FRAZER For my sake! George!

(FRAZER *hurls the revolver on the floor and sinks into the chair by the table, hiding his face in his hands and sobbing heavily.* MRS. FRAZER *goes to him and puts her arm around his shoulder. He makes a feeble effort to shake her off.* BENTON *creeps stealthily over and picks up the revolver*)

ROYLSTON (*Severely*) You may go, Benton.

(BENTON *looks at him irresolutely, then goes out.* FRAZER *finally regains his composure somewhat and turns his grief-stricken face to his wife*)

FRAZER Ethel—why? My God!

MRS. FRAZER (*Distractedly*) Will this misunderstanding never be cleared up!

ROYLSTON Yes, I will clear it up.

FRAZER (*Furiously*) Shut up, you— You lie! I know what I know. You have done me harm enough without trying to treat me like a fool. I'd have shot you for the skulking liar you are—but—it wasn't for your sake I didn't—

ROYLSTON (*With calm dignity*) I choose to ignore your insults for the present, Mr. Frazer. When you are calmer you will hear what I have to say and this ludicrous melodrama will end.

(*He turns to go out the door in back*)

MRS. FRAZER No, please stay; you must. (ROYLSTON *remains standing by the door*)

MRS. FRAZER (*Her voice trembling*) George, how did you find out?

FRAZER I always knew you'd wind up here sooner or later. Before you left, when I was certain you didn't care for me any more, I suspected you were in love with this (*With bitter scorn*) gentleman. His books, his plays all over the place, his photograph on the middle of your dresser. (MRS. FRAZER *flushes.* ROYLSTON *looks at her in astonishment*) That was why I had you followed.

MRS. FRAZER (*With a frown*) I thought you had given up spying on me.

FRAZER (*Pleadingly*) It wasn't spying. You mustn't think that, Ethel. It was for your own sake I did it.

MRS. FRAZER (*With a hard laugh*) For my sake!

FRAZER I wanted to protect you. You don't know the world. I knew you'd do something foolish sooner or later with your head full of his crazy ideas. You don't know the game these gentlemen play.

ROYLSTON (*Angrily*) Oh!

(*He turns and goes out the door in back*)

MRS. FRAZER So I was followed to this house?

FRAZER Yes.

MRS. FRAZER When I came—last night?

FRAZER (*With a groan*) Yes.

MRS. FRAZER How is it you gave up waiting for me? Why haven't you tried to see me yourself—it's nearly two months.

FRAZER I could see you didn't want me bothering you—and I've been sick.

MRS. FRAZER (*Alarmed*) Sick?

FRAZER (*Lightly*) Nothing serious—overwork—nervous breakdown, the doctor said. Had to go to bed—he prescribed perfect rest. (*Ironically*) Perfect rest!

MRS. FRAZER (*With tender anxiety*) But you're all right now, de— (*She bites back the term of endearment at his wondering look*) George?

FRAZER (*Sarcastically*) Fine—as you can see.

MRS. FRAZER Why couldn't you have sent me word? It would have changed things so.

FRAZER You mean you wouldn't be here? Well, I couldn't. I didn't want you to come back because you pitied me. (*Bitterly*) I didn't think you'd care.

MRS. FRAZER (*Wincing*) Oh. (*After a pause*) Why did you come here this morning?

FRAZER The detective telephoned me—when he was sure. I wanted to kill this man and you too, at first. I didn't know what I was doing.

MRS. FRAZER (*Sadly*) And now I suppose it's all over —forever—between us. You can't want me any longer—believing what you do.

FRAZER (*Turning away from her to hide his emotion*) Don't say that, Ethel. I can't give you up—this way. Life is too hard to bear—without you. I can't help loving you—in spite of everything. I shouldn't —I suppose—now. (MRS. FRAZER *is looking at him with eyes full of tenderness*) If you'd only—love me a little—I could forget this foolishness—not your fault—if we'd had children—you were always alone—my fault.

(*A sob shakes his shoulders*)

MRS. FRAZER (*Softly*) So you still want me—to come back?

FRAZER Yes, that's why I came—to ask you—if you would.

MRS. FRAZER (*Kneeling down beside him—eagerly*) Then look into my eyes quick—now! (*He looks down at her*) I swear to you I am innocent—that I love you more now than I ever did, even on our honeymoon; and I am as innocent of wrong now as I was then. Can you believe me?

FRAZER (*Wonderingly*) Then you don't love him?

MRS. FRAZER No, no, a thousand times no! I love you, and he loves his wife. My presence here is folly, nothing more. Let me explain the whole thing to you.

FRAZER (*Joyfully*) No, no, I believe you without that.

(*He takes her into his arms and kisses her.* MRS. ROYLSTON *enters from the door on the left. She has a small traveling bag in her hand. Her eyes are red from weeping. She stops in astonishment and her bag drops from her hand when she sees the* FRAZERS)

MRS. ROYLSTON (*Timidly*) I beg your pardon.

(*Startled, they both jump to their feet and face* MRS. ROYLSTON *in confusion*)

MRS. FRAZER (*Joyfully*) I want you to meet my husband, Mrs. Roylston. George, this is Mrs. Roylston.

MRS. ROYLSTON (*Astonished*) I'm very happy—

FRAZER A great pleasure—

MRS. FRAZER Mrs. Roylston is the most wonderful woman in the world. (MRS. ROYLSTON *smiles feebly*) If you don't believe me, ask her husband. (*As* FRAZER *stammers and* MRS. ROYLSTON *is equally nonplussed*) And now you and I will be going—home! (*She walks over toward the door on the left*) Good-bye, Mrs. Roylston. I hope when you understand everything you will become my friend. (*She holds out her hand, which* MRS. ROYLSTON *takes uncertainly as if in a daze*) Come, George, out into the open air. I have so much to say to you.

(*She goes out.* FRAZER *follows her but stops at the door and turns to* MRS. ROYLSTON)

FRAZER Mrs. Roylston, will you tell your husband I wish to take back all I said to him a while ago. He'll understand.

MRS. ROYLSTON (*Dully*) I'll tell him.

FRAZER Thank you; good-bye.

(*He goes out. A moment later the front door is heard closing*)

MRS. ROYLSTON (*Mechanically*) Good-bye.

(*She takes her bag and sets it down beside the table; then sinks wearily into the chair and leans both elbows on the table, holding her face in her hands in an attitude of deep dejection.* ROYLSTON *enters from the door in the rear. He gives a joyful exclamation on seeing his wife*)

ROYLSTON (*Coming over quickly, he stands beside her*) Alice.

MRS. ROYLSTON (*Startled, she turns and looks up at him —dully*) Yes.

ROYLSTON They have gone—Mr. and Mrs. Frazer—together?

MRS. ROYLSTON Yes.

ROYLSTON (*Jubilantly*) Good! And without hearing my explanation! That is a proof of love and trust on his part which I would hardly have expected of him. You see, Alice, the most ludicrous part of this whole misunderstanding is the fact that I did not spend last night in this house.

MRS. ROYLSTON (*Slowly—as if she could not believe her ears*) You—were not here?

ROYLSTON No. After I directed Mrs. Frazer to her room I ran away—spent the night at the roadhouse. I was afraid to stay, I must confess—afraid of myself—afraid of how the situation might be misconstrued. I didn't want to be the cause of any more trouble to Mrs. Frazer, who had suffered enough already.

MRS. ROYLSTON (*Her eyes brimming with happy tears*) Oh, I'm so glad!

ROYLSTON I want you to prove my statement—to be completely satisfied that I am speaking the truth. My name is on the register at the roadhouse and they all know me and can testify to my story. I wanted to explain before but your doubts hurt my obstinate pride—I had boasted to Mrs. Frazer that you would not judge by appearances, you know. As for Frazer's detective, he must have taken everything for granted—as you and all the rest did. I'll have to write to Frazer and tell him. In spite of his fine confidence there might be some secret suspicions in the back of his mind.

MRS. ROYLSTON David—forgive me.

ROYLSTON (*Impetuously*) Forgive you? What nonsense! (*He bends down to kneel beside her and knocks his knee against her bag. He holds it up wonderingly*) What's this? Your bag all packed! Then you were really going to leave me?

MRS. ROYLSTON (*Tremblingly*) I thought you loved her. I wanted you to be happy.

ROYLSTON And the children?

MRS. ROYLSTON I had no right— It was best for them to stay.

ROYLSTON You were going to leave them, too—and all for my sake! Good heavens! And you ask for forgiveness! (*Kneeling down beside her and putting his arms around her*) Ah, my dear, my dear, how deeply you make me feel my unworthiness! I am the one who must plead for pardon, pardon for a lifetime of selfish neglect, of vain posing, of stupid conceit—

MRS. ROYLSTON (*Kissing him*) Ssshhh!

ROYLSTON (*His voice vibrating with tenderness*) Dear, the future will be all that the past has not been, I swear it. We start on our honeymoon today—a lifelong honeymoon. (*Jumping to his feet, with mock severity*) But haven't you read your husband's books, you wonderful, foolish woman? Don't you know it was your duty to claim your right as an individual, to shake off the shackles my insufferable egotism had forced upon you? Don't you understand that you have stifled your own longings, given up your own happiness that I might feel self-satisfied.

MRS. ROYLSTON (*Interrupting him—softly and tenderly*) That was my happiness.

(*He bends down and kisses her reverently*)

Curtain

ABORTION

A Play in One Act

Characters

JACK TOWNSEND
JOHN TOWNSEND, *his father*
MRS. TOWNSEND, *his mother*
LUCY TOWNSEND, *his sister*
EVELYN SANDS, *his fiancée*
DONALD (BULL) HERRON, *his roommate*
JOE MURRAY, *a machinist*
STUDENTS OF THE UNIVERSITY

SCENE—*The study of the suite of rooms occupied by* JACK TOWNSEND *and* DONALD HERRON *on the ground floor of a dormitory in a large eastern university of the United States. The left wall is composed almost entirely of a large bow window looking out on the campus, forming a window seat which is piled high with bright-colored cushions. In the middle of the far side, a door opening into a hallway of the dormitory. On either side of the door, leather-covered divans with leather cushions. In the right corner to the rear, a writing desk with an electric drop-light hanging over it. In the middle of the right wall, a fireplace. In the extreme right foreground, a door opening into a bedroom. In the center of the room, a table with an electric reading lamp wired from the chandelier above. Books, periodicals, pipes, cigarette boxes, ashtrays, etc., are also on the table. The walls of the room are hung with flags, class banners, framed photographs of baseball and football teams, college posters, etc. Two Morris chairs and several rockers are grouped about the table.*

It is about eight o'clock in the evening of a warm day in June. At first the windows on the left are gray with the dim glow of the dying twilight, but as the action progresses this slowly disappears.

A sound of voices comes from the hall. The door in the rear is opened and MRS. TOWNSEND *and* LUCY *enter, escorted by* HERRON. *Their figures can be vaguely made out in the dusk of the room.*

LUCY (*Feeling her way toward the table*) Do put on the lights, Bull! I know I'm going to break my neck in a minute.

(MRS. TOWNSEND *remains standing by the doorway*)

HERRON (*Cheerfully*) One minute, one minute! (*Striking his shin against the corner of the divan —wrathfully*) Oh—

(*He bites his tongue just in time*)

LUCY (*With a gurgling laugh*) Say it! Say it!

HERRON (*Leaning over the divan and feeling on the wall for the electric switch—softly*) Oh darn!

LUCY Hypocrite! That isn't what you were going to say.

HERRON Oh gosh, then. (*Finding the switch*) There! (*Turning on all the lights except the drop-light*) Let there be light!

LUCY (*She is a small, vivacious blond, nineteen years old, gushing with enthusiasm over everything and everybody. She wears an immense bouquet of flowers at the waist of her dark blue dress and carries a flag*) Don't stand there posing, Bull. (*She *flings herself into one of the Morris chairs*) You look much more like a god of darkness than one of light.

MRS. TOWNSEND (*She is a sweet-faced, soft-spoken, gray-haired lady in her early fifties. She is dressed in dark gray. She turns to* LUCY *with smiling remonstrance*) Lucy! (*To* HERRON, *who clumsily arranges a cushion at the back of a rocking chair for her*) Thank you, Donald. (HERRON *winces at the "Donald"*)

LUCY (*Contemptuously*) Donald!

HERRON (*Chuckling. He is a huge, swarthy six-footer with a bull neck and an omnipresent grin, slow to anger and to understanding but—an All-American tackle. His immense frame is decked out in white flannels which make him look gigantic*) I don't care much for the "Donald" myself.

LUCY And I still claim, Mother, that Donald, alias Bull, resembles Pluto more than any other divinity. It is true, judging from the pictures I have seen, that Pluto was not as fat (*As* HERRON *slouches into a sitting position on the divan*) nor as clumsy, but—

HERRON (*Grinning*) What have I done today? What have I done? Didn't I purchase candy and beautiful flowers? And now I reap nothing but abuse. I appeal to you, Mrs. Townsend. She is breaking me on the wheel.

LUCY Poor butterfly! (*Convulsed with laughter*) Ha ha ha! Poor, delicate, fragile butterfly!

HERRON There you go again! (*Appealingly*) You see, Mrs. Townsend? Every word of mine is turned to mockery.

(*He sighs explosively*)

MRS. TOWNSEND (*Smiling*) Never mind, Donald; you ought to hear the nice things she says behind your back.

LUCY (*Indignantly*) Mother!

HERRON I find it hard to believe.

LUCY Mother is fibbing so as not to hurt your feelings. (*With a roguish smile*) I never, never in all my life said a good word about you. You don't deserve it.

MRS. TOWNSEND Why, Lucy, what a thing to say!

(*While she is speaking* JOE MURRAY *appears in the doorway to the rear. He is a slight, stoop-shouldered, narrow-chested young fellow of eighteen, with large, feverish black eyes, thin lips, pasty complexion, and the sunken cheeks of a tuberculosis victim. He wears a shabby dark suit. He peers blinkingly around the room and knocks, but they do not hear him*)

LUCY (*Glancing toward the door and seeing him*) Someone to see you, Bull.

HERRON (*Turning to* MURRAY) Anything you want?

MURRAY (*Aggressively*) I wanna see Townsend, Jack Townsend.

HERRON He's not here.

MURRAY D'yuh know when he'll be in?

HERRON Any minute; but I advise you not to wait. He won't have any time for you tonight. If you want to leave a message I'll give it to him.

MURRAY (*Truculently*) He'll find time for me all right.

HERRON (*Staring at him*) You think so? Suit yourself. (*Pointedly*) You can wait for him *outside*.

(MURRAY'*s face pales with rage. He starts to say something, then turns abruptly and disappears into the hallway*)

HERRON Pleasant little man!

LUCY Don't you know who it was?

HERRON Never saw him before; probably some fresh "townie" who thinks Jack's indebted to him because he recovered a stolen baseball bat or something, and wants to put the acid on him for a dollar or two. Jack's such a good-natured slob—

LUCY (*With a giggle*) Listen to who is talking.

MRS. TOWNSEND (*Proudly*) Jack always has been so good-hearted.

HERRON (*With a smile*) He's only stingy with base hits. Great game he pitched today. Star players usually fall down when they're captains of teams and it's their last year in college; but not old Jack —only three hits off him.

MRS. TOWNSEND This game we saw today decides the championship, doesn't it?

LUCY Certainly, Mother. You don't suppose I'd have yelled my whole voice away if it wasn't, do you? I can hardly speak.

MRS. TOWNSEND (*With a sly wink at* HERRON) I hadn't noticed that, Lucy.

(HERRON *shakes with suppressed mirth*)

LUCY (*Pouting*) Oh, Mother, how unkind!

MRS. TOWNSEND I must confess I'm not much of a fan— Is that what you call it? I do not understand the game and if it wasn't for Jack playing I'm afraid I would find it rather wearisome.

HERRON Jack is the big man of the college tonight, all

right. The president is a mere nonentity beside him. Add to our list of athletic heroes one Jack Townsend, captain and pitcher.

MRS. TOWNSEND How they carried him around the field after the game!

LUCY And cheered him!

HERRON You bet we did. I had a hold of one leg. But I agree with you, Mrs. Townsend. If Jack didn't play I wouldn't take much interest in baseball myself. (*Enthusiastically*) Football is the real game.

LUCY Of course you'd say that.

MRS. TOWNSEND That's beyond me, too. I've heard it's so rough, that so many players are injured. When John first entered college his father and I made him promise not to go in for it on any account.

HERRON (*Regretfully*) You spoiled a fine player. (*There is a noise of voices from the hall*) Speaking of the—hm—angel.

(EVELYN SANDS *enters followed by* JACK TOWNSEND. EVELYN *is a tall, dark-haired, beautiful girl about twenty years old. Her eyes are large and brown; her mouth full-lipped, resolute; her figure lithe and graceful. She is dressed simply but stylishly in white.* JACK *is a well-built handsome young fellow about twenty-two years old, with blond hair brushed straight back from the forehead, intelligent blue eyes, a good-natured, self-indulgent mouth and ruddy, tanned complexion. He has the easy, confident air of one who has, through his prowess in athletics, become a figure of note in college circles and is accustomed to the deference of those around him. He wears a dark coat, white soft shirt with a bright-colored tie, flannel trousers and white tennis shoes*)

LUCY Hail to the hero!

(EVELYN *comes over and sits on the arm of* LUCY'S *chair.* JACK *stands beside his mother*)

MRS. TOWNSEND (*Smiling fondly up at him*) Where is your father?

JACK Right outside, talking to Professor Simmons. After dinner, as we were following you out of the Inn, we ran into the Prof and he walked down with us. Did you think we were lost?

LUCY (*With a mischievous glance at* EVELYN) We thought you might have forestalled the forthcoming happy event by eloping.

(EVELYN *blushes*)

JACK (*Laughing*) With Father for chaperon?

LUCY Well, don't you dare do it! I'd never forgive you spoiling my chance to wear my gown. I'm going to be just the most stunning bridesmaid. Am I not, Mother?

MRS. TOWNSEND Of course, dear. (*To* JACK) Why didn't you ask the professor to come in?

JACK I did, Mother, but he's on his way somewhere or other.

HERRON By the way, Jack, there was a "townie" in here asking to see you a few minutes ago.

JACK (*Starting nervously*) A "townie"? Did he give any name?

HERRON No. A fresh little shrimp; said he'd wait. Wasn't he outside?

JACK (*Visibly uneasy*) I didn't see anyone.

HERRON He'll be back probably; and look out for a touch.

(*The singing of a distant quartet sounds faintly from the campus*)

LUCY (*Springing up*) I hear them singing on the campus. I'm going out. Bull, when does the big P'rade start?

HERRON Pretty soon; you can hear the clans gathering now.

LUCY I'm going to march beside them all the way to the lake.

MRS. TOWNSEND The lake?

LUCY There's going to be a canoe carnival, and bonfires, and dancing, and everything, Mother. You've simply got to come, all of you, in honor of hero Jack.

JACK (*Embarrassed*) Come, come, Sis, praise from you is rare indeed.

HERRON (*Emphatically*) Indeed!

LUCY (*Archly, to* HERRON) Indeed?

MRS. TOWNSEND (*Getting quickly from her chair—with a girlish laugh*) I'm going with you. I'll show you young people I can celebrate with the best of you.

JACK Are you sure it isn't too much for you, Mother?

MRS. TOWNSEND (*Her face flushed with excitement*) Nonsense, Jack!

JACK (*Putting his arm around her affectionately*) Dear old Mother—young Mother, I should say.

LUCY Come on, everybody!

JACK You people go on ahead and I'll catch up with you.

(MRS. TOWNSEND *goes out*)

LUCY (*To* HERRON) Come on, Jumbo.

HERRON (*Groaning*) Jumbo! And Bull! Lucy thinks I'm a menagerie.

(*He and* LUCY *go out.* EVELYN *starts to follow them but* JACK *stops her and takes her in his arms*)

JACK We won't be alone again for ages.

(*He kisses her*)

EVELYN (*Smiling up into his face*) I'm so proud of you, Jack dear.

JACK (*Laughingly puts his fingers across her lips*) Ssshhh! You'll give me an awful attack of exaggerated ego if you go on talking like that.

EVELYN But it's true, dear.

JACK Then for the good of my soul don't tell me. Praise from Sis is wonder enough for one day.

EVELYN (*Moving a few steps away from him*) I wish I could tell you how proud I felt when I sat in the grandstand and watched you. (*With a laugh*) It was a horrid sort of selfish pride, too, for I couldn't help saying to myself from time to time: "He loves me, *me!* He belongs to *me!*" And I thought of how jealous all the girls around me who were singing his praises would be if they knew.

JACK (*His face suddenly grows serious, as if at some painful memory*) Please, Evelyn! You make me feel so mean—and contemptible when you talk like that.

EVELYN (*Astonished*) Mean? Contemptible? How foolish you are, Jack. (*Excitedly*) I felt like standing on my seat and shouting to all of them: "What right have you to think of him? He is *mine, mine!*" (*Laughing at her own enthusiasm, adds in a matter-of-fact tone*) Or will be in three months.

JACK (*His voice thrilling with emotion*) In three months! (*Jokingly*) Do you know those three months are going to seem like three years?

EVELYN (*Gaily*) Three centuries; but I was telling you how splendid you were this afternoon.

JACK (*Protestingly*) Ssshhh, Evelyn!

(*He tries to put his arms around her*)

EVELYN (*Backing away and avoiding him*) You were so cool, so brave. It struck me as symbolic of the way you would always play, in the game of life—fairly, squarely, strengthening those around you, refusing to weaken at critical moments, advancing others by sacrifices, fighting the good fight for the cause, the team, and always, always, whether vanquished or victor, reserving a hearty, honest cheer for the other side. (*Breaking off breathlessly*) Oh, Jack dear, I loved you so!

JACK (*A strong note of pain in his voice, he puts his hands over his ears, and forces a laugh*) I won't listen any longer. I positively refuse.

EVELYN (*Smiling*) It's all over. I'm through. I simply had to tell you.

(*She holds out both hands to him. He draws her into his arms and kisses her*)

JACK (*With deep feeling*) I shall try—with all my strength—in the future, Evelyn—to live as you have said and become worthy of you. Today was nothing. One does one's best for the sake of the game, for the love of the struggle. Our best happened to be luckier, more skillful, perhaps, than the other fellow's—that's all.

EVELYN It's so like you to say that. You're a dear.

(*She kisses him.* JACK*'s father,* JOHN TOWNSEND, *appears in the doorway. He is a tall, kindly old man of sixty or so with a quantity of white hair. He is erect, well-preserved, energetic, dressed immaculately but soberly. He laughs and shakes a finger at* EVELYN)

TOWNSEND Caught in the act. (EVELYN *smiles and blushes*) Evelyn, they're waiting for you outside and Lucy threatens to come in and drag you out if my persuasive powers have no effect. They want to make a start for the Steps and see the P'rade form. It's due to start shortly.

(*While he is speaking he comes forward, puts his straw hat on the table and sits down in one of the Morris chairs*)

EVELYN (*Eagerly*) I wouldn't miss it for worlds. (*She goes to the door; then turns and looks at* JACK *irresolutely*) Aren't you coming with us, both of you?

(JACK *looks at his father uncertainly*)

TOWNSEND We'll join you there; or, better still— (*To* JACK) The P'rade passes right by here, doesn't it? They always used to in the old days.

JACK Yes, Dad.

TOWNSEND Then you go ahead with the others, Evelyn, and since Lucy tells me you're going to follow the P'rade, we'll be able to join you when you pass by. (*Explanatively*) I've seen and taken part in so many of these affairs that their novelty has sort of worn off for me; and Jack—if they were to discover the hero of the day at this stage of the game he wouldn't have a rag to his back, eh, Jack?

JACK (*Smiling*) I'm black and blue all over from their fond caresses this afternoon.

EVELYN (*Gaily*) I'm off, then. (*Looking at* JACK) You'll surely join us when we pass?

JACK Sure thing.

EVELYN (*Waving her hand*) Bye-bye.

(*She goes out.* JACK *sits down near his father*)

TOWNSEND (*He takes out a cigar and lights it.* JACK *watches him uneasily as if he foresees what his father is going to say and dreads it.* TOWNSEND *avoids his eyes. There is an uncomfortable silence. Then* TOWNSEND *begins vaguely*) It certainly removes the burden of the years from my shoulders to come out to the old college in the spring and live the old days over in memory and hobnob with some of the old-timers who were young-timers with me. It becomes more difficult every year, I find. All the old landmarks are disappearing one by one.

JACK (*Perfunctorily*) Yes, even in my time there have been great changes.

TOWNSEND (*Very palpably talking to gain time*) It gives me a painful heart-throb every time I come back and look for some old place and find it renovated or torn down.

JACK (*Shortly*) I can well understand that.

TOWNSEND You don't realize what this college comes to mean to you in after years; how it becomes inseparably woven into the memories of one's lost youth until the two become identical.

JACK (*Impatiently*) Yes, I suppose so.

TOWNSEND (*More and more vaguely*) Happiest days of my life, of anyone's life—

JACK (*Abruptly*) Come to the point, Dad.

TOWNSEND (*Confused*) What? Eh?

JACK (*Firmly*) You didn't send Evelyn away in order that you might wax reminiscent; you know that, Dad.

TOWNSEND (*Heaving a sigh of relief*) You are quite right, I did not; but what I ought to speak about is such a deuced painful subject for both of us that I hardly dare speak of it—especially on your day of triumph when I should be the last one to bring up any unpleasantness.

JACK (*Kindly*) Never mind that, Dad.

TOWNSEND You see, I didn't know when I'd have another opportunity of seeing you without arousing your mother's suspicions.

JACK I understand.

TOWNSEND And the thing has caused me much worry, I simply had to hear from your own lips that everything was all right.

JACK Then I will set your mind at rest immediately. Everything *is* all right.

TOWNSEND (*Fervently*) Thank God for that! Why haven't you written to me?

JACK Until a few days ago I had nothing new to tell you.

TOWNSEND When was the operation performed?

JACK Last Monday.

TOWNSEND And you've heard from her since?

JACK I received a short note from her that night. It was all over and everything was all right, she said. She told me I needn't worry any longer.

TOWNSEND That was five days ago. You haven't had any word since then?

JACK No.

TOWNSEND That's a favorable sign. If any further complications had cropped up she would surely have let you know, wouldn't she?

JACK Yes, I think she would. I imagine she's frightened to death and doesn't want any more to do with me. I'm sure I hope so. And then, you see, I never answered her letter or telephoned.

TOWNSEND (*Gravely*) You were wrong there, my boy.

JACK (*Excitedly*) I know it, I know it, Dad; but I had just received a letter from Evelyn telling me she was coming out for Commencement Week and the game, and— Oh, when I thought of her the other affair seemed so horrible and loathsome, I swore I'd never speak or write again. When I was certain she was in no danger I judged it best for both of us to break off once and for all.

TOWNSEND Listen, my boy, are you sure—you know one's vanity blinds one in such cases—are you sure, absolutely sure, you were the father of this child which would have been born to her?

JACK (*Emphatically*) Yes, I am certain of it, as certain as one can possibly be. (*Wildly*) Oh, I wish to God I had grounds for some suspicion of the sort. What a salve it would be for my conscience! But no, no! To even think such is an insult to a sweet girl. (*Defiantly*) For she is a sweet, lovely girl in spite of everything, and if I had loved her the least particle, if I had not been in love with Evelyn, I should certainly have married her.

TOWNSEND Hm—if you did not love this girl, why did you—why, in the first place—?

JACK (*Leaning toward his father and fixing his eyes upon him searchingly*) Why? Why? Who knows why or who, that does know, has the courage to confess it, even to himself. Be frank, Dad! Judging from several anecdotes which your friend Professor Simmons has let slip about your four years here, you were no St. Anthony. Turn your mind back to those days and then answer your own question: Why, in the first place?

TOWNSEND (*Staring at the floor in moody retrospection—a pause*) We've retained a large portion of the original mud in our make-up. That's the only answer I can think of.

JACK (*Ironically*) That's it! Do you suppose it was the same man who loves Evelyn who did this other thing? No, a thousands time no, such an idea is abhorrent. It was the male beast who ran gibbering through the forest after its female thousands of years ago.

TOWNSEND Come, Jack, that is pure evasion. You are responsible for the Mr. Hyde in you as well as for the Dr. Jekyll. Restraint—

JACK (*Scornfully*) Restraint? Ah, yes, everybody preaches it but who practices it? And could they if they wanted to? Some impulses are stronger than we are, have proved themselves so throughout the world's history. Is it not rather our ideals of conduct, of Right and Wrong, our ethics, which are unnatural and monstrously distorted? Is society not suffering from a case of the evil eye which sees evil where there is none? Isn't it our moral laws which force me into evasions like the one which you have just found fault with?

TOWNSEND You're delving too deep for me, my boy. Save your radical arguments for the younger generation. I cannot see them in the same light you do (*Grumblingly*) and if I could, I wouldn't. What I cannot understand is how you happened to get in with this young woman in the first place. You'll pardon me, Jack, but it seems to me to show a lack of judgment on your part, and—er—good taste.

JACK (*Shrugging his shoulders*) Such things usually are errors in taste.

TOWNSEND This young woman was hardly of the class you have been accustomed to associate with, I presume.

JACK She is a working girl, a stenographer.

HERRON Has she any immediate relations who would be liable to discover the unfortunate termination of your (*Sarcastically*) love affair?

JACK Her father is dead. Her mother is a silly woman who would be the last to suspect anything. She has two sisters, both youngsters under ten, and one brother about eighteen, a machinist or something of the sort who is only home for weekends.

TOWNSEND And she and her brother support the others?

JACK (*Avoiding his father's eyes*) So I believe.

TOWNSEND (*His expression stern and accusing; he starts to say something but restrains himself*) Ah.

JACK (*Glancing at his father*) Yes, yes, I know it, Dad. I have played the scoundrel all the way through. I realize that now. Why couldn't I have felt this way before, at the start? Then this would never have happened. But at that time the whole thing seemed just a pleasant game we were playing; its serious aspects appeared remote, unreal. I never gave them a thought. I have paid for it since then, I want you to believe that. I have had my glance into the abyss. In loss of confidence and self-respect, in bitter self-abasement I have paid, and I am sure the result of it all will be to make me a better man, a man more worthy to be Evelyn's husband.

TOWNSEND (*Huskily*) God grant it, my boy. (*He gets to his feet*) I want to thank you for the confidence you placed in your father by making a frank appeal to me when you got in this trouble. It shows you regard me not only as a father but as a friend; and that is the way I would have it.

JACK You have always urged me to come to you and be frank about everything; and I always have and always will. I had to have the money and I thought I owed it to you to be open and above board and not start in deceiving you at this late day. I couldn't get it in any other way very well. Two hundred dollars is quite a sum for a college student to raise at a moment's notice.

TOWNSEND (*Restored to good humor*) The wages of sin are rather exorbitant.

JACK He was the only doctor I could find who would

do that sort of thing. He knew I was a college student and probably made inquiries about your financial rating—and there you are. There was nothing for me to do but grin and pay. But as I said in my letter, this money is a loan. It would be unfair for me to make you shoulder my—mistakes.

TOWNSEND (*Cheerfully*) Let's forget all about it. (*He holds out his hand to* JACK, *who clasps it heartily*) All's well that ends well. You've learned your lesson. (*The sound of a college cheer comes faintly through the open window*) And now shall we join the others? That cheer wakens the old fever in me. I want to follow the band and get singed by the Roman candles.

(*He picks his straw hat from the table*)

JACK (*Eagerly*) Yes, let's do that.

(*They are going toward the door in the rear when* JOE MURRAY *appears in the doorway.* JACK *cannot repress an exclamation of alarm and his face grows pale*)

MURRAY (*Fixing his eyes on* JACK *with an expression of furious hatred*) Look here, Townsend, I gotta see yuh for a minute.

JACK (*Unwillingly*) All right, Murray. You join the others, Dad, and I'll catch you in a few minutes.

(TOWNSEND, *struck by the change in his son's voice, looks questioningly at him, asking an explanation.* JACK *turns away from him*)

JACK Come in, Murray, and have a seat.

(TOWNSEND *goes out.* MURRAY *slouches to the middle of the room but does not sit down. His fingers fumble nervously at the buttons of his coat. He notices this and plunges his hands into his coat pockets. He seems endeavoring to restrain the hatred and rage which the spasmodic working of his features show to be boiling within him*)

JACK (*He appears occupied in arranging the things on the table*) Well?

MURRAY (*Chokingly*) Well!

(*He can go no further*)

JACK (*Coldly, without looking at him*) Anything I can do for you?

MURRAY (*In strangled tones*) Anything you can do for *me*!

JACK (*Hurriedly*) Yes. I'm in rather a hurry and if it's nothing very important I'd be just as well pleased if you'd come some other time.

MURRAY Important? *You* mayn't think so. It's not important to *you*, yuh—

(*He is stopped by a fit of violent coughing which racks his thin body*)

JACK (*Irritably*) You've come here looking for trouble, Murray. You better wait until you've cooled off. (*Then, more kindly*) What is it you want to say to me? Out with it!

MURRAY (*Wiping his mouth on his coat sleeve—angrily*) I'll out with it, damn yuh! Standing there so cool—dressed in swell clothes—and all these other goils— (*Choking*) and Nellie—and Nellie—

JACK (*Leaning toward him*) Yes—Nellie?

MURRAY (*Sobbing*) She's dead. (*In a transport of rage*) You killed her, yuh dirty murderer!

JACK (*Dully, as if he did not understand*) Dead? No, no, you don't mean that. She wrote to me everything was all right. Dead?

(*As he speaks he backs away from* MURRAY *in horror and stumbles against one of the Morris chairs. He sits down in it mechanically*)

MURRAY (*Shrilly*) She's dead—Nellie, my sister—she's dead.

JACK (*Half to himself*) No, it's impossible. (*Fiercely*) It's a lie! What scheme is this of yours? You're trying to frighten me.

MURRAY (*Raging*) She's dead, I tell yuh, dead! She died this morning.

JACK (*Forced to believe*) She died this morning? (*In a dazed voice*) But why didn't she—I didn't know —(*Stares straight before him*) God!

MURRAY Why didn't she let yuh know, yuh mean? She wrote to yuh, she told me she did; and yuh knew she was sick and never answered it. She might'a lived if she thought yuh cared, if she heard from yuh; but she knew yuh were trying to git rid of her.

JACK (*In agony*) Stop, for God's sake! I know I should have written. I meant to write but—

MURRAY She kept sayin': "I wanta die. I don't wanta live!" (*Furiously*) But I'll fix yuh! I'll make yuh pay.

JACK (*Startled, he turns to him quickly*) What do you mean?

MURRAY Don't give me any of that. Yuh know what I mean. Yuh know how she died. (*Fiercely*) Yuh know who killed her.

JACK (*His voice trembling—not looking at* MURRAY) How she died? Killed her? I don't understand—

MURRAY Yuh lie! She was murdered and yuh know it.

JACK (*Horror-struck*) Murdered?

MURRAY Yes, and *you* murdered her.

JACK (*Shuddering*) I? What? I murdered? Are you crazy?

MURRAY You and your dirty skunk of a doctor.

JACK (*Sinking back in his chair with a groan*) Ooh!

MURRAY (*With fierce scorn*) Yuh thought yuh was safe, didn't yuh, with me away from home? Yuh c'd go out and pitch the championship game—and she lyin' dead! Yuh c'd ruin her and throw her down and no one say a word because yuh're a swell college guy and captain of the team, and she ain't good enough for yuh to marry. She's goin' to have a kid, *your* kid, and because yuh're too rotten to act like a man, yuh send her to a faker of a doctor to be killed; and she does what yuh say because she loves yuh; and yuh don't even think enough of her to answer her letter (*Sobbing*) when she's dyin' on account of *you!*

JACK (*Speaking with difficulty*) She—told you—all this?

MURRAY Not a word! (*Proudly*) She died game; she wasn't no coward. I tried every way I knew how to git her to tell me but she wouldn't. Not a word outa her against you. (*Choking with angry sobs*) And *you*—and *you*—yuh dirty coward!—playin' ball!

JACK (*Dully*) I did what I thought was best for her.

MURRAY Yuh sneaked out like a coward because yuh thought she wasn't good enough. (*With a sneer*) Yuh think yuh c'n get away with that stuff and then marry some goil of your own kind, I s'pose—some goil like I seen yuh come in with tonight. (*Vindictively*) But yuh won't; not if I have to go to hell for it!

(*A pause.* JACK *is silent, breathing hard. His eyes are haunted, full of despair, as he vainly seeks to escape from the remorse which is torturing him. The faint sound of a college cheer, then of the band, comes from the open window. From this point to the end these sounds are continuous, the band only being silenced to permit the giving of the cheer, and as the action progresses they become more and more distinct*)

MURRAY (*Continuing in the same vindictive tones*) I've always hated yuh since yuh come to the house. I've always hated all your kind. Yuh come here to school and yuh think yuh c'n do as yuh please with us town people. Yuh treat us like servants, an' what are *you*, I'd like to know? A lot of lazy no-good dudes spongin' on your old men; and the goils, our goils, think yuh're grand!

(JACK *is staring at the floor, his head bowed, and does not seem to hear him*)

MURRAY I knew somethin' would happen. I told Nellie to look out, and she laughed. When the old lady sent for me and I come home and saw Nellie and she wouldn't leave me go for a doctor, I had a hunch what was wrong. She wouldn't say nothin' but I got our doc, not the one *you* sent her to, and he told me just what I thought and said she was goin' to die. (*Raging*) If I'd seen yuh that minute I'd killed yuh. I knew it was *you* but I couldn't prove it. Then one of the kids got scared and told me Nellie'd sent her to your doc for medicine when she first took sick. I bought a gun and the kid showed me where he was. I shoved the gun in his face and he owned up and told me about you. He offered me money, lots of it, to keep my mouth shut, and I took it—the money he'd got from you—blood money! (*With a savage grin*) An' I'll keep my mouth shut—maybe!

JACK (*His eyes lighting up with a gleam of hope, he turns eagerly to* MURRAY) Listen, Murray! This affair is unspeakably horrible, and I am—everything you say; but I want you—you must believe I honestly thought I was acting for the best in having the operation performed. That it has turned out so tragically is terrible. You cannot realize how I am suffering. I feel as if I were what you called me—a murderer. (*Brokenly*) It is horrible, horrible! The thought of it will torture me all my life.

MURRAY That don't bring her back to life. Yuh're too late!

JACK (*Frenziedly*) Too late! What do you mean? You haven't told anyone? You haven't—

MURRAY When I left his office I went home and—she was dead. Then I come up here lookin' for *you.* I wanted to kill yuh, but—I been thinkin'—yuh're not worth gittin' hung for. (*With a cruel grin*) I c'n see a better way of fixin' yuh—one that'll get yuh right.

JACK (*Half to himself*) You haven't told anyone?

MURRAY What's the difference? There's plenty of time. *I* know.

JACK (*Trying to steady his voice, which is trembling with apprehension*) Murray, for your own sake, for your dead sister's good name, for your family's sake, you must keep this thing quiet. I do not plead for myself. I am willing to have you punish me individually in any way you see fit; but there are others, innocent ones, who will suffer.

MURRAY She was innocent, too, before you—

JACK (*Interrupting him*) My mother and father, my sister, Ev—(*Bites back the name*) This would kill my mother if she knew. They are innocent. Do not revenge yourself on them.

MURRAY (*Inflexibly*) You killed my sister.

JACK Why will you keep saying that? You know it was an accident; that I would gladly have given my own life rather than have it happen. And you must keep silent. I will do anything you want, I tell you! (*He goes close to* MURRAY) You say the doctor gave you money? I'll give you ten times as much as he did. (MURRAY's *face grows livid*) I'll see that you get so much a year for the rest of your life. My father is rich. We'll get you a good position, do everything you wish. (*Breaking down*) Only do not punish the innocent.

MURRAY (*Slowly*) You want—to pay me—for Nellie!

(*With a terrible cry of rage he pulls a revolver from the pocket of his coat. Before he can pull the trigger* JACK *seizes his wrist. There is a short struggle.* JACK *takes the revolver away from him and lays it on the table.* MURRAY *has a violent attack of coughing. He recovers and is slinking toward the door when* JACK *suddenly picks up the revolver from the table and holds it out to him*)

JACK (*Steadily*) Here, take it! I was a fool to stop you. Let the thing end with me and leave the innocent alone.

MURRAY (*Malevolently*) It's too good for yuh. (*He has edged stealthily nearer and nearer the door and with a final spring gains the safety of the hallway. He shouts back*) I'm goin' to the p'lice station. D'yuh hear, yuh dirty ba - rd! To the p'lice station!

(*His quick footsteps can be heard as he runs out.* JACK *makes a movement as if to follow him but stops and sits down heavily by the table, laying the revolver on it. He hears the band and the cheers of the paraders, who have evidently just invaded that section of the campus. He hurries to the windows, closes them and pulls down the shades. The band is playing a march song and the students are singing.* JACK *groans and hides his face in his hands. The parade is about to pass by his windows. The glare of the red fire glows dully on the right. Several students crowd in the doorway from the hall*)

ONE STUDENT He's not here.

ANOTHER STUDENT He ran away.

(*All go out laughing and shouting. The band stops playing.* JACK *comes out from the bedroom, his face drawn with agony. The cheerleader's voice can be heard shouting: "He ran away but if we give him a cheer, he'll hear us. A long cheer for Townsend, fellows! Hip! Hip!"* JACK *staggers toward the window, crying brokenly: "No! No! For God's sake!" The first part of the cheer booms out. He reels to the table and sees the revolver lying there. He snatches it up and presses it to his temple. The report is drowned by the cheering. He falls forward on his face, twitches, is still*)

THE STUDENTS (*Winding up the nine long rahs*) Rah! Rah! Rah! Townsend! Townsend! Townsend! (*The band strikes up "For He's a Jolly Good Fellow." The students commence to sing. The parade moves off again.* EVELYN *appears in the doorway to the rear*)

EVELYN Jack! It's all right now, dear. You can come out of hiding. (*She blinks for a moment, blinded by the light; then comes into the room and sees the body—in terror*) Jack! What's the matter?

(*She rushes over and kneels beside him; then faints as she sees the blood on his temples, the revolver still clutched in his right hand. She falls on the floor beside him*)

THE STUDENTS (*Their voices growing gradually fainter*) "For he's a jolly good fellow, which nobody can deny."

Curtain

THE MOVIE MAN

A Comedy in One Act

Characters

HENRY (HEN) ROGERS, *Representative of Earth Motion Picture Company*
AL DEVLIN, *photographer for the same company*
PANCHO GOMEZ, *Commander-in-Chief of the Constitutionalist Army*
LUIS VIRELLA, *General of a Division*
ANITA FERNANDEZ
A SENTRY

SCENE—*The main room of a house in the suburb of a large town in northern Mexico. To the left, a white-washed wall of adobe with a small black crucifix hanging from a nail. In the rear wall, a doorway opening on the street. On either side of the doorway, an open window. On the right side of the room, another door which is closed. On the wall above it, a faded lithograph of the Virgin. In the left-hand corner several Mauser carbines are stacked, and bandoleers of cartridges are thrown on the dirt floor beside them. In the right-hand corner several saddles are lying. Near the door, another saddle. In the middle of the room, a rickety table with a pen, paper and ink on it. Three or four stiff cane-bottomed chairs are placed about the table.*

HEN ROGERS *and* AL DEVLIN *are sitting by the table. Both are smoking pipes. Both are dressed in khaki shirts, riding breeches, puttees, etc. Their wide-brimmed Stetson hats are on the table beside them.* ROGERS *is tall, blond, clean-shaven, in his early thirties.* DEVLIN *is short, dark, with a good-natured irregular face, middle-aged.*

A sentry in a filthy, ragged olive-drab uniform lolls in the doorway leaning on his rifle. He wears the wide sombrero of the Mexican peon, and is barefooted. He is smoking a cigarette and watching the two Americans with an expression of bored indifference.

It is in the early hours of a sultry tropic night.

DEVLIN (*Singing in a cracked falsetto*) Mexico, my nice cool Mexico!

ROGERS (*Mopping the perspiration from his forehead with a bandana handkerchief*) Have a heart, Al, have a heart, and kill the canary-bird stuff. If you see anything to be merry over in this flea-bitten cluster of shanties, you got something on me.

DEVLIN (*Chuckling*) Lovely little spot to spend the summer!

ROGERS (*Dryly*) Ideal is the word. And speaking of fleas, on the level, I never knew what a poor dog has to put up with until I hit this one-horse country.

DEVLIN They don't bother me any.

ROGERS No, they've got some class, you gotta hand it to them.

DEVLIN Is *that* so?

ROGERS "Discretion is the better part of valor"—any well-bred Mexican flea is hep to that. Those are the first words in the Mexican Constitution, and every man and beast in this country swears by them. If they didn't we'd have been in Mexico City months ago, and right now I'd be down at Manhattan Beach in God's Country with a large mint julep, full of ice—

DEVLIN (*With a groan*) Help! Help! I'm a nut!

ROGERS When this cruel war is over and on the films I'm going to quit the picture business and go way up north, marry an Esquimau, and start housekeeping on an exclusive, refined, accordion-pleated, little iceberg.

DEVLIN (*Whistling shrilly to the sentry, who grabs his rifle in alarm*) Boy, page an iceberg for Mr. Rogers!

THE SENTRY (*With lazy scorn*) *Muy loco!*

ROGERS What's that he said, Al? Look it up in your little book. It sounded almost like real talk.

DEVLIN (*With a laugh*) I don't have to look that up. He means we're crazy.

ROGERS (*To the sentry—approvingly*) You said something then, Mike. We sure are as nutty as a fruitcake or we wouldn't be here. Phew, but it's hot! (*After a short pause—musingly*) Say, Al, did you ever notice the happy, contented expression on a polar bear's face?

DEVLIN (*Laughing*) *Basta! Basta!*

(*The sentry instinctively springs to attention, then lapses into indifference again as he realizes it is only the crazy American speaking*)

ROGERS Say, you're getting to be a regular talker of spigoty! Slip me the answer to that word *basta*, will you? I hear friend General pulling it all the time; and just to show you what a fine little guesser I am, I'll bet you a case-note it means when.

DEVLIN Come across with that peso. It doesn't mean when; it means enough.

ROGERS Same thing. I knew it—I never yet heard him say it when I was pouring him out a drink.

DEVLIN You owe me a peso, don't forget it.

ROGERS (*Grumblingly*) I'm not liable to with you around. (*An excited babble of voices is heard from the door on the right*) Listen to those boobs, will you! What do you suppose they're framing up in there?

DEVLIN Who is it—Gomez?

ROGERS Yes. He and all his little generals are having some sort of a confab. I'll bet you that smack back again he's going to try and capture the town tomorrow.

DEVLIN What's this you're springing on me—inside information?

ROGERS Nope; but this afternoon I gave him that case of Scotch I promised him when he signed our contract, and he's feeling some brave this evening.

DEVLIN Say, Hen, about that contract, I forgot to tell you, you wanta hand a call to this Gomez guy. He is playing the game. You remember the other day when they were going after that fort on the outskirts?

ROGERS Sure—good stuff—plenty of real live action that day.

DEVLIN (*Indignantly*) It was good stuff all right, but I missed all the first part of it on account of that simp General Virella. He was just waving his sword and ordering 'em to charge when I came up. "Here, you!" I said to him. "Wait a minute. Can't you see I'm not ready for you yet?" And what do you think that greaser said to me? You know he speaks good English. He says: "Shall my glorious soldiers be massacred waiting for your machine?" And away he runs with all his yellow-bellies after him. What d'you know about that?

ROGERS (*Frowning*) He's a fresh guy, that Virella. I'll have Gomez stick him back in the rear after this. He's a mean little worm, too. He's the one who's nagged Gomez into croaking old Fernandez.

DEVLIN What! Are they going to shoot Fernandez?

ROGERS At sunrise tomorrow they stand him against the wall and—curtain.

DEVLIN It's a damn shame—just because they can't get any more coin out of him. He's a good fellow —Fernandez. Went to school in the States—Cornell or some place. Can't you get him off?

ROGERS Nix. Virella has a grudge against him and Gomez needs Virella. Anyway, I've got no license to butt in on their little scraps. Besides, it'll make a great picture. Be sure and get it.

DEVLIN I'll be there. Say, have them hold it till a little later, will you? The light isn't any good so early.

ROGERS How'll eight o'clock do?

DEVLIN Great!

ROGERS All right, I'll tell Gomez to postpone it till then. (*A shrill voice is heard shouting* "Viva" *from the room on the right*) That's Virella, now. I'd like to take just one swing at that guy. They'd carry him home in a white-pine kimono. (*Another cheer from the room next door*) Full of booze and patriotism! Gee, I wish I was a war correspondent. I'd send in a little notice like this: "The courage and spirits of the troops were never better. A trainload of rum arrived today. We will be in Mexico City in two weeks."

DEVLIN (*Picking his hat from the table, he gets to his feet*) I think I'll take a look around and see what's doing.

ROGERS Oho! I've got your number all right!

DEVLIN (*Laughing*) What do you mean: got my number?

ROGERS Have a care, little one, have a care! Some one of these Mexican dolls you're googooing at will carve her initials on your back with the bread knife some one of these days.

DEVLIN I should fret!

ROGERS (*Disgustedly*) What you can see in these skirts has got me beat. They're so homely the mules shy at them.

DEVLIN Is *that* so? Well, let me tell you, there's some class to some of the dames down here. You ought to have seen the bear I lamped this afternoon. Some queen, take it from me.

ROGERS Load that noise in one of the cannons and fire it off!

DEVLIN On the level, Hen, she had the swellest lamps I've ever seen on a dame; and a figure—my boy! my boy!

ROGERS Captain Sweeney of the Marines, please listen! And I suppose you copped her and dated her up?

DEVLIN Nothing like it, Hen. She was doing a sob act on one of the benches in that little park out here, and I asked her in my best Spanish what was the matter. Phew! Talk about the icy onceover! She looked at me as if I was a wet dog. I turned and beat it like a little man.

ROGERS You were wise, for once. She'd have operated on you with her stiletto in another second. I wouldn't trust one of these dolls as far as I could hit Walter Johnson's fast one.

DEVLIN But what d'you suppose she was doing a weep about?

ROGERS (*Dryly*) Maybe one of her husbands got killed in the war.

DEVLIN What sweet thoughts you have! S'long, Hen. Don't forget to have Gomez postpone that shooting thing.

(*He goes to the door in the rear*)

ROGERS I won't; and you come back early—if you're still alive. I want you to scratch my back before I hit the hay. I'd have to be a contortionist or a centipede to follow this flea-game properly.

DEVLIN (*Laughing*) They'll take your mind off your worries. Be good!

(*He passes the sentry and disappears in the darkness. Another cheer is heard from the next room.* ROGERS *grunts disgustedly and attempts to scratch the middle of his back. The sentry's head falls forward on his chest as he dozes in the doorway.*

ANITA FERNANDEZ *appears outside the door and creeps stealthily by the sentry into the room. She is a beautiful young Mexican girl with a mass of black hair and great black eyes. She stumbles over the saddle by the door and utters a little cry of pain. The sentry wakes up, rushes over to her and grabs her furiously by the arm. He drags her toward the door.* ROGERS *springs from his chair and yells at the sentry*)

ROGERS Hey, you, Mike, what are you doing? Let go of that dame!

(*The sentry scowls uncertainly at him.* ROGERS *makes a threatening gesture and the sentry releases* ANITA *and returns to his post by the doorway.* ANITA *sinks into a chair by the table and, hiding her face in her hands, commences to sob.* ROGERS *stands beside her not knowing what to do*)

ROGERS What'll I say to her? (*Sees the English-Spanish book of* DEVLIN'*s on the table*) Here's Al's Spanish book. Let's see. (*Turning over the pages*) "What do you want?"—I wonder how you say it? Oh, here it is. (*He repeats the line to himself, then bends down to* ANITA) *Que quere, señorita?* (*He pronounces it "Kwi query, seenorita?" She raises her head and stares at him with a puzzled expression*) She doesn't make me at all—oh hell!

ANITA (*Haughtily*) Pleese to not swear, *señor.*

ROGERS (*Confused*) Excuse me—awfully sorry—tongue slipped. (*With a sigh of relief*) Thank Go—heavens, you speak English.

ANITA But most badly, *señor.*

ROGERS (*Sitting down across the table from her*) No, very good, just as good as mine. Who was it you wanted to see?

ANITA El Generalissimo Gomez.

ROGERS (*Shaking his head*) You better wait. He'll be all lit up like a torch tonight.

ANITA (*Mystified*) *Señor?*

ROGERS You know what I mean—he's soused, pickled, stewed, boiled—

ANITA (*In puzzled accents*) Es-stewed? Boiled? (*In horrified tones*) You mean he is cooking—the General? But no, *señor*, I onderstand Eenglish veree badly. For one year alone, I estudy in the convent in Nueva York—Noo York. Then *mi madre*—my mothair—die and I must come home to the house of my fathair becose I have more years —I am older than my sisters.

(*There is a ringing "Viva" from the next room.* ANITA *turns pale*)

ROGERS (*Making a motion with his hand as if he were taking a drink and nodding toward the room*) You understand now? He's drinking, and—

ANITA (*Shuddering*) Ah, he es drunk, no?

ROGERS I'm afraid he will be before he leaves that room—if he isn't already.

ANITA (*The tears starting to her eyes*) *Mi padre!*

ROGERS You better wait until tomorrow to see him.

ANITA Eet ees not possible. I must—tonight!

ROGERS (*Earnestly*) Don't do it, kid! Don't you know Gomez is a bad guy—man—for a young girl to come and see at night—specially when he's drunk?

ANITA (*Flushing*) I know, *si, señor,* but eet must be.

ROGERS Won't you tell me why?

ANITA (*Her voice trembling*) *Si,* I will tell you. Eet ees not long to tell, *señor.* You have heard—you know Ernesto Fernandez?

ROGERS You mean the Fernandez who is going to be shot tomorrow morning?

ANITA (*Shuddering*) *Si, señor,* he eet ess I mean. He ees my fathair.

ROGERS (*Astounded*) Your father! Good God!

ANITA I must see the General Gomez tonight to ask him to save my fathair.

ROGERS He will not do it.

ANITA (*Faintly*) You know that, *señor?*

ROGERS Virella is with him—in there—now!

ANITA (*Terrified*) Virella? He is the most bad enemy of my fathair.

ROGERS You might buy Gomez off; pay him to set your father free. He'll do anything for money. Have you any money?

ANITA Alas, no, *señor;* Gomez has taken from us everything.

ROGERS Too bad, too bad! Hm— Well, you mustn't stay here any longer. They're liable to come out any minute. Go home now, and I'll see what I can do with Gomez.

ANITA (*Resolutely*) *Gracias,* I thank you, *señor;* you are very kind—but I must see Gomez.

ROGERS (*Deliberately—looking steadily into her eyes*) Don't you know what Gomez will want—the price he will make you pay if he finds you here?

ANITA (*Closing her eyes and swaying weakly on her feet*) For the life—of my fathair—

(*She sobs softly*)

ROGERS (*Looking at her in admiration*) God!

ANITA (*Fiercely*) I would keel myself to save him!

ROGERS But even if he said he'd free your father you couldn't believe him. What is Gomez' word worth? No, you must let me fix this for you.

ANITA (*Doubtfully*) But you—Gomez ees veree powerful, *señor*—ess it possible for you to do?

ROGERS (*Decisively*) I'll save your old man if I have to start a revolution of my own to do it.

ANITA (*Her eyes shining with gratitude*) Ah, thank you, *señor*—but if you should fail?

ROGERS (*Emphatically*) I won't fail. You just watch me start something!

(*He has scarcely finished speaking when the door to the right is thrown open and* GOMEZ *and* VIRELLA *enter the room. They are both in a state of great excitement and show they have been drinking.* VIRELLA *is an undersized man with shifty, beady black eyes and a black mustache.* GOMEZ *is tall and heavily built, with a bloated, dissipated-looking face and a bristly black mustache. Both are dressed in new uniforms of olive-drab and wear military caps. Cartridge belts with automatic revolvers in leather holsters are strapped about their waists over their coats.*

ANITA *stares at them for a moment with horrified loathing; then shrinks away into the far corner of the room.* GOMEZ *turns to shout an "Adiós" to the officers who are still carousing in the room he has just left; then bangs the door shut behind him.* VIRELLA *sees* ANITA *and walks toward her with a drunken leer on his flushed face*)

VIRELLA *Buenas noches, señorita.*

ROGERS (*Steps forward and places himself in front of* VIRELLA, *whom he grasps by the shoulders and forcibly turns in the direction of the door*) Now beat it, snake-in-the-grass!

VIRELLA (*Struggling to free himself*) Pig of a Gringo!

ROGERS General Gomez and I want to have a talk in private, don't we, Gomez?

(*He glances at* GOMEZ *with a commanding air*)

GOMEZ (*Uncertainly*) *Por cierto, amigo,* if you like eet.

VIRELLA (*Frothing at the mouth with rage*) Dog! Pig!

ROGERS (*Calmly*) Those are hard words, my pet—and you hear what your General commands?

(*He turns to* GOMEZ)

GOMEZ *Si*, Virella, I command eet.

ROGERS (*To* VIRELLA, *contemptuously*) Now blow before I crown you!

(*He draws back his fist threateningly.* VIRELLA *shrinks away from him, salutes* GOMEZ *and slinks out of the door in the rear*)

GOMEZ (*Forcing a laugh*) Ees thees the way you treat my generals?

ROGERS You ought to shoot that little scorpion—before he shoots you.

GOMEZ (*Frowning*) Eet ees true, *amigo*, what you say, and pairhaps soon—but—now he ees to me necessary. (*He notices* ANITA *for the first time and turns to* ROGERS *with a chuckle*) Excuse me, *señorita!* (*He takes his cap off and makes her a gallant bow*) Ah, Señor Rogers, you are—how you call eet?—a man of—ladies, no? (*He walks over to* ANITA, *who shrinks back to the wall in terror*) Have you fear of me, *chiquita?* Of Gomez? But Pancho Gomez, he loav the ladies, that ees well known. Ask el señor Rogers.

(*He chucks her under the chin*)

ROGERS (*Stepping between them—quietly*) This young lady is *my* friend, Gomez.

GOMEZ (*Biting his lips*) I say in fun only. (*He walks back to the table and remarks sullenly to* ROGERS, *who is following him*) She ees *muy hermosa*, veree preety, your *señorita*.

ROGERS She is the daughter of Ernesto Fernandez.

GOMEZ (*Surprised*) *Que dice?* What you say?

ROGERS She's the daughter of the man you're going to have shot in the morning. She came to ask you—

GOMEZ (*Emphatically*) No, *hombre*, no! I know what you will say. I cannot do. Eet ees not possible! (ANITA *rushes forward and throws herself at his feet*) No, no, no, *señorita*, I must go.

(*He strides toward the door in the rear.* ANITA *lies where she has thrown herself, sobbing hopelessly*)

ROGERS One minute, Gomez! Where are you going?

GOMEZ To prepare the attack. Ah, I forget! I have not tole you. (*Excitedly*) Tonight, *amigo*, we storm the town. We catch them asleep, no? and before they wake they are—(*He makes a motion across his neck with his forefinger*) dead, how you call eet?—as a nail. (*Proudly*) Eet ees a plan sublime, most glorious—eet ees the plan of Gomez! In one small week, *hombre*, we shall be in Mexico City.

ROGERS That Scotch is great stuff. One more drink and old Napoleon would be a piker.

GOMEZ (*Puzzled*) What you say?

ROGERS Nothing, nothing. (*His face lighting up with a ray of hope*) A night attack, eh?

GOMEZ *Si, hombre*, at twelve hours—twelve o'clock.

ROGERS (*Calmly*) Who said so?

GOMEZ I say it, I, Pancho Gomez!

ROGERS (*Emphatically*) Well, you just listen to me, Gomez; I say you can't do it. There'll be no night attack in this war when I'm around. (GOMEZ *is stupefied*) How do you expect us to get pictures at night? You didn't think of that, eh?

GOMEZ (*Bewildered*) But, *amigo*—

ROGERS Nix on the night attacks, do you get me? (*Pulling a paper out of his pocket*) Here's a copy of your contract giving us rights to all your fights—*all*, do you hear, all! And we got one clause especially for night attacks. (*Reads*) "The party of the second part hereby agrees to fight no battles at night or on rainy days or at any time whatsoever when the light is so poor as to make the taking of motion pictures impracticable. Failure to comply with these conditions will constitute a breach of contract and free the party of the first part from all the obligations entered into by this contract." (*He hands the contract to* GOMEZ) Here it is, black and white, English and Spanish both, with your signature at the bottom with mine. Read for yourself.

(GOMEZ *glances at the paper mechanically and hands it back*)

GOMEZ (*With a defiant snarl*) And if I say to hell, you! Then what you do, eh?

ROGERS (*Mimicking the* GENERAL'*s tone*) Who buys and sends you most of your ammunition, eh? Who pays you and the other generals and the German in charge of your artillery—the only man who savvys how to use the guns right, eh? Who has promised to see that you get siege guns for Mexico City and twenty more machine guns with men, real men, to run them for you, eh? Your soldiers'll desert you if you don't pay them soon, and you know it. Well, who has agreed to loan you the money to give them their back pay, eh? And, above all, who has promised to help you become President when you reach Mexico City? (*Impressively*)

We have—The Earth Motion Picture Company! Well, you break this contract and all that stops, see?—and goes to the other side.

GOMEZ (*Softly—fingering his revolver*) *Bueno;* but I can also have you shot, *hombre.*

ROGERS Nix on that rough stuff! You wouldn't dare. You've got to keep on the right side of the U.S.A. or your revolution isn't worth the powder to blow it to—Mexico.

GOMEZ (*Pleadingly*) But, *amigo,* permit eet this once. The plan is fine, the town will be ours, my soldiers will steal and no more grumble against Gomez. Tomorrow I will shoot all the prisoners for your pictures, I promise eet.

ROGERS (*Kindly*) I'd like to do you a favor, Gomez, but I don't see my way to do this, unless—

GOMEZ (*With a smile*) Aha, tell me, *hombre,* your price.

ROGERS (*Firmly*) The life of Ernesto Fernandez!

(ANITA *jumps to her feet and stretches out her arms beseechingly to* GOMEZ. *He twirls his mustache thoughtfully for a moment*)

GOMEZ *Bueno,* my friend, I accept your terms. (*He goes to the table and hurriedly scratches a few lines which he hands to* ANITA) *Su padre de uste*—your father, he ees free, *señorita.* For this thank my fine friend Señor Rogers. (*He claps* ROGERS *jovially on the back*) Now must I have shot the General Virella, who will never forgive me your father should live, *señorita.* Mexico ees too es-small for those two *hombres*—both alive. (*He pulls a flask from his pocket and offers it to* ROGERS, *who refuses with a smile*) Señor Rogers—how you call eet?—here ees looking at you! (*He drinks*) And now I must to prepare the attack. (*He goes to the door; then turns and remarks grandiloquently*) Should anyone wish me, *señor,* tell them that een the hour of battle, Pancho Gomez, like the immortal Juarez, will ever be found at the head of his brave soldiers. *Adiós!*

(*He makes a sweeping bow and goes out past the saluting sentry*)

ROGERS (*With a long whistle of amusement—turning to* ANITA) Some bull! Honest, you've got to hand it to that guy, at that.

ANITA And now I, too, must go—to my poor fathair.

ROGERS Can't I take you there? You know, there's lots of drunken soldiers around and—

ANITA No, no, *señor,* you are too kind. Eet ees but two steps to the carcel—the prison. Eet ees not necessary. (*Indicating the paper in her hand*) The name of Gomez is most sufficient. (*Holding out her hand to him with a shy smile*) *Muchísima gracias, señor*—with all my heart do I thank you. My fathair and I, we will be at the home tomorrow—eet ees the first hacienda beyond the hill—you will come, *señor?* As a brother, my father's son, shall you be to us!

ROGERS (*Holding her hand and looking into her eyes*) Only—a brother?

ANITA (*Drawing her hand away in confusion, she runs to the door; then turns*) *Quién sabe, señor?* Who knows?

(*She hurries out*)

ROGERS (*He does a few Spanish dance steps, snapping his fingers and humming. The sentry grins at him*) What are you grinning at, Mike?

SENTRY (*With a contemptuous smile he makes a gesture of turning a wheel near his head*) *Muy loco!*

ROGERS I got you the first time, Mike. Crazy is the right word. (*He commences to sing*) "Mexico, my bright-eyed Mexico."

(DEVLIN *appears in the doorway and scowls darkly at him*)

DEVLIN Kill it, kill it, you bone! (*He comes in and throws his hat irritably on the table.* ROGERS *looks at him with an amused smile*) What're you chirping about? Are you soused, too? Where have you hidden the joy-water? Everyone in this bush-league army seems all corned up tonight except me. Say, I just got another flash at that dame I was telling you about. She looked right through me at something behind my back. Some nerve to that greaser chicken giving a real white man the foot! (*Scornfully*) I got a good slant at her this time. She isn't much to look at after all. Back in God's Country we'd use her photo for a before-taking ad.

ROGERS (*Indignantly*) Al, you always were a simp! (*Grumblingly*) Better get a pair of cheaters for those bum lamps of yours. (*Cheerfully*) Cheer up, Al, you're all wrong, my son, you're all wrong!

(DEVLIN *gapes at him in open-mouthed amazement.* ROGERS *commences to sing again: "Mexico, my bright-eyed Mexico." The sentry grunts contemptuously*)

Curtain

THE SNIPER

A Play in One Act

Characters

ROUGON, *a Belgian peasant*
THE VILLAGE PRIEST
A GERMAN CAPTAIN OF INFANTRY
FOUR PRIVATES OF THE REGIMENT
JEAN, *a peasant boy*

SCENE—*The main room of a ruined cottage on the outskirts of a small Belgian village. The rear wall has two enormous breaches made by the shells of the artillery. The right wall is partly hidden by a mass of wreckage from the roof, which has caved in leaving a jagged hole through which the sky can be seen. The ceiling slants drunkenly downward toward the right, ending abruptly in a ragged edge of splintered boards and beams which forms a fantastic fretwork against the sky. The floor is littered with all kinds of debris.*

In the rear wall near the right corner, a window, its panes of glass all broken, with a torn white curtain. No trace of the doorway to the road remains. The larger breach in the rear wall is used as exit and entrance.

The left wall, with a door in the middle, is uninjured. Over the door a large black crucifix hangs from a nail.

In the center of the room, an overturned table. A solitary chair, the only thing left standing, is beside it. On the right of the table, a smashed armchair.

The time is about sundown on a September day. Through the breaches in the wall a dark green vista of rolling fields can be seen. Where they meet the horizon they are already shimmering in the golden dust of the sunset. Muffled and far-off, the booming of distant cannon reverberates slowly over the fields.

The sound of shuffling footsteps is heard from the road before the cottage and a great hulking old man of sixty-five or so appears at the larger breach in the rear wall. He is dressed in the usual peasant fashion and wears wooden sabots on his feet. He is bent under some burden, which, as he enters the room, is seen to be the body of a young man dressed in the uniform of a Belgian infantryman. He lays the body down carefully in a cleared space between the table and the left wall, pillowing the soldier's head upon his knapsack. The body lies with its feet toward the rear wall.

He stands looking down at the still form, his attitude one of abject despair. A heavy sob shakes his round shoulders. He murmurs brokenly: "Charles! My little one!"; then turns abruptly and stumbles to the middle of the room, where he mechanically rights the overturned table. He sits down on the chair and stares at the ruins about him with an expression of dazed bewilderment on his broad face, his round, childlike eyes wandering dully from one object to another. His gaze finally rests on the smashed armchair on the other side of the table, and suddenly overcome by a flood of anguished horror, he hides his face in his hands, rocking from side to side on his chair, moaning to himself like a wounded animal.

The slight black-robed figure of a priest appears on the road outside. He casts a quick glance into the room and, seeing the bowed figure on the chair, quickly picks his way to the peasant's side. The priest is old, white-haired, with a kindly, spiritual face.

PRIEST Rougon!

ROUGON (*Not hearing him*) God, oh God!

PRIEST (*Laying a thin white hand compassionately on* ROUGON'*s broad back*) There, there, my son! It is the will of God.

ROUGON (*Startled by the sound of a voice, he jumps up from his chair*) Eh?

(*He stares at the priest with dazed eyes*)

PRIEST (*With a sad smile*) Oh, come now, it isn't possible that you've forgotten me.

ROUGON (*Snatching off his cap respectfully*) Pardon, Father. I was—I didn't know—you see—all this—

PRIEST (*Gently*) I have heard of your loss. I understand.

ROUGON But take the chair, Father. (*Bitterly*) I am lucky to have it left to offer you.

PRIEST (*Sitting down*) You must not brood over your misfortunes. Many, a great many, have suffered even more than you. You must learn to bear these burdens as they come, at such a dreadful time as this, and pray to God for strength. We must all bow ourselves before His will.

ROUGON His will? Ha! No, the good God would not punish me so—I, who have harmed no one. (*Furiously*) It is all these cursed Pruss—

PRIEST Ssshh! (*After a pause*) Such thoughts may rest in the heart, but to let them rise to the lips is hardly wise—now.

ROUGON What matter if they should hear? I am finished, me! They can do no more but kill me.

(*He sits on the edge of the table. A heavy sob shakes his bowed shoulders*)

PRIEST (*After a pause during which he gazes sadly at the face of the dead young soldier*) You must not mourn his loss so bitterly. He has given his life for his country. He is at rest with God. You should feel proud of him.

ROUGON (*Dully*) Yes, he is—at rest—in heaven. And look you, Father, you remember, this was the day —today he was to have been married.

PRIEST (*In accents of deep grief*) True, true, I had forgotten. Poor boy, poor boy—and poor Louise!

ROUGON And my poor old woman. Ah, good God, what have we done? All this—in one day!

PRIEST Your wife—she doesn't know?

ROUGON No. This morning, look you, I sent her away. It was Charles who came to me this morning—in his new uniform—he who lies there so still now —he whom they have murdered, those cursed Prussians!

PRIEST Ssshh! Would you bring more misfortune upon yourself?

ROUGON (*Springing to his feet in a frenzy*) Ah, how I would love to slaughter them, to grind my heel in their fat faces, to—to—

PRIEST Calm yourself, for the love of heaven, my good Rougon! Will it improve matters, think you, to have you, too, shot? Do not forget your poor old wife. You must be careful for her sake, if for nothing else.

ROUGON (*Sullenly slouching back to his seat on the table*) It is hard, name of a dog, it is hard. I feel like a coward, me, to stand by and do nothing.

PRIEST (*In low tones*) Be comforted. The hour of retribution will yet strike. The end is not yet. Your son Charles will be avenged.

ROUGON (*Shaking his head doubtfully*) There are so many.

PRIEST But you were telling me about your wife. You sent her away this morning?

ROUGON If the good God so pleases, she is in Brussels by now. For, look you, Charles came to me this morning. "My father," he said, "I am afraid there will be fighting here today. I have warned the family of Louise and she is to flee with them to Brussels. I have arranged that Mother should go with them; and you, too, my father." "But no," I said. "It is right for your mother. She shall go. As you say, it will be no place for women if there be fighting. But me, no, I shall stay." "Mind you, then, Father, no shooting!" Charles said as he kissed me good-bye and ran to join the regiment on the village place. "Or they will shoot you like a dog."

PRIEST You see! Your son gave you the best advice. Remember you are not a soldier.

ROUGON (*Proudly*) If I were not too old I should have been in a uniform this long time gone. Too old! The fools! As if I could not shoot straighter than all these boys!

PRIEST There are other things to consider, my poor Rougon. Someone must gather in the harvest if we are not all to starve.

ROUGON (*Fiercely*) The harvest? What is there left?

First it is the French who take away my two fine horses that I have saved up every centime two years to buy—and leave me a scrap of paper; then—

PRIEST The French are our friends; in due time you shall be paid.

ROUGON Bah, promises!

PRIEST (*Earnestly*) At a time like this all must bear their share of sacrifice.

ROUGON All who wanted war, yes; but we who desired nothing more than to be left in peace to till our fields? Look you, my Father, why should we be robbed and plundered and our homes blown apart by their accursed cannon?

PRIEST (*Shaking his head sadly*) God knows. Our poor country is a lamb among wolves.

ROUGON (*Raising his voice excitedly*) The first shell that burst in our village—do you know where it struck?

PRIEST No.

ROUGON Out there—on my barn—setting it in flames—killing my two cows, one of which I was to have given Charles, with half of my farm, as a wedding present—burning up all my hay I had gathered for the winter. (*Stamping his foot in his rage*) Ah, those dirty beasts!

PRIEST Ssshh! They are all around.

ROUGON And then, look you, the cavalry ride over my fields trampling my grain beneath their horses, the artillery wheels tear up the earth, the cannon blow my home to pieces—as you see. (*Bitterly*) Harvest? There is nothing left to harvest but dirt and stones!

PRIEST (*To change the subject which is rapidly infuriating the old man*) You may well give thanks to the good God that your wife is safe in Brussels.

ROUGON They started early this morning, as I have said, and the family of Louise has relatives in Brussels. She is safe, God be thanked. (*With a grief-stricken glance at the body of his son*) But when she knows—and Louise, who also loved him so— Oh, my God!

(*He chokes back a sob*)

PRIEST God give them strength to bear it.

ROUGON (*Indicating his son*) He wanted me to go with them. He was afraid I would do something rash if I stayed. But I have been calm. But, name of a dog, it has been hard—when I saw them trampling my wheat—those pigs—when I saw the ashes which had been my barn—and this house, as you see, where I had lived so many years—this finger itched to press the trigger and send at least one to hell for payment.

PRIEST My son, my son!

ROUGON Your pardon, my Father. Had it not been for the promise I had given Charles, I would have taken the old rifle from where I have it hidden in there (*He indicates with a nod of his head the room on the left*) and—

PRIEST (*Casting an apprehensive glance toward the street*) Ssshh! Be careful what you say in so loud a tone. Their soldiers are everywhere. But where were you when all this fighting was taking place?

ROUGON I was hiding in the well. I had placed a board across, on which I could stand and see what took place through the chinks in the stones. I wanted to see—him.

PRIEST See—Charles? How could—

ROUGON His part of the regiment was behind the wall in the orchard not one hundred meters away. I could watch him clearly.

PRIEST (*To himself, half-aloud*) Poor man!

ROUGON At first it was all right. Their infantry came up so close to each other that not even a child could have missed them. Bang! and they were toppled over before they had even reached the foot of the hill. I laughed. I thought it was all finished. I could see Charles laughing and talking with his comrades—and then—

(*He stops, shaking his head despondently*)

PRIEST And then?

ROUGON One of their devilish flying machines which look like the great birds flew overhead, far up. All shot at it but it was too far away. It flew back to them, and a minute later, look you, I saw white puffs of smoke on all the hills over to the west; then bang! crash! I could not hear; my ears were cracked with the din. There was dust, and falling walls, and my barn blazing. Ah, those accursed cannon! I climbed out of the well and ran to the barn.

PRIEST In the midst of all those bursting shells?

ROUGON I trembled with rage. I had no fear of their cannon. I remembered only the cow, the pretty little cow I was to give to Charles. But I could do nothing. Not all the fire engines in Belgium could have saved it. I ran back to the well. Ssszzz! went the bullets all round. As I was climbing over I was stunned by a terrible crash. The roof of this house tumbled in—as you see.

PRIEST And you remained in the well all during the battle?

ROUGON Yes—until I saw Charles fall. He was just aiming his rifle over the wall when I saw him throw up his hands, spin around like a top, and fall on his face. I ran down and carried him back on my shoulders to the well—but it was too late. He was dead. (*He stops abruptly, choking back a sob*)

PRIEST (*After a pause*) *Requiescat in pace.* His life was ever a happy one. He never knew the cares and worries that come with the years and the ceaseless struggle for bread. He loved and was loved. He died the death of the brave. (*Gently*) Is it not better after all—as it is? (ROUGON *does not answer*) Can you not console yourself with that thought?

ROUGON Perhaps. Who knows? But, look you, it is hard for me—and for Louise—and most of all for his mother whose baby he was.

PRIEST You all loved him, did everything in your power to make him happy. You have nothing with which to reproach yourselves.

ROUGON But now—what shall I do? Look you, it was for him we worked and saved, his mother and I; that he might never have to know, as we had known, what it is to be poor and hungry. (*Despondently*) And now we are old—what use to work? There is nothing left but death.

PRIEST You have each other.

ROUGON Yes, we have each other. Were it not for the thought of my poor Margot, I had let these butchers kill me before this.

PRIEST (*Sternly*) I do not like to hear you talk in that manner. You must realize well, that in its time of stress, your country has need of you; as much need of you as of her soldiers. You must not be rash. You must live and help and bear your part of her burden as best you can. It is your duty.

ROUGON Yes, yes, I well know it; but—

PRIEST Above all, you have to exercise control over your hasty temper. You must realize that you will best serve your country and revenge your personal wrongs by living and helping, not by willfully seeking death. You must remember you are a civilian and, according to the rules of war, you have no right to fight. Your part lies elsewhere. Let others shoot the guns.

ROUGON (*Disgustedly*) Bah! The children they have as soldiers cannot shoot. With my little rifle in there I could pick off more Prussian swine than a whole regiment of youngsters like my poor Charles. (*Scornfully*) Yet they tell me I am too old to enlist! Dolts!

PRIEST (*Rising and laying his hand on* ROUGON'*s back—with solemn earnestness*) My son, before I leave, I want you to swear to me before the God who watches over us, that you will remember what I have said and not allow your temper to force you to violence.

ROUGON (*Sullenly*) I promise. I swear it.

PRIEST (*Patting him on the back*) There, now you are sensible, more like yourself. (*He stands looking down at* CHARLES) I would advise you as to the burial of Charles. (ROUGON *groans*) Let it be done as secretly as possible. Let us avoid all provocation, and on their heads be it if misfortune happens. Perhaps tonight would be best.

ROUGON Ah, no, no, no! Please, my Father, not yet! Tonight let him remain here in his home, the house he was born in, with me.

PRIEST So be it. Tomorrow night then. You will let me know what time you wish it to be.

ROUGON Very well, my Father.

PRIEST And now I must go; but first let us kneel down and humbly offer up a prayer for the repose of his soul. (*They kneel down beside the dead body. The* PRIEST *commences to intone a prayer in which the words "Almighty God," "Merciful," "Infinite justice," "Infinite love," Infinite pity," "Thy son Jesus," "We, Thy children," "Praise Thy infinite goodness" stand out from the general mumble of sing-song sentences. Perhaps a sense of the crushing irony of this futile prayer penetrates the sorrow-numbed brain of* ROUGON *and proves the last straw which breaks down his self-control; for he interrupts the droning supplications of the* PRIEST *with a groan of agony, throws himself beside the young soldier's body and sobs brokenly: "Charles, Charles, my little one! Oh, why did not God take me instead!" The* PRIEST, *after a pause, wipes the tears from his eyes with his large handkerchief*) Come, come, it is hard, I know, but you must bear it like a man. God's will be done! He, too, had a Son who died for others. Pray to Him and He will comfort you in your affliction.

ROUGON (*Placing his hand gently on his son's face*) Cold! Cold! He who was so alive and smiling only this morning.

(*A step is heard on the road outside. The two get hastily to their feet as a young man in the gray uniform of a German captain of infantry appears at one of the gaps of the wall.*)

CAPTAIN (*Entering and turning to the* PRIEST) Are you the— (*Seeing the body on the floor*) I beg your pardon.

PRIEST (*Coldly*) What is your wish?

CAPTAIN (*Twirling his blond mustache fiercely to hide his embarrassment*) Again, I ask pardon. I meant no disrespect. (*Taking off his helmet impressively. He is a very young captain*) I honor the brave dead on whichever side they fall.

PRIEST (*Indicating* ROUGON, *who has slunk off to the other side of the table and is controlling his hatred and rage with very apparent effort*) It is his son.

CAPTAIN Ah! Too bad! The fortunes of war. Today, him; tomorrow, me, perhaps. Are you the *curé* of the village?

PRIEST I am.

CAPTAIN I have been seeking you ever since we occupied the place.

PRIEST I returned but a short time ago from Brussels, where I had been called to make my report to the Bishop. I knew nothing of the fighting here or I should have returned sooner. (*Sadly*) There were many, perhaps, who died needing me. But what is it you wish?

CAPTAIN I was sent by the Colonel to find you and deliver his orders. There seems to be no one of civil authority left in the village—else I should not intrude upon you.

PRIEST I am listening.

CAPTAIN (*Oratorically*) It is the Colonel's wish that you warn the inhabitants against committing any violence against our soldiers. Civilians caught with arms will be immediately shot. (*The* PRIEST *casts a significant glance at* ROUGON, *who scowls and mutters to himself*) Is that clear?

PRIEST Quite.

CAPTAIN On the other hand, all we demand of you will be paid for in cash. Let all your parishioners return to their work without fear of molestation. We make no war upon the helpless. (*With complacent pride*) I hope I make my meaning clear. I flatter myself my French is not so bad.

PRIEST (*With cold politeness*) You speak it very well, *monsieur*. You may tell your colonel that I will do all in my power to impress his words upon the minds of my people—not that I respect his orders or admit his right to give them to a man of peace, but because I have the welfare of my people at heart.

CAPTAIN Good. I will tell him. And now I will say *au revoir*, for I, too, have my duties to perform. We march from here immediately.

PRIEST (*Significantly*) *Adieu.*

(*The* CAPTAIN *goes out*)

ROUGON (*Raging*) Dog of a Prussian!

PRIEST Silence! Are you a fool?

(*While he is speaking, an awkward peasant boy of about fifteen with a broad face appears at the breach in the rear wall. His clothes are mud-stained and ragged and he is trembling with fear. He breathes in great shuddering gasps. There is a cut on his forehead beneath which the blood has dried in reddish-brown streaks*)

ROUGON (*Hears the noise*) What's that?

(*They both turn and see the boy*)

PRIEST Why, it's Jean! Whatever are you doing skulking around like that?

JEAN (*Stopping uneasily as if he intended to run away again*) Nothing, nothing.

PRIEST Come over here. (JEAN *does not move but stares at him with frightened eyes*) Don't you hear me speaking to you? What is the matter with you?

JEAN (*Faintly*) I am afraid.

PRIEST Of me? Come, this is ridiculous.

JEAN (*His lips trembling*) I am afraid—of them. Everything—blows up.

ROUGON Come to the good Father when he speaks to you, stupid dolt! Or I shall find a good strong stick and—

PRIEST Hush, you are only frightening him. Come to me, Jean, like a good boy. (JEAN *goes slowly to the* PRIEST, *who puts an arm about his shoulders*) Why, you're trembling like a leaf! Did the battle frighten you?

JEAN No, no, no! I don't know.

ROUGON (*Contemptuously*) The battle? He was never near the fighting. It was bad enough for we others without having this half-witted calf around. So we sent him away with the women this morning. (*To* JEAN) Answer me, you, how is it you are back here?

JEAN (*Trembling*) I don't know.

ROUGON (*Roughly*) Name of a dog, what do you know? Did we send you away with the women this morning or didn't we?

JEAN (*Uncertainly*) Yes—I went away—this morning.

PRIEST Hush, Rougon, you are only frightening the poor fellow. Jean, listen to me and stop trembling. I shall not let anyone hurt you. I have always been your good friend, have I not?

JEAN Yes—you are my friend.

PRIEST Of course I am; and while I am around, there is nothing you need fear. Come now, tell me like a good lad; you went away with the others this morning, didn't you?

JEAN Yes, Father.

PRIEST Then how do you happen to be here now? Why did you return to the village? Your clothes are in a shocking state. Where have you been hiding and how did you get that cut on your forehead?

JEAN (*Feeling the cut on his forehead with a dazed air*) It hurts.

PRIEST You will come home with me presently and we will wash that nasty cut and wrap it up in a nice clean bandage. Then you may be sure you will no longer feel any hurt at all. But first tell me—

JEAN I don't know. I ran and ran—and I came here.

PRIEST But something must have happened to make you run. Come, tell us, what was it?

JEAN (*Vaguely*) We left here and walked a long, long ways. Some rode in wagons but I was walking.

ROUGON And did you see Mother Rougon there, and Louise?

JEAN (*In a strange tone—with a shudder*) Yes, I saw them, I saw them.

(ROUGON *gives a grunt of satisfaction*)

PRIEST Go on, my son, tell us what happened next.

JEAN We could hear shots. We hurried faster. The horses galloped. The women commenced to scream and cry. Always the firing was louder. We didn't see any soldiers for a long time. Then we came upon lots of bodies—men from our army and others dressed in gray.

ROUGON (*In growing alarm*) Name of a dog, why didn't you turn back, eh?

JEAN (*Vaguely*) I don't know. (*He drones on in his expressionless voice*) The women were praying. They were afraid. They wanted us to hurry up and get to Brussels. We beat the horses. The hills were covered with white spots like—like daisies; and they floated way up in the air.

(*He makes a queer awkward gesture upward*)

ROUGON Idiot! What is all this foolish talk?

PRIEST (*Gently*) It was the smoke from the guns you saw, my child.

JEAN (*Very slowly—trying his best to imitate the exact sound*) Boom! Boom! Boom! I couldn't hear what anyone was saying.

(*He pauses*)

ROUGON Why do you stop, stupid? Go on, go on, or—

(*He shakes his clenched fist at the boy*)

PRIEST Silence, Rougon! Give the poor lad a chance.

JEAN (*In flat, monotonous tones*) Something blew up in a field by the road and threw dirt and stones on us. The horses were afraid. They ran faster. Then we came to the top of a hill. Lots of the soldiers in our army were there hiding in a long ditch. They shouted for us to run away. Then—then—then—

PRIEST (*Anxiously*) Yes?

(ROUGON *stands tensely with averted face as if afraid to listen*)

JEAN (*Throwing both his arms into the air with a wild gesture*) Then everything around blew up. (*In flat tones*) Something hit me on the head. I laid down for a while. When I got up I couldn't see any of the rest. There were bodies all around. I saw Mother Rougon—

PRIEST (*Clinging to a last shred of hope*) Alive and unharmed?

(*But* ROUGON *has guessed the worst and stands as if in a stupor, clenching and unclenching his big red hands, his features working convulsively*)

JEAN She was lying on the ground. She had a big hole here (*Pointing to his chest*) and blood all over—bright and red like—like flowers.

ROUGON (*Dully*) Dead! She, too!

JEAN And Louise had a hole in her head, here (*Pointing to his forehead*) and—

PRIEST (*Distracted with horror*) Enough! Stop! We have heard all we care to, do you hear?

JEAN So I ran, and ran, and ran, and ran, and ran.

(*His words die away into a murmur. He stares straight

before him like one in a trance)

PRIEST Merciful God, have pity!

ROUGON *(Slowly—as if the meaning of* JEAN'*s words were just commencing to dawn on him)* So—they are gone, too—the old woman—and Louise— *(Licks his lips with his dry tongue)* Everything is gone.

(There is a long silence. The PRIEST *dabs with his big handkerchief at the tears which are welling into his eyes.* JEAN *wanders over to the breach in the wall and stands looking down the road. A loud bugle call is heard.* JEAN *darts back into the room)*

JEAN *(Waving his arms, cries in terrified tones)* They are coming. They are coming this way!

(He runs to the right corner of the room and crouches there trembling, seeking to hide himself in the fallen ruins)

ROUGON So—*they* are coming?

(He strides resolutely across the room and enters the room on left)

PRIEST *(Alarmed by the expression on* ROUGON'*s face)* Rougon! Rougon! What are you going to do? *(He receives no answer. A moment later* ROUGON *re-enters the room carrying a long-barreled rifle. The* PRIEST *seizes him by the arm)* No, no, I beseech you!

ROUGON *(Roughly throwing the* PRIEST *aside)* Let me alone! *(He half-kneels beside one of the breaches in the wall—then speaks in a voice of deadly calmness)* They will not pass here. They are going to turn off at the fork in the road. It is near enough, however.

(The rhythmic tramp of the marching troops can be faintly heard)

PRIEST *(In agony)* In the name of God I implore you—

ROUGON Bah, God! *(He takes careful aim and fires)* That for Margot! *(He loads and fires again)* That for Louise!

(Cries of rage and running footsteps are heard. ROUGON *is reloading his rifle when the* CAPTAIN *and four German privates rush in.* ROUGON *struggles but is disarmed and forced back to the wall. He stands proudly, calmly awaiting his fate. One of the soldiers seizes the* PRIEST*)*

SOLDIER *(To the* CAPTAIN*)* *Was mit dem Priester?*

ROUGON *(To the* CAPTAIN*)* The good Father did nothing. He but did his best to hold my arm and stop me. It is I alone who did the shooting, dog of a Prussian!

CAPTAIN Is this true, priest?

PRIEST It is as he tells you. I tried to restrain him—not for your sakes, but for his own.

CAPTAIN *(To the soldier)* *Las den Priester gehen!* *(The soldier releases the* PRIEST*. The* CAPTAIN *turns to* ROUGON*)* If you have a prayer to say, be quick!

(The four soldiers line up in front of ROUGON *and face him across the body of* CHARLES*)*

ROUGON *(With angry scorn)* I want no prayers!

PRIEST Rougon!

ROUGON *(Furiously)* To hell with your prayers!

PRIEST *(Supplicatingly)* Make your peace with God, my son!

ROUGON *(Spitting on the floor, fiercely)* That for your God who allows such things to happen! *(To the* CAPTAIN*)* I am ready, pig!

CAPTAIN *(To the soldiers)* *Gewehr! Heraus!* *(The soldiers take aim)*

PRIEST May God have mercy on—

CAPTAIN *Feuer!* *(There is a crashing report.* ROUGON *pitches forward on his face, quivers for a moment, is still. The soldiers file out to the road. The* CAPTAIN *turns to the horrified* PRIEST*)*

CAPTAIN *(Shrugging his shoulders)* It is the law. *(He follows the soldiers)*

PRIEST *(Looking down with infinite compassion at the still bodies of father and son)* Alas, the laws of men!

(The sun has set. The twilight is fading grayly into night. From the heap of wreckage in the right corner comes the sound of stifled weeping)

Curtain

BEFORE BREAKFAST

A Play in One Act

SCENE. *A small room serving both as kitchen and dining-room in a flat in Christopher Street, New York City. In the rear, to the right, a door leading to the outer hall. On the left of the doorway, a sink, and a two-burner gas stove. Over the stove, and extending to the left wall, a wooden cupboard for dishes, etc. On the left, two windows looking out on a fire-escape where several potted plants are dying of neglect. Before the windows, a table covered with oilcloth. Two cane-bottomed chairs are placed by the table. Another stands against the wall to the right of door in rear. In the right wall, rear, a doorway leading into a bedroom. Farther forward, different articles of a man's and a woman's clothing are hung on pegs. A clothes line is strung from the left corner, rear, to the right wall, forward.*

It is about eight-thirty in the morning of a fine, sunshiny day in the early autumn.

Mrs. Rowland enters from the bedroom, yawning, her hands still busy putting the finishing touches on a slovenly toilet by sticking hairpins into her hair which is bunched up in a drab-coloured mass on top of her round head. She is of medium height and inclined to a shapeless stoutness, accentuated by her formless blue dress, shabby and worn. Her face is characterless, with small regular features and eyes of a nondescript blue. There is a pinched expression about her eyes and nose and her weak, spiteful mouth. She is in her early twenties but looks much older.

She comes to the middle of the room and yawns, stretching her arms to their full length. Her drowsy eyes stare about the room with the irritated look of one to whom a long sleep has not been a long rest. She goes wearily to the clothes hanging on the right and takes an apron from a hook. She ties it about her waist, giving vent to an exasperated "damn" when the knot fails to obey her clumsy fingers. Finally gets it tied and goes slowly to the gas stove and lights one burner. She fills the coffee-pot at the sink and sets it over the flame. Then slumps down into a chair by the table and puts a hand over her forehead as if she were suffering from headache. Suddenly her face brightens as though she had remembered something, and she casts a quick glance at the dish cupboard; then looks sharply at the bedroom door and listens intently for a moment or so.

MRS. ROWLAND (*in a low voice*). Alfred! Alfred! (*There is no answer from the next room and she continues suspiciously in a louder tone.*) You needn't pretend you're asleep.

(*There is no reply to this from the bedroom, and, reassured, she gets up from her chair and tiptoes cautiously to the dish cupboard. She slowly opens one door, taking great care to make no noise, and slides out, from their hiding place behind the dishes, a bottle of Gordon gin and a glass. In doing so she disturbs the top dish, which rattles a little. At this sound she starts guiltily and looks with sulky defiance at the doorway to the next room.*)

(*Her voice trembling.*) Alfred!

(*After a pause, during which she listens for any sound, she takes the glass and pours out a large drink and gulps it down; then hastily returns the bottle and glass to their hiding-place. She closes the cupboard door with the same care as she had opened it, and, heaving a great sigh of relief, sinks down into her chair again. The large dose of alcohol she has taken has an almost immediate effect. Her features become more animated, she seems to gather energy, and she looks at the bedroom door with a hard, vindictive smile on her lips. Her eyes glance quickly about the room and are fixed on a man's coat and waistcoat which hang from a hook at right. She moves stealthily over to the open doorway and stands there, out of sight of anyone inside, listening for any movement.*)

(*Calling in a half-whisper.*) Alfred!

(*Again there is no reply. With a swift movement she takes the coat and waistcoat from the hook and returns with them to her chair. She sits down and takes the various articles out of each pocket but quickly puts them back again. At last, in the inside pocket of the vest, she finds a letter.*)

(*Looking at the handwriting – slowly to herself.*) Hmm! I knew it.

(*She opens the letter and reads it. At first her expression is one of hatred and rage, but as she goes on to the end it changes to one of triumphant malignity. She remains in deep thought for a moment, staring before her, the letter in her hands, a cruel smile on her lips. Then she puts the letter back in the pocket of the waistcoat, and still careful not to awaken the sleeper, hangs the clothes up again on the same hook, and goes to the bedroom door and looks in.*)

(*In a loud, shrill voice.*) Alfred! (*Still louder.*) Alfred! (*There is a muffled, yawning groan from the next room.*) Don't you think it's about time you got up? Do you want to stay in bed all day? (*Turning around and coming back to her chair.*) Not that I've got any doubts about your being lazy enough to stay in bed for ever. (*She sits down and looks out of the window, irritably.*) Goodness knows what time it is. We haven't even got any way of telling the time since you pawned your watch like a fool. The last valuable thing we had, and you knew it. It's been nothing but pawn, pawn, pawn, with you – anything to put off getting a job, anything to get out of going to work like a man. (*She taps the floor with her foot nervously, biting her lips.*) (*After a short pause.*) Alfred! Get up, do you hear me? I want to make that bed before I go out. I'm sick of having this place in a continual mess on your account. (*With a certain vindictive satisfaction.*) Not that we'll be here long unless you manage to get some money somehow. Heaven knows I do my part – and more – going out to sew every day while you play the gentleman and loaf around bar rooms with that good-for-nothing lot of artists from the Square.

(*A short pause during which she plays nervously with a cup and saucer on the table.*)

And where are you going to get money, I'd like to know? The rent's due this week and you know what the landlord is. He won't let us stay a minute over our time. You say you *can't* get a job. That's a lie and you know it. You never even look for one. All you do is moon around all day writing silly poetry and stories that no one will buy – and no wonder they won't. I notice I can always get a position, such as it is; and it's only that which keeps us from starving to death.

(*Gets up and goes over to the stove – looks into the coffee-pot to see if the water is boiling; then comes back and sits down again.*)

You'll have to get money to-day somehow. I can't do it all, and I won't do it all. You've got to come to your senses. You've got to beg, borrow, or steal it somewheres. (*With a contemptuous laugh.*) But where, I'd like to know? You're too proud to beg, and you've borrowed the limit, and you haven't the nerve to steal.

(*After a pause – getting up angrily.*) Aren't you up yet, for heaven's sake? It's just like you to go to sleep again, or pretend to. (*She goes to the bedroom door and looks in.*) Oh, you are up. Well, it's about time. You needn't look at me like that. Your airs don't fool me a bit any more. I know you too well – better than you think I do – you and your goings-on. (*Turning away from the door – meaningly.*) I know a lot of things, my dear. Never mind what I know, now. I'll tell you before I go, you needn't worry.

(*She comes to the middle of the room and stands there, frowning.*)

(*Irritably.*) Hmm! I suppose I might as well get breakfast ready – not that there's anything much to get. (*Questioningly.*) Unless you have some money? (*She pauses for an answer from the next room which does not come.*) Foolish question! (*She gives a short, hard laugh.*) I ought to know you better than that by this time. When you left here in such a huff last night I knew what would happen. You can't be trusted for a second. A nice condition you came home in! The fight we had was only an excuse for you to make a beast of yourself. What was the use pawning your watch if all you wanted with the money was to waste it in buying drink?

(*Goes over to the dish cupboard and takes out plates, cups, etc., while she is talking.*)

Hurry up! It don't take long to get breakfast these days, thanks to you. All we got this morning is bread and butter and coffee; and you wouldn't even have that if it wasn't for me sewing my fingers off. (*She slams the loaf of bread on the table with a bang.*)

The bread's stale. I hope you'll like it. *You* don't deserve any better, but I don't see why *I* should suffer.

(*Going over to the stove.*) The coffee'll be ready in a minute, and you needn't expect me to wait for you.

(*Suddenly with great anger.*) What on earth are you doing all this time? (*She goes over to the door and looks in.*) Well, you're *almost* dressed at any rate. I expected to find you back in bed. That'd be just like you. How awful you look this morning! For heaven's sake, shave! You're disgusting! You look like a tramp. No wonder no one will give you a job. I don't blame them – when you don't even look half-way decent. (*She goes to the stove.*) There's plenty of hot water right here. You've got no excuse. (*Gets a bowl and pours some of the water from the coffee-pot into it.*) Here.

(*He stretches his hand into the room for it. It is a sensitive hand with slender fingers. It trembles and some of the water spills on the floor.*)

(*Tauntingly.*) Look at your hand tremble! You'd better give up drinking. You can't stand it. It's just your kind that get the D.T.'s. *That would be* the last straw! (*Looking down at the floor.*) Look at the mess you've made of this floor – cigarette ends and ashes all over the place. Why can't you put them on a plate? No, you wouldn't be considerate enough to do that. You never think of me. You don't have to sweep the room and that's all you care about.

(*Takes the broom and commences to sweep viciously, raising a cloud of dust. From the inner room comes the sound of a razor being stropped.*)

(*Sweeping.*) Hurry up! It must be nearly time for me to go. If I'm late I'm liable to lose my position, and then I couldn't support you any longer. (*As an afterthought she adds sarcastically.*) And then you'd have to go to work or something dreadful like that. (*Sweeping under the table.*) What I want to know is whether you're going to look for a job to-day or not. You know your family won't help us any more. They've had enough of you, too. (*After a moment's silent sweeping.*) I'm about sick of all this life. I've a good notion to go home, if I wasn't too proud to let them know what a failure you've been – you, the millionaire Rowland's only son, the Harvard graduate, the poet, the catch of the town – Huh! (*With bitterness.*) There wouldn't be many of them now envy my catch if they knew the truth. What has our marriage been, I'd like to know? Even before your *millionaire* father died owing every one in the world money, you certainly never wasted any of your time on your wife. I suppose you thought I'd ought to be glad you were *honourable* enough to marry me – after getting me into trouble. You were ashamed of me with your fine friends because my father's only a grocer, that's what you were. At least he's honest, which is more than anyone could say about yours. (*She is sweeping steadily toward the door. Leans on her broom for a moment.*)

You hoped every one'd think you'd been forced to marry me, and pity you, didn't you? You didn't hesitate much about telling me you loved me, and making me believe your lies, before it happened, did you? You made me think you didn't want your father to buy me off as he tried to do. I know better now. I haven't lived with you all this time for nothing. (*Sombrely.*) It's lucky the poor thing was born dead, after all. What a father you'd have been!

(*Is silent, brooding moodily for a moment – then she continues with a sort of savage joy.*)

But I'm not the only one who's got you to thank for being unhappy. There's one other, at least, and *she* can't hope to marry you now. (*She puts her head into the next room.*) How about Helen? (*She starts back from the doorway, half frightened.*)

Don't look at me that way! Yes, I read her letter. What about it? I got a right to. I'm your wife. And I know all there is to know, so don't lie. You needn't stare at me so. You can't bully me with your superior airs any longer. Only for me you'd be going without breakfast this very morning. (*She sets the broom back in the corner – whiningly.*) You never did have any gratitude for what I've done. (*She comes to the stove and puts the coffee into the pot.*) The coffee's ready. I'm not going to wait for you. (*She sits down in her chair again.*)

(*After a pause – puts her hand to her head – fretfully.*) My head aches so this morning. It's a shame I've got to go to work in a stuffy room all day in my condition. And I wouldn't if you were half a man. By rights I ought to be lying on my back instead of you. You know how sick I've been this last year; and yet you object when I take a little something to keep up my spirits. You even didn't want me to take that tonic I got at the drug store. (*With a hard laugh.*) I know you'd be glad to have me dead and out of your way; then you'd be free to run after all these silly girls that think you're such a wonderful, misunderstood person – this Helen and the others. (*There is a sharp exclamation of pain from the next room.*)

(*With satisfaction*). There! I knew you'd cut yourself. It'll be a lesson to you. You know you oughtn't to be running around nights drinking with your nerves in such an awful shape. (*She goes to the door and looks in.*)

What makes you so pale? What are you staring at yourself in the mirror that way for? For goodness' sake, wipe that blood off your face! (*With a shudder.*) It's horrible. (*In relieved tones.*) There, that's better. I never could stand the sight of blood. (*She shrinks back from the door a little.*) You better give up trying and go to a barber shop. Your hand shakes dreadfully. Why do you stare at me like that? (*She turns away from the door.*) Are you still mad at me about that letter? (*Defiantly.*) Well, I had a right to read it. I'm your wife. (*She comes to the chair and sits down again. After a pause.*)

I knew all the time you were running around with some one. Your lame excuses about spending the time at the library didn't fool me. Who is this Helen, anyway? One of those artists? Or does she write poetry, too? Her letter sounds that way. I'll bet she told you your things were the best ever, and you believed her, like a fool. Is she young and pretty? I was young and pretty, too, when you fooled me with your fine, poetic talk; but life with you would soon wear anyone down. What I've been through!

(*Goes over and takes the coffee off the stove.*) Breakfast is ready. (*With a contemptuous glance.*) Breakfast! (*Pours out a cup of coffee for herself and puts the pot on the table.*) Your coffee'll be cold. What are you doing – still shaving, for heaven's sake? You'd better give it up. One of these mornings you'll give yourself a serious cut. (*She cuts off bread and butters it. During the following speeches she eats and sips her coffee.*)

I'll have to run as soon as I've finished eating. One of us has got to work. (*Angrily.*) Are you going to look for a job to-day or aren't you? I should think some of your fine friends would help you, if they really think you're so much. But I guess they just like to hear you talk. (*Sits in silence for a moment.*)

I'm sorry for this Helen, whoever she is. Haven't you got any feelings for other people? What will her family say? I see she mentions them in her letter. What is she going to do – have the child – or go to one of those doctors? That's a nice thing, I must say. Where can she get the money? Is she rich? (*She waits for some answer to this volley of questions.*)

Hmm! You won't tell me anything about her, will you? Much I care. Come to think of it, I'm not so sorry for her after all. She knew what she was doing. She isn't any school-girl, like I was, from the looks of her letter. Does she know you're married? Of course, she must. All your friends know about your unhappy marriage. I know they pity you, but they don't know my side of it. They'd talk different if they did.

(*Too busy eating to go on for a second or so.*)

This Helen must be a fine one, if she knew you were married. What does she expect, then? That I'll divorce you and let her marry you? Does she think I'm crazy enough for that – after all you've made me go through? I guess not! And you can't get a divorce from me and you know it. No one can say *I've* ever done anything wrong. (*Drinks the last of her cup of coffee.*)

She deserves to suffer, that's all I can say. I'll tell you what I think; I think your Helen is no better than a common street-walker, that's what I think. (*There is a stifled groan of pain from the next room.*)

Did you cut yourself again? Serves you right. (*Gets up and takes off her apron.*) Well, I've got to run along. (*Peevishly.*) This is a fine life for me to be leading! I won't stand for your loafing any longer. (*Something catches her ear and she pauses and listens intently.*) There! You've overturned the water all over everything. Don't say you haven't. I can hear it dripping on the floor. (*A vague expression of fear comes over her face.*) Alfred! Why don't you answer me?

(*She moves slowly toward the room. There is the noise of a chair being overturned and something crashes heavily to the floor. She stands, trembling with fright.*)

Alfred! Alfred! Answer me! What is it you knocked over? Are you still drunk? (*Unable to stand the tension a second longer she rushes to the door of the bedroom.*)

Alfred!

(*She stands in the doorway looking down at the floor of the inner room, transfixed with horror. Then she shrieks wildly and runs to the other door, unlocks it and frenziedly pulls it open, and runs shrieking madly into the outer hall.*)

Curtain

ILE

A Play in One Act

Characters

BEN, *the cabin boy*
THE STEWARD
CAPTAIN KEENEY
SLOCUM, *second mate*
MRS. KEENEY
JOE, *a harpooner*
MEMBERS OF THE CREW OF THE STEAM WHALER "ATLANTIC QUEEN"

The action of the play takes place in the years preceding the outbreak of World War I

SCENE. *Captain Keeney's cabin on board the steam whaling ship Atlantic Queen—a small, square compartment about eight feet high with a skylight in the centre looking out on the poop deck. On the left (the stern of the ship) a long bench with rough cushions is built in against the wall. In front of the bench, a table. Over the bench, several curtained port-holes.*

In the rear, left, a door leading to the captain's sleeping quarters. To the right of the door a small organ, looking as if it were brand new, is placed against the wall.

On the right, to the rear, a marble-topped sideboard. On the sideboard, a woman's sewing basket. Farther forward, a doorway leading to the companion-way and past the officers' quarters to the main deck.

In the centre of the room, a stove. From the middle of the ceiling a hanging lamp is suspended. The walls of the cabin are painted white.

There is no rolling of the ship, and the light which comes through the skylight is sickly and faint, indicating one of those grey days of calm when ocean and sky are alike dead. The silence is unbroken except for the measured tread of some one walking up and down on the poop deck overhead.

It is nearing two bells—one o'clock—in the afternoon of a day in the year 1895.

At the rise of the curtain there is a moment of intense silence. Then the Steward enters and commences to clear the table of the few dishes which still remain on it after the Captain's dinner. He is an old, grizzled man dressed in dungaree trousers, a sweater, and a woollen cap with ear flaps. His manner is sullen and angry. He stops stacking up the plates and casts a quick glance upward at the skylight; then tiptoes over to the closed door in rear and listens with his ear pressed to the crack. What he hears makes his face darken and he mutters a furious curse. There is a noise from the doorway on the right and he darts back to the table.

Ben enters. He is an overgrown, gawky boy with a long, pinched face. He is dressed in sweater, fur cap, etc. His teeth are chattering with the cold and he hurries to the stove, where

he stands for a moment shivering, blowing on his hands, slapping them against his sides, on the verge of crying.

THE STEWARD (*in relieved tones—seeing who it is*). Oh, 'tis you, is it? What're ye shiverin' 'bout? Stay by the stove where ye belong and ye'll find no need of chatterin'.

BEN. It's c-c-cold. (*Trying to control his chattering teeth—derisively.*) Who d'ye think it were—the Old Man?

THE STEWARD (*makes a threatening move—Ben shrinks away*). None o' your lip, young un', or I'll learn ye. (*More kindly.*) Where was it ye've been all o' the time—the fo'c'sle?

BEN. Yes.

THE STEWARD. Let the Old Man see ye up for'ard monkeyshinin' with the hands and ye'll get a hidin' ye'll not forget in a hurry.

BEN. Aw, he don't see nothin'. (*A trace of awe in his tones—he glances upward.*) He just walks up and down like he didn't notice nobody—and stares at the ice to the no'the'ard.

THE STEWARD (*the same tone of awe creeping into his voice*). He's always starin' at the ice. (*In a sudden rage, shaking his fist at the skylight.*) Ice, ice, ice! Damn him and damn the ice! Holdin' us in for nigh on a year—nothin' to see but ice—stuck in it like a fly in molasses!

BEN (*apprehensively*). Ssshh! He'll hear ye.

THE STEWARD (*raging*). Aye, damn him, and damn the Arctic seas, and damn this stinkin' whalin' ship of his, and damn me for a fool to ever ship on it! (*Subsiding as if realizing the uselessness of this outburst—shaking his head—slowly, with deep conviction.*) He's a hard man—as hard a man as ever sailed the seas.

BEN (*solemnly*). Aye.

THE STEWARD. The two years we all signed up for are done this day. Blessed Christ! Two years o' this dog's life, and no luck in the fishin', and the hands half starved with the food runnin' low, rotten as it is; and not a sign of him turnin' back for home! (*Bitterly.*) Home! I begin to doubt if ever I'll set foot on land again. (*Excitedly.*) What is it he thinks he' goin' to do? Keep us all up here after our time is worked out till the last man of us is starved to death or frozen? We've grub enough hardly to last out the voyage back if we started now. What are the men goin' to do 'bout it? Did ye hear any talk in the fo'c'sle?

BEN (*going over to him—in a half whisper*). They said if he don't put back south for home to-day they're goin' to mutiny.

THE STEWARD (*with grim satisfaction*). Mutiny? Aye, 'tis the only thing they can do; and serve him right after the manner he's treated them—'s if they wern't no better nor dogs.

BEN. The ice is all broke up to s'uth'ard. They's clear water 's far 's you can see. He ain't got no excuse for not turnin' back for home, the men says.

THE STEWARD (*bitterly*). He won't look nowheres but no'the'ard where they's only the ice to see. He don't want to see no clear water. All he thinks on is gittin' the ile—'s if it was our fault he ain't had good luck with the whales. (*Shaking his head.*) I think the man's mighty nigh losin' his senses.

BEN (*awed*). D'you really think he's crazy?

THE STEWARD. Aye, it's the punishment o' God on him. Did ye ever hear of a man who wasn't crazy do the things he does? (*Pointing to the door in rear.*) Who but a man that's mad would take his woman—and as sweet a woman as ever was—on a stinkin' whalin' ship to the Arctic seas to be locked in by the rotten ice for nigh on a year, and maybe lose her senses forever—for it's sure she'll never be the same again.

BEN (*sadly*). She useter be awful nice to me before—(*his eyes grow wide and frightened*)—she got—like she is.

THE STEWARD. Aye, she was good to all of us. 'Twould have been hell on board without her; for he's a hard man—a hard, hard man—a driver if there ever was one. (*With a grim laugh.*) I hope he's satisfied now—drivin' her on till she's near lost her mind. And who could blame her? 'Tis a God's wonder we're not a ship full of crazed people—with the damned ice all the time, and the quiet so thick you're afraid to hear your own voice.

BEN (*with a frightened glance toward the door on right*). She don't never speak to me no more—jest looks at me 's if she didn't know me.

THE STEWARD. She don't know no one—but him. She talks to him—when she does talk—right enough.

BEN. She does nothin' all day long now but sit and sew—and then she cries to herself without makin' no noise. I've seen her.

THE STEWARD. Aye, I could hear her through the door a while back.

BEN (*tiptoes over to the door and listens*). She's cryin' now.

THE STEWARD (*furiously—shaking his fist*). God send his soul to hell for the devil he is!

(*There is the noise of some one coming slowly down the companionway stairs. The Steward hurries to his stacked-up dishes. He is so nervous from fright that he knocks off the top one, which falls and breaks on the floor. He stands aghast, trembling with dread. Ben is violently rubbing off the organ with a piece of cloth which he has snatched from his pocket. Captain Keeney appears in the doorway on right and comes into the cabin, removing his fur cap as he does so. He is a man of about forty, five feet ten in height, but looking much shorter on account of the enormous proportions of his shoulders and chest. His face is massive and deeply lined, with grey-blue eyes of a bleak hardness, and a tightly clenched, thin-lipped mouth. His thick hair is long and grey. He is dressed in a heavy blue jacket and blue trousers stuffed into his sea-boots.*)

(*He is followed into the cabin by the Second Mate, a lanky six-footer with a lean weather-beaten face. The Mate is dressed about the same as the Captain. He is a man of thirty or so.*)

KEENEY (*comes toward the Steward—with a stern look on his face. The Steward is visibly frightened and the stack of dishes rattles in his trembling hands. Keeney draws back his fist and the Steward shrinks away. The fist is gradually lowered and Keeney speaks slowly*). 'Twould be like hitting a worm. It is nigh on two bells, Mr. Steward, and this truck not cleared yet.

THE STEWARD (*stammering*). Y-y-yes, sir.

KEENEY. Instead of doin' your rightful work ye've been below here gossipin' old woman's talk with that boy. (*To Ben, fiercely.*) Get out o' this, you! Clean up the chart room. (*Ben darts past the Mate to the open doorway.*) Pick up that dish, Mr. Steward!

THE STEWARD (*doing so with difficulty*). Yes, sir.

KEENEY. The next dish you break, Mr. Steward, you take a bath in the Bering Sea at the end of a rope.

THE STEWARD (*tremblingly*). Yes, sir. (*He hurries out. The Second Mate walks slowly over to the Captain.*)

MATE. I warn't 'specially anxious the man at the wheel should catch what I wanted to say to you, sir. That's why I asked you to come below.

KEENEY (*impatiently*). Speak your say, Mr. Slocum.

MATE (*unconsciously lowering his voice*). I'm afeard there'll be trouble with the hands by the look o' things. They'll likely turn ugly, every blessed one o' them, if you don't put back. The two years they signed up for is up to-day.

KEENEY. And d'you think you're tellin' me somethin' new, Mr. Slocum? I've felt it in the air this long time past. D'you think I've not seen their ugly looks and the grudgin' way they worked?

(*The door in rear is opened and Mrs. Keeney stands in the doorway. She is a slight, sweet-faced little woman primly dressed in black. Her eyes are red from weeping and her face drawn and pale. She takes in the cabin with a frightened glance and stands as if fixed to the spot by some nameless dread, clasping and unclasping her hands nervously. The two men turn and look at her.*)

KEENEY (*with rough tenderness*). Well, Annie?

MRS. KEENEY (*as if awakening from a dream*). David, I—— (*She is silent. The Mate starts for the doorway.*)

KEENEY (*turning to him—sharply*). Wait!

MATE. Yes, sir.

KEENEY. D'you want anything, Annie?

MRS. KEENEY (*after a pause, during which she*

seems to be endeavouring to collect her thoughts). I thought maybe—I'd go up on deck, David, to get a breath of fresh air. (*She stands humbly awaiting his permission. He and the Mate exchange a significant glance.*)

KEENEY. It's too cold, Annie. You'd best stay below to-day. There's nothing to look at on deck—but ice.

MRS. KEENEY (*monotonously*). I know—ice, ice, ice! But there's nothing to see down here but these walls. (*She makes a gesture of loathing.*)

KEENEY. You can play the organ, Annie.

MRS. KEENEY (*dully*). I hate the organ. It puts me in mind of home.

KEENEY (*a touch of resentment in his voice*). I got it jest for you.

MRS. KEENEY (*dully*). I know. (*She turns away from them and walks slowly to the bench on left. She lifts up one of the curtains and looks through a port-hole; then utters an exclamation of joy.*) Ah, water! Clear water! As far as I can see! How good it looks after all these months of ice! (*She turns round to them, her face transfigured with joy.*) Ah, now I must go upon deck and look at it, David.

KEENEY (*frowning*). Best not to-day, Annie. Best wait for a day when the sun shines.

MRS. KEENEY (*desperately*). But the sun never shines in this terrible place.

KEENEY (*a tone of command in his voice*). Best not to-day, Annie.

MRS. KEENEY (*crumbling before this command—abjectly*). Very well, David.

(*She stands there staring straight before her as if in a daze. The two men look at her uneasily.*)

KEENEY (*sharply*). Annie!

MRS. KEENEY (*dully*). Yes, David.

KEENEY. Me and Mr. Slocum has business to talk about—ship's business.

MRS. KEENEY. Very well, David.

(*She goes slowly out, rear, and leaves the door three-quarters shut behind her.*)

KEENEY. Best not have her on deck if they's goin' to be any trouble.

MATE. Yes, sir.

KEENEY. And trouble they's goin' to be. I feel it in my bones. (*Takes a revolver from the pocket of his coat and examines it.*) Got your'n?

MATE. Yes, sir.

KEENEY. Not that we'll have to use 'em—not if I know their breed of dog—jest to frighten 'em up a bit. (*Grimly.*) I ain't never been forced to use one yit; and trouble I've had by land and by sea's long as I kin remember, and will have till my dyin' day, I reckon.

MATE (*hesitatingly*). Then you ain't goin'—to turn back?

KEENEY. Turn back! Mr. Slocum, did you ever hear o' me pointin' s'uth for home with only a measly four hundred barrel of ile in the hold?

MATE (*hastily*). No, sir—but the grub's gittin' low.

KEENEY. They's enough to last a long time yit, if they're careful with it; and they's plenty o' water.

MATE. They say it's not fit to eat—what's left; and the two years they signed on fur is up to-day. They might make trouble for you in the courts when we git home.

KEENEY. To hell with 'em! Let them make what law trouble they kin. I don't give a damn 'bout the money. I've got to git the ile! (*Glancing sharply at the Mate.*) You ain't turnin' no damned sea lawyer, be you, Mr. Slocum?

MATE (*flushing*). Not by a hell of a sight, sir.

KEENEY. What do the fools want to go home fur now? Their share o' the four hundred barrel wouldn't keep 'em in chewin' terbacco.

MATE (*slowly*). They wants to git back to their folks an' things, I s'pose.

KEENEY (*looking at him searchingly*). 'N' you want to turn back, too. (*The Mate looks down confusedly before his sharp gaze.*) Don't lie, Mr. Slocum. It's writ down plain in your eyes. (*With grim sarcasm.*) I hope, Mr. Slocum, you ain't agoin' to jine the men agin me.

MATE (*indignantly*). That ain't fair, sir, to say sich things.

KEENEY (*with satisfaction*). I warn't much afeard o' that, Tom. You been with me nigh on ten year and I've learned ye whalin'. No man kin say I ain't a good master, if I be a hard one.

MATE. I warn't thinkin' of myself, sir—'bout turnin' home, I mean. (*Desperately.*) But Mrs. Keeney, sir—seems like she ain't jest satisfied up here, ailin' like—what with the cold an' bad luck an' the ice an' all.

KEENEY (*his face clouding—rebukingly but not severely*). That's my business, Mr. Slocum. I'll thank you to steer a clear course o' that. (*A pause.*) The ice'll break up soon to no'th'ard. I could see it startin' to-day. And when it goes and we git some sun Annie'll perk up. (*Another pause—then he bursts forth.*) It ain't the damned money what's keepin' me up in the Northern seas, Tom. But I can't go back to Homeport with a measly four hundred barrel of ile. I'd die fust. I ain't never come back home in all my days without a full ship. Ain't that truth?

MATE. Yes, sir; but this voyage you been ice-bound, an'——

KEENEY (*scornfully*). And d'you s'pose any of 'em would believe that—any o' them skippers I've beaten voyage after voyage? Can't you hear 'em laughin' and sneerin'—Tibbots 'n' Harris 'n' Simms and the rest—and all o' Homeport makin' fun o' me: "Dave Keeney what boasts he's the best whalin' skipper out o' Homeport comin' back with a measly four hundred barrel of ile"? (*The thought of this drives him into a frenzy, and he smashes his fist down on the marble top of the sideboard.*) Hell! I got to git the ile, I tell you. How could I figger on this ice? It's never been so bad before in the thirty year I been acomin' here. And now it's breakin' up. In a couple o' days it'll be all gone. And they's whale here, plenty of 'em. I know they is and I ain't never gone wrong yit. I got to git the ile! I got to git it in spite of all hell, and by God, I ain't agoin' home till I do git it!

(*There is the sound of subdued sobbing from the door in rear. The two men stand silent for a moment, listening. Then Keeney goes over to the door and looks in. He hesitates for a moment as if he were going to enter—then closes the door softly. Joe, the harpooner, an enormous six-footer with a battered ugly face, enters from right and stands waiting for the Captain to notice him.*)

KEENEY (*turning and seeing him*). Don't be standin' there like a gawk, Harpooner. Speak up!

JOE (*confusedly*). We want—the men, sir—they wants to send a depitation aft to have a word with you.

KEENEY (*furiously*). Tell 'em to go to—— (*Checks himself and continues grimly.*) Tell 'em to come. I'll see 'em.

JOE. Aye, aye, sir. (*He goes out.*)

KEENEY (*with a grim smile*). Here it comes, the trouble you spoke of, Mr. Slocum, and we'll make short shrift of it. It's better to crush such things at the start than let them make headway.

MATE (*worriedly*). Shall I wake up the First and Fourth, sir? We might need their help.

KEENEY. No, let them sleep. I'm well able to handle this alone, Mr. Slocum.

(*There is the shuffling of footsteps from outside and five of the crew crowd into the cabin, led by Joe. All are dressed alike—sweaters, sea-boots, etc. They glance uneasily at the Captain, twirling their fur caps in their hands.*)

KEENEY (*after a pause*). Well? Who's to speak fur ye?

JOE (*stepping forward with an air of bravado*). I be.

KEENEY (*eyeing him up and down coldly*). So you be. Then speak your say and be quick about it.

JOE (*trying not to wilt before the Captain's glance and avoiding his eyes*). The time we signed up for is done to-day.

KEENEY (*icily*). You're tellin' me nothin' I don't know.

JOE. You ain't pintin' fur home yit, far's we kin see.

KEENEY. No, and I ain't agoin' to till this ship is full of ile.

JOE. You can't go no further no'the with the ice afore ye.

KEENEY. The ice is breaking up.

JOE (*after a slight pause during which the others mumble angrily to one another*). The grub we're gittin' now is rotten.

KEENEY. It's good enough fur ye. Better men than ye are have eaten worse.

(*There is a chorus of angry exclamations from the crowd.*)

JOE (*encouraged by this support*). We ain't agoin' to work no more less you puts back for home.

KEENEY (*fiercely*). You ain't, ain't you ?

JOE. No ; and the law courts'll say we was right.

KEENEY. To hell with your law courts ! We're at sea now and I'm the law on this ship. (*Edging up toward the harpooner.*) And every mother's son of you what don't obey orders goes in irons.

(*There are more angry exclamations from the crew. Mrs. Keeney appears in the doorway in rear and looks on with startled eyes. None of the men notice her.*)

JOE (*with bravado*). Then we're agoin' to mutiny and take the old hooker home ourselves. Ain't we, boys ?

(*As he turns his head to look at the others, Keeney's fist shoots out to the side of his jaw. Joe goes down in a heap and lies there. Mrs. Keeney gives a shriek and hides her face in her hands. The men pull out their sheath knives and start a rush, but stop when they find themselves confronted by the revolvers of Keeney and the Mate.*)

KEENEY (*his eyes and voice snapping*). Hold still ! (*The men stand huddled together in a sullen silence. Keeney's voice is full of mockery.*) You've found out it ain't safe to mutiny on this ship, ain't you ? And now git for'ard where ye belong, and—— (*He gives Joe's body a contemptuous kick.*) Drag him with you. And remember the first man of ye I see shirkin' I'll shoot dead as sure as there's a sea under us, and you can tell the rest the same. Git for'ard now ! Quick ! (*The men leave in cowed silence, carrying Joe with them. Keeney turns to the Mate with a short laugh and puts his revolver back in his pocket.*) Best get up on deck, Mr. Slocum, and see to it they don't try none of their skulkin' tricks. We'll have to keep an eye peeled from now on. I know 'em.

MATE. Yes, sir.

(*He goes out, right. Keeney hears his wife's hysterical weeping and turns around in surprise—then walks slowly to her side.*)

KEENEY (*putting an arm around her shoulder —with gruff tenderness*). There, there, Annie. Don't be afeard. It's all past and gone.

MRS. KEENEY (*shrinking away from him*). Oh, I can't bear it ! I can't bear it any longer !

KEENEY (*gently*). Can't bear what, Annie ?

MRS. KEENEY (*hysterically*). All this horrible brutality, and these brutes of men, and this terrible ship, and this prison cell of a room, and the ice all around, and the silence.

(*After this outburst she calms down and wipes her eyes with her handkerchief.*)

KEENEY (*after a pause during which he looks down at her with a puzzled frown*). Remember, I warn't hankerin' to have you come on this voyage, Annie.

MRS. KEENEY. I wanted to be with you, David, don't you see ? I didn't want to wait back there in the house all alone as I've been doing these last six years since we were married—waiting, and watching, and fearing—with nothing to keep my mind occupied—not able to go back teaching school on account of being Dave Keeney's wife. I used to dream of sailing on the great, wide, glorious ocean. I wanted to be by your side in the danger and vigorous life of it all. I wanted to see you the hero they make you out to be in Homeport. And instead—— (*Her voice grows tremulous.*) All I find is ice and cold—and brutality ! (*Her voice breaks.*)

KEENEY. I warned you what it'd be, Annie. " Whalin' ain't no ladies' tea party," I says to you, and " you better stay to home where you've got all your woman's comforts." (*Shaking his head.*) But you was so set on it.

MRS. KEENEY (*wearily*). Oh, I know it isn't your fault, David. You see, I didn't believe you. I guess I was dreaming about the old Vikings in the story books and I thought you were one of them.

KEENEY (*protestingly*). I done my best to make it as cosy and comfortable as could be. (*Mrs. Keeney looks around her in wild scorn.*) I even sent to the city for that organ for ye, thinkin' it might be soothin' to ye to be playin' it times when they was calms and things was dull like.

MRS. KEENEY (*wearily*). Yes, you were very kind, David. I know that. (*She goes to left and lifts the curtains from the port-hole and looks out—then suddenly bursts forth.*) I won't stand it—I can't stand it—pent up by these walls like a prisoner. (*She runs over to him and throws her arms around him, weeping. He puts his arm protectingly over her shoulders.*) Take me away from here, David! If I don't get away from here, out of this terrible ship, I'll go mad! Take me home, David! I can't think any more. I feel as if the cold and the silence were crushing down on my brain. I'm afraid. Take me home!

KEENEY (*holds her at arm's length and looks at her face anxiously*). Best go to bed, Annie. You ain't yourself. You got fever. Your eyes look so strange like. I ain't never seen you look this way before.

MRS. KEENEY (*laughing hysterically*). It's the ice and the cold and the silence—they'd make any one look strange.

KEENEY (*soothingly*). In a month or two, with good luck, three at the most, I'll have her filled with ile and then we'll give her everything she'll stand and pint for home.

MRS. KEENEY. But we can't wait for that—I can't wait. I want to get home. And the men won't wait. They want to get home. It's cruel, it's brutal for you to keep them. You must sail back. You've got no excuse. There's clear water to the south now. If you've a heart at all you've got to turn back.

KEENEY (*harshly*). I can't, Annie.

MRS. KEENEY. Why can't you?

KEENEY. A woman couldn't rightly understand my reason.

MRS. KEENEY (*wildly*). Because it's a stupid, stubborn reason. Oh, I heard you talking with the second mate. You're afraid the other captains will sneer at you because you didn't come back with a full ship. You want to live up to your silly reputation even if you do have to beat and starve men and drive me mad to do it.

KEENEY (*his jaw set stubbornly*). It ain't that, Annie. Them skippers would never dare sneer to my face. It ain't so much what any one'd say—but—— (*He hesitates, struggling to express his meaning.*) You see—I've always done it—since my first voyage as skipper. I always come back—with a full ship—and—it don't seem right not to—somehow. I been always first whalin' skipper out o' Homeport, and—— Don't you see my meanin', Annie? (*He glances at her. She is not looking at him but staring dully in front of her, not hearing a word he is saying.*) Annie! (*She comes to herself with a start.*) Best turn in, Annie, there's a good woman. You ain't well.

MRS. KEENEY (*resisting his attempts to guide her to the door in rear*). David! Won't you please turn back?

KEENEY. (*gently*). I can't, Annie—not yet awhile. You don't see my meanin'. I got to git the ile.

MRS. KEENEY. It'd be different if you needed the money, but you don't. You've got more than plenty.

KEENEY (*impatiently*). It ain't the money I'm thinkin' of. D'you think I'm as mean as that?

MRS. KEENEY (*dully*). No—I don't know—I can't understand—— (*Intensely.*) Oh, I want to be home in the old house once more and see my own kitchen again, and hear a woman's voice talking to me and be able to talk to her. Two years! It seems so long ago—as if I'd been dead and could never go back.

KEENEY (*worried by her strange tone and the far-away look in her eyes*). Best go to bed, Annie. You ain't well.

MRS. KEENEY (*not appearing to hear him*). I used to be lonely when you were away. I used to think Homeport was a stupid, monotonous place. Then I used to go down on the beach, especially when it was windy and the breakers were rolling in, and I'd dream of the fine free life you must be leading. (*She gives a laugh which is half a sob.*) I used to love the sea then. (*She pauses; then continues with slow intensity.*) But now—I don't ever want to see the sea again.

KEENEY (*thinking to humour her*). 'Tis no fit

place for a woman, that's sure. I was a fool to bring ye.

MRS. KEENEY (*after a pause—passing her hand over her eyes with a gesture of pathetic weariness*). How long would it take us to reach home—if we started now?

KEENEY (*frowning*). 'Bout two months, I reckon, Annie, with fair luck.

MRS. KEENEY (*counts on her fingers—then murmurs with a rapt smile*). That would be August, the latter part of August, wouldn't it? It was on the twenty-fifth of August we were married, David, wasn't it?

KEENEY (*trying to conceal the fact that her memories have moved him—gruffly*). Don't *you* remember?

MRS. KEENEY (*vaguely—again passes her hand over her eyes*). My memory is leaving me—up here in the ice. It was so long ago. (*A pause—then she smiles dreamily.*) It's June now. The lilacs will be all in bloom in the front yard—and the climbing roses on the trellis to the side of the house—they're budding.

(*She suddenly covers her face with her hands and commences to sob.*)

KEENEY (*disturbed*). Go in and rest, Annie. You're all wore out cryin' over what can't be helped.

MRS. KEENEY (*suddenly throwing her arms around his neck and clinging to him*). You love me, don't you, David?

KEENEY (*in amazed embarrassment at this outburst*). Love you? Why d'you ask me such a question, Annie?

MRS. KEENEY (*shaking him—fiercely*). But you do, don't you, David? Tell me!

KEENEY. I'm your husband, Annie, and you're my wife. Could there be aught but love between us after all these years?

MRS. KEENEY (*shaking him again—still more fiercely*). Then you do love me. Say it!

KEENEY (*simply*). I do, Annie.

MRS. KEENEY (*gives a sigh of relief—her hands drop to her sides. Keeney regards her anxiously. She passes her hand across her eyes and murmurs half to herself.*) I sometimes think if we could only have had a child. (*Keeney turns away from her, deeply moved. She grabs his arm and turns him around to face her—intensely.*) And I've always been a good wife to you, haven't I, David?

KEENEY (*his voice betraying his emotion*). No man has ever had a better, Annie.

MRS. KEENEY. And I've never asked for much from you, have I, David? Have I?

KEENEY. You know you could have all I got the power to give ye, Annie.

MRS. KEENEY (*wildly*). Then do this this once for my sake, for God's sake—take me home! It's killing me, this life—the brutality and cold and horror of it. I'm going mad. I can feel the threat in the air. I can hear the silence threatening me—day after grey day and every day the same. I can't bear it. (*Sobbing.*) I'll go mad, I know I will. Take me home, David, if you love me as you say. I'm afraid. For the love of God, take me home!

(*She throws her arms around him, weeping against his shoulder. His face betrays the tremendous struggle going on within him. He holds her out at arm's length, his expression softening. For a moment his shoulders sag, he becomes old, his iron spirit weakens as he looks at her tear-stained face.*)

KEENEY (*dragging out the words with an effort*). I'll do it, Annie—for your sake—if you say it's needful for ye.

MRS. KEENEY (*with wild joy—kissing him*). God bless you for that, David!

(*He turns away from her silently and walks toward the companionway. Just at that moment there is a clatter of footsteps on the stairs and the Second Mate enters the cabin.*)

MATE (*excitedly*). The ice is breakin' up to no'the'ard, sir. There's a clear passage through the floe, and clear water beyond, the look-out says.

(*Keeney straightens himself like a man coming out of a trance. Mrs. Keeney looks at the Mate with terrified eyes.*)

KEENEY (*dazedly—trying to collect his thoughts*). A clear passage? To no'the'ard?

MATE. Yes, sir.

KEENEY (*his voice suddenly grim with determination*). Then get her ready and we'll drive her through.

MATE. Aye, aye, sir.

MRS. KEENEY (*appealingly*). David!

KEENEY (*not heeding her*). Will the men turn to willin' or must we drag 'em out?

MATE. They'll turn to willin' enough. You put the fear o' God into 'em, sir. They're meek as lambs.

KEENEY. Then drive 'em—both watches. (*With grim determination.*) They's whale t'other side o' this floe and we're going to git 'em.

MATE. Aye, aye, sir.

(*He goes out hurriedly. A moment later there is the sound of scuffling feet from the deck outside and the Mate's voice shouting orders.*)

KEENEY (*speaking aloud to himself—derisively*). And I was agoin' home like a yaller dog!

MRS. KEENEY (*imploringly*). David!

KEENEY (*sternly*). Woman, you ain't adoin' right when you meddle in men's business and weaken 'em. You can't know my feelin's. I got to prove a man to be a good husband for ye to take pride in. I got to git the ile, I tell ye.

MRS. KEENEY (*supplicatingly*). David! Aren't you going home?

KEENEY (*ignoring this question—commandingly*). You ain't well. Go and lay down a mite. (*He starts for the door.*) I got to git on deck. (*He goes out. She cries after him in anguish.*) David!

(*A pause. She passes her hand across her eyes—then commences to laugh hysterically and goes to the organ. She sits down and starts to play wildly an old hymn. Keeney re-enters from the doorway to the deck and stands looking at her angrily. He comes over and grabs her roughly by the shoulder.*)

KEENEY. Woman, what foolish mockin' is this? (*She laughs wildly and he starts back from her in alarm.*) Annie! What is it? (*She doesn't answer him. Keeney's voice trembles.*) Don't you know me, Annie?

(*He puts both hands on her shoulders and turns her around so that he can look into her eyes. She stares up at him with a stupid expression, a vague smile on her lips. He stumbles away from her, and she commences softly to play the organ again.*)

KEENEY (*swallowing hard—in a hoarse whisper, as if he had difficulty in speaking*). You said—you was a-goin' mad—God! (*A long wail is heard from the deck above.*) Ah bl-o-o-o-ow! (*A moment later the Mate's face appears through the skylight. He cannot see Mrs. Keeney.*)

MATE (*in great excitement*). Whales, sir—a whole school of 'em—off the star'b'd quarter 'bout five mile away—big ones!

KEENEY (*galvanized into action*). Are you lowerin' the boats?

MATE. Yes, sir.

KEENEY (*with grim decision*). I'm a-comin' with ye.

MATE. Aye, aye, sir. (*Jubilantly.*) You'll git the ile now right enough, sir. (*His head is withdrawn and he can be heard shouting orders.*)

KEENEY (*turning to his wife*). Annie! Did you hear him! I'll git the ile. (*She doesn't answer or seem to know he is there. He gives a hard laugh, which is almost a groan.*) I know you're foolin' me, Annie. You ain't out of your mind—(*anxiously*)—be you? I'll git the ile now right enough—jest a little while longer, Annie—then we'll turn hom'ard. I can't turn back now, you see that, don't ye? I've got to git the ile. (*In sudden terror.*) Answer me! You ain't mad, be you?

(*She keeps on playing the organ, but makes no reply. The Mate's face appears again through the skylight.*)

MATE. All ready, sir.

(*Keeney turns his back on his wife and strides to the doorway, where he stands for a moment and looks back at her in anguish, fighting to control his feelings.*)

MATE. Comin', sir?

KEENEY (*his face suddenly grown hard with determination*). Aye.

(He turns abruptly and goes out. Mrs. Keeney *does not appear to notice his departure. Her whole attention seems centred in the organ. She sits with half-closed eyes, her body swaying a little from side to side to the rhythm of the hymn. Her fingers move faster and faster and she is playing wildly and discordantly as*

THE CURTAIN FALLS

IN THE ZONE

A Play in One Act

Characters

SMITTY
DAVIS
SWANSON
SCOTTY
IVAN
PAUL
JACK
DRISCOLL
COCKY

(Seamen on the British tramp steamer, "Glencairn")

SCENE. *The seamen's forecastle. On the right above the bunks three or four port-holes covered with black cloth can be seen. On the floor near the doorway is a pail with a tin dipper. A lantern in the middle of the floor, turned down very low, throws a dim light around the place. Five men, Scotty, Ivan, Swanson, Smitty and Paul, are in their bunks apparently asleep. It is about ten minutes to twelve on a night in the autumn of the year* 1915.

Smitty turns slowly in his bunk and, leaning out over the side, looks from one to another of the men as if to assure himself that they are asleep. Then he climbs carefully out of his bunk and stands in the middle of the forecastle fully dressed, but in his stocking feet, glancing around him suspiciously. Reassured, he leans down and cautiously pulls out a suit-case from under the bunks in front of him.

Just at this moment Davis appears in the doorway, carrying a large steaming coffee-pot in his hand. He stops short when he sees Smitty. A puzzled expression comes over his face, followed by one of suspicion, and he retreats farther back in the alleyway, where he can watch Smitty without being seen.

All the latter's movements indicate a fear of discovery. He takes out a small bunch of keys and unlocks the suit-case, making a slight noise as he does so. Scotty wakes up and peers at him over the side of the bunk. Smitty opens the suit-case and takes out a small black tin box, carefully places this under his mattress, shoves the suit-case back under the bunk, climbs into his bunk again, closes his eyes and begins to snore loudly.

Davis enters the forecastle, places the coffee-pot beside the lantern, and goes from one to the other of the sleepers and shakes them vigorously, saying to each in a low voice : Near eight bells, Scotty. Arise and shine, Swanson. Eight bells, Ivan. *Smitty yawns loudly with a great pretence of having been dead asleep. All the rest of the men tumble out of their bunks, stretching and gaping, and commence to pull on their shoes. They go one by one to the cupboard near the open door, take out their cups and spoons, and sit down together on the benches. The coffee-pot is passed around. They munch their biscuits and sip their coffee in dull silence.*

DAVIS (*suddenly jumping to his feet—nervously*). Where's that air comin' from ? (*All are startled and look at him wonderingly.*)

SWANSON (*a squat, surly-faced Swede—grumpily*). What air? I don't feel nothing.

DAVIS (*excitedly*). I kin feel it—a draught. (*He stands on the bench and looks around—suddenly exploding.*) Damn fool square-head! (*He leans over the upper bunk in which Paul is sleeping and slams the port-hole shut.*) I got a good notion to report him. Serve him bloody well right! What's the use o' blindin' the ports when that thick-head goes an' leaves 'em open?

SWANSON (*yawning—too sleepy to be aroused by anything—carelessly*). Dey don't see what little light go out yust one port.

SCOTTY (*protestingly*). Dinna be a loon, Swanson! D'ye no ken the dangerr o' showin' a licht wi' a pack o' submarrines lyin' aboot?

IVAN (*shaking his shaggy ox-like head in an emphatic affirmative*). Dot's right, Scotty. I don' li-ike blow up, no, by devil!

SMITTY (*his manner slightly contemptuous*). I don't think there's much danger of meeting any of their submarines, not until we get into the War Zone, at any rate.

DAVIS (*he and Scotty look at Smitty suspiciously—harshly*). You don't, eh? (*He lowers his voice and speaks slowly.*) Well, we're in the war zone right this minit if you wants to know.

(*The effect of this speech is instantaneous. All sit bolt upright on their benches and stare at Davis.*)

SMITTY. How do you know, Davis?

DAVIS (*angrily*). 'Cos Drisc heard the First send the Third below to wake the skipper when we fetched the zone—'bout five bells, it was. Now whata y' got to say?

SMITTY (*conciliatingly*). Oh, I wasn't doubting your word, Davis; but you know they're not pasting up bulletins to let the crew know when the zone is reached—especially on ammunition ships like this.

IVAN (*decidedly*). I don't li-ike dees voyage. Next time I ship on windjammer Boston to River Plate, load with wood only so it float, by golly!

SWANSON (*fretfully*). I hope British navy blow 'em to hell, those submarines, py damn!

SCOTTY (*looking at Smitty, who is staring at the doorway in a dream, his chin on his hands. Meaningly*). It is no' the submarrines only we've to fear, I'm thinkin'.

DAVIS (*assenting eagerly*). That's no lie, Scotty.

SWANSON. You mean the mines?

SCOTTY. I wasna thinkin' o' mines eitherr.

DAVIS. There's many a good ship blown up and at the bottom of the sea, what never hit no mine or torpedo.

SCOTTY. Did ye neverr read of the Gerrman spies and the dirrty work they're doin' all the war?

(*He and Davis both glance at Smitty, who is deep in thought and is not listening to the conversation.*)

DAVIS. An' the clever way they fool you!

SWANSON. Sure; I read it in paper many time.

DAVIS. Well—(*he is about to speak but hesitates and finishes lamely*)—you got to watch out, that's all I says.

IVAN (*drinking the last of his coffee and slamming his fist on the bench explosively*). I tell you dis rotten coffee give me belly-ache, yes! (*They all look at him in amused disgust.*)

SCOTTY (*sardonically*). Dinna fret about it, Ivan. If we blow up ye'll no' be mindin' the pain in your middle.

(*Jack enters. He is a young American with a tough, good-natured face. He wears dungarees and a heavy jersey.*)

JACK. Eight bells, fellers.

IVAN (*stupidly*). I don't hear bell ring.

JACK. No, and yuh won't hear any ring, yuh boob—(*lowering his voice unconsciously*)—now we're in the war zone.

SWANSON (*anxiously*). Is the boats all ready?

JACK. Sure; we can lower 'em in a second.

DAVIS. A lot o' good the boats'll do, with us loaded deep with all kinds o' dynamite and stuff the like o' that! If a torpedo hits this hooker we'll all be in hell b'fore you could wink your eye.

JACK. They ain't goin' to hit us, see? That's my dope. Whose wheel is it?

IVAN (*sullenly*). My wheel. (*He lumbers out.*)

JACK. And whose look-out?

SWANSON. Mine, I tink. (*He follows Ivan.*)

JACK (*scornfully*). A hell of a lot of use keepin' a look-out! We couldn't run away or fight if we wanted to. (*To Scotty and Smitty.*) Better look up the bo'sun or the Fourth, you two, and let 'em see you're awake.

(*Scotty goes to the doorway and turns to wait for Smitty, who is still in the same position, head on hands, seemingly unconscious of everything. Jack slaps him roughly on the shoulder and he comes to with a start.*)

Aft and report, Duke! What's the matter with yuh—in a dope dream? (*Smitty goes out after Scotty without answering. Jack looks after him with a frown.*) He's a queer guy. I can't figger him out.

DAVIS. Nor no one else. (*Lowering his voice—meaningly.*) An' he's liable to turn out queerer than any of us think if we ain't careful.

JACK (*suspiciously*). What d'yuh mean?

(*They are interrupted by the entrance of Driscoll and Cocky.*)

COCKY (*protestingly*). Blimey if I don't fink I'll put in this 'ere watch ahtside on deck. (*He and Driscoll go over and get their cups.*) I down't want to be caught in this 'ole if they 'its us. (*He pours out coffee.*)

DRISCOLL (*pouring his*). Divil a bit ut wud matther where ye arre. Ye'd be blown to smithereens b'fore ye cud say your name. (*He sits down, overturning as he does so the untouched cup of coffee which Smitty had forgotten and left on the bench. They all jump nervously as the tin cup hits the floor with a bang. Driscoll flies into an unreasoning rage.*) Who's the dirty scut left this cup where a man 'ud sit on ut?

DAVIS. It's Smitty's.

DRISCOLL (*kicking the cup across the forecastle*). Does he think he's too much av a bloody gentleman to put his own away loike the rist av us? If he does I'm the bye'll beat that noshun out av his head.

COCKY. Be the airs 'e puts on you'd think 'e was the Prince of Wales. Wot's 'e doin' on a ship, I arsks yer? 'E ain't now good as a sailor, is 'e?—dawdlin' abaht on deck like a chicken wiv 'is 'ead cut orf!

JACK (*good-naturedly*). Aw, the Duke's all right. S'posin' he did ferget his cup—what's the dif? (*He picks up the cup and puts it away—with a grin.*) This war zone stuff's got yer goat, Drisc—and yours too, Cocky—and I ain't cheerin' much fur it myself, neither.

COCKY (*with a sigh*). Blimey, it ain't no bleedin' joke, yer first trip, to know as there's a ship full of shells li'ble to go orf in under your bloomin' feet, as you might say, if we gets 'it be a torpedo or mine. (*With sudden savagery.*) Calls theyselves 'uman bein's, too! Blarsted 'Uns!

DRISCOLL (*gloomily*). 'Tis me last trip in the bloody zone, God help me. The divil take their twenty-foive per cent. bonus—and be drowned like a rat in a trap in the bargain, maybe.

DAVIS. Wouldn't be so bad if she wasn't carryin' ammunition. Them's the kind the subs is layin' for.

DRISCOLL (*irritably*). Fur the love av hivin, don't be talkin' about ut. I'm sick wid thinkin' and jumpin' at iviry bit av a noise.

(*There is a pause during which they all stare gloomily at the floor.*)

JACK. Hey, Davis, what was you sayin' about Smitty when they come in?

DAVIS (*with a great air of mystery*). I'll tell you in a minit. I want to wait an' see if he's comin' back. (*Impressively.*) You won't be callin' him all right when you hears what I seen with my own eyes. (*He adds with an air of satisfaction.*) An' you won't be feelin' no safer, neither.

(*They all look at him with puzzled glances full of a vague apprehension.*)

DRISCOLL. God blarst ut!

(*He fills his pipe and lights it. The others, with an air of remembering something they had forgotten, do the same. Scotty enters.*)

SCOTTY (*in awed tones*). Mon, but it's clear outside the nicht! Like day.

DAVIS (*in low tones*). Where's Smitty, Scotty?

SCOTTY. Out on the hatch starin' at the moon like a mon half-daft.

DAVIS. Kin you see him from the doorway?

SCOTTY (*goes to doorway and carefully peeks out*). Aye; he's still there.

DAVIS. Keep your eyes on him for a moment. I've got something I wants to tell the boys and I don't want him walkin' in in the middle of it. Give a shout if he starts this way.

SCOTTY (*with suppressed excitement*). Aye, I'll watch him. And I've somethin' myself to tell aboot his Lordship.

DRISCOLL (*impatiently*). Out wid ut! You're talkin' more than a pair av auld women wud be standin' in the road, and gittin' no further along.

DAVIS. Listen! You 'member when I went to git the coffee, Jack?

JACK. Sure, I do.

DAVIS. Well, I brings it down here same as usual and got as far as the door there when I sees him.

JACK. Smitty?

DAVIS. Yes, Smitty! He was standin' in the middle of the fo'c'sle there—(*pointing*)—lookin' around sneakin'-like at Ivan and Swanson and the rest 's if he wants to make certain they're asleep.

(*He pauses significantly, looking from one to the other of his listeners. Scotty is nervously dividing his attention between Smitty on the hatch outside and Davis' story, fairly bursting to break in with his own revelations.*)

JACK (*impatiently*). What of it?

DAVIS. Listen! He was standin' right there —(*pointing again*)—in his stockin' feet—no shoes on, mind, so he wouldn't make no noise!

JACK (*spitting disgustedly*). Aw!

DAVIS (*not heeding the interruption*). I seen right away somethin' on the queer was up, so I slides back into the alleyway where I kin see him but he can't see me. After he makes sure they're all asleep he goes in under the bunks there—bein' careful not to raise a noise, mind!—an' takes out his bag there. (*By this time every one, Jack included, is listening breathlessly to his story.*) Then he fishes in his pocket an' takes out a bunch o' keys an' kneels down beside the bag an' opens it.

SCOTTY (*unable to keep silent longer*). Mon, didn't I see him do that same thing wi' these two eyes. 'Twas just that moment I woke and spied him.

DAVIS (*surprised, and a bit nettled to have to share his story with any one*). Oh, you seen him, too, eh? (*To the others.*) Then Scotty kin tell you if I'm lyin' or not.

DRISCOLL. An' what did he do whin he'd the bag opened?

DAVIS. He bends down and reaches out his hand sort o' scared-like, like it was somethin' dang'rous he was after, an' feels round in under his duds—hidden in under his duds an' wrapped up in 'em, it was—an' he brings out a black iron box!

COCKY (*looking around him with a frightened glance*). Gawd blimey!

(*The others likewise betray their uneasiness, shuffling their feet nervously.*)

DAVIS. Ain't that right, Scotty!

SCOTTY. Right as rain, I'm tellin' ye!

DAVIS (*to the others with an air of satisfaction*). There you are! (*Lowering his voice.*) An' then what d'you suppose he did? Sneaks to his bunk an' slips the black box in under his mattress—in under his mattress, mind!

JACK. And it's there now?

DAVIS. Course it is!

(*Jack starts toward Smitty's bunk. Driscoll grabs him by the arm.*)

DRISCOLL. Don't be touchin' ut, Jack!

JACK. Yuh needn't worry. I ain't goin' to touch it. (*He pulls up Smitty's mattress and looks down. The others stare at him, holding their breaths. He turns to them, trying hard to assume a careless tone.*) It's there, aw right.

COCKY (*miserably upset*). I'm gointer 'op it aht on deck. (*He gets up, but Driscoll pulls him down again. Cocky protests.*) It fair guvs me the trembles sittin' still in 'ere.

DRISCOLL (*scornfully*). Are ye frightened, ye toad? 'Tis a hell av a thing fur grown men to be shiverin' loike childer at a bit av a black box. (*Scratching his head in uneasy perplexity.*) Still, ut's damn queer, the looks av ut.

DAVIS (*sarcastically*). A bit of a black box, eh?

How big d'you think them—(*he hesitates*)—things has to be—big as this fo'c'sle?

JACK (*in a voice meant to be reassuring*). Aw, hell! I'll bet it ain't nothin' but some coin he's saved he's got locked up in there.

DAVIS (*scornfully*). That's likely, ain't it? Then why does he act so s'picious? He's been on ship near two year, ain't he? He knows damn well there ain't no thiefs in this fo'c'sle, don't he? An' you know 's well 's I do he didn't have no money when he came on board an' he ain't saved none since. Don't you? (*Jack doesn't answer.*) Listen! D'you know what he done after he put that thing in under his mattress?—an' Scotty'll tell you if I ain't speakin' truth. He looks round to see if any one's woke up——

SCOTTY. I clapped my eyes shut when he turned round.

DAVIS. An' then he crawls into his bunk an shut his eyes, an' starts in *snorin'*, *pretendin'* he was asleep, mind!

SCOTTY. Aye, I could hear him.

DAVIS. An' when I goes to call him I don't even shake him. I just says, "Eight bells, Smitty," in a'most a whisper-like, an' up he gets yawnin' an' stretchin' fit to kill hisself 's if he'd been dead asleep.

COCKY. Gawd blimey!

DRISCOLL (*shaking his head*). Ut looks bad, divil a doubt av ut.

DAVIS (*excitedly*). An' now I come to think of it, there's the port-hole. How'd it come to git open, tell me that? I know'd well Paul never opened it. Ain't he grumblin' about bein' cold all the time?

SCOTTY. The mon that opened it meant no good to this ship, whoever he was.

JACK (*sourly*). What port-hole? What're yuh talkin' about?

DAVIS (*pointing over Paul's bunk*). There. It was open when I come in. I felt the cold air on my neck an' shut it. It woulda been clear's a lighthouse to any sub that was watchin'—an' we s'posed to have all the ports blinded! Who'd do a dirty trick like that? It wasn't none of us, nor Scotty here, nor Swanson, nor Ivan. Who would it be, then?

COCKY (*angrily*). Musta been 'is bloody Lordship.

DAVIS. For all we know he mighta been signallin' with it. They does it like that by winkin' a light. Ain't you read how they gets caught doin' it in London an' on the coast?

COCKY (*firmly convinced now*). An' wots 'e doin' aht alone on the 'atch—keepin' 'isself clear of us like 'e was afraid?

DRISCOLL. Kape your eye on him, Scotty.

SCOTTY. There's no' a move oot o' him.

JACK (*in irritated perplexity*). But, hell, ain't he an Englishman? What'd he wanta——

DAVIS. English? How d'we know he's English? Cos he talks it? That ain't no proof. Ain't you read in the papers how all them German spies they been catchin' in England has been livin' there for ten, often as not twenty years, an' talks English as good's any one? An' look here, ain't you noticed he don't talk natural? He talks it too damn good, that's what I mean. He don't talk exactly like a toff, does he, Cocky?

COCKY. Not like any toff as I ever met up wiv.

DAVIS. No; an' he don't talk it like us, that's certain. An' he don't look English. An' what d'we know about him when you come to look at it? Nothin'! He ain't ever said where he comes from or why. All we knows is he ships on here in London 'bout a year b'fore the war starts, as an A.B.—stole his papers most lik'ly—when he don't know how to box the compass, hardly. Ain't that queer in itself? An' was he ever open with us like a good shipmate? No; he's always had that sly air about him 's if he was hidin' somethin'.

DRISCOLL (*slapping his thigh—angrily*). Divil take me if I don't think ye have the truth av ut, Davis.

COCKY (*scornfully*). Lettin' on be 'is silly airs, and all, 'e's the son of a blarsted earl or somethink!

DAVIS. An' the name he calls hisself—Smith! I'd risk a quid of my next pay day that his real name is Schmidt, if the truth was known.

JACK (*evidently fighting against his own conviction*). Aw, say, you guys give me a pain! What'd they want puttin' a spy on this old tub for?

DAVIS (*shaking his head sagely*). They're deep ones, an' there's a lot o' things a sailor'll see in the ports he puts in ought to be useful to 'em. An' if he kin signal to 'em an' they blows us up it's one ship less, ain't it? (*Lowering his voice and indicating Smitty's bunk.*) Or if he blows us up hisself.

SCOTTY (*in alarmed tones*). Hush, mon! Here he comes!

(*Scotty hurries over to a bench and sits down. A thick silence settles over the forecastle. The men look from one to another with uneasy glances. Smitty enters and sits down beside his bunk. He is seemingly unaware of the dark glances of suspicion directed at him from all sides. He slides his hand back stealthily over his mattress and his fingers move, evidently feeling to make sure the box is still there. The others follow this movement carefully with quick looks out of the corners of their eyes. Their attitudes grow tense as if they were about to spring at him. Satisfied the box is safe, Smitty draws his hand away slowly and utters a sigh of relief.*)

SMITTY (*in a casual tone which to them sounds sinister*). It's a good light night for the subs if there's any about.

(*For a moment he sits staring in front of him. Finally he seems to sense the hostile atmosphere of the forecastle and looks from one to the other of the men in surprise. All of them avoid his eyes. He sighs with a puzzled expression and gets up and walks out of the doorway. There is silence for a moment after his departure and then a storm of excited talk breaks loose.*)

DAVIS. Did you see him feelin' if it was there?

COCKY. 'E ain't 'arf a sly one wiv 'is talk of submarines, Gawd blind 'im!

SCOTTY. Did ye see the sneakin' looks he gave us?

DRISCOLL. If ivir I saw black shame on a man's face 'twas on his whin he sat there!

JACK (*thoroughly convinced at last*). He looked bad to me. He's a crook, aw right.

DAVIS (*excitedly*). What'll we do? We gotter do somethin' quick, or——

(*He is interrupted by the sound of something hitting against the port side of the forecastle with a dull, heavy thud. The men start to their feet in wild-eyed terror and turn as if they were going to rush for the deck. They stand that way for a strained moment, scarcely breathing and listening intently.*)

JACK (*with a sickly smile*). Hell! It's on'y a piece of driftwood or a floatin' log. (*He sits down again.*)

DAVIS (*sarcastically*). Or a mine that didn't go off—that time—or a piece o' wreckage from some ship they've sent to Davy Jones.

COCKY (*mopping his brow with a trembling hand*). Blimey! (*He sinks back weakly on a bench.*)

DRISCOLL (*furiously*). God blarst ut! No man at all cud be puttin' up wid the loike av this—an' I'm not wan to be fearin' anything or any man in the worrld'll stand up to me face to face; but this divil's trickery in the darrk—— (*He starts for Smitty's bunk.*) I'll throw ut out wan av the port-holes an' be done wid ut. (*He reaches toward the mattress.*)

SCOTTY (*grabbing his arm—wildly*). Arre ye daft, mon?

DAVIS. Don't monkey with it, Drisc. I knows what to do. Bring the bucket o' water here, Jack, will you? (*Jack gets it and brings it over to Davis.*) An' you, Scotty, see if he's back on the hatch.

SCOTTY (*cautiously peering out*). Aye, he's sittin' there the noo.

DAVIS. Sing out if he makes a move. Lift up the mattress, Drisc—careful now! (*Driscoll does so with infinite caution.*) Take it out, Jack—careful—don't shake it now, for Christ's sake! Here—put it in the water—easy! There, that's fixed it! (*They all sit down with great sighs of relief.*) The water'll git in and spoil it.

DRISCOLL (*slapping Davis on the back*). Good wurrk for ye, Davis, ye scut! (*He spits on his hands aggressively.*) An' now what's to be done wid that black-hearted thraitor?

COCKY (*belligerently*). Guv 'im a shove in the marf and 'eave 'im over the side!

DAVIS. An' serve him right!

JACK. Aw, say, give him a chance. Yuh can't prove nothin' till yuh find out what's in there.

DRISCOLL (*heatedly*). Is ut more proof ye'd be needin' afther what we've seen an' heard? Then listen to me—an' ut's Driscoll talkin'—if there's divilmint in that box an' we see plain 'twas his plan to murrdher his own shipmates that have served him fair—— (*He raises his fist.*) I'll choke his rotten hearrt out wid me own hands, an' over the side wid him, and one man missin' in the mornin'.

DAVIS. An' no one the wiser. He's the balmy kind what commits suicide.

COCKY. They 'angs spies ashore.

JACK (*resentfully*). If he's done what yuh think I'll croak him myself. Is that good enough for yuh?

DRISCOLL (*looking down at the box*). How'll we be openin' this, I wonder?

SCOTTY (*from the doorway—warningly*). He's standin' up.

DAVIS. We'll take his keys away from him when he comes in. Quick, Drisc! You an' Jack get beside the door and grab him. (*They get on either side of the door. Davis snatches a small coil of rope from one of the upper bunks.*) This'll do for me an' Scotty to tie him.

SCOTTY. He's turrnin' this way—he's comin'! (*He moves away from the door.*)

DAVIS. Stand by to lend a hand, Cocky.

COCKY. Right-o!

(*As Smitty enters the forecastle he is seized roughly from both sides and his arms pinned behind him. At first he struggles fiercely, but seeing the uselessness of this, he finally stands calmly and allows Davis and Scotty to tie up his arms.*)

SMITTY (*when they have finished—with cola contempt*). If this is your idea of a joke I'll have to confess it's a bit too thick for me to enjoy.

COCKY (*angrily*). Shut yer marf, 'ear!

DRISCOLL (*roughly*). Ye'll find ut's no joke, me bucko, b'fore we're done wid you. (*To Scotty.*) Kape your eye peeled, Scotty, and sing out if any one's comin'. (*Scotty resumes his post at the door.*)

SMITTY (*with the same icy contempt*). If you'd be good enough to explain——

DRISCOLL (*furiously*). Explain, is ut? 'Tis you'll do the explainin'—an' damn quick, or we'll know the reason why. (*To Jack and Davis.*) Bring him here, now. (*They push Smitty over to the bucket.*) Look here, ye murrdherin' swab. D'you see ut? (*Smitty looks down with an expression of amazement which rapidly changes to one of anguish.*)

DAVIS (*with a sneer*). Look at him! S'prised, ain't you? If you wants to try your dirty spyin' tricks on us you've gotter git up earlier in the mornin'.

COCKY. Thorght yer weren't 'arf a fox, didn't yer?

SMITTY (*trying to restrain his growing rage*). What—what do you mean? That's only—How dare—What are you doing with my private belongings?

COCKY (*sarcastically*). Ho yus! Private b'longings!

DRISCOLL (*shouting*). What is ut, ye swine? Will you tell us to our faces? What's in ut?

SMITTY (*biting his lips—holding himself in check with a great effort*). Nothing but—— That's my business. You'll please attend to your own.

DRISCOLL. Oho, ut is, is ut? (*Shaking his fist in Smitty's face.*) Talk aisy now if ye know what's best for you. Your business, indade! Then we'll be makin' ut ours, I'm thinkin'. (*To Jack and Davis.*) Take his keys away from him an' we'll see if there's one'll open ut, maybe. (*They start in searching Smitty, who tries to resist and kicks out at the bucket. Driscoll leaps forward and helps them push him away.*) Try to kick ut over, wud ye? Did ye see him then? Tryin' to murrdher us all, the scut! Take that pail out av his way, Cocky.

(*Smitty struggles with all of his strength and keeps them busy for a few seconds. As Cocky grabs the pail Smitty makes a final effort and, lunging forward, kicks again at the bucket, but only succeeds in hitting Cocky on the shin. Cocky immediately sets down the pail with a bang and, clutching his knee in both hands, starts hopping around the forecastle, groaning and swearing.*)

COCKY. Ooow! Gawd strike me pink! Kicked me, 'e did! Bloody, bleedin', rotten Dutch 'og! (*Approaching Smitty, who has given up the fight and is pushed back against the wall near the doorway with Jack and Davis holding him on either side—wrathfully, at the top of his lungs.*) Kick me, will yer? I'll show yer what for, yer bleedin' sneak! (*He draws back his fist. Driscoll pushes him to one side.*)

DRISCOLL. Shut your mouth! D'you want to wake the whole ship? (*Cocky grumbles and retires to a bench, nursing his sore shin.*)

JACK (*taking a small bunch of keys from Smitty's pocket.*) Here yuh are, Drisc.

DRISCOLL (*taking them*). We'll soon be knowin'.

(*He takes the pail and sits down, placing it on the floor between his feet. Smitty again tries to break loose, but he is too tired and is easily held back against the wall.*)

SMITTY (*breathing heavily and very pale*). Cowards!

JACK (*with a growl*). Nix on the rough talk, see! That don't git yuh nothin'.

DRISCOLL (*looking at the lock on the box in the water and then scrutinizing the keys in his hand*). This'll be ut, I'm thinkin'. (*He selects one and gingerly reaches his hand in the water.*)

SMITTY (*his face grown livid—chokingly*). Don't you open that box, Driscoll. If you do, so help me God, I'll kill you if I have to hang for it.

DRISCOLL (*pausing—his hand in the water*). Whin I open this box I'll not be the wan to be kilt, me sonny bye! I'm no dirty spy.

SMITTY (*his voice trembling with rage. His eyes are fixed on Driscoll's hand*). Spy? What are you talking about? I only put that box there so I could get it quick in case we were torpedoed. Are you all mad? Do you think I'm—— (*Chokingly.*) You stupid curs! You cowardly dolts! (*Davis claps his hand over Smitty's mouth.*)

DAVIS. That'll be enough from you!

(*Driscoll takes the dripping box from the water and starts to fit in the key. Smitty springs forward furiously, almost escaping from their grasp, and drags them after him half-way across the forecastle.*)

DRISCOLL. Hold him, ye divils!

(*He puts the box back in the water and jumps to their aid. Cocky hovers on the outskirts of the battle, mindful of the kick he received.*)

SMITTY (*raging*). Cowards! Damn you! Rotten curs! (*He is thrown to the floor and held there.*) Cowards! Cowards!

DRISCOLL. I'll shut your dirty mouth for you. (*He goes to his bunk and pulls out a big wad of waste and comes back to Smitty.*)

SMITTY. Cowards! Cowards!

DRISCOLL (*with no gentle hand slaps the waste over Smitty's mouth*). That'll teach you to be misnamin' a man, ye sneak. Have ye a handkerchief, Jack? (*Jack hands him one and he ties it tightly around Smitty's head over the waste.*) That'll fix your gab. Stand him up, now, and tie his feet, too, so he'll not be movin'. (*They do so and leave him with his back against the wall near Scotty. Then they all sit down beside Driscoll, who again lifts the box out of the water and sets it carefully on his knees. He picks out the key, then hesitates, looking from one to the other uncertainly.*) We'd best be takin' this to the skipper, d'you think, maybe?

JACK (*irritably*). To hell with the Old Man. This is our game and we c'n play it without no help.

COCKY. Now bleedin' horficers, I says!

DAVIS. They'd only be takin' all the credit and makin' heroes of theyselves.

DRISCOLL (*boldly*). Here goes, thin! (*He slowly turns the key in the lock. The others instinctively turn away. He carefully pushes the cover back on its hinges and looks at what he sees inside with an expression of puzzled astonishment. The others crowd up close. Even Scotty leaves his post to take a look.*) What is ut, Davis?

DAVIS (*mystified*). Looks funny, don't it? Somethin' square tied up in a rubber bag. Maybe it's dynamite—or somethin'—you can't never tell.

JACK. Aw, it ain't got no works so it ain't no bomb, I'll bet.

DAVIS (*dubiously*). They makes them all kinds, they do.

JACK. Open it up, Drisc.

DAVIS. Careful now!

(*Driscoll takes a black rubber bag resembling a large tobacco pouch from the box and unties the string which is wound tightly around the top. He opens it and takes out a small packet of letters also tied up with string. He turns these over in his hands and looks at the others questioningly.*)

JACK (*with a broad grin*). On'y letters! (*Slapping Davis on the back.*) Yuh're a hell of a Sherlock Holmes, ain't yuh? Letters from his best girl too, I'll bet. Let's turn the Duke loose, what d'yuh say? (*He starts to get up.*)

DAVIS (*fixing him with a withering look*). Don't be so damn smart, Jack. Letters, you says, 's if there never was no harm in 'em. How d'you s'pose spies gets their orders and sends back what they finds out if it ain't by letters and such things? There's many a letter is worser'n any bomb.

COCKY. Right-o! They ain't as innercent as they looks, I'll take me oath, when you read 'em. (*Pointing at Smitty.*) Not 'is Lordship's letters; not be no means!

JACK (*sitting down again*). Well, read 'em and find out.

(*Driscoll commences untying the packet. There is a muffled groan of rage and protest from Smitty.*)

DAVIS (*triumphantly*). There! Listen to him! Look at him tryin' to git loose! Ain't that proof enough? He knows well we're findin' him out. Listen to me! Love letters, you says, Jack, 's if they couldn't harm nothin'. Listen! I was readin' in some magazine in New York on'y two weeks back how some German spy in Paris was writin' love letters to some woman spy in Switzerland who sent 'em on to Berlin, Germany. To read 'em you wouldn't s'pect nothin'—just mush and all. (*Impressively.*) But they had a way o' doin' it—a damn sneakin' way. They had a piece o' plain paper with pieces cut out of it an' when they puts it on top o' the letter they sees on'y the words what tells them what they wants to know. An' the Frenchies gets beat in a fight all on account o' that letter.

COCKY (*awed*). Gawd blimey! They ain't 'arf smart bleeders!

DAVIS (*seeing his audience is again all with him*). An' even if these letters of his do sound all right they may have what they calls a code. You can't never tell. (*To Driscoll, who has finished untying the packet.*) Read one of 'em, Drisc. My eyes is weak.

DRISCOLL (*takes the first one out of its envelope and bends down to the lantern with it. He turns up the wick to give him a better light.*) I'm no hand to be readin', but I'll try ut.

(*Again there is a muffled groan from Smitty as he strains at his bonds.*)

DAVIS (*gloatingly*). Listen to him! He knows. Go ahead, Drisc!

DRISCOLL (*his brow furrowed with concentration*). Ut begins: Dearest Man—— (*His eyes travel down the page.*) An' thin there's a lot av blarney tellin' him how much she misses him now she's gone away to singin' school—an' how she hopes he'll settle down to rale worrk an' not be skylarkin' around now that she's away loike he used to before she met up wid him—and ut ends: "I love you betther than anythin' in the worrld. You know that, don't you, dear? But b'fore I can agree to live out my life wid you, you must prove to me that the black shadow—I won't menshun uts hateful name, but you know what I mean—which might wreck both our lives, does not exist for you. You can do that, can't you, dear? Don't you see you must for my sake?" (*He pauses for a moment—then adds gruffly.*) Uts signed: "Edith."

(*At the sound of the name, Smitty, who has stood tensely with his eyes shut as if he were undergoing torture during the reading, makes a muffled sound like a sob and half turns his face to the wall.*)

JACK (*sympathetically*). Hell! What's the use of readin' that stuff even if——

DAVIS (*interrupting him sharply*). Wait! Where's that letter from, Drisc?

DRISCOLL. There's no address on the top av ut.

DAVIS (*meaningly*). What'd I tell you? Look at the postmark, Drisc,—on the envelope.

DRISCOLL. The name that's written is Sidney Davidson, wan hundred an'——

DAVIS. Never mind that. O' course it's a false name. Look at the postmark.

DRISCOLL. There's a furrin stamp on ut by the looks av ut. The mark's blurred so it's hard to read. (*He spells it out laboriously.*) B-e-r—the nixt is an l, I think—i—an' an n.

DAVIS (*excitedly*). Berlin! What did I tell you? I knew them letters was from Germany.

COCKY (*shaking his fist in Smitty's direction*). Rotten 'ound!

(*The others look at Smitty as if this last fact had utterly condemned him in their eyes.*)

DAVIS. Give me the letter, Drisc. Maybe I kin make somethin' out of it. (*Driscoll hands the letter to him.*) You go through the others, Drisc, and sing out if you sees anythin' queer. (*He bends over the first letter as if he were determined to figure out its secret meaning. Jack, Cocky and Scotty look over his shoulder with eager curiosity. Driscoll takes out some of the other letters, running his eyes quickly down the pages. He looks curiously over at Smitty from time to time, and sighs frequently with a puzzled frown.*)

DAVIS (*disappointedly*). I gotter give it up. It's too deep for me, but we'll turn 'em over to the perlice when we docks at Liverpool to look through. This one I got was written a year before the war started, anyway. Find anythin' in yours, Drisc?

DRISCOLL. They're all the same as the first—lovin' blarney, an' how her singin' is doin', and the great things the Dutch teacher says about her voice, an' how glad she is that her Sidney bye is worrkin' harrd an' makin' a man av himself for her sake.

(*Smitty turns his face completely to the wall.*)

DAVIS (*disgustedly*). If we on'y had the code!

DRISCOLL (*taking up the bottom letter*). Hullo! Here's wan addressed to this ship—s.s. *Glencairn*, ut says—whin we was in Cape Town sivin months ago—— (*Looking at the postmark.*) Ut's from London.

DAVIS (*eagerly*). Read it! (*There is another choking groan from Smitty.*)

DRISCOLL (*reads slowly—his voice becomes lower and lower as he goes on*). Ut begins wid simply the name Sidney Davidson—no dearest or sweetheart to this wan. "Ut is only from your chance meetin' wid Harry—whin you were drunk—that I happen to know where to reach you. So you have run away to sea loike the coward you are because you knew I had found out the truth—the truth you have covered over with your mean little lies all the time I was away in Berlin and blindly trusted you. Very well, you have chosen. You have shown that your drunkenness means more to you than any love or faith av mine. I am sorry—for I loved you, Sidney Davidson—but this is the end. I lave you—the mem'ries; an' if ut is any satisfaction to you I lave you the real-i-zation that you have wrecked my loife as you have wrecked your own. My one remainin' hope is that nivir in God's worrld will I ivir see your face again. Good-bye. Edith."

(*As he finishes there is a deep silence, broken only by Smitty's muffled sobbing. The men cannot look at each other. Driscoll holds the rubber bag limply in his hand and some small white object falls out of it and drops noiselessly on the floor. Mechanically Driscoll leans over and picks it up, and looks at it wonderingly.*)

DAVIS (*in a dull voice*). What's that?

DRISCOLL (*slowly*). A bit av a dried-up flower,—a rose, maybe.

(*He drops it into the bag and gathers up the letters and puts them back. He replaces the bag in the box, and locks it and puts it back under Smitty's mattress. The others follow him with their eyes. He steps softly over to Smitty and cuts the ropes about his arms and ankles with his sheath knife, and unties the handkerchief over the gag. Smitty does not turn around, but covers his face with his hands and leans his head against the wall. His shoulders continue to heave spasmodically, but he makes no further sound.*)

DRISCOLL (*stalks back to the others—there is a moment of silence, in which each man is in agony with the hopelessness of finding a word he can say—then Driscoll explodes*). God stiffen us, are we never goin' to turn in fur a wink av sleep?

(*They all start as if awakening from a bad dream and gratefully crawl into their bunks, shoes and all, turning their faces to the wall, and pulling their blankets up over their shoulders. Scotty tiptoes past Smitty out into the darkness. Driscoll turns down the light and crawls into his bunk as*)

THE CURTAIN FALLS

THE LONG VOYAGE HOME

A Play in One Act

Characters

FAT JOE, *proprietor of a low public-house*
NICK, *a crimp*
MAG, *a barmaid*
OLSON, DRISCOLL, COCKY, IVAN — *Seaman of the British tramp steamer, "Glencairn"*
KATE
FREDA
TWO ROUGHS

The action of the play takes place in the years preceding the outbreak of World War I

SCENE. *The bar of a low public-house near the London docks—a squalid, dingy room, dimly lighted by oil lamps placed in brackets on the walls. On the left, the bar. In front of it, a door leading to a side room. On the right, tables with chairs round them. In the rear, a door leading to the street.*

A slovenly barmaid with a stupid face sodden with drink is mopping up the bar. Her arm moves back and forth mechanically and her eyes are half shut as if she were dozing on her feet. At the far end of the bar stands Fat Joe, the proprietor, a gross bulk of a man with an enormous stomach. His face is red and bloated, his little piggish eyes being almost concealed by rolls of fat. The thick fingers of his big hands are loaded with cheap rings and a gold watch-chain of cable-like proportions stretches across his checked waistcoat.

At one of the tables, front, a round-shouldered young fellow is sitting, smoking a cigarette. His face is pasty, his mouth weak, his eyes shifting and cruel. He is dressed in a shabby suit, which must have once been cheaply flashy, and wears a muffler and cap.

It is about nine o'clock in the evening.

JOE (*yawning*). Blimey if bizness ain't 'arf slow to-night. I donnow wot's 'appened. The place is like a bleedin' tomb. Where's all the sailor men, I'd like to know? (*Raising his voice.*) Ho, you Nick! (*Nick turns round listlessly.*) Wot's the name o' that wessel put in at the dock below jest arter noon?

NICK (*laconically*). *Glencairn*—from Bewnezerry (Buenos Aires).

JOE. Ain't the crew been paid orf yet?

NICK. Paid orf this arternoon, they tole me. I 'opped on board of 'er an' seen 'em. 'Anded 'em some o' yer cards, I did. They promised faithful they'd 'appen in to-night—them as whose time was done.

JOE. Any two-year men to be paid orf?

NICK. Four—three Britishers an' a square-'ead.

JOE (*indignantly*). An' yer popped orf an' left 'em? An' me a-payin' yer to 'elp an' bring 'em in 'ere!

NICK (*grumblingly*). Much you pays me! An' I ain't slingin' me 'ook abaht the 'ole bleedin' town fur now man. See?

JOE. I ain't speakin' on'y fur meself. Down't I always give yer yer share, fair an' square, as man to man?

NICK (*with a sneer*). Yus—b'cause you 'as to.

JOE. 'As to? Listen to 'im! There's many'd be 'appy to 'ave your berth, me man!

NICK. Yus? Wot wiv the peelers li'ble to put me away in the bloody jail fur crimpin', an' all?

JOE (*indignantly*). We down't do no crimpin'.

NICK (*sarcastically*). Ho, now! Not 'arf!

JOE (*a bit embarrassed*). Well, on'y a bit now an' agen when there ain't no reg'lar trade. (*To hide his confusion he turns to the barmaid angrily. She is still mopping up the bar, her chin on her breast, half-asleep.*) 'Ere, me gel, we've 'ad enough o' that. You been a-moppin', an' a-moppin', an' a-moppin' the blarsted bar fur a 'ole 'our. 'Op it aht o' this! You'd fair guv a bloke the shakes a-watchin' yer.

MAG (*beginning to sniffle*). Ow, you do frighten me when you 'oller at me, Joe. I ain't a bad gel, I ain't. Gawd knows I tries to do me best fur you. (*She bursts into a tempest of sobs.*)

JOE (*roughly*). Stop yer grizzlin'! An' 'op it aht of 'ere!

NICK (*chuckling*). She's drunk, Joe. Been 'ittin' the gin, eh, Mag?

MAG (*ceases crying at once and turns on him furiously*). You little crab, you! Orter wear a muzzle, you ort! A-openin' of your ugly mouth to a 'onest woman what ain't never done you no 'arm. (*Commencing to sob again.*) H'abusin' me like a dawg cos I'm sick an' orf me oats, an' all.

JOE. Orf yer go, me gel! Go hupstairs and 'ave a sleep. I'll wake yer if I wants yer. An' wake the two gels when yer goes hup. It's 'arpas' nine an' time as some one was a-comin' in, tell 'em. D'yer 'ear me?

MAG (*stumbling around the bar to the door on left—sobbing*). Yus, yus, I 'ears you. Gawd knows wot's goin' to 'appen to me, I'm that sick. Much you cares if I dies, down't you? (*She goes out.*)

JOE (*still brooding over Nick's lack of diligence—after a pause*). Four two-year men paid orf wiv their bloody pockets full o' sovereigns—an' yer lorst 'em. (*He shakes his head sorrowfully.*)

NICK (*impatiently*). Stow it! They promised faithful they'd come, I tells yer. They'll be walkin' in in 'arf a mo'. There's lots o' time yet. (*In a low voice.*) 'Ave yer got the drops? We might wanter use 'em.

JOE (*taking a small bottle from behind the bar*). Yus; 'ere it is.

NICK (*with satisfaction*). Right-o! (*His shifty eyes peer about the room searchingly. Then he beckons to Joe, who comes over to the table and sits down.*) Reason I arst yer about the drops was 'cause I seen the capt'n of the *Amindra* this arter-noon.

JOE. The *Amindra*? Wot ship is that?

NICK. Bloody windjammer—skys'l yarder—full rigged—painted white—been layin' at the dock above 'ere fur a month. You knows 'er.

JOE. Ho, yus. I knows now.

NICK. The capt'n says as 'e wants a man special bad—ter-night. They sails at daybreak ter-morrer.

JOE. There's plenty o' 'ands lyin' abaht waitin' fur ships, I should fink.

NICK. Not fur this ship, ole buck. The capt'n an' mate are bloody slave-drivers, an' they'r bound down round the 'Orn. They 'arf starved the 'ands on the larst trip 'ere, an' no one'll dare ship on 'er. (*After a pause.*) I promised the capt'n faithful I'd get 'im one, and ter-night.

JOE (*doubtfully*). An' 'ow are yer goin' to git 'im?

NICK (*with a wink*). I was thinkin' as one of em from the *Glencairn*'d do—them as was paid orf an' is comin' 'ere.

JOE (*with a grin*). It'd be a good 'aul, that's the troof. (*Frowning.*) If they comes 'ere.

NICK. They'll come, an' they'll all be rotten drunk, wait an' see. (*There is the noise of loud, boisterous singing from the street.*) Sounds like 'em, now. (*He opens the street door and looks out.*) Gawd blimey if it ain't the four of 'em! (*Turning to Joe in triumph.*) Naw, what d'yer say? They're lookin' for the place. I'll go aht an' tell 'em.

(*He goes out. Joe gets into position behind the bar, assuming his most oily smile. A moment later the door is opened, admitting Driscoll, Cocky, Ivan and Olson. Driscoll is a tall, powerful Irishman; Cocky, a wizened runt of a man with a straggling grey moustache; Ivan, a hulking oaf of a peasant; Olson, a stocky, middle-aged Swede with round, childish blue eyes. The first three are all very drunk, especially Ivan, who is managing his legs with difficulty. Olson is perfectly sober. All are dressed in their ill-fitting shore clothes and look very uncomfortable. Driscoll has unbuttoned his stiff collar and its ends stick out sideways. He has lost his tie. Nick slinks into the room after them and sits down at a table in rear. The seamen come to the table, front.*)

JOE (*with affected heartiness*). Ship ahoy, mates! 'Appy to see yer 'ome safe an' sound.

DRISCOLL (*turns round, swaying a bit, and peers at him across the bar*). So ut's you, is ut? (*He looks about the place with an air of recognition.*) 'An the same damn rat's-hole, sure enough. I remimber foive or six years back 'twas here I was sthripped av me last shillin' whin I was aslape. (*With sudden fury.*) God stiffen ye, come none av your dog's thricks on me this trip or I'll—— (*He shakes his fist at Joe.*)

JOE (*hastily interrupting*). Yer must be mistaiken. This is a 'onest place, this is.

COCKY (*derisively*). Ho, yus! An' you're a bleedin' angel, I s'pose?

IVAN (*vaguely taking off his hat and putting it on again—plaintively*). I don' li-ike dis place.

DRISCOLL (*going over to the bar—as genial as he was furious a moment before*). Well, no matther, 'tis all past an' gone an' forgot. I'm not the man to be holdin' harrd feelin's on me first night ashore, an' me dhrunk as a lord. (*He holds out his hand, which Joe takes very gingerly.*) We'll all be havin' a dhrink, I'm thinkin'. Whiskey for the three av us—*Irish* whiskey!

COCKY (*mockingly*). An' a glarse o' ginger beer fur our blarsted love-child 'ere. (*He jerks his thumb at Olson.*)

OLSON (*with a good-natured grin*). I bane a good boy dis night, for one time.

DRISCOLL (*bellowing, and pointing to Nick as Joe brings the drinks to the table*). An' see what that crimpin' son av a crimp'll be wantin'—an' have your own pleasure. (*He pulls a sovereign out of his pocket and slams it on the bar.*)

NICK. Guv me a pint o' beer, Joe.

(*Joe draws the beer and takes it down to the far end of the bar. Nick comes over to get it and Joe gives him a significant wink and nods toward the door on the left. Nick signals back that he understands.*)

COCKY (*drink in hand—impatiently*). I'm that bloody dry! (*Lifting his glass to Driscoll.*) Cheero, ole dear, cheero!

DRISCOLL (*pocketing his change without looking at it*). A toast for ye: Hell roast that divil av a bo'sun! (*He drinks.*)

COCKY. Right-o! Gawd strike 'im blind! (*He drains his glass.*)

IVAN (*half-asleep*). Dot's gude.

(*He tosses down his drink in one gulp. Olson sips his ginger ale. Nick takes a swallow of his beer and then comes round the bar and goes out the door on left.*)

COCKY (*producing a sovereign*). Ho there, you Fatty! Guv us another!

JOE. The saime, mates?

COCKY. Yus.

DRISCOLL. No, ye scut! I'll be havin' a pint av beer. I'm dhry as a loime kiln.

IVAN (*suddenly getting to his feet in a befuddled manner and nearly upsetting the table*). I don' li-ike dis place! I wan' see girls—plenty girls. (*Pathetically.*) I don' li-ike dis place. I wan' dance with girl.

DRISCOLL (*pushing him back on his chair with a

thud). Shut up, ye Rooshan baboon! A foine Romeo you'd make in your condishun. (*Ivan blubbers some incoherent protest—then suddenly falls asleep.*)

JOE (*bringing the drinks—looks at Olson*). An' you, matey?

OLSON (*shaking his head*). Noting dis time, thank you.

COCKY (*mockingly*). A-saivin' of 'is money, 'e is! Goin' back to 'ome an' mother. Goin' to buy a bloomin' farm an' punch the blarsted dirt, that's wot 'e is! (*Spitting disgustedly.*) There's a funny bird of a sailor man for yer, Gawd blimey!

OLSON (*wearing the same good-natured grin*). Yust what I like, Cocky. I wus on farm long time when I wus kid.

DRISCOLL. Lave him alone, ye bloody insect! 'Tis a foine sight to see a man wid some sense in his head instead av a damn fool the loike av us. I only wisht I'd a mother alive to call me own. I'd not be dhrunk in this divil's hole this minute, maybe.

COCKY (*commencing to weep dolorously*). Ow, down't talk, Drisc! I can't bear to 'ear you. I ain't never 'ad no mother, I ain't——

DRISCOLL. Shut up, ye ape, an' don't be makin' that squealin'. If ye cud see your ugly face, wid the big red nose av ye all screwed up in a knot, ye'd never shed a tear the rist av your loife. (*Roaring into song.*) We ar-re the byes av We-e-exford who fought wid hearrt an' hand! (*Speaking.*) To hell wid Ulster! (*He drinks and the others follow his example.*) An' I'll strip to any man in the city av London won't dhrink to that toast.

(*He glares truculently at Joe, who immediately downs his beer. Nick enters again from the door on the left and comes up to Joe and whispers in his ear. The latter nods with satisfaction.*)

DRISCOLL (*glowering at them*). What divil's thrick are ye up to now, the two av ye? (*He flourishes a brawny fist.*) Play fair wid us or ye deal wid me!

JOE (*hastily*). No trick, shipmate! May Gawd kill me if that ain't troof!

NICK (*indicating Ivan, who is snoring*). On'y your mate there was arskin' fur gels an' I thorght as 'ow yer'd like 'em to come dawhn and 'ave a wet wiv yer.

JOE (*with a smirking wink*). Pretty, 'olesome gels they be, ain't they, Nick?

NICK. Yus.

COCKY. Aar! I knows the gels you 'as, not 'arf! They'd fair blind yer, they're that 'omely. None of yer bloomin' gels fur me, ole Fatty. Me an' Drisc knows a place, down't we, Drisc?

DRISCOLL. Divil a lie, we do. An' we'll be afther goin' there in a minute. There's music there an' a bit av a dance to liven a man.

JOE. Nick, 'ere, can play yer a tune, can't yer, Nick?

NICK. Yus.

JOE. An' yer can 'ave a dance in the side room 'ere.

DRISCOLL. Hurroo! Now you're talkin'. (*The two women, Freda and Kate, enter from the left. Freda is a little, sallow-faced blonde. Kate is stout and dark.*)

COCKY (*in a loud aside to Driscoll*). Gawd blimey, look at 'em! Ain't they 'orrible? (*The women come forward to the table, wearing their best set smiles.*)

FREDA (*in a rasping voice*). 'Ullo, mates.

KATE. 'Ad a good voyage?

DRISCOLL. Rotten; but no matther. Welcome, as the sayin' is, an' sit down, an' what'll ye be takin' for your thirst? (*To Kate.*) You'll be sittin' by me, darlin'—what's your name?

KATE (*with a stupid grin*). Kate. (*She stands by his chair.*)

DRISCOLL (*putting his arm around her*). A good Irish name, but you're English by the trim av ye, an' be damned to you. But no matther. Ut's fat ye are, Katy dear, an' I never cud endure skinny wimin. (*Freda favours him with a viperish glance and sits down by Olson.*) What'll ye have?

OLSON. No, Drisc. Dis one bane on me.

(*He takes out a roll of notes from his inside pocket and lays one on the table. Joe, Nick, and the women look at the money with greedy eyes. Ivan gives a particularly violent snore.*)

FREDA. Waike up your fren'. Gawd, 'ow I 'ates to 'ear snorin'.

DRISCOLL (*springing to action, smashes Ivan's hat over his ears*). D'you hear the lady talkin' to ye, ye Rooshan swab? (*The only reply to this is a snore. Driscoll pulls the battered remains of the hat off Ivan's head and smashes it back again.*) Arise an' shine, ye dhrunken swine!

(*Another snore. The women giggle. Driscoll throws the beer left in his glass into Ivan's face. The Russian comes to in a flash, spluttering. There is a roar of laughter.*)

IVAN (*indignantly*). I tell you—dot's someting I don' li-ike!

COCKY. Down't waste good beer, Drisc.

IVAN (*grumblingly*). I tell you—dot is not ri-ight.

DRISCOLL. Ut's your own doin', Ivan. Ye was moanin' for girrls an' whin they come you sit gruntin' loike a pig in a sty. Have ye no manners? (*Ivan seems to see the women for the first time and grins foolishly.*)

KATE (*laughing at him*). Cheero, ole chum, 'ows Russha?

IVAN (*greatly pleased—putting his hand in his pocket*). I buy a drink.

OLSON. No; dis one bane on me. (*To Joe.*) Hey, you faller!

JOE. Wot'll it be, Kate?

KATE. Gin.

FREDA. Brandy.

DRISCOLL. An' Irish whiskey for the rist av us—wid the excipshun av our timperance friend, God pity him!

FREDA (*to Olson*). You ain't drinkin'?

OLSON (*half-ashamed*). No.

FREDA (*with a seductive smile*). I down't blame yer. You got sense, you 'ave. I on'y tike a nip o' brandy now an' agen fur my 'ealth.

(*Joe brings the drinks and Olson's change. Cocky gets unsteadily to his feet and raises his glass in the air.*)

COCKY. 'Ere's a toff toast for yer: The ladies, Gawd—(*he hesitates—then adds in a grudging tone*)—bless 'em.

KATE (*with a silly giggle*). Oo-er! That wasn't what you was goin' to say, you bad Cocky, you! (*They all drink.*)

DRISCOLL (*to Nick*). Where's the tune ye was promisin' to give us?

NICK. Come ahn in the side 'ere an' you'll 'ear it.

DRISCOLL (*getting up*). Come on, all av ye. We'll have a tune an' a dance if I'm not too dhrunk to dance, God help me.

(*Cocky and Ivan stagger to their feet. Ivan can hardly stand. He is leering at Kate and snickering to himself in a maudlin fashion. The three, led by Nick, go out by the door on the left. Kate follows them. Olson and Freda remain seated.*)

COCKY (*calling over his shoulder*). Come on an' dance, Ollie.

OLSON. Yes, I come.

(*He starts to get up. From the side room comes the sound of an accordion and a boisterous whoop from Driscoll, followed by a heavy stamping of feet.*)

FREDA. Ow, down't go in there. Stay 'ere an' 'ave a talk wiv me. They're all drunk an' you ain't drinkin'. (*With a smile up into his face.*) I'll think yer don't like me if yer goes in there.

OLSON (*confused*). You wus wrong, Miss Freda. I don't—I mean I do like you.

FREDA (*smiling—puts her hand over his on the table*). An' I likes you. Yer a genelman. You don't get drunk an' hinsult poor gels wot 'as a 'ard an' uneppy life.

OLSON (*pleased, but still more confused—wriggling his feet*). I bane drunk many time, Miss Freda.

FREDA. Then why ain't yer drinkin' now? (*She exchanges a quick, questioning glance with Joe, who nods back at her—then she continues persuasively.*) Tell me somethin' abaht yeself.

OLSON (*with a grin*). There ain't noting to say, Miss Freda. I bane poor devil sailor man, dat's all.

FREDA. Where was you born—Norway? (*Olson shakes his head.*) Denmark?

OLSON. No. You guess once more.

FREDA. Then it must be Sweden.

OLSON. Yes. I wus born in Stockholm.

FREDA (*pretending great delight*). Ow, ain't

that funny! I was born there, too—in Stockholm.

OLSON (*astonished*). You wus born in Sweden?

FREDA. Yes; you wouldn't think it, but it's Gawd's troof. (*She claps her hands delightedly.*)

OLSON (*beaming all over*). You speak Swedish?

FREDA (*trying to smile sadly*). Now. Y'see my ole man an' woman come 'ere to England when I was on'y a baby an' they was speakin' English b'fore I was old enough to learn. Sow I never knew Swedish. (*Sadly.*) Wisht I 'ad! (*With a smile.*) We'd 'ave a bloomin' lark of it if I 'ad, wouldn't we?

OLSON. It sounds nice to hear the old talk yust once in a time.

FREDA. Right-o! No place like yer 'ome, I says. Are yer goin' up to—to Stockholm b'fore yer ship's away agen?

OLSON. Yes. I go home from here to Stockholm. (*Proudly.*) As passenger!

FREDA. An' you'll git another ship up there arter you've 'ad a 'oliday?

OLSON. No. I don't never ship on sea no more. I got all sea I want for my life—too much hard work for little money. Yust work, work, work on ship. I don't want more.

FREDA. Ow, I see. That's why you give up drinkin'.

OLSON. Yes. (*With a grin.*) If I drink I yust get drunk and spend all money.

FREDA. But if you ain't gointer be a sailor no more, what'll yer do? You been a sailor all yer life, ain't yer?

OLSON. No. I work on farm till I am eighteen. I like it, too—it's nice—work on farm.

FREDA. But ain't Stockholm a city same's London? Ain't no farms there, is there?

OLSON. We live—my brother and mother live—my father iss dead—on farm yust a little way from Stockholm. I have plenty money, now. I go back with two years' pay and buy more land yet; work on farm. (*Grinning.*) No more sea, no more bum grub, no more storms—yust nice work.

FREDA. Ow, ain't that luv'ly! I s'pose you'll be gittin' married, too?

OLSON (*very much confused*). I don't know. I like to, if I find nice girl, maybe.

FREDA. Ain't yer got some gel back in Stockholm? I bet yer 'as.

OLSON. No. I got nice girl once before I go on sea. But I go on ship, and I don't come back, and she marry other faller. (*He grins sheepishly.*)

FREDA. Well, it's nice for yer to be goin' 'ome, anyway.

OLSON. Yes. I tank so.

(*There is a crash from the room on left and the music abruptly stops. A moment later Cocky and Driscoll appear, supporting the inert form of Ivan between them. He is in the last stage of intoxication, unable to move a muscle. Nick follows them and sits down at the table in rear.*)

DRISCOLL (*as they zigzag up to the bar*). Ut's dead he is, I'm thinkin', for he's as limp as a blarsted corpse.

COCKY (*puffing*). Gawd, 'e ain't 'arf 'eavy!

DRISCOLL (*slapping Ivan's face with his free hand*). Wake up, ye divil, ye. Ut's no use. Gabriel's trumpet itself cudn't rouse him. (*To Joe.*) Give us a dhrink, for I'm perishing wid the thirst. 'Tis harrd worrk, this.

JOE. Whiskey?

DRISCOLL. *Irish* whiskey, ye swab.

(*He puts down a coin on the bar. Joe serves Cocky and Driscoll. They drink and then swerve over to Olson's table.*)

OLSON. Sit down and rest for time, Drisc.

DRISCOLL. No, Ollie, we'll be takin' this lad home to his bed. Ut's late for wan so young to be out in the night. An' I'd not trust him in this hole as dhrunk as he is, an' him wid a full pay day on him. (*Shaking his fist at Joe.*) Oho, I know your games, me sonny bye!

JOE (*with an air of grievance*). There yer goes again—hinsultin' a 'onest man!

COCKY. Ho, listen to 'im! Guv 'im a shove in the marf, Drisc.

OLSON (*anxious to avoid a fight—getting up*). I help you take Ivan to boarding house.

FREDA (*protestingly*). Ow, you ain't gointer leave me, are yer? An' we 'avin' sech a nice talk, an' all.

DRISCOLL (*with a wink*). Ye hear what the lady says, Ollie. Ye'd best stay here, me timperance lady's man. An' we need no help. 'Tis only a bit av a way and we're two strong men if we are dhrunk. Ut's no hard shift to take the remains home. But ye can open the door for us, Ollie. (*Olson goes to the door and opens it.*) Come on, Cocky, an' don't be fallin' aslape yourself. (*They lurch toward the door. As they go out Driscoll shouts back over his shoulder.*) We'll be comin' back in a short time, surely. So wait here for us, Ollie.

OLSON. All right. I wait here, Drisc.

(*He stands in the doorway uncertainly. Joe makes violent signs to Freda to bring him back. She goes over and puts her arm around Olson's shoulder. Joe motions to Nick to come to the bar. They whisper together excitedly.*)

FREDA (*coaxingly*). You ain't gointer leave me, are yer, dearie? (*Then irritably.*) Fur Gawd's sake, shet that door! I'm fair freezin' to death wiv the fog.

(*Olson comes to himself with a start and shuts the door.*)

OLSON (*humbly*). Excuse me, Miss Freda.

FREDA (*leading him back to the table—coughing*). Buy me a drink o' brandy, will yer? I'm sow cold.

OLSON. All you want, Miss Freda, all you want. (*To Joe, who is still whispering instructions to Nick.*) Hey, Yoe! Brandy for Miss Freda. (*He lays a coin on the table.*)

JOE. Right-o! (*He pours out her drink and brings it to the table.*) 'Avin' somethink yeself, shipmate?

OLSON. No. I don't tank so. (*He points to his glass with a grin.*) Dis iss only belly-wash, no? (*He laughs.*)

JOE (*hopefully*). 'Ave a man's drink.

OLSON. I would like to—but no. If I drink one I want drink one tousand. (*He laughs again.*)

FREDA (*responding to a vicious nudge from Joe's elbow*). Ow, tike somethin'. I ain't gointer drink all be meself.

OLSON. Den give me a little yinger beer—small one.

(*Joe goes back of the bar, making a sign to Nick to go to their table. Nick does so and stands so that the sailor cannot see what Joe is doing.*)

NICK (*to make talk*). Where's yer mates popped orf ter?

(*Joe pours the contents of the little bottle into Olson's glass of ginger beer.*)

OLSON. Dey take Ivan, dat drunk faller, to bed. They come back.

(*Joe brings Olson's drink to the table and sets it before him.*)

JOE (*to Nick—angrily*). 'Op it, will yer? There ain't no time to be dawdlin'. See? 'Urry!

NICK. Down't worry, ole bird, I'm orf. (*He hurries out the door. Joe returns to his place behind the bar.*)

OLSON (*after a pause—worriedly*). I tank I should go after dem. Cocky iss very drunk, too, and Drisc——

FREDA. Aar! The big Irish is all right. Don't yer 'ear 'im say as 'ow they'd surely come back 'ere, an' fur you to wait fur 'em?

OLSON. Yes; but if dey don't come soon I tank I go see if dey are in boarding house all right.

FREDA. Where is the boardin' 'ouse?

OLSON. Yust little way back from street here.

FREDA. You stayin' there, too?

OLSON. Yes—until steamer sail for Stockholm—in two day.

FREDA (*she is alternately looking at Joe and feverishly trying to keep Olson talking so he will forget about going away after the others*). Yer mother won't be 'arf glad to see yer agen, will she? (*Olson smiles.*) Does she know yer comin'?

OLSON. No. I tought I would yust give her surprise. I write to her from Bonos Eres but I don't tell her I come home.

FREDA. Must be old, ain't she, yer ole lady?

OLSON. She iss eighty-two. (*He smiles reminiscently.*) You know, Miss Freda, I don't see my mother or my brother in—let me tank—(*he counts laboriously on his fingers*)—must be more than ten year. I write once in while and she write many time; and my brother he write me, too. My mother say in all letter I should come home right away. My brother he write same ting, too. He want me to help him on farm. I write back always I come soon; and I mean all time to go back home at end of voyage. But I come ashore, I take one drink, I take many drinks, I get drunk, I spend all money, I have to ship away for other voyage. So dis time I say to myself: Don't drink one drink, Ollie, or, sure, you don't get home. And I want go home dis time. I feel homesick for farm and to see my people again. (*He smiles.*) Yust like little boy, I feel homesick. Dat's why I don't drink noting to-night but dis—belly-wash! (*He roars with childish laughter, then suddenly becomes serious.*) You know, Miss Freda, my mother get very old, and I want see her. She might die and I would never——

FREDA (*moved a lot in spite of herself*). Ow, don't talk like that! I jest 'ates to 'ear any one speakin' abaht dyin'.

(*The door to the street is opened and Nick enters, followed by two rough-looking, shabbily-dressed men, wearing mufflers, with caps pulled down over their eyes. They sit at the table nearest to the door. Joe brings them three beers, and there is a whispered consultation, with many glances in the direction of Olson.*)

OLSON (*starting to get up—worriedly*). I tank I go round to boarding house. I tank someting go wrong with Drisc and Cocky.

FREDA. Ow, down't go. They kin take care of theyselves. They ain't babies. Wait 'arf a mo'. You ain't 'ad yer drink yet.

JOE (*coming hastily over to the table, indicates the men in the rear with a jerk of his thumb*). One of them blokes wants yer to 'ave a wet wiv 'im.

FREDA. Right-o! (*To Olson.*) Let's drink this. (*She raises her glass. He does the same.*) 'Ere's a toast fur yer: Success to yer bloomin' farm an' may yer live long an' 'appy on it. Skoal!

(*She tosses down her brandy. He swallows half his glass of ginger beer and makes a wry face.*)

OLSON. Skoal! (*He puts down his glass.*)

FREDA (*with feigned indignation*). Down't yer like my toast?

OLSON (*grinning*). Yes. It iss very kind, Miss Freda.

FREDA. Then drink it all like I done.

OLSON. Well—— (*He gulps down the rest.*) Dere! (*He laughs.*)

FREDA. Done like a sport!

ONE OF THE ROUGHS (*with a laugh*). *Amindra* ahoy!

NICK (*warningly*). Sssshh!

OLSON (*turns around in his chair*). *Amindra?* Iss she in port? I sail on her once long time ago—three mast, full rig, skys'l yarder? Iss dat ship you mean?

THE ROUGH (*grinning*). Yus; right you are.

OLSON (*angrily*). I know dat damn ship—worst ship dat sail to sea. Rotten grub and dey make you work all time—and the Captain and Mate wus Bluenose devils. No sailor who know anyting ever ship on her. Where iss she bound from here?

THE ROUGH. Round Cape 'Orn—sails at daybreak.

OLSON. Py yingo, I pity poor fallers make dat trip round Cape Stiff dis time year. I bet you some of dem never see port once again. (*He passes his hand over his eyes in a dazed way. His voice grows weaker.*) Py golly, I feel dizzy. All the room go round and round like I wus drunk. (*He gets weakly to his feet.*) Good night, Miss Freda. I bane feeling sick. Tell Drisc—I go home. (*He takes a step forward and suddenly collapses over a chair, rolls to the floor, and lies there unconscious.*)

JOE (*from behind the bar*). Quick, nawh!

(*Nick darts forward with Joe following. Freda is already beside the unconscious man and has taken the roll of money *from his inside pocket. She strips off a note furtively and shoves it into her bosom, trying to conceal her action, but Joe sees her. She hands the roll to Joe, who pockets it. Nick goes through all the other pockets and lays a handful of change on the table.)*

JOE (*impatiently*). 'Urry, 'urry, can't yer? The other blokes'll be 'ere in 'arf a mo'. (*The two roughs come forward.*) 'Ere, you two, tike 'im in under the arms like 'e was drunk. (*They do so.*) Tike 'im to the *Amindra*—yer knows that, don't yer?—two docks above. Nick'll show yer. An' you, Nick, down't yer leave the bleedin' ship till the capt'n guvs yer this bloke's advance —full month's pay—five quid, d'yer 'ear?

NICK. I knows me bizness, ole bird.

(*They support Olson to the door.*)

THE ROUGH (*as they are going out*). This silly bloke'll 'ave the s'prise of 'is life when 'e wakes up on board of 'er.

(*They laugh. The door closes behind them. Freda moves quickly for the door on the left, but Joe gets in her way and stops her.*)

JOE (*threateningly*). Guv us what yer took!

FREDA. Took? I guv yer all 'e 'ad.

JOE. Yer a liar! I seen yer a-playin' yer sneakin' tricks, but yer can't fool Joe. I'm too old a 'and. (*Furiously.*) Guv it to me, yer bloody cow! (*He grabs her by the arm.*)

FREDA. Lemme alone! I ain't got no——

JOE (*hits her viciously on the side of the jaw. She crumples up on the floor.*) That'll learn yer!

(*He stoops down and fumbles in her bosom and pulls out the bank-note, which he stuffs into his pocket with a grunt of satisfaction. Kate opens the door on the left and looks in—then rushes to Freda and lifts her head up in her arms.*)

KATE (*gently*). Pore dearie! (*Looking at Joe angrily.*) Been 'ittin' 'er agen, 'ave yer, yer cowardly swine!

JOE. Yus; an' I'll 'it you, too, if yer don't keep yer marf shut. Tike 'er aht of 'ere!

(*Kate carries Freda into the next room. Joe goes behind the bar. A moment later the outer door is opened and Driscoll and Cocky come in.*)

DRISCOLL. Come on, Ollie. (*He suddenly sees that Olson is not there, and turns to Joe.*) Where is ut he's gone to?

JOE (*with a meaning wink*). 'E an' Freda went aht t'gether 'bout five minutes past. 'E's fair gone on 'er, 'e is.

DRISCOLL (*with a grin*). Oho, so that's ut, is ut? Who'd think Ollie'd be sich a divil wid the wimin? 'Tis lucky he's sober or she'd have him stripped to his last ha'penny. (*Turning to Cocky, who is blinking sleepily.*) What'll ye have, ye little scut? (*To Joe.*) Give me whiskey, *Irish* whiskey!

CURTAIN

THE MOON OF THE CARIBBEES

A Play in One Act

Characters

YANK, DRISCOLL, OLSON, DAVIS, COCKY, SMITTY, PAUL — *Seaman of the British tramp steamer, "Glencairn"*
LAMPS, *the lamptrimmer*
CHIPS, *the carpenter*
OLD TOM, *the donkeyman*
BIG FRANK, DICK, MAX, PADDY — *Firemen on the "Glencairn"*
BELLA, SUSIE, VIOLET, PEARL — *West Indian Negresses*
THE FIRST MATE
Two other seamen – SCOTTY and IVAN – and several other members of the stokehole-engine-room crew

The action of the play takes place in the years preceding the outbreak of World War I

SCENE. *A forward section of the main deck of the British tramp steamer Glencairn, at anchor off an island in the West Indies. The full moon, half-way up the sky, throws a clear light on the deck. The sea is calm and the ship motionless.*

On the left two of the derrick booms of the foremast jut out at an angle of forty-five degrees, black against the sky. In the rear the dark outline of the port bulwark is sharply defined against a distant strip of coral beach, white in the moonlight, fringed with coco palms whose tops rise clear of the horizon. On the right is the forecastle with an open doorway in the centre leading to the seamen's and firemen's quarters. On either side of the doorway are two closed doors opening on the quarters of the Bo'sun, the ship's carpenter, the messroom steward, and the donkeyman—what might be called the petty officers of the ship. Near each bulwark there is also a short staircase, like a section of fire escape, leading up to the forecastle head (the top of the forecastle)—the edge of which can be seen on the right.

In the centre of the deck, and occupying most of the space, is the large, raised square of the number one hatch, covered with canvas, battened down for the night.

A melancholy negro chant, faint and far-off, drifts, crooning, over the water.

Most of the seamen and firemen are reclining

or sitting on the hatch. Paul is leaning against the port bulwark, the upper part of his stocky figure outlined against the sky. Smitty and Cocky are sitting on the edge of the forecastle head with their legs dangling over. Nearly all are smoking pipes or cigarettes. The majority are dressed in patched suits of dungaree. Quite a few are in their bare feet and some of them, especially the firemen, have nothing on but a pair of trousers and a vest. A good many wear caps.

There is the low murmur of different conversations going on in the separate groups as the curtain rises. This is followed by a sudden silence in which the singing from the land can be plainly heard.

DRISCOLL (*a powerfully built Irishman who is sitting on the edge of the hatch, front—irritably*). Will ye listen to them naygurs? I wonder now, do they call that keenin' a song?

SMITTY (*a young Englishman with a blond moustache. He is sitting on the forecastle head looking out over the water with his chin supported on his hands*). It doesn't make a chap feel very cheerful, does it? (*He sighs.*)

COCKY (*a wizened runt of a man with a straggling grey moustache—slapping Smitty on the back*). Cheero, ole dear! Down't be ser dawhn in the marf, Duke. She loves yer.

SMITTY (*gloomily*). Shut up, Cocky! (*He turns away from Cocky and falls to dreaming again, staring toward the spot on shore where the singing seems to come from.*)

BIG FRANK (*a huge fireman sprawled out on the right of the hatch—waving a hand towards the land*). They bury somebody—py chimminy Christmas, I tink so from way it sound.

YANK (*a rather good-looking rough who is sitting beside Driscoll*). What d'yuh mean, bury? They don't plant 'em down here, Dutchy. They eat 'em to save fun'ral expenses. I guess this guy went down the wrong way an' they got indigestion.

COCKY. Indigestion! Ho yus, not 'arf! Down't yer know as them blokes 'as two stomachs like a bleedin' camel?

DAVIS (*a short, dark man seated on the right of hatch*). An' you seen the two, I s'pect, ain't you?

COCKY (*scornfully*). Down't be showin' yer igerance be tryin' to make a mock o' me what has seen more o' the world than yeself ever will.

MAX (*a Swedish fireman—from the rear of hatch*). Spin dat yarn, Cocky.

COCKY. It's Gawd's troof, what I tole yer. I 'eard it from a bloke what was captured pris'ner by 'em in the Solomon Islands. Shipped wiv 'im one voyage. 'Twas a rare treat to 'ear 'im tell what 'appened to 'im among 'em. (*Musingly.*) 'E was a funny bird, 'e was—'ailed from Mile End, 'e did.

DRISCOLL (*with a snort*). Another lyin' Cockney, the loike av yourself!

LAMPS (*a fat Swede who is sitting on a campstool in front of his door talking with Chips*). Where you meet up with him, Cocky?

CHIPS (*a lanky Scotchman—derisively*). In New Guinea, I'll lay my oath!

COCKY (*defiantly*). Yus! It *was* in New Guinea, time I was shipwrecked there. (*There is a perfect storm of groans and laughter at this speech.*)

YANK (*getting up*). Yuh know what we said yuh'd get if yuh sprung any of that lyin' New Guinea dope on us again, don't yuh? Close that trap if yuh don't want a duckin' over the side.

COCKY. Ow, I was on'y tryin' to edicate yer a bit. (*He sinks into dignified silence.*)

YANK (*nodding toward the shore*). Don't yuh know this is the West Indies, yuh crazy mut? There ain't no cannibals here. They're only common niggers.

DRISCOLL (*irritably*). Whativir they are, the divil take their cryin'. It's enough to give a man the jigs listenin' to 'em.

YANK (*with a grin*). What's the matter, Drisc? Yuh're as sore as a boil about somethin'.

DRISCOLL. I'm dyin' wid impatience to have a dhrink; an' that blarsted bumboat naygur woman took her oath she'd bring back rum enough for the lot av us whin she came back on board to-night.

BIG FRANK (*overhearing this—in a loud eager voice*). You say the bumboat voman vill bring booze?

DRISCOLL (*sarcastically*). That's right—tell the Old Man about ut, an' the Mate, too. (*All of the crew have edged nearer to Driscoll and are listening to the conversation with an air of suppressed excitement. Driscoll lowers his voice impressively and addresses them all.*) She said she cud snake ut on board in the bottoms av thim baskets av fruit they're goin' to bring wid 'em to sell to us for'ard.

THE DONKEYMAN (*an old grey-headed man with a kindly, wrinkled face. He is sitting on a camp-stool in front of his door, right front*). She'll be bringin' some black women with her this time—or times has changed since I put in here last.

DRISCOLL. She said she wud—two or three—more, maybe, I dunno. (*This announcement is received with great enthusiasm by all hands.*)

COCKY. Wot a bloody lark!

OLSON. Py yingo, we have one hell of a time!

DRISCOLL (*warningly*). Remimber ye must be quiet about ut, ye scuts—wid the dhrink, I mane—ivin if the bo'sun is ashore. The Old Man ordered her to bring no booze on board or he wudn't buy a thing off av her for the ship.

PADDY (*a squat, ugly Liverpool Irishman*). To the divil wid him!

BIG FRANK (*turning on him*). Shud up, you tamn fool, Paddy! You vant make trouble? (*To Driscoll.*) You und me, ve keep dem quiet, Drisc.

DRISCOLL. Right ye are, Dutchy. I'll split the skull av the first wan av ye starts to foight. (*Three bells are heard striking.*)

DAVIS. Three bells. When's she comin', Drisc?

DRISCOLL. She'll be here any minute now, surely. (*To Paul, who has returned to his position by the bulwark after hearing Driscoll's news.*) D'you see 'em comin', Paul?

PAUL. I don't see anyting like bumboat.

(*They all set themselves to wait, lighting pipes, cigarettes, and making themselves comfortable. There is a silence broken only by the mournful singing of the negroes on shore.*)

SMITTY (*slowly—with a trace of melancholy*). I wish they'd stop that song. It makes you think of—well—things you ought to forget. Rummy go, what?

COCKY (*slapping him on the back*). Cheero, ole love! We'll be 'avin' our rum in arf a mo', Duke. (*He comes down to the deck, leaving Smitty alone on the forecastle head.*)

BIG FRANK. Sing someting, Drisc. Den ve don't hear dot yelling.

DAVIS. Give us a chanty, Drisc.

PADDY. Wan all av us knows.

MAX. We all sing in on chorus.

OLSON. "Rio Grande," Drisc.

BIG FRANK. No, ve don't know dot. Sing "Viskey Johnny."

CHIPS. "Flyin' Cloud."

COCKY. Now! Guv us "Maid o' Amsterdam."

LAMPS. "Santa Anna" iss good one.

DRISCOLL. Shut your mouths, all av you. (*Scornfully.*) A chanty is ut ye want? I'll bet me whole pay day there's not wan in the crowd 'ceptin' Yank here, an' Ollie, an' meself, an' Lamps an' Cocky, maybe, wud be sailors enough to know the main from the mizzen on a windjammer. Ye've heard the names av chanties but divil a note av the tune or a loine av the words do ye know. There's hardly a rale deep-water sailor lift on the seas, more's the pity.

YANK. Give us "Blow the Man Down." We all know some of that. (*A chorus of assenting voices: Yes!—Righto!—Let 'er drive!—Start 'er, Drisc! etc.*)

DRISCOLL. Come in then, all av ye. (*He sings.*) As I was a-roamin' down Paradise Street—

ALL. Wa-a-ay, blow the man down!

DRISCOLL. As I was a-roamin' down Paradise Street—

ALL. Give us some time to blow the man down!

CHORUS

Blow the man down, boys, oh, blow
the man down!
Wa-a-ay, blow the man down!
As I was a-roamin' down Paradise
Street—
Give us some time to blow the
man down!

DRISCOLL. A pretty young maiden I chanced for to meet.

ALL. Wa-a-ay, blow the man down!

DRISCOLL. A pretty young maiden I chanced for to meet.

ALL. Give us some time to blow the man down!

CHORUS

Blow the man down, boys, oh, blow
the man down!
Wa-a-ay, blow the man down!
A pretty young maiden I chanced
for to meet.
Give us some time to blow the
man down!

PAUL (*just as Driscoll is clearing his throat preparatory to starting the next verse*). Hay, Drisc! Here she come, I tink. Some bumboat comin' dis way. (*They all rush to the side and look toward the land.*)

YANK. There's five or six of them in it--and they paddle like skirts.

DRISCOLL (*wildly elated*). Hurroo, ye scuts! 'Tis thim right enough. (*He does a few jig steps on the deck.*)

OLSON (*after a pause during which all are watching the approaching boat*). Py yingo, I see six in boat, yes, sir.

DAVIS. I kin make out the baskets. See 'em there amidships?

BIG FRANK. Vot kind booze dey bring—viskey?

DRISCOLL. Rum, foine West Indy—wid a kick in ut loike a mule's hoind leg.

LAMPS. Maybe she don't bring any; maybe skipper scare her.

DRISCOLL. Don't be throwin' cold water, Lamps. I'll skin her black hoide off av her if she goes back on her worrd.

YANK. Here they come. Listen to 'em gigglin'. (*Calling.*) Oh, you kiddo! (*The sound of women's voices can be heard talking and laughing.*)

DRISCOLL (*calling*). Is ut you, Mrs. Old Black Joe?

A WOMAN'S VOICE. 'Ullo, mike! (*There is loud feminine laughter at this retort.*)

DRISCOLL. Shake a leg an' come abord thin.

THE WOMAN'S VOICE. We're a-comin'.

DRISCOLL. Come on, Yank. You an' me'd best be goin' to give 'em a hand wid their truck. 'Twill put 'em in good spirits.

COCKY (*as they start off left*). Ho, you ain't 'arf a fox, Drisc. Down't drink it all afore we sees it.

DRISCOLL (*over his shoulder*). You'll be havin' yours, me sonny bye, don't fret. (*He and Yank go off left.*)

COCKY (*licking his lips*). Gawd blimey, I can do wiv a wet.

DAVIS. Me, too!

CHIPS. I'll bet there ain't none of us'll let any go to waste.

BIG FRANK. I could trink a whole barrel mineself, py chimminy Christmas!

COCKY. I 'opes all the gels ain't as bloomin' ugly as 'er. Looked like a bloody organ-grinder's monkey, she did. Gawd, I couldn't put up wiv the likes of 'er!

PADDY. Ye'll be lucky if any of thim looks at ye, ye squint-eyed runt.

COCKY (*angrily*). Ho, yus? You ain't no bleedin' beauty prize yeself, me man. A 'airy ape, I calls yer.

PADDY (*walking toward him—truculently*). Whot's thot? Say ut again if ye dare.

COCKY (*his hand on his sheath knife—snarling*). 'Airy ape! That's wot I says! (*Paddy tries to reach him, but the others keep them apart.*)

BIG FRANK (*pushing Paddy back*). Vot's the matter mit you, Paddy? Don't you hear vat Driscoll say—no fighting?

PADDY (*grumblingly*). I don't take no back talk from that deck-scrubbin' shrimp.

COCKY. Blarsted coal-puncher! (*Driscoll appears wearing a broad grin of satisfaction. The fight is immediately forgotten by the crowd who gather around him with exclamations of eager curiosity. How is it, Drisc? Any luck? Vot she bring, Drisc? Where's the gels? etc.*)

DRISCOLL (*with an apprehensive glance back at the bridge*). Not so loud, for the love av hivin! (*The clamour dies down.*) Yis, she has ut wid her. She'll be here in a minute wid a pint bottle or two for each wan av ye—three shillin's a bottle. So don't be impashunt.

COCKY (*indignantly*). Three bob! The bloody cow!

SMITTY (*with an ironic smile*). Grand larceny, by God! (*They all turn and look up at him, surprised to hear him speak.*)

OLSON. Py yingo, we don't pay so much.

BIG FRANK. Tamn black tief!

PADDY. We'll take ut away from her and give her nothin'.

THE CROWD (*growling*). Dirty thief! Dot's right! Give her nothin'! Not a bloomin' 'apenny! *etc.*

DRISCOLL (*grinning*). Ye can take ut or lave ut, me sonny byes. (*He casts a glance in the direction of the bridge and then reaches inside his shirt and pulls out a pint bottle.*) 'Tis foine rum, the rale stuff. (*He drinks.*) I slipped this wan out av wan av the baskets whin they wasn't lookin'. (*He hands the bottle to Olson who is nearest him.*) Here ye are, Ollie. Take a small sup an' pass ut to the nixt. 'Tisn't much but 'twill serve to take the black taste out av your mouths if ye go aisy wid ut. An' there's buckets more av ut comin'.

(*The bottle passes from hand to hand, each man taking a sip and smacking his lips with a deep "Aaah" of satisfaction.*)

DAVIS. Where's she now, Drisc?

DRISCOLL. Up havin' a worrd wid the skipper, makin' arrangements about the money, I s'pose.

DAVIS. An' where's the other gels?

DRISCOLL. Wid her. There's foive av thim she took aboard—two swate little slips av things, near as white as you an' me are, for that grey-whiskered auld fool, an' the mates—an' the engineers too, maybe. The rist av thim'll be comin' for'ard whin she comes.

COCKY. 'E ain't 'arf a funny ole bird, the skipper. Gawd blimey! 'Member when we sailed from 'ome 'ow 'e stands on the bridge lookin' like a bloody ole sky pilot? An' 'is missus dawhn on the bloomin' dock 'owlin' fit to kill 'erself? An' 'is kids 'owlin' an' wavin' their 'andkerchiefs? (*With great moral indignation.*) An' 'ere 'e is makin' up to a bleedin' nigger! There's a captain for yer! Gawd blimey! Bloody crab, I calls 'im!

DRISCOLL. Shut up, ye insect! Sure, it's not you should be talkin', an' you wid a woman an' childer weepin' for ye in iviry divil's port in the wide worrld, if we can believe your own tale av ut.

COCKY (*still indignant*). I ain't no bloomin' captain, I ain't. I ain't got no missus—reg'lar married, I means. I ain't——

BIG FRANK (*putting a huge paw over Cocky's mouth*). You ain't going talk so much, you hear? (*Cocky wriggles away from him.*) Say, Drisc, how ve pay dis voman for booze? Ve ain't got no cash.

DRISCOLL. It's aisy enough. Each girl'll have a slip av paper wid her an' whin you buy anythin' you write ut down and the price beside ut and sign your name. If ye can't write have some one who can do ut for ye. An' rimimber this: Whin ye buy a bottle av dhrink or (*with a wink*) somethin' else forbid, ye must write down tobaccy or fruit or somethin' the loike av that. Whin she laves the skipper'll pay what's owin' on the paper an' take ut out av your pay. Is ut clear to ye now?

ALL. Yes—Clear as day—Aw right, Drisc—Righto—Sure, *etc.*

DRISCOLL. An' don't forgit what I said about bein' quiet wid the dhrink, or the Mate'll be down on our necks an' spile the fun. (*A chorus of assent.*)

DAVIS (*looking aft*). Ain't this them comin'? (*They all look in that direction. The silly laughter of a woman is heard.*)

DRISCOLL. Look at Yank, wud ye, wid his arrm around the middle av wan av thim. That lad's not wastin' any toime.

(*The four women enter from the left, giggling and whispering to each other. The first three carry baskets on their heads. The youngest and best-looking comes last. Yank has his arm about her waist and is carrying her basket in his other hand. All four are distinct negro types. They wear light-coloured, loose-fitting clothes and have bright bandana handkerchiefs on their heads. They put down their baskets on the hatch and sit down beside them. The men crowd around, grinning.*)

BELLA (*she is the oldest, stoutest, and homeliest of the four—grinning back at them*). 'Ullo, boys.

THE OTHER GIRLS. 'Ullo, boys.

THE MEN. Hello, yourself—Evenin'—Hello—How are you? *etc.*

BELLA (*genially*). Hope you had a nice voyage. My name's Bella, this here's Susie, yander's Violet, and her there (*pointing to the girl with Yank*) is Pearl. Now we all knows each other.

PADDY (*roughly*). Never mind the girls. Where's the dhrink?

BELLA (*tartly*). You're a hawg, ain't you? Don't talk so loud or you don't git any—you nor no man. Think I wants the ole captain to put me off the ship, do you?

YANK. Yes, nix on hollerin', you! D'yuh wanta queer all of us?

BELLA (*casting a quick glance over her shoulder*). Here! Some of you big strapping boys sit back of us on the hatch there so's them officers can't see what we're doin'. (*Driscoll and several of the others sit and stand behind the girls on the hatch. Bella turns to Driscoll.*) Did you tell 'em they gotter sign for what they gits—and *how* to sign?

DRISCOLL. I did—what's your name again—oh, yis—Bella, darlin'.

BELLA. Then it's all right; but you boys has gotter go inside the fo'castle when you gits your bottle. No drinkin' out here on deck. I ain't takin' no chances. (*An impatient murmur of assent goes up from the crowd.*) Ain't that right, Mike?

DRISCOLL. Right as rain, darlin'. (*Big Frank leans over and says something to him in a low voice. Driscoll laughs and slaps his thigh.*) Listen, Bella, I've somethin' to ask ye for my little friend here who's bashful. Ut has to do wid the ladies so I'd best be whisperin' ut to ye meself to kape them from blushin'. (*He leans over and asks her a question.*)

BELLA (*firmly*). Four shillin's.

DRISCOLL (*laughing*). D'you hear that, all av ye? Four shillin's ut is.

PADDY (*angrily*). To hell wid this talkin'. I want a dhrink.

BELLA. Is everything all right, Mike?

DRISCOLL (*after a look back at the bridge*). Sure. Let her droive!

BELLA. All right, girls. (*The girls reach down in their baskets in under the fruit which is on top and each pulls out a pint bottle. Four of the men crowd up and take the bottles.*) Fetch a light, Lamps, that's a good boy. (*Lamps goes to his room and returns with a candle. This is passed from one girl to another as the men sign the sheets of paper for their bottles.*) Don't you boys forget to mark down cigarettes or tobacco or fruit, remember! Three shillin's is the price. Take it into the fo'castle. For Gawd's sake, don't stand out here drinkin' in the moonlight. (*The four go into the forecastle. Four more take their places. Paddy plants himself in front of Pearl who is sitting by Yank with his arm still around her.*)

PADDY (*gruffly*). Gimme thot! (*She holds out a bottle which he snatches from her hand. He turns to go away.*)

YANK (*sharply*). Here, you! Where d'yuh get that stuff? You ain't signed for that yet.

PADDY (*sullenly*). I can't write me name.

YANK. Then I'll write it for yuh. (*He takes the paper from Pearl and writes.*) There ain't goin' to be no welchin' on little Bright Eyes here—not when I'm around, see? Ain't I right, kiddo?

PEARL (*with a grin*). Yes, suh.

BELLA (*seeing all four are served*). Take it into the fo'castle, boys. (*Paddy defiantly raises his bottle and gulps down a drink in the full moonlight. Bella sees him.*) Look at 'im! Look at the dirty swine! (*Paddy slouches into the forecastle.*) Wants to git me in trouble. That settles it! We all got to git inside, boys, where we won't git caught. Come on, girls.

(*The girls pick up their baskets and follow Bella. Yank and Pearl are the last to reach the doorway. She lingers behind him, her eyes fixed on Smitty, who is still sitting on the forecastle head, his chin on his hands, staring off into vacancy.*)

PEARL (*waving a hand to attract his attention*). Come ahn in, pretty boy. Ah likes you.

SMITTY (*coldly*). Yes; I want to buy a bottle, please.

(*He goes down the steps and follows her into the forecastle. No one remains on deck but the Donkeyman, who sits smoking his pipe in front of his door. There is the subdued babble of voices from the crowd inside, but the mournful cadence of the song from the shore can again be faintly heard. Smitty reappears and closes the door to the forecastle after him. He shudders and shakes his shoulders as if flinging off something which disgusted him. Then he lifts the bottle which is in his hand to his lips and gulps down a long drink. The Donkeyman watches him impassively. Smitty sits down on the hatch facing him. Now that the closed door has shut off nearly all the noise the singing from shore comes clearly over the moonlit water.*)

SMITTY (*listening to it for a moment*). Damn that song of theirs. (*He takes another big drink.*) What do you say, Donk?

THE DONKEYMAN (*quietly*). Seems nice an' sleepy-like.

SMITTY (*with a hard laugh*). Sleepy! If I listened to it long—sober—I'd never go to sleep.

THE DONKEYMAN. 'Tain't sich bad music, is it? Sounds kinder pretty to me—low an' mournful—same as listenin' to the organ outside o' church of a Sunday.

SMITTY (*with a touch of impatience*). I didn't mean it was bad music. It isn't. It's the beastly memories the damn thing brings up—for some reason. (*He takes another pull at the bottle.*)

THE DONKEYMAN. Ever hear it before?

SMITTY. No; never in my life. It's just a something about the rotten thing which makes me think of—well—oh, the devil! (*He forces a laugh.*)

THE DONKEYMAN (*spitting placidly*). Queer things, mem'ries. I ain't ever been bothered much by 'em.

SMITTY (*looking at him fixedly for a moment—with quiet scorn*). No, you wouldn't be.

THE DONKEYMAN. Not that I ain't had my share o' things goin' wrong; but I puts 'em out o' me mind, like, an' fergets 'em.

SMITTY. But suppose you couldn't put them out of your mind? Suppose they haunted you when you were awake and when you were asleep—what then?

THE DONKEYMAN (*quietly*). I'd git drunk, same's you're doin'.

SMITTY (*with a harsh laugh*). Good advice. (*He takes another drink. He is beginning to show the effects of the liquor. His face is flushed and he talks rather wildly.*) We're poor little lambs who have lost our way, eh, Donk? Damned from here to eternity, what? God have mercy on such as we! True, isn't it, Donk?

THE DONKEYMAN. Maybe; I dunno. (*After a slight pause.*) Whatever set you goin' to sea? You ain't made for it.

SMITTY (*laughing wildly*). My old friend in the bottle here, Donk.

THE DONKEYMAN. I done my share o' drinkin' in my time. (*Regretfully.*) Them was good times, those days. Can't hold up under drink no more. Doctor told me I'd got to stop or die. (*He spits contentedly.*) So I stops.

SMITTY (*with a foolish smile*). Then I'll drink one for you. Here's your health, old top! (*He drinks.*)

THE DONKEYMAN (*after a pause*). S'pose there's a gel mixed up in it some place, ain't there?

SMITTY (*stiffly*). What makes you think so?

THE DONKEYMAN. Always is when a man lets music bother 'im. (*After a few puffs at his pipe.*) An' she said she threw you over 'cause you was drunk; an' you said you was drunk 'cause she threw you over. (*He spits leisurely.*) Queer thing, love, ain't it?

SMITTY (*rising to his feet with drunken dignity*). I'll trouble you not to pry into my affairs, Donkeyman.

THE DONKEYMAN (*unmoved*). That's everybody's affair, what I said. I been through it many's the time. (*Genially.*) I always hit 'em a whack on the ear an' went out and got drunker'n ever. When I come home again they always had somethin' special nice cooked fur me to eat. (*Puffing at his pipe.*) That's the on'y way to fix 'em when they gits on their high horse. I don't s'pose you ever tried that?

SMITTY (*pompously*). Gentlemen don't hit women.

THE DONKEYMAN (*placidly*). No; that's why they has mem'ries when they hears music. (*Smitty does not deign to reply to this, but sinks into a scornful silence. Davis and the girl Violet come out of the forecastle and close the door behind them. He is staggering a bit and she is laughing shrilly.*)

DAVIS (*turning to the left*). This way, Rose, or Pansy, or Jessamine, or Black Tulip, or Violet, or whatever the hell flower your name is. No one'll see us back here. (*They go off left.*)

THE DONKEYMAN. There's love at first sight for you—an' plenty more o' the same in the fo'c'sle. No mem'ries jined with that.

SMITTY (*really repelled*). Shut up, Donk. You're disgusting. (*He takes a long drink.*)

THE DONKEYMAN (*philosophically*). All depends on how you was brung up, I s'pose. (*Pearl comes out of the forecastle. There is a roar of voices from inside. She shuts the door behind her, sees Smitty on the hatch, and comes over and sits beside him and puts her arm over his shoulder.*)

THE DONKEYMAN (*chuckling*). There's love for you, Duke.

PEARL (*patting Smitty's face with her hand*). 'Ullo, pretty boy. (*Smitty pushes her hand away coldly.*) What you doin' out here all alone by yourself?

SMITTY (*with a twisted grin*). Thinking and—(*he indicates the bottle in his hand*)—drinking to stop thinking. (*He drinks and laughs maudlinly. The bottle is three-quarters empty.*)

PEARL. You oughtn't drink so much, pretty boy. Don' you know dat? You have big, big headache come mawnin'.

SMITTY (*dryly*). Indeed?

PEARL. Tha's true. Ah knows what Ah say. (*Cooingly.*) Why you run 'way from me, pretty boy? Ah likes you. Ah don' like them other fellahs. They act too rough. You ain't rough. You're a genelman. Ah knows. Ah can tell a genelman fahs Ah can see 'im.

SMITTY. Thank you for the compliment; but you're wrong, you see. I'm merely—a ranker. (*He adds bitterly.*) And a rotter.

PEARL (*patting his arm*). No, you ain't. Ah knows better. You're a genelman. (*Insinuatingly.*) Ah wouldn't have nothin' to do with them other men, but (*she smiles at him enticingly*) you is diff'rent. (*He pushes her away from him disgustedly. She pouts.*) Don' you like me, pretty boy?

SMITTY (*a bit ashamed*). I beg your pardon. I didn't mean to be rude, you know, really. (*His politeness is drunkenly exaggerated.*) I'm a bit off colour.

PEARL (*brightening up.*) Den you do like me—little ways?

SMITTY (*carelessly*). Yes, yes, why shouldn't I? (*He suddenly laughs wildly and puts his arm around her waist and presses her to him.*) Why not? (*He pulls his arm back quickly with a shudder of disgust, and takes a drink. Pearl looks at him curiously, puzzled by his strange actions. The door from the forecastle is kicked open and Yank comes out. The uproar of shouting, laughing and singing voices has increased in violence. Yank staggers over toward Smitty and Pearl.*)

YANK (*blinking at them*). What the hell—oh, it's you, Smitty the Duke. I was goin' to turn one loose on the jaw of any guy'd cop my dame, but seein' it's you—— (*Sentimentally.*) Pals is pals and any pal of mine c'n have anythin' I got, see? (*Holding out his hand.*) Shake, Duke. (*Smitty takes his hand and he pumps it up and down.*) You'n me's frens. Ain't I right?

SMITTY. Right it is, Yank. But you're wrong about this girl. She isn't with me. She was just going back to the fo'c'sle to you. (*Pearl looks at him with hatred gathering in her eyes.*)

YANK. Tha' right?

SMITTY. On my word!

YANK (*grabbing her arm*). Come on then, you, Pearl! Le's have a drink with the bunch. (*He pulls her to the entrance where she shakes off his hand long enough to turn on Smitty furiously.*)

PEARL. You swine! You can go to hell! (*She goes in the forecastle, slamming the door.*)

THE DONKEYMAN (*spitting calmly*). There's love for you. They're all the same—white, brown, yeller 'n' black. A whack on the ear's the only thing'll learn 'em.

(*Smitty makes no reply, but laughs harshly and takes another drink; then sits staring before him, the almost empty bottle tightly clutched in one hand. There is an increase in volume of the muffled clamour from the forecastle and a mo-*

ment later the door is thrown open and the whole mob, led by Driscoll, pours out on deck. All of them are very drunk and several of them carry bottles in their hands. Bella is the only one of the women who is absolutely sober. She tries in vain to keep the men quiet. Pearl drinks from Yank's bottle every moment or so, laughing shrilly, and leaning against Yank, whose arm is about her waist. Paul comes out last, carrying an accordion. He staggers over and stands on top of the hatch, his instrument under his arm.)

DRISCOLL. Play us a dance, ye square-head swab !—a rale, Godforsaken son av a turkey trot wid guts to ut.

YANK. Straight from the old Barbary Coast in 'Frisco !

PAUL. I don' know. I try. (*He commences tuning up.*)

YANK. Ataboy ! Let 'er rip ! (*Davis and Violet come back and join the crowd. The Donkeyman looks on them all with a detached, indulgent air. Smitty stares before him and does not seem to know there is anyone on deck but himself.*)

BIG FRANK. Dance ? I don't dance. I trink ! (*He suits the action to the word and roars with meaningless laughter.*)

DRISCOLL. Git out av the way thin, ye big hulk, an' give us some room. (*Big Frank sits down on the hatch, right. All of the others who are not going to dance either follow his example or lean against the port bulwark.*)

BELLA (*on the verge of tears at her inability to keep them in the forecastle or make them be quiet now they are out*). For Gawd's sake, boys, don't shout so loud ! Want to git me in trouble ?

DRISCOLL (*grabbing her*). Dance wid me, me cannibal quane. (*Some one drops a bottle on deck and it smashes.*)

BELLA (*hysterically*). There they goes ! There they goes ! Captain'll hear that ! Oh, my Lawd !

DRISCOLL. Be damned to him ! Here's the music ! Off ye go !

(*Paul starts playing " You Great Big Beautiful Doll " with a note left out every now and then. The four couples commence dancing—a jerk-shouldered version of the old Turkey Trot as it was done in the sailor-town dives, made more grotesque by the fact that all the couples are drunk and keep lurching into each other every moment. Two of the men start dancing together, intentionally bumping into the others. Yank and Pearl come around in front of Smitty and, as they pass him, Pearl slaps him across the side of the face with all her might, and laughs viciously. He jumps to his feet with his fists clenched, but sees who hit him and sits down again, smiling bitterly. Yank laughs boisterously.*)

YANK. Wow ! Some wallop ! One on you, Duke.

DRISCOLL (*hurling his cap at Paul*). Faster, ye toad ! (*Paul makes frantic efforts to speed up and the music suffers in the process.*)

BELLA (*puffing*). Let me go. I'm wore out with you steppin' on my toes, you clumsy Mick. (*She struggles, but Driscoll holds her tight.*)

DRISCOLL. God blarst you for havin' such big feet, thin. Aisy, aisy, Mrs. Old Black Joe ! 'Tis dancin'll take the blubber off ye.

(*He whirls her around the deck by main force. Cocky, with Susie, is dancing near the hatch, right, when Paddy, who is sitting on the edge with Big Frank, sticks his foot out and the wavering couple stumble over it and fall flat on the deck. A roar of laughter goes up. Cocky rises to his feet, his face livid with rage, and springs at Paddy, who promptly knocks him down. Driscoll hits Paddy and Big Frank hits Driscoll. In a flash a wholesale fight has broken out and the deck is a surging crowd of drink-maddened men hitting out at each other indiscriminately, although the general idea seems to be a battle between seamen and firemen. The women shriek and take refuge on top of the hatch, where they huddle in a frightened group. Finally there is the flash of a knife held high in the moonlight and a loud yell of pain.*)

DAVIS (*somewhere in the crowd*). Here's the Mate comin'! Let's git out o' this!

(*There is a general rush for the forecastle. In a moment there is no one left on deck but the little group of women on the hatch; Smitty, still dazedly rubbing his cheek; The Donkeyman quietly smoking on his stool; and Yank and Driscoll, their faces battered up considerably, their vests in shreds, bending over the still form of Paddy, which lies stretched out on the deck between them. In the silence the mournful chant from the shore creeps slowly out to the ship.*)

DRISCOLL (*quickly—in a low voice*). Who knoifed him?

YANK (*stupidly*). I didn't see it. How do I know? Cocky, I'll bet. (*The First Mate enters from the left. He is a tall, strongly-built man, dressed in a plain blue uniform.*)

THE MATE (*angrily*). What's all this noise about? (*He sees the man lying on the deck.*) Hello! What's this? (*He bends down on one knee beside Paddy.*)

DRISCOLL (*stammering*). All av us—was in a bit av a harmless foight, sir,—an'—I dunno—— (*The Mate rolls Paddy over and sees a knife wound on his shoulder.*)

THE MATE. Knifed, by God. (*He takes an electric flash from his pocket and examines the cut.*) Lucky it's only a flesh wound. He must have hit his head on deck when he fell. That's what knocked him out. This is only a scratch. Take him aft and I'll bandage him up.

DRISCOLL. Yis, sor.

(*They take Paddy by the shoulders and feet and carry him off left. The Mate looks up and sees the women on the hatch for the first time.*)

THE MATE (*surprised*). Hello! (*He walks over to them.*) Go to the cabin and get your money and clear off. If I had my way, you'd never—— (*His foot hits a bottle. He stoops down and picks it up and smells of it.*) Rum, by God! So that's the trouble! I thought their breaths smelled damn queer. (*To the women, harshly.*) You needn't go to the skipper for any money. You won't get any. That'll teach you to smuggle rum on a ship and start a riot.

BELLA. But, Mister——

THE MATE (*sternly*). You know the agreement—rum—no money.

BELLA (*indignantly*). Honest to Gawd, Mister, I never brung no——

THE MATE (*fiercely*). You're a liar! And none of your lip or I'll make a complaint ashore to-morrow and have you locked up.

BELLA (*subdued*). Please, Mister——

THE MATE. Clear out of this, now! Not another word out of you! Tumble over the side damn quick! The two others are waiting for you. Hop, now! (*They walk quickly—almost run—off to the left. The Mate follows them, nodding to The Donkeyman, and ignoring the oblivious Smitty.*)

(*There is absolute silence on the ship for a few moments. The melancholy song of the negroes drifts crooning over the water. Smitty listens to it intently for a time; then sighs heavily, a sigh that is half a sob.*)

SMITTY. God! (*He drinks the last drop in the bottle and throws it behind him on the hatch.*)

THE DONKEYMAN (*spitting tranquilly*). More mem'ries? (*Smitty does not answer him. The ship's bell tolls four bells. The Donkeyman knocks out his pipe.*) I think I'll turn in. (*He opens the door to his cabin, but turns to look at Smitty—kindly.*) You can't hear it in the fo'c'sle—the music, I mean—an' there'll likely be more drink in there, too. Good night. (*He goes in and shuts the door.*)

SMITTY. Good night, Donk.

(*He gets wearily to his feet and walks with bowed shoulders, staggering a bit, to the forecastle entrance and goes in. There is silence for a second or so, broken only by the haunted, saddened voice of that brooding music, faint and far-off, like the mood of the moonlight made audible.*)

CURTAIN

THE ROPE

A Play in One Act

Characters

ABRAHAM BENTLEY
ANNIE, *his daughter*
PAT SWEENEY, *her husband*
MARY, *their child*
LUKE BENTLEY, *Abe's son by a second marriage*

The action of the play takes place in the years preceding the outbreak of World War I

SCENE. *The interior of an old barn situated on top of a high headland of the sea coast. In the rear, to the left, a stall in which lumber is stacked up. To the right of it, an open double doorway looking out over the ocean. Outside the doorway, the faint trace of what was once a road leading to the barn. Beyond the road, the edge of a cliff which rises sheer from the sea below. On the right of the doorway, three stalls with mangers and hay-racks. The first of these is used as a wood-bin and is half full of piled-up cordwood. Near this bin, a chopping-block with an axe driven into the top of it.*

The left section of the barn contains the hay loft, which extends at a height of about twelve feet from the floor as far to the right as the middle of the doorway. The loft is bare except for a few scattered mounds of dank-looking hay. From the edge of the loft, half-way from the door, a rope about five feet long with an open running noose at the end is hanging. A rusty plough and various other farming implements, all giving evidence of long disuse, are lying on the floor near the left wall. Farther forward an old cane-bottomed chair is set back against the wall.

In front of the stalls on the right stands a long, roughly constructed carpenter's table, evidently home-made. Saws, a lathe, a hammer, a chisel, a keg containing nails, and other tools of the carpentry trade are on the table. Two benches are placed, one in front, one to the left of it.

The right side of the barn is a bare wall.

It is between six and half-past in the evening of a day in early spring. At the rising of the curtain some trailing clouds near the horizon, seen through the open doorway, are faintly tinged with gold by the first glow of the sunset. As the action progresses, this reflected light gradually becomes brighter, and then slowly fades into a smoky crimson. The sea is a dark slate colour. From the rocks below the headland sounds the muffled monotone of breaking waves.

As the curtain rises, Mary is discovered squatting cross-legged on the floor, her back propped against the right side of the doorway, her face in profile. She is a skinny, overgrown girl of ten with thin, carroty hair worn in a pig-tail. She wears a shabby gingham dress. Her face is stupidly expressionless. Her hands flutter about aimlessly in relaxed, flabby gestures.

She is staring fixedly at a rag doll which she has propped up against the doorway opposite her. She hums shrilly to herself.

At a sudden noise from outside she jumps to her feet, peeps out, and quickly snatches up the doll, which she hugs fiercely to her breast. Then, after a second's fearful hesitation, she runs to the carpenter's table and crawls under it.

As she does so Abraham Bentley appears in the doorway and stands, blinking into the shadowy barn. He is a tall, lean, round-shouldered old man of sixty-five. His thin legs, twisted by rheumatism, totter feebly under him as he shuffles slowly along by the aid of a thick cane. His face is gaunt, chalky-white, furrowed with wrinkles, surmounted by a shiny bald scalp fringed with scanty wisps of white hair. His eyes peer weakly from beneath bushy black brows. His mouth is a sunken line drawn in under his large beak-like nose. A two weeks' growth of stubby patches of beard covers his jaws and chin. He has on a threadbare brown overcoat, but wears no hat.

BENTLEY (*comes slowly into the barn, peering around him suspiciously. As he reaches the table and leans one hand on it for support, Mary darts from underneath and dashes out through the doorway. Bentley is startled ; then shakes his cane after her*). Out o' my sight, you Papist brat ! Spawn o' Satan ! Spyin' on me ! They set her to it. Spyin' to watch me ! (*He limps to the door and looks out cautiously. Satisfied, he turns back into the barn.*) Spyin' to see—what they'll never know. (*He stands staring up at the rope and taps it testingly several times with his stick, talking to himself as he does so.*) It's tied strong—strong as death—— (*He cackles with satisfaction.*) They'll see, then ! They'll see ! (*He laboriously creeps over to the bench and sits down wearily. He looks toward the sea and his voice quavers in a doleful chant.*) " Woe unto us ! for the day goeth away, for the shadows of the evening are stretched out." (*He mumbles to himself for a moment—then speaks clearly.*) Spyin' on me ! Spawn o' the Pit ! (*He renews his chant.*) " They hunt our steps that we cannot go in our streets : our end is near, our days are fulfilled ; for our end is come."

(*As he finishes, Annie enters. She is a thin, slovenly, worn-out looking woman of about forty with a drawn, pasty face. Her habitual expression is one of a dulled irritation. She talks in a high-pitched sing-song whine. She wears a faded gingham dress and a torn sun-bonnet.*)

ANNIE (*comes over to her father, but warily keeps out of range of his stick*). Paw ! (*He doesn't answer or appear to see her.*) Paw ! You ain't fergittin' what the doctor told you when he was here last, be you ? He said you was to keep still and not go a-walkin' round. Come on back to the house, Paw. It's gittin' near supper-time and you got to take your medicine b'fore it, like he says.

BENTLEY (*his eyes fixed in front of him*). " The punishment of thine iniquity is accomplished, O daughter of Zion : he will visit thine iniquity, O daughter of Edom ; he will discover thy sins."

ANNIE (*waiting resignedly until he has finished—wearily*). You better take watch on your health, Paw, and not be sneakin' up to this barn no more. Lord sakes, soon's ever my back is turned you goes sneakin' off agen. It's enough to drive a body outa their right mind.

BENTLEY. " Behold, every one that useth proverbs shall use this proverb against thee, saying, As is the mother, so is her daughter ! " (*He cackles to himself.*) So is her daughter !

ANNIE (*her face flushing with anger*). And if I am, I'm glad I take after her and not you, y'old wizard ! (*Scornfully.*) A fine one you be to be shoutin' Scripture in a body's ears all the livelong day—you that druv Maw to her death with your naggin', and pinchin', and miser stinginess. If you've a mind to pray, it's down in the medder you ought to go, and kneel down by her grave, and ask God to forgive you for the meanness you done to her all her life.

BENTLEY (*mumbling*). " As is the mother, so is her daughter."

ANNIE (*enraged by the repetition of this quotation*). *You* quotin' Scripture ! Why, Maw wasn't cold in the earth b'fore you was down in the port courtin' agen—courtin' that harlot that was the talk o' the whole town ! And then you disgraces yourself and me by marryin' her—*her*—and bringin' her back home with you ; and me still goin' every day to put flowers on Maw's grave that you'd fergotten. (*She glares at him vindictively, pausing for breath.*) And between you you'd have druv me into the grave like you done Maw if I hadn't married Pat Sweeney so's I could git away and live in peace. Then you took on so high and mighty 'cause he was a Cath'lic—*you* gittin' religion all of a moment just for spite on me 'cause I'd left—and b'cause she egged you on against me; *you* sayin' it was a sin to marry a Papist, after not bein' at Sunday meetin' yourself for more'n twenty years!

BENTLEY (*loudly*). "He will visit thine iniquity ——"

ANNIE (*interrupting*). And the carryin's-on you had the six years at home after I'd left you—the shame of the whole county! Your wife, indeed, with a child she *claimed* was your'n, and her goin' with this farmer and that, and even men off the ships in the port, and you blind to it! And then when she got sick of you and ran away—only to meet her end at the hands of God a year after—she leaves you alone with that—*your* son, Luke, *she* called him—and him only five years old!

BENTLEY (*babbling*). Luke? Luke?

ANNIE (*tauntingly*). Yes, Luke! "As is the mother, so is her son"—that's what you ought to preach 'stead of puttin' curses on me. You was glad enougl to git me back home agen, and Pat with me, to tend the place, and help bring up that brat of hers. (*Jealously.*) You was fond enough of him all them years—and how did he pay you back? Stole your money and ran off and left you just when he was sixteen and old enough to help. Told you to your face he'd stolen and was leavin'. He only laughed when you was took crazy and cursed him; and he only laughed harder when you hung up that silly rope there—(*she points*)—and told him to hang himself on it when he ever came home agen.

BENTLEY (*mumbling*). You'll see, then. You'll see!

ANNIE (*wearily—her face becoming dull and emotionless again*). I s'pose I'm a bigger fool than you be to argy with a half-witted body. But I tell you agen that Luke of yours ain't comin' back; and if he does he ain't the kind to hang himself, more's the pity. He's like her. He'd hang *you* more likely if he s'pected you had any money. So you might 's well take down that ugly rope you've had tied there since he run off. He's probably dead anyway by this.

BENTLEY (*frightened*). No! No!

ANNIE. Them as bad as him comes to a sudden end. (*Irritably.*) Land sakes, Paw, here I am argyin' with your lunatic notions and the supper not ready. Come on and git your medicine. You can see no one ain't touched your old rope. Come on! You can sit 'n' read your Bible. (*He makes no movement. She comes closer to him and peers into his face—uncertainly.*) Don't you hear me? I do hope you ain't off in one of your fits when you don't know nobody. D'you know who's talkin'? This is Annie—your Annie, Paw.

BENTLEY (*bursting into senile rage*). None o' mine! Spawn o' the Pit! (*With a quick movement he hits her viciously over the arm with his stick. She gives a cry of pain and backs away from him, holding her arm.*)

ANNIE (*weeping angrily*). That's what I git for tryin' to be kind to you, you ugly old devil!

(*The sound of a man's footstep is heard from outside and Sweeney enters. He is a stocky, muscular, sandy-haired Irishman, dressed in patched corduroy trousers, shoved down into high laced boots, and a blue flannel shirt. The bony face of his bullet head has a pressed-in appearance except for his heavy jaw, which sticks out pugnaciously. There is an expression of mean cunning and cupidity about his mouth and his small, round, blue eyes. He has evidently been drinking and his face is flushed and set in an angry scowl.*)

SWEENEY. Have ye no supper at all made, ye lazy slut? (*Seeing that she has been crying.*) What're you blubberin' about?

ANNIE. It's all his fault. I was tryin' to git him home, but he's that set I couldn't budge him; and he hit me on the arm with his cane when I went near him.

SWEENEY. He did, did he? I'll soon learn him better. (*He advances toward Bentley threateningly.*)

ANNIE (*grasping his arm*). Don't touch him, Pat. He's in one of his fits and you might kill him.

SWEENEY. An' good riddance!

BENTLEY (*hissing*). Papist! (*Chants.*) "Pour out thy fury upon the heathen that know thee not, and upon the families that call not on thy name: for they have eaten up Jacob, and devoured him, and consumed him, and made his habitation desolate."

SWEENEY (*instinctively crosses himself—then scornfully*). Spit curses on me till ye choke. It's not likely the Lord God'll be listenin' to a wicked auld sinner the like of you. (*To Annie.*) What's got into him to be roamin' up here? When I left for the town he looked too weak to lift a foot.

ANNIE. Oh, it's the same crazy notion he's had ever since Luke left. He wanted to make sure the rope was still here.

BENTLEY (*pointing to the rope with his stick*). He-he! Luke'll come back. Then you'll see. You'll see!

SWEENEY (*nervously*). Stop that mad cacklin' for the love of heaven! (*With a forced laugh.*) It's great laughter I should be havin' at you, mad as you are, for thinkin' that thief of a son of yours would come back to hang himself on account of your curses. It's five years he's been gone, and not a sight of him; an' you, cursin' an' callin' down the wrath o' God on him by day an' by night. That shows you what God thinks of your curses—an' Him deaf to you!

ANNIE. It's no use talkin' to him, Pat.

SWEENEY. I've small doubt but that Luke is hung long since—by the police. He's come to no good end, that lad. (*His eyes on the rope.*) I'll be pullin' that thing down, so I will; an' the auld loon'll stay in the house, where he belongs, then, maybe.

(*He reaches up for the rope as if to try and yank it down. Bentley waves his stick frantically in the air, and groans with rage.*)

ANNIE (*frightened*). Leave it alone, Pat. Look at him. He's liable to hurt himself. Leave his rope be. It don't do no harm.

SWEENEY (*reluctantly moves away*). It looks ugly hangin' there open like a mouth. (*The old man sinks back into a relieved immobility. Sweeney speaks to his wife in a low tone.*) Where's the child? Get her to take him out o' this. I want a word with you he'll not be hearin'. (*She goes to the door and calls out.*) Ma-ry! Ma-ry! (*A faint, answering cry is heard and a moment later Mary rushes breathlessly into the barn. Sweeney grabs her roughly by the arm. She shrinks away, looking at him with terrified eyes.*) You're to take your grandfather back to the house—an' see to it he stays there.

ANNIE. And give him his medicine.

SWEENEY (*as the child continues to stare at him silently with eyes stupid from fear, he shakes her impatiently*). D'you hear me, now? (*To his wife.*) It's soft-minded she is, like I've always told you, an' stupid; and you're not too firm in the head yourself at times, God help you! An' look at him! It's the curse is in the wits of your family, not mine.

ANNIE. You've been drinkin' in town or you wouldn't talk that way.

MARY (*whining*). Maw! I'm skeered!

SWEENEY (*lets go of her arm and approaches Bentley*). Get up out o' this, ye auld loon, an' go with Mary. She'll take you to the house. (*Bentley tries to hit him with the cane.*) Oho, ye would, would ye? (*He wrests the cane from the old man's hands.*) Bad cess to ye, you're the treach'rous one! Get up, now! (*He jerks the old man to his feet.*) Here, Mary, take his hand. Quick now! (*She does so tremblingly.*) Lead him to the house.

ANNIE. Go on, Paw! I'll come and git your supper in a minute.

BENTLEY (*stands stubbornly and begins to intone*). "O Lord, thou hast seen my wrong; judge thou my cause. Thou hast seen all their vengeance and all their imaginations against me——"

SWEENEY (*pushing him toward the door. Bentley tries to resist. Mary pulls at his hand in a sudden fit of impish glee, and laughs shrilly*). Get on now an' stop your cursin'.

BENTLEY. "Render unto them a recompense, O Lord, according to the work of their hands."

SWEENEY. Shut your loud quackin'! Here's your cane. (*He gives it to the old man as they come to the doorway and quickly steps back out of reach.*) An' mind you don't touch the child with it or I'll beat you to a jelly, old as ye are.

BENTLEY (*resisting Mary's efforts to pull him out, stands shaking his stick at Sweeney and his wife*).

"Give them sorrow of heart, thy curse unto them. Persecute and destroy them in anger from under the heavens of the Lord."

MARY (*tugging at his hand and bursting again into shrill laughter*). Come on, gran'paw. (*He allows himself to be led off, right.*)

SWEENEY (*making the sign of the cross furtively—with a sigh of relief*). He's gone, thank God! What a snake's tongue he has in him! (*He sits down on the bench to the left of table.*) Come here, Annie, till I speak to you. (*She sits down on the bench in front of table. Sweeney winks mysteriously.*) Well, I saw him, sure enough.

ANNIE (*stupidly*). Who?

SWEENEY (*sharply*). Who? Who but Dick Waller, the lawyer, that I went to see. (*Lowering his voice.*) An' I've found out what we was wishin' to know. (*With a laugh.*) Ye said I'd been drinkin'—which is true; but 'twas all in the plan I'd made. I've a head for strong drink, as ye know, but he hasn't. (*He winks cunningly.*) An' the whiskey loosened his tongue till he'd told all he knew.

ANNIE. He told you—about Paw's will?

SWEENEY. He did. (*Disappointedly.*) But for all the good it does us we might as well be no wiser than we was before. (*He broods for a moment in silence—then hits the table furiously with his fist.*) God's curse on the auld miser!

ANNIE. What did he tell you?

SWEENEY. Not much at the first. He's a cute one, an' he'd be askin' a fee to tell you your own name, if he could get it. His practice is all dribbled away from him lately on account of the drink. So I let on I was only payin' a friendly call, havin' known him for years. Then I asked him out to have a drop o' drink, knowin' his weakness; an' we had rashers of them, an' I payin' for it. Then I come out with it straight and asked him about the will—because the auld man was crazy an' on his last legs, I told him, an' he was the lawyer made out the will when Luke was gone. So he winked at me an' grinned—he was drunk by this—an' said: "It's no use, Pat. He left the farm to the boy." "To hell with the farm," I spoke back. "It's mortgaged to the teeth; but how about the money?" "The money?" an' he looks at me in surprise, "What money?" "The cash he has," I says. "You're crazy," he says. "There wasn't any cash—only the farm." "D'you mean to say he made no mention of money in his will?" I asked. You could have knocked me down with a feather. "He did not—on my oath," he says. (*Sweeney leans over to his wife—indignantly.*) Now what d'you make o' that? The auld divil!

ANNIE. Maybe Waller was lyin'.

SWEENEY. He was not. I could tell by his face. He was surprised to hear me talkin' of money.

ANNIE. But the thousand dollars Paw got for the mortgage just before that woman ran away ——

SWEENEY. An' that I've been slavin' me hands off to pay the int'rist on!

ANNIE. What could he have done with that? He ain't spent it. It was in twenty-dollar gold pieces he got it, I remember Mr. Kellar of the bank tellin' me once.

SWEENEY. Divil a penny he's spent. Ye know as well as I do if it wasn't for my hammerin', an' sawin', an' nailin', he'd be in the poor house this minute—or the mad house, more likely.

ANNIE. D'you suppose that harlot ran off with it?

SWEENEY. I do not; I know better—an' so do you. D'you not remember the letter she wrote tellin' him he could support Luke on the money he'd got on the mortgage she'd signed with him; for he'd made the farm over to her when he married her. An' where d'you suppose Luke got the hundred dollars he stole? The auld loon must have had cash with him then, an' it's only five years back.

ANNIE. He's got it hid some place in the house most likely.

SWEENEY. Maybe you're right. I'll dig in the cellar this night when he's sleepin'. He used to be down there a lot recitin' Scripture in his fits.

ANNIE. What else did Waller say?

SWEENEY. Nothin' much; except that we should put notices in the papers for Luke, an' if he didn't come back by sivin years from when he'd left—two years from now, that'd be—the courts would say he was dead an' give us the farm.

Divil a lot of use it is to us now with no money to fix it up ; an' himself ruinin' it years ago by sellin' everythin' to buy that slut new clothes.

ANNIE. Don't folks break wills like his'n in the courts ?

SWEENEY. Waller said 'twas no use. The auld divil was plain in his full senses when he made it ; an' the courts cost money.

ANNIE (*resignedly*). There ain't nothin' we can do then ?

SWEENEY. No—except wait an' pray that young thief is dead an' won't come back ; an' try an' find where it is the auld man has the gold hid, if he has it yet. I'd take him by the neck an' choke him till he told it, if he wasn't your father. (*He takes a full quart flask of whiskey from the pocket of his coat and has a big drink.*) Aahh ! If we'd on'y the thousand we'd stock the farm good an' I'd give up this dog's game—(*he indicates the carpentry outfit scornfully*)—an' we'd both work hard with a man or two to help, an' in a few years we'd be rich ; for 'twas always a payin' place in the auld days.

ANNIE. Yes, yes, it was always a good farm then.

SWEENEY. He'll not last long in his senses, the doctor told me. His next attack will be very soon an' after it he'll be a real lunatic with no legal claims to anythin'. If we on'y had the money —— 'Twould be the divil an' all if the auld fool should forget where he put it, an' him takin' leave of his senses altogether. (*He takes another nip at the bottle and puts it back in his pocket—with a sigh.*) Ah, well, I'll save what I can an' at the end of two years, with good luck in the trade, maybe we'll have enough.

(*They are both startled by the heavy footsteps of some one approaching outside. A shrill burst of Mary's laughter can be heard and the deep voice of a man talking to her.*)

SWEENEY (*uneasily*). It's Mary ; but who could that be with her ? It's not himself.

(*As he finishes speaking, Luke appears in the doorway, holding the dancing Mary by the hand. He is a tall, strapping young fellow, about twenty-five, with a coarse-featured, rather handsome face bronzed by the sun. What his face lacks in intelligence is partly forgiven for his good-natured, half-foolish grin, his hearty laugh, his curly dark hair, a certain devil-may-care recklessness and irresponsible youth in voice and gesture. But his mouth is weak and characterless ; his brown eyes are large but shifty and acquisitive. He wears a dark blue jersey, patched blue trousers, rough sailor shoes, and a grey cap. He advances into the stable with a mocking smile on his lips until he stands directly under the rope. The man and woman stare at him in petrified amazement.*)

ANNIE. Luke !

SWEENEY (*crossing himself*). Glory be to God—it's him !

MARY (*hopping up and down wildly*). It's Uncle Luke, Uncle Luke, Uncle Luke ! (*She runs to her mother, who pushes her away angrily.*)

LUKE (*regarding them both with an amused grin*). Sure, it's Luke—back after five years of bummin' round the rotten old earth in ships and things. Paid off a week ago—had a bust-up—and then took a notion to come out here—bummed my way—and here I am. And you're both of you tickled to death to see me, ain't yuh ?—like hell ! (*He laughs and walks over to Annie.*) Don't yuh even want to shake flippers with your dear, long-lost brother, Annie ? I remember you and me used to git on so fine together—like hell !

ANNIE (*giving him a venomous look of hatred*). Keep your hands to yourself.

LUKE (*grinning*). You ain't changed, that's sure —on'y yuh're homlier'n ever. (*He turns to the scowling Sweeney.*) How about you, brother Pat ?

SWEENEY. I'd not lower myself to take the hand of a——

LUKE (*with a threat in his voice*). Easy goes with that talk ! I'm not so soft to lick as I was when I was a kid ; and don't forget it.

ANNIE (*to Mary, who is playing catch with a silver dollar which she has had clutched in her hand—sharply*). Mary ! What have you got there ? Where did you get it ? Bring it here to me this minute !

(*Mary presses the dollar to her breast and remains standing by the doorway in stubborn silence.*)

LUKE. Aw, let her alone! What's bitin' yuh? That's on'y a silver dollar I give her when I met her front of the house. She told me you was up here; and I give her that as a present to buy candy with. I got it in 'Frisco—cart-wheels, they call 'em. There ain't none of them in these parts I ever seen, so I brung it along on the voyage.

ANNIE (*angrily*). I don't know or care where you got it—but I know you ain't come by it honest. Mary! Give that back to him this instant! (*As the child hesitates, she stamps her foot furiously.*) D'you hear me? (*Mary starts to cry softly, but comes to Luke and hands him the dollar.*)

LUKE (*taking it—with a look of disgust at his half-sister*). I was right when I said you ain't changed, Annie. You're as stinkin' mean as ever. (*To Mary, consolingly.*) Quit bawlin', kid. You'n' me'll go out on the edge of the cliff here and chuck some stones in the ocean same's we useter, remember?

(*Mary's tears immediately cease. She looks up at him with shining eyes, and claps her hands.*)

MARY (*pointing to the dollar he has in his hand*). Throw that! It's flat 'n' it'll skip.

LUKE (*with a grin*). That's the talk, kid. That's all it's good for—to throw away; not buryin' it like your miser folks'd tell you. Here! You take it and chuck it away. It's your'n. (*He gives her the dollar and she hops to the doorway. He turns to Pat with a grin.*) I'm learnin' your kid to be a sport, Tight-Wad. I hope you ain't got no objections.

MARY (*impatiently*). Come on, Uncle Luke. Watch me throw it.

LUKE. Aw right. (*To Pat.*) I'll step outside a second and give you two a chanct to git all the dirty things yuh're thinkin' about me off your chest. (*Threateningly.*) And then I'm gointer come and talk turkey to you, see? I didn't come back here for fun, and the sooner you gets that in your beans, the better.

MARY. Come on and watch me!

LUKE. Aw right, I'm comin'.

(*He walks out and stands, leaning his back against the doorway, left. Mary is about six feet beyond him on the other side of the road. She is leaning down, peering over the edge of the cliff and laughing excitedly.*)

MARY. Can I throw it now? Can I?

LUKE. Don't git too near the edge, kid. The water's deep down there, and you'd be a drowned rat if you slipped. (*She shrinks back a step.*) You chuck it when I say three. Ready, now! (*She draws back her arm.*) One! Two! Three! (*She throws the dollar away and bends down to see it hit the water.*)

MARY (*clapping her hands and laughing*). I seen it! I seen it splash! It's deep down now, ain't it?

LUKE. Yuh betcher it is! Now watch how far I kin chuck rocks.

(*He picks up a couple and goes to where she is standing. During the following conversation between Sweeney and his wife he continues to play this way with Mary. Their voices can be heard, but the words are indistinguishable.*)

SWEENEY (*glancing apprehensively toward the door—with a great sigh*). Speak of the divil an' here he is! (*Furiously.*) Flingin' away dollars, the dirty thief, an' us without——

ANNIE (*interrupting him*). Did you hear what he said? A thief like him ain't come back for no good. (*Lowering her voice.*) D'you s'pose he knows about the farm bein' left to him?

SWEENEY (*uneasily*). How could he? An' yet—I dunno——(*With sudden decision.*) You'd best lave him to me to watch out for. It's small sense you have to hide your hate from him. You're as looney as the rist of your breed. An' he needs to be blarneyed round to fool him an' find out what he's wantin'. I'll pritind to make friends with him, God roast his soul! An' do you run to the house an' break the news to the auld man; for if he seen him suddin it's likely the little wits he has left would leave him; an' the thief could take the farm from us to-morrow if himself turned a lunatic.

ANNIE (*getting up*). I'll tell him a little at a time till he knows.

SWEENEY. Be careful, now, or we'll lose the farm this night. (*She starts towards the doorway. Sweeney speaks suddenly in a strange, awed voice.*) Did you see Luke when he first came in to us? He stood there with the noose of the rope almost touchin' his head. I was almost wishin'—— (*He hesitates.*)

ANNIE (*viciously*). I was wishin' it was round his neck chokin' him, that's what I was—hangin' him just as Paw says.

SWEENEY. Ssshh! He might hear ye. Go along, now. He's comin' back.

MARY (*pulling at Luke's arm as he comes back to the doorway*). Lemme throw 'nother! Lemme throw 'nother!

LUKE (*enters just as Annie is going out and stops her*). Goin' to the house? Do we get any supper? I'm hungry.

ANNIE (*glaring at him, but restraining her rage*). Yes.

LUKE (*jovially*). Good work! And tell the old man I'm here and I'll see him in a while. He'll be glad to see me, too—like hell! (*He comes forward. Annie goes off, right.*)

MARY (*in an angry whine, tugging at his hand*). Lemme throw 'nother. Lemme——

LUKE (*shaking her away*). There's lots of rocks, kid. Throw them. Dollars ain't so plentiful.

MARY (*screaming*). No! No! I don't wanter throw rocks. Lemme throw 'nother o' them.

SWEENEY (*severely*). Let your uncle in peace, ye brat! (*She commences to cry.*) Run help your mother now or I'll give ye a good hidin'. (*Mary runs out of the door, whimpering. Pat turns to Luke and holds out his hand.*)

LUKE (*looking at it in amazement*). Ahoy, there! What's this?

SWEENEY (*with an ingratiating smile*). Let's let bygones be bygones. I'm harbourin' no grudge agen you these past years. Ye was only a lad when ye ran away an' not to be blamed for it. I'd have taken your hand a while back, an' glad to, but for her bein' with us. She has the divil's own tongue, as ye know, an' she can't forget the rowin' you an' her used to be havin'.

LUKE (*still looking at Sweeney's hand*). So that's how the wind blows! (*With a grin.*) Well, I'll take a chanct.

(*They shake hands and sit down by the table, Sweeney on the front bench and Luke on the left one.*)

SWEENEY (*pulls the bottle from his coat pocket—with a wink*). Will ye have a taste? It's real stuff.

LUKE. Yuh betcher I will! (*He takes a big gulp and hands the bottle back.*)

SWEENEY (*after taking a drink himself, puts bottle on table*). I wasn't wishin' herself to see it or I'd have asked ye sooner. (*There is a pause, during which each measures the other with his eyes.*)

LUKE. Say, how's the old man now?

SWEENEY (*cautiously*). Oh, the same as ivir—older an' uglier, maybe.

LUKE. I thought he might be in the bughouse by this time.

SWEENEY (*hastily*). Indeed not; he's foxy to pritind he's looney, but he's his wits with him all the time.

LUKE (*insinuatingly*). Is he as stingy with his coin as he used to be?

SWEENEY. If he owned the ocean he wouldn't give a fish a drink; but I doubt if he's any money left at all. Your mother got rid of it all, I'm thinkin'. (*Luke smiles a superior, knowing smile.*) He has on'y the farm, an' that mortgaged. I've been payin' the int'rist an' supportin' himself an' his doctor's bills by the carpentryin' these five years past.

LUKE (*with a grin*). Huh! Yuh're slow. Yuh oughter get wise to yourself.

SWEENEY (*inquisitively*). What d'ye mean by that?

LUKE (*aggravatingly*). Aw, nothing. (*He turns around and his eyes fix themselves on the rope.*) What the hell—— (*He is suddenly convulsed with laughter and slaps his thigh.*) Hahaha! If that don't beat the Dutch! The old nut!

SWEENEY. What?

LUKE. That rope. Say, has he had that hangin' there ever since I skipped?

SWEENEY (*smiling*). Sure; an' he thinks you'll

be comin' home to hang yourself.

LUKE. Hahaha! Not this chicken! And you say he ain't crazy! Gee, that's too good to keep. I got to have a drink on that. (*Sweeney pushes the bottle toward him. He raises it toward the rope.*) Here's how, old chum! (*He drinks. Sweeney does likewise.*) Say, I'd a'most forgotten about that. Remember how hot he was that day when he hung that rope up and cussed me for pinchin' the hundred? He was standin' there shakin' his stick at me, and I was laughin' 'cause he looked so funny with the spit dribblin' outa his mouth like he was a mad dog. And when I turned round and beat it he shouted after me: "Remember, when you come home again there's a rope waitin' for yuh to hang yourself on, yuh bastard!" (*He spits contemptuously.*) What a swell chanct. (*His manner changes and he frowns.*) The old slave-driver! That's a hell of a fine old man for a guy to have!

SWEENEY (*pushing the bottle toward him*). Take a sup an' forgit it. 'Twas a long time past.

LUKE. But the rope's there yet, ain't it? And he keeps it there. (*He takes a large swallow. Sweeney also drinks.*) But I'll git back at him aw right, yuh wait 'n' see. I'll git every cent he's got this time.

SWEENEY (*slyly*). If he has a cent. I'm not wishful to discourage ye, but—— (*He shakes his head doubtfully, at the same time fixing Luke with a keen glance out of the corner of his eye.*)

LUKE (*with a cunning wink*). Aw, he's got it aw right. You watch me! (*He is beginning to show the effects of the drink he has had. He pulls out tobacco and a paper and rolls a cigarette and lights it. As he puffs he continues boastfully.*) You country jays oughter wake up and see what's goin' on. Look at me. I was green as grass when I left here, but bummin' round the world, and bein' in cities, and meetin' all kinds, and keepin' your two eyes open—that's what'll learn yuh a cute trick or two.

SWEENEY. No doubt but you're right. Us country folks is stupid in most ways. We've no chance to learn the things a travellin' lad like you'd be knowin'.

LUKE (*complacently*). Well, you watch me and I'll learn yuh. (*He snickers.*) So yuh think the old man's flat broke, do yuh?

SWEENEY. I do so.

LUKE. Then yuh're simple; that's what—simple! You're lettin' him kid yuh.

SWEENEY. If he has any, it's well hid, I know that. He's a sly old bird.

LUKE. And I'm a slyer bird. D'yuh hear that? I c'n beat his game any time. You watch me!

(*He reaches out his hand for the bottle. They both drink again. Sweeney begins to show signs of getting drunk. He hiccoughs every now and then and his voice grows uncertain and husky.*)

SWEENEY. It'd be a crafty one who'd find where he'd hidden it, sure enough.

LUKE. You watch me! I'll find it. I betcher anything yuh like I find it. You watch me! Just wait till he's asleep and I'll show yuh—ter-night. (*There is a noise of shuffling footsteps outside and Annie's whining voice raised in angry protest.*)

SWEENEY. Ssshh! It's himself comin' now.

(*Luke rises to his feet and stands, waiting in a defensive attitude, a surly expression on his face. A moment later Bentley appears in the doorway, followed by Annie. He leans against the wall, in an extraordinary state of excitement, shaking all over, gasping for breath, his eyes devouring Luke from head to foot.*)

ANNIE. I couldn't do nothin' with him. When I told him *he'd* come back there was no holdin' him. He was a'most frothin' at the mouth till I let him out. (*Whiningly.*) You got to see to him, Pat, if you want any supper. I can't——

SWEENEY. Shut your mouth! We'll look after him.

ANNIE. See that you do. I'm goin' back.

(*She goes off, right. Luke and his father stand looking at each other. The surly expression disappears from Luke's face, which gradually expands in a broad grin.*)

LUKE (*jovially*). Hello, old sport! I s'pose

yuh're tickled to pieces to see me—like hell! (*The old man stutters and stammers incoherently as if the very intensity of his desire for speech had paralysed all power of articulation. Luke turns to Pat.*) I see he ain't lost the old stick. Many a crack on the nut I used to get with that.

BENTLEY (*suddenly finding his voice—chants.*) "Bring forth the best robe, and put it on him; and put a ring on his hand, and shoes on his feet: And bring hither the fatted calf, and kill it; and let us eat, and be merry: For this my son was dead, and is alive again; he was lost, and is found." (*He ends up with a convulsive sob.*)

LUKE (*disapprovingly*). Yuh're still spoutin' the rotten old Word o' God same's ever, eh? Say, give us a rest on that stuff, will yuh? Come on and shake hands like a good sport. (*He holds out his hand. The old man totters over to him, stretching out a trembling hand. Luke seizes it and pumps it up and down.*) That's the boy!

SWEENEY (*genuinely amazed*). Look at that, would ye—the two-faced auld liar.

(*Bentley passes his trembling hand all over Luke, feeling his arms, his chest, his back. An expression of overwhelming joy suffuses his worn features.*)

LUKE (*grinning at Sweeney*). Say, watch this. (*With tolerant good-humour.*) On the level I b'lieve the old boy's glad to see me at that. He looks like he was tryin' to grin; and I never seen him grin in my life, I c'n remember. (*As Bentley attempts to feel his face.*) Hey, cut it out! (*He pushes his hand away, but not roughly.*) I'm all here, yuh needn't worry. Yuh needn't be scared I'm a ghost. Come on and sit down before yuh fall down. Yuh ain't got your sea-legs workin' right. (*He guides the old man to the bench at left of table.*) Squat here for a spell and git your wind. (*Bentley sinks down on the bench. Luke reaches for the bottle.*) Have a drink to my makin' port. It'll buck yuh up.

SWEENEY (*alarmed*). Be careful, Luke. It might likely end him.

LUKE (*holds the bottle up to the old man's mouth, supporting his head with the other hand. Bentley gulps, the whiskey drips over his chin, and he goes into a fit of convulsive coughing. Luke laughs.*) Hahaha! Went down the wrong way, did it? I'll show yuh the way to do it. (*He drinks.*) There yuh are—smooth as silk. (*He hands the bottle to Sweeney, who drinks and puts it back on the table.*)

SWEENEY. He must be glad to see ye or he'd not drink. 'Tis dead against it he's been these five years past. (*Shaking his head.*) An' him cursin' you day an' night! I can't put head or tail to it. Look out he ain't meanin' some bad to ye underneath. He's crafty at pretendin'.

LUKE (*as the old man makes signs to him with his hand*). What's he after now? He's lettin' on he's lost his voice again. What d'yuh want?

(*Bentley points with his stick to the rope. His lips move convulsively as he makes a tremendous effort to utter words.*)

BENTLEY (*mumbling incoherently*). Luke—Luke—rope—Luke—hang.

SWEENEY (*appalled*). There ye are! What did I tell you? It's to see you hang yourself he's wishin', the auld fiend!

BENTLEY (*nodding*). Yes—Luke—hang.

LUKE (*taking it as a joke—with a loud guffaw*). Hahaha! If that don't beat the Dutch! The old nanny-goat! Aw right, old sport. Anything to oblige. Hahaha!

(*He takes the chair from left and places it under the rope. The old man watches him with eager eyes and seems to be trying to smile. Luke stands on the chair.*)

SWEENEY. Have a care, now! I'd not be foolin' with it in your place.

LUKE. All out for the big hangin' of Luke Bentley by hisself. (*He puts the noose about his neck with an air of drunken bravado and grins at his father. The latter makes violent motions for him to go on.*) Look at him, Pat. By God, he's in a hurry. Hahaha! Well, old sport, here goes nothin'. (*He makes a movement as if he were going to jump and kick the chair from under him.*)

SWEENEY (*half starts to his feet—horrified.*) Luke! Are ye gone mad?

LUKE (*stands staring at his father, who is still making gestures for him to jump. A scowl slowly replaces his good-natured grin*). D'yuh really mean it—that yuh want to see me hangin' myself? (*Bentley nods vigorously in the affirmative. Luke *glares at him for a moment in silence.*) Well, I'll be damned! (*To Pat.*) An' I thought he was only kiddin'. (*He removes the rope gingerly from his neck. The old man stamps his foot and gesticulates wildly, groaning with disappointment. Luke jumps to the floor and looks at his father for a second. Then his face grows white with a vicious fury.*) I'll fix your hash, you stinkin' old murderer! (*He grabs the chair by its back and swings it over his head as if he were going to crush Bentley's skull with it. The old man cowers on the bench in abject terror.*)

SWEENEY (*jumping to his feet with a cry of alarm*). Luke! For the love of God!

(*Luke hesitates; then hurls the chair behind him under the loft, and stands menacingly in front of his father, his hands on his hips.*)

LUKE (*grabbing Bentley's shoulder and shaking him—hoarsely*). Yuh wanted to see me hangin' there in real earnest, didn't yuh? You'd hang me yourself if yuh could, wouldn't yuh? And you my own father! Yuh damned son of a gun! Yuh would, would yuh? I'd smash your brains out for a nickel! (*He shakes the old man more and more furiously.*)

SWEENEY. Luke! Look out! You'll be killin' him next.

LUKE (*giving his father one more shake, which sends him sprawling on the floor*). Git outa here! Git outa this b'fore I kill yuh dead! (*Sweeney rushes over and picks the terrified old man up.*) Take him outa here, Pat! (*His voice rises to a threatening roar.*) Take him outa here, or I'll break every bone in his body! (*He raises his clenched fists over his head in a frenzy of rage.*)

SWEENEY. Ssshh! Don't be roarin'! I've got him. (*He steers the whimpering, hysterical Bentley to the doorway.*) Come out o' this, now. Get down to the house! Hurry now! Ye've made enough trouble for one night. (*They disappear off right. Luke flings himself on a bench, breathing heavily. He picks up the bottle and takes a long swallow. Sweeney re-enters from rear. He comes over and sits down in his old place.*) Thank God he's off down to the house, scurryin' like a frightened hare as if he'd never a kink in his legs in his life. He was moanin' out loud so you could hear him a long ways. (*With a sigh.*) It's a murd'rous auld loon he is, sure enough.

LUKE (*thickly*). The damned son of a gun!

SWEENEY. I thought you'd be killin' him that time with the chair.

LUKE (*violently*). Serve him damn right if I done it.

SWEENEY. An' you laughin' at him a moment sooner! I thought 'twas jokin' ye was.

LUKE (*sullenly*). So I was kiddin'; but I thought he was tryin' to kid me, too. And then I seen by the way he acted he really meant it. (*Banging the table with his fist.*) Ain't that a hell of a fine old man for yuh!

SWEENEY. He's a mean auld swine.

LUKE. He meant it aw right, too. Yuh shoulda seen him lookin' at me. (*With sudden lugubriousness.*) Ain't he a hell of a nice old man for a guy to have? Ain't he?

SWEENEY (*soothingly*). Hush! It's all over now. Don't be thinkin' about it.

LUKE (*on the verge of drunken tears*). How kin I help thinkin'—and him my own father? After me bummin' and starvin' round the rotten earth, and workin' myself to death on ships and things—and when I come home he tries to make me bump off—wants to see me a corpse—my own father, too! Ain't he a hell of an old man to have? The rotten son of a gun!

SWEENEY. It's past an' done. Forgit it. (*He slaps Luke on the shoulder and pushes the bottle toward him.*) Let's take a drop more. We'll be goin' to supper soon.

LUKE (*takes a big drink—huskily*). Thanks. (*He wipes his mouth on his sleeve with a snuffle.*) But I'll tell yuh something you can put in your pipe and smoke. It ain't past and done, and it ain't goin' to be! (*More and more aggressively.*) And I ain't goin' to forget it, either! Yuh kin betcher life on that, pal. And *he* ain't goin' to forget it—not if he lives a million—not by a damned sight! (*With sudden fury.*) I'll fix his hash! I'll git even with him, the old skunk! You watch me! And this very night, too!

SWEENEY. How d'you mean?

LUKE. You just watch me, I tell yuh! (*Banging the table.*) I said I'd git even and I will git even—this same night, with no long waits, either! (*Frowning.*) Say, you don't stand up for him, do yuh?

SWEENEY (*spitting—vehemently*). That's child's talk. There's not a day passed I've not wished him in his grave.

LUKE (*excitedly*). Then we'll both git even on him—you 'n' me. We're pals, ain't we?

SWEENEY. Sure.

LUKE. And yuh kin have half what we gits. That's the kinda feller I am! That's fair enough, ain't it?

SWEENEY. Surely.

LUKE. I don't want no truck with this rotten farm. You kin have my share of that. I ain't made to be no damned dirt puncher—not me! And I ain't goin' to loaf round here more'n I got to, and when I goes this time I ain't never comin' back. Not me! Not to punch dirt and milk cows. You kin have the rotten farm for all of me. What I wants is cash—regular coin yuh kin spend—not dirt. I want to show the gang a real time, and then ship away to sea agen or go bummin' agen. I want coin yuh kin throw away—same's your kid chucked that dollar of mine overboard, remember? A real dollar, too! She's a sport, aw right!

SWEENEY (*anxious to bring him back to the subject*). But where d'you think to find his money?

LUKE (*confidently*). Don't yuh fret. I'll show yuh. You watch me! I know his hidin' places. I useter spy on him when I was a kid—— Maw used to make me—and I seen him many a time at his sneakin'. (*Indignantly.*) He used to hide stuff from the old lady. What d'yuh know about him—the mean skunk.

SWEENEY. That was a long time back. You don't know——

LUKE (*assertively*). But I do know, see! He's got two places. One was where I swiped the hundred.

SWEENEY. It'll not be there, then.

LUKE. No; but there's the other place; and he never knew I was wise to that. I'd have left him clean on'y I was a kid and scared to pinch more. So you watch me! We'll git even on him, you 'n' me, and go halfs, and yuh kin start the rotten farm goin' agen and I'll beat it where there's some life.

SWEENEY. But if there's no money in that place, what'll you be doin' to find out where it is, then?

LUKE. Then you 'n' me 'ull make him tell!

SWEENEY. Oho, don't think it! 'Tis not him'd be tellin'.

LUKE. Aw, say, you're simple! You watch me! I know a trick or two about makin' people tell what they don't wanter. (*He picks up the chisel from the table.*) Yuh see this? Well, if he don't answer up nice and easy we'll show him! (*A ferocious grin settles over his face.*) We'll git even on him, you 'n' me—and he'll tell where it's hid. We'll just shove this into the stove till it's red hot and take off his shoes and socks and warm the bottoms of his feet for him. (*Savagely.*) He'll tell then—anything we wants him to tell.

SWEENEY. But Annie?

LUKE. We'll shove a rag in her mouth so's she can't yell. That's easy.

SWEENEY (*his head lolling drunkenly—with a cruel leer*). 'Twill serve him right to heat up his hoofs for him, the limpin', auld miser!—if ye don't hurt him too much.

LUKE (*with a savage scowl*). We won't hurt him—more'n enough. (*Suddenly raging.*) I'll pay him back aw right! He won't want no more people to hang themselves when I git through with him. I'll fix his hash! (*He sways to his feet, the chisel in his hand.*) Come on! Let's git to work. Sooner we starts the sooner we're rich. (*Sweeney rises. He is steadier on his feet than Luke. At this moment Mary appears in the doorway.*)

MARY. Maw says supper's ready. I had mine. (*She comes into the room and jumps up, trying to grab hold of the rope.*) Lift me, Uncle Luke. I wanter swing.

LUKE (*severely*). Don't yuh dare touch that rope, d'yuh hear?

MARY (*whining*). I wanter swing.

LUKE (*with a shiver*). It's bad, kid. Yuh leave it alone, take it from me.

SWEENEY. She'll get a good whalin' if I catch her jumpin' at it.

LUKE. Come on, pal. T'hell with supper. We got work to do first. (*They go to the doorway.*)

SWEENEY (*turning back to the sulking Mary*). And you stay here, d'you hear, ye brat, till we call ye —or I'll skin ye alive.

LUKE. And ter-morrer mornin', kid, I'll give yuh a whole handful of them shiny, bright things yuh chucked in the ocean—and yuh kin be a real sport.

MARY (*eagerly*). Gimme 'em now ! Gimme 'em now, Uncle Luke. (*As he shakes his head—whiningly.*) Gimme one ! Gimme one !

LUKE. Can't be done, kid. Ter-morrer. Me 'n' your old man is goin' to git even now—goin' to make him pay for——

SWEENEY (*interrupting—harshly*). Hist with your noise ! D'you think she's no ears ? Don't be talkin' so much. Come on, now.

LUKE (*permitting himself to be pulled out the doorway*). Aw right ! I'm with yuh. We'll git even—you 'n' me. The damned son of a gun ! (*They lurch off to the right.*)

(*Mary skips to the doorway and peeps after them for a moment. Then she comes back to the centre of the floor and looks around her with an air of decision. She sees the chair in under the loft and runs over to it, pulling it back and setting it on its legs directly underneath the noose of the rope. She climbs and stands on the top of the chair and grasps the noose with both her upstretched hands. Then with a shriek of delight she kicks the chair from under her and launches herself for a swing. The rope seems to part where it is fixed to the beam. A dirty grey bag tied to the end of the rope falls to the floor with a muffled, metallic thud. Mary sprawls forward on her hands and knees, whimpering. Straggly wisps from the pile of rank hay fall silently to the floor in a mist of dust. Mary, discovering she is unhurt, glances quickly around and sees the bag. She pushes herself along the floor and, untying the string at the top, puts in her hand. She gives an exclamation of joy at what she feels and, turning the bag upside down, pours its contents in her lap. Giggling to herself, she gets to her feet and goes to the doorway, where she dumps what she has in her lap in a heap on the floor just inside the barn. They lie there in a little glittering pile, shimmering in the faint sunset glow—fifty twenty-dollar gold pieces. Mary claps her hands and sings to herself :* " Skip—skip—skip." *Then she quickly picks up four or five of them and runs out to the edge of the cliff. She throws them one after another into the ocean as fast as she can and bends over to see them hit the water. Against the background of horizon clouds still tinted with blurred crimson she hops up and down in a sort of grotesque dance, clapping her hands and laughing shrilly. After the last one is thrown she rushes back into the barn to get more.*)

MARY (*picking up a handful—giggling ecstatically*). Skip ! Skip ! (*She turns and runs out to throw them as*

THE CURTAIN FALLS)

THE DREAMY KID

A Play in One Act

Characters

MAMMY SAUNDERS
ABE, *her grandson,* (THE DREAMY KID)
CEELY ANN
IRENE

SCENE. *Mammy Saunders' bedroom in a house just off Carmine Street, New York City. The left of the room, forward, is taken up by a heavy, old-fashioned wooden bedstead with a feather mattress. A gaudy red-and-yellow quilt covers the other bedclothes. Behind the bed, a chest of drawers placed against the left wall. On top of the chest, a small lamp. A rocking-chair stands beside the head of the bed on the right. In the rear wall, toward the right, a low window with ragged white curtains. In the right corner, a washstand with bowl and pitcher. Bottles of medicine, a spoon, a glass, etc., are also on the stand. Farther forward, a door opening on the passage and staircase.*

It is soon after nightfall of a day in early winter. The room is in shadowy half darkness, the only light being a pale glow that seeps through the window from the arc lamp on the street corner, and by which the objects in the room can be dimly discerned. The vague outlines of Mammy Saunders' figure lying in the bed can be seen, and her black face stands out in sharp contrast from the pillows that support her head.

MAMMY (*weakly*). Ceely Ann! (*With faint querulousness.*) Light de lamp, will you? Hit's mighty dark in yere. (*After a slight pause.*) Ain't you dar, Ceely Ann?

(*Receiving no reply she sighs deeply and her limbs move uneasily under the bedclothes. The door is opened and shut and the stooping form of another coloured woman appears in the semi-darkness. She goes to the foot of the bed sobbing softly, and stands there evidently making an effort to control her emotion.*)

MAMMY. Dat you, Ceely Ann?

CEELY (*huskily*). Hit ain't no yuther, Mammy.

MAMMY. Light de lamp, den. I can't see nowhars.

CEELY. Des one second till I finds a match. (*She wipes her eyes with her handkerchief – then goes to the chest of drawers and feels around on the top of it – pretending to grumble.*) Hit beat all how dem pesky little sticks done hide umse'fs. Shoo! Yere dey is. (*She fumbles with the lamp.*)

MAMMY (*suspiciously*). You ain't been cryin', is you?

CEELY (*with feigned astonishment*). Cryin'? I clar' ter goodness you does git de mos' fool notions lyin' dar.

MAMMY (*in a tone of relief*). I mos' thought I yeard you.

CEELY (*lighting the lamp*). 'Deed you ain't.

(*The two women are revealed by the light. Mammy Saunders is an old, white-haired negress about ninety with a wizened face furrowed by wrinkles and withered by old age and sickness. Ceely is a stout woman of fifty or so with grey hair and a round fat face. She wears a loose-fitting gingham dress and a shawl thrown over her head.)*

CEELY (*with attempted cheeriness*). Bless yo' soul, I ain't got nothin' to cry 'bout. Yere. Lemme fix you so you'll rest mo' easy. (*She lifts the old woman gently and fixes the pillows.*) Dere. Now, ain't you feelin' better?

MAMMY (*dully*). My strenk don' all went. I can't lift a hand.

CEELY (*hurriedly*). Dat'll all come back ter you de doctor tole me des now when I goes down to de door with him. (*Glibly.*) He say you is de mos' strongest 'oman fo' yo' years ever he sees in de worl'; and he tell me you gwine ter be up and walkin' agin fo' de week's out. (*As she finds the old woman's eyes fixed on her she turns away confusedly and abruptly changes the subject.*) Hit ain't too wa'm in dis room, dat's a fac'.

MAMMY (*shaking her head – in a half whisper*). No, Ceely Ann. Hit ain't no use'n you tellin' me nothin' but de trufe. I feels mighty poo'ly. En I knows hit's on'y wid de blessin' er God I kin las' de night out.

CEELY (*distractedly*). Ain't no sich a thing! Hush yo' noise, Mammy!

MAMMY (*as if she hadn't heard – in a crooning sing-song*). I'se gwine soon fum dis wicked yearth – and may de Lawd have mercy on dis po' ole sinner. (*After a pause – anxiously.*) All I'se prayin' fer is dat God don' take me befo' I sees Dreamy agin. Whar's Dreamy, Ceely Ann? Why ain't he come yere? Ain't you done sent him word I'se sick like I tole you?

CEELY. I tole dem boys ter tell him speshul, and dey swar dey would soon's dey find him. I s'pose dey ain't kotch him yit. Don' you pester yo'se'f worryin'. Dreamy 'ull come fo' ve'y long.

MAMMY (*after a pause – weakly*). Dere's a feelin' in my haid like I was a-floatin' yander whar I can't see nothin', or 'member nothin', or know de sight er any pusson I knows; en I wants ter see Dreamy agin befo' –

CEELY (*quickly*). Don' waste yo' strenk talkin'. You git a wink er sleep en I wake you when he comes, you heah me?

MAMMY (*faintly*). I does feel mighty drowsy.

(*She closes her eyes. Ceely goes over to the window and pulling the curtains aside stands looking down into the street as if she were watching for some one coming. A moment later there is a noise of footfalls from the stairs in the hall, followed by a sharp rap on the door.*)

CEELY (*turning quickly from the window*). Ssshh! Ssshh!

(*She hurries to the door, glancing anxiously toward Mammy. The old woman appears to have fallen asleep. Ceely cautiously opens the door a bare inch or so and peeps out. When she sees who it is she immediately tries to slam it shut again, but a vigorous shove from the outside forces her back and Irene pushes her way defiantly into the room. She is a young, good-looking negress, highly rouged and powdered, dressed in gaudy, cheap finery.*)

IRENE (*in a harsh voice – evidently worked up to a great state of nervous excitement*). No you don't, Ceely Ann! I said I was comin' here and it'll take mo'n you to stop me!

CEELY (*almost speechless with horrified indignation – breathing heavily*). Yo' bad 'oman! Git back ter yo' bad-house whar yo' b'longs!

IRENE (*raising her clenched hand – furiously*). Stop dat talkin' to me, nigger, or I'll split yo' fool head! (*As Ceely shrinks away Irene lowers her hand and glances quickly around the room.*) Whar's Dreamy?

CEELY (*scornfully*). Yo' ax me dat! Whar's Dreamy? Ax yo'se'f. Yo's de one ought ter know whar he is.

IRENE. Den he ain't come here?

CEELY. I ain't tellin' de likes er you wedder he is or not.

IRENE (*pleadingly*). Tell me, Ceely Ann, ain't he been here? He'd be sure to come here 'count of Mammy dyin', dey said.

CEELY (*pointing to Mammy – apprehensively*). Ssshh! (*Then lowering her voice to a whisper – suspiciously.*) Dey said? Who said?

IRENE (*equally suspicious*). None o' your business who said. (*Then pleading again.*) Ceely Ann, I jest got ter see him dis minute, dis secon'! He's in bad, Dreamy is, and I knows somep'n I gotter tell him, somep'n I jest heard –

CEELY (*uncomprehendingly*). In bad? What you jest heah?

IRENE. I ain't tellin' no one but him. (*Desperately.*) For Gawd's sake, tell me whar he is, Ceely!

CEELY. I don' know no mo'n you.

IRENE (*fiercely*). You's lyin', Ceely! You's lyin' ter me jest 'cause I'se bad.

CEELY. De good Lawd bar witness I'se tellin' you de trufe!

IRENE (*hopelessly*). Den I gotter go find him, high and low, somewheres. (*Proudly.*) You ain't got de right not ter trust me, Ceely, where de Dreamy's mixed in it. I'd go ter hell for Dreamy!

CEELY (*indignantly*). Hush yo' wicked cussin'! (*Then anxiously.*) Is Dreamy in trouble?

IRENE (*with a scornful laugh*). Trouble? Good Lawd, it's worser'n dat! (*Then in surprise.*) Ain't you heerd what de Dreamy done last night, Ceely?

CEELY (*apprehensively*). What de Dreamy do? Tell me, gal. Somep'n bad?

IRENE (*with the same scornful laugh*). Bad? Worser'n bad, what he done!

CEELY (*lamenting querulously*). Oh good Lawd, I knowed it! I knowed with all his carryin's-on wid dat passel er tough young niggers – him so uppity 'cause he's de boss er de gang – sleepin' all de day 'stead er workin' an' Lawd knows what he does in de nights – fightin' wid white folks, an' totin' a pistol in his pocket – (*with a glance of angry resentment at Irene*) – an' as fo' de udder company he's been keepin' –

IRENE (*fiercely*). Shut your mouth, Ceely! Dat ain't your business.

CEELY. Oh, I knowed Dreamy'd be gittin' in trouble fo' long! De lowflung young trash! An' here's his ole Mammy don' know no dif'frunt but he's de mos' innercent young lamb in de worl'. (*In a strained whisper.*) What he do? Is he been stealin' somep'n?

IRENE (*angrily*). You go ter hell, Ceely Ann! You ain't no fren' of de Dreamy's, you talk dat way, and I ain't got no time ter waste argyin' wid your fool notions. (*She goes to the door.*) Dreamy'll go ter his death sho's yo' born, if I don't find him an' tell him quick!

CEELY (*terrified*). Oh Lawd!

IRENE (*anxiously*). He'll sho'ly try ter come here and see his ole Mammy befo' she dies, don't you think, Ceely?

CEELY. Fo' Gawd I hopes so! She's been a-prayin' all de day –

IRENE (*opening the door*). You hopes so, you fool nigger! I tells you it's good-bye to de Dreamy, he come here! I knows! I gotter find an' stop him. If he come here, Ceely, you tell him git out quick and hide, he don't wanter git pinched. You hear? You tell him dat, Ceely, for Gawd's sake! I'se got ter go – find him – high an' low.

(*She goes out leaving Ceely staring at her in speechless indignation.*)

CEELY (*drawing a deep breath*). Yo' street gal! I don' b'lieve one word you says – stuffin' me wid yo' bad lies so's you kin keep de Dreamy frum leavin' you! (*Mammy Saunders awakes and groans faintly. Ceely hurries over to her bedside.*) Is de pain hurtin' agin, Mammy?

MAMMY (*vaguely*). Dat you, Dreamy?

CEELY. No, Mammy, dis is Ceely. Dreamy's comin' soon. Is you restin' easy?

MAMMY (*as if she hadn't heard*). Dat you, Dreamy?

CEELY (*sitting down in the rocker by the bed and taking one of the old woman's hands in hers*). No. Dreamy's comin'.

MAMMY (*after a pause – suddenly*). Does you 'member yo' dead Mammy, chile?

CEELY (*mystified*). My dead Mammy?

MAMMY. Didn' I heah yo' talkin' jest now, Dreamy?

CEELY (*very worried*). I clar ter goodness, she don' know me ary bit. Dis is Ceely Ann talkin' ter yo', Mammy.

MAMMY. Who was yo' talkin' wid, Dreamy?

CEELY (*shaking her head – in a trembling voice*). Hit can't be long befo' de en'. (*In a louder tone.*) Hit was me talkin' wid a pusson fum ovah de way. She say tell you Dreamy comin' heah ter see yo' right away. You heah dat, Mammy? (*The old woman sighs but does not answer. There is a pause.*)

MAMMY (*suddenly*). Does yo' 'member yo' dead Mammy, chile? (*Then with a burst of religious exaltation.*) De Lawd have mercy!

CEELY (*like an echo*). Bless de Lawd! (*Then in a frightened half-whisper to herself.*) Po' thing! Her min's done leavin' her jest like de doctor said.

(*She looks down at the old woman helplessly. The door on the right is opened stealthily and the Dreamy Kid slinks in on tiptoe.*)

CEELY (*hearing a board creak, turns quickly toward the door and gives a frightened start*). Dreamy!

DREAMY (*puts his fingers to his lips – commandingly*). Ssshh!

(*He bends down to a crouching position and holding the door about an inch open, peers out into the passage in an attitude of tense waiting, one hand evidently clutching some weapon in the side pocket of his coat. After a moment he is satisfied of not being followed, and, after closing the door carefully and locking it, he stands up and walks to the centre of the room casting a look of awed curiosity at the figure in the bed. He is a well-built, good-looking young negro, light in colour. His eyes are shifty and hard, their expression one of tough, scornful defiance. His mouth is cruel and perpetually drawn back at the corners into a snarl. He is dressed in well-fitting clothes of a flashy pattern. A light cap is pulled down on the side of his head.*)

CEELY (*coming from the bed to meet him*). Bless de Lawd, here you is at las'!

DREAMY (*with a warning gesture*). Nix on de loud talk! Talk low, can't yuh! (*He glances back at the door furtively – then continues with a sneer.*) Yuh're a fine nut, Ceely Ann! What for you sendin' out all ober de town for me like you was crazy! D'yuh want ter git me in de cooler? Don' you know dey're after me for what I done last night?

CEELY (*fearfully*). I heerd somep'n – but – what you done, Dreamy?

DREAMY (*with an attempt at a careless bravado*). I croaked a guy, dat's what! A white man.

CEELY (*in a frightened whisper*). What you mean – croaked?

DREAMY (*boastfully*). I shot him dead, dat's what! (*As Ceely shrinks away from him in horror – resentfully.*) Aw say, don' gimme none o' dem looks o' yourn. 'T'warn't my doin' nohow. He was de one lookin' for trouble. I wasn't seekin' for no mess wid him dat I could help. But he told folks he was gwine ter git me for a fac', and dat fo'ced my hand. I had ter git him ter pertect my own life. (*With cruel satisfaction.*) And I got him right, you b'lieve me!

CEELY (*putting her hands over her face with a low moan of terror*). May de good Lawd pardon yo' wickedness! Oh Lawd! What yo' po' ole Mammy gwine say if she hear tell – an' she never knowin' how bad you's got.

DREAMY (*fiercely*). Hell! You ain't tole her, is you?

CEELY. Think I want ter kill her on the instant? An' I didn' know myse'f – what you done – till you tells me. (*Frightenedly.*) Oh, Dreamy, what you gwine do now? How you gwine git away? (*Almost wailing.*) Good Lawd, de perlice don' kotch you suah!

DREAMY (*savagely*). Shut yo' loud mouth, damn you! (*He stands tensely listening for some sound from the hall. After a moment he points to the bed.*) Is Mammy sleepin'?

CEELY (*tiptoes to the bed*). Seems like she is. (*She comes back to him.*) Dat's de way wid her – sleep fo' a few minutes, den she wake, den sleep again.

DREAMY (*scornfully*). Aw, dere ain't nothin' wrong wid her 'ceptin' she's ole. What yuh wanter send de word tellin' me she's croakin', and git me comin' here at de risk o' my life, and den find her sleepin'. (*Clenching his fist threateningly.*) I gotter mind ter smash yo' face for playin' de damn fool and makin' me de goat. (*He turns toward the door.*) Ain't no us'en me stayin' here when dey'll likely come lookin' for me. I'm gwine out where I gotta chance ter make my git-away. De boys is all fixin' it up for me. (*His hand on the doorknob.*) When Mammy wakes, you tell her I couldn't wait, you hear ?

CEELY (*hurrying to him and grabbing his arm – pleadingly*). Don' yo' go now, Dreamy – not jest yit. Fo' de good Lawd's sake, don' you go befo' you speaks wid her! If yo' knew how she's been a-callin' an' a-prayin' for yo' all de day –

DREAMY (*scornfully but a bit uncertainly*). Aw, she

don' need none o' me. What good kin I do watchin' her do a kip? It'd be dif'frunt if she was croakin' on de level.

CEELY (*in an anguished whisper*). She's gwine wake up in a secon' an' den she call: "Dreamy. Whar's Dreamy?" – an' what I gwine tell her den? An' yo' Mammy is dyin', Dreamy, sho's fate! Her min' been wanderin' an' she don' even recernize me no mo', an' de doctor say when dat come it ain't but a sho't time befo' de en'. Yo' gotter stay wid yo' Mammy long 'nuff ter speak wid her, Dreamy. Yo' jest gotter stay wid her in her las' secon's on dis yearth when she's callin' ter yo'. (*With conviction as he hesitates.*) Listen heah, yo' Dreamy! Yo' don' never git no bit er luck in dis worril ary agin, yo' leaves her now. De perlice gon' kotch yo' suah.

DREAMY (*with superstitious fear*). Ssshh! Can dat bull, Ceely! (*Then boastfully.*) I wasn't pinin' to beat it up here, git me? De boys was all persuadin' me not ter take de chance. It's takin' my life in my hands, dat's what. But when I heerd it was ole Mammy croakin' and axin' ter see me, I says ter myse'f: "Dreamy, you gotter make good wid old Mammy no matter what come – or you don' never git a bit of luck in yo' life no mo'." And I was game and come, wasn't I? Nary body in dis worril kin say de Dreamy ain't game ter de core, n'matter what. (*With sudden decision walks to the foot of the bed and stands looking down at Mammy. A note of fear creeps into his voice.*) Gawd, she's quiet 'nuff. Maybe she done passed away in her sleep like de ole ones does. You go see, Ceely; an' if she's on'y sleepin', you wake her up. I wanter speak wid her quick – an' den I'll make a break outa here. You make it fast, Ceely Ann, I tells yo'.

CEELY (*bends down beside the bed*). Mammy! Mammy! Here's de Dreamy.

MAMMY (*opens her eyes – drowsily and vaguely, in a weak voice*). Dreamy?

DREAMY (*shuffling his feet and moving around the bed*). Here I is, Mammy.

MAMMY (*fastening her eyes on him with fascinated joy*). Dreamy! Hit's yo'! (*Then uncertainly.*) I ain't dreamin' nor seein' ha'nts, is I?

DREAMY (*coming forward and taking her hand*). 'Deed I ain't no ghost. Here I is, sho' 'nuff.

MAMMY (*clutching his hand tight and pulling it down on her breast – in an ecstasy of happiness*). Didn' I know you'd come! Didn' I say: "Dreamy ain't gwine let his ole Mammy die all lone by he'se'f an' him not dere wid her." I knows yo'd come. (*She starts to laugh joyously, but coughs and sinks back weakly.*)

DREAMY (*shudders in spite of himself as he realizes for the first time how far gone the old woman is – forcing a tone of joking reassurance*). What's dat foolishness I hears you talkin', Mammy? Wha' d' yuh mean pullin' dat bull 'bout croakin' on me? Shoo! Tryin' ter kid me, ain't you? Shoo! You live ter plant de flowers on my grave, see if you don'.

MAMMY (*sadly and very weakly*). I knows! I knows! Hit ain't long now. (*Bursting into a sudden weak hysteria.*) Yo' stay heah, Dreamy! Yo' stay heah by me, yo' stay heah – till de good Lawd takes me home. Yo' promise me dat! Yo' do dat fo' po' ole Mammy, won't yo'?

DREAMY (*uneasily*). 'Deed I will, Mammy, 'deed I will.

MAMMY (*closing her eyes with a sigh of relief – calmly*). Bless de Lawd for dat. Den I ain't skeered no mo'. (*She settles herself comfortably in the bed as if preparing for sleep.*)

CEELY (*in a low voice*). I gotter go home fo' a minute, Dreamy. I ain't been dere all de day and Lawd knows what happen. I'll be back yere befo' ve'y long.

DREAMY (*his eyes fixed on Mammy*). Aw right, beat it if yuh wanter. (*Turning to her – in a fierce whisper.*) On'y don' be long. I can't stay here an' take dis risk, you hear?

CEELY (*frightenedly*). I knows, chile. I come back, I swar!

(*She goes out quietly. Dreamy goes quickly to the window and cautiously searches the street below with his eyes.*)

MAMMY (*uneasily*). Dreamy. (*He hurries back and takes her hand again.*) I got de mos' 'culiar feelin' in my head. Seems like de years done all roll away an' I'm back down home in de ole place whar you was bo'n. (*After a short pause.*) Does yo' 'member yo' own mammy, chile?

DREAMY. No.

MAMMY. Yo' was too young, I s'pec'. Yo' was on'y a baby w'en she tuck 'n' die. My Sal was a mighty fine 'oman, if I does say hit m'se'f.

DREAMY (*fidgeting nervously*). Don' you talk, Mammy. Better you'd close yo' eyes an' rest.

MAMMY (*with a trembling smile – weakly*). Shoo! W'at is I done come ter wid my own gran' chile bossin' me 'bout. I wants ter talk. You knows you ain't give me much chance ter talk wid yo' dese las' years.

DREAMY (*sullenly*). I ain't had de time, Mammy; but you knows I was always game ter give you anything I got. (*A note of appeal in his voice.*) You knows dat, don' you, Mammy?

MAMMY. Sho'ly I does. Yo' been a good boy, Dreamy; an' if dere's one thing more'n 'nother makes me feel like I mighter done good in de sight er de Lawd, hits dat I raised yo' fum a baby.

DREAMY (*clearing his throat gruffly*). Don' you talk so much, Mammy.

MAMMY (*querulously*). I gotter talk, chile. Come times – w'en I git thinkin' yere in de bed – w'at's gwine ter come ter me a'mos' b'fore I knows hit – like de thief in de night – en den I gits skeered. But w'en I talks wid yo' I ain't skeered a bit.

DREAMY (*defiantly*). You ain't got nothin' to be skeered of – not when de Dreamy's here.

MAMMY (*after a slight pause – faintly*). Dere's a singin' in my ears all de time. (*Seized by a sudden religious ecstasy.*) Maybe hit's de singin' hymns of de blessed angels I done heah fum above. (*Wildly.*) Bless Gawd! Bless Gawd! Pity dis po' ole sinner.

DREAMY (*with an uneasy glance at the door*). Ssshh, Mammy! Don' shout so loud.

MAMMY. De pictures keep a whizzin' fo' my eyes like de thread in a sewing machine. Seem 's if all my life done fly back ter me all ter once. (*With a flickering smile – weakly.*) Does you know how yo' come by dat nickname dey alls call yo' – de Dreamy? Is I ever tole yo' dat?

DREAMY (*evidently lying*). No, Mammy.

MAMMY. Hit was one mawnin' b'fo' we come No'th. Me an' yo' mammy – yo' was des a baby in arms den –

DREAMY (*hears a noise from the hall*). Ssshh, Mammy! For God's sake, don't speak for a minute. I hears somep'n. (*He stares at the door, his face hardening savagely, and listens intently.*)

MAMMY (*in a frightened tone*). W'at's de matter, chile?

DREAMY. Ssshh! Somebody comin'. (*A noise of footsteps comes from the hall staircase. Dreamy springs to his feet.*) Leggo my hand, Mammy – jest for a secon'. I come right back to you.

(*He pulls his hand from the old woman's grip. She falls back on the pillows moaning. Dreamy pulls a large automatic revolver from his coat pocket and tiptoes quickly to the door. As he does so there is a sharp rap. He stands listening at the crack for a moment, then noiselessly turns the key, unlocking the door. Then he crouches low down by the wall so that the door, when opened, will hide him from the sight of anyone entering. There is another and louder rap on the door.*)

MAMMY (*groaning*). W'at's dat, Dreamy? Whar is yo'?

DREAMY. Ssshh! (*Then muffling his voice he calls.*) Come in.

(*He raises the revolver in his hand. The door is pushed open and Irene enters, her eyes peering wildly about the room. Her bosom is heaving as if she had been running and she is trembling all over with terrified excitement.*)

IRENE (*not seeing him calls out questioningly*). Dreamy?

DREAMY (*lowering his revolver and rising to his feet roughly*). Close dat door!

IRENE (*whirling about with a startled cry*). Dreamy!

DREAMY (*shutting the door and locking it – aggressively*). Shut yo' big mouth, gal, or I'll bang it shut for you! You wanter let de whole block know where I is?

IRENE (*hysterical with joy – trying to put her arms around him*). Bless God, I foun' you at last!

DREAMY (*pushing her away roughly*). Leggo o' me! Why you come here follerin' me? Ain't yo' got 'nuff sense in yo' fool head ter know de bulls is liable ter shadow you when dey knows you's my gal? Is you pinin' ter git me kotched an' sent to de chair?

IRENE (*terrified*). No, no!

DREAMY (*savagely*). I gotter mind ter hand you

one you won't ferget! (*He draws back his fist.*)

IRENE (*shrinking away*). Don' you hit me, Dreamy! Don' you beat me up now! Jest lemme 'xplain, dat's all.

MAMMY (*in a frightened whimper*). Dreamy! Come yere to me. Whar is yo'? I'se skeered!

DREAMY (*in a fierce whisper to Irene*). Can dat bull or I'll fix you. (*He hurries to the old woman and pats her hand.*) Here I is, Mammy.

MAMMY. Who dat yo's a-talkin' wid?

DREAMY. On'y a fren' o' Ceely Ann's, Mammy, askin' where she is. I gotter talk wid her some mo' yit. You sleep, Mammy. (*He goes to Irene.*)

MAMMY (*feebly*). Don' yo' leave me, Dreamy.

DREAMY. I'se right here wid you. (*Fiercely, to Irene.*) You git the hell outa here, you Reeny, you heah – quick! Dis ain't no place for de likes o' you wid ole Mammy dyin'.

IRENE (*with a horrified glance at the bed*). Is she dyin' – honest?

DREAMY. Ssshh! She's croakin', I tells yo' – an' I gotter stay wid her fo' a while – an' I ain't got no time ter be pesterin' wid you. Beat it, now! Beat it outa here befo' I knocks yo' cold, git me?

IRENE. Jest wait a secon' for de love o' Gawd. I got somep'n ter tell you –

DREAMY. I don' wanter hear yo' fool talk. (*He gives her a push toward the door.*) Git outa dis, you hear me?

IRENE. I'll go. I'm going soon – soon's ever I've had my say. Lissen, Dreamy! It's about de coppers I come ter tell you.

DREAMY (*quickly*). Why don' you say dat befo'? What you know, gal?

IRENE. Just befo' I come here to find you de first time, de Madam sends me out to Murphy's ter git her a bottle o' gin. I goes in de side door but I ain't rung de bell yet. I hear yo' name spoken an' I stops ter lissen. Dey was three or four men in de back room. Dey don't hear me open de outside door, an' dey can't see me, 'course. It was Big Sullivan from de Central Office talkin'. He was talkin' 'bout de killin' you done last night and he tells dem odders he's heerd 'bout de ole woman gittin' so sick, and dat if dey don't fin' you none of de udder places dey's lookin', dey's goin' wait for you here. Dey s'pecs you come here say good-bye to Mammy befo' you make yo' git-away.

DREAMY. It's aw right den. Dey ain't come yit. Twister Smith done tole me de coast was clear befo' I come here.

IRENE. Dat was den. It ain't now.

DREAMY (*excitedly*). What you mean, gal?

IRENE. I was comin' in by de front way when I sees some pusson hidin' in de doorway 'cross de street. I gits a good peek at him and when I does – it's a copper, Dreamy, suah's yo' born, in his plain clo'se, and he's a watchin' de door o' dis house like a cat.

DREAMY (*goes to the window and stealthily crouching by the dark side peeps out. One glance is enough. He comes quickly back to Irene*). You got de right dope, gal. It's dat Mickey. I knows him even in de dark. Dey're waitin' – so dey ain't wise I'm here yit, dat's suah.

IRENE. But dey'll git wise befo' long.

DREAMY. He don' pipe you comin' in here?

IRENE. I skulked roun' and sneaked in by de back way froo de yard. Dey ain't none o' dem dar yit. (*Raising her voice – excitedly.*) But dere will be soon. Dey're boun' to git wise to dat back door. You ain't got no time to lose, Dreamy. Come on wid me now. Git back where yo' safe. It's de cooler for you certain if you stays here. Dey'll git you like a rat in de trap. (*As Dreamy hesitates.*) For de love of Gawd, Dreamy, wake up to youse'f!

DREAMY (*uncertainly*). I can't beat it – wid Mammy here alone. My luck done turn bad all my life, if I does.

IRENE (*fiercely*). What good's you gittin' pinched and sent to de chair gwine do her? Is you crazy mad? Come away wid me, I tells you!

DREAMY (*half-persuaded – hesitatingly*). I gotter speak wid her. You wait a secon'.

IRENE (*wringing her hands*). Dis ain't no time now for fussin' wid her.

DREAMY (*gruffly*). Shut up! (*He makes a motion for her to remain where she is and goes over to the bed – in a low voice.*) Mammy.

MAMMY (*hazily*). Dat you, Dreamy? (*She tries to reach out her hand and touch him.*)

DREAMY. I'm gwine leave you – jest for a moment, Mammy. I'll send de word for Ceely Ann –

MAMMY (*wideawake in an instant – with intense alarm*). Don' yo' do dat! Don' yo' move one step out er yere or yo'll be sorry, Dreamy.

DREAMY (*apprehensively*). I gotter go, I tells you. I'll come back.

MAMMY (*with wild grief*). O good Lawd! W'en I's drawin' de las' bre'fs in dis po' ole body — (*Frenziedly.*) De Lawd have mercy! Good Lawd have mercy!

DREAMY (*fearfully*). Stop dat racket, Mammy! You bring all o' dem down on my head! (*He rushes over and crouches by the window again to peer out — in relieved tones.*) He ain't heerd nothin'. He's dar yit.

IRENE (*imploringly*). Come on, Dreamy! (*Mammy groans with pain.*)

DREAMY (*hurrying to the bed*). What's de matter, Mammy?

IRENE (*stamping her foot*). Dreamy! Fo' Gawd's sake!

MAMMY. Lawd have mercy! (*She groans.*) Gimme yo' han', chile. Yo' ain't gwine leave me now, Dreamy? Yo' ain't, is yo'? Yo' ole Mammy won't bodder yo' long. Yo' know w'at yo' promise me, Dreamy! Yo' promise yo' sacred word yo' stay wid me till de en'. (*With an air of sombre prophecy — slowly.*) If yo' leave me now, yo' ain't gwine git no bit er luck s'long's yo' live, I tells yo' dat!

DREAMY (*frightened — pleadingly*). Don' you say dat, Mammy!

IRENE. Come on, Dreamy!

DREAMY (*slowly*). I can't. (*In awed tones.*) Don' you hear de curse she puts on me if I does?

MAMMY (*her voice trembling with weak tears*). Don' go, chile!

DREAMY (*hastily*). I won't leave dis room, I swar ter you! (*Relieved by the finality in his tones, the old woman sighs and closes her eyes. Dreamy frees his hand from hers and goes to Irene. He speaks with a strange calm.*) De game's up, gal. You better beat it while de goin's good.

IRENE (*aghast*). You gwine stay?

DREAMY. I gotter, gal. I ain't gwine agin her dyin' curse. No, suh!

IRENE (*pitifully*). But dey'll git you suah!

DREAMY (*slapping the gun in his pocket significantly*). Dey'll have some gittin'. I git some o' dem fust. (*With gloomy determination.*) Dey don't git dis chicken alive! Lawd Jesus, no suh. Not de Dreamy!

IRENE (*helplessly*). Oh, Lawdy, Lawdy! (*She goes to the window — with a short cry.*) He's talkin' wid some one. Dere's two o' dem. (*Dreamy hurries to her side.*)

DREAMY. I knows him — de udder. It's Big Sullivan. (*Pulling her away roughly.*) Come out o' dat! Dey'll see you. (*He pushes her toward the door.*) Dey won't wait down dere much longer. Dey'll be comin' up here soon. (*Prayerfully, with a glance at the bed.*) I hopes she's croaked by den', fo' Christ I does!

IRENE (*as if she couldn't believe it*). Den you ain't gwine save youse'f while dere's time? (*Pleadingly.*) Oh, Dreamy, you can make it yit!

DREAMY. De game's up, I tole you. (*With gloomy fatalism.*) I s'pect it hatter be. Yes, suh. Dey'd git me in de long run anyway — and wid her curse de luck'd be agin me. (*With sudden anger.*) Git outa here, you Reeny! You ain't aimin' ter get shot up too, is you? Ain't no sense in dat.

IRENE (*fiercely*). I'se stayin' too, here wid you!

DREAMY. No you isn't! None o' dat bull! You ain't got no mix in dis jamb.

IRENE. Yes, I is! Ain't you my man?

DREAMY. Don' make no dif. I don't wanter git you in Dutch more'n you is. It's bad 'nuff fo' me. (*He pushes her toward the door.*) Blow while you kin, I tells you!

IRENE (*resisting him*). No, Dreamy! What I care if dey kills me? I'se gwine stick wid you.

DREAMY (*gives her another push*). No, you isn't, gal. (*Unlocking the door — relentlessly.*) Out wid you!

IRENE (*hysterically*). You can't turn me out. I'm gwine stay.

DREAMY (*gloomily*). On'y one thing fo' me ter do den. (*He hits her on the side of the face with all his might, knocking her back against the wall where she sways as if about to fall. Then he opens the door and grabs her two arms from behind.*) Out wid you, gal!

IRENE (*moaning*). Dreamy! Dreamy! Lemme stay wid you! (*He pushes her into the passage and holds her there at arm's length.*) Fo' Gawd's sake, Dreamy!

MAMMY (*whimperingly*). Dreamy! I'se skeered!

IRENE (*from the hall*). I'se gwine stay right here at de door. You might s'well lemme in.

DREAMY (*frowning*). Don' do dat, Reeny. (*Then with a sudden idea.*) You run roun' and tell de gang what's up. Maybe dey git me outa dis, you hear?

IRENE (*with eager hope*). You think dey kin?

DREAMY. Never kin tell. You hurry – through de back yard, 'member – an' don' git pinched, now.

IRENE (*eagerly*). I'm gwine! I'll bring dem back!

DREAMY (*stands listening to her retreating footsteps – then shuts and locks the door – gloomily to himself*). Ain't no good. Dey dassent do nothin' – but I hatter git her outa dis somehow.

MAMMY (*groaning*). Dreamy!

DREAMY. Here I is. Jest a secon'. (*He goes to the window.*)

MAMMY (*weakly*). I feels – like – de en's comin'. Oh, Lawd, Lawd!

DREAMY (*absent-mindedly*). Yes, Mammy. (*Aloud to himself.*) Dey're sneakin' cross de street. Dere's anudder of 'em. Dat's tree.

(*He glances around the room quickly – then hurries over and takes hold of the chest of drawers. As he does so the old woman commences to croon shrilly to herself.*)

DREAMY. Stop dat noise, Mammy! Stop dat noise!

MAMMY (*wanderingly*). Dat's how come yo' got dat – dat nickname – Dreamy.

DREAMY. Yes, Mammy.

(*He puts the lamp on the floor to the rear of the door, turning it down low. Then he carries the chest of drawers over and places it against the door as a barricade.*)

MAMMY (*rambling as he does this – very feebly*). Does yo' know – I gives you dat name – w'en yo's des a baby – lyin' in my arms –

DREAMY. Yes, Mammy.

MAMMY. Down by de crik – under de ole willow – whar I uster take yo' – wid yo' big eyes a-chasin' – de sun flitterin' froo de grass – an' out on de water –

DREAMY (*takes the revolver from his pocket and puts it on top of the chest of drawers*). Dey don' git de Dreamy alive – not for de chair! Lawd Jesus, no suh!

MAMMY. An' yo' was always – a-lookin' – an' a-thinkin' ter yo'se'f – an' yo' big eyes jest a-dreamin' an' a-dreamin' – an' dat's w'en I gives yo' dat nickname – Dreamy – Dreamy –

DREAMY. Yes, Mammy. (*He listens at the crack of the door – in a tense whisper.*) I don' hear dem – but dey're comin' sneakin' up de stairs, I knows it.

MAMMY (*faintly*). Whar is yo', Dreamy? I can't – ha'dly – breathe – no mo'. Oh, Lawd have mercy!

DREAMY (*goes over to the bed*). Here I is, Mammy.

MAMMY (*speaking with difficulty*). Yo' – kneel down – chile – say a pray'r – Oh, Lawd!

DREAMY. Jest a secon', Mammy. (*He goes over and gets his revolver and comes back.*)

MAMMY. Gimme – yo' hand – chile. (*Dreamy gives her his left hand. The revolver is in his right. He stares nervously at the door.*) An' yo' kneel down – pray fo' me. (*Dreamy gets on one knee beside the bed. There is a sound from the passage as if some one had made a misstep on the stairs – then silence. Dreamy starts and half aims his gun in the direction of the door. Mammy groans weakly.*) I'm dyin', chile. Hit's de en'. You pray for me – out loud – so's I can heah. Oh, Lawd! (*She gasps to catch her breath.*)

DREAMY (*abstractedly, not having heard a word she has said*). Yes, Mammy. (*Aloud to himself with an air of grim determination as if he were making a pledge.*) Dey don't git de Dreamy! Not while he's 'live! Lawd Jesus, no suh!

MAMMY (*falteringly*). Dat's right – yo' pray – Lawd Jesus – Lawd Jesus – (*There is another slight sound of movement from the hallway.*)

Curtain

BEYOND THE HORIZON

A Play in Three Acts

TO AGNES

Characters

JAMES MAYO, *a farmer*
KATE MAYO, *his wife*
CAPTAIN DICK SCOTT, *of the barque "Sunda", her brother*
ANDREW MAYO } *sons of James Mayo*
ROBERT MAYO } *sons of James Mayo*
RUTH ATKINS
MRS. ATKINS, *her widowed mother*
MARY
BEN, *a farm-hand*
DOCTOR FAWCETT

(The "right" and "left" of the stage directions are the audience's)

Scenes

ACT ONE

SCENE ONE The road. Sunset of a day in spring.
SCENE TWO The farm-house. The same night.

ACT TWO

(Three years later)

SCENE ONE The farm-house. Noon of a summer day.
SCENE TWO The top of a hill on the farm overlooking the sea. The following day.

ACT THREE

(Five years later)

SCENE ONE The farm-house. Dawn of a day in late fall.
SCENE TWO The road. Sunrise.

ACT ONE SCENE ONE

SCENE. *A section of country highway. The road runs diagonally from the left, forward, to the right, rear, and can be seen in the distance winding toward the horizon like a pale ribbon between the low, rolling hills with their freshly ploughed fields clearly divided from each other, checker-board fashion, by the lines of stone walls and rough snake-fences.*

The forward triangle cut off by the road is a section of a field from the dark earth of which myriad bright-green blades of fall-sown rye are sprouting. A straggling line of piled rocks, too low to be called a wall, separates this field from the road.

To the rear of the road is a ditch with a sloping, grassy bank on the far side. From the centre of this an old, gnarled apple tree, just budding into leaf, strains its twisted branches heavenwards, black against the pallor of distance. A snake-fence sidles from left to right along the top of the bank, passing beneath the apple tree.

The hushed twilight of a day in May is just beginning. The horizon hills are still rimmed by a faint line of flame, and the sky above them glows with the crimson flush of the sunset. This fades gradually as the action of the scene progresses.

At the rise of the curtain, Robert Mayo is discovered sitting on the fence. He is a tall, slender young man of twenty-three. There is a touch of the poet about him expressed in his high forehead and wide, dark eyes. His features are delicate and refined, leaning to weakness in the mouth and chin. He is dressed in grey corduroy trousers pushed into high laced boots, and a blue flannel shirt with a bright coloured tie. He is reading a book by the fading sunset light. He shuts this, keeping a finger in to mark the place, and turns his head toward the horizon, gazing out over the fields and hills. His lips move as if he were reciting something to himself.

His brother Andrew comes along the road from the right, returning from his work in the fields. He is twenty-seven years old, an opposite type to Robert – husky, sun-bronzed, handsome in a large-featured, manly fashion – a son of the soil, intelligent in a shrewd way, but with nothing of the intellectual about him. He wears overalls, leather boots, a grey flannel shirt open at the neck, and a soft, mud-stained hat pushed back on his head. He stops to talk to Robert, leaning on the hoe he carries.

ANDREW (*seeing Robert has not noticed his presence – in a loud shout*). Hey there! (*Robert turns with a start. Seeing who it is, he smiles.*) Gosh, you do take the prize for day-dreaming! And I see you've carted one of the old books along with you. Want to bust your eyesight reading in this light?

ROBERT (*glancing at the book in his hand with a rather shamefaced air*). I wasn't reading – just then, Andy.

ANDREW. No, but you have been. Shucks, you never will get any sense, Rob. (*He crosses the ditch and sits on the fence near his brother.*) What is it this time – poetry, I'll bet. (*He reaches for the book.*) Let me see.

ROBERT (*handing it to him rather reluctantly*). Yes, it's poetry. Look out you don't get it full of dirt.

ANDREW (*glancing at his hands*). That isn't dirt – it's good clean earth; but I'll be careful of the old thing. I just wanted to take a peep at it. (*He turns over the pages.*)

ROBERT (*slyly*). Better look out for your eyesight, Andy.

ANDREW. Huh! If reading this stuff was the only way to get blind, I'd see for ever. (*His eyes read something and he gives an exclamation of disgust.*) Hump! (*With a provoking grin at his brother he reads aloud in a doleful, sing-song voice.*) "I have loved wind and light, and the bright sea. But holy and most sacred night, not as I love and have loved thee." (*He hands the book back.*) Here! Take it and bury it. Give me a good magazine any time.

ROBERT (*with a trace of irritation*). The Farm Journal?

ANDREW. Sure; anything sensible. I suppose it's that year in college gave you a liking for that kind of stuff. I'm darn glad I stopped with High School, or maybe I'd been crazy too. (*He grins and slaps Robert on the back affectionately.*) Imagine me reading poetry and ploughing at the same time. The team'd run away, I'll bet.

ROBERT (*laughing*). Or picture me ploughing. That'd be worse.

ANDREW (*seriously*). Pa was right never to sick you on to the farm. You surely were never cut out for a farmer, that's a fact – even if you'd never been took sick. (*With concern.*) Say, how'd you feel now, anyway? I've lost track of you. Seems as if I never did get a chance to have a talk alone with you these days, 'count of the work. But you're looking fine as silk.

ROBERT. Why, I feel great – never better.

ANDREW. That's bully. You've surely earned it. You certainly had enough sickness in the old days to last you the rest of your life.

ROBERT. A healthy animal like you, you brute, can hardly understand what I went through – although you saw it. You remember – sick one day and well the next – always weak – never able to last through a whole term at school 'til I was years behind every one my age – not able to get in any games – it was hell! These last few years of comparative health have been heaven to me.

ANDREW. I know; they must have been. (*After a pause.*) You should have gone back to college last fall, like I know you wanted to. You're fitted for that sort of thing – just as I ain't.

ROBERT. You know why I didn't go back, Andy. Pa didn't like the idea, even if he didn't say so, and I know he wanted the money to use improving the farm. And besides, I had pretty much all I cared for in that one year. I'm not keen on being a student, just because you see me reading books all the time. What I want to do now is keep on moving, so that I won't take root in any one place.

ANDREW. Well, the trip you're leaving on to-morrow will keep you moving all right. (*At this mention of the trip they both fall silent. There is a pause. Finally Andrew goes on, awkwardly attempting to speak casually.*) Uncle says you'll be gone three years.

ROBERT. About that, he figures.

ANDREW (*moodily*). That's a long time.

ROBERT. Not so long when you come to consider it. You know the *Sunda* sails around the Horn for Yokohama first, and that's a long voyage on a sailing ship, and if we go to any of the other places Uncle Dick mentions – India, or Australia, or South Africa, or South America – they'll be long voyages, too.

ANDREW. You can have all those foreign parts for all of me. A trip to the port once in a while, or maybe down to New York a couple of times a year – that's all the travel I'm hankering after. (*He looks down the road to the right.*) Here comes Pa.

(*The noise of a team of horses coming slowly down the road is heard, and a man's voice urging them on. A moment later James Mayo enters, driving the two weary horses which have been unhitched from the plough. He is his son Andrew over again in body and face – an Andrew sixty-five years old, with a short, square, white beard. He is dressed much the same as Andrew.*)

MAYO (*checking his horses when he sees his sons*). Whoa there! Hello boys! What are you two doin' there roostin' on the fence like a pair of hens?

ROBERT (*laughing*). Oh, just talking things over, Pa.

ANDREW (*with a sly wink*). Rob's trying to get me into reading poetry. He thinks my education's been neglected.

MAYO (*chuckling*). That's good! You kin go out and sing it to the stock at nights to put 'em to sleep. What's that he's got there – 'nother book? Good Lord, I thought you'd read every book there was in the world, Robert, and here you go and finds 'nother one!

ROBERT (*with a smile*). There's still a few left, Pa.

ANDREW. He's learning a new poem about the "bright sea" so he'll be all prepared to recite when he gets on the boat to-morrow.

MAYO (*a bit rebukingly*). He'll have plenty of time to be thinkin' 'bout the water in the next years. No need to bother 'bout it yet.

ROBERT (*gently*). I wasn't. That's just Andy's fooling.

MAYO (*changing the subject abruptly; turns to Andrew*). How are things lookin' up to the hill lot, Andy?

ANDREW (*enthusiastically*). Fine as silk for this early in the year. Those oats seem to be coming along great.

MAYO. I'm most done ploughin' up the old medder – figger I ought to have it all up by to-morrow noon; then you kin start in with the harrowin'.

ANDREW. Sure. I expect I'll be through up above by then. There ain't but a little left to do.

MAYO (*to the restive team*). Whoa there! You'll get your supper soon enough, you hungry critters. (*Turning again to Andrew.*) It looks like a good year for us, son, with fair luck on the weather – even if it's hard work gettin' things started.

ANDREW (*with a grin of satisfaction*). I can stand my share of the hard work, I guess – and then some.

MAYO. That's the way to talk, son. Work never done a man harm yet – leastways, not work done out in the open. (*Robert has been trying to pretend an interest in their conversation, but he can't help showing that it bores him. Andrew notices this.*)

ANDREW. But farming ain't poetry, is it, Rob? (*Robert smiles but remains silent.*)

MAYO (*seriously*). There's more satisfaction in the earth than ever was in any book, and Robert'll find it out sooner or later. (*A twinkle comes into his eyes.*) When he's grown up and got some sense.

ROBERT (*whimsically*). I'm never going to grow up – if I can help it.

MAYO. Time'll tell. Well, I'll be movin' along home. Don't you two stay gossipin' too long. (*He winks at Robert.*) 'Specially you, Andy. Ruth and her Maw is comin' to supper, and you'd best be hurryin' to wash up and put on your best Sunday-go-to-meetin' clothes. (*He laughs. Robert's face contracts as if he were wincing at some pain, but he forces a smile. Andrew grows confused and casts a quick side glance at his brother.*)

ANDREW. I'll be along in a minute, Pa.

MAYO. And you, Robert, don't you stay moonin' at the sky longer'n is needful. You'll get lots o' time for that the next three years you're out on the sea. Remember this is your last night at home, and you've got to make an early start to-morrow (*he hesitates, then finishes earnestly*), 'n' your Ma'll be wantin' to see all she kin o' you the little time left.

ROBERT. I'm not forgetting, Pa. I'll be home right away.

MAYO. That's right. I'll tell your Maw you're acomin'. (*He chucks to the horses.*) Giddap, old bones! Don't you want no supper to-night?

(*The horses walk off, and he follows them. There is a pause. Andrew and Robert sit silently, without looking at each other.*)

ANDREW (*after a while*). Ma's going to miss you a lot, Rob.

ROBERT. Yes – and I'll miss her.

ANDREW. And Pa ain't feeling none too happy to have you go – though he's been trying not to show it.

ROBERT. I can see how he feels.

ANDREW. And you can bet that I'm not giving any cheers about it. (*He puts one hand on the fence near Robert.*)

ROBERT (*putting one hand on top of Andrew's with a gesture almost of shyness*). I know that too, Andy.

ANDREW. I'll miss you as much as anybody, I guess. I know how lonesome the old place was winter before last when you was away at college – and even then you used to come home once in a while; but this time — (*He stops suddenly.*)

ROBERT. Let's not think about it – 'til afterward. We'll only spoil this last night if we do.

ANDREW. That's good advice. (*But after a pause, he returns to the subject again.*) You see, you and I ain't like most brothers – always fighting and separated a lot of the time, while we've always been together – just the two of us. It's different with us. That's why it hits so hard, I guess.

ROBERT (*with feeling*). It's just as hard for me, Andy – believe that! I hate to leave you and the old folks – but – I feel I've got to. There's something calling me – (*He points to the horizon*) calling to me from over there, beyond – and I feel as if – no matter what happens – Oh, I can't just explain it to you, Andy.

ANDREW. No need to, Rob. (*Angry at himself.*) You needn't try to explain. It's all just as it ought to be. Hell! You want to go. You feel you ought to, and you *got* to! – that's all there is to it; and I wouldn't have you miss this chance for the world.

ROBERT. It's fine of you to feel that way, Andy.

ANDREW. Huh! I'd be a nice son-of-a-gun if I didn't, wouldn't I? When I know how you need this sea trip to make a new man of you – in the body, I mean – and give you your full health back.

ROBERT (*a trifle impatiently*). All of you seem to keep harping on my health. You were so used to seeing me lying around the house in the old days that you never will get over the notion that I'm a chronic invalid, and have to be looked after like a baby all the time, or wheeled round in a chair like Mrs. Atkins. You don't realize how I've bucked up in the past few years. Why, I bet right now I'm just as healthy as you are – I mean just as sound in wind and limb; and if I was staying on at the farm, I'd prove it to you. You're suffering from a fixed idea about my delicateness – and so are Pa and Ma. Every time I've offered to help, Pa has stared at me as if he thought I was contemplating suicide.

ANDREW (*conciliatingly*). Nobody claimed the undertaker was taking your measurements. All I was saying was the sea trip would be bound to do anybody good.

ROBERT. If I had no other excuse for going on Uncle Dick's ship but just my health, I'd stay right here and start in ploughing.

ANDREW. Can't be done. No use in your talking that way, Rob. Farming ain't your nature. There's all the difference shown in just the way us two feel about the farm. I like it, all of it, and you – well, you like the home part of it, I expect; but as a place to work and grow things, you hate it. Ain't that right?

ROBERT. Yes, I suppose it is. I've tried to take an interest but – well, you're the Mayo branch of the family, and I take after Ma and Uncle Dick. It's natural enough when you come to think of it. The Mayos have been farmers from way back, while the Scotts have been mostly seafaring folks, with a school teacher thrown in now and then on the woman's side – just as Ma was before her marriage.

ANDREW. You do favour Ma. I remember she used always to have her nose in a book when I was a kid; but she seems to have given it up of late years.

ROBERT (*with a trace of bitterness*). The farm has claimed her in spite of herself. That's what I'm afraid it might do to me in time, and that's why I feel I ought to get away. (*Fearing he has hurt Andrew's feelings.*) You mustn't misunderstand me, Andy. For you it's a different thing. You're a Mayo through and through. You're wedded to the soil. You're as much a product of it as an ear of corn is, or a tree. Father is the same. This farm is his life-work, and he's happy in knowing that another Mayo, inspired by the same love, will take up the work where he leaves off. I can understand your attitude, and Pa's, and I think it's wonderful and sincere. But I – well, I'm not made that way.

ANDREW. No, you ain't; but when it comes to understanding, I guess I realize that you've got your own angle of looking at things.

ROBERT (*musingly*). I wonder if you do, really.

ANDREW (*confidently*). Sure I do. You've seen a bit of the world, enough to make the farm seem small, and you've got the itch to see it all.

ROBERT. It's more than that, Andy.

ANDREW. Oh, of course. I know you're going to learn navigation, and all about a ship, so's you can be an officer. That's natural, too. There's fair pay in it, I expect, when you consider that you've always got a home and grub thrown in; and if you're set on travelling, you can go anywhere you've a mind to, without paying fare.

ROBERT (*with a smile that is half-sad*). It's more than that, Andy.

ANDREW. Sure it is. There's always a chance of a good thing coming your way in some of those foreign ports or other. I've heard there are great opportunities for a young fellow with his eyes open in some of those new countries that are just being opened up. And with your education you ought to pick up the language quick. (*Jovially.*) I'll bet that's what you've been turning over in your mind under all your quietness! (*He slaps his brother on the back with a laugh.*) Well, if you get to be a millionaire all of a sudden, call 'round once in a while and I'll pass the plate to you. We could use a lot of money right here on the farm without hurting it any.

ROBERT (*forced to laugh*). I've never considered that practical side of it for a minute, Andy. (*As Andrew looks incredulous.*) That's the truth.

ANDREW. Well, you ought to.

ROBERT. No, I oughtn't. You're trying to wish an eye-for-business on me I don't possess. (*Pointing to the horizon – dreamily.*) Supposing I was to tell you that it's just Beauty that's calling me, the beauty of the far off and unknown, the mystery and spell of the East, which lures me in the books I've read, the need of the freedom of great wide spaces, the joy of wandering on and on – in quest of the secret which is hidden just over there, beyond the horizon? Suppose I told you that was the one and only reason for my going?

ANDREW. I should say you were nutty.

ROBERT. Then I must be – because it's so.

ANDREW. I don't believe it. You've got that idea out of your poetry books. A good dose of sea-sickness will get that out of your system.

ROBERT (*frowning*). Don't, Andy. I'm serious.

ANDREW. Then you might as well stay right here, because we've got all you're looking for right on this farm. There's wide space enough, Lord knows, and you can have all the sea you want by walking a mile down to the beach, and there's plenty of horizon to look at, and beauty enough for anyone, except in the winter. (*He grins.*) As for the mystery and spell, and other things you mentioned, I haven't met 'em yet, but they're probably lying around somewheres. I'll have you understand this is a first-class farm with all the fixings. (*He laughs.*)

ROBERT (*joining in the laughter in spite of himself*). It's no use talking to you, you chump!

ANDREW. Maybe; but you'll see I'm right before you've gone far. You're not as big a nut as you'd like to make out. You'd better not say anything to Uncle Dick about spells and things when you're on the ship. He'll likely chuck you overboard for a Jonah. (*He jumps down from fence.*) I'd better run along. I've got to wash up some as long as Ruth's Ma is coming over for supper.

ROBERT (*pointedly – almost bitterly*). And Ruth.

ANDREW (*confused – looking everywhere except at Robert – trying to appear unconcerned*). Yes, Pa did say she was staying too. Well, I better hustle, I guess, and — (*He steps over the ditch to the road while he is talking.*)

ROBERT (*who appears to be fighting some strong inward emotion – impulsively*). Wait a minute, Andy! (*He jumps down from the fence.*) There is something I want to — (*He stops abruptly, biting his lips, his face colouring.*)

ANDREW (*facing him; half-defiantly*). Yes?

ROBERT (*confusedly*). No – never mind – it doesn't matter, it was nothing.

ANDREW (*after a pause, during which he stares fixedly at Robert's averted face*). Maybe I can guess – what you were going to say – but I guess you're right not to talk about it. (*He pulls Robert's hand from his side and grips it tensely; the two brothers stand looking into each other's eyes for a minute.*) We can't help those things, Rob. (*He turns away, suddenly releasing Robert's hand.*) You'll be coming along shortly, won't you?

ROBERT (*dully*). Yes.

ANDREW. See you later, then.

(*He walks off down the road to the left. Robert stares after him for a moment; then climbs to the fence rail again, and looks out over the hills, an expression of deep grief on his face. After a moment or so, Ruth enters hurriedly from the left. She is a healthy, blonde, out-of-door girl of twenty, with a graceful, slender figure. Her face, though inclined to roundness, is undeniably pretty, its large eyes of a deep blue set off strikingly by the sun-bronzed complexion. Her small, regular features are marked by a certain strength – an underlying, stubborn fixity of purpose hidden in the frankly-appealing charm of her fresh youthfulness. She wears a simple white dress but no hat.*)

RUTH (*seeing him*). Hello, Rob!

ROBERT (*startled*). Hello, Ruth!

RUTH (*jumps the ditch and perches on the fence beside him*). I was looking for you.

ROBERT (*pointedly*). Andy just left here.

RUTH. I know. I met him on the road a second ago. He told me you were here. (*Tenderly playful.*) I wasn't looking for Andy, Smarty, if that's what you mean. I was looking for *you*.

ROBERT. Because I'm going away to-morrow?

RUTH. Because your mother was anxious to have you come home and asked me to look for you. I just wheeled Ma over to your house.

ROBERT (*perfunctorily*). How is your mother?

RUTH (*a shadow coming over her face*). She's about the same. She never seems to get any better or any worse. Oh, Rob, I do wish she'd pick up a little or – or try to make the best of things that can't be helped.

ROBERT. Has she been nagging at you again?

RUTH (*nods her head, and then breaks forth rebelliously*). She never stops nagging. No matter what I do for her she finds fault. She's growing more irritable every day. Oh, Rob, you've no idea how hard it is living there alone with her in that big lonely house. It's enough to drive anyone mad. If only Pa was still living — (*She stops as if ashamed of her outburst.*) I suppose I shouldn't complain this way. I wouldn't to anyone but you. (*She sighs.*) Poor Ma, Lord knows it's hard enough for her – having to be wheeled around in a chair ever since I was born. I suppose it's natural to be cross when you're not able ever to walk a step. But why should she be in a temper with me all the time? Oh, I'd like to be going away some place – like you!

ROBERT. It's hard to stay – and equally hard to go, sometimes.

RUTH. There! If I'm not the stupid body! I swore I wasn't going to speak about your trip – until after you'd gone, and there I go, first thing!

ROBERT. Why didn't you want to speak of it?

RUTH. Because I didn't want to spoil this last night you're here. Oh, Rob, I'm going to – we're all going to miss you so awfully. Your mother is going around looking as if she'd burst out crying any minute. You ought to know how I feel. Andy and you and I – why, it seems as if we'd always been together.

ROBERT (*with a wry attempt at a smile*). You and Andy will still have each other. It'll be harder for me without anyone.

RUTH. But you'll have new sights and new people to take your mind off; while we'll be here with the old, familiar place to remind us every minute of the day. It's a shame you're going – just at this time, in spring, when everything is getting so nice. (*With a sigh.*) I oughtn't to talk that way when I know going's the best thing for you – on account of your health. The sea trip's bound to do you so much good, every one says.

ROBERT (*with a half-resentful grimace*). Don't tell me *you* think I'm a hopeless invalid, too! I've heard enough of that talk from the folks. Honestly, Ruth, I feel better than I ever did in my life. I'm disgustingly healthy. I wouldn't even consider my health an excuse for this trip.

RUTH (*vaguely*). Of course you're bound to find all sorts of opportunities to get on, your father says.

ROBERT (*heatedly*). I don't give a damn about that! I wouldn't take a voyage across the road for the best opportunity in the world of the kind Pa thinks of. I'd run away from it instead. (*He smiles at his own irritation.*) Excuse me, Ruth, for getting worked up over it; but Andy gave me an overdose of the practical considerations.

RUTH (*slowly puzzled*). Well, then, if it isn't any of those reasons — (*With sudden intensity.*) Oh, Rob, why *do* you want to go?

ROBERT (*turning to her quickly, in surprise – slowly*). Why do you ask that, Ruth?

RUTH (*dropping her eyes before his searching glance*). Because — (*Lamely.*) It seems such a shame.

ROBERT (*insistently*). Why?

RUTH. Oh, because – everything.

ROBERT. I could hardly back out now, even if I wanted to. And I'll be forgotten before you know it.

RUTH (*indignantly*). You won't! I'll never forget — (*She stops and turns away to hide her confusion.*)

ROBERT (*softly*). Will you promise me that?

RUTH (*evasively*). Of course. It's mean of you to think that any of us would forget so easily.

ROBERT (*disappointedly*). Oh!

RUTH (*with an attempt at lightness*). But you haven't told me your reason for leaving yet? Aren't you going to?

ROBERT (*moodily*). I doubt if you'll understand. It's difficult to explain, even to myself. It's more an instinctive longing that won't stand dissection. Either you feel it, or you don't. The cause of it all is in the blood and the bone, I guess, not in the brain, although imagination plays a large part in it. I can remember being conscious of it first when I was only a kid – you haven't forgotten what a sickly specimen I was then, in those days, have you?

RUTH (*with a shudder*). They're past. Let's not think about them.

ROBERT. You'll have to, to understand. Well, in those days, when Ma was fixing meals, she used to get me out of the way by pushing my chair to the west window and telling me to look out and be quiet. That wasn't hard. I guess I was always quiet.

RUTH (*compassionately*). Yes, you always were – and you suffering so much, too!

ROBERT (*musingly*). So I used to stare out over the fields to the hills, out there – (*He points to the horizon*) and somehow after a time I'd forget any pain I was in, and start dreaming. I knew the sea was over beyond those hills – the folks had told me – and I used to wonder what the sea was like, and try to form a picture of it in my mind. (*With a smile.*) There was all the mystery in the world to me then about that – far-off sea – and there still is! It called to me then just as it does now. (*After a slight pause.*) And other times my eyes would follow this road, winding off into the distance, toward the hills, as if it, too, was searching for the sea. And I'd promise myself that when I grew up and was strong, I'd follow that road, and it and I would find the sea together. (*With a smile.*) You see, my making this trip is only keeping that promise of long ago.

RUTH (*charmed by his low, musical voice telling the dreams of his childhood*). Yes, I see.

ROBERT. Those were the only happy moments of my life then, dreaming there at the window. I liked to be all alone – those times. I got to know all the different kinds of sunsets by heart – the clear ones and the cloudy ones, and all the colour schemes of their countless variations – although I could hardly name more than three or four colours correctly. And all those sunsets took place over there – (*He points*) beyond the horizon. So gradually I came to believe that all the wonders of the world happened on the other side of those hills. There was the home of the good fairies who performed beautiful miracles. (*He smiles.*) I believed in fairies then, although I suppose I ought to have been ashamed of it from a boy's standpoint. But you know how contemptuous of all religion Pa's always been – even the mention of it in the house makes him angry.

RUTH. Yes. (*Wearily.*) It's just the opposite to our house.

ROBERT. He'd bullied Ma into being ashamed of believing in anything and he'd forbidden her to teach Andy or me. There wasn't much about our home but the life on the farm. I didn't like that, so I *had* to believe in fairies. (*With a smile.*) Perhaps I still do believe in them. Anyway, in those days they were real enough, and sometimes – I suppose the mental science folks would explain it by self-hypnosis – I could actually hear them calling to me in soft whispers to come out and play with them, dance with them down the road in the dusk in a game of hide-and-seek to find out where the sun was hiding himself. They sang their little songs to me, songs that told of all the wonderful things they had in their home on the other side of the hills, and they promised to show me all of them, if I'd only come, come! But I couldn't come then, and I used to cry sometimes and Ma would think I was in pain. (*He breaks off suddenly with a laugh.*) That's why I'm going now, I suppose. For I can still hear them calling, although I'm a man and have seen the other side of many hills. But the horizon is as far away and as luring as ever. (*He turns to her – softly.*) Do you understand now, Ruth?

RUTH (*spellbound, in a whisper*). Yes.

ROBERT. You feel it then?

RUTH. Yes, yes, I do! (*Unconsciously she snuggles close against his side. His arm steals about her as if he were not aware of the action.*) Oh, Rob, how could I help feeling it? You tell things so beautifully!

ROBERT (*suddenly realizing that his arm is around her, and that her head is resting on his shoulder, gently takes his arm away. Ruth, brought back to herself, is overcome with confusion.*) So now you know why I'm going. It's for that reason – that and one other.

RUTH. You've another? Then you must tell me that, too.

ROBERT (*looking at her searchingly. She drops her eyes before his gaze*). I wonder if I ought to. I wonder if you'd really care to hear it – if you knew. You'll promise not to be angry – whatever it is?

RUTH (*softly, her face still averted*). Yes, I promise.

ROBERT (*simply*). I love you. That's the other reason.

RUTH (*hiding her face in her hands*). Oh, Rob!

ROBERT. You must let me finish now I've begun. I wasn't going to tell you, but I feel I have to. It can't matter to you now that I'm going so far away, and for so long – perhaps for ever. I've loved you all these years, but the realization of it never came to me 'til I agreed to go away with Uncle Dick. Then I thought of leaving you, and the pain of that thought revealed the truth to me in a flash – that I loved you, *had* loved you as long as I could remember. (*He gently pulls one of Ruth's hands away from her face.*) You mustn't mind my telling you this, Ruth. I realize how impossible it all is – and I understand; for the revelation of my own love seemed to open my eyes to the love of others. I saw Andy's love for you – and I knew that you must love him.

RUTH (*breaking out stormily*). I don't! I don't love Andy! I don't! (*Robert stares at her in stupia astonishment. Ruth weeps hysterically.*) Whatever – put such a fool notion into – into your head? (*She suddenly throws her arms about his neck and hides her head on his shoulder.*) Oh, Rob! Don't go away! Please! You mustn't, now! You can't! I won't let you! It'd break my – my heart!

ROBERT (*the expression of stupid bewilderment giving way to one of overwhelming joy. He presses her close to him – slowly and tenderly*). Do you mean that – that you love me?

RUTH (*sobbing*). Yes, yes – of course I do – what d'you s'pose? (*She lifts up her head and looks into his eyes with a tremulous smile.*) You stupid thing! (*He kisses her.*) I've loved you right along.

ROBERT (*mystified*). But you and Andy were always together!

RUTH. Because you never seemed to want to go any place with me. You were always reading an old book, and not paying any attention to me. I was too proud to let you see I cared because I thought the year you had away to college had made you stuck-up, and you thought yourself too educated to waste any time on me.

ROBERT (*kissing her*). And I was thinking — (*With a laugh.*) What fools we've both been!

RUTH (*overcome by a sudden fear*). You won't go away on the trip, will you, Rob? You'll tell them you can't go on account of me, won't you? You can't go now! You can't!

ROBERT (*bewildered*). Perhaps – you can come too.

RUTH. Oh, Rob, don't be so foolish. You know I can't. Who'd take care of Ma? She has no one in the world but me. I can't leave her – the way she is. It'd be different if she was well and healthy like other people. Don't you see I couldn't go – on her account?

ROBERT (*vaguely*). I could go – and then send for you both – when I'd settled some place out there.

RUTH. Ma never could. She'd never leave the farm for anything, and she couldn't make a trip anywhere 'til she got better – if she ever does. And oh, Rob, I wouldn't want to live in any of those outlandish places you were going to. I couldn't stand it there, I know I couldn't – not knowing anyone. It makes me afraid just to think of it. I've never been away from here, hardly and – I'm just a home body, I'm afraid. (*She clings to him imploringly.*) Please don't go – not now. Tell them you've decided not to. They won't mind. I know your mother and father'll be glad. They'll all be. They don't want you to go so far away from them. Please, Rob! We'll be so happy here together where it's natural and we know things. Please tell me you won't go!

ROBERT (*face to face with a definite, final decision, betrays the conflict going on within him*). But – Ruth – I – Uncle Dick —

RUTH. He won't mind when he knows it's for your happiness to stay. How could he? (*As Robert remains silent she bursts into sobs again.*) Oh, Rob! And you said – you loved me!

ROBERT (*conquered by this appeal – an irrevocable decision in his voice*). I won't go, Ruth. I promise you. There! Don't cry! (*He presses her to him, stroking her hair tenderly. After a pause he speaks with happy hopefulness.*) Perhaps after all Andy was right – righter than he knew – when he said I could find all the things I was seeking for here, at home on the farm. The mystery and the wonder – our love should bring them home to us. I think love must have been the secret – the secret that called to me from over the world's rim – the secret beyond every horizon; and when I did not come, it came to me. (*He clasps Ruth to him fiercely.*) Oh, Ruth, you are right! Our love is sweeter than any distant dream. It is the meaning of all life, the whole world. The kingdom of heaven is within – *us!*

(*He kisses her passionately and steps to the ground, lifting Ruth in his arms and carrying her to the road, where he puts her down.*)

RUTH (*with a happy laugh*). My, but you're strong!

ROBERT. Come! We'll go and tell them at once.

RUTH (*dismayed*). Oh no, don't, Rob, not 'til after I've gone. Then you can tell your folks and I'll tell Ma when I get her home. There'd be bound to be such a scene with them all together.

ROBERT (*kissing her – gaily*). As you like – little Miss Common Sense!

RUTH. Let's go, then.

(*She takes his hand, and they start to go off left. Robert suddenly stops and turns as though for a last look at the hills and the dying sunset flush.*)

ROBERT (*looking upward and pointing*). See! The first star. (*He bends down and kisses her tenderly.*) *Our* star!

RUTH (*in a soft murmur*). Yes. Our very own star. (*They stand for a moment looking up at it, their arms around each other. Then Ruth takes his hand again and starts to lead him away.*) Come, Rob, let's go. (*His eyes are fixed again on the horizon as he half-turns to follow her. Ruth urges.*) We'll be late for supper, Rob.

ROBERT (*shakes his head impatiently, as though he were throwing off some disturbing thought – with a laugh*). All right. We'll run then. Come on! (*They run off laughing as*

The Curtain Falls)

ACT ONE SCENE TWO

SCENE. *The sitting-room of the Mayo farm-house about nine o'clock the same night. On the left, two windows looking out on the fields. Against the wall between the windows, an old-fashioned walnut desk. In the left corner, rear, a sideboard with a mirror. In the rear wall to the right of the sideboard, a window looking out on the road. Next to the window a door leading out into the yard. Farther right, a black horse-hair sofa, and another door opening on a bedroom. In the corner, a straight-backed chair. In the right wall, near the middle, an open doorway leading to the kitchen. Farther forward a double-heater stove with coal-scuttle, etc. In the centre of the newly carpeted floor, an oak dining-room table with a red cover. In the centre of the table, a large oil reading-lamp. Four chairs, three rocking with crocheted tidies on their backs, and one straight-backed, are placed about the table. The walls are papered a dark red with a scrolly figured pattern.*

Everything in the room is clean, well-kept, and in its exact place, yet there is no suggestion of primness about the whole. Rather the atmosphere is one of the orderly comfort of a simple, hard-earned prosperity, enjoyed and maintained by the family as a unit.

James Mayo, his wife, her brother, Captain Dick Scott, and Andrew are discovered. Mrs. Mayo is a slight, round-faced, rather prim-looking woman of fifty-five, who had once been a school teacher. The labours of a farmer's wife have bent but not broken her, and she retains a certain refinement of movement and expression foreign to the Mayo part of the family. Whatever of resemblance Robert has to his parents may be traced to her. Her brother, the Captain, is short and stocky, with a weather-beaten, jovial face and a white moustache – a typical old salt, loud of voice and given to gesture. He is fifty-eight years old.

James Mayo sits in front of the table. He wears spectacles, and a farm journal which he has been reading lies in his lap. The Captain leans forward from a chair in the rear, his hands on the table in front of him. Andrew is tilted back on the straight-backed chair to the left, his chin sunk forward on his chest, staring at the carpet, preoccupied and frowning.

As the curtain rises the Captain is just finishing the relation of some sea episode. The others are pretending an interest which is belied by the absent-minded expressions on their faces.

THE CAPTAIN (*chuckling*). And that mission woman, she hails me on the dock as I was acomin' ashore, and she says – with her silly face all screwed up serious as judgment – "Captain," she says, "would you be so kind as to tell me where the sea-gulls sleeps at nights?" Blow me if them warn't her exact words! (*He slaps the table with the palms of his hands and laughs loudly. The others force smiles.*) Ain't that just like a fool woman's question? And I looks at her serious as I could, "Ma'm," says I, "I couldn't rightly answer that question. I ain't never seed a sea-gull in his bunk yet. The next time I hears one snorin'," I says, "I'll make a note of where he's turned in, and write you a letter 'bout it." And then she calls me a fool real spiteful and tacks away from me quick. (*He laughs again uproariously.*) So I got rid of her that way. (*The others smile but immediately relapse into expressions of gloom again.*)

MRS. MAYO (*absent-mindedly – feeling that she has to say something*). But when it comes to that, where *do* sea-gulls sleep, Dick?

SCOTT (*slapping the table*). Ho! Ho! Listen to her, James. 'Nother one! Well, if that don't beat all hell – 'scuse me for cussin', Kate.

MAYO (*with a twinkle in his eyes*). They unhitch their wings, Katey, and spreads 'em out on a wave for a bed.

SCOTT. And then they tells the fish to whistle to 'em when it's time to turn out. Ho! Ho!

MRS. MAYO (*with a forced smile*). You men folks are too smart to live, aren't you? (*She resumes her knitting. Mayo pretends to read his paper; Andrew stares at the floor.*)

SCOTT (*looks from one to the other of them with a puzzled air. Finally he is unable to bear the thick silence a minute longer, and blurts out:*) You folks look as if you was settin' up with a corpse. (*With exaggerated concern.*) God A'mighty, there ain't anyone dead, be there?

MAYO (*sharply*). Don't play the dunce, Dick! You know as well as we do there ain't no great cause to be feelin' chipper.

SCOTT (*argumentatively*). And there ain't no cause to be wearin' mourning, either, I can make out.

MRS. MAYO (*indignantly*). How can you talk that way, Dick Scott, when you're taking our Robbie away from us, in the middle of the night, you might say, just to get on that old boat of yours on time! I think you might wait until morning when he's had his breakfast.

SCOTT (*appealing to the others hopelessly*). Ain't that a woman's way o' seein' things for you? God A'mighty, Kate, I can't give orders to the tide that it's got to be high just when it suits me to have it. I ain't gettin' no fun out o' missin' sleep and leavin' here at six bells myself. (*Protestingly.*) And the *Sunda* ain't an old ship – leastways, not very old – and she's good's she ever was. Your boy Robert'll be as safe on board o' her as he'd be home in bed here.

MRS. MAYO. How can you say that, Dick, when we read in almost every paper about wrecks and storms, and ships being sunk.

SCOTT. You've got to take your chances with such things. They don't happen often – not nigh as often as accidents do ashore.

MRS. MAYO (*her lips trembling*). I wish Robbie weren't going – not so far away and for so long.

MAYO (*looking at her over his glasses – consolingly*). There, Katey!

MRS. MAYO (*rebelliously*). Well, I *do* wish he wasn't! It'd be different if he'd ever been away from home before for any length of time. If he was healthy and strong too, it'd be different. I'm so afraid he'll be taken down ill when you're miles from land, and there's no one to take care of him.

MAYO. That's the very reason you was willin' for him to go, Katey – 'count o' your bein' 'fraid for his health.

MRS. MAYO (*illogically*). But he seems to be all right now without Dick taking him away.

SCOTT (*protestingly*). You'd think to hear you, Kate, that I was kidnappin' Robert agin your will. Now I ain't asayin' I ain't tickled to death to have him along, because I be. It's a'mighty lonesome for a captain on a sailin' vessel at times, and Robert'll be company for me. But what I'm sayin' is, I didn't propose it. I never even suspicioned that he was hankerin' to ship out, or that you'd let him go 'til you and James speaks to me 'bout it. And now you blames me for it.

MAYO. That's so. Dick's speaking the truth, Katey.

SCOTT. You shouldn't be taking it so hard, 's far as I kin see. This vige'll make a man of him. I'll see to it he learns how to navigate, 'n' study for a mate's c'tificate right off – and it'll give him a trade for the rest of his life, if he wants to travel.

MRS. MAYO. But I don't want him to travel all his life. You've got to see he comes home when this trip is over. Then he'll be all well, and he'll want to – to marry – (*Andrew sits forward in his chair with an abrupt movement*) – and settle down right here.

SCOTT. Well, in any case it won't hurt him to learn things when he's travellin'. And then he'll get to see a lot of the world in the ports we put in at, 'n' that'll help him afterwards, no matter what he takes up.

MRS. MAYO (*staring down at the knitting in her lap – as if she hadn't heard him*). I never realized how hard it was going to be for me to have Robbie go – or I wouldn't have considered it a minute. (*On the verge of tears.*) Oh, if only he wouldn't go!

SCOTT. It ain't no good goin' on that way, Kate, now it's all settled.

MRS. MAYO (*half-sobbing*). It's all right for *you* to talk. You've never had any children of your own, and you don't know what it means to be parted from them – and Robbie my youngest, too. (*Andrew frowns and fidgets in his chair.*)

MAYO (*a trace of command in his voice*). No use takin' on so, Katey! It's best for the boy. We've got to take that into consideration – no matter how much we hate to lose him. (*Firmly.*) And like Dick says, it's all settled now.

ANDREW (*suddenly turning to them*). There's one thing none of you seem to take into consideration – that Rob wants to go. He's dead set on it. He's been dreaming over this trip ever since it was first talked about. It wouldn't be fair to him not to have him go. (*A sudden thought seems to strike him and he continues doubtfully.*) At least, not if he still feels the same way about it he did when he was talking to me this evening.

MAYO (*with an air of decision*). Andy's right, Katey. Robert wants to go. That ends all argyment, you can see that.

MRS. MAYO (*faintly, but resignedly*). Yes. I suppose it must be, then.

MAYO (*looking at his big silver watch*). It's past nine. Wonder what's happened to Robert. He's been gone long enough to wheel the widder home, certain. He can't be out dreamin' at the stars his last night.

MRS. MAYO (*a bit reproachfully*). Why didn't you wheel Mrs. Atkins back to-night, Andy? You usually do when she and Ruth come over.

ANDREW (*avoiding her eyes*). I thought maybe Robert wanted to go to-night. He offered to go right away when they were leaving.

MRS. MAYO. He only wanted to be polite.

ANDREW (*gets to his feet*). Well, he'll be right back, I guess. (*He turns to his father.*) Guess I'll go take a look at the black cow, Pa – see if she's ailing any.

MAYO. Yes – better had, son. (*Andrew goes into the kitchen on the right.*)

SCOTT (*as he goes out – in a low tone*). *There's* the boy that would make a good, strong seafarin' man – if he'd a mind to.

MAYO (*sharply*). Don't you put no such fool notions in Andy's head, Dick – or you 'n' me's goin' to fall out. (*Then he smiles.*) You couldn't tempt him, no ways. Andy's a Mayo bred in the bone, and he's a born farmer, and a damn good one, too. He'll live and die right here on this farm, like I expect to. (*With proud confidence.*) And he'll make this one of the slickest, best-payin' farms in the state, too, afore he gits through!

SCOTT. Seems to me it's a pretty slick place right now.

MAYO (*shaking his head*). It's too small. We need more land to make it amount to much, and we ain't got the capital to buy it.

(*Andrew enters from the kitchen. His hat is on, and he carries a lighted lantern in his hand. He goes to the door in the rear leading out.*)

ANDREW (*opens the door and pauses*). Anything else you can think of to be done, Pa?

MAYO. No, nothin' I know of. (*Andrew goes out, shutting the door.*)

MRS. MAYO (*after a pause*). What's come over Andy to-night, I wonder? He acts so strange.

MAYO. He does seem sort o' glum and out of sorts. It's 'count o' Robert leavin', I s'pose. (*To Scott.*) Dick, you wouldn't believe how them boys o' mine sticks together. They ain't like most brothers. They've been thick as thieves all their lives, with nary a quarrel I kin remember.

SCOTT. No need to tell me that. I can see how they take to each other.

MRS. MAYO (*pursuing her train of thought*). Did you notice, James, how queer every one was at supper? Robert seemed stirred up about something, and Ruth was so flustered and giggly, and Andy sat there dumb, looking as if he'd lost his best friend, and all of them only nibbled at their food.

MAYO. Guess they was all thinkin' about to-morrow, same as us.

MRS. MAYO (*shaking her head*). No. I'm afraid somethin's happened – somethin' else.

MAYO. You mean – 'bout Ruth?

MRS. MAYO. Yes.

MAYO (*after a pause – frowning*). I hope her and Andy ain't had a serious fallin'-out. I always sorter hoped they'd hitch up together sooner or later. What d'you say, Dick? Don't you think them two'd pair up well?

SCOTT (*nodding his head approvingly*). A sweet, wholesome couple they'd make.

MAYO. It'd be a good thing for Andy in more ways than one. I ain't what you'd call calculatin' generally, and I b'lieve in lettin' young folks run their affairs to suit themselves; but there's advantages for both o' them in this match you can't overlook in reason. The Atkins' farm is right next to ourn. Jined together they'd make a jim-dandy of a place, with plenty o' room to work in. And bein' a widder with only a daughter, and laid up all the time to boot, Mrs. Atkins can't do nothin' with the place as it ought to be done. Her hired help just goes along as they pleases, in spite o' her everlastin' complainin' at 'em. She needs a man, a first-class farmer, to take hold o' things, and Andy's just the one.

MRS. MAYO (*abruptly*). I don't think Ruth loves Andy.

MAYO. You don't? Well, maybe a woman's eyes is sharper in such things, but – they're always together. And if she don't love him now, she'll likely come around to it in time.

MAYO (*as Mrs. Mayo shakes her head*). You seem mighty fixed in your opinion, Katey. How d'you know?

MRS. MAYO. It's just – what I feel.

MAYO (*a light breaking over him*). You don't mean to say – (*Mrs. Mayo nods. Mayo chuckles scornfully*). Shucks! I'm losin' my respect for your eyesight, Katey. Why, Robert ain't got no time for Ruth, 'cept as a friend!

MRS. MAYO (*warningly*). Sss-h-h!

(*The door from the yard opens, and Robert enters. He is smiling happily, and humming a song to himself, but as he comes into the room an undercurrent of nervous uneasiness manifests itself in his bearing.*)

MAYO. So here you be at last! (*Robert comes forward and sits on Andy's chair. Mayo smiles slyly at his wife.*) What have you been doin' all this time – countin' the stars to see if they all come out right and proper?

ROBERT. There's only one I'll ever look for any more, Pa.

MAYO (*reproachfully*). You might've even not wasted time lookin' for that one – your last night.

MRS. MAYO (*as if she were speaking to a child*). You ought to have worn your coat a sharp night like this, Robbie.

ROBERT. I wasn't cold, Ma. It's beautiful and warm on the road.

SCOTT (*disgustedly*). God A'mighty, Kate, you treat Robert as if he was one year old!

ROBERT (*with a smile*). I'm used to that, Uncle.

SCOTT (*with joking severity*). You'll learn to forget all that baby coddlin' nights down off the Horn when you're haulin' hell-bent on the braces with a green sea up to your neck, and the old hooker doin' summersaults under you. That's the stuff'll put iron in your blood, eh Kate?

MRS. MAYO (*indignantly*). What are you trying to do, Dick Scott – frighten me out of my senses? If you can't say anything cheerful, you'd better keep still.

SCOTT. Don't take on, Kate. I was only joshin' him and you.

MRS. MAYO. You have strange notions of what's a joke, I must say! (*She notices Robert's nervous uneasiness.*) You look all worked up over something, Robbie. What is it?

ROBERT (*swallowing hard, looks quickly from one to the other of them – then begins determinedly*). Yes, there *is* something – something I must tell you – all of you. (*As he begins to talk Andrew enters quietly from the rear, closing the door behind him, and setting the lighted lantern on the floor. He remains standing by the door, his arms folded, listening to Robert with a repressed expression of pain on his face. Robert is so much taken up with what he is going to say that he does not notice Andrew's presence.*) Something I discovered only this evening – very beautiful and wonderful – something I did not take into consideration previously because I hadn't dared to hope that such happiness could ever come to me. (*Appealingly.*) You must all remember that fact, won't you?

MAYO (*frowning*). Let's get to the point, son.

ROBERT. You were offended because you thought I'd been wasting my time star-gazing on my last night at home. (*With a trace of defiance.*) Well, the point is this, Pa; it *isn't* my last night at home. I'm not going – I mean – I can't go to-morrow with Uncle Dick – or at any future time, either.

MRS. MAYO (*with a sharp sigh of joyful relief*). Oh, Robbie, I'm so glad!

MAYO (*astounded*). You ain't serious, be you, Robert?

ROBERT. Yes, I mean what I say.

MAYO (*severely*). Seems to me it's a pretty late hour in the day for you to be upsettin' all your plans so sudden!

ROBERT. I asked you to remember that until this evening I didn't know myself – the wonder which makes everything else in the world seem sordid and pitifully selfish by comparison. I had never dared to dream —

MAYO (*irritably*). Come to the point. What is this foolishness you're talkin' of?

ROBERT (*flushing*). Ruth told me this evening that – she loved me. It was after I'd confessed I loved her. I told her I hadn't been conscious of my love until after the trip had been arranged, and

I realized it would mean – leaving her. That was the truth. I *didn't* know until then. (*As if justifying himself to the others.*) I hadn't intended telling her anything but – suddenly – I felt I must. I didn't think it would matter, because I was going away, and before I came back I was sure she'd have forgotten. And I thought she loved – some one else. (*Slowly – his eyes shining.*) And then she cried and said it was I she'd loved all the time, but I hadn't seen it. (*Simply.*) So we're going to be married – very soon – and I'm happy – and that's all there is to say. (*Appealingly.*) But you see, I couldn't go away now – even if I wanted to.

MRS. MAYO (*getting up from her chair*). Of course not! (*Rushes over and throws her arms about him.*) I knew it! I was just telling your father when you came in – and, oh, Robbie, I'm so happy you're not going!

ROBERT (*kissing her*). I knew you'd be glad, Ma.

MAYO (*bewilderedly*). Well, I'll be damned! You do beat all for gettin' folks' minds all tangled up, Robert. And Ruth too! Whatever got into her of a sudden? Why, I was thinkin' —

MRS. MAYO (*hurriedly – in a tone of warning*). Never mind what you were thinking, James. It wouldn't be any use telling us that now. (*Meaningly.*) And what you were hoping for turns out just the same almost, doesn't it?

MAYO (*thoughtfully – beginning to see this side of the argument*). Yes; I suppose you're right, Katey. (*Scratching his head in puzzlement.*) But how *it* ever come about! It do beat anything ever I heard. (*Finally he gets up with a sheepish grin and walks over to Robert.*) We're glad you ain't goin', your Ma and I, for we'd have missed you terrible, that's certain and sure; and we're glad you've found happiness. Ruth's a fine girl and'll make a good wife to you.

ROBERT (*much moved*). Thank you, Pa. (*He grips his father's hand in his.*)

ANDREW (*his face tense and drawn comes forward and holds out his hand, forcing a smile*). I guess it's my turn to offer congratulations, isn't it?

ROBERT (*with a startled cry when his brother appears before him so suddenly*). Andy! (*Confused.*) Why – I – I didn't see you. Were you here when—.

ANDREW. I heard everything you said; and here's wishing you every happiness, you and Ruth. You both deserve the best there is.

ROBERT (*taking his hand*). Thanks, Andy, it's fine of you to — (*His voice dies away as he sees the pain in Andrew's eyes.*)

ANDREW (*giving his brother's hand a final grip*). Good luck to you both!

(*He turns away and goes back to the rear, when he bends over the lantern, fumbling with it to hide his emotion from the others.*)

MRS. MAYO (*to the Captain, who has been too flabbergasted by Robert's decision to say a word*). What's the matter, Dick? Aren't you going to congratulate Robbie?

SCOTT (*embarrassed*). Of course I be! (*He gets to his feet and shakes Robert's hand, muttering a vague*) Luck to you, boy.

(*He stands beside Robert as if he wanted to say something more but doesn't know how to go about it.*)

ROBERT. Thanks, Uncle Dick.

SCOTT. So you're not acomin' on the *Sunda* with me? (*His voice indicates disbelief.*)

ROBERT. I can't, Uncle – not now. I'm very grateful to you for having wanted to take me. I wouldn't miss it for anything else in the world under any other circumstances. (*He sighs unconsciously.*) But you see I've found – a bigger dream.

SCOTT (*gruffly*). Bring the girl along with you. I'll fix it so there's room.

MRS. MAYO (*sharply*). How can you propose such a crazy idea, Dick – to take a young girl on a sail-boat all over the world and not a woman on the boat but herself. Have you lost your senses?

ROBERT (*regretfully*). It would be wonderful if we could both go with you, Uncle – but it's impossible. Ruth couldn't go on account of her mother, and besides, I'm afraid she doesn't like the idea of the sea.

SCOTT (*putting all his disapproval into an exclamation*). Humph!

(*He goes back and sits down at the table.*)

ROBERT (*in joyous high spirits*). I want you all to understand one thing – I'm not going to be a loafer on your hands any longer. This means the beginning of a new life for me in every way. I'm sick and disgusted at myself for sitting around and seeing every one else hard at work, while all I've been doing is keep the accounts – a couple of hours' work a week! I'm going to settle right down and take a real interest in the farm, and do my share. I'll prove to you, Pa, that I'm as good a Mayo as you are – or Andy, when I want to be.

MAYO (*kindly but sceptically*). That's the right spirit, Robert, but it ain't needful for you to—

MRS. MAYO (*interrupting him*). No one said you weren't doing your part, Robbie. You've got to look out for —

ROBERT. I know what you're going to say, and that's another false idea you've got to get out of your heads. It's ridiculous for you to persist in looking on me as an invalid. I'm as well as anyone, and I'll prove it to you if you'll give me half a chance. Once I get the hang of it, I'll be able to do as hard a day's work as anyone. You wait and see.

MAYO. Ain't none of us doubts your willin'ness, but you ain't never learned —

ROBERT. Then I'm going to start learning right away, and you'll teach me, won't you?

MAYO (*mollifyingly*). Of course I will, boy, and be glad to, only you'd best go easy at first.

ROBERT. With the two farms to look after, you'll need me; and when I marry Ruth I'll have to know how to take care of things for her and her mother.

MAYO. That's so, son.

SCOTT (*who has listened to this conversation in mingled consternation and amazement*). You don't mean to tell me you're goin' to let him stay, do you, James?

MAYO. Why, things bein' as they be, Robert's free to do as he's a mind to.

MRS. MAYO. *Let him!* The very idea!

SCOTT (*more and more ruffled*). Then all I got to say is, you're a soft, weak-willed critter to be permittin' a boy – and women, too – to be layin' your course for you wherever they damn pleases.

MAYO (*slyly amused*). It's just the same with me as 'twas with you, Dick. You can't order the tides on the seas to suit you, and I ain't pretendin' I can reg'late love for young folks.

SCOTT (*scornfully*). Love! They ain't old enough to know love when they sight it! Love! I'm ashamed of you, Robert, to go lettin' a little huggin' and kissin' in the dark spile your chances to make a man out o' yourself. It ain't common sense – no sirree, it ain't – not by a hell of a sight!

(*He pounds the table with his fists in exasperation.*)

ROBERT (*smiling*). I'm afraid I can't help it, Uncle.

SCOTT. Humph! You ain't got any sand, that's what! And you, James Mayo, lettin' boys and women run things to the devil and back – you've got less sense than he has!

MAYO (*with a grin*). If Robert can't help it, I'm sure I ain't able, Dick.

MRS. MAYO (*laughing provokingly at her brother*). A fine one you are to be talking about love, Dick – an old cranky bachelor like you. Goodness sakes!

SCOTT (*exasperated by their joking*). I've never been a damn fool like most, if that's what you're steerin' at.

MRS. MAYO (*tauntingly*). Sour grapes, aren't they, Dick? (*She laughs. Robert and his father chuckle. Scott sputters with annoyance.*) Good gracious, Dick, you do act silly, flying into a temper over nothing.

SCOTT (*indignantly*). Nothin'! Is that what you call it – nothin'? You talk as if I wasn't concerned nohow in this here business. Seems to me I've got a right to have my say. Ain't I gone to all sorts o' trouble gettin' the sta'b'd cabin all cleaned out and painted and fixed up so's that Robert o' yours'd be comfortable? Ain't I made all arrangements with the owners and stocked up with some special grub all on Robert's account?

ROBERT. You've been fine, Uncle Dick; and I appreciate it. Truly.

MAYO. 'Course; we all does, Dick.

MRS. MAYO. And don't spoil it now by getting angry at us.

SCOTT (*unplacated*). It's all right for you to say don't this and don't that; but you ain't seen things from my side of it. I've been countin' sure on havin' Robert for company on this vige – to sorta talk to and show things to, and teach, kinda, and I got my mind so set on havin' him I'm goin' to be double lonesome this vige. (*He pounds on the table, attempting to cover up this confession of weakness.*) Darn all this silly lovin' business, anyway.

MRS. MAYO (*touched*). It's too bad you have to be

so lonesome, Dick. Why don't you give up the old boat? You've been on the sea long enough, heaven knows. Why don't you make up your mind and settle down here with us?

SCOTT (*emphatically*). And go diggin' up the dirt and plantin' things? Not by a hell of a sight! You can have all the darned dirt in the earth for all o' me. I ain't sayin' it ain't all right – if you're made that way – but *I ain't*. No settlin' down for me. No sirree! (*Irritably.*) But all this talk ain't tellin' me what I'm to do with that sta'b'd cabin I fixed up. It's all painted white, an' a bran new mattress on the bunk, 'n' new sheets 'n' blankets 'n' things. And Chips built in a book-case so's Robert could take his books along – with a slidin' bar fixed across't it, mind, so's they couldn't fall out no matter how she rolled. (*With excited consternation.*) What d'you suppose my officers is goin' to think when there's no one comes aboard to occupy that sta'b'd cabin? And the men what did the work on it – what'll *they* think? (*He shakes his finger indignantly.*) They're liable as not to suspicion it was a *woman* I'd planned to ship along, and that she gave me the go-by at the last moment! (*He wipes his perspiring brow in anguish at this thought.*) Gawd A'mighty! They're only lookin' to have the laugh on me for something like that. They're liable to b'lieve anything, those fellers is!

MAYO (*with a wink*). Then there's nothing to it but for you to get right out and hunt up a wife somewheres for that spic 'n' span cabin. She'll have to be a pretty one, too, to match it. (*He looks at his watch with exaggerated concern.*) You ain't got much time to find her, Dick.

SCOTT (*as the others smile – sulkily*). You kin go to thunder, Jim Mayo!

ANDREW (*comes forward from where he has been standing by the door, rear, brooding. His face is set in a look of grim determination*). You needn't worry about that spare cabin, Uncle Dick, if you've a mind to take me in Robert's place.

ROBERT (*turning to him quickly*). Andy! (*He sees at once the fixed resolve in his brother's eyes, and realizes immediately the reason for it – in consternation.*) Andy, you mustn't!

ANDREW. You've made your decision, Rob, and now I've made mine. You're out of this, remember.

ROBERT (*hurt by his brother's tone*). But Andy—

ANDREW. Don't interfere, Rob – that's all I ask. (*Turning to his uncle.*) You haven't answered my question, Uncle Dick.

SCOTT (*clearing his throat, with an uneasy side glance at James Mayo, who is staring at his elder son as if he thought he had suddenly gone mad.* O' course, I'd be glad to have you, Andy.

ANDREW. It's settled then. I can pack the little I want to take in a few minutes.

MRS. MAYO. Don't be a fool, Dick. Andy's only joking you. He wouldn't go for anything.

SCOTT (*disgruntledly*). It's hard to tell who's jokin' and who's not in this house.

ANDREW (*firmly*). I'm not joking, Uncle Dick – and since I've got your permission, I'm going with you. (*As Scott looks at him uncertainly.*) You needn't be afraid I'll go back on my word. When I say I'll go, I'll go.

ROBERT (*hurt by the insinuation he feels in Andrew's tone*). Andy! That isn't fair!

MRS. MAYO (*beginning to be disturbed*). But I know he must be fooling us. Aren't you, Andy?

ANDREW. No, Ma, I'm not.

MAYO (*frowning*). Seems to me this ain't no subject to joke over – not for Andy.

ANDREW (*facing his father*). I agree with you, Pa, and I tell you again, once and for all, that I've made up my mind to go.

MAYO (*dumbfounded – unable to doubt the determination in Andrew's voice – helplessly*). But why, son? Why?

ANDREW (*evasively*). I've always wanted to go, even if I ain't said anything about it

ROBERT. Andy!

ANDREW (*half-angrily*). You shut up, Rob! I told you to keep out of this. (*Turning to his father again.*) I didn't ever mention it because as long as Rob was going I knew it was no use; but now Rob's staying on here, and Uncle Dick wants some one along with him, there isn't any reason for me not to go.

MAYO (*breathing hard*). No reason? Can you stand there and say that to me, Andrew?

MRS. MAYO (*hastily – seeing the gathering storm*). He doesn't mean a word of it, James.

MAYO (*making a gesture to her to keep silence*). Let

me talk, Katey. (*In a more kindly tone.*) What's come over you so sudden, Andy? You know's well as I do that it wouldn't be fair o' you to run off at a moment's notice right now when we're up to our necks in hard work.

ANDREW (*avoiding his eyes*). Rob'll hold his end up as soon as he learns.

MAYO. You know that ain't so. Robert was never cut out for a farmer, and you was.

ANDREW. You can easily get a man to do my work.

MAYO (*restraining his anger with an effort*). It sounds strange to hear you, Andy, that I always thought had good sense, talkin' crazy like that. And you don't believe yourself one bit of what you've been sayin' – not 'less you've suddenly gone out of your mind. (*Scornfully.*) Get a man to take your place? Where'd I get him, tell me, with the shortage of farm labour hereabouts? And if I could get one, what int'rest d'you suppose he'd take beyond doin' as little work as he could for the money I paid him? You ain't been workin' here for no hire, Andy, that you kin give me your notice to quit like you've done. The farm is your'n as well as mine. You've always worked on it with that understanding; and what you're sayin' you intend doin' is just skulkin' out o' your rightful responsibility.

ANDREW (*looking at the floor – simply*). I'm sorry, Pa. (*After a slight pause.*) It's no use talking any more about it.

MRS. MAYO (*in relief*). There! I knew Andy'd come to his senses!

ANDREW. Don't get the wrong idea, Ma. I'm not backing out.

MAYO. You mean you're goin' in spite of – everythin'?

ANDREW. Yes. I'm going. I want to – and – I've got to. (*He looks at his father defiantly.*) I feel I oughtn't to miss this chance to go out into the world and see things, and – I want to go.

MAYO (*with bitter scorn*). So – you want to go out into the world and see thin's! (*His voice raised and quivering with anger.*) I never thought I'd live to see the day when a son o' mine'd look me in the face and tell a barefaced lie! (*Bursting out.*) You're a liar, Andy Mayo, and a mean one to boot!

MRS. MAYO. James!

ROBERT. Pa!

SCOTT. Steady there, Jim!

MAYO (*waving their protests aside*). He is and he knows it.

ANDREW (*his face flushed*). I won't argue with you, Pa. You can think as badly of me as you like. I can't help that. Let's not talk about it any more. I've made up my mind, and nothing you can say will change it.

MAYO (*shaking his finger at Andy, in a cold rage*). You know I'm speakin' truth – that's why you're afraid to argy! You lie when you say you want to go 'way – and see things! You ain't got no likin' in the world to go. Your place is right here on this farm – the place you was born to by nature – and you can't tell me no different. I've watched you grow up, and I know your ways, and they're my ways. You're runnin' against your own nature, and you're goin' to be a'mighty sorry for it if you do. You're tryin' to pretend to me something that don't fit in with your make-up, and it's damn fool pretendin' if you think you're foolin' me. 'S if I didn't know your real reason for runnin' away! And runnin' away's the only words to fit it. You're runnin' away 'cause you're put out and riled 'cause your own brother's got Ruth 'stead o' you, and—

ANDREW (*his face crimson – tensely*). Stop, Pa! I won't stand hearing that – not even from you!

MRS. MAYO (*rushing to Andy and putting her arms about him protectingly*). Don't mind him, Andy dear. He don't mean a word he's saying!

(*Robert stands rigidly, his hands clenched, his face contracted by pain. Scott sits dumbfounded and open-mouthed. Andrew soothes his mother, who is on the verge of tears.*)

MAYO (*in angry triumph*). It's the truth, Andy Mayo! And you ought to be bowed in shame to think of it!

ROBERT (*protestingly*). Pa! You've gone far enough. It's a shame for you to talk that way!

MRS. MAYO (*coming from Andrew to his father; puts her hands on his shoulders as though to try and push him back in the chair from which he has risen*). Won't you be still, James? Please won't you?

MAYO (*looking at Andrew over his wife's shoulder – stubbornly*). The truth – God's truth!

MRS. MAYO. Sh-h-h! (*She tries to put a finger across his lips, but he twists his head away.*)

ANDREW (*who has regained control over himself*). You're wrong, Pa, it isn't truth. (*With defiant assertiveness.*) I don't love Ruth. I never loved her, and the thought of such a thing never entered my head.

MAYO (*with an angry snort of disbelief*). Hump! You're pilin' lie on lie!

ANDREW (*losing his temper – bitterly*). I suppose it'd be hard for you to explain anyone's wanting to leave this blessed farm except for some outside reason like that. You think these few measly acres are heaven, and that none'd want to ever do nothing in all their lives but stay right here and work like a dog all the time. But I'm sick and tired of it – whether you want to believe me or not – and that's why I'm glad to get a chance to move on. I've been sick and tired of farm life for a long time, and if I hadn't said anything about it, it was only to save your feelings. Just because you love it here, you've got your mind set that I like it, too. You want mc to stay on so's you can know that I'll be taking care of the rotten farm after you're gone. Well, Rob'll be here, and he's a Mayo, too. You can leave it in his hands.

ROBERT. Andy! Don't! You're only making it worse.

ANDREW (*sulkily*). I don't care. I've done my share of work here. I've earned my right to quit when I want to. (*Suddenly overcome with anger and grief; with rising intensity.*) I'm sick and tired of the whole damn business. I hate the farm and every inch of ground in it. I'm sick of digging in the dirt and sweating in the sun like a slave without getting a word of thanks for it. (*Tears of rage starting to his eyes – hoarsely.*) I'm through, through for good and all; and if Uncle Dick won't take me on his ship, I'll find another. I'll get away somewhere, somehow.

MRS. MAYO (*in a frightened voice*). Don't you answer him, James. He doesn't know what he's saying to you. Don't say a word to him 'til he's in his right senses again. Please James, don't—

MAYO (*pushes her away from him; his face is drawn and pale with the violence of his passion. He glares at Andrew as if he hated him*). You dare to – you dare to speak like that to me? You talk like that 'bout this farm – the Mayo farm – where you was born – you – you— (*He clenches his fist above his head and advances threateningly on Andrew.*) You damned whelp!

MRS. MAYO (*with a shriek*). James!

(*She covers her face with her hands and sinks weakly into Mayo's chair. Andrew remains standing motionless, his face pale and set.*)

SCOTT (*starting to his feet and stretching his arms across the table toward Mayo*). Easy there, Jim!

ROBERT (*throwing himself between father and brother*). Stop! Are you mad?

MAYO (*grabs Robert's arm and pushes him aside – then stands for a moment gasping for breath before Andrew. He points to the door with a shaking finger*). Yes – go! – go! – You're no son o' mine – no son o' mine! You can go to hell if you want to! Don't let me find you here – in the mornin' – or – or – I'll *throw* you out!

ROBERT. Pa! For God's sake!

(*Mrs. Mayo bursts into noisy sobbing.*)

SCOTT (*placatingly*). Ain't you goin' too far, Jim?

MAYO (*turning on him furiously*). Shut up, you – you Dick! It's your fault – a lot o' this – you and your cussed ship! Don't you take him – if you do – don't you dare darken this door again. Let him go by himself and learn to starve – *starve!* (*He gulps convulsively and turns again to Andrew.*) And you go – to-morrow mornin' – and by God – don't come back – don't dare come back – by God, not while I'm livin' – or I'll – I'll—

(*He shakes over his muttered threat and strides toward the door rear, right.*)

MRS. MAYO (*rising and throwing her arms around him – hysterically*). James! James! Where are you going?

MAYO (*incoherently*). I'm goin' – to bed, Katey. It's late, Katey – it's late. (*He goes out.*)

MRS. MAYO (*following him, pleading hysterically*). James! Take back what you've said to Andy. James!

(*She follows him out. Robert and the Captain stare after them with horrified eyes. Andrew stands rigidly looking straight in front of him, his fists clenched at his sides.*)

SCOTT (*the first to find his voice – with an explosive sigh*). Well, if he ain't the devil himself when he's roused! You oughtn't to have talked to him that way, Andy, 'bout the damn farm, knowin' how touchy he is about it. (*With another sigh.*) Well, you won't mind what he's said in anger. He'll be sorry for it when he's calmed down a bit.

ANDREW (*in a dead voice*). No, he won't. You don't know him. (*Defiantly.*) What's said is said and can't be unsaid; and I've chosen.

SCOTT (*uncertainly*). You don't mean – you're still a mind to go – go with me, do you?

ANDREW (*stubbornly*). I haven't said I've changed my mind, have I? There's all the reason in the world for me to go – now. And I'm going if you're not afraid to take me after what he said.

ROBERT (*with violent protest*). Andy! You can't! Don't be a fool! This is all so stupid – and terrible.

ANDREW (*coldly*). I'll talk to you in a minute, Rob, when we're alone. This is between Uncle and me. (*Crushed by his brother's cold indifference, Robert sinks down into a chair, holding his head in his hands. Andrew turns again to Scott.*) If you don't want to take me, it's all right – there's no hard feelings. I can understand you don't like to fall out with Pa.

SCOTT (*indignantly*). Gawd A'mighty, Andy, I ain't scared o' your Pa, nor no man livin', I want t'have you come along! Only I was thinkin' o' Kate. We don't want her to have to suffer from his contrariness. Let's see. (*He screws up his brows in thought.*) S'posing we both lie a little, eh? I'll tell 'em you're not comin' with me, and you tell 'em you're goin' to the port to get another ship. We can leave here in the team together. That's natural enough. They can't suspect nothin' from that. And then you can write home the first port we touch and explain things. (*He winks at Andrew cunningly.*) Are you on to the course?

ANDREW (*frowning*). Yes – if you think it's best.

SCOTT. For your Ma's sake. I wouldn't ask it, else.

ANDREW (*shrugging his shoulders*). All right then.

SCOTT (*with a great sigh of relief – comes and slaps Andrew on the back – beaming*). I'm damned glad you're shippin' on, Andy. I like your spirit, and the way you spoke up to him. (*Lowering his voice to a cautious whisper.*) You was right not to want to waste your life ploughin' dirt and pattin' it down again. The sea's the place for a young feller like you that isn't half dead 'n' alive. (*He gives Andy a final approving slap.*) You 'n' me'll get along like twins, see if we don't. I'm durned glad you're comin', boy.

ANDREW (*wearily*). Let's not talk about it any more, Uncle. I'm tired of talking.

SCOTT. Right! I'm goin' aloft to turn in, and leave you two alone. Don't forget to pack your dunnage. And git some sleep, if you kin. We'll want to sneak out extra early b'fore they're up. It'll do away with more argyments. Robert can drive us down to the town, and bring back the team. (*He goes to the door in the rear, left.*) Well, good night.

ANDREW. Good night. (*Scott goes out. The two brothers remain silent for a moment. Then Andrew comes over to his brother and puts a hand on his back. He speaks in a low voice, full of feeling.*) Buck up, Rob. It ain't any use crying over spilt milk; and it'll all turn out for the best – let's hope. It couldn't be helped – what's happened.

ROBERT (*wildly*). But it's a lie, Andy, a lie!

ANDREW. Of course it's a lie. You know it and I know it – but that's all ought to know it.

ROBERT. Pa'll never forgive you. Oh, why did you want to anger him like that? You know how he feels about the farm. Oh, the whole affair is so senseless – and tragic. Why did you think you must go away?

ANDREW. You know better than to ask that. You know why. (*Fiercely.*) I can wish you and Ruth all the good luck in the world, and I do, and I mean it; but you can't expect me to stay around here and watch you two together, day after day – and me alone. You couldn't expect that! I couldn't stand it – not after all the plans I'd made to happen on this place thinking— (*His voice breaks.*) Thinking she cared for me.

ROBERT (*putting a hand on his brother's arm*). God! It's horrible! I feel so guilty – to think that I should be the cause of your suffering, after we've been such pals all our lives. If I could have foreseen what'd happen, I swear to you I'd have never said a word to Ruth. I swear I wouldn't have, Andy.

ANDREW. I know you wouldn't; and that

would've been worse, for Ruth would've suffered then. (*He pats his brother's shoulder.*) It's best as it is. It had to be, and I've got to stand the gaff, that's all. Pa'll see how I felt – after a time (*as Robert shakes his head*) – and if he don't – well, it can't be helped.

ROBERT. But think of Ma! God, Andy, you can't go! You can't!

ANDREW (*fiercely*). I've got to go – to get away! I've got to, I tell you. I'd die here. I'd kill myself! Can't you understand what it'd mean to me, how I'd suffer? You don't know how I'd planned – for Ruth and me – the hopes I'd had about what the future'd be like. You can't blame me to go. You'd do the same yourself. I'd go crazy here, bein' reminded every second of the day how my life's been smashed, and what a fool I'd made of myself. I'd have nothing to hope or live for. I've got to get away and try and forget, if I can. I never could stay here – seeing her. And I'd hate the farm if I stayed, hate it for bringin' things back. I couldn't take interest in the work any more, work with no purpose in sight. Can't you see what a hell it'd be? You love her too, Rob. Put yourself in my place, and remember I haven't stopped loving her, and couldn't if I was to stay. Would that be fair to you or to her? Put yourself in my place. (*He shakes his brother fiercely by the shoulder.*) What'd you do then? Tell me the truth! You love her. What'd you do? In spite of all hell, what'd you do?

ROBERT (*chokingly*). I'd – I'd go, Andy! (*He buries his face in his hands with a shuddering sob.*) God!

ANDREW (*seeming to relax suddenly all over his body – in a low, steady voice.*) Then you know why I got to go; and there's nothing more to be said.

ROBERT (*in a frenzy of rebellion*). Why did this have to happen to us? It's damnable!

(*He looks about him wildly, as if his vengeance were seeking the responsible Fate.*)

ANDREW (*soothingly – again putting his hands on his brother's shoulder*). It's no use fussing any more, Rob. It's done. (*Affectionately.*) You'll forget anything I said to hurt when I was mad, won't you? I wanted to keep you out of it.

ROBERT. Oh, Andy, it's me who ought to be asking your forgiveness for the suffering I've brought on you.

ANDREW (*forcing a smile*). I guess Ruth's got a right to have who she likes; you ain't to blame for that. She made a good choice – and God bless her for it!

ROBERT. Andy! Oh, I wish I could tell you half I feel of how fine you are!

ANDREW (*interrupting him quickly*). Shut up! Let's go to bed. We've talked long enough, and I've got to be up long before sun-up. You, too, if you're going to drive us down.

ROBERT. Yes. Yes.

ANDREW (*turning down the lamp*). And I've got to pack yet. (*He yawns with utter weariness.*) I'm as tired as if I'd been ploughing twenty-four hours at a stretch. (*Dully.*) I feel – dead. (*Robert covers his face again with his hands. Andrew shakes his head as if to get rid of his thoughts, and continues with a poor attempt at cheery briskness.*) I'm going to douse the light. Come on. (*He slaps his brother on the back. Robert does not move. Andrew bends over and blows out the lamp. His voice comes from the darkness.*) Don't sit there mourning, Rob. It'll all come out in the wash. Come on and get some sleep. Everything'll turn out all right in the end.

(*Robert can be heard stumbling to his feet, and the dark figures of the two brothers can be seen groping their way toward the doorway in the rear as*

The Curtain Falls)

ACT TWO SCENE ONE

SCENE. *Same as Act One, Scene Two. Sitting-room of the farm-house about half-past twelve in the afternoon of a hot, sun-baked day in midsummer, three years later. All the windows are open, but no breeze stirs the soiled white curtains. A patched screen door is in the rear. Through it the yard can be seen, its small stretch of lawn divided by the dirt path leading to the door from the gate in the white picket fence which borders the road.*

The room has changed, not so much in its outward appearance as in its general atmosphere. Little significant details give evidence of carelessness, of inefficiency, of an industry gone to seed. The chairs appear shabby from lack of paint; the table cover is spotted and askew; holes show in the curtains; a child's doll, with one arm gone, lies under the table; a hoe stands in a corner; a man's coat is flung on the couch in the rear; the desk is cluttered up with odds and ends; a number of books are piled carelessly on the sideboard. The noon enervation of the sultry, scorching day seems to have penetrated indoors, causing even inanimate objects to wear an aspect of despondent exhaustion.

A place is set at the end of the table, left, for some one's dinner. Through the open door to the kitchen comes the clatter of dishes being washed, interrupted at intervals by a woman's irritated voice and the peevish whining of a child.

At the rise of the curtain Mrs. Mayo and Mrs. Atkins are discovered sitting facing each other, Mrs. Mayo to the rear, Mrs. Atkins to the right of the table. Mrs. Mayo's face has lost all character, disintegrated, become a weak mask wearing a helpless, doleful expression of being constantly on the verge of comfortless tears. She speaks in an uncertain voice, without assertiveness, as if all power of willing had deserted her. Mrs. Atkins is in her wheel chair. She is a thin, pale-faced, unintelligent-looking woman of about forty-eight, with hard, bright eyes. A victim of partial paralysis for many years, condemned to be pushed from day to day of her life in a wheel chair, she has developed the selfish irritable nature of the chronic invalid. Both women are dressed in black. Mrs. Atkins knits nervously as she talks. A ball of unused yarn, with needles stuck through it, lies on the table before Mrs. Mayo.

MRS. ATKINS (*with a disapproving glance at the place set on the table*). Robert's late for his dinner again, as usual. I don't see why Ruth puts up with it, and I've told her so. Many's the time I've said to her "It's about time you put a stop to his nonsense. Does he suppose you're runnin' an hotel – with no one to help with things?" But she don't pay no attention. She's as bad as he is, a'most – thinks she knows better than an old, sick body like me.

MRS. MAYO (*dully*). Robbie's always late for things. He can't help it, Sarah.

MRS. ATKINS (*with a snort*). Can't help it! How you do go on, Kate, findin' excuses for him! Anybody can help anything they've a mind to – as long as they've got health, and ain't rendered helpless like me (*she adds as a pious afterthought*) – through the will of God.

MRS. MAYO. Robbie can't.

MRS. ATKINS. Can't! It do make me mad, Kate Mayo, to see folks that God gave all the use of their limbs to potterin' round and wastin' time doin' everything the wrong way – and me powerless to help and at their mercy, you might say. And it ain't that I haven't pointed the right way to 'em. I've talked to Robert thousands of times and told him how things ought to be done. You know that, Kate Mayo. But d'you s'pose he takes any notice of what I say? Or Ruth, either – my own daughter? No, they think I'm a crazy, cranky old woman, half-dead a'ready, and the sooner I'm in the grave and out o' their way the better it'd suit them.

MRS. MAYO. You mustn't talk that way, Sarah. They're not as wicked as that. And you've got years and years before you.

MRS. ATKINS. You're like the rest, Kate. You don't know how near the end I am. Well, at least I can go to my eternal rest with a clear conscience. I've done all a body could do to avert ruin from this house. On their heads be it!

MRS. MAYO (*with hopeless indifference*). Things might be worse. Robert never had any experience in farming. You can't expect him to learn in a day.

MRS. ATKINS (*snappily*). He's had three years to learn, and he's gettin' worse 'stead of better. He hasn't got it in him, that's what; and I do say it to you, Kate Mayo, even if he is your son. He doesn't want to learn. Everything I've told him he's that pig-headed he's gone and done the exact opposite. And now look where things are! They couldn't be worse, spite o' what you say. Not on'y your place but mine too is driftin' to rack and ruin, and I can't do nothin' to prevent, 'cause Ruth backs him up in his folly and shiftlessness.

MRS. MAYO (*with a spark of assertiveness*). You

can't say but Robbie works hard, Sarah.

MRS. ATKINS. What good's workin' hard if it don't accomplish anythin', I'd like to know?

MRS. MAYO. Robbie's had bad luck against him.

MRS. ATKINS. Say what you've a mind to, Kate, the proof of the puddin's in the eatin'; and you can't deny that things have been goin' from bad to worse ever since your husband died two years back.

MRS. MAYO (*wiping tears from her eyes with her handkerchief*). It was God's will that he should be taken.

MRS. ATKINS (*triumphantly*). It was God's punishment on James Mayo for the blasphemin' and denyin' of God he done all his sinful life! (*Mrs. Mayo begins to weep softly.*) There, Kate, I shouldn't be remindin' you, I know. He's at peace, poor man, and forgiven, let's pray.

MRS. MAYO (*wiping her eyes – simply*). James was a good man.

MRS. ATKINS (*ignoring this remark*). What I was sayin' was that since Robert's been in charge things've been goin' downhill steady. You don't know *how* bad they are. Robert don't let on to you what's happinin'; and you'd never see it yourself if 'twas under your nose. But, thank God, Ruth still comes to me once in a while for advice when she's worried near out of her senses by his goin's-on. Do you know what she told me last night? But I forgot, she said not to tell you – still I think you've got a right to know, and it's my duty not to let such things go on behind your back.

MRS. MAYO (*wearily*). You can tell me if you want to.

MRS. ATKINS (*bending over toward her – in a low voice*). Ruth was almost crazy about it. Robert told her he'd have to mortgage the farm – said he didn't know how he'd pull through 'til harvest without it, and he can't get money any other way. (*She straightens up – indignantly.*) Now what do you think of your Robert?

MRS. MAYO (*resignedly*). If it has to be—

MRS. ATKINS. You don't mean to say you're goin' to sign away your farm, Kate Mayo – after me warnin' you?

MRS. MAYO. I'll do what Robbie says is needful.

MRS. ATKINS (*holding up her hands*). Well, of all the foolishness! – well, it's your farm, not mine, and I've nothin' more to say.

MRS. MAYO. Maybe Robbie'll manage till Andy gets back and sees to things. It can't be long now.

MRS. ATKINS (*with keen interest*). Ruth says Andy ought to turn up any day. When does Robert figger he'll get here?

MRS. MAYO. He says he can't calculate exactly on account o' the *Sunda* being a sail-boat. Last letter he got was from England, the day they were sailing for home. That was over a month ago, and Robbie thinks they're overdue now.

MRS. ATKINS. We can give praise to God then that he'll be back in the nick o' time. I've got confidence in Andy and always did have, when it comes to farmin'; and he ought to be tired of travellin' and anxious to get home and settle down to work again.

MRS. MAYO. Andy *has* been working. He's head officer on Dick's boat, he wrote Robbie. You know that.

MRS. ATKINS. That foolin' on ships is all right for a spell, but he must be right sick of it by this. Andy's got to the age where it's time he took hold of things serious and got this farm workin' as it ought to be again.

MRS. MAYO (*musingly*). I wonder if he's changed much. He used to be so fine-looking and strong. (*With a sigh.*) Three years! It seems more like three hundred. (*Her eyes filling – piteously.*) Oh, if James could only have lived 'til he came back – and forgiven him!

MRS. ATKINS. He never would have – not James Mayo! Didn't he keep his heart hardened against him till the last in spite of all you and Robert did to soften him?

MRS. MAYO (*with a feeble flash of anger*). Don't you dare say that! (*Brokenly.*) Oh, I know deep down in his heart he forgave Andy, though he was too stubborn ever to own up to it. It was that brought on his death – breaking his heart just on account of his stubborn pride.

(*She wipes her eyes with her handkerchief and sobs.*)

MRS. ATKINS (*piously*). It was the will of God. (*The whining crying of the child sounds from the kitchen. Mrs. Atkins frowns irritably.*) Drat that young one! Seems as if she cries all the time on purpose to set a body's nerves on edge.

MRS. MAYO (*wiping her eyes*). It's the heat upsets her. Mary doesn't feel any too well these days, poor little child!

MRS. ATKINS. She gets it right from her Pa – bein' sickly all the time. You can't deny Robert was always ailin' as a child. (*She sighs heavily.*) It was a crazy mistake for them two to get married. I argyed against it at the time, but Ruth was so spelled with Robert's wild poetry notions she wouldn't listen to sense. Andy was the one would have been the match for her. I always thought so in those days, same as your James did; and I know she liked Andy. Then 'long comes Robert with his book-learnin' and high-fangled talk – and off she goes and marries him.

MRS. MAYO. I've often thought since it might have been better the other way. But Ruth and Robbie seem happy enough together.

MRS. ATKINS. At any rate it was God's work – and His will be done.

(*The two women sit in silence for a moment. Ruth enters from the kitchen, carrying in her arms her two-year-old daughter, Mary, a pretty but sickly and anæmic-looking child with a tear-stained face. Ruth has aged appreciably. Her face has lost its youth and freshness. There is a trace in her expression of something hard and spiteful. She sits in the rocker in front of the table and sighs wearily. She wears a gingham dress with a soiled apron tied around her waist.*)

RUTH. Land sakes, if this isn't a scorcher! That kitchen's like a furnace. Phew!

(*She pushes the damp hair back from her forehead.*)

MRS. MAYO. Why didn't you call me to help with the dishes?

RUTH (*shortly*). No. The heat in there'd kill you.

MARY (*sees the doll under the table and struggles on her mother's lap*). Mary wants Dolly, Mamma! Give Mary Dolly!

RUTH (*pulling her back*). It's time for your nap. You can't play with Dolly now.

MARY (*commencing to cry whiningly*). Mary wants Dolly!

MRS. ATKINS (*irritably*). Can't you keep that child still? Her racket's enough to split a body's ears. Put her down and let her play with the doll if it'll quiet her.

RUTH (*lifting Mary to the floor*). There! I hope you'll be satisfied and keep still. You're only to play for a minute, remember. Then you've got to take your nap. (*Mary sits down on the floor before the table and plays with the doll in silence. Ruth glances at the place set on the table.*) It's a wonder Rob wouldn't try to get to meals on time once in a while. Does he think I've nothing to do on a hot day like this but stand in that kitchen washing dishes?

MRS. MAYO (*dully*). Something must have gone wrong again.

RUTH (*wearily*). I s'pose so. Something's always going wrong these days, it looks like.

MRS. ATKINS (*snappily*). It wouldn't if you possessed a bit of spunk. The idea of you permittin' him to come in to meals at all hours – and you doin' the work! You ought to force him to have more consideration. I never heard of such a thin'. You mind my words and let him go to the kitchen and get his own once in a while, and see if he don't toe the mark. You're too easy goin', that's the trouble.

RUTH. Do stop your nagging at me, Ma! I'm sick of hearing you. I'll do as I please about it; and thank you for not interfering. (*She wipes her moist forehead – wearily.*) Phew! It's too hot to argue. Let's talk of something pleasant. (*Curiously.*) Didn't I hear you speaking about Andy a while ago?

MRS. MAYO. We were wondering when he'd get home.

RUTH (*brightening*). Rob says any day now he's liable to drop in and surprise us – him and the Captain. I wonder if he's changed much – what he'll be like. It'll certainly look natural to see him around the farm again.

MRS. ATKINS. Let's hope the farm'll look more natural, too, when he's had a hand at it. The way thin's are now!

RUTH (*irritably*). Will you stop harping on that, Ma? We all know things aren't as they might be. What's the good of your complaining all the time?

MRS. ATKINS. There, Kate Mayo! Ain't that just what I told you? I can't say a word of advice to my own daughter even, she's that stubborn and self-willed.

RUTH (*putting her hands over her ears – in exasperation*). For goodness sakes, Ma!

MRS. MAYO (*dully*). Never mind. Andy'll fix everything when he comes.

RUTH (*hopefully*). Oh yes, I know he will. He always did know just the right thing ought to be done. (*With weary vexation.*) It's a shame for him to come home and have to start in with things in such a topsy-turvy.

MRS. MAYO. Andy'll manage.

RUTH (*sighing*). I s'pose it isn't Rob's fault things go wrong with him.

MRS. ATKINS (*scornfully*). Hump! (*She fans herself nervously.*) Land o' Goshen, but it's bakin' in here! Let's go out in under the trees in back where there's a breath of fresh air. Come, Kate. (*Mrs. Mayo gets up obediently and starts to wheel the invalid's chair toward the screen door.*) You better come too, Ruth. It'll do you good. Learn him a lesson and let him get his own dinner. Don't be such a fool.

RUTH (*going and holding the screen door open for them – listlessly*). He wouldn't mind. He tells me never to wait – but he wouldn't know where to find anything.

MRS. ATKINS. Let him go hungry then – and serve him right.

RUTH. He wouldn't mind that, either. He doesn't eat much. But I can't go anyway. I've got to put baby to bed.

MRS. ATKINS. Let's go, Kate. I'm boilin' in here.

(*Mrs. Mayo wheels her out and off left. Ruth comes back and sits down in her chair.*)

RUTH (*mechanically*). Come and let me take off your shoes and stockings, Mary, that's a good girl. You've got to take your nap now.

(*The child continues to play as if she hadn't heard, absorbed in her doll. An eager expression comes over Ruth's tired face. She glances toward the door furtively – then gets up and goes to the desk. Her movements indicate a guilty fear of discovery. She takes a letter from a pigeonhole and retreats swiftly to her chair with it. She opens the envelope and reads the letter with great interest, a flush of excitement coming to her cheeks. Robert walks up the path and opens the screen door quietly and comes into the room. He, too, has aged. His shoulders are stooped as if under too great a burden. His eyes are dull and lifeless, his face burned by the sun and unshaven for days. Streaks of sweat have smudged the layer of dust on his cheeks. His lips, drawn down at the corners, give him a hopeless, resigned expression. The three years have accentuated the weakness of his mouth and chin. He is dressed in overalls, laced boots, and a flannel shirt open at the neck.*)

ROBERT (*throwing his hat over on the sofa – with a great sigh of exhaustion*). Phew! The sun's hot today!

(*Ruth is startled. At first she makes an instinctive motion as if to hide the letter in her bosom. She immediately thinks better of this and sits with the letter in her hands looking at him with defiant eyes. He bends down and kisses her.*)

RUTH (*feeling her cheek – irritably*). Why don't you shave? You look awful.

ROBERT (*indifferently*). I forgot – and it's too much trouble this weather.

MARY (*throwing aside her doll, runs to him with a happy cry*). Dadda! Dadda!

ROBERT (*swinging her up above his head – lovingly*). And how's this little girl of mine this hot day, eh?

MARY (*screeching happily*). Dadda! Dadda!

RUTH (*in annoyance*). Don't do that to her! You know it's time for her nap and you'll get her all waked up; then I'll be the one that'll have to sit beside her till she falls asleep.

ROBERT (*sitting down in the chair on the left of table and cuddling Mary on his lap*). You needn't bother. I'll put her to bed.

RUTH (*shortly*). You've got to get back to your work, I s'pose.

ROBERT (*with a sigh*). Yes, I was forgetting. (*He glances at the open letter on Ruth's lap.*) Reading Andy's letter again? I should think you'd know it by heart by this time.

RUTH (*colouring as if she'd been accused of something – defiantly*). I've got a right to read it, haven't I? He says it's meant for all of us.

ROBERT (*with a trace of irritation*). Right? Don't be so silly. There's no question of right. I was only saying that you must know all that's in it after so many readings.

RUTH. Well, I don't. (*She puts the letter on the table and gets wearily to her feet.*) I s'pose you'll be wanting your dinner now.

ROBERT (*listlessly*). I don't care. I'm not hungry. It's almost too hot to eat.

RUTH. And here I been keeping it hot for you!

ROBERT (*irritably*). Oh, all right then. Bring it in and I'll try to eat.

RUTH. I've got to get her to bed first. (*She goes to lift Mary off his lap.*) Come, dear. It's after time and you can hardly keep your eyes open now.

MARY (*crying*). No, no, I don't wanter sleep! (*Appealing to her father.*) Dadda! No!

RUTH (*accusingly to Robert*). There! Now see what you've done! I told you not to —

ROBERT (*shortly*). Let her alone, then. She's all right where she is. She'll fall asleep on my lap in a minute if you'll stop bothering her.

RUTH (*hotly*). She'll not do any such thing! She's got to learn to mind me, that she has! (*Shaking her finger at Mary.*) You naughty child! Will you come with Mamma when she tells you for your own good?

MARY (*clinging to her father*). No, Dadda!

RUTH (*losing her temper*). A good spanking's what you need, my young lady – and you'll get one from me if you don't mind better, d'you hear? (*Mary starts to whimper frightenedly.*)

ROBERT (*with sudden anger*). Leave her alone! How often have I told you not to threaten her with whipping? It's barbarous, and I won't have it. That's got to be understood. (*Soothing the wailing Mary.*) There! There, little girl! Baby mustn't cry. Dadda won't like you if you do. Dadda'll hold you and you must promise to go to sleep like a good little girl. Will you when Dadda asks you?

MARY (*cuddling up to him*). Yes, Dadda.

RUTH (*looking at them, her pale face set and drawn*). I won't be ordered by you! She's my child as much as yours. A fine one you are to be telling folks how to do things, you — (*She bites her lips. Husband and wife look into each other's eyes with something akin to hatred in their expressions; then Ruth turns away with a shrug of affected indifference.*) All right, take care of her then, if you think it's so easy. You'll be whipping her yourself inside of a week. (*She walks away into the kitchen.*)

ROBERT (*smoothing Mary's hair – tenderly*). We'll show Mamma you're a good little girl, won't we?

MARY (*crooning drowsily*). Dadda, Dadda.

ROBERT. Let's see: Does your mother take off your shoes and stockings before your nap?

MARY (*nodding with half-shut eyes*). Yes, Dadda.

ROBERT (*taking off her shoes and stockings*). We'll show Mamma we know how to do those things, won't we? There's one old shoe off – and there's the other old shoe – and here's one old stocking – and there's the other old stocking. There we are, all nice and cool and comfy. (*He bends down and kisses her.*) And now will you promise to go right to sleep if Dadda takes you to bed? (*Mary nods sleepily.*) That's the good little girl.

(*He gathers her up in his arms carefully and carries her into the bedroom. His voice can be heard faintly as he lulls the child to sleep. Ruth comes out of the kitchen and gets the plate from the table. She hears the voice from the room and tiptoes to the door to look in. Then she starts for the kitchen but stands for a moment thinking, a look of ill-concealed jealousy on her face. At a noise from inside she hurriedly disappears into the kitchen. A moment later Robert reenters. He comes forward and picks up the shoes and stockings which he shoves carelessly under the table. Then, seeing no one about, he goes to the sideboard and selects a book. Coming back to his chair, he sits down and immediately becomes absorbed in reading. Ruth returns from the kitchen bringing his plate heaped with food, and a cup of tea. She sets those before him and sits down in her former place. Robert continues to read, oblivious to the food on the table.*)

RUTH (*after watching him irritably for a moment*).

For heaven's sakes, put down that old book! Don't you see your dinner's getting cold?

ROBERT (*closing his book*). Excuse me, Ruth. I didn't notice.

(*He picks up his knife and fork and begins to eat gingerly, without appetite.*)

RUTH. I should think you might have some feeling for me, Rob, and not always be late for meals. If you think it's fun sweltering in that oven of a kitchen to keep things warm for you, you're mistaken.

ROBERT. I'm sorry, Ruth, really I am.

RUTH. That's what you always say; but you keep coming late just the same.

ROBERT. I know; and I can't seem to help it. Something crops up every day to delay me. I mean to be here on time.

RUTH (*with a sigh*). Mean-tos don't count.

ROBERT (*with a conciliating smile*). Then punish me, Ruth. Let the food get cold and don't bother about me. Just set it to one side. I won't mind.

RUTH. I'd have to wait just the same to wash up after you.

ROBERT. But I can wash up.

RUTH. A nice mess there'd be then!

ROBERT (*with an attempt at lightness*). The food is lucky to be able to get cold this weather.

(*As Ruth doesn't answer or smile he opens his book and resumes his reading, forcing himself to take a mouthful of food every now and then. Ruth stares at him in annoyance.*)

RUTH. And besides, you've got your own work that's got to be done.

ROBERT (*absent-mindedly, without taking his eyes from the book*). Yes, of course.

RUTH (*spitefully*). Work you'll never get done by reading books all the time.

ROBERT (*shutting the book with a snap*). Why do you persist in nagging at me for getting pleasure out of reading? Is it because — (*He checks himself abruptly.*)

RUTH (*colouring*). Because I'm too stupid to understand them, I s'pose you were going to say.

ROBERT (*shamefacedly*). No – no. (*In exasperation.*) Oh, Ruth, why do you want to pick quarrels like this? Why do you goad me into saying things I don't mean? Haven't I got my share of troubles trying to work this cursed farm without your adding to them? You know how hard I've tried to keep things going in spite of bad luck —

RUTH (*scornfully*). Bad luck!

ROBERT. And my own very apparent unfitness for the job, I was going to add; but you can't deny there's been bad luck in it, too. You know how unsuited I am to the work and how I hate it; and I've managed to fight along somehow. Why don't you take things into consideration? Why can't we pull together? We used to. I know it's hard on you also. Then why can't we help each other instead of hindering? That's the only way we can make life bearable for each other.

RUTH (*sullenly*). I do the best I know how.

ROBERT (*gets up and puts his hand on her shoulder*). I know you do. But let's both of us try to do better. We can both improve. Say a word of encouragement once in a while when things go wrong, even if it is my fault. You know the odds I've been up against since Pa died. I'm not a farmer. I've never claimed to be one. But there's nothing else I can do under the circumstances, and I've got to pull things through somehow. With your help, I can do it. With you against me — (*He shrugs his shoulders. There is a pause. Then he bends down and kisses her hair – with an attempt at cheerfulness.*) So you promise that; and I'll promise to be here when the clock strikes – and anything else you tell me to. Is it a bargain?

RUTH (*dully*). I s'pose so.

ROBERT. The reason I was late to-day – it's more bad news, so be prepared.

RUTH (*as if this was only what she expected*). Oh! (*They are interrupted by the sound of a loud knock at the kitchen door.*) There's some one at the kitchen door. (*She hurries out. A moment later she reappears.*) It's Ben. He says he wants to see you.

ROBERT (*frowning*). What's the trouble now, I wonder? (*In a loud voice.*) Come on in here, Ben. (*Ben slouches in from the kitchen. He is a hulking, awkward young fellow with a heavy, stupid face and shifty, cunning eyes. He is dressed in overalls, boots, etc., and wears a broad-brimmed hat of coarse straw pushed back on his head.*) Well, Ben, what's the matter?

BEN (*drawlingly*). The mowin' machine's bust.

ROBERT. Why, that can't be. The man fixed it only last week.

BEN. It's bust just the same.

ROBERT. And can't you fix it?

BEN. No. Don't know what's the matter with the goll-darned thing. 'Twon't work, anyhow.

ROBERT (*getting up and going for his hat*). Wait a minute and I'll go look it over. There can't be much the matter with it.

BEN (*impudently*). Don't make no diff'rence t'me whether there be or not. I'm quittin'.

ROBERT (*anxiously*). You're quitting? You don't mean you're throwing up your job here?

BEN. That's what! My month's up to-day and I want what's owin' t'me.

ROBERT. But why are you quitting now, Ben, when you know I've so much work on hand? I'll have a hard time getting another man at such short notice.

BEN. That's for you to figger. I'm quittin'.

ROBERT. But what's your reason? You haven't any complaint to make about the way you've been treated, have you?

BEN. No. 'Tain't that. (*Shaking his finger.*) Look-a-here. I'm sick o' bein' made fun at, that's what; an' I got a job up to Timms' place; an' I'm quittin' here.

ROBERT. Being made fun of? I don't understand you. Who's making fun of you?

BEN. They all do. When I drive down with the milk in the mornin' they all laughs and jokes at me – that boy up at Harris' and the new feller up at Slocum's, and Bill Evans down at Meade's, and all the rest of 'em.

ROBERT. That's a queer reason for leaving me flat. Won't they laugh at you just the same when you're working for Timms?

BEN. They wouldn't dare to. Timms is the best farm hereabouts. They was laughin' at me for workin' for *you*, that's what! "How're things up at the Mayo place?" they hollers every mornin'. "What's Robert doin' now – pasturin' the cattle in the corn-lot? Is he seasonin' his hay with rain this year, same as last?" they shouts. "Or is he inventin' some 'lectrical milkin' engine to fool them dry cows o' his into givin' hard cider?" (*Very much ruffled.*) That's like they talks; and I ain't goin' to put up with it no longer. Every one's always knowd me as a first-class hand hereabouts, and I ain't wantin' 'em to get no different notion. So I'm quittin' you. And I wants what's comin' to me.

ROBERT (*coldly*). Oh, if that's the case, you can go to the devil.

BEN. This farm'd take me there quick 'nuff if I was fool 'nuff to stay.

ROBERT (*angrily*). None of your damned cheek! You'll get your money to-morrow when I get back from town – not before!

BEN (*turning to doorway to kitchen*). That suits me. (*As he goes out he speaks back over his shoulder.*) And see that I do get it, or there'll be trouble.

(*He disappears and the slamming of the kitchen door is heard.*)

ROBERT (*as Ruth comes from where she has been standing by the doorway and sits down dejectedly in her old place*). The stupid damn fool! And now what about the haying? That's an example of what I'm up against. No one can say I'm responsible for that.

RUTH. Yes you are! He wouldn't dare act that way with anyone else. They do like they please with you, because you don't know how to treat 'em. They think you're easy – and you are!

ROBERT (*indignantly*). I suppose I ought to be a slave driver like the rest of the farmers – stand right beside them all day watching every move they make, and work them to their last ounce of strength? Well, I can't do it, and I won't do it!

RUTH. It's better to do that than have to ask your Ma to sign a mortgage on the place.

ROBERT (*distractedly*). Oh, damn the place! (*He walks to the window on left and stands looking out.*)

RUTH (*after a pause, with a glance at Andrew's letter on the table*). It's lucky Andy's coming back.

ROBERT (*coming back and sitting down*). Yes, Andy 'll see the right thing to do in a jiffy. He has the knack of it; and he ought to be home any time now. The *Sunda's* overdue. Must have met with head winds all the way across.

RUTH (*anxiously*). You don't think – anything's happened to the boat?

ROBERT. Trust Uncle Dick to bring her through all right! He's too good a sailor to be caught napping. Besides, we'll never know the ship's here till

Andy steps in the door. He'll want to surprise us. (*With an affectionate smile.*) I wonder if the old chump's changed much? He doesn't seem to from his letters, does he? Still the same practical hard-head. (*Shaking his head.*) But just the same, I doubt if he'll want to settle down to a humdrum farm life, after all he's been through.

RUTH (*resentfully*). Andy's not like you. He likes the farm.

ROBERT (*immersed in his own thoughts – enthusiastically*). Gad, the things he's seen and experienced! Think of the places he's been! Hong-Kong, Yokohama, Batavia, Singapore, Bangkok, Rangoon, Bombay – all the marvellous East! And Honolulu, Sydney, Buenos Aires! All the wonderful far places I used to dream about! God, how I envy him! What a trip!

(*He springs to his feet and instinctively goes to the window and stares out at the horizon.*)

RUTH (*bitterly*). I s'pose you're sorry now you didn't go?

ROBERT (*too occupied with his own thoughts to hear her – vindictively*). Oh, those cursed hills out there that I used to think promised me so much! How I've grown to hate the sight of them! They're like the walls of a narrow prison yard shutting me in from all the freedom and wonder of life! (*He turns back to the room with a gesture of loathing.*) Sometimes I think if it wasn't for you, Ruth, and – (*his voice softening*) – little Mary, I'd chuck everything up and walk down the road with just one desire in my heart – to put the whole rim of the world between me and those hills, and be able to breathe freely once more! (*He sinks down into his chair and smiles with bitter self-scorn.*) There I go dreaming again – my old fool dreams.

RUTH (*in a low, repressed voice – her eyes smouldering*). You're not the only one!

ROBERT (*buried in his own thoughts – bitterly*). And Andy, who's had the chance – what has he got out of it? His letters read like the diary of a – of a farmer! "We're in Singapore now. It's a dirty hole of a place and hotter than hell. Two of the crew are down with fever, and we're short-handed on the work. I'll be damn glad when we sail again, although tacking back and forth in these blistering seas is a rotten job too!" (*Scornfully.*) That's about the way he summed up his impressions of the East. Every port they touched at he found the same silly fault with. God! The only place he appeared to like was Buenos Aires – and that only because he saw the business opportunities in a booming country like Argentine.

RUTH (*her repressed voice trembling*). You needn't make fun of Andy.

ROBERT. Perhaps I am too hard on him; but when I think – but what's the use? You know I wasn't making fun of Andy personally. No one loves him better than I do, the old chump! But his attitude toward things is – is rank, in my estimation.

RUTH (*her eyes flashing – bursting into uncontrollable rage*). You was too making fun of him! And I ain't going to stand for it! You ought to be ashamed of yourself! A fine one you be! (*Robert stares at her in amazement. She continues furiously.*) A fine one to talk about anyone else – after the way you've ruined everything with your lazy loafing! – and the stupid way you do things!

ROBERT (*angrily*). Stop that kind of talk, do you hear?

RUTH. You findin' fault – with your own brother who's ten times the man you ever was or ever will be – a thing like you to be talking. You're jealous, that's what! Jealous because he's made a man of himself, while you're nothing but a – but a — (*She stutters incoherently, overcome by rage.*)

ROBERT. Ruth! Ruth! Don't you dare —! You'll be sorry for talking like that.

RUTH. I won't! I won't never be sorry! I'm only saying what I've been thinking for years.

ROBERT (*aghast*). Ruth! You can't mean that!

RUTH. What do you think – living with a man like you – having to suffer all the time because you've never been man enough to work and do things like other people. But no! You never own up to that. You think you're so much better than other folks, with your college education, where you never learned a thing, and always reading your stupid books instead of working. I s'pose you think I ought to be *proud* to be your wife – a poor, ignorant thing like me! (*Fiercely.*) But I'm not. I hate it! I hate the sight of you! Oh, if I'd only known! If I hadn't been such a fool to listen to your cheap, silly, poetry talk that you learned out of books! If I could have seen how you were in your true self – like you are now – I'd have killed myself before I'd have married you! I was sorry for it before we'd been together a month. I knew what you were really like – when it was too late.

ROBERT (*his voice raised loudly*). And now – I'm finding out what you're really like – what a – a creature I've been living with. (*With a harsh laugh.*) God! It wasn't that I haven't guessed how mean and small you are – but I've kept on telling myself that I must be wrong – like a fool! – like a damned fool!

RUTH. You were saying you'd go out on the road if it wasn't for me. Well, you can go, and the sooner the better! I don't care! I'll be glad to get rid of you! The farm 'll be better off too. There's been a curse on it ever since you took hold. So go! Go and be a tramp, like you've always wanted. It's all you're good for. I can get along without you, don't you worry. I'll get some peace. (*Exulting fiercely.*) And Andy's coming back, don't forget that! He'll attend to things like they should be. He'll show what a man can do! I don't need you. Andy's coming!

ROBERT (*they are both standing. Robert grabs her by the shoulders and glares into her eyes*). What do you mean? (*He shakes her violently.*) What are you thinking of? What's in your evil mind, you – you —? (*His voice is a harsh shout.*)

RUTH (*in a defiant scream*). Yes, I do mean it! I'd say it if you was to kill me! I do love Andy. I do! I do! I always loved him. (*Exultantly.*) And he loves me! He loves me! I know he does. He always did! And you know he did, too! So go! Go if you want to!

ROBERT (*throwing her away from him. She staggers back against the table – thickly*). You – you slut!

(*He stands glaring at her as she leans back, supporting herself by the table, gasping for breath. A loud frightened whimper sounds from the awakened child in the bedroom. It continues. The man and woman stand looking at one another in horror, the extent of their terrible quarrel suddenly brought home to them. A pause. The noise of a horse and carriage comes from the road before the house. The two, suddenly struck by the same premonition, listen to it breathlessly, as to a sound heard in a dream. It stops. They hear Andy's voice from the road shouting a long hail –* "Ahoy there!")

RUTH (*with a strangled cry of joy*). Andy! Andy!

(*She rushes and grabs the knob of the screen door, about to fling it open.*)

ROBERT (*in a voice of command that forces obedience*). Stop! (*He goes to the door and gently pushes the trembling Ruth away from it. The child's crying rises to a louder pitch.*) I'll meet Andy. You better go in to Mary, Ruth.

(*She looks at him defiantly for a moment, but there is something in his eyes that makes her turn and walk slowly into the bedroom.*)

ANDY'S VOICE (*in a louder shout*). Ahoy there, Rob!

ROBERT (*in an answering shout of forced cheeriness*). Hallo, Andy!

(*He opens the door and walks out as*

The Curtain Falls)

ACT TWO SCENE TWO

SCENE. *The top of a hill on the farm. It is about eleven o'clock the next morning. The day is hot and cloudless. In the distance the sea can be seen.*

The top of the hill slopes downward slightly toward the left. A big boulder stands in the centre toward the rear. Farther right, a large oak tree. The faint trace of a path leading upward to it from the left foreground can be detected through the bleached, sun-scorched grass.

Robert is discovered sitting on the boulder, his chin resting on his hands, staring out toward the horizon seaward. His face is pale and haggard, his expression one of utter despondency. Mary is sitting on the grass near him in the shade, playing with her doll, singing happily to herself. Presently she casts a curious glance at her father, and, propping her doll up against the tree, comes over and clambers to his side.

MARY (*pulling at his hand – solicitously*). Is Dadda sick?

ROBERT (*looking at her with a forced smile*). No, dear. Why?

MARY. Then why don't he play with Mary?

ROBERT (*gently*). No, dear, not to-day. Dadda doesn't feel like playing to-day.

MARY (*protestingly*). Yes, please, Dadda!

ROBERT. No, dear. Dadda does feel sick – a little. He's got a bad headache.

MARY. Let Mary see. (*He bends his head. She pats his hair.*) Bad head.

ROBERT (*kissing her – with a smile*). There! It's better now, dear, thank you.

(*She cuddles up close against him. There is a pause during which each of them looks out seaward.*)

MARY (*pointing toward the sea*). Is that all wa-wa, Dadda?

ROBERT. Yes, dear.

MARY (*amazed by the magnitude of this conception*). Oh-oh! (*She points to the horizon.*) And it all stops there, over farver?

ROBERT. No, it doesn't stop. That line you see is called the horizon. It's where the sea and sky meet. Just beyond that is where the good fairies live. (*Checking himself – with a harsh laugh.*) But you mustn't ever believe in fairies. It's bad luck. And besides, there aren't any good fairies.

(*Mary looks up into his face with a puzzled expression.*)

MARY. Then if fairies don't live there, what lives there?

ROBERT (*bitterly*). God knows! Mocking devils, I've found them. (*Mary frowns in puzzlement, turning this over in her mind. There is a pause. Finally Robert turns to her tenderly.*) Would you miss Dadda very much if he went away?

MARY. Far – far away?

ROBERT. Yes. Far, far away.

MARY. And Mary wouldn't see him, never?

ROBERT. No; but Mary'd forget him very soon, I'm sure.

MARY (*tearfully*). No! No! Dadda mustn't go 'way. No, Dadda, no!

ROBERT. Don't you like Uncle Andy – the man that came yesterday – not the old man with the white moustache – the other?

MARY. But Dadda mustn't go 'way. Mary loves Dadda.

ROBERT (*with fierce determination*). He won't go away, baby. He was only joking. He couldn't leave his little Mary. (*He presses the child in his arms.*)

MARY (*with an exclamation of pain*). Oh! Dadda hurts!

ROBERT. I'm sorry, little girl. (*He lifts her down to the grass.*) Go play with Dolly, that's a good girl; and be careful to keep in the shade.

(*She reluctantly leaves him and takes up her doll again. A moment later she points down the hill to the left.*)

MARY. Here comes mans, Dadda.

ROBERT (*looking that way*). It's your Uncle Andy.

MARY. Will he play wiv me, Dadda?

ROBERT. Not now, dear. You mustn't bother him. After awhile he will, maybe.

(*A moment later Andrew comes up from the left, whistling cheerfully. He has changed but little in appearance, except for the fact that his face has been deeply bronzed by his years in the tropics; but there is a decided change in his manner. The old easy-going good-nature seems to have been partly lost in a breezy, business-like briskness of voice and gesture. There is an authoritative note in his speech as though he were accustomed to give orders and have them obeyed as a matter of course. He is dressed in the simple blue uniform and cap of a merchant ship's officer.*)

ANDREW. Here you are, eh?

ROBERT. Hallo, Andy.

ANDREW (*going over to Mary*). And who's this young lady I find you all alone with, eh? Who's this pretty young lady? (*He tickles the laughing, squirming Mary, then lifts her up at arm's length over his head.*) Upsy – daisy! (*He sets her down on the ground again.*) And there you are! (*He walks over and sits down on the boulder beside Robert who moves to one side to make room for him.*) Ruth told me I'd probably find you up top-side here; but I'd have guessed it, anyway. (*He digs his brother in the ribs affectionately.*) Still up to your old tricks, you old beggar! I can remember how you used to come up here to mope and dream in the old days.

ROBERT (*with a smile*). I come up here now because it's the coolest place on the farm. I've given up dreaming.

ANDREW (*grinning*). I don't believe it. You can't have changed that much.

ROBERT (*wearily*). One gets tired of dreaming – when they never come true.

ANDREW (*scrutinizing his brother's face*). You've changed in looks all right. You look all done up, as if you'd been working too hard. Better let up on yourself for awhile.

ROBERT. Oh, I'm all right!

ANDREW. Take a fool's advice and go it easy. You remember – your old trouble. You wouldn't want that coming back on you, eh? It pays to keep top-notch in your case.

ROBERT (*betraying annoyance*). Oh, that's all a thing of the past, Andy. Forget it!

ANDREW. Well – a word to the wise does no harm? Don't be touchy about it. (*Slapping his brother on the back.*) You know I mean well, old man, even if I do put my foot in it.

ROBERT. Of course, Andy. I'm not touchy about it. I don't want you to worry about dead things, that's all. I've a headache to-day, and I expect I do look done up.

ANDREW. Mum's the word, then! (*After a pause – with boyish enthusiasm.*) Say, it sure brings back old times to be up here with you having a chin all by our lonesomes again. I feel great being back home.

ROBERT. It's great for us to have you back.

ANDREW (*after a pause – meaningly*). I've been looking over the old place with Ruth. Things don't seem to be —

ROBERT (*his face flushing – interrupts his brother shortly*). Never mind the damn farm! There's nothing about it we don't both know by heart. Let's talk about something interesting. This is the first chance I've had to have a word with you alone. To the devil with the farm for the present. They think of nothing else at home. Tell me about your trip. That's what I've been anxious to hear about.

ANDREW (*with a quick glance of concern at Robert*). I suppose you do get an overdose of the farm at home. (*Indignantly.*) Say, I never realized that Ruth's mother was such an old rip till she talked to me this morning. (*With a grin.*) Phew! I pity you, Rob, when she gets on her ear!

ROBERT. She is – difficult sometimes; but one must make allowances. (*Again changing the subject abruptly.*) But this isn't telling me about the trip.

ANDREW. Why, I thought I told you everything in my letters.

ROBERT (*smiling*). Your letters were – sketchy, to say the least.

ANDREW. Oh, I know I'm no author. You needn't be afraid of hurting my feelings. I'd rather go through a typhoon again than write a letter.

ROBERT (*with eager interest*). Then you were through a typhoon?

ANDREW. Yes – in the China Sea. Had to run before it under bare poles for two days. I thought we were bound down for Davy Jones, sure. Never dreamed waves could get so big or the wind blow so hard. If it hadn't been for Uncle Dick being such a good skipper we'd have gone to the sharks, all of us. As it was we came out minus a main top-mast, and had to beat back to Hong-Kong for repairs. But I must have written you all this.

ROBERT. You never mentioned it.

ANDREW. Well, there was so much dirty work getting things ship-shape again I must have forgotten about it.

ROBERT (*looking at Andrew – marvelling*). Forget a typhoon? (*With a trace of scorn.*) You're a strange combination, Andy. And is what you've told me all you remember about it?

ANDREW. Oh, I could give you your bellyful of details if I wanted to turn loose on you; but they're not the kind of things to fit in with your pretty notions of life on the ocean wave, I'll give you that straight.

ROBERT (*earnestly*). Tell me. I'd like to hear them – honestly!

ANDREW. What's the use? They'd make a man want to live in the middle of America without even a river in a hundred miles of him so he'd feel safe. It was rotten, that's what it was! Talk about work! I was wishin' the ship 'd sink and give me a rest, I was so dog tired toward the finish. We didn't get a warm thing to eat for nearly two weeks. There was enough China Sea in the galley to float the stove, and the fo'c'sle was flooded, too. And you couldn't sleep a wink. No place on the darned old tub stayed still long enough for you to lie on it. And every one was soaked to the skin all the time, with green seas boiling over the deck keeping you busy jumping for the rat-lines to keep from being washed over. Oh, it was all-wool-and-a-yard-wide-Hell, I'll tell you. You ought to have been there. I remember thinking about you at the worst of it when you couldn't force a breath out against the wind, and saying to myself: "This'd cure Rob of them ideas of his about the beautiful sea, if he could see it." And it would have too, you bet! (*He nods emphatically.*)

ROBERT. And you don't see any romance in that?

ANDREW. Romance be blowed! It was hell! (*As an afterthought.*) Oh, I was forgetting! One of the men *was* washed overboard – a Norwegian – Ollie we called him. (*With a grin of sarcasm.*) I suppose that's romance, eh? Well, it might be for a fish, but not for me, old man!

ROBERT (*dryly*). The sea doesn't seem to have impressed you very favourably.

ANDREW. I should say it didn't! It's a dog's life. You work like the devil and put up with all kinds of hardships – for what? For a rotten wage you'd be ashamed to take on shore.

ROBERT. Then you're not going to – follow it up?

ANDREW. Not me! I'm through! I'll never set foot on a ship again if I can help it – except to carry me some place I can't get to by train. No. I've had enough. Dry land is the only place for me.

ROBERT. But you studied to become an officer!

ANDREW. Had to do something or I'd gone mad. The days were like years. Nothing to look at but sea and sky. No place to go. A regular prison. (*He laughs.*) And as for the East you used to rave about – well, you ought to see it, and *smell* it! And the Chinks and Japs and Hindus and the rest of them – you can have them! One walk down one of their filthy narrow streets with the tropic sun beating on it would sicken you for life with the "wonder and mystery" you used to dream of. I can say one thing for it though – it certainly has the stink market cornered.

ROBERT (*shrinking from his brother with a glance of aversion*). So all you found in the East was a stench?

ANDREW. *A* stench! Ten thousand of them! That and the damned fever! You can have the tropics, old man. I never want to see them again. At that, there's lots of money to be made down there – for a white man. The natives are too lazy to work, that's the only trouble.

ROBERT. But you did like some of the places, judging from your letters – Sydney, Buenos Aires —

ANDREW. Yes, Sydney's a good town. (*Enthusiastically.*) But Buenos Aires – there's the place for you. Argentine's a country where a fellow has a chance to make good. You're right I liked it. And I'll tell you, Rob, that's right where I'm going just as soon as I've seen you folks awhile and can get a ship. I don't intend to pay for my passage now I can get a berth as second officer, and I'll jump the ship when I get there. I'll need every cent of the wages Uncle's paid me to get a start at something in B.A.

ROBERT (*staring at his brother – slowly*). So you're not going to stay on the farm.

ANDREW. Why sure not! Did you think I was? There wouldn't be any sense. One of us is enough to run this little place.

ROBERT. I suppose it does seem small to you now.

ANDREW (*not noticing the sarcasm in Robert's tone*). You've no idea, Rob, what a splendid place Argentine is. I went around Buenos Aires quite a lot and got to know people – English-speaking people, of course. The town is full of them. It's foreign capital that's developed the country, you know. I had a letter from a marine insurance chap that I'd made friends with in Hong-Kong to his brother, who's in the grain business in Buenos Aires. He took quite a fancy to me, and what's more important, he offered me a job if I'd come back there. I'd have taken it on the spot, only I couldn't leave Uncle Dick in the lurch, and I'd promised you folks to come home. But I'm going back there very soon, you bet, and then you watch me get on! (*He slaps Robert on the back.*) But don't you think it's a big chance, Rob?

ROBERT. It's fine – for you, Andy.

ANDREW. We call this a farm – but you ought to hear about the farms down there – ten square miles where we've got an acre. It's a new country where big things are opening up – and I want to get in on something big before I die. That job

I'm offered 'll furnish the wedge. I'm no fool when it comes to farming, and I know something about grain. I've been reading up a lot on it, too, lately. (*He notices Robert's absent-minded expression and laughs.*) Wake up, you old poetry book-worm, you! I know my talking about business makes you want to choke me, doesn't it?

ROBERT (*with an embarrassed smile*). No, Andy, I – I just happened to think of something else. (*Frowning.*) There've been lots of times lately that I've wished I had some of your faculty for business.

ANDREW (*soberly*). There's something I want to talk about, Rob – the farm. You don't mind, do you?

ROBERT. No.

ANDREW. I walked over it this morning with Ruth – and she told me about things – (*evasively*) – the hard luck you'd had and how things stood at present – and about your thinking of raising a mortgage.

ROBERT (*bitterly*). It's all true, I guess, and probably worse than she told you.

ANDREW. I could see the place had run down; but you mustn't blame yourself. When luck's against anyone —

ROBERT. Don't, Andy! It *is* my fault – my inability. You know it as well as I do. The best I've ever done was to make ends meet, and this year I can't do that without the mortgage.

ANDREW (*after a pause*). You mustn't raise the mortgage, Rob. I've got over a thousand saved, and you can have that.

ROBERT (*firmly*). No. You need that for your start in Buenos Aires.

ANDREW. I don't. I can —

ROBERT (*determinedly*). No, Andy! Once and for all, no! I won't hear of it!

ANDREW (*protestingly*). You obstinate old son of a gun! (*There is a pause.*) Well, I'll do the best I can while I'm here. I'll get a real man to superintend things for you – if he can be got. That'll relieve you some. If he gets results, you can afford to pay him.

ROBERT. Oh, everything 'll be on a sound footing after harvest. Don't worry about it.

ANDREW (*doubtfully*). Maybe. The prospects don't look so bad.

ROBERT. And then I can pay the mortgage off again. It's just to tide over.

ANDREW (*after a pause*). I wish you'd let me help, Rob.

ROBERT (*with a tone of finality*). No. Please don't suggest it any more. My mind's made up on that point.

ANDREW (*slapping his brother on the back – with forced joviality*). Well, anyway, you've got to promise to let me step in when I've made my pile, and I'll make it down there, I'm certain, and it won't take me long, either.

ROBERT. I've no doubt you will with your determination.

ANDREW. I'll be able to pay off all the mortgages you can raise! Still, a mortgage isn't such a bad thing at that – it makes a place heaps easier to sell – and you may want to cut loose from this farm some day – come down and join me in Buenos Aires, that's the ticket.

ROBERT. If I had only myself to consider —

ANDREW. Yes, I suppose they wouldn't want to come. (*After a pause.*) It's too bad Pa couldn't have lived to see things through. (*With feeling.*) It cut me up a lot – hearing he was dead. Tell me about it. You didn't say much in your letter.

ROBERT (*evasively*). He's at peace, Andy. It'll only make you feel bad to talk of it.

ANDREW. He never – softened up, did he – about me, I mean?

ROBERT. He never understood, that's a kinder way of putting it. He does now.

ANDREW (*after a pause*). You've forgotten all about what – caused me to go, haven't you, Rob? (*Robert nods but keeps his face averted.*) I was a slushier damn fool in those days than you were. But it was an act of Providence I did go. It opened my eyes to how I'd been fooling myself. Why, I'd forgotten all about – that – before I'd been at sea six months.

ROBERT (*turns and looks into Andrew's eyes searchingly*). You're speaking of – Ruth?

ANDREW (*confused*). Yes. I didn't want you to get false notions in your head, or I wouldn't say anything. (*Looking Robert squarely in the eyes.*) I'm telling you the truth when I say I'd forgotten long ago. It don't sound well for me, getting over things so easy, but I guess it never really amounted to more than a kid idea I was letting rule me. I'm certain now I never was in love – I was getting fun out of thinking I was – and being a hero to myself. (*He heaves a great sigh of relief.*) There! Gosh, I'm glad that's off my chest. I've been feeling sort of awkward ever since I've been home, thinking of what you two might think. (*A trace of appeal in his voice.*) You've got it all straight now, haven't you, Rob?

ROBERT (*in a low voice*). Yes, Andy.

ANDREW. And I'll tell Ruth, too, if I can get up the nerve. She must feel kind of funny having me round – after what used to be – and not knowing how I feel about it.

ROBERT (*slowly*). Perhaps – for her sake – you'd better not tell her.

ANDREW. For her sake? Oh, you mean she wouldn't want to be reminded of my foolishness? Still, I think it'd be worse if —

ROBERT (*breaking out – in an agonized voice*). Do as you please, Andy; but for God's sake, let's not talk about it! (*There is a pause. Andrew stares at Robert in hurt stupefaction. Robert continues after a moment in a voice which he vainly attempts to keep calm.*) Excuse me, Andy. This rotten headache has my nerves shot to pieces.

ANDREW (*mumbling*). It's all right, Rob – long as you're not sore at me.

ROBERT. Where did Uncle Dick disappear to this morning?

ANDREW. He went down to the port to see to things on the *Sunda*. He said he didn't know exactly when he'd be back. I'll have to go down and tend to the ship when he comes. That's why I dressed up in these togs.

MARY (*pointing down the hill to the left*). See Dadda! Mamma! Mamma!

(*She jumps to her feet and starts to run down the path.*)

ANDREW (*standing and looking down*). Yes, here comes Ruth. Must be looking for you, I guess. (*Jumping forward and stopping Mary.*) Hey up! You mustn't run downhill like that, little girl. You'll take a bad fall, don't you know it?

ROBERT. Stay here and wait for your mother. Mary.

MARY (*struggling to her feet*). No! No! Mamma! Dadda!

ANDREW. Here she is!

(*Ruth appears at left. She is dressed in white, shows she has been fixing up. She looks pretty, flushed and full of life.*)

MARY (*running to her mother*). Mamma!

RUTH (*kissing her*). Hello, dear! (*She walks toward the rock and addresses Robert coldly.*) Jake wants to see you about something. He finished working where he was. He's waiting for you at the road.

ROBERT (*getting up – wearily*). I'll go down right away.

(*As he looks at Ruth, noting her changed appearance, his face darkens with pain.*)

RUTH. And take Mary with you, please. (*To Mary.*) Go with Dadda, that's a good girl. Grandma has your dinner most ready for you.

ROBERT (*shortly*). Come, Mary!

MARY (*taking his hand and dancing happily beside him*). Dadda! Dadda! (*They go down the hill to the left. Ruth looks after them for a moment, frowning – then turns to Andy with a smile.*) I'm going to sit down. Come on, Andy. It'll be like old times. (*She jumps lightly to the top of the rock and sits down.*) It's so fine and cool up here after the house.

ANDREW (*half-sitting on the side of the boulder*). Yes. It's great.

RUTH. I've taken a holiday in honour of your arrival – from work in the kitchen. (*Laughing excitedly.*) I feel so free I'd like to have wings and fly over the sea. You're a man. You can't know how awful and stupid it is – cooking and washing dishes all the time.

ANDREW (*making a wry face*). I can guess.

RUTH. Besides, your mother just insisted on getting your first dinner at home, she's that happy at having you back. You'd think I was planning to poison you the flurried way she shooed me out of the kitchen.

ANDREW. That's just like Ma, bless her!

RUTH. She's missed you terrible. We all have. And you can't deny the farm has, after what I showed you and told you when we was looking over the place this morning.

ANDREW (*with a frown*). Things are run down, that's a fact! It's too darn hard on poor old Rob.

RUTH (*scornfully*). It's his own fault. He never

takes any interest in things.

ANDREW (*reprovingly*). You can't blame him. He wasn't born for it; but I know he's done his best for your sake and the old folks and the little girl.

RUTH (*indifferently*). Yes, I suppose he has. (*Gaily.*) But thank the Lord, all those days are over now. The "hard luck" Rob's always blaming won't last long when you take hold, Andy. All the farm's ever needed was some one with the knack of looking ahead and preparing for what's going to happen.

ANDREW. Yes, Rob hasn't got that. He's frank to own up to that himself. I'm going to try and hire a good man for him – an experienced farmer – to work the place on a salary and percentage. That'll take it off of Rob's hands, and he needn't be worrying himself to death any more. He looks all worn out, Ruth. He ought to be careful.

RUTH (*absent-mindedly*). Yes, I s'pose. (*Her mind is filled with premonitions by the first part of his statement.*)

ANDREW. It would be a good idea if Rob could pull out of here – get a job in town on a newspaper, or something connected with writing – and this plan of mine'd give him a chance.

RUTH (*vaguely*). He's always wanted to get away. (*Suspiciously.*) Why do you want to hire a man to oversee things? Seems as if now that you're back it wouldn't be needful.

ANDREW. Oh, of course I'll attend to everything while I'm here. I mean after I'm gone.

RUTH (*as if she couldn't believe her ears*). Gone!

ANDREW. Yes. When I leave for the Argentine again.

RUTH (*aghast*). You're going away to sea again!

ANDREW. Not to sea, no; I'm through with the sea for good as a job. I'm going down to Buenos Aires to get in the grain business.

RUTH. But – that's way far off – isn't it?

ANDREW (*easily*). Six thousand miles more or less. It's quite a trip. (*With enthusiasm.*) I've got a peach of a chance down there, Ruth. Ask Rob if I haven't. I've just been telling him all about it. I won't bother you by repeating. Rob can tell you.

RUTH (*a flush of anger coming over her face*). And didn't he try to stop you from going?

ANDREW (*in surprise*). No, of course not. Why?

RUTH (*slowly and vindictively*). That's just like him – not to.

ANDREW (*resentfully*). Rob's too good a chum to try and stop me when he knows I'm set on a thing. And he could see just as soon's I told him what a good chance it was. You ask him about it.

RUTH (*dazedly*). And you're bound on going?

ANDREW. Sure thing. Oh, I don't mean right off. I'll have to wait for a ship sailing there for quite a while, likely. Anyway, I want to stay at home and visit with you folks a spell before I go.

RUTH (*dumbly*). I s'pose. (*With sudden anguish.*) Oh, Andy, you can't go! You can't. Why we've all thought – we've all been hoping and praying you was coming home to stay, to settle down on the farm and see to things. You mustn't go! Think of how your Ma'll take on if you go – and how the farm'll be ruined if you leave it to Rob to look after. You can see that.

ANDREW (*frowning*). Rob hasn't done so bad. When I get a man to direct things the farm'll be safe enough.

RUTH (*insistently*). But your Ma – think of her.

ANDREW. She's used to me being away. She won't object when she knows it's best for her and all of us for me to go. You ask Rob. In a couple of years down there I'll make my pile, see if I don't, and then I'll come back and settle down and turn this farm to the crackiest place in the whole state. In the meantime, I can help you both from down there. (*Earnestly.*) I tell you, Ruth, I'm going to make good right from the minute I land, if working hard and a determination to get on can do it, and I *know* they can! I'll have money and lots of it before long, and none of you'll have to worry about this pesky little farm any more. (*Excitedly – in a rather boastful tone.*) I tell you, I feel ripe for bigger things than settling down here. The trip did that for me, anyway. It showed me the world in a larger proposition than ever I thought it was in the old days. I couldn't be content any more stuck here like a fly in molasses. There ain't enough to do. It all seems trifling, somehow. You ought to be able to understand what I feel.

RUTH (*dully*). Yes – I s'pose I ought.

ANDREW. I felt sure you'd see, and wait till Rob tells you about —

RUTH (*a dim suspicion forming in her mind – interrupting him*). What did he tell you – about me?

ANDREW. Tell? About you? Why, nothing.

RUTH (*staring at him intensely*). Are you telling me the truth, Andy Mayo? Didn't he say – I — (*She stops confusedly.*)

ANDREW (*surprised*). No, he didn't mention you, I can remember. Why? What made you think he did?

RUTH (*wringing her hands*). Oh, I wish I could tell if you're lying or not!

ANDREW (*indignantly*). What're you talking about? I didn't used to lie to you, did I? And what in the name of God is there to lie for?

RUTH (*still unconvinced*). Are you sure – will you swear – it isn't the reason — (*She lowers her eyes and half-turns away from him.*) The same reason that made you go last time that's driving you away again? 'Cause if it is – I was going to say – you mustn't go – on that account. (*Her voice sinks to a tremulous, tender whisper as she finishes.*)

ANDREW (*confused – forces a laugh*). Oh, is *that* what you're driving at? Well, you needn't worry about that no more — (*Soberly.*) I don't blame you, Ruth, feeling embarrassed having me around again, after the way I played the dumb fool about going away last time. You'll have to put it down to me just being young and foolish and not responsible for my actions – and forgive me and forget it. Will you?

RUTH (*in anguish buries her face in her hands*). Oh, Andy!

ANDREW (*misunderstanding*). I know I oughtn't to talk about such foolishness to you. Still I figure it's better to get it out of my system so's we three can be together same's years ago, and not be worried thinking one of us might have the wrong notion. No, don't you fret about me having any such reason for going this time. I'm not a calf any more. Why honest, Ruth, before the ship got to Hong Kong I'd near forgat all that part of it. All I remembered was the awful scrap I'd had with Pa – and I was darned cut up about that.

RUTH. Andy! Please! Don't!

ANDREW. Let me finish now that I've started. It'll help clear things up. I don't want you to think once a fool always a fool, and be upset all the time I'm here on my fool account. I want you to believe I put all that silly nonsense back of me a long time ago – and now – it seems – well – as if you'd always been my sister, that's what, Ruth.

RUTH (*at the end of her endurance – laughing hysterically*). For God's sake, Andy – won't you please stop talking!

(*She again hides her face in her hands, her bowed shoulders trembling.*)

ANDREW (*ruefully*). Seem's if I put my foot in it whenever I open my mouth to-day. Rob shut me up with almost them same words when I tried speaking to him about it.

RUTH (*fiercely*). You told him – what you've told me?

ANDREW (*astounded*). Why sure! Why not?

RUTH (*shuddering*). Oh, my God!

ANDREW (*alarmed*). Why? Shouldn't I have?

RUTH (*hysterically*). Oh, I don't care what you do! I don't care! Leave me alone!

(*Andrew gets up and walks down the hill to the left, embarrassed, hurt, and greatly puzzled by her behaviour.*)

ANDREW (*after a pause – pointing down the hill*). Hello! Here they come back – and the Captain's with them. How'd he come to get back so soon, I wonder? That means I've got to hustle down to the port and get on board. Rob's got the baby with him. (*He comes back to the boulder. Ruth keeps her face averted from him.*) Gosh, I never saw a father so tied up in a kid as Rob is! He just watches every move she makes. And I don't blame him. You both got a right to feel proud of her. She's surely a little winner. (*He glances at Ruth to see if this very obvious attempt to get back in her good graces is having any effect.*) I can see the likeness to Rob standing out all over her, can't you? But there's no denying she's your young one, either. There's something about her eyes —

RUTH (*piteously*). Oh, Andy, I've a headache! I don't want to talk! Leave me alone, won't you, please?

ANDREW (*stands staring at her for a moment – then walks away, saying in a hurt tone*). Everybody hereabouts seems to be on edge to-day. I begin to feel as if I'm not wanted around.

(*He stands near the path, left, kicking at the grass with the toe of his shoe. A moment *later Captain Dick Scott enters, followed by Robert carrying Mary. The Captain seems scarcely to have changed at all from the jovial, booming person he was three years before. He wears a uniform similar to Andrew's. He is puffing and breathless from his climb and mops wildly at his perspiring countenance. Robert casts a quick glance at Andrew, noticing the latter's discomfited look, and then turns his eyes on Ruth who, at their approach, has moved so her back is toward them, her chin resting on her hands as she stares out seaward.*)

MARY. Mamma! Mamma!

(*Robert puts her down and she runs to her mother. Ruth turns and grabs her up in her arms with a sudden fierce tenderness, quickly turning away again from the others. During the following scene she keeps Mary in her arms.*)

SCOTT (*wheezily*). Phew! I got great news for you, Andy. Let me get my wind first. Phew! God A'mighty, mountin' this damned hill is worser'n goin' aloft to the skys'l yard in a blow. I got to lay to a while.

(*He sits down on the grass, mopping his face.*)

ANDREW. I didn't look for you this soon, Uncle.

SCOTT. I didn't figger it, neither; but I run across a bit o' news down to the Seamen's Home made me 'bout ship and set all sail back here to find you.

ANDREW (*eagerly*). What is it, Uncle?

SCOTT. Passin' by the Home I thought I'd drop in an' let 'em know I'd be lackin' a mate next trip count o' your leavin'. Their man in charge o' the shippin' asked after you 'special curious. 'Do you think he'd consider a berth as Second on a steamer, Captain?' he asks. I was goin' to say no when I thinks o' you wantin' to get back down south to the Plate agen; so I asks him: 'What is she and where's she bound?' 'She's the *El Paso*, a brand-new tramp,' he says, 'and she's bound for Buenos Aires.'

ANDREW (*his eyes lighting up – excitedly*). Gosh, that is luck! When does she sail?

SCOTT. To-morrow mornin'. I didn't know if you'd want to ship away agen so quick an' I told him so. 'Tell him I'll hold the berth open for him until late this afternoon,' he says. So I said I'd tell you, an' I catches the first car back to town. So there you be, an' you can make your own choice.

ANDREW. I'd like to take it. There may not be another ship for Buenos Aires with a vacancy in months. (*His eyes roving from Robert to Ruth and back again – uncertainly.*) Still – damn it all – to-morrow morning *is* soon. I wish she wasn't leaving for a week or so. That'd give me a chance – it seems hard to go right away again when I've just got home. And yet it's a chance in a thousand — (*Appealing to Robert.*) What do you think, Rob? What would you do?

ROBERT (*forcing a smile*). He who hesitates, you know. (*Frowning.*) It's a piece of good luck thrown in your way – and – from what you've told me of your plans – I think you owe it to yourself to jump at it. But don't ask me to decide for you.

RUTH (*turning to look at Andrew – in a tone of fierce resentment*). Yes, go, Andy!

(*She turns quickly away again. There is a moment of embarrassed silence.*)

ANDREW (*thoughtfully*). Yes, I guess I will. It'll be the best thing for all of us in the end, don't you think so, Rob? (*Robert nods but remains silent.*)

SCOTT (*getting to his feet*). Then, that's settled.

ANDREW (*now that he has definitely made a decision his voice rings with hopeful strength and energy*). Yes, I'll take the berth. The sooner I go the sooner I'll be back, that's a certainty, and I won't come back with empty hands next time. You bet I won't!

SCOTT. You ain't got so much time, Andy. To make sure you'd best leave here soon's you kin. You can't put too much trust in them fellers. I got to get right back aboard. You'd best come with me.

ANDREW. I'll go to the house and repack my bag right away.

ROBERT (*quietly*). You'll both be here for dinner, won't you?

ANDREW (*worriedly*). I don't know. Will there be time? What time is it now, I wonder?

ROBERT (*reproachfully*). Ma's been getting dinner especially for you, Andy.

ANDREW (*flushing – shamefacedly*). Hell! And I was forgetting! I'm a damn fool. Of course I'll stay for dinner if I missed every damned ship in the world. (*He turns to the Captain – briskly.*) Come on, Uncle. Walk down with me to the house and you can tell me more about this berth on the way. I've got to pack before dinner. (*He and the Captain start down to the left. Andrew calls back over his shoulder.*) You're coming soon, aren't you, Rob?

ROBERT. Yes. I'll be right down.

(*Andrew and the Captain leave. Ruth puts Mary on the ground and hides her face in her hands. Her shoulders shake as if she were sobbing. Robert stares at her with a grim, sombre expression. Mary walks backward toward Robert, her wondering eyes fixed on her mother.*)

MARY (*her voice vaguely frightened, taking her father's hand*). Dadda, Mamma's cryin', Dadda.

ROBERT (*bending down and stroking her hair – in a voice he endeavours to keep from being harsh*). No, she isn't, little girl. The sun hurts her eyes, that's all. Aren't you beginning to feel hungry, Mary?

MARY (*decidedly*). Yes, Dadda.

ROBERT (*meaningly*). It must be your dinner time now.

RUTH (*in a muffled voice*). I'm coming, Mary. (*She wipes her eyes quickly and, without looking at Robert, comes and takes Mary's hand – in a dead voice.* Come on and I'll get your dinner for you.

(*She walks out left, her eyes fixed on the ground, the skipping Mary tugging at her hand. Robert waits a moment for them to get ahead and then slowly follows as*

The Curtain Falls)

ACT THREE SCENE ONE

SCENE. *Same as Act Two, Scene One. The sitting-room of the farm house about six o'clock in the morning of a day toward the end of October five years later. It is not yet dawn, but as the action progresses the darkness outside the windows gradually fades to grey.*

The room, seen by the light of the shadeless oil lamp with a smoky chimney which stands on the table, presents an appearance of decay, of dissolution. The curtains at the windows are torn and dirty and one of them is missing. The closed desk is grey with accumulated dust as if it had not been used in years. Blotches of dampness disfigure the wall-paper. Threadbare trails, leading to the kitchen and outer doors, show in the faded carpet. The top of the coverless table is stained with the imprints of hot dishes and spilt food. The rung of one rocker has been clumsily mended with a piece of plain board. A brown coating of rust covers the unblacked stove. A pile of wood is stacked up carelessly against the wall by the stove.

The whole atmosphere of the room, contrasted with that of former years, is one of an habitual poverty too hopelessly resigned to be any longer ashamed or even conscious of itself.

At the rise of the curtain Ruth is discovered sitting by the stove, with hands outstretched to the warmth as if the air in the room were damp and cold. A heavy shawl is wrapped about her shoulders, half-concealing her dress of deep mourning. She has aged horribly. Her pale, deeply lined face has the stony lack of expression of one to whom nothing more can ever happen, whose capacity for emotion has been exhausted. When she speaks her voice is without timbre, low and monotonous. The negligent disorder of her dress, the slovenly arrangement of her hair, now streaked with grey, her muddied shoes run down at the heel, give full evidence of the apathy in which she lives.

Her mother is asleep in her wheel chair beside the stove toward the rear, wrapped up in a blanket.

There is a sound from the open bedroom door in the rear as if some one were getting out of bed. Ruth turns in that direction with a look of dull annoyance. A moment later Robert appears in the doorway, leaning weakly against it for support. His hair is long and unkempt, his face and body emaciated. There are bright patches of crimson over his cheek-bones and his eyes are burning with fever. He is dressed in corduroy pants, a flannel shirt, and wears worn carpet slippers on his bare feet.

RUTH (*dully*). S-s-s-h-h! Ma's asleep.

ROBERT (*speaking with an effort*). I won't wake her.

(*He walks weakly to a rocker by the side of the table and sinks down in it exhausted.*)

RUTH (*staring at the stove*). You better come near the fire where it's warm.

ROBERT. No. I'm burning up now.

RUTH. That's the fever. You know the doctor told you not to get up and move round.

ROBERT (*irritably*). That old fossil! He doesn't know anything. Go to bed and stay there – that's his only prescription.

RUTH (*indifferently*). How are you feeling now?

ROBERT (*buoyantly*). Better! Much better than I've felt in ages. Really I'm quite healthy now – only very weak. It's the turning-point, I guess. From now on I'll pick up so quick I'll surprise you – and no thanks to that old fool of a country quack, either.

RUTH. He's always tended to us.

ROBERT. Always helped us to die, you mean! He "tended" to Pa and Ma and – (*his voice breaks*) – and to – Mary.

RUTH (*dully*). He did the best he knew, I s'pose. (*After a pause.*) Well, Andy's bringing a specialist with him when he comes. That ought to suit you.

ROBERT (*bitterly*). Is that why you're waiting up all night?

RUTH. Yes.

ROBERT. For Andy?

RUTH (*without a trace of feeling*). Somebody had got to, when he's bringing that doctor with him. You can't tell when he might get here if he's coming from the port in an auto like he telegraphed us. And besides, it's only right for some one to meet him after he's been gone five years.

ROBERT (*with bitter mockery*). Five years! It's a long time.

RUTH. Yes.

ROBERT (*meaningly*). To *wait*!

RUTH (*indifferently*). It's past now.

ROBERT. Yes, it's past. (*After a pause.*) Have you got his two telegrams with you? (*Ruth nods.*) Let me see them, will you? My head was so full of fever when they came I couldn't make head or tail of them. (*Hastily.*) But I'm feeling fine now. Let me read them again.

(*Ruth takes them from the bosom of her dress and hands them to him.*)

RUTH. Here. The first one's on top.

ROBERT (*opening it*). New York. "Just landed from steamer. Have important business to wind up here. Will be home as soon as deal is completed." (*He smiles bitterly.*) Business first was always Andy's motto. (*He reads.*) "Hope you are all well. Andy." (*He repeats ironically.*) "Hope you are all well!"

RUTH (*dully*). He couldn't know you'd been took sick till I answered that and told him.

ROBERT (*contritely*). Of course he couldn't. You're right. I'm a fool. I'm touchy about nothing lately. Just what did you say in your reply? I forget.

RUTH (*inconsequentially*). I had to send it collect. (*Robert frowns.*) I wrote you were pretty low and for him to hurry up here.

ROBERT (*irritably*). He'll think I'm dying or some such foolishness. What an idiotic exaggeration! What did you say was the matter with me? Did you mention that?

RUTH. I wrote you had lung trouble – just those two words. (*Dully.*) The boy said it wouldn't cost any more for two words.

ROBERT (*flying into a petty temper*)- You *are* a fool! How often have I explained to you that it's *pleurisy* is the matter with me. You can't seem to get it in your head that the pleura is outside the lungs, not in them!

RUTH (*callously*). I only wrote what Doctor Smith told me.

ROBERT (*angrily*). He's a damned ignoramus!

RUTH (*dully*). Makes no difference. I had to tell Andy something, didn't I?

ROBERT (*after a pause, opening the other telegram*). He sent this last evening. Let's see. (*He reads.*) "Leave for home on midnight train. Just received your wire. Am bringing specialist to see Rob. Will motor to farm from Port." (*He calculates.*) The midnight gets in the Port about four-thirty, I think, or five. It should take a car an hour or more to get here. What time is it now?

RUTH. Round six, must be.

ROBERT. He ought to be here soon. I'm glad he's bringing a doctor who knows something. I'm tired of being at the mercy of that cheap old quack. A specialist will tell you in a second that there's nothing the matter with my lungs.

RUTH (*stolidly*). You've been coughing an awful lot lately.

ROBERT (*irritably*). What nonsense! For God's sake, haven't you ever had a bad cold yourself? (*Ruth stares at the stove in silence. Robert fidgets in his chair. There is a pause. Finally Robert's eyes are fixed on the sleeping Mrs. Atkins.*) Your mother is lucky to be able to sleep so soundly.

RUTH. Ma's tired. She's been sitting up with me most of the night.

ROBERT (*mockingly*). Is she waiting for Andy, too? (*There is a pause. Robert sighs.*) I couldn't get to sleep to save my soul. I counted ten million sheep if I counted one. No use! My brain kept pounding out thoughts as if its life depended on it. I gave up trying finally and just laid there in the dark thinking. (*He pauses, then continues in a tone of tender sympathy.*) I was thinking about you, Ruth – of how hard these last years must have been for you. (*Appealingly.*) I'm sorry, Ruth.

RUTH (*in a dead voice*). I don't know. They're past now. They were hard on all of us.

ROBERT. Yes; on all of us but Andy. (*With a flash of sick jealousy.*) Andy's made a big success of himself – the kind he wanted. He's got lots of money and, I suppose, a reputation for being a sharp business man. (*Mockingly.*) What else is there in life to wish for, eh, Ruth? And now he's coming home to let us admire his greatness. (*Frowning – irritably.*) What does it matter? What am I talking about? My brain must be sick, too. (*After a pause.*) Yes, these years have been terrible for both of us. (*His voice is lowered to a trembling whisper.*) Especially the last eight months since Mary – died. (*He forces back a sob with a convulsive shudder – then breaks out in a passionate agony.*) Our last hope of happiness! I could curse God from the bottom of my soul – if there was a God!

(*He is racked by a violent fit of coughing and hurriedly puts his handkerchief to his lips.*)

RUTH (*without looking at him*). Mary's better off – being dead.

ROBERT (*gloomily*). We'd all be better off for that matter. (*With sudden exasperation.*) You tell that mother of your she's got to stop saying that Mary's death was due to a weak constitution inherited from me. (*On the verge of tears of weakness.*) It's got to stop, I tell you!

RUTH (*sullenly*). She's only saying what Doctor Smith said.

ROBERT (*fiercely*). He's an old ass, and I'll tell him if —

RUTH (*sharply*). S-h-h! You'll wake her, and then she'll nag at me – not you.

ROBERT (*coughs and lies back in his chair weakly – a pause*). It's all because your mother's down on me for not begging Andy for help when things got worse here.

RUTH (*resentfully*). You might have. He's got plenty, if what he says is true.

ROBERT. How can *you* of all people think of taking money from *him*?

RUTH (*dully*). I don't see the harm. He's your own brother.

ROBERT (*shrugging his shoulders*). What's the use of talking to you? Well, *I* couldn't. (*Proudly.*) And I've managed to keep things going, thank God. You can't deny that without help I've succeeded in — (*He breaks off with a bitter laugh.*) My God, what am I boasting of? Debts to this one and that, taxes, interest unpaid! I'm a fool! (*He lies back in his chair closing his eyes for a moment, then speaks in a low voice.*) I'll be frank, Ruth. I've been an utter failure, and I've dragged you with me. I couldn't blame you in all justice – for hating me.

RUTH (*without feeling*). I don't hate you. It's been my fault too, I s'pose.

ROBERT. No. You couldn't help loving – Andy.

RUTH (*dully*). I don't love anyone.

ROBERT (*waving her remark aside*). You needn't deny it. It doesn't matter. (*After a pause – with a tender smile.*) Do you know, Ruth, what I've been dreaming back there in the dark? (*With a short laugh.*) It may sound silly of me but – I was planning our future when I get well. (*He looks at her with appealing eyes as if afraid she will sneer at him. Her expression does not change. She stares at the stove. His voice takes on a note of eagerness.*) After all, why shouldn't we have a future? We're young yet. If we can only shake off the curse of this farm! It's the farm that's ruined our lives, damn it! And now that Andy's coming back – I'm going to sink my foolish pride, Ruth! I'll borrow the money from him to give us a good start in the city. We'll go where people live instead of stagnating, and start all over again. (*Confidently.*) I won't be the failure there that I've been here, Ruth. You won't need to be ashamed of me there. I'll prove to you the reading I've done can be put to some use. (*Vaguely.*) I'll write, or something of that sort. I've always wanted to write. (*Pleadingly.*) You'll want to do that, won't you, Ruth?

RUTH (*dully*). There's Ma.

ROBERT. She can come with us.

RUTH. She wouldn't.

ROBERT (*angrily*). So that's your answer! (*He trembles with violent passion. His voice is so strange that Ruth turns to look at him in alarm.*) You're lying, Ruth! Your mother's just an excuse. You want to stay here. You think that because Andy's coming back that — (*He chokes and has an attack of coughing.*)

RUTH (*getting up – in a frightened voice*). What's the matter? (*She goes to him.*) I'll go with you, Rob. I don't care for Andy like you think. Stop that coughing for goodness' sake! It's awful bad for you. (*She soothes him in dull tones.*) I'll go with you to the city – soon's you're well again. Honest I will, Rob, I promise! (*Rob lies back and closes his eyes. She stands looking down at him anxiously*). Do you feel better now?

ROBERT. Yes. (*Ruth goes back to her chair. After a pause he opens his eyes and sits up in his chair. His face is flushed and happy.*) Then you *will* go, Ruth?

RUTH. Yes.

ROBERT (*excitedly*). We'll make a new start, Ruth – just you and I. Life owes us some happiness after what we've been through. (*Vehemently.*) It must! Otherwise our suffering would be meaningless – and that is unthinkable.

RUTH (*worried by his excitement*). Yes, yes, of course, Rob, but you mustn't —

ROBERT. Oh, don't be afraid. I feel completely well, really I do – now that I can hope again. Oh, if you knew how glorious it feels to have something to look forward to – not just a dream, but something tangible, something already within our grasp! Can't you feel the thrill of it, too – the vision of a new life opening up after all the horrible years?

RUTH. Yes, yes, but do be —

ROBERT. Nonsense! I won't be careful. I'm getting back all my strength. (*He gets lightly to his feet.*) See! I feel light as a feather. (*He walks to her chair and bends down to kiss her smilingly.*) One kiss – the first in years, isn't it? – to greet the dawn of a new life together.

RUTH (*submitting to his kiss – worriedly*). Sit down, Rob, for goodness' sake!

ROBERT (*with tender obstinacy – stroking her hair*). I won't sit down. You're silly to worry. (*He rests one hand on the back of her chair.*) Listen. All our suffering has been a test through which we had to pass to prove ourselves worthy of a finer realization. (*Exultingly.*) And we did pass through it! It hasn't broken us! And now the dream is to come true! Don't you see?

RUTH (*looking at him with frightened eyes as if she thought he had gone mad*). Yes, Rob, I see; but won't you go back to bed now and rest?

ROBERT. No. I'm going to see the sun rise. It's an augury of good fortune. (*He goes quickly to the window in the rear, left, and pushing the curtains aside, stands looking out. Ruth springs to her feet and comes quickly to the table, left, where she remains watching Robert in a tense, expectant attitude. As he peers out his body seems gradually to sag, to grow limp and tired. His voice is mournful as he speaks.*) No sun yet. It isn't time. All I can see is the black rim of the damned hills outlined against a creeping greyness. (*He turns around, letting the curtains fall back, stretching a hand out to the wall to support himself. His false strength of a moment has evaporated, leaving his face drawn and hollow eyed. He makes a pitiful attempt to smile.*) That's not a very happy augury, is it? But the sun'll come – soon. (*He sways weakly.*)

RUTH (*hurrying to his side and supporting him*). Please go to bed, won't you, Rob? You don't want to be all wore out when the specialist comes, do you?

ROBERT (*quickly*). No. That's right. He mustn't think I'm sicker than I am. And I feel as if I could sleep now – (*cheerfully.*) – a good, sound, restful sleep.

RUTH (*helping him to the bedroom door*). That's what you need most. (*They go inside. A moment later she reappears, calling back*). I'll shut this door so's you'll be quiet. (*She closes the door and goes quickly to her mother and shakes her by the shoulder.*) Ma! Ma! Wake up!

MRS. ATKINS (*coming out of her sleep with a start*). Glory be! What's the matter with you?

RUTH. It was Rob. He's just been talking to me out here. I put him back to bed. (*Now that she is sure her mother is awake her fear passes and she relapses into dull indifference. She sits down in her chair and stares at the stove – dully.*) He acted – funny; and his eyes looked so – so wild like.

MRS. ATKINS (*with asperity*). And is that all you woke me out of a sound sleep for, and scared me near out of my wits?

RUTH. I was afraid. He talked so crazy – staring out of the window as if he saw – something – and speaking about the hills, and wanting to see the sun rise – and all such notions. I couldn't quiet him. It was like he used to talk – only mad, kind of. I didn't want to be alone with him that way. Lord knows what he might do.

MRS. ATKINS (*scornfully*). Humph! A poor help I'd be to you and me not able to move a step! Why didn't you run and get Jake?

RUTH (*dully*). Jake isn't here. I thought I'd told you. He quit last night. He hasn't been paid in three months. You can't blame him.

MRS. ATKINS (*indignantly*). No, I can't blame him when I come to think of it. What decent person'd want to work on a place like this? (*With sudden exasperation.*) Oh, I wish you'd never married that man!

RUTH (*wearily*). You oughtn't to talk about him now when he's sick in his bed.

MRS. ATKINS (*working herself into a fit of rage*). It's lucky for me and you, too, I took my part of the place out of his hands years ago. You know very well, Ruth Mayo, if it wasn't for me helpin' you on the sly out of my savin's, you'd both been in the poor house – and all 'count of his pig-headed pride in not lettin' Andy know the state thin's were in. A nice thing for me to have to support him out of what I'd saved for my last days – and me an invalid with no one to look to!

RUTH. Andy'll pay you back, Ma. I can tell him so's Rob'll never know.

MRS. ATKINS (*with a snort*). What'd Rob think you and him was livin' on, I'd like to know?

RUTH (*dully*). He didn't think about it, I s'pose. (*After a slight pause.*) He said he'd made up his mind to ask Andy for help when he comes. (*As a clock in the kitchen strikes six.*) Six o'clock. Andy ought to get here directly.

MRS. ATKINS. D'you think this special doctor'll do Rob any good?

RUTH (*hopelessly*). I don't know. (*The two women remain silent for a time staring dejectedly at the stove.*)

MRS. ATKINS (*shivering irritably*). For goodness' sake put some wood on that fire. I'm most freezin'!

RUTH (*pointing to the door in the rear*). Don't talk so loud. Let him sleep if he can.

(*She gets wearily from the chair and puts a few pieces of wood in the stove. Then she tiptoes to the bedroom door and listens.*)

MRS. ATKINS (*in a sharp whisper*). Is he sleepin'?

RUTH (*coming back*). I couldn't hear him move. I s'pose he is. (*She puts another stick in the stove.*) This is the last of the wood in the pile. I don't know who'll cut more now that Jake's left. (*She sighs and walks to the window in the rear, left, pulls the curtains aside, and looks out.*) It's getting grey out. It'll be light soon and we can put out that lamp. (*She comes back to the stove.*) Looks like it'd be a nice day. (*She stretches out her hands to warm them.*) Must've been a heavy frost last night. We're paying for the spell of warm weather we've been having. (*The throbbing whine of a motor sounds from the distance outside.*)

MRS. ATKINS (*sharply*). S-h-h! Listen! Ain't that an auto I hear?

RUTH (*without interest*). Yes. It's Andy, I s'pose.

MRS. ATKINS (*with nervous irritation*). Don't sit there like a silly goose. Look at the state of this room! What'll this strange doctor think of us? Look at that lamp chimney all smoke! Gracious sakes, Ruth—

RUTH (*indifferently*). I've got a lamp all cleaned up in the kitchen.

MRS. ATKINS (*peremptorily*). Wheel me in there this minute. I don't want him to see me looking a sight. I'll lay down in the room the other side. You don't need me now and I'm dead for sleep. I'll have plenty of time to see Andy.

(*Ruth wheels her mother off right. The noise of the motor grows louder and finally ceases as the car stops on the road before the farm-house. Ruth returns from the kitchen with a lighted lamp in her hand which she sets on the table beside the other. The sound of footsteps on the path is heard – then a sharp rap on the door. Ruth goes and opens it. Andrew enters, followed by Doctor Fawcett carrying a small black bag. Andrew has changed greatly. His face seems to have grown high-strung, hardened by the look of decisiveness which comes from being constantly under a strain where judgments on the spur of the moment are compelled to be accurate. His eyes are keener and more alert. There is even a suggestion of ruthless cunning about them. At present, however, his expression is one of tense anxiety. Doctor Fawcett is a short, dark, middle-aged man with a Vandyke beard. He wears glasses.)*

RUTH. Hello, Andy! I've been waiting—

ANDREW (*kissing her hastily*). I know. I got here as soon as I could. (*He throws off his cap and heavy overcoat on the table, introducing Ruth and the Doctor as he does so. He is dressed in an expensive business suit and appears stouter.*) My sister-in-law, Mrs. Mayo – Doctor Fawcett. (*They bow to each other silently. Andrew casts a quick glance about the room.*) Where's Rob?

RUTH (*pointing*). In there.

ANDREW. I'll take your coat and hat, Doctor. (*As he helps the Doctor with his things.*) Is he very bad, Ruth?

RUTH (*dully*). He's been getting weaker.

ANDREW. Damn! This way, Doctor. Bring the lamp, Ruth.

(*He goes into the bedroom, followed by the Doctor and Ruth carrying the clean lamp. Ruth reappears almost immediately closing the door behind her, and goes slowly to the outside door, which she opens, and stands in the doorway looking out. The sound of Andrew's and Robert's voices comes from the bedroom. A moment later Andrew re-enters, closing the door softly. He comes forward and sinks down on the rocker on the right of table, leaning his head on his hand. His face is drawn in a shocked expression of great grief. He sighs heavily, staring mournfully in front of him. Ruth turns and stands watching him. Then she shuts the door and returns to her chair by the stove, turning it so she can face him.*)

ANDREW (*glancing up quickly – in a harsh voice*). How long has this been going on?

RUTH. You mean – how long has he been sick?

ANDREW (*shortly*). Of course! What else?

RUTH. It was last summer he had a bad spell first, but he's been ailin' ever since Mary died – eight months ago.

ANDREW (*harshly*). Why didn't you let me know – cable me? Do you want him to die, all of you? I'm damned if it doesn't look that way! (*His voice breaking.*) Poor old chap! To be sick in this out-of-the-way hole without anyone to attend to him but a country quack! It's a damned shame!

RUTH (*dully*). I wanted to send you word once, but he only got mad when I told him. He was too proud to ask anything, he said.

ANDREW. Proud? To ask *me*? (*He jumps to his feet and paces nervously back and forth.*) I can't understand the way you've acted. Didn't you see how sick he was getting? Couldn't you realize – why, I nearly dropped in my tracks when I saw him! He looks (*he shudders.*) – terrible! (*With fierce scorn.*) I suppose you're so used to the idea of his being delicate that you took his sickness as a matter of course. God, if I'd only known!

RUTH (*without emotion*). A letter takes so long to get where you were – and we couldn't afford to telegraph. We owed every one already, and I couldn't ask Ma. She'd been giving me money out of her savings for the last two years till she hadn't much left. Don't say anything to Rob about it. I never told him. He'd only be mad at me if he knew. But I had to, because – God knows how we'd have got on if I hadn't.

ANDREW. You mean to say — (*His eyes seem to take in the poverty-stricken appearance of the room for the first time.*) You sent that telegram to me collect. Was it because — (*Ruth nods silently. Andrew pounds on the table with his fist.*) Good God! And all this time I've been – why I've had everything! (*He sits down in his chair and pulls it close to Ruth's – impulsively.*) But – I can't get it through my head. Why? Why? What has happened? How did it ever come about? Tell me!

RUTH (*dully*). There's nothing much to tell. Things kept getting worse, that's all – and Rob didn't seem to care.

ANDREW. But hasn't he been working the farm?

RUTH. He never took any interest since way back when your Ma died. After that he got men to take charge, and they nearly all cheated him – he couldn't tell – and left one after another. And then there'd be times when there was no one to see to it, when he'd be looking to hire some one new. And the hands wouldn't stay. It was hard to get them. They didn't want to work here, and as soon as they'd get a chance to work some other place they'd leave. Then after Mary died he didn't pay no heed to anything any more – just stayed indoors and took to reading books again. So I had to ask Ma if she wouldn't help us some.

ANDREW (*surprised and horrified*). Why, damn it, this is frightful! Rob must be mad not to have let me know. Too proud to ask help of *me*! It's an insane idea! It's crazy! And for Rob, of all people, to feel that way! What's the matter with him in God's name? He didn't appear to have changed when I was talking to him a second ago. He seemed the same old Rob – only very sick physically. (*A sudden, horrible suspicion entering his mind.*) Ruth! Tell me the truth. His mind hasn't gone back on him, has it?

RUTH (*dully*). I don't know. Mary's dying broke him up terrible – but he's used to her being gone by this, I s'pose.

ANDREW (*looking at her queerly*). Do you mean to say *you're* used to it?

RUTH (*in a dead tone*). There's a time comes – when you don't mind any more – anything.

ANDREW (*looks at her fixedly for a moment – with great pity*). I'm sorry I talked the way I did just now, Ruth – if I seemed to blame you. I didn't realize — The sight of Rob lying in bed there, so gone to pieces – it made me furious at every one. Forgive me, Ruth.

RUTH. There's nothing to forgive. It doesn't matter.

ANDREW (*springing to his feet again and pacing up and down*). Thank God I came back before it was too late. This doctor will know exactly what to do to bring him back to health. That's the first thing to think of. When Rob's on his feet again we can get the farm working on a sound basis once more. I'll see to it so that you'll never have any more trouble – before I leave.

RUTH. You're going away again?

ANDREW. Yes. Back to Argentine. I've got to.

RUTH. You wrote Rob you was coming back to stay this time.

ANDREW. I expected to – until I got to New York. Then I learned certain facts that make it necessary. (*With a short laugh.*) To be candid, Ruth, I'm not the rich man you've probably been led to believe by my letters – not now. I was when I wrote them. I made money hand over fist as long as I stuck to legitimate trading; but I wasn't content with that. I wanted it to come easier, so like all the rest of the idiots, I tried speculation. It was funny, too. I'd always been dead set against that form of gambling before. I guess there's still enough of the farmer in me to make me feel squeamish about Wheat Pits. But I got into it just the same, and it seemed as if I never had a chance to get out. Oh, I won all right! Several times I've been almost a millionaire – on paper – and then come down to earth again with a bump. Finally the strain was too much. I got disgusted with myself and made up my mind to get out and come home and forget it and really live again. I got out – with just a quarter of a million dollars more than I'd had when I landed there five years before. (*He gives a harsh laugh.*) And now comes the funny part. The day before the steamer sailed I saw what I thought was a chance to become a millionaire again. (*He snaps his fingers.*) That easy! I plunged. Then, before things broke, I left – I was so confident I couldn't be wrong – and I left explicit orders to *friends.* (*Bitterly.*) Friends! Well, maybe it wasn't their fault. A fool deserves what he gets. Anyway, when I landed in New York – I wired you I had business to wind up, didn't I? Well, it was the business that wound me up! (*He smiles grimly, pacing up and down, his hands in his pockets.*)

RUTH (*dully*). You found – you'd lost everything?

ANDREW (*sitting down again*). Practically. (*He takes a cigar from his pocket, bites the end off, and lights it.*) Oh, I don't mean I'm dead broke. I've saved ten thousand from the wreckage, maybe twenty. But that's a poor showing for five years' hard work. That's why I'll have to go back. (*Confidently.*) I can make it up in a year or so down there – and I don't need but a shoestring to start with. (*A weary expression comes over his face and he sighs heavily.*) I wish I didn't have to. I'm sick of it all. And I'd made so many plans about converting this place into a real home for all of us, and a working proposition that'd pay big at the same time. (*With another sigh.*) It'll have to wait.

RUTH. It's too bad – things seem to go wrong so.

ANDREW (*shaking off his depression – briskly*). They might be much worse. There's enough left to fix the farm O.K. before I go. I won't leave 'til Rob's on his feet again. In the meantime I'll make things fly around here. (*With satisfaction.*) I need a rest, and the kind of rest I need is hard work in the open – just like I used to do in the old days. I'll organize things on a working basis and get a real man to carry out my plans while I'm away – what I intended to do the last time. (*Stopping abruptly and lowering his voice cautiously.*) Not a word to Rob about my losing money! Remember that, Ruth! You can see why. If he's grown so touchy he'd never accept a cent if he thought I was hard up; see?

RUTH. Yes, Andy.

(*After a pause, during which Andrew puffs at his cigar abstractedly, his mind evidently busy with plans for the future, the bedroom door is opened and Doctor Fawcett enters, carrying a bag. He closes the door quietly behind him and comes forward, a grave expression on his face. Andrew springs out of his chair.*)

ANDREW. Ah, Doctor! (*He pushes a chair between his own and Ruth's.*) Won't you have a chair?

FAWCETT (*glancing at his watch*). I must catch the nine o'clock back to the city. It's imperative. I have only a moment. (*Sitting down and clearing his throat – in a perfunctory, impersonal voice.*) The case of your brother, Mr. Mayo, is — (*He stops and glances at Ruth and says meaningly to Andrew.*) Perhaps it would be better if you and I —

RUTH (*with dogged resentment*). I know what you mean, Doctor; but I'm not going. I'm his wife, and I've got a right to hear what you're going to say. (*Dully.*) Don't be afraid I can't stand it. I'm used to bearing trouble by this; and I can guess what you've found out. Don't you s'pose I could see it staring out of his eyes at me these last days? (*She hesitates for a moment – then continues in a monotonous voice.*) Rob's going to die.

ANDREW (*angrily*). Ruth!

FAWCETT (*raising his hand as if to command silence*). In view of what you have said, Mrs. Mayo, I see no reason to withhold the facts from you. (*He turns to Andrew.*) I am afraid my diagnosis of your brother's condition forces me to the same conclusion as Mrs. Mayo's.

ANDREW (*groaning*). But Doctor, surely —

FAWCETT (*calmly*). I am concerned only with facts, my dear sir, and this is one of them. Your brother has not long to live – perhaps a few days, perhaps only a few hours. I would not dare to venture a prediction on that score. It is a marvel that he is alive at this moment. My examination revealed that both of his lungs are terribly affected. A hæmorrhage, resulting from any exertion or merely through the unaided progress of the disease itself, will undoubtedly prove fatal.

ANDREW (*brokenly*). Good God! (*Ruth keeps her eyes fixed on her lap in a trance-like stare.*)

FAWCETT. I am sorry I have to tell you this, sorry my trip should prove to be of such little avail. If there was anything that could be done —

ANDREW. There isn't anything?

FAWCETT (*shaking his head*). I am afraid not. It is too late. Six months ago there might have —

ANDREW (*in anguish*). But if we were to take him to the mountains – or to Arizona – or —

FAWCETT. That might have prolonged his life six months ago. (*Andrew groans.*) But now — (*He shrugs his shoulders significantly.*) I would only be raising a hope in you foredoomed to disappointment if I encouraged any belief that a change of air could accomplish the impossible. He could not make a journey. The excitement, the effort required, would inevitably bring on the end.

ANDREW (*appalled by a sudden thought*). Good heavens, you haven't told him this, have you, Doctor?

FAWCETT. No. I lied to him. I said a change of

climate to the mountains, the desert would bring about a cure. (*Perplexedly.*) He laughed at that. He seemed to find it amusing for some reason or other. I am sure he knew I was lying. A clear foresight seems to come to people as near death as he is. (*He sighs.*) One feels foolish lying to them; and yet one feels one ought to do it, I don't know why. (*He looks at his watch again nervously.*) I must take my leave of you. It is really imperative that I take no risk of missing — (*He gets up.*)

ANDREW (*getting to his feet – insistently*). But there must still be a chance for him, isn't there, Doctor?

FAWCETT (*as if he were reassuring a child*). There is always that last chance – the miracle. We doctors see it happen too often to disbelieve in it. (*He puts on his hat and coat – bowing to Ruth.*) Good-bye, Mrs. Mayo.

RUTH (*without raising her eyes – dully*). Good-bye.

ANDREW (*mechanically*). I'll walk to the car with you, Doctor. (*They go out the door. Ruth sits motionlessly. The motor is heard starting and the noise gradually recedes into the distance. Andrew re-enters and sits down in his chair, holding his head in his hands.*) Ruth! (*She lifts her eyes to his.*) Hadn't we better go in and see him? God! I'm afraid to! I know he'll read it in my face. (*The bedroom door is noiselessly opened and Robert appears in the doorway. His cheeks are flushed with fever, and his eyes appear unusually large and brilliant. Andrew continues with a groan.*) It can't be, Ruth. It can't be as hopeless as he said. There's always a fighting chance. We'll take Rob to Arizona. He's *got* to get well. There *must* be a chance!

ROBERT (*in a gentle tone*). Why must there, Andy? (*Ruth turns and stares at him with terrified eyes.*)

ANDREW (*whirling around*). Rob! (*Scoldingly.*) What are you doing out of bed? (*He gets up and goes to him.*) Get right back now and obey the Doc, or you're going to get a licking from me!

ROBERT (*ignoring these remarks*). Help me over to the chair, please, Andy.

ANDREW. Like hell I will! You're going right back to bed, that's where you're going, and stay there! (*He takes hold of Robert's arm.*)

ROBERT (*mockingly*). Stay there 'til I die, eh, Andy? (*Coldly.*) Don't behave like a child. I'm sick of lying down. I'll be more rested sitting up. (*As Andrew hesitates – violently.*) I swear I'll get out of bed every time you put me there. You'll have to sit on my chest, and that wouldn't help my health any. Come on, Andy. Don't play the fool. I want to talk to you, and I'm going to. (*With a grim smile.*) A dying man has some rights, hasn't he?

ANDREW (*with a shudder*). Don't talk that way, for God's sake! I'll only let you sit down if you'll promise that. Remember. (*He helps Rob to the chair between his own and Ruth's.*) Easy now! There you are! Wait, and I'll get a pillow for you. (*He goes into the bedroom. Robert looks at Ruth who shrinks away from him in terror. Robert smiles bitterly. Andrew comes back with the pillow which he places behind Robert's back.*) How's that?

ROBERT (*with an affectionate smile*). Fine! Thank you! (*As Andrew sits down.*) Listen, Andy. You've asked me not to talk – and I won't after I've made my position clear. (*Slowly.*) In the first place I know I'm dying.

(*Ruth bows her head and covers her face with her hands. She remains like this all during the scene between the two brothers.*)

ANDREW. Rob! That isn't so!

ROBERT (*wearily*). It *is* so! Don't lie to me. It's useless and it irritates me. After Ruth put me to bed before you came, I saw it clearly for the first time. (*Bitterly.*) I'd been making plans for our future – Ruth's and mine – so it came hard at first – the realization. Then when the Doctor examined me, I knew – although he tried to lie about it. And then to make sure I listened at the door to what he told you. So, for my sake, don't mock me with fairy tales about Arizona, or any such rot as that. Because I'm dying is no reason you should treat me as an imbecile or a coward. Now that I'm sure what's happening I can say Kismet to it with all my heart. It was only the silly uncertainty that hurt. (*There is a pause. Andrew looks around in impotent anguish, not knowing what to say. Robert regards him with an affectionate smile.*)

ANDREW (*finally blurts out*). It isn't foolish. You *have* got a chance. If you heard all the Doctor said that ought to prove it to you.

ROBERT. Oh, you mean when he spoke of the possibility of a miracle? (*Dryly.*) The Doctor and I disagree on that point. I don't believe in miracles – in my case. Beside, I know more than any doctor in earth *could* know – because I *feel* what's coming. (*Dismissing the subject.*) But we've agreed not to talk of it. Tell me about yourself, Andy, and what you've done all these years. That's what I'm interested in. Your letters were too brief and far apart to be illuminating.

ANDREW. I meant to write oftener.

ROBERT (*with a faint trace of irony*). I judge from them you've accomplished all you set out to do five years ago?

ANDREW. That isn't much to boast of.

ROBERT (*surprised*). Have you really, honestly reached that conclusion?

ANDREW. Well, it doesn't seem to amount to much now.

ROBERT. But you're rich, aren't you?

ANDREW (*with a quick glance at Ruth*). Yes, I s'pose so.

ROBERT. I'm glad. You can do to the farm all I've undone. (*With a smile.*) Do you know I was too proud to ask you for money when things went bad here? You'll have to forgive me for that, Andy.

ANDREW. I knew it wasn't like you to feel that way.

ROBERT. But what did you do down there? Tell me. You went in the grain business with that friend of yours?

ANDREW. Yes. After two years I had a share in it. I sold out last year. (*He is answering Rob's questions with great reluctance.*)

ROBERT. And then?

ANDREW. I went in on my own

ROBERT. Your own business?

ANDREW. I s'pose you'd call it that.

ROBERT. Still in grain?

ANDREW. Yes.

ROBERT. What's the matter? What's there to be ashamed of? You look as if I was accusing you of crimes.

ANDREW. I'm proud enough of the first four years. It's after that I'm not boasting of. You see, I couldn't make money easy enough that way, so I took to speculating.

ROBERT. In wheat?

ANDREW. Yes.

ROBERT. And you made money – gambling?

ANDREW. Yes.

ROBERT. I can't imagine you as the easy-come-easy-go kind.

ANDREW. I'm not. I'm sick of it.

ROBERT (*thoughtfully*). I've been wondering what the great change was in you. I can see now. It's your eyes. There's an expression about them as if you were constantly waiting to hear a cannon go off, and wincing at the bang beforehand.

ANDREW (*grimly*). I've felt just that way all the past year.

ROBERT (*after a pause during which his eyes search Andrew's face*). Why haven't you ever married?

ANDREW. Never wanted to. Didn't have time to think of it, I guess.

ROBERT (*after a pause*). You – a farmer – to gamble in a wheat pit with scraps of paper. There's a spiritual significance in that picture, Andy. (*He smiles bitterly.*) I'm a failure, and Ruth's another – but we can both justly lay some of the blame for our stumbling on God. But you're the deepest-dyed failure of the three, Andy. You've spent eight years running away from yourself. Do you see what I mean? You used to be a creator when you loved the farm. You and life were in harmonious partnership. And now — (*He stops as if seeking vainly for words.*) My brain is muddled. But part of what I mean is that your gambling with the thing you used to love to create proves how far astray you've gotten from the truth. So you'll be punished. You'll have to suffer to win back — (*His voice grows weaker and he sighs wearily.*) It's no use. I can't say it.

(*He lies back and closes his eyes, breathing pantingly.*)

ANDREW (*slowly*). I think I know what you're driving at, Rob – and it's true, I guess.

(*Robert smiles gratefully and stretches out his hand, which Andrew takes in his.*)

ROBERT. I want you to promise me to do one thing, Andy, after —

ANDREW. I'll promise anything, as God is my Judge!

ROBERT. Remember, Andy, Ruth has suffered double her share, and you haven't suffered at all. (*His voice faltering with weakness.*) Only through contact with suffering, Andy, will you – awaken.

Listen. You must marry Ruth – afterwards.

RUTH (*with a cry*). Rob! (*Robert lies back, his eyes closed, gasping heavily for breath.*)

ANDREW (*making signs to her to humour him – gently*). You're tired out, Rob. You shouldn't have talked so much. You better lie down and rest a while, don't you think? We can talk later on.

ROBERT (*with a mocking smile*). Later on! You always were an optimist, Andy! (*He sighs with exhaustion.*) Yes, I'll go and rest a while. (*As Andrew comes to help him.*) It must be near sunrise, isn't it? It's getting grey out.

ANDREW. Yes – pretty near. It's after six.

ROBERT (*as Andrew helps him to the bedroom*). Pull the bed around so it'll face the window, will you, Andy? I can't sleep, but I'll rest and forget if I can watch the rim of the hills and dream of what is waiting beyond. (*They go into the bedroom.*) And the shut door, Andy. I want to be alone.

(*Andrew reappears and shuts the door softly. He comes and sits down on his chair again, supporting his head on his hands. His face is drawn with the intensity of his dry-eyed anguish.*)

RUTH (*glancing at him – fearfully*). He's out of his mind now, isn't he?

ANDREW. He may be a little delirious. The fever would do that. (*With impotent rage.*) God, what a shame! And there's nothing we can do but sit and – wait! (*He springs from his chair and walks to the stove.*)

RUTH (*dully*). He was talking – wild – like he used to – only this time it sounded – unnatural, don't you think?

ANDREW. I don't know. The things he said to me had truth in them – even if he did talk them way up in the air, like he always sees things. Still — (*He glances down at Ruth keenly.*) Why do you suppose he wanted us to promise we'd — (*Confusedly.*) You know what he said.

RUTH (*dully*). His mind was wandering, I s'pose.

ANDREW (*with conviction*). No – there was something back of it.

RUTH. He wanted to make sure I'd be all right – after he'd gone, I expect.

ANDREW. No, it wasn't that. He knows very well I'd naturally look after you without – anything like that.

RUTH. He might be thinking of – something happened five years back, the time you came home from the trip.

ANDREW. What happened? What do you mean?

RUTH (*dully*). It was the day you came. We had a fight.

ANDREW. A fight? What has that to do with me?

RUTH. It was about you – in a way.

ANDREW (*amazed*). About *me*?

RUTH. Yes, mostly. You see I'd found out I'd made a mistake about Rob soon after we were married – when it was too late.

ANDREW. Mistake? (*Slowly.*) You mean – you found out you didn't love Rob?

RUTH. Yes.

ANDREW. Good God!

RUTH. And then I thought that when Mary came it'd be different, and I'd love him; but it didn't happen that way. And I couldn't bear with his blundering and book-reading – and I grew to hate him, almost.

ANDREW. Ruth!

RUTH. I couldn't help it. No woman could. It had to be because I loved some one else, I'd found out. (*She sighs wearily.*) It can't do no harm to tell you now – when it's all past and gone – and dead. *You* were the one I really loved – only I didn't come to the knowledge of it 'til too late.

ANDREW (*stunned*). Ruth! Do you know what you're saying?

RUTH. It was true – then. (*With sudden fierceness.*) How could I help it? No woman could.

ANDREW. Then – you loved me – that time I came home?

RUTH. Yes.

ANDREW. But – couldn't you see – I didn't love you – that way?

RUTH (*doggedly*). Yes – I saw then; but I'd known your real reason for leaving home the first time – everybody knew it – and for three years I'd been thinking —

ANDREW. That I loved you?

RUTH. Yes. Then that day on the hill you laughed about what a fool you'd been for loving me once – and I knew it was all over.

ANDREW. Good God, but I never thought — (*He stops, shuddering at his remembrance.*) And did Rob —

RUTH. That was what I'd started to tell. We'd had a fight just before you came and I got crazy mad – and I told him all I've told you.

ANDREW (*gaping at her speechlessly for a moment*). You told Rob – you loved me?

RUTH. Yes.

ANDREW (*shrinking away from her in horror*). You – you – you mad fool, you! How could you do such a thing?

RUTH. I couldn't help it. I'd got to the end of bearing things – without talking.

ANDREW. And the thought of the child – his child and yours – couldn't keep your mouth shut?

RUTH. I was crazy mad at him – when I told.

ANDREW. Then Rob must have known every moment I stayed here! And yet he never said or showed – God, how he must have suffered! Didn't you know how much he loved you?

RUTH (*dully*). Yes. I knew he liked me.

ANDREW. Liked you! How can you talk in that cold tone – now – when he's dying! What kind of a woman are you? I'd never believe it was in you to be so — Couldn't you have kept silent – no matter what you felt or thought? Did you have to torture him? No wonder he's dying. I don't see how he's lived through it as long as he has. I couldn't. No. I'd have killed myself – or killed you.

RUTH (*dully*). I wish he had – killed me.

ANDREW. And you've lived together for five years with this horrible secret between you?

RUTH. We've lived in the same house – not as man and wife.

ANDREW. But what does he feel about it now? Tell me! Does he still think —

RUTH. I don't know. We've never spoke a word about it since that day. Maybe, from the way he went on, he s'poses I care for you yet. Maybe that's one reason he said what he did.

ANDREW. But you don't. You can't. It's outrageous. It's stupid! You don't love me!

RUTH (*slowly*). I wouldn't know how to feel love, even if I tried, any more.

ANDREW (*brutally*). And I don't love you, that's sure! (*He sinks into his chair, his head between his hands.*) It's damnable such a thing should be between Rob and me – we that have been pals ever since we were born, almost. Why, I love Rob better'n anybody in the world and always did. There isn't a thing on God's green earth I wouldn't have done to keep trouble away from him. And now I have to be the very one – it's admnable! How am I going to face him again? What can I say to him now? (*He groans with anguished rage. After a pause.*) He asked me to promise – what am I going to do?

RUTH. You can promise – so's it'll ease his mind – and not mean anything.

ANDREW. What? Lie to him now – when he's dying? Can you believe I'd descend as low as that? And there's no sense in my lying. He knows I don't love you. (*Determinedly.*) No! It's *you* who'll have to do the lying, since it must be done. You're the cause of all this. You've got to! You've got a chance now to undo some of all the suffering you've brought on Rob. Go in to him! Tell him you never loved me – it was all a mistake. Tell him you only said so because you were mad and didn't know what you were saying, and you've been ashamed to own up to the truth before this. Tell him something, anything, that'll bring him peace and make him believe you've loved him all the time.

RUTH (*dully*). It's no good. He wouldn't believe me.

ANDREW (*furiously*). You've got to make him believe you, do you hear? You've got to – now – hurry – you never know when it may be too late. (*As she hesitates – imploringly.*) For God's sake, Ruth! Don't you see you owe it to him? You'll never forgive yourself if you don't.

RUTH (*dully*). I'll go. (*She gets wearily to her feet and walks slowly toward the bedroom.*) But it won't do any good. (*Andrew's eyes are fixed on her anxiously. She opens the door and steps inside the room. She remains standing there for a minute. Then she calls in a frightened voice.*) Rob! Where are you?

(*Then she hurries back, trembling with fright.*) Andy! Andy! He's gone!

ANDREW (*misunderstanding her – his face pale with dread*). He's not —

RUTH (*interrupting him – hysterically*). He's gone! He isn't in there. The bed's empty. The window's wide open. He must have crawled out into the yard!

ANDREW (*springing to his feet. He rushes into the bedroom and returns immediately with an expression of alarmed amazement on his face*). Come! He can't have gone far! We've got to find him! (*Grabbing his hat he takes Ruth's arm and shoves her toward the door.*) Come on! (*Opening the door.*) Let's hope to God — (*The door closes behind them, cutting off his words as*

The Curtain Falls)

ACT THREE SCENE TWO

SCENE. *Same as Act One, Scene One. A section of country highway. The sky to the east is already alight with bright colour and a thin, quivering line of flame is spreading slowly along the horizon rim of the dark hills. The roadside, however, is still steeped in the greyness of the dawn, shadowy and vague. The field in the foreground has a wild uncultivated appearance as if it had been allowed to remain fallow the preceding summer. Parts of the snake-fence in the rear have been broken down. The apple tree is leafless and seems dead.*

Robert staggers weakly in from the left. He stumbles into the ditch and lies there for a moment; then crawls with a great effort to the top of the bank where he can see the sun rise, and collapses weakly. Ruth and Andrew come hurriedly along the road from the left.

ANDREW (*stopping and looking about him*). There he is! I knew it! I knew we'd find him here.

ROBERT (*trying to raise himself to a sitting position as they hasten to his side – with a wan smile.*) I thought I'd given you the slip.

ANDREW (*with kindly bullying*). Well, you didn't, you old scoundrel, and we're going to take you right back where you belong – in bed. (*He makes a motion to lift Robert.*) What d'you mean by running away like this, eh?

ROBERT. Don't, Andy. Don't, I tell you! I can't bear it!

ANDREW. You're in pain?

ROBERT (*simply*). No. I'm dying. (*He falls back weakly. Ruth sinks down beside him with a sob and pillows his head on her lap.*) Don't try to move me, Andy. It would mean — I had a bad hæmorrhage – trying to get here. I knew then – it was only – a few minutes more. (*Andrew stands looking down at him helplessly. Robert moves his head restlessly on Ruth's lap.*) There! Just so I can see – the sun. I couldn't stand it back there in the room. It seemed as if all my life – I'd been cooped in a room. So I thought I'd try to end as I might have – if I'd had the courage to live my dream. Alone – in a ditch by the open road – watching the sun rise.

ANDREW. Rob! Don't talk. You're wasting your strength. Rest a while and then we'll carry you —

ROBERT. Still hoping, Andy? Don't. I know. (*There is a pause during which he breathes heavily, straining his eyes toward the horizon.*) The sun comes so slowly. I haven't long – to wait. (*With an ironical smile.*) The Doctor told me to go to the far-off places – and I'd be cured. He was right. That was always the cure for me. It's too late – for this world – but in the next I'll not miss – the secret. (*He has a fit of coughing which racks his body.*)

ANDREW (*with a hoarse sob*). Rob! (*He clenches his fists in an impotent rage against Fate.*) God! God!

(*Ruth sobs brokenly and wipes Robert's lips with her handkerchief.*)

ROBERT (*in a voice which is suddenly ringing with the happiness of hope*). You mustn't feel sorry for me. It's ridiculous! Don't you see I'm happy at last – because I'm making a start to the far-off places – free – free! – freed from the farm – free to wander on and on – eternally! Even the hills are powerless to shut me in now. (*He raises himself on his elbow, his face radiant, and points to the horizon.*) Look! Isn't it beautiful beyond the hills? I can hear the old voices calling me to come — (*Exultantly.*) And this time I'm going – I'm free! It isn't the end. It's a free beginning – the start of my voyage! Don't you see? I've won to my trip – the right of release – beyond the horizon! Oh, you ought to be glad – glad – for my sake! (*He collapses weakly.*) Andy! (*Andrew bends down to him.*) Remember Ruth —

ANDREW. I'll take care of her, I swear to you, Rob!

ROBERT. Ruth has suffered – and for your own sake and hers – remember, Andy – only through sacrifice – the secret beyond there — (*He suddenly raises himself with his last remaining strength and points to the horizon where the edge of the sun's disc is rising from the rim of the hills.*) The sun! (*He remains with his eyes fixed on it for a moment. A rattling noise throbs from his throat. He mumbles:*) Remember!

(*And falls back and is still. Ruth gives a cry of horror and springs to her feet, shuddering, her hands over her eyes. Andrew bends on one knee beside the body, placing a hand over Robert's heart, then he kisses his brother reverentially on the forehead and stands up.*)

ANDREW (*facing Ruth, the body between them – in a dead voice*). He's dead. (*With a sudden burst of fury.*) God damn you, you never told him!

RUTH (*piteously*). He was so happy without my lying to him.

ANDREW (*pointing to the body – trembling with the violence of his rage*). This is your doing, you damn woman, you coward, you murderess! He's dead because you've killed him, do you hear?

RUTH (*sobbing*). Don't, Andy! Stop! I couldn't help it – and he knew how I'd suffered, too. He told you – to remember.

ANDREW (*stares at her for a moment, his rage ebbing away, an expression of deep pity gradually coming over his face. Then he glances down at his brother and speaks brokenly in a compassionate voice*). Forgive me, Ruth – for his sake. I know he was right – and I'll remember what he said. (*Ruth lets her hands fall from her face and looks at him uncomprehendingly. He lifts his eyes to hers and forces out falteringly:*) I – you – we've both made such a mess of things! We must try to help each other – and – in time – we'll come to know what's right to do — (*Desperately.*) And perhaps we —

(*But Ruth, if she is aware of his words, gives no sign. She remains silent, gazing at him dully with the sad humility of exhaustion, her mind already sinking back into that spent calm beyond the further troubling of any hope.*)

Curtain

WHERE THE CROSS IS MADE

A Play in One Act

Characters

CAPTAIN ISAIAH BARTLETT
NAT BARTLETT, *his son*
SUE BARTLETT, *his daughter*
DOCTOR HIGGINS

SILAS HORNE, *mate*
CATES, *bo'sun*
JIMMY KANAKA, *harpooner*
} *of the schooner "Mary Allen"*

The action of the play takes place in the years preceding the outbreak of World War I

SCENE. *Captain Bartlett's "cabin"—a room erected as a look-out post at the top of his house situated on a high point of land on the California coast. The inside of the compartment is fitted up like the captain's cabin of a deep-sea sailing vessel. On the left, forward, a port-hole. Farther back, the stairs of the companionway. Still farther, two more port-holes. In the rear, left, a marble-topped sideboard with a ship's lantern on it. In the rear, centre, a door opening on stairs which lead to the lower house. A cot with a blanket is placed against the wall to the right of the door. In the right wall, five port-holes. Directly under them, a wooden bench. In front of the bench, a long table with two straight-backed chairs, one in front, the other to the left of it. A cheap, dark-coloured rug is on the floor. In the ceiling, mid-way from front to rear, a skylight extending from opposite the door to above the left edge of the table. In the right extremity of the sky-light is placed a floating ship's compass. The light from the binnacle sheds over this from above and filters down into the room, casting a vague globular shadow of the compass on the floor.*

The time is an early hour of a clear windy night in the autumn of the year 1900. *Moon-light, winnowed by the wind which moans in the stubborn angles of the old house, creeps wearily in through the port-holes and rests like tired dust in circular patches upon the floor and table. An insistent monotone of thundering surf, muffled and far off, is borne upward from the beach below.*

After the curtain rises the door in the rear is opened slowly and the head and shoulders of Nat Bartlett appear over the sill. He casts a quick glance about the room, and seeing no one there, ascends the remaining steps and enters. He makes a sign to some one in the darkness beneath: "All right, Doctor." *Doctor Higgins follows him into the room and, closing the door, stands looking with great curiosity around him. He is a slight, medium-sized professional-looking man of about thirty-five. Nat Bartlett is very tall, gaunt, and loose-framed. His right arm has been amputated at the shoulder and the sleeve on that side of the heavy pea-jacket he wears hangs flabbily or flaps against his body as he moves. He appears much older than his thirty years. His shoulders have a weary stoop as if worn down by the burden of his *massive head with its heavy shock of tangled, black hair. His face is long, bony, and sallow with deep-set black eyes, a large aquiline nose, a wide, thin-lipped mouth shadowed by an unkempt bristle of moustache. His voice is low and deep with a penetrating, hollow, metallic quality. In addition to the pea-jacket, he wears corduroy trousers stuffed down into high laced boots.*

NAT. Can you see, Doctor?

HIGGINS (*in the too-casual tones which betray an inward uneasiness*). Yes—perfectly—don't trouble. The moonlight is so bright——

NAT. Luckily. (*Walking slowly toward the table.*) He doesn't want any light—lately—only the one from the binnacle there.

HIGGINS. He? Ah—you mean your father?

NAT (*impatiently*). Who else?

HIGGINS (*a bit startled—gazing around him in embarrassment*). I suppose this is all meant to be like a ship's cabin?

NAT. Yes—as I warned you.

HIGGINS (*in surprise*). Warned me? Why, warned? I think it's very natural—and interesting—this whim of his.

NAT (*meaningly*). Interesting, it may be.

HIGGINS. And he lives up here, you said—never comes down?

NAT. Never—for the past three years. My sister brings his food up to him. (*He sits down in the chair to the left of the table.*) There's a lantern on the sideboard there, Doctor. Bring it over and sit down. We'll make a light. I'll ask your pardon for bringing you to this room on the roof—but—no one'll hear us here; and by seeing for yourself the mad way he lives—— Understand that I want you to get all the facts—just that, facts!—and for that light is necessary. Without that—they become dreams up here—dreams, Doctor.

HIGGINS (*with a relieved smile carries over the lantern*). It is a trifle spooky.

NAT (*not seeming to notice this remark*). He won't take any note of this light. His eyes are too busy—out there. (*He flings his left arm in a wide gesture seaward.*) And if he does notice—well, let him come down. You're bound to see him sooner or later. (*He scratches a match and lights the lantern.*)

HIGGINS. Where is—he?

NAT (*pointing upward*). Up on the poop. Sit down, man! He'll not come—yet awhile.

HIGGINS (*sitting gingerly on the chair in front of table*). Then he has the roof, too, rigged up like a ship?

NAT. I told you he had. Like a deck, yes. A wheel, compass, binnacle light, the companionway there,—(*he points*)—a bridge to pace up and down on—*and keep watch.* If the wind wasn't so high you'd hear him now—back and forth—all the livelong night. (*With a sudden harshness.*) Didn't I tell you he's mad?

HIGGINS (*with a professional air*). That was nothing new. I've heard that about him from all sides since I first came to the asylum yonder. You say he only walks at night—up there?

NAT. Only at night, yes. (*Grimly.*) The things he wants to see can't be made out in daylight—dreams and such.

HIGGINS. But just what is he trying to see? Does any one know? Does he tell?

NAT (*impatiently*). Why, every one knows what Father looks for, man! The ship, of course.

HIGGINS. What ship?

NAT. His ship—the *Mary Allen*—named for my dead mother.

HIGGINS. But—I don't understand—— Is the ship long overdue—or what?

NAT. Lost in a hurricane off the Celebes with all on board—three years ago!

HIGGINS (*wonderingly*). Ah. (*After a pause.*) But your father still clings to a doubt——

NAT. There is no doubt for him or any one else to cling to. She was sighted bottom up, a complete wreck, by the whaler *John Slocum.* That was two weeks after the storm. They sent a boat out to read her name.

HIGGINS. And hasn't your father ever heard——

NAT. He was the first to hear, naturally. Oh, he *knows* right enough, if that's what you're driving at. (*He bends toward the doctor—intensely.*) He *knows*, Doctor, he *knows*—but he won't *believe.* He can't—and keep living.

HIGGINS (*impatiently*). Come, Mr. Bartlett, let's get down to brass tacks. You didn't drag me up here to make things more obscure, did you? Let's have the facts you spoke of. I'll need them to give sympathetic treatment to his case when we get him to the asylum.

NAT (*anxiously lowering his voice*). And you'll come to take him away to-night—for sure?

HIGGINS. Twenty minutes after I leave here I'll be back in the car. That's positive.

NAT. And you know your way through the house?

HIGGINS. Certainly, I remember—but I don't see——

NAT. The outside door will be left open for you. You must come right up. My sister and I will be here—with him. And you understand —— Neither of us knows anything about this. The authorities have been complained to—not by us, mind—but by some one. He must never know——

HIGGINS. Yes, yes—but still I don't—— Is he liable to prove violent?

NAT. No—no. He's quiet always—too quiet; but he might do something—anything—if he knows——

HIGGINS. Rely on me not to tell him, then; but I'll bring along two attendants in case—— (*He breaks off and continues in matter-of-fact tones.*) And now for the facts in this case, if you don't mind, Mr. Bartlett.

NAT (*shaking his head—moodily*). There are cases where facts—— Well, here goes—the brass tacks. My father was a whaling captain as his father before him. The last trip he made was seven years ago. He expected to be gone two years. It was four before we saw him again. His ship had been wrecked in the Indian Ocean. He and six others managed to reach a small island on the fringe of the Archipelago—an island barren as hell, Doctor—after seven days in an open boat. The rest of the whaling crew never were heard from again—gone to the sharks. Of the six who reached the island with my father only three were alive when a fleet of Malay canoes picked them up, mad from thirst and starvation, the four of them. These four men finally reached 'Frisco. (*With great emphasis.*) They were my father; Silas Horne, the mate; Cates, the bo'sun, and Jimmy Kanaka, a Hawaiian harpooner. Those four! (*With a forced laugh.*) There are facts for you. It was all in the papers at the time—my father's story.

HIGGINS. But what of the other three who were on the island?

NAT (*harshly*). Died of exposure, perhaps. Mad and jumped into the sea, perhaps. That was the told story. Another was whispered—killed and eaten, perhaps! But gone—vanished—that, undeniably. That was the fact. For the rest—who knows? And what does it matter?

HIGGINS (*with a shudder*). I should think it would matter—a lot.

NAT (*fiercely*). We're dealing with facts, Doctor! (*With a laugh.*) And here are some more for you. My father brought the three down to this house with him—Horne and Cates and Jimmy Kanaka. We hardly recognized my father. He had been through hell and looked it. His hair was white. But you'll see for yourself—soon. And the others—they were all a bit queer, too—mad, if you will. (*He laughs again.*) So much for the facts, Doctor. They leave off there and the dreams begin.

HIGGINS (*doubtfully*). It would seem—the facts are enough.

NAT. Wait. (*He resumes deliberately.*) One day my father sent for me and in the presence of the others told me the dream. I was to be heir to the secret. Their second day on the island, he said, they discovered in a sheltered inlet the rotten, water-logged hulk of a Malay prau—a proper war prau such as the pirates used to use. She had been there rotting—God knows how long. The crew had vanished—God knows where, for there was no sign on the island that man had ever touched there. The Kanakas went over the prau—they're devils for staying under water, you know—and they found—in two chests—(*he leans back in his chair and smiles ironically*)—Guess what, Doctor?

HIGGINS (*with an answering smile*). Treasure, of course.

NAT (*leaning forward and pointing his finger accusingly at the other*). You see! The root of belief is in you, too! (*Then he leans back with a hollow chuckle.*) Why, yes. Treasure, to be sure. What else? They landed it and—you can guess the rest, too—diamonds, emeralds, gold ornaments—innumerable, of course. Why limit the stuff of dreams? Ha-ha! (*He laughs sardonically as if mocking himself.*)

HIGGINS (*deeply interested*). And then?

NAT. They began to go mad—hunger, thirst, and the rest—and they began to forget. Oh, they forgot a lot, and lucky for them they did, probably. But my father realizing, as he told me, what was happening to them, insisted that while they still knew what they were doing they should—guess again now, Doctor. Ha-ha!

HIGGINS. Bury the treasure?

NAT (*ironically*). Simple, isn't it? Ha-ha! And then they made a map—the same old dream, you see—with a charred stick, and my father had care of it. They were picked up soon after, mad as hatters, as I have told you, by some Malays. (*He drops his mocking and adopts a calm, deliberate tone again.*) But the map isn't a dream, Doctor. We're coming back to facts again. (*He reaches into the pocket of his pea-jacket and pulls out a crumpled paper.*) Here. (*He spreads it out on the table.*)

HIGGINS (*craning his neck eagerly*). Dammit! This is interesting. The treasure, I suppose, is where——

NAT. Where the cross is made.

HIGGINS. And here are the signatures, I see. And that sign?

NAT. Jimmy Kanaka's. He couldn't write.

HIGGINS. And below? That's yours, isn't it?

NAT. As heir to the secret, yes. We all signed it here the morning the *Mary Allen*, the schooner my father had mortgaged this house to fit out, set sail to bring back the treasure. Ha-ha!

HIGGINS. The ship he's still looking for—that was lost three years ago?

NAT. The *Mary Allen*, yes. The other three men sailed away on her. Only father and the mate knew the approximate location of the island—and I—as heir. It's—— (*He hesitates, frowning.*) No matter. I'll keep the mad secret. My father wanted to go with them—but my mother was dying. I dared not go either.

HIGGINS. Then you wanted to go? You believed in the treasure then?

NAT. Of course. Ha-ha! How could I help it? I believed until my mother's death. Then *he* became mad, entirely mad. He built this cabin—to wait in—and he suspected my growing doubt as time went on. So, as final proof, he gave me a thing he had kept hidden from them all—a sample of the richest of the treasure. Ha-ha! Behold!

(*He takes from his pocket a heavy bracelet thickly studded with stones and throws it on the table near the lantern.*)

HIGGINS (*picking it up with eager curiosity—as if in spite of himself*). Real jewels?

NAT. Ha-ha! You want to believe, too. No—paste and brass—Malay ornaments.

HIGGINS. You had it looked over?

NAT. Like a fool, yes. (*He puts it back in his pocket and shakes his head as if throwing off a burden.*) Now you know why he's mad—waiting for that ship—and why in the end I had to ask you to take him away where he'll be safe. The mortgage—the price of that ship—is to be foreclosed. We have to move, my sister and I. We can't take him with us. She is to be married soon. Perhaps away from the sight of the sea he may——

HIGGINS (*perfunctorily*). Let's hope for the best. And I fully appreciate your position. (*He gets up, smiling.*) And thank you for the interesting story. I'll know how to humour him when he raves about treasure.

NAT (*sombrely*). He is quiet always—too quiet. He only walks to and fro—watching——

HIGGINS. Well, I must go. You think it's best to take him to-night?

NAT (*persuasively*). Yes, Doctor. The neighbours—they're far away, but—for my sister's sake—you understand.

HIGGINS. I see. It must be hard on her—this sort of thing. Well—(*he goes to the door, which Nat opens for him*)—I'll return presently. (*He starts to descend.*)

NAT (*urgently*). Don't fail us, Doctor. And come right up. He'll be here.

(*He closes the door and tiptoes carefully to the companionway. He ascends it a few *steps and remains for a moment listening for some sound from above. Then he goes over to the table, turning the lantern very low, and sits down, resting his elbow, his chin on his hand, staring sombrely before him. The door in the rear is slowly opened. It creaks slightly and Nat jumps to his feet—in a thick voice of terror.)* Who's there? *(The door swings wide open, revealing Sue Bartlett. She ascends into the room and shuts the door behind her. She is a tall, slender woman of twenty-five, with a pale, sad face framed in a mass of dark red hair. This hair furnishes the only touch of colour about her. Her full lips are pale; the blue of her wistful wide eyes is fading into a twilight grey. Her voice is low and melancholy. She wears a dark wrapper and slippers.)*

SUE *(stands and looks at her brother accusingly).* It's only I. What are you afraid of?

NAT *(averts his eyes and sinks back on his chair again).* Nothing. I didn't know—I thought you were in your room.

SUE *(comes to the table).* I was reading. Then I heard some one come down the stairs and go out. Who was it? *(With sudden terror.)* It wasn't—Father?

NAT. No. He's up there—watching—as he always is.

SUE *(sitting down—insistently).* Who was it?

NAT *(evasively).* A man—I know.

SUE. What man? What is he? You're holding something back. Tell me.

NAT *(raising his eyes defiantly).* A doctor.

SUE *(alarmed).* Oh! *(With quick intuition.)* You brought him up here—so that I wouldn't know!

NAT *(doggedly).* No. I took him up here to see how things were—to ask him about Father.

SUE *(as if afraid of the answer she will get).* Is he one of them—from the asylum? Oh, Nat, you haven't——

NAT *(interrupting her—hoarsely).* No, no! Be still.

SUE. That would be—the last horror.

NAT *(defiantly).* Why? You always say that. What could be more horrible than things as they are? I believe—it would be better for him—away—where he couldn't see the sea. He'll forget his mad idea of waiting for a lost ship and a treasure that never was. *(As if trying to convince himself—vehemently.)* I believe this!

SUE *(reproachfully).* You don't, Nat. You know he'd die if he hadn't the sea to live with.

NAT *(bitterly).* And you know old Smith will foreclose the mortgage. Is that nothing? We cannot pay. He came yesterday and talked with me. He knows the place is his—to all purposes. He talked as if we were merely his tenants, curse him! And he swore he'd foreclose immediately unless——

SUE *(eagerly).* What?

NAT *(in a hard voice).* Unless we have—Father—taken away.

SUE *(in anguish).* Oh! But why, why? What is Father to him?

NAT. The value of the property—our home which is his, Smith's. The neighbours are afraid. They pass by on the road at nights coming back to their farms from the town. They see *him* up there walking back and forth—waving his arms against the sky. They're afraid. They talk of a complaint. They say for his own good he must be taken away. They even whisper the house is haunted. Old Smith is afraid of his property. He thinks that *he* may set fire to the house—do anything——

SUE *(despairingly).* But you told him how foolish that was, didn't you? That Father is quiet, always quiet.

NAT. What's the use of telling—when they believe—when they're afraid? *(Sue hides her face in her hands—a pause—Nat whispers hoarsely.)* I've been afraid myself—at times.

SUE. Oh, Nat! Of what?

NAT *(violently).* Oh, him and the sea he calls to! Of the damned sea he forced me on as a boy—the sea that robbed me of my arm and made me the broken thing I am!

SUE *(pleadingly).* You can't blame Father—for your misfortune.

NAT. He took me from school and forced me

on his ship, didn't he? What would I have been now but an ignorant sailor like him if he had had his way? No. It's the sea I should not blame, that foiled him by taking my arm and then throwing me ashore—another one of *his* wrecks!

SUE (*with a sob*). You're bitter, Nat—and hard. It was so long ago. Why can't you forget?

NAT (*bitterly*). Forget! You can talk! When Tom comes home from this voyage you'll be married and out of this with life before you—a captain's wife as our mother was. I wish you joy.

SUE (*supplicatingly*). And you'll come with us, Nat—and father, too—and then——

NAT. Would you saddle your young husband with a madman and a cripple? (*Fiercely.*) No, no, not I! (*Vindictively.*) And not him, either! (*With sudden meaning—deliberately.*) I've got to stay here. My book is three-fourths done—my book that will set me free! But I know, I feel, as sure as I stand here living before you, that I must finish it here. It could not live for me outside of this house where it was born. (*Staring at her fixedly.*) So I will stay—in spite of hell! (*Sue sobs hopelessly. After a pause he continues.*) Old Smith told me I could live here indefinitely without paying—as caretaker—if——

SUE (*fearfully—like a whispered echo*). If?

NAT (*staring at her—in a hard voice*). If I have *him* sent—where he'll no longer harm himself—nor others.

SUE (*with horrified dread*). No—no, Nat! For our dead mother's sake.

NAT (*struggling*). Did I say I had? Why do you look at me—like that?

SUE. Nat! Nat! For our mother's sake!

NAT (*in terror*). Stop! Stop! She's dead—and at peace. Would you bring her tired soul back to him again to be bruised and wounded?

SUE. Nat!

NAT (*clutching at his throat as though to strangle something within him—hoarsely*). Sue! Have mercy! (*His sister stares at him with dread foreboding. Nat calms himself with an effort and continues deliberately.*) Smith said he would give two thousand cash if I would sell the place to him—and he would let me stay, rent free, as caretaker.

SUE (*scornfully*). Two thousand! Why, over and above the mortgage it's worth——

NAT. It's not what it's worth. It's what one can get, cash—for my book—for freedom!

SUE. So that's why he wants Father sent away, the wretch! He must know the will Father made——

NAT. Gives the place to me. Yes, he knows. I told him.

SUE (*dully*). Ah, how vile men are!

NAT (*persuasively*). If it were to be done—if it were, I say—there'd be half for you for your wedding portion. That's fair.

SUE (*horrified*). Blood money! Do you think I could touch it?

NAT (*persuasively*). It would be only fair. I'd give it you.

SUE. My God, Nat, are you trying to bribe me?

NAT. No. It's yours in all fairness. (*With a twisted smile.*) You forget I'm heir to the treasure, too, and can afford to be generous. Ha-ha!

SUE (*alarmed*). Nat! You're so strange. You're sick, Nat. You couldn't talk this way if you were yourself. Oh, we must go away from here—you and father and I! Let Smith foreclose. There'll be something over the mortgage; and we'll move to some little house—by the sea so that father——

NAT (*fiercely*). Can keep up his mad game with me—whispering dreams in my ear—pointing out to sea—mocking me with stuff like this! (*He takes the bracelet from his pocket. The sight of it infuriates him and he hurls it into a corner, exclaiming in a terrible voice.*) No! No! It's too late for dreams now. It's too late! I've put them behind me to-night—forever!

SUE (*looks at him and suddenly understands that what she dreads has come to pass—letting her head fall on her outstretched arms with a long moan.*) Then—you've done it! You've sold him! Oh, Nat, you're cursed!

NAT (*with a terrified glance at the roof above*).

Ssshh ! What are you saying ? He'll be better off—away from the sea.

SUE (*dully*). You've sold him.

NAT (*wildly*). No ! No ! (*He takes the map from his pocket.*) Listen, Sue ! For God's sake, listen to me ! See ! The map of the island. (*He spreads it out on the table.*) And the treasure—where the cross is made. (*He gulps and his words pour out incoherently.*) I've carried it about for years. Is that nothing ? You don't know what it means. It stands between me and my book. It's stood between me and life—driving me mad ! *He* taught me to wait and hope with him—wait and hope—day after day. He made me doubt my brain and give the lie to my eyes—when hope was dead—when I knew it was all a dream—I couldn't kill it ! (*His eyes starting from his head.*) God forgive me, I still believe ! And that's mad—mad, do you hear ?

SUE (*looking at him with horror*). And that is why—you hate him !

NAT. No, I don't—— (*Then in a sudden frenzy.*) Yes ! I do hate him ! He's stolen my brain ! I've got to free myself, can't you see, from him—and his madness.

SUE (*terrified—appealingly*). Nat ! Don't ! You talk as if——

NAT (*with a wild laugh*). As if I were mad ? You're right—but I'll be mad no more ! See ! (*He opens the lantern and sets fire to the map in his hand. When he shuts the lantern again it flickers and goes out. They watch the paper burn with fascinated eyes as he talks.*) See how I free myself and become sane. And now for facts, as the doctor said. I lied to you about him. He was a doctor from the asylum. See how it burns ! It must all be destroyed—this poisonous madness. Yes, I lied to you—see—it's gone—the last speck—and the only other map is the one Silas Horne took to the bottom of the sea with him. (*He lets the ash fall to the floor and crushes it with his foot.*) Gone ! I'm free of it—at last ! (*His face is very pale, but he goes on calmly.*) Yes, I sold him, if you will—to save my soul. They're coming from the asylum to get him—— (*There is a loud, muffled cry from above, which sounds like* "Sail-ho," *and a stamping of feet. The slide to the companion-way above is slid back with a bang. A gust of air tears down into the room. Nat and Sue have jumped to their feet and stand petrified. Captain Bartlett tramps down the stairs.*)

NAT (*with a shudder*). God ! Did he hear ?

SUE. Ssshh !

(*Captain Bartlett comes into the room. He bears a striking resemblance to his son, but his face is more stern and formidable, his form more robust, erect and muscular. His mass of hair is pure white, his bristly moustache the same, contrasting with the weather-beaten leather colour of his furrowed face. Bushy grey brows overhang the obsessed glare of his fierce dark eyes. He wears a heavy, double-breasted blue coat, trousers of the same material, and rubber boots turned down from the knee.*)

BARTLETT (*in a state of mad exultation strides toward his son and points an accusing finger at him. Nat shrinks backward a step*). Bin thinkin' me mad, did ye ? Thinkin' it for the past three years, ye bin—ever since them fools on the *Slocum* tattled their damn lie o' the *Mary Allen* bein' a wreck.

NAT (*swallowing hard—chokingly*). No—Father—I——

BARTLETT. Don't lie, ye whelp ! You that I'd made my heir—aimin' to git me out o' the way! Aimin' to put me behind the bars o' the jail for mad folk !

SUE. Father—no !

BARTLETT (*waving his hand for her to be silent*). Not you, girl, not you. You're your mother.

NAT (*very pale*). Father—do you think—I——

BARTLETT (*fiercely*). A lie in your eyes ! I bin a-readin' 'em. My curse on you !

SUE. Father ! Don't !

BARTLETT. Leave me be, girl. He believed, didn't he ? And ain't he turned traitor—mockin' at me and sayin' it's all a lie—mockin' at himself, too, for bein' a fool to believe in dreams, as he calls 'em.

NAT (*placatingly*). You're wrong, Father. I do believe.

BARTLETT (*triumphantly*). Aye, now ye do !

Who wouldn't credit their own eyes?

NAT (*mystified*). Eyes?

BARTLETT. Have ye not seen her, then? Did ye not hear me hail?

NAT (*confusedly*). Hail? I heard a shout. But—hail what?—seen what?

BARTLETT (*grimly*). Aye, now's your punishment, Judas. (*Explosively.*) The *Mary Allen*, ye blind fool, come back from the Southern Seas—come back as I swore she must!

SUE (*trying to soothe him*). Father! Be quiet. It's nothing.

BARTLETT (*not heeding her—his eyes fixed hypnotically on his son's*). Turned the pint a half-hour back—the *Mary Allen*—loaded with gold as I swore she would be—carryin' her lowers—not a reef in 'em—makin' port, boy, as I swore she must—too late for traitors, boy, too late!—droppin' her anchor just when I hailed her.

NAT (*a haunted, fascinated look in his eyes, which are fixed immovably on his father's*). The *Mary Allen*! But how do you know?

BARTLETT. Not know my own ship! 'Tis you're mad!

NAT. But at night—some other schooner——

BARTLETT. No other, I say! The *Mary Allen*—clear in the moonlight. And heed this: D'you call to mind the signal I gave to Silas Horne if he made this port o' a night?

NAT (*slowly*). A red and a green light at the mainmast-head.

BARTLETT (*triumphantly*). Then look out if ye dare! (*He goes to the port-hole, left forward.*) Ye can see it plain from here. (*Commandingly.*) Will ye believe your eyes? Look—and then call me mad! (*Nat peers through the port-hole and starts back, a dumbfounded expression on his face.*)

NAT (*slowly*). A red and a green at the mainmast-head. Yes—clear as day.

SUE (*with a worried look at him*). Let me see. (*She goes to the port-hole.*)

BARTLETT (*to his son with fierce satisfaction*). Aye, ye see now clear enough—too late for you. (*Nat stares at him spellbound.*) And from above I saw Horne and Cates and Jimmy Kanaka plain on the deck in the moonlight lookin' up at me. Come!

(*He strides to the companionway, followed by Nat. The two of them ascend. Sue turns from the port-hole, an expression of frightened bewilderment on her face. She shakes her head sadly. A loud "Mary Allen, ahoy!" comes from above in Bartlett's voice, followed like an echo by the same hail from Nat. Sue covers her face with her hands, shuddering. Nat comes down the companionway, his eyes wild and exulting.*)

SUE (*brokenly*). He's bad to-night, Nat. You're right to humour him. It's the best thing.

NAT (*savagely*). Humour him? What in hell do you mean?

SUE (*pointing to the port-hole*). There's nothing there, Nat. There's not a ship in harbour.

NAT. You're a fool—or blind! The *Mary Allen's* there in plain sight of any one, with the red and the green signal lights. Those fools lied about her being wrecked. And I've been a fool, too.

SUE. But, Nat, there's nothing. (*She goes over to the port-hole again.*) Not a ship. See.

NAT. I saw, I tell you! From above it's all plain. (*He turns from her and goes back to his seat by the table. Sue follows him, pleading frightenedly.*

SUE. Nat! You mustn't let this—— You're all excited and trembling, Nat. (*She puts a soothing hand on his forehead.*)

NAT (*pushing her away from him roughly*). You blind fool!

(*Bartlett comes down the steps of the companionway. His face is transfigured with the ecstasy of a dream come true.*)

BARTLETT. They've lowered a boat—the three—Horne and Cates and Jimmy Kanaka. They're a-rowin' ashore. I heard the oars in the locks. Listen! (*A pause.*)

NAT (*excitedly*). I hear!

SUE (*who has taken the chair by her brother—in a warning whisper*). It's the wind and sea you hear, Nat. Please!

BARTLETT (*suddenly*). Hark! They've landed.

They're back on earth again as I swore they'd come back. They'll be a-comin' up the path now.

(*He stands in an attitude of rigid attention. Nat strains forward in his chair. The sound of the wind and sea suddenly ceases and there is a heavy silence. A dense green glow floods slowly in rhythmic waves like a liquid into the room—as of great depths of the sea faintly penetrated by light.*)

NAT (*catching at his sister's hand—chokingly*). See how the light changes! Green and gold! (*He shivers.*) Deep under the sea! I've been drowned for years! (*Hysterically.*) Save me! Save me!

SUE (*patting his hand comfortingly*). Only the moonlight, Nat. It hasn't changed. Be quiet, dear, it's nothing. (*The green light grows deeper and deeper.*)

BARTLETT (*in a crooning, monotonous tone*). They move slowly—slowly. They're heavy, I know, heavy—the two chests. Hark! They're below at the door. You hear?

NAT (*starting to his feet*). I hear! I left the door open.

BARTLETT. For them?

NAT. For them.

SUE (*shuddering*). Ssshh! (*The sound of a door being heavily slammed is heard from downstairs.*)

NAT (*to his sister—excitedly*). There! You hear?

SUE. A shutter in the wind.

NAT. There is no wind.

BARTLETT. Up they come! Up, bullies! They're heavy—heavy! (*The paddling of bare feet sounds from the floor below—then comes up the stairs.*)

NAT. You hear them now?

SUE. Only the rats running about. It's nothing, Nat.

BARTLETT (*rushing to the door and throwing it open*). Come in, lads, come in!—and welcome home!

(*The forms of Silas Horne, Cates, and Jimmy Kanaka rise noiselessly into the room from the stairs. The last two carry heavy inlaid chests. Horne is a parrot-nosed angular old man dressed in grey cotton trousers and a singlet torn open across his hairy chest. Jimmy is a tall, sinewy, bronzed young Kanaka. He wears only a breech cloth. Cates is squat and stout and is dressed in dungaree trousers and a torn white sailor's jumper, stained with iron rust. All are in their bare feet. Water drips from their soaked and rotten clothes. Their hair is matted, intertwined with slimy strands of sea-weed. Their eyes, as they glide silently into the room, stare frightfully wide at nothing. Their flesh in the green light has the suggestion of decomposition. Their bodies sway limply, nervelessly, rhythmically as if to the pulse of long swells of the deep sea.*)

NAT (*making a step toward them*). See! (*Frenziedly.*) Welcome home, boys!

SUE (*grabbing his arm*). Sit down, Nat. It's nothing. There's no one there. Father—sit down!

BARTLETT (*grinning at the three and putting his finger to his lips*). Not here, boys, not here—not before him. (*He points to his son.*) He has no right, now. Come. The treasure is ours only. We'll go away with it together. Come. (*He goes to the companionway. The three follow. At the foot of it Horne puts a swaying hand on his shoulder and with the other holds out a piece of paper to him. Bartlett takes it and chuckles exultantly.*) That's right—for him—that's right! (*He ascends. The figures sway up after him.*)

NAT (*frenziedly*). Wait! (*He struggles toward the companionway.*)

SUE (*trying to hold him back*). Nat—don't! Father—come back!

NAT. Father!

(*He flings her away from him and rushes up the companionway. He pounds against the slide, which seems to have been shut down on him.*)

SUE (*hysterically—runs wildly to the door in rear*). Help! Help!

(*As she gets to the door, Doctor Higgins appears, hurrying up the stairs.*)

HIGGINS (*excitedly*). Just a moment, Miss. What's the matter?

SUE (*with a gasp*). My father—up there!

HIGGINS. I can't see—where's my flash? Ah.

(*He flashes it on her terror-stricken face, then quickly around the room. The green glow disappears. The wind and sea are heard again. Clear moonlight floods through the port-holes. Higgins springs to the companionway. Nat is still pounding.*)

Here, Bartlett. Let me try.

NAT (*coming down—looking dully at the doctor*). They've locked it. I can't get up.

HIGGINS (*looks up—in an astonished voice*). What's the matter, Bartlett? It's all open. (*He starts to ascend.*)

NAT (*in a voice of warning*). Look out, man! Look out for them!

HIGGINS (*calls down from above*). Them? Who? There's no one here. (*Suddenly—in alarm.*) Come up! Lend a hand here! He's fainted!

(*Nat goes up slowly. Sue goes over and lights the lantern, then hurries back to the foot of the companionway with it. There is a scuffling noise from above. They reappear, carrying Captain Bartlett's body.*)

HIGGINS. Easy now! (*They lay him on the couch in rear. Sue sets the lantern down by the couch. Higgins bends and listens for a heart-beat. Then he rises, shaking his head.*) I'm sorry——

SUE (*dully*). Dead?

HIGGINS (*nodding*). Heart failure, I should judge. (*With an attempt at consolation.*) Perhaps it's better so, if——

NAT (*as if in a trance*). There was something Horne handed him. Did you see?

SUE (*wringing her hands*). Oh, Nat, be still! He's dead. (*To Higgins with pitiful appeal.*) Please go—go——

HIGGINS. There's nothing I can do?

SUE. Go—please—— (*Higgins bows stiffly and goes out. Nat moves slowly to his father's body, as if attracted by some irresistible fascination.*)

NAT. Didn't you see? Horne handed him something.

SUE (*sobbing*). Nat! Nat! Come away! Don't touch him, Nat! Come away.

(*But her brother does not heed her. His gaze is fixed on his father's right hand, which hangs downward over the side of the couch. He pounces on it and forcing the clenched fingers open with a great effort, secures a crumpled ball of paper.*)

NAT (*flourishing it above his head with a shout of triumph*). See! (*He bends down and spreads it out in the light of the lantern.*) The map of the island! Look! It isn't lost for me after all! There's still a chance—*my* chance! (*With mad, solemn decision.*) When the house is sold I'll go—and I'll find it! Look! It's written here in his handwriting: "The treasure is buried where the cross is made."

SUE (*covering her face with her hands—brokenly*). Oh, God! Come away, Nat! Come away!

CURTAIN

THE STRAW

Characters

BILL CARMODY
MARY, NORA, TOM, BILLY — *his children*
DOCTOR GAYNOR
FRED NICHOLLS
EILEEN CARMODY, *Bill's eldest child*
STEPHEN MURRAY
MISS HOWARD, *a nurse in training*
MISS GILPIN, *superintendent of the Infirmary*
DOCTOR STANTON, *of the Hill Farm Sanatorium*
DOCTOR SIMMS, *his assistant*
MR. SLOAN
PETERS, *a patient*
MRS. TURNER, *matron of the Sanatorium*
MISS BAILEY, MRS. ABNER, FLYNN — *patients*
OTHER PATIENTS OF THE SANATORIUM
MRS. BRENNAN

Scenes

ACT ONE

SCENE ONE The kitchen of the Carmody home. Evening.

SCENE TWO The reception room of the Infirmary, Hill Farm Sanatorium. An evening a week later.

ACT TWO

SCENE ONE Assembly Room of the main building at the Sanatorium. A morning four months later.

SCENE TWO A crossroads near the Sanatorium. Midnight of the same day.

ACT THREE

An isolation room and porch at the Sanatorium. An afternoon four months later.

TIME: 1910

Act One, Scene One

The kitchen of the Carmody home on the outskirts of a manufacturing town in Connecticut. On the left, forward, the sink. Farther back, two windows looking out on the yard. In the left corner, rear, the icebox. Immediately to the right of it, in the rear wall, a window opening on the side porch. To the right of this, a china cupboard, and a door leading into the hall where the main front entrance to the house and the stairs to the floor above are situated. On the right, to the rear, a door opening on to the dining room. Further forward, the kitchen range with scuttle, wood box, etc. In the centre of the room, a table with a red and white cloth. Four cane-bottomed chairs are pushed under the table. In front of the stove, two battered wicker rocking chairs. The floor is partly covered by linoleum strips. The walls are papered a light cheerful colour. Several old framed picture-supplement prints hang from nails. Everything has a clean, neatly-kept appearance. The supper dishes are piled in the sink ready for washing. A saucepan of water simmers on the stove.

It is about eight o'clock in the evening of a bitter cold day in late February of the year 1912.

As the curtain rises, Bill Carmody is discovered sitting in a rocker by the stove, reading a newspaper and smoking a blackened clay pipe. He is a man of fifty, heavy-set and round-shouldered, with long muscular arms and swollen-veined, hairy hands. His face is bony and ponderous; his nose short and squat; his mouth large, thick-lipped and harsh; his complexion mottled—red, purple-streaked, and freckled; his hair, short and stubby with a bald spot on the crown. The expression of his small, blue eyes is one of selfish cunning. His voice is loud and hoarse. He wears a flannel shirt, open at the neck, criss-crossed by red braces; black, baggy trousers grey with dust; muddy brogues.

His youngest daughter, Mary, is sitting on a chair by the table, front, turning over the pages of a picture book. She is a delicate, dark-haired, blue-eyed, quiet little girl about eight years old.

CARMODY (*after watching the child's preoccupation for a moment, in a tone of half exasperated amusement*). Well, but you're the quiet one, surely! (*Mary looks up at him with a shy smile, her eyes still full of dreams.*) Glory be to God, I'd not know a soul was alive in the room, barrin' myself. What is it you're at, Mary, that there's not a word out of you?

MARY. I'm looking at the pictures.

CARMODY. It's the dead spit and image of your sister Eileen you are, with your nose always in a book; and you're like your mother, too, God rest her soul. (*He crosses himself with pious unction and Mary also does so.*) It's Nora and Tom has the high spirits in them like their father; and Billy, too,—if he is a lazy, shiftless divil—has the fightin' Carmody blood like me. You're a Cullen like your mother's people. They always was dreamin' their lives out. (*He lights his pipe and shakes his head with ponderous gravity*) There's no good in too many books, I'll tell you. It's out rompin' and playin' with your brother and sister you ought to be at your age, not carin' a fig for books. (*With a glance at the clock.*) Is that auld fool of a doctor stayin' the night? If he had his wits about him he'd know in a jiffy 'tis only a cold has taken Eileen, and give her the medicine. Run out in the hall, Mary, and see if you hear him. He may have sneaked away by the front door.

MARY (*goes out into the hall, rear, and comes back*). He's upstairs. I heard him talking to Eileen.

CARMODY. Close the door, ye little divil! There's a freezin' draught comin' in. (*She does so and comes back to her chair. Carmody continues with a sneer.*) It's mad I am to be thinkin' he'd go without gettin' his money—the like of a doctor! (*Angrily.*) Rogues and thieves they are, the lot of them, robbin' the poor like us! I've no use for their drugs at all. They only keep you sick to pay more visits. I'd not have sent for this bucko if Eileen didn't scare me by faintin'.

MARY (*anxiously*). Is Eileen very sick, Papa?

CARMODY (*spitting—roughly*). If she is, it's her own fault entirely—weakenin' her health by readin' here in the house. This'll be a lesson for her, and for you, too. (*Irritably.*) Put down that book on the table and leave it be. I'll have no more readin' in this house, or I'll take the strap to you!

MARY (*laying the book on the table*). It's only pictures.

CARMODY. No back talk! Pictures or not, it's all the same mopin' and lazin' in it. (*After a pause—morosely.*) It's the bad luck I've been havin' altogether this last year since your mother died. Who's to do the work and look after Nora and Tom and yourself, if Eileen is bad took and has to stay in her bed? I'll have to get Mrs. Brennan come look after the house. That means money, too, and where's it to come from? All that I've saved from slavin' and sweatin' in the sun with a gang of lazy Dagoes'll be up the spout in no time. (*Bitterly.*) What a fool a man is to be raisin' a raft of children and him not a millionaire! (*With lugubrious self-pity.*) Mary, dear, it's a black curse God put on me when he took your mother just when I needed her most. (*Mary commences to sob. Carmody starts and looks at her angrily.*)

What are you sniffin' at?

MARY (*tearfully*). I was thinking—of Mamma.

CARMODY (*scornfully*). It's late you are with your tears, and her cold in her grave for a year. Stop it, I'm tellin' you! (*Mary gulps back her sobs.*)

(*There is a noise of childish laughter and screams from the street in front. The outside door is opened and slammed, footsteps pound along the hall. The door in the rear is pushed open, and Nora and Tom rush in breathlessly. Nora is a bright, vivacious, red-haired girl of eleven—pretty after an elfish, mischievous fashion—light-hearted and robust.*)

(*Tom resembles Nora in disposition and appearance. A healthy, good-humoured youngster with a shock of sandy hair. He is a year younger than Nora. They are followed into the room, a moment later, by their brother Billy, who is evidently loftily disgusted with their antics. Billy is a fourteen-year-old replica of his father, whom he imitates even to the hoarse, domineering tone of voice.*)

CARMODY (*grumpily*). Ah, here you are, the lot of you. Shut that door after you! What's the use in me spendin' money for coal if all you do is to let the cold night in the room itself?

NORA (*hopping over to him—teasingly*). Me and Tom had a race, Papa. I beat him. (*She sticks her tongue out at her younger brother.*) Slow poke!

TOM. You didn't beat me, neither!

NORA. I did, too!

TOM. You did not! You didn't play fair. You tripped me comin' up the steps. Brick-top! Cheater!

NORA (*flaring up*). You're a liar! You stumbled over your own big feet, clumsy bones! And I beat you fair Didn't I, Papa?

CARMODY (*with a grin*). You did, darlin', and fair, too. (*Tom slinks back to the chair in the rear of table, sulking. Carmody pats Nora's red hair with delighted pride.*) Sure it's you can beat the divil himself!

NORA (*sticks out her tongue again at Tom.*) See? Liar! (*She goes and perches on the table near Mary, who is staring sadly in front of her.*)

CARMODY (*to Billy—irritably*). Did you get the plug for me I told you?

BILLY. Sure. (*He takes a plug of tobacco from his pocket and hands it to his father. Nora slides down off her perch and disappears, unnoticed, under the table.*)

CARMODY. It's a great wonder you didn't forget it—and me without a chew. (*He bites off a piece and tucks it into his cheek.*)

TOM (*suddenly clutching at his leg with a yell*). Ouch! Darn you! (*He kicks frantically at something under the table, but Nora scrambles out at the other end, grinning.*)

CARMODY (*angrily*). Shut your big mouth! What is the matter with you at all?

TOM (*indignantly*). She pinched me—hard as she could, too—and look at her laughin'!

NORA (*hopping on the table again*). Cry-baby! I owed you one.

TOM. I'll fix you. I'll tell Eileen, wait 'n' see!

NORA. Tattle-tale! I don't care. Eileen's sick.

TOM. That's why you dast do it. You dasn't if she was up. I'll get even, you bet!

CARMODY (*exasperated*). Shut up your noise! Go up to bed, the two of you, and no more talk, and you go with them, Mary.

NORA (*giving a quick tug at Mary's hair*). Come on, Mary. Wake up.

MARY. Ow! (*She begins to cry.*)

CARMODY (*raising his voice furiously*). Hush your noise, you soft, weak thing, you! It's nothin' but blubberin' you do be doin' all the time. (*He stands up threateningly.*) I'll have a moment's peace, I will! Off to bed with you before I get the strap! It's crazy mad you all get the moment Eileen's away from you. Go on, now! (*They scurry out of the rear door.*) And be quiet or I'll be up to you!

NORA (*sticks her head back in the door*). Can I say good-night to Eileen, Papa?

CARMODY. No. The doctor's with her yet. (*Then he adds hastily.*) Yes, go in to her, Nora. It'll drive himself out of the house maybe, bad cess to him, and him stayin' half the night. (*Nora waits to hear no more but darts back, shutting the door behind her. Billy takes the chair in front of the table. Carmody sits down again with a groan.)* The rheumatics are in my leg again. *(Shakes his head.)* If Eileen's in bed long those brats'll have the house down.

BILLY. Eileen ain't sick very bad, is she ?

CARMODY *(easily).* It's a cold only she has. *(Then mournfully.)* Your poor mother died of the same. *(Billy looks awed.)* Ara, well, it's God's will, I suppose, but where the money'll come from, I dunno. *(With a disparaging glance at his son.)* They'll not be raisin' your wages soon, I'll be bound.

BILLY *(surlily).* Naw. The old boss never gives no one a raise, 'less he has to. He's a tight-wad for fair.

CARMODY *(still scanning him with contempt).* Five dollars a week—for a strappin' lad the like of you! It's shamed you should be to own up to it. A divil of a lot of good it was for me to go against Eileen's wish and let you leave off your schoolin' this year like you wanted, thinkin' the money you'd earn at work would help with the house.

BILLY. Aw, goin' to school didn't do me no good. The teachers was all down on me. I couldn't learn nothin' there.

CARMODY *(disgustedly).* Nor any other place, I'm thinkin', you're that thick. *(There is a noise from the stairs in the hall.)* Whisht! It's the doctor comin' down from Eileen. What'll he say, I wonder ? *(The door in the rear is opened and Doctor Gaynor enters. He is a stout, bald, middle-aged man, forceful of speech, who in the case of patients of the Carmodys' class dictates rather than advises. Carmody adopts a whining tone.)* Aw, Doctor, and how's Eileen now ? Have you got her cured of the weakness ?

GAYNOR *(does not answer this but comes forward into the room holding out two slips of paper—dictatorially).* Here are two prescriptions that'll have to be filled immediately.

CARMODY *(frowning).* You take them, Billy, and run round to the drug store. *(Gaynor hands them to Billy.)*

BILLY. Give me the money, then.

CARMODY *(reaches down into his trousers pocket with a sigh).* How much will they come to, Doctor ?

GAYNOR. About a dollar, I guess.

CARMODY *(protestingly).* A dollar! Sure it's expensive medicines you're givin' her for a bit of a cold. *(He meets the doctor's cold glance of contempt and he wilts—grumblingly, as he peels a dollar bill off a small roll and gives it to Billy.)* Bring back the change—if there is any. And none of your tricks, for I'll stop at the drug store myself to-morrow and ask the man how much it was.

BILLY. Aw, what do you think I am ? *(He takes the money and goes out.)*

CARMODY *(grudgingly).* Take a chair, Doctor, and tell me what's wrong with Eileen.

GAYNOR *(seating himself by the table—gravely).* Your daughter is very seriously ill.

CARMODY *(irritably).* Aw, Doctor, didn't I know you'd be sayin' that, anyway!

GAYNOR *(ignoring this remark — coldly).* Your daughter has tuberculosis of the lungs.

CARMODY *(with puzzled awe).* Too-ber-c'losis ?

GAYNOR. Consumption, if that makes it plainer to you.

CARMODY *(with dazed terror—after a pause).* Consumption ? Eileen ? *(With sudden anger.)* What lie is it you're tellin' me ?

GAYNOR *(icily).* Look here, Carmody! I'm not here to stand for your insults!

CARMODY *(bewilderingly).* Don't be angry, now, at what I said. Sure I'm out of my wits entirely. Eileen to have the consumption! Ah, Doctor, sure you must be mistaken!

GAYNOR. There's no chance for a mistake, I'm sorry to say. Her right lung is badly affected.

CARMODY *(desperately).* It's a bad cold only, maybe.

GAYNOR *(curtly).* Don't talk nonsense. *(Carmody groans. Gaynor continues authoritatively.)* She will have to go to a sanatorium at once. She ought to have been sent to one months ago. The girl's been keeping up on her nerve when she should have been in bed, and it's given the disease a chance to develop. *(Casts a look of indignant scorn at Carmody, who is sitting staring at the floor with an expression of angry stupor on his face.)* It's a wonder to me you didn't see the condition she was in and force her to take care of herself. Why, the girl's nothing but skin and bone!

CARMODY *(with vague fury).* God blast it!

GAYNOR. No, your kind never realises things till the crash comes—usually when it's too late. She kept on doing her work, I suppose—taking care of her brothers and sisters, washing, cooking, sweeping, looking after your comfort—worn out—when she should have been in bed—and—— (*He gets to his feet with a harsh laugh.*) But what's the use of talking? The damage is done. We've got to set to work to repair it at once. I'll write to-night to Dr. Stanton of the Hill Farm Sanatorium and find out if he has a vacancy. And if luck is with us we can send her there at once. The sooner the better.

CARMODY (*his face growing red with rage*). Is it sendin' Eileen away to a hospital you'd be? (*Exploding.*) Then you'll not! You'll get that notion out of your head damn quick. It's all nonsense you're stuffin' me with, and lies, makin' things out to be the worst in the world. I'll not believe a word of Eileen having the consumption at all. It's doctors' notions to be always lookin' for a sickness that'd kill you. She'll not move a step out of here, and I say so, and I'm her father!

GAYNOR (*who has been staring at him with contempt—coldly angry*). You refuse to let your daughter go to a sanatorium?

CARMODY. I do.

GAYNOR (*threateningly*). Then I'll have to report her case to the Society for the Prevention of Tuberculosis of this county, and tell them of your refusal to help her.

CARMODY (*wavering a bit*). Report all you like, and be damned to you!

GAYNOR (*ignoring the interruption—impressively*). A majority of the most influential men of this city are behind the Society. Do you know that? (*Grimly.*) We'll find a way to move you, Carmody, if you try to be stubborn.

CARMODY (*thoroughly frightened, but still protesting*). Ara, Doctor, you don't see the way of it at all. If Eileen goes to the hospital, who's to be takin' care of the others, and mindin' the house when I'm off to work?

GAYNOR. You can easily hire some woman.

CARMODY (*at once furious again*). Hire? D'you think I'm a millionaire itself?

GAYNOR (*contemptuously*). That's where the shoe pinches, eh? (*In a rage.*) I'm not going to waste any more words on you, Carmody, but I'm damn well going to see this thing through! You might as well give in first as last.

CARMODY (*wailing*). But where's the money comin' from?

GAYNOR (*brutally*). That's your concern. Don't lie about your poverty. You've a steady well-paid job, and plenty of money to throw away on drunken sprees, I'll bet. The weekly fee at the Hill Farm is only seven dollars. You can easily afford that—the price of a few rounds of drinks.

CARMODY. Seven dollars! And I'll have to pay a woman to come in—and the four of the children eatin' their heads off! Glory be to God, I'll not have a penny saved for me old age—and then it's the poor-house!

GAYNOR (*curtly*). Don't talk nonsense!

CARMODY. Ah, doctor, it's the truth I'm tellin' you!

GAYNOR. Well, perhaps I can get the Society to pay half for your daughter—if you're really as hard up as you pretend. They're willing to do that where it seems necessary.

CARMODY (*brightening*). Ah, Doctor, thank you.

GAYNOR (*abruptly*). Then it's all settled?

CARMODY (*grudgingly—trying to make the best of it*). I'll do my best for Eileen, if it's needful—and you'll not be tellin' them people about it at all, Doctor?

GAYNOR. Not unless you force me to.

CARMODY. And they'll pay the half, surely?

GAYNOR. I'll see what I can do—for your daughter's sake, not yours, understand!

CARMODY. God bless you, Doctor! (*Grumblingly.*) It's the whole of it they ought to be payin', I'm thinkin', and them with bags of money. 'Tis them builds the hospitals and why should they be wantin' the poor like me to support them?

GAYNOR (*disgustedly*). Bah! (*Abruptly.*) I'll telephone to Doctor Stanton to-morrow morning. Then I'll know something definite when I come to see your daughter in the afternoon.

CARMODY (*darkly*). You'll be comin' again to-morrow? (*Half to himself.*) Leave it to the likes of you to be drainin' a man dry.

(*Gaynor has gone out to the hall in rear and does not hear this last remark. There is a loud knock from the outside door. The Doctor comes back into the room carrying his hat and overcoat.*)

GAYNOR. There's someone knocking.

CARMODY. Who'll it be? Ah, it's Fred Nicholls, maybe. (*In a low voice to Gaynor who has started to put on his overcoat.*) Eileen's young man, Doctor, that she's engaged to marry, as you might say.

GAYNOR (*thoughtfully*). H'mm—yes—she spoke of him.

(*As another knock sounds Carmody hurries to the rear. Gaynor, after a moment's indecision, takes off his overcoat again and sits down. A moment later Carmody re-enters, followed by Fred Nicholls, who has left his overcoat and hat in the hallway. Nicholls is a young fellow of twenty-three, stockily built, fair-haired, handsome in a commonplace, conventional mould. His manner is obviously an attempt at suave gentility; he has an easy, taking smile and a ready laugh, but there is a petty, calculating expression in his small, observing, blue eyes. His well-fitting, ready-made clothes are carefully pressed. His whole get-up suggests an attitude of man-about-small-town complacency.*)

CARMODY (*as they enter*). I had a mind to phone to your house, but I wasn't wishful to disturb you, knowin' you'd be comin' to call to-night.

NICHOLLS (*with disappointed concern*). It's nothing serious, I hope.

CARMODY (*grumblingly*). Ah, who knows? Here's the doctor. You've not met him?

NICHOLLS (*politely, looking at Gaynor, who inclines his head stiffly*). I haven't had the pleasure. Of course, I've heard——

CARMODY. It's Doctor Gaynor. This is Fred Nicholls, Doctor. (*The two men shake hands with conventional greetings.*) Sit down, Fred, that's a good lad, and be talkin' to the Doctor a moment while I go upstairs and see how is Eileen. She's all alone up there.

NICHOLLS. Certainly, Mr. Carmody. Go ahead—and tell her how sorry I am to learn she's under the weather.

CARMODY. I will so. (*He goes out.*)

GAYNOR (*after a pause in which he is studying Nicholls*). Do you happen to be any relative to the Albert Nicholls who is superintendent over at the Downs Manufacturing Company?

NICHOLLS (*smiling*). He's sort of a near relative—my father.

GAYNOR. Ah, yes?

NICHOLLS (*with satisfaction*). I work for the Downs Company myself—bookkeeper——

GAYNOR. Miss Carmody—the sick girl upstairs—she had a position there also, didn't she, before her mother died?

NICHOLLS. Yes. She had a job as stenographer for a time. When she graduated from the business college course—I was already working at the Downs—and through my father's influence—you understand. (*Gaynor nods curtly.*) She was getting on finely, too, and liked the work. It's too bad—her mother's death, I mean—forcing her to give it up and come home to take care of those kids.

GAYNOR. It's a damn shame. That's the main cause of her breakdown.

NICHOLLS (*frowning*). I've noticed she's been looking badly lately. So that's the trouble? Well, it's all her father's fault—and her own, too, because whenever I raised a kick about his making a slave of her, she always defended him. (*With a quick glance at the Doctor—in a confidential tone.*) Between us, Carmody's as selfish as they make 'em, if you want my opinion.

GAYNOR (*with a growl*). He's a hog on two legs.

NICHOLLS (*with a gratified smile*). You bet! (*With a patronising air.*) I hope to get Eileen away from all this as soon as—things pick up a little. (*Making haste to explain his connection with the dubious household.*) Eileen and I have gone around together for years—went to Grammar and High School together—in different classes, of course. She's really a corker—very different from the rest of the family you've seen—like her mother. She's really educated and knows a lot—used to carry off all the prizes at school. My folks like her awfully well. Of course, they'd never stand for—him.

GAYNOR. You'll excuse my curiosity—I've a good reason for it—but you and Miss Carmody are engaged, aren't you? Carmody said you were.

NICHOLLS (*embarrassed*). Why, yes, in a way—but nothing definite—no official announcement or anything of that kind. It's all in the future. We have to wait, you know. (*With a sentimental smile.*) We've been sort of engaged for years, you might say. It's always been sort of understood between us. (*He laughs awkwardly.*)

GAYNOR (*gravely*). Then I can be frank with you. I'd like to be because I may need your help. I don't put much faith in any promise Carmody makes. Besides, you're bound to know anyway. She'd tell you.

NICHOLLS (*a look of apprehension coming over his face*). Is it—about her sickness?

GAYNOR. Yes.

NICHOLLS. Then—it's serious?

GAYNOR. It's pulmonary tuberculosis — consumption.

NICHOLLS (*stunned*). Consumption? Good heavens! (*After a dazed pause—lamely.*) Are you sure, Doctor?

GAYNOR. Positive. (*Nicholls stares at him with vaguely frightened eyes.*) It's had a good start—thanks to her father's blind selfishness—but let's hope that can be overcome. The important thing is to ship her off to a sanatorium immediately. Carmody wouldn't hear of it at first. However, I managed to bully him into consenting; but I don't trust his word. That's where you can be of help. It's up to you to convince him that it's imperative she be sent away at once—for the safety of those around her as well as her own.

NICHOLLS (*confusedly*). I'll do my best, Doctor. (*As if he couldn't yet believe his ears—shuddering.*) Good heavens! She never said a word about—being so ill. She's had a cold. But, Doctor—do you think this sanatorium will——?

GAYNOR (*with hearty hopefulness*). Most certainly. She has every chance. The Hill Farm has a really surprising record of arrested cases—as good as any place in the country. Of course, she'll never be able to live as carelessly as before, even after the most favourable results. She'll have to take care of herself. (*Apologetically.*) I'm telling you all this as being the one most intimately concerned. I don't count Carmody. You are the one who will have to assume responsibility for her welfare when she returns to everyday life.

NICHOLLS (*answering as if he were merely talking to screen the thoughts in his mind*). Yes—certainly. Where is this sanatorium, Doctor—very far away?

GAYNOR. Half an hour by train to the town. The sanatorium is two miles out on the hills—a nice drive. You'll be able to see her whenever you've a day off. It's a pleasant trip.

NICHOLLS (*a look of horrified realisation has been creeping into his eyes*). You said—Eileen ought to be sent away—for the sake of those around her——?

GAYNOR. That's obvious. T.B. is extremely contagious, you must know that. Yet I'll bet she's been fondling and kissing those brothers and sisters of hers regardless. (*Nicholls fidgets uneasily on his chair.*) And look at this house sealed tight against the fresh air! Not a window open an inch! (*Fuming.*) That's what we're up against in the fight with T.B.—a total ignorance of the commonest methods of prevention——

NICHOLLS (*his eyes shiftily avoiding the doctor's face*). Then the kids might have gotten it—by kissing Eileen?

GAYNOR. It stands to reason that's a common means of communication.

NICHOLLS (*very much shaken*). Yes. I suppose it must be. But that's terrible, isn't it? (*With sudden volubility, evidently extremely anxious to wind up this conversation and conceal his thoughts from Gaynor.*) I'll promise you, Doctor, I'll tell Carmody straight what's what. He'll pay attention to me or I'll know the reason why.

GAYNOR (*getting to his feet and picking up his overcoat*). Good boy! You've probably saved me a disagreeable squabble. I won't wait for Carmody. The sight of him makes me lose my temper. Tell him I'll be back to-morrow with definite information about the sanatorium.

NICHOLLS (*helping him on with his overcoat, anxious to have him go*). All right, Doctor.

GAYNOR (*puts on his hat*). And do your best to cheer the patient up when you talk to her. Give her confidence in her ability to get well. That's half the battle. And she'll believe it, coming from you.

NICHOLLS (*hastily*). Yes, yes, I'll do all I can.

GAYNOR (*turns to the door and shakes Nicholls' hand sympathetically*). And don't take it to heart too much yourself. There's every hope, remember that. In six months she'll come back to you her old self again.

NICHOLLS (*nervously*). It's hard on a fellow—so suddenly—but I'll remember—and—(*abruptly*). Good night, Doctor.

GAYNOR. Good night.

(*He goes out. The outer door is heard shutting behind him. Nicholls closes the door, rear, and comes back and sits in the chair in front of table. He rests his chin on his hands and stares before him, a look of desperate, frightened calculation coming into his eyes. Carmody is heard clumping heavily down the stairs. A moment later he enters. His expression is glum and irritated.*)

CARMODY (*coming forward to his chair by the stove*). Has he gone away?

NICHOLLS (*turning on him with a look of repulsion*). Yes. He told me to tell you he'd be back to-morrow with definite information—about the sanatorium business.

CARMODY (*darkly*). Oho, he did, did he? Maybe I'll surprise him. I'm thinkin' it's lyin' he is about Eileen's sickness, and her lookin' as fresh as a daisy with the high colour in her cheeks when I saw her now.

NICHOLLS (*impatiently*). That's silly, Mr. Carmody. Gaynor knows his business. (*After a moment's hesitation.*) He told me all about Eileen's sickness.

CARMODY (*resentfully*). Did he now, the auld monkey! Small thanks to him to be tellin' our secrets to the town.

NICHOLLS (*exasperated*). I didn't want to learn your affairs. He only told me because you'd said I and Eileen were engaged You're the one who was telling—secrets.

CARMODY (*irritated*). Ara, don't be talkin'! That's no secret at all with the whole town watchin' Eileen and you spoonin' together from the time you was kids.

NICHOLLS (*vindictively*). Well, the whole town is liable to find out—— (*He checks himself.*)

CARMODY (*too absorbed in his own troubles to notice this threat*). To hell with the town and all in it! I've troubles enough of my own. So he told you he'd send Eileen away to the hospital? I've half a mind not to let him—and let him try to make me! (*With a frown.*) But Eileen herself says she's wantin' to go, now. (*Angrily.*) It's all that divil's notion he put in her head that the children'd be catchin' her sickness that makes her willin' to go.

NICHOLLS (*with a superior air*). From what he told me, I should say it was the only thing for Eileen to do if she wants to get well quickly. (*Spitefully.*) And I'd certainly not go against Gaynor, if I was you. He told me he'd make it hot for you if you did. He will, too, you can bet on that. He's that kind.

CARMODY (*worriedly*). He's a divil. But what can he do—him and his Sasiety? I'm her father.

NICHOLLS (*seeing Carmody's uneasiness, with revengeful satisfaction*). Oh, he'll do what he says, don't worry! You'll make a mistake if you think he's bluffing. It'd probably get in all the papers about you refusing. Every one would be down on you. (*As a last jab—spitefully.*) You might even lose your job over it, people would be so sore.

CARMODY (*jumping to his feet*). Ah, divil take him! Let him send her where he wants, then. I'll not be sayin' a word.

NICHOLLS (*as an afterthought*). And, honestly, Mr. Carmody, I don't see how you can object for a second—after he's told you it's absolutely necessary for Eileen to go away. (*Seeing Carmody's shaken condition, he finishes boldly.*) You've some feeling for your own daughter, haven't you? You'd be a fine father if you hadn't!

CARMODY (*apprehensively*). Whisht! She might hear you. But you're right. Let her do what she's wishful to, *and* get well soon.

NICHOLLS (*complacently—feeling his duty in the matter well done*). That's the right spirit. I knew you'd see it that way. And you and I'll do all we can to help her. (*He gets to his feet.*) Well, I guess I'll have to go. Tell Eileen——

CARMODY. You're not goin'? Sure, Eileen is puttin' on her clothes to come down and have a look at you. She'll be here in a jiffy. Sit down now, and wait for her.

NICHOLLS (*suddenly panic-stricken by the prospect of facing her*). No—no—I can't stay—I only came for a moment—I've got an appointment—honestly. Besides, it isn't right for her to be up. She's too weak. It'll make her worse. You should have told her.

(*The door in the rear is opened and Eileen enters. She is just over eighteen. Her wavy mass of dark hair is parted in the middle and combed low on her forehead, covering her ears, to a knot at the back of her head. The oval of her face is spoiled by a long, rather heavy Irish jaw contrasting with the delicacy of her other features. Her eyes are large and blue, confident in their compelling candour and sweetness; her lips, full and red, half-open over strong, even teeth, droop at the corners into an expression of wistful sadness; her clear complexion is unnaturally striking in its contrasting colours, rose and white; her figure is slight and undeveloped. She wears a plain black dress with a bit of white at the neck and wrists. She stands looking appealingly at Nicholls, who avoids her glance. Her eyes have a startled, stunned expression as if the doctor's verdict were still in her ears.*)

EILEEN (*faintly—forcing a smile*). Good evening, Fred. (*Her eyes search his face anxiously.*)

NICHOLLS (*confusedly*). Hello, Eileen. I'm so sorry to—— (*Clumsily trying to cover up his confusion, he goes over and leads her to a chair.*) You must sit down. You've got to take care of yourself. You never ought to have got up to-night.

EILEEN (*sits down*). I wanted to talk to you. (*She raises her face with a pitiful smile. Nicholls hurriedly moves back to his own chair.*)

NICHOLLS (*almost brusquely*). I could have talked to you from the hall. You're silly to take chances just now.

(*Eileen's eyes show her hurt at his tone.*)

CARMODY (*seeing his chance—hastily*). You'll be stayin' a while now, Fred? I'll take a walk down the road. I'm needin' a drink to clear my wits. (*He goes to the door in rear.*)

EILEEN (*reproachfully*). You won't be long, Father? And please don't—you know.

CARMODY (*exasperated*). Sure who wouldn't get drunk with all the sorrows of the world piled on him? (*He stamps out. A moment later the outside door bangs behind him. Eileen sighs. Nicholls walks up and down with his eyes on the floor.*)

NICHOLLS (*furious at Carmody for having left him in this situation.*) Honestly, Eileen, your father is the limit. I don't see how you stand for him. He's the most selfish——

EILEEN (*gently*). Sssh! You mustn't, Fred. He's not to blame. He just doesn't understand. (*Nicholls snorts disdainfully.*) Don't! Let's not talk about him now. We won't have many more evenings together for a long, long time. Did father or the Doctor tell you—— (*She falters.*)

NICHOLLS (*not looking at her—glumly*). Everything there was to tell, I guess.

EILEEN (*hastening to comfort him*). You mustn't worry, Fred. Please don't! It'd make it so much worse for me if I thought you did. I'll be all right. I'll do exactly what they tell me, and in a few months I'll be back so fat and healthy you won't know me.

NICHOLLS (*lamely*). Oh, there's no doubt of that. No one's worrying about your not getting well quick.

EILEEN. It won't be long. We can write often, and it isn't far away. You can come out and see me every Sunday—if you want to.

NICHOLLS (*hastily*). Of course I will!

EILEEN (*looking at his face searchingly*). Why do you act so funny? Why don't you sit down—here, by me? Don't you want to?

NICHOLLS (*drawing up a chair by hers—flushing guiltily*). I—I'm all flustered, Eileen. I don't know what I'm doing.

EILEEN (*putting her hand on his knee*). Poor Fred! I'm so sorry I have to go. I didn't want to at first. I knew how hard it would be on father and the kids—especially little Mary. (*Her voice trembles a bit.*) And then the doctor said if I stayed I'd be putting them all in danger. He even ordered me not to kiss them any more. (*She bites her lip to restrain a sob—then coughs, a soft, husky cough. Nicholls shrinks away from her to the edge of his chair, his eyes shifting nervously with fright. Eileen continues gently.*) So I've got to go and get well, don't you see?

NICHOLLS (*wetting his dry lips*). Yes—it's better.

EILEEN (*sadly*). I'll miss the kids so much. Taking

care of them has meant so much to me since mother died. (*With a half-sob she suddenly throws her arms about his neck and hides her face on his shoulder. He shudders and fights against an impulse to push her away.*) But I'll miss you most of all, Fred. (*She lifts her lips towards his, expecting a kiss. He seems about to kiss her—then averts his face with a shrinking movement, pretending he hasn't seen. Eileen's eyes grow wide with horror. She throws herself back into her chair, staring accusingly at Nicholls. She speaks chokingly.*) Fred! Why—why didn't you kiss—what is it? Are you—afraid? (*With a moaning sound.*) Oooh!

NICHOLLS (*goaded by this accusation into a display of manhood, seizes her fiercely by the arms.*) No! What—what d'you mean? (*He tries to kiss her, but she hides her face.*)

EILEEN (*in a muffled voice of hysterical self-accusation, pushing his head away*). No, no, you mustn't! I was wrong. The doctor told you not to, didn't he? Please don't, Fred! It would be awful if anything happened to you—through me. (*Nicholls gives up his attempts, recalled to caution by her words. She raises her face and tries to force a smile through her tears.*) But you can kiss me on the forehead, Fred. That can't do any harm. (*His face crimson, he does so. She laughs hysterically.*) It seems so silly—being kissed that way—by you. (*She gulps back a sob and continued to attempt to joke.*) I'll have to get used to it, won't I?

CURTAIN

Act One, Scene Two.

The reception room of the Infirmary, a large, high-ceilinged room painted white, with oiled, hard wood floor. In the left wall, forward, a row of four windows. Farther back, the main entrance from the drive, and another window. In the rear wall left, a glass partition looking out on the sleeping porch. A row of white beds, with the faces of patients barely peeping out from under piles of heavy bed-clothes, can be seen. To the right of this partition, a bookcase, and a door leading to the hall past the patients' rooms. Farther right, another door opening on the examining room. In the right wall, rear, a door to the office. Farther forward, a row of windows. In front of the windows, a long dining-table with chairs. On the left of the table, towards the centre of the room, a chimney with two open fire-places, facing left and right. Several wicker armchairs are placed around the fire-place on the left in which a cheerful wood fire is crackling. To the left of centre, a round reading and writing table with a green-shaded electric lamp. Other electric lights are in brackets around the walls. Easy chairs stand near the table, which is stacked with magazines. Rocking chairs are placed here and there about the room, near the windows, etc. A gramophone stands near the left wall, forward.

It is nearing eight o'clock of a cold evening about a week later.

At the rise of the curtain Stephen Murray is discovered sitting in a chair in front of the fire-place, left. Murray is thirty years old—a tall, slender, rather unusual-looking fellow with a pale face, sunken under high cheek bones, lined about the eyes and mouth, jaded and worn for one still so young. His intelligent, large hazel eyes have a tired, dispirited expression in repose, but can quicken instantly with a concealed mechanism of mocking, careless humour whenever his inner privacy is threatened. His large mouth aids this process of protection by a quick change from its set apathy to a cheerful grin of cynical good nature. He gives off the impression of being somehow dissatisfied with himself, but not yet embittered enough by it to take it out on others. His manner, as revealed by his speech—nervous, inquisitive, alert—seems more an acquired quality than any part of his real nature. He stoops a trifle, giving him a slightly round-shouldered appearance. He is dressed in a shabby dark suit, baggy at the knees. He is staring into the fire, dreaming, an open book lying unheeded on the arm of his chair. The gramophone is whining out the last strains of Dvorak's Humoresque. In the doorway to the office, Miss Gilpin stands talking to Miss Howard. The former is a slight, middle-aged woman with black hair, and a strong, intelligent face, its expression of resolute efficiency softened and made kindly by her warm, sympathetic grey eyes. Miss Howard is tall, slender and blonde—decidedly pretty and pro-

vokingly conscious of it, yet with a certain air of seriousness underlying her apparent frivolity. She is twenty years old. The elder woman is dressed in the all-white of a full-fledged nurse. Miss Howard wears the grey-blue uniform of one still in training. The record finishes. Murray sighs with relief, but makes no move to get up and stop the grinding needle. Miss Howard hurries across to the machine. Miss Gilpin goes back into the office.

MISS HOWARD (*takes off the record, glancing at Murray with amused vexation.*) It's a wonder you wouldn't stop this machine grinding itself to bits, Mr. Murray.

MURRAY (*with a smile.*) I was hoping the darn thing would bust. (*Miss Howard sniffs. Murray grins at her teasingly.*) It keeps you from talking to me. That's the real music.

MISS HOWARD (*comes over to his chair laughing*). It's easy to see you've got Irish in you. Do you know what I think? I think you're a natural born kidder. All newspaper reporters are like that, I've heard.

MURRAY. You wrong me terribly. (*Then frowning.*) And it isn't charitable to remind me of my job. I hoped to forget all about it up here.

MISS HOWARD (*surprised*). I think it's great to be able to write. I wish I could. You ought to be proud of it.

MURRAY (*glumly*). I'm not. You can't call it writing—not what I did—small town stuff. (*Changing the subject.*) But I wanted to ask you something. Do you know when I'm to be moved away to the huts?

MISS HOWARD. In a few days, I guess. Don't be impatient. (*Murray grunts and moves nervously on his chair.*) What's the matter? Don't you like us here at the Sanatorium?

MURRAY (*smiling*). Oh — you — yes! (*Then seriously.*) I don't care for the atmosphere, though. (*He waves his hand towards the partition looking out on the porch.*) All those people in bed out there on the porch seem so sick. It's depressing. I can't do anything for them—and—it makes me feel so helpless.

MISS HOWARD. Well, it's the rules, you know. All the patients have to come here first until Doctor Stanton finds out whether they're well enough to be sent out to the huts and cottages. And remember you're a patient just like the ones in bed out there—even if you are up and about.

MURRAY. I know it. But I don't feel as I were—really sick like them.

MISS HOWARD (*wisely*). None of them do, either.

MURRAY (*after a moment's reflection—cynically*). Yes, I suppose it's that pipe dream that keeps us all going, eh?

MISS HOWARD. Well, you ought to be thankful. You're very lucky, if you knew it. (*Lowering her voice.*) Shall I tell you a secret? I've seen your chart and *you've* no cause to worry. Doctor Stanton joked about it. He said you were too uninteresting—there was so little the matter with you.

MURRAY (*pleased, but pretending indifference*). Humph! He's original in that opinion.

MISS HOWARD. I know it's hard your being the only one up the week since you've been here, with no one to talk to; but there's another patient due to-day. Maybe she'll be well enough to be around with you. (*With a quick glance at her wrist watch.*) She can't be coming unless she got in on the last train.

MURRAY (*interestedly*). It's a she, eh?

MISS HOWARD. Yes.

MURRAY (*grinning provokingly*). Young?

MISS HOWARD. Eighteen, I believe. (*Seeing his grin—with feigned pique.*) I suppose you'll be asking if she's pretty next! Oh, you men are all alike, sick or well. Her name is Carmody, that's the only other thing I know. So there!

MURRAY. Carmody?

MISS HOWARD. Oh, you don't know her. She's from another part of the state from your town.

MISS GILPIN (*appearing in the office doorway*). Miss Howard.

MISS HOWARD. Yes, Miss Gilpin. (*In an aside to Murray as she leaves him.*) It's time for those horrid diets.

(*She hurries back into the office. Murray stares into the fire. Miss Howard reappears from the office and goes out by the door to the hall, rear. Carriage wheels are heard from the drive in front of the house on the left. They stop. After a pause there is a sharp rap on the door and a bell rings insistently. Men's muffled voices are heard in argument. Murray turns curiously in his chair. Miss Gilpin comes from the office and walks quickly to the door, unlocking and opening it. Eileen enters, followed by Nicholls, who is carrying her suit-case, and by her father.)*

EILEEN. I'm Miss Carmody. I believe Doctor Gaynor wrote——

MISS GILPIN (*taking her hand—with kind affability*). We've been expecting you all day. How do you do? I'm Miss Gilpin. You came on the last train, didn't you?

EILEEN (*heartened by the other woman's kindness*). Yes. This is my father, Miss Gilpin—and Mr. Nicholls.

(*Miss Gilpin shakes hands cordially with the two men who are staring about the room in embarrassment. Carmody has very evidently been drinking. His voice is thick and his face puffed and stupid. Nicholls' manner is that of one who is accomplishing a necessary but disagreeable duty with the best grace possible, but is frightfully eager to get it over and done with. Carmody's condition embarrasses him acutely and when he glances at him it is with hatred and angry disgust.*)

MISS GILPIN (*indicating the chairs in front of the windows on the left, forward*). Won't you gentlemen sit down? (*Carmody grunts sullenly and plumps himself into the one nearest the door. Nicholls hesitates, glancing down at the suit-case he carries. Miss Gilpin turns to Eileen.*) And now we'll get you settled immediately. Your room is all ready for you. If you'll follow me—— (*She turns toward the door in rear, centre.*)

EILEEN. Let me take the suit-case now, Fred.

MISS GILPIN (*as he is about to hand it to her—decisively*). No, my dear, you mustn't. Put the case right down there, Mr. Nicholls. I'll have it taken to Miss Carmody's room in a moment. (*She shakes her finger at Eileen with kindly admonition.*) That's the first rule you'll have to learn. Never exert yourself or tax your strength. It's very important. You'll find laziness is a virtue instead of a vice with us.

EILEEN (*confused*). I—— I didn't know——

MISS GILPIN (*smiling*). Of course you didn't. And now if you'll come with me I'll show you your room. We'll have a little chat there and I can explain all the other important rules in a second. The gentlemen can make themselves comfortable in the meantime. We won't be gone more than a moment.

NICHOLLS (*feeling called upon to say something*). Yes—we'll wait—certainly, we're all right.

(*Carmody remains silent, glowering at the fire. Nicholls sits down beside him. Miss Gilpin and Eileen go out. Murray switches his chair so that he can observe the two men out of the corner of his eye while pretending to be absorbed in his book.*)

CARMODY (*looking about shiftily and reaching for the inside pocket of his overcoat*). I'll be havin' a nip now we're alone, and that cacklin' hen gone. I'm feelin' sick in the pit of the stomach. (*He pulls out a pint flask, half full.*)

NICHOLLS (*excitedly*). For God's sake, don't! Put that bottle away! (*In a whisper.*) Don't you see that fellow in the chair there?

CARMODY (*taking a big drink*). Ah, I'm not mindin' a man at all. Sure I'll bet it's himself would be likin' a taste of the same. (*He appears about to get up and invite Murray to join him, but Nicholls grabs his arm.*)

NICHOLLS (*with a frightened look at Murray who appears buried in his book*). Stop it, you—— Don't you know he's probably a patient and they don't allow them——

CARMODY (*scornfully*). A sick one, and him readin' a book like a dead man without a civil word out of him! It's queer they'd be allowin' the sick ones to read books, when I'll bet it's the same lazy readin' in the house brought the half of them down with the consumption itself. (*Raising his voice.*) I'm thinking this whole shebang is a big, thievin' fake—and I've always thought so.

NICHOLLS (*furiously*). Put that bottle away, damn it! And don't shout. You're not in a public-house.

CARMODY (*with provoking calm*). I'll put it back when I'm ready, not before, and no lip from you!

NICHOLLS (*with fierce disgust*). You're drunk now. It's disgusting.

CARMODY (*raging*). Drunk, am I? Is it the like of a young jackass like you that's still wet behind the ears to be tellin' me I'm drunk?

NICHOLLS (*half-rising from his chair—pleadingly*). For heaven's sake, Mr. Carmody, remember where we are and don't raise any rumpus. What'll Eileen say? Do you want to make trouble for her at the start?

CARMODY (*puts the bottle away hastily, mumbling to himself—then glowers about the room scornfully with blinking eyes*). It's a grand hotel this is, I'm thinkin', for the rich to be takin' their ease, and not a hospital for the poor, but the poor has to pay for it.

NICHOLLS (*fearful of another outbreak*). Sssh!

CARMODY. Don't be shshin' at me? I'm tellin' you the truth. I'd make Eileen come back out of this to-night if that divil of a doctor didn't have me by the throat.

NICHOLLS (*glancing at him nervously*). I wonder how soon she'll be back? The carriage is waiting for us. We'll have to hurry to make that last train back. If we miss it—it means two hours on the damn tram.

CARMODY (*angrily*). Is it anxious to get out of her sight you are, and you engaged to marry and pretendin' to love her? (*Nicholls flushes guiltily. Murray pricks up his ears and stares over at Nicholls. The latter meets his glance, scowls, and hurriedly averts his eyes. Carmody goes on accusingly.*) Sure, it's no heart at all you have—and her your sweetheart for years—and her sick with the consumption—and you wild to run away from her and leave her alone.

NICHOLLS (*springing to his feet—furiously*). That's a——! (*He controls himself with an effort. His voice trembles.*) You're not responsible for the idiotic things you're saying or I'd——. (*He turns away, seeking some escape from the old man's tongue.*) I'll see if the man is still there with the carriage. (*He walks to the door on left and goes out.*)

CARMODY (*following him with his eyes*). Go to hell, for all I'm preventin' You've got no guts of a man in you. (*He addresses Murray with the good nature inspired by the flight of Nicholls.*) Is it true you're one of the consumptives, young fellow?

MURRAY (*delighted by this speech—with a grin*). Yes, I'm one of them.

CARMODY. My name's Carmody. What's yours, then?

MURRAY. Murray.

CARMODY (*slapping his thigh*). Irish as Paddy's pig! (*Murray nods. Carmody brightens and grows confidential.*) I'm glad to be knowin' you're one of us. You can keep an eye on Eileen. That's my daughter that came with us. She's got consumption like yourself.

MURRAY. I'll be glad to do all I can.

CARMODY. Thanks to you—though it's a grand life she'll be havin' here from the fine look of the place. (*With whining self-pity.*) It's me it's hard on, God help me, with four small children and me widowed, and havin' to hire a woman to come in and look after them and the house now that Eileen's sick; and payin' for her curin' in this place, and me with only a bit of money in the bank for my old age. That's hard, now, on a man, and who'll say it isn't?

MURRAY (*made uncomfortable by this confidence*). Hard luck always comes in bunches. (*To head off Carmody who is about to give vent to more woe—quickly, with a glance towards the door from the hall.*) If I'm not mistaken, here comes your daughter now.

CARMODY (*as Eileen comes into the room*). I'll make you acquainted. Eileen! (*She comes over to them, embarrassed to find her father in his condition so chummy with a stranger. Murray rises to his feet.*) This is Mr. Murray, Eileen. I want you to meet. He's Irish and he'll put you on to the ropes of the place. He's got the consumption, too, God pity him.

EILEEN (*distressed*). Oh, Father, how can you——(*With a look at Murray which pleads for her father.*) I'm glad to meet you, Mr. Murray.

MURRAY (*with a straight glance at her which is so frankly admiring that she flushes and drops her eyes.*) I'm glad to meet you. (*The front door is opened and Nicholls re-appears, shivering with the cold. He stares over at the others with ill-concealed irritation.*)

CARMODY (*noticing him—with malicious satisfaction*). Oho, here you are again. (*Nicholls scowls and turns away. Carmody addresses his daughter with a sly wink at Murray.*) I thought Fred was slidin' down hill to the train with his head bare to the frost, and him so desperate hurried to get away from here. Look at the knees on him clappin' together with the cold, and with the great fear that's in him he'll be catchin' a sickness in this place! (*Nicholls, his guilty conscience stabbed to the quick, turns pale with impotent rage.*)

EILEEN (*remonstrating pitifully*). Father! Please! (*She hurries over to Nicholls.*) Oh, please don't mind him, Fred. You know what he is when he's drinking. He doesn't mean a word he's saying.

NICHOLLS (*thickly*). That's all right—for you to say. But I won't forget—I'm sick and tired standing for—I'm not used to—such people.

EILEEN (*shrinking from him*). Fred!

NICHOLLS (*with a furious glance at Murray*). Before that cheap slob, too—letting him know everything!

EILEEN (*faintly*). He seems—very nice.

NICHOLLS. You've got your eyes set on him already, have you? Leave it to you! No fear of your not having a good time of it out here!

EILEEN. Fred!

NICHOLLS. Well, go ahead if you want to. I don't care. I'll—— (*Startled by the look of anguish which comes over her face, he hastily swallows his words. He takes out his watch—fiercely.*) We'll miss that train, damn it!

EILEEN (*in a stricken tone*). Oh, Fred! (*Then forcing back her tears she calls to Carmody in a strained voice.*) Father! You'll have to go now. Miss Gilpin told me to tell you you'd have to go right away to catch the train.

CARMODY (*shaking hands with Murray*). I'll be goin'. Keep your eye on her. I'll be out soon to see her and you and me'll have another talk.

MURRAY. Glad to. Good-bye for the present. (*He walks to windows on the far right, turning his back considerately on their leave-taking.*)

EILEEN (*comes to Carmody and hangs on his arm as they proceed to the door*). Be sure and kiss them all for me—Billy and Tom and Nora and little Mary—and bring them out to see me as soon as you can, father, please! And you come often, too, won't you? And don't forget to tell Mrs. Brennan all the directions I gave you coming out on the train. I told her, but she mightn't remember—about Mary's bath—and to give Tom his——

CARMODY (*impatiently*). Hasn't she brought up brats of her own, and doesn't she know the way of it? Don't be worryin' now, like a fool.

EILEEN (*helplessly*). Never mind telling her, then. I'll write to her.

CARMODY. You'd better not. Leave her alone. She'll not wish you mixin' in with her work and tellin' her how to do it.

EILEEN (*aghast*). *Her* work! (*She seems at the end of her tether—wrung too dry for any further emotion. She kisses her father at the door with indifference and speaks calmly.*) Good-bye, father.

CARMODY (*in a whining tone of injury*). A cold kiss! And never a small tear out of her! Is your heart a stone? (*Drunken tears well from his eyes and he blubbers.*) And your own father going back to a lone house with a stranger in it!

EILEEN (*wearily, in a dead voice*). You'll miss your train, father.

CARMODY (*raging in a second*). I'm off, then! Come on, Fred. It's no welcome we have with her here in this place—and a great curse on this day I brought her to it! (*He stamps out.*)

EILEEN (*in the same dead tone*). Good-bye, Fred.

NICHOLLS (*repenting his words of a moment ago—confusedly*). I'm sorry, Eileen—for what I said. I didn't mean—you know what your father is—excuse me, won't you?

EILEEN (*without feeling*). Yes.

NICHOLLS. And I'll be out soon—in a week if I can make it. Well then,—good-bye for the present. (*He bends down as if to kiss her, but she shrinks back out of his reach.*)

EILEEN (*a faint trace of mockery in her weary voice*). No, Fred. Remember you mustn't now.

NICHOLLS (*in an instant huff*). Oh, if that's the way you feel about——

(*He strides out and slams the door viciously behind him. Eileen walks slowly back towards the fire-place, her face fixed in a dead calm of despair. As she sinks into one of the armchairs, the strain becomes too much. She breaks down, hiding her face in her hands, her frail shoulders heaving with the violence of her sobs.*

At this sound, Murray turns from the windows and comes over near her chair.)

MURRAY (*after watching her for a moment—in an embarrassed tone of sympathy*). Come on, Miss Carmody, that'll never do. I know it's hard at first —but—getting yourself all worked up is bad for you. You'll run a temperature and then they'll keep you in bed—which isn't pleasant. Take hold of yourself! It isn't so bad up here—really—once you get used to it! (*The shame she feels at giving way in the presence of a stranger only adds to her loss of control and she sobs heartbrokenly. Murray walks up and down nervously, visibly nonplussed and upset. Finally he hits upon something.*) One of the nurses will be in any minute. You don't want them to see you like this.

EILEEN (*chokes back her sobs and finally raises her face and attempts a smile*). I'm sorry—to make such a sight of myself. I just couldn't help it.

MURRAY (*jocularly*). Well, they say a good cry does you a lot of good.

EILEEN (*forcing a smile*). I do feel—better.

MURRAY (*staring at her with a quizzical smile—cynically*). You shouldn't take those lovers' squabbles so seriously. To-morrow he'll be sorry—you'll be sorry. He'll write begging forgiveness—you'll do ditto. Result—all serene again.

EILEEN (*a shadow of pain on her face—with dignity*). Don't—please.

MURRAY (*angry at himself—hanging his head contritely*). I'm a fool. Pardon me. I'm rude sometimes—before I know it. (*He shakes off his confusion with a renewed attempt at a joking tone.*) You can blame your father for any breaks I make. He made me your guardian, you know—told me to see that you behaved.

EILEEN (*with a genuine smile*). Oh, father! (*Flushing.*) You mustn't mind anything he said to-night.

MURRAY (*thoughtlessly*). Yes, he was well lit up. I envied him. (*Eileen looks very shame-faced. Murray sees it and exclaims in exasperation at himself.*) Darn! There I go again putting my foot in it! (*With an irrepressible grin.*) I ought to have my tongue operated on—that's what's the matter with me. (*He laughs and throws himself in a chair.*)

EILEEN (*forced in spite of herself to smile with him*). You're candid, at any rate, Mr. Murray.

MURRAY. Don't misunderstand me. Far be it from me to cast slurs at your father's high spirits. I said I envied him his jag and that's the truth. The same candour compels me to confess that I was pickled to the gills myself when I arrived here. Fact! I made love to all the nurses and generally disgraced myself—and had a wonderful time.

EILEEN. I suppose it does make you forget your troubles—for a while.

MURRAY (*waving this aside*). I didn't want to forget—not for a second. I wasn't drowning my sorrow. I was hilariously celebrating.

EILEEN (*astonished—by this time quite interested in this queer fellow to the momentary forgetfulness of her own grief*). Celebrating—coming here? But—aren't you sick?

MURRAY. T. B.? Yes, of course. (*Confidentially.*) But it's only a matter of time when I'll be all right again. I hope it won't be too soon. I was dying for a rest—a good, long rest with time to think about things. I'm due to get what I wanted here. That's why I celebrated.

EILEEN (*with wide eyes*). I wonder if you really mean——

MURRAY. What I've been sayin'? I sure do—every word of it!

EILEEN (*puzzled*). I can't understand how anyone could—— (*With a worried glance over her shoulder.*) I think I'd better look for Miss Gilpin, hadn't I? She may wonder—— (*She half rises from her chair.*)

MURRAY (*quickly*). No. Please don't go yet. Sit down. Please do. (*She glances at him irresolutely, then resumes her chair.*) They'll give you your diet of milk and shoo you off to bed on that freezing porch soon enough, don't worry. I'll see to it that you don't fracture any rules. (*Hitching his chair nearer hers—impulsively.*) In all charity to me you've got to stick awhile. I haven't had a chance to really talk to a soul for a week. You found what I said a while ago hard to believe, didn't you?

EILEEN (*with a smile*). Isn't it? You said you hoped you wouldn't get well too soon!

MURRAY. And I meant it! This place is honestly

like heaven to me—a lonely heaven till your arrival. (*Eileen looks embarrassed.*) And why wouldn't it be? I've no fear for my health—eventually. Just let me tell you what I was getting away from—— (*With a sudden laugh full of a weary bitterness.*) Do you know what it means to work from seven at night till three in the morning as a reporter on a morning newspaper in a town of twenty thousand people—for *ten years?* No. You don't. You can't. No one could who hadn't been through the mill. But what it did to me—it made me happy—yes, happy!—to get out here—T. B. and all, notwithstanding.

EILEEN (*looking at him curiously*). But I always thought being a reporter was so interesting.

MURRAY (*with a cynical laugh*). Interesting? On a small town rag? A month of it, perhaps, when you're a kid and new to the game. But ten years. Think of it! With only a raise of a couple of dollars every blue moon or so, and a weekly spree on Saturday night to vary the monotony. (*He laughs again.*) Interesting, eh? Getting the dope on the Social of the Queen Esther Circle in the basement of the Methodist Episcopal Church, unable to sleep through a meeting of the Common Council on account of the noisy oratory caused by John Smith's application for a permit to build a house; making a note that a tugboat towed two barges loaded with coal up the river, that Mrs. Perkins spent a week-end with relatives in Hickville, that John Jones—— Oh help! Why go on? Ten years of it! I'm a broken man. God, how I used to pray that our Congressman would commit suicide, or the Mayor murder his wife—just to be able to write a real story!

EILEEN (*with a smile*). Is it as bad as that? But weren't there other things in the town—outside your work—that were interesting?

MURRAY (*decidedly*). No Never anything new—and I knew everyone and every thing in town by heart years ago (*With sudden bitterness.*) Oh, it was my own fault Why didn't I get out of it? Well, I didn't. I was always going to—to-morrow—and to-morrow never came. I got in a rut—and stayed put. People seem to get that way, somehow—in that town. It's in the air. All the boys I grew up with—nearly all, at least—took root in the same way. It took pleurisy, followed by T. B., to blast me loose.

EILEEN (*wonderingly*). But—your family—didn't they live there?

MURRAY. I haven't much of a family left. My mother died when I was a kid. My father—he was a lawyer—died when I was nineteen, just about to go to college. He left nothing, so I went to work on the paper instead. And there I've been ever since. I've two sisters, respectably married and living in another part of the state. We don't get along—but they are paying for me here, so I suppose I've no kick. (*Cynically.*) A family wouldn't have changed things. From what I've seen that blood-thicker-than-water dope is all wrong. It's thinner than table-d'hôte soup. You may have seen a bit of that truth in your own case already.

EILEEN (*shocked*). How can you say that? You don't know——

MURRAY. Don't I, though? Wait till you've been here three months or four—when the gap you left has been comfortably filled. You'll see then!

EILEEN (*angrily, her lips trembling*). You must be crazy to say such things! (*Fighting back her tears.*) Oh, I think it's hateful—when you see how badly I feel!

MURRAY (*in acute confusion. Stammering*). Look here, Miss Carmody, I didn't mean to——. Listen—don't feel mad at me, please. My tongue ran away with me. I was only talking. I'm like that. You mustn't take it seriously.

EILEEN (*still resentful*). I don't see how you can talk. You don't—you can't know about these things—when you've just said you had no family of your own, really.

MURRAY (*eager to return to her good graces*). No. Of course I don't know. I was just talking regardless for the fun of listening to it.

EILEEN (*after a pause*). Hasn't either of your sisters any children?

MURRAY. One of them has—two of them—ugly, squally little brats.

EILEEN (*disapprovingly*). You don't like babies?

MURRAY (*bluntly*). No. (*Then with a grin at her shocked face.*) I don't get them. They're something I can't seem to get acquainted with.

EILEEN (*with a smile, indulgently*). You're a funny person. (*Then with a superior, motherly air.*) No wonder you couldn't understand how badly I feel. (*With a tender smile.*) I've four of them—my brothers and sisters—though they're not what you'd call babies, except to me. Billy is fourteen, Nora eleven, Tom ten, and even little Mary is eight. I've been a mother to them now for a whole year—ever since our mother died (*Sadly.*) And I don't know how they'll ever get along while I'm away.

MURRAY (*cynically*). Oh, they'll—— (*He checks what he was going to say and adds lamely*)——get along somehow.

EILEEN (*with the same superior tone*). It's easy for you to say that. You don't know how children grow to depend on you for everything. You're not a woman.

MURRAY (*with a grin*). Are you? (*Then with a chuckle.*) You're as old as the pyramids, aren't you? I feel like a little boy. Won't you adopt me, too?

EILEEN (*flushing, with a shy smile*). Someone ought to. (*Quickly changing the subject.*) Do you know, I can't get over what you said about hating your work so. I should think it would be wonderful—to be able to write things.

MURRAY. My job had nothing to do with writing. To write—really write—yes, that's something worth trying for. That's what I've always meant to have a stab at. I've run across ideas enough for stories—that sounded good to me, anyway. (*With a forced laugh.*) But—like everything else—I never got down to it. I started one or two—but—either I thought I didn't have the time or—— (*He shrugs his shoulders.*)

EILEEN. Well, you've plenty of time now, haven't you?

MURRAY (*instantly struck by this suggestion*). You mean—— I could write—up here? (*She nods. His face lights up with enthusiasm.*) Say! That is an idea! Thank you! I'd never have had sense enough to have thought of that myself. (*Eileen flushes with pleasure.*) Sure there's time—nothing but time up here——

EILEEN. Then you seriously think you'll try it?

MURRAY (*determinedly*). Yes. Why not? I've got to try and do something real some time, haven't I? I've no excuse not to, now. My mind isn't sick.

EILEEN (*excitedly*). That'll be wonderful!

MURRAY (*confidently*). Listen. I've had ideas for a series of short stories for the last couple of years—small town experiences, some of them actual. I know that life—too darn well. I ought to be able to write about it. And if I can sell one—to the *Post*, say—I'm sure they'd take the others, too. And then——I should worry! It'd be easy sailing. But you must promise to help—play critic for me—read them and tell me where they're rotten.

EILEEN (*pleased, but protesting*). Oh, no, I'd never dare. I don't know anything——

MURRAY. Yes, you do. You're the public. And you started me off on this thing—if I'm really starting at last. So you've got to back me up now. (*Suddenly.*) Say, I wonder if they'd let me have a typewriter up here?

EILEEN. It'd be fine if they would. I'd like to have one, too—to practice. I learned stenography at a business college and then I had a position for a year—before my mother died.

MURRAY. We could hire one—I could. I don't see why they wouldn't allow it. I'm to be sent to one of the men's huts within the next few days, and you'll be shipped to one of the women's cottages within ten days. You're not sick enough to be kept here in bed, I'm sure of that.

EILEEN. I—— I don't know——

MURRAY. Here! None of that! You just think you're not and you won't be. Say, I'm keen on that typewriter idea. They couldn't kick if we only used it during recreation periods. I could have it a week, and then you a week.

EILEEN (*eagerly*). And I could type your stories after you've written them! I *could* help that way.

MURRAY (*smiling*). But I'm quite able—— (*Then seeing how interested she is he adds hurriedly.*) That'd be great! It'd save so much time. I've always been a fool at a machine. And I'd be willing to pay whatever—— (*Miss Gilpin enters from the rear and walks towards them.*)

EILEEN (*quickly*). Oh, no! I'd be glad to get the practice. I wouldn't accept—— (*She coughs slightly.*)

MURRAY (*with a laugh*). Maybe, after you've read

my stuff, you won't type it at any price.

MISS GILPIN. Miss Carmody, may I speak to you for a moment, please.

(She takes Eileen aside and talks to her in low tones of admonition. Eileen's face falls. She nods a horrified acquiescence. Miss Gilpin leaves her and goes into the office, rear.)

MURRAY *(as Eileen comes back. Noticing her perturbation. Kindly)*. Well? Now, what's the trouble?

EILEEN *(her lips trembling)*. She told me I mustn't forget to shield my mouth with my handkerchief when I cough.

MURRAY *(consolingly)*. Yes, that's one of the rules, you know.

EILEEN *(falteringly)*. She said they'd give me—a—cup to carry around—— *(She stops, shuddering.)*

MURRAY *(easily)*. It's not as horrible as it sounds. They're only little paste-board things you carry in your pocket.

EILEEN *(as if speaking to herself)*. It's so horrible *(She holds out her hand to Murray.)* I'm to go to my room now. Good night, Mr. Murray.

MURRAY *(holding her hand for a moment—earnestly)*. Don't mind your first impressions here. You'll look on everything as a matter of course in a few days. I felt your way at first. *(He drops her hand and shakes his finger at her.)* Mind your guardian, now! *(She forces a trembling smile.)* See you at breakfast. Good night.

(Eileen goes out to the hall in rear. Miss Howard comes in from the door just after her, carrying a glass of milk.)

MISS HOWARD. Almost bedtime, Mr. Murray. Here's your diet. *(He takes the glass. She smiles at him provokingly.)* Well, is it love at first sight, Mr. Murray?

MURRAY *(with a grin)*. Sure thing! You can consider yourself heartlessly jilted. *(He turns and raises his glass towards the door through which Eileen has just gone, as if toasting her.)*

"A glass of milk, and thou
Coughing beside me in the wilderness——
Ah—wilderness were Paradise enow!"

(He takes a sip of milk.)

MISS HOWARD *(peevishly)*. That's old stuff, Mr. Murray. A patient at Saranac wrote that parody.

MURRAY *(maliciously)*. Aha, you've discovered it's a parody, have you, you sly minx! *(Miss Howard turns from him huffily and walks back towards the office, her chin in the air.)*

CURTAIN

Act Two, Scene One

The assembly room of the main building of the sanatorium—early in the morning of a fine day in June, four months later. The room is large, light and airy, painted a fresh white. On the left forward, an armchair. Farther back, a door opening on the main hall. To the rear of this door, a pianola on a raised platform. At back of the pianola, a door leading into the office. In the rear wall, a long series of French windows looking out on the lawn, with wooded hills in the far background. Shrubs in flower grow immediately outside the windows Inside, there is a row of potted plants. In the right wall, rear, four windows. Farther forward, a long well-filled bookcase, and a doorway leading into the dining-room. Following the walls, but about five feet out from them a stiff line of chairs placed closely against each other forms a sort of right-angled auditorium of which the large, square table that stands at centre, forward, would seem to be the stage.

From the dining-room comes the clatter of dishes, the confused murmur of many voices, male and female—all the mingled sounds of a crowd of people at a meal.

After the curtain rises, Doctor Stanton enters from the hall, followed by a visitor, Mr. Sloan, and the assistant physician, Doctor Simms. Doctor Stanton is a handsome man of forty-five or so with a grave, care-lined, studious face lightened by a kindly, humorous smile. His grey eyes, saddened by the suffering they have witnessed, have the sympathetic quality of real understanding. The look they give is full of companionship, the courage-

renewing, human companionship of a hope which is shared. He speaks with a slight Southern accent, soft and slurring. Doctor Simms is a tall, angular young man with a long sallow face and a sheepish, self-conscious grin. Mr. Sloan is fifty, short and stout, well dressed—one of the successful business men whose endowments have made the Hill Farm a possibility.

STANTON (*as they enter*). This is what you might call the general assembly room, Mr. Sloan—where the patients of both sexes are allowed to congregate together after meals, for diets, and in the evening.

SLOAN (*looking around him*). Couldn't be more pleasant, I must say—light and airy. (*He walks to where he can take a peep into the dining-room.*) Ah, they're all at breakfast, I see.

STANTON (*smiling*). Yes, and with no lack of appetite, let me tell you. (*With a laugh of proud satisfaction.*) They'd sure eat us out of house and home at one sitting, if we'd give them the opportunity. (*To his assistant.*) Wouldn't they, Doctor?

SIMMS (*with his abashed grin*). You bet they would, sir.

SLOAN (*with a smile*). That's fine. (*With a nod towards the dining-room.*) The ones in there are the sure cures, aren't they?

STANTON (*a shadow coming over his face*). Strictly speaking, there are no sure cures in this disease, Mr. Sloan. When we permit a patient to return to take up his or her activities in the world, the patient is what we call an arrested case. The disease is overcome, quiescent; the wound is healed over. It's then up to the patient to so take care of himself that this condition remains permanent. It isn't hard for them to do this, usually. Just ordinary, bull-headed common sense—added to what they've learned here—is enough for their safety. And the precautions we teach them to take don't diminish their social usefulness in the slightest, either, as I can prove by our statistics of former patients. (*With a smile.*) It's rather early in the morning for statistics, though.

SLOAN (*with a wave of the hand*). Oh, you needn't. Your reputation in that respect, Doctor—— (*Stanton inclines his head in acknowledgment. Sloan jerks his thumb towards the dining-room*). But the ones in there *are* getting well, aren't they?

STANTON. To all appearances, yes. You don't dare swear to it, though. Sometimes, just when a case looks most favourably, there's a sudden, unforeseen breakdown, and they have to be sent back to bed, or, if it's very serious, back to the Infirmary again. These are the exceptions, however, not the rule. You can bank on most of those eaters being out in the world and usefully employed within six months.

SLOAN. You couldn't say more than that (*Abruptly*). But—the unfortunate ones—do you have many deaths?

STANTON (*with a frown*). No. We're under a very hard, almost cruel imperative which prevents that. If, at the end of six months, a case shows no response to treatment, continues to go down hill—if, in a word, it seems hopeless—we send them away, to one of the State Farms if they have no private means. (*Apologetically.*) You see, this sanatorium is overcrowded and has a long waiting list, most of the time, of others who demand their chance for life. We have to make places for them. We have no time to waste on incurables. There are other places for them—and sometimes, too, a change is beneficial and they pick up in new surroundings. You never can tell. But we're bound by the rule. It may seem cruel—but it's as near justice to all concerned as we can come.

SLOAN (*soberly*). I see. (*His eyes fall on the pianola—in surprise.*) Ah—a piano.

STANTON (*replying to the other's thought*). Yes, the patients play and sing. (*With a smile.*) If you'd call the noise they make by those terms. They'd dance, too, if we permitted it. There's only one song taboo—Home, Sweet Home. We forbid that—for obvious reasons.

SLOAN. I see. (*With a final look around.*) Did I understand you to say this is the only place where the sexes are permitted to mingle?

STANTON. Yes, sir.

SLOAN (*with a smile*). Not much chance for a love affair then.

STANTON (*seriously*). We do our best to prevent them. We even have a strict rule which allows us to step in and put a stop to any intimacy which grows beyond the casual. People up here, Mr. Sloan, are expected to put aside all ideas except the one—getting well.

SLOAN (*somewhat embarrassed*). A damn good rule, too, I should say, under the circumstances.

STANTON (*with a laugh*). Yes, we're strictly anti-Cupid, sir, from top to bottom. (*Turning to the door to the hall.*) And now, if you don't mind, Mr. Sloan, I'm going to turn you loose to wander about the grounds on an unconducted tour. To-day is my busy morning—Saturday. We weigh each patient immediately after breakfast.

SLOAN. Every week?

STANTON. Every Saturday. You see we depend on fluctuations in weight to tell us a lot about the patient's condition. If they gain, or stay at normal, all's usually well. If they lose week after week without any reason we can definitely point to, we keep careful watch. It's a sign that something's wrong. We're forewarned by it and on our guard.

SLOAN (*with a smile*). Well, I'm certainly learning things. (*He turns to the door.*) And you just shoo me off wherever you please and go on with the good work. I'll be glad of a ramble in the open on such a glorious morning.

STANTON. After the weighing is over, sir, I'll be free to——

(*His words are lost as the three go out. A moment later, Eileen enters from the dining-room. She has grown stouter, her face has more of a healthy, out-of-door colour, but there is still about her the suggestion of being worn down by a burden too oppressive for her courage. She is dressed in blouse and dark skirt. She goes to the armchair, left forward, and sinks down on it. She is evidently in a state of nervous depression; she twists her fingers together in her lap; her eyes stare sadly before her; she clenches her upper lip with her teeth to prevent its trembling. She has hardly regained control over herself when Stephen Murray comes in hurriedly from the dining-room and, seeing her at his first glance, walks quickly over to her chair. He is the picture of health, his figure has filled out solidly, his tanned face beams with suppressed exultation.*)

MURRAY (*excitedly*). Eileen! I saw you leave your table. I've something to tell you. I didn't get a chance last night after the mail came. You'd gone to the cottage. Just listen, Eileen—it's too good to be true—but on that mail—guess what?

EILEEN (*forgetting her depression—with an excited smile*). I know! You've sold your story!

MURRAY (*triumphantly*). Go to the head of the class. What d'you know about that for luck! My first, too—and only the third magazine I sent it to! (*He cuts a joyful caper.*)

EILEEN (*happily*). Isn't that wonderful, Stephen! But I knew all the time you would. The story's so good.

MURRAY. Well, you might have known, but I didn't think there was a chance in the world. And as for being good—— (*With superior air*)——wait till I turn loose with the real big ones, the kind I'm going to write. Then I'll make them sit up and take notice. They can't stop me now. This money gives me a chance to sit back and do what I please for a while. And I haven't told you the best part. The editor wrote saying how much he liked the yarn and asked me for more of the same kind.

EILEEN. And you've the three others about the same person—just as good, too! Why, you'll sell them all! (*She clasps her hands delightedly.*)

MURRAY. And I can send them out right away. They're all typed, thanks to you. That's what's brought me luck, I know. I never had a bit by myself. (*Then, after a quick glance around to make sure they are alone, he bends down and kisses her.*) There! A token of gratitude—even if it is against the rules.

EILEEN (*flushing—with timid happiness*). Stephen! You mustn't! They'll see.

MURRAY (*boldly*). Let them!

EILEEN. But you know—they've warned us against being so much together, already.

MURRAY. Let them! We'll be out of this prison soon. (*Eileen shakes her head sadly, but he does not notice.*) Oh, I wish you could leave when I do. We'd have some celebration together.

EILEEN (*her lips trembling*). I was thinking last night—that you'd soon be going away. You look so well. Do you think—they'll let you go—soon?

MURRAY. You bet I do. I'm bound to go now. It's ridiculous keeping me here when I'm as healthy as a pig. I caught Stanton in the hall last night and asked him if I could go.

EILEEN (*anxiously*). What did he say?

MURRAY. He only smiled and said: "We'll see if you gain weight to-morrow." As if that mattered now! Why, I'm way above normal as it is! But you know Stanton—always putting you off. But I could tell by the way he said it he'd be willing to consider——

EILEEN (*slowly*). Then—if you gain to-day——

MURRAY. He'll let me go. Yes, I know he will. I'm going to insist on it.

EILEEN. Then—you'll leave——?

MURRAY. Right away. The minute I can get packed.

EILEEN (*trying to force a smile*). Oh, I'm so glad—for your sake; but- I'm selfish—it'll be so lonely here without you.

MURRAY (*consolingly*). You'll be going away yourself before long. (*Eileen shakes her head. He goes on without noticing, wrapped in his own success.*) Oh, Eileen, you can't imagine all it opens up for me—selling that story. I don't have to go back home to stagnate. I can go straight to New York, and live, and meet real people who are doing things. I can take my time, and try and do the work I hope to. (*Feelingly.*) You don't know how grateful I am to you, Eileen—how you've helped me. Oh, I don't mean just the typing, I mean your encouragement, your faith! I'd never have had guts enough to stick to it myself. The stories would never have been written if it hadn't been for you.

EILEEN (*choking back a sob*). I didn't do—anything.

MURRAY (*staring down at her—with rough kindliness*). Here, here, that'll never do! You're not weeping about it, are you, silly? (*He pats her on the shoulder.*) What's the matter, Eileen? You didn't eat a thing this morning. I was watching you. (*With kindly severity.*) That's no way to gain weight, you know. You'll have to feed up. Do you hear what your guardian commands, eh?

EILEEN (*with dull hopelessness*). I know I'll lose again. I've been losing steadily the past three weeks.

MURRAY. Here! Don't you dare talk that way! I won't stand for it. Why, you've been picking up wonderfully—until just lately. You've made such a game fight for four months. Even the old Doc has told you how much he admired your pluck, and how much better you were getting. You're not going to quit now, are you?

EILEEN (*despairingly*). Oh, I don't care! I don't care—now.

MURRAY. Now? What do you mean by that? What's happened to make things any different?

EILEEN (*evasively*). Oh—nothing. Don't ask me, Stephen.

MURRAY (*with sudden anger*). I don't have to ask you. I can guess. Another letter from home—or from that ass, eh?

EILEEN (*shaking her head*). No, it isn't that. (*She looks at him as if imploring him to comprehend.*)

MURRAY (*furiously*). Of course, you'd deny it. You always do. But don't you suppose I've got eyes? It's been the same damn thing all the time you've been here. After every nagging letter—thank God they don't write often any more!—you've been all in; and after their Sunday visits—you can thank God they've been few, too—you're utterly knocked out. It's a shame! The selfish swine!

EILEEN. Stephen!

MURRAY (*relentlessly*). Don't be sentimental, Eileen. You know it's true. From what you've told me of their letters, their visits—from what I've seen and suspected—they've done nothing but worry and torment you and do their best to keep you from getting well.

EILEEN (*faintly*). You're not fair, Stephen.

MURRAY. Rot! When it isn't your father grumbling about expense, it's the kids, or that stupid housekeeper, or that slick Aleck, Nicholls, with his cowardly lies. Which is it this time?

EILEEN (*pitifully*). None of them.

MURRAY (*explosively*). But him, especially—the dirty cad! Oh, I've got a rich notion to pay a call on that gentleman when I leave and tell him what I think of him.

EILEEN (*quickly*). No—you mustn't ever! He's not to blame. If you knew—— (*She stops, lowering *her eyes in confusion.)*

MURRAY (*roughly*). Knew what? You make me sick, Eileen—always finding excuses for him. I never could understand what a girl like you could see—— But what's the use? I've said all this before. You're wasting yourself on a—— (*Rudely.*) Love must be blind. And yet you say you don't love him, really?

EILEEN (*shaking her head—helplessly*). But I do—like Fred. We've been good friends so many years. I don't want to hurt him—his pride——

MURRAY. That's the same as answering no to my question. Then, if you don't love him, why don't you write and tell him to go to——break it off? (*Eileen bows her head, but doesn't reply. Irritated, Murray continues brutally.*) Are you afraid it would break his heart? Don't be a fool! The only way you could do that would be to deprive him of his meals.

EILEEN (*springing to her feet—distractedly*). Please stop, Stephen! You're cruel! And you've been so kind—the only real friend I've had up here. Don't spoil it all now.

MURRAY (*remorsefully*). I'm sorry, Eileen. I was only talking. I won't say another word. (*Irritably.*) Still, someone ought to say or do something to put a stop to——

EILEEN (*with a broken laugh*). Never mind Everything will stop—soon, now!

MURRAY (*suspiciously*) What do you mean?

EILEEN (*with an attempt at a careless tone*). Nothing. If you can't see—— (*She turns to him with sudden intensity.*) Oh, Stephen, if you only knew how wrong you are about everything you've said. It's all true; but it isn't that—any of it—any more——that's—— Oh, I can't tell you!

MURRAY (*with great interest*). Please do, Eileen!

EILEEN (*with a helpless laugh*). No.

MURRAY. Please tell me what it is! Let me help you.

EILEEN. No. It wouldn't be any use, Stephen.

MURRAY (*offended*). Why do you say that? Haven't I helped before?

EILEEN. Yes—but this——

MURRAY. Come now! 'Fess up! What is "this"?

EILEEN. No. I couldn't speak of it here, anyway. They'll all be coming out soon

MURRAY (*insistently*). Then when? Where?

EILEEN. Oh, I don't know—perhaps never, nowhere. I don't know—— Sometime before you leave, maybe.

MURRAY. But I may go to-morrow morning—if I gain weight and Stanton lets me.

EILEEN (*sadly*). Yes, I was forgetting—you were going right away. (*Dully.*) Then nowhere, I suppose—never. (*Glancing towards the dining-room.*) They're all getting up. Let's not talk about it any more—now.

MURRAY (*stubbornly*). But you'll tell me later, Eileen? You must.

EILEEN (*vaguely*). Perhaps. It depends——

(*The patients, about forty in number, straggle in from the dining-room by twos and threes, chatting in low tones. The men and women with few exceptions separate into two groups, the women congregating in the left right angle of chairs, the men sitting or standing in the right right angle. In appearance, most of the patients are tanned, healthy, and cheerful-looking. The great majority are under middle age. Their clothes are of the cheap, ready-made variety. They are all distinctly of the wage-earning class. They might well be a crowd of cosmopolitan factory workers gathered together after a summer vacation. A hollow-chestedness and a tendency to round shoulders may be detected as a common characteristic. A general air of tension, marked by frequent bursts of laughter in too high a key, seems to pervade the throng. Murray and Eileen, as if to avoid contact with the others, come over to the right in front of the dining-room door.*)

MURRAY (*in a low voice*). Listen to them laugh. Did you ever notice—perhaps it's my imagination—how forced they act on Saturday mornings before they're weighed?

EILEEN (*dully*). No.

MURRAY. Can't you tell me that secret now? No one'll hear.

EILEEN (*vehemently*). No, no, how could I? Don't speak of it!

(*A sudden silence falls on all the groups at once. Their eyes, by a common impulse, turn quickly towards the door to the hall.*)

A WOMAN (*nervously—as if this moment's silent pause oppressed her.*) Play something, Peters. They ain't coming yet.

(*Peters, a stupid-looking young fellow with a sly, twisted smirk which gives him the appearance of perpetually winking his eye, detaches himself from a group on the right. All join in with urging exclamations: "Go on, Peters! Go to it! Pedal up, Pete! Give us a rag! That's the boy, Peters!" etc.*)

PETERS. Sure, if I got time.

(*He goes to the pianola and puts in a roll. The mingled conversation and laughter bursts forth again as he sits on the bench and starts pedalling.*)

MURRAY (*disgustedly*). It's sure good to think I won't have to listen to that old tin-pan being banged much longer!

(*The music interrupts him—a quick rag. The patients brighten, hum, whistle, sway their heads or tap their feet in time to the tune. Doctor Stanton and Doctor Simms appear in the doorway from the hall. All eyes are turned on them.*)

STANTON (*raising his voice*). They all seem to be here, Doctor. We might as well start.

(*Mrs. Turner, the matron, comes in behind them—a stout, motherly, capable-looking woman with grey hair. She hears Stanton's remark.*)

MRS. TURNER. And take temperatures after, Doctor?

STANTON. Yes, Mrs. Turner. I think that's better to-day.

MRS. TURNER. All right, Doctor.

(*Stanton and the assistant go out. Mrs. Turner advances a step or so into the room and looks from one group of patients to the other, inclining her head and smiling benevolently. All force smiles and nod in recognition of her greeting. Peters, at the pianolo, lets the music slow down, glancing questioningly at the matron to see if she is going to order it stopped. Then, encouraged by her smile, his feet pedal harder than ever.*)

MURRAY Look at old Mrs. Grundy's eyes pinned on us! She'll accuse us of being too familiar again, the old wench!

EILEEN. Ssshh. You're wrong. She's looking at me, not at us.

MURRAY. At you? Why?

EILEEN. I ran a temperature yesterday. It must have been over a hundred last night.

MURRAY (*with consoling scepticism*). You're always looking for trouble, Eileen. How do you know you ran a temp? You didn't see the stick, I suppose?

EILEEN. No—but—I could tell. I felt feverish and chilly. It must have been way up.

MURRAY. Bosh! If it was you'd have been sent to bed.

EILEEN. That's why she's looking at me. (*Piteously.*) Oh, I do hope I won't be sent back to bed! I don't know what I'd do. If I could only gain this morning. If my temp has only gone down! (*Hopelessly.*) But I feel—— I didn't sleep a wink—thinking——

MURRAY (*roughly*). You'll persuade yourself you've got leprosy in a second. Don't be silly! It's all imagination, I tell you. You'll gain. Wait and see if you don't.

(*Eileen shakes her head. A metallic rumble and jangle comes from the hallway. Everyone turns in that direction with nervous expectancy.*)

MRS. TURNER (*admonishingly*). Mr. Peters!

PETERS. Yes, ma'am.

(*He stops playing and rejoins the group of men on the right. In the midst of a silence broken only by hushed murmurs of conversation, Doctor Stanton appears in the hall doorway. He turns to help his assistant wheel in a Fairbanks scale on castors. They place the scale against the wall immediately to the rear of the doorway. Doctor Simms adjusts it to a perfect balance.*)

DOCTOR STANTON (*takes a pencil from his pocket and opens the record book he has in his hand*). All ready, Doctor?

DOCTOR SIMMS. Just a second, sir.

(*A chorus of coughs comes from the impatient crowd, and handkerchiefs are hurriedly produced to shield mouths.*)

MURRAY (*with a nervous smile*). Well, we're all set. Here's hoping!

EILEEN. You'll gain, I'm sure you will. You look so well.

MURRAY. Oh—I—I wasn't thinking of myself, I'm a sure thing. I was betting on you. I've simply got to gain to-day, when so much depends on it.

EILEEN. Yes, I hope you—— (*She falters brokenly and turns away from him.*)

DOCTOR SIMMS (*straightening up*). All ready, Doctor?

STANTON (*nods and glances at his book—without raising his voice—distinctly*). Mrs. Abner.

(*A middle-aged woman comes and gets on the scale. Simms adjusts it to her weight of the previous week, which Stanton reads to him from the book in a low voice, and weighs her.*)

MURRAY (*with a relieved sigh*). They're off. (*Noticing Eileen's downcast head and air of dejection.*) Here! Buck up, Eileen! Old Lady Grundy's watching you—and it's your turn in a second.

(*Eileen raises her head and forces a frightened smile. Mrs. Abner gets down off the scale with a pleased grin. She has evidently gained. She rejoins the group of women, chattering volubly in low tones. Her exultant "gained half a pound" can be heard. The other women smile their perfunctory congratulations, their eyes absent-minded, intent on their own worries. Stanton writes down the weight in the book.*)

STANTON. Miss Bailey. (*A young girl goes to the scales.*)

MURRAY. Bailey looks bad, doesn't she?

EILEEN (*her lips trembling*). She's been losing, too.

MURRAY. Well, *you're* going to gain to-day. Remember, now!

EILEEN (*with a feeble smile*). I'll try to obey your orders.

(*Miss Bailey goes down off the scales. Her eyes are full of despondency although she tries to make a brave face of it, forcing a laugh as she joins the women. They stare at her with pitying looks and murmur consoling phrases.*)

EILEEN. She's lost again. Oh, I wish I didn't have to get weighed——

STANTON. Miss Carmody.

(*Eileen starts nervously.*)

MURRAY (*as she leaves him*). Remember now! Break the scales!

(*She walks quickly to the scales, trying to assume an air of defiant indifference. The balance stays down as she steps up. Eileen's face shows her despair at this. Simms weighs her and gives the poundage in a low voice to Stanton. Eileen steps down mechanically, then hesitates as if not knowing where to turn, her anguished eyes flitting from one group to another.*)

MURRAY (*savagely*). Damn!

(*Doctor Stanton writes the figures in his book, glances sharply at Eileen, and then nods significantly to Mrs. Turner who is standing beside him.*)

STANTON (*calling the next*). Miss Doeffler.

(*Another woman comes to be weighed.*)

MRS. TURNER. Miss Carmody! Will you come here a moment, please?

EILEEN (*her face growing very pale*). Yes, Mrs. Turner.

(*The heads of the different groups bend together. Their eyes follow Eileen as they whisper. Mrs. Turner leads her down front, left. Behind them the weighing of the women continues briskly. The great majority have gained. Those who have not have either remained stationary or lost a negligible fraction of a pound. So, as the weighing proceeds, the general air of smiling satisfaction rises among the groups of women. Some of them, their ordeal over, go out through the hall doorway by twos and threes with suppressed *laughter and chatter. As they pass behind Eileen they glance at her with pitying curiosity. Doctor Stanton's voice is heard at regular intervals calling the names in alphabetical order: Mrs. Elbing, Miss Finch, Miss Grimes, Miss Haines, Miss Hayes, Miss Jutner, Miss Linowski, Mrs. Marini, Mrs. McCoy, Miss McElroy, Miss Nelson, Mrs. Nott, Mrs. O'Brien, Mrs. Olson, Miss Paul, Miss Petrovski, Mrs. Quinn, Miss Robersi, Mrs. Stattler, Miss Unger.)*

MRS. TURNER (*putting her hand on Eileen's shoulder—kindly*). You're not looking so well lately, my dear, do you know it?

EILEEN (*bravely*). I feel—fine. (*Her eyes, as if looking for encouragement, seek Murray, who is staring at her worriedly.*)

MRS. TURNER (*gently*). You lost weight again, you know.

EILEEN. I know—but——

MRS. TURNER. This is the fourth week.

EILEEN. I—— I know it is——

MRS. TURNER. I've been keeping my eye on you. You seem—worried. Are you upset about—something we don't know?

EILEEN (*quickly*). No, no! I haven't slept much lately. That must be it.

MRS. TURNER. Are you worrying about your condition? Is that what keeps you awake?

EILEEN. No.

MRS. TURNER. You're sure it's not that?

EILEEN. Yes, I'm sure it's not, Mrs. Turner.

MRS. TURNER. I was going to tell you if you were: Don't do it! You can't expect it to be all smooth sailing. Even the most favourable cases have to expect these little setbacks. A few days' rest in bed will start you on the right trail again.

EILEEN (*in anguish, although she had realised this was coming*). Bed? Go back to bed? Oh, Mrs. Turner!

MRS. TURNER (*gently*). Yes, my dear, Doctor Stanton thinks it best. So when you go back to your cottage——

EILEEN. Oh, please—not to-day—not right away!

MRS. TURNER. You had a temperature and a high pulse yesterday, didn't you realise it? And this morning you look quite feverish. (*She tries to put her hand on Eileen's forehead, but the latter steps away defensively.*)

EILEEN. It's only—not sleeping last night. I was nervous. Oh, I'm sure it'll go away.

MRS. TURNER (*consolingly*). When you lie still and have perfect rest, of course it will.

EILEEN (*with a longing look over at Murray*). But not to-day—please, Mrs. Turner.

MRS. TURNER (*looking at her keenly*). There is something upsetting you. You've something on your mind that you can't tell me, is that it? (*Eileen maintains a stubborn silence.*) But think—*can't* you tell me? (*With a kindly smile.*) I'm used to other people's troubles. I've been playing mother-confessor to the patients for years now, and I think I've usually been able to help them. Can't you confide in me, child? (*Eileen drops her eyes, but remains silent. Mrs. Turner glances meaningly over at Murray, who is watching them whenever he thinks the matron is not aware of it—a note of sharp rebuke in her voice.*) I think I can guess your secret, my dear, even if you're too stubborn to tell. This setback is your own fault. You've let other notions become more important to you than the idea of getting well. And you've no excuse for it. After I had to warn you a month ago, I expected *that* silliness to stop instantly.

EILEEN (*her face flushed—protesting*). There never was anything. Nothing like that has anything to do with it.

MRS. TURNER (*sceptically*). What is it that has, then?

EILEEN (*lying determinedly*). It's my family. They keep writing—and worrying me—and—— That's what it is, Mrs. Turner.

MRS. TURNER (*not exactly knowing whether to believe this or not—probing the girl with her eyes*). Your father?

EILEEN. Yes, all of them. (*Suddenly seeing a way to discredit all of the matron's suspicions—excitedly.*) And principally the young man I'm engaged to—the one who came to visit me several times——

MRS. TURNER (*surprised*). So—you're engaged?

(*Eileen nods. Mrs. Turner immediately dismisses her suspicions.*) Oh, pardon me. I didn't know that, you see, or I wouldn't—— (*She pats Eileen on the shoulder comfortingly.*) Never mind. You'll tell me all about it, won't you?

EILEEN (*desperately*). Yes. (*She seems about to go on, but the matron interrupts her.*)

MRS. TURNER. Oh, not here, my dear. Now now. Come to my room—let me see—I'll be busy all the morning—some time this afternoon. Will you do that?

EILEEN. Yes. (*Joyfully.*) Then I needn't go to bed right away?

MRS. TURNER. No—on one condition. You mustn't take any exercise. Stay in your recliner all day and rest and remain in bed to-morrow morning. And promise me you will rest and not worry any more about things we can easily fix up between us.

EILEEN. I promise, Mrs. Turner.

MRS. TURNER (*smiling in dismissal*). Very well, then. I must speak to Miss Bailey. I'll see you this afternoon.

EILEEN. Yes, Mrs. Turner.

(*The matron goes to the rear where Miss Bailey is sitting with Mrs. Abner. She beckons to Miss Bailey, who gets up with a scared look, and they go to the far left corner of the room. Eileen stands for a moment hesitating—then starts to go to Murray, but just at this moment Peters comes forward and speaks to Murray.*)

PETERS (*with his sly twisted grin*). Say, Carmody musta lost fierce. Did yuh see the Old Woman handin' her an earful? Sent her back to bed, I betcha. What d'yuh think?

MURRAY (*impatiently, showing his dislike*). How the hell do I know?

PETERS (*sneeringly*). Huh, you don't know nothin' 'bout her, I s'pose? Where d'yuh get that stuff? Think yuh're kiddin' me?

MURRAY (*with cold rage before which the other slinks away*). Peters, the more I see of you the better I like a skunk! If it wasn't for other people losing weight you couldn't get any joy out of life, could you? (*Roughly.*) Get away from me! (*He makes a threatening gesture.*)

PETERS (*beating a snarling retreat*). Wait'n' see if yuh don't lose too, yuh stuck-up boob!

(*Seeing that Murray is alone again, Eileen starts towards him, but this time she is intercepted by Mrs. Abner, who stops on her way out. The weighing of the women is now finished, and that of the men, which proceeds much quicker, begins.*)

STANTON. Anderson!

(*Anderson comes to the scales. The men all move down to the left to wait their turn, with the exception of Murray, who remains by the dining-room door, fidgeting impatiently, anxious for a word with Eileen.*)

MRS. ABNER (*taking Eileen's arm*). Coming over to the cottage, dearie?

EILEEN. Not just this minute, Mrs. Abner. I have to wait——

MRS. ABNER. For the Old Woman? You lost to-day, didn't you? Is she sendin' you to bed, the old devil?

EILEEN. Yes, I'm afraid I'll have to——

MRS. ABNER. She's a mean one, ain't she? I gained this week—half a pound. Lord, I'm gittin' fat! All my clothes are gittin' too small for me. Don't know what I'll do. Did you lose much, dearie?

EILEEN. Three pounds.

MRS. ABNER. Ain't that awful! (*Hastening to make up for this thoughtless remark.*) All the same, what's three pounds! You can git them back in a week after you're resting more. You been runnin' a temp, too, ain't you? (*Eileen nods.*) Don't worry about it, dearie. It'll go down. Worryin's the worst. Me, I don't never worry none. (*She chuckled with satisfaction—then soberly.*) I just been talkin' with Bailey. She's got to go to bed, too, I guess. She lost two pounds. She ain't runnin' no temp though.

STANTON. Barnes! (*Another man comes to the scales.*)

MRS. ABNER (*in a mysterious whisper*). Look at Mr. Murray, dearie. Ain't he nervous to-day? I don't know as I blame him, either. I heard the doctor said he'd let him go home if he gained to-day. Is it true, d'you know?

EILEEN (*dully*). I don't know.

MRS. ABNER. Gosh, I wish it was me! My old man's missin' me like the dickens, he writes. (*She starts to go.*) You'll be over to the cottage in a while, won't you? Me'n' you'll have a game of casino, eh?

EILEEN (*happy at this deliverance*). Yes, I'll be glad to.

STANTON. Cordero!

(*Mrs. Abner goes out. Eileen again starts towards Murray, but this time Flynn, a young fellow with a brick-coloured, homely, good-natured face, and a shaven-necked haircut, slouches back to Murray. Eileen is brought to a halt in front of the table where she stands, her face working with nervous strain, clasping and unclasping her trembling hands.*)

FLYNN (*curiously*). Say, Steve, what's this bull about the Doc lettin' yuh beat it if yuh gain to-day? Is it straight goods?

MURRAY. He said he might, that's all. (*Impatiently.*) How the devil did that story get travelling around?

FLYNN (*with a grin*). Wha' d'yuh expect with this gang of skirts chewin' the fat? Well, here's hopin' yuh come home a winner, Steve.

MURRAY (*gratefully*). Thanks. (*With confidence.*) Oh, I'll gain all right; but whether he'll let me go or not—— (*He shrugs his shoulders.*)

FLYNN. Make 'em believe. I wish Stanton'd ask waivers on me. (*With a laugh.*) I oughter gain a ton to-day. I ate enough spuds for breakfast to plant a farm.

STANTON. Flynn!

FLYNN. Me to the plate! (*He strides to the scales.*)

MURRAY. Good luck!

(*He starts to join Eileen, but Miss Bailey, who has finished her talk with Mrs. Turner, who goes out to the hall, approaches Eileen at just this moment. Murray stops in his tracks, fuming. He and Eileen exchange a glance of helpless annoyance.*)

MISS BAILEY (*her thin face full of the satisfaction of misery finding company—plucks at Eileen's sleeve*). Say, Carmody, she sent you back to bed, too, didn't she?

EILEEN (*absent-mindedly*). I suppose——

MISS BAILEY. You suppose? Don't you know? Of course she did. I got to go, too. (*Pulling Eileen's sleeve.*) Come on. Let's get out of here. I hate this place, don't you?

STANTON (*calling the next*). Hopper!

FLYNN (*shouts to Murray as he is going out to the hall*). I hit 'er for a two-bagger, Steve. Come on now, Bo, and bring me home! 'Atta, boy! (*Grinning gleefully, he slouches out. Doctor Stanton and all the patients laugh.*)

MISS BAILEY (*with irritating persistence*). Come on, Carmody. You've got to go to bed, too.

EILEEN (*at the end of her patience—releasing her arm from the other's grasp*). Let me alone, will you? I don't have to go to bed now—not till to-morrow morning.

MISS BAILEY (*despairingly, as if she couldn't believe her ears*). You don't have to go to bed?

EILEEN. Not now—no.

MISS BAILEY (*in a whining rage*). Why not? You've been running a temp, too, and I haven't. You must have a pull, that's what! It isn't fair. I'll bet you lost more than I did, too! What right have you got—— Well, I'm not going to bed if you don't. Wait 'n' see!

EILEEN (*turning away, revolted*). Go away! Leave me alone, please.

STANTON. Lowenstein!

MISS BAILEY (*turns to the hall door, whining*). All right for you! I'm going to find out. It isn't square. I'll write home.

(*She disappears in the hallway. Murray strides over to Eileen, whose strength seems to have left her and who is leaning weakly against the table.*)

MURRAY. Thank God—at last! Isn't it hell—all these fools! I couldn't get to you. What did Old Lady Grundy have to say to you? I saw her giving me a hard look. Was it about us—the old stuff? (*Eileen nods with downcast eyes.*) What did she say? Never mind now. You can tell me in a minute. It's my turn next. (*His eyes glance towards the scales.*)

EILEEN (*intensely*). Oh, Stephen, I wish you weren't going away!

MURRAY (*excitedly*). Maybe I'm not. It's exciting—like gambling—if I win——

STANTON. Murray!

MURRAY. Wait here, Eileen.

(He goes to the scales. Eileen keeps her back turned. Her body stiffens rigidly in the intensity of her conflicting emotions. She stares straight ahead, her eyes full of anguish. Murray steps on the scales nervously. The balance rod hits the top smartly. He has gained. His face lights up and he heaves a great sigh of relief. Eileen seems to sense this outcome and her head sinks, her body sags weakly and seems to shrink to a smaller size Murray gets off the scales, his face beaming with a triumphant smile. Doctor Stanton smiles and murmurs something to him in a low voice. Murray nods brightly; then turns back to Eileen.)

STANTON. Nathan! *(Another patient advances to the scales.)*

MURRAY *(trying to appear casual)*. Well—three rousing cheers! Stanton told me to come to his office at eleven. That means a final exam—and release!

EILEEN *(dully)*. So you gained?

MURRAY. Three pounds.

EILEEN. Funny—I lost three. *(With a pitiful effort at a smile)*. I hope you gained the ones I lost. *(Her lips tremble.)* So you're surely going away.

MURRAY *(his joy fleeing as he is confronted with her sorrow—slowly)*. It looks that way, Eileen.

EILEEN *(in a trembling whisper broken by rising sobs)*. Oh—I'm so glad—you gained—the ones I lost, Stephen—— So glad! *(She breaks down, covering her face with her hands, stifling her sobs.)*

MURRAY *(alarmed)*. Eileen! What's the matter? *(Desperately.)* Stop it! Stanton'll see you!

CURTAIN

Act Two, Scene Two

Midnight of the same day. A cross-road near the sanatorium. The main road comes down forward from the right. A smaller road, leading down from the left, joins it towards left centre.

Dense woods rise sheer from the grass and bramble-grown ditches at the roadsides. At the junction of the two roads there is a signpost, its arms pointing towards the right and the left, rear. A pile of round stones is at the road corner, left forward. A full moon, riding high overhead, throws the roads into white, shadowless relief and masses the woods into walls of compact blackness. The trees lean heavily together, their branches motionless, unstirred by any trace of wind.

As the curtain rises, Eileen is discovered standing in the middle of the road, front centre. Her face shows white and clear in the bright moonlight as she stares with anxious expectancy up the road to the left. Her body is fixed in an attitude of rigid immobility as if she were afraid the slightest movement would break the spell of silence and awaken the unknown. She has shrunk instinctively as far away as she can from the mysterious darkness which rises at the roadsides like an imprisoning wall. A sound of hurried footfalls, muffled by the dust, comes from the road she is watching. She gives a startled gasp. Her eyes strain to identify the oncomer. Uncertain, trembling with fright, she hesitates a second; then darts to the side of the road and crouches down in the shadow.

Stephen Murray comes down the road from the left. He stops by the signpost and peers about him. He wears a cap, the peak of which casts his face into shadow. Finally he calls in a low voice.)

MURRAY. Eileen!

EILEEN *(coming out quickly from her hiding-place—with a glad little cry)*. Stephen! At last! *(She runs to him as if she were going to fling her arms about him, but stops abashed. He reaches out and takes her hands.)*

MURRAY. At last? It can't be twelve yet. *(He leads her to the pile of stones on the left.)* I haven't heard the village clock.

EILEEN. I must have come early. It seemed as if I'd been waiting for ages. I was so anxious——

MURRAY. How your hands tremble! Were you frightened?

EILEEN (*forcing a smile*). A little. The woods are so black—and queer-looking. I'm all right now.

MURRAY. Sit down. You must rest. (*In a tone of annoyed reproof.*) I'm going to read you a lecture, young lady. You shouldn't ever have done this—running a temp and—— Good heavens, don't you want to get well?

EILEEN (*dully*). I don't know——

MURRAY (*irritably*). You make me ill when you talk that way, Eileen. It doesn't sound like you at all. What's come over you lately? Get a grip on yourself, for God's sake. I was—knocked out—when I read the note you slipped me after supper. I didn't get a chance to read it until late, I was so busy packing, and by that time you'd gone to your cottage. If I could have reached you any way I'd have refused to come here, I tell you straight. But I couldn't—and I knew you'd be here waiting—and —still, I feel guilty. Damn it, this isn't the thing for you! You ought to be in bed asleep. Can't you look out for yourself?

EILEEN (*humbly*). Please, Stephen, don't scold me.

MURRAY. How the devil did you ever get the idea —meeting me here at this ungodly hour?

EILEEN. You'd told me about your sneaking out that night to go to the village, and I thought there'd be no harm this one night—the last night.

MURRAY. But I'm well. I've been well. It's different. You—— Honest, Eileen, you shouldn't lose sleep and tax your strength.

EILEEN. Don't scold me, please. I'll make up for it. I'll rest all the time—after you're gone. I just had to see you some way—somewhere where there weren't eyes and ears on all sides—when you told me after dinner that Doctor Stanton had examined you and said you could go to-morrow—— (*A clock in the distant village begins striking.*) Ssshh! Listen.

MURRAY. That's twelve now. You see I was early.

(*In a pause of silence they wait motionlessly until the last mournful note dies in the hushed woods.*)

EILEEN (*in a stifled voice*). It isn't to-morrow now, is it? It's to-day—the day you're going.

MURRAY (*something in her voice making him avert his face and kick at the heap of stones on which she is sitting—brusquely*). Well, I hope you took precautions so you wouldn't be caught sneaking out.

EILEEN. I did just what you'd told me you did—stuffed the pillows under the clothes so the watchman would think I was there.

MURRAY. None of the patients on your porch saw you leave, did they?

EILEEN. No. They were all asleep.

MURRAY. That's all right, then. I wouldn't trust any of that bunch of women. They'd be only too glad to squeal on you. (*There is an uncomfortable pause. Murray seems waiting for her to speak. He looks about him at the trees, up into the moonlit sky, breathing in the fresh air with a healthy delight. Eileen remains with downcast head, staring at the road.*) It's beautiful to-night, isn't it? Worth losing sleep for.

EILEEN (*dully*). Yes. (*Another pause—finally she murmurs faintly.*) Are you leaving early?

MURRAY. The ten-forty. Leave the San at ten, I guess.

EILEEN. You're going home?

MURRAY. Home? You mean to the town? No. But I'm going to see my sisters—just to say hello. I've got to, I suppose. I won't stay more than a few days, if I can help it.

EILEEN. I'm sure—I've often felt—you're unjust to your sisters. (*With conviction.*) I'm sure they must both love you.

MURRAY (*frowning*). Maybe, in their own way. But what's love without a glimmer of understanding —a nuisance! They have never seen the real me and never have wanted to—that's all.

EILEEN (*as if to herself*). What is—the real you? (*Murray kicks at the stones impatiently without answering. Eileen hastens to change the subject.*) And then you'll go to New York?

MURRAY (*interested at once*). Yes. You bet.

EILEEN. And write more?

MURRAY. Not in New York, no. I'm going there to take a vacation, and live, really enjoy myself for a while. I've enough money for that as it is, and if the other stories you typed sell—I'll be as rich as Rockefeller. I might even travel—— No, I've got to make good with my best stuff first. I'll save the travelling as a reward, a prize to gain. That'll keep me at it. I know what I'll do. When I've had enough of New York, I'll rent a place in the country —some old farmhouse—and live alone there and work. (*Lost in his own plans—with pleasure.*) That's the right idea, isn't it ?

EILEEN (*trying to appear enthused*). It ought to be fine for your work. (*After a pause.*) They're fine, those stories you wrote here. They're—so much like you. I'd know it was you wrote them even if—I didn't know.

MURRAY (*pleased*). Wait till you read the others I'm going to do! (*After a slight pause—with a good-natured grin*). Here I am talking about myself again! Why don't you call me down when I start that drivel ? But you don't know how good it is to have your dreams coming true. It'd make an egotist out of anyone.

EILEEN (*sadly*). No. I don't know. But I love to hear you talk of yours.

MURRAY (*with an embarrassed laugh*). Thanks. Well, I've certainly told you all of them. You're the only one—— (*He stops and abruptly changes the subject.*) You said in your note that you had something important to tell me. (*He sits down beside her, crossing his legs.*) Is it about your interview with Old Mrs. Grundy this afternoon ?

EILEEN. No, that didn't amount to anything. She seemed mad because I told her so little. I think she guessed I only told her what I did so she'd let me stay up, maybe—your last day,—and to keep her from thinking what she did—about us.

MURRAY (*quickly, as if he wishes to avoid this subject*). What is it you wanted to tell me, then ?

EILEEN (*sadly*). It doesn't seem so important now, somehow. I suppose it was silly of me to drag you out here, just for that. It can't mean anything to you—much.

MURRAY (*encouragingly*). How do you know it can't ?

EILEEN (*slowly*). I only thought—you might like to know.

MURRAY (*interestedly*). Know what ? What is it ? If I can help——

EILEEN. No. (*After a moment's hesitation.*) I wrote to him this afternoon.

MURRAY. Him ?

EILEEN. The letter you've been advising me to write.

MURRAY (*as if the knowledge of this alarmed him—haltingly*). You mean—Fred Nicholls ?

EILEEN. Yes.

MURRAY (*after a pause—uncomfortably*). You mean —you broke it all off ?

EILEEN. Yes—for good. (*She looks up at his averted face. He remains silent. She continues apprehensively.*) You don't say anything. I thought—you'd be glad. You've always told me it was the honourable thing to do.

MURRAY (*gruffly*). I know. I say more than my prayers, damn it! (*With sudden eagerness.*) Have you mailed the letter yet ?

EILEEN. Yes. Why ?

MURRAY (*shortly*). Humph. Oh—nothing.

EILEEN (*with pained disappointment*). Oh, Stephen, you don't think I did wrong, do you—now—after all you've said ?

MURRAY (*hurriedly*). Wrong ? No, not if you were convinced it was the right thing to do yourself —if you know you don't love him. But I'd hate to think you did it just on my advice. I shouldn't't—— I didn't mean to interfere. I don't know enough about your relations for my opinion to count.

EILEEN (*hurt*). You know all there is to know.

MURRAY. I didn't mean—anything like that. I know you've been frank. But him—I don't know him. How could I, just meeting him once ? He may be quite different from my idea. That's what I'm getting at. I don't want to be unfair to him.

EILEEN (*bitterly scornful*). You needn't worry. You weren't unfair. And you needn't be afraid you were responsible for my writing. I'd been going to for a long time before you ever spoke.

MURRAY (*with a relieved sigh*). I'm glad of that—honestly, Eileen. I felt guilty. I shouldn't have knocked him behind his back without knowing him at all.

EILEEN. You said you could read him like a book from his letters I showed you.

MURRAY (*apologetically*). I know. I'm a fool.

EILEEN (*angrily*). What makes you so considerate of Fred Nicholls all of a sudden ? What you thought about him was right.

MURRAY (*vaguely*). I don't know. One makes mistakes.

EILEEN (*assertively*). Well, I know! You needn't waste pity on him. He'll be only too glad to get my letter. He's been anxious to be free of me ever since I was sent here, only he thought it wouldn't be decent to break it off himself while I was sick. He was afraid of what people would say about him when they found it out. So he's just gradually stopped writing and coming for visits, and waited for me to realise. And if I didn't, I know he'd have broken it off himself the first day I got home. I've kept persuading myself that, in spite of the way he's acted, he did love me as much as he could love anyone, and that it would hurt him if I—— But now I know that he never loved me, that he couldn't love anyone but himself. Oh, I don't hate him for it. He can't help being what he is. And all people seem to be—like that, mostly. I'm only going to remember that he and I grew up together, and that he was kind to me then when he thought he liked me—and forget all the rest. (*With agitated impatience.*) Oh, Stephen, you know all this I've said about him. Why don't you admit it? You've read his letters.

MURRAY (*haltingly*). Yes, I'll admit that was my opinion—only I wanted to be sure you'd found out for yourself.

EILEEN (*defiantly*). Well, I have! You see that now, don't you?

MURRAY. Yes; and I'm glad you're free of him, for your own sake. I knew he wasn't the person. (*With an attempt at a joking tone.*) You must get one of the right sort—next time.

EILEEN (*springing to her feet with a cry of pain*). Stephen!

(*He avoids her eyes, which search his face pleadingly.*)

MURRAY (*mumbling*). He wasn't good enough—to lace your shoes—nor anyone else, either.

EILEEN (*with a nervous laugh*). Don't be silly. (*After a pause, during which she waits hungrily for some word from him—with a sigh of despair—faintly.*) Well, I've told you—all there is. I might as well go back.

MURRAY (*not looking at her—indistinctly*). Yes. You mustn't lose too much sleep. I'll come to your cottage in the morning to say good-bye. They'll permit that, I guess.

EILEEN (*stands looking at him imploringly, her face convulsed with anguish, but he keeps his eyes fixed on the rocks at his feet. Finally she seems to give up and takes a few uncertain steps up the road towards the right—in an exhausted whisper*). Good night, Stephen.

MURRAY (*his voice choked and husky*). Good night, Eileen.

EILEEN (*walks weakly up the road, but, as she passes the signpost, she suddenly stops and turns to look again at Murray, who has not moved or lifted his eyes. A great shuddering sob shatters her pent-up emotions. She runs back to Murray, her arms outstretched, with a choking cry*). Stephen!

MURRAY (*startled, whirls to face her and finds her arms thrown around his neck—in a terrified tone*). Eileen!

EILEEN (*brokenly*). I love you, Stephen—you! That's what I wanted to tell!

(*She gazes up into his eyes, her face transfigured by the joy and pain of this abject confession.*)

MURRAY (*wincing as if this were the thing he had feared to hear*). Eileen!

EILEEN (*pulling down his head with fierce strength and kissing him passionately on the lips*). I love you! I will say it! There! (*With sudden horror.*) Oh, I know I shouldn't kiss you! I mustn't! You're all well—and I——

MURRAY (*protesting frenziedly*). Eileen! Damn it! Don't say that! What do you think I am!

(*He kisses her fiercely two or three times until she forces a hand over her mouth.*)

EILEEN (*with a hysterically happy laugh*). No! Just hold me in your arms—just a little while—before——

MURRAY (*his voice trembling*). Eileen! Don't talk that way! You're—it's killing me. I can't stand it!

EILEEN (*with soothing tenderness*). Listen, dear—listen—and you won't say a word—I've so much to say—till I get through—please, will you promise?

MURRAY (*between clinched teeth*). Yes—anything, Eileen!

EILEEN. Then I want to say—I know your secret. You don't love me—Isn't that it? (*Murray groans.*) Ssshh! It's all right, dear. You can't help what you don't feel. I've guessed you didn't—right along. And I've loved you—such a long time now—always, it seems. And you've sort of guessed—that I did—didn't you? No, don't speak! I'm sure you've guessed—only you didn't want to know—that—did you?—when you didn't love me. That's why you were lying—but I saw, I knew! Oh, I'm not blaming you, darling. How could I—never! You mustn't look so—so frightened. I know how you felt, dear. I've—I've watched you. It was just a flirtation for you at first. Wasn't it? Oh, I know. It was just fun, and—— Please don't look at me so. I'm not hurting you, am I? I wouldn't for worlds, dear—you know—hurt you! And then afterwards—you found we could be such good friends—helping each other—and you wanted it to stay just like that always, didn't you?—I know—and then I had to spoil it all—and fall in love with you—didn't I? Oh, it was stupid—I shouldn't—I couldn't help it, you were so kind and—and different—and I wanted to share in your work and—and everything. I knew you wouldn't want to know I loved you—when you didn't—and I tried hard to be fair and hide my love so you wouldn't see—and I did, didn't I, dear? You never knew till just lately—maybe not till just to-day—did you?—when I knew you were going away so soon—and couldn't help showing it. You never knew before, did you? Did you?

MURRAY (*miserably*). No. Oh, Eileen—Eileen, I'm so sorry!

EILEEN (*in heart-broken protest*). Sorry? Oh, no, Stephen, you mustn't be! It's been beautiful—all of it—for me! That's what makes your going—so hard. I had to see you to-night—I'd have gone—crazy—if I didn't know you knew, if I hadn't made you guess. And I thought—if you knew about my writing to Fred—that—maybe—it'd make some difference. (*Murray groans—and she laughs hysterically.*) I must have been crazy to think that—mustn't I? As if that could—when you don't love me. Sshh! Please! Let me finish. You mustn't feel sad—or anything. It's made me happier than I've ever been—loving you—even when I did know—you didn't. Only now—you'll forgive me telling you all this, won't you, dear? Now, it's so terrible to think I won't see you any more. I'll feel so—without anybody.

MURRAY (*brokenly*). But I'll—come back. And you'll be out soon—and then——

EILEEN (*brokenly*). Sshh! Let me finish. You don't know how alone I am now. Father—he'll marry that housekeeper—and the children—they've forgotten me. None of them need me any more. They've found out how to get on without me—and I'm a drag—dead to them—no place for me home any more—and they'll be afraid to have me back—afraid of catching—I know she won't want me back. And Fred—he's gone—he never mattered, anyway. Forgive me, dear—worrying you—only I want you to know how much you've meant to me—so you won't forget—ever—after you've gone.

MURRAY (*in grief-stricken tones*). Forget? Eileen! I'll do anything in God's world——

EILEEN. I know—you like me a lot even if you can't love me—don't you? (*His arms tighten about her as he bends down and forces a kiss on her lips again.*) Oh, Stephen! That was for good-bye. You mustn't come to-morrow morning. I couldn't bear having you—with people watching. But you'll write after—often—won't you? (*Heart-brokenly.*) Oh, please do that, Stephen!

MURRAY. I will! I swear! And when you get out I'll—we'll—I'll find something. (*He kisses her again.*)

EILEEN (*breaking away from him with a quick movement and stepping back a few feet*). Good-bye, darling. Remember me—and perhaps—you'll find out after a time—I'll pray God to make it so! Oh, what am I saying? Only—I'll hope—I'll hope—till I die!

MURRAY (*in anguish*). Eileen!

EILEEN (*her breath coming in tremulous heaves of her bosom*). Remember, Stephen—if ever you want—I'll do anything—anything you want—no matter what—I don't care—there's just you and—don't hate me, dear. I love you—love you—remember! (*She suddenly turns and runs away up the road.*)

MURRAY. Eileen! (*He starts to run after her, but stops by the signpost and stamps on the ground furiously, his fists clenched in impotent rage at himself and at fate. He curses hoarsely.*) Christ!

CURTAIN

Act Three

Four months later. An isolation room at the Infirmary with a sleeping porch at the right of it. Late afternoon of a Sunday towards the end of October. The room, extending two-thirds of the distance from left to right, is, for reasons of space economy, scantily furnished with the bare necessities—a bureau with mirror in the left corner, rear—two straight-backed chairs—a table with a glass top in the centre. The floor is varnished hardwood. The walls and furniture are painted white. On the left, forward, a door to the hall. On the right, rear, a double glass door opening on the porch. Farther front two windows. The porch, a screened-in continuation of the room, contains only a single iron bed, painted white, and a small table placed beside the bed.

The woods, the leaves of the trees rich in their autumn colouring, rise close about this side of the Infirmary. Their branches almost touch the porch on the right. In the rear of the porch they have been cleared away from the building for a narrow space, and through this opening the distant hills can be seen with the tree tops glowing in the sunlight.

As the curtain rises, Eileen is discovered lying in the bed on the porch, propped up into a half-sitting position by pillows under her back and head. She seems to have grown much thinner. Her face is pale and drawn, with deep hollows under her cheek-bones. Her eyes are dull and lustreless. She gazes straight before her into the wood with the unseeing stare of apathetic indifference. The door from the hall in the room behind her is opened, and Miss Howard enters, followed by Bill Carmody, Mrs. Brennan, and Mary. Carmody's manner is unwontedly sober and subdued. This air of respectable sobriety is further enhanced by a black suit, glaringly new and stiffly pressed, a new black derby hat, and shoes polished like a mirror. His expression is full of a bitter, if suppressed, resentment. His gentility is evidently forced upon him in spite of himself and correspondingly irksome. Mrs. Brennan is a tall, stout woman of fifty, lusty and loud-voiced, with a broad, snub-nosed, florid face, a large mouth, the upper lip darkened by a suggestion of moustache, and little round blue eyes, hard and restless with a continual fuming irritation. She is got up regardless in her ridiculous Sunday-best. Mary appears tall and skinny-legged in a starched, outgrown frock. The sweetness of her face has disappeared, giving way to a hang-dog sullenness, a stubborn silence, with sulky, furtive glances of rebellion directed at her step-mother.

MISS HOWARD (*pointing to the porch*). She's out there on the porch.

MRS. BRENNAN (*with dignity*). Thank you, ma'am.

MISS HOWARD (*with a searching glance at the visitors as if to appraise their intentions*). Eileen's been very sick lately, you know, so be careful not to worry her about anything. Do your best to cheer her up.

CARMODY (*mournfully*). We'll try to put life in her spirits, God help her. (*With an uncertain look at Mrs. Brennan.*) Won't we, Maggie ?

MRS. BRENNAN (*turning sharply on Mary, who has gone over to examine the things on the bureau*). Come away from that, Mary. Curiosity killed a cat. Don't be touchin' her things. Remember what I told you. Or is it admirin' your mug in the mirror you are ? (*Turning to Miss Howard as Mary moves away from the bureau, hanging her head—shortly.*) Don't you worry, ma'am. We won't trouble Eileen at all.

MISS HOWARD. Another thing. You mustn't say anything to her of what Miss Gilpin just told you about her being sent away to the State Farm in a few days. Eileen isn't to know till the very last minute. It would only disturb her.

CARMODY (*hastily*). We'll not say a word of it.

MISS HOWARD (*turning to the hall door*). Thank you.

(*She goes out, shutting the door.*)

MRS. BRENNAN (*angrily*). She has a lot of impudent gab, that one, with her don't do this and don't do that ! It's a wonder you wouldn't speak up to her and shut her mouth, you great fool, and you payin' money to give her her job. (*Disgustedly.*) You've no guts in you.

CARMODY (*placatingly*). Would you have me raisin' a shindy when Eileen's leavin' here in a day or more ? What'd be the use ?

MRS. BRENNAN. In the new place she's goin' you'll

not have to pay a cent, and that's a blessing! It's small good they've done her here for all the money they've taken. (*Gazing about the room critically.*) It's neat and clean enough; and why shouldn't it, a tiny room and the lot of them nothing to do all day but scrub. (*Scornfully.*) Two sticks of chairs and a table! They don't give much for the money.

CARMODY. Catch them! It's a good thing she's clearin' out of this, and her worse off after them curin' her eight months than she was when she came. She'll maybe get well in the new place.

MRS. BRENNAN (*indifferently*). It's God's will, what'll happen. (*Irritably.*) And I'm thinkin' it's His punishment she's under now for having no heart in her and never writin' home a word to you or the children in two months or more. If the doctor hadn't wrote us himself to come see her, she was sick, we'd have been no wiser.

CARMODY. Whisht! Don't be blamin' a sick girl.

MARY (*who has drifted to one of the windows at right—curiously*). There's somebody in bed out there. I can't see her face. Is it Eileen?

MRS. BRENNAN. Don't be goin' out there till I tell you, you imp! I must speak to your father first. (*Coming closer to him and lowering her voice.*) Are you going to tell her about it?

CARMODY (*pretending ignorance*). About what?

MRS. BRENNAN. About what, indeed! Don't pretend you don't know. About our marryin' two weeks back, of course. What else?

CARMODY (*uncertainly*). Yes—I disremembered she didn't know. I'll have to tell her, surely.

MRS. BRENNAN (*flaring up*). You speak like you wouldn't. Is it shamed of me you are? Are you afraid of a slip of a girl? Well, then, I'm not! I'll tell her to her face soon enough.

CARMODY (*angry in his turn—assertively*). You'll not, now! Keep your mouth out of this and your rough tongue! I tell you I'll tell her.

MRS. BRENNAN (*satisfied*). Let's be going out to her, then. (*They move towards the door to the porch.*) And keep your eye on your watch. We mustn't miss the train. Come with us, Mary, and remember to keep your mouth shut.

(*They go out on the porch and stand just outside the door waiting for Eileen to notice them; but the girl in bed continues to stare into the woods, oblivious to their presence.*)

MRS. BRENNAN (*nudging Carmody with her elbow—in a harsh whisper*). She don't see us. It's a dream she's in with her eyes open. Glory be, it's bad she's lookin'. The look on her face'd frighten you. Speak to her, you!

(*Eileen stirs uneasily as if this whisper had disturbed her unconsciously.*)

CARMODY (*wetting his lips and clearing his throat huskily*). Eileen.

EILEEN (*startled, turns and stares at them with frightened eyes. After a pause she ventures uncertainly, as if she were not sure but what these figures might be creatures of her dream*). Father. (*Her eyes shift to Mrs. Brennan's face and she shudders.*) Mrs. Brennan.

MRS. BRENNAN (*quickly—in a voice meant to be kindly*). Here we are, all of us, come to see you. How is it you're feelin' now, Eileen?

(*While she is talking she advances to the bedside, followed by Carmody, and takes one of the sick girl's hands in hers. Eileen withdraws it as if stung and holds it out to her father. Mrs. Brennan's face flushes angrily and she draws back from the bedside.*)

CARMODY (*moved—with rough tenderness patting her hand*). Ah, Eileen, sure it's a sight for sore eyes to see you again! (*He bends down as if to kiss her, but, struck by a sudden fear, hesitates, straightens himself, and shamed by the understanding in Eileen's eyes, grows red and stammers confusedly.*) How are you now? Sure it's the picture of health you're lookin'.

(*Eileen sighs and turns her eyes away from him with a resigned sadness.*)

MRS. BRENNAN. What are you standin' there for like a stick, Mary? Haven't you a word to say to your sister?

EILEEN (*twisting her head around and seeing Mary for the first time—with a glad cry.*) Mary! I—why, I didn't see you before! Come here.

(*Mary approaches gingerly with apprehensive side glances at Mrs. Brennan, who watches her grimly. Eileen's arms reach *out for her hungrily. She grasps her about the waist and seems trying to press the unwilling child to her breast.)*

MARY (*fidgeting nervously—suddenly in a frightened whine.*) Let me go! (*Eileen releases her, looks at her face dazedly for a second, then falls back limply with a little moan and shuts her eyes. Mary, who has stepped back a pace, remains fixed there as if fascinated with fright by her sister's face. She stammers.*) Eileen—you look so—so funny.

EILEEN (*without opening her eyes—in a dead voice*). You, too! I never thought you—— Go away, please.

MRS. BRENNAN (*with satisfaction*). Come here to me, Mary, and don't be botherin' your sister.

(*Mary avoids her step-mother, but retreats to the far end of the porch where she stands shrunk back against the wall, her eyes fixed on Eileen with the same fascinated horror.*)

CARMODY (*after an uncomfortable pause, forcing himself to speak*). Is the pain bad, Eileen?

EILEEN (*dully—without opening her eyes*). There's no pain. (*There is another pause—then she murmurs indifferently*). There are chairs in the room you can bring out if you want to sit down.

MRS. BRENNAN (*sharply*). We've not time to be sittin'. We've the train back to catch.

EILEEN (*in the same lifeless voice*). It's a disagreeable trip. I'm sorry you had to come.

CARMODY (*fighting against an oppression he cannot understand, bursts into a flood of words*). Don't be talking of the trip. Sure we're glad to take it to get a sight of you. It's three months since I've had a look at you, and I was anxious. Why haven't you written a line to us? You could do that without trouble, surely. Don't you ever think of us at all any more? (*He waits for an answer, but Eileen remains silent with her eyes closed. Carmody starts to walk up and down, talking with an air of desperation.*) You're not asking a bit of news from home. I'm thinkin' the people out here have taken all the thought of us out of your head. We're all well, thank God. I've another good job on the streets from Murphy and one that'll last a long time, praise be! I'm needin' it surely, with all the expenses—but no matter. Billy had a raise from his old skinflint of a boss a month back. He's gettin' seven a week now and proud as a turkey. He was comin' out with us to-day, but he'd a date with his girl. Sure, he's got a girl now, the young bucko! What d'you think of him? It's old Malloy's girl he's after—the pop-eyed one with glasses, you remember—as ugly as a blind sheep, only he don't think so. He said to give you his love. (*Eileen stirs and sighs wearily, a frown appearing for an instant on her forehead.*) And Tom and Nora was comin' out too, but Father Fitz had some doin's or other up to the school, and he told them to be there, so they wouldn't come with us, but they sent their love to you, too. They're growin' so big you'd not know them. Tom's no good at the school. He's like Billy was. I've had to take the strap to him often. He's always playin' hooky and roamin' the streets. And Nora. (*With pride.*) There's the divil for you! Up to everything she is and no holdin' her high spirits. As pretty as a picture, and the smartest girl in her school, Father Fitz says. Am I lyin', Maggie?

MRS. BRENNAN (*grudgingly*). She's smart enough—and too free with her smartness.

CARMODY (*pleased*). Ah, don't be talkin'! She'll know more than the lot of us before she's grown even. (*He pauses in his walk and stares down at Eileen, frowning.*) Are you sick, Eileen, that you're keepin' your eyes shut without a word out of you?

EILEEN (*wearily*). No. I'm tired, that's all.

CARMODY (*resuming his walk*). And who else is there, let me think? Oh, Mary—she's the same as ever, you can see for yourself.

EILEEN (*bitterly*). The same? Oh, no!

CARMODY. She's grown, you mean? I suppose. You'd notice, not seeing her so long?

(*He can think of nothing else to say, but walks up and down with a restless, uneasy expression.*)

MRS. BRENNAN (*sharply*). What time is it gettin'?

CARMODY (*fumbles for his watch*). Half-past four, a bit after.

MRS. BRENNAN. We'll have to leave soon. It's a long jaunt down that hill in that buggy.

(*She catches his eye and makes violent signs to him to tell Eileen what he has come to tell.*)

CARMODY (*after an uncertain pause—clenching his fists and clearing his throat*). Eileen.

EILEEN. Yes.

CARMODY (*irritably*). Can't you open your eyes on me? It's like talkin' to myself I am.

EILEEN (*looking at him—dully*). What is it?

CARMODY (*stammering—avoiding her glance*). It's this, Eileen—me and Maggie—Mrs. Brennan, that is—we——

EILEEN (*without surprise*). You're going to marry her?

CARMODY (*with an effort*). Not goin' to. It's done.

EILEEN (*without a trace of feeling*). Oh, so you've been married already?

(*Without further comment, she closes her eyes.*)

CARMODY. Two weeks back we were, by Father Fitz.

(*He stands staring down at his daughter, irritated, perplexed and confounded by her silence, looking as if he longed to shake her.*)

MRS. BRENNAN (*angry at the lack of enthusiasm shown by Eileen*). Let us get out of this, Bill. We're not wanted, that's plain as the nose on your face. It's little she's caring about you, and little thanks she has for all you've done for her and the money you've spent.

CARMODY (*with a note of pleading*). Is that a proper way to be treatin' your father, Eileen, after what I've told you? Have you no heart in you at all? Is it nothin' to you you've a good, kind woman now for mother?

EILEEN (*fiercely, her eyes flashing open on him*). No, no! Never!

MRS. BRENNAN (*plucking at Carmody's elbow. He stands looking at Eileen helplessly, his mouth open, a guilty flush spreading over his face*). Come out of here, you big fool, you! Is it to listen to insults to your livin' wife you're waiting? Am I to be tormented and you never raise a hand to stop her?

CARMODY (*turning on her threateningly*). Will you shut your gab?

EILEEN (*with a moan*). Oh, go away, Father! Please! Take her away!

MRS. BRENNAN (*pulling at his arm*). Take me away this second or I'll go on without you and never speak again to you till the day I die!

CARMODY (*pushes her violently away from him—raging, his fist uplifted*). Shut your gab, I'm saying!

MRS. BRENNAN. The divil mend you and yours then! I'm leavin' you. (*She starts for the door.*)

CARMODY (*hastily*). Wait a bit, Maggie. I'm comin'. (*She goes into the room, slamming the door, but once inside the stands still, trying to listen. Carmody glares down at his daughter's pale twitching face with the closed eyes. Finally he croaks in a whining tone of fear.*) Is your last word a cruel one to me this day, Eileen?

(*She remains silent. His face darkens. He turns and strides out of the door. Mary darts after him with a frightened cry of "Papa." Eileen covers her face with her hands and a shudder of relief runs over her body.*)

MRS. BRENNAN (*as Carmody enters the room—in a mollified tone*). So you've come, have you? Let's go, then? (*Carmody stands looking at her in silence, his expression full of gloomy rage. She bursts out impatiently.*) Are you comin' or are you goin' back to her? (*She grabs Mary's arm and pushes her towards the door to the hall.*) Are you comin' or not, I'm askin'?

CARMODY (*sombrely—as if to himself*). There's something wrong in the whole of this—that I can't make out. (*With sudden fury he brandishes his fists as though defying someone and growls threateningly.*) And I'll get drunk this night—dead, rotten drunk! (*He seems to detect disapproval in Mrs. Brennan's face, for he shakes his fist at her and repeats like a solemn oath.*) I'll get drunk this night, I'm sayin'! I'll get drunk if my soul roasts for it—and no one in the whole world is strong enough to stop me!

(*Mrs. Brennan turns from him with a disgusted shrug of her shoulders and hustles Mary out of the door. Carmody, after a second's pause, follows them. Eileen lies still, looking out into the woods with empty, desolate eyes. Miss Howard comes into the room from the hall and goes to the porch, carrying a glass of milk in her hand.*)

MISS HOWARD. Here's your diet, Eileen. I forgot it until just now. Sundays are awful days, aren't they? They get me all mixed up in my work, with all these visitors around. Did you have a nice visit with your folks?

EILEEN (*forcing a smile*). Yes.

MISS HOWARD. You look worn out. I hope they didn't worry you over home affairs?

EILEEN. No.

(*She sips her milk and sets it back on the table with a shudder of disgust.*)

MISS HOWARD (*with a smile*). What a face! You'd think you were taking poison.

EILEEN. I hate it! (*With deep passion.*) I wish it was poison!

MISS HOWARD (*jokingly*). Oh, come now! That isn't a nice way to feel on the Sabbath. (*With a meaning smile.*) I've some news that'll cheer you up, I bet. (*Archly.*) Guess who's here on a visit?

EILEEN (*startled—in a frightened whisper*). Who?

MISS HOWARD. Mr. Murray. (*Eileen closes her eyes wincingly for a moment and a shadow of pain comes over her face.*) He just came about the time your folks did. I saw him for a moment, not to speak to. He was going to the main building—to see Doctor Stanton, I suppose. (*Beaming—with a certain curiosity.*) What do you think of that for news?

EILEEN (*trying to conceal her agitation and assume a casual tone*). He must have come to be examined.

MISS HOWARD (*with a meaning laugh*). Oh, I'd hardly say that was his main reason. He does look much thinner and very tired, though. I suppose he's been working too hard. (*In business-like tones.*) Well, I've got to get back on the job. (*She turns to the door calling back jokingly.*) He'll be in to see you, of course, so look your prettiest.

(*She goes out and shuts the door to the porch. Eileen gives a frightened gasp and struggles up in bed as if she wanted to call the nurse to return. Then she lies back in a state of great nervous excitement, twisting her head with eager, fearful glances towards the door, listening, clasping and unclasping her thin fingers on the white spread. As Miss Howard walks across the room to the hall door, it is opened and Stephen Murray enters. A great change is visible in his face. It is much thinner and the former healthy tan has faded to a sallow pallor. Puffy shadows of sleeplessness and dissipation are marked under his heavy-lidded eyes. He is dressed in a well-fitting, expensive dark suit, a white shirt with a soft collar and bright-coloured tie.*)

MISS HOWARD (*with pleased surprise, holding out her hand*). Hello, Mr. Murray.

MURRAY (*shaking her hand—with a forced pleasantness*). How are you, Miss Howard?

MISS HOWARD. Fine as ever. It certainly looks natural to see you around here again—not that I hope you're here to stay, though. (*With a smile.*) I suppose you're on your way to Eileen now. Well, I won't keep you. I've stacks of work to do. (*She opens the hall door. He starts for the porch.*) Oh, I was forgetting—Congratulations! I've read those stories—all of us have. They're great. We're all so proud of you. You're one of our graduates, you know.

MURRAY (*indifferently*). Oh,—that stuff.

MISS HOWARD (*gaily*). Don't be so modest. Well, see you later, I hope.

MURRAY. Yes. Doctor Stanton invited me to stay for supper and I may——

MISS HOWARD. Fine! Be sure to!

(*She goes out. Murray walks to porch door and steps out. He finds Eileen's eyes waiting for him. As their eyes meet she gasps involuntarily and he stops short in his tracks. For a moment they remain looking at each other in silence.*)

EILEEN (*dropping her eyes—faintly*). Stephen.

MURRAY (*much moved, strides to her bedside and takes her hands awkwardly*). Eileen. (*Then after a second's pause, in which he searches her face and is shocked by the change illness has made—anxiously.*) How are you feeling, Eileen? (*He grows confused by her gaze and his eyes shift from hers, which search his face with wild yearning.*)

EILEEN (*forcing a smile*). Oh, I'm all right. (*Eagerly.*) But you, Stephen? How are you? (*Excitedly.*) Oh, it's good to see you again! (*Her *eyes continue fixed on his face pleadingly, questioningly.)*

MURRAY (*haltingly*). And it's sure great to see you again, Eileen. (*He releases her hand and turns away.*) And I'm fine and dandy. I look a little done up, I guess, but that's only the result of too much New York.

EILEEN (*sensing from his manner that whatever she has hoped for from his visit is not to be, sinks back on the pillows, shutting her eyes hopelessly, and cannot control a sigh of pain.*)

MURRAY (*turning to her anxiously*). What's the matter, Eileen? You're not in pain, are you?

EILEEN (*wearily*). No.

MURRAY. You haven't been feeling badly lately, have you? Your letters suddenly stopped—not a line for the past three weeks—and I——

EILEEN (*bitterly*). I got tired of writing and never getting any answer, Stephen.

MURRAY (*shame-faced*). Come, Eileen, it wasn't as bad as that. You'd think I never—and I did write, didn't I?

EILEEN. Right after you left here, you did, Stephen. Lately——

MURRAY. I'm sorry, Eileen. It wasn't that I didn't mean to—but—in New York it's so hard. You start to do one thing and something else interrupts you. You never seem to get any one thing done when it ought to be. You can understand that, can't you, Eileen?

EILEEN (*sadly*). Yes. I understand everything now.

MURRAY (*offended*). What do you mean by everything? You said that so strangely. You mean you don't believe—— (*But she remains silent with her eyes shut. He frowns and takes to pacing up and down beside the bed.*) Why have they got you stuck out here on this isolation porch, Eileen?

EILEEN (*dully*). There was no room on the main porch, I suppose.

MURRAY. You never mentioned in any of your letters——

EILEEN. It's not very cheerful to get letters full of sickness. I wouldn't like to, I know.

MURRAY (*hurt*). That isn't fair, Eileen. You know I—— How long have you been back in the Infirmary?

EILEEN. About a month.

MURRAY (*shocked*). A month! But you were up and about—on exercise, weren't you—before that?

EILEEN. No. I had to stay in bed while I was at the cottage.

MURRAY. You mean—ever since that time they sent you back—the day before I left?

EILEEN. Yes.

MURRAY. But I thought from the cheery tone of your letters that you were——

EILEEN (*uneasily*). Getting better? I am, Stephen. I'm strong enough to be up now, but Doctor Stanton wants me to take a good long rest this time so that when I do get up again I'll be sure—— (*She breaks off impatiently.*) But don't let's talk about it. I'm all right. (*Murray glances down at her face worriedly. She changes the subject.*) You've been over to see Doctor Stanton, haven't you?

MURRAY. Yes.

EILEEN. Did he examine you?

MURRAY. Yes. (*Carelessly.*) Oh, he found me O.K. I'm fine and dandy, as I said before.

EILEEN. I'm glad, Stephen. (*After a pause.*) Tell about yourself—what you've been doing. You've written a lot lately, haven't you?

MURRAY (*frowning*). No. I haven't been able to get down to it—somehow. There's so little time to yourself once you get to know people in New York. The sale of the stories you typed put me on easy street as far as money goes, so I've felt no need—— (*He laughs weakly.*) I guess I'm one of those who have to get down to hard pan before they get the kick to drive them to hard work.

EILEEN (*surprised*). Was it hard work writing them up here? You used to seem so happy just in doing them.

MURRAY. I was—happier than I've been before or afterwards. (*Cynically.*) But—I don't know—it was a new game to me then and I was chuck full of illusions about the glory of it. (*He laughs half-heartedly.*) Now I'm hardly a bit more enthusiastic over it than I used to be over newspaper work. It's like everything else, I guess. When you've got it, you find you don't want it.

EILEEN (*looking at him wonderingly—disturbed*). But isn't just the writing itself worth while?

MURRAY (*as if suddenly ashamed of himself—quickly*) Yes. Of course it is. I'm talking like a fool. I'm sore at everything because I'm dissatisfied with my own cussedness and laziness—and I want to pass the buck. (*With a smile of cheerful confidence.*) It's only a fit. I'll come out of it all right and get down to brass tacks again.

EILEEN (*with an encouraging smile*). That's the way you ought to feel. It'd be wrong—I've read the two stories that have come out so far over and over. They're fine, I think. Every line in them sounds like you, and at the same time sounds natural and like people and things you see every day. Everybody thinks they're fine, Stephen.

MURRAY (*pleased, but pretending cynicism*). Then they must be rotten. (*Then with self-assurance*). Well, I've plenty more of those stories in my head. Every time I think of my home town there seems to be a new story in someone I've known there. (*Spiritedly.*) Oh, I'll pound them out some time when the spirit moves; and I'll make them so much better than what I've done so far, you won't recognise them. I feel it's in me to do it. (*Smiling.*) Darn it, do you know just talking about it makes me feel as if I could sit right down now and start in on one. Is it the fact I've worked here before—or is it seeing you, Eileen. (*Gratefully.*) I really believe it's you. I haven't forgotten how you helped me before.

EILEEN (*in a tone of pain*). Don't, Stephen. I didn't do anything.

MURRAY (*eagerly*). Yes, you did. You made it possible. I can't tell you what a help you were. And since I've left the San, I've looked forward to your letters to boost up my spirits. When I felt down in the mouth over my own idiocy, I used to re-read them, and they always were good medicine. I can't tell you how grateful I've felt, honestly!

EILEEN (*faintly*). You're kind to say so, Stephen—but it was nothing, really.

MURRAY. And I can't tell you how I've missed those letters for the past three weeks. They left a big hole in things. I was worried about you—not having heard a word. (*With a smile.*) So I came to look you up.

EILEEN (*faintly. Forcing an answering smile*). Well, you see now I'm all right.

MURRAY (*concealing his doubt*). Yes, of course you are. Only I'd a darn sight rather see you up and about. We could take a walk, then—through the woods. (*A wince of pain shadows Eileen's face. She closes her eyes. Murray continues softly, after a pause.*) You haven't forgotten that last night—out there—Eileen?

EILEEN (*her lips trembling—trying to force a laugh*). Please don't remind me of that, Stephen. I was so silly and so sick, too. My temp was so high it must have made me—completely crazy—or I'd never dreamed of doing such a stupid thing. My head must have been full of wheels because I don't remember anything I did or said, hardly.

MURRAY (*his pride taken down a peg by this—in a hurt tone*). Oh! Well—I haven't forgotten and I never will, Eileen. (*Then his face clears up as if a weight had been taken off his conscience.*) Well—I rather thought you wouldn't take it seriously—afterwards. You were all up in the air that night. And you never mentioned it in your letters——

EILEEN (*pleadingly*). Don't talk about it! Forget it ever happened. It makes me feel— (*with a half-hysterical laugh*)—like a fool!

MURRAY (*worried*). All right, Eileen. I won't. Don't get worked up over nothing. That isn't resting, you know. (*Looking down at her closed eyes—solicitously.*) Perhaps all my talking has tired you out? Do you feel done up? Why don't you try and take a nap now?

EILEEN (*dully*). Yes, I'd like to sleep.

MURRAY (*clasps her hands gently*). I'll leave you then. I'll drop back to say good-bye and stay awhile before I go. I won't leave until the last train. (*As she doesn't answer.*) Do you hear, Eileen?

EILEEN (*weakly*). Yes. You'll come back—to say good-bye.

MURRAY. Yes. I'll be back sure.

(*He presses her hand and after a kindly glance of sympathy down at her face, tiptoes to the door and goes into the room, shutting the door behind him. When she hears the door shut Eileen struggles up in bed and stretches her arms after him with an agonised sob "Stephen!" She hides her face in her hands and sobs brokenly.*

Murray walks across to the hall door and is about to go out when the door is opened and Miss Gilpin enters.)

MISS GILPIN (*hurriedly*). How do you do, Mr. Murray. Doctor Stanton just told me you were here.

MURRAY (*as they shake hands—smiling*). How are you, Miss Gilpin?

MISS GILPIN. He said he'd examined you, and that you were O.K. I'm glad. (*Glancing at him keenly.*) You've been talking to Eileen?

MURRAY. Just left her this second. She wanted to sleep for a while.

MISS GILPIN (*wonderingly*). Sleep? (*Then hurriedly.*) It's too bad. I wish I'd known you were here sooner. I wanted very much to talk to you before you saw Eileen. You see, I knew you'd pay us a visit some time. (*With a worried smile.*) I still think I ought to have a talk with you.

MURRAY. Certainly, Miss Gilpin.

MISS GILPIN (*takes a chair and places it near the hall door*). Sit down. She can't hear us here. Goodness knows this is hardly the place for confidences, but there are visitors all over and it'll have to do. Did you close the door tightly? She mustn't hear me above all. (*She goes to the porch door and peeps out for a moment; then comes back to him with flashing eyes.*) She's crying! What have you been saying to her? Oh, it's too late, I know! The fools shouldn't have permitted you to see her before I—— What has happened out there? Tell me! I must know.

MURRAY (*stammering*). Happened? Nothing. She's crying? Why, Miss Gilpin—you know I wouldn't hurt her for worlds.

MISS GILPIN (*more calmly*). Intentionally. I know you wouldn't. But something has happened. (*Then briskly.*) We're talking at cross purposes. Since you don't seem inclined to confide in me, I'll have to in you. You noticed how badly she looks, didn't you?

MURRAY. Yes, I did.

MISS GILPIN (*gravely*). She's been going down hill steadily—(*meaningly*)—ever since you left. She's in a very serious state, let me impress you with that. We've all loved her, and felt so sorry for her and admired her spirit so—that's the only reason she's been allowed to stay here so long after her time. We've kept hoping she'd start to pick up—in another day—in another week. But now that's all over. Doctor Stanton has given up hope of her improving here, and her father is unwilling to pay for her elsewhere now he knows there's a cheaper place—the State Farm. So she's to be sent there in a day or so.

MURRAY (*springing to his feet—horrified*). To the State Farm!

MISS GILPIN. Her time here is long past. You know the rule—and she isn't getting better.

MURRAY (*appalled*). That means——!

MISS GILPIN (*forcibly*). Death! That's what it means for her!

MURRAY (*stunned*). Good God, I never dreamed——

MISS GILPIN. With others it might be different. They might improve under changed surroundings. In her case, it's certain. She'll die. And it wouldn't do any good to keep her here, either. She'd die here. She'll die anywhere. She'll die because lately she's given up hope, she hasn't wanted to live any more. She's let herself go—and now it's too late.

MURRAY. Too late? You mean there's no chance—now? (*Miss Gilpin nods. Murray is overwhelmed—after a pause—stammering.*) Isn't there—anything—we can do?

MISS GILPIN (*sadly*). I don't know. I should have talked to you before you—— You see, she's seen you now. She knows. (*As he looks mystified she continues slowly.*) I suppose you know that Eileen loves you, don't you?

MURRAY (*as if defending himself against an accusation—with confused alarm*). No—Miss Gilpin. You're wrong, honestly. She may have felt something like that—once—but that was long ago before I left the San. She's forgotten all about it since, I know she has. (*Miss Gilpin smiles bitterly.*) Why, she never even alluded to it in any of her letters—all these months.

MISS GILPIN. Did you in yours?

MURRAY. No, of course not. You don't understand. Why—just now—she said that part of it had all been so silly she felt she'd acted like a fool and didn't ever want to be reminded of it.

MISS GILPIN. She saw that you didn't love her—

any more than you did in the days before you left. Oh, I used to watch you then. I sensed what was going on between you. I would have stopped it then out of pity for her, if I could have, if I didn't know that any interference would only make matters worse. And then I thought that it might be only a surface affair—that after you were gone it would end for her. (*She sighs—then after a pause.*) You'll have to forgive me for speaking to you so boldly on a delicate subject. But, don't you see, it's for her sake. I love Eileen. We all do. (*Averting her eyes from his—in a low voice.*) I know how Eileen feels, Mr. Murray. Once—a long time ago—I suffered as she is suffering—from this same mistake. But I had resources to fall back upon that Eileen hasn't got—a family who loved me and understood—friends—so I pulled through. But it spoiled my life for a long time. (*Looking at him again and forcing a smile.*) So I feel that perhaps I have a right to speak for Eileen who has no one else.

MURRAY (*huskily—much moved*). Say anything to me you like, Miss Gilpin.

MISS GILPIN (*after a pause—sadly*). You don't love her—do you?

MURRAY. No—I—— I don't believe I've ever thought much of loving anyone—that way.

MISS GILPIN (*sadly*). Oh, it's too late, I'm afraid. If we had only had this talk before you had seen her! I meant to talk to you frankly and if I found out you didn't love Eileen—there was always the forlorn hope that you might—I was going to tell you not to see her, for her sake—not to let her face the truth. For I am sure she continued to hope in spite of everything, and always would—to the end—if she didn't see you. I was going to implore you to stay away, to write her letters that would encourage her hope, and in that way she would never learn the truth. I thought of writing you all this—but—it's so delicate a matter—I didn't have the courage. (*With intense grief.*) And now Doctor Stanton's decision to send her away makes everything doubly hard. When she knows *that*—she will throw everything that holds her to life—out of the window! And think of it—her dying there alone!

MURRAY (*very pale*). Don't! That shan't happen. I can at least save her from that. I have money enough—I'll make more—to send her to any place you think——

MISS GILPIN. That is something—but it doesn't touch the source of her unhappiness. If there were only some way to make her happy in the little time that is left to her! She has suffered so much through you. Oh, Mr. Murray, can't you tell her you love her?

MURRAY (*after a pause—slowly*). But she'll never believe me, I'm afraid, now.

MISS GILPIN (*eagerly*). But you must make her believe! And you must ask her to marry you. If you're engaged it will give you the right in her eyes to take her away. You can take her to some private San. There's a small place, but a very good one, at White Lake. It's not too expensive, and it's a beautiful spot, out of the world, and you can live and work near by. And she'll be happy to the very last. Don't you think that's something—the best you have—the best you can give in return for her love for you?

MURRAY (*slowly—deeply moved*). Yes. (*Then determinedly.*) But I won't go into this thing by halves. It isn't fair to her. I'm going to marry her—yes, I mean it. I owe her that if it will make her happy. But to ask her without really meaning it—knowing she—no, I can't do that.

MISS GILPIN (*with a sad smile*). I'm glad you feel that way. It shouldn't be hard now for you to convince her. But I know Eileen. She will never consent—for your sake—until she is well again. And stop and think, Mr. Murray. Even if she did consent to marry you right now the shock—the excitement—it would be suicide for her. I would have to warn her against it myself; and you wouldn't propose it if you knew the danger to her in her present condition. She hasn't long to live, at best. I've talked with Dr. Stanton. I know. God knows I would be the first one to hold out hope if there was any. There isn't. It's merely a case of prolonging the short time left to her and making it happy. You must bear that in mind—as a fact!

MURRAY (*dully*). All right. I'll remember. But it's hell to realise—— (*He turns suddenly towards the porch door.*) I'll go out to her now while I feel—that—yes, I know I can make her believe me now.

MISS GILPIN. You'll tell me—later on?

MURRAY. Yes. (*He opens the door to the porch and goes out. Miss Gilpin stands for a moment looking *after him worriedly. Then she sighs helplessly and goes out to the hall. Murray steps noiselessly out on the porch. Eileen is lying motionless with her eyes closed. Murray stands looking at her, his face showing the emotional stress he is under, a great pitying tenderness in his eyes. Then he seems to come to a revealing decision on what is best to do for he tiptoes to the bed-side and bending down with a quick movement, takes her in his arms and kisses her.*) Eileen!

EILEEN (*startled at first, resists automatically for a moment*). Stephen! (*Then she succumbs and lies back in his arms with a happy sigh, putting both hands to the sides of his face and staring up at him adoringly.*) Stephen, dear!

MURRAY (*quickly questioning her before she can question him*). You were fibbing—about that night—weren't you? You do love me, don't you, Eileen?

EILEEN (*breathlessly*). Yes—I—but you, Stephen—you don't love me. (*She makes a movement as if to escape from his embrace.*)

MURRAY (*genuinely moved—with tender reassurance*). Why do you suppose I came up here if not to tell you I did? But they warned me—Miss Gilpin—that you were still weak and that I mustn't excite you in any way. And I—I didn't want—but I had to come back and tell you in spite of them.

EILEEN (*convinced—with a happy laugh*). And is that why you acted so strange—and cold? Aren't they silly to tell you that! As if being happy could hurt me! Why, it's just that, just you I've needed!

MURRAY (*his voice trembling*). And you'll marry me, Eileen?

EILEEN (*a shadow of doubt crossing her face momentarily*). Are you sure—you want me, Stephen?

MURRAY (*a lump in his throat—huskily*). Yes. I do want you, Eileen.

EILEEN (*happily*). Then I will—after I'm well again, of course. (*She kisses him.*)

MURRAY (*chokingly*). That won't be long now, Eileen.

EILEEN (*joyously*). No—not long—now that I'm happy for once in my life. I'll surprise you, Stephen, the way I'll pick up and grow fat and healthy. You won't know me in a month. How can you ever love such a skinny homely thing as I am now! (*With a laugh.*) I couldn't if I was a man—love such a fright.

MURRAY. Ssshh!

EILEEN (*confidently*). But you'll see now. I'll make myself get well. We won't have to wait long, dear. And can't you move up to the town near here where you can see me every day, and you can work and I can help you with your stories just as I used to—and I'll soon be strong enough to do your typing again. (*She laughs.*) Listen to me—talking about helping you—as if they weren't all your own work, those blessed stories!—as if I had anything to do with it!

MURRAY (*hoarsely*). You had! You did! They're yours. (*Trying to calm himself.*) But you mustn't stay here, Eileen. You'll let me take you away, won't you?—to a better place—not far away—White Lake, it's called. There's a small private sanatorium there. Doctor Stanton says it's one of the best. And I'll live near by—it's a beautiful spot—and see you every day.

EILEEN (*in the seventh heaven*). And did you plan out all this for me beforehand, Stephen? (*He nods with averted eyes. She kisses his hair.*) You wonderful, kind dear! And it's a small place—this White Lake? Then we won't have so many people around to disturb us, will we? We'll be all to ourselves. And you ought to work so well up there. I know New York wasn't good for you—alone—without me. And I'll get well and strong so quick! And you say it's a beautiful place? (*Intensely.*) Oh, Stephen, any place in the world would be beautiful to me—if you were with me! (*His face is hidden in the pillow beside her. She is suddenly startled by a muffled sob—anxiously.*) Why—Stephen—you're—you're crying! (*The tears start to her own eyes.*)

MURRAY (*raising his face which is this time alight with a passionate awakening—a revelation*). Oh, I do love you, Eileen. I do! I love you, love you!

EILEEN (*thrilled by the depth of his present sincerity—but with a teasing laugh*). Why, you say that as if you'd just made the discovery, Stephen!

MURRAY. Oh, what does it matter, Eileen! I love you! Oh, what a blind, selfish ass I've been! I love you! You are my life—everything! I love you, Eileen! I do! I do! And we'll be married——

(*Suddenly his face grows frozen with horror as he remembers the doom. For the first time the grey spectre of Death confronts him face to face as a menacing reality.*)

EILEEN (*terrified by the look in his eyes*). What is it, Stephen? What——?

MURRAY (*with a groan—protesting half-aloud in a strangled voice*). No! No! It can't be——! My God! (*He clutches her hands and hides his face in them.*)

EILEEN (*with a cry*). Stephen! What is the matter? (*Her face suddenly betrays apprehension, an intuitive sense of the truth.*) Oh—Stephen—— (*Then with a childish whimper of terror.*) Oh, Stephen, I'm going to die! I'm going to die!

MURRAY (*lifting his tortured face—wildly*). No!

EILEEN (*her voice sinking to a dead whisper*). I'm going to die.

MURRAY (*seizing her in his arms in a passionate frenzy and pressing his lips to hers*). No, Eileen, no, my love, no! What are you saying? What could have made you think it? You—die? Why, of course, we're all going to die—but—Good God! What damned nonsense! You're getting well—every day. Everyone — Miss Gilpin — Stanton — everyone told me that. I swear before God, Eileen, they did! You're still weak, that's all. They said—it won't be long. You mustn't think that—not now.

EILEEN (*miserably—unconvinced*). But why did you look at me—that way—with that awful look in your eyes——?

(*While she is speaking Miss Gilpin enters the room from the corridor. She appears worried, agitated. She hurries towards the porch, but stops inside the doorway, arrested by Murray's voice.*)

MURRAY (*takes Eileen by the shoulders and forces her to look into his eyes*). I wasn't thinking about you then—— No, Eileen—not you. I didn't mean you—but me—yes, me! I couldn't tell you before. They'd warned me—not to excite you—and I knew that would—if you loved me.

EILEEN (*staring at him with frightened amazement*). You mean you—— you're sick again?

MURRAY (*desperately striving to convince her*). Yes. I saw Stanton. I lied to you before—about that. It's come back on me, Eileen—you see how I look—I've let myself go. I don't know how to live without you, don't you see? And you'll—marry me now—without waiting—and help me to get well—you and I together—and not mind their lies—what they say to prevent you? You'll do that, Eileen?

EILEEN. I'll do anything for you—— And I'd be so happy—— (*She breaks down.*) But, Stephen, I'm so afraid. I'm all mixed up. Oh, Stephen, I don't know what to believe!

MISS GILPIN (*who has been listening thunderstruck to Murray's wild pleading, at last summons up the determination to interfere—steps out on the porch—in a tone of severe remonstrance*). Mr. Murray!

MURRAY (*starts to his feet with wild, bewildered eyes—confusedly*). Oh—you—— (*Miss Gilpin cannot restrain an exclamation of dismay as she sees his face wrung by despair. Eileen turns her head away with a little cry, as if she would hide her face in the bedclothes. A sudden fierce resolution lights up Murray's countenance—hoarsely.*) You're just in the nick of time, Miss Gilpin! Eileen! Listen! You'll believe Miss Gilpin, won't you? She knows all about it. (*Eileen turns her eyes questioningly on the bewildered nurse.*)

MISS GILPIN. What——?

MURRAY (*determinedly*). Miss Gilpin, Doctor Stanton has spoken to you since he examined me. He must have told you the truth about me. Eileen doesn't believe me—when I tell her I've got T. B. again. She thinks—I don't know what. I know you're not supposed to, but can't you make an exception—in this case? Can't you tell Eileen the truth?

MISS GILPIN (*stunned by being thus defiantly confronted—stammeringly*). Mr. Murray! I—I—how can you ask——

MURRAY (*quickly*). Eileen has a right to know. She loves me—and I—I—love her! (*He holds her eyes and speaks with a passion of sincerity that compels belief.*) I love her, do you hear?

MISS GILPIN (*falteringly*). You—love—Eileen?

MURRAY. Yes! I do! (*Entreatingly.*) So—tell her—won't you?

MISS GILPIN (*swallowing hard, her eyes full of pity and sorrow fixed on Eileen*). Yes—Eileen—it's true. (*She turns away slowly towards the door.*)

EILEEN (*with a little cry of alarmed concern, stretches out her hands to Murray protectingly*). Poor Stephen—dear! (*He grasps her hands and kisses them.*)

MISS GILPIN (*in a low voice*). Mr. Murray. May I speak to you for a moment?

MURRAY (*with a look of questioning defiance at her*). Certainly.

MISS GILPIN (*turns to Eileen with a forced smile*).

I won't steal him away for more than a moment, Eileen. (*Eileen smiles happily.*)

MURRAY (*follows Miss Gilpin into the room. She leads him to the far end of the room near the door to the hall, after shutting the porch door carefully behind him. He looks at her defiantly*). Well?

MISS GILPIN (*in low agitated tones*). What has happened? What is the meaning—I feel as if I may have done a great wrong to myself—to you—to her—by that lie. And yet—something impelled me.

MURRAY (*moved*). Don't regret it, Miss Gilpin! It has saved her—us. Oh, how can I explain what happened? I suddenly saw—how beautiful and sweet and good she is—how I couldn't bear the thought of life without her—her love—— That's all. (*Determinedly.*) She must marry me at once and I will take her away—the far West—any place Stanton thinks can help. And she can take care of me—as she thinks—and I know she will grow well as I seem to grow well. Oh Miss Gilpin, don't you see? No half and half measures—no promises—no conditional engagements—can help us—help her. We love too much! (*Fiercely, as if defying her.*) But we'll win together. We can! We must! There are things your doctors cannot value—cannot know the strength of! (*Exultantly.*) You'll see! I'll make Eileen get well, I tell you! Happiness will cure! Love is stronger than—— (*He suddenly breaks down before the pitying negation she cannot keep from her eyes. He sinks on a chair, shoulders bowed, face hidden in his hands, with a groan of despair.*) Oh, why did you give me a hopeless hope?

MISS GILPIN (*putting her hand on his shoulder—with tender compassion—sadly*). Isn't everything we know—just that—when you think of it? (*Her face lighting up with a consoling revelation.*) But there must be something behind it—some promise of fulfilment,—somehow—somewhere—in the spirit of hope itself.

MURRAY (*dully*). Yes—but what do words mean to me now? (*Then suddenly starting to his feet and flinging off her hand with disdainful strength—violently and almost insultingly.*) What damned rot! I tell you we'll win! We must! Oh, I'm a fool to waste words on you! What can you know? Love isn't in the materia medica. Your predictions—all the verdicts of all the doctors—what do they matter to me? This is—beyond you! And we'll win in spite of you! (*Scornfully.*) How dare you use the word hopeless—as if it were the last! Come now, confess, damn it! There's always hope, isn't there? What do you *know?* Can you say you *know* anything?

MISS GILPIN (*taken aback by his violence for a moment, finally bursts into a laugh of helplessness which is close to tears*). I? I know nothing—absolutely nothing! God bless you both!

(*She raises her handkerchief to her eyes and hurries out to the corridor without turning her head. Murray stands looking after her for a moment; then strides out to the porch.*)

EILEEN (*turning and greeting him with a shy smile of happiness as he comes and kneels by her bedside*). Stephen! (*He kisses her. She strokes his hair and continues in a tone of motherly, self-forgetting solicitude.*) I'll have to look out for you, Stephen, won't I? From now on? And see that you rest so many hours a day—and drink your milk when I drink mine—and go to bed at nine sharp when I do—and obey everything I tell you—and——

CURTAIN

GOLD

A Play in Four Acts

Characters

CAPTAIN ISAIAH BARTLETT, *of the whaling ship, "Triton"*
SILAS HORNE, *boatswain of the "Triton"*
BEN CATES } *of the "Triton's" crew*
JIMMY KANAKA, *an Islander* } *of the "Triton's" crew*
BUTLER, *cook of the "Triton"*
ABEL, *the ship's boy*
SARAH ALLEN BARTLETT, *the captain's wife*
SUE, *their daughter*
NAT, *their son*
DANIEL DREW, *officer of a freight steamer*
DOCTOR BERRY

Scenes

ACT ONE

A barren coral island on the fringe of the Malay Archipelago. Noon.

ACT TWO

Interior of a boat-shed on the wharf of the Bartlett place on the California coast. An afternoon six months later.

ACT THREE

Exterior of the Bartlett house. Dawn of the following morning.

ACT FOUR

Bartlett's "cabin" – his look-out post – at the top of the house. A night one year later.

TIME: about the year 1900

ACT ONE

SCENE. *A small, barren coral island on the southern fringe of the Malay Archipelago. The coral sand, blazing white under the full glare of the sun, lifts in the right foreground to a long hummuck a few feet above sea-level. A stunted coco palm rises from the centre of this elevation, its bunch of scraggly leaves drooping motionlessly, casting a small circular patch of shadow directly beneath on the ground about the trunk. About a hundred yards in the distance the lagoon is seen, its vivid blue contrasting with the white coral beach which borders its circular outline. The far horizon to seaward is marked by a broad band of purplish haze which separates the bright blue of the water from the metallic grey-blue of the sky. The island bakes. The intensity of the sun's rays is flung back skyward in a quivering mist of heat-waves which distorts the outlines of things, giving the visible world an intangible eerie quality, as if it were floating submerged in some colourless molten fluid.*

As the curtain rises, Abel is discovered lying

asleep, curled up in the patch of shade beneath the coco palm. He is a runty, under-sized boy of fifteen, with a shrivelled old face, tanned to parchment by the sun. He has on a suit of dirty dungarees, man's size, much too large for him, which hang in loose folds from his puny frame. A thatch of brown hair straggles in limp wisps from under the peaked canvas cap he wears. He looks terribly exhausted. His dreams are evidently fraught with terror, for he twitches convulsively and moans with fright. Butler enters hurriedly, panting, from the right, rear. He is a tall man of over middle age, dressed in the faded remainder of what was once a brown suit. The coat, the buttons of which have been torn off, hangs open, revealing his nakedness beneath. A cloth cap covers his bald head, with its halo of dirty thin grey hair. His body is emaciated. His face, with its round, blue eyes, is weathered and cracked by the sun's rays. The wreck of a pair of heavy shoes flop about his bare feet. He looks back cautiously, as if he were afraid of being followed; then satisfied that he is not, he approaches the sleeping boy, and bending down, puts his hand on Abel's forehead. Abel groans and opens his eyes. He stares about furtively, as if seeking some one whose presence he dreads to find.

ABEL (*in a husky voice*). Where's Capt'n and the rest, Butts?

BUTLER (*in a hoarse, cracked whisper*). On the beach – down there.

(*He makes an exhausted gesture, right, and then sinks with a groan at the foot of the tree, leaning back against the trunk, trying vainly to hunch his long legs up so as to be completely in the shade.*)

ABEL. What're they doin'? (*With avid eyes.*) They ain't found no water yet?

BUTLER (*shaking his head, his eyes closing wearily*). No. How would they – when there ain't any – not on this devil's island – dry as a bone, my sonny – sand and sun – that's all.

ABEL (*remonstratingly – his lips trembling a little*). Aw – maybe – you don't know no different.

BUTLER. No. Might as well look the devil in the face, sonny. There's no water here. Not a damn drop. No – nor a scrap to eat, neither. Only the damn sun. (*Weakly – touching the skin of his face with trembling fingers.*) God! My face is like the raw inside of a wet hide! If it'd only rain! (*After a pause – kindly.*) But how are you, eh? Had a good sleep?

ABEL. I was dreamin' awful. (*With a sudden, shrill agony – his lips twitching.*) I need a drink of water – something awful! My mouth's burnin' up. (*With tremulous pleading.*) Say, ain't you got 'nother drink left? – honest, ain't you?

BUTLER (*looking around him cautiously*). Not so loud! (*Fixing his eyes sternly on the boy.*) This is a dead secret, mind! You'll swear you won't blab – not to him?

ABEL. Sure, Butts, sure! Gawd strike me dead!

BUTLER (*takes a pint bottle from the hip-pocket of his pants. It is about half-full of water*). He don't know I've got this, remember! He – and the rest – they'd kill me like a dog – and you too, sonny – remember that!

ABEL. Sure! I ain't goin' to tell 'em, Butts. (*Stretching out his hands frenziedly.*) Aw, give it to me, Butts! Give me a drink, for Christ's sake!

BUTLER. No, you don't! I'll hold it for you. Only a few drops. You'd have it all down your throat. And we've got to be careful. It's got to last 'til the ship comes past that'll pick us up. That's the only hope. (*Holding the bottle at arm's length from the boy.*) Hands down, now – or you don't get a drop! (*The boy lets his hands drop to his sides. Butler puts the bottle carefully to his lips, and allows the boy two gulps – then snatches it away.*) That's all now. More later.

(*He takes one gulp himself, and making a tremendous effort of will, jerks the bottle from his lips, and corking it quickly, thrusts it back in his pocket and heaves a shuddering sigh.*)

ABEL. Aw, more! Just another swaller —

BUTLER (*determinedly*). No!

ABEL (*crying weakly*). Yuh dirty mut!

BUTLER (*quietly*). There! Don't get riled. It only makes you hotter – and thirstier. (*The boy sinks back exhausted and closes his eyes. Butler begins to talk in a more assured voice, as if the sip of water had renewed his courage.*) That'll save us yet, that bit of water. A lucky notion of mine to think of it – at the last moment. They were just lowering the boats. I could hear you calling to me to hurry and come. They didn't care if I went down with that stinking whaling ship or not, damn them! What did the dirty cook matter to them? But I thought of filling this bottle. It'd been lying there in the galley for two years almost. I'd had it on my hip, full of whisky, that night in Oakland when I was shanghaied. So I filled it out of a bucket before I ran to the boat. Lucky I did, son – for you and me – not for them – damn 'em!

ABEL (*struggling to a sitting posture, evidently strengthened by his drink*). Gee, if the Old Man was wise you got it —

BUTLER. He won't know – nor Horne, nor Cates, nor Jimmy Kanaka, neither. (*As if in self-justification.*) Why should I tell 'em, eh? Did I ever get anything better than a kick or a curse from one of them? (*Vindictively.*) Would they give it to me if they had it? They'd see me in hell first! And besides, it's too late for them. They're mad as hatters right now, the four of them. They ain't had a drop since three nights back, when the water in the cask gave out and we rowed up against this island in the dark. Think of it, and them out walking and roasting in the sun all day, looking for water where there ain't any. Wouldn't you be crazy? (*Suddenly he laughs queerly.*) Didn't you hear them shouting and yelling like lunatics just before I came?

ABEL. I thought I heard something – on'y maybe I was dreamin'.

BUTLER. It's them that are doing the dreaming. I was with them. I had to go. (*With rising anger.*) He kicked me awake – and every time I tried to get away he beat me back. He's strong yet – (*with threatening vindictiveness.*) – but he can't last long, damn him! (*Controlling himself, goes on with his story excitedly.*) Well, we went looking for water – on this sand pile. Then Jimmy Kanaka saw a boat sunk half under down inside the reef – a Malay canoe, only bigger. They got down in her the best way they could, up to their waists in water. They thought there might be something to drink on her. I was trying to sneak off, scared to go in on account of sharks. All of a sudden they gave an awful yell. I thought they'd found something to drink and ran back. They was all standing about a box they'd forced open, yelling and cursing and out of their heads completely. When I looked I seen the box was full of all sorts of metal junk – bracelets and bands and necklaces that I guess the Malays wear. Nothing but brass and copper, and bum imitations of diamonds and things – not worth a damn; and there they were, shouting with joy and slapping each other on the back. And that hellion of a skipper shouts at me: "Get out of this! No share here for a stinking cook!" he yells. I didn't say nothing but just picked up some of the stuff to make sure. Then I told him straight. "This ain't gold. It's brass and copper – not worth a damn." God, he got wild! I had to run, or he'd knifed me – then and there. That was when I woke you up.

ABEL. And ain't it worth nothin', honest? How'd you know it ain't?

BUTLER. D'you think I ain't learned to know gold in my time? And polished enough copper and brass to know them, too? Just as if it was gold it'd do 'em any good! You can't drink gold, can you? (*With sudden violence.*) It serves 'em right, all that's happened and going to happen. Kicks and smacks in the face if I even winked an eye – two years of it! And me shanghaied when I was drunk – taken away from a good job and forced to cook the swill on a rotten whaler. Oh, I'll pay him back for it! His damn ship is wrecked and lost to him – that's the first of it. I'll see him rot and die – and the three with him! But you and me'll be saved! D'you know why I've let you go halves on this water, instead of hogging it all myself? It's because you were the only one on board that didn't treat me like a dog – and they kicked and beat you, too. We were in the same boat. And now we'll get even! Them and their dirty box of junk! (*He sinks back, exhausted by this outburst.*)

ABEL (*suddenly, in a piteous voice*). Gee, I wisht I was back home again!

BUTLER. You'll get back. We both will. (*He closes his eyes. After a pause – weakly.*) When I close my eyes, everything gets to rocking under me, like I was in that open boat again. I won't forget these four days in a hurry. Up and down — Nothing but sun and water.

(*They are both silent, leaning with closed eyes against the bole of the tree, panting exhaustedly. A murmur of men's voices comes from the right, rear, and gradually gets nearer.*)

ABEL (*opening his eyes with a start*). Butts! I hear 'em comin'!

BUTLER (*listening, wide-eyed, for a moment*). Yes, it's them. (*He gets to his feet weakly.*) Come, let's get out of this. (*Abel staggers to his feet. They both move to the left. Butler shades his eyes with his hands and looks toward the beach.*) Look! They're dragging along that box of junk with 'em, the damn fools! (*Warningly.*) They're crazy as hell. Don't give 'em no chance to pick on you, d'you hear? They'd stop at nothing when they're this way.

(*There is a scuffling of heavy footsteps in the sand, and Captain Bartlett appears, followed by Horne, who in turn is followed by Cates and Jimmy Kanaka. Bartlett is a tall, huge-framed figure of a man, dressed in a blue double-breasted coat, trousers of the same material, and rubber sea-boots turned down from the knees. In spite of the ravages of hunger and thirst there is still a suggestion of immense strength in his heavy-muscled body. His head is massive, thickly covered with tangled, iron-grey hair. His face is large, bony, and leather-tanned, with a long aquiline nose and a gash of a mouth shadowed by a bristling grey moustache. His broad jaw sticks out at an angle of implacable stubbornness. Bushy grey brows overhang the obsessed glare of his sombre dark eyes. Silas Horne is a thin, parrot-nosed, angular old man, his lean face marked by a lifetime of crass lusts and mean cruelty. He is dressed in grey cotton trousers, and a singlet torn open across his hairy chest. The exposed skin of his arms and shoulders and chest has been blistered and seared by the sun. A cap is on his head. Cates is squat and broad-chested, with thick. stumpy legs and arms. His square, stupid face, with its greedy pig's eyes, is terribly pock-marked. He is gross and bestial, an unintelligent brute. He is dressed in dungaree trousers and a dirty white sailor's blouse, and wears a brown cap. Jimmy Kanaka is a tall, sinewy, bronzed young Islander. He wears only a loin cloth and a leather belt with a sheath-knife. The last two are staggering beneath the weight of a heavy inlaid chest. The eyes of the three white men are wild. They pant exhaustedly, their legs trembling with weakness beneath them. Their lips are puffed and cracked, their voices muffled by their swollen tongues. But there is a mad air of happiness, of excitement, about their scorched faces.*)

BARTLETT (*in a crooning, monotonous voice*). It's heavy, I know, heavy – that chest. Up, bullies! Up with her! (*He flings himself in the shade, resting his back against the tree, and points to the sand at his feet.*) Put 'er there, bullies – there where I kin see!

HORNE (*echoing his words mechanically*). Put 'er there!

CATES (*in thick, stupid tones*). Aye, aye, sir! Down she goes, Jimmy! (*They set the chest down.*)

BARTLETT. Sit down, lads, sit down. Ye've earned your spell of rest.

(*The three men throw themselves on the sand in attitudes of spent weariness. Bartlett's eyes are fixed gloatingly on the chest. There is a silence suddenly broken by Cates, who leaps to a kneeling position with a choked cry.*)

CATES (*his eyes staring at the Captain with fierce insistence*). I want a drink – water!

(*The others are startled into a rigid, dazed attention. Horne's lips move painfully in a soundless repetition of the word. There is a pause. Then Bartlett strikes the side of his head with his fist, as if to drive this obsession from his brain. Butler and Abel stand looking at them with frightened eyes.*)

BARTLETT (*having regained control over himself, in a determined voice, deep-toned and menacing*). If ye speak that word ever again, Ben Cates – if ye say it once again – ye'll be food for the sharks! Ye hear?

CATES (*terrified*). Yes, sir.

(*He collapses limply on the sand again. Horne and the Kanaka relax hopelessly.*)

BARTLETT (*with heavy scorn*). Are ye a child to take on like a sick woman – cryin' for what ye know we've not got? Can't ye stand up under a little thirst like a man? (*Resolutely.*) There'll be water enough – if ye'll wait and keep a stiff upper lip on ye. We'll all be picked up to-day. I'll stake my word on it. This state o' things can't last. (*His eyes fall on the chest.*) Ye ought to be singin' 'stead o' cryin' – after the find we've made. What's the lack of water amount to – when ye've gold before you? (*With mad exultation.*) Gold! Enough of it in your share alone to buy ye rum, and wine, and women, too, for the rest o' your life!

CATES (*straightening up to a sitting posture – his small eyes staring at the box fascinatedly – in a stupid mumble.*) Aye – aye – rum and wine!

BARTLETT (*half-closing his eyes as if the better to enjoy his vision.*) Yes, rum and wine and women for you and Horne and Jimmy. No more hard work on the dirty sea for ye, bullies, but a full payday in your pockets to spend each day o' the year. (*The three strain their ears, listening eagerly. Even Butler and Abel advance a step or two toward him, as if they, too, were half-hypnotized.*) And Cates grumbling because he's thirsty! I'd be the proper one to complain – if complainin' there was to do! Ain't I lost my ship and the work o' two years with her? And what have ye lost, all three, but a few rags o' clothes? (*With savage emphasis.*) I tell ye, I be glad the *Triton* went down! (*He taps the box with his fingers.*) They's more in this than ever was earned by all the whalin' ships afloat. They's gold – heavy and solid – and diamonds and emeralds and rubies! – red and green, they be.

CATES (*licking his lips*). Aye, I seen 'em there – and emeralds be green, I know, and sell for a ton of gold!

BARTLETT (*as if he hadn't heard and was dreaming out loud to himself*). Rum and wine for you three, and rest for me. Aye, I'll rest at home 'til the day I die. Aye, woman, I be comin' home now for good. Aye, Nat and Sue, your father be comin' home for the rest o' his life! No more stinkin' blubber on the deck. I'll give up whalin' like ye've always been askin' me, Sarah. Aye, I'll go to meetin' with ye on a Sunday like ye've always prayed I would. We'll make the damn neighbours open their eyes, curse 'em! Carriages and silks for ye – they'll be nothin' too good – and for Sue and the boy. I've been dreamin' o' this in my sleep for years. I never give a damn 'bout the oil – that's just trade – but I always hoped on some voyage I'd pick up ambergris – a whole lot of it – and that's worth gold!

HORNE (*his head bobbing up from his chest – drowsily*). Aye, ambergris! It's costly truck.

BUTLER (*in a whisper to the boy – cautiously*). There! Wasn't I right? Mad as hatters, all of 'em! Come on away!

ABEL (*staring at the Captain fascinatedly*). No. I wanter see 'em open it.

BUTLER. Look out! You'll be going batty yourself, first thing you know. (*But he also stays.*)

BARTLETT (*his voice more and more that of a somnambulist*). It's time I settled down to home with ye, Sarah, after twenty years o' whalin'. They's plenty o' big trees on my place, bullies, and shade and green grass, and a cool wind off the sea. (*He shakes off the growing drowsiness and glares about him in a rage.*) Hell's fire! What crazy truck be I thinkin' of? (*But he and the others sink back immediately into stupor. After a pause he begins to relate a tale in a droning voice.*) Years ago, when I was whalin' out o' New Bedford – just after I got my first ship, it was – a man come to me – Spanish-looking, he was – and wanted to charter my ship and me go shares. He showed me a map o' some island off the coast of South America somewhere. They was a cross marked on it where treasure had been buried by the old pirates. That was what he said. But I was a fool. I didn't believe him. I didn't see's I could take a chance. He got old Scott's schooner – finally. She sailed and never was heard o' since. But I've never forgot him and his map. And often I've thought if I'd 'a' went that vige —— (*He straightens up and shouts with aggressive violence.*) But here she be! Run right into it – without no map nor nothin'. Gold and diamonds and all – all them things he said was there – there they be in front o' our eyes! (*To the now alert Jimmy.*) Open 'er up, Jimmy!

JIMMY (*getting up – in his soft voice*). Aye, Captain. (*He reaches down to lift the lid.*)

BARTLETT (*a sudden change of feeling comes over him, and he knocks Jimmy's arm aside savagely*). Hands off, ye dog! I'm takin' care o' this chest, and no man's hand's goin' to touch it but mine!

JIMMY (*stepping back docilely – in the same unmoved, soft tone*). Aye, Captain.

(*He squats down to the left of the chest.*)

BARTLETT (*seeming suddenly to notice the cook for the

first time). So there you be, eh? (*His voice growing thick with rage.*) I ain't forgot what ye said down by the shore there! Lucky for ye I didn't catch ye then! "Brass and copper – junk," ye said – "not gold! Not worth a damn," ye said! Ye blasted son o' a liar! No share for ye! I'll not forget. And keep your distance o' me if ye want your hide! (*Looking at Abel.*) Ye've been tellin' that boy your lies too, I kin tell by the look o' him. (*Sternly.*) Come here, boy!

ABEL (*advances with faltering steps*). Y-yes, s-sir?

BARTLETT. Open up that chest! Open it up, ye brat! (*With a desperate movement of fear Abel reaches down and flings open the lid of the chest. As he does so, Bartlett's huge hand fastens on the collar of his coat, and holds him with face bent over the box. Horne, Cates, and Jimmy Kanaka pull themselves close, their necks craning for a look inside. Butler takes a few steps toward them.*)

BUTLER (*in a low uncertain tone*). Maybe I was wrong, Captain Bartlett, sir.

BARTLETT (*shaking the terror-stricken boy*). What d'ye see there, ye little swab? What d'ye see there?

ABEL. Aw – leggo – I'm chokin'!

BARTLETT (*grimly*). Ye'll choke in earnest if ye don't answer me. What d'ye see? Is it gold? Answer me – is it gold?

ABEL (*stutteringly*). Yes – sure – gold – I see it!

BARTLETT (*thrusts him away. The boy staggers and falls to the sand. Bartlett turns to Butler triumphantly*). Ye see, ye liar? Gold! Gold! Even a child can tell it at a look. (*With a sombre menace in his tone.*) But ye – don't believe – do ye?

BUTLER (*frightenedly*). Maybe I was wrong, sir. I – didn't – look very careful.

BARTLETT. Come here! (*He stands up, his back against the tree.*) Come here!

BUTLER. Yes, sir. (*But he looks about him shiftily, as if to run away.*)

BARTLETT. Jimmy! (*The Kanaka leaps to his feet.*) Knife him, Jimmy, if he tries to run.

JIMMY (*his hand goes to his knife, his dark eyes lighting up with savagery – in his soft voice*). Aye, Captain!

BARTLETT (*to the trembling cook*). Come here!

BUTLER (*goes to him with the courage of desperation*). Yes, sir.

BARTLETT (*pointing to the contents of the chest*). Is it gold – or not?

BUTLER. If I can feel of one —

BARTLETT. Pick one up.

BUTLER (*picks up a heavy anklet encrusted with coloured glass, looks at it for a minute – then feigning great assurance*). I was wrong, Captain. It's gold all right enough – worth all kinds of money, I bet.

BARTLETT (*with mad triumph*). Ha! Ye've come to your senses, have ye? Too late, ye swab! No share for ye! And here's to teach ye for lyin' to me before!

(*His fist jerks out from his side, and Butler is knocked sprawling on the sand, where he lies groaning for a moment, the anklet still clutched in his hand. The boy gives a gasp of fright and scampers off, left.*)

That'll learn ye! (*He sits down beside the chest. The others crouch close. Bartlett shoves in both of his hands – in a tone of mad gloating.*) Gold! Better'n whaling, ain't she, boys? Better'n ambergris, even if I ever had luck to find any!

(*Butler staggers to his feet. He examines the anklet with contemptuous scorn and even bites it to make sure. Then he edges stealthily toward the left. A sudden transformation comes over his face and he glowers at the Captain with hatred, his features distorted with fury.*)

JIMMY KANAKA (*pointing to Butler*). He got him, Captain!

BARTLETT (*glancing at the cook with contemptuous scorn*). Sneakin' away with that piece o' the gold, be ye? Ye thievin' swine! Ye know right enough it's gold now, don't ye? Well, ye kin keep it – for your share for speakin' the truth that once.

HORNE (*his cupidity protesting*). Don't give it to him, sir! It's so much the less for us that worked for it when he did nothin'!

BUTLER (*overcome by hysterical rage – stammering*). Who asked you for it – eh? Who – wants the damn thing? Not me! No! You damned lunatics! You oughter all be in the asylum? (*Holding the anklet out contemptuously.*) Gold? Ha-ha! This junk? I just bit it to make sure. Gold? Brass, that's what – and pieces of glass! Junk! Not worth a damn. Here! Take it! You can have it! (*He flings it on the sand before them. Bartlett snatches it up protectingly.)*

BARTLETT (*in a frenzy*). Jimmy!

(*But Butler runs off left with a terrified cry. Jimmy springs to his feet and stands with his hand on his knife, waiting for a further order.*)

JIMMY (*eagerly*). I go catch – go stick him, Captain?

BARTLETT (*pausing – with a frown*). No. They's time enough for that – if need be. Sit down. (*Jimmy sits down again with a childish air of sulking. Bartlett stares at the treasure, continuing to frown, as if Butler's action had made him uneasy, bewildered and confused him. He mutters half to himself.*) Queer! Queer! He threw it back as if 'twas a chunk of mud! He knew – and yet he said he didn't want it. Junk, he called it – and he knows it's gold! He said 'twas gold himself a second back. He's queer. Why would he say junk when he knows it's gold? D'ye think – he don't believe?

HORNE. He was mad because you knocked him down.

BARTLETT (*shaking his head grimly*). It ain't the first time I've knocked him down; but he never spoke up to me – like that – before. No, it's somethin' else is wrong with him – somethin'.

HORNE. No share for him, you told him, sir. That's what wrong with him.

BARTLETT (*again shaking his head*). No. His eyes — It's somethin' he's got in his head – somethin' he's hidin'! His share – maybe he thinks he'll get his share anyway, in spite o' us! Maybe he thinks his share wouldn't be all he wants! Maybe he thinks we'll die o' hunger and thirst before we get picked up – and that he'll live – and then – he'll come in for the whole chestful! (*Suddenly springing to his feet in a rage, convinced that he has found the truth.*) Hell's fire! That's it, bullies! That's his sneakin' plan! To watch us die – and steal it from us!

CATES (*rising to his knees and shaking his hand threateningly above his head*). Tell Jimmy to knife him, sir! Tell Jimmy – I ain't got a knife, or I'd do it myself. (*He totters weakly to his feet.*)

JIMMY (*eagerly*). You speak, I stick him, Captain. I stick boy, too.

CATES (*weakening*). I'm weak, but I kin do for him yet. I'm weak — (*His knees sag under him. He pleads piteously.*) If I'd only a drink to put some strength in me! If I'd only a sup o' water, I'd do for him! (*Turning, as if to stagger down toward the beach.*) There must be water. Let's look again. I'll go look —

(*But the effort he makes is too much for his strength and he falls to the sand, panting with open mouth.*)

BARTLETT (*summoning his strength – sternly*). Put a clapper on that jaw of yours, Cates, or I'll do it for ye!

CATES (*blubbering*). If we don't find water – he'll watch us die.

JIMMY (*insinuatingly*). Better me knife cook fella – kill boy, too!

BARTLETT. Will killin' 'em give us drink, ye fools? (*After a pause, he shakes his head as if to drive off some thought, and mutters.*) No more o' that! (*Suddenly, in a tone of sharp command.*) No more o' that, I say! We're keepin' no right watch for ships. Go aloft on that tree, Jimmy – and damn quick! Take a look and see if ye can sight a sail.

(*Kanaka shins quickly up the bole of the coco palm to the top and looks out on all sides of him. The others rise painfully to their feet and gaze up at him with awakened hope.*)

JIMMY (*suddenly, in a glad voice*). I see um – see sail, Captain.

CATES (*waving his arms frenziedly*). Sail – ho!

JIMMY. Look plenty like trade schooner, Captain. She no change course she fetch plenty close by here. She make full sail, she got plenty fella wind out there, she come quick.

HORNE (*clapping Cates on the back*). Headin' straight for us, Cates, d'you hear?

BARTLETT. How far d'ye reckon she be?

JIMMY. She's five, six fella mile, Captain.

BARTLETT. Come down. (*The Islander slides down. Bartlett exclaims exultantly.*) Didn't I tell ye? In the nick o' time. When she makes in close we'll go down to the reef and yell and wave at her. They'll see! The luck's with us to-day! (*His eyes fall on the treasure and he starts.*) But now – what's to do with this chest – the gold?

HORNE (*quickly*). You ain't going to tell them on

the schooner about it?

CATES. They'd claim to share with us.

HORNE. More like they'd steal it and knife us in the bargain. I know the kind on them schooners.

BARTLETT (*scornfully*). D'ye think I'm cracked? No, we'll bury it here.

CATES (*regretfully*). Leave it behind for anyone to find?

BARTLETT. We'll bury it deep, where hell itself won't find it – and we'll make a map o' this island. (*He takes a sheet of paper and a stub of pencil from his pocket – pointing to the foot of the tree.*) Dig a hole here – you, Horne and Jimmy – and dig it deep. (*The two bend down and commence to hollow out the sand with their hands. Bartlett draws on the paper.*) There's the lagoon – and the reef – and here's this tree – the only one on the island – 't would be hard to miss. (*To Cates, who is peering over his shoulder.*) And here where the tree is, d'ye see, Cates, I'll make a cross where the gold is hid.

HORNE (*over his shoulder, without ceasing his work*). How d'ye know the lay o' this island – to find it again?

BARTLETT. By the last reckonin' o' the *Triton's*. It's writ on a page I tore from the log-book. And from there we headed due north in the boat, unless the compass lied – four days – a hundred-and-fifty miles, I reckon. (*Exultantly.*) Oh, all hell'd not stop me from findin' this place again when I know the gold's here. Let us once get home and I'll fit out a small schooner the four of us can sail, and we'll come back here to dig it up. It won't be long, I swear to ye!

HORNE (*straightening up*). This deep enough, sir?

BARTLETT. It looks to be.

JIMMY (*who has straightened up and is looking off left – suddenly points excitedly*). He look, Captain! Cook fella, he look here! Boy he look, too! They look plenty too much, Captain!

(*All four stand staring off at Butler and the boy, whose presence on the island they have forgotten in their mad excitement.*)

CATES (*in stupid dismay*). They'll know where it's hid, sir!

HORNE. They'll tell 'em on the schooner!

CATES (*wildly*). We've got to do for 'em, Captain! Gimme your knife, Jimmy – your knife —

(*He stumbles toward the Islander, who pushes him aside brusquely, looking questioningly toward the Captain.*)

BARTLETT (*who has been standing motionless, as if stunned by this forgotten complication – slowly*). There they be watchin' us, the sneakin' dogs! Sit down, an' they won't see. (*They all squat in the sand.*) I was forgettin' they was here. (*Striking his knee with clenched fist.*) We've got to do somethin' damn quick! That schooner'll be up soon where they kin sight her – and they'll wave and yell then – and she'll see 'em!

HORNE. And good-bye to the gold for us!

JIMMY (*eagerly*). You say fella word, Captain, me kill um quick. They no make plenty cry for schooner! They keep damn still plenty too much!

BARTLETT (*looking at the Islander with mad cunning but replying only to Horne*). Aye, it's good-bye to the gold, Horne. That scum of a cook – he's made a mock o' us – sayin' it wasn't gold when he knew it was – he'll tell 'em – he'll get joy o' tellin' 'em!

HORNE. And that scrub of a boy – he's no better. He'll be in with him neck and crop.

CATES (*hoarsely*). Knife 'em – and be done with it – I say!

BARTLETT. Or, if they don't tell the schooner's skipper it'll only be because they're plannin' to come back themselves – before we kin – and dig it up. That cook – there's somethin' queer in his mind – somethin' he was hidin' – pretendin' not to believe. What d'ye think, Horne?

HORNE. I think – time's gettin' short – and talkin' won't do no good. (*Insinuatingly.*) They'd do for us soon enough if *they* was able.

BARTLETT. Aye, murder was plain in his eyes when he looked at me.

HORNE (*lowering his voice to a whisper*). Tell Jimmy – Captain Bartlett – is what I say!

BARTLETT. It's agin the law, Silas Horne!

HORNE. The law don't reach to this island.

BARTLETT (*monotonously*). It's against the law a captain's sworn to keep wherever he sails. They ain't refused duty – nor mutinied.

HORNE. Who'll know they ain't? They're trying to steal what's yours – that's worse'n mutiny. (*As a final persuasion.*) And Jimmy's a nigger –

and under no laws. And he's stronger'n you are. You couldn't stop 'im.

BARTLETT. Aye – I couldn't prevent —

JIMMY (*eagerly*). I fix um, Captain, they no tell!

(*Bartlett doesn't answer, but stares at the treasure. Horne makes violent motions to Jimmy to go. The Islander stares at his master's face. Then, seeming to read the direct command there, he grunts with satisfaction, and pulling his knife from its sheath, he goes stealthily off left. Cates raises himself on his haunches to watch the Islander's movements. Horne and Bartlett sit still in a strained immobility, their eyes on the chest.*)

CATES (*in an excited whisper*). I see 'em! They're sittin' with their backs this way! (*A slight pause.*) There's Jimmy. He's crawlin' on his hands behind 'em. They don't notice – he's right behind – almost atop o' them. (*A pause. Cates gives a fiendish grunt.*) Ugh! (*Butler's muffled cry comes from the left.*) Right in the middle of the back! The cook's done! The boy's runnin'!

(*There is a succession of quick screams from the boy, the padding of feet running toward them, the fall of a body, and the boy's dying groan.*)

HORNE (*with satisfaction*). It's done, sir!

BARTLETT (*slowly*). I spoke no word, remember that, Silas Horne!

HORNE (*cunningly*). Nor me neither, sir. Jimmy took it on himself. If blame there is – and who'd blame him for it? – it's on him.

BARTLETT (*gloomily*). I spoke no word! (*Jimmy returns noiselessly from the left.*)

JIMMY (*grinning with savage pride*). I fix um fella plenty, Captain. They no tell. They no open mouth plenty too much!

CATES (*maudlinly*). You're a man, Jimmy – a man with guts to him – even if you're a — (*He babbles incoherently.*)

JIMMY (*as the Captain does not look at him*). I go climb fella tree, Captain? I make look for schooner?

BARTLETT (*rousing himself with an effort*). Yes – go up. (*The Islander climbs the tree.*)

HORNE (*getting to his feet – eagerly*). Where away, Jimmy?

JIMMY. She come, Captain, she come plenty quick.

HORNE (*looking in the direction Jimmy indicates*). I kin see her tops'ls from here, sir. Look!

BARTLETT (*getting to his feet – stares out to sea*). Aye! There she be – and makin' towards us fast. (*In a flash his sombre preoccupation is gone, and he is commander once more. He puts the anklet in his hand into his coat pocket – harshly.*) Come down out o' that? They's work to do. (*Jimmy clambers down.*) Did ye leave – them – lyin' in plain sight on the open sand?

JIMMY. Yes. I no touch um, Captain.

BARTLETT. Then ye'll touch 'em now. Go, bury 'em, cover 'em up with sand. And mind ye make a good job o' it that none'll see. Jump now!

JIMMY (*obediently*). I go, Captain. (*He hurries off left.*)

BARTLETT. Down to the reef with ye, Horne! (*Giving the prostrate Cates a kick.*) Up out o' that, Cates! Go with Horne, and when ye see the schooner hull up, wave to 'em, and yell like mad, d'ye hear?

HORNE. Aye, aye, sir!

BARTLETT. I'll stay here and bury the gold. It's best to be quick about it! They may turn a spyglass on us when they raise the island from deck! Off with ye! (*He gives Cates another kick.*)

CATES (*groaning*). I'm sick! (*Incoherently.*) Can't – report for duty – this watch. (*With a shout.*) Water!

BARTLETT (*contemptuously*). Ye dog! Give him a hand, Horne.

HORNE (*putting a hand under his shoulder*). Up, man! We're to signal the schooner. There'll be water on board o' her – barrels of it!

CATES (*aroused, scrambles to his feet, violently shaking off Horne's hand*). Water aboard o' her! (*His staring eyes catch the schooner's sails on the horizon. He breaks into a staggering run and disappears down toward the beach, right rear, waving his arms wildly and shouting.*) Ahoy! Ahoy! Water! (*Horne walks out quickly after him. Left alone, Bartlett, after a quick glance around, sinks on his knees beside the chest and shoves both hands into it. From the chest comes *a metallic clink as he fingers the pieces in his hands gloatingly.*) Ye're safe now! There's none to tell left livin'! He's dead – damn him! – that lied about ye. And ye'll rest safe here till I come back for ye! (*In a dreaming tone, his eyes fixed before him in an ecstatic vision.*) No more whalin' on the dirty seas! Rest at home! Gold! I've been dreamin' o' it all my life! Aye – we'll rest now, Sarah! Your father be a rich man, Nat and Sue! (*Shaking himself – savagely.*) Ye fool! What drivel be ye talkin'? Loosin' your senses, be ye? Time ye was picked up! Lucky! (*He shoves down the lid and places the chest in the hole. He pushes the sand in on top of it, whispering hoarsely.*) Lay safe, d'ye hear. For I'll be back for ye! Aye – in spite of hell I'll dig ye up again! (*The voices of Horne and Jimmy can be heard from the distance shouting as*

The Curtain Falls)

ACT TWO

SCENE. *Interior of an old boat-shed on the wharf of the Bartlett place on the California coast. In the rear, a double doorway looking out over the end of the wharf to the bay with the open sea beyond. On the left, two windows, and another door, opening on the dock. Near this door, a cot with blankets and a pillow without a slip. In the centre, front, a table with a bottle and glasses on it, and three cane-bottomed chairs. On the right, a fishing dory. Here and there about the shed all sorts of odds and ends pertaining to a ship – old anchors, ropes, tackle, paint-pots, old spars, etc.*

It is late afternoon of a day six months later. Sunlight filters feebly through the stained, cobwebby window-panes.

As the curtain rises, Bartlett and Silas Horne are discovered. Horne is in working clothes of paint-stained dungaree. If his sufferings on the island have left any marks on his dry wizened face, they are undiscoverable. In Bartlett, however, the evidence is marked. His hair has turned white. There are deep hollows under his cheek-bones. His jaw and tight-lipped mouth express defiant determination, as if he were fighting back some weakness inside himself, a weakness found in his eyes, which have something in them of fear, of a wishing to avoid other eyes. He is dressed much the same as when on the island. He sits by the table, centre, his abstracted gaze bent on the floor before him.

HORNE (*who is evidently waiting for the Captain to say something – after a pause, glancing at him uneasily.*) I'd best be gettin' back aboard the schooner, sir.

(*Receiving no answer he starts for the door on the left.*)

BARTLETT (*rousing himself with an effort*). Wait. (*After a pause.*) The full tide's at dawn to-morrow, ye said?

HORNE. Yes, sir.

BARTLETT. They know we'll be sailin' then, don't they – Cates and Jimmy?

HORNE. Yes, sir. They're all ready. Oh, Cates and Jimmy'll be glad o' the word – and me, too, sir. (*With a greedy grin.*) It's all we've been talking of since ye brought us down here – diggin' up the gold!

BARTLETT (*passionately*). Aye, the gold! We'll have it before long, now, I reckon. That schooner – the way we've fitted her up – she'd take a man safe to the Pole and back! We'll drop anchor here with the chest on board in six months, unless — (*Hesitates.*)

HORNE (*uneasily*). What, sir?

BARTLETT (*brusquely*). The weather, ye fool! Can ye take count before o' storms an' calms?

HORNE. We'll trust to luck for that. (*Glancing at the Captain curiously.*) And speakin' o' luck, sir – the schooner ain't been christened yet.

BARTLETT (*betraying a sudden, fierce determination*). She will be!

HORNE. There'd be no luck for a ship sailin' out without a name.

BARTLETT. She'll have a name, I tell ye! A name that'll take all curse away and leave her clean. She'll be named the Sarah Allen, and Sarah'll christen her herself.

HORNE. It oughter been done, by rights, when we launched her a month back.

BARTLETT (*sternly*). I know that as well as ye.

(*After a pause.*) She wasn't willin' to do it then. Women has queer notions – when they're sick, like. (*Defiantly – as if he were addressing some one outside of the room.*) But Sarah'll be willin' now! She'll be willin' in spite o' — (*Catching himself and abruptly lowering his voice.*) The schooner'll be christened to-morrow at dawn afore she sails.

HORNE. Yes, sir. (*He again turns to go, as if he were anxious to get away.*)

BARTLETT. Wait! There's somethin' else I want to ask ye. Nat, he's been hangin' round the schooner all his spare time o' late. I seen him talkin' to you and Cates and Jimmy. (*With rising anger.*) I hope ye've remembered what I ordered ye, all three. Not a word o' it to him! I said I'd keep him out o' this, for his own good, mind! And if I thought any of ye — (*His fist is raised threateningly, and he glares savagely at Horne.*)

HORNE (*retreating a step – hastily*). No fear o' that, sir! We've been keerful. But it's hard. He's a sharp one, Nat is. And when we tells him the schooner's fitted out for tradin' in the islands, he just laughs. He's gettin' the wind on somethin' – without any o' us sayin' a word.

BARTLETT (*in relieved tones*). Let him s'spect all he's a mind to – as long as he don't know. It ain't that I'm afeerd to tell him o' the gold, Silas Horne. He'll share that, anyway. (*Slowly.*) It's them – other things – I'd keep him clear of.

HORNE (*immediately guessing what he means – reassuringly*). We was all out o' our heads with thirst and sun when them things happened, sir.

BARTLETT. Mad? Aye! But I ain't forgot – them two. (*Harshly.*) I'd rather be you nor me, Silas Horne. You be too rotten bad to care. And I'd rather be Cates or Jimmy. Cates be too dull to remember, and Jimmy be proud as a boy o' what he done. (*He represses a shudder – then goes on slowly.*) Do they ever come back to you – when you're asleep, I mean?

HORNE (*pretending mystification*). Who's that, sir?

BARTLETT (*with sombre emphasis*). That cook and that boy. They come to me. I'm gettin' to be afeerd o' goin' to sleep – not 'feered o' them, I don't mean. (*With sudden defiant bravado.*) Not all the ghosts out o' hell kin keep me from a thing I've set my mind on. (*Collecting himself.*) But I've waked up talkin' out loud – to them – and I'm afeerd there might be some one hear me. That's why I've been sleepin' down here at the boathouse all alone.

HORNE (*uneasily – with an attempt to be reassuring*). You ain't all cured o' that sun and thirst on the island yet, sir.

BARTLETT (*evidently reassured – roughly*). O' course! D'ye think I'd really believe in things in nightmares? (*With an attempt at conviviality.*) Sit down a bit, Horne, and take a grog.

(*Horne does so. Bartlett pours out a half-tumbler full of rum for himself and shoves the bottle over to Horne.*)

HORNE. Luck to our vige, sir.

BARTLETT. Aye, luck! (*They drink. Bartlett leans over and taps Horne on the arm.*) Aye, it takes time to get cured o' thirst and sun! Lucky that tradin' schooner picked us up the time she did.

HORNE. If she hadn't – we'd been as dead men – as them two.

BARTLETT (*sombrely – after a pause*). I spoke no word, Silas Horne, d'ye remember?

HORNE. Nor me. Jimmy did it alone. (*Craftily.*) We'd all three swear Bible oaths to that in any court. And even if ye'd given the word, there ain't no good thinkin' more o' it, sir. Didn't they deserve all they got – that thief o' a cook and that boy? Wasn't they plottin' on the sly to steal the gold?

BARTLETT (*his eyes gleaming*). Aye!

HORNE. And when you said he'd get no share of it, didn't he lie to your face that it wasn't gold, thinkin' we'd leave it be and he'd git it all for himself?

BARTLETT (*with sudden rage*). Aye, brass and junk, he said, the lyin' scum! That's what he keeps sayin' when I see him in sleep! He didn't believe – makin' a mock o' me – an' then he owned up himself 'twas gold! He knew! He lied a-purpose! He was a cunnin' rat – a thief ashore afore they shipped him with us, I reckon.

HORNE (*eagerly*). Most like, sir.

BARTLETT (*rising to his feet – with confident defiance*). They deserved no better nor they got. Let 'em rot! (*Pouring out another drink for himself and Horne.*) We'll drink, an' then ye get back to the ship. Tell Cates and Jimmy we sail at dawn – sure! (*He drinks.*)

HORNE. Luck, sir! (*He drinks. There is a knock at the door on the left, followed by Mrs. Bartlett's voice calling feebly,* "ISAIAH! ISAIAH!" *Bartlett starts but makes no answer. He seems suddenly sunk in gloom again. Horne turns to him questioningly.*) It's Mrs. Bartlett, sir. Shall I open the door?

BARTLETT. No. I ain't aimin' to see her – yet awhile. (*Then with sudden reasonless rage.*) Let her in, damn ye!

(*Horne goes and unhooks the door. Mrs. Bartlett enters. She is a slight, slender little woman of fifty. Sickness, or the inroads of a premature old age, have bowed her shoulders, whitened her hair, and forced her to walk feebly with the aid of a cane. A resolute spirit still flashes from her eyes, however, and there is a look of fixed determination on her face. She stands gazing at her husband. There is something accusing in her stare.*)

BARTLETT (*avoiding her eyes – brusquely*). Well? What is it ye want o' me, Sarah?

MRS. B. I want to speak with you alone, Isaiah.

HORNE. I'll be gettin' back aboard, sir. (*Starts to go.*)

BARTLETT (*in a tone almost of fear*). Wait. I'm goin' with ye. (*Turning to his wife – with a certain rough tenderness.*) Ye oughtn't to walk down the hill here, Sarah. The doctor told ye to rest in the house and save your strength.

MRS. B. I want to speak to you alone, Isaiah. You never come home no more, hardly, so I had to come to ye. (*Accusingly.*) You know it ain't walkin is sappin' my strength, Isaiah.

BARTLETT (*very uneasily*). I've got to work on the schooner, Sarah. That's why I've no time at home.

MRS. B. She'll be sailin' soon?

BARTLETT (*suddenly turning on her defiantly*). Tomorrow at dawn!

MRS. B. (*with her eyes fixed accusingly on his*). And you be goin' with her?

BARTLETT (*in the same defiant tone*). Yes, I be! Who else'd captain her?

MRS. B. On a craft without a name.

BARTLETT. She'll have that name.

MRS. B. No.

BARTLETT. She'll have that name, I tell ye.

MRS. B. No.

BARTLETT (*thoroughly aroused, his will tries to break hers, but finds her unbending. He mutters menacingly*). Ye'll see! We'll talk o' that later, you and me. (*With sudden apprehension.*) But not now. They's plenty o' time yet for that. Come on, Horne, we'll get aboard.

(*Without a further glance at his wife he strides past her and disappears through the doorway, followed by Horne. Mrs. Bartlett sinks down in the chair by the table. She appears suddenly weak and crushed. Then from outside comes a girl's laughing voice. Mrs. Bartlett does not seem to hear, nor to notice Sue and Drew when they enter. Sue is a slender, pretty girl of about twenty, with large blue eyes, reddish-brown hair, and a healthy, sun-tanned, out-of-door complexion. In spite of the slightness of her figure there is a suggestion of great vitality and nervous strength about her. Drew is a well-set-up, tall young fellow of thirty. Not in any way handsome, his boyish face, tanned to a deep brown, possesses an engaging character of healthy, cheerful forcefulness that has its compelling charm. There would be no chance of mistaking him for anything but the ship's officer he is. It is written on his face, his walk, his voice, his whole bearing.*)

SUE (*as they enter*). He'll either be here or on the schooner, Danny. (*Then she sees her mother, with startled amazement.*) Ma! Good heavens, what are you doing here? (*Throwing her arms around her neck and kissing her.*) Don't you know you shouldn't —

MRS. B. (*with a start – turning to her daughter with a forced smile*). There, Sue, now! Don't go scoldin' me. (*Then seeing Drew – in a tone of forced gaiety.*) And if there ain't Danny Drew – back home in port at last! You can kiss an old woman, Danny – without makin' her jealous, I reckon.

DREW (*kissing her – with a smile*). I don't know about that, Ma Bartlett. (*Heartily.*) It certainly seems good to see you again – and be back again myself.

MRS. B. We've been expectin' you right along this past month. Then we read in the paper t'other day where your ship'd reached San Francisco, and we knew you'd be down any day. Sue's been on pins and needles ever since.

SUE (*protestingly*). Ma!

DREW. We were delayed in Valparaiso, waiting for cargo. (*With a grin.*) It's a long time to be away from Sue – four months.

SUE (*laughing*). It seems more like four years!

DREW. You remember, Ma, I left just after the big excitement here – when Captain Bartlett turned up after we'd all heard the *Triton* was wrecked and given him up for lost. That was sure a wonderful surprise when he walked into the house that day.

MRS. B. (*her face clouding – in a tone of deep sorrow*). Yes. (*Drew is surprised and glances at Sue questioningly. She sighs. Mrs. Bartlett gets to her feet with difficulty, assisted by Drew. She forces a smile.*) I've taken on a third leg since you was here, Danny!

SUE. We'll help you back to the house. You can't climb that steep hill alone.

MRS. B. Shucks! I'm sick o' the house. I need sun and fresh air, and to-day's so nice I couldn't stay indoors. I'll take your arm to hold on to, Danny. No, I ain't goin' up to the house yet awhile, so don't you try to bully me into it, Sue. I'm goin' to set in the shade o' this shed out on the wharf and watch your Pa workin' on the schooner. Ain't much time left to see her, Sue. They're sailin' to-morrow at dawn, your Pa says.

SUE. To-morrow! Then – you're going to christen her?

MRS. B. (*with grim determination*). No, I ain't, Sue! (*Catching Drew's glance fixed on her with puzzled curiosity, she immediately attempts to resume her joking tone.*) Shucks! Here's Danny wonderin' what silliness we're talkin' of. It's just this, Danny. Captain Bartlett, he's got a crazy notion in his head that just because his ship was wrecked last vige he'll give up whalin' for life. He's fitted out this little schooner for tradin' in the Islands. More money in that, he says. But I don't agree with no such lunatic notions, and I'm just that stubborn I'm not goin' to set my approval on his craziness by christenin' his ship with my name, like he wants me to. He'd ought to stick to whalin', like he's done all his life. Don't you think so, Danny?

DREW (*embarrassed*). Why, sure – he's rated one of the smartest whaling skippers here on the coast – and I should think —

MRS. B. Just what I tell him – only he's that stubborn. I'd best get out quick while it's still sunny and warm. It's damp in here for an old body.

(*Drew helps her to the door on the left, opens it, and the two go out, followed by Sue, who carries a chair. After a pause, Sue and Drew return. Sue carefully shuts the door after them. Her face is troubled.*)

DREW (*looks at her for a minute, then comes and puts his arm around her and kisses her*). What's the trouble, Sue?

SUE (*trying to force a smile*). Nothing, Danny.

DREW. Oh yes there is! No use putting me off that way. Why, I've felt it hanging about in the air ever since I first looked at your mother.

SUE. Yes, she's failed terribly since you saw her last.

DREW. Oh, I don't mean just sickness – only – did you notice how she had to – force herself – to joke about things? She used to be so cheerful natural. (*Scratching his head in honest puzzlement.*) But – that ain't what I mean, either. What is it, Sue? Maybe I can help somehow. You look worried, too. Pshaw! You can tell me, can't you?

SUE. Why, yes, Danny – of course – if I could tell – only I'm just as puzzled as you over what it comes from.

DREW (*persuasively*). Well, you sit down and tell me what's happened since I've been away. Then maybe we can put our heads together and figure out what's wrong, and turn to to get things shipshape again. (*Sue sits down but does not speak. Drew remarks as if to get her started.*) That schooner's a smart little craft for sailing, I should say. I didn't notice no one about working, though.

SUE. No. They're probably below in the cabin, drinking. That's all they've been doing lately. The schooner's been ready to sail for two weeks – but Pa has kept waiting – I don't know what for. Yes, I do know, too – I think I guess. He's been waiting for Ma to give in and christen the ship with her name. But she won't give in. You heard her.

DREW. Well, I suppose she does take it to heart that he'd give up the business he's been in all his life to go in for something new – at his age.

SUE. He mortgaged the house to get money to buy and fit out this schooner. You know he lost most everything when the *Triton* was wrecked. He'd only had her two years, and she cost him a pile of money. Then, too, he's lost a lot all his life – since he and Ma moved out here from the East – investing in all sorts of silly mining ventures – gold mines that always turned out to be only holes in the ground. As far back as I can remember he's never seemed to care about the whaling business – the oil. Ambergris was what he was after. Finding one chunk of that meant more to him than a full cargo of oil.

DREW (*with a grin*). "Old Ambergris." That's what they call him along the coast – behind his back, of course. I reckon he was sort of prospecting the Pacific Ocean looking for an ambergris mine. (*Apologetically.*) Sounds as if I was making fun of him, but you remember how you'n' me 'n' Nat used to laugh about it together.

SUE. It's past a laughing matter now, Danny.

DREW. And what do you reckon the real trouble is?

SUE. Something between him and Ma – something that only the two of them know. It all seemed to start one morning after you'd left – about a week after he'd come home with those three awful men. During that first week he acted all right – just like he used to – only he'd get talking kind of wild now and then about being glad the *Triton* was lost, and promising we'd all be millionaires once he started making trips on the schooner. Ma didn't seem to mind his going in for trading then. Then, the night of the day he bought the schooner, something must have happened between them. Neither of them came down to breakfast. I went up to Ma, and found her so sick we sent for the doctor. He said she'd suffered a great shock of some kind, although she wouldn't tell him a word. I found Pa down in this shed. He'd moved that cot down here, and said he'd have to sleep here after that because he wanted to be near the schooner. It's been that way ever since. He's slept down here and never come up to the house except at meal-times. He's never been alone with Ma one second since then, I don't believe. And she – she's been trying to corner him, to get him alone. I've noticed it, although she does her best to hide it from Nat and me. And she's been failing, growing weaker and sicker looking every day. (*Breaking down.*) Oh, Danny, these last months have been terrible! I'm so glad you're back again.

DREW (*soothing her*). There! It'll all come out right.

SUE. I'm sure that's why she's crept down here to-day. She's bound she'll see him alone before he sails.

DREW. Well, maybe it's for the best. Maybe when they've had it out, things'll clear up.

SUE. Yes, perhaps. But I can't help feeling – it'll only make it worse.

DREW (*frowning*). Seems to me it must be all your Pa's fault, Sue – whatever it is. Have you tried to talk to him?

SUE. Yes – a good many times; but all he's ever said was: "There's things you wouldn't take interest in, Sue. You'll know when it's time to know." – and then he'd break off by asking me what I'd like most to have in the world if he had piles of money. And then, one time, he seemed to be terribly afraid of something, and he said to me: "You hustle up and marry Danny, Sue. You marry him and get out of this."

DREW (*with an affectionate grin*). That does sound crazy – any man wanting to get rid of you that way. (*A note of entreaty in his voice.*) But I surely wish you'd take his advice, Sue! (*He kisses her.*)

SUE (*with intense longing*). Oh, I wish I could, Danny.

DREW. I've quite considerable saved now, Sue, and it won't be so long before I get my own ship, I'm hoping, now that I've got my master's certificate. I was hoping at the end of this voyage —

SUE. So was I, Danny – but it can't be this time. With Ma so weak, and no one to take care of her but me — (*Shaking her head – in a tone of decision.*) I couldn't leave home now, Danny. It wouldn't be right. I couldn't feel really happy – until this thing – whatever it is – is settled between Pa and Ma and they're just as they used to be again. (*Pleadingly.*) You understand, don't you, Danny?

DREW (*soberly*). Why – surely I do, Sue. (*He pats her hand.*) Only, it's hard waiting. (*He sighs.*)

SUE. I know. It's just as hard for me.

DREW. I thought maybe I could help; but this isn't anything anyone outside your family could mix in. (*Sue shakes her head. He goes on gloomily after a pause.*) What's the matter with Nat? Seems as if he ought to be able to step in and talk turkey to your Pa.

SUE (*slowly*). You'll find Nat changed, too, Danny – changed terribly. He's caught the disease – whatever it is. You know how interested in his work he's been ever since they put him in the designing department down in the shipyard?

DREW. Yes.

SUE (*with emphasis*). Well, all that's changed. He hates it now, or at least he says he does. And when he comes home, he spends all his time prowling around the dock here, talking with those three awful men. And what do you think he told me only the other day? That he was bound he'd throw up his job and make this voyage on the schooner. He even asked me to ask Pa to let him go.

DREW. Your Pa doesn't want him to, eh?

SUE. Why, of course not! Leave a fine position he worked so hard to get just for this crazy notion! Pa'd never let him. He's even ordered him to keep off the schooner and not to talk to those men.

DREW. Funny Nat'd like to go to sea. He's always seemed to want to fight shy of it.

SUE. The terrible part is, he's got Ma worried to death – as if she wasn't upset enough already. She's so afraid he'll go – that Pa'll let him at the last moment. She's always pleading with Nat not to think of it – so that he keeps out of her way, too. Poor Ma! She's only got me to talk to.

DREW. Maybe I can help after all. I can talk to Nat.

SUE (*shaking her head*). He's not the same Nat, Danny.

DREW (*trying to be consoling*). Pshaw, Sue! I think you just get to imagining things. (*As he finishes speaking, the door in the rear opens and Nat appears. He is a tall, loose-framed boy of eighteen, who bears a striking resemblance to his father. His face, like his father's, is large and bony, with deep-set black eyes, an aquiline nose, and a wide, thin-lipped mouth. There is no suggestion in Nat, however, of the older man's physical health and great strength. He appears an indoor product, undeveloped in muscle, with a sallow complexion and stooped shoulders. His thick hair is a deep black. His voice recalls his father's, hollow and penetrating. He is dressed in a grey flannel shirt and corduroy trousers. Drew calls out to him heartily.*) Hello, Nat! Speak of the Devil! Sue and I were just talking about you. (*He goes toward Nat, his hand outstretched.*)

NAT (*comes toward them, meets Drew, and shakes his hand with evident pleasure*). Hello, Danny! You're a sight for sore eyes! (*His manner undergoes a sudden change. He casts a quick, suspicious glance from Drew to his sister.*) You were talking about me? What about?

SUE (*quickly – with a warning glance at Drew*). About your work down at the shipyard.

NAT (*disgustedly*). Oh, that. (*In a tone of reasonless irritation.*) For God's sake, Sue, let me alone about my work. Don't I have to live with the damn thing all day, without your shoving it in my face the minute I get home? I want to forget it – get away!

DREW. Go to sea, eh?

NAT (*suspiciously*). Maybe. Why? What do you mean?

DREW (*warned by a glance from Sue, says carelessly*). Well, that's where you'd be apt to go, isn't it?

NAT (*suspiciously*). That isn't what you were thinking, Danny. (*Turning to his sister – angrily.*) What have you been telling Danny?

SUE. I was talking about the schooner – telling him that she sails to-morrow.

NAT (*dumbfounded*). To-morrow? (*Overcome by sudden, nervous excitement.*) It can't be. How do you know? Who told you?

SUE. Ma. Pa told her.

NAT. Then she's been talking to him – telling him not to take me, I'll bet. (*Angrily.*) Oh, I wish Ma'd mind her own business!

SUE. Nat!

NAT. Well, Sue, how would you like it? I'm not a little boy any more. I know what I want to do. I want to go with them. I want to go more than I've ever wanted anything else in my life before. He – he doesn't want me. He's afraid I — But I think I can force him to — (*He glances at Drew's amazed face and stops abruptly – sullenly.*) Where is Pa?

SUE. He's aboard the schooner.

NAT (*disappointedly*). Then it's no good trying to

see him now. I'll have to wait.

DREW. Sound's funny to hear you talking about going to sea. Why, you always used —

NAT (*wearily*). I know. This is different.

DREW. You want to see the Islands, I suppose?

NAT (*suspiciously*). Maybe. Why not?

DREW. What group is your Pa heading for first?

NAT (*more suspiciously*). You'll have to ask him. Why do you want to know? (*Abruptly.*) You better be getting up to the house, Sue – if we're to have any supper. Danny must be hungry. (*He turns his back on them. They exchange meaning glances.*)

SUE (*with a sigh*). It must be getting late. Come on, Danny. You can see Pa later on. (*They go toward the door in the rear.*) Aren't you coming, Nat?

NAT. No. I'll wait. (*Impatiently.*) Go ahead. I'll be up before long.

DREW. See you later, then, Nat.

NAT. Yes.

(*They go out, rear. Nat paces up and down in a great state of excitement. The door on the left is opened and Bartlett enters. His eyes are wild, as if he had been drinking heavily, but he shows no other effects. Father and son stand looking at one another for a second. Nat takes a step backward as if in fear, then straightens up defiantly.*)

BARTLETT (*slowly*). Is this the way ye mind my orders, boy? I've told ye time an' again not to be sneakin' and spyin' around this wharf.

NAT. I'm not sneaking and spying. I wanted to talk to you, Pa.

BARTLETT (*sits down by the table*). Well, here I be.

NAT. Sue said the schooner sails to-morrow.

BARTLETT. Aye!

NAT (*resolutely*). I want to go with you, Pa.

BARTLETT (*briefly – as if dismissing the matter*). Ye can't. I've told ye that before. Let this be the last time ye ask it.

NAT. But why? Why can't I go?

BARTLETT. Ye've your own work to do – good work. Attend to that and leave me to mine.

NAT. But you always wanted me to go on voyages to learn whaling with you.

BARTLETT. This be different.

NAT (*with excited indignation*). Yes, this is different! Don't I know it? Do you think you can hide that from me? It is different, and that's why I want to go.

BARTLETT. Ye can't, I say.

NAT (*pleadingly*). But why not, Pa? I'm not a boy. I can do a man's work on a ship, or anywhere else.

BARTLETT (*roughly*). Let's have done with talk! Your place is here, with Sue and your Ma, and here you'll stay.

NAT (*angrily*). That isn't any reason. But I know your real one. You're afraid —

BARTLETT (*half-rising to his feet*). Ye say that to me? (*Recovering himself with an effort and settling down again.*) Keep a clapper on your jaw, boy. That's talk I'll not put up with. (*With a touch of uneasiness – forcing a scornful laugh.*) Afeerd! Afeerd o' what? Did ye ever know me to be afeerd?

NAT. Afraid of what I know, of what I might find out if I went with you.

BARTLETT (*with the same forced, uneasy scorn*). And what d'ye think ye'd find out, Nat?

NAT. First of all that it's not a trading venture you're going on. Oh, I'm not a fool! That story is all right to fool the neighbours and girls like Sue. But I know better.

BARTLETT. What d'ye know?

NAT. You're going for something else.

BARTLETT. What would that be?

NAT. I don't know – exactly. Something – on that island.

BARTLETT. What?

NAT. I don't know. But I could guess a lot of things. (*With sudden excitement.*) Ambergris! That's it! Is that it? It must be. That's what you've been hunting for years.

BARTLETT. Aye – and never found! (*He gets to his feet with a forced burst of laughter.*) Ambergris! Ye fool of a boy! Ye got that notion out o' some fool book ye've been reading, didn't ye? And I thought ye'd growed to be a man! (*More and more wild in his forced scorn.*) Ye'll be tellin' me next it's buried treasure I be sailin' after – pirates' gold buried on that island – all in a chest – and a map to guide me with a cross marked on it where the gold is hid! And then they be ghosts guardin' it, ben't they – spirits o' murdered men? They always be, in the books. (*He laughs scornfully.*)

NAT (*gazing at him with fascinated eyes*). No, not that last. That's silly – but I did think you might have found —

BARTLETT (*laughing again*). Treasure? Gold? (*With forced sternness.*) Nat, I be ashamed of ye. Ye've had schoolin', and ye've been doin' a man's work in the world, and doin' it well, and I'd hoped ye'd take my place here to home when I be away, and look after your Ma and Sue. But ye've owned up to bein' little better nor a boy in short britches, dreamin' o' pirates' gold that never was 'cept in books.

NAT. But you – you're to blame. When you first came home you did nothing but talk mysteriously of how rich we'd all be when the schooner got back.

BARTLETT (*roughly*). But what's that to do with silly dreams? It's in the line o' trade I meant.

NAT. But why be so mysterious about trade? There's something you're hiding. You can't say no, because I feel it.

BARTLETT (*insinuatingly – with a crafty glance at his son*). Supposin' in one of them Eastern trading ports I'd run across a bit o' business with a chance for a fortune in it for a man that wasn't afeerd of the law, and could keep his mouth shut?

NAT (*disappointed*). You mean illegal trading?

BARTLETT. I mean what I mean, Nat – and I'd be a fool to tell an overgrown boy, or two women – or any man in the world, for the matter o' that – what I do mean.

NAT (*turning toward the door in the rear – disgustedly*). If it's only that, I don't want to hear it. (*He walks toward the door – stops and turns again to his father.*) No, I don't believe it. That's not like you. You're not telling the truth, Pa.

BARTLETT (*rising to his feet – with a savage sternness in which there is a wild note of entreaty*). I've listened to your fool's talk enough. Get up to the house where ye belong! I'll stand no more o' your meddling in business o' mine. I've been patient with ye, but there's an end to that! Take heed o' what I'm sayin', if ye know what's good for ye! I'd rather see ye dead to-night than sail on that schooner at dawn. I'd kill ye with my own hands first! (*With a sort of sombre pride.*) I'll stand alone in this business and finish it out alone if I go to hell for it. Ye hear me?

NAT (*alarmed by this outburst – submissively*). Yes, Pa.

BARTLETT. Then see that ye heed. (*After a pause – as Nat lingers.*) They'll be waitin' for ye at the house.

NAT. All right. I'll go. (*He turns to the doorway on the left, but before he gets to it, the door is pushed open and Mrs. Bartlett enters. Nat stops, startled*). Ma!

MRS. BARTLETT (*with a forced smile*). Run along, Nat. It's all right. I want to speak with your Pa.

BARTLETT (*uneasily*). You'd best go up with Nat, Sarah. I've work to do.

MRS. BARTLETT (*fixing her eyes on her husband*). I want to talk with you alone, Isaiah.

BARTLETT (*grimly – as if he were accepting a challenge*). As ye like, then.

MRS. BARTLETT (*dismissing Nat with a feeble attempt at a smile*). Tell Sue I'll be comin' up directly, Nat.

NAT (*hesitates for a moment, looking from one to the other uneasily*). All right, Ma. (*He goes out.*)

BARTLETT (*waits for Nat to get out of hearing*). Won't ye set, Sarah? (*She comes forward and sits by the table. He sits by the other side.*)

MRS. BARTLETT (*shuddering as she sees the bottle on the table*). Will drinkin' this poison make you forget, Isaiah?

BARTLETT (*gruffly*). I've naught to forget – leastways naught that's in your mind. But they's things about the stubborn will o' woman I'd like to forget. (*They look at each other across the table. There is a pause. Finally he cannot stand her accusing glance. He looks away, gets to his feet, walks about, then sits down again, his face set determinedly – with a grim smile.*) Well, here we be, Sarah – alone together for the first time since —

MRS. BARTLETT (*quickly*). Since that night, Isaiah.

BARTLETT (*as if he hadn't heard*). Since I come back to you, almost. Did ye ever stop to think o' how strange it be we'd ever come to this? I never dreamed a day'd come when ye'd force me to sleep away from ye, alone in a shed like a mangy dog!

MRS. BARTLETT (*gently*). I didn't drive you away, Isaiah. You came o' your own will.

BARTLETT. Because o' your naggin' tongue, woman – and the wrong ye thought o' me.

MRS. BARTLETT (*shaking her head, slowly*). It wasn't me you ran from, Isaiah. You ran away from your own self – the conscience God put in you that you think you can fool with lies.

BARTLETT (*starting to his feet – angrily*). Lies?

MRS. BARTLETT. It's the truth, Isaiah, only you be too weak to face it.

BARTLETT (*with defiant bravado*). Ye'll find I be strong enough to face anything, true or lie! (*Then protestingly.*) What call have ye to think evil o' me, Sarah? It's mad o' ye to hold me to account for things I said in my sleep – for the damned nightmares that set me talkin' wild when I'd just come home and my head was still cracked with the thirst and the sun I'd borne on that island. Is that right, woman, to be blamin' me for mad dreams?

MRS. BARTLETT. You confessed the rest of what you said was true – of the gold you'd found and buried there.

BARTLETT (*with a sudden fierce exultation*). Aye – that be true as Bible, Sarah. When I've sailed back in the schooner, ye'll see for yourself. There be a big chest o' it, yellow and heavy, and fixed up with diamonds, emeralds and sech, that be worth more, even, nor the gold. We'll be rich, Sarah – rich like I've always dreamed we'd be! There'll be silks and carriages for ye – all the woman's truck in the world ye've a mind to want – and all that Nat and She'll want, too.

MRS. BARTLETT (*with a shudder*). Are you tryin' to bribe me, Isaiah – with a treasure that's been cursed by God?

BARTLETT (*as if he hadn't heard*). D'ye remember long ago, back East, just after we was married, and I was skipper o' my first whalin' ship, how that foreigner come to me with the map o' the pirates' gold and asked me to charter the ship? D'ye remember o' how I'd talk to ye o' findin' ambergris, a pile o' it on one vige that'd make us rich? Ye used to take interest then, and all th' vige with me ye'd be hopin' I'd find it, too.

MRS. BARTLETT. That was my sin o' greed that I'm bein' punished for now.

BARTLETT (*again as if he hadn't heard*). And now when it's come to us at last – bigger nor I ever dreamed on – ye drive me away from ye and say it's cursed.

MRS. BARTLETT (*inexorably*). Cursed with the blood o' the man and boy ye murdered!

BARTLETT (*in a mad rage*). Ye lie, woman! I spoke no word!

MRS. BARTLETT. That's what you kept repeatin' in your sleep, night after night that first week you was home, till I knew the truth, and could bear no more. "I spoke no word!" you kept sayin', as if 'twas your own soul had you at the bar of judgment. And "That cook, he didn't believe 'twas gold," you'd say, and curse him.

BARTLETT (*wildly*). He was lyin', the thief! Lyin' so's he and the boy could steal th' gold. I made him own up he was lyin'. What if it's all true, what ye heard? Hadn't we the right to do away with two thieves? And we was all mad with thirst and sun. Can ye hold madmen to account for the things they do?

MRS. BARTLETT. You wasn't so crazed but you remember.

BARTLETT. I remember I spoke no word, Sarah – as God's my judge!

MRS. BARTLETT. But you could have prevented it with a word, couldn't you, Isaiah? That heathen savage lives in the fear of you. He'd not have done it if —

BARTLETT (*gloomily*). That's woman's talk. There be three o' us can swear in any court I spoke no word.

MRS. BARTLETT. What are courts? Can you swear it to yourself? You can't, and it's that's drivin' you mad, Isaiah. Oh, I'd never have believed it of you for all you said in sleep, if it wasn't for the way you looked and acted out of sleep. I watched you that first week, Isaiah, till the fear of it had me down sick. I had to watch you, you was so strange and fearful to me. At first I kept sayin', 'twas only you wasn't rid o' the thirst and the sun yet. But then, all to once, God gave me sight, and I saw 'twas guilt written on your face, on the queer stricken way you acted, and guilt in your eyes. (*She stares into them.*) I see it now, as I always see it when you look at me. (*She covers her face with her hands with a sob.*)

BARTLETT (*his face haggard and drawn – hopelessly, as if he were too beaten to oppose her further – in a hoarse whisper*). What would ye have me do, Sarah?

MRS. BARTLETT (*taking her hands from her face – her eyes lighting up with religious fervour*). Confess your sin, Isaiah! Confess to God and men, and make your peace and take your punishment. Forget that gold that's cursed and the voyage you be settin' out on, and make your peace. (*Passionately.*) I ask you to do this for my sake and the children's, and your own most of all! I'll get down on my knees, Isaiah, and pray you to do it, as I've prayed to God to send you his grace! Confess and wash your soul of the stain o' blood that's on it. I ask you that, Isaiah – and God asks you – to make your peace with Him.

BARTLETT (*his face tortured by the inward struggle – as if the word strangled him*). Confess and let some one steal the gold! (*This thought destroys her influence over him in a second. His obsession regains possession of him instantly, filling him with rebellious strength. He laughs harshly.*) Ye'd make an old woman o' me, would ye, Sarah? – an old, Sunday go-to-meetin' woman snivvelin' and prayin' to God for pardon! Pardon for what? Because two sneakin' thieves are dead and done for? I spoke no word, I tell ye – but if I had, I'd not repent it. What I've done I've done, and I've never asked pardon o' God or men for aught I've done, and never will. Confess, and give up the gold I've dreamed of all my life that I've found at last! By thunder, ye must think I'm crazed.

MRS. BARTLETT (*seeming to shrivel up on her chair as she sees she has lost – weakly*). You be lost, Isaiah – no one can stop you.

BARTLETT (*triumphantly*). Aye, none'll stop me. I'll go my course alone. I'm glad ye see that, Sarah.

MRS. BARTLETT (*feebly trying to get to her feet*). I'll go home.

BARTLETT. Ye'll stay, Sarah. Ye've had your say, and I've listened to ye; now I'll have mine and ye listen to me. (*Mrs. Bartlett sinks back in her chair exhaustedly. Bartlett continues slowly.*) The schooner sails at dawn on the full tide. I ask ye again and for the last time, will ye christen her with your name afore she sails?

MRS. BARTLETT (*firmly*). No.

BARTLETT (*menacingly*). Take heed, Sarah, o' what ye're sayin'! I'm your husband ye've sworn to obey. By right I kin order ye, not ask.

MRS. BARTLETT. I've never refused in anything that's right – but this be wicked wrong.

BARTLETT. It's only your stubborn woman's spite makes ye refuse. Ye've christened every ship I've ever been skipper on, and it's brought me luck o' a kind, though not the luck I wanted. And we'll christen this one with your own name to bring me the luck I've always been seekin'.

MRS. BARTLETT (*resolutely*). I won't, Isaiah.

BARTLETT. Ye will, Sarah, for I'll make ye. Ye force me to it.

MRS. BARTLETT (*again trying to get up*). Is this the way you talk to me who've been a good wife to you for more than thirty years?

BARTLETT (*commandingly*). Wait! (*Threateningly.*) If ye don't christen her afore she sails, I'll take Nat on the vige along with me. (*Mrs. Bartlett sinks back in her chair, stunned.*) He wants to go, ye know it. He's asked me a hundred times. He s'spects – 'bout the gold – but he don't know for sartin. But I'll tell him the truth o' it, and he'll come with me, unless —

MRS. BARTLETT (*looking at him with terror-stricken eyes – imploringly*). You won't do that, Isaiah? You won't take Nat away from me and drag him into sin? I know he'll go if you give him the word, in spite of what I say. (*Pitifully.*) You be only frightenin' me! You can't be so wicked cruel as that.

BARTLETT. I'll do it, I take my oath – unless —

MRS. BARTLETT (*with hysterical anger*). Then I'll tell him myself – of the murders you did, and —

BARTLETT (*grimly*). And I'll say 'twas done in fair fight to keep them from stealin' the gold! I'll tell him your's is a woman's notion, and he'll believe me, not you. He's his father's son, and he's set to go. Ye know it, Sarah. (*She falls back in the chair hopelessly staring at him with horrified eyes. He turns away and adds after a pause.*) So ye'll christen the Sarah Allen in the mornin' afore she sails, won't ye, Sarah?

MRS. BARTLETT (*in a terrified tone*). Yes – if it's needful to save Nat – and God'll forgive me when He sees my reason. But you – Oh, Isaiah! (*She shudders and then breaks down, sobbing.*)

BARTLETT (*after a pause, turns to her humbly as if asking her forgiveness*). Ye mustn't think hard o' me that I want your name. It's because it's a good woman's name, and I know it'll bring luck to our vige. I'd find it hard to sail without it – the way things be.

MRS. BARTLETT (*getting to her feet – in a state of feverish fear of him*). I'm goin' home.

BARTLETT (*going to her*). I'll help ye to the top o' the hill, Sarah.

MRS. BARTLETT (*shrinking from him in terror*). No. Don't you touch me! Don't you touch me!

(*She hobbles quickly out of the door in the rear, looking back frightenedly over her shoulder to see if he is following as*

The Curtain Falls)

ACT THREE

SCENE. *Dawn of the following morning – exterior of the Bartlett home, showing the main entrance, facing left, toward the harbour. On either side of the door, two large windows, their heavy green shutters tightly closed. In front of the door, a small porch, the roof supported by four white columns. A flight of three steps goes up to this porch from the ground. Two paths lead to the steps through the straggly patches of grass, one around the corner of the house to the rear, the other straight to the left to the edge of the cliff where there is a small projecting iron platform, fenced in by a rail. The top of a steel ladder can be seen. This ladder leads up the side of the cliff from the shore below to the platform. The edge of the cliff extends from the left corner front, half-diagonally back to the right, rear-centre.*

In the grey half-light of the dawn, Horne, Cates, and Jimmy Kanaka are discovered. Horne is standing on the steel platform looking down at the shore below. Cates is sprawled on the ground near by. Jimmy squats on his haunches, his eyes staring out to sea as if he were trying to pierce the distance to the warm islands of his birth. Cates wears dungarees, Jimmy dungaree trousers and a black jersey; Horne the same as in ACT TWO.

CATES (*with sluggish indifference*). Ain't she finished with it yet?

HORNE (*irritably*). No, damn her! I kin see 'em all together on the wharf at the bow o' the schooner. That old crow o' a woman o' his! Why the hell don't she christen her and be done with it and let us make sail?

CATES (*after a pause*). Funny, ain't it – his orderin' us to come up here and wait till it's all done.

HORNE (*angrily*). That's her doin', too. She thinks we ain't good enough to be where she is. (*After a pause.*) But there's nothin' funny to me that he does no more. He's still out o' his head, d'ye know that, Cates?

CATES (*stupidly*). I ain't noticed nothin' diff'rent 'bout him.

HORNE (*scornfully*). He axed me if I ever seen them two in my sleep – that cook and the boy o' the *Triton*. Said he did often.

CATES (*immediately protesting uneasily as if he had been accused*). They was with us in the boat b'fore we fetched the island, that's all 'bout 'em I remember. I was crazy, after.

HORNE (*looking at him with contempt*). So was we all crazy, for the matter o' that. I'll not call ye a liar, Cates, but – a hell o' a man ye be! You wasn't so out o' your head that ye forgot the gold, was ye?

CATES (*his eyes glistening*). That's diff'rent. Any man'd remember that, even if he was crazy.

HORNE (*with a greedy grin*). Aye. That's the one thing I see in my sleep. (*Gloatingly.*) We'll dig it up soon now. In three months we'd ought to be there – an' then we'll be rich, by Christ! (*There is the faint sound of cries from the beach below. Horne starts and turns to look down again.*) They must 'a' finished it. (*Cates and Jimmy come to the edge to look down.*)

JIMMY (*suddenly – with an eager childish curiosity*). That fella wife Captain she make strong fella spell on ship, we sail fast, plenty good wind?

HORNE (*contemptuously*). Aye, that's as near as ye'll come to it. She's makin' a spell. Ye stay here, Jimmy, and tell us when the Old Man is comin'. (*Jimmy remains looking down. Horne motions Cates to follow him, front – then in a low voice, disgustedly.*) Did ye hear that damn fool nigger?

CATES (*grumblingly*). Why the hell is the Old Man givin' him a full share? One piece o' it'd be enough for a nigger like him.

HORNE (*craftily*). There's a way to get rid o' him – if it comes to that. He knifed them two, ye remember.

CATES. Aye.

HORNE. The two o' us can take oath to that in any court.

CATES. Aye.

HORNE (*after a calculating look into his companion's greedy eyes – meaningly*). We're two sane men, Cates – and the other two to share is a lunatic and a nigger. The skipper's showed me where there's a copy o' his map o' the island locked up in the cabin – in case anything happens to him I'm to bring back the gold to his woman, he says. (*He laughs harshly.*) Bring it back! Catch me! The fool! I'll be open with ye, Cates. If I could navigate and find the island myself I wouldn't wait for a cracked man to take me there. No, be damned if I would! Me and you'd chance it alone some way or other.

CATES (*greedily*). The two o' us – share and share alike! (*Then shaking his head warningly.*) But he's a hard man to git the best on.

HORNE (*grimly*). And I be a hard man, too. And he's not right in his head. We'll keep our eyes peeled for a chance. Something may turn up – and maybe —

JIMMY (*turning to them*). Captain, he come.

(*Cates and Horne separate hastily. Bartlett climbs into sight up the ladder to the platform. He is breathing heavily, but his expression is one of triumphant exultation..*)

BARTLETT (*motions with his arms*). Down with ye and git aboard. The schooner's got a name now – a name that'll bring us luck. We'll sail on this tide.

HORNE. Aye – aye, sir.

BARTLETT. I got to wait here till they climb up the path. I'll be aboard afore long. See that ye have her ready to cast off by then.

HORNE. Aye – aye, sir. (*He and Cates disappear down the ladder. Jimmy lingers, looking sidewise at his Captain.*)

BARTLETT (*noticing him – gruffly but almost kindly*). What are ye waitin' for?

JIMMY (*volubly*). That old fella wife belong you, Captain, she make strong fella spell for wind blow plenty? She catch strong devil charm for schooner, Captain?

BARTLETT (*scowling*). What's that, ye brown devil? (*Then suddenly laughing harshly.*) Yes – a strong spell to bring us luck. (*Roughly.*) Git aboard, ye dog! Don't let her find ye here with me.

(*Jimmy disappears hurriedly down the ladder. Bartlett remains at the edge looking down after him. There is a sound of voices from the right and presently Mrs. Bartlett, Sue, Drew and Nat enter, coming around the house from the rear. Nat and Drew walk at either side of Mrs. Bartlett, who is in a state of complete collapse, so that they are practically carrying her. Sue follows, her handkerchief to her eyes. Nat keeps his eyes on the ground, his expression fixed and gloomy. Drew casts a glance of angry indignation at the Captain, who, after one indifferent look at them, has turned back to watch the operations on the schooner below.*)

BARTLETT (*as they reach the steps of the house – intent on the work below – makes a megaphone of his hands and shouts in stentorian tones*). Look lively there, Horne!

SUE (*protestingly*). Pa!

BARTLETT (*wheels about. When he meets his daughter's eyes he controls his angry impatience and speaks gently*). What d'ye want, Sue?

SUE (*pointing to her mother who is being assisted through the door – her voice trembling*). You mustn't shout. She's very sick.

BARTLETT (*dully, as if he didn't understand*). Sick?

SUE (*turning to the door*). Wait. I'll be right back.

(*She enters the house. As soon as she is gone all of Bartlett's excitement returns. He paces up and down with nervous impatience. Nat comes out of the house.*)

NAT (*in a tone of anxiety*). Ma seems bad. We can't do anything. I'm going for the doctor. (*As his father doesn't seem to hear him – tapping him on the shoulder, his voice breaking.*) Why did you make her do it, Pa? It was too much for her strength.

Wouldn't anyone else or any other name have done just as well?

BARTLETT (*impatiently*). No. It had to be.

NAT. When she spoke the words – and fell back in a faint – I thought she was dead.

BARTLETT (*vaguely*). Weakness. She'll be all right again after a rest. (*He draws Nat's attention to the schooner.*) Smart lines on that schooner, boy. She'll sail hell bent in a breeze. I knowed what I was about when I bought her.

NAT (*staring down fascinatedly*). How long will the voyage take?

BARTLETT (*preoccupied*). How long?

NAT (*insinuatingly*). To get to the island.

BARTLETT. Three months at most – with fair luck. (*Exultantly*). And I'll have luck now!

NAT. Then in six months you may be back – with *it*?

BARTLETT. Aye, with — (*Stopping abruptly, turns and stares into his son's eyes – angrily*). With what? What boy's foolishness be ye talkin'?

NAT (*pleading fiercely*). I want to go, Pa! There's no good in my staying here any more. I can't think of anything but — Oh, why don't you be fair and let me sail with you!

BARTLETT (*sternly, to conceal his uneasiness*). Keep clear o' this, boy, I've warned ye!

SUE (*appearing in doorway – indignantly*). Nat! Haven't you gone for the doctor yet?

NAT (*shamefacedly*). I forgot.

SUE. Forgot!

NAT (*starting off*). I'm going, Sue. (*Then over his shoulder.*) You won't sail before I come back, Pa? (*Bartlett does not answer. Nat stands miserably hesitating.*)

SUE. Nat! For heaven's sake!

(*Nat hurries off around the corner of the house, rear. Sue comes to her father who is watching her with a queer, humble, hunted expression.*)

BARTLETT. Well, Sue?

SUE (*her voice trembling*). Oh, Pa, how can you do such terrible things. How could you drag Ma out of bed at dawn to christen your old boat – when you knew how sick she's been!

BARTLETT (*avoiding her eyes*). It's only weakness. She'll get well o' it soon.

SUE. Pa! How can you say things like that – as if you didn't care! (*Accusingly.*) The way you've acted ever since you've been home almost, anyone would think – you *hated* her!

BARTLETT (*wincing*). No!

SUE. Oh, Pa, what is it that has come between you? Can't you tell me? Can't I help to set things right again?

BARTLETT (*mumblingly*). Nothin' – nothin' ye kin help – nor me. Keep clear o' it, Sue. Danny – ye think o' him, that's enough for ye.

SUE. But things can't go on like this. Don't you see how it's killing Ma?

BARTLETT. She'll forget her stubborn notions, now I be sailin' away.

SUE. But you're not – not going for a while now, are you?

BARTLETT. Ain't I been sayin' I'd sail at dawn to-day? They're makin' her ready to cast off. I'm waitin' for Horne to hail.

SUE (*looking at him for a moment with shocked amazement*). But – you can't mean – right now!

BARTLETT (*keeping his face averted*). Aye – or we'll miss this tide.

SUE (*putting her hands on his shoulders and trying to look into his face*). Pa! You can't mean that! (*His face is set with his obsessed determination. She lets her hands fall with a shudder.*) You can't be as cruel as that! Why, I thought, of course, you'd put off — (*Wildly.*) You have, haven't you, Pa? You did tell those men you couldn't sail when you saw how sick Ma was, didn't you – when she fainted down on the wharf?

BARTLETT (*implacably*). I said I was sailin' by this tide – and sail I will, by thunder!

SUE. Pa! (*Then pleadingly.*) When the doctor comes and you hear what he says —

BARTLETT (*roughly*). I ain't stoppin' on his word nor any man's. I know what's best to do. (*Intensely.*) That schooner's been fit to sail these two weeks past. I been waitin' on her stubborn will (*he gestures toward the house*), eatin' my heart out day and night. Then I swore I'd sail to-day. I tell ye, Sue, I got a feelin' in my bones if I don't put out now I never will. Aye, I feel it deep down inside me. (*In a tone of superstitious awe.*) And when she christened the schooner – jest to the minute, mind ye! – a fair breeze sprung up and come down out o' the land to blow her out to sea – like a sign o' good luck.

SUE (*aroused to angry indignation*). What kind of a man have you become – to think of such things now! Oh, I can't believe you're the same man who used to be my father!

BARTLETT. Sue!

SUE. To talk cold-bloodedly of sailing away on a long voyage when Ma's inside – dying for all you seem to know or care! Oh, I hate you when you're like this! You're not the father I love! You've changed into some one else – hateful and cruel – and I hate him, I hate him! (*She breaks down, sobbing hysterically.*)

BARTLETT (*who has listened to her with a face suddenly stricken by fear and torturing remorse*). Sue! Ye don't know what ye be sayin', do ye?

SUE. I do! You're not the same to me any more – or to any of us. I'm afraid of you. And when you coldly propose to go away – now – I hate you, yes I do! And I hate those three awful men who make you act this way. I hate the schooner! I wish she and they were at the bottom of the sea!

BARTLETT (*frenziedly – putting his hand over her mouth to stop her words*). Stop, girl! Don't ye dare —

SUE (*shrinking away from him – frightenedly*). Pa!

BARTLETT (*bewilderedly, pleading for forgiveness*). Don't heed that, Sue – I didn't mean – ye git me so riled – I'd not hurt ye for all the gold in the world. But don't ye talk wrong o' things ye can't know on.

SUE. Oh, Pa, what kind of things must they be – when you're ashamed to tell them!

BARTLETT. I ain't ashamed. It ain't that. On'y they be things a girl's no call to meddle in. They be men's business and I be man enough to carry 'em out alone. Ye'll know all they be to know – and your Ma and Nat, too – when I come back from this vige. And the sooner I sail, the quicker I'll be back to ye. Oh, ye'll be glad enough then – when ye see with your own eyes! Ye'll bless me then 'stead o' turning agin me! (*Hesitating for a second – then sombrely.*) On'y now – till it's all over and done – ye'd best keep clear o' it.

SUE (*passionately*). I don't care – I don't want to know anything about it. What I do know is that you can't sail now. Oh, Pa, don't you see you can't? Haven't you any heart at all? Can't you see how bad Ma is?

BARTLETT. It's the sight o' me sickens her. She'll git better with me away from her.

SUE. No. She needs you. She doesn't want you to go. She called your name just a while ago – the only word she's spoken since she christened the ship. Come in to her, Pa! Tell her you won't go!

BARTLETT (*desperately*). I got to git away from her, I tell ye, Sue! She's been houndin' me ever since I got back – houndin' me with her stubborn tongue till she's druv me mad, a'most! Ye've been on'y givin' thought to her, not me. They's my side to it, too!

SUE. I'll talk to her, Pa. She can't realize she's hurting you or she wouldn't — And then everything will be just the same as it used to be again.

BARTLETT (*shaking his head*). They be too much between. The only chance for that be my plan – to sail away and come back with – what I be seekin'. Then she'll give over her stubborn naggin' – if she's human woman. It's for her sake as much as my own I'm goin' – for her and you and Nat. (*With a sudden return of his old resolution.*) I've made up my mind, I tell ye, and in the end ye'll know I be right. (*A hail in Horne's voice comes thinly up from the shore below. Bartlett starts, his eyes gleaming.*) Ye hear? It's Horne hailin' me to come. They be ready to cast off. I'll git aboard. (*He starts for the ladder.*)

SUE. Pa! After all I've said – without one word of good-bye to Ma! (*Hysterically.*) Oh, what can I do, what can I say to stop you! She hasn't spoken but that one call for you. She hardly seems to breathe. If it weren't for her eyes I'd believe she was dead – but her eyes look for you. She'll die if you go, Pa!

BARTLETT. No!

SUE. You might just as well kill her now in cold blood as murder her that way!

BARTLETT (*shaken – raising his hands as if to put them over his ears to shut out her words – hoarsely*). No! Ye lie! She'll live till I git back and all'll be as it was again!

DREW (*appearing in the doorway, his face working with grief and anger – harshly*). Captain Bartlett! (*Then lowering his voice as he sees Sue.*) Mrs. Bartlett is asking to see you, Captain, before you go.

SUE. There! Didn't I tell you, Pa!

BARTLETT (*struggling with himself – dully*). She's wantin' to hound me again, that be all.

SUE (*seeing him weakening – grasps his hand persuasively*). Pa! Come with me. She won't hound you. How silly you are! Come! (*Hesitatingly, head bowed, he follows her toward the door.*)

BARTLETT (*as he comes to Drew he stops and looks into the young man's angry, accusing face. He mutters half-mockingly*). So ye, too, be agin me, Danny?

DREW (*unable to restrain his indignation*). What man that's a real man wouldn't be against you, sir?

SUE (*frightenedly*). Danny! Pa!

BARTLETT (*in a sudden rage draws back his fist threateningly. Drew stares into his eyes unflinchingly – Bartlett controls himself with an effort and lets his arm fall to his side – scornfully*). Big words from a boy, Danny. I'll forget them this time – on account o' Sue. (*He turns to her.*) I'm goin' in to her to please ye, Sue – but if ye think any words that she kin say'll change my mind, ye make a mistake – for I be sailin' out as I planned I would in spite o' all hell! (*He walks resolutely into the house. Sue follows him after exchanging a hopeless glance with Danny.*)

DREW (*to himself – with a shudder*). He's mad, damn him!

(*He paces up and down. Horne appears on the ladder from below, followed by Cates.*)

HORNE (*coming forward and addressing Drew*). Is the skipper about?

DREW (*curtly*). He's in the house. You can't speak to him now.

HORNE. She's ready to cast off. I hailed him from below, but I 'spect he didn't hear. (*As Drew makes no comment – impatiently.*) If he don't shake a leg, we'll miss the tide. There's a bit o' fair breeze, too.

DREW (*glancing at him resentfully*). Don't count on his sailing to-day. It's just as likely he'll change his mind.

HORNE (*angrily*). Change his mind again? After us waitin' and wastin' time for weeks! (*To Cates in a loud tone so Drew can hear.*) What did I tell ye, Cates? He's crazy as hell.

DREW (*sharply*). What's that?

HORNE. I was tellin' Cates the skipper's not right in his head. (*Angrily.*) What man in his senses'd do the way he does?

DREW (*letting his resentment escape him*). That's no lie, damn it!

HORNE (*surprised*). Aye, ye've seen it, too, have ye? (*After a pause.*) Now I axe ye, as a sailor, how'd ye like to be puttin' out on a vige with a cracked man for skipper?

(*Sue comes out of the door, stops with a shudder of disgust as she sees the two sailors, and stands listening. They do not notice her presence.*)

DREW. It seems to me a crazy voyage all round. What kind of trading is it you're to do?

HORNE (*suspiciously*). Ye'll have to ask the skipper that.

DREW (*with a scornful shrug*). I was forgetting it's such a dead secret. That the craziest part, eh? (*With sudden interest as if a new idea had come to him.*) But you know all about it, don't you – what the Captain plans to do on this voyage – and all that?

HORNE (*dryly*). Aye, as well as himself – but I'm tellin' no man.

DREW. And I'm not asking. What do you suppose I care about any sneaking trade deal in the Islands he may have up his sleeve? What I want to find out is: Do you know enough about this business to make this one voyage alone and attend to everything – in case the Captain can't go?

HORNE (*exchanging a quick glance with Cates – trying to hide his eagerness*). Aye, I could do as well as any man alive. I've been sailin' this sea for twenty year or more and I know the Island trade inside and out. He could trust me for it – and I'd make more money for him than he's likely to make with his head out o' gear. (*Then scowling.*) On'y trouble is, who'd captain her if he ain't goin'?

DREW (*disappointedly*). Then you don't know navigation enough for that?

HORNE. I've never riz above bo'sun. (*Then after a pause in which he appears to be calculating something – curiously.*) Why d'ye ask me them questions? (*Insinuatingly – almost in a whisper.*) It can't be done 'less we got an officer like you aboard.

DREW (*angrily*). Eh? What're you driving at? D'you think I —

SUE (*who has been listening with aroused interest*). Danny! (*She comes down to him. Horne and Cates bob their heads respectfully and move back near the platform. Horne watches Sue and Drew out of the corner of his eye.*) Danny, I've been listening to what you were saying, but I don't understand. What are you thinking of?

DREW (*excitedly*). I was thinking — Listen, Sue! Seems to me from what I saw your Pa's out of his right mind, and, being that way, he's sure bound to go unless some one or something steps in to stop him. D'you think your Ma — ?

SUE (*shaking her head – sadly*). No, I'm afraid anything she says will only make things worse.

DREW. Then you've no hope — ? No more have I. Something's got to be done to keep him home in spite of himself. Even leaving your Ma out of it, he's not in any fit state to take a ship to sea; and I was thinking if we could fix it some way so that fellow Horne could take her out on this voyage —

SUE. But, Danny, Pa'd never give in to that.

DREW. I wasn't thinking he would. It'd have to be done on the sly. We – you'd have to give the word – and keep him in the house somehow – and then when he did come out it'd be too late. The schooner'd be gone.

SUE (*disturbed, but showing that his plan has caught her mind*). But – would it be fair? – he'd never forgive —

DREW. When he's back in his right mind again, he would. (*Earnestly.*) I'm not fond of lying and tricks myself, Sue, but this is a case where you can't pick and choose. You can't let him sail, and wreck his ship and himself in the bargain, likely. Then, there's your Ma —

SUE. No, no, we can't let him. (*With a glance at Horne and Cates.*) But I don't trust those men.

DREW. No more do I; but it would be better to chance them than — (*Suddenly interrupting himself – with a shrug of his shoulders.*) But there's no good talking of that. I was forgetting. None of them can navigate. They couldn't take her out.

SUE. But didn't I hear him say – if they had an officer on board – like you —

DREW. Yes, but where'll you find one at a second's notice?

SUE (*meaningly*). And you told me, didn't you, that you'd just got your master's papers. Then you're a captain by rights.

DREW (*looking at her with stunned astonishment*). Sue! D'you mean —

SUE (*a light coming over her face*). Oh, Danny, we could trust you! He'd trust you! And after he'd calmed down I know he wouldn't mind so much. Oh, Danny, it'll break my heart to have you go, to send you away just after you've come back. But I don't see any other way. I wouldn't ask – if it wasn't for Ma being this way – and him — Oh, Danny, can't you see your way to do it – for my sake?

DREW (*bewilderedly*). Why, Sue, I – I never thought — (*Then as he sees the look of disappointment which comes over her face at his hesitancy – resolutely.*) Why sure, Sue, I'll do it – if you want me to. I'll do it if it can be done. But we've got to hustle. You stand in the door, Sue. You've got to keep him in the house some way if he aims to come out. And I'll talk to them.

(*Sue goes to the doorway. Drew goes over to Horne and Cates.*)

SUE (*after listening*). He's still in with Ma. It's all right.

DREW (*to Horne, with forced joviality*). How would you like me for skipper on this one voyage?

HORNE (*craftily*). Ye got your skipper's papers all reg'lar?

DREW. Yes, that part of it's all right and square. Listen here. Miss Sue's decided her father isn't in a fit state to captain this trip. It'd mean danger for him and the schooner – and for you.

HORNE. That's no lie.

CATES (*to Horne protestingly*). But if we git ketched the Old Man'll take it out o' our hides, not his'n.

HORNE (*savagely*). Shut up, ye fool! (*To Drew, craftily.*) Cates is right, jest the same. Ye are as good as his married son and she's his daughter. He'd not blame you if things went wrong. He'd take it out on us.

DREW (*impatiently*). I'll shoulder all that risk, man!

SUE (*earnestly*). No harm will come to any of you, I promise you. This is all my plan, and I'll tell my father I'm alone to blame.

HORNE (*in the tone of one clinching a bargain*).

Then we'll chance it. (*Warningly.*) But it's got to be done smart, sir. Ye'd best look lively.

DREW. I've got to get my dunnage. I'll be right back and we'll tumble aboard. (*He goes to the door.*) Hold him, Sue, on some excuse if he's coming. Only a second now and it'll all be safe. (*He goes into the house. She follows him in.*)

CATES (*with stupid anger*). This is a hell o' a mess we're gettin' in, if ye axe me.

HORNE. And I tell ye it's a great stroke o' luck. It couldn't o' come out better.

CATES. He'll be aboard to spy on us.

HORNE. Let him! What does he know? He thinks we're goin' tradin', and there's no one to tell him diff'rent but me.

CATES. He'll know better afore long. He'll s'pect —

HORNE. 'Bout the gold? He ain't that kind. He's a soft young swab o' a lady steamer's mate. Leave me to fool him. And when the time comes to git rid o' him, I'll find a means some way or other. But can't ye see, ye fool, it's luck to have him with us till we git clear o' civilized ports? He kin navigate and he's got skipper's papers that'll come in handy if there's any trouble. And if anythin' goes wrong at the start and we're brung back, him and the girl'll take the blame.

CATES (*stupidly*). S'long as he don't git no share o' the gold —

HORNE (*contemptuously*). Share, ye dumbhead! I'd see him in hell first – and send him there myself.

(*Drew comes out of the house carrying his bag which he hands to Cates. Sue follows him.*)

DREW. Look lively now! Let's hustle aboard and get her under way.

HORNE. Aye – aye, sir. (*He and Cates clamber hurriedly down the ladder.*)

SUE (*throwing her arms around his neck and kissing him*). Good-bye, Danny. It's so fine of you to do this for us! I'll never forget —

DREW (*tenderly*). Ssssh! It's nothing, Sue.

SUE (*tearfully*). Oh, Danny, I hope I'm doing right! I'll miss you so dreadfully! But you'll come back just as soon as you can —

DREW. Of course!

SUE. Danny! Danny! I love you so!

DREW. And I guess you know I love you, don't you? (*Kisses her.*) And we'll be married when I come back this time *sure?*

SUE. Yes – yes – Danny – sure!

DREW. I've got to run. Good-bye, Sue.

SUE. Good-bye, dear.

(*They kiss for the last time and he disappears down the ladder. She stands at the top, sobbing, following him with her eyes. Nat comes around the house from the rear and goes to the front door.*)

NAT (*seeing his sister*). Sue! He hasn't gone yet, has he?

(*She doesn't hear him. He hesitates in the doorway for a moment, listening for the sound of his father's voice from inside. Then, very careful to make no noise, he tiptoes carefully into the house. Sue waves her hand to Drew who has evidently now got aboard the ship. Then she covers her face with her hands, sobbing. Nat comes out of the house again and goes to his sister. As she sees him approaching, she dries her eyes hastily, trying to smile.*)

SUE. Did you get the doctor, Nat?

NAT. Yes, he's coming right away, he promised. (*Looking at her face.*) What – have you been crying?

SUE. No.

(*She walks away from the edge of the cliff, drawing him with her.*)

NAT. Yes, you have. Look at your eyes.

SUE. Oh, Nat, everything's so awful! (*She breaks down again.*)

NAT (*trying to comfort her in an absent-minded way*). There, don't get worked up. Ma'll be all right as soon as the doctor comes. (*Then curiously.*) Pa's inside with her. They were arguing – have they made it up, d'you think?

SUE. Oh, Nat, I don't know. I don't think so.

NAT. The strain's been too much for him – waiting and hiding his secret from all of us. What do you suppose it is, Sue – ambergris?

SUE (*wildly*). I don't know and I don't care! (*Noticing the strange preoccupied look in his eyes – trying to bring him back to earth – scornfully.*)

Ambergris! Are you going crazy? Don't you remember you've always been the first one to laugh at that silly idea?

NAT. Well, there's something — (*Starts for the platform. Sue does her best to interpose to hold him back.*) Are they all ready on the schooner. He'll have to hurry if she's going to sail on this tide. (*With sudden passion.*) Oh, I've got to go! I can't stay here! (*Pleadingly.*) Don't you think, Sue, if you were to ask him for me he'd — You're the only one he seems to act sane with or care about any more.

SUE. No! I won't! I can't!

NAT (*angrily*). Haven't you any sense? Wouldn't it be better for every one if I went in his place?

SUE. No. You know that's a lie. Ma would lose her mind if you went.

NAT. And I'll lose mine if I stay! (*Half-aware of Sue's intention to keep him from looking down at the schooner – irritably.*) What are you holding my arm for, Sue? I want to see what they're doing. (*He pushes her aside and goes to the platform – excitedly.*) Hello, they've got the fores'l and mains'l set. They're setting the stays'l. (*In amazement.*) Why – they're casting off! She's moving away from the wharf! (*More and more excitedly.*) I see four of them on board! Who – who is that, Sue?

SUE. It's Danny.

NAT (*furiously*). Danny! What right has he – when I can't! Sue, call Pa! They're sailing, I tell you, you little fool!

SUE (*trying to calm him – her voice trembling*). Nat! Don't be such a donkey! Danny's only going a little way – just trying the boat to see how she sails while they're waiting for Pa.

NAT (*uncertainly*). Oh. (*Then bitterly.*) I was never allowed to do even that – his own son! Look, Sue, that must be Danny at the stern waving.

SUE (*brokenly*). Yes.

(*She waves her handkerchief over her head – then breaks down, sobbing again. There is the noise of Bartlett's voice from inside and a moment later he appears in the doorway. He seems terribly shattered, at the end of his tether. He hesitates uncertainly, looking about him wildly as if he didn't know what to do or where to go.*)

SUE (*after one look at his face, runs to him and flings her arms about his neck*). Pa! (*She weeps on his shoulder.*)

BARTLETT. Sue, ye did wrong beggin' me to see her. I knowed it'd do no good. Ye promised she'd not hound me — "Confess," she says – when they be naught to tell that couldn't be swore to in any court. "Don't go on this vige," she says, "there be the curse o' God on it." (*With a note of baffled anguish.*) She kin say that after givin' the ship her own name! (*With wild, haggard defiance.*) But curse or no curse, I be goin'!

(*He moves toward the platform, Sue clinging to his arm.*)

SUE (*frightenedly*). Pa! Go back in the house, won't you?

BARTLETT. I be sorry to go agin your will, Sue, but it's got to be. Ye'll know the reason some day – and be glad o' it. And now good-bye to ye. (*With a sudden strange tenderness he bends and kisses his daughter. Then as she seems about to protest further, his expression becomes stern and inflexible.*) No more o' talk, Sue! I be bound out. (*He takes her hand off his arm and strides to the platform. One look down at the harbour and he stands transfixed – in a hoarse whisper.*) What damned trick be this? (*He points to the schooner and turns to Nat bewilderedly.*) Ain't that my schooner, boy – the *Sarah Allen* – reachin' toward the p'int?

NAT (*surprised*). Yes, certainly. Didn't you know? Danny's trying her to see how she sails while they're waiting for you.

BARTLETT (*with a tremendous sigh of relief*). Aye. (*Then angrily.*) He takes a lot o' rope to himself without askin' leave o' me. Don't he know they's no time to waste on boy's foolin'? (*Then with admiration.*) She sails smart, don't she, boy? I knowed she'd show a pair o' heels.

NAT (*with enthusiasm*). Yes, she's a daisy! Say, Danny's taking her pretty far out, isn't he?

BARTLETT (*anxiously*). He'd ought to come about now if he's to tack back inside the p'int. (*Furiously.*) Come about, damn ye! The swab! That's what comes o' steamer trainin'. I'd sooner trust Sue to sail her nor him. (*Waves his arm and shouts.*) Come about!

NAT (*bitterly*). He seems to be heading straight for the open sea. He's taking quite a sail, it seems to me.

BARTLETT (*as if he couldn't believe his eyes*). He's passed the p'int – and now – headin' her out to sea – so'east by east. By God, that be the course I charted for her! (*Sue bursts out sobbing. He wheels on her, his mouth fallen open, his face full of a stupid despair.*) They be somethin' wrong here. What be it, Sue? What be it, Nat? (*His voice has begun to quiver with passion.*) That schooner – she's sailin' without me — (*He suddenly springs at Nat and grabs him by the throat – with hoarse fury, shaking him.*) What be it, ye whelp? It's your doin' – because I wouldn't let ye go. Answer me!

SUE (*rushing to them with a scream*). Pa!

(*She tugs frantically at his hands. Bartlett lets them fall to his side, stepping back from Nat who sinks weakly to the ground, gasping for breath. Bartlett stands looking at him wildly.*)

Nat didn't know, Pa. It's all my fault. I had to do it. There was no other way —

BARTLETT (*raging*). What d'ye mean, girl? What is it ye've done? Tell me, I say! Tell me or I'll —

SUE (*unflinchingly*). You had to be stopped from going some way. You wouldn't listen to reason. So I asked Danny if he wouldn't make the trip in your place. He's just got his captain's papers – and oh, Pa, you can trust him, you know that! That man Horne said he knows about everything you wanted done, and he promised to tell Danny, and Danny'll come back —

BARTLETT (*chokingly*). So – that be it — (*Shaking his clenched fist at the sky as if visualizing the fate he feels in all of this.*) Curse ye! Curse ye!

(*He subsides weakly, his strength spent, his hand falls limply at his side.*)

MRS. BARTLETT (*appears in the doorway. Her face is pale with anguish. She gives a cry of joy when she sees her son.*) Nat! (*Then with a start of horror as her eyes fall on her husband.*) Isaiah! (*He doesn't seem to hear.*) Then – you ain't sailed yet?

SUE (*going to her – gently*). No, Ma, he isn't going to sail. He's going to stay home with you. But the schooner's gone. See.

(*She points and her mother's eyes turn seaward.*)

BARTLETT (*aloud to himself – in a tone of groping superstitious awe and bewildered fear*). They be somethin' queer – somethin' wrong – they be a curse in this somewhere —

MRS. BARTLETT (*turning accusing eyes on him – with a sort of fanatical triumph*). I'm glad to hear you confess that, Isaiah. Yes, there be a curse – God's curse on the wicked sinfulness o' men – and I thank God He's saved you from the evil of that voyage, and I'll pray Him to visit His punishment and His curse on them three men on that craft you forced me to give my name —

(*She has raised her hand as if calling down retribution on the schooner she can dimly see.*)

SUE (*terrified*). Ma!

BARTLETT (*starting toward his wife with an insane yell of fury*). Stop it, I tell ye!

(*He towers over her with upraised fist as if to crush her.*)

SUE. Pa!

NAT (*starting to his feet from where he has been sitting on the ground – hoarsely*). Pa! For God's sake!

MRS. BARTLETT (*gives a weak, frightened gasp*). Would you murder me too, Isaiah?

(*She closes her eyes and collapses in Sue's arms.*)

SUE (*tremblingly*). Nat! Help me! Quick! We must carry her to bed.

(*They take their mother in their arms, carrying her inside the house.*)

BARTLETT (*while they are doing this, rushes in his mad frenzy to the platform over the edge of the cliff. He puts his hands to his mouth, megaphone-fashion, and yells with despairing rage*). Ahoy! Ahoy! *Sarah Allen!* Put back! Put back! (*as*

The Curtain Falls)

ACT FOUR

SCENE. *About nine o'clock of a moonlight night one year later – Captain Bartlett's "cabin," a room erected on the top of his house as a look-out post. The interior is fitted up like the cabin of a sailing vessel. On the left, forward, a porthole. Farther back, the stairs of the companionway. Still farther, two more portholes. In the rear, left, a marble-topped sideboard. In the rear, centre, a door opening on stairs which lead to the lower house. A cot with a blanket is placed against the wall to the right of door. In the right wall, five portholes. Directly under them, a wooden bench. In front of the bench, a long table with two chairs placed, one in front, one to the left of it. A cheap, dark-coloured rug is on the floor. In the ceiling, midway from front to rear, a skylight extending from opposite the door to above the left edge of the table. In the right extremity of the skylight is placed a floating ship's compass. The light from the binnacle sheds down over this and seeps into the room, casting a vague globular shadow of the compass on the floor. Moonlight creeps in through the portholes on the right. A lighted lantern is on the table.*

As the curtain rises, Sue and Doctor Berry are discovered sitting by the table. The doctor is a man of sixty or so, hale and hearty-looking, his white hair and moustache setting off his ruddy complexion. His blue eyes have a gentle expression, his smile is kindly and sympathetic. His whole manner toward Sue is that of the old family doctor and friend, not the least of whose duties is to play father-confessor to his patients. She is dressed in deep mourning. She looks much older. Her face is pale and plainly marked by the ravages of suffering and grief. But there is an excited elation in her face at present, her eyes are alight with some unexpected joy.

SUE (*excitedly*). And here is Danny's letter, Doctor – to prove it's all true. (*She takes a letter from the bosom of her dress and holds it out to him.*)

DOCTOR (*takes it with a smile, patting her hand*). I can't say how glad I am, Susan. Coming after we'd all given him up for lost – it's like a miracle. Eh, well, I can hardly believe —

SUE (*smiling happily*). Read what he says. Then you won't doubt.

DOCTOR (*hesitating – playfully*). I don't know that it's right for me – love-letters at my age!

SUE. Go ahead. I want you to read it. (*He reaches in his pocket for his spectacles. Sue continues gratefully.*) As if I could have any secrets from you after all you've done for us since Ma died. You've been the only friend — (*She stops, her lips trembling.*)

DOCTOR. Tut-tut. (*He adjusts his spectacles and peers at her over them.*) Who wouldn't be of all the service he could to a brave girl like you – and I who've known you since you were so high! Eh, well, my dear girl, this past year – with your mother's death – the state your father's in – and then the news of the schooner being reported lost – one damn thing on top of another! You've borne the whole brunt of it on your shoulders and stood up like a major. I'll tell Danny when he comes he ought to get down on his knees and thank God for getting such a wife!

SUE (*flushing*). You're too good. I don't deserve it. It was just a case where some one had to carry things on.

DOCTOR. Not many could have stood it – living in this house with him the way he is – even if he was their father.

SUE (*glancing up at the skylight – apprehensively*). Ssshh! He might hear you.

DOCTOR (*listening intently*). Not him. There he goes pacing up and down up there in the night, looking out to sea for that ship that will never come back! And your brother Nat is getting just as bad. (*Shaking himself.*) Brrr! This house of mad dreams! It's the crowning wonder to me you haven't lost your balance too – spending nearly all of your time in this crazy cabin – afraid to go out – afraid of what he might do —

SUE. Don't you think Pa'll come to realize the schooner is lost as time goes by and she doesn't come back?

DOCTOR. If he was going to realize that, the report of the facts five months ago would have convinced him. There it was, plain as the nose on your face. British freighter reports finding derelict schooner. Steams near enough to read the name on the stern – *Sarah Allen*, Harbourport. Well, who could get around that evidence except a man with an obsession? No, your father won't let himself look the facts in the face. If he did, probably the shock of it would kill him. That darn dream of his has become his life. No, Susan, as time goes on he'll believe in it harder and harder. After observing him for the past year – and I speak for his own sake, too, as his good friend for twenty years or more – my final advice is the same: Send him to an asylum.

SUE (*with a shudder*). No, Doctor.

DOCTOR (*shaking his head*). You'll have to come to it in time. He's getting worse. No one can tell – he might get violent —

SUE. How can you say that? You know how gentle and sane he is with me – just like he used to be in the old days.

DOCTOR. You're his last connecting link with things as they are – but that can't last. On the other hand, I think that if we got him away from the sea, from this house, especially from this crazy cabin and the ship's deck he had built up there – (*he nods upward*) – that perhaps —

SUE (*with conviction*). No. It would kill him to leave it.

DOCTOR. Eh, well, my dear, one thing you've got to realize: Your father and Nat must be separated somehow. Nat's going to pieces. He's lost his job, he moons about this house, he takes no interest in anything but this craziness. I'll bet he doesn't believe that schooner is lost any more than your father does.

SUE. You mean he still hopes it may not be true. That's only natural. He's in San Francisco now tracing down the report again. He saw in the papers where the British freighter that found the derelict was in port again and he went to talk with the people on board. I'm hoping he'll come back fully convinced, with the whole thing out of his mind.

DOCTOR (*shaking his head – gravely*). I've watched him and talked with him — Why, even your father seems to realize, in his twisted way, that he has a bad effect on Nat.

SUE. Yes, as I've told you before, he hasn't spoken to Nat alone since the schooner sailed a year ago. And Nat sneaks about trying to spy on him – and I have to be always on the watch to keep them apart — It's terrible.

DOCTOR. You've got to persuade Nat to go away, Susan.

SUE. He won't heed me – but I was thinking that now Danny is coming back, I'd get him —

DOCTOR. There's another thing. You can't continue to play slave to these two after you're married.

SUE (*miserably.*) We'll have to wait a while longer —

DOCTOR (*roughly*). Rats! You can't sacrifice any more of your life and Danny's to mad dreams.

SUE (*helplessly*). I don't know — (*Then brightening.*) That'll all be decided when the time comes. Just now it's enough to know Danny's alive and coming back. Read his letter, Doctor. You've been holding it in your hand all this time.

DOCTOR. Yes, yes, let's see. (*He takes the letter from the envelope.*)

SUE. Poor Danny! He's been through terrible things.

DOCTOR. Hmm! Rangoon.

SUE. Yes, he's still in the hospital there. You'll see.

DOCTOR (*reads the letter – grunts with astonishment – angrily*). By Gad! The damn scoundrels!

SUE (*shuddering*). Yes, wasn't it hideous – those awful men stabbing him and leaving him for dead in that out-of-the-way native settlement! The natives nursed him back to life, have you got that far yet? And then he was laid up for four months there waiting for a vessel to touch and take him back to civilization. And then, think of it, getting the fever on top of all that and nearly dying in the hospital in Rangoon!

DOCTOR. A terrible time of it! He's lucky to be alive. Hmm. I see he foresaw the wreck of the schooner. Those brutes couldn't navigate. (*Folding the letter and putting it back.*) He doesn't seem to have found out what the purpose of that mad trip was. Horne hid it from him to the last, he says. Well, it's queer – damn queer. But I'm glad to know those wretches have gone to their final accounting.

SUE (*with a shudder*). I was always afraid of them. They looked like – murderers. (*At a noise from below they both start. Steps can be heard climbing the stairs. Sue jumps to her feet frightenedly.*) Why – do you hear – who can that be? (*There is a soft rap on the door. The Doctor jumps to his feet. Sue turns to him with a half-hysterical laugh.*) Shall I open? I don't know why – but I'm afraid.

DOCTOR. Tut-tut! I'll see who it is. (*He opens the door and Nat is discovered on the stairs outside.*) Why hello, boy. You gave us a scare. Susan thought it was a ghost knocking.

NAT (*comes into the room. He has aged, grown thin, his face gaunt and drawn from continual mental strain, his eyes moody and preoccupied. He glances up at the skylight apprehensively, then turns to Sue*). I didn't find you downstairs, so I — (*Then to the*

Doctor.) Yes, you do grow to look for ghosts in this house, don't you? (*Again glancing upward.*) He's up there as usual, I suppose – looking for a ship that'll *never, never come now!*

DOCTOR (*with a grunt of approval*). I'm glad to hear you acknowledge that.

SUE (*who is just recovering from her fright*). But Nat, I didn't expect you — Did you find out — ?

NAT. Yes, I talked with several of the men who were on board at the time. They said they steamed in so close to the schooner it was easy to read the name with the naked eye. All agreed – *Sarah Allen*, Harbourport. They even remembered how her taffrail was painted. There's no chance for mistake. The *Sarah Allen* is gone. (*With great emphasis.*) And I'm glad – damn glad! I feel as if a weight of lead had been taken off my brain. I feel free again, and I can go back to work – but not here. I've got to go away – start new altogether.

SUE (*happily, coming and putting her arms around him*). It's so good to hear you talk like your old self again.

DOCTOR (*earnestly*). Yes, Nat, by Gad, that's sound sense. Get out of this.

NAT (*giving him a queer look*). I suppose you thought I was doomed, eh? – like him. (*He makes a motion upward – then with an uncertain laugh.*) A doctor's always looking for trouble where there isn't any. (*In a tone of finality.*) Well, it's all over, anyway.

SUE (*snatching the letter from the table*). Oh, I was forgetting, Nat. Read this. I got it yesterday.

NAT (*turns it over in his hands suspiciously*). Who from?

SUE. Open it and see.

NAT (*does so and turns over the pages to read the signature – he gives a start – hoarsely*). Danny! It can't be! But it's his writing, sure enough! (*He exclaims with a sudden wild exultation.*) Then they must have been lying to me!

SUE. No, the *Sarah Allen* was wrecked all right, but that was afterwards. He wasn't on board then. Read it. You'll see.

(*Nat sinks back on a chair, evidently depressed by this information. He starts to read the letter with unconcealed indifference, then becomes engrossed, excited, the paper trembling in his hands. The Doctor shakes his head at Sue, indicating his disapproval of her giving him the letter. Nat finishes and springs to his feet – angrily.*)

NAT. The stupid fool! He let Horne pull the wool over his eyes in fine shape. He deserved all he got for being so dumb!

SUE (*indignantly*). Nat!

NAT (*unheedingly*). Oh, if I could only have gone in his place! I knew the kind Horne was. He couldn't have played that trick on me. I'd have forced the secret out of him if I had to — (*He raises his clenched fist in a gesture of threat like his father's – then lets it fall and sits down again – disgustedly.*) But what's the use? And what's the use of this? (*Tosses the letter contemptuously on the table.*) He might just as well not have written. We're no wiser than we were before.

SUE (*snatching up the letter – deeply hurt*). Aren't you even glad to hear Danny's alive?

NAT (*turning to her at once – with remorseful confusion*). Yes – yes – of course, Sue – I don't have to say that, do I? What I mean is, he never found out from Horne – and we're no wiser.

DOCTOR (*briskly – with a significant glance at Sue*). Well, Susan – Nat – I've got to run along — (*Meaningly.*) I'll be over again to-morrow, Susan.

SUE. Yes, do come. (*Goes with him to the door.*) Can you see your way?

DOCTOR. Yes. Good night.

SUE. Good night.

(*She closes the door and comes back to Nat. The Doctor's footsteps die out.*)

NAT (*savagely*). That damned old fool! What is he doing, sneaking around here all the time? I've grown to hate the sight of him.

SUE. Nat! You can't mean that. Think of how kind he's been.

NAT. Yes – kindness with a purpose.

SUE. Don't be silly. What purpose could he have except wanting to help us?

NAT. To find out things, of course, you simpleton. To pump Pa when he's not responsible for what he's saying.

SUE (*indignantly*). Nat!

NAT. Much good it's done him! I know Pa.

Sane or not, he won't tell *that* to anyone – not even you or me, Sue. (*With sudden fury.*) I'm going away – but before I go I'm going to make him tell me! He won't refuse this time when he knows I'm leaving for good. He'll be glad then. He's been so afraid I'd find out, so scared to speak to me even – locking himself up here. But I'll make him tell – yes, I will!

SUE. Careful, Nat. He'll hear you if you shout like that.

NAT. But we have a right to know – his own children. What if he dies without ever speaking?

SUE (*uneasily*). Be sensible, Nat. There's nothing to tell except in your imagination. (*Taking his arm – persuasively.*) Come on downstairs. I'll get you something to eat. You must be starved, aren't you?

NAT. No – I don't know – I suppose I ought to be. (*He gets to his feet and glances around with a shudder.*) What a place for him to build to wait in – like the cabin of a ship sunk deep under the sea – like the *Sarah Allen's* cabin as it is now, probably. (*With a shiver.*) There's a chill comes over you. No wonder he's mad. (*He listens.*) Hear him. A year ago to-day she sailed. I wonder if he knows that. Back and forth, always staring out to sea for the *Sarah Allen*. Ha-ha! God! It would be funny if it didn't make your flesh creep. (*Brusquely.*) Come on. Let's leave him and go down where there's light and warmth.

(*They go down the stairs, closing the door behind them. There is a pause. Then the door of the companionway above is heard being opened and shut. A gust of wind sweeps down into the room. Bartlett stamps down the stairs. The madness which has taken almost complete possession of him in the past year is clearly stamped on his face, particularly in his eyes which seem to stare through and beyond objects with a hunted, haunted expression. His movements suggest an automaton obeying invisible wires. They are quick, jerky, spasmodic. He appears to be labouring under a state of extraordinary excitement. He stands for a second at the foot of the stairs, peering about him suspiciously. Then he goes to the table and sits down on the edge of a chair, his chin supported on his hands.*)

BARTLETT (*takes a folded piece of paper from his pocket and spreads it out on the table in the light of the lantern – pointing with his finger – mumblingly*). Where the cross be – ye'll not forget that, Silas Horne. Ye had a copy o' this – no chance for a mistake, bullies – the gold's there, restin' safe – back to me and we'll share it fair and square. A year ago to-day – ye remember the orders I wrote ye, Horne. (*Threateningly.*) Ye'll not be gone more nor a year or I'll – and if ye make port home here at night, hang a red and a green light at the mainm'st-head so I'll see ye comin'. A red and a green — (*He springs up suddenly and goes to a porthole to look out at the sea – disappointedly.*) No light be there – but they'll come. The year be up to-day and ye've got to come or I'll — (*He sinks back on the chair, his head in his hands. Suddenly he starts and stares straight in front of him as if he saw something in the air – with angry defiance.*) Aye, there ye be again – the two o' ye! Makin' a mock o' me! Brass and junk, ye say, not worth a damn! Ye don't believe, do ye? I'll show ye! (*He springs to his feet and makes a motion as if grabbing some one by the throat and shaking them – savagely.*) Ye lie! Is it gold or no? Answer me! (*With a mocking laugh.*) Aye, ye own up to it now, right enough. Too late, ye swabs! No share for ye! (*He sinks back on the chair again – after a pause, dully.*) Jimmy's gone. Let them rot. But I spoke no word, Silas Horne, remember! (*Then in a tone of fear.*) Be ye dyin', Sarah? No, ye must live – live to see your ship come home with the gold – and I'll buy ye all in the world ye set your heart on. No, not ambergris, Sarah – gold and diamonds and sech! We're rich at last! (*Then with great anguish.*) What woman's stubborn talk be this? Confess, ye say? But I spoke no word, I swear to ye! Why will ye hound me and think evil o' what I done? Men's business, I tell ye. They would have killed us and stolen the gold, can't ye see? (*Wildly.*) Enough o' talk, Sarah! I'll sail out in spite o' ye!

(*He gets to his feet and paces up and down the room. The door in the rear is opened and Nat re-enters. He glances at his father, then looks down the stairs behind him cautiously to see if he is followed. He comes in and closes the door behind him carefully.*)

NAT (*in a low voice*). Pa! (*Then as his father does not appear to notice his presence – louder.*) Pa!

BARTLETT (*stops short and stares at his son as if he were gradually awakening from a dream – slowly*). Be that ye, Nat?

NAT (*coming forward*). Yes. I want to talk with you.

BARTLETT (*struggling to bring his thoughts under control*). Talk? Ye want to talk – to me? Men's business – no room for a boy in it – keep clear o' this.

NAT (*defiantly*). That's what you've always said. But I won't be put off any longer. I won't, do you hear?

BARTLETT (*angrily*). I've ordered ye not to set foot in this cabin o' mine. Git below where ye belong. Where's Sue? I told her to keep ye away.

NAT. She can't prevent me this time. I've made up my mind. Listen, Pa. I'm going away to-morrow.

BARTLETT (*uncertainly*). Goin' away?

NAT. Yes, and I'm never coming back. I'm going to start a new life. That's why I want a final talk with you – before I go.

BARTLETT (*dully*). I've naught to say to ye.

NAT. You will have. Listen. I've absolute proof the *Sarah Allen* is lost.

BARTLETT (*fiercely*). Ye lie!

NAT (*curiously*). Why do you say that? You know it's true. It's just that you *won't believe.*

BARTLETT (*wanderingly – the word heading his mind into another channel*). Believe? Aye, he wouldn't believe. Brass and junk, he said, not worth a damn – but in the end I made him own up 'twas gold.

NAT (*repeating the word fascinatedly*). Gold?

BARTLETT. A year ago to-day she sailed. Ye lie! Ye don't believe either, do ye? – like him. But I'll show ye! I'll make ye own up as I made him! (*With mad exultation.*) She's comin' home to-night as I ordered Horne she must! I kin feel her makin' for home, I tell ye! A red an' a green at the mainm'st-head if ye make port o' night, I ordered Horne. Ye'll see!

(*He goes to look out of a porthole. Nat, as if under a spell, goes to another.*)

NAT (*turning away disappointedly – making an effort to throw off his thoughts – without conviction.*) Nonsense. There's nothing there – no lights – and I don't believe there ever will be.

BARTLETT (*his wild eyes fixed on his son's with an intense effort of will as if he were trying to break down his resistance*). Ye'll see, I tell ye – a red and a green! It ain't time yet, boy, but when it be they'll be plain in the night afore your eyes.

(*He goes and sits down by the table. Nat follows him and sits down in the other chair. He sees the map and stares at it fascinatedly.*)

NAT. What is this – the map of the island? (*He reaches out his hand for it.*)

BARTLETT (*snatching it up – with a momentary return to reason – frightenedly*). Not for ye, boy. Keep clear o' this for your own good. (*Then with a crazed triumph.*) Aye! Ye'd believe this soon enough, wouldn't ye?

NAT (*intensely*). I've always believed there was something – and a moment ago you mentioned gold. (*Triumphant in his turn.*) So you needn't try to hide the secret any longer. I know now. It's gold – gold you found on that island – gold you fitted out the *Sarah Allen* to sail back for – gold you buried where I saw that cross marked on the map! (*Passionately.*) Why have you been afraid to confide in me, your own son? Why didn't you let me sail back in your place? Were you afraid I'd give the secret away? Did you think I wouldn't believe — ?

BARTLETT (*with a mad chuckle*). Aye, ye believe now, right enough.

NAT. I always believed, I tell you. (*Pleadingly.*) And now that I know so much why can't you tell me the rest? I must know! I have a right to be heir to the secret. Why don't you confess —

BARTLETT (*interrupting – his brain catching at the word*). Confess? Confess, did ye say, Sarah? To Nat, did ye mean? Aye, Sarah, I'll tell him all and leave it to him to say if I did wrong. (*His gleaming eyes fixed on his son's.*) I'll tell ye, boy, from start to finish o' it. I been eatin' my heart to tell some one – some one who'd believe – some one that'd say I did no wrong. Listen, boy, ye know o' our four days in an open boat after the *Triton* went down. I told ye o' that when I come home. But what I didn't tell ye was they was six o' us in that boat, not four.

NAT. Six? There were you and Horne and Cates and Jimmy —

BARTLETT. The cook o' the *Triton* and the ship's boy. We'd been on the island two days – an island barren as hell, mind – without food or drink. We was roasted by the sun and nigh mad with thirst. Then, on the second day, I seed a Malay canoe – a proper war canoe such as the pirates use – sunk down inside the reef. I sent Jimmy down to go over her thinkin' they might be some cask o' water in her the sea'd not got to. (*With impressive emphasis.*) He found no water, boy, but he did find – d'ye know what, boy?

NAT (*exultantly*). The gold, of course!

BARTLETT (*laughing harshly*). Ha-ha! Ye do believe right enough, don't ye! Aye, the gold – in a chest. We hauled her up ashore and forced the lid open. (*Gloatingly.*) And there it was afore our eyes in the sun – gold bracelets and rings and ornaments o' all sorts fixed up fancy with diamonds and emeralds and rubies and sech – red and green – shinin' in the sun! (*He stops impressively.*)

NAT (*fascinatedly*). Diamonds and — But how did they get there?

BARTLETT. Looted treasure o' some Chinese junk, likely. What matter how it come about? There it was afore our eyes. And then, mind ye, that thief o' a cook came runnin' up from where he'd been shirkin' to look at what we'd found. "No share for ye, ye swab," I yelled at him; and then he says: "It ain't gold – brass and junk," he says and run off for fear o' me. Aye, he run off to the boy and told him to jine with his sneakin' plan to steal the gold from us!

NAT (*savagely*). But why didn't you stop him? Why didn't you — ?

BARTLETT. I be comin' to that, boy, and ye'll see if I did wrong. We carried the chest to the shade o' a palm and there was that thief o' a cook an' the boy waitin'. I collared 'em both and made 'em look at the gold. "Look and tell me if it's gold or no," I says. (*Triumphantly.*) They was afeerd to lie. Even that thief o' a cook owned up 'twas gold. Then when I turned 'em loose, because he knowed he'd git no share, he shouted again: "Brass and junk. Not worth a damn."

NAT (*furiously*). But why did you allow — Why didn't you —

BARTLETT (*with mad satisfaction*). Aye, ye be seein' the way o' it, boy. It was just then we sighted the schooner that picked us up after. We made a map and was buryin' the gold when we noticed them two thieves sneakin' about to see where we'd hide it. I saw 'em plain, the scum! That thief o' a cook was thinkin' he'd tell the folks on the schooner and go shares with them – and leave us on the island to rot; or he was thinkin' he and the boy'd be able to come back and dig it up afore I could. We had to do somethin' quick to spile their plan afore the schooner come. (*In a tone of savage satisfaction.*) And so – though I spoke no word to him – Jimmy knifed 'em both and covered 'em up with sand. But I spoke no word, d'ye hear? Their deaths be on Jimmy's head alone.

NAT (*passionately*). And what if you had? They deserved what they got.

BARTLETT. Then ye think I did no wrong?

NAT. No! Any man – I'd have done the same myself.

BARTLETT (*gripping his son's hand tensely*). Ye be true son o' mine, Nat. I ought to told ye before. (*Exultantly.*) Ye hear, Sarah? Nat says I done no wrong.

NAT. The map! Can I see it?

BARTLETT. Aye.

(*He hands it to Nat, who spreads it out on the table and pores over it.*)

NAT (*excitedly*). Why, with this I – we – can go back – even if the *Sarah Allen* is lost.

BARTLETT. She ain't lost, boy – not her. Don't heed them lies ye been hearin'. She's due now. I'll go up and look. (*He goes up the companionway stairs. Nat does not seem to notice his going, absorbed in the map. Then there is a loud muffled hail in Bartlett's voice.*) *Sarah Allen*, ahoy!

(*Nat starts, transfixed – then rushes to one of the portholes to look. He turns back, passing his hand over his eyes, frowning bewilderedly. The door above is flung open and slammed shut and Bartlett stamps down the stairs.*)

BARTLETT (*fixing Nat hypnotically with his eyes – triumphantly*). What did I tell ye? D'ye believe now she'll come back? D'ye credit your own eyes?

NAT (*vaguely*). Eyes? I looked. I didn't see —

BARTLETT. Ye lie! The *Sarah Allen*, ye blind

fool, come back from the Southern Seas as I swore she must! Loaded with gold as I swore she would be! – makin' port! – droppin' her anchor just when I hailed her.

NAT (*feebly, his will crumbling*). But – how do you know? – some other schooner —

BARTLETT. Not know my own ship – and the signal I'd ordered Horne to make!

NAT (*mechanically*). I know – a red and a green at the mainm'st-head.

BARTLETT. Then look out if ye dare! (*He goes to a porthole.*) Ye kin see it plain from here. (*Commandingly.*) Will ye believe your eyes? Look!

(*Nat comes to him slowly – looks through the porthole – and starts back, a possessed expression coming over his face.*)

NAT (*slowly*). A red and a green – clear as day!

BARTLETT (*his face is now transfigured by the ecstasy of a dream come true*). They've lowered a boat – the three – Horne an' Cates and Jimmy Kanaka. They're rowin' ashore. Listen. I hear the oars in the locks. Listen!

NAT (*staring into his father's eyes – after a pause during which he appears to be straining his hearing to the breaking point – excitedly*). I hear!

BARTLETT. Listen! They've landed. They'll be comin' up the path now. (*In a crooning, monotonous tone.*) They move slowly – slowly. It be heavy, I know – that chest. (*After a pause.*) Hark! They're below at the door in front.

NAT. I hear!

BARTLETT. Ye'll see it now in a moment, boy – the gold. Up with it, bullies! Up ye come! Up, bullies! It's heavy, heavy!

NAT (*madly*). I hear them! They're on the floor below! They're coming! I'll open the door. (*He springs to the door and flings it open, shouting.*) Welcome home, boys!

(*Sue is discovered outside just climbing up the stairs from below. She steps inside, then stops, looking with amazement and horror from father to brother. Nat pushes her roughly aside to look behind her down the stairs.*)

SUE. Nat!

NAT (*turning to his father*). I'll go down to the wharf. They must be there or —

(*The rest of his words are lost as he hurries down the stairs. Bartlett steps back, shrinking away from his daughter, and sinks on a chair by the table with a groan, his hands over his eyes.*)

SUE (*comes to him and shakes him by the shoulder – alarmed*). Pa! What has happened? What is the matter with Nat? What have you told him? (*With bitter despair.*) Oh, can't you see you're driving him mad, too?

BARTLETT (*letting his hands fall and staring at her haggardly – falteringly, as if reason were slowly filtering back into his brain*). Sue – ye said – drivin' him mad, *too*! Then ye think I be — ? (*He staggers to his feet. Sue breaks down, sobbing. Bartlett falters on.*) But I seen her – the *Sarah Allen* – the signal lights —

SUE. Oh, Pa, there's nothing there! You know it! She was lost months ago.

BARTLETT. Lost? (*He stumbles over to a porthole and looks out. His body sags as if he were going to fall. He turns away and cries hopelessly in a tone of heart-rending grief.*) Lost! Aye, they be no *Sarah Allen* there – no lights – nothin'!

SUE (*pleading fiercely*). Pa, you've got to save Nat! He won't heed anyone else. Can't you tell him the truth – the whole truth whatever it is – now when I'm here and you're yourself again – and set him free from this crazy dream!

BARTLETT (*with wild grief*). Confess, ye mean? Sue, ye be houndin' me like your Ma did to her dyin' hour! Confess – that I spoke the word to Jimmy – in my mind! Confess – brass and junk – not worth a damn! (*In frenzied protest.*) No! Ye lie!

SUE. Oh, Pa, I don't know what you mean. Tell Nat the truth! Save him!

BARTLETT. The truth? It's a lie! (*As Sue tries to bar his way to the companionway – sternly.*) Out o' my way, girl!

(*He pulls himself feebly up the stairs. The door is heard slamming above. Sue sits down in a chair in a hopeless, exhausted attitude. After a pause Nat re-enters. He is panting heavily from his exertions. His pale face is set in an expression of despair.*)

NAT (*looking about the room wildly*). Where is he? Sue! (*He comes forward and falls on his knees beside *her chair, hiding his face in her lap like a frightened child. He sobs hoarsely.*) Sue! What does it all mean? I looked. There was nothing there – no schooner – nothing.

SUE (*soothing him as if he were a little boy*). Of course there wasn't. Did you expect there would be, you foolish boy? Come, you know better than that. Why, Nat, you told the doctor and I that you were absolutely convinced the *Sarah Allen* was lost.

NAT (*dully*). Yes, I know – but I don't believe – like him —

SUE. Sshhhh! You know the state Pa is in. He doesn't realize what he's saying half the time. You ought to have better sense than to pay any attention —

NAT (*excitedly*). But he told me all he's been hiding from us – all about the gold!

SUE (*looking at him with alarm – mystified*). Gold? (*Then forcing a smile.*) Don't be silly, Nat. It doesn't exist except in his poor, deranged mind.

NAT (*fiercely*). That's a lie, Sue! I saw the map, I tell you – the map of the island with a cross marked on it where they buried the gold.

SUE. He showed a map to you – a real map? (*Gently.*) Are you sure you're not just imagining that, too?

NAT. I had it in my hands, you fool, you! There – on the table. (*He springs to his feet, sees the map on the table, and snatches it up with an exclamation of joy – showing it to Sue.*) See! Now will you believe me! (*She examines the map perplexedly. Nat paces up and down – excitedly.*) I tell you it's all true. You can't deny it now. It's lucky for us I forced him to confess. He might have died keeping the secret and then we'd have lost – I'll tell you what I'm going to do now, Sue. I'm going to raise the money somewhere, somehow, and fit out another schooner and this time I'll sail on her myself. No trusting to Danny or anyone else! Yes, Sue, we'll come into our own yet, even if the *Sarah Allen* is lost — (*He stops – then in accents of bewildered fear.*) But – she can't be lost – I saw the lights, Sue – red and green – as plain as I see you now — (*He goes to one of the portholes again.*)

SUE (*who has been watching him worriedly, puts the map back on the table, gets up and, assuming a brisk, matter-of-fact tone, she goes over and takes him by the arm*). Come downstairs, Nat. Don't think any more about it to-night. It's late and you're worn out. You need rest and a good sleep.

NAT (*following her toward the door – confusedly*). But Sue – I saw them — (*From above in the night comes the muffled hail in Bartlett's voice.*) *Sarah Allen*, ahoy!

(*Nat stops, tortured, his hands instinctively raised up to cover his ears. Sue gives a startled cry. The door above is slammed and Bartlett comes down the stairs, his face revealing that the delusion has again full possession of his mind.*)

BARTLETT (*pointing his finger at his son and fixing him with his eyes – in ringing, triumphant tones.*) The *Sarah Allen*, boy – in the harbour below – a red and a green plain afore my eyes! What did I tell ye, boy? Come back from the Southern Seas as I swore she must! Loaded with gold as I swore she would be!

(*Nat again seems to crumble – to give way to the stronger will. He takes a step toward his father, his eyes lighting up. Sue looks at his face – then rushes to her father.*)

SUE (*putting her hands to her father's head and forcing him to look down into her face – intensely.*) Pa! Stop, do you hear me! It's all mad! You're driving Nat mad, too! (*As she sees her father hesitate, the wild light dying out of his eyes, she summons all her power to a fierce pleading.*) For my sake, Pa! For Ma's sake! Think of how she would feel if she were alive and saw you acting this way with Nat! Tell him! Tell him now – before me – tell him it's all a lie!

BARTLETT (*trying in an agony of conflict to get hold of his reason – incoherently*). Yes, Sue – I hear ye – confess – aye, Sarah, your dyin' words – keep Nat clear o' this – but – red and green – I seen 'em plain — (*Then suddenly after a tremendous struggle, lifting his tortured face to Nat's – in tones of despair.*) Nothin' there, boy! Don't ye believe! No red and green! She'll never come! Derelict and lost, boy, the *Sarah Allen*. (*After another struggle with himself.*) And I lied to ye, boy. I gave the word – in my mind – to kill them two. I murdered 'em in cold blood.

SUE (*shrinking from him in horror*). Pa! You don't know what you're saying.

BARTLETT. The truth, girl. Ye said – confess —

NAT (*bewilderedly*). But – it was right. They were trying to steal —

BARTLETT (*overcome by the old obsession for a moment – savagely.*) Aye, that's it! The thievin' scum! They was tryin' — (*He stops short, throwing his head back, his whole body tense and quivering with the effort he makes to force this sustaining lie out of his brain – then, broken but self-conquering, he looks again at Nat – gently.*) No, Nat. That be the lie I been tellin' myself ever since. That cook – he said 'twas brass — But I'd been lookin' for ambergris – gold – the whole o' my life – and when we found that chest – I *had* to believe, I tell ye! I'd been dreamin' o' it all my days! But he said brass and junk, and told the boy – and I give the word to murder 'em both and cover 'em up with sand.

NAT (*very pale – despairingly*). But he lied, didn't he? It is gold – real gold – isn't it?

BARTLETT (*slowly takes the studded anklet from his pocket and holds it out to Nat. The latter brings it to the light of the lantern. Bartlett sits on a chair, covering his face with his hands – in a tone of terrible suffering*). Ye'll tell me, boy – if it's gold or no. I've had it by me all this time – but I've been afeerd to show —

NAT (*in a tone of wild scorn*). Why, it's brass, of course! The cheapest kind of junk – not worth a damn!

(*He flings it savagely into a corner of the room. Bartlett groans and seems to shrink up and turn into a figure of pitiable feebleness.*)

SUE (*pityingly*). Don't, Nat.

(*She puts her arms around her father's shoulders protectingly.*)

NAT (*in a stifled voice*). What a damned fool I've been!

(*He flings himself down on the cot, his shoulders heaving.*)

BARTLETT (*uncovers his grey face on which there is now settling an expression of strange peace – stroking his daughter's hand*). Sue – don't think hard o' me. (*He takes the map.*) An end to this!

(*He slowly tears it into small pieces, seeming to grow weaker and weaker as he does so. Finally as he lets the fragments filter through his fingers, his whole frame suddenly relaxes. He sighs, his eyes shut, and sags back in his chair, his head bent forward limply on his chest.*)

SUE (*alarmed*). Pa! (*She sinks to her knees beside him and looks up into his face.*) Pa! Speak to me! It's Sue! (*Then turning toward her brother – terrifiedly.*) Nat! Run – get the doctor — (*Nat starts to a sitting position. Sue tries with trembling hands to feel of her father's pulse, his heart – then begins to sob hysterically.*) Oh, Nat – he's dead, I think he's dead!

Curtain

ANNA CHRISTIE

Characters

"JOHNNY-THE-PRIEST"
TWO LONGSHOREMEN
A POSTMAN
LARRY, *bar-tender*
CHRIS CHRISTOPHERSON, *Captain of the barge "Simeon Winthrop"*
MARTHY OWEN
ANNA CHRISTOPHERSON, *Chris's daughter*
THREE MEN OF A STEAMER'S CREW
MAT BURKE, *a stoker*
JOHNSON, *deckhand on the barge*

Scenes

ACT ONE

"Johnny-the-Priest's" saloon near the water-front, New York City.

ACT TWO

The barge, *Simeon Winthrop*, at anchor in the harbour of Provincetown, Mass. Ten days later.

ACT THREE

Cabin of the barge, at dock in Boston. A week later.

ACT FOUR

The same. Two days later.

TIME: about 1910

Act I

SCENE. *"Johnny-the-Priest's" saloon near South Street, New York City. The stage is divided into two sections, showing a small back room on the right. On the left, forward, of the bar-room, a large window looking out on the street. Beyond it, the main entrance—a double swinging door. Farther back, another window. The bar runs from left to right nearly the whole length of the rear wall. In back of the bar, a small showcase displaying a few bottles of goods, for which there is evidently little call. The remainder of the rear space in front of the large mirrors is occupied by half-barrels of cheap whisky of the "nickel-a-shot" variety, from which the liquor is drawn by means of spigots. On the right is an open doorway leading to the back room. In the back room are four round wooden tables with five chairs grouped about each. In the rear, a family entrance opening on a side street.*

It is late afternoon of a day in Autumn.

As the curtain rises, Johnny is discovered. "Johnny-the-Priest" deserves his nickname. With his pale, thin, clean-shaven face, mild blue eyes and white hair, a cassock would seem more suited to him than the apron he wears. Neither his voice nor his general manner dispel this illusion which has made him a personage of the water-front. They are soft and bland. But beneath all his mildness one senses the man behind the mask—cynical, callous, hard as nails. He is lounging at ease behind the bar, a pair of spectacles on his nose, reading an evening paper.

Two longshoremen enter from the street, wearing their working aprons, the button of the Union pinned conspicuously on the caps pulled sideways on their heads at an aggressive angle.

FIRST LONGSHOREMAN (*as they range themselves at the bar*). Gimme a shock. Number Two. (*He tosses a coin on the bar.*)

SECOND LONGSHOREMAN. Same here.

(*Johnny sets two glasses of barrel whisky before them.*)

FIRST LONGSHOREMAN. Here's luck!

(*The other nods. They gulp down their whisky.*)

SECOND LONGSHOREMAN (*putting money on the bar*). Give us another.

FIRST LONGSHOREMAN. Gimme a scoop this time—lager and porter. I'm dry.

SECOND LONGSHOREMAN. Same here.

(*Johnny draws the lager and porter and sets the big, foaming tankards before them. They drink down half the contents and start to talk together hurriedly in low tones. The door on the left is swung open and Larry enters. He is a boyish, red-cheeked, rather good-looking young fellow of twenty or so.*)

LARRY (*nodding to Johnny—cheerily*). Hallo, boss!

JOHNNY. Hallo, Larry! (*With a glance at his watch.*) Just on time.

(*Larry goes to the right, behind the bar, takes off his coat, and puts on an apron.*)

FIRST LONGSHOREMAN (*abruptly*). Let's drink up and get back to it.

(*They finish their drinks and go out left. The Postman enters as they leave. He exchanges nods with Johnny and throws a letter on the bar.*)

THE POSTMAN. Addressed care of you, Johnny. Know him?

JOHNNY (*picks up the letter, adjusting his spectacles. Larry comes and peers over his shoulders. Johnny reads very slowly*). Christopher Christopherson.

THE POSTMAN (*helpfully*). Square-head name.

LARRY. Old Chris—that's who.

JOHNNY. Oh, sure. I was forgetting Chris carried a hell of a name like that. Letters come here for him sometimes before, I remember now. Long time ago, though.

THE POSTMAN. It'll get him all right, then?

JOHNNY. Sure thing. He comes here whenever he's in port.

THE POSTMAN (*turning to go*). Sailor, eh?

JOHNNY (*with a grin*). Captain of a coal barge.

THE POSTMAN (*laughing*). Some job! Well, s'long.

JOHNNY. S'long. I'll see he gets it. (*The Postman goes out. Johnny scrutinizes the letter.*) You got good eyes, Larry. Where's it from?

LARRY (*after a glance*). St. Paul. That'll be in Minnesota, I'm thinkin'. Looks like a woman's writing, too, the old divil!

JOHNNY. He's got a daughter somewheres out West, I think he told me once. (*He puts the letter on the cash register.*) Come to think of it, I ain't seen old Chris in a dog's age. (*Putting his overcoat on, he comes around the end of the bar.*) Guess I'll be gettin' home. See you to-morrow.

LARRY. Good night to ye, boss.

(*As Johnny goes toward the street door, it is pushed open and Christopher Christopherson enters. He is a short, squat, broad-shouldered man of about fifty, with a round, weather-beaten, red face from which his light-blue eyes peer short-sightedly, twinkling with a simple good humour. His large mouth, overhung by a thick, drooping, yellow moustache, is childishly self-willed and weak, of an obstinate kindliness. A thick neck is jammed like a post into the heavy trunk of his body. His arms, with their big, hairy, freckled hands, and his stumpy legs terminating in large, flat feet, are awkwardly short and muscular. He walks with a clumsy, rolling gait. His voice, when not raised in a hollow boom, is toned down to a sly, confidential half-whisper with something vaguely plaintive in its quality. He is dressed in a wrinkled, ill-fitting, dark suit of shore clothes, and wears a faded cap of grey cloth over his mop of grizzled, blond hair. Just now his face beams with a too-blissful happiness, and he has evidently been drinking. He reaches his hand out to Johnny.)*

CHRIS. Hallo, Yohnny! Have drink on me. Come on, Larry. Give us drink. Have one yourself. (*Putting his hand in his pocket.*) Ay gat money—plenty money.

JOHNNY (*shakes Chris by the hand*). Speak of the devil. We was just talkin' about you.

LARRY (*coming to the end of the bar*). Hallo, Chris! Put it there. (*They shake hands.*)

CHRIS (*beaming*). Give us drink.

JOHNNY (*with a grin*). You got a half-snootful now. Where'd you get it?

CHRIS (*grinning*). Oder fallar on oder barge—Irish fallar—he gat bottle vhisky and we drank it, yust us two. Dot vhisky get kick, by yingo! Ay yust come ashore. Give us drink, Larry. Ay vas little drunk, not much. Yust feel good. (*He laughs and commences to sing in a nasal, high-pitched quaver:*)

"My Yosephine, come board de ship. Long time
Ay vait for you.
De moon, she shi-i-i-ine. She looka yust like you.
Tchee-tchee, tchee-tchee, tchee-tchee, tchee-tchee."

(*To the accompaniment of this last he waves his hand as if he were conducting an orchestra.*)

JOHNNY (*with a laugh*). Same old Yosie, eh, Chris?

CHRIS. You don't know good song when you hear him. Italian fallar on oder barge, he learn me dat. Give us drink. (*He throws change on the bar.*)

LARRY (*with a professional air*). What's your pleasure, gentlemen?

JOHNNY. Small beer, Larry.

CHRIS. Vhisky—Number Two.

LARRY (*as he gets their drinks*). I'll take a cigar on you.

CHRIS (*lifting his glass*). Skoal! (*He drinks.*)

JOHNNY. Drink hearty.

CHRIS (*immediately*). Have oder drink.

JOHNNY. No. Some other time. Got to go home now. So you've just landed? Where are you in from this time?

CHRIS. Norfolk. Ve make slow voyage—dirty vedder—yust fog, fog, fog, all bloody time! (*There is an insistent ring from the door-bell at the family entrance in the back room. Chris gives a start—hurriedly.*) Ay go open, Larry. Ay forgat. It vas Marthy. She come with me. (*He goes into the back room.*)

LARRY (*with a chuckle*). He's still got that same cow livin' with him, the old fool!

JOHNNY (*with a grin*). A sport, Chris is. Well, I'll beat it home. S'long. (*He goes to the street door.*)

LARRY. So long, boss.

JOHNNY. Oh—don't forget to give him his letter

LARRY. I won't.

(*Johnny goes out. In the meantime, Chris has opened the family entrance door, admitting Marthy. She might be forty or fifty. Her jowly, mottled face, with its thick, red nose, is streaked with interlacing purple veins. Her thick, grey hair is piled anyhow in a greasy mop on top of her round head. Her figure is flabby and fat; her breath comes in wheezy gasps; she speaks in a loud, mannish voice, punctuated by explosions of hoarse laughter. But there still twinkles in her blood-shot blue eyes a youthful lust for life which hard usage has failed to stifle, a sense of humour, mocking, but good-tempered. She wears a man's cap, double-breasted man's jacket, and a grimy, calico skirt. Her bare feet are encased in a man's shoes several sizes too large for her, which gives her a shuffling, wobbly gait.*)

MARTHY (*grumblingly*). What yuh tryin' to do, Dutchy—keep me standin' out there all day? (*She comes forward and sits at the table in the right corner, front.*)

CHRIS (*mollifyingly*). Ay'm sorry, Marthy. Ay talk to Yohnny. Ay forgat. What you goin' take for drink?

MARTHY (*appeased*). Gimme a scoop of lager an' ale.

CHRIS. Ay go bring him back. (*He returns to the bar.*) Lager and ale for Marthy, Larry. Vhisky for me. (*He throws change on the bar.*)

LARRY. Right you are. (*Then remembering, he takes the letter from in back of the bar.*) Here's a letter for you—from St. Paul, Minnesota—and a lady's writin'. (*He grins.*)

CHRIS (*quickly—taking it*). Oh, den it come from my daughter, Anna. She live dere. (*He turns the letter over in his hands uncertainly.*) Ay don't gat letter from Anna—must be a year.

LARRY (*jokingly*). That's a fine fairy tale to be tellin'—your daughter! Sure, I'll bet it's some tart.

CHRIS (*soberly*). No. Dis come from Anna. (*Engrossed by the letter in his hand—uncertainly.*) By golly, Ay tank Ay'm too drunk for read dis letter from Anna. Ay tank Ay sat down for a minute. You bring drinks in back room, Larry. (*He goes into the room on right.*)

MARTHY (*angrily*). Where's my larger an' ale, yuh big stiff?

CHRIS (*preoccupied*). Larry bring him.

He sits down opposite her. Larry brings in the drinks and sets them on the table. He and Marthy exchange nods of recognition. Larry stands looking at Chris curiously. Marthy takes a long draught of her tankard and heaves a huge sigh of satisfaction, wiping her mouth with the back of her hand. Chris stares at the letter for a moment—slowly opens it, and squinting his eyes, commences to read laboriously, his lips moving as he spells out the words. As he reads his face lights up with an expression of mingled joy and bewilderment.)

LARRY. Good news?

MARTHY (*her curiosity also aroused*). What's that yuh got—a letter, fur Gawd's sake?

CHRIS (*pauses for a moment, after finishing the letter, as if to let the news sink in—then suddenly pounds his fist on the table with happy excitement*). Py yiminy! Yust tank, Anna say she's comin' here right avay! She gat sick on yob in St. Paul, she say. It's short letter, don't tal me much more'n dat. (*Beaming.*) Py golly, dat's good news all at one time for ole fallar! (*Then turning to Marthy, rather shamefacedly.*) You know, Marthy, Ay've tole you Ay don't see my Anna since she vas little gel in Sveden five year ole.

MARTHY. How old'll she be now?

CHRIS. She must be—lat me see—she must be twenty year ole, py Yo!

LARRY (*surprised*). You've not seen her in fifteen years?

CHRIS (*suddenly growing sombre—in a low tone*). No. Ven she vas little gel, Ay vas bo'sun on vindjammer. Ay never gat home only few time dem year. Ay'm fool sailor fallar. My voman—Anna's mother—she gat tired vait all time Sveden for me ven Ay don't never come. She come dis country, bring Anna, dey go out Minnesota, live with her cousins on farm. Den ven her mo'der die ven Ay vas on voyage, Ay tank it's better dem cousins keep Anna. Ay tank it's better Anna live on farm, den she don't know dat ole davil, sea, she don't know fader like me.

LARRY (*with a wink at Marthy*). This girl, now'll be marryin' a sailor herself, likely. It's in the blood.

CHRIS (*suddenly springing to his feet and smashing his fist on the table in a rage*). No, py God! She don't do dat!

MARTHY (*grasping her tankard hastily—angrily*). Hey, look out, yuh nut! Wanta spill my suds for me?

LARRY (*amazed*). Oho, what's up with you? Ain't you a sailor yourself now, and always been?

CHRIS (*slowly*). Dat's yust vhy Ay say it. (*Forcing a smile.*) Sailor vas all right fallar, but not for marry gel. No. Ay know dat. Anna's mo'der, she know it, too.

LARRY (*as Chris remains sunk in gloomy reflection*). When is your daughter comin'? Soon?

CHRIS (*roused*). Py yiminy, Ay forgat. (*Reads through the letter hurriedly.*) She say she come right avay, dat's all.

LARRY. She'll maybe be comin' here to look for you, I s'pose.

(*He returns to the bar, whistling. Left alone with Marthy, who stares at him with a twinkle of malicious humour in her eyes, Chris suddenly becomes desperately ill at ease. He fidgets, then gets up hurriedly.*)

CHRIS. Ay gat speak with Larry. Ay be right back. (*Mollifyingly.*) Ay bring you oder drink.

MARTHY (*emptying her glass*). Sure. That's me. (*As he retreats with the glass she guffaws after him derisively.*)

CHRIS (*to Larry in an alarmed whisper*). Py yingo, Ay gat gat Marthy shore off barge before Anna come ! Anna raise hell if she find dat out. Marthy raise hell, too, for go, py golly !

LARRY (*with a chuckle*). Serve ye right, ye old divil—havin' a woman at your age !

CHRIS (*scratching his head in a quandary*). You tal me lie for tal Marthy, Larry, so's she gat off barge quick.

LARRY. She knows your daughter's comin'. Tell her to get the hell out of it.

CHRIS. No. Ay don't like make her feel bad.

LARRY. You're an old mush ! Keep your girl away from the barge, then. She'll likely want to stay ashore, anyway. (*Curiously.*) What does she work at, your Anna ?

CHRIS. She stay on dem cousins' farm till two year ago. Dan she gat yob nurse gel in St. Paul. (*Then shaking his head resolutely.*) But Ay don't vant for her gat yob now. Ay vant for her stay with me.

LARRY (*scornfully*). On a coal barge ! She'll not like that, I'm thinkin'.

MARTHY (*shouts from next room*). Don't I get that bucket o' suds, Dutchy ?

CHRIS (*startled—in apprehensive confusion*). Yes, Ay come, Marthy.

LARRY (*drawing the lager and ale, hands it to Chris—laughing*). Now you're in for it ! You'd better tell her straight to get out !

CHRIS (*shaking in his boots*). Py golly. (*He takes her drink in to Marthy and sits down at the table. She sips it in silence. Larry moves quietly close to the partition to listen, grinning with expectation. Chris seems on the verge of speaking, hesitates, gulps down his whisky desperately as if seeking for courage. He attempts to whistle a few bars of "Yosephine" with careless bravado, but the whistle peters out futilely. Marthy stares at him keenly, taking in his embarrassment with a malicious twinkle of amusement in her eye. Chris clears his throat.*) Marthy—

MARTHY (*aggressively*). Wha's that ? (*Then, pretending to fly into a rage, her eyes enjoying Chris's misery.*) I'm wise to what's in back of your nut, Dutchy. Yuh want to git rid o' me, huh ?—now she's comin'. Gimme the rush ashore, huh ? Lemme tell yuh, Dutchy, there ain't a square-head workin' on a boat man enough to git away with that. Don't start nothin' yuh can't finish !

CHRIS (*miserably*). Ay don't start nutting, Marthy.

MARTHY (*glares at him for a second—then cannot control a burst of laughter*). Ho-ho ! Yuh're a scream, Square-head—an honest-ter-Gawd knockout ! Ho-ho ! (*She wheezes, panting for breath.*)

CHRIS (*with childish pique*). Ay don't see nutting for laugh at.

MARTHY. Take a slant in the mirror and yuh'll see. Ho-ho ! (*Recovering from her mirth—chuckling, scornfully.*) A square-head tryin' to kid Marthy Owen at this late day !—after me campin' with barge-men the last twenty years. I'm wise to the game, up, down, and sideways. I ain't been born and dragged up on the water-front for nothin'. Think I'd make trouble, huh ? Not me ! I'll pack up me duds an' beat it. I'm quittin' yuh, get me ? I'm tellin' yuh I'm sick of stickin' with yuh, and I'm leavin' yuh flat, see ? There's plenty of other guys on other barges waitin' for me. Always was, I always found. (*She claps the astonished Chris on the back.*) So cheer up, Dutchy ! I'll be offen the barge before she comes. You'll be rid o' me for good—and me o' you—good riddance for both of us. Ho-ho !

CHRIS (*seriously*). Ay don' tank dat. You vas good gel, Marthy.

MARTHY (*grinning*). Good girl ? Aw, can the bull ! Well, yuh treated me square, yuhself. So it's fifty-fifty. Nobody's sore at nobody. We're still good frien's, huh ?

(*Larry returns to bar.*)

CHRIS (*beaming now that he sees his troubles disappearing*). Yes, py golly.

MARTHY. That's the talkin' ! In all my time

I tried never to split with a guy with no hard feelin's. But what was yuh so scared about—that I'd kick up a row? That ain't Marthy's way. (*Scornfully.*) Think I'd break my heart to loose yuh? Commit suicide, huh? Ho-ho! Gawd! The world's full o' men if that's all I'd worry about! (*Then with a grin, after emptying her glass.*) Blow me to another scoop, huh? I'll drink your kid's health for yuh.

CHRIS (*eagerly*). Sure tang. Ay go gat him. (*He takes the two glasses into the bar.*) Oder drink. Same for both.

LARRY (*getting the drinks and putting them on the bar*). She's not such a bad lot, that one.

CHRIS (*jovially*). She's good gel, Ay tal you! Py golly, Ay calabrate now! Give me vhisky here at bar, too. (*He puts down money. Larry serves him.*) You have drink, Larry?

LARRY (*virtuously*). You know I never touch it.

CHRIS. You don't know what you miss. Skoal! (*He drinks—then begins to sing loudly:*)
" My Yosephine, come board de ship——"
(*He picks up the drinks for Marthy and himself and walks unsteadily into the back room, singing:*)
" De moon, she shi-i-i-ine. She looks yust like you.
Tche-tchee, tchee-tchee, tchee-tchee, tchee-tchee."

MARTHY (*grinning, hands to ears*). Gawd!

CHRIS (*sitting down*). Ay'm good singer, yes? Ve drink, eh? Skoal! Ay calabrate! (*He drinks.*) Ay calabrate 'cause Anna's coming home. You know, Marthy, Ay never write for her to come, 'cause Ay tank Ay'm no good for her. But all time Ay hope like hell some day she vant for see me and den she come. And dat's vay it happen now, py yiminy! (*His face beaming.*) What you tank she look like, Marthy? Ay bet you she's fine, good, strong gel, pooty like hell! Living on farm made her like dat. And Ay bet you some day she marry good, steady land fallar here in East, have home all her own, have kits—and dan Ay'm ole grandfader, py golly! And Ay go visit dem every time Ay gat in port near! (*Bursting with joy.*) By yiminy crickens, Ay calabrate dat! (*Shouts.*) Bring oder drink, Larry! (*He smashes his fist on the table with a bang.*)

LARRY (*coming in from bar—irritably*). Easy there! Don't be breakin' the table, you old goat!

CHRIS (*by way of reply, grins foolishly and begins to sing*). " My Yosephine comes board de ship—"

MARTHY (*touching Chris's arm persuasively*). You're soused to the ears, Dutchy. Go out and put a feed into you. It'll sober you up. (*Then as Chris shakes his head obstinately.*) Listen, yuh old nut! Yuh don't know what time your kid's liable to show up. Yuh want to be sober when she comes, don't yuh?

CHRIS (*aroused—gets unsteadily to his feet*). Py golly, yes.

LARRY. That's good sense for you. A good beef stew'll fix you. Go round the corner.

CHRIS. All right. Ay be back soon, Marthy. (*Chris goes through the bar and out the street door.*)

LARRY. He'll come round all right with some grub in him.

MARTHY. Sure.

(*Larry goes back to the bar and resumes his newspaper. Marthy sips what is left of her tankard reflectively. There is the ring of the family entrance bell. Larry comes to the door and opens it a trifle—then, with a puzzled expression, pulls it wide. Anna Christopherson enters. She is a tall, blonde, fully-developed girl of twenty, handsome after a large, Viking-daughter fashion, but now run down in health and plainly showing all the outward evidences of belonging to the world's oldest profession. Her youthful face is already hard and cynical beneath its layer of make-up. Her clothes are the tawdry finery of peasant stock turned prostitute. She comes and sinks wearily in a chair by the table, left front.*)

ANNA. Gimme a whisky—ginger ale on the side. (*Then, as Larry turns to go, forcing a winning smile at him.*) And don't be stingy, baby.

LARRY (*sarcastically*). Shall I serve it in a pail?

ANNA (*with a hard laugh*). That suits me down to the ground. (*Larry goes into the bar. The two women size each other up with frank stares. Larry comes back with the drink, which he sets before Anna and returns to the bar again. Anna downs her drink at a gulp. Then, after a moment, as the alcohol begins to rouse her, she turns to Marthy with a friendly smile.*) Gee, I needed that bad, all right, all right!

MARTHY (*nodding her head sympathetically*). Sure—yuh look all in. Been on a bat?

ANNA. No—travelling—day and a half on the train. Had to sit up all night in the dirty coach too. Gawd, I thought I'd never get here!

MARTHY (*with a start—looking at her intently*). Where'd yuh come from, huh?

ANNA. St. Paul—out in Minnesota.

MARTHY (*staring at her in amazement—slowly*). So—yuh're— (*She suddenly bursts out into hoarse, ironical laughter.*) Gawd!

ANNA. All the way from Minnesota, sure. (*Flaring up.*) What you laughing at? Me?

MARTHY (*hastily*). No, honest, kid. I was thinkin' of somethin' else.

ANNA (*mollified—with a smile*). Well, I wouldn't blame you, at that. Guess I do look rotten—yust out of the hospital two weeks. I'm going to have another 'ski. What d'you say? Have something on me?

MARTHY. Sure I will. T'anks. (*She calls.*) Hey, Larry! Little service! (*He comes in.*)

ANNA. Same for me.

MARTHY. Same here.

(*Larry takes their glasses and goes out.*)

ANNA. Why don't you come sit over here, be sociable. I'm a dead stranger in this burg—and I ain't spoke a word with no one since day before yesterday.

MARTHY. Sure thing.

(*She shuffles over to Anna's table and sits down opposite her. Larry brings the drinks and Anna pays him.*)

ANNA. Skoal! Here's how! (*She drinks.*)

MARTHA. Here's luck! (*She takes a gulp from her tankard.*)

ANNA (*taking a package of Sweet Caporal cigarettes from her bag*). Let you smoke in here, won't they?

MARTHY (*doubtfully*). Sure. (*Then with evident anxiety*). On'y trow it away if yuh hear some one comin'.

ANNA (*lighting one and taking a deep inhale*). Gee, they're fussy in this dump, ain't they? (*She puffs, staring at the table top. Marthy looks her over with a new penetrating interest, taking in every detail of her face. Anna suddenly becomes conscious of this appraising stare—resentfully*). Ain't nothing wrong with me, is there? You're looking hard enough.

MARTHY (*irritated by the other's tone—scornfully*). Ain't got to look much. I got your number the minute you stepped in the door.

ANNA (*her eyes narrowing*). Ain't you smart! Well, I got yours, too, without no trouble. You're me forty years from now. That's you! (*She gives a hard little laugh.*)

MARTHY (*angrily*). Is that so? Well, I'll tell you straight, kiddo, that Marthy Owen never— (*She catches herself up short—with a grin.*) What are you and me scrappin' over? Let's cut it out, huh? Me, I don't want no hard feelin's with no one. (*Extending her hand.*) Shake and forget it, huh?

ANNA (*shakes her hand gladly*). Only too glad to. I ain't looking for trouble. Let's have 'nother. What d'you say?

MARTHY (*shaking her head*). Not for mine. I'm full up. And you—had anythin' to eat lately?

ANNA. Not since this morning on the train.

MARTHY. Then yuh better go easy on it, hadn't yuh?

ANNA (*after a moment's hesitation*). Guess you're right. I got to meet some one, too. But my nerves is on edge after that rotten trip.

MARTHY. Yuh said yuh was just outa the hospital?

ANNA. Two weeks ago. (*Leaning over to Marthy confidentially.*) The joint I was in out in St. Paul got raided. That was the start. The judge give all us girls thirty days. The others didn't seem to mind being in the cooler much. Some of 'em was used to it. But me, I couldn't stand it. It got my goat right—couldn't eat or sleep or nothing. I never could stand being caged up nowheres. I got good and sick and they had to send me to the hospital. It was nice there. I was sorry to leave it, honest!

MARTHY (*after a slight pause*). Did yuh say yuh got to meet some one here?

ANNA. Yes. Oh, not what you mean. It's my Old Man I got to meet. Honest! It's funny, too. I ain't seen him since I was a kid—don't even know what he looks like—yust had a letter every now and then. This was always the only address he give me to write him back. He's yanitor of some building here now—used to be a sailor.

MARTHY (*astonished*). Janitor!

ANNA. Sure. And I was thinking maybe, seeing he ain't never done a thing for me in my life, he might be willing to stake me to a room and eats till I get rested up. (*Wearily.*) Gee, I sure need that rest! I'm knocked out. (*Then resignedly.*) But I ain't expecting much from him. Give you a kick when you're down, that's what all men do. (*With sudden passion.*) Men, I hate 'em—all of 'em! And I don't expect he'll turn out no better than the rest. (*Then with sudden interest.*) Say, do you hang out around this dump much?

MARTHY. Oh, off and on.

ANNA. Then maybe you know him—my Old Man—or at least seen him?

MARTHY. It ain't old Chris, is it?

ANNA. Old Chris?

MARTHY. Chris Christopherson, his full name is.

ANNA (*excitedly*). Yes, that's him! Anna Christopherson—that's my real name—only out there I called myself Anna Christie. So you know him, eh?

MARTHY (*evasively*). Seen him about for years.

ANNA. Say, what's he like, tell me—honest?

MARTHY. Oh, he's short and—

ANNA (*impatiently*). I don't care what he looks like. What kind is he?

MARTHY (*earnestly*). Well, yuh can bet your life, kid, he's as good an old guy as ever walked on two feet. That goes!

ANNA (*pleased*). I'm glad to hear it. Then you thinks he'll stake me to that rest cure I'm after?

MARTHY (*emphatically*). Surest thing you know. (*Disgustedly.*) But where'd yuh get the idea he was a janitor?

ANNA. He wrote me he was himself.

MARTHY. Well, he was lyin'. He ain't. He's captain of a barge—five men under him.

ANNA (*disgusted in her turn*). A barge? What kind of a barge?

MARTHY. Coal, mostly.

ANNA. A coal barge! (*With a harsh laugh.*) If that ain't a swell job to find your long-lost Old Man working at! Gee, I knew something'd be bound to turn out wrong—always does with me. That puts my idea of his giving me a rest up the spout.

MARTHY. What d'yuh mean?

ANNA. I s'pose he lives on the boat, don't he?

MARTHY. Sure. What about it? Can't you live on it, too?

ANNA (*scornfully*). Me? On a dirty coal barge! What d'you think I am?

MARTHY (*resentfully*). What d'yuh know about barges, huh? Bet yuh ain't never seen one. That's what comes of his bringing yuh up inland—away from the old divil sea—where yuh'd be safe—Gawd! (*The irony of it strikes her sense of humour and she laughs hoarsely.*)

ANNA (*angrily*). His bringing me up! Is that what he tells people! I like his nerve! He let them cousins of my Old Woman's keep me on their farm and work me to death like a dog.

MARTHY. Well, he's got queer notions on some things. I've heard him say a farm was the best place for a kid.

ANNA. Sure. That's what he'd always answer back—and a lot of crazy stuff about staying away from the sea—stuff I couldn't make head or tail to. I thought he must be nutty.

MARTHY. He is on that one point. (*Casually.*) So yuh didn't fall for life on the farm, huh?

ANNA. I should say not! The old man of the family, his wife, and four sons—I had to slave for all of 'em. I was only a poor relation, and they treated me worse than they dare treat a hired girl. (*After a moment's hesitation—sombrely.*) It was one of the sons—the youngest—started me—when I was sixteen. After that, I hated 'em so I'd killed 'em all if I'd stayed. So I run away—to St. Paul.

MARTHY (*who has been listening sympathetically*). I've heard Old Chris talkin' about your bein' a nurse girl out there. Was that all a bluff yuh put up when yuh wrote him?

ANNA. Not on your life, it wasn't. It was true for two years. I didn't go wrong all at one jump. Being a nurse girl was yust what finished me. Taking care of other people's kids, always listening to their bawling and crying, caged in, when you're only a kid yourself and want to go out and see things. At last I got the chance—to get into that house. And you bet your life I took it! (*Defiantly.*) And I ain't sorry neither. (*After a pause—with bitter hatred.*) It was all men's fault—the whole business. It was men on the farm ordering and beating me—and giving me the wrong start. Then when I was a nurse, it was men again hanging around, bothering me, trying to see what they could get. (*She gives a hard laugh.*) And now it's men all the time. Gawd, I hate 'em all, every mother's son of 'em! Don't you?

MARTHY. Oh, I dunno. There's good ones and bad ones, kid. You've just had a run of bad luck with 'em, that's all. Your Old Man, now—old Chris—he's a good one.

ANNA (*sceptically*). He'll have to show me.

MARTHY. Yuh kept right on writing him yuh was a nurse girl still, even after yuh was in the house, didn't yuh?

ANNA. Sure. (*Cynically*). Not that I think he'd care a darn.

MARTHY. Yuh're all wrong about him, kid. (*Earnestly.*) I know Old Chris well for a long time. He's talked to me 'bout you lots o' times. He thinks the world o' you, honest he does.

ANNA. Aw, quit the kiddin'!

MARTHY. Honest! Only, he's a simple old guy, see? He's got nutty notions. But he means well, honest. Listen to me, kid— (*She is interrupted by the opening and shutting of the street door in the bar and by hearing Chris's voice.*) Ssshh!

ANNA. What's up?

CHRIS (*who has entered the bar. He seems considerably sobered up*). Py golly, Larry, dat grub taste good. Marthy in back?

LARRY. Sure—and another tramp with her.

(*Chris starts for the entrance to the back room.*)

MARTHY (*to Anna in a hurried, nervous whisper*). That's him now. He's comin' in here. Brace up!

ANNA. Who?

(*Chris opens the door.*)

MARTHY (*as if she were greeting him for the first time*). Why hallo, Old Chris. (*Then before he can speak, she shuffles hurriedly past him into the bar, beckoning him to follow her.*) Come here. I wanta tell yuh somethin'. (*He goes out to her. She speaks hurriedly in a low voice.*) Listen! I'm goin' to beat it down to the barge—pack up me duds and blow. That's her in there—your Anna—just come—waitin' for yuh. Treat her right, see? She's been sick. Well, s'long! (*She goes into the back room—to Anna.*) S'long, kid. I gotta beat it now. See yuh later.

ANNA (*nervously*). So long.

(*Martha goes quickly out of the family entrance.*)

LARRY (*looking at the stupefied Chris curiously*). Well, what's up now?

CHRIS (*vaguely*). Nutting—nutting. (*He stands before the door to the back room in an agony of embarrassed emotion—then he forces himself to a bold decision, pushes open the door and walks in. He stands there, casts a shy glance at Anna, whose brilliant clothes, and, to him, high-toned appearance, awe him terribly. He looks about him with pitiful nervousness as if to avoid the appraising look with which she takes in his face, his clothes, etc.—his voice seeming to plead for her forbearance.*) Anna!

ANNA (*acutely embarrassed in her turn*). Hallo—father. She told me it was you. I yust got here a little while ago.

CHRIS (*goes slowly over to her chair*). It's good—for see you—after all dem years, Anna. (*He bends down over her. After an embarrassed struggle they manage to kiss each other.*)

ANNA (*a trace of genuine feeling in her voice*). It's good to see you, too.

CHRIS (*grasps her arms and looks into her face—then overcome by a wave of fierce tenderness*). Anna lilla! Anna lilla! (*Takes her in his arms.*)

ANNA (*shrinks away from him, half frightened*). What's that—Swedish? I don't know it. (*Then as if seeking relief from the tension in a voluble chatter.*) Gee, I had an awful trip coming here. I'm all in. I had to sit up in the dirty coach all night—couldn't get no sleep, hardly—and then I had a hard job finding this place. I never been in New York before, you know, and—

CHRIS (*who has been staring down at her face admiringly, not hearing what she says—impulsively*). You know you vas awful pooty gel, Anna? Ay bet all men see you fall in love with you, py yiminy!

ANNA (*repelled—harshly*). Cut it! You talk same as they all do.

CHRIS (*hurt—humbly*). Ain't no harm for your fader talk dat vay, Anna.

ANNA (*forcing a short laugh*). No—course not. Only—it's funny to see you and not remember nothing. You're like—a stranger.

CHRIS (*sadly*). Ay s'pose. Ay never come home only few times ven you vas kit in Sveden. You don't remember dat?

ANNA. No. (*Resentfully.*) But why didn't you never come home them days? Why didn't you never come out West to see me?

CHRIS (*slowly*). Ay tank, after your mo'der die, ven Ay vas avay on voyage, it's better for you you don't never see me! (*He sinks down in the chair opposite her dejectedly—then turns to her—sadly.*) Ay don't know, Anna, vhy Ay never come home Sveden in ole year. Ay vant come home end of every voyage. Ay vant see your mo'der, your two bro'der before dey vas drowned, you ven you vas born—but—Ay—don't go. Ay sign on oder ships—go South America, go Australia, go China, go every port all over world many times—but Ay never go aboard ship sail for Sveden. Ven Ay gat money for pay passage home as passenger den—(*He bows his head guiltily.*) Ay forgat and Ay spend all money. Ven Ay tank again, it's too late. (*He sighs.*) Ay don't know vhy, but dat's vay with most sailor fallar, Anna. Dat ole davil sea make dem crazy fools with her dirty tricks. It's so.

ANNA (*who has watched him keenly while he has been speaking—with a trace of scorn in her voice*). Then you think the sea's to blame for everything, eh? Well, you're still workin' on it, ain't you, spite of all you used to write me about hating it. That dame was here told me you was captain of a coal barge—and you wrote me you was yanitor of a building!

CHRIS (*embarrassed but lying glibly*). Oh, Ay work on land long time as yanitor. Yust short time ago Ay got dis yob cause Ay was sick, need open air.

ANNA (*sceptically*). Sick? You? You'd never think it.

CHRIS. And, Anna, dis ain't real sailor yob. Dis ain't real boat on sea. She's yust ole tub—like piece of land with house on it dat float. Yob on her ain't sea yob. No. Ay don't gat yob on sea, Anna, if Ay die first. Ay swear dat, ven your mo'der die. Ay keep my word, py yingo!

ANNA (*perplexed*). Well, I can't see no difference. (*Dismissing the subject.*) Speaking of being sick, I been there myself—yust out of the hospital two weeks ago.

CHRIS (*immediately all concern*). You, Anna? Py golly! (*Anxiously.*) You feel better now, dough, don't you? You look little tired, dat's all!

ANNA (*wearily*). I am. Tired to death. I need a long rest and I don't see much chance of getting it.

CHRIS. What you mean, Anna?

ANNA. Well, when I made up my mind to come to see you, I thought you was a yanitor—that you'd have a place where, maybe, if you didn't mind having me, I could visit a while and rest up—till I felt able to get back on the job again.

CHRIS (*eagerly*). But Ay gat place, Anna—nice place. You rest all you want, py yiminy! You don't never have to vork as nurse gel no more. You stay with me, py golly!

ANNA (*surprised and pleased by his eagerness—with a smile*). Then you're really glad to see me—honest?

CHRIS (*pressing one of her hands in both of his*). Anna, Ay like see you like hell, Ay tal you! And don't you talk no more about gatting yob. You stay with me. Ay don't see you for long time, you don't forgat dat. (*His voice trembles.*) Ay'm gatting ole. Ay gat no one in vorld but you.

ANNA (*touched—embarrassed by this unfamiliar emotion*). Thanks. It sounds good to hear some one—talk to me that way. Say, though—if you're so lonely—it's funny—why ain't you ever married again?

CHRIS (*shaking his head emphatically—after a pause*). Ay love your mo'der too much for ever do dat, Anna.

ANNA (*impressed—slowly*). I don't remember nothing about her. What was she like? Tell me.

CHRIS. Ay tal you all about everytang—and you

tal me all tangs happen to you. But not here now. Dis ain't good place for young gel, anyway. Only no good sailor fallar come here for gat drunk. (*He gets to his feet quickly and picks up her bag.*) You come with me, Anna. You need lie down, gat rest.

ANNA (*half rises to her feet, then sits down again*). Where're you going ?

CHRIS. Come. Ve gat on board.

ANNA (*disappointedly*). On board your barge, you mean ? (*Dryly.*) Nix for mine ! (*Then seeing his crestfallen look—forcing a smile.*) Do you think that's a good place for a young girl like me—a coal barge ?

CHRIS (*dully*). Yes, Ay tank. (*He hesitates—then continues more and more pleadingly.*) You don't know how nice it's on barge, Anna. Tug come and ve gat towed out on voyage—yust water all round, and sun, and fresh air, and good grub for make you strong, healthy gel. You see many tangs you don't see before. You gat moonlight at night, maybe ; see steamer pass ; see schooner make sail—see everytang dat's pooty. You need take rest like dat. You work too hard for young gel already. You need vacation, yes !

ANNA (*who has listened to him with a growing interest—with an uncertain laugh*). It sounds good to hear you tell it. I'd sure like a trip on the water, all right. It's the barge idea has me stopped. Well, I'll go down with you and have a look—and maybe I'll take a chance. Gee, I'd do anything once.

CHRIS (*picks up her bag again*). Ve go, eh ?

ANNA. What's the rush ? Wait a second. (*Forgetting the situation for a moment, she relapses into the familiar form and flashes one of her winning trade smiles at him.*) Gee, I'm thirsty.

CHRIS (*sets down her bag immediately—hastily*). Ay'm sorry, Anna. What you tank you like for drink, eh ?

ANNA (*promptly*). I'll take a— (*Then suddenly reminded—confusedly.*) I don't know. What's they got here ?

CHRIS (*with a grin*). Ay don't tank dey got much fancy drink for young gel in dis place, Anna. Yinger ale—sas'prilla, maybe.

ANNA (*forcing a laugh herself*). Make it sas, then.

CHRIS (*coming up to her—with a wink*). Ay tal you, Anna, ve calabrate, yes—dis one time because ve meet after many year. (*In a half whisper, embarrassedly.*) Dey gat good port wine, Anna. It's good for you, Ay tank—little bit—for give you appetite. It ain't strong, neider. One glass don't go to your head, Ay promise.

ANNA (*with a half-hysterical laugh*). All right. I'll take port.

CHRIS. Ay go gat him. (*He goes out to the bar. As soon as the door closes, Anna starts to her feet.*)

ANNA (*picking up her bag—half-aloud—stammeringly*). Gawd, I can't stand this ! I better beat it. (*Then she lets her bag drop, stumbles over to her chair again, and covering her face with her hands, begins to sob.*)

LARRY (*putting down his paper as Chris comes up—with a grin*). Well, who's the blonde ?

CHRIS (*proudly*). Dat vas Anna, Larry.

LARRY (*in amazement*). Your daughter, Anna ?

(*Chris nods. Larry lets a long, low whistle escape him and turns away embarrassedly.*)

CHRIS. Don't you tank she vas pooty gel, Larry ?

LARRY (*rising to the occasion*). Sure ! A peach !

CHRIS. You bet you ! Give me drink for take back—one port vine for Anna—she calabrate dis one time with me—and small beer for me.

LARRY (*as he gets the drinks*). Small beer for you, eh ? She's reformin' you already.

CHRIS (*pleased*). You bet ! (*He takes the drinks. As she hears him coming, Anna hastily dries her eyes, tries to smile. Chris comes in and sets the drinks down on the table—stares at her for a second anxiously—patting her hand.*) You look tired, Anna. Vell, Ay make you take good long rest now. (*Picking up his beer.*) Come, you drink vine. It put new life in you. (*She lifts her glass—he grins.*) Skoal, Anna ! You know dat Svedish word ?

ANNA. Skoal ! (*downing her port at a gulp like a drink of whisky—her lips trembling*). Skoal ? Guess I know that word, all right, all right !

Curtain

Act II

SCENE. *Ten days later. The stern of the deeply-laden barge, " Simeon Winthrop," at anchor in the outer harbour of Provincetown, Mass. It is ten o'clock at night. Dense fog shrouds the barge on all sides, and she floats motionless on a calm. A lantern set up on an immense coil of thick hawser sheds a dull, filtering light on objects near it—the heavy steel bits for making fast the tow-lines, etc. In the rear is the cabin, its misty windows glowing wanly with the light of a lamp inside. The chimney of the cabin stove rises a few feet above the roof. The doleful tolling of bells, on Long Point, on ships at anchor, breaks the silence at regular intervals.*

As the curtain rises, Anna is discovered standing near the coil of rope on which the lantern is placed. She looks healthy, transformed, the natural colour has come back to her face. She has on a black, oilskin coat, but wears no hat. She is staring out into the fog astern with an expression of awed wonder. The cabin door is pushed open and Chris appears. He is dressed in yellow oilskins—coat, trousers, sou'wester—and wears high sea-boots.

CHRIS (*the glare from the cabin still in his eyes, peers blinkingly astern*). Anna ! (*Receiving no reply, he calls again, this time with apparent apprehension.*) Anna !

ANNA (*with a start—making a gesture with her hand as if to impose silence—in a hushed whisper*). Yes, here I am. What d'you want ?

CHRIS (*walks over to her—solicitously*). Don't you come turn in, Anna ? It's late—after four bells. It ain't good for you stay out here in fog, Ay tank.

ANNA. Why not ? (*With a trace of strange exultation.*) I love this fog ! Honest ! It's so—(*she hesitates, groping for a word*)—funny and still. I feel as if I was—out of things altogether.

CHRIS (*spitting disgustedly*). Fog's vorst one of her dirty tricks, py yingo !

ANNA (*with a short laugh*). Beefing about the sea again ? I'm getting so's I love it, the little I've seen.

CHRIS (*glancing at her moodily*). Dat's foolish talk, Anna. You see her more, you don't talk dat vay. (*Then seeing her irritation, he hastily adopts a more cheerful tone.*) But Ay'm glad you like it on barge. Ay'm glad it makes you feel good again. (*With a placating grin.*) You like live like dis alone with ole fa'der, eh ?

ANNA. Sure I do. Everything's been so different from anything I ever come across before. And now—this fog—Gee, I wouldn't have missed it for nothing. I never thought living on ships was so different from land. Gee, I'd yust love to work on it, honest I would, if I was a man. I don't wonder you always been a sailor.

CHRIS (*vehemently*). Ay ain't sailor, Anna. And dis ain't real sea. You only see nice part. (*Then as she doesn't answer, he continues hopefully.*) Vell, fog lift in morning, Ay tank.

ANNA (*the exultation again in her voice*). I love it ! I don't give a rap if it never lifts ! (*Chris fidgets from one foot to the other worriedly. Anna continues slowly, after a pause.*) It makes me feel clean —out here—'s if I'd taken a bath.

CHRIS (*after a pause*). You better go in cabin—read book. Dat put you to sleep.

ANNA. I don't want to sleep. I want to stay out here—and think about things.

CHRIS (*walks away from her toward the cabin—then comes back*). You act funny to-night, Anna.

ANNA (*her voice rising angrily*). Say, what're you trying to do—make things rotten ? You been kind as kind can be to me and I certainly appreciate it—only don't spoil it all now. (*Then, seeing the hurt expression on her father's face, she forces a smile.*) Let's talk of something else. Come. Sit down here. (*She points to the coil of rope.*)

CHRIS (*sits down beside her with a sigh*). It's gatting pooty late in night, Anna. Must be near five bells.

ANNA (*interestedly*). Five bells ? What time is that ?

CHRIS. Half-past ten.

ANNA. Funny I don't know nothing about sea talk—but those cousins was always talking crops and that stuff. Gee, wasn't I sick of it—and of them !

CHRIS. You don't like live on farm, Anna?

ANNA. I've told you a hundred times I hated it. (*Decidedly.*) I'd rather have one drop of ocean than all the farms in the world! Honest! And you wouldn't like a farm, neither. Here's where you belong. (*She makes a sweeping gesture seaward.*) But not on a coal barge. You belong on a real ship, sailing all over the world.

CHRIS (*moodily*). Ay've done dat many year, Anna, when Ay vas damn fool.

ANNA (*disgustedly*). Oh, rats! (*After a pause she speaks musingly.*) Was the men in our family always sailors—as far back as you know about?

CHRIS (*shortly*). Yes. Damn fools! All men in our village on coast, Sveden, go to sea. Ain't nutting else for dem to do. My fa'der die on board ship in Indian Ocean. He's buried at sea. Ay don't never know him only little bit. Den my tree bro'der, older'n me, dey go on ships. Den Ay go, too. Den my mo'der she's left all 'lone. She die pooty quick after dat—all 'lone. Ve was all avay on voyage when she die. (*He pauses sadly.*) Twc my bro'der dey gat lost on fishing boat same like your bro'ders vas drowned. My oder bro'der, he save money, give up sea, den he die home in bed. He's only one dat ole davil don't kill. (*Defiantly.*) But me, Ay bet you Ay die ashore in bed, too!

ANNA. Were all of 'em yust plain sailors?

CHRIS. Able body seaman, most of dem. (*With a certain pride.*) Dey vas all smart seaman, too—AI. (*Then after hesitating a moment—shyly.*) Ay vas bos'n.

ANNA. Bos'n?

CHRIS. Dat's kind of officer.

ANNA. Gee, that was fine. What does he do?

CHRIS (*after a second's hesitation, plunged into gloom again by his fear of her enthusiasm*). Hard vork all time. It's rotten, Ay tal you, for go to sea. (*Determined to disgust her with sea life—volubly.*) Dey're all fool fallar, dem fallar in our family. Dey all york rotten yob on sea for nutting, don't care nutting but yust gat big pay-day in pocket, gat drunk, gat robbed, ship avay again on oder voyage. Dey don't come home. Dey don't do anytang like good man do. And dat ole davil, sea, sooner, later she svallow dem up.

ANNA (*with an excited laugh*). Good sports, I'd call 'em. (*Then hastily.*) But say—listen—did all the women of the family marry sailors?

CHRIS (*eagerly—seeing a chance to drive home his point*). Yes—and it's bad on dem like hell vorst of all. Dey don't see deir men only once in long while. Dey set and vait all 'lone. And vhen deir boys grows up, go to sea, dey sit and vait some more. (*Vehemently.*) Any gel marry sailor, she's crazy fool! Your mo'der she tal you same tang if she vas alive. (*He relapses into an attitude of sombre brooding.*)

ANNA (*after a pause—dreamily*). Funny! I do feel sort of—nutty, to-night. I feel old.

CHRIS (*mystified*). Ole?

ANNA. Sure—like I'd been living a long, long time—out here in the fog. (*Frowning perplexedly.*) I don't know how to tell you yust what I mean. It's like I'd come home after a long visit away some place. It all seems like I'd been here before lots of times—on boats—in this same fog. (*With a short laugh.*) You must think I'm off my base.

CHRIS (*gruffly*). Anybody feel funny dat vay in fog.

ANNA (*persistently*). But why d'you s'pose I feel so—so—like I'd found something I'd missed and been looking for—'s if this was the right place for me to fit in? And I seem to have forgot—everything that's happened—like it didn't matter no more. And I feel clean, somehow—like you feel yust after you've took a bath. And I feel happy for once—yes, honest!—happier than I ever been anywhere before! (*As Chris makes no comment but a heavy sigh, she continues wonderingly.*) It's nutty for me to feel that way, don't you think?

CHRIS (*a grim foreboding in his voice*). Ay tank Ay'm damn fool for bring you on voyage, Anna.

ANNA (*impressed by his tone*). You talk—nutty to-night yourself. You act's if you was scared something was going to happen.

CHRIS. Only God know dat, Anna.

ANNA (*half-mockingly*). Then it'll be Gawd's will, like the preachers say—what does happen.

CHRIS (*starts to his feet with fierce protest*). No! Dat ole davil, sea, she ain't God! (*In the pause of silence that comes after his defiance a hail in a man's husky, exhausted voice comes faintly out of the fog to port.* "Ahoy!" *Chris gives a startled exclamation.*)

ANNA (*jumping to her feet*). What's that?

CHRIS (*who has regained his composure—sheepishly*). Py golly, dat scare me for minute. It's only some fallar hail, Anna—loose his course in fog. Must be fisherman's power boat. His engine break down, Ay guess. (*The* "Ahoy" *comes again through the wall of fog, sounding much nearer this time. Chris goes over to the port bulwark.*) Sound from dis side. She come in from open sea. (*He holds his hands to his mouth, megaphone-fashion, and shouts back.*) Ahoy, dere! Vhat's trouble?

THE VOICE (*this time sounding nearer but up forward toward the bow*). Heave a rope when we come alongside. (*Then irritably.*) Where are ye, ye scut?

CHRIS. Ay hear dem rowing. Dey come up by bow, Ay tank. (*Then shouting out again.*) Dis vay!

THE VOICE. Right ye are! (*There is a muffled sound of oars in row-locks.*)

ANNA (*half to herself—resentfully*). Why don't that guy stay where he belongs?

CHRIS (*hurriedly*). Ay go up bow. All hands asleep 'cepting fallar on vatch. Ay gat heave line to dat fallar. (*He picks up a coil of rope and hurries off toward the bow. Anna walks back toward the extreme stern as if she wanted to remain as much isolated as possible. She turns her back on the proceedings and stares out into the fog. The Voice is heard again shouting* "Ahoy" *and Chris answering* "Dis vay." *Then there is a pause—the murmur of excited voices—then the scuffling of feet. Chris appears from around the cabin to port. He is supporting the limp form of a man dressed in dungarees, holding one of the man's arms around his neck. The deckhand, Johnson, a young, blond Swede, follows him, helping along another exhausted man similar fashion. Anna turns to look at them. Chris stops for a second—volubly.*) Anna! You come help, vill you? You find vhisky in cabin. Dese fallars need drink for fix dem. Dey vas near dead.

ANNA (*hurrying to him*). Sure—but who are they? What's the trouble?

CHRIS. Sailor fallars. Deir steamer gat wrecked. Dey been five days in open boat—four fallars—only one left able stand up. Come, Anna. (*She precedes him into the cabin, holding the door open while he and Johnson carry in their burdens. The door is shut, then opened again as Johnson comes out. Chris's voice shouts after him.*) Go gat oder fallar, Yohnson.

JOHNSON. Yes, sir.

(*He goes. The door is closed again. Mat Burke stumbles in around the port side of the cabin. He moves slowly, feeling his way uncertainly, keeping hold of the port bulwark with his right hand to steady himself. He is stripped to the waist, has on nothing but a pair of dirty dungaree trousers. He is a powerful, broad-chested six-footer, his face handsome in a hard, rough, bold, defiant way. He is about thirty, in the full power of his heavy-muscled, immense strength. His dark eyes are bloodshot and wild from sleeplessness. The muscles of his arms and shoulders are lumped in knots and bunches, the veins of his forearms stand out like blue cords. He finds his way to the coil of hawser and sits down on it facing the cabin, his back bowed, head in his hands in an attitude of spent weariness.*)

BURKE (*talking aloud to himself*). Row, ye divil! Row! (*Then lifting his head and looking about him.*) What's this tub? Well, we're safe, anyway—with the help of God. (*He makes the sign of the cross mechanically. Johnson comes along the deck to port, supporting the fourth man, who is babbling to himself incoherently. Burke glances at him disdainfully.*) Is it losing the small wits ye iver had, ye are? Deck-scrubbing scut! (*They pass him and go into the cabin, leaving the door open. Burke sags forward wearily.*) I'm bate out—bate out entirely.

ANNA (*comes out of the cabin with a tumbler quarter-full of whisky in her hand. She gives a start when she sees Burke so near her, the light from the open door falling full on him. Then, overcoming what is evidently a feeling of repulsion, she comes up beside him*). Here you are. Here's a drink for you. You need it, I guess.

BURKE (*lifting his head slowly—confusedly*). Is it dreaming I am?

ANNA (*half smiling*). Drink it and you'll find it ain't no dream.

BURKE. To hell with the drink—but I'll take it just the same. (*He tosses it down.*) Aah! I'm needin' that—and 'tis fine stuff. (*Looking up at her with frank, grinning admiration.*) But 'twasn't the booze I meant when I said, was I dreaming. I thought you was some mermaid out of the sea come to torment me. (*He reaches out to feel of her arm.*) Aye, rale flesh and blood, divil a less.

ANNA (*coldly. Stepping back from him*). Cut that.

BURKE. But tell me, isn't this a barge I'm on—or isn't it?

ANNA. Sure.

BURKE. And what is a fine, handsome woman the like of you doing on this scow?

ANNA (*coldly*). Never you mind. (*Then half amused in spite of herself.*) Say, you're a great one, honest—starting right in kidding after what you been through.

BURKE (*delighted—proudly*). Ah, it was nothing—aisy for a rale man with guts to him, the like of me. (*He laughs.*) All in the day's work, darlin'. (*Then, more seriously, but still in a boastful tone, confidentially.*) But I won't be denying 'twas a damn narrow squeak. We'd all ought to be with Davy Jones at the bottom of the sea, be rights. And only for me, I'm telling you, and the great strength and guts is in me, we'd be being scoffed by the fishes this minute!

ANNA (*contemptuously*). Gee, you hate yourself, don't you? (*Then turning away from him indifferently.*) Well, you'd better come in and lie down. You must want to sleep.

BURKE (*stung—rising unsteadily to his feet with chest out and head thrown back—resentfully*). Lie down and sleep, is it? Divil a wink I'm after having for two days and nights and divil a bit I'm needing now. Let you not be thinking I'm the like of them three weak scuts come in the boat with me. I could lick the three of them sitting down with one hand tied behind me. They may be bate out, but I'm not—and I've been rowing the boat with them lying in the bottom not able to raise a hand for the last two days we was in it. (*Furiously, as he sees this is making no impression on her.*) And I can lick all hands on this tub, wan be wan, tired as I am!

ANNA (*sarcastically*). Gee, ain't you a hard guy! (*Then, with a trace of sympathy, as she notices him swaying from weakness.*) But never mind that fight talk. I'll take your word for all you've said. Go on and sit down out here, anyway, if I can't get you to come inside. (*He sits down weakly.*) You're all in, you might as well own up to it.

BURKE (*fiercely*). The hell I am!

ANNA (*coldly*). Well, be stubborn then for all I care. And I must say I don't care for your language. The men I know don't pull that rough stuff when ladies are around.

BURKE (*getting unsteadily to his feet again—in a rage*). Ladies! Ho-ho! Divil mend you! Let you not be making game of me. What would ladies be doing on this bloody hulk? (*As Anna attempts to go to the cabin, he lurches into her path.*) Aisy, now! You're not the old Square-head's woman, I suppose you'll be telling me next—living in his cabin with him, no less! (*Seeing the cold, hostile expression on Anna's face, he suddenly changes his tone to one of boisterous joviality.*) But I do be thinking, iver since the first look my eyes took at you, that it's a fool you are to be wasting yourself—a fine, handsome girl—on a stumpy runt of a man like that old Swede. There's too many strapping great lads on the sea would give their heart's blood for one kiss of you!

ANNA (*scornfully*). Lads like you, eh?

BURKE (*grinning*). Ye take the words out o' my mouth. I'm the proper lad for you, if it's meself do be saying it. (*With a quick movement he puts his arms about her waist.*) Whisht, now, me daisy! Himself's in the cabin. It's wan of your kisses I'm needing to take the tiredness from me bones. Wan kiss, now! (*He presses her to him and attempts to kiss her.*)

ANNA (*struggling fiercely*). Leggo of me, you big mut!

(*She pushes him away with all her might. Burke, weak and tottering, is caught off his guard. He is thrown down backward, and, in falling, hits his head a hard thump against the bulwark. He lies there still, knocked out for the moment. Anna stands for a second, looking down at him anxiously. Then she kneels down beside him and raises his head to her knee, staring into his face for some sign of life.*)

BURKE (*stirring a bit—mutteringly*). God stiffen it! (*He opens his eyes and blinks up at her with vague wonder.*)

ANNA (*letting his head sink back on the deck, rising to her feet with a sigh of relief*). You're coming to all right, eh? Gee, I was scared for a moment I'd killed you.

BURKE (*with difficulty rising to a sitting position—scornfully*). Killed, is it? It'd take more than a bit of a blow to crack my thick skull. (*Then looking at her with the most intense admiration.*) But, glory be, it's a power of strength is in them two fine arms of yours. There's not a man in the world can say the same as you, that he seen Mat Burke lying at his feet and him dead to the world.

ANNA (*rather remorsefully*). Forget it. I'm sorry it happened, see? (*Burke rises and sits on bench. Then severely.*) Only you had no right to be getting fresh with me. Listen, now, and don't go getting any more wrong notions. I'm on this barge because I'm making a trip with my father. The captain's my father. Now you know.

BURKE. The old square—the old Swede, I mean?

ANNA. Yes.

BURKE (*rising—peering at her face*). Sure, I might have known it, if I wasn't a bloody fool from birth. Where else'd you get that fine yellow hair is like a golden crown on your head.

ANNA (*with an amused laugh*). Say, nothing stops you, does it? (*Then attempting a severe tone again.*) But don't you think you ought to be apologizing for what you said and done yust a minute ago, instead of trying to kid me with that mush?

BURKE (*indignantly*). Mush! (*Then bending forward toward her with very intense earnestness.*) Indade, and I will ask your pardon a thousand times—and on my knees, if ye like. I didn't mean a word of what I said or did. (*Resentful again for a second.*) But divil a woman in all the ports of the world has iver made a great fool of me that way before!

ANNA (*with amused sarcasm*). I see. You mean you're a lady-killer and they all fall for you.

BURKE (*offended. Passionately*). Leave off your fooling! 'Tis that is after getting my back up at you. (*Earnestly.*) 'Tis no lie I'm telling you about the women. (*Ruefully.*) Though it's a great jackass I am to be mistaking you, even in anger, for the like of them cows on the water-front is the only women I've met up with since I was growed to a man. (*As Anna shrinks away from him at this, he hurries on pleadingly.*) I'm a hard, rough man, and I'm not fit, I'm thinking, to be kissing the shoesoles of a fine, dacent girl the like of yourself. 'Tis only the ignorance of your kind made me see you wrong. So you'll forgive me, for the love of God, and let us be friends from this out. (*Passionately.*) I'm thinking I'd rather be friends with you than have my wish for anything else in the world. (*He holds out his hand to her shyly.*)

ANNA (*looking queerly at him, perplexed and worried, but moved and pleased in spite of herself—takes his hand uncertainly*). Sure.

BURKE (*with boyish delight*). God bless you! (*In his excitement he squeezes her hand tight.*)

ANNA. Ouch!

BURKE (*hastily dropping her hand—ruefully*). Your pardon, Miss. 'Tis a clumsy ape I am. (*Then simply—glancing down his arm proudly.*) It's great power I have in my hand and arm, and I do be forgetting it at times.

ANNA (*nursing her crushed hand and glancing at his arm, not without a trace of his own admiration*). Gee, you're some strong, all right.

BURKE (*delighted*). It's no lie, and why shouldn't I be, with me shovelling a million tons of coal in the stokeholes of ships since I was a lad only. (*He pats the coil of hawser invitingly.*) Let you sit down, now, Miss, and I'll be telling you a bit of myself, and you'll be telling me a bit of yourself, and in an hour we'll be as old friends as if we was born in the same house. (*He pulls at her sleeve shyly.* Sit down now, if you plaze.

ANNA (*with a half-laugh*). Well— (*She sits down.*) But we won't talk about me, see? You tell me about yourself and about the wreck.

BURKE (*flattered*). I'll tell you, surely. But can I be asking you one question, Miss, has my head in a puzzle?

ANNA (*guardedly*). Well—I dunno—what is it?

BURKE. What is it you do when you're not taking a trip with the Old Man? For I'm thinking a fine girl the like of you ain't living always on this tub.

ANNA (*uneasily*). No—of course I ain't. (*She searches his face suspiciously, afraid there may be some hidden insinuation in his words. Seeing his simple frankness, she goes on confidently.*) Well, I'll tell you. I'm a governess, see? I take care of kids for people and learn them things.

BURKE (*impressed*). A governess, is it? You must be smart, surely.

ANNA. But let's not talk about me. Tell me about the wreck, like you promised me you would.

BURKE (*importantly*). 'Twas this way, Miss. Two weeks out we ran into the divil's own storm, and she sprang wan hell of a leak up for'ard. The skipper was hoping to make Boston before another blow would finish her, but ten days back we met up with another storm the like of the first, only worse. Four days we was in it with green seas raking over her from bow to stern. That was a terrible time, God help us. (*Proudly.*) And if 'twasn't for me and my great strength, I'm telling you—and it's God's truth—there'd been mutiny itself in the stokehole. 'Twas me held them to it, with a kick to wan and a clout to another, and they not caring a damn for the engineers any more, but fearing a clout of my right arm more than they'd fear the sea itself. (*He glances at her anxiously, eager for her approval.*)

ANNA (*concealing a smile—amused by this boyish boasting of his*). You did some hard work, didn't you?

BURKE (*promptly*). I did that! I'm a divil for sticking it out when them that's weak give up. But much good it did anyone! 'Twas a mad, fightin' scramble in the last seconds with each man for himself. I disremember how it come about, but there was the four of us in wan boat, and when we was raised high on a great wave I took a look about and divil a sight there was of ship or men on top of the sea.

ANNA (*in a subdued voice*). Then all the others was drowned?

BURKE. They was, surely.

ANNA (*with a shudder*). What a terrible end!

BURKE (*turns to her*). A terrible end for the like of them swabs does live on land, maybe. But for the like of us does be roaming the seas, a good end, I'm telling you—quick and clane.

ANNA (*struck by the word*). Yes, clean. That's yust the word for—all of it—the way it makes me feel.

BURKE. The sea, you mean? (*Interestedly.*) I'm thinking you have a bit of it in your blood, too. Your Old Man wasn't only a barge rat—begging your pardon—all his life, by the cut of him.

ANNA. No, he was bo'sun on sailing ships for years. And all the men on both sides of the family have gone to sea as far back as he remembers, he says. All the women have married sailors, too.

BURKE (*with intense satisfaction*). Did they, now? They had spirit in them. It's only on the sea you'd find rale men with guts is fit to wed with fine, high-tempered girls—(*then he adds half-boldly*)—the like of yourself.

ANNA (*with a laugh*). There you go kiddin' again. (*Then seeing his hurt expression—quickly.*) But you was going to tell me about yourself. You're Irish, of course I can tell that.

BURKE (*stoutly*). Yes, thank God, though I've not seen a sight of it in fifteen years or more.

ANNA (*thoughtfully*). Sailors never do go home hardly, do they? That's what my father was saying.

BURKE. He wasn't telling no lie. (*With sudden melancholy.*) It's a hard and lonesome life, the sea is. The only women you'd meet in the ports of the world who'd be willing to speak you a kind word isn't woman at all. You know the kind I mane, and they're a poor, wicked lot, God forgive them. They're looking to steal the money from you only.

ANNA (*her face averted—rising to her feet—agitatedly*). I think—I guess I'd better see what's doing inside.

BURKE (*afraid he has offended her—beseechingly*). Don't go, I'm saying! Is it I've given you offence with my talk of the like of them? Don't heed it at all! I'm clumsy in my wits when it comes to talking proper with a girl the like of you. And why wouldn't I be? Since the day I left home for to go to sea punching coal, this is the first time I've had a word with a rale, dacent woman. So don't turn your back on me now, and we beginning to be friends.

ANNA (*turning to him again—forcing a smile*). I'm not sore at you, honest.

BURKE (*gratefully*). God bless you!

ANNA (*changing the subject abruptly*). But if you honestly think the sea's such a rotten life, why don't you get out of it?

BURKE (*surprised*). Work on land, is it? (*She nods. He spits scornfully.*) Digging spuds in the muck from dawn to dark, I suppose? (*Vehemently.*) I wasn't made for it, Miss.

ANNA (*with a laugh*). I thought you'd say that.

BURKE (*argumentatively*). But there's good jobs and bad jobs at sea, like there'd be on land. I'm thinking if it's in the stokehole of a proper liner I was, I'd be able to have a little house and be home to it wan week out of four. And I'm thinking that maybe then I'd have the luck to find a fine dacent girl—the like of yourself, now—would be willing to wed with me.

ANNA (*turning away from him with a short laugh—uneasily*). Why, sure. Why not?

BURKE (*edging up close to her—exultantly*). Then you think a girl the like of yourself might maybe not mind the past at all but only be seeing the good herself put in me?

ANNA (*in the same tone*). Why, sure.

BURKE (*passionately*). She'd not be sorry for it, I'd take my oath! 'Tis no more drinking and roving about I'd be doing then, but giving my pay-day into her hand and staying at home with her as meek as a lamb each night of the week I'd be in port.

ANNA (*moved in spite of herself and troubled by this half-concealed proposal—with a forced laugh*). All you got to do is find the girl.

BURKE. I have found her!

ANNA (*half-frightened—trying to laugh it off*). You have? When? I thought you was saying—

BURKE (*boldly and forcefully*). This night. (*Hanging his head—humbly.*) If she'll be having me. (*Then raising his eyes to hers—simply.*) 'Tis you I mean.

ANNA (*is held by his eyes for a moment—then shrinks back from him with a strange, broken laugh*). Say—are you—going crazy? Are you trying to kid me? Proposing—to me!—for Gawd's sake!—on such short acquaintance?

(*Chris comes out of the cabin and stands staring blinkingly astern. When he makes out Anna in such intimate proximity to this strange sailor, an angry expression comes over his face.*)

BURKE (*following her—with fierce, pleading insistence*). I'm telling you there's the will of God in it that brought me safe through the storm and fog to the wan spot in the world where you was! Think of that now, and isn't it queer—

CHRIS. Anna! (*He comes toward them, raging, his fists clenched.*) Anna, you gat in cabin, you hear!

ANNA (*all her emotions immediately transformed into resentment at his bullying tone*). Who d'you think you're talking to—a slave?

CHRIS (*hurt—his voice breaking—pleadingly*). You need gat rest, Anna. You gat sleep. (*She does not move. He turns on Burke furiously.*) What you doing here, you sailor fallar? You ain't sick like oders. You gat in fo'c'sle. Dey give you bunk. (*Threateningly.*) You hurry, Ay tal you!

ANNA (*impulsively*). But he is sick. Look at him. He can hardly stand up.

BURKE (*straightening and throwing out his chest—with a bold laugh*). Is it giving me orders ye are, me bucko? Let you look out, then! With wan hand, weak as I am, I can break ye in two and fling the pieces over the side—and your crew after you. (*Stopping abruptly.*) I was forgetting. You're her Old Man, and I'd not raise a fist to you for the world.

(*His knees sag, he wavers and seems about to fall. Anna utters an exclamation of alarm and hurries to his side.*)

ANNA (*taking one of his arms over her shoulder*). Come on in the cabin. You can have my bed if there ain't no other place.

BURKE (*with jubilant happiness—as they proceed toward the cabin*). Glory be to God, is it holding my arm about your neck you are! Anna! Anna! Sure, it's a sweet name is suited to you.

ANNA (*guiding him carefully*). Sssh! Sssh!

BURKE. Whisht, is it? Indade, and I'll not. I'll be roaring it out like a fog horn over the sea! You're the girl of the world, and we'll be marrying soon, and I don't care who knows it!

ANNA (*as she guides him through the cabin door*). Ssshh! Never mind that talk. You go to sleep.

(*They go out of sight in the cabin. Chris, who has been listening to Burke's last words with open-mouthed amazement, stands looking after them helplessly.*)

CHRIS (*turns suddenly and shakes his fist out at the sea—with bitter hatred*). Dat's your dirty trick, damn ole davil, you! (*Then in a frenzy of rage.*) But, py God, you don't do dat! Not while Ay'm living! No, py God, you don't!

Curtain

Act III

SCENE. *The interior of the cabin on the barge, "Simeon Winthrop" (at dock in Boston)—a narrow, low-ceilinged compartment, the walls of which are painted a light brown with white trimmings. In the rear on the left, a door leading to the sleeping quarters. In the far left corner, a large locker-closet, painted white, on the door of which a mirror hangs on a nail. In the rear wall, two small square windows and a door opening out on the deck toward the stern. In the right wall, two more windows looking out on the port deck. White curtains, clean and stiff, are at the windows. A table with two cane-bottomed chairs stands in the centre of the cabin. A dilapidated, wicker rocker, painted brown, is also by the table.*

It is afternoon of a sunny day about a week later. From the harbour and docks outside, muffled by the closed door and windows, comes the sound of steamers' whistles and the puffing snort of the donkey engines of some ship unloading near by.

As the curtain rises, Chris and Anna are discovered. Anna is seated in the rocking-chair by the table, with a newspaper in her hands. She is not reading but staring straight in front of her. She looks unhappy, troubled, frowningly concentrated on her thoughts. Chris wanders about the room, casting quick, uneasy side glances at her face, then stopping to peer absent-mindedly out of the window. His attitude betrays an overwhelming, gloomy anxiety which has him on tenterhooks. He pretends to be engaged in setting things shipshape, but this occupation is confined to picking up some object, staring at it stupidly for a second, then aimlessly putting it down again. He clears his throat and starts to sing to himself in a low, doleful voice : "My Yosephine, come aboard de ship. Long time Ay vait for you."

ANNA (*turning on him, sarcastically*). I'm glad some one's feeling good. (*Wearily.*) Gee, I sure wish we was out of this dump and back in New York.

CHRIS (*with a sigh*). Ay'm glad when ve sail again, too. (*Then, as she makes no comment, he goes on with a ponderous attempt at sarcasm.*) Ay don't see vhy you don't like Boston, dough. You have good time here, Ay tank. You go ashore all time, every day and night veek ve've been here. You go to movies, see show, gat all kinds fun— (*His eyes hard with hatred.*) All with that damn Irish fallar !

ANNA (*with weary scorn*). Oh, for heaven's sake, are you off on that again ? Where's the harm in his taking me around ? D'you want me to sit all day and night in this cabin with you—and knit ? Ain't I got a right to have as good a time as I can ?

CHRIS. It ain't right kind of fun—not with that fallar, no.

ANNA. I been back on board every night by eleven, ain't I ? (*Then struck by some thought—looks at him with keen suspicion—with rising anger.*) Say, look here, what d'you mean by what you yust said ?

CHRIS (*hastily*). Nutting but what Ay say, Anna.

ANNA. You said " ain't right " and you said it funny. Say, listen here, you ain't trying to insinuate that there's something wrong between us, are you ?

CHRIS (*horrified*). No, Anna ! No, Ay svear to God, Ay never tank dat !

ANNA (*mollified by his very evident sincerity—sitting down again*). Well, don't you never think it neither if you want me ever to speak to you again. (*Angrily again.*) If I ever dreamt you thought that, I'd get the hell out of this barge so quick you couldn't see me for dust.

CHRIS (*soothingly*). Ay wouldn't never dream—(*Then, after a second's pause, reprovingly.*) You vas gatting learn to svear. Dat ain't nice for young gel, you tank ?

ANNA (*with a faint trace of a smile*). Excuse me. You ain't used to such language, I know. (*Mockingly.*) That's what your taking me to sea has done for me.

CHRIS (*indignantly*). No, it ain't me. It's dat damn sailor fallar learn you bad tangs.

ANNA. He ain't a sailor. He's a stoker.

CHRIS (*forcibly*). Dat vas million times vorse, Ay tal you ! Dem fallars dat vork below shovelling coal vas de dirtiest, rough gang of no-good fallars in vorld !

ANNA. I'd hate to hear you say that to Mat.

CHRIS. Oh, Ay tal him same tang. You don't gat it in head Ay'm scared of him yust 'cause he vas stronger'n Ay vas. (*Menacingly.*) You don't gat for fight with fists with dem fallars. Dere's oder vay for fix him.

ANNA (*glancing at him with sudden alarm*). What d'you mean?

CHRIS (*sullenly*). Nutting.

ANNA. You'd better not. I wouldn't start no trouble with him if I was you. He might forget some time that you was old and my father—and then you'd be out of luck.

CHRIS (*with smouldering hatred*). Vell, yust let him! Ay'm ole bird maybe, but Ay bet Ay show him trick or two.

ANNA (*suddenly changing her tone—persuasively*). Aw come on, be good. What's eating you, anyway? Don't you want no one to be nice to me except yourself?

CHRIS (*placated—coming to her—eagerly*). Yes, Ay do, Anna—only not fallar on sea. But Ay like for you marry steady fallar got good yob on land. You have little home in country all your own—

ANNA (*rising to her feet—brusquely*). Oh, cut it out! (*Scornfully.*) Little home in the country! I wish you could have seen the little home in the country where you had me in jail till I was sixteen! (*With rising irritation.*) Some day you're going to get me so mad with that talk, I'm going to turn loose on you and tell you—a lot of things that'll open your eyes.

CHRIS (*alarmed*). Ay don't vant—

ANNA. I know you don't; but you keep on talking yust the same.

CHRIS. Ay don't talk no more den, Anna.

ANNA. Then promise me you'll cut out saying nasty things about Mat Burke every chance you get.

CHRIS (*evasive and suspicious*). Vhy? You like dat fallar—very much, Anna?

ANNA. Yes, I certainly do! He's a regular man, no matter what faults he's got. One of his fingers is worth all the hundreds of men I met out there—inland.

CHRIS (*his face darkening*). Maybe you tank you love him, den?

ANNA (*defiantly*). What of it if I do.

CHRIS (*scowling and forcing out the words*). Maybe —you tank you—marry him?

ANNA (*shaking her head*). No! (*Chris's face lights up with relief. Anna continues slowly, a trace of sadness in her voice.*) If I'd met him four years ago—or even two years ago—I'd have jumped at the chance, I tell you that straight. And I would now—only he's such a simple guy—a big kid—and I ain't got the heart to fool him. (*She breaks off suddenly.*) But don't never say again he ain't good enough for me. It's me ain't good enough for him.

CHRIS (*snorts scornfully*). Py yiminy, you go crazy, Ay tank!

ANNA (*with a mournful laugh*). Well, I been thinking I was myself the last few days. (*She goes and takes a shawl from a hook near the door and throws it over her shoulders.*) Guess I'll take a walk down to the end of the dock for a minute and see what's doing. I love to watch the ships passing. Mat'll be along before long, I guess. Tell him where I am, will you?

CHRIS (*despondently*). All right, Ay tal him.

(*Anna goes out the doorway on rear. Chris follows her out and stands on the deck outside for a moment looking after her. Then he comes back inside and shuts the door. He stands looking out of the window—mutters*—"Dirty ole davil, you." *Then he goes to the table, sets the cloth straight mechanically, picks up the newspaper Anna has let fall to the floor and sits down in the rocking-chair. He stares at the paper for a while, then puts it on table, holds his head in his hands and sighs drearily. The noise of a man's heavy footsteps comes from the deck outside and there is a loud knock on the door. Chris starts, makes a move as if to get up and go to the door, then thinks better of it and sits still. The knock is repeated—then as no answer comes, the door is flung open and Mat Burke appears. Chris scowls at the intruder and his hand instinctively goes back to the sheath knife on his hip. Burke is dressed up—wears a cheap blue suit, a striped cotton shirt with a black tie, and black shoes newly shined. His face is beaming with good humour.*)

BURKE (*as he sees Chris—in a jovial tone of mockery*). Well, God bless who's here! (*He bends down and squeezes his huge form through the narrow doorway.*) And how is the world treating you this afternoon, Anna's father?

CHRIS (*sullenly*). Pooty goot—if it ain't for some fallars.

BURKE (*with a grin*). Meaning me, do you? (*He laughs.*) Well, if you ain't the funny old crank of a man! (*Then soberly.*) Where's herself? (*Chris sits dumb, scowling, his eyes averted. Burke is irritated by this silence.*) Where's Anna, I'm after asking you?

CHRIS (*hesitating—then grouchily*). She go down end of dock.

BURKE. I'll be going down to her, then. But first I'm thinking I'll take this chance when we're alone to have a word with you. (*He sits down opposite Chris at the table and leans over toward him.*) And that word is soon said. I'm marrying your Anna before this day is out, and you might as well make up your mind to it whether you like it or no.

CHRIS (*glaring at him with hatred and forcing a scornful laugh*). Ho-ho! Dat's easy for say!

BURKE. You mean I won't? (*Scornfully.*) Is it the like of yourself will stop me, are you thinking?

CHRIS. Yes, Ay stop it, if it come to vorst.

BURKE (*with scornful pity*). God help you!

CHRIS. But ain't no need for me do dat. Anna—

BURKE (*smiling confidently*). Is it Anna you think will prevent me?

CHRIS. Yes.

BURKE. And I'm telling you she'll not. She knows I'm loving her, and she loves me the same, and I know it.

CHRIS. Ho-ho! She only have fun. She make big fool of you, dat's all!

BURKE (*unshaken—pleasantly*). That's a lie in your throat, divil mend you!

CHRIS. No, it ain't lie. She tal me yust before she go out she never marry fallar like you.

BURKE. I'll not believe it. 'Tis a great old liar you are, and a divil to be making a power of trouble if you had your way. But 'tis not trouble I'm looking for, and me sitting down here. (*Earnestly.*) Let us be talking it out now as man to man. You're her father, and wouldn't it be a shame for us to be at each other's throats like a pair of dogs, and I married with Anna. So out with the truth, man alive. What is it you're holding against me at all?

CHRIS (*a bit placated, in spite of himself, by Burke's evident sincerity—but puzzled and suspicious*). Vell—Ay don't vant for Anna gat married. Listen, you fallar. Ay'm a ole man. Ay don't see Anna for fifteen year. She vas all Ay gat in vorld. And now ven she come on first trip—you tank Ay vant her leave me 'lone again?

BURKE (*heartily*). Let you not be thinking I have no heart at all for the way you'd be feeling.

CHRIS (*astonished and encouraged—trying to plead persuasively*). Den you do right tang, eh? You ship avay again, leave Anna alone. (*Cajolingly.*) Big fallar like you dat's on sea, he don't need vife. He gat new gel in every port, you know dat.

BURKE (*angry for a second*). God stiffen you! (*Then controlling himself—calmly.*) I'll not be giving you the lie on that. But divil take you, there's a time comes to every man, on sea or land, that isn't a born fool, when he's sick of the lot of them cows, and wearing his heart out to meet up with a fine dacent girl, and have a home to call his own and be rearing up children in it. 'Tis small use you're asking me to leave Anna. She's the wan woman of the world for me, and I can't live without her now, I'm thinking.

CHRIS. You forgat all about her in one veek out of port, Ay bet you!

BURKE. You don't know the like I am. Death itself wouldn't make me forget her. So let you not be making talk to me about leaving her. I'll not, and be damned to you! It won't be so bad for you as you'd make out at all. She'll be living here in the States, and her married to me. And you'd be seeing her often so—a sight more often than ever you saw her the fifteen years she was growing up in the West. It's quare you'd be the one to be making great trouble about her leaving you when you never laid eyes on her once in all them years.

CHRIS (*guiltily*). Ay taught it vas better Anna stay avay, grow up inland where she don't ever know ole davil, sea.

BURKE (*scornfully*). Is it blaming the sea for your troubles ye are again, God help you? Well,

Anna knows it now. 'Twas in her blood, anyway.

CHRIS. And Ay don't vant she ever know no-good fallar on sea—

BURKE. She knows one now.

CHRIS (*banging the table with his fist—furiously*). Dat's yust it! Dat's yust what you are—no-good, sailor fallar! You tank Ay lat her life be made sorry by you like her mo'der's vas by me! No, Ay swear! She don't marry you if Ay gat kill you first!

BURKE (*looks at him a moment, in astonishment—then laughing uproariously*). Ho-ho! Glory be to God, it's bold talk you have for a stumpy runt of a man!

CHRIS (*threateningly*). Vell—you see!

BURKE (*with grinning defiance*). I'll see, surely! I'll see myself and Anna married this day, I'm telling you! (*Then with contemptuous exasperation.*) It's quare fool's blather you have about the sea done this and the sea done that. You'd ought to be shamed to be saying the like, and you an old sailor yourself. I'm after hearing a lot of it from you and a lot more that Anna's told me you do be saying to her, and I'm thinking it's a poor weak thing you are, and not a man at all!

CHRIS (*darkly*). You see if Ay'm man—maybe quicker'n you tank.

BURKE (*contemptuously*). Yerra, don't be boasting. I'm thinking 'tis out of your wits you've got with fright of the sea. You'd be wishing Anna married to a farmer, she told me. That'd be a swate match, surely! Would you have a fine girl the like of Anna lying down at nights with a muddy scut stinking of pigs and dung? Or would you have her tied for life to the like of them skinny, shrivelled swabs does be working in cities?

CHRIS. Dat's lie, you fool!

BURKE. 'Tis not. 'Tis your own mad notions I'm after telling. But you know the truth in your heart, if great fear of the sea has made you a liar and coward itself. (*Pounding the table.*) The sea's the only life for a man with guts in him isn't afraid of his own shadow! 'Tis only on the sea he's free, and him roving the face of the world, seeing all things, and not giving a damn for saving up money, or stealing from his friends, or any of the black tricks that a landlubber'd waste his life on. 'Twas yourself knew it once, and you a bo'sun for years.

CHRIS (*sputtering with rage*). You vas crazy fool, Ay tal you!

BURKE. You've swallowed the anchor. The sea give you a clout once knocked you down, and you're not man enough to get up for another, but lie there for the rest of your life howling bloody murder. (*Proudly.*) Isn't it myself the sea has nearly drowned, and me battered and bate till I was that close to hell I could hear the flames roaring, and never a groan out of me till the sea gave up and it seeing the great strength and guts of a man was in me?

CHRIS (*scornfully*). Yes, you vas hell of fallar, hear you tal it!

BURKE (*angrily*). You'll be calling me a liar once too often, me old bucko! Wasn't the whole story of it and my picture itself in the newspapers of Boston a week back? (*Looking Chris up and down belittlingly.*) Sure, I'd like to see you in the best of your youth do the like of what I done in the storm and after. 'Tis a mad lunatic, screeching with fear, you'd be this minute!

CHRIS. Ho-ho! You vas young fool! In ole years when Ay was on windyammer, Ay vas through hundred storms vorse'n dat! Ships vas ships den—and men dat sail on dem vas real men. And now what you gat on steamers? You gat fallars on deck don't know ship from mudscow. (*With a meaning glance at Burke.*) And below deck you gat fallars yust know how for shovel coal—might yust as vell vork on coal vagon ashore!

BURKE (*stung—angrily*). Is it casting insults at the men in the stokehole ye are, ye old ape? God stiffen you! Wan of them is worth any ten stock-fish-swilling Square-heads ever shipped on a wind-bag!

CHRIS (*his face working with rage, his hand going back to the sheath-knife on his hip*). Irish svine, you!

BURKE (*tauntingly*). Don't ye like the Irish, ye old babboon? 'Tis that you're needing in your family, I'm telling you—an Irishman and a man of the stokehole—to put guts in it so that you'll not be having grandchildren would be fearful cowards and jackasses the like of yourself!

CHRIS (*half rising from his chair—in a voice choked with rage*). You look out!

BURKE (*watching him intently—a mocking smile on his lips*). And it's that you'll be having, no matter what you'll do to prevent; for Anna and me'll be married this day, and no old fool the like of you will stop us when I've made up my mind.

CHRIS (*with a hoarse cry*). You don't!

(*He throws himself at Burke, knife in hand, knocking his chair over backwards. Burke springs to his feet quickly in time to meet the attack. He laughs with the pure love of battle. The old Swede is like a child in his hands. Burke does not strike or mistreat him in any way, but simply twists his right hand behind his back and forces the knife from his fingers. He throws the knife into a far corner of the room—tauntingly.*)

BURKE. Old men is getting childish shouldn't play with knives. (*Holding the struggling Chris at arm's length—with a sudden rush of anger, drawing back his fist.*) I've half a mind to hit you—a great clout will put sense in your square head. Kape off me now, I'm warning you! (*He gives Chris a push with the flat of his hand which sends the old Swede staggering back against the cabin wall, where he remains standing, panting heavily, his eyes fixed on Burke with hatred, as if he were only collecting his strength to rush at him again. Warningly*). Now don't be coming at me again, I'm saying, or I'll flatten you on the floor with a blow, if 'tis Anna's father you are itself! I've no patience left for you. (*Then with an amused laugh.*) Well, 'tis a bold old man you are just the same, and I'd never think it was in you to come tackling me alone. (*A shadow crosses the cabin windows. Both men start. Anna appears in the doorway.*)

ANNA (*with pleased surprise as she sees Burke*). Hallo, Mat. Are you here already? I was down — (*She stops, looking from one to the other, sensing immediately that something has happened.*) What's up? (*Then noticing the overturned chair—in alarm.*) How'd that chair get knocked over? (*Turning on Burke reproachfully.*) You ain't been fighting with him, Mat—after you promised?

BURKE (*his old self again*). I've not laid a hand on him, Anna. (*He goes and picks up the chair, then turning on the still questioning Anna—with a reassuring smile.*) Let you not be worried at all. 'Twas only a bit of an argument we was having to pass the time till you'd come.

ANNA. It must have been some argument when you got to throwing chairs. (*She turns on Chris.*) Why don't you say something? What was it about?

CHRIS (*relaxing at last—avoiding her eyes—sheepishly*). Ve vas talking about ships and fallars on sea.

ANNA (*with a relieved smile*). Oh—the old stuff, eh?

BURKE (*suddenly seeming to come to a bold decision—with a defiant grin at Chris*). He's not after telling you the whole of it. We was arguing about you mostly.

ANNA (*with a frown*). About me?

BURKE. And we'll be finishing it out right here and now in your presence if you're willing. (*He sits down at the left of table.*)

ANNA (*uncertainly—looking from him to her father*). Sure. Tell me what it's all about.

CHRIS (*advancing toward the table—protesting to Burke*). No! You don't do dat, you! You tal him you don't vant for hear him talk, Anna.

ANNA. But I do. I want this cleared up.

CHRIS (*miserably afraid now*). Vell, not now, anyvay. You vas going ashore, yes? You ain't got time—

ANNA (*firmly*). Yes, right here and now. (*She turns to Burke.*) You tell me, Mat, since he don't want to.

BURKE (*draws a deep breath—then plunges in boldly*). The whole of it's in a few words only. So's he'd make no mistake, and him hating the sight of me, I told him in his teeth I loved you. (*Passionately.*) And that's God truth, Anna, and well you know it!

CHRIS (*scornfully—forcing a laugh*). Ho-ho! He tal same tang to gel every port he go!

ANNA (*shrinking from her father with repulsion—resentfully*). Shut up, can't you? (*Then to Burke—feelingly.*) I know it's true, Mat. I don't mind what he says.

BURKE (*humbly grateful*). God bless you!

ANNA. And then what?

BURKE. And then— (*Hesitatingly.*) And then I said— (*He looks at her pleadingly.*) I said I was sure—I told him I thought you have a bit of love for me, too. (*Passionately.*) Say you do, Anna! Let you not destroy me entirely, for the love of God! (*He grasps both her hands in his two.*)

ANNA (*deeply moved and troubled—forcing a trembling laugh*). So you told him that, Mat? No wonder he was mad. (*Forcing out the words.*) Well, maybe it's true, Mat. Maybe I do. I been thinking and thinking—I didn't want to, Mat, I'll own up to that—I tried to cut it out—but— (*She laughs helplessly.*) I guess I can't help it anyhow. So I guess I do, Mat. (*Then with a sudden joyous defiance.*) Sure I do! What's the use of kidding myself different? Sure I love you, Mat!

CHRIS (*with a cry of pain*). Anna! (*He sits crushed.*)

BURKE (*with a great depth of sincerity in his humble gratitude*). God be praised!

ANNA (*assertively*). And I ain't never loved a man in my life before, you can always believe that—no matter what happens.

BURKE (*goes over to her and puts his arms around her*). Sure I do be believing ivery word you iver said or iver will say. And 'tis you and me will be having a grand, beautiful life together to the end of our days!

(*He tries to kiss her. At first she turns away her head—then, overcome by a fierce impulse of passionate love, she takes his head in both her hands and holds his face close to hers, staring into his eyes. Then she kisses him full on the lips.*)

ANNA (*pushing him away from her—forcing a broken laugh*). Good-bye.

(*She walks to the doorway in rear—stands with her back toward them, looking out. Her shoulders quiver once or twice as if she were fighting back her sobs.*)

BURKE (*too in the seventh heaven of bliss to get any correct interpretation of her word—with a laugh*). Good-bye, is it? The divil you say! I'll be coming back at you in a second for more of the same! (*To Chris, who has quickened to instant attention at his daughter's good-bye, and has looked back at her with a stirring of foolish hope in his eyes.*) Now, me old bucko, what'll you be saying? You heard the words from her own lips. Confess I've bate you. Own up like a man when you're bate fair and square. And here's my hand to you— (*Holds out his hand.*) And let you take it and we'll shake and forget what's over and done, and be friends from this out.

CHRIS (*with implacable hatred*). Ay don't shake hands with you fallar—not vhile Ay live!

BURKE (*offended*). The back of my hand to you then, if that suits you better. (*Growling.*) 'Tis a rotten bad loser you are, divil mend you!

CHRIS. Ay don't lose— (*Trying to be scornful and self-convincing.*) Anna say she like you little bit, but you don't hear her say she marry you, Ay bet. (*At the sound of her name Anna has turned round to them. Her face is composed and calm again, but it is the dead calm of despair.*)

BURKE (*scornfully*). No, and I wasn't hearing her say the sun is shining either.

CHRIS (*doggedly*). Dat's all right. She don't say it, yust same.

ANNA (*quietly—coming forward to them*). No, I didn't say it, Mat.

CHRIS (*eagerly*). Dere! You hear!

BURKE (*misunderstanding her—with a grin*). You're waiting till you do be asked, you mane? Well, I'm asking you now. And we'll be married this day, with the help of God!

ANNA (*gently*). You heard what I said, Mat—after I kissed you?

BURKE (*alarmed by something in her manner*). No—I disremember.

ANNA. I said good-bye. (*Her voice trembling.*) That kiss was for good-bye, Mat.

BURKE (*terrified*). What d'you mane?

ANNA. I can't marry you, Mat—and we've said good-bye. That's all.

CHRIS (*unable to hold back his exultation*). Ay know it! Ay know dat vas so!

BURKE (*jumping to his feet—unable to believe his ears*). Anna! Is it making game of me you'd be? 'Tis a quare time to joke with me, and don't be doing it, for the love of God.

ANNA (*looking him in the eyes—steadily*). D'you think I'd kid you now? No, I'm not joking, Mat. I mean what I said.

BURKE. Ye don't! Ye can't! 'Tis mad you are, I'm telling you!

ANNA (*fixedly*). No, I'm not.

BURKE (*desperately*). But what's come over you

so sudden? You was saying you loved me—

ANNA. I'll say that as often as you want me to. It's true.

BURKE (*bewildered*). Then why—what, in the divil's name— Oh, God help me, I can't make head or tail to it at all!

ANNA. Because it's the best way out I can figure, Mat. (*Her voice catching.*) I been thinking it over and thinking it over day and night all week. Don't think it ain't hard on me, too, Mat.

BURKE. For the love of God, tell me then, what is it that's preventing you wedding me when the two of us has love? (*Suddenly getting an idea and pointing at Chris—with exasperation.*) Is it giving heed to the like of that old fool ye are, and him hating me and filling your ears full of bloody lies against me?

CHRIS (*getting to his feet—raging triumphantly before Anna has a chance to get in a word*). Yes, Anna, believe me, not you! She know her old fa'der don't lie like you.

ANNA (*turning on her father angrily*). You sit down, d'you hear? Where do you come in butting in and making things worse? You're like a devil, you are! (*Harshly.*) Good Lord, and I was beginning to like you, beginning to forget all I've got held up against you!

CHRIS (*crushed—feebly*). You ain't got nutting for hold against me, Anna.

ANNA. Ain't I yust! Well, lemme tell you—(*She glances at Burke and stops abruptly.*) Say, Mat, I'm s'prised at you. You didn't think anything he'd said—

BURKE (*glumly*). Sure, what else would it be?

ANNA. Think I've ever paid any attention to all his crazy bull? Gee, you must take me for a five-year-old kid.

BURKE (*puzzled and beginning to be irritated at her too*). I don't know how to take you, with your saying this one minute and that the next.

ANNA. Well, he has nothing to do with it.

BURKE. Then what is it has? Tell me, and don't keep me waiting and sweating blood.

ANNA (*resolutely*). I can't tell you—and I won't. I got a good reason—and that's all you need to know. I can't marry you, that's all there is to it. (*Distractedly.*) So, for Gawd's sake, let's talk of something else.

BURKE. I'll not! (*Then fearfully.*) Is it married to some one else you are—in the West maybe?

ANNA (*vehemently*). I should say not.

BURKE (*regaining his courage*). To the divil with all other reasons then. They don't matter with me at all. (*He gets to his feet confidently, assuming a masterful tone.*) I'm thinking you're the like of them women can't make up their mind till they're drove to it. Well, then, I'll make up your mind for you bloody quick. (*He takes her by the arms, grinning to soften his serious bullying.*) We've had enough of talk! Let you be going into your room now and be dressing in your best and we'll be going ashore.

CHRIS (*aroused—angrily*). No, py God, she don't do that! (*Takes hold of her arm.*)

ANNA (*who has listened to Burke in astonishment. She draws away from him, instinctively repelled by his tone, but not exactly sure if he is serious or not—a trace of resentment in her voice*). Say, where do you get that stuff?

BURKE (*imperiously*). Never mind, now! Let you go get dressed, I'm saying. (*Then turning to Chris.*) We'll be seeing who'll win in the end—me or you.

CHRIS (*to Anna—also in an authoritative tone*). You stay right here, Anna, you hear!

(*Anna stands looking from one to the other of them as if she thought they had both gone crazy. Then the expression of her face freezes into the hardened sneer of her experience.*)

BURKE (*violently*). She'll not! She'll do what I say! You've had your hold on her long enough. It's my turn now.

ANNA (*with a hard laugh*). Your turn? Say, what am I, anyway?

BURKE. 'Tis not what you are, 'tis what you're going to be this day—and that's wedded to me before night comes. Hurry up now with your dressing.

CHRIS (*commandingly*). You don't do one tang he say, Anna! (*Anna laughs mockingly.*)

BURKE. She will, so!

CHRIS. Ay tal you she don't! Ay'm her fa'der.

BURKE. She will in spite of you. She's taking my orders from this out, not yours.

ANNA (*laughing again*). Orders is good!

BURKE (*turning to her impatiently*). Hurry up now, and shake a leg. We've no time to be wasting. (*Irritated as she doesn't move.*) Do you hear what I'm telling you?

CHRIS. You stay dere, Anna!

ANNA (*at the end of her patience—blazing out at them passionately*). You can go to hell, both of you! (*There is something in her tone that makes them forget their quarrel and turn to her in a stunned amazement. Anna laughs wildly.*) You're just like all the rest of them—you two! Gawd, you'd think I was a piece of furniture! I'll show you! Sit down now! (*As they hesitate—furiously.*) Sit down and let me talk for a minute. You're all wrong, see? Listen to me! I'm going to tell you something—and then I'm going to beat it. (*To Burke—with a harsh laugh.*) I'm going to tell you a funny story, so pay attention. (*Pointing to Chris.*) I've been meaning to turn it loose on him every time he'd get my goat with his bull about keeping me safe inland. I wasn't going to tell you, but you've forced me into it. What's the dif? It's all wrong anyway, and you might as well get cured that way as any other. (*With hard mocking.*) Only don't forget what you said a minute ago about it not mattering to you what other reason I got so long as I wasn't married to no one else.

BURKE (*manfully*). That's my word, and I'll stick to it!

ANNA (*laughing bitterly*). What a chance! You make me laugh, honest! Want to bet you will? Wait'n see! (*She stands at the table rear, looking from one to the other of the two men with her hard, mocking smile. Then she begins, fighting to control her emotion and speak calmly.*) First thing is, I want to tell you two guys something. You was going on's if one of you had got to own me. But nobody owns me, see?—'cepting myself. I'll do what I please, and no man, I don't give a hoot who he is, can tell me what to do! I ain't asking either of you for a living. I can make it myself—one way or other. I'm my own boss. So put that in your pipe and smoke it! You and your orders!

BURKE (*protestingly*). I wasn't meaning it that way at all and well you know it. You've no call to be raising this rumpus with me. (*Pointing to Chris.*) 'Tis him you've a right—

ANNA. I'm coming to him. But you—you did mean it that way, too. You sounded—yust like all the rest. (*Hysterically.*) But, damn it, shut up! Let me talk for a change!

BURKE. 'Tis quare, rough talk, that—for a dacent girl the like of you!

ANNA (*with a hard laugh*). Decent? Who told you I was? (*Chris is sitting with bowed shoulders, his head in his hands. She leans over in exasperation and shakes him violently by the shoulder.*) Don't go to sleep, Old Man! Listen here, I'm talking to you now!

CHRIS (*straightening up and looking about as if he were seeking a way to escape—with frightened foreboding in his voice*). Ay don't vant for hear it. You vas going out of head, Ay tank, Anna.

ANNA (*violently*). Well, living with you is enough to drive anyone off their nut. Your bunk about the farm being so fine! Didn't I write you year after year how rotten it was and what a dirty slave them cousins made of me? What'd you care? Nothing! Not even enough to come out and see me! That crazy bull about wanting to keep me away from the sea don't go down with me! You yust didn't want to be bothered with me! You're like all the rest of 'em!

CHRIS (*feebly*). Anna! It ain't so—

ANNA (*not heeding his interruption—revengefully*). But one thing I never wrote you. It was one of them cousins that you think is such nice people—the youngest son—Paul—that started me wrong. (*Loudly.*) It wasn't none of my fault. I hated him worse'n hell, and he knew it. But he was big and strong—(*pointing to Burke*)—like you!

BURKE (*half springing to his feet—his fists clenched*). God blarst it! (*He sinks slowly back in his chair again, the knuckles showing white on his clenched hands, his face tense with the effort to suppress his grief and rage.*)

CHRIS (*in a cry of horrified pain*). Anna!

ANNA (*to him—seeming not to have heard their interruptions*). That was why I run away from the farm. That was what made me get a yob as nurse girl in St. Paul. (*With a hard, mocking laugh.*) And you think that was a nice yob for a girl, too, don't you? (*Sarcastically.*) With all them nice inland fellers yust looking for a chance to marry me, I s'pose. Marry me? What a chance! They wasn't looking for marrying. (*As Burke lets a groan of fury escape him—desperately.*) I'm owning up to everything fair and square. I was caged in, I tell you—yust like in yail—taking care of other people's kids—listening to 'em bawling and crying day and night—when I wanted to be out—and I was lonesome as hell! (*With a sudden weariness in her voice.*) So I give up finally. What was the use? (*She stops and looks at the two men. Both are motionless and silent. Chris seems in a stupor of despair, his house of cards fallen about him. Burke's face is livid with the rage that is eating him up, but he is too stunned and bewildered yet to find a vent for it. The condemnation she feels in their silence goads Anna into a harsh, strident defiance.*) You don't say nothing—either of you—but I know what you're thinking. You're like all the rest! (*To Chris—furiously.*) And who's to blame for it, me or you? If you'd even acted like a man—if you'd even been a regular father and had me with you—maybe things would be different!

CHRIS (*in agony*). Don't talk dat vay, Anna! Ay go crazy! Ay von't listen! (*Puts his hands over his ears.*)

ANNA (*infuriated by his action—stridently*). You will listen though! (*She leans over and pulls his hands from his ears—with hysterical rage.*) You—keeping me safe inland—I wasn't no nurse girl the last two years—I lied when I wrote you—I was in a house, that's what!—yes, that kind of a house—the kind sailors like you and Mat goes to in port—and your nice inland men, too—and all men, God damn 'em! I hate 'em! Hate 'em! (*She breaks into hysterical sobbing, throwing herself into the chair and hiding her face in her hands on the table. The two men have sprung to their feet.*)

CHRIS (*whimpering like a child*). Anna! Anna! It's lie! It's lie! (*He stands wringing his hands together and begins to weep.*)

BURKE (*his whole great body tense like a spring—dully and gropingly*). So that's what's in it!

ANNA (*raising her head at the sound of his voice—with extreme mocking bitterness*). I s'pose you remember your promise, Mat? No other reason was to count with you so long as I wasn't married already. So I s'pose you want me to get dressed and go ashore, don't you? (*She laughs.*) Yes, you do!

BURKE (*on the verge of his outbreak—stammering*). God stiffen you!

ANNA (*trying to keep up her hard, bitter tone, but gradually letting a note of pitiful pleading creep in*). I s'pose if I tried to tell you I wasn't—that—no more you'd believe me, wouldn't you? Yes, you would! And if I told you that yust getting out in this barge, and being on the sea had changed me and made me feel different about things, 's if all I'd been through wasn't me and didn't count and was yust like it never happened—you'd laugh, wouldn't you? And you'd die laughing sure if I said that meeting you that funny way that night in the fog, and afterwards seeing that you was straight goods stuck on me, had got me to thinking for the first time, and I sized you up as a different kind of man—a sea-man as different from the ones on land as water is from mud—and that was why I got stuck on you, too. I wanted to marry you and fool you, but I couldn't. Don't you see how I'd changed? I couldn't marry you with you believing a lie—and I was shamed to tell you the truth—till the both of you forced my hand, and I seen you was the same as all the rest. And now, give me a bawling out and beat it, like I can tell you're going to. (*She stops, looking at Burke. He is silent, his face averted, his features beginning to work with fury. She pleads passionately.*) Will you believe it if I tell you that loving you has made me—clean? It's the straight goods, honest! (*Then as he doesn't reply—bitterly.*) Like hell you will! You're like all the rest!

BURKE (*blazing out—turning on her in a perfect frenzy of rage—his voice trembling with passion*). The rest, is it? God's curse on you! Clane, is it? You slut, you, I'll be killing you now! (*He picks up the chair on which he has been sitting, and, swinging it high over his shoulder, springs toward her. Chris rushes forward with a cry of alarm, trying to ward off the blow from his daughter. Anna looks up into Burke's eyes with the fearlessness of despair. Burke checks himself, the chair held in the air.*)

CHRIS (*wildly*). Stop, you crazy fool! You vant for murder her!

ANNA (*pushing her father away brusquely, her eyes still holding Burke's*). Keep out of this, you! (*To Burke—dully.*) Well, ain't you got the nerve to do it? Go ahead! I'll be thankful to you, honest. I'm sick of the whole game.

BURKE (*throwing the chair away into a corner of the room—helplessly*). I can't do it, God help me, and your two eyes looking at me. (*Furiously.*) Though I do be thinking I'd have a good right to smash your skull like a rotten egg. Was there iver a woman in the world had the rottenness in her that you have, and was there iver a man the like of me was made the fool of the world, and me thinking thoughts about you, and having great love for you, and dreaming dreams of the fine life we'd have when we'd be wedded! (*His voice high pitched in a lamentation that is like a keen.*) Yerra, God help me! I'm destroyed entirely and my heart is broken in bits! I'm asking God Himself, was it for this He'd have me roaming the earth since I was a lad only, to come to black shame in the end, where I'd be giving a power of love to a woman is the same as others you'd meet in any hooker-shanty in port, with red gowns on them and paint on their grinning mugs, would be sleeping with any man for a dollar or two!

ANNA (*in a scream*). Don't, Mat! For Gawd's sake! (*Then raging and pounding on the table with her hands.*) Get out of here! Leave me alone! Get out of here!

BURKE (*his anger rushing back on him*). I'll be going, surely! And I'll be drinking sloos of whisky will wash that black kiss of yours off my lips; and I'll be getting dead rotten drunk so I'll not remember if 'twas iver born you was at all; and I'll be shipping away on some boat will take me to the other end of the world where I'll never see your face again! (*He turns toward the door.*)

CHRIS (*who has been standing in a stupor—suddenly grasping Burke by the arm—stupidly*). No, you don't go. Ay tank maybe it's better Anna marry you now.

BURKE (*shaking Chris off—furiously*). Lave go of me, ye old ape! Marry her, is it? I'd see her roasting in hell first! I'm shipping away out of this, I'm telling you! (*Pointing to Anna—passionately.*) And my curse on you and the curse of Almighty God and all the Saints! You've destroyed me this day, and may you lie awake in the long nights, tormented with thoughts of Mat Burke and the great wrong you've done him!

ANNA (*in anguish*). Mat! (*But he turns without another word and strides out of the doorway. Anna looks after him wildly, starts to run after him, then hides her face in her outstretched arms, sobbing. Chris stands in a stupor, staring at the floor.*)

CHRIS (*after a pause, dully*). Ay tank Ay go ashore, too.

ANNA (*looking up, wildly*). Not after him! Let him go! Don't you dare—

CHRIS (*sombrely*). Ay go for gat drink.

ANNA (*with a harsh laugh*). So I'm driving you to drink, too, eh? I s'pose you want to get drunk so's you can forget—like him?

CHRIS (*bursting out angrily*). Yes, Ay vant! You tank Ay like hear dem tangs. (*Breaking down—weeping.*) Ay tank you vasn't dat kind of gel, Anna.

ANNA (*mockingly*). And I s'pose you want me to beat it, don't you? You don't want me here disgracing you, I s'pose?

CHRIS. No, you stay here! (*Goes over and pats her on the shoulder, the tears running down his face.*) Ain't your fault, Anna, Ay know dat. (*She looks up at him, softened. He bursts into rage.*) It's dat ole davil, sea, do this to me! (*He shakes his fist at the door.*) It's her dirty tricks! It vas all right on barge with yust you and me. Den she bring dat Irish fallar in fog, she make you like him, she make you fight with me all time! If dat Irish fallar don't never come, you don't never tal me dem tangs, Ay don't never know, and everytang's all right. (*He shakes his fist again.*) Dirty ole davil!

ANNA (*with spent weariness*). Oh, what's the use? Go on ashore and get drunk.

CHRIS (*goes into room on left and gets his cap. He goes to the door, silent and stupid—then turns*). You vait here, Anna?

ANNA (*dully*). Maybe—and maybe not. Maybe I'll get drunk, too. Maybe I'll— But what the hell do you care what I do? Go on and beat it. (*Chris turns stupidly and goes out. Anna sits at the table, staring straight in front of her.*)

Curtain

Act IV

SCENE. *Same as Act III, about nine o'clock of a foggy night two days later. The whistles of steamers in the harbour can be heard. The cabin is lighted by a small lamp on the table. A suit-case stands in the middle of the floor. Anna is sitting in the rocking-chair. She wears a hat, is all dressed up as in Act I. Her face is pale, looks terribly tired and worn, as if the two days just past had been ones of suffering and sleepless nights. She stares before her despondently, her chin in her hands. There is a timid knock on the door in rear. Anna jumps to her feet with a startled exclamation and looks toward the door with an expression of mingled hope and fear.*

ANNA (*faintly*). Come in. (*Then summoning her courage—more resolutely.*) Come in. (*The door is opened and Chris appears in the doorway. He is in a very bleary, bedraggled condition, suffering from the after-effects of his drink. A tin pail full of foaming beer is in his hand. He comes forward, his eyes avoiding Anna's. He mutters stupidly.*) It's foggy.

ANNA (*looking him over with contempt*). So you come back at last, did you? You're a fine-looking sight! (*Then jeeringly.*) I thought you'd beaten it for good on account of the disgrace I'd brought on you.

CHRIS (*wincing—faintly*). Don't say dat, Anna, please! (*He sits in a chair by the table, setting down the can of beer, holding his head in his hands.*)

ANNA (*looks at him with a certain sympathy* What's the trouble? Feeling sick?

CHRIS (*dully*). Inside my head feel sick.

ANNA. Well, what d'you expect after being soused for two days? (*Resentfully.*) It serves you right. A fine thing—you leaving me alone on this barge all that time!

CHRIS (*humbly*). Ay'm sorry, Anna.

ANNA (*scornfully*). Sorry!

CHRIS. But Ay'm not sick inside head vay you mean. Ay'm sick from tank too much about you, about me.

ANNA. And how about me? D'you suppose I ain't been thinking, too?

CHRIS. Ay'm sorry, Anna. (*He sees her bag and gives a start*). You pack your bag, Anna? You vas going—

ANNA (*forcibly*). Yes, I was going right back to what you think.

CHRIS. Anna!

ANNA. I went ashore to get a train for New York. I'd been waiting and waiting till I was sick of it. Then I changed my mind and decided not to go to-day. But I'm going first thing to-morrow, so it'll all be the same in the end.

CHRIS (*raising his head—pleadingly*). No, you never do dat, Anna!

ANNA (*with a sneer*). Why not, I'd like to know?

CHRIS. You don't never gat to do—dat way—no more, Ay tal you. Ay fix dat up all right.

ANNA (*suspiciously*). Fix what up?

CHRIS (*not seeming to have heard her question—sadly*). You vas vaiting, you say? You vasn't vaiting for me, Ay bet.

ANNA (*callously*). You'd win.

CHRIS. For dat Irish fallar?

ANNA (*defiantly*). Yes—if you want to know! (*Then with a forlorn laugh.*) If he did come back it'd only be 'cause he wanted to beat me up or kill me, I suppose. But even if he did, I'd rather have him come than not show up at all. I wouldn't care what he did.

CHRIS. Ay guess it's true you vas in love with him all right.

ANNA. You guess!

CHRIS (*turning to her earnestly*). And Ay'm sorry for you like hell he don't come, Anna!

ANNA (*softened*). Seems to me you've changed your tune a lot.

CHRIS. Ay've been tanking, and Ay guess it vas all my fault—all bad tangs dat happen to you. (*Pleadingly.*) You try for not hate me, Anna. Ay'm crazy ole fool, dat's all.

ANNA. Who said I hated you?

CHRIS. Ay'm sorry for everytang Ay do wrong for you, Anna. Ay vant for you be happy all rest of your life for make up! It make you happy marry dat Irish fallar, Ay vant it, too.

ANNA (*dully*). Well, there ain't no chance. But

I'm glad you think different about it, anyway.

CHRIS (*supplicatingly*). And you tank—maybe—you forgive me sometime?

ANNA (*with a wan smile*). I'll forgive you right now.

CHRIS (*seizing her hand and kissing it—brokenly*). Anna lilla! Anna lilla!

ANNA (*touched but a bit embarrassed*). Don't bawl about it. There ain't nothing to forgive, anyway. It ain't your fault, and it ain't mine, and it ain't his neither. We're all poor nuts, and things happen, and we yust get mixed in wrong, that's all.

CHRIS (*eagerly*). You say right tang, Anna, py golly! It ain't nobody's fault! (*Shaking his fist.*) It's dat ole davil, sea!

ANNA (*with an exasperated laugh*). Gee, won't you ever can that stuff? (*Chris relapses into injured silence. After a pause Anna continues curiously.*) You said a minute ago you'd fixed something up—about me. What was it?

CHRIS (*after a hesitating pause*). Ay'm shipping avay on sea again, Anna.

ANNA (*astounded*). You're—what?

CHRIS. Ay sign on steamer sail to-morrow. Ay gat my ole yob—bos'n. (*Anns stares at him. As he goes on, a bitter smile comes over her face.*) Ay tank dat's best tang for you. Ay only bring you bad luck, Ay tank. Ay make your mo'der's life sorry. Ay don't vant make yours dat way, but Ay do yust same. Dat ole davil, sea, she make me Yonah man ain't no good for nobody. And Ay tank now it ain't no use fight with sea. No man dat live going to beat her, py yingo!

ANNA (*with a laugh of helpless bitterness*). So that's how you've fixed me, is it?

CHRIS. Yes, Ay tank if dat ole davil gat me back she leave you alone den.

ANNA (*bitterly*). But, for Gawd's sake, don't you see, you're doing the same thing you've always done? Don't you see— (*But she sees the look of obsessed stubbornness on her father's face and gives it up helplessly.*) But what's the use of talking. You ain't right, that's what. I'll never blame you for nothing no more. But how you could figure out that was fixing me—

CHRIS. Dat ain't all. Ay gat dem fallars in steamship office to pay you all money coming to me every month vhile Ay'm avay.

ANNA (*with a hard laugh*). Thanks. But I guess I won't be hard up for no small change.

CHRIS (*hurt—humbly*). It ain't much, Ay know, but it's plenty for keep you so you never gat go back—

ANNA (*shortly*). Shut up, will you? We'll talk about it later, see?

CHRIS (*after a pause—ingratiatingly*). You like Ay go ashore look for dat Irish fallar, Anna?

ANNA (*angrily*). Not much! Think I want to drag him back?

CHRIS (*after a pause—uncomfortably*). Py golly, dat booze don't go vell. Give me fever, Ay tank. Ay feel hot like hell. (*He takes off his coat and lets it drop on the floor. There is a loud thud.*)

ANNA (*with a start*). What you got in your pocket, for Pete's sake—a ton of lead? (*She reaches down, takes the coat and pulls out a revolver—looks from it to him in amazement.*) A gun? What were you doing with this?

CHRIS (*sheepishly*). Ay forgat. Ain't nutting. Ain't loaded, anyway.

ANNA (*breaking it open to make sure—then closing it again—looking at him suspiciously.*) That ain't telling me why you got it?

CHRIS (*sheepishly*). Ay'm ole fool. Ay gat it vhen Ay go ashore first. Ay tank den it's all fault of dat Irish fallar.

ANNA (*with a shudder*). Say, you're crazier than I thought. I never dreamt you'd go that far.

CHRIS (*quickly*). Ay don't. Ay gat better sense right avay. Ay don't never buy bullets even. It ain't his fault, Ay know.

ANNA (*still suspicious of him*). Well, I'll take care of this for a while, loaded or not. (*She puts it in the drawer of table and closes the drawer.*)

CHRIS (*placatingly*). Throw it overboard if you vant. Ay don't care. (*Then after a pause.*) Py golly, Ay tank Ay go lie down. Ay feel sick. (*Anna takes a magazine from the table. Chris hesitates by her chair.*) Ve talk again before Ay go, yes?

ANNA (*dully*). Where's this ship going to?

CHRIS. Cape Town. Dat's in South Africa. She's British steamer called "Londonderry." (*He stands hesitatingly—finally blurts out.*) Anna—you forgive me sure?

ANNA (*wearily*). Sure I do. You ain't to blame. You're yust—what you are—like me.

CHRIS (*pleadingly*). Den—you lat me kiss you again once?

ANNA (*raising her face—forcing a wan smile*). Sure. No hard feelings.

CHRIS (*kisses her—brokenly*). Anna lilla! Ay—(*he fights for words to express himself, but finds none—miserably—with a sob*)—Ay can't say it. Good night, Anna.

ANNA. Good night. (*He picks up the can of beer and goes slowly into the room on left, his shoulders bowed, his head sunk forward dejectedly. He closes the door after him. Anna turns over the pages of the magazine, trying desperately to banish her thoughts by looking at the pictures. This fails to distract her, and flinging the magazine back on the table, she springs to her feet and walks about the cabin distractedly, clenching and unclenching her hands. She speaks aloud to herself in a tense, trembling voice.*) Gawd, I can't stand this much longer! What am I waiting for, anyway?—like a damn fool! (*She laughs helplessly, then checks herself abruptly, as she hears the sound of heavy footsteps on the deck outside. She appears to recognize these and her face lights up with joy. She gasps:*) Mat!

(*A strange terror seems suddenly to seize her. She rushes to the table, takes the revolver out of drawer and crouches down in the corner, left, behind the cupboard. A moment later the door is flung open and Mat Burke appears in the doorway. He is in bad shape—his clothes torn and dirty, covered with sawdust as if he had been grovelling or sleeping on bar-room floors. There is a red bruise on his forehead over one of his eyes, another over one cheekbone, his knuckles are skinned and raw—plain evidence of the fighting he has been through on his "bat." His eyes are bloodshot and heavy-lidded, his face has a bloated look. But beyond these appearances—the results of heavy drinking—there is an expression in his eyes of wild mental turmoil, of impotent animal rage baffled by its own abject misery.*)

BURKE (*peers blinkingly about the cabin—hoarsely*). Let you not be hiding from me, whoever's here—though 'tis well you know I'd have a right to come back and murder you. (*He stops to listen. Hearing no sound, he closes the door behind him and comes forward to the table. He throws himself into the rocking-chair—despondently.*) There's no one here, I'm thinking, and 'tis a great fool I am to be coming. (*With a sort of dumb, uncomprehending anguish.*) Yerra, Mat Burke, 'tis a great jackass you've become and what's got into you at all, at all? She's gone out of this long ago, I'm telling you, and you'll never see her face again. (*Anna stands up, hesitating, struggling between joy and fear. Burke's eyes fall on Anna's bag. He leans over to examine it.*) What's this? (*Joyfully.*) It's hers. She's not gone! But where is she? Ashore? (*Darkly.*) What would she be doing ashore on this rotten night? (*His face suddenly convulsed with grief and rage.*) 'Tis that, is it? Oh, God's curse on her! (*Raging.*) I'll wait till she comes and choke her dirty life out.

(*Anna starts, her face grows hard. She steps into the room, the revolver in her right hand by her side.*)

ANNA (*in a cold, hard tone*). What are you doing here?

BURKE (*wheeling about with a terrified gasp*). Glory be to God! (*They remain motionless and silent for a moment, holding each other's eyes.*)

ANNA (*in the same hard voice*). Well, can't you talk?

BURKE (*trying to fall into an easy, careless tone*). You've a year's growth scared out of me, coming at me so sudden and me thinking I was alone.

ANNA. You've got your nerve butting in here without knocking or nothing. What d'you want?

BURKE (*airily*). Oh, nothing much. I was wanting to have a last word with you, that's all. (*He moves a step toward her.*)

ANNA (*sharply—raising the revolver in her hand*). Careful now! Don't try getting too close. I heard what you said you'd do to me.

BURKE (*noticing the revolver for the first time*). Is it murdering me you'd be now, God forgive you? (*Then with a contemptuous laugh.*) Or is it thinking I'd be frightened by that old tin whistle? (*He walks straight for her.*)

ANNA (*wildly*). Look out, I tell you!

BURKE (*who has come so close that the revolver is almost touching his chest*). Let you shoot, then!

(*Then with sudden wild grief.*) Let you shoot, I'm saying, and be done with it! Let you end me with a shot and I'll be thanking you, for it's a rotten dog's life I've lived the past two days since I've known what you are, till I'm after wishing I was never born at all!

ANNA (*overcome—letting the revolver drop to the floor, as if her fingers had no strength to hold it—hysterically*). What d'you want coming here? Why don't you beat it? Go on! (*She passes him and sinks down in the rocking-chair.*)

BURKE (*following her—mournfully*). 'Tis right you'd be asking why did I come. (*Then angrily.*) 'Tis because 'tis a great weak fool of the world I am, and me tormented with the wickedness you'd told of yourself, and drinking oceans of booze that'd make me forget. Forget? Divil a word I'd forget, and your face grinning always in front of my eyes, awake or asleep, till I do be thinking a mad-house is the proper place for me.

ANNA (*glancing at his hands and face—scornfully*). You look like you ought to be put away some place. Wonder you wasn't pulled in. You been scrapping, too, ain't you?

BURKE. I have—with every scut would take off his coat to me! (*Fiercely.*) And each time I'd be hitting one a clout in the mug, it wasn't his face I'd be seeing at all, but yours, and me wanting to drive you a blow would knock you out of this world where I wouldn't be seeing or thinking more of you.

ANNA (*her lips trembling pitifully*). Thanks!

BURKE (*walking up and down—distractedly*). That's right, make game of me! Oh, I'm a great coward surely, to be coming back to speak with you at all. You've a right to laugh at me.

ANNA. I ain't laughing at you, Mat.

BURKE (*unheeding*). You to be what you are, and me to be Mat Burke, and me to be drove back to look at you again! 'Tis black shame is on me!

ANNA (*resentfully*). Then get out. No one's holding you!

BURKE (*bewilderedly*). And me to listen to that talk from a woman like you and be frightened to close her mouth with a slap! Oh, God help me, I'm a yellow coward for all men to spit at! (*Then furiously.*) But I'll not be getting out of this till I've had me word. (*Raising his fist threateningly.*) And let you look out how you'd drive me! (*Letting his fist fall helplessly.*) Don't be angry now! I'm raving like a real lunatic, I'm thinking, and the sorrow you put on me has my brains drownded in grief. (*Suddenly bending down to her and grasping her arm intensely.*) Tell me it's a lie, I'm saying! That's what I'm after coming to hear you say.

ANNA (*dully*). A lie? What?

BURKE (*with passionate entreaty*). All the badness you told me two days back. Sure it must be a lie! You was only making game of me, wasn't you? Tell me 'twas a lie, Anna, and I'll be saying prayers of thanks on my two knees to the Almighty God!

ANNA (*terribly shaken—faintly*). I can't, Mat. (*As he turns away—imploringly.*) Oh, Mat, won't you see that no matter what I was I ain't that any more? Why, listen! I packed up my bag this afternoon and went ashore. I'd been waiting here all alone for two days, thinking maybe you'd come back—thinking maybe you'd think over all I'd said—and maybe—oh, I don't know what I was hoping! But I was afraid to even go out of the cabin for a second, honest—afraid you might come and not find me here. Then I gave up hope when you didn't show up and I went to the railroad station. I was going to New York. I was going back—

BURKE (*hoarsely*). God's curse on you!

ANNA. Listen, Mat! You hadn't come, and I'd gave up hope. But—in the station—I couldn't go. I'd bought my ticket and everything. (*She takes the ticket from her dress and tries to hold it before his eyes.*) But I got to thinking about you—and I couldn't take the train—I couldn't! So I come back here—to wait some more. Oh, Mat, don't you see I've changed? Can't you forgive what's dead and gone—and forget it?

BURKE (*turning on her—overcome by rage again*). Forget, is it? I'll not forget till my dying day, I'm telling you, and me tormented with thoughts. (*In a frenzy.*) Oh, I'm wishing I had wan of them fornenst me this minute and I'd beat him with my fists till he'd be a bloody corpse! I'm wishing the whole lot of them will roast in hell till the Judgment Day—and yourself along with them, for you're as bad as they are.

ANNA (*shuddering*). Mat! (*Then after a pause—in a voice of dead, stony calm.*) Well, you've had your say. Now you better beat it.

BURKE (*starts slowly for the door—hesitates—then after a pause*). And what'll you be doing?

ANNA. What difference does it make to you?

BURKE. I'm asking you!

ANNA (*in the same tone*). My bag's packed and I got my ticket. I'll go to New York to-morrow.

BURKE (*helplessly*). You mean—you'll be doing the same again?

ANNA (*stonily*). Yes.

BURKE (*in anguish*). You'll not! Don't torment me with that talk! 'Tis a she-devil you are sent to drive me mad entirely!

ANNA (*her voice breaking*). Oh, for Gawd's sake, Mat, leave me alone! Go away! Don't you see I'm licked? Why d'you want to keep on kicking me?

BURKE (*indignantly*). And don't you deserve the worst I'd say, God forgive you?

ANNA. All right. Maybe I do. But don't rub it in. Why ain't you done what you said you was going to? Why ain't you got that ship was going to take you to the other side of the earth where you'd never see me again?

BURKE. I have.

ANNA (*startled*). What—then you're going—honest?

BURKE. I signed on to-day at noon, drunk as I was—and she's sailing to-morrow.

ANNA. And where's she going to?

BURKE. Cape Town.

ANNA (*the memory of having heard that name a little while before coming to her—with a start, confusedly*). Cape Town? Where's that. Far away?

BURKE. 'Tis at the end of Africa. That's far for you.

ANNA (*forcing a laugh*). You're keeping your word all right, ain't you? (*After a slight pause—curiously.*) What's the boat's name?

BURKE. The "Londonderry."

ANNA (*it suddenly comes to her that this is the same ship her father is sailing on*). The "Londonderry"! It's the same—oh, this is too much! (*With wild, ironical laughter.*) Ha-ha-ha!

BURKE. What's up with you now!

ANNA. Ha-ha-ha! It's funny, funny! I'll die laughing!

BURKE (*irritated*). Laughing at what?

ANNA. It's a secret. You'll know soon enough. It's funny. (*Controlling herself—after a pause—cynically.*) What kind of a place is this Cape Town? Plenty of dames there, I suppose?

BURKE. To hell with them! That I may never see another woman to my dying hour!

ANNA. That's what you say now, but I'll bet by the time you get there you'll have forgot all about me and start in talking the same old bull you talked to me to the first one you meet.

BURKE (*offended*). I'll not, then! God mend you, is it making me out to be the like of yourself you are, and you taking up with this one and that all the years of your life?

ANNA (*angrily assertive*). Yes, that's yust what I do mean! You been doing the same thing all your life, picking up a new girl in every port. How're you any better than I was?

BURKE (*thoroughly exasperated*). Is it no shame you have at all? I'm a fool to be wasting talk on you and you hardened in badness. I'll go out of this and lave you alone for ever. (*He starts for the door—then stops to turn on her furiously.*) And I suppose 'tis the same lies you told them all before that you told to me?

ANNA (*indignantly*). That's a lie! I never did!

BURKE (*miserably*). You'd be saying that, anyway.

ANNA (*forcibly, with growing intensity*). Are you trying to accuse me—of being in love—really in love—with them?

BURKE. I'm thinking you were, surely.

ANNA (*furiously, as if this were the last insult—advancing on him threateningly*). You mutt, you! I've stood enough from you. Don't you dare. (*With scornful bitterness.*) Love 'em! Oh, my Gawd! You damn thick-head! Love 'em? (*Savagely.*) I hated 'em, I tell you! Hated 'em, hated 'em, hated 'em! And may Gawd strike me dead this minute and my mother, too, if she was alive, if I ain't telling you the honest truth!

BURKE (*immensely pleased by her vehemence—a light beginning to break over his face—but still uncertain, torn between doubt and the desire to believe—helplessly*). If I could only be believing you now!

ANNA (*distractedly*). Oh, what's the use? What's

the use of me talking? What's the use of anything? (*Pleadingly.*) Oh, Mat, you mustn't think that for a second! You mustn't! Think all the other bad about me you want to, and I won't kick, 'cause you've a right to. But don't think that! (*On the point of tears.*) I couldn't bear it! It'd be yust too much to know you was going away where I'd never see you again—thinking that about me!

BURKE (*after an inward struggle—tensely—forcing out the words with difficulty*). If I was believing—that you'd never had love for any other man in the world but me—I could be forgetting the rest, maybe.

ANNA (*with a cry of joy*). Mat!

BURKE (*slowly*). If 'tis truth you're after telling, I'd have a right, maybe, to believe you'd changed—and that I'd changed you myself till the thing you'd been all your life wouldn't be you any more at all.

ANNA (*hanging on his words—breathlessly*). Oh, Mat! That's what I been trying to tell you all along!

BURKE (*simply*). For I've a power of strength in me to lead men the way I want, and women, too, maybe, and I'm thinking I'd change you to a new woman entirely, so I'd never know, or you either, what kind of woman you'd been in the past at all.

ANNA. Yes, you could, Mat! I know you could!

BURKE. And I'm thinking 'twasn't your fault, maybe, but having that old ape for a father that left you to grow up alone, made you what you was. And if I could be believing 'tis only me you—

ANNA (*distractedly*). You got to believe it, Mat! What can I do? I'll do anything, anything you want to prove I'm not lying!

BURKE (*suddenly seems to have a solution. He feels in the pocket of his coat and grasps something—solemnly*). Would you be willing to swear an oath, now—a terrible, fearful oath would send your soul to the divils in hell if you was lying?

ANNA (*eagerly*). Sure, I'll swear, Mat—on anything!

BURKE (*takes a small, cheap old crucifix from his pocket and holds it up for her to see*). Will you swear on this?

ANNA (*reaching out for it*). Yes. Sure I will. Give it to me.

BURKE (*holding it away*). 'Tis a cross was given me by my mother, God rest her soul. (*He makes the sign of the cross mechanically.*) I was a lad only, and she told me to keep it by me if I'd be waking or sleeping and never lose it, and it'd bring me luck. She died soon after. But I'm after keeping it with me from that day to this, and I'm telling you there's great power in it, and 'tis great bad luck it's saved me from and me roaming the seas, and I having it tied round my neck when my last ship sunk, and it bringing me safe to land when the others went to their death. (*Very earnestly.*) And I'm warning you now, if you'd swear an oath on this, 'tis my old woman herself will be looking down from Hivin above, and praying Almighty God and the Saints to put a great curse on you if she'd hear you swearing a lie!

ANNA (*awed by his manner—superstitiously*). I wouldn't have the nerve—honest—if it was a lie. But it's the truth and I ain't scared to swear. Give it to me.

BURKE (*handing it to her—almost frightened, as if he feared for her safety*). Be careful what you'd swear, I'm saying.

ANNA (*holding the cross gingerly*). Well—what do you want me to swear? You say it.

BURKE. Swear I'm the only man in the world ivir you felt love for.

ANNA (*looking into his eyes steadily*). I swear it.

BURKE. And that you'll be forgetting from this day all the badness you've done and never do the like of it again.

ANNA (*forcibly*). I swear it! I swear it by God!

BURKE. And may the blackest curse of God strike you if you're lying. Say it now!

ANNA. And may the blackest curse of God strike me if I'm lying!

BURKE (*with a stupendous sigh*). Oh, glory be to God, I'm after believing you now! (*He takes the cross from her hand, his face beaming with joy, and puts it back in his pocket. He puts his arm about her waist and is about to kiss her when he stops, appalled by some terrible doubt.*)

ANNA (*alarmed*). What's the matter with you?

BURKE (*with sudden fierce questioning*). Is it Catholic ye are?

ANNA (*confused*). No. Why?

BURKE (*filled with a sort of bewildered foreboding*). Oh, God, help me! (*With a dark glance of suspicion at her.*) There's some divil's trickery in it, to be swearing an oath on a Catholic cross and you wan of the others.

ANNA (*distractedly*). Oh, Mat, don't you believe me?

BURKE (*miserably*). If it isn't a Catholic you are—

ANNA. I ain't nothing. What's the difference? Didn't you hear me swear?

BURKE (*passionately*). Oh, I'd a right to stay away from you—but I couldn't! I was loving you in spite of it all, and wanting to be with you, God forgive me, no matter what you are. I'd go mad if I'd not have you! I'd be killing the world— (*He seizes her in his arms and kisses her fiercely.*)

ANNA (*with a gasp of joy*). Mat!

BURKE (*suddenly holding her away from him and staring into her eyes as if to probe into her soul—slowly*). If your oath is no proper oath at all, I'll have to be taking your naked word for it and have you anyway, I'm thinking—I'm needing you that bad!

ANNA (*hurt—reproachfully*). Mat! I swore, didn't I?

BURKE (*defiantly, as if challenging fate*). Oath or no oath, 'tis no matter. We'll be wedded in the morning, with the help of God. (*Still more defiantly.*) We'll be happy now, the two of us, in spite of the divil!

(*He crushes her to him and kisses her again. The door on the left is pushed open and Chris appears in the doorway. He stands blinking at them. At first the old expression of hatred of Burke comes into his eyes instinctively. Then a look of resignation and relief takes its place. His face lights up with a sudden happy thought. He turns back into the bedroom—reappears immediately with the tin can of beer in his hand—grinning.*)

CHRIS. Ve have drink on this, py golly! (*They break away from each other with startled exclamations.*)

BURKE (*explosively*). God stiffen it! (*He takes a step toward Chris threateningly.*)

ANNA (*happily—to her father*). That's the way to talk! (*With a laugh.*) And say, it's about time for you and Mat to kiss and make up. You're going to be shipmates on the "Londonderry," did you know it?

BURKE (*astounded*). Shipmates— Has himself—

CHRIS (*equally astounded*). Ay vas bos'n on her.

BURKE. The divil! (*Then angrily.*) You'd be going back to sea and leaving her alone, would you?

ANNA (*quickly*). It's all right, Mat. That's where he belongs, and I want him to go. You got to go, too; we'll need the money. (*With a laugh, as she gets the glasses.*) And as for me being alone, that runs in the family, and I'll get used to it. (*Pouring out their glasses.*) I'll get a little house somewhere, and I'll make a regular place for you two to come back to—wait and see. And now you drink up and be friends.

BURKE (*happily—but still a bit resentful against the old man*). Sure! (*Clinking his glass against Chris's.*) Here's luck to you! (*He drinks.*)

CHRIS (*subdued—his face melancholy*). Skoal. (*He drinks.*)

BURKE (*to Anna, with a wink*). You'll not be lonesome long. I'll see to that, with the help of God. 'Tis himself here will be having a grandchild to ride on his foot, I'm telling you!

ANNA (*turning away in embarrassment*). Quit the kidding, now.

(*She picks up her bag and goes into the room on left. As soon as she is gone Burke relapses into an attitude of gloomy thought. Chris stares at his beer absentmindedly. Finally Burke turns on him.*)

BURKE. Is it any religion at all you have, you and your Anna?

CHRIS (*surprised*). Vhy yes. Ve vas Lutheran in ole country.

BURKE (*horrified*). Luthers, is it? (*Then with a grim resignation, slowly, aloud to himself.*) Well, I'm damned then surely. Yerra, what's the difference? 'Tis the will of God, anyway.

CHRIS (*moodily preoccupied with his own thoughts—speaks with sombre premonition as Anna re-enters from the left*). It's funny. It's queer, yes—you and me shipping on same boat dat vay. It ain't right. Ay don't know—it's dat funny vay ole davil sea do her vorst dirty tricks, yes. It's so. (*He gets up and goes back, and opening the door, stares out into the darkness.*)

BURKE (*nodding his head in gloomy acquiescence—with a great sigh*). I'm fearing maybe you have the right of it for once, divil take you.

ANNA (*forcing a laugh*). Gee, Mat, you ain't agreeing with him, are you? (*She comes forward and puts her arm about his shoulder—with a determined gaiety.*) Aw say, what's the matter? Cut out the gloom. We're all fixed now, ain't we, me and you? (*Pours out more beer into his glass and fills one for herself—slaps him on the back.*) Come on! Here's to the sea, no matter what! Be a game sport and drink to that! Come on! (*She gulps down her glass. Burke banishes his superstitious premonitions with a defiant jerk of his head grins up at her, and drinks to her toast.*)

CHRIS (*looking out into the night—lost in his sombre preoccupation—shakes his head and mutters*). Fog, fog, fog, all bloody time. You can't see vhere you vas going, no. Only dat ole davil, sea—she knows! (*The two stare at him. From the harbour comes the muffled, mournful wail of steamers' whistles.*)

Curtain

THE EMPEROR JONES

Characters

BRUTUS JONES, *Emperor*
HENRY SMITHERS, *A Cockney trader*
AN OLD NATIVE WOMAN
LEM, *A native chief*
SOLDIERS, *adherents of Lem*

The Little Formless Fears, Jeff, The Negro Convicts, The Prison Guard, The Planters, the Auctioneer, The Slaves, The Congo Witch-Doctor, The Crocodile God

The action of the play takes place on an island in the West Indies as yet not self-determined by White Mariners. The form of native government is, for the time being, an Empire.

Scene One

The audience chamber in the palace of the Emperor—a spacious, high-ceilinged room with bare, white-washed walls. The floor is of white tiles. In the rear, to the left of centre, a wide archway giving out on a portico with white pillars. The palace is evidently situated on high ground for beyond the portico nothing can be seen but a vista of distant hills, their summits crowned with thick groves of palm trees. In the right wall, centre, a smaller arched doorway leading to the living quarters of the palace. The room is bare of furniture with the exception of one huge chair made of uncut wood which stands at centre, its back to rear. This is very apparently the Emperor's throne. It is painted a dazzling, eye-smiting scarlet. There is a brilliant orange cushion on the seat and another smaller one is placed on the floor to serve as a foot-stool. Strips of matting, dyed scarlet, lead from the foot of the throne to the two entrances.

It is late afternoon, but the yellow sunlight still blazes beyond the portico and there is an oppressive burden of exhausting heat in the air.

As the curtain rises, a native negro woman sneaks in cautiously from the entrance on the right. She is very old, dressed in cheap calico, bare-footed, a red bandana handkerchief covering all but a few stray wisps of white hair. A bundle bound in coloured cloth is carried over her shoulder on the end of a stick. She hesitates beside the doorway, peering back as if in extreme dread of being discovered. Then she begins to glide noiselessly, a step at a time, towards the doorway in the rear. At this moment Smithers appears beneath the portico.

Smithers is a tall man, round-shouldered, about forty. His bald head, perched on a long neck with an enormous Adam's apple, looks like an egg. The tropics have tanned his naturally pasty face with its small, sharp features to a sickly yellow, and native rum has painted his pointed nose to a startling red. His little washy-blue eyes are red-rimmed and dart about him like a ferret's. His expression is one of unscrupulous meanness, cowardly and dangerous. He is dressed in a worn riding suit of dirty white drill, puttees, spurs, and wears a white cork helmet. A cartridge belt with an automatic revolver is around his waist. He carries a riding whip in his hand. He sees the woman and stops to watch her suspiciously. Then, making up his mind, he steps quickly on tiptoe into the room. The woman, looking back over her shoulder continually, does not see him until it is too late. When she does Smithers springs forward and grabs her firmly by the shoulder. She struggles to get away, fiercely but silently.

SMITHERS (*tightening his grasp—roughly*). Easy! None o' that, me birdie. You can't wriggle out now. I got me 'ooks on yer.

WOMAN (*seeing the uselessness of struggling, gives way to frantic terror, and sinks to the ground, embracing his knees supplicatingly*). No tell him! No tell him, Mister!

SMITHERS (*with great curiosity*). Tell 'im? (*Then scornfully.*) Oh, you mean 'is bloomin' Majesty. What's the game, any 'ow? What are you sneakin' away for? Been stealin' a bit, I s'pose. (*He taps her bundle with his riding whip significantly.*)

WOMAN (*shaking her head vehemently*). No, me no steal.

SMITHERS. Bloody liar! But tell me what's up. There's somethin' funny goin' on. I smelled it in the air first thing I got up this mornin'. You blacks are up to some devilment. This palace of 'is is like a bleedin' tomb. Where's all the 'ands? (*The woman keeps sullenly silent. Smithers raises his whip threateningly.*) Ow, yer won't, won't yer? I'll show yer what's what.

WOMAN (*coweringly*). I tell, Mister. You no hit. They go—all go. (*She makes a sweeping gesture towards the hills in the distance.*)

SMITHERS. Run away—to the 'ills?

WOMAN. Yes, Mister. Him Emperor—Great Father. (*She touches her forehead to the floor with a quick mechanical jerk.*) Him sleep after eat. Then they go—all go. Me old woman. Me left only. Now me go too.

SMITHERS (*his astonishment giving way to an immense, mean satisfaction*). Ow! So that's the ticket! Well, I know bloody well wot's in the air—when they runs orf to the 'ills. The tom-tom 'll be thumping out there bloomin' soon. (*With extreme vindictiveness.*) And I'm bloody glad of it, for one! Serve 'im right! Puttin' on airs, the stinkin' nigger! 'Is Majesty! Gawd blimey! I only hopes I'm there when they takes 'im out to shoot 'im. (*Suddenly.*) 'E's still 'ere all right, ain't 'e?

WOMAN. Yes. Him sleep.

SMITHERS. 'E's bound to find out soon as 'e wakes up. 'E's cunnin' enough to know when 'is time's come. (*He goes to the doorway on right and whistles shrilly with his fingers in his mouth. The old woman springs to her feet and runs out of the doorway, rear. Smithers goes after her, reaching for his revolver.*) Stop or I'll shoot! (*Then stooping—indifferently.*) Pop orf then, if yer like, yer black cow. (*He stands in the doorway, looking after her.*)

(*Jones enters from the right. He is a tall, powerfully-built, full-blooded negro of middle age. His features are typically negroid, yet there is something decidedly distinctive about his face—an underlying strength of will, a hardy, self-reliant confidence in himself that inspires respect. His eyes are alive with a keen, cunning intelligence. In manner he is shrewd, suspicious, evasive. He wears a light blue uniform coat, sprayed with brass buttons, heavy gold chevrons on his shoulders, gold braid on the collar, cuffs, etc. His trousers are bright red with a light blue stripe down the side. Patent leather laced boots with brass spurs, and a belt with a long-barrelled, pearl-handled revolver in a holster complete his attire. Yet there is something not altogether ridiculous about his grandeur. He has a way of carrying it off.*)

JONES (*not seeing anyone—greatly irritated and blinking sleepily—shouts*). Who dare whistle dat way in my palace? Who dare wake up de Emperor? I'll git de hide flayed off some o' you niggers sho'!

SMITHERS (*showing himself—in a manner half-afraid and half-defiant*). It was me whistled to yer. (*As Jones frowns angrily.*) I got news for yer.

JONES (*putting on his suavest manner, which fails to cover up his contempt for the white man.*) Oh, it's you, Mister Smithers. (*He sits down on his throne with easy dignity.*) What news you got to tell me?

SMITHERS (*coming close to enjoy his discomfiture*). Don't yer notice nothin' funny to-day?

JONES (*coldly*). Funny? No. I ain't perceived nothin' of de kind!

SMITHERS. Then yer ain't so foxy as I thought yer was. Where's all your court? (*Sarcastically.*) The Generals and the Cabinet Ministers and all?

JONES (*imperturbably*). Where dey mostly runs to minute I closes my eyes—drinkin' rum and talkin' big down in de town. (*Sarcastically.*) How come you don't know dat? Ain't you carousing with 'em most every day?

SMITHERS (*stung, but pretending indifference—with a wink*). That's part of the day's work. I got ter—ain't I—in my business?

JONES (*contemptuously*). Yo' business!

SMITHERS (*imprudently enraged*). Gawd blimey, you was glad enough for me ter take yer in on it when you landed here first. You didn't 'ave no 'igh and mighty airs in them days!

JONES (*his hand going to his revolver like a flash—menacingly*). Talk polite, white man! Talk polite, you heah me! I'm boss heah now, is you fergettin'?

(*The Cockney seems about to challenge this last statement with the facts, but something in the other's eyes holds and cowers him.*)

SMITHERS (*in a cowardly whine*). No 'arm meant, old top.

JONES (*condescendingly*). I accepts yo' apology. (*Lets his hand fall from his revolver.*) No use'n you rakin' up ole times. What I was den is one thing. What I is now 's another. You didn't let me in on yo' crooked work out o' no kind feelin's dat time. I done de dirty work fo' you—and most o' de brain work, too, fo' dat matter—and I was wu'th money to you, dat's de reason.

SMITHERS. Well, blimey, I give yer a start, didn't I—when no one else would. I wasn't afraid to 'ire yer like the rest was—'count of the story about your breakin' jail back in the States.

JONES. No, you didn't have no s'cuse to look down on me fo' dat. You been in jail you'self more'n once.

SMITHERS (*furiously*). It's a lie! (*Then trying to pass it off by an attempt at scorn*). Garn! Who told yer that fairy tale?

JONES. Dey's some tings I ain't got to be tole. I kin see 'em in folk's eyes. (*Then after a pause—meditatively.*) Yes, you sho' give me a start. And it didn't take long from dat time to git dese fool woods' niggers right where I wanted dem. (*With pride.*) From stowaway to Emperor in two years! Dat's goin' some!

SMITHERS (*with curiosity*). And I bet you got yer pile o' money 'id safe some place.

JONES (*with satisfaction*). I sho' has! And it's in a foreign bank where no pusson don't ever git it out but me no matter what come. You didn't s'pose I was holdin' down dis Emperor job for de glory in it, did you? Sho'! De fuss and glory part of it, dat's only to turn de heads o' de low-flung bush niggers dat's here. Dey wants de big circus show for deir money. I gives it to 'em an' I gits de money. (*With a grin.*) De long green, dat's me every time! (*Then rebukingly.*) But you ain't got no kick agin me, Smithers. I'se paid you back all you done for me many times. Ain't I pertected you and winked at all de crooked tradin' you been doin' right out in de broad day. Sho' I has—and me makin' laws to stop it at de same time! (*He chuckles.*)

SMITHERS (*grinning*). But, meanin' no' 'arm, you been grabbin' right and left yourself, ain't yer? Look at the taxes you've put on 'em! Blimey! You've squeezed 'em dry!

JONES (*chuckling*). No, dey ain't *all* dry yet. I'se still heah, ain't I?

SMITHERS (*smiling at his secret thought.*) They're dry right now, you'll find out. (*Changing the subject abruptly.*) And as for me breakin' laws, you've broke 'em all yerself just as fast as yer made 'em.

JONES. Ain't I de Emperor? De laws don't go for him. (*Judicially.*) You heah what I tells you, Smithers. Dere's little stealin' like you does, and dere's big stealin' like I does. For de little stealin' dey gits you in jail soon or late. For de big stealin' dey makes you Emperor and puts you in de Hall o' Fame when you croaks. (*Reminiscently.*) If dey's one thing I learns in ten years on de Pullman ca's listenin' to de white quality talk, it's dat same fact. And when I gits a chance to use it I winds up Emperor in two years.

SMITHERS (*unable to repress the genuine admiration of the small fry for the large*). Yes, yer turned the bleedin' trick, all right. Blimey, I never seen a bloke 'as 'ad the bloomin' luck you 'as.

JONES (*severely*). Luck? What you mean—luck?

SMITHERS. I suppose you'll say as that swank about the silver bullet ain't luck—and that was what first got the fool blacks on yer side the time of the revolution, wasn't it?

JONES (*with a laugh*). Oh, dat silver bullet! Sho' was luck! But I makes dat luck, you heah? I loads de dice! Yessuh! When dat murderin' nigger ole Lem hired to kill me takes aim ten feet away and his gun misses fire and I shoots him dead, what you heah me say?

SMITHERS. You said yer'd got a charm so's no lead bullet'd kill yer. You was so strong only a silver bullet could kill yer, you told 'em. Blimey, wasn't that swank for yer, and plain, fat-'eaded luck?

JONES (*proudly*). I got brains and I uses 'em quick. Dat ain't luck.

SMITHERS. Yer know they wasn't 'ardly liable to get no silver bullets. And it was luck 'e didn't 'it you that time.

JONES (*laughing*). And dere all dem fool bush niggers was kneelin' down and bumpin' deir heads on de ground like I was a miracle out o' de Bible. Oh Lawd, from dat time on I has dem all eatin' out of my hand. I cracks de whip and dey jumps through.

SMITHERS (*with a sniff*). Yankee bluff done it.

JONES. Ain't a man's talkin' big what makes him big—long as he makes folks believe it? Sho', I talks large when I ain't got nothin' to back it up, but I ain't talkin' wild just de same. I knows I kin fool 'em—I *knows* it—and dat's backin' enough fo' my game. And ain't I got to learn deir lingo and teach some of dem English befo' I kin talk to em? Ain't dat wuk? You ain't never learned any word of it, Smithers in de ten years you been heah, dough you' knows it's money in yo' pocket tradin' wid 'em if you does. But you'se too shiftless to take de trouble.

SMITHERS (*flushing*). Never mind about me. What's this I've 'eard about yer really 'avin' a silver bullet moulded for yourself?

JONES. It's playin' out my bluff. I has de silver bullet moulded and I tells 'em when de time comes I kills myself wid it. I tells 'em dat's 'cause I'm de on'y man in de world big enuff to git me. No use'n deir tryin'. And dey falls down and bumps deir heads. (*He laughs.*) I does dat so's I kin take a walk in peace widout no jealous nigger gunnin' at me from behind de trees.

SMITHERS (*astonished*). Then you 'ad it made—'onest?

JONES. Sho' did. Heah she be. (*He takes out his revolver, breaks it, and takes the bullet out of one chamber.*) Five lead an' dis silver baby at de last. Don't she shine pretty? (*He holds it in his hand, looking at it admiringly, as if strangely fascinated.*)

SMITHERS. Let me see. (*Reaches out his hand for it.*)

JONES (*harshly*). Keep yo' hands whar dey b'long, white man. (*He replaces it in the chamber and puts the revolver back on his hip.*)

SMITHERS (*snarling*). Gawd blimey! Think I'm a bleedin' thief, you would.

JONES. No, 'tain't dat. I knows you'se scared to steal from me. On'y I ain't 'lowin' nary body to touch dis baby. She's my rabbit's foot.

SMITHERS (*sneering*). A bloomin' charm, wot? (*Venomously.*) Well, you'll need all the bloody charms you 'as before long, s' 'elp me!

JONES (*judicially*). Oh, I'se good for six months yit 'fore dey gits sick o' my game. Den, when I sees trouble comin', I makes a move.

SMITHERS. Ho! You got it all planned, ain't yer?

JONES. I ain't no fool. I knows dis Emperor's time is sho't. Dat why I make hay when de sun shine. Was you thinkin' I'se aimin' to hold down dis job for life? No, suh! What good is gittin' money if you stays back in dis raggedy country? I wants action when I spends. And when I sees dese niggers gittin' up deir nerve to tu'n me out, and I'se got all de money in sight, I resigns on de spot and gets away quick.

SMITHERS. Where to?

JONES. None o' yo' business.

SMITHERS. Not back to the bloody States, I'll lay my oath.

JONES (*suspiciously*). Why don't I? (*Then with an easy laugh.*) You mean 'count of dat story 'bout me breakin' from jail back dere? Dat's all talk.

SMITHERS (*sceptically*). Ho, yes!

JONES (*sharply*). You ain't 'sinuatin' I'se a liar, is you?

SMITHERS (*hastily*). No, Gawd strike me! I was only thinkin' o' the bloody lies you told the blacks 'ere about killin' white men in the States.

JONES (*angered*). How come dey're lies?

SMITHERS. You'd 'ave been in jail if you 'ad, wouldn't yer then? (*With venom.*) And from what I've 'eard, it ain't 'ealthy for a black to kill a white man in the States. They burns 'em in oil, don't they?

JONES (*with cool deadliness*). You mean lynchin' 'd scare me? Well, I tells you, Smithers, maybe I does kill one white man back dere. Maybe I does. And maybe I kills another right heah 'fore long if he don't look out.

SMITHERS (*trying to force a laugh*). I was on'y spoofin' yer. Can't yer take a joke? And you was just sayin' you'd never been in jail.

JONES (*in the same tone—slightly boastful*). Maybe I goes to jail dere for gettin' in an argument wid razors ovah a game of dice. Maybe I gits twenty years when dat coloured man die. Maybe I gits in 'nother argument wid de prison guard and de overseer ovah us when we're wukin' de roads. Maybe he hits me wid a whip and I splits his head wid a shovel and runs away and files de chain off my leg and gits away safe. Maybe I does all dat an' maybe I don't. It's a story I tells you so's you knows I'se de kind of man dat if you evah repeats one word of it, I ends yo' stealin' on dis yearth mighty damn quick!

SMITHERS (*terrified*). Think I'd peach on yer? Not me! Ain't I always been yer friend?

JONES (*suddenly relaxing*). Sho' you has—and you better be.

SMITHERS (*recovering his composure—and with it his malice*). And just to show yer I'm yer friend, I'll tell yer that bit o' news I was goin' to.

JONES. Go ahead! Must be bad news from de happy way you look.

SMITHERS (*warningly*). Maybe it's gettin' time for you to resign—with that bloomin' silver bullet, wot? (*He finishes with a mocking grin.*)

JONES (*puzzled*). What's dat you say? Talk plain.

SMITHERS. Ain't noticed any of the guards or servants about the place to-day, I 'aven't.

JONES (*carelessly*). Dey're all out in de garden sleepin' under de trees. When I sleeps, dey sneaks a sleep too, and I pretends I never suspicions it. All I got to do is to ring de bell and dey come flyin', makin' a bluff dey was wukin' all de time.

SMITHERS (*in the same mocking tone*). Ring the bell now an' you'll bloody well see what I mean.

JONES (*startled to alertness, but preserving the same careless tone*). Sho' I rings.

(*He reaches below the throne and pulls out a big common dinner bell which is painted the same vivid scarlet as the throne. He rings this vigorously—then stops to listen. Then he goes to both doors, rings again, and looks out.*)

SMITHERS (*watching him with malicious satisfaction, after a pause—mockingly*). The bloody ship is sinkin' an' the bleedin' rats 'as slung their 'ooks.

JONES (*in a sudden fit of anger flings the bell clattering into a corner*). Low-flung bush niggers! (*Then catching Smithers' eye on him, he controls himself and suddenly bursts into a low chuckling laugh.*) Reckon I overplays my hand dis once! A man can't take de pot on a short-tailed flush all de time. Was I sayin' I'd sit it six months mo'? Well, I'se changed my mind den. I gives in and resigns de job of Emperor right dis minute.

SMITHERS (*with real admiration*). Blimey, but you're a cool bird, and no mistake.

JONES. No use'n fussin'. When I knows de game's up I kisses it good-bye widout no long waits. Dey've all run off to de hills, ain't dey?

SMITHERS. Yes—every bleedin' man jack of 'em.

JONES. Den de revolution is at de door. And de Emperor better git his feet movin' up de trail. (*He starts for the door in rear.*)

SMITHERS. Goin' out to look for your 'orse? Yer won't find any. They steals the 'orses first thing. Mine was gone when I went for 'im this mornin'. That's wot first give me a suspicion of wot was up.

JONES (*alarmed for a second, scratches his head, then philosophically*). Well, den I hoofs it. Feet, do yo' duty! (*He pulls out a gold watch and looks at it.*)

Three-thuty. Sundown's at six-thuty or dereabouts. (*Puts his watch back—with cool confidence.*) I got plenty o' time to make it easy.

SMITHERS. Don't be so bloomin' sure of it. They'll be after you 'ot and 'eavy. Ole Lem is at the bottom o' this business an' 'e 'ates you like 'ell. 'E'd rather do for you than eat 'is dinner, 'e would!

JONES (*scornfully*). Dat fool no-count nigger! Does you think I'se scared o' him? I stands him on his thick head more'n once befo' dis, and I does it again if he comes in my way—— (*Fiercely.*) And dis time I leave him a dead nigger fo' sho'!

SMITHERS. You'll 'ave to cut through the big forest—an' these blacks 'ere can sniff and follow a trail in the dark like 'ounds. You'd 'ave to 'ustle to get through that forest in twelve hours even if you knew all the bloomin' paths like a native.

JONES (*with indignant scorn*). Look-a-heah, white man! Does you think I'se a natural bo'n fool? Give me credit fo' havin' some sense, fo' Lawd's sake! Don't you s'pose I'se looked ahead and made sho' of all de chances? I'se gone out in dat big forest, pretendin' to hunt, so many times dat I knows it high an' low like a book. I could go through on dem paths wid my eyes shut. (*With great contempt.*) Think dese ig'nerent bush niggers dat ain't got brains enuff to know deir own names even, can catch Brutus Jones? Huh, I s'pects not! Not on yo' life! Why, man, de white men went after me wid bloodhounds, where I come from an' I jes' laughs at 'em. It's a shame to fool dese black trash around heah, dey're so easy. You watch me, man'. I'll make dem look sick, I will. I'll be 'cross de plain to de edge of de forest by time dark comes. Once in de woods in de night, dey got a fine chance o' findin' dis baby! Dawn to-morrow I'll be out at de oder side and on de coast whar dat French gunboat is stayin'. She picks me up, take me to the Martinique when she go dar, and dere I is safe wid a mighty big bankroll in my pocket. It's easy as rollin' off a log.

SMITHERS (*maliciously*). But s'posin' somethin' 'appens wrong an' they do nab yer?

JONES (*decisively*). Dey don't—dat's de answer.

SMITHERS. But, just for argyment's sake—what'd you do?

JONES (*frowning*). I'se got five lead bullets in dis gun good enuff fo' common bush niggers—and after dat I got de silver bullet left to cheat 'em out o' gittin' me.

SMITHERS (*jeeringly*). Ho, I was fergettin' that silver bullet. You'll bump yourself orf in style, won't yer? Blimey!

JONES (*gloomily*). You kin bet yo' whole money on one thing, white man. Dis baby plays out his string to de end and when he quits, he quits wid a bang de way he ought. Silver bullet ain't none too good for him when he go, dat's a fac'! (*Then shaking off his nervousness—with a confident laugh.*) Sho'! What is I talkin' about? Ain't come to dat yit and I never will—not wid trash niggers like dese yere. (*Boastfully.*) Silver bullet bring me luck anyway. I kin outguess, outrun, outfight, an' outplay de whole lot o' dem all ovah de board any time o' de day er night! You watch me!

(*From the distant hills comes the faint, steady thump of a tom-tom, low and vibrating. It starts at a rate exactly corresponding to normal pulse beat—72 to the minute—and continues at a gradually accelerating rate from this point uninterruptedly to the very end of the play.*)

(*Jones starts at the sound. A strange look of apprehension creeps into his face for a moment as he listens. Then he asks, with an attempt to regain his most casual manner*). What's dat drum beatin' fo'?

SMITHERS (*with a mean grin*). For you. That means the bleedin' ceremony 'as started. I've 'eard it before and I knows.

JONES. Cer'mony? What cer'mony?

SMITHERS. The blacks is 'oldin' a bloody meetin', 'avin' a war dance, gettin' their courage worked up b'fore they starts after you.

JONES. Let dem! Dey'll sho' need it!

SMITHERS. And they're there 'oldin' their 'eathen religious service—makin' no end of devil spells and charms to 'elp 'em against your silver bullet. (*He guffaws loudly.*) Blimey, but they're balmy as 'ell!

JONES (*a tiny bit awed and shaken in spite of himself*). Huh! Takes more'n dat to scare dis chicken!

SMITHERS (*scenting the other's feeling—maliciously*). Ternight when it's pitch black in the forest, they'll 'ave their pet devils and ghosts 'oundin' after you.

You'll find yer bloody 'air 'll be standin' on end before termorrow morning'. (*Seriously.*) It's a bleedin' queer place, that stinkin' forest, even in daylight. Yer don't know what might 'appen in there, it's that rotten still. Always sends the cold shivers down my back minute I gets in it.

JONES (*with a contemptuous sniff*). I ain't no white-liver like you is. Trees an' me, we'se friends, and dar's a full moon comin' bring me light. And let dem po' niggers make all de fool spells dey'se a min' to. Does yo' s'pect I'se silly enuff to b'lieve in ghosts an' ha'nts an' all dat ole woman's talk? G'long, white man! You ain't talkin' to me. (*With a chuckle.*) Doesn't you know dey's got to do wid a man who was member in good standin' o' de Baptist Church? Sho' I was dat when I was porter on de Pullmans, befo' I gits into my little trouble. Let dem try deir heathen tricks. De Baptist Church done pertect me and land dem all in hell. (*Then with more confident satisfaction.*) And I'se got little silver bullet o' my own, don't forgit.

SMITHERS. Ho! You 'aven't give much 'eed to your Baptist Church since you been down 'ere. I've 'eard myself you 'ad turned yer coat an' was takin' up with their blarsted witch-doctors, or whatever the 'ell yer calls the swine.

JONES (*vehemently*). I pretends to! Sho' I pretends! Dat's part o' my game from de fust. If I finds out dem niggers believes dat black is white, den I yells it out louder 'n deir loudest. It don't git me nothin' to do missionary work for de Baptist Church. I'se after de coin, an' I lays my Jesus on de shelf for de time bein'. (*Stops abruptly to look at his watch—alertly.*) But I ain't got de time to waste no more fool talk wid you. I'se gwine away from heah dis secon'. (*He reaches in under the throne and pulls out an expensive Panama hat with a bright multi-coloured band and sets it jauntily on his head.*) So long, white man! (*With a grin.*) See you in jail some time, maybe!

SMITHERS. Not me, you won't. Well, I wouldn't be in yer bloody boots for no bloomin' money, but 'ere's wishin' yer luck just the same.

JONES (*contemptuously*). You're de frightenedest man evah I see! I tells you I'se safe's 'f I was in New York City. It takes dem niggers from now to dark to git up de nerve to start somethin'. By dat time, I'se got a head start dey never kotch up wid.

SMITHERS (*maliciously*). Give my regards to any ghosts yer meets up with.

JONES (*grinning*). If dat ghost got money, I'll tell him never ha'nt you less'n he wants to lose it.

SMITHERS (*flattered*). Garn! (*Then curiously.*) Ain't yer takin' no luggage with yer?

JONES. I travels light when I wants to move fast. And I got tinned grub buried on de edge o' de forest. (*Boastfully.*) Now say dat I don't look ahead an' use my brains! (*With a wide, liberal gesture.*) I will all dat's left in de palace to you—and you better grab all you kin sneak away wid befo' dey gits here.

SMITHERS (*gratefully*). Righto—and thanks ter yer. (*As Jones walks towards the door in rear—cautioningly*). Say! Look 'ere, you ain't goin' out that way, are yer?

JONES. Does you think I'd slink out de back door like a common nigger? I'se Emperor yit, ain't I? And de Emperor Jones leaves de way he comes, and dat black trash don't dare stop him—not yit, leastways. (*He stops for a moment in the doorway, listening to the far-off but insistent beat of the tom-tom.*) Listen to dat roll-call, will you? Must be mighty big drum carry dat far. (*Then with a laugh.*) Well, if dey ain't no whole brass band to see me off, I sho' got de drum part of it. So long, white man.

(*He puts his hands in his pockets and with studied carelessness, whistling a tune, he saunters out of the doorway and off to left.*)

SMITHERS (*looks after him with a puzzled admiration*). 'E's got 'is bloomin' nerve with 'im, s'elp me! (*Then angrily.*) Ho—the bleedin' nigger—puttin' on 'is bloody airs! I 'opes they nabs 'im an' gives 'im what's what! (*Then putting business before the pleasure of this thought, looking around him with cupidity.*) A bloke ought to find a 'ole lot in this palace that'd go for a bit of cash. Let's take a look, 'Arry, me lad. (*He starts for the doorway on right as*

THE CURTAIN FALLS

Scene Two: Nightfall

The end of the plain where the Great Forest begins. The foreground is sandy, level ground dotted by a few stones and clumps of stunted bushes cowering close against the earth to escape the buffeting of the trade wind. In the rear the forest is a wall of darkness dividing the world. Only when the eye becomes accustomed to the gloom can the outlines of separate trunks of the nearest trees be made out, enormous pillars of deeper blackness. A sombre monotone of wind lost in the leaves moans in the air. Yet this sound serves but to intensify the impression of the forest's relentless immobility, to form a background throwing into relief its brooding, implacable silence.

(*Jones enters from the left, walking rapidly. He stops as he nears the edge of the forest, looks around him quickly, peering into the dark as if searching for some familiar landmark. Then, apparently satisfied that he is where he ought to be, he throws himself on the ground, dog-tired.*)

Well, heah I is. In de nick o' time, too! Little mo' an' it'd be blacker'n de ace of spades heah-abouts. (*He pulls a bandana handkerchief from his hip pocket and mops off his perspiring face.*) Sho'! Gimme air! I'se done up sho' 'nuff. Dat soft Emperor job ain't no trainin' for' a long dash ovah dat plain in de brilin' sun. (*Then with a chuckle.*) Cheah up, nigger, de worst is yet to come. (*He lifts his head and stares at the forest. His chuckle peters out abruptly. In a tone of awe.*) My goodness, look at dem woods, will you? Dat no-count Smithers said dey'd be black an' he sho' called de turn. (*Turning away from them quickly and looking down at his feet, he snatches at a chance to change the subject—solicitously.*) Feet, you is holdin' up yo' end fine an' I sutinly hopes you ain't blisterin'. It's time you git a rest. (*He takes off his shoes, his eyes studiously avoiding the forest. He feels the soles of his feet gingerly.*) You is still in de pink—on'y a little mite feverish. Cool yo'selfs. Remember you got a long journey yit before you. (*He sits in a weary attitude, listening to the rhythmic beating of the tom-tom. He grumbles in a loud tone to cover up a growing uneasiness.*) Bush niggers! Wonder dey wouldn' git sick o' beatin' dat drum. Sounds louder, seem like. I wonder if dey's startin' after me? (*He scrambles to his feet, looking back across the plain.*) Couldn't see dem now, nohow, if dey was hundred feet away. (*Then shaking himself like a wet dog to get rid of these depressing thoughts.*) Sho', dey's miles an' miles behind. What you gittin' fidgety about? (*But he sits down and begins to lace up his shoes in great haste, all the time muttering reassuringly.*) You know what? Yo' belly is empty, dat's what's de matter wid you. Come time to eat! Wid nothin' but wind on yo' stumach, o' course you feels jiggedy. Well, we eats right heah an' now soon's I gits dese here shoes laced up. (*He finishes lacing up his shoes.*) Dere! Now le's see! (*Gets on his hands and knees and searches the ground around him with his eyes.*) White stone, white stone, where is you? (*He sees the first white stone and crawls to it—with satisfaction.*) Heah you is! I knowed dis was de right place. Box of grub, come to me. (*He turns over the stone and feels in under it—in a tone of dismay.*) Ain't heah! Gorry, is I in de right place or isn't I? Dere's 'nother stone. Guess dat's it. (*He scrambles to the next stone and turns it over.*) Ain't heah, neither! Grub, whar is you? Ain't heah. Gorry, has I got to go hungry into dem woods—all de night? (*While he is talking he scrambles from one stone to another, turning them over in frantic haste. Finally he jumps to his feet excitedly.*) Is I lost de place? Must have! But how dat happen when I was followin' de trail across de plain in broad daylight? (*Almost plaintively.*) I'se hungry, I is! I gotta git my feed. Whar's my strength gonna come from if I doesn't? Gorry, I gotta find dat grub high an' low somehow! Why it come dark so quick like dat? Can't see nothin'. (*He scratches a match on his trousers and peers about him. The rate of the beat of the far-off tom-tom increases perceptibly as he does so. He mutters in a bewildered voice.*) How come all dese white stones come heah when I only remembers one? (*Suddenly, with a frightened gasp, he flings the match on the ground and stamps on it.*) Nigger, is you gone crazy mad? Is you lightin' matches to show dem whar you is? Fo' Lawd's sake, use yo' haid. Gorry, I'se got to be careful! (*He stares at the plain behind him apprehensively, his hand on his revolver.*) But how come all dese white stones?

And whar's dat tin box o' grub I hid all wrapped up in oil cloth ?

(While his back is turned, the Little Formless Fears creep out from the deeper blackness of the forest. They are black, shapeless, only their glittering little eyes can be seen. If they have any describable form at all it is that of a grubworm about the size of a creeping child. They move noiselessly, but with deliberate, painful effort, striving to raise themselves on end, failing and sinking prone again. Jones turns about to face the forest. He stares up at the tops of the trees, seeking vainly to discover his whereabouts by their conformation.)

Can't tell nothin' from dem trees ! Gorry, nothin' 'round heah look like I evah seed it befo'. I'se gone lost de place sho' 'nuff. *(With mournful foreboding.)* It's mighty queer ! It's mighty queer ! *(With sudden forced defiance—in an angry tone.)* Woods, is you tryin' to put somethin' ovah on me ?

(From the formless creatures on the ground in front of him comes a tiny gale of low mocking laughter like a rustling of leaves. They squirm upward towards him in twisted attitudes. Jones looks down, leaps backwards with a yell of terror, pulling out his revolver as he does so—in a quavering voice.) What's dat. Who's dar ? What is you ? Git away from me befo' I shoots ! You don't ?——

(He fires. There is a flash, a loud report, then silence broken only by the far-off quickened throb of the tom-tom. The formless creatures have scurried back into the forest. Jones remains fixed in his position listening intently. The sound of the shot, the reassuring feel of the revolver in his hand, have somewhat restored his shaken nerve. He addresses himself with renewed confidence.)

Dey're gone. Dat shot fix 'em. Dey was only little animals—little wild pigs, I reckon. Dey've maybe rooted out yo' grub an' eat it. Sho', you fool nigger, what you think dey is—ha'nts. *(Excitedly.)* Gorry, you give de game away when you fire dat shot. Dem niggers heah dat fo' su'tin ! Time you beat it in de woods widout no long waits. *(He starts for the forest—hesitates before the plunge—then urging himself in with manful resolution.)* Git in, nigger ! What you skeered at ? Ain't nothin' dere but de trees ! Git in ! *(He plunges boldly into the forest.)*

Scene Three

Nine o'clock. In the forest. The moon has just risen. Its beams, drifting through the canopy of leaves, make a barely perceptible, suffused, eerie glow. A dense low wall of underbrush and creepers is in the nearer foreground, fencing in a small triangular clearing. Beyond this is the massed blackness of the forest like an encompassing barrier. A path is dimly discerned leading down to the clearing from left, rear, and winding away from it again towards the right. As the scene opens nothing can be distinctly made out. Except for the beating of the tom-tom, which is a trifle louder and quicker than in the previous scene, there is silence, broken every few seconds by a queer, clicking sound. Then gradually the figure of the negro, Jeff, can be discerned crouching on his haunches at the rear of the triangle. He is middle-aged, thin, brown in colour, is dressed in a Pullman porter's uniform, cap, etc. He is throwing a pair of dice on the ground before him, picking them up, shaking them, casting them out with the regular, rigid, mechanical movements of an automaton. The heavy, plodding footsteps of someone approaching along the trail from the left are heard and Jones' voice, pitched in a slightly higher key and strained in a cheering effort to overcome its own tremors.

De moon's rizen. Does you heah dat, nigger ? You gits more light from dis forrard. No mo' buttin' yo' fool head agin' de trunks an' scratchin' de hide off yo' legs in de bushes. Now you sees whar you'se gwine. So cheer up ! From now on you has it easy. *(He steps just to the rear of the triangular clearing and mops off his face on his sleeve. He has lost his Panama hat. His face is scratched, his brilliant uniform shows several large rents.)* What time's it gittin' to be, I wonder ? I dassent light no match to find out. Phoo'. It's wa'm an' dats a fac' ! *(Wearily.)* How long I been makin' trampin' dese woods ? Must be hours an' hours. Seems like fo'evah ! Yit can't be, when de moon's jes' riz. Dis am a long night fo' yo', yo' Majesty! (*With a mournful chuckle.*) Majesty! Der ain't much majesty 'bout dis baby now. (*With attempted cheerfulness.*) Never min'. It's all part o' de game. Dis night come to an end like everything else. And when you gits dar safe and has dat bankroll in yo' hands you laughs at all dis. (*He starts to whistle, but checks himself abruptly.*) What yo' whistlin' for, you po' fool! Want all de worl' to heah you? (*He stops talking to listen.*) Heah dat ole drum! Sho' gits nearer from de sound. Dey're takin' it along wid 'em. Time fo' me to move. (*He takes a step forward, then stops—worriedly.*) What's dat odder queer clicketty sound I heah? Dere it is! Sound close! Sound like—sound like—Fo' God sake, sound like some nigger was shootin' dice! (*Frightenedly.*) I better get on quick when I gits dem notions. (*He walks quickly into the clear space —then stands transfixed as he sees Jeff—in a terrified gasp.*) Who dar? Who dat? Is dat you, Jeff? (*Starting towards the other, forgetful for a moment of his surroundings and really believing it is a living man that he sees—in a tone of happy relief.*) Jeff! I'se sho' mighty glad to see you! Dey tols me you done died from dat razor cut I give' you. (*Stopping suddenly, bewildered*). But how you come to be heah, nigger? (*He stares fascinatedly at the other who continues his mechanical play with the dice. Jones' eyes began to roll wildly. He stutters.*) Ain't you gwine—look up—can't you speak to me? Is you—is you—a ha'nt? (*He jerks out his revolver in a frenzy of terrified rage.*) Nigger, I kills you dead once. Has I got to kill you agin? You take it den. (*He fires. When the smoke clears away Jeff has disappeared. Jones stands trembling—then with a certain reassurance.*) He's gone, anyway. Ha'nt or no ha'nt, dat shot fix him. (*The beat of the far-off tom-tom is perceptibly louder and more rapid. Jones becomes conscious of it—with a start, looking back over his shoulder.*) Dey's gittin' near! Dey'se comin' fast! And heah I is shootin' shots to let 'em know jes' whar I is. Oh, Gorry, I'se got to run. (*Forgetting the path he plunges wildly into the underbrush in the rear and disappears in the shadow.*)

Scene Four

Eleven o'clock. In the forest. A wide dirt road runs diagonally from right, front, to left, rear. Rising sheer on both sides the forest walls it in. The moon is now up. Under its light the road glimmers ghastly and unreal. It is as if the forest has stood aside momentarily to let the road pass through and accomplish its veiled purpose. This done, the forest will fold in upon itself again and the road will be no more. Jones stumbles in from the forest on the right. His uniform is ragged and torn. He looks about him with numbed surprise when he sees the road, his eyes blinking in the bright moonlight. He flops down exhaustedly and pants heavily for a while. Then with sudden anger.

I'm meltin' wid heat! Runnin' an' runnin' an' runnin'! Damn dis heah coat! Like a strait jacket! (*He tears off his coat and flings it away from him, revealing himself stripped to the waist.*) Dere! Dat's better! Now I kin breathe! (*Looking down at his feet, the spurs catch his eye.*) And to hell wid dese high-fangled spurs. Dey're what's been a-trippin' me up an' breakin' me neck. (*He unstraps them and flings them away disgustedly.*) Dere! I gits rid o' dem frippety Emperor trappin's an' I travels lighter. Lawd! I'se tired! (*After a pause, listening to the insistent beat of the tom-tom in the distance.*) I must 'a put some distance between myself an' dem—runnin' like dat—and yit—dat damn drum sound jes' de same—nearer, even. Well, I guess I a'most holds my lead anyhow. Dey won't never catch up. (*With a sigh.*) If on'y my fool legs stands up. Oh, I'se sorry I evah went in for dis. Dat Emperor job is sho' hard to shake. (*He looks around him suspiciously.*) How'd dis road evah git heah? Good level road, too. I never remembers seein' if befo'. (*Shaking his head apprehensively.*) Dese woods is sho' full o' de queerest things at night. (*With a sudden terror.*) Lawd God, don't let me see no more o' dem ha'nts! Dey gits me scared! (*Then trying to talk himself into confidence.*) Ha'nts! You fool nigger, dey ain't no such things! Don't de Baptist parson tell you dat many time? Is you civilised, or is you like dese ign'rent black niggers heah? Sho'! Dat was all in yo' own head. Wasn't nothin' dere. Wasn't no Jeff! Know what? You jus' get seein' dem things 'cause yo' belly's empty and you's sick wid hunger inside. Hunger 'fects yo' head and yo' eyes. Any fool know dat. (*Then pleading fervently.*) But bless God, I don't come across no more o' dem, whatever dey is! (*Then cautiously.*) Rest! Don't talk! Rest! You needs it. Den you gits on yo' way again. (*Looking at the moon.*) Night's half gone a'most. You hits de coast in de mawning! Den you'se all safe.

(*From the right forward a small gang of negroes enter. They are dressed in striped convict suits, their heads are shaven, one leg drags limpingly, shackled to a heavy ball and chain. Some carry picks, the others shovels. They are followed by a white man dressed in the uniform of a prison guard. A Winchester rifle is slung across his shoulders and he carries a heavy whip. At a signal from the guard they stop on the road opposite where Jones is sitting. Jones, who has been staring up at the sky, unmindful of their noiseless approach, suddenly looks down and sees them. His eyes pop out, he tries to get to his feet and fly, but sinks back, too numbed by fright to move. His voice catches in a choking prayer.*)

Lawd Jesus!

(*The prison guard cracks his whip—noiselessly —and at that signal all the convicts start at work on the road. They swing their picks, they shovel, but not a sound comes from their labour. Their movements, like those of Jeff in the preceding scene, are those of automatons—rigid, slow, and mechanical. The prison guard points sternly at Jones with his whip, motions him to take his place among the other shovellers. Jones gets to his feet in a hypnotised stupor. He mumbles subserviently.*)

Yes, suh! Yes, suh! I'se comin'.

(*As he shuffles, dragging one foot, over to his place, he curses under his breath with rage and hatred.*)

God damn yo' soul, I gits even wid you yit, some time.

(*As if there were a shovel in his hands he goes through weary, mechanical gestures of digging up dirt, and throwing it to the roadside. Suddenly the guard approaches him angrily, threateningly. He raises his whip and lashes Jones viciously across the shoulders with it. Jones winces with pain and cowers abjectly. The guard turns his back on him and walks away contemptuously. Instantly Jones straightens up. With arms upraised as if his shovel were a club in his hands he springs murderously at the unsuspecting guard. In the act of crashing down his shovel on the white man's skull, Jones suddenly becomes aware that his hands are empty. He cries despairingly.*)

Whar's my shovel? Gimme my shovel 'till I splits his damn head! (*Appealing to his fellow convicts.*) Gimme a shovel, one o' you, fo' God's sake!

(*They stand fixed in motionless attitudes, their eyes on the ground. The guard seems to wait expectantly, his back turned to the attacker. Jones bellows with baffled, terrified rage, tugging frantically at his revolver.*)

I kills you, you white debil, if it's de last thing I evah does! Ghost or debil, I kill you agin!

(*He frees the revolver and fires point blank at the guard's back. Instantly the walls of the forest close in from both sides, the road and the figures of the convict gang are blotted out in an enshrouding darkness. The only sounds are a crashing in the underbrush as Jones leaps away in mad flight and the throbbing of the tom-tom, still far distant, but increased in volume of sound and rapidity of beat.*)

Scene Five

One o'clock. A large circular clearing, enclosed by the serried ranks of gigantic trunks of tall trees whose tops are lost to view. In the centre is a big dead stump worn by time into a curious resemblance to an auction block. The moon floods the clearing with a clear light. Jones forces his way in through the forest on the left. He looks wildly about the clearing with hunted, fearful glances. His trousers are in tatters, his shoes cut and misshapen, flapping about his feet. He slinks cautiously to the stump in the centre and sits down in a tense position, ready for instant flight. Then he holds his head in his hands and rocks back and forth, moaning to himself miserably.)

Oh Lawd, Lawd! Oh Lawd, Lawd! (*Suddenly he throws himself on his knees and raises his clasped hands to the sky—in a voice of agonised pleading.*) Lawd Jesus, heah my prayer! I'se a po' sinner, a po' sinner! I knows I done wrong, I knows it! When I cotches Jeff cheatin' wid loaded dice my anger overcomes me and I kills him dead! Lawd, I done wrong! When dat guard hits me wid de whip, my anger overcomes me, and I kills him dead. Lawd, I done wrong! And down heah whar dese fool bush niggers raises me up to the seat o' de mighty, I steals all I could grab. Lawd, I done wrong! I knows it! I'se sorry! Forgive me, Lawd! Forgive dis po' sinner! (*Then beseeching terrifiedly.*) And keep dem away, Lawd! Keep dem away from me! And stop dat drum soundin' in my ears! Dat begin to sound ha'nted, too. (*He gets to his feet, evidently slightly reassured by his prayer—with attempted confidence.*) De Lawd'll preserve me from dem ha'nts after dis. (*Sits down on the stump again.*) I ain't skeered o' real men. Let dem come. But dem odders—— (*He shudders—then looks down at his feet, working his toes inside the shoes—with a groan.*) Oh, my po' feet! Dem shoes ain't no use no more 'ceptin' to hurt. I'se better off widout dem. (*He unlaces them and pulls them off—holds the wrecks of the shoes in his hands and regards them mournfully.*) You was real, A-one patin' leather, too. Look at you now. Emperor, you'se gittin' mighty low!

(He sighs dejectedly and remains with bowed shoulders, staring down at the shoes in his hands as if reluctant to throw them away. While his attention is thus occupied, a crowd of figures silently enter the clearing from all sides. All are dressed in Southern costumes of the period of the fifties of the last century. There are middle-aged men who are evidently well-to-do planters. There is one spruce, authoritative individual—the Auctioneer. There are a crowd of curious spectators, chiefly young belles and dandies who have come to the slave-market for diversion. All exchange courtly greetings in dumb show and chat silently together. There is something stiff, rigid, unreal, marionettish about their movements. They group themselves about the stump. Finally a batch of slaves are led in from the left by an attendant—three men of different ages, two women, one with a baby in her arms, nursing. They are placed to the left of the stump, beside Jones.

The white planters look them over appraisingly as if they were cattle. The dandies point their fingers and make witty remarks. The belles titter bewitchingly. All this in silence save for the ominous throb of the tom-tom. The Auctioneer holds up his hand, taking his place at the stump. The groups strain forward. He touches Jones on the shoulder peremptorily, motioning for him to stand on the stump—the auction block.

Jones looks up, sees the figures on all sides, looks wildly for some opening to escape, sees none, screams and leaps madly to the top of the stump to get as far away from them as possible. He stands there, cowering, paralysed with horror. The Auctioneer begins his silent speech. He points to Jones, appeals to the planters to see for themselves. Here is a good field hand, sound in wind and limb as they can see. Very strong still in spite of his being middle-aged. Look at that back. Look at those shoulders. Look at the muscles in his arms and his sturdy legs. Capable of any amount of hard labour. Moreover of a good disposition, intelligent and tractable. Will any gentleman start the bidding? The planters raise their fingers, make their bids. They are apparently all eager to possess Jones. The bidding is lively, the crowd interested. While this has been going on, Jones has been seized by the courage of desperation. He dares to look down and around him. Over his face abject terror gives way to mystification, to gradual realisation—stutteringly.)

What you all doin', white folks? What's all dis? What you all lookin' at me fo'? What you doin' wid me, anyhow? (*Suddenly convulsed with raging hatred and fear.*) Is dis a auction? Is you sellin' me like dey uster befo' de war? (*Jerking out his revolver just as the Auctioneer knocks him down to one of the planters—glaring from him to the purchaser.*) And *you* sells me? And *you* buys me? I shows you I'se a free nigger, damn yo' souls!

(*He fires at the Auctioneer and at the planter with such rapidity that the two shots are almost simultaneous. As if this were a signal the walls of the forest fold in. Only blackness remains and silence broken by Jones as he rushes off, crying with fear—and by the quickened, ever louder beat of the tom-tom.*)

Scene Six

Three o'clock. A cleared space in the forest. The limbs of the trees meet over it forming a low ceiling about five feet from the ground. The interlocked ropes of creepers reaching upward to entwine the tree trunks gives an arched appearance to the sides. The space thus enclosed is like the dark, noisome hold of some ancient vessel. The moonlight is almost completely shut out and only a vague, wan light filters through. There is the noise of someone approaching from the left, stumbling and crawling through the undergrowth. Jones' voice is heard between chattering moans.

Oh, Lawd, what I gwine do now? Ain't got no bullet left on'y de silver one. If mo' o' dem ha'nts come after me, how I gwine skeer dem away? Oh, Lawd, on'y de silver one left—an' I gotta save dat fo' luck. If I shoots dat one I'm a goner sho'! Lawd, it's black heah! Whar's de moon? Oh, Lawd, don't dis night evah come to an end? (*By the sounds, he is feeling his way cautiously forward.*) Dere! Dis feels like a clear space. I gotta lie down an' rest. I don't care if dem niggers does cotch me. I gotta rest.

(*He is well forward now where his figure can be dimly made out. His trousers have been so torn away that what is left of them is no better than a loin cloth. He flings himself full length, face downward on the ground, panting with exhaustion. Gradually it seems to grow lighter in the enclosed space and two rows of seated figures can be seen behind Jones. They are sitting in crumpled, despairing attitudes, hunched, facing one another with their backs touching the forest walls as if they were shackled to them. All are negroes naked save for loin cloths. At first they are silent and motionless. Then they begin to sway slowly forward towards each and back again, in unison, as if they were laxly letting themselves follow the long roll of a ship at sea. At the same time a low, melancholy murmur rises among them, increasing gradually by rhythmic degrees which seem to be directed and controlled by the throb of the tom-tom in the distance, to a long, tremulous wail of despair that reaches a certain pitch, unbearably acute, then falls by slow gradations of tone into silence and is taken up again. Jones starts, looks up, sees the figures, and throws himself down again to shut out the sight. A shudder of terror shakes his whole body as the wail rises up about him again. But the next time his voice, as if under some uncanny compulsion, starts with the others. As their chorus lifts he rises to a sitting posture similar to the others, swaying back and forth. His voice reaches the highest pitch of sorrow, of desolation. The light fades out, the other voices cease, and only darkness is left. Jones can be heard scrambling to his feet and running off, his voice sinking down the scale and receding as he moves farther and farther away in the forest. The tom-tom beats louder, quicker, with a more insistent, triumphant pulsation.*)

Scene Seven

Five o'clock. The foot of a gigantic tree by the edge of a great river. A rough structure of boulders, like an altar, is by the tree. The raised river bank is in the nearer background. Beyond this the surface of the river spreads out, brilliant and unruffled in the moonlight, blotted out and merged into a veil of bluish mist in the distance. Jones' voice is heard from the left rising and falling in the long, despairing wail of the chained slaves, to the rhythmic beat of the tom-tom. As his voice sinks into silence, he enters the open space. The expression of his face is fixed and stony, his eyes have an obsessed glare, he moves with a strange deliberation like a sleep-walker or one in a trance. He looks around at the tree, the rough stone altar, the moonlit surface of the river beyond, and passes his hand over his head with a vague gesture of puzzled bewilderment. Then, as if in obedience to some obscure impulse, he sinks into a kneeling, devotional posture before the altar. Then he seems to come to himself partly, to have an uncertain realisation of what he is doing, for he straightens up and stares about him horrifiedly—in an incoherent mumble.

What—what is I doin'? What is—dis place? Seems like—seems like I know dat tree—an' dem stones—an' de river. I remember—seems like I been heah befo'. (*Tremblingly.*) Oh, Gorry, I'se skeered in dis place! I'se skeered! Oh, Lawd, pertect dis sinner!

(*Crawling away from the altar, he cowers close to the ground, his face hidden, his shoulders heaving with sobs of hysterical fright. From behind the trunk of the tree, as if he had sprung out of it, the figure of the Congo Witch-Doctor appears. He is wizened and old, naked except for the fur of some small animal tied about his waist, its bushy tail hanging down in front. His body is stained all over a bright red. Antelope horns are on each side of his head, branching upward. In one hand he carries a bone rattle, in the other a charm stick with a bunch of white cockatoo feathers tied to the end. A great number of glass beads and bone ornaments are about his neck, ears, wrists, and ankles. He struts noiselessly with a queer prancing step to a position in the clear ground between Jones and the altar. Then with a preliminary, summoning stamp of his foot on the earth, he begins to dance and to chant. As if in response to his summons the beating of the tom-tom grows to a fierce, exultant boom whose throbs seem to fill the air with vibrating rhythm. Jones looks up, starts to spring to his feet, reaches a half-kneeling, half-squatting position and remains rigidly fixed there, paralysed with awed fascination by this new apparition. The Witch-Doctor sways, stamping with his foot, his bone rattle clicking the time. His voice rises and falls in a weird, monotonous croon, without articulate word divisions. Gradually his dance becomes clearly one of a narrative in pantomime, his croon is an incantation, a charm to allay the fierceness of some implacable deity demanding sacrifice. He flees, he is pursued by devils, he hides, he flees again. Ever wilder and wilder becomes his flight, nearer and nearer draws the pursuing evil, more and more the spirit of terror gains possession of him. His croon, rising to intensity, is punctuated by shrill cries. Jones has become completely hypnotised. His voice joins in the incantation, in the cries, he beats time with his hands and sways his body to and fro from the waist. The whole spirit and meaning of the dance has entered into him, has become his spirit. Finally the theme of the pantomime halts on a howl of despair, and is taken up again in a note of savage hope. There is a salvation. The forces of evil demand sacrifice. They must be appeased. The Witch-Doctor points with his wand to the sacred tree, to the river beyond, to the altar, and finally to Jones with a ferocious command. Jones seems to sense the meaning of this. It is he who must offer himself for sacrifice. He beats his forehead abjectly to the ground, moaning hysterically.)*

Mercy, oh Lawd! Mercy! Mercy on dis po' sinner.

(The Witch-Doctor springs to the river bank. He stretches out his arms and calls to some god within its depths. Then he starts backward slowly, his arms remaining out. A huge head of a crocodile appears over the bank and its eyes, glittering greenly, fasten upon Jones. He stares into them fascinatedly. The Witch-Doctor prances up to him, touches him with his wand, motions with hideous command towards the waiting monster. Jones squirms on his belly nearer and nearer, moaning continually.)

Mercy, Lawd! Mercy!

(The crocodile heaves more of his enormous hulk on to the land. Jones squirms towards him. The Witch-Doctor's voice shrills out in furious exultation, the tom-tom beats madly. Jones cries out in a fierce, exhausted spasm of anguished pleading.)

Lawd, save me! Lawd Jesus, heah my prayer!

(Immediately, in answer to his prayer, comes the thought of the one bullet left him. He snatches at his hip, shouting defiantly.)

De silver bullet! You don't git me yit!

(He fires at the green eyes in front of him. The head of the crocodile sinks back behind the river bank, the Witch-Doctor springs behind the sacred tree and disappears. Jones lies with his face to the ground, his arms outstretched, whimpering with fear as the throb of the tom-tom fills the silence about him with a sombre pulsation, a baffled but revengeful power.)

Scene Eight

Dawn. Same as Scene Two, the dividing line of forest and plain. The nearest tree trunks are dimly revealed, but the forest behind them is still a mass of glooming shadow. The tom-tom seems on the very spot, so loud and continuously vibrating are its beats. Lem enters from the left, followed by a small squad of his soldiers, and by the Cockney trader, Smithers. Lem is a heavy-set, ape-faced old savage of the extreme African type, dressed only in a loin cloth. A revolver and cartridge belt are about his waist. His soldiers are in different degrees of rag-concealed nakedness. All wear broad palm-leaf hats. Each one carries a rifle. Smithers is the same as in Scene One. One of the soldiers, evidently a tracker, is peering about keenly on the ground. He grunts and points to the spot where Jones entered the forest. Lem and Smithers come to look.

SMITHERS *(after a glance, turns away in disgust)*. That's where 'e went in right enough. Much good it'll do yer. 'E's miles orf by this an' safe to the coast, damn 's 'ide! I tole yer yer'd lose 'im, didn't I?—wastin' the 'ole bloomin' night beatin' yer bloody drum and castin' yer silly spells! Gawd blimey, wot a pack!

LEM *(gutturally)*. We cotch him. You see. *(He makes a motion to his soldiers who squat down on their haunches in a semi-circle.)*

SMITHERS *(exasperatedly)*. Well, ain't yer goin' in an' 'unt 'im in the woods? What the 'ell's the good of waitin'?

LEM *(imperturbably—squatting down himself)*. We cotch him.

SMITHERS *(turning away from him contemptuously)*. Aw! Garn! 'E's a better man than the lot o' you put together. I 'ates the sight o' 'im, but I'll say that for 'im.

(A sound of snapping twigs comes from the forest. The soldiers jump to their feet, cocking their rifles alertly. Lem remains sitting with an imperturbable expression, but listening intently. The sound from the woods is repeated. Lem makes a quick signal with his hand. His followers creep quickly but noiselessly

into the forest, scattering so that each enters at a different spot.)

SMITHERS (*in the silence that follows—in a contemptuous whisper*). You ain't thinkin' that would be 'im, I 'ope?

LEM (*calmly*). We cotch him.

SMITHERS. Blarsted fat 'eads! (*Then after a second's thought—wonderingly*). Still, after all, it might 'appen. If 'e lost 'is bloody way in these stinkin' woods 'e'd likely turn in a circle without 'is knowin' it. They all does.

LEM (*peremptorily*). Ssshh! (*The reports of several rifles sound from the forest, followed a second later by savage, exultant yells. The beating of the tom-tom abruptly ceases. Lem looks up at the white man with a grin of satisfaction.*) We cotch him. Him dead.

SMITHERS (*with a snarl*). 'Ow d'yer know it's 'im, an' 'ow d'yer know 'e's dead?

LEM. My mens dey got 'um silver bullets. Dey kill him shure.

SMITHERS (*astonished*). They got silver bullets?

LEM. Lead bullet no kill him. He got um strong charm. I cook um money, make um silver bullet, make um strong charm, too.

SMITHERS (*light breaking upon him*). So that's wot you was up to all night, wot? You was scared to put after 'im till you'd moulded silver bullets, eh?

LEM (*simply stating a fact*). Yes. Him got strong charm. Lead no good.

SMITHERS (*slapping his thigh and guffawing*). Haw-haw! If yer don't beat all 'ell! (*Then recovering himself—scornfully.*) I'll bet yer it ain't 'im they shot at all, yer bleedin' looney!

LEM (*calmly*). Dey come bring him now. (*The soldiers come out of the forest, carrying Jones's limp body. There is a little reddish-purple hole under his left breast. He is dead. They carry him to Lem, who examines his body with great satisfaction. Smithers leans over his shoulder—in a tone of frightened awe.*) Well, they did for yer right enough, Jonesy, me lad! Dead as a bloater! (*Mockingly.*) Where's yer 'igh an' mighty airs now, yer bloomin' Majesty? (*Then with a grin.*) Silver bullets! Gawd blimey, but yer died in the 'eighth o' style, any'ow! (*Lem makes a motion to the soldiers to carry the body out, left. Smithers speaks to him sneeringly.*)

SMITHERS. And I s'pose you think it's yer bleedin' charms and yer silly beatin' the drum that made 'im run in a circle when 'e'd lost 'imself, don't yer? (*But Lem makes no reply, does not seem to hear the question, walks out, left, after his men. Smithers looks after him with contemptuous scorn.*) Stupid as 'ogs, the lot of 'em! Blarsted niggers!

CURTAIN

DIFF'RENT

Characters

CAPTAIN CALEB WILLIAMS
EMMA CROSBY
CAPTAIN JOHN CROSBY, *her father*
MRS. CROSBY, *her mother*
JACK CROSBY, *her brother*
HARRIET WILLIAMS, *Caleb's sister (later Mrs. Rogers)*
ALFRED ROGERS
BENNY ROGERS, *their son*

Scenes

ACT ONE

Parlour of the Crosby home on a side-street of a seaport village in New England. Mid-afternoon of a day in late spring in the year 1890.

ACT TWO

The same. Late afternoon of a day in the early spring of the year 1920.

Act One

Parlour of the Crosby home. The room is small and low-ceilinged. Everything has an aspect of scrupulous neatness. On the left, forward, a stiff plush-covered chair. Farther back, in order, a window looking out on a vegetable garden, a black horsehair sofa, and another window. In the far left corner, an old mahogany chest of drawers. To the right of it, in rear, a window looking out on the front garden. To the right of this window is the front door, reached by a gravel path through the small lawn which separates the house from the street. To the right of door, another window. In the far right corner, a diminutive, old-fashioned piano with a stool in front of it. Near the piano on the right, a door leading to the next room. On this side of the room are also a small book-case half filled with old volumes, a big open fireplace, and another plush-covered chair. Over the fireplace a mantelpiece with marble clock and figure groups either side. The walls are papered a brown colour. The floor is covered with a dark carpet. In the centre of the room there is a clumsy, marble-topped table. On the table a large china lamp, a bulky Bible with a brass clasp, and books that look like cheap novels. Near the table, three plush covered chairs, two of which are rockers. Several enlarged photos of uncomfortable stern-looking people are hung on the walls.

It is mid-afternoon of a fine day in late spring of the year 1890. Bright sunlight streams through the windows on the left. Through the window and the screen door in the rear the fresh green of the lawn and of the elm trees that line the street can be seen. Stiff white curtains are at all the windows.

As the curtain rises Emma Crosby and Caleb Williams are discovered. Emma is a slender girl of twenty, rather under medium height. Her face, in spite of plain features, gives an impression of prettiness, due to large, soft blue eyes which have an incongruous quality of romantic dreaminess about them. Her mouth and chin are heavy, full of a self-willed stubbornness. Although her body is slight, there is a quick, nervous vitality about her movements that reveals an underlying constitution of reserve power and health. She has light brown hair, thick and heavy. She is dressed soberly and neatly in her black Sunday best style of the period.

Caleb Williams is tall and powerfully built, about thirty. Black hair, keen dark eyes, face rugged and bronzed, mouth obstinate but good-natured. He also is got up in black Sunday best and is uncomfortably self-conscious and stiff therein.

They are sitting on the horsehair sofa, side by side. His arm is about her waist. She holds one of his big hands in both of hers, her head leaning back against his shoulder, her eyes half closed in a dreamy contentedness. He stares before him rigidly, his whole attitude wooden and fixed as if he were posing for a photograph; yet his eyes are expressively tender and protecting when he glances down at her diffidently out of the corners without moving his head.

EMMA (*sighing happily*). Gosh, I wish we could sit this way for ever! (*Then after a pause, as he makes no comment except a concurring squeeze.*) Don't you, Caleb?

CALEB (*with another squeeze—emphatically*). Hell, yes! I'd like it, Emmer.

EMMA (*softly*). I do wish you wouldn't swear so awful much, Caleb.

CALEB. S'cuse me, Emmer, it jumped out o' my mouth afore I thought. (*Then with a grin.*) You'd ought to be used to that part o' men's wickedness—with your Pa and Jack cussin' about the house all the time.

EMMA (*with a smile*). Oh, I haven't no strict religious notions about it. I'm hardened in sin so far's they're concerned. Goodness me, how would Ma and me ever have lived in the same house with them two if we wasn't used to it? I don't even notice their cussing no more. And I don't mind hearing it from the other men, either. Being sea-faring men, away from their women folks most of the time, I know it just gets to be part of their natures and they ain't responsible. (*Decisively.*) But you're diff'rent. You just got to be diff'rent from the rest.

CALEB (*amused by her seriousness*). Diff'rent? Ain't I a sea-farin' man, too?

EMMA. You're diff'rent just the same. That's what made me fall in love with you 'stead of any of them. And you've got to stay di'ffrent. Promise me, Caleb, that you'll always stay diff'rent from them—even after we're married years and years.

CALEB (*embarrassed*). Why—I promise to do my best by you, Emmer. You know that, don't ye? On'y don't git the notion in your head I'm any better'n the rest. They're all good men—most of 'em, anyway. Don't tell me, for instance, you think I'm better'n your Pa or Jack—'cause I ain't. And I don't know as I'd want to be, neither.

EMMA (*excitedly*). But you got to want to be—when I ask it.

CALEB (*surprised*). Better'n your Pa?

EMMA (*struggling to convey her meaning*). Why, Pa's all right. He's a fine man—and Jack's all right, too. I wouldn't hear a bad word about them for anything. And the others are all right in their way, too, I s'pose. Only—don't you see what I mean?—I look on you as diff'rent from all of them. I mean there's things that's all right for them to do that wouldn't be for you—in my mind, anyway.

CALEB (*puzzled and a bit uneasy*). Sailors ain't plaster saints, Emmer—not a darn one of 'em ain't!

EMMA (*hurt and disappointed*). Then you won't promise me to stay diff'rent for my sake?

CALEB (*with rough tenderness*). Oh, hell, Emmer, I'll do any cussed thing in the world you want me to, and you know it!

EMMA (*lovingly*). Thank you, Caleb. It means a lot to me—more'n you think. And don't you think I'm diff'rent, too—not just the same as all the other girls hereabouts?

CALEB 'Course you be! Ain't I always said that? You're wo'th the whole pack of 'em put together.

EMMA. Oh, I don't mean I'm any better. I mean I just look at things diff'rent from what they do—getting married, for example, and other things, too. And so I've got it fixed in my head that you and me ought to make a married couple—diff'rent from the rest—not that they ain't all right in their way.

CALEB (*puzzled—uncertainly*). Waal—it's bound to

be from your end of it, you bein' like you are. But I ain't so sure o' mine.

EMMA. Well, I am!

CALEB (*with a grin*). You got me scared, Emmer. I'm scared you'll want me to live up to one of them high-fangled heroes you been readin' about in them books. (*He indicates the novels on the table.*)

EMMA. No, I don't. I want you to be just like yourself, that's all.

CALEB. That's easy. It ain't hard bein' a plain, ordinary cuss.

EMMA. You are not!

CALEB (*with a laugh*). Remember, I'm warnin' you, Emmer; and after we're married and you find me out, you can't say I got you under no false pretences.

EMMA (*laughing*). I won't. I won't ever need to. (*Then after a pause.*) Just think, it's only two days more before you and me'll be man and wife.

CALEB (*squeezing her*). Waal, it's about time, ain't it?—after waitin' three years for me to git enough money saved—and us not seein' hide or hair of each other the last two of 'em. (*With a laugh.*) Shows ye what trust I put in you, Emmer, when I kin go off on a two year whalin' vige and leave you all 'lone for all the young fellers in town to make eyes at.

EMMA. But lots and lots of the others does the same thing without thinking nothing about it.

CALEB (*with a laugh*). Yes, but I'm diff'rent, like you says.

EMMA (*laughing*). Oh, you're poking fun now.

CALEB (*with a wink*). And you know as well's me that some o' the others finds out some funny things that's been done when they was away.

EMMA (*laughing at first*). Yes, but you know I'm diff'rent, too. (*Then frowning.*) But don't let's talk about that sort o' ructions. I hate to think of such things—even joking. I ain't like that sort.

CALEB. Thunder, I know you ain't, Emmer. I was on'y jokin'.

EMMA. And I never doubted you them two years; and I won't when you sail away again, neither.

CALEB (*with a twinkle in his eye*). No, even a woman'd find it hard to git jealous of a whale!

EMMA (*laughing*). I wasn't thinking of whales, silly! But there's plenty of diversion going on in the ports you touched, if you'd a mind for it.

CALEB. Waal, I didn't have no mind for it, that's sartin. My fust vige as skipper, you don't s'pose I had time for no monkey-shinin', do ye? Why, I was that anxious to bring back your Pa's ship with a fine vige that'd make him piles o' money. I didn't even think of nothin' else.

EMMA. 'Cepting me, I hope?

CALEB. O' course! What was my big aim in doin' it if it wasn't so's we'd git married when I come to home? And then, s'far as ports go, we didn't tech at one the last year—'ceptin' when that durn tempest blowed us south and we put in at one o' the islands for water.

EMMA. What island? You never told me nothing about that.

CALEB (*growing suddenly very embarrassed as if some memory occurred to him*). Ain't nothin' to tell, that's why. Just an island near the Line, that's all. On'y naked heathen livin' there—brown coloured savages that ain't even Christians. (*He gets to his feet abruptly and pulls out his watch.*) Gittin' late, must be. I got to go down to the store and git some things for Harriet afore I forgets 'em.

EMMA (*rising also and putting her hands on his shoulders*). But you did think of me and miss me all the time you was gone, didn't you?—same as I did you.

CALEB. 'Course I did. Every minute.

EMMA (*nestling closer to him—softly*). I'm glad of that, Caleb. Well, good-bye for a little while.

CALEB. I'll step in again for a spell afore supper—that is, if you want me to.

EMMA. Yes, course I do, Caleb. Good-bye. (*She lifts her face to his.*)

CALEB. Good-bye, Emmer.

(*He kisses her and holds her in his arms for a moment. Jack comes up the walk to the screen door. They do not notice his approach.*)

JACK (*peering in and seeing them—in a joking bellow*). Belay there!

(*They separate with startled exclamations. Jack comes in grinning. He is a hulking stocky-built young fellow of 25. His heavy face is sunburned, handsome in a coarse, good-natured, animal fashion. His small blue eyes twinkle with the unconsciously malicious humour of the born practical joker. He wears thigh sea-boots turned down from the knees, dirty cotton shirt and pants, and a yellow sou'wester pushed jauntily on the back of his head, revealing his dishevelled, curly blonde hair. He carries a string of cod heads.*)

JACK (*laughing at the embarrassed expression on their faces*). Caught ye that time, by gum! Go ahead! Kiss her again, Caleb. Don't mind me.

EMMA (*with flurried annoyance*). You got a head on you just like one of them cod heads you're carrying—that stupid! I should think you'd be ashamed at your age—shouting to scare folks as if you was a little boy.

JACK (*putting his arm about her waist*). There, kitty, don't git to spittin'. (*Stroking her hair.*) Puss, puss, puss! Nice kitty! (*He laughs.*)

EMMA (*forced to smile—pushing him away*). Get away! You'll never get sense. Land sakes, what a brother to have!

JACK. Oh, I dunno. I ain't so bad, as brothers go—eh, Caleb?

CALEB (*smiling*). I reckon you'll do, Jack.

JACK. See there! Listen to Caleb. You got to take his word—love, honour, and *obey*, ye know, Emmer.

EMMA (*laughing*). Leave it to men folks to stick up for each other, right or wrong.

JACK (*cockily*). Waal, I'm willin' to leave it to the girls, too. Ask any of 'em you knows if I ain't a jim-dandy to have for a brother. (*He winks at Caleb who grins back at him.*)

EMMA (*with a sniff*). I reckon you don't play much brother with them—the kind you knows. You may fool 'em into believing you're some pumpkins, but they'd change their minds if they had to live in the same house with you playing silly jokes all the time.

JACK (*provokingly*). A good lot on 'em 'd be on'y too damn glad to git me in the same house—if I was fool enough to git married.

EMMA. "Pride goeth before a fall." But what's the good paying any attention to you. (*She smiles at him affectionately.*)

JACK (*exaggeratedly*). You see, Caleb? See how she misuses me—her lovin' brother. Now you know what you'll be up against for the rest o' your natural days.

CALEB. Don't see no way but what I got to bear it, Jack.

EMMA. Caleb needn't fear. He's diff'rent.

JACK (*with a sudden guffaw*). Oh, hell, yes! I was forgittin'. Caleb's a Sunday go-to-meetin' Saint, ain't he? Yes, he is!

EMMA (*with real resentment*). He's better'n what you are, if that's what you mean.

JACK (*with a still louder laugh*). Ho-ho! Caleb's one o' them goody-goody heroes out o' them story books you're always readin', ain't he?

CALEB (*soberly—a bit disturbed*). I was tellin' Emmer not to take me that high.

JACK. No use, Caleb. She won't hear of it. She's got her head set t'other way. You'd ought to heard her argyin' when you was gone about what a parson's pet you was. Butter won't melt in your mouth, no siree! Waal, love is blind—and deaf, too, as the feller says—and I can't argy no more 'cause I got to give Ma these heads. (*He goes to the door on right—then glances back at his sister maliciously and says meaningly.*) You ought to have a talk with Jim Benson, Emmer. Oughtn't she, Caleb. (*He winks ponderously and goes off laughing uproariously.*)

CALEB (*his face worried and angry*). Jack's a durn fool at times, Emmer,—even if he is your brother. He needs a good lickin'.

EMMA (*staring at him—uneasily*). What'd he mean about Jim Benson, Caleb?

CALEB (*frowning*). I don't know—exzactly. Makin' up foolishness for a joke, I reckon.

EMMA. You don't know—*exactly?* Then there is—something?

CALEB (*quickly*). Not as I know on. On'y Jim Benson's one o' them slick jokers, same's Jack; can't keep their mouths shet or mind their own business.

EMMA. Jim Benson was mate with you this last trip, wasn't he?

CALEB. Yes.

EMMA. Didn't him and you get along?

CALEB (*a trifle impatiently*). 'Course we did. Jim's all right. We got along fust rate. He just can't keep his tongue from waggin', that's all's the matter with him.

EMMA (*uneasily*). What's it got to wag about? You ain't done nothing wrong, have you?

CALEB. Wrong? No, nothin' a man'd rightly call wrong.

EMMA. Nothing you'd be shamed to tell me?

CALEB (*awkwardly*). Why—no, Emmer.

EMMA (*pleadingly*). You'd swear that, Caleb?

CALEB (*hesitating for a second—then firmly*). Yes, I'd swear. I'd own up to everything fair and square I'd ever done, if it comes to that p'int. I ain't shamed o' anything I ever done, Emmer. On'y—women folks ain't got to know everything, have they?

EMMA (*turning away from him—frightenedly*). Oh, Caleb!

CALEB (*preoccupied with his own thoughts—going to the door in rear*). I'll see you later, Emmer. I got to go up street now more'n ever. I want to give that Jim Benson a talkin' to he won't forgit in a hurry—that is, if he's been tellin' tales. Good-bye, Emmer.

EMMA (*faintly*). Good-bye, Caleb. (*He goes out. She sits in one of the rockers by the table, her face greatly troubled, her manner nervous and uneasy. Finally she makes a decision, goes quickly to the door on the right and calls.*) Jack! Jack!

JACK (*from the kitchen*). What you want?

EMMA. Come here a minute, will you?

JACK. Jest a second. (*She comes back by the table, fighting to conceal her agitation. After a moment Jack comes in from the right. He has evidently been washing up, for his face is red and shiny, his hair wet. He looks around for Caleb.*) Where's Caleb?

EMMA. He had to go up street. (*Then coming to the point abruptly—with feigned indifference.*) What's that joke about Jim Benson, Jack? It seemed to get Caleb all riled up.

JACK (*with a chuckle*). You got to ask Caleb about that, Emmer.

EMMA. I did. He didn't seem to want to own up it was anything.

JACK (*with a laugh*). 'Course he wouldn't. He don't 'preciate a joke when it's on him.

EMMA. How'd you come to hear of it?

JACK. From Jim. Met him this afternoon and me and him had a long talk. He was tellin' me all 'bout their vige.

EMMA. Then it was on the vige this joke happened?

JACK. Yes. It was when they put in to git water at them South Islands where the tempest blowed 'em.

EMMA. Oh. (*Suspiciously.*) Caleb didn't seem willing to tell me much about their touching there.

JACK (*chuckling*). 'Course he didn't. Wasn't I sayin' the joke's on him? (*Coming closer to her—in a low, confidential tone, chucklingly.*) We'll fix up a joke on Caleb, Emmer, what d'ye say?

EMMA (*tortured by foreboding—resolved to find out what is behind all this by hook or crook—forcing a smile*). All right, Jack. I'm willing.

JACK. Then I'll tell you what Jim told me. And you put it up to Caleb, see, and pertend you're madder'n hell. (*Unable to restrain his mirth.*) Ho! ho! It'll git him wild if you do that. On'y I didn't tell ye, mind! You heard it from someone else. I don't want to git Caleb down on me. And you'd hear about it from someone sooner or later 'cause Jim and the rest o' the boys has been tellin' the hull town.

EMMA (*taken aback—frowning*). So all the town knows about it?

JACK. Yes, and they're all laffin' at Caleb. Oh, it ain't nothin' so out o' the ordinary. Most o' the whalin' men hereabouts have run up against it in their time. I've heard Pa and all the others tellin' stories like it out o' their experience. On'y with Caleb it ended up so damn funny! (*He laughs.*) Ho-ho! Jimminy!

EMMA (*in a strained voice*). Well, ain't you going to tell me?

JACK. I'm comin' to it. Waal, seems like they all went ashore on them islands to git water and the native brown women, all naked a'most, come round to meet 'em same as they always does—wantin' to swap for terbaccer and other tradin' stuff with straw mats and whatever other junk they'd got. Them brown gals was purty as the devil, Jim says—that is, in their heathen, outlandish way—and the boys got makin' up to 'em; and then, o' course, everything happened like it always does, and even after they'd got all the water they needed aboard, it took 'em a week to round up all hands from where they was foolin' about with them nigger women.

EMMA (*in anguish*). Yes—but Caleb—he ain't like them others. He's diff'rent.

JACK (*with a sly wink*). Oho, is he? I'm comin' to Caleb. Waal, seems s'if he kept aboard mindin' his own business and winkin' at what the boys was doin'. And one o' them gals—the purtiest on 'em, Jim says—she kept askin', where's the captain? She wouldn't have nothin' to do with any o' the others. She thought on'y the skipper was good enough for her, I reckon. So one night jest afore they sailed some o' the boys, bein' drunk on native rum they'd stole, planned to put up a joke on Caleb and on that brown gal, too. So they tells her the captain had sent for her and she was to swim right out and git aboard the ship where he was waitin' for her alone. That part of it was true enough 'cause Caleb was alone, all hands havin' deserted, you might say.

EMMA (*letting an involuntary exclamation escape her*). Oh!

JACK. Waal, that fool brown gal b'lieved 'em and she swum right off, tickled to death. What happened between 'em when she got aboard, nobody knows. Some thinks one thing and some another. And I ain't sayin' nothin' 'bout it (*with a wink*) but I know damn well what I'd 'a done in Caleb's boots, and I guess he ain't the cussed old woman you makes him out. But that part of it's got nothin' to do with the joke nohow. The joke's this: that brown gal took an awful likin' to Caleb and when she saw the ship was gittin' ready to sail she raised ructions, standin' on the beach howlin' and screamin', and beatin' her chest with her fists. And when they ups anchor, she dives in the water and swims out after 'em. There's no wind hardly and she kin swim like a fish and catches up to 'em and tries to climb aboard. At fust, Caleb tries to treat her gentle and argy with her to go back. But she won't listen, she gits wilder and wilder, and finally he gits sick of it and has the boys push her off with oars while he goes and hides in the cabin. Even this don't work. She keeps swimmin' round and yellin' for Caleb. And finally they has to p'int a gun at her and shoot in the water near her afore the crazy cuss gives up and swims back to home, howlin' all the time. (*With a chuckle.*) And Caleb lyin' low in the cabin skeered to move out, and all hands splittin' their sides! Gosh, I wish I'd been there! It must have been funnier'n hell! (*He laughs loudly—then noticing his sister's stony expression, stops abruptly.*) What're you pullin' that long face for, Emmer? (*Offendedly.*) Hell, you're a nice one to tell a joke to!

EMMA (*after a pause—forcing the words out slowly*). Caleb's comin' back here, Jack. I want you to see him for me. I want you to tell him——

JACK. Not me! You got to play this joke on him yourself or it won't work.

EMMA (*tensely*). This ain't a joke, Jack—what I mean. I want you to tell him I've changed my mind and I ain't going to marry him.

JACK. What!

EMMA. I been thinking things over, tell him—and I take back my promise—and he can have back his ring—and I ain't going to marry him.

JACK (*flabbergasted—peering into her face anxiously*). Say—what the hell——? Are you tryin' to josh me, Emmer? Or are you gone crazy all of a sudden?

EMMA. I ain't joking nor crazy neither. You tell him what I said.

JACK (*vehemently*). I will like ———. Say, what's come over you, anyhow?

EMMA. My eyes are opened, that's all, and I ain't going to marry him.

JACK. Is it—'count of that joke about Caleb I was tellin' you?

EMMA (*her voice trembling*). It's 'count of something I got in my own head. What you told only goes to prove I was wrong about it.

JACK (*greatly perturbed now*). Say, what's the matter? Can't you take a joke? Are you mad at him 'count o' that brown gal?

EMMA. Yes, I am—and I ain't going to marry him and that's all there is to it.

JACK (*argumentatively*). Jealous of a brown heathen woman that ain't no better'n a nigger? God sakes, Emmer, I didn't think you was so big a fool. Why them kind o' women ain't women like you. They don't count like folks. They ain't Christians—nor nothin'!

EMMA. That ain't it. I don't care what they are.

JACK. And it wasn't Caleb, anyhow. It was all her fixin'. And how'd you know he had anything to do with her—like that? I ain't said he did. Jim couldn't swear he did neither. And even if he did—what difference does it make? It ain't rightly none o' your business what he does on a vige. He didn't ask her to marry him, did he?

EMMA. I don't care. He'd ought to have acted diff'rent.

JACK. Oh, golly, there you go agen makin' a durned creepin' saint out of him! What d'you want to marry, anyhow—a man or a sky-pilot? Caleb's a man, ain't he?—and a damn good man and as smart a skipper as there be in these parts! What more d'you want, anyhow?

EMMA (*violently*). I want you to shet up! You're too dumb stupid and bad yourself to ever know what I'm thinking.

JACK (*resentfully*). Go to the devil, then! I'm goin' to tell Ma and set her on to you. You'll maybe listen to her and git some sense. (*He stamps out, right, while he is speaking. Emma bursts into sobs and throws herself on a chair, covering her face with her hands. Harriet Williams and Alfred Rogers come up the path to the door in rear. Peering through the screen and catching sight of Emma, Harriet calls.*) Emmer!

(*Emma leaps to her feet and dabs at her eyes with a handkerchief in a vain effort to conceal traces of her tears. Harriet has come in, followed by Rogers. Caleb's sister is a tall, dark girl of twenty. Her face is plainly homely and yet attracts the eye by a certain boldly-appealing vitality of self-confident youth. She wears an apron and has evidently just come out of the kitchen. Rogers is a hefty young fisherman of 24, washed and got up in his ill-fitting best.*)

ROGERS. Hello, Emmer.

EMMA (*huskily, trying to force a smile*). Hello, Harriet. Hello, Alfred. Won't you set?

HARRIET. No, I jest run over from the house a second to see if—— Where's Caleb, Emmer?

EMMA. He's gone up street.

HARRIET. And here I be waitin' in the kitchen for him to bring back the things so's I can start his supper. (*With a laugh and a roguish look at Rogers.*) Dearie me, it ain't no use dependin' on a man to remember nothin' when he's in love.

ROGERS (*putting his arm about her waist and giving her a squeeze—grinning*). How 'bout me? Ain't I in love and ain't I as reliable as an old hoss?

HARRIET. Oh, you! You're the worst of 'em all.

ROGERS. You don't think so. (*He tries to kiss her.*)

HARRIET. Stop it. Ain't you got no manners? What'll Emmer think?

ROGERS. Emmer can't throw stones. Her and Caleb is worser at spoonin' than what we are. (*Harriet breaks away from him laughingly and goes to Emma.*)

HARRIET (*suddenly noticing the expression of misery on Emma's face—astonished*). Why, Emmer Crosby, what's the matter? You look as if you'd lost your best friend.

EMMA (*trying to smile*). Nothing. It's nothing.

HARRIET. It is, too! Why, I do believe you've been crying!

EMMA. No, I ain't.

HARRIET. You have, too! (*Putting her arms about Emma.*) Goodness, what's happened? You and Caleb ain't had a tiff, have you, with your weddin' only two days off?

EMMA (*with quick, resentful resolution*). There ain't going to be any wedding.

HARRIET What!

ROGERS (*pricking up his ears—inquisitively*). Huh?

EMMA. Not in two days nor no time.

HARRIET (*dumbfounded*). Why, Emmer Crosby, whatever's got into you? You and Caleb must have had an awful set to!

ROGERS (*with a man-of-the-world attitude of cynicism*). Don't take her so dead serious, Harriet. Emmer'll git over it like you all does.

EMMA (*angrily*). You shet up, Alf Rogers!

(*Mrs. Crosby enters bustlingly from the right. She is a large, fat, florid woman of fifty. In spite of her two hundred and more pounds she is surprisingly active, and the passive, lazy expression of her round moon face is belied by her quick, efficient movements. She exudes an atmosphere of motherly good nature. She wears an apron on which she is drying her hands as she enters. Jack follows her into the room. He has changed to a dark suit, and is ready for "up street."*)

MRS CROSBY (*smiling at Harriet and Rogers*). After noon, Harriet—and Alf.

HARRIET. Afternoon, Ma.

ROGERS. Afternoon.

JACK (*grinning*). There she be, Ma. (*Points to Emma.*) Don't she look like she'd scratch a feller's eyes out! Phew! Look at her back curve! Meow? Sptt-sptt! Nice puss!

(*He gives a vivid imitation of a cat fight at this last. Then he and Rogers roar with laughter and Harriet cannot restrain a giggle and Mrs. Crosby smiles. Emma stares stonily before her as if she didn't hear.*)

MRS. CROSBY (*good-naturedly*). Shet up your foolin', Jack.

JACK (*pretending to be hurt*). Nobody in this house kin take a joke. (*He grins and beckons to Rogers.*) Come along, Alf. You kin 'preciate a joke. Come on in here and I'll tell you.

(*The grinning Rogers follows him into the next room, where they can be heard talking and laughing during the following scene.*)

MRS. CROSBY (*smiling, puts her arms around Emma*). Waal, Emmer, what's this foolishness Jack's been tellin' about——

EMMA (*resentfully*). It ain't foolishness, Ma. I've made up my mind. I tell you that right here and now.

MRS. CROSBY (*after a quick glance at her face—soothingly*). There, there! Let's set down and be comfortable. Me, I don't relish roostin' on my feet. (*She pushes Emma gently into a rocker—then points to a chair on the other side of the table.*) Set down, Harriet.

HARRIET (*torn between curiosity and a sense of being one too many*). Maybe I'd best go home and leave you two alone?

MRS. CROSBY. Bosh! Ain't you like one o' the family—Caleb's sister and livin' right next door ever since you was all children playin' together. We ain't got no secrets from you. Set down. (*Harriet does so with an uncertain glance at the frozen Emma. Mrs. Crosby has efficiently bustled another rocker beside her daughter's and sits down with a comfortable sigh.*) There. (*She reaches over and takes one of her daughter's hands in hers.*) And now, Emmer, what's all this fuss over? (*As Emma makes no reply.*) Jack says as you've sworn you was breakin' with Caleb. Is that true?

EMMA. Yes.

MRS. CROSBY. Hmm. Caleb don't know this yet, does he?

EMMA. No. I asked Jack to tell him when he comes back.

MRS. CROSBY. Jack says he won't.

EMMA. Then I'll tell him myself. Maybe that's better, anyhow. Caleb'll know what I'm driving at and see my reason (*bitterly*)—which nobody else seems to.

MRS. CROSBY. Hmm. You ain't tried me yet. (*After a pause.*) Jack was a dumb fool to tell you 'bout them goin's-on at them islands they teched. Ain't no good repeatin' sech things.

EMMA (*surprised*). Did you know about it before Jack——

MRS. CROSBY. Mercy, yes. Your Pa heard it from Jim Benson fust thing they landed here, and Pa told me that night.

EMMA (*resentfully*). And you never told me!

MRS. CROSBY. Mercy, no. Course I didn't. They's trouble enough in the world without makin' more. If you was like most folks I'd told it to you. Me, I thought it was a good joke on Caleb.

EMMA (*with a shudder*). It ain't a joke to me.

MRS. CROSBY. That's why I kept my mouth shet. I knowed you was touchy and diff'rent from most.

EMMA (*proudly*). Yes, I am diff'rent—and that's just what I thought Caleb was, too—and he ain't.

HARRIET (*breaking in excitedly*). Is it that story about Caleb and that heathen brown woman you're talking about? Is that what you're mad at Caleb for, Emmer?

MRS. CROSBY (*as Emma remains silent*). Yes, Harriet, that's it.

HARRIET (*astonished*). Why, Emmer Crosby, how can you be so silly? You don't s'pose Caleb took it serious, do you, and him makin' them fire shots round her to scare her back to land and get rid of her? Good gracious! (*A bit resentfully.*) I hope you ain't got it in your head my brother Caleb would sink so low as to fall in love serious with one of them critters?

EMMA (*harshly*). He might just as well.

HARRIET (*bridling*). How can you say sech a thing! (*Sarcastically.*) I ain't heard that Caleb offered to marry her, have you? Then you might have some cause—— But d'you s'pose he's ever give her another thought? Not Caleb! I know him better'n that. He'd forgot all about the hull thing before they was out o' sight of land, I'll bet, and if them fools hadn't started this story going, he'd never remembered it again.

MRS. CROSBY (*nodding*). That's jest it. Harriet's right, Emmer.

EMMA. Ma!

MRS. CROSBY. Besides, you don't know there was anythin' wrong happened. Nobody kin swear that for sartin. Ain't that so, Harriet?

HARRIET (*hesitating—then frankly*). I don't know. Caleb ain't no plaster saint and I reckon he's as likely to sin that way as any other man. He wasn't married then and I s'pose he thought he was free to do as he's a mind to till he was hitched up. Goodness sakes, Emmer, all the men thinks that—and a lot of 'em after they're married, too.

MRS. CROSBY. Harriet's right, Emmer. If you've been wide awake to all that's happened in this town since you was old enough to know, you'd ought to realise what men be.

HARRIET (*scornfully*). Emma'd ought to fallen in love with a minister, not a sailor. As for me, I wouldn't give much thought of a man that was too goody-goody to raise Cain once in a while—before he married me, I mean. Why, look at Alf Rogers, Emmer. I'm going to marry him some day, ain't I? But I know right well all the foolin' he's done—and still is doing, I expect. I ain't sayin' I like it, but I do like him, and I got to take him the way he is, that's all. If you're looking for saints, you got to die first and go to heaven. A girl'd never git married hereabouts if she expected too much.

MRS. CROSBY. Harriet's right, Emmer.

EMMA (*resentfully*). Maybe she is, Ma, from her side. I ain't claiming she's wrong. Her and me just looks at things diff'rent, that's all. And she can't understand the way I feel about Caleb

HARRIET. Well, there's one thing certain, Emmer. You won't find a man in a day's walk is any better'n Caleb—or as good.

EMMA (*wearily*). I know that, Harriet.

HARRIET. Then it's all right. You'll make up with him, and I s'pose I'm a fool to be takin' it so serious. (*As Emma shakes her head.*) Oh, yes, you will. You wouldn't want to get him all broke up, would you? (*As Emma keeps silent—irritably.*) Story-book notions, that's the trouble with you, Emmer. You're gettin' to think you're better'n the rest of us.

EMMA (*vehemently*). No, I don't! Can't you see——

MRS. CROSBY. Thar, now! Don't you two git to fightin'—to make things worse.

HARRIET (*repentantly, coming and putting her arms around Emma and kissing her*). I'm sorry, Emmer. You know I wouldn't fall out with you for nothing or nobody, don't you? Only it gits me riled to think of how awful broke up Caleb'd be if—— But you'll make it all up with him when he comes, won't you?

(*Emma stares stubbornly before her. Before she has a chance to reply a roar of laughter comes from the next room as Jack winds up his tale.*)

ROGERS (*from the next room*). Gosh, I wished I'd been there! (*He follows Jack into the room. Both are grinning broadly. Rogers says teasingly.*) Reckon I'll take to whalin' 'stead o' fishin' after this. You won't mind, Harriet? From what I hears o' them brown women, I'm missin' a hull lot by stayin' at home.

HARRIET (*in a joking tone—with a meaning glance at Emma*). Go on, then! There's plenty of fish in the sea. Anyhow, I'd never git jealous of your foolin' with one of them heathen critters. They ain't worth notice from a Christian.

JACK. Oho, ain't they! They're purty as pictures, Benson says. (*With a wink.*) And mighty accommodatin' in their ways. (*He and Rogers roar delightedly. Emma shudders with revulsion.*)

MRS. CROSBY (*aware of her daughter's feeling—smilingly but firmly*). Get out o' this, Jack. You, too, Alf. Go on up street if you want to joke. You're in my way.

JACK. Aw right, Ma. Come on up street, Alf.

HARRIET. Wait. I'll go with you a step. I got to see if Caleb's got back with them supper things. (*They all go to the door in rear. Jack and Rogers pass out, talking and laughing. Harriet turns in the doorway—sympathetically.*) I'll give Caleb a talking to before he comes over. Then it'll be easy for you to finish him. Treat him firm but gentle and you'll see he won't never do it again in a hurry. After all, he wasn't married, Emmer—and he's a man—and what can you expect? Good-bye. (*She goes.*)

EMMA (*inaudibly*). Good-bye.

MRS. CROSBY (*after a pause in which she rocks back and forth studying her daughter's face—placidly.*) Harriet's right, Emmer. You give him a good talkin'-to and he won't do it again.

EMMA (*coldly*). I don't care whether he does or not. I ain't going to marry him.

MRS. CROSBY (*uneasy—persuasively*). Mercy, you can't act like that, Emmer. Here's the weddin' on'y two days off, and everythin' fixed up with the minister, and your Pa and Jack has bought new clothes speshul for it, and I got a new dress——

EMMA (*turning to her mother—pleadingly*). You wouldn't want me to keep my promise to Caleb if you knew I'd be unhappy, would you, Ma?

MRS. CROSBY (*hesitatingly*). N-no, Emmer. (*Then decisively.*) 'Course I wouldn't. It's because I know he'll make you happy. (*As Emma shakes her head.*) Shaw, Emmer, you can't tell me you've got over all likin' for him jest 'count o' this one foolishness o' his'n.

EMMA. I don't love him—what he is now. I loved—what I thought he was.

MRS. CROSBY (*more and more uneasy*). That's all your queer notions, and I don't know where you gits them from. Caleb ain't changed, neither have you. Why, Emmer, it'd be jest like goin' agen an act of Nature for you not to marry him. Ever since you was children you been livin' side by side, goin' round together, and neither you nor him ever did seem to care for no one else. Bosh, Emmer, you'll git me to lose patience with you if you act that stubborn. You'd ought to remember all he's been to you and forget this one little wrong he's done.

EMMA. I can't, Ma. It makes him another person—not Caleb, but someone just like all the others.

MRS. CROSBY. Waal, is the others so bad? Men is men the world over, I reckon.

EMMA. No, they ain't bad. I ain't saying that. Don't I like 'em all? If it was one of the rest—like Jim Benson or Jack, even—had done this I'd thought it was a joke, too. I ain't strict in judging 'em and you know it. But—can't you see, Ma?—Caleb always seemed diff'rent—and I thought he was.

MRS. CROSBY (*somewhat impatiently*). Waal, if he ain't, he's a good man jest the same, as good as any sensible girl'd want to marry.

EMMA (*slowly*). I don't want to marry nobody no more. I'll stay single.

MRS. CROSBY (*tauntingly*). An old maid! (*Then resentfully.*) Emmer, d'you s'pose if I'd had your high-fangled notions o' what men ought to be when I was your age, d'you s'pose you'd ever be settin' there now?

EMMA (*slowly*). No. I know from what I can guess from his own stories, Pa never was no saint.

MRS. CROSBY (*in a tone of finality, as if this settled the matter*). There, now! And ain't he been as good a husband to me as ever lived, and a good father to you and Jack? You'll find out Caleb'll turn out the same. You think it over. (*She gets up—bustlingly.*) And now I got to git back in the kitchen.

EMMA (*wringing her hands—desperately*). Oh, Ma, why can't you see what I feel? Of course, Pa's good—as good as good can be——

CAPTAIN CROSBY (*from outside the door, which he has approached without their noticing him—in a jovial bellow*). What's that 'bout Pa bein' good? (*He comes in laughing. He is a squat, bow-legged, powerful man, almost as broad as he is long—sixty years old, but still in the prime of health and strength, with a great, red, weather-beaten face seamed by sun wrinkles. His sandy hair is thick and dishevelled. He is dressed in an old baggy suit much the worse for wear—striped cotton shirt open at the neck. He pats Emma on the back with a playful touch that almost jars her off her feet.*) Thunderin' Moses, that's the fust time ever I heerd good o' myself by listenin'! Most times it's: "Crosby? D'you mean that drunken, good-for-nothin', mangy old cuss?" That's what I hears usual. Thank ye, Emmer. (*Turning to his wife.*) What ye got to say now, Ma? Here's Emmer tellin' you the truth after you hair-pullin' me all these years 'cause you thought it wa'n't. I always told ye I was good, ain't I—good as hell I be! (*He shakes with laughter and kisses his wife a resounding smack.*)

MRS. CROSBY (*teasing lovingly*). Emmer don't know you like I do.

CROSBY (*turning back to Emma again*). Look-a-here, Emmer, I jest seen Jack. He told me some fool story 'bout you fallin' out with Caleb. Reckon he was joshin' wa'n't he?

MRS. CROSBY (*quickly*). Oh, that's all settled, John. Don't you go stirrin' it up again. (*Emma seems about to speak, but stops helplessly after one glance at her father.*)

CROSBY. An' all 'count o' that joke they're tellin' 'bout him and that brown female critter, Jack says. Hell, Emmer, you ain't a real Crosby if you takes a joke like that serious. Thunderin' Moses, what the hell d'you want Caleb to be—a durned, he-virgin, missionary? Caleb's a man wo'th ten o' most, and, spite o' his bein' on'y a boy yit, he's the smartest skipper out o' this port and you'd ought to be proud you'd got him. And as for them islands, all whalin' men knows 'em. I've teched thar for water more'n once myself, and I know them brown females like a book. And I tells you, after a year or more aboard ship, a man'd have to be a goll-durned geldin' if he don't——

MRS. CROSBY (*glancing uneasily at Emma*). Ssshh! You come out in the kitchen with me, Pa, and leave Emmer be.

CROSBY. God A'mighty, Ma, I ain't sayin' nothin' agen Emmer, be I? I knows Emmer ain't that crazy. If she ever got religion that bad, I'd ship her off as female missionary to the damned yellow Chinks. (*He laughs.*)

MRS. CROSBY (*taking his arm*). You come with me. I want to talk with you 'bout somethin'.

CROSBY (*going*). Aye-aye, skipper! You're boss aboard here. (*He goes out right with her, laughing. Emma stands for a while, staring stonily before her. She sighs hopelessly, clasping and unclasping her hands, looking around the room as if she longed to escape from it. Finally she sits down helplessly and remains fixed in a strained attitude, her face betraying the conflict that is tormenting her. Slow steps sound from the path in front of the house. Emma recognises them and her face freezes into an expression of obstinate intolerance. Caleb appears outside the screen door. He looks in, coughs—then asks uncertainly.*) It's me, Emmer. Kin I come in?

EMMA (*coldly*). Yes

CALEB (*comes in and walks down beside her chair. His face is set emotionlessly, but his eyes cannot conceal a worried bewilderment, a look of uncomprehending hurt. He stands uncomfortably, fumbling with his hat, waiting for her to speak or look up. As she does neither, he finally blurts out*). Kin I set a while?

EMMA (*in the same cold tone*). Yes. (*He lowers himself carefully to a wooden posture on the edge of a rocker near hers.*)

CALEB (*after a pause*). I seen Jim Benson. I give him hell. He won't tell no more tales, I reckon. (*Another pause.*) I stepped in home on the way back from the store. I seen Harriet. She says Jack'd told you that story they're all tellin' as a joke on me. (*Clenching his fists—angrily.*) Jack's a durn fool. He needs a good lickin' from someone.

EMMA (*resentfully*). Don't try to put the blame on Jack. He only told me the truth, didn't he? (*Her voice shows that she hopes against hope for a denial.*)

CALEB (*after a long pause—regretfully*). Waal, I guess what he told is true enough.

EMMA (*wounded*). Oh!

CALEB. But that ain't no good reason for tellin' it. Them sort o' things ought to be kept among men. (*After a pause—gropingly.*) I didn't want nothin' like that to happen, Emmer. I didn't mean it to. I was thinkin' o' how you might feel—even down there. That's why I stayed aboard all the time when the boys was ashore. I wouldn't have b'lieved it could happen—not to me. (*A pause.*) I wish you could see them islands, Emmer, and be there for a time. Then you might see—— It's hard's hell to explain, and you havin' never seen 'em. Everything is diff'rent down there—the weather, and the trees and water. You git lookin' at it all, and you git to feel diff'rent from what you do at home here. It's purty hereabouts sometimes—like now, in spring—but it's purty there all the time—and down there you notice it and you git feelin'—diff'rent. And them native women—they're diff'rent. A man don't think of 'em as women—like you. But they're purty—in their fashion—and at night they sings—and it's all diff'rent like something you'd see in a painted picture. (*A pause.*) That night when she swum out and got aboard when I was alone, she caught me by s'prise. I wasn't expectin' nothin' o' that sort. I tried to make her git back to land at fust—but she wouldn't go. She couldn't understand enough English for me to tell her how I felt—and I reckon she wouldn't have seed my p'int anyhow, her bein' a native. (*A pause.*) And then I was afeerd she'd catch cold goin' round all naked and wet in the moonlight—though it was warm—and I wanted to wrap a blanket round her (*He stops as if he had finished.*)

EMMA (*after a long, tense pause—dully*). Then you own up—there really was something happened?

CALEB (*after a pause*). I was sorry for it, after. I locked myself in the cabin and left her to sleep out on deck.

EMMA (*after a pause—fixedly*). I ain't going to marry you, Caleb.

CALEB. Harriet said you'd said that; but I didn't b'lieve you'd let a slip like that make—such a diff'rence.

EMMA (*with finality*). Then you can believe it now, Caleb.

CALEB (*after a pause*). You got queer, strict notions, Emmer. A man'll never live up to 'em—with never one slip. But you got to act accordin' to your lights, I expect. It sort o' busts everythin' to bits for me—— (*His voice betrays his anguish for a second, but he instantly regains his iron control.*) But o' course, if you ain't willin' to take me the way I be, there's nothin' to do. And whatever you think is best, suits me.

EMMA (*after a pause—gropingly*). I wish I could explain my side of it—so's you'd understand. I ain't got any hard feelings against you, Caleb—not now. It ain't plain jealousy—what I feel. It ain't even that I think you've done nothing terrible wrong. I think I can understand—how it happened—and make allowances. I know that most any man would do the same, and I guess all of 'em I ever met has done it.

CALEB (*with a glimmer of eager hope*). Then—you'll forgive it, Emmer?

EMMA. Yes, I forgive it. But don't think that my forgiving is going to make any diff'rence—'cause I ain't going to marry you, Caleb. That's final. (*After a pause—intensely.*) Oh, I wish I could make you see—my reason. You don't. You never will, I expect. What you done is just what any other man would have done—and being like them is exactly what'll keep you from ever seeing my meaning. (*After a pause—in a last effort to make him understand.*) Maybe it's my fault more'n your'n. It's like this, Caleb. Ever since we was little I guess I've always had the idea that you was—diff'rent. And when we growed up and got engaged I thought that more and more. And you was diff'rent, too! And that was why I loved you. And now you've proved you ain't. And so how can I love you any more? I don't, Caleb, and that's all there is to it. You've busted something way down inside me—and I can't love you no more.

CALEB (*gloomily*). I've warned you often, ain't I, you was settin' me up where I'd no business to be. I'm human like the rest and always was. I ain't diff'rent. (*After a pause—uncertainly.*) I reckon there ain't no use sayin' nothing' more. I'll go home. (*He starts to rise.*)

EMMA. Wait. I don't want you to go out of here with no hard feelings. You 'n' me, Caleb, we've been too close all our lives to ever get to be enemies. I like you, Caleb, same's I always did. I want us to stay friends. I want you to be like one of the family same's you've always been. There's no reason you can't. I don't blame you—as a man—for what I wouldn't hold against any other man. If I find I can't love you—that way—no more or be your wife, it's just that I've decided—things being what they be and me being what I am—I won't marry no man. I'll stay single. (*Forcing a smile.*) I guess there's worse things than being an old maid.

CALEB. I can't picture you that, Emmer. It's natural in some, but it ain't in you. (*Then with a renewal of hope.*) And o' course I want to stay friends with you, Emmer. There's no hard feelin's on my side. You got a right to your own way—even if—— (*Hopefully.*) And maybe if I show you what I done wasn't natural to me—by never doin' it again—maybe the time'll come when you'll be willin' to forget——

EMMA (*shaking her head—slowly*). It ain't a question of time, Caleb. It's a question of something being dead. And when a thing's died, time can't make no diff'rence.

CALEB (*sturdily*). You don't know that for sure, Emmer. You're human, too, and as liable to make mistakes as any other. Maybe you on'y think it's dead, and when I come back from the next vige and you ve had two years to think it over, you'll see diff'rent and know I ain't as bad as I seem to ye now.

EMMA (*helplessly*). But you don't seem bad, Caleb. And two years can't make no change in me—that way.

CALEB (*feeling himself somehow more and more heartened by hope*). I ain't givin' up hope, Emmer, and you can't make me. Not by a hell of a sight. (*With emphasis.*) I ain't never goin' to marry no woman but you, Emmer. You can trust my word for that. And I'll wait for ye to change your mind, I don't care a durn how long it'll take—till I'm sixty years old—thirty years if it's needful! (*He rises to his feet as he is speaking this last.*)

EMMA (*with a mournful smile*). You might just as well say for life, Caleb. In thirty years we'll both be dead and gone, probably. And I don't want you to think it's needful for you to stay single 'cause I——

CALEB. I ain't goin' to stay single. I'm goin' to wait for you. And some day when you realise men was never cut out for angels you'll——

EMMA (*helplessly*). Me 'n' you'll never understand each other, Caleb, so long as we live. (*Getting up and holding out her hand.*) Good-bye, Caleb. I'm going up and lie down a while.

CALEB (*made hopeless again by her tone—clasps her hand mechanically—dully*). Good-bye, Emmer. (*He goes to the door in the rear, opens it, then hesitates and looks back at her as she goes out the door on the right without turning around. Suddenly he blurts out despairingly.*) You'll remember what I told ye 'bout waitin', Emmer?

(*She is gone, makes no reply. His face sets in its concealment mask of emotionlessness and he turns slowly and goes out the door as*

THE CURTAIN FALLS

Act Two

Thirty years after—the scene is the same but not the same. The room has a grotesque aspect of old age turned flighty and masquerading as the most empty-headed youth. There is an obstreperous newness about everything. Orange curtains are at the windows. The carpet has given way to a varnished hardwood floor, its glassy surface set off by three small, garish-coloured rugs, placed with precision in front of the two doors and under the table. The wall-paper is now a cream colour sprayed with pink flowers. Eye-aching seascapes, of the painted-to-order quality, four in number, encased in gilded frames, are hung on the walls at mathematically spaced intervals. The plush-covered chairs are gone, replaced by a set of varnished oak. The horse-hair sofa has been relegated to the attic. A cane-bottomed affair with fancy cushions serves in its stead. A gramophone is where the old mahogany chest had been. A brand new piano shines resplendently in the far right corner by the door, and a bookcase with glass doors that pull up and slide in, flanks the fireplace. This bookcase is full of instalment-plan sets of uncut volumes. The table at centre is of varnished oak. On it are piles of fashion magazines and an electric reading lamp. Only the old Bible, which still preserves its place of honour on the table, and the marble clock on the mantel, have survived the renovation and serve to emphasise it all the more by contrast.

It is late afternoon of a day in the early spring of the year 1920.

As the curtain rises, Emma and Benny Rogers are discovered. She is seated in a rocker by the table. He is standing by the gramophone which is playing a jazz band record. He whistles, goes through the motions of dancing to the music. He is a young fellow of twenty-three, a replica of his father in Act One, but coarser, more hardened and cocksure. He is dressed in the khaki uniform of a private in the United States Army. The thirty years have transformed Emma into a withered, scraggy woman. But there is something revoltingly incongruous about her, a pitiable sham, a too-apparent effort to cheat the years by appearances. The white dress she wears is too frilly, too youthful for her; so are the high-heeled shoes and clocked silk stockings. There is an absurd suggestion of rouge on her tight cheeks and thin lips, of pencilled make-up about her eyes. The black of her hair is brazenly untruthful. Above all there is shown in her simpering, self-consciously coquettish manner that laughable—and at the same time irritating and disgusting—mockery of undignified age snatching greedily at the empty similitude of youth. She resembles some passé stock actress of fifty made up for a heroine of twenty.

BENNY (*as the record stops—switches off the machine*). Oh, baby! Some jazz!

EMMA (*smiling lovingly at his back*). I'm glad you like it. It's one of them you picked out on the list.

BENNY. Oh, I'm a smart little picker, aw right. (*Turning to her.*) Say, you're a regular feller—gettin' them records for me.

EMMA (*coquettishly*). Well, if that ain't just like a man! Who told you I git them just for you?

BENNY. Well, didn't you?

EMMA. No indeed! I only took your advice on what to get. I knew you'd know, being growed to a man of the world now since you was overseas. But I got 'em because I like them jazz tunes myself. They put life and ginger in an old lady like me—not like them slow, old-time tunes.

BENNY (*bends over chair—kiddingly*). You ain't old. That's all bunk.

EMMA (*flattered*). Now, now, Benny!

BENNY. You ain't. You're a regular up-to-date sport—the only live one in this dead dump. (*With a grin.*) And if you fall for that jazz stuff, all you got to do now is learn to dance to it.

EMMA (*giggling*). I will—if you'll teach me.

BENNY (*struggling with a guffaw*). Oh, oui! Sure I will. We'll have a circus, me an' you. Say, you're sure one of the girls aw right, Aunt Emmer.

EMMA. Oh, you needn't think we're *all* so behind the times at home here just because you've been to France and all over.

BENNY. *You* ain't, I'll say, Aunt Emmer.

EMMA. And how often have I got to tell you not to call me Aunt Emmer?

BENNY (*with a grin*). Oh, oui! My foot slipped. 'Scuse me, Emmer.

EMMA (*delighted by his coarse familiarity*). That's better. Why, you know well enough I ain't your aunt anyway.

BENNY. I got to get used to the plain Emmer. They taught me to call you "aunt" when I was a kid. (*Emma looks displeased at this remark and Benny hastens to add cajolingly.*) And you almost was my aunt-in-law one time from what I've heard. (*Winks at her cunningly.*)

EMMA (*flustered*). That was ages ago. (*Catching herself quickly.*) Not so awful long really, but it's all so dead and gone it seems a long while.

BENNY (*unthinkingly*). It was before I was born, wasn't it? (*Seeing her expression he hurries on.*) Well, that ain't so darned long. Say, here's something I never could make out—how did you ever come to fall for Uncle Caleb?

EMMA (*bridling—quickly*). I never did. That's all talk, Benny. We was good friends and still are. I was young and foolish and got engaged to him—and then discovered I didn't like him that way. That's all there ever was to it.

BENNY (*resentfully*). I can't figure how anybody'd ever like him anyway. He's a darn stingy, ugly old cuss, if you want my opinion of him. I can't stand him at all. I've hated him ever since Pa died and Ma and me had to go live next door to him.

EMMA. You oughtn't to say that. He's kind at bottom, spite of his rough ways, and he's brought you up.

BENNY (*grumpily*). Dragged me up, you mean. (*With a calculating look at her out of the corners of his eyes.*) He's a tight-wad and I hate folks that're tight with their coin. Spend and be a good sport, that's my motto. (*Flattering.*) He'd ought to be more like you that way, Emmer.

EMMA (*pleased—condescendingly*). Your Uncle Caleb's an old man, remember. He's set in his ways and believes in being strict with you—too strict, I've told him.

BENNY. He's got piles of money hoarded in the bank, but he's too mean even to retire from whalin' himself—goes right on makin' vige after vige to grab more and never spends a penny less'n he has to. It was always like pryin' open a safe for me to separate him from a cent. (*With extreme disgust.*) Aw, he's a miser. I hate him and I always did!

EMMA (*looking towards the door apprehensively*). Ssshh!

BENNY. What you scared of? He don't get in from New Bedford till the night train and even if he's got to the house by this he'll be busy as a cock bird for an hour getting himself dolled up to pay you a call.

EMMA (*perfunctorily*). I hope he's had a good vige and is in good health.

BENNY (*roughly*). You needn't worry. He's too

mean ever to get real sick. Gosh, I wish Pa'd lived—or Uncle Jack. They wasn't like him. I was only a kid when they got drowned, but I remember enough about 'em to know they was good sports. Wasn't they?

EMMA (*rather primly*). They was too sporty for their own good.

BENNY. Don't you hand me that. That don't sound like you. You're a sport yourself. (*After a pause.*) Say, it's nutty when you come to think of it—Uncle Caleb livin' next door all these years and comin' to call all the time when he ain't at sea.

EMMA. What's funny about that? We've always been good friends.

BENNY (*with a grin*). It's just as if the old guy was still mashin' you. And I'll bet anything he's as stuck on you as he ever was—the old fool!

EMMA (*with a coquettish titter*). Gracious, Benny, a body'd think you were actually jealous of your uncle the way you go on.

BENNY (*with a mocking laugh*). Jealous! Oh, oui! Sure I am! Kin you blame me? (*Then seriously, with a calculating look at her.*) No, all kiddin' aside, I know he'll run me down first second he sees you. Ma'll tell him all her tales, and he'll be sore at me right off. He's always hated me anyway He was glad when I enlisted, 'cause that got him rid of me. All he was hopin' was that some German'd get me for good. Then when I come back he wouldn't do nothin' for me so I enlisted again.

EMMA (*chiding—playfully*). Now, Benny! Didn't you tell me you enlisted again 'cause you were sick o' this small place and wanted to be out where there was more fun?

BENNY. Well o' course it was that, too. But I could have a swell time even in this dump if he'd loosen out and give me a bit. (*Again with the calculating look at her.*) Why, look here, right now there's a pal of mine wants me to meet him in Boston and he'll show me a good time, and if I had a hundred dollars——

EMMA. A hundred dollars! That's an awful lot to spend, Benny.

BENNY (*disgustedly*). Now you're talkin' tight like him.

EMMA (*hastily*). Oh, no, Benny. You know better'n that. What was you sayin'—if you had a hundred dollars——?

BENNY. That ain't such a deal these days with everything gone up so. If I went to Boston I'd have to get dolled up and everything. And this pal of mine is a sport and a spender. Easy come, easy go is his motto. His folks ain't tight 'uns like mine. And I couldn't show myself up by travellin' 'round with him and just spongin' on him. (*With the calculating glance to see what effect his words are having—pretending to dismiss the subject.*) But what's the good of talkin'? I got some hopes tellin' that to Uncle Caleb. He'd give me one look and then put a double padlock on his purse. But it ain't fair just the same. Here I'm sweatin' blood in the army after riskin' my life in France and when I get a leave to home, everyone treats me like an unwanted dog.

EMMA (*softly*). Do you mean me, too, Benny?

BENNY—No, not you. You're diff'rent from the rest. You're regular—and you ain't any of my real folks either, and ain't got any reason.

EMMA (*coquettishly*). Oh, yes, I have a reason. I like you very, very much, Benny—better than anyone in the town—especially since you've been home these last few times and come to call so often and I feel I've growed to know you. When you first came back from France I never would have recognised you as Harriet's Benny, you was so big and strong and handsome.

BENNY (*uncomfortably*). Aw, you're kiddin'. But you can tell how good I think you are from me bein' over here so much—so you know I ain't lyin'. (*Made more and more uncomfortable by the ardent looks Emma is casting at him.*) Well, guess I'll be movin' along.

EMMA (*pleadingly*). Oh, you mustn't go yet! Just when we're gettin' so friendly!

BENNY. Uncle Caleb'll be over soon and I don't want him to catch me here—nor nowhere else till he gets calmed down after hearin' Ma's kicks about me. So I guess I better get up street.

EMMA. He won't come for a long time yet. I know when to expect him. (*Pleading ardently and kittenishly.*) Do set down a while, Benny! Lord, I hardly get a sight of you before you want to run away again. I'll begin to think you're only pretending to like me.

BENNY (*seeing his calculations demand it*). Aw right—jest for a second. (*He looks about him, seeking a neutral subject for conversation.*) Gee, you've had this old place fixed up swell since I was home last.

EMMA (*coquettishly*). Guess who I had it all done for, mostly?

BENNY. For yourself, of course.

EMMA (*shaking her head roguishly*). No, not for me, not for me! Not that I don't like it, but I'd never have gone to the trouble and expense for myself. (*With a sigh.*) I s'pose poor Ma and Pa turned over in their graves when I ordered it to be done.

BENNY (*with a sly grin*). Who d'you have it done for, then?

EMMA. For you! Yes, for you, Benny—so's you'd have a nice up-to-date place to came to when you was on vacation from the horrid old army.

BENNY (*embarrassed*). Well, it's quite aw right. And it sure looks swell—nothing cheap about it.

EMMA (*delighted*). As long as you like it, I'm satisfied. (*Then suddenly, wagging an admonishing finger at him and hiding beneath a joking manner an undercurrent of uneasiness.*) I was forgetting I got a bone to pick with you, young man! I heard them sayin' at the store that you'd been up callin' on that Tilly Small evenin' before last.

BENNY (*with a lady-killer's carelessness*). Aw, I was passin' by and she called me in, that's all.

EMMA (*frowning*). They said you had the piano goin' and was singing and no end of high jinks.

BENNY. Aw, these small town folk think you're raising hell if you're up after eleven.

EMMA (*excitedly*). I ain't blamin' you. But her —she ought to have better sense—at her age, too, when she's old enough to be your mother.

BENNY. Aw, say, she ain't half as old——(*Catching himself.*) Oh, she's an old fool, you're right there, Emmer.

EMMA (*severely*). And I hope you know the kind of woman she is and has been since she was a girl.

BENNY (*with a wink*). I wasn't born yesterday. I got her number long ago. I ain't in my cradle, get me! I'm in the army! Oui! (*Chuckles.*)

EMMA (*fidgeting nervously*). What'd you—what'd you do when you was there?

BENNY. Why, nothing'. I told her to cut the rough work and behave—and a nice time was had by all. (*He grins provokingly.*)

EMMA (*springs to her feet nervously*). I don't know what to think—when you act so queer about it.

BENNY (*carelessly*). Well, don't think nothing wrong—'cause there wasn't. Bill Tinker was with me and we was both wishin' we had a drink. And Bill says, "Let's go see Tilly Small. She always has some buried and if we hand her a line of talk maybe she'll drag out the old bottle." So we did—and she did. We kidded her for a couple of drinks. (*He snickers.*)

EMMA (*standing in front of him—fidgeting*). I want you to promise you won't go to see her no more. If you —if you want liquor now and again, maybe I—maybe I can fix it so's I can get some to keep here for you.

BENNY (*eagerly*). Say, that'd be great! Will you? (*She nods. He goes on carelessly.*) And sure I'll promise not to see Tilly no more. Gosh, what do you think I care about her? Or about any dame in this town, for that matter—'ceptin' you. These small town skirts interest me nothin'. (*With a grin.*) You forgot I was in France—and after the dames over there these birds here look some guys.

EMMA (*sits down—wetting her lips*). And what—what are those French critters like?

BENNY (*with a wink*). Oh, boy! They're some pippins! It ain't so much that they're better lookin' as that they've got a way with 'em—lots of ways. (*He laughs with a lascivious smirk.*)

EMMA (*unconsciously hitches her chair nearer his. The turn the conversation has taken seems to have aroused a hectic, morbid intensity in her. She continually wets her lips and pushes back her hair from her flushed face as if it were stifling her.*) What do you mean, Benny? What kind of ways have they got—them French girls?

BENNY (*smirking mysteriously*). Oh, ways of dressin' and doin' their hair—and lots of ways.

EMMA (*eagerly*). Tell me! Tell me all about 'em. You needn't be scared—to talk open with me. I ain't as strict as I seem—about hearin' things. Tell me! I've heard French girls was awful wicked.

BENNY. I don't know about wicked, but they're darned good sports. They'd do anything a fellow asks 'em. Oui, tooty sweet! (*Laughs foolishly.*)

EMMA. And what—what'd you ask 'em, for instance?

BENNY (*with a wink*). Curiosity killed a cat! Ask me no questions and I'll tell you no lies.

EMMA (*with queer, stupid insistence*). But won't you tell me? Go on!

BENNY. Can't be did, Aunt Emmer, can't be did! (*With a silly laugh.*) You're too young. No, all I'll say is, that to the boys who've knocked around over there the girls in town here are just rank amatoors. They don't know how to love, and that's a fact. (*He gets to his feet.*) And as for an old dud like Tilly—not me! Well, I guess I'll get along——

EMMA (*getting up and putting a hand on his arm—feverishly*). No, don't go. Not yet—not yet. No, don't go.

BENNY (*stepping away with an expression of repulsion*). Why not? What's the matter with you, Aunt Emmer? You look 's if you was gettin' sick. (*Before she can reply, Harriet's voice is heard calling.*)

HARRIET. Benny! Benny! (*This acts like a pail of cold water on Emma who moves away from Benny quickly.*)

EMMA. That's Harriet. It's your Ma calling, Benny.

BENNY (*impatiently*). I know. That means Uncle Caleb has come and she's told him her stories and it's up to me to go catch hell. (*Stopping Emma as she goes towards the door as if to answer Harriet's hail.*) Don't answer, Aunt Emmer. Let her come over here to look. I want to speak to her and find out how I stand before he sees me.

EMMA (*doubtfully*). I don't know as she'll come. She's been actin' funny to me lately, Harriet has, and she ain't put her foot in my door the last month.

BENNY (*as his mother's voice is heard much nearer, calling "Benny!"*). There! Sure she's comin'.

EMMA (*flustered*). Gracious, I can't let her see me this way. I got to run upstairs and tidy myself a little. (*She starts for the door at right.*)

BENNY (*flatteringly*). Aw, you look swell. Them new clothes you got looks great.

EMMA (*turning in the doorway—coquettishly*). Oh, them French girls ain't the only ones knows how to fix up.

(*She flounces out. Benny stands looking after her with a derisive grin of contempt. There is a sharp knock on the door in the rear. Benny goes to open it, his expression turning surly and sullen. Harriet enters. She wears an apron over her old-fashioned black dress with a brooch at the neck. Her hair is grey, her face thin, lined and careworn, with a fretful, continuously irritated expression. Her shoulders stoop, and her figure is flabby and ugly. She stares at her son with resentful annoyance.*)

HARRIET. Ain't you got sense enough, you big lump, to answer me when I call, and not have me shouting my lungs out?

BENNY. I never heard you callin'.

HARRIET. You're lyin' and you know it. (*Then severely.*) Your uncle's to home. He's waitin' to talk to you.

BENNY. Let him wait. (*In a snarling tone.*) I s'pose you've been givin' him an earful of lies about me?

HARRIET. I told him the truth, if that's what you mean. How you stole the money out of the bureau drawer——

BENNY (*alarmed, but pretending scorn*). Aw, you don't know it was me. You don't know nothin' about it.

HARRIET (*ignoring this*). And about your disgracin' him and me with your drunken carryin's-on with that harlot, Tilly Small, night after night.

BENNY. Aw, wha'd you know about that?

HARRIET. And last but not least, the sneakin' way you're makin' a silly fool out of poor Emmer Crosby.

BENNY (*with a grin*). You don't notice her kickin' about it, do you? (*Brusquely.*) Why don't you mind your own business, Ma?

HARRIET (*violently*). It's a shame, that's what it is! That I should live to see the day when a son of mine'd descend so low he'd tease an old woman to get money out of her, and her alone in the world. Oh, you're low, you're low all through like your Pa was—and since you been in the army you got bold so you ain't even ashamed of your dirtiness no more!

BENNY (*in a snarling whisper*). That's right! Blame it all on me. I s'pose she ain't got nothin' to do with it. (*With a wink.*) You oughter see her perform sometimes. You'd get wise to something then.

HARRIET. Shut up! You've the same filthy mind your Pa had. As for Emmer, I don't hold her responsible. She's been gettin' flighty the past two years. She couldn't help it, livin' alone the way she does, shut up in this house all her life. You ought to be 'shamed to take advantage of her condition—but shame ain't in you.

BENNY. Aw, give us a rest!

HARRIET (*angrily*). Your Uncle Caleb'll give you a rest when he sees you! Him and me's agreed not to give you another single penny if you was to get down on your knees for it. So there! You can git along on your army pay from this onward.

BENNY (*worried by the finality in her tone—placatingly.*) Aw, say, Ma, what's worryin' you? What 'ave I done that's so bad? Gosh, you oughta know some of the gang I know in the army. You'd think I was a saint if you did. (*Trying a confidential tone.*) Honest, Ma, this here thing with Aunt Emmer ain't my fault. How can I help it if she goes cranky in her old age and gets sweet about me? (*With a sly grin—in a whisper.*) Gee, Ma, you oughter see her to-day. She's a scream, honest! She's upstairs now gettin' calmed down. She was gettin' crazy when you're callin' stopped her. Wait till she comes down and you git a look! She'll put your eye out—all dolled up like a kid of sixteen and enough paint on her face for a Buffalo Bill Indian——

HARRIET (*staring at him with stern condemnation*). You're a worthless loafer, Benny Rogers, same as your Pa was.

BENNY (*frustrated and furious*). Aw, g'wan with that bunkum! (*He turns away from her.*)

HARRIET. And I'm goin' to tell Emmer about you and try to put some sense back into her head.

BENNY. Go ahead. You'll get fat runnin' me down to her!

HARRIET. And if my word don't have no influence, I'll tell your Uncle Caleb everything, and get him to talk to her. She'll mind him.

BENNY (*defiantly*). You just try it, that's all!

HARRIET. I've been scared to do more'n hint about it to him. I'm hopin' any day Emmer'll come out of this foolishness, and he'll never know.

BENNY. Aw!

HARRIET. If shame was in you, you'd remember your Uncle Caleb's been in love with Emmer all his life and waited for her year after year hopin' in the end she'd change her mind and marry him. And she will, too, I believe, if she comes out of this fit into her sane mind—which she won't if you keep fussin' with her.

BENNY (*with revengeful triumph*). She'll never marry the old cuss—I'll fix that!

HARRIET. Now you're showin' yourself up for what you are! And I kin see it's come to the p'int where I got to tell your Uncle Caleb everythin' no matter how it breaks him up. I got to do it for Emmer's sake as well as his'n. We got to get her cured of your bad influence once and for all. It's the on'y hope for the two of 'em.

BENNY. You just try it!

HARRIET. And as for you, you get back to the army where you b'long! And don't never expect another cent from me or Caleb 'cause you won't get it! And don't never come to see us again till you've got rid of the meanness and filth that's the Rogers part of you and found the honesty and decency that's the Williams part—if you got any of me in you at all, which I begin to doubt. (*Goes to the door in rear.*) And now I'm goin' back to Caleb—and you better not let him find you here when he comes less'n you want a good hidin' for once in your life. (*She goes out.*)

BENNY (*stammering between fear and rage—shouting after her*). G'wan! Tell him! What the hell do I care? I'll fix him! I'll spill the beans for both of you, if you try to fix me! (*He stands in the middle of the room hesitating whether to run away or stay, concentrating his thoughts on finding some way to make good his bluff. Suddenly his face lights up with a cruel grin and he mutters to himself with savage satisfaction.*) By God, that's it! I'll bet I kin work it, too! By God, that'll fix 'em! (*He chuckles and goes quickly to the door on right and calls up to the floor above.*) Emmer! Emmer!

EMMA (*her voice faintly heard answering*). Yes, Benny, I'm coming.

BENNY (*he calls quickly*). Come down! Come down quick! (*He comes back to the centre of the room where he stands waiting, planning his course of action*)

EMMA (*appears in the doorway. Her face is profusely powdered—with nervous excitement*). Benny! What's the matter? You sounded so—why, where's your Ma?

BENNY. Gone. Gone back home.

EMMA (*offendedly*). Without waiting to see me? Why, I only sat down for a minute to give you a chance to talk to her. I was coming right down. Didn't she want to see me? Whatever's got into Harriet lately?

BENNY. She's mad as thunder at you 'cause I come over here so much 'stead of stayin' home with her.

EMMA (*pleased*). Oh, is that why? Well, if she ain't peculiar! (*She sits in a rocker by the table.*)

BENNY (*with a great pretence of grief, taking one of her hands in his*). Say, Emmer—what I called you down for was—— I want to say good-bye and thank you for all you've done——

EMMA (*frightenedly*). Good-bye? How can you say that! What——?

BENNY. Good-bye for good this time.

EMMA. For good?

BENNY. Yes. I've got to beat it. I ain't got no home here no more. Ma and Uncle Caleb, they've chucked me out.

EMMA. Good gracious, what're you saying?

BENNY. That's what Ma come over to tell me—that Uncle Caleb'd said I'd never get another cent from him, alive or after he's dead, and she told me to git back to the army and never to come home again.

EMMA (*gasping*). She was only joking. She—they couldn't mean it.

BENNY. If you'd heard her you wouldn't think she was joking.

EMMA (*as he makes a movement as if to go away*). Benny! You can't go! Go, and me never see you again, maybe! You can't! I won't have it!

BENNY. I got to, Emmer. What else is there for me to do when they've throwed me out? I don't give a damn about leaving them—but I hate to leave you and never see you again.

EMMA (*excitedly—grabbing his arm*). You can't! I won't let you go!

BENNY. I don't want to—but what can I do?

EMMA. You can stay here with me.

BENNY (*his eyes gleaming with satisfaction*). No, I couldn't. You know this sort of a town. Folks would be sayin' all sorts of bad things in no time. I don't care for myself. They're all down on me anyway because I'm diff'rent from small-town boobs like them and they hate me for it.

EMMA. Yes, you are diff'rent. And I'll show 'em I'm diff'rent, too. You can stay with me—and let 'em gossip all they've a mind to!

BENNY. No, it wouldn't be actin' square with you. I got to go. And I'll try to save up my pay and send you back what I've borrowed now and again.

EMMA (*more and more wrought up*). I won't hear of no such thing. Oh, I can't understand your Ma and your Uncle Caleb bein' so cruel!

BENNY. Folks have been lyin' to her about me, like I told you, and she's told him. He's only too glad to believe it, too, long as it's bad.

EMMA. I can talk to your Uncle Caleb. He's always minded me more'n her.

BENNY (*hastily*). Don't do that, for God's sake! You'd only make it worse and get yourself up against him, too!

EMMA (*bewilderedly*). But—I—don't see——

BENNY (*roughly*). Well, he's still stuck on you, ain't he?

EMMA. (*with a flash of coquetry*). Now, Benny!

BENNY. I ain't kiddin'. This is dead serious. He's stuck on you and you know it.

EMMA (*coyly*). I haven't given him the slightest reason to hope in thirty years.

BENNY. Well, he hopes just the same. Sure he does! Why, Ma said when she was here just now she'd bet you and him'd be married some day yet

EMMA. No such thing! Why, she must be crazy!

BENNY. Oh, she ain't so crazy Ain't he spent every durn evenin' of the time he's home between trips, over here with you—for the last thirty years?

EMMA. When I broke my engagement I said I wanted to stay friends like we'd been before, and we always have; but every time he'd even hint at bein' engaged again I'd always tell him we was friends only and he'd better leave it be that way. There's never been nothing else between us. (*With a coy smile.*) And besides, Benny, you know how little time he's had at home between viges.

BENNY. I kin remember the old cuss marchin' over here every evenin' he was home since I was a kid.

EMMA (*with a titter of delight*). D'you know, Benny, I do actually believe you're jealous!

BENNY (*loudly—to lend conviction*). Sure I'm jealous! But that ain't the point just now. The point is *he's* jealous of me—and you can see what chance you've got of talkin' him over now, can't you! You'd on'y make him madder.

EMMA (*embarrassedly*). He's getting foolish. What cause has he got——

BENNY. When Ma tells him the lies about us——

EMMA (*excitedly*). What lies?

BENNY. I ain't goin' to repeat 'em to you, but you kin guess, can't you, me being so much over here?

EMMA (*springing to her feet—shocked but pleased*). Oh!

BENNY (*turning away from her*). And now I'm going to get out. I'll stay at Bill Grainger's to-night and get the morning train.

EMMA (*grabbing his arm*). No such thing! You'll stay right here!

BENNY. I can't—Emmer. If you was really my aunt, things'd be diff'rent and I'd tell 'em all to go to hell.

EMMA (*smiling at him coquettishly*). But I'm glad I ain't your aunt.

BENNY. Well, I mean if you was related to me in some way. (*At some noise he hears from without, he starts frightenedly.*) Gosh, that sounded like our front door slamming. It's him and he's coming over. I got to get out the back way. (*He starts for the door on the right.*)

EMMA (*clinging to him*). Benny! Don't go! You musn't go!

BENNY (*inspired by alarm and desire for revenge suddenly blurts out*). Say, let's me 'n' you git married, Emmer—to-morrow, eh? Then I kin stay! That'll stop 'em, damn 'em, and make 'em leave me alone.

EMMA (*dazed with joy*). Married? You 'n' me? Oh, Benny, I'm too old. (*She hides her head on his shoulder.*)

BENNY (*hurriedly, with one anxious eye on the door*). No, you ain't! Honest, you ain't! You're the best girl in this town! (*Shaking her in his anxiety.*) Say yes, Emmer! Say you will—first thing to-morrow.

EMMA (*choking with emotion*). Yes—I will—if I'm not too old for you.

BENNY (*jubilantly*). Tell him. Then he'll see where he gets off! Listen! I'm goin' to the kitchen and wait. You come and tell me when he's gone. (*A knock comes at the door. He whispers.*) That's him. I'm goin'.

EMMA (*embracing him fiercely*). Oh, Benny! (*She kisses him on the lips. He ducks away from her and disappears off right. The knock is repeated. Emma dabs tremblingly at her cheeks with a handkerchief. Her face is beaming with happiness and looks indescribably silly. She trips lightly to the door and opens it—forcing a light, careless tone.*) Oh, it's you, Caleb. Come right in and set. I was kind of expecting you. Benny—I'd heard that you was due home to-night.

(*He comes in and shakes the hand she holds out to him in a limp, vague, absent-minded manner. In appearance, he has changed but little in the thirty years save that his hair is now nearly white and his face more deeply lined and wrinkled. His body is still erect, strong and vigorous. He wears dark clothes, much the same as he was dressed in Act One.*)

CALEB (*mechanically*). Hello, Emmer.

(*Once inside the door, he stands staring about the room, frowning. The garish strangeness of everything evidently repels and puzzles him. His face wears its set expression of an emotionless mask, but his eyes cannot conceal an inward struggle, a baffled and painful attempt to comprehend, a wounded look of bewildered hurt.*)

EMMA (*blithely indifferent to this—pleasantly*). Are you looking at the changes I've made? You ain't seen this room since, have you? Of course not. What am I thinking of? They only got through with the work two weeks ago. Well, what d' you think of it?

CALEB (*frowning—hesitatingly*). Why—it's—all right, I reckon.

EMMA. It was so gloomy and old-timey before, I just couldn't bear it. Now it's light and airy and young-looking, don't you think? (*With a sigh.*) I suppose Pa and Ma turned over in their graves.

CALEB (*grimly*). I reckon they did, too.

EMMA. Why, you don't mean to tell me you don't like it neither, Caleb? (*Then as he doesn't reply—resentfully.*) Well, you always was a silly, old-fashioned critter, Caleb Williams, same as they was. (*She plumps herself into a rocker by the table—then, noticing the lost way in which he is looking about him.*) Gracious, why don't you set, Caleb? You give me the fidgets standing that way! You ain't a stranger that's got to be invited, are you? (*Then suddenly realising the cause of his discomfiture, she smiles pityingly, not without a trace of malice.*) Are you looking for your old chair you used to set in? Is that it? Well, I had it put up in the attic. It didn't fit in with them new things.

CALEB (*dully*). No, I s'pose it wouldn't.

EMMA (*indicating a chair next to hers*). Do set down and make yourself at home. (*He does so gingerly. After a pause she asks perfunctorily.*) Did you have good luck this voyage?

CALEB (*again dully*). Oh, purty fair.

(*He begins to look at her as if he were seeing her for the first time, noting every detail with a numb, stunned astonishment.*)

EMMA. You're looking as well as ever.

CALEB (*dully*). Oh, I ain't got nothin' to complain of.

EMMA. You're the same as me, I reckon. (*Happily.*) Why, I seem to get feelin' younger and more lively every day, I declare I do. (*She becomes uncomfortably aware of his examination—nervously.*) Gracious, what you starin' at so?

CALEB (*brusquely blurting out his disapproval*). You've changed, Emmer—changed so I wouldn't know you, hardly.

EMMA (*resentfully*). Well, I hope you think it's for the best.

CALEB (*evasively*). I ain't enough used to it yet—to tell.

EMMA (*offended*). I ain't old-timey and old-maidy like I was, I guess that's what you mean. Well, I just got tired of mopin' alone in this house, waiting for death to take me and not enjoyin' anything. I was gettin' old before my time. And all at once I saw what was happenin' and I made up my mind I was going to get some fun out of what Pa'd left me while I was still in the prime of life, as you might say.

CALEB (*severely*). Be that paint and powder you got on your face, Emmer?

EMMA (*embarrassed by this direct question*). Why, yes—I got a little mite—it's awful good for your complexion, they say—and in the cities now all the women wears it.

CALEB (*sternly*). The kind of women I've seed in cities wearin' it—— (*He checks himself and asks abruptly*). Warn't your hair turnin' grey last time I was home?

EMMA (*flustered*). Yes—yes—so it was—but then it started to come in again black as black all of a sudden.

CALEB (*glancing at her shoes, stockings and dress*). You're got up in them things like a young girl goin' to a dance.

EMMA (*forcing a defiant laugh*). Maybe I will go soon's I learn—and Benny's goin' to teach me.

CALEB (*keeping his rage in control—heavily*). Benny——

EMMA (*suddenly bursting into hysterical tears*). And I think it's real mean of you, Caleb—nasty mean to come here on your first night home—and—make—fun—of—my—clothes—and everything. (*She hides her face in her hands and sobs.*)

CALEB (*overcome by remorse—forgetting his rage instantly—gets up and pats her on the shoulder—with rough tenderness*). Thar, thar, Emmer! Don't cry, now! I didn't mean nothin'. Don't pay no 'tention to what I said. I'm a durned old fool! What the hell do I know o' women's fixin's anyhow? And I reckon I be old-fashioned and set in my ideas.

EMMA (*reassured—pressing one of his hands gratefully*). It hurts—hearing you say—me 'n' you such old friends and——

CALEB. Forgit it, Emmer. I won't say no more about it. (*She dries her eyes and regains her composure. He goes back to his seat, his face greatly softened, looking at her with the blind eyes of love. There is a pause. Finally, he ventures in a gentle tone*). D'you know what time this be, Emmer?

EMMA (*puzzled*). I don't know exactly, but there's a clock in the next room.

CALEB (*quickly*). Hell, I don't mean that kind o' time. I mean—it was thirty years ago this spring.

EMMA (*hastily*). Gracious, don't let's talk of that. It only gets me thinking how old I am.

CALEB (*with an affectionate smile*). We both got to realise now and then that we're gettin' old.

EMMA (*bridling*). That's all right for you to say. You're twelve years older 'n me, don't forget, Caleb.

CALEB (*smiling*). Waal, even that don't make you out no spring chicken, Emmer.

EMMA (*stiffly*). A body's as old as they feels—and I feel right young.

CALEB. Waal, so do I as far as health goes. I'm as able and sound as ever. (*After a pause.*) But, what I meant was, d'you remember what happened thirty years back.

EMMA. I suppose I do.

CALEB. D'you remember what I said that day?

EMMA (*primly*). You said a lot that it's better to forget, if you ask me.

CALEB. I don't mean—that part of it. I mean when I was sayin' good-bye, I said—— (*He gasps—*

then blurts it out.) I said I'd wait thirty years—if need be. (*After a pause.*) I know you told me time and again not to go back to that. On'y—I was thinkin' all this last vige—that maybe—now when the thirty years are past—I was thinkin' that maybe—— (*He looks at her humbly, imploring some encouragement. She stares straight before her, her mouth set thinly. He sighs forlornly and blunders on.*) Thirty years—that's a hell of a long time to wait, Emmer—makin' vige after vige always alone—and feelin' even more alone in between times when I was home, livin' right next door to you and callin' on you every evenin'. (*A pause.*) I've made money enough, I know—but what the hell good's that to me—long as you're out of it? (*A pause.*) Seems to me, Emmer, thirty o' the best years of a man's life ought to be proof enough to you to make you forget—that one slip o' mine.

EMMA (*rousing herself—forcing a careless tone*). Lord sakes, I forgot all about that long ago. And here you go remindin' me of it!

CALEB (*doggedly*). You ain't answered what I was drivin' at, Emmer. (*A pause; then, as if suddenly afraid of what her answer will be, he breaks out quickly.*) And I don't want you to answer right now, neither I want you to take time to think it all over.

EMMA (*feebly evasive*). All right, Caleb, I'll think it over.

CALEB (*after a pause*). Somehow—seems to me's if—you might really *need* me now. You never did before.

EMMA (*suspiciously*). Why should I need you now any more'n any other time.

CALEB (*embarrassedly*). Oh, I just feel that way.

EMMA. It ain't count o' nothin' Harriet's been tellin' you, is it? (*Stiffly.*) Her 'n' me ain't such good friends no more, if you must know.

CALEB (*frowning*). Her 'n' me nearly had a fight right before I came over here. (*Emma starts.*) Harriet lets her tongue run away with her and says dumb fool things she don't really mean. I didn't pay much 'tention to what she was sayin'—but it riled me jest the same. She won't repeat such foolishness after the piece o' my mind I gave her.

EMMA. What did she say?

CALEB. Oh, nothin' worth tellin'. (*A pause.*) But neither you nor me ought to get mad at Harriet serious. We'd ought, by all rights, to make allowances for her. You know's well as me what a hard time she's had. Bein' married to Alf Rogers for five years'd p'izin any woman's life.

EMMA. No, he wasn't much good, there's no denyin'.

CALEB. And now there's Benny drivin' her crazy.

EMMA (*instantly defensive*). Benny's all right!

CALEB (*staring at her sharply—after a pause*). No, that's jest it. He ain't all right, Emmer.

EMMA. He is, too! He's as good as gold!

CALEB (*frowning—with a trace of resentment*). You kin say so, Emmer, but the facts won't bear you out.

EMMA (*excitedly*). What facts, Caleb Williams? If you mean the nasty lies the folks in this town are mean enough to gossip about him, I don't believe any of 'em. I ain't such a fool.

CALEB (*bitterly*). Then you've changed, Emmer. You didn't stop about believin' the fool stories they gossiped about me that time.

EMMA. You owned up yourself that was true!

CALEB. And Benny'd own up if he was half the man I was! (*Angrily.*) But he ain't a man no ways. He's a mean skunk from top to bottom!

EMMA (*springing to her feet*). Oh!

CALEB (*vehemently*). I ain't judged him by what folks have told me. But I've watched him grow up from a boy and every time I've come home I've seed he was gittin' more 'n' more like his Pa—and you know what a low dog Alf Rogers turned out to be and what a hell he made for Harriet. Waal, I'm sayin' this boy Benny is just Alf all over again—on'y worse!

EMMA. Oh!

CALEB. There ain't no Williams' blood left in Benny. He's a mongrel Rogers! (*Trying to calm himself a little and be convincing.*) Listen, Emmer, You don't suppose I'd be sayin' it, do you, if it wasn't so? Ain't he Harriet's boy? Ain't I brought him up in my own house since he was knee-high? Don't you know I got some feelin's 'bout it and I wouldn't hold nothing agen him less'n I knowed it was true?

EMMA (*harshly*). Yes, you would! You're only too anxious to believe all the bad you can about him. You've always hated him, he says—and I can see it's so.

CALEB (*roughly*). You know damned well it ain't, you mean! Ain't I talked him over with you and asked your advice about him whenever I come home? Ain't I always aimed to do all I could to help him git on right? You know damned well I never hated him! It's him that's always hated me! (*Vengefully.*) But I'm beginning to hate him now—and I've good cause for it!

EMMA (*frightened*). What cause?

CALEB (*ignoring her question*). I seed what he was comin' to years back. Then I thought when the war come, and he was drafted into it, that the army and strict discipline 'd maybe make a man o' him. But it ain't! It's made him worse! It's killed whatever mite of decency was left in him. And I reckon now that if you put a coward in one of them there uniforms, he thinks it gives him the privilege to be a bully! Put a sneak in one and it gives him the courage to be a thief! That's why when the war was over Benny enlisted again 'stead o' goin' whalin' with me. He thinks he's found a good shield to cover up his natural-born laziness—and crookedness!

EMMA (*outraged*). You can talk that way about him that went way over to France to shed his blood for you and me!

CALEB. I don't need no one to do my fightin' for me—against German or devil. And you know durned well he was only in the Quartermaster's Department unloadin' and truckin' groceries, as safe from a gun as you and me be this minute. (*With heavy scorn.*) If he shed any blood, he must have got a nose bleed.

EMMA. Oh, you do hate him, I can see it! And you're just as mean as mean, Caleb Williams! All you've said is a wicked lie and you've got no cause——

CALEB. I ain't, eh? I got damned good cause, I tell ye! I ain't minded his meanness to me. I ain't even give as much heed to his meanness to Harriet as I'd ought to have, maybe. But when he starts in his sneakin' thievery with you, Emmer, I put my foot down on him for good and all!

EMMA. What sneakin' thievery with me? How dare you say such things?

CALEB. I got proof it's true. Why, he's even bragged all over town about bein' able to borrow all the money from you he'd a mind to—boastin' of what an old fool he was makin' of you, with you fixin' up your house all new to git him to comin' over.

EMMA (*scarlet—blazing*). It's a lie! He never said it! You're makin' it all up—'cause you're—'cause you're——

CALEB. 'Cause I'm what, Emmer?

EMMA (*flinging it at him like a savage taunt*). 'Cause you're jealous of him, that's what! Any fool can see that!

CALEB (*getting to his feet and facing her—slowly*). Jealous? Of Benny? How—I don't see your meanin' rightly.

EMMA (*with triumphant malice*). Yes, you do! Don't pretend you don't! You're jealous 'cause you know I care a lot about him.

CALEB (*slowly*). Why would I be jealous 'count o' that? What kind o' man d'you take me for? Don't I know you must care for him when you've been a'most as much a mother to him for years as Harriet was?

EMMA (*wounded to the quick—furiously*). No such thing! You're a mean liar! I ain't never played a mother to him. He's never looked at me that way—never! And I don't care for him that way at all. Just because I'm a mite older 'n him—can't them things happen just as well as any other—what d'you suppose—can't I care for him same as any woman cares for a man? And I do! I care more'n I ever did for you! And that's why you're lying about him! You're jealous of that!

CALEB (*staring at her with stunned eyes—in a hoarse whisper*). Emmer! Ye don't know what you're sayin', do ye?

EMMA. I do, too!

CALEB. Harriet said you'd been actin' out o' your right senses.

EMMA. Harriet's mad because she knows Benny loves me better'n her. And he does love me! He don't mind my bein' older. He's said so! And I love him, too!

CALEB (*stepping back from her in horror.*) Emmer!

EMMA. And he's asked me to marry him to-morrow. And I'm going to! Then you can all lie all you've a mind to!

CALEB. You're—going to—marry Benny?

EMMA. First thing to-morrow. And since you've throwed him out of his house in your mad jealousness, I've told him he can stay here with me to-night. And he's going to!

CALEB (*his fists clenching—tensely*). Where—where is the skunk now?

EMMA (*hastily*). Oh, he ain't here. He's gone up street.

CALEB (*starting for the door in rear*). I'm goin' to find the skunk.

EMMA (*seizing his arms—frightened*). What're you going to do?

CALEB (*between his clenched teeth*). I don't know, Emmer—I don't know—— On'y he ain't goin' to marry you, by God!

EMMA. Caleb! (*She tries to throw her arms about him to stop his going. He pushes her firmly but gently aside. She shrieks.*) Caleb! (*She flings herself on her knees and wraps her arms around his legs in supplicating terror.*) Caleb! You ain't going to kill him, Caleb? You ain't going to hurt him, be you? Say you ain't! Tell me you won't hurt him! (*As she thinks she sees a relenting softness come into his face as he looks down at her.*) Oh, Caleb, you used to say you loved me! Don't hurt him then, Caleb—for my sake! I love him, Caleb! Don't hurt him—just because you think I'm an old woman ain't no reason—and I won't marry you, Caleb. I won't—not even if you have waited thirty years. I don't love you. I love him! And I'm going to marry him—to-morrow. So you won't hurt him, will you, Caleb—not when I ask you on my knees!

CALEB (*breaking away from her with a shudder of disgust.*) No, I won't touch him. If I was wantin' to git even with ye, I wouldn't dirty my hands on him. I'd let you marry the skunk and set and watch what happened—or else I'd offer him money not to marry ye—more money than the little mite you kin bring him—and let ye see how quick he'd turn his back on ye!

EMMA (*getting to her feet—frenziedly*). It's a lie! He never would!

CALEB (*unheeding—with a sudden ominous calm*). But I ain't goin' to do neither. You ain't worth it—and he ain't—and no one ain't, nor nothin'. Folks be all crazy and rotten to the core and I'm done with the whole kit and caboodle of 'em. I kin only see one course out for me and I'm goin' to take it. "A dead whale or a stove boat?" we says in whalin'—and my boat is stove! (*He strides away from her, stops, and turns back—savagely.*) Thirty o' the best years of my life flung for a yeller dog like him to feed on. God! You used to say you was diff'rent from the rest o' folks. By God, if you are, it's just you're a mite madder'n they be! By God, that's all! (*He goes, letting the door slam to behind him.*)

EMMA (*in a pitiful whimper*). Caleb!

(*She sinks into a chair by the table sobbing hysterically. Benny sneaks through the door on right, hesitates for a while, afraid that his uncle may be coming back.*)

BENNY (*finally, in a shrill whisper*). Aunt Emmer!

EMMA (*raising her face to look at him for a second*). Oh, Benny! (*She falls to weeping again.*)

BENNY. Say, you don't think he's liable to come back, do you?

EMMA. No—he'll—never—come back here—no more. (*Sobs bitterly.*)

BENNY (*his courage returning, comes forward into the room*). Say, he's 'way up in the air, ain't he? (*With a grin.*) Say, that was some ballin' out he give you!

EMMA. You—heard what he said?

BENNY. Sure thing. When you got to shoutin' I sneaked out o' the kitchen into there to hear what was goin' on. (*With a complacent grin.*) Say, you certainly stood up for me all right. You're a good old scout at that, d'you know it?

EMMA (*raising her absurd, besmeared face to his, as if expecting him to kiss her*). Oh, Benny, I'm giving up everything I've held dear all my life for your sake.

BENNY (*turning away from her with a look of aversion.*) Well, what about it? Ain't I worth it? Ain't I worth a million played-out old cranks like him? (*She stares at him bewilderedly. He takes a handful of almonds from his pocket and begins cracking and eating them, throwing the shells on the floor with an impudent carelessness.*) Hope you don't mind my havin' a feed? I found them in the kitchen and helped myself.

EMMA (*pitifully*). You're welcome to anything that's here, Benny.

BENNY (*insolently*). Sure, I know you're a good scout. Don't rub it in. (*After a pause—boastfully.*) Where did you get that stuff about askin' him not to hurt me? He'd have a swell chance! There's a lot of hard guys in the army have tried to get funny with me till I put one over on 'em. I'd like to see him start something! I could lick him with my hands handcuffed.

EMMA (*revolted*). Oh!

BENNY (*resentfully*). Think I'm bluffin'? I'll show you some time. (*He swaggers about the room—finally stopping beside her. With a cunning leer.*) Say, I been thinkin' it over and I guess I'll call his bluff.

EMMA (*confusedly*). What—do you mean?

BENNY. I mean what he said just before he beat it—that he could get me not to marry you if he offered me more coin than you got. (*Very interestedly.*) Say, d'you s'pose the old miser really was serious about that?

EMMA (*dazedly—as if she could not realise the significance of his words.*) I—I—don't know, Benny.

BENNY (*swaggering about again*). If I was on'y sure he wasn't stallin'! If I could get the old cuss to shell out that way! (*With a tickled chuckle.*) Gosh, that'd be the real stunt aw right, aw right. Oui, oui! Maybe he wasn't kiddin' at that, the old simp! It's worth takin' a stab at, damned if it ain't. I ain't got nothin' to lose.

EMMA (*frightenedly*). What—what're you talkin' about, Benny?

BENNY. Say, I think I'll go over and talk to Ma after a while. You can go over first to make sure he ain't there. I'll get her to put it up to him straight. If he's willin' to dig into his pocket for some real coin—real dough, this time!—I'll agree to beat it and not spill the beans for him with you. (*Threateningly*). And if he's too tight, I'll go right through with what I said I would, if only to spite him! That's me!

EMMA. You mean—if he's willing to bribe you with money, you won't marry me to-morrow?

BENNY. Sure! If he'll put up enough money. I won't stand him otherwise.

EMMA (*whimpering*). Oh, Benny, you're only jokin', ain't you? You can't—you can't mean it!

BENNY (*with careless effrontery*). Why can't I? Sure I mean it!

EMMA (*hiding her face in her hands—with a tortured moan*). Oh, Benny!

BENNY (*disgustedly*). Aw, don't go ballin'! (*After a pause—a bit embarrassedly.*) Aw, say, what d'you think, anyway? What're you takin' it so damned serious for—me askin' you to marry me, I mean? I was on'y sort of kiddin' anyway—just so you'd tell him and get him ragin'. (*As she looks up at him with agonised despair. With a trace of something like pity showing in his tone.*) Say, honest, Aunt Emmer, you didn't believe—you didn't think I was really struck on you, did you? Ah, say, how could I? Have a heart! Why, you're as old as Ma is, ain't you, Aunt Emmer? (*He adds ruthlessly.*) And I'll say you look it, too!

EMMA (*cowering—as if he had struck her*). Oh! Oh!

BENNY (*a bit irritated*). What's the use of blubberin', for God's sake? Can't you take it like a sport? Hell, I ain't lookin' to marry no one, if I can help it. What do I want a wife for? There's too many others. (*After a pause—as she still sobs—calculatingly.*) Aw, come on, be a sport—and say, listen, if he ain't willin' to come across, I'll marry you all right, honest I will. (*More and more calculatingly.*) Sure! If they mean that stuff about kickin' me out of home—sure I'll stay here with you! I'll do anything you want. If you want me to marry you, all you've got to do is say so—any time! Only not to-morrow, we'd better wait and see——

EMMA (*hysterically*). Oh, go away! Go away!

BENNY (*looking down at her disgustedly*). Aw, come up for air, can't you? (*He slaps her on the back.*) Buck up! Be a pal! Tell me where your drink is. This thing's got me so balled up I don't know how I stand. (*With sudden fury.*) Damn his hide! I bet he'll go and leave all he's got to some lousy orphan asylum now.

EMMA. Oh, go away! Go away!

BENNY (*viciously*). So you're givin' me the gate, too, eh? I'd like to see you try it! You asked me to stay and I'll stick. It's all your fool fault that's got me in wrong. And now you want to shake me! This is what I get for foolin' around with an old hen like you that oughta been planted in the cemetery long ago! Paintin' your old mush and dressin' like a kid! Christ A'mighty!

EMMA (*in a cry of despair*). Don't! Stop! Go away.

BENNY (*suddenly alert—sharply*). Sh! I hear someone coming. (*Shaking her.*) Stop—now, Emmer! Damn it, you gotta go to the door. Maybe it's him.

(*He scurries into the room on right. There is a faint knock at the door. Emma lifts her head. She looks horribly old and worn out. Her face is frozen into an expressionless mask, her eyes are red-rimmed, dull and lifeless. The knock is repeated more sharply. Emma rises like a weary automaton and goes to the door and opens it. Harriet is revealed standing outside.)*

HARRIET (*making no movement to come in—coldly*). I want to speak to Caleb.

EMMA (*dully*). He ain't here. He left a while back—said he was goin' up street—I think.

HARRIET (*worriedly*). Oh, dear! (*Then hostilely*). Do you know where Benny is?

EMMA (*dully*). Yes, he's here.

HARRIET (*contemptuously*). I might have guessed that! (*Icily formal.*) Would you mind tellin' him I want to see him?

EMMA (*turns and calls*). Benny! Here's your Ma!

BENNY (*comes from the next room*). Aw right. (*In a fierce whisper as he passes Emma.*) What d'you tell her I was here for, you old fool.

(*Emma gives no sign of having heard him, but comes back to her chair and sits down. Benny slouches to the door—sullenly*). What d'you want, Ma?

HARRIET (*coldly*). I wanted your Uncle Caleb, not you, but you'll have to do, bein' the only man about.

BENNY (*suspiciously*). What is it?

HARRIET (*a bit frightenedly*). I just heard a lot of queer noises down to the barn. Someone's in there, Benny, sure as I'm alive. They're stealin' the chickens, must be.

BENNY (*carelessly*). It's only the rats.

HARRIET (*angrily*). Don't play the idiot! This was a big thumpin' noise no rat'd make.

BENNY. What'd any guy go stealin' this early—(*As Harriet turns away angrily—placatingly.*) Aw right, I'm coming. I'll have a look if that'll satisfy you. Don't go gettin' sore at me again.

(*While he is speaking he goes out and disappears after his mother. Emma sits straight and stiff in her chair for a while, staring before her with waxy eyes. Then she gets to her feet and goes from window to window taking down all the curtains with quick mechanical movements. She throws them on a pile in the middle of the floor. She lifts down the framed pictures from the walls and piles them on the curtains. She takes the cushions and throws them on; pushes the rugs to the pile with her feet; sweeps everything off the table on to the floor. She does all this without a trace of change in her expression—rapidly, but with no apparent effort. There is the noise of running footsteps from outside and Benny bursts into the room panting for breath. He is terribly excited and badly frightened.*)

BENNY (*stops short as he sees the pile on the floor*). What the hell——

EMMA (*dully*). The tally man's coming for them in the morning.

BENNY (*too excited to be surprised*). To hell with that! Say, listen, Aunt Emmer, he's hung himself—Uncle Caleb—in the barn—he's dead!

EMMA (*slowly letting the words fall—like a beginner on the typewriter touching two new letters*). Caleb—dead!

BENNY (*voluble now*). Dead as a door nail! Neck's busted. I just cut him down and carried him home. Say, you've got to come over and help look after Ma. She's goin' on alarmin'. I can't do nothin' with her.

EMMA (*as before*). Caleb hanged himself—in the barn?

BENNY. Yes—and made a sure job of it. (*With morbid interest in the details.*) Know how he did it? You know our barn. The same as yourn a'most. Well, he got a halter—same as you got on your cow—and he made a noose of the rope for his neck and climbed up in the loft and hitched the leather end to a beam and then let himself drop. He must have kicked in that quick! (*He snaps his fingers—then urgently.*) Say, come on. Come on over 'n' help me with Ma, can't you? She's goin' wild. I can't do nothin'!

EMMA (*vaguely*). I'll be over—in a minute. (*Then with a sudden air of having decided something irrevocably.*) I got to go down to the barn.

BENNY. Barn? Say, are you crazy? He ain't there now. I told you I carried him home.

EMMA. I mean—my barn. I got to go down——

BENNY (*exasperated*). Oh, hell! You're as bad as Ma! Everyone's lost their heads but me. Well, I got to get someone else, that's all. (*He rushes out rear, slamming the door behind him.*)

EMMA (*after a tense pause—with a sudden outburst of wild grief*). Caleb! (*Then in a strange whisper.*) Wait, Caleb, I'm going down to the barn. (*She moves like a sleep-walker towards the door in the rear as*

THE CURTAIN FALLS)

THE FIRST MAN

A Play in Four Acts

Characters

CURTIS JAYSON
MARTHA, *his wife*
JOHN JAYSON, *his father, a banker*
JOHN, JR., *his brother*
RICHARD, *his brother*
ESTHER (MRS. MARK SHEFFIELD), *his sister*
LILY, *his sister*
MRS. DAVIDSON, *his father's aunt*
MARK SHEFFIELD, *a lawyer*
EMILY, *John Jr.'s wife*
RICHARD BIGELOW
A MAID
A TRAINED NURSE

Scenes

ACT ONE

Living-room in the house of Curtis Jayson, Bridgetown, Conn. An afternoon in early fall.

ACT TWO

Curtis's study. Morning of the following day.

ACT THREE

The same. Three o'clock in the morning of a day in early spring of the next year.

ACT FOUR

Same as Act One. Three days later.

TIME: the present

Act I

SCENE. *Living-room of Curtis Jayson's house in Bridgetown, Conn.*

A large, comfortable room. On the left, an arm-chair, a big open fire-place, a writing-desk with chair in far left corner. On this side there is also a door leading into Curtis's study. In the rear, centre, a double doorway opening on the hall and the entrance. Book-cases are built into the wall on both sides of this doorway. In the far right corner, a grand piano. Three large windows looking out on the lawn, and another arm-chair, front, are on this right side of the room. Opposite the fire-place is a couch, facing front. Opposite the windows on the right is a long table with magazines, reading lamp, etc. Four chairs are grouped about the table. The walls and ceiling are in a French grey colour. A great rug covers most of the hardwood floor.

It is around four o'clock of a fine afternoon in early Autumn.

As the curtain rises, Martha, Curtis and Bigelow are discovered. Martha is a healthy, fine-looking woman of thirty-eight. She does not appear this age, for her strenuous life in the open has kept her young and fresh. She possesses the frank, clear, direct quality of outdoors, outspoken and generous. Her wavy hair is a dark brown, her eyes blue-grey. Curtis Jayson is a tall, broad-shouldered man of thirty-seven. While spare, his figure has an appearance of rugged health, of great nervous strength held in reserve. His square-jawed, large-featured face retains an eager, boyish enthusiasm in spite of its prevailing expression of thoughtful, preoccupied aloofness. His crisp dark hair is greying at the temples. Edward Bigelow is a large, handsome man of thirty-nine. His face shows culture and tolerance, a sense of humour, a lazy unambitious contentment. Curtis is reading an article in some scientific periodical, seated by the table. Martha and Bigelow are sitting near by, laughing and chatting.

BIGELOW (*is talking with a comically worried but earnest air*). Do you know, I'm getting so I'm actually afraid to leave them alone with that governess. She's too romantic. I'll wager she's got a whole book full of ghost stories, superstitions, and yellow-journal horrors up her sleeve.

MARTHA. Oh, pooh ! Don't go milling around for trouble. When I was a kid I used to get fun out of my horrors.

BIGELOW. But I imagine you were more courageous than most of us.

MARTHA. Why ?

BIGELOW. Well, Nevada—the Far West at that time—I should think a child would have grown so accustomed to violent scenes—

MARTHA (*smiling*). Oh, in the mining camps ; but you don't suppose my father lugged me along on his prospecting trips, do you ? Why, I never saw any rough scenes until I'd finished with school and went to live with father in Goldfield.

BIGELOW (*smiling*). And then you met Curt.

MARTHA. Yes—but I didn't mean he was a rough scene. He was very mild even in those days. Do tell me what he was like at Cornell.

BIGELOW. A romanticist—and he still is !

MARTHA (*pointing at Curtis with gay mischief*). What ! That sedate man ! Never !

CURTIS (*looking up and smiling at them both affectionately—lazily*). Don't mind him, Martha. He always was crazy.

BIGELOW (*to Curt—accusingly*). Why did you elect to take up mining engineering at Cornell instead of a classical degree at the Yale of your fathers and brothers ? Because you had been reading Bret Harte in prep. school and mistaken him for a modern realist. You devoted four years to grooming yourself for another outcast of Poker Flat. (*Martha laughs.*)

CURTIS (*grinning*). It was you who were hypnotized by Harte—so much so that his West of the past is still your blinded New England-movie idea of the West at present. But go on. What next ?

BIGELOW. Next ? You get a job as engineer in that Goldfield mine—but you are soon disillusioned by a laborious life where six-shooters are as rare as nuggets. You try prospecting. You find nothing but different varieties of pebbles. But it is necessary to your nature to project romance into these stones, so you go in strong for geology. As a geologist, you become a slave to the Romance of the Rocks. It is but a step from that to anthropology—the last romance of all. There you find yourself—because there is no farther to go. You win fame as the most proficient of young skull-hunters—and wander over the face of the globe, digging up bones like an old dog.

CURTIS (*with a laugh*). The man is mad, Martha.

BIGELOW. Mad ! What an accusation to come from one who is even now considering setting forth on a five-year excavating contest in search of the remains of our gibbering ancestor, the First Man !

CURTIS (*with sudden seriousness*). I'm not considering it any longer. I've decided to go.

MARTHA (*starting—the hurt showing in her voice*). When did you decide ?

CURTIS. I only really came to a decision this morning. (*With a seriousness that forces Bigelow's interested attention.*) It's a case of got to go. It's a tremendous opportunity that it would be a crime for me to neglect.

BIGELOW. And a big honour, too, isn't it, to be picked as a member of such a large affair ?

CURTIS (*with a smile*). I guess it's just that they want all the men with considerable practical experience they can get. There are bound to be hardships, and they know I'm hardened to them. (*Turning to his wife with an affectionate smile.*) We haven't roughed it in the queer corners for the last ten years without knowing how it's done, have we, Martha?

MARTHA (*dully*). No, Curt.

CURTIS (*with an earnest enthusiasm*). And this expedition *is* what you call a large affair, Big. It's the largest thing of its kind ever undertaken. The possibilities, from the standpoint of anthropology, are limitless.

BIGELOW (*with a grin*). Aha! Now we come to the Missing Link!

CURTIS (*frowning*). Darn your Barnum and Bailey circus lingo, Big. This isn't a thing to mock at. I should think the origin of man would be something that would appeal even to your hot-house imagination. Modern science believes—knows—that Asia was the first home of the human race. That's where we're going, to the great Central Asian plateau north of the Himalayas.

BIGELOW (*more soberly*). And there you hope to dig up—our first ancestor?

CURTIS. It's a chance in a million, but I believe we may, myself—at least find authentic traces of him so that we can reconstruct his life and habits. I was up in that country a lot while I was mining adviser to the Chinese Government—did some of my own work on the side. The extraordinary results I obtained with the little means at my disposal convinced me of the riches yet to be uncovered. The First Man may be among them.

BIGELOW (*turning to Martha*). And you were with him on that Asian plateau?

MARTHA. Yes, I've always been with him.

CURTIS. You bet she has. (*He goes over and puts his hand on his wife's shoulder affectionately.*) Martha's more efficient than a whole staff of assistants and secretaries. She knows more about what I'm doing than I do half the time. (*He turns toward his study.*) Well, I guess I'll go in and work some.

MARTHA (*quietly*). Do you need me now, Curt?

BIGELOW (*starting up*). Yes, if you two want to work together, why just shoo me—

CURTIS (*puts both hands on his shoulders and forces him to his seat again*). No. Sit down, Big. I don't need Martha now. (*Coming over to her, bends down and kisses her—rather mockingly.*) I couldn't deprive Big of an audience for his confessions of a fond parent.

BIGELOW. Aha! Now it's you who are mocking at something you know nothing about. (*An awkward silence follows this remark.*)

CURTIS (*frowning*). I guess you're forgetting, aren't you, Big? (*He turns and walks into his study, closing the door gently behind him.*)

MARTHA (*after a pause—sadly*). Poor Curt.

BIGELOW (*ashamed and confused*). I had forgotten—

MARTHA. The years have made me reconciled. They haven't Curt. (*She sighs—then turns to Bigelow with a forced smile.*) I suppose it's hard for any of you back here to realize that Curt and I ever had any children.

BIGELOW (*after a pause*). How old were they when—

MARTHA. Three years and two—both girls. (*She goes on sadly.*) We had a nice little house in Goldfield. (*Forcing a smile.*) We were very respectable home folks then. The wandering came later, after— It was a Sunday in winter when Curt and I had gone visiting some friends. The nurse girl fell asleep—or something—and the children sneaked out in their underclothes and played in the snow. Pneumonia set in—and a week later they were both dead.

BIGELOW (*shocked*). Good heavens!

MARTHA. We were real lunatics for a time. And then when we'd calmed down enough to realize—how things stood with us—we swore we'd never have children again—to steal away their memory. It wasn't what you thought—romanticism—that set Curt wandering—and me with him. It was a longing to lose ourselves—to forget. He flung himself with all his power into every new study that interested him. He couldn't keep still, mentally or bodily—and I followed. He needed me—then—so dreadfully!

BIGELOW. And is it that keeps driving him on now?

MARTHA. Oh no. He's found himself. His work has taken the place of the children.

BIGELOW. And with you, too?

MARTHA (*with a wan smile*). Well, I've helped—all I could. His work has me in it, I like to think—and I have him.

BIGELOW (*shaking his head*). I think people are

foolish to stand by such an oath as you took—for ever. (*With a smile.*) Children are a great comfort in one's old age, I've tritely found.

MARTHA (*smiling*). Old age!

BIGELOW. I'm knocking at the door of fatal forty.

MARTHA (*with forced gaiety*). You're not very tactful, I must say. Don't you know I'm thirty-eight?

BIGELOW (*gallantly*). A woman is as old as she looks. You're not thirty yet.

MARTHA (*laughing*). After that nice remark I'll have to forgive you everything, won't I?

(*Lily Jayson comes in from the rear. She is a slender, rather pretty girl of twenty-five. The stamp of college student is still very much about her. She rather insists on a superior, intellectual air, is full of nervous, thwarted energy. At the sight of them sitting on the couch together, her eyebrows are raised.*)

LILY (*coming into the room—breezily*). Hallo, Martha. Hallo, Big. (*They both get up with answering* "Hallos.") I walked right in regardless. Hope I'm not interrupting.

MARTHA. Not at all.

LILY (*sitting down by the table as Martha and Bigelow resume their seats on the lounge*). I must say it sounded serious. I heard you tell Big you'd forgive him everything, Martha. (*Dryly—with a mocking glance at Bigelow.*) You're letting yourself in for a large proposition.

BIGELOW (*displeased but trying to smile it off*). The past is never past for a dog with a bad name, eh, Lily? (*Lily laughs. Bigelow gets up.*) If you want to reward me for my truthfulness, Mrs. Jayson, help me take the kids for an airing in the car. I know it's an imposition, but they've grown to expect you. (*Glancing at his watch.*) By Jove, I'll have to run along. I'll get them and then pick you up here. Is that all right?

MARTHA. Fine.

BIGELOW. I'll run, then. Good-bye, Lily. (*She nods. Bigelow goes out rear.*)

MARTHA (*cordially*). Come on over here, Lily.

LILY (*sits on couch with Martha—after a pause—with a smile*). You were forgetting, weren't you?

MARTHA. What?

LILY. That you'd invited all the family over here to tea this afternoon. I'm the advance guard.

MARTHA (*embarrassed*). So I was! How stupid!

LILY (*with an inquisitive glance at Martha's face but with studied carelessness*). Do you like Bigelow?

MARTHA. Yes, very much. And Curt thinks the world of him.

LILY. Oh, Curt is the last one to be bothered by anyone's morals. Curt and I are the unconventional ones of the family. The trouble with Bigelow, Martha, is that he was too careless to conceal his sins—and that won't go down in this Philistine small town. You have to hide and be a fellow hypocrite, or they revenge themselves on you. Bigelow didn't. He flaunted his love-affairs in every one's face. I used to admire him for it. No one exactly blamed him, in their secret hearts. His wife was a terrible, strait-laced creature. No man could have endured her. (*Disgustedly.*) After her death he suddenly acquired a bad conscience. He'd never noticed the children before. I'll bet he didn't even know their names. And then, presto, he's about in our midst giving an imitation of a wet hen with a brood of ducks. It's a bore, if you ask me.

MARTHA (*flushing*). I think it's very fine of him.

LILY (*shaking her head*). His reform is too sudden. He's joined the hypocrites, I think.

MARTHA. I'm sure he's no hypocrite. When you see him with the children—

LILY. Oh, I know he's a good actor. Lots of women have been in love with him. (*Then suddenly.*) You won't be furious if I'm very, very frank, will you, Martha?

MARTHA (*surprised*). No, of course not, Lily.

LILY. Well, I'm the bearer of a message from the Jayson family.

MARTHA (*astonished*). A message? For me?

LILY. Don't think that I have anything to do with it. I'm only a gramophone record of their misgivings. Shall I switch it going? Well, then, father thinks, brother John and wife, sister Esther, and husband all think that you are unwisely intimate with this same Bigelow.

MARTHA (*stunned*). I? Unwisely intimate—(*Suddenly laughing with amusement.*) Well, you sure are funny people!

LILY. No, we're not funny. We'd be all right if we were. On the contrary, we're very dull and deadly. Bigelow really has a villainous rep. for philandering. But, of course, you didn't know that.

MARTHA (*beginning to feel resentful—coldly*). No, I didn't—and I don't care to know it now.

LILY (*calmly*). I told them you wouldn't relish their silly advice. (*In a very confidential, friendly tone.*) Oh, I hate their narrow small-town ethics as much as you do, Martha. I sympathize with you, indeed I do. But I have to live with them, and so, for comfort's sake, I've had to make compromises. And you're going to live in our midst from now on, aren't you? Well, then, you'll have to make compromises, too—if you want any peace.

MARTHA. But—compromises about what? (*Forcing a laugh.*) I refuse to take it seriously. How anyone could think—it's too absurd.

LILY. What set them going was Big's being around such an awful lot the weeks Curt was in New York, just after you'd settled down here. You must acknowledge he was—very much present then, Martha.

MARTHA. But it was on account of his children. They were always with him.

LILY. The town doesn't trust this sudden fond parenthood, Martha. We've known him too long, you see.

MARTHA. But he's Curt's oldest and best friend.

LILY. We've found they always are.

MARTHA (*springing to her feet—indignantly*). It's a case of evil minds, it seems to me—and it would be extremely insulting if I didn't have a sense of humour. (*Resentfully.*) You can tell your family, that as far as I'm concerned, the town may—

LILY. Go to the devil. I knew you'd say that. Well, fight the good fight. You have all my best wishes. (*With a sigh*). I wish I had something worth fighting for. Now that I'm through with college, my occupation's gone. All I do is read book after book. The only live people are the ones in books, I find, and the only live life.

MARTHA (*immediately sympathetic*). You're lonely, that's what, Lily.

LILY (*dryly*). Don't pity me, Martha—or I'll join the enemy.

MARTHA. I'm not. But I'd like to help you if I could. (*After a pause.*) Have you ever thought of marrying?

LILY (*with a laugh*). Martha! How banal! The men I see are enough to banish that thought if I ever had it.

MARTHA. Marriage isn't only the man. It's children. Wouldn't you like to have children?

LILY (*turning to her bluntly*). Wouldn't you?

MARTHA (*confused*). But—Lily—

LILY. Oh, I know it wasn't practicable as long as you elected to wander with Curt—but why not now when you've definitely settled down here? I think that would solve things all round. If you could present father with a grandson, I'm sure he'd fall on your neck. He feels piqued at the John and Esther families because they've had a run of girls. A male Jayson! Aunt Davidson would weep with joy. (*Suddenly.*) You're thirty-eight, aren't you, Martha?

MARTHA. Yes.

LILY. Then why don't you—before it's too late? (*Martha, struggling with herself, does not answer. Lily goes on slowly.*) You won't want to tag along with Curt to the ends of the earth for ever, will you? (*Curiously.*) Wasn't that queer life like any other? I mean, didn't it get to pall on you?

MARTHA (*as if confessing it reluctantly*). Yes—perhaps—in the last two years.

LILY (*decisively*). It's time for both of you to rest on your laurels. Why can't Curt keep on with what he's doing now—stay home and write his books?

MARTHA. Curt isn't that kind. The actual work—the romance of it—that's his life.

LILY. But if he goes and you have to stay, you'll be lonesome—(*meaningly*)—alone.

MARTHA. Horribly. I don't know what I'll do.

LILY. Then why—why? Think, Martha. If

Curt knew—that was to happen—he'd want to stay here with you. I'm sure he would.

MARTHA (*shaking her head sadly*). No. Curt has grown to dislike children. They remind him of—ours that were taken. He adored them so—he's never become reconciled.

LILY. If you confronted Curt with the actual fact, he'd be reconciled soon enough, and happy in the bargain.

MARTHA (*eagerly*). Do you really think so?

LILY. And you, Martha—I can tell from the way you've talked that you'd like to.

MARTHA (*excitedly*). Yes, I—I never thought I'd ever want to again. For many years after they died I never once dreamed of it. But lately—the last years—I've felt—and when we came to live here—and I saw all around me—homes—and children, I— (*She hesitates as if ashamed at having confessed so much.*)

LILY (*putting an arm around her—affectionately*). I know. (*Vigorously.*) You must, that's all there is to it! If you want my advice, you go right ahead and don't tell Curt until it's a fact he'll have to learn to like, willy-nilly. You'll find, in his inmost heart, he'll be tickled to death.

MARTHA (*forcing a smile*). Yes, I—I'll confess I thought of that. In spite of my fear, I—I've—I mean—I— (*She flushes in a shamed confusion.*)

LILY (*looking at her searchingly*). Why, Martha, what— (*Then suddenly understanding—with excited pleasure.*) Martha! I know! It is so, isn't it? It is!

MARTHA (*in a whisper*). Yes.

LILY (*kissing her affectionately*). You dear, you! (*Then after a pause.*) How long have you known?

MARTHA. For over two months. (*There is a ring from the front door bell in the hall.*)

LILY (*jumping up*). I'll bet that's we Jaysons now. (*She runs to the door in the rear and looks down the hall to the right.*) Yes, it's Esther and husband and Aunt Davidson. (*She comes back to Martha laughing excitedly. The Maid is seen going to the door.*) The first wave of attack, Martha! Be brave! The Young Guard dies but never surrenders!

MARTHA (*displeased but forcing a smile*). You make me feel terribly ill at ease when you put it that way, Lily. (*She rises now and goes to greet the visitors, who enter. Mrs. Davidson is seventy-five years old—a thin, sinewy old lady, old-fashioned, unbending and rigorous in manner. She is dressed aggressively in the fashion of a bygone age. Esther is a stout, middle-aged woman with the round, unmarked, sentimentally-contented face of one who lives unthinkingly from day to day, sheltered in an assured position in her little world. Mark, her husband, is a lean, tall, stooping man of about forty-five. His long face is alert, shrewd, cautious, full of the superficial craftiness of the lawyer mind. Martha kisses the two women, shakes hands with Mark, uttering the usual meaningless greetings in a forced tone. They reply in much the same spirit. There is the buzz of this empty chatter while Martha gets them seated. Lily stands looking on with a cynical smile of amusement. Mrs. Davidson is in the chair at the end of table, left, Esther sits by Martha on couch, Mark in chair at front of table.*) Will you have tea now or shall we wait for the others?

ESTHER. Let's wait. They ought to be here any moment.

LILY (*maliciously*). Just think, Martha had forgotten you were coming. She was going motoring with Bigelow. (*There is a dead silence at this—broken diplomatically by Sheffield.*)

SHEFFIELD. Where is Curt, Martha?

MARTHA. Hard at work in his study. I'm afraid he's there for the day.

SHEFFIELD (*condescendingly*). Still plugging away at his book, I suppose. Well, I hope it will be a big success.

LILY (*irritated by his smugness*). As big a success as the brief you're writing to restrain the citizens from preventing the Traction Company robbing them, eh, Mark? (*Before anyone can reply, she turns suddenly on her aunt who is sitting rigidly on her chair, staring before her stonily like some old lady in a daguerreotype—in a loud challenging tone.*) You don't mind if I smoke, aunt? (*She takes a cigarette out of case and lights it.*)

ESTHER (*smiling*). Lily!

MRS. DAVIDSON (*fixes Lily with her stare—in a tone of irrevocable decision*). We'll get you married, young lady, and that very soon. What you need to bring you down to earth is a husband and the responsibility of children. (*Turning her glance to Martha, a challenge in her question.*) Every woman who is able should have children. Don't you believe that, Martha Jayson? (*She accentuates the full name.*)

MARTHA (*taken aback for a moment but restraining her resentment—gently*). Yes, I do, Mrs. Davidson.

MRS. DAVIDSON (*seemingly placated by this reply—in a milder tone*). You must call me aunt, my dear. (*Meaningly.*) All the Jaysons do.

MARTHA (*simply*). Thank you, aunt.

LILY (*as if all of this aroused her irritation—in a nervous fuming*). Why don't the others come, darn 'em? I'm dying for my tea. (*The door from the study is opened and Curt appears. They all greet him.*)

CURTIS (*absent-mindedly*). Hallo, everybody. (*Then with a preoccupied air to Martha.*) Martha, I don't want to interrupt you—but—

MARTHA (*getting up briskly*). You want my help?

CURTIS (*with the same absent-minded air*). Yes—not for long—just a few notes before I forget them. (*He goes back into the study.*)

MARTHA (*seemingly relieved by this interruption and glad of the chance it gives to show them her importance to Curt*). You'll excuse me for a few moments, all of you, won't you? (*They all nod.*)

MRS. DAVIDSON (*rather harshly*). Why doesn't Curt hire a secretary? That is no work for his wife.

MARTHA (*quietly*). A paid secretary could hardly give the sympathy and understanding Curt needs, Mrs. Davidson. (*Proudly.*) And she would have to study for years, as I have done, in order to take my place. (*To Lily.*) If I am not here by the time the others arrive, will you see about the tea, Lily—

LILY (*eagerly*). Sure. I love to serve drinks. If I were a man, I'd be a bar-tender—in Mexico or Canada.

MARTHA (*going toward the study*). I'll be with you again in a minute, I hope. (*She goes in and shuts the door behind her.*)

ESTHER (*pettishly*). Even people touched by a smattering of science seem to get rude, don't they?

MRS. DAVIDSON (*harshly*). I have heard much silly talk of this being an age of free women, and I have always said it was tommyrot. (*Pointing to the study.*) She is an example. She is more of a slave to Curt's hobbies than any of my generation were to anything but their children. (*Still more harshly.*) Where are her children?

LILY. They died, aunt, as children have a bad habit of doing. (*Then meaningly.*) However, I wouldn't despair if I were you. (*Mrs. Davidson stares at her fixedly.*)

ESTHER (*betraying a sudden frightened jealousy*). What do you mean, Lily? What are you so mysterious about? What did she say? What—

LILY (*mockingly*). Mark, your frau seems to have me on the stand. Can I refuse to answer? (*There is a ring at the bell. Lily jumps to her feet excitedly.*) Here comes the rest of our Grand Fleet. Now I'll have my tea. (*She darts out to the hallway.*)

ESTHER (*shaking her head*). Goodness, Lily is trying to the nerves.

Jayson, his two sons, John and Dick, and John's wife, Emily, enter from the hall in rear. Jayson, the father, is a short, stout, bald-headed man of sixty. A typical, small-town, New England best-family banker, reserved in pose, unobtrusively important—a placid exterior hiding querulousness and a fussy temper. John Jr. is his father over again in appearance, but pompous, obtrusive, purse-and-family-proud, extremely irritating in his self-complacent air of authority, emptily assertive and loud. He is about forty. Richard, the other brother, is a typical young Casino and country club member, college-bred, good looking, not unlikable. He has been an officer in the war, and has not forgotten it. Emily, John Jr.'s wife, is one of those small, mouse-like women who conceal beneath an outward aspect of gentle, unprotected innocence a very active envy, a silly pride, and a mean malice. The people in the room with the exception of Mrs. Davidson rise to greet them. All exchange familiar, perfunctory greetings. Sheffield relinquishes his seat in front of the table to Jayson, going to the chair, right front, himself. John and Dick take the two chairs to the rear of table. Emily joins Esther on the couch and they whisper together excitedly, Esther doing most of the talking. The men remain in uncomfortable silence for a moment.)

DICK (*with gay mockery*). Well, the gang's all here. Looks like the League of Nations. (*Then with impatience.*) Let's get down to cases, folks. I want to know why I've been summoned here. I'm due for tournament mixed-doubles at the Casino at five. Where's the tea?—and has Curt a stick in the cellar to put in it?

LILY (*appearing in the doorway*). Here's tea—but no stick for you, sot. (*The Maid brings in tray with tea-things.*)

JOHN (*heavily*). It seems it would be more to the point to inquire where our hostess—

JAYSON (*rousing himself again*). Yes. And where is Curt?

LILY. Working at his book. He called Martha to take notes on something.

ESTHER (*with a trace of resentment*). She left us as if she were glad of the excuse.

LILY. Stuff, Esther! She knows how much Curt depends on her—and we don't.

EMILY (*in her quiet, lisping voice—with the most innocent air*). Martha seems to be a model wife. (*But there is some quality to the way she says it that makes them all stare at her uneasily.*)

LILY (*insultingly*). How well you say what you don't mean, Emily! Twinkle, twinkle, little bat! But I'm forgetting to do the honours. Tea, everybody? (*Without waiting for any answer.*) Tea, everybody! (*The tea is served.*)

JAYSON (*impatiently*). Stop fooling, Lily. Let's get to our muttons. Did you talk with Martha?

LILY (*briskly*). I did, sir.

JAYSON (*in a lowered voice*). What did she say?

LILY. She said you could all go to the devil! (*They all look shocked and insulted. Lily enjoys this, then adds quietly.*) Oh, not in those words. Martha is a perfect lady. But she made it plain she will thank you to mind your own business.

ESTHER (*volubly*). And just imagine, she'd even forgotten she'd asked us here this afternoon and was going motoring with Bigelow.

LILY. With his three children, too, don't forget.

EMILY (*softly*). They have become such well-behaved and intelligent children, they say. (*Again all the others hesitate, staring at her suspiciously.*)

LILY (*sharply*). You'd better let Martha train yours for a while, Emily. I'm sure she'd improve their manners—though, of course, she couldn't give them any intelligence.

EMILY (*with the pathos of outraged innocence*). Oh!

DICK (*interrupting*). So it's Bigelow you're up in the air about? (*He gives a low whistle—then frowns angrily.*) The deuce you say!

LILY (*mockingly*). Look at our soldier boy home from the wars getting serious about the family honour! It's too bad this is a rough, untutored country where they don't permit duelling, isn't it, Dick?

DICK (*his pose crumbling—angrily*). Go to the devil!

SHEFFIELD (*with a calm, judicious air*). This wrangling is getting us nowhere. You say she was resentful about our well-meant word to the wise?

JAYSON (*testily*). Surely she must realize that some consideration is due the position she occupies in Bridgetown as Curt's wife.

LILY. Martha is properly unimpressed by big frogs in tiny puddles. And there you are.

MRS. DAVIDSON (*outraged*). The idea! She takes a lot upon herself—the daughter of a Wild Western coal-miner.

LILY (*mockingly*). Gold miner, aunt.

MRS. DAVIDSON. It makes no difference—a common miner!

SHEFFIELD (*keenly inquisitive*). Just before the others came, Lily, you gave out some hints—very definite hints, I should say—

ESTHER (*excitedly*). Yes, you did, Lily. What did you mean?

LILY (*uncertainly*). Perhaps I shouldn't have. It's not my secret. (*Enjoying herself immensely now that she holds the spotlight—after a pause, in a stage whisper.*) Shall I tell you? Yes, I can't help telling. Well, Martha is going to have a son. (*They are all stunned and flabbergasted and stare at her speechlessly.*)

MRS. DAVIDSON (*her face lighting up—joyously*). A son! Curt's son!

JAYSON (*pleased by the idea, but bewildered*). A son?

DICK (*smartly*). Lily's kidding you. How can she know it's a son—unless she's a clairvoyant?

ESTHER (*with glad relief*). Yes, how stupid!

LILY. I am clairvoyant in this case. Allah is great, and it will be a son—if only to make you and Emily burst with envy among your daughters.

ESTHER. Lily!

EMILY. Oh!

JAYSON (*testily*). Keep still for a moment, Lily, for God's sake. This is no subject to joke about, remember.

LILY. Martha told me. I know that.

JAYSON. And does Curt know this?

LILY. No, not yet. Martha has been afraid to tell him.

JAYSON. Ah, that explains matters. You know I asked Curt some time ago—and he said it was impossible.

EMILY (*with a lift of her eyebrows*). Impossible? Why, what a funny thing to say.

SHEFFIELD (*keenly lawyer-like*). And why is Martha afraid to tell him, Lily?

LILY. It's all very simple. When the two died years ago, they said they would never have one again. Martha thinks Curt is still haunted by their memory, and is afraid he will resent another as an intruder. I told her that was all foolishness—that a child was the one thing to make Curt settle down for good at home here and write his books.

JAYSON (*eagerly*). Yes, I believe that myself. (*Pleased.*) Well, this is fine news.

EMILY. Still, it was her duty to tell Curt, don't you think? I don't see how she could be afraid of Curt—for those reasons. (*They all stare at her.*)

ESTHER (*resentfully*). I don't, either. Why, Curt's the biggest-hearted and kindest—

EMILY. I wonder how long she's known—this?

LILY (*sharply*). Two months, she said.

EMILY. Two months? (*She lets this sink in.*)

JOHN (*quickly scenting something—eagerly*). What do you mean, Emily? (*Then as if he read her mind.*) Two months? But before that—Curt was away in New York almost a month!

LILY (*turning on Emily fiercely*). So! You got some one to say it for you as you always do, Poison Mind! Oh, I wish the ducking stool had never been abolished!

EMILY (*growing crimson—falteringly*). I—I didn't mean—

JOHN (*furiously*). Where the honour of the family is at stake—

LILY (*fiercely*). Ssshh, you empty barrel! I think I hear—

(*The door from the study is opened and Martha comes in in the midst of a heavy silence. All the gentlemen rise stiffly. Martha is made immediately self-conscious and resentful by the feeling that they have been discussing her unfavourably.*)

MARTHA (*coming forward—with a forced cordiality*). How do you do, everybody? So sorry I wasn't here when you came. I hope Lily made proper excuses for me. (*She goes from one to the other of the four latest comers with* "So glad you came," *etc. They reply formally and perfunctorily. Martha finally finds a seat on the couch between Emily and Esther.*) I hope Lily—but I see you've all had tea.

LILY (*trying to save the situation—gaily*). Yes. You can trust me as understudy for the part of hostess any time.

MARTHA (*forcing a smile*). Well, I'm glad to know I wasn't missed.

EMILY (*sweetly*). We were talking about you—at least, we were listening to Lily talk about you.

MARTHA (*stiffening defensively*). About me?

EMILY. Yes—about how devoted you were to Curt's work. (*Lily gives her a venomous glance of scorn.*)

MARTHA (*pleased but inwardly uneasy*). Oh, but you see I consider it my work, too, I've helped him with it so long now.

JAYSON (*in a forced tone*). And how is Curt's book coming, Martha?

MARTHA (*more and more stung by their strained attitudes and inquisitive glances. Coldly and cuttingly*). Finely, thank you. The book will cause quite a stir, I believe. It will make the name of Jayson famous in the big world outside of Bridgetown.

MRS. DAVIDSON (*indignantly*). The name of Jayson has been—

JAYSON (*pleadingly*). Aunt Elizabeth!

LILY. Aunt means it's world-famous already, Martha. (*Pointing to the sullen John.*) John was once a substitute on the Yale Freshman soccer team, you know. If it wasn't for his weak shins he would have made the team, fancy!

DICK (*this tickles his sense of humour and he bursts into laughter*). Lily wins! (*As his brother glares at him—looking at his watch.*) Heavens, I'll have to hustle! (*Gets to his feet.*) I'm due at the Casino. (*Comes and shakes Martha's hand formally.*) I'm sorry I can't stay.

MARTHA. So glad you came. Do come in again any time. We keep open house, you know—Western fashion. (*She accentuates this.*)

DICK (*hurriedly*). Delighted to. (*He starts for the door in rear.*)

LILY (*as if suddenly making up her mind*). Wait a second! I'm coming with you—

DICK. Sure thing—only hurry, darn you! (*He goes out.*)

LILY (*stops at the door in rear and catching Martha's eye, looks meaningly at the others*). Phew! I need fresh air!

(*She makes an encouraging motion as if pummelling some one to Martha, indicating her assembled family as the victim—then goes out laughing. A motor is heard starting—running off.*)

ESTHER (*with a huge sigh of relief*). Thank goodness, she's gone. What a vixen! What would you do if you had a sister like that, Martha?

MARTHA. I'd love her—and try to understand her.

SHEFFIELD (*meaningly*). She's a bad ally to rely on—this side of the fence one day, and that the next.

MARTHA. Is that why you advised her to become a lawyer, Mr. Sheffield?

SHEFFIELD (*stung, but maintaining an unruffled front*). Now, now, that remark must be catalogued as catty.

MARTHA (*defiantly*). It seems to be in the Bridgetown atmosphere. I never was—not the least bit—in the open air.

JAYSON (*conciliatingly*). Oh, Bridgetown isn't so bad, Martha, once you get used to us.

JOHN. It's one of the most prosperous and wealthy towns in the U.S.—and that means in the world, nowadays.

EMILY (*with her sugary smile*). That isn't what Martha means, you silly. I know what she's thinking about us, and I'm not sure that I don't agree with her—partly. She feels that we're so awfully strict—about certain things. It must be so different in the Far West—I suppose—so much freer.

MARTHA (*acidly*). Then you believe broad-mindedness and clean thinking are a question of locality? I can't agree with you. I know nothing of the present Far West, not having lived there for ten years, but Curt and I have lived in the Far East and I'm sure he'd agree with me in saying that Chinese ancestor worship is far more dignified than ours. After all, you know, theirs is religion, not snobbery. (*There is a loud honking of a motor horn before the house. Martha starts, seems to come to a quick decision, and announces with studied carelessness.*) That must be Mr. Bigelow. I suppose Lily told you I had an engagement to go motoring with him. So sorry I must leave. But I'm like Lily. I need fresh air. (*She walks to the study door as she is talking.*) I'll call Curt. (*She raps loudly on the door and calls.*) Curt! Come out! It's important. (*She turns and goes to the door, smiling fixedly.*) He'll be out when he's through swearing. (*She goes out, rear.*)

JOHN (*exploding*). Well, of all the damned cheek!

ESTHER. She shows her breeding, I must say.

EMILY (*with horror*). Oh, how rude—and insulting.

MRS. DAVIDSON (*rising rigidly to her feet*). I will never set foot in this house again!

JAYSON (*jumping up to restrain her—agitatedly*). Now, Aunt Elizabeth, do keep your head! We must have no scandal of any sort. Remember there are servants about. Do sit down. (*The old lady refuses in stubborn silence.*)

SHEFFIELD (*judiciously*). One must make allowances for one in her condition, aunt.

JAYSON (*snatching at this*). Exactly. Remember her condition, aunt,—(*testily*)—and do sit down. (*The old lady plumps herself down again angrily.*)

EMILY (*in her lisp of hidden meanings*). Yes, the family mustn't forget—her condition.

(*The door from the study is opened and Curt appears. His face shows his annoyance at being interrupted, his eyes are preoccupied. They all turn and greet him with embarrassment. He nods silently and comes slowly down front.*)

CURTIS (*looking around*). Where's Martha? What's the important thing she called me out for?

ESTHER (*forcing gaiety*). To play host, you big bear, you! Don't you think we came to see you, too? Sit down here and be good. (*He sits on sofa.*)

EMILY (*softly*). Martha had to leave us to go motoring with Mr. Bigelow.

ESTHER (*hastily*). And the three children.

CURTIS (*frowning grumpily*). Hm! Big and his eternal kids. (*He sighs. They exchange meaning glances. Curt seems to feel ashamed of his grumpiness and tries to fling it off—with a cheerful smile.*) But what the deuce! I must be getting selfish to grudge Martha her bit of fresh air. You don't know what it means to outdoor animals like us to be pent up. (*He springs to his feet and paces back and forth nervously.*) We're used to living with the sky for a roof— (*Then with interest.*) Did Martha tell you I'd definitely decided to go on the five-year Asian expedition?

ESTHER. Curt! You're not!

EMILY. And leave Martha here—all alone—for five years?

JAYSON. Yes, you can't take Martha with you this time, you know.

CURTIS (*with a laugh*). No? What makes you so sure of that? (*As they look mystified, he continues confidentially.*) I'll let you in on the secret—only you must all promise not to breathe a word to Martha—until to-morrow. To-morrow is her birthday, you know, and this is a surprise I've saved for her. (*They all nod.*) I've been intriguing my damnedest for the past month to get permission for Martha to go with me. It was difficult because women are supposed to be barred. (*Happily.*) But I've succeeded. The letter came this morning. How tickled to death she'll be when she hears! I know she's given up hope. (*Thoughtfully.*) I suppose it's that has been making her act so out of sorts lately.

JAYSON (*worriedly*). Hmm! But would you persist in going—alone—if you knew it was impossible for her—

CURTIS (*frowning*). I can't imagine it without her. You people can't have any idea what a help—a chum—she's been. You can't believe that a woman could be—so much that—in a life of that kind—how I've grown to depend on her. The thousand details—she attends to them all. She remembers everything. Why, I'd be lost. I wouldn't know how to start. (*With a laugh.*) I know this sounds like a confession of weakness, but it's true just the same. (*Frowning again.*) However, naturally my work must always be the first consideration. Yes, absolutely! (*Then with glad relief.*) But what's the use of rambling on this way? We can both go, thank heaven!

MRS. DAVIDSON (*sternly*). No. *She* cannot go. And it is *your* duty—

CURTIS (*interrupting her with a trace of impatience*). Oh, come! That's all nonsense, aunt. You don't understand the kind of woman Martha is.

MRS. DAVIDSON (*harshly*). The women I understand prefer rearing their children to selfish gallivanting over the world.

CURTIS (*impatiently*). But we have no children now, aunt.

MRS. DAVIDSON. I know that, more's the pity. But later—

CURTIS (*emphatically*) No, I tell you! It's impossible!

MRS. DAVIDSON (*grimly*). I have said my last word. Go your own road and work your own ruin.

CURTIS (*brusquely*). I think I'll change my togs and go for a walk. Excuse me for a second. I'll be right down again. (*He goes out, rear.*)

EMILY (*with her false air of innocence*). Curt acts so funny, doesn't he? Did you notice how emphatic he was about it's being impossible? And he said Martha seemed to him to be acting queer lately—with him, I suppose he meant.

ESTHER. He certainly appeared put out when he heard she'd gone motoring with Big.

JAYSON (*moodily*). This dislike of the very mention of children. It isn't like Curt, not a bit.

JOHN. There's something rotten in Denmark somewhere. This family will yet live to regret having accepted a stranger—

SHEFFIELD (*mollifyingly—with a judicial air*). Come now! This is all only suspicion. There is no evidence; you have no case; and the defendant is innocent until you have proved her guilty, remember. (*Getting to his feet.*) Well, let's break up. Esther, you and I ought to be getting home. (*They all rise.*)

JAYSON (*testily*). Well, if I were sure it would all blow over without any open scandal, I'd offer up a prayer of thanks.

Curtain

Act II

SCENE. *Curtis Jayson's study.*

On the left, forward, a gun rack in which are displayed several varieties of rifles and shot-guns. Farther back, three windows looking out on the garden. In the rear wall, an open fire-place with two leather arm-chairs in front of it. To right of fire-place, a door leading into the living-room. In the far right corner, another chair. In the right wall, three windows looking out on the lawn and garden. On this side, front, a typewriting table with machine and chair. Opposite the windows on the right, a bulky leather couch, facing front. In front of the windows on the left, a long table with stacks of paper piled here and there on it, reference books, etc. On the left of table, a swivel chair. Grey oak bookcases are built into the cream rough plaster walls which are otherwise almost hidden from view by a collection of all sorts of hunters' trophies, animal heads of all kinds. The floor is covered with animal skins—tiger, polar bear, leopard, lion, etc. Skins are also thrown over the backs of the chairs. The sections of the bookcase not occupied by scientific volumes have been turned into a specimen case for all sorts of zoological, geological, anthropological oddities.

It is mid-morning, sunny and bright, of the following day.

Curtis and Bigelow are discovered. Curtis is half-sitting on the corner of the table, left, smoking a pipe. Bigelow is lying sprawled on the couch. Through the open windows on the right come the shouts of children playing. Martha's voice joins in with theirs.

BIGELOW. Listen to that rumpus, will you! The kids are having the time of their lives. (*He goes to the window and looks out—delightedly.*) Your wife is playing hide and seek with them. Come and look.

CURTIS (*with a trace of annoyance*). Oh, I can see well enough from here.

BIGELOW (*with a laugh*). She seems to get as much fun out of it as they do. (*As a shriek comes from outside—excitedly.*) Ah, Eddy discovered her behind the tree. Isn't he tickled now! (*He turns back from the window and lights a cigarette—enthusiastically.*) Jove, what a hand she is with children!

CURTIS (*as if the subject bored him*). Oh, Martha gets along well with anyone.

BIGELOW (*sits on the couch again—with a sceptical smile*). You think so? With every one?

CURTIS (*surprised*). Yes—with every one we've ever come in contact with—even aboriginal natives.

BIGELOW. With the aboriginal natives of Bridgetown? With the well-known Jayson family, for example?

CURTIS (*getting to his feet—frowning*). Why, everything's all right between Martha and them, isn't it? What do you mean, Big? I certainly imagined—but I'll confess this damn book has had me so preoccupied—

BIGELOW. Too darn preoccupied, if you'll pardon my saying so. It's not fair to leave her to fight it alone.

CURTIS (*impatiently*). Fight what? Martha has a sense of humour. I'm sure their petty prejudices merely amuse her.

BIGELOW (*sententiously*). A mosquito is a ridiculous, amusing creature, seen under a microscope;

but when a swarm has been stinging you all night—

CURTIS (*a broad grin coming over his face*). You speak from experience, eh?

BIGELOW (*smiling*). You bet I do. Touch me anywhere and you'll find a bite. This, my native town, did me the honour of devoting its entire leisure attention for years to stinging me to death.

CURTIS. Well, if I am to believe one-tenth of the family letters I used to receive on the subject of my old friend, Bigelow, they sure had just cause.

BIGELOW. Oh, I'll play fair. I'll admit they did—then. But it's exasperating to know they never give you credit for changing—I almost said, reforming. One ought to be above the gossip of a town like this—but say what you like, it does get under your skin.

CURTIS (*with an indulgent smile*). So you'd like to be known as a reformed character, eh?

BIGELOW (*rather ruefully*). Et tu! Your tone is sceptical. But I swear to you, Curt, I'm an absolutely new man since my wife's death, since I've grown to love the children. Before that I hardly knew them. They were hers, not mine, it seemed. (*His face lighting up.*) Now we're the best of pals, and I've commenced to appreciate life from a different angle. I've found a career at last—the children—the finest career a man could have, I believe.

CURTIS (*indifferently*). Yes, I suppose so—if you're made that way.

BIGELOW. Meaning you're not?

CURTIS. Not any more. (*Frowning.*) I tried that once.

BIGELOW (*after a pause—with a smile*). But we're wandering from the subject of Martha versus the mosquitoes.

CURTIS (*with a short laugh*). Oh, to the deuce with that! Trust Martha to take care of herself. Besides, I'll have her out of this stagnant hole before so very long—six months, to be exact.

BIGELOW. Where do you think of settling her then?

CURTIS. No settling about it. I'm going to take her with me.

BIGELOW (*surprised*). On the Asian expedition?

CURTIS. Yes. I haven't told her yet, but I'm going to to-day. It's her birthday—and I've been saving the news to surprise her with.

BIGELOW. Her birthday? I wish the children and I had known—but it's not too late yet.

CURTIS (*with a grin*). Thirty-nine candles, if you're thinking of baking a cake!

BIGELOW (*meaningly*). That's not old—but it's not young either, Curt.

CURTIS (*disgustedly*). You talk like an old woman, Big. What have years to do with it? Martha is young in spirit and always will be. (*There is a knock at the door and Martha's voice calling:* "May I come in, people?") Sure thing!

(*Bigelow jumps to open the door and Martha enters. She is flushed, excited, full of the joy of life, panting from her exertions.*)

MARTHA (*laughing*). I've had to run away and leave them with the governess. They're too active for me. (*She throws herself on the couch.*) Phew! I'm all tired out. I must be getting old.

CURTIS (*with a grin*). Big was just this minute remarking that, Martha. (*Bigelow looks embarrassed.*)

MARTHA (*laughing at him*). Well, I declare! Of all the horrid things to hear—

BIGELOW (*still embarrassed but forcing a joking tone*). He—prevaricates, Mrs. Jayson.

MARTHA. There now, Curt! I'm sure it was you who said it. It sounds just like one of your horrid facts.

BIGELOW. And how can I offer my felicitations now? But I do, despite your husband's calumny. May your shadow never grow less!

MARTHA. Thank you. (*She shakes his proffered hand heartily.*)

BIGELOW. And now I'll collect my flock and go home.

CURTIS. So long, Big. Be sure you don't mislay one of your heirs!

BIGELOW. No fear—but they might mislay me. (*He goes. Curt sits down on couch. Martha goes to the window right, and looks out—after a pause, waving her hand.*)

MARTHA. There they go. What darlings they are! (*Curtis grunts perfunctorily. Martha comes back and sits beside Curt on the couch—with a sigh.*) Whoever did say it was right, Curt. I am getting old.

CURTIS (*taking one of her hands and patting it*). Nonsense!

MARTHA (*shaking her head and smiling with a touch of sadness*). No. I feel it.

CURTIS (*puts his arms around her protectingly*). Nonsense! You're not the sort that ever grows old.

MARTHA (*nestling up to him*). I'm afraid we're all that sort, dear. Even you. (*She touches the white hair about his temples playfully.*) Circumstantial evidence. I'll have to dye it when you're asleep some time—and then nobody'll know.

CURTIS (*looking at her*). You haven't any silver threads. (*Jokingly.*) Am I to suspect—

MARTHA. No, I don't. Honest, cross my heart, I wouldn't even conceal that from you, if I did. But grey hairs prove nothing. I am actually older than you, don't forget.

CURTIS. One whole year! That's frightful, isn't it?

MARTHA. I'm a woman, remember; so that one means at least six. Ugh! Let's not talk about it. Do you know, it really fills me with a queer panic sometimes?

CURTIS (*squeezing her*). Silly girl!

MARTHA (*snuggling close to him*). Will you always love me—even when I'm old and ugly and feeble and you're still young and strong and handsome?

CURTIS (*kisses her—tenderly*). Martha! What a foolish question, sweetheart. If we ever have to grow old, we'll do it together just as we've always done everything.

MARTHA (*with a happy sigh*). That's my dream of happiness, Curt. (*Enthusiastically.*) Oh, it has been a wonderful, strange life we've lived together, Curt, hasn't it? You're sure you've never regretted—never had the weest doubt that it might have been better with—some one else?

CURTIS (*kisses her again—tenderly reproachful*). Martha!

MARTHA. And I have helped—really helped you, haven't I?

CURTIS (*much moved*). You've been the best wife a man could ever wish for, Martha. You've been—you are wonderful. I owe everything to you—your sympathy and encouragement. Don't you know I realize that? (*She kisses him gratefully.*)

MARTHA (*musing happily*). Yes, it's been a wonderful, glorious life. I'd live it over again if I could, every single second of it—even the terrible suffering—the children.

CURTIS (*wincing*). Don't. I wouldn't want that over again. (*Then changing the subject abruptly.*) But why have you been putting all our life into the past tense? It seems to me the most interesting part is still ahead of us.

MARTHA (*softly*). I mean—together—Curt.

CURTIS. So do I!

MARTHA. But you're going away—and I can't go with you this time.

CURTIS (*smiling to himself over her head*). Yes, that does complicate matters, doesn't it?

MARTHA (*hurt—looking up at him*). Curt! How indifferently you say that—as if you didn't care!

CURTIS (*avoiding her eyes—teasingly*). What do you think you'll do all the time I'm gone?

MARTHA. Oh, I'll be lost—dead—I won't know what to do. I'll die of loneliness—(*yearning creeping into her voice*)—unless—

CURTIS (*inquisitively*). Unless what?

MARTHA (*burying her face on his shoulder—passionately*). Oh, Curt, I love you so! Swear that you'll always love me no matter what I do—no matter what I ask—

CURTIS (*vaguely uneasy now, trying to peer into her face*). But, sweetheart—

MARTHA (*giving way weakly to her feelings for a moment—entreatingly*). Then don't go!

CURTIS (*astonished*). Why, I've got to go. You know that.

MARTHA. Yes, I suppose you have. (*Vigorously, as if flinging off a weakness.*) Of course you have!

CURTIS. But, Martha—you said you'd be lonely unless—unless what?

MARTHA. Unless I—— (*She hesitates, blushing and confused.*) I mean we—oh, I'm so afraid of what you'll—hold me close, very close to you and I'll whisper it. (*She pulls his head down and whispers in his ear. A look of disappointment and aversion forces itself on his face.*)

CURTIS (*almost indignantly*). But that's impossible, Martha!

MARTHA (*pleadingly*). Now don't be angry with me, Curt—not till you've heard everything. (*With a trace of defiance.*) It isn't impossible, Curt. It's so! It's happened! I was saving it as a secret—to tell you to-day—on my birthday.

CURTIS (*stunned*). You mean it—is a fact?

MARTHA. Yes. (*Then pitifully.*) Oh, Curt, don't look that way! You seem so cold—so far away from me. (*Straining her arms about him.*) Why don't you hold me close to you? Why don't you say you're glad—for my sake?

CURTIS (*agitatedly*). But, Martha—you don't understand. How can I pretend gladness when— (*Vehemently.*) Why, it would spoil all our plans!

MARTHA. Plans? *Our* plans? What do you mean?

CURTIS (*excitedly*). Why, you're going with me, of course! I've obtained official permission. I've been working for it for months. The letter came yesterday morning.

MARTHA (*stunned*). Permission—to go with you—

CURTIS (*excitedly*). Yes. I couldn't conceive going without you. And I knew how you must be wishing—

MARTHA (*in pain*). Oh!

CURTIS (*distractedly—jumping to his feet and staring at her, bewildered*). Martha! You don't mean to tell me you weren't!

MARTHA (*in a crushed voice*). I was wishing you would finally decide not to go—to stay at home.

CURTIS (*betraying exasperation*). But you must realize that's impossible. Martha, are you sure you've clearly understood what I've told you? You can go with me, do you hear? Everything is arranged. And I've had to fight so hard—I was running the risk of losing my own chance by my insistence that I couldn't go without you.

MARTHA (*weakly and helplessly*). I understand all that, Curt.

CURTIS (*indignantly*). And yet—you hesitate! Why, this is the greatest thing of its kind ever attempted! There are unprecedented possibilities! A whole new world of knowledge may be opened up—the very origin of Man himself! And you will be the only woman—

MARTHA. I realize all that, Curt.

CURTIS. You can't—and hesitate! And then—think, Martha!—it will mean that you and I won't have to be separated. We can go on living the old, free life together.

MARTHA (*growing calm now*). You are forgetting—what I told you, Curt. You must face the fact. I cannot go.

CURTIS (*overwhelmed by the finality of her tone—after a pause*). How long have you known—this?

MARTHA. Two months, about.

CURTIS. But why didn't you tell me before?

MARTHA. I was afraid you wouldn't understand—and you haven't, Curt. But why didn't you tell me before—what you were planning?

CURTIS (*eagerly*). You mean—then—you would have been glad to go—before this had happened?

MARTHA. I would have accepted it.

CURTIS (*despairingly*). Martha, how could you ever have allowed this to happen? Oh, I suppose I'm talking foolishness. It wasn't your seeking, I know.

MARTHA. Yes it was, Curt. I wished it. I sought it.

CURTIS (*indignantly*). Martha! (*Then in a hurt tone.*) You have broken the promise we made when they died. We were to keep their memories inviolate. They were to be always—our only children.

MARTHA (*gently*). They forgive me, Curt. And you will forgive me, too—when you see him—and love him.

CURTIS. Him?

MARTHA. I know it will be a boy.

CURTIS (*sinking down on the couch beside her—dully*). Martha! You have blown my world to bits.

MARTHA (*taking one of his hands in hers—gently*). You must make allowances for me, Curt, and forgive me. I *am* getting old. No, it's the truth. I've reached the turning point. Will you listen to my side of it, Curt, and try to see it—with sympathy—with true understanding—(*with a trace of bitterness*)—forgetting your work for the moment?

CURTIS (*miserably*). That's unfair, Martha. I think of it as *our* work—and I have always believed you did, too.

MARTHA (*quickly*). I did, Curt! I do! All in the past is our work. It's my greatest pride to think so. But, Curt, I'll have to confess frankly—during the past two years I've felt myself—feeling as if I wasn't complete—with that alone.

CURTIS. Martha! (*Bitterly.*) And all the time I believed that more and more it was becoming the aim of your life, too.

MARTHA (*with a sad smile*). I'm glad of that, dear. I tried my best to conceal it from you. It would have been so unfair to let you guess while we were still in harness. But oh, how I kept looking forward to the time when we would come back—and rest—in our own home! You know—you said that was your plan—to stay here and write your books—and I was hoping—

CURTIS (*with a gesture of aversion*). I loathe this book-writing. It isn't my part, I realize now. But when I made the plans you speak of, how could I know that then?

MARTHA (*decisively*). You've got to go. I won't try to stop you. I'll help all in my power—as I've always done. Only—I can't go with you any more. And you must help me—to do my work—by understanding it. (*He is silent, frowning, his face agitated, preoccupied. She goes on intensely.*) Oh, Curt, I wish I could tell you what I feel, make you feel with me the longing for a child. If you had just the tiniest bit of feminine in you—(*Forcing a smile.*) But you're so utterly masculine, dear! That's what has made me love you, I suppose—so I've no right to complain of it. (*Intensely.*) I don't. I wouldn't have you changed one bit! I love you! And I love the things you love—your work—because it's a part of you. And that's what I want you to do—to reciprocate—to love the creator in me—to desire that I, too, should complete myself with the thing nearest my heart!

CURTIS (*intensely preoccupied with his own struggle—vaguely*). But I thought—

MARTHA. I know; but, after all, your work is yours, not mine. I have been only a helper, a good comrade, too, I hope, but—somehow—outside of it all. Do you remember two years ago when we were camped in Yunnan, among the aboriginal tribes? It was one night there when we were lying out in our sleeping-bags up in the mountains along the Tibetan frontier. I couldn't sleep. Suddenly I felt oh, so tired—utterly alone—out of harmony with you—with the earth under me. I became horribly despondent—like an outcast who suddenly realizes the whole world is alien. And all the wandering about the world, and all the romance and excitement I'd enjoyed in it, appeared an aimless, futile business, chasing around in a circle in an effort to avoid touching reality. Forgive me, Curt. I meant myself, not you, of course. Oh, it was horrible, I tell you, to feel that way. I tried to laugh at myself, to fight it off, but it stayed and grew worse. It seemed as if I were the only creature alive—who was not alive. And all at once the picture came of a tribeswoman who stood looking at us in a little mountain village as we rode by. She was nursing her child. Her eyes were so curiously sure of herself. She was horribly ugly, poor woman, and yet—as the picture came back to me—I appeared to myself the ugly one while she was beautiful. And I thought of our children who had died—and such a longing for another child came to me that I began sobbing. You were asleep. You didn't hear. (*She pauses—then proceeds slowly.*) And when we came back here—to have a home at last, I was so happy because I saw my chance of fulfilment—before it was too late. (*In a gentle, pleading voice.*) Now can you understand, dear? (*She puts her hand on his arm.*)

CURTIS (*starting as if awaking from a sleep*). Understand? No, I can't understand, Martha.

MARTHA (*in a gasp of unbearable hurt*). Curt! I don't believe you heard a word I was saying.

CURTIS (*bursting forth as if releasing all the pent-up struggle that has been gathering within him*). No, I can't understand. I cannot, cannot! It seems like treachery to me.

MARTHA. Curt!

CURTIS. I've depended on you. This is the crucial point—the biggest thing of my life—and you desert me!

MARTHA (*resentment gathering in her eyes*). If you had listened to me—if you had even tried to feel—

CURTIS. I feel that you are deliberately ruining my highest hope. How can I go on without you? I've been trying to imagine myself alone. I can't! Even with my work—who can I get to take your place? Oh, Martha, why do you have to bring this new element into our lives at this late day? Haven't we been sufficient, you and I together? Isn't that a more difficult, beautiful happiness to achieve than—children? Every one has children. Don't I love you as much as any man could love a woman? Isn't that enough for you? Doesn't it mean anything to you that I need you so terribly—for myself, for my work—for everything that is best and worthiest in me? Can you expect me to be glad when you propose to introduce a stranger who will steal away your love, your interest—who will separate us and deprive me of you! No, no, I cannot! It's asking the impossible. I am only human.

MARTHA. If you were human you would think of my life as well as yours.

CURTIS. I do! It is *our* life I am fighting for, not mine—*our* life that you want to destroy.

MARTHA. Our life seems to mean your life to you, Curt—and only your life. I have devoted fifteen years to that. Now I must fight for my own.

CURTIS (*aghast*). You talk as if we were enemies, Martha! (*Striding forward and seizing her in his arms.*) No, you don't mean it! I love you so, Martha! You've made yourself part of my life, my work—I need you so! I can't share you with anyone! I won't! Martha, my own! Say that you won't, dear? (*He kisses her passionately again and again.*)

MARTHA (*all her love and tenderness aroused by his kisses and passionate sincerity—weakening*). Curt! Curt! (*Pitiably.*) It won't separate us, dear. Can't you see he will be a link between us—even when we are away from each other—that he will bring us together all the closer?

CURTIS. But I can't be away from you!

MARTHA (*miserably*). Oh, Curt, why won't you look the fact in the face—and learn to accept it with joy? Why can't you for my sake? I would do that for you.

CURTIS (*breaking away from her—passionately*). You will not do what I have implored you—for me! And I am looking the fact in the face—the fact that there must be no fact! (*Avoiding her eyes—as if defying his own finer feelings.*) There are doctors who—

MARTHA (*shrinking back from him*). Curt! You propose that—to me! (*With overwhelming sorrow.*) Oh, Curt! When I feel him—his life within me—like a budding of my deepest soul—to flower and continue me—you say what you have just said! (*Grief-stricken.*) Oh, you never, never, never will understand!

CURTIS (*shamefacedly*). Martha, I—(*distractedly*)—I don't know what I'm saying! This whole situation is so unbearable! Why, why does it have to happen now?

MARTHA (*gently*). It must be now—or not at all—at my age, dear. (*Then after a pause—staring at him, frightened—sadly.*) You have changed, Curt. I remember it used to be your happiness to sacrifice yourself for me.

CURTIS. I had no work then—no purpose beyond myself. To sacrifice oneself is easy. But when your only meaning becomes as a searcher for knowledge—you cannot sacrifice that, Martha. You must sacrifice everything for that—or lose all sincerity.

MARTHA. I wonder where your work leaves off and you begin. Hasn't your work become you?

CURTIS. Yes and no. (*Helplessly.*) You can't understand, Martha! . . .

MARTHA. Nor you.

CURTIS (*with a trace of bitter irony*). And you and your work? Aren't they one and the same?

MARTHA. So you think mine is selfish, too? (*After a pause—sadly.*) I can't blame you, Curt. It's all my fault. I've spoiled you by giving up my life so completely to yours. You've forgotten I have one. Oh, I don't mean that I was a martyr. I know that in you alone lay my happiness and fulfilment in those years—after the children died. But we are no longer what we were then. We must, both of us, re-learn to love and respect—what we have become.

CURTIS (*violently*). Nonsense! You talk as if love were an intellectual process— (*Taking her into his arms—passionately.*) I love you—always and for ever! You are me and I am you. What use is all this vivisecting? (*He kisses her fiercely. They look into each other's eyes for a second—then instinctively fall back from one another.*)

MARTHA (*in a whisper*). Yes, you love me. But who am I? There is no recognition in your eyes. You don't know.

CURTIS (*frightened*). Martha! Stop! This is terrible! (*They continue to be held by each other's fearfully questioning eyes.*)

Curtain

ACT III

SCENE. *Same as Act II.*

As the curtain rises, Jayson is discovered sitting in an arm-chair by the fire-place, in which a log fire is burning fitfully. He is staring into the flames, a strained, expectant expression on his face. It is about three o'clock in the morning. There is no light but that furnished by the fire which fills the room with shifting shadows. The door in the rear is opened and Richard appears, his face harried by the stress of unusual emotion. Through the opened doorway, a low, muffled moan of anguish sounds from the upper part of the house. Jayson and Richard both shudder. The latter closes the door behind him quickly as if anxious to shut out the noise.

JAYSON (*looking up anxiously*). Well?

RICHARD (*involuntarily straightening up as if about to salute and report to a superior officer*). No change, sir. (*Then, as if remembering himself, comes to the fire-place and slumps down in a chair—agitatedly.*) God, dad, I can't stand her moaning and screaming! It's got my nerves shot to pieces. I thought I was hardened. I've heard them out in No Man's Land—dying by inches—when you couldn't get to them or help—but this is worse—a million times! After all, that was war—and they were men—

JAYSON. Martha is having an exceptionally hard ordeal.

RICHARD. Since three o'clock this morning—yesterday morning, I should say. It's a wonder she isn't dead.

JAYSON (*after a pause*). Where is Curt?

RICHARD (*harshly*). Still out in the garden, walking around bareheaded in the cold like a lunatic.

JAYSON. Why didn't you make him come in?

RICHARD. Make him! It's easy to say. He's in a queer state, dad, I can tell you! There's something torturing him besides her pain—

JAYSON (*after a pause*). Yes, there's a lot in all this we don't know about.

RICHARD. I suppose the reason he's so down on the family is because we've rather cut her since that tea affair.

JAYSON. He shouldn't blame us. She acted abominably, and has certainly caused enough talk since then—always about with Bigelow—

RICHARD (*with a sardonic laugh*). And yet he keeps asking every one to send for Bigelow—says he wants to talk to him—not us. *We* can't understand! (*He laughs bitterly.*)

JAYSON. I'm afraid Curt knows we understand too much. (*Agitatedly.*) But why does he want Bigelow, in God's name? In his present state—with the suspicions he must have—there's liable to be a frightful scene.

RICHARD. Don't be afraid of a scene. (*With pitying scorn.*) The hell of it is he seems to regard Bigelow as his best friend. Damned if I can make it out.

JAYSON. I gave orders that they were always to tell Curt Bigelow was out of town and couldn't be reached. (*With a sigh.*) What a frightful situation for all of us! (*After a pause.*) It may sound cruel of me—but—I can't help wishing for all our sakes that this child will never—

RICHARD. Yes, dad, I know what you're thinking. It would be the best thing for it, too—although I hate myself for saying it.

(*There is a pause. Then the door in rear is opened and Lily appears. She is pale and agitated. Leaving the door open behind her she comes forward and flings herself on the lounge.*)

JAYSON (*anxiously*). Well?

LILY (*irritably, getting up and switching on the lights*). Isn't everything gloomy enough? (*Sits down.*) I couldn't bear it upstairs one second longer. Esther and Emily are coming down, too. It's too much for them—and they've had personal experience. (*Trying to mask her agitation by a pre-

tence at flippancy.) I hereby become a life-member of the birth-control league. Let's let humanity cease—if God can't manage its continuance any better than that!

RICHARD (*seriously*). Second the motion.

JAYSON (*peevishly*). You're young idiots. Keep your blasphemous nonsense to yourself, Lily!

LILY (*jumping up and stamping her foot—hysterically*). I can't stand it. Take me home, Dick, won't you? We're doing no good waiting here. I'll have a fit—or something—if I stay.

RICHARD (*glad of the excuse to go himself—briskly*). That's how I feel. I'll drive you home. Come along.

(*Esther and Emily enter, followed by John.*)

LILY (*excitedly*). I'll never marry or have a child! Never, never! I'll go into Mark's office to-morrow and make myself independent of marriage.

ESTHER. Sssh! Lily! Don't you know you're shouting? And what silly talk!

LILY. I'll show you whether it's silly! I'll—

RICHARD (*impatiently*). Are you coming or not?

LILY (*quickly*). Yes—wait—here I am. (*She pushes past the others and follows Richard out rear. Esther and Emily sit on couch—John on chair, right rear.*)

ESTHER (*with a sigh*). I thought I went through something when mine were born—but this is too awful.

EMILY. And, according to John, Curt actually says he hates it! Isn't that terrible? (*After a pause—meaningly.*) It's almost as if her suffering was a punishment, don't you think?

ESTHER. If it is, she's being punished enough, Heaven knows. It can't go on this way much longer or something dreadful will happen.

EMILY. Do you think the baby—

ESTHER. I don't know. I shouldn't say it, but perhaps it would be better if—

EMILY. That's what I think.

ESTHER. Oh, I wish I didn't have such evil suspicions—but the way Curt goes on—how can you help feeling there's something wrong?

JAYSON (*suddenly*). How is Curt?

EMILY. John just came in from the garden. (*Turning around to where John is dozing in his chair—sharply.*) John! Well I never! If he isn't falling asleep! John! (*He jerks up his head and stares at her, blinking stupidly. She continues irritably.*) A nice time to pick out for a nap, I must say.

JOHN (*surlily*). Don't forget I have to be at the bank in the morning.

JAYSON (*testily*). I have to be at the bank, too—and you don't notice me sleeping. Tell me about Curt. You just left him, didn't you?

JOHN (*irritably*). Yes, and I've been walking around that damned garden half the night watching over him. Isn't that enough to wear anyone out? I can feel I've got a terrible cold coming on—

ESTHER (*impatiently*). For goodness' sake, don't you start to pity yourself!

JOHN (*indignantly*). I'm not. I think I've showed my willingness to do everything I could. If Curt was only the least bit grateful! He isn't. He hates us all and wishes we were out of his home. I would have left long ago if I didn't want to do my part in saving the family name from disgrace.

JAYSON (*impatiently*). Has he quieted down, that's what I want to know?

JOHN (*harshly*). Not the least bit. He's out of his head—and I'd be out of mine if a child was being born to my wife that—

JAYSON (*angrily*). Keep that to yourself! Remember you have no proof. (*Morosely.*) Think all you want—but don't talk.

EMILY (*pettishly*). The whole town knows it, anyway; I'm sure they must.

JAYSON. There's only been gossip—no real scandal. Let's do our united best to keep it at that. (*After a pause.*) Where's Aunt Elizabeth? We'll have to keep an eye on her, too, or she's quite liable to blurt out the whole business before all comers.

ESTHER. You needn't be afraid. She's forgotten all about the scandalous part. No word of it has come to her out in the country, and she hasn't set foot in town since that unfortunate tea, remember. And at present she's so busy wishing the child will be a boy, that she hasn't a thought for another thing.

(*The door in the rear is opened and Mark Sheffield enters. He comes up to the fire to warm himself. The others watch him in silence for a moment.*)

JAYSON (*impatiently*). Well, Mark? Where's Curt?

SHEFFIELD (*frowning*). Inside. I think he'll be with us in a minute. (*With a scornful smile.*) Just now he's 'phoning to Bigelow. (*The others gasp.*)

JAYSON (*furiously*). For God's sake, couldn't you stop him?

SHEFFIELD. Not without a scene. Your aunt persuaded him to come into the house—and he rushed for the 'phone. I think he guessed we had been lying to him—

JAYSON (*after a pause*). Then he—Bigelow—will be here soon?

SHEFFIELD (*dryly*). It depends on his sense of decency. As he seems lacking in that quality, I've no doubt he'll come.

JOHN (*rising to his feet—pompously*). Then I, for one, will go. Come, Emily. Since Curt seems bound to disgrace every one concerned, I want it thoroughly understood that we wash our hands of the whole disgraceful affair.

EMILY (*snappishly*). Go if you want to! I won't! (*Then with a sacrificing air.*) I think it is our duty to stay.

JAYSON (*exasperated*). Sit down. Wash your hands, indeed! Aren't you as much concerned as any of us?

SHEFFIELD (*sharply*). Sshh! I think I hear Curt now.

(*John sits down abruptly. All stiffen into stony attitudes. The door is opened and Curt enters. He is incredibly drawn and haggard, a tortured, bewildered expression in his eyes. His hair is dishevelled, his boots caked with mud. He stands at the door staring from one to the other of his family with a wild, contemptuous scorn and mutters.*)

CURTIS. Liars! Well, he's coming now. (*Then, bewildered.*) Why didn't you want him to come, eh? He's my oldest friend. I've got to talk to some one—and I can't to you. (*Wildly.*) What do you want here, anyway? Why don't you go? (*A scream of Martha's is heard through the doorway. Curt shudders violently, slams the door to with a crash, putting his shoulders against it as if to bar out the sound inexorably—in anguish.*) God, why must she go through such agony? Why? Why?

(*He goes to the fire-place as Mark makes way for him, flings himself exhaustedly on a chair, his shoulders bowed, his face hidden in his hands. The others stare at him pityingly. There is a long silence. Then the two women whisper together, get up and tiptoe out of the room, motioning for the others to follow them. John does so. Sheffield starts to go, then notices the preoccupied Jayson who is staring moodily into the fire.*)

SHEFFIELD. Sstt! (*As Jayson looks up—in a whisper*). Let's go out and leave him alone. Perhaps he'll sleep.

JAYSON (*starting to follow Sheffield, hesitates and puts a hand on his son's shoulder*). Curt. Remember I'm your father. Can't you confide in me? I'll do anything to help.

CURTIS (*harshly*). No, dad. Leave me alone.

JAYSON (*piqued*). As you wish. (*He starts to go.*)

CURTIS. And send Big in to me as soon as he comes.

JAYSON (*stops, appears about to object—then remarks coldly*). Very well—if you insist.

(*He switches off the lights. He hesitates at the door uncertainly, then opens it and goes out. There is a pause. Then Curt lifts his head and peers about the room. Seeing he is alone he springs to his feet and begins to pace back and forth, his teeth clenched, his features working convulsively. Then, as if attracted by an irresistible impulse, he goes to the closed door and puts his ear to the crack. He evidently hears his wife's moans, for he starts away—in agony.*)

CURTIS. Oh, Martha, Martha! Martha, darling! (*He flings himself in the chair by the fire-place—hides his face in his hands and sobs bitterly. There is a ring from somewhere in the house. Soon after there is a knock at the door. Curtis doesn't hear at first, but when it is repeated he mutters huskily.*) Come in. (*Bigelow enters. Curt looks up at him.*) Close that door, Big, for God's sake!

BIGELOW (*does so—then taking off his overcoat, hat, and throwing them on the lounge comes quickly over to Curt*). I got over as soon as I could. (*As he sees Curt's face he starts and says sympathetically.*) By Jove, old man, you look as though you'd been through hell!

CURTIS (*grimly*). I have. I am.

BIGELOW (*slapping his back*). Buck up! (*Then anxiously*). How's Martha?

CURTIS. She's in hell, too—

BIGELOW (*attempting consolation*). You're surely not worrying, are you? Martha is so strong and healthy there's no doubt of her pulling through in fine shape.

CURTIS. She should never have attempted this. (*After a pause.*) I've a grudge against you, Big. It was you bringing your children over here that first planted this in her mind.

BIGELOW (*after a pause*). I've guessed you thought that. That's why you haven't noticed me—or them—over here so much lately. I'll confess that I felt you— (*Angrily.*) And the infernal gossip—I'll admit I thought that you—oh, damn this rotten town, anyway!

CURTIS (*impatiently*). Oh, for God's sake! (*Bitterly.*) I didn't want you here to discuss Bridgetown gossip.

BIGELOW. I know, old man, forgive me.

(*In spite of the closed door one of Martha's agonized moans is heard. They both shudder.*)

CURTIS (*in a dead, monotonous tone*). She has been moaning like that hour after hour. I shall have those sounds in my ears until the day I die. Nothing can ever make me forget—nothing.

BIGELOW (*trying to distract him*). Deuce take it, Curt, what's the matter with you? I never thought you'd turn morbid.

CURTIS (*darkly*). I've changed, Big—I hardly know myself any more.

BIGELOW. Once you're back on the job again, you'll be all right. You're still determined to go on this expedition, aren't you?

CURTIS. Yes. I was supposed to join them this week in New York, but I've arranged to catch up with them in China—as soon as it's possible for us to go.

BIGELOW. Us? You mean you still plan to take—

CURTIS (*angrily aggressive*). Yes, certainly! Why not? Martha ought to be able to travel in a month or so.

BIGELOW. Yes, but—do you think it would be safe to take the child?

CURTIS (*with a bitter laugh*). Yes—I was forgetting the child, wasn't I? (*Viciously.*) But perhaps— (*Then catching himself with a groan.*) Oh, damn all children, Big!

BIGELOW (*astonished*). Curt!

CURTIS (*in anguish*). I can't help it—I've fought against it. But it's there—deep down in me—and I can't drive it out. I can't!

BIGELOW (*bewildered*). What, Curt?

CURTIS. Hatred! Yes, hatred! What's the use of denying it? I must tell some one, and you're the only one who might understand. (*With a wild laugh.*) For you—hated your wife, didn't you?

BIGELOW (*stunned*). Good God, you don't mean you hate—Martha?

CURTIS (*raging*). Hate Martha? How dare you, you fool! I love Martha—love her with every miserable drop of blood in me—with all my life—all my soul! She is my whole world—everything! Hate Martha! God, man, have you gone crazy to say such a mad thing? (*Savagely.*) No. I hate it. It!

BIGELOW (*shocked*). Curt! Don't you know you can't talk like that—now—when—

CURTIS (*harshly*). It has made us both suffer torments—not only now—every day, every hour, for months and months. Why shouldn't I hate it, eh?

BIGELOW (*staring at his friend's wild, distorted face with growing horror*). Curt! Can't you realize how horrible—

CURTIS. Yes, it's horrible. I've told myself that a million times. (*With emphasis.*) But it's true!

BIGELOW (*severely*). Shut up! You're not yourself. Come, think for a moment. What would Martha feel if she heard you going on this way? Why—it would kill her!

CURTIS (*with a sobbing groan*). Oh, I know, I know! (*After a pause.*) She read it in my eyes. Yes, it's horrible, but when I saw her there suffering so frightfully—I couldn't keep it out of my eyes. I tried to force it back—for her sake—but I couldn't. I was holding her hands and her eyes searched mine with such a longing question in them—and she read only my hatred there, not my love for her. And she screamed and seemed to try to push me away. I wanted to kneel down and pray for forgiveness—to tell her it was only my love for her—that I couldn't help it. And then the doctors told me to leave—and now the door is locked against me— (*He sobs.*)

BIGELOW (*greatly moved*). This is only your damned imagination. They put you out because you were in their way, that's all. And as for Martha, she was probably suffering so much—

CURTIS. No. She read it in my eyes. I saw that look in hers—of horror—horror of me!

BIGELOW (*gruffly*). You're raving, damn it!

CURTIS (*unheeding*). It came home to her then—the undeniable truth. (*With a groan.*) Isn't it fiendish that I should be the one to add to her torture—in spite of myself—in spite of all my will to conceal it! She will never forgive me, never! And how can I forgive myself?

BIGELOW (*distractedly*). For God's sake, don't think about it! It's absurd—ridiculous!

CURTIS (*growing more calm—in a tone of obsession*). She's guessed it ever since that day when we quarrelled—her birthday. Oh, you can have no idea of the misery there has been in our lives since then. You haven't seen or guessed the reason. No one has. It has been—the thought of *it*.

BIGELOW. Curt!

CURTIS (*unheeding*). For years we had welded our lives together so that we two were sufficient, each to each. There was no room for a third. And it was a fine, free life we had made—a life of new worlds, of discovery, of knowledge invaluable to mankind. Isn't such a life worth all the sacrifice it must entail?

BIGELOW. But that life was your life, Curt—

CURTIS (*vehemently*). No, it was her life, too—her work as well as mine. She had made the life, our life—the work, our work. Had she the right to repudiate what she had built because she suddenly has a fancy for a home, children, a miserable ease! I had thought I was her home, her children. I had tried to make my life worthy of being that to her. And I had failed. I was not enough.

BIGELOW. Curt!

CURTIS. Oh, I tried to become reconciled. I tried my damnedest. I tried to love this child as I had loved those that died. But I couldn't. And so, this being estranged us. We loved as intensely as ever but *it* pushed us apart. I grew to dread the idea of this intruder. She saw this in me. I denied it—but she knew. There was something in each of us the other grew to hate. And still we loved as never before, perhaps, for we grew to pity each other's helplessness.

BIGELOW. Curt! Are you sure you ought to tell anyone this?

CURTIS (*waving his remark aside*). One day, when I was trying to imagine myself without her, and finding nothing but hopelessness—yet knowing I must go—a thought suddenly struck me—a horrible but fascinating possibility that had never occurred to me before. (*With feverish intensity.*) Can you guess what it was?

BIGELOW. No. And I think you've done enough morbid raving, if you ask me.

CURTIS. The thought that came to me was that if a certain thing happened, Martha could still go with me. And I knew, if it did happen, that she would want to go, that she would fling herself into the spirit of our work to forget, that she would be mine more than ever.

BIGELOW (*afraid to believe the obvious answer*). Curt!

CURTIS. Yes. My thought was that the child might be born dead.

BIGELOW (*repelled—sternly*). Damn it, man, do you know what you're saying? (*Relentingly.*) No, Curt, old boy, do stop talking. If you don't I'll send for a doctor, damned if I won't. That talk belongs in an asylum. God, man, can't you realize this is your child—yours as well as hers?

CURTIS. I've tried. I cannot. There is some inexorable force in me—

BIGELOW (*coldly*). Do you realize how contemptible this confession makes you out? (*Angrily.*) Why, if you had one trace of human kindness in you—one bit of unselfish love for your wife—one particle of pity for her suffering—

CURTIS (*anguished*). I have—all the love and pity in the world for her! That's why I can't help hating—the cause of her suffering.

BIGELOW. Have you never thought that you might repay Martha for giving up all her life to you by devoting the rest of yours to her?

CURTIS (*bitterly*). She can be happy without me. She will have this child—to take my place. (*Intensely.*) You think I would not give up my work for her? But I would! I will stay here—do anything she wishes—if only we can make a new beginning again—together—*alone*!

BIGELOW (*agitated*). Curt, for God's sake, don't return to that! Why, good God, man—even now—while you're speaking—don't you realize what may be happening? And you can talk as if you were wishing—

CURTIS (*fiercely*). I can't help but wish it!

BIGELOW (*distractedly*). For the love of God, if you have such thoughts, keep them to yourself. I won't listen! You make me despise life!

CURTIS. And would you have me love life? (*The door in the rear is opened and Jayson enters, pale and unnerved. A succession of quick, piercing shrieks is heard before he can close the door behind him. Shuddering.*) My God! My God! (*With a fierce cry.*) Will—this—never—end!

JAYSON (*tremblingly*). Shhh, they say this is the crisis. (*Puts his arm around Curt.*) Bear up, my boy. it will soon be over now.

(*He sits down in the chair Bigelow has vacated, pointedly ignoring the latter. The door is opened again, and Emily, Esther, John and Sheffield file in quickly as if escaping from the cries of the woman upstairs. They are all greatly agitated. Curt groans, pressing his clenched fists against his ears. The two women sit on the lounge. Mark comes forward and stands by Jayson's chair, John sits by the door as before. Bigelow retreats behind Curt's chair, aware of their hostility. There is a long pause.*)

ESTHER (*suddenly*). She has stopped— (*They all listen.*)

JAYSON (*huskily*). Thank God, it's over at last.

(*The door is opened and Mrs. Davidson enters. The old lady is radiant, weeping tears of joy.*)

MRS. DAVIDSON (*calls out exultantly between sobs*). A son, Curt—a son. (*With rapt fervour—falling on her knees.*) Let us all give thanks to God!

CURTIS (*in a horrible cry of rage and anguish*). No! No! You lie! (*They all cry out in fright and amazement:* "Curt!" *The door is opened and the Nurse appears.*)

NURSE (*looking at Curt—in a low voice*). Mr. Jayson, your wife is asking for you.

BIGELOW (*promptly slapping Curt on the back*). There! What did I tell you? Run, you chump!

CURTIS (*with a gasp of joy*). Martha! Darling, I'm coming— (*He rushes out after the Nurse.*)

BIGELOW (*comes forward to get his hat and coat from the sofa—coldly*). Pardon me, please. (*They shrink away from him.*)

EMILY (*as he goes to the door—cuttingly*). Some people seem to have no sense of decency!

BIGELOW (*stung, stops at the door and looks from one to the other of them—bitingly*). No, I quite agree with you. (*He goes out, shutting the door. They all gasp angrily.*)

JOHN. Scoundrel!

JAYSON (*testily—going to Mrs. Davidson, who is still on her knees praying*). Do get up, Aunt Elizabeth! How ridiculous! What a scene if anyone should see you like that. (*He raises her to her feet and leads her to a chair by the fire. She obeys unresistingly, seemingly unaware of what she is doing.*)

ESTHER (*unable to restrain her jealousy*). So it's a boy.

EMILY. Did you hear Curt—how he yelled out "No"? It's plain as the nose on your face he didn't want—

ESTHER. How awful!

JOHN. Well, can you blame him?

EMILY. And the awful cheek of that Bigelow person—coming here—

ESTHER. They appeared as friendly as ever when we came in.

JOHN (*scornfully*). Curt is a blind simpleton—and that man is a dyed-in-the-wool scoundrel.

JAYSON (*frightened*). Shhh! Suppose we were overheard!

EMILY. When Curt leaves we can put her in her proper place. I'll soon let her know she hasn't fooled me, for one. (*While she is speaking Mrs. Davidson has gotten up and is going silently toward the door.*)

JAYSON (*testily*). Aunt Elizabeth, where are you going?

MRS. DAVIDSON (*tenderly*). I must see him again, the dear! (*She goes out.*)

ESTHER (*devoured by curiosity—hesitatingly*). I think I—come on, Emily. Let's go up and see—

EMILY. Not I! I never want to lay eyes on it.

JOHN. Nor I.

ESTHER. I was only thinking—every one will think it funny if we don't.

JAYSON (*hastily*). Yes, yes. We must keep up appearances. (*Getting to his feet.*) Yes, I think we had better all go up—make some sort of inquiry about Martha, you know. It's expected of us and—

(*They are all standing, hesitating, when the door in the rear is opened and the Nurse appears, supporting Curt. The latter is like a corpse. His face is petrified with grief, his body seems limp and half-paralysed.*)

NURSE (*her eyes flashing, indignantly*). It's a wonder some of you wouldn't come up—here, help me! Take him, can't you? I've got to run back!

(*Jayson and Sheffield spring forward and lead Curt to a chair by the fire.*)

JAYSON (*anxious*). Curt! Curt, my boy! What is it, son?

EMILY (*catching the Nurse as she tries to go*). Nurse! What is the matter?

NURSE (*slowly*). His wife is dead. (*They are all still, stunned.*) She lived just long enough to recognize him.

EMILY. And—the baby?

NURSE (*with a professional air*). Oh, it's a fine, healthy baby—eleven pounds—that's what made it so difficult. (*She goes. The others all stand in silence.*)

ESTHER (*suddenly sinking on the couch and bursting into tears*). Oh, I'm so sorry I said—or thought—anything wrong about her. Forgive me, Martha!

SHEFFIELD (*honestly moved but unable to resist this opportunity for Latin—solemnly*). De mortuis nil nisi bonum.

JAYSON (*who has been giving all his attention to his son*). Curt! Curt!

EMILY. Hadn't the doctor better—

JAYSON. Shhh! He begins to recognize me. Curt!

CURTIS (*looking around him with bewilderment*). Yes. (*Suddenly remembrance comes and a spasm of intolerable pain contracts his features. He presses his hands to the side of his head and groans brokenly.*) Martha! Gone! Dead! Oh! (*He appeals wildly to the others.*) Her eyes—she knew me—she smiled—she whispered—forgive me, Curt,—forgive her—when it was I who should have said forgive me—but before I could—she— (*He falters brokenly.*)

EMILY (*looking from one to the other meaningly as if this justified all their suspicions*). Oh!

CURTIS (*a sudden triumph in his voice*). But she loved me again—only me—I saw it in her eyes! She had forgotten—*it*. (*Raging.*) Never let me see it! Never let it come near me! It has murdered her! (*Springing to his feet.*) I hate it from the bottom of my soul—I will never see it—never—never—I take my oath! (*As his father takes his arm—shaking him off.*) Let me go! I am going back to her! (*He strides out of the door in a frenzy of grief and rage. They all stand transfixed, looking at each other, bewildered.*)

EMILY (*putting all her venomous gratification into one word*). Well!

Curtain

Act IV

SCENE. *Same as Act I. It is afternoon of a fine day three days later. Motors are heard coming up the drive in front of the house. There is the muffled sound of voices. The maid is seen going along the hall to the front door. Then the family enter from the rear. First come Jayson and Esther with Mrs. Davidson—then Lily, Dick and Sheffield—then John and his wife. All are dressed in mourning. The only one who betrays any signs of sincere grief is Mrs. Davidson. The others all have a strained look, irritated, worried, or merely gloomy. They seem to be thinking "The worst is yet to come."*

JAYSON (*leading Mrs. Davidson, who is weeping softly, to the chair at left of table—fretfully*). Please do sit down, aunt. (*She does so mechanically.*) And do stop crying.

(*He sits down in front of table. Esther goes to couch where she is joined by Emily. Mark goes over and stands at the back of them. Dick and John sit at rear of table. Lily comes down front and walks about nervously. She seems in a particularly fretful, upset mood.*)

LILY (*trying to conceal her feelings under a forced flippancy*). What ridiculous things funerals are, anyway! That stupid minister—whining away through his nose! Why does the Lord show such a partiality for men with adenoids, I wonder?

JAYSON (*testily*). Shhh! Have you no respect for anything?

LILY (*resentfully*). If I had, I'd have lost it when I saw all of you pulling such long faces in the church where you knew you were under observation. Pah! Such hypocrisy! And then, to cap it all, Emily has to force out a few crocodile tears at the grave!

EMILY (*indignantly*). When I saw Curt—that's why I cried—not for her!

JAYSON. What a scene Curt made! I actually believe he wanted to throw himself into the grave!

DICK. You *believe* he wanted to! Why, it was all Mark and I could do to hold him, wasn't it, Mark? (*Sheffield nods.*)

JAYSON. Intolerable! I never expected he'd turn violent like that. He's seemed calm enough the past three days.

LILY. Calm! Yes, just like a corpse is calm!

JAYSON (*distractedly*). And now this perfectly mad idea of going away to-day to join that infernal expedition—leaving that child on our hands—the child he has never even looked at! Why, it's too monstrously flagrant! He's deliberately flaunting this scandal in every one's face!

JOHN (*firmly*). He must be brought to time.

SHEFFIELD. Yes, we must talk to him—quite openly, if we're forced to. After all, I guess he realizes the situation more keenly than any of us.

LILY (*who has wandered to window on right*). You mean you think he believes— Well, I don't. And you had better be careful not to let him guess what you think. (*Pointing outside.*) There's my proof. There he is walking about with Bigelow. Can you imagine Curt doing that—if he thought for a moment—

DICK. Oh, I guess Curt isn't all fool. He knows that's the very best way to keep people from suspecting.

ESTHER (*indignantly*). But wouldn't you think that Bigelow person— It's disgusting, his sticking to Curt like this.

SHEFFIELD. Well, for one, I'm becoming quite resigned to Bigelow's presence. In the first place, he seems to be the only one who can bring Curt to reason. Then again, I feel that it is to Bigelow's own interest to convince Curt that he mustn't provoke an open scandal by running away without acknowledging this child.

LILY (*suddenly bursting forth hysterically*). Oh, I hate you, all of you! I loathe your suspicions—and I loathe myself because I'm beginning to be poisoned by them, too.

EMILY. Really, Lily, at this late hour—after the way Curt has acted—and her last words when she was dying—

LILY (*distractedly*). I know! Shut up! Haven't you told it a million times already?

(*Mrs. Davidson gets up and walks to the door, rear. She has been crying softly during this scene, oblivious to the talk around her.*)

JAYSON (*testily*). Aunt Elizabeth! Where are

you going? (*As she doesn't answer but goes out into the hall.*) Esther, go with her and see that she doesn't—

ESTHER (*gets up with a jealous irritation*). She's only going up to see the baby. She's simply forgotten everything else in the world!

LILY (*indignantly*). She probably realizes what we are too mean to remember—that the baby, at least, is innocent. Wait, Esther. I'll come with you.

JAYSON. Yes, hurry, she shouldn't be left alone. (*Esther and Lily follow the old lady out, rear.*)

DICK (*after a pause—impatiently*). Well, what next? I don't see what good we are accomplishing. May I run along? (*He gets up restlessly as he is speaking and goes to the window.*)

JAYSON (*severely*). You will stay, if you please. There's to be no shirking on anyone's part. It may take all of us to induce Curt—

SHEFFIELD. I wouldn't worry. Bigelow is taking that job off our hands, I imagine.

DICK (*looking out of the window*). He certainly seems to be doing his damnedest. (*With a sneer.*) The stage missed a great actor in him.

JAYSON (*worriedly*). But, if Bigelow should fail—

SHEFFIELD. Then we'll succeed. (*With a grim smile.*) By God, we'll have to.

JAYSON. Curt has already packed his trunks and had them taken down to the station—told me he was leaving on the five o'clock train.

SHEFFIELD. But didn't you hint to him there was now this matter of the child to be considered in making his plans?

JAYSON (*lamely*). I started to. He simply flared up at me with insane rage.

DICK (*looking out the window*). Say, I believe they're coming in.

JAYSON. Bigelow?

DICK. Yes, they're both making for the front door.

SHEFFIELD. I suggest we beat a retreat to Curt's study and wait there.

JAYSON. Yes, let's do that—come on, all of you.

(*They all retire grumbling but precipitately to the study, closing the door behind them. The front door is heard opening and a moment later Curt and Bigelow enter the room. Curt's face is set in an expression of stony grief. Bigelow is flushed, excited, indignant.*)

BIGELOW (*as Curt sinks down on the couch—pleading indignantly*). Curt, damn it, wake up! Are you made of stone? Has everything I've said gone in one ear and out the other? I know it's hell for me to torment you at this particular time, but it's your own incredibly unreasonable actions that force me to. I know how terribly you must feel, but—damn it, man, postpone this going away! Face this situation like a man! Be reconciled to your child; stay with him at least until you can make suitable arrangements—

CURTIS (*fixedly*). I will never see it! Never!

BIGELOW. How can you keep repeating that—with Martha hardly cold in her grave! I ask you again, what would she think, how would she feel—If you would only consent to see this baby, I know you'd realize how damnably mad and cruel you are. Won't you—just for a second?

CURTIS. No. (*Then raging.*) If I saw it I'd be tempted to— (*Then brokenly.*) No more of that talk, Big. I've heard enough. I've reached the limit.

BIGELOW (*restraining his anger with difficulty—coldly*). That's your final answer, eh? Well, I'm through. I've done all I could. If you want to play the brute—to forget all that was most dear in the world to Martha—to go your own damn selfish way—well, there's nothing more to be said. You will be punished for it, believe me! (*He takes a step toward the door.*) And I—I want you to understand that all friendship ceases between us from this day. You are not the Curt I thought I knew—and I have nothing but a feeling of repulsion—good-bye. (*He starts for the door.*)

CURTIS (*dully*). Good-bye, Big.

BIGELOW (*stops, his features working with grief, and looks back at his friend—then suddenly goes back to him—penitently*). Curt! Forgive me! I ought to know better. This isn't you. You'll come to yourself when you've had time to think it over. The memory of Martha—she'll tell you what you must do. (*He wrings Curt's hand.*) Good-bye, old scout.

CURTIS (*dully*). Good-bye. (*Bigelow hurries out, rear. Curt sits in a dumb apathy for a while—then groans broken-heartedly.*) Martha! Martha!

(*He springs to his feet distractedly. The door of the study is slowly opened and Sheffield peers out cautiously—then comes into the room, followed by the others. They all take seats as before. Curt ignores them.*)

SHEFFIELD (*clearing his throat*). Curt—

CURTIS (*suddenly*). What time is it, do you know?

SHEFFIELD (*looking at his watch*). Two minutes to four.

CURTIS (*impatiently*). Still an hour more of this!

JAYSON (*clearing his throat*). Curt—

(*Before he starts what he intends to say, there is the sound of voices from the hall. Esther and Lily help in Mrs. Davidson to her former chair. The old lady's face is again transformed with joy. Esther joins Emily on the couch. Lily sits in chair—front right. There is a long, uncomfortable pause during which Curt paces up and down.*)

MRS. DAVIDSON (*suddenly murmuring aloud to herself—happily*). He's such a dear! I could stay watching him for ever.

JAYSON (*testily*). Shhh, Aunt! (*Then clearing his throat again.*) Surely you're not still thinking of going on the five o'clock train, are you, Curt?

CURTIS. Yes.

SHEFFIELD (*dryly*). Then Mr. Bigelow didn't persuade you—

CURTIS (*coldly and impatiently*). I'm not to be persuaded by Big or anyone else. And I'll thank you not to talk any more about it. (*They all stiffen resentfully at his tone.*)

JAYSON (*to Curt—in a pleading tone*). You mustn't be unreasonable, Curt. After all, we are your family—your best friends in the world—and we are only trying to help you—

CURTIS (*with nervous vehemence*). I don't want your help. You will help me most by keeping silent.

EMILY (*with a meaning look at the others—sneeringly*). Yes, no doubt.

ESTHER. Shhh, Emily!

JAYSON (*helplessly*). But, you see, Curt—

SHEFFIELD (*with his best judicial air*). If you'll all allow me to be the spokesman, I think perhaps that I— (*They all nod and signify their acquiescence.*) Well, then, will you listen to me, Curt? (*This last somewhat impatiently as Curt continues to pace, eyes on the floor.*)

CURTIS (*without looking at him—harshly*). Yes, I'm listening. What else can I do when you've got me cornered? Say what you like and let's get this over.

SHEFFIELD. First of all, Curt, I hope it is needless for me to express how very deeply we all feel for you in your sorrow. But we sincerely trust that you are aware of our heartfelt sympathy. (*They all nod. A bitter, cynical smile comes over Lily's face.*)

ESTHER (*suddenly breaking down and beginning to weep*). Poor Martha! (*Sheffield glances at his wife, impatient at this interruption. The others also show their irritation.*)

EMILY (*pettishly*). Esther! For goodness' sake!

(*Curt hesitates, stares at his sister frowningly as if judging her sincerity—then bends down over her and kisses the top of her bowed head impulsively—seems about to break down himself—grits his teeth and forces it back—glances around at the others defiantly and resumes his pacing. Esther dries her eyes, forcing a trembling smile. The cry has done her good.*)

SHEFFIELD (*clearing his throat*). I may truthfully say we all feel—as Esther does—even if we do not give vent— (*With an air of sincere sympathy.*) I know how terrible a day this must be for you, Curt. We all do. And we feel guilty in breaking in upon the sanctity of your sorrow in any way But, if you will pardon my saying so, your own course of action—the suddenness of your plans—have made it imperative that we come to an understanding about certain things—about one thing in particular, I might say. (*He pauses. Curt goes on pacing back and forth as if he hadn't heard.*)

JAYSON (*placatingly*). Yes, it is for the best, Curt.

ESTHER. Yes, Curt dear, you mustn't be unreasonable.

DICK (*feeling called upon to say something*). Yes, old man, you've got to face things like a regular. Facts are facts. (*This makes everybody uneasy.*)

LILY (*springing to her feet*). Phew! it's close in here. I'm going out in the garden. You can call me when these—orations—are finished. (*She sweeps out scornfully.*)

JAYSON (*calling after her imperiously*). Lily! (*But she doesn't answer and he gives it up with a hopeless sigh.*)

CURTIS (*harshly*). What time is it?

SHEFFIELD. You have plenty of time to listen to what I—I should rather say we—have to ask you, Curt. I promise to be brief. But first let me again impress upon you that I am talking in a spirit of the deepest friendliness and sympathy with you—as a fellow-member of the same family, I may say—and with the highest ideals and the honour of that family always in view. (*Curt makes no comment. Sheffield unconsciously begins to adopt the alert keenness of the cross-examiner.*) First, let me ask you, is it your intention to take that five o'clock train to-day?

CURTIS (*harshly*). I've told you that.

SHEFFIELD. And then you'll join this expedition to Asia?

CURTIS. You know that.

SHEFFIELD. To be gone five years?

CURTIS (*shrugging his shoulders*). More or less.

SHEFFIELD. Is it your intention to return here at any time before you leave for Asia?

CURTIS. No!

SHEFFIELD. And your determination on these plans is irrevocable?

CURTIS. Irrevocable! Exactly. Please remember that.

SHEFFIELD (*sharply*). That being your attitude, I will come bluntly to the core of the whole matter—the child whose coming into the world cost Martha her life.

CURTIS (*savagely*). Her murderer! You are right! (*They all look shocked, suspicious.*)

SHEFFIELD (*remonstratingly but suspiciously*). You can hardly hold the child responsible for the terrible outcome. Women die every day from the same cause. (*Keenly.*) Why do you attribute guilt to the child in this case, Curt?

CURTIS. It lives and Martha is gone—but enough! I've said I never wanted it mentioned to me. Will you please remember that?

SHEFFIELD (*sharply*). Its name is Jayson, Curt—in the eyes of the law. Will *you* please remember that?

CURTIS (*distractedly*). I don't want to remember anything! (*Wildly.*) Please, for God's sake, leave me alone!

SHEFFIELD (*coldly*). I am sorry, Curt, but you cannot act as if you were alone in this affair.

CURTIS. Why not? Am I not alone—more alone this minute than any creature on God's earth?

SHEFFIELD (*soothingly*). In your great grief. Yes, yes, of course. We all appreciate—and we hate to— (*Persuasively.*) Yes, it would be much wiser to postpone these practical considerations until you are in a calmer mood. And if you will only give us the chance—why not put off this precipitate departure—for a month, say—and in the meantime—

CURTIS (*harshly*). I am going when I said I was. I must get away from this horrible hole—as far away as I can. I must get back to my work, for only in it will I find Martha again. But you—you can't understand that. What is the good of all this talking which leads nowhere?

SHEFFIELD (*coldly*). You're mistaken. It leads to this: Do you understand that your running away from this child—on the very day of its mother's funeral!—will have a very queer appearance in the eyes of the world?

EMILY. And what are you going to do with the baby, Curt? Do you think you can run off regardless and leave it here—on our hands?

CURTIS (*distractedly*). I'll give it this home. And some one—anyone—Esther, Lily—can appoint a nurse to live here and— (*Breaking down.*) Oh, don't bother me!

SHEFFIELD (*sharply*). In the world's eyes, it will appear precious like a desertion on your part.

CURTIS. Oh, arrange it to suit yourselves—anything you wish—

SHEFFIELD (*quickly*). I'll take you at your word. Then let us arrange it this way. You will remain here a month longer at least—

CURTIS. No!

SHEFFIELD (*ignoring the interruption*). You can make plans for the child's future in that time, become reconciled to it—

CURTIS. No!

JAYSON (*pleadingly*). Curt—please—for all our sakes—when the honour of the family is at stake.

DICK. Yes, old man, there's that about it, you know.

CURTIS. No!

EMILY. Oh, he's impossible!

SHEFFIELD. Perhaps Curt misunderstood me. (*Meaningly.*) Be reconciled to it in the eyes of the public, Curt. That's what I meant. Your own private feelings in the matter—are no one's business but your own, of course.

CURTIS (*with bewilderment*). But—I don't see— Oh, damn your eyes of the public!

EMILY (*breaking in*). It's all very well for you to ignore what people in town think—you'll be in China or heaven knows where. The scandal won't touch you—but we've got to live here, and have our position to consider.

CURTIS (*mystified*). Scandal? What scandal? (*Then with a harsh laugh.*) Oh, you mean the imbecile busybodies will call me an unnatural father. Well, let them! I suppose I am. But they don't know—

EMILY (*spitefully*). Perhaps they know more than you think they do.

CURTIS (*turning on her—sharply*). Just what do you mean by that, eh?

ESTHER. Emily! Shhh!

JAYSON (*flurriedly*). Be still, Emily. Let Mark do the talking.

SHEFFIELD (*interposing placatingly*). What Emily means is simply this, Curt: you haven't even been to look at this child since it has been born—not once, have you?

CURTIS. No, and I never intend—

SHEFFIELD (*insinuatingly*). And don't you suppose the doctors and nurses—and the servants—have noticed this? It is not the usual procedure, you must acknowledge, and they wouldn't be human if they didn't think your action—or lack of action—peculiar and comment on it outside.

CURTIS. Well, let them! Do you think I care a fiddler's curse how people judge me?

SHEFFIELD. It is hardly a case of their judging—you. (*Breaking off as he catches Curt's tortured eyes fixed on him wildly.*) This is a small town, Curt, and you know as well as I do, gossip is not the least of its faults. It doesn't take long for such things to get started. (*Persuasively.*) Now I ask you frankly, is it wise to provoke deliberately what may easily be set at rest by a little—I'll be frank—a little pretence on your part?

JAYSON. Yes, my boy. As a Jayson, I know you don't wish—

ESTHER (*with a sigh*). Yes, you really must think of us, Curt.

CURTIS (*in an acute state of muddled confusion*). But—I—you—how are you concerned? Pretence? You mean you want me to stay and pretend—in order that you won't be disturbed by any silly tales they tell about me? (*With a wild laugh.*) Good God, this is too much! Why does a man have to be maddened by fools at such a time! (*Raging.*) Leave me alone! You're like a swarm of poisonous flies.

JAYSON. Curt! This is—really—when we've tried to be so considerate—

JOHN (*bursting with rage*). It's an outrage to allow such insults!

DICK. You're not playing the game, Curt.

EMILY (*spitefully*). It seems to me it's much more for Martha's sake, we're urging you than for our own. After all, the town can't say anything against us.

CURTIS (*turning on her*). Martha's sake? (*Brokenly.*) Martha is gone. Leave her out of this.

SHEFFIELD (*sharply*). But unfortunately, Curt, others will not leave her out of this. They will pry and pry—you know what they are—and—

EMILY. Curt couldn't act the way he is doing if he ever really cared for her.

CURTIS. You dare to say that! (*Then controlling

himself a bit—with scathing scorn.) What do you know of love—women like you? You call your little rabbit-hutch emotions love—your bread-and-butter passions—and you have the effrontery to judge—

EMILY (*shrinking from him, frightened*). Oh, John!

JOHN (*getting to his feet*). I protest! I cannot allow even my own brother—

DICK (*grabbing his arm*). Keep your head, old boy.

SHEFFIELD (*peremptorily*). You are making a fool of yourself, Curt—and you are damned insulting in the bargain. I think I may say that we've all about reached the end of our patience. What Emily said is for your own best interest, if you had the sense to see it. And I put it to you once and for all: Are you or are you not willing to act like a man of honour to protect your own good name, the family name, the name of this child, and your wife's memory? Let me tell you, your wife's good name is more endangered by your stubbornness than anything else.

CURTIS (*trembling with rage*). I—I begin to think—you—all of you—are aiming at something against Martha in this. Yes—at the back of your words—your actions—I begin to feel— (*Raging.*) Go away! Get out of this house—all of you! Oh, I know your meanness! I've seen how you've tried to hurt her ever since we came—because you resented in your small minds her evident superiority—

EMILY (*scornfully*). Superiority, indeed!

CURTIS. Her breadth of mind and greatness of soul that you couldn't understand. I've guessed all this, and if I haven't interfered it's only because I knew she was too far above you to notice your sickening malice—

EMILY (*furiously*). You're only acting—acting for our benefit because you think we don't—

CURTIS (*turning on her—with annihilating contempt*). Why, you—you poor little nonentity! (*John struggles to get forward but Dick holds him back.*)

EMILY (*insane with rage—shrilly*). But we know—and the whole town knows—and you needn't pretend you've been blind. You've given the whole thing away yourself—the silly way you've acted—telling every one how you hated that baby—letting every one see—

JAYSON. Emily! (*The others are all frightened, try to interrupt her. Curt stares at her in a stunned bewilderment.*)

EMILY (*pouring forth all her venom regardless*). But you might as well leave off your idiotic pretending. It doesn't fool us—or anyone else—your sending for Bigelow that night—your hobnobbing with him ever since—your pretending he's as much your friend as ever. They're all afraid of you—but I'm not! I tell you to your face—it's all acting you're doing—just cheap acting to try and pull the wool over our eyes until you've run away like a coward—and left us to face the disgrace for you with this child on our hands!

ESTHER (*trying to silence her—excitedly*). Emily! Keep still, for heaven's sake! (*The others all utter exclamations of caution, with fearful glances at Curt.*)

EMILY (*becoming exhausted by her outburst—more faintly*). Well, some one had to show him his place. He thinks he's so superior to us just because—telling us how much better she was than—But I won't stand for that. I've always had a clean name—and always will—and my children, too, thank God! (*She sinks down on the couch exhausted, panting but still glaring defiantly at Curt.*)

CURTIS (*an awareness of her meaning gradually forcing itself on his mind*). Bigelow! Big? Pretending he's as much my friend— (*With a sudden gasp of sickened understanding.*) Oh! (*He sways as if he were about to fall, shrinking away from Emily, all horror.*) Oh, you—you—you—filth!

JOHN (*his fists clenched, tries to advance on his brother*). How dare you insult my wife! (*He is restrained, held back by his remonstrating father and Dick.*)

MRS. DAVIDSON (*as if suddenly coming out of a dream—frightened*). What is the matter? Why is John mad at Curt?

CURTIS (*his hands over his eyes, acting like a person stricken with a sudden attack of nausea, weakly*). So—that's—what has been in your minds. Oh, this is bestial—disgusting! And there is nothing to be done. I feel defenceless. One would have to be as low as you are— She would have been defenceless, too. It is better she is dead. (*He stares about him—wildly.*) And you think—you all think—

ESTHER (*pityingly*). Curt, dear, we don't think anything except what you've made us think with your crazy carrying-on.

CURTIS (*looking from one to the other of them*). Yes—all of you—it's on your faces. (*His eyes fix themselves on his aunt.*) No you don't—you don't—

MRS. DAVIDSON. I? Don't what, Curtis? My, how sick you look, poor boy!

CURTIS. You—don't believe—this child—

MRS. DAVIDSON. He's the sweetest baby I ever saw—(*proudly*)—and Jayson right to the tips of his toes.

CURTIS. Ah, I know you— (*Looking around at the others with loathing and hatred.*) But look at them— (*With a burst of fierce determination.*) Wait! I'll give you the only answer—

(*He dashes for the door in rear, shakes off his father and Dick, who try to stop him, and then is heard bounding up the stairs in hall. Dick runs after him, Jayson as far as the doorway. Esther gives a stifled scream. There is a tense pause. Then Dick reappears.*)

DICK. It's all right. I saw him go in.

JAYSON (*frightened*). But—good God—he's liable—why didn't you follow him?

DICK. The doctor and nurse are there. They would have called out, wouldn't they, if—

MRS. DAVIDSON (*getting angrier and angrier as her puzzlement has grown greater—in a stern tone*). I understand less and less of this. Where has Curtis gone? Why did he act so sick? What is the matter with all of you?

ESTHER. Nothing, aunt dear, nothing!

MRS. DAVIDSON. No, you'll not hush me up! (*Accusingly.*) You all look guilty. Have you been saying anything against Curtis's baby? That was what Curtis seemed to think. A fine time you've picked out—with his wife not cold in her grave!

JAYSON. Aunt!

MRS. DAVIDSON. I never liked that woman. I never understood her. But now—now I love her and beg her forgiveness. She died like a true woman in the performance of her duty. She died gloriously—and I will always respect her memory. (*Suddenly flying into a passion.*) I feel that you are all hostile to her baby—poor, little, defenceless creature! Yes, you'd hate the idea of Curtis's having a son—you and your girls! Well, I'll make you bitterly regret the day you— (*She plumps herself down in her chair again, staring stubbornly and angrily before her.*)

EMILY (*spitefully*). I fear it will be necessary to tell aunt—

JAYSON. Shhh! You have made enough trouble with your telling already! (*Miserably.*) It should never have come to this pass. Curt will never forgive us—never!

ESTHER (*resentfully to Emily*). See what not holding your tongue has done—and my children will have to suffer for it, too!

SHEFFIELD (*severely*). If Emily had permitted me to conduct this business uninterruptedly, this would never have occurred.

EMILY. That's right! All pick on me! Cowards! (*She breaks down and sobs.*)

DICK (*from the doorway. Coming back into the room*). Sstt! Here he comes!

CURTIS (*re-enters. There is a look of strange exultation on his face. He looks from one to the other of them. He stammers*). Well—my answer to you—your rotten world—I kissed him—he is mine! He looked at me—it was as if Martha looked at me—through his eyes.

ESTHER (*voicing the general relief. Joyfully*). Oh, Curt! You won't go now? You'll stay?

CURTIS (*staring at her, then from one to another of the rest with a withering scorn*). Ha! Now you think you have conquered, do you? No, I'm not going to stay! Do you think your vile slander could influence me to give up my work? And neither shall you influence the life of my son. I leave him here. I must. But not to your tender mercies. No, no! Thank God, there still remains one Jayson with unmuddled integrity to whom I can appeal. (*He goes to Mrs. Davidson.*) I will leave him in your care, aunt—while I am gone.

MRS. DAVIDSON (*delighted*). It will be a great happiness. He will be—the one God never granted me. (*Her lips trembling.*) God has answered my prayer at last.

CURTIS. I thank you, aunt. (*Kisses her reverentially.*)

MRS. DAVIDSON (*pleased but morally bound to grumble at him*). But I cannot approve of your running away like this. It isn't natural. (*Then with selfish haste, fearing her words may change his mind and she will lose the baby.*) But you always were a queer person—and a man must do faithfully the work ordained for him.

CURTIS (*gladly*). Yes, I must go! What would I be for him—or anyone—if I stayed? Thank God, you understand. But I will come back. (*The light of an ideal beginning to shine in his eyes.*) When he is old enough, I will teach him to know and love a big, free life. Martha used to say that he would take her part in time. My goal shall be his goal, too. Martha shall live again for me in him. And you, aunt, swear to keep him with you—out there in the country—never to let him know this obscene little world. (*He indicates his relatives.*)

MRS. DAVIDSON. Yes, I promise, Curtis. Let anyone dare—! (*She glares about her. The noise of a motor is heard from the drive. It stops in front of the house.*)

CURTIS. I must go. (*He kisses his aunt.*) Teach him his mother was the most beautiful soul that ever lived. Good-bye, Aunt.

MRS. DAVIDSON. Good-bye, Curtis!

(*Without looking at the others, he starts for the door, rear. They all break out into conscience-stricken protestations.*)

JAYSON (*miserably*). Curt! You're not leaving us that way?

ESTHER. Curt—you're going—without a word! (*They all say this practically together and crowd toward him. John and Emily remain sullenly apart. Curt turns to face them.*)

LILY (*enters from the rear*). You're not going, Curt?

CURTIS (*turning to her*). Yes. Good-bye, Lily. (*He kisses her.*) You loved her, didn't you? You are not like— Take my advice and get away before you become— (*He has been staring into her face. Suddenly he pushes her brusquely away from him—coldly.*) But I see in your face it's too late.

LILY (*miserably*). No, Curt—I swear—

CURTIS (*facing them all defiantly*). Yes, I am going without a word—because I cannot find the fitting one. Be thankful I can't. It would shrivel up your souls like flame. (*He again turns and strides to the door.*)

JAYSON (*his grief overcoming him*). My boy! We are wrong—we know—but—at least say you forgive us.

CURTIS (*wavers with his back towards them—then turns and forces the words out*). Ask forgiveness of her. She—yes—she was so fine—I feel she—so you are forgiven. Good-bye. (*He goes. The motor is heard driving off. There is a tense pause.*)

LILY. Then he did find out? Oh, a fine mess you've made of everything! But no—I should say "we," shouldn't I? Curt guessed that. Oh, I hate you—and myself! (*She breaks down.*)

(*There is a strained pause during which they are all silent, their eyes avoiding each other, fixed in dull, stupid stares. Finally, Dick fidgets uncomfortably, heaves a noisy sigh, and blurts out with an attempt at comforting reassurance.*)

DICK. Well, it isn't as bad as it might have been, anyway. He did acknowledge the kid—before witnesses, too.

JAYSON (*testily*). Keep your remarks to yourself, if you please! (*But most of his family are already beginning to look relieved.*)

Curtain

THE HAIRY APE

A Comedy of Ancient and Modern Life

Characters

ROBERT SMITH, "YANK"
PADDY
LONG
MILDRED DOUGLAS
HER AUNT
SECOND ENGINEER
A GUARD
A SECRETARY OF AN ORGANIZATION
STOKERS, LADIES, GENTLEMEN, *etc.*

Scenes

SCENE ONE The firemen's forecastle of an ocean liner. An hour after sailing from New York.
SCENE TWO Section of promenade deck, two days out. Morning.
SCENE THREE The stokehole. A few minutes later.
SCENE FOUR Same as Scene One. Half an hour later.
SCENE FIVE Fifth Avenue, New York. Three weeks later.
SCENE SIX An island near the city. The next night.
SCENE SEVEN In the city. About a month later.
SCENE EIGHT In the city. Twilight of the next day.

TIME: the modern

Scene I

SCENE. *The firemen's forecastle of a transatlantic liner an hour after sailing from New York for the voyage across. Tiers of narrow, steel bunks, three deep, on all sides. An entrance in rear. Benches on the floor before the bunks. The room is crowded with men, shouting, cursing, laughing, singing—a confused, inchoate uproar swelling into a sort of unity, a meaning—the bewildered, furious, baffled defiance of a beast in a cage. Nearly all the men are drunk. Many bottles are passed from hand to hand. All are dressed in dungaree trousers and heavy ugly shoes. Some wear vests, but the majority are stripped to the waist.*

The treatment of this scene, or of any other scene in the play, should by no means be naturalistic. The effect sought after is a cramped space in the bowels of a ship, imprisoned by white steel. The lines of bunks, the uprights supporting them, cross each other like the steel framework of a cage. The ceiling crushes down upon the men's heads. They cannot stand upright. This accentuates the natural stooping posture which shovelling coal and the resultant over-development of back and shoulder muscles have given them. The men themselves should resemble those pictures in which the appearance of Neanderthal Man is guessed at. All are hairy-chested, with long arms of tremendous power, and low, receding brows above their small, fierce, resentful eyes. All the civilized white races are represented, but except for the slight differentiation in colour of hair, skin, eyes, all these men are alike.

The Curtain rises on a tumult of sound. Yank is seated in the foreground. He seems broader, fiercer, more truculent, more powerful, more sure of himself than the rest. They respect his superior strength—the grudging respect of fear. Then, too, he represents to them a self-expression, the very last word in what they are, their most highly developed individual.

VOICES. Gif me trink dere, you!
'Ave a wet!
Salute!
Gesundheit!
Skoal!
Drunk as a lord, God stiffen you!
Here's how!
Luck!
Pass back that bottle, damn you!
Pourin' it down his neck!
Ho, Froggy! Where the devil have you been?
La Touraine.
I hit him smash in yaw, py Gott!
Jenkins—the First—he's a rotten swine—
And the coppers nabbed him—and I run—
I like peer better. It don't pig head gif you.
A slut, I'm sayin'! She robbed me aslape—
To hell with 'em all!
You're a bloody liar!
Say dot again! (*Commotion. Two men about to fight are pulled apart.*)
No scrappin' now!
To-night—
See who's the best man!
Bloody Dutchman!
To-night on the for'ard square.
I'll bet on Dutchy.
He packa da wallop, I tella you!
Shut up, Wop!
No fightin', maties. We're all chums, ain't we?

(*A voice starts bawling a song.*)

"Beer, beer, glorious beer!
Fill yourselves right up to here."

YANK (*for the first time seeming to take notice of the uproar about him, turns around threateningly—in a tone of contemptuous authority*). Choke off dat noise! Where d'yuh get dat beer stuff? Beer, hell! Beer's for goils—and Dutchmen. Me for somep'n wit a kick to it! Gimme a drink, one of youse guys. (*Several bottles are eagerly offered. He takes a tremendous gulp at one of them; then, keeping the bottle in his hand, glares belligerently at the owner, who hastens to acquiesce in this robbery by saying:*) All right-o, Yank. Keep it and have another. (*Yank contemptuously turns his back on the crowd again. For a second there is an embarrassed silence. Then—*)

VOICES. We must be passing the Hook.
She's beginning to roll to it.
Six days in hell—and then Southampton.
Py Yesus, I vish somepody take my first vatch for me!
Gittin' seasick, Square-head?
Drink up and forget it!
What's in your bottle?
Gin.
Dot's nigger trink.
Absinthe? It's doped. You'll go off your chump, Froggy!
Cochon!
Whisky, that's the ticket!
Where's Paddy?
Going asleep.
Sing us that whisky song, Paddy.

(*They all turn to an old, wizened Irishman who is dozing, very drunk, on the benches forward. His face is extremely monkey-like with all the sad, patient pathos of that animal in his small eyes.*)

Singa da song, Caruso Pat!
He's gettin' old. The drink is too much for him.
He's too drunk.

PADDY (*blinking about him, starts to his feet resentfully, swaying, holding on to the edge of a bunk*). I'm never too drunk to sing. 'Tis only when I'm dead to the world I'd be wishful to sing at all. (*With a sort of sad contempt.*) "Whisky, Johnny," ye want? A chanty, ye want? Now that's a queer wish from the ugly like of you, God help you. But no matther. (*He starts to sing in a thin, nasal, doleful tone:*)

Oh, whisky is the life of man!
Whisky! O Johnny! (*They all join in on this.*)

Oh, whisky is the life of man!
  Whisky for my Johnny! (*Again chorus.*)
Oh, whisky drove my old man mad!
  Whisky! O Johnny!
Oh, whisky drove my old man mad!
  Whisky for my Johnny!

YANK (*again turning around scornfully*). Aw hell! Nix on dat old sailing-ship stuff! All dat bull's dead, see? And you're dead, too, yuh damned old Harp, on'y yuh don't know it. Take it easy, see. Give us a rest. Nix on de loud noise. (*With a cynical grin.*) Can't youse see I'm tryin' to tink?

ALL (*repeating the word after him as one with the same cynical amused mockery*). Think! (*The chorused word has a brazen, metallic quality, as if their throats were phonograph horns. It is followed by a general uproar of hard, barking laughter.*)

VOICES. Don't be cracking your head wid ut, Yank.
You gat headache, py yingo!
One thing about it—it rhymes with drink!
Ha, ha, ha!
Drink, don't think!
Drink, don't think!
Drink, don't think!

(*A whole chorus of voices has taken up this refrain, stamping on the floor, pounding on the benches with fists.*)

YANK (*taking a gulp from his bottle—good-naturedly*). Aw right. Can de noise. I got yuh de foist time. (*The uproar subsides. A very drunken sentimental tenor begins to sing:*)

"Far away in Canada,
  Far across the sea,
There's a lass who fondly waits
  Making a home for me—"

YANK (*fiercely contemptuous*). Shut up, yuh lousey boob! Where d'yuh get dat tripe? Home? Home, hell! I'll make a home for yuh! I'll knock yuh dead. Home! T'hell wit home! Where d'yuh get dat tripe? Dis is home, see? What d'yuh want wit home? (*Proudly.*) I runned away from mine when I was a kid. On'y too glad to beat it, dat was me. Home was lickings for me, dat's all. But yuh can bet your shoit no one ain't never licked me since! Wanter try it, any of youse? Huh! I guess not. (*In a more placated but still contemptuous tone.*) Goils waitin' for yuh, huh? Aw, hell! Dat's all tripe. Dey don't wait for no one. Dey'd double-cross yuh for a nickel. Dey're all tarts, get me? Treat 'em rough, dat's me. To hell wit 'em. Tarts, dat's what, de whole bunch of 'em.

LONG (*very drunk, jumps on a bench excitedly, gesticulating with a bottle in his hand*). Listen 'ere, Comrades! Yank 'ere is right. 'E says this 'ere stinkin' ship is our 'ome. And 'e says as 'ome is 'ell. And 'e's right! This is 'ell. We lives in 'ell, Comrades—and right enough we'll die in it. (*Raging.*) And who's ter blame, I arsks yer? We ain't. We wasn't born this rotten way. All men is born free and ekal. That's in the bleedin' Bible, maties. But what d'they care for the Bible—them lazy, bloated swine what travels first cabin? Them's the ones. They dragged us down till we're on'y wage slaves in the bowels of a bloody ship, sweatin', burnin' up, eatin' coal-dust! Hit's them's ter blame—the damned capitalist clarss! (*There had been a gradual murmur of contemptuous resentment rising among the men until now he is interrupted by a storm of catcalls, hisses, boos, hard laughter.*)

VOICES. Turn it off!
Shut up!
Sit down!
Closa da face!
Tamn fool! (*Etc.*)

YANK (*standing up and glaring at Long*). Sit down before I knock yuh down! (*Long makes haste to efface himself. Yank goes on contemptuously.*) De Bible, huh? De Cap'tlist class, huh? Aw nix on dat Salvation Army-Socialist bull. Git a soap-box! Hire a hall! Come and be saved, huh? Jerk us to Jesus, huh? Aw g'wan! I've listened to lots of guys like you, see. Yuh're all wrong. Wanter know what I tink? Yuh ain't no good for no one. Yuh're de bunk. Yuh ain't got no noive, get me? Yuh're yellow, dat's what. Yellow, dat's you. Say! What's dem slobs in de foist cabin got to do wit us? We're better men dan dey are, ain't we? Sure! One of us guys could clean up de whole mob wit one mit. Put one of 'em down here for one watch in de stokehole, what'd happen? Dey'd carry him off on a stretcher. Dem boids don't amount to nothin'. Dey're just baggage. Who makes dis old tub run? Ain't it us guys? Well den, we belong, don't we? We belong and dey don't. Dat's all. (*A loud chorus of approval. Yank goes on.*) As for dis bein' hell

—aw, nuts! Yuh lost your noive, dat's what. Dis is a man's job, get me? It belongs. It runs dis tub. No stiffs need apply. But yuh're a stiff, see? Yuh're yellow, dat's you.

VOICES (*with a great hard pride in them*).
Right-o!
A man's job!
Talk is cheap, Long.
He never could hold up his end.
Divil take him!
Yank's right. We make it go.
Py Gott, Yank say right ting!
We don't need no one cryin' over us.
Makin' speeches.
Throw him out!
Yellow!
Chuck him overboard!
I'll break his jaw for him!

(*They crowd around Long threateningly.*)

YANK (*half good-natured again—contemptuously*). Aw, take it easy. Leave him alone. He ain't woith a punch. Drink up. Here's how, whoever owns dis. (*He takes a long swallow from his bottle. All drink with him. In a flash all is hilarious amiability again, back-slapping, loud talk, etc.*)

PADDY (*who has been sitting in a blinking, melancholy daze—suddenly cries out in a voice full of old sorrow*). We belong to this, you're saying? We make the ship to go, you're saying? Yerra then, that Almighty God have pity on us! (*His voice runs into the wail of a keen, he rocks back and forth on his bench. The men stare at him, startled and impressed in spite of themselves.*) Oh, to be back in the fine days of my youth, ochone! Oh, there was fine beautiful ships them days—clippers wid tall masts touching the sky—fine strong men in them—men that was sons of the sea as if 'twas the mother that bore them. Oh, the clean skins of them, and the clear eyes, the straight backs and full chests of them! Brave men they was, and bold men surely! We'd be sailing out, bound down round the Horn maybe. We'd be making sail in the dawn, with a fair breeze, singing a chanty song wid no care to it. And astern the land would be sinking low and dying out, but we'd give it no heed but a laugh, and never a look behind. For the day that was, was enough, for we was free men—and I'm thinking 'tis only slaves do be giving heed to the day that's gone or the day to come—until they're old like me. (*With a sort of religious exaltation.*) Oh, to be scudding south again wid the power of the Trade Wind driving her on steady through the nights and the days! Full sail on her! Nights and days! Nights when the foam of the wake would be flaming wid fire, when the sky'd be blazing and winking wid stars. Or the full of the moon maybe. Then you'd see her driving through the grey night, her sails stretching aloft all silver and white, not a sound on the deck, the lot of us dreaming dreams, till you'd believe 'twas no real ship at all you was on but a ghost ship like the Flying Dutchman they say does be roaming the seas for evermore widout touching a port. And there was the days, too. A warm sun on the clean decks. Sun warming the blood of you, and wind over the miles of shiny green ocean like strong drink to your lungs. Work—aye, hard work—but who'd mind that at all? Sure, you worked under the sky, and 'twas work wid skill and daring to it. And wid the day done, in the dog-watch, smoking me pipe at ease, the look out would be raising land maybe, and we'd see the mountains of South Americy wid the red fire of the setting sun painting their white tops and the clouds floating by them! (*His tone of exaltation ceases. He goes on mournfully.*) Yerra, what's the use of talking? 'Tis a dead man's whisper. (*To Yank resentfully.*) 'Twas them days men belonged to ships, not now. 'Twas them days a ship was part of the sea, and a man was part of a ship, and the sea joined all together and made it one. (*Scornfully.*) Is it one wid this you'd be, Yank—black smoke from the funnels smudging the sea, smudging the decks—the bloody engines pounding and throbbing and shaking—wid divil a sight of sun or a breath of clean air—choking our lungs wid coal-dust—breaking our backs and hearts in the hell of the stokehole—feeding the bloody furnace—feeding our lives along wid the coal, I'm thinking—caged in by steel from a sight of the sky like bloody apes in the Zoo! (*With a harsh laugh.*) Ho-ho, divil mend you! Is it to belong to that you're wishing? Is it a flesh and blood wheel of the engines you'd be?

YANK (*who has been listening with a contemptuous sneer, barks out the answer*). Sure ting! Dat's me! What about it?

PADDY (*as if to himself—with great sorrow*). Me time is past due. That a great wave wid sun in the heart of it may sweep me over the side sometime I'd be dreaming of the days that's gone!

YANK. Aw, yuh crazy Mick! (*He springs to

his feet and advances on Paddy threateningly—then stops, fighting some queer struggle within himself—lets his hands fall to his sides—contemptuously.) Aw, take it easy. Yuh're aw right at dat. Yuh're bugs, dat's all—nutty as a cuckoo. All dat tripe yuh been pullin'—Aw, dat's all right. On'y it's dead, get me ? Yuh don't belong no more, see. Yuh don't get de stuff. Yuh're too old. (*Disgustedly.*) But aw say, come up for air onct in a while, can't yuh ? See what's happened since yuh croaked. (*He suddenly bursts forth vehemently, growing more and more excited.*) Say ! Sure ! Sure I meant it ! What de hell— Say, lemme talk ! Hey ! Hey, you old Harp ! Hey, youse guys ! Say, listen to me—wait a moment—I gotter talk, see. I belong and he don't. He's dead but I'm livin'. Listen to me ! Sure I'm part of de engines ! Why de hell not ! Dey move, don't dey ? Dey're speed, ain't dey ? Dey smash trou, don't dey ? Twenty-five knots a' hour ! Dat's goin' some ! Dat's new stuff ! Dat belongs ! But him, he's too old. He gets dizzy. Say, listen. All dat crazy tripe about nights and days ; all dat crazy tripe about stars and moons ; all dat crazy tripe about suns and winds, fresh air and de rest of it —aw hell, dat's all a dope dream ! Hittin' de pipe of de past, dat's what he's doin'. He's old and don't belong no more. But me, I'm young ! I'm in de pink ! I move wit it ! It, get me ! I mean de ting dat's de guts of all dis. It ploughs trou all de tripe he's been sayin'. It blows dat up ! It knocks dat dead ! It slams dat offen de face of de oith ! It, get me ! De engines and de coal and de smoke and all de rest of it ! He can't breathe and swallow coal-dust, but I kin, see ? Dat's fresh air for me ! Dat's food for me ! I'm new, get me ? Hell in de stokehole ? Sure ! It takes a man to work in hell. Hell, sure, dat's my fav'rite climate. I eat it up ! I git fat on it ! It's me makes it hot ! It's me makes it roar ! It's me makes it move ! Sure, on'y for me everyting stops. It all goes dead, get me ? De noise and smoke and all de engines movin' de woild, dey stop. Dere ain't nothin' no more ! Dat's what I'm sayin'. Everyting else dat makes de woild move, somep'n makes it move. It can't move witout somep'n else, see ? Den yuh get down to me. I'm at de bottom, get me ! Dere ain't nothin' foither. I'm de end ! I'm de start ! I start somep'n and de woild moves ! It—dat's me !—de new dat's moiderin' de old ! I'm de ting in coal dat makes it boin ; I'm steam and oil for de engines ; I'm de ting in noise dat makes yuh hear it ; I'm smoke and express trains and steamers and factory whistles ; I'm de ting in gold dat makes it money ! And I'm what makes iron into steel ! Steel, dat stands for de whole ting ! And I'm steel —steel—steel ! I'm de muscles in steel, de punch behind it ! (*As he says this he pounds with his fist against the steel bunks. All the men, roused to a pitch of frenzied self-glorification by his speech, do likewise. There is a deafening metallic roar, through which Yank's voice can be heard bellowing.*) Slaves, hell ! We run de whole woiks. All de rich guys dat t'ink dey're somep'n, dey ain't nothin' ! Dey don't belong. But us guys, we're in de move, we're at de bottom, de whole ting is us ! (*Paddy from the start of Yank's speech has been taking one gulp after another from his bottle, at first frightenedly, as if he were afraid to listen, then desperately, as if to drown his senses, but finally has achieved complete indifferent, even amused, drunkenness. Yank sees his lips moving. He quells the uproar with a shout.*) Hey, youse guys, take it easy ! Wait a moment ! De nutty Harp is sayin' somep'n.

PADDY (*is heard now—throws his head back with a mocking burst of laughter*). Ho-ho-ho-ho-ho—

YANK (*drawing back his fist, with a snarl*). Aw ! Look out who yuh're givin' the bark !

PADDY (*begins to sing the "Miller of Dee" with enormous good-nature*) :

> " I care for nobody, no, not I,
> And nobody cares for me."

YANK (*good-natured himself in a flash, interrupts Paddy with a slap on the bare back like a report*). Dat's de stuff ! Now yuh're gettin' wise to somep'n. Care for nobody, dat's de dope ! To hell wit 'em all ! And nix on nobody else carin'. I kin care for myself, get me ! (*Eight bells sound, muffled, vibrating through the steel walls as if some enormous brazen gong were embedded in the heart of the ship. All the men jump up mechanically, file through the door silently close upon each other's heels in what is very like a prisoners' lockstep. Yank slaps Paddy on the back.*) Our watch, yuh old Harp ! (*Mockingly.*) Come on down in hell. Eat up de coal-dust. Drink in de heat. It's it, see ! Act like yuh liked it, yuh better—or croak yuhself.

PADDY (*with jovial defiance*). To the divil wid it ! I'll not report this watch. Let thim log me and be damned. I'm no slave the like of you. I'll be sittin' here at me ease, and drinking, and thinking, and dreaming dreams.

YANK (*contemptuously*). T'inkin' and dreamin',

what'll that get yuh? What's t'inkin' got to do wit it? We move, don't we? Speed, ain't it? Fog, dat's all you stand for. But we drive trou dat, don't we? We split dat up and smash trou—twenty-five knots a' hour! (*Turns his back on Paddy scornfully.*) Aw, yun make me sick! Yuh don't belong! (*He strides out the door in rear. Paddy hums to himself, blinking drowsily.*)

Curtain.

Scene II

SCENE. *Two days out. A section of the promenade deck. Mildred Douglas and her aunt are discovered reclining in deck-chairs. The former is a girl of twenty, slender, delicate, with a pale, pretty face marred by a self-conscious expression of disdainful superiority. She looks fretful, nervous and discontented, bored by her own anæmia. Her aunt is a pompous and proud—and fat—old lady. She is a type even to the point of a double chin and lorgnettes. She is dressed pretentiously, as if afraid her face alone would never indicate her position in life. Mildred is dressed all in white.*

The impression to be conveyed by this scene is one of the beautiful, vivid life of the sea all about—sunshine on the deck in a great flood, the fresh sea wind blowing across it. In the midst of this, these two, incongruous, artificial figures, inert and disharmonious, the elder like a grey lump of dough touched up with rouge, the younger looking as if the vitality of her stock had been sapped before she was conceived, so that she is the expression not of its life energy but merely of the artificialities that energy had won for itself in the spending.

MILDRED (*looking up with affected dreaminess*). How the black smoke swirls back against the sky! Is it not beautiful?

AUNT (*without looking up*). I dislike smoke of any kind.

MILDRED. My great-grandmother smoked a pipe—a clay pipe.

AUNT (*ruffling*). Vulgar!

MILDRED. She was too distant a relative to be vulgar. Time mellows pipes.

AUNT (*pretending boredom but irritated*). Did the sociology you took up at college teach you that—to play the ghoul on every possible occasion, excavating old bones? Why not let your great-grandmother rest in her grave?

MILDRED (*dreamily*). With her pipe beside her—puffing in Paradise.

AUNT (*with spite*). Yes, you are a natural born ghoul. You are even getting to look like one, my dear.

MILDRED (*in a passionless tone*). I detest you, aunt. (*Looking at her critically.*) Do you know what you remind me of? Of a cold pork pudding against a background of linoleum tablecloth in the kitchen of a—but the possibilities are wearisome. (*She closes her eyes.*)

AUNT (*with a bitter laugh*). Merci for your candour. But since I am and must be your chaperone—in appearance, at least—let us patch up some sort of armed truce. For my part you are quite free to indulge any pose of eccentricity that beguiles you—as long as you observe the amenities—

MILDRED (*drawling*). The inanities?

AUNT (*going on as if she hadn't heard*). After exhausting the morbid thrills of social service work on New York's East Side—how they must have hated you, by the way, the poor that you made so much poorer in their own eyes!—you are now bent on making your slumming international. Well, I hope Whitechapel will provide the needed nerve tonic. Do not ask me to chaperone you there, however. I told your father I would not. I loathe deformity. We will hire an army of detectives and you may investigate everything—they allow you to see.

MILDRED (*protesting with a trace of genuine earnestness*). Please do not mock at my attempts to discover how the other half lives. Give me credit for some sort of groping sincerity in that at least. I would like to help them. I would like to be some use in the world. Is it my fault I don't know how? I would like to be sincere, to touch life somewhere. (*With weary bitterness.*) But I'm afraid I have neither the vitality nor integrity. All that was burnt out in our stock before I was born. Grandfather's blast furnaces, flaming to the sky, melting steel, making millions—then father keeping those home fires burning, making more millions—and little me at the tail-end of it all. I'm a waste product in the Bessemer process—like the millions. Or rather, I inherit the acquired trait of the by-product, wealth, but none of the energy, none of the strength of the steel that made it. I am sired by gold and dammed by it, as they say at the race track—damned in more ways than one. (*She laughs mirthlessly.*)

AUNT (*unimpressed—superciliously*). You seem to be going in for sincerity to-day. It isn't becoming to you, really—except as an obvious pose. Be as artificial as you are, I advise. There's a sort of sincerity in that, you know. And, after all, you must confess you like that better.

MILDRED (*again affected and bored*). Yes, I suppose I do. Pardon me for my outburst. When a leopard complains of its spots, it must sound rather grotesque. (*In a mocking tone.*) Purr, little leopard. Purr, scratch, tear, kill, gorge yourself and be happy—only stay in the jungle where your spots are camouflage. In a cage they make you conspicuous.

AUNT. I don't know what you are talking about.

MILDRED. It would be rude to talk about anything to you. Let's just talk. (*She looks at her wrist watch.*) Well, thank goodness, it's about time for them to come for me. That ought to give me a new thrill, aunt.

AUNT (*affectedly troubled*). You don't mean to say you're really going? The dirt—the heat must be frightful—

MILDRED. Grandfather started as a puddler. I should have inherited an immunity to heat that would make a salamander shiver. It will be fun to put it to the test.

AUNT. But don't you have to have the captain's—or some one's—permission to visit the stokehole?

MILDRED (*with a triumphant smile*). I have it—both his and the chief engineer's. Oh, they didn't want to at first, in spite of my social service credentials. They didn't seem a bit anxious that I should investigate how the other half lives and works on a ship. So I had to tell them that my father, the president of Nazareth Steel, chairman of the board of directors of this line, had told me it would be all right.

AUNT. He didn't.

MILDRED. How naïve age makes one! But I said he did, aunt. I even said he had given me a letter to them—which I had lost. And they were afraid to take the chance that I might be lying. (*Excitedly.*) So it's ho! for the stokehole. The second engineer is to escort me. (*Looking at her watch again.*) It's time. And here he comes, I think.

(*The Second Engineer enters. He is a fine-looking man of thirty-five or so. He stops before the two and tips his cap, visibly embarrassed and ill at ease.*)

SECOND ENGINEER. Miss Douglas?

MILDRED. Yes. (*Throwing off her rugs and getting to her feet.*) Are we all ready to start?

SECOND ENGINEER. In just a second, ma'am. I'm waiting for the Fourth. He's coming along.

MILDRED (*with a scornful smile*). You don't care to shoulder this responsibility alone, is that it?

SECOND ENGINEER (*forcing a smile*). Two are better than one. (*Disturbed by her eyes, glances out to sea—blurts out.*) A fine day we're having.

MILDRED. Is it?

SECOND ENGINEER. A nice warm breeze—

MILDRED. It feels cold to me.

SECOND ENGINEER. But it's hot enough in the sun—

MILDRED. Not hot enough for me. I don't like Nature. I was never athletic.

SECOND ENGINEER (*forcing a smile*). Well, you'll find it hot enough where you're going.

MILDRED. Do you mean hell?

SECOND ENGINEER (*flabbergasted, decides to laugh*). Ho-ho! No, I mean the stokehole.

MILDRED. My grandfather was a puddler. He played with boiling steel.

SECOND ENGINEER (*all at sea—uneasily*). Is that so? Hum, you'll excuse me, ma'am, but are you intending to wear that dress?

MILDRED. Why not?

SECOND ENGINEER. You'll likely rub against oil and dirt. It can't be helped.

MILDRED. It doesn't matter. I have lots of white dresses.

SECOND ENGINEER. I have an old coat you might throw over—

MILDRED. I have fifty dresses like this. I will throw this one into the sea when I come back. That ought to wash it clean, don't you think?

SECOND ENGINEER (*doggedly*). There's ladders to climb down that are none too clean—and dark alley-ways—

MILDRED. I will wear this very dress and none other.

SECOND ENGINEER. No offence meant. It's none of my business. I was only warning you—

MILDRED. Warning? That sounds thrilling.

SECOND ENGINEER (*looking down the deck—with a sigh of relief*). There's the Fourth now. He's waiting for us. If you'll come—

MILDRED. Go on. I'll follow you. (*He goes. Mildred turns a mocking smile on her aunt.*) An oaf—but a handsome, virile oaf.

AUNT (*scornfully*). Poser!

MILDRED. Take care. He said there were dark alley-ways—

AUNT (*in the same tone*). Poser!

MILDRED (*biting her lips angrily*). You are right. But would that my millions were not so anæmically chaste!

AUNT. Yes, for a fresh pose I have no doubt you would drag the name of Douglas in the gutter!

MILDRED. From which it sprang. Good-bye, aunt. Don't pray too hard that I may fall into the fiery furnace.

AUNT. Poser!

MILDRED (*viciously*). Old hag! (*She slaps her aunt insultingly across the face and walks off, laughing gaily.*)

AUNT (*screams after her*). I said poser!

Curtain.

Scene III

SCENE. *The stokehole. In the rear, the dimly-outlined bulks of the furnaces and boilers. High overhead one hanging electric bulb sheds just enough light through the murky air laden with coal-dust to pile up masses of shadows everywhere. A line of men, stripped to the waist, is before the furnace doors. They bend over, looking neither to right nor left, handling their shovels as if they were part of their bodies, with a strange, awkward, swinging rhythm. They use the shovels to throw open the furnace doors. Then from these fiery round holes in the black a flood of terrific light and heat pours full upon the men who are outlined in silhouette in the crouching, inhuman attitudes of chained gorillas. The men shovel with a rhythmic motion, swinging as on a pivot from the coal which lies in heaps on the floor behind to hurl it into the flaming mouths before them. There is a tumult of noise—the brazen clang of the furnace doors as they are flung open or slammed shut, the grating, teeth-gritting grind of steel against steel, of crunching coal. This clash of sounds stuns one's ears with its rending dissonance. But there is order in it, rhythm, a mechanical, regulated recurrence, a tempo. And rising above all, making the air hum with the quiver of liberated energy, the roar of leaping flames in the furnaces, the monotonous throbbing beat of the engines.*

As the curtain rises, the furnace doors are shut. The men are taking a breathing spell. One or two are arranging the coal behind them, pulling it into more accessible heaps. The others can be dimly made out leaning on their shovels in relaxed attitudes of exhaustion.

PADDY (*from somewhere in the line—plaintively*). Yerra, will this divil's own watch nivir end? Me back is broke. I'm destroyed entirely.

YANK (*from the centre of the line—with exuberant scorn*). Aw, yuh make me sick! Lie down and croak, why don't yuh? Always beefin', dat's you! Say, dis is a cinch! Dis was made for me! It's my meat, get me! (*A whistle is blown—a thin, shrill note from somewhere overhead in the darkness. Yank curses without resentment.*) Dere's de damn engineer crackin' de whip. He tinks we're loafin'.

PADDY (*vindictively*). God stiffen him!

YANK (*in an exultant tone of command*). Come on, youse guys! Git into de game! She's gittin' hungry! Pile some grub in her! Trow it into her belly! Come on now, all of youse! Open her up! (*At this last all the men, who have followed his movements of getting into position, throw open their furnace doors with a deafening clang. The fiery light floods over their shoulders as they bend round for the coal. Rivulets of sooty sweat have traced maps on their backs. The enlarged muscles form bunches of high light and shadow.*)

YANK (*chanting a count as he shovels without seeming effort*). One—two—tree— (*His voice rising exultantly in the joy of battle.*) Dat's de stuff! Let her have it! All togedder now! Sling it into her! Let her ride! Shoot de piece now! Call de toin on her! Drive her into it! Feel her move! Watch her smoke! Speed, dat's her middle name! Give her coal, youse guys! Coal, dat's her booze! Drink it up, baby! Let's see yuh sprint! Dig in and gain a lap! Dere she go-o-es. (*This last in the chanting formula of the gallery gods at the six-day bike race. He slams his furnace door shut. The others do likewise with as much unison as their wearied bodies will permit. The effect is of one fiery eye after another being blotted out with a series of accompanying bangs.*)

PADDY (*groaning*). Me back is broke. I'm bate out—bate— (*There is a pause. Then the inexorable whistle sounds again from the dim regions above the electric light. There is a growl of cursing rage from all sides.*)

YANK (*shaking his fist upward—contemptuously*). Take it easy dere, you! Who d'yuh tinks runnin' dis game, me or you? When I git ready, we move. Not before! When I git ready, get me!

VOICES (*approvingly*). That's the stuff!
Yank tal him, py golly!
Yank ain't affeerd.
Goot poy, Yank!
Give him hell!
Tell 'im 'e's a bloody swine!
Bloody slave-driver!

YANK (*contemptuously*). He ain't got no noive. He's yellow, get me? All de engineers is yellow. Dey got streaks a mile wide. Aw, to hell wit him! Let's move, youse guys. We had a rest. Come on, she needs it! Give her pep! It ain't for him. Him and his whistle, dey don't belong. But we belong, see! We gotter feed de baby! Come on!

(*He turns and flings his furnace door open. They all follow his lead. At this instant the Second and Fourth Engineers enter from the darkness on the left with Mildred between them. She starts, turns paler, her pose is crumbling, she shivers with fright in spite of the blazing heat, but forces herself to leave the engineers and take a few steps nearer the men. She is right behind Yank. All this happens quickly while the men have their backs turned.*)

Come on, youse guys! (*He is turning to get coal when the whistle sounds again in a peremptory, irritating note. This drives Yank into a sudden fury. While the other men have turned full around and stopped dumbfounded by the spectacle of Mildred standing there in her white dress, Yank does not turn far enough to see her. Besides, his head is thrown back, he blinks upward through the murk trying to find the owner of the whistle, he brandishes his shovel murderously over his head in one hand, pounding on his chest, gorilla-like, with the other, shouting:*) Toin off dat whistle! Come down outa dere, yuh yellow, brass-buttoned, Belfast scut, yuh! Come down and I'll knock yer brains out! Yuh lousey, stinkin', yellow mut of a Catholic-moiderin' bastard! Come down and I'll moider yuh! Pullin' dat whistle on me, huh? I'll show yuh! I'll crash yer skull in! I'll drive yer teet' down yer troat! I'll slam yer nose trou de back of yer head! I'll cut yer guts out for a nickel, yuh lousey boob, yuh dirty, crummy, muck-eatin' son of a— (*Suddenly he becomes conscious of all the other men staring at something directly behind his back. He whirls defensively with a snarling, murderous growl, crouching to spring, his lips drawn back over his teeth, his small eyes gleaming ferociously. He sees Mildred, like a white apparition in the full light from the open furnace doors. He glares into her eyes, turned to stone. As for her, during his speech she has listened, paralysed with horror, terror, her whole personality crushed, beaten in, collapsed, by the terrific impact of this unknown, abysmal brutality, naked and shameless. As she looks at his gorilla face, as his eyes bore into hers, she utters a low, choking cry and shrinks away from him, putting both hands up before her eyes to shut out the sight of his face, to protect her own. This startles Yank to a reaction. His mouth falls open, his eyes grow bewildered.*)

MILDRED (*about to faint—to the Engineers, who now have her one by each arm—whimperingly*). Take me away! Oh, the filthy beast! (*She faints. They carry her quickly back, disappearing in the darkness at the left, rear. An iron door clangs shut. Rage and bewildered fury rush back on Yank. He feels himself insulted in some unknown fashion in the very heart of his pride. He roars:* God damn yuh! *And hurls his shovel after them at the door which has just closed. It hits the steel bulkhead with a clang and falls clattering on the steel floor. From overhead the whistle sounds again in a long, angry, insistent command.*)

Curtain

Scene IV

SCENE. *The firemen's forecastle. Yank's watch has just come off duty and had dinner. Their faces and bodies shine from a soap and water scrubbing, but around their eyes, where a hasty dousing does not touch, the coal-dust sticks like black make-up, giving them a queer, sinister expression. Yank has not washed either face or body. He stands out in contrast to them, a blackened, brooding figure. He is seated forward on a bench in the exact attitude of Rodin's "The Thinker." The others, most of them smoking pipes, are staring at Yank half-apprehensively, as if fearing an outburst; half-amusedly, as if they saw a joke somewhere that tickled them.*

VOICES. He ain't ate nothin'.
Py golly, a fallar gat gat grub in him.
Divil a lie.
Yank feeda da fire, no feeda da face.
Ha-ha.
He ain't even washed hisself.
He's forgot.
Hey, Yank, you forgot to wash.

YANK (*sullenly*). Forgot nothin'! To hell wit washin'.

VOICES. It'll stick to you.
It'll get under your skin.
Give yer the bleedin' itch, that's wot.
It makes spots on you—like a leopard.
Like a piebald nigger, you mean.
Better wash up, Yank.
You sleep better.
Wash up, Yank.
Wash up! Wash up!

YANK (*resentfully*). Aw say, youse guys. Lemme alone. Can't youse see I'm tryin' to tink?

ALL (*repeating the word after him as one with cynical mockery*). Think! (*The word has a brazen, metallic quality as if their throats were phonograph horns. It is followed by a chorus of hard, barking laughter.*)

YANK (*springing to his feet and glaring at them belligerently*). Yes, tink! Tink, dat's what I said! What about it! (*They are silent, puzzled by his sudden resentment at what used to be one of his jokes. Yank sits down again in the same attitude of "The Thinker."*)

VOICES. Leave him alone.
He's got a grouch on.
Why wouldn't he?

PADDY (*with a wink at the others*). Sure I know what's the matther. 'Tis aisy to see. He's fallen in love, I'm telling you.

ALL (*repeating the word after him as one with cynical mockery*). Love! (*The word has a brazen, metallic quality as if their throats were phonograph horns. It is followed by a chorus of hard, barking laughter.*)

YANK (*with a contemptuous snort*). Love, hell! Hate, dat's what. I've fallen in hate, get me?

PADDY (*philosophically*). 'Twould take a wise man to tell one from the other. (*With a bitter, ironical scorn, increasing as he goes on.*) But I'm telling you it's love that's in it. Sure what else but love for us poor bastes in the stokehole would be bringing a fine lady, dressed like a white quane, down a mile of ladders and steps to be havin' a look at us? (*A growl of anger goes up from all sides.*)

LONG (*jumping on a bench—hecticly*). Hinsultin' us! Hinsultin' us, the bloody cow! And them bloody engineers! What right 'as they got to be exhibitin' us 's if we was bleedin' monkeys in a menagerie? Did we sign for hinsults to our dignity as 'onest workers? Is that in the ship's articles? You kin bloody well bet it ain't! But I knows why they done it. I arsked a deck steward 'o she was and 'e told me. 'Er old man's a bleedin' millionaire, a bloody Capitalist! 'E's got enuf bloody gold to sink this bleedin' ship! 'E makes arf the bloody steel in the world! 'E owns this bloody boat! And you and me, comrades, we're 'is slaves! And the skipper and mates and engineers, they're 'is slaves! And she's 'is bloody daughter and we're all 'er slaves, too! And she gives 'er orders as 'ow she wants to see the bloody animals below decks and down they takes 'er! (*There is a roar of rage from all sides.*)

YANK (*blinking at him, bewildered*). Say! Wait a moment! Is all dat straight goods?

LONG. Straight as string! The bleedin' steward as waits on 'em, 'e told me about 'er. And what're we goin' ter do, I arsks yer? 'Ave we got ter swaller 'er hinsults like dogs? It ain't in the ship's articles. I tell yer we got a case. We kin go ter law—

YANK (*with abysmal contempt*). Hell! Law!

ALL (*repeating the word after him as one with cynical mockery*). Law! (*The word has a brazen, metallic quality as if their throats were phonograph horns. It is followed by a chorus of hard, barking laughter.*)

LONG (*feeling the ground slipping from under his feet—desperately*). As voters and citizens we kin force the bloody Governments—

YANK (*with abysmal contempt*). Hell! Governments!

ALL (*repeating the word after him as one with cynical mockery*). Governments! (*The word has a brazen, metallic quality as if their throats were phonograph horns. It is followed by a chorus of hard, barking laughter.*)

LONG (*hysterically*). We're free and equal in the sight of God—

YANK (*with abysmal contempt*). Hell! God!

ALL (*repeating the word after him as one with cynical mockery*). God! (*The word has a brazen, metallic quality as if their throats were phonograph horns. It is followed by a chorus of hard, barking laughter.*)

YANK (*witheringly*). Aw, join de Salvation Army!

ALL. Sit down! Shut up! Damn fool! Sea-lawyer! (*Long slinks back out of sight.*)

PADDY (*continuing the trend of his thoughts as if he had never been interrupted—bitterly*). And there she was standing behind us, and the Second pointing at us like a man you'd hear in a circus would be saying: In this cage is a queerer kind of baboon than ever you'd find in darkest Africy. We roast them in their own sweat—and be damned if you won't hear some of thim saying they like it! (*He glances scornfully at Yank.*)

YANK (*with a bewildered, uncertain growl*). Aw!

PADDY. And there was Yank roarin' curses and turning round wid his shovel to brain her—and she looked at him, and him at her—

YANK (*slowly*). She was all white. I tought she was a ghost. Sure.

PADDY (*with heavy, biting sarcasm*). 'Twas love at first sight, divil a doubt of it! If you'd seen the endearin' look on her pale mug when she shrivelled away with her hands over her eyes to shut out the sight of him! Sure, 'twas as if she'd seen a great hairy ape escaped from the Zoo!

YANK (*stung—with a growl of rage*). Aw!

PADDY. And the loving way Yank heaved his shovel at the skull of her, only she was out the door! (*A grin breaking over his face.*) 'Twas touching, I'm telling you! It put the touch of home, swate home in the stokehole. (*There is a roar of laughter from all.*)

YANK (*glaring at Paddy menacingly*). Aw, choke dat off, see!

PADDY (*not heeding him—to the others*). And her grabbin' at the Second's arm for protection. (*With a grotesque imitation of a woman's voice.*) Kiss me, Engineer dear, for it's dark down here and me old man's in Wall Street making money! Hug me tight, darlin', for I'm afeerd in the dark and me mother's on deck makin' eyes at the skipper! (*Another roar of laughter.*)

YANK (*threateningly*). Say! What yuh tryin' to do, kid me, yuh old Harp?

PADDY. Divil a bit! Ain't I wishin' myself you'd brained her?

YANK (*fiercely*). I'll brain her! I'll brain her yet, wait'n see! (*Coming over to Paddy—slowly.*) Say, is dat what she called me—a hairy ape?

PADDY. She looked it at you if she didn't say the word itself.

YANK (*grinning horribly*). Hairy ape, huh? Sure! Dat's de way she looked at me, aw right. Hairy ape! So dat's me, huh? (*Bursting into rage—as if she were still in front of him.*) Yuh skinny tart! Yuh white-faced slut, yuh! I'll show yuh who's a ape! (*Turning to the others, bewilderment seizing him again.*) Say, youse guys. I was bawlin' him out for pullin' de whistle on us. You heard me. And den I seen youse lookin' at somep'n and I tought he'd sneaked down to come up in back of me, and I hopped round to knock him dead wit de shovel. And dere she was wit de light on her! Christ, yuh could a-pushed me over with a finger! I was scared, get me? Sure! I tought she was a ghost, see? She was all in white like dey wrap around stiffs. You seen her. Kin yuh blame me? She didn't belong, dat's what. And den when I come to and seen it was a real skoit and seen de way she was lookin' at me—like Paddy said—Christ, I was sore, get me? I don't stand for dat stuff from nobody. And I flung de shovel—on'y she'd beat it. (*Furiously.*) I wished it'd banged her! I wished it'd knocked her block off!

LONG. And be 'anged for murder or 'lectrocuted? She ain't bleedin' well worth it.

YANK. I don't give a damn what! I'd be square wit her, wouldn't I? Tink I wanter let her put somep'n over on me? Tink I'm going to let her git away wit dat stuff? Yuh don't know me! No one ain't never put nothin' over on me and got away wit it, see!—not dat kind of stuff—no guy and no skoit neither! I'll fix her! Maybe she'll come down again—

VOICE. No chance, Yank. You scared her out of a year's growth.

YANK. I scared her? Why de hell should I scare her? Who de hell is she? Ain't she de same as me? Hairy ape, huh? (*With his old confident bravado.*) I'll show her I'm better'n her, if she on'y knew it. I belong and she don't, see! I move and she's dead! Twenty-five knots a hour, dats me! Dat carries her, but I make dat. She's on'y baggage. Sure! (*Again, bewildered.*) But, Christ, she was funny lookin'! Did yuh pipe her hands? White and skinny. Yuh could see de bones trough 'em. And her mush, dat was dead white, too. And her eyes, dey was like dey'd seen a ghost. Me, dat was! Sure! Hairy ape! Ghost, huh? Look at dat arm! (*He extends his right arm, swelling out the great muscles.*) I could a-took her wit dat, wit' just my little finger even, and broke her in two. (*Again, bewildered.*) Say, who is dat skoit, huh? What is she? What's she come from? Who made her? Who give her de noive to look at me like dat? Dis ting's got my goat right. I don't get her. She's new to me. What does a skoit like her mean, huh? She don't belong, get me! I can't see her. (*With growing anger.*) But one ting I'm wise to, aw right, aw right! Youse all kin bet your shoits I'll git even wit her. I'll show her if she tinks she— She grinds de organ and I'm on de string, huh? I'll fix her! Let her come down again and I'll fling her in de furnace! She'll move den! She won't shiver at nothin', den! Speed, dat'll be her! She'll belong den! (*He grins horribly.*)

PADDY. She'll never come. She's had her belly-full, I'm telling you. She'll be in bed now, I'm thinking, wid ten doctors and nurses feedin' her salts to clean the fear out of her.

YANK (*enraged*). Yuh tink I made her sick, too, do yuh? Just lookin' at me, huh? Hairy ape, huh? (*In a frenzy of rage.*) I'll fix her! I'll tell her where to git off! She'll git down on her knees and take it back or I'll bust de face offen her! (*Shaking one fist upward and beating on his chest with the other.*) I'll find yuh! I'm comin', d'you hear? I'll fix yuh, God damn yuh! (*He makes a rush for the door.*)

VOICES. Stop him!
He'll get shot!
He'll murder her!
Trip him up!
Hold him!
He's gone crazy!
Gott, he's strong!
Hold him down!
Look out for a kick!
Pin his arms!

(*They have all piled on him and, after a fierce struggle, by sheer weight of numbers have borne him to the floor just inside the door.*)

PADDY (*who has remained detached*). Kape him down till he's cooled off. (*Scornfully.*) Yerra, Yank, you're a great fool. Is it payin' attention at all you are to the like of that skinny sow widout one drop of rale blood in her?

YANK (*frenziedly, from the bottom of the heap*). She done me doit! She done me doit, didn't she? I'll git square wit her! I'll get her some way! Git offen me, youse guys! Lemme up! I'll show her who's a ape!

Curtain

Scene V

SCENE. *Three weeks later. A corner of Fifth Avenue on a fine Sunday morning. A general atmosphere of clean, well-tidied, wide street; a flood of mellow, tempered sunshine; gentle, genteel breezes. In the rear, the show windows of two shops, a jewellery establishment on the corner, a furrier's next to it. Here the adornments of extreme wealth are tantalizingly displayed. The jeweller's window is gaudy with glittering diamonds, emeralds, rubies, pearls, etc., fashioned in ornate tiaras, crowns, necklaces, collars, etc. From each piece hangs an enormous tag from which a dollar sign and numerals in intermittent electric lights wink out the incredible prices. The same in the furrier's. Rich furs of all varieties hang there bathed in a downpour of artificial light. The general effect is of a background of magnificence cheapened and made grotesque by commercialism, a background in tawdry disharmony with the clear light and sunshine on the street itself.*

Up the side street Yank and Long come swaggering. Long is dressed in shore clothes, wears a black tie and cloth cap. Yank is in his dirty dungarees. A fireman's cap with black peak is cocked defiantly on the side of his head. He has not shaved for days, and around his fierce, resentful eyes—as around those of Long to a lesser degree—the black smudge of coal-dust still sticks like make-up. They hesitate and stand together at the corner, swaggering, looking about them with a forced, defiant contempt.

LONG (*indicating it all with an oratorical gesture*). Well, 'ere we are. Fif' Avenoo. This 'ere's their bleedin' private lane, as yer might say. (*Bitterly.*) We're trespassers 'ere. Proletarians keep orf the grass!

YANK (*dully*). I don't see no grass, yuh boob. (*Staring at the pavement.*) Clean, ain't it? Yuh could eat a fried egg offen it. The white wings got some job sweepin' dis up. (*Looking up and down the avenue—surlily.*) Where's all de white-collar stiffs yuh said was here—and de skoits—*her* kind?

LONG. In church, blarst 'em! Arskin' Jesus to give 'em more money.

YANK. Choich, huh? I useter go to choich onct—sure—when I was a kid. Me old man and woman, dey made me. Dey never went demselves, dough. Always got too big a head on Sunday mornin', dat was dem. (*With a grin.*) Dey was scrappers for fair, bot' of dem. On Satiday nights when dey bot' got a skinful dey could put up a bout oughter been staged at de Garden. When dey got trough dere wasn't a chair or table wit a leg under it. Or else dey bot' jumped on me for somep'n. Dat was where I loined to take punishment. (*With a grin and a swagger.*) I'm a chip offen de old block, get me?

LONG. Did yer old man follow the sea?

YANK. Naw. Worked along shore. I runned away when me old lady croaked wit de tremens. I helped at truckin' and in de market. Den I shipped in de stokehole. Sure. Dat belongs. De rest was nothin'. (*Looking around him.*) I ain't never seen dis before. De Brooklyn waterfront, dat was where I was dragged up. (*Taking a deep breath.*) Dis ain't so bad at dat, huh?

LONG. Not bad? Well, we pays for it wiv our bloody sweat, if yer wants to know!

YANK (*with sudden angry disgust*). Aw, hell! I don't see no one, see—like her. All dis gives me a pain. It don't belong. Say, ain't dere a back-room around dis dump? Let's go shoot a ball. All dis is too clean and quiet and dolled-up, get me! It gives me a pain.

LONG. Wait and yer'll bloody well see—

YANK. I don't wait for no one. I keep on de move. Say, what yuh drag me up here for, anyway? Tryin' to kid me, yuh simp, yuh?

LONG. Yer wants to get back at her, don't yer? That's what yer been saying' every bloomin' 'our since she hinsulted yer.

YANK (*vehemently*). Sure ting I do! Didn't I try to git even wit her in Southampton? Didn't I sneak on de dock and wait for her by de gangplank? I was goin' to spit in her pale mug, see! Sure, right in her pop-eyes! Dat would a-made me even, see? But no chanct. Dere was a whole army of plain clothes bulls around. Dey spotted me and gimme de rush. I never seen her. But I'll git square wit her yet, you watch! (*Furiously.*) De lousey tart! She tinks she kin get away wit moider—but not wit me! I'll fix her! I'll tink of a way!

LONG (*as disgusted as he dares to be*). Ain't that why I brought yer up 'ere—to show yer? Yer been lookin' at this 'ere 'ole affair wrong. Yer been actin' an' talkin's if it was all a bleedin' personal matter between yer and that bloody cow. I wants to convince yer she was on'y a representative of 'er clarss. I wants to awaken yer bloody clarss consciousness. Then yer'll see it's 'er clarss yer've got to fight, not 'er alone. There's a 'ole mob of 'em like 'er, Gawd blind 'em!

YANK (*spitting on his hands—belligerently*). De more de merrier when I gits started. Bring on de gang!

LONG. Yer'll see 'em in arf a mo', when that church lets out. (*He turns and sees the window display in the two stores for the first time.*) Blimey! Look at that, will yer? (*They both walk back and stand looking in the jeweller's. Long flies into a fury.*) Just look at this 'ere bloomin' mess! Just look at it! Look at the bleedin' prices on 'em—more'n our 'old bloody stokehole makes in ten voyages sweatin' in 'ell! And they—her and her bloody clarss—buys 'em for toys to dangle on 'em! One of these 'ere would buy grub for a starvin' family for a year!

YANK. Aw, cut de sob stuff! T' hell wit de starvin' family! Yuh'll be passin' de hat to me next. (*With naïve admiration.*) Say, dem tings is pretty, huh? Bet yuh dey'd hock for a piece of change aw right. (*Then turning away, bored.*) But, aw hell, what good are dey? Let her have 'em. Dey don't belong no more'n she does. (*With a gesture of sweeping the jeweller's into oblivion.*) All dat don't count, get me?

LONG (*who has moved to the furrier's—indignantly*). And I s'pose this 'ere don't count neither—skins of poor, 'armless animals slaughtered so as 'er and 'ers can keep their bleedin' noses warm!

YANK (*who has been staring at something inside—with queer excitement*). Take a slant at dat! Give it de once-over! Monkey fur—two t'ousand bucks! (*Bewildered.*) Is dat straight goods—monkey fur? What de hell—

LONG (*bitterly*). It's straight enuf. (*With grim humour.*) They wouldn't bloody well pay that for a 'airy ape's skin—no, nor for the 'ole livin' ape with all 'is 'ead, and body, and soul thrown in!

YANK (*clenching his fists, his face growing pale with rage as if the skin in the window were a personal insult*). Trowin' it up in my face! Christ! I'll fix her!

LONG (*excitedly*). Church is out. 'Ere they come, the bleedin' swine. (*After a glance at Yank's lowering face—uneasily.*) Easy goes, Comrade. Keep yer bloomin' temper. Remember force defeats itself. It ain't our weapon. We must impress our demands through peaceful means—the votes of the on-marching proletarians of the bloody world!

YANK (*with abysmal contempt*). Votes, hell! Votes is a joke, see. Votes for women! Let dem do it!

LONG (*still more uneasily*). Calm, now. Treat 'em wiv the proper contempt. Observe the bleedin' parasites, but 'old yer 'orses.

YANK (*angrily*). Git away from me! Yuh're yellow, dat's what. Force, dat's me! De punch, dat's me every time, see!

(*The crowd from church enter from the right, sauntering slowly and affectedly, their heads held stiffly up, looking neither to right nor left, talking in toneless, simpering voices. The women are rouged, calcimined, dyed, overdressed to the nth degree. The men are in tail coats, tall hats, spats, canes, etc. A procession of gaudy marionettes, yet with something of the relentless horror of Frankensteins in their detached, mechanical unawareness.*)

VOICES. Dear Doctor Caiaphas! He is so sincere!
What was the sermon? I dozed off.
About the radicals, my dear—and the false doctrines that are being preached.
We must organize a hundred per cent American bazaar.
And let every one contribute one one-hundredth per cent of their income tax.
What an original idea!
We can devote the proceeds to rehabilitating the veil of the temple.
But that has been done so many times.

YANK (*glaring from one to the other of them—with an insulting snort of scorn*). Huh! Huh!

(*Without seeming to see him, they make wide detours to avoid the spot where he stands in the middle of the pavement.*)

LONG (*frightened*). Keep yer bloomin' mouth shut, I tells yer.

YANK (*viciously*). G'wan! Tell it to Sweeney! (*He swaggers away and deliberately lurches into a top-hatted gentleman, then glares at him pugnaciously.*) Say, who d'yuh tink yuh're bumpin'? Tink yuh own de oith?

GENTLEMAN (*coldly and affectedly*). I beg your pardon. (*He has not looked at Yank and passes on without a glance, leaving him bewildered.*)

LONG (*rushing up and grabbing Yank's arm*). 'Ere! Come away! This wasn't what I meant. Yer'll 'ave the bloody coppers down on us.

YANK (*savagely—giving him a push that sends him sprawling*). G'wan!

LONG (*picks himself up—hysterically*). I'll pop orf then. This ain't what I meant. And whatever 'appens, yer can't blame me. (*He slinks off left.*)

YANK. T' hell wit youse! (*He approaches a lady—with a vicious grin and a smirking wink.*) Hallo, Kiddo. How's every little ting? Got anyting on for to-night? I know an old boiler down to de docks we kin crawl into. (*The lady stalks by without a look, without a change of pace. Yank turns to others—insultingly.*) Holy smokes, what a mug! Go hide yuhself before de horses shy at yuh. Gee, pipe de heinie on dat one! Say, youse, yuh look like de stoin of a ferryboat. Paint and powder! All dolled up to kill! Yuh look like stiffs laid out for de boneyard! Aw, g'wan, de lot of youse! Yuh give me de eyeache. Yuh don't belong, get me! Look at me, why don't youse dare? I belong, dat's me! (*Pointing to a skyscraper across the street which is in process of construction—with bravado.*) See dat building goin' up dere? See de steel work? Steel, dat's me! Youse guys live on it and tink yuh're somep'n. But I'm *in* it, see! I'm de hoistin' engine dat makes it go up! I'm it—de inside and bottom of it! Sure! I'm steel and steam and smoke and de rest of it! It moves—speed—twenty-five stories up—and me at de top and bottom—movin'! Youse simps don't move. Yuh're on'y dolls I winds up to see'm spin. Yuh're de garbage, get me—de leavin's—de ashes we dump over de side! Now, what a-yuh got to say? (*But as they seem neither to see nor hear him, he flies into a fury.*) Pigs! Tarts! Bitches! (*He turns in a rage on the men, bumping viciously into them but not jarring them the least bit. Rather it is he who recoils after each collision. He keeps growling.*) Git off de oith! G'wan! Look where yuh're goin', can't yuh? Git out a-here! Fight, why don't yuh? Put up yer mits! Don't be a dog! Fight, or I'll knock yuh dead! (*But, without seeming to see him, they all answer with mechanical, affected politeness:*) I beg your pardon. (*Then at a cry from one of the women, they all scurry to the furrier's window.*)

THE WOMAN (*ecstatically, with a gasp of delight*). Monkey fur! (*The whole crowd of men and women chorus after her in the same tone of affected delight.*) Monkey fur!

YANK (*with a jerk of his head back on his shoulders, as if he had received a punch full in the face—raging*). I see yuh, all in white! I see yuh, yuh white-faced tart, yuh! Hairy ape, huh? I'll hairy ape yuh!

(*He bends down and grips at the street kerbing as if to pluck it out and hurl it. Foiled in this, snarling with passion, he leaps to the lamp-post on the corner and tries to pull it up for a club. Just at that moment a bus is heard rumbling up. A fat, high-hatted, spatted gentleman runs out from the side street. He calls out plaintively:* "Bus! Bus! Stop there!" *and runs full tilt into the bending, straining Yank, who is bowled off his balance.*)

YANK (*seeing a fight—with a roar of joy as he springs to his feet*). At last! Bus, huh? I'll bust yuh!

(*He lets drive a terrific swing, his fist landing full on the fat gentleman's face. But the gentleman stands unmoved as if nothing had happened.*)

GENTLEMAN. I beg your pardon. (*Then irritably.*) You have made me lose my bus. (*He claps his hands and begins to scream:*) Officer! Officer!

(*Many police whistles shrill out on the instant, and a whole platoon of policemen rush in on Yank from all sides. He tries to *fight, but is clubbed to the pavement and fallen upon. The crowd at the window have not moved or noticed this disturbance. The clanging gong of the patrol wagon approaches with a clamouring din.)*

Curtain

Scene VI

SCENE. *Night of the following day. A row of cells in the prison on Blackwells Island. The cells extend back diagonally from right front to left rear They do not stop, but disappear in the dark background as if they ran on, numberless, into infinity. One electric bulb from the low ceiling of the narrow corridor sheds its light through the heavy steel bars of the cell at the extreme front and reveals part of the interior. Yank can be seen within, crouched on the edge of his cot in the attitude of Rodin's "The Thinker." His face is spotted with black and blue bruises. A blood-stained bandage is wrapped around his head.*

YANK (*suddenly starting as if awakening from a dream, reaches out and shakes the bars—aloud to himself, wonderingly*). Steel. Dis is de Zoo, huh? (*A burst of hard, barking laughter comes from the unseen occupants of the cells, runs back down the tier, and abruptly ceases.*)

VOICES (*mockingly*). The Zoo? That's a new name for this coop—a damn good name!
Steel, eh? You said a mouthful. This is the old iron house.
Who is that boob talkin'?
He's the bloke they brung in out of his head. The bulls had beat him up fierce.

YANK (*dully*). I must a-been dreamin'. I tought I was in a cage at de Zoo—but de apes don't talk, do dey?

VOICES (*with mocking laughter*). You're in a cage aw right.
A coop!
A pen!
A sty!
A kennel! (*Hard laughter—a pause.*)
Say, guy! Who are you? No, never mind lying. What are you?
Yes, tell us your sad story. What's your game?
What did they jug yuh for?

YANK (*dully*). I was a fireman—stokin' on de liners. (*Then with sudden rage, rattling his cell bars.*) I'm a hairy ape, get me? And I'll bust youse all in de jaw if yuh don't lay off kiddin' me.

VOICES. Huh! You're a hard-boiled duck, ain't you!
When you spit, it bounces! (*Laughter.*)
Aw, can it. He's a regular guy. Ain't you?
What did he say he was—a ape?

YANK (*defiantly*). Sure ting! Ain't dat what youse all are—apes? (*A silence. Then a furious rattling of bars from down the corridor.*)

A VOICE (*thick with rage*). I'll show yuh who's a ape, yuh mut!

VOICES. Ssshh! Nix!
Can de noise!
Piano!
You'll have the guard down on us!

YANK (*scornfully*). De guard? Yuh mean de keeper, don't yuh? (*Angry exclamations from all the cells.*)

VOICE (*placatingly*). Aw, don't pay no attention to him. He's off his nut from the beatin'-up he got. Say, you guy! We're waitin' to hear what they landed you for—or ain't yuh tellin'?

YANK. Sure, I'll tell youse. Sure! Why de hell not? On'y—youse won't get me. Nobody gets me but me, see? I started to tell de Judge and all he says was: "Toity days to tink it over." Tink it over! Christ, dat's all I been doin' for weeks! (*After a pause.*) I was tryin' to git even wit some one, see?—some one dat done me doit.

VOICES (*cynically*). De old stuff, I bet. Your goil, huh?
Give yuh the double-cross, huh?
That's them every time!
Did yuh beat up de odder guy?

YANK (*disgustedly*). Aw, yuh're all wrong! Sure, dere was a skoit in it—but not what youse mean, not dat old tripe. Dis was a new kind of skoit. She was dolled up all in white—in de stokehole. I tought she was a ghost. Sure. (*A pause.*)

VOICES (*whispering*). Gee, he's still nutty.
Let him rave. It's fun listenin'.

YANK (*unheeding—groping in his thoughts*). Her hands—dey was skinny and white like dey wasn't real but painted on somep'n. Dere was a million miles from me to her—twenty-five knots a hour. She was like some dead ting de cat brung in. Sure, dat's what. She didn't belong. She belonged in de window of a toy store, or on de top of a garbage can, see! Sure! (*He breaks out angrily.*) But would yuh believe it, she had de noive to do me doit. She lamped me like she was seein' somep'n broke loose from de menagerie. Christ, yuh'd oughter seen her eyes! (*He rattles the bars of his cell furiously.*) But I'll get back at her yet, you watch! And if I can't find her I'll take it out on de gang she runs wit. I'm wise to where dey hangs out now. I'll show her who belongs! I'll show her who's in de move and who ain't. You watch my smoke!

VOICES (*serious and joking*). Dat's de talkin'!
Take her for all she's got!
What was this dame, anyway? Who was she, eh?

YANK. I dunno. First cabin stiff. Her old man's a millionare, dey says—name of Douglas.

VOICES. Douglas? That's the President of the Steel Trust, I bet.
Sure. I seen his mug in de papers.
He's filthy with dough.

VOICE. Hey, feller, take a tip from me. If you want to get back at that dame, you better join the Wobblies. You'll get some action then.

YANK. Wobblies? What de hell's dat?

VOICE. Ain't you ever heard of the I.W.W.?

YANK. Naw. What is it?

VOICE. A gang of blokes—a tough gang. I been readin' about 'em to-day in the paper. The guard give me the "Sunday Times." There's a long spiel about 'em. It's from a speech made in the Senate by a guy named Senator Queen. (*He is in the cell next to Yank's. There is a rustling of paper.*) Wait'll I see if I got light enough and I'll read you. Listen. (*He reads:*) "There is a menace existing in this country to-day which threatens the vitals of our fair Republic—as foul a menace against the very life-blood of the American Eagle as was the foul conspiracy of Cataline against the eagles of ancient Rome!"

VOICE (*disgustedly*). Aw hell! Tell him to salt de tail of dat eagle!

VOICE (*reading*). "I refer to that devil's brew of rascals, jailbirds, murderers and cut-throats who libel all honest working-men by calling themselves the Industrial Workers of the World; but in the light of their nefarious plots, I call them the Industrious *Wreckers* of the World!"

YANK (*with vengeful satisfaction*). Wreckers, dat's de right dope! Dat belongs! Me for dem!

VOICE. Ssshh! (*Reading.*) "This fiendish organization is a foul ulcer on the fair body of our Democracy—"

VOICE. Democracy, hell! Give him the boid, fellers—the raspberry! (*They do.*)

VOICE. Ssshh! (*Reading:*) "Like Cato I say to this Senate, the I.W.W. must be destroyed! For they represent an ever-present dagger pointed at the heart of the greatest nation the world has ever known, where all men are born free and equal, with equal opportunities to all, where the Founding Fathers have guaranteed to each one happiness, where Truth, Honour, Liberty, Justice, and the Brotherhood of Man are a religion absorbed with one's mother's milk, taught at our father's knee, sealed, signed, and stamped upon in the glorious Constitution of these United States!" (*A perfect storm of hisses, catcalls, boos, and hard laughter.*)

VOICES (*scornfully*). Hurrah for de Fort' of July!
Pass de hat!
Liberty!
Justice!
Honour!
Opportunity!
Brotherhood!

ALL (*with abysmal scorn*). Aw, hell!

VOICE. Give that Queen Senator guy the bark! All togedder now—one—two—tree— (*A terrific chorus of barking and yapping.*)

GUARD (*from a distance*). Quiet there, youse—or I'll git the hose. (*The noise subsides.*)

YANK (*with growling rage*). I'd like to catch dat senator guy alone for a second. I'd loin him some trute!

VOICE. Ssshh ! Here's where he gits down to cases on the Wobblies. (*Reads :*) " They plot with fire in one hand and dynamite in the other. They stop not before murder to gain their ends, nor at the outraging of defenceless womanhood. They would tear down society, put the lowest scum in the seats of the mighty, turn Almighty God's revealed plan for the world topsy-turvy, and make of our sweet and lovely civilization a shambles, a desolation, where man, God's masterpiece, would soon degenerate back to the ape ! "

VOICE (*to* YANK). Hey, you guy. There's your ape stuff again.

YANK (*with a growl of fury*). I got him. So dey blow up tings, do dey ? Dey turn tings round, do dey ? Hey, lend me dat paper, will yuh ?

VOICE. Sure. Give it to him. On'y keep it to yourself, see. We don't wanter listen to no more of that slop.

VOICE. Here you are. Hide it under your mattress.

YANK (*reaching out*). Tanks. I can't read much, but I kin manage. (*He sits, the paper in the hand at his side, in the attitude of Rodin's " The Thinker." A pause. Several snores from down the corridor. Suddenly Yank jumps to his feet with a furious groan as if some appalling thought had crashed on him.*) Sure—her old man—President of de Steel Trust—makes half de steel in de world—steel—where I tought I belonged—drivin' trou—movin'—in dat—to make *her*—and cage me in for her to spit on ! Christ. (*He shakes the bars of his cell door till the whole tier trembles. Irritated, protesting exclamations from those awakened or trying to get to sleep.*) He made dis—dis cage ! Steel ! *It* don't belong, dat's what ! Cages, cells, locks, bolts, bars—dat's what it means !—holdin' me down wit him at de top ! But I'll drive trou ! Fire, dat melts it ! I'll be fire—under de heap—fire dat never goes out—hot as hell—breakin' out in de night—

(*While he has been saying this last he has shaken his cell door to a clanging accompaniment. As he comes to the " breakin' out " he seizes one bar with both hands and, putting his two feet up against the others so that his position is parallel to the floor like a monkey's, he gives a great wrench backwards. The bar bends like a liquorice stick under his tremendous strength. Just at this moment the Prison Guard rushes in, dragging a hose behind him.*)

GUARD (*angrily*). I'll loin youse to wake me up ! (*Sees Yank.*) Hallo, it's you, huh ? Got the D.T's, hey ? Well, I'll cure 'em. I'll drown your snakes for yuh ! (*Noticing the bar.*) Hell, look at dat bar bended ! On'y a bug is strong enough for dat !

YANK (*glaring at him*). Or a hairy ape, yuh big yellow scut ! Look out ! Here I come ! (*He grabs another bar.*)

GUARD (*scared now—yelling off left*). Toin de hoose on, Ben !—full pressure ! And call de others—and a strait-jacket ! (*The curtain is falling. As it hides Yank from view, there is a splattering smash as the stream of water hits the steel of Yank's cell.*)

Curtain

Scene VII

SCENE. *Nearly a month later. An I.W.W. local near the waterfront, showing the interior of a front room on the ground-floor, and the street outside. Moonlight on the narrow street, buildings massed in black shadow. The interior of the room, which is general assembly room, office and reading room, resembles some dingy settlement boys' club. A desk and high stool are in one corner. A table with papers, stacks of pamphlets, chairs about it, is at centre. The whole is decidedly cheap, banal, commonplace and unmysterious as a room could well be. The secretary is perched on the stool making entries in a large ledger. An eye-shade casts his face into shadows. Eight or ten men, longshoremen, iron workers, and the like, are grouped about the table. Two are playing checkers. One is writing a letter. Most of them are smoking pipes. A big signboard is on the wall at the rear, " Industrial Workers of the World—Local No. 57."*

Yank comes down the street outside. He is dressed as in Scene V. He moves cautiously, mysteriously. He comes to a point opposite the door ; tiptoes softly up to it, listens, is impressed by the silence within, knocks carefully, as if he were guessing at the password to some secret rite.

Listens. No answer. Knocks again a bit louder. No answer. Knocks impatiently, much louder.

SECRETARY (*turning around on his stool*). What the devil is that—some one knocking? (*Shouts:*) Come in, why don't you?

(*All the men in the room look up. Yank opens the door slowly, gingerly, as if afraid of an ambush. He looks around for secret doors, mystery, is taken aback by the commonplaceness of the room and the men in it, thinks he may have gotten in the wrong place, then sees the signboard on the wall and is reassured.*)

YANK (*blurts out*). Hallo!

MEN (*reservedly*). Hallo!

YANK (*more easily*). I tought I'd bumped into de wrong dump.

SECRETARY (*scrutinizing him carefully*). Maybe you have. Are you a member?

YANK. Naw, not yet. Dat's what I come for—to join.

SECRETARY. That's easy. What's your job—longshore?

YANK. Naw. Fireman—stoker on de liners.

SECRETARY (*with satisfaction*). Welcome to our city. Glad to know you people are waking up at last. We haven't got many members in your line.

YANK. Naw. Dey're all dead to de woild.

SECRETARY. Well, you can help to wake 'em. What's your name? I'll make out your card.

YANK (*confused*). Name? Lemme tink.

SECRETARY (*sharply*). Don't you know your own name?

YANK. Sure; but I been just Yank for so long—Bob, dat's it—Bob Smith.

SECRETARY (*writing*). Robert Smith. (*Fills out the rest of card.*) Here you are. Cost you half a dollar.

YANK. Is dat all—four bits? Dat's easy. (*Gives the Secretary the money.*)

SECRETARY (*throwing it in drawer*). Thanks. Well, make yourself at home. No introductions needed. There's literature on the table. Take some of those pamphlets with you to distribute aboard ship. They may bring results. Sow the seed, only go about it right. Don't get caught and fired. We got plenty out of work. What we need is men who can hold their jobs—and work for us at the same time.

YANK. Sure. (*But he still stands, embarrassed and uneasy.*)

SECRETARY (*looking at him—curiously*). What did you knock for? Think we had a coon in uniform to open doors?

YANK. Naw. I tought it was locked—and dat yuh'd wanter give me the once-over trou a peep-hole or somep'n to see if I was right.

SECRETARY (*alert and suspicious, but with an easy laugh*). Think we were running a crap game? That door is never locked. What put that in your nut?

YANK (*with a knowing grin, convinced that this is all camouflage, a part of the secrecy*). Dis burg is full of bulls, ain't it?

SECRETARY (*sharply*). What have the cops got to do with us? We're breaking no laws.

YANK (*with a knowing wink*). Sure. Youse wouldn't for woilds. Sure. I'm wise to dat.

SECRETARY. You seem to be wise to a lot of stuff none of us knows about.

YANK (*with another wink*). Aw, dat's aw right, see. (*Then made a bit resentful by the suspicious glances from all sides.*) Aw, can it! Youse needn't put me trou de toid degree. Can't youse see I belong? Sure! I'm reg'lar. I'll stick, get me? I'll shoot de woiks for youse. Dat's why I wanted to join in.

SECRETARY (*breezily, feeling him out*). That's the right spirit. Only are you sure you understand what you've joined? It's all plain and above board; still, some guys get a wrong slant on us. (*Sharply.*) What's your notion of the purpose of the I.W.W.?

YANK. Aw, I know all about it.

SECRETARY (*sarcastically*). Well, give us some of your valuable information.

YANK (*cunningly*). I know enough not to speak out-a my toin. (*Then resentfully again.*) Aw, say! I'm reg'lar. I'm wise to de game. I know yuh got to watch your step wit a stranger. For all youse know, I might be a plain-clothes dick, or somep'n, dat's what yuh're tinkin', huh? Aw, forget it! I belong, see? Ask any guy down to de docks if I don't.

SECRETARY. Who said you didn't?

YANK. After I'm 'nitiated, I'll show yuh.

SECRETARY (*astounded*). Initiated? There's no initiation.

YANK (*disappointed*). Ain't there no password—no grip nor nothin'?

SECRETARY. What'd you think this is—the Elks—or the Black Hand?

YANK. De Elks, hell! De Black Hand, dey're a lot of yellow backstickin' Ginees. Naw. Dis is a man's gang, ain't it?

SECRETARY. You said it! That's why we stand on our two feet in the open. We got no secrets.

YANK (*surprised but admiringly*). Yuh mean to say yuh always run wide open—like dis?

SECRETARY. Exactly.

YANK. Den yuh sure got your noive wit youse!

SECRETARY (*sharply*). Just what was it made you want to join us? Come out with that straight.

YANK. Yuh call me? Well, I got noive, too! Here's my hand. Yuh wanter blow tings up don't yuh? Well, dat's me! I belong!

SECRETARY (*with pretended carelessness*). You mean, change the unequal conditions of society by legitimate direct action—or with dynamite?

YANK. Dynamite! Blow it offen de oith—steel—all de cages—all de factories, steamers, buildings, jails—de Steel Trust and all dat makes it go.

SECRETARY. So—that's your idea, eh? And did you have any special job in that line you wanted to propose to us?

(*He makes a sign to the men, who get up cautiously one by one and group behind Yank.*)

YANK (*boldly*). Sure, I'll come out wit it. I'll show youse I'm one of de gang. Dere's dat millionaire guy, Douglas—"

SECRETARY. President of the Steel Trust, you mean? Do you want to assassinate him?

YANK. Naw, dat don't get yuh nothin'. I mean blow up de factory, de woiks, where he makes de steel. Dat's what I'm after—to blow up de steel, knock all de steel in de woild up to de moon. Dat'll fix tings! (*Eagerly, with a touch of bravado.*) I'll do it by me lonesome! I'll show yuh! Tell me where his woiks is, how to git there, all de dope. Gimme de stuff, de old butter—and watch me do de rest! Watch de smoke and see it move! I don't give a damn if dey nab me—long as it's done! I'll soive life for it—and give 'em de laugh! (*Half to himself.*) And I'll write her a letter and tell her de hairy ape done it. Dat'll square tings.

SECRETARY (*stepping away from Yank*). Very interesting.

(*He gives a signal. The men, huskies all, throw themselves on Yank, and before he knows it they have his legs and arms pinioned. But he is too flabbergasted to make a struggle, anyway. They feel him over for weapons.*)

MAN. No gat, no knife. Shall we give him what's what and put the boots to him?

SECRETARY. No. He isn't worth the trouble we'd get into. He's too stupid. (*He comes closer and laughs mockingly in Yank's face.*) Ho-ho! By God, this is the biggest joke they've put up on us yet. Hey, you Joke! Who sent you—Burns or Pinkerton? No, by God, you're such a bonehead I'll bet you're in the Secret Service! Well, you dirty spy, you rotten agent provocator, you can go back and tell whatever skunk is paying you blood-money for betraying your brothers that he's wasting his coin. You couldn't catch a cold. And tell him that all he'll ever get on us, or ever has got, is just his own sneaking plots that he's framed up to put us in jail. We are what our manifesto says we are, neither more nor less—and we'll give him a copy of that any time he calls. And as for you—(*He glares scornfully at Yank, who is sunk in an oblivious stupor.*) Oh, hell, what's the use of talking? You're a brainless ape.

YANK (*aroused by the word to fierce but futile struggles*). What's dat, yuh Sheeny, yuh!

SECRETARY. Throw him out, boys.

(*In spite of his struggles, this is done with gusto and éclat. Propelled by several parting kicks, Yank lands sprawling in the middle of the narrow cobbled street. With a growl he starts to get up and storm the closed door, but stops bewildered by the confusion in his brain, pathetically impotent. He sits there, brooding, in as near to the attitude of Rodin's "Thinker" as he can get in his position.*)

YANK (*bitterly*). So dem boids don't tink I belong, neider. Aw, to hell wit 'em! Dey're in de wrong pew—de same old bull—soapboxes and Salvation Army—no guts! Cut out an hour offen de job a day and make me happy! Gimme a dollar more a day and make me happy! Tree square a day, and cauliflowers in de front yard—ekal rights—a woman and kids—a lousey vote—and I'm all fixed for Jesus, huh? Aw, hell! What does dat get yuh? Dis ting's in your inside, but it ain't your belly. Feedin' your face—sinkers and coffee—dat don't touch it. It's way down—at de bottom. Yuh can't grab it, and yuh can't stop it. It moves, and everyting moves. It stops and de whole woild stops. Dat's me now—I don't tick, see?—I'm a busted Ingersoll, dat's what. Steel was me, and I owned de woild. Now I ain't steel, and de woild owns me. Aw, hell! I can't see—it's all dark, get me? It's all wrong! (*He turns a bitter, mocking face up like an ape gibbering at the moon.*) Say, youse up dere, Man in de Moon, yuh look so wise, gimme de answer, huh? Slip me de inside dope, de information right from de stable—where do I get off at, huh?

A POLICEMAN (*who has come up the street in time to hear this last—with grim humour*). You'll get off at the station, you boob, if you don't get up out of that and keep movin'.

YANK (*looking up at him—with a hard, bitter laugh*). Sure! Lock me up! Put me in a cage! Dat's de on'y answer yuh know. G'wan, lock me up!

POLICEMAN. What you been doin'?

YANK. Enuf to gimme life for! I was born, see? Sure, dat's de charge. Write it in de blotter. I was born, get me!

POLICEMAN (*jocosely*). God pity your old woman! (*Then matter-of-fact.*) But I've no time for kidding. You're soused. I'd run you in but it's too long a walk to the station. Come on now, get up, or I'll fan your ears with this club. Beat it now! (*He hauls Yank to his feet.*)

YANK (*in a vague, mocking tone*). Say, where do I go from here?

POLICEMAN (*giving him a push—with a grin indifferently*). Go to hell.

Curtain

Scene VIII

SCENE. *Twilight of the next day. The monkey-house at the Zoo. One spot of clear, grey light falls on the front of one cage so that the interior can be seen. The other cages are vague, shrouded in shadow from which chatterings pitched in a conversational tone can be heard. On the one cage a sign from which the word "gorilla" stands out. The gigantic animal himself is seen squatting on his haunches on a bench in much the same attitude as Rodin's "Thinker." Yank enters from the left. Immediately a chorus of angry chattering and screeching breaks out. The gorilla turns his eyes, but makes no sound or move.*

YANK (*with a hard, bitter laugh*). Welcome to your city, huh? Hail, hail, de gang's all here! (*At the sound of his voice the chattering dies away into an attentive silence. Yank walks up to the gorilla's cage and, leaning over the railing, stares in at its occupant, who stares back at him, silent and motionless. There is a pause of dead stillness. Then Yank begins to talk in a friendly, confidential tone, half-mockingly, but with a deep undercurrent of sympathy.*) Say, yuh're some hard-lookin' guy, ain't yuh? I seen lots of tough nuts dat de gang called gorillas, but yuh're de foist real one I ever seen. Some chest yuh got, and shoulders, and dem arms and mits! I bet yuh got a punch in eider fist dat'd knock 'em all silly! (*This with genuine admiration. The gorilla, as if he understood, stands upright, swelling out his chest and pounding on it with his fist. Yank grins sympathetically.*) Sure, I get yuh. Yuh challenge de whole woild, huh? Yuh got what I was sayin' even if yuh muffed de woids. (*Then bitterness creeping in.*) And why wouldn't yuh get me? Ain't we both members of de same club—de Hairy Apes? (*They stare at each other—a pause—then Yank goes on slowly and bitterly.*) So yuh're what she seen when she looked at me, de white-faced tart! I was you to her, get me? On'y outa de cage—broke out—free to moider her, see? Sure! Dat's what she tought. She wasn't wise dat I was in a cage, too—worser'n yours—sure—a damn sight—'cause you got some chanct to bust loose—

but me— (*He grows confused.*) Aw, hell! It's all wrong, ain't it? (*A pause.*) I s'pose yuh wanter know what I'm doin' here, huh? I been warmin' a bench down to de Battery—ever since last night. Sure. I seen de sun come up. Dat was pretty, too—all red and pink and green. I was lookin' at de skyscrapers—steel—and all de ships comin' in, sailin' out, all over de oith—and dey was steel, too. De sun was warm, dey wasn't no clouds, and dere was a breeze blowin'. Sure, it was great stuff. I got it aw right—what Paddy said about dat bein' de right dope—on'y I couldn't get *in* it, see? I couldn't belong in dat. It was over my head. And I kept tinkin'—and den I beat it up here to see what youse was like. And I waited till dey was all gone to git yuh alone. Say, how d'yuh feel sittin' in dat pen all de time, havin' to stand for 'em comin' and starin' at yuh—de white-faced, skinny tarts and de boobs what marry 'em—makin' fun of yuh, laughin' at yuh, gittin' scared of yuh—damn 'em! (*He pounds on the rail with his fist. The gorilla rattles the bars of his cage and snarls. All the other monkeys set up an angry chattering in the darkness. Yank goes on excitedly.*) Sure! Dat's de way it hits me, too. On'y yuh're lucky, see? Yuh don't belong wit 'em and yuh know it. But me, I belong wit 'em—but I don't, see? Dey don't belong wit me, dat's what. Get me? Tinkin' is hard— (*He passes one hand across his forehead with a painful gesture. The gorilla growls impatiently. Yank goes on gropingly.*) It's dis way, what I'm drivin' at. Youse can sit and dope dream in de past, green woods, de jungle, and de rest of it. Den yuh belong and dey don't. Den yuh kin laugh at 'em, see? Yuh're de champ of de woild. But me—I ain't got no past to tink in, nor nothin' dat's comin', on'y what's now—and dat don't belong. Sure, you're de best off! Yuh can't tink, can yuh? Yuh can't talk neider. But I kin make a bluff at talkin' and tinkin'—a'most git away wit it—a'most!—and dat's where de joker comes in. (*He laughs.*) I ain't on oith and I ain't in Heaven, get me? I'm in de middle tryin' to separate 'em, takin' all de woist punches from bot' of 'em. Maybe dat's what dey call Hell, huh? But you, yuh're at de bottom. You belong! Sure! Yuh're de on'y one in de woild dat does, yuh lucky stiff! (*The gorilla growls proudly.*) And dat's why dey gotter put yuh in a cage, see? (*The gorilla roars angrily.*) Sure! Yuh get me. It beats it when you try to tink it or talk it—it's way down—deep—behind—you'n me we feel it. Sure! Bot' members of dis club! (*He laughs—then in a savage tone.*) What de hell! T' hell wit it! A little action, dat's our meat! Dat belongs! Knock 'em down and keep bustin' 'em till dey croaks yuh wit a gat—wit steel! Sure! Are yuh game? Dey've looked at youse, ain't dey—in a cage? Wanter git even? Wanter wind up like a sport 'stead of croakin' slow in dere? (*The gorilla roars an emphatic affirmative. Yank goes on with a sort of furious exaltation.*) Sure! Yuh're reg'lar! Yuh'll stick to de finish! Me'n you, huh?—bot' members of this club! We'll put up one last star bout dat'll knock 'em offen deir seats! Dey'll have to make de cages stronger after we're trou! (*The gorilla is straining at his bars, growling, hopping from one foot to the other. Yank takes a jimmy from under his coat and forces the lock on the cage door. He throws this open.*) Pardon from de governor! Step out and shake hands! I'll take yuh for a walk down Fif' Avenoo. We'll knock 'em offen de oith and croak wit de band playin'. Come on, Brother. (*The gorilla scrambles gingerly out of his cage. Goes to Yank and stands looking at him. Yank keeps his mocking tone—holds out his hand.*) Shake—de secret grip of our order. (*Something, the tone of mockery, perhaps, suddenly enrages the animal. With a spring he wraps his huge arms around Yank in a murderous hug. There is a crackling snap of crushed ribs—a gasping cry, still mocking, from Yank.*) Hey, I didn't say kiss me. (*The gorilla lets the crushed body slip to the floor; stands over it uncertainly, considering; then picks it up, throws it in the cage, shuts the door, and shuffles off menacingly into the darkness at left. A great uproar of frightened chattering and whimpering comes from the other cages. Then Yank moves, groaning, opening his eyes, and there is silence. He mutters painfully.*) Say—dey oughter match him—wit Zybszko. He got me, aw right. I'm trou. Even him didn't tink I belonged. (*Then, with sudden, passionate despair.*) Christ, where do I get off at? Where do I fit in? (*Checking himself as suddenly.*) Aw, what de hell! No squakin', see! No quittin', get me! Croak wit your boots on! (*He grabs hold of the bars of the cage and hauls himself painfully to his feet—looks around him, bewildered—forces a mocking laugh.*) In de cage, huh? (*In the strident tones of a circus barker.*) Ladies and gents, step forward and take a slant at de one and only—(*his voice weakening*)—one and original—Hairy Ape from de wilds of— (*He slips in a heap on the floor and dies. The monkeys set up a chattering, whimpering wail. And, perhaps, the Hairy Ape at last belongs.*

Curtain

THE FOUNTAIN

Characters

IBNU ASWAD, *a Moorish chieftain*
JUAN PONCE DE LEON
PEDRO, *his servant*
MARIA DE CORDOVA
LUIS DE ALVAREDO
YUSEF, *a Moorish minstrel*
DIEGO MENENDEZ, *a Franciscan*
VICENTE DE CORDOVA, *Maria's husband*
ALONZO DE OVIEDO, MANUEL DE CASTILLO, CRISTOVAL DE MENDOZA — *nobles*
A SOLDIER
FRIAR QUESADA, *a Franciscan*
BEATRIZ DE CORDOVA, *daughter of Maria and Vicente*
NANO, *an Indian chief*
A CHIEF OF THE INDIANS IN FLORIDA
A MEDICINE MAN
A FIGURE
A POET OF CATHAY
AN OLD INDIAN WOMAN OF THE BAHAMAS
A DOMINICAN MONK
FATHER SUPERIOR OF THE DOMINICANS IN CUBA
JUAN, *nephew of Juan Ponce de Leon*
Nobles, Monks, Soldiers, Sailors, Captive Indians of Porto Rico, Indians in Florida

Scenes

PART ONE

SCENE ONE Courtyard of the house of Ibnu Aswad, Granada, Spain. The night of the Moorish capitulation, 1492.

SCENE TWO Columbus's flagship on the last day of his second voyage, 1493.

PART TWO

SCENE THREE Courtyard of the Government House, Porto Rico, an afternoon twenty years or more later.

SCENE FOUR Cabinet of Bishop Menendez in the Government House. An evening three months later.

SCENE FIVE A prisoner's cell in the Government House. The same time.

SCENE SIX Same as Scene Three. Immediately follows Scene Five.

PART THREE

SCENE SEVEN A strip of beach on the Florida coast. A night four months later.

SCENE EIGHT The same. Noon the following day.

SCENE NINE A clearing in the forest. That night.

SCENE TEN The same, some hours later.

SCENE ELEVEN Courtyard of a Dominican monastery in Cuba. Several months later.

TIME: late fifteenth and early sixteenth centuries

SCENE ONE

SCENE. *Courtyard of Ibnu Aswad's palace in Granada.*

The section forms a right triangle, its apex at the rear, right. In the left, centre, a massive porte-cochère opens on the street. On the right, a door leading into the house itself. In the centre of the courtyard, a large splendid fountain of green marble with human and animal figures in gilt bronze. The peristyle of the gallery running around the court is supported by slender columns of polished marble, partly gilded. The interspaces above the horseshoe arches springing from the columns are filled with arabesques, texts from the Koran, red, blue and gold in colour. Above are the latticed windows of the women's apartments. Over the house-top a sky with stars can be seen. It is early night.

As the curtain rises, the court is empty and there is silence except for the splash of the fountain. Then a loud, imperious knocking, as of someone pounding with the hilt of a sword, is heard from the porte-cochère. Ibnu Aswad enters from the right. He is an elderly, noble-looking Moor, the lower part of his face covered by a long, white beard. His expression is one of great pride borne down by sorrow and humiliation. He goes out through the porte-cochère, and returns ushering in Juan Ponce de Leon and his servant, Pedro. Juan is a tall, handsome Spanish noble of thirty-one, dressed in full uniform. His countenance is haughty, full of a romantic adventurousness and courage; yet he gives the impression of disciplined ability, of a confident self-mastery – a romantic dreamer governed by the ambitious thinker in him. Pedro is a dull-looking young fellow.

JUAN (*as they enter*) (*to Aswad*). Your pardon, Sir Moor.

ASWAD (*haughtily*). You are quartered here? (*Juan bows in affirmation.*) Welcome then, since it is the will of Allah that you should conquer.

JUAN (*graciously*). I am no conqueror here. I am a stranger grateful for hospitality.

ASWAD (*unbending a bit*). You are kind. I have seen you in action on the field. You are brave. Defeat loses its bitterness when the foe is noble. (*Moodily and bitterly – staring at the fountain.*) The waters of the fountain fall – but ever they rise again, Sir Spaniard. Such is the decree of destiny. (*With fervour.*) Blessed be Allah who exalteth and debaseth the kings of the earth, according to his divine will, in whose fulfilment consists eternal justice. (*Fiercely and defiantly.*) Whosoever the victor, there is no conqueror but Allah!

JUAN (*stiffening – coldly*). Your fortitude does you honour. (*By way of dismissing the subject – abruptly.*) I am expecting friends. Will that disturb your household? If so –

ASWAD (*coldly*). My house is your house. It is decreed. (*He bows with stately grace and goes out, right.*)

JUAN (*makes a movement as if to detain him – then shrugs his shoulders*). What can I do for him? (*Ironically repeating Ibnu's inflexion.*) It is decreed by Spain if not by Allah. (*Seeing Pedro lolling against the wall, drowsily staring at the fountain – amused.*) Lazy lout! Does the fountain cause you, too, to dream? (*In a tone of command.*) Bring the wine. They will be here soon.

PEDRO. Yes, sir. (*He goes. Juan paces back and forth, humming to himself. Pedro returns and approaches his master cautiously – in a mysterious whisper.*) A lady, sir.

JUAN (*frowning*). Is she alone? (*Pedro nods, Juan smiles cynically.*) Surely you have mistaken her calling. Tell her I am not here.

(*As Pedro turns to go, Maria de Cordova appears in the arch of the porte-cochère. A heavy black veil is thrown over her face.*)

MARIA (*her voice forced and trembling*). Juan!

JUAN (*immediately the gallant cavalier, makes a motion for Pedro to leave, and bows low – mockery in his voice*). Beautiful lady, you do me an unmerited honour.

MARIA (*wearily*). Spare me your mockery, Juan.

(*She throws back her veil. She is a striking-looking woman of thirty-eight or forty, but discontent and sorrow have marked her age clearly on her face.*)

JUAN (*astonished*). Maria! (*Then with genuine alarm.*) In God's name!

MARIA (*her voice breaking*). Juan, I had to come.

JUAN (*sternly*). Your husband is my brother in arms. To-night – here – he is to be among my guests. I feel that every word we speak now degrades me in my honour.

MARIA (*in a tone of great grief*). You are cruel! I had to speak with you alone. This is my one chance. I leave the Court to-morrow.

JUAN (*with evident relief*). Ah.

MARIA (*stares at him with a pitiful appeal. He avoids her eyes*). Oh, what a fool I am – (*with a half-sob, as if the confession were wrung from her*) – to love you, Juan!

(*She makes a movement toward him, but he steps back, aloof and cold.*)

JUAN (*frowning*). That word – we have never uttered it before. You have always been – my friend. (*After a pause, with deep earnestness.*) Why must you ruin our rare friendship for a word that every minstrel mouths? (*Then with irritation.*) Love, love, love we chatter everlastingly. We pretend love alone is why we live! Bah! Life is nobler than the weak lies of poets – or it's nothing!

MARIA (*wounded and indignant*). If you had had to fight for love as you have fought for glory! –

JUAN (*struck by the pain in her tone, kneels and kisses her hand – remorsefully*). Forgive me! I would die rather than bring sorrow to a heart as kind as yours. Keep me for ever in that heart, I beg – but as a friend – as it has always been.

MARIA (*with a gasp of pain*). Ah! (*Taking her hand from his – with a deep sigh.*) God give you knowledge of the heart!

JUAN (*rises – plainly endeavouring to change the subject*). You are leaving the Court?

MARIA. The Queen has granted my wish to retire to Cordova. (*Passionately.*) I'm sick of the Court! I long for simple things! I pray to become worthy again of that pure love of God I knew as a girl. I must seek peace in Him! (*After a pause.*) Granada is ours. The Moors are driven from Spain. The wars are over. What will you do now, Juan?

JUAN. Peace means stagnation – a slack ease of cavaliers and songs and faded roses. I must go on.

MARIA. Where will you go?

JUAN (*smiles half-whimsically at an idea*). Perhaps with the Genoese, Christopher Columbus, when he sails to find the western passage to Cathay.

MARIA (*disturbed*). But they say he is mad.

JUAN (*seriously now*). Mad or not, he dreams of glory. I have heard he plans to conquer for Spain that immense realm of the Great Khan which Marco Polo saw.

MARIA. What! Abandon your career at Court now when your exploits have brought you in such favour? No one would ruin himself so senselessly save in despair! (*Jealously.*) It must be from love you are fleeing! (*Fiercely mocking.*) Is a woman avenging women? Tell me her name!

JUAN (*with a mocking laugh*). Love, love, and always love! Can no other motive exist for you? God pity women!

MARIA (*after a pause – sadly*). God pity me – because pity is what you offer me. (*As Juan seems about to protest wearily.*) Don't deny it, Juan. It sneers at me in your pretended scorn of love – You wish to comfort my humiliation! Am I a fool? Have you not loved others? I could name ten –

JUAN. Maria!

MARIA. Do you imagine I haven't guessed the truth? Those others had youth – while I – And my love seems to you – pitiable!

JUAN (*kneeling and taking her hand – with passionate earnestness*). No, dear friend, no! I swear to you! (*After a pause.*) What you call loves – they were merely moods – dreams of a night or two – lustful adventures – gestures of vanity, perhaps – but I have never loved. Spain is the mistress to whom I give my heart, Spain and my own ambitions, which are Spain's. Now do you understand?

MARIA (*sadly*). No, Juan. (*He rises.*) I understand that I am growing old – that love has passed for me – and that I suffer in my loneliness. Perhaps if God had granted me a child – But His justice punishes. He has seen my secret sin. I have loved you, Juan, for years. But it was only in the last year when my heart, feeling youth die, grew desperate that I dared let you see. And now, farewell, until God's will be done in death. We must not meet again.

JUAN (*sternly*). No. (*Passionately.*) I wish to God you had not told me this!

MARIA (*gently*). If you are still my friend you will not wish it. It was my final penance – that you should know. And, having told you, I am free, for my heart is dead. There is only my soul left that knows the love of God which blesses and does not torture. Farewell once more, Juan. (*He kneels and kisses her hand. She puts the other on his head as if blessing him.*) You are noble, the soul of courage, a man of men. You will go far, soldier of iron – and dreamer. God pity you if those two selves should ever clash! You shall have all my prayers for your success – but I shall add, Dear Saviour, let him know tenderness to recompense him when his hard youth dies! (*She turns quickly and goes out.*)

JUAN (*looks after her in melancholy thought for a while – then sighs deeply and shrugs his shoulders*). Time tarnishes even the pure, difficult things with common weakness.

(*Luis de Alvaredo enters through the porte-cochère. He is a dissipated-looking noble, a few years older than Juan. His face is homely but extremely fetching in its nobility, its expression of mocking fun and raillery. He is dressed carelessly, is slightly drunk.*)

LUIS (*mockingly*). Lover of glory, beloved of women, hail! (*He comes to the startled Juan as voices are heard from the porte-cochère – in a hurried, cautioning whisper.*) The devil, Juan! Have you lost your wits – or has she? I recognized her – and Vicente was only ten paces behind. (*Then again mockingly.*) Discretion, my stainless knight, discretion!

JUAN (*sternly*). Stop! You wrong her and me. (*Sounds of a loud, angry dispute are heard from without.*) What is that brawling?

LUIS. My Moor. (*Explaining hurriedly to Juan.*) A fellow poet – a minstrel of their common folk. We found him running amuck about the streets declaiming to the stars that their king, Abdallah, had sold his soul to hell when he surrendered. (*With admiration.*) By God, Juan, how he cursed! Oh, he's a precious songster, and as poet to poet I collared him and dragged him with us. Our friend, Diego, would have cut his throat for the Church's glory had I not interfered.

JUAN (*smiling*). As madman for madman, eh? But why bring him here to howl?

LUIS. He has a lute. It is my whim he should sing some verses (*With an amused grin.*) The dog speaks only Arabic. If he is wily, he will chant such curses on our heads as will blight that fountain dry – and no one of us but me will understand. (*With great glee.*) It will be sport, Juan! (*The clamour from outside grows more violent.*) By God, Diego will murder my minstrel – after all my pains. (*Starts to hurry out – stops in the entrance.*) Remember, Juan. Vicente may have recognized – the lady.

JUAN (*nods, frowning*). The devil take all women! (*Luis goes out. Pedro enters, carrying two large baskets full of bottles and sets them down, rear.*) Drink and forget sad nonsense. Bring out cushions. We will sit beside the fountain.

(*Pedro goes into the house, right. Luis re-enters, holding Yusef by the arm – a wizened old Moor dressed in the clothes of the common people, but wearing the turban signifying that he has made the pilgrimage to Mecca. His deep-set eyes smoulder with hatred, but physically he is so exhausted as to seem resigned to his fate. They are followed by Diego Menendez, a Franciscan monk, about the same age as Juan and Luis. He has a pale, long face, the thin, cruel mouth, the cold, self-obsessed eyes of the fanatic. Just now he is full of helpless fury and indignation. Accompanying him is Vicente de Cordova, a grey-haired, stern, soldierly noble of forty-five. Following them are the three nobles, Oviedo, Castillo and Mendoza. They are the type of adventurous cavaliers of the day – cruel, courageous to recklessness, practically uneducated – knights of the true Cross, ignorant of and despising every first principle of real Christianity – yet carrying the whole off with a picturesque air.*)

MENENDEZ (*angrily*). I protest to you, Juan. It is heresy to suffer this dog's presence when we offer thanks to God for victory.

JUAN (*stares at the Moor interestedly for a moment*

– then carelessly). I see no desecration, Diego – if he will sing, not howl. (*Turning to Vicente, scrutinizing his face keenly – carelessly.*) What do you say, Vicente?

VICENTE (*gives him a dark look of suspicion – coldly and meaningly*). I say nothing – now.

JUAN. Ah! (*He and Luis exchange a look.*)

OVIEDO. Well, I say let him remain. We may have sport with him.

CASTILLO (*with a cruel smile*). Perhaps with a sword-point we can persuade him to sing where the townsfolk hid their gold.

MENDOZA. Your words are inspired, Manuel!

LUIS (*scornfully*). Materialists! You would sack heaven and melt the moon for silver. Juan, where is your wine?

(*Pedro appears, bringing cushions and goblets for each. He uncorks the bottles and pours their goblets full. Scorning a goblet, Luis snatches a bottle from him and drinks from that.*)

JUAN (*keeping a wary eye on Vicente*). Let us drink. (*Takes a goblet from Pedro.*) To our most Gracious Sovereigns and to Spain! (*He drinks.*)

MENENDEZ. And to the Church! (*Angrily.*) But I will not drink until that infidel is moved apart!

VICENTE. I agree.

JUAN (*impatiently*). Let the Moor go, Luis – since Diego takes himself so seriously.

VICENTE (*coldly resentful*). And I? (*Juan is about to reply irritably when Luis breaks in hurriedly.*)

LUIS. Shhh! I'll sing a song for you. (*Releasing the Moor and pointing to the rear.*) Go, brother bard, and take your ease.

(*The Moor goes to the right, rear, and squats down in the shadow by the wall. Luis sings.*)

Love is a flower
For ever blooming.
Life is a fountain
For ever leaping
Upward to catch the golden sunlight,
Striving to reach the azure heaven;
Failing, falling,
Ever returning
To kiss the earth that the flower may live.

(*They all applaud as he finishes.*)

JUAN. Charming, Sir Poet – but a lie. (*Mockingly.*) Love, and love, and always love! The devil seize your flower! Do fountains flow only to nourish flowers that bloom a day and die?

LUIS. Roar, lion! You will not wake my dream that life is love!

JUAN. Listen to him, Diego! We know his only love is his old mother; and yet, to judge from his songs, you would think him a greater philanderer than – than –

VICENTE (*interrupting sneeringly*). Than you, Don Juan?

JUAN (*turning on him – coldly*). Gossip gives many a false name – but gossip only deludes old women.

VICENTE (*growing pale*). Do you intend that insult?

(*Their hands go to the hilt of their swords. The three nobles quicken to excited interest. Luis leaps between them.*)

LUIS. For God's sake! Is either of you a Moor? (*Raises his bottle.*) Let us drink again to Spain!

OVIEDO. And to the next war!

CASTILLO. May it be soon!

MENDOZA. With a world to sack! Sing us a song of that, Luis!

LUIS. I am too thirsty. But come, I was forgetting our infidel. Let me use persuasion –

(*He goes back to the Moor, and can be heard talking to him in Arabic.*)

JUAN. We were speaking of wars to come. With whom?

OVIEDO. With anyone!

JUAN. But guess. I think it will be in lands beyond strange seas – Cipango and Cathay – the cities of gold that Marco Polo saw.

OVIEDO. But who will lead us there?

JUAN. Why, Christopher Columbus. (*They all laugh.*)

CASTILLO. That Genoese mongrel! – to lead Spaniards!

MENDOZA. He's mad. He claims the earth is round – like an egg! (*They all laugh.*)

JUAN (*impressively*). I saw him to-day. He was riding his flea-bitten mule as if he were a Cæsar in a triumph. His eyes were full of golden cities.

CASTILLO. Bah, Juan, you romance! The man's an idiot!

LUIS (*coming back*). The more fool you to think so! He will yet find for Spain the Western Passage to the East.

CASTILLO. Or fall off the world's edge! I will wager you would not go with him for all the gold in Indies!

LUIS. You would lose!

JUAN. I'm planning to go. (*All are astonished.*) But not on his first voyage. Before I pledge my sword I must have proof that it can serve Spain's glory. There is no profit in staking life for dreams.

LUIS. There is no profit in anything but that! You're from the East, Moor. Tell us of the Great Khan, of Cipango and Cathay and Cambuluc, of golden roofs and emerald-studded lintels to the doors. Your people must have heard these wonders.

MENDOZA. Yes, let him sing of treasure. (*But the Moor remains silent.*)

LUIS. Wait, I'll talk to him. (*He goes back and speaks to the Moor in Arabic. The latter replies.*)

MENENDEZ (*furiously*). This is all treasonable. The dog had broken the peace. The punishment is death.

JUAN (*mockingly*). Let him sing of treasure, Diego. Even the Church loves gold.

LUIS (*coming back – exultantly*). He consents, Juan – because I am a colleague. He will sing of treasure in the East – a tale told to his father by some wandering poet who came from Cathay with a caravan. (*All except the outraged Diego and the sullen, preoccupied Vicente quicken to interested attention. The Moor strikes a few notes on his lute.*) Hush!

(*The Moor begins a crooning chant of verses, accompanying himself on the lute. At first they are all held by its strange rhythm, then they begin to betray impatience.*)

OVIEDO. By God, our wolf turns into a sick shepherd.

LUIS. Hush!

CASTILLO (*impatiently*). What does he sing?

LUIS (*enrapt – vaguely*). Hush, hush.

MENENDEZ (*rising to his feet as the Moor's recitative abruptly ends – harshly*). This is the service in a devil's mass!

LUIS (*passes his hand across his eyes, then stares into the fountain dreamily*). He sang of treasure – but strange to your longing. There is in some far country of the East – Cathay, Cipango, who knows – a spot that Nature has set apart from men and blessed with peace. It is a sacred grove where all things live in the old harmony they knew before man came. Beauty resides there and is articulate. Each sound is music, and every sight a vision. The trees bear golden fruit. And in the centre of the grove, there is a fountain – beautiful beyond human dreams, in whose rainbows all of life is mirrored. In that fountain's waters, young maidens play and sing and tend it everlastingly, for very joy in being one with it. This is the Fountain of Youth, he said. The wise men of that far-off land have known it many ages. They make it their last pilgrimage when sick with years and weary of their lives. Here they drink, and the years drop from them like a worn-out robe. Body and mind know youth again, and these young men, who had been old, leap up and join the handmaids' dance. Then they go back to life, but with hearts purified, and the old discords trouble them no more, but they are holy and the folk revere them. (*With a sigh.*) That's his tale, my friends – but he added it is hard to find that fountain. Only to the chosen does it reveal itself.

MENENDEZ (*furiously*). Idolatry!

OVIEDO. Is this his treasure! By God, he mocks us!

LUIS. Fools! Beauty is lost on you. Your souls clink like coppers. (*Menendez slinks back step by step toward the Moor. Luis grabs a bottle.*) Come, let us drink! We'll all to Cathay with Don Christopher. You can burrow for dung there – but I will search for this fountain.

JUAN (*drinking – a bit tipsily*). Drink and forget sad nonsense! The devil! His song beguiled me until you tricked it into that old woman's mumble. Youth! Is youth a treasure? Then are we all – except Vicente – priceless rich; and yet, God's blood, one has but to look to see how poor we are!

LUIS. Poor in spirit! I understand you, Juan.

JUAN. Fountain of youth, God help us, with love to boot! I wish he'd sung instead of the armies and power of the Great Khan! (*Then half-aside to Luis.*) The tale is always told to the wrong person. There was one here not long ago who would have given pearls for drops from that same fountain!

VICENTE (*who has crept vengefully toward Juan in time to hear these last words – with cold fury*). A moment ago you taunted me with age – and now you dare – (*He slaps Juan across the face. They draw their swords.*)

LUIS (*trying to intervene*). For God's sake, friends!

OVIEDO (*with excited interest*). A duel!

(*The others echo this. Suddenly there is a harsh shriek from the rear. Menendez appears from the shadow, dagger in hand, a look of fanatical triumph on his face. Forgetting the duel, the others stand appalled.*)

MENENDEZ (*sheathing the dagger*). I have slain the dog. It was high time.

LUIS. Miserable bigot!

(*Raging, he tries to throw himself at the monk, but Juan grasps him and forces him down on a cushion. He breaks down, weeping.*)

MENENDEZ (*coldly scornful*). What! A soldier of Christ weep for an infidel!

JUAN (*sternly*). Be still, Diego! (*Then frowning – curtly, in a tone of dismissal which silences all protest.*) Our revelling is under an ill star. There is blood upon it. Good-night. (*Turning to Vicente.*) Until to-morrow.

(*Vicente bows and goes, accompanied by Menendez. The young nobles troop out behind, disputing noisily about the coming duel.*)

JUAN (*comes over and puts his hand on Luis' shoulder – in a mocking, but comforting tone*). Come, Luis. Your brother romancer is dead. Tears will not help him. Perhaps even now he drinks of that Fountain of Youth in Dreamland – if he is not in hell.

LUIS (*raising his head*). Juan, why do you always sneer at beauty – while your heart calls you liar?

JUAN (*frowning*). I have Spain in my heart – and my ambition. All else is weakness. (*Changing his tone – carelessly.*) Well, you were right. Vicente recognized – and so, a duel. I'll prick him in the thigh and send him home to bed. She will nurse and love him then – and hate me for a murderer. Thus, all works out for the best in this fair world! But – a rare thing dies – and I'm sad, Luis. (*Shaking himself and taking a goblet of wine.*) Come, forget sad nonsense. We will drink to voyaging with Don Christopher – and to the battles before those golden cities of Cathay!

LUIS (*recovering his spirits – grabbing a bottle*). Lucifer fire your cities! I drink to my fountain!

JUAN. Your health, Sir Lying Poet!

LUIS. And yours, Sir Glory-Glutton!

(*They laugh, clink goblet and bottle, and drink as*

The Curtain Falls)

SCENE TWO

SCENE. *About a year later – Columbus's flagship on the last day of his second voyage. The section of the vessel shown reveals the main deck amidships, the mainmast, the mainsail with its Maltese Cross, the two higher decks of the poop, the lateen sail on the mizzenmast, etc. Wooden stairs on the starboard, near the bulwark, are the means of getting from one deck to another.*

It is the time just preceding the dawn. The ship is sailing steadily on a calm sea. There is a large lantern at the centre of the main deck, another low down in the rigging on the port side, another over the cross which hangs over the stern from the high poop. The ship is crowded with people. On the main deck are the nobles. They are dressed in rich uniforms, in armour. Most of them are asleep, lying sprawled on the deck, wrapped in their cloaks – or huddled in hunched attitudes, their backs propped against the mast or the bulwarks. But one small group has apparently been awake all night. They are sitting cross-legged, throwing dice by the light of the lantern. The faces of the gamesters are haggard and drawn, their eyes feverish. Prominent among them are Oviedo, Castillo, Mendoza and Luis.

On the first deck of the poop, the monks, all Franciscans, are lying asleep. Here, also, are four of the converted Indians Columbus is bringing back. They are dressed in incongruous costumes, half savage and half civilized. They are huddled in the right corner, not asleep, but frozen in a helpless apathy.

On the highest deck Juan is seen standing by the pilot who tends the helm.

LUIS (*excitedly*). Double or quits!

OVIEDO. Done. (*They play. Luis loses.*)

LUIS. I am ruined again! (*With a comical groan of despair.*) Fortune is a damned mercenary wench. She scorns the poor. (*Takes up the dice to throw.*) Once more!

OVIEDO (*grumblingly*). No. You owe me more than you can pay.

LUIS. I will soon be rich as Crœsus. Don Columbus says we will sight land to-day – the Indies, Isles of Spice, Cipango, Cathay, who knows what? I will stake my future wealth against yours. Come! One more cast for anything you wish.

OVIEDO (*dryly*). For gold – gold I can see and touch.

LUIS (*disgustedly*). The devil! I must borrow from Juan then. (*He gets to his feet.*)

OVIEDO. He will not thank you to wake him on a beggar's errand.

LUIS. Do you imagine he sleeps with his Promised Land so near? He is astern on the Admiral's poop keeping a watch of his own – for fear the lookout will miss Cathay!

CASTILLO. Juan is over-eager. He will make the Genoese jealous.

MENDOZA. Has already. It is plain Columbus slights him.

OVIEDO. From policy. He knows Juan is in disgrace at Court since the duel. Our admiral trims his sails to the wind.

CASTILLO. Juan paid dearly for Vicente's wound – a pin-prick that hardly drew blood.

MENDOZA. It was the scandal.

LUIS (*indignantly*). All false – the malice of envious tongues! Vicente himself apologized to Juan. As for the lady, when I was home in Cordova I saw her with Vicente. You could not find a more married pair. It was even rumoured they were to have a child – (*Juan has come down from the Admiral's poop, passed through the sleeping monks and now appears by the light of the lamp in the rigging at the head of the stairs to the main deck. Luis breaks off suddenly.*) Is that you, Juan? Come, be a brother. This son of luck (*he indicates Oviedo*) has won everything but my skin.

JUAN (*with a laugh*). Then stake the Fountain of Youth which you will find – to-morrow! Sold by the cask it should make you the richest man in Spain. (*The nobles laugh.*)

LUIS (*with real aversion*). What trader's scheming – from you! (*Then jokingly.*) Take care! When the pox of old age is on you will come begging to me! (*Then rattling the dice.*) But come, loan me gold for a last cast of revenge. (*Then with a sudden idea.*) And you throw for me. My star is behind a cloud.

OVIEDO. Not fair. Juan always wins.

JUAN (*frowning*). This is no time for gaming.

LUIS (*insistently*). Just once, Juan.

JUAN (*consenting unwillingly*). Only once. The stakes are yours. Let the cast be an augury for me.

(*He takes gold from his purse. He and Oviedo play. Oviedo wins and there is a murmur of astonishment.*)

OVIEDO (*exultantly*). I win. The first time I have ever beat you, Juan.

JUAN (*getting up*). A poor omen. (*Then mockingly.*) But here on the under side of earth these signs must run by opposites.

MENDOZA (*half frightenedly*). Can we be hanging head down and not know it?

CASTILLO. Bah! The Genoese made his first voyage safely. We cannot fall off, it seems.

OVIEDO. Columbus may be a liar.

MENDOZA (*savagely*). A low-born braggart! He displayed his origin in the hoggish demands he made on the crown. What could the Sovereigns be thinking of – to make this foreign upstart an Admiral and a Viceroy?

JUAN (*sternly rebuking*). It is not for us to question. (*He pauses – then adds.*) His enterprise has served Spain well. He is our commander. That is enough to know.

(*He turns his back on them and walks to the port side where he stands by the rigging looking out to sea. The nobles look after him for a moment in an abashed silence.*)

CASTILLO (*mockingly*). You are a perfect Christian, Juan – to love your enemy.

OVIEDO (*yawns*). Put out the lantern. Let us sleep. The dawn will wake us.

(*Mendoza puts out the lantern. All except Luis wrap themselves in their robes and lie down on the deck. Luis comes over to Juan.*)

LUIS (*scornfully*). Look at those clods. They would snore through the Last Judgment. (*Then as Juan is silent.*) What are you dreaming of – Cathay and glory?

JUAN. No. (*Then suddenly.*) When I came down I heard Vicente's name – and mention of a child. What were you saying?

LUIS. Gossip of Cordova. My mother told me Maria was having masses said that she might bear an heir – and the rumour was her prayers were answered.

JUAN (*with deep sincerity*). God grant it. She will be happy then. (*With an ironical laugh.*) Did I not tell you that night our duel would reconcile them? (*Soberly.*) But I pay. Well, what matter the cost if Maria wins happiness?

LUIS (*reassuringly*). One exploit and the Court will be at your feet again.

JUAN (*shaking his head*). We will be far from Spain – out of sight and mind. Columbus will be king here, and he and I are by nature antagonistic.

(*There is a noise from the higher deck of the poop. A tall figure can be made out coming up on deck there from the companionway. He moves back until the light from the lantern above the cross reveals him. It is Columbus. He is in full uniform but wears no hat on his long, white hair. A commanding figure of noble presence, the face full of the ardent, fixed enthusiasm of the religious devotee.*)

LUIS (*pulling Juan back into the shadow*). Speak the devil's name! (*They stand, watching and listening, but hidden from the poop.*)

COLUMBUS (*to the helmsman*). Have you held the course?

HELMSMAN. South-west by west, sir.

COLUMBUS (*peering about him*). Will the dawn never come? (*He comes to the edge of the deck and calls down where the monks are – in a low voice.*) Father Menendez. Are you awake?

MENENDEZ (*gets up quickly from among the sleeping monks*). I am here, your Excellency. (*He mounts to the deck above and stands waiting respectfully.*)

COLUMBUS (*begins in a blunt, perfunctory tone*). Toscanelli's map must be in error. We should have sighted land before. (*A pause. He paces back and forth.*) The sun will soon be up. It leaps from the darkness in these parts. (*A pause, then with evident irritation.*) A weary voyage, Father! The spirit of these nobles is perverse. They look on this voyage as an escapade in search of easy riches, not as a crusade for the glory of God.

MENENDEZ (*curtly*). They are brave. Many of them have proven their ability in war – Juan Ponce de Leon, for one.

COLUMBUS (*resentfully*). A bravo! A duellist!

LUIS (*in an indignant whisper*). The devil seize him!

JUAN (*grimly*). Another aftermath of that cursed duel!

MENENDEZ (*shortly*). You are unjust, Excellency.

COLUMBUS. Oh, I admit he possesses all the attributes but the one which alone gives them virtue – an humble piety. On this great quest there is no place for egotists who seek only selfish ends. We must all feel ourselves unworthy servants of God's Holy Will. (*Then breaking off – abruptly.*) But I did not call you to speak of him. (*After a pause – despondently.*) My soul is overburdened, Father.

MENENDEZ (*dryly*). You wish to confess?

COLUMBUS (*surprised*). Confess? (*Then in a loud, ringing tone.*) Yes, to all men! Their mouths are full of lies against me. They say the demands I made for my share of discovery prove my low-minded avarice. Knaves! What can they know of my heart? Is it for myself I desire wealth? No! But as a chosen instrument of God, Who led me to His Indies, I need the power that wealth can give. I need it for God's glory, not my own! (*More and more exaltedly.*) I have a dream, Father! Listen! From my earliest youth I have hated the infidel. I fought on the ships of Genoa against their corsairs and as I saw my city's commerce with the East cut off by their ruthlessness, I prayed for one glorious last Crusade that would reclaim the Mediterranean for Christendom and, most fervent prayer of all, regain from profanation the Holy Sepulchre of our Lord Jesus! (*He crosses himself. Menendez also. Then he hurries on exultantly.*) And now an answer is granted! With my share of the wealth from Indies, from Cipango and Cathay, I will fit out an army – the Last Crusade! I have promised it to His Holiness, the Pope – fifty thousand men, four thousand horse, with a like force to follow after five years. I shall reconquer the Blessed Tomb of Christ for the True Faith! And to that sacred end I devote my life and all my wealth and power! (*He stands looking up to heaven with the rapt gaze of a devotee.*)

MENENDEZ (*dryly*). Such a pious ambition does you honour.

JUAN (*unable to restrain himself, calls mockingly*). The Crusades are dead – and the wealth of the East is still unwon.

COLUMBUS (*stung – indignantly*). Who dares – ?

JUAN (*proudly*). A noble of Spain who thinks of her greatness while you dream of Genoa and Rome; a soldier of the present, not the ghost of a Crusader! (*Then with exasperated mockery.*) God's blood, have all our leaders become half monk? There was a time for that when we fought the Moor, but now a new era of world empire dawns for Spain. By living in the past you will consecrate her future to fanaticism!

COLUMBUS (*angrily*). Insolent!

JUAN (*vehemently*). No. I respect you, Columbus – but I have my vision, too. Spain can become the mistress of the world, greater than ancient Rome, if she can find leaders who will weld conquest to her, who will dare to govern with tolerance. (*He laughs a bitter, mocking laugh.*) But what a time to speak! Look at the men of this fleet – now when the East dawns for them! I agree with you, Don Christopher – a weary voyage! Adventurers lusting for loot to be had by a murder or two; nobles of Spain dreaming greedy visions of wealth to be theirs by birthright; monks itching for the rack to torture useful subjects of the Crown into slaves of the Church! And for leader to have you, Don Christopher – you who will pillage to resurrect the Crusades! Looters of the land, one and all! There is not one who will see it as an end to build upon! We will loot and loot and, weakened by looting, be easy prey for stronger looters. God pity this land until all looters perish from the earth! (*While he is speaking it has grown perceptibly lighter.*)

COLUMBUS (*furiously*). Who are you? Stand forth! You dare not!

JUAN (*jumps up to the lower level of the poop and advances to the ladder to the Admiral's poop – proudly*). It is I – Juan Ponce de Leon! Why should I not dare? Do you want men under your command – or lackeys?

COLUMBUS (*striving to control his rage*). Silence!

(*A wailing cry of "Land Ho" comes from the mainmast head. Immediately the same cry can be heard coming over the water from the other vessels of the fleet. Instantly all is confusion. Every one jumps to their feet, half awake, peering about bewilderedly. The four Indians sense what has happened and hang over the bulwark, staring over the seas with intense longing. A crowd of half-dressed sailors and rabble pour up from below decks. There is a babble of excited shouts. Columbus looks upward to see where the lookout is pointing, then turns to the horizon off the starboard bow. Juan leaps to the ratlines.*)

THE CROWD. Land! Land! Where? I heard the call. He shouted land! Is it Cathay? Where is he pointing? Look where the Admiral looks. When the sun comes – (*Suddenly the ship is flooded by shafts of golden crimson light. They all cry.*) The sun!

JUAN (*pointing*). There! I see! In a haze of gold and purple – Greater Spain!

ALL (*crowd to the starboard side and to the front.*

The Indians are pushed away, jostled, thrown aside contemptuously with imprecations until they are hunched disconsolately in the background in dumb terror and bewilderment). Where? I see! Where? There! There! Cathay. Cipango. Is it Cathay? Where are the golden cities? Where are the golden roofs? Is it Cipango? The Indies! The Isles of Spice! Marco Polo's land!

(*They all crowd, pushing and elbowing each other, craning their necks, the eyes of all, rabble, soldiers, nobles, priests, straining with the same greedy longing, the lust to loot.*)

JUAN (*exultantly*). Cathay or Cipango or the Isles of Spice, what difference? It shall be Greater Spain! (*The crowd cheers vociferously.*)

COLUMBUS (*trying to quell the tumult*). Silence, I say! (*Fixing his eyes sternly on Juan with undisguised hostility – rebukingly.*) The earth is God's! Give thanks to Him! Kneel, I command you! Raise the cross!

(*The monks raise their cross. They kneel, but the nobles and soldiers hesitate waiting for Juan as if they saw in him their true commander.*)

JUAN (*leaps down from the rigging, drawing his sword – with fierce exultance*). This is a cross too, a soldier's cross – the cross of Spain!

(*He sticks his sword-point into the deck before him. He kneels before it. All the nobles and soldiers do likewise with a great flourish of gestures and excited shouts. They are all kneeling with their quivering cross swords, hilts rising above their heads.*)

COLUMBUS (*from his knees – looking up to heaven devoutly*). Te Deum!

(*The monks begin to chant. All join in, their pent-up excitement giving to the hymn a hectic, nervous quality. Juan does not sing but stares at the land on the distant horizon.*)

Curtain

SCENE THREE

SCENE. *Twenty years or so later – the courtyard of the Governor's palace, Porto Rico. Flowers, shrubs, a coco-palm, orange and banana trees. A large, handsome fountain closely resembling that of Scene One, is at centre. Two marble benches are at front and rear of fountain. A narrow paved walk encircles the fountain basin, with other walks leading from it to the different entrances. Doors to the interior of the house are at left and right. The main entrance to the courtyard, opening on the road, is at rear centre.*

It is in the late, languid hours of a torrid afternoon. The courtyard bakes in the heat, the fountain shimmering in the heat-waves.

Juan is seated on the stone bench in front of the basin. He is dressed in the full uniform of his authority as Governor. His face is aged, lined, drawn. His hair and beard are grey. His expression and attitude are full of great weariness. His eyes stare straight before him blankly in a disillusioned dream. The lines about his compressed lips are bitter.

Luis enters from the left, rear. He is dressed in the robe of a Dominican monk. His face shows the years but it has achieved a calm, peaceful expression as if he were at last in harmony with himself. He comes down to Juan and puts a hand on his shoulder.

JUAN (*starts – then greets his friend with a smile*). Ah, it's you, reverend Father. (*He accents this last mockingly.*)

LUIS (*good-naturedly*). Yes, illustrious Governor. (*He sits beside Juan – with a laugh.*) You are like a sulky child, Juan. Come, is it not time, after five years, you forgave me for being a Dominican?

JUAN (*bitterly*). My friend deserting to my enemy!

LUIS (*protestingly*). Come, come! (*Then after a pause, with a sigh.*) You have always had the dream of Cathay. What had I? What had I done with life? – an aimless, posing rake, neither poet nor soldier, without place nor peace! I had no meaning even to myself until God awakened me to His Holy Will. Now I live in truth. You must renounce in order to possess.

JUAN. The world would be stale indeed if that were true! (*After a pause – irritably.*) I fight the battles; you monks steal the spoils! I seek to construct; you bind my hands and destroy!

LUIS (*remonstrating*). You speak of Diego and his kind.

JUAN (*frowning*). Whether you convert by clemency or he by cruelty, the result is the same. All this baptizing of Indians, this cramming the cross down their throats has proved a ruinous error. It crushes their spirits and weakens their bodies. They become burdens for Spain instead of valuable servitors.

LUIS. Your army crushed them first –

JUAN. They had to be conquered, but there I would have stopped. (*Then irritably.*) God's blood, here we are arguing about this same issue – for the thousandth time! It is too late. Talk is useless. (*With a weary sigh.*) We do what we must – and sand covers our bodies and our deeds. (*With a smile.*) And the afternoon is too hot, besides. Tell me some news. Will the fleet from Spain make port to-day?

LUIS. Just now I saw them rounding the point under full sail. They should anchor soon.

(*They are interrupted by the noise of several people approaching from outside. Oviedo and Friar Quesada, a Franciscan, enter, followed by the Indian chief, Nano, who is guarded by two soldiers with drawn swords. Quesada is a thin young monk with the sallow, gaunt face and burning eyes of a fanatic. Oviedo is aged but gives no evidence of having changed in character. Nano is a tall, powerfully built Indian of fifty or so. Although loaded down with chains, he carries himself erect with an air of aloof, stoical dignity. He wears a head-dress of feathers. His face and body are painted, ornaments are about his neck. He is naked except for a loin-cloth and moccasins.*)

QUESADA (*fiercely and arrogantly*). I demand justice on this dog!

JUAN (*freezing – proudly*). Demand?

QUESADA (*with ill-concealed hatred but awed by Juan's manner*). Pardon my zeal in the service of God, Your Excellency. I ask justice. (*Then defiantly.*) But it is not the Church's custom to be a suppliant.

JUAN. So much the worse – (*Sternly.*) What is this Indian's crime?

QUESADA. His tribe will not pay the tithes – and he himself has dared to refuse baptism!

JUAN (*coldly*). I'll question him. (*Then as Quesada hesitates, raging inwardly – sternly.*) You may go.

QUESADA (*controlling his rage, bows*). Yes, Your Excellency. (*He goes.*)

JUAN (*to Oviedo with a certain contempt*). You also have a charge against this Indian?

OVIEDO (*angrily*). A plea for justice! These dogs will not pay their taxes. And we who own estates cannot get them to work except by force, which you have arbitrarily curtailed. Then why not punish them by leasing their labour to us until their debt's wiped out? Thus the Government will be paid, and we will have workers for our mines and fields.

JUAN (*disgustedly*). Your brain is not inventive, Oviedo! You are well aware that is the same blunder which failed on Espaniola. It means slavery. It defeats its purpose. The Indians die under the lash – and your labour dies with them. (*Contemptuously.*) Do you think I am Columbus that you ask this folly of me?

OVIEDO (*haughtily*). You refuse? (*He goes to the rear where he turns – threateningly.*) Take care, Juan! There will come a day of reckoning – when Diego returns from Spain. (*He goes out.*)

JUAN (*frowning*). Diego? What do you mean?

OVIEDO (*with a revengeful smile*). Nothing. Adios, Don Juan. (*He goes out.*)

JUAN (*with a bitter laugh*). There you have it! Bah! What use – ? (*He suddenly seems to see Nano for the first time. They stare at each other.*) I was forgetting you. Are you not Nano, chief of the last tribe I conquered? (*As the Indian is silent – imperiously.*) Speak!

NANO. The devils were with you. Our villages were burned. Women and children were killed – my wives, my children!

JUAN (*frowning*). Contrary to my command.

But, again, what use? The dead are dead. It is too late. (*After a pause – with a sort of weary self-mockery.*) Have you ever heard of Cathay – Cipango? Do you know of vast countries to the west – many peoples – great villages with high walls – much gold?

NANO. I have heard.

JUAN (*surprised – eagerly*). Ah! Where are they? (*Nano points west.*)

LUIS (*amusedly*). Where the fountain of youth of my drunken days is located – in dreamland!

JUAN (*with a certain seriousness*). Do you know, they say there is a similar fountain legend among these tribes. (*Then to Nano with a mocking smile.*) My friend here is growing impatient waiting for immortality in heaven and would rather gain it here on earth –

LUIS. Juan!

JUAN. So tell him, O Mighty Chief, if there is not over there – a fountain – a spring – in which old men bathe or drink and become young warriors again?

NANO (*to both their surprise*). The tale is told. Not here. In my home – a land that never ends. Our priests told the tale. I was young then. I was captured in war and brought here. I was adopted. I have never returned.

JUAN (*lost in thought*). So? Where is this land, your home? (*Nano points as before.*) Where Cathay is? And the fountain – the spring – is there?

NANO (*after a moment's hesitation*). Yes. My people call it the Spring of Life.

LUIS (*whimsically*). A pretty title, indeed. (*Sceptically.*) But none can find it, I suppose?

NANO. Those the Gods love can find it.

JUAN (*scornfully*). Aha, that old trick of poets – evasion of facts! (*Turning to Luis.*) Do you remember the Moor that night in Granada? "Only to the chosen." Here is the echo! Bah! What jugglery! (*Then thoughtfully.*) But it is strange. Where there is so much smoke, there must be a spark of fire. The Moor traced his myth back to the East – Cathay – and now we discover it again – still in Cathay – circling the world – (*Then, as if ashamed of himself for taking it so seriously – carelessly.*) At all events, it is added evidence that Cathay is near. (*The boom of a cannon comes from the harbour.*)

LUIS. The fleet has anchored. Diego will soon be here. If you can give this Indian into my keeping I will attempt his conversion.

JUAN (*impatiently*). Until his case is investigated, he must go to prison. You may see him there. (*To Nano, sternly.*) If it is proven you have encouraged rebellion against Spain, you will be hung. Against any other charge I will try to save you. (*Summoning the soldiers.*) Guard. (*They salute and lead Nano out, left. Juan paces up and down in frowning thought.*) Diego! Did you hear Oviedo threaten me with him? What mischief will he bring from Spain this time, I wonder? The cursed spider! His intriguing will destroy all my work here – (*With impotent anger.*) And the fight is hopeless. His weapons are whispers. A man of honour stands disarmed. (*Intensely.*) Would to God this fleet brought me the King's patent to discover new lands! I would sail tomorrow for Cathay – or for the moon!

LUIS (*firmly*). Fight your battle here! This is your land. You conquered it.

JUAN. Columbus discovered it; and I still feel his influence, like a black fog, stifling me!

LUIS (*mollifyingly*). He is dead. Forgive. He suffered too much injustice to be just.

JUAN. How can my pride forgive? For years I held his solitary outposts; I suffered wounds and fevers; I fought the Indians for him while he went sailing for the Garden of Eden, the mines of Solomon, his Bible-crazed chimeras! He knew my honour would not permit my conspiring against him as others did. So he ignored my services and deliberately condemned me to obscurity! Never one mention of my name in his reports to Spain! It is only since his downfall – (*Breaking off.*) But this, too, is an old story. (*Then with sudden exasperation.*) Why should I not sail to find Cathay? He failed in that – but I would succeed! I am no visionary chasing rainbows. (*Desperately.*) I tell you I loathe this place! I loathe my petty authority! By God, I could sink all Porto Rico under the sea for one glimpse of Cathay!

LUIS (*alarmed*). Juan!

JUAN (*after a pause – ironically*). Well, do not fear that I will leave your precious island. The patent will never come – and if it did, there is a flaw – (*Despondently, with a great weariness.*) It is too late. Cathay is too far. I am too weary. I have fought small things so long that I am small. My spirit has rusted in chains for twenty years. Now it tends to accept them – to gain peace. (*With passionate yearning.*) If I could only feel again my old fire, my energy of heart and mind – ! If I could be once more the man who fought before Granada – ! But the fire smoulders. It merely warms my will to dream of the past. It no longer catches flame in deeds. (*With a desolate smile of self-pity.*) I begin to dread – another failure. I am too old to find Cathay.

(*Menendez appears in rear in time to hear this last. He is dressed in a Bishop's robes. He looks his years, but his expression of rabid fanaticism has changed to one, not less cruel, of the crafty schemer made complacent by a successful career, the oily intriguer of Church politics. He hesitates with a suspicious, inquisitive glance from one to the other – then advances with a forced air of joviality.*) What is this I hear? Too old? Tut-tut! This is heresy, Juan. (*The two turn, startled. Juan stares at him resentfully. Menendez exchanges a cold bow of condescension with Luis, then comes to Juan with outstretched hands, smiling oilily.*) Have you no greeting for me, old friend?

JUAN (*takes his hands perfunctorily – then sarcastically*). Who would expect you unattended – like any eavesdropping monk?

MENENDEZ (*unruffled*). My eagerness to see you. I have great news. I often spoke to the King about you. He now holds you in the highest esteem, and as a proof of his favour I bring you – (*Then with a sly smile.*) But, on second thought, I should not say, I bring you. That is reserved for a worthier hand!

JUAN (*impatiently*). I dislike mysteries.

MENENDEZ (*provokingly*). I will give you this hint out of respect for the old age you were lamenting! Prepare to welcome youth – and a prize you have sought for all your life in the Indies – a gift more welcome to you than wine was to Luis before he repented! (*With this parting gibe, he turns away.*) Pardon me if I leave you. I must make preparations – for this event. (*He bows mockingly and goes off right.*)

JUAN (*angrily*). Schemer! (*He paces up and down.*)

LUIS (*after pondering a moment – suddenly*). I have it! It must be your patent to explore! He has obtained it from the King – because he wishes to get rid of you here! You stand in his way – your policy of clemency. He wants to be dictator to introduce torture and slavery! Yet he is afraid to fight you openly, so what craftier scheme than to send you away contented, grateful for a gift, bribed without knowing it?

JUAN (*resentfully*). Then I will fool the fox! There is no compulsion in such a patent. (*Then confused.*) But – it would be my highest hope come true – too late! Too late! I am too old. (*With an attempt at a railing tone.*) God's blood, I need to find Cathay – if your Fountain of Youth is there!

LUIS. I hear a crowd coming. I must go. It adds to their spleen to find us together. (*He presses Juan's hand.*) Whatever comes, be firm, old friend.

(*He goes out left. The murmur of the crowd increases. Juan sinks on the bench before the fountain, oblivious to it, lost in gloomy thought. Beatriz de Cordova appears, attended by her duenna and a crowd of richly dressed nobles. She is a beautiful young girl of eighteen or so, the personification of youthful vitality, charm and grace. The nobles point out Juan to her. She dismisses them, motioning for them to be quiet – then comes in and approaches Juan, keeping the fountain between them. She holds a sealed document in her hand. Finally she calls in a trembling, eager voice.*)

BEATRIZ. Don Juan!

(*Juan whirls on his bench and stares through the fountain at her. He utters a stunned exclamation as if he saw a ghost. His eyes are held fascinated by her beauty. Then suddenly she laughs – a gay, liquid, clear note – and coming quickly around confronts him.*) It is I, Don Juan.

JUAN (*stares at her still fascinated – then, reminded, springs to his feet and bows low with his old mocking gallantry*). Pardon! I am bewitched! I thought you were the spirit of the fountain. (*Then more mockingly.*) Beautiful lady, you do me unmerited honour!

BEATRIZ (*hurt and confused by his tone*). You don't know me? Why, I'm Beatriz. (*As he bows but shows no recognition.*) Has Bishop Menendez not told you – ?

JUAN (*suspiciously*). Nothing of you, my lady.

BEATRIZ. I am Beatriz de Cordova –

JUAN (*guessing – amazed, stares at her – a pause, slowly*). Maria's child! – you!

BEATRIZ (*letting it all pour forth regardless*). She died a year ago – and – I am your ward now. It was her last wish. My father was dead. There was no near relative whom she would trust. I asked the King to send me here to you. He bade me wait until the Bishop could escort me. He made me the bearer of this gift for you – your dearest wish, he said. (*She gives him the document.*)

JUAN (*unrolls it – a pause as he stares at it dully, then bitterly*). The patent – to find Cathay!

BEATRIZ. Yes! And you can find it where the others failed, I know! You were my dear mother's ideal of Spanish chivalry, of a true knight of the Cross! That was her prophecy, that you would be the first to reach Cathay!

JUAN. She spoke of the man she knew. (*Staring at her fascinatedly – eagerly.*) She sends me you – and you are youth! Is it in mockery?

BEATRIZ (*suddenly*). Oh, Don Juan, I recall something she said I must remember when we should meet. "Bring him tenderness," she said. "That will repay the debt I owe him for saving me for you." She said these words were secrets to tell you alone. What did she mean, Don Juan?

JUAN (*deeply moved*). Tenderness? Do you bring me that, Beatriz? (*Then as if recalling himself.*) No, do not – for it means weakness. Bring me the past instead. Give me back – the man your mother knew.

BEATRIZ (*who has been scrutinizing him without paying attentionto his words*). You are older than I dreamed, Don Juan.

JUAN (*wounded – with harsh violence*). No tenderness there! Youth! A cuirass of shining steel! A glittering sword! Laughter above the battle! (*Then seeing her look of frightened astonishment at his wild words, he controls himself and adds with a melancholy bitterness.*) It was so long ago, Beatriz – that night in Granada – a dimly-remembered dream – (*Then with a sudden return of his mockingly gallant manner.*) Forgive me. I have become a savage lost to manners. (*He kneels and kisses her hand with all his old-time gallantry.*) Welcome, dear ward, to Porto Rico!

(*She looks down at his bowed head, blushing with pleasure and naïve embarrassment, as*

The Curtain Falls)

SCENE FOUR

SCENE. *Three months later – Menendez' official study in the palace – a large, high-ceilinged, bare room with a heavy table at centre. The colour scheme is dark and gloomy, the atmosphere that of a rigid, narrow ecclesiasticism. In one corner is an altar with high candles burning before it. Heavy hangings shut out the light from the lofty, arched windows. An enormous crucifix hangs on the wall in rear. The room is like an exaggerated monk's cell, but it possesses a sombre power over the imagination by the force of its concentration. There is a main entrance at rear, centre, and a smaller side door at left, hidden by curtains.*

It is early evening. Menendez is seated at the table. He is frowningly impatient, listening and waiting for some one. There is the sound of approaching footsteps. Menendez turns eagerly in his chair. Quesada enters through the hangings on the left. His face is ominous and set. He wears a sword and pistols over his robe which is tucked up over high riding boots and spurs. He is covered with dust, and has evidently been riding hard. He bows respectfully to Menendez.

MENENDEZ. I had begun to think you would never come. (*Then with anxiety.*) What news?

QUESADA. The meeting is being held. They have gathered in the fort outside the town.

MENENDEZ. Good! It is moving according to my plan, then.

QUESADA. They all agree that Don Juan must resign his patent.

MENENDEZ. Unless he sails to find Cathay at once?

QUESADA. Yes. They are all mad for the gold (*with a sneer*) over there, the report of which I have had rumoured about, as you directed.

MENENDEZ. Good. Then we shall be rid of Juan and all the discontented spirits on the island at one stroke!

QUESADA (*excitedly*). But they also demand that first the Indian, Nano, must be burned at the stake. They believe he has bewitched the Governor. They know of Don Juan's secret interviews with him.

MENENDEZ (*angrily*). Who told them?

QUESADA (*after a moment's hesitation – defiantly*). I did.

MENENDEZ (*angrily*). Fool!

QUESADA (*alarmed – humbly*). But the dog still refuses baptism.

MENENDEZ (*sternly*). Is this a time to consider one Indian? Idiot! You know as well as I that my intention has been to attack Juan on one issue, and only one – his failure to sail for Cathay now that he has the King's patent. What have all the Nanos, hung or unhung, to do with that?

QUESADA. Much! If Don Juan were not bewitched by Nano's spells, he would have sailed long since.

MENENDEZ. And you told the rabble that? God pardon you! Was it any part of my orders that you should play upon the mob's lust for blood? I have worked for a peaceable revolt that would awaken Juan to his weakness and shame him into leaving. You have dared to evoke a madness which might easily sweep away all recognized authority. Quick! What was the rabble's mood when you left? (*Quesada avoids his eyes. Menendez pounds the table.*) Answer me!

QUESADA (*evasively*). They had been drinking –

MENENDEZ (*furiously, a note of alarm creeping in*). Ah!

QUESADA (*now thoroughly cowed*). They were clamouring to march on the palace. Don Oviedo was trying to restrain them –

MENENDEZ (*fiercely – with bitter scorn*). You cursed blunderer! No, I am the dolt for having trusted you!

QUESADA (*kneeling – cowed*). Forgive me, Your Grace!

MENENDEZ. Your action was treachery to me! And I shall punish you! When this expedition sails for that golden fable, Cathay, you shall go with it. Then blunder all you like! (*He rises and strides to the window at rear.*)

QUESADA (*humbly*). I humbly accept my penance.

MENENDEZ (*bitterly*). Behold the first fruits of your excessive piety! (*He points.*) The southern horizon is aflame!

QUESADA (*rising*). They must have set fire to the Indian villages.

MENENDEZ. Blood and fire! Your merry dance begins well! (*He lets the curtains fall back.*) Only Juan can control them now – if he would only promise them to sail at once – but no, he is too proud. He will fight armed rebellion to the last – and we will all go down in the same ruin!

QUESADA (*scornfully*). He is not the man he was – since Nano bewitched him.

MENENDEZ (*disgustedly*). Bah! You fool! (*Then intently.*) Yet there is truth in what you say. He has grown weak – between Luis' influence and the girl's meddling – (*Abruptly.*) Come! There is still a chance. Summon Don Juan to me at once! (*This last in a shout of impatience.*)

JUAN (*from outside, rear, mockingly*). There is no need for messengers.

(*He enters. In the three months he has aged greatly. His hair and beard have grown perceptibly white. Beneath the bitter, mocking mask there is an expression of deep, hidden conflict and suffering on his face as if he were at war with himself.*)

MENENDEZ (*startled, afraid of what Juan may have overheard*). You heard – ?

JUAN (*scornfully*). Only what you shouted. Am I a monk to listen at keyholes? (*This with a glance at Quesada.*) But I know your intrigues. This meeting of yapping curs – you see, I have heard the rumour – you would have me sail at their bidding, and thus you would be free to rule this island in God's Holy Name! Is it not so?

MENENDEZ (*controlling his anger*). You have lost your senses. You will not realize that things have reached a crisis! The government has slipped through your fingers while you played at being a loving father –

JUAN (*stung – fiercely*). It's a lie! (*Controlling himself.*) I tell you again, Diego, I will sail at my pleasure, not yours.

MENENDEZ (*persuasively*). You have kept repeating that – and meanwhile your apathy has ruined us. Your soldiers and sailors are in open mutiny. The mob has risen. (*Urgently.*) Juan, do you want rebellion to overwhelm us? You promised them Cathay –

JUAN (*proudly*). It was you who promised them in my name, you mean, to make certain you would be rid of me!

MENENDEZ (*tauntingly – noting Juan's reactions craftily*). I promised because I thought you were still Juan Ponce de Leon. But you are not. You have become merely a slave to a girl's sentimental whims! You are too feeble to govern here and too weak for Cathay. (*Juan's hand goes to his sword. Menendez continues cuttingly.*) Then for the sake of Spain, resign your office and surrender your patent for discovery to some one with the youth and courage to dare!

JUAN (*infuriated, half drawing his sword*). Take care, Diego! Your cloth cannot condone such insults!

MENENDEZ (*in a softened, oily tone*). Forgive me, Juan. I insult you for your own sake! Push on to your greatest victory! Do not wait here in a stupor for inglorious defeat!

JUAN (*shaken*). I shall sail – but first I must know – know for a certainty, beyond all doubt – exactly where – (*He stops abruptly.*)

MENENDEZ (*inquisitively*). What?

JUAN (*suspiciously*). Nothing.

QUESADA (*who has been listening with feverish interest – points to Juan accusingly*). He has gone to Nano every day. Look at his eyes! He is bewitched! (*Juan starts guiltily but tries to ignore him contemptuously.*)

MENENDEZ. Be still, Quesada! (*He looks at Juan.*) These interviews *are* mysterious, Juan.

JUAN (*quickly – half turning away and averting his eyes – with forced carelessness*). I need accurate information for my voyage that only Nano can give me. That is why I have delayed.

MENENDEZ (*looking at him sharply*). So? I had thought it might be affection for Beatriz that held you.

JUAN (*vehemently*). No!

MENENDEZ (*keenly*). Why are you so vehement? It would be natural enough. You have lived alone. To find a daughter in your declining years –

JUAN (*pale with rage and agony*). Daughter? How could she look upon me – ?

MENENDEZ (*soothingly but with a taunting intent*). She used to regard you as her hero, her great commander. She must wonder now at this old man's weakness in you.

JUAN (*frenziedly*). Do you dare taunt me in her name? I *will* sail, I say! I will sail the very first day after I discover – (*Then distractedly, shaken.*) Enough, Diego! I shall do what I wish and when it pleases me!

(*He rushes out rear as if furies were hounding him. Menendez looks after him, a sneering smile of satisfaction gradually coming over his face as if something were proven to him.*)

MENENDEZ (*half to himself, half to Quesada*). I should have guessed it before. Yet, who would have thought – He is bewitched, certainly.

QUESADA (*eagerly*). Yes!

MENENDEZ (*dryly*). But you are blaming the wrong witch. The guilty one is sinless. (*Quesada puzzles over this paradox with open eyes. Menendez ponders for a moment, then he turns to Quesada.*) Bring the Lady Beatriz.

QUESADA. Yes, Your Grace. (*He bows and hurries out, left. Menendez sits thoughtfully, evidently planning out his campaign. A moment later Beatriz enters. She bows respectfully.*)

BEATRIZ (*reservedly*). You wish to see me, Your Grace?

MENENDEZ (*nods and motions her to a chair. He scrutinizes her face carefully for a moment, then begins in a playful, ironical tone*). Beauty did not leave a stone on stone of ancient Troy. Are you another Helen, Beatriz?

BEATRIZ (*confused*). I – don't understand.

MENENDEZ (*coldly and brusquely*). Not understand that rebellion is seething in Porto Rico? – a rebellion that will deal destruction to us all!

BEATRIZ (*bewildered*). Rebellion? (*Then spiritedly.*) Who would dare rebel against Don Juan?

MENENDEZ (*belittlingly*). Juan is powerless. His own soldiers have taken the lead against him. He is facing ruin! Do you understand? I wish I had words of fire to brand it on your brain! For I tell you on my conscience, as God's minister, you are the one responsible!

BEATRIZ (*stunned*). I? I? You are jesting! (*Then with haughty resentment.*) I harm Don Juan, who is my second father!

MENENDEZ (*seeming to grow more icy under her anger*). Who has done most in influencing him to softness and lax discipline –

BEATRIZ (*indignantly*). You mean because I have pitied the suffering of the Indians – ?

MENENDEZ (*dryly*). Let us judge your pity by its results. These heathen no longer fear. They defy our Holy Faith. They sneer at baptism. These Indians shirk their labour. And because Don Juan spends his time with you, he has forgotten not only his duty to govern but his oath to seek Cathay. The soldiers and sailors have waited too long in idleness. Now they revere him no longer as a daring general who will lead them to glory but despise him for a dissembler, delaying because he has lost the courage for action! And so they have conspired. Those are the facts. Will you deny your influence is deep at the root of them? (*Beatriz is too overwhelmed by the ruthlessness of his attack to reply. He pushes his advantage.*) And can you deny that a great change has come over Don Juan since your arrival? You cannot have helped but notice this!

BEATRIZ. He has seemed – to become despondent at times.

MENENDEZ (*vehemently*). Spiritless! Infirm! His thoughts wander like a senile old man's! I believe his mind is failing him!

BEATRIZ (*horrified*). No! No!

MENENDEZ. You must face the truth! (*Sternly.*) When you take a life's ambition from a man like Juan, the man withers away. You have made him forget Cathay. Why? Why have you not urged him to go – for his own sake? When you brought out the patent, you dreamed of him as he dreams of himself – a conqueror and hero!

BEATRIZ (*hesitatingly*). Father Luis told me we must keep him here – or else his good work would be undone –

MENENDEZ. This uprising will undo it in an hour! (*Then soothingly.*) Father Luis is a good man – but blind. You are a girl – and inexperienced – Come. (*He pauses, watching her keenly, then takes her hand, and leading her to the window, pulls back the curtain.*) Look!

BEATRIZ (*with a shudder of horror*). Ah!

MENENDEZ. Now do you believe in the rebellion – in Juan's danger?

BEATRIZ (*horrified*). Fire!

MENENDEZ. And murder! In the Indian villages. See what your pity for them has done! And it will not stop there. That is only the first spark of revolution. They'll march here! (*Impressively.*) Beatriz, you can save Don Juan. He loves you – as his daughter. Urge him to sail at once! Rouse the hero in him! Give him back his sanity! He is my old friend. I implore you for his sake, Beatriz!

BEATRIZ (*bewilderedly*). Yes – yes – but give me time to think – to pray for guidance –

(*She kneels before the altar.*)

MENENDEZ (*impatiently*). There is no time!

(*There is a noise of hurrying steps and Oviedo enters. He is booted, spurred, covered with dust, his face betraying anxiety and alarm.*)

OVIEDO (*without stopping to see who is there, bursts forth*). Diego! I tried to check them, but they have gone mad! They are marching on the town! Juan will be lost!

MENENDEZ (*to Beatriz who has turned around in terror*). You hear!

OVIEDO. The time has come to abandon that sick fool! We must openly lead this rebellion!

BEATRIZ (*springs to her feet and faces him – her

eyes flashing). Coward! (*He falls back, his hand on his sword, glaring at her.*)

MENENDEZ (*urgently*). Go, Beatriz!

(*She passes Oviedo with a scathing glance, and goes out rear. Menendez turns to Oviedo with an ironical but worried smile.*)

MENENDEZ. If she will but speak to Juan as she did to you, we may still win, my friend!

Curtain

SCENE FIVE

SCENE. *Nano's dungeon – a circular cavern, hollowed out by Nature and cut out by man in the solid rock under the Government house. The enclosed space is narrow but lofty, cylindrical in form. A cut-in flight of steps leads from the floor in rear to a trap-door above. The high wall glistens with moisture. A small bench is at right. A lantern stands on one of the lower steps. In the middle of the floor stands a soldier, thick-set, brutal-looking, his sleeves rolled up over his muscular arms. He is blowing with a bellows on a charcoal brazier, glowing red-hot, in which are thrust several irons. On the wall in the rear, his toes barely touching the floor, Nano hangs with his arms outstretched over his head, the wrists bound by chains to iron sockets in the rock. His head hangs on one side as if he were in a state of semi-consciousness. His body is thin and wasted.*

The trap-door is opened and a circular patch of grey light falls on the stairs. This is obscured as some one descends. It is Juan. He shuts the trap-door behind him and comes down. He stops when he is opposite Nano's head, and, leaning over, stares at the savage's face. The latter opens his eyes. His head stiffens proudly erect on his shoulders. He and Juan stare into each other's eyes. Juan drops his guiltily, turns away and descends to the floor, where the soldier is standing at attention.

JUAN (*harshly*). Has he spoken?

SOLDIER. Not one word, sir.

JUAN. Then you have not obeyed –

SOLDIER (*indicates the irons in the fire*). I have tried every trick I know – but he's made of iron.

JUAN (*looks up at Nano with intense hatred*). Dog! (*Then he turns to the soldier.*) Go and keep guard above.

SOLDIER. Yes, sir. (*He bends down to pick up the brazier.*)

JUAN (*harshly*). No.

SOLDIER (*with a glance at him – understandingly*). Yes, sir.

(*He goes up the stairs, opens the trap-door and disappears, letting it fall shut behind him. Juan sinks on the stone bench at right and stares up at Nano, who looks back at him with unflinching defiance. A pause.*)

JUAN (*his eyes now fixed dully on the floor – half-aloud to himself*). Diego did not lie. The storm is gathering. (*With bitter hopelessness.*) What matter? I could pray that it might be a deluge annihilating mankind – but for Beatriz. (*He groans, then raises his eyes again to Nano.*) Why do you look at me? I can never read your eyes. They see in another world. What are you? Flesh, but not our flesh. Earth. I come after – or before – but lost, blind in a world where my eyes deflect on surfaces. What values give you your loan of life? Answer! I must know the terms in which to make appeal! (*The savage is silent, motionless. A pause. Then Juan, as if suddenly reminded, jumps to his feet in a frenzy of impatience.*) Answer me, dog! I must find the will to act – or be dishonoured!

NANO (*solemnly – in a faint voice*). The Gods are angry.

JUAN (*with wild joy*). You speak! At last! Nano, why have you kept dumb while I implored – ?

NANO. The Gods have stopped your ears.

JUAN (*going on obsessed, regardless*). Juan Ponce de Leon – to torture a helpless captive! Why did you bring me to such shame? Why would you not answer my question?

NANO (*with contempt*). My tongue grew weary. For a moon I answered every day.

JUAN (*fiercely*). But you lied! Tell me the truth now! Where is the fountain?

NANO (*indifferently, shutting his eyes*). Only the Gods know.

JUAN. The same lie! You told me at first that men of your former tribe knew! You must know! This is your revenge – for the death of your wives and children! Must I swear to you again they were killed in spite of my strict orders? Come! Forget them! I will give you your choice of all your women on the island – your freedom – I will petition the King to honour you – give you back your lands – anything if you will answer me! (*Nano remains silent. Juan utters a furious cry and, rushing to the brazier, takes a red-hot coal with the tongs and holds it before the Indian's eyes.*) Dog! I will burn that scorn from your eyes! (*The Indian stares at the hot iron immovably. Juan lets it fall to the floor with a desperate groan of misery.*) Pardon! Forgiveness in Christ's name! It is you who torture me! Nano, I burn to hell! I love! (*He suddenly stops, chilled to despair by the implacable isolation in the savage's face. He throws himself down on the bench in an apathy. Finally he slowly draws his sword and speaks in a dead voice.*) Either you speak or you die. I swear it.

NANO (*with aloof contempt*). What is death?

JUAN (*dully*). I will die, too. Perhaps in the grave there is oblivion and peace. (*After a pause.*) You are a fool, Nano. If you would help me I could make you pilot of the fleet to guide us to your land. The fountain once found, you would be free. No harm should come to your people. Do you never long for your old home?

NANO (*who has been listening with quickened interest*). Home? To the land of flowers. My home of many warriors. (*After a pause.*) You will let me guide the great winged canoes – to my home?

JUAN (*eagerly*). Yes. (*In great suspense.*) Will you help me? Tell me! (*He has sprung to his feet.*)

NANO. Only the Gods – (*He checks himself abruptly.*)

JUAN (*frenziedly*). Ah! (*He raises his sword as if to run the savage through.*)

NANO (*looking into Juan's eyes without noticing the threat*). The tongues of the white devils are false. How can I trust your word?

JUAN. I take my sacred oath! (*He raises his hand.*)

NANO. Your God is a God of lies.

JUAN (*wildly*). By your God then – since mine has forsaken me!

NANO (*lifts his head and murmurs some supplication, as if begging forgiveness – then looks at Juan with savage triumph*). I will guide you – but remember the way is long!

JUAN (*triumphantly*). At last! What does it matter how long or difficult! (*Raising his arms.*) Ah, God's blood, I already feel new life, the will to live! I can conquer now! (*A pounding of a sword-butt on the trap-door. Then it is flung open.*)

SOLDIER. Pardon, Excellency –

BEATRIZ' VOICE (*calls down*). Don Juan! Don Juan!

JUAN (*exultantly*). Her voice! A happy omen! (*He hurries up the stairs.*)

NANO (*again lifting his eyes to heaven – with religious fervour*). Great Spirit, forgive my lie. His blood shall atone!

Curtain

SCENE SIX

SCENE. *Same as Scene Three – Courtyard of the Governor's house – a stifling twilight. The sky is darkening with clouds.*

Beatriz' voice – from the left – calls down as at the end of preceding scene.

BEATRIZ. Don Juan! Don Juan!

(*His voice is heard, "Beatriz." She enters, pale and agitated, runs to rear and looks for signs of the insurrection – then hurries back just in time to meet Juan, who enters, left. He is in a tense state of hectic excitement, his face ghastly pale, his obsessed eyes burning feverishly, his drawn sword still in his hand. She starts back from him, frightened by his appearance.*)

JUAN (*in a strained, high-pitched tone*). Was it

the fountain called – or you, Beatriz? You, for you are the fountain! (*He takes her hand impetuously and kisses it.*)

BEATRIZ (*flurriedly*). I came to warn you –

JUAN (*with a sharp glance*). Warn? Then you have seen Diego? Bah! (*He makes a gesture of contempt with his sword as if brushing all revolutions aside.*) When the hour comes, I shall be strong. The will breathes in me again. Forget all else, Beatriz. Give me your thoughts! Have you been happy here with me?

BEATRIZ (*not knowing what to say or do*). Yes – yes. (*Trying to return to her mission.*) But –

JUAN. You came as a benediction – that cursed me. (*Abruptly.*) Have you not noticed how much older I have grown?

BEATRIZ (*convinced he is out of his head – resolved to humour him – frightened but pityingly*). You can become young again.

JUAN (*exultantly*). I will! (*Then mysteriously.*) This is a strange world with many wonders still undiscovered.

BEATRIZ (*seeing a chance to bring in her point – quickly*). Then discover them. The search will make you young.

JUAN (*deeply and superstitiously impressed*). From your own lips! It is another blessed augury! (*Eagerly.*) But pretend I am young. What then?

BEATRIZ. Why then you would be happy.

JUAN (*intensely*). You promise – ? Have you never loved?

BEATRIZ (*bewildered*). Loved?

JUAN. Since you speak of happiness.

BEATRIZ. I loved my mother – my father – I love you, Don Juan.

JUAN (*avidly*). Ah, say that again! Those words are blood to my heart!

BEATRIZ (*earnestly*). I love you as I loved my father –

JUAN (*brusquely – wounded to the quick*). Has love never stolen into your dreams? You are no nun. Come, tell me the image of the one you dream of as a lover.

BEATRIZ (*resolved to pass this off jestingly*). It is a great secret. You insist? Well then, it is your double – (*Juan utters a cry of joy, bending toward her. She adds hastily.*) You as my mother described you in the wars before Granada.

JUAN (*bitterly*). When I had youth. But I loved only glory then. Did she not tell you that?

BEATRIZ. Why then – that is why she said, bring him tenderness.

JUAN (*sombrely*). You have fulfilled her wish – or was it her revenge? (*Then abruptly.*) And what if I should myself become that double? – the knight of Granada with your gift of tenderness – what then?

BEATRIZ (*frightened by his strangeness*). Ah, now, you are jesting, Don Juan. (*She forces a laugh.*)

JUAN (*passionately*). No, Beatriz! (*She instinctively shrinks away from him. He calms himself.*) No more now. I fear your laughter. First let the consummation – Then you will not laugh. You – (*Trying to read her mystified eyes – miserably uncertain.*) What will you do?

BEATRIZ (*controlling her timidity – softly persuasive*). You are ill, Don Juan. Will you listen to my cure for you?

JUAN. Yes.

BEATRIZ (*with energy*). Sail and find Cathay!

JUAN (*with a start, tormentedly*). You, too, condemn me! But I swear to you I have longed to go! I have hated my own cowardice! I have played the traitor to every dream, every great hope – But, Beatriz, when I go, I will leave my life behind with you. So – until I knew – I was afraid of losing what I have – (*Then with a quick change to something approaching triumphant decision.*) But that is past! My will has risen from the dead. It is decreed by your own lips. I shall sail at once!

BEATRIZ. Oh, I am glad!

JUAN (*sadly*). Glad I am leaving you?

BEATRIZ. No, I shall be sad and lonely. It is for your own welfare –

JUAN. But promise me one boon –

BEATRIZ (*eagerly*). Anything!

JUAN. Promise you will not marry until I return – or you hear I am dead?

BEATRIZ (*confused*). I have never even thought of marrying.

JUAN (*in deadly earnest in spite of his pitiful pretence at a joking tone*). Until I present my double to you – ?

BEATRIZ (*relieved and laughing easily*). Why, I

might change my mind then, Don Juan.

JUAN. Will you seal that pledge with a kiss? (*He forces a smile to conceal his longing.*)

BEATRIZ (*uncertainly – forcing a laugh*). Yes, Don Juan. (*She lifts her face to him. He starts to kiss her on the lips, but something in her face stops him and he ends by kissing her reverentially on the forehead – forcing a smile.*)

JUAN. There – upon your forehead – for remembrance. The other – for tenderness – is still a promise of my dream.

(*There is a sound of hurrying steps and Juan moves away from Beatriz guiltily. Luis enters from the rear. His face is agitated, full of alarm and anxiety.*)

BEATRIZ (*greeting him eagerly, glad of the interruption*). Father Luis.

LUIS. Juan! I bring you terrible news. (*He sees Juan's drawn sword.*) Ah, you know! It is time you drew your sword.

JUAN (*scornfully*). You mean the scum rises? When I tell them the fleet sails to-morrow –

LUIS. Will you give them Nano to burn at the stake? That is their first demand. (*Beatriz gives a horrified cry.*)

JUAN (*stunned – unbelievingly*). Surrender Nano? No, it is impossible. You have heard rumours –

LUIS. Quesada has roused their cruelty to frenzy. (*He points to where a red glow is mounting up in the sky.*) See! They are burning the Indian quarter. May God have mercy!

JUAN (*in a rage*). Kill Nano? The curs! I shall order a company of my guard –

LUIS (*looking at him pityingly*). Your guard is leading the mob! (*Reproachfully.*) Juan, Juan, why have you lived in a dream! I warned you time after time. If you had been governor in anything but name –

JUAN (*sinking on the bench – stupidly*). Call the guard. I must order them to disperse.

BEATRIZ (*pityingly*). His mind is sick –

LUIS (*rather peremptorily*). Will you leave us, Beatriz?

BEATRIZ (*obediently*). Yes, Father. (*Then excitedly.*) I must see Bishop Menendez – (*She hurries out, right.*)

LUIS (*comes and slaps Juan on the back – sternly*). Juan! Awake, in God's name!

JUAN (*startled to action, springs to his feet*). I shall protect his life with my own!

LUIS. In order to torture him yourself?

JUAN (*vehemently but guiltily*). A lie! (*Suspicious – resentfully.*) Have you seen him? I gave orders –

LUIS. It is weeks since I was permitted to see him; and you have avoided meeting me. Why?

JUAN (*harshly*). I have no patience with your converting. I need Nano as he is.

LUIS. Because you prefer his heathen myths –

JUAN (*controlling an outburst of rage*). Myths? Why myths? Cathay is there. (*He points.*)

LUIS. I was not speaking of Cathay. You are sailing to-morrow? Does this mean you have finally wrung from this poor Indian's agonies a faith in magic fountains – ?

JUAN (*losing control of himself – raging*). Fool! You are like those dullards who, when Columbus said the earth was round, brayed at him for blaspheming! Listen to me! I do not believe Nano, I believe in Nature. Nature is part of God. She can perform miracles. Since this land was discovered have we not found wonders undreamed of before? The points in Nano's story hold true to the facts we know. His home is a beautiful mainland – "A land of flowers," in his own words. Is not Cathay also known as the "Flowery Land"? There are great walled cities with roofs of gold inland to the West. Is not that Marco Polo's land beyond all doubt? And the fountain is in Cathay. All the evidence from around the world proves that! And I shall find it!

LUIS (*pityingly*). But this evidence is merely fable, legend, the dreams of poets!

JUAN (*furiously*). Have praying and fasting made you an imbecile? What evidence had Columbus? And you – you believe Christ lived and died. Well, have you talked with men who saw Him in the manger, or on the cross?

LUIS. Juan, this is blasphemy!

JUAN (*with bitter despair*). Then let it be! I have prayed to Him in vain.

LUIS. Juan!

JUAN (*with all the power of his will in the words*). Let me be damned for ever if Nature will only grant me youth upon this earth again!

LUIS (*horrified*). Juan! You defy your God!

JUAN. There is no God but Love – no heaven but youth!

LUIS (*looks at his tortured face intently – suddenly realizes – in a tone of great pity*). So that is it – I have been blind. I thought your love saw in her – a child, a daughter!

JUAN (*intensely*). A child – yes – for a time – but one morning standing by the fountain she was a woman. More than a woman! She was the Spirit of Youth, Hope, Ambition, Power to dream and dare! She was all that I had lost. She was Love and the Beauty of Love! So I loved her, loved her with all the intensity of Youth's first love – when youth was dead! Oh, it was monstrous folly, I admit. I called myself a senile fool! I suffered with the damned. I lived in hell without the recompense of being dead! And I loved her more – and more! (*His head sinks down on his hands. A great sob racks his whole body.*)

LUIS (*overcome by compassion, his voice trembling*). Old friend – God in His Mercy have pity on you! (*He is interrupted by the hurried entrance of Beatriz from the right.*)

BEATRIZ (*indignantly*). Bishop Menendez says he can do nothing – that you must give Nano up! (*The angry tumult of a mob marching is heard from the distance. Frightenedly.*) Listen! Oh, Don Juan, you will save him, will you not?

JUAN (*starting up – in a voice in which rage and apprehension are blended*). I must! (*He listens to the rising murmur of the mob. As he does so his whole body stiffens into defiant determination. He becomes in an instant the commander again.*) Cowardly rabble! (*He springs to the entrance on the left and shouts to the soldier on guard.*) Bring Nano! (*He comes back to where Beatriz and Luis are standing and looks around the courtyard as if measuring his position.*) I shall face them here. Take Beatriz away, Luis.

BEATRIZ. I wish to stay with you!

MENENDEZ (*enters from the right*). Juan! (*Seeing his drawn sword – apprehensively.*) What? You will defy them? Then you are lost! Yield to them, I advise you. Give Nano to justice. (*While he is speaking Nano is half carried in by the soldiers. He is limp and exhausted.*)

JUAN (*with wild scorn*). Ah, High Priest! Deliver him up, eh?

MENENDEZ. Juan! You are impious! (*Angrily.*) It is sacrilege – to compare this Indian dog – you mock our Blessed Saviour! You are cursed – I wash my hands – His will be done! (*He turns and strides back into the house, right.*)

LUIS (*at a nearer roar from the mob*). Juan! Escape! There is still time –

JUAN. Run from jackals! Is my honour dead?

LUIS (*as a smashing battering sounds from outside*). They are at the outer gate! Come, Beatriz, in God's name!

(*She struggles, but he succeeds in getting her as far as the entrance, right. A last crashing smash is heard as the outer gate gives way. A moment later the advance guard of the mob pour in – all of the lower rabble, these. Some wave torches above their heads. All are armed with pikes, knives, and various crude weapons that they have picked up or stolen.*)

JUAN (*in a roar of command*). Back!

(*They hesitate for a moment. Then they see Nano and with yells of fury rush for him around the fountain. Juan springs to meet them. With quick thrusts and cuts of his sword he kills or wounds four of the foremost, who drop to the ground. The rest fall back frightened and awed for the moment. In this lull the remainder of the mob pour in from the rear, crowding and jostling each other. They are a nondescript crowd, ranging from nobles, richly dressed, soldiers, sailors, to the riff-raff of the criminal element in bright-coloured rags. There are a number of monks among them, Franciscans who urge them on, a few Dominicans who plead for restraint.*)

THE MOB. Don Juan! It's the Governor – push back there! – To the flames with the Indian dog! Seize him! Stand aside, Don Juan! Heretic! He's bewitched! The dog refused baptism! Torture!

JUAN (*sternly*). I will kill the man who touches this Indian! (*He walks up and down before them, his sword ready to thrust, looking from eye to eye – scathingly.*) Scoundrels! Where is your valour now? Prick up your courage! (*Mockingly.*) Come! Who wishes to die?

A NOBLE. We demand justice!

(*Yells of approval from the crowd. They push in closer. Juan levels his sword at the breast of the nearest who springs back with a frightened cry. The mob sways and surges, close packed and indecisive, cowed by Juan's eyes.*)

QUESADA (*suddenly pushing his way to the front of the crowd – pointing at Nano, frantically*). Give him up! You are bewitched!

(*The mob are again aroused. There are cries of "To the stake! Torture!" etc.*)

JUAN. No! (*Yells of rage. The mob surges forward. Juan raises his sword.*) I will kill the first one who – (*They recoil again, all but Quesada. With his free hand Juan sweeps him to one side contemptuously – then fiercely threatening the crowd.*) Will you rebel against the Governor of your King? Then you are traitors to Spain! And, by God's blood, I will hang one of you on every tree!

(*The crowd gives way by inches, sullenly, their yells reduced for the moment to a rebellious muttering: "The King will remove you! Hang the Indians! Hang them! Hang Nano!" etc.*)

A SOLDIER. We mean no harm to you, Don Juan. Keep your word to us. Order the fleet to sail. (*A yell of acclamation from the soldiers and sailors.*)

QUESADA. And give over that dog! The Inquisition shall know you protect infidels!

JUAN. I am Spain's soldier, not the Inquisition's! Soldiers and sailors! I tell you it is in Spain's service this Indian's life is spared. The fleet sails to-morrow – and we need Nano to pilot our voyage! (*A tumult from the bewildered crowd. Shouts of various nature: "The fleet sails! To-morrow! Hurrah! He jokes! He mocks us! Spare him? No luck with a heathen on board! What does he mean? Guide us? No! The curse of the Church!" But the mob is puzzled, blundering, and Juan continues with a sort of condescension as if he were speaking to children.*) Silence! Since you are so stupid, I must explain. This Nano was born on the mainland – Cathay! – our goal, do you understand? – and I have put off sailing while I questioned him. We must have his knowledge. He must be our pilot. (*With a fierce glance at Nano as if to let his threat strike home.*) And if he fails in his promise to me, I will gladly give him to you for punishment.

QUESADA (*furiously*). You say this to save him!

JUAN. Soldiers, sailors, I appeal to you! Can this mad monk lead you to conquest? You must decide between us. (*The crowd are all turning his way, becoming greedily enthusiastic. Juan sees the psychological moment to play a trump card.*) But to convince you finally, listen to Nano. Speak, Nano! Tell them what you told me – of the golden cities. Speak! (*Then under cover of the crowd's shouts of "Down with the dog! Torture! Hear! Let him speak! Don Juan says let him!" etc., he adds in a fierce whisper to the Indian.*) If you wish ever to see your home again!

NANO (*mechanically, in a clear monotonous voice, with expressionless face*). A big land – far mighty cities – gold –

JUAN. You hear? The cities of gold! (*The crowd murmurs excitedly.*)

NANO. There is much gold. The houses have gold on them.

A SOLDIER. Cipango! We'll storm their cities for them!

A SAILOR. Loot, my bullies!

JUAN. Glory and gold for all of you! And now go! (*The crowd are jubilant. Shouts of "Up anchor! Ahoy Cathay! At last! We sail! Sack! Riches! Gold!" etc. Juan shouts above the tumult.*) Go! Disperse! To-morrow we sail! (*A voice cries, "Long live Don Juan!" The whole mob takes it up. Juan begins to give way under the strain – wearily.*) Go. Go.

THE MOB (*led by a sailor, takes up a sort of chanty song in mighty chorus, dancing wildly, waving their torches, crowding out, rear*).

The Cities of Gold
In far Cathay –
Their great Khan is old,
And his wealth untold
In prize for our bold
Who sail away.
Aye!

His gold for our bold who sail away!!

BEATRIZ (*as the last of the mob disappear – rushing up to Juan with great admiration*). You have saved him! What they have said of you is true indeed – lion by nature as well as name!

JUAN (*bitterly*). Lion? No! Tricky politician! If I had been the Juan of long ago, I would not have pleaded or bargained with such curs. I would have –

(*He raises his sword threateningly – then lets his arm sink limply. The sword slips from his fingers and falls to the ground.*)

BEATRIZ (*kneels quickly and presents its hilt to him*). I give you back your sword – to bring good fortune. Now you must find the golden cities!

JUAN (*taking it – longingly*). I care only for the one, Beatriz – the golden city of Youth, where you are queen.

(*She looks into his face smilingly, mystified as –*

The Curtain Falls)

SCENE SEVEN

SCENE. *Four months later – a strip of beach on the Florida coast – a bright, moonlight night. The forest runs diagonally from right, front, to left, rear – a wall of black shadow. The sand gleams a pallid white in the moonlight. The rhythmic ebb and flow of waves is heard – their voice on a windless night of calm.*

As the curtain rises, an Indian is discovered, standing in the moonlight, just out of the shadow of the forest. He is old, but still erect and warrior-like, a chief by his demeanour. His body, naked save for a piece of deerskin at his waist, is elaborately painted, as is his face. A knot of feathers is in his hair. A tomahawk and flint knife are at his waist. He is motionless and silent as a statue, one hand clasping his unslung bow as if it were a staff, but he peers intently at some object in the ocean before him. Finally, he gives an ejaculation of surprise and makes a motion of summons to the forest behind him. The Medicine Man glides out of the darkness to his side. This latter is incredibly old and shrunken, daubed with many insignia in paint, wearing many ornaments of bone and shell. They confer together in low tones with much pantomime. A man is evidently swimming toward them from some strange object out at sea. Other Indians steal from the forest, form a group in the shadow behind the two, point out to sea, gesticulate. At a sharp command from the Chief, they unsling their bows, fit arrows to strings, crouch in an ambush in the shadow. The Chief does likewise and stands waiting, prepared for what may come. Nano walks up the beach from front, left. His naked body glistens with drops of water. He sees the Chief and stops, raising his right hand above his head. The Chief makes a sign. The other Indians dart from their ambush and surround Nano.

CHIEF. Bind him.

NANO (*calmly*). Is a brother an enemy? (*They all start with surprise at hearing their own langauge. Nano goes on.*) This is the land of my fathers. I am Nano, a son of Boanu, who was a chief. (*They all stare at him. The Chief makes a sign to the Medicine Man, who comes forward and examines Nano's face intently.*)

MEDICINE MAN. His words are truth. He is Nano – or an evil spirit in his body. (*He shakes a charm at him.*) Are you from the Land of the Dead?

NANO. I am of the living. They did not chain me. They think I fear the sea. I come to warn you. I swam from the great canoes. They are the warships of the Spaniards.

CHIEF (*mystified*). What are Spaniards? Their winged canoes are like the boats of Gods.

NANO. These are no Gods. They are men who die from wounds. Their faces are white, but they are evil. They wear shirts that arrows cannot pierce. They have strange sticks that spit fire and kill. Their devils make them strong. But they are not true warriors. They are thieves and rapers of women.

CHIEF. Have they no God?

NANO (*with scorn*). Their God is a thing of

earth! It is this! (*He touches a gold ornament that the Chief wears.*)

MEDICINE MAN (*mystified*). Gold? Gold is sacred to the Sun. It can be no God itself.

NANO (*contemptuously*). They see only things, not the spirit behind things. Their hearts are muddy as a pool in which deer have trampled. Listen. Their Medicine Men tell of a God who came to them long ago in the form of a man. He taught them to scorn things. He taught them to look for the spirit behind things. In revenge, they killed him. They tortured him as a sacrifice to their Gold Devil. They crossed two big sticks. They drove little sticks through his hands and feet and pinned him on the others – thus.

(*He illustrates. A murmur of horror and indignation goes up among them.*)

MEDICINE MAN. To torture a God! How did they dare?

NANO. Their devils protected them. And now each place they go, they carry that figure of a dying God. They do this to strike fear. They command you to submit when you see how even a God who fought their evil was tortured. (*Proudly.*) But I would not.

MEDICINE MAN (*suspiciously*). If you defied them, how are you alive?

NANO. I am craftier than they. They have an old chief who is cursed with madness. Him I told of the Spring of Life. I said I would find it for him.

MEDICINE MAN. Only the Gods can reveal it. Why have you told this lie?

NANO (*fiercely*). Revenge! I have made a plan. Is there a spring near?

CHIEF (*mystified*). Yes. In the forest.

NANO (*with satisfaction*). Good! Listen. This mad chief is the mightiest among them. Without him they would turn cowards. To-morrow night I will lead him to the spring. You must lie hidden. We will kill him there. Is this clear?

CHIEF. Yes.

NANO. I will swim back now. I escaped to tell you of my plan and warn you. They would lay waste your land as they did mine. They killed my wives and children. They burned. They tortured. They chained warriors neck to neck. They beat them with a whip to dig in the fields like squaws. This old chief led them. My heart is fire. Until he dies, it will know no peace.

CHIEF. I begin to feel your hatred.

NANO. Then remember to hide by the spring.

CHIEF. We will not forget.

NANO. It is well.

(*He turns and strides down to the sea. They stand watching him in silence.*)

MEDICINE MAN (*uneasily, thoughtful*). Only devils could build great canoes that fly with wings. My brothers, they are evil spirits. Nano has made war with them. They have beaten him. Can we trust his plan?

CHIEF. What is your counsel?

MEDICINE MAN. I have heard the voice of the Great Spirit speaking in the night. Let us first try to propitiate their devils.

CHIEF. I do not know how to war with devils. That is your duty. Let us summon the council.

(*He makes a sign at which his followers disappear silently into the wood. He and the Medicine Man follow as –*

The Curtain Falls)

SCENE EIGHT

SCENE. *The same. High noon of the following day – glaring sunlight on the beach, an atmosphere of oppressive heat and languor. The earth seems dead, preserved in some colourless, molten fluid. The forest is a matted green wall. The sound of the sea has the quality of immense exhaustion.*

On the beach, a sort of makeshift altar is being erected – two round boulders supporting a flat slub of rock. On top of the slab is placed a shallow bowl made of bark. A group of Indians, under the direction of the Medicine Man, are hurriedly putting on the finishing touches to this shrine. They keep casting awed apprehensive glances seaward. The Medicine Man is binding two branches of a tree together in the form of a cross. All the Indians are feathered and painted as for an unusual solemn occasion.

THE INDIANS (*their eyes on the sea as they work—frightenedly*). The small canoes leave the great winged ones. They are coming! The sun gleams on their shirts that arrows cannot pierce. Their fire-sticks glitter in the sun. Their faces are turned. Their faces are pale! They are watching us!

MEDICINE MAN (*finishing his work*). Keep your hearts brave! (*Giving the cross to two Indians.*) Here. This is their totem pole. Stand it there. (*They dig a hole in the sand before the altar and set the cross there; but they make the mistake of setting it head down. The Medicine Man grunts with satisfaction.*) They will think we adore the same devil. They will leave us in peace.

INDIAN (*his eyes on the sea*). The last canoe has left the great ships. (*He gives a cry of fear echoed by the others.*) Aie! Fire and smoke!

(*They cower. The hollow boom of a cannon fired in salute reverberates over the sea. They all shrink with terror, bowing their heads.*)

INDIAN (*awestruck*). The Thunder fights with them!

INDIAN. They are white Gods!

MEDICINE MAN (*frightened himself, but rallying his followers sternly*). You have the hearts of squaws. Quick! Where is the gold?

(*An Indian comes to him with an earthenware vessel. He empties it out on the bowl on the top of the altar. It is full of gold nuggets of different sizes. They form a heap glowing in the sun.*)

INDIANS. They come! They come!

MEDICINE MAN (*sternly*). Pretend to worship their gold devil but pray to our Great Father, the Sun. He can defeat all devils. Pray to him! (*An Indian starts to beat rhythmically on the small drum. The Medicine Man lifts his shrill voice in the first strains of the chant. Immediately the others all join in as if hypnotized.*) Great Father, Mighty One, Ruler of Earth. Maker of Days. Ripener of the Corn. Creator of Life. Look down upon us out of your Sky-Tent. Let our song rise to you. Let it enter your heart. Mighty One, hear us. Hide not your face in clouds. Bless us at the dawn. And at the day's end.

(*They form a circle and dance about the altar, their eyes raised to the sun overhead. Their chant hides the noise of the Spaniards landing. Then the Spaniards appear from the left, front. First comes Juan, his face wild and haggard, his eyes obsessed. He is accompanied by Luis. Following him are a squad of Soldiers, guarding Nano, who is in chains. Then come four Franciscan Monks, led by Quesada, who wears a sword and pistol over his robe. The others carry crosses. Following them is a group of Nobles, richly dressed. Then come ranks of Soldiers. They all stare at this Indian ceremony with contemptuous scorn.*)

JUAN (*irritably*). Make them cease their accursed noise, Luis. Let Nano speak to them.

LUIS (*advancing toward the Indians—in a loud but friendly voice, raising his right hand*). Peace, brothers.

(*The Indians stop, petrified, staring with awe at the white men. The Medicine Man lifts his right hand and advances a step toward Luis. Quesada notices the cross, utters a furious exclamation, strides forward to verify his suspicion. When he sees that it is indeed upside down his face grows livid with fury.*)

QUESADA. The cross head down! The black mass! (*He pulls out his pistol.*) Blaspheming dog!

(*He fires. The Medicine Man falls. The other Indians who have shrunk back toward the woods in terror at his first move, now turn tail in panic and flee.*)

LUIS (*in horror*). Stop, Quesada!

(*Quesada pulls up the cross and is setting it back upright when the Medicine Man, by a last dying effort, draws his knife, and writhing to his feet, plunges it into Quesada's back. They both fall together, the Indian dead. Quesada shudders and is still. A yell of rage goes up from the Spaniards. They rush forward toward the woods as if to pursue the Indians, but Juan shouts a command.*)

JUAN. Halt! Fools! (*They stop prudently but sullenly. Juan turns to Luis, who is kneeling beside Quesada.*) Is he dead?

LUIS. Yes. (*Crossing himself.*) May his soul rest in peace. (*All echo this, crossing themselves.*)

JUAN. An eye for an eye, a tooth for a tooth. (*Mockingly.*) And now it is his eye, his tooth. (*Then with a shudder.*) Take him away. This is a bloody baptism for Cathay. (*Turning to Nano as the Soldiers carry the bodies aside.*) Is this the land, Nano?

NANO (*his eyes smouldering with hate*). Yes.

JUAN. You said it was a wonder land – a land of flowers. I see no flowers.

NANO (*in a sinister tone*). In the forest – flowers grow by a spring –

JUAN (*harshly – with an apprehensive glance about*). Silence!

A NOBLE (*from the group that has been stirring impatiently*). Your Excellency. The banners of Castile and Aragon wait on your pleasure.

JUAN (*making a confused gesture as if wiping cobwebs from his brain*). Yes – yes – I must take possession. Bring the banners. (*He kneels on one knee. They all do likewise.*) In the name of Jesus Christ, Our Lord, and of his most gracious Majesty, the sovereign of Castile and Aragon, I do hereby annex to his dominions this land and all its environs. And I call the land Florida.

(*He bends and kisses the sand. The banners are planted in the ground, where they hang motionless from their poles. Juan, having made this effort, seems to fall into a stupor.*)

A NOBLE (*in a mocking whisper*). A pretty name!

A NOBLE. He has grown imbecile. Will he go spring-hunting here, too? My faith, with all the water he has drunk in the past four months, he must be flooded. (*They all snicker at this.*)

A NOBLE (*impatiently*). Will he never get off his knees and let us rise?

LUIS (*sensing what is going on behind their backs – to Juan – who seems to be praying with bowed head – plucking his sleeve*). Juan! Come!

JUAN (*vaguely*). I was praying – to what God who knows?

(*He rises to his feet weakly. At this, they all rise.*)

A NOBLE (*pointing excitedly*). Look! In that bowl on the stones. Is it not gold? (*They all rush forward to the altar. The Noble picks up a piece of it – his voice hoarse with greedy triumph.*) Gold! (*They all grab at the bowl, upsetting its contents on the sand. They bend down and clutch for it crying.*) Gold! This must be a rich land! There must be more! The Golden Cities are near! Cathay at last!

(*The Soldiers forget discipline, break ranks, form a disorderly, pushing crowd about their leaders. Even the Monks edge forward inquisitively.*)

LUIS (*urgently*). Juan! Look! This is disgraceful!

JUAN (*coming to himself with a start – in a furious tone of command*). Get back to your ranks! A brave example you set, nobles of Spain! (*His personality is compelling. They all slink to their former order again, muttering rebelliously. Juan seems suddenly seized with a wild exultation.*) Cathay! We have found Cathay! This is the land – the Flowery Land! Our dreams lie hidden here! Sing the Te Deum! Sing!

(*There is an oppressive silence for a moment, in which the heat, the sun glaring on the beach, the green of the forest, all nature seems to lay upon these men a mysterious spell, a sudden exhausted recognition of their own defeat. Then the Franciscan Monks raise their voices mechanically and spiritlessly in the Te Deum. Other listless voices gradually join theirs as –*

The Curtain Falls)

SCENE NINE

SCENE. *About midnight – in the forest. Gigantic tree-trunks, entwined with vines in flower, are in the foreground. Festoons of Spanish moss hang clear to the ground from the branches. Through the network one sees a circular clearing, grass-grown, flooded with moonlight. There is the soft murmur of a spring which bubbles from the ground in the centre of this open space. Indians are crouched in ambush among the trees, motionless, their eyes fixed on the clearing.*

The stillness is broken by the whistled call of a bird. The Indians stir alertly. One of them whistles in answer to the call. An Indian creeps swiftly in from the left. The Chief comes from his place of ambush to meet him.

CHIEF. He comes?

INDIAN. He has entered the forest.

CHIEF. I will give Nano the signal when we are ready. Go. Hide.

(*The Indian takes a place with the others. The Chief fits an arrow to his bow and crouches in the shadow. There is a pause of silence – then the noise of some one pushing his way through the woods at the rear of the clearing. Nano appears there, followed by Juan.*)

JUAN. Why do you stop?

NANO. This is the place.

JUAN (*looking around him disappointedly*). This?

NANO. There is the spring.

JUAN (*stepping forward to look at it – with growing anger*). It looks a common spring like any other. Beware, dog! In these past months you have shown me many springs –

NANO (*quickly*). The voyage was long. There were many islands. You forced me to lead you to a spring on each. But I told you the Spring of Life was here.

JUAN. I feared your revenge might lie. (*Relapsed into a mood of sombre preoccupation – bitterly.*) I drank of every one. I closed my eyes. I felt the stirring of rebirth. Fool! Always the mirror in the spring showed me the same loathsome blighted face – (*He groans – then with a harsh laugh.*) A sacred grove, the legend says! Some of those springs bubbled from sandy water! Beautiful maidens? There were none. At one place I found an old hag filling her bowl, who drank and mumbled at me. (*Then in a harsh tone of command.*) Nano! I command you to tell me if you have lied. (*Distractedly.*) I must have certainty, be it of faith or despair!

NANO. This is the spring.

JUAN (*looking around him*). But where are the trees with golden fruit, the maidens, the fountain – ? (*Bewildered, staring – grasping at hope.*) And yet – this spot has singular beauty. I feel enchantment. But why do I shudder? (*A low whistled signal comes from the Chief hidden on the edge of the clearing. Juan starts.*) Sssh! What was that?

NANO. A bird (*Insistently*). It is a magic spring. Drink!

JUAN (*bending over the spring*). A mirror of moonlight. The dead eyes of a corpse stare back in mine. (*He kneels by the spring as if fascinated.*) I dare not drink. To whom can I pray? Beatriz! Oh, to hear your voice once more, to see your face! And yet I see you everywhere. Your spirit inspires all things wherever there is beauty. I hear you call in the song of the waves, the wind is your breath, the trees reach out with your arms, the dawn and sunset promise with your lips! You are everywhere and nowhere – part of all life but mine! (*He breaks off, turning distrustful, harried eyes on the impatient Nano – bitterly.*) I am a spectacle for laughter, eh? A grotesque old fool!

NANO (*in a fierce tone of command*). Drink!

JUAN (*hectically – goading himself to action*). The test. Spirit of Eternal Youth, I pray to you! Beatriz!

(*He bends down and drinks. As he does so Nano darts away from him to the woods in front.*)

NANO (*hurriedly*). Kill when he stands again! (*The Indians can be seen raising their bows, taking aim.*)

JUAN (*having drunk, remains kneeling by the spring – in a trembling tone of hesitating joy*). New life thrills in me! Is it youth? Do I dream? Then let me never wake till the end of time! (*Then harshly.*) Coward! How often have you looked death in the face. Are you afraid of life? Open! Open and see! (*He opens his eyes and stares down into the spring. A terrible groan tears from his breast.*) O God! (*His grief is turned immediately into a frenzy of rage.*) Treacherous dog. You betrayed me.

(*He leaps to his feet, drawing his sword. There is a twanging of many bows, the whiz of a flight of arrows. Juan falls, clutches at the grass, is still. The Indians pour out into the clearing but keep a cautious distance from Juan.)*

NANO (*with more courage than they, he bends down over the body*). He wore no shining shirt. He is dead. (*He does a wild dance of savage triumph beside the body – then stops as suddenly.*) Quick. To their camp. The great Spirit has made them helpless. Be brave and kill!

(*He runs swiftly into the woods, followed by the whole band, brandishing their weapons. There is a pause. Then the fierce yells of the savages as they fall upon the sleeping camp, the howls of terror of the Spaniards, the screams of the dying, a few futile musket-shots.*)

Curtain

SCENE TEN

SCENE. *The same clearing in the woods some hours later. There is no intervening fringe of trees in this scene, the open space is in full view. The Spring is at centre. The wall of forest forms a semicircular background. As the curtain rises, there is a pitch-blackness and silence except for the murmur of the Spring. Then the sound of some one struggling to rise from the ground, falling back again with a groan of pain. Juan's voice comes out of the darkness.*

JUAN (*as if he had just regained consciousness – then with a groan of rage and pain as memory returns*). Fool! Why did I look? I might have died in my dream. (*A pause – weakly.*) Sleep seems humming in my ears. Or is it – death! – death, the Merciful One! (*He stirs and his voice suddenly grows strident.*) No, No! Why have I lived! To die alone like a beast in the wilderness? (*With a bitter mocking despair.*) O Son of God, is this Thy justice? Does not the Saviour of Man know magnanimity? True, I prayed for a miracle which was not Thine. Let me be damned then, but (*passionately*) let me believe in Thy Kingdom! Show me Thy miracle – a sign – a word – a second's vision of what I am that I should have lived and died! A test, Lord God of Hosts! (*He laughs with a scornful bravado.*) Nothing! (*But even as he speaks a strange unearthly light begins to flood down upon a spot on the edge of the clearing on the right. Startled in spite of himself.*) This light – the moon has waned – (*Beneath the growing light a form takes shape – a tall woman's figure, like a piece of ancient sculpture, shrouded in long draperies of a blue that is almost black. The face is a pale mask with features indistinguishable save for the eyes that stare straight ahead with a stony penetration that sees through and beyond things. Her arms are rigid at her sides, the palms of the hands turned outward. Juan stares at her, defiance striving with his awe.*) What are you? (*Forcing a sneer.*) An angel in answer to my prayer? (*He cannot control a shudder – tries to calm himself. He stares at the figure – after a pause, boldly.*) Or are you Death? Why then I have often laughed in your eyes! (*Tauntingly.*) Off with your mask, coward! (*Mockingly but uneasy.*) Delightful Lady, you are enigmatic. One must embrace you with bold arms, tear off your masquerade. That was my pastime once – to play at love as gaming. Were I the Juan of long ago – but you see I am old now and wounded. (*He pauses. The figure is frozen. He asks a bit falteringly.*) Are you – death? Then wait – (*In passionate invocation.*) O Beatriz! Let me hear your voice again in mercy of farewell! (*As if in answer to this the voice of Beatriz sings from the darkness.*)

VOICE. Love is a flower
For ever blooming
Life is a fountain
For ever leaping
Upward to catch the golden sunlight
Upward to reach the azure heaven
Failing, falling,
Ever returning,
To kiss the earth that the flower may live.

JUAN (*raptly*). Youth! (*As the song is sung, the same mystical light floods down slowly about the Spring, which is transformed into a gigantic fountain, whose waters, arched with rainbows, seem to join earth and sky, forming a shimmering veil, which hides the background of forest. Juan and the Figure are left at the edge of this, on the outside. The form of Beatriz appears within as if rising from the spring. She dances in ecstasy – the personified spirit of the fountain. Juan cries with a voice trembling with joy.)* The Fountain! Let me drink! *(He tries to drag himself to it but cannot – in anguish.)* Must I die –? *(Making a furious gesture of defiance at the Figure and struggling to rise.)* No! I defy you! *(Exhausted, he sinks back crying beseechingly.)* Beatriz! *(But she seems not to see or hear him. Juan half sobs in despair.)* She will not see! She will not hear! Fountain, cruel as the heart of youth, what mercy have you for the old and wounded? *(He sinks down overcome by weakness. Beatriz vanishes from the fountain. In her place appears the form of a Chinese poet. He is a venerable old man with the mild face of a dreamer and scholar. He carries a block and writes upon it with a brush, absorbed in contemplation. Juan looking up and seeing him – startled.)* What are you? *(Groping at some clue in his memory.)* I know – that night in Granada – the Moor's tale – *(Excitedly.)* Of the poet from the East who told his father the Fountain lie! Are you not that poisoner of life? *(The Poet raises his hand as if in summons. The form of the Moorish minstrel of Scene One appears at his side.)* The Moor! *(Raging.)* Infidel dog! Your lie has cursed me! *(The form of Nano appears at the other side of the Chinese poet. Juan struggles to reach his sword in a fury.)* Murderer! *(Then his eyes are caught by a fourth figure which materializes beside the Moor. It is Luis as he was in Scene One. With a cry of joy.)* Luis – old friend – *(Then as Luis seems neither to see nor hear him, he sinks back helplessly.)* No – another mocking phantom! *(He watches the Chinese poet, who seems to be reading what he has written to all of them.)* See! The dead lie to the living. It passes on – from East to West – round the round world – from old worlds to new – cheating the old and wounded – Ha!

(He laughs harshly and wildly. The Chinese poet takes the Indian by one hand, the Moor by the other. These latter stretch out their hands to Luis, who takes them, thus completing the circle. Beatriz' voice can be heard singing.)

VOICE.
Life is a field
For ever growing
Beauty a fountain
For ever flowing
Upward beyond the source of sunshine
Upward beyond the azure heaven,
Born of God but
Ever returning
To merge with earth that the field may live.

(As she sings, the four forms disappear as if they were dissolved in the fountain).

JUAN *(lost in the ecstasy of her song).* Sing on, Youth! *(With a start as the song stops – stupidly.)* The ghosts are gone. What is the answer to their riddle? I am no poet. I have striven for what the hand can grasp. What is left when Death makes the hand powerless? *(Addresses the Figure pitifully, trying to mock.)* O Mighty Relaxer of hands, have you no vision for the graspers of earth? *(The Figure raises a summoning hand. One by one, within the fountain, solemn figures materialize. First the Chinese poet, now robed as a Buddhist priest; then the Moorish minstrel, dressed as a priest of Islam; and then the Medicine Man as he was in Scene Eight, decked out in all the paint and regalia of his office; lastly, Luis, the Dominican monk of the present. Each one carries the symbol of his religion before him. They appear clearly for a moment, then fade from sight, seeming to dissolve in the fountain. Juan has stared at them with straining eyes – in a bewildered voice.)* All faiths – they vanish – are one and equal – within – *(Awe and reverence creeping into his voice.)* What are you, Fountain? That from which all life springs and to which it must return – God! Are all dreams of you but the one dream? *(Bowing his head miserably.)* I do not know. Come back, Youth. Tell me this secret! *(For a moment the voice of Beatriz is heard from the darkness.)*

Death is a mist
Veiling sunrise.

(Juan seems to fall into a rapt spell. The form of an old Indian woman appears from the left. She falters forward, a wooden bowl under her arm, as if she were going to fill it at the fountain.)

JUAN *(recognizing her aghast).* Damned hag! I remember you waited beside a spring to mock me! Begone! *(But the old woman stretches out her hands to him with a mysterious beseeching. Juan shudders – then after a struggle with himself, gets to his feet painfully.)* So be it. Sit here by me. I am old, too – and, poor woman, you cannot fill your bowl there. Come. *(He grasps her hands. In a flash her mask of age disappears. She is Beatriz. Juan gazes at her in an ecstasy – faltering, his mind groping.*) Beatriz! Age – Youth – They are the same rhythm of eternal life! (*Without his noticing it, Beatriz recedes from him and vanishes in the Fountain. He raises his face to the sky – with halting joy.*) Light comes! Light creeps into my soul! (*Then he sees the Figure walk slowly from its place and vanish in the Fountain.*) Death is no more! (*The Figure materializes again within the Fountain but this time there is no mask, the face is that of Beatriz, her form grown tall, majestic, vibrant with power. Her arms are raised above her head. Her whole body soars upward. A radiant, dancing fire, proceeding from the source of the Fountain, floods over and envelops her until her figure is like the heart of its flame. Juan stares at this vision for a moment, then sinks on his knees – exultantly.*) I see! Fountain Everlasting, time without end! Soaring flame of the spirit transfiguring Death! All is within! All things dissolve, flow on eternally! O aspiring fire of life, sweep the dark soul of man! Let us burn in thy unity! (*Beatriz' voice rises triumphantly.*)

VOICE. God is a flower
For ever blooming
God is a fountain
For ever flowing.

(*The song ceases. The light fades. There is darkness. Juan's voice is heard sobbing with happiness.*)

JUAN. O God, Fountain of Eternity, Thou art the All in One, the One in All – the Eternal Becoming which is Beauty! (*He falls unconscious. A pause. Then the faint misty light of the dawn floats over the clearing. Juan is seen lying where he had fallen. There is the noise of some one approaching from the woods in the rear, Luis and a brother Dominican enter from the forest.*)

LUIS (*seeing Juan*). God be praised! (*He rushes forward and kneels by Juan's body. Juan stirs and groans.*) He moves! Juan! It's Luis! Our friends were murdered. A boat from the fleet is waiting –

JUAN (*in a dreaming ecstasy*). God – Thou art all –

DOMINICAN. He prays.

LUIS. Delirium. Let us carry him. We'll sail for the nearest settlement –

JUAN (*as they raise him*). Light! I see and know!

LUIS. It is the dawn, Juan.

JUAN (*exultantly*). The dawn!

(*They carry him out as –*

The Curtain Falls)

SCENE ELEVEN

SCENE. *Some months later. The courtyard of a Dominican monastery in Cuba. A crude little home-made fountain is in centre. This is the only adornment of the quadrangle of bald, sun-baked earth, enclosed on the left and in the rear by a high white wall, on the right by the monastery building itself. The entrance to this is an arched doorway surmounted by a crucifix of carved wood. Two niches on either side of this door shelter primitive wooden figures of the Holy Family and Saint Dominic. In the wall, centre, is another arched door with a cross above it. Beyond the wall nature can be seen and felt – vivid, colourful, burgeoning with the manifold, compelling life of the tropics. Palm trees lean over the wall casting their graceful shadows within. Vines in flower have climbed to the top and are starting to creep down inside.*

A sunset sky of infinite depth glows with mysterious splendour.

As the curtain rises, Juan and the Father Superior are discovered. Juan is asleep, reclining on a sort of improvised invalid's chair, his cloak wrapped around him, facing the fountain. He is pale and emaciated but his wasted countenance has gained an entirely new quality, the calm of a deep spiritual serenity. The Father Superior is a portly monk with a simple round face, grey hair and beard. His large eyes have the opaque calm of a ruminating cow's. The door in the rear is opened and Luis enters. He closes the door carefully and tiptoes forward.

LUIS (*in a whisper*). He is sleeping?

FATHER SUPERIOR. As you see, Father.

LUIS (*looking down at Juan*). How calm his face is – as if he saw a vision of peace.

FATHER SUPERIOR. It is a blessed miracle he has lived so long.

LUIS. He has been waiting. (*Sadly.*) And now, I am afraid his desire is fulfilled – but not as he dreamed. Rather the cup of gall and wormwood –

FATHER SUPERIOR (*mystified*). You mean the caravel brings him bad tidings?

LUIS. Yes; and I must wake him to prepare his mind.

FATHER SUPERIOR. I will leave you with him. It is near vesper time. (*He turns and goes into the monastery.*)

LUIS (*touching Juan on the arm – gently*). Juan, awake. (*Juan opens his eyes.*) The caravel has anchored.

JUAN. From Porto Rico?

LUIS. Yes.

JUAN (*with an air of certainty – with exultant joy*). Then Beatriz is here!

LUIS (*disturbed – evasively*). There has been a frightful insurrection of the Indians. Diego was killed. (*Hastily.*) But I will not trouble you with that. (*Then slowly.*) Beatriz comes to nurse you – (*With warning emphasis*) – her second father, those were her words.

JUAN (*smiling*). You need not emphasize. I know her heart. (*Then earnestly.*) But I must tell her my truth. (*Then with a sort of pleading for assurance.*) It is for that I have waited, to tell her of the love I bore her – now – as farewell – when she cannot misunderstand. (*Proudly.*) My love was no common thing. It was the one time Beauty touched my life. I wish to live in her memory as what she was to me. (*Sinking back – with a flickering smile, weakly.*) Come, old friend, are you grown so ascetic you deny my right to lay this Golden City – the only one I ever conquered – at the feet of Beauty?

LUIS (*kindly persuasive*). Silence is better, Juan. You should renounce –

JUAN (*gently*). All is renounced. But do you begrudge a traveller if he begs a flower from this earth, a last token of the world's grace, to lend farewell the solace of regret?

LUIS (*more and more troubled*). Juan – I – I speak because – you have suffered – and now – I would not have you suffer more, dear friend. (*Then blurting out most brusquely.*) The caravel brings you a surprise. Your nephew, Juan, has arrived from Spain and comes from Porto Rico to greet you.

JUAN (*vaguely*). My nephew? (*The sound of voices comes from inside the monastery.*) Beatriz!

(*The Father Superior appears in the doorway ushering in Beatriz and Juan's nephew. They are followed by the Duenna and the Nephew's Servant, who carries his master's cloak and a lute. During the following scene these two remain standing respectfully by the doorway for a time, then go back into the monastery, the Servant leaving the cloak and lute on the ground beside the doorway. The Father Superior retires immediately. Luis, after a clasp of Juan's hand, also withdraws, exchanging greetings as he passes the Nephew and Beatriz. Beatriz glows with fulfilment, is very apparently deeply in love. The Nephew is a slender, graceful young cavalier. He is dressed richly.*)

BEATRIZ (*halting a moment with a shocked exclamation as she sees Juan's wasted face – then rushing forward and flinging herself on her knees beside his chair. Hastily*). Don Juan! Oh, this is happiness – to find you still – recovered from your wounds! Oh, I'll say prayers of thanksgiving! (*Impulsively she kisses him.*)

JUAN (*thrilled – choked – unable to say but one word*). Beatriz! Beatriz!

NEPHEW (*kneels and kisses Juan's hand. Startled, Juan's eyes search his face keenly, apprehensive of what he, too, plainly sees there*). I greet you, sir. God grant you may soon be strong again.

JUAN (*weakly*). Soon – I shall be strong – against all wounds. (*After a pause.*) And so your name is Juan, too?

NEPHEW. In your honour. Though I can add no honour to it, I hope to bear it worthily.

JUAN (*hostility creeping into his tone*). You come out here adventuring?

NEPHEW. I come to serve Spain!

JUAN (*harshly*). A heart as steeled as your

sword. Have you that?

BEATRIZ (*eagerly – somewhat hurt by Juan's reception*). Oh, he is brave! When the mob tried to storm the palace it was Juan who led the defenders.

JUAN (*more and more agitated – trying to hide his growing resentment under effusive amiability*). Bravely done! But you have doubtless heard great tales of mountains of jewels – Golden Cities of Cathay – you hope to grow rich.

NEPHEW (*proudly*). I do not care for riches; and as for Golden Cities, I only wish to plant Spain's banner on their citadels!

JUAN (*inspired by respect in spite of himself*). Brave dreams! Echoes blown down the wind of years.

BEATRIZ (*looking at the Nephew with great pride as Juan searches her face*). He is as you were in my mother's tales. (*She and the Nephew are held by each other's eyes.*)

JUAN (*after a conquering struggle with his bitterness – fatalistically*). So – thus old heart – in silence. (*Then rousing himself – intensely.*) But with joy! with joy! (*They look at him in puzzled alarm. He smiles gently at Beatriz.*) Then you have found him at last – my double?

BEATRIZ (*blushing, confusedly*). I – I do not know, Don Juan.

JUAN. Then I know. (*Musing a bit sadly.*) You have stolen my last gesture. An old man had a tale to tell you – oh, so brave a tale! – but now he sees that if youth cannot, age must keep its secrets! A sad old ghost to haunt your memory, that would be a poor wedding gift. (*They again look from him to each other, mystified and apprehensive. Juan suddenly looks up at them – with a startling directness.*) You love each other! (*He hurries on with feverish gaiety.*) Forgive – I'm a rough soldier – and there is need for haste. Quick. Do you not ask my blessing?

BEATRIZ (*falling on her knees beside him – happily*). Oh, yes, good Don Juan. (*The Nephew kneels beside her.*)

JUAN (*he raises his hands over their heads*). Youth of this earth – love – hail – and farewell! May you be blessed for ever!

(*He touches their heads with his hands – then sinks back, closing his eyes. They rise and stand looking down at him uncertainly.*)

NEPHEW (*after a pause – in a whisper*). He wishes to sleep.

BEATRIZ (*as they walk apart, in a whisper, the tears in her eyes*). Oh, Juan, I'm afraid – and yet – I am not sad.

NEPHEW (*takes her in his arms passionately*). My life! My soul! (*He kisses her.*)

BEATRIZ. My love!

NEPHEW. Life is beautiful! The earth sings for us! Let us sing, too!

(*He strides over to where the lute is and picks it up.*)

BEATRIZ (*happily*). Yes – (*Then reminded.*) Ssshh! (*She points at Juan.*)

NEPHEW (*urgingly*). He is asleep. We can go out beyond the walls.

(*He puts his arms around her and leads her out through the door in rear.*)

JUAN (*opening his eyes and looking after them, a tender smile on his lips*). Yes! Go where Beauty is! Sing!

(*From outside the voices of Beatriz and his Nephew are heard mingling in their version of the fountain song*)

Love is a flower
For ever blooming
Beauty a fountain
For ever flowing
Upward into the source of sunshine,
Upward into the azure heaven;
One with God but
Ever returning
To kiss the earth that the flower may live.

(*Juan listens in an ecstasy, bows his head, weeps. Then he sinks back with closed eyes exhaustedly. Luis enters from the monastery.*)

LUIS (*hurries forward in alarm*). Juan! (*He hears the song and is indignant.*) Have they lost all feeling? I will soon stop – (*He starts for the door in rear.*)

JUAN (*in a ringing voice*). No! I am that song! One must accept, absorb, give back, become oneself a symbol! Juan Ponce de Leon is past! He is resolved into the thousand moods of beauty that make up happiness – colour of the sunset, of to-morrow's dawn, breath of the great Trade wind – sunlight on grass, an insect's song, the rustle of leaves, an ant's ambitions. (*In an ecstasy.*) Oh, Luis, I begin to know eternal youth! I have found my Fountain! O Fountain of Eternity, take back this drop, my soul!

(*He dies. Luis bows his head and weeps.*)

FATHER SUPERIOR (*enters from the right*). Vespers. (*Then in a voice of awe as he stares at Juan.*) Is he – dead?

LUIS (*aroused – exaltedly*). No! He lives in God! Let us pray.

(*Luis sinks on his knees beside Juan's body, the Father Superior beside him. He lifts his eyes and clasped hands to heaven and prays fervently. The voices of Beatriz and the Nephew in the fountain song seem to rise to an exultant pitch. Then the chant of the monks swells out, deep and vibrant. For a moment the two strains blend into harmony, fill the air in an all-comprehending hymn of the mystery of life as*

The Curtain Falls)

WELDED

A Play in Three Acts

Characters

MICHAEL CAPE
ELEANOR OWEN, *his wife*
JOHN DARNTON
A WOMAN

Scenes

ACT ONE

SCENE The Capes' apartment.

ACT TWO

SCENE ONE Library, Darnton's home.
SCENE TWO A room.

ACT THREE

SCENE Same as Act One.

ACT I

SCENE. *The Capes' studio apartment on Fifty-ninth Street, New York City—a large room with a high ceiling. In the rear there is a balcony with a stairway at centre leading down to the studio floor. This balcony is the second story of the apartment, on which are situated the bedrooms, bathroom, etc. The section of the studio beneath the balcony is used as a dining-room. The studio proper is a combination of tasteful comfort with the practicability of a workroom. Well-filled bookcases line the walls. There is a typewriting table with a machine on it, a big desk, a reading- and writing-table with books, magazines, etc. Easy chairs, a chaise-longue, rugs, etc.*

It is about eleven-thirty. The room is in darkness except for the reading-lamp on the table. The chaise-longue has been pulled up within the circle of light and Eleanor is lying back on this, reading from a manuscript. She is a woman of thirty. Her figure is tall, with the lithe lines of nervous strength. Her face, with its high, rather prominent cheek-bones, lacks harmony; but each feature is in itself arresting. It is dominated by passionate, blue-grey eyes, restrained by a high forehead from which the mass of her dark brown hair is combed straight back. The first impression of her whole personality is one of charm, partly innate, partly imposed by years of self-discipline. The motions of her body are free and sure. Each movement is a complete reason for itself. The low notes of her voice are disturbing. She is something of every character she has ever played, of every woman one has ever met.

She reads, puts the script down, and her lips move as if she were memorizing. She hesitates, frowns, utters an exclamation of annoyance, looks at the script, finally flings it on the table with a sigh of irritation at her mistakes, gets up, lights a cigarette, resumes her former position, starts to take up the script again, but instead, with a sudden impulse which has something in it of girlish embarrassment, picks up a letter from the table. This she opens and reads, an expression of delight and love coming over her face. She kisses the letter impulsively—then gives a gay laugh at herself. She lets the letter fall on her lap and stares straight before her, lost in a sentimental reverie.

The door at right, underneath the balcony, is noiselessly opened and Cape appears. He is thirty-five, tall and dark. His unusual face impresses one. It is older and wiser than he, a harrowed battlefield of super-sensitiveness, the features at war with one another though the general effect is of a handsome face. He has the forehead of a thinker, the eyes of a dreamer, the nose and mouth of a sensualist. One feels a powerful imagination tinged with sombre sadness—a driving force of creation which can be sympathetic and cruel at the same time. His manner is extraordinarily nervous and self-conscious. He is never at ease, is always watching himself. There is something tortured about him. Yet at moments he can be astonishingly boyish and outpouring. His body is gracefully made, but his nervousness gives his movements an unco-ordinated quality. One feels perpetual strain about him, a passionate tension, a self-protecting and intellectually arrogant defiance of life and his own weakness, a deep need to love and be loved, for a faith in which to relax.

He has a suitcase, hat, and overcoat which he sets inside on the floor by wall to rear of door, glancing toward his wife, trying not to make the slightest noise. But she suddenly becomes aware of some presence in the room, starts nervously, then turns boldly to face it. She gives an exclamation of delighted astonishment when she sees Cape and jumps up to meet him as he strides toward her.

ELEANOR. Michael!

CAPE (*with a boyish grin*). You've spoiled it, Nelly; I wanted a kiss to announce me. (*They are in each other's arms. He kisses her tenderly.*)

ELEANOR (*kissing him—joyfully*). This *is* a surprise!

CAPE (*straining her in his arms and kissing her passionately*). Own little wife!

ELEANOR. Dearest! (*They look into each other's eyes for a long moment.*)

CAPE (*tenderly*). Happy?

ELEANOR. Yes, yes! Why do you always ask? You know. (*She kisses him again and nestles her face against his shoulder.*)

CAPE (*pressing her to him*). Darling!

ELEANOR (*suddenly pushing him to arms' length—with a happy laugh*). It's positively immoral for an old married couple to act this way. (*She leads him by the hand to the chaise-longue.*) And you must explain. You wrote not to expect you till the end of the week. (*She sits down.*) Get a cushion. Sit down here. (*He puts a cushion on the floor beside the chaise-longue and sits down.*) Tell me all about it.

CAPE (*notices the letter lying on the floor*). Were you reading my letter? (*She nods. He gives a happy grin.*) Do you mean to say you still read them over—after five years of me?

ELEANOR (*with a tender smile*). Oh—sometimes.

CAPE (*kissing her hand*). Sweetheart! (*Smiling.*) What were you dreaming about when I intruded?

ELEANOR. Never mind. You're enough of an egotist already. (*Her hand caressing his face and hair.*) I've been feeling so lonely—and it's only been a few weeks, hasn't it?—but it's seemed—ages. (*She laughs.*) How was everything in the country? (*Suddenly kissing him.*) Oh, I'm so happy you're back. (*With mock severity.*) But ought I? Have you finished the fourth act? You know you promised not to return until you did.

CAPE. This afternoon!

ELEANOR. That's splendid!

CAPE. When I wrote you last it was dragging damnably—then suddenly everything cleared and there was nothing to do but write like the devil. (*With smiling elation.*) From then on it rode me unmercifully to the finish!

ELEANOR. You're sure you didn't force it—

(*with a tender smile at him*)—because you were lonely, too?

CAPE (*with a sudden change in manner that is almost stern*). No. I wouldn't—I couldn't—— You know that.

ELEANOR (*her face showing a trace of hurt in spite of herself*). I was only fooling. (*Then rousing herself as if conquering a growing depression.*) Tell me about the last act. I'm terribly anxious to hear what you've done.

CAPE (*enthusiastically*). It's *real*, Nelly! You'll see when I read you—— The whole play has power and truth, I know it! And you're going to be marvellous! I could see you in it every second I was writing! It's going to be the finest thing we've ever done!

ELEANOR (*kissing him impulsively*). Dear! I love you for saying "we." But the "we" is you. I only—(*with a smile of ironical self-pity*)—act a part you've created.

CAPE (*impetuously*). Nonsense! You're an artist. Each performance of yours has taught me something new. Why, my women used to be—death masks. But now I flatter myself they're as alive as you are—(*with a sudden grin*)—at least, when you play them, Wonderful! (*He kisses her hand.*)

ELEANOR (*her eyes shining with excited pleasure*). You don't know how much it means to have you talk like that! Oh, I'm going to work so hard on this play, Michael! I've been studying the first three acts—— (*Impetuously.*) You've simply got to read me that last act right now!

CAPE (*jumping to his feet eagerly*). All right. (*He walks toward his bag—then stops when he is half-way and, hesitating, turns slowly and comes back. He bends down and lifts her face to his and kisses her tenderly, looking into her eyes—with a loving smile, slowly.*) No, on second thoughts, I won't read it now.

ELEANOR (*disappointed—but tenderly*). Oh, why not, dear?

CAPE (*with a smile*). Because——

ELEANOR (*smiling*). Plagiarist!

CAPE. Because I've been hoping for this night as our own. Let's forget the actress and playwright. Let's just be—us—lovers.

ELEANOR (*with a tender smile—musingly*). We *have* remained lovers—in spite of marriage—haven't we?

CAPE (*with a grin*). Fights and all.

ELEANOR (*with a little frown*). We don't fight so much.

CAPE (*frowning himself*). Too much.

ELEANOR (*forcing a smile*). Perhaps that's the price.

CAPE (*with a wry smile*). Don't grow fatalistic—just when I was about to propose reform.

ELEANOR (*smiling—quickly*). Oh, I'll promise to be good—if you will. (*Gently reproachful.*) Do you think I enjoy fighting with you? (*Intensely.*) Don't you realize how it destroys me?

CAPE (*with deep seriousness*). Then let's resolve—once and for all—to refuse to wound each other again—— (*With passion.*) It's wrong, Nelly. It's evil! We love too deeply.

ELEANOR. Ssshh! We promise, dear.

CAPE (*kissing her; then, hesitatingly*). We've been taking each other too much for granted. That may do very well with the earthly loves of the world—but ours has a God in it! And when the worshippers nod, the God deserts their shrine. (*He suddenly laughs with awkward self-consciousness.*) I'm afraid that sounds like preaching. (*He suddenly pulls her head down and kisses her impulsively.*) But you understand! Oh, Nelly, I love you—love you with all my soul!

ELEANOR (*deeply moved*). And I love you, Michael—always and for ever! (*They sit close, she staring dreamily before her, he watching her face.*)

CAPE (*after a pause*). What are you thinking?

ELEANOR (*with a tender smile*). Of the first time we met—at rehearsal, remember? I was thinking of how mistakenly I had pictured you before that. (*She pauses—then frowning a little.*) I'd heard such a lot of gossip about your love affairs.

CAPE (*with a wry grin*). You must have been disappointed if you expected Don Juan. (*A pause

—*then forcing a short laugh.*) I also had heard a lot of rumours about your previous—— (*He stops abruptly with an expression of extreme bitterness.*)

ELEANOR (*sharply*). Don't! (*A pause—then she goes on sadly.*) It was only our past together I wanted to remember. (*A pause—then with a trace of scornful resentment.*) I was forgetting your morbid obsession——

CAPE (*with gloomy irritation*). Obsession? Why——? (*Then determinedly throwing off this mood—reproachfully forcing a joking tone.*) We're not "starting something" now, are we—after our promise?

ELEANOR (*impulsively kissing him and straining her arms around him*). No, no—of course not! Dearest!

CAPE (*after a pause—a bit awkwardly*). But you guessed my desire, at that. I wanted to dream with you in our past—to find together in our old love—a new faith——

ELEANOR (*smiling—a bit mockingly*). Another Grand Ideal for our marriage?

CAPE (*frowning*). Don't mock.

ELEANOR (*smiling teasingly*). But you're such a relentless idealist. You needn't frown. That was exactly what drew me to you in those first days. (*Earnestly.*) I had lost faith in everything. Your love saved me. Your work saved mine. (*Intensely.*) I owe you myself, Michael! (*She kisses him. Then she goes on intensely.*) Do you remember—our first night together?

CAPE (*kissing her hand—tenderly reproachful*). Do you imagine I could've forgotten?

ELEANOR (*continuing as if she hadn't heard*). The play was such a marvellous success! I knew I had finally won recognition—through your work. I loved myself! I loved you! You came to me—and my whole being strained out —— (*More and more intensely.*) Oh, it was beautiful madness! I found and lost myself, I began living in you. I wanted to die and become you!

CAPE (*passionately*). And I, you!

ELEANOR (*softly*). And do you remember the dawn creeping in—and how we began to discuss our future? (*He kisses her hand. She exclaims impulsively.*) Oh, I'd give anything in the world to live those days over again!

CAPE (*smiling reproachfully*). Why? Hasn't our marriage kept the spirit of that time—with a growth of something deeper—finer——

ELEANOR. Yes,—but—— Oh, you know what I mean! It was revelation, then—a miracle out of the sky.

CAPE (*insistently*). But haven't we realized the ideal we conceived of our marriage—— (*Smiling, but with deep earnestness nevertheless.*) We approached our wedding extremely cautiously, if you'll remember, even after months of successful living together. Not for us the convenient sanction, the family rite. We swore to have a true sacrament—our own—or nothing! Our marriage must be a consummation of creative love, demanding and combining the best in each of us! Hard, difficult, guarded from the commonplace, kept sacred as the outward form of our deep, inner harmony! (*With an awkward sense of having become rhetorical he adds self-mockingly.*) We'd tend our flame on an altar, not in a kitchen range! (*He forces a grin—then abruptly changing again, with a sudden fierce pleading.*) It has been what we dreamed, hasn't it, Nelly?

ELEANOR (*thoughtfully*). Our ideal was difficult —for human beings. But even when we've hurt each other most cruelly—I've always known——

CAPE (*putting his arms about her and straining her to him*). We must learn to love even the things we hate in each other. We must accept each other wholly, as we are, as we must become!

ELEANOR (*sadly*). Sometimes I think we have loved too intensely—demanded too much of each other. Now there's nothing left but that something which can't give itself. And I blame you for this—because I can neither take more nor give more—and you blame me! (*She smiles tenderly.*) And then we fight!

CAPE (*excitedly*). Then let's be proud of our fight! It's the penalty of a love that strives to surpass itself—by regaining unity. It began with the splitting of a cell a hundred million years ago into you and me, leaving an eternal yearning to become one life again.

ELEANOR (*kissing him passionately*). At moments —we do.

CAPE. Yes! Yes! (*He kisses her—then intensely.*) You and I—year after year—together—forms of our two bodies coalescing into one form; rhythm of our separate lives beating against each other, forming slowly the one rhythm—the life of Us—our life created by us—outside, beyond, above! (*With sudden furious anger.*) God, what I feel of the truth of this—the beauty!—but how can I express it?

ELEANOR (*kissing him*). I understand.

CAPE (*straining her to him with fierce passion*). Oh, My Own, My Own—and I your own—to the end of time! I love you! I love you!

ELEANOR (*returning his kisses*). I love you!

CAPE (*with passionate exultance*). Why do you regret our first days? Their fire still burns in us—but deeper—more sacred. Don't you feel that? (*Kissing her again and again.*) My Own! My Own! I have become you! You have become me! One heart! One blood! Ours! (*He pulls her to her feet and kisses her.*) My wife—— Come!

ELEANOR (*almost swooning in his arms*). My lover—yes—— My lover——

CAPE. Come! (*With his arms around her he leads her to the stairway. As they get to the foot, there is a noise from the hall. She hears it, starts, seems suddenly brought back to herself. Cape is oblivious and continues up the stairs. She stands swaying, holding on to the banister as if in a daze. At the top, Cape turns in surprise at not finding her, as if he had felt her behind him. He looks down passionately, stretching out his arms, his eyes glowing.*) Come!

ELEANOR (*weakly*). Ssshh! A moment—— Listen!

CAPE (*bewilderingly*). What? What is it?

ELEANOR. Ssshh! Listen! Someone—— (*She speaks in an unnatural, mechanical tone. A knock comes at the door. She gives a sort of gasp of relief.*) There.

CAPE (*still bewilderedly as if something mysterious were happening that he cannot grasp*). What—what——! (*Then as she takes a slow, mechanical step toward the door—with tense pleading.*) Nelly! Come here! (*She turns to look at him and is held by his imploring eyes. She sways irresolutely toward him, again reaching to the banister for support. Then a sharper knock comes at the door. It acts like a galvanic shock on her. Her eyes move in that direction, she takes another jerky step. Cape stammers in a fierce whisper.*) No! Don't go!

ELEANOR (*without looking at him—mechanically*). I must.

CAPE (*frantically*). They'll go away. Nelly, don't! Don't!

(*Again she stops irresolutely like a hypnotized person torn by two conflicting suggestions. The knock is repeated, this time with authority, assurance. Her body reacts as if she were throwing off a load.*)

ELEANOR (*with a return to her natural tone—but hysterically*). Please—don't be silly, Michael. It might be—something important. (*She hurries to the door.*)

CAPE (*rushing down the stairs—frantically*). No! No! (*He just gets to the bottom as she opens the door. He stands there fixed, disorganized, trembling all over.*)

ELEANOR (*as she sees who it is—in a relieved tone of surprise*). Why, hello, John! Come in! Here's Michael. Michael, it's John.

(*Darnton steps into the room. He is a man of about fifty, tall, loose-limbed, a bit stoop-shouldered, with iron-grey hair, and a long, gaunt, shrewd face. He is not handsome, but his personality compels affection. His eyes are round and childlike. They seem to understand sorrow without ever having known it. They see every one with understanding, they never judge. The whole man has the quality of steadfastness. You feel he will always be there, unchanged, unchangeable, always serene and kindly, a cool rock for the fevered. He has no nerves. His voice is low and calming. He is dressed negligently but in expensive tweed.*)

DARNTON (*shaking Eleanor by the hand*). Hello, Nelly! I was on my way home from the theatre and I thought I'd drop in for a second. Hello, Michael! When'd you get in? Glad to see you back.

(*He comes to him and shakes his hand which Cape extends jerkily, as if in spite of himself, without a word.*)

ELEANOR (*after a glance at her husband—in a forced tone*). We're so glad you've come. Sit down.

DARNTON (*he becomes aware of the disharmonious atmosphere his appearance has created*). I can't stay a second. (*To Cape.*) I wanted some news of the big play. I thought Nelly'd probably have heard from you. (*He slaps Cape on the back with jovial familiarity.*) Well, how's it coming?

CAPE (*in a frozen tone*). Oh, all right—all right.

ELEANOR (*uneasily*). Won't you have a cigarette, John? (*She takes the box from the table and holds it out to him.*)

DARNTON (*taking one*). Thanks, Nelly. (*He half sits on the arm of a chair. She holds out a light to him.*) Thanks.

ELEANOR (*nervously*). Why don't you sit down, Michael? (*He doesn't answer. She goes to him with the cigarettes.*) Don't you want a cigarette?

(*Cape stares at her with a hot glance of scorn. She recoils from it, turning quickly away from him, visibly shaken. Without appearing to notice, Darnton scrutinizes their faces keenly, sizing up the situation.*)

DARNTON (*breaking in matter-of-factly*). You look done up, Michael.

CAPE (*with a guilty start*). I—I—I'm tired out.

ELEANOR (*with a forced air*). He's been working too hard. He finished the last act only this afternoon.

DARNTON (*with a grunt of satisfaction*). Glad to hear it—mighty glad. (*Abruptly.*) When can I see it?

CAPE. In a day or so—I want to go over——

DARNTON. All right. (*Getting to his feet.*) Well, that's that. I'll run along.

ELEANOR (*almost frightenedly*). Do stay. Why don't you read us the last act now, Michael?

CAPE (*fiercely*). No! It's rotten! I hate the whole play!

DARNTON (*easily*). Suffering from the reaction. This play's the finest thing you've done. (*He comes to Cape and slaps him on the back reassuringly.*) And it's the biggest chance the lady here has ever had. It'll be a triumph for you both, wait and see. So cheer up—and get a good night's rest. (*Cape smiles with bitter irony.*) Well, good night. (*Cape nods without speaking. Darnton goes to the door, Eleanor accompanying him.*) Good night, Nelly. Better start on your part—only don't you overdo it, too. (*He pats her on the back.*) Good night.

ELEANOR. Good night.

(*She closes the door after him. She remains there for a moment staring at the closed door, afraid to turn and meet Cape's fiercely accusing eyes which she feels fixed upon her. Finally, making an effort of will, she walks back to the table, avoiding his eyes, assuming a careless air.*)

CAPE (*suddenly explodes in furious protest*). Why did you do that?

ELEANOR (*with an assumed surprise, but with a guilty air, turning over the pages of a magazine*). Do what?

CAPE (*tensely, clutching her by the arm*). You know what I mean! (*Unconsciously he grips her tighter, almost shaking her.*)

ELEANOR (*coldly*). You are hurting me. (*A bit shamefacedly, Cape lets go of her arm. She glances quickly at his face, then speaks with a kind of dull remorse.*) I suppose I can guess—my going to the door?

CAPE. He would have gone away—— (*With anguish.*) Nelly, why did you?

ELEANOR (*defensively*). Wasn't it important you should see John?

CAPE (*with helpless anger*). Don't evade! (*With deep feeling.*) I should think you'd be ashamed.

ELEANOR (*after a pause—dully*). Perhaps—I am. (*A pause.*) I couldn't help myself.

CAPE (*intensely*). You should have been oblivious to everything! (*Miserably.*) I—I can't understand!

ELEANOR. That's you, Michael. The other is me—or a part of me—I hardly understand myself.

CAPE (*sinking down on a chair, his head in his hands*). After all we'd been to each other tonight——! (*With bitter despondency.*) Ruined now—gone—a rare moment of beauty! It seems at times as if some jealous demon of the commonplace were mocking our love—— (*With a violent gesture of loathing.*) Oh, how intolerably insulting life can be! (*Then brokenly.*) Nelly, why, why did you?

ELEANOR (*dully*). I—I don't know. (*Then after a pause she comes over and puts her hand on his shoulder.*) Don't brood, dear. I'm sorry. I hate myself. (*A pause. She looks down at him, seeming to make up her mind to something—in a forced tone.*) But—why is it gone—irrevocably—our beautiful moment? (*She strokes his hair.*) We have the whole night—— (*He stares up at her wonderingly. She forces a smile, half turning away.*)

CAPE (*in wild protest*). Nelly, what are you offering me—a sacrifice? Please!

ELEANOR (*revolted*). Michael! (*Then hysterically.*) No, forgive me! I'm the disgusting one! Forgive me!

(*She turns away from him and throws herself on a chair, staring straight before her. Their chairs are side by side, each facing front, so near that by a slight movement each could touch the other, but during the following scene they stare straight ahead and remain motionless. They speak, ostensibly to the other, but showing by their tone it is a thinking aloud to oneself, and neither appears to hear what the other has said.*)

CAPE (*after a long pause*). More and more frequently. There's always some knock at the door, some reminder of the life outside which calls you away from me.

ELEANOR. It is so beautiful—and then—suddenly I'm being crushed. I feel a cruel presence in you paralysing me, creeping over my body, possessing it so it is no longer my body—then grasping at some last inmost thing which makes me—me—my soul—demanding to have that, too! I have to rebel with all my strength—seize any pretext! Just now at the foot of the stairs—the knock on the door was—liberation. (*In anguish.*) And yet I love you! It's because I love you! If I am destroyed, what is left to love you, what is left for you to love?

CAPE. I've grown inward into our life. But you keep trying to escape as if it were a prison. You feel the need of what is outside. I am not enough for you.

ELEANOR. Why is it I can never know you? I love you—and you're strange. I try to know you and I can't. I desire to take all of you into my heart, but there is a great alien force—— I hate that unknown power in you which would destroy me. (*Pleadingly.*) Haven't I a right to myself as you have to yourself?

CAPE. You fight against me as if I were your enemy. Every word or action of mine which affects you, you resent. At every turn you feel your individuality invaded—while at the same time you are jealous of any separateness in me. You demand more and more while you give less and less. And I have to acquiesce. Have to? Yes, because I love you. I cannot live without you! You realize that! You take advantage of it while you despise me for my helplessness! (*This seems to goad him to desperation.*) But look out! I still have the strength to——! (*He turns his head and stares at her challengingly.*)

ELEANOR (*as before*). You insist that I have no life at all outside you. Even my work must exist only as an echo of yours. You hate my need of easy, casual associations. You think that weakness. You hate my friends. You are jealous of everything and everybody. You would wall me in—— (*Resentfully.*) I have to fight. You are too severe. Your ideal is too inhuman. Why can't you understand and be generous—be just! (*She turns to meet his eyes, staring back with resentful accusation. They look at each other in this manner for a long moment.*)

CAPE (*averting his eyes and addressing her directly in a cold, sarcastic tone*). Strange—that Darnton should pop in on us suddenly like that.

ELEANOR (*resentfully*). I don't see anything strange about it.

CAPE. It's past twelve——

ELEANOR. You're in New York now.

CAPE (*sharply*). I'm quite aware of that. Nevertheless——

ELEANOR (*shortly*). He explained. Didn't you hear him? He wanted news of the play and thought I might have a letter——

CAPE. That's just the point. He had no idea he would find me here.

ELEANOR (*about to fly at him, checks herself after a pause, coldly*). Why shouldn't he come to see me? He's the oldest friend I've got. He gave me my first chance and he's always helped me since. I owe whatever success I've made of my acting to his advice and direction.

CAPE (*stung—sarcastically*). Oh, undoubtedly!

ELEANOR. I suppose you think I ought to have said it's to you I owe everything?

CAPE (*dryly*). I'd prefer to say it was to yourself, and no one else. (*After a pause—attempting a casual tone.*) Has he been in the habit of calling here while I've been gone? (*Hurriedly.*) Don't misunderstand me. I'm merely asking a question.

ELEANOR (*scornfully*). Oh! (*A pause. She bites her lips—then coldly.*) Yes, he's been here once before. (*Mockingly.*) And after the theatre, too! Think of that!

CAPE (*sneeringly*). The same insatiable curiosity about my play?

ELEANOR (*angrily*). Michael! (*A pause—then scornfully.*) Don't tell me you're becoming jealous of John again!

CAPE (*meaningly*). Again. That's just it.

ELEANOR (*springing from her chair—excitedly.*) This is insufferable! (*Then calming herself with an effort—with a forced laugh.*) Please don't be so ridiculous, Michael. I'll only lose my temper if you keep on. (*Then suddenly she makes up her mind and comes to him.*) Please stop, dear. We've made up our minds not to quarrel. Let's drop it. (*She pats his head with a friendly smile.*)

CAPE (*impulsively takes her hand and kisses it*). All right. Forgive me. I'm all unstrung. His breaking in on us like that——

(*He relapses into frowning brooding again. She sits down, this time facing him, and looks at him uneasily.*)

ELEANOR (*after a pause—rather irritably*). It's too absolutely silly, your being jealous of John.

CAPE. I'm not jealous of him. I'm jealous of you—the perverse something in you that repulses our love—the stranger in you.

ELEANOR (*with a short laugh*). I should think after five years——

CAPE (*unheeding*). And what makes me hate you at those times is that I know you like to make me jealous, that my suffering pleases you, that it satisfies some craving in you—for revenge!

ELEANOR (*scornfully*). Can't you realize how absurd you are? (*Then with a forced placating laugh.*) No, really, Michael, it would be funny—if it weren't so exasperating.

CAPE (*after a pause—sombrely*). You mentioned our years together as proof. What of the years that preceded?

ELEANOR (*challengingly*). Well, what of them?

CAPE. By their light, I have plausible grounds for jealousy in Darnton's case. Or don't you acknowledge that?

ELEANOR. I deny it absolutely!

CAPE. Why, you've told me yourself he was in love with you for years, that he once asked you to marry him!

ELEANOR. Well, did I marry him?

CAPE. But he still loves you.

ELEANOR. Don't be stupid!

CAPE. He does, I tell you!

ELEANOR. If you had any sense you'd know

that his love has become purely that of an old friend. And I refuse to give up his friendship for your silly whims.

CAPE (*after a pause in which they each brood resentfully—sarcastically*). You were a shining exception, it appears. The other women he helped could hardly claim he had remained—merely their friend.

ELEANOR (*vehemently*). It's a lie! You're repeating low Broadway scandal. And even if it were true, you'd find it was they who offered themselves.

CAPE (*significantly*). Ah! (*Then after a pause.*) Perhaps because they felt it necessary for their careers.

ELEANOR (*dryly*). Perhaps. (*Then after a pause.*) But they discovered their mistake, then. John isn't that type.

CAPE (*suddenly*). Why do you act so jealous—of those others?

ELEANOR (*flushing angrily*). I don't. It's your stupid imagination.

CAPE. Then why lose your temper?

ELEANOR. Because I resent your superior attitude that John had to bribe women to love him. Isn't he as worthy of love—as you are?

CAPE (*sarcastically*). If I am to believe your story, you didn't think so.

ELEANOR (*irritably*). Then let's stop arguing, for Heaven's sake! Why do you always have to rake up the past? For the last year or so you've begun to act more and more as you did when we first lived together—jealous and suspicious of everything and everybody! (*Hysterically.*) I can't bear it, Michael!

CAPE (*ironically*). You used to love me for it then.

ELEANOR (*calming herself*). Well, I can't endure it now. It's too degrading. I have a right to your complete faith. (*Reaching over and grasping his hands—earnestly.*) You know I have in your heart of hearts. You know I love you, that there can never be anyone but you. Forget the past. It wasn't us. For your peace—and mine, Michael!

CAPE (*moved—pressing her hands*). All right. Let's stop. It's only that I've thought I've felt you drawing away——! Perhaps it's all my supersensitiveness—— (*Patting her hand and forcing a smile.*) Let's talk of something else. (*Cheerfully—after a pause.*) You can't imagine how wonderful it's been up in the country. There's just enough winter in the air to make one energetic. No summer fools about. Solitude and work. I was happy—that is, as happy as I ever can be without you.

ELEANOR (*withdrawing her hands from his with a quick movement—sarcastically*). Thanks for that afterthought—but do you expect me to believe it? When you're working I might die and you'd never know it.

CAPE (*amused, but irritated*). There you go! You denounce my jealousy, but it seems to me your brand of it is much more ridiculous.

ELEANOR (*sharply*). You imagine I'm jealous of your work? You—you flatter yourself!

CAPE (*stung—bitingly*). It's an unnatural passion certainly—in your case. And an extremely ungrateful passion, I might add!

ELEANOR (*losing her temper completely*). You mean I ought to be grateful for—— I suppose you think that without your work I—— (*Springing to her feet.*) Your egotism is making a fool of you! You're becoming so exaggeratedly conceited no one can stand you! Every one notices it!

CAPE (*angrily*). You know that's untrue. You only say it to be mean. As for my work, you've acknowledged a million times——

ELEANOR. If I have—but please remember there are other playwrights in the world!

CAPE (*bitingly*). You were on the stage seven years before I met you. Your appearance in the work of other playwrights—you must admit you were anything but successful!

ELEANOR (*with a sneer of rage*). And I suppose you were?

CAPE. Yes! Not in your Broadway sense, perhaps, but——

ELEANOR. You're contemptible! You know

that's the very last thing you can say of me. It was exactly because I wasn't that kind—because I was an artist—that I found it so hard!

CAPE (*unheeding*). My plays had been written. The one you played in first was written three years before. The work was done. That's the proof.

ELEANOR (*scathingly*). That's absurd! You know very well if it hadn't been for John, you——

CAPE (*violently*). Nonsense! There were other managers who——

ELEANOR. They didn't want your work, you know it!

CAPE (*enraged*). I see what you're driving at! You'd like to pretend I was as much dependent on Darnton as you were! (*Trembling all over with the violence of his passion.*) I should think you'd be ashamed to boast so brazenly—to me!—of what he had done for you!

ELEANOR. Why should I be ashamed of my gratitude?

CAPE. To drag that relationship out of the past and throw it in my face!

ELEANOR (*very pale—tensely*). What relationship?

CAPE (*incoherently, strangled by his passion*). Ask anyone—here—to Forty-second Street! (*Then suddenly with anguished remorse.*) No, no! I don't mean that! (*Torturedly.*) Wounds! Wounds! For God's sake, let's stop!

ELEANOR (*trembling with rage*). I'll never forget you said that! You cur!

CAPE (*stung—in a passion again at once*). Cur? Because I resent that man's being here—late at night—when I was away? I would be a cur if I didn't! Oh, I don't mean I suspect you—now——

ELEANOR (*viciously*). What noble faith! Maybe you're going to discover I don't deserve it!

CAPE (*unheeding*). But there was scandal enough about you and him, and if you had any respect for me——

ELEANOR. I've lost it now!

CAPE. You wouldn't deliberately open the way——

ELEANOR (*tensely*). So you believe—that gutter gossip? You think I——? Then all these years you've really believed——? Oh, you mean hypocrite!

CAPE (*stung—bitingly*). Don't act moral indignation! What else could I have thought? When we first fell in love, you confessed frankly you had had lovers—not Darnton, but others——

ELEANOR (*brokenly—with mingled grief and rage*). I was an idiot! I should have lied to you! But I thought you'd understand—that I'd been searching for something—that I needed love—something I found at last in you! I tried to make you see the truth—the truth!—that those experiences had only served to make me appreciate you all the more when I found you! I told you how little these men had meant to me. I tried to convince you that in the state of mind I had been in it had no significance either one way or the other, and that such an attitude is possible for a woman without her being base. I thought you understood. But you didn't, you're not big enough for that! By your own experiences in the past you had made sex a degradation to yourself—and physical virtue the highest virtue in women! (*With a gesture of loathing.*) Always the physical! As if there could be only one attitude toward it for women!

CAPE (*angrily protesting*). What has all this silly generalizing to do with us? You forget that when we conceived the ideal of our marriage we *both* agreed that unfaithfulness would be the unpardonable sin—not because we regarded it as a crime in itself, but because it was a symbol of our separate weak attitudes toward love in the past—a sin against love, do you hear?—our love which we wished to make unique, beautiful, finer than other loves!

ELEANOR (*with a wild ironical laugh*). Words! Now I know why the women in your plays are so wooden! You ought to get down on your knees and thank me for breathing life into them!

CAPE (*furiously*). Good God, how dare you criticize creative work, actress!

ELEANOR (*violently*). You deny that I create——? Perhaps if I'd consent to give up the stage, have children and a home, take up knitting—— (*She laughs wildly.*) I'd be safe then, wouldn't I?—reliable, guaranteed not to——

(*Her face seems suddenly to congeal.*) So you think that I was Darnton's mistress—that I loved him—or do you believe I just sold myself for a career?

CAPE (*in agony*). No, no! For God's sake, stop! I may have thought you once loved——

ELEANOR (*frozenly*). Well, it was—that—just that! When he first engaged me—I'd heard the gossip—I thought he expected—and I agreed with myself—it meant nothing to me one way or the other—nothing meant anything then but a chance to do my work, live my life—yes, I agreed—but you see he didn't, he didn't agree. He loved me, but he saw I didn't love him—that way—and he's a finer man than you dream!

CAPE (*hoarsely*). You're lying! (*Bewilderedly.*) I can't believe——

ELEANOR (*fiercely*). Oh, yes, you can! You want to! You do! And you're glad! It makes me seem a lower creature than you thought, but you're glad to know it just the same! You're glad because now you can really believe that—nothing ever happened between us! (*She stares into his eyes and seems to read some confirmation of her statement there, for she cries with triumphant bitterness.*) It's true! You can't deny it!

CAPE (*wildly*). No! You devil, you, you read thoughts into my mind!

ELEANOR (*with wild hysterical scorn*). It's true! How can I love you? How could I ever love you?

CAPE (*clutching her in his arms fiercely*). Stop! Stop! You do love me! (*He kisses her frantically. For a moment she submits, appears even to return his kisses in spite of herself. Cape cries triumphantly.*) You do!

(*She suddenly pushes him away and glares at him at arms' length. Her features are working convulsively. Her whole tortured face expresses an abysmal self-loathing, a frightful hatred for him.*)

ELEANOR (*as if to herself—in a strangled voice*). No! You cannot crush—my loathing! (*Her face becomes deadly calm. She speaks with intense, cold hatred.*) Don't kiss me. I despise you! I love him. He was—my lover—when you were away!

CAPE (*stares dumbly into her eyes for a long moment—hoarsely, in agony*). You lie! You lie! You only want to torture——

ELEANOR (*deathly calm*). It's true!

(*Cape stares at her another second—then, with a snarl of fury like an animal's, he seizes her about the throat with both hands. He chokes her, forcing her down to her knees. She does not struggle, but continues to look into his eyes with the same defiant hate. At last he comes to himself with a shudder and steps away from her. She remains where she is, only putting out her hand on the floor to support herself.*)

CAPE (*in a terrible state, sobbing with rage and anguish*). Gone! Dead! All our beauty gone! Oh, how I hate you! And you don't love him! You lie! You did this out of hatred for me! You dragged our ideal in the gutter—with delight! (*Wildly.*) And you pride yourself you've killed it, do you, you actress, you barren soul? (*With savage triumph.*) But I tell you only a creator can really destroy! (*With a climax of frenzy.*) And I will! I will! I won't give your hatred the satisfaction of seeing our love live on in me—to torture me! I'll drag it lower than you! I'll stamp it into the vilest depth! I'll leave it dead! I'll murder it—and be free!

(*Again he threatens her, his hands twitching back toward her neck—then he rushes out of the door as if furies were pursuing him, slamming it shut behind him.*)

ELEANOR (*with a cry of despair*). Michael! (*She stops as hatred and rage overpower her again—leaps up and runs to the door—opens it and screams after him violently.*) Go! Go! I'm glad! I hate you. I'll go, too! I'm free! I'll go——

(*She turns and runs up the stairs. She disappears for a moment, then comes back with a hat and coat on and, hurrying down the stairs again, rushes out, leaving the door open behind her.*)

Curtain

ACT II Scene I

SCENE—*Library of John Darnton's home in Connecticut, an hour or so from the city. The room is spacious, furnished in excellent taste. The rear wall is lined with bookshelves. On the wall above the shelves are hung framed photographs of stage-sets. A door is in the rear, toward right. A grand piano on the left of the door. Near it a round table with a bronze lamp. A smaller table with another lamp is in the left corner. In the right corner a big cushioned chair and an expensive gramophone. In the right wall, French windows opening on a porch. In the left wall, an open fireplace in which logs are burning. Before the fireplace, a double couch facing left and right. The lamp in the left corner is the only one lit. Over the fireplace, a framed, enlarged portrait study of Eleanor, evidently taken some years before.*

As the curtain rises, John Darnton is discovered. He is sitting in front of the fireplace lost in an apathetic dream. His body is bent over wearily, the shoulders bowed, his long arms resting on his knees, his hands dangling. He sits on the extreme edge in the exact middle of the big couch, and this heightens the sense of loneliness about him, of a man growing old among dreams which become profitless as he feels the lack of a love that could understand and share them.

Suddenly he starts as the sound of a motor comes from the driveway. The car is heard driving up ; it stops before the front door ; its door is slammed, it drives off ; a ringing of the door-bell sounds from somewhere back in the house. Darnton has got up, gone toward the door in the rear, exclaiming irritably as the bell continues to ring—All right, damn it ! Who the devil—— ? (*He is heard opening the front door—in blank amazement.*) Nelly ! (*Then her voice in a strained, hysterical pitch.*) John ! I—— (*The rest is lost incoherently. Then his voice soothingly.*) Come in by the fire ! Come in. (*He follows her into the room. Her face is pale, distraught, desperate. She comes quickly to the couch and flings herself down in one corner, staring into the fire. He stands near by uncertainly, watching her. His face holds a confused mixture of alarm, tenderness, perplexity, passionate hope.*)

DARNTON. You're shivering. Come close to the fire.

ELEANOR (*with a startled movement*). No—I—I'm warm. (*A pause. He waits for her to speak, not knowing what to think. She gradually collects herself. Memory crowds back on her and her face twitches with pain which turns to hatred and rage. She becomes conscious of Darnton's eyes, forces this back, her face growing mask-like and determined. She looks up at Darnton and forces the words out slowly.*) John—you said, if ever—— You once said I might always come——

DARNTON (*his face lights up for a second with a joy that is incongruously savage—at once controlling this—simply*). Yes, Nelly.

ELEANOR (*a bit brokenly now*). I hope—you meant that.

DARNTON (*simply*). Yes, I meant it.

ELEANOR. I mean—that you still mean it——?

DARNTON (*forcing an awkward smile*). Then—now—for ever after, amen—any old time at all, Nelly. (*Then overcome by a rush of bewildered joy—stammering.*) Why—you ought to know—— !

ELEANOR (*smiling tensely*). Would I still be welcome if I'd come—to stay ?

DARNTON (*his voice quivering*). Nelly ! (*He starts toward her, then stops—in a low, uncertain voice.*) And Michael ?

ELEANOR (*with an exclamation of pain*). Don't ! (*Quickly recovering herself—in a cold, hard voice.*) That's—dead ! (*Darnton lets a held-back breath of suspense escape him. Eleanor stammers a bit hysterically.*) Don't talk of him ! I've forgotten—as if he'd never lived ! Do you still love me ? Do you ? Then tell me ! I must know some one——

DARNTON (*still uncertain, but coming nearer to her—simply*). You knew once. Since then—— My God, you've guessed, haven't you ?

ELEANOR. I need to hear. You've never spoken—for years——

DARNTON. There was—Michael.

ELEANOR (*wildly putting her hands up to her ears as if to shut out the name*). Don't!

DARNTON. You loved him.

ELEANOR (*intensely*). I hate him! And he hates me! (*She shudders—then, driven by a desperate determination, forces a twisted smile.*) Why do you stand there? Are you afraid? I'm beginning to suspect—perhaps, you've only imagined you loved me——

DARNTON. Nelly! (*He seizes one of her hands awkwardly and covers it with kisses—confusedly, with deep emotion*). I—— You know—— Don't joke—— You know I love you!

ELEANOR (*with the same fixed smile*). You must put your arms around me—and kiss me—on the lips——

DARNTON (*takes her in his arms awkwardly and kisses her on the lips—with passionate incoherence*). Nelly! I'd given up hoping—I—I can't believe —— (*She submits to his kisses with closed eyes, her face like a mask, her body trembling with revulsion. Suddenly he seems to sense something disharmonious—confusedly.*) But you—you don't care for me!

ELEANOR (*still with closed eyes—dully*). Yes. (*With a spurt of desperate energy she kisses him wildly several times, then sinks back again, closing her eyes.*) I'm so tired, John—so tired!

DARNTON (*immediately all concern*). You're trembling all over. I'm an idiot not to have seen —— Forgive me. (*He puts his hand on her forehead.*) You're feverish. You'd better go to bed, young lady, right away. Come. (*He raises her to her feet.*)

ELEANOR (*wearily*). Yes, I'm tired. (*Bitterly.*) Oh, it's good to be loved by someone who is unselfish and kind—after all the hate——

DARNTON. Ssshh! (*Forcing a joking tone.*) I'm cast for the Doctor now. Doctor's orders: don't talk, don't think, sleep. Come, I'll show you your room.

ELEANOR (*dully*). Yes. (*As if she were not aware of what she is doing, she allows him to lead her to the door at right, rear. There she suddenly starts as if awakening—frightenedly.*) Where are we going?

DARNTON (*with gentle bullying*). You're going upstairs to bed.

ELEANOR (*with a shudder—incoherently*). No, no! Not now—no—wait—you must wait—— (*Then calming herself and trying to speak matter-of-factly.*) I'd rather stay up and sit with you. I must have gotten chilled. I want to sit by the fire.

DARNTON (*worriedly, but giving in to her at once*). All right. Whatever suits you. (*They go back to the fire. She sits in a chair which he pushes near it. He puts a cushion in behind her.*) How's that?

ELEANOR (*with a wan, grateful smile*). You're so kind, John. You've always been kind. You're so different—— (*She checks herself, her face growing hard, and stares into the fire. Darnton watches her face. There is a long pause.*)

DARNTON (*finally—in a gentle tone*). Nelly, don't you think it'd help if you told me—everything that's happened?

ELEANOR (*with a shudder*). No! It was all horror—and hatred—and disgust! (*Wildly resentful.*) Why do you make me remember? I've come to you. Why do you ask for reasons? (*With a harsh laugh.*) Are you jealous—of him?

DARNTON (*quietly*). I've always envied Michael.

ELEANOR. If you'd seen him to-night, you wouldn't envy him. You'd despise him as I do. He is mean and contemptible! He makes everything as low as he is! He went away threatening, boasting he would—— (*Hysterically.*) Why do you make me think of him? I hate him, I tell you! I want to be yours—yours! (*She throws herself into his arms.*)

DARNTON (*straining her to him—with awkward passion*). Nelly! Yes—yes—— (*Under his kisses her face again becomes mask-like, her body rigid, her eyes closed. Darnton suddenly grows aware of this. He stares down at her face, his own growing bewildered and afraid. He stammers.*) Nelly! What is it?

ELEANOR (*opening her eyes—in alarm*). What ——?

DARNTON (*with a sigh of relief*). You gave me a scare. You were like a corpse.

ELEANOR (*breaks away from him and bends over the fire with her trembling hands spread out to it*). I—I'm so cold. I believe I do feel ill. I'll go to bed. (*She moves toward the door.*)

DARNTON (*uneasily—with a forced heartiness*). Now you're talking sense. Come on. (*He leads the way into the hall. She goes as far as the doorway—then stops. A queer struggle is apparent in her face, her whole body, as if she were fighting with all her will to overcome some invisible barrier which bars her way. Darnton is watching her keenly now, a sad foreboding coming into his eyes. He steps past her back into the room, saying kindly but with a faint trace of bitterness.*) It's the first door upstairs on your right—if you'd rather go alone.

(*He walks still farther away, then turns to watch her, his face growing more and more aware and melancholy.*)

ELEANOR (*vaguely*). No—you don't understand—— (*She stands swaying, reaching out her hand to the side of the doorway for support—dully.*) The first door to the right—upstairs?

DARNTON. Yes.

ELEANOR (*struggles with herself, confused and impotent, trying to will—finally turns to Darnton like a forlorn child.*) John. Can't you help me?

DARNTON (*gravely*). No—not now when I do understand. You must do it alone.

ELEANOR (*with a desperate cry*). I can! I'm as strong as he! I do!

(*This breaks the spell which has chained her. She grows erect and strong. She walks through the doorway.*)

DARNTON (*with a triumphant exclamation of joy*). Ah! (*He strides toward the doorway—then stops as he notices that she also has stopped at the bottom of the stairs, one foot on the first stair, looking up at the top. Then she wavers and suddenly bolts back into the room, gropingly, her face strained and frightened. Darnton questions her with fierce disappointment.*) What is it? Why did you stop?

ELEANOR (*forcing a twisted smile—wildly*). You're right. I must be feverish. (*Trying to control herself—self-mockingly.*) Seeing spooks, that's pretty far gone, isn't it? (*Laughing hysterically.*) Yes—I swear I saw him—standing at the head of the stairs waiting for me—just as he was standing when you knocked at our door,—remember? (*She laughs.*) Really, it was too ridiculous—so plain——

DARNTON. Ssshh! (*Glancing at her worriedly.*) Won't you lie down here? Try and rest.

ELEANOR (*allowing him to make her comfortable on the couch before the fire*). Yes. (*Her eyes glance up into his bewilderedly.*)

DARNTON (*after a long pause—slowly*). You don't love me, Nelly!

ELEANOR (*pitifully protesting*). But I do, John! I do! You're kind! You're unselfish and fine! I do love you!

DARNTON (*with a wry smile*). That isn't me. You don't love me.

ELEANOR (*desperately defiant, leaps to her feet*). I do! (*She takes his face between her hands and bringing her own close to it, stares into his eyes. He looks back into hers. She mutters fiercely between her clenched teeth.*) I do! I do love you!

(*For a long moment they remain there, as she brings her face nearer and nearer, striving with all her will to kiss him on the lips. Finally her eyes falter, her body grows limp, she turns away and throws herself on the couch in a fit of abandoned sobbing.*)

DARNTON (*with a sad smile*). You see?

ELEANOR (*her voice muffled—between sobs*). But I—want to! And I will—I know—some day—I promise!

DARNTON (*forcing a light tone*). Well, I'll be resigned to wait and hope then—and trust in your good intentions. (*After a pause—in a calming, serious tone.*) You're calmer now? Tell me what happened between you and Michael.

ELEANOR. No! Please!

DARNTON (*smiling, but earnestly*). It'll relieve your mind, Nelly—and besides, how can I help you otherwise?

ELEANOR (*after a pause—with resigned dullness*). We've quarrelled, but never like this before. This was final! (*She shudders—then suddenly bursts out wildly.*) Oh, John, for God's sake don't ask me! I want to forget! We tore each other to pieces, we destroyed one another! I realized I hated him! I couldn't restrain my hate! I had to crush him as he was crushing me! (*After a pause—dully again.*) And so that was the end.

DARNTON (*tensely, hoping again now—pleadingly*). You're sure, Nelly? You're sure your love is dead——

ELEANOR (*fiercely*). I hate him!

DARNTON (*after a pause—earnestly*). Then stay here. I think I can help you forget. Never mind what people say. Make this your home—and maybe—in time—— (*He forces a smile.*) You see, I'm already starting to nurse along that crumb of hope you gave. (*She is looking down, preoccupied with her own thoughts. He looks at her embarrassedly, then goes on gently, timidly persuasive.*) I don't mind waiting. I'm used to it. And I've been hoping ever since I first met you—eight years ago, isn't it? (*Forcing a half-laugh.*) I'll admit when you married him the waiting and hoping seemed excess labour. I tried to fire them—thought I had—but when you came to-night—there they were right on to the job again! (*He laughs—then catching himself awkwardly.*) But hell! I don't want to bother you now. Forget me. Will you stay here and rest up—treat this as your house? That's the point.

ELEANOR (*in a bland, absent-minded tone which wounds him*). You're so kind, John. (*Then following her own line of thought, she breaks out savagely.*) I told him I'd been your mistress while he was away!

DARNTON (*amazed*). Nelly!

ELEANOR. I had to tell that lie! He was degrading me! I had to revenge myself!

DARNTON. But certainly he could never believe——

ELEANOR (*with fierce triumph*). Oh, I made him believe! (*Then dully.*) Then—he went away. He said he would kill our love as I had—worse—— (*With a twisted smile.*) That's what he's doing now. He has gone to one of those women he lived with before—— (*Laughing harshly.*) No! They wouldn't be vile enough—for his beautiful revenge on me! He has a wonderful imagination. Every one acknowledges that! (*She laughs with wild bitterness—this is transformed into a frenzy of rage.*) Oh, how I loathe him! (*Then in agony.*) My God, why do I think——! Help me, John! Help me to forget—to love you!

DARNTON (*after a pause—with a sad, bitter helplessness*). You mean—to hate him! Help you—to revenge yourself! But don't you realize I can't—you can't—because—I see this damn clear now, so don't deny it!—because you still love him!

ELEANOR (*fiercely*). No! (*After a pause—brokenly.*) Don't! I know! I hate myself for loving him! I hate him because I love him! (*She sobs heart-brokenly.*)

DARNTON (*after a pause, as her sobbing grows quieter—sadly*). Go home.

ELEANOR. No! (*After a pause, brokenly.*) He hates me.

DARNTON (*with a grim smile*). Because he loves you.

ELEANOR. He'll never come back now.

DARNTON (*with bitter humour*). Oh, yes, he will; take my word for it. I know—because I happen to love you, too.

ELEANOR (*faintly*). And do you—hate me?

DARNTON (*after a pause—with melancholy self-disgust*). No. I'm too soft. That's why you've always liked me and never loved me. (*Bitterly.*) I ought to hate you! Twice now you've treated my love with the most humiliating contempt—— Once, years ago, when you were willing to endure it as the price of a career—again to-night, when you try to give yourself out of hate and love—love—for him! (*In sudden furious revolt.*) Christ! What am I, eh? (*Then checking his anger and forcing a wry smile.*) I think your treatment has been rather hard to take, Nelly—and even now I'm not cured, at that! (*He laughs harshly and turns away to conceal his real hurt.*)

ELEANOR (*with deep grief*). Forgive me.

DARNTON (*as if to himself—reassuringly*). Still—I would have been the poorest slave. I couldn't have fought you like Michael. Perhaps, deep down, I'm glad——

ELEANOR. Don't say that! If I could have loved you—if I could love you now—I'd be happy.

DARNTON. You'd have grown to despise a slave long ago. (*Then bluntly.*) You'd better go home right away.

ELEANOR (*dully*). Even if he has——

DARNTON (*brusquely*). You know you've got to—no matter what!

ELEANOR. How can I have faith? And how can I ever make him believe I lied about you? How can he ever trust me about us—here—to-night? (*Miserably.*) Oh, don't you see how impossible——?

DARNTON (*impatiently*). But evidently you must. Face the truth in yourself. Must you—or mustn't you?

ELEANOR (*after a moment's defiant struggle with herself—forlornly.*) Yes. (*After a pause, with a gesture toward the door and a weary, beaten smile.*) Upstairs—if I could have gone—I'd have been free. But he's trained me too well in his ideal. And I love him. From the depths of my humiliation I love him! (*Despairingly.*) But when I think of what he's doing, of what he will do to crush——! I hate him! I hate him so terribly that——! (*She stops, trembling with passion, her face convulsed—then, shrugging her shoulders, fatalistically.*) It's broken me. I'm no longer anything. So what does it matter how weak I am? Let him win. (*A slight pause.*) I begin to know—something. (*With a sudden queer exultant pride.*) I love him! But my love for him is my own, not his! My love for him he can never possess! It is *my* own! It is *my* life! (*She turns to Darnton determinedly.*) I must go home now.

DARNTON (*wonderingly*). Good. I'll drive you back. (*He starts for the door.*)

ELEANOR (*suddenly grasping his arm*). Wait. (*Affectionately.*) I was forgetting you—as usual. How can you forgive me? What can I do——?

DARNTON (*with a wry smile*). Forget, Nelly. Remember me as a manager. Study your part; help Michael; and we'll all three be enormously successful! (*He laughs mockingly.*)

ELEANOR (*tenderly*). I'll always believe Fate should have let me love you, instead.

DARNTON (*with the same wry smile*). While I begin to suspect that in a way I'm lucky—to be heart-broken. Our might-have-beens are more enjoyable—as dreams, eh? (*With a laugh.*) Curtain! You'll want to go upstairs and powder your nose. There's no angel with a flaming sword there now, is there? (*He points to the doorway.*)

ELEANOR (*with a tired smile*). No.

(*She goes to the doorway. He follows her. They both stop there for a moment instinctively and smile forlornly at each other.*)

DARNTON (*impulsively*). One question: That time you stood here and called to me for help—if I could have given you a push, mental, moral, physical——?

ELEANOR (*smiling*). Might-have-beens, John! (*Then earnestly.*) You didn't because you couldn't. It wouldn't have helped, anyway. The angel was here. (*She touches her breast.*)

DARNTON (*with a sigh*). Thanks. That saves me a lifelong regret.

ELEANOR (*earnestly—gripping his right hand in hers and holding his eyes*). There must be no regrets—ever—between old friends.

DARNTON (*gripping her hand in turn*). No, I promise, Nelly. (*Then letting her hand drop and turning away to conceal his emotion—forcing a joking tone.*) After all, friendship is sounder, saner—more in the picture for my type, eh?

ELEANOR (*absent-minded again now—vaguely*). I don't know. (*Then briskly.*) We must hurry. I'll be right down. (*She goes out and up the stairway in the hall.*)

DARNTON (*stares up after her for a second, then smiling grimly*). Well, business of living on as usual. (*He passes his arm here and there in the *open doorway as if he were a magician—with bitter irony.*) You see—nothing there! Invisible cobwebs—cast-iron cobwebs! (*He laughs harshly.*) Catching title for a play. I'll tell Michael! (*He laughs again—checks himself—then walks out, calling up the stairs.*) I'm going to get the car, Nelly!

Curtain

Scene 2

SCENE—*A dingy bedroom in a Sixth Avenue "bed house." In the rear, centre, a door leading into the hall. A chair to left of door. In the left corner, a washstand with bowl, pitcher, towels, etc. In the left wall, centre, a small window with a torn dark shade pulled down. On the right, a bed. A filthy threadbare carpet on the floor. Ugly wall-paper, dirty, stained, criss-crossed with match-strokes.*

When the curtain rises, the room is in darkness except for a faint glow on the window shade from some street lamp. Then the door is opened and a woman's figure is silhouetted against the dim, yellow light of the hall. She turns and speaks to someone who is following her. Her voice is heavy and slow with the strong trace of a foreign intonation, although the words are clearly enough defined.

WOMAN. Got a match?

(*A man's figure appears behind hers. He fumbles in his pockets, hands her a match without speaking. She strikes it on the wall, lights the gas-jet near the door. The room is revealed in sordid detail in the tarnished yellow light. The Woman is fairly young. Her face, rouged, powdered, pencilled, is broad and stupid. Her small eyes have a glazed look. Yet she is not ugly—rather pretty for her bovine, stolid type—and her figure is still attractive, although its movements just now are those of a tired charwoman's. She takes off her coat, hangs it on a hook, then goes to a mirror on the wall over the washstand and removes her hat.*

The man is Michael Cape. He is bare-headed, his hair dishevelled, his eyes wild, his face has a feverish, mad expression. He stands in the doorway watching each movement of the Woman's with an unnatural preoccupied concentration.)

WOMAN (*having removed her hat and put it on the washstand, turns to him impatiently*). Ain't you comin' in? (*He starts and nods stupidly, moving his lips as if answering, but not making a sound.*) Come in! Shut the door.

(*He does so and locks it mechanically—then looks from her around the room with a frightened, puzzled glance as if he were aware of his surroundings for the first time.*)

WOMAN (*forcing a trade smile—with an attempt at lightness*). Well, here we are, dearie. (*Then with a sigh of physical weariness as she sits on the side of the bed.*) Gawd, I'm tired! My feet hurt fierce! I been walkin' miles. I got corns, too. (*She sighs again, this time with a sort of restful content.*) It's good 'n' warm in this dump, I'll hand it that. (*A pause.*) I'd gave up hope and was beatin' it gome when you come along. (*A pause during which she takes him in calculatingly.*) How'd you lose your hat? (*He starts, passes a trembling hand through his hair bewilderedly, but does not answer. A pause—then the Woman sighs and yawns wearily—bored.*) Can't you say nothin'? You was full enough of bull when you met me. Gawd, I thought you'd get us both pinched. You acted like you was crazy. Remember kissing me on the corner with a whole mob pipin' us off?

CAPE (*with a start—evidently answering some train of thought in his mind—with a wild laugh*). Remember?

(*He sinks on the chair with his head in his hands. There is a pause.*)

WOMAN (*insinuatingly*). Goin' to stay all night? (*He glances up at her stupidly, but doesn't answer. The Woman insists dully.*) Say, you got ear-muffs on? I ast you, d'you wanta stay all night?

CAPE (*after a moment's groping, nods emphatically again and again, swallowing hard several times as if he were striving to get control of his voice—finally blurts out in a tone of desperation*). Yes—yes—of course! Where else would I go?

WOMAN. Home. (*Indifferently.*) That's where most of 'em goes—afterwards.

CAPE (*with a sudden burst of wild laughter*). Ha-ha-ha! Home! Is that your private brand of revenge—to go with men with homes? I congratulate you! (*He laughs to himself with bitter irony—then suddenly deadly calm.*) Yes, I have a home, come to think of it—from now on hell is my home! I suspect we're fellow-citizens. (*He laughs.*)

WOMAN (*superstitiously*). You oughtn't to say them things.

CAPE (*with dull surprise*). Why?

WOMAN. Somep'n might happen. (*A pause.*) Don't you believe in no God?

CAPE. I believe in the Devil!

WOMAN (*frightened*). Say! (*Then after a pause, forcing a smile.*) I'm wise to what's wrong with you. You been lappin' up some bum hooch.

CAPE (*jerkily*). No. I'm not drunk. I thought of that—but—it's evasion. (*Wildly.*) And I must be conscious—fully conscious, do you understand?—of what I do! I will this act as a symbol of release—of the end of all things! (*He stops, shuddering. She looks at him stolidly. A pause. He presses his hands to his forehead.*) My brain burns up! (*Suddenly striking his head with both fists—in a frenzy.*) Stop thinking, damn you! Stop! (*Then after a pause—dully.*) How long——? What time is it?

WOMAN. Little after two, I guess.

CAPE (*amazed*). Only that? (*She nods.*) Only two hours since——? (*A pause.*) I remember streets—lights—dead faces—— Then you—your face alone was alive for me, alive with my deliverance! That was why I kissed you. You shall avenge me!

WOMAN (*looking at him queerly*). Say, you talk nutty. Been dopin' up on coke, I bet you.

CAPE (*with an abrupt exclamation*). Ha! (*He stares at her with unnatural intensity.*) You seem to take it quite casually that men must be either drunk or doped—otherwise——! Marvellous! You—you are the last depth—— (*With a strange, wild exultance, leaps to his feet.*) You are my salvation! You have the power—and the right—to defile beauty and murder love! You can satisfy hate and exhaust it! Will you let me kiss you again? (*He strides over to her.*)

WOMAN (*in a stupid state of bewilderment, feeling she has been insulted, but not exactly knowing by what or how to resent it—angrily, pushing him away*). No! Get away from me! (*Then afraid she may lose his trade by this rebuff.*) Aw, all right. Sure you can. (*Making a tremendous visible effort he kisses her on the lips, then shrinks back with a shudder and forces a harsh laugh. She stares at him and mutters resentfully.*) On'y don't get so fresh, see? I don't like your line of talk. (*He slumps down on the chair again, sunk in a sombre stupor. She watches him. She yawns. Finally she asks insinuatingly.*) Ain't you gettin' sleepy?

CAPE (*starting—with wild scorn*). Sleep! Do you think I——! (*Staring at her.*) Oh—I see—you mean, what did I come here for?

WOMAN (*in same tone*). It's gettin' late.

CAPE (*dully, with no meaning to his question—like an automaton.*) A little after two?

WOMAN. Yes. (*She yawns.*) You better let me go to bed and come yourself.

CAPE (*again staring at her with strange intensity—suddenly with a queer laugh.*) How long have you and I been united in the unholy bonds of—bedlock? (*He chuckles sardonically at his own play on words.*)

WOMAN (*with a puzzled grin*). Say!

CAPE. Ten thousand years—about—isn't it? Or twenty? Don't you remember?

WOMAN (*keeping her forced grin*). Tryin' to kid me, ain't you?

CAPE. Don't lie about your age! You were beside the cradle of love, and you'll dance dead drunk on its grave!

WOMAN. I'm only twenty-six, honest.

CAPE (*with a wild laugh*). A fact! You're right. Thoughts keep alive. Only facts kill—deeds! (*He starts to his feet.*) Then hate will let me alone. Love will be dead. I will be as ugly as the world. My dreams will be low dreams. I'll "lay me down among the swine." Will you promise me this, you?

WOMAN (*vaguely offended—impatiently*). Sure, I'll promise anything. (*She gets up to start undressing. She has been pulling the pins out of her hair and, as she rises, it falls over her shoulders in a peroxided flood. She turns to him, smiling with childish pride.*) D'you like my hair, kid? I got a lot of it, ain't I?

CAPE (*laughing sardonically*). "O love of mine, let down your hair and I will make my shroud of it."

WOMAN (*coquettishly pleased*). What's that—po'try? (*Then suddenly reminded of something, she regards him calculatingly—after a pause, coldly.*) Say, you ain't broke, are you? Is that what's troubling you?

CAPE (*startled—then with bitter mockery*). Ha! I see you're a practical person. (*He takes a bill from his pocket and holds it out to her—contemptuously.*) Here!

WOMAN (*stares from the bill to him, flushing beneath her rouge*). Say! I don't like the way you act. (*Proudly.*) I don't take nothin' for nothin'—not from you, see!

CAPE (*surprised and ashamed*). I'll leave it here, then. (*He puts it on top of the washstand and turns to her—embarrassedly.*) I didn't mean—to offend you.

WOMAN (*her face clearing immediately*). Aw, never mind. It's all right.

CAPE (*staring at her intently—suddenly deeply moved*). Poor woman!

WOMAN (*stung—excitedly*). Hey, none of that! Nix! Cut it out! I don't stand for that from nobody! (*She sits down on the bed angrily.*)

CAPE (*with unnatural intensity*). Do you know what you are? You're a symbol. You're all the tortures man inflicts on woman—and you're the revenge of woman! You're love revenging itself upon itself! You're the suicide of love—of my love—of all love since the world began! (*Wildly.*) Listen to me! Two hours ago—— (*Then he beats his head with both clenched hands—distractedly.*) Leave me alone! Leave me alone, damn you!

(*He flings himself on the chair in a violent outburst of dry sobbing.*)

WOMAN (*bewilderedly*). Say! Say! (*Then touched, she comes to him and puts her arms around his shoulders, on the verge of tears herself.*) Aw, come on, kid. Quit it. It's all right. Everything's all right, see. (*As his sobbing grows quieter—helpfully.*) Say, maybe you ain't ate nothin', huh? Maybe soup'd fix you. S'posin' I go round the corner, huh? Sure, all I got to do is put up my hair——

CAPE (*controlling hysterical laughter—huskily*). No—thanks. (*Then his bitter memories rush back agonizingly. He stammers wildly.*) She confessed—with hate! She was proud of her hate! She was proud of my torture. She screamed: "I hate you! I'll go too." Go where? Did she go? Yes, she must——! Oh, my God! Stop! Stop! (*He springs up, his face distorted, and clutches the Woman fiercely in his arms.*) Save me, you! Help me to kill this beauty which she defiled! Help me to gain the peace which is the death of love. (*He kisses her again and again frenziedly. She submits stolidly. Finally with a groan he pushes her away, shuddering with loathing, and sinks back on the chair.*) No! I can't—I can't!

WOMAN (*wiping her lips with the back of her hand—a vague comprehension coming into her face—scornfully*). Huh! I got a hunch now what's eatin' you. (*Then with a queer sort of savage triumph.*) Well, I'm glad one of youse guys got paid back like you oughter!

CAPE (*with dull impotent rage*). I can't! I love her! (*As if he were defying himself by this confession.*) Yes, I still love her! And I can't! I only hate because I love—I'm the weaker. Our love must live on in me. There is no death for it. There is no freedom—while I live. (*Struck by a sudden thought.*) Then, why——? (*A pause.*) An end of loathing—in a second, peace—no wounds, no memories—sleep!

WOMAN (*with a shudder*). Say, you're beginning to give me the creeps.

CAPE (*startled—with a forced laugh*). Am I? Well, never mind. (*He shakes his head as if to drive some thought from his mind and forces a trembling, mocking smile.*) That's over. The great temptation, isn't it? I suppose you've known it. But also the great evasion. Too simple for the complicated—too weak for the strong, too strong for the weak. One must go on, eh?—even wounded, on one's knees—if only out of curiosity to see what will happen—to oneself. (*He laughs harshly and turns with a quick movement toward the door.*) Well, good-bye, and forgive me. It isn't you, you know. You're the perfect death—but I'm too strong, or weak—no, merely I'm myself—and that myself can't, you understand—can't! So, good-bye. (*He goes to the door.*)

WOMAN (*frightenedly*). Say! What're you goin' to do?

CAPE. Go on in the dark.

WOMAN. You better beat it home, that's what.

CAPE (*violently*). No! (*Then, bitterly.*) I came home once to-night——

WOMAN (*wearily*). Aw, forget it. She's your wife, ain't she?

CAPE. How do you know? (*He comes back to her, curiously attracted.*)

WOMAN (*cynically*). Aw, I'm wise. Stick to her, see? You'll get over it. You can get used to anything, take it from me!

CAPE (*in anguish*). Don't! But it's true—it's the insult we all swallow as the price of life. (*Rebelliously.*) But I——!

WOMAN (*with a sort of forlorn chuckle*). Oh, you'll go back, aw right! Don't kid yourself. You'll go back no matter what, and you'll learn to like it. Don't I know? You love her, don't you? Well, then! There's no use buckin' that game. Go home. Kiss and make up. Ferget it. It's easy to ferget—when you got to! (*She finishes up with a cynical, weary scorn.*)

CAPE (*very pale—stammering*). You—you make life despicable.

WOMAN (*angrily*) Say! (*Then with groping, growing resentment.*) I don't like your talk! You've pulled a lot of bum cracks about—about—never mind, I got you, anyhow! You ain't got no right—— What'd you wanter pick me up for, anyway? Wanter just get me up here to say rotten things? Wanter use me to pay her back? Say! Where do I come in? Guys go with me 'cause they like my looks, see?—what I am, understand?—but you, you don't want nothin'. You ain't drunk, neither! You just don't like me. And you was beatin' it leavin' your money there—without nothin'. I was goin' to let you then, I ain't now. (*She suddenly gives him a furious push which sends him reeling back against the wall.*) G'wan! Take your lousy coin and beat it! I wouldn't take nothin', nor have nothin' to do with you if you was to get down on your knees!

CAPE (*stares at her—an expression comes as if he were seeing her for the first time—with great pity.*) So—it still survives in you. They haven't killed it—that lonely life of one's own which suffers in solitude. (*Shamefacedly.*) I should have known. Can you forgive me?

WOMAN (*defensively*). No!

CAPE. Through separate ways love has brought us both to this room. As one suffering, lonely human being to another, won't you——?

WOMAN (*struggling with herself—harshly*). No!

CAPE (*gently*). Not even if I ask it on my knees? (*He kneels before her, looking up into her face.*)

WOMAN (*bewildered, with hysterical fierceness*). No! Git up, you——! Don't do that, I tell you! Git up or I'll brain yuh! (*She raises her fist threateningly over his head.*)

CAPE (*gently*). Not until you——

WOMAN (*exhaustedly*). Aw right—aw right—I forgive——

CAPE (*gets up and takes her face between his hands and stares into her eyes—then he kisses her on the forehead.*) Sister!

WOMAN (*with a half-sob*). Nix! Lay off of me, can't you!

CAPE. But I learned that from you.

WOMAN (*stammering*). What?—loined what? (*She goes away from him and sinks on the bed exhaustedly.*) Say, you better beat it.

CAPE. I'm going. (*He points to the bill on the washstand.*) You need this money. You'll accept it from me now, won't you?

WOMAN (*dully*). Sure. Leave it there.

CAPE (*in the same gentle tone*). You'll have to give it to him in the morning?

WOMAN (*dully*). Sure.

CAPE. All of it?

WOMAN. Sure.

CAPE. Or he'd beat you?

WOMAN. Sure. (*Then suddenly grinning.*) Maybe he'll beat me up, anyway—just for the fun of it.

CAPE. But you love him, don't you?

WOMAN. Sure. I'm lonesome.

CAPE. Yes. (*After a slight pause.*) Why did you smile when you said he'd beat you, anyway?

WOMAN. I was thinkin' of the whole game. It's funny, ain't it?

CAPE (*slowly*). You mean—life and love?

WOMAN. Sure. You got to laugh, ain't you? Sure! You got to loin to like it!

CAPE (*this makes an intense impression on him. He nods his head several times*). Yes! That's it! That's exactly it! That goes deeper than wisdom. To learn to love the truth of life—to accept it and be exalted—that's the one faith left to us! (*Then with a tremulous smile.*) Good-bye, I've joined your church. I'm going home.

WOMAN (*with a grin that is queerly affectionate*). Sure. That's the stuff. Close your eyes and your feet'll take you there.

CAPE (*impressed again*). Yes! Yes! Of course they would! They've been walking there for thousands of years—blindly. However, I'll keep my eyes open—(*he smiles back at her affectionately*)—and learn to like it!

WOMAN (*grinning*). Sure. Good luck.

CAPE. Good-bye.

(*He goes out, closing the door after him. She stares at the door for a moment, listening to his footsteps as they die out down the stairs. Then she takes a comb from her bag and, going to the mirror, starts to comb her hair. She is preoccupied and her hand suddenly stops.*)

WOMAN (*confusedly*). Say——?

(*She stares at herself with a vaguely-troubled, ruminating stolidity. Then with a sigh she goes on combing her hair.*)

Curtain

ACT III

SCENE—*Same as Act I, the Capes' apartment, about five o'clock the same morning. The door to the hall is still open, the reading-lamp alight, everything exactly as at the close of Act I.*

Eleanor is standing by the table, leaning her back against it, facing the door, her whole attitude strained, expectant, but frightened, tremblingly uncertain whether to run and hide from, or run forward and greet Cape, who is standing in the doorway. For a long, tense moment they remain fixed, staring into each other's eyes with an apprehensive questioning. Then, as if unconsciously, falteringly, with trembling smiles, they come toward each other. Their lips move as if they were trying to speak. When they come close, they instinctively reach out their hands in a strange conflicting gesture of a protective warding off and at the same time a seeking possession. Their hands clasp and they again stop, searching each other's eyes. Finally their lips force out words.

ELEANOR (*penitently*). Michael!

CAPE (*humbly*). Nelly! (*They smile with a queer understanding, their arms move about each other, their lips meet. They seem in a forgetful, happy trance at finding each other again. They touch each other testingly as if each cannot believe the other is really there. They act for the moment like two persons of different races, deeply in love, but separated by a barrier of language.)*

ELEANOR (*rambling tenderly*). Michael—I—— Dearest—I was afraid——

CAPE (*stammering*). Nelly—it's so good! I thought—my own—you'd gone—— (*They stare at each other—a pause.*)

ELEANOR (*beginning to be aware—a bit bewilderedly, breaking away from him with a little shiver—stupidly*). I feel—there's a draught, isn't there?

CAPE (*becoming aware in his turn—heavily*). I'll shut the door. (*He goes and does so. She walks to her chair and sits down. He comes and sits beside her. They are now side by side as in Act I. A pause. They stare ahead, each frowningly abstracted. Then each, at the same moment, steals a questioning side glance at the other. Their eyes meet, they look away, then back, they stare at each other with a peculiar dull amazement, recognition yet non-recognition. They seem about to speak, then turn away again. Their faces grow sad, their eyes begin to suffer, their bodies become nervous and purposeless. Finally Cape exclaims with a dull resentment, directed not at her, but at life.*) What is—it? (*He makes a gesture of repulsing something before him.*)

ELEANOR (*in his tone*). I don't know.

CAPE (*harshly*). A moment ago—there—— (*He indicates where they had stood in an embrace.*) We knew everything. We understood!

ELEANOR (*eagerly*). Oh, yes!

CAPE (*bitterly*). Now—we must begin to think—to continue going on, getting lost——

ELEANOR (*sadly*). It was happy to forget. Let's not think—yet.

CAPE (*grimly*). We've begun. (*Then with a harsh laugh.*) One must explain. Thinking explains. It eliminates the unexplainable—by which we live.

ELEANOR (*warningly*). By which we love. Ssshh! (*A pause.*)

CAPE (*wonderingly—not looking at her*). You have learned that, too?

ELEANOR (*with a certain exultance*). Oh, yes, Michael—yes! (*She clasps his hand. A pause. Then she murmurs.*) Now—we know peace. (*Their hands drop apart. She sighs.*)

CAPE (*slowly*). Peace isn't our meaning.

ELEANOR (*suddenly turns and addresses him directly in a sad, sympathetic tone*). You've something you want to ask me, Michael?

CAPE (*turns to her with an immediate affirmative on his lips, checks it as he meets her eyes, turns away—a pause—then he turns back humbly*). No.

ELEANOR (*her head has been averted since he turned away—without looking at him*). Yes.

CAPE (*decisively*). No, Nelly. (*She still keeps her head averted. After a pause he asks simply.*) Why? Is there something you want to ask me?

ELEANOR. No. (*After a pause—with a trace of bitter humour.*) I can't be less magnanimous than you, can I?

CAPE. Then there is something——?

ELEANOR. Haven't you something you want to tell?

CAPE (*looks at her. Their eyes meet again*). Yes—the truth—if I can. And you?

ELEANOR. Yes, I wish to tell you the truth. (*They look into each other's eyes. Suddenly she laughs with a sad self-mockery.*) Well, we've both been noble. I haven't asked you; you haven't asked me; and yet—— (*She makes a helpless gesture with her hands. A pause. Then abruptly and mechanically.*) I'll begin at the beginning. I left here right after you did.

CAPE (*with an involuntary start*). Oh! (*He checks himself.*)

ELEANOR (*her eyes reading his—after a pause—a bit dryly*). You thought I'd stayed here all the time? (*Mockingly.*) Waiting for you?

CAPE (*wounded*). Don't! (*After a pause—painfully.*) When I found you—perhaps I hoped——

ELEANOR (*dully*). I had only been back a few minutes. (*After a pause.*) Was that why you seemed so happy—there——? (*She points to the spot where they had stood embraced.*)

CAPE (*indignantly*). No, no! Don't think

that! I'm not like that—not any more! (*Without looking at her he reaches out and clasps her hand.*)

ELEANOR (*looks at him—after a pause, understandingly*). I'm sorry——

CAPE (*self-defensively*). Of course, I knew you must have gone, you'd have been a fool to stay. (*Excitedly.*) And it doesn't matter—not a damn! I've gotten beyond that.

ELEANOR (*misunderstanding—coldly*). I'm glad. (*A pause. She asks coldly.*) Shall I begin again?

CAPE (*struggling with himself—disjointedly*). No—not unless—I don't need—— I've changed. That doesn't matter. I—— (*With a sudden twisted grin.*) I'm learning to like it, you see.

ELEANOR (*looks at him, strangely impressed—a pause—slowly*). I think I know what you mean. We're both learning.

CAPE (*wonderingly*). You——? (*She has turned away from him. He turns to stare at her.*)

ELEANOR (*after a pause, taking up her story matter-of-factly*). I went to John.

CAPE (*trying with agony to take this stoically—mumbling stupidly*). Yes—of course—I supposed——

ELEANOR (*in the same mechanical tone*). He drove me back here in his car. He predicted you'd be back any moment, so he went right home again.

CAPE (*a wild, ironical laugh escapes his control*). Shrewd—ha!

ELEANOR (*after a pause—rebukingly*). John is a good man.

CAPE (*startled, turns and stares at her averted face—then miserably humble, stammers*). Yes, yes—I know—I acknowledge—good—— (*He breaks down, cursing pitiably at himself.*) God damn you!

ELEANOR. Oh!

CAPE. Not you! Me! (*Then he turns to her—with fierce defiance.*) I love John!

ELEANOR (*moved, without looking at him reaches and clasps his hand*). That—is beautiful, Michael. (*A pause.*)

CAPE (*begins to frown sombrely—lets go of her hand*). It's hard—after what you confessed——

ELEANOR (*frightenedly*). Ssshh! (*Then calmly.*) That was a lie. I lied to make you suffer more than you were making me suffer. (*A pause—then she turns to him.*) Can you believe this?

CAPE (*humbly*). I want to believe——

ELEANOR (*immediately turning away—significantly*). Oh!

CAPE (*fiercely—as if to himself*). I will believe! But what difference does it make—believing or not believing? I've changed, I tell you! I accept!

ELEANOR. I can't be a lie you live with!

CAPE (*turning to her resentfully*). Well, then—— (*As if she were goading him to something against his will—threateningly.*) Shall I tell you what happened to me?

ELEANOR (*facing him defiantly*). Yes. (*He turns away. Immediately her brave attitude crumbles. She seems about to implore him not to speak.*)

CAPE (*after a pause—hesitatingly*). You said that years ago you had offered yourself—to him—— (*He turns suddenly—hopefully.*) Was that a lie, too?

ELEANOR. No.

CAPE (*turns away with a start of pain*). Ah! (*A pause. Suddenly his face grows convulsed. He turns back to her, overcome by a craving for revenge—viciously.*) Then I may as well tell you I—— (*He checks himself and turns away.*)

ELEANOR (*defensively—with feigned indifference*). I don't doubt—you kept your threat.

CAPE (*glares at her wildly*). Oho, you don't doubt that, do you? You saw I'd changed, eh?

ELEANOR. I saw—something.

CAPE (*with bitter irony*). God! (*A pause.*)

ELEANOR (*turning on him doggedly as if she were impersonally impelled to make the statement*). I want to tell you that to-night—John and I—nothing you may ever suspect—— (*She falters, turns away with a bitter smile.*) I only tell you this for my own satisfaction. I don't expect you to believe it.

CAPE (*with a wry grin*). No. How could you? (*Then turning to her—determinedly—after a pause.*) But it doesn't matter.

ELEANOR. I wanted revenge as much as you. I wanted to destroy—and be free of our love for ever!

CAPE. As I did.

ELEANOR (*after a pause—simply*). I couldn't.

CAPE (*turns and stares at her—a pause—then he asks wonderingly, eagerly*). Why couldn't you? Tell me that.

ELEANOR (*after a pause—simply*). Something stronger.

CAPE (*with a passionate triumph*). Love! (*With intense pleading.*) Nelly! Will you believe that I, too——? (*He tries to force her eyes to return to his.*)

ELEANOR (*after a pause—looking before her—sadly*). You should have been generous sooner.

CAPE. It's the truth, Nelly! (*Desperately.*) I swear to you——!

ELEANOR (*after a pause—wearily*). We've sworn to so much.

CAPE. Everything is changed, I tell you! Something extraordinary happened to me—a revelation!

ELEANOR (*with bitter cynicism*). A woman?

CAPE (*wounded, turns away from her*). Don't. (*Then after a pause—with deep feeling.*) Yes—she was a woman. And I had conceived of her only as revenge—the lowest of the low!

ELEANOR (*with a shudder*). Ah!

CAPE (*with feeling*). Don't judge, Nelly. She was—good!

ELEANOR (*with another shudder*). Not her! You!

CAPE (*desperately*). I tell you I——! (*He checks himself helplessly. She gives no sign. Then he asks sadly.*) If you can think that, how could you come back?

ELEANOR (*stammering hysterically*). How? How? (*Bursting into tears.*) Because I love you! (*Then turning on him fiercely as if defying him.*) I love you! I love you!

CAPE (*starting up from his chair and trying to take her in his arms—exultantly*). Nelly!

ELEANOR (*pushing him away—violently*). No! I didn't come back to you! I came back to my love which is mine—mine! It conquered me, not you! Something in me—myself—not you! (*She stares him in the eyes defiantly, triumphantly.*)

CAPE (*gently*). It doesn't matter. (*After a pause.*) Did I come back to you?

ELEANOR (*taken aback, turning away*). No, I suppose—— (*Cape stares at her uncertainly, then sits down in his chair again.*)

CAPE (*after a pause, looking before him—assertively, as if taking a pledge*). But I have faith!

ELEANOR (*wearily*). Now—for a moment.

CAPE. No!

ELEANOR. Yes. We shall believe—and disbelieve We are—that.

CAPE (*protestingly*). Nelly! (*For a time they both sit staring bleakly before them. Suddenly he turns to her—desperately*). If there is nothing left but—resignation!—what use is there?

ELEANOR. I know I love.

CAPE (*bitterly—beginning to work himself into a passion*). How can we endure having our dream perish in this?

ELEANOR. Have we any choice?

CAPE (*intensely*). No! It's not Fate! Fate lives—moves on! We are merely victims of our dead selves. (*He seems to collect all his forces and turns on her with a fierce challenge.*) We can choose—an end!

ELEANOR (*shudders instinctively as she reads his meaning*). Michael! (*A pause—then looking into his eyes—as a calm counter-challenge.*) Yes—if *you* wish.

CAPE (*with passionate self-scorn*). We! We have become ignoble.

ELEANOR. As *you* wish. (*She again accents the you.*)

CAPE. I ?

ELEANOR. I accept. I can live—or I can die. (*A pause—gently.*) I love you. You must not suffer too much. (*She reaches out her hand and clasps his comfortingly.*) It is I who have changed most, Michael. (*Then she speaks sadly but firmly as if she had come to a decision.*) There is only one way we can give life to each other. We must redeem our love from ourselves !

CAPE (*sharply*). How ?

ELEANOR. By releasing each other.

CAPE (*with a harsh laugh*). Are you forgetting we tried that once to-night ?

ELEANOR. With hate. This would be because we loved.

CAPE (*violently*). Don't be a fool ! (*Controlling himself—forcing a smile.*) Forgive me. (*Excitedly.*) But, my God, what solution—— ?

ELEANOR. It will give you peace for your work—freedom——

CAPE. Nonsense !

ELEANOR. I will continue to love you. I'll work for you ! We'll no longer stand between each other. Then I can really give you my soul and possess yours. (*Rising to her feet in a pitch of dreamy enthusiasm.*) Oh, Michael, isn't that a finer love than the old ?

CAPE (*controlling himself with difficulty*). You're talking rot !

ELEANOR (*hurt*). Michael !

CAPE. You're mad ! (*Then, suddenly glaring at her suspiciously.*) Why did you come back ? Why do you want to go ? What are you hiding behind all this ?

ELEANOR (*wounded*). Your faith ? You see ?

CAPE (*brokenly*). I — I didn't mean—— (*Then after a struggle with desperate bitterness.*) Well—I accept ! I love you enough for that. Go—if you want to !

ELEANOR (*hurt*). Michael ! It isn't—— (*Then determinedly.*) But even if you misunderstand, I must be strong for you !

CAPE (*almost tauntingly*). Then go—go now if you can—if you're strong enough. (*Harshly.*) Let me see you act nobility ! (*Then suddenly remorseful, catching her hand and covering it with kisses.*) No ! I love you ! Go now before—— Do whatever seems good. Be strong ! Be free ! I—I cannot !

ELEANOR (*brokenly*). We can try—— (*She bends down swiftly and kisses his head, turns away quickly.*) Good-bye.

CAPE (*in a strangled voice*). Good-bye. (*He sits in anguish, in a tortured restraint. She grabs her cloak from the chair, goes quickly to the door, puts her hand on the knob—then stops as tense as he. Suddenly he can stand it no longer, he leaps to his feet and jumps toward the door with a pleading cry.*) Nelly !

(*He stands fixed as he sees her before the door as if he had expected to find her gone. She does not turn, but remains staring at the door in front of her. Finally she raises her hand and knocks on the door softly—then stops to listen.*)

ELEANOR (*in a queer far-away voice*). No. Never again. "Come out." (*She opens the door and turns to Cape with a strange smile.*) It opens inward, Michael. (*She closes it again, smiles to herself and walks back to the foot of the stairway. Then she turns to face Cape. She looks full of some happy certitude. She smiles at him and speaks with a tender weariness.*) It must be nearly dawn. I'll say good night instead of good-bye.

(*They stare into each other's eyes. It is as if now by a sudden flash from within they recognized themselves, shorn of all the ideas, attitudes, cheating gestures which constitute the vanity of personality. Everything, for this second, becomes simple for them—serenely unquestionable. It becomes impossible that they should ever deny life, through each other, again.*)

ELEANOR (*with a low tender cry as if she were awakening to maternity*). Michael !

CAPE (*passionately sure of her now—in a low voice*). Nelly ! (*Then unable to restrain his triumphant exultance.*) You've failed !

ELEANOR (*smiling at him simply*). Yes. Again.

(*Smiling dimly at herself.*) My acting—didn't convince me.

CAPE. We've failed!

ELEANOR. Are we weak? (*Dreamily.*) I'm happy.

CAPE. Strong! We've passed through! We can live again!

ELEANOR (*with a strange dreamy exultance*). We love!

CAPE (*exultantly—but as if testing her, warningly*). But we'll hate!

ELEANOR (*in her same tone*). Yes!

CAPE. And we'll torture and tear, and clutch for each other's souls!

ELEANOR (*nodding her head in a simple emphasis of agreement*). Yes.

CAPE. We'll have to strive on for perfect union—fight each other—fail again—blame each other—fail and hate again—(*he raises his voice in aggressive triumph*)—but!—fail and hate *with pride*—with joy!

ELEANOR (*exulted by his exultation rather than by his words*). Yes!

CAPE. *Our* life is to bear together our burden which is our goal—on and up!

ELEANOR (*dreamily*). Your dream.

CAPE. Above the world, beyond its vision—our height—our love—our meaning!

ELEANOR (*her eyes fixed on him—passionately*). My love!

CAPE (*half sobbing as the intensity of his passion breaks the spell of his exultation*). Oh, Nelly, Nelly, I want to say so much that I feel, but I can only stutter like an idiot! (*He has fallen on his knees before her.*)

ELEANOR (*intensely moved—passionately*). Like an angel! My lover! I know! (*She bends over and kisses him.*)

CAPE (*straining passionately for expression*). Listen! Often I wake up in the night—terrified—in a black world, alone in time—a hundred million years of darkness. I feel like crying out to God for mercy because life lives! Then instinctively I seek you—my hand touches you! You are there—beside me—alive—with you I become a whole, a truth! Life guides me back through the hundred million years to you. It reveals a beginning in unity that I may have faith in the unity of the end! (*He bows his head and kisses her feet ecstatically.*) I love you! Forgive me all I've ever done, all I'll ever do.

ELEANOR (*brokenly*). No. Forgive me—my child, you! (*She begins to sob softly.*)

CAPE (*looking at her—gently*). Why do you cry?

ELEANOR. Because I'm happy. (*Then with a sudden tearful gaiety.*) You be happy! You ought to be! Isn't our future as hard as you could wish? Haven't we your old dreams back again?

CAPE. Deeper and more beautiful!

ELEANOR (*smiling*). Deeper and more beautiful! (*She ascends the stairs slowly.*) Come! (*She reaches the top of the stairway and stands there looking down at him—then stretches out her arms with a passionate, tender gesture.*) Come!

CAPE (*leaping to his feet—intensely*). My Own!

ELEANOR (*dreamily*). Love—and sleep. (*With deep, passionate tenderness.*) My lover!

CAPE. My wife! (*His eyes fixed on her, he ascends. As he does so her arms move back until they are stretched out straight to right and left, forming a cross. Cape stops two steps below her—in a low, wondering tone.*) Why do you stand like that?

ELEANOR (*her head thrown back, her eyes shut—slowly, dreamily*). Perhaps I'm praying. I don't know. I love.

CAPE (*deeply moved*). I love you!

ELEANOR (*as if from a great distance*). We love!

(*He moves close to her and his hands reach out for hers. For a moment as their hands touch they form together one cross. Then their arms go about each other and their lips meet.*)

Curtain

ALL GOD'S CHILLUN GOT WINGS

Characters

JIM HARRIS
MRS. HARRIS, *his mother*
HATTIE, *his sister*
ELLA DOWNEY
SHORTY
JOE
MICKEY
WHITES AND NEGROES

Scenes

ACT ONE

SCENE ONE A corner in lower New York. Years ago. End of an afternoon in spring.

SCENE TWO The same. Nine years later. End of an evening in spring.

SCENE THREE The same. Five years later. A night in spring.

SCENE FOUR The street before a church in the same ward. A morning some weeks later.

ACT TWO

SCENE ONE A flat in the same ward. A morning two years later.

SCENE TWO The same. At twilight some months later.

SCENE THREE The same. A night some months later.

ACT I Scene 1

SCENE. *A corner in lower New York, at the edge of a coloured district. Three narrow streets converge. A triangular building in the rear, red brick, four-storied, its ground floor a grocery. Four-story tenements stretch away down the sky-line of the two streets. The fire escapes are crowded with people. In the street leading left, the faces are all white ; in the street leading right, all black. It is hot Spring. On the sidewalk are eight children, four boys and four girls. Two of each sex are white, two black. They are playing marbles. One of the black boys is Jim Harris. The little blonde girl, her complexion rose and white, who sits behind his elbow and holds his marbles is Ella Downey. She is eight. They play the game with concentrated attention for a while. People pass, black and white, the Negroes frankly participants in the spirit of Spring, the whites laughing constrainedly, awkward in natural emotion. Their words are lost. One only hears their laughter. It expresses the difference in race. There are street noises—the clattering roar of the Elevated, the puff of its locomotives, the ruminative lazy sound of a horse-car, the hoofs of its team clacking on the cobbles. From the street of the whites a high-pitched, nasal tenor sings the chorus of "Only a Bird in a Gilded Cage." On the street of the blacks a Negro strikes up the chorus of : "I Guess I'll Have to Telegraph My Baby." As this singing ends, there is laughter, distinctive in quality, from both streets. Then silence. The light in the street begins to grow brilliant with the glow of the setting sun. The game of marbles goes on.*

WHITE GIRL (*tugging at the elbow of her brother*). Come on, Mickey!

HER BROTHER (*roughly*). Aw, gwan, youse!

WHITE GIRL. Aw right, den. You kin git a lickin' if you wanter. (*Gets up to move off.*)

HER BROTHER. Aw, git off de eart'!

WHITE GIRL. De old woman'll be madder'n hell!

HER BROTHER (*worried now*). I'm comin', ain't I! Hold your horses.

BLACK GIRL (*to a black boy*). Come on, you Joe. We gwine git frailed too, you don't hurry.

JOE. Go long!

MICKEY. Bust up de game, huh? I gotta run! (*Jumps to his feet.*)

OTHER WHITE BOY. Me, too! (*Jumps up.*)

OTHER BLACK GIRL. Lawdy, it's late!

JOE. Me for grub!

MICKEY (*to* JIM HARRIS). You's de winner, Jim Crow. Yeh gotta play tomorrer.

JIM (*readily*). Sure t'ing, Mick. Come one, come all! (*He laughs.*)

OTHER WHITE BOY. Me too! I gotta git back at yuh.

JIM. Aw right, Shorty.

LITTLE GIRLS. Hurry! Come on, come on!

(*The six start off together. Then they notice that Jim and Ella are hesitating, standing awkwardly and shyly together. They turn to mock.*)

JOE. Look at dat Jim Crow! Land sakes, he got a gal! (*He laughs. They all laugh.*)

JIM (*ashamed*). Ne're mind, you Chocolate!

MICKEY. Look at de two softies, will yeh! Mush! Mush! (*He and the two other boys take this up.*)

LITTLE GIRLS (*pointing their fingers at Ella*). Shame! Shame! Everybody knows your name! Painty Face! Painty Face!

ELLA (*hanging her head*). Shut up!

LITTLE WHITE GIRL. He's been carrying her books!

COLOURED GIRL. Can't you find nuffin' better'n him, Ella? Look at de big feet he got! (*She laughs. They all laugh. Jim puts one foot on top of the other, looking at Ella.*)

ELLA. Mind yer own business, see! (*She strides toward them angrily. They jump up and dance in an ecstasy, screaming and laughing.*)

ALL. Found yeh out! Found yeh out!

MICKEY. Mush-head! Jim Crow de Sissy! Stuck on Painty Face!

JOE. Will Painty Face let you hold her doll, boy?

SHORTY. Sissy! Softy! (*Ella suddenly begins to cry. At this they all howl.*)

ALL. Cry-baby! Cry-baby! Look at her! Painty Face!

JIM (*suddenly rushing at them, with clenched fists, furiously*). Shut yo' moufs! I kin lick de hull of you! (*They all run away, laughing, shouting, and jeering, quite triumphant now that they have made him, too, lose his temper. He comes back to Ella, and stands beside her sheepishly, stepping on one foot after the other. Suddenly he blurts out:*) Don't bawl no more. I done chased 'em.

ELLA (*comforted, politely*). T'anks.

JIM (*swelling out*). It was a cinch. I kin wipe up de street wid any one of dem. (*He stretches out his arms, trying to bulge out his biceps.*) Feel dat muscle!

ELLA (*does so gingerly—then with admiration*). My!

JIM (*protectingly*). You mustn't never be scared when I'm hanging round, Painty Face.

ELLA. Don't call me that, Jim—please!

JIM (*contritely*). I didn't mean nuffin'. I didn't know you'd mind.

ELLA. I do—more'n anything.

JIM. You oughtn't to mind. Dey's jealous, dat's what.

ELLA. Jealous? Of what?

JIM (*pointing to her face*). Of dat. Red 'n' white. It's purty.

ELLA. I hate it!

JIM. It's purty. Yes, it's—it's purty. It's—outa sight!

ELLA. I hate it. I wish I was black like you.

JIM (*sort of shrinking*). No, you don't. Dey'd call you Crow, den—or Chocolate—or Smoke.

ELLA. I wouldn't mind.

JIM (*sombrely*). Dey'd call you nigger sometimes, too.

ELLA. I wouldn't mind.

JIM (*humbly*). You wouldn't mind?

ELLA. No, I wouldn't mind. (*An awkward pause.*)

JIM (*suddenly*). You know what, Ella? Since I been tuckin' yo' books to school and back, I been drinkin' lots o' chalk 'n' water three times a day. Dat Tom, de barber, he tole me dat make me white, if I drink enough. (*Pleadingly.*) Does I look whiter?

ELLA (*comfortingly*). Yes — maybe — a little bit——

JIM (*trying a careless tone*). Reckon dat Tom's a liar, an' de joke's on me! Dat chalk only makes me feel kinder sick inside.

ELLA (*wonderingly*). Why do you want to be white?

JIM. Because—just because—I lak dat better.

ELLA. I wouldn't. I like black. Let's you and me swap. I'd like to be black. (*Clapping her hands.*) Gee, that'd be fun, if we only could!

JIM (*hesitatingly*). Yes—maybe——

ELLA. Then they'd call me Crow, and you'd be Painty Face!

JIM. They wouldn't never dast call you nigger, you bet! I'd kill 'em! (*A long pause. Finally she takes his hand shyly. They both keep looking as far away from each other as possible.*)

ELLA. I like you.

JIM. I like you.

ELLA. Do you want to be my feller?

JIM. Yes.

ELLA. Then I'm your girl.

JIM. Yes. (*Then grandly.*) You kin bet none o' de gang gwine call you Painty Face from dis out! I lam' 'em good! (*The sun has set. Twilight has fallen on the street. An organgrinder comes up to the corner and plays "Annie Rooney." They stand hand-in-hand and listen. He goes away. It is growing dark.*)

ELLA (*suddenly*). Golly, it's late! I'll git a lickin'!

JIM. Me, too.

ELLA. I won't mind it much.

JIM. Me nuther.

ELLA. See you going to school to-morrow?

JIM. Sure.

ELLA. I gotta skip now.

JIM. Me, too.

ELLA. I like you, Jim.

JIM. I like you.

ELLA. Don't forget.

JIM. Don't you.

ELLA. Good-bye.

JIM. So long. (*They run away from each other—then stop abruptly, and turn as at a signal.*)

ELLA. Don't forget.

JIM. I won't, you bet!

ELLA. Here! (*She kisses her hand at him, then runs off in frantic embarrassment.*)

JIM (*overcome*). Gee! (*Then he turns and darts away, as*)

The Curtain Falls)

Scene 2

SCENE. *The same corner. Nine years have passed. It is again late Spring at a time in the evening which immediately follows the hour of Scene 1. Nothing has changed much. One street is still all white, the other all black. The fire escapes are laden with drooping human beings. The grocery store is still at the corner. The street noises are now more rhythmically mechanical, electricity having taken the place of horse and steam. People pass, white and black. They laugh as in Scene 1. From the street of the whites the high-pitched nasal tenor sings, "Gee, I Wish That I Had a Girl," and the Negro replies with, "All I Got Was Sympathy." The singing is followed again by laughter from both streets. Then silence. The dusk grows darker. With a spluttering flare the arc-lamp at the corner is lit and sheds a pale glare over the street. Two young roughs slouch up to the corner, as tough in manner as they can make themselves. One is the Shorty of Scene 1; the other the Negro, Joe. They stand loafing. A boy of seventeen or so passes by, escorting a girl of about the same age. Both are dressed in their best, the boy in black with stiff collar, the girl in white.*

SHORTY (*scornfully*). Hully cripes! Pipe who's here. (*To the girl, sneeringly.*) Wha's matter, Liz? Don't yer recernize yer old fr'en's?

GIRL (*frightenedly*). Hello, Shorty.

SHORTY. Why de glad rags? Goin' to graduation? (*He tries to obstruct their way, but, edging away from him, they turn and run.*)

JOE. Har-har! Look at dem scoot, will you! (*Shorty grins with satisfaction.*)

SHORTY (*looking down other street*). Here comes Mickey.

JOE. He won de semi-final last night easy?

SHORTY. Knocked de bloke out in de thoid.

JOE. Dat boy's suah a-comin'! He'll be de champeen yit.

SHORTY (*judicially*). Got a good chanct—if he leaves de broads alone. Dat's where he's wide open.

(*Mickey comes in from the left. He is dressed loudly, a straw hat with a gaudy band cocked over one cauliflower ear. He has acquired a typical "pug's" face, with the added viciousness of a natural bully. One of his eyes is puffed, almost closed, as a result of his battle the night before. He swaggers up.*)

BOTH. Hello, Mickey!

MICKEY. Hello!

JOE. Hear you knocked him col'.

MICKEY. Sure. I knocked his block off. (*Changing the subject.*) Say. Seen 'em goin' past to de graduation racket?

SHORTY (*with a wink*). Why? You int'rested?

JOE (*chuckling*). Mickey's gwine roun' git a good conduct medal.

MICKEY. Sure. Dey kin pin it on de seat o' me pants. (*They laugh.*) Listen. Seen Ella Downey goin'?

SHORTY. Painty Face? No, she ain't been along.

MICKEY (*with authority*). Can dat name, see! Want a bunch o' fives in yer kisser? Den nix! She's me goil, understan'?

JOE (*venturing to joke*). Which one? Yo' number ten?

MICKEY (*flattered*). Sure. De real K.O. one.

SHORTY (*pointing right—sneeringly*). Gee! Pipe Jim Crow all dolled up for de racket.

JOE (*with disgusted resentment*). You mean tell me dat nigger's graduatin'?

SHORTY. Ask him. (*Jim Harris comes in. He is dressed in black, stiff white collar, etc.—a quiet-mannered Negro boy with a queerly-baffled, sensitive face.*)

JIM (*pleasantly*). Hello, fellows! (*They grunt in reply, looking over him scornfully.*)

JOE (*staring resentfully*). Is you graduatin' to-night?

JIM. Yes.

JOE (*spitting disgustedly*). Fo' Gawd's sake! You *is* gittin' high-falutin'!

JIM (*smiling deprecatingly*). This is my second try. I didn't pass last year.

JOE. What de hell does it git you, huh? Whatever is you gwine do wid it now you gits it? Live lazy on yo' ol' woman?

JIM (*assertively*). I'm going to study and become a lawyer.

JOE (*with a snort*). Fo' Chris' sake, nigger!

JIM (*fiercely*). Don't you call me that—not before them!

JOE (*pugnaciously*). Does you deny you's a nigger? I shows you——

MICKEY (*gives them both a push—truculently*). Cut it out, see! I'm runnin' dis corner. (*Turning to Jim insultingly.*) Say, you! Painty Face's gittin' her ticket to-night, ain't she?

JIM. You mean Ella——

MICKEY. Painty Face Downey, dat's who I mean! I don't have to be perlite wit' her. She's me goil!

JIM (*glumly*). Yes, she's graduating.

SHORTY (*winks at Mickey*). Smart, huh?

MICKEY (*winks back—meaningly*). Willin' to loin, take it from me! (*Jim stands tensely as if a struggle were going on in him.*)

JIM (*finally blurts out*). I want to speak to you, Mickey—alone.

MICKEY (*surprised—insultingly*). Aw, what de hell——!

JIM (*excitedly*). It's important, I tell you!

MICKEY. Huh? (*Stares at him inquisitively—then motions the others back carelessly and follows Jim down front.*)

SHORTY. Some noive!

JOE (*vengefully*). I gits dat Jim alone, you wait!

MICKEY. Well, spill de big news. I ain't got all night. I got a date.

JIM. With—Ella?

MICKEY. What's dat to you?

JIM (*the words tumbling out*). What—I wanted to say! I know—I've heard—all the stories—what you've been doing around the ward—with other girls—it's none of my business, with them—but she—Ella—it's different—she's not that kind——

MICKEY (*insultingly*). Who told yuh so, huh?

JIM (*draws back his fist threateningly*). Don't you dare——! (*Mickey is so paralysed by this effrontery that he actually steps back.*)

MICKEY. Say, cut de comedy! (*Beginning to feel insulted.*) Listen, you Jim Crow! Ain't you wise I could give yuh one poke dat'd knock yuh into next week?

JIM. I'm only asking you to act square, Mickey.

MICKEY. What's it to yuh? Why, yuh lousy goat, she wouldn't spit on yuh even! She hates de sight of a coon.

JIM (*in agony*). I—I know—but once she didn't mind—we were kids together——

MICKEY. Aw, ferget dat! Dis is *now!*

JIM. And I'm still her friend always—even if she don't like coloured people——

MICKEY. *Coons*, why don't yuh say it right! De trouble wit' yoh is yuh're gittin' stuck up, dat's what! Stay where yeh belong, see! Yer old man made coin at de truckin' game and yuh're tryin' to buy yerself white—graduatin' and law, for hell's sake! Yuh're gittin' yerself in Dutch wit' everyone in de ward—and it ain't cause yer a coon neider. Don't de gang all train wit' Joe dere and lots of others? But yuh're tryin' to buy white and it won't git yuh no place, see!

JIM (*trembling*). Some day—I'll show you——

MICKEY (*turning away*). Aw, gwan!

JIM. D'you think I'd change—be you—your dirty white——!

MICKEY (*whirling about*). What's dat?

JIM (*with hysterical vehemence*). You act square with her—or I'll show you up—I'll report you—I'll write to the papers—the sporting writers—I'll let them know how white you are!

MICKEY (*infuriated*). Yuh damn nigger, I'll bust yer jaw in! (*Assuming his ring pose he weaves toward Jim, his face set in a cruel scowl. Jim waits helplessly but with a certain dignity.*)

SHORTY. Cheese it! A couple bulls! And here's de Downey skoit comin', too.

MICKEY. I'll get yuh de next time!

(*Ella Downey enters from the right. She is seventeen, still has the same rose-and-white complexion, is pretty but with a rather repelling bold air about her.*)

ELLA (*smiles with pleasure when she sees Mickey*). Hello, Mick! Am I late? Say, I'm so glad you won last night. (*She glances from one to the other as she feels something in the air.*) Hello! What's up?

MICKEY. Dis boob. (*He indicates Jim scornfully.*)

JIM (*diffidently*). Hello, Ella!

ELLA (*shortly, turning away*). Hello! (*Then to Mickey.*) Come on, Mick. Walk down with me. I got to hurry.

JIM (*blurts out*). Wait—just a second. (*Painfully.*) Ella, do you hate—coloured people?

MICKEY. Aw, shut up!

JIM. Please answer.

ELLA (*forcing a laugh*). Say! What is this—another exam?

JIM (*doggedly*). Please answer.

ELLA (*irritably*). Of course I don't! Haven't I been brought up alongside—— Why, some of my oldest—the girls I've been to public school the longest with——

JIM. Do you hate me, Ella?

ELLA (*confusedly and more irritably*). Say, is he drunk? Why should I? I don't hate anyone.

JIM. Then why haven't you ever hardly spoken to me—for years?

ELLA (*resentfully*). What would I speak about? You and me've got nothing in common any more.

JIM (*desperately*). Maybe not any more—but—right on this corner—do you remember once——?

ELLA. I don't remember nothing! (*Angrily.*) Say! What's got into you to be butting into my business all of a sudden like this? Because you finally managed to graduate, has it gone to your head?

JIM. No, I—only want to help you, Ella.

ELLA. Of all the nerve! You're certainly forgetting your place! Who's asking you for help, I'd like to know? Shut up and stop bothering me!

JIM (*insistently*). If you ever need a friend—a true friend——

ELLA. I've got lots of friends among my own—kind, I can tell you. (*Exasperatedly.*) You make me sick! Go to—hell! (*She flounces off. The three men laugh. Mickey follows her. Jim is stricken. He goes and sinks down limply on a box in front of the grocery store.*)

SHORTY. I'm going to shoot a drink. Come on, Joe, and I'll blow yuh.

JOE (*who has never ceased to follow every move of Jim's with angry, resentful eyes.*) Go long. I'se gwine stay here a secon'. I got a lil' argyment. (*He points to Jim.*)

SHORTY. Suit yerself. Do a good job. See yuh later. (*He goes, whistling.*)

JOE (*stands for a while glaring at Jim, his fierce little eyes peering out of his black face. Then he spits on his hands aggressively and strides up to the oblivious Jim. He stands in front of him, gradually working himself into a fury at the other's seeming indifference to his words.*) Listen to me, nigger: I got a heap to whisper in yo' ear! Who is you, anyhow? Who does you think you is? Don't yo' old man and mine work on de docks togidder befo' yo' old man gits his own truckin' business? Yo' ol' man swallers his nickels, my ol' man buys him beer wid dem and swallers dat—dat's the on'y diff'rence. Don't you 'n' me drag up togidder?

JIM (*dully*). I'm your friend, Joe.

JOE. No, you isn't! I ain't no fren' o' yourn!

I don't even know who you is ! What's all dis schoolin' you doin' ? What's all dis dressin' up and graduatin' an' sayin' you gwine study be a lawyer ? What's all dis fakin' an' pretendin' and swellin' out grand an' talkin' soft and perlite ? What's all dis denyin' you's a nigger—an' wid de white boys listenin' to you say it ! Is you aimin' to buy white wid yo' ol' man's dough like Mickey say ? What is you ? (*In a rage at the other's silence.*) You don't talk ? Den I takes it out o' yo' hide ! (*He grabs Jim by the throat with one hand and draws the other fist back.*) Tell me befo' I wrecks yo' face in ! Is you a nigger or isn't you ? (*Shaking him.*) Is you a nigger, Nigger ? Nigger, is you a nigger ?

JIM (*looking into his eyes—quietly*). Yes. I'm a nigger. We're both niggers. (*They look at each other for a moment. Joe's rage vanishes. He slumps on to a box beside Jim's. He offers him a cigarette. Jim takes it. Joe scratches a match and lights both their cigarettes.*)

JOE (*after a puff, with full satisfaction*). Man, why didn't you 'splain dat in de fust place ?

JIM. We're both niggers. (*The same hand-organ man of Scene 1 comes to the corner. He plays the chorus of "Bonbon Buddie," the "Chocolate Drop." They both stare straight ahead listening. Then the organ man goes away. A silence. Joe gets to his feet.*)

JOE. I'll go get me a cold beer. (*He starts to move off—then turns.*) Time you was graduatin', ain't it ? (*He goes, Jim remains sitting on his box staring straight before him as*

The Curtain Falls.)

Scene 3

SCENE. *The same corner five years later. Nothing has changed much. It is a night in Spring. The arc-lamp discovers faces with a favourless cruelty. The street noises are the same but more intermittent and dulled with a quality of fatigue. Two people pass, one black and one white. They are tired. They both yawn, but neither laughs. There is no laughter from the two streets. From the street of the whites the tenor, more nasal than ever and a bit drunken, wails in high barber-shop falsetto the last half of the chorus of "When I Lost You." The Negro voice, a bit maudlin in turn, replies with the last half of "Waiting for the Robert E. Lee." Silence. Shorty enters. He looks tougher than ever, the typical gangster. He stands waiting, singing a bit drunkenly, peering down the street.*

SHORTY (*indignantly*). Yuh bum ! Ain't yuh ever comin' ? (*He begins to sing : "And sewed up in her yeller kimona, She had a blue-barrelled forty-five gun, For to get her man Who'd done her wrong." Then he comments scornfully.*) Not her, dough ! No gat for her. She ain't got de noive. A little sugar. Dat'll fix her.

(*Ella enters. She is dressed poorly, her face is pale and hollow-eyed, her voice cold and tired.*)

SHORTY. Yuh got de message ?

ELLA. Here I am.

SHORTY. How yuh been ?

ELLA. All right. (*A pause. He looks at her puzzledly.*)

SHORTY (*a bit embarrassedly*). Well, I s'pose yuh'd like me to give yuh some dope on Mickey, huh ?

ELLA. No.

SHORTY. Mean to say yuh don't wanter know where he is or what he's doin' ?

ELLA. No.

SHORTY. Since when ?

ELLA. A long time.

SHORTY (*after a pause—with a rat-like viciousness*). Between you'n me, kid, you'll get even soon—you'n all de odder dames he's tossed. I'm on de inside. I've watched him trainin'. His next scrap, watch it ! He'll go ! It won't be de odder guy. It'll be all youse dames he's kidded—and de ones what's kidded him. Youse'll all be in de odder guy's corner. He won't need no odder seconds. Youse'll trow water on him, and sponge his face, and take de kinks out of his socker—and Mickey'll catch it on de button—and he won't be able to take it no more—'cause all your weight—you and de odders—'ll be behind dat punch. Ha, ha! (*He laughs an evil laugh.*) And Mickey'll go—down to his knees first—— (*He sinks to his knees in the attitude of a groggy boxer.*)

ELLA. I'd like to see him on his knees!

SHORTY. And den—flat on his pan—dead to de world—de boidies singin' in de trees—ten—out! (*He suits his action to the words, sinking flat on the pavement, then rises and laughs the same evil laugh.*)

ELLA. He's been out—for me—a long time. (*A pause.*) Why did you send for me?

SHORTY. He sent me.

ELLA. Why?

SHORTY. To slip you this wad o' dough. (*He reluctantly takes a roll of bills from his pocket and holds it out to her.*)

ELLA (*looks at the money indifferently*). What for?

SHORTY. For you.

ELLA. No.

SHORTY. For de kid den.

ELLA. The kid's dead. He took diphtheria.

SHORTY. Hell yuh say! When?

ELLA. A long time.

SHORTY. Why didn't you write Mickey——?

ELLA. Why should I? He'd only be glad.

SHORTY (*after a pause*). Well—it's better.

ELLA. Yes.

SHORTY. You made up wit yer family?

ELLA. No chance.

SHORTY. Livin' alone?

ELLA. In Brooklyn.

SHORTY. Workin'?

ELLA. In a factory.

SHORTY. You're a sucker. There's lots of softer snaps for you, kid——

ELLA. I know what you mean. No.

SHORTY. Don't yuh wanter step out no more—have fun—live?

ELLA. I'm through.

SHORTY (*mockingly*). Jump in de river, huh? T'ink it over, baby. I kin start yuh right in my stable. No one'll bodder yuh den. I got influence.

ELLA (*without emphasis*). You're a dirty dog. Why doesn't someone kill you?

SHORTY. Is dat so! What're you? They say you been travellin' round with Jim Crow.

ELLA. He's been my only friend.

SHORTY. A nigger!

ELLA. The only white man in the world! Kind and white. You're all black—black to the heart.

SHORTY. Nigger-lover! (*He throws the money in her face. It falls to the street.*) Listen, you! Mickey says he's off of yuh for keeps. Dis is de finish! Dat's what he sent me to tell you. (*Glances at her searchingly—a pause.*) Yuh won't make no trouble?

ELLA. Why should I? He's free. The kid's dead. I'm free. No hard feelings—only—I'll be there in spirit at his next fight, tell him! I'll take your tip—the other corner—second the punch—nine—ten—out! He's free! That's all. (*She grins horribly at Shorty.*) Go away, Shorty.

SHORTY (*looking at her and shaking his head—maudlinly*). Groggy! Groggy! We're all groggy! Gluttons for punishment! Me for a drink. So long.

(*He goes. A Salvation Army band comes toward the corner. They are playing and singing "Till We Meet at Jesus' Feet." They reach the end as they enter and stop before Ella. The Captain steps forward.*)

CAPTAIN. Sister——

ELLA (*picks up the money and drops it in his hat—mockingly*). Here. Go save yourself. Leave me alone.

A WOMAN SALVATIONIST. Sister——

ELLA. Never mind that. I'm not in your line—yet. (*As they hesitate, wonderingly.*) I want to be alone.

(*To the thud of the big drum they march off. Ella sits down on a box, her hands hanging at her sides. Presently Jim Harris comes in. He has grown into a quietly-dressed, studious-looking Negro with an intelligent yet queerly-baffled face.*)

JIM (*with a joyous but bewildered cry*). Ella! I just saw Shorty——

ELLA (*smiling at him with frank affection*). He had a message from Mickey.

JIM (*sadly*). Ah!

ELLA (*pointing to the box behind her*). Sit down. (*He does so. A pause—then she says indifferently.*) It's finished. I'm free, Jim.

JIM (*wearily*). We're never free—except to do what we have to do.

ELLA. What are you getting gloomy about all of a sudden?

JIM. I've got the report from the school. I've flunked again.

ELLA. Poor Jim!

JIM. Don't pity me. I'd like to kick myself all over the block. Five years—and I'm still plugging away where I ought to have been at the end of two.

ELLA. Why don't you give it up?

JIM. No!

ELLA. After all, what's being a lawyer?

JIM. A lot—to me—what it means. (*Intensely.*) Why, if I was a Member of the Bar right now, Ella, I believe I'd almost have the courage to——

ELLA. What?

JIM. Nothing. (*After a pause—gropingly.*) I can't explain—just—but it hurts like fire. It brands me in my pride. I swear I know more'n any member of my class. I ought to, I study harder. I work like the devil. It's all in my head—all fine and correct to a T. Then when I'm called on—I stand up—all the white faces looking at me—and I can feel their eyes—I hear my own voice sounding funny, trembling—and all of a sudden it's all gone in my head—there's nothing remembered—and I hear myself stuttering—and give up—sit down—— They don't laugh, hardly ever. They're kind. They're good people. (*In a frenzy.*) They're considerate, damn them! But I feel branded!

ELLA. Poor Jim!

JIM (*going on painfully*). And it's the same thing in the written exams. For weeks before I study all night. I can't sleep, anyway. I learn it all, I see it, I understand it. Then they give me the paper in the exam room. I look it over, I know each answer—perfectly. I take up my pen. On all sides are white men starting to write. They're so sure—even the ones that I know know nothing. But I know it all—but I can't remember any more—it fades—it goes—it's gone. There's a blank in my head—stupidity—I sit like a fool fighting to remember a little bit here, a little bit there—not enough to pass—not enough for anything—when I know it all!

ELLA (*compassionately*). Jim, it isn't worth it. You don't need to——

JIM. I need it more than anyone ever needed anything. I need it to live.

ELLA. What'll it prove?

JIM. Nothing at all much—but everything to me.

ELLA. You're so much better than they are in every other way.

JIM (*looking up at her*). Then—you understand?

ELLA. Of course. (*Affectionately.*) Don't I know how fine you've been to me! You've been the only one in the world who's stood by me—the only understanding person—and all after the rotten way I used to treat you.

JIM. But before that—way back so high—you treated me good. (*He smiles.*)

ELLA. You've been white to me, Jim. (*She takes his hand.*)

JIM. White—to you!

ELLA. Yes.

JIM. All love is white. I've always loved you. (*This with the deepest humility.*)

ELLA. Even now—after all that's happened!

JIM. Always.

ELLA. I like you, Jim—better than anyone else in the world.

JIM. That's more than enough, more than I ever hoped for. (*The organgrinder comes to the corner. He plays the chorus of "Annie Laurie." They sit listening, hand-in-hand.*) Would you ever want to marry me, Ella?

ELLA. Yes, Jim.

JIM (*as if this quick consent alarmed him*). No, no, don't answer now. Wait! Turn it over in your mind! Think what it means to you! Consider it—over and over again! I'm in no hurry, Ella. I can wait months—years——

ELLA. I'm alone. I've got to be helped. I've got to help someone—or it's the end—one end or another.

JIM (*eagerly*). Oh, I'll help—I know I can help—I'll give my life to help you—that's what I've been living for——

ELLA. But can I help you? Can I help you?

JIM. Yes! Yes! We'll go abroad where a man is a man—where it don't make that difference—where people are kind and wise to see the soul under skins. I don't ask you to love me—I don't dare to hope nothing like that! I don't want nothing—only to wait—to know you like me—to be near you—to keep harm away—to make up for the past—to never let you suffer any more—to serve you—to lie at your feet like a dog that loves you—to kneel by your bed like a nurse that watches over you sleeping—to preserve and protect and shield you from evil and sorrow—to give my life and my blood and all the strength that's in me to give you peace and joy—to become your slave!—yes, be your slave—your black slave that adores you as sacred!

(*He has sunk to his knees. In a frenzy of self-abnegation, as he says the last words he beats his head on the flagstones.*)

ELLA (*overcome and alarmed*). Jim! Jim! You're crazy! I want to help you, Jim—I want to help——

Curtain

Scene 4

SCENE.—*Some weeks or so later. A street in the same ward in front of an old brick church. The church stands back from the sidewalk in a yard enclosed by a rusty iron railing with a gate at centre. On each side of this yard are tenements. The buildings have a stern, forbidding look. All the shades on the windows are drawn down, giving an effect of staring, brutal eyes that pry callously at human beings without acknowledging them. Even the two tall, narrow church windows on either side of the arched door are blanked with dull green shades. It is a bright sunny morning. The district is unusually still, as if it were waiting, holding its breath.*

From the street of the blacks to the right a Negro tenor sings in a voice of shadowy richness—the first stanza with a contented, childlike melancholy—

Sometimes I feel like a mourning dove,
Sometimes I feel like a mourning dove,
I feel like a mourning dove.

The second with a dreamy, boyish exultance—

Sometimes I feel like an eagle in the air,
Sometimes I feel like an eagle in the air,
I feel like an eagle in the air.

The third with a brooding, earthbound sorrow—

Sometimes I wish that I'd never been born,
Sometimes I wish that I'd never been born,
I wish that I'd never been born.

As the music dies down there is a pause of waiting stillness. This is broken by one startling, metallic clang of the church-bell. As if it were a signal, people—men, women, children—pour from the two tenements, whites from the tenement to the left, blacks from the one to the right. They hurry to form into two racial lines on each side of the gate, rigid and unyielding, staring across at each other with bitter hostile eyes. The halves of the big church door swing open and Jim and Ella step out from the darkness within into the sunlight. The doors slam behind them like wooden lips of an idol that has spat them out. Jim is dressed in black. Ella in white, both with extreme plainness. They stand in the sunlight, shrinking and confused. All the hostile eyes are now concentrated on them. They become aware of the two lines through which they must pass ; they hesitate and tremble ; then stand there staring back at the people as fixed and immovable as they are. The organgrinder comes in from the right. He plays the chorus of " Old Black Joe." As he finishes the bell of the church clangs one more single stroke, insistently dismissing.

JIM (*as if the sound had awakened him from a trance, reaches out and takes her hand*). Come. Time we got to the steamer. Time we sailed away over the sea. Come, Honey ! (*She tries to answer, but her lips tremble ; she cannot take her eyes off the eyes of the people ; she is unable to move. He sees this and, keeping the same tone of profound, affectionate kindness, he points upward in the sky, and gradually persuades her eyes to look up.*) Look up, Honey ! See the sun ! Feel his warm eye lookin' down ! Feel how kind he looks ! Feel his blessing deep in your heart, your bones ! Look up, Honey ! (*Her eyes are fixed on the sky now. Her face is calm. She tries to smile bravely back at the sun. Now he pulls her by the hand, urging her gently to walk with him down through the yard and gate, through the lines of people. He is maintaining an attitude to support them through the ordeal only by a terrible effort, which manifests itself in the hysteric quality of ecstasy which breaks into his voice.*) And look at the sky ! Ain't it kind and blue ? Blue for hope. Don't they say blue's for hope ? Hope ! That's for us, Honey. All those blessings in the sky ! What's it the Bible says ? Falls on just and unjust alike ? No, that's the sweet rain. Pshaw, what am I saying ! All mixed up. There's no unjust about it. We're all the same—equally just—under the sky—under the sun—under God—sailing over the sea—to the other side of the world—the side where Christ was born—the kind side that takes count of the soul—over the sea—the sea's blue, to—— Let's not be late—let's get that steamer ! (*They have reached the kerb now, passed the lines of people. She is looking up to the sky with an expression of trance-like calm and peace. He is on the verge of collapse, his face twitching, his eyes staring. He calls hoarsely :*) Taxi ! Where is he ? Taxi !

Curtain

ACT II Scene I

SCENE. *Two years later. A flat of the better sort in the Negro district near the corner of Act* I. *This is the parlour. Its furniture is a queer clash. The old pieces are cheaply ornate, naïvely, childishly gaudy—the new pieces give evidence of a taste that is diametrically opposed, severe to the point of sombreness. On one wall, in a heavy gold frame, is a coloured photograph—the portrait of an elderly Negro with an able, shrewd face, but dressed in outlandish lodge regalia, a get-up adorned with medals, sashes, a cocked hat with frills—the whole effect as absurd to contemplate as one of Napoleon's Marshals in full uniform. In the left corner, where a window lights it effectively, is a Negro primitive mask from the Congo—a grotesque face, inspiring obscure, dim connotations in one's mind, but beautifully done, conceived in a true religious spirit. In this room, however, the mask acquires an arbitrary accentuation. It dominates by a diabolical quality that contrast imposes upon it.*

There are two windows on the left looking out in the street. In the rear, a door to the hall of the building. In the right, a doorway with red and gold portières leading into the bedroom and the rest of the flat. Everything is cleaned and polished. The dark brown wall-paper is new, the brilliantly figured carpet also. There is a round mahogany table at centre. In a rocking-chair by the table Mrs. Harris is sitting. She is a mild-looking, grey-haired Negress of sixty-five, dressed in an old-fashioned Sunday-best dress. Walking about the room nervously is Hattie, her daughter, Jim's sister, a woman of about thirty with a high-strung, defiant face—an intelligent head showing both power and courage. She is dressed severely, mannishly.

It is a fine morning in Spring. Sunshine comes through the windows at the left.

MRS. HARRIS. Time dey was here, ain't it?

HATTIE (*impatiently*). Yes.

MRS. HARRIS (*worriedly*). You ain't gwine ter kick up a fuss, is you—like you done wid Jim befo' de weddin'?

HATTIE. No. What's done is done.

MRS. HARRIS. We mustn't let her see we hold it agin' her—de bad dat happened to her wid dat no-count fighter.

HATTIE. I certainly never give that a thought. It's what she's done to Jim—making him run away and give up his fight——!

MRS. HARRIS. Jim loves her a powerful lot, must be.

HATTIE (*after a pause—bitterly*). I wonder if she loves Jim!

MRS. HARRIS. She must, too. Yes, she must, too. Don't you forget dat it was hard for her—mighty, mighty hard—harder for de white dan for de black!

HATTIE (*indignantly*). Why should it be?

MRS. HARRIS (*shaking her head*). I ain't talkin' of shoulds. It's too late for shoulds. Dey's on'y one should. (*Solemnly.*) De white and de black shouldn't mix dat close. Dere's one road where de white goes on alone; dere's anudder road where de black goes on alone——

HATTIE. Yes, if they'd only leave us alone!

MRS. HARRIS. Dey leaves your Pa alone. He comes to de top till he's got his own business, lots o' money in de bank, he owns a building even befo' he die. (*She looks up proudly at the picture. Hattie sighs impatiently—then her mother goes on.*) Dey leaves me alone. I bears four children into dis worl', two dies, two lives. I helps you two grow up fine an' healthy and eddicated wid schoolin' and money fo' yo' comfort——

HATTIE (*impatiently*). Ma!

MRS. HARRIS. I does de duty God set for me in dis worl'. Dey leaves me alone. (*Hattie goes to the window to hide her exasperation. The mother broods for a minute—then goes on.*) The worl' done change. Dey ain't no satisfaction wid nuffin' no more.

HATTIE. Oh! (*Then after a pause.*) They'll be here any minute now.

MRS. HARRIS. Why didn't you go meet 'em at de dock like I axed you?

HATTIE. I couldn't. My face and Jim's among those hundreds of white faces—— (*With a harsh laugh.*) It would give her too much advantage!

MRS. HARRIS (*impatiently*). Don't talk dat way! What makes you so proud? (*Then after a pause—sadly.*) Hattie!

HATTIE (*turning*). Yes, Ma.

MRS. HARRIS. I want to see Jim again—my only boy—but—all de same I'd ruther he stayed away. He say in his letter he's happy, she's happy, dey likes it dere, de folks don't think nuffin' but what's natural at seeing 'em married. Why don't dey stay?

HATTIE (*vehemently*). No! They were cowards to run away. If they believe in what they've done, then let them face it out, live it out here, be strong enough to conquer all prejudice!

MRS. HARRIS. Strong? Dey ain't many strong. Dey ain't many happy neider. Dey was happy ovah yondah.

HATTIE. We don't deserve happiness till we've fought the fight of our race and won it! (*In the pause that follows there is a ring from back in the flat.*) It's the door bell! You go, Ma. I—I—I'd rather not. (*Her mother looks at her rebukingly and goes out agitatedly through the portières. Hattie waits, nervously walking about, trying to compose herself. There is a long pause. Finally the portières are parted and Jim enters. He looks much older, graver, worried.)*

JIM. Hattie!

HATTIE. Jim! (*They embrace with great affection.*)

JIM. It's great to see you again! You're looking fine.

HATTIE (*looking at him searchingly*). You look well, too—thinner maybe—and tired. (*Then as she sees him frowning.*) But where's Ella?

JIM. With Ma. (*Apologetically.*) She sort of—broke down—when we came in. The trip wore her out.

HATTIE (*coldly*). I see.

JIM. Oh, it's nothing serious. Nerves. She needs a rest.

HATTIE. Wasn't living in France restful?

JIM. Yes, but—too lonely—especially for her.

HATTIE (*resentfully*). Why? Didn't the people there want to associate——?

JIM (*quickly*). Oh, no indeed, they didn't think anything of that. (*After a pause.*) But—she did. For the first year it was all right. Ella liked everything a lot. She went out with French folks and got so she could talk it a little—and I learned it—a little. We were having a right nice time. I never thought then we'd ever want to come back here.

HATTIE (*frowning*). But—what happened to change you?

JIM (*after a pause—haltingly*). Well—you see—the first year—she and I were living around—like friends—like a brother and sister—like you and I might.

HATTIE (*her face becoming more and more drawn and tense*). You mean—then——? (*She shudders—then after a pause.*) She loves you, Jim?

JIM. If I didn't know that I'd have to jump in the river.

HATTIE. Are you sure she loves you?

JIM. Isn't that why she's suffering?

HATTIE (*letting her breath escape through her clenched teeth*). Ah!

JIM (*suddenly springs up and shouts almost hysterically*). Why d'you ask me all those damn questions? Are you trying to make trouble between us?

HATTIE (*controlling herself—quietly*). No, Jim.

JIM (*after a pause—contritely*). I'm sorry, Hattie. I'm kind of on edge to-day. (*He sinks down on his chair—then goes on as if something forced him to speak.*) After that we got to living housed in. Ella didn't want to see nobody, she said just the two of us was enough. I was happy then—and I really guess she was happy, too—in a way—for a while. (*Again a pause.*) But she never did get to wanting to go out any place again. She got to saying she felt she'd be sure to run into someone she knew—from over here. So I moved us out to the country where no tourist ever comes—but it didn't make any difference to her. She got to avoiding the French folks the same as if they were Americans and I couldn't get it out of her mind. She lived in the house and got paler and paler, and more and more nervous and scarey, always imagining things—until I got to imagining things, too. I got to feeling blue. Got to sneering at myself that I wasn't any better than a quitter because I sneaked away right after getting married, didn't face nothing, gave up trying to become a Member of the Bar—and I got to suspecting Ella must feel that way about me, too—that I wasn't a *real man*!

HATTIE (*indignantly*). She couldn't!

JIM (*with hostility*). You don't need to tell me! All this was only in my own mind. We never quarrelled a single bit. We never said a harsh word. We were as close to each other as could be. We were all there was in the world to each other. We were alone together! (*A pause.*) Well, one day I got so I couldn't stand it. I could see she couldn't stand it. So I just up and said: Ella, we've got to have a plain talk, look everything straight in the face, hide nothing, come out with the exact truth of the way we feel.

HATTIE. And you decided to come back!

JIM. Yes. We decided the reason we felt sort of ashamed was we'd acted like cowards.

We'd run away from the thing—and taken it with us. We decided to come back and face it and live it down in ourselves, and prove to ourselves we were strong in our love—and then, and that way only, by being brave we'd free ourselves, and gain confidence, and be really free inside and able then to go anywhere and live in peace and equality with ourselves and the world without any guilty uncomfortable feeling coming up to rile us. (*He has talked himself now into a state of happy confidence.*)

HATTIE (*bending over and kissing him*). Good for you! I admire you so much, Jim! I admire both of you! And are you going to begin studying right away and get admitted to the Bar?

JIM. You bet I am!

HATTIE. You must, Jim! Our race needs men like you to come to the front and help—— (*As voices are heard approaching she stops, stiffens, and her face grows cold.*)

JIM (*noticing this—warningly*). Remember Ella's been sick! (*Losing control—threateningly.*) You be nice to her, you hear!

(*Mrs. Harris enters, showing Ella the way. The coloured woman is plainly worried and perplexed. Ella is pale, with a strange, haunted expression in her eyes. She runs to Jim as to a refuge, clutching his hands in both of hers, looking from Mrs. Harris to Hattie with a frightened defiance.*)

MRS. HARRIS. Dere he is, child, big's life! She was afraid we'd done kidnapped you away, Jim.

JIM (*patting her hand*). This place ought to be familiar, Ella. Don't you remember playing here with us sometimes as a kid?

ELLA (*queerly—with a frown of effort*). I remember playing marbles one night—but that was on the street.

JIM. Don't you remember Hattie?

HATTIE (*coming forward with a forced smile*). It was a long time ago—but I remember Ella. (*She holds out her hand.*)

ELLA (*taking it—looking at Hattie with the same queer defiance*). I remember. But you've changed so much.

HATTIE (*stirred to hostility by Ella's manner—condescendingly*). Yes, I've grown older, naturally. (*Then in a tone which, as if in spite of herself, becomes bragging.*) I've worked so hard. First I went away to college, you know—then I took up post-graduate study—when suddenly I decided I'd accomplish more good if I gave up learning and took up teaching. (*She suddenly checks herself, ashamed, and stung by Ella's indifference.*) But this sounds like stupid boasting. I don't mean that. I was only explaining——

ELLA (*indifferently*). I didn't know you'd been to school so long. (*A pause.*) Where are you teaching? In a coloured school, I suppose. (*There is an indifferent superiority in her words that is maddening to Hattie.*)

HATTIE (*controlling herself*). Yes. A private school endowed by some wealthy members of our race.

ELLA (*suddenly—even eagerly*). Then you must have taken lots of examinations and managed to pass them, didn't you?

HATTIE (*biting her lips*). I always passed with honours!

ELLA. Yes, we both graduated from the same High School, didn't we? That was dead easy for me. Why, I hardly even looked at a book. But Jim says it was awfully hard for him. He failed one year, remember?

(*She turns and smiles at Jim—a tolerant, superior smile, but one full of genuine love. Hattie is outraged, but Jim smiles.*)

JIM. Yes, it was hard for me, Honey.

ELLA. And the law school examinations Jim hardly ever could pass at all. Could you? (*She laughs lovingly.*)

HATTIE (*harshly*). Yes, he could! He can! He'll pass them now—if you'll give him a chance!

JIM (*angrily*). Hattie!

MRS. HARRIS. Hold yo' fool tongue!

HATTIE (*sullenly*). I'm sorry.

(*Ella has shrunk back against Jim. She regards Hattie with a sort of wondering hatred. Then she looks away about the room. Suddenly her eyes fasten on the primitive mask and she gives a stifled scream.*)

JIM. What's the matter, Honey?

ELLA (*pointing*). That! For God's sake, what is it?

HATTIE (*scornfully*). It's a Congo mask. (*She goes and picks it up.*) I'll take it away if you wish. I thought you'd like it. It was my wedding present to Jim.

ELLA. What is it?

HATTIE. It's a mask which used to be worn in religious ceremonies by my people in Africa. But, aside from that, it's beautifully made, a work of Art by a real artist—as real in his way as your Michael Angelo. (*Forces Ella to take it.*) Here. Just notice the workmanship.

ELLA (*defiantly*). I'm not scared of it if you're not. (*Looking at it with disgust.*) Beautiful? Well, some people certainly have queer notions! It looks ugly to me and stupid—like a kid's game—making faces! (*She slaps it contemptuously.*) Pooh! You needn't look hard at me. I'll give you the laugh. (*She goes to put it back on the stand.*)

JIM. Maybe, if it disturbs you, we better put it in some other room.

ELLA (*defiantly aggressive*). No. I want it here where I can give it the laugh! (*She sets it there again—then turns suddenly on Hattie with aggressive determination.*) Jim's not going to take any more examinations! I won't let him!

HATTIE (*bursting forth*). Jim! Do you hear that? There's white justice!—their fear for their superiority——!

ELLA (*with a terrified pleading*). Make her go away, Jim!

JIM (*losing control—furiously to his sister*). Either you leave here—or we will!

MRS. HARRIS (*weeping—throws her arms around Hattie*). Let's go, chile! Let's go!

HATTIE (*calmly now*). Yes, Ma. All right.

(*They go through the portières. As soon as they are gone, Jim suddenly collapses into a chair and hides his head in his hands. Ella stands beside him for a moment. She stares distractedly about her, at the portrait, at the mask, at the furniture, at Jim. She seems fighting to escape from some weight on her mind. She throws this off and, completely her old self for the moment, kneels by Jim and pats his shoulder.*)

ELLA (*with kindness and love*). Don't, Jim! Don't cry, please! You don't suppose I really meant that about the examinations, do you? Why, of course, I didn't mean a word! I couldn't mean it! I want you to take the examinations! I want you to pass! I want you to be a lawyer! I want you to be the best lawyer in the country! I want you to show 'em—all the dirty sneaking, gossiping liars that talk behind our backs—what a man I married. I want the whole world to know you're the whitest of the white! I want you to climb and climb—and step on 'em, stamp right on their mean faces! I love you, Jim. You know that!

JIM (*calm again—happily*). I hope so, Honey—and I'll make myself worthy.

HATTIE (*appears in the doorway—quietly*). We're going now, Jim.

ELLA. No. Don't go.

HATTIE. We were going to, anyway. This is your house—Mother's gift to you, Jim.

JIM (*astonished*). But I can't accept——Where are you going?

HATTIE. We've got a nice flat in the Bronx—(*with bitter pride*) in the heart of the Black Belt—the Congo—among our own people!

JIM (*angrily*). You're crazy—I'll see Ma——

(*He goes out. Hattie and Ella stare at each other with scorn and hatred for a moment, then Hattie goes. Ella remains kneeling for a moment by the chair, her eyes dazed and strange as she looks about her. Then she gets to her feet and stands before the portrait of Jim's father—with a sneer.*)

ELLA. It's his Old Man—all dolled up like a circus horse! Well, they can't help it. It's in the blood, I suppose. They're ignorant, that's all there is to it. (*She moves to the mask—forcing a mocking tone.*) Hello, sport! Who d'you think you're scaring? Not me! I'll give you the laugh. He won't pass, you wait and see. Not in a thousand years! (*She goes to the window and looks down at the street and mutters.*) All black! Every one of them! (*Then with sudden excitement.*) No, there's one. Why, it's Shorty! (*She throws the window open and calls.*) Shorty! Shorty! Hello, Shorty! (*She leans out and waves—then stops, remains there for a moment looking down, then comes back into the room suddenly as if she wanted to hide—her whole face in an anguish.*) Say! Say! I wonder?—No, he didn't hear you. Yes, he did, too! He must have! I yelled so loud you could hear me in Jersey! No, what are you talking about? How would he hear with all kids yelling down there? He never heard a word, I tell you! He did, too! He didn't want to hear you! He didn't want to let anyone know he knew you! Why don't you acknowledge it? What are you lying about? I'm not! Why shouldn't he? Where does he come in to—for God's sake, who is Shorty, anyway? A pimp! Yes, and a dope-pedlar, too! D'you mean to say he'd have the nerve to hear me call him and then deliberately—— ? Yes, I mean to say it! I do say it! And it's true, and you know it, and you might as well be honest for a change and admit it! He heard you, but he didn't want to hear you! He doesn't want to know you any more. No, not even him! He's afraid it'd get him in wrong with the old gang. Why? You know well enough! Because you married a—a—a—well, I won't say it, but you know without my mentioning names! (*Ella springs to her feet in horror and shakes off her obsession with a frantic effort.*) Stop! (*Then whimpering like a frightened child.*) Jim! Jim! Jim! Where are you? I want you, Jim! (*She runs out of the room as*

The Curtain Falls.)

Scene 2

SCENE. *The same. Six months later. It is evening. The walls of the room appear shrunken in, the ceiling lowered, so that the furniture, the portrait, the mask, look unnaturally large and domineering. Jim is seated at the table studying, law books piled by his elbows. He is keeping his attention concentrated only by a driving physical effort which gives his face the expression of a runner's near the tape. His forehead shines with perspiration. He mutters one sentence from Blackstone over and over again, tapping his forehead with his fist in time to the rhythm he gives the stale words. But, in spite of himself, his attention wanders, his eyes have an uneasy, hunted look, he starts at every sound in the house or from the street. Finally, he remains rigid, Blackstone forgotten, his eyes fixed on the portières with tense grief. Then he groans, slams the book shut, goes to the window and throws it open and sinks down beside it, his arms on the sill, his head resting wearily on his arms, staring out into the night, the pale glare from the arc-lamp on the corner throwing his face into relief. The portières on the right are parted and Hattie comes in.*

HATTIE (*not seeing him at the table*). Jim! (*Discovering him.*) Oh, there you are! What're you doing?

JIM (*turning to her*). Resting. Cooling my head. (*Forcing a smile.*) These law books certainly are a sweating proposition! (*Then, anxiously.*) How is she?

HATTIE. She's asleep now. I felt it was safe to leave her for a minute. (*After a pause.*) What did the doctor tell you, Jim?

JIM. The same old thing. She must have rest, he says, her mind needs rest—— (*Bitterly.*) But he can't tell me any prescription for that rest—leastways not any that'd work.

HATTIE (*after a pause*). I think you ought to leave her, Jim—or let her leave you—for a while, anyway.

JIM (*angrily*). You're like the doctor. Everything's so simple and easy. Do this and that happens. Only it don't. Life isn't simple like that—not in this case, anyway—no, it isn't simple a bit. (*After a pause.*) I can't leave her. She can't leave me. And there's a million little reasons combining to make one big reason why we can't. (*A pause.*) For her sake—if it'd do her good—I'd go—I'd leave—I'd do anything—because I love her. I'd kill myself even—jump out of this window this second—I've thought it over, too—but that'd only make matters worse for her. I'm all she's got in the world! Yes, that isn't bragging or fooling myself. I know that for a fact! Don't you know that's true? (*There is a pleading for the certainty he claims.*)

HATTIE. Yes, I know she loves you, Jim. I know that now.

JIM (*simply*). Then we've got to stick together to the end, haven't we, whatever comes—and hope and pray for the best? (*A pause—then hopefully.*) I think maybe this is the crisis in her mind. Once she settles this in herself, she's won to the other side. And me—once I become a Member of the Bar—then I win, too! We're both free—by our own fighting down our own weakness! We're both really, truly free! Then we can be happy with ourselves here or anywhere. She'll be proud then! Yes, she's told me again and again, she says she'll be actually proud!

HATTIE (*turning away to conceal her emotion*). Yes, I'm sure—but you mustn't study too hard, Jim! You mustn't study too awfully hard!

JIM (*gets up and goes to the table and sits down wearily*). Yes, I know. Oh, I'll pass easily. I haven't got any scarey feeling about that any more. And I'm doing two years' work in one here alone. That's better than schools, eh?

HATTIE (*doubtfully*). It's wonderful, Jim.

JIM (*his spirit evaporating*). If I can only hold out! It's hard! I'm worn out. I don't sleep. I get to thinking and thinking. My head aches and burns like fire with thinking. Round and round my thoughts go chasing like crazy chickens hopping and flapping before the wind. It gets me crazy mad—'cause I can't stop!

HATTIE (*watching him for a while and seeming to force herself to speak*). The doctor didn't tell you all, Jim.

JIM (*dully*). What's that?

HATTIE. He told me you're liable to break down too, if you don't take care of yourself.

JIM (*abjectly weary*). Let 'er come! I don't care what happens to me. Maybe if I get sick she'll get well. There's only so much bad luck allowed to one family, maybe. (*He forces a wan smile.*)

HATTIE (*hastily*). Don't give in to that idea, for the Lord's sake!

JIM. I'm tired—and blue—that's all.

HATTIE (*after another long pause*). I've got to tell you something else, Jim.

JIM (*dully*). What?

HATTIE. The doctor said Ella's liable to be sick like this a very long time.

JIM. He told me that, too—that it'd be a long time before she got back her normal strength. Well, I suppose that's got to be expected.

HATTIE (*slowly*). He didn't mean convalescing—what he told me. (*A long pause.*)

JIM (*evasively*). I'm going to get other doctors in to see Ella—specialists. This one's a damn fool.

HATTIE. Be sensible, Jim. You'll have to face the truth—sooner or later.

JIM (*irritably*). I know the truth about Ella better'n any doctor.

HATTIE (*persuasively*). She'd get better so much sooner if you'd send her away to some nice sanatorium——

JIM. No! She'd die of shame there!

HATTIE. At least until after you've taken your examinations——

JIM. To hell with me!

HATTIE. Six months. That wouldn't be long to be parted.

JIM. What are you trying to do—separate us? (*He gets to his feet—furiously.*) Go on out! Go on out!

HATTIE (*calmly*). No, I won't. (*Sharply.*) There's something that's got to be said to you and I'm the only one with the courage—— (*Intensely.*) Tell me, Jim, have you heard her raving when she's out of her mind?

JIM (*with a shudder*). No!

HATTIE. You're lying, Jim. You must have—if you don't stop your ears—and the doctor says she may develop a violent mania, dangerous for you—get worse and worse until—Jim, you'll go crazy, too—living this way. To-day she raved on about "Black! Black!" and cried because she said her skin was turning black—that you had poisoned her——

JIM (*in anguish*). That's only when she's out of her mind.

HATTIE. And then she suddenly called me a dirty nigger.

JIM. No! She never said that ever! She never would!

HATTIE. She did—and kept on and on! (*A tense pause.*) She'll be saying that to you soon.

JIM (*torturedly*). She don't mean it! She isn't responsible for what she's saying!

HATTIE. I know she isn't—yet she is just the same. It's deep down in her or it wouldn't come out.

JIM. Deep down in her people—not deep in her.

HATTIE. I can't make such distinctions. The race in me, deep in me, can't stand it. I can't play nurse to her any more, Jim,—not even for your sake. I'm afraid—afraid of myself—afraid sometime I'll kill her dead to set you free! (*She loses control and begins to cry.*)

JIM (*after a long pause—sombrely*). Yes, I guess you'd better stay away from here. Good-bye.

HATTIE. Who'll you get to nurse her, Jim,—a white woman?

JIM. Ella'd die of shame. No, I'll nurse her myself.

HATTIE. And give up your studies?

JIM. I can do both.

HATTIE. You can't! You'll get sick yourself! Why, you look terrible even as it is—and it's only beginning!

JIM. I can do anything for her! I'm all she's got in the world! I've got to prove I can be all to her! I've got to prove worthy! I've got to prove she can be proud of me! I've got to prove I'm the whitest of the white!

HATTIE (*stung by this last—with rebellious bitterness*). Is that the ambition she's given you? Oh, you soft, weak-minded fool, you traitor to your race! And the thanks you'll get—to be called a dirty nigger—to hear her cursing you because she can never have a child because it'll be born black——!

JIM (*in a frenzy*). Stop!

HATTIE. I'll say what must be said even though you kill me, Jim. Send her to an asylum before you both have to be sent to one together.

JIM (*with a sudden wild laugh*). Do you think you're threatening me with something dreadful now? Why, I'd like that. Sure, I'd like that! Maybe she'd like it better, too. Maybe we'd both find it all simple then—like you think it is now. Yes. (*He laughs again.*)

HATTIE (*frightenedly*). Jim!

JIM. Together! You can't scare me even with hell fire if you say she and I go together. It's heaven then for me! (*With sudden savagery.*) You go out of here! All you've ever been aiming to do is to separate us so we can't be together!

HATTIE. I've done what I did for your own good.

JIM. I have no own good. I only got a good together with her. I'm all she's got in the world! Let her call me nigger! Let her call me the whitest of the white! I'm all she's got in the world, ain't I? She's all I've got! You with your fool talk of the black race and the white race! Where does the human race get a chance to come in? I suppose that's simple for you. You lock it up in asylums and throw away the key! (*With fresh violence.*) Go along! There isn't going to be no more people coming in here to separate—excepting the doctor. I'm going to lock the door, and it's going to stay locked, you hear? Go along, now!

HATTIE (*confusedly*). Jim !

JIM (*pushes her out gently and slams the door after her—vaguely*). Go along ! I got to study. I got to nurse Ella, too. Oh, I can do it ! I can do anything for her !

(*He sits down at the table and, opening the book, begins again to recite the lines from Blackstone in a meaningless rhythm, tapping his forehead with his fist. Ella enters noiselessly through the portières. She wears a red dressing-gown over her night-dress but is in her bare feet. She has a carving-knife in her right hand. Her eyes fasten on Jim with a murderous mania. She creeps up behind him. Suddenly he senses something and turns. As he sees her he gives a cry, jumping up and catching her wrist. She stands fixed, her eyes growing bewildered and frightened.*)

JIM (*aghast*). Ella ! For God's sake ! Do you want to murder me ? (*She does not answer. He shakes her.*)

ELLA (*whimperingly*). They kept calling me names as I was walking along—I can't tell you what, Jim—and then I grabbed a knife——

JIM. Yes ! See ! This ! (*She looks at it frightenedly.*)

ELLA. Where did I—— ? I was having a nightmare—— Where did they go—I mean, how did I get here ? (*With sudden terrified pleading—like a little girl.*) Oh, Jim—don't ever leave me alone ! I have such terrible dreams, Jim—promise you'll never go away !

JIM. I promise, Honey.

ELLA (*her manner becoming more and more childishly silly*). I'll be a little girl—and you'll be old Uncle Jim who's been with us for years and years—— Will you play that ?

JIM. Yes, Honey. Now you better go back to bed.

ELLA (*like a child*). Yes, Uncle Jim. (*She turns to go. He pretends to be occupied by his book. She looks at him for a second—then suddenly asks in her natural woman's voice.*) Are you studying hard, Jim ?

JIM. Yes, Honey. Go to bed now. You need to rest, you know.

ELLA (*stands looking at him, fighting with herself. A startling transformation comes over her face. It grows mean, vicious, full of jealous hatred. She cannot contain herself, but breaks out harshly with a cruel, venomous grin.*) You dirty nigger !

JIM (*starting as if he'd been shot*). Ella ! For the good Lord's sake !

ELLA (*coming out of her insane mood for a moment, aware of something terrible, frightened*). Jim ! Jim ! Why are you looking at me like that ?

JIM. What did you say to me just then ?

ELLA (*gropingly*). Why, I—I said—I remember saying, are you studying hard, Jim ? Why ? You're not mad at that, are you ?

JIM. No, Honey. What made you think I was mad ? Go to bed now.

ELLA (*obediently*). Yes, Jim. (*She passes behind the portières. Jim stares before him. Suddenly her head is thrust out at the side of the portières. Her face is again that of a vindictive maniac.*) Nigger ! (*The face disappears—she can be heard running away, laughing with cruel satisfaction. Jim bows his head on his outstretched arms, but he is too stricken for tears.*)

Curtain

Scene 3

SCENE. *The same, six months later. The sun has just gone down. The Spring twilight sheds a vague, grey light about the room, picking out the Congo mask on the stand by the window. The walls have shrunken in still more, the ceiling now barely clears the people's heads, the furniture and the characters appear enormously magnified. Law books are stacked in two great piles on each side of the table. Ella comes in from the right, the carving-knife in her hand. She is pitifully thin, her face is wasted, but her eyes glow with a mad energy, her movements are abrupt and spring-like. She looks stealthily about the room, then advances and stands before the mask, her arms akimbo, her attitude one of crazy mockery, fear and bravado. She is dressed in the red dressing-gown, grown dirty and ragged now, and is in her bare feet.*

ELLA. I'll give you the laugh, wait and see! (*Then in a confidential tone.*) He thought I was asleep! He called, Ella, Ella—but I kept my eyes shut, I pretended to snore. I fooled him good. (*She gives a little hoarse laugh.*) This is the first time he's dared to leave me alone for months and months. I've been wanting to talk to you every day, but this is the only chance—— (*With sudden violence—flourishing her knife.*) What're you grinning about, you dirty nigger, you? How dare you grin at me? I guess you forget what you are! That's always the way. Be kind to you, treat you decent, and in a second you've got a swelled head, you think you're somebody, you're all over the place putting on airs. Why, it's got so I can't even walk down the street without seeing niggers, niggers everywhere. Hanging around, grinning, grinning—going to school—pretending they're white—taking examinations—— (*She stops, arrested by the word, then suddenly.*) That's where he's gone—down to the mail-box—to see if there's a letter from the Board—telling him—— But why is he so long? (*She calls pitifully.*) Jim! (*Then in a terrified whimper.*) Maybe he's passed! Maybe he's passed! (*In a frenzy.*) No! No! He can't! I'd kill him! I'd kill myself! (*Threatening the Congo mask.*) It's you who're to blame for this! Yes, you! Oh, I'm on to you! (*Then appealingly.*) But why d'you want to do this to us? What have I ever done wrong to you? What have you got against me? I married you, didn't I? Why don't you let Jim alone? Why don't you let him be happy as he is—with me? Why don't you let me be happy? He's white, isn't he—the whitest man that ever lived? Where do you come in to interfere? Black! Black! Black as dirt! You've poisoned me! I can't wash myself clean! Oh, I hate you! I hate you! Why don't you let Jim and I be happy?

(*She sinks down in his chair, her arms outstretched on the table. The door from the hall is slowly opened and Jim appears. His bloodshot, sleepless eyes stare from deep hollows. His expression is one of crushed numbness. He holds an open letter in his hand.*)

JIM (*seeing Ella—in an absolutely dead voice*). Honey—I thought you were asleep.

ELLA (*starts and wheels about in her chair*). What's that? You got—you got a letter——?

JIM (*turning to close the door after him*). From the Board of Examiners for admission to the Bar, State of New York—God's country! (*He finishes up with a chuckle of ironic self-pity so spent as to be barely audible.*)

ELLA (*writhing out of her chair like some fierce animal, the knife held behind her—with fear and hatred*). You didn't—you didn't—you didn't pass, did you?

JIM (*looking at her wildly*). Pass? Pass? (*He begins to chuckle and laugh between sentences and phrases, rich, Negro laughter, but heart-breaking in its mocking grief.*) Good Lord, child, how come you can ever imagine such a crazy idea? Pass? Me? Jim Crow Harris? Nigger Jim Harris—become a full-fledged Member of the Bar! Why, the mere notion of it is enough to kill you with laughing! It'd be against all natural laws, all human right and justice. It'd be miraculous, there'd be earthquakes and catastrophes, the Seven Plagues'd come again and locusts'd devour all the money in the banks, the second Flood'd come roaring and Noah'd fall overboard, the sun'd drop out of the sky like a ripe fig, and the Devil'd perform miracles, and God'd be tipped head first right out of the Judgment Seat! (*He laughs, maudlinly uproarious.*)

ELLA (*her face beginning to relax, to light up*). Then you—you didn't pass?

JIM (*spent—giggling and gasping idiotically*). Well, I should say not! I should certainly say not!

ELLA (*with a cry of joy, pushes all the law books crashing to the floor—then with childish happiness she grabs Jim by both hands and dances up and down*). Oh, Jim, I knew it! I knew you couldn't! Oh, I'm so glad, Jim! I'm so happy! You're still my old Jim—and I'm so glad! (*He looks at her dazedly, a fierce rage slowly gathering on his face. She dances away from him. His eyes follow her. His hands clench. She stands in front of the mask—triumphantly.*) There! What did I tell you? I told you I'd give you the laugh! (*She begins to laugh with wild unrestraint, grabs the mask from its place, sets it in the middle of the table and plunging the knife down through it pins it to the table.*) There! Who's got the laugh now?

JIM (*his eyes bulging—hoarsely*). You devil! You white devil woman! (*In a terrible roar, raising his fists above her head.*) You devil!

ELLA (*looking up at him with a bewildered cry of terror*). Jim! (*Her appeal recalls him to himself. He lets his arms slowly drop to his sides, bowing his head. Ella points tremblingly to the mask*). It's all right, Jim! It's dead. The devil's dead. See! It couldn't live—unless you passed. If you'd passed it would have lived in you. Then I'd have had to kill you, Jim, don't you see—or it would have killed me. But now I've killed it. (*She pats his hand.*) So you needn't ever be afraid any more, Jim.

JIM (*dully*). I've got to sit down, Honey. I'm tired. I haven't had much chance for sleep in so long—— (*He slumps down in the chair by the table.*)

ELLA (*sits down on the floor beside him and holds his hand. Her face is gradually regaining an expression that is happy, childlike, and pretty*). I know, Jim! That was my fault. I wouldn't let you sleep. I couldn't let you. I kept thinking if he sleeps good then he'll be sure to study good and then he'll pass—and the devil'll win!

JIM (*with a groan*). Don't, Honey!

ELLA (*with a childish grin*). That was why I carried that knife around—(*she frowns—puzzled*)—one reason—to keep you from studying and sleeping by scaring you.

JIM. I wasn't scared of being killed. I was scared of what they'd do to you after.

ELLA (*after a pause—like a child*). Will God forgive me, Jim?

JIM. Maybe He can forgive what you've done to me; and maybe He can forgive what I've done to you; but I don't see how He's going to forgive—Himself.

ELLA. I prayed and prayed. When you were away taking the examinations and I was alone with the nurse, I closed my eyes and pretended to be asleep, but I was praying with all my might: O God, don't let Jim pass!

JIM (*with a sob*). Don't, Honey, don't! For the good Lord's sake! You're hurting me!

ELLA (*frightenedly*). How, Jim? Where? (*Then after a pause—suddenly.*) I'm sick, Jim. I don't think I'll live long.

JIM (*simply*). Then I won't either. Somewhere yonder maybe—together—our luck'll change. But I wanted—here and now—before you—we—I wanted to prove to you—to myself—to become a full-fledged Member—so you could be proud—— (*He stops. Words fail and he is beyond tears.*)

ELLA (*brightly*). Well, it's all over, Jim. Everything'll be all right now. (*Chattering along.*) I'll be just your little girl, Jim—and you'll be my little boy—just as we used to be, remember, when we were beaux; and I'll put shoe blacking on my face and pretend I'm black, and you can put chalk on your face and pretend you're white, just as we used to do—and we can play marbles—only you mustn't all the time be a boy. Sometimes you must be my old kind Uncle Jim who's been with us for years and years. Will you, Jim?

JIM (*with utter resignation*). Yes, Honey.

ELLA. And you'll never, never, never, never leave me, Jim?

JIM. Never, Honey.

ELLA. 'Cause you're all I've got in the world—and I love you, Jim. (*She kisses his hand as a child might, tenderly and gratefully.*)

JIM (*suddenly throws himself on his knees and raises his shining eyes, his transfigured face*). Forgive me, God—and make me worthy! Now I see Your Light again! Now I hear Your Voice! (*He begins to weep in an ecstasy of religious humility.*) Forgive me, God, for blaspheming You! Let this fire of burning suffering purify me of selfishness and make me worthy of the child You send me for the woman You take away!

ELLA (*jumping to her feet—excitedly*). Don't cry, Jim! You mustn't cry! I've got only a little time left and I want to play. Don't be old Uncle Jim now. Be my little boy, Jim. Pretend you're Painty Face and I'm Jim Crow. Come and play!

JIM (*still deeply exalted*). Honey, Honey, I'll play right up to the gates of heaven with you! (*She tugs at one of his hands, laughingly trying to pull him up from his knees as*

The Curtain Falls.)

DESIRE UNDER THE ELMS

A Play in Three Parts

Characters

EPHRAIM CABOT
SIMEON } *his sons*
PETER } *his sons*
EBEN } *his sons*

ABBIE PUTNAM
Young Girl, Two Farmers, The Fiddler, A Sheriff, and other people from the surrounding farms

General Scene

The action of the entire play takes place in, and immediately outside of, the Cabot farm-house in New England, in the year 1850. The south end of the house faces a stone wall with a wooden gate at centre opening on a country road. The house is in good condition, but in need of paint. Its walls are a sickly greyish, the green of the shutters faded. Two enormous elms are on each side of the house. They bend their trailing branches down over the roof – they appear to protect and at the same time subdue; there is a sinister maternity in their aspect, a crushing, jealous absorption. When the wind does not keep them astir, they develop from their intimate contact with the life of man in the house an appalling humaneness. They brood oppressively over the house, they are like exhausted women resting their sagging breasts and hands and hair on its roof, and when it rains their tears trickle down monotonously and rot on the shingles.

There is a path running from the gate around the right corner of the house to the front door. A narrow porch is on this side. The end wall facing us has two windows in its upper storey, two larger ones on the floor below. The two upper are those of the father's bedroom and that of the brothers. On the left, ground floor, is the kitchen – on the right, the parlour, the blinds of which are always pulled down.

PART I Scene 1

Exterior of the Farm-house. It is sunset of a day at the beginning of summer in the year 1850. There is no wind and everything is still. The sky above the roof is suffused with deep colours, the green of the elms glows, but the house is in shadow, seeming pale and washed out by contrast.

A door opens and Eben Cabot comes to the end of the porch and stands looking down the road to the right. He has a large bell in his hand and this he swings mechanically, awakening a deafening clangour. Then he puts his hands on his hips and stares up at the sky. He sighs with a puzzled awe and blurts out with halting appreciation.

EBEN. God! Purty!

(*His eyes fall and he stares about him frowningly. He is twenty-five, tall and sinewy. His face is well formed, good-*

looking, but its expression is resentful and defensive. His defiant dark eyes remind one of a wild animal's in captivity. Each day is a cage in which he finds himself trapped, but inwardly unsubdued. There is a fierce repressed vitality about him. He has black hair, moustache, a thin curly trace of beard. He is dressed in rough farm clothes.

He spits on the ground with intense disgust, turns and goes back into the house.

Simeon and Peter come in from their work in the fields. They are tall men, much older than their half-brother (Simeon is thirty-nine and Peter thirty-seven), built on a squarer, simpler model, fleshier in body, more bovine and homelier in face, shrewder and more practical. Their shoulders stoop a bit from years of farm work. They clump heavily along in their clumsy thick-soled boots caked with earth. Their clothes, their faces, hands, bare arms and throats are earth-stained. They smell of earth. They stand together for a moment in front of the house and, as if with the one impulse, stare dumbly up at the sky, leaning on their hoes. Their faces have a compressed, unresigned expression. As they look upward, this softens.)

SIMEON (*grudgingly*). Purty.

PETER. Ay-eh.

SIMEON (*suddenly*). Eighteen year ago.

PETER. What?

SIMEON. Jenn. My woman. She died.

PETER. I'd fergot.

SIMEON. I rec'lect—now an' agin. Makes it lonesome. She'd hair long's a hoss's tail—an' yaller like gold!

PETER. Waal—she's gone. (*This with indifferent finality—then after a pause.*) They's gold in the West, Sim.

SIMEON (*still under the influence of sunset—vaguely*). In the sky?

PETER. Waal—in a manner o' speakin'—thar's the promise. (*Growing excited.*) Gold in the sky—in the west—Golden Gate—Californi-a!—Golden West!—fields o' gold!

SIMEON (*excited in his turn*). Fortunes layin' just atop o' the ground waitin' t' be picked! Solomon's mines, they says! (*For a moment they continue looking up at the sky—then their eyes drop.*)

PETER (*with sardonic bitterness*). Here—it's stones atop o' the ground—stones atop o' stones—makin' stone walls—year atop o' year—him 'n' yew 'n' me 'n' then Eben—makin' stone walls fur him to fence us in!

SIMEON. We've wuked. Give our strength. Give our years. Ploughed 'em under in the ground (*he stamps rebelliously*)—rottin'—makin' soil for his crops! (*A pause.*) Waal—the farm pays good for hereabouts.

PETER. If we ploughed in Californi-a, they'd be lumps o' gold in the furrow——!

SIMEON. Californi-a's t'other side o' earth, a'most. We got t' calc'late——

PETER (*after a pause*). 'Twould be hard fur me, too, to give up what we've 'arned here by our sweat. (*A pause. Eben sticks his head out of the dining-room window, listening.*)

SIMEON. Ay-eh. (*A pause.*) Mebbe—he'll die soon.

PETER (*doubtfully*). Mebbe.

SIMEON. Mebbe—fur all we knows—he's dead now.

PETER. Ye'd need proof——

SIMEON. He's been gone two months—with no word.

PETER. Left us in the fields an evenin' like this. Hitched up an' druv off into the West. That's plumb onnateral. He hain't never been off this farm 'ceptin' t' the village in thirty year or more, not since he married Eben's maw. (*A pause. Shrewdly.*) I calc'late we might git him declared crazy by the court.

SIMEON. He skinned 'em too slick. He got the best o' all on 'em. They'd never b'lieve him crazy. (*A pause.*) We got t' wait—till he's under ground.

EBEN (*with a sardonic chuckle*). Honour thy father! (*They turn, startled, and stare at him. He grins, then scowls.*) I pray he's died. (*They stare at him. He continues matter-of-factly.*) Supper's ready.

SIMEON *and* PETER (*together*). Ay-eh.

EBEN (*gazing up at the sky*). Sun's downin' purty.

SIMEON *and* PETER (*together*). Ay-eh. They's gold in the West.

EBEN. Ay-eh. (*Pointing.*) Yonder atop o' the hill pasture, ye mean?

SIMEON *and* PETER (*together*). In Californi-a!

EBEN. Hunh? (*Stares at them indifferently for a second, then drawls.*) Waal—supper's gittin' cold. (*He turns back into kitchen.*)

SIMEON (*startled—smacks his lips*). I air hungry!

PETER (*sniffing*). I smells bacon!

SIMEON (*with hungry appreciation*). Bacon's good!

PETER (*in same tone*). Bacon's bacon!

(*They turn, shouldering each other, their bodies bumping and rubbing together as they hurry clumsily to their food, like two friendly oxen toward their evening meal. They disappear around the right corner of house and can be heard entering the door.*)

Curtain

PART I Scene 2

The colour fades from the sky. Twilight begins. The interior of the kitchen is now visible. A pine table is at centre, a cooking-stove in the right rear corner, four rough wooden chairs, a tallow candle on the table. In the middle of the rear wall is fastened a big advertising poster with a ship in full sail and the word "California" in big letters. Kitchen utensils hang from nails. Everything is neat and in order, but the atmosphere is of a men's camp kitchen rather than that of a home.

Places for three are laid. Eben takes boiled potatoes and bacon from the stove and puts them on the table, also a loaf of bread and a crock of water. Simeon and Peter shoulder in, slump down in their chairs without a word. Eben joins them. The three eat in silence for a moment, the two elder as naturally unrestrained as beasts of the field, Eben picking at his food without appetite, glancing at them with a tolerant dislike.

SIMEON (*suddenly turns to Eben*). Looky here! Ye'd oughtn't t' said that, Eben.

PETER. 'Twa'n't righteous.

EBEN. What?

SIMEON. Ye prayed he'd die.

EBEN. Waal—don't yew pray it? (*A pause.*)

PETER. He's our Paw.

EBEN (*violently*). Not mine!

SIMEON (*dryly*). Ye'd not let no one else say that about yer Maw! Ha! (*He gives one abrupt sardonic guffaw. Peter grins.*)

EBEN (*very pale*). I meant—I hain't his'n—I hain't like him—he hain't me——

PETER (*dryly*). Wait till ye've growed his age!

EBEN (*intensely*). I'm Maw—every drop of blood! (*A pause. They stare at him with indifferent curiosity.*)

PETER (*reminiscently*). She was good t' Sim 'n' me. A good step-maw's scurse.

SIMEON. She was good t' every one.

EBEN (*greatly moved, gets to his feet and makes an awkward bow to each of them—stammering*). I be thankful t' ye. I'm her. Her heir. (*He sits down in confusion.*)

PETER (*after a pause—judicially*). She was good even t' him.

EBEN (*fiercely*). An' fur thanks he killed her!

SIMEON (*after a pause*). No one never kills nobody. It's allus somethin'. That's the murderer.

EBEN. Didn't he slave Maw t' death?

PETER. He's slaved himself t' death. He's slaved Sim 'n' me 'n' yew t' death—on'y none o' us hain't died—yit.

SIMEON. It's somethin'—drivin' him—t' drive us——

EBEN (*vengefully*). Waal—I hold him t' jedgment! (*Then scornfully.*) Somethin'! What's somethin'?

SIMEON. Dunno.

EBEN (*sardonically*). What's drivin' yew to Californi-a, mebbe? (*They look at him in surprise.*) Oh, I've heerd ye! (*Then, after a pause.*) But ye'll never go t' the gold-fields!

PETER (*assertively*). Mebbe!

EBEN. Whar'll ye git the money?

PETER. We kin walk. It's an a'mighty ways—Californi-a—but if yew was t' put all the steps we've walked on this farm end t' end we'd be in the moon!

EBEN. The Injuns'll skulp ye on the plains.

SIMEON (*with grim humour*). We'll mebbe make 'em pay a hair fur a hair!

EBEN (*decisively*). But 'tain't that. Ye won't never go because ye'll wait here fur yer share o' the farm, thinkin' allus he'll die soon.

SIMEON (*after a pause*). We've a right.

PETER. Two-thirds belongs t' us.

EBEN (*jumping to his feet*). Ye've no right! She wa'n't yewr Maw! It was her farm! Didn't he steal it from her? She's dead. It's my farm.

SIMEON (*sardonically*). Tell that t' Paw—when he comes! I'll bet ye a dollar he'll laugh—fur once in his life. Ha! (*He laughs himself in one single mirthless bark.*)

PETER (*amused in turn, echoes his brother*). Ha!

SIMEON (*after a pause*). What've ye got held agin us, Eben? Year arter year it's skulked in yer eye—somethin'.

PETER. Ay-eh.

EBEN. Ay-eh. They's somethin'. (*Suddenly exploding.*) Why didn't ye never stand between him 'n' my Maw when he was slavin' her to her grave—t' pay her back fur the kindness she done t' yew? (*There is a long pause. They stare at him in surprise.*)

SIMEON. Waal—the stock'd got t' be watered.

PETER. 'R they was woodin' t' do.

SIMEON. 'R ploughin'.

PETER. 'R hayin'.

SIMEON. 'R spreadin' manure.

PETER. 'R weedin'.

SIMEON. 'R prunin'.

PETER. 'R milkin'.

EBEN (*breaking in harshly*). An' makin' walls—stone atop o' stone—makin' walls till yer heart's a stone ye heft up out o' the way o' growth on to a stone wall t' wall in yer heart!

SIMEON (*matter-of-factly*). We never had no time t' meddle.

PETER (*to Eben*). Yew was fifteen afore yer Maw died—an' big fur yer age. Why didn't ye never do nothin'?

EBEN (*harshly*). They was chores t' do, wa'n't they? (*A pause—then slowly.*) It was on'y arter she died I come to think o' it. Me cookin'—doin' her work—that made me know her, suffer her sufferin'—she'd come back t' help—come back t' bile potatoes—come back t' fry bacon—come back t' bake biscuits—come back all cramped up t' shake the fire, an' carry ashes, her eyes weepin' an' bloody with smoke an' cinders same's they used t' be. She still comes back—stands by the stove thar in the evenin'—she can't find it nateral sleepin' an' restin' in peace. She can't git used t' bein' free—even in her grave.

SIMEON. She never complained none.

EBEN. She'd got too tired. She'd got too used t' bein' too tired. That was what he done.

(*With vengeful passion.*) An' sooner'r later, I'll meddle. I'll say the thin's I didn't say then t' him! I'll yell 'em at the top o' my lungs. I'll see t' it my Maw gits some rest an' sleep in her grave! (*He sits down again, relapsing into a brooding silence. They look at him with a queer indifferent curiosity.*)

PETER (*after a pause*). Whar in tarnation d'ye s'pose he went, Sim?

SIMEON. Dunno. He druv off in the buggy, all spick an' span, with the mare all breshed an' shiny, druv off clackin' his tongue an' wavin' his whip. I remember it right well. I was finishin' ploughin', it was spring an' May an' sunset, an' gold in the West, an' he druv off into it. I yells "Whar ye goin', Paw?" an' he hauls up by the stone wall a jiffy. His old snake's eyes was glitterin' in the sun like he'd been drinkin' a jugful an' he says with a mule's grin: "Don't ye run away till I come back!"

PETER. Wonder if he knowed we was wantin' fur Californi-a?

SIMEON. Mebbe. I didn't say nothin' and he says, lookin' kinder queer an' sick: "I been hearin' the hens cluckin' an' the roosters crowin' all the durn day. I been listenin' t' the cows lowin' an' everythin' else kickin' up till I can't stand it no more. It's spring an' I'm feelin' damned," he says. "Damned like an old bare hickory tree fit on'y fur burnin'," he says. An' then I calc'late I must've looked a mite hopeful, fur he adds real spry and vicious: "But don't git no fool idee I'm dead. I've sworn t' live a hundred an' I'll do it, if on'y t' spite yer sinful greed! An' now I'm ridin' out t' learn God's message t' me in the spring, like the prophets done. An' yew git back t' yer ploughin'," he says. An' he druv off singin' a hymn. I thought he was drunk—'r I'd stopped him goin'.

EBEN (*scornfully*). No, ye wouldn't! Ye're scared o' him. He's stronger—inside—than both o' ye put together!

PETER (*sardonically*). An' yew—be yew Samson?

EBEN. I'm gittin' stronger. I kin feel it growin' in me—growin' an' growin'—till it'll bust out——! (*He gets up and puts on his coat and a hat. They watch him, gradually breaking into grins. Eben avoids their eyes sheepishly.*) I'm goin' out fur a spell—up the road.

PETER. T' the village?

SIMEON. T' see Minnie?

EBEN (*defiantly*). Ay-eh!

PETER (*jeeringly*). The Scarlet Woman!

SIMEON. Lust—that's what's growin' in ye!

EBEN. Waal—she's purty!

PETER. She's been purty fur twenty year!

SIMEON. A new coat o' paint'll make a heifer out of forty.

EBEN. She hain't forty!

PETER. If she hain't, she's teeterin' on the edge.

EBEN (*desperately*). What d'yew know——?

PETER. All they is . . . Sim knew her—an' then me arter——

SIMEON. An' Paw kin tell yew somethin', too! He was fust!

EBEN. D'ye mean t' say he——?

SIMEON (*with a grin*). Ay-eh! We air his heirs in everythin'!

EBEN (*intensely*). That's more to it! That grows on it! It'll bust soon! (*Then violently.*) I'll go smash my fist in her face! (*He pulls open the door in rear violently.*)

SIMEON (*with a wink at Peter—drawlingly*). Mebbe—but the night's wa'm—purty—by the time ye git thar mebbe ye'll kiss her instead!

PETER. Sart'n he will!

(*They both roar with coarse laughter. Eben rushes out and slams the door—then the outside front door—comes around the corner of the house and stands still by the gate, staring up at the sky.*)

SIMEON (*looking after him*). Like his Paw!

PETER. Dead spit an' image!

SIMEON. Dog'll eat dog!

PETER. Ay-eh. (*Pause. With yearning.*) Mebbe a year from now we'll be in Californi-a.

SIMEON. Ay-eh. (*A pause. Both yawn.*) Let's git t' bed.

(*He blows out the candle. They go out door in rear. Eben stretches his arms up to the sky—rebelliously.*)

EBEN. Waal—thar's a star, an' somewhar's they's him, an' here's me, an' thar's Min up the road—in the same night. What if I does kiss her? She's like t'night, she's soft 'n' wa'm, her eyes kin wink like a star, her mouth's wa'm, her arms're wa'm, she smells like a wa'm ploughed field, she's purty. . . . Ay-eh! By God A'mighty she's purty, an' I don't give a damn how many sins she's sinned afore mine or who she's sinned 'em with, my sin's as purty as any one on 'em! (*He strides off down the road to the left.*)

PART I Scene 3

It is the pitch darkness just before dawn. Eben comes in from the left and goes around to the porch, feeling his way, chuckling bitterly and cursing half-aloud to himself.

EBEN. The cussed old miser! (*He can be heard going in the front door. There is a pause as he goes upstairs, then a loud knock on the bedroom door of the brothers.*) Wake up!

SIMEON (*startled*). Who's thar?

EBEN (*pushing open the door and coming in, a lighted candle in his hand. The bedroom of the brothers is revealed. Its ceiling is the sloping roof. They can stand upright only close to the centre dividing wall of the upstairs. Simeon and Peter are in a double bed, front. Eben's cot is to the rear. Eben has a mixture of silly grin and vicious scowl on his face.*) I be!

PETER (*angrily*). What in hell fire——?

EBEN. I got news fur ye! Ha! (*He gives one abrupt sardonic guffaw.*)

SIMEON (*angrily*). Couldn't ye hold it 'till we'd got our sleep?

EBEN. It's nigh sun up. (*Then explosively.*) He's gone an' married agen!

SIMEON *and* PETER (*explosively*). Paw?

EBEN. Got himself hitched to a female 'bout thirty-five—an' purty, they says——

SIMEON (*aghast*). It's a durn lie!

PETER. Who says?

SIMEON. They been stringin' ye!

EBEN. Think I'm a dunce, do ye? The hull village says. The preacher from New Dover, he brung the news—told it t' our preacher—New Dover, that's whar the old loon got himself hitched—that's whar the woman lived——

PETER (*no longer doubting—stunned*). Waal . . . !

SIMEON (*the same*). Waal . . . !

EBEN (*sitting down on a bed—with vicious hatred*). Ain't he a devil out o' hell? It's jest t' spite us—the damned old mule!

PETER (*after a pause*). Everythin'll go t' her now.

SIMEON. Ay-eh. (*A pause—dully.*) Waal—if it's done——

PETER. It's done us. (*Pause—then persuasively.*) They's gold in the fields o' Californi-a, Sim. No good a-stayin' here now.

SIMEON. Jest what I was a-thinkin'. (*Then with decision.*) 'S well fust's last! Let's lightout and git this mornin'.

PETER. Suits me.

EBEN. Ye must like walkin'.

SIMEON (*sardonically*). If ye'd grow wings on us we'd fly thar!

EBEN. Ye'd like ridin' better—on a boat, wouldn't ye? (*Fumbles in his pocket and takes out a crumpled sheet of foolscap.*) Waal, if ye sign this ye kin ride on a boat. I've had it writ out an' ready in case ye'd ever go. It says fur three hundred dollars t' each ye agree yewr shares o' the farm is sold t' me. (*They look suspiciously at the paper. A pause.*)

SIMEON (*wonderingly*). But if he's hitched agen——

PETER. An' whar'd yew git that sum o' money, anyways?

EBEN (*cunningly*). I know whar it's hid. I been waitin'—Maw told me. She knew whar it lay fur years, but she was waitin'. . . . It's her'n—the money he hoarded from her farm an' hid from Maw. It's my money by rights now.

PETER. Whar's it hid?

EBEN (*cunningly*). Whar yew won't never find it without me. Maw spied on him—'r she'd never knowed. (*A pause. They look at him suspiciously, and he at them.*) Waal, is it fa'r trade?

SIMEON. Dunno.

PETER. Dunno.

SIMEON (*looking at window*). Sky's greyin'.

PETER. Ye better start the fire, Eben.

SIMEON. An' fix some vittles.

EBEN. Ay-eh. (*Then with a forced jocular heartiness.*) I'll git ye a good one. If ye're startin' t' hoof it t' California ye'll need somethin' that'll stick t' yer ribs. (*He turns to the door, adding meaningly.*) But ye kin ride on a boat if ye'll swap. (*He stops at the door and pauses. They stare at him.*)

SIMEON (*suspiciously*). Whar was ye all night?

EBEN (*defiantly*). Up t' Min's. (*Then slowly.*) Walkin' thar, fust I felt 's if I'd kiss her; then I got a-thinkin' o' what ye'd said o' him an' her an' I says, I'll bust her nose fur that! Then I got t' the village an' heerd the news an' I got madder'n hell an' run all the way t' Min's not knowin' what I'd do—— (*He pauses—then sheepishly but more defiantly.*) Waal—when I seen her, I didn't hit her—nor I didn't kiss her nuther—I begun t' beller like a calf an' cuss at the same time, I was so durn mad—an' she got scared—an' I jest grabbed holt an' tuk her! (*Proudly.*) Yes, sirree! I tuk her. She may've been his'n—an' your'n, too—but she's mine now!

SIMEON (*dryly*). In love, air yew?

EBEN (*with lofty scorn*). Love! I don't take no stock in sech slop!

PETER (*winking at Simeon*). Mebbe Eben's aimin' t' marry, too.

SIMEON. Min'd make a true faithful he'pmeet—fur the army! (*They snicker.*)

EBEN. What do I care fur her—'ceptin' she's round an' wa'm? The p'int is she was his'n—an' now she b'longs t' me! (*He goes to the door—then turns—rebelliously.*) An' Min hain't sech a bad un. They's worse'n Min in the world, I'll bet ye! Wait'll we see this cow the Old Man's hitched t'! She'll beat Min, I got a notion! (*He starts to go out.*)

SIMEON (*suddenly*). Mebbe ye'll try t' make her your'n, too?

PETER. Ha! (*He gives a sardonic laugh of relish at this idea.*)

EBEN (*spitting with disgust*). Her—here—sleepin' with him—stealin' my Maw's farm! I'd as soon pet a skunk 'r kiss a snake! (*He goes out. The two stare after him suspiciously. A pause. They listen to his steps receding.*)

PETER. He's startin' the fire.

SIMEON. I'd like t' ride t' Californi-a—but——

PETER. Min might 'a' put some scheme in his head.

SIMEON. Mebbe it's all a lie 'bout Paw marryin'. We'd best wait an' see the bride.

PETER. An' don't sign nothin' till we does——

SIMEON. Nor till we've tested it's good money! (*Then with a grin.*) But if Paw's hitched we'd be sellin' Eben somethin' we'd never git nohow!

PETER. We'll wait an' see. (*Then with sudden vindictive anger.*) An' till he comes, let's yew 'n' me not wuk a lick, let Eben tend to thin's if he's a mind t', let's us jest sleep an' eat an' drink likker, an' let the hull damned farm go t' blazes!

SIMEON (*excitedly*). By God, we've 'arned a rest! We'll play rich fur a change. I hain't a-goin' to stir outa bed till breakfast's ready.

PETER. An' on the table!

SIMEON (*after a pause—thoughtfully*). What d'ye calc'late she'll be like—our new Maw? Like Eben thinks?

PETER. More'n likely.

SIMEON (*vindictively*). Waal—I hope she's a she-devil that'll make him wish he was dead an' livin' in the pit o' hell fur comfort!

PETER (*fervently*). Amen!

SIMEON (*imitating his father's voice*). "I'm ridin' out t' learn God's message t' me in the spring like the prophets done," he says. I'll bet right then an' thar he knew plumb well he was goin' whorin', the stinkin' old hypocrite!

PART I Scene 4

Same as Scene 2—shows the interior of the kitchen, with a lighted candle on table. It is grey dawn outside. Simeon and Peter are just finishing their breakfast. Eben sits before his plate of untouched food, brooding frowningly.

PETER (*glancing at him rather irritably*). Lookin' glum don't help none.

SIMEON (*sarcastically*). Sorrowin' over his lust o' the flesh.

PETER (*with a grin*). Was she yer fust?

EBEN (*angrily*). None o' yer business. (*A pause.*) I was thinkin' o' him. I got a notion he's gittin' near—I kin feel him comin' on like yew kin feel malaria chill afore it takes ye.

PETER. It's too early yet.

SIMEON. Dunno. He'd like t' catch us nappin'—jest t' have somethin' t' hoss us 'round over.

PETER (*mechanically gets to his feet. Simeon does the same*). Waal—let's git t' wuk. (*They both plod mechanically toward the door before they realize. Then they stop short.*)

SIMEON (*grinning*). Ye're a cussed fool, Pete—and I be wuss! Let him see we hain't wukin'! We don't give a durn!

PETER (*as they go back to the table*). Not a damned durn! It'll serve t' show him we're done with him. (*They sit down again. Eben stares from one to the other with surprise.*)

SIMEON (*grins at him*). We're aimin' t' start bein' lilies o' the field.

PETER. Nary a toil 'r spin 'r lick o' wuk do we put in!

SIMEON. Ye're sole owner—till he comes—that's what ye wanted. Waal, ye got t' be sole hand, too.

PETER. The cows air bellerin'. Ye better hustle at the milkin'.

EBEN (*with excited joy*). Ye mean ye'll sign the paper?

SIMEON (*dryly*). Mebbe.

PETER. Mebbe.

SIMEON. We're considerin'. (*Peremptorily.*) Ye better git t' wuk.

EBEN (*with queer excitement*). It's Maw's farm agen! It's my farm! Them's my cows! I'll milk my durn fingers off fur cows o' mine! (*He goes out door in rear, they stare after him indifferently.*)

SIMEON. Like his Paw.

PETER. Dead spit 'n' image!

SIMEON. Waal—let dog eat dog!

(*Eben comes out of front door and around the corner of the house. The sky is beginning to grow flushed with sunrise. Eben stops by the gate and stares around him with glowing, possessive eyes. He takes in the whole farm with his embracing glance of desire.*)

EBEN. It's purty! It's damned purty! It's mine! (*He suddenly throws his head back boldly and glares with hard, defiant eyes at the sky.*) Mine, d'ye hear? Mine! (*He turns and walks quickly *off left, rear, toward the barn. The two brothers light their pipes.*)

SIMEON (*putting his muddy boots up on the table, tilting back his chair, and puffing defiantly*). Waal—this air solid comfort—fur once.

PETER. Ay-eh. (*He follows suit. A pause Unconsciously they both sigh.*)

SIMEON (*suddenly*). He never was much o' a hand at milkin', Eben wa'n't.

PETER (*with a snort*). His hands air like hoofs! (*A pause.*)

SIMEON. Reach down the jug thar! Let's take a swaller. I'm feelin' kind o' low.

PETER. Good idee! (*He does so—gets two glasses—they pour out drinks of whisky.*) Here's t' gold in Californi-a!

SIMEON. An' luck t' find it! (*They drink—puff resolutely—sigh—take their feet down from the table.*)

PETER. Likker don't 'pear t' sot right.

SIMEON. We hain't used t' it this early. (*A pause. They become very restless.*)

PETER. Gittin' close in this kitchen.

SIMEON (*with immense relief*). Let's git a breath o' air.

(*They arise briskly and go out rear—appear around house and stop by the gate. They stare up at the sky with a numbed appreciation.*)

PETER. Purty!

SIMEON. Ay-eh. Gold's t' the East now.

PETER. Sun's startin' with us fur the Golden West.

SIMEON (*staring around the farm, his compressed lips tightened, unable to conceal his emotion*). Waal—it's our last mornin'—mebbe.

PETER (*the same*). Ay-eh.

SIMEON (*stamps his foot on the earth and addresses it desperately*). Waal—ye've thirty year o' me buried in ye—spread out over ye—blood an' bone an' sweat—rotted away—fertilizin' ye—richin' yer soul—prime manure, by God, that's what I been t' ye!

PETER. Ay-eh! An' me!

SIMEON. An' yew, Peter. (*He sighs—then spits.*) Waal—no use'n cryin' over spilt milk.

PETER. They's gold in the West—an' freedom mebbe. We been slaves t' stone walls here.

SIMEON (*defiantly*). We hain't nobody's slaves from this out—nor no thin's slaves nuther. (*A pause—restlessly.*) Speakin' o' milk, wonder how Eben's managin'?

PETER. I s'pose he's managin'.

SIMEON. Mebbe we'd ought t' help—this once.

PETER. Mebbe. The cows knows us.

SIMEON. An' likes us. They don't know him much.

PETER. An' the hosses, an' pigs, an' chickens. They don't know him much.

SIMEON. They knows us like brothers—an' likes us! (*Proudly.*) Hain't we raised 'em t' be fust-rate, number one prize stock?

PETER. We hain't—not no more.

SIMEON (*dully*). I was fergittin'. (*Then resignedly.*) Waal, let's go help Eben a spell an' git waked up.

PETER. Suits me.

(*They are starting off down left, rear, for the barn when Eben appears from there hurrying toward them, his face excited.*)

EBEN (*breathlessly*). Waal—har they be! The old mule an' the bride! I seen 'em from the barn down below at the turnin'.

PETER. How could ye tell that far?

EBEN. Hain't I as far-sight as he's near-sight? Don't I know the mare 'n' buggy, an' two people settin' in it? Who else . . . ? An' I tell ye I kin feel 'em a-comin', too! (*He squirms as if he had the itch.*)

PETER (*beginning to be angry*). Waal—let him do his own unhitchin'!

SIMEON (*angry in his turn*). Let's hustle in an' git our bundles an' be a-goin' as he's a-comin'. I don't want never t' step inside the door agen arter he's back.

(*They both start back around the corner of the house. Eben follows them.*)

EBEN (*anxiously*). Will ye sign it afore ye go?

PETER. Let's see the colour o' the old skinflint's money an' we'll sign.

(*They disappear left. The two brothers clump upstairs to get their bundles. Eben appears in the kitchen, runs to window, peers out, comes back and pulls up a strip of flooring under stove, takes out a canvas bag and puts it on table, then sets the floor-board back in place. The two brothers appear a moment after. They carry old carpet bags.*)

EBEN (*puts his hand on bag guardingly*). Have ye signed?

SIMEON (*shows paper in his hand*). Ay-eh. (*Greedily.*) Be that the money?

EBEN (*opens bag and pours out pile of twenty-dollar gold pieces*). Twenty-dollar pieces—thirty on 'em. Count 'em. (*Peter does so, arranging them in stacks of five, biting one or two to test them.*)

PETER. Six hundred. (*He puts them in bag and puts it inside his shirt carefully.*)

SIMEON (*handing paper to Eben*). Har ye be.

EBEN (*after a glance, folds it carefully and hides it under his shirt—gratefully*). Thank yew.

PETER. Thank yew fur the ride.

SIMEON. We'll send ye a lump o' gold fur Christmas. (*A pause. He stares at them and they at him.*)

PETER (*awkwardly*). Waal—we're a-goin'.

SIMEON. Comin' out t' the yard?

EBEN. No. I'm waitin' in here a spell. (*Another silence. The brothers edge awkwardly to door in rear—then turn and stand.*)

SIMEON. Waal—good-bye.

PETER. Good-bye.

EBEN. Good-bye.

(*They go out. He sits down at the table, faces the stove and pulls out the paper. He looks from it to the stove. His face, lighted up by the shaft of sunlight from the window, has an expression of trance. His lips move. The two brothers come out to the gate.*)

PETER (*looking off toward barn*). Thar he be—unhitchin'.

SIMEON (*with a chuckle*). I'll bet ye he's riled!

PETER. An' thar she be.

SIMEON. Let's wait 'n' see what our new Maw looks like.

PETER (*with a grin*). An' give him our partin' cuss!

SIMEON (*grinning*). I feel like raisin' fun. I feel light in my head an' feet.

PETER. Me, too. I feel like laffin' till I'd split up the middle.

SIMEON. Reckon it's the likker?

PETER. No. My feet feel itchin' t' walk an' walk—an' jump high over thin's—an'——

SIMEON. Dance? (*A pause.*)

PETER (*puzzled*). It's plumb onnateral.

SIMEON (*a light coming over his face*). I calc'late it's 'cause school's out. It's holiday. Fur once we're free!

PETER (*dazedly*). Free?

SIMEON. The halter's broke—the harness is busted—the fence bars is down—the stone walls air crumblin' an' tumblin'! We'll be kickin' up an' tearin' away down the road!

PETER (*drawing a deep breath—oratorically*). Anybody that wants this stinkin' old rock-pile of a farm kin hev it. 'Tain't our'n, no sirree!

SIMEON (*takes the gate off its hinges and puts it under his arm*). We harby 'bolishes shet gates, an' open gates, an' all gates, by thunder!

PETER. We'll take it with us fur luck an' let 'er sail free down some river.

SIMEON (*as a sound of voices comes from left, rear*). Har they comes !

(*The two brothers congeal into two stiff, grim-visaged statues. Ephraim Cabot and Abbie Putnam come in. Cabot is seventy-five, tall and gaunt, with great, wiry, concentrated power, but stoop-shouldered from toil. His face is as hard as if it were hewn out of a boulder, yet there is a weakness in it, a petty pride in its own narrow strength. His eyes are small, close together, and extremely near-sighted, blinking continually in the effort to focus on objects, their stare having a straining, ingrowing quality. He is dressed in his dismal black Sunday suit. Abbie is thirty-five, buxom, full of vitality. Her round face is pretty, but marred by its rather gross sensuality. There is strength and obstinacy in her jaw, a hard determination in her eyes, and about her whole personality the same unsettled, untamed, desperate quality which is so apparent in Eben.*)

CABOT (*as they enter—a queer strangled emotion in his dry cracking voice*). Har we be t' hum, Abbie.

ABBIE (*with lust for the word*). Hum ! (*Her eyes gloating on the house without seeming to see the two stiff figures at the gate.*) It's purty—purty ! I can't b'lieve it's r'ally mine.

CABOT (*sharply*). Yewr'n ? Mine ! (*He stares at her penetratingly. She stares back. He adds relentingly.*) Our'n—mebbe ! It was lonesome too long. I was growin' old in the spring. A hum's got t' hev a woman.

ABBIE (*her voice taking possession*). A woman's got t' hev a hum !

CABOT (*nodding uncertainly*). Ay-eh. (*Then irritably.*) Whar be they ? Ain't thar nobody about—'r wukin'—'r nothin' ?

ABBIE (*sees the brothers. She returns their stare of cold appraising contempt with interest—slowly*). Thar's two men loafin' at the gate an' starin' at me like a couple o' strayed hogs.

CABOT (*straining his eyes*). I kin see 'em—but I can't make out——

SIMEON. It's Simeon.

PETER. It's Peter.

CABOT (*exploding*). Why hain't ye wukin' ?

SIMEON (*dryly*). We're waitin' t' welcome ye hum—yew an' the bride !

CABOT (*confusedly*). Hunh ? Waal—this be yer new Maw, boys. (*She stares at them and they at her.*)

SIMEON (*turns away and spits contemptuously*). I see her !

PETER (*spits also*). An' I see her !

ABBIE (*with the conqueror's conscious superiority*). I'll go in an' look at *my* house. (*She goes slowly around to porch.*)

SIMEON (*with a snort*). *Her* house !

PETER (*calls after her*). Ye'll find Eben inside. Ye better not tell him it's *yewr* house.

ABBIE (*mouthing the name*). Eben. (*Then quietly.*) I'll tell Eben.

CABOT (*with a contemptuous sneer*). Ye needn't heed Eben. Eben's a dumb fool—like his Maw—soft an' simple !

SIMEON (*with his sardonic burst of laughter*). Ha ! Eben's a chip o' yew—spit 'n' image—hard 'n' bitter's a hickory tree ! Dog'll eat dog. He'll eat ye yet, old man !

CABOT (*commandingly*). Ye git t' wuk !

SIMEON (*as Abbie disappears in house—winks at Peter and says tauntingly*). So that thar's our new Maw, be it ? Whar in hell did ye dig her up ? (*He and Peter laugh.*)

PETER. Ha ! Ye'd better turn her in the pen with the other sows. (*They laugh uproariously, slapping their thighs.*)

CABOT (*so amazed at their effrontery that he stutters in confusion*). Simeon ! Peter ! What's come over ye ? Air ye drunk ?

SIMEON. We're free, old man—free o' yew an' the hull damned farm ! (*They grow more and more hilarious and excited.*)

PETER. An' we're startin' out fur the gold-fields o' Californi-a!

SIMEON. Ye kin take this place an' burn it!

PETER. An' bury it—fur all we cares!

SIMEON. We're free, old man! (*He cuts a caper.*)

PETER. Free! (*He gives a kick in the air.*)

SIMEON (*in a frenzy*). Whoop!

PETER. Whoop! (*They do an absurd Indian war dance about the old man, who is petrified between rage and the fear that they are insane.*)

SIMEON. We're free as Injuns! Lucky we don't skulp ye!

PETER. An' burn yer barn an' kill the stock!

SIMEON. An' rape yer new woman! Whoop! (*He and Peter stop their dance, holding their sides, rocking with wild laughter.*)

CABOT (*edging away*). Lust fur gold—fur the sinful, easy gold o' Californi-a! It's made ye mad!

SIMEON (*tauntingly*). Wouldn't ye like us to send ye back some sinful gold, ye old sinner?

PETER. They's gold besides what's in Californi-a! (*He retreats back beyond the vision of the old man and takes the bag of money and flaunts it in the air above his head, laughing.*)

SIMEON. And sinfuller, too!

PETER. We'll be voyagin' on the sea! Whoop! (*He leaps up and down.*)

SIMEON. Livin' free! Whoop! (*He leaps in turn.*)

CABOT (*suddenly roaring with rage*). My cuss on ye!

SIMEON. Take our'n in trade fur it! Whoop!

CABOT. I'll hev ye both chained up in the asylum!

PETER. Ye old skinflint! Good-bye!

SIMEON. Ye old blood-sucker! Good-bye!

CABOT. Go afore I——!

PETER. Whoop! (*He picks a stone from the road. Simeon does the same.*)

SIMEON. Maw'll be in the parlour.

PETER. Ay-eh! One! Two!

CABOT (*frightened*). What air ye——?

PETER. Three! (*They both throw, the stones hitting the parlour window with a crash of glass, tearing the shade.*)

SIMEON. Whoop!

PETER. Whoop!

CABOT (*in a fury now, rushing toward them*). If I kin lay hand on ye—I'll break yer bones fur ye!

(*But they beat a capering retreat before him, Simeon with the gate still under his arm. Cabot comes back, panting with impotent rage. Their voices as they go off take up the song of the gold-seekers to the old tune of* "Oh, Susannah!")

"I jumped aboard the Liza ship,
And travelled on the sea,
And every time I thought of home
I wished it wasn't me!
Oh! Californi-a,
That's the land fur me!
I'm off to Californi-a!
With my wash-bowl on my knee."

(*In the meantime the window of the upper bedroom on right is raised and Abbie sticks her head out. She looks down at Cabot—with a sigh of relief.*)

ABBIE. Waal—that's the last o' them two, hain't it? (*He doesn't answer. Then in possessive tones.*) This here's a nice bedroom, Ephraim. It's a r'al nice bed. Is it my room, Ephraim?

CABOT (*grimly—without looking up*). Our'n! (*She cannot control a grimace of aversion and pulls back her head slowly and shuts the window. A sudden horrible thought seems to enter Cabot's head.*) They been up to somethin'! Mebbe—mebbe they've pizened the stock—'r somethin'!

(*He almost runs off down toward the barn. A moment later the kitchen door is slowly pushed open and Abbie enters. For a moment she stands looking at

Eben. He does not notice her at first. Her eyes take him in penetratingly with a calculating appraisal of his strength as against hers. But under this her desire is dimly awakened by his youth and good looks. Suddenly he becomes conscious of her presence and looks up. Their eyes meet: He leaps to his feet, glowering at her speechlessly.)

ABBIE (*in her most seductive tones which she uses all through this scene*). Be you—Eben? I'm Abbie—— (*She laughs.*) I mean, I'm yer new Maw.

EBEN (*viciously*). No, damn ye!

ABBIE (*as if she hadn't heard—with a queer smile*). Yer Paw's spoke a lot o' yew——

EBEN. Ha!

ABBIE. Ye mustn't mind him. He's an old man. (*A long pause. They stare at each other.*) I don't want t' pretend playin' Maw t' ye, Eben. (*Admiringly.*) Ye're too big an' too strong fur that. I want t' be fren's with ye. Mebbe with me fur a fren' ye'd find ye'd like livin' here better. I kin make it easy fur ye with him, mebbe. (*With a scornful sense of power.*) I calc'late I kin git him t' do most anythin' fur me.

EBEN (*with bitter scorn*). Ha! (*They stare again, Eben obscurely moved, physically attracted to her—in forced stilted tones.*) Yew kin go t' the devil!

ABBIE (*calmly*). If cussin' me does ye good, cuss all ye've a mind t'. I'm all prepared t' have ye agin me—at fust. I don't blame ye nuther. I'd feel the same at any stranger comin' t' take my Maw's place. (*He shudders. She is watching him carefully.*) Yew must've cared a lot fur yewr Maw, didn't ye? My Maw died afore I'd growed. I don't remember her none. (*A pause.*) But yew won't hate me long, Eben. I'm not the wust in the world—an' yew an' me've got a lot in common. I kin tell that by lookin' at ye. Waal—I've had a hard life, too—oceans o' trouble an' nuthin' but wuk fur reward. I was a' orphan early an' had t' wuk fur others in others' hums. Then I married, an' he turned out a drunken spreer an' so he had to wuk fur others an' me too agen in others' hums, an' the baby died, an' my husband got sick an' died too, an' I was glad, sayin' now I'm free fur once, on'y I diskivered right away all I was free fur was t' wuk agen in others' hums, doin' others' wuk in others' hums till I'd most give up hope o' ever doin' my own wuk in my own hum, an' then your Paw come——

(*Cabot appears, returning from the barn. He comes to the gate and looks down the road the brothers have gone. A faint strain of their retreating voices is heard;* "Oh, Californi-a! That's the place for me." *He stands glowering, his fist clenched, his face grim with rage.*)

EBEN (*fighting against his growing attraction and sympathy—harshly*). An' bought yew—like a harlot! (*She is stung and flushes angrily. She has been sincerely moved by the recital of her troubles. He adds furiously.*) An' the price he's payin' ye—this farm—was my Maw's, damn ye!—an' mine now!

ABBIE (*with a cool laugh of confidence*). Yewr'n? We'll see 'bout that! (*Then strongly.*) Waal—what if I did need a hum? What else'd I marry an old man like him fur?

EBEN (*maliciously*). I'll tell him ye said that!

ABBIE (*smiling*). I'll say ye're lyin' a-purpose—an' he'll drive ye off the place!

EBEN. Ye devil!

ABBIE (*defying him*). This be my farm—this be my hum—this be my kitchen——!

EBEN (*furiously, as if he were going to attack her*). Shut up, damn ye!

ABBIE (*walks up to him—a queer coarse expression of desire in her face and body—slowly*). An' upstairs—that be my bedroom—an' my bed! (*He stares into her eyes, terribly confused and torn. She adds softly.*) I hain't bad nor mean—'ceptin' fur an enemy—but I got t' fight fur what's due me out o' life, if I ever 'spect t' git it. (*Then putting her hand on his arm—seductively.*) Let's yew 'n' me be fren's, Eben.

EBEN (*stupidly—as if hypnotized*). Ay-eh. (*Then furiously flinging off her arm.*) No, ye durned old witch! I hate ye! (*He rushes out the door.*)

ABBIE (*looks after him, smiling satisfiedly—then*

half to herself, mouthing the word). Eben's nice. (*She looks at the table, proudly.*) I'll wash up *my* dishes now. (*Eben appears outside, slamming the door behind him. He comes around corner, stops on seeing his father, and stands staring at him with hate.*)

CABOT (*raising his arms to Heaven in the fury he can no longer control*). Lord God o' Hosts, smite the undutiful sons with Thy wust cuss.

EBEN (*breaking in violently*). Yew 'n' yewr God! Allus cussin' folks—allus naggin' em!

CABOT (*oblivious to him—summoningly*). God o' the old! God o' the lonesome!

EBEN (*mockingly*). Naggin' His sheep t' sin! T' hell with yewr God!

CABOT (*wrathfully*). "The days air prolonged and every vision faileth!"

EBEN (*spitting*). Good enuf fur ye! (*Cabot turns. He and Eben glower at each other.*)

CABOT (*harshly*). So it's yew. I might've knowed it. (*Shaking his finger threateningly at him.*) Blasphemin' fool! (*Then quickly.*) Why hain't ye t' wuk?

EBEN. Why hain't yew? They've went. I can't wuk it all alone.

CABOT (*contemptuously*). Nor noways! I'm wuth ten o' ye yit, old's I be! Ye'll never be more'n half a man! (*Then, matter-of-factly.*) Waal—let's git t' the barn.

(*They go. A last faint note of the* "California" *song is heard from the distance. Abbie is washing the dishes.*)

Curtain

PART II Scene I

The exterior of the farm-house, as in Part I—a hot Sunday afternoon two months later. Abbie, dressed in her best, is discovered sitting in a rocker at the end of the porch. She rocks listlessly, enervated by the heat, staring in front of her with bored, half-closed eyes.

Eben sticks his head out of his bedroom window. He looks around furtively and tries to see—or hear—if anyone is on the porch, but although he has been careful to make no noise, Abbie has sensed his movement. She stops rocking, her face grows animated and eager, she waits attentively. Eben seems to feel her presence, he scowls back his thoughts of her and spits with exaggerated disdain—then withdraws back into the room. Abbie waits, holding her breath as she listens with passionate eagerness for every sound within the house.

Eben comes out. Their eyes meet. His falter, he is confused, he turns away and slams the door resentfully. At this gesture, Abbie laughs tantalizingly, amused, but at the same time piqued and irritated. He scowls, strides off the porch to the path and starts to walk past her to the road with a grand swagger of ignoring her existence. He is dressed in his store suit, spruced up, his face shines from soap and water. Abbie leans forward on her chair, her eyes hard and angry now, and, as he passes her, gives a sneering, taunting chuckle.

EBEN (*stung—turns on her furiously*). What air yew cacklin' 'bout?

ABBIE (*triumphant*). Yew!

EBEN. What about me?

ABBIE. Ye look all slicked up like a prize bull.

EBEN (*with a sneer*). Waal—ye hain't so durned purty yerself, be ye? (*They stare into each other's eyes, his held by hers in spite of himself, hers glowingly possessive. Their physical attraction becomes a palpable force quivering in the hot air.*)

ABBIE (*softly*). Ye don't mean that, Eben. Ye may think ye mean it, mebbe, but ye don't. Ye can't. It's agin nature, Eben. Ye been fightin' yer nature ever since the day I come—tryin' t' tell yerself I hain't purty t' ye. (*She laughs a low humid laugh without taking her eyes from his. A pause—her body squirms desirously—she murmurs languorously.*) Hain't the sun strong an' hot? Ye kin feel it burnin' into the earth—Nature—makin' thin's grow—bigger 'n' bigger—burnin' inside ye—makin' ye want t' grow—into somethin' else—till ye're jined with it—an' it's your'n —but it owns ye, too—an' makes ye grow bigger —like a tree—like them elums—— (*She laughs again softly, holding his eyes. He takes a step toward her, compelled against his will.*) Nature'll beat ye, Eben. Ye might's well own up t' it fust 's last.

EBEN (*trying to break from her spell—confusedly*). If Paw'd hear ye goin' on . . . (*Resentfully.*) But ye've made such a damned idjit out o' the old devil. . . . (*Abbie laughs.*)

ABBIE. Waal—hain't it easier fur yew with him changed softer?

EBEN (*defiantly*). No. I'm fightin' him—fightin' yew—fightin' fur Maw's rights t' her hum! (*This breaks her spell for him. He glowers at her.*) An' I'm on to ye. Ye hain't foolin' me a mite. Ye're aimin' t' swaller up everythin' an' make it your'n. Waal, you'll find I'm a heap sight bigger hunk nor yew kin chew! (*He turns from her with a sneer.*)

ABBIE (*trying to regain her ascendancy—seductively*). Eben!

EBEN. Leave me be! (*He starts to walk away.*)

ABBIE (*more commandingly*). Eben!

EBEN (*stops—resentfully*). What d'ye want?

ABBIE (*trying to conceal a growing excitement*). Whar air ye goin'?

EBEN (*with malicious nonchalance*). Oh—up the road a spell.

ABBIE. T' the village?

EBEN (*airily*). Mebbe.

ABBIE (*excitedly*). T' see that Min, I s'pose?

EBEN. Mebbe.

ABBIE (*weakly*). What d'ye want t' waste time on her fur?

EBEN (*revenging himself now—grinning at her*). Ye can't beat Nature, didn't ye say? (*He laughs and again starts to walk away.*)

ABBIE (*bursting out*). An ugly old hake!

EBEN (*with a tantalizing sneer*). She's purtier'n yew be!

ABBIE. That every wuthless drunk in the country has. . . .

EBEN (*tauntingly*). Mebbe—but she's better'n yew. She owns up f'ar 'n' squ'ar t' her doin's.

ABBIE (*furiously*). Don't ye dare compare——

EBEN. She don't go sneakin' an' stealin'—what's mine.

ABBIE (*savagely seizing on his weak point*). Your'n? Yew mean—my farm?

EBEN. I mean the farm yew sold yerself fur like any other old whore—my farm!

ABBIE (*stung—fiercely*). Ye'll never live t' see the day when even a stinkin' weed on it 'll belong t' ye! (*Then in a scream.*) Git out o' my sight! Go on t' yer slut—disgracin' yer Paw 'n' me! I'll git yer Paw t' horsewhip ye off the place if I want t'! Ye're only livin' here 'cause I tolerate ye! Git along! I hate the sight o' ye! (*She stops, panting and glaring at him.*)

EBEN (*returning her glance in kind*). An' I hate the sight o' yew!

(*He turns and strides off up the road. She follows his retreating figure with concentrated hate. Old Cabot appears coming up from the barn. The hard, grim expression of his face has changed. He seems in some queer way softened, mellowed. His eyes have taken on a strange, incongruous dreamy quality. Yet there is no hint of physical weakness about him—rather he looks more robust and younger. Abbie sees him and turns away quickly with unconcealed aversion. He comes slowly up to her.*)

CABOT (*mildly*). War yew an' Eben quarrellin' agin?

ABBIE (*shortly*). No.

CABOT. Ye was talkin' a'mighty loud. . . . (*He sits down on the edge of porch.*)

ABBIE (*snappishly*). If ye heerd us they hain't no need askin' questions.

CABOT. I didn't hear what ye said.

ABBIE (*relieved*). Waal—it wa'n't nothin' t' speak on.

CABOT (*after a pause*). Eben's queer.

ABBIE (*bitterly*). He's the dead spit 'n' image o' yew !

CABOT (*queerly interested*). D'ye think so, Abbie ? (*After a pause, ruminatingly.*) Me 'n' Eben's allus fit 'n' fit. I never could b'ar him noways. He's so thunderin' soft—like his Maw.

ABBIE (*scornfully*). Ay-eh ! 'Bout as soft as yew be !

CABOT (*as if he hadn't heard*). Mebbe I been too hard on him.

ABBIE (*jeeringly*). Waal—ye're gittin' soft now —soft as slop ! That's what Eben was sayin'.

CABOT (*his face instantly grim and ominous*). Eben was sayin' ? Waal, he'd best not do nothin' t' try me 'r he'll soon diskiver. . . . (*A pause. She keeps her face turned away. His gradually softens. He stares up at the sky.*) Purty, hain't it ?

ABBIE (*crossly*). I don't see nothin' purty.

CABOT. The sky. Feels like a warm field up thar.

ABBIE (*sarcastically*). Air yew aimin' t' buy up over the farm, too ? (*She snickers contemptuously.*)

CABOT (*strangely*). I'd like t' own my place up thar. (*A pause.*) I'm getting old, Abbie. I'm gittin' ripe on the bough. (*A pause. She stares at him mystified. He goes on.*) It's allus lonesome cold in the house—even when it's bilin' hot outside. Hain't yew noticed ?

ABBIE. No.

CABOT. It's warm down t' the barn—nice smellin' an' warm—with the cows. (*A pause.*) Cows is queer.

ABBIE. Like yew !

CABOT. Like Eben. (*A pause.*) I'm gittin' t' feel resigned t' Eben—jest as I got t' feel 'bout his Maw. I'm gittin' t' learn to b'ar his softness —jest like her'n. I calc'late I c'd a'most take t' him—if he wa'n't sech a dumb fool ! (*A pause.*) I s'pose it's old age a-creepin' in my bones.

ABBIE (*indifferently*). Waal—ye hain't dead yet.

CABOT (*roused*). No, I hain't, yew bet—not by a hell of a sight—I'm sound 'n' tough as hickory ! (*Then moodily.*) But arter three score and ten the Lord warns ye t' prepare. (*A pause.*) That's why Eben's come in my head. Now that his cussed sinful brothers is gone their path t' hell, they's no one left but Eben.

ABBIE (*resentfully*). They's me, hain't they ? (*Agitatedly.*) What's all this sudden likin' ye've tuk to Eben ? Why don't ye say nothin' 'bout me ? Hain't I yer lawful wife ?

CABOT (*simply*). Ay-eh. Ye be. (*A pause—he stares at her desirously—his eyes grow avid—then with a sudden movement he seizes her hands and squeezes them, declaiming in a queer camp-meeting preacher's tempo.*) Yew air my Rose o' Sharon ! Behold, yew air fair ; yer eyes air doves ; yer lips air like scarlet ; yer two breasts air like two fawns ; yer navel be like a round goblet ; yer belly be like a heap o' wheat. . . . (*He covers her hand with kisses. She does not seem to notice. She stares before her with hard angry eyes.*)

ABBIE (*jerking her hands away—harshly*). So ye're plannin' t' leave the farm t' Eben, air ye ?

CABOT (*dazedly*). Leave . . . ? (*Then with resentful obstinacy.*) I hain't a-givin' it t' no one !

ABBIE (*remorselessly*). Ye can't take it with ye.

CABOT (*thinks a moment—then reluctantly*). No, I calc'late not. (*After a pause—with a strange passion.*) But if I could, I would, by the Etarnal ! 'R if I could, in my dyin' hour, I'd set it afire an' watch it burn—this house an' every ear o' corn an' every tree down t' the last blade o' hay ! I'd sit an' know it was all a-dying with me an' no one else'd ever own what was mine, what I'd made out o' nothin' with my own sweat 'n' blood ! (*A pause—then he adds with a queer affection.*) 'Ceptin' the cows. Them I'd turn free.

ABBIE (*harshly*). An' me ?

CABOT (*with a queer smile*). Ye'd be turned free, too.

ABBIE (*furiously*). So that's the thanks I git fur marryin' ye—t' have ye change kind to Eben who hates ye, an' talk o' turnin' me out in the road.

CABOT (*hastily*). Abbie! Ye know I wa'n't. . . .

ABBIE (*vengefully*). Just let me tell ye a thing or two 'bout Eben! Whar's he gone? T' see that harlot, Min! I tried fur t' stop him. Disgracin' yew an' me—on the Sabbath, too!

CABOT (*rather guiltily*). He's a sinner—nateral-born. It's lust eatin' his heart.

ABBIE (*enraged beyond endurance—wildly vindictive*). An' his lust fur me! Kin ye find excuses fur that?

CABOT (*stares at her—after a dead pause*). Lust—fur yew?

ABBIE (*defiantly*). He was tryin' t' make love t' me—when ye heerd us quarrellin'.

CABOT (*stares at her—then a terrible expression of rage comes over his face—he springs to his feet shaking all over*). By the A'mighty God—I'll end him!

ABBIE (*frightened now for Eben*). No! Don't ye!

CABOT (*violently*). I'll git the shotgun an' blow his soft brains t' the top o' them elums!

ABBIE (*throwing her arms around him*). No, Ephraim!

CABOT (*pushing her away violently*). I will, by God!

ABBIE (*in a quieting tone*). Listen, Ephraim. T'wa'n't nothin' bad—on'y a boy's foolin'—t'wa'n't meant serious—jest jokin' an' teasin'. . . .

CABOT. Then why did ye say—lust?

ABBIE. It must hev sounded wusser'n I meant. An' I was mad at thinkin'—ye'd leave him the farm.

CABOT (*quieter, but still grim and cruel*). Waal then, I'll horsewhip him off the place if that much'll content ye.

ABBIE (*reaching out and taking his hand*). No. Don't think o' me! Ye mustn't drive him off. T'ain't sensible. Who'll ye get to help ye on the farm? They's no one hereabouts.

CABOT (*considers this—then nodding his appreciation*). Ye got a head on ye. (*Then irritably.*) Waal, let him stay. (*He sits down on the edge of the porch. She sits beside him. He murmurs contemptuously.*) I oughtn't t' git riled so—at that 'ere fool calf. (*A pause.*) But har's the p'int. What son o' mine'll keep on here t' the farm—when the Lord does call me? Simeon an' Peter air gone t' hell—an Eben's follerin' 'em——

ABBIE. They's me.

CABOT. Ye're on'y a woman.

ABBIE. I'm yewr wife.

CABOT. That hain't me. A son is me—my blood—mine. Mine ought t' git mine. An' then it's still mine—even though I be six foot under. D'ye see?

ABBIE (*giving him a look of hatred*). Ay-eh. I see. (*She becomes very thoughtful, her face growing shrewd, her eyes studying Cabot craftily.*)

CABOT. I'm gittin' old—ripe on the bough. (*Then with a sudden forced reassurance.*) Not but what I hain't a hard nut t' crack even yet—an' fur many a year t' come! By the Etarnal, I kin break most o' the young fellers' backs at any kind o' work any day o' the year!

ABBIE (*suddenly*). Mebbe the Lord'll give *us* a son.

CABOT (*turns and stares at her eagerly*). Ye mean—a son—t' me 'n' yew?

ABBIE (*with a cajoling smile*). Ye're a strong man yet, hain't ye? 'Tain't noways impossible, be it? We know that. Why d'ye stare so? Hain't ye never thought o' that afore? I been thinkin' o' it all along. Ay-eh—an' I been prayin' it'd happen, too.

CABOT (*his face growing full of joyous pride and a sort of religious ecstasy*). Ye been prayin', Abbie?—fur a son?—t' us?

ABBIE. Ay-eh. (*With a grim resolution.*) I want a son now.

CABOT (*excitedly clutching both of her hands in his*). It'd be the blessin' o' God, Abbie—the blessin' o' God A'mighty on me—in my old age—in my lonesomeness! They hain't nothin' I wouldn't do fur ye then, Abbie. Ye'd hev on'y t' ask it—anythin' ye'd a mind t'——

ABBIE (*interrupting*). Would ye will the farm t' me then—t' me an' it—— ?

CABOT (*vehemently*). I'd do anythin' ye axed, I tell ye! I swear it! May I be everlastin' damned t' hell if I wouldn't! (*He sinks to his knees, pulling her down with him. He trembles all over with the fervour of his hopes.*) Pray t' the Lord agin, Abbie. It's the Sabbath! I'll jine ye! Two prayers air better nor one. "An' God hearkened unto Rachel an' she conceived an' bore a son." An' God hearkened unto Abbie! Pray, Abbie! Pray fur Him to hearken! (*He bows his head, mumbling. She pretends to do likewise, but gives him a side glance of scorn and triumph.*)

PART II Scene 2

About eight in the evening. The interior of the two bedrooms on the top floor is shown. Eben is sitting on the side of his bed in the room on the left. On account of the heat he has taken off everything but his undershirt and pants. His feet are bare. He faces front, brooding moodily, his chin propped on his hands, a desperate expression on his face.

In the other room Cabot and Abbie are sitting side by side on the edge of their bed, an old four-poster with feather mattress. He is in his night-shirt, she in her night-dress. He is still in the queer excited mood into which the notion of a son has thrown him. Both rooms are lighted dimly and flickeringly by tallow candles.

CABOT. The farm needs a son.

ABBIE. I need a son.

CABOT. Ay-eh. Sometimes ye air the farm an' sometimes the farm be yew. That's why I clove t' ye in my lonesomeness. (*A pause. He pounds his knee with his fist.*) Me an' the farm has got t' beget a son!

ABBIE. Ye'd best go t' sleep. Ye're gittin' thin's all mixed.

CABOT (*with an impatient gesture*). No, I hain't. My mind's clear's a well. Ye don't know me, that's it. (*He stares hopelessly at the floor.*)

ABBIE (*indifferently*). Mebbe.

(*In the next room Eben gets up and paces up and down distractedly. Abbie hears him. Her eyes fasten on the intervening wall with concentrated attention. Eben stops and stares. Their hot glances seem to meet through the wall. Unconsciously he stretches out his arms for her and she half rises. Then aware, he mutters a curse at himself and flings himself face downward on the bed, his clenched fists above his head, his face buried in the pillow. Abbie relaxes with a faint sigh, but her eyes remain fixed on the wall, she listens with all her attention for some movement from Eben.*)

CABOT (*suddenly raises his head and looks at her—scornfully*). Will ye ever know me—'r will any man 'r woman? (*Shaking his head.*) No. I calc'late 't wa'n't t' be. (*He turns away. Abbie looks at the wall. Then, evidently unable to keep silent about his thoughts, without looking at his wife, he puts out his hand and clutches her knee. She starts violently, looks at him, sees he is not watching her, concentrates again on the wall and pays no attention to what he says.*) Listen, Abbie. When I come here fifty odd year ago—I was jest twenty an' the strongest an' hardest ye ever seen—ten times as strong an' fifty times as hard as Eben. Waal—this place was nothin' but fields o' stones. Folks laughed when I tuk it. They couldn't know what I knowed. When ye kin make corn sprout out o' stones, God's livin' in yew. They wa'n't strong enuf fur that! They reckoned God was easy. They laughed. They don't laugh no more. Some died hereabouts. Some went West an' died. They're all under ground—fur follerin' arter an easy God. God hain't easy. (*He shakes his head slowly.*) An' I growed hard. Folks kept allus sayin', "He's a hard man," like 'twas sinful t' be hard, so's at last I said back at 'em, "Waal then, by thunder, ye'll git me hard an' see how ye like it!" (*Then suddenly.*) But I give in t' weakness once. 'Twas arter I'd been here two year. I got weak—despairful—they was so many stones. They was a party leavin', givin' up, goin' West. I jined 'em. We tracked on 'n on. We come t' broad medders, plains, whar the soil was black an' rich as gold. Nary a stone. Easy. Ye'd on'y to plough an' sow an' then set an' smoke yer pipe an' watch thin's grow. I could o' been a rich man—but somethin' in me fit me an' fit me—the voice o' God sayin', "This hain't wuth nothin' t' Me. Git ye back t' hum!" I got afeered o' that voice an' I lit out back t' hum here, leavin' my claim an' crops t' whoever'd a mind t' take 'em. Ay-eh. I actooly give up what was rightful mine! God's hard, not easy! God's in the stones! Build My church on a rock—out o' stones an' I'll be in them. That's what He meant t' Peter! (*He sighs heavily—a pause.*) Stones. I picked 'em up an' piled 'em into walls. Ye kin read the years o' my life in them walls, every day a hefted stone, climbin' over the hills up and down, fencing in the fields that was mine, whar I'd made thin's grow out o' nothin'—like the will o' God, like the servant o' His hand. It wa'n't easy. It was hard an' He made me hard fur it. (*He pauses.*) All the time I kept gittin' lonesomer. I tuk a wife. She bore Simeon an' Peter. She was a good woman. She wuked hard. We was married twenty year. She never knowed me. She helped, but she never knowed what she was helpin'. I was allus lonesome. She died. After that it wa'n't so lonesome fur a spell. (*A pause.*) I lost count o' the years. I had no time t' fool away countin' 'em. Sim an' Peter helped. The farm growed. It was all mine! When I thought o' that I didn't feel lonesome. (*A pause.*) But ye can't hitch yer mind t' one thin' day an' night. I tuk another wife—Eben's Maw. Her folks was contestin' me at law over my deeds t' the farm—my farm! That's why Eben keeps a-talking his fool talk o' this bein' his Maw's farm. She bore Eben. She was purty—but soft. She tried t' be hard. She couldn't. She never knowed me nor nothin'. It was lonesomer 'n hell with her. After a matter o' sixteen odd years, she died. (*A pause.*) I lived with the boys. They hated me 'cause I was hard. I hated them 'cause they was soft. They coveted the farm without knowin' what it meant. It made me bitter 'n wormwood. It aged me—them coveting what I'd made fur mine. Then this spring the call come—the voice o' God cryin' in my wilderness, in my lonesomeness—t' go out an' seek an' find! (*Turning to her with strange passion.*) I sought ye an' I found ye! Yew air my Rose o' Sharon! Yer eyes air like. . . . (*She has turned a blank face, resentful eyes to his. He stares at her for a moment—then harshly.*) Air ye any the wiser fur all I've told ye?

ABBIE (*confusedly*). Mebbe.

CABOT (*pushing her away from him—angrily*). Ye don't know nothin'—nor never will. If ye don't hev a son t' redeem ye . . . (*This in a tone of cold threat.*)

ABBIE (*resentfully*). I've prayed, hain't I?

CABOT (*bitterly*). Pray agin—fur understandin'!

ABBIE (*a veiled threat in her tone*). Ye'll have a son out o' me I promise ye.

CABOT. How can ye promise?

ABBIE. I got second-sight, mebbe. I kin foretell. (*She gives a queer smile.*)

CABOT. I believe ye have. Ye give me the chills sometimes. (*He shivers.*) It's cold in this house. It's oneasy. They's thin's pokin' about in the dark—in the corners. (*He pulls on his trousers, tucking in his night-shirt, and pulls on his boots.*)

ABBIE (*surprised*). Whar air ye goin'?

CABOT (*queerly*). Down whar it's restful—whar it's warm—down t' the barn. (*Bitterly.*) I kin talk t' the cows. They know. They know the farm an' me. They'll give me peace. (*He turns to go out the door.*)

ABBIE (*a bit frightenedly*). Air ye ailin' to-night, Ephraim?

CABOT. Growin'. Growin' ripe on the bough. (*He turns and goes, his boots clumping down the stairs. Eben sits up with a start, listening. Abbie is conscious of his movement and stares at the wall. Cabot comes out of the house around the corner and stands by the gate, blinking at the sky. He stretches up his hands in a tortured gesture.*) God A'mighty, call from the dark!

(*He listens as if expecting an answer. Then*

his arms drop, he shakes his head and plods off toward the barn. Eben and Abbie stare at each other through the wall. Eben sighs heavily and Abbie echoes it. Both become terribly nervous, uneasy. Finally Abbie gets up and listens, her ear to the wall. He acts as if he saw every move she was making; he becomes resolutely still. She seems driven into a decision—goes out the door in rear determinedly. His eyes follow her. Then as the door of his room is opened softly, he turns away, waits in an attitude of strained fixity. Abbie stands for a second staring at him, her eyes burning with desire. Then with a little cry she runs over and throws her arms about his neck, she pulls his head back and covers his mouth with kisses. At first, he submits dumbly; then he puts his arms about her neck and returns her kisses, but finally, suddenly aware of his hatred, he hurls her away from him, springing to his feet. They stand speechless and breathless, panting like two animals.)

ABBIE (*at last—painfully*). Ye shouldn't, Eben —ye shouldn't—I'd make ye happy!

EBEN (*harshly*). I don't want happy—from yew!

ABBIE (*helplessly*). Ye do, Eben! Ye do! Why d'ye lie?

EBEN (*viciously*). I don't take t' ye, I tell ye! I hate the sight o' ye!

ABBIE (*with an uncertain troubled laugh*). Waal, I kissed ye anyways—an' ye kissed back—yer lips was burnin'—ye can't lie 'bout that! (*Intensely.*) If ye don't care, why did ye kiss me back—why was yer lips burnin'?

EBEN (*wiping his mouth*). It was like pizen on 'em. (*Then tauntingly.*) When I kissed ye back, mebbe I thought 'twas someone else.

ABBIE (*wildly*). Min?

EBEN. Mebbe.

ABBIE (*torturedly*). Did ye go t' see her? Did ye r'ally go? I thought ye mightn't. Is that why ye throwed me off jest now?

EBEN (*sneeringly*). What if it be?

ABBIE (*raging*). Then ye're a dog, Eben Cabot!

EBEN (*threateningly*). Ye can't talk that way t' me!

ABBIE (*with a shrill laugh*). Can't I? Did ye think I was in love with ye—a weak thin' like yew? Not much! I on'y wanted ye fur a purpose o' my own—an' I'll hev ye fur it yet 'cause I'm stronger'n yew be!

EBEN (*resentfully*). I knowed well it was on'y part o' yer plan t' swaller everythin'!

ABBIE (*tauntingly*). Mebbe!

EBEN (*furious*). Git out o' my room!

ABBIE. This air my room an' ye're on'y hired help!

EBEN (*threateningly*). Git out afore I murder ye!

ABBIE (*quite confident now*). I hain't a mite afeerd. Ye want me, don't ye? Yes, ye do! An yer Paw's son'll never kill what he wants! Look at yer eyes! They's lust fur me in 'em, burnin' 'em up! Look at yer lips now! They're tremblin' an' longin' t' kiss me, an' yer teeth t' bite! (*He is watching her now with a horrible fascination. She laughs a crazy triumphant laugh.*) I'm a-goin' t' make all o' this hum my hum! They's one room hain't mine yet, but it's a-goin' t' be to-night. I'm a-goin' down now an' light up! (*She makes him a mocking bow.*) Won't ye come courtin' me in the best parlour, Mister Cabot?

EBEN (*staring at her—horribly confused—dully*). Don't ye dare! It hain't been opened since Maw died an' was laid out thar! Don't ye . . . (*But her eyes are fixed on his so burningly that his will seems to wither before hers. He stands swaying toward her helplessly.*)

ABBIE (*holding his eyes and putting all her will into her words as she backs out the door*). I'll expect ye afore long, Eben.

EBEN (*stares after her for awhile, walking toward the door. A light appears in the parlour window. He murmurs.*) In the parlour? (*This seems to *arouse connections, for he comes back and puts on his white shirt, collar, half ties the tie mechanically, puts on coat, takes his hat, stands barefooted looking about him in bewilderment, mutters wonderingly.)* Maw! Whar air yew? (*Then goes slowly toward the door in rear.*)

PART II Scene 3

A few minutes later. The interior of the parlour is shown. A grim, repressed room like a tomb in which the family has been interred alive. Abbie sits on the edge of the horsehair sofa. She has lighted all the candles and the room is revealed in all its preserved ugliness. A change has come over the woman. She looks awed and frightened now, ready to run away.

The door is opened and Eben appears. His face wears an expression of obsessed confusion. He stands staring at her, his arms hanging disjointedly from his shoulders, his feet bare, his hat in his hand.

ABBIE (*after a pause—with a nervous, formal politeness*). Won't ye set?

EBEN (*dully*). Ay-eh. (*Mechanically he places his hat carefully on the floor near the door and sits stiffly beside her on the edge of the sofa. A pause. They both remain rigid, looking straight ahead with eyes full of fear.*)

ABBIE. When I fust come in—in the dark—they seemed somethin' here.

EBEN (*simply*). Maw.

ABBIE. I kin still feel—somethin'——

EBEN. It's Maw.

ABBIE. At fust I was feered o' it. I wanted t' yell an' run. Now—since yew come—seems like it's growin' soft an' kind t' me. (*Addressing the air—queerly.*) Thank yew.

EBEN. Maw allus loved me.

ABBIE. Mebbe it knows I love ye, too. Mebbe that makes it kind t' me.

EBEN (*dully*). I dunno. I should think she'd hate ye.

ABBIE (*with certainty*). No. I kin feel it don't —not no more.

EBEN. Hate ye fur stealin' her place—here in her hum—settin' in her parlour whar she was laid. . . . (*He suddenly stops, staring stupidly before him.*)

ABBIE. What is it, Eben?

EBEN (*in a whisper*). Seems like Maw didn't want me t' remind ye.

ABBIE (*excitedly*). I knowed, Eben! It's kind t' me! It don't b'ar me no grudges fur what I never knowed an' couldn't help!

EBEN. Maw b'ars him a grudge.

ABBIE. Waal, so does all o' us.

EBEN. Ay-eh. (*With passion.*) I does, by God!

ABBIE (*taking one of his hands in hers and patting it*). Thar! Don't git riled thinkin' o' him. Think o' yer Maw who's kind t' us. Tell me about yer Maw, Eben.

EBEN. They hain't nothin' much. . . . She was kind. She was good.

ABBIE (*putting one arm over his shoulder. He does not seem to notice—passionately*). I'll be kind an' good t' ye!

EBEN. Sometimes she used t' sing fur me.

ABBIE. I'll sing fur ye!

EBEN. This was her hum. This was her farm.

ABBIE. This is my hum. This is my farm.

EBEN. He married her t' steal 'em. She was soft an' easy. He couldn't 'preciate her.

ABBIE. He can't 'preciate me!

EBEN. He murdered her with his hardness.

ABBIE. He's murderin' me!

EBEN. She died. (*A pause.*) Sometimes she used to sing fur me. (*He bursts into a fit of sobbing.*)

ABBIE (*both her arms around him—with wild passion*). I'll sing fur ye! I'll die fur ye! (*In spite of her overwhelming desire for him, there is a sincere maternal love in her manner and voice—a horribly frank mixture of lust and mother-love.*) Don't cry, Eben! I'll take yer Maw's place! I'll be everythin' she was t' ye! Let me kiss ye, Eben! (*She pulls his head around. He makes a bewildered pretence of resistance. She is tender.*) Don't be afeered! I'll kiss ye pure, Eben—same 's if I was a Maw t' ye—an' ye kin kiss me back 's if yew was my son—my boy—sayin' good night t' me! Kiss me, Eben. (*They kiss in restrained fashion. Then suddenly wild passion overcomes her. She kisses him lustfully again and again and he flings his arms about her and returns her kisses. Suddenly, as in the bedroom, he frees himself from her violently and springs to his feet. He is trembling all over, in a strange state of terror. Abbie strains her arms toward him with fierce pleading.*) Don't ye leave me, Eben! Can't ye see it hain't enuf—lovin' ye like a Maw—can't ye see it's got t' be that an' more—much more—a hundred times more—fur me t' be happy—fur yew t' be happy?

EBEN (*to the presence he feels in the room*). Maw! Maw! What d'ye want? What air ye tellin' me?

ABBIE. She's tellin' ye t' love me. She knows I love ye an' I'll be good t' ye. Can't ye feel it? Don't ye know? She's tellin ye t' love me, Eben!

EBEN. Ay-eh. I feel—mebbe she—but—I can't figger out—why—when ye've stole her place—here in her hum—in the parlour whar she was. . . .

ABBIE (*fiercely*). She knows I love ye!

EBEN (*his face suddenly lighting up with a fierce triumphant grin*). I see it! I sees why. It's her vengeance on him—so's she kin rest quiet in her grave!

ABBIE (*wildly*). Vengeance o' her on him! Vengeance o' her on me—an' mine on yew—an' yourn on me—an' ourn on him! Vengeance o' God on the hull o' us! What d' we give a durn? I love ye, Eben! God knows I love ye! (*She stretches out her arms for him.*)

EBEN (*throws himself on his knees beside the sofa and grabs her in his arms—releasing all his pent-up passion*). An' I love yew, Abbie!—now I kin say it! I been dyin' fur want o' ye—every hour—since ye come! I love ye! (*Their lips meet in a fierce, bruising kiss.*)

PART II Scene 4

Exterior of the farm-house. It is just dawn. The front door at right is opened and Eben comes out and walks around to the gate. He is dressed in his working clothes. He seems changed. His face wears a bold and confident expression, he is grinning to himself with evident satisfaction. As he gets near the gate, the window of the parlour is heard opening and the shutters are flung back and Abbie sticks her head out. Her hair tumbles over her shoulders in disarray, her face is flushed, she looks at Eben with tender, languorous eyes and calls softly.)

ABBIE. Eben. (*As he turns—playfully.*) Jest one more kiss afore ye go. I'm goin' t' miss ye fearful all day.

EBEN. An me yew, ye kin bet! (*He goes to her. They kiss several times. He draws away, laughingly.*) Thar. That's enuf, hain't it? Ye won't hev none left fur next time.

ABBIE. I got a million 'on 'em left fur ye! (*Then a bit anxiously.*) D'ye r'ally love me, Eben?

EBEN (*emphatically*). I like ye better'n any gal I ever knowed! That's gospel!

ABBIE. Likin' hain't lovin'.

EBEN. Waal then—I love ye. Now air yew satisfied?

ABBIE. Ay-eh, I be. (*She smiles at him adoringly.*)

EBEN. I better git t' the barn. The old critter's liable t' suspicion an' come sneakin' up.

ABBIE (*with a confident laugh*). Let him! I

kin allus pull the wool over his eyes. I'm goin' t' leave the shutters open and let in the sun 'n' air. This room's been dead long enuf. Now it's goin' t' be my room.

EBEN (*frowning*). Ay-eh.

ABBIE (*hastily*). I meant—our room.

EBEN. Ay-eh.

ABBIE. We made it our'n last night, didn't we? We give it life—our lovin' did. (*A pause.*)

EBEN (*with a strange look*). Maw's gone back t' her grave. She kin sleep now.

ABBIE. May she rest in peace! (*Then tenderly rebuking.*) Ye oughtn't t' talk o' sad thin's—this mornin'.

EBEN. It jest come up in my mind o' itself.

ABBIE. Don't let it. (*He doesn't answer. She yawns.*) Waal, I'm a-goin' t' steal a wink o' sleep. I'll tell the Old Man I hain't feelin' pert. Let him git his own vittles.

EBEN. I see him comin' from the barn. Ye better look smart an' git upstairs.

ABBIE. Ay-eh. Good-bye. Don't ferget me.

(*She throws him a kiss. He grins—then squares his shoulders and awaits his father confidently. Cabot walks slowly up from the left, staring up at the sky with a vague face.*)

EBEN (*jovially*). Mornin', Paw. Star-gazin' in daylight?

CABOT. Purty, hain't it?

EBEN (*looking around him possessively*). It's a durned purty farm.

CABOT. I mean the sky.

EBEN (*grinning*). How d'ye know? Them eyes o' your'n can't see that fur. (*This tickles his humour and he slaps his thigh and laughs.*) Ho-ho! That's a good un!

CABOT (*grimly sarcastic*). Ye're feelin' right chipper, hain't ye? Whar'd ye steal the likker?

EBEN (*good-naturedly*). 'Tain't likker. Jest life. (*Suddenly holding out his hand—soberly.*) Yew 'n' me is quits. Let's shake hands.

CABOT (*suspiciously*). What's come over ye?

EBEN. Then don't. Mebbe it's jest as well. (*A moment's pause.*) What's come over me? (*Queerly.*) Didn't ye feel her passin'—goin' back t' her grave?

CABOT (*dully*). Who?

EBEN. Maw. She kin rest now an' sleep content. She's quits with ye.

CABOT (*confusedly*). I rested. I slept good—down with the cows. They know how t' sleep. They're teachin' me.

EBEN (*suddenly jovial again*). Good fur the cows! Waal—ye better git t' work.

CABOT (*grimly amused*). Air yew bossin' me, ye calf?

EBEN (*beginning to laugh*). Ay-eh! I'm bossin' yew! Ha-ha-ha! See how ye like it! Ha-ha-ha! I'm the prize rooster o' this roost. Ha-ha-ha! (*He goes off toward the barn laughing.*)

CABOT (*looks after him with scornful pity*). Soft-headed. Like his Maw. Dead spit 'n' image. No hope in him! (*He spits with contemptuous disgust.*) A born fool! (*Then matter-of-factly.*) Waal—I'm gittin' peckish. (*He goes toward door.*)

PART III Scene I

A night in late spring the following year. The kitchen and the two bedrooms upstairs are shown. The two bedrooms are dimly lighted by a tallow candle in each. Eben is sitting on the side of the bed in his room, his chin propped on his fists, his face a study of the struggle he is making to understand his conflicting emotions. The noisy laughter and music from below where a kitchen dance is in progress annoy and distract him. He scowls at the floor.

In the next room a cradle stands beside the double bed.

In the kitchen all is festivity. The stove has been taken down to give more room to the dancers. The chairs, with wooden benches added, have been pushed back against the walls. On these are seated, squeezed in tight against one another, farmers and their wives and their young folks of both sexes from the neighbouring farms. They are all chattering and laughing loudly. They evidently have some secret joke in common. There is no end of winking, of nudging, of meaning nods of the head toward Cabot who, in a state of extreme hilarious excitement increased by the amount he has drunk, is standing near the rear door where there is a small keg of whisky and serving drinks to all the men. In the left corner, front, dividing the attention with her husband, Abbie is sitting in a rocking chair, a shawl wrapped about her shoulders. She is very pale, her face is thin and drawn, her eyes are fixed anxiously on the open door in rear as if waiting for someone.

The musician is tuning up his fiddle, seated in the far right corner. He is a lanky young fellow with a long weak face. His pale eyes blink incessantly and he grins about him slyly with a greedy malice.

ABBIE (*suddenly turning to a young girl on her right*). Whar's Eben?

YOUNG GIRL (*eyeing her scornfully*). I dunno, Mrs. Cabot. I hain't seen Eben in ages. (*Meaningly.*) Seems like he's spent most o' his time t' hum since yew come.

ABBIE (*vaguely*). I tuk his Maw's place.

YOUNG GIRL. Ay-eh. So I've heerd.

(*She turns away to retail this bit of gossip to her mother sitting next to her. Abbie turns to her left to a big stoutish middle-aged man whose flushed face and starting eyes show the amount of "likker" he has consumed.*)

ABBIE. Ye hain't seen Eben, hev ye?

MAN. No, I hain't. (*Then he adds with a wink.*) If yew hain't, who would?

ABBIE. He's the best dancer in the county. He'd ought t' come an' dance.

MAN (*with a wink*). Mebbe he's doin' the dutiful an' walkin' the kid t' sleep. It's a boy, hain't it?

ABBIE (*nodding vaguely*). Ay-eh—born two weeks back—purty's a picter——

MAN. They all is—t' their Maws. (*Then in a whisper with a nudge and a leer.*) Listen, Abbie—if ye ever git tired o' Eben, remember me! Don't fergit now! (*He looks at her uncomprehending face for a second—then grunts disgustedly.*) Waal—guess I'll likker agin. (*He goes over and joins Cabot, who is arguing noisily with an old farmer over cows. They all drink.*)

ABBIE (*this time appealing to nobody in particular*). Wonder what Eben's a-doin'? (*Her remark is repeated down the line with many a guffaw and titter until it reaches the fiddler. He fastens his blinking eyes on Abbie.*)

FIDDLER (*raising his voice*). Bet I kin tell ye, Abbie, what Eben's doin'! He's down t' the church offerin' up prayers o' thanksgivin'. (*They all titter expectantly.*)

A MAN. What fur? (*Another titter.*)

FIDDLER. 'Cause unto him a—(*he hesitates just long enough*)—brother is born!

(*A roar of laughter. They all look from Abbie to Cabot. She is oblivious, staring at the door. Cabot, although he hasn't heard the words, is irritated by the laughter, and steps forward, glaring about him. There is an immediate silence.*)

CABOT. What're ye all bleatin' about—like a flock o' goats? Why don't ye dance, damn ye? I axed ye here t' dance—t' eat, drink an' be merry—an' thar ye set cacklin' like a lot o' wet hens with the pip! Ye've swilled my likker an' guzzled my vittles like hogs, hain't ye? Then dance fur me, can't ye? That's fa'r an' squa'r, hain't it? (*A grumble of resentment goes around, but they are all evidently in too much awe of him to express it openly.*)

FIDDLER (*slyly*). We're waitin' fur Eben. (*A suppressed laugh.*)

CABOT (*with a fierce exultation*). T' hell with Eben! Eben's done fur now! I got a new son!

(*His mood switching with drunken suddenness.*) But ye needn't t' laugh at Eben, none o' ye! He's my blood, if he be a dumb fool. He's better nor any o' yew! He kin do a day's work a'most up t' what I kin—an' that'd put any o' yew pore critters t' shame!

FIDDLER. An' he kin do a good night's work, too! (*A roar of laughter.*)

CABOT. Laugh, ye damn fools! Ye're right just the same, Fiddler. He kin work day an' night, too, like I kin, if need be!

OLD FARMER (*from behind the keg where he is weaving drunkenly back and forth—with great simplicity*). They hain't many t' touch ye, Ephraim —a son at seventy-six. That's a hard man fur ye! I be on'y sixty-eight an' I couldn't do it. (*A roar of laughter, in which Cabot joins uproariously.*)

CABOT (*slapping him on the back*). I'm sorry fur ye, Hi. I'd never suspicion sech weakness from a boy like yew!

OLD FARMER. An' I never reckoned yew had it in ye nuther, Ephraim. (*Another laugh.*)

CABOT (*suddenly grim*). I got a lot in me—a hell of a lot—folks don't know on. (*Turning to the fiddler.*) Fiddle 'er up, durn ye! Give 'em somethin' t' dance t'! What air ye, an ornament? Hain't this a celebration? Then grease yer elbow an' go it!

FIDDLER (*seizes a drink which the Old Farmer holds out to him and downs it*). Here goes!

(*He starts to fiddle* "Lady of the Lake." *Four young fellows and four girls form in two lines and dance a square dance. The Fiddler shouts directions for the different movements, keeping his words in the rhythm of the music and interspersing them with jocular personal remarks to the dancers themselves. The people seated along the walls stamp their feet and clap their hands in unison. Cabot is especially active in this respect. Only Abbie remains apathetic, staring at the door as if she were alone in a silent room.*)

FIDDLER. Swing your partner t' the right! That's it, Jim! Give her a b'ar hug! Her Maw hain't lookin'. (*Laughter.*) Change partners! That suits ye, don't it, Essie, now ye got Reub afore ye? Look at her redden up, will ye? Waal, life is short an' so's love, as the feller says. (*Laughter.*)

CABOT (*excitedly, stamping his foot*). Go it, boys! Go it, gals!

FIDDLER (*with a wink at the others*). Ye're the spryest seventy-six ever I sees, Ephraim! Now, if ye'd on'y good eyesight . . .! (*Suppressed laughter. He gives Cabot no chance to retort, but roars.*) Promenade! Ye're walkin' like a bride down the aisle, Sarah! Waal, while they's life they's allus hope, I've heerd tell. Swing your partner to the left! Gosh A'mighty, look at Johnny Cook high-steppin'! They hain't goin' t' be much strength left fur howin' in the corn lot t'-morrow. (*Laughter.*)

CABOT. Go it! Go it! (*Then suddenly, unable to restrain himself any longer, he prances into the midst of the dancers, scattering them, waving his arms about wildly.*) Ye're all hoofs! Git out o' my road! Give me room! I'll show ye dancin'. Ye're all too soft! (*He pushes them roughly away. They crowd back toward the walls, muttering, looking at him resentfully.*)

FIDDLER (*jeeringly*). Go it, Ephraim! Go it! (*He starts* "Pop Goes the Weasel," *increasing the tempo with every verse until at the end he is fiddling crazily as fast as he can go.*)

CABOT (*starts to dance, which he does very well and with tremendous vigour. Then he begins to improvise, cuts incredibly grotesque capers, leaping up and cracking his heels together, prancing around in a circle with body bent in an Indian war dance, then suddenly straightening up and kicking as high as he can with both legs. He is like a monkey on a string. And all the while he intersperses his antics with shouts and derisive comments*). Whoop! Here's dancin' fur ye! Whoop! See that! Seventy-six, if I'm a day! Hard as iron yet! Beatin' the young 'uns like I allus done! Look at me! I'd invite ye t' dance on my hundredth birthday on'y ye'll all be dead by then. Ye're a sickly generation! Yer hearts air pink, not red! Yer veins is full o' mud an' water! I be the on'y man in the county! Whoop! See that! I'm a Injun! I've killed Injuns in the West afore ye was born— an' skulped 'em, too! They's a arrer wound on my backside I c'd show ye! The hull tribe chased me. I outrun 'em all—with the arrer stuck in me! An' I tuk vengeance on 'em. Ten eyes fur an eye, that was my motter! Whoop! Look at me! I kin kick the ceilin' off the room! Whoop!

FIDDLER (*stops playing—exhaustedly*). God A'mighty, I got enuf. Ye got the devil's strength in ye.

CABOT (*delightedly*). Did I beat yew, too? Waal, ye played smart. Hev a swig.

(*He pours whisky for himself and Fiddler. They drink. The others watch Cabot silently with cold, hostile eyes. There is a dead pause. The Fiddler rests. Cabot leans against the keg, panting, glaring around him confusedly. In the room above, Eben gets to his feet and tiptoes out the door in rear, appearing a moment later in the other bedroom. He moves silently, even frightenedly, toward the cradle and stands there looking down at the baby. His face is as vague as his reactions are confused, but there is a trace of tenderness, of interested discovery. At the same moment that he reaches the cradle, Abbie seems to sense something. She gets up weakly and goes to Cabot.*)

ABBIE. I'm goin' up t' the baby.

CABOT (*with real solicitation*). Air ye able fur the stairs? D'ye want me t' help ye, Abbie?

ABBIE. No. I'm able. I'll be down agin soon.

CABOT. Don't ye git wore out! He needs ye, remember—our son does! (*He grins affectionately, patting her on the back. She shrinks from his touch.*)

ABBIE (*dully*). Don't—tech me. I'm goin'—up. (*She goes. Cabot looks after her. A whisper goes around the room. Cabot turns. It ceases. He wipes his forehead streaming with sweat. He is breathing pantingly.*)

CABOT. I'm a-goin' out t' git fresh air. I'm feelin' a mite dizzy. Fiddle up thar! Dance, all o' ye! Here's likker fur them as wants it. Enjoy yerselves. I'll be back. (*He goes, closing the door behind him.*)

FIDDLER (*sarcastically*). Don't hurry none on our account! (*A suppressed laugh. He imitates Abbie.*) Whar's Eben? (*More laughter.*)

A WOMAN (*loudly*). What's happened in this house is plain as the nose on yer face! (*Abbie appears in the doorway upstairs and stands looking in surprise and adoration at Eben, who does not see her.*)

A MAN. Ssshh! He's li'ble t' be listenin' at the door. That'd be like him.

(*Their voices die to an intensive whispering. Their faces are concentrated on this gossip. A noise as of dead leaves in the wind comes from the room. Cabot has come out from the porch and stands by the gate, leaning on it, staring at the sky blinkingly. Abbie comes across the room silently. Eben does not notice her until quite near.*)

EBEN (*starting*). Abbie!

ABBIE. Ssshh! (*She throws her arms around him. They kiss—then bend over the cradle together.*) Ain't he purty?—dead spit 'n' image o' yew!

EBEN (*pleased*). Air he? I can't tell none.

ABBIE. E-zactly like!

EBEN (*frowningly*). I don't like this. I don't like lettin' on what's mine's his'n. I been doin' that all my life. I'm gittin' t' the end o' b'arin' it!

ABBIE (*putting her finger on his lips*). We're doin' the best we kin. We got t' wait. Somethin's bound t' happen. (*She puts her arms around him.*) I got t' go back.

EBEN. I'm goin' out. I can't b'ar it with the fiddle playin' an' the laughin'.

ABBIE. Don't git feelin' low. I love ye, Eben. Kiss me. (*He kisses her. They remain in each other's arms.*)

CABOT (*at the gate, confusedly*). Even the music can't drive it out—somethin'—ye kin feel it droppin' off the elums, climbin' up the roof, sneakin' down the chimney, pokin' in the corners. . . . They's no peace in houses, they's no rest livin' with folks. Somethin's always livin' with ye. (*With a deep sigh.*) I'll go t' the barn an' rest a spell. (*He goes wearily toward the barn.*)

FIDDLER (*tuning up*). Let's celebrate the old skunk gittin' fooled! We kin have some fun now he's went. (*He starts to fiddle* "Turkey in the Straw." *There is real merriment now. The young folks get up to dance.*)

PART III Scene 2

A half-hour later—exterior—Eben is standing by the gate looking up at the sky, an expression of dumb pain bewildered by itself on his face. Cabot appears, returning from the barn, walking wearily, his eyes on the ground. He sees Eben and his whole mood immediately changes. He becomes excited, a cruel, triumphant grin comes to his lips, he strides up and slaps Eben on the back. From within comes the whining of the fiddle and the noise of stamping feet and laughing voices.

CABOT. So har ye be!

EBEN (*startled, stares at him with hatred for a moment—then dully*). Ay-eh.

CABOT (*surveying him jeeringly*). Why hain't ye been in 't' dance? They was all axin' fur ye.

EBEN. Let 'em ax!

CABOT. They's a hull passel o' purty gals——

EBEN. T' hell with 'em!

CABOT. Ye'd ought t' be marryin' one o' 'em soon.

EBEN. I hain't marryin' no one.

CABOT. Ye might 'arn a share o' a farm that way.

EBEN (*with a sneer*). Like yew did, ye mean? I hain't that kind.

CABOT (*stung*). Ye lie! 'Twas yer Maw's folks aimed t' steal my farm from me.

EBEN. Other folks don't say so. (*After a pause—defiantly.*) An' I got a farm, anyways!

CABOT (*derisively*). Whar?

EBEN (*stamps a foot on the ground*). Har.

CABOT (*throws his head back and laughs coarsely*). Ho-ho! Ye hev, hev ye? Waal, that's a good 'un!

EBEN (*controlling himself—grimly*). Ye'll see.

CABOT (*stares at him suspiciously, trying to make him out—a pause—then with scornful confidence*). Ay-eh. I'll see. So'll ye. It's ye what's blind—blind as a mole underground. (*Eben suddenly laughs, one short sardonic bark:* "Ha." *A pause. Cabot peers at him with renewed suspicion.*) What air ye hawin' 'bout? (*Eben turns away without answering. Cabot grows angry.*) God A'mighty, yew air a dumb dunce! They's nothin' in that thick skull o' your'n but noise—like a empty keg it be! (*Eben doesn't seem to hear. Cabot's rage grows.*) Yewr farm! God A'mighty! If ye wa'n't a born donkey ye'd know ye'll never own stick nor stone on it, specially now arter him bein' born. It's his'n, I tell ye—his'n arter I die—but I'll live a hundred jest t' fool ye all—an' he'll be growed then—yewr age a'most! (*Eben laughs again his sardonic* "Ha." *This drives Cabot into a fury.*) Ha? Ye think ye kin git 'round that someways, do ye? Waal, it'll be her'n, too—Abbie's—ye won't git 'round her—she knows yer tricks—she'll be too much fur ye—she wants the farm her'n—she was afeerd o' ye—she told me ye was sneakin' 'round tryin' t' make love t' her t' git her on yer side . . . ye . . . ye mad fool, ye! (*He raises his clenched fists threateningly.*)

EBEN (*is confronting him, choking with rage*). Ye lie, ye old skunk! Abbie never said no sech thing!

CABOT (*suddenly triumphant when he sees how shaken Eben is*). She did. An' I says, I'll blow his brains t' the top o' them elums—an' she says no, that hain't sense, who'll ye git t' help ye on the farm in his place—an' then she says yew'n me ought t' have a son—I know we kin, she says—an' I says, if we do, ye kin have anythin' I've got ye've a mind t'. An' she says, I wants Eben cut off so's this farm'll be mine when ye die! (*With terrible gloating.*) An' that's what's happened, hain't it? An' the farm's her'n! An' the dust o' the road—that's your'n! Ha! Now who's hawin'?

EBEN (*has been listening, petrified with grief and rage—suddenly laughs wildly and brokenly*). Ha-ha-ha! So that's her sneakin' game—all along!—like I suspicioned at fust—t' swaller it all—an' me, too . . . ! (*Madly.*) I'll murder her! (*He springs toward the porch, but Cabot is quicker and gets in between.*)

CABOT. No, ye don't!

EBEN. Git out o' my road!

(*He tries to throw Cabot aside. They grapple in what becomes immediately a murderous struggle. The old man's concentrated strength is too much for Eben. Cabot gets one hand on his throat and presses him back across the stone wall. At the same moment, Abbie comes out on the porch. With a stifled cry she runs toward them.*)

ABBIE. Eben! Ephraim! (*She tugs at the hand on Eben's throat.*) Let go, Ephraim! Ye're chokin' him!

CABOT (*removes his hand and flings Eben sideways full length on the grass, gasping and choking. With a cry, Abbie kneels beside him, trying to take his head on her lap, but he pushes her away. Cabot stands looking down with fierce triumph*). Ye needn't t've fret, Abbie, I wa'n't aimin' t' kill him. He hain't wuth hangin' fur—not by a hell of a sight! (*More and more triumphantly.*) Seventy-six an' him not thirty yit—an' look whar he be fur thinkin' his Paw was easy! No, by God, I hain't easy! An' him upstairs, I'll raise him t' be like me! (*He turns to leave them.*) I'm goin' in an' dance!—sing an' celebrate! (*He walks to the porch—then turns with a great grin.*) I don't calc'late it's left in him, but if he gits pesky, Abbie, ye jest sing out. I'll come a-runnin' an', by the Etarnal, I'll put him across my knee an' birch him! Ha-ha-ha! (*He goes into the house laughing. A moment later his loud* "Whoop" *is heard.*)

ABBIE (*tenderly*). Eben! Air ye hurt? (*She tries to kiss him, but he pushes her violently away and struggles to a sitting position.*)

EBEN (*gaspingly*). T' hell—with ye!

ABBIE (*not believing her ears*). It's me, Eben—Abbie—don't ye know me?

EBEN (*glowering at her with hatred*). Ay-eh—I know ye—now! (*He suddenly breaks down, sobbing weakly.*)

ABBIE (*fearfully*). Eben—what's happened t' ye—why did ye look at me 's if ye hated me?

EBEN (*violently, between sobs and gasps*). I do hate ye! Ye're a whore—a damn trickin' whore!

ABBIE (*shrinking back horrified*). Eben! Ye don't know what ye're sayin'!

EBEN (*scrambling to his feet and following her—accusingly*). Ye're nothin' but a stinkin' passel o' lies! Ye've been lyin' t' me every word ye spoke, day an' night, since we fust—done it. Ye've kept sayin' ye loved me. . . .

ABBIE (*frantically*). I do love ye! (*She takes his hand, but he flings hers away.*)

EBEN (*unheeding*). Ye've made a fool o' me—a sick, dumb fool—a-purpose! Ye've been on'y playin' yer sneakin', stealin' game all along—gittin' me t' lie with ye so's ye'd hev a son he'd think was his'n, an' makin' him promise he'd give ye the farm and let me eat dust, if ye did git him a son! (*Staring at her with anguished, bewildered eyes.*) They must be a devil livin' in ye! 'Tain't human t' be as bad as that be!

ABBIE (*stunned—dully*). He told yew . . . ?

EBEN. Hain't it true? It hain't no good in yew lyin'. . . .

ABBIE (*pleadingly*). Eben, listen—ye must listen—it was long ago—afore we done nothin'—yew was scornin' me—goin' t' see Min—when I was lovin' ye—an' I said it t' him t' git vengeance on ye!

EBEN (*unheedingly. With tortured passion*). I wish ye was dead! I wish I was dead along with ye afore this come! (*Ragingly.*) But I'll git my vengeance, too! I'll pray Maw t' come back t' help me—t' put her cuss on yew an' him!

ABBIE (*brokenly*). Don't ye, Eben! Don't ye! (*She throws herself on her knees before him, weeping.*) I didn't mean t' do bad t' ye! Fergive me, won't ye?

EBEN (*not seeming to hear her—fiercely*). I'll git squar' with the old skunk—an' yew! I'll tell him the truth 'bout the son he's so proud o'!

Then I'll leave ye here t' pizen each other—with Maw comin' out o' her grave at nights—an' I'll go t' the gold-fields o' Californi-a whar Sim an' Peter be. . . .

ABBIE (*terrified*). Ye won't—leave me? Ye can't!

EBEN (*with fierce determination*). I'm a-goin', I tell ye! I'll git rich thar an' come back an' fight him fur the farm he stole—an' I'll kick ye both out in the road—t' beg an' sleep in the woods—an' yer son along with ye—t' starve an' die! (*He is hysterical at the end.*)

ABBIE (*with a shudder—humbly*). He's yewr son, too, Eben.

EBEN (*torturedly*). I wish he never was born! I wish he'd die this minit! I wish I'd never sot eyes on him! It's him—yew havin' him—a-purpose t' steal—that's changed everythin'!

ABBIE (*gently*). Did ye believe I loved ye—afore he come?

EBEN. Ay-eh—like a dumb ox!

ABBIE. An' ye don't believe no more?

EBEN. B'lieve a lyin' thief! Ha!

ABBIE (*shudders—then humbly*). An' did ye really love me afore?

EBEN (*brokenly*). Ay-eh—an' ye was trickin' me!

ABBIE. An' ye don't love me no more!

EBEN (*violently*). I hate ye, I tell ye!

ABBIE. An' ye're truly goin' West—goin' t' leave me—all on account o' him bein' born?

EBEN. I'm a-goin' in the mornin'—or may God strike me t' hell!

ABBIE (*after a pause—with a dreadful cold intensity—slowly*). If that's what his comin's done t' me—killin' yewr love—takin' ye away—my on'y joy—the on'y joy I ever knowed—like heaven t' me—purtier'n heaven—then I hate him, too, even if I be his Maw!

EBEN (*bitterly*). Lies! Ye love him! He'll steal the farm fur ye! (*Brokenly.*) But 'tain't the farm so much—not no more—it's yew foolin' me—gittin' me t' love ye—lyin' yew loved me—jest t' steal . . . !

ABBIE (*distractedly*). He won't steal! I'd kill him fust! I do love ye! I'll prove t' ye——!

EBEN (*harshly*). 'Tain't no use lyin' no more. I'm deaf t' ye! (*He turns away.*) I hain't seein' ye agen. Good-bye!

ABBIE (*pale with anguish*). Hain't ye even goin' t' kiss me—not once—arter all we loved——?

EBEN (*in a hard voice*). I hain't wantin' t' kiss ye never again! I'm wantin' t' forgit I ever sot eyes on ye!

ABBIE. Eben!—ye mustn't—wait a spell—I want t' tell ye . . .

EBEN. I'm a-goin' in t' git drunk. I'm a-goin' t' dance.

ABBIE (*clinging to his arm—with passionate earnestness*). If I could make it—'s if he'd never come up between us—if I could prove t' ye I wa'n't schemin' t' steal from ye—so's everythin' could be jest the same with us, lovin' each other jest the same, kissin' an' happy the same's we've been happy all along—if I could do it—ye'd love me agen, wouldn't ye? Ye'd kiss me agen? Ye wouldn't never leave me, would ye?

EBEN (*moved*). I calc'late not. (*Then shaking her hand off his arm—with a bitter smile.*) But ye hain't God, be ye?

ABBIE (*exultantly*). Remember ye've promised! (*Then with strange intensity.*) Mebbe I kin do one thin' God does!

EBEN (*peering at her*). Ye're gittin' cracked, hain't ye? (*Then going towards door.*) I'm a-goin' t' dance.

ABBIE (*calls after him intensely*). I'll prove t' ye! I'll prove I love ye better'n . . . (*He goes in the door, not seeming to hear. She remains standing where she is, looking after him—then she finishes desperately.*) Better'n everythin' else put t'gether!

PART III Scene 3

Just before dawn in the morning—shows the kitchen and Cabot's bedroom. In the kitchen, by the light of a tallow candle on the table, Eben is sitting, his chin propped on his hands, his drawn face blank and expressionless. His carpet bag is on the floor beside him. In the bedroom, dimly lighted by a small whale-oil lamp, Cabot lies asleep. Abbie is bending over the cradle, listening, her face full of terror, yet with an undercurrent of desperate triumph. Suddenly, she breaks down and sobs, appears about to throw herself on her knees beside the cradle, but the old man turns restlessly, groaning in his sleep, and she controls herself, and, shrinking away from the cradle with a gesture of horror, backs swiftly toward the door in rear and goes out. A moment later she comes into the kitchen and, running to Eben, flings her arms about his neck and kisses him wildly. He hardens himself, he remains unmoved and cold, he keeps his eyes straight ahead.

ABBIE (*hysterically*). I done it, Eben! I told ye I'd do it! I've proved I love ye—better'n everythin'—so's ye can't never doubt me no more!

EBEN (*dully*). Whatever ye done, it hain't no good now.

ABBIE (*wildly*). Don't ye say that! Kiss me, Eben, won't ye? I need ye t' kiss me arter what I done! I need ye t' say ye love me!

EBEN (*kisses her without emotion—dully*). That's fur good-bye. I'm a-goin' soon.

ABBIE. No! No! Ye won't go—not now!

EBEN (*going on with his own thoughts*). I been a-thinkin'—an' I hain't goin' t' tell Paw nothin'. I'll leave Maw t' take vengeance on ye. If I told him, the old skunk'd jest be stinkin' mean enuf to take it out on that baby. (*His voice showing emotion in spite of him.*) An' I don't want nothin' bad t' happen t' him. He hain't t' blame fur yew. (*He adds with a certain queer pride.*) An' he looks like me! An', by God, he's mine! An' some day I'll be a-comin' back an'——

ABBIE (*too absorbed in her own thoughts to listen to him—pleadingly*). They's no cause fur ye t' go now—they's no sense—it's all the same's it was—they's nothin' come b'tween us now—arter what I done!

EBEN (*something in her voice arouses him. He stares at her a bit frightenedly*). Ye look mad, Abbie. What did ye do?

ABBIE. I—I killed him, Eben.

EBEN (*amazed*). Ye killed him?

ABBIE (*dully*). Ay-eh.

EBEN (*recovering from his astonishment—savagely*). An' serves him right! But we got t' do somethin' quick t' make it look 's if the old skunk'd killed himself when he was drunk. We kin prove by 'em all how drunk he got.

ABBIE (*wildly*). No! No! Not him! (*Laughing distractedly.*) But that's what I ought t' done, hain't it? I oughter killed him instead! Why didn't ye tell me?

EBEN (*appalled*). Instead? What d'ye mean?

ABBIE. Not him.

EBEN (*his face grown ghastly*). Not—not that baby!

ABBIE (*dully*). Ay-eh!

EBEN (*falls to his knees as if he'd been struck—his voice trembling with horror*). Oh, God A'mighty! A'mighty God! Maw, whar was ye, why didn't ye stop her?

ABBIE (*simply*). She went back t' her grave that night we fust done it, remember! I hain't felt her about since. (*A pause. Eben hides his head in his hands, trembling all over as if he had the ague. She goes on dully.*) I left the piller over his little face. Then he killed himself. He stopped breathin'. (*She begins to weep softly.*)

EBEN (*rage beginning to mingle with grief*). He looked like me. He was mine, damn ye!

ABBIE (*slowly and brokenly*). I didn't want t' do it. I hated myself fur doin' it. I loved him. He was so purty—dead spit 'n' image o' yew. But I loved yew more—an' yew was goin' away—

far off whar I'd never see ye agen, never kiss ye, never feel ye pressed agin me agen—an' ye said ye hated me fur havin' him—ye said ye hated him an' wished he was dead—ye said if it hadn't been fur him comin' it'd be the same's afore between us.

EBEN (*unable to endure this, springs to his feet in a fury, threatening her, his twitching fingers seeming to reach out for her throat*). Ye lie! I never said—I never dreamed ye'd—— I'd cut off my head afore I'd hurt his finger!

ABBIE (*piteously, sinking on her knees*). Eben, don't ye look at me like that—hatin' me—not after what I done fur ye—fur us—so's we could be happy agen——

EBEN (*furiously now*). Shut up, or I'll kill ye! I see yer game now—the same old sneakin' trick—ye're aimin' t' blame me fur the murder ye done!

ABBIE (*moaning—putting her hands over her ears*). Don't ye, Eben! Don't ye! (*She grasps his legs.*)

EBEN (*his mood suddenly changing to horror, shrinks away from her*). Don't ye tech me! Ye're pizen! How could ye—t' murder a pore little critter—— Ye must've swapped yer soul t' hell! (*Suddenly raging.*) Ha! I kin see why ye done it! Not the lies ye jest told—but 'cause ye wanted t' steal agen—steal the last thin' ye'd left me—my part o' him—no, the hull o' him—ye saw he looked like me—ye knowed he was all mine—an' ye couldn't b'ar it—I know ye! Ye killed him fur bein' mine! (*All this has driven him almost insane. He makes a rush past her for the door—then turns—shaking both fists at her, violently.*) But I'll take vengeance now! I'll git the Sheriff! I'll tell him everythin'! Then I'll sing, "I'm off to Californi-a!" an' go—gold—Golden Gate—gold sun—fields o' gold in the West! (*This last he half shouts, half croons incoherently, suddenly breaking off passionately.*) I'm a-goin' fur the Sheriff t' come an' git ye! I want ye tuk away, locked up from me! I can't stand t' luk at ye! Murderer an' thief 'r not, ye still tempt me! I'll give ye up t' the Sheriff!

(*He turns and runs out, around the corner of house, panting and sobbing, and breaks into a swerving sprint down the road.*)

ABBIE (*struggling to her feet, runs to the door, calling after him*). I love ye, Eben! I love ye! (*She stops at the door weakly, swaying, about to fall.*) I don't care what ye do—if ye'll on'y love me agen! (*She falls limply to the floor in a faint.*)

PART III Scene 4

About an hour later. Same as Scene 3. Shows the kitchen and Cabot's bedroom. It is after dawn. The sky is brilliant with the sunrise. In the kitchen, Abbie sits at the table, her body limp and exhausted, her head bowed down over her arms, her face hidden. Upstairs, Cabot is still asleep, but awakens with a start. He looks toward the window and gives a snort of surprise and irritation—throws back the covers and begins hurriedly pulling on his clothes. Without looking behind him, he begins talking to Abbie, whom he supposes beside him.

CABOT. Thunder 'n' lightnin', Abbie! I hain't slept this late in fifty year! Looks 's if the sun was full riz a'most. Must've been the dancin' an' likker. Must be gittin' old. I hope Eben's t' wuk. Ye might've tuk the trouble t' rouse me, Abbie. (*He turns—sees no one there—surprised.*) Waal—whar air she? Gittin' vittles, I calc'late (*He tiptoes to the cradle and peers down—proudly.*) Mornin', sonny. Purty's a picter! Sleepin' sound. He don't beller all night like most on 'em. (*He goes quietly out the door in rear—a few moments later enter kitchen—sees Abbie—with satisfaction.*) So thar ye be. Ye got any vittles cooked?

ABBIE (*without moving*). No.

CABOT (*coming to her, almost sympathetically*). Ye feelin' sick?

ABBIE. No.

CABOT (*pats her on shoulder. She shudders*). Ye'd best lie down a spell. (*Half jocularly.*) Yer son'll be needin' ye soon. He'd ought t' wake up with a gnashin' appetite, the sound way he's sleepin'.

ABBIE (*shudders—then in a dead voice*). He hain't never goin' t' wake up.

CABOT (*jokingly*). Takes after me this mornin'. I hain't slept so late in——

ABBIE. He's dead.

CABOT (*stares at her—bewilderedly*). What——?

ABBIE. I killed him.

CABOT (*stepping back from her—aghast*). Air ye drunk—'r crazy—'r——?

ABBIE (*suddenly lifts her head and turns on him—wildly*). I killed him, I tell ye! I smothered him. Go up an' see if ye don't b'lieve me!

(*Cabot stares at her a second, then bolts out the rear door, can be heard bounding up the stairs, and rushes into the bedroom and over to the cradle. Abbie has sunk back lifelessly into her former position. Cabot puts his hand down on the body in the crib. An expression of fear and horror comes over his face.*)

CABOT (*shrinking away—trembling*). God A'mighty! God A'mighty. (*He stumbles out the door—in a short while returns to the kitchen—comes to Abbie, the stunned expression still on his face—hoarsely.*) Why did ye do it? Why? (*As she doesn't answer, he grabs her violently by the shoulder and shakes her.*) I ax ye why ye done it! Ye'd better tell me 'r——

ABBIE (*gives him a furious push which sends him staggering back and springs to her feet—with wild rage and hatred*). Don't ye dare tech me! What right hev ye t' question me 'bout him? He wa'n't yewr son! Think I'd have a son by yew? I'd die fust! I hate the sight o' ye an' allus did! It's yew I should've murdered, if I'd had good sense! I hate ye! I love Eben. I did from the fust. An' he was Eben's son—mine an' Eben's—not your'n!

CABOT (*stands looking at her dazedly—a pause—finding his words with an effort—dully*). That was it—what I felt—pokin' round the corners—while ye lied—holdin' yerself from me—sayin' ye'd a'ready conceived. . . . (*He lapses into crushed silence—then with a strange emotion.*) He's dead, sart'n. I felt his heart. Pore little critter! (*He blinks back one tear, wiping his sleeve across his nose.*)

ABBIE (*hysterically*). Don't ye! Don't ye! (*She sobs unrestrainedly.*)

CABOT (*with a concentrated effort that stiffens his body into a rigid line and hardens his face into a stony mask—through his teeth to himself*). I got t' be—like a stone—a rock o' jedgment! (*A pause. He gets complete control over himself—harshly.*) If he was Eben's, I be glad he air gone! An' mebbe I suspicioned it all along. I felt they was somethin' onnateral—somewhars—the house got so lonesome—an' cold—drivin' me down t' the barn—t' the beasts o' the field. . . . Ay-eh. I must've suspicioned—somethin'. Ye didn't fool me—not altogether, leastways—I'm too old a bird—growin' ripe on the bough. . . . (*He becomes aware he is wandering, straightens again, looks at Abbie with a cruel grin.*) So ye'd liked t' hev murdered me 'stead o' him, would ye? Waal, I'll live to a hundred! I'll live t' see ye hung! I'll deliver ye up t' the jedgment o' God an' the law! I'll git the Sheriff now. (*Starts for the door.*)

ABBIE (*dully*). Ye needn't. Eben's gone fur him.

CABOT (*amazed*). Eben—gone fur the Sheriff?

ABBIE. Ay-eh.

CABOT. T' inform agen ye?

ABBIE. Ay-eh.

CABOT (*considers this—a pause—then in a hard voice*). Waal, I'm thankful fur him savin' me the trouble. I'll git t' wuk. (*He goes to the door—then turns—in a voice full of strange emotion.*) He'd ought t' been my son, Abbie. Ye'd ought t' loved me. I'm a man. If ye'd loved me, I'd never told no Sheriff on ye, no matter what ye did, if they was t' brile me alive!

ABBIE (*defensively*). They's more to it nor yew know, makes him tell.

CABOT (*dryly*). Fur yewr sake, I hope they be. (*He goes out—comes around to the gate—stares up at the sky. His control relaxes. For a moment he is old and weary. He murmurs despairingly.*) God A'mighty, I be lonesomer'n ever! (*He hears running footsteps from the left, immediately is himself again. Eben runs in, panting exhaustedly, wild-eyed and mad-looking. He lurches through the gate. Cabot grabs him by the shoulder. Eben stares at him dumbly.*) Did ye tell the Sheriff?

EBEN (*nodding stupidly*). Ay-eh.

CABOT (*gives him a push away that sends him sprawling—laughing with withering contempt*). Good fur ye ! A prime chip o' yer Maw ye be ! (*He goes toward the barn, laughing harshly. Eben scrambles to his feet. Suddenly Cabot turns—grimly threatening.*) Git off this farm when the Sheriff takes her—or, by God, he'll have t' come back an' git me fur murder, too !

(*He stalks off. Eben does not appear to have heard him. He runs to the door and comes into the kitchen. Abbie looks up with a cry of anguished joy. Eben stumbles over and throws himself on his knees beside her—sobbing brokenly.*)

EBEN. Fergive me !

ABBIE (*happily*). Eben ! (*She kisses him and pulls his head over against her breast.*)

EBEN. I love ye ! Fergive me !

ABBIE (*ecstatically*). I'd fergive ye all the sins in hell fur sayin' that ! (*She kisses his head, pressing it to her with a fierce passion of possession.*)

EBEN (*brokenly*). But I told the Sheriff. He's comin' fur ye !

ABBIE. I kin b'ar what happens t' me—now !

EBEN. I woke him up. I told him. He says, "Wait 'till I git dressed." I was waiting. I got to thinkin' o' yew. I got to thinkin' how I'd loved ye. It hurt like somethin' was bustin' in my chest an' head. I got t' cryin'. I knowed sudden I loved ye yet, an' allus would love ye !

ABBIE (*caressing his hair—tenderly*). My boy, hain't ye ?

EBEN. I begun t' run back. I cut across the fields an' through the woods. I thought ye might have time t' run away—with me—an'——

ABBIE (*shaking her head*). I got t' take my punishment—t' pay fur my sin.

EBEN. Then I want t' share it with ye.

ABBIE. Ye didn't do nothin'.

EBEN. I put it in yer head. I wisht he was dead ! I as much as urged ye t' do it !

ABBIE. No. It was me alone !

EBEN. I'm as guilty as yew be ! He was the child o' our sin.

ABBIE (*lifting her head as if defying God*). I don't repent that sin ! I hain't askin' even God t' fergive that !

EBEN. Nor me—but it led up t' the other—an' the murder ye did, ye did 'count o' me—an' it's my murder, too, I'll tell the Sheriff—an' if ye deny it, I'll say we planned it t'gether—an' they'll all b'lieve me, fur they suspicion everythin' we've done, an' it'll seem likely an' true to 'em. An' it is true—way down—I did help ye—somehow.

ABBIE (*laying her head on his—sobbing*). No ! I don't want yew t' suffer !

EBEN. I got t' pay fur my part o' the sin ! An' I'd suffer wuss leavin' ye, goin' West, thinkin' o' ye day an' night, bein' out when yew was in . . . (*Lowering his voice.*) 'R bein' alive when yew was dead. (*A pause.*) I want t' share with ye, Abbie—prison 'r death 'r hell 'r anythin' ! (*He looks into her eyes and forces a trembling smile.*) If I'm sharin' with ye, I won't feel lonesome, leastways.

ABBIE (*weakly*). Eben ! I won't let ye ! I can't let ye !

EBEN (*kissing her—tenderly*). Ye can't he'p yerself. I got ye beat fur once !

ABBIE (*forcing a smile—adoringly*). I hain't beat—s'long's I got ye !

EBEN (*hears the sound of feet outside*). Ssshh ! Listen ! They've come t' take us !

ABBIE. No, it's him. Don't give him no chance to fight ye, Eben. Don't say nothin'—no matter what he says. An' I won't, neither. (*It is Cabot. He comes up from the barn in a great state of excitement and strides into the house and then into the kitchen. Eben is kneeling beside Abbie, his arm around her, hers around him. They stare straight ahead.*)

CABOT (*stares at them, his face hard. A long pause—vindictively*). Ye make a slick pair o' murderin' turtle-doves ! Ye'd ought t' be both hung on the same limb an' left thar t' swing in the breeze an' rot—a warnin' t' old fools like me t' b'ar their lonesomeness alone—an' fur young fools like ye t' hobble their lust. (*A pause. The excitement returns to his face, his eyes snap, he looks a bit crazy.*) I couldn't work to-day. I couldn't take no interest. T' hell with the farm ! I'm leavin' it ! I've turned the cows an' other stock loose ! I've druv 'em into the woods whar they kin be free ! By freein' 'em, I'm freein' myself ! I'm quittin' here to-day ! I'll set fire t' house an' barn an' watch 'em burn, an' I'll leave yer Maw t' haunt the ashes, an' I'll will the fields back t' God, so that nothin' human kin never touch 'em ! I'll be a-goin' to Californi-a—t' jine Simeon an' Peter —true sons o' mine if they be dumb fools—an' the Cabots 'll find Solomon's Mines t'gether ! (*He suddenly cuts a mad caper.*) Whoop ! What was the song they sung ? " Oh, Californi-a ! That's the land fur me." (*He sings this—then gets on his knees by the floor-board under which the money was hid.*) An' I'll sail thar on one o' the finest clippers I kin find ! I've got the money ! Pity ye didn't know whar this was hidden so's ye could steal . . . (*He has pulled up the board. He stares—feels—stares again. A pause of dead silence. He slowly turns, slumping into a sitting position on the floor, his eyes like those of a dead fish, his face the sickly green of an attack of nausea. He swallows painfully several times—forces a weak smile at last.*) So—ye did steal it !

EBEN (*emotionlessly*). I swapped it t' Sim an' Peter fur their share o' the farm—t' pay their passage t' Californi-a.

CABOT (*with one sardonic laugh*). Ha ! (*He begins to recover. Gets slowly to his feet—strangely.*) I calc'late God give it to 'em—not yew ! God's hard, not easy ! Mebbe they's easy gold in the West, but it hain't God's gold. It hain't fur me. I kin hear His voice warnin' me agen t' be hard an' stay on my farm. I kin see His hand usin' Eben t' steal t' keep me from weakness. I kin feel I be in the palm o' His hand, His fingers guidin' me. (*A pause—then he mutters sadly.*) It's a-goin' t' be lonesomer now than ever it war afore—an' I'm gittin' old, Lord—ripe on the bough. . . . (*Then stiffening.*) Waal—what d'ye want ? God's lonesome, hain't He ? God's hard an' lonesome ! (*A pause. The Sheriff with two men come up the road from the left. They move cautiously to the door. The Sheriff knocks on it with the butt of his pistol.*)

SHERIFF. Open in the name o' the law ! (*They start.*)

CABOT. They've come fur ye. (*He goes to the rear door.*) Come in, Jim ! (*The three men enter. Cabot meets them in doorway.*) Jest a minit, Jim. I got 'em safe here. (*The Sheriff nods. He and his companions remain in the doorway.*)

EBEN (*suddenly calls*). I lied this mornin', Jim. I helped her do it. Ye kin take me, too.

ABBIE (*brokenly*). No !

CABOT. Take 'em both. (*He comes forward—stares at Eben with a trace of grudging admiration.*) Purty good—fur yew ! Waal, I got t' round up the stock. Good-bye.

EBEN. Good-bye.

ABBIE. Good-bye.

(*Cabot turns and strides past the men—comes out and around the corner of the house, his shoulders squared, his face stony, and stalks grimly toward the barn. In the meantime the Sheriff and men have come into the room.*)

SHERIFF (*embarrassed*). Waal—we'd best start.

ABBIE. Wait. (*Turns to Eben.*) I love ye, Eben.

EBEN. I love ye, Abbie. (*They kiss. The three men grin and shuffle embarrassedly.*)

EBEN (*to the Sheriff*). Now. (*He takes Abbie's hand.*) Come. (*They go out the door in rear, the men following, and come from the house, walking hand-in-hand to the gate. Eben stops there and points to the sunrise sky.*) Sun's a-risin'. Purty, hain't it ?

ABBIE. Ay-eh. (*They both stand for a moment looking up raptly in attitudes strangely aloof and devout.*)

SHERIFF (*looking around at the farm enviously—to his companion*). It's a jim-dandy farm, no denyin'. Wish I owned it !

Curtain

MARCO MILLIONS

FOREWORD

This play is an attempt to render poetic justice to one long famous as a traveller, unjustly world-renowned as a liar, but sadly unrecognized by posterity in his true eminence as a man and a citizen – Marco Polo of Venice. The failure to appraise Polo at a fair valuation is his own fault. He dictated the book of his travels but left the traveller out. He was no author. He stuck to a recital of what he considered facts and the world called him a liar for his pains. Even in his native Venice, he was scoffingly nicknamed 'the millionaire', or 'Marco Millions'. They could not take seriously his impressive statistics about the 'millions' of this and the 'millions' of that in the East. Polo, the man of brass tacks, became celebrated as an extravagant romancer and ever since has travelled down the prejudiced centuries, a prophet without honour, or even notoriety, save in false whiskers. This has moved me to an indignant crusade between the lines of his book, the bars of his prison, in order to whitewash the good soul of that maligned Venetian.

Characters

CHRISTIANS (in the order in which they appear)

A TRAVELLER
MARCO POLO
DONATA
NICOLO POLO, *Marco's father*
MAFFEO POLO, *Marco's uncle*
TEDALDO, *Legate of Syria (afterward Pope Gregory X)*
A DOMINICAN MONK
A KNIGHT-CRUSADER
A PAPAL COURIER
PAULO LOREDANO, *Donata's father, a gentleman from Venice*
Ladies and gentlemen of Venice, soldiers, people of Acre, musicians, servants, *etc.*

HEATHENS (in the order in which they appear)

A MAGIAN TRAVELLER
A BUDDHIST TRAVELLER
A MAHOMETAN CAPTAIN OF GHAZAN'S ARMY
THE ALI BROTHERS, *Mahometan merchants*
A PROSTITUTE
A DERVISH
TWO BUDDHIST MERCHANTS
TWO TARTAR MERCHANTS
A MONGOL PRIEST
EMISSARY FROM KUBLAI
KUBLAI, THE GREAT KAAN
PRINCESS KUKACHIN, *his granddaughter*
CHU-YIN, *a Cathayan sage*
GENERAL BAYAN
A MESSENGER FROM PERSIA
GHAZAN, KHAN OF PERSIA
A BUDDHIST PRIEST
A TAOIST PRIEST
A CONFUCIAN PRIEST
A MOSLEM PRIEST
A TARTAR CHRONICLER
People of Persia, India, Mongolia, Cathay, courtiers, nobles, ladies, wives, warriors of Kublai's court, musicians, dancers, Chorus of Mourners

Scenes

PROLOGUE

A sacred tree in Persia near the confines of India toward the close of the thirteenth century.

ACT ONE

SCENE ONE Exterior of Donata's house, Venice. Twenty-three years earlier.

SCENE TWO Palace of the Papal Legate of Syria at Acre. Six months later.

SCENE THREE Persia. Four months later.

SCENE FOUR India. Eight months later.

SCENE FIVE Mongolia. Eleven months later.

SCENE SIX Cathay. The Grand Throne Room in Kublai's palace at Cambaluc. One month later.

ACT TWO

SCENE ONE The Little Throne Room in Kublai's summer palace at Xanadu, 'the city of Peace'. Fifteen years later.

SCENE TWO The royal wharf at the seaport of Zayton. Several weeks later.

SCENE THREE Deck of the royal junk of the Princess Kukachin at anchor in the harbour of Hormuz, Persia. Two years later.

ACT THREE

SCENE ONE The Grand Throne Room in the Imperial Palace at Cambaluc. One year later – and later the dining room of the Polo home in Venice at the same time.

SCENE TWO The Grand Throne Room at Cambaluc. One year later.

EPILOGUE

The theatre.

PROLOGUE

SCENE. *A sacred tree on a vast plain in Persia near the confines of India. Votive offerings, pieces of cloth torn from clothing, bangles, armlets, ornaments, tapers, have been nailed on the trunk or tied to the branches. The heavy limbs spread out to a great distance from the trunk. Beneath them is deep cool shade, contrasting with the blinding glare of the noon sun on the sandy plain in the background. A merchant carrying in each hand a strapped box that resembles a modern sample case, plods wearily to the foot of the tree. He puts the boxes down and takes out a handkerchief to mop his forehead. He is a white Christian, middle-aged, average-looking, with a moustache and beard beginning to show grey. His clothes in the style of the Italian merchant class of the thirteenth century are travel-worn. He sighs, tired and hot.*

CHRISTIAN. Phoo!

(*From the left a Magian, a Persian, dressed in the fashion of a trader, comes in. He carries a small, square bag. He also is hot, weary, and dust-covered. In age and appearance, making allowance for the difference in race, he closely resembles the Christian. He and the latter stare at each other, then bow perfunctorily. The Magian sets down his bag and wipes his brow.*)

CHRISTIAN (*sympathetically*). Hot as hell!

MAGIAN (*grimly*). Hotter!

(*They both chuckle. A Buddhist, a Kashmiri travelling merchant, comes in, puffing and sweating, from the right. He has a pack strapped on his back. He resembles the other two in the essential character of his body and face. He stops on seeing them. After eyeing him for an appraising second, the two bow and the Buddhist comes forward to set his pack beside the bags of the others.)*

BUDDHIST (*with relief*). Phoo! (*Then breaking the ice.*) The sun would cook you!

MAGIAN. It is hot certainly.

CHRISTIAN (*as they all sit down to rest, looks from one to the other – jovially*). Funny! You'd think we three had an appointment here. Your faces look familiar. Haven't I seen you somewhere before?

MAGIAN. In the house of the courtesans at Shiraz. You were drunk.

BUDDHIST. I happened to be there that night, too. You danced and sang lewd songs.

CHRISTIAN (*a bit embarrassed, but grinning*). Humn – oh, yes – I remember. It was my birthday and I'd taken a drop too much – a very unusual thing for me. (*Then abruptly changing the subject.*) How are conditions down your way?

BUDDHIST (*pursing his lips*). Slow. I come from Delhi. There is a new import tax and trade is very unsettled. We make prayer beads.

MAGIAN (*gloomily*). And I, for my sins, am hawking a novelty, a block-printed book, for an Arab house. It contains one thousand Arabian lies, with one over for good measure, all full of lechery – at least so they instructed me to tell people to get them to buy.

CHRISTIAN. Did your trip take you down around Ispahan way?

MAGIAN. I just came from there. It is a sad city now. All the bazaars have been closed by an imperial edict in mourning for Queen Kukachin.

CHRISTIAN (*bounding to his feet as if a wasp had stung him*). Is Queen Kukachin dead? (*Stunned.*) Why, I've got a letter of introduction to her from the head of my firm – Marco Polo of Polo Brothers and Son, Venice. He acted as her official escort, and took her from Cathay to Persia to be married! Why, I was counting on selling her and her husband a whole fleet load of goods!

MAGIAN (*suddenly, pointing off left*). What makes that cloud of dust? (*They all stare and begin to grow worried.*)

CHRISTIAN. It doesn't look like camels.

BUDDHIST (*fearfully*). It has a strange look!

CHRISTIAN. It's coming directly this way.

MAGIAN. These plains are haunted by evil spirits.

CHRISTIAN (*very frightened, but striving to put up a brave front*). I've heard those rumours. And I know for a fact that people are sometimes possessed by devils, but I don't believe –

BUDDHIST (*suddenly, pointing to the tree*). I am going to offer a prayer for protection to this tree sacred to Buddha.

CHRISTIAN, MAGIAN (*in chorus – irritably*). Sacred to Buddha?

BUDDHIST. Certainly! Do you not know the legend of how the Holy Sakya picked a twig to cleanse his teeth, and then throwing it away, it took root, and sprang up into this mighty tree to testify for ever to his miraculous power?

CHRISTIAN (*resentfully*). You're absolutely all wrong! This tree was the staff of our first father, Adam. It was handed down to Moses who used it to tap water out of stones and finally planted it. The cross our Lord was crucified on was made of this wood. And ever since this tree has been sacred to Him!

MAGIAN (*cuttingly*). You have both of you been duped by childish lies! This tree is sacred to the founder of the one true religion, Zoroaster, who brought a shoot of the Tree of Life down from Paradise and planted it here!

BUDDHIST (*scornfully*). You are a pair of superstitious sheep!

CHRISTIAN. You are a couple of idolatrous dogs!

MAGIAN. The two of you are blasphemous hogs!

(*They glare at each other insultingly, their hands on their daggers. Suddenly they hear a noise from the left. Their eyes at once are turned in that direction and, forgetting personal animosities, they give a startled exclamation at what they see.*)

BUDDHIST. They are pulling a chariot!

CHRISTIAN. They must be slaves. See how the driver lashes them!

BUDDHIST. But what can that be on the wagon? – like a coffin!

CHRISTIAN. It must be treasure!

MAGIAN. No. It is a coffin. (*Trembling.*) Ssst! I have a foreboding of evil.

(*They prostrate themselves, their faces to the ground. A moment later, preceded by shouts, a cracking of whips, and the dull stamping of feet, a double file of thirty men of different ages, stripped to the waist, harnessed to each other waist-to-waist and to the long pole of a two-wheeled wagon, stagger in, straining forward under the lashes of two soldiers who run beside them and the long whips of the Captain and a Corporal who are riding on the wagon, the Captain driving. As they reach the middle of the shade they stop. Lashed on the wagon is a coffin covered with a white pall.*)

CAPTAIN (*a brutal, determined-looking man of forty, bellows*). Halt! (*The files of bleeding and sweating men collapse in panting, groaning heaps. The Soldiers sprawl down beside them. The Captain springs off the wagon.*) Phoo! This shade is grateful. (*He looks at the tree – then in an awed tone.*) This must be the Holy Tree which was once the staff of Mahomet and, passing down through generations, was buried in the grave of Abu Abdallah where it struck root and grew by the will of Allah into this tree. (*He makes obeisance and prays to the tree as do the Soldiers. He gets up and takes a gulp of water – then, looking around, notices the three merchants – with startled surprise, drawing his sword.*) Ho! What are you? Get up! (*They do so fearfully. He stares at them and laughs coarsely with relief.*) By all the demons, you startled me! But you traders are like fleas, one finds you everywhere! (*Then with a scowl.*) Three dogs of unbelievers, too! (*Sharply.*) Give an account of yourselves!

BUDDHIST. I was proceeding westward on a business venture, good sir.

MAGIAN. And I to the northward.

CHRISTIAN. And I to the court of Ghazan Khan to present this letter to Queen Kukachin. But I hear she's dead.

(*He hands him the letter but the Captain backs away superstitiously.*)

CAPTAIN. Allah forbid I touch what belongs to a corpse. (*Then with forced laughter.*) You need not journey farther. She is in there! (*His voice has dropped, he points toward the coffin. The others stare at it, dumbfounded and awed. The Captain goes on dryly.*) You cannot cheat her now, Christian! (*Then lowering his voice as if afraid he will be overheard.*) And yet, to look at her face you would think her only sleeping.

CHRISTIAN (*astonished*). What? Can you look at her?

CAPTAIN. Her coffin is glass. Her body was anointed by Egyptians so that she preserves the appearance of life. This was done by command of her grandfather Kublai, the Great Kaan. She is being taken home to Cathay for burial – and under penalty of torture I must transport her over the first stage by dark to-night! (*Suddenly lamenting.*) But Allah afflicted me! When I reached the last village with my camels foundering, I found the accursed villagers had driven off their beasts to escape requisition. But the dogs could not balk me. I hitched them to the pole instead. (*He looks at the moaning figures with a cruel appraising eye.*) But will they last till night? Hi, there! Water to revive them!

(*The Soldiers carry around jugs of water which the panting men reach out for avidly, then sink back. But three of the more elderly men are too spent to move.*)

CHRISTIAN (*timorously – anxious to change the subject*). Was the Queen very beautiful?

CAPTAIN (*with bravado*). Would you care to see? You had a letter to her. It can do no harm – and it is a very great wonder!

CHRISTIAN (*reassuringly, because he is now extremely curious*). Dead Queens in the West usually lie in state.

CAPTAIN. You pull back the cloth then, since that is your custom.

(*The Christian goes to the wagon and gingerly pulls back the pall from the head of the coffin – then retreats with an exclamation as Kukachin's face, that of a beautiful Tartar princess of twenty-three, is revealed inside the glass. Her calm expression seems to glow with the intense peace of a life beyond death, the eyes are shut as if she were asleep. The men stare, fascinated.*)

CHRISTIAN (*after a pause – crossing himself awedly*). Are you certain she's dead?

CAPTAIN (*in an awed whisper*). In the palace I commanded the company who guarded her coffin at night. I could not take my eyes from her face. It seemed that any moment she must awake and speak!

(*While they have been speaking, unnoticed by them, it has grown dark. An unearthly glow, like a halo, lights up the face of Kukachin. From the branches of the tree comes a sound of sweet sad music as if the leaves were tiny harps strummed by the wind. The face of Kukachin becomes more and more living. Finally her lips part and her eyes open to look up at the tree.*)

(*Kneeling down to pray.*) Allah, be pitiful!

BUDDHIST. Buddha, protect Thy servant!

MAGIAN. Mithra, All-Powerful One!

CHRISTIAN. Jesus, have mercy!

(*A voice which is Kukachin's, and yet more musical than a human voice, comes from the coffin as her lips are seen to move.*)

KUKACHIN. Say this, I loved and died. Now I am love, and live. And living, have forgotten. And loving, can forgive. (*Here her lips part in a smile of beautiful pity.*) Say this for me in Venice!

(*A sound of tender laughter, of an intoxicating, supernatural gaiety, comes from her lips and is taken up in chorus in the branches of the tree as if every harp-leaf were laughing in music with her. The laughter recedes heavenward and dies as the halo of light about her face fades and noonday rushes back in a blaze of baking plain. Everyone is prostrate, the harnessed wretches in the exhausted attitudes of sleep, the others visibly trembling with superstitious horror.*)

CHRISTIAN (*the first to recover – with bewilderment*). Venice! It must have been a message she wished me to take back to Marco Polo!

CAPTAIN (*his terror going and rage taking its place, leaps to his feet*). It was the voice of some Christian devil you summoned! It bewitched even me until Allah drove it back to hell! (*He draws his sword.*) Cover her face, accursed sorcerer!

CHRISTIAN (*pulls the covering over the head of the coffin with indecent haste*). I pledge you my word, good Captain –!

CAPTAIN (*to his Soldiers*). Attention! Kick them up! We must get away from here! (*With blows and kicks the Soldiers get their human beasts to their feet. There are groans and curses and cries of pain. But three cannot be roused. The Captain growls savagely at the Christian to keep up his courage.*) Pig of an infidel! (*Then glaring at the Buddhist and Magian.*) You too! You were in league with him! (*He grips his sword.*)

ALL THREE (*kneeling – pitiably*). Mercy! Spare us!

A CORPORAL (*comes up and salutes*). We cannot get three of them up, sir.

CAPTAIN (*raging*). Lash them!

CORPORAL. They are dead, sir.

CAPTAIN (*glumly*). Oh. (*Then an idea comes – with cruel satisfaction.*) Three, did you say? That is fortunate. Allah has provided! Cut them out and put these in their places!

(*At a sign, the Soldiers fall upon the three merchants, strip off their upper clothes, untie the dead men, and hitch them in their places. All the time the three set up miserable screams of protest, punctuated by the blows and kicks they receive. The others look on with exhausted indifference.*)

CHRISTIAN (*making himself heard above the tumult*). My letter! It was to the Queen! When Polo Brothers hear of this outrage they'll get the Kaan to flay you alive!

CAPTAIN (*taken aback a moment – then craftily*). Show me your letter again!

CHRISTIAN (*holding it out with frantic eagerness*). Here! Now set me free!

CAPTAIN (*takes it and calmly tears it up*). I cannot read, but I think you are lying. At any rate, now you have no letter! (*The Christian sets up a wailing cry and receives a blow. The Captain and Corporals spring up on the wagon.*) And now forward march!

(*With a great cracking of whips and shouts of pain the wagon is pulled swiftly away.*

On the ground under the sacred tree three bodies lie in crumpled heaps. The same sweet sad music comes from the tree again as if its spirit were playing on the leaves a last lamenting farewell to the dead Princess. It rises softly and as softly dies away until it is nothing but a faint sound of wind rustling the leaves.)

Curtain

ACT ONE SCENE ONE

SCENE. *Twenty-three years earlier. A fresh boy's voice is heard singing a love song in a subdued tone. The light slowly reveals the exterior of Donata's home on a canal, Venice. Marco Polo, a boy of fifteen, youthfully handsome and well made, is standing in a gondola beneath a barred window of the house, a guitar over his shoulder. The song finished, he waits anxiously. A hand is thrust out to him through the bars. He kisses it passionately. It is hurriedly withdrawn. Donata's face appears pressed against the bars. She is a girl of twelve, her face pale and pretty in the moonlight.*

DONATA (*coyly and tenderly*). You mustn't, Mark.

MARCO. There's no harm in that – just kissing your hand!

DONATA (*demurely*). It's a sin, I'm sure of it.

MARCO (*with a quick movement of his own hand, captures hers through the bars*). Then I'll have to steal it, and that's a worse sin. (*He pulls her willing hand down toward his lips.*)

DONATA. You're hurting my fingers.

MARCO (*boldly now*). Then I know how to cure them. (*He kisses them one by one.*) There!

DONATA (*tenderly*). You silly boy! Why do you do that?

MARCO (*very seriously*). You know, Donata.

DONATA. Know what? (*Softly.*) Go on and tell me, Mark.

MARCO (*blurts out gruffly*). I love you, that's what! I've loved you ever since I can remember. And you've known it right along, too, so there's no good pretending.

DONATA (*softly*). I wasn't sure.

MARCO (*recklessly*). And how about you? Do you love me? You've got to answer me that!

DONATA. You know – without my saying it.

MARCO. Please say it!

DONATA (*in a whisper*). I love you. There, silly!

MARCO. And you'll promise to marry me when I come back?

DONATA. Yes, but you'll have to ask my parents.

MARCO (*easily*). Don't worry about them. They'll be glad, and my folks, too. It'll bring the two firms into closer contact.

DONATA (*practically*). Yes, I think so, too.

(*A pause. Songs and music come from near and far-off in the night about them. Marco has gained possession of her two hands now and his face is closer to the bars of her window.*)

MARCO (*with a sigh*). It's beautiful to-night. I wish I hadn't got to go away.

DONATA. I wish, too! Must you really!

MARCO. Yes. And I want to, too – all but leaving you. I want to travel and see the world and all the different people, and get to know their habits and needs from first-hand knowledge. You've got to do that if you want to become really big and important. That's what Father says – and Uncle.

DONATA. But won't this trip so very far away be full of danger?

MARCO (*boastfully*). I can take care of myself. Uncle says taking chances – *necessary* chances, of course – is the best schooling for a real merchant; and Father has a saying that where there's nothing risked, there's nothing gained. And they ought to know, oughtn't they, after spending nine years at the court of the Great Kaan and travelling there and back?

DONATA. Is that where you're going?

MARCO. Yes. He's the richest king in the world and Uncle and Father are personal friends of his. They did a lot of work for him. I'll be on the right side of him from the start, and Father and

Uncle both say there's millions to be made in his service if you're not afraid of work and keep awake to opportunity.

DONATA. I'm sure you'll succeed. But I wish you weren't going for so long.

MARCO. I'll miss you as much as you miss me. (*Huskily.*) I hate to leave you, Donata – but I've got to make my own way – so that we can marry –

DONATA (*hurriedly*). Yes – of course – only come back as soon as you can.

MARCO. But you'll wait, won't you, no matter how long?

DONATA (*solemnly*). Yes, I swear to, Mark.

MARCO. And I swear by God I'll come back and marry you, and I'll always be true and never forget or do anything –

DONATA (*startled by a noise from within*). Ssshh! There's some one moving inside. You'll have to go. Here. (*She hands him a locket.*) It's a medallion of me painted by an artist who owed Father for spices and couldn't pay with money. Will you keep looking at this all the time you're away and never forget me?

MARCO (*kissing it passionately*). Every day!

DONATA. And you'll write to me?

MARCO. I promise. Every chance I get.

DONATA (*hesitatingly*). Will you write me – a poem? I won't care how short it is if it's only a poem.

MARCO. I'll try, Donata. I'll do my best.

DONATA. I'll just love it to death, Mark! (*Startledly.*) Ssshh! I hear it again. It must be Father. I've got to sneak back.

MARCO (*desperately*). Won't you kiss me – let me really kiss you – just once – for good-bye?

DONATA. I mustn't.

MARCO. Just once – when I'm going so far away? (*Desperately.*) I – I – I'll die if you don't!

DONATA. Well – just once. (*The moonlight fades into darkness as their lips meet. Then from the darkness are their voices heard in hushed tones.*) Good-bye, Mark.

MARCO. Good-bye, Donata.

(*The sentimental singing voices and guitars are heard from all corners of the night in celebration of love. The sound gradually grows fainter and fainter, receding into the distance, as if Marco were already leaving Venice behind him.*)

DARKNESS

ACT ONE SCENE TWO

SCENE. *Six months later. The tolling of a church bell is first heard. Then the interior of the Papal Legate's palace at Acre is revealed – a combination of church and government building.*

The Legate, Tedaldo, a man of sixty with a strong, intelligent face, is seated on a sort of throne placed against the rear wall. On his right, stands a warrior noble, a Knight-Crusader, in full armour, leaning on his sword. On his left, a Dominican Monk, his adviser. On the left of the room is an altar with candles burning. On the right, an open portal with a sentry pacing up and down, spear in hand.

The two elder Polos, Nicolo and Maffeo, stand in attitudes of patient servility before the throne. Marco's father, Nicolo, is a small thin middle-aged man, with a dry, shrewd face. Maffeo, Marco's uncle, is about the same age, but he is tall and stout with a round, jovial face and small, cunning eyes. There is a strong general resemblance between both of them and Marco. Marco is sitting on a stool in the foreground, his body all screwed up into an awkward intensity, striving with all his might to compose a poem to Donata, but constantly distracted in spite of himself.

TEDALDO (*bored but tolerantly*). What can I do except advise you to be patient? I'm sure the Conclave of Cardinals must soon select a Pope.

NICOLO. Two years in session! (*Then suddenly – consoled.*) Well, it's a new world's record, anyway.

MAFFEO (*shaking his head*). This uncertainty is bad for trade.

TEDALDO (*with a bored yawn*). No doubt. (*Then rather impatiently.*) Then, when your business so evidently calls you to the East, why delay longer? Why not simply explain to the Great Kaan, Kublai, that there was no Pope to whom you could deliver his message?

NICOLO. He mightn't understand. His instructions to us were pretty emphatic.

MAFFEO. To request the Pope to send him a hundred wise men of the West –

TEDALDO (*dryly*). This Kublai is an optimist!

MAFFEO. – to argue with his Buddhists and Taoists and Confucians which religion in the world is best.

MONK (*outraged*). Impudent ignoramus! Does he imagine the Church would stoop to such bickering?

TEDALDO (*with a weary smile*). I begin to think Kublai is a humorist, too.

MAFFEO (*craftily*). It'd pay to convert him. He's the richest king in the world. He rules over millions of subjects, his empire covers millions of square miles of great undeveloped natural resources, his personal wealth in cash and jewels and goods alone easily runs into millions of millions!

MARCO (*stares at his uncle – then mutters, fascinatedly.*) Millions! (*Then, shaking away this interruption, bends to his writing again.*)

TEDALDO (*wearily*). I am bored with your millions, Messrs. Polo. Even if they are true, it is too much effort to conceive them. (*They bow humbly and retire backward. His eyes following them listlessly Tedaldo sees Marco, who at this moment is scratching himself, twisting and turning his legs and feet, tearing his hair in a perfect frenzy of balked inspiration. Tedaldo smiles and addresses him in an affectionate, humorous tone.*) God's mercy on you, Master Marco! Are you suddenly possessed by a devil – or is it only these infernal Mahometan fleas the Almighty sends us for our sins?

MARCO (*coming out of his fit – sheepishly*). I'm only writing something.

MAFFEO. Mark is surprisingly quick at figures.

NICOLO. But still heedless. A dreamer! (*To Marco, with a condescending paternal air.*) What are you writing, son? (*He and Maffeo draw near Marco.*)

MARCO (*more confused*). Nothing, sir – just – something. (*He tries to hide it.*)

MAFFEO. Why are you so mysterious? Come, let's see.

MARCO. No – please, Uncle.

MAFFEO (*with a sudden cunning motion, he snatches it from Marco's hand, glances at it and bursts into laughter*). Look, Nicolo, look!

MARCO (*rebelliously*). Give that back!

NICOLO (*sternly*). Behave yourself, Mark! (*To Maffeo.*) What is it?

MAFFEO. See for yourself. (*He hands it to him.*) Did you know you'd hatched a nightingale? (*He laughs coarsely. Nicolo reads, a scornful grin coming to his lips.*)

TEDALDO. Surely it cannot be a song he has written?

NICOLO (*going to him – laughing*). A rhyme! A love poem, no less!

TEDALDO (*severely, as he takes the poem*). Do not mock at him! Rather be grateful if a thistle can bring forth figs. (*Marco remains sullenly apart, shamefaced and angry, his fists clenched. Tedaldo reads – frowns – laughs – then smilingly to Nicolo.*) Your fear that this is a poem is – hum – exaggerated! (*He reads with amusement as Marco squirms.*)

'You are lovely as the gold in the sun
Your skin is like silver in the moon
Your eyes are black pearls I have won.
I kiss your ruby lips and you swoon,
Smiling your thanks as I promise you
A large fortune if you will be true,
While I am away earning gold
And silver so when we are old
I will have a million to my credit
And in the meantime can easily afford
A big wedding that will do us credit
And start having children, bless the Lord!'

(*There is a roar of laughter in which Tedaldo joins. Marco looks about for a hole into which to crawl. Tedaldo addresses him amusedly but with kindness.*) Come, Marco. Here is your poem. Your lady is a bit too mineral, your heaven of love a trifle monetary – but, never mind, you will be happier as a Polo than as a poet. Here. (*He gives it to Marco. The latter fiercely crumples it up and throws it on the floor and stamps on it.*)

NICOLO (*approvingly*). Sensibly done, my boy.

TEDALDO (*looking searchingly at Marco's face – gently*). Perhaps I was too critical. Your poem had merits of its own. I am sure it would touch your lady's heart.

MARCO (*with a great bluster of manliness*). Oh, I don't mind your making fun. I can take a joke. It *was* silly. Poetry's all stupid, anyway. I was only trying it for fun, to see if I could. You won't catch me ever being such a fool again!

MONK (*as a noise of shouting comes toward them*). Ssstt! What's that?

(*The Knight hurries to the portal.*)

KNIGHT. Some one is running here, and a crowd behind. I hear them shouting 'Pope.'

MONK. Then the Conclave has chosen!

POLOS (*joyfully*). At last!

(*The cries of many voices. The Sentinel and Knight admit the Messenger but push back the others.*)

MESSENGER (*exhausted – falls on his knees before Tedaldo, holding out a sealed paper*). I come from the Conclave. You were chosen. Your Holiness – (*He falls fainting. The crowds cheer and sweep in.*)

TEDALDO (*rising – pale and trembling*). What does he say?

MONK (*has picked up the document – joyfully*). See! The official seal! You are the Pope! (*He kneels humbly.*) Your Holiness, let me be the first –

(*He kisses Tedaldo's hand. All are kneeling now, their heads bowed. The bells of the churches begin to ring.*)

TEDALDO (*raising his hands to heaven – dazed*). Lord, I am not worthy! (*Then to those about him – tremblingly.*) Leave me. I must pray to God for strength – for guidance!

CROWD (*in a clamour*). Your blessing!

(*Tedaldo, with a simple dignity and power, blesses them. They back out slowly, the Monk and Knight last. The Polos group together in the foreground, holding a whispered conference. Tedaldo kneels before the altar.*)

MAFFEO. Now that he's the Pope, if we could get an answer from him, we could start right away.

NICOLO. We couldn't hope for better weather.

MAFFEO. He seems to have taken a fancy to Mark. You speak to him, Mark.

MARCO (*unwillingly*). He's praying.

MAFFEO. He'll have time enough for that, but with us time is money. (*Giving the unwilling Marco a push.*) This will test your nerve, Mark! Don't shirk!

MARCO (*gritting his teeth*). All right. I'll show you I'm not scared! (*He advances boldly toward the altar, stands there for a moment awkwardly as Tedaldo remains oblivious – then he falls on his knees – humbly but insistently.*) Your Holiness. Forgive me, Your Holiness –

TEDALDO (*turns to him and springs to his feet – imperiously*). I wish to be alone! (*Then as Marco is shrinking back – more kindly.*) Well, what is it? I owe you a recompense, perhaps – for an injury.

MARCO (*stammeringly*). Your Holiness – if you could give us some answer to deliver to the Great Kaan – we could start now – with such favourable weather –

TEDALDO (*amused in spite of himself*). On the last day one of your seed will interrupt Gabriel to sell him another trumpet! (*Then sardonically to the elder Polos.*) I have no hundred wise men – nor one! Tell the Great Kaan he must have been imposed upon by your patriotic lies, or he could never make such a request.

POLOS (*terrified*). But, Your Holiness, we dare not repeat – He'd have us killed!

TEDALDO. I will send him a monk or two. That is quite sufficient to convert a Tartar barbarian!

MAFFEO. But, Your Holiness, he's not a barbarian! Why, every plate on his table is solid gold!

TEDALDO (*smiling*). And has he millions of plates, too? (*Then with a sudden whimsicality.*) But if the monks fail, Master Marco can be my missionary. Let him set an example of virtuous Western manhood amid all the levities of paganism, shun the frailty of poetry, have a million to his credit, as he so beautifully phrased it, and I will wager a million of something or other myself that the Kaan will soon be driven to seek spiritual salvation somewhere! Mark my words, Marco will be worth a million wise men – in the cause of wisdom! (*He laughs gaily, raising his hand over Marco's head.*) Go with my blessing! But what need have you for a blessing? You were born with success in your pocket! (*With a last gesture he turns, going quickly out of the door in rear.*)

MAFFEO (*as he goes – approvingly*). Mark is making a good impression already!

NICOLO. Well, he's got a head on him!

MARCO (*beginning to swell out a bit matter-of-factly*). Never mind about me. When do we start?

POLOS (*hurriedly*). At once. Let's go and pack. (*They go out left.*) Come, Mark! Hurry!

MARCO. I'm coming. (*He waits, looks after them, picks up the crumpled poem, starts to hide it in his jacket, stops, mutters with brave self-contempt.*) Aw! You damn fool!

(*He throws the poem down again, starts to go, hesitates, suddenly turns back, picks it up, crams it into his doublet and runs wildly out of the door. The scene fades into darkness. For a time the church bells, which have never ceased ringing, are heard acclaiming the new Pope; but the Polos proceed speedily on their journey and the sound is soon left behind them.*)

DARKNESS

ACT ONE SCENE THREE

SCENE. *Light comes, gradually revealing the scene. In the rear is the front of a Mahometan mosque. Before the mosque is a throne on which sits a Mahometan ruler. On the right, the inevitable warrior – on his left, the inevitable priest – the two defenders of the State. At the ruler's feet his wives crouch like slaves. Everything is jewelled, high-coloured, gorgeous in this background. Squatted against the side walls, forming a sort of semi-circle with the throne at* C., *counting from left to right consecutively, are a mother nursing a baby, two children playing a game, a young girl and a young man in a loving embrace, a middle-aged couple, an aged couple, a coffin. All these Mahometan figures remain motionless. Only their eyes move, staring fixedly but indifferently at the Polos, who are standing at centre. Marco is carrying in each hand bags which curiously resemble modern sample cases. He sets these down and gazes around with a bewildered awe.*

NICOLO (*turning on him – genially*). Well, son, here we are in Islam.

MARCO (*round-eyed*). A man told me that Noah's Ark is still somewhere around here on top of a mountain. (*Eagerly.*) And he proved it to me, too. Look! (*He shows them a piece of wood.*) He broke this off of the Ark. See, it's got Noah's initials on it!

MAFFEO (*grimly*). How much did you pay him for it?

MARCO. Ten soldi in silver.

NICOLO (*dashing it out of Marco's hand – bitterly*). Muttonhead! Do you suppose Almighty God would allow infidels to cut up Noah's Ark into souvenirs to sell to Christians?

MAFFEO (*teasingly*). Your son and your money are soon parted, Brother. (*Then placatingly.*) But he's only a boy. He'll learn. And before we go farther, Nicolo, we had better read him from the notes we made on our last trip all there is to remember about this corner of the world.

NICOLO (*they take out note-books closely resembling a modern business man's diary and read*). We're now passing through Kingdoms where they worship Mahomet.

MAFFEO. There's one kingdom called Musul and in it a district of Baku where there's a great fountain of oil. There's a growing demand for it. (*Then speaking.*) Make a mental note of that.

MARCO. Yes, sir.

NICOLO. Merchants make great profits. The people are simple creatures. It's very cold in winter. The women wear cotton drawers. This they do to look large in the hips, for the men think that a great beauty.

(*The two Mahometan Merchants enter from the left. Maffeo recognizes them immediately – in a swift aside to his brother.*)

MAFFEO. There's those damned Ali brothers. They'll cut under our prices with their cheap junk as usual. (*The Ali brothers have seen the Polos and a whispered aside, evidently of the same nature, passes between them. Then simultaneously the two firms advance to meet each other, putting on expressions of the utmost cordiality.*) Well, well. You folks are a welcome sight!

ONE ALI. My dear, dear friends! Praise be to Allah! (*They embrace.*)

MAFFEO (*with a cunning smirk*). Selling a big bill of goods hereabouts, I'll wager, you old rascals?

THE OLDER ALI (*airily*). My dear friend, don't speak of business. But you, you are on a venture to the court of the Great Kaan, we hear?

MAFFEO. What lies get around! Nothing in it – absolutely nothing!

NICOLO. For Heaven's sake, let's not talk business! Let's have a nice friendly chat. (*The four squat together in a circle.*)

MAFFEO (*with a wink*). I'll tell you a good one an Armenian doily-dealer told me down in Bagdad. (*They all bend their heads toward him with expectant grins. He looks around – then begins in a cautious lowered tone.*) Well, there was an old Jew named Ikey and he married a young girl named Rebecca –

(*He goes on telling the rest of the story with much exaggerated Jewish pantomime but in a voice too low to be heard. In the meantime, Marco has slipped off, full of curiosity and wonder, to look at this strange life. He goes first to the left, stops before the mother and baby, smiles down at it uncertainly, then bends down to take hold of its hand.*)

MARCO. Hello! (*Then to the mother.*) He's fat as butter! (*Both remain silent and motionless, staring at him from a great distance with indifferent calm. Marco is rebuffed, grows embarrassed, turns away to the children, who, frozen in the midst of their game of jackstraws, are looking at him. Marco adopts a lofty condescending air.*) Humh! Do you still play that game here? I remember it – when I was a kid. (*They stare silently. He mutters disgustedly.*) Thick-heads! (*And turns to the lovers, who, with their arms about each other, cheek to cheek, stare at him. He looks at them, fascinated and stirred, and murmurs enviously.*) She's pretty. I suppose they're engaged – like Donata and me. (*He fumbles and pulls out the locket which is hung around his neck on a ribbon.*) Donata's prettier. (*Then, with embarrassment, he holds it out for them to see.*) Don't you think she's pretty? She and I are going to be married some day. (*They do not look except into his eyes. He turns away, hurt and angry.*) Go to the devil, you infidels! (*He stuffs the locket back – stops before the throne – tries to stare insolently at the king but, awed in spite of himself, makes a grudging bow and passes on, stops before the family group, sneers and passes on, stops before the old couple and cannot restrain his curiosity.*) Would you tell me how old you are?

(*He passes on, rebuffed again, stops as if fascinated before the coffin, leans out and touches it with defiant daring, shudders superstitiously and shrinks away, going to the merchant group who are roaring with laughter as Maffeo ends his story.*)

THE OLDER ALI (*to Nicolo*). Your son?

NICOLO. Yes, and a chip of the old block.

THE OLDER ALI. Will he follow in your footsteps?

NICOLO (*jocosely*). Yes, and you'd better look out then! He's as keen as a hawk already.

THE OLDER ALI (*with a trace of a biting smile*). He greatly resembles a youth I saw back on the road buying a piece of Noah's Ark from a wayside sharper.

MAFFEO (*hastily coming to the rescue as Nicolo cannot hide his chagrin – boastfully*). It wasn't Mark. Mark would have sold him the lions of St. Mark's for good mousers!

(*The Prostitute enters from the right. She is painted, half-naked, alluring in a brazen, sensual way. She smiles at Marco enticingly.*)

MARCO (*with a gasp*). Look! Who's that?

(*They all turn, and, recognizing her, laugh with coarse familiarity.*)

MAFFEO (*jokingly*). So here you are again. You're like a bad coin – always turning up.

PROSTITUTE (*smiling*). Shut up. You can bet it

isn't old fools like you that turn me.

NICOLO (*with a lecherous grin at her*). No? But it's the old who have the money.

PROSTITUTE. Money isn't everything, not always. Now I wouldn't ask money from him. (*She points to Marco.*)

NICOLO (*crossly and jealously*). Leave him alone, you filth!

MAFFEO (*broad-mindedly*). Come, come, Nicolo. Let the boy have his fling.

PROSTITUTE (*her eyes on Marco*). Hello, Handsome.

MARCO (*bewildered*). You've learned our language?

PROSTITUTE. I sell to all nations.

MARCO. What do you sell?

PROSTITUTE (*mockingly*). A precious jewel. Myself. (*Then desirously.*) But for you I'm a gift. (*Putting her hands on his shoulders and lifting her lips.*) Why don't you kiss me?

MARCO (*terribly confused – strugglingly*). I – I don't know – I mean, I'm sorry but – you see I promised some one I'd never – (*Suddenly freeing himself – frightened.*) Leave go! I don't want your kisses.

(*A roar of coarse taunting laughter from the men. Marco runs away, off* L.)

NICOLO (*between his teeth*). What a dolt!

MAFFEO (*slapping the Prostitute on the bare shoulder*). Better luck next time. He'll learn!

PROSTITUTE (*trying to hide her pique – forcing a cynical smile*). Oh, yes, but I won't be a gift then. I'll make him pay, just to show him!

(*She laughs harshly and goes out* L. *A pause. All four squat again in silence.*)

THE OLDER ALI (*suddenly*). Many wonders have come to pass in these regions. They relate that in old times three kings from this country went to worship a Prophet that was born and they carried with them three manner of offerings – Gold and Frankincense and Myrrh – and when they had come to the place where the Child was born, they marvelled and knelt before him.

MAFFEO. That's written in the Bible. The child was Jesus Christ, our Lord. (*He crosses himself, Nicolo does likewise.*)

THE OLDER ALI. Your Jesus was a great prophet.

NICOLO (*defiantly*). He was the Son of God!

BOTH ALIS (*stubbornly*). There is no God but Allah!

(*A strained pause. A dervish of the desert runs in shrieking and begins to whirl. No one is surprised except the two Polos, who get up to gape at him with the thrilled appreciation inspired by a freak in a sideshow. Marco comes back and joins them.*)

MAFFEO (*with appreciation*). If we had him in Venice we could make a mint of money exhibiting him. (*Nicolo nods.*)

MARCO. I'll have to write Donata all about this. (*Wonderingly.*) Is he crazy?

MAFFEO (*in a low aside to him*). My boy, all Mahometans are crazy. That's the only charitable way to look at it.

(*Suddenly the call to prayer sounds from Muezzins in the minarets of the mosque. The Dervish falls on his face. Everyone sinks into the attitude of prayer except the Polos who stand embarrassed, not knowing what to do.*)

MARCO. Are they praying?

NICOLO. Yes, they call it that. Much good it does them!

MAFFEO. Ssshh! Come! This is a good time to move on again. Marco! Wake up!

(*They go quickly out* R., *Marco following with the sample cases. The scene fades quickly into darkness as the call of the Muezzins is heard again.*)

DARKNESS

ACT ONE SCENE FOUR

SCENE. *The slowly-rising light reveals an Indian snake-charmer squatted on his haunches at* C. *A snake is starting to crawl from the basket in front of him, swaying its head to the thin, shrill whine of a gourd. Otherwise, the scene, in the placing of its people and the characters and types represented, is the exact duplicate of the last except that here the locale is Indian. The background for the ruler's throne is now a Buddhist temple instead of a mosque. The motionless staring figures are all Indians. Looming directly above and behind the ruler's throne is an immense Buddha. The Polos stand at centre as before, Marco still lugging the sample cases. He is seventeen now. Some of the freshness of youth has worn off. They stare at the snake-charmer, the two older men cynically. Marco gasps with enthralled horror.*

MARCO. Look at that deadly snake!

MAFFEO (*cynically*). He's a fake, like everything else here. His fangs have been pulled out.

MARCO (*disillusioned*). Oh! (*He turns away. The snake-charmer glares at them, stops playing, pushes his snake back into the box and carries it off, after spitting on the ground at their feet with angry disgust. Marco sits on one of the cases and glances about with a forced scorn; looks finally at the Buddha – in a superior tone.*) So that is Buddha!

NICOLO (*begins to read from his note-book*). These people are idolaters. The climate is so hot that if you put an egg in their rivers it will be boiled.

MAFFEO (*taking up the reading from his book in the same tone*). The merchants make great profits. Ginger, pepper, and indigo. Largest sheep in the world. Diamonds of great size. The Kings have five hundred wives apiece.

MARCO (*disgustedly*). It's too darn hot here!

MAFFEO (*warningly*). Sshhh! Don't let the natives hear you. Remember any climate is healthy where trade is brisk.

MARCO (*walks sullenly off to left. At the same moment two merchants, this time Buddhists, come in. The same interplay goes on with them as with the Ali Brothers in the previous scene, only this time it is all done in pantomime until the loud laughter at the end of Maffeo's story. As Maffeo tells the story, Marco is looking at the people, but this time he assumes the casual, indifferent attitude of the worldly-wise. He makes a silly gesture to attract the baby's attention, passes by the two children with only a contemptuous glance, but stops and stares impudently at the lovers – finally spits with exaggerated scorn*). Where do you think you are – home with the light out? Why don't you charge admission? (*He stalks on – pauses before the middle-aged couple who have a bowl of rice between them – in astonishment as though this evidence of a humanity common with his struck him as strange.*) Real rice! (*He ignores the throne, passes quickly by the old people with a glance of aversion and very obviously averts his head from the coffin. As he returns to the group at centre, Maffeo has just finished his story. There is a roar of laughter. Grinning eagerly.*) What was it, Uncle?

MAFFEO (*grinning teasingly*). You're too young.

MARCO (*boastfully*). Is that so?

NICOLO (*severely*). Mark!

(*The Prostitute, the same but now in Indian garb, has entered from left and comes up behind Marco.*)

PROSTITUTE. A chip of the old block, Nicolo!

NICOLO (*angrily*). You again!

MARCO (*pleased to see her, but embarrassed*). Why, hello!

PROSTITUTE (*cynically*). I knew you'd want to see me. (*She raises her lips.*) Will you kiss me now? (*As he hesitates.*) Forget your promise. You know you want to.

MAFFEO (*grinning*). There's no spirit in the youngsters nowadays. I'll bet he won't.

PROSTITUTE (*her eyes on Marco's*). How much will you bet?

MAFFEO. Ten –

(*Marco suddenly kisses her.*)

PROSTITUTE (*turning to Maffeo*). I win, Uncle.

MARCO (*with a grin*). No. I kissed you before he said ten what.

MAFFEO. That's right! Good boy, Mark!

PROSTITUTE (*turning to Marco – cynically*). You're

learning, aren't you? You're becoming shrewd even about kisses. You need only me now to make you into a real man – for ten pieces of gold.

MARCO (*genuinely overcome by a sudden shame*). No, please – I – I didn't mean it. It was only in fun.

PROSTITUTE (*with a sure smile*). Later, then – when we meet again. (*She walks off* L.)

MARCO (*looks after her. As she evidently turns to look back at him, he waves his hand and grins – then abashed*). She's pretty. It's too bad she's – what she is.

MAFFEO. Don't waste pity. Her kind are necessary evils. All of us are human.

(*A long pause.*)

THE OLDER BUDDHIST MERCHANT (*suddenly*). The Buddha taught that one's loving-kindness should embrace all forms of life, that one's compassion should suffer with the suffering, that one's sympathy should understand all things, and last that one's judgment should regard all persons and things as of equal importance.

NICOLO (*harshly*). Who was this Buddha?

THE OLDER BUDDHIST MERCHANT. The Incarnation of God.

NICOLO. You mean Jesus?

THE OLDER BUDDHIST MERCHANT (*unheedingly*). He was immaculately conceived. The Light passed into the womb of Maya, and she bore a son who, when he came to manhood, renounced wife and child, riches and power, and went out as a beggar on the roads to seek the supreme enlightenment which would conquer birth and death; and at last he attained the wisdom where all desire has ended and experienced the heaven of peace, Nirvana. And when he died he became a God again.

(*The temple bells begin to ring in chorus. All except the Polos prostrate themselves before the Buddha.*)

MARCO (*to his uncle – in a whispered chuckle*). Died and became a God? So that's what they believe about that stone statue, is it?

MAFFEO. They're all crazy, like the Mahometans. They're not responsible.

MARCO (*suddenly*). I saw two of them with a bowl of rice –

MAFFEO. Oh, yes. They eat the same as we do. (*Then abruptly.*) Come on! This is our chance to make a start. Don't forget our cases, Mark.

(*They go out* L. *followed by Marco with the sample cases. The scene fades into darkness. The clamour of the temple bells slowly dies out in the distance.*)

DARKNESS

ACT ONE SCENE FIVE

SCENE. *From the darkness comes the sound of a small Tartar kettledrum, its beats marking the rhythm for a crooning, nasal voice, rising and falling in a wordless chant.*

The darkness gradually lifts. In the rear is a section of the Great Wall of China with an enormous shut gate. It is late afternoon, just before sunset. Immediately before the gate is a rude throne on which sits a Mongol ruler with warrior and sorcerer to right and left of him. At the sides are Mongol circular huts. The motionless figures sit before these. The Minstrel, squatting at centre, is the only one whose body moves. In the back of the throne and above it is a small idol made of felt and cloth. The clothes of the ruler and his court are of rich silk stuffs, lined with costly furs. The squatting figures of the people are clothed in rough robes.

The Polos stand at centre, Marco still lugging the battered sample cases. He is now nearly eighteen, a self-confident young man, assertive and talkative. All the Polos are weary and their clothes shabby and travel-worn.)

MARCO (*setting down the bags with a thump and staring about with an appraising contempt*). Welcome to that dear old Motherland, Mongolia!

MAFFEO (*wearily takes out his guide-book and begins to read in the monotone of a boring formula*). Flocks – goats – horses – cattle. The women do all the buying and selling. Business is all in cattle and crops. In short, the people live like beasts.

NICOLO (*reading from his book*). They have two Gods – a God of Heaven to whom they pray for health of mind, and a God of Earth who watches over their earthly goods. They pray to him also and do many other stupid things.

MARCO (*bored*). Well – let them!

(*He walks away and makes the circuit of the figures, but now he hardly glances at them. The Two Tartar Merchants enter and there is the same pantomime of greeting between them and the Polos as with the Buddhist Merchants in the previous scene. Marco joins them. It is apparent the whole company is extremely weary. They yawn and prepare to lie down.*)

MAFFEO. We'll have time to steal a nap before they open the Gate.

MARCO (*with an assertive importance*). Just a moment! I've got a good one an idol-polisher told me in Tibet. This is the funniest story you ever heard! It seems an Irishman got drunk in Tangut and wandered into a temple where he mistook one of the female statues for a real woman and –

(*He goes on, laughing and chuckling to himself, with endless comic pantomime. The two Tartar Merchants fall asleep. Nicolo stares at his son bitterly, Maffeo with contemptuous pity. Finally Marco finishes to his own uproarious amusement.*)

NICOLO (*bitterly*). Dolt!

MAFFEO (*mockingly. With a yawn*). Youth will have its laugh!

(*Marco stops open-mouthed and stares from one to the other.*)

MARCO (*faintly*). What's the matter?

NICOLO (*pettishly*). Unless your jokes improve you'll never sell anything.

MAFFEO. I'll have to give Marco some lessons in how to tell a short story. (*Warningly.*) And until I pronounce you graduated, mum's the word, understand! The people on the other side of that wall may look simple but they're not.

(*The Prostitute enters, dressed now as a Tartar. She comes and puts her hand on Marco's head.*)

PROSTITUTE. What has this bad boy been doing now?

MAFFEO. He's getting too witty! (*He rests his head on his arms and goes to sleep.*)

PROSTITUTE. Shall I expect you again to-night?

MARCO. No. You've got all my money. (*Suddenly gets to his feet and faces her – disgusted.*) And I'm through with you, anyway.

PROSTITUTE (*with a scornful smile*). And I with you – now that you're a man. (*She turns away.*)

MARCO (*angrily*). Listen here! Give me back what you stole! I know I had it on a ribbon around my neck last night and this morning it was gone. (*Threateningly.*) Give it to me, you, or I'll make trouble!

PROSTITUTE (*takes a crumpled paper from her bosom*). Do you mean this?

MARCO (*tries to snatch it*). No!

PROSTITUTE (*she unfolds it and reads*).

'I'll have a million to my credit
And in the meantime can easily afford
A big wedding that will do us credit
And start having children, Bless the Lord!'

(*She laughs.*) Are you a poet, too?

MARCO (*abashed and furious*). I didn't write that.

PROSTITUTE. You're lying. You must have. Why deny it? Don't sell your soul for nothing. That's bad business. (*She laughs, waving the poem in her upraised hand, staring mockingly.*) Going! Going! Gone! (*She lets it fall and grinds it under her feet into the earth – laughing.*) Your soul! Dead and buried! You strong man! (*She laughs.*)

MARCO (*threateningly*). Give me what was wrapped up in that, d'you hear!

PROSTITUTE (*scornfully. Takes the miniature from her bosom*). You mean this? I was bringing it back to you. D'you think I want her ugly face around? Here! (*She throws it at his feet. He leans down and picks it up, polishing it on his sleeve remorsefully. The Prostitute, walking away, calls back over her shoul-*

der.) I kissed it so you'd remember my kiss whenever you kiss her!

(*She laughs. Marco starts as if to run after her angrily. Suddenly a shout rises from the lips of all the Tartars, the Minstrel and his drum become silent, and with one accord they raise their arms and eyes to the sky. Then the Minstrel chants.*)

MINSTREL. God of the Heaven, be in our souls! (*Then they all prostrate themselves on the ground as he chants.*) God of the Earth, be in our bodies!

(*The Tartars sit up. The Minstrel begins again his drum-beat, crooning in a low monotone. The Polos rise and stretch sleepily.*)

MARCO (*inquisitively*). Two Gods? Are they in one Person like our Holy Trinity?

MAFFEO (*shocked*). Don't be impious! These are degraded pagans – or crazy, that's a more charitable way to –

(*From behind the wall comes the sound of martial Chinese music. The gate opens. The blinding glare of the setting sun floods in from beyond. A file of soldiers, accompanying a richly-dressed Court Messenger, comes through. He walks directly up to the Polos and bows deeply.*)

MESSENGER. The Great Kaan, Lord of the World, sent me – (*He looks around.*) But where are the hundred wise men of the West?

NICOLO (*confusedly*). We had two monks to start with – but they left us and went back.

MAFFEO (*warningly*). Ssst!

MESSENGER (*indifferently*). You will explain to the Kaan. I was ordered to arrange a welcome for them.

MAFFEO (*claps him on the back*). Well, here we are – and hungry as hunters! So your welcome will be welcome, Brother. (*The Messenger bows, starts back, the Polos following him, Maffeo calling.*) Get on the job, Mark! (*They pass through the gate.*)

MARCO (*wearily picks up the cases – then goading himself on*). Giddap! Cathay or bust!

(*He struggles through the gate. For a second he is framed in it, outlined against the brilliant sky, tugging a sample case in each hand. Then the gate shuts, the light fades out. The drum-beat and the chanting recede into the distance.*)

DARKNESS

ACT ONE SCENE SIX

SCENE. *Music from full Chinese and Tartar bands crashes up to a tremendous blaring crescendo of drums, gongs, and the piercing shrilling of flutes. The light slowly comes to a pitch of blinding brightness. Then, as light and sound attain their highest point, there is a sudden dead silence. The scene is revealed as the Grand Throne Room in the palace of Kublai, the Great Kaan, in the city of Cambaluc, Cathay – an immense octagonal room, the lofty walls adorned in gold and silver. In the far rear wall, within a deep recess like the shrine of an idol, is the throne of the Great Kaan. It rises in three tiers, three steps to a tier. On golden cushions at the top Kublai sits dressed in his heavy gold robes of state. He is a man of sixty but still in the full prime of his powers, his face proud and noble, his expression tinged with an ironic humour and bitterness yet full of a sympathetic humanity. In his person are combined the conquering indomitable force of a descendant of Chinghiz with the humanizing culture of the conquered Chinese who have already begun to absorb their conquerors.*

On the level of the throne below Kublai are: on his right a Mongol warrior in full armour with shield and spear, his face grim, cruel and fierce. On his left Chu-Yin, the Cathayan sage and adviser to the Kaan, a venerable old man with white hair, dressed in a simple black robe.

On the main floor, grouped close to the throne, are: on the right, the sons of the Kaan. Farther away, the nobles and warriors of all degrees with their wives behind them. On the left, the wives and concubines of the Kaan, then the courtiers, officers, poets, scholars, etc. – all the non-military officials and hangers-on of government, with their women beside them.

Marco stands, a sample case in each hand, bewildered and dazzled, gawking about him on every side. His father and uncle, bowing, walk to the foot of the throne and kneel before the Kaan. They make frantic signals to Marco to do likewise but he is too dazed to notice. All the people in the room are staring at him. The Kaan is looking at the two brothers with a stern air. An usher of the palace comes quietly to Marco and makes violent gestures to him to kneel down.

MARCO (*misunderstanding him – gratefully*). Thank you, Brother. (*He sits down on one of the sample cases, to the gasping horror of all the Court. The Kaan is still looking frowningly at the two Polos as he listens to the report of their Messenger escort. He does not notice. An outraged Chamberlain rushes over to Marco and motions him to kneel down. Bewilderedly.*) What's the trouble now?

KUBLAI (*dismissing the Messenger, having heard his report – addresses the Polos coldly*). I bid you welcome, Messrs. Polo. But where are the hundred wise men of the West who were to dispute with my wise men of the sacred teachings of Lao-Tseu and Confucius and the Buddha and Christ?

MAFFEO (*hurriedly*). There was no Pope elected until just before –

NICOLO. And he had no wise men, anyway.

(*The Kaan now sees Marco and a puzzled expression of interest comes over his face.*)

KUBLAI. Is he with you?

NICOLO (*hesitantly*). My son, Marco, your Majesty – still young and graceless.

KUBLAI. Come here, Marco Polo.

(*Marco comes forward, trying feebly to assume a bold, confident air.*)

MAFFEO (*in a loud, furious aside*). Kneel, you ass!

(*Marco flounders to his knees.*)

KUBLAI (*with a smile*). I bid you welcome, Master Marco.

MARCO. Thank you, sir – I mean, your Lordship – your – (*Then suddenly.*) Before I forget – the Pope gave me a message for you, sir.

KUBLAI (*smiling*). Are you his hundred wise men?

MARCO (*confidently*). Well – almost. He sent me in their place. He said I'd be worth a million wise men to you.

NICOLO (*hastily*). His Holiness meant that Marco, by leading an upright life – not neglecting the practical side, of course – might set an example that would illustrate, better than wise words, the flesh and blood product of our Christian civilization.

KUBLAI (*with a quiet smile*). I shall study this apotheosis with unwearied interest, I foresee it.

MARCO (*suddenly – with a confidential air*). Wasn't that just a joke, your asking for the wise men? His Holiness thought you must have a sense of humour. Or that you must be an optimist.

KUBLAI (*with a smile of appreciation*). I am afraid your Holy Pope is a most unholy cynic. (*Trying to solve a riddle in his own mind – musingly.*) Could he believe this youth possesses that thing called soul which the West dreams lives after death – and might reveal it to me? (*Suddenly to Marco.*) Have you an immortal soul?

MARCO (*in surprise*). Of course! Any fool knows that.

KUBLAI (*humbly*). But I am not a fool. Can you prove it to me?

MARCO. Why, if you had no soul, what would happen when you die?

KUBLAI. What, indeed?

MARCO. Why, nothing. You'd be dead – just like an animal.

KUBLAI. Your logic is irrefutable.

MARCO. Well, I'm not an animal, am I? That's certainly plain enough. (*Then proudly.*) No, sir! I'm a man made by Almighty God in His Own Image for His greater glory!

KUBLAI (*staring at him for a long moment with appalled appreciation – ecstatically.*) So you are the Image of God! There is certainly something about you, something complete and unanswerable – but wait – a test!

(*He claps his hands, pointing to Marco. Soldiers with drawn swords leap forward and seize him, trussing up his hands behind his back.*)

MAFFEO (*grovelling*). Mercy! He is only a boy!

NICOLO (*grovelling*). Mercy! He is only a fool!

KUBLAI (*sternly*). Silence! (*To Marco, with inhuman calm.*) Since you possess eternal life, it can do you no harm to cut off your head. (*He makes a sign to a soldier, who flourishes his sword.*)

MARCO (*trying to conceal his fear under a quavering, joking tone*). I might – catch – cold!

KUBLAI. You jest, but your voice trembles. What! Are you afraid to die, immortal youth? Well, then, if you will confess that your soul is a stupid invention of your fear and that when you die you will be dead as a dead dog is dead –

MARCO (*with sudden fury*). You're a heathen liar! (*He glares defiantly. His father and uncle moan with horror.*)

KUBLAI (*laughs and claps his hands. Marco is freed. The Kaan studies his sullen but relieved face with amusement*). Your pardon, Marco! I suspected a flaw, but you are perfect. You cannot imagine your death. You are a born hero. I must keep you near me. You shall tell me about your soul and I will listen as to a hundred wise men from the West! Is it agreed?

MARCO (*hesitatingly*). I know it's a great honour, sir – but, forgetting the soul side of it, I've got to eat.

KUBLAI (*astonished*). To eat?

MARCO. I mean, I'm ambitious. I've got to succeed, and – (*Suddenly blurts out.*) What can you pay me?

KUBLAI. Ha! Well, you will find me a practical man, too. I can start you upon any career you wish. What is your choice?

MAFFEO (*interposing eagerly*). If I might speak to the boy in private a minute – give him my humble advice – he is so young – (*Maffeo and Nicolo hurriedly lead Marco down to the foreground.*) You've made a favourable impression – God knows why – but strike while the iron is hot, you ninny! Ask to be appointed a Second Class government commission-agent.

MARCO (*offended*). No! I'll be first-class or nothing!

MAFFEO. Don't be a fool! A First Class agent is all brass buttons and no opportunities. A Second Class travels around, is allowed his expenses, gets friendly with all the dealers, scares them into letting him in on everything – and gets what's rightfully coming to him! (*Then with a crafty look and a nudge in the ribs.*) And, being always in the secret, you'll be able to whisper to us in time to take advantage –

MARCO (*a bit flustered – with bluff assertion*). I don't know. The Kaan's been square with me. After all, honesty's the best policy, isn't it?

MAFFEO (*looking him over scathingly*). You'd think I was advising you to steal – I, Maffeo Polo, whose conservatism is unquestioned!

MARCO (*awed*). I didn't mean –

MAFFEO (*solemnly*). Do you imagine the Kaan is such a Nero as to expect you to live on your salary?

MARCO (*uncertainly*). No, I suppose not. (*He suddenly looks at Maffeo with a crafty wink.*) When I do give you a tip, what do I get from Polo Brothers?

MAFFEO (*between appreciation and dismay*). Ha! You learn quickly, don't you? (*Then hastily.*) Why, we – we've already thought of that – trust us to look after your best interests – and decided to – to make you a junior partner in the firm – eh, Nick? – Polo Brothers and Son – doesn't that sound solid, eh?

MARCO (*with a sly grin*). It's a great honour – a very great honour. (*Then meaningly.*) But as neither of you are Neros, naturally you'll also offer me –

MAFFEO (*grinning in spite of himself*). Hmm! Hmm! You Judas!

MARCO. A fair commission –

NICOLO (*blustering – but his eyes beaming with paternal pride*). You young scamp!

MAFFEO (*laughing*). Ha-ha! Good boy, Mark! Polos will be Polos!

(*They all embrace laughingly. Kublai, who has been observing them intently, turns to Chu-Yin and they both smile.*)

KUBLAI. Did their Pope mean that a fool is a wiser study for a ruler of fools than a hundred wise men could be? This Marco touches me, as a child might, but at the same time there is something warped, deformed – Tell me, what shall I do with him?

CHU-YIN. Let him develop according to his own

inclination and give him also every opportunity for true growth if he so desires. And let us observe him. At least, if he cannot learn, we shall.

KUBLAI (*smilingly*). Yes. And be amused. (*He calls commandingly.*) Marco Polo! (*Marco turns rather frightened and comes to the throne and kneels.*) Have you decided?

MARCO (*promptly*). I'd like to be appointed a commission-agent of the Second Class.

KUBLAI (*somewhat taken aback, puzzled*). You are modest enough!

MARCO (*manfully*). I want to start at the bottom!

KUBLAI (*with mocking grandeur*). Arise then, Second Class Marco! You will receive your agent's commission at once. (*Then with a twinkle in his eye.*) But each time you return from a journey you must relate to me all the observations and comments of your soul on the East. Be warned and never fail me in this!

MARCO (*confused but cocksurely*). I won't. I'll take copious notes. (*Then meaningly.*) And I can memorize any little humorous incidents –

MAFFEO (*apprehensively*). Blessed Saviour! (*He gives a violent fit of coughing.*)

MARCO (*looks around at him questioningly*). Hum? (*Misinterpreting his signal.*) And may I announce to your Majesty that a signal honour has just been conferred on me? My father and uncle have taken me into the firm. It will be Polo Brothers and Son from now on, and any way we can serve your Majesty –

KUBLAI (*a light coming over his face*). Aha! I begin to smell all the rats in Cathay! (*The two elder Polos are bowed to the ground, trembling with apprehension. Kublai laughs quietly.*) Well, I am sure you wish to celebrate this family triumph together, so you may go. And accept my congratulations, Marco!

MARCO. Thank you, your Majesty. You will never regret it. I will always serve your best interests, so help me God!

(*He goes grandly, preceded hurriedly by the trembling Nicolo and Maffeo. Kublai laughs and turns to Chu-Yin, who is smiling.*)

CURTAIN

ACT TWO SCENE ONE

SCENE. *The Little Throne Room in the bamboo summer palace of the Kaan at Xanadu, the City of Peace – smaller, more intimate than the one at Cambaluc, but possessing an atmosphere of aloof dignity and simplicity fitting to the philosopher ruler who retreats here to contemplate in peace the vanity of his authority.*

About fifteen years have elapsed. It is a beautiful sunlit morning in late June. The Kaan reclines comfortably on his cushioned bamboo throne. His face has aged greatly. The expression has grown mask-like, full of philosophic calm. He has the detached air of an idol. Kukachin, a beautiful young girl of twenty, pale and delicate, is sitting at his feet. Her air is grief-stricken. A flute player in the garden is playing a melancholy air. Kukachin recites in a low tone:

KUKACHIN. My thoughts in this autumn are lonely and sad,
A chill wind from the mountain blows in the garden.
The sky is grey, a snowflake falls, the last chrysanthemum
Withers beside the deserted summer-house.
I walk along the path in which weeds have grown.
My heart is bitter and tears blur my eyes.
I grieve for the days when we lingered together
In this same garden, along these paths between flowers.
In the spring we sang of love and laughed with youth
But now we are parted by many leagues and years
And I weep that never again shall I see your face.

(*She finishes and relapses into her attitude of broken resignation. The flute player ceases his playing. Kublai looks down at her tenderly.*)

KUBLAI (*musingly*). Sing while you can. When the voice fails, listen to song. When the heart fails, be sung asleep. (*Chidingly.*) That is a sad poem, Little Flower. Are you sad because you must soon become Queen of Persia? But Arghun is a great hero, a Khan of the blood of Chinghiz. You will be blessed with strong sons able to dare the proud destiny of our blood.

KUKACHIN (*dully*). Your will is my law.

KUBLAI. Not my will. The will of life to continue the strong. (*Forcing a consoling tone.*) Come, Little Flower. You have been fading here. See how pale you have grown! Your eyes are listless! Your lips droop even in smiling! But life at the Court of Persia is gay. There will be feasts, celebrations, diverting pleasures. You will be their Queen of Beauty.

KUKACHIN (*with a sigh*). A Queen may be only a woman who is unhappy.

KUBLAI (*teasingly*). What despair! You talk like the ladies in poems who have lost their lovers! (*Kukachin gives a violent start which he does not notice and a spasm of pain comes over her face.*) But, never mind, Arghun of Persia is a hero no woman could fail to love.

KUKACHIN (*starting to her feet – desperately*). No! I can bear his children, but you cannot force me to – (*She breaks down, weeping.*)

KUBLAI (*astonished – gazing at her searchingly*). Have I ever forced you to anything? (*Then resuming his tone of tender teasing.*) I would say, rather, that ever since you were old enough to talk, the Ruler of Earth, as they innocently call your grandfather, has been little better than your slave.

KUKACHIN (*taking his hand and kissing it*). Forgive me. (*Then smiling at him.*) Have I been so bad as that? Has my love for you, who have been both father and mother to me, brought you no happiness?

KUBLAI (*with deep emotion*). You have been a golden bird singing beside a black river. You took your mother's place in my heart when she died. I was younger then. The river was not so black – the river of man's life so deep and silent – flowing with an insane obsession – whither? – and why? (*Then suddenly forcing a smile.*) Your poem has made me melancholy. And I am too old, if not too wise, to afford anything but optimism! (*Then sadly.*) But now you in your turn must leave me, the river seems black indeed! (*Then after a pause – tenderly.*) If it will make you unhappy, you need not marry Arghun Khan.

KUKACHIN (*recovering herself – resolutely*). No. Your refusal would insult him. It might mean war. (*Resignedly.*) And Arghun is as acceptable as any other. Forgive my weakness. You once told me a Princess must never weep. (*She forces a smile.*) It makes no difference whether I stay or go, except that I shall be homesick for you. (*She kisses his hand again.*)

KUBLAI (*gratefully*). My little one. (*He strokes her hair. After a pause during which he looks at her thoughtfully – tenderly.*) We have never had secrets from each other, you and I. Tell me, can you have fallen in love?

KUKACHIN (*after a pause – tremblingly*). You must not ask that – if you respect my pride! (*With a pitiful smile.*) You see – he does not even know –

(*She is blushing and hanging her head with confusion. Chu-Yin enters hurriedly from the right. He is very old but still upright. He is a bit breathless from haste, but his face is wreathed in smiles.*)

CHU-YIN (*making an obeisance*). Your Majesty, do you hear that martial music? His Honour, Marco Polo, Mayor of Yang-Chau, seems about to visit you in state! (*The strains of a distant band can be heard.*)

KUBLAI (*still looking at Kukachin, who has started violently at the mention of Marco's name – worriedly*). Impossible! In love? . . . (*Then to Chu-Yin – preoccupiedly.*) Eh? Marco? I have given no order for him to return.

CHU-YIN (*ironically*). No doubt he comes to refresh your humour with new copious notes on his exploits. Our Marco has made an active mayor. Yang-Chau, according to the petition for mercy you have received from its inhabitants, is the most governed of all your cities. I talked recently with a poet who had fled from there in horror. Yang-Chau used to have a soul, he said. Now it has a brand new Court House. And another, a man of wide culture, told me, our Christian mayor is exterminating our pleasures and our rats as if they were twin breeds of vermin!

KUBLAI (*irritably*). He is beginning to weary me with his grotesque antics. A jester inspires mirth only so long as his deformity does not revolt one.

Marco's spiritual hump begins to disgust me. He has not even a mortal soul, he has only an acquisitive instinct. We have given him every opportunity to learn. He has memorized everything and learned nothing. He has looked at everything and seen nothing. He has lusted for everything and loved nothing. He is only a shrewd and crafty greed. I shall send him home to his native wallow.

CHU-YIN (*in mock alarm*). What? Must we lose our clown?

KUKACHIN (*who has been listening with growing indignation*). How dare you call him a clown? Just because he is not a dull philosopher you think –

KUBLAI (*astounded – admonishingly*). Princess!

KUKACHIN (*turns to him – on the verge of tears – rebelliously*). Why are you both so unjust? Has he not done well everything he was ever appointed to do? Has he not always succeeded where others failed? Has he not by his will-power and determination risen to the highest rank in your service? (*Then, her anger dying – faltering.*) He is strange, perhaps, to people who do not understand him, but that is because he is so different from other men, so much stronger! And he has a soul! I know he has!

KUBLAI (*whose eyes have been searching her face – aghast*). Kukachin! (*She sees he has guessed her secret and at first she quails and shrinks away, then stiffens regally and returns his gaze unflinchingly. Chu-Yin looks from one to the other comprehendingly. Finally Kublai addresses her sternly.*) So, because I have allowed this fool a jester's latitude, because I permitted him to amuse you when you were a little girl, and since then, on his returns, to speak with you – a Princess! – (*Then brusquely.*) I shall inform the ambassadors you will be ready to sail for Persia within ten days. You may retire.

(*She bows with a proud humility and walks off* L. *Kublai sits in a sombre study, frowning and biting his lips. The blaring of Marco's band grows steadily nearer.*)

CHU-YIN (*gently*). Is intolerance wisdom? (*A pause. Then he goes on.*) I have suspected her love for him for a long time.

KUBLAI. Why didn't you warn me?

CHU-YIN. Love is to wisdom what wisdom seems to love – a folly. I reasoned, love comes like the breath of wind on water and is gone, leaving calm and reflection. I reasoned, but this is an enchanted moment for her and it will remain a poignant memory to recompense her when she is no longer a girl but merely a Queen. And I reasoned, who knows but some day this Marco may see into her eyes and his soul may be born, and that will make a very interesting study – for Kukachin, and her grandfather, the Son of Heaven and Ruler of the World! (*He bows mockingly.*) And for the old fool who is I!

KUBLAI (*bewilderedly*). I cannot believe it! Why, since she was a little girl, she has only talked to him once or twice every two years or so!

CHU-YIN. That was unwise, for thus he has remained a strange, mysterious dream-knight from the exotic West, an enigma with something about him of a likable boy who brought her home each time a humble, foolish, touching little gift! And also remember that on each occasion he returned in triumph, having accomplished a task – a victor, more or less, acting the hero. (*The band has crashed and dinned its way into the courtyard.*) As now! Listen! (*He goes to the window and looks down – with ironical but intense amusement.*) Ah! He wears, over his Mayor's uniform, the regalia of Cock of Paradise in his secret fraternal order of the Mystic Knights of Confucius! The band of the Xanadu lodge is with him as well as his own! He is riding on a very fat white horse. He dismounts, aided by the steps of your Imperial Palace! He slaps a policeman on the back and asks his name! He chucks a baby under the chin and asks the mother its name. She lies and says 'Marco' although the baby is a girl. He smiles. He is talking loudly so that everyone can overhear. He gives the baby one yen to start a savings account and encourage its thrift. The mother looks savagely disappointed. The crowd cheers. He keeps his smile frozen as he notices an artist sketching him. He shakes hands with a one-legged veteran of the Manzi campaign and asks his name. The veteran is touched. Tears come to his eyes. He tells him – but the Polo forgets his name even as he turns to address the crowd. He waves one hand for silence. The band stops. It is the hand on which he wears five large jade rings. The other hand rests upon – and pats – the head of a bronze dragon, our ancient symbol of Yang, the celestial, male principle of the Cosmos. He clears his throat, the crowd stands petrified, he is about to draw a deep breath and open his mouth carefully in position one of the five phonetic exercises – (*Here Chu-Yin chuckles*). But I am an old man full of malice and venom and it embitters me to see others unreasonably happy, so – (*Here, just as Marco is heard starting to speak, he throws open the window and calls in a loud, commanding tone.*) Messer Polo, His Imperial Majesty commands that you stop talking, dismiss your followers, and repair to his presence at once!

MARCO'S VOICE (*very faint and crestfallen*). Oh – all right – I'll be right there.

KUBLAI (*cannot control a laugh in spite of himself – helplessly*). How can one deal seriously with such a child-actor?

CHU-YIN (*coming back from the window – ironically.*) Most women, including Kukachin, love children – and all women must take acting seriously in order to love at all.

(*Just as he finishes speaking, Kukachin enters from* L. *She is terribly alarmed. She throws herself at Kublai's feet.*)

KUKACHIN. Why did you summon him? I told you he does not know. It is all my fault! Punish me, if you will! But promise me you will not harm him!

KUBLAI (*looking down at her – sadly*). Is it my custom to take vengeance? (*Then as people are heard approaching – quickly.*) Compose yourself! Remember again, Princesses may not weep! (*She springs to her feet, turns away for a moment, then turns back, her face rigidly calm and emotionless. Kublai nods with appreciation of her control.*) Good. You will make a Queen. (*She bows and retires backward to the left side of the throne. At the same moment, Nicolo and Maffeo Polo enter ceremoniously from* R. *They wear the regalia of officers in the Mystic Knights of Confucius over their rich merchants' robes.* (*This costume is a queer jumble of stunning effects that recall the parade uniforms of our modern Knights Templar, of Columbus, of Pythias, Mystic Shriners, the Klan, etc.*) *They are absurdly conscious and proud of this get-up – like two old men in a children's play. Kublai and Chu-Yin regard them with amused astonishment. Even Kukachin cannot restrain a smile. They prostrate themselves at the foot of the throne. Then just at the right moment, preceded by a conscious cough, Marco Polo makes his entrance. Over his gorgeous uniform of Mayor, he wears his childishly fantastic regalia as chief of the Mystic Knights of Confucius. As he steps on, he takes off his gilded, laced hat with its Bird of Paradise plumes and bows with a mechanical dignity on all sides. He has the manner and appearance of a successful movie star at a masquerade ball, disguised so that no one can fail to recognize him. His regular, good-looking, well-groomed face is carefully arranged into the grave responsible expression of a Senator from the South of the United States of America about to propose an amendment to the Constitution restricting the migration of non-Nordic birds into Texas, or prohibiting the practice of the laws of biology within the twelve-mile limit. He moves in stately fashion to the throne and prostrates himself before the Kaan. Kukachin stares at him with boundless admiration, hoping to catch his eye. The Kaan looks from her to him and his face grows stern. Chu-Yin is enjoying himself.*) Rise. (*Marco does so. Kublai continues dryly.*) To what do I owe the honour of this unexpected visit?

MARCO (*hastily, but with full confidence*). Well, I was sending in to your treasury the taxes of Yang-Chau for the fiscal year, and I knew you'd be so astonished at the unprecedented amount I had sweated out of them that you'd want to know how I did it – so here I am. (*An awkward pause. Marco is disconcerted at the Kaan's steady impersonal stare. He glances about – sees the Princess – welcomes this opportunity for diverting attention. Bowing with humble respect.*) Pardon me, Princess. I didn't recognize you before, you've so grown up. (*Flatteringly.*) You look like a Queen.

KUKACHIN (*falteringly*). I bid you welcome, Your Honour.

KUBLAI (*as a warning to Kukachin to control her emotion*). The Princess will soon be Queen of Persia.

MARCO (*flustered and awed, bowing to her again – flatteringly*). Then – Your Majesty – if I may be humbly permitted (*bowing to Kublai*) – to offer my congratulations – and before I settle down to discussing business – if Her Highness – Majesty – will accept a small token of my esteem – (*Here he stamps his foot. An African Slave, dressed in a pink livery with green hat and shoes and stockings and carrying a golden wicker basket, enters. He kneels, presents the basket to Marco, who lifts the cover and pulls out a small Chow puppy with a pink ribbon tied around its neck. He steps forward and offers this to *the Princess, with a boyish grin.*) A contribution to your zoo – from your most humble servant!

KUKACHIN (*taking it – flushing with pleasure*). Oh, what a little darling! (*She cuddles the puppy in her arms.*)

MARCO (*boastfully*). He's a genuine, pedigreed pup. I procured him at great cost – I mean he's extra well-bred.

KUKACHIN. Oh, thank you so much, Marco Polo! (*Stammering.*) I mean, Your Honour.

KUBLAI (*warningly*). His Honour wishes to talk business, Princess.

KUKACHIN (*controlling herself*). I ask pardon. (*She bows and retires to* L.R., *where she stands fondling the puppy and watching Marco.*)

MARCO (*plunging in confidently on what he thinks is a sure point of attack*). My tax scheme, Your Majesty, that got such wonderful results, is simplicity itself. I simply reversed the old system. For one thing, I found they had a high tax on excess profits. Imagine a profit being excess! Why, it isn't humanly possible! I repealed it. And I repealed the tax on luxuries. I found out that the great majority in Yang-Chau couldn't afford luxuries. The tax wasn't democratic enough to make it pay! I crossed it off and I wrote on the statute books a law that taxes every necessity in life, a law that hits every man's pocket equally, be he beggar or banker! And I got results!

CHU-YIN (*gravely*). In beggars?

KUBLAI (*with a chilling air*). I have received a petition from the inhabitants of Yang-Chau enumerating over three thousand cases of your gross abuse of power!

MARCO (*abashed only for a moment*). Oh, so they've sent that vile slander to you, have they? That's the work of a mere handful of radicals –

KUBLAI (*dryly*). Five hundred thousand names are signed to it. (*Still more dryly.*) Half a million citizens accuse you of endeavouring to stamp out their ancient culture!

MARCO. What! Why, I even had a law passed that anyone caught interfering with culture would be subject to a fine! It was Section One of a blanket statute that every citizen must be happy or go to jail. I found it was the unhappy ones who were always making trouble and getting discontented. You see, here's the way I figure it; if a man's good, he's happy – and if he isn't happy, it's a sure sign he's no good to himself or anyone else and he had better be put where he can't do harm.

KUBLAI (*a bit helplessly now*). They complain that you have entirely prohibited all free expression of opinion.

MARCO (*feelingly*). Well, when they go to the extreme of circulating such treasonable opinions against me, isn't it time to protect your sovereignty by strong measures? (*Kublai stares at this effrontery with amazement. Marco watches this impression and hurries on with an injured dignity.*) I can't believe, Your Majesty, that this minority of malcontents can have alienated your long-standing high regard for me!

KUBLAI (*conquered – suddenly overpowered by a great smile*). Not so! You are the marvel of mankind! And I would be lost without you!

MARCO (*flattered but at the same time nonplussed*). I thank you! (*Hesitatingly.*) But, to tell the truth, I want to resign, anyhow. I've done all I could. I've appointed five hundred committees to carry on my work and I retire confident that with the system I've instituted everything will go on automatically and brains are no longer needed. (*He adds as a bitter afterthought.*) And it's lucky they're not, or Yang-Chau would soon be a ruin!

KUBLAI (*with mock seriousness*). In behalf of the population of Yang-Chau I accept your resignation, with deep regret for the loss of your unique and extraordinary services. (*Then suddenly in a strange voice.*) Do you still possess your immortal soul, Marco Polo?

MARCO (*flustered*). Ha-ha! Yes, of course – at least I hope so. But I see the joke. You mean that Yang-Chau used to be a good place to lose one. Well, you wouldn't know the old town now. Sin is practically unseen. (*Hurrying on to another subject – boisterously.*) But however much I may have accomplished there, it's nothing to the big surprise I've got in reserve for you. May I demonstrate? (*Without waiting for permission, takes a piece of printed paper like a dollar bill from his pocket.*) What is it? Paper. Correct! What is it worth? Nothing. That's where you're mistaken. It's worth ten yen. No, I'm not a liar! See ten yen written on it, don't you? Well, I'll tell you the secret. This is money, legally valued at ten yens' worth of anything you wish to buy, by order of His Imperial Majesty, the Great Kaan! Do you see my point? Its advantages over gold and silver coin are obvious. It's light, easy to carry – (*Here he gives a prodigious wink*) wears out quickly, can be made at very slight expense, and yields enormous profit. Think of getting ten yen for this piece of paper. Yet it can be done. If you make the people believe it's worth it, it is! After all, when you stop to think, who was it first told them gold was money? I'll bet anything it was some quick-thinker who'd just discovered a gold mine! (*Kublai and Chu-Yin stare at him in petrified incredulity. He mistakes it for admiration and is flattered. Bows and lays his paper money on the Kaan's knee.*) You're stunned, I can see that. It's so simple – and yet, who ever thought of it before me? I was amazed myself. Think it over, Your Majesty, and let the endless possibilities dawn on you! And now I want to show another little aid to government that I thought out. (*He makes a sign to his uncle and father. The former takes a mechanical contrivance out of a box and sets it up on the floor. It is a working model of a clumsy cannon. Nicolo, meanwhile, takes children's blocks out of his box and builds them into a fortress wall. Marco is talking. His manner and voice have become grave and portentous.*) It all came to me, like an inspiration, last Easter Sunday when Father and Uncle and I were holding a little service. Uncle read a prayer which spoke of Our Lord as the Prince of Peace. Somehow, that took hold of me. I thought to myself, well, it's funny, there always have been wars and there always will be, I suppose, because I've never read much in any history about heroes who waged peace. Still, that's wrong. War is a waste of money which eats into the profits of life like thunder! Then why war, I asked myself? But how are you going to end it? Then the flash came! There's only one workable way, and that's to conquer everybody else in the world so they'll never dare fight you again! An impossible task, you object? Not any more! This invention you see before you makes conquering easy. Let me demonstrate with these models. On our right, you see the fortress wall of a hostile capital. Under your present system with battering rams, to make an effective breach in this wall would cost you the lives of ten thousand men. Valuing each life conservatively at ten yen, this amounts to one hundred thousand yen! This makes the cost of breaching prohibitive. But all of this waste can be saved. How? Just keep your eyes on your right and permit my exclusive invention to solve this problem. (*He addresses the fortress in a matter-of-fact tone.*) So you won't surrender, eh? (*Then in a mock-heroic falsetto, answering himself like a ventriloquist.*) We die but we never surrender! (*Then matter-of-factly.*) Well, Brother, those heroic sentiments do you a lot of credit, but this is war and not a tragedy. You're up against new methods this time, and you'd better give in and avoid wasteful bloodshed. (*Answering himself.*) No! Victory or Death! (*Then again.*) All right, Brother, don't blame me. Fire! (*His uncle fires the gun. There is a bang, and a leaden ball is shot out which knocks a big breach in the wall of blocks. Marco beams. Kukachin gives a scream of fright, then a gasp of delight, and claps her hands. Marco bows to her the more gratefully as Kublai and Chu-Yin are staring at him with a queer appalled wonder that puzzles him although he cannot imagine it is not admiration.*) I see you are stunned again. What made it do that, you're wondering? This! (*He takes a little package out of his pocket and pours some black powder out of it on his palm.*) It's the same powder they've been using here in children's fireworks. They've had it under their noses for years without a single soul ever having creative imagination enough to visualize the enormous possibilities. But you can bet I did! It was a lad crying with a finger half blown off where he held a fire-cracker too long that first opened my eyes. I learned the formula, improved on it, experimented in secret, and here's the gratifying result! (*He takes the cannon ball from his father who has retrieved it.*) You see? Now just picture this little ball magnified into one weighing twenty pounds or so and then you'll really grasp my idea. The destruction of property and loss of life would be tremendous! No one could resist you!

KUBLAI (*after a pause – musingly*). I am interested in the hero of that city who preferred death to defeat. Did you conquer his immortal soul?

MARCO (*with frankness*). Well, you can't consider souls when you're dealing with soldiers, can you? (*He takes his model and places it on the Kaan's knee with the paper money.*) When you have time, I wish you'd look this over. In fact – and this is the big idea I've been saving for the last – consider these two inventions of mine in combination. You conquer the world with this – (*He pats the cannon-model*) and you pay for it with this. (*He pats *the paper money – rhetorically.)* You become the bringer of peace on earth and good-will to men, and it doesn't cost you a yen hardly. Your initial expense – my price – is as low as I can possibly make it out of my deep affection for your Majesty – only a million yen.

KUBLAI *(quickly)*. In paper?

MARCO *(with a grin and a wink)*. No. I'd prefer gold, if you don't mind. *(Silence. Marco goes on meaningly.)* Of course, I don't want to force them on you. I'm confident there's a ready market for them elsewhere.

KUBLAI *(grimly smiling)*. Oh, I quite realize that in self-protection I've got to buy them – or kill you!

MARCO *(briskly)*. Then it's a bargain? But I've still got one proviso – that you give us permission to go home. *(Kukachin gives a little gasp. Marco goes on feelingly.)* We're homesick, Your Majesty. We've served you faithfully, and frankly now that we've made our fortune we want to go home and enjoy it. There's no place like home, Your Majesty! I'm sure even a King in his palace appreciates that.

KUBLAI *(with smiling mockery)*. But – who can play your part? And your mission – your example! What will your Pope say when you tell him I'm still unconverted?

MARCO *(confidently)*. Oh, you will be – on your death-bed, if not before – a man of your common sense.

KUBLAI *(ironically)*. Courtier! *(Then solemnly.)* But my last objection is insurmountable. You haven't yet proved you have an immortal soul!

MARCO. It doesn't need proving.

KUBLAI. If you could only bring forward one reliable witness.

MARCO. My Father and Uncle can swear –

KUBLAI. They think it is a family trait. Their evidence is prejudiced.

MARCO *(worried now – looks at Chu-Yin hopefully)*. Mr. Chu-Yin ought to be wise enough to acknowledge –

CHU-YIN *(smiling)*. But I believe that what can be proven cannot be true.

(Marco stands puzzled, irritated, looking stubborn, frightened and foolish. His eyes wander about the room, finally resting appealingly on Kukachin.)

KUKACHIN *(suddenly steps forward – flushed but proudly)*. I will bear witness he has a soul.

(Kublai looks at her with a sad wonderment, Chu-Yin smilingly, Marco with gratitude, Nicolo and Maffeo exchange a glance of congratulation.)

KUBLAI. How can you know, Princess?

KUKACHIN. Because I have seen it – once, when he bound up my dog's leg, once when he played with a slave's baby, once when he listened to music over water and I heard him sigh, once when he looked at sunrise, another time at sunset, another at the stars, another at the moon, and each time he said that Nature was wonderful. And all the while, whenever he has been with me I have always felt – something strange and different – and that something must be His Honour's soul, must it not?

KUBLAI *(with wondering bitterness)*. The eye sees only its own sight.

CHU-YIN. But a woman may feel life in the unborn.

KUBLAI *(mockingly but sadly)*. I cannot contest the profound intuitions of virgins and mystics. Go home, Your Honour, Immortal Marco, and live for ever! *(With forced gaiety.)* And tell your Pope your example has done much to convert me to wisdom – if I could find the true one!

KUKACHIN *(boldly now)*. And may I humbly request, since His Honour, and his father and uncle, are experienced masters of navigation, that they be appointed, for my greater safety, to attend me and command the fleet on my voyage to Persia?

KUBLAI *(astonished at her boldness – rebukingly)*. Princess!

KUKACHIN *(returning his look – simply)*. It is the last favour I shall ever ask. I wish to be converted to wisdom, too – one or another – before I become a name.

KUBLAI *(bitterly)*. I cannot deny your last request, even though you wish your own unhappiness. *(To the Polos.)* You will accompany the Princess.

MARCO *(jubilantly)*. I'll be only too glad! *(Turn-*

ing to the Princess.) It'll be a great pleasure! (*Then briskly.*) And have we your permission to trade in the ports along the way?

KUKACHIN (*to Marco – embarrassed*). As you please, Your Honour.

MARCO (*bowing low*). I'll promise it won't disturb you. It's really a scheme to while away the hours, for I warn you in advance this is liable to be a mighty long trip.

KUKACHIN (*impulsively*). I do not care how long – (*She stops in confusion.*)

MARCO. Now if I had the kind of ships we build in Venice to work with I could promise you a record passage, but with your tubby junks it's just as well to expect the worst and you'll never be disappointed. (*Familiarly.*) And the trouble with any ship, for a man of action, is that there's so little you can do. I hate idleness where there's nothing to occupy your mind but thinking. I've been so used to being out, overcoming obstacles, getting things done, creating results where there weren't any before, going after the impossible – well – (*Here he gives a little deprecating laugh*) all play and no work makes Jack a dull boy. I'm sure I'd make a pretty dull person to have around if there wasn't plenty to do. You might not believe it, but when I'm idle I actually get gloomy sometimes!

KUKACHIN (*eagerly*). But we shall have dancers on the ship and actors who will entertain us with plays –

MARCO (*heartily*). That'll be grand. There's nothing better than to sit down in a good seat at a good play after a good day's work in which you know you've accomplished something, and after you've had a good dinner, and just take it easy and enjoy a good wholesome thrill or a good laugh and get your mind off serious things until it's time to go to bed.

KUKACHIN (*vaguely*). Yes. (*Then, eager to have him pleased.*) And there will be poets to recite their poems –

MARCO (*not exactly overjoyed*). That'll be nice. (*Then very confidentially – in a humorous whisper.*) I'll tell you a good joke on me, Your Highness. I once wrote a poem myself; would you ever believe it, to look at me?

KUKACHIN (*smiling at him as at a boy – teasingly*), No?

MARCO (*smiling back like a boy*). Yes, I did too, when I was young and foolish. It wasn't bad stuff either, considering I'd had no practice. (*Frowning with concentration.*) Wait! Let me see if I can remember any – oh, yes – 'You are lovely as the gold in the sun.' (*He hesitates.*)

KUKACHIN (*thrilled*). That is beautiful!

MARCO. That's only the first line. (*Then jokingly.*) You can consider yourself lucky. I don't remember the rest.

KUKACHIN (*dropping her eyes – softly*). Perhaps on the voyage you may be inspired to write another.

KUBLAI (*who has been staring at them with weary amazement*). Life is so stupid, it is mysterious!

DARKNESS

ACT TWO SCENE TWO

SCENE: *The wharves of the Imperial Fleet at the seaport of Zayton – several weeks later. At the left, stern to, is an enormous junk, the flagship. The wharf extends out, rear, to the right of her. At the right is a warehouse, from a door in which a line of half-naked slaves, their necks, waists, and right ankles linked up by chains, form an endless chain which revolves mechanically, as it were, on sprocket wheels in the interiors of the shed and the junk. As each individual link passes out of the shed it carries a bale on its head, moved with mechanical precision across the wharf, disappears into the junk, and reappears a moment later, having dumped its load, and moves back into the shed. The whole process is a man-power original of the modern devices with bucket scoops that dredge, load coal, sand, etc. By the side of the shed, a foreman sits with a drum and gong with which he marks a perfect time for the slaves, a four-beat rhythm, three beats of the drum, the fourth a bang on the gong as one slave at each end loads and unloads. The effect is like the noise of a machine.*

A bamboo stair leads up to the high poop of the junk from front, left. It is just getting dawn. A forest of masts, spars, sails of woven bamboo laths, shuts out all view of the harbour at the end of the wharf. At the foot of the stairs, Chu-Yin stands like a sentinel. Above on top of the poop, the figures of Kublai and Kukachin are outlined against the lightening sky.

KUBLAI (*brokenly*). I must go. (*He takes her in his arms.*) We have said all we can say. Little Daughter, all rare things are secrets which cannot be revealed to anyone. That is why life must be so lonely. But I love you more dearly than anything on earth. And I know you love me. So perhaps we do not need to understand. (*Rebelliously.*) Yet I wish some Power could give me assurance that in granting your desire I am acting for your happiness, and for your eventual deliverance from sorrow to acceptance and peace. (*He notices she is weeping – in self-reproach.*) Old fool! I have made you weep again! I am death advising life how to live! Be deaf to me! Strive after what your heart desires! Who can ever know which are the mistakes we make? One should be either sad or joyful. Contentment is a warm sty for the eaters and sleepers! (*Impulsively.*) Do not weep! Even now I can refuse your hand to Arghun. Let it mean war!

KUKACHIN (*looking up and controlling herself – with a sad finality*). You do not understand. I wish to take this voyage.

KUBLAI (*desperately*). But I could keep Polo here. (*With impotent anger.*) He shall pray for his soul on his knees before you!

KUKACHIN (*with calm sadness*). Do I want a slave? (*Dreamily.*) I desire a captain of my ship on a long voyage in dangerous, enchanted seas.

KUBLAI (*with a fierce defiance of fate*). I am the Great Kaan! I shall have him killed! (*A pause.*)

CHU-YIN (*from below, recites in a calm, soothing tone*). The noble man ignores self. The wise man ignores action. His truth acts without deeds. His knowledge venerates the unknowable. To him birth is not the beginning nor is death the end. (*Kublai's head bends in submission. Chu-Yin continues tenderly.*) I feel there are tears in your eyes. The Great Kaan, Ruler of the World, may not weep.

KUBLAI (*brokenly*). Ruler? I am my slave! (*Then controlling himself – forcing an amused teasing tone.*) Marco will soon be here, wearing the self-assurance of an immortal soul and his new admiral's uniform! I must fly in retreat from what I can neither laugh away nor kill. Write when you reach Persia. Tell me – all you can tell – particularly what his immortal soul is like! (*Then tenderly.*) Farewell, Little Flower! Live. There is no other advice possible from one human being to another.

KUKACHIN. Live – and love!

KUBLAI (*trying to renew his joking tone*). One's ancestors, particularly one's grandfather. Do not forget me!

KUKACHIN. Never! (*They embrace.*)

KUBLAI (*chokingly*). Farewell. (*He hurries down the ladder – to Chu-Yin.*) You remain – see him – bring me word – (*He turns his head up to Kukachin.*) For the last time, farewell, Little Flower of my life! May you know happiness! (*He turns quickly and goes.*)

KUKACHIN. Farewell! (*She bows her head on the rail and weeps.*)

CHU-YIN (*after a pause*). You are tired, Princess. Your eyes are red from weeping and your nose is red. You look old – a little homely, even. The Admiral Polo will not recognize you. (*Kukachin dries her eyes hastily.*)

KUKACHIN (*half-smiling and half-weeping at his teasing*). I think you are a very horrid old man!

CHU-YIN. A little sleep, Princess, and you will be beautiful. The old dream passes. Sleep and awake in the new. Life is perhaps most wisely regarded as a bad dream between two awakenings, and every day is a life in miniature.

KUKACHIN (*wearily and drowsily*). Your wisdom makes me sleep. (*Her head sinks back on her arms and she is soon asleep.*)

CHU-YIN (*after a pause – softly*). Kukachin! (*He sees she is asleep – chuckles.*) I have won a convert. (*Then speculatively.*) Youth needs so much sleep and old age so little. Is that not a proof that from birth to death one grows steadily closer to complete life? Hum.

(*He ponders on this. From the distance comes the sound of Polo's band playing the same martial air as in the previous scene. Chu-Yin starts – then smiles. The music quickly grows louder. The Princess awakes with a start.*)

KUKACHIN (*startled*). Chu-Yin! Is that the Admiral coming?

CHU-YIN (*dryly*). I suspect so. It is like him not to neglect a person in the city when saying goodbye.

KUKACHIN (*flurriedly*). I must go to my cabin for a moment. (*She hurries back.*)

CHU-YIN (*listens with a pleased, ironical smile as the band gets rapidly nearer. Finally it seems to turn a corner near by, and a moment later, to a deafening clangour, Marco enters, dressed in a gorgeous Admiral's uniform. Two paces behind, side by side, walk Maffeo and Nicolo, dressed only a trifle less gorgeously as Commodores. Behind them comes the band. Marco halts as he sees Chu-Yin, salutes condescendingly, and signals the band to be silent. Chu-Yin bows gravely and remarks as if answering an argument in his own mind*). Still, even though they cannot be housebroken, I prefer monkeys because they are so much less noisy.

MARCO (*with a condescending grin*). What's that – more philosophy? (*Clapping him on the back.*) Well, I like your determination. (*He wipes his brow with a handkerchief.*) Phew! I'll certainly be glad to get back home where I can hear some music that I can keep step to. My feet just won't give in to your tunes. (*With a grin.*) And look at the Old Man and Uncle. They're knock-kneed for life. (*Confidentially.*) Still, I thought the band was a good idea – to sort of cheer up the Princess, and let people know she's leaving at the same time. (*As people begin to come in and stare at the poop of the ship.*) See the crowd gather? I got them out of bed, too!

CHU-YIN (*ironically*). You also woke up the Princess. You sail at sunrise?

MARCO (*briskly – taking operations in hand*). Thank you for reminding me. I've got to hurry. (*To his Father and Uncle.*) You two better get aboard your ships and be ready to cast off when I signal. (*They go off. He suddenly bawls to some one in the ship.*) Much more cargo to load?

A VOICE. Less than a hundred bales, sir.

MARCO. Good. Call all hands on deck and stand by to put sail on her.

A VOICE. Aye-aye, sir.

MARCO. And look lively, damn your lazy souls! (*To Chu-Yin – complacently.*) You've got to impose rigid discipline on shipboard.

CHU-YIN (*inquisitively*). I suppose you feel your heavy responsibility as escort to the future Queen of Persia?

MARCO (*soberly*). Yes, I do. I'll confess I do. If she were a million yens' worth of silk or spices I wouldn't worry an instant, but a Queen, that's a different matter. However, when you give my last word to His Majesty, you can tell him that I've always done my duty by him and I won't fail him this time. As long as I've a breath in me, I'll take care of her!

CHU-YIN (*with genuine appreciation*). That is bravely spoken.

MARCO. I don't know anything about brave speaking. I'm by nature a silent man, and I let my actions do the talking. But, as I've proved to you people in Cathay time and again, when I say I'll do a thing, I do it!

CHU-YIN (*suddenly with a sly smile to himself*). I was forgetting. His Majesty gave me some secret last instructions for you. You are, at some time every day of the voyage, to look carefully and deeply into the Princess's eyes and note what you see there.

MARCO. What for? (*Then brightly.*) Oh, he's afraid she'll get fever in the tropics. Well, you tell him I'll see to it she keeps in good condition. I'll do what's right by her without considering fear or favour. (*Then practically.*) Then, of course, if her husband thinks at the end of the voyage that my work deserves a bonus – why, that's up to him. (*Inquisitively.*) She's never seen him, has she?

CHU-YIN. No.

MARCO (*with an air of an independent thinker*). Well, I believe in love matches myself, even for Kings and Queens. (*With a grin.*) Come to think of it, I'll be getting married to Donata myself when I get home.

CHU-YIN. Donata?

MARCO (*proudly*). The best little girl in the world! She's there waiting for me.

CHU-YIN. You have heard from her?

MARCO. I don't need to hear. I can trust her. And I've been true to her, too. I haven't ever thought of loving anyone else. Of course, I don't mean I've been any he-virgin. I've played with concubines at odd moments when my mind needed relaxation – but that's only human nature. (*His eyes glistening reminiscently.*) Some of them were beauties, too! (*With a sigh.*) Well, I've had my fun and I suppose it's about time I settled down.

CHU-YIN. Poor Princess!

MARCO. What's that? Oh, I see, yes, I sympathize with her, too – going into a harem. If there's one thing more than another that proves you in the East aren't responsible, it's that harem notion. (*With a grin.*) Now in the West we've learned by experience that one at a time is trouble enough.

CHU-YIN (*dryly*). Be sure and converse on love and marriage often with the Princess. I am certain you will cure her.

MARCO (*mystified*). Cure her?

CHU-YIN. Cure her mind of any unreasonable imaginings.

MARCO (*easily*). Oh, I'll guarantee she'll be contented, if that's what you mean. (*The human chain in back finishes its labours and disappears into the shed. The crowd of people has been steadily augmented by new arrivals, until a small multitude is gathered standing in silence staring up at the poop. Marco says with satisfaction.*) Well, cargo's all aboard, before schedule, too. We killed six slaves but, by God, we did it! And look at the crowd we've drawn, thanks to my band!

CHU-YIN (*disgustedly*). They would have come without noise. They love their Princess.

MARCO (*cynically*). Maybe, but they love their sleep, too. I know 'em!

(*A cry of adoration goes up from the crowd. With one movement they prostrate themselves as the Princess comes from the cabin dressed in a robe of silver and stands at the rail looking down.*)

THE CROWD (*in a long, ululating whisper*). Farewell – farewell – farewell – farewell!

KUKACHIN (*silences them with a motion of her hand*). I shall know the long sorrow of an exile
As I sail over the green water and the blue water
Alone under a strange sky amid alien flowers and faces.
My eyes shall be ever red with weeping, my heart bleeding,
While I long for the land of my birth and my childhood
Remembering with love the love of my people.
(*A sound of low weeping comes from the crowd.*) Farewell!

THE CROWD. Farewell – farewell – farewell – farewell!

MARCO (*feeling foolish because he is moved*). Damn it! Reciting always makes me want to cry about something. Poetry acts worse on me than wine that way. (*He calls up – very respectfully.*) Princess! We'll be sailing at once. Would you mind retiring to your cabin? I'm afraid you're going to catch cold standing bareheaded in the night air.

KUKACHIN (*tremulously – grateful for his solicitude*). I am in your charge, Admiral. I am grateful that you should think of my health, and I obey.

(*She turns and goes back into her cabin. The crowd silently filters away, leaving only the band.*)

MARCO (*proudly and fussily*). You can't have women around when you're trying to get something done. I can see where I'll have to be telling her what to do every second. Well, I hope she'll take it in good part and not forget I'm acting in her husband's interests, not my own. (*Very confidentially.*) You know, apart from her being a Princess, I've always respected her a lot. She's not haughty and she's – well, human, that's what I mean. I'd do anything I could for her, Princess or not! Yes, sir!

CHU-YIN (*wonderingly*). There may be hope – after all.

MARCO. What's that?

CHU-YIN. Nothing. Enigma!

MARCO. There's always hope! Don't be a damned pessimist! (*Clapping him on the back.*) Enigma, eh? Well, if that isn't like a philosopher – to start in on riddles just at the last moment! (*He ascends half-way up the ladder to the poop, then turns back to Chu-Yin with a chuckle.*) Take a fool's advice and don't think so much or you'll get old before your time! (*More oratorically.*) If you look before you leap, you'll decide to sit down. Keep on going ahead and you can't help being right! You're bound to get somewhere! (*He suddenly breaks into a grin again.*) There! Don't ever say I never gave you good advice! (*He springs swiftly to the top deck and bellows.*) Cast off there amidships! Where the hell are you – asleep? Set that foresail! Hop, you kidney-footed gang of thumb-fingered infidels! (*He turns with a sudden fierceness on the band, who are standing stolidly, awaiting orders.*) Hey you! Didn't I tell you to strike up when I set foot on the deck? What do you think I paid you in advance for – to wave me good-bye? (*The band plunges madly into it. A frenzied cataract of sound results. Chu-Yin covers his ears and moves away, shaking his head, as Marco leans over the rail and bawls after him.*) And tell the Kaan – anything he wants – write me – just Venice – they all know me there – and if they don't, by God, they're going to!

DARKNESS

ACT TWO SCENE THREE

SCENE: *Poop deck of the royal junk of the Princess Kukachin at anchor in the harbour of Hormuz, Persia – a moonlight night some two years later. On a silver throne at* C. *Kukachin is sitting dressed in a gorgeous golden robe of ceremony. Her beauty has grown more intense, her face has undergone a change, it is the face of a woman who has known real sorrow and suffering. In the shadow of the highest deck in rear her women-in-waiting are in a group, sitting on cushions. On the highest deck in rear Sailors lower and furl the sail of the mizzenmast, every movement being carried out in unison with a machine-like rhythm. The bulwarks of the junk are battered and splintered, the sail is frayed and full of jagged holes and patches. In the foreground (the port side of deck) the two elder Polos are squatting. Each has a bag of money before him from which they are carefully counting gold coins and packing stacks of these into a chest that stands between them.*

MARCO (*his voice, hoarse and domineering, comes from the left just before the curtain rises*). Let go that anchor!

(*A meek 'Aye-aye, sir,' is heard replying and then a great splash and a long rattling of chains. The curtain then rises, discovering the scene as above. Marco's voice is again heard, 'Lower that mizzensail! Look lively now!'*)

BOATSWAIN (*with the sailors*). Aye-aye, sir! (*They lower the sail, and begin to tie it up trimly.*)

MAFFEO (*looking up and straightening his cramped back – with a relieved sigh*). Here's Persia! I'll be glad to get on dry land again. Two years on this foreign tub are too much.

NICOLO (*with a grunt, intent on the money*). Keep counting if you want to finish before we go ashore. It's nine hundred thousand now in our money, isn't it?

MAFFEO (*nods – counting again*). This lot will bring it to a million. (*He begins stacking and packing again.*)

BOATSWAIN (*chanting as his men work*).

Great were the waves,
Volcanoes of foam
Ridge after ridge
To the rim of the world!
Great were the waves!

CHORUS OF SAILORS. Great were the waves!

BOATSWAIN. Fierce were the winds!
Demons screamed!
Their claws rended
Sails into rags,
Fierce were the winds!

CHORUS. Fierce were the winds!

BOATSWAIN. Fire was the sun!
Boiled the blood black,
Our veins hummed
Like bronze kettles.
Fire was the sun!

CHORUS. Fire was the sun!

BOATSWAIN. Long was the voyage!
Life drifted becalmed,
A dead whale awash
In the toil of tides.
Long was the voyage!

CHORUS. Long was the voyage!

BOATSWAIN. Many have died!
Sleep in green water.
Wan faces at home
Pray to the sea.
Many have died!

CHORUS. Many have died!

KUKACHIN (*chants the last line after them – sadly*).
Many have died!

(*After a brooding pause she rises and chants in a low voice.*)

If I were asleep in green water,
No pang could be added to my sorrow,
Old grief would be forgotten,
I would know peace.

SAILORS. There is peace deep in the sea
But the surface is sorrow.

WOMEN. Kukachin will be a Queen!
A Queen may not sorrow
Save for her King!

KUKACHIN. When love is not loved it loves death.
When I sank drowning, I loved Death.
When the pirate's knife gleamed, I loved Death.
When fever burned me, I loved Death.
But the man I love saved me.

SAILORS. Death lives in a silent sea,
Grey and cold under cold grey sky,
Where there is neither sun nor wind
Nor joy nor sorrow!

WOMEN. Kukachin will be a wife.
A wife must not sorrow
Save for her man.

KUKACHIN. A hero is merciful to women.
Why could not this man see or feel or know?
Then he would have let me die.

SAILORS. There are harbours at every voyage-end
Where we rest from the sorrows of the sea.

WOMEN. Kukachin will be a mother.
A mother may not sorrow
Save for her son.

(*Kukachin bows her head in resignation. A pause of silence. Marco Polo enters briskly from below on* L. *He is dressed in full uniform, looking spick and span and self-conscious. His face wears an expression of humorous scorn. He bows ceremoniously to the Princess, his attitude a queer mixture of familiarity and an uncertain awe.*)

MARCO. Your Highness – (*Then ingratiatingly*) – or I suppose I'd better say Majesty now that we've reached Persia – I've got queer news for you. A boat just came from the shore with an official notification that your intended husband, Arghun Khan, is dead and I'm to hand you over to his son, Ghazan, to marry. (*He hands her a sealed paper.*) See!

KUKACHIN (*letting the paper slip from her hand without a glance – dully*). What does it matter?

MARCO (*admiringly – as he picks it up*). I must say you take it coolly. Of course, come to think of it, never having seen either, one's as good as another. (*He winds up philosophically.*) And you'll be Queen just the same, that's the main thing.

KUKACHIN (*with bitter irony*). So you think that is happiness? (*Then, as Marco stares at her uncertainly, she turns away and looks out over the sea with a sigh – after a pause.*) There, where I see the lights, is that Hormuz?

MARCO. Yes. And I was forgetting, the messenger said Ghazan Khan would come to take you ashore to-night.

KUKACHIN (*with sudden fear*). So soon? To-night? (*Then rebelliously.*) Is the granddaughter of the Great Kublai no better than a slave? I will not go until it pleases me!

MARCO. Good for you! That's the spirit! (*Then alarmed at his own temerity – hastily.*) But don't be rash! The Khan probably meant whenever you were willing. And don't mind what I just said.

KUKACHIN (*looks at him with a sudden dawning of hope – gently*). Why should you be afraid of what you said?

MARCO (*offended*). I'm not afraid of anything – when it comes to the point!

KUKACHIN. What point?

MARCO (*nonplussed*). Why – well – when I feel some one's trying to steal what's rightfully mine, for instance.

KUKACHIN. And now – here – you do not feel that?

MARCO (*with a forced laugh, thinking she is joking*). Ha! Well – (*Uncertainly.*) That is – I don't catch your meaning – (*Then changing the subject abruptly.*) But here's something I want to ask you. Your grandfather entrusted you to my care. He relied on me to prove equal to the task of bringing you safe and sound to your husband. Now I want to ask you frankly if you yourself won't be the first to acknowledge that in spite of typhoons, shipwrecks, pirates and every other known form of bad luck, I've brought you through in good shape?

KUKACHIN (*with an irony almost hysterical*). More than anyone in the world, I can appreciate your devotion to duty! You have been a prodigy of heroic accomplishment! In the typhoon when a wave swept me from the deck, was it not you who swam to me as I was drowning?

MARCO (*modestly*). It was easy. Venetians make the best swimmers in the world.

KUKACHIN (*even more ironically*). When the pirates attacked us, was it not your brave sword that warded off their curved knives from my breast and struck them dead at my feet?

MARCO. I was out of practice, too. I used to be one of the crack swordsmen of Venice – and they're the world's foremost, as everyone knows.

KUKACHIN (*with a sudden change – softly*). And when the frightful fever wasted me, was it not you who tended me night and day, watching by my bedside like a gentle nurse, even brewing yourself the medicines that brought me back to life?

MARCO (*with sentimental solemnity*). My mother's recipes. Simple home remedies – from the best friend I ever had!

KUKACHIN (*a trifle wildly*). Oh, yes, you have been a model guardian, Admiral Polo!

MARCO (*quickly*). Thank you, Princess. If I have satisfied you – then if I might ask you a favour, that you put in writing all you've just said in your first letter to the Great Kaan, and also tell your husband?

KUKACHIN (*suddenly wildly bitter*). I will assuredly! I will tell them both of your heroic cruelty in saving me from death! (*Intensely.*) Why could you not let me die?

MARCO (*confusedly*). You're joking. You certainly didn't want to die, did you?

KUKACHIN (*slowly and intensely*). Yes!

MARCO (*puzzled and severe*). Hum! You shouldn't talk that way.

KUKACHIN (*longingly*). I would be asleep in green water!

MARCO (*worried – suddenly reaches out and takes her hand*). Here now, young lady! Don't start getting morbid!

KUKACHIN (*with a thrill of love*). Marco!

MARCO. I believe you're feverish. Let me feel your pulse!

KUKACHIN (*violently*). No! (*She draws her hand from his as if she had been stung.*)

MARCO (*worried*). Please don't be unreasonable. There'd be the devil to pay if you should suffer a relapse of that fever after I sweated blood to pull you through once already! Do you feel hot?

KUKACHIN (*wildly*). No! Yes! On fire!

MARCO. Are your feet cold?

KUKACHIN. No! Yes! I don't know!

(*Gravely Marco kneels, removes a slipper, and feels the sole of her foot – then pats her foot playfully.*)

MARCO. No. They're all right. (*He gets up – professionally.*) Any cramps?

KUKACHIN. You fool! No! Yes! My heart feels as if it were bursting!

MARCO. It burns?

KUKACHIN. Like a red ember flaring up for the last time before it chills into grey ash for ever!

MARCO. Then something must have disagreed with you. Will you let me see your tongue?

KUKACHIN (*in a queer hysterical state where she delights in self-humiliation*). Yes! Yes! Anything! I am a Princess of the Imperial blood of Chinghiz and you are a dog! Anything! (*She sticks out her tongue, the tears streaming down her face as he looks at it.*)

MARCO (*shakes his head*). No sign of biliousness. There's nothing seriously wrong. If you would only try to sleep a while –

KUKACHIN. O Celestial God of the Heavens! What have I done that Thou shouldst torture me? (*Then wildly to Marco.*) I wished to sleep in the depths of the sea. Why did you awaken me?

MARCO (*worried again*). Perhaps it's brain fever. Does your head ache?

KUKACHIN. No! Does your immortal soul?

MARCO. Don't blaspheme! You're talking as if you were delirious! (*Then pleadingly.*) For Heaven's sake, try and be calm, Princess! What if your husband, Ghazan Khan, should find you in such a state?

KUKACHIN (*calming herself with difficulty – after a pause, bitterly*). I suppose you are relieved to get me here alive and deliver me – like a cow!

MARCO (*injuredly*). I've only carried out your own grandfather's orders!

KUKACHIN (*forcing a smile*). Won't you miss being my guardian? (*Striving pitifully to arouse his jealousy.*) When you think of Ghazan protecting me and nursing me when I am sick – and – and loving me? Yes! I will compel him to love me, even though I never love him! He shall look into my eyes and see that I am a woman and beautiful!

MARCO. That's a husband's privilege.

KUKACHIN. Or a man's – a man who has a soul! (*Mockingly but intensely.*) And that reminds me, Admiral Polo! You are taking advantage of this being the last day to shirk your duty!

MARCO. Shirk! No one can ever say –!

KUKACHIN. It was my grandfather's special command, given to you by Chu-Yin, you told me, that every day you should look into my eyes.

MARCO (*resignedly*). Well, it isn't too late yet, is it?

(*He moves toward her with a sigh of half-impatience with her whims.*)

KUKACHIN. Wait. This is the one part of your duty in which I shall have to report you incompetent.

MARCO (*hurt*). I've done my best. I never could discover anything out of the way.

KUKACHIN. There must be something he wished you to find. I myself feel there is something, something I cannot understand, something you must interpret for me! And remember this is your last chance! There is nothing in life I would not give – nothing I would not do – even now it is not too late! See my eyes as those of a woman and not a Princess! Look deeply! I will die if you do not see what is there! (*She finishes hysterically and beseechingly.*)

MARCO (*worried – soothingly*). There! There! Certainly, Princess! Of course, I'll look. And will you promise me that afterwards you'll lie down?

KUKACHIN. Look! See! (*She throws her head back, her arms outstretched. He bends over and looks into her eyes. She raises her hands slowly above his head as if she were going to pull it down to hers. Her lips part, her whole being strains out to him. He looks for a moment critically, then he grows tense, his face moves hypnotically toward hers, their lips seem about to meet in a kiss. She murmurs.*) Marco!

MARCO (*his voice thrilling for this second with oblivious passion.*) Kukachin!

MAFFEO (*suddenly slapping a stack of coins into the chest with a resounding clank*). One million!

MARCO (*with a start, comes to himself and backs away from the Princess in terror*). What, Uncle? Did you call?

MAFFEO. One million in God's money! (*He and Nicolo lock and fasten the box jubilantly.*)

KUKACHIN (*in despair*). Marco!

MARCO (*flustered*). Yes, Princess. I saw something queer! It made me feel feverish too! (*Recovering a bit – with a sickly smile.*) Oh, there's trouble there, all right! You must be delirious! I advise you to go to sleep.

KUKACHIN (*with wild despair pulls out a small dagger from the bosom of her dress*). I obey! I shall sleep for ever!

(*But Marco, the man of action, springs forward and wresting the dagger from her hand, flings it over the side. She confronts him defiantly, her eyes wild with grief and rage. He stares at her, dumbfounded and bewildered.*)

MARCO (*bewildered*). I never believed people – sane people – ever seriously tried –

KUKACHIN (*intensely*). I implored an ox to see my soul! I no longer can endure the shame of living!

MARCO (*sheepishly*). You mean it was a terrible insult when I called you – by your name?

KUKACHIN (*bursting into hysterical laughter*). Yes! How dared you!

MARCO (*hastily*). I ask pardon, Princess! Please forgive me! My only excuse is, I forgot myself. I'll have to stop overworking or I'll suffer a nervous breakdown. I felt like one of those figures in a puppet show with some one jerking the wires. It wasn't me, you understand. My lips spoke without me saying a word. And here's the funniest part of it all, and what'll explain matters in full, if you can believe it. It wasn't you I was seeing and talking to, not a Princess at all, you'd changed into some one else, some one I've got a good right to – just a girl –

KUKACHIN (*again clutching at hope*). A girl – a woman – you saw in me?

MARCO (*enthusiastically, groping in his shirt front*). Yes. Here she is! (*He jerks the locket out of an under pocket and presents it to her proudly.*) The future Mrs. Marco Polo! (*The Princess takes it mechanically and stares at it in a stupor as Marco rambles on.*) You may believe it or not, but like a flash she was standing there in your place and I was talking to her, not you at all!

KUKACHIN (*dully*). But it was my name you spoke.

MARCO (*confused*). I meant to say Donata. That's her name. We're going to be married as soon as I get home. (*Then as she stares at the miniature – proudly.*) Pretty, isn't she?

KUKACHIN (*dully*). She may have married another.

MARCO (*confidently*). No. Her family needs an alliance with our house.

KUKACHIN. She may have had lovers.

MARCO (*simply*). Oh, no. She's not that kind.

KUKACHIN (*staring at the picture*). She will be middle-aged – fat – and stupid!

MARCO (*with a grin*). Well, I don't mind a wife being a bit plump – and who wants a great thinker around the house? Sound common sense and a home where everything runs smooth, that's what I'm after.

KUKACHIN (*looks from him to the miniature*). There is no soul even in your love, which is no better than a mating of swine! And I –! (*A spasm of pain covers her face – then with hatred and disdain.*) Pig of a Christian! Will you return to this sow and boast that a Princess and a Queen –? (*With rage.*) Shall I ask as my first wedding present from Ghazan Khan that he have you flayed and thrown into the street to be devoured by dogs?

MAFFEO AND NICOLO (*who have pricked up their ears at this last, rush to the Princess, dragging their box between them, and prostrate themselves at her feet*). Mercy! Mercy!

(*She seems not to hear or to see them but stares ahead stonily. Marco beckons Maffeo to one side.*)

MARCO (*in a whisper*). Don't be afraid. She doesn't mean a word of it. She's hysterical. Listen, I just noticed the royal barge coming. I'll go and meet the Khan. You keep her from doing anything rash until he gets here.

MAFFEO. Yes.

(*He goes back and crouches again before the Princess, keeping a wary eye on her, but she seems turned to stone. Marco comes down and goes off* L. *There is the blare of a trumpet, the reflections of lanterns and torches, the sound of running about on deck and Marco's voice giving commands. The Women come out to attend the Princess. She remains rigid, giving no sign.*)

WOMEN (*in chorus*).
The lover comes,
Who becomes a husband,
Who becomes a son,
Who becomes a father –
In this contemplation lives the woman

KUKACHIN (*her face now a fatalistic mask of acceptance*).
I am not.
Life is.
A cloud hides the sun.
A life is lived.
The sun shines again.
Nothing has changed.
Centuries wither into tired dust.
A new dew freshens the grass.
Somewhere this dream is being dreamed.

(*From* L. *Marco comes escorting Ghazan Khan, attended by a train of nobles and slaves with lights. He can be heard saying: 'She is a little feverish – the excitement –' All are magnificently dressed, glittering with jewels. Ghazan is a young man, not handsome but noble and manly looking. He comes forward and bows low before her, his attendants likewise. Then he looks into her face and stands fascinated by her beauty. She *looks back at him with a calm indifference.)*

GHAZAN (*after a pause – his voice thrilling with admiration*). If it were possible for a son who loved a noble father to rejoice at that father's death, then I should be that guilty son! (*As she makes no reply.*) You have heard? Arghun Khan is dead. You must bear the humiliation of accepting his son for husband, a crow to replace an eagle! Forgive me. But with your eyes to watch I may become at least a shadow of his greatness.

KUKACHIN (*calmly*). What am I? I shall obey the eternal will which governs your destiny and mine.

GHAZAN (*impetuously*). You are more beautiful than I had dared to dream! It shall not be I who rules, but you! I shall be your slave! Persia shall be your conquest and everywhere where songs are sung they shall be in praise of your beauty! You shall be Queen of Love –!

KUKACHIN (*sharply, with pain*). No!

(*She drops the locket on the floor and grinds it into pieces under her foot.*)

MARCO (*excitedly*). Princess! Look out! You're stepping on –

(*She kicks it away from her. Marco stoops on his knees and begins picking up the wreckage in his handkerchief. Kukachin turns to Ghazan and points to Marco.*)

KUKACHIN. My first request of you, my Lord, is that you reward this Christian who has brought me here in safety. I ask, as a fitting tribute to his character, that you give an immense feast in his honour. Let there be food in tremendous amounts! He is an exquisite judge of quantity. Let him be urged to eat and drink until he can hold no more, until he becomes his own ideal figure, an idol of stuffed self-satisfaction! Will you do this? (*She is a trifle hectic now and her manner has grown wilder.*)

GHAZAN. Your wish is my will!

KUKACHIN (*pointing to a magnificent lion in diamonds on his breast*). What is that wonderful glittering beast?

GHAZAN. It is the emblem of the Order of the Lion, which only great heroes and kings of men may wear.

KUKACHIN (*gives a laugh of wild irony*). Great heroes – kings of men? (*Then eagerly.*) Will you give it to me? I implore you! (*Ghazan, fascinated, yet with a wondering glance, unpins it and hands it to her without a word. She prods Marco, who is still collecting the pieces of the locket, with her foot.*) Arise! Let me give you the noble Order of the Lion! (*She pins the blazing diamond figure on the breast of the stunned Marco, laughing with bitter mockery.*) How well it is set off on the bosom of a sheep! (*She laughs more wildly.*) Kneel again! Bring me a chest of gold! (*Ghazan makes a sign. Two slaves bring a chest of gold coins to her. She takes handfuls and throws them over the kneeling forms of the Polos, laughing.*) Here! Guzzle! Grunt! Wallow for our amusement!

(*The two elder are surreptitiously snatching at the coins, but Marco jumps to his feet, his face flushing.*)

MARCO (*in a hurt tone*). I don't see why you're trying to insult me – just at the last moment. What have I done? (*Then suddenly forcing a smile.*) But I realize you're not yourself.

GHAZAN (*sensing something*). Has this man offended you? Shall he be killed?

KUKACHIN (*wearily*). No. He has amused me. Let him be fed. Stuff him with food and gold and send him home. And you, My Lord, may I ask that this first night I be allowed to remain on board alone with my women? I am weary!

GHAZAN. Again your wish is my will, even though I will not live until I see you again!

KUKACHIN (*exhaustedly*). I am humbly grateful. Good night, My Lord.

(*She bows. Ghazan and the Court bow before her. They retire toward* L., *Marco talking earnestly to the oblivious Ghazan, whose eyes are riveted on the Princess, who has turned away from them. The two elder Polos, carrying their chest, their pockets stuffed, trudge along last.*)

MARCO. The close confinement of a long voyage. I think probably her spleen is out of order.

(*They are gone from sight. Kukachin's shoulders quiver as, her head bowed in her hands, she sobs quietly. The ship can be heard making off.*)

WOMEN. Weep, Princess of the Wounded
Heart,
Weeping heals the wounds of sorrow
Till only the scars remain
And the heart forgets.

KUKACHIN (*suddenly runs up to the upper deck and stands outlined against the sky, her arms outstretched – in a voice which is a final, complete renunciation, calls*). Farewell, Marco Polo!

MARCO (*his voice comes from over the water, cheery and relieved*). Good-bye, Your Majesty – and all best wishes for long life and happiness!

(*The Princess sinks to her knees, her face hidden in her arms on the bulwark.*)

CURTAIN

ACT THREE SCENE ONE

SCENE: *One year later.*

The Grand Throne Room in the Imperial palace at Cambaluc. Kublai squats on his throne, aged and sad, listening with an impassive face to General Bayan who, dressed in the full military uniform and armour of the Commander-in-Chief, is explaining earnestly with several maps in his hand. On Kublai's left stands Chu-Yin, who is reading. Behind Bayan are grouped at attention all the generals of his army with a multitude of young staff officers, all gorgeously uniformed and armoured. From the room on the right, the ballroom, a sound of dance music and laughter comes through the closed doors.

BAYAN (*impressively – pointing to the map*). Here, Your Majesty, is the line of the river Danube which marks the Western boundary of your Empire. Beyond it, lies the West. Our spies report their many petty states are always quarrelling. So great is their envy of each other that we could crush each singly and the rest would rejoice. We can mobilize one million horsemen on the Danube within a month. (*Proudly.*) We would ride their armies down into the sea! Your Empire would extend from ocean to ocean!

KUBLAI (*wearily*). It is much too large already. Why do you want to conquer the West? It must be a pitiful land, poor in spirit and material wealth. We have everything to lose by contact with its greedy hypocrisy. The conqueror acquires first of all the vices of the conquered. Let the West devour itself.

BAYAN (*helplessly*). But – everywhere in the East there is peace!

KUBLAI (*with hopeless irony*). Ah! And you are becoming restless?

BAYAN (*proudly*). I am a Mongol – a man of action!

KUBLAI (*looking at him with musing irony*). Hum! You have already conquered the West, I think.

BAYAN (*puzzled*). What, Your Majesty? (*Then persuasively.*) The West may not be strong, but it is crafty. Remember how that Christian, Polo, invented the engine to batter down walls? It would be better to wipe out their cunning now before they make too many engines to weaken the power of men. (*Then with a sudden inspiration.*) And it would be a righteous war! We would tear down their Christian Idols and set up the image of the Buddha!

KUBLAI. Buddha, the Prince of Peace?

BAYAN (*bowing his head, as do all his retinue*). The Gentle One, The Good, The Kind, The Pitiful, The Merciful, The Wise, The Eternal Contemplative One!

KUBLAI. In His Name?

BAYAN (*fiercely*). Death to those who deny Him!

ALL (*with a great fierce shout and a clanking of swords*). Death!

KUBLAI (*looks up at the ceiling quizzically*). A thunderbolt? (*Waits.*) No? Then there is no God! (*Then to Bayan with a cynical, bitter smile.*) August Commander, if you must have war, let it be one without fine phrases – a practical war of few words, as that Polo you admire would say. Leave the West alone. Our interests do not conflict – yet. But there is a group of islands whose silk industry is beginning to threaten the supremacy of our own. Lead your gallant million there – and see to it your war leaves me in peace!

BAYAN. I hear and I obey! (*He turns to his staff exultantly.*) His Majesty has declared war!

ALL (*with a fierce cheer*). Down with the West!

BAYAN (*hastily*). No. Not yet. Down with Japan! (*They cheer with equal enthusiasm – then he harangues them with the air of a patriotic exhorter.*) His Majesty's benevolence and patience have been exhausted by the continued outrages against our silk nationals perpetrated by unscrupulous Japanese trade-pirates who, in spite of his protests, are breeding and maintaining silkworms for purposes of aggression! We fight in the cause of moral justice, that our silk-makers may preserve their share of the eternal sunlight! (*A long cheer.*)

KUBLAI (*smiling – distractedly*). War without rhetoric, please! Polo has infected you with cant! The West already invades us! Throw open the doors! Music! (*The doors are thrown open. The dance music sounds loudly.*) Go in and dance, everyone! You, too, General! I revoke my declaration of war – unless you learn to dance and be silent! (*They all go into the ballroom, Bayan stalking majestically with an injured mien.*) But dancing makes me remember Kukachin whose little dancing feet –! Shut the doors! Music brings back her voice singing! (*Turning to Chu-Yin – harshly.*) Wisdom! No, do not read! What good are wise writings to fight stupidity? One must have stupid writings that men can understand. In order to live even wisdom must be stupid!

A CHAMBERLAIN (*enters hurriedly and prostrates himself*). A courier from Persia!

KUBLAI (*excitedly*). From Kukachin! Bring him here! (*The Chamberlain dashes to the door and a moment later the Courier enters, travel-stained and weary. He sinks into a heap before the throne. Kublai shouts at him impatiently.*) Have you a letter?

COURIER (*with a great effort holds out a letter*). Here!

(*He collapses. Chu-Yin hands the letter up to Kublai, who takes it eagerly from him. He begins to read at once. The Chamberlain comes back with a cup of wine. The Courier is revived and gets to his knees, waiting humbly.*)

CHU-YIN (*goes back to Kublai, who has finished reading the short note and is staring sombrely before him*). And did the Little Flower save his Immortal Soul? (*Kublai does not look at him, but mutely hands him the letter. Chu-Yin becomes grave. He reads aloud.*) 'Arghun had died. I am the wife of his son, Ghazan. It does not matter. He is kind, but I miss my home and you. I doubt if I shall be blessed with a son. I do not care. I have lost my love of life. My heart beats more and more wearily. Death woos me. You must not grieve. You wish me to be happy, do you not? And my body may resist Death for a long time yet. Too long. My soul he has already possessed. I wish to commend the unremitting attention to his duty of Admiral Polo. He saved my life three times at the risk of his own. He delivered me to Ghazan. Send him another million. You were right about his soul. What I had mistaken for one I discovered to be a fat woman with a patient virtue. By the time you receive this they will be married in Venice. I do not blame him. But I cannot forgive myself – nor forget – nor believe again in any beauty in the world. I love you the best in life. And tell Chu-Yin I love him too.'

(*He lets the letter in his hand drop to his side, his eyes filling, his voice grown husky. Kublai stares bleakly ahead of him.*)

KUBLAI (*at last rouses himself – harshly to the Courier*). Did the Queen give you this in person?

COURIER. Yes, Your Majesty – with a generous gift.

KUBLAI. I can be generous too. Did she appear – ill?

COURIER. Yes. I could scarcely hear her voice.

KUBLAI. You brought no other word?

COURIER. Not from the Queen. I came privately from her. But Admiral Polo suspected my departure and gave me a verbal message which he caused me to memorize.

KUBLAI (*harshly – his eyes beginning to gleam with anger*). Ha! Go on! Repeat!

COURIER (*stopping for a moment to freshen his memory*). He said, tell the Great Kaan that 'in spite of perils too numerous to relate, I have delivered my charge safely to Ghazan Khan. In general, she gave but little trouble on the voyage, for although flighty in temper and of a passionate disposition, she never refused to heed my advice for her welfare, and as I informed His Majesty, King Ghazan, the responsibilities of marriage and the duties of motherhood will sober her spirit and she will settle down as a sensible wife should. This much I further add, that in humble obedience to your final instructions given me by Mr. Chu-Yin, I looked daily into her eyes.'

KUBLAI (*bewilderedly to Chu-Yin*). What? Did you –?

CHU-YIN (*miserably*). Forgive an old fool! I meant it partly in jest as a last chance – to cure her – or to awaken him.

COURIER (*continuing*). 'But I have never noted any unnatural change in them except toward the termination of our trip, particularly on the last day, when I noticed a rather strained expression, but this I took to be fever due to her Highness's spleen being sluggish after the long confinement on shipboard.'

KUBLAI (*choking with wrath*). O God of the Sombre Heavens!

COURIER. And he gave me no money for delivering the message, but he promised that you would reward me nobly.

KUBLAI (*with wild laughter*). Ha-ha-ha! Stop! Do you dare to madden me? (*Then suddenly raging.*) Out of my sight, dog, before I have you impaled! (*The terror-stricken Courier scrambles out like a flash. Kublai stands up with flashing eyes – revengefully.*) I have reconsidered! I shall conquer the West! I shall lead my armies in person! I shall not leave one temple standing nor one Christian alive who is not enslaved! Their cities shall vanish in flame, their fields shall be wasted! Famine shall finish what I leave undone! And of the city of Venice not one vestige shall remain! And of the body of Marco Polo there shall not be a fragment of bone nor an atom of flesh which will not have shrieked through ten days' torture before it died!

CHU-YIN. Master! (*He throws himself on his face at Kublai's feet.*) Do not torture yourself! Is this Wisdom? Is this the peace of the soul?

KUBLAI (*distractedly*). To revenge oneself – that brings a kind of peace!

CHU-YIN. To revenge equally the wrong of an equal perhaps, but this –? Can you confess yourself weaker than his stupidity?

KUBLAI. He has murdered her!

CHU-YIN. She does not accuse him. What would be her wish?

KUBLAI (*his anger passing – wearily and bitterly, after a pause*). Rise, my old friend, it is I who should be at your feet, not you at mine! (*He sinks dejectedly on his throne again. After a pause, sadly.*) She will die. Why is this? What purpose can it serve? My hideous suspicion is that God is only an infinite, insane energy which creates and destroys without other purpose than to pass eternity in avoiding thought. Then the stupid man becomes the Perfect Incarnation of Omnipotence and the Polos are the true children of God! (*He laughs bitterly.*) Ha! How long before we shall be permitted to die, my friend? I begin to resent life as the insult of an ignoble inferior with whom it is a degradation to fight! (*Broodingly – after a pause.*) I have had a foreboding she would die. Lately, to while away time, I experimented with the crystal. I do not believe the magic nonsense about it, but I do consider that, given a focus, the will can perhaps overcome the limits of the senses. Whatever the explanation be, I looked into the crystal and willed to see Kukachin in Persia and she appeared, sitting alone in a garden, beautiful and sad, apart from life, waiting – (*Brokenly.*) My eyes filled with tears. I cried out to her – and she was gone! (*Then suddenly – to the Chamberlain.*) Bring me the crystal! (*To Chu-Yin as the Chamberlain goes.*) Marco, the true ruler of the world, will have come to Venice by this time. My loathing grows so intense I feel he must jump into the crystal at my bidding. And – in the cause of wisdom, say – we must see what he is doing now. (*The Chamberlain returns with the crystal. Kublai takes it eagerly from his hand and stares fixedly into it.*)

CHU-YIN (*protestingly*). Why do you wish to hurt yourself further?

KUBLAI (*staring fixedly*). I shall observe dispassionately. It is a test of myself I want to make as a penalty for my weakness a moment ago. (*He sees something.*) Ah – it begins. (*A pause. The light grows dimmer and dimmer on the stage proper as it begins to come up on the extreme foreground.*) I see – a city whose streets are canals – it is evening – a house. I begin to see through the walls – Ah!

(*The lights come up again on the back stage as the forestage is fully revealed. The Kaan on his throne and Chu-Yin are seen dimly, behind and above, like beings on another plane. At the centre of the forestage is a great banquet table garishly set with an ornate gold service. A tall major-domo in a gorgeous uni-*

form enters and stands at attention as the procession begins. First come the Guests, male and female, a crowd of good substantial bourgeois, who stare about with awe and envy and are greatly impressed by the gold plate.)

A MAN. They've laid out a pile of money here!

A WOMAN. Is that gold service really gold?

ANOTHER. Absolutely. I can tell without biting it.

A MAN. They must have cash, whoever they are.

A WOMAN. Do you think they're really the Polos?

ANOTHER. They looked like greasy Tartars to me.

ANOTHER. That was their queer clothes.

A MAN. And remember they've been gone twenty-odd years.

ANOTHER. In spite of that, I thought I could recognize Maffeo.

A WOMAN. Will Donata know Marco, I wonder?

A MAN. What's more to her point, will he recognize her?

A WOMAN. Imagine her waiting all this time!

ANOTHER. How romantic! He must be terribly rich – if it's really him.

A MAN. We'll soon know. That's why we were invited.

A WOMAN. Ssshh! Here comes Donata now. How old she's getting to look!

ANOTHER. And how fat in the hips!

A MAN (*jokingly*). That's the way I like 'em, and perhaps Marco –

(*Donata enters on the arm of her father, a crafty, wizened old man. She has grown into a stout middle-age, but her face is unlined and still pretty in a bovine, good-natured way. All bow and they return this salutation.*)

ALL. Congratulations, Donata!

(*She blushes and turns aside in an incongruous girlish confusion.*)

FATHER (*proud but pretending querulousness*). Don't tease her now! The girl's nervous enough already. And it may not be Marco after all, but only a joke some one's put up on us.

A WOMAN. No one could be so cruel!

ALL (*suddenly with a great gasp*). Oh, listen! (*An orchestra vigorously begins a flowery, sentimental Italian tune. This grows into quite a blare as the musicians enter from the right, six in number, in brilliant uniforms.*) Oh, look! (*The musicians form a line, three on each side by the stairs on right.*) Oh, see! (*A procession of servants begins to file one by one through the ranks of musicians, each carrying on his head or upraised hand an enormous platter on which are whole pigs, fowl of all varieties, roasts, vegetables, salads, fruits, nuts, dozens of bottles of wine. The servants arrange these on the table, in symmetrical groups, with the trained eye for display of window-dressers, until the table, with the bright light flooding down on it, closely resembles the front of a pretentious delicatessen store. Meanwhile*) See! What a turkey! Such a goose! The fattest pig I ever saw! What ducks! What vegetables! Look at the wine! A feast for the gods! And all those servants! An army! And the orchestra! What expense! Lavish! They must be worth millions! (*The three Polos make their grand entrance from the stairs on right, walking with bursting self-importance between the files of musicians who now blare out a triumphant march. The two elder precede Marco. All three are dressed in long robes of embroidered crimson satin reaching almost to the ground. The guests give a new united gasp of astonishment.*) Is it they? Is that old Nicolo? That's Maffeo's nose! No! It isn't them at all! Well, if it's a joke, I don't see the point. But such robes! Such hand embroidery! Such material! They must be worth millions!

DONATA (*falteringly*). Is that him, father? I can't tell. (*She calls faintly.*) Marco!

(*But he pretends not to hear. He gives a sign at which the three take off their robes and hand them to the servants. They have even more gorgeous blue ones underneath. Marco addresses the servants in a false voice.*)

MARCO. My good men, you may sell these rich robes and divide the proceeds among yourselves! And here is a little something extra.

(*He tosses a handful of gold to the servants and another to the musicians. A mad scramble results. The guests gasp. They seem inclined to join in the scramble.*)

GUESTS. How generous! What prodigality! What indifference to money! They throw it away like dirt. They must be worth millions!

MARCO (*in the same false voice*). Our guests look thirsty. Pass around the wine. (*The servants do so. The guests gaze, smell, taste.*)

ALL. What a vintage! What flavour! What bouquet! How aged! It must have cost twenty lire a bottle! (*At another signal the three Polos take off their blue robes.*)

MARCO (*regally*). Give those to the musicians! (*They are revealed now in their old dirty, loose Tartar travelling dress, and look quite shabby. The guests gape uncertainly. Then Marco declares grandly.*) You look astonished, good people, but this is a moral lesson to teach you not to put too much faith in appearances, for behold!

(*He slits up the wide sleeves of his own robe, as do his father and uncle, and now the three, standing beside a big empty space which has been purposely left at the very centre of the table at the front, lower their opened sleeves, and, as the musicians, obeying this signal, start up a great blare, let pour from them a perfect stream of precious stones which forms a glittering multi-coloured heap. This is the final blow. The guests stare pop-eyed, open-mouthed, speechless for a second. Then their pent-up admiration breaks forth.*)

ALL. Extraordinary! Jewels! Gems! Rubies! Emeralds! Diamonds! Pearls! A king's ransom! Millions!

MARCO (*suddenly with his hail-fellow-well-met joviality*). Well, folks, are you all tongue-tied? Isn't one of you going to say welcome home? And Miss Donata, don't I get a kiss? I'm still a bachelor!

(*Immediately with mad shouts of 'Bravo!' 'Welcome home!' 'Hurrah for the Polos!' etc., etc., the guests bear down on them in a flood. There is a confused whirl of embraces, kisses, back-slaps, handshakes and loud greetings of all sorts. Marco manages to get separated and pulls Donata down front to the foreground.*)

DONATA (*half swooning*). Marco!

MARCO (*moved*). My old girl! (*They kiss, then he pushes her away.*) Here! Let me get a good look at you! Why, you're still as pretty as a picture and you don't look a day older!

DONATA (*exaltedly*). My beloved prince!

MARCO (*jokingly*). No, if I was a prince I'd never have remained single all these years in the East! I'm a hero, that's what! And all the twenty-odd years I kept thinking of you, and I was always intending to write – (*He pulls the pieces of the miniature wrapped in the handkerchief out of his pocket.*) Here's proof for you! Look at yourself! You're a bit smashed, but that was done in a hand-to-hand fight with pirates. Now don't I deserve another kiss?

DONATA (*giving it*). My hero! (*Then jealously.*) But I know all the heathen women must have fallen in love with you.

MARCO. Oh, maybe one or two or so – but I didn't have time to waste on females. I kept my nose to the grindstone every minute. (*Proudly.*) And I got results. I don't mind telling you, Donata, I'm worth over two millions! How's that for keeping my promise? Worth while your waiting, eh? (*He slaps her on the back.*)

DONATA. Yes, my wonder boy! (*Then worriedly.*) You said there were one or two women? But you were true in spite of them, weren't you?

MARCO. I tell you I wouldn't have married the prettiest girl in Cathay! (*This with emphasis. Then abruptly.*) But never mind any other girl. (*He chucks her under the chin.*) What I want to know is when this girl is going to marry me?

DONATA (*softly*). Any time!

(*They hug. The guests group about them kittenishly, pointing and murmuring, 'What a romance! What a romance!'*)

DONATA'S FATHER (*seizing the opportunity*). Friends, I take this opportunity to announce publicly the betrothal of my daughter, Donata, to

Marco Polo of this City! (*Another wild round of congratulations, kisses, etc.*)

MARCO (*his voice sounding above the hubbub*). Let's eat, friends! (*They swirl to their places behind the long table. When they stand their faces can be seen above the piles of food, but when they sit they are out of sight.*) No ceremony among friends. Just pick your chair. All ready? Let's sit down then! (*With one motion they disappear.*)

VOICE OF DONATA'S FATHER. But, first, before we regale ourselves with your cheer, won't you address a few words to your old friends and neighbours who have gathered here on this happy occasion?

(*Applause. Marco is heard expostulating, but finally he gives in.*)

MARCO. All right, if you'll promise to go ahead and eat and not wait for me. (*His head appears, his expression full of importance. Servants flit about noisily. He coughs and begins with dramatic feeling.*) My friend and neighbours of old, your generous and wholehearted welcome touches me profoundly. I would I had the gift of oratory to thank you fittingly, but I am a simple man, an ordinary man, I might almost say, – a man of affairs used to dealing in the hard facts of life, a silent man given to deeds not words – (*Here he falters fittingly.*) And so now – forgive my emotion – words fail me – (*Here he clears his throat with an important cough and bursts forth into a memorized speech in the grand Chamber of Commerce style.*) But I'll be glad to let you have a few instructive facts about the silk industry as we observed it in the Far East, laying especial emphasis upon the keystone of the whole silk business – I refer to the breeding of worms! (*A few hungry guests start to eat. Knives and forks and spoons rattle against plates. Soup is heard. Marco strikes a good listening attitude so that he will be sure not to miss a word his voice utters, and warms to his work.*) Now, to begin with, there are millions upon millions of capital invested in this industry, millions of contented slaves labour unremittingly millions of hours per annum to obtain the best results in the weaving and dyeing of the finished product, but I don't hesitate to state that all this activity is relatively unimportant beside the astounding fact that in the production of the raw material there are constantly employed millions upon millions upon millions of millions of worms!

ONE VOICE (*rather muffled by roast pig*). Hear!

(*But the rest are all absorbed in eating and a perfect clamour of knives and forks resounds. Marco begins again, but this time the clamour is too great, his words are lost, only the one he lays such emphasis upon can be distinguished.*)

MARCO. Millions! . . . millions! . . . millions! . . . millions!

KUBLAI (*who from the height of his golden throne, crystal in hand, has watched all this with fascinated disgust while Chu-Yin has sat down to read again, now turns away with a shudder of loathing – and in spite of himself, a shadow of a smile – and lets the crystal fall from his hand and shatter into bits with a loud report. Instantly there is darkness and from high up in the darkness Kublai's voice speaking with a pitying scorn*). The Word became their flesh, they say. Now all is flesh! And can their flesh become the Word again?

DARKNESS

ACT THREE SCENE TWO

SCENE. *Grand Throne Room in the Imperial Palace at Cambaluc, about two years later. The walls tower majestically in shadow, their elaborate detail blurred into a background of half-darkness.*

Kublai sits at the top of his throne, cross-legged in the posture of an idol, motionless, wrapped in contemplation. He wears a simple white robe without adornment of any sort. A brilliant light floods down upon him in one concentrated ray. His eyes are fixed on a catafalque, draped in heavy white silk, which stands in the centre of the room, emphasized by another downpouring shaft of light.

Chu-Yin stands on the level below, on Kublai's left. On the main floor are the nobles and people of the Court, grouped as in Act One, Scene Six.

There is a long pause clamorous with the pealing of the thousands of bells in the city, big and little, near and far. Every figure in the room is as motionless as the Kaan himself. Their eyes are kept on him with the ardent humility and respect of worship. Behind their impassive faces, one senses a tense expectancy of some sign from the throne. At last, Kublai makes a slight but imperious motion of command with his right hand. Immediately the women all turn with arms outstretched toward the catafalque. Their voices rise together in a long, rhythmic wail of mourning; their arms with one motion move slowly up; their voices attain a prolonged note of unbearable poignancy; their heads are thrown back, their arms appeal to Heaven in one agonized gesture of despair. Here the Kaan makes the same barely perceptible sign of command again. The voices are instantly silenced. With one motion, the women throw themselves prostrate on the floor. The bells, except for one slow deep-toned one in the palace itself, are almost instantly hushed. At the same instant, from outside, at first faint, but growing momentarily in volume, comes the sound of funeral music. A moment later the funeral procession enters. The men sink to the cross-legged position of prayer, their heads bowed.

First come the musicians, nine in number, men in robes of bright red. They are followed by the chorus of nine singers, five men and four women, all of them aged, with bent bodies, their thin, cracked voices accompanying the music in queer, breaking waves of lamentation. These are masked, the men with a male mask of grief, the women with a female. All are dressed in deep black with white edging to their robes. After them comes a troupe of young girls and boys, dressed in white with black edging, moving slowly backward in a gliding, interweaving dance pattern. Their faces are not masked but are fixed in a disciplined, traditional expression of bewildered, uncomprehending grief that is like a mask. They carry silver censers which they swing in unison toward the corpse of the Princess Kukachin, carried on a bier directly behind them on the shoulders of eight princes of the blood in black armour.

Accompanying the bier, one at each corner, are four priests – the foremost two, a Confucian and a Taoist, the latter two, a Buddhist and a Moslem. Each walks with bent head, reading aloud to himself from his Holy Book.

The princes lift the bier of Kukachin to the top of the catafalque. Her body is wrapped in a winding sheet of deep blue, a jewelled golden head-dress is on her black hair, her face is white and clear as a statue's. The young boys and girls place their smoking censers about the catafalque, the incense ascending in clouds about the Princess as if it were bearing her soul with it. The music and the singing cease as the dancers, singers, and musicians form on each side, and to the rear, of the catafalque and sink into attitudes of prayer.

Kublai speaks to the priests in a voice of command in which is weariness and disbelief.

KUBLAI. Peace! She does not need your prayers. She was a prayer! (*With one motion they shut their books, raise their heads and stare before them in silence Kublai continues – sadly.*) Can words recall life to her beauty? (*To the Priest of Tao.*) Priest of Tao, will you conquer death by your mystic Way?

PRIEST OF TAO (*bowing his head in submission – fatalistically*). Which is the greater evil, to possess or to be without? Death is.

CHORUS (*in an echo of vast sadness*). Death is.

KUBLAI (*to the Confucian*). Follower of Confucius, the Wise, have you this wisdom?

PRIEST OF CONFUCIUS (*slowly*). Before we know life, how can we know death? (*Then as the Taoist, submissively.*) Death is.

CHORUS (*as before*). Death is.

KUBLAI (*to the Buddhist Priest*). Worshipper of Buddha, can your self-overcoming overcome that greatest overcomer of self?

BUDDHIST PRIEST. This is a thing which no god can bring about: that what is subject to death should not die. (*Then as the others, submissively.*) Death is.

CHORUS (*as before*). Death is.

KUBLAI (*wearily*). And your answer, priest of Islam?

PRIEST OF ISLAM. It is the will of Allah! (*Submissively.*) Death is.

CHORUS. Death is. Death is. Death is. (*Their voices die away.*)

KUBLAI (*after a pause*). What is death? (*A long pause. His eyes rest in loving contemplation on the body of Kukachin. Finally he speaks tenderly to her with a sad smile.*) Girl whom we call dead, whose beauty is even in death more living than we, smile with infinite silence upon our speech, smile with infinite forbearance upon our wisdom, smile with infinite remoteness upon our sorrow, smile as a star smiles! (*His voice appears about to break. A muffled sound of sobbing comes from the prostrate women. Kublai regains control over his weakness and rises to his feet – with angry self-contempt.*) No more! That is for poets! (*With overstressed arrogance – assertively.*) I am the Great Kaan!

(*Everyone in the room rises with one motion of assertion.*)

CHORUS (*accompanied by a clangour of brass from the musicians – recite with discordant vigour*).

Greatest of the Great!
Son of Heaven!
Lord of Earth!
Sovereign of the World!
Ruler over Life and Death!

KUBLAI (*silences them by an imperious gesture – and now even the great palace bell is stilled – half-mockingly but assertively*). The Son of Heaven? Then I should know a prayer. Sovereign of the World? Then I command the World to pray! (*With one motion all sink to the position of prayer.*) In silence! Prayer is beyond words! Contemplate the eternal life of Life! Pray thus! (*He himself sinks to the position of prayer – a pause – then slowly.*) In silence – for one concentrated moment – be proud of life! Know in your heart that the living of life can be noble! Know that the dying of death can be noble! Be exalted by life! Be inspired by death! Be humbly proud! Be proudly grateful! Be immortal because life is immortal. Contain the harmony of womb and grave within you! Possess life as a lover – then sleep requited in the arms of death! If you awake, love again! If you sleep on, rest in peace! Who knows which? What does it matter? It is nobler not to know!

(*A pause of silence. He rises to his feet. With one motion all do likewise. Kublai sits back on his cushions again, withdrawing into contemplation. The Mongol Chronicler comes forward to fulfil his function of chanting the official lament for the dead. He declaims in a high, wailing voice accompanied by the musicians and by the Chorus who sway rhythmically and hum a rising and falling mourning accompaniment.*)

CHRONICLER. We lament the shortness of life.
Life at its longest is brief enough.
Too brief for the wisdom of joy, too long for the knowledge of sorrow.
Sorrow becomes despair when death comes to the young, untimely.
Oh that her beauty could live again, that her youth could be born anew.
Our Princess was young as Spring, she was beautiful as a bird or flower.
Cruel when Spring is smitten by Winter, when birds are struck dead in full song, when the budding blossom is blighted!
Alas that our Princess is dead, she was the song of songs, the perfume of perfumes, the perfect one!
Our sobs stifle us, our tears wet the ground, our lamentations sadden the wind from the West. (*Bows submissively – speaks.*)
Yet we must bow humbly before the Omnipotent.

CHORUS. We must be humble.

CHRONICLER. Against Death all Gods are powerless.

CHORUS. All Gods are powerless. (*Their voices die into silence.*)

KUBLAI (*after a pause – wearily*). Leave her in peace. Go. (*The Court leaves silently at his command in a formal, expressionless order. The four priests go first, beginning to pray silently again. They are followed by the nobles and officials with their women coming after. Finally the young boys and girls take up their censers and dance their pattern out backward, preceded by the musicians. Only the Chorus remain, grouped in a semi-circle behind the catafalque, motionless, and Chu-Yin who stays at the left hand of Kublai. The music fades away. Kublai takes his eyes from the dead girl with a sigh of bitter irony.*) Oh, Chu-Yin, my Wise Friend, was the prayer I taught them wisdom?

CHU-YIN. It was the wisdom of pride. It was thy wisdom.

CHORUS (*echoing sadly*). Thy wisdom.

KUBLAI. Was it not truth?

CHU-YIN. It was the truth of power. It was thy truth.

CHORUS (*as before*). Thy truth.

KUBLAI. My pride, my power? My wisdom, my truth? For me there remains only – her truth! (*Then after staring at Kukachin for a second, bitterly.*) Her truth! She died for love of a fool!

CHU-YIN. No. She loved love. She died for beauty.

KUBLAI. Your words are hollow echoes of the brain. Do not wound me with wisdom. Speak to my heart! (*Sadly – his eyes again on Kukachin.*) Her little feet danced away the stamp of armies. Her smile made me forget the servile grin on the face of the World. In her eyes' mirror I watched myself live protected from life by her affection – a simple old man dying contentedly a little, day after pleasant day.

CHU-YIN (*bowing – compassionately*). Then weep, old man. Be humble and weep for your child. The old should cherish sorrow. (*He bows again and goes out silently.*)

KUBLAI (*after a pause, gets up and descending from his throne, slowly approaches the catafalque, speaking to the dead girl softly as he does so – with a trembling smile.*) I think you are hiding your eyes, Kukachin. You are a little girl again. You are playing hide-and-seek. You are pretending. Did we not once play such games together, you and I? You have made your face still, you have made your face cold, you have set your lips in a smile so remote – you are pretending even that you are dead! (*He is very near her now. His voice breaks – more and more intensely.*) Let us stop playing! It is late. It is time you were asleep. Open your eyes and laugh! Laugh now that the game is over. Take the blindfold from my dim eyes. Whisper your secret in my ear. I – I am dead and you are living! Weep for me, Kukachin! Weep for the dead! (*He stretches his arms out to her beseechingly – pauses, standing beside the body, staring down at her; then, after a moment, he passes his hand over her face – tremblingly – with a beautiful tenderness of grief.*) So, little Kukachin – so, Little Flower – you have come back – they could not keep you – you were too homesick – you wanted to return – to gladden my last days – (*He no longer tries to control his grief. He sobs like a simple old man, bending and kissing his granddaughter on the forehead – with heart-breaking playfulness.*) I bid you welcome home, Little Flower! I bid you welcome home! (*He weeps, his tears falling on her calm white face.*)

CURTAIN

EPILOGUE

The play is over. The lights come up brilliantly in the theatre. In an aisle seat in the first row a Man rises, conceals a yawn in his palm, stretches his legs as if they had become cramped by too long an evening, takes his hat from under the seat and starts to go out slowly with the others in the audience. But although there is nothing out of the ordinary in his actions, his appearance excites general comment and surprise, for he is dressed as a Venetian merchant of the later Thirteenth Century. In fact, it is none other than Marco Polo himself, looking a bit sleepy, a trifle puzzled, and not a little irritated as his thoughts, in spite of himself, cling for a passing moment to the play just ended. He appears quite unaware of being unusual and walks in the crowd without self-consciousness, very much as one of them. Arrived in the lobby his face begins to clear of all disturbing memories of what had happened on the stage. The noise, the lights of the streets, recall him at once to himself. Impatiently he waits for his car, casting a glance here and there at faces in the groups around him, his eyes impersonally speculative, his bearing stolid with the dignity of one who is sure of his place in the world. His car, a luxurious limousine, draws up at the curb. He gets in briskly, the door is slammed, the car edges away into the traffic and Marco Polo, with a satisfied sigh at the sheer comfort of it all, resumes his life.

THE END

THE GREAT GOD BROWN

Characters

WILLIAM A. BROWN
HIS FATHER, *a contractor*
HIS MOTHER
DION ANTHONY
HIS FATHER, *a builder*
HIS MOTHER
MARGARET
HER THREE SONS
CYBEL
TWO DRAUGHTSMEN } *in Brown's office*
A STENOGRAPHER }

Scenes

PROLOGUE

The pier of the Casino. Moonlight in middle June.

ACT ONE

SCENE ONE Sitting-room, Margaret Anthony's apartment. Afternoon, seven years later.
SCENE TWO Billy Brown's office. The same afternoon.
SCENE THREE Cybel's parlour. That night.

ACT TWO

SCENE ONE Cybel's parlour. Seven years later. Dusk.
SCENE TWO Drafting-room, William A. Brown's office. That evening.
SCENE THREE Library, William A. Brown's home. That night.

ACT THREE

SCENE ONE Brown's office, a month later. Morning.
SCENE TWO Library, Brown's home. That evening.
SCENE THREE Sitting-room, Margaret's home. That night.

ACT FOUR

SCENE ONE Brown's office, weeks later. Late afternoon.
SCENE TWO Library, Brown's house, hours later. The same night.

EPILOGUE

The pier of the Casino. Four years later.

PROLOGUE

SCENE. *A cross-section of the pier of the Casino. In the rear, built out beyond the edge, is a rectangular space with benches on the three sides. A rail encloses the entire wharf at the back.*

It is a moonlight night in mid-June. From the Casino comes the sound of the school quartet rendering "Sweet Adeline" with many ultra-sentimental quavers. There is a faint echo of the ensuing hand-clapping – then nothing but the lapping of ripples against the piles and their swishing on the beach – then footsteps on the boards and Billy Brown walks along from right with his mother and father. The mother is a dumpy woman of forty-five, overdressed in black lace and spangles. The father is fifty or more, the type of bustling, genial, successful, provincial business man, stout and hearty in his evening dress.

Billy Brown is a handsome, tall and athletic boy of nearly eighteen. He is blond and blue-eyed, with a likeable smile and a frank good-humoured face, its expression already indicating a disciplined restraint. His manner has the easy self-assurance of a normal intelligence. He is in evening dress.

They walk arm in arm, the mother between.

MOTHER (*always addressing the father*). This Commencement dance is badly managed. Such singing! Such poor voices! Why doesn't Billy sing?

BILLY (*to her*). Mine is a regular fog horn! (*He laughs.*)

MOTHER (*to the air*). I had a pretty voice, when I was a girl. (*Then, to the father, caustically.*) Did you see young Anthony strutting around the ballroom in dirty flannel trousers?

FATHER. He's just showing off.

MOTHER. Such impudence! He's as ignorant as his father.

FATHER. The old man's all right. My only kick against him is he's been too damned conservative to let me branch out.

MOTHER (*bitterly*). He has kept you down to his level – out of pure jealousy.

FATHER. But he took me into partnership, don't forget –

MOTHER (*sharply*). Because you were the brains! Because he was afraid of losing you! (*A pause.*)

BILLY (*admiringly*). Dion came in his old clothes for a bet with me. He's a real sport. He wouldn't have been afraid to appear in his pyjamas! (*He grins with appreciation.*)

MOTHER. Isn't the moonlight clear! (*She goes and sits on the centre bench. Billy stands at the left corner, forward, his hand on the rail, like a prisoner at the bar, facing the judge. His father stands in front of the bench on right. The mother announces, with finality.*) After he's through college, Billy must study for a profession of some sort, I'm determined on that! (*She turns to her husband, defiantly, as if expecting opposition.*)

FATHER (*eagerly and placatingly*). Just what I've been thinking, my dear. Architecture! How's that? Billy a first-rate number-one architect! That's my proposition! What I've always wished I could have been myself. Only I never had the opportunity. But Billy – we'll make him a partner in the firm after. Anthony, Brown *and Son, architects* and builders – instead of *contractors* and builders!

MOTHER (*yearning for the realization of a dream*). And we won't lay sidewalks – or dig sewers – ever again?

FATHER (*a bit ruffled*). I and Anthony can build anything your pet can draw – even if it's a church. (*Then, selling his idea.*) It's a great chance for him! He'll design – expand us – make the firm famous.

MOTHER (*to the air – musingly*). When you proposed, I thought your future promised success – my future – (*with a sigh*) – Well, I suppose we've been comfortable. Now, it's his future. How would Billy like to be an architect? (*She does not look at him.*)

BILLY (*to her*). All right, Mother. (*Then sheepishly.*) I guess I've never bothered much about what I'd like to do after college – but architecture sounds all right to me, I guess.

MOTHER (*to the air – proudly*). Billy used to draw houses when he was little.

FATHER (*jubilantly.*) Billy's got the stuff in him to win, if he'll only work hard enough.

BILLY (*dutifully*). I'll work hard, Dad.

MOTHER. Billy can do anything!

BILLY (*embarrassed*). I'll try, Mother. (*There is a pause.*)

MOTHER (*with a sudden shiver*). The nights are so much colder than they used to be! Think of it, I once went moonlight bathing in June when I was a girl – but the moonlight was so warm and beautiful in those days, do you remember, Father?

FATHER (*puts his arm around her affectionately*). You bet I do, Mother. (*He kisses her. The orchestra at the Casino strikes up a waltz.*) There's the music. Let's go back and watch the young folks dance. (*They start off, leaving Billy standing there.*)

MOTHER (*suddenly calls back over her shoulder*). I want to watch Billy dance.

BILLY (*dutifully*). Yes, Mother!

(*He follows them. For a moment the faint sound of the music and the lapping of waves is heard. Then footsteps again and the three Anthonys come in. First come the father and mother, who are not masked. The father is a tall lean man of fifty-five or sixty, with a grim, defensive face, obstinate to the point of stupid weakness. The mother is a thin, frail, faded woman, her manner perpetually nervous and distraught, but with a sweet and gentle face that had once been beautiful. The father wears an ill-fitting black suit, like a mourner. The mother wears a cheap, plain, black dress. Following them, as if he were a stranger, walking alone, is their son, Dion. He is about the same height as young Brown, but lean and wiry, without repose, continually in restless nervous movement. His face is masked. The mask is a fixed forcing of his own face – dark, spiritual, poetic, passionately supersensitive, helplessly unprotected in its childlike, religious faith in life – into the expression of a mocking, reckless, defiant, gaily scoffing and sensual young Pan. He is dressed in a grey flannel shirt, open at the neck, rubber-soled shoes over bare feet, and soiled white flannel trousers. The father strides to the centre bench and sits down. The mother, who has been holding to his arm, lets go and stands by the bench at the right. They both stare at Dion, who, with a studied carelessness, takes his place at the rail, where young Brown had stood. They watch him, with queer, puzzled eyes.*)

MOTHER (*suddenly – pleading*). You simply must send him to college.

FATHER. I won't. I don't believe in it. Colleges turn out lazy loafers to sponge on their poor old fathers! Let him slave like I had to! That'll teach him the value of a dollar! College'll only make him a bigger fool than he is already! I never got above grammar school but I've made money and established a sound business. Let him make a man out of himself like I made of myself!

DION (*mockingly – to the air*). This Mr. Anthony is my father, but he only imagines he is God the Father. (*They both stare at him.*)

FATHER (*with angry bewilderment*). What – what – what's that?

MOTHER (*gently remonstrating to her son*). Dion, dear! (*Then to her husband – tauntingly*). Brown takes all the credit! He tells every one the success is all due to his energy – that you're only an old stick-in-the-mud!

FATHER (*stung, harshly*). The damn fool! He knows better'n anyone if I hadn't held him down to common sense, with his crazy wild-cat notions, he'd have had us ruined long ago!

MOTHER. He's sending Billy to college – Mrs. Brown just told me – going to have him study architecture afterwards, too, so's he can help expand your firm!

FATHER (*angrily*). What's that? (*Suddenly turns on Dion furiously.*) Then you can make up your mind to go too! And you'll learn to be a better architect than Brown's boy or I'll turn you out in the gutter without a penny! You hear?

DION (*mockingly – to the air*). It's difficult to choose – but architecture sounds less laborious.

MOTHER (*fondly*). You ought to make a wonderful architect, Dion. You've always painted pictures so well –

DION (*with a start – resentfully*). Why must she lie? Is it my fault? She knows I only try to paint. (*Passionately.*) But I will, some day! (*Then quickly, mocking again.*) On to college! Well, it won't be home, anyway, will it? (*He laughs queerly and approaches them. His father gets up defensively. Dion bows to him.*) I thank Mr. Anthony for this splendid opportunity to create myself – (*He kisses his mother, who bows with a strange humility as if she were a servant being saluted by the young master – then adds lightly*) – in my mother's image, so she may feel her life comfortably concluded.

(*He sits in his Father's place at centre and his mask stares with a frozen mockery before him. They stand on each side, looking dumbly at him.*)

MOTHER (*at last, with a shiver*). It's cold. June didn't use to be cold. I remember the June when I was carrying you, Dion – three months before you were born. (*She stares up at the sky.*) The moonlight was warm, then. I could feel the night wrapped around me like a grey velvet gown lined with warm sky and trimmed with silver leaves!

FATHER (*gruffly – but with a certain awe*). My mother used to believe the full of the moon was the time to sow. She was terrible old-fashioned. (*With a grunt.*) I can feel it's bringing on my rheumatism. Let's go back indoors.

DION (*with intense bitterness*). Hide! Be ashamed! (*They both start and stare at him.*)

FATHER (*with bitter hopelessness. To his wife – indicating their son*). Who is he? You bore him!

MOTHER (*proudly*). He's my boy! He's Dion!

DION (*bitterly resentful*). What else, indeed! The identical son. (*Then, mockingly.*) Are Mr. Anthony and his wife going in to dance! The nights grow cold! The days are dimmer than they used to be! Let's play hide-and-seek! Seek the monkey in the moon!

(*He suddenly cuts a grotesque caper, like a harlequin, and darts off, laughing with forced abandon. They stare after him – then slowly follow. Again there is silence except for the sound of the lapping waves. Then Margaret comes in, followed by the humbly worshipping Billy Brown. She is almost seventeen, pretty and vivacious, blonde, with big romantic eyes, her figure lithe and strong, her facial expression intelligent but youthfully dreamy, especially now in the moonlight. She is in a simple white dress. On her entrance, her face is masked with an exact, almost transparent reproduction of her own features, but giving her the abstract quality of a Girl instead of the individual Margaret.*)

MARGARET (*looking upward at the moon and singing in low tone as they enter*). " Ah, moon of my delight that knowest no wane!"

BILLY (*eagerly*). I've got that record – John McCormack. It's a peach! Sing some more. (*She looks upward in silence. He keeps standing respectfully behind her, glancing embarrassedly toward her averted face. He tries to make conversation.*) I think the *Rubáiyát's* great stuff, don't you? I never could memorize poetry worth a darn. Dion can recite lots of Shelley's poems by heart.

MARGARET (*slowly takes off her mask – to the moon*). Dion! (*A pause.*)

BILLY (*fidgeting*). Margaret!

MARGARET (*to the moon*). Dion is so wonderful!

BILLY (*blunderingly*). I asked you to come out here because I wanted to tell you something.

MARGARET (*to the moon*). Why did Dion look at me like that? It made me feel so crazy!

BILLY. I wanted to ask you something, too.

MARGARET. That one time he kissed me – I can't forget it! He was only joking – but I felt – and he saw and just laughed.

BILLY. Because that's the uncertain part. My end of it is a sure thing, and has been for a long time, and I guess everybody in town knows it – they're always kidding me – so it's a cinch you must know – how I feel about you.

MARGARET. Dion's so different from all the others. He can paint beautifully and write poetry and he plays and sings and dances so marvellously. But he's sad and shy, too, just like a baby sometimes, and he understands what I'm really like inside – and – and I'd love to run my fingers through his hair – and I love him! Yes, I love him! (*She stretches out her arms to the moon*). Oh, Dion, I love you!

BILLY. I love you, Margaret.

MARGARET. I wonder if Dion – I saw him looking at me again to-night – Oh, I wonder . . .!

BILLY (*takes her hand and blurts out*). Can't you love me? Won't you marry me – after college –

MARGARET. Where is Dion, now, I wonder?

BILLY (*shaking her hand in an agony of uncertainty*). Margaret! Please answer me!

MARGARET (*her dream broken, puts on her mask and turns to him – matter-of-factly*). It's getting chilly. Let's go back and dance, Billy.

BILLY (*desperately*). I love you! (*He tries clumsily to kiss her.*)

MARGARET (*with an amused laugh*). Like a brother! You can kiss me if you like. (*She kisses him.*) A big-brother kiss. It doesn't count. (*He steps back crushed, with head bowed. She turns away and takes off her mask – to the moon.*) I wish Dion would kiss me again!

BILLY (*painfully*). I'm a poor boob. I ought to know better. I'll bet I know. You're in love with

Dion. I've seen you look at him. Isn't that it?

MARGARET. Dion! I love the sound of it!

BILLY (*huskily*). Well – he's always been my best friend – I'm glad it's him – and I guess I know how to lose – (*He takes her hand and shakes it*) – so here's wishing you all the success and happiness in the world, Margaret – and remember I'll always be your best friend! (*He gives her hand a final shake – swallows hard – then manfully.*) Let's go back in!

MARGARET (*to the moon – faintly annoyed*). What is Billy Brown doing here? I'll go down to the end of the dock and wait. Dion is the moon and I'm the sea. I want to feel the moon kissing the sea. I want Dion to leave the sky to me. I want the tides of my blood to leave my heart and follow him! (*She whispers like a little girl.*) Dion! Margaret! Peggy! Peggy is Dion's girl – Peggy is Dion's little girl – (*She sings laughingly, elfishly.*) Dion is my Daddy-O! (*She is walking toward the end of the dock, off left.*)

BILLY (*who has turned away*). I'm going. I'll tell Dion you're here.

MARGARET (*more and more strongly and assertively, until at the end she is a wife and a mother*). And I'll be Mrs. Dion – Dion's wife – and he'll be my Dion – my own Dion – my little boy – my baby! The moon is drowned in the tides of my heart, and peace sinks deep through the sea!

(*She disappears off left, her upturned unmasked face like that of a rapturous visionary. There is silence again, in which the dance music is heard. Then this stops and Dion comes in. He walks quickly to the bench at centre, and throws himself on it, hiding his masked face in his hands. After a moment, he lifts his head, peers about, listens huntedly, then slowly takes off his mask. His real face is revealed in the bright moonlight, shrinking, shy and gentle, full of a deep sadness.*)

DION (*with a suffering bewilderment.*) Why am I afraid to dance, I who love music and rhythm and grace and song and laughter? Why am I afraid to live, I who love life and the beauty of flesh and the living colours of earth and sky and sea? Why am I afraid of love, I who love love? Why am I afraid, I who am not afraid? Why must I pretend to scorn in order to pity? Why must I hide myself in self-contempt in order to understand? Why must I be so ashamed of my strength, so proud of my weakness? Why must I live in a cage like a criminal, defying and hating, I who love peace and friendship? (*Clasping his hands above in supplication.*) Why was I born without a skin, O God, that I must wear armour in order to touch or to be touched?

(*A second's pause of waiting silence – then he suddenly claps his mask over his face again, with a gesture of despair, and his voice becomes bitter and sardonic.*) Or rather, Old Graybeard, why the devil was I ever born at all?

(*Steps are heard from the right. Dion stiffens and his mask stares straight ahead. Billy comes in from the right. He is shuffling along disconsolately. When he sees Dion, he stops abruptly and glowers resentfully – but at once the "good loser" in him conquers this.*)

BILLY (*embarrassedly*). Hello, Dion. I've been looking all over for you. (*He sits down on the bench at right, forcing a joking tone.*) What are you sitting here for, you nut – trying to get more moon-struck? (*A pause – awkwardly.*) I just left Margaret –

DION (*gives a start – immediately defensively mocking*). Bless you, my children!

BILLY (*gruffly and slangily*). I'm out of it – she gave me the gate. You're the original white-haired boy. Go on in and win! We've been chums ever since we were kids, haven't we? – and – I'm glad it's you, Dion. (*This huskily – he fumbles for Dion's hand and gives it a shake.*)

DION (*letting his hand fall back – bitterly*). Chums? Oh no, Billy Brown would despise me!

BILLY. She's waiting for you now, down at the end of the dock.

DION. For me? Which? Who? Oh no, girls only allow themselves to look at what is seen!

BILLY. She's in love with you.

DION (*moved – a pause – stammers*). Miracle? I'm afraid! (*He chants flippantly.*) I love, thou lovest, he loves, she loves! She loves, she loves – what?

BILLY. And I know damn well, underneath your nuttiness, you're gone on her.

DION (*moved*). Underneath? I love love! I'd love to be loved! But I'm afraid! (*Then aggressively.*) *Was* afraid! Not now! Now I can make love – to anyone! Yes, I love Peggy! Why not? Who is she? Who am I? We love, you love, they love, one loves! No one loves! All the world loves a lover, God loves us all and we love Him! Love is a word – a shameless ragged ghost of a word – begging at all doors for life at any price!

BILLY (*always as if he hadn't listened to what the other said*). Say, let's you and me room together at college –

DION. Billy wants to remain by her side!

BILLY. It's a bet, then! (*Forcing a grin.*) You can tell her I'll see that you behave! (*Turns away.*) So long. Remember she's waiting. (*He goes.*)

DION (*dazedly, to himself*). Waiting – waiting for me! (*He slowly removes his mask. His face is torn and transfigured by joy. He stares at the sky raptly.*) O God in the moon, did you hear? She loves me! I am not afraid! I am strong! I can love! She protects me! Her arms are softly around me! She is warmly around me! She is my skin! She is my armour! Now I am born – I – the I! – one and indivisible – I who love Margaret! (*He glances at his mask triumphantly – in tones of deliverance.*) You are outgrown! I am beyond you! (*He stretches out his arms to the sky.*) O God, now I believe! (*From the end of the wharf, her voice is heard.*)

MARGARET. Dion!

DION (*raptly*). Margaret!

MARGARET (*nearer*). Dion!

DION. Margaret!

MARGARET. Dion! (*She comes running in, her mask in her hands. He springs toward her with outstretched arms, but she shrinks away with a frightened shriek and hastily puts on her mask. Dion starts back. She speaks coldly and angrily.*) Who are you? Why are you calling me? I don't know you!

DION (*heart-brokenly*). I love you!

MARGARET (*freezingly*). Is this a joke – or are you drunk?

DION (*with a final pleading whisper*). Margaret! (*But she only glares at him contemptuously. Then with a sudden gesture he claps his mask on and laughs wildly and bitterly.*) Ha-ha-ha! That's one on you, Peg!

MARGARET (*with delight, pulling off her mask*). Dion! How did you ever – Why, I never knew you!

DION (*puts his arm around her boldly*). How? It's the moon – the crazy moon – the monkey in the moon – playing jokes on us! (*He kisses her with his masked face with a romantic actor's passion again and again.*) You love me! You know you do! Say it! Tell me! I want to hear! I want to feel! I want to know! I want to want! To want you as you want me!

MARGARET (*in ecstasy*). Oh, Dion, I do! I do love you!

DION (*with ironic mastery – rhetorically*). And I love you! Oh, madly! Oh, for ever and ever, amen! You are my evening star and all my Pleiades! Your eyes are blue pools in which gold dreams glide, your body is a young white birch leaning backward beneath the lips of spring. So! (*He has bent her back, his arms supporting her, his face above hers.*) So! (*He kisses her.*)

MARGARET (*with overpowering passionate languor*). Oh, Dion! Dion! I love you!

DION (*with more and more mastery in his tone*). I love, you love, we love! Come! Rest! Relax! Let go your clutch on the world! Dim and dimmer! Fading out in the past behind! Gone! Death! Now! Be born! Awake! Live! Dissolve into dew – into silence – into night – into earth – into space – into peace – into meaning – into joy – into God – into the Great God Pan! (*While he has been speaking, the moon has passed gradually behind a black cloud, its light fading out. There is a moment of intense blackness and silence. Then the light gradually comes on again. Dion's voice, at first in a whisper, then increasing in volume with the light, is heard.*) Wake up! Time to get up! Time to exist! Time for school! Time to learn! Learn to pretend! Cover your nakedness! Learn to lie! Learn to keep step! Join the procession! Great Pan is dead! Be ashamed!

MARGARET (*with a sob*). Oh, Dion, I am ashamed!

DION (*mockingly*). Sssshh! Watch the monkey in the moon! See him dance! His tail is a piece of string that was left when he broke loose from

Jehovah and ran away to join Charley Darwin's circus!

MARGARET. I know you must hate me now! (*She throws her arms around him and hides her head on his shoulder.*)

DION (*deeply moved*). Don't cry! Don't – ! (*He suddenly tears off his mask – in a passionate agony.*) Hate you? I love you with all my soul! Love me! Why can't you love me, Margaret?

(*He tries to kiss her but she jumps to her feet with a frightened cry, holding up her mask before her face protectingly.*)

MARGARET. Don't! Please! I don't know you. You frighten me!

DION (*puts on his mask again – quietly and bitterly*). All's well. I'll never let you see again. (*He puts his arm around her – gently mocking.*) By proxy, I love you. There! Don't cry! Don't be afraid! Dion Anthony will marry you some day. (*He kisses her.*) "I take this woman – " (*Tenderly joking.*) Hello, woman! Do you feel older by æons? Mrs. Dion Anthony, shall we go in and may I have the next dance?

MARGARET (*tenderly*). You crazy child. (*Then, laughing with joy.*) Mrs. Dion Anthony! It sounds wonderful, doesn't it?

(*They go out as*

The Curtain Falls)

ACT ONE

SCENE ONE

SCENE. *Seven years later.*

The sitting-room of Mrs. Dion Anthony's half of a two-family house in the residential quarter of the town – one of those one-design districts that daze the eye with multiplied ugliness. The four pieces of furniture shown are in keeping – an arm-chair at left, a table with a chair behind it at centre, a sofa at right. The same court-room effect of the arrangement of benches in Act One is held to here. The background is a backdrop on which the rear wall is painted with the intolerable lifeless realistic detail of the stereotyped paintings which usually adorn the sitting-rooms of such houses. It is late afternoon of a grey day in winter.

Dion is sitting behind the table, staring before him. The mask hangs on his breast below his neck, giving the effect of two faces. His real face has aged greatly, grown more strained and tortured, but at the same time, in some queer way, more selfless and ascetic, more fixed in its resolute withdrawal from life. The mask, too, has changed. It is older, more defiant and mocking, its sneer more forced and bitter, its Pan quality becoming Mephistophelean. It has already begun to show the ravages of dissipation.

DION (*suddenly reaches out and takes up a copy of the New Testament which is on the table and, putting a finger in at random, opens and reads aloud the text at which it points*). "Come unto me all ye who are heavy laden and I will give you rest." (*He stares before him in a sort of trance, his face lighted up from within but painfully confused – in an uncertain whisper.*) I will come – but where are you, Saviour? (*The noise of the outer door shutting is heard. Dion starts and claps the mocking mask on his face again. He tosses the Testament aside contemptuously.*) Blah! Fixation on old Mamma Christianity! You infant blubbering in the dark, you!

(*He laughs, with a bitter self-contempt. Footsteps approach. He picks up a newspaper and hides behind it hurriedly. Margaret enters. She is dressed in stylish, expensive clothes and a fur coat, which look as if they had been remodelled and seen service. She has grown mature and maternal, in spite of her youth. Her pretty face is still fresh and healthy but there is the beginning of a permanently worried, apprehensive expression about the nose and mouth – an uncomprehending hurt in her eyes. Dion pretends to be engrossed in his paper. She bends down and kisses him.*)

MARGARET (*with a forced gaiety*). Good morning – at four in the afternoon! You were snoring when I left!

DION (*puts his arms around her with a negligent, accustomed gesture – mockingly*). The Ideal Husband!

MARGARET (*already preoccupied with another*

thought – comes and sits in chair on left). I was afraid the children would disturb you, so I took them over to Mrs. Young's to play. (*A pause. He picks up the paper again. She asks anxiously.*) I suppose they'll be all right over there, don't you? (*He doesn't answer. She is more hurt than offended.*) I wish you'd try to take more interest in the children, Dion.

DION (*mockingly*). Become a father – before breakfast? I'm in too delicate a condition. (*She turns away, hurt. Penitently he pats her hand – vaguely.*) All right. I'll try.

MARGARET (*squeezing his hand – with possessive tenderness*). Play with them. You're a bigger kid than they are – underneath.

DION (*self-mockingly – flipping the Bible*). Underneath – I'm becoming downright infantile! "Suffer these little ones!"

MARGARET (*keeping to her certainty*). You're my oldest.

DION (*with mocking appreciation*). She puts the Kingdom of Heaven in its place!

MARGARET (*withdrawing her hand*). I was serious.

DION. So was I – about something or other. (*He laughs.*) This domestic diplomacy! We communicate in code – when neither has the other's key!

MARGARET (*frowns confusedly – then forcing a playful tone*). I want to have a serious talk with you, young man! In spite of your promises, you've kept up the hard drinking and gambling you started the last year abroad.

DION. From the time I realized it wasn't in me to be an artist – except in living – and not even in that! (*He laughs bitterly.*)

MARGARET (*with conviction*). But you *can* paint, Dion – beautifully!

DION (*with deep pain*). No! (*He suddenly takes her hand and kisses it gratefully.*) I love Margaret! Her blindness surpasseth all understanding! (*Then bitterly*) – or is it pity?

MARGARET. We've only got about one hundred dollars left in the bank.

DION (*with dazed surprise*). What? Is all the money from the sale of the house gone?

MARGARET (*wearily*). Every day or so you've been cashing cheques. You've been drinking – you haven't counted –

DION (*irritably*). I know! (*A pause – soberly.*) No more estate to fall back on, eh? Well, for five years it kept us living abroad in peace. It bought us a little happiness – of a kind – didn't it? – living and loving and having children – (*A slight pause – bitterly*) – thinking one was creating before one discovered one couldn't!

MARGARET (*this time with forced conviction*). But you *can* paint – beautifully!

DION (*angrily*). Shut up! (*A pause – then jeeringly.*) So my wife thinks it behoves me to settle down and support my family in the meagre style to which they'll have to become accustomed?

MARGARET (*shamefacedly*). I didn't say – still – something's got to be done.

DION (*harshly*). Will Mrs. Anthony helpfully suggest what?

MARGARET. I met Billy Brown on the street. He said you'd have made a good architect, if you'd stuck to it.

DION. Flatterer! Instead of leaving college when my Old Man died? Instead of marrying Peggy and going abroad and being happy?

MARGARET (*as if she hadn't heard*). He spoke of how well you used to draw.

DION. Billy was in love with Margaret at one time.

MARGARET. He wanted to know why you've never been in to see him.

DION. He's bound heaven-bent for success. It's the will of Mammon! Anthony and Brown, contractors and builders – death subtracts Anthony and I sell out – Billy graduates – Brown and Son, architects and builders – old man Brown perishes of paternal pride – and now we have William A. Brown, architect! Why his career itself already has an architectural design! One of God's mud pies!

MARGARET. He particularly told me to ask you to drop in.

DION (*springs to his feet – assertively*). No! Pride! I have been alive!

MARGARET. Why don't you have a talk with him?

DION. Pride in my failure.

MARGARET. You were always such close friends.

DION (*more and more desperately*). The pride which came after man's fall – by which he laughs as a creator at his self-defeats!

MARGARET. Not for my sake – but for your own – and, above all, for the children's!

DION (*with terrible despair*). Pride! Pride without which the Gods are worms!

MARGARET (*after a pause, meekly and humbly*). You don't want to? It would hurt you? All right, dear. Never mind. We'll manage somehow – you mustn't worry – you must start your beautiful painting again – and I can get that position in the library – it would be such fun for me working there! . . . (*She reaches out and takes his hand – tenderly.*) I love you, dear. I understand.

DION (*slumps down into his chair, crushed, his face averted from hers, as hers is from him, although their hands are still clasped – in a trembling, expiring voice*). Pride is dying! (*As if he were suffocating, he pulls the mask from his resigned, pale, suffering face. He prays like a Saint in the desert, exorcizing a demon.*) Pride is dead! Blessed are the meek! Blessed are the poor in spirit!

MARGARET (*without looking at him – in a comforting motherly tone*). My poor boy!

DION (*resentfully – clapping on his mask again and springing to his feet – derisively*). Blessed are the meek for they shall inherit graves! Blessed are the poor in spirit for they are blind! (*Then with tortured bitterness.*) All right! Then I ask my wife to go and ask Billy Brown – that's more deadly than if I went myself! (*With wild mockery.*) Ask him if he can't find an opening for a talented young man who is only honest when he isn't sober – implore him, beg him in the name of old love, old friendship – to be a generous hero and save the woman and her children! (*He laughs with a sort of diabolical, ironical glee now, and starts to go out.*)

MARGARET (*meekly*). Are you going up street, Dion?

DION. Yes.

MARGARET. Will you stop at the butcher's and ask them to send two pounds of pork chops?

DION. Yes.

MARGARET. And stop at Mrs. Young's and tell the children to hurry right home?

DION. Yes.

MARGARET. Will you be back for dinner, Dion?

DION. No. (*He goes, the outer door slams. Margaret sighs with a tired incomprehension and goes to the window and stares out.*)

MARGARET (*worriedly*). I hope they'll be careful, crossing the street.

Curtain

ACT ONE SCENE TWO

SCENE. *Billy Brown's Office, at five in the afternoon. At centre, a fine mahogany desk with a swivel chair behind it. To the left of desk, an office armchair. To the right of desk, an office lounge. The background is a backdrop of an office wall, treated similarly to that of Scene One in its over-meticulous representation of detail.*

Billy Brown is seated at the desk looking over a blue print by the light of a desk lamp. He has grown into a fine-looking, well-dressed, capable, college-bred American business man, boyish still and with the same engaging personality.

The telephone rings.

BROWN (*answering it*). Yes? Who? (*This in surprise – then with eager pleasure.*) Ask her to come right in.

(*He gets up and goes to the door, expectant and curious. Margaret enters. Her face is concealed behind the mask of the pretty young matron, still hardly a woman, who cultivates a naïvely innocent and bravely hopeful attitude toward things and acknowledges no wound to the world. She is dressed as in Scene One but with an added touch of effective primping here and there.*)

MARGARET (*very gaily*). Hello, Billy Brown!

BROWN (*awkward in her presence, shakes her hand*). Come in. Sit down. This is a pleasant surprise, Margaret.

(*She sits down on the lounge. He sits in his chair behind the desk, as before.*)

MARGARET (*looking around*). What lovely offices! My, but Billy Brown is getting grand!

BROWN (*pleased*). I've just moved in. The old place was too stuffy.

MARGARET. It looks so prosperous – but then, Billy is doing so wonderfully well, every one says.

BROWN (*modestly*). Well, to be frank, it's been mostly luck. Things have come my way without my doing much about it. (*Then, with an abashed pride.*) Still – I have done a little something myself. (*He picks the plan from the desk.*) See this? It's my design for the New Municipal Building. It's just been accepted – provisionally – by the Committee.

MARGARET (*taking it – vaguely*). Oh? (*She looks at it abstractedly. There is a pause. Suddenly.*) You mentioned the other day how well Dion used to draw –

BROWN (*a bit stiffly*). Yes, he certainly did. (*He takes the drawing from her and at once becomes interested and squints at it frowningly.*) Did you notice that anything seemed lacking in this?

MARGARET (*indifferently*). Not at all.

BROWN (*with a cheerful grin*). The Committee want it made a little more American. It's too much of a conventional Greco-Roman tomb, they say. (*Laughs.*) They want an original touch of modern novelty stuck in to liven it up and make it look different from other town halls. (*Putting the drawing back on his desk.*) And I've been figuring out how to give it to them, but my mind doesn't seem to run that way. Have you any suggestion?

MARGARET (*as if she hadn't heard*). Dion certainly draws well, Billy Brown was saying?

BROWN (*trying not to show his annoyance*). Why, yes – he did – and still can, I expect. (*A pause. He masters what he feels to be an unworthy pique and turns to her generously.*) Dion would have made a cracking good architect.

MARGARET (*proudly*). I know. He could be anything he wanted to.

BROWN (*a pause – embarrassedly*). Is he working at anything these days?

MARGARET (*defensively*). Oh, yes! He's painting wonderfully! But he's just like a child, he's so impractical. He doesn't try to have an exhibition anywhere, or anything.

BROWN (*surprised*). The one time I ran into him, I thought he told me he'd destroyed all his pictures – that he'd got sick of painting and completely given it up.

MARGARET (*quickly*). He always tells people that. He doesn't want anyone even to look at his things, imagine! He keeps saying they're rotten – when they're really too beautiful! He's too modest for his own good, don't you think? But it is true he hasn't done so much lately since we've been back. You see the children take up such a lot of his time. He just worships them! I'm afraid he's becoming a hopeless family man, just the opposite of what anyone would expect who knew him in the old days.

BROWN (*painfully embarrassed by her loyalty and his knowledge of the facts*). Yes, I know. (*He coughs self-consciously.*)

MARGARET (*aroused by something in his manner*). But I suppose the gossips are telling the same silly stories about him they always did. (*She forces a laugh.*) Poor Dion! Give a dog a bad name! (*Her voice breaks a little in spite of herself.*)

BROWN (*hastily*). I haven't heard any stories – (*he stops uncertainly, then decides to plunge in*) – except about money matters.

MARGARET (*forcing a laugh*). Oh, perhaps they're true enough. Dion is such a generous fool with his money, like all artists.

BROWN (*with a certain doggedness*). There's a rumour that you've applied for a position at the Library.

MARGARET (*forcing a gay tone*). Yes, indeed! Won't it be fun! Maybe it'll improve my mind! And one of us has got to be practical, so why not me? (*She forces a gay, girlish laugh.*)

BROWN (*impulsively reaches out and takes her hand – awkwardly*). Listen, Margaret. Let's be perfectly frank, will you? I'm such an old friend, and I want like the deuce to. . . . You know darn well I'd do anything in the world to help you – or Dion.

MARGARET (*withdrawing her hand, coldly*). I'm afraid I – don't understand, Billy Brown.

BROWN (*acutely embarrassed*). Well, I – I just meant – you know, if you needed – (*A pause. He looks questioningly at her averted face – then ventures on another tack, matter-of-factly.*) I've got a proposition to make to Dion – if I could ever get hold of him. It's this way: business has been piling up on me – a run of luck – but I'm short-handed. I need a crack chief draughtsman darn badly – or I'm liable to lose out. Do you think Dion would consider it – as a temporary stop-gap – until he felt in the painting mood again?

MARGARET (*striving to conceal her eagerness and relief – judicially*). Yes – I really do. He's such a good sport and Billy and he were such pals once. I know he'd be only too tickled to help him out.

BROWN (*diffidently*). I thought he might be sensitive about working for – I mean, with me – when, if he hadn't sold out to Dad he'd be my partner now – (*earnestly*) – and, by jingo, I wish he was! (*Then, abruptly.*) Let's try to nail him down right away, Margaret. Is he home now? (*He reaches for the 'phone.*)

MARGARET (*hurriedly*). No, he – he went out for a long walk.

BROWN. Perhaps I can locate him later around town somewhere.

MARGARET (*with a note of pleading*). Please don't trouble. It isn't necessary. I'm sure when I talk to him – he's coming home to dinner – (*Getting up.*) Then it's all settled, isn't it? Dion will be so glad to be able to help an old friend – he's so terribly loyal, and he's always liked Billy Brown so much! (*Holding out her hand.*) I really must go now!

BROWN (*shakes her hand*). Good-bye, Margaret. I hope you'll be dropping in on us a lot when Dion gets here.

MARGARET. Yes. (*She goes.*)

BROWN (*sits at his desk again, looking ahead in a not unsatisfying melancholy reverie. He mutters admiringly but pityingly*). Poor Margaret! She's a game sport, but it's pretty damn tough on her! (*Indignantly.*) By God, I'm going to give Dion a good talking-to one of these days!

Curtain

ACT ONE SCENE THREE

SCENE. *Cybel's parlour. An automatic, penny-in-the-slot player-piano is at centre, rear. On its right is a dirty gilt second-hand sofa. At the left is a bald-spotted crimson plush chair. The backdrop for the rear wall is cheap wall-paper of a dull yellow-brown, resembling a blurred impression of a fallow field in early spring. There is a cheap alarm clock on top of the piano. Beside it her mask is lying.*

Dion is sprawled on his back, fast asleep on the sofa. His mask has fallen down on his chest. His pale face is singularly pure, spiritual and sad.

The player-piano is groggily banging out a sentimental medley of "Mother – Mammy" tunes.

Cybel is seated on the stool in front of the piano. She is a strong, calm, sensual, blonde girl of twenty or so, her complexion fresh and healthy, her figure full-breasted and wide-hipped, her movements slow and solidly languorous like an animal's, her large eyes dreamy with the reflected stirring of profound instincts. She chews gum like a sacred cow forgetting time with an eternal end. Her eyes are fixed, incuriously, on Dion's pale face.

CYBEL (*as the tune runs out, glances at the clock, which indicates midnight, then goes slowly over to Dion and puts her hand gently on his forehead*). Wake up!

DION (*stirs, sighs and murmurs dreamily*). "And He laid his hands on them and healed them." (*Then with a start he opens his eyes and, half sitting up, stares at her bewilderedly.*) What – where – who are you? (*He reaches for his mask and claps it on defensively.*)

CYBEL (*placidly*). Only another female. You was camping on my steps, sound asleep. I didn't want to run any risk getting into more trouble with the cops pinching you there and blaming me, so I took you in to sleep it off.

DION (*mockingly*). Blessed are the pitiful, Sister! I'm broke – but you will be rewarded in Heaven!

CYBEL (*calmly*). I wasn't wasting my pity. Why should I? You were happy, weren't you?

DION (*approvingly*). Excellent! You're not a moralist, I see.

CYBEL (*going on*). And you look like a good boy,

too – when you're asleep. Say, you better beat it home to bed or you'll be locked out.

DION (*mockingly*). Now you're becoming maternal, Miss Earth. Is that the only answer – to pin my soul into every vacant diaper? (*She stares down at his mask, her face growing hard. He laughs.*) But please don't stop stroking my aching brow. Your hand is a cool mud poultice on the sting of thought!

CYBEL (*calmly*). Stop acting. I hate ham fats. (*She looks at him as if waiting for him to remove his mask – then turns her back indifferently and goes to the piano.*) Well, if you simply got to be a regular devil like all the other visiting sports, I s'pose I got to play with you. (*She takes her mask and puts it on – then turns. The mask is the rouged and eye-blackened countenance of the hardened prostitute. In a coarse, harsh voice.*) Kindly state your dishonourable intentions, if any! I can't sit up all night keeping company! Let's have some music! (*She puts a plug in the machine. The same sentimental medley begins to play. The two masks stare at each other. She laughs.*) Shoot! I'm all set! It's your play, Kid Lucifer!

DION (*slowly removes his mask. She stops the music with a jerk. His face is gentle and sad – humbly*). I'm sorry. It has always been such agony for me to be touched!

CYBEL (*taking off her mask – sympathetically as she comes back and sits down on her stool*). Poor kid! I've never had one, but I can guess. They hug and kiss you and take you on their laps and pinch you and want to see you getting dressed and undressed – as if they owned you – I bet you I'd never let them treat one of mine that way!

DION (*turning to her*). You're lost in blind alleys, too. (*Suddenly holding out his hand to her.*) But you're strong. Let's be friends.

CYBEL (*with a strange sternness, searches his face*). And never nothing more?

DION (*with a strange smile*). Let's say, never anything less!

(*She takes his hand. There is a ring at the outside door bell. They stare at each other. There is another ring.*)

CYBEL (*puts on her mask, Dion does likewise. Mockingly*). When you got to love to live it's hard to love living. I better join the A.F. of L. and soap-box for the eight-hour night! Got a nickel, baby? Play a tune. (*She goes out. Dion puts a nickel in. The same sentimental tune starts. Cybel returns, followed by Billy Brown. His face is rigidly composed, but his superior disgust for Dion can be seen. Dion jerks off the music and he and Billy look at each other for a moment, Cybel watching them both – then, bored, she yawns.*) He's hunting for you. Put out the lights when you go. I'm going to sleep. (*She starts to go – then, as if reminded of something – to Dion.*) Life's all right, if you let it alone. (*Then mechanically flashing a trade smile at Billy.*) Now you know the way, Handsome, call again! (*She goes.*)

BROWN (*after an awkward pause*). Hello, Dion! I've been looking all over town for you. This place was the very last chance. . . . (*Another pause – embarrassedly.*) Let's take a walk.

DION (*mockingly*). I've given up exercise. They claim it lengthens your life.

BROWN (*persuasively*). Come on, Dion, be a good fellow. You're certainly not staying here –

DION. Billy would like to think me taken in *flagrante delicto*, eh?

BROWN. Don't be a damn fool! Listen to me! I've been looking you up for purely selfish reasons. I need your help.

DION (*astonished*). What?

BROWN. I've a proposition to make that I hope you'll consider favourably out of old friendship. To be frank, Dion, I need you to lend me a hand down at the office.

DION (*with a harsh laugh*). So it's the job, is it? Then my poor wife did a-begging go!

BROWN (*repelled – sharply*). On the contrary, I had to beg her to beg you to take it! (*More angrily.*) Look here, Dion! I won't listen to you talk that way about Margaret! And you wouldn't if you weren't drunk! (*Suddenly shaking him.*) What in hell has come over you, anyway! You didn't use to be like this! What the devil are you going to do with yourself – sink into the gutter and drag Margaret with you? If you'd heard her defend you, lie about you, tell me how hard you were working, what beautiful things you were painting, how you stayed at home and idolized the children! – when every one knows you've been out every night sousing and gambling away the last of your estate. . . . (*He stops, ashamed, con-*

trolling himself.)

DION (*wearily*). She was lying about her husband, not me, you fool! But it's no use explaining. (*Then, in a sudden, excitable passion.*) What do you want? I agree to anything – except the humiliation of yelling secrets at the deaf!

BROWN (*trying a bullying tone – roughly*). Bunk! Don't try to crawl out! There's no excuse and you know it. (*Then as Dion doesn't reply – penitently.*) But I know I shouldn't talk this way, old man! It's only because we're such old pals – and I hate to see you wasting yourself – you who had more brains than any of us! But, damn it, I suppose you're too much of a rotten cynic to believe I mean what I've just said!

DION (*touched*). I know Billy was always Dion Anthony's friend.

BROWN. You're damn right, I am – and I'd have proved it long ago if you'd only given me half a chance! After all, I couldn't keep chasing after you and be snubbed every time. A man has some pride!

DION (*bitterly mocking*). Dead wrong! Never more! None whatever! It's unmoral! Blessed are the poor in spirit, Brother! When shall I report?

BROWN (*eagerly*). Then you'll take the – you'll help me?

DION (*wearily bitter*). I'll take the job. One must do something to pass away the time, while one is waiting – for one's next incarnation.

BROWN (*jokingly*). I'd say it was a bit early to be worrying about that. (*Trying to get Dion started.*) Come along, now. It's pretty late.

DION (*shakes his hand off his shoulder and walks away from him – after a pause*). Is my father's chair still there?

BROWN (*turns away – embarrassed*). I – I don't really remember, Dion – I'll look it up.

DION (*taking off his mask – slowly*). I'd like to sit where he spun what I have spent. What aliens we were to each other! When he lay dead, his face looked so familiar that I wondered where I had met that man before. Only at the second of my conception. After that, we grew hostile with concealed shame. And my mother? I remember a sweet, strange girl, with affectionate, bewildered eyes as if God had locked her in a dark closet without any explanation. I was the sole doll our ogre, her husband, allowed her and she played mother and child with me for many years in that house until at last through two tears I watched her die with the shy pride of one who has lengthened her dress and put up her hair. And I felt like a forsaken toy and cried to be buried with her, because her hands alone had caressed without clawing. She lived long and aged greatly in the two days before they closed her coffin. The last time I looked, her purity had forgotten me, she was stainless and imperishable, and I knew my sobs were ugly and meaningless to her virginity; so I shrank away, back into life, with naked nerves jumping like fleas, and in due course of nature another girl called me her boy in the moon and married me and became three mothers in one person, while I got paint on my paws in an endeavour to see God! (*He laughs wildly – claps on his mask.*) But that Ancient Humorist had given me weak eyes, so now I'll have to foreswear my quest for Him and go in for the Omnipresent Successful Serious One, the Great God Mr. Brown, instead! (*He makes him a sweeping, mocking bow.*)

BROWN (*repelled but cajolingly*). Shut up, you nut! You're still drunk. Come on! Let's start! (*He grabs Dion by the arm and switches off the light.*)

DION (*from the darkness – mockingly*). I am thy shorn, bald, nude sheep! Lead on, Almighty Brown, thou Kindly Light!

Curtain

ACT TWO SCENE ONE

SCENE. *Cybel's parlour – about sunset in spring seven years later. The arrangement of furniture is the same but the chair and sofa are new, bright-coloured, costly pieces. The old automatic piano at centre looks exactly the same. The cheap alarm clock is still on top of it. On either side of the clock, the masks of Dion and Cybel are lying. The background backdrop is brilliant, stunning wall-paper, on which crimson and purple flowers and fruits tumble over one another in a riotously profane lack of any apparent design.*

Dion sits in the chair on left, Cybel on the sofa. A card-table is between them. Both are playing solitaire. Dion is now prematurely grey. His face is that of an ascetic, a martyr, furrowed by pain and self-torture, yet lighted from within by a spiritual calm and human kindliness.

Cybel has grown stouter and more voluptuous, but her face is still unmarked and fresh, her calm more profound. She is like an unmoved idol of Mother Earth.

The piano is whining out its same old sentimental medley. They play their cards intently and contentedly. The music stops.

CYBEL (*musingly*). I love those rotten old sob tunes. They make me wise to people. That's what's inside them – what makes them love and murder their neighbour – crying jags set to music!

DION (*compassionately*). Every song is a hymn. They keep trying to find the Word in the Beginning.

CYBEL. They try to know too much. It makes them weak. I never puzzled over them myself. I gave them a Tart. They understood her and knew their parts and acted naturally. And on both sides we were able to keep our real virtue, if you get me. (*She plays her last card – indifferently.*) I've made it again.

DION (*smiling*). Your luck is uncanny. It never comes out for me.

CYBEL. You keep getting closer, but it knows you still want to win – a little bit – and it's wise all I care about is playing. (*She lays out another game.*) Speaking of my canned music, our Mr. Brown hates that old box. (*At the mention of Brown, Dion trembles as if suddenly possessed, has a terrible struggle with himself, then while she continues to speak, gets up like an automaton and puts on his mask. The mask is now terribly ravaged. All of its Pan quality has changed into a diabolical Mephistophelean cruelty and irony.*) He doesn't mind the music inside. That gets him somehow. But he thinks the case looks shabby and he wants it junked. But I told him that just because he's been keeping me so long, he needn't start bossing like a husband or I'll – (*She looks up and sees the masked Dion standing by the piano – calmly.*) Hello! Getting jealous again?

DION (*jeeringly*). Are you falling in love with your keeper, old Sacred Cow?

CYBEL (*without taking offence*). Cut it! You've been asking me that for years. Be yourself! He's healthy and handsome – but he's too guilty. What makes you pretend you think love is so important, anyway? It's just one of a lot of things you do to keep life living.

DION (*in same tone*). Then you've lied when you've said you loved me, have you, Old Filth?

CYBEL (*affectionately*). You'll never grow up! We've been friends, haven't we, for seven years? I've never let myself want you nor you me. Yes, I love you. It takes all kinds of love to make a world! Ours is the living cream, I say, living rich and high! (*A pause. Coaxingly.*) Stop hiding. I know you.

DION (*taking off his mask, wearily comes and sits down at her feet and lays his head in her lap – with a grateful smile*). You're strong. You always give. You've given my weakness strength to live.

CYBEL (*tenderly, stroking his hair maternally.*) You're not weak. You were born with ghosts in your eyes and you were brave enough to go looking into your own dark – and you got afraid. (*After a pause.*) I don't blame your being jealous of Mr. Brown sometimes. I'm jealous of your wife, even though I know you do love her.

DION (*slowly*). I love Margaret. I don't know who my wife is.

CYBEL (*after a pause – with a queer broken laugh*). Oh, God, sometimes the truth hits me such a sock between the eyes I can see the stars! – and then I'm so damn sorry for the lot of you, every damn mother's son-of-a-gun of you, that I'd like to run out naked into the street and love the whole mob to death like I was bringing you all a new brand of dope that'd make you forget everything that ever was for good! (*Then, with a twisted smile.*) But they wouldn't see me, any more than they see each other. And they keep right on moving along and dying without my help anyway.

DION (*sadly*). You've given me strength to die.

CYBEL. You may be important but your life's not. There's millions of it born every second. Life can cost too much even for a sucker to afford it – like everything else. And it's not sacred – only the you inside is. The rest is earth.

DION (*gets to his knees and with clasped hands

looks up raptly and prays with an ascetic fervour). "Into thy hands, O Lord," . . . (*Then suddenly, with a look of horror.*) Nothing! To feel one's life blown out like the flame of a cheap match . . .! (*He claps on his mask and laughs harshly.*) To fall asleep and know you'll never, never be called to get on the job of existence again! "Swift be thine approaching flight! Come soon – soon!" (*He quotes this last with a mocking longing.*)

CYBEL (*pats his head maternally*). There, don't be scared. It's born in the blood. When the time comes, you'll find it's easy.

DION (*jumps to his feet and walks about excitedly*). It won't be long. My wife dragged in a doctor the day before yesterday. He says my heart is gone – booze – He warned me, never another drop or – (*Mockingly.*) What say? Shall we have a drink?

CYBEL (*like an idol*). Suit yourself. It's in the pantry. (*Then, as he hesitates.*) What set you off on this bat? You were raving on about some cathedral plans. . . .

DION (*wildly mocking*). They've been accepted – Mr. Brown's designs! My designs really! You don't need to be told that. He hands me one mathematically correct barn after another and I doctor them up with cute allurements so that fools will desire to buy, sell, breed, sleep, love, hate, curse and pray in them! I do this with devilish cleverness to their entire delight! Once I dreamed of painting wind on the sea and the skimming flight of cloud shadows over the tops of trees! Now . . . (*He laughs.*) But pride is a sin – even in a memory of the long deceased! Blessed are the poor in spirit! (*He subsides weakly on his chair, his hand pressed to his heart.*)

CYBEL (*like an idol*). Go home and sleep. Your wife'll be worried.

DION. She knows – but she'll never admit to herself that her husband ever entered your door. (*Mocking.*) Aren't women loyal – to their vanity and their other things!

CYBEL. Brown is coming soon, don't forget.

DION. He knows too and can't admit. Perhaps he needs me here – unknown. What first aroused his passion to possess you exclusively, do you think? Because he knew you loved me and he felt himself cheated. He wanted what he thought was my love of the flesh! He feels I have no right to love. He'd like to steal it as he steals my ideas – complacently – righteously. Oh, the good Brown!

CYBEL. But you like him, too! You're brothers, I guess, somehow. Well, remember he's paying, he'll pay – in some way or other.

DION (*raises his head as if starting to remove the mask*). I know. Poor Billy! God forgive me the evil I've done him!

CYBEL (*reaches out and takes his hand*). Poor boy!

DION (*presses her convulsively – then with forced harshness*). Well, homeward Christian Soldier! I'm off! By-bye, Mother Earth. (*He starts to go off right. She seems about to let him go.*)

CYBEL (*suddenly starts and calls with deep grief*). Dion! (*He looks at her. A pause. He comes slowly back. She speaks strangely in a deep, far-off voice – and yet like a mother talking to her little son.*) You mustn't forget to kiss me before you go, Dion. (*She removes his mask.*) Haven't I told you to take off your mask in the house? Look at me, Dion. I've – just – seen – something. I'm afraid you're going away a long, long way. I'm afraid I won't see you again for a long, long time. So it's good-bye, dear. (*She kisses him gently. He begins to sob. She hands him back his mask.*) Here you are. Don't get hurt. Remember, it's all a game, and after you're asleep I'll tuck you in.

DION (*in a choking, heart-broken cry*). Mother! (*Then he claps on his mask with a terrible effort of will – mockingly.*) Go to the devil, you sentimental old pig! See you to-morrow! (*He goes, whistling, slamming the door.*)

CYBEL (*like an idol again*). What's the good of bearing children? What's the use of giving birth to death? (*She sighs wearily, turns, puts a plug in the piano, which starts up its old sentimental tune. At the same moment Brown enters quietly from the left. He is the ideal of the still youthful, good-looking, well-groomed, successful provincial American of forty. Just now, he is plainly perturbed. He is not able to see either Cybel's face or her mask.*)

BROWN. Cybel! (*She starts, jams off the music and reaches for her mask, but has no time to put it on.*) Wasn't that Dion I just saw going out – after all your promises never to see him! (*She turns like an idol, holding the mask behind her. He stares, bewildered – stammers.*) I – I beg your pardon – I thought –

CYBEL (*in her strange voice*). Cybel's gone out to dig in the earth and pray.

BROWN (*with more assurance*). But – aren't those her clothes?

CYBEL. Cybel doesn't want people to see me naked. I'm her sister. Dion came to see me.

BROWN (*relieved*). So that's what he's up to, is it? (*Then with a pitying sigh.*) Poor Margaret! (*Then with playful reproof.*) You really shouldn't encourage him. He's married and got three big sons.

CYBEL. And you haven't.

BROWN (*stung*). No, I'm not married.

CYBEL. He and I were friends.

BROWN (*with a playful wink*). Yes, I can imagine how the platonic must appeal to Dion's pure, innocent type! It's no good your kidding me about Dion. We've been friends since we were kids. I know him in and out. I've always stood up for him whatever he's done – so you can be perfectly frank. I only spoke as I did on account of Margaret – his wife – it's pretty tough on her.

CYBEL. You love his wife.

BROWN (*scandalized*). What? What are you talking about? (*Then uncertainly.*) Don't be a fool! (*A pause – then as if impelled by an intense curiosity.*) So Dion is your lover, eh? That's very interesting. (*He pulls his chair closer to hers.*) Sit down. Let's talk. (*She continues to stand, the mask held behind her.*) Tell me – I've always been curious – what is it that makes Dion so attractive to women – especially certain types of women, if you'll pardon me? He always has been and yet I never could see exactly what they saw in him. Is it his looks – or because he's such a violent sensualist – or because he poses as artistic and temperamental – or because he's so wild – or just what is it?

CYBEL. He's alive!

BROWN (*suddenly takes one of her hands and kisses it – insinuatingly*). Well, don't you think I'm alive, too? (*Eagerly.*) Listen. Would you consider giving up Dion – and letting me take care of you under a similar arrangement to the one I've made with Cybel? I like you, you can see that. I won't bother you much – I'm much too busy – you can do what you like – lead your own life – except for seeing him. (*He stops. A pause. She stares ahead unmoved as if she hadn't heard. He pleads.*) Well – what do you say? Please do!

CYBEL (*her voice very weary*). Cybel asked me to tell you she'd be back next week, Mr. Brown.

BROWN (*with queer agony*). You mean you won't? Don't be so cruel! I love you! (*She walks away. He clutches at her, pleadingly.*) At least – I'll give you anything you ask! – please promise me you won't see Dion Anthony again!

CYBEL (*with deep grief*). He will never see me again, I promise you. Good-bye!

BROWN (*jubilantly, kissing her hand – politely*). Thank you! Thank you! I'm exceedingly grateful. (*Tactfully.*) I won't disturb you any further. Please forgive my intrusion, and remember me to Cybel when you write. (*He bows, turns, and goes off left.*)

Curtain

ACT TWO SCENE TWO

SCENE. *The draughting-room in Brown's office. Dion's draughting table with a high stool in front is at centre. Another stool is to the left of it. At the right is a bench. It is in the evening of the same day. The black wall drop has windows painted on it with a dim, street-lighted view of black houses across the way.*

Dion is sitting on the stool behind the table, reading aloud from the "Imitation of Christ" by Thomas à Kempis to his mask, which is on the table before him. His own face is gentler, more spiritual, more saintlike and ascetic than ever before.

DION (*like a priest, offering up prayers for the dying*). "Quickly must thou be gone from hence, see then how matters stand with thee. Ah, fool – learn now to die to the world that thou mayst begin to live with Christ! Do now, beloved, do now all thou canst because thou knowest not when thou shalt die; nor dost thou know what shall befall thee after death. Keep thyself as a pilgrim, and a stranger upon earth, to whom the affairs of this world do not – belong! Keep thy heart free and raised upwards to God because thou hast not here a lasting abode. 'Because at what hour you know not the Son of Man will come!'" Amen. (*He raises his hand over the mask as if he were blessing it, closes the book and puts it back in his pocket. He raises the mask in his hands and stares at it with a pitying tenderness.*) Peace, poor tortured one, brave pitiful pride of man, the hour of our deliverance comes. To-morrow we may be with Him in Paradise! (*He kisses it on the lips and sets it down again. There is the noise of footsteps climbing the stairs in the hallway. He grabs up the mask in a sudden panic and, as a knock comes on the door, he claps it on and calls mockingly.*) Come in, Mrs. Anthony, come in!

(*Margaret enters. In one hand behind her, hidden from him, is the mask of the brave face she puts on before the world to hide her suffering and disillusionment, and which she has just taken off. Her own face is still sweet and pretty, but lined, drawn and careworn for its years, sad, resigned, but a bit querulous.*)

MARGARET (*wearily reproving*). Thank goodness I've found you! Why haven't you been home the last two days? It's bad enough your drinking again without your staying away and worrying us to death!

DION (*bitterly*). My ears knew her footsteps. One gets to recognize everything – and to see nothing!

MARGARET. I finally sent the boys out looking for you and came myself. (*With tired solicitude.*) I suppose you haven't eaten a thing, as usual. Won't you come home and let me fry you a chop?

DION (*wonderingly*). Can Margaret still love Dion Anthony? Is it possible she does?

MARGARET (*forcing a tired smile*). I suppose so, Dion. I certainly oughtn't to, ought I?

DION (*in same tone*). And I love Margaret! What haunted, haunting ghosts we are! We dimly remember so much it will take us so many million years to forget! (*He comes forward, putting one arm around her bowed shoulders, and they kiss.*)

MARGARET (*patting his hand affectionately*). No, you certainly don't deserve it. When I stop to think of all you've made me go through in the years since we settled down here . . . ! I really don't believe I could ever have stood it if it weren't for the boys! (*Forcing a smile.*) But perhaps I would, I've always been such a big fool about you.

DION (*a bit mockingly*). The boys! Three strong sons! Margaret can afford to be magnanimous!

MARGARET. If they didn't find you, they were coming to meet me here.

DION (*with sudden wildness – torturedly, sinking on his knees beside her*). Margaret! Margaret! I'm lonely! I'm frightened! I'm going away! I've got to say good-bye!

MARGARET (*patting his hair*). Poor boy! Poor Dion! Come home and sleep.

DION (*springs up frantically*). No! I'm a man. I'm a lonely man! I can't go back! I have conceived myself! (*Then with desperate mockery.*) Look at me, Mrs. Anthony! It's the last chance! To-morrow I'll have moved on to the next hell! Behold your man – the snivelling, cringing, life-denying Christian slave you have so nobly ignored in the father of your sons! Look! (*He tears the mask from his face, which is radiant with a great pure love for her and a great sympathy and tenderness.*) O woman – my love – that I have sinned against in my sick pride and cruelty – forgive my sins – forgive my solitude – forgive my sickness – forgive me! (*He kneels and kisses the hem of her dress.*)

MARGARET (*who has been staring at him with terror, raising her mask to ward off his face*). Dion! Don't! I can't bear it! You're like a ghost. You're dead! Oh, my God! Help! Help! (*She falls back fainting on the bench. He looks at her – then takes her hand which holds her mask and looks at that face – gently.*) And now I am permitted to understand and love you, too! (*He kisses the mask first – then kisses her face, murmuring.*) And you, sweetheart! Blessed, thrice blessed are the meek!

(*There is a sound of heavy, hurrying footsteps on the stairs. He puts on his mask in haste. The three sons rush into the room. The Eldest is about fourteen, the two others thirteen and twelve. They look healthy, normal, likeable boys, with much the same quality as Billy Brown's in Act One, Scene One. They stop short and stiffen all in a row, staring from the woman on the bench to their father, accusingly.*)

ELDEST. We heard some one yell. It sounded like Mother.

DION (*defensively*). No. It was this lady – my wife.

ELDEST. But hasn't Mother come yet?

DION (*going to Margaret*). Yes. Your Mother is here. (*He stands between them and puts her mask over Margaret's face – then steps back.*) She has fainted. You'd better bring her to.

BOYS. Mother! (*They run to her side, kneel and rub her wrists. The Eldest smooths back her hair.*)

DION (*watching them*). At least I am leaving her well provided for. (*He addresses them directly.*) Tell your mother she'll get word from Mr. Brown's house. I must pay him a farewell call. I am going. Good-bye. (*They stop, staring at him fixedly, with eyes a mixture of bewilderment, distrust and hurt.*)

ELDEST (*awkwardly and shamefacedly*). Honest, I think you ought to have . . .

SECOND. Yes, honest you ought . . .

YOUNGEST. Yes, honest . . .

DION (*in a friendly tone*). I know. But I couldn't. That's for you who can. You must inherit the earth for her. Don't forget now, boys. Good-bye.

BOYS (*in the same awkward, self-conscious tone, one after another*). Good-bye – good-bye – good-bye. (*Dion goes.*)

Curtain

ACT TWO SCENE THREE

SCENE. *The library of William Brown's home – night of the same day. A backdrop of carefully painted, prosperous, bourgeois culture, book-cases filled with sets, etc. The heavy table at centre is expensive. The leather arm-chair at left of it and the couch at right are opulently comfortable. The reading lamp on the table is the only light.*

Brown sits in the chair at left reading an architectural periodical. His expression is composed and gravely receptive. In outline, his face suggests a Roman consul on an old coin. There is an incongruous distinction about it, the quality of unquestioning faith in the finality of its achievement.

There is a sudden loud thumping on the front door and the ringing of the bell. Brown frowns and listens as a servant answers. Dion's voice can be heard, raised mockingly.

DION. Tell him it's the devil come to conclude a bargain.

BROWN (*suppressing annoyance, calls out with forced good nature*). Come on in, Dion. (*Dion enters. He is in a wild state. His clothes are dishevelled, his masked face has a terrible deathlike intensity, its mocking irony becomes so cruelly malignant as to give him the appearance of a real demon, tortured into torturing others.*) Sit down.

DION (*stands and sings*). William Brown's soul lies mouldering in the crib, but his body goes marching on!

BROWN (*maintaining the same indulgent, big-brotherly tone, which he tries to hold throughout the scene.*) Not so loud, for Pete's sake! I don't mind – but I've got neighbours.

DION. Hate them! Fear thy neighbour as thyself! That's the leaden rule for the safe and sane. (*Then advancing to the table with a sort of deadly calm.*) Listen! One day when I was four years old, a boy sneaked up behind when I was drawing a picture in the sand he couldn't draw and hit me on the head with a stick and kicked out my picture and laughed when I cried. It wasn't what he'd done that made me cry, but him! I had loved and trusted him and suddenly the good God was disproved in his person and the evil and injustice of Man was born! Every one called me cry-baby, so I became silent for life and designed a mask of the Bad Boy Pan in which to live and rebel against that other boy's God and protect myself from His cruelty. And that other boy, secretly he felt ashamed but he couldn't acknowledge it; so from that day he instinctively developed into the good boy, the good friend, the good man, William Brown!

BROWN (*shamefacedly*). I remember now. It was a dirty trick. (*Then with a trace of resentment.*)

Sit down. You know where the booze is. Have a drink, if you like. But I guess you've had enough already.

DION (*looks at him fixedly for a moment – then strangely*). Thanks be to Brown for reminding me. I must drink. (*He goes and gets a bottle of whisky and a glass.*)

BROWN (*with a good-humoured shrug*). All right. It's your funeral.

DION (*returning and pouring out a big drink in the tumbler*). And William Brown's! When I die, he goes to hell! Shöal! (*He drinks and stares malevolently. In spite of himself, Brown is uneasy. A pause.*)

BROWN (*with forced casualness*). You've been on this toot for a week now.

DION (*tauntingly*). I've been celebrating the acceptance of *my* design for the cathedral.

BROWN (*humorously*). You certainly helped me a lot on it.

DION (*with a harsh laugh*). O perfect Brown! Never mind! I'll make him look in my mirror yet – and drown in it! (*He pours out another big drink.*)

BROWN (*rather tauntingly*). Go easy. I don't want your corpse on my hands.

DION. But I do. (*He drinks.*) Brown will still need me – to reassure him he's alive! I've loved, lusted, won and lost, sung and wept! I've been life's lover! I've fulfilled her will and if she's through with me now it's only because I was too weak to dominate her in turn. It isn't enough to be her creature, you've got to create her or she requests you to destroy yourself.

BROWN (*good-naturedly*). Nonsense. Go home and get some sleep.

DION (*as if he hadn't heard – bitingly*). But to be neither creature nor creator! To exist only in her indifference! To be unloved by life! (*Brown stirs uneasily.*) To be merely a successful freak, the result of some snide neutralizing of life forces – a spineless cactus – a wild boar of the mountains altered into a packer's hog eating to become food – a Don Juan inspired to romance by a monkey's glands – and to have Life not even think you funny enough to see!

BROWN (*stung – angrily*). Bosh!

DION. Consider Mr. Brown. His parents bore him on earth as if they were thereby entering him in a baby parade with prizes for the fattest – and he's still being wheeled along in the procession, too fat now to learn to walk, let alone to dance or run, and he'll never live until his liberated dust quickens into earth!

BROWN (*gruffly*). Rave on! (*Then with forced good-nature.*) Well, Dion, at any rate, I'm satisfied.

DION (*quickly and malevolently*). No! Brown isn't satisfied! He's piled on layers of protective fat, but vaguely, deeply he feels at his heart the gnawing of a doubt ! And I'm interested in that germ which wriggles like a question mark of insecurity in his blood, because it's part of the creative life Brown's stolen from me!

BROWN (*forcing a sour grin*). Steal germs? I thought you caught them.

DION (*as if he hadn't heard*). It's mine – and I'm interested in seeing it thrive and breed and become multitudes and eat until Brown is consumed!

BROWN (*cannot restrain a shudder*). Sometimes when you're drunk, you're positively evil; do you know it?

DION (*sombrely*). When Pan was forbidden the light and warmth of the sun he grew sensitive and self-conscious and proud and revengeful – and became Prince of Darkness.

BROWN (*jocularly*). You don't fit the rôle of Pan, Dion. It sounds to me like Bacchus, alias the Demon Rum, doing the talking. (*Dion recovers from his spasm with a start and stares at Brown with terrible hatred. There is a pause. In spite of himself, Brown squirms and adopts a placating tone.*) Go home. It's all well enough celebrating our design being accepted, but –

DION (*in a steely voice*). I've been the brains! I've been the design! I've designed even his success – drunk and laughing at him – laughing at his career! Not proud! Sick! Sick of myself and him! Designing and getting drunk? Saving my woman and children! (*He laughs.*) Ha! And this cathedral is my masterpiece! It will make Brown the most eminent architect in this state of God's Country. I put a lot into it – what was left of my life! It's one vivid blasphemy from pavement to the tips of its spires! – but so concealed that the fools will never know. They'll kneel and worship the ironic Silenus who tells them the best good is never to be born! (*He laughs triumphantly.*) Well, blasphemy is faith, isn't it? In self-preservation the devil must believe! But Mr. Brown, the Great Brown, has no faith! He couldn't design a cathedral without it looking like the First Supernatural Bank! He only believes in the immortality of the moral belly! (*He laughs wildly – then sinks down in his chair, gasping, his hands pressed to his heart. Then suddenly becomes deadly calm and pronounces like a cruel malignant condemnation.*) From now on, Brown will never design anything. He will devote his life to renovating the house of my Cybel into a home for my Margaret!

BROWN (*springing to his feet, his face convulsed with strange agony*). I've stood enough! How dare you . . .!

DION (*his voice like a probe*). Why has no woman ever loved him? Why has he always been the Big Brother, the Friend? Isn't their trust – a contempt?

BROWN. You lie!

DION. Why has he never been able to love – since my Margaret? Why has he never married? Why has he tried to steal Cybel, as he once tried to steal Margaret? Isn't it out of revenge – and envy?

BROWN (*violently*). Rot! I wanted Cybel, and I bought her!

DION. Brown bought her for me! She has loved me more than he will ever know!

BROWN. You lie! (*Then furiously.*) I'll throw her back on the street!

DION. To me! To her fellow-creature! Why hasn't Brown had children – he who loves children – he who loves *my* children – he who envies me *my* children?

BROWN (*brokenly*). I'm not ashamed to envy you them!

DION. They like Brown, too – as a friend – as an equal – as Margaret has always liked him –

BROWN (*brokenly*). And as I've liked her!

DION. How many million times Brown has thought how much better for her it would have been if she'd chosen him instead!

BROWN (*torturedly*). You lie! (*Then with sudden frenzied defiance.*) All right! If you force me to say it, I do love Margaret! I always have loved her and you've always known I did!

DION (*with a terrible composure*). No! That is merely the appearance, not the truth! Brown loves me! He loves me because I have always possessed the power he needed for love, because I am love!

BROWN (*frenziedly*). You drunken fool! (*He leaps on Dion and grabs him by the throat.*)

DION (*triumphantly, staring into his eyes*). Ah! Now he looks into the mirror! Now he sees his face!

(*Brown lets go of him and staggers back to his chair, pale and trembling.*)

BROWN (*humbly*). Stop, for God's sake! You're mad!

DION (*sinking in his chair, more and more weakly*). I'm done. My heart, not Brown – (*Mockingly.*) My last will and testament! I leave Dion Anthony to William Brown – for him to love and obey – for him to become me – then my Margaret will love me – my children will love me – Mr. and Mrs. Brown and sons, happily ever after! (*Staggering to his full height and looking upward defiantly.*) Nothing more – but Man's last gesture – by which he conquers – to laugh! Ha – (*He begins, stops as if paralysed, and drops on his knees by Brown's chair, his mask falling off, his Christian Martyr's face at the point of death.*) Forgive me, Billy. Bury me, hide me, forget me for your own happiness! May Margaret love you! May you design the Temple of Man's Soul! Blessed are the meek and the poor in spirit! (*He kisses Brown's feet – then more and more weakly and childishly.*) What was the prayer, Billy? I'm getting so sleepy. . . .

BROWN (*in a trancelike tone*). "Our Father who art in Heaven."

DION (*drowsily*). "Our Father." . . .

(*He dies. A pause. Brown remains in a stupor for a moment – then stirs himself, puts his hand on Dion's breast.*)

BROWN (*dully*). He's dead – at last. (*He says this mechanically, but the last two words awaken him – wonderingly.*) At last? (*Then with triumph.*) At last! (*He stares at Dion's real face contemptuously.*) So that's the poor weakling you really were! No wonder you hid! And I've always been afraid of you – yes, I'll confess it now, in awe of you! Paugh! (*He picks up the mask from the floor.*) No, not of you! Of this! Say what you like, it's strong if it is bad! And this is what Margaret loved, not you! Not you! This man! – this man who willed himself to me! (*Struck by an idea, he jumps to his feet.*) By God! (*He slowly starts to put the mask on. A knocking comes on the street door. He starts guiltily, laying the mask on the table. Then he picks it up again quickly, takes the dead body and carries it off left. He reappears immediately and goes to the front door as the knocking recommences – gruffly.*) Hello! Who's there?

MARGARET. It's Margaret, Billy. I'm looking for Dion.

BROWN (*uncertainly*). Oh – all right – (*Unfastening door.*) Come in. Hello, Margaret. Hello, Boys! He's here. He's asleep. I – I was just dozing off too.

(*Margaret enters. She is wearing her mask. The three sons are with her.*)

MARGARET (*seeing the bottle, forcing a laugh*). Has he been celebrating?

BROWN (*with strange glibness now*). No. I was. He wasn't. He said he'd sworn off to-night – for ever – for your sake – and the kids!

MARGARET (*with amazed joy*). Dion said that? (*Then hastily defensive.*) But of course he never does drink much. Where is he?

BROWN. Upstairs. I'll wake him. He felt bad. He took off his clothes to take a bath before he lay down. You just wait here.

(*She sits in the chair where Dion had sat and stares straight before her. The Sons group around her, as if for a family photo. Brown hurries out left.*)

MARGARET. It's late to keep you boys up. Aren't you sleepy?

BOYS. No, Mother.

MARGARET (*proudly*). I'm glad to have three such strong boys to protect me.

ELDEST (*boastingly*). We'd kill anyone that touched you, wouldn't we?

NEXT. You bet! We'd make him wish he hadn't!

YOUNGEST. You bet!

MARGARET. You're Mother's brave boys! (*She laughs fondly – then curiously.*) Do you like Mr. Brown?

ELDEST. Sure thing! He's a regular fellow.

NEXT. He's all right!

YOUNGEST. Sure thing!

MARGARET (*half to herself*). Your father claims he steals his ideas.

ELDEST (*with a sheepish grin*). I'll bet father said that when he was – just talking.

NEXT. Mr. Brown doesn't have to steal, does he?

YOUNGEST. I should say not! He's awful rich.

MARGARET. Do you love your father?

ELDEST (*scuffling – embarrassed*). Why – of course –

NEXT (*ditto*). Sure thing!

YOUNGEST. Sure I do.

MARGARET (*with a sigh*). I think you'd better start on before – right now – before your father comes – He'll be very sick and nervous and he'll want to be quiet. So run along!

BOYS. All right.

(*They file out and close the front door as Brown, dressed in Dion's clothes and wearing his mask, appears at left.*)

MARGARET (*taking off her mask, gladly*). Dion! (*She stares wonderingly at him and he at her; goes to him and puts an arm around him.*) Poor dear, do you feel sick? (*He nods.*) But you look – (*squeezing his arms*) – why, you actually feel stronger and better already! Is it true what Billy told me – about your swearing off for ever? (*He nods. She exclaims intensely.*) Oh, if you'll only – and get well – we can still be so happy! Give Mother a kiss. (*They kiss. A shudder passes through both of them. She breaks away laughing with aroused desire.*) Why, Dion? Aren't you ashamed? You haven't kissed me like that for ages!

BROWN (*his voice imitating Dion's and muffled by the mask*). I've wanted to, Margaret!

MARGARET (*gaily and coquettishly now*). Were you afraid I'd spurn you? Why, Dion, something has happened. It's like a miracle! Even your voice is changed! It actually sounds younger; do you know it? (*Then, solicitously.*) But you must be worn out. Let's go home. (*With an impulsive movement she flings her arms wide open, throwing her mask away from her as if suddenly no longer needing it.*) Oh, I'm beginning to feel so happy, Dion – so happy!

BROWN (*stifledly*). Let's go home. (*She puts her arm around him. They walk to the door.*)

Curtain

ACT THREE SCENE ONE

SCENE. *The draughting-room and private office of Brown are both shown. The former is on the left, the latter on the right of a dividing wall at the centre. The arrangement of furniture in each room is the same as in previous scenes. It is ten in the morning of a day about a month later. The backdrop for both rooms is of plain wall with a few tacked-up designs and blue prints painted on it.*

Two Draughtsmen, a middle-aged and a young man, both stoop-shouldered, are sitting on stools behind what was formerly Dion's table. They are tracing plans. They talk as they work.

OLDER DRAUGHTSMAN. W. B. is late again.

YOUNGER DRAUGHTSMAN. Wonder what's got into him the last month? (*A pause. They work silently.*)

OLDER DRAUGHTSMAN. Yes, ever since he fired Dion. . . .

YOUNGER DRAUGHTSMAN. Funny his firing him all of a sudden like that. (*A pause. They work.*)

OLDER DRAUGHTSMAN. I haven't seen Dion around town since then. Have you?

YOUNGER DRAUGHTSMAN. No, not since Brown told us he'd sacked him. I suppose he's off drowning his sorrow!

OLDER DRAUGHTSMAN. I heard some one had seen him at home and he was sober and looking fine. (*A pause. They work.*)

YOUNGER DRAUGHTSMAN. What got into Brown? They say he fired all his old servants that same day and only uses his house to sleep in.

OLDER DRAUGHTSMAN (*with a sneer*). Artistic temperament, maybe – the real name of which is swelled head! (*There is a noise of footsteps from the hall. Warningly.*) Ssstt!

(*They bend over their table. Margaret enters. She does not need to wear a mask now. Her face has regained the self-confident spirit of its youth, her eyes shine with happiness.*)

MARGARET (*heartily*). Good morning! What a lovely day!

BOTH (*perfunctorily*). Good morning, Mrs. Anthony.

MARGARET (*looking around*). You've been changing around in here, haven't you? Where is Dion? (*They stare at her.*) I forgot to tell him something important this morning and our phone's out of order. So if you'll tell him I'm here – (*They don't move. A pause. Margaret says stiffly.*) Oh, I realize Mr. Brown has given strict orders Dion is not to be disturbed, but surely. . . . (*Sharply.*) Where is my husband, please?

OLDER DRAUGHTSMAN. We don't know.

MARGARET. You don't know?

YOUNGER DRAUGHTSMAN. We haven't seen him.

MARGARET. Why, he left home at eight-thirty!

OLDER DRAUGHTSMAN. To come here?

YOUNGER DRAUGHTSMAN. This morning?

MARGARET (*provoked*). Why, of course, to come here – as he does every day! (*They stare at her. A pause.*)

OLDER DRAUGHTSMAN (*evasively*). We haven't seen him.

MARGARET (*with asperity*). Where is Mr. Brown?

YOUNGER DRAUGHTSMAN (*at a noise of footsteps from the hall – sulkily.*) Coming now.

(*Brown enters. He is now wearing a mask which is an exact likeness of his face as it was in the last scene – the self-assured success. When he sees Margaret, he starts back apprehensively.*)

BROWN (*immediately controlling himself – breezily*). Hello, Margaret! This is a pleasant surprise! (*He holds out his hand.*)

MARGARET (*hardly taking it – reservedly*). Good morning.

BROWN (*turning quickly to the Draughtsmen*). I hope you explained to Mrs. Anthony how busy Dion . . .

MARGARET (*interrupting him – stiffly*). I certainly can't understand –

BROWN (*hastily*). I'll explain. Come in here and be comfortable. (*He throws open the door and ushers her into his private office.*)

OLDER DRAUGHTSMAN. Dion must be putting

over some bluff on her.

YOUNGER DRAUGHTSMAN. Pretending he's still here – and Brown's helping him. . . .

OLDER DRAUGHTSMAN. But why should Brown, after he . . .?

YOUNGER DRAUGHTSMAN. Well, I suppose — Search me. (*They work.*)

BROWN. Have a chair, Margaret. (*She sits on the chair stiffly. He sits behind the desk.*)

MARGARET (*coldly*). I'd like some explanation. . . .

BROWN (*coaxingly*). Now, don't get angry, Margaret! Dion is hard at work on his design for the new State Capitol, and I don't want him disturbed, not even by you! So be a good sport! It's for his own good, remember! I asked him to explain to you.

MARGARET (*relenting*). He told me you'd agreed to ask me and the boys not to come here – but then, we hardly ever did.

BROWN. But you might! (*Then with confidential friendliness.*) This is for his sake, Margaret. I know Dion. He's got to be able to work without distractions. He's not the ordinary man; you appreciate that. And this design means his whole future! He's to get full credit for it, and as soon as it's accepted, I take him into partnership. It's all agreed. And after that I'm going to take a long vacation – go to Europe for a couple of years – and leave everything here in Dion's hands! Hasn't he told you all this?

MARGARET (*jubilant now*). Yes – but I could hardly believe . . . (*Proudly.*) I'm sure he can do it. He's been like a new man lately, so full of ambition and energy! It's made me so happy! (*She stops in confusion.*)

BROWN (*deeply moved, takes her hand impulsively*). And it has made me happy, too!

MARGARET (*confused – with an amused laugh*). Why, Billy Brown! For a moment, I thought it was Dion, your voice sounded so much . . .!

BROWN (*with sudden desperation*). Margaret, I've got to tell you! I can't go on like this any longer! I've got to confess. . . .! There's something. . .!

MARGARET (*alarmed*). Not – not about Dion?

BROWN (*harshly*). To hell with Dion! To hell with Billy Brown! (*He tears off his mask and reveals a suffering face that is ravaged and haggard, his own face tortured and distorted by the demon of Dion's mask.*) Think of me! I love you, Margaret! Leave him! I've always loved you! Come away with me! I'll sell out here! We'll go abroad and be happy!

MARGARET (*amazed*). Billy Brown, do you realize what you're saying? (*With a shudder.*) Are you crazy? Your face – is terrible. You're sick! Shall I phone for a doctor?

BROWN (*turning away slowly and putting on his mask – dully.*) No. I've been on the verge – of a breakdown – for some time. I get spells. . . . I'm better now. (*He turns back to her.*) Forgive me! Forget what I said! But, for all our sakes, don't come here again.

MARGARET (*coldly*). After this – I assure you . . . ! (*Then looking at him with pained incredulity.*) Why, Billy – I simply won't believe – after all these years. . . .!

BROWN. It will never happen again. Good-bye.

MARGARET. Good-bye. (*Then, wishing to leave on a pleasant change of subject – forcing a smile.*) Don't work Dion to death! He's never home for dinner any more.

(*She goes out past the Draughtsmen and off right, rear. Brown sits down at his desk, taking off the mask again. He stares at it with bitter, cynical amusement.*)

BROWN. You're dead, William Brown, dead beyond hope of resurrection! It's the Dion you buried in your garden who killed you, not you him! It's Margaret's husband who . . . (*He laughs harshly.*) Paradise by proxy! Love by mistaken identity! God! (*This is almost a prayer – then fiercely defiant.*) But it *is* paradise! I *do* love!

(*As he is speaking, a well-dressed, important, stout man enters the draughting-room. He is carrying a rolled-up plan in his hand. He nods condescendingly and goes directly to Brown's door, on which he raps sharply, and, without waiting for an answer, turns the knob. Brown has just time to turn his head and get his mask on*).

MAN (*briskly*). Ah, good morning! I came right in. Hope I didn't disturb . . .?

BROWN (*the successful architect now – urbanely*). Not at all, sir. How are you? (*They shake hands.*) Sit down. Have a cigar. And now what can I do for you this morning?

MAN (*unrolling his plan*). It's your plan. My wife and I have been going over it again. We like it – and we don't – and when a man plans to lay out half a million, why he wants everything exactly right, eh? (*Brown nods.*) It's too cold, too spare, too like a tomb, if you'll pardon me, for a liveable home. Can't you liven it up, put in some decorations, make it fancier and warmer – you know what I mean. (*Looks at him a bit doubtfully.*) People tell me you had an assistant, Anthony, who was a real shark on these details but that you've fired him –

BROWN (*suavely*). Gossip! He's still with me but, for reasons of his own, doesn't wish it known. Yes, I trained him and he's very ingenious. I'll turn this right over to him and instruct him to carry out your wishes.

Curtain

ACT THREE SCENE TWO

SCENE. *The same as Act Two, Scene Three – the library of Brown's home about eight the same night. He can be heard feeling his way in through the dark. He switches on the reading lamp on the table. Directly under it on a sort of stand is the mask of Dion, its empty eyes staring front.*

Brown takes off his own mask and lays it on the table before Dion's. He flings himself down in the chair and stares without moving into the eyes of Dion's mask. Finally, he begins to talk to it in a bitter, mocking tone.)

BROWN. Listen! To-day was a narrow escape – for us! We can't avoid discovery much longer. We must get our plot to working! We've already made William Brown's will, leaving you his money and business. We must hustle off to Europe now – and murder him there! (*A bit tauntingly.*) Then you – the I in you – *I* will live with Margaret happily ever after. (*More tauntingly.*) She will have children by me! (*He seems to hear some mocking denial from the mask. He bends toward it.*) What? (*Then with a sneer.*) Anyway, that doesn't matter! Your children already love me more than they ever loved you! And Margaret loves me more! You think you've won, do you – that I've got to vanish into you in order to live? Not yet, my friend! Never! Wait! Gradually Margaret will love what is beneath – me! Little by little I'll teach her to know me, and then finally I'll reveal myself to her, and confess that I stole your place out of love for her, and she'll understand and forgive and love me! And you'll be forgotten! Ha! (*Again he bends down to the mask as if listening – torturedly.*) What's that? She'll never believe? She'll never see? She'll never understand? You lie, devil! (*He reaches out his hands as if to take the mask by the throat, then shrinks back with a shudder of hopeless despair.*) God have mercy! Let me believe! Blessed are the merciful! Let me obtain mercy! (*He waits, his face upturned – pleadingly.*) Not yet? (*Despairingly.*) Never? (*A pause. Then, in a sudden panic of dread, he reaches out for the mask of Dion like a dope fiend after a drug. As soon as he holds it, he seems to gain strength and is able to force a sad laugh.*) Now I am drinking your strength, Dion – strength to love in this world and die and sleep and become fertile earth, as you are becoming now in my garden – your weakness the strength of my flowers, your failure as an artist painting their petals with life! (*Then, with bravado.*) Come with me while Margaret's bridegroom dresses in your clothes, Mr. Anthony! I need the devil when I'm in the dark! (*He goes off left, but can be heard talking.*) Your clothes begin to fit me better than my own! Hurry, Brother! It's time we were home. Our wife is waiting! (*He reappears, having changed his coat and trousers.*) Come with me and tell her again I love her! Come and hear her tell me how she loves you! (*He suddenly cannot help kissing the mask.*) I love you because she loves you! My kisses on your lips are for her! (*He puts the mask over his face and stands for a moment, seeming to grow tall and proud – then with a laugh of bold self-assurance.*) Out by the back way! I mustn't forget I'm a desperate criminal, pursued by God, and by myself! (*He goes out right, laughing with amused satisfaction.*)

Curtain

ACT THREE SCENE THREE

SCENE. *Is the same as Scene One of Act One – the sitting-room of Margaret's home. It is about half an hour after the last scene. Margaret sits on the sofa, waiting with the anxious, impatient expectancy of one deeply in love. She is dressed with a careful, subtle extra touch to attract the eye. She looks young and happy. She is trying to read a book. The front door is heard opening and closing. She leaps up and runs back to throw her arms around Brown as he enters from right, rear. She kisses him passionately.*

MARGARET (*as he recoils with a sort of guilt – laughingly*). Why, you hateful old thing, you! I really believe you were trying to avoid kissing me! Well, just for that, I'll never . . .

BROWN (*with fierce, defiant passion, kisses her again and again*). Margaret!

MARGARET. Call me Peggy again. You used to when you really loved me. (*Softly.*) Remember the school commencement dance – you and I on the dock in the moonlight?

BROWN (*with pain*). No. (*He takes his arms from around her.*)

MARGARET (*still holding him – with a laugh*). Well, I like that! You old bear, you! Why not?

BROWN (*sadly*). It was so long ago.

MARGARET (*a bit melancholy*). You mean you don't want to be reminded that we're getting old?

BROWN. Yes. (*He kisses her gently.*) I'm tired. Let's sit down. (*They sit on the sofa, his arm about her, her head on his shoulder.*)

MARGARET (*with a happy sigh*). I don't mind remembering – now I'm happy. It's only when I'm unhappy that it hurts – and I've been so happy lately, dear – and so grateful to you! (*He stirs uneasily. She goes on joyfully.*) Everything's changed! I'd got pretty resigned to – and sad and hopeless, too – and then all at once you turn right around and everything is the same as when we were first married – much better even, for I was never sure of you then. You were always so strange and aloof and alone, it seemed I was never really touching you. But now I feel you've become quite human – like me – and I'm so happy, dear! (*She kisses him.*)

BROWN (*his voice trembling*). Then I have made you happy – happier than ever before – no matter what happens? (*She nods.*) Then – that justifies everything! (*He forces a laugh.*)

MARGARET. Of course it does! I've always known that. But you – you wouldn't be – or you couldn't be – and I could never help you – and all the time I knew you were so lonely! I could always hear you calling to me that you were lost, but I couldn't find the path to you because I was lost, too! That's an awful way for a wife to feel! (*She laughs – joyfully.*) But now you're here! You're mine! You're my long-lost lover, and my husband, and my big boy, too!

BROWN (*with a trace of jealousy*). Where are your other big boys to-night?

MARGARET. Out to a dance. They've all acquired girls, I'll have you know.

BROWN (*mockingly*). Aren't you jealous?

MARGARET (*gaily*). Of course! Terribly! But I'm diplomatic. I don't let them see. (*Changing the subject.*) Believe me, they've noticed the change in you! The eldest was saying to me to-day: "It's great not to have Father so nervous, any more. Why, he's a regular sport when he gets started!" And the other two said very solemnly: "You bet!" (*She laughs.*)

BROWN (*brokenly*). I – I'm glad.

MARGARET. Dion! You're crying!

BROWN (*stung by the name, gets up – harshly*). Nonsense! Did you ever know Dion to cry about anyone?

MARGARET (*sadly*). You couldn't – then. You were too lonely. You had no one to cry to.

BROWN (*goes and takes a rolled-up plan from the table drawer – dully*). I've got to do some work.

MARGARET (*disappointedly*). What, has that old Billy Brown got you to work at home again, too?

BROWN (*ironically*). It's for Dion's good, you know – and yours.

MARGARET (*making the best of it – cheerfully*). All right, I won't be selfish. It really makes me proud for you to be so ambitious. Let me help.

(*She brings his drawing-board, which he puts on the table and pins his plan upon. She sits on sofa and picks up her book.*)

BROWN (*carefully casual*). I hear you were in to see me to-day?

MARGARET. Yes, and Billy wouldn't hear of it! I was quite furious until he convinced me it was all for the best. When is he going to take you into partnership?

BROWN. Very soon now.

MARGARET. And will he really give you full charge when he goes abroad?

BROWN. Yes.

MARGARET (*practically*). I'd pin him down if I could. Promises are all right, but – (*she hesitates*) I don't trust him.

BROWN (*with a start, sharply*). What makes you say that?

MARGARET. Oh, something that happened to-day.

BROWN. What?

MARGARET. I don't mean I blame him, but – to be frank, I think the Great God Brown, as you call him, is getting a bit queer and it's time he took a vacation. Don't you?

BROWN (*his voice a bit excited – but guardedly*). But why? What did he do?

MARGARET (*hesitatingly*). Well – it's really too silly – he suddenly got awfully strange. His face scared me. It was like a corpse. Then he raved on some nonsense about he'd always loved me. He went on like a perfect fool! (*She looks at Brown, who is staring at her. She becomes uneasy.*) Maybe I shouldn't tell you this. He simply wasn't responsible. Then he came to himself and was all right and begged my pardon and seemed dreadfully sorry, and I felt sorry for him. (*Then with a shudder.*) But honestly, Dion, it was just too disgusting for words to hear him! (*With kind, devastating contempt.*) Poor Billy!

BROWN (*with a show of tortured derision*). Poor Billy! Poor Billy the Goat! (*With mocking frenzy.*) I'll kill him for you! I'll serve you his heart for breakfast!

MARGARET (*jumping up – frightenedly*). Dion!

BROWN (*waving his pencil knife with grotesque flourishes*). I tell you I'll murder this God-damned disgusting Great God Brown who stands like a fatted calf in the way of our health and wealth and happiness!

MARGARET (*bewilderedly, not knowing how much is pretending, puts an arm about him*). Don't, dear! You're being horrid and strange again. It makes me afraid you haven't really changed, after all.

BROWN (*unheeding*). And then my wife can be happy! Ha! (*He laughs. She begins to cry. He controls himself – pats her head – gently.*) All right, dear. Mr. Brown is now safely in hell. Forget him!

MARGARET (*stops crying – but still worriedly*). I should never have told you – but I never imagined you'd take it seriously. I've never thought of Billy Brown except as a friend, and lately not even that! He's just a stupid old fool!

BROWN. Ha-ha! Didn't I say he was in hell? They're torturing him! (*Then controlling himself again – exhaustedly.*) Please leave me alone now. I've got to work.

MARGARET. All right, dear. I'll go into the next room and anything you want, just call. (*She pats his face – cajolingly.*) Is it all forgotten?

BROWN. Will you be happy?

MARGARET. Yes.

BROWN. Then it's dead, I promise! (*She kisses him and goes out. He stares ahead, then shakes off his thoughts and concentrates on his work – mockingly.*) Our beautiful new Capitol calls you, Mr. Dion! To work! We'll adroitly hide old Silenus on the cupola! Let him dance over their law-making with his eternal leer! (*He bends over his work.*)

Curtain

ACT FOUR SCENE ONE

SCENE. *Same as Scene One of Act Three – the draughting-room and Brown's office. It is dusk of a day about a month later.*

The two draughtsmen are bent over their table, working.

Brown, at his desk, is working feverishly over a plan. He is wearing the mask of Dion. The mask of William Brown rests on the desk beside him. As he works, he chuckles with malicious glee – finally flings down his pencil with a flourish.

BROWN. Done! In the name of the Almighty Brown, amen, amen! Here's a wondrous fair capitol! The design would do just as well for a Home for Criminal Imbeciles! Yet to them, such is my art, it will appear to possess a pure commonsense, a fat-bellied finality, as dignified as the suspenders of an assemblyman! Only to me will that pompous façade reveal itself as the wearily ironic grin of Pan as, his ears drowsy with the crumbling hum of past and future civilizations, he half-listens to the laws passed by his fleas to enslave him! Ha-ha-ha! (*He leaps grotesquely from behind his desk and cuts a few goatish capers, laughing with lustful merriment.*) Long live Chief of Police Brown! District Attorney Brown! Alderman Brown! Assemblyman Brown! Mayor Brown! Congressman Brown! Governor Brown! Senator Brown! President Brown! (*He chants.*) Oh, how many persons in one God make up the good God Brown? Hahahaha! (*The two Draughtsmen in the next room have stopped work and are listening.*)

YOUNGER DRAUGHTSMAN. Drunk as a fool!

OLDER DRAUGHTSMAN. At least Dion used to have the decency to stay away from the office –

YOUNGER DRAUGHTSMAN. Funny how it's got hold of Brown so quick!

OLDER DRAUGHTSMAN. He was probably hitting it up on the Q.T. all the time.

BROWN (*has come back to his desk, laughing to himself and out of breath*). Time to become respectable again! (*He takes off the Dion mask and reaches out for the William Brown one – then stops, with a hand on each, staring down on the plan with fascinated loathing. His real face is now sick, ghastly, tortured, hollow-cheeked and feverish-eyed.*) Ugly! Hideous! Despicable! Why must the demon in me pander to cheapness – then punish me with self-loathing and life-hatred? Why am I not strong enough to perish – or blind enough to be content? (*To heaven, bitterly but pleadingly.*) Give me the strength to destroy this! – and myself! – and him! – and I will believe in Thee! (*While he has been speaking there has been a noise from the stairs. The two Draughtsmen have bent over their work. Margaret enters, closing the door behind her. At this sound, Brown starts. He immediately senses who it is – with alarm.*) Margaret! (*He grabs up both masks and goes into room off right.*)

MARGARET (*she looks healthy and happy, but her face wears a worried, solicitous expression – pleasantly to the staring Draughtsmen.*) Good morning. Oh, you needn't look worried, it's Mr. Brown I want to see, not my husband.

YOUNGER DRAUGHTSMAN (*hesitatingly*). He's locked himself in – but maybe if you'll knock –

MARGARET (*knocks – somewhat embarrassedly*). Mr. Brown!

(*Brown enters his office, wearing the William Brown mask. He comes quickly to the other door and unlocks it.*)

BROWN (*with a hectic cordiality*). Come on, Margaret! Enter! This is delightful! Sit down! What can I do for you?

MARGARET (*taken aback – a bit stiffly*). Nothing much.

BROWN. Something about Dion, of course. Well, your darling pet is all right – never better!

MARGARET (*coldly*). That's a matter of opinion. I think you're working him to death.

BROWN. Oh, no, not him. It's Brown who is to die. We've agreed on that.

MARGARET (*giving him a queer look*). I'm serious.

BROWN. So am I. Deadly serious! Hahaha!

MARGARET (*checking her indignation*). That's what I came to see you about. Really, Dion has acted so hectic and on edge lately I'm sure he's on the verge of a breakdown.

BROWN. Well, it certainly isn't drink. He hasn't had a drop. He doesn't need it! Haha! And I haven't either, although the gossips are beginning to say I'm soused all the time! It's because I've started to laugh! Hahaha! They can't believe in joy in this town except by the bottle! What funny little people! Hahaha! When you're the Great God Brown, eh, Margaret? Hahaha!

MARGARET (*getting up – uneasily*). I'm afraid I –

BROWN. Don't be afraid, my dear! I won't make love to you again! Honour bright! I'm too near the grave for such folly! But it must have been funny for you when you came here the last time – watching a disgusting old fool like me, eh? – too funny for words! Hahaha! (*Then with a sudden movement he flourishes the design before her.*)

Look! We've finished it! Dion has finished it! His fame is made!

MARGARET (*tartly*). Really, Billy, I believe you are drunk!

BROWN. Nobody kisses me – so you can all believe the worst! Hahaha!

MARGARET (*chillingly*). Then if Dion is through, why can't I see him?

BROWN (*crazily*). See Dion? See Dion? Well, why not? It's an age of miracles. The streets are full of Lazaruses. Pray! I mean – wait a moment, if you please.

(*Brown disappears into the room off right. A moment later he reappears in the mask of Dion. He holds out his arms and Margaret rushes into them. They kiss passionately. Finally he sits with her on the lounge.*)

MARGARET. So you've finished it.

BROWN. Yes. The Committee is coming to see it soon. I've made all the changes they'll like, the fools!

MARGARET (*lovingly*). And can we go on that second honeymoon, right away now?

BROWN. In a week or so, I hope – as soon as I've got Brown off to Europe.

MARGARET. Tell me – isn't he drinking hard?

BROWN (*laughing as Brown did*). Haha! Soused to the ears all the time! Soused on life! He can't stand it! It's burning his insides out!

MARGARET (*alarmed*). Dear! I'm worried about you. You sound as crazy as he did – when you laugh! You must rest!

BROWN (*controlling himself*). I'll rest in peace – when he's gone!

MARGARET (*with a queer look*). Why, Dion, that isn't your suit. It's just like –

BROWN. It's his! We're getting to be like twins. I'm inheriting his clothes already! (*Then calming himself as he sees how frightened she is.*) Don't be worried, dear. I'm just a trifle elated, now the job's done. I guess I'm a bit soused on life, too!

(*The Committee, three important-looking, average personages, come into the draughting-room.*)

MARGARET (*forcing a smile.*) Well, don't let it burn *your* insides out!

BROWN. No danger! Mine were tempered in hell! Hahaha!

MARGARET (*kissing him, coaxingly*). Come home, dear – please!

OLDER DRAUGHTSMAN (*knocks on the door*). The Committee is here, Mr. Brown.

BROWN (*hurriedly to Margaret*). You receive them. Hand them the design. I'll get Brown. (*He raises his voice.*) Come right in, gentlemen.

(*He goes off right, as the Committee enter the office. When they see Margaret, they stop in surprise.*)

MARGARET (*embarrassedly*). Good afternoon. Mr. Brown will be right with you. (*They bow. Margaret holds out the design to them.*) This is my husband's design. He finished it to-day.

COMMITTEE. Ah! (*They crowd around to look at it – with enthusiasm.*) Perfect! Splendid! Couldn't be better! Exactly what we suggested.

MARGARET (*joyfully*). Then you accept it? Mr. Anthony will be so pleased!

MEMBER. Mr. Anthony?

ANOTHER. Is he working here again?

THIRD. Did I understand you to say this was your husband's design?

MARGARET (*excitedly*). Yes! Entirely his! He's worked like a dog – (*Appalled.*) You don't mean to say – Mr. Brown never told you? (*They shake their heads in solemn surprise.*) Oh, the contemptible cad! I hate him!

BROWN (*appearing at right – mockingly*). Hate me, Margaret? Hate Brown? How superfluous! (*Oratorically.*) Gentlemen, I have been keeping a secret from you in order that you might be the more impressed when I revealed it. That design is entirely the inspiration of Mr. Dion Anthony's genius. I had nothing to do with it.

MARGARET (*contritely*). Oh, Billy! I'm sorry! Forgive me!

BROWN (*ignoring her, takes the plan from the Committee and begins unpinning it from the board – mockingly*). I can see by your faces you have approved this. You are delighted, aren't you? And why not, my dear sirs? Look at it, and look at you! Hahaha! It'll immortalize you, my good men! You'll be as death-defying a joke as any in Joe Miller! (*Then with a sudden complete change of tone – angrily.*) You damn fools! Can't you see this is an insult – a terrible, blasphemous insult! – that this embittered failure Anthony is hurling in the teeth of our success – an insult to you, to me, to you, Margaret – and to Almighty God ! (*In a frenzy of fury.*) And if you are weak and cowardly enough to stand for it, I'm not!

(*He tears the plan into four pieces. The Committee stand aghast. Margaret runs forward.*)

MARGARET (*in a scream*). You coward! Dion! Dion! (*She picks up the plan and hugs it to her bosom.*)

BROWN (*with a sudden goatish caper*). I'll tell him you're here. (*He disappears, but reappears almost immediately in the mask of Dion. He is imposing a terrible discipline on himself to avoid dancing and laughing. He speaks suavely.*) Everything is all right – all for the best – you mustn't get excited! A little paste, Margaret! A little paste, gentlemen! And all will be well. Life is imperfect, Brothers! Men have their faults, Sister! But with a few drops of glue much may be done! A little dab of pasty resignation here and there – and even broken hearts may be repaired to do yeoman service! (*He has edged toward the door. They are all staring at him with petrified bewilderment. He puts his finger to his lips.*) Ssssh! This is Daddy's bedtime secret for to-day: Man is born broken. He lives by mending. The grace of God is glue! (*With a quick prancing movement, he has opened the door, gone through, and closed it after him silently, shaking with suppressed laughter. He springs lightly to the side of the petrified Draughtsmen – in a whisper.*) They will find him in the little room. Mr. William Brown is dead!

(*With light leaps he vanishes, his head thrown back, shaking with silent laughter. The sound of his feet leaping down the stairs, five at a time, can be heard. Then a pause of silence. The people in the two rooms stare. The Younger Draughtsman is the first to recover.*)

YOUNGER DRAUGHTSMAN (*rushing into the next room, shouts in terrified tones*). Mr. Brown is dead!

COMMITTEE. He murdered him!

They all run into the little room off right. Margaret remains, stunned with horror. They return in a moment, carrying the mask of William Brown, two on each side, as if they were carrying a body by the legs and shoulders. They solemnly lay him down on the couch and stand looking down at him.)

FIRST COMMITTEEMAN (*with a frightened awe*). I can't believe he's gone.

SECOND COMMITTEEMAN (*in same tone*). I can almost hear him talking. (*As if impelled, he clears his throat and addresses the mask importantly.*) Mr. Brown – (*then stops short.*)

THIRD COMMITTEEMAN (*shrinking back*). No. Dead, all right! (*Then suddenly, hysterically angry and terrified.*) We must take steps at once to run Anthony to earth!

MARGARET (*with a heart-broken cry*). Dion's innocent!

YOUNGER DRAUGHTSMAN. I'll phone for the police, sir! (*He rushes to the phone.*)

Curtain

ACT FOUR SCENE TWO

SCENE. *The same as Scene Two of Act Three – the library of William Brown's home. The mask of Dion stands on the table beneath the light, facing front.*

On his knees beside the table, facing front, stripped naked except for a white cloth around his loins, is Brown. The clothes he has torn off in his agony are scattered on the floor. His eyes, his arms, his whole body strain upward, his muscles writhe with his lips as they pray silently in their agonized supplication. Finally a voice seems torn out of him.

BROWN. Mercy, Compassionate Saviour of Man! Out of my depths I cry to you! Mercy on thy poor clod, thy clot of unhallowed earth, thy clay, the Great God Brown! Mercy, Saviour!

(*He seems to wait for an answer – then leaping to his feet he puts out one hand to touch the mask like a frightened child reaching out for its nurse's hand – then with immediate mocking despair.*) Bah! I am sorry, little children, but your kingdom is empty. God has become disgusted and moved away to some far ecstatic star where life is a dancing flame! We must die without him. (*Then – addressing the mask – harshly.*) Together, my friend! You, too! Let Margaret suffer! Let the whole world suffer as I am suffering!

(*There is a sound of a door being pushed violently open, padding feet in slippers, and Cybel, wearing her mask, runs into the room. She stops short on seeing Brown and the mask, and stares from one to the other for a second in confusion. She is dressed in a black kimono robe and wears slippers over her bear feet. Her yellow hair hangs down in a great mane over her shoulders. She has grown stouter, has more of the deep objective calm of an idol.*)

BROWN (*staring at her – fascinated – with great peace as if her presence comforted him*). Cybel! I was coming to you! How did you know?

CYBEL (*takes off her mask and looks from Brown to the Dion mask, now with a great understanding*). So that's why you never came to me again! You are Dion Brown!

BROWN (*bitterly*). I am the remains of William Brown! (*He points to the mask of Dion.*) I am his murderer and his murdered!

CYBEL (*with a laugh of exasperated pity*). Oh, why can't you ever learn to leave yourselves alone and leave me alone.

BROWN (*boyishly and naïvely*). I am Billy.

CYBEL (*immediately, with a motherly solicitude*). Then run, Billy, run! They are hunting for some one! They came to my place, hunting for a murderer, Dion! They must find a victim! They've got to quiet their fears, to cast out their devils, or they'll never sleep soundly again! They've got to absolve themselves by finding a guilty one! They've got to kill some one now, to live! You're naked! You must be Satan! Run, Billy, run! They'll come here! I ran here to warn – some one! So run away if you want to live!

BROWN (*like a sulky child*). I'm too tired. I don't want to.

CYBEL (*with motherly calm*). All right, you needn't, Billy. Don't sulk. (*As a noise comes from outside.*) Anyway, it's too late. I hear them in the garden now.

BROWN (*listening, puts out his hand and takes the mask of Dion – as he gains strength, mockingly*). Thanks for this one last favour, Dion! Listen! Your avengers! Standing on your grave in the garden! Hahaha! (*He puts on the mask and springs to the left and makes a gesture as if flinging French windows open. Gaily mocking.*) Welcome, dumb worshippers! I am your great God Brown! I have been advised to run from you but it is my almighty whim to dance into escape over your prostrate souls!

(*Shouts from the garden and a volley of shots. Brown staggers back and falls on the floor by the couch, mortally wounded.*)

CYBEL (*runs to his side, lifts him on to the couch and takes off the mask of Dion*). You can't take this to bed with you. You've got to go to sleep alone.

(*She places the mask of Dion back on its stand under the light and puts on her own, just as, after a banging of doors, crashing of glass, trampling of feet, a Squad of Police with drawn revolvers, led by a grizzly, brutal-faced Captain, run into the room. They are followed by Margaret, still distractedly clutching the pieces of the plan to her breast.*)

CAPTAIN (*pointing to the mask of Dion – triumphantly*). Got him! He's dead!

MARGARET (*throws herself on her knees, takes the mask and kisses it – heart-brokenly*). Dion! Dion!

(*Her face hidden in her arms, the mask in her hands above her bowed head, she remains, sobbing with deep, silent grief.*)

CAPTAIN (*noticing Cybel and Brown – startled*). Hey! Look at this! What're you doin' here? Who's he?

CYBEL. You ought to know. You croaked him!

CAPTAIN (*with a defensive snarl – hastily*). It was Anthony! I saw his mug! This feller's an accomplice, I bet yuh! Serves him right! Who is he? Friend o' yours! Crook! What's his name? Tell me or I'll fix yuh!

CYBEL. Billy.

CAPTAIN. Billy what?

CYBEL. I don't know. He's dying. (*Then suddenly.*) Leave me alone with him and maybe I'll get him to squeal it.

CAPTAIN. Yuh better! I got to have a clean report. I'll give yuh a couple o' minutes.

(*He motions to the Policemen, who follow him off left. Cybel takes off her mask and sits down by Brown's head. He makes an effort to raise himself toward her and she helps him, throwing her kimono over his bare body, drawing his head on to her shoulder.*)

BROWN (*snuggling against her – gratefully*). The earth is warm.

CYBEL (*soothingly, looking before her like an idol*). Ssshh! Go to sleep, Billy.

BROWN. Yes, Mother. (*Then explainingly.*) It was dark and I couldn't see where I was going and they all picked on me.

CYBEL. I know. You're tired.

BROWN. And when I wake up . . .?

CYBEL. The sun will be rising again.

BROWN. To judge the living and the dead! (*Frightenedly.*) I don't want justice. I want love.

CYBEL. There is only love.

BROWN. Thank you, Mother. (*Then feebly.*) I'm getting sleepy. What's the prayer you taught me – Our Father – ?

CYBEL (*with calm exultance*). Our Father Who Art!

BROWN (*taking her tone – exultantly*). Who art! Who art! (*Suddenly – with ecstasy.*) I know! I have found Him! I hear Him speak! "Blessed are they that weep, for they shall laugh!" Only he that has wept can laugh! The laughter of Heaven sows earth with a rain of tears, and out of Earth's transfigured birth-pain the laughter of Man returns to bless and play again in innumerable dancing gales of flame upon the knees of God! (*He dies.*)

CYBEL (*gets up and arranges his body on the couch. She bends down and kisses him gently – she straightens up and looks into space – with a profound pain*). Always spring comes again bearing life! Always again! Always, always for ever again! – Spring again! – life again! – summer and autumn and death and peace again! – (*with agonized sorrow*) – but always, always, love and conception and birth and pain again – spring bearing the intolerable chalice of life again! – (*then with agonized exultance*) – bearing the glorious, blazing crown of life again! (*She stands like an idol of Earth, her eyes staring out over the world.*)

MARGARET (*lifting her head adoringly to the mask – triumphant tenderness mingled with her grief*). My lover! My husband! My boy! (*She kisses the mask.*) Good-bye. Thank you for happiness! And you're not dead, sweetheart! You can never die till my heart dies! You will live for ever! You will sleep under my heart! I will feel you stirring in your sleep, for ever under my heart! (*She kisses the mask again. There is a pause.*)

CAPTAIN (*comes just into sight at left and speaks front without looking at them – gruffly*). Well, what's his name?

CYBEL. Man!

CAPTAIN (*taking a grimy notebook and an inch-long pencil from his pocket*). How d'yuh spell it?

Curtain

EPILOGUE

SCENE. *Four years later.*

The same spot on the same pier as in Prologue on another moonlight night in June. The sound of the waves and of distant dance music.

Margaret and her three sons appear from the right. The eldest is now eighteen. All are dressed in the height of correct school elegance. They are all tall, athletic, strong and handsome-looking. They loom up around the slight figure of their mother like protecting giants, giving her a strange aspect of lonely, detached, small femininity. She wears her mask of the proud, indulgent Mother. She has grown appreciably older. Her hair is now a beautiful grey. There is about her manner and voice the sad but contented feeling of one who knows her life-purpose well accomplished but is at the same time a bit empty and comfortless with the finality of it. She is wrapped in a grey cloak.

ELDEST. Doesn't Bee look beautiful to-night, Mother?

NEXT. Don't you think Mabel's the best dancer in there, Mother?

YOUNGEST. Aw, Alice has them both beat, hasn't she, Mother?

MARGARET (*with a sad little laugh*). Each of you is right. (*Then, with strange finality.*) Good-bye, boys.

BOYS (*surprised*). Good-bye.

MARGARET. It was here on a night just like this your father first – proposed to me. Did you ever know that?

BOYS (*embarrassedly*). No.

MARGARET (*yearningly*). But the nights now are so much colder than they used to be. Think of it, I went in for moonlight-bathing in June when I was a girl. It was so warm and beautiful in those days. I remember the Junes when I was carrying you boys – (*A pause. They fidget uneasily. She asks pleadingly.*) Promise me faithfully never to forget your father!

BOYS (*uncomfortably*). Yes, Mother.

MARGARET (*forcing a joking tone*). But you mustn't waste June on an old woman like me! Go in and dance. (*As they hesitate dutifully.*) Go on. I really want to be alone – with my Junes.

BOYS (*unable to conceal their eagerness*). Yes, Mother. (*They go away.*)

MARGARET (*slowly removes her mask, laying it on the bench, and stares up at the moon with a wistful, resigned sweetness*). So long ago! And yet I'm still the same Margaret. It's only our lives that grow old. We *are* where centuries only count as seconds and after a thousand lives our eyes begin to open – (*she looks around her with a rapt smile*) – and the moon rests in the sea! I want to feel the moon at peace in the sea! I want Dion to leave the sky for me! I want him to sleep in the tides of my heart! (*She slowly takes from under her cloak, from her bosom, as if from her heart, the mask of Dion as it was at the last and holds it before her face.*) My lover! My husband! My boy! You can never die till my heart dies! You will live for ever! You are sleeping under my heart! I feel you stirring in your sleep, for ever under my heart. (*She kisses him on the lips with a timeless kiss.*)

Curtain

LAZARUS LAUGHED

A Play for an Imaginative Theatre

Characters

LAZARUS OF BETHANY
HIS FATHER
HIS MOTHER
MARTHA } *his sisters*
MARY }
MIRIAM, *his wife*
SEVEN GUESTS, *neighbours of Lazarus*
CHORUS OF OLD MEN
AN ORTHODOX PRIEST
CHORUS OF LAZARUS' FOLLOWERS
A CENTURION
GAIUS CALIGULA
CRASSUS, *a Roman general*
CHORUS OF GREEKS
SEVEN CITIZENS OF ATHENS
CHORUS OF ROMAN SENATORS
SEVEN SENATORS
CHORUS OF LEGIONARIES
FLAVIUS, *a centurion*
MARCELLUS, *a patrician*
CHORUS OF THE GUARD
TIBERIUS CÆSAR
POMPEIA
CHORUS OF YOUTHS AND GIRLS
CHORUS OF THE ROMAN POPULACE
CROWDS

Scenes

ACT ONE

SCENE ONE Lazarus' home in Bethany. A short time after the miracle.

SCENE TWO Months later. Outside the House of Laughter in Bethany. Late evening.

ACT TWO

SCENE ONE A street in Athens. A night months later.

SCENE TWO A temple immediately inside the walls of Rome. Midnight. Months later.

ACT THREE

SCENE ONE Garden of Tiberius' palace. A night a few days later.

SCENE TWO Inside the palace. Immediately after.

ACT FOUR

SCENE ONE The same. A while after.

SCENE TWO Interior of a Roman theatre. Dawn of the same night.

ACT ONE SCENE ONE

SCENE. *Exterior and interior of Lazarus' home at Bethany. The main room at the front end of the house is shown—a long, low-ceilinged, sparely furnished chamber, with white walls grey in the fading daylight that enters from three small windows at the left. To the left of centre several long tables placed lengthwise to the width of the room, around which many chairs for guests have been placed. In the rear wall, right, a door leading into the rest of the house. On the left, a doorway opening on a road where a crowd of men has gathered. On the right, another doorway leading to the yard where there is a crowd of women.*

Inside the house, on the men's side, seven male Guests are grouped by the door, watching Lazarus with frightened awe, talking hesitantly in low whispers. The Chorus of Old Men, seven in number, is drawn up in a crescent, in the far corner, right, facing Lazarus.

[*All of these people are masked in accordance with the following scheme: There are seven periods of life shown: Boyhood (or Girlhood), Youth, Young Manhood (or Womanhood), Manhood (or Womanhood), Middle Age, Maturity, and Old Age; and each of these periods is represented by seven different masks of general types of character as follows: The Simple, Ignorant; the Happy, Eager; the Self-Tortured, Introspective; the Proud, Self-Reliant; the Servile, Hypocritical; the Revengeful, Cruel; the Sorrowful, Resigned. Thus in each crowd (this includes among the men the Seven Guests who are composed of one male of each period-type as period one—type one, period two—type two, and so on up to period seven—type seven) there are forty-nine different combinations of period and type. Each type has a distinct predominant colour for its costumes, which varies in kind according to its period. The masks of the Chorus of Old Men are double the size of the others. They are all seven in the Sorrowful, Resigned type of Old Age.*]

On a raised platform at the middle of the one table placed lengthwise at centre sits Lazarus, his head haloed and his body illumined by a soft radiance as of tiny phosphorescent flames.

Lazarus, freed now from the fear of death, wears no mask.

In appearance Lazarus is tall and powerful, about fifty years of age, with a mass of grey-black hair and a heavy beard. His face recalls that of a statue of a divinity of Ancient Greece in its general structure, and particularly in its quality of detached serenity. It is dark-complected, ruddy and brown, the colour of rich earth upturned by the plough, calm but furrowed deep with the marks of former suffering endured with a grim fortitude that had never softened into resignation. His forehead is broad and noble, his eyes black and deep-set. Just now he is staring straight before him as if his vision were still fixed beyond life.

Kneeling beside him with bowed heads are his wife, Miriam; his sisters, Martha and Mary; and his Father and Mother.

Miriam is a slender, delicate woman of thirty-five, dressed in deep black, who holds one of his hands in both of hers, and keeps her lips pressed to it. The upper part of her face is covered by a mask which conceals her forehead, eyes and nose, but leaves her mouth revealed. The mask is the pure pallor of marble, the expression that of a statue of Woman, of her eternal acceptance of the compulsion of motherhood, the inevitable cycle of love into pain into joy, and new love into separation and pain again, and the loneliness of age. The eyes of the mask are almost closed. Their gaze turns within, oblivious to the life outside, as they dream down on the child forever in memory at her breast. The mouth of Miriam is sensitive and sad, tender with an eager, understanding smile of self-forgetful love, the lips still fresh and young. Her skin, in contrast to the mask, is sunburned and earth-coloured like that of Lazarus. Martha, Mary, and the two parents all wear full masks which broadly reproduce their own characters. Martha is a buxom middle-aged housewife, plain and pleasant. Mary is young and pretty, nervous and high-strung. The Father is a small, thin, feeble old man of over eighty, meek and pious. The Mother is tall and stout, over sixty-five, a gentle, simple woman.

All the masks of these Jews of the first two scenes of the play are pronouncedly Semitic.

A background of twilight sky. A dissolving touch of sunset still lingers on the horizon.

It is some time after the miracle and Jesus has gone away.

CHORUS OF OLD MEN (*in a quavering rising and falling chant—their arms outstretched toward Lazarus*). Jesus wept!

Behold how he loved him!
He that liveth,
He that believeth,
Shall never die!

CROWD (*on either side of house, echo the chant*).

He that believeth

Shall never die!
Lazarus, come forth!

FIRST GUEST (*a Simple Boy—in a frightened whisper after a pause of dead silence*). That strange light seems to come from within him! (*With awe.*) Think of it! For four days he lay in the tomb! (*Turns away with a shudder.*)

SECOND GUEST (*a Happy Youth—with reassuring conviction*). It is a holy light. It came from Jesus.

FIFTH GUEST (*an Envious, Middle-Aged Man*). Maybe if the truth were known, our friend there never really died at all!

FOURTH GUEST (*a Defiant Man, indignantly*). Do you doubt the miracle? I tell you I was here in this house when Lazarus died!

SEVENTH GUEST (*an Aged, Sorrowful Man*). And I used to visit him every day. He knew himself his hour was near.

FOURTH GUEST. He wished for death! He said to me one day: "I have known my fill of life and the sorrow of living. Soon I shall know peace." And he smiled. It was the first time I had seen him smile in years.

THIRD GUEST (*a Self-Tortured Man—gloomily*). Yes, of late years his life had been one long misfortune. One after another his children died——

SIXTH GUEST (*a Mature Man with a cruel face—with a harsh laugh*). They were all girls. Lazarus had no luck.

SEVENTH GUEST. The last was a boy, the one that died at birth. You are forgetting him.

THIRD GUEST. Lazarus could never forget. Not only did his son die, but Miriam could never bear him more children.

FIFTH GUEST (*practically*). But he could not blame bad luck for everything. Take the loss of his father's wealth since he took over the management. That was his own doing. He was a bad farmer, a poor breeder of sheep, and a bargainer so easy to cheat it hurt one's conscience to trade with him!

SIXTH GUEST (*with a sneer—maliciously*). You should know best about that!

(*A suppressed laugh from those around him.*)

FIRST GUEST (*who has been gazing at Lazarus—softly*). Ssssh! Look at his face!

(*They all stare. A pause.*)

SECOND GUEST (*with wondering awe*). Do you remember him, neighbours, before he died? He used to be pale even when he worked in the fields. Now he seems as brown as one who has laboured in the earth all day in a vineyard beneath the hot sun!

(*A pause.*)

FOURTH GUEST. The whole look of his face has changed. He is like a stranger from a far land. There is no longer any sorrow in his eyes. They must have forgotten sorrow in the grave.

FIFTH GUEST (*grumblingly*). I thought we were invited here to eat—and all we do is stand and gape at him!

FOURTH GUEST (*sternly*). Be silent! We are waiting for him to speak.

THIRD GUEST (*impressively*). He did speak once. And he laughed!

ALL THE GUESTS (*amazed and incredulous*). Laughed?

THIRD GUEST (*importantly*). Laughed! I heard him! It was a moment after the miracle——

MIRIAM (*her voice, rich with sorrow, exultant now*). Jesus cried, "Lazarus, come forth!"

(*She kisses his hand. He makes a slight movement, a stirring in his vision. The Guests stare. A frightened pause.*)

FIFTH GUEST (*nudging the Second—uneasily*). Go on with your story!

THIRD GUEST. Just as he appeared in the opening of the tomb, wrapped in his shroud——

SECOND GUEST (*excitedly—interrupting*). My heart stopped! I fell on my face! And all the women screamed! (*Sceptically.*) You must have sharp ears to have heard him laugh in that uproar!

THIRD GUEST. I helped to pry away the stone, so I was right beside him. I found myself kneeling, but between my fingers I watched Jesus and Lazarus. Jesus looked into his face for what seemed a long time, and suddenly Lazarus said "Yes," as if he were answering a question in Jesus' eyes.

ALL THE GUESTS (*mystified*). Yes? What could he mean by yes?

THIRD GUEST. Then Jesus smiled sadly but with tenderness, as one who from a distance of years of sorrow remembers happiness. And then Lazarus knelt and kissed Jesus' feet and both of them smiled and Jesus blessed him and called him "My Brother" and went away; and Lazarus, looking after Him, began to laugh softly like a man in love with God! Such a laugh I never heard! It made my ears drunk! It was like wine! And though I was half-dead with fright I found myself laughing, too!

MIRIAM (*with a beseeching summons*). Lazarus, come forth!

CHORUS (*chanting*). Lazarus! Come forth!

CROWD (*on either side of the house—echoing the chant*). Come forth! Come forth!

LAZARUS (*suddenly in a deep voice—with a wonderful exultant acceptance in it*). Yes!

(*The Guests in the room, the Crowds outside, all cry out in fear and joy and fall on their knees.*)

CHORUS (*chanting exultantly*). The stone is taken away!
The spirit is loosed!
The soul let go!

LAZARUS (*rising and looking around him at everyone and everything—with an all-embracing love—gently*). Yes!

(*His family and the Guests in the room now throng about Lazarus to embrace him. The Crowds of men and women on each side push into the room to stare at him. He is in the arms of his Mother and Miriam while his Sisters and Father kiss and press his hands. The five are half-hysterical with relief and joy, sobbing and laughing.*)

FATHER. My son is reborn to me!

CHORUS. Hosanna!

ALL (*with a great shout*). Hosanna!

FATHER. Let us rejoice! Eat and drink! Draw up your chairs, friends! Music! Bring wine!

(*Music begins in the room off right rear—a festive dance tune. The company sit down in their places, the Father and Mother at Lazarus' right and left, Miriam next to the Mother, Martha and Mary beside the Father. But Lazarus remains standing. And the Chorus of Old Men remain in their formation at the rear. Wine is poured and all raise their goblets toward Lazarus—then suddenly they stop, the music dies out, and an awed and frightened stillness prevails, for Lazarus is a strange, majestic figure whose understanding smile seems terrible and enigmatic to them.*)

FATHER (*pathetically uneasy*). You frighten us, my son. You are strange—standing there—(*In the midst of a silence more awkward than before he rises to his feet, goblet in hand—forcing his voice, falteringly.*) A toast, neighbours!

CHORUS (*in a forced echo*). A toast!

ALL (*echoing them*). A toast!

FATHER. To my son, Lazarus, whom a blessed miracle has brought back from death!

LAZARUS (*suddenly laughing softly out of his vision, as if to himself, and speaking with a strange unearthly calm in a voice that is like a loving whisper of hope and confidence*). No! There is no death!

(*A moment's pause. The people remain with goblets uplifted, staring at him. Then all repeat after him questioningly and frightenedly.*)

ALL. There—is—no—death?

SIXTH GUEST (*suddenly blurts out the question which is in the minds of all*). What did you find beyond there, Lazarus?

(*A pause of silence.*)

LAZARUS (*smiles gently and speaks as if to a group of inquisitive children*). O Curious Greedy Ones, is not one world in which you know not how to live enough for you?

SIXTH GUEST (*emboldened*). Why did you say yes, Lazarus?

FOURTH GUEST. Why did you laugh?

ALL THE GUESTS (*with insistent curiosity but in low awed tones*). What is beyond there, Lazarus?

CHORUS (*in a low murmur*). What is beyond there? What is beyond?

CROWD (*carrying the question falteringly back into silence*). What is beyond?

LAZARUS (*suddenly again—now in a voice of loving

exultation). There is only life! I heard the heart of Jesus laughing in my heart; "There is Eternal Life in No," it said, "and there is the same Eternal Life in Yes! Death is the fear between!" And my heart reborn to love of life cried "Yes!" and I laughed in the laughter of God!

(*He begins to laugh, softly at first—a laugh so full of a complete acceptance of life, a profound assertion of joy in living, so devoid of all self-consciousness or fear, that it is like a great bird song triumphant in depths of sky, proud and powerful, infectious with love, casting on the listener an enthralling spell. The crowd in the room are caught by it. Glancing sideways at one another, smiling foolishly and self-consciously, at first they hesitate, plainly holding themselves in for fear of what the next one will think.*)

CHORUS (*in a chanting murmur*). Lazarus laughs!
Our hearts grow happy!
Laughter like music!
The wind laughs!
The sea laughs!
Spring laughs from the earth!
Summer laughs in the air!
Lazarus laughs!

LAZARUS (*on a final note of compelling exultation*). Laugh! Laugh with me! Death is dead! Fear is no more! There is only life! There is only laughter!

CHORUS (*chanting exultingly now*). Laugh! Laugh!
Laugh with Lazarus!
Fear is no more!
There is no death!

(*They laugh in a rhythmic cadence dominated by the laughter of Lazarus.*)

CROWD (*who, gradually, joining in by groups or one by one—including Lazarus' family with the exception of Miriam, who does not laugh but watches and listens to his laughter with a tender smile of being happy in his happiness—have now all begun to laugh in rhythm with the Chorus—in a great, full-throated pæan as the laughter of Lazarus rises higher and higher*). Laugh! Laugh!
Fear is no more!
There is no death!

CHORUS. Laugh! Laugh!
There is only life!
There is only laughter!
Fear is no more!
Death is dead!

CROWD (*in a rhythmic echo*). Laugh! Laugh!
Death is dead!
There is only laughter!

(*The room rocks, the air outside throbs with the rhythmic beat of their liberated laughter—still a bit uncertain of its freedom, harsh, discordant, frenzied, desperate and drunken, but dominated and inspired by the high, free, aspiring, exulting laughter of Lazarus.*)

CURTAIN

SCENE TWO

SCENE. *Some months later. Exterior of Lazarus' home in Bethany, now known as the House of Laughter. It is a clear bright night, the sky sparkling with stars. At the extreme front is a road. Between this and the house is a small raised terrace. The house is low, of one story only, its walls white. Four windows are visible with a closed door in the middle of the wall. Steps lead up to this door, and to the left of door a flight of stairs goes up to the balustraded roof. The windows shine brilliantly with the flickering light of many candles which gives them a throbbing star-like effect. From within comes the sound of flutes and dance music. The dancers can be seen whirling swiftly by the windows. There is continually an overtone of singing laughter emphasizing the pulsing rhythm of the dance.*

On the road in the foreground, at left and right, two separate groups of Jews are gathered. They are not divided according to sex as in the previous scene. Each is composed about equally of men and women, forty-nine in each, masked and costumed as before. It is religious belief that now divides them. The adherents of Jesus, the Nazarenes, among whom may be noted Martha and Mary, are on the left; the Orthodox, among whom are Lazarus' Father and Mother and a Priest, are at right. Between the two hostile groups is the same Chorus of Old Men, in a formation like a spearhead, whose point is placed at the foot of the steps leading to the terrace. All these people are staring fascinatedly at the house, listening entranced, their feet moving, their bodies swaying to the music's beat, stiffly, constrainedly, compelled against their wills. Then the music suddenly stops and the chant of youthful voices is heard:

FOLLOWERS OF LAZARUS (*from within the house*).
Laugh! Laugh!
There is only life!
There is only laughter!

CHORUS OF OLD MEN (*as if they were subjects moved by hypnotic suggestion—miserably and discordantly*). Ha-ha-ha-ha!
There is only laughter!
Ha-ha——

CROWD (*in the same manner*). Ha-ha——

MARY. Ha— (*Then frantically—half-weeping with indignant rage—to the Nazarenes.*) Stop! Oh, how can we laugh! We are betraying Jesus! My brother Lazarus has become a devil!

THE ORTHODOX PRIEST (*his mask is that of a religious fanatic. He is sixty or so*). Ha—ha— (*Tearing his beard and stamping with rage.*) Stop it, you fools! It is a foul sin in the sight of Jehovah! Why do you come here every night to listen and watch their abominations? The Lord God will punish you!

MARY (*echoing him—to her people*). Jesus will never forgive you!

THE PRIEST (*angrily*). Jesus?

(*He turns to look at the Nazarenes disdainfully and spits on the ground insultingly.*)

(*The members of the two groups begin to glare at each other. The Chorus falls back, three on each side, leaving one neutral figure before the steps. The Priest goes on tauntingly.*)

Did you hear her, friends? These renegade Nazarenes will soon deny they are Jews at all! They will begin to worship in filthy idolatry the sun and stars and man's body—as Lazarus in there (*points to the house*), the disciple of their Jesus, has so well set them the example!

(*This is followed by an outburst of insulting shouts of accusation and denial from both sides.*)

A NAZARENE (*the Fourth Guest of Scene One*). You lie! Lazarus is no disciple! He is a traitor to Jesus! We scorn him!

PRIEST (*sneeringly*). But your pretended Messiah did not scorn him. According to your stupid lies, he raised him from the dead! And answer me, has your Jesus ever denied Lazarus, or denounced his laughter? No! No doubt he is laughing, too, at all you credulous fools—for if Lazarus is not his disciple, in the matter of the false miracle he was his accomplice!

(*This provokes a furious protest from the Nazarenes and insulting hoots and jeers from the Orthodox, penetrated by a piercing scream from Lazarus' Mother, who, crushed in the crowd, sinks fainting to the ground. The Father bends over her. The group of the Orthodox falls back from them. With frightened cries Martha and Mary run from the group of Nazarenes and kneel beside her.*)

FATHER (*pitifully*). Rachel! Darling! Speak to me!

MARTHA (*practically*). She has only fainted.

MARY. She is opening her eyes! Mother, dear!

MOTHER (*weakly*). Did I fall? (*Recognizing Martha and Mary.*) Martha—and Mary—my dear ones! (*They embrace her, weeping.*) I have not kissed you since you left home to follow that Jesus—— Oh, if we were only at home again—and if, also, my poor boy, Lazarus—— (*She sobs.*)

FATHER (*gruffly*). You must not speak of him!

MARTHA. Do not worry your head about Lazarus. He is not worth it!

MARY (*with surprising vindictiveness*). He is accursed! He has betrayed our Lord!

PRIEST (*to those around him—mockingly*). Do you hear? They already call the Nazarene "Lord"!

A Lord who is in the common prison at Jerusalem, I heard to-day! A fine Lord whom our High Priests have had arrested like a thief!

MARY (*with fanatic fervour*). He is a king! Whenever He chooses He will gather a great army and He will seize His kingdom and all who deny Him shall be crucified!

PRIEST (*tauntingly*). Now their jail-bird is a king, no less! Soon they will make him a god, as the Romans do their Cæsars!

MARY (*her eyes flashing*). He is the Messiah!

PRIEST (*furiously*). The Messiah! May Jehovah smite you in your lies! Step back among your kind! You defile us! (*As she stands defiantly he appeals to the Father.*) Have you no authority? She called him the Messiah—that common beggar, that tramp! Curse her!

FATHER (*confused, pitifully harried, collecting his forces*). Wait! Go back, Mary! You chose to follow that impostor——

MARY (*defiantly*). The Messiah!

MARTHA (*trying to calm her*). Ssssh! Remember he is our father!

MARY (*fanatically*). I deny him! I deny all who deny Jesus!

MOTHER (*tearfully*). And me, darling?

MARY. You must come to us, Mother! You must believe in Jesus and leave all to follow Him!

FATHER (*enraged*). So! You want to steal your mother away, to leave me lonely in my old age! You are an unnatural daughter! I disown you! Go, before I curse——

MOTHER (*beseechingly*). Father!

MARTHA (*pulling Mary away*). Mary! Jesus teaches to be kind.

MARY (*hysterically*). He teaches to give up all and follow Him! I want to give Him everything! I want my father to curse me!

FATHER (*frenziedly*). Then I do curse you! No—not you—but the devil in you! And the devil in Martha! And the great mocking devil that dwells in Lazarus and laughs from his mouth! I curse these devils and that Prince of Devils, that false prophet, Jesus! It is he who has brought division to my home and many homes that were happy before. I curse him! I curse the day he called my good son, Lazarus, from the grave to walk again with a devil inside him! It was not my son who came back but a devil! My son is dead! And you, my daughters, are dead! I am the father only of devils! (*His voice has risen to a wailing lament.*) My children are dead!

LAZARUS (*his voice rings from within the house in exultant denial*). Death is dead! There is only laughter! (*He laughs.*)

(*The voices of all his Followers echo his laughter. They pour in a laughing rout from the doorway on to the terrace. At the same moment the Chorus of Followers appears on the roof and forms along the balustrade, facing front.*)

(*These Followers of Lazarus, forty-nine in number, composed about equally of both sexes, wear a mask that, while recognizably Jewish, is a Lazarus mask, resembling him in its expression of fearless faith in life, the mouth shaped by laughter. The Chorus of Followers, seven in number, all men, have identical masks of double size, as before. The Period of all these masks is anywhere between Youth and Manhood (or Womanhood).*)

(*The music continues to come from within. Laughing, the Followers dance to it in weaving patterns on the terrace. They are dressed in bright-coloured diaphanous robes. Their chorused laughter, now high and clear, now dying to a humming murmur, stresses the rhythmic flow of the dance.*)

CHORUS OF FOLLOWERS. Laugh! Laugh!
There is no death!
There is only laughter!

FOLLOWERS. There is only laughter!
Death is dead!
Laugh! Laugh!

CROWD (*the two groups of Nazarenes and Orthodox, on the appearance of the Followers, immediately forget their differences and form into one mob, led by their Chorus of Old Men, whose jeering howls they echo as one voice*). Yaah! Yaah! Yaah!

(*But they cannot keep it up. The music and

laughter rise above their hooting. They fall into silence. Then they again begin to feel impelled by the rhythm and laughter, their feet move, their bodies sway. Their lips quiver, their mouths open as if to laugh. Their Chorus of Old Men are the first to be affected. It is as if this reaction were transmitted through the Chorus to the Crowd.)

PRIEST (*his mouth twitching—fighting against the compulsion in him—stammers*). Brothers—listen —we must unite—in one cause—to—stamp out —this abomination !

(*It is as if he can no longer control his speech. He presses his hand over his mouth convulsively.*)

AN AGED ORTHODOX JEW (*the Seventh Guest of Scene One—starts to harangue the crowd. He fights the spell but cannot control his jerking body nor his ghastly, spasmodic laughter*). Neighbours ! Our young people are corrupted ! They are leaving our farms—to dance and sing ! To laugh ! Ha—! Laugh at everything ! Ha-ha—— ! (*He struggles desperately to control himself.*)

CHORUS OF OLD MEN (*a barking laugh forced from them*). Ha-ha—— !

CROWD (*echoing this*). Ha-ha—— !

THE AGED JEW. They have no respect for life ! When I said in kindness, "You must go back to work," they laughed at me ! Ha— ! "We desire joy. We go to Lazarus," they said—and left my fields ! I begged them to stay—with tears in my eyes ! I even offered them more money ! They laughed ! "What is money ? Can the heart eat gold ?" They laughed at money ! Ha-ha—— ! (*He chokes with exasperated rage.*)

CHORUS OF OLD MEN (*echoing him*). Ha-ha—— !

CROWD (*echoing the Chorus*). Ha-ha !——

AGED JEW (*shaking his fist at Lazarus' Followers*). That loafer taught them that ! They come to him and work for nothing ! For nothing ! And they are glad, these undutiful ones ! While they sow, they dance ! They sing to the earth when they are ploughing ! They tend his flocks and laugh toward the sun ! Ha-ha-ha—— ! (*He struggles again.*)

CHORUS OF OLD MEN (*as before*). Ha-ha-ha——

CROWD (*as before*). Ha-ha-ha——

AGED JEW. How can we compete with labour for laughter ! We will have no harvest. There will be no food ! Our children will starve ! Our race will perish ! And he will laugh ! Ha-ha-ha-ha ! (*He howls with furious, unconstrained laughter.*)

CHORUS OF OLD MEN (*echoing his tone*). Our children will starve !
Our race will perish !
Lazarus laughs !
Ha-ha-ha-ha ! Ha-ha-ha-ha !

CROWD (*as before*). Ha-ha-ha-ha! Ha-ha-ha-ha!

(*Their former distinctions of Nazarenes and Orthodox are now entirely forgotten. The members of Lazarus' family are grouped in the centre as if nothing had ever happened to separate them. The Chorus of Old Men is again joined in its spearhead formation at the stairs. Apparent first in this Chorus, a queer excitement begins to pervade this mob. They begin to weave in and out, clasping each other's hands now and then, moving mechanically in jerky steps to the music in a grotesque sort of marionettes' country dance. At first this is slow but it momentarily becomes more hectic and peculiar. They raise clenched fists or hands distended into threatening talons. Their voices sound thick and harsh and animal-like with anger as they mutter and growl, each one aloud to himself or herself.*)

CHORUS OF OLD MEN (*threateningly, gradually rising to hatred*). Hear them laugh !
See them dance !
Shameless ! Wanton !
Dirty ! Evil !
Infamous ! Bestial !
Madness ! Blood !
Adultery ! Murder !
We burn !
We kill !
We crucify !
Death ! Death !
Beware, Lazarus ! (*This last in a wild frenzy.*)

CROWD (*frenziedly*). Beware, Lazarus !
We burn ! We kill !

We crucify !
Death ! Death !

(*They crowd toward the gateway, their arms stretched out as if demanding Lazarus for a sacrificial victim. Meanwhile they never cease to hop up and down, to mill around, to twist their bodies toward and away from each other in bestial parody of the dance of the Followers.*)

(*The tall figure of Lazarus, dressed in a white robe, suddenly appears on the roof of the house. He stands at the balustrade in the middle of the Chorus. Beside him, a little behind, Miriam appears dressed in black, her face upturned, her lips praying. She appears to have grown older, to be forty now. Lazarus' body is softly illumined by its inner light. The change in him is marked. He seems ten years younger, at the prime of forty. His body has become less angular and stiff. His movements are graceful and pliant. The change is even more noticeable in his face, which has filled out, become purer in outline, more distinctly Grecian. His complexion is the red-brown of rich earth, the grey in his black, curly beard has almost disappeared.*)

(*He makes a sign and the music ceases. His Followers remain fixed in their dancing attitudes like figures in a frieze. Each member of the mob remains frozen in a distorted posture. He stares down at the mob pityingly, his face calm.*)

LAZARUS (*speaks amid a profound silence. His voice releases his own dancers and the mob from their fixed attitudes. The music begins to play again within the house, very soft and barely audible, swelling up and down like the sound of an organ from a distant church*). You laugh, but your laughter is guilty ! It laughs a hyena laughter, spotted, howling its hungry fear of life ! That day I returned did I not tell you your fear was no more, that there is no death ? You believed then—for a moment ! You laughed—discordantly, hoarsely, but with a groping toward joy. What ! Have you so soon forgotten, that now your laughter curses life again as of old ? (*He pauses—then sadly*). That is your tragedy ! You forget ! You forget the God in you ! You wish to forget ! Remembrance would imply the high duty to live as a son of God—generously !—with love !—with pride !—with laughter ! This is too glorious a victory for you, too terrible a loneliness ! Easier to forget, to become only a man, the son of a woman, to hide from life against her breast, to whimper your fear to her resigned heart and be comforted by her resignation ! To live by denying life ! (*Then exhortingly.*) Why are your eyes always either fixed on the ground in weariness of thought, or watching one another with suspicion ? Throw your gaze upward ! To Eternal Life ! To the fearless and deathless ! The everlasting ! To the stars ! (*He stretches out his arms to the sky—then suddenly points.*) See ! A new star has appeared ! It is the one that shone over Bethlehem ! (*His voice becomes a little bitter and mocking.*) The Master of Peace and Love has departed this earth. Let all stars be for you henceforth symbols of Saviours—Sons of God who appeared on worlds like ours to tell the saving truth to ears like yours, inexorably deaf ! (*Then exaltedly*). But the greatness of Saviours is that they may not save ! The greatness of Man is that no god can save him—until he becomes a god !

(*He stares up at the stars, rapt in contemplation, oblivious to all around him now.*)

(*Rapidly approaching from the left a man's voice jarring in high-pitched cruel laughter is heard. They all listen, huddled together like sheep.*)

MESSENGER (*the Third Guest of Scene One rushes in breathlessly, shouting*). The Nazarene has been crucified !

PRIEST (*with fierce triumph*). Jehovah is avenged ! Hosanna !

ORTHODOX. Hosanna ! The false prophet is dead ! The pretended Messiah is dead !

(*They jump and dance, embracing one another. The Nazarenes stand paralysed and stunned. The two groups mechanically separate to right and left again, the Chorus of Old Men dividing itself as before.*)

MARY (*in a frenzy of grief*). Do not believe him ! Jesus could not die !

(*But at this moment a Nazarene youth,*

exhausted by grief and tears, staggers in from the left.)

MESSENGER (*Second Guest of Scene One*). Jesus is dead! Our Lord is murdered!

(*He sinks on his knees sobbing. All the Nazarenes do likewise, wailing, rending their garments, tearing their hair, some even beating their heads on the ground in the agony of their despair.*)

MARY (*insane with rage now*). They have murdered Him! (*To her followers—savagely.*) An eye for an eye! Avenge the Master!

(*Their frenzy of grief turned into rage, the Nazarenes leap to their feet threateningly. Concealed swords and knives are brought out by both sides.*)

MIRIAM (*leaning over the balustrade—in a voice of entreaty*). Mary! Brothers!

(*But none heed her or seem to see her. Lazarus and his Followers remain oblivious to men, arms upstretched toward the stars, their heads thrown back.*)

MARY (*wildly*). Vengeance! Death to His murderers!

PRIEST (*fiercely to his followers*). Death to the Nazarenes!

(*With cries of rage the two groups rush on one another. There is a confused tumult of yells, groans, curses, the shrieks of women, the sounds of blows as they meet in a pushing, whirling, struggling mass in which individual figures are indistinguishable. Knives and swords flash above the heads of the mass, hands in every tense attitude of striking, clutching, tearing are seen upraised. As the fight is at its height a Roman Centurion and a squad of eight Soldiers come tramping up at the double-quick. They all are masked. These Roman masks now and henceforth in the play are carried out according to the same formula of Seven Periods, Seven Types, as those of the Jews seen previously, except that the basis of each face is Roman—heavy, domineering, self-complacent, the face of a confident dominant race. The Centurion differs from his soldiers only in being more individualized. He is middle-aged, his soldiers belong to the Period of Manhood. All are of the Simple, Ignorant Type.*)

CENTURION (*shouts commandingly*). Disperse! (*But no one hears him—with angry disgust to his Soldiers.*) Charge! Cut them down!

(*The Soldiers form a wedge and charge with a shout. They soon find it necessary to use their swords, and strike down everyone in their way.*)

MIRIAM. Mercy, Romans! (*As they pay no attention to her, in desperation she embraces Lazarus beseechingly, forcing his attention back to earth.*) Lazarus! Mercy!

LAZARUS (*looks down upon the struggling mass and cries in a ringing voice*). Hold!

(*Each person stands transfixed, frozen in the last movement, even the Roman Soldiers and the Centurion himself. Ten dead and mortally wounded lie on the ground, trampled by the feet of friend and foe alike. Lazarus looks at the Crowd. To each he seems to look at him or her alone. His eyes are accusing and stern. As one head, the headsof all are averted. Even the Centurion stares at the ground humbly, in spite of himself. Finally Lazarus speaks in a voice of infinite disdain.*)

Sometimes it is hard to laugh—even *at* men!

(*He turns his eyes from them, staring straight before him. This seems to release them from their fixed positions. The Nazarenes and the Orthodox separate and slink guiltily apart. The Chorus of Old Men forms again, the apex at the centre of the steps as before. A low wail of lamentation arises from them. The two crowds of Nazarenes and Orthodox echo this.*)

CHORUS OF OLD MEN (*in a wailing chant*). Woe unto Israel!
Woe unto thee, Jerusalem!
O divided house,
Thou shalt crumble to dust,
And swine shall root
Where thy Temple stood!
Woe unto us!

CROWD (*in a great echoing cry*). Woe unto us!

CENTURION (*gruffly to hide his embarrassment at being awed by Lazarus*). Here, you! Drag your carcasses away! (*From each side men and women come forward to identify and mourn their dead. The wail of lamentation rises and falls. The Centurion looks up at Lazarus—harshly.*) You, there! Are you he whom they call the Laugher?

LAZARUS (*without looking at him—his voice seeming to come from some dream within him*). I am Lazarus.

CENTURION. Who was brought back from death by enchantment?

LAZARUS (*looking down at him now—with a smile, simply*). No. There is no death!

CHORUS OF FOLLOWERS (*chanting joyously*). There is no death!

FOLLOWERS (*echoing*). There is no death!

AN ORTHODOX MAN (*bending beside the body of Lazarus' father*). Here is your father, Lazarus. He is dead.

AN ORTHODOX WOMAN. This is your mother, Lazarus. She is dead.

A NAZARENE. Here is your sister, Martha, Lazarus. She is dead.

A NAZARENE WOMAN. And this is Mary, Lazarus. She is dead.

MIRIAM (*suddenly—with deep grief*). And Jesus who was the Son of Man, who loved you and gave you life again, has died, Lazarus—has died!

LAZARUS (*in a great triumphant voice*). Yes! Yes!! Yes!!! Men die! Even a Son of Man must die to show men that Man may live! But there is no death!

CENTURION (*at first in a tone of great awe—to his Soldiers*). Is he a god? (*Then gruffly, ashamed of his question.*) Come down, Jew! I have orders to bring you to Rome to Cæsar!

LAZARUS (*as if he were answering not the Centurion but the command of his fate from the sky*). Yes! (*He walks down the narrow stairs and, Miriam following him, comes down the path to the road. He goes and kneels for a moment each beside the bodies of his Father, Mother, and Sisters, and kisses each in turn on the forehead. For a moment the struggle with his grief can be seen in his face. Then he looks up to the stars and, as if answering a question, again says simply and acceptingly*). Yes! (*Then exultantly.*) Yes!! (*And begins to laugh from the depths of his exalted spirit. The laughter of his Chorus and then of his Followers echoes his. The music and dancing begin again.*)

(*The Centurion grins sheepishly. The Soldiers chuckle. The Centurion laughs awkwardly. The Soldiers laugh. The music from the house and the laughter of the Followers grow louder. The infection spreads to the Chorus of Old Men whose swaying grief falls into the rhythm of the laughter and music as does that of the mourners.*)

LAZARUS' FOLLOWERS (*led by their Chorus*).
Laugh! Laugh!

CHORUS OF OLD MEN (*torn by the conflict—torturedly*). Ha-ha-ha—
Woe to us, woe!

CROWD (*beside the bodies*). Woe to us, woe!
Ha-ha——!

CENTURION (*laughingly*). You are brave, you Laugher! Remember Tiberius never laughs! And boast not to Cæsar there is no death, or he will invent a new one for you!

LAZARUS (*with a smile*). But all death is men's invention! So laugh!

(*He laughs, and the Centurion and Soldiers laugh with him, half dancing clumsily now to the beat of the music.*)

CHORUS OF LAZARUS' FOLLOWERS. Laugh! Laugh!
Fear is no more!
There is no death!
There is only life!
There is only laughter!

FOLLOWERS (*dancing*). Laugh! Laugh!
Fear is no more!
Death is dead!

CHORUS OF OLD MEN (*forgetting their grief—their eyes on Lazarus now, their arms outstretched to him as are those of the crowd grouped around the bodies but forgetting them*). Death is no more!
Death is dead!
Laugh!

CROWD. Laugh! Laugh!
Death is no more!

CENTURION (*laughing, to his laughing Soldiers*).
Forward!

(*They tramp, dancing, off.*)

(*Lazarus and Miriam start to follow.*)

MIRIAM (*suddenly pointing to his Followers who are dancing and laughing obliviously—pityingly*). But your faithful ones who love you, Lazarus?

LAZARUS (*simply, with a trace of a sad sternness*). This is their test. Their love must remember—or it must forget. Come!

(*With a last gesture back like a blessing on all he is leaving, he goes. The laughter of the Soldiers recedes. That of the Chorus of Old Men and of the Crowd falters and breaks into lamenting grief again, guilt-stricken because of its laughter.*)

CHORUS OF OLD MEN. Laugh! Laugh!
Death is dead!
Laugh!—But woe!
There lie our dead!
Oh shame and guilt!
We forget our dead!

CROWD (*with fierce remorseful grief*). Woe to us, woe!
There lie our dead!

CHORUS OF LAZARUS FOLLOWERS (*their voices and the music growing more and more hesitating and faint*). Laugh! Laugh!
There is only life!
There is only—
Laugh— (*Their dance is faltering and slow now.*)
Fear is no—
Death is—
Laugh—

(*The music and dancing and voices cease. The lights in the windows, which have been growing dim, go out. There is a second of complete, death-like silence. The mourning folk in the foreground are frozen figures of grief. Then a sudden swelling chorus of forlorn bewilderment, a cry of lost children, comes from the Chorus of Followers and the Followers themselves. They huddle into groups on the roof and on the terrace. They stretch their arms out in every direction supplicatingly.*)

CHORUS OF FOLLOWERS. Oh, Lazarus, laugh!
Do not forsake us!
We forget!
Where is thy love fled?
Give back thy laughter,
Thy fearless laughter!
We forget!

FOLLOWERS. Give back thy laughter!
We forget!

CHORUS OF FOLLOWERS (*with dull, resigned terror now*). Death slinks out
Of his grave in the heart!
Ghosts of fear
Creep back in the brain!
We remember fear!
We remember death!

FOLLOWERS. Death in the heart!
Fear in the brain!
We remember fear!
We remember death!

CHORUS OF FOLLOWERS (*wailing hopelessly now*). Forgotten is laughter!
We remember
Only death!
Fear is God!
Forgotten is laughter!
Life is death!

FOLLOWERS. Forgotten is laughter!
Life is death!

ALL (*the Chorus of Old Men and the Crowd joining in*). Life is a fearing,
A long dying,
From birth to death!
God is a slayer!
Life is death!

CURTAIN

ACT TWO SCENE ONE

SCENE. *Some months later. A square in Athens about ten o'clock at night. In the rear, pure and beautiful in the light of a full moon, is the façade of a temple. An excited crowd of Greeks of both sexes is gathered in the square as if for some public festival. They are masked according to the scheme of Seven Periods in Seven Types of Character for each sex. Here, of course, the foundation of the mask is the Grecian type of face.*

On the left, the Chorus of Greeks is grouped, seven in number, facing front, in the spearhead formation. As before, the Chorus wears masks double the life size of the Crowd masks. They are all of the Proud Self-Reliant type, in the period of Young Manhood.

These seven are clad in goat skins, their tanned bodies and masks daubed and stained with wine lees, in imitation of the old followers of Dionysus. Rumour has led them to hope and believe that Lazarus may be the reincarnation of this deity.

The people in the crowd are holding themselves in restraint with difficulty, they stir and push about restlessly with an eager curiosity and impatience. All eyes are fixed off left. A buzz of voices hums in the air.

Acting as police, a number of Roman legionaries (masked like the soldiers of Scene Two) armed with staves, keep back the crowd from the line of the street that runs from left to right, front. They resent this duty, which has already kept them there a long time, and are surly and quick-tempered with the Greeks.

At front, pacing impatiently up and down, is a young Roman noble of twenty-one, clad richly, wearing beautifully wrought armour and helmet. This is Gaius, the heir of Tiberius Cæsar, nicknamed Caligula by the soldiers, in whose encampments he was born and where he spent his childhood. His body is bony and angular, almost malformed with wide, powerful shoulders and long arms and hands, and short, skinny, hairy legs like an ape's. He wears a half-mask of crimson, dark with a purplish tinge, that covers the upper part of his face to below the nose. This mask accentuates his bulging, prematurely wrinkled forehead, his hollow temples and his bulbous, sensual nose. His large troubled eyes, of a glazed greenish-blue, glare out with a shifty feverish suspicion at every one. Below his mask his own skin is of an anæmic transparent pallor. Above it, his hair is the curly blond hair of a child of six or seven. His mouth also is childish, the red lips soft and feminine in outline. Their expression is spoiled, petulant and self-obsessed, weak but domineering. In combination with the rest of the face there is an appalling morbid significance to his mouth. One feels that its boyish cruelty, encouraged as a manly attribute in the coarse brutality of camps, has long ago become naïvely insensitive to any human suffering but its own.

Walking with Caligula is Cneius Crassus, a Roman general—a squat, muscular man of sixty, his mask that of a heavy battered face full of coarse humour.

CHORUS OF GREEKS (*intoning solemnly*). Soon the God comes!
Redeemer and Saviour!
Dionysus, Son of Man and a God!

GREEK CROWD (*echoing*). Soon the God comes!
Redeemer and Saviour!
Dionysus!

FIRST GREEK. They say an unearthly flame burns in this Lazarus!

SECOND GREEK. The sacred fire! He must be the Fire-born, the son of Zeus!

THIRD GREEK. Many who have seen him swear he is Dionysus, re-arisen from Hades!

FOURTH GREEK (*importantly*). I saw Lazarus at Antioch where the galley on which they were taking him to Rome had been thrice blown back by a storm. Fear of this warning omen is why they now march with him by land.

FIRST GREEK. Does he truly resemble a god?

FOURTH GREEK (*impressively*). One look in his eyes while his laughter sings in your ears and you forget sorrow! You dance! You laugh! It is as if a heavy weight you had been carrying all your life without knowing it suddenly were lifted. You are like a cloud, you can fly, your mind reels with laughter, you are drunk with joy! (*Solemnly.*) Take my word for it, he is indeed a god. Everywhere the people have acclaimed him. He heals the sick, he raises the dead, by laughter.

SEVENTH GREEK. But I have heard that when he has gone people cannot remember his laughter, that the dead are dead again and the sick die, and the sad grow more sorrowful.

FIFTH GREEK. Well, we shall soon see with our own eyes. But why should the god return in the body of a Jew?

SIXTH GREEK. What better disguise if he wishes to remain unknown? The fools of

Romans will never suspect him!

THIRD GREEK (*laughing*). Never! They are beginning to claim he is a Roman!

FIFTH GREEK. So much the better! He will be in their confidence!

FOURTH GREEK. He will lead us against Rome! He will laugh our tyrants into the sea! Ha!

(*He turns toward the Romans and laughs sneeringly. This is taken up by the Crowd—unpleasant, resentful laughter. They push forward aggressively and almost sweep the Soldiers from their feet.*)

CRASSUS (*angrily*). Drive them back!

CALIGULA (*suddenly with a distorted warped smile*). Order them to use their swords, Cneius. Let the scum look at their dead and learn respect for us!

SOLDIERS (*shoving and whacking*). Back! Step back! Back there!

(*The crowd push back to their former line. There are muttered curses, groans, protests, which subside into the former hum of expectancy.*)

CALIGULA (*with the same smile*). The sword, my old hyena! Corpses are so educational!

CRASSUS (*surlily*). I would like to, I promise you! When I see how they hate us——!

CALIGULA (*carelessly*). Let them hate—so long as they fear us! We must keep death dangling (*he makes the gesture of doing so*) before their eyes! (*He gives a soft, cruel laugh.*) Will you not sacrifice in my honour? What are a few Greeks? (*Queerly.*) I like to watch men die.

CRASSUS. I dare not, Caligula. Cæsar has forbidden bloodshed.

CALIGULA. Tiberius is a miser. He wants to hoard all of death for his own pleasure! (*He laughs again.*)

CRASSUS (*with rough familiarity*). I wager no one will make that complaint against you when you are Cæsar! (*He chuckles.*)

CALIGULA (*with the sudden grandiose posturing of a bad actor unintentionally burlesquing grandeur*). When I, Gaius Caligula, am Cæsar, I— (*Then superstitiously looking up at the sky with cringing foreboding*). But it brings bad luck to anticipate fate. (*He takes off his helmet and spits in it—then with a grim smile.*) The heirs of a Cæsar take sick so mysteriously! Even with you who used to ride me on your knee, I do not eat nor drink until you have tasted first.

CRASSUS (*nodding approvingly*). You are sensible. I suppose I, too, have my price—if they were only clever enough to discover it! (*He laughs hoarsely.*)

CALIGULA (*steps back from him with an uneasy shudder*). You are honest, at least—too honest, Cneius! (*Grimly.*) If my father Germanicus had had you for his counsellor, he might have escaped their poison. (*Then gloomily.*) I must fear everyone. The world is my enemy.

CRASSUS. Kill it then! (*He laughs again.*)

CHORUS (*stretching out their arms in the direction from which Lazarus is expected—supplicatingly*). Son of the Lightning!
Deadly thy vengeance!
Swift thy deliverance!
Beholding thy Mother,
Greece, our Mother,
Her beauty in bondage,
Her pride in chains!
Hasten, Redeemer!

CROWD (*as before—echoing the chant*). Hasten, Redeemer!
Son of the Lightning!
Deadly thy vengeance!
Swift thy deliverance!

CALIGULA (*disdainfully*). What clods! Mob is the same everywhere, eager to worship any new charlatan! They have already convinced themselves this Lazarus is a reincarnation of Dionysus! A Jew become a god! By the breasts of Venus that *is* a miracle.! (*He laughs.*)

CRASSUS (*seriously*). But he must be expert in magic. He was buried four days and came out unharmed. Maybe he is not a Jew. Some say his father was really a legionary of our garrison in Judea. And he teaches people to laugh at death. That smacks of Roman blood!

CALIGULA (*ironically*). Better still! He tells them there is no death at all! Hence the multitude of fools who have acclaimed him everywhere since he left his own country—and why Tiberius has begun to fear his influence.

CRASSUS (*sententiously*). Whom Cæsar fears—disappears !

CALIGULA. Yes, the dupes who follow Lazarus will be killed. But Tiberius believes this Lazarus may know a cure for death or for renewing youth, and the old lecher hopes he can worm the secret out of him—before he kills him. (*He laughs ironically, then disgustedly.*) That is why I must escort this Jew to Rome—as a special honour ! (*With fierce, haughty resentment.*) I, the heir of Cæsar ! (*Savagely.*) Oh, if I were Cæsar—— !

CRASSUS (*with a coarse, meaning smirk*). Patience. Tiberius is old.

CALIGULA (*suddenly becoming terribly uneasy at some thought*). Cneius ! What if this Lazarus has really discovered a cure for old age and should reveal it to Tiberius ! (*His lips tremble, his eyes are terrified, he shrinks against Crassus for protection—with boyish pleading.*) Oh, Cneius, what could I do then ?

CRASSUS (*matter-of-factly*). Kill him before Cæsar can talk to him.

CALIGULA (*almost in tears*). But if he knows a charm against death, how could he be slain, old fool ?

CRASSUS (*gruffly*). Bah ! (*Then with grim humour.*) Death in bed I suspect, but when men are killed I know they stay dead ! (*Disgustedly.*) A moment ago you were laughing at him ! (*Scornfully.*) Do you fear him now ?

CALIGULA (*rather shamefacedly pulls himself together—then broodingly*). I fear every one who lives. Even you. As you advised me. (*He turns away.*)

CRASSUS (*contemptuously*). Well, maybe he can teach you to laugh at fear. You would welcome him then, eh, cry baby ?

CALIGULA (*with sudden passionate intensity but only half aloud, as if to himself*). I would love him, Cneius ! As a father ! As a god !

(*He stands staring before him strangely, There is a new stir from the crowd, who again push forward.*)

CRASSUS (*pointing off right*). Look ! I see a great crowd ! Your Lazarus must be coming at last !

CHORUS (*chanting in a deep rhythmic monotone, like the rising and falling cadences of waves on a beach*). He comes, the Redeemer and Saviour !
Laughing along the mountains !
To give back our lost laughter,
To raise from the dead our freedom,
To free us from Rome !

CROWD (*echoing this chant*). Fire-born ! Redeemer ! Saviour !
Raise from the dead our freedom !
Give back our lost laughter !
Free us from Rome !

(*They have been pushing forward, more and more fiercely and defiantly. The Roman Soldiers in spite of their efforts are pushed backward step by step.*)

SOLDIERS (*angrily*). Back ! Back !

(*The Soldiers work with a will, dealing out blows with their staves at every one in reach. But now these blows seem only to infuriate the Crowd, which steadily pushes them back into the street. At the same time the distant sound of exultant music, singing and laughter becomes steadily louder. Both Soldiers and Crowd are inspired to battle by these strains without their knowing it. Caligula is listening spell-bound, his mouth open, his body swaying and twitching. Even Crassus stares off at the oncomers, forgetful of the growing plight of his Soldiers.*)

CROWD (*led by their Chorus—angrily*). Cowards ! Pigs !
Strike ! Hit !
Stones ! Knives !
Stab ! Kill !
Death to the Romans !
Death !

A SOLDIER (*alarmed, calls to Crassus*). General ! Let us use our swords !

SOLDIERS (*enraged—eagerly*). Yes ! Swords !

CROWD. Death !

CRASSUS (*turning—uneasy, but afraid to give any drastic order*). Bah ! Staves are enough. Crack their skulls !

CROWD (*led by the Chorus—defiantly*). Death to Crassus !

Drunkard! Coward!
Death to him!

(*They continue to push forward, hooting and jeering.*)

CRASSUS (*exploding for a second*). By the gods— ! (*To the Soldiers.*) Draw your swords!

(*The troops do so eagerly. The Crowd sag back momentarily with exclamations of fear.*)

CALIGULA (*listening as in a trance to the music and what is going on behind him—in a queer whisper*). Kill, Cneius! Let me dance! Let me sing! (*The music and crashing of cymbals and the ferment of passions around him cause him to lose all control over himself. He gives a crazy leap in the air and begins to dance grotesquely and chant in a thick voice.*) He is coming! Death, the Deliverer! Kill, soldiers! I command you! I, Caligula! I will be Cæsar! Death!

CROWD (*led by the Chorus—savage now*). Beast! Cur!
Death to Caligula!

(*They crowd forward.*)

CALIGULA (*drawing his sword and flourishing it drunkenly—his eyes glazed*). Death!

CRASSUS (*drawing his own sword in a frenzy*). Strike! Death!

(*His Soldiers raise their swords. The Crowd have raised whatever weapons they have found—knives, clubs, daggers, stones, bare fists.*)

CHORUS (*chanting fiercely*). Death!

ALL (*Romans and Greeks alike as one great voice*). Death!

(*The chorused word beats down all sound into a stricken silence. The wild joyous music ceases. The Romans and Greeks seem to lean back from one another and collect strength to leap forward. At this moment the voice of Larazus comes ringing through the air like a command from the sky.*)

LAZARUS. There is no death!

(*The Soldiers and Greeks remain frozen in their attitudes of murderous hate. Following his words the laughter of Lazarus is heard, exultant and gaily mocking, filling them with the sheepish shame of children caught in mischief. Their hands hang, their arms sink to their sides. The music starts once more with a triumphant clash of cymbals, Lazarus' laughter is echoed from the throats of the multitude of his Followers who now come dancing into the square, preceded by a band of masked musicians and by their Chorus.*)

(*This Chorus wears, in double size, the laughing mask of Lazarus' Followers in the same Period and Type as in the preceding scene, except that here the mask of each member of the Chorus has a different racial basis—Egyptian, Syrian, Cappadocian, Lydian, Phrygian, Cilician, Parthian. The Followers are costumed and masked as in the preceding scene, seven Types in seven Periods, except that, as in the Chorus, racially there are many nations represented. All have wreaths of ivy in their hair, and flowers in their hands which they scatter about. They whirl in between the Soldiers and Crowd, forcing them back from each other, teasing them, sifting into the Crowd, their Chorus in a half-circle, confronting the Chorus of Greeks.*)

CHORUS OF FOLLOWERS. Laugh! Laugh!
There is no death!
There is only life!
There is only laughter!

FOLLOWERS (*echoing*). Laugh! Laugh!
There is no death!

(*Caligula and Crassus are swept to one side, left. Then the cries and laughter of all become mingled into one exclamation:*)

ALL. Lazarus! Lazarus!

(*The squad of Roman Soldiers led by the Centurion who had taken Lazarus prisoner, march in with dancers' steps, like a proud guard of honour now, laughing, pulling a chariot in which Lazarus stands dressed in a tunic of white and gold, his bronzed face and limbs radiant in the halo of his own glowing light.*)

(*Lazarus now looks less than thirty-five. His countenance now might well be that of the positive masculine Dionysus, closest to the soil of the Grecian gods, a Son of Man, born of a mortal. Not the coarse, drunken Dionysus, nor the effeminate god, but Dionysus in his middle period, more comprehensive in his symbolism, the soul of the recurring seasons, of living and dying as processes in eternal growth, of the wine of life stirring forever in the sap and blood and loam of things. Miriam is beside him, dressed in black, smiling the same sad tender smile, holding Lazarus' arm as if for protection and in protection. She appears older, a woman over forty-five.*)

CHORUS OF GREEKS (*rushing to Lazarus' car*).
Hail, Dionysus !
Iacchus !
Lazarus !
Hail !

(*They surround him, throw over his shoulders and head the finely dressed hide of a bull with great gilded horns, force into his right hand the mystic rod of Dionysus with a pine cone on top, then prostrate themselves.*)

Hail, Saviour !
Redeemer !
Conqueror of Death !

ALL (*in a repeated chorus which finally includes even the Roman Soldiers, raising their arms to him*). Hail, Lazarus !
Redeemer !
Hail !

(*They are silent. Lazarus looks at them, seeming to see each and all at the same time, and his laughter, as if in answer to their greetings, is heard rising from his lips like a song.*)

CRASSUS (*awed*). Look ! He is more than man !

CALIGULA (*trembling, in a queer agitation*). I dare not look !

CRASSUS. Do you hear his laughter ?

CALIGULA (*chokingly—puts his hands over his ears*). I will not hear !

CRASSUS. But you must welcome him in Cæsar's name !

CALIGULA (*his teeth chattering*). I must kill him !

LAZARUS (*looking directly at him—gaily mocking*). Death is dead, Caligula ! (*He begins to laugh again softly.*)

CALIGULA (*with an hysterical cry of defiant terror*). You lie ! (*Sword in hand he whirls to confront Lazarus, but at the first sight of his face he stops in his tracks, trembling, held fascinated by Lazarus' eyes, mumbling with a last pitiful remainder of defiance.*) But you lie—whatever you are ! I say there *must* be death ! (*The sword has fallen to his side. He stares open-mouthed at Lazarus. There is something of a shy, wondering child about his attitude now. Lazarus looks at him, laughing with gentle understanding. Caligula suddenly drops his sword, and covering his face with his hands weeps like a boy who has been hurt.*) You have murdered my only friend, Lazarus ! Death would have been my slave when I am Cæsar. He would have been my jester and made me laugh at fear ! (*He weeps bitterly.*)

LAZARUS (*gaily*). Be your own jester instead, O Caligula ! Laugh at yourself, O Cæsar-to-be !

(*He laughs. The Crowd now all join in with him.*)

(*Caligula suddenly uncovers his face, grins his warped grin, gives a harsh cackle which cracks through the other laughter with a splitting discord, cuts a hopping caper like some grotesque cripple which takes him to the side of Lazarus' chariot, where he squats on his hams and, stretching out his hand, fingers Lazarus' robe inquisitively and stares up into his face in the attitude of a chained monkey.*)

CALIGULA (*with a childish, mischievous curiosity*). Then if there is no death, O Teacher, tell me why I love to kill ?

LAZARUS. Because you fear to die ! (*Then gaily mocking.*) But what do you matter, O Deathly-Important One ? Put yourself that question—as a jester ! (*Exultantly.*) Are you a speck of dust danced in the wind ? Then laugh, dancing ! Laugh yes to your insignificance !

Thereby will be born your new greatness! As Man, Petty Tyrant of Earth, you are a bubble pricked by death into a void and a mocking silence! But as dust, you are eternal change, and everlasting growth, and a high note of laughter soaring through chaos from the deep heart of God! Be proud, O Dust! Then you may love the stars as equals! (*Then mockingly again.*) And then perhaps you may be brave enough to love even your fellow-men without fear of their vengeance!

CALIGULA (*dully*). I cannot understand. I hate men. I am afraid of their poison and their swords and the cringing envy in their eyes that only yields to fear!

LAZARUS (*gaily mocking*). Tragic is the plight of the tragedian whose only audience is himself! Life is for each man a solitary cell whose walls are mirrors. Terrified is Caligula by the faces he makes! But I tell you to laugh in the mirror, that seeing your life gay, you may begin to live as a guest, and not as a condemned one! (*Raising his hands for silence—with a playful smile.*) Listen! In the dark peace of the grave the man called Lazarus rested. He was still weak, as one who recovers from a long illness—for, living, he had believed his life a sad one! (*He laughs softly, and softly they all echo his laughter.*) He lay dreaming to the croon of silence, feeling as the flow of blood in his own veins the past re-enter the heart of God to be renewed by faith into the future. He thought: "Men call this death"—for he had been dead only a little while and he still remembered. Then, of a sudden, a strange gay laughter trembled from his heart as though his life, so long repressed in him by fear, had found at last its voice and a song for singing. "Men call this death," it sang. "Men call life death and fear it. They hide from it in horror. Their lives are spent in hiding. Their fear becomes their living. They worship life as death!"

CHORUS OF FOLLOWERS (*in a chanting echo*). Men call life death and fear it.
They hide from it in horror.
Their lives are spent in hiding.
Their fear becomes their living.
They worship life as death!

LAZARUS. And here the song of Lazarus' life grew pitiful. "Men must learn to live," it mourned. "Before their fear invented death they knew, but now they have forgotten. They must be taught to laugh again!" And Lazarus answered "Yes!" (*He now addresses the crowd—especially Caligula, directly, laughingly.*) Thus sang his life to Lazarus while he lay dead! Man must learn to live by laughter! (*He laughs.*)

CHORUS OF FOLLOWERS. Laugh! Laugh!
There is only life!
There is only laughter!
Fear is no more!
Death is dead!

CHORUS OF GREEKS. Laugh! Laugh!
Hail, Dionysus!
Fear is no more!
Thou hast conquered death!

ALL (*laughing—in a great laughing chorus*). Laugh! Laugh!
Fear is no more!
Death is dead!

LAZARUS (*as to a crowd of children—laughingly*). Out with you! Out into the woods! Upon the hills! Cities are prisons wherein man locks himself from life. Out with you under the sky! Are the stars too pure for your sick passions? Is the warm earth smelling of night too desirous of love for your pale introspective lusts? Out! Let laughter be your new clean lust and sanity! So far man has only learned to snicker meanly at his neighbour! Let a laughing away of self be your new right to live for ever! Cry in your pride, "I am Laughter, which is Life, which is the Child of God!"

(*He laughs, and again his voice leads and dominates the rhythmic chorus of theirs. The music and dancing begin again.*)

THE TWO CHORUSES (*chanting in unison*). Laugh! Laugh!
There is only God!
We are His Laughter!

ALL (*echoing*). There is only God!
We are His Laughter!
Laugh! Laugh!

(*They take hold of his chariot traces, and as he had come, in the midst of a happy multitude, now augmented by all the Greeks, and the Roman Soldiers who had awaited him, dancing, playing, singing, laughing, he is escorted off. The noise of their passing recedes. Caligula and Crassus are left in the empty square, the former squatting on his hams, monkey-wise, and brooding sombrely.)*

CRASSUS (*is swaying and staggering, like a man in a drunken stupor, in a bewildered, stubborn struggle to control himself. He stammers after the Soldiers*). Ha-ha-ha— Halt! Halt, I say! No use—they are gone—mutiny—Halt! (*He continues to stumble toward left.*) Ha-ha— Stop it, curse you! Am I laughing? Where am I going? After Lazarus? Thirty years of discipline and I— Halt, traitor! Remember Cæsar! Remember Rome! Halt, traitor! (*He faints with the violence of his struggle and falls in a limp heap.*)

CALIGULA (*startled by his fall, terrified, hops to his feet and snatches up his sword defensively, glancing over his shoulder and whirling around as if he expected someone to stab him in the back. Then, forcing a twisted grin of self-contempt—harshly*). Coward! What do I fear—if there is no death? (*As if he had to cut something, he snatches up a handful of flowers—desperately.*) You must laugh, Caligula! (*He starts to lop off the flowers from their stems with a savage intentness.*) Laugh! Laugh! Laugh! (*Finally, impatiently, he cuts off all the remaining with one stroke.*) Laugh! (*He grinds the petals under his feet and breaks out into a terrible hysterical giggle.*) Ha-ha——

CURTAIN

SCENE TWO

SCENE. *A midnight, months later. Immediately inside the walls of Rome. In the foreground is the portico of a temple between whose massive columns one looks across a street on a lower level to the high wall of Rome at the extreme rear. In the centre of the wall is a great metal gate. The night is thick and oppressive. In the sky overhead lightning flashes and thunder rumbles and crashes but there is no rain.*

Within the portico on rows of chairs placed on a series of wide steps which are on each side, members of the Senate are seated in their white robes. High hanging lamps cast a wan light over their faces. They are all masked in the Roman mask, refined in them by nobility of blood but at the same time with strength degenerated, corrupted by tyranny and debauchery to an exhausted cynicism. The three periods of Middle Age, Maturity and Old Age are represented in the types of the Self-Tortured, Introspective; Proud, Self-Reliant; the Servile, Hypocritical; the Cruel, Revengeful; and the Resigned, Sorrowful. The Senators are divided into two groups on each side, thirty in each. Seated in the middle of the lower of the three high broad stairs that lead to the level from which the columns rise is the Chorus of Senators, seven in number, facing front, in double-sized masks of the Servile, Hypocritical type of Old Age.

Lazarus, in his robe of white and gold, the aura of light surrounding his body seeming to glow more brightly than ever, stands in the rear at the edge of the portico, centre, gazing upward into the pall of sky beyond the wall. His figure appears in its immobility to be the statue of the god of the temple. Near him, but to the rear and to the left of him, facing right, Miriam is kneeling in her black robes, swaying backward and forward, praying silently with moving lips like a nun who asks for mercy for the sins of the world. She has grown much older, her hair is grey, her shoulders are bowed.

On the other side, placed similarly in relation to Lazarus and facing Miriam, Caligula is squatting on his hams on a sort of throne-chair of ivory and gold. He is dressed with foppish richness in extreme bright colours, a victory wreath around his head. He stares blinkingly and inquisitively at Lazarus, then at Miriam. He is half-drunk. A large figured goblet of gold is in his hand. A slave with an amphora of wine crouches on the steps by his chair. The slave wears a black negroid mask.

At the opening of the scene there is heard the steady tramp of departing troops, whose masks, helmets and armoured shoulders can be seen as they pass through the street before Lazarus to the gate beyond. Finally with a metallic clash the gate is shut behind them and there is a heavy and oppressive silence in which only the murmured prayers of Miriam are heard.

CHORUS OF THE SENATE (*intones wearily, as if under a boring compulsion*). The Roman Senate.

Is the Roman Senate
The Mighty Voice
Of the Roman People,
As long as Rome is Rome.

CALIGULA (*as if he hadn't heard—sings hoarsely an old camp song of the Punic Wars, pounding with his goblet*). A bold legionary am I!
March, oh march on!
A Roman eagle was my daddy,
My mother was a drunken drabby.
Oh, march on to the wars!

Since lived that lady Leda—
March, oh march on!
Women have loved high-fliers,
And we are eagles of Rome!
Oh march on to the wars!

Comrades, march to the wars!
There's pretty girls in Carthage,
And wine to swill in Carthage,
So we must capture Carthage
And fight for Mother Rome!

(*Holds out his goblet to be refilled. There is silence again. He stares at Lazarus with a sombre intentness. He says thickly.*)

The legions have gone, Lazarus.

(*Lazarus gives no evidence of having heard him. Caligula gulps at his wine. The Senators begin to talk to each other in low voices.*)

FIRST SENATOR. How does that Jew make that light come from him, I wonder? It is a well-contrived bit of magic.

SECOND SENATOR. What are we waiting for? A messenger came to me with Cæsar's command that the Senate meet here at midnight.

THIRD SENATOR (*bored*). Some new whim of Tiberius, naturally—(*with a meaning titter*)—of rather I should say, unnaturally!

FOURTH SENATOR. Perhaps Cæsar has decided to abolish our august body by a massacre in mass!

THIRD SENATOR (*yawning*). There was a feast at Cinna's last night that lasted until this evening. I could welcome my own murder as an excuse for sleeping!

FIFTH SENATOR (*pompously*). Tiberius would not dare harm the Senate. He may mistreat individual Senators, but the Roman Senate is the Roman Senate!

CHORUS OF THE SENATE (*as before—wearily as if under a boring compulsion—intones*). While Rome is Rome
The Senate is the Senate—
The Mighty Voice of the Roman People.

FIRST SENATOR (*with the ghost of a laugh—wearily*). The Senate is an empty name—a pack of degenerate cowards with no trace of their ancient nobility or courage remaining—that and no more!

THIRD SENATOR (*flippantly*). You are too severe with yourself, Lucius!

(*A titter of laughter.*)

FIRST SENATOR (*wearily*). A degenerate coward. I am, I confess it. So are you too, Sulpicius—a hundred fold!—whether you admit it or not.

(*Sulpicius laughs weakly, without taking offence.*)

SIXTH SENATOR (*after a pause—sighing*). In truth, the Senate is not what it used to be. I can remember——

FIRST SENATOR. Let us forget, if we can! (*Then impatiently.*) What are we doing here?

SECOND SENATOR. I imagine it has something to do with the followers of this Lazarus encamped outside the wall. Probably the legions are to butcher them in their sleep.

SEVENTH SENATOR. And what part do we play—official witnesses? But how can we witness at night and through a wall? (*With bored resignation.*) Ah well, the moods of Tiberius are strange, to say the least. But Cæsar is Cæsar.

CHORUS (*again with bored weariness as before*). Hail!
Cæsar is Cæsar—
The August One,
Prince of the Senate,
Tribune over Tribunes,
Consul of Consuls,
Supreme Pontiff,
Emperor of Rome,
God among gods.
Hail!

FIRST SENATOR (*after a pause of silence—dryly*). Cæsar is a beast—and a madman!

FIFTH SENATOR (*pompously*). Respect, sir! More respect for Cæsar!

THIRD SENATOR (*mockingly*). Or caution, Lucius. One of us might repeat your opinion to him.

FIRST SENATOR. You would if it would pay you. But all my money is squandered. My death is worthless to Tiberius. He would not reward you. Moreover, you would not be revenged on me, for I long for death.

THIRD SENATOR (*dryly*). Your stomach must be out of order.

FIRST SENATOR. The times are out of order. But let us change the subject. Is it true Tiberius has fled to Capri?

FOURTH SENATOR. Yes. He was terrified by the multitude of laughing idiots who appeared to-day with that charlatan. (*He points to Lazarus.*)

SECOND SENATOR. There are thousands of them outside the wall. Cæsar refused to let them enter the city. The story is, this Lazarus was dead four days and then restored himself to life by magic.

FIRST SENATOR. I have a mind to question him. (*Calls as to a slave.*) You, there! Jew, turn round! In the name of the Senate!

(*Lazarus seems not to hear him. Lucius remarks with a weary smile.*)

So much for our authority!

SIXTH SENATOR (*with injured dignity*). What insolence! (*In a rage.*) Ho, barbarian cur, turn round! The Senate commands you!

(*Lazarus does not seem to hear, but Caligula turns on them fiercely.*)

CALIGULA. Silence! Leave him alone! (*With insulting scorn.*) I, Caligula, command *you*!

(*The Senators seem to shrink back from him in fear, all but Lucius, who answers with a mocking servility.*)

FIRST SENATOR. At least, grant us the boon to see this corpse's face, O gracious Gaius!

CALIGULA (*fixing his cruel, burning eyes on him—softly*). I heard you wish for death, Lucius. When I am Cæsar you shall scream and pray for it!

FIRST SENATOR (*dryly and haughtily*). You were bred in camp, Gaius. You should have learned more courage there along with your coarseness. But accept my gratitude for your warning. I shall take care to die before you become Cæsar—and life becomes too idiotic!

CALIGULA (*his grin becoming ferocious with cruelty*). No. You are too weak to kill yourself. Look at me, Lucius! I am imagining what I shall have done to you!

(*The Senators are now trembling. Even Lucius cannot repress a shudder of horror at the face glaring at him. Suddenly Caligula throws the cup from him and springs to his feet.*)

What good is wine if it cannot kill thought? Lazarus! It is time. I must give the signal! The legions are waiting. It is Cæsar's command that they spare none of your followers. (*He has walked toward Lazarus.*)

MIRIAM (*stretches out her hands to Caligula imploringly*). Mercy! Spare them who are so full of life and joy!

CALIGULA (*harshly*). For their joy I will revenge myself upon them! Mercy? If there is no death, then death is a mercy! Ask that man! (*He points accusingly to Lazarus.*) And why should you plead for them, Jewess? There are few Jews among them. They are mostly those whom your people call idolators and would gladly see murdered.

MIRIAM (*with deep grief*). I am a mother of dead children. I plead for the mothers of those about to die.

CALIGULA (*contemptuously*). Pah! (*He turns from her and puts his hand on Lazarus' shoulder.*) Lazarus! Do you hear? I must signal to the legions!

LAZARUS (*turns. He has grown more youthful. He seems no more than thirty. His face is exalted and calm and beautiful. His eyes shine with an unearthly glory. The Senators lean forward in their seats, fascinated by his face. A low murmur of admiration comes from them. Lazarus speaks commandingly*). Wait! I will awaken my beloved ones that their passing may be a symbol to the world that there is no death!

(*He turns, throwing back his head and stretching up his arms, and begins to laugh low and tenderly, like caressing music at first, but gradually gaining in volume, becoming more and more intense and insistent, finally ending up on a triumphant, blood-stirring call to that ultimate attainment in which all prepossession with self is lost in an ecstatic affirmation of Life. The voices of his

Followers from beyond the wall, at first one by one, then several at a time, then multitudes, join in his laughter. Even the Senators are drawn into it. Now every one of these is standing up, stretching out his arms toward Lazarus, laughing harshly and discordantly and awkwardly in his attempt to laugh. Terrific flashes of lightning and crashes of thunder seem a responsive accompaniment from the heavens to this laughter of thousands which throbs in beating waves of sound in the air. Mingled with the laughing from beyond the wall comes the sound of singing and the music of flutes and cymbals. Miriam has crawled on her knees to the edge of the portico where her black figure of grief is outlined below and to the left of Lazarus, her arms raised outward like the arms of a cross.)

FOLLOWERS OF LAZARUS (*in a great chanting singing chorus*). Laugh! Laugh!

There is only God!
Life is His Laughter!
We are His Laughter!
Fear is no more!
Death is dead!

CHORUS OF SENATORS (*taking it up in a tone between chanting and their old solemn intoning*). Laugh! Laugh!

Fear is no more!
Death is dead!

ALL (*the multitude beyond the wall, all the Senators, every one except the never-laughing Miriam and Caligula and the Men of the Legions*). Laugh! Laugh!

Death is dead!

CALIGULA (*in a queer state of mingled exaltation and fear—hopping restlessly about from foot to foot—shouting*). The signal! Shall I give the signal to kill, Lazarus?

MEN OF THE LEGIONS (*following a brazen trumpet call, are suddenly heard from beyond the wall beginning to laugh their hoarse, bass laughter, a deeper note than all the others*). Laugh! Laugh!

CALIGULA (*listening—with dismay*). I hear the legions, Lazarus! They are laughing with them! (*He cries with a strange pitifulness and beseeching.*) You are playing me false, Lazarus! You are trying to evade death! You are trying to spare your people! You are small and weak like other men when the test comes! You give way to pity! Your great laughter becomes pitiful! (*Working himself into a rage.*) You are a traitor, Lazarus! You betray Cæsar! Have you forgotten I will be Cæsar? You betray me, Lazarus! (*He rushes to the edge and, making a megaphone of his hands, bellows.*) You on the wall! Sentry! It is I, Caligula! Kill!

(*The brazen trumpets of the Legions sound from beyond the wall. He springs near Lazarus again, in a fiendish ecstasy, dancing a hopping grotesque sword dance behind him, chanting as he does so.*)

Kill! Kill laughter! Kill those who deny Cæsar! I will be Cæsar! Kill those who deny Death! I will be Death! My face will be bright with blood! My laughing face, Lazarus! Laughing because men fear me! My face of victorious Fear! Look at me! I am laughing, Lazarus! *My* laughter! Laughter of gods and Cæsars! Ha-ha-ha-ha!

(*He laughs, his laughter fanatically cruel and savage, forced from his lips with a desperate, destroying abandon. For a moment, above all the chorus of other sounds, his voice fights to overcome that of Lazarus, whose laughter seems now to have attained the most exultant heights of spiritual affirmation. Then Caligula's breaks into a cry of fear and a sob, and, casting his sword aside, he hides his face in his hands and cries beseechingly.*)

Forgive me! I love you, Lazarus! Forgive me!

(*At this second the blaring trumpets of the Legions are heard approaching and their great bass chorus of marching tramping laughter.*)

MEN OF THE LEGIONS (*chanting*). Laugh! Laugh! Laugh!

Fear, no more!
Death, no more!
Death is dead!

(*There is now no sound of the singing or the laughter or music of Lazarus' Followers. Miriam rocks to and fro and raises a low wail of lamentation. The Senators cheer and shout as at a triumph.*)

CHORUS OF SENATORS (*saluting Lazarus*). Hail, Victor!
Hail, Divine One!
Thou hast slain fear!
Thou hast slain death!
Hail! Triumph!

SENATORS. Hail! Hail!
Slayer of Fear!
Slayer of Death!

(*The gate in the wall is clanged open. The returning Legions burst through and gather in a dense mob in the street below Lazarus, who looks down upon them, silent but smiling gently now. They stare at him with admiration. Only a sea of their masks can be seen, their eyes shining exultantly. Crassus, their general, ascends the steps until he stands a little below Lazarus. Their Chorus of Legionaries in double-sized masks climb to the step below Crassus, forming behind him. They are in the Period of Manhood, of the Simple, Ignorant Type. No weapons can be seen—only their masks and helmets and armour gleaming in the lightning flashes and in the flickering light of torches. Their laughter seems to shake the walls and make the pillars of the temple dance.*)

CHORUS OF THE LEGIONS. Fear, no more!
Death, no more!
Death is dead!

LEGIONARIES (*echoing*). Laugh! Laugh! Laugh!
Death is dead!

CRASSUS (*raising his hand*). Silence! (*They obey. He turns to Lazarus and bows his head, falling on one knee, raising his right arm.*) Hail!

LEGIONARIES (*as one man—raising their arms*). Hail!

CALIGULA (*suddenly pushes forward impudently and strikes a grandiose attitude*). I am here, my brave ones!

(*There is a roar of mocking laughter from the Legionaries.*)

CRASSUS (*not unkindly*). Not you, Little Killer! We hail the Great Laugher!

CALIGULA (*harshly*). Have you killed all his followers?

CRASSUS. No. They died. They did not wait for our attack. They charged upon us, laughing! They tore our swords away from us, laughing, and we laughed with them! They stabbed themselves, dancing as though it were a festival! They died, laughing, in one another's arms! We laughed, too, with joy because it seemed it was not they who died but death itself they killed! (*He stops uncertainly, bowing to Lazarus, awkwardly.*) I do not understand this. I am a soldier. But there is a god in it somewhere! For I know they were drunk, and so were we, with a happiness no mortal ever felt on earth before! And death was dead! (*In a sudden outburst as if he were drunk with excitement, he takes off his helmet and waves it.*) Hail, Deliverer! Death is dead! We left our swords with them! What virtue in killing when there is no death? Your foe laughs. The joke is on you. What a fool's game, eh? One can only laugh! Now we want peace to laugh in—to laugh at war! Let Cæsars fight—that is all they are good for—and not much good for that!

CALIGULA (*frenziedly*). Silence, impious traitor!

CRASSUS (*smiling drunkenly*). Shut up, yourself, camp-brat! Though you were Cæsar this minute I would laugh at you! Your death is dead! We will make Lazarus Cæsar! What say you? (*He appeals to the Soldiers.*)

CALIGULA. No!

CHORUS OF THE LEGIONS (*with laughing intoxication*). Hail, Lazarus Cæsar! Hail!

LEGIONARIES. Lazarus Cæsar, hail!

CRASSUS (*appealing to Senate*). And you, Senators!

CHORUS OF SENATORS (*with the same joyous intoxication as the Soldiers*). Hail, Lazarus Cæsar! Hail!

SENATORS. Lazarus Cæsar, hail!

CALIGULA (*piteously*). No, Lazarus! Say no for my sake!

LAZARUS (*with gay mockery*). What is—Cæsar?

(*He begins to laugh with mockery. All except Caligula and Miriam join in this laughter.*)

CRASSUS. Ha-ha! What is Cæsar? You

are right! You deserve better from us. A god? How is that? We will build you a temple, Lazarus, and make you a god!

LAZARUS (*laughingly*). When men make gods, there is no God! (*He laughs. They all laugh.*)

CRASSUS (*with puzzled good-nature*). I do not understand. But there is a god in it somewhere—a god of peace—a god of happiness! Perhaps you are already he, eh? Are you? Well, never mind now, remember our offer. Give us your answer to-morrow. Good night to you!

LAZARUS (*as the Soldiers start to march away behind Crassus, and the Senators turn to retire, he stops them all for a moment with a gesture—with a deep earnestness*). Wait! When you awake to-morrow, try to remember! Remember that death is dead! Remember to laugh!

ALL (*as if taking an oath with one voice*). We will remember, Lazarus!

CRASSUS (*making a sign to the regimental musicians jovially*). And we will laugh! Play there!

(*The bands crash out. The Legions tramp away.*)

CHORUS OF THE LEGIONS (*chanting to the music*).
Laugh! Laugh! Laugh!
Cæsar, no more!
War, no more!
Wounds, no more!
Death is dead!
Dead! Dead! Dead!

LEGIONARIES. Laugh! Laugh! Laugh!
Death is dead!
Dead! Dead! Dead!

CHORUS OF SENATORS (*following them*). Cæsar, no more!
Fear, no more!
Death, no more!
Laugh! Laugh! Laugh!

SENATE (*elated, excited as a crowd of schoolboys going on a vacation. Marching after them*).
Laugh! Laugh! Laugh!
Death is dead!

(*Lazarus, Miriam and Caligula remain.*)

LAZARUS (*with a great yearning*). If men would remember! If they could! (*He stares after them compassionately.*)

CALIGULA (*crouching beside Lazarus. Plucks at his robe humbly*). You will not laugh at Cæsar, Lazarus, will you—when I am Cæsar? You will not laugh at gods when they make me a god?

(*Lazarus does not answer. Caligula forces a cruel vindictive smile.*)

I swear you shall not laugh at death when I am Death! Ha-ha—— (*He starts to laugh harshly—then suddenly, terrified, slinks away and sidles off at right.*)

MIRIAM (*from where she kneels bowed with grief—brokenly*). Those who have just died were like your children, Lazarus. They believed in you and loved you.

LAZARUS. And I loved them!

MIRIAM. Then how could you laugh when they were dying?

LAZARUS (*exultingly*). Did they not laugh? That was their victory and glory! (*With more and more of a passionate, proud exultation.*) Eye to eye with the Fear of Death, did they not laugh with scorn? "Death to old Death," they laughed! "Once as squirming specks we crept from the tides of the sea. Now we return to the sea! Once as quivering flecks of rhythm we beat down from the sun. Now we re-enter the sun! Cast aside is our pitiable pretence, our immortal ego-hood, the holy lantern behind which cringed our Fear of the Dark! Flung off is that impudent insult to life's nobility which gibbers: 'I, this Jew, this Roman, this noble or this slave, must survive in my pettiness for ever!' Away with such cowardice of spirit! We will to die! We will to change! Laughing we lived with our gift, now with laughter give we back that gift to become again the Essence of the Giver! Dying we laugh with the Infinite! We are the Giver and the Gift! Laughing, we will our own annihilation! Laughing, we give our lives for Life's sake—! (*He laughs up to heaven ecstatically.*) This must Man will as his end and his new beginning! He must conceive and desire his own passing as a mood of eternal laughter and cry with pride, "Take back, O God, and accept in turn a gift from me, my grateful blessing for Your gift—and see, O God, now I am laughing with You! I am Your laughter—and You are mine!" (*He laughs again, his laughter dying lingeringly and tenderly on his lips like a strain of music receding into the silence over still waters.*)

MIRIAM (*with a sigh—meekly*). I cannot understand, Lazarus. (*Sadly.*) They were like your children—and they have died. Must you not mourn for them?

LAZARUS (*gently*). Mourn? When they laughed?

MIRIAM (*sadly*). They are gone from us. And their mothers weep.

LAZARUS (*puts his arm around her and raises her to her feet—tenderly*). But God, their Father, laughs! (*He kisses her on the forehead.*)

CURTAIN

ACT THREE SCENE ONE

SCENE. *Some days later—exterior of Tiberius' villa-palace at Capri. It is about two in the morning of a clear, black night. In the rear, the walls of the villa, which is built entirely of marble on the brow of a cliff, loom up with a startling clarity against the sky. The rear foreground is a marble terrace at the middle of which is a triumphal arch. On each side, leading up to it, are massive marble columns standing like the mummies of legionaries at attention. In the exact centre of the arch itself a cross is set up on which a full-grown male lion has been crucified. A lamp reflecting downward has been fixed at the top of the cross to light up an inscription placed over the lion's head. Below the steps to the terrace, in a line facing front, on each side of the cross, is the Chorus of the Guard in their double masks and gorgeous uniforms and armour. Their masks are the same as the Legionary Chorus of the previous scene.*

The windows of the palace glow crimson-purple with the reflection of many shaded lamps. The sound of music in a strained theme of that joyless abandon which is vice is heard above a confused drunken clamour of voices, punctuated by the high, staccato laughter of women and youths. A squad of the Guard in the same uniforms as the Chorus, masked as all the Roman Soldiers previously, enter from the left, front, climbing up from the beach below. They are commanded by a Centurion, Flavius. His mask is that of a typical young patrician officer. They are followed by Lazarus and Miriam. Caligula walks behind, his drawn sword in his hand. He is in a state of queer conflicting emotion, seeming to be filled with a nervous dread and terror of everything about him, while at the same time perversely excited and elated by his own morbid tension. Lazarus, looking no more than twenty-five, haloed in his own mystic light, walks in a deep, detached serenity.

Miriam, in black, her hair almost white now, her figure bowed and feeble, seems more than ever a figure of a sad, resigned mother of the dead. The soldiers form in line with the columns.

FLAVIUS (*saluting Caligula—with an awed glance at Lazarus*). I will announce your coming—(*as if in spite of himself he bows awkwardly to Lazarus*)—and that of this man. Cæsar was not expecting you so soon, I think.

CALIGULA (*forcing a light tone*). Lazarus laughed and the galley slaves forgot their fetters and made their oars fly as if they were bound for the Blessed Isles of Liberty! (*Then with an ironic smile.*) But you need not tell Tiberius that, good Flavius. Say it was due to my extreme zeal.

FLAVIUS (*smiles with respectful understanding. Caligula nods in dismissal. Flavius turns to go—apologetically*). You may have to wait. I dare not speak before he questions me.

(*Flavius salutes and hastens to the villa, walking under an arm of the cross unconcernedly without an upward glance. As they follow him with their eyes Caligula and Miriam see the lion for the first time. He steps back with a startled exclamation. She gives a cry of horror and covers her eyes with her hands to shut out the sight.*)

LAZARUS (*immediately puts his arms around her protectingly*). What is it, Beloved?

(*She hides her face on his breast, pointing toward the lion with a trembling hand.*)

CALIGULA (*pointing—curiously now, but with entire callousness*). This lion they have crucified.

Are you frightened, Jewess? (*With a cruel laugh.*) My grandfather frequently plants whole orchards of such trees, but usually they bear human fruit!

MIRIAM (*with a shudder*). Monster!

CALIGULA (*with genuine surprise—turning to her*). Who? Why? (*He approaches the cross and stares at it moodily.*) But why did he have it placed here where he knew you must pass? Tiberius does not go to such pains to frighten women. (*His eyes fasten on the inscription above the lion's head.*) Aha! I see! (*He reads.*) "From the East, land of false gods and superstition, this lion was brought to Rome to amuse Cæsar." (*A silence. Caligula shrugs his shoulders, turning away—lightly.*) A lesson for you, Lazarus. An example for other lions—not to roar—or laugh—at Cæsar! (*He gives a harsh laugh.*) Tiberius must be terribly afraid of you. (*Then sombrely.*) You should never have come here. I would have advised you not to—but what are you to me? My duty, if I wish to become Cæsar, is to Cæsar. Besides, you are no fool. Evidently you must desire your own death. Last night *you* might have been Cæsar. The legions were yours.

LAZARUS (*smiling without bitterness—with a sad comprehension*). But this morning the legions had forgotten. They only remembered—to go out and pick up their swords! They also pillaged the bodies a little, as their right, believing now that they had slain them! (*This last a bit bitterly.*)

CALIGULA (*tauntingly*). The legions did slay them! It was only by some magician's trick you made them think your followers killed themselves.

LAZARUS (*not answering him—ironically to himself*). It is too soon. Men still need their swords to slash at ghosts in the dark. Men, those haunted heroes! (*He laughs softly.*)

CALIGULA (*irritably*). What are you laughing at?

LAZARUS. At Lazarus when I find him feeling wronged because men are men! (*He laughs again, softly and musically.*)

CALIGULA (*again taunting brutally*). You may be in his place soon! (*He points to the lion.*) Will you laugh then?

(*Miriam gives a cry of terror.*)

LAZARUS (*calmly*). Yes. (*Then humbly, bowing his head.*) I will laugh with the pride of a beggar set upon the throne of Man!

CALIGULA (*sneeringly*). You boast. (*Then as Lazarus does not answer, touching the lion with intentional provoking brutality.*) This one from Africa seems almost gone. They do not last as long as men.

LAZARUS (*walks up the steps to the cross and, stretching to his full height, gently pushes the lion's hair out of its eyes—tenderly*). Poor brother! Cæsar avenges himself on you because of me. Forgive me your suffering!

CALIGULA (*with a start backward—with frightened awe*). Gods! He licks your hand! I could swear he smiles—with his last breath! (*Then with relief.*) Now he is dead!

LAZARUS (*gently*). There is no death.

CALIGULA (*pointing to the lion*). What is that then?

LAZARUS. Your fear of life.

CALIGULA (*impatiently*). Bah! (*Then sombrely.*) A little fear is useful even for lions—or teachers of laughter if they wish to laugh long! (*Then with a sudden exasperation.*) Escape now, you fool, while there is still time!

LAZARUS (*laughing softly*). Escape—what?

CALIGULA (*in a frenzy*). You know, you ass, you lunatic! Escape death! Death! Death! (*To Miriam.*) You, woman! Talk to him! Do you want him nailed up like that?

MIRIAM (*with a pitiful cry*). Lazarus! Come! Caligula will help us!

CALIGULA (*harshly*). You presume, Jewess! I have no wish to die! (*Then with his wry smile.*) But I will turn my back—and shut my eyes—— (*He walks away to left.*)

MIRIAM (*beseechingly*). Lazarus! I could no bear that aching hunger of my empty heart if you should die again!

LAZARUS (*coming to her—tenderly*). I will not leave you! Believe in me! (*He kisses her forehead tenderly.*)

MIRIAM (*after a pause—slowly and lamentingly*). I wish we were home, Lazarus. This Roman world is full of evil. These skies threaten.

These hearts are heavy with hatred. There is a taint of blood in the air that poisons the breath of the sea. These columns and arches and thick walls seem waiting to fall, to crush these rotten men and then to crumble over the bones that raised them until both are dust. It is a world deadly to your joy, Lazarus. Its pleasure is a gorging of dirt, its fulfilled desire a snoring in a sty in the mud among swine. Its will is so sick that it must kill in order to be aware of life at all. I wish we were home, Lazarus. I begin to feel horror gnawing at my breast. I begin to know the torture of the fear of death, Lazarus—not of my death but of yours—not of the passing of your man's body but of the going away from me of your laughter which is to me as my son, my little boy!

LAZARUS (*soothing her*). Be comforted, Beloved. Your fear shall never be!

MIRIAM. On the hills near Bethany you might pray at noon and laugh your boy's laughter in the sun and there would be echoing laughter from the sky and up from the grass and distantly from the shining sea. We would adopt children whose parents the Romans had butchered, and their laughter would be around me in my home where I cooked and weaved and sang. And in the dawn at your going out, and in the evening on your return, I would hear in the hushed air the bleating of sheep and the tinkling of many little bells and your voice. And my heart would know peace.

LAZARUS (*tenderly*). Only a little longer! There is God's laughter on the hills of space, and the happiness of children, and the soft healing of innumerable dawns and evenings, and the blessing of peace!

CALIGULA (*looks around at Lazarus impatiently. Then he makes a beckoning gesture to Miriam*). Ssstt!

(*Wonderingly she leaves Lazarus' side and follows him. Lazarus remains, his eyes fixed on the cross, directly in front of it. Caligula speaks gruffly to Miriam with a sneer.*)

Jewess, your Lazarus is mad, I begin to think. (*Then confusedly but helplessly inquisitive and confiding—bursting out.*) What is it troubles me about him? What makes me dream of him? Why should I—love him, Jewess? Tell me! You love him, too. I do not understand this. Why, wherever he goes, is there joy? You heard even the galley slaves laugh and clank time with their chains! (*Then with exasperation.*) And yet why can I not laugh, Jewess?

MIRIAM (*in a tone of hushed grief*). I may not laugh either. My heart remains a little dead with Lazarus in Bethany. The miracle could not revive all his old husband's life in my wife's heart.

CALIGULA (*disgustedly*). What answer is that to me? (*Then brusquely.*) But I called you to put you on your guard. (*He points.*) There is death in there—Tiberius' death, a kind from which no miracles can recall one! (*He smiles his twisted smile.*) Since Lazarus will not help himself, you must protect him. I will not, for once in there I am (*mockingly*) the heir of Cæsar, and you are scum whom I will kill at his order as I would two beetles! So keep watch! Taste first of what he eats—even were I the one to give it to him!

LAZARUS (*suddenly laughs softly*). Why do you delight in believing evil of yourself, Caligula?

CALIGULA (*flying into a queer rage*). You lie! I am what I am! (*With grandiose pride.*) What could you know of a Cæsar?

LAZARUS (*still laughing with an affectionate understanding.*) What—I know!

(*As he finishes speaking all the sound of music and voices from the house ceases abruptly and there is a heavy silence.*)

MIRIAM (*shaking her head and turning away sadly*). This is too far, Lazarus. Let us go home.

CALIGULA (*harshly*). Sst! Do you hear? Flavius has told Cæsar. (*Grimly forcing a harsh snicker.*) Now we will soon know——

(*There is the sudden blaring of a trumpet from within the palace. A wide door is flung open and a stream of reddish light comes out against which the black figures of several men are outlined. The door is shut again quickly. Several Slaves bearing lamps on poles escort the patrician, Marcellus, forward to the arch. He passes under the crucified lion without a glance—then stands, cool and disdainful, to look about him. He is a man of about thirty-five, wearing the type mask of a Roman patrician to which are added the dissipated courtier's characteristics of one who leans to evil more through weakness than any instinctive urge. He is dressed richly. His smile is hypocritical and his eyes are hard and cold, but when they come to rest on Lazarus he gives a start of genuine astonishment.)*

CALIGULA *(who has moved to Lazarus' side defensively—in a quick whisper)*. Beware of this man, Lazarus! *(Then advancing—with a condescending hauteur.)* Greeting, Marcellus!

MARCELLUS *(in an ingratiating tone)*. Greeting, Gaius. I have a message from Cæsar for the man called Lazarus.

LAZARUS *(calmly)*. I am Lazarus.

MARCELLUS *(makes a deep bow—flatteringly)*. I had surmised it, sir. Although I cannot pretend to virtue in myself at least I may claim the merit of recognizing it in others. *(He advances toward Lazarus, smiling, with one hand kept hidden beneath his cloak.)*

CALIGULA *(stepping between them—sharply)*. What is your message?

MARCELLUS *(surprised—placatingly)*. I am sorry, Gaius, but it was Cæsar's command I speak to Lazarus alone.

CALIGULA *(fiercely)*. And then, Marcellus?

(Marcellus shrugs his shoulders and smiles deprecatingly.)

LAZARUS *(with a compelling dignity)*. Let him speak. *(Inclining his head to Marcellus—strangely.)* Over here where it is dark you will not be seen—nor see yourself. *(He walks to the darkness at right.)*

CALIGULA *(turning his back on them, with angry boyish resentfulness that is close to tears)*. Idiot! Go and die, then!

MIRIAM *(with a terrified cry)*. Lazarus! *(She starts to go to him.)*

LAZARUS *(motioning her to remain where she is—gently)*. Believe, Beloved! *(He turns his back on them all and stands waiting.)*

MARCELLUS *(stares at Lazarus—then over his shoulder at Caligula—uncertainly)*. What does he mean, Gaius? *(Then suddenly putting on a brave front, he strides up behind Lazarus.)* Cæsar wished me to bid you welcome, to tell you how much regard he has for you, but he desired me to ask whether you propose to laugh here—in Cæsar's palace? He has heard that you laugh at death—that you have caused others to laugh—even his legionaries. *(A pause, Marcellus remains behind Lazarus' back, the latter standing like a victim.)* Briefly, Cæsar requires your pledge that you will not laugh. Will you give it? *(He frees his dagger from under his robe. A pause. Arrogantly.)* I am waiting! Answer when Cæsar commands! *(Then angrily, baffled.)* I will give you while I count three—or take your silence as a refusal! One! Two! Three!

(He raises his hand to stab Lazarus in the back. Miriam stifles a scream. At the same instant, Lazarus begins to laugh, softly and affectionately. Marcellus stops, frozen in mid-action, the dagger upraised. Caligula has whirled around and stands staring, a smile gradually coming to his face. Lazarus turns, his laughter grown a trifle louder, and faces Marcellus. The latter steps back from him, staring open-mouthed, fascinated. His arm sinks to his side. The dagger falls from his fingers. He smiles back at Lazarus—the curious, sheepish, bashful smile of one who has fallen in love and been discovered.)

LAZARUS *(going to him, puts both hands on his shoulders and looks in his eyes, laughing affectionately—then quizzically.)* Here is another one who believes in death! But soon you will laugh with life! I see it in your eyes. Farewell, Marcellus!

(He turns away from him and walks, laughing, toward the arch in rear. With bowed head the black-robed figure of Miriam follows him. Marcellus hides his face in his hands, half-sobbing, and half-laughing hysterically. Lazarus pauses before the cross for a moment—raises his hand as if blessing the dead lion, then passes below it, moving slowly on toward the palace in the rear. His laughter rises with more and more summoning power. The files of the Guard, as he passes them, two by two join in his laughter, saluting him as if in spite of themselves.)

CALIGULA (*sidling up to Marcellus, cruel and mocking*). Are you weeping, Marcellus? Laugh at that blundering fool, yourself! What will Cæsar say? Will he laugh when he has your body broken one bone at a time with hammers? Why did you not kill? For shame! A patrician exposed to laughter by a Jew! Poor craven! Why could you not strike? There *must* be death! Coward! Why did you not stab? (*Then in a queer awed whisper.*) I know! Was it not because of a sudden you loved him and could not?

MARCELLUS (*suddenly—eagerly*). Yes! That was it! I loved him!

CALIGULA (*craftily and cruelly*). You were about to murder him!

MARCELLUS (*tortured with remorse*). No! No! How could I? What infamy! (*Cries tearfully.*) Forgive me, Lazarus!

CALIGULA (*with vindictive insistence*). Judge yourself! (*He takes up the dagger.*) Here is your dagger! Avenge him on yourself!

MARCELLUS (*trying to laugh*). Ha-ha— Yes! (*He stabs himself and falls. Suddenly his laughter is released.*) I laugh! You are a fool, Caligula! There is no death! (*He dies, laughing up at the sky.*)

CALIGULA (*kicks his body with savage cruelty*). You lie! (*Then suddenly kneels and bends over it imploringly.*) Tell me you lie, Marcellus! Do me that mercy!—and when I am Cæsar, I——

(*He begins to weep like a frightened boy, his head in his hands. Meanwhile Lazarus has arrived with Miriam at the steps before the door of the palace. As he starts to ascend these, the crimson-purple lights of the many windows of the palace go out one by one as if fleeing in terror from the laughter which now beats at the walls.*)

CHORUS OF THE GUARD. Fear, no more!
Death, no more!
Laugh! Laugh! Laugh!
Death is dead!

ALL THE GUARDS (*now all in a great chorus, raising their spears aloft and saluting Lazarus as if they were his own triumphal bodyguard*).
Laugh! Laugh! Laugh!
Death is dead!

(*Lazarus has ascended the steps. He walks into the black archway of the darkened palace, his figure radiant and unearthly in his own light. Miriam follows him. They disappear in the darkness. There is a pause of dead silence.*)

CALIGULA (*raises his head uneasily, looks back toward the palace, jumps to his feet in a panic of terror, and runs toward the palace door, calling*). Lazarus! Wait! I will defend you! There is death inside there—death! Beware, Lazarus!

CHORUS OF THE GUARD (*as the laughter of Lazarus is heard again from the dark palace*).
Laugh! Laugh! Laugh!
Death is dead!

ALL THE GUARDS. Dead! Dead! Dead!
Death is dead!

CURTAIN

SCENE TWO

SCENE. *The banquet hall in the palace of Tiberius—an immense high-ceilinged room. In the rear, centre, is a great arched doorway. Smaller arches in the middle of the side walls lead into other rooms. Long couches are placed along the walls at right and left, and along the rear wall on either side of the arch. Before these couches, a series of narrow tables is set. In the centre of the room on a high dais is the ivory and gold chair of Cæsar, a table in front of it, couches for him to recline on at either side. On this table, and on all the tables for his guests, gold lamps with shades of crimson-purple are placed.*

Reclining on the couches on the right are young women and girls, on the left, youths of an equal number.

The masks are based on the Roman masks of the periods of Boyhood (or Girlhood), Youth, and Young Manhood (or Womanhood), and there are seven individuals of each period and sex in each of the three types of the Introspective,

Self-Tortured; the Servile, Hypocritical; and the Cruel, Revengeful—a crowd of forty-two in all. There is a distinctive character to the masks of each sex, the stamp of an effeminate corruption on all the male, while the female have a bold, masculine expression. The male masks are a blotched heliotrope in shade. These youths wear female wigs of curled wire like frizzed hair of a yellow gold. They are dressed in women's robes of pale heliotrope, they wear anklets and bracelets and necklaces. The women are dressed as males in crimson or deep purple. They also wear wire wigs but of straight hair cut in short boyish mode, dyed either deep purple or crimson. Those with crimson hair are dressed in purple, and vice versa. The female voices are harsh, strident, mannish—those of the youths affected, lisping, effeminate. The whole effect of these two groups is of sex corrupted and warped, of invented lusts and artificial vices.

The Chorus in this scene and the next is composed of three males and four females—the males in the period of Youth, one in each of the types represented, and three of the females in similar type-period masks. The fourth female is masked in the period of Womanhood in the Proud, Self-Reliant type. They sit, facing front in their double-sized masks, on the side steps of the dais, four on right, three on left.

Pompeia, a Roman noblewoman, the favourite mistress of Cæsar, sits at front, right.

She wears a half-mask on the upper part of her face, olive-coloured with the red of blood smouldering through, with great, dark, cruel eyes—a dissipated mask of intense evil beauty, of lust and perverted passion. Beneath the mask, her own complexion is pale, her gentle, girlish mouth is set in an expression of agonized self-loathing and weariness of spirit. Her body is strong and beautiful. Her wig and dress are purple.

Tiberius Cæsar stands on the dais, dressed in deep purple, fringed and ornamented with crimson and gold. An old man of seventy-six, tall, broad and corpulent but of great muscular strength still despite his age, his shiny white cranium rises like a polished shell above his half-masked face. This mask is a pallid purple blotched with darker colour, as if the imperial blood in his veins had been sickened by age and debauchery. The eyes are protuberant, leering, cynical slits, the long nose, once finely modelled, now gross and thickened, the forehead lowering and grim. Beneath the mask, his own mouth looks as incongruous as Caligula's. The lips are thin and stern and self-contained—the lips of an able soldier-statesman of rigid probity. His chin is forceful and severe. The complexion of his own skin is that of a healthy old campaigner.

As the curtain rises, slaves are hurriedly putting out the many lamps. From outside, the laughter of Lazarus rises on the deep ground swell of the Guard's laughter. The walls and massive columns seem to reverberate with the sound. In the banquet-room all are listening fascinatedly. Every reaction, from the extreme of panic fear or hypnotized ecstasy to a feigned cynical amusement or a pretended supercilious indifference, is represented in their frozen attitudes. Tiberius stands, shrinking back, staring at the doorway in the rear with superstitious dread. A squad of the Guard surround the dais, commanded by Flavius.

TIBERIUS (*in a strained voice shaken by apprehension and awe*). Marcellus! Strike him down! Stab him!

SOLDIERS OF THE GUARD (*from without*). Laugh! Laugh! Laugh!
Death is dead!

TIBERIUS (*as he suddenly sees the shining figure of Lazarus appear at the end of the dark hall beyond the archway*). Gods! Flavius, look! (*He points with a shaking finger. Flavius has leaped up to his side.*)

FLAVIUS (*not without dread himself*). That is the man, Cæsar.

TIBERIUS. Man? Say a dæmon! (*To the slaves who are turning out the few remaining lamps.*) Quick! Darkness! (*He puts out the lamp on his table himself. Then as nothing is seen but the light from the approaching Lazarus.*) Flavius! Stand here in my place! It will think you are Cæsar! (*He clumps heavily down the steps of the dais.*) Guards! Here! Cover me with your shields!

(*He goes to the extreme right corner, front, and crouches there. His Guards follow him. They hold their shields so that they form a wall around him and half over him. Then Caligula's voice is heard screaming above the chorus of laughter as he enters the hall behind Lazarus.)*

CALIGULA. Beware of death! I will defend you, Lazarus! (*He is seen to rush past Lazarus, flourishing his sword and comes running into the room, shouting.*) Cæsar! Dare not to murder Lazarus! (*He leaps to the dais and up its steps in a frenzy.*) Dare not, I say! (*He stabs Flavius with a savage cry.*) Ah! (*Then as the body of Flavius falls heavily and rolls down the steps at right, he begins to laugh, at first a clear laughter of selfless joy, sounding startlingly incongruous from him.*) I have saved you, Lazarus—at the risk of my own life—and now, hear me, I can laugh!

(*Lazarus appears in the archway, Miriam behind him. He stops laughing and immediately there is silence, except for Caligula. Lazarus casts a luminous glow over the whole room in which the masked faces appear distorted and livid. Caligula stands with upraised sword by the chair of Cæsar. Suddenly his laughter cracks, changes, becomes full of his old fear and blood-lust.*)

CALIGULA. Ha-ha-ha! See, Lazarus! (*He points to the body of Flavius with his sword.*) Welcome in the name of Cæsar, now Cæsar is slain and I am Cæsar!

(*He assumes the absurd grandiose posture of his imperial posing. No one looks at him or hears him. Their eyes are on Lazarus as he moves directly to where Tiberius crouches behind the shields of the Guards. Miriam follows him. Caligula turns and stares toward him, and then down at the body of Flavius and back, in a petrified, bewildered stupor. Lazarus steps up beside Tiberius. The Guards make way for him fearfully.*)

TIBERIUS (*feeling his nearness—straightening himself with a certain dignity*). Strike! I have been a soldier. Thou canst not make me fear death, Dæmon! (*He draws his toga over his face.*)

LAZARUS (*smiling gently*). Then fear not fear, Tiberius!

(*He reaches out and pulls back the toga from his face. Tiberius looks into his eyes, at first shrinkingly, then with growing reassurance, his own masked face clearly revealed now in the light from Lazarus.*)

TIBERIUS (*at first falteringly*). So—thou art not evil? Thou art not come to contrive my murder? (*As Lazarus smilingly shakes his head, Tiberius frowns.*) Then why dost thou laugh against Cæsar? (*Then bitterly—with a twisted attempt at a smile.*) Yet I like thy laughter. It is young. Once I laughed somewhat like that—so I pardon thee. I will even laugh at thee in return. Ha-ha! (*His laughter is cold, cruel and merciless as the grin of a skeleton.*)

CALIGULA (*who has been staring in a bewildered stupor from Tiberius, whom he thought he had killed, to the body of Flavius—quaking with terror now as if this laugh was meant for him, drops to his knees, his sword clattering down the steps to the floor*). Mercy, Tiberius! I implore you forgive your Caligula!

TIBERIUS (*not understanding. Fixing his eyes on Caligula with a malevolent irony*). Come down from my throne, Caligula. (*Caligula slinks down warily.*) You are too impatient. But I must pardon you, too—for where could I find another heir so perfect for serving my spite upon mankind? (*He has walked toward the throne while he is speaking, Caligula backing away from him. Lazarus remains where he is, Miriam beside and to the rear of him. Tiberius, his eyes fixed on Caligula, stumbles against the body of Flavius. He gives a startled gasp and shrinks back, calling.*) Lights! A light here! (*A crowd of masked slaves obey his orders. One runs to him with a lantern. He looks down at Flavius' corpse—half to himself.*) I did wisely to stand him in my place. (*To Caligula—with sinister emphasis.*) Too impatient, my loving grandchild! Take care lest I become impatient also—with your impatience!

(*Caligula shudders and backs away to the extreme left corner, front, where he crouches on his haunches as inconspicuously as possible. Tiberius suddenly whirls around as if he felt a dagger at his back.*)

TIBERIUS. Where—? (*Seeing Lazarus where*

he had been—with relief—staring at his face now that the room is flooded with the purplish-crimson glow from all the lamps.) Ah, you are there. More lights! Darkness leads men into error. My heir mistakes a man for Cæsar, and Cæsar, it appears, has mistaken a man for a dæmon! (*Scrutinizing him—with sinister finality.*) I can deal with men. I know them well. Too well! (*He laughs grimly.*) Therefore I hate them. (*He mounts the steps of the dais and sits on the couch at left of table—staring at Lazarus, wonderingly.*) But you seem—something other than man! That light! (*Then he forces a harsh laugh.*) A trick! I had forgotten you are a magician. (*Arrogantly.*) Stand there, Jew. I would question you about your magic. (*Smilingly Lazarus ascends to where Tiberius points at the top of the dais. Miriam remains standing at the foot. Tiberius stares for a while with sombre intensity at Lazarus.*) They say you died and have returned from death?

LAZARUS (*smiling—as if he were correcting a child*). There is no death, Cæsar.

TIBERIUS (*with a sneer of scepticism but with an underlying eagerness*). I have heard you teach that folly. (*Then threateningly.*) You shall be given full opportunity to prove it! (*A pause—then in a low voice, bending down toward Lazarus.*) Do you foretell the future? (*Trembling but with a pretence of carelessness.*) Must I die soon?

LAZARUS (*simply*). Yes, Cæsar.

TIBERIUS (*jumping up with a shuddering start*). Soon? Soon? (*Then his fear turning to rage.*) What do you say? Vile Jew, do you dare threaten me with death! (*Lazarus, looking into his eyes, begins to laugh softly. Tiberius sinks back on his couch, fighting to control himself—confusedly.*) Laugh not, I ask you. I am old. It is not seemly. (*Lazarus ceases his low laughter. A pause. Tiberius broods—then suddenly.*) And you were really dead? (*He shudders.*) Come nearer. I need to watch your face. I have learned to read the lies in faces. A Cæsar gets much practice—from childhood on—too much! (*With awe.*) Your eyes are dark with death. While I watch them, answer me, what cured thee of death?

LAZARUS (*gently*). There is only life, Cæsar. (*Then gaily mocking but compellingly.*) And laughter! Look! Look well into my eyes, old Reader of Lies, and see if you can find aught in them that is not life—and laughter!

(*He laughs softly. A ripple of soft laughter from the motionless figures about the room echoes his. Tiberius stares into his eyes. In the silence that ensues Pompeia gets up and walks over to the dais. She stops to stare for a moment with cruel contempt at Miriam, then stands and looks up at Lazarus, trying in vain to attract his or Cæsar's attention. Failing in this, she passes over and sits beside Caligula, whose attention is concentrated on Lazarus.*)

POMPEIA. I admire your strange magician, Caligula.

CALIGULA (*without looking at her*). He is no magician. He is something like a god.

POMPEIA (*longingly*). His laughter is like a god's. He is strong. I love him.

CALIGULA (*turning to her—coarsely*). Do not waste your lust. He is faithful to his wife, I warn you.

POMPEIA (*she points to Miriam*). Not that ugly slave?

CALIGULA. Yes. And yet, on our journey, whole herds of women—and many as beautiful as you, Pompeia—threw themselves on him and begged for his love.

POMPEIA (*her voice hardening*). And he?

CALIGULA. He laughed—and passed on. (*She starts. Caligula goes on wonderingly.*) But they seemed as happy as if his laughter had possessed them! You are a woman. Tell me, how could that be?

POMPEIA (*her voice cruel*). He shall not laugh at me!

CALIGULA (*tauntingly*). I will bet a string of pearls against your body for a night that he does.

POMPEIA (*defiantly*). Done! (*Then she laughs—a low, cruel laugh—staring at Miriam.*) So he loves that woman?

CALIGULA (*curiously*). What are you planning?

POMPEIA. I shall offer her the fruit Cæsar preserves for those he fears.

CALIGULA (*with a careless shrug*). You will not

win his love by killing her.

POMPEIA. I no longer want his love. I want to see him suffer, to hear his laughter choke in his throat with pain! (*She speaks with more and more voluptuous satisfaction.*) Then *I* shall laugh! (*She laughs softly and steps forward.*)

CALIGULA (*concernedly*). Stop. I am his protector. (*Then suddenly.*) But what is the Jewess to me? (*With more and more of a spirit of perverse cruelty.*) Do it, Pompeia! His laughter is too cruel to us! We must save death from him!

POMPEIA (*walks to the dais which she ascends slowly until she stands by Cæsar's couch behind him, confronting Lazarus. But the two men remain unmindful of her presence. Tiberius continues to stare into Lazarus' eyes. His whole body is now relaxed, at rest, a dreamy smile softens his thin, compressed mouth. Pompeia leans over and takes a peach from the bowl of fruit on Cæsar's table and, taking Tiberius' hand in her other, she kisses it and calls insistently*). Cæsar. It is I, Pompeia.

(*Lazarus does not look at her. She stares at him defiantly. Tiberius blinks his eyes in a daze.*)

TIBERIUS (*dreamily*). Yes! A cloud came from a depth of sky—around me, softly, warmly, and the cloud dissolved into the sky, and the sky into peace! (*Suddenly springing to his feet and staring about him in a confused rage—clutching Pompeia by the shoulder and forcing her to her knees.*) What are you doing here?

POMPEIA. Forgive your loving slave! I grew afraid this magician had put you under a spell. (*She stares at Lazarus, her words challenging him.*)

TIBERIUS (*confusedly, sinking back on his couch and releasing her*). A spell? Could it be he laid a dream of death upon me, leading me to death? (*He trembles timorously—appealing to Lazarus.*) Whatever magic thou didst to me, Dæmon, I beseech thee undo it!

LAZARUS (*smiling*). Do you fear peace?

POMPEIA (*harshly and insolently*). Mock not at Cæsar, dog! (*Lazarus continues to smile. His eyes remain on Cæsar. He seems absolutely unaware of Pompeia. This enrages her the more against him. She speaks tauntingly to Tiberius.*) Surely, Cæsar, this magician must have powerful charms, since he dares to mock Tiberius to his face!

TIBERIUS (*stung*). Be still! (*Then in a low tone to her.*) Do you not know this Lazarus died and then by his magic rose from his tomb.

POMPEIA (*scornfully*). To believe that, I must have seen it, Cæsar!

TIBERIUS (*impatiently*). Do you think I would believe without good evidence? I have had them take the statements of many witnesses. The miracle was done in conjunction with another Jew acting as this man's tool. This other Jew, the report states, could not possibly have possessed any magic power Himself, for Pilate crucified Him a short time after and He died in pain and weakness within a few hours. But this Lazarus laughs at death!

LAZARUS (*looks up, smiling with ironical bitterness*). Couldst Thou but hear, Jesus! And men shall keep on in panic nailing Man's soul to the cross of their fear until in the end they do it to avenge Thee, for Thine Honour and Glory! (*He sighs sadly—then after a struggle overcoming himself—with exultance.*) Yes! (*His eyes fall again to Tiberius and he smiles.*) Yes! Yes to the stupid as to the wise! To what is understood and to what cannot be understood! Known and unknown! Over and over! For ever and ever! Yes! (*He laughs softly to himself.*)

TIBERIUS (*with superstitious dread*). What dost thou mean, Dæmon?

POMPEIA (*with indignant scorn*). Let him prove there is no death, Cæsar! (*She appeals to the company, who straighten up on their couches with interest.*)

CHORUS (*chant demandingly*). Let him prove
there is no death!
We are bored!

CROWD (*echoing*). Prove there is no death!
We are bored, Cæsar!

TIBERIUS (*waits to see what Lazarus will say—then as he says nothing, plucking up his courage—his cruelty aroused*). Do you hear, Lazarus?

POMPEIA. Make him perform his miracle again!

CHORUS (*as before*). Let him perform a
miracle!
We are bored, Cæsar!

CROWD (*they now stand up and coming from behind their tables, move forward toward the dais*). A miracle !
We are bored !

POMPEIA. Let him raise someone from the dead !

CHORUS (*chanting with a pettish insistence*). Raise the dead !
We are bored !

CROWD (*echoing—grouping in a big semicircle as of spectators in a theatre, around and to the sides of the dais, one sex on each side. Caligula moves in from the left in front of them. They form in three ranks, the first squatting on their hams like savages (as Caligula does), the second rank crouching over them, the third leaning over the second, all with a hectic, morbid interest*). We are bored !
Raise the dead !

POMPEIA (*with a cruel smile*). I have thought of a special test for him, Cæsar. (*She whispers in Cæsar's ear and points to Miriam and the fruit in her hand.*) And he must laugh !

TIBERIUS (*with a harsh, cruel chuckle*). Yes, I shall command him to laugh ! (*Then disgustedly.*) But she is sad and old. I will be only doing him a favour.

CALIGULA (*rocking back and forth on his haunches —looking at Lazarus with taunting cruelty*). No, Cæsar ! I know he loves her !

LAZARUS. Yes ! (*He steps down from the dais to Miriam's side and taking her head in both his hands, he kisses her on the lips.*)

TIBERIUS (*with a malignant grin*). Give her the fruit !

POMPEIA (*advances and offers the peach to Miriam —with a hard, cruel little laugh*). Cæsar invites you to eat !

MIRIAM (*to Lazarus—requesting meekly but longingly*). May I accept, Lazarus ? Is it time at last ? My love has followed you over long roads among strangers and each league we came from home my heart has grown older. Now it is too old for you, a heart too weary for your loving laughter. Ever your laughter has grown younger, Lazarus ! Upward it springs like a lark from a field, and sings ! Once I knew your laughter was my child, my son of Lazarus ; but then it grew younger and I felt at last it had returned to my womb—and ever younger and younger—until, to-night, when I spoke to you of home, I felt new birth-pains as your laughter, grown too young for me, flew back to the unborn—a birth so like a death ! (*She sobs and wipes her eyes with her sleeve—then humbly, reaching out for the fruit.*) May I accept it, Lazarus ? You should have new-born laughing hearts to love you. My old one labours with memories and its blood is sluggish with the past. Your home on the hills of space is too far away. My heart longs for the warmth of close walls of earth baked in the sun. Our home in Bethany, Lazarus, where you and my children lived and died. Our tomb near our home, Lazarus, in which you and my children wait for me. Is it time at last ?

LAZARUS (*deeply moved*). Poor lonely heart ! It has been crueller for you than I remembered. Go in peace—to peace ! (*His voice trembles in spite of himself.*) I shall be lonely, dear one. (*With a note of pleading.*) You have never laughed with my laughter. Will you call back—Yes !—when you know—to tell me you understand and laugh with me at last ?

MIRIAM (*not answering him, to Pompeia, taking the peach and making a humble courtesy before her*). I thank you, pretty lady.

(*She raises the peach toward her mouth. Involuntarily one of Lazarus' hands half-reaches out as if to stop her.*)

POMPEIA (*with savage triumph, pointing*). See ! He would stop her ! He is afraid of death !

CHORUS (*pointing—jeeringly*). He is afraid of death ! Ha-ha-ha-ha !

CROWD (*jeeringly*). Ha-ha-ha-ha !

MIRIAM (*bites into the peach and, chewing, begins, as if immediately affected, to talk like a garrulous old woman, her words coming quicker and quicker as her voice becomes fainter and fainter*). Say what you like, it is much better I should go home first, Lazarus. We have been away so long, there will be so much to attend to about the house. And all the children will be waiting. You would be as helpless as a child, Lazarus. Between you and the children, things would soon be in a fine state ! (*More and more confused.*) No, no ! You cannot help me, dearest one. You are only in my way. No, I will make the fire. When you laid it the last time, we all had to run for our lives, choking, the smoke poured from the windows, the neighbours thought the house was burning! (*She laughs—a queer, vague little inward laugh.*) You are so impractical. The neighbours all get the best of you. Money slips through your fingers. If it was not for me— (*She sighs—then brightly and lovingly.*) But, dearest husband, why do you take it so to heart? Why do you feel guilty because you are not like other men? That is why I love you so much. Is it a sin to be born a dreamer? But God, He must be a dreamer, too, or how would we be on earth? Do not keep saying to yourself so bitterly, you are a failure in life! Do not sit brooding on the hilltop in the evening like a black figure of Job against the sky! (*Her voice trembling.*) Even if God has taken our little ones—yes, in spite of sorrow—have you not a good home I make for you, and a wife who loves you? (*She forces a chuckle.*) Be grateful, then—for me! Smile, my sad one! Laugh a little once in a while! Come home, bringing me laughter of the wind from the hills! (*Swaying, looking at the peach in her hand.*) What a mellow, sweet fruit! Did you bring it home for me?

(*She falls back into his arms. Gently he lets her body sink until it rests against the steps of the dais. Tiberius rises from his couch to bend over with cruel gloating. Pompeia steps nearer to Lazarus, staring at him mockingly. Caligula hops to her side, looking from Lazarus to Miriam. The half-circle of masked figures moves closer, straining forward and downward as if to overwhelm the two figures at the foot of the dais with their concentrated death wish.*)

TIBERIUS (*thickly*). She is dead, and I do not hear you laugh!

LAZARUS (*bending down—supplicatingly*). Miriam! Call back to me! Laugh! (*He pauses. A second of dead silence. Then, with a sound that is very like a sob, he kisses her on the lips.*) I am lonely!

POMPEIA (*with savage malice—jeeringly*). See! He weeps, Cæsar! (*She bursts into strident laughter.*) Ha-ha-ha-ha!

CHORUS (*echoing her laughter*). Ha-ha-ha-ha!
There is fear!
There is death!

CROWD. There is death!
Ha-ha-ha-ha!

CALIGULA (*in a frenzy of despairing rage, hopping up and down*). Liar! Charlatan! Weakling! How you have cheated Caligula! (*He suddenly slaps Lazarus viciously across the face.*) There is death! Laugh, if you dare!

TIBERIUS (*standing—in a sinister cold rage, the crueller because his dream of a cure for death is baffled, yet feeling his power as Cæsar triumphant nevertheless*). And I thought you might be a dæmon. I thought you might have a magic cure— (*With revengeful fury.*) But death is, and death is mine! I shall make you pray for death! And I shall make Death laugh at you! Ha-ha-ha-ha! (*In a frenzy as Lazarus neither makes a sound nor looks up.*) Laugh, Lazarus! Laugh at yourself! Laugh with me! (*Then to his soldiers.*) Scourge him! Make him laugh!

CALIGULA (*running to soldiers—fiercely*). Give me a scourge!

POMPEIA (*running to the soldiers—hysterically*). Ha-ha-ha-ha! Let me beat him, Cæsar!

(*They group behind him. The rods and scourges are up-lifted over his back to strike, when in the dead expectant silence, Miriam's body is seen to rise in a writhing tortured last effort.*)

MIRIAM (*in a voice of unearthly sweetness*). Yes! There is only life! Lazarus, be not lonely! (*She laughs and sinks back and is still.*)

(*A shuddering murmur of superstitious fear comes from them as they shrink back swiftly from Lazarus, remaining huddled one against the other. Pompeia runs to the feet of Tiberius and crouches down on the steps below him, as if for protection, her terrified eyes on Miriam. Caligula runs to her and crouches beside and beneath her.*)

LAZARUS (*kisses Miriam again and raises his head. His face is radiant with new faith and joy. He smiles with happiness and speaks to himself with a mocking affection as if to an amusing child*). That much remained hidden in me of the sad old Lazarus who died of self-pity—his loneliness! Lonely no more! Man's loneliness is but his fear of life! Lonely no more! Millions of laughing stars there are around me! And laughing dust, born once of woman on this earth, now freed to dance! New stars are born of dust eternally! The old, grown mellow with God, burst into flaming seed! The fields of infinite space are sown—and grass for sheep springs up on the hills of earth! But there is no death, nor fear, nor loneliness! There is only God's Eternal Laughter! His Laughter flows into the lonely heart!

(He begins to laugh, his laughter clear and ringing—the laughter of a conqueror arrogant with happiness and the pride of a new triumph. He bends and picks up the body of Miriam in his arms and, his head thrown back, laughing, he ascends the dais and places her on the table as on a bier. He touches one hand on her breast, as if he were taking an oath to life on her heart, looks upward and laughs, his voice ringing more and more with a terrible unbearable power and beauty that beats those in the room into an abject submissive panic.)

(Tiberius grovels half under the table, his hands covering his ears, his face on the floor; he is laughing with the agony and terror of death. Pompeia lies face down on the first step and beats it with her fists; she is laughing with horror and self-loathing. Caligula, his hands clutching his head, pounds it against the edge of the steps; he is laughing with grief and remorse. The rest, soldiers, slaves and the prostitutes of both sexes, writhe and twist distractedly, seeking to hide their heads against each other, beating each other and the floor with clenched hands. An agonized moan of supplicating laughter comes from them all.)

ALL. Ha-ha-ha-ha! Ha-ha-ha-ha!
Let us die, Lazarus!
Mercy, Laughing One!
Mercy of death!
Ha-ha-ha-ha! Ha-ha-ha-ha!

(But the laughter of Lazarus is as remote now as the laughter of a god.)

CURTAIN

ACT FOUR
SCENE ONE

SCENE. *The same as previous scene—the same night a short while later. All the lamps are out except the one on the table on the dais which, placed beside the head of Miriam, shines down upon the white mask of her face. In the half-darkness, the walls are lost in shadow, the room seems immense, the dais nearer.*

Lazarus sits on the couch at the right on the dais. His face is strong and proud, although his eyes are fixed down on the face of Miriam. He seems more youthful still now, like a young son who keeps watch by the body of his mother, but at the same time retaining the aloof serenity of the statue of a god. His face expresses sorrow and a happiness that transcends sorrow.

On the other side of the table, at the end of the couch, Tiberius sits facing front, his elbows on his knees, his large hands with bloated veins hanging loosely. He keeps his gaze averted from the corpse. He talks to Lazarus half over his shoulder.

On the top step, Pompeia sits, facing right, her hands clasped about one knee, the other leg stretched down to the lower step. Her head is thrown back and she is gazing up into Lazarus' face.

On the step below her, Caligula squats on his haunches, his arms on his knees, his fists pressed to his temples. He is staring straight before him. Only these four people are in the room now.

TIBERIUS *(gloomily)*. Was she dead, Dæmon, and was it thy power that recalled life to her body for that moment? Or was she still living and her words only the last desire of her love to comfort you, Lazarus? *(Lazarus does not reply.)* If thou dost not tell me, I must always doubt thee, Dæmon.

POMPEIA *(with a sigh of bewildered happiness, turns to Caligula)*. I am glad he laughed, Caligula! Did I say I loved him before? Then it was only my body that wanted a slave. Now it is my heart that desires a master! Now I know love for the first time in my life!

CALIGULA *(bitterly)*. Fool! What does he

care for love? (*Sombrely.*) He loves every one—but no one—not even me! (*He broods frowningly.*)

POMPEIA (*following her own thoughts*). And now that hag is dead he will need a woman, young and beautiful, to protect and comfort him, to make him a home and bear his children! (*She dreams, her eyes again fixed on Lazarus—then suddenly turning to Caligula.*) I am glad I lost our bet. But you must accept some other payment. Now I know love, I may not give myself to any man save him!

CALIGULA. I do not want you! What are you but another animal! Faugh! (*With a grimace of disgust.*) Pleasure is dirty and joyless! Or we who seek it are, which comes to the same thing. (*Then grimly.*) But our bet can rest. This is not the end. There may still be a chance for you to laugh at him!

POMPEIA. No! Now I could not! I should weep for his defeat!

TIBERIUS (*gloomily arguing, half to himself*). His laughter triumphed over me, but he has not brought her back to life. I think he knows no cure for another's death, as I had hoped. And I must always doubt that it was not some trick—(*harshly*) until I have tested him with his own life! He cannot cheat me then! (*A pause—arguing to himself.*) But he was dead—that much has been proved—and before he died he was old and sad. What did he find beyond there? (*Suddenly—turning to Lazarus now.*) What did you find beyond death, Lazarus?

LAZARUS (*exaltedly*). Life! God's Eternal Laughter!

TIBERIUS (*shaking his head*). I want hope—for me, Tiberius Cæsar.

LAZARUS. What is—you? But there is hope for Man! Love is Man's hope—love for his life on earth, a noble love above suspicion and distrust! Hitherto Man has always suspected his life, and in revenge and self-torture his love has been faithless! He has even betrayed Eternity, his mother, with his slave he calls Immortal Soul! (*He laughs softly, gaily, mockingly—then to Tiberius directly.*) Hope for you, Tiberius Cæsar? Then dare to love Eternity without your fear desiring to possess her! Be brave enough to be possessed!

TIBERIUS (*strangely*). My mother was the wife of Cæsar. (*Then dully.*) I do not understand.

LAZARUS. Men are too cowardly to understand! And so the worms of their little fears eat them and grow fat and terrible and become their jealous gods they must appease with lies!

TIBERIUS (*wearily*). Your words are meaningless, Lazarus. You are a fool. All laughter is malice, all gods are dead, and life is a sickness.

LAZARUS (*laughs pityingly*). So say the race of men, whose lives are long dyings! They evade their fear of death by becoming so sick of life that by the time death comes they are too lifeless to fear it! Their disease triumphs over death—a noble victory called resignation! "We are sick," they say, "therefore there is no God in us, therefore there is no God!" Oh, if men would but interpret that first cry of man fresh from the womb as the laughter of one who even then says to his heart, "It is my pride as God to become Man. Then let it be my pride as Man to recreate the God in me!" (*He laughs softly but with exultant pride.*)

POMPEIA (*laughing with him—proudly*). He will create a god in me! I shall be proud!

CALIGULA (*pounding his temples with his fists—tortured*). I am Caligula. I was born in a camp among soldiers. My father was Germanicus, a hero, as all men know. But I do not understand this—and though I burst with pride, I cannot laugh with joy!

TIBERIUS (*gloomily*). Obscurities! I have found nothing in life that merits pride. I am not proud of being Cæsar—and what is a god but a Cæsar over Cæsars? If fools kneel and worship me because they fear me, should I be proud? But Cæsar is a fact, and Tiberius, a man, is one, and I cling to these certainties—and I do not wish to die! If I were sure of eternal sleep beyond there, deep rest and forgetfulness of all I have ever seen or heard or hated or loved on earth, I would gladly die! But surely, Lazarus, nothing is sure—peace the least sure of all—and I fear there is no rest beyond there, that one remembers there as here and cannot sleep, that the mind goes on eternally the same—a long insomnia of memories and regrets and the ghosts of dreams one has poisoned to death passing with white bodies spotted by the leprous fingers of one's lusts. (*Bitterly.*) I fear the long nights now in which I lie awake and listen to Death dancing round me in the darkness, prancing to the drum beat of my heart! (*He shudders.*) And I am afraid, Lazarus—afraid that there is no sleep beyond there, either!

LAZARUS. There is peace!

(*His words are like a benediction he pronounces upon them. Soothed in a mysterious, childlike way, they repeat the word after him, wonderingly.*)

POMPEIA. Peace?

CALIGULA. Peace?

TIBERIUS. Peace? (*For a long moment there is complete silence. Then Tiberius sighs heavily, shaking his head.*) Peace! Another word is blurred into a senseless sigh by men's longing! A bubble of froth blown from the lips of the dying toward the stars! No! (*He grins bitterly—then looks at Lazarus—sombrely contemptuous and threatening.*) You are pleased to act the mysterious, Jew, but I shall solve you! (*Then with a lawyer-like incisiveness.*) There is one certainty about you and I must know the cause—for there must be a cause and a rational explanation! You were fifty when you died——

LAZARUS (*smiling mockingly*). Yes. When I died.

TIBERIUS (*unheeding*). And now your appearance is of one younger by a score. Not alone your appearance! You *are* young. I see the fact, the effect. And I demand an explanation of the cause without mystic nonsense or evasion. (*Threateningly.*) And I warn you to answer directly in plain words—and not to laugh, you understand!—not to dare!—or I shall lose patience with you and—(*with a grim smile*) I can be terrible! (*Lazarus smiles gently at him. He turns away with confused annoyance, then back to Lazarus, resuming his lawyer-like manner.*) What was it restored your youth? How did you contrive that your body reversed the natural process and grows younger? Is it a charm by which you invoke a supernatural force? Or is it a powder you dissolve in wine? Or a liquid? Or an unguent you rub into the skin to revitalize the old bones and tissues? Or—what is it, Lazarus?

LAZARUS (*gently*). I know that age and time are but timidities of thought.

TIBERIUS (*broodingly—as if he had not heard—persuasively*). Perhaps you ask yourself, what would Tiberius do with youth? Then, because you must have heard rumours of my depravity, you will conclude the old lecher desires youth for his lusts! (*He laughs harshly.*) Ha! Why, do not my faithful subjects draw pictures of an old buck goat upon the walls and write above them, Cæsar? And they are just. In self-contempt of Man I have made this man, myself, the most swinish and contemptible of men! Yes! In all this empire there is no man so base a hog as I! (*He grins bitterly and ironically.*) My claim to this excellence, at least, is not contested! Every one admits therein Tiberius is by right their Cæsar! (*He laughs bitterly.*) Ha! So who would believe Tiberius if he said, I want youth again because I loathe lust and long for purity!

LAZARUS (*gently*). I believe you, Cæsar.

TIBERIUS (*stares at him—deeply moved*). You—believe—? (*Then gruffly.*) You lie! You are not mad—and only a madman would believe another man! (*Then confidingly, leaning over toward Lazarus.*) I know it is folly to speak—but—one gets old, one becomes talkative, one wishes to confess, to say the thing one has always kept hidden, to reveal one's unique truth—and there is so little time left—and one is alone! Therefore the old—like children—talk to themselves, for they have reached that hopeless wisdom of experience which knows that though one were to cry it in the streets to multitudes, or whisper it in the kiss to one's beloved, the only ears that can ever hear one's secret are one's own! (*He laughs bitterly.*) And so I talk aloud, Lazarus! I talk to my loneliness!

LAZARUS (*simply*). I hear, Tiberius.

TIBERIUS (*again moved and confused—forcing a mocking smile*). Liar! Eavesdropper! You merely—listen! (*Then he turns away.*) My mother, Livia, that strong woman, giving birth to me, desired not a child, but a Cæsar—just as, married to Augustus, she loved him not but loved herself as Cæsar's wife. She made me feel, in the proud questioning of her scornful eyes, that to win her mother love I must become Cæsar. She poisoned Prince Marcellus and young Gaius and Lucius that the way might be clear for me. I used to see their blood dance in red specks before my eyes when I looked at the sky. Now—(*he brushes his hand before his eyes*)—it is all a red blot! I cannot distinguish. There have been too many. My mother—her blood is in that blot, for I revenged myself on her. I did not kill her, it is true, but I deprived her of her power and she died, as I knew she must, that powerful woman who bore me as a weapon! The murder was subtle and cruel—how cruel only that passionate, deep-breasted woman unslaked by eighty years of devoured desires could know! Too cruel! I did not go to her funeral. I was afraid her closed eyes might open and look at me! (*Then with almost a cry.*) I want youth, Lazarus, that I may play again about her feet with the love I felt for her before I learned to read her eyes! (*He half sobs, bowing his head. A pause.*)

CALIGULA (*nudging Pompeia—with a crafty whisper*). Do you hear? The old lecher talks to himself. He is becoming senile. He will soon die. And I shall be Cæsar. Then I shall laugh!

POMPEIA (*staring up at Lazarus' face, hearing only Caligula's words without their meaning*). No. My Lazarus does not laugh now. See. His mouth is silent—and a little sad, I think.

LAZARUS (*gently and comfortingly*). I hear, Tiberius.

TIBERIUS (*harshly*). I hated that woman, my mother, and I still hate her! Have you ever loved, Lazarus? (*Then with a glance at Miriam's body and a shuddering away from it—vaguely.*) I was forgetting her. I killed your love, too, did I not? Well, I must! I envy those who are loved. Where I can, I kill love—for retribution's sake—but much of it escapes me. (*Then harshly again.*) I loved Agrippina. We were married. A son was born to us. We were happy. Then that proud woman, my mother, saw my happiness. Was she jealous of my love? Or did she know no happy man would wish to be Cæsar? Well, she condemned my happiness to death. She whispered to Augustus and he ordered me to divorce Agrippina. I should have opened her veins and mine, and died with her. But my mother stayed by me, Agrippina was kept away, my mother spoke to me and spoke to me and even wept, that tall woman, strong as a great man, and I consented that my love be murdered. Then my mother married me to a whore. Why? The whore was Cæsar's daughter, true—but I feel that was not all of it, that my mother wished to keep me tortured that I might love her alone and long to be Cæsar! (*He laughs harshly.*) Ha! In brief, I married the whore, she tortured me, my mother's scheming prospered—that subtle and crafty woman!—and many years passed in being here and there, in doing this and that, in growing full of hate and revengeful ambition to be Cæsar. At last, Augustus died. I was Cæsar. Then I killed that whore, my wife, and I starved my mother's strength to death until she died, and I began to take pleasure in vengeance upon men, and pleasure in taking vengeance on myself. (*He grins horribly.*) It is all very simple, as you see! (*He suddenly starts to his feet—with harsh arrogance and pride, threateningly.*) Enough! Why do I tell you these old tales? Must I explain to you why I want youth? It is my whim! I am Cæsar! And now I must lie down and try to sleep! And it is my command that you reveal the secret of your youth to me when I awake, or else—(*with malignant cruelty*)—I will have to revenge the death of a hope on you—and a hope at my age demands a terrible expiation on its slayer! (*He walks down and starts to go off, right—then turns and addresses Lazarus with grim irony.*) Good night to you, Lazarus. And remember there shall be death while I am Cæsar! (*He turns to go.*)

LAZARUS (*smiling affectionately at him, shakes his head*). Cæsar must believe in death. But does the husband of Agrippina?

TIBERIUS (*stops short and stares at Lazarus, confused and stuttering*). What—what—do you mean, Lazarus?

LAZARUS. I have heard your loneliness.

TIBERIUS (*cruelly and grimly again*). So much the more reason why my pride should kill you! Remember that! (*He turns and strides off into the darkness at right.*)

CALIGULA (*peers after him until sure he is gone—then gets up and begins a grotesque, hopping dance, singing a verse of the legionary's song.*)

A bold legionary am I
March, oh march on!
A Roman eagle was my daddy,
My mother was a drunken drabby,

Oh, march on to the wars!

(*He laughs gratingly, posturing and gesticulating up at Lazarus.*)

Ha-ha-ha! He is gone! I can breathe! His breath in the same air suffocates me! The gods grant mine do the same for him! But he is failing! He talks to himself like a man in second childhood. His words are a thick babble I could not hear. They well from his lips like clots of blood from a reopened wound. I kept listening to the beating of his heart. It sounded slow, slower than when I last heard it. Did you detect that, Lazarus? Once or twice I thought it faltered— (*He draws in his breath with an avid gasp—then laughs gratingly.*) Ha-ha-ha— (*Grandiloquently.*) Tiberius, the old buck-goat, will soon be gone, my friends, and in his place you will be blessed with the beautiful young god, Caligula! Hail to Caligula! Hail! Ha-ha-ha——

(*His laughter suddenly breaks off into a whimper, and he stands staring around him in a panic of fear that he has been overheard. He slinks noiselessly up the steps of the dais and squats coweringly at Lazarus' feet, blinking up at his face in monkey-wise, clutching Lazarus' hand in both of his. His teeth can be heard chattering together in nervous fear.*)

(*Pompeia, whose gaze has remained fixed on Lazarus' throughout, has gradually moved closer to him until she, too, is at his feet, half-kneeling beneath the table on which Miriam lies, side by side with Caligula but as oblivious of him as he is of her.*)

(*Having grown calmer now, Caligula speaks again—mournful and bewildered.*)

CALIGULA. Why should I love you, Lazarus? Your laughter taunts me! It insults Cæsar! It denies Rome! But I will warn you again. Escape! To-night Tiberius' mood is to play sentimental, but to-morrow he will jeer while hyenas gnaw at your skull and lick your brain. And then—there is pain, Lazarus! There is pain!

POMPEIA (*pressing her hand to her own heart—with a shudder*). Yes, there is pain!

LAZARUS (*smiling down on them—gently*). If you can answer Yes to pain, there is no pain!

POMPEIA (*passionately*). Yes! Yes! I love Lazarus!

CALIGULA (*with a bitter grin*). Do not take pain away from us! It is our one truth. Without pain there is nothing—a nothingness in which even your laughter, Lazarus, is swallowed at one gulp like a whining gnat by the cretin's silence of immensity! Ha-ha! No, we must keep pain! Especially Cæsar must! Pain must twinkle with a mad mirth in a Cæsar's eyes—men's pain—or they would become dissatisfied and disrespectful! Ha-ha! (*He stops his grating laughter abruptly and continues mournfully.*) I am sick, Lazarus, sick of cruelty and lust and human flesh and all the imbecilities of pleasure—the unclean antics of half-witted children! (*With a mounting agony of longing.*) I would be clean! If I could only laugh your laughter, Lazarus! That would purify my heart. For I could wish to love all men, as you love them—as I love you! If only I did not fear them and despise them! If I could only believe—believe in them—in life—in myself!—believe that one man or woman in the world knew and loved the real Caligula—then I might have faith in Caligula myself—then I might laugh your laughter!

LAZARUS (*suddenly, in a quiet but compelling voice*). I, who know you, love you, Caligula. (*Gently patting his head.*) I love Caligula.

CALIGULA (*staring up at him in pathetic confusion*). You? You? You, Lazarus? (*He begins to tremble all over as if in a seizure—chokingly.*) Beware! It is not good—not just—to make fun of me—to laugh at my misery—saying you love— (*In a frenzy, he jumps to his feet threatening Lazarus.*) Are you trying to fool me, hypocrite? Do you think I have become so abject that you dare—? Because I love you, do you presume—? Do you think I am your slave, dog of a Jew, that you can—insult—to my face—the heir of Cæsar—— (*He stutters and stammers with rage, hopping up and down grotesquely, shaking his fist at Lazarus, who smiles at him affectionately as at a child in a tantrum.*)

LAZARUS (*catching his eyes and holding them with his glance—calmly*). Believe, Caligula!

CALIGULA (*again overcome—stuttering with strange terror*). Believe? But I cannot! I must not!

You cannot know me, if— You are a holy man! You are a god in a mortal body—you can laugh with joy to be alive—while I— Oh, no, you cannot love me! There is nothing in me at bottom but a despising and an evil eye! You cannot! You are only being kind! (*Hysterically.*) I do not want your kindness! I hate your pity! I am too proud! I am too strong! (*He collapses weepingly, kneeling and clutching Lazarus' hand in both of his.*)

LAZARUS (*smiling*). You are so proud of being evil! What if there is no evil? What if there are only health and sickness? Believe in the healthy god called Man in you! Laugh at Caligula, the funny clown who beats the backside of his shadow with a bladder and thinks thereby he is Evil, the Enemy of God! (*He suddenly lifts the face of Caligula and stares into his eyes.*) Believe! What if you are a man and men are despicable? Men are also unimportant! Men pass! Like rain into the sea! The sea remains! Man remains! Man slowly arises from the past of the race of men that was his tomb of death! For Man death is not! Man, Son of God's Laughter, *is*! (*He begins to laugh triumphantly, staring deep into Caligula's eyes.*) *Is*, Caligula! Believe in the laughing god within you!

CALIGULA (*bursting suddenly into choking, joyful laughter—like a visionary*). I believe! I believe there is love even for Caligula! I can laugh—now—Lazarus! Free laughter! Clean! No sickness! No lust for death! My corpse no longer rots in my heart! The tomb is full of sunlight! I am alive! I who love Man, I who can love and laugh! Listen, Lazarus! I dream! When I am Cæsar, I will devote my power to your truth. I will decree that there must be kindness and love! I will make the Empire one great Blessed Isle! Rome shall know happiness, it shall believe in life, it shall learn to laugh your laughter, Lazarus, or I—— (*He raises his hand in an imperial autocratic gesture.*)

LAZARUS (*gaily mocking*). Or you will cut off its head?

CALIGULA (*fiercely*). Yes! I will—! (*Then meeting Lazarus' eyes, he beats his head with his fists crazily.*) Forgive me! I forget! I forget!

LAZARUS. Go out under the sky! Let your heart climb on laughter to a star! Then make it look down at earth, and watch Caligula commanding Life under pain of death to do his will! (*He laughs.*)

CALIGULA (*laughing*). I will! I do! I laugh at him! Caligula is a trained ape, a humped cripple! Now I take him out under the sky, where I can watch his monkey tricks, where there is space for laughter and where this new joy, your love of me, may dance!

(*Laughing clearly and exultantly, he runs out through the arched doorway at rear.*)

LAZARUS (*stops laughing—shaking his head, almost sadly*). They forget! It is too soon for laughter! (*Then grinning at himself.*) What, Lazarus? Are you, too, thinking in terms of time, old fool so soon to re-enter infinity? (*He laughs with joyous self-mockery.*)

POMPEIA (*who has crept to his feet, kisses his hand passionately*). I love you, Lazarus!

LAZARUS (*stops laughing, and looks down at her gently*). And I love you, woman.

POMPEIA (*with a gasp of delight*). You? (*She stares up into his eyes doubtingly, raising her face toward his.*) Then—put your arms around me. (*He does so, smiling gently.*) And hold me to you. (*He presses her closer to him.*) And kiss me. (*He kisses her on the forehead.*) No, on the lips! (*He kisses her. She flings her arms about his neck. passionately and kisses him again and again—then slowly draws away—remains looking into his eyes a long time, shrinking back from him with bewildered pain which speedily turns to rage and revengeful hatred.*) No! No! It is *my* love, not Love! I want you to know *my* love, to give me back love —for me—only for me—Pompeia—my body, my heart—me, a woman—not Woman, women! Do I love Man, men? I hate men! I love you, Lazarus—a man—a lover—a father to children! I want love—as you loved that woman there (*she points to Miriam*) that I poisoned for love of you! But did you love her—or just Woman, wife and mother of men? (*She stares—then as if reading admission in his eyes, she springs to her feet.*) Liar! Cheat! Hypocrite! Thief! (*Half hysterical with rage, pain and grief, she bends over Miriam and smoothes the hair back from her forehead.*) Poor wife! Poor woman! How he must have tortured you! Now I remember the pity in your eyes when you looked at me!

Oh, how his soothing grey words must have pecked at the wound in your heart like doves with bloody beaks ! (*Then with sudden harshness.*) But perhaps you were too dull to understand, too poor and tired and ugly and old to care, too slavish—! Pah ! (*She turns away with contempt and faces Lazarus with revengeful hatred.*) Did you think I would take her place—become your slave, wait upon you, give you love and passion and beauty in exchange for phrases about man and gods—you who are neither a man nor a god but a dead thing without desire ! You dared to hope I would give my body, my love, to you ! (*She spits in his face and laughs harshly.*) You insolent fool ! I shall punish you ! You shall be tortured as you have tortured ! (*She laughs wildly—then steps down from the dais and goes off right, crying distractedly.*) Cæsar ! This man has made you a fool before all the world ! Torture him, Cæsar ! Now ! Let the people witness ! Send heralds to wake them ! Torture him, Cæsar, the man who laughs at you ! Ha-ha-ha-ha !

(*Her laughter is caught up by all the Girls and Youths of the palace, who, as she disappears, led by their Chorus, pour in from each side of the room and dance forward to group themselves around the dais as in the previous scene, staring at Lazarus, laughing cruelly, falsely, stridently.*)

CHORUS (*tauntingly*). Ha-ha-ha-ha !

Laugh now, Lazarus !
Let us see you laugh !
Ha-ha-ha-ha !

CROWD (*echoing*). Ha-ha-ha-ha !

Ha-ha-ha-ha !

LAZARUS (*moves, and immediately there is silence. He bends down and kisses Miriam and picks her up in his arms. Talking down to her face—with a tender smile*). Farewell ! You are home ! And now I will take your body home to earth ! Space is too far away, you said ! Home in the Earth ! There will be so much for you to do there ! Home ! Earth ! (*His voice trembling a bit.*) Farewell, body of Miriam. My grief is a lonely cry wailing in the home in my heart that you have left for ever ! (*Then exultantly.*) But what am I ? Now your love has become Eternal Love ! Now, since your life passed, I feel Eternal Life made nobler by your selflessness ! Love has grown purer ! The laughter of God is more profoundly tender ! (*He looks up in an ecstasy and descends the dais, carrying her.*) Yes, that is it ! That is it, my Miriam ! (*Laughing softly and tenderly, he walks around the dais and carries the body out through the doorway in rear.*)

(*The Chorus and Youths and Girls make way for him in awed silence—then scurry around to right and left, forming an aisle through which he passes—then after he has gone out through the arch, they close into a semicircular group again, staring after him, and a whisper of strange, bewildered, tender laughter comes from them.*)

CHORUS (*in this whisper*). That is it !

Love is pure !
Laughter is tender !
Laugh !

CROWD (*echoing*). Laugh ! Laugh !

CURTAIN

SCENE TWO

SCENE. *The arena of an amphitheatre. It is just before dawn of the same night. Cæsar's throne is on the left at the extreme front, facing right, turned a little toward front. It is lighted by four immense lamps. In front of the throne is a marble railing that tops the wall that encloses the arena. In the rear the towering pile of the circular amphitheatre is faintly outlined in deeper black against the dark sky.*

Tiberius sits on the throne, his eyes fixed on the middle of the arena off right, where, bound to a high stake after he had been tortured, Lazarus is now being burnt alive over a huge pile of faggots. The crackling of the flames is heard. Their billowing rise and fall is reflected on the masked faces of the multitude who sit on the banked tiers of marble behind and to the rear of the throne, with their Chorus, seven men masked in Middle Age in the Servile, Hypocritical type, grouped on each side of the throne of Cæsar on a lower tier.

Half-kneeling before Tiberius, her chin resting on her hands on top of the marble rail, Pompeia also stares at Lazarus.

Before the curtain, the crackle of the flames and an uproar of human voices from the multitude, jeering, hooting, laughing at Lazarus in cruel mockery of his laughter. This sound has risen to its greatest volume as the curtain rises.

CHORUS (*chanting mockingly*). Ha-ha-ha-ha !
Burn and laugh !
Laugh now, Lazarus !
Ha-ha-ha-ha !

CROWD (*chanting with revengeful mockery*). Ha-ha-ha-ha !

TIBERIUS. Who laughs now, Lazarus—thou or Cæsar ? Ha-ha—! (*With awe.*) His flesh melts in the fire but his eyes shine with peace !

POMPEIA. How he looks at me ! (*Averting her eyes with a shudder.*) Command them to put out his eyes, Cæsar !

TIBERIUS (*harshly*). No. I want to read his eyes when they see death ! (*Then averting his face—guiltily.*) He is looking at me, not you. I should not have listened to your cries for his death.

POMPEIA (*turning to him again with a shudder of agony—beseechingly*). Have them put out his eyes, Cæsar ! They call to me !

TIBERIUS (*as if not hearing her—to himself*). Why do I feel remorse ? His laughter dies and is forgotten, and the hope it raised dies—(*With sudden excitement.*) And yet—he must know something—and if he would—even now he could tell— (*Suddenly rising to his feet he calls imploringly.*) Lazarus !

CHORUS (*chanting in a great imploring chorus now*). Lazarus !

CROWD (*echoing*). Lazarus !

SOLDIER'S VOICE (*calling from off beside the stake*). You had us gag him, Cæsar, so he might not laugh. Shall we cut away the gag ?

POMPEIA (*in terror*). No, Cæsar ! He will laugh ! And I will go to him ! (*Desperately.*) He will laugh at you, Cæsar—and the mob will laugh with him !

TIBERIUS (*struggles with himself—then calls*). Lazarus ! If you hear let your eyes answer, and I will grant the mercy of death to end your agony ! Is there hope of love somewhere for men on earth ?

CHORUS (*intoning as before*). Is there hope of love
For us on earth ?

CROWD. Hope of love
For us on earth !

SOLDIER'S VOICE. His eyes laugh, Cæsar !

TIBERIUS (*in a strange frenzy now*). Hear me, thou Dæmon of Laughter ! Hear and answer, I beseech thee, who alone hath known joy ! (*More and more wildly.*) How must we live ? Wherein lies happiness ?

CHORUS. Wherein lies happiness ?

CROWD. Wherein, happiness ?

TIBERIUS. Why are we born ? To what end must we die ?

CHORUS. Why are we born to die ?

CROWD. Why are we born ?

SOLDIER'S VOICE. His eyes laugh, Cæsar ! He is dying ! He would speak !

CHORUS AND CROWD (*in one great cry*). Cæsar ! Let Lazarus speak !

POMPEIA (*terrified*). No, Cæsar ! He will laugh—and you will die—and I will go to him !

TIBERIUS (*torn—arguing with his fear*). But—he may know some hope— (*Then making his decision, with grim fatalism.*) Hope—or nothing ! (*Calls to the Soldiers.*) Let him speak !

CHORUS AND CROWD (*cheering*). Hail, Cæsar !

LAZARUS (*his voice comes, recognizably the voice of Lazarus, yet with a strange, fresh, clear quality of boyhood, gaily mocking with life*). Hail, Cæsar !

CROWD (*frantic with hope*). Hail, Lazarus !

TIBERIUS. Pull away the fire from him ! I see death in his eyes ! (*The flaming reflections in the banked, masked faces dance madly as the Soldiers rake back the fire from the stake. With a forced, taunting mockery.*) What do you say now, Lazarus ? You are dying !

CHORUS AND CROWD (*taking his tone—mockingly*).

You are dying, Lazarus!

LAZARUS (*his voice a triumphant assertion of the victory of life over pain and death*). Yes!

TIBERIUS (*triumphant yet disappointed—with scorn and rage*). Ha! You admit it, do you, coward! Craven! Knave! Duper of fools! Clown! Liar! Die! I laugh at you! Ha-ha-ha-ha—— (*His voice breaks chokingly.*)

CROWD (*led by their Chorus—in the same frenzy of disappointment, with all sorts of grotesque and obscene gestures and noises, thumbing their fingers to their noses, wagging them at their ears, sticking out their tongues, slapping their behinds, barking, crowing like roosters, howling, and hooting in every conceivable manner*). Yah! Yah! Yellow Gut! Bung-kisser! Muckheel! Scumwiper! Liar! Pig! Jackal! Die! We laugh at you! Ha-ha-ha—— (*Their voices, too, break.*)

POMPEIA (*rising to her feet like one in a trance, staring toward Lazarus*). They are tormenting him. I hear him crying to me! (*She moves to the top of the steps leading to the arena.*)

LAZARUS (*his voice thrilling with exultance*). O men, fear not life! You die—but there is no death for Man!

(*He begins to laugh, and at the sound of his laughter, a great spell of silence settles upon all his hearers—then as his laughter rises, they begin to laugh with him.*)

POMPEIA (*descending the steps like a sleep-walker*). I hear his laughter calling. I must go to him.

TIBERIUS (*as if he realized something was happening that was against his will—trying feebly to be imperial*). I command you not to laugh! Cæsar commands—— (*Calling feebly to the Soldiers.*) Put back the gag! Stop his laughter!

(*The laughter of Lazarus gaily and lovingly mocks back at him.*)

SOLDIER'S VOICE (*his voice gently remonstrating*). We may not, Cæsar. We love his laughter!

(*They laugh with him.*)

CHORUS AND CROWD (*in a soft, dreamy murmur*).
We love his laughter!
We laugh!

TIBERIUS (*dreamily*). Then—pile the fire back around him. High and higher! Let him blaze to the stars! I laugh with him!

SOLDIER'S VOICE (*gently and gravely*). That is just, Cæsar. We love men flaming toward the stars! We laugh with him!

CHORUS AND CROWD (*as the flames, piled back and fed anew by the Soldiers, flare upward and are reflected on their masks in dancing waves of light*).
We love men flaming toward the stars!
We laugh!

POMPEIA (*in the arena*). The fire calls me. My burning heart calls for the fire!

(*She laughs softly and passes swiftly across the arena toward Lazarus.*)

TIBERIUS (*in a sort of childish complaint*). You must pardon me, Lazarus. This is my Cæsar's duty—to kill you! You have no right to laugh—before all these people—at Cæsar. It is not kind. (*He sobs snuffingly—then begins to laugh at himself.*)

(*Suddenly the flames waver, die down, then shoot up again and Pompeia's laughter is heard for a moment, rising clear and passionately with that of Lazarus, then dying quickly out.*)

SOLDIER'S VOICE. A woman has thrown herself in the flames, Cæsar! She laughs with Lazarus!

TIBERIUS (*in a sudden panicky flurry—feverishly*). Quick, Lazarus! You will soon be silent! Speak!—in the name of man's solitude—his agony of farewell—what is beyond there, Lazarus? (*His voice has risen to a passionate entreaty.*)

CHORUS (*in a great pleading echo*). What is beyond there, Lazarus?

CROWD. What is beyond?

LAZARUS (*his voice speaking lovingly, with a surpassing clearness and exaltation*). Life! Eternity! Stars and dust! God's Eternal Laughter!

(*His laughter bursts forth now in its highest pitch of ecstatic summons to the feast and sacrifice of Life, the Eternal.*)

(*The crowds laugh with him in a frenzied rhythmic chorus. Led by the Chorus, they pour down from the banked walls of the amphitheatre and dance in the flaring reflection of the flames strange wild measures of liberated joy. Tiberius stands on the raised dais laughing great shouts of clear, fearless laughter.)*

CHORUS (*chanting as they dance*). Laugh! Laugh!
We are stars!
We are dust!
We are gods!
We are laughter!

CROWD. We are dust!
We are gods!
Laugh! Laugh!

CALIGULA (*enters from behind Tiberius. His aspect is wild, his hair dishevelled, his clothes torn, He is panting as if exhausted by running. He stares toward the flames stupidly—then screams despairingly above the chant*). Lazarus! I come to save you! Do you still live, Lazarus?

TIBERIUS (*has been speaking. His words are now heard as the tumult momentarily dies down*). I have lived long enough! I will die with Lazarus! I no longer fear death! I laugh! I laugh at Cæsar! I advise you, my brothers, fear not Cæsars! Seek Man in the brotherhood of the dust! Cæsar is your fear of Man! I counsel you, laugh away your Cæsars!

CALIGULA (*with resentful jealousy and rage—in a voice rising to a scream*). What do I hear, Lazarus? You laugh with your murderer? You give him your laughter? You have forgotten me—my love—you make him love you—you make him laugh at Cæsars—at me! (*Suddenly springs on Tiberius in a fury and grabbing him by the throat chokes him, forcing him back on the throne—screaming.*) Die, traitor! Die! (*Tiberius' body relaxes in his hands, dead, and slips from the chair. Caligula rushes madly down the stairs into the midst of the oblivious, laughing, dancing crowd, screaming.*) You have betrayed me, dog of a Jew! You have betrayed Cæsar! (*Beginning to be caught by the contagion of the laughter.*) Ha-ah— No! I will not laugh! I will kill you! Give me a spear! (*He snatches a spear from a soldier and fights his way drunkenly toward the flames, like a man half overcome by a poisonous gas, shouting, half-laughing in spite of himself, half-weeping with rage.*) Ha-ha— The gods be with Cæsar Caligula! O Immortal Gods, give thy brother strength! You shall die, Lazarus—die— Ha-ha——! (*He disappears toward the flames, his spear held ready to stab.*)

CHORUS AND CROWD (*who have been entirely oblivious of him—chanting*). Laugh! Laugh!
We are gods!
We are dust!

LAZARUS (*at his first word there is a profound silence in which each dancer remains frozen in the last movement*). Hail, Caligula Cæsar! Men forget! (*He laughs with gay mockery as at a child.*)

CHORUS AND CROWD (*starting to laugh*). Laugh! Laugh!

(*Then there is a fierce cry of rage from Caligula and Lazarus' laughter ceases, and with it the laughter of the crowd turns to a wail of fear and lamentation.*)

CALIGULA (*dashes back among them waving his bloody spear and rushing up to the throne stands on it and strikes a grandiose pose*) I have killed God! I am Death! Death is Cæsar!

CHORUS AND CROWD (*turning and scurrying away—huddled in fleeing groups, crouching close to the ground like a multitude of terrified rats, their voices squeaky now with fright*). Hail, Cæsar! Hail to Death!

(*They are gone.*)

CALIGULA (*keeping his absurd majestic pose, turns and addresses with rhetorical intoning, and flowing gestures, the body of Lazarus, high upon its stake, the flames below it now flickering fitfully*). Hail, Caligula! Hero of heroes, conqueror of the Dæmon, Lazarus, who taught the treason that fear and death were dead! But I am Lord of Fear! I am Cæsar of Death! And you, Lazarus, are carrion! (*Then in a more conversational tone, putting aside his grandiose airs, confidentially.*) I had to kill you, Lazarus! Surely your good sense tells you— You heard what the old fool, Tiberius, told the mob. A moment more and there would have been a revolution—no more Cæsars—and my dream—! (*He stops—bewilderedly.*) My dream? Did I kill laughter? I had just learned to laugh—with love! (*More confusedly.*) I must be a little mad, Lazarus. It was one terror too many, to have been laughing your laughter in the night, to have been dreaming great yearning dreams of all the good my love might do for men when I was Cæsar—and then, to hear the old howling of mob lust, and to run here—and there a high white flame amidst the fire—you, Lazarus !—dying !—laughing with him—Tiberius—betraying me—who loved you, Lazarus ! Yes, I became mad ! I am mad ! And I can laugh my own mad laughter, Lazarus—my own ! Ha-ha-ha-ha ! (*He laughs with a wild triumphant madness and again rhetorically, with sweeping gestures and ferocious capers.*) And all of men are vile and mad, and I shall be their madmen's Cæsar ! (*He turns as if addressing an amphitheatre full of his subjects.*) O my good people, my faithful scum, my brother swine, Lazarus is dead and we have murdered great laughter, and it befits our madness to have done so, and it is befitting above all to have Caligula for Cæsar ! (*Then savagely.*) Kneel down ! Abase yourselves ! I am your Cæsar and your God ! Hail ! (*He stands saluting himself with a crazy intensity that is not without grandeur. A pause. Suddenly the silence seems to crush down upon him ; he is aware that he is alone in the vast arena ; he whirls about, looking around him as if he felt an assassin at his back ; he lunges with his spear at imaginary foes, jumping, dodging from side to side, yelping.*) Ho, there ! Help ! Help ! Your Cæsar calls you ! Help, my people ! To the rescue ! (*Suddenly throwing his spear away and sinking on his knees, his face toward Lazarus, supplicatingly.*) Lazarus ! Forgive me ! Help me ! Fear kills me ! Save me from death ! (*He is grovelling in a paroxysm of terror, grinding his face in his fists as if to hide it.*)

LAZARUS (*his voice is heard in a gentle, expiring sigh of compassion, followed by a faint dying note of laughter that rises and is lost in the sky like the flight of his soul back into the womb of Infinity.*) Fear not, Caligula ! There is no death !

CALIGULA (*lifts his head at the first sound and rises with the laughter to his feet, until, as it is finally lost, he is on tip-toes, his arms straining upward to the sky, a tender, childish laughter of love on his lips*). I laugh, Lazarus ! I laugh with you ! (*Then grief-stricken.*) Lazarus ! (*He hides his face in his hands, weeping.*) No more ! (*Then beats his head with his fists.*) I will remember ! I will ! (*Then suddenly, with a return to grotesqueness—harshly.*) All the same, I killed him and I proved there is death ! (*Immediately overcome by remorse, grovelling and beating himself.*) Fool ! Madman ! Forgive me, Lazarus ! Men forget !

CURTAIN

STRANGE INTERLUDE

Characters

CHARLES MARSDEN
PROFESSOR HENRY LEEDS
NINA LEEDS, *his daughter*
EDMUND DARRELL
SAM EVANS
MRS. AMOS EVANS, *Sam's mother*
GORDON EVANS
MADELINE ARNOLD

Scenes

FIRST PART

ACT ONE Library, the Leeds' home in a small university town of New England. An afternoon in late summer.

ACT TWO The same. Fall of the following year. Night.

ACT THREE Dining-room of the Evans' homestead in northern New York state. Late spring of the next year. Morning.

ACT FOUR The same as Acts One and Two. Fall of the same year. Evening.

ACT FIVE Sitting-room of small house Evans has rented in a seashore suburb near New York. The following April. Morning.

SECOND PART

ACT SIX The same. A little over a year later. Evening.

ACT SEVEN Sitting-room of the Evans' apartment on Park Avenue. Nearly eleven years later. Early afternoon.

ACT EIGHT Section of afterdeck of the Evans' cruiser anchored near the finish line at Poughkeepsie. Ten years later. Afternoon.

ACT NINE A terrace on the Evans' estate on Long Island. Several months later. Late afternoon.

FIRST PART, ACT ONE

SCENE: *The library of Professor Leeds' home in a small university town in New England. This room is at the front part of his house with windows opening on the strip of lawn between the house and the quiet residential street. It is a small room with a low ceiling. The furniture has been selected with a love for old New England pieces. The walls are lined almost to the ceiling with glassed-in bookshelves. These are packed with books, principally editions, many of them old and rare, of the ancient classics in the original Greek and Latin, of the later classics in French and German and Italian, of all the English authors who wrote while* s *was still like an* ſ *and a few since then, the most modern probably being Thackeray. The atmosphere of the room is that of a cosy, cultured retreat, sedulously built as a sanctuary where, secure with the culture of the past at his back, a fugitive from reality can view the present safely from a distance, as a superior with condescending disdain, pity, and even amusement.*

There is a fair-sized table, a heavy arm-chair, a rocker, and an old bench made comfortable with cushions. The table, with the Professor's arm-chair at its left, is arranged toward the left of the room, the rocker is at centre, the bench at right.

There is one entrance, a door in the right wall, rear.

It is late afternoon of a day in August. Sunshine, cooled and dimmed in the shade of trees, fills the room with a soothing light.

The sound of a maid's voice – a middle-aged woman – explaining familiarly but respectfully from the right, and Marsden enters. He is a tall thin man of thirty-five, meticulously well dressed in tweeds of distinctly English tailoring, his appearance that of an Anglicized New England gentleman. His face is too long for its width, his nose is high and narrow, his forehead broad, his mild blue eyes those of a dreamy self-analyst, his thin lips ironical and a bit sad. There is an indefinable feminine quality about him, but it is nothing apparent in either appearance or act. His manner is cool and poised. He speaks with a careful ease as one who listens to his own conversation. He has long fragile hands, and the stooping shoulders of a man weak muscularly, who has never liked athletics and has always been regarded as of delicate constitution. The main point about his personality is a quiet charm, a quality of appealing, inquisitive friendliness, always willing to listen, eager to sympathize, to like and to be liked.

MARSDEN

(*Standing just inside the door, his tall, stooped figure leaning back against the books – nodding back at the maid and smiling kindly.*)

I'll wait in here, Mary.

(*His eyes follow her for a second, then return to gaze around the room slowly with an appreciative relish for the familiar significance of the books. He smiles affectionately and his amused voice recites the words with a rhetorical resonance.*)

Sanctum Sanctorum!

(*His voice takes on a monotonous musing quality, his eyes stare idly at his drifting thoughts.*)

How perfectly the Professor's unique haven! . . .

(*He smiles.*)

Primly classical . . . when New Englander meets Greek! . . .

(*Looking at the books now.*)

He hasn't added one book in years . . . how old was I when I first came here? . . . six . . . with my father . . . father . . . how dim his face has grown! . . . he wanted to speak to me just before he died . . . the hospital . . . smell of iodoform in the cool halls . . . hot summer . . . I bent down . . . his voice had withdrawn so far away . . . I couldn't understand him . . . what son can ever understand? . . . always too near, too soon, too distant, or too late! . . .

(*His face has become sad with a memory of the bewildered suffering of the adolescent boy he had been at the time of his father's death. Then he shakes his head, flinging off his thoughts, and makes himself walk about the room.*)

What memories on such a smiling afternoon! . . . this pleasant old town after three months . . . I won't go to Europe again . . . couldn't write a line there . . . how answer the fierce question of all those dead and maimed? . . . too big a job for me! . . .

(*He sighs – then self-mockingly.*)

But back here . . . it is the interlude that gently questions . . . in this town dozing . . . decorous bodies moving with circumspection through the afternoons . . . their habits affectionately chronicled . . . an excuse for weaving amusing words . . . my novels . . . not of cosmic importance, hardly . . .

(*Then self-reassuringly.*)

but there is a public to cherish them, evidently . . . and I can write! . . . more than one can say of these modern sex-yahoos! . . . I must start work to-morrow . . . I'd like to use the Professor in a novel some time . . . and his wife . . . seems impossible she's been dead six years . . . so aggressively his wife! . . . poor Professor! now it's Nina who bosses him . . . but that's different . . . she has bossed me, too, ever since she was a baby . . . she's a woman now . . . known love and death . . . Gordon brought down in flames . . . two days before the armistice . . . what fiendish irony! . . . his wonderful athlete's body . . . her lover . . charred bones in a cage of twisted steel . . . no wonder she broke down . . . Mother said she's become quite queer lately . . . Mother seemed jealous of my concern . . . why have I never fallen in love with Nina? . . . could I? . . . that way . . . used to dance her on my knee . . . sit her on my lap . . . even now she'd never think anything about it . . . but sometimes the scent of her hair and skin . . . like a dreamy drug . . . dreamy! . . . there's the rub! . . . all dreams with me! . . . my sex life among the phantoms! . . .

(*He grins torturedly.*)

Why? . . . oh, this digging in gets nowhere . . . to the devil with sex! . . . our impotent pose of to-day to beat the loud drum on fornication! . . . boasters . . . eunuchs parading with the phallus! . . . giving themselves away . . . whom do they fool? . . . not even themselves! . . .

(*His face suddenly full of an intense pain and disgust.*)

Ugh! . . . always that memory! . . . why can't I ever forget? . . . as sickeningly clear as if it were yesterday . . . prep school . . . Easter vacation . . . Fatty Boggs and Jack Frazer . . . that house of cheap vice . . . one dollar! . . . why did I go? . . . Jack, the dead game sport . . . how I admired him! . . . afraid of his taunts . . . he pointed to the Italian girl . . . "Take her!" . . . daring me . . . I went . . . miserably frightened . . . what a pig she was! . . . pretty vicious face under caked powder and rouge . . . surly and contemptuous . . . lumpy body . . . short legs and thick ankles . . . slums of Naples . . . "What you gawkin' about? Git a move on, kid" . . . kid! . . . I *was* only a kid! . . . sixteen . . . test of manhood . . . ashamed to face Jack again unless . . . fool! . . . I might have lied to him! . . . but I honestly thought that wench would feel humiliated if I . . . oh, stupid kid! . . . back at the hotel I waited till they were asleep . . . then sobbed . . . thinking of Mother . . . feeling I had defiled her . . . and myself . . . for ever! . . .

(*Mocking bitterly.*)

"Nothing half so sweet in life as love's young dream," what? . . .

(*He gets to his feet impatiently.*)

Why does my mind always have to dwell on that? . . . too silly . . . no importance really . . . an incident such as any boy of my age . . .

(*He hears someone coming quickly from the right and*

turns expectantly. Professor Leeds enters, a pleased relieved expression fighting the flurried worry on his face. He is a small, slender man of fifty-five, his hair grey, the top of his head bald. His face, prepossessing in spite of its too-small, over-refined features, is that of a retiring, studious nature. He has intelligent eyes and a smile that can be ironical. Temperamentally timid, his defence is an assumption of his complacent, superior manner of the classroom toward the world at large. This defence is strengthened by a natural tendency toward a prim provincialism where practical present-day considerations are concerned (though he is most liberal – even radical – in his tolerant understanding of the manners and morals of Greece and Imperial Rome!) This classroom poise of his, however, he cannot quite carry off outside the classroom. There is an unconvincing quality about it that leaves his larger audience – and particularly the Professor himself – subtly embarrassed. As Marsden is one of his old students, whom, in addition, he has known from childhood, he is perfectly at ease with him.)

MARSDEN

(Holding out his hand – with unmistakable liking.)

Here I am again, Professor!

PROFESSOR LEEDS

(Shaking his hand and patting him on the back – with genuine affection.)

So glad to see you, Charlie! A surprise, too! We didn't expect you back so soon!

(He sits in his chair on the left of the table while Marsden sits in the rocker.)

(Looking away from Marsden a moment, his face now full of selfish relief as he thinks.)

Fortunate, his coming back . . . always calming influence on Nina . .

MARSDEN

And I never dreamed of returning so soon. But Europe, Professor, is the big casualty they were afraid to set down on the list.

PROFESSOR LEEDS

(His face clouding.)

Yes, I suppose you found everything completely changed since before the war.

(He thinks resentfully.)

The war . . . Gordon! . . .

MARSDEN

Europe has "gone west" –

(He smiles whimsically.)

to America, let's hope!

(Then frowningly.)

I couldn't stand it. There were millions sitting up with the corpse already, who had a family right to be there –

(Then matter-of-factly.)

I was wasting my time, too. I couldn't write a line.

(Then gaily.)

But where's Nina? I must see Nina!

PROFESSOR LEEDS

She'll be right in. She said she wanted to finish thinking something out – You'll find Nina changed, Charlie, greatly changed!

(He sighs – thinking with a trace of guilty alarm.)

The first thing she said at breakfast . . . "I dreamed of Gordon" . . . as if she wanted to taunt me! . . . how absurd! . . . her eyes positively glared! . . .

(Suddenly blurting out resentfully.)

She dreams about Gordon.

MARSDEN

(Looking at him with amused surprise.)

Well, I'd hardly call that a change, would you?

PROFESSOR LEEDS

(Thinking, oblivious to this remark.)

But I must constantly bear in mind that she's not herself . . that she's a sick girl . . .

MARSDEN

(Thinking.)

The morning news of Gordon's death came . . . her face like grey putty . . . beauty gone . . . no face can afford intense grief . . . it's only later when sorrow . . .

(With concern.)

Just what do you mean by changed, Professor? Before I left she seemed to be coming out of that horrible numbed calm.

PROFESSOR LEEDS

(Slowly and carefully.)

Yes, she has played a lot of golf and tennis this summer, motored around with her friends, and even danced a good deal. And she eats with a ravenous appetite.

(Thinking frightenedly.)

Breakfast . . . "dreamed of Gordon" . . . what a look of hate for me in her eyes! . . .

MARSDEN

But that sounds splendid! When I left she wouldn't see anyone or go anywhere.

(Thinking pityingly.)

Wandering from room to room . . . her thin body and

pale lost face . . . gutted, love-abandoned eyes! . . .

PROFESSOR LEEDS

Well, now she's gone to the opposite extreme! Sees everyone – bores, fools – as if she'd lost all discrimination or wish to discriminate. And she talks interminably, Charlie – intentional nonsense, one would say! Refuses to be serious! Jeers at everything!

MARSDEN

(*Consolingly.*)

Oh, that's all undoubtedly part of the effort she's making to forget.

PROFESSOR LEEDS

(*Absent-mindedly.*)

Yes.

(*Arguing with himself.*)

Shall I tell him? . . . no . . . it might sound silly . . . but it's terrible to be so alone in this . . . if Nina's mother had lived . . . my wife . . . dead! . . . and for a time I actually felt released! . . . wife! . . . helpmate! . . . now I need help! . . . no use! . . . she's gone! . . .

MARSDEN

(*Watching him – thinking with a condescending affection.*)

Good little man . . . he looks worried . . . always fussing about something . . . he must get on Nina's nerves. . . .

(*Reassuringly.*)

No girl could forget Gordon in a hurry, especially after the shock of his tragic death.

PROFESSOR LEEDS

(*Irritably.*)

I realize that.

(*Thinking resentfully.*)

Gordon . . . always Gordon with everyone! . .

MARSDEN

By the way, I located the spot near Sedan where Gordon's machine fell. Nina asked me to, you know.

PROFESSOR LEEDS

(*Irritated – expostulatingly.*)

For heaven's sake, don't remind her! Give her a chance to forget if you want to see her well again. After all, Charlie, life must be lived and Nina can't live with a corpse for ever!

(*Trying to control his irritation and talk in an objective tone.*)

You see, I'm trying to see things through clearly and unsentimentally. If you'll remember, I was as broken up as anyone over Gordon's death. I'd become so reconciled to Nina's love for him – although, as you know, I was opposed at first, and for fair reasons, I think, for the boy, for all his good looks and prowess in sport and his courses, really came of common people and had no money of his own except as he made a career for himself.

MARSDEN

(*A trifle defensively.*)

I'm sure he would have had a brilliant career.

PROFESSOR LEEDS

(*Impatiently.*)

No doubt. Although you must acknowledge, Charlie, that college heroes rarely shine brilliantly in after life. Unfortunately, the tendency to spoil them in the university is a poor training –

MARSDEN

But Gordon was absolutely unspoiled, I should say.

PROFESSOR LEEDS

(*Heatedly.*)

Don't misunderstand me, Charlie! I'd be the first to acknowledge –

(*A bit pathetically.*)

It isn't Gordon, Charlie. It's his memory, his ghost, you might call it, haunting Nina, whose influence I have come to dread because of the terrible change in her attitude toward me.

(*His face twitches as if he were on the verge of tears – he thinks desperately.*)

I've got to tell him . . . he will see that I acted for the best . . . that I was justified. . . .

(*He hesitates – then blurts out.*)

It may sound incredible, but Nina has begun to act as if she hated me!

MARSDEN

(*Startled.*)

Oh, come now!

PROFESSOR LEEDS

(*Insistently.*)

Absolutely! I haven't wanted to admit it. I've refused to believe it, until it's become too appallingly obvious in her whole attitude toward me!

(*His voice trembles.*)

MARSDEN

(*Moved – expostulating.*)

Oh, now you're becoming morbid! Why, Nina has always idolized you! What possible reason – ?

PROFESSOR LEEDS

(*Quickly.*)

I can answer that, I think. She has a reason. But why she should blame me when she must know I acted for the best – You probably don't know, but just before he sailed for the front Gordon wanted their marriage to take place, and Nina consented. In fact, from the insinuations she lets drop now, she must have been most eager, but at the time – However, I felt it was ill-advised and I took Gordon aside and pointed out to him that such a precipitate marriage would be unfair to Nina, and scarcely honourable on his part.

MARSDEN

(*Staring at him wonderingly.*)

You said that to Gordon?

(*Thinking cynically.*)

A shrewd move! . . . Gordon's proud spot, fairness and honour! . . . but was it honourable of you? . . .

PROFESSOR LEEDS

(*With a touch of asperity.*)

Yes, I said it, and I gave him my reason. There *was* the possibility he might be killed, in the flying service rather more than a possibility, which, needless to say, I did not point out, but which Gordon undoubtedly realized, poor boy! If he were killed, he would be leaving Nina a widow, perhaps with a baby, with no resources, since he was penniless, except what pension she might get from the Government; and all this while she was still at an age when a girl, especially one of Nina's charm and beauty, should have all of life before her. Decidedly, I told him, in justice to Nina, they must wait until he had come back and begun to establish his position in the world. That was the square thing. And Gordon was quick to agree with me!

MARSDEN

(*Thinking.*)

The square thing! . . . but we must all be crooks where happiness is concerned! . . . steal or starve! . . .

(*Then rather ironically.*)

And so Gordon told Nina he'd suddenly realized it wouldn't be fair to her. But I gather he didn't tell her it was your scruple originally?

PROFESSOR LEEDS

No, I asked him to keep what I said strictly confidential.

MARSDEN

(*Thinking ironically.*)

Trusted to his honour again! . . . old fox! . . . poor Gordon! . . .

But Nina suspects now that you – ?

PROFESSOR LEEDS

(*Startled.*)

Yes. That's exactly it. She knows in some queer way. And she acts toward me exactly as if she thought I had deliberately destroyed her happiness, that I had hoped for Gordon's death and been secretly overjoyed when the news came!

(*His voice is shaking with emotion.*)

And there you have it, Charlie – the whole absurd mess!

(*Thinking with a strident accusation.*)

And it's true, you contemptible . . . !

(*Then miserably defending himself.*)

No! . . . I acted unselfishly . . . for her sake! . . .

MARSDEN

(*Wonderingly.*)

You don't mean to tell me she has accused you of all this?

PROFESSOR LEEDS

Oh, no, Charlie! Only by hints – looks – innuendos. She knows she has no real grounds, but in the present state of her mind the real and the unreal become confused –

MARSDEN

(*Thinking cynically.*)

As always in all minds . . . or how could men live? . . .

(*Soothingly.*)

That's just what you ought to bear in your mind – the state of hers – and not get so worked up over what I should say is a combination of imagination on both your parts.

(*He gets to his feet as he hears voices from the right.*)

Buck up! This must be Nina coming.

(*The Professor gets to his feet, hastily composing his features into his bland, cultured expression.*)

(*Thinking self-mockingly, but a bit worried about himself.*)

My heart pounding! . . . seeing Nina again! . . . how sentimental . . . how she'd laugh if she knew! . . . and quite rightly . . . absurd for me to react as if I loved . . . that way . . . her dear old Charlie . . . ha! . . .

(*He smiles with bitter self-mockery.*)

PROFESSOR LEEDS

(*Thinking worriedly.*)

I hope she won't make a scene . . . she's seemed on the verge all day . . . thank God, Charlie's like one of the family . . . but what a life for me! . . . with the opening of the new term only a few weeks off! . . . I can't do it . . . I'll have to call in a nerve specialist . . . but the last one did her no good . . . his outrageous fee . . . he can take it to court . . . I absolutely refuse . . . but if he should bring suit? . . . what a scandal . . . no, I'll have to pay . . . somehow . . . borrow . . . he has me in a corner, the robber! . . .

NINA

(Enters and stands just inside the doorway looking directly at her father with defiant eyes, her face set in an expression of stubborn resolve. She is twenty, tall, with broad square shoulders, slim strong hips and long beautifully developed legs – a fine athletic girl of the swimmer, tennis player, golfer type. Her straw-blond hair, framing her sunburned face, is bobbed. Her face is striking, handsome rather than pretty, the bone structure prominent, the forehead high, the lips of her rather large mouth clearly modelled above the firm jaw. Her eyes are beautiful and bewildering, extraordinarily large and a deep greenish blue. Since Gordon's death they have a quality of continually shuddering before some terrible enigma, of being wounded to their depths and made defiant and resentful by their pain. Her whole manner, the charged atmosphere she gives off, is totally at variance with her healthy outdoor physique. It is strained, nerve-racked, hectic, a terrible tension of will alone maintaining self-possession. She is dressed in smart sport clothes. Too preoccupied with her resolve to remember or see Marsden, she speaks directly to her father in a voice tensely cold and calm.)

I have made up my mind, Father.

PROFESSOR LEEDS

(Thinking distractedly.)

What does she mean? . . . oh, God help me! . . .

(Flustered – hastily.)

Don't you see Charlie, Nina?

MARSDEN

(Troubled – thinking.)

She has changed . . . what has happened? . . .

(He comes forward toward her – a bit embarrassed, but affectionately using his pet name for her.)

Hallo, Nina Cara Nina! Are you trying to cut me dead, young lady?

NINA

(Turning her eyes to Marsden, holding out her hand for him to shake, in her cool, preoccupied voice.)

Hallo, Charlie!

(Her eyes immediately return to her father.)

Listen, Father!

MARSDEN

(Standing near her, concealing his chagrin.)

That hurts! . . . I mean nothing! . . . but she's a sick girl . . . I must make allowance . . .

PROFESSOR LEEDS

(Thinking distractedly.)

That look in her eyes! . . . hate! . . .

(With a silly giggle.)

Really, Nina, you're absolutely rude! What has Charlie done?

NINA

(In her cool tone.)

Why, nothing. Nothing at all.

(She goes to him with a detached, friendly manner.)

Did I seem rude, Charlie? I didn't mean to be.

(She kisses him with a cool, friendly smile.)

Welcome home.

(Thinking wearily.)

What has Charlie done? . . . nothing . . . and never will . . . Charlie sits beside the fierce river, immaculately timid, cool and clothed, watching the burning, frozen naked swimmers drown at last. . . .

MARSDEN

(Thinking torturedly.)

Cold lips . . . the kiss of contempt! . . . for dear old Charlie! . . .

(Forcing a good-natured laugh.)

Rude? Not a bit!

(Banteringly.)

As I've often reminded you, what can I expect when the first word you ever spoke in this world was an insult to me. "Dog" you said, looking right at me – at the age of one!

(He laughs. The Professor laughs nervously. Nina smiles perfunctorily.)

NINA

(Thinking wearily.)

The fathers laugh at little daughter Nina . . . I must get away! . . . nice Charlie doggy . . . faithful . . . fetch and carry . . . bark softly in books at the deep night. . . .

PROFESSOR LEEDS

(Thinking.)

What is she thinking? . . . I can't stand living like this! . . .

(Giggle gone to a twitching grin.)

You are a cool one, Nina! You'd think you'd just seen Charlie yesterday!

NINA

(*Slowly – coolly and reflectively.*)

Well, the war is over. Coming back safe from Europe isn't such an unusual feat now, is it?

MARSDEN

(*Thinking bitterly.*)

A taunt . . . I didn't fight . . . physically unfit . . . not like Gordon . . . Gordon in flames . . . how she must resent my living! . . . thinking of me, scribbling in Press Bureau . . . louder and louder lies . . . drown the guns and the screams . . . deafen the world with lies . . . hired choir of liars! . . .

(*Forcing a joking tone.*)

Little you know the deadly risks I ran, Nina! If you'd eaten some of the food they gave me on my renovated transport, you'd shower me with congratulations!

(*The Professor forces a snicker.*)

NINA

(*Coolly.*)

Well, you're here, and that's that.

(*Then suddenly expanding in a sweet, genuinely affectionate smile.*)

And I *am* glad, Charlie, always glad you're here! You know that.

MARSDEN

(*Delighted and embarrassed.*)

I hope so, Nina!

NINA

(*Turning on her father – determinedly.*)

I must finish what I started to say, Father. I've thought it all out and decided that I simply must get away from here at once – or go crazy! And I'm going on the nine-forty tonight.

(*She turns to Marsden with a quick smile.*)

You'll have to help me pack, Charlie!

(*Thinking with weary relief.*)

Now that's said . . . I'm going . . . never come back . . . oh, how I loathe this room! . . .

MARSDEN

(*Thinking with alarm.*)

What's this? . . . going? . . . going to whom? . . .

PROFESSOR LEEDS

(*Thinking – terrified.*)

Going? . . . never come back to me? . . . no! . . .

(*Desperately putting on his prim severe manner toward an unruly pupil.*)

This is rather a sudden decision, isn't it? You haven't mentioned before that you were considering – in fact, you've led me to believe that you were quite contented here – that is, of course I mean for the time being, and I really think –

MARSDEN

(*Looking at Nina – thinking with alarm.*)

Going away to whom? . . .

(*Then watching the Professor with a pitying shudder.*)

He's on the wrong tack with his professor's manner . . . her eyes seeing cruelly through him . . . with what terrible recognition! . . . God, never bless me with children! . . .

NINA

(*Thinking with weary scorn.*)

The Professor of Dead Languages is talking again . . . a dead man lectures on the past of living . . . since I was born I have been in his class, loving-attentive, pupil-daughter Nina . . my ears numb with spiritless messages from the dead . . . dead words droning on . . . listening because he is my cultured father . . . a little more inclined to deafness than the rest (let me be just) because he is my father . . . father? . . . what is father? . . .

PROFESSOR LEEDS

(*Thinking – terrified.*)

I must talk her out of it! . . . find the right words! . . . oh, I know she won't hear me! . . . oh, wife, why did you die, you would have talked to her, she would have listened to you! . . .

(*Continuing in his professor's superior manner.*)

– and I really think, in justice to yourself above all, you ought to consider this step with great care before you definitely commit yourself. First and foremost, there is your health to be taken into consideration. You've been very ill, Nina, how perilously so perhaps you're not completely aware, but I assure you, and Charlie can corroborate my statement, that six months ago the doctors thought it might be years before – and yet, by staying home and resting and finding healthy outdoor recreation among your old friends, and keeping your mind occupied with the routine of managing the household –

(*He forces a prim playful smile.*)

and managing me, I might add! – you have wonderfully improved, and I think it most ill-advised in the hottest part of August, while you're really still a convalescent –

NINA

(*Thinking.*)

Talking! . . . his voice like a fatiguing dying tune droned on a beggar's organ . . . his words arising from the tomb of a soul in puffs of ashes . . .

(*Torturedly.*)

Ashes! . . . oh, Gordon, my dear one! . . . oh, lips on my lips, oh, strong arms around me, oh, spirit so brave and generous and gay! . . . ashes dissolving into mud! . . . mud and ashes! . . . that's all! . . . gone! . . . gone for ever from me! . . .

PROFESSOR LEEDS

(Thinking angrily.)

Her eyes . . . I know that look . . . tender, loving . . . not for me . . . damn Gordon! . . . I'm glad he's dead! . . .

(A touch of asperity in his voice.)

And at a couple of hours' notice to leave everything in the air, as it were –

(Then judicially.)

No, Nina, frankly, I can't see it. You know I'd gladly consent to anything in the world to benefit you, but – surely, you can't have reflected!

NINA

(Thinking torturedly.)

Gordon darling, I must go away where I can think of you in silence! . . .

(She turns on her father, her voice trembling with the effort to keep it in control – icily.)

It's no use talking, Father. I *have* reflected and I am going!

PROFESSOR LEEDS

(With asperity.)

But I tell you it's quite impossible! I don't like to bring up the money consideration, but I couldn't possibly afford – And how will you support yourself, if I may ask? Two years in the University, I am sorry to say, won't be much use to you when applying for a job. And even if you had completely recovered from your nervous breakdown, which it's obvious to anyone you haven't, then I most decidedly think you should finish out your science course and take your degree before you attempt –

(Thinking desperately.)

No use! . . . she doesn't hear . . . thinking of Gordon . . . she'll defy me . . .

NINA

(Thinking desperately.)

I must keep calm . . . I mustn't let go or I'll tell him everything . . . and I mustn't tell him . . . he's my father . . .

(With the same cold calculating finality.)

I've already had six months' training for a nurse. I will finish my training. There's a doctor I know at a sanatorium for crippled soldiers – a friend of Gordon's. I wrote to him and he answered that he'll gladly arrange it.

PROFESSOR LEEDS

(Thinking furiously.)

Gordon's friend . . . Gordon again! . . .

(Severely.)

You seriously mean to tell me you, in your condition, want to nurse in a soldiers' hospital! Absurd!

MARSDEN

(Thinking with indignant revulsion.)

Quite right, Professor! . . . her beauty . . . all those men . . . in their beds . . . it's too revolting! . . .

(With a persuasive quizzing tone.)

Yes, I must say I can't see you as a peace-time Florence Nightingale, Nina!

NINA

(Coolly, struggling to keep control, ignoring these remarks.)

So you see, Father, I've thought of everything and there's not the slightest reason to worry about me. And I've been teaching Mary how to take care of you. So you won't need me at all. You can go along as if nothing had happened – and really, nothing will have happened that hasn't already happened.

PROFESSOR LEEDS

Why, even the manner in which you address me – the tone you take – proves conclusively that you're not yourself!

NINA

(Her voice becoming a bit uncanny, her thoughts breaking through.)

No, I'm not myself yet. That's just it. Not all myself. But I've been becoming myself. And I must finish!

PROFESSOR LEEDS

(With angry significance – to Marsden.)

You hear her, Charlie? She's a sick girl!

NINA

(Slowly and strangely.)

I'm not sick. I'm too well. But they are sick and I must give my health to help them to live on, and to live on myself.

(With a sudden intensity in her tone.)

I must pay for my cowardly treachery to Gordon! You should understand this, Father, you who –

(She swallows hard, catching her breath.)

(Thinking desperately.)

I'm beginning to tell him! . . . I mustn't! . . . he's my father! . . .

PROFESSOR LEEDS

(In a panic of guilty fear, but defiantly.)

What do you mean? I am afraid you're not responsible for what you're saying.

NINA

(*Again with the strange intensity.*)

I must pay! It's my plain duty! Gordon is dead! What use is my life to me or anyone? But I must make it of use – by giving it!

(*Fiercely.*)

I must learn to give myself, do you hear – give and give until I can make that gift of myself for a man's happiness without scruple, without fear, without joy except in his joy! When I've accomplished this I'll have found myself, I'll know how to begin living my own life again!

(*Appealing to them with a desperate impatience.*)

Don't you see? In the name of the commonest decency and honour, I owe it to Gordon!

PROFESSOR LEEDS

(*Sharply.*)

No, I can't see – nor anyone else!

(*Thinking savagely.*)

I hope Gordon is in hell! . . .

MARSDEN

(*Thinking.*)

Give herself? . . . can she mean her body? . . . beautiful body . . . to cripples? . . . for Gordon's sake? . . . damn Gordon! . . .

(*Coldly.*)

What do you mean, you owe it to Gordon, Nina?

PROFESSOR LEEDS

(*Bitterly.*)

Yes, how ridiculous! It seems to me when you gave him your love, he got more than he could ever have hoped –

NINA

(*With fierce self-contempt.*)

I gave him? What did I give him? It's what I didn't give! That last night before he sailed – in his arms until my body ached – kisses until my lips were numb – knowing all that night – something in me knowing he would die, that he would never kiss me again – knowing this so surely yet with my cowardly brain lying, no, he'll come back and marry you, you'll be happy ever after and feel his children at your breasts looking up with eyes so much like his, possessing eyes so happy in possessing you!

(*Then violently.*)

But Gordon never possessed me! I'm still Gordon's silly virgin! And Gordon is muddy ashes! And I've lost my happiness for ever! All that last night I knew he wanted me. I knew it was only the honourable code-bound Gordon, who kept commanding from his brain, no, you mustn't, you must respect her, you must wait till you have a marriage licence!

(*She gives a mocking laugh.*)

PROFESSOR LEEDS

(*Shocked.*)

Nina! This is really going too far!

MARSDEN

(*With a superior sneer – repelledly.*)

Oh, come now, Nina! You've been reading books. Those don't sound like your thoughts.

NINA

(*Without looking at him, her eyes on her father's – intensely.*)

Gordon wanted me! I wanted Gordon! I should have made him take me! I knew he would die and I would have no children, that there would be no big Gordon or little Gordon left to me, that happiness was calling me, never to call again if I refused! And yet I did refuse! I didn't make him take me! I lost him for ever! And now I am lonely and not pregnant with anything at all, but – but loathing!

(*She hurls this last at her father – fiercely.*)

Why did I refuse? What was that cowardly something in me that cried, no, you mustn't, what would your father say?

PROFESSOR LEEDS

(*Thinking – furiously.*)

What an animal! . . . and my daughter! . . . she doesn't get it from me! . . . was her mother like that? . . .

(*Distractedly.*)

Nina! I really can't listen!

NINA

(*Savagely.*)

And that's exactly what my father did say! Wait, he told Gordon! Wait for Nina till the war's over, and you've got a good job and can afford a marriage licence!

PROFESSOR LEEDS

(*Crumbling pitifully.*)

Nina! I – !

MARSDEN

(*Flurriedly – going to him.*)

Don't take her seriously, Professor!

(*Thinking with nervous repulsion.*)

Nina has changed . . . all flesh now . . . lust . . . who would dream she was so sensual? . . . I wish I were out of this! . . . I wish I hadn't come here to-day! . . .

NINA

(*Coldly and deliberately.*)

Don't lie any more, Father! To-day I've made up my mind to face things. I know now why Gordon suddenly dropped all idea of marriage before he left, how unfair to me he suddenly decided it would be! Unfair to me! Oh, that's humorous! To think I might have had happiness, Gordon, and now Gordon's child . . .

(*Then directly accusing him.*)

You told him it'd be unfair, you put him on his honour, didn't you?

PROFESSOR LEEDS

(*Collecting himself – woodenly.*)

Yes. I did it for your sake, Nina.

NINA

(*In the same voice as before.*)

It's too late for lies!

PROFESSOR LEEDS

(*Woodenly.*)

Let us say then that I *persuaded* myself it was for your sake. That may be true. You are young. You think one can live with truth. Very well. It is also true I was jealous of Gordon. I was alone and I wanted to keep your love. I hated him as one hates a thief one may not accuse nor punish. I did my best to prevent your marriage. I was glad when he died. There! Is that what you wish me to say?

NINA

Yes. Now I begin to forget I've hated you. You were braver than I, at least.

PROFESSOR LEEDS

I wanted to live comforted by your love until the end. In short, I am a man who happens to be your father.

(*He hides his face in his hands and weeps softly.*)

Forgive that man!

MARSDEN

(*Thinking timidly.*)

In short, forgive us our possessing as we forgive those who possessed before us . . . Mother must be wondering what keeps me so long . . . it's time for tea . . . I must go home . . .

NINA

(*Sadly.*)

Oh, I forgive you. But do you understand now that I must somehow find a way to give myself to Gordon still, that I must pay my debt and learn to forgive myself?

PROFESSOR LEEDS

Yes.

NINA

Mary will look after you.

PROFESSOR LEEDS

Mary will do very well, I'm sure.

MARSDEN

(*Thinking.*)

Nina has changed . . . this is no place for me . . . Mother is waiting tea. . . .

(*Then venturing on an uncertain tone of pleasantry.*)

Quite so, you two. But isn't this all nonsense? Nina will be back with us in a month, Professor, what with the depressing heat and humidity, and the more depressing halt and the lame!

PROFESSOR LEEDS

(*Sharply.*)

She must stay away until she gets well. This time I do speak for her sake.

NINA

I'll take the nine-forty.

(*Turning to Marsden – with a sudden girlishness.*)

Come on upstairs, Charlie, and help me pack!

(*She grabs him by the hand and starts to pull him away.*)

MARSDEN

(*Shrugging his shoulders – confusedly.*)

Well – I don't understand this!

NINA

(*With a strange smile.*)

But some day I'll read it all in one of your books, Charlie; and it'll be so simple and easy to understand that I won't be able to recognize it, Charlie, let alone understand it!

(*She laughs teasingly.*)

Dear old Charlie!

MARSDEN

(*Thinking in agony.*)

God damn in hell . . . dear old Charlie! . . .

(*Then with a genial grin.*)

I'll have to propose, Nina, if you continue to be my severest critic! I'm a stickler for these little literary conventions, you know!

NINA

All right. Propose while we pack!

(*She leads him off, right.*)

PROFESSOR LEEDS

(*Blows his nose, wipes his eyes, sighs, clears his throat, squares his shoulders, pulls his coat down in front, sets his tie straight, and starts to take a brisk turn about the room. His face is washed blandly clean of all emotion.*)

Three weeks now . . . new term . . . I shall have to be looking over my notes. . . .

(*He looks out of window, front.*)

Grass parched in the middle . . . Tom forgotten the sprinkler . . . careless . . . ah, there goes Mr. Davis of the bank . . . bank . . . my salary will go farther now . . . books I really need . . . all bosh two can live as cheaply as one . . . there are worse things than being a trained nurse . . . good background of discipline . . . she needs it . . . she may meet rich fellow there . . . mature . . . only students here for her . . . and their fathers never approve if they have anything. . . .

(*He sits down with a forced sigh of peace.*)

I am glad we had it out . . . his ghost will be gone now . . . no more Gordon, Gordon, Gordon, love and praise and tears, all for Gordon! . . . Mary will do very well by me . . . I shall have more leisure and peace of mind . . . and Nina will come back home . . . when she is well again . . . the old Nina! . . . my little Nina! . . . she knows and she forgave me . . . she said so . . . said! . . . but could she really? . . . don't you imagine? . . . deep in her heart? . . . she still must hate? . . . oh, God! . . . I feel cold! . . . alone! . . . this home is abandoned! . . . the house is empty and full of death! . . . there is a pain about my heart! . . .

(*He calls hoarsely, getting to his feet.*)

Nina!

NINA'S VOICE

(*Her voice, fresh and girlish, calls from upstairs.*)

Yes, Father. Do you want me?

PROFESSOR LEEDS

(*Struggling with himself – goes to door and calls with affectionate blandness.*)

No. Never mind. Just wanted to remind you to call for a taxi in good time.

NINA'S VOICE

I won't forget.

PROFESSOR LEEDS

(*Looks at his watch.*)

Five-thirty just . . . nine-forty, the train . . . then . . . Nina no more! . . . four hours more . . . she'll be packing . . . then good-bye . . . a kiss . . . nothing more ever to say to each other . . . and I'll die in here some day . . . alone . . . gasp, cry out for help . . . the president will speak at the funeral . . . Nina will be here again . . . Nina in black . . . too late! . . .

(*He calls hoarsely.*)

Nina!

(*There is no answer.*)

In other room . . . doesn't hear . . . just as well . . .

(*He turns to the bookcase and pulls out the first volume his hands come on and opens it at random and begins to read aloud sonorously like a child whistling to keep up his courage in the dark.*)

"Stetit unus in arcem
Erectus capitis victorque ad sidera mittit
Sidereos oculos propiusque adspectat Olympum
Inquiritque Iovem;" . . .

Curtain

ACT TWO

SCENE: *The same as Scene One, Professor Leeds' study. It is about nine o'clock of a night in early fall, over a year later. The appearance of the room is unchanged except that all the shades, of the colour of pale flesh, are drawn down, giving the windows a suggestion of lifeless closed eyes and making the room seem more withdrawn from life than before. The reading lamp on the table is lit. Everything on the table, papers, pencils, pens, etc., is arranged in meticulous order.*

Marsden is seated on the chair at centre. He is dressed carefully in an English made suit of blue serge so dark as to seem black, which, combined with the gloomy brooding expression of his face, strongly suggests one in mourning. His tall, thin body sags wearily in the chair, his head is sunk forward, the chin almost touching his chest, his eyes stare sadly at nothing.

MARSDEN

(*His thoughts at ebb, without emphasis, sluggish and melancholy.*)

Prophetic Professor! . . . I remember he once said . . . shortly after Nina went away . . . "someday, in here, . . . you'll find me" . . . did he foresee? . . . no . . . everything in life is so contemptuously accidental! . . . God's sneer at our self-importance! . . .

(*Smiling grimly.*)

Poor Professor! he was horribly lonely . . . tried to hide it . . . always telling you how beneficial the training at the hospital would be for her . . . poor old chap! . . .

(*His voice grows husky and uncertain – he controls it – straightens himself.*)

What time is it? . . .

(*He takes out his watch mechanically and looks at it.*)

Ten past nine. . . . Nina ought to be here. . . .

(*Then with sudden bitterness.*)

Will she feel any real grief over his death, I wonder? . . .

I doubt it! . . . but why am I so resentful? . . . the two times I've visited the hospital she's been pleasant enough . . . pleasantly evasive! . . . perhaps she thought her father had sent me to spy on her . . . poor Professor! . . . at least she answered his letters . . . he used to show them to me . . . pathetically overjoyed . . . newsy, loveless scripts, telling nothing whatever about herself . . . well, she won't have to compose them any more . . . she never answered mine . . . she might at least have acknowledged them. . . . Mother thinks she's behaved quite inexcusably . . .

(*Then jealously.*)

I suppose every single damned inmate has fallen in love with her! . . . her eyes seemed cynical . . . sick with men . . . as though I'd looked into the eyes of a prostitute . . . not that I ever have . . . except that once . . . the dollar house . . . hers were like patent leather buttons in a saucer of blue milk! . . .

(*Getting up with a movement of impatience.*)

The devil! . . . what beastly incidents our memories insist on cherishing! . . . the ugly and disgusting . . . the beautiful things we have to keep diaries to remember! . . .

(*He smiles with a wry amusement for a second – then bitterly.*)

That last night Nina was here . . . she talked so brazenly about giving herself . . . I wish I knew the truth of what she's been doing in that house full of men . . . particularly that self-important young ass of a doctor! . . . Gordon's friend! . . .

(*He frowns at himself, determinedly puts an end to his train of thought and comes and sits down again in the chair – in sneering, conversational tones as if he were this time actually addressing another person.*)

Really, it's hardly a decent time, is it, for that kind of speculation . . . with her father lying dead upstairs? . . .

(*A silence as if he had respectably squelched himself – then he pulls out his watch mechanically and stares at it. As he does so a noise of a car is heard approaching, stopping at the kerb beyond the garden. He jumps to his feet and goes towards the door – then hesitates confusedly.*)

No, let Mary go . . . I shouldn't know what to do . . . take her in my arms? . . . kiss her? . . . right now? . . . or wait until she? . . .

(*A bell rings insistently from the back of the house. From the front voices are heard, first Nina's, then a man's. Marsden starts, his face suddenly angry and dejected.*)

Someone with her! . . . a man! . . . I thought she'd be alone! . . .

(*Mary is heard shuffling to the front door, which is opened. Immediately, as Mary sees Nina, she breaks down and there is the sound of her uncontrolled sobbing and choking, incoherent words drowning out Nina's voice, soothing her.*)

NINA

(*As Mary's grief subsides a trifle, her voice is heard, flat and toneless.*)

Isn't Mr. Marsden here, Mary?

(*She calls.*)

Charlie!

MARSDEN

(*Confused – huskily.*)

In here – I'm in the study, Nina.

(*He moves uncertainly toward the door.*)

NINA

(*Comes in and stands just inside the doorway. She is dressed in a nurse's uniform with cap, a raglan coat over it. She appears older than in the previous scene, her face is pale and much thinner, her cheek bones stand out, her mouth is taut in hard lines of a cynical scorn. Her eyes try to armour her wounded spirit with a defensive stare of disillusionment. Her training has also tended to coarsen her fibre a trifle, to make her insensitive to suffering, to give her the nurse's professionally callous attitude. In her fight to regain control of her nerves she has overstriven after the cool and efficient poise, but she is really in a more highly strung, disorganized state than ever, although she is now more capable of suppressing and concealing it. She remains strikingly handsome and her physical appeal is enhanced by her pallor and the mysterious suggestion about her of hidden experience. She stares at Marsden blankly and speaks in queer flat tones.*)

Hallo, Charlie! He's dead, Mary says.

MARSDEN

(*Nodding his head several times – stupidly.*)

Yes.

NINA

(*In same tones.*)

It's too bad. I brought Doctor Darrell. I thought there might be a chance.

(*She pauses and looks about the room.*)

(*Thinking confusedly.*)

His books . . . his chair . . . he always sat there . . . there's his table . . . little Nina was never allowed to touch anything . . . she used to sit on his lap . . . cuddle against him . . . dreaming into the dark beyond the windows . . . warm in his arms before the fireplace . . . dreams like sparks soaring up to die in the cold dark . . . warm in his love, safe-drifting into sleep . . . "Daddy's girl, aren't you?" . . .

(*She looks around and then up and down.*)

His home . . . my home . . . he was my father . . . he's dead . . .

(*She shakes her head.*)

Yes, I hear you, little Nina, but I don't understand one word of it. . . .

(*She smiles with a cynical self-contempt.*)

I'm sorry, Father! . . . you see you've been dead for me a long time . . . when Gordon died, all men died . . . what did you feel for me then? . . . nothing . . . and now I feel nothing . . . it's too bad . . .

MARSDEN

(*Thinking woundedly.*)

I hoped she would throw herself in my arms . . . weeping . . . hide her face on my shoulder . . . "Oh, Charlie, you're all I've got left in the world . . ."

(*Then angrily.*)

Why did she have to bring that Darrell with her?

NINA

(*Flatly.*)

When I said good-bye that night I had a premonition I'd never see him again.

MARSDEN

(*Glad of this opening for moral indignation.*)

You've never tried to see him, Nina!

(*Then overcome by disgust with himself – contritely.*)

Forgive me! It was rotten of me to say that!

NINA

(*Shaking her head – flatly.*)

I didn't want him to see what he would have thought was me.

(*Ironically.*)

That's the other side of it you couldn't dissect into words from here, Charlie!

(*Then suddenly asking a necessary question in her nurse's cool, efficient tones.*)

Is he upstairs?

(*Marsden nods stupidly.*)

I'll take Ned up. I might as well.

(*She turns and walks out briskly.*)

MARSDEN

(*Staring after her – dully.*)

That isn't Nina. . . .

(*Indignantly.*)

They've killed her soul down there! . . .

(*Tears come to his eyes suddenly and he pulls out his handkerchief and wipes them, muttering huskily.*)

Poor old Professor! . . .

(*Then suddenly jeering at himself.*)

For God's sake, stop acting! . . . it isn't the Professor! . . . dear old Charlie is crying because she didn't weep on his shoulder . . . as he had hoped! . . .

(*He laughs harshly – then suddenly sees a man outside the doorway and stares – then calls sharply.*)

Who's that?

EVANS

(*His voice embarrassed and hesitating comes from the hall.*)

It's all right.

(*He appears in the doorway, grinning bashfully.*)

It's me – I, I mean – Miss Leeds told me to come in here.

(*He stretches out his hand awkwardly.*)

Guess you don't remember me, Mr. Marsden. Miss Leeds introduced us one day at the hospital. You were leaving just as I came in. Evans is my name.

MARSDEN

(*Who has been regarding him with waning resentment, forces a cordial smile and shakes hands.*)

Oh, yes. At first I couldn't place you.

EVANS

(*Awkwardly.*)

I sort of feel I'm butting in.

MARSDEN

(*Beginning to be taken by his likable boyish quality.*)

Not at all. Sit down.

(*He sits in the rocker at centre as Evans goes to the bench at right.*)

(*Evans sits uncomfortably hunched forward, twiddling his hat in his hands. He is above the medium height, very blond, with guileless, diffident blue eyes, his figure inclined to immature lumbering outlines. His face is fresh and red-cheeked, handsome in a boyish fashion. His manner is bashful with women or older men, coltishly playful with his friends. There is a lack of self-confidence, a lost and strayed appealing air about him, yet with a hint of some unawakened obstinate force beneath his apparent weakness. Although he is twenty-five and has been out of college three years, he still wears the latest in collegiate clothes, and as he looks younger than he is, he is always mistaken for an undergraduate, and likes to be. It keeps him placed in life for himself.*)

MARSDEN

(*Studying him keenly – amused.*)

This is certainly no giant intellect . . . overgrown boy . . . likable quality though . . .

EVANS

(*Uneasy under Marsden's eyes.*)

Giving me the once-over . . . seems like good egg . . . Nina says he is . . . suppose I ought to say something about his books, but I can't even remember a title of one . . .

(*He suddenly blurts out.*)

You've known Nina – Miss Leeds – ever since she was a kid, haven't you?

MARSDEN

(*A bit shortly.*)

Yes. How long have you known her?

EVANS

Well – really only since she's been at the hospital, although I met her once years ago at a Prom with Gordon Shaw.

MARSDEN

(*Indifferently.*)

Oh, you knew Gordon?

EVANS

(*Proudly.*)

Sure thing! I was in his class!

(*With admiration amounting to hero-worship.*)

He sure was a wonder, wasn't he?

MARSDEN

(*Cynically.*)

Gordon über alles and for ever! . . . I begin to appreciate the Professor's viewpoint . . .

(*Casually.*)

A fine boy! Did you know him well?

EVANS

No. The crowd he went with were mostly fellows who were good at sports – and I always was a dud.

(*Forcing a smile.*)

I was always one of the first to get bounced off the squad in any sport.

(*Then with a flash of humble pride.*)

But I never quit trying, anyway!

MARSDEN

(*Consolingly.*)

Well, the sport hero usually doesn't star after college.

EVANS

Gordon did!

(*Eagerly – with intense admiration.*)

In the war! He was an ace! And he always fought just as cleanly as he'd played football! Even the Huns respected him!

MARSDEN

(*Thinking cynically.*)

This Gordon worshipper must be the apple of Nina's eye! . . .

(*Casually.*)

Were you in the army?

EVANS

(*Shamefacedly.*)

Yes – infantry – but I never got to the front – never saw anything exciting.

(*Thinking glumly.*)

Won't tell him I tried for flying service . . . wanted to get in Gordon's outfit . . . couldn't make the physical exam. . . . never made anything I wanted . . . suppose I'll lose out with Nina, too . . .

(*Then rallying himself.*)

Hey, you! . . . what's the matter with you? . . . don't quit! . . .

MARSDEN

(*Who has been staring at him inquisitively.*)

How did you happen to come out here to-night?

EVANS

I was calling on Nina when your wire came. Ned thought I better come along, too – might be of some use.

MARSDEN

(*Frowning.*)

You mean Doctor Darrell?

(*Evans nods.*)

Is he a close friend of yours?

EVANS

(*Hesitatingly.*)

Well, sort of. Roomed in the same dorm with me at college. He was a senior when I was a freshman. Used to help me along in lots of ways. Took pity on me, I was so green. Then about a year ago when I went to the hospital to visit a fellow who'd been in my outfit I ran into him again.

(*Then with a grin.*)

But I wouldn't say Ned was close to anyone. He's a dyed-in-the-wool doc. He's only close to whatever's the matter with you!

(*He chuckles – then hastily.*)

But don't get me wrong about him. He's the best egg ever! You know him, don't you?

MARSDEN

(*Stiffly.*)

Barely. Nina introduced us once.

(*Thinking bitterly.*)

He's upstairs alone with her . . . I hoped it would be I who . . .

EVANS

Don't want him to get the wrong idea of Ned . . . Ned's my best friend . . . doing all he can to help me with Nina . . . he thinks she'll marry me in the end . . . God, if she only would! . . . I wouldn't expect her to love me at first . . . be happy only to take care of her . . . cook her breakfast . . . bring it up to her in bed . . . tuck the pillows behind her . . . comb her hair for her . . . I'd be happy just to kiss her hair! . . .

MARSDEN

(Agitated – thinking suspiciously.)

What are Darrell's relations with Nina? . . . close to what's the matter with her? . . . damned thoughts! . . . why should I care? . . . I'll ask this Evans . . . pump him while I have a chance . . .

(With forced indifference.)

Is your friend, the Doctor, "close" to Miss Leeds? She's had quite a lot the matter with her since her breakdown, if that's what interests him!

(He smiles casually.)

EVANS

(Gives a start, awakening from his dream.)

Oh – er – yes. He's always trying to bully her into taking better care of herself, but she only laughs at him.

(Soberly.)

It'd be much better if she'd take his advice.

MARSDEN

(Suspiciously.)

No doubt.

EVANS

(Pronounces with boyish solemnity.)

She isn't herself, Mr. Marsden. And I think nursing all those poor guys keeps the war before her when she ought to forget it. She ought to give up nursing and be nursed for a change, that's my idea.

MARSDEN

(Struck by this – eagerly.)

Exactly my opinion.

(Thinking.)

If she'd settle down here . . . I could come over every day . . . I'd nurse her . . . Mother home . . . Nina here . . . how I could work then! . . .

EVANS

(Thinking.)

He certainly seems all for me . . . so far! . . .

(Then in a sudden flurry.)

Shall I tell him? . . . he'll be like her guardian now . . . I've got to know how he stands . . .

(He starts with a solemn earnestness.)

Mr. Marsden, I – there's something I ought to tell you, I think. You see, Nina's talked a lot about you. I know how much she thinks of you. And now her old man –

(He hesitates in confusion.)

I mean, her father's dead –

MARSDEN

(In a sort of panic – thinking.)

What's this? . . . proposal? . . . in form? . . . for her hand? . . . to me? . . . Father Charlie now, eh? . . . ha! . . . God, what a fool! . . . does he imagine she'd ever love him? . . . but she might . . . not bad-looking . . . likable, innocent . . . something to mother . . .

EVANS

(Blundering on regardless now.)

I know it's hardly the proper time –

MARSDEN

(Interrupting – dryly.)

Perhaps I can anticipate. You want to tell me you're in love with Nina?

EVANS

Yes, sir, and I've asked her to marry me.

MARSDEN

What did she say?

EVANS

(Sheepishly.)

Nothing. She just smiled.

MARSDEN

(With relief.)

Ah.

(Then harshly.)

Well, what could you expect? Surely you must know she still loves Gordon?

EVANS

(Manfully.)

Sure I know it – and I admire her for it! Most girls forget too easily. She ought to love Gordon for a long time yet. And I know I'm an awful wash-out compared to him – but I love her as much as he did, or anyone could! And I'll work my way up for her – I know I can! – so I can give her everything she wants. And I wouldn't ask for anything in return except the right to take care of her.

(Blurts out confusedly.)

I never think of her – that way – she's too beautiful and wonderful – not that I don't hope she'd come to love me in time –

MARSDEN

(Sharply.)

And just what do you expect me to do about all this?

EVANS

(*Taken aback.*)

Why – er – nothing, sir. I just thought you ought to know.

(*Sheepishly he glances up at ceiling, then down at floor, twiddling his hat.*)

MARSDEN

(*Thinking – at first with a grudging appreciation and envy.*)

He thinks he means that . . . pure love! . . . it's easy to talk . . . he doesn't know life . . . but he might be good for Nina . . . if she were married to this simpleton would she be faithful? . . . and then I? . . . what a vile thought! . . . I don't mean that! . . .

(*Then forcing a kindly tone.*)

You see, there's really nothing I can do about it.

(*With a smile.*)

If Nina will, she will – and if she won't, she won't. But I can wish you good luck.

EVANS

(*Immediately all boyish gratitude.*)

Thanks! That's darn fine of you, Mr. Marsden!

MARSDEN

But I think we'd better let the subject drop, don't you? We're forgetting that her father –

EVANS

(*Guiltily embarrassed.*)

Yes – sure – I'm a damn fool! Excuse me!

(*There is the noise of steps from the hall and Doctor Edmund Darrell enters. He is twenty-seven, short, dark, wiry, his movements rapid and sure, his manner cool and observant, his dark eyes analytical. His head is handsome and intelligent. There is a quality about him, provoking and disturbing to women, of intense passion which he has rigidly trained himself to control and set free only for the objective satisfaction of studying his own and their reactions: and so he has come to consider himself as immune to love through his scientific understanding of its real sexual nature. He sees Evans and Marsden, nods at Marsden silently, who returns it coldly, goes to the table and taking a prescription pad from his pocket, hastily scratches on it.*)

MARSDEN

(*Thinking sneeringly.*)

Amusing, these young doctors! . . . perspire with the effort to appear cool! . . . writing a prescription . . . cough medicine for the corpse, perhaps! . . . good-looking? . . . more or less . . . attractive to women, I dare say. . . .

DARRELL

(*Tears it off – hands it to Evans.*)

Here, Sam. Run along up the street and get this filled.

EVANS

(*With relief.*)

Sure. Glad of the chance for a walk.

(*He goes out, rear.*)

DARRELL

(*Turning to Marsden.*)

It's for Nina. She's got to get some sleep to-night.

(*He sits down abruptly in the chair at centre. Marsden unconsciously takes the Professor's place behind the table. The two men stare at each other for a moment, Darrell with a frank probing, examining look that ruffles Marsden and makes him all the more resentful toward him.*)

This Marsden doesn't like me . . . that's evident . . . but he interests me . . . read his books . . . wanted to know his bearing on Nina's case . . . his novels just well-written surface . . . no depth, no digging underneath . . . why? . . . has the talent but doesn't dare . . . afraid he'll meet himself somewhere . . . one of those poor devils who spend their lives trying not to discover which sex they belong to! . . .

MARSDEN

Giving me the fishy, diagnosing eye they practise at medical school . . . like freshmen from Ioway cultivating broad A's at Harvard! . . . what is his specialty? . . . neurologist, I think . . . I hope not psychoanalyst . . . a lot to account for, Herr Freud! . . . punishment to fit his crimes, be forced to listen eternally during breakfast while innumerable plain ones tell him dreams about snakes . . . pah, what an easy cure-all! . . . sex the philosopher's stone . . . "O Oedipus, O my king! The world is adopting you!" . . .

DARRELL

Must pitch into him about Nina . . . have to have his help . . . damn little time to convince him . . . he's the kind you have to explode a bomb under to get them to move . . . but not too big a bomb . . . they blow to pieces easily . . .

(*Brusquely.*)

Nina's gone to pot again! Not that her father's death is a shock in the usual sense of grief. I wish to God it were! No, it's a shock because it's finally convinced her she can't feel anything any more. That's what she's doing upstairs now – trying to goad herself into feeling something!

MARSDEN

(*Resentfully.*)

I think you're mistaken. She loved her father –

DARRELL

(*Shortly and dryly.*)

We can't waste time being sentimental, Marsden! She'll be down any minute, and I've got a lot to talk over with you.

(*As Marsden seems again about to protest.*)

Nina has a real affection for you and I imagine you have for her. Then you'll want as much as I do to get her straightened out. She's a corking girl. She ought to have every chance for a happy life.

(*Then sharply driving his words in.*)

But the way she's conditioned now, there's no chance. She's piled on too many destructive experiences. A few more and she'll dive for the gutter just to get the security that comes from knowing she's touched bottom and there's no farther to go!

MARSDEN

(*Revolted and angry, half springs to his feet.*)

Look here, Darrell, I'll be damned if I'll listen to such a ridiculous statement!

DARRELL

(*Curtly – with authority.*)

How do you know it's ridiculous? What do you know of Nina since she left home? But she hadn't been nursing with us three days before I saw she really ought to be a patient; and ever since then I've studied her case. So I think it's up to you to listen.

MARSDEN

(*Freezingly.*)

I'm listening.

(*With apprehensive terror.*)

Gutter . . . has she . . . I wish he wouldn't tell me! . . .

DARRELL

(*Thinking.*)

How much need I tell him? . . . can't tell him the raw truth about her promiscuity . . . he isn't built to face reality . . . no writer is outside of his books . . . have to tone it down for him . . . but not too much! . . .

Nina has been giving way more and more to a morbid longing for martyrdom. The reason for it is obvious. Gordon went away without – well, let's say marrying her. The war killed him. She was left suspended. Then she began to blame herself and to want to sacrifice herself and at the same time give happiness to various fellow war-victims by pretending to love them. It's a pretty idea, but it hasn't worked out. Nina's a bad actress. She hasn't convinced the men of her love – or herself of her good intentions. And each experience of this kind has only left her more a prey to a guilty conscience than before and more determined to punish herself!

MARSDEN

(*Thinking.*)

What does he mean? . . . how far did she? . . . how many? . . .

(*Coldly and sneeringly.*)

May I ask on what specific actions of hers this theory of yours is based?

DARRELL

On her evident craving to make an exhibition of kissing, necking, petting – whatever you call it – spooning in general – with any patient in the institution who got a case on her!

(*Ironically – thinking.*)

Spooning! . . . rather a mild word for her affairs . . . but strong enough for this ladylike soul. . . .

MARSDEN

(*Bitterly.*)

He's lying! . . . what's he trying to hide? . . . was he one of them? . . . her lover? . . . I must get her away from him . . . get her to marry Evans! . . .

(*With authority.*)

Then she mustn't go back to your hospital, that's certain!

DARRELL

(*Quickly.*)

You're quite right. And that brings me to what I want you to urge her to do.

MARSDEN

(*Thinking suspiciously.*)

He doesn't want her back . . . I must have been wrong . . . but there might be many reasons why he'd wish to get rid of her . . .

(*Coldly.*)

I think you exaggerate my influence.

DARRELL

(*Eagerly.*)

Not a bit. You're the last link connecting her with the girl she used to be before Gordon's death. You're closely associated in her mind with that period of happy security, of health and peace of mind. I know that from the way she talks about you. You're the only person she still respects – and really loves.

(*As Marsden starts guiltily and glances at him in confusion – with a laugh.*)

Oh, you needn't look frightened. I mean the sort of love she'd feel for an uncle.

MARSDEN

(*Thinking in agony.*)

Frightened? . . . was I? . . . only person she loves . . . and then he said "love she'd feel for an uncle" . . . Uncle Charlie now! . . . God damn him! . . .

DARRELL

(*Eyeing him.*)

Looks damnably upset . . . wants to evade all responsibility for her, I suppose . . . he's that kind . . . all the better! . . . he'll be only too anxious to get her safely married. . . .

(*Bluntly.*)

And that's why I've done all this talking. You've got to help snap her out of this.

MARSDEN

(*Bitterly.*)

And how, if I may ask?

DARRELL

There's only one way I can see. Get her to marry Sam Evans.

MARSDEN

(*Astonished.*)

Evans?

(*He makes a silly gesture toward the door.*)
(*Thinking confusedly.*)

Wrong again . . . why does he want her married to . . . it's some trick. . . .

DARRELL

Yes, Evans. He's in love with her. And it's one of those unselfish loves you read about. And she is fond of him. In a maternal way, of course – but that's just what she needs now, someone she cares about to mother and boss and keep her occupied. And still more important, this would give her a chance to have children. She's got to find normal outlets for her craving for sacrifice. She needs normal love objects for the emotional life Gordon's death blocked up in her. Now marrying Sam ought to do the trick. Ought to. Naturally, no one can say for certain. But I think his unselfish love, combined with her real liking for him, will gradually give her back a sense of security and a feeling of being worth something to life again, and once she's got that, she'll be saved!

(*He has spoken with persuasive feeling. He asks anxiously.*)

Doesn't that seem good sense to you?

MARSDEN

(*Suspicious – dryly non-committal.*)

I'm sorry, but I'm in no position to say. I don't know anything about Evans, for one thing.

DARRELL

(*Emphatically.*)

Well, I do. He's a fine healthy boy, clean and unspoiled. You can take my word for that. And I'm convinced he's got the right stuff in him to succeed, once he grows up and buckles down to work. He's only a big kid now, but all he needs is a little self-confidence and a sense of responsibility. He's holding down a fair job, too, considering he's just started in the advertising game – enough to keep them living.

(*With a slight smile.*)

I'm prescribing for Sam, too, when I boost this wedding.

MARSDEN

(*His snobbery coming out.*)

Do you know his family – what sort of people? –

DARRELL

(*Bitingly.*)

I'm not acquainted with their social qualifications, if that's what you mean! They're up-state country folks – fruit growers and farmers, well off, I believe. Simple, healthy people, I'm sure of that although I've never met them.

MARSDEN

(*A bit shamefacedly – changing the subject hastily.*)

Have you suggested this match to Nina?

DARRELL

Yes, a good many times lately in a half-joking way. If I were serious she wouldn't listen, she'd say I was prescribing. But I think what I've said has planted it in her mind as a possibility.

MARSDEN

(*Thinking suspiciously.*)

Is this Doctor her lover? . . . trying to pull the wool over my eyes? . . . use me to arrange a convenient triangle for him? . . .

(*Harshly – but trying to force a joking tone.*)

Do you know what I'm inclined to suspect, Doctor? That you may be in love with Nina yourself!

DARRELL

(*Astonished.*)

The deuce you do! What the devil makes you think that? Not that any man mightn't fall in love with Nina. Most of them do. But I didn't happen to. And what's more I never could. In my mind she always belongs to Gordon. It's probably a reflection of her own silly fixed idea about him.

(*Suddenly, dryly and harshly.*)

And I couldn't share a woman – even with a ghost!

(*Thinking cynically.*)

Not to mention the living who have had her! . . . Sam doesn't know about them . . . and I'll bet he couldn't believe it of her even if she confessed! . . .

MARSDEN

(Thinking baffledly.)

Wrong again! . . . he isn't lying . . . but I feel he's hiding something . . . why does he speak so resentfully of Gordon's memory? . . . why do I sympathize? . . .

(In a strange mocking ironic tone.)

I can quite appreciate your feeling about Gordon. I wouldn't care to share with a ghost-lover myself. That species of dead is so invulnerably alive! Even a doctor couldn't kill one, eh?

(He forces a laugh – then in a friendly confidential tone.)

Gordon is too egregious for a ghost. That was the way Nina's father felt about him, too.

(Suddenly reminded of the dead man – in penitently sad tones.)

You didn't know her father, did you? A charming old fellow!

DARRELL

(Hearing a noise from the hall – warningly.)

Sstt!

(Nina enters slowly. She looks from one to the other with a queer, quick, inquisitive stare, but her face is a pale expressionless mask drained of all emotional response to human contacts. It is as if her eyes were acting on their own account as restless, prying, recording instruments. The two men have risen and stare at her anxiously. Darrell moves back and to one side until he is standing in relatively the same place as Marsden had occupied in the previous scene, while Marsden is in her father's place, and she stops where she had been. There is a pause. Then just as each of the men is about to speak, she answers as if they had asked a question.)

NINA

(In a queer flat voice.)

Yes, he's dead – my father – whose passion created me – who began me – he is ended. There is only his end living – his death. It lives now to draw nearer me, to draw me nearer, to become my end!

(Then with a strange twisted smile.)

How we poor monkeys hide from ourselves behind the sounds called words!

MARSDEN

(Thinking frightenedly.)

How terrible she is! . . . who is she? . . . not my Nina! . . .

(As if to reassure himself – timidly.)

Nina!

(Darrell makes an impatient gesture for him to let her go on. What she is saying interests him and he feels talking it out will do her good. She looks at Marsden for a moment startledly as if she couldn't recognize him.)

NINA

What?

(Then placing him – with real affection that is like a galling goad to him.)

Dear old Charlie!

MARSDEN

Dear damned Charlie! . . . She loves to torture! . . .

(Then forcing a smile – soothingly.)

Yes, Nina Cara Nina! Right here!

NINA

(Forcing a smile.)

You look frightened, Charlie. Do I seem queer? It's because I've suddenly seen the lies in the sounds called words. You know – grief, sorrow, love, father – those sounds our lips make and our hands write. You ought to know what I mean. You work with them. Have you written another novel lately? But, stop to think, you're just the one who couldn't know what I mean. With you the lies have become the only truthful things. And I suppose that's the logical conclusion to the whole evasive mess, isn't it? Do you understand me, Charlie? Say lie –

(She says it, drawing it out.)

L-i-i-e! Now say life. L-i-i-f-e! You see! Life is just a long drawn out lie with a sniffling sigh at the end!

(She laughs.)

MARSDEN

(In strange agony.)

She's hard! . . . like a whore! . . . tearing your heart with dirty finger nails! . . . my Nina! . . . cruel bitch! . . . some day I won't bear it! . . . I'll scream out the truth about every woman! . . . no kinder at heart than dollar tarts! . . .

(Then in a passion of remorse.)

Forgive me, Mother! . . . I didn't mean all! . . .

DARRELL

(A bit worried himself now – persuasively.)

Why not sit down, Nina, and let us two gentlemen sit down?

NINA

(Smiling at him swiftly and mechanically.)

Oh, all right, Ned.

(She sits at centre. He comes and sits on the bench. Marsden sits by the table. She continues sarcastically.)

Are you prescribing for me again, Ned? This is my pet doctor, Charlie. He couldn't be happy in heaven unless God called him in because He'd caught something! Did you ever know a young scientist, Charlie? He believes if you pick a lie to pieces, the pieces are the truth! I like him because he's so inhuman. But once he kissed me – in a moment of carnal weakness! I was as startled as if a mummy had done it! And then he looked so disgusted with himself! I had to laugh!

(She smiles at him with a pitying scorn.)

DARRELL

(Good-naturedly smiling.)

That's right! Rub it in!

(Ruffled but amused in spite of it.)

I'd forgotten about that kiss . . . I was sore at myself afterwards . . . she was so damned indifferent! . . .

NINA

(Wanderingly.)

Do you know what I was doing upstairs? I was trying to pray. I tried hard to pray to the modern science God. I thought of a million light years to a spiral nebula – one other universe among innumerable others. But how could that God care about our trifling misery of death-born-of-birth? I couldn't believe in Him, and I wouldn't if I could! I'd rather imitate His indifference and prove I had that one trait at least in common!

MARSDEN

(Worriedly.)

Nina, why don't you lie down?

NINA

(Jeeringly.)

Oh, let me talk, Charlie! They're only words, remember! So many, many words have jammed up into thoughts in my poor head! You'd better let them overflow or they'll burst the dam! I wanted to believe in any God at any price – a heap of stones, a mud image, a drawing on a wall, a bird, a fish, a snake, a baboon – or even a good man preaching the simple platitudes of truth, those Gospel words we love the sound of but whose meaning we pass on to spooks to live by!

MARSDEN

(Again – half rising – frightenedly.)

Nina! You ought to stop talking. You'll work yourself into –

(He glances angrily at Darrell as if demanding that, as a doctor, he do something.)

NINA

(With bitter hopelessness.)

Oh, all right!

DARRELL

(Answering his look – thinking.)

You poor fool! . . . it'll do her good to talk this out of her system . . . and then it'll be up to you to bring her around to Sam . . .

(Starts toward the door.)

Think I'll go out and stretch my legs.

MARSDEN

(Thinking – in a panic.)

I don't want to be alone with her! . . . I don't know her! . . . I'm afraid! . . .

(Protestingly.)

Well – but – hold on – I'm sure Nina would rather –

NINA

(Dully.)

Let him go. I've said everything I can ever say – to him. I want to talk to you, Charlie.

(Darrell goes out noiselessly with a meaning look at Marsden – a pause.)

MARSDEN

(Thinking tremblingly.)

Here . . . now . . . what I hoped . . . she and I alone . . . she will cry . . . I will comfort her . . . why am I so afraid? . . . whom do I fear? . . . is it she? . . . or I? . . .

NINA

(Suddenly, with pity yet with scorn.)

Why have you always been so timid, Charlie? Why are you always afraid? What are you afraid of?

MARSDEN

(Thinking in a panic.)

She sneaked into my soul to spy! . . .

(Then boldly.)

Well, then, a little truth for once in a way! . . .

(Timidly.)

I'm afraid of – of life, Nina.

NINA

(Nodding slowly.)

I know.

(After a pause – queerly.)

The mistake began when God was created in a male image. Of course, women would see Him that way, but men should have been gentlemen enough, remembering their mothers, to make God a woman! But the God of gods – the Boss – has always been a man. That makes life so perverted, and death so unnatural. We should have imagined life as created in the birth-pain of God the Mother. Then we would understand why we, Her children, have inherited pain, for we would know that our life's rhythm beats from Her great heart, torn with the agony of love and birth. And we would feel that death meant reunion with Her, a passing back into Her substance, blood of Her blood again, peace of Her peace!

(Marsden has been listening to her fascinatedly. She gives a strange little laugh.)

Now wouldn't that be more logical and satisfying than having God a male whose chest thunders with egotism and is too hard for tired heads and thoroughly comfortless? Wouldn't it, Charlie?

MARSDEN

(With a strange passionate eagerness.)

Yes! It would, indeed! It would, Nina!

NINA

(Suddenly jumping to her feet and going to him – with a horrible moaning desolation.)

Oh, God, Charlie, I want to believe in something! I want to believe so I can feel! I want to feel that he is dead – my father! And I can't feel anything, Charlie! I can't feel anything at all!

(She throws herself on her knees beside him and hides her face in her hands on his knees and begins to sob – stifled torn sounds.)

MARSDEN

(Bends down, pats her head with trembling hands, soothes her with uncertain trembling words.)

There – there – don't – Nina, please – don't cry – you'll make yourself sick – come now – get up – do!

(His hands grasping her arms he half raises her to her feet, but, her face still hidden in her hands, sobbing, she slips on to his lap like a little girl and hides her face on his shoulder. His expression becomes transported with a great happiness.)

(In an ecstatic whisper.)

As I dreamed . . . with a deeper sweetness! . . .

(He kisses her hair with a great reverence.)

There . . . this is all my desire . . . I am this kind of lover . . . this is my love . . . she is my girl . . . not woman . . . my little girl . . . and I am brave because of her little girl's pure love . . . and I am proud . . . no more afraid . . . no more ashamed of being pure! . . .

(He kisses her hair again tenderly and smiles at himself.)

(Then soothingly with a teasing incongruous gaiety.)

This will never do, Nina Cara Nina – never, never do, you know – I can't permit it!

NINA

(In a muffled voice, her sobbing beginning to ebb away into sighs – in a young girl's voice.)

Oh, Charlie, you're so kind and comforting! I've wanted you so!

MARSDEN

(Immediately disturbed.)

Wanted? . . . wanted? . . . not that kind of wanted . . . can she mean? . . .

(Questioning hesitatingly.)

You've wanted me, Nina?

NINA

Yes, – awfully! I've been so homesick. I've wanted to run home and 'fess up, tell how bad I've been, and be punished! Oh, I've got to be punished, Charlie, out of mercy for me, so I can forgive myself! And now Father dead, there's only you. You will, won't you – or tell me how to punish myself? You've simply got to, if you love me!

MARSDEN

(Thinking intensely.)

If I love her! . . . oh, I do love her! . . .

(Eagerly.)

Anything you wish, Nina – anything!

NINA

(With a comforted smile, closing her eyes and cuddling up against him.)

I knew you would. Dear old Charlie!

(As he gives a wincing start.)

What is it?

(She looks up into his face.)

MARSDEN

(Forcing a smile – ironically.)

Twinge – rheumatics – getting old, Nina.

(Thinking with wild agony.)

Dear old Charlie! . . . descended again into hell! . . .

(Then in a flat voice.)

What do you want to be punished for, Nina?

NINA

(In a strange, far-away tone, looking up not at him but at the ceiling.)

For playing the silly slut, Charlie. For giving my cool

clean body to men with hot hands and greedy eyes which they called love! Ugh!

(*A shiver runs over her body.*)

MARSDEN

(*Thinking with sudden agony.*)
Then she did! . . . the little filth! . . .
(*In his flat voice.*)

You mean you –

(*Then pleadingly.*)

But not – Darrell?

NINA

(*With simple surprise.*)

Ned? No, how could I? The war hadn't maimed him. There would have been no point in that. But I did with others – oh, four or five or six or seven men, Charlie. I forget – and it doesn't matter. They were all the same. Count them all as one, and that one a ghost of nothing. That is, to me. They were important to themselves, if I remember rightly. But I forget.

MARSDEN

(*Thinking in agony.*)
But why? . . . the dirty little trollop! . . . why? . . .
(*In his flat voice.*)

Why did you do this, Nina?

NINA

(*With a sad little laugh.*)

God knows, Charlie! Perhaps I knew at the time, but I've forgotten. It's all mixed up. There was a desire to be kind. But it's horribly hard to give anything, and frightful to receive! And to give love – oneself – not in this world! And men are difficult to please, Charlie. I seemed to feel Gordon standing against a wall with eyes bandaged and these men were a firing squad whose eyes were also bandaged – and only I could see! No, I was the blindest! I would not see! I knew it was a stupid, morbid business, that I was more maimed than they were, really, that the war had blown my heart and insides out! And I knew too that I was torturing these tortured men, morbidly supersensitive already, that they loathed the cruel mockery of my gift! Yet I kept on, from one to one, like a stupid, driven animal until one night not long ago I had a dream of Gordon diving down out of the sky in flames and he looked at me with such sad burning eyes, and all my poor maimed men, too, seemed staring out of his eyes with a burning pain, and I woke up crying, my own eyes burning. Then I saw what a fool I'd been – a guilty fool! So be kind and punish me!

MARSDEN

(*Thinking with bitter confusion.*)

I wish she hadn't told me this . . . it has upset me terribly! . . . I positively must run home at once . . . Mother is waiting up . . . oh, how I'd love to hate this little whore! . . . then I could punish! . . . I wish her father were alive . . . "now he's dead there's only you," she said . . . "I've wanted you" . . .

(*With intense bitterness.*)

Dear old Father Charlie now! . . . ha! . . . that's how she wants me! . . .

(*Then suddenly in a matter-of-fact tone that is mockingly like her father's.*)

Then, under the circumstances, having weighed the pros and cons, so to speak, I should say that decidedly the most desirable course –

NINA

(*Drowsily – her eyes shut.*)

You sound so like Father, Charlie.

MARSDEN

(*In the tone like her father's.*)

– is for you to marry that young Evans. He is a splendid chap, clean and boyish, with real stuff in him, too, to make a career for himself if he finds a helpmate who will inspire him to his best efforts and bring his latent ability to the surface.

NINA

(*Drowsily.*)

Sam is a nice boy. Yes, it would be a career for me to bring a career to his surface. I would be busy – surface life – no more depths, please God! But I don't love him, Father.

MARSDEN

(*Blandly – in the tone like her father's.*)

But you like him, Nina. And he loves you devotedly. And it's time you were having children – and when children come, love comes, you know.

NINA

(*Drowsily.*)

I want children. I must become a mother so I can give myself. I am sick of sickness.

MARSDEN

(*Briskly.*)

Then it's all settled?

NINA

(*Drowsily.*)

Yes.

(*Very sleepily.*)

Thank you, Father. You've been so kind. You've let me off too easily. I don't feel as if you'd punished me hardly at all. But I'll never, never do it again, I promise – never, never! –

(*She falls asleep and gives a soft little snore.*)

MARSDEN

(*Still in her father's tones – very paternally – looking down.*)

She's had a hard day of it, poor child! I'll carry her up to her room.

(*He rises to his feet with Nina sleeping peacefully in his arms. At this moment Sam Evans enters from the right with the package of medicine in his hand.*)

EVANS

(*Grinning respectfully.*)

Here's the –

(*As he sees Nina.*)

Oh!

(*Then excitedly.*)

Did she faint?

MARSDEN

(*Smiling kindly at Evans – still in her father's tones.*)

Sssh! She's asleep. She cried and then she fell asleep – like a little girl.

(*Then benignantly.*)

But first we spoke a word about you, Evans, and I'm sure you have every reason to hope.

EVANS

(*Overcome, his eyes on his shuffling feet and twiddling cap.*)

Thanks – I – I really don't know how to thank –

MARSDEN

(*Going to door – in his own voice now.*)

I've got to go home. My mother is waiting up for me. I'll just carry Nina upstairs and put her on her bed and throw something over her.

EVANS

Can't I help you, Mr. Marsden?

MARSDEN

(*Dully.*)

No. I cannot help myself.

(*As Evans looks puzzled and startled he adds with an ironical, self-mocking geniality.*)

You'd better call me just Charlie after this.

(*He smiles bitterly to himself as he goes out.*)

EVANS

(*Looks after him for a moment – then cannot restrain a joyful, coltish caper – gleefully.*)

Good egg! Good old Charlie!

(*As if he had heard or guessed, Marsden's bitter laugh comes back from the end of the hallway.*)

Curtain

ACT THREE

SCENE: *Seven months or so later – the dining-room of the Evans' homestead in northern New York state – about nine o'clock in the morning of a day in late spring of the following year.*

The room is one of those big, misproportioned dining-rooms that are found in the large, jigsaw country houses scattered around the country as a reult of the rural taste for grandeur in the 'eighties. There is a cumbersome hanging lamp suspended from chains over the exact centre of the ugly table with its set of straight-backed chairs set back at spaced intervals against the walls. The wall-paper, a repulsive brown, is stained at the ceiling line with damp blotches of mildew, and here and there has started to peel back where the strips join. The floor is carpeted in a smeary brown with a dark red design blurred into it. In the left wall is one window with starched white curtains looking out on a covered side porch, so that no sunlight ever gets to this room, and the light from the window, although it is a beautiful warm day in the flower garden beyond the porch, is cheerless and sickly. There is a door in the rear, to left of centre, that leads to a hall opening on the same porch. To the right of door a heavy side-board, a part of the set, displaying some "company" china and glassware. In the right wall, a door leading to the kitchen.

Nina is seated at the foot of the table, her back to the window, writing a letter. Her whole personality seems changed, her face has a contented expression, there is an inner calm about her. And her personal appearance has changed in kind, her face and figure have filled out, she is prettier in a conventional way and less striking and unusual; nothing remains of the strange fascination of her face except her unchangeably mysterious eyes.

NINA

(*Reading over to herself what she has just written.*)

It's a queer house, Ned. There is something wrong with its psyche, I'm sure. Therefore you'd simply adore it. It's a hideous old place, a faded gingerbread with orange fixin's and numerous lightning rods. Around it are acres and acres of apple trees in full bloom, all white and pinkish and beautiful, like brides just tripping out of church with the bridegroom, Spring, by the arm.

Which reminds me, Ned, that it's over six months since Sam and I were married and we haven't seen hide nor hair of you since the ceremony. Do you think that is any nice way to act? You might at least drop me a line. But I'm only joking. I know how busy you must be now that you've got the chance: you've always wanted to do research work. Did you get our joint letter of congratulation written after we read of your appointment?

But to get back to this house. I feel it has lost its soul and grown resigned to doing without it. It isn't haunted by anything at all – and ghosts of some sort are the only normal life a house has – like our minds, you know. So although last evening when we got here at first I said "obviously haunted" to myself, now that I've spent one night in it I know that whatever spooks there may once have been have packed up their manifestations a long time ago and drifted away over the grass, wisps of mist between the apple trees, without one backward glance of regard or recollection. It's incredible to think Sam was born and spent his childhood here. I'm glad he doesn't show it! We slept last night in the room he was born in. Or rather he slept, I couldn't. I lay awake and found it difficult to breathe, as if all the life in the air had long since been exhausted in keeping the dying living a little longer. It was hard to believe anyone had ever been born alive there. I know you're saying crossly "She's still morbid," but I'm not. I've never been more normal. I feel contented and placid.

(*Looking up from the letter, thinking embarrassedly.*)

Should I have told him? . . . no . . . my own secret . . . tell no one . . . not even Sam . . . why haven't I told Sam? . . . it'd do him much good . . . he'd feel so proud of himself, poor dear . . . no . . . I want to keep it just my baby . . . only mine . . . as long as I can . . . and it will be time enough to let Ned know when I go to New York . . . he can suggest a good obstetrician . . . how delighted he'll be when he hears! . . . he always said it would be the best thing for me . . . well, I do feel happy when I think . . . and I love Sam now . . . in a way . . . it will be his baby too . . .

(*Then with a happy sigh, turns back to letter.*)

But speaking of Sam's birth, you really must meet his mother some time. It's amazing how little she is like him, a strange woman from the bit I saw of her last night. She has been writing Sam regularly once a week ever since she's known we were married, the most urgent invitations to visit her. They were really more like commands, or prayers. I suspect she is terribly lonely all by herself in this big house. Sam's feeling toward her puzzles me. I don't believe he ever mentioned her until her letters began coming or that he'd ever have come to see the poor woman if I hadn't insisted. His attitude rather shocked me. It was just as though he'd forgotten he had a mother. And yet as soon as he saw her he was sweet enough She seemed dreadfully upset to see Charlie with us, until we'd explained it was thanks to his kindness and in his car we were taking this deferred honeymoon. Charlie's like a fussy old woman about his car, he's afraid to let Sam or me drive it –

MARSDEN

(*Enters from the rear. He is spruce, dressed immaculately, his face a bit tired and resigned, but smiling kindly. He has a letter in his hand.*)

Good morning.

(*She gives a start and instinctively covers the letter with her hand.*)

NINA

Good morning.

(*Thinking amusedly.*)

If he knew what I'd just written . . . poor old Charlie! . . .

(*Then indicating the letter he carries.*)

I see you're an early correspondent, too.

MARSDEN

(*With sudden jealous suspicion.*)

Why did she cover it up like that? . . . who's she writing to? . . .

(*Coming toward her.*)

Just a line to Mother to let her know we've not all been murdered by rum-bandits. You know how she worries.

NINA

(*Thinking with a trace of pitying contempt.*)

Apron strings . . . still his devotion to her is touching . . . I hope if mine is a boy he will love me as much . . . oh, I hope it is a boy . . . healthy and strong and beautiful . . . like Gordon! . . .

(*Then suddenly sensing Marsden's curiosity – perfunctorily.*)

I'm writing to Ned Darrell. I've owed him one for ages.

(*She folds it up and puts it aside.*)

MARSDEN

(*Thinking glumly.*)

I thought she'd forgotten him . . . still, I suppose it's just friendly . . . and it's none of my business now she's married. . . .

(*Perfunctorily.*)

How did you sleep?

NINA

Not a wink. I had the strangest feeling.

MARSDEN

Sleeping in a strange bed, I suppose.

(*Jokingly.*)

Did you see any ghosts?

NINA

(*With a sad smile.*)

No, I got the feeling the ghosts had all deserted the house and left it without a soul – as the dead so often leave the living –

(*She forces a little laugh.*)

if you get what I mean.

MARSDEN

(*Thinking worriedly.*)

Slipping back into that morbid tone . . . first time in a long while . . .

(*Teasingly.*)

Hallo! Do I hear graveyards yawning from their sleep – and yet I observe it's a gorgeous morning without, the flowers are flowering, the trees are treeing with one another, and you, if I mistake not, are on your honeymoon!

NINA

(*Immediately gaily mocking.*)

Oh, very well, old thing! "God's in his heaven, all's right with the world!" And Pippa's cured of the pip!

(*She dances up to him.*)

MARSDEN

(*Gallantly.*)

Pippa is certainly a pippin this morning!

NINA

(*Kisses him quickly.*)

You deserve one for that! All I meant was that ghosts remind me of men's smart crack about women, you can't live with them and can't live without them.

(*Stands still and looks at him teasingly.*)

But there you stand proving me a liar by every breath you draw! You're ghostless and womanless – and as sleek and satisfied as a pet seal!

(*She sticks out her tongue at him and makes a face of superior scorn.*)

Bah! That for you, 'Fraid-cat Charlie, you slacker bachelor!

(*She runs to the kitchen door.*)

I'm going to bum some more coffee! How about you?

MARSDEN

(*With a forced smile.*)

No, thank you.

(*She disappears into the kitchen.*)

(*Thinking with bitter pain.*)

Ghostless! . . . if she only knew . . . that joking tone hides her real contempt! . . .

(*Self-mockingly.*)

"But when the girls began to play 'Fraid-cat Charlie ran away!"

(*Then rallying himself.*)

Bosh! . . . I haven't had such thoughts . . . not since their marriage . . . happy in her happiness . . . but is she happy? . . . in the first few months she was obviously playing a part . . . kissed him too much . . . as if she'd determined to make herself a loving wife . . . and then all of a sudden she became contented . . . her face filled out . . . her eyes lazily examined peace . . . pregnant . . . yes, she must be . . I hope so . . . why? . . . for her sake . . . my own, too . . . when she has a child I know I can entirely accept . . . forget I have lost her . . . lost her? . . . silly ass! . . . how can you lose what you never possessed? . . . except in dreams! . . .

(*Shaking his head exasperatedly.*)

Round and round . . . thoughts . . . damn pests! . . . mosquitoes of the soul . . . whine, sting, suck one's blood . . . why did I invite Nina and Sam on this tour . . . it's a business trip with me, really . . . I need a new setting for my next novel . . . "Mr. Marsden departs a bit from his familiar field" . . . well, there they were stuck in the Professor's house . . . couldn't afford a vacation . . . never had a honeymoon . . . I've pretended to be done up every night so they could . . . I've gone to bed right after dinner so they could be alone and . . . I wonder if she can really like him . . . that way? . . .

(*The sound of Evans' voice and his mother's is heard from the garden. Marsden goes over and carefully peers out.*)

Sam with his mother . . . peculiar woman . . . strong . . . good character for a novel . . . no, she's too sombre . . . her eyes are the saddest . . . and, at the same time, the grimmest . . . they're coming in . . . I'll drive around the country a bit . . . give them a chance for a family conference . . . discuss Nina's pregnancy, I suppose . . . does Sam know? . . . he gives no indication . . . why do wives hide it from their husbands? . . . ancient shame . . . guilty of continuing life, of bringing fresh pain into the world . . .

(*He goes out, rear. The outside door in the hall is heard being opened and Evans and his mother evidently meet Marsden as he is about to go out. Their voices, his voice explaining, are heard, then the outer door being opened and shut again as Marsden departs. A moment later Evans and his mother enter the dining-room. Sam looks timorously happy, as if he could not quite believe in his good fortune and had constantly to reassure himself about it, yet he is riding the crest of the wave, he radiates love and devotion and boyish adoration. He is a charming-looking fresh boy now. He wears a sweater and linen knickers, collegiate to the last degree. His mother is a tiny woman with a frail figure, her head and face, framed in iron-grey hair, seeming much too large for her body, so that at first glance she gives one the impression of a wonderfully made, life-like doll. She is only about forty-five, but she looks at least sixty. Her face with its delicate features must have once been of a romantic, tender, clinging-vine beauty, but what has happened to her has compressed its defenceless curves into planes, its mouth into the thin line around a locked door, its gentle chin has been forced out aggressively by a long reliance on clenched teeth. She is very pale. Her big dark eyes are grim with the prisoner-pain of a walled-in soul. Yet a sweet lovingkindness, the ghost of an old faith and trust in life's goodness, hovers girlishly, fleetingly, about the corners of her mouth and softens into deep sorrow the shadowy grimness of her eyes. Her voice jumps startlingly in tone from a caressing gentleness to a blunted flat assertiveness, as if what she said then was merely a voice on its own without human emotion to inspire it.)*

EVANS

(As they come in – rattling on in the cocksure boastful way of a boy showing off his prowess before his mother, confident of thrilled adulation.)

In a few years you won't have to worry one way or another about the darned old apple crop. I'll be able to take care of you then. Wait and see! Of course, I'm not making so much now. I couldn't expect to. I've only just started. But I'm making good, all right, all right – since I got married – and it's only a question of time when – Why, to show you, Cole – he's the manager and the best egg ever – called me into his office and told me he'd had his eye on me, that my stuff was exactly what they wanted, and he thought I had the makings of a real find.

(Proudly.)

How's that? That's certainly fair enough, isn't it?

MRS. EVANS

(Vaguely – she has evidently not heard much of what he said.)

That's fine, Sammy.

(Thinking apprehensively.)

I do hope I'm wrong! . . . but that old shiver of dread took me the minute she stepped in the door! . . . I don't think she's told Sammy, but I got to make sure. . . .

EVANS

(Seeing her preoccupation now – deeply hurt – testily.)

I'll bet you didn't hear a word I said! Are you still worrying about how the darn old apples are going to turn out?

MRS. EVANS

(With a guilty start – protestingly.)

Yes, I did hear you, Sammy – every word! That's just what I was thinking about – how proud I am you're doing so wonderful well!

EVANS

(Mollified but still grumbling.)

You'd never guess it from the gloomy way you looked!

(But encouraged to go on.)

And Cole asked me if I was married – seemed to take a real personal interest – said he was glad to hear it because marriage was what put the right kind of ambition into a fellow – unselfish ambition – working for his wife and not just himself –

(Then embarrassedly.)

He even asked me if we were expecting an addition to the family.

MRS. EVANS

(Seeing this is her chance – quickly – forcing a smile.)

I've been meaning to ask you that myself, Sammy.

(Blurts out apprehensively.)

She – Nina – she isn't going to have a baby, is she?

EVANS

(With an indefinable guilty air – as if he were reluctant to admit it.)

I – why – you mean, is she now? I don't think so, Mother.

(He strolls over the window whistling with an exaggeratedly casual air, and looks out.)

MRS. EVANS

(Thinking with grim relief.)

He don't know . . . there's that much to be thankful for, anyway. . . .

EVANS

(Thinking with intense longing.)

If that'd only happen! . . . soon! . . . Nina's begun to love me . . . a little . . . I've felt it the last two months . . . God, it's made me happy! . . . before that she didn't . . . only liked me . . . that was all I asked . . . never dared hope she'd come to love me . . . even a little . . . so soon . . . sometimes I feel it's too good to be true . . . don't deserve it . . . and now . . . if that'd happen . . . then I'd feel sure . . . it'd be there . . . half Nina, half me . . . living proof! . . .

(Then an apprehensive note creeping in.)

And I know she wants a baby so much . . . one reason why she married me . . . and I know she's felt right along that then she'd love me . . . really love me . . .

(*Gloomily.*)

I wonder why . . . ought to have happened before this . . . hope it's nothing wrong . . . with me! . . .

(*He starts, flinging off this thought – then suddenly clutching at a straw, turns hopefully to his mother.*)

Why did you ask me that, Mother? D'you think – ?

MRS. EVANS

(*Hastily.*)

No, indeed! I don't think she is! I wouldn't say so at all!

EVANS

(*Dejectedly.*)

Oh – I thought perhaps –

(*Then changing the subject.*)

I suppose I ought to go up and say hallo to Aunt Bessie.

MRS. EVANS

(*Her face becoming defensive – in blunted tones, a trifle pleadingly.*)

I wouldn't, Sammy. She hasn't seen you since you were eight. She wouldn't know you. And you're on your honeymoon, and old age is always sad to young folks. Be happy while you can!

(*Then pushing him toward door.*)

Look here! You catch that friend, he's just getting his car out. You drive to town with him, give me a chance to get to know my daughter-in-law, and call her to account for how she's taking care of you!

(*She laughs forcedly.*)

EVANS

(*Bursting out passionately.*)

Better than I deserve! She's an angel, Mother! I know you'll love her!

MRS. EVANS

(*Gently.*)

I do already, Sammy! She's so pretty and sweet!

EVANS

(*Kisses her – joyously.*)

I'll tell her that. I'm going out this way and kiss her goodbye.

(*He runs out through the kitchen door.*)

MRS. EVANS

(*Looking after him – passionately.*)

He loves her! . . . he's happy! . . . that's all that counts! . . . being happy! . . .

(*Thinking apprehensively.*)

If only she isn't going to have a baby . . . if only she doesn't care so much about having one . . . I got to have it out with her . . . got to! . . . no other way . . . in mercy . . . in justice . . . this has got to end with my boy . . . and he's got to live happy! . . .

(*At the sound of steps from the kitchen she straightens up in her chair stiffly.*)

NINA

(*Comes in from the kitchen, a cup of coffee in her hand, smiling happily.*)

Good morning –

(*She hesitates – then shyly.*)

Mother.

(*She comes over and kisses her – slips down and sits on the floor beside her.*)

MRS. EVANS

(*Flusteredly – hurriedly.*)

Good morning! It's a real fine day, isn't it? I ought to have been here and got your breakfast, but I was out gallivanting round the place with Sammy. I hope you found everything you wanted.

NINA

Indeed I did! And I ate so much I'm ashamed of myself!

(*She nods at the cup of coffee and laughs.*)

See, I'm still at it!

MRS. EVANS

Good for you!

NINA

I ought to apologize for coming down so late. Sam should have called me. But I wasn't able to get to sleep until after daylight somehow.

MRS. EVANS

(*Strangely.*)

You couldn't sleep? Why? Did you feel anything funny – about this house?

NINA

(*Struck by her tone – looks up.*)

No. Why?

(*Thinking.*)

How her face changes! . . . what sad eyes! . . .

MRS. EVANS

(Thinking in an agony of apprehension.)

Got to start in to tell her . . . got to . . .

NINA

(Apprehensive herself now.)

That sick dead feeling . . . when something is going to happen . . . I felt it before I got the cable about Gordon . . .

(Then taking a sip of coffee, and trying to be pleasantly casual.)

Sam said you wanted to talk to me.

MRS. EVANS

(Dully.)

Yes. You love my boy, don't you?

NINA

(Startled – forcing a smile, quickly.)

Why, of course!

(Reassuring herself.)

No, it isn't a lie . . . I do love him . . . the father of my baby . . .

MRS. EVANS

(Blurts out.)

Are you going to have a baby, Nina?

NINA

(She presses Mrs. Evans' hand.)

(Simply.)

Yes, Mother.

MRS. EVANS

(In her blunt flat tones – with a mechanical rapidity to her words.)

Don't you think it's too soon? Don't you think you better wait until Sammy's making more money? Don't you think it'll be a drag on him and you? Why don't you just go on being happy together, just you two?

NINA

(Thinking frightenedly.)

What is behind what she's saying? . . . that feeling of death again! . . .

(Moving away from her – repulsed.)

No, I don't think any of those things, Mrs. Evans. I want a baby – beyond everything! We both do!

MRS. EVANS

(Hopelessly.)

I know.

(Then grimly.)

But you can't! You've got to make up your mind you can't!

(Thinking fiercely – even with satisfaction.)

Tell her! . . . make her suffer what I was made to suffer! . . . I've been too lonely! . . .

NINA

(Thinking with terrified foreboding.)

I knew it! . . . Out of a blue sky . . . black! . . .

(Springing to her feet – bewilderedly.)

What do you mean? How can you say a thing like that?

MRS. EVANS

(Reaching out her hand tenderly, trying to touch Nina.)

It's because I want Sammy – and you, too, child – to be happy.

(Then as Nina shrinks away from her hand – in her blunted tones.)

You just can't.

NINA

(Defiantly.)

But I can! I have already! I mean – I am, didn't you understand me?

MRS. EVANS

(Gently.)

I know it's hard.

(Then inexorably.)

But you can't go on!

NINA

(Violently.)

I don't believe you know what you're saying! It's too terrible for you – Sam's own mother – how would you have felt if someone – when you were going to have Sam – came to you and said –?

MRS. EVANS

(Thinking fiercely.)

Now's my chance! . . .

(Tonelessly.)

They did say it! Sam's own father did – my husband! And I said it to myself! And I did all I could, all my husband could think of, so's I wouldn't – but we didn't know enough. And right to the time the pains come on, I prayed Sammy'd be born dead, and Sammy's father prayed, but Sammy was born healthy and smiling, and we just had to love him, and live in fear. He doubled the torment of fear we lived in.

And that's what you'd be in for. And Sammy, he'd go the way his father went. And your baby, you'd be bringing it into torment.

(*A bit violently.*)

I tell you it'd be a crime – a crime worse than murder!

(*Then recovering – commiseratingly.*)

So you just can't, Nina!

NINA

(*Who has been listening distractedly – thinking.*)

Don't listen to her! . . . feeling of death! . . . what is it? . . . she's trying to kill my baby! . . . oh, I hate her! . . .

(*Hysterically resentful.*)

What do you mean? Why don't you speak plainly?

(*Violently.*)

I think you're horrible! Praying your baby would be born dead! That's a lie! You couldn't!

MRS. EVANS

(*Thinking.*)

I know what she's doing now . . . just what I did . . . trying not to believe . . .

(*Fiercely.*)

But I'll make her! . . . she's got to suffer, too! . . . I been too lonely! . . . she's got to share and help me save my Sammy! . . .

(*With an even more blunted flat relentless tonelessness.*)

I thought I was plain, but I'll be plainer. Only remember it's a family secret, and now you're one of the family. It's the curse on the Evanses. My husband's mother – she was an only child – died in an asylum, and her father before her. I know that for a fact. And my husband's sister, Sammy's aunt, she's out of her mind. She lives on the top floor of this house, hasn't been out of her room in years, I've taken care of her. She just sits, doesn't say a word, but she's happy, she laughs to herself a lot, she hasn't a care in the world. But I remember when she was all right, she was always unhappy, she never got married, most people around here were afraid of the Evanses in spite of their being rich for hereabouts. They knew about the craziness going back, I guess, for heaven knows how long. I didn't know about the Evanses until after I'd married my husband. He came to the town I lived in, no one there knew about the Evanses. He didn't tell me until after we were married. He asked me to forgive him, he said he loved me so much he'd have gone mad without me, said I was his only hope of salvation. So I forgave him. I loved him an awful lot. I said to myself, I'll be his salvation – and maybe I could have been if we hadn't had Sammy born. My husband kept real well up to then. We'd swore we'd never have children, we never forgot to be careful for two whole years. Then one night we'd both gone to a dance, we'd both had a little punch to drink, just enough – to forget – driving home in the moonlight – that moonlight! – such little things at the back of big things!

NINA

(*In a dull moan.*)

I don't believe you! I won't believe you!

MRS. EVANS

(*Drones on.*)

My husband, Sammy's father, in spite of all he and I fought against it, he finally gave in to it when Sammy was only eight, he couldn't keep up any more living in fear for Sammy, thinking any minute the curse might get him, every time he was sick, or had a headache, or bumped his head, or started crying, or had a nightmare and screamed, or said something queer like children do naturally.

(*A bit stridently.*)

Living like that with that fear is awful torment! I know that! I went through it by his side! It nearly drove me crazy, too – but I didn't have it in my blood! And that's why I'm telling you! You got to see you can't, Nina!

NINA

(*Suddenly breaking out – frenziedly.*)

I don't believe you! I don't believe Sam would ever have married me if he knew – !

MRS. EVANS

(*Sharply.*)

Who said Sammy knew? He don't know a single thing about it! That's been the work of my life, keeping him from knowing. When his father gave up and went off into it I sent Sammy right off to boarding school. I told him his father was sick, and a little while after I sent word his father was dead, and from then on until his father did really die during Sammy's second year to college, I kept him away at school in winter and camp in summers and I went to see him, I never let him come home.

(*With a sigh.*)

It was hard, giving up Sammy, knowing I was making him forget he had a mother. I was glad taking care of them two kept me so busy I didn't get much chance to think then. But here's what I've come to think since, Nina: I'm certain sure my husband might have kept his mind with the help of my love if I hadn't had Sammy. And if I'd never had Sammy I'd never have loved Sammy – or missed him, would I? – and I'd have kept my husband.

NINA

(*Not heeding this last – with wild mockery.*)

And I thought Sam was so normal – so healthy and sane –

not like me! I thought he'd give me such healthy, happy children and I'd forget myself in them and learn to love him!

MRS. EVANS

(Horrified, jumping to her feet.)

Learn to? You told me you did love Sammy!

NINA

No! Maybe I almost have – lately – but only when I thought of his baby! Now I hate him!

(She begins to weep hysterically. Mrs. Evans goes to her and puts her arms around her. Nina sobs out.)

Don't touch me! I hate you, too! Why didn't you tell him he must never marry?

MRS. EVANS

What reason could I give, without telling him everything? And I never heard about you till after you were married. Then I wanted to write to you, but I was scared he might read it. And I couldn't leave her upstairs to come away to see you. I kept writing Sammy to bring you here right off, although having him come frightened me to death for fear he might get to suspect something. You got to get him right away from here, Nina! I just kept hoping you wouldn't want children right away – young folks don't nowadays – until I'd seen you and told you everything. And I thought you'd love him like I did his father, and be satisfied with him alone.

NINA

(Lifting her head – wildly.)

No! I don't! I won't! I'll leave him!

MRS. EVANS

(Shaking her – fiercely.)

You can't! He'd go crazy sure then! You'd be a devil! Don't you see how he loves you?

NINA

(Breaking away from her – harshly.)

Well, I don't love him! I only married him because he needed me – and I needed children! And now you tell me I've got to kill my – oh, yes, I see I've got to, you needn't argue any more! I love it too much to make it run that chance! And I hate it too, now, because it's sick, it's not my baby, it's his!

(With terrible ironic bitterness.)

And still you can dare to tell me I can't even leave Sam!

MRS. EVANS

(Very sadly and bitterly.)

You just said you married him because he needed you. Don't he need you now – more'n ever? But I can't tell you not to leave him, not if you don't love him. But you oughtn't to have married him when you didn't love him. And it'll be your fault, what'll happen.

NINA

(Torturedly.)

What will happen? – what do you mean? – Sam will be all right – just as he was before – and it's not my fault, anyway! – it's not my fault!

(Then thinking conscience-strickenly.)

Poor Sam . . . she's right . . . it's not his fault . . . it's mine . . . I wanted to use him to save myself . . . I acted the coward again . . . as I did with Gordon . . .

MRS. EVANS

(Grimly.)

You know what'll happen to him if you leave him – after all I've told you!

(Then breaking into intense pleading.)

Oh, I'd get down on my knees to you, don't make my boy run that risk! You got to give one Evans, the last one, a chance to live in this world! And you'll learn to love him, if you give up enough for him!

(Then with a grim smile.)

Why, I even love that idiot upstairs, I've taken care of her so many years, lived her life for her with my life, you might say. You give your life to Sammy, then you'll love him same as you love yourself. You'll have to! That's sure as death!

(She laughs a queer gentle laugh full of amused bitterness.)

NINA

(With a sort of dull stupid wonderment.)

And you've found peace? –

MRS. EVANS

(Sardonically.)

There's peace in the green fields of Eden, they say! You got to die to find out!

(Then proudly.)

But I can say I feel proud of having lived fair to them that gave me love and trusted in me!

NINA

(Struck – confusedly.)

Yes – that's true, isn't it?

(*Thinking strangely.*)

Lived fair . . . pride . . . trust . . . play the game! . . . who is speaking to me . . . Gordon! . . . oh, Gordon, do you mean I must give Sam the life I didn't give you? . . . Sam loved you, too . . . he said, if we have a boy, we'll call him Gordon in Gordon's honour . . . Gordon's honour! . . . what must I do now in your honour, Gordon? . . . yes! . . . I know! . . .

(*Speaking mechanically in a dull voice.*)

All right, Mother. I'll stay with Sam. There's nothing else I can do, is there, when it isn't his fault, poor boy!

(*Then suddenly snapping and bursting out in a despairing cry.*)

But I'll be so lonely! I'll have lost my baby!

(*She sinks down on her knees at Mrs. Evans' feet – piteously.*)

Oh, Mother, how can I keep on living?

MRS. EVANS

(*Thinking miserably.*)

Now she knows my suffering . . . now I got to help her . . . she's got a right to have a baby . . . another baby . . . sometime . . . somehow . . . she's giving her life to save my Sammy . . . I got to save her! . . .

(*Stammeringly.*)

Maybe, Nina –

NINA

(*Dully and resentfully again now.*)

And how about Sam? You want him to be happy, don't you? It's just as important for him as it is for me that I should have a baby! If you know anything at all about him, you ought to see that!

MRS. EVANS

(*Sadly.*)

I know that. I see that in him, Nina.

(*Gropingly.*)

There must be a way – somehow. I remember when I was carrying Sam, sometimes I'd forget I was a wife, I'd only remember the child in me. And then I used to wish I'd gone out deliberate in our first year, without my husband knowing, and picked a man, a healthy male to breed by, same's we do with stock, to give the man I loved a healthy child. And if I didn't love that other man nor him me where would be the harm? Then God would whisper: "It'd be a sin, adultery, the worst sin!" But after He'd gone I'd argue back again to myself, then we'd have a healthy child, I needn't be afraid! And maybe my husband would feel without ever knowing how he felt it, that I wasn't afraid and that child wasn't cursed and so he needn't fear and I could save him.

(*Then scornfully.*)

But I was too afraid of God then to have ever done it!

(*Then very simply.*)

He loved children so, my poor husband did, and the way they took to him, you never saw anything like it, he was a natural born father. And Sammy's the same.

NINA

(*As from a distance – strangely.*)

Yes, Sammy's the same. But I'm not the same as you.

(*Defiantly.*)

I don't believe in God the Father!

MRS. EVANS

(*Strangely.*)

Then it'd be easy for you.

(*With a grim smile.*)

And I don't believe in Him, neither, not any more. I used to be a great one for worrying about what's God and what's devil, but I got richly over it living here with poor folks that was being punished for no sins of their own, and me being punished with them for no sin but loving much.

(*With decision.*)

Being happy, that's the nearest we can ever come to knowing what's good! Being happy, that's good! The rest is just talk!

(*She pauses – then with a strange austere sternness.*)

I love my boy, Sammy. I could see how much he wants you to have a baby. Sammy's got to feel sure you love him – to be happy. Whatever you can do to make him happy is good – is good, Nina! I don't care what! You've got to have a healthy baby – some time – so's you can both be happy! It's your rightful duty!

NINA

(*Confusedly – in a half-whisper.*)

Yes, Mother.

(*Thinking longingly.*)

I want to be happy! . . . it's my right . . . and my duty! . . .

(*Then suddenly in guilty agony.*)

Oh, my baby . . . my poor baby . . . I'm forgetting you . . . desiring another after you are dead! . . . I feel you beating against my heart for mercy . . . oh! . . .

(*She weeps with bitter anguish.*)

MRS. EVANS

(*Gently and with deep sympathy.*)

I know what you're suffering. And I wouldn't say what I just said now only I know us two mustn't see each other ever again. You and Sammy have got to forget me.

(As Nina makes a motion of protest – grimly and inexorably.)

Oh, yes, you will – easy. People forget everything. They got to, poor people! And I'm saying what I said about a healthy baby so's you will remember it when you need to, after you've forgotten – this one.

NINA

(Sobbing pitifully.)

Don't! Please, Mother!

MRS EVANS

(With sudden tenderness – gathering Nina up in her arms, brokenly.)

You poor child! You're like the daughter of my sorrow! You're closer to me now than ever Sammy could be! I want you to be happy!

(She begins to sob, too, kissing Nina's bowed head.)

Curtain

ACT FOUR

SCENE: *An evening early in the following winter about seven months later. The Professor's study again. The books in the cases have never been touched, their austere array shows no gaps, but the glass separating them from the world is grey with dust, giving them a blurred ghostly quality. The table, although it is the same, is no longer the Professor's table, just as the other furniture in the room, by its disarrangement, betrays that the Professor's well-ordered mind no longer trims it to his personality. The table has become neurotic. Volumes of the "Encyclopædia Britannica" mixed up with popular treatises on "Mind Training for Success," etc., looking startlingly modern and disturbing against the background of classics in the original, are slapped helter-skelter on top of each other on it. The titles of these books face in all directions, no one volume is placed with any relation to the one beneath it – the effect is that they have no connected meaning. The rest of the table is littered with an ink bottle, pens, pencils, erasers, a box of typewriting paper, and a typewriter at the centre before the chair, which is pushed back, setting the rug askew. On the floor beside the table are an overflowing waste paper basket, a few sheets of paper and the rubber cover for the typewriter like a collapsed tent. The rocking chair is no longer at centre but has been pulled nearer the table, directly faces it with its back to the bench. This bench in turn has been drawn much closer, but is now placed more to the rear and half faces front, its back squarely to the door in the corner.*

Evans is seated in the Professor's old chair. He has evidently been typing, or is about to type, for a sheet of paper can be seen in the machine. He smokes a pipe, which he is always re-lighting whether it needs it or not, and which he bites and shifts about and pulls in and out and puffs at nervously. His expression is dispirited, his eyes shift about, his shoulders are collapsed submissively. He seems much thinner, his face drawn and sallow. The collegiate clothes are no longer natty, they need pressing and look too big for him.

EVANS

(Turns to his typewriter and pounds out a few words with a sort of aimless desperation – then tears the sheet out of the machine with an exclamation of disgust, crumples it up and throws it violently on the floor, pushing his chair back and jumping to his feet.)

Hell!

(He begins pacing up and down the room, puffing at his pipe, thinking tormentedly.)

No use . . . can't think of a darn thing . . . well, who could dope out a novel ad on another powdered milk, anyway? . . . all the stuff been used already . . . Tartars conquering on dried mare's milk . . . Metchnikoff, eminent scientist . . . been done to death . . . but simply got to work out something or . . . Cole said, what's been the matter with you lately? . . . you started off so well . . . I thought you were a real find, but your work's fallen off to nothing . . .

(He sits down on the edge of the bench near by, his shoulders hunched – despondently.)

Couldn't deny it . . . been going stale ever since we came back from that trip home . . . no ideas . . . I'll get fired . . . sterile . . .

(With a guilty terror.)

in more ways than one, I guess! . . .

(He springs to his feet as if this idea were a pin stuck in him – lighting his already lighted pipe, walks up and down again, forcing his thoughts into other channels.)

Bet the old man turns over in his grave at my writing ads in his study . . . maybe that's why I can't . . . bum influence . . . try to-morrow in my bedroom . . . sleeping alone . . . since Nina got sick . . . some woman's sickness . . . wouldn't tell me . . . too modest . . . still, there are some things a husband has a right to know . . . especially when we haven't . . . in five months . . . doctor told her she mustn't, she said . . . what doctor? . . . she's never said . . . what the hell's the matter with you, do you think Nina's lying? . . . no . . . but . . .

(Desperately.)

If I was only sure it was because she's really sick . . . not just sick of me! . . .

(He sinks down in the rocking chair despondently.)

Certainly been a big change in her . . . since that visit home . . . what happened between Mother and her? . . . she says nothing . . . they seemed to like each other . . . both of them cried when we left . . . still, Nina insisted on going that same day and Mother seemed anxious to get rid of us . . . can't make it out . . . next few weeks Nina couldn't be loving enough . . . I never was so happy . . . then she crashed . . . strain of waiting and hoping she'd get pregnant . . . and nothing happening . . . that's what did it . . . my fault! . . . how d'you know? . . . you can't tell that! . . .

(He jumps to his feet again – walks up and down again distractedly.)

God, if we'd only have a kid! . . . then I'd show them all what I could do! . . . Cole always used to say I had the stuff, and Ned certainly thought so. . . .

(With sudden relieved excitement.)

By gosh, I was forgetting! . . . Ned's coming out to-night . . . forgot to tell Nina . . . mustn't let her get wise I got him to come to look her over . . . she'd hate me for swallowing my pride after he's never been to see us . . . but I had to . . . this has got my goat . . . I've got to know what's wrong . . . and Ned's the only one I can trust . . .

(He flings himself on chair in front of desk and, picking up a fresh sheet of paper, jams it into the machine.)

Gosh, I ought to try and get a new start on this before it's time . . .

(He types a sentence or two, a strained frown of concentration on his face. Nina comes silently through the door and stands just inside it looking at him. She has grown thin again, her face is pale and drawn, her movements are those of extreme nervous tension.)

NINA

(Before she can stifle her immediate reaction of contempt and dislike.)

How weak he is! . . . he'll never do anything . . . never give me my desire . . . if he'd only fall in love with someone else . . . go away . . . not be here in my father's room . . . I even have to give him a home . . . if he'd disappear . . . leave me free . . . if he'd die . . .

(Checking herself – remorsefully.)

I must stop such thoughts . . . I don't mean it . . . poor Sam! . . . trying so hard . . . loving me so much . . . I give so little in return . . . he feels I'm always watching him with scorn . . . I can't tell him it's with pity . . . how can I help watching him? . . . help worrying over his worry because of what it might lead to . . . after what his mother . . . how horrible life is! . . . he's worried now . . . he doesn't sleep . . . I hear him tossing about . . . I must sleep with him again soon . . . he's only home two nights a week . . . it isn't fair of me . . . I must try . . . I must! . . . he suspects my revulsion . . . it's hurting him . . . oh, poor dead baby I dared not bear, how I might have loved your father for your sake! . . .

EVANS

(Suddenly feeling her presence, jerks himself to his feet – with a diffident guilty air which is noticeable about him now whenever he is in her presence.)

Hallo, dear! I thought you were lying down.

(Guiltily.)

Did the noise of my typing bother you? I'm terribly sorry!

NINA

(Irritated in spite of herself.)

Why is he always cringing? . . .

(She comes forward to the chair at centre and sits down – forcing a smile.)

But there's nothing to be terribly sorry about!

(As he stands awkard and confused, like a schoolboy who has been called on to recite and cannot and is being "bawled out" before the class, she forces a playful tone.)

Goodness, Sam, how tragic you can get about nothing at all!

EVANS

(Still forced to justify himself – contritely.)

I know it isn't pleasant for you having me drag my work out here, trying to pound out rotten ads.

(With a short laugh.)

Trying to is right!

(Blurts out.)

I wouldn't do it except that Cole gave me a warning to buck up – or get out.

NINA

(Stares at him, more annoyed, her eyes hardening, thinking.)

Yes! . . . he'll always be losing one job, getting another, starting with a burst of confidence each time, then . . .

(Cutting him with a careless sneering tone.)

Well, it isn't a job to worry much about losing, is it?

EVANS

(Wincing pitiably.)

No, not much money. But I used to think there was a fine chance to rise there – but of course that's my fault, I haven't made good –

(He finishes miserably.)

somehow.

NINA

(Her antagonism giving way to remorseful pity.)

What makes me so cruel? . . . he's so defenceless . . . his mother's baby . . . poor sick baby! . . . poor Sam! . . .

(She jumps to her feet and goes over to him.)

EVANS

(As she comes – with a defensive, boastful bravery.)

Oh, I can get another job just as good, all right – maybe a lot better.

NINA

(Reassuringly.)

Certainly, you can! And I'm sure you're not going to lose this one. You're always anticipating trouble.

(She kisses him and sits on the arm of his chair, putting an arm around his neck and pulling his head on to her breast.)

And it isn't your fault, you big goose, you! It's mine. I know how hard it makes everything for you, being tied to a wife who's too sick to be a wife. You ought to have married a big strapping, motherly –

EVANS

(In the seventh heaven now – passionately.)

Bunk! All the other women in the world aren't worth your little finger! It's you who ought to have married some one worth while, not a poor fish like me! But no one could love you more than I do, no matter what he was!

NINA

(Presses his head on her breast, avoiding his eyes, kisses him on the forehead.)

And I love you, Sam.

(Staring out over his head – with loving pity, thinking.)

I almost do . . . poor unfortunate boy! . . . at these moments . . . as his mother loves him . . . but that isn't enough for him . . . I can hear his mother saying, "Sammy's got to feel sure you love him . . . to be happy." . . . I must try to make him feel sure . . .

(Speaking gently.)

I want you to be happy, Sam.

EVANS

(His face transformed with happiness.)

I am – a hundred times more than I deserve!

NINA

(Presses his head down on her breast so he cannot see her eyes – gently.)

Ssshh!

(Thinking sadly.)

I promised her . . . but I couldn't see how hard it would be to let him love me . . . after his baby . . . was gone . . . it was hard even to keep on living . . . after that operation . . . Gordon's spirit followed me from room to room . . . poor reproachful ghost! . . .

(With bitter mockery.)

Oh, Gordon, I'm afraid this is a deeper point of honour than any that was ever shot down in flames! . . . what would your honour say now? . . . "Stick to him! . . . play the game!" . . . oh, yes, I know . . . I'm sticking . . . but he isn't happy . . . I'm trying to play the game . . . then why do I keep myself from him? . . . but I was really sick . . . for a time after . . . since then, I couldn't . . . but . . . oh, I'll try . . . I'll try soon . . .

(Tenderly – but having to force herself to say it.)

Doesn't my boy want to sleep with me again – some time soon?

EVANS

(Passionately – hardly able to believe his ears.)

Oh, it'd be wonderful, Nina! But are you sure you really want me to – that you'll feel well enough?

NINA

(Repeats his words as if she were memorizing a lesson.)

Yes, I want you to. Yes, I'll feel well enough.

(He seizes her hand and kisses it in a passionately grateful silence.)

(She thinks with resigned finality.)

There, Sammy's mother and Gordon . . . I'll play the game . . . it will make him happy for a while . . . as he was in those weeks after we'd left his mother . . . when I gave myself with a mad pleasure in torturing myself for his pleasure! . . .

(Then with weary hopelessness.)

He'll be happy until he begins to feel guilty again because I'm not pregnant . . .

(With a grim bitter smile.)

Poor Sam, if he only knew the precautions . . . as if I wouldn't die rather than take the slightest chance of that happening! . . . ever again . . . what a tragic joke it was on both of us! . . . I wanted my baby so! . . . oh, God! . . . his mother said . . . "You've got to have a healthy baby . . . some time . . . it's your rightful duty" . . . that seemed right then . . . but now . . . it seems cowardly . . . to betray poor Sam . . . and vile to give myself . . . without love or desire . . . and yet I've given myself to men before without a thought, just to give them a moment's happiness . . . can't I do that again? . . . when it's a case of Sam's happiness? . . . and my own? . . .

(She gets up from beside him with a hunted movement.)

It must be half-past eight. Charlie's coming to bring his suggestions on my outline for Gordon's biography.

EVANS

(His bliss shattered – dejectedly.)

Always happens . . . just as we get close . . . something comes between . . .

(Then confusedly.)

Say, I forgot to tell you Ned's coming out to-night.

NINA

(Astonished.)

Ned Darrell?

EVANS

Sure. I happened to run into him the other day and invited him and he said Saturday evening. He couldn't tell what train. Said never mind meeting him.

NINA

(Excitedly.)

Why didn't you tell me before, you big booby?

(She kisses him.)

There, don't mind. But it's just like you. Now someone'll have to go down to the store. And I'll have to get the spare room ready.

(She hurries to the doorway. He follows her.)

EVANS

I'll help you.

NINA

You'll do nothing of the kind! You'll stay right downstairs and bring them in here and cover up my absence. Thank heavens, Charlie won't stay long if Ned is here.

(The door-bell rings – excitedly.)

There's one of them now. I'll run upstairs. Come up and tell me if it's Ned – and get rid of Charlie.

(She kisses him playfully and hurries out.)

EVANS

(Looking after her – thinks.)

She seems better to-night . . . happier . . . she seems to love me . . . if she'll only get all well again, then everything will . . .

(The bell rings again.)

I must give Ned a good chance to talk to her . . .

(He goes out to the outer door – returns a moment later with Marsden. The latter's manner is preoccupied and nervous. His face has an expression of anxiety which he tries to conceal. He seems a prey to some inner fear he is trying to hide even from himself and is resolutely warding off from his consciousness. His tall, thin body stoops as if a part of its sustaining will had been removed.)

EVANS

(With a rather forced welcoming note.)

Come on in, Charlie. Nina's upstairs lying down.

MARSDEN

(With marked relief.)

Then by all means don't disturb her. I just dropped in to bring back her outline with the suggestions I've made.

(He has taken some papers out of his pocket and hands them to Evans.)

I couldn't have stayed but a minute in any event. Mother is a bit under the weather these days.

EVANS

(Perfunctorily.)

Too bad.

(Thinking vindictively.)

Serve her right, the old scandal-monger, after the way she's gossiped about Nina! . . .

MARSDEN

(With assumed carelessness.)

Just a little indigestion. Nothing serious, but it annoys her terribly.

(Thinking frightenedly.)

That dull pain she complains of . . . I don't like it . . . and she won't see anyone but old Doctor Tibbetts . . . she's sixty-eight . . . I can't help fearing . . . no! . . .

EVANS

(Bored – vaguely.)

Well, I suppose you've got to be careful of every little thing when you get to her age.

MARSDEN

(Positively bristling.)

Her age? Mother isn't so old!

EVANS

(Surprised.)

Over sixty-five, isn't she?

MARSDEN

(Indignantly.)

You're quite out there! She's still under sixty-five – and in health and spirits she isn't more than fifty! Everyone remarks that!

(Annoyed at himself.)

Why did I lie to him about her age? . . . I must be on edge . . . Mother is rather difficult to live with these days, getting me worried to death, when it's probably nothing . . .

EVANS

(Annoyed in his turn – thinking.)

Why all the fuss? . . . as if I gave a damn if the old girl was a million! . . .

(Indicating the papers.)

I'll give these to Nina first thing in the morning.

MARSDEN

(Mechanically.)

Right-o! Thank you.

(He starts to go toward door – then turns – fussily.)

But you'd better take a look while I'm here and see if it's clear. I've written on the margins. See if there's anything you can't make out.

(Evans nods helplessly and begins reading the sheets, going back beneath the lamp.)

MARSDEN

(Looking around him with squeamish disapproval.)

What a mess they've made of this study! . . . poor Professor! . . . dead and forgotten . . . and his tomb desecrated . . . does Sam write his ads here of a week-end now? . . . the last touch! . . . and Nina labours with love at Gordon's biography . . . whom the Professor hated! . . . "life is so full of a number of things!" . . . why does everyone in the world think they can write? . . . but I've only myself to blame . . . why the devil did I ever suggest it to her? . . . because I hoped my helping her while Sam was in the city would bring us alone together? . . . but I made the suggestion before she had that abortion performed! . . . how do you know she did? . . . because I know! . . . there are psychic affinities . . . her body confessed . . . and since then, I've felt an aversion . . . as if she were a criminal . . . she is! . . . how could she? . . . why? . . . I thought she wanted a child . . . but evidently I don't know her . . . I suppose, afraid it would spoil her figure . . . her flesh . . . her power to enslave men's senses . . . mine . . . and I had hoped . . . looked forward to her becoming a mother . . . for my peace of mind. . . .

(Catching himself – violently.)

Shut up! . . . what a base creature I'm becoming! . . . to have such thoughts when Mother is sick and I ought to be thinking only of her! . . . and it's none of my damn business, anyway! . . .

(Glaring at Evans resentfully as if he were to blame.)

Look at him! . . . he'll never suspect anything! . . . what a simple-simon! . . . he adored Gordon as a newsboy does a champion pugilist! . . . and Nina writes of Gordon as if he had been a demi-god! . . . when actually he came from the commonest people! . . .

(He suddenly speaks to Evans with a really savage satisfaction.)

Did I tell you I once looked up Gordon's family in Beachampton? A truly deplorable lot! When I remembered Gordon and looked at his father I had either to suspect a lover in the wood pile or to believe in an Immaculate Conception . . . that is, until I saw his mother! Then a stork became the only conceivable explanation!

EVANS

(Who has only half heard and hasn't understood, says vaguely.)

I never saw his folks.

(Indicating the papers.)

I can make this all out all right.

MARSDEN

(Sarcastically.)

I'm glad it's understandable!

EVANS

(Blunderingly.)

I'll give it to Nina – and I hope your mother is feeling better to-morrow.

MARSDEN

(Piqued.)

Oh, I'm going. Why didn't you tell me if I was interrupting – your writing!

EVANS

(Immediately guilty.)

Oh, come on, Charlie, don't get peevish, you know I didn't mean –

(The bell rings. Evans stammers in confusion, trying at a nonchalant air.)

Hallo! That must be Ned. You remember Darrell? He's coming out for a little visit. Excuse me.

(He blunders out of the door.)

MARSDEN

(Looking after him with anger mixed with alarmed suspicion and surprise.)

Darrell? . . . what's he doing here? . . . have they been meeting? . . . perhaps he was the one who performed the . . . no, his idea was she ought to have a child . . . but if she came and begged him? . . . but why should Nina beg not to have a baby? . . .

(Distractedly.)

Oh, I don't know! . . . it's all a sordid mess! . . . I ought to be going home! . . . I don't want to see Darrell! . . .

(He starts for the door – then struck by a sudden thought, stops.)

Wait . . . I could ask him about Mother . . . yes . . . good idea . . .

(He comes back to the middle of the room, front, and is standing there when Darrell enters, followed by Evans. Darrell has not changed in appearance except that his expression is graver and more thoughtful. His manner is more convincingly authoritative, more mature. He takes in Marsden from head to foot with one comprehensive glance.)

EVANS

(Awkwardly.)

Ned, you remember Charlie Marsden?

MARSDEN

(Holding out his hand, urbanely polite.)

How are you, Doctor?

DARRELL

(Shaking his hand – briefly.)

Hallo!

EVANS

I'll go up and tell Nina you're here, Ned.

(He goes, casting a resentful glance at Marsden.)

MARSDEN

(*Awkwardly, as Darrell sits down in the chair at centre, goes over and stands by the table.*)

I was on the point of leaving when you rang. Then I decided to stop and renew our acquaintance.

(*He stoops and picks up one sheet of paper, and puts it back carefully on the table.*)

DARRELL

(*Watching him – thinking.*)

Neat . . . suspiciously neat . . . he's an old maid who seduces himself in his novels . . . so I suspect . . . I'd like a chance to study him more closely. . . .

MARSDEN

(*Thinking resentfully.*)

What a boor! . . . he might say something! . . .

(*Forcing a smile.*)

And I wanted to ask a favour of you, a word of advice as to the best specialist, the very best, it would be possible to consult –

DARRELL

(*Sharply.*)

On what?

MARSDEN

(*Almost naïvely.*)

My mother has a pain in her stomach.

DARRELL

(*Amused – dryly.*)

Possibly she eats too much.

MARSDEN

(*As he bends and carefully picks another sheet from the floor to place it as carefully on the table.*)

She doesn't eat enough to keep a canary alive. It's a dull, constant pain, she says. She's terribly worried. She's terrified by the idea of cancer. But, of course, that's perfect rot, she's never been sick a day in her life and –

DARRELL

(*Sharply.*)

She's showing more intelligence about her pain than you are.

MARSDEN

(*Bending down for another sheet, his voice trembling with terror.*)

I don't understand – quite. Do you mean to say you think – ?

DARRELL

(*Brutally.*)

It's possible.

(*He has pulled out his pen and a card and is writing.*)
(*Thinking grimly.*)

Explode a bomb under him, as I did once before . . . only way to get him started doing anything. . . .

MARSDEN

(*Angrily.*)

But – that's nonsense!

DARRELL

(*With satisfaction – unruffledly.*)

People who are afraid to face unpleasant possibilities until it's too late commit more murders and suicides than –

(*Holds out a card.*)

Doctor Schultz is your man. Take her to see him – to-morrow!

MARSDEN

(*Bursting out in anger and misery.*)

Damn it, you're condemning her without – !

(*He breaks down chokingly.*)

You've no damn right – !

(*He bends down, trembling all over, to pick up another piece of paper.*)

DARRELL

(*Genuinely astonished and contrite.*)

And I thought he was so ingrown he didn't care a damn about anyone! . . . his mother . . . now I begin to see him . . .

(*He jumps from his chair and going to Marsden puts a hand on his shoulder – kindly.*)

I beg your pardon, Marsden. I only wanted to drive it in that all delay is dangerous. Your mother's pain may be due to any number of harmless causes, but you owe it to her to make sure. Here.

(*He hands out the card.*)

MARSDEN

(*Straightens up and takes it, his eyes grateful now – humbly.*)

Thank you. I'll take her to see him to-morrow.

(*Evans comes in.*)

EVANS

(*To Marsden, blunderingly.*)

Say, Charlie, I don't want to hurry you, but Nina wants some things at the store before it closes, and if you'd give me a lift –

MARSDEN

(*Dully.*)

Of course. Come along.

(*He shakes hands with Darrell.*)

Good night, Doctor – and thank you.

DARRELL

Good night.

(*Marsden goes, followed by Evans.*)

EVANS

(*Turns in the doorway and says meaningly.*)

Nina'll be right down. For Pete's sake, have a good heart-to-heart talk with her, Ned!

DARRELL

(*Frowning – impatiently.*)

Oh – all right! Run along.

(*Evans goes.*)

(*Darrell remains standing near the table looking after them, thinking about Marsden.*)

Queer fellow, Marsden . . . mother's boy still . . . if she dies what will he do? . . .

(*Then dismissing Marsden with a shrug of his shoulders.*)

Oh, well, he can always escape life in a new book. . . .

(*He moves around the table examining its disorder critically, then sits down in arm-chair – amused.*)

Evidences of authorship . . . Sam's ads? . . . isn't making good, he said . . . was I wrong in thinking he had stuff in him? . . . hope not . . . always liked Sam, don't know why exactly . . . said Nina'd gotten into a bad state again . . . what's happened to their marriage? . . . I felt a bit sorry for myself at their wedding . . . not that I'd ever fallen . . . but I did envy him in a way . . . she always had strong physical attraction for me . . . that time I kissed her . . . one reason I've steered clear since . . . take no chances on emotional didos . . . need all my mind on my work . . . got rid of even that slight suspicion . . . I'd forgotten all about her . . . she's a strange girl . . . interesting case . . . I should have kept in touch on that account . . . hope she'll tell me about herself . . . can't understand her not having child . . . it's so obviously the sensible thing . . .

(*Cynically.*)

Probably why . . . to expect common sense of people proves you're lacking in it yourself! . . .

NINA

(*Enters silently. She has fixed herself up, put on her best dress, arranged her hair, rouged, etc. – but it is principally her mood that has changed her, making her appear a younger, prettier person for the moment. Darrell immediately senses her presence, and, looking up, gets to his feet with a smile of affectionate admiration. She comes quickly over to him saying with frank pleasure:*)

Hallo, Ned! I'm certainly glad to see you again – after all these years!

DARRELL

(*As they shake hands – smiling.*)

Not as long as all that, is it?

(*Thinking admiringly.*)

Wonderful-looking as ever . . . Sam is a lucky devil! . . .

NINA

(*Thinking.*)

Strong hands like Gordon's . . . take hold of you . . . not like Sam's . . . yielding fingers that let you fall back into yourself . . .

(*Teasingly.*)

I ought to cut you dead after the shameful way you've ignored us!

DARRELL

(*A bit embarrassedly.*)

I've really meant to write.

(*His eyes examining her keenly.*)

Been through a lot since I saw her . . . face shows it . . . nervous tension pronounced . . . hiding behind her smile . . .

NINA

(*Uneasy under his glance.*)

I hate that professional look in his eyes . . . watching symptoms . . . without seeing me . . .

(*With resentful mockery.*)

Well, what do you suspect is wrong with the patient now, Doctor?

(*She laughs nervously.*)

Sit down, Ned. I suppose you can't help your diagnosing stare.

(*She turns from him and sits down in the rocker at centre.*)

DARRELL

(*Quickly averting his eyes – sits down – jokingly.*)

Same old unjust accusation! You were always reading diagnosis into me, when what I was really thinking was what fine eyes you had, or what a becoming gown, or –

NINA

(*Smiling.*)

Or what a becoming alibi you could cook up! Oh, I know you!

(*With a sudden change of mood she laughs gaily and naturally.*)

But you're forgiven – that is, if you can explain why you've never been to see us.

DARRELL

Honestly, Nina, I've been so rushed with work I haven't had a chance to go anywhere.

NINA

Or an inclination!

DARRELL

(*Smiling.*)

Well – maybe.

NINA

Do you like the Institute so much?

(*He nods gravely.*)

Is it the big opportunity you wanted?

DARRELL

(*Simply.*)

I think it is.

NINA

(*With a smile.*)

Well, you're the taking kind for whom opportunities are made!

DARRELL

(*Smiling.*)

I hope so.

NINA

(*Sighing.*)

I wish that could be said of more of us –

(*Then quickly.*)

– meaning myself.

DARRELL

(*Thinking with a certain satisfaction.*)

Meaning Sam . . . that doesn't look hopeful for future wedded bliss! . . .

(*Teasingly.*)

But I heard you were "taking an opportunity" to go in for literature – collaborating with Marsden.

NINA

No, Charlie is only going to advise. He'd never deign to appear as co-author. And, besides, he never appreciated the real Gordon. No one did except me.

DARRELL

(*Thinking caustically.*)

Gordon myth strong as ever . . . root of her trouble still . . .

(*Keenly inquisitive.*)

Sam certainly appreciated him, didn't he?

NINA

(*Not remembering to hide her contempt.*)

Sam? Why, he's the exact opposite in every way!

DARRELL

(*Caustically thinking.*)

These heroes die hard . . . but perhaps she can write him out of her system. . . .

(*Persuasively.*)

Well, you're going ahead with the biography, aren't you? I think you ought to.

NINA

(*Dryly.*)

For my soul, Doctor?

(*Listlessly.*)

I suppose I will. I don't know. I haven't much time. The duties of a wife –

(*Teasingly.*)

By the way, if it isn't too rude to inquire, aren't you getting yourself engaged to some fair lady or other?

DARRELL

(*Smiling – but emphatically.*)

Not on your life! Not until after I'm thirty-five, at least!

NINA

(*Sarcastically.*)

Then you don't believe in taking your own medicine? Why, Doctor! Think of how much good it would do you! –

(*Excitedly with a hectic sarcasm.*)

– if you had a nice girl to love – or was it learn to love? – and take care of – whose character you could shape and whose life you could guide and make what you pleased, in whose unselfish devotion you could find peace!

(*More and more bitterly sarcastic.*)

And you ought to have a baby, Doctor! You will never know what life is, you'll never be really happy until you've had a baby, Doctor – a fine, healthy baby!

(*She laughs a bitter, sneering laugh.*)

DARRELL

(*After a quick, keen glance, thinking.*)

Good! . . . she's going to tell . . .

(*Meekly.*)

I recognize my arguments. Was I really wrong on every point, Nina?

NINA

(*Harshly.*)

On every single point, Doctor!

DARRELL

(*Glancing at her keenly.*)

But how? You haven't given the baby end of it a chance yet, have you?

NINA

(*Bitterly.*)

Oh, haven't I?

(*Then bursts out with intense bitterness.*)

I'll have you know I'm not destined to bear babies, Doctor!

DARRELL

(*Startledly.*)

What's that? . . . why not? . . .

(*Again with a certain satisfaction.*)

Can she mean Sam? . . . that he . . .

(*Soothingly – but plainly disturbed.*)

Why don't you begin at the beginning and tell me all about it? I feel responsible.

NINA

(*Fiercely.*)

You are!

(*Then wearily.*)

And you're not. No one is. You didn't know. No one could know.

DARRELL

(*In same tone.*)

Know what?

(*Thinking with the same eagerness to believe something he hopes.*)

She must mean no one could know that Sam wasn't . . . but I might have guessed it . . . from his general weakness . . . poor unlucky devil! . . .

(*Then as she remains silent – urgingly.*)

Tell me. I want to help you, Nina.

NINA

(*Touched.*)

It's too late, Ned.

(*Then suddenly.*)

I've just thought – Sam said he happened to run into you. That isn't so, is it? He went to see you and told you how worried he was about me and asked you out to see me, didn't he?

(*As Darrell nods.*)

Oh, I don't mind! It's even rather touching.

(*Then mockingly.*)

Well, since you're out here professionally, and my husband wants me to consult you, I might as well give you the whole case history!

(*Wearily.*)

I warn you it isn't pretty, Doctor! But then life doesn't seem to be pretty, does it? And, after all, you aided and abetted God the Father in making this mess. I hope it'll teach you not to be so cocksure in future.

(*More and more bitterly.*)

I must say you proceeded very unscientifically, Doctor!

(*Then suddenly starts her story in a dull monotonous tone recalling that of Evans' mother in the previous Act.*)

When we went to visit Sam's mother I'd known for two months that I was going to have a baby.

DARRELL

(*Startled – unable to hide a trace of disappointment.*)

Oh, then you actually were?

(*Thinking disappointedly and ashamed of himself for being disappointed.*)

All wrong, what I thought . . . she was going to . . . then why didn't she? . . .

NINA

(*With a strange happy intensity.*)

Oh, Ned, I loved it more than I've ever loved anything in my life – even Gordon! I loved it so it seemed at times that Gordon must be its real father, that Gordon must have come to me in a dream while I was lying asleep beside Sam! And I was happy! I almost loved Sam then! I felt he was a good husband!

DARRELL

(*Instantly repelled – thinking with scornful jealousy.*)

Ha! . . . the hero again! . . . comes to her bed! . . . puts horns on poor Sam! . . . becomes the father of his child! . . . I'll be damned if hers isn't the most idiotic obsession I ever . . .

NINA

(*Her voice suddenly becoming flat and lifeless.*)

And then Sam's mother told me I couldn't have my baby. You see, Doctor, Sam's great-grandfather was insane, and Sam's grandmother died in an asylum, and Sam's father had lost his mind for years before he died, and an aunt who is still alive is crazy. So of course I had to agree it would be wrong – and I had an operation.

DARRELL

(*Who has listened with amazed horror – profoundly shocked and stunned.*)

Good God! Are you crazy, Nina? I simply can't believe! It would be too hellish! Poor Sam, of all people!

(*Bewilderedly.*)

Nina! Are you absolutely sure?

NINA

(*Immediately defensive and mocking.*)

Absolutely, Doctor! Why? Do you think it's I who am crazy? Sam looks so healthy and sane, doesn't he? He fooled you completely, didn't he? You thought he'd be an ideal husband for me! And poor Sam's fooling himself too because he doesn't know anything about all this – so you can't blame him, Doctor!

DARRELL

(Thinking in a real panic of horror – and a flood of protective affection for her.)

God, this is too awful! . . . on top of all the rest! . . . how did she ever stand it! . . . she'll lose her mind, too! . . . and it's my fault! . . .

(Getting up, comes to her and puts his hand on her shoulders, standing behind her – tenderly.)

Nina! I'm so damn sorry! There's only one possible thing to do now. You'll have to make Sam give you a divorce.

NINA

(Bitterly.)

Yes? Then what do you suppose will be his finish? No, I've enough guilt in my memory now, thank you! I've got to stick to Sam!

(Then with a strange monotonous insistence.)

I've promised Sam's mother I'd make him happy! He's unhappy now because he thinks he isn't able to give me a child. And I'm unhappy because I've lost my child. So I must have another baby – somehow – don't you think, Doctor? – to make us both happy?

(She looks up at him pleadingly. For a moment they stare into each other's eyes – then both turn away in guilty confusion.)

DARRELL

(Bewilderedly thinking.)

That look in her eyes . . . what does she want me to think? . . . why does she talk so much about being happy? . . . am I happy? . . . I don't know . . what is happiness? . . .

(Confusedly.)

Nina, I don't know what to think.

NINA

(Thinking strangely.)

That look in his eyes . . . what did he mean? . . .

(With the same monotonous insistence.)

You must know what to think. I can't think it out myself any more. I need your advice – your *scientific* advice this time, if you please, Doctor. I've thought and thought about it. I've told myself it's what I ought to do. Sam's own mother urged me to do it. It's sensible and kind and just and good. I've told myself this a thousand times and yet I can't quite convince something in me that's afraid of something. I need the courage of someone who can stand outside and reason it out as if Sam and I were no more than guinea-pigs. You've got to help me, Doctor! You've got to show me what's the sane – the truly sane, you understand! – thing I must do for Sam's sake, and my own.

DARRELL

(Thinking confusedly.)

What do I have to do? . . . this was all my fault . . . I owe her something in return . . . I owe Sam something . . . I owe them happiness! . . .

(Irritably.)

Damn it, there's a humming in my ears! . . . I've caught some fever . . . I swore to live coolly . . . let me see . . .

(In a cold, emotionless professional voice, his face like a mask of a doctor.)

A doctor must be in full possession of the facts, if he is to advise. What is it precisely that Sam's wife has thought so much of doing?

NINA

(In the same insistent tone.)

Of picking out a healthy male about whom she cared nothing and having a child by him that Sam would believe was his child, whose life would give him confidence in his own living, who would be for him a living proof that his wife loved him.

(Confusedly, strangely and purposefully.)

This doctor is healthy. . . .

DARRELL

(In his ultra-professional manner – like an automaton of a doctor.)

I see. But this needs a lot of thinking over. It isn't easy to prescribe –

(Thinking.)

I have a friend who has a wife . . . I was envious at his wedding . . . but what has that to do with it? . . . damn it, my mind won't work! . . . it keeps running away to her . . . it wants to mate with her mind . . . in the interest of Science? . . . what damned rot I'm thinking! . . .

NINA

(Thinking as before.)

This doctor is nothing to me but a healthy male . . . when he was Ned he once kissed me . . . but I cared nothing about him . . . so that's all right, isn't it, Sam's Mother?

DARRELL

(Thinking.)

Let me see. . . . I am in the laboratory and they are guinea-pigs . . . in fact, in the interest of Science, I can be, for the purpose of this experiment, a healthy guinea-pig myself and still remain an observer . . . I observe my pulse is high, for example, and that's obviously because I am stricken with a recurrence of an old desire . . . desire is a natural male reaction to the beauty of the female . . . her husband is my friend. . . . I have always tried to help him . . .

(*Coldly.*)

I've been considering what Sam's wife told me and her reasoning is quite sound. The child can't be her husband's.

NINA

Then you agree with Sam's mother? She said: "Being happy is the nearest we can ever come to knowing what good is!"

DARRELL

I agree with her decidedly. Sam's wife should find a healthy father for Sam's child at once. It is her sane duty to her husband.

(*Worriedly thinking.*)

Have I ever been happy? . . . I have studied to cure the body's unhappiness . . . I have watched happy smiles form on the lips of the dying . . . I have experienced pleasure with a number of women I desired but never loved . . . I have known a bit of honour and a trifle of self-satisfaction . . . this talk of happiness seems to me extraneous . . .

NINA

(*Beginning to adopt a timid, diffident, guilty tone.*)

This will have to be hidden from Sam so he can never know! Oh, Doctor, Sam's wife is afraid!

DARRELL

(*Sharply professional.*)

Nonsense! This is no time for timidity! Happiness hates the timid! So does Science! Certainly Sam's wife must conceal her action! To let Sam know would be insanely cruel of her – and stupid, for then no one could be the happier for her act!

(*Anxiously thinking.*)

Am I right to advise this? . . . yes, it is clearly the rational thing to do . . . but this advice betrays my friend! . . . no, it saves him! . . . it saves his wife . . . and if a third party should know a little happiness . . . is he any poorer, am I any the less his friend because I saved him? . . . no, my duty to him is plain . . . and my duty as an experimental searcher after truth . . . to observe these three guinea-pigs, of which I am one . . .

NINA

(*Thinking determinedly.*)

I must have my baby! . . .

(*Timidly – gets from her chair and half turns toward him – pleadingly.*)

You must give his wife courage, Doctor. You must free her from her feeling of guilt.

DARRELL

There can only be guilt when one deliberately neglects one's manifest duty to life. Anything else is rot! This woman's duty is to save her husband and herself by bearing a healthy child!

(*Thinking guiltily and instinctively moving away from her.*)

I am healthy . . . but he is my friend . . . there is such a thing as honour! . . .

NINA

(*Determinedly.*)

I must take my happiness! . . .

(*Frightenedly – comes after him.*)

But she is ashamed. It's adultery. It's wrong.

DARRELL

(*Moving away again – with a cold sneering laugh of impatience.*)

Wrong! Would she rather see her husband wind up in an asylum? Would she rather face the prospect of going to pot herself, mentally, morally and physically, through year after year of devilling herself and him? Really, Madame, if you can't throw overboard all such irrelevant moral ideas, I'll have to give up this case here and now!

(*Thinking frightenedly.*)

Who is talking? . . . is he suggesting me? . . . but you know very well I can't be the one, Doctor! . . . why not, you're healthy and it's a friendly act for all concerned. . . .

NINA

(*Thinking determinedly.*)

I must have my baby! . . .

(*Going further toward him – she can now touch him with her hand.*)

Please, Doctor, you must give her strength to do this right thing that seems to her so right and then so wrong!

(*She puts out her hand and takes one of his.*)

DARRELL

(*Thinking frightenedly.*)

Whose hand is this? . . . it burns me . . . I kissed her once . . . her lips were cold . . . now they would burn with happiness for me! . . .

NINA

(*Taking his other hand and slowly pulling him around to face her, although he does not look at her – pleadingly.*)

Now she feels your strength. It gives her the courage to ask you, Doctor, to suggest the father. She has changed, Doctor, since she became Sam's wife. She can't bear the thought now of giving herself to any man she could neither desire nor respect. So each time her thoughts come to the man she must select they are afraid to go on! She needs your courage to choose!

DARRELL

(As if listening to himself.)

Sam is my friend . . . well, and isn't she your friend? . . . her two hands are so warm! . . . I must not even hint at my desire! . . .

(Judicially calm.)

Well, the man must be someone who is not unattractive to her physically, of course.

NINA

Ned always attracted her.

DARRELL

(Thinking frightenedly.)

What's that she said? . . . Ned? . . . attracts? . . .

(In same tone.)

And the man should have a mind that can truly understand – a scientific mind superior to the moral scruples that cause so much human blundering and unhappiness.

NINA

She always thought Ned had a superior mind.

DARRELL

(Thinking frightenedly.)

Did she say Ned? . . . she thinks Ned . . . ?

(In same tone.)

The man should like and admire her, he should be her good friend and want to help her, but he should not love her – although he might, without harm to anyone, desire her.

NINA

Ned does not love her – but he used to like her and, I think, desire her. Does he now, Doctor?

DARRELL

(Thinking.)

Does he? . . . who is he? . . . he is Ned! . . . Ned is I! . . . I desire her! . . . I desire happiness! . . .

(Trembling now – gently.)

But, Madame, I must confess the Ned you are speaking of is I, and I am Ned.

NINA

(Gently.)

And I am Nina, who wants her baby.

(Then she reaches out and turns his head until his face faces hers, but he keeps his eyes down – she bends her head meekly and submissively – softly.)

I should be so grateful, Ned.

(He starts, looks up at her wildly, makes a motion as though to take her in his arms, then remains fixed for a moment in that attitude, staring at her bowed head as she repeats submissively:)

I should be so humbly grateful.

DARRELL

(Suddenly falling on his knees and taking her hand in both of his and kissing it humbly – with a sob.)

Yes – yes, Nina – yes – for your happiness – in that spirit!

(Thinking – fiercely triumphant.)

I shall be happy for a while! . . .

NINA

(Raising her head – thinking – proudly triumphant.)

I shall be happy! . . . I shall make my husband happy! . . .

Curtain

ACT FIVE

SCENE: *The sitting-room of a small house Evans has rented in a seashore suburb near New York. It is a bright morning in the following April.*

The room is a typical sitting-room of the quantity-production bungalow type. Windows on the left look out on a broad porch. A double doorway in rear leads into the hall. A door on right, to the dining-room. Nina has tried to take the curse of offensive, banal newness off the room with some of her own things from her old home, but the attempt has been half-hearted in the face of such overpowering commonness, and the result is a room as disorganized in character as was the Professor's study in the last Act.

The arrangement of the furniture follows the same pattern as in preceding scenes. There is a Morris chair and a round golden oak table at left of centre, an upholstered chair, covered with bright chintz at centre, a sofa covered with the same chintz at right.

Nina is sitting in the chair at centre. She has been trying to read a book, but has let this drop listlessly on her lap. A great change is noticeable in her face and bearing. She is again the pregnant woman of Act Three, but this time there is a triumphant strength about her expression, a ruthless self-confidence in her eyes. She has grown stouter, her face has filled out. One gets no impression of neurotic strain from her now, she seems nerveless and deeply calm.

NINA

(*As if listening for something within her – joyfully.*)

There! . . . that can't be my imagination . . . I felt it plainly . . . life . . . my baby . . . my only baby . . . the other never really lived . . . this is the child of my love! . . . I love Ned! . . . I've loved him ever since that first afternoon . . . when I went to him . . . so scientifically! . . .

(*She laughs at herself.*)

Oh, what a goose I was! . . . then love came to me . . . in his arms . . . happiness! . . . I hid it from him . . . I saw he was frightened . . . his own joy frightened him . . . I could feel him fighting with himself . . . during all those afternoons . . . our wonderful afternoons of happiness! . . . and I said nothing . . . I made myself be calculating . . . so when he finally said . . . dreadfully disturbed . . . "Look here, Nina, we've done all that is necessary, playing with fire is dangerous" . . . I said, "You're quite right, Ned, of all things I don't want to fall in love with you!" . . .

(*She laughs.*)

He didn't like that! . . . he looked angry . . . and afraid . . . then for weeks he never even 'phoned . . . I waited . . . it was prudent to wait . . . but every day I grew more terrified . . . then just as my will was breaking, his broke . . . he suddenly appeared again . . . but I held him to his aloof doctor's pose and sent him away, proud of his will power . . . and sick of himself with desire for me! . . . every week since then he's been coming out here . . . as my doctor . . . we've talked about our child wisely, dispassionately . . . as if it were Sam's child . . . we've never given in to our desire . . . and I've watched love grow in him until I'm sure . . .

(*With sudden alarm.*)

But am I? . . . he's never once mentioned love . . . perhaps I've been a fool to play the part I've played . . . it may have turned him against me . . .

(*Suddenly with calm confidence.*)

No . . . he does . . . I feel it . . . it's only when I start thinking I begin to doubt . . .

(*She settles back and stares dreamily before her – a pause.*)

There . . . again . . . his child! . . . my child moving in my life . . . my life moving in my child . . . the world is whole and perfect . . . all things are each other's . . . life is . . . and the is is beyond reason . . . questions die in the silence of this peace . . . I am living a dream within the great dream of the tide . . . breathing in the tide I dream and breathe back my dream into the tide . . . suspended in the movement of the tide, I feel life move in me, suspended in me . . . no whys matter . . . there is no why . . . I am a mother . . . God is a Mother . . .

(*She sighs happily, closing her eyes. A pause.*)

(*Evans enters from the hallway in rear. He is dressed carefully but his clothes are old ones – shabby collegiate gentility – and he has forgotten to shave. His eyes look pitiably harried, his manner has become a distressingly obvious attempt to cover up a chronic state of nervous panic and guilty conscience. He stops inside the doorway and looks at her with a pitiable furtiveness, arguing with himself, trying to get up his courage.*)

EVANS

Tell her! . . . go on! . . . you made up your mind to, didn't you? . . . don't quit now! . . . tell her you've decided . . . for her sake . . . to face the truth . . . that she can't love you . . . she's tried . . . she's acted like a good sport . . . but she's beginning to hate you . . . and you can't blame her . . . she wanted children . . . and you haven't been able . . .

(*Protesting feebly.*)

But I don't know for certain . . . that that's my fault . . .

(*Then bitterly.*)

Aw, don't kid yourself, if she'd married someone else . . . if Gordon had lived and married her . . . I'll bet in the first month she'd . . . you'd better resign from the whole game . . . with a gun! . . .

(*He swallows hard as if he were choking back a sob – then savagely.*)

Stop whining! . . . go on and wake her up! . . . say you're willing to give her a divorce so she can marry some real guy who can give her what she ought to have! . . .

(*Then with sudden terror.*)

And if she says yes? . . . I couldn't bear it! . . . I'd die without her! . . .

(*Then with a sombre alien forcefulness.*)

All right . . . good riddance! . . . I'd have the guts to bump off then, all right! . . . that'd set her free . . . come on now! . . . ask her! . . .

(*But his voice begins to tremble uncertainly again as he calls.*)

Nina!

NINA

(*Opens her eyes and gazes calmly, indifferently at him.*)

Yes?

EVANS

(*Immediately terrified and beaten – thinking.*)

I can't! . . . the way she looks at me! . . . she'd say yes! . . .

(*Stammering.*)

I hate to wake you up, but – it's about time for Ned to come, isn't it?

NINA

(*Calmly.*)

I wasn't asleep.

(*Thinking as if she found it hard to concentrate on him, to realize his existence.*)

This man is my husband . . . it's hard to remember that . . . people will say he's the father of my child. . . .

(*With revulsion.*)

That's shameful! . . . and yet that's exactly what I wanted! . . . wanted! . . . not now! . . . now I love Ned! . . . I won't lose him! . . . Sam must give me a divorce . . . I've sacrificed enough of my life . . . what has he given me? . . . not even a home . . . I had to sell my father's home to get money so we could move near his job . . . and then he lost his job! . . . now he's depending on Ned to help him get another! . . . my love! . . . how shameless! . . .

(*Then contritely.*)

Oh, I'm unjust . . . poor Sam doesn't know about Ned . . . and it was I who wanted to sell the place . . . I was lonely there . . . I wanted to be near Ned. . . .

EVANS

(Thinking in agony.)

What's she thinking? . . . probably lucky for me I don't know! . . .

(Forcing a brisk air as he turns away from her.)

I hope Ned brings that letter he promised me to the manager of the Globe Company. I'm keen to get on the job again.

NINA

(With scornful pity.)

Oh, I guess Ned will bring the letter. I asked him not to forget.

EVANS

I hope they'll have an opening right off. We can use the money.

(Hanging his head.)

I feel rotten, living on you when you've got so little.

NINA

(Indifferently but with authority, like a governess to a small boy.)

Now, now!

EVANS

(Relieved.)

Well, it's true.

(Then coming to her – humbly ingratiating.)

You've felt a lot better lately, haven't you, Nina?

NINA

(With a start – sharply.)

Why?

EVANS

You look ever so much better. You're getting fat.

(He forces a grin.)

NINA

(Curtly.)

Don't be absurd, please! As a matter of fact, I don't feel a bit better.

EVANS

(Thinking despondently.)

Lately, she jumps on me every chance she gets . . . as if everything I did disgusted her! . . .

(He strays over to the window and looks out listlessly.)

I thought we'd get some word from Charlie this morning saying if he was coming down or not. But I suppose he's still too broken up over his mother's death to write.

NINA

(Indifferently.)

He'll probably come without bothering to write.

(Vaguely – wonderingly.)

Charlie . . . dear old Charlie! . . . I've forgotten him, too. . . .

EVANS

I think that's Ned's car now. Yes. It's stopping. I'll go out and meet him.

(He starts for the door in rear.)

NINA

(Sharply, before she can restrain the impulse.)

Don't be such a fool!

EVANS

(Stops – stammers confusedly.)

What – what's the matter?

NINA

(Controlling herself – but irritably.)

Don't mind me. I'm nervous.

(Thinking guiltily.)

One minute I feel ashamed of him for making such a fool of himself over my lover . . . the next minute something hateful urges me to drive him into doing it! . . .

(The maid has answered the ring and opened the outer door. Ned Darrell comes in from the rear. His face looks older. There is an expression of defensive bitterness and self-resentment about his mouth and eyes. This vanishes into one of desire and joy as he sees Nina.)

DARRELL

(He starts toward her impulsively.)

Nina!

(Then stops short as he sees Evans.)

NINA

(Forgetting Evans, gets to her feet as if to receive Darrell in her arms – with love.)

Ned!

EVANS

(Affectionately and gratefully.)

Hallo, Ned!

(He holds out his hand, which Darrell takes mechanically.)

DARRELL

(Trying to overcome his guilty embarrassment.)

Hallo! Sam. Didn't see you.

(Hurriedly reaching in his coat pocket.)

Before I forget, here's that letter. I had a talk over the 'phone with Appleby yesterday. He's pretty sure there's an opening –

(*With a condescension he can't help.*)

– but you'll have to get your nose on the grindstone to make good with him.

EVANS

(*Flushing guiltily – forcing a confident tone.*)

You bet I will!

(*Then gratefully and humbly.*)

Gosh, Ned, I can't tell you how grateful I am!

DARRELL

(*Brusquely, to hide his embarrassment.*)

Oh, shut up! I'm only too glad.

NINA

(*Watching Evans with a contempt that is almost gloating – in a tone of curt dismissal.*)

You'd better go and shave, hadn't you, if you're going to town?

EVANS

(*Guiltily, passing his hand over his face – forcing a brisk, purposeful air.*)

Yes, of course. I forgot I hadn't. Excuse me, will you?

(*This to Darrell. Evans hurries out, rear.*)

DARRELL

(*As soon as he is out of earshot – turning on Nina accusingly.*)

How can you treat him that way? It makes me feel – like a swine!

NINA

(*Flushing guiltily – protestingly.*)

What way?

(*Then inconsequentially.*)

He's always forgetting to shave lately.

DARRELL

You know what I mean, Nina!

(*Turns away from her – thinking bitterly.*)

What a rotten liar I've become! . . . and he trusts me absolutely! . . .

NINA

(*Thinking frightenedly.*)

Why doesn't he take me in his arms? . . . oh, I feel he doesn't love me now! . . . he's so bitter! . . .

(*Trying to be matter-of-fact.*)

I'm sorry, Ned. I don't mean to be cross, but Sam does get on my nerves.

DARRELL

(*Thinking bitterly.*)

Sometimes I almost hate her! . . . if it wasn't for her I'd have kept my peace of mind . . . no good for anything lately, damn it! . . . but it's idiotic to feel guilty . . . if Sam only didn't trust me! . . .

(*Then impatiently.*)

Bosh! . . . sentimental nonsense! . . . end justifies means! . . . this will have a good end for Sam, I swear to that! . . . why doesn't she tell him she's pregnant? . . . what's she waiting for? . . .

NINA

(*Thinking passionately, looking at him.*)

Oh, my lover, why don't you kiss me? . . .

(*Imploringly.*)

Ned! Don't be cross with me, please!

DARRELL

(*Fighting to control himself – coldly.*)

I'm not cross, Nina. Only you must admit these triangular scenes are, to say the least, humiliating.

(*Resentfully.*)

I won't come out here again!

NINA

(*With a cry of pain.*)

Ned!

DARRELL

(*Thinking exultingly at first.*)

She loves me! . . . she's forgotten Gordon! . . . I'm happy! . . . do I love her? . . . no! . . . I won't! . . . I can't! . . . think what it would mean to Sam! . . . to my career! . . . be objective about it! . . . you guinea-pig! . . . I'm her doctor . . . and Sam's . . . I prescribed child for them . . . that's all there is to it! . . .

NINA

(*Torn between hope and fear.*)

What is he thinking? . . . he's fighting his love . . . oh, my lover! . . .

(*Again with longing.*)

Ned!

DARRELL

(*Putting on his best professional air, going to her.*)

How do you feel to-day? You look as if you might have a little fever.

(*He takes her hand as if to feel her pulse.*)

(*Her hand closes over his. She looks up into his face. He keeps his turned away.*)

NINA

(Straining up toward him – with intense longing – thinking.)

I love you! . . . take me! . . . what do I care for anything in the world but you! . . . let Sam die! . . .

DARRELL

(Fighting himself – thinking.)

Christ! . . . touch of her skin! . . . her nakedness! . . . those afternoons in her arms! happiness! . . . what do I care for anything else! . . . to hell with Sam! . . .

NINA

(Breaking out passionately.)

Ned! I love you! I can't hide it any more! I won't! I love you, Ned!

DARRELL

(Suddenly taking her in his arms and kissing her frantically.)

Nina! Beautiful!

NINA

(Triumphantly – between kisses.)

You love me, don't you? Say you do, Ned!

DARRELL

(Passionately.)

Yes! Yes!

NINA

(With a cry of triumph.)

Thank God! At last you've told me! You've confessed it to yourself! Oh, Ned, you've made me so happy!

(There is a ring from the front-door bell. Darrell hears it. It acts like an electric shock on him. He tears himself away from her. Instinctively she gets up too and moves to the lounge at right.)

DARRELL

(Stupidly.)

Someone – at the door.

(He sinks down in the chair by the table at left.)
(Thinking torturedly.)

I said I loved her! . . . she won! . . . she used my desire! . . . but I don't love her! . . . I won't! . . . she can't own my life! . . .

(Violently – almost shouts at her.)

I don't, Nina! I tell you I don't!

NINA

(The maid has just gone to the front door.)

Sshh!

(Then in a triumphant whisper.)

You do, Ned! You do!

DARRELL

(With dogged stupidity.)

I don't!

(The front door has been opened. Marsden appears in the rear, walks slowly and woodenly like a man in a trance into the room. He is dressed immaculately in deep mourning. His face is pale, drawn, haggard with loneliness and grief. His eyes have a dazed look as if he were still too stunned to comprehend clearly what has happened to him. He does not seem conscious of Darrell's presence at first. His shoulders are bowed, his whole figure droops.)

NINA

(Thinking – in a strange superstitious panic.)

Black . . . in the midst of happiness . . . black comes . . . again . . . death . . . my father . . . comes between me and happiness! . . .

(Then recovering herself, scornfully.)

You silly coward! . . . it's only Charlie! . . .

(Then furious with resentment.)

The old fool! . . . what does he mean coming in on us without warning? . . .

MARSDEN

(Forcing a pitiful smile to his lips.)

Hallo, Nina! I know it's an imposition – but – I've been in such a terrible state since Mother –

(He falters, his face becomes distorted into an ugly mask of grief, his eyes water.)

NINA

(Immediately sympathetic, gets up and goes to him impulsively.)

There's no question of imposition, Charlie. We were expecting you.

(She has come to him and put her arms around him. He gives way and sobs, his head against her shoulder.)

MARSDEN

(Brokenly.)

You don't know, Nina – how terrible – it's terrible! –

NINA

(Leading him to the chair at centre, soothingly.)

I know, Charlie.

(Thinking with helpless annoyance.)

Oh, dear, what can I say? . . . his mother hated me . . .

I'm not glad she's dead . . . but neither am I sorry . . .

(*With a trace of contempt.*)

Poor Charlie! . . . he was so tied to her apron strings . . .

(*Then kindly but condescendingly, comforting him.*)

Poor old Charlie!

MARSDEN

(*The words and the tone shock his pride to life. He raises his head and half pushes her away – resentfully, thinking.*)

Poor old Charlie! . . . damn it, what am I to her? . . . her old dog who's lost his mother? . . . Mother hated her . . . no, poor dear Mother was so sweet, she never hated anyone . . . she simply disapproved . . .

(*Coldly.*)

I'm all right, Nina. Quite all right now, thank you. I apologize for making a scene.

DARRELL

(*Has got up from his chair – with relief – thinking.*)

Thank God for Marsden . . . I feel sane again . . .

(*He comes to Marsden – cordially.*)

How are you, Marsden?

(*Then offering conventional consolation, pats Marsden's shoulder.*)

I'm sorry, Marsden.

MARSDEN

(*Startled, looks up at him in amazement.*)

Darrell!

(*Then with instant hostility.*)

There's nothing to be sorry about that I can discover!

(*Then as they both look at him in surprise he realizes what he has said – stammeringly.*)

I mean – sorry – is hardly the right word – hardly – is it?

NINA

(*Worriedly.*)

Sit down, Charlie. You look so tired.

(*He slumps down in the chair at centre mechanically. Nina and Darrell return to their chairs. Nina looks across him at Darrell – triumphantly – thinking.*)

You do love me, Ned! . . .

DARRELL

(*Thinking – answering her look – defiantly.*)

I don't love you! . . .

MARSDEN

(*Stares intensely before him. Thinking suspiciously – morbidly agitated.*)

Darrell! . . . and Nina! . . . there's something in this room! . . . something disgusting! . . . like a brutal, hairy hand, raw and red, at my throat! . . . stench of human life! . . . heavy and rank! . . . outside it's April . . . green buds on the slim trees . . . the sadness of spring . . . my loss at peace in Nature . . . her sorrow of birth consoling my sorrow of death . . . something human and unnatural in this room! . . . love and hate and passion and possession! . . . cruelly indifferent to my loss! . . . mocking my loneliness! . . . no longer any love for me in any room! . . . lust in this room! . . . lust with a loathsome jeer taunting my sensitive timidities! . . . my purity! . . . purity? . . . ha! yes, if you say prurient purity! . . . lust ogling me for a dollar with oily shoe-button Italian eyes! . . .

(*In terror.*)

What thoughts! . . . what a low scoundrel you are! . . . and your mother dead only two weeks! . . . I hate Nina! . . . that Darrell in this room! . . . I feel their desires! . . . where is Sam? . . . I'll tell him! . . . no, he wouldn't believe . . . he's such a trusting fool . . . I must punish her some other way . . .

(*Remorsefully.*)

What? . . . punish Nina? . . . my little Nina? . . . why, I want her to be happy! . . . even with Darrell? . . . it's all so confused! . . . I must stop thinking! . . . I must talk! . . . forget! . . . say something! . . . forget everything! . . .

(*He suddenly bursts into a flood of garrulity.*)

Mother asked for you, Nina – three days before the end. She said, "Where is Nina Leeds now, Charlie? When is she going to marry Gordon Shaw?" Her mind was wandering, poor woman! You remember how fond she always was of Gordon? She used to love to watch the football games when he was playing. He was so handsome and graceful, she always thought. She always loved a strong, healthy body. She took such strict care of her own, she walked miles every day, she loved bathing and boating in the summer even after she was sixty, she was never sick a day in her life until –

(*He turns on Darrell – coldly.*)

You were right, Doctor Darrell. It was cancer.

(*Then angrily.*)

But the doctor you sent me to, and the other he called in, could do nothing for her – absolutely nothing! I might just as well have imported some witch doctors from the Solomon Islands! They at least would have diverted her in her last hours with their singing and dancing, but your specialists were a total loss!

(*Suddenly with an insulting, ugly sneer, raising his voice.*)

I think you doctors are a pack of God-damned ignorant liars and hypocrites!

NINA

(*Sharply.*)

Charlie!

MARSDEN

(*Coming to himself – with a groan – shamefacedly.*)

Don't mind me. I'm not myself, Nina. I've been through hell!

(*He seems about to sob – then abruptly springs to his feet, wildly.*)

It's this room! I can't stand this room! There's something repulsive about it!

NINA

(*Soothingly.*)

I know it's ugly, Charlie. I haven't had a chance to fix it up yet. We've been too broke.

MARSDEN

(*Confusedly.*)

Oh, it's all right. I'm ugly, too! Where's Sam?

NINA

(*Eagerly.*)

Right upstairs. Go on up. He'll be delighted to see you.

MARSDEN

(*Vaguely.*)

Very well.

(*He goes to the door, then stops mournfully.*)

But from what I saw on that visit to his home, he doesn't love his mother much. I don't think he'll understand, Nina. He never writes to her, does he?

NINA

(*Uneasily.*)

No – I don't know.

MARSDEN

She seemed lonely. He'll be sorry for it some day after she –

(*He gulps.*)

Well –

(*He goes.*)

NINA

(*In a sudden pause – thinking.*)

Sam's mother! . . . "Make my boy, Sammy, happy!" . . . I promised . . . oh, why did Charlie have to remember her? . . .

(*Then resolutely.*)

I can't remember her now! . . . I won't! . . . I've got to be happy! . . .

DARRELL

(*Uneasily trying to force a casual conversation.*)

Poor Marsden is completely knocked off balance, isn't he?

(*A pause.*)

My mother died when I was away at school. I hadn't seen her for some time, so her death was never very real to me; but in Marsden's case –

NINA

(*With a possessive smile of tolerance.*)

Never mind Charlie, Ned. What do I care about Charlie? I love you! And you love me!

DARRELL

(*Apprehensively, forcing a tone of annoyed rebuke.*)

But I don't! And you don't! You're simply letting your romantic imagination run away with you –

(*Showing his jealous resentment in spite of himself.*)

– as you did once before with Gordon Shaw!

NINA

(*Thinking.*)

He is jealous of Gordon! . . . how wonderful that is! . . .

(*With provoking calm.*)

I loved Gordon.

DARRELL

(*Irritably ignoring this as if he didn't want to hear it.*)

Romantic imagination! It has ruined more lives than all the diseases! Other diseases, I should say! It's a form of insanity!

(*He gets up forcefully and begins to pace about the room.*)

(*Thinking uneasily.*)

Mustn't look at her . . . find an excuse and get away . . . and this time never come back! . . .

(*Avoiding looking at her, trying to argue reasonably – coldly.*)

You're acting foolishly, Nina – and very unfairly. The agreement we made has no more to do with love than a contract for building a house. In fact, you know we agreed it was essential that love mustn't enter into it. And it hasn't, in spite of what you say.

(*A pause. He walks about. She watches him.*)

(*Thinking.*)

She's got to come back to earth! . . . I've got to break with her! . . . bad enough now! . . . but to go on with it! . . . what a mess it'd make of all our lives! . . .

NINA

(*Thinking tenderly.*)

Let his pride put all the blame on me! . . . I'll accept it gladly! . . .

DARRELL

(*Irritably.*)

Of course, I realize I've been to blame, too. I haven't

been able to be as impersonal as I thought I could be. The trouble is there's been a dangerous physical attraction. Since I first met you, I've always desired you physically. I admit that now.

NINA

(Smiling tenderly – thinking.)
Oh, he admits that, does he? . . . poor darling! . . .
(Enticingly.)

And you still do desire me, don't you, Ned?

DARRELL

(Keeping his back turned to her – roughly.)

No! That part of it is finished!

(Nina laughs softly, possessively. He whirls around to face her – angrily.)

Look here! You're going to have the child you wanted, aren't you?

NINA

(Implacably.)

My child wants its father!

DARRELL

(Coming a little toward her – desperately.)

But you're crazy! You're forgetting Sam! It may be stupid, but I've got a guilty conscience! I'm beginning to think we've wronged the very one we were trying to help!

NINA

You were trying to help me, too, Ned!

DARRELL

(Stammering.)

Well – all right – let's say that part of it was all right then. But it's got to stop! It can't go on!

NINA

(Implacably.)

Only your love can make me happy now! Sam must give me a divorce so I can marry you.

DARRELL

(Thinking suspiciously.)
Look out! . . . there it is! . . . marry! . . . own me! . . . ruin my career! . . .
(Scornfully.)

Marry? Do you think I'm a fool? Get that out of your head quick! I wouldn't marry anyone – no matter what!

(As she continues to look at him with unmoved determination – pleadingly.)

Be sensible, for God's sake! We're absolutely unsuited to each other! I don't admire your character! I don't respect you! I know too much about your past!

(Then indignantly.)

And how about Sam? Divorce him? Have you forgotten all his mother told you? Do you mean to say you'd deliberately – ? And you expect me to – ? What do you think I am?

NINA

(Inflexibly.)

You're my lover! Nothing else matters. Yes, I remember what Sam's mother said. She said, "being happy is the nearest we can come to knowing what good is." And I'm going to be happy! I've lost everything in life so far because I didn't have the courage to take it – and I've hurt everyone around me. There's no use trying to think of others. One human being can't think of another. It's impossible.

(Gently and caressingly.)

But this time I'm going to think of my own happiness – and that means you – and our child! That's quite enough for one human being to think of, dear, isn't it?

(She reaches out and takes his hand. A pause. With her other hand she gently pulls him around until he is forced to look into her eyes.)

DARRELL

(Thinking fascinatedly.)
I see my happiness in her eyes . . . the touch of her soft skin! . . . those afternoons! . . . God, I was happy! . . .
(In a strange dazed voice – as if it were forced out of him by an impulse stronger than his will.)

Yes, Nina.

NINA

(In a determined voice.)

I've given Sam enough of my life! And it hasn't made him happy, not the least bit! So what's the good? And how can we really know that his thinking our child was his would do him any good? We can't! It's all guesswork. The only thing sure is that we love each other.

DARRELL

(Dazedly.)

Yes.

(A noise from the hall and Evans comes in from the rear. He sees their two hands together, but mistakes their meaning.)

EVANS

(Genially – with a forced self-confident air.)

Well, Doc, how's the patient? I think she's much better, don't you? – although she won't admit it.

DARRELL

(At the first sound of Evans' voice, pulls his hand from Nina's as if it were a hot coal – avoiding Evans' eyes, moving away from her jerkily and self-consciously.)

Yes. Much better.

EVANS

Good!

(He pats Nina on the back. She shrinks away. His confidence vanishes in a flash.)

(Thinking miserably.)

Why does she shrink away . . . if I even touch her? . . .

NINA

(Matter-of-factly.)

I must see how lunch is coming on. You'll stay, of course, Ned?

DARRELL

(Struggling – shakenly.)

No, I think I'd better –

(Thinking desperately.)

Got to go! . . . can't go! . . . got to go! . . .

EVANS

Oh, come on, old man!

NINA

(Thinking.)

He must stay . . . and after lunch we'll tell Sam. . . .

(With certainty.)

He'll stay.

(Meaningly.)

And we want to have a long talk with you after lunch, Sam – don't we, Ned?

(Darrell does not answer. She goes out, right.)

EVANS

(Vaguely making talk.)

I got Charlie to lie down. He's all in, poor guy.

(Then trying to face Darrell, who keeps looking away from him.)

What did Nina mean, you want a long talk with me? Or is it a secret, Ned?

DARRELL

(Controlling an impulse toward hysterical laughter.)

A secret? Yes, you bet it's a secret!

(He flings himself in the chair at left, keeping his face averted.)

(His thoughts bitter and desperate like a cornered fugitive's.)

This is horrible! . . . Sam thinks I'm finest fellow in world . . . and I do this to him! . . . as if he hadn't enough! . . . born under a curse! . . . I finish him! . . . a doctor! . . . God damn it! . . . I can see his end! . . . never forgive myself! . . . never forget! . . . break me! . . . ruin my career! . . .

(More desperately.)

Got to stop this! . . . while there's time! . . . she said . . . after lunch, talk . . . she meant, tell him . . . that means kill him . . . then she'll marry me! . . .

(Beginning to be angry.)

By God, I won't! . . . she'll find out! . . . smiling! . . . got me where she wants me! . . . then be as cruel to me as she is to him! . . . love me? . . . liar! . . . still loves Gordon! . . . her body is a trap! . . . I'm caught in it! . . . she touches my hand, her eyes get in mine, I lose my will! . . .

(Furiously.)

By God, she can't make a fool of me that way! . . . I'll go away to some place! . . . go to Europe! . . . study! . . . forget her in work! . . . keep hidden until boat sails so she can't reach me! . . .

(He is in a state of strange elation by this time.)

Go now! . . . no! . . . got to spike her guns with Sam! . . . by God, I see! . . . tell him about baby! . . . that'll stop her! . . . when she knows I've told him that, she'll see it's hopeless! . . . she'll stick to him! . . . poor Nina! . . . I'm sorry! . . . she does love me! . . . hell! . . . she'll forget! . . . she'll have her child! . . . she'll be happy! . . . and Sam'll be happy! . . .

(He suddenly turns to Evans, who has been staring at him, puzzledly – in a whisper.)

Look here, Sam. I can't stay to lunch. I haven't time, I've got a million things to do. I'm sailing for Europe in a few days.

EVANS

(Surprised.)

You're sailing?

DARRELL

(Very hurriedly.)

Yes – going to study over there for a year or so. I haven't told anyone. I came out to-day to say good-bye. You won't be able to reach me again. I'll be out of town visiting.

(Then elatedly.)

And now for your secret! It ought to make you very happy, Sam. I know how much you've wished for it, so I'm going to tell you, although Nina'll be furious with me. She was saving it to surprise you with at her own proper time –

(Still more elatedly.)

– but I'm selfish enough to want to see you happy before I go!

EVANS

(Not daring to believe what he hopes – stammering.)

What – what is it, Ned?

DARRELL

(Clapping him on the back – with strange joviality.)

You're going to be a father, old scout, that's the secret!

(Then as Evans just stares at him dumbly in a blissful satisfaction, he rattles on.)

And now I've got to run. See you again in a year or so. I've said good-bye to Nina. Good-bye, Sam.

(He takes his hand and clasps it.)

Good luck! Buckle down to work now! You've got the stuff in you! When I get back I'll expect to hear you're on the highroad to success! And tell Nina I'll expect to find you both happy in your child – both of you, tell her! – happy in your child! Tell her that, Sam!

(He turns and goes to the door.)
(Thinking as he goes.)

That does it! . . . honourably! . . . I'm free! . . .

(He goes out – then through the front door – a moment later his motor is heard starting – dies away.)

EVANS

(Stares after him dumbly in the same state of happy stupefaction – mumbles.)

Thank you – Ned!

(Thinking disjointedly.)

Why did I doubt myself? . . . now she loves me . . . she's loved me right along . . . I've been a fool . . .

(He suddenly falls on his knees.)

O God, I thank you!

(Nina comes in from the kitchen. She stops in amazement when she sees him on his knees. He jumps to his feet and takes her in his arms with confident happiness and kisses her.)

Oh, Nina, I love you so! And now I know you love me! I'll never be afraid of anything again!

NINA

(Bewildered and terror-stricken, trying feebly to push him away – thinking.)

Has he . . . has he gone crazy? . . .

(Weakly.)

Sam! What's come over you, Sam?

EVANS

(Tenderly.)

Ned told me – the secret – and I'm so happy, dear!

(He kisses her again.)

NINA

(Stammering.)

Ned told you – what?

EVANS

(Tenderly.)

That we're going to have a child, dear. You mustn't be sore at him. Why did you want to keep it a secret from me? Didn't you know how happy it would make me, Nina?

NINA

He told you we – we – you, the father – ?

(Then suddenly breaking from him – wildly.)

Ned! Where is Ned?

EVANS

He left a moment ago.

NINA

(Stupidly.)

Left? Call him back. Lunch is ready.

EVANS

He's gone. He couldn't stay. He's got so much to do getting ready to sail.

NINA

Sail?

EVANS

Didn't he tell you he was sailing for Europe? He's going over for a year or so to study.

NINA

A year or so!

(Wildly.)

I've got to call him up! No, I'll go in and see him right now!

(She takes a wavering step toward the door.)
(Thinking in anguish.)

Go! . . . go to him! . . . find him! . . . my lover! . . .

EVANS

He won't be there, I'm afraid. He said we couldn't reach him, that he'd be visiting friends out of town until he sailed.

(Solicitously.)

Why, do you have to see him about something important, Nina? Perhaps I could locate –

NINA

(Stammering and swaying.)

No.

(She stifles an hysterical laugh.)

No, nothing – nothing important – nothing is important – ha – !

(She stifles another laugh – then on the verge of fainting, weakly.)

Sam! Help me –

EVANS

(Rushes to her, supports her to sofa at right.)

Poor darling! Lie down and rest.

(She remains in a sitting position, staring blankly before her. He chafes her wrists.)

Poor darling!

(Thinking jubilantly.)

Her condition . . . this weakness comes from her condition! . . .

NINA

(Thinking in anguish.)

Ned doesn't love me! . . . he's gone! . . . gone for ever! . . . like Gordon! . . . no, not like Gordon! . . . like a sneak, a coward! . . . a liar! . . . oh, I hate him! . . . O Mother God, please let me hate him! . . . he must have been planning this! . . . he must have known it to-day when he said he loved me! . . .

(Thinking frenziedly.)

I won't bear it! . . . he thinks he has palmed me off on Sam for ever! . . . and his child! . . . he can't! . . . I'll tell Sam he was lying! . . . I'll make Sam hate him! . . . I'll make Sam kill him! . . . I'll promise to love Sam if he kills him! . . .

(Suddenly turns to Evans – savagely.)

He lied to you!

EVANS

(Letting her wrists drop – appalled – stammers.)

You mean – Ned lied about – ?

NINA

(In same tone.)

Ned lied to you!

EVANS

(Stammers.)

You're not – going to have a child –

NINA

(Savagely.)

Oh, yes! Oh, yes, I am! Nothing can keep me from that! But you're – you're – I mean, you . . .

(Thinking in anguish.)

I can't say that to him! . . . I can't tell him without Ned to help me! . . . I can't! . . . look at his face! . . . oh, poor Sammy! . . . poor little boy! . . . poor little boy! . . .

(She takes his head and presses it to her breast and begins to weep.)

(Weeping.)

I mean, you weren't to know about it, Sammy.

EVANS

(Immediately on the crest again – tenderly.)

Why? Don't you want me to be happy, Nina?

NINA

Yes – yes, I do, Sammy.

(Thinking strangely.)

Little boy! . . . little boy! . . . one gives birth to little boys! . . . one doesn't drive them mad and kill them! . . .

EVANS

(Thinking.)

She's never called me Sammy before . . . someone used to . . . oh, yes, Mother. . . .

(Tenderly and boyishly.)

And I'm going to make you happy from now on, Nina. I tell you, the moment Ned told me, something happened to me! I can't explain it, but – I'll make good now, Nina! I know I've said that before, but I was only boasting. I was only trying to make myself think so. But now I say it knowing I can do it!

(Softly.)

It's because we're going to have a child, Nina. I knew that you'd never really come to love me without that. That's what I was down on my knees for when you came in. I was thanking God – for our baby!

NINA

(Tremblingly.)

Sammy! Poor boy!

EVANS

Ned said when he came back he'd expect to find us both happy – in our baby. He said to tell you that. You will be happy now, won't you, Nina?

NINA

(Brokenly and exhaustedly.)

I'll try to make you happy, Sammy.

(He kisses her, then hides his head on her breast. She stares out over his head. She seems to grow older.)

(Thinking as if she were repeating the words of some inner voice of life.)

Not Ned's child! . . . not Sam's child! . . . mine! . . . there! . . . again! . . . I feel my child live . . . moving in my life . . . my life moving in my child . . . breathing in the tide I dream and breathe my dream back into the tide . . . God is a Mother! . . .

(Then with sudden anguish.)

Oh, afternoons . . . dear wonderful afternoons of love with you, my lover! . . . you are lost . . . gone from me for ever! . . .

Curtain

SECOND PART ACT SIX

SCENE: *The same – an evening a little over a year later. The room has undergone a significant change. There is a comfortable, homy atmosphere as though now it definitely belonged to the type of person it was built for. It has a proud air of modest prosperity.*

It is soon after dinner – about eight o'clock. Evans is sitting by the table at left, glancing through a newspaper at headlines and reading an article here and there. Nina is in the chair at centre, knitting a tiny sweater. Marsden is sitting on the sofa at right, holding a book which he pretends to be looking through, but glancing wonderingly at Evans and Nina.

There is a startling change in Evans. He is stouter, the haggard look of worry and self-conscious inferiority has gone from his face, it is full and healthy and satisfied. There is also, what is more remarkable, a decided look of solidity about him, of a determination moving toward ends it is confident it can achieve. He has matured, found his place in the world.

The change in Nina is also perceptible. She looks noticeably older, the traces of former suffering are marked on her face, but there is also an expression of present contentment and calm.

Marsden has aged greatly. His hair is grey, his expression one of a deep grief that is dying out into a resignation resentful of itself. He is dressed immaculately in dark tweed.

NINA

(*Thinking.*)

I wonder if there's a draught in the baby's room? . . . maybe I'd better close the window? . . . oh, I guess it's all right . . . he needs lots of fresh air . . . little Gordon . . . he does remind me of Gordon . . . something in his eyes . . . my romantic imagination? . . . Ned said that . . . why hasn't Ned ever written? . . . it's better he hasn't . . . how he made me suffer! . . . but I forgive him . . . he gave me my baby . . . the baby certainly doesn't look like him . . . every one says he looks like Sam . . . how absurd! . . . but Sam makes a wonderful father . . . he's become a new man in the past year . . . and I've helped him . . . he asks me about everything . . . I have a genuine respect for him now . . . I can give myself without repulsion . . . I am making him happy . . . I've written his mother I'm making him happy . . . I was proud to be able to write her that . . . how queerly things work out! . . . all for the best . . . and I don't feel wicked . . . I feel good . . .

(*She smiles strangely.*)

MARSDEN

(*Thinking.*)

What a change! . . . the last time I was here the air was poisoned . . . Darrell . . . I was sure he was her lover . . . but I was in a morbid state . . . why did Darrell run away? . . . Nina could have got Sam to divorce her if she really loved Darrell . . . then it's evident she couldn't have loved him . . . and she was going to have Sam's baby . . . Darrell's love must have seemed like treachery . . . so she sent him away . . . that must be it! . . .

(*With satisfaction.*)

Yes, I've got it straight now. . . .

(*With contemptuous pity.*)

Poor Darrell . . . I have no use for him, but I did pity him when I ran across him in Munich . . . he was going the pace . . . looked desperate. . . .

(*Then gloomily.*)

My running away was about as successful as his . . . as if one could leave one's memory behind! . . . I couldn't forget Mother . . . she haunted me through every city of Europe . . .

(*Then irritatedly.*)

I must get back to work! . . . not a line written in over a year! . . . my public will be forgetting me! . . . a plot came to me yesterday . . . my mind is coming around again . . . I am beginning to forget, thank God! . . .

(*Then remorsefully.*)

No, I don't want to forget you, Mother! . . . but let me remember . . . without pain! . . .

EVANS

(*Turning over a page of his paper.*)

There's going to be the biggest boom before long this country has ever known, or I miss my guess, Nina.

NINA

(*With great seriousness.*)

Do you think so, Sammy?

EVANS

(*Decidedly.*)

I'm dead sure of it.

NINA

(*With a maternal pride and amusement.*)

Dear Sam . . . I can't quite believe in this self-confident business man yet . . . but I have to admit he's proved it . . . he asked for more money and they gave it without question . . . they're anxious to keep him . . . they ought to be . . . how he's slaved! . . . for me and my baby! . . .

EVANS

(*Has been looking at Marsden surreptitiously over his paper.*)

Charlie's mother must have hoarded up a half-million . . . he'll let it rot in Government bonds . . . wonder what he'd say if I proposed that he back me? . . . he's always taken a friendly interest . . . well, it's worth a bet, anyway . . . he'd be an easy partner to handle . . .

MARSDEN

(*Staring at Evans wonderingly.*)

What a changed Sam! . . . I preferred him the old way . . . futile, but he had a sensitive quality . . . now he's hardened . . . a little success . . . oh, he'll succeed all right . . . his kind are inheriting the earth . . . hogging it, cramming it down their tasteless gullets! . . . and he's happy! . . . actually happy! . . . he has Nina . . . a beautiful baby . . . a comfortable home . . . no sorrow, no tragic memories . . . and I have nothing . . . but utter loneliness! . . .

(*With grieving self-pity.*)

If only Mother had lived! . . . how horribly I miss her! . . . my lonely home . . . who will keep house for me now? . . . it has got to be done sympathetically or I shan't be able to work . . . I must write to Jane . . . she'll probably be only too glad . . .

(*Turning to Nina.*)

I think I'll write to my sister in California and ask her to come and live with me. She's alone now that her youngest daughter is married, and she has very little money. And my hands are tied as far as sharing the estate with her is concerned. According to Mother's will, I'm cut off too if I give her a penny. Mother never got over her bitter feeling about Jane's marriage. In a way, she was right. Jane's husband wasn't much – no family or position or ability – and I doubt if she was ever happy with him.

(*Sarcastically.*)

It was one of those love matches!

NINA

(*Smiling – teasingly.*)

There's no danger of your ever making a love match, is there, Charlie?

MARSDEN

(*Wincing – thinking.*)

She can't believe any woman could possibly love me! . . .

(*Caustically.*)

I trust I'll never make that kind of a fool of myself, Nina!

NINA

(*Teasingly.*)

Pooh! Aren't you the superior bachelor! I don't see anything to be so proud of! You're simply shirking, Charlie!

MARSDEN

(*Wincing, but forcing a teasing air.*)

You were my only true love, Nina. I made a vow of perpetual bachelorhood when you threw me over in Sam's favour!

EVANS

(*Has listened to this last – jokingly.*)

Hallo! What's this? I never knew you were my hated rival, Charlie!

MARSDEN

(*Dryly.*)

Oh – didn't you really?

(*But Evans has turned back to his paper.*)

(*Thinking savagely.*)

That fool, too! . . . he jokes about it! . . . as if I were the last one in the world he could imagine . . .

NINA

(*Teasingly.*)

Well, if I'm responsible, Charlie, I feel I ought to do something about it. I'll pick out a wife for you – guaranteed to suit! She must be at least ten years older than you, large and matronly and placid, and a wonderful cook and housekeeper –

MARSDEN

(*Sharply.*)

Don't be stupid!

(*Thinking angrily.*)

She picks someone beyond the age! . . . she never imagines sex could enter into it! . . .

NINA

(*Placatingly – seeing he is really angry.*)

Why, I was only picking out a type I thought would be good for you, Charlie – and for your work.

MARSDEN

(*Sneeringly – with a meaning emphasis.*)

You didn't mention chaste. I couldn't respect a woman who hadn't respected herself!

NINA

(*Thinking – stung.*)

He's thinking of those men in the hospital . . . what a fool I was ever to tell him! . . .

(*Cuttingly.*)

Oh, so you think you deserve an innocent virgin!

MARSDEN

(*Coldly – controlling his anger.*)

Let's drop me, if you please.

(*With a look at her that is challenging and malicious.*)

Did I tell you I ran into Doctor Darrell in Munich?

NINA

(*Startled – thinking frightenedly and confusedly.*)

Ned! . . . he saw Ned! . . . why hasn't he told me before? . . . why did he look at me like that? . . . does he suspect? . . .

(*Trying to be calm, but stammering.*)

You saw – Ned?

MARSDEN

(*With savage satisfaction.*)

That struck home! . . . look at her! . . . guilty! . . . then I was right that day! . . .

(*Casually.*)

Yes, I chanced to run into him.

NINA

(*More calmly now.*)

Why on earth didn't you tell us before, Charlie?

MARSDEN

(*Coolly.*)

Why? Is it such important news? You knew he was there, didn't you? I supposed he'd written you.

EVANS

(*Looking up from his paper – affectionately.*)

How was the old scout?

MARSDEN

(*Maliciously.*)

He seemed in fine feather – said he was having a gay time. When I saw him he was with a startling-looking female – quite beautiful, if you like that type. I gathered they were living together.

NINA

(*Cannot restrain herself – breaks out.*)

I don't believe it!

(*Then immediately controlling herself and forcing a laugh.*)

I mean, Ned was always so serious-minded it's hard to imagine him messed up in that sort of thing.

(*Thinking in a queer state of jealous confusion.*)

Hard to imagine! . . . my lover! . . . oh, pain again! . . . why? . . . I don't love him now . . . be careful! . . . Charlie's staring at me. . . .

MARSDEN

(*Thinking – jealously.*)

Then she did love him! . . . does she still? . . .

(*Hopefully.*)

Or is it only pique? . . . no woman likes to lose a man even when she no longer loves him. . . .

(*With malicious insistence.*)

Why is that hard to imagine, Nina? Darrell never struck me as a Galahad. After all, why shouldn't he have a mistress?

(*Meaningly.*)

He has no tie over here to remain faithful to, has he?

NINA

(*Struggling with herself – thinking pitiably.*)

He's right . . . why shouldn't Ned? . . . is that why he's never written? . . .

(*Airily.*)

I don't know what ties he has or hasn't got. It's nothing to me if he has fifty mistresses. I suppose he's no better than the rest of you.

EVANS

(*Looking over at her – tenderly reproachful.*)

That isn't fair, Nina.

(*Thinking-proudly.*)

I'm proud of that . . . never anyone before her . . .

NINA

(*Looking at him – with real gratitude.*)

I didn't mean you, dear.

(*Thinking – proudly.*)

Thank God for Sammy! . . . I know he's mine . . . no jealousy . . . no fear . . . no pain . . . I've found peace . . .

(*Then distractedly.*)

Oh, Ned, why haven't you written? . . . stop it! . . . what a fool I am! . . . Ned's dead for me! . . . oh, I hate Charlie! . . . why did he tell me? . . .

MARSDEN

(*Looking at Evans – contemptuously thinking.*)

What a poor simpleton Sam is! . . . boasting of his virtue! . . . as if women loved you for that! . . . they despise it! . . . I don't want Nina to think I've had no experiences with women. . . .

(*Mockingly.*)

So then it's Sam who is the Galahad, eh? Really, Nina, you should have him put in the Museum among the prehistoric mammals!

EVANS

(*Pleased – comes back teasingly.*)

Well, I never had your chances, Charlie! I couldn't run over to Europe and get away with murder the way you have!

MARSDEN

(*Foolishly pleased – admitting while denying.*)

Oh, I wasn't quite as bad as all that, Sam!

(*Scornfully ashamed of himself – thinking.*)

Poor sick ass that I am! . . . I want them to think I've been a Don Juan! . . . how pitiful and disgusting! . . . I wouldn't have a mistress if I could! . . . if I could? . . . of course I could! . . . I've simply never cared to degrade myself! . . .

NINA

(*Thinking – tormentedly.*)

The thought of that woman! . . . Ned forgetting our

afternoons in nights with her! . . . stop these thoughts! . . . I won't give in to them! . . . why did Charlie want to hurt me? . . . is he jealous of Ned? . . . Charlie has always loved me in some queer way of his own . . . how ridiculous! . . . look at him! . . . he's so proud of being thought a Don Juan! . . . I'm sure he never even dared to kiss a woman except his mother! . . .

(Mockingly.)

Do tell us about all your various mistresses in foreign parts, Charlie!

MARSDEN

(In confusion now.)

I – I really don't remember, Nina!

NINA

Why, you're the most heartless person I've ever heard of, Charlie! Not remember even one! And I suppose there are little Marsdens – and you've forgotten all about them, too!

(She laughs maliciously – Evans laughs with her.)

MARSDEN

(Still more confused – with a silly idiotic smirk.)

I can't say about that, Nina. It's a wise father who knows his own child, you know!

NINA

(Frightenedly – thinking.)

What does he mean? . . . does he suspect about the baby, too? . . . I must be terribly careful of Charlie! . . .

EVANS

(Looking up from his paper again.)

Did Ned say anything about coming back?

NINA

(Thinking – longingly.)

Come back? . . . oh, Ned, how I wish! . . .

MARSDEN

(Looking at her – meaningly.)

No, he didn't say. I gathered he was staying over indefinitely.

EVANS

I'd sure like to see him again.

NINA

(Thinking.)

He has forgotten me . . . if he did come, he'd probably avoid me. . . .

MARSDEN

He spoke of you. He asked if I'd heard whether Nina had had her baby yet or not. I told him I hadn't.

EVANS

(Heartily.)

Too bad you didn't know. You could have told him what a world-beater we've got! Eh, Nina?

NINA

(Mechanically.)

Yes.

(Joyfully – thinking.)

Ned asked about my baby! . . . then he hadn't forgotten! . . . if he came back he'd come to see his baby! . . .

EVANS

(Solicitously.)

Isn't it time to nurse him again?

NINA

(Starts to her feet automatically.)

Yes, I'm going now.

(She glances at Marsden, thinking calculatingly.)

I must win Charlie over again . . . I don't feel safe . . .

(She stops by his chair and takes his hand and looks into his eyes gently and reproachfully.)

MARSDEN

(Thinking shamefacedly.)

Why have I been trying to hurt her? . . . my Nina! . . . I am nearer to her than anyone! . . . I'd give my life to make her happy! . . .

NINA

(Triumphantly.)

How his hand trembles! . . . what a fool to be afraid of Charlie! . . . I can always twist him round my finger! . . .

(She runs her hand through his hair, and speaks as though she were hiding a hurt reproach beneath a joking tone.)

I shouldn't like you any more, you know, after you've practically admitted you've philandered all over Europe! And I thought you were absolutely true to me, Charlie!

MARSDEN

(So pleased he can hardly believe his ears.)

Then she did believe me! . . . she's actually hurt! . . . but I can't let her think . . .

(With passionate earnestness, clasping her hand in both of his, looking into her eyes.)

No, Nina! I swear to you!

NINA

(Thinking – cruelly.)

Pah! . . . how limp his hands are! . . . his eyes are so shrinking! . . . is it possible he loves me? . . . like that? . . . what a sickening idea! . . . it seems incestuous somehow! . . . no, it's too absurd! . . .

(Smiling, gently releases her hand.)

All right. I forgive you, Charlie.

(Then matter-of-factly.)

Excuse me, please, while I go up and feed my infant, or we're due to hear some lusty howling in a moment.

(She turns away, then impulsively turns back and kisses Marsden with real affection.)

You're an old dear, do you know it, Charlie? I don't know what I'd do without you!

(Thinking.)

It's true, too! . . . he's my only dependable friend . . . I must never lose him . . . never let him suspect about little Gordon . . .

(She turns to go.)

EVANS

(Jumping up, throwing his paper aside.)

Wait a second. I'll come with you. I want to say good night to him.

(He comes, puts his arm about her waist, kisses her and they go out together.)

MARSDEN

(Thinking excitedly.)

I almost confessed I loved her! . . . a queer expression came over her face . . . what was it? . . . was it satisfaction? . . . she didn't mind? . . . was it pleasure? . . . then I can hope? . . .

(Then miserably.)

Hope for what? . . . what do I want? . . . If Nina were free, what would I do? . . . would I do anything? . . . would I wish to? . . . what would I offer her? . . . money? . . . she could get that from others . . . myself? . . .

(Bitterly.)

What a prize! . . . my ugly body . . . there's nothing in me to attract her . . . my fame? . . . God, what a shoddy, pitiful! . . . but I might have done something big . . . I might still . . . if I had the courage to write the truth . . . but I was born afraid . . . afraid of myself . . . I've given my talent to making fools feel pleased with themselves in order that they'd feel pleased with me . . . and like me . . . I'm neither hated nor loved . . . I'm liked . . . women like me . . . Nina likes me! . . .

(Resentfully.)

She can't help letting the truth escape her! . . . "You're an old dear, do you know it, Charlie?" Oh, yes, I know it . . . too damned well! . . . dear old Charlie! . . .

(In anguish.)

Dear old Rover, nice old doggie, we've had him for years, he's so affectionate and faithful, but he's growing old, he's getting cross, we'll have to get rid of him soon! . . .

(In a strange rage, threateningly.)

But you won't get rid of me so easily, Nina! . . .

(Then confusedly and shamefacedly.)

Good God, what's the matter with me! . . . since Mother's death I've become a regular idiot! . . .

EVANS

(Comes back from the right, a beaming look of proud parenthood on his face.)

He was sleeping so soundly an earthquake wouldn't have made him peep!

(He goes back to his chair – earnestly.)

He sure is healthy and husky, Charlie. That tickles me more than anything else. I'm going to start in training him as soon as he's old enough – so he'll be a crack athlete when he goes to college – what I wanted to be and couldn't. I want him to justify the name of Gordon and be a bigger star than Gordon ever was, if that's possible.

MARSDEN

(With a sort of pity – thinking.)

His is an adolescent mind . . . he'll never grow up . . . well, in this adolescent country, what greater blessing could he wish for? . . .

(Forcing a smile.)

How about training his mind?

EVANS

(Confidently.)

Oh, that'll take care of itself. Gordon was always near the top in his studies, wasn't he? And with Nina for a mother, his namesake ought to inherit a full set of brains.

MARSDEN

(Amused.)

You're the only genuinely modest person I know, Sam.

EVANS

(Embarrassed.)

Oh – me – I'm the boob of the family.

(Then hastily.)

Except when it comes to business. I'll make the money.

(Confidently.)

And you can bet your sweet life I will make it!

MARSDEN

I'm quite sure of that.

EVANS

(Very seriously – in a confidential tone.)

I couldn't have said that two years ago – and believed it. I've changed a hell of a lot! Since the baby was born, I've felt as if I had a shot of dynamite in each arm. They can't pile on the work fast enough.

(He grins – then seriously.)

It was about time I got hold of myself. I wasn't much for Nina to feel proud about having around the house in those days. Now – well – at least I've improved. I'm not afraid of my own shadow any more.

MARSDEN

(Thinking strangely.)

Not to be afraid of one's shadow! . . . that must be the

highest happiness of heaven! . . .
(*Flatteringly.*)

Yes, you've done wonders in the past year.

EVANS

Oh, I haven't even started yet. Wait till I get my chance!

(*Glances at Marsden sharply, makes up his mind and leans forward toward him confidentially.*)

And I see my real chance, Charlie – lying right ahead, waiting for me to grab it – an agency that's been allowed to run down and go to seed. Within a year or so they'll be willing to sell out cheap. One of their people who's become a good pal of mine told me that in confidence, put it up to me. He'd take it on himself but he's sick of the game. But I'm not! I love it! It's great sport!

(*Then putting the brake on this exuberance – matter-of-factly.*)

But I'll need a hundred thousand – and where will I get it?

(*Looking at Marsden keenly, but putting on a joking tone.*)

Any suggestion you can make, Charlie, will be gratefully received.

MARSDEN

(*Thinking suspiciously.*)

Does he actually imagine I . . . ? and a hundred thousand, no less! . . . over one-fifth of my entire . . . by Jove, I'll have to throw cold water on that fancy! . . .
(*Shortly.*)

No, Sam, I can't think of anyone. Sorry.

EVANS

(*Without losing any confidence – with a grin.*)

Check! . . . That's that! . . . Charlie's out . . . till the next time! . . . but I'll keep after him! . . .
(*Contemplating himself with pride.*)
Gee, I have changed all right! I can remember when a refusal like that would have ruined my confidence for six months!
(*Heartily.*)

Nothing to be sorry about, old man. I only mentioned it on the off chance you might know of someone.

(*Trying a bold closing stroke – jokingly.*)

Why don't you be my partner, Charlie? Never mind the hundred thousand. We'll get that elsewhere. I'll bet you might have darn fine original ideas to contribute.

(*Thinking – satisfied.*)

There! . . . That'll keep my proposition pinned up in his mind! . . .
(*Then jumping to his feet – briskly.*)

What do you say to a little stroll down to the shore and back? Come on – do you good.

(*Taking his arm and hustling him genially toward the door.*)

What you need is exercise. You're soft as putty. Why don't you take up golf?

MARSDEN

(*With sudden resistance pulls away – determinedly.*)

No, I won't go, Sam. I want to think out a new plot.

EVANS

Oh, all right! If it's a case of work, go to it! See you later.

(*He goes out. A moment later the front door is heard closing.*)

MARSDEN

(*Looks after him with a mixture of annoyance and scornful amusement.*)

What a fount of meaningless energy he's tapped! . . . always on the go . . . typical terrible child of the age . . . universal slogan, keep moving . . . moving where? . . . never mind that . . . don't think of ends . . . the means are the end . . . keep moving! . . .

(*He laughs scornfully and sits down in Evans' chair, picking up the paper and glancing at it sneeringly.*)

It's in every headline of this daily newer testament . . . going . . . going . . . never mind the gone . . . we won't live to see it . . . and we'll be so rich, we can buy off the deluge, anyway! . . . even our new God has His price! . . . must have! . . . aren't we made in His image? . . . or vice versa? . . .

(*He laughs again, letting the paper drop disdainfully – then bitterly.*)

But why am I so superior? . . . where am I going? . . . to the same nowhere! . . . worse! . . . I'm not even going! . . . I'm there! . . .

(*He laughs with bitter self-pity – then begins to think with amused curiosity.*)

Become Sam's partner? . . . there's a grotesque notion! . . . it might revive my sense of humour about myself, at least . . . I'm the logical one to help him . . . I helped him to Nina . . . logical partner . . . partner in Nina? . . . what inane thoughts! . . .

(*With a sigh.*)

No use trying to think out that plot to-night . . . I'll try to read. . . .

(*He sees the book he has been reading on the couch and gets up to get it. There is a ring from the front door. Marsden turns toward it uncertainly. A pause. Then Nina's voice calls down the stairs.*)

NINA

The maid's out. Will you go to the door, Charlie?

MARSDEN

Surely.

(*He goes out and opens the front door. A pause. Then he can be heard saying resentfully:*)

Hallo, Darrell.

(And some one answering "Hallo, Marsden." and coming in and the door closing.)

NINA

(From upstairs, her voice strange and excited.)

Who is it, Charlie?

DARRELL

(Comes into view in the hall, opposite the doorway, at the foot of the stairs – his voice trembling a little with suppressed emotion.)

It's I, Nina – Ned Darrell.

NINA

(With a glad cry.)

Ned!

(Then in a voice which shows she is trying to control herself, and is frightened now.)

I – make yourself at home. I'll be down – in a minute or two.

(Darrell remains standing looking up the stairs in a sort of joyous stupor. Marsden stares at him.)

MARSDEN

(Sharply.)

Come on in and sit down.

(Darrell starts, comes into the room, plainly getting a grip on himself. Marsden follows him, glaring at his back with enmity and suspicion. Darrell moves as far away from him as possible, sitting down on the sofa at right. Marsden takes Evans' chair by the table. Darrell is pale, thin, nervous, unhealthy looking. There are lines of desperation in his face, puffy shadows of dissipation and sleeplessness under his restless, harried eyes. He is dressed carelessly, almost shabbily. His eyes wander about the room, greedily taking it in.)

DARRELL

(Thinking disjointedly.)

Here again! . . . dreamed of this house . . . from here, ran away . . . I've come back . . . my turn to be happy! . . .

MARSDEN

(Watching him – savagely.)

Now I know! . . . absolutely! . . . his face! . . . her voice! . . . they did love each other! . . . they do now! . . .

(Sharply.)

When did you get back from Europe?

DARRELL

(Curtly.)

This morning on the "Olympic."

(Thinking – cautiously.)

Look out for this fellow . . . always had it in for me . . . like a woman . . . smells out love . . . he suspected before . . .

(Then boldly.)

Well, who gives a damn now? . . . all got to come out! . . . Nina wanted to tell Sam . . . now I'll tell him myself! . . .

MARSDEN

(Righteously indignant.)

What has brought him back? . . . what a devilish, cowardly trick to play on poor unsuspecting Sam! . . .

(Revengefully.)

But I'm not unsuspecting! . . . I'm not their fool! . . .

(Coldly.)

What brought you back so soon? When I saw you in Munich you weren't intending –

DARRELL

(Shortly.)

My father died three weeks ago. I've had to come back about his estate.

(Thinking.)

Lie . . . Father's death just gave me an excuse to myself . . . wouldn't have come back for that . . . came back because I love her! . . . damn his questions! . . . I want to think . . . before I see her . . . sound of her voice . . . seemed to burn inside my head . . . God, I'm licked! . . . no use fighting it . . . I've done my damnedest . . . work . . . booze . . . other women . . . no use . . . I love her! . . . always! . . . to hell with pride! . . .

MARSDEN

(Thinking.)

He has two brothers . . . they'll probably all share equally . . . his father noted Philadelphia surgeon . . . rich, I've heard . . .

(With a bitter grin.)

Wait till Sam hears that! . . . he'll ask Darrell to back him . . . and Darrell will jump at it . . . chance to avert suspicion . . . conscience money, too! . . . it's my duty to protect Sam . . .

(As he hears Nina coming down the stairs.)

I must watch them . . . it's my duty to protect Nina from herself . . . Sam is a simpleton . . . I'm all she has . . .

DARRELL

(Hearing her coming – in a panic – thinking.)

Coming! . . . in a second I'll see her! . . .

(Terrified.)

Does she still love me? . . . she may have forgotten . . . no, it's my child . . . she can never forget that! . . .

(Nina comes in from the rear. She has put on a fresh dress, her hair is arranged, her face newly rouged and powdered, she looks extremely pretty and this is heightened by the feverish state of mind she is in – a mixture of love, of triumphant egotism in knowing her lover has come back to

her, and of fear and uncertainty in feeling her new peace, her certainties, her contented absorption in her child failing her. She hesitates just inside the door, staring into Darrell's eyes, thinking a fierce question.)

NINA

Does he still love me? . . .

(Then triumphantly as she reads him.)

Yes! . . . he does! . . . he does! . . .

DARRELL

(Who has jumped to his feet – with a cry of longing.)

Nina!

(Thinking with alarm now.)

She's changed! . . . changed! . . . can't tell if she loves! . . .

(He has started to go to her. Now he hesitates.)

(His voice taking on a pleading uncertain quality.)

Nina!

NINA

(Thinking triumphantly – with a certain cruelty.)

He loves me! . . . he's mine . . . now more than ever! . . . he'll never dare leave me again! . . .

(Certain of herself now, she comes to him and speaks with confident pleasure.)

Hallo, Ned! This is a wonderful surprise! How are you?

(She takes his hand.)

DARRELL

(Taken aback – confusedly.)

Oh – all right, Nina.

(Thinking in a panic.)

That tone! . . . as if she didn't care! . . . can't believe that! . . . she's playing a game to fool Marsden! . . .

MARSDEN

(Who is watching them keenly – thinking.)

She loves his love for her . . . she's cruelly confident . . . much as I hate this man I can't help feeling sorry . . . I know her cruelty . . . it's time I took a hand in this . . . what a plot for a novel! . . .

(Almost mockingly.)

Darrell's father died, Nina. He had to come home to see about the estate.

DARRELL

(With a glare at Marsden – protestingly.)

I was coming home anyway. I only intended to stay a year, and it's over that since –

(Intensely.)

I was coming back anyway, Nina!

NINA

(Thinking with triumphant happiness.)

You dear, you! . . . as if I didn't know that! . . . oh, how I'd love to take you in my arms! . . .

(Happily.)

I'm awfully glad you've come, Ned. We've missed you terribly.

DARRELL

(Thinking – more and more at sea.)

She looks glad . . . but she's changed . . . I don't understand her . . . "we've missed" . . . that means Sam . . . what does that mean? . . .

(Intensely, pressing her hand.)

And I've missed you – terribly!

MARSDEN

(Sardonically.)

Yes, indeed, Darrell, I can vouch for their missing you – Sam in particular. He was asking about you only a short while ago – how things were going with you when I saw you in Munich.

(Maliciously.)

By the way, who was the lady you were with that day? She was certainly startling-looking.

NINA

(Thinking – triumphantly mocking.)

A miss, Charlie! . . . he loves me! . . . what do I care about that woman? . . .

(Gaily.)

Yes, who was the mysterious beauty, Ned? Do tell us!

(She moves away from him and sits down at centre. Darrell remains standing.)

DARRELL

(Glaring at Marsden, sullenly.)

Oh, I don't remember –

(Thinking apprehensively with a bitter resentment.)

She doesn't give a damn! . . . if she loved me she'd be jealous! . . . but she doesn't give a damn! . .

(He blurts out resentfully at Nina.)

Well, she was my mistress – for a time – I was lonely.

(Then with sudden anger, turning on Marsden.)

But what's all this to you, Marsden?

MARSDEN

(Coolly.)

Absolutely nothing. Pardon me. It was a tactless question.

(Then with continued open malice.)

But I was starting to say how Sam had missed you, Darrell.

It's really remarkable. One doesn't encounter such friendship often in these slack days. Why, he'd trust you with anything!

NINA

(*Wincing – thinking.*)

That hurts . . . hurts Ned . . . Charlie is being cruel! . . .

DARRELL

(*Wincing – in a forced tone.*)

And I'd trust Sam with anything.

MARSDEN

Of course. He is a person one can trust. They are rare. You're going to be amazed at the change in Sam, Darrell. Isn't he, Nina? He's a new man. I never saw such energy. If ever a man was bound for success Sam is. In fact, I'm so confident he is that as soon as he thinks the time is ripe to start his own firm I'm going to furnish the capital and become his silent partner.

DARRELL

(*Puzzled and irritated – thinking confusedly.*)

What's he driving at? . . . why the hell doesn't he get out and leave us alone? . . . but I'm glad Sam is on his feet . . . makes it easier to tell him the truth. . . .

NINA

(*Thinking – worriedly.*)

What's Charlie talking about? . . . it's time I talked to Ned . . . Oh, Ned, I do love you! . . . you can be my lover! . . . we won't hurt Sam! . . . he'll never know! . . .

MARSDEN

Yes, ever since the baby was born Sam's been another man – in fact, ever since he knew there was going to be a baby, isn't it, Nina?

NINA

(*Agreeing as if she had only half heard him.*)

Yes.

(*Thinking.*)

Ned's baby! . . . I must talk to him about our baby. . . .

MARSDEN

Sam is the proudest parent I've ever seen!

NINA

(*As before.*)

Yes, Sam makes a wonderful father, Ned.

(*Thinking.*)

Ned doesn't care for children . . . I know what you're hoping, Ned . . . but if you think I'm going to take Sam's baby from him, you're mistaken! . . . or if you think I'll run away with you and leave my baby . . .

MARSDEN

(*With the same strange driving insistence.*)

If anything happened to that child I actually believe Sam would lose his reason! Don't you think so, Nina?

NINA

(*With emphasis.*)

I know I'd lose mine! Little Gordon has become my whole life.

DARRELL

(*Thinking – with a sad bitter irony.*)

Sam . . . wonderful father . . . lose his reason . . . little Gordon! . . . Nina called my son after Gordon! . . . romantic imagination! . . . Gordon is still her lover! . . Gordon, Sam and Nina! . . . and my son! . . . closed corporation! . . . I'm forced out! . . .

(*Then rebelling furiously.*)

No! . . . not yet, by God! . . . I'll smash it up! . . . I'll tell Sam the truth no matter what! . . .

NINA

(*Thinking with a strange calculation.*)

I couldn't find a better husband than Sam . . . and I couldn't find a better lover than Ned . . . I need them both to be happy . . .

MARSDEN

(*With sudden despairing suspicion.*)

Good God . . . after all, is it Sam's child? . . . mightn't it be Darrell's! . . . why have I never thought of that? . . . No! . . . Nina couldn't be so vile! . . . to go on living with Sam, pretending . . . and, after all, why should she, you fool? . . . there's no sense! . . . she could have gone off with Darrell, couldn't she? . . . Sam would have given her a divorce . . . there was no possible reason for her staying with Sam, when she loved Darrell, unless exactly because this was Sam's baby . . . for its sake . . .

(*Hectically relieved.*)

Of course! . . . of course! . . . that's all right! . . . I love that poor baby now! . . . I'll fight for its sake against these two! . . .

(*Smilingly gets to his feet – thinking.*)

I can leave them alone now . . . for they won't be alone, thanks to me! . . . I leave Sam and his baby in this room with them . . . and their honour . . .

(*Suddenly raging.*)

Their honour! . . . what an obscene joke! . . . the honour of a harlot and a pimp! . . . I hate them! . . . if only God would strike them dead! . . . now! . . . and I could see them die! . . . I would praise His justice! . . . His kindness and mercy to me! . . .

NINA

(*Thinking – with horrified confusion.*)

Why doesn't Charlie go? . . . What is he thinking? . . . I suddenly feel afraid of him! . . .

(*She gets to her feet with a confused pleading cry.*)

Charlie!

MARSDEN

(Immediately urbane and smiling.)

It's all right. I'm going out to find Sam. When he knows you're here he'll come on the run, Darrell.

(He goes to the door. They watch him suspiciously.)

And you two probably have a lot to talk over.

(He chuckles pleasantly and goes into the hall – mockingly warning.)

We'll be back before long.

(The front door is heard slamming. Nina and Darrell turn and look at each other guiltily and frightenedly. Then he comes to her and takes both of her hands uncertainly.)

DARRELL

(Stammeringly.)

Nina – I – I've come back to you – do you – do you still care – Nina?

NINA

(Giving way to his love passionately, as if to drown her fears.)

I love you, Ned!

DARRELL

(Kisses her awkwardly – stammering.)

I – I didn't know – you seemed so cold – damn Marsden! – he suspects, doesn't he? – but it makes no difference now, does it?

(Then in a flood of words.)

Oh, it's been hell, Nina! I couldn't forget you! Other women – they only made me love you more! I hated them and loved you even at the moment when – that's honest! It was always you in my arms – as you used to be – those afternoons – God, how I've thought of them – lying awake – recalling every word you said, each movement, each expression on your face, smelling your hair, feeling your soft body –

(Suddenly taking her in his arms and kissing her again and again – passionately.)

Nina! I love you so!

NINA

And I've longed for you so much! Do you think I've forgotten those afternoons?

(Then in anguish.)

Oh, Ned, why did you run away? I can never forgive that! I can never trust you again!

DARRELL

(Violently.)

I was a fool! I thought of Sam! And that wasn't all! Oh, I wasn't all noble, I'll confess! I thought of myself and my career! Damn my career! A lot of good that did it! I didn't study! I didn't live! I longed for you – and suffered! I paid in full, believe me, Nina! But I know better now! I've come back. The time for lying is past! You've got to come away with me!

(He kisses her.)

NINA

(Letting herself go, kissing him passionately.)

Yes! My lover!

(Then suddenly resisting and pushing him away.)

No! You're forgetting Sam – and Sam's baby!

DARRELL

(Staring at her wildly.)

Sam's baby? Are you joking? Ours, you mean! We'll take him with us, of course!

NINA

(Sadly.)

And Sam?

DARRELL

Damn Sam! He's got to give you a divorce! Let him be generous for a change!

NINA

(Sadly but determinedly.)

He would be. You must be just to Sam. He'd give his life for my happiness. And this would mean his life. Could we be happy then? You know we couldn't! And I've changed, Ned. You've got to realize that. I'm not your old mad Nina. I still love you. I shall always love you. But now I love my baby, too. His happiness comes first with me!

DARRELL

But – he's mine, too!

NINA

No! You gave him to Sam to save Sam!

DARRELL

To hell with Sam! It was to make you happy!

NINA

So I could make Sam happy! That was in it, too! I was sincere in that, Ned! If I hadn't been, I could never have gone to you that first day – or if I had, I'd never have forgiven myself. But as it is I don't feel guilty or wicked. I have made Sam happy! and I'm proud! I love Sam's happiness! I love the devoted husband and father in him! And I feel it's his baby – that we've made it his baby!

DARRELL

(*Distractedly.*)

Nina! For God's sake! You haven't come to love Sam, have you! Then – I'll go – I'll go away again – I'll never come back – I tried not to this time – but I had to, Nina!

NINA

(*Taking him in her arms – with sudden alarm.*)

No, don't go away, Ned – ever again. I don't love Sam! I love you!

DARRELL

(*Miserably.*)

But I don't understand! Sam gets everything – and I have nothing!

NINA

You have my love!

(*With a strange, self-assured smile at him.*)

It seems to me you're complaining unreasonably!

DARRELL

You mean – I can be – your lover again?

NINA

(*Simply, even matter-of-factly.*)

Isn't that the nearest we can come to making everyone happy? That's all that counts.

DARRELL

(*With a harsh laugh.*)

And is that what you call playing fair to Sam?

NINA

(*Simply.*)

Sam will never know. The happiness I have given him has made him too sure of himself ever to suspect me now. And as long as we can love each other without danger to him, I feel he owes that to us for all we've done for him.

(*With finality.*)

That's the only possible solution, Ned, for all our sakes, now you've come back to me.

DARRELL

(*Repulsed.*)

Nina! How can you be so inhuman and calculating!

NINA

(*Stung – mockingly.*)

It was you who taught me the scientific approach, Doctor!

DARRELL

(*Shrinking back from her – threateningly.*)

Then I'll leave again! I'll go back to Europe! I won't endure –!

(*Then in a queer, futile rage.*)

You think I'll stay – to be your lover – watching Sam with my wife and my child – you think that's what I came back to you for? You can go to hell, Nina!

NINA

(*Calmly – sure of him.*)

But what else can I do, Ned?

(*Then warningly.*)

I hear them coming, dear. It's Sam, you know.

DARRELL

(*In a frenzy.*)

What else can you do? Liar! But I can do something else! I can smash your calculating game for you! I can tell Sam – and I will – right now – by God, I will!

NINA

(*Quietly.*)

No. You won't, Ned. You can't do that to Sam.

DARRELL

(*Savagely.*)

Like hell I can't!

(*The front door is opened. Evans' voice is immediately heard, even before he bounds into the room. He rushes up to Ned hilariously, shakes his hand and pounds his back, oblivious of Darrell's wild expression.*)

EVANS

You old son of a gun! Why didn't you let a guy know you were coming? We'd have met you at the dock, and brought the baby. Let me have a look at you! You look thinner. We'll fatten you up, won't we, Nina? Let us do the prescribing this time! Why didn't you let us know where you were, you old bum? We wanted to write you about the baby. And I wanted to boast about how I was getting on! You're the only person in the world – except Nina and Charlie – I would boast about that to.

NINA

(*Affectionately.*)

Mercy, Sam, give Ned a chance to get a word in!

(*Looking at Ned pityingly but challengingly.*)

He wants to tell you something, Sam.

DARRELL

(*Crushed – stammers.*)

No – I mean, yes – I want to tell you how damn glad I am . . .

(*He turns away, his face is screwed up in his effort to hold back his tears.*)

(*Thinking miserably.*)

I can't tell him! . . . God damn him, I can't! . . .

NINA

(*With a strange triumphant calm.*)

There! . . . that's settled for all time! . . . poor Ned! . . . how crushed he looks! . . . I mustn't let Sam look at him! . . .

(*She steps between them protectingly.*)

Where's Charlie, Sam?

MARSDEN

(*Appearing from the hall.*)

Here, Nina. Always here!

(*He comes to her, smiling with assurance.*)

NINA

(*Suddenly with a strange unnatural elation – looking from one to the other with triumphant possession.*)

Yes, you're here, Charlie – always! And you, Sam – and Ned!

(*With a strange gaiety.*)

Sit down, all of you! Make yourselves at home! You are my three men! This is your home with me!

(*Then in a strange half-whisper.*)

Ssshh! I thought I heard the baby. You must all sit down and be very quiet. You must not wake our baby.

(*Mechanically the three sit down, careful to make no noise – Evans in his old place by the table, Marsden at centre, Darrell on the sofa at right. They sit staring before them in silence. Nina remains standing, dominating them, a little behind and to the left of Marsden.*)

DARRELL

(*Thinking abjectly.*)

I couldn't! . . . there are things one may not do and live with oneself afterwards . . . there are things one may not say . . . memory is too full of echoes! . . . there are secrets one must not reveal . . . memory is lined with mirrors! . . . he was too happy! . . . to kill happiness is a worse murder than taking life! . . . I gave him that happiness! . . . Sam deserves my happiness! . . . God bless you, Sam! . . .

(*Then in a strange objective tone – thinking.*)

My experiment with the guinea-pigs has been a success . . . the ailing ones, Sam, and the female, Nina, have been restored to health and normal function . . . only the other male, Ned, seems to have suffered deterioration. . . .

(*Then bitterly humble.*)

Nothing left but to accept her terms . . . I love her . . . I can help to make her happy . . . half a loaf is better . . . to a starving man. . . .

(*Glancing over at Evans – bitterly gloating.*)

And your child is mine! . . . your wife is mine! . . . your happiness is mine! . . . may you enjoy my happiness, her husband! . . .

EVANS

(*Looking at Darrell affectionately.*)

Sure good to see Ned again . . . a real friend if there ever was one . . . looks blue about something . . . oh, that's right, Charlie said his old man had kicked in . . . his old man was rich . . . that's an idea . . . I'll bet he'd put up that capital . . .

(*Then ashamed of himself.*)

Aw hell, what's the matter with me? . . . he's no sooner here than I start . . . he's done enough . . . forget it! . . . now, anyway . . . he looks pretty dissipated . . . too many women . . . ought to get married and settle down . . . tell him that if I didn't think he'd laugh at me giving him advice . . . but he'll soon realize I'm not the old Sam he knew . . . I suppose Nina's been boasting about that already . . . she's proud . . . she's helped me . . . she's a wonderful wife and mother . . .

(*Looking up at her – solicitously.*)

She acted a bit nervous just now . . . queer . . . like she used to . . . haven't noticed her that way for a long time . . . suppose it's the excitement of Ned turning up . . . mustn't let her get over-excited . . . bad for the baby's milk. . . .

MARSDEN

(*Glancing furtively over his shoulder at Nina – broodingly thinking.*)

She's the old queer Nina now . . . the Nina I could never fathom . . . her three men! . . . and we are! . . . I? . . . yes, more deeply than either of the others since I serve for nothing . . . a queer kind of love, maybe . . . I am not ordinary! . . . our child . . . what could she mean by that? . . . child of us three? . . . on the surface, that's insane . . . but I felt when she said it there was something in it . . . she has strange devious intuitions that tap the hidden currents of life . . . dark intermingling currents that become the one stream of desire . . . I feel, with regard to Nina, my life queerly identified with Sam's and Darrell's . . . her child is the child of our three loves for her . . . I would like to believe that . . . I would like to be her husband in a sense . . . and the father of a child, after my fashion . . . I could forgive her everything . . . permit everything . . .

(*Determinedly.*)

And I do forgive! . . . and I will not meddle hereafter more than is necessary to guard her happiness, and Sam's and our baby's . . . as for Darrell, I am no longer jealous of him . . . she is only using his love for her own happiness . . . he can never take her away from me! . . .

NINA

(*More and more strangely triumphant.*)

My three men! . . . I feel their desires converge in me! . . . to form one complete beautiful male desire which I absorb . . . and am whole . . . they dissolve in me, their life is my life . . . I am pregnant with the three! . . . husband! . . . lover! . . . father! . . . and the fourth man! . . . little man! . . . little Gordon! . . . he is mine, too! . . . that makes it perfect! . . .

(*With an extravagant suppressed exultance.*)

Why, I should be the proudest woman on earth! . . . I should be the happiest woman in the world! . . .

(*Then suppressing an outbreak of hysterical triumphant laughter only by a tremendous effort.*)

Ha-ha . . . only I better knock wood . . .

(*She raps with both knuckles in a fierce tattoo on the table.*)

before God the Father hears my happiness! . . .

EVANS

(*As the three turn to her – anxiously.*)

Nina? What's the matter?

NINA

(*Controlling herself with a great effort comes to him – forcing a smile – puts her arms around him affectionately.*)

Nothing, dear. Nerves, that's all. I'm over-tired, I guess.

EVANS

(*Bullying her – with loving authority.*)

Then you go right to bed, young lady! We'll excuse you.

NINA

(*Quietly and calmly now.*)

All right, dear. I guess I do need to rest.

(*She kisses him as she might kiss a big brother she loved – affectionately.*)

Good night, you bossy old thing, you!

EVANS

(*With deep tenderness.*)

Good night, darling.

NINA

(*She goes and kisses Charlie dutifully on the cheek as she might her father – affectionately.*)

Good night, Charlie.

MARSDEN

(*With a touch of her father's manner.*)

That's a good girl! Good night, dear.

NINA

(*She goes and kisses Darrell lovingly on the lips as she would kiss her lover.*)

Good night, Ned.

DARRELL

(*Looks at her with grateful humility.*)

Thank you. Good night.

(*She turns and walks quietly out of the room. The eyes of the three men follow her.*)

Curtain

ACT SEVEN

SCENE: *Nearly eleven years later. The sitting-room of the Evans' apartment on Park Avenue, New York City – a room that is a tribute to Nina's good taste. It is a large, sunny room, the furniture expensive but extremely simple. The arrangement of the furniture shown is as in previous scenes except there are more pieces. Two chairs are by the table at left. There is a smaller table at centre, and a* chaise longue. *A large, magnificently comfortable sofa is at right.*

It is about one in the afternoon of a day in early fall. Nina and Darrell and their son, Gordon, are in the room. Nina is reclining on the chaise longue *watching Gordon who is sitting on the floor near her, turning over the pages of a book. Darrell is sitting by the table at left, watching Nina.*

Nina is thirty-five, in the full bloom of her womanhood. She is slimmer than in the previous scene. Her skin still retains a trace of summer tan and she appears in the pink of physical condition. But as in the first act of the play, there is beneath this a sense of great mental strain. One notices the many lines in her face at second glance. Her eyes are tragically sad in repose and her expression is set and mask-like.

Gordon is eleven – a fine boy with, even at this age, the figure of an athlete. He looks older than he is. There is a grave expression on his face. His eyes are full of a quick-tempered sensitiveness. He does not noticeably resemble his mother. He looks nothing at all like his father. He seems to have sprung from a line distinct from any of the people we have seen.

Darrell has aged greatly. His hair is streaked with grey. He has grown stout. His face is a bit jowly and puffy under the eyes. The features have become blurred. He has the look of a man with no definite aim or ambition to which he can relate his living. His eyes are embittered and they hide his inner self-resentment behind a pose of cynical indifference.

GORDON

(*Thinking – resentfully.*)

I wish Darrell'd get out of here! . . . why couldn't Mother let me run my own birthday? . . . I'd never had him here, you bet! . . . what's he always hanging 'round for? . . . why don't he go off on one of his old trips again? . . . last time he was gone more'n a year . . . I was hoping he'd died! . . . what makes Mother like him so much? . . . she makes me sick! . . . I'd think she'd get sick of the old fool and tell him to get out and never come back! . . . I'd kick him out if I was big enough! . . . it's good for him he didn't bring me any birthday present or I'd smash it first chance I got! . . .

NINA

(*Watching him – brooding with loving tenderness – sadly.*)

No longer my baby . . . my little man . . . eleven . . . I can't believe it . . . I'm thirty-five . . . five years more . . . at forty a woman has finished living . . . life passes by her . . . she rots away in peace! . . .

(*Intensely.*)

I want to rot away in peace! . . . I'm sick of the fight for happiness! . . .

(*Smiling with a wry amusement at herself.*)

What ungrateful thoughts on my son's birthday! . . . my love for him has been happiness . . . how handsome he is! . . . not at all like Ned . . . when I was carrying him I was fighting to forget Ned . . . hoping he might be like Gordon . . . and he is . . . poor Ned, I've made him suffer a great deal . . . !

(*She looks over at Darrell – self-mockingly.*)

My lover! . . . so very rarely now, those interludes of passion . . . what has bound us together all these years? . . . love? . . . if he could only have been contented with what I was able to give him! . . . but he has always wanted more . . . yet never had the courage to insist on all or nothing . . . proud without being proud enough! . . . he has shared me for his comfort's sake with a little gratitude and a big bitterness . . . and sharing me has corrupted him! . . .

(*Then bitterly.*)

No, I can't blame myself! . . . no woman can make a man happy who has no purpose in life! . . . why did he give up his career? . . . because I had made him weak? . . .

(*With resentful scorn.*)

No, it was I who shamed him into taking up biology and starting the station at Antigua . . . if I hadn't he'd simply have hung around me year after year, doing nothing . . .

(*Irritatedly.*)

Why does he stay so long? . . . over six months . . . I can't stand having him around me that long any more! . . . why doesn't he go back to the West Indies? . . . I always get a terrible feeling after he's been back a while that he's waiting for Sam to die! . . . or go insane! . . .

DARRELL

(*Thinking – with an apathetic bitterness.*)

What is she thinking? . . . we sit together in silence, thinking . . . thoughts that never know the other's thoughts . . . our love has become the intimate thinking together of thoughts that are strangers . . . our love! . . . well, whatever it is that has bound us together, it's strong! . . . I've broken with her, run away, tried to forget her . . . running away to come back each time more abject! . . . or, if she saw there was some chance I might break loose, she'd find some way to call me back . . . and I'd forget my longing for freedom, I'd come wagging my tail . . . no, guinea-pigs have no tails . . . I hope my experiment has proved something! . . . Sam . . . happy and wealthy . . . and healthy! . . . I used to hope he'd break down . . . I'd watch him and read symptoms of insanity into every move he made . . . despicable? . . . certainly, but love makes one either noble or despicable! . . . he only grew healthier . . . now I've given up watching him . . . almost entirely . . . now I watch him grow fat and I laugh! . . . the huge joke has dawned on me! . . . Sam is the only normal one! . . . we lunatics! . . . Nina and I! . . . have made a sane life for him out of our madness! . . .

(*Watching Nina – sadly.*)

Always thinking of her son . . . well, I gave him to her . . . Gordon . . . I hate that name . . . why do I continue hanging around here? . . . each time after a few months my love changes to bitterness . . . I blame Nina for the mess I've made of life . . .

NINA

(*Suddenly turning on him.*)

When are you going back to the West Indies, Ned?

DARRELL

(*Determinedly.*)

Soon!

GORDON

(*Stops playing to listen – thinking.*)

Gosh, I'm glad! . . . How soon, I wonder? . . .

NINA

(*With a trace of a sneer.*)

I don't see how you can afford to leave your work for such long periods. Don't you grow rusty?

DARRELL

(*Looking at her meaningly.*)

My life work is to rust – nicely and unobtrusively!

(*He smiles mockingly.*)

NINA

(*Sadly – thinking.*)

To rot away in peace . . . that's all he wants now, too! . . . and this is what love has done to us! . . .

DARRELL

(*Bitterly.*)

My work was finished twelve years ago. As I believe you know, I ended it with an experiment which resulted so successfully that any further meddling with human lives would have been superfluous!

NINA

(*Pityingly.*)

Ned!

DARRELL

(*Indifferent and cynical.*)

But you meant my present dabbling about. You know better than to call that work. It's merely my hobby. Our backing Sam has made Marsden and me so wealthy that we're forced to take up hobbies. Marsden goes in for his old one of dashing off genteel novels, while I play at biology. Sam argued that golf would be healthier and less nonsensical for me, but you insisted on biology. And give it its due, it has kept me out in the open air and been conducive to travelling and broadening my mind!

(*Then forcing a smile.*)

But I'm exaggerating. I really am interested, or I'd never keep financing the Station. And when I'm down there I do work hard, helping Preston. He's doing remarkable work already, and he's still in his twenties. He'll be a big man –

(*His bitterness cropping up again.*)

at least if he takes my advice and never carries his experiments as far as human lives!

NINA

(*In a low voice.*)

How can you be so bitter, Ned – on Gordon's birthday?

DARRELL

(*Thinking cynically.*)

She expects me to love the child she deliberately took from me and gave to another man! . . . no, thank you, Nina! . . . I've been hurt enough! . . . I'll not leave myself open there! . . . .

(*Regarding his son bitterly.*)

Every day he gets more like Sam, doesn't he?

GORDON

(*Thinking.*)

He's talking about me . . . he better look out! . . .

NINA

(*Resentfully.*)

I don't think Gordon resembles Sam at all. He reminds me a great deal of his namesake.

DARRELL

(*Touched on a sore spot – with a nasty laugh – cuttingly.*)

Gordon Shaw? Not the slightest bit in the world! And you ought to thank God he doesn't! It's the last thing I'd wish for a boy of mine – to be like that rah-rah hero!

GORDON

(*Thinking contemptuously.*)

Boy of his! . . . He hasn't got a boy! . . .

NINA

(*Amused and pleased by his jealousy.*)

Poor Ned! . . . isn't he silly? . . . at his age, after all we've been through, to feel jealous still . . .

DARRELL

I'd much rather have him

(*Pointing to Gordon.*)

grow up to be an exact duplicate of the esteemed Samuel!

GORDON

(*Thinking resentfully.*)

He's always making fun of my father! . . . he better look out! . . .

DARRELL

(*More and more mockingly.*)

And what could be fairer? The good Samuel is an A 1 success. He has a charming wife and a darling boy, and a Park Avenue apartment and a membership in an expensive golf club. And, above all, he rests so complacently on the proud assurance that he is self-made!

NINA

(*Sharply.*)

Ned! You ought to be ashamed! You know how grateful Sam has always been to you!

DARRELL

(*Bitingly.*)

Would he be grateful if he knew how much I'd really done for him?

NINA

(*Sternly.*)

Ned!

GORDON

(*Suddenly jumps up and confronts Darrell, his fists clenched, trembling with rage, stammers.*)

You – shut up – making fun of my father!

NINA

(*In dismay.*)

Gordon!

DARRELL

(*Mockingly.*)

My dear boy, I wouldn't make fun of your father for the world!

GORDON

(*Baffledly – his lips trembling.*)

You – you did, too!

(*Then intensely.*)

I hate you!

NINA

(*Shocked and indignant.*)

Gordon! How dare you talk like that to your Uncle Ned!

GORDON

(*Rebelliously.*)

He's not my uncle! He's not my anything!

NINA

Not another word or you'll be punished, whether it's your birthday or not! If you can't behave better than that, I'll have to 'phone to all your friends they mustn't come here this afternoon, that you've been so bad you can't have a party!

(*Thinking remorsefully.*)

Is this my fault? . . . I've done my best to get him to love Ned! . . . but it only makes him worse! . . . it makes him turn against me! . . . turn from me to Sam! . . .

GORDON

(*Sullenly.*)

I don't care! I'll tell Dad!

NINA

(*Peremptorily.*)

Leave the room! And don't come near me again, do you hear, until you've apologized to Uncle Ned!

(*Thinking angrily.*)

Dad! . . . It's always Dad with him now! . . .

DARRELL

(*Boredly.*)

Oh, never mind, Nina!

GORDON

(*Going out – mutters.*)

I won't 'pologize – never!

(*Thinking vindictively.*)

I hate her too when she sides with him! . . . I don't care if she is my mother! . . . she has no right! . . .

(*He goes out, rear.*)

DARRELL

(*Irritably.*)

What if he does hate me? I don't blame him! He suspects what I know – that I've acted like a coward and a weakling toward him! I should have claimed him no matter what happened to other people! Whose fault is it if he hates me, and I dislike him because he loves another father? Ours! You gave him to Sam and I consented! All right! Then don't blame him for acting like Sam's son!

NINA

But he shouldn't say he hates you.

(*Thinking bitterly.*)

Sam's! . . . he's becoming all Sam's! . . . I'm getting to mean nothing! . . .

DARRELL

(*Sardonically.*)

Perhaps he realizes subconsciously that I am his father, his rival in your love; but I'm not his father ostensibly, there are no taboos, so he can come right out and hate me to his heart's content!

(*Bitterly.*)

If he realized how little you love me any more, he wouldn't bother!

NINA

(*Exasperatedly.*)

Oh, Ned, do shut up! I can't stand hearing those same old reproaches I've heard a thousand times before! I can't bear to hear myself making the same old bitter counter-accusations. And then there'll be the same old terrible scene of hate and you'll run away – it used to be to drink and women, now it's to the Station. Or I'll send you away, and then after a time I'll call you back, because I'll have got so lonely again living this lonely lie of my life, with no one to speak to except Sam's business friends and their deadly wives.

(*She laughs helplessly.*)

Or else you'll get lonely in your lie a little before I do and come back again of your own desire! And then we'll kiss and cry and love each other again!

DARRELL

(*With an ironical grimace.*)

Or I might cheat myself into believing I'd fallen in love with some nice girl and get myself engaged to be married again as I did once before! And then you'd be jealous again and have to find some way of getting me to break it off!

NINA

(*Forlornly amused.*)

Yes – I suppose the thought of a wife taking you away from me would be too much – again!

(*Then helplessly.*)

Oh, Ned, when are we ever going to learn something about each other? We act like such brainless fools – with our love. It's always so wonderful when you first come back, but you always stay too long – or I always keep you too long! You never leave before we've come to the ugly bitter stage when we blame each other!

(*Then suddenly forlornly tender.*)

Is it possible you can still love me, Ned?

DARRELL

(*Mournfully smiling.*)

I must, or I'd never act this fool way, would I?

NINA

(*Smiling back.*)

And I must love you.

(*Then seriously.*)

After all, I can never forget that Gordon is the child of your love, Ned.

DARRELL

(*Sadly.*)

You'd better forget that, for his sake and your own. Children have sure intuitions. He feels cheated of your love – by me. So he's concentrating his affections on Sam whose love he knows is secure, and withdrawing from you.

NINA

(*Frightened – angrily.*)

Don't be stupid, Ned! That isn't so at all! I hate you when you talk that way!

DARRELL

(*Cynically.*)

Hate me, exactly. As he does! That's what I'm advising you to do if you want to keep his love!

(*He smiles grimly.*)

NINA

(*Sharply.*)

If Gordon doesn't love you it's because you've never made the slightest attempt to be lovable to him! There's no earthly reason why he should like you, when you come right down to it, Ned! Take to-day, for instance. It's his birthday, but you'd forgotten, or didn't care! You never even brought him a present.

DARRELL

(*With bitter sadness.*)

I did bring him a present. It's out in the hall. I bought him a costly delicate one so he could get full satisfaction and yet not strain himself when he smashed it, as he's smashed every present of mine in the past! And I left it out in the hall, to be given to him after I've gone because, after all, he is my son and I'd prefer he didn't smash it before my eyes!

(*Trying to mock his own emotion back – with savage bitterness.*)

I'm selfish, you see! I don't want my son to be too happy at my expense, even on his birthday!

NINA

(*Tormented by love and pity and remorse.*)

Ned! For God's sake! How can you torture us like that! Oh, it's too dreadful – what I have done to you! Forgive me, Ned!

DARRELL

(*His expression changing to one of pity for her – goes to her and puts his hand on her head – tenderly.*)

I'm sorry.

(*With remorseful tenderness.*)

Dreadful, what you've done, Nina? Why, you've given me the only happiness I've ever known! And no matter what I may say or do in bitterness, I'm proud – and grateful, Nina!

NINA

(*Looks up at him with deep tenderness and admiration.*)

Dearest, it's wonderful of you to say that!

(*She gets up and puts her hands on his shoulders and looks into his eyes – tenderly in a sort of pleading.*)

Can't we be brave enough – for you to go away – now, on this note – sure of our love – with no ugly bitterness for once?

DARRELL

(*Joyfully.*)

Yes! I'll go – this minute if you wish!

NINA

(*Playfully.*)

Oh, you needn't go this minute! Wait and say good-bye to Sam. He'd be terribly hurt if you didn't.

(*Then seriously.*)

And will you promise to stay away two years – even if I call you back before then – and work this time, really work?

DARRELL

I'll try, Nina!

NINA

And then – surely come back to me!

DARRELL

(*Smiling.*)

Surely – again!

NINA

Then good-bye, dear!

(*She kisses him.*)

DARRELL

Again!

(*He smiles and she smiles and they kiss again. Gordon appears in the doorway at rear and stands for a moment in a passion of jealousy and rage and grief, watching them.*)

GORDON

(*Thinking with a strange tortured shame.*)

I mustn't see her! . . . pretend I didn't see her! . . mustn't never let her know I saw her! . . .

(*He vanishes as silently as he had come.*)

NINA

(*Suddenly moving away from Darrell, looking around her uneasily.*)

Ned, did you see – ? I had the queerest feeling just then that someone –

GORDON

(*His voice sounds from the hall with a strained casualness.*)

Mother! Uncle Charlie's downstairs. Shall he come right up?

NINA

(*Startled, her own voice straining to be casual.*)

Yes, dear – of course!

(*Then worriedly.*)

His voice sounded funny. Did it to you? Do you suppose he – ?

DARRELL

(*With a wry smile.*)

It's possible. To be on the safe side, you'd better tell him you kissed me good-bye to get rid of me!

(*Then angrily.*)

So Marsden's here again! The damned old woman! I simply can't stand him any more, Nina! Why Gordon should take such a fancy to that old sissy is beyond me!

NINA

(*Suddenly struck – thinking.*)

Why, he's jealous of Gordon liking Charlie! . . .

(*Immediately all affectionate pity.*)

Then he must love Gordon a little! . . .

(*Letting her pity escape her.*)

Poor Ned!

(*She makes a movement toward him.*)

DARRELL

(*Startled and afraid she may have guessed something he doesn't acknowledge to himself.*)

What? why do you say that?

(*Then rudely defensive.*)

Don't be silly!

(*Resentfully.*)

You know well enough what I've always held against him! I wanted to put up all the money to back Sam when he started. I wanted to do it for Sam's sake – but especially for my child's sake. Why did Marsden absolutely insist on Sam letting him in equally? It isn't that I begrudge him the money he's made, but I know there was something queer in his mind and that he did it intentionally to spite me!

(*From the hallway comes the sound of Marsden's voice and Gordon's greeting him vociferously as he lets him into the apartment. As Darrell listens his expression becomes furious again. He bursts out angrily.*)

You're letting that old ass spoil Gordon, you fool, you!

(*Marsden comes in from the rear, smiling, immaculately dressed as usual. He looks hardly any older except that his hair is greyer and his tall figure more stooped. His expression and the general atmosphere he gives out are more nearly like those of Act One. If not happy, he is at least living in comparative peace with himself and his environment.*)

MARSDEN

(*Comes straight to Nina.*)

Hallo, Nina Cara Nina! Congratulations on your son's birthday!

(*He kisses her.*)

He's grown so much bigger and stronger in the two months since I've seen him.

(*He turns and shakes hands with Darrell coldly – with a trace of a patronizing air.*)

Hallo, Darrell! Last time I was here you were leaving for the West Indies in a week, but I see you're still around.

DARRELL

(*Furious – with a mocking air.*)

And here you are around again yourself! You're looking comfortable these days, Marsden. I hope your sister is well. It must be a great comfort, having her to take your mother's place!

(*Then with a harsh laugh.*)

Yes, we're two bad pennies, eh, Marsden? – counterfeits – fakes – Sam's silent partners!

NINA

(*Thinking irritably.*)

Ned's getting hateful again! . . . Poor Charlie! . . . I won't have him insulted! . . . he's become such a comfort . . . he understands so much . . . without my having to tell him . . .

(*Looking rebukingly at Darrell.*)

Ned is sailing this week, Charlie.

MARSDEN

(*Thinking triumphantly.*)

He's trying to insult me . . . I know all he means . . . but what do I care what he says . . . she's sending him away! . . . intentionally before me! . . . it means he's finished! . . .

DARRELL

(*Thinking resentfully.*)

Is she trying to humiliate me before him? . . . I'll teach her! . . .

(*Then struggling with himself – remorsefully.*)

No . . . not this time . . . I promised . . . no quarrel . . . remember . . .

(*Acquiescing – with a pleasant nod to Marsden.*)

Yes, I'm going this week and I expect to be gone at least two years this time – two years of hard work.

MARSDEN

(*Thinking with scornful pity.*)

His work! . . . what a pretence! . . . a scientific dilettante! . . . could anything be more pitiable? . . . poor chap! . . .

(*Perfunctorily.*)

Biology must be an interesting study. I wish I knew more about it.

DARRELL

(*Stung yet amused by the other's tone – ironically.*)

Yes, so do I wish you did, Marsden! Then you might write more about life and less about dear old ladies and devilish bachelors! Why don't you write a novel about life some time, Marsden?

(*He turns his back on Marsden with a glance of repulsion and walks to the window and stares out.*)

MARSDEN

(*Confusedly.*)

Yes – decidedly – but hardly in my line –

(*Thinking in anguish – picking up a magazine and turning over the pages aimlessly.*)

That . . . is . . . true! . . . he's full of poison! . . . I've never married the word to life! . . . I've been a timid bachelor of Arts, not an artist! . . . my poor pleasant books! . . . all is well! . . . is this well, the three of us? . . . Darrell has become less and less her lover . . . Nina has turned more and more to me . . . we have built up a secret life of subtle sympathies and confidences . . . she has known I have understood about her mere physical passion for Darrell . . . what woman could be expected to love Sam passionately? . . . someday she'll confide all about Darrell to me . . . now that he's finished . . . she knows that I love her without my telling . . . she even knows the sort of love it is. . . .

(*Passionately – thinking.*)

My love is finer than any she has known! . . . I do not lust for her! . . . I would be content if our marriage should be purely the placing of our ashes in the same tomb . . . our urns side by side and touching one another . . . could the others say as much, could they love so deeply? . . .

(*Then suddenly miserably self-contemptuous.*)

What! . . . platonic heroics at my age! . . . do I believe a word of that? . . . look at her beautiful eyes! . . . wouldn't I give anything in life to see them desire me? . . . and the intimacy I'm boasting about, what more does it mean than that I've been playing the dear old Charlie of her girlhood again? . . .

(*Thinking in anguish.*)

Damned coward and weakling! . . .

NINA

(*Looking at him – pityingly – thinking.*)

What does he always want of me? . . . me? . . . I am the only one who senses his deep hurt . . . I feel how life has wounded him . . . is that partly my fault, too? . . . I have wounded everyone . . . poor Charlie, what can I do for you? . . . if giving myself to you would bring you a moment's happiness, could I? . . . the idea used to be revolting . . . now, nothing about love seems important enough to be revolting . . . poor Charlie, he only thinks he ought to desire me! . . . dear Charlie, what a perfect lover he would make for one's old age! . . . what a perfect lover when one was past passion! . . .

(*Then with sudden scornful revulsion.*)

These men make me sick! . . . I hate all three of them! . . . they disgust me! . . . the wife and mistress in me has been killed by them! . . . thank God, I am only a mother now! . . . Gordon is my little man, my only man! . . .

(*Suddenly.*)

I've got a job for you, Charlie – make the salad dressing for lunch. You know, the one I'm so crazy about.

MARSDEN

(*Springs to his feet.*)

Right-o!

(*He puts his arm about her waist and they go out together laughingly, without a glance at Darrell.*)

DARRELL

(*Thinking dully.*)

I mustn't stay to lunch . . . ghost at my son's feast! . . . I better go now . . . why wait for Sam? . . . what is there to say to him I can say? . . . and there's nothing about him I want to see . . . he's as healthy as a pig . . . and as sane . . . I was afraid once his mother had lied to Nina . . . I went up-state and investigated . . . true, every word of it

. . . his great-grandfather, his grandmother, his father, were all insane . . .

(Moving uneasily.)

Stop it! . . . time to go when those thoughts come . . . sail on Saturday . . . not come here again . . . Nina will soon be fighting Sam for my son's love! . . . I'm better out of that! . . . O Christ, what a mess it all is! . . .

GORDON

(Appears in the doorway in rear. He carries a small, expensive model of a yacht with the sails set. He is in a terrific state of conflicting emotions, on the verge of tears yet stubbornly determined.)

I got to do it! . . . Gosh, it's awful . . . this boat is so pretty . . . why did it have to come from him? . . . I can get Dad to buy me another boat . . . but now I love this one . . . but he kissed Mother . . . she kissed him . . .

(He walks up defiantly and confronts Darrell, who turns to him in surprise.)

Hey – Darrell – did you – ?

(He stops chokingly.)

DARRELL

(Immediately realizing what is coming – thinking with sombre anguish.)

So this has to happen! . . . what I dreaded! . . . my fate is merciless, it seems! . . .

(With strained kindliness.)

Did what?

GORDON

(Growing hard – stammers angrily.)

I found this – out in the hall. It can't be from anybody else. Is this – your present?

DARRELL

(Hard and defiant himself.)

Yes.

GORDON

(In a rage – tremblingly.)

Then – here's what – I think of you!

(Beginning to cry, he breaks off the mast, bowsprit, breaks the mast in two, tears the rigging off and throws the dismantled hull at Darrell's feet.)

There! You can keep it!

DARRELL

(His anger overcoming him for an instant.)

You – you mean little devil, you! You don't get that from me –

(He has taken a threatening step forward. Gordon stands white-faced, defying him. Darrell pulls himself up short – then in a trembling voice of deeply wounded affection.)

You shouldn't have done that, son. What difference do I make? It was never my boat. But it was your boat. You should consider the boat, not me. Don't you like boats for themselves? It was a beautiful little boat, I thought. That's why I –

GORDON

(Sobbing miserably.)

It was awful pretty! I didn't want to do it!

(He kneels down and gathers up the boat into his arms again.)

Honest I didn't. I love boats! But I hate you!

(This last with passionate intensity.)

DARRELL

(Dryly.)

So I've observed.

(Thinking with angry anguish.)

He hurts, damn him! . . .

GORDON

No, you don't know! More'n ever now! More'n ever!

(The secret escaping him.)

I saw you kissing Mother! I saw Mother, too!

DARRELL

(Startled, but immediately forcing a smile.)

But I was saying good-bye. We're old friends. You know that.

GORDON

You can't fool me! This was different!

(Explosively.)

It would serve you good and right – and Mother, too – if I was to tell Dad on you!

DARRELL

Why, I'm Sam's oldest friend. Don't make a little fool of yourself!

GORDON

You are not his friend. You've always been hanging around cheating him – hanging around Mother!

DARRELL

Rubbish! What do you mean cheating him?

GORDON

I don't know. But I know you aren't his friend. And some time I'm going to tell him I saw you –

DARRELL

(*With great seriousness now – deeply moved.*)

Listen! There are things a man of honour doesn't tell anyone – not even his mother or father. You want to be a man of honour, don't you?

(*Intensely.*)

There are things we don't tell, you and I!

(*He has put his hand around Gordon's shoulder impulsively.*)

This is my son! . . . I love him! . . .

GORDON

(*Thinking – terribly torn.*)

Why do I like him now? . . . I like him awful! . . .

(*Crying.*)

We? – who d'you mean? – I've got honour! – more'n you! – you don't have to tell me! – I wasn't going to tell Dad, anyway, honest I wasn't! We? – what d'you mean, we? – I'm not like you! I don't want to be ever like you!

(*There is the sound of a door being flung open and shut and Evans' hearty voice.*)

EVANS

(*From the entrance hall.*)

Hallo, everybody!

DARRELL

(*Slapping Gordon on the back.*)

Buck up, son! Here he is! Hide that boat or he'll ask questions.

(*Gordon runs and hides the boat under the sofa. When Evans enters, Gordon is entirely composed and runs to him joyfully. Evans has grown stouter, his face is heavy now, he has grown executive and used to command, he automatically takes charge wherever he is. He does not look his age except that his hair has grown scanty and there is a perceptible bald spot on top. He is expensively tailored.*)

EVANS

(*Hugging Gordon to him – lovingly.*)

How's the old son? How's the birthday coming along?

GORDON

Fine, Dad!

EVANS

Hallo, Ned! Isn't this kid of mine a whopper for his age, though?

DARRELL

(*Smiling strainedly.*)

Yes.

(*Writhing – thinking.*)

It hurts now! . . . to see my son his son! . . . I've had enough! . . . get out! . . . any excuse! . . . I can 'phone afterwards! . . . I'll yell out the whole business if I stay! . . .

I was just going, Sam. I've got to step around and see a fellow who lives near – biologist.

(*He has gone to the door.*)

EVANS

(*Disappointedly.*)

Then you won't be here for lunch?

DARRELL

(*Thinking.*)

I'll yell the truth into your ears if I stay a second longer . . . you damned lunatic! . . .

Can't stay. Sorry. This is important. I'm sailing in a few days – lots to do – see you later, Sam. So long – Gordon.

(*He goes out with awkward haste.*)

GORDON

Good-bye – Uncle Ned.

(*Thinking confusedly.*)

Why did I call him that when I said I never would? . . . I know . . . must be because he said he's sailing and I'm glad . . .

EVANS

So long, Ned.

(*Thinking – good-naturedly superior.*)

Ned and his biology! . . . He takes his hobby pretty seriously! . . .

(*With satisfaction.*)

Well, he can afford to have hobbies now! . . . his investment with me has made him a pile. . . .

Where's Mother, son?

GORDON

Out in the kitchen with Uncle Charlie.

(*Thinking.*)

I hope he never comes back! . . . why did I like him then? . . . it was only for a second . . . I didn't really . . . I never could! . . . why does he always call me Gordon as if he hated to? . . .

EVANS

(*Sitting down at left.*)

I hope lunch is ready soon. I'm hungry as the devil, aren't you?

GORDON

(*Absent-mindedly.*)

Yes, Dad.

EVANS

Come over here and tell me about your birthday.

(Gordon comes over. Evans pulls him up on his lap.)

How'd you like your presents? What'd you get from Uncle Ned?

GORDON

(Evasively.)

They were all dandy.

(Suddenly.)

Why was I named Gordon?

EVANS

Oh, you know all about that – all about Gordon Shaw. I've told you time and again.

GORDON

You told me once he was Mother's beau – when she was a girl.

EVANS

(Teasingly.)

What do you know about beaux? You're growing up!

GORDON

Did Mother love him a lot?

EVANS

(Embarrassedly.)

I guess so.

GORDON

(Thinking keenly.)

That's why Darrell hates me being called Gordon . . . he knows Mother loved Gordon better'n she does him . . . now I know how to get back at him . . . I'll be just like Gordon was and Mother'll love me better'n him! . . .

And then that Gordon was killed, wasn't he? Am I anything like him?

EVANS

I hope you are. If when you go to college you can play football or row like Gordon did, I'll – I'll give you anything you ask for! I mean that!

GORDON

(Dreamily.)

Tell me about him again, will you, Dad – about the time he was stroking the crew and the fellow who was Number Seven began to crack, and he couldn't see him but he felt him cracking somehow, and he began talking back to him all the time and sort of gave him his strength so that when the race was over and they'd won Gordon fainted and the other fellow didn't.

EVANS

(With a fond laugh.)

Why, you know it all by heart! What's the use of my telling you?

NINA

(Comes in from the rear while they are talking. She comes forward slowly.)

(Thinking resentfully.)

Does he love Sam more than he does me? . . . oh, no, he can't! . . . but he trusts him more! . . . he confides in him more! . . .

GORDON

Did you ever used to fight fellows, Dad?

EVANS

(Embarrassedly.)

Oh, a little – when I had to.

GORDON

Could you lick Darrell?

NINA

(Thinking frightenedly.)

Why does he ask that? . . .

EVANS

(Surprised.)

Your Uncle Ned? What for? We've always been friends.

GORDON

I mean, if you weren't friends, could you?

EVANS

(Boastfully.)

Oh, yes, I guess so. Ned was never as strong as I was.

NINA

(Thinking contemptuously.)

Ned is weak. . . .

(Then apprehensively.)

But you're getting too strong, Sam. . . .

GORDON

But Gordon could have licked you, couldn't he?

EVANS

You bet he could!

GORDON

(*Thinking.*)

She must have loved Gordon better'n Dad even! . . .

NINA

(*She comes forward to the chair at centre, forcing a smile.*)

What's all this talk about fighting? That's not nice. For heaven's sake, Sam, don't encourage him –

EVANS

(*Grinning.*)

Never mind the women, Gordon. You've got to know how to fight to get on in this world.

NINA

(*Thinking pityingly.*)

You poor booby! . . . how brave you are now! . . .

(*Softly.*)

Perhaps you're right, dear.

(*Looking around.*)

Has Ned gone?

GORDON

(*Defiantly.*)

Yes – and he's not coming back – and he's sailing soon!

NINA

(*With a shudder.*)

Why does he challenge me that way? . . . and cling to Sam? . . . he must have seen Ned and me . . . he doesn't offer to come to my lap . . . he used to . . . Ned was right . . . I've got to lie to him . . . get him back . . . here . . . on my lap! . . .

(*With a sneer – to Evans.*)

I'm glad Ned's gone. I was afraid he was going to be on our hands all day.

GORDON

(*Eagerly, half getting down from his father's lap.*)

You're glad – ?

(*Then cautiously thinking.*)

She's cheating . . . I saw her kiss him. . . .

NINA

Ned's getting to be an awful bore. He's so weak. He can't get started on anything unless he's pushed.

GORDON

(*Moving a little nearer – searching her face – thinking.*)

She doesn't seem to like him so much . . . but I saw her kiss him! . . .

EVANS

(*Surprised.*)

Oh, come now, Nina, aren't you being a little hard on Ned? It's true he's sort of lost his grip in a way, but he's our best friend.

GORDON

(*Moving away from his father again – resentfully – thinking.*)

What's Dad standing up for him to her for? . . .

NINA

(*Thinking triumphantly.*)

That's right, Sam . . . just what I wanted you to say! . . .

(*Boredly.*)

Oh, I know he is, but he gets on my nerves hanging around all the time. Without being too rude, I urged him to get back to his work, and made him promise me he wouldn't return for two years. Finally he promised – and then he became silly and sentimental and asked me to kiss him good-bye for good luck! So I kissed him to get rid of him! The silly fool!

GORDON

(*Thinking – overjoyed.*)

Then! . . . that's why! . . . that's why! . . . and he'll be gone two years! . . . oh, I'm so glad! . . .

(*He goes to her and looks up into her face with shining eyes.*)

Mother!

NINA

Dear!

(*She takes him up on her lap and hugs him in her arms.*)

GORDON

(*Kisses her.*)

There!

(*Triumphantly thinking.*)

That makes up for his kiss! . . . That takes it off her mouth. . . .

EVANS

(*Grinning.*)

Ned must be falling for you – in his old age!

(*Then sentimentally.*)

Poor guy! He's never married, that's the trouble. He's lonely. I know how he feels. A fellow needs a little feminine encouragement to help him keep his head up.

NINA

(*Snuggling Gordon's head against hers – laughing teasingly.*)

I think your hard-headed Dad is getting mushy and silly! What do you think, Gordon?

GORDON

(Laughing with her.)

Yes, he's mushy, Mother! He's silly!

(He kisses her and whispers.)

I'm going to be like Gordon Shaw, Mother!

(She hugs him fiercely to her, triumphantly happy.)

EVANS

(Grinning.)

You two are getting too hard-boiled for me.

(He laughs. They all laugh happily together.)

NINA

(Suddenly overcome by a wave of conscience-stricken remorse and pity.)

Oh, I am hard on Ned! . . . poor dear generous Ned! . . . you told me to lie to your son against you . . . for my sake . . . I'm not worthy of your love! . . . I'm low and selfish! . . . but I do love you! . . . this is the son of our love in my arms! . . . oh, Mother God, grant my prayer that some day we may tell our son the truth and he may love his father! . . .

GORDON

(Sensing her thoughts, sits up in her lap and stares into her face, while she guiltily avoids his eyes – in fear and resentment.)

(Thinking.)

She's thinking about that Darrell now! . . . I know! . . . she likes him, too! . . . she can't fool me! . . . I saw her kissing! . . . she didn't think he was a silly fool then! . . . she was lying to Dad and me! . . .

(He pushes off her lap and backs away from her.)

NINA

(Thinking frightenedly.)

He read my thoughts! . . . I mustn't even think of Ned when he's around! . . . poor Ned! . . . no, don't think of him! . . .

(Leaning forward toward Gordon with her arms stretched out entreatingly but adopting a playful tone.)

Why, Gordon, what's come over you? You jumped off my lap as though you'd sat on a tack!

(She forces a laugh.)

GORDON

(His eyes on the floor – evasively.)

I'm hungry. I want to see if lunch is nearly ready.

(He turns abruptly and runs out.)

EVANS

(In a tone of superior manly understanding, kindly but laying down the law to womanly weakness.)

He's sick of being babied, Nina. You forget he's getting to be a big boy. And we want him to grow up a real he-man and not an old lady like Charlie.

(Sagaciously.)

That's what's made Charlie like he is, I'll bet. His mother never stopped babying him.

NINA

(Submissively – but with a look of bitter scorn at him.)

Perhaps you're right, Sam.

EVANS

(Confidently.)

I know I am!

NINA

(Thinking with a look of intense hatred.)

Oh, Mother God, grant that I may some day tell this fool the truth! . . .

Curtain

ACT EIGHT

SCENE: *Late afternoon in late June, ten years later – the afterdeck of the Evans' motor-cruiser anchored in the lane of yachts near the finish line at Poughkeepsie. The bow and amidship of the cruiser are off right, pointed upstream. The portside rail is in the rear, the curve of the stern at left, the rear of the cabin with broad windows and a door is at right. Two wicker chairs are at left and a* chaise longue *at right. A wicker table with another chair is at centre. The afterdeck is in cool shade, contrasted with the soft golden haze of late afternoon sunlight that glows on the river.*

Nina is sitting by the table at centre, Darrell in the chair farthest left, Marsden in the chaise longue *at right. Evans is leaning over the rail just behind Nina, looking up the river through a pair of binoculars. Madeline Arnold is standing by his side.*

Nina's hair has turned completely white. She is desperately trying to conceal the obvious inroads of time by an over-emphasis on make-up that defeats its end by drawing attention to what it would conceal. Her face is thin, her cheeks taut, her mouth drawn with forced smiling. There is little left of her face's charm except her eyes, which now seem larger and more deeply mysterious than ever. But she has kept her beautiful figure. It has the tragic effect of making her face seem older and more worn-out by contrast. Her general manner recalls instantly the Nina of Act Four, neurotic, passionately embittered and torn. She is dressed in a white yachting costume.

Darrell seems to have "thrown back" to the young doctor we had seen at the house of Nina's father in Act Two. He has again the air of the cool, detached scientist regarding himself and the people around him as interesting phenomena. In appearance, he is once more sharply defined, his face and body have grown lean and well-conditioned, the puffiness and jowls of the previous Act are gone. His skin is tanned almost black by his years in the tropics. His thick hair is iron-grey. He wears flannel pants, a blue coat, white buckskin shoes. He looks his fifty-one years, perhaps, but not a day more. Marsden has aged greatly. The stoop of his tall figure is accentuated, his hair has grown whitish. He is an older image of the Marsden of Act Five, who was so prostrated by his mother's death. Now it is his sister's death two months before that has plunged him into despair. His present grief, however, is more resigned to its fate than the old. He is dressed immaculately in black, as in Act Five.

Evans is simply Evans, his type logically developed by ten years of continued success and accumulating wealth, jovial and simple and good-natured as ever, but increasingly stubborn and self-opinionated. He has grown very stout. His jowly broad face has a heavy, flushed, apoplectic look. His head has grown quite bald on top. He is wearing a yachting cap, blue yachting coat, white flannel pants, buckskin shoes.

Madeline Arnold is a pretty girl of nineteen, with dark hair and eyes. Her skin is deeply tanned, her figure tall and athletic, reminding us of Nina's when we first saw her. Her personality is direct and frank. She gives the impression of a person who always knows exactly what she is after and generally gets it, but is also generous and a good loser, a good sport who is popular with her own sex as well as sought after by men. She is dressed in a bright-coloured sports costume.

EVANS

(*Nervous and excited – on pins and needles – lowering his binoculars impatiently.*)

Can't see anything up there! There's a damned haze on the river!

(*Handing the binoculars to Madeline.*)

Here, Madeline. You've got young eyes.

MADELINE

(*Eagerly.*)

Thank you.

(*She looks up the river through the glasses.*)

NINA

(*Thinking – bitterly.*)

Young eyes! . . . they look into Gordon's eyes! . . . he sees love in her young eyes! . . . mine are old now! . . .

EVANS

(*Pulling out his watch.*)

Soon be time for the start.

(*Comes forward – exasperatedly.*)

Of course, the damned radio has to pick out this time to go dead! Brand new one I had installed especially for this race, too! Just my luck!

(*Coming to Nina and putting his hand on her shoulder.*)

Gosh, I'll bet Gordon's some keyed-up right at this moment, Nina!

MADELINE

(*Without lowering the glasses.*)

Poor kid! I'll bet he is!

NINA

(*Thinking with intense bitterness.*)

That tone in her voice! . . . her love already possesses him! . . . my son! . . .

(*Vindictively.*)

But she won't! . . . as long as I live! . . .

(*Flatly.*)

Yes, he must be nervous.

EVANS

(*Taking his hand away, sharply.*)

I didn't mean nervous. He doesn't know what it is to have nerves. Nothing's ever got him rattled yet.

(*This last with a resentful look down at her as he moves back to the rail.*)

MADELINE

(*With the calm confidence of one who knows.*)

Yes, you can bank on Gordon never losing his nerve.

NINA

(*Coldly.*)

I'm quite aware my son isn't a weakling –

(*Meaningly, with a glance at Madeline.*)

even though he does do weak things sometimes.

MADELINE

(*Without lowering the glasses from her eyes – thinking good-naturedly.*)

Ouch! . . . that was meant for me! . . .

(*Then hurt.*)

Why does she dislike me so? . . . I've done my best, for Gordon's sake, to be nice to her. . . .

EVANS

(*Looking back at Nina resentfully – thinking.*)

Another nasty crack at Madeline! . . . Nina's certainly

become the prize bum sport! . . . I thought once her change of life was over she'd be ashamed of her crazy jealousy . . . instead of that it's got worse . . . but I'm not going to let her come between Gordon and Madeline . . . he loves her and she loves him . . . and her folks have got money and position, too . . . and I like her a lot . . . and, by God, I'm going to see to it their marriage goes through on schedule, no matter how much Nina kicks up! . . .

DARRELL

(*Keenly observant – thinking.*)

Nina hates this young lady . . . of course! . . . Gordon's girl . . . she'll smash their engagement if she can . . . as she did mine once . . . once! . . . thank God my slavery is over! . . . how did she know I was back in town? . . . I wasn't going to see her again . . . but her invitation was so imploring . . . my duty to Gordon, she wrote . . . what duty? . . . pretty late in the day! . . . that's better left dead, too! . . .

EVANS

(*Looking at his watch again.*)

They ought to be lined up at the start any minute now.

(*Pounding his fist on the rail – letting his pent-up feelings explode.*)

Come on, Gordon!

NINA

(*Startled – with nervous irritation.*)

Sam! I told you I have a splitting headache!

(*Thinking intensely.*)

You vulgar boor! . . . Gordon's engagement to her is all your fault! . . .

EVANS

(*Resentfully.*)

I'm sorry. Why don't you take some aspirin?

(*Thinking irritably.*)

Nina in the dumps! . . . Charlie in mourning! . . . what a pair of killjoys! . . . I wanted to bring Gordon and his friends on board to celebrate . . . no chance! . . . have to take Madeline . . . stage a party in New York . . . leave this outfit flat . . . Nina'll be sore as the devil, but she'll have to like it . . .

DARRELL

(*Examining Nina critically – thinking.*)

She's got into a fine neurotic state . . . reminds me of when I first knew her . . .

(*Then exultantly.*)

Thank God, I can watch her objectively again . . . these last three years away have finally done it . . . complete cure! . . .

(*Then remorsefully.*)

Poor Nina! . . . we're all deserting her . . .

(*Then glancing at Marsden – with a trace of a sneer.*)

Even Marsden seems to have left her for the dead! . . .

MARSDEN

(*Vaguely irritated – thinking.*)

What am I doing here? . . . what do I care about this stupid race? . . . why did I let Nina bully me into coming? . . . I ought to be alone . . . with my memories of dear Jane . . . it will be two months on Saturday since she died . . .

(*His lips tremble, tears come to his eyes.*)

MADELINE

(*With an impatient sigh, lowering the glasses.*)

It's no use, Mr. Evans, I can't see a thing.

EVANS

(*With angry disgust.*)

If only that damned radio was working!

NINA

(*Exasperatedly.*)

For heaven's sake, stop swearing so much!

EVANS

(*Hurt – indignantly.*)

What about it if I am excited? Seems to me you could show a little more interest without it hurting you, when it's Gordon's last race, his last appearance on a 'varsity!

(*He turns away from her.*)

MADELINE

(*Thinking.*)

He's right . . . she's acting rotten . . . if I were Gordon's mother, I certainly wouldn't . . .

EVANS

(*Turning back to Nina – resentfully.*)

You used to cheer loud enough for Gordon Shaw! And our Gordon's got him beat a mile, as an oarsman, at least!

(*Turning to Darrell.*)

And that isn't father stuff either, Ned! All the experts say so!

DARRELL

(*Cynically.*)

Oh, come on, Sam! Surely no one could ever touch Shaw in anything!

(*He glances at Nina with a sneer.*)

(*Immediately angry at himself.*)

What an idiot! . . . that popped out of me! . . . old habit! . . . For years I haven't loved her! . . .

NINA

(*Thinking indifferently.*)

Ned still feels jealous . . . that no longer pleases me . . .

I don't feel anything . . . except that I must get him to help me.

(She turns to Darrell bitterly.)

Sam said "our" Gordon. He means his. Gordon's become so like Sam, Ned, you won't recognize him!

MADELINE

(Thinking indignantly.)

She's crazy! . . . he's nothing like his father! . . . he's so strong and handsome! . . .

EVANS

(Good-naturedly, with a trace of pride.)

You flatter me, Nina. I wish I thought that. But he isn't a bit like me, luckily for him. He's the living image of Gordon Shaw at his best.

MADELINE

(Thinking.)

Shaw . . . I've seen his picture in the gym . . . my Gordon is better looking . . . he once told me Shaw was an old beau of his mother's . . . they say she was beautiful once . . .

NINA

(Shaking her head – scornfully.)

Don't be modest, Sam. Gordon *is* you. He may be a fine athlete like Gordon Shaw, because you've held that out to him as your ideal, but there the resemblance ceases. He isn't really like him at all, not the slightest bit!

EVANS

(Restraining his anger with difficulty – thinking.)

I'm getting sick of this! . . . she's carrying her jealousy too far! . . .

(Suddenly exploding, pounds his fist on the rail.)

Damn it, Nina, if you had any feeling you couldn't – right at the moment when he's probably getting into the shell –

(He stops, trying to control himself, panting, his face red.)

NINA

(Staring at him with repulsion – with cool disdain.)

I didn't say anything so dire, did I – merely that Gordon resembles you in character.

(With malice.)

Don't get so excited. It's bad for your high blood pressure. Ask Ned if it isn't.

(Intensely – thinking.)

If he'd only die! . . .

(Thinking – immediately.)

Oh, I don't mean that . . . I mustn't . . .

DARRELL

(Thinking keenly.)

There's a death wish . . . things have gone pretty far . . . Sam does look as if he might have a bad pressure . . . what hope that would have given me at one time! . . . no more, thank God! . . .

(In a joking tone.)

Oh, I guess Sam's all right, Nina.

EVANS

(Gruffly.)

I never felt better.

(He jerks out his watch again.)

Time for the start. Come on in the cabin, Ned, and have a drink. We'll see if McCabe's getting the damned radio fixed.

(Passing by Marsden he claps him on the shoulder exasperatedly.)

Come on, Charlie! Snap out of it!

MARSDEN

(Startled out of his trance – bewilderedly.)

Eh? – what is it? – are they coming?

EVANS

(Recovering his good nature – with a grin, taking his arm.)

You're coming to have a drink. You need about ten, I think, to get you in the right spirit to see the finish!

(To Darrell, who has got up but is still standing by his chair.)

Come on, Ned.

NINA

(Quickly.)

No, leave Ned with me. I want to talk to him. Take Madeline – and Charlie.

MARSDEN

(Looking at her appealingly.)

But I'm perfectly contented sitting –

(Then after a look in her eyes – thinking.)

She wants to be alone with Darrell . . . all right . . . doesn't matter now . . . their love is dead . . . but there's still some secret between them she's never told me . . . never mind . . . she'll tell me some time . . . I'm all she will have left . . . soon. . . .

(Then stricken with guilt.)

Poor dear Jane! . . . how can I think of anyone but you! . . . God, I'm contemptible! . . . I'll get drunk with that fool! . . . that's all I'm good for! . . .

MADELINE

(Thinking resentfully.)

She takes a fine do-this-little-girl tone toward me! . . . I'll give in to her now . . . but once I'm married! . . .

EVANS

Come on then, Madeline. We'll give you a small one.

(Impatiently.)

Charlie! Head up!

MARSDEN

(With hectic joviality.)

I hope it's strong poison!

EVANS

(Laughing.)

That's the spirit! We'll make a sport out of you yet!

MADELINE

(Laughing, goes and takes Marsden's arm.)

I'll see you get home safe, Mr. Marsden!

(They go into the cabin, Evans following them. Nina and Darrell turn and look at each other wonderingly, inquisitively, for a long moment. Darrell remains standing and seems to be a little uneasy.)

DARRELL

(Thinking with melancholy interest.)

And now? . . . what? . . . I can look into her eyes . . . strange eyes that will never grow old . . . without desire or jealousy or bitterness . . . was she ever my mistress? . . . can she be the mother of my child? . . . is there such a person as my son? . . . I can't think of these things as real any more . . . they must have happened in another life. . . .

NINA

(Thinking sadly.)

My old lover . . . how well and young he looks! . . . now we no longer love each other at all . . . our account with God the Father is settled . . . afternoons of happiness paid for with years of pain . . . love, passion, ecstasy . . . in what a far-off life were they alive! . . . the only living life is in the past and future . . . the present is an interlude . . . strange interlude in which we call on past and future to bear witness we are living! . . .

(With a sad smile.)

Sit down, Ned. When I heard you were back I wrote you because I need a friend. It has been so long since we loved each other we can now be friends again. Don't you feel that?

DARRELL

(Gratefully.)

Yes. I do.

(He sits down in one of the chairs at left, drawing it up closer to her.)

(Thinking cautiously.)

I want to be her friend . . . but I will never . . .

NINA

(Thinking cautiously.)

I must keep very cool and sensible or he won't help me. . . .

(With a friendly smile.)

I haven't seen you look so young and handsome since I first knew you. Tell me your secret.

(Bitterly.)

I need it! I'm old! Look at me! And I was actually looking forward to being old! I thought it would mean peace. I've been sadly disillusioned!

(Then forcing a smile.)

So tell me what fountain of youth you've found.

DARRELL

(Proudly.)

That's easy. Work! I've become as interested in biology as I once was in medicine. And not selfishly interested, that's the difference. There's no chance of my becoming a famous biologist and I know it. I'm very much a worker in the ranks. But our Station is a "huge success," as Sam would say. We've made some damned important discoveries. I say "we." I really mean Preston. You may remember I used to write you about him with enthusiasm. He's justified it. He *is* making his name world-famous. He's what I might have been – I did have the brains, Nina! – if I'd had more guts and less vanity, if I'd hewn to the line!

(Then forcing a smile.)

But I'm not lamenting. I've found myself in helping him. In that way I feel I've paid my debt – that his work is partly my work. And he acknowledges it. He possesses the rare virtue of gratitude.

(With proud affection.)

He's a fine boy, Nina! I suppose I should say man now he's in his thirties.

NINA

(Thinking with bitter sorrow.)

So, Ned . . . you remember our love . . . with bitterness! . . . as a stupid mistake! . . . the proof of a gutless vanity that ruined your career! . . . oh! . . .

(Then controlling herself – thinking cynically.)

Well, after all, how do I remember our love? . . . with no emotion at all, not even bitterness! . . .

(Then with sudden alarm.)

He's forgotten Gordon for this Preston! . . .

(Thinking desperately.)

I must make him remember Gordon is his child or I can never persuade him to help me! . . .

(Reproachfully.)

So you have found a son while I was losing mine – who is yours, too!

DARRELL

(Struck by this – impersonally interested.)

That's never occurred to me, but now I think of it –

(*Smiling.*)

Yes, perhaps unconsciously Preston is a compensating substitute. Well, it's done both of us good and hasn't harmed anyone.

NINA

(*With bitter emphasis.*)

Except your real son – and me – but we don't count, I suppose!

DARRELL

(*Coolly.*)

Harmed Gordon? How? He's all right, isn't he?

(*With a sneer.*)

I should say from all I've been hearing that he was your ideal of college hero – like his never-to-be-forgotten namesake!

NINA

(*Thinking resentfully.*)

He's sneering at his own son! . . .

(*Then trying to be calculating.*)

But I mustn't get angry . . . I must make him help me. . . .

(*Speaking with gentle reproach.*)

And am I the ideal of a happy mother, Ned?

DARRELL

(*Immediately moved by pity and ashamed of himself.*)

Forgive me, Nina. I haven't quite buried all my bitterness, I'm afraid.

(*Gently.*)

I'm sorry you're unhappy, Nina.

NINA

(*Thinking with satisfaction.*)

He means that . . . he still does care a little . . . if only it's enough to . . .

(*Speaking sadly.*)

I've lost my son, Ned! Sam has made him all his. And it was done so gradually that, although I realized what was happening, there was never any way I could interfere. What Sam advised seemed always the best thing for Gordon's future. And it was always what Gordon himself wanted, to escape from me to boarding school and then to college, to become Sam's athletic hero –

DARRELL

(*Impatiently.*)

Oh, come now, Nina, you know you've always longed for him to be like Gordon Shaw!

NINA

(*Bursting out in spite of herself – violently.*)

He's not like Gordon! He's forgotten me for that – !

(*Trying to be more reasonable.*)

What do I care whether he's an athlete or not? It's such nonsense, all this fuss! I'm not the slightest bit interested in this race to-day, for example! I wouldn't care if he came in last!

(*Stopping herself – thinking frightenedly.*)

Oh, if he should ever guess I said that! . . .

DARRELL

(*Thinking keenly.*)

Hallo! . . . she said that as if she'd like to see him come last! . . why? . . .

(*Then vindictively.*)

Well, so would I! . . . it's time these Gordons took a good licking from life! . . .

MADELINE

(*Suddenly appears in the doorway of the cabin, her face flushed with excitement.*)

They're off! Mr. Evans is getting something – it's terribly faint, but – Navy and Washington are leading – Gordon's third!

(*She disappears again in the cabin.*)

NINA

(*Looking after her with hatred.*)

Her Gordon! . . . she is so sure! . . . how I've come to detest her pretty face! . . .

DARRELL

(*Thinking with a sneer.*)

"Gordon's third"! . . . you might think there was no one else pulling the shell! . . . what idiots women make of themselves about these Gordons! . . . she's pretty, that Madeline! . . . she's got a figure like Nina's when I first loved her . . . those afternoons . . . age is beginning to tell on Nina's face . . . but she's kept her wonderful body! . . .

(*With a trace of malice – dryly.*)

There's a young lady who seems to care a lot whether Gordon comes in last or not!

NINA

(*Trying to be sorrowful and appealing.*)

Yes. Gordon is hers now, Ned.

(*But she cannot bear this thought – vindictively.*)

That is, they're engaged. But, of course, that doesn't necessarily mean – Can you imagine him throwing himself away on a little fool like that? I simply can't believe he really loves her! Why, she's hardly even pretty and she's deadly stupid. I thought he was only flirting with her – or merely indulging in a passing physical affair.

(*She winces.*)

At his age, one has to expect – even a mother must face

nature. But for Gordon to take her seriously, and propose marriage – it's too idiotic for words!

DARRELL

(*Thinking cynically.*)

Oh, so you'll compromise on his sleeping with her . . . if you have to . . . but she must have no real claim to dispute your ownership, eh? . . . you'd like to make her the same sort of convenient slave for him that I was for you! . . .

(*Resentfully.*)

I can't agree with you. I find her quite charming. It seems to me if I were in Gordon's shoes I'd do exactly what he has done.

(*In confusion – thinking bitterly.*)

In Gordon's shoes! . . . I always was in Gordon Shaw's shoes! . . . and why am I taking this young Gordon's part? . . . what is he to me, for God's sake? . . .

NINA

(*Unheedingly.*)

If he marries her, it means he'll forget me! He'll forget me as completely as Sam forgot his mother! She'll keep him away from me! Oh, I know what wives can do! She'll use her body until she persuades him to forget me! My son, Ned! And your son, too!

(*She suddenly gets up and goes to him and takes one of his hands in both of hers.*)

The son of our old love, Ned!

DARRELL

(*Thinking with a strange shudder of mingled attraction and fear as she touches him.*)

Our love . . . old love . . . old touch of her flesh . . . we're old . . . it's silly and indecent . . . does she think she still can own me? . . .

NINA

(*In the tone a mother takes in speaking to her husband about their boy.*)

You'll have to give Gordon a good talking to, Ned.

DARRELL

(*Still more disturbed – thinking.*)

Old . . . but she's kept her wonderful body . . . how many years since? . . . she has the same strange influence over me . . . touch of her flesh . . . it's dangerous . . . bosh, I'm only humouring her as a friend . . . as her doctor . . . and why shouldn't I have a talk with Gordon? . . . a father owes something to his son . . . he ought to advise him. . . .

(*Then alarmed.*)

But I was never going to meddle again . . .

(*Sternly.*)

I swore I'd never again meddle with human lives, Nina!

NINA

(*Unheedingly.*)

You must keep him from ruining his life.

DARRELL

(*Doggedly – struggling with himself.*)

I won't touch a life that has more than one cell!

(*Harshly.*)

And I wouldn't help you in this, anyway! You've got to give up owning people, meddling in their lives as if you were God and had created them!

NINA

(*Strangely forlorn.*)

I don't know what you mean, Ned. Gordon is my son, isn't he?

DARRELL

(*With a sudden strange violence.*)

And mine! Mine, too!

(*He stops himself.*)

(*Thinking.*)

Shut up, you fool! . . . is that the way to humour her? . . .

NINA

(*With strange quiet.*)

I think I still love you a little, Ned.

DARRELL

(*In her tone.*)

And I still love you a little, Nina.

(*Then sternly.*)

But I will not meddle in your life again!

(*With a harsh laugh.*)

And you've meddled enough with human love, old lady! Your time for that is over! I'll send you a couple of million cells you can torture without harming yourself!

(*Regaining control – shamefacedly.*)

Nina! Please forgive me!

NINA

(*Starts as if out of a dream – anxiously.*)

What were you saying, Ned?

(*She lets go of his hand and goes back to her chair.*)

DARRELL

(*Dully.*)

Nothing.

NINA

(*Strangely.*)

We were talking about Sam, weren't we? How do you think he looks?

DARRELL

(*Confusedly casual.*)

Fine. A bit too fat, of course. He looks as though his blood pressure might be higher than it ought to be. But that's not unusual in persons of his build and age. It's nothing to hope – I meant, to worry over!

(*Then violently.*)

God damn it, why did you make me say hope?

NINA

(*Calmly.*)

It may have been in your mind, too, mayn't it?

DARRELL

No! I've nothing against Sam. I've always been his best friend. He owes his happiness to me.

NINA

(*Strangely.*)

There are so many curious reasons we dare not think about for thinking things!

DARRELL

(*Rudely.*)

Thinking doesn't matter a damn! Life is something in one cell that doesn't need to think!

NINA

(*Strangely.*)

I know! God the Mother!

DARRELL

(*Excitedly.*)

And all the rest is gutless egotism! But to hell with it! What I started to say was, what possible reason could I have for hoping for Sam's death?

NINA

(*Strangely.*)

We're always desiring death for ourselves or others, aren't we – while we while away our lives with the old surface ritual of coveting our neighbour's ass?

DARRELL

(*Frightenedly.*)

You're talking like the old Nina now – when I first loved you. Please don't! It isn't decent – at our age!

(*Thinking in terror.*)

The old Nina! . . . am I the old Ned? . . . then that means? . . . but we must not meddle in each other's lives again! . . .

NINA

(*Strangely.*)

I am the old Nina! And this time I will not let my Gordon go from me for ever!

EVANS

(*Appears in the doorway of the cabin – excited and irritated.*)

Madeline's listening in now. It went dead on me.

(*Raising the binoculars as he goes to the rail, he looks up the river.*)

Last I got, Gordon third, Navy and Washington leading. They're the ones to fear, he said – Navy especially.

(*Putting down the glasses – with a groan.*)

Damned haze! My eyes are getting old.

(*Then suddenly with a grin.*)

You ought to see Charlie! He started throwing Scotch into him as if he were drinking against time. I had to take the bottle away from him. It's hit him an awful wallop.

(*Then looking from one to the other – resentfully.*)

What's the matter with you two? There's a race going on, don't you know it? And you sit like dead clams!

DARRELL

(*Placatingly.*)

I thought someone'd better stay out here and let you know when they get in sight.

EVANS

(*Relieved.*)

Oh, sure, that's right! Here, take the glasses. You always had good eyes.

(*Darrell gets up and takes the glasses and goes to the rail and begins adjusting them.*)

DARRELL

Which crew was it you said Gordon feared the most?

EVANS

(*Has gone back to the cabin doorway.*)

Navy.

(*Then proudly.*)

Oh, he'll beat them! But it'll be damn close. I'll see if

Madeline's getting –

(*He goes into the cabin.*)

DARRELL

(*Looking up the river – with vindictive bitterness – thinking.*)

Come on, Navy! . . .

NINA

(*Thinking bitterly.*)

Madeline's Gordon! . . . Sam's Gordon! . . . the thanks I get for saving Sam at the sacrifice of my own happiness! . . . I won't have it! . . . what do I care what happens to Sam now? . . . I hate him! . . . I'll tell him Gordon isn't his child! . . . and threaten to tell Gordon, too, unless! . . . he'll be in deadly fear of that! . . . he'll soon find some excuse to break their engagement! . . . he can! . . . he has the strangest influence over Gordon! . . . but Ned must back me up or Sam won't believe me! . . . Ned must tell him, too! . . . but will Ned? . . . he'll be afraid of the insanity! . . . I must make him believe Sam's in no danger . . .

(*Intensely.*)

Listen, Ned, I'm absolutely sure, from things she wrote me before she died, that Sam's mother must have been deliberately lying to me about the insanity that time. She was jealous because Sam loved me and she simply wanted to be revenged, I'm sure.

DARRELL

(*Without lowering glasses – dryly.*)

No. She told you the truth. I never mentioned it, but I went up there once and made a thorough investigation of his family.

NINA

(*With resentful disappointment.*)

Oh – I suppose you wanted to make sure so you could hope he'd go insane?

DARRELL

(*Simply.*)

I needed to be able to hope that, then. I loved you horribly at that time, Nina – horribly!

NINA

(*Putting her hands on his arm.*)

And you don't – any more, Ned?

(*Thinking intensely.*)

Oh, I must make him love me again . . . enough to make him tell Sam! . . .

DARRELL

(*Thinking strangely – struggling with himself.*)

She'd like to own me again . . . I wish she wouldn't touch me . . . what is this tie of old happiness between our flesh? . . .

(*Harshly – weakly struggling to shake off her hands, without lowering the glasses.*)

I won't meddle again with human lives, I told you!

NINA

(*Unheeding, clinging to him.*)

And I loved you horribly! I still do love you, Ned! I used to hope he'd go insane myself because I loved you so! But look at Sam! He's sane as a pig! There's absolutely no danger now!

DARRELL

(*Thinking – alarmed.*)

What is she after now . . . what does she want me for? . . .

(*Stiffly.*)

I'm no longer a doctor, but I should say he's a healthy miss of Nature's. It's a thousand to one against it at this late day.

NINA

(*With sudden fierce intensity.*)

Then it's time to tell him the truth, isn't it? We've suffered all our lives for his sake! We've made him rich and happy! It's time he gave us back our son!

DARRELL

(*Thinking.*)

Aha . . . so that's it! . . . tell Sam the truth? . . . at last! . . . by God, I'd like to tell him, at that! . . .

(*With a sneer.*)

Our son? You mean yours, my dear! Kindly count me out of any further meddling with –

NINA

(*Unruffledly – obsessed.*)

But Sam won't believe me if I'm the only one to tell him! He'll think I'm lying for spite, that it's only my crazy jealousy! He'll ask you! You've got to tell him too, Ned!

DARRELL

(*Thinking.*)

I'd like to see his face when I told him this famous oarsman isn't his son but mine! . . . that might pay me back a little for all he's taken from me! . . .

(*Harshly.*)

I've stopped meddling in Sam's life, I tell you!

NINA

(*Insistently.*)

Think of what Sam has made us go through, of how he's

made us suffer! You've got to tell him! You still love me a little, don't you, Ned? You must when you remember the happiness we've known in each other's arms! You were the only happiness I've ever known in life!

DARRELL

(*Struggling weakly – thinking.*)

She lies! . . . there was her old lover, Gordon! . . . he was always first! . . . then her son, Gordon! . . .

(*With desperate rancour – thinking.*)

Come on, Navy! . . . beat her Gordons for me! . . .

NINA

(*Intensely.*)

Oh, if I'd only gone away with you that time when you came back from Europe! How happy we would have been, dear! How our boy would have loved you – if it hadn't been for Sam!

DARRELL

(*Thinking – weakly.*)

Yes, if it hadn't been for Sam I would have been happy! . . . I would have been the world's greatest neurologist! . . . my boy would have loved me and I'd have loved him! . . .

NINA

(*With a crowning intensity to break down his last resistance.*)

You must tell him, Ned! For my sake! Because I love you! Because you remember our afternoons – our mad happiness! Because you love me!

DARRELL

(*Beaten – dazedly.*)

Yes – what must I do? – meddle again?

(*The noise of Madeline's excited voice cheering and clapping her hands, of Marsden's voice yelling drunkenly, of Evans', all shouting, "Gordon! Gordon! Come on, Gordon!" comes from the cabin. Marsden appears swaying in the cabin doorway yelling, "Gordon!" He is hectically tipsy. Darrell gives a violent shudder as if he were coming out of a nightmare and pushes Nina away from him.*)

DARRELL

(*Thinking – dazedly still, but in a tone of relief.*)

Marsden again! . . . thank God! . . . he's saved me! . . . from her! . . . and her Gordons! . . .

(*Turning on her triumphantly.*)

No, Nina – sorry – but I can't help you. I told you I'd never meddle again with human lives!

(*More and more confidently.*)

Besides, I'm quite sure Gordon isn't my son, if the real deep core of the truth were known! I was only a body to you. Your first Gordon used to come back to life. I was never more to you than a substitute for your dead lover! Gordon is really Gordon's son! So you see I'd be telling Sam a lie if I boasted that I – And I'm a man of honour! I've proved that, at least!

(*He raises his glasses and looks up the river.*)

(*Thinking exultantly.*)

I'm free! . . . I've beaten her at last! . . . now come on, Navy! . . . you've got to beat her Gordons for me! . . .

NINA

(*After staring at him for a moment – walking away from him – thinking with a dull fatalism.*)

I've lost him . . . he'll never tell Sam now . . . is what he said right? . . . is Gordon Gordon's? . . . oh, I hope so! . . . oh, dear, dead Gordon, help me to get back your son! . . . I must find some way. . . .

(*She sits down again.*)

MARSDEN

(*Who has been staring at them with a foolish grin.*)

Hallo, you two! Why do you look so guilty? You don't love each other any more! It's all nonsense! I don't feel the slightest twinge of jealousy. That's proof enough, isn't it?

(*Then blandly apologetic.*)

Pardon me if I sound a bit pipped – a good bit! Sam said ten and then took the bottle away when I'd had only five! But it's enough! I've forgotten sorrow! There's nothing in life worth grieving about, I assure you, Nina! And I've got interested in this race now.

(*He sings raucously.*)

"Oh, we'll row, row, row, right down the river! And we'll row, row, row –" Remember that old tune – when you were a little girl, Nina? Oh, I'm forgetting Sam said to tell you Gordon was on even terms with the leaders! A gallant spurt did it! Touch and go now! I don't care who wins – as long as it isn't Gordon! I don't like him since he's grown up! He thinks I'm an old woman!

(*Sings.*)

"Row, row, row." The field against Gordon!

DARRELL

(*Hectically.*)

Right!

(*He looks through the glasses – excitedly.*)

I see a flashing in the water way up there! Must be their oars! They're coming! I'll tell Sam!

(*He hurries into the cabin.*)

NINA

(*Thinking dully.*)

He'll tell Sam . . . no, he doesn't mean that . . . I must find some other way . . .

MARSDEN

(Walks a bit uncertainly to Nina's chair.)

Gordon really should get beaten to-day – for the good of his soul, Nina. That Madeline is pretty, isn't she? These Gordons are too infernally lucky – while we others –

(He almost starts to blubber – angrily.)

we others have got to beat him to-day!

(He slumps clumsily down to a sitting position on the deck by her chair and takes her hand and pats it.)

There, there, Nina Cara Nina! Don't worry your pretty head! It will all come out all right! We'll only have a little while longer to wait and then you and I'll be quietly married!

(Thinking frightenedly.)

The devil! . . . what am I saying? . . . I'm drunk! . . . all right, all the better! . . . I've wanted all my life to tell her! . . .

Of course, I realize you've got a husband at present, but never mind, I can wait. I've waited a lifetime already; but for a long while now I've had a keen psychic intuition that I wasn't born to die before –

(Evans and Madeline and Darrell come rushing out of the cabin. They all have binoculars. They run to the rail and train their glasses up the river.)

MADELINE

(Excitedly.)

I see them!

(Grabbing his arm and pointing.)

Look, Mr. Evans – there – don't you see?

EVANS

(Excitedly.)

No – not yet – Yes! Now I see them!

(Pounding on the rail.)

Come on, Gordon boy!

MADELINE

Come on, Gordon!

(The whistles and sirens from the yachts up the river begin to be heard. This grows momentarily louder as one after another other yachts join in the chorus as the crews approach nearer and nearer until toward the close of the scene there is a perfect pandemonium of sound.)

NINA

(With bitter hatred – thinking.)

How I hate her! . . .

(Then suddenly with a deadly calculation – thinking.)

Why not tell her? . . . as Sam's mother told me . . . of the insanity? . . . she thinks Gordon is Sam's son. . . .

(With a deadly smile of triumph.)

That will be poetic justice! . . . that will solve everything! . . . she won't marry him! . . . he will turn to me for comfort! . . . but I must plan it out carefully! . . .

MARSDEN

(Driven on – extravagantly.)

Listen, Nina! After we're married I'm going to write a novel – my first real novel! All the twenty odd books I've written have been long-winded fairy tales for grown-ups – about dear old ladies and witty, cynical bachelors and quaint characters with dialects, and married folk who always admire and respect each other, and lovers who avoid love in hushed whispers! That's what I've been, Nina – a hush-hush whisperer of lies! Now I'm going to give an honest healthy yell – turn on the sun into the shadows of lies – shout "This is life and this is sex, and here are passion and hatred and regret and joy and pain and ecstasy, and these are men and women and sons and daughters whose hearts are weak and strong, whose blood is blood and not a soothing syrup!" Oh, I can do it, Nina! I can write the truth! I've seen it in you, your father, my mother, sister, Gordon, Sam, Darrell, and myself. I'll write the book of us! But here I am talking while my last chapters are in the making – right here and now –

(Hurriedly.)

You'll excuse me, won't you, Nina? I must watch – my duty as an artist!

(He scrambles to his feet and peers about him with a hectic eagerness. Nina pays no attention to him.)

EVANS

(Exasperatedly, taking down his glasses.)

You can't tell a damn thing – which is which or who's ahead – I'm going to listen in again.

(He hurries into the cabin.)

NINA

(With a smile of cruel triumph – thinking.)

I can tell her . . . confidentially . . . I can pretend I'm forced to tell her . . . as Sam's mother did with me . . . because I feel it's due to her happiness and Gordon's . . . it will explain my objection to the engagement . . . oh, it can't help succeeding . . . my Gordon will come back! . . . I'll see he never gets away again! . . .

(She calls.)

Madeline!

MARSDEN

(Thinking.)

Why is she calling Madeline? . . . I must watch all this carefully! . . .

EVANS

(*Comes rushing out in wild alarm.*)

Bad news! Navy has drawn ahead – half a length – looks like Navy's race, he said –

(*Then violently.*)

But what does he know, that damn fool announcer – some poor boob – !

MADELINE

(*Excitedly.*)

He doesn't know Gordon! He's always best when he's pushed to the limit!

NINA

(*She calls more sharply.*)

Madeline!

DARRELL

(*Turns around to stare at her – thinking.*)

Why is she calling Madeline? . . . she's bound she'll meddle in their lives . . . I've got to watch her . . . well, let's see.

(*He touches Madeline on the shoulder.*)

Mrs. Evans is calling you, Miss Arnold.

MADELINE

(*Impatiently.*)

Yes, Mrs. Evans. But they're getting closer. Why don't you come and watch?

NINA

(*Not heeding – impressively.*)

There's something I must tell you.

MADELINE

(*In hopeless irritation.*)

But – Oh, all right!

(*She hurries over to her, glancing eagerly over her shoulder toward the river.*)

Yes, Mrs. Evans?

DARRELL

(*Moves from the rail toward them – thinking keenly.*)

I must watch this . . . she's in a desperate meddling mood! . . .

NINA

(*Impressively.*)

First, give me your word of honour that you'll never reveal a word of what I'm going to tell you to a living soul – above all not to Gordon!

MADELINE

(*Looking at her in amazement – soothingly.*)

Couldn't you tell me later, Mrs. Evans – after the race?

NINA

(*Sternly – grabbing her by the wrist.*)

No, now! Do you promise?

MADELINE

(*With helpless annoyance.*)

Yes, Mrs. Evans.

NINA

(*Sternly.*)

For the sake of your future happiness and my son's I've got to speak! Your engagement forces me to! You've probably wondered why I objected. It's because the marriage is impossible. You can't marry Gordon! I speak as your friend! You must break your engagement with him at once!

MADELINE

(*Cannot believe her ears – suddenly panic-stricken.*)

But why – why?

DARRELL

(*Who has come closer – resentfully thinking.*)

She wants to ruin my son's life as she ruined mine! . . .

NINA

(*Relentlessly.*)

Why? Because –

DARRELL

(*Steps up suddenly beside them – sharply and sternly commanding.*)

No, Nina!

(*He taps Madeline on the shoulder and draws her aside. Nina lets go of her wrist and stares after them in a sort of stunned stupor.*)

Miss Arnold, as a doctor I feel it my duty to tell you that Mrs. Evans isn't herself. Pay no attention to anything she may say to you. She's just passed through a critical period in a woman's life and she's morbidly jealous of you and subject to queer delusions!

(*He smiles kindly at her.*)

So get back to the race! And God bless you!

(*He grips her hand, strangely moved.*)

MADELINE

(*Gratefully.*)

Thank you. I understand, I think. Poor Mrs. Evans!

(*She hurries back to the rail, raising her glasses.*)

NINA

(*Springing to her feet and finding her voice – with despairing accusation.*)

Ned!

DARRELL

(*Steps quickly to her side.*)

I'm sorry, Nina, but I warned you not to meddle.

(*Then affectionately.*)

And Gordon is – well – sort of my stepson, isn't he? I really want him to be happy.

(*Then smiling good-naturedly.*)

All the same, I can't help hoping he'll be beaten in this race. As an oarsman he recalls his father, Gordon Shaw, to me.

(*He turns away and raises his glasses, going back to the rail. Nina slumps down in her chair again.*)

EVANS

Damn! They all look even from here! Can you tell which is which, Madeline?

MADELINE

No – not yet – oh, dear, this is awful! Gordon!

NINA

(*Looking about her in the air – with a dazed question.*)

Gordon?

MARSDEN

(*Thinking.*)

Damn that Darrell! . . . if he hadn't interfered Nina would have told . . . something of infinite importance, I know! . . .

(*He comes and again sits on the deck by her chair and takes her hand.*)

Because what, Nina – my dear little Nina Cara Nina – because what? Let me help you!

NINA

(*Staring before her as if she were in a trance – simply, like a young girl.*)

Yes, Charlie. Yes, Father. Because all of Sam's father's family have been insane. His mother told me so that I wouldn't have his baby. I was going to tell Madeline so that she wouldn't marry Gordon. But it would have been a lie because Gordon isn't really Sam's child at all, he's Ned's. Ned gave him to me and I gave him to Sam so Sam could have a healthy child and be well and happy. And Sam is well and happy, don't you think?

(*Childishly.*)

So I haven't been such an awfully wicked girl, have I, Father?

MARSDEN

(*Horrified and completely sobered by what he has heard – stares at her with stunned eyes.*)

Nina! Good God! Do you know what you're saying?

MADELINE

(*Excitedly.*)

There! The one on this side! I saw the colour on their blades just now!

EVANS

(*Anxiously.*)

Are you sure? Then he's a little behind the other two!

DARRELL

(*Excitedly.*)

The one in the middle seems to be ahead! Is that the Navy?

(*But the others pay no attention to him. All three are leaning over the rail, their glasses glued to their eyes, looking up the river. The noise from the whistle is now very loud. The cheering from the observation trains can be heard.*)

MARSDEN

(*Stares into her face with great pity now.*)

Merciful God, Nina! Then you've lived all these years – with this horror! And you and Darrell deliberately – ?

NINA

(*Without looking at him – to the air.*)

Sam's mother said I had a right to be happy, too.

MARSDEN

And you didn't love Darrell then – ?

NINA

(*As before.*)

I did afterwards. I don't now. Ned is dead, too.

(*Softly.*)

Only you are alive now, Father – and Gordon.

MARSDEN

(*Gets up and bends over her paternally, stroking her hair with a strange, wild, joyous pity.*)

Oh, Nina – poor little Nina – my Nina – how you must have suffered! I forgive you! I forgive you everything! I forgive even your trying to tell Madeline – you wanted to keep Gordon – oh, I understand that – and I forgive you!

NINA

(As before – affectionately and strangely.)

And I forgive you, Father. It was all your fault in the beginning, wasn't it? You mustn't ever meddle with human lives again!

EVANS

(Wildly excited.)

Gordon's sprinting, isn't he? He's drawing up on that middle one!

MADELINE

Yes! Oh, come on, Gordon!

DARRELL

(Exultantly.)

Come on, Navy!

EVANS

(Who is standing next to Ned, whirls on him in a furious passion.)

What's that? What the hell's the matter with you?

DARRELL

(Facing him – with a strange friendliness slaps him on the back.)

We've got to beat these Gordons, Sam! We've got to beat –

EVANS

(Raging.)

You – !

(He draws back his fist – then suddenly horrified at what he is doing, but still angry, grabs Darrell by both shoulders and shakes him.)

Wake up! What the hell's got into you? Have you gone crazy?

DARRELL

(Mockingly.)

Probably! It runs in my family! All of my father's people were happy lunatics – not healthy, country folk like yours, Sam! Ha!

EVANS

(Staring at him.)

Ned, old man, what's the trouble? You said "Navy."

DARRELL

(Ironically – with a bitter hopeless laugh.)

Slip of the tongue! I meant Gordon! Meant Gordon, of course! Gordon is always meant – meant to win! Come on, Gordon! It's fate!

MADELINE

Here they come! They're both spurting! I can see Gordon's back!

EVANS

(Forgetting everything else, turns back to the race.)

Come on, boy! Come on, son!

(The chorus of noise is now a bedlam as the crews near the finish line. The people have to yell and scream to make themselves heard.)

NINA

(Getting up – thinking with a strange, strident, wild passion.)

I hear the Father laughing! . . . O Mother God, protect my son! . . . let Gordon fly to you in heaven! . . . quick, Gordon! . . . love is the Father's lightning! . . . Madeline will bring you down in flames! . . . I hear His screaming laughter! . . . fly back to me! . . .

(She is looking desperately up into the sky as if some race of life and death were happening there for her.)

EVANS

(Holding on to a stanchion and leaning far out at the imminent risk of falling in.)

One spurt more will do it! Come on, boy, come on! It took death to beat Gordon Shaw! You can't be beaten either, Gordon! Lift her out of the water, son! Stroke! Stroke! He's gaining! Now! Over the line, boy! Over with her! Stroke! That's done it! He's won! He's won!

MADELINE

(Has been shrieking at the same time.)

Gordon! Gordon! He's won! Oh, he's fainted! Poor dear darling!

(She remains standing on the rail, looking out dangerously, holding on with one hand, looking down longingly toward his shell.)

EVANS

(Bounding back to the deck, his face congested and purple with a frenzy of joy, dancing about.)

He's won! By God, it was close! Greatest race in the history of rowing! He's the greatest oarsman God ever made!

(Embracing Nina and kissing her frantically.)

Aren't you happy, Nina? Our Gordon! The greatest ever!

NINA

(Torturedly – trying incoherently to force out a last despairing protest.)

No! – not yours! – mine! – and Gordon's! – Gordon is Gordon's! – he was my Gordon! – his Gordon is mine!

EVANS

(Soothingly, humouring her – kissing her again.)

Of course he's yours, dear – and a dead ringer for Gordon Shaw, too! Gordon's body! Gordon's spirit! Your body and spirit, too, Nina! He's not like me, lucky for him! I'm a poor boob! I never could row worth a damn!

(He suddenly staggers as if he were very drunk, leaning on Marsden – then gives a gasp and collapses inertly to the deck, lying on his back.)

MARSDEN

(Stares down at him stupidly – then thinking strangely.)

I knew it! . . . I saw the end beginning! . . .

(He touches Nina's arm – in a low voice.)

Nina – your husband!

(Touching Darrell who has stood staring straight before him, with a bitter ironical smile on his lips.)

Ned – your friend! Doctor Darrell – a patient!

NINA

(Stares down at Evans – slowly, as if trying to bring her mind back to him.)

My husband?

(Suddenly with a cry of pain, sinks on her knees beside the body.)

Sam!

DARRELL

(Looking down at him – thinking yearningly.)

Is her husband dead . . . at last? . . .

(Then with a shudder at his thoughts.)

No! . . . I don't hope! . . . I don't! . . .

(He cries:)

Sam!

(He kneels down, feels at his heart, pulse, looks into his face – with a change to a strictly professional manner.)

He's not dead. Only a bad stroke.

NINA

(With a cry of grief.)

Oh, Ned, did all our old secret hopes do this at last?

DARRELL

(Professionally, staring at her coldly.)

Bosh, Mrs. Evans! We're not in the Congo that we can believe in evil charms!

(Sternly.)

In his condition, Mr. Evans must have absolute quiet and peace of mind or – And perfect care! You must tend him night and day! And I will! We've got to keep him happy!

NINA

(Dully.)

Again?

(Then sternly in her turn, as if swearing a pledge to herself.)

I will never leave his side! I will never tell him anything that might disturb his peace!

MARSDEN

(Standing above them – thinking exultantly.)

I shall not have long to wait now! . . .

(Then ashamed.)

How can I think such things . . . poor Sam! . . . he was . . . I mean he is my friend . . .

(With assertive loyalty.)

A rare spirit! A pure and simple soul! A good man – yes, a good man! God bless him!

(He makes a motion over the body like a priest blessing.)

DARRELL

(His voice suddenly breaking with a sincere human grief.)

Sam, old boy! I'm so damned sorry! I would give my life to save you!

NINA

(In dull anguish.)

Save – again?

(Then lovingly, kissing Evans' face.)

Dear husband, you have tried to make me happy, I will give you my happiness again! I will give you Gordon to give to Madeline!

MADELINE

(Still standing on the rail, staring after Gordon's shell.)

Gordon! . . . dear lover . . . how tired . . . but you'll rest in my arms . . . your head will lie on my breast . . . soon! . . .

Curtain

ACT NINE

SCENE: *Several months later. A terrace on the Evans' estate on Long Island. In the rear, the terrace overlooks a small harbour with the ocean beyond. On the right is a side entrance of the pretentious villa. On the left is a hedge with an arched gateway leading to a garden. The terrace is paved with rough stone. There is a stone bench at centre, a* chaise longue *at right, a wicker table and arm-chair at left.*

It is late afternoon of a day in early fall. Gordon Evans is sitting on the stone bench, his chin propped on his hands, Madeline standing behind him, her arm about his shoulders. Gordon is over six feet tall with the figure of a trained athlete. His sun-bronzed face is extremely handsome after the fashion of the magazine-cover American-collegian. It is a strong face but of a strength wholly material in quality. He has been too thoroughly trained to progress along a certain groove to success ever to question it or be dissatisfied with its rewards. At the same time, although entirely an unimaginative code-bound gentleman of his groove, he is boyish and likable, of an even, modest, sporting disposition. His expression is boyishly forlorn, but he is making a manly effort to conceal his grief.

Madeline is much the same as in the previous Act except that there is now a distinct maternal older feeling in her attitude toward Gordon as she endeavours to console him.

MADELINE

(Tenderly, smoothing his hair.)

There, dear! I know how horribly hard it is for you. I loved him, too. He was so wonderful and sweet to me.

GORDON

(His voice trembling.)

I didn't really realize he was gone – until out at the cemetery –

(His voice breaks.)

MADELINE

(Kissing his hair.)

Darling! Please don't!

GORDON

(Rebelliously.)

Damn it, I don't see why he had to die!

(With a groan.)

It was that constant grind at the office! I ought to have insisted on his taking better care of himself. But I wasn't home enough, that's the trouble. I couldn't watch him.

(Then bitterly.)

But I can't see why Mother didn't!

MADELINE

(Reprovingly but showing she shares his feeling.)

Now! You mustn't start feeling bitter toward her.

GORDON

(Contritely.)

I know I shouldn't.

(But returning to his bitter tone.)

But I can't help remembering how unreasonably she's acted about our engagement.

MADELINE

Not since your father was taken sick, she hasn't, dear. She's been wonderfully nice.

GORDON

(In the same tone.)

Nice? Indifferent, you mean! She doesn't seem to care a damn one way or the other any more!

MADELINE

You could hardly expect her to think of anyone but your father. She's been with him every minute. I never saw such devotion.

(Thinking.)

Will Gordon ever get old and sick like that? . . . oh, I hope we'll both die before! . . . but I'd nurse him just as she did his father . . . I'll always love him! . . .

GORDON

(Consoled – proudly.)

Yes, she sure was wonderful to him, all right!

(Then coming back to his old tone.)

But – this may sound rotten of me – I always had a queer feeling she was doing it as a duty. And when he died, I felt her grief was – not from love for him – at least, only the love of a friend, not a wife's love.

(As if under some urgent compulsion from within.)

I've never told you, but I've always felt, ever since I was a little kid, that she didn't really love Dad. She liked him and respected him. She was a wonderful wife. But I'm sure she didn't love him.

(Blurting it out as if he couldn't help it.)

I'll tell you, Madeline! I've always felt she cared a lot for – Darrell.

(Hastily.)

Of course, I might be wrong.

(Then bursting out.)

No, I'm not wrong! I've felt it too strongly, ever since I was a kid. And then when I was eleven – something happened. I've been sure of it since then.

MADELINE

(Thinking in amazement, but not without a queer satisfaction.)

Does he mean that she was unfaithful to his father? . . . no, he'd never believe that . . . but what else could he mean? . . .

(Wonderingly.)

Gordon! Do you mean you've been sure that your mother was –

GORDON

(Outraged by something in her tone – jumping to his feet and flinging her hand off – roughly.)

Was what? What do you mean, Madeline?

MADELINE

(Frightened – placatingly puts her arms around him.)

I didn't mean anything, dear. I simply thought you meant –

GORDON

(Still indignant.)

All I mean was that she must have fallen in love with Darrell long after she was married – and then she sent him away for Dad's sake – and mine, too, I suppose. He kept coming back every couple of years. He didn't have guts enough to stay away for good! Oh, I suppose I'm unfair. I suppose it was damned hard on him. He fought it down, too, on account of his friendship for Dad.

(Then with a bitter laugh.)

I suppose they'll be getting married now! And I'll have to wish them good luck. Dad would want me to. He was game.

(With a bitter gloomy air.)

Life is damn queer, that's all I've got to say!

MADELINE

(Thinking with a sort of tender, loving scorn for his boyish naïveté.)

How little he knows her! . . . Mr. Evans was a fine man but . . . Darrell must have been fascinating once . . . if she loved anyone she isn't the kind who would hesitate . . . any more than I have with Gordon . . . oh, I'll never be unfaithful to Gordon . . . I'll love him always! . . .

(She runs her fingers through his hair caressingly – comfortingly.)

You must never blame them, dear. No one can help love. We couldn't, could we?

(She sits beside him. He takes her in his arms. They kiss each other with rising passion. Marsden comes in noiselessly from the garden, a bunch of roses and a pair of shears in his hands. He looks younger, calm and contented. He is dressed in his all black, meticulous, perfectly tailored mourning costume. He stands looking at the two lovers, a queer agitation coming into his face.)

MARSDEN

(Scandalized as an old maid – thinking.)

I must say! . . . his father hardly cold in his grave! . . . it's positively bestial! . . .

(Then struggling with himself – with a defensive self-mockery.)

Only it wasn't his father . . . what is Sam to Darrell's son? . . . and even if he were Sam's son, what have the living to do with the dead? . . . his duty is to love that life may keep on living . . . and what has their loving to do with me? . . . my life is cool green shade wherein comes no scorching zenith sun of passion and possession to wither the heart with bitter poisons . . . my life gathers roses, coolly crimson, in sheltered gardens, on late afternoons in love with evening . . . roses heavy with after-blooming of the long day, desiring evening . . . my life is an evening . . . Nina is a rose, my rose, exhausted by the long, hot day, leaning wearily toward peace. . . .

(He kisses one of the roses with a simple sentimental smile – then still smiling, makes a gesture toward the two lovers.)

That is on another planet, called the world . . . Nina and I have moved on to the moon. . . .

MADELINE

(Passionately.)

Dear one! Sweetheart!

GORDON

Madeline! I love you!

MARSDEN

(Looking at them – gaily mocking – thinking.)

Once I'd have felt jealous . . . cheated . . . swindled by God out of joy! . . . I would have thought bitterly, "The Gordons have all the luck!" . . . but now I know that dear old Charlie . . . yes, poor dear old Charlie! – passed beyond desire, has all the luck at last! . . .

(Then matter-of-factly.)

But I'll have to interrupt their biological preparations . . . there are many things still to be done this evening . . . Age's terms of peace, after the long interlude of war with life, have still to be concluded . . . Youth must keep decently away . . . so many old wounds may have to be unbound, and old scars pointed to with pride, to prove to ourselves we have been brave and noble! . . .

(He lets the shears drop to the ground. They jump startledly and turn around. He smiles quietly.)

Sorry to disturb you. I've been picking some roses for your mother, Gordon. Flowers really have the power to soothe grief. I suppose it was that discovery that led to their general use at funerals – and weddings!

(He hands a rose to Madeline.)

Here, Madeline, here's a rose for you. Hail, Love, we who have died, salute you!

(He smiles strangely. She takes the rose automatically, staring at him uncomprehendingly.)

MADELINE

(Thinking suspiciously.)

What a queer creature! . . there's something uncanny!

. . . oh, don't be silly! . . . it's only poor old Charlie! . . .
(She makes him a mocking curtsy.)

Thank you, Uncle Charlie!

GORDON

(Thinking with sneering pity.)
Poor old guy! . . . he means well . . . Dad liked him. . . .
(Pretending an interest in the roses.)

They're pretty.

(Then suddenly.)

Where's Mother – still in the house?

MARSDEN

She was trying to get rid of the last of the people. I'm going in. Shall I tell her you want to see her? It would give her an excuse to get away.

GORDON

Yes. Will you?

(Marsden goes into the house on right.)

MADELINE

You'd better see your mother alone. I'll go down to the 'plane and wait for you. You want to fly back before dark, don't you?

GORDON

Yes, and we ought to get started soon.
(Moodily.)

Maybe it would be better if you weren't here. There are some things I feel I ought to say to her – and Darrell. I've got to do what I know Dad would have wanted. I've got to be fair. He always was to everyone all his life.

MADELINE

You dear, you! You couldn't be unfair to anyone if you tried!

(She kisses him.)

Don't be too long.

GORDON

(Moodily.)

You bet I won't! It won't be so pleasant I'll want to drag it out!

MADELINE

Good-bye for a while then.

GORDON

So long!
(He looks after her lovingly as she goes out right, rear, around the corner of the house.)
(Thinking.)
Madeline's wonderful! . . . I don't deserve my luck . . . but, God, I sure do love her! . . .
(He sits down on the bench again, his chin on his hands.)
It seems rotten and selfish to be happy . . . when Dad . . . oh, he understands, he'd want me to be . . . it's funny how I got to care more for Dad than for Mother . . . I suppose it was finding out she loved Darrell . . . I can remember that day seeing her kiss him . . . it did something to me I never got over . . . but she made Dad happy . . . she gave up her own happiness for his sake . . . that was certainly damn fine . . . that was playing the game . . . I'm a hell of a one to criticize . . . my own mother! . . .
(Changing the subject of his thoughts abruptly.)
Forget it! . . . think of Madeline . . . we'll be married . . . then two months' honeymoon in Europe . . . God, that'll be great! . . . then back and dive into the business . . . Dad relied on me to carry on where he left off . . . I'll have to start at the bottom, but I'll get to the top in a hurry, I promise you that, Dad! . . .
(Nina and Darrell come out of the house on the right. He hears the sound of the door and looks around.)
(Thinking resentfully.)
Funny! . . . I can't stand it even now! . . . when I see him with Mother! . . . I'd like to beat him up! . . .
(He gets to his feet, his face unconsciously becoming older and cold and severe. He stares accusingly at them as they come slowly toward him in silence. Nina looks much older than in the preceding Act. Resignation has come into her face, a resignation that uses no make-up, that has given up the struggle to be sexually attractive and look younger. She is dressed in deep black. Darrell's deep sunburn of the tropics has faded, leaving his skin a Mongolian yellow. He, too, looks much older. His expression is sad and bitter.)

NINA

(Glancing at Gordon searchingly – thinking sadly.)
He sent for me to say good-bye . . . really good-bye for ever this time . . . he's not my son now, nor Gordon's son, nor Sam's, nor Ned's . . . he has become that stranger, another woman's lover. . . .

DARRELL

(Also after a quick keen glance at Gordon's face – thinking.)
There's something up . . . some final accounting . . .
(Thinking resignedly.)
Well, let's get it over . . . then I can go back to work. . . . I've stayed too long up here . . . Preston must be wondering if I've deserted him. . . .
(Then with a wondering sadness.)
Is that my son? . . . my flesh and blood? . . . staring at me with such cold enmity? . . . how sad and idiotic this all is! . . .

NINA

(Putting on a tone of joking annoyance.)

Your message was a godsend, Gordon. Those stupid people

with their social condolences were killing me. Perhaps I'm morbid, but I always have the feeling that they're secretly glad someone is dead – that it flatters their vanity and makes them feel superior because they're living.

(*She sits wearily on the bench. Darrell sits on side of the* chaise longue *at right.*)

GORDON

(*Repelled by this idea – stiffly.*)

They were all good friends of Dad's. Why shouldn't they be sincerely sorry? His death ought to be a loss to everyone who knew him.

(*His voice trembles. He turns away and walks to the table.*)

(*Thinking bitterly.*)

She doesn't care a damn! . . . she's free to marry Darrell now! . . .

NINA

(*Thinking sadly, looking at his back.*)

He's accusing me because I'm not weeping . . . well, I did weep . . . all I could . . . there aren't many tears left . . . it was too bad Sam had to die . . . living suited him . . . he was so contented with himself . . . but I can't feel guilty . . . I helped him to live . . . I made him believe I loved him . . . his mind was perfectly sane to the end . . . and just before he died, he smiled at me . . . so gratefully and forgivingly, I thought . . . closing our life together with that smile . . . that life is dead . . . its regrets are dead . . . I am sad, but there's comfort in the thought that now I am free at last to rot away in peace . . . I'll go and live in Father's old home . . . Sam bought that back . . . I suppose he left it to me . . . Charlie will come in every day to visit . . . he'll comfort and amuse me . . . we can talk together of the old days . . . when I was a girl . . . when I was happy . . . before I fell in love with Gordon Shaw and all this tangled mess of love and hate and pain and birth began! . . .

DARRELL

(*Staring at Gordon's back resentfully.*)

It gets under my skin to see him act so unfeelingly toward his mother! . . . if he only knew what she's suffered for his sake! . . . the Gordon Shaw ideal passed on through Sam has certainly made my son an insensitive clod! . . .

(*With disgust.*)

Bah, what has that young man to do with me? . . . compared to Preston he's only a well-muscled, handsome fool! . . .

(*With a trace of anger.*)

But I'd like to jolt his stupid self-complacency! . . . if he knew the facts about himself, he wouldn't be sobbing sentimentally about Sam . . . he'd better change his tune or I'll certainly be tempted to tell him . . . there's no reason for his not knowing now . . .

(*His face is flushed. He has worked himself into a real anger.*)

GORDON

(*Suddenly, having got back his control, turns to them – coldly.*)

There are certain things connected with Dad's will I thought I ought to –

(*With a tinge of satisfied superiority.*)

I don't believe Dad told you about his will, did he, Mother?

NINA

(*Indifferently.*)

No.

GORDON

Well, the whole estate goes to you and me, of course. I didn't mean that.

(*With a resentful look at Darrell.*)

But there is one provision that is peculiar, to say the least. It concerns you, Doctor Darrell – a half-million for your Station to be used in biological research work.

DARRELL

(*His face suddenly flushing with anger.*)

What's that? That's a joke, isn't it?

(*Thinking furiously.*)

It's worse! . . . it's a deliberate insult! . . . a last sneer of ownership! . . . of my life! . . .

GORDON

(*Coldly sneering.*)

I thought it must be a joke myself – but Dad insisted.

DARRELL

(*Angrily.*)

Well, I won't accept it – and that's final!

GORDON

(*Coldly.*)

It's not left to you, but to the Station. Your supervision is mentioned, but I suppose if you won't carry on, whoever is in real charge down there will be only too glad to accept it.

DARRELL

(*Stupefied.*)

That means Preston! But Sam didn't even know Preston – except from hearing me talk about him! What had Sam to do with Preston? Preston is none of his business! I'll advise Preston to refuse it!

(*Thinking torturedly.*)

But it's for Science! . . . he has no right to refuse! . . . I have no right to ask him to! . . . God damn Sam! . . . wasn't it enough for him to own my wife, my son, in his lifetime? . . . now in death he reaches out to steal Preston! . . . to steal my work! . . .

NINA

(*Thinking bitterly.*)

Even in death Sam makes people suffer . . .

(*Sympathetically.*)

It isn't for you – nor for Preston. It's for Science, Ned. You must look at it that way.

GORDON

(*Thinking resentfully.*)

What a tender tone she takes toward him! . . . she's forgotten Dad already! . . .

(*With a sneer.*)

You'd better accept. Half-millions aren't being thrown away for nothing every day.

NINA

(*In anguish – thinking.*)

How can Gordon insult poor Ned like that! . . . his own father! . . . Ned has suffered too much! . . .

(*Sharply.*)

I think you've said about enough, Gordon!

GORDON

(*Bitterly, but trying to control himself – meaningly.*)

I haven't said all I'm going to say, Mother!

NINA

(*Thinking – at first frightenedly.*)

What does he mean? . . . does he know about Ned being . . . ?

(*Then with a sort of defiant relief.*)

Well, what does it matter what he thinks of me? . . . he's hers now, anyway. . . .

DARRELL

(*Thinking vindictively.*)

I hope he knows the truth, for if he doesn't, by God, I'll tell him! . . . if only to get something back from Sam of all he's stolen from me! . . .

(*Authoritatively – as Gordon hesitates.*)

Well, what have you got to say? Your mother and I are waiting.

GORDON

(*Furiously, taking a threatening step toward him.*)

Shut up, you! Don't take that tone with me or I'll forget your age –

(*Contemptuously.*)

and give you a spanking!

NINA

(*Thinking hysterically.*)

Spanking! . . . the son spanks the father! . . .

(*Laughing hysterically.*)

Oh, Gordon, don't make me laugh! It's all so funny!

DARRELL

(*Jumps from his chair and goes to her – solicitously.*

Nina! Don't mind him! He doesn't realize –

GORDON

(*Maddened, comes closer.*)

I realize a lot! I realize you've acted like a cur!

(*He steps forward and slaps Darrell across the face viciously. Darrell staggers back from the force of the blow, his hands to his face. Nina screams and flings herself on Gordon, holding his arms.*)

NINA

(*Piteously – hysterically.*)

For God's sake, Gordon! What would your father say? You don't know what you're doing! You're hitting your father!

DARRELL

(*Suddenly breaking down – chokingly.*)

No – it's all right, son – all right – you didn't know –

GORDON

(*Crushed, overcome by remorse for his blow.*)

I'm sorry – sorry – you're right, Mother – Dad would feel as if I'd hit him – just as bad as if I'd hit him!

DARRELL

It's nothing, son – nothing!

GORDON

(*Brokenly.*)

That's damn fine, Darrell – damn fine and sporting of you! It was a rotten, dirty trick! Accept my apology, Darrell, won't you?

DARRELL

(*Staring at him stupidly – thinking.*)

Darrell? . . . he calls me Darrell! . . . but doesn't he know? . . . I thought she told him. . . .

NINA

(*Laughing hysterically – thinking.*)

I told him he hit his father . . . but he can't understand me! . . . why, of course he can't! . . . how could he? . . .

GORDON

(*Insistently holding out his hand.*)

I'm damned sorry! I didn't mean it! Shake hands, won't you?

DARRELL

(*Doing so mechanically – stupidly.*)

Only too glad – pleased to meet you – know you by reputation – the famous oarsman – great race you stroked last June – but I was hoping the Navy would give you a beating.

NINA

(*Thinking in desperate hysterical anguish.*)

Oh, I wish Ned would go away and stay away for ever! . . . I can't bear to watch him suffer any more! . . . it's too frightful! . . . yes, God the Father, I hear you laughing . . . you see the joke . . . I'm laughing, too . . . it's all so crazy, isn't it? . . .

(*Laughing hysterically.*)

Oh, Ned! Poor Ned! You were born unlucky!

GORDON

(*Making her sit down again – soothing her.*)

Mother! Stop laughing! Please! It's all right – all right between us! I've apologized!

(*As she has grown calmer.*)

And now I want to say what I was going to say. It wasn't anything bad. It was just that I want you to know how fine I think you've both acted. I've known ever since I was a kid that you and Darrell were in love with each other. I hated the idea on Father's account – that's only natural, isn't it? – but I knew it was unfair, that people can't help loving each other any more than Madeline and I could have helped ourselves. And I saw how fair you both were to Dad – what a good wife you were, Mother – what a true friend you were, Darrell – and how damn much he loved you both! So all I wanted to say is, now he's dead, I hope you'll get married and I hope you'll be as happy as you both deserve –

(*Here he breaks down, kissing her and then breaking away.*)

I've got to say good-bye – got to fly back before dark – Madeline's waiting.

(*He takes Darrell's hand and shakes it again. They have both been staring at him stupidly.*)

Good-bye, Darrell! Good luck!

DARRELL

(*Thinking sufferingly.*)

Why does he keep on calling me Darrell? . . . he's my boy. . . I'm his father . . . I've got to make him realize I'm his father! . . .

(*Holding Gordon's hand.*)

Listen, son. It's my turn. I've got to tell you something –

NINA

(*Thinking torturedly.*)

Oh, he mustn't! . . . I feel he mustn't! . . .

(*Sharply.*)

Ned! First, let me ask Gordon a question.

(*Then looking her son in the eyes, slowly and impressively.*)

Do you think I was ever unfaithful to your father, Gordon?

GORDON

(*Startled, stares at her – shocked and horrified – then suddenly he blurts out indignantly.*)

Mother, what do you think I am – as rotten-minded as that!

(*Pleadingly.*)

Please, Mother, I'm not as bad as that! I know you're the best woman that ever lived – the best of all! I don't even except Madeline!

NINA

(*With a sobbing triumphant cry.*)

My dear Gordon! You do love me, don't you?

GORDON

(*Kneeling beside her and kissing her.*)

Of course!

NINA

(*Pushing him away – tenderly.*)

And now go! Hurry! Madeline is waiting! Give her my love! Come to see me once in a while in the years to come! Good-bye, dear!

(*Turning to Darrell, who is standing with a sad resigned expression – imploringly.*)

Did you still want to tell Gordon something, Ned?

DARRELL

(*Forcing a tortured smile.*)

Not for anything in the world! Good-bye, son.

GORDON

Good-bye, sir.

(*He hurries off around the corner of the house at left, rear, thinking troubledly.*)

What does she think I am? . . . I've never thought that! . . . I couldn't! . . . my own mother! I'd kill myself if I ever even caught myself thinking . . . !

(*He is gone.*)

NINA

(*Turns to Ned, gratefully taking his hand and pressing it.*)

Poor dear Ned, you've always had to give! How can I ever thank you?

DARRELL

(*With an ironical smile – forcing a joking tone.*)

By refusing me when I ask you to marry me! For I've got

to ask you! Gordon expects it! And he'll be so pleased when he knows you turned me down.

(*Marsden comes out of the house.*)

Hallo, here comes Charlie! I must hurry. Will you marry me, Nina?

NINA

(*With a sad smile.*)

No. Certainly not. Our ghosts would torture us to death!

(*Then forlornly.*)

But I wish I did love you, Ned! Those were wonderful afternoons long ago! The Nina of those afternoons will always live in me, will always love her lover, Ned, the father of her baby!

DARRELL

(*Lifting her hand to his lips – tenderly.*)

Thank you for that! And that Ned will always adore his beautiful Nina! Remember him! Forget me! I'm going back to work.

(*He laughs softly and sadly.*)

I leave you to Charlie. You'd better marry him, Nina – if you want peace. And after all, I think you owe it to him for his lifelong devotion.

MARSDEN

(*Thinking uneasily.*)

They're talking about me . . . why doesn't he go? . . . she doesn't love him any more . . . even now he's all heat and energy and the tormenting drive of noon . . . can't he see she is in love with evening? . . .

(*Clearing his throat uneasily.*)

Do I hear my name taken in vain?

NINA

(*Looking at Marsden with a strange yearning.*)

Peace! . . . yes . . . that is all I desire . . . I can no longer imagine happiness . . . Charlie has found peace . . . he will be tender . . . as my father was when I was a girl . . . when I could imagine happiness . . .

(*With a girlish coquettishness and embarrassment – making way for him on the bench beside her – strangely.*)

Ned's just proposed to me. I refused him, Charlie. I don't love him any more.

MARSDEN

(*Sitting down beside her.*)

I suspected as much. Then whom do you love, Nina Cara Nina?

NINA

(*Sadly smiling.*)

You, Charlie, I suppose. I have always loved your love for me.

(*She kisses him – wistfully.*)

Will you let me rot away in peace?

MARSDEN

(*Strongly.*)

All my life I've waited to bring you peace.

NINA

(*Sadly teasing.*)

If you've waited that long, Charlie, we'd better get married to-morrow. But I forgot. You haven't asked me yet, have you? Do you want me to marry you, Charlie?

MARSDEN

(*Humbly.*)

Yes, Nina.

(*Thinking with a strange ecstasy.*)

I knew the time would come at last when I would hear her ask that! . . . I could never have said it, never! . . . oh, russet-golden afternoon, you are a mellow fruit of happiness ripely falling! . . .

DARRELL

(*Amused – with a sad smile.*)

Bless you, my children!

(*He turns to go.*)

NINA

I don't suppose we'll ever see you again, Ned.

DARRELL

I hope not, Nina. A scientist shouldn't believe in ghosts.

(*With a mocking smile.*)

But perhaps we'll become part of cosmic positive and negative electric charges and meet again.

NINA

In our afternoons – again?

DARRELL

(*Smiling sadly.*)

Again. In our afternoons.

MARSDEN

(*Coming out of his day dream.*)

We'll be married in the afternoon, decidedly. I've already picked out the church, Nina – a grey ivied chapel, full of restful shadow, symbolical of the peace we have found. The crimsons and purples in the windows will stain our faces with faded passion. It must be in the hour before sunset when the earth dreams in afterthoughts and mystic premonitions of life's beauty. And then we'll go up to your old home to live. Mine wouldn't be suitable for us. Mother and Jane live there in memory. And I'll work in your father's old study. He won't mind me.

(From the bay below comes the roaring hum of an aeroplane motor. Nina and Darrell jump startledly and go to the rear of the terrace to watch the 'plane ascend from the water, standing side by side. Marsden remains oblivious.)

NINA

(With anguish.)

Gordon! Good-bye, dear!

(Pointing as the 'plane climbs higher, moving away off to the left – bitterly.)

See, Ned! He's leaving me without a backward look!

DARRELL

(Joyfully.)

No! He's circling. He's coming back!

(The roar of the engine grows steadily nearer now.)

He's going to pass directly over us!

(Their eyes follow the 'plane as it comes swiftly nearer and passes directly over them.)

See! He's waving to us!

NINA

Oh, Gordon! My dear son!

(She waves frantically.)

DARRELL

(With a last tortured protest.)

Nina! Are you forgetting? He's my son, too!

(He shouts up at the sky.)

You're my son, Gordon! You're my –

(He controls himself abruptly – with a smile of cynical self-pity.)

He can't hear! Well, at least I've done my duty!

(Then with a grim fatalism – with a final wave of his hand at the sky.)

Good-bye, Gordon's son!

NINA

(With tortured exultance.)

Fly up to heaven, Gordon! Fly with your love to heaven! Fly always! Never crash to earth like my old Gordon! Be happy, dear! You've got to be happy!

DARRELL

(Sardonically.)

I've heard that cry for happiness before, Nina! I remember hearing myself cry it – once – it must have been long ago! I'll get back to my cells – sensible unicellular life that floats in the sea and has never learned the cry for happiness! I'm going, Nina.

(As she remains oblivious, staring after the 'plane – thinking fatalistically.)

She doesn't hear, either. . . .

(He laughs up at the sky.)

Oh, God, so deaf and dumb and blind! . . . teach me to be resigned to be an atom! . . .

(He walks off, right, and enters the house.)

NINA

(Finally lowering her eyes – confusedly.)

Gone! My eyes are growing dim. Where is Ned? Gone, too. And Sam is gone. They're all dead. Where are Father and Charlie?

(With a shiver of fear she hurries over and sits on the bench beside Marsden, huddling against him.)

Gordon is dead, Father. I've just had a cable. What I mean is, he flew away to another life – my son, Gordon, Charlie. So we're alone again – just as we used to be.

MARSDEN

(Putting his arm around her – affectionately.)

Just as we used to be, dear Nina Cara Nina, before Gordon came.

NINA

(Looking up at the sky – strangely.)

My having a son was a failure, wasn't it? He couldn't give me happiness. Sons are always their fathers. They pass through the mother to become their father again. The Sons of the Father have all been failures! Failing they died for us, they flew away to other lives, they could not stay with us, they could not give us happiness!

MARSDEN

(Paternally – in her father's tone.)

You had best forget the whole affair of your association with the Gordons. After all, dear Nina, there was something unreal in all that has happened since you first met Gordon Shaw, something extravagant and fantastic, the sort of thing that isn't done, really, in our afternoons. So let you and me forget the whole distressing episode, regard it as an interlude, of trial and preparation, say, in which our souls have been scraped clean of impure flesh and made worthy to bleach in peace.

NINA

(With a strange smile.)

Strange interlude! Yes, our lives are merely strange dark interludes in the electrical display of God the Father!

(Resting her head on his shoulder.)

You're so restful, Charlie. I feel as if I were a girl again and you were my father and the Charlie of those days made into one. I wonder is our old garden the same? We'll pick flowers together in the ageing afternoons of spring and summer, won't we? It will be a comfort to get home – to be old and to be home again at last – to be in love with peace together – to love each other's peace – to sleep with peace together –!

(She kisses him – then shuts her eyes with a deep sigh of requited weariness.)

– to die in peace! I'm so contentedly weary with life!

MARSDEN

(With a serene peace.)

Rest, dear Nina.

(Then tenderly.)

It has been a long day. Why don't you sleep now – as you used to, remember? – for a little while?

NINA

(Murmurs with drowsy gratitude.)

Thank you, Father – have I been wicked? – you're so good – dear old Charlie!

MARSDEN

(Reacting automatically and wincing with pain – thinking mechanically.)

God damn dear old . . . !

(Then with a glance down at Nina's face, with a happy smile.)

No, God bless dear old Charlie . . . who, passed beyond desire, has all the luck at last! . . .

(Nina has fallen asleep. He watches with contented eyes the evening shadows closing in around them.)

Curtain

DYNAMO

Characters

REVEREND HUTCHINS LIGHT
AMELIA, *his wife*
REUBEN, *their son*
RAMSAY FIFE, *superintendent of a hydro-electric plant*
MAY, *his wife*
ADA, *their daughter*
JENNINGS, *an operator at the plant*

Scenes

ACT ONE

SCENE ONE The Light sitting-room and Reuben's bedroom above it.
SCENE TWO The Fife sitting-room with Ramsay's and May's bedroom on the floor above.
SCENE THREE The Light and Fife sitting-rooms.
SCENE FOUR Reuben's bedroom.

ACT TWO

SCENE ONE Same as Act One. Fifteen months later. The Light sitting-room.
SCENE TWO Reuben's bedroom. Night of the same day.
SCENE THREE Exterior of the hydro-electric power plant near the town. Half an hour later.

ACT THREE

GENERAL SCENE The hydro-electric power plant near the town. Four months later.
SCENE ONE Exterior of the plant.
SCENE TWO Interiors of the upper and lower switch galleries.
SCENE THREE Interiors of the two switch galleries, the switchboard room, and the dynamo room.

General Scene

The exterior of the homes of the Lights and the Fifes in a small town in Connecticut. These houses stand side by side, facing front, on the street. They are set close together, separated by narrow strips of lawn, with a lilac hedge at centre marking the boundary-line between the two properties, and a row of tall maples in the background behind the yards and the two houses. The Fife house, a small brownish-tinted modern stucco bungalow type, recently built, is at left; the Light home, a little old New England white frame cottage with green shutters, at right. Only the half-sections of the two houses are visible which are nearest to each other, the one containing the Fife sitting-room, with Ramsay's and May's bedroom directly above it, and the section of the Lights' home in which are their sitting-room and Reuben's bedroom on the floor above.

As the separate scenes of Part One require, the front walls of these rooms are removed to show the different interiors. All these rooms are small, the ones in the Light home particularly so.

It is the month of May of the present day. The lilacs are in bloom, the grass is a fresh green.

ACT ONE SCENE ONE

SCENE. *It is evening. In the background between the two houses the outlines of the maples are black against a sky pale with the light of a quarter-moon. Now and then there is a faint flash of lightning from far off and a low mumble of thunder.*

The Light sitting-room and Reuben's bedroom are revealed. Both are sparsely furnished with the bare necessities. Reuben's bedroom contains an old four-poster bed, front, facing left, a small table on which are stacked his textbooks, and a chair in left corner, front. In the left wall is a window. A washstand with bowl and pitcher is in the left corner, rear, and an old-fashioned bureau in the middle of the rear wall. To the right of this is the door of a clothes closet. The door to the hall and the stairs is at right, rear. There is a lighted kerosene lamp on the table.

In the sitting-room below there is a table at centre, front. The minister's arm-chair is beside this on the left. His wife's rocker is at the right of the table. Farther right is another chair. Three small hooked rugs are on the floor. Several framed prints of scenes from the Bible hang on the walls. The minister's small desk is placed against the left wall beside the window. On the table at centre are a cheap oil reading-lamp, a Bible, and some magazines. There is a door to the hall in the right wall, rear.

The ceilings of both rooms are low, the wall-paper so faded that the ugliness of its colour and design has been toned down into a neutral blur. But everything in this home is spotlessly clean and in order, the old furniture and floors are oiled and polished.

The Reverend Hutchins Light is seated in his arm-chair, his wife in her rocker. He is a man in his early sixties, slightly under medium height, ponderously built. His face is square, ribbed with wrinkles, the forehead low, the nose heavy, the eyes small and grey blue, the reddish hair grizzled and bushy, the stubborn jaw weakened by a big indecisive mouth. His voice is the bullying one of a sermonizer who is the victim of an inner uncertainty that compensates itself by being boomingly over-assertive.

His wife, Amelia, is fifteen years his junior and appears even younger. Her stout figure is still firm and active, with large breasts and broad, round hips. She must have been pretty as a girl. Even now her dark-complexioned face, with its big brown eyes and wavy black hair, retains its attractiveness although it has grown fleshy. Her expression is one of virtuous resignation. Only her mouth is rebellious. It is a thin small mouth, determined and stubborn, sensual and selfish.

In the bedroom above, their son, Reuben, is sitting in his shirt-sleeves on the side of his bed. He is seventeen, tall and thin. His eyes are large, shy and sensitive, of the same grey blue as his father's. His mouth is like his father's. His jaw is stubborn, his thick hair curly and reddish-blond. He speaks timidly and hesitatingly, as a much younger boy might. His natural voice has an almost feminine gentleness. In intercourse with the world, however, he instinctively imitates his father's tone, booming self-protectively.

Hutchins Light has a pad on which he has been trying to make notes for his next sermon, but his mind is abstracted. He stares before him with the resentful air of one brooding over a wrong done him and unsuccessfully plotting revenge. His wife is pretending to read, but her thoughts are actively elsewhere, and she glances inquisitively at her husband from under lowered lids.

In the bedroom above, Reuben's eyes are turned toward the window, his face eager with dreams.

LIGHT (*arguing tormentedly within himself*). What did he mean about Reuben? . . . that foul-mouthed scoundrel! . . . "Better call in your son or some night I might mistake his odour of sanctity for a skunk's and fill his" . . . filthy word belching from his grinning mouth! . . . "full of buckshot" . . . I heard the corner loafers laugh . . . and I had to slink by and pretend not to hear! . . . If it weren't for my cloth I'd have beaten his face to a bloody pulp! . . . I'd . . . ! (*Suddenly horrified at himself.*) A murderer's thoughts! . . . Lord God, forgive me! . . .

MRS. LIGHT (*glances at him and speaks in a gentle tone that carries a challenging quality*). Hutchins, do you realize Reuben will graduate from school in less than a month?

LIGHT (*oblivious*). But, Lord, Thou knowest what a thorn in the flesh that atheist, Fife, has been since the devil brought him next door! . . . (*Protesting petulantly to his God.*) How long, O Lord? . . . does not his foul ranting begin to try Thy patience? . . . is not the time ripe to smite this blasphemer who defies Thee publicly to strike him dead? . . . Lord God of Hosts, why dost Thou not strike him? . . . If Thou didst, I would proclaim the awful warning of it over all America! . . . I would convert multitudes, as it was once my dream to do! . . .

MRS. LIGHT. Hutchins, please pay attention to what I'm saying. Don't you think we ought to decide definitely about Reuben's future?

LIGHT (*turns to her with a frown*). I have decided. He shall follow in my footsteps—mine and those of my father before me, and his father before him. It is God's manifest will! (*He presses his lips tightly together—an effort to appear implacable that gives his face the expression of a balky animal's.*)

MRS. LIGHT (*thinks scornfully*). He is always so sure of what God wills! . . . but Reuben'll never be a minister if I can prevent it! . . . I'd rather see him dead than go through the poverty and humiliation I've had to face! . . . Reuben's got to go to college . . . then into business . . . marry a nice girl with money . . . he doesn't care anything about girls yet, thank goodness!

(*She speaks in a meek persuasive tone.*) Each of us must judge about Reuben according to the light vouchsafed by God. He doesn't feel any call to the ministry and I think it would be a great sin if——

LIGHT (*his voice booming*). And I tell you, Amelia, it is God's will!

REUBEN (*hearing his father's voice, jumps to his feet and stares down toward the room with an expression of boyish apprehension*). What's he shouting about? . . . has he heard about Ada and me? . . . he'll raise the roof! . . . but Mother'll take my side against him . . . she's always sided with me . . . and she won't hate Ada when she knows I love her . . . (*Then resentfully.*) What do I care about him anyway? . . . he hates Fife because he's scared of him . . . he's scared to take up Fife's challenge to debate about whether there's a God or not . . . when Fife took out his watch and said if there was a God let Him prove it by striking him dead in five minutes, why was it nothing happened? . . . I should think if . . . (*He looks around uneasily, afraid of where his thoughts are leading him. A faint flash of lightning from the distant storm flickers through his window. He starts guiltily and hastily makes a reassuring declaration of faith.*) Of course there's a God! . . . He wouldn't pay any attention to a fool like Fife, that's all! . . .

LIGHT. I believe that storm must be coming this way. (*He gets to his feet—a bit shamefacedly.*) I think I'll close the shutters.

MRS. LIGHT. But it'll make it so dreadfully close in here! (*Then seeing his ashamed look, she smiles.*) Oh, all right, close them if you're getting scared.

LIGHT (*his dignity ruffled, turns his back on her and goes to the window*). Lightning gets on lots of people's nerves without their being afraid of it.

REUBEN. Aw, what's the matter with me? . . . that lightning had nothing to do with what I was thinking . . . (*He goes to the window and looks over toward the Fife home.*) She said she'd put a record on the Victrola as soon as she was free . . . then I was to meet her down by the lilacs . . . (*He breathes in the spring.*) Gee, those lilacs smell sweet! . . . I wish she'd hurry up! . . . I've got to get up my nerve and tell her I love her . . .

LIGHT (*stands by the window and sniffs the air*). Can you smell the perfume of the lilacs, Amelia? Do you remember our first spring here?

MRS. LIGHT. Of course. (*Then, after a pause, her voice turned bitter.*) Twenty-three years! It's a long time to live in this awful little house! Hutchins, are you ever going to insist that they instal electric lighting here? It's a shame the way they deny you the ordinary comforts of life!

LIGHT (*turns away and leans out of the window, staring into the night.*) Comforts of life! . . . she has always desired the comfortable path . . . where the spirit decays in the sinful sloth of the flesh . . .

(*From the open, curtained windows of the Fife

living-room a burst of laughter is heard— Fife's voice, sardonic and malicious. Light draws back into the room, muttering viciously.) Scum of the earth! *(Then turning on his wife.)* Tell me, has Reuben been having anything to do with that cursed pack next door? That scoundrel called something at me on the street to-day that made me think——

MRS. LIGHT *(impatiently).* Don't you know that man well enough by this time not to pay attention to his trying to rile you?

LIGHT. Then answer me this: why has Reuben taken such a sudden notion to going out in the evening lately?

MRS. LIGHT. Do you expect a boy of his age to stay in like a poor stick-in-the-mud just because he happens to be a minister's son—especially when it's spring!

LIGHT. I remembered that it's spring—and I've just remembered that Fife has a daughter!

MRS. LIGHT. That painted flapper with her skirts hitched up over her knees! Do you think for one moment that Reuben, who never looks at girls anyway—and knowing what her father is!—Really, Hutchins, you're getting just too stupid!

(From the Fife house comes the sound of a Victrola starting a jazz record.)

REUBEN *(starts from his dream by the window upstairs).* That's her signal! . . . *(He hurriedly puts on his coat.)* I better sneak out the back . . . *(He blows out the light and makes his way carefully out the bedroom door in right, rear.)*

LIGHT *(listening to the Victrola, fixes his eyes on his wife combatively).* You may call me as stupid as you like, but I insist there was something back of what that Fife said about Reuben. He sneered that we'd better keep him home at night and insinuated he was hanging around their place. The thought of that girl of his never entered my head until a moment ago—but what else could he mean? I'm going to face Reuben with it right now and we'll see what he has to say for himself!

MRS. LIGHT *(sharply).* Now don't you go preaching at him again! You better let me talk to him first. He's never lied to me. *(She goes toward the door in rear, plainly worried now, but trying to make little of it.)* You're always so ready to believe the worst of him! I know it's all nonsense! *(She goes out.)*

LIGHT *(sits thinking gloomily).* Never lied to her . . . she means he does to me . . . why? . . . have I been too stern? . . . but even when he was little I sensed in him his mother's rebellious spirit . . . and now . . . if it is Fife's daughter . . . what a feather in that blasphemer's cap to corrupt my son! . . . how the gossips would sneer at me! . . . *(This thought drives him frantic—he paces up and down trying vainly to calm himself.)* No, no! . . . Reuben could never be guilty of so base a treachery! . . . *(He sits down by the table and, picking up his Bible, begins to read in a determined effort to get his mind off the subject.)*

MRS. LIGHT *(can be dimly made out entering the bedroom above just as Reuben, coming from the back door of the house, slinks stealthily around the rear corner across the patch of moonlit lawn to the shadow of the lilacs. Keeping in this shadow he moves down until he comes to a small gap that is almost at the end of the hedge, front. He stands by this, waiting nervously, peering through the gap at the Fife house. Mrs. Light thinks worriedly).* Gone to bed? . . . so early? . . . was he sick and didn't tell me? . . . *(She has come to the bed—with sudden fear.)* He's not here! . . . he must have sneaked out! . . . the first time he ever did such a thing! . . . but how do I know it's the first? . . . all the evenings I thought he was here studying! . . . it can only mean one thing! . . . a girl! . . . not a good girl! . . . it must be that Fife girl! . . . but I simply can't believe! . . . *(She goes to the window, peering out but keeping her head carefully inside—with fierce jealousy.)* That dirty little . . . I'd like to see her try to catch my Reuben! . . . *(There is a strong flash of distant lightning that suddenly reveals Reuben in his hiding-place by the hedge. She gives a gasp.)* Oh! . . . there he is! . . . watching their house! . . . I've got to make sure! . . . Oh, Reuben, I can't believe it, you've never noticed girls! . . .

There is darkness for a moment—(as if the moon had passed behind a cloud)—to mark the end of SCENE ONE. *No time elapses between* SCENES ONE *and* TWO.

SCENE TWO

SCENE. *When it grows light again the outer walls of the two rooms in the Light home have been replaced, while the interiors of the Fife sitting-room and the couple's bedroom above it are now revealed. There is one small window on the top floor front of the Light home, two on the ground floor. Mrs. Light's head can be seen peering out of the side bedroom window at Reuben, crouched in the shadow of the lilacs. The two rooms in the Fife home, bright with all their electric lights on, are of a glaring newness. There is a table at centre, front, in the sitting-room, a Victrola in the rear corner, left, near the door in the left wall which leads to the hall. In the right wall are three windows looking out on the lawn toward the lilac hedge and the Light home. These windows are repeated in the same series in the bedroom above. The bed is at left, front, its head against the left wall. In the same wall to the rear of the bed, is the door. There is a dressing table with a big mirror against the rear wall, right, near the windows.*

Ramsay Fife is seated at the left of the table, glancing through the pages of a technical book on Hydro-Electric Engineering. His wife is lying back in a chaise longue that she has pushed close to the windows on the right so she can stare up at the sky.

Fife is a small wiry man of fifty, of Scotch-Irish origin, with a sharp face and keen black eyes. His thin mouth is full of the malicious humour of the practical joker. He has a biting tongue, but at bottom is a good-natured man except where the religious bigotry of his atheism is concerned.

His wife is tall and stout, weighing well over two hundred. Her face must have once been one of those rosy-cheeked pretty doll-like faces, and in spite of its fat, it has kept its girlish naïveté and fresh complexion. Her figure is not formless nor flabby. It suggests, rather, an inert strength. A mass of heavy copper-coloured hair is piled without apparent design around her face. Her mouth is small, with full lips. Her eyes are round and dark blue. Their expression is blank and dreamy. Her voice is sentimental and wondering. She is about forty years old.

Their daughter, Ada, sixteen, who is upstairs in the bedroom putting on a heavy make-up of rouge and mascara, resembles her father more than her mother. She has his alert quality. Her pretty face, with her mother's big blue eyes, is alive and keen, her mouth has a touch of her father's malicious humour. Her brown hair is boyishly bobbed. Her manner is self-assertive and consciously slangy. She is at the stage where being a hardened flapper is her frank ambition as her short skirts and obtrusive make-up give evidence. Beneath her flip talk, however, one senses a strong trace of her mother's sentimentality.

MRS. FIFE (*dreaming sentimentally*). I hear Ada upstairs . . . she's primping up before my mirror . . . she's falling in love . . . it's nice to be in love in May . . . I love May better than any other month . . . May is when I first met Ramsay . . . it's warm to-night . . . I mustn't forget to make Ramsay change to his summer underwear this week . . . he always wears his heavies too long and gets prickly heat and then he's terrible cross . . .

FIFE (*reading—disgustedly*). "Hydro-Electric engineering" . . . it's studying this stuff gives those stuck-up engineers their diplomas . . . "Frequency and number of phases" . . . "Inherent Regulations" . . . "Parallel Working" . . . "Wave Form" . . . diagrams and equations ! . . . "The kinetic energy of a rotor of diameter D and axial length L, running at a speed of rotation *n*, is theoretically proportional to D4 L*n*2" . . . arrh ! . . . the devil take their theories ! . . . when anything goes wrong at the plant it's me who fixes it without any theory ! . . . (*He tosses the book on the table and speaks to his wife.*) I wish Townsend wouldn't go forcing his books on me, telling me I owe it to myself to pass for engineer's papers. (*With a chuckle.*) Him arguing with me and at the same time admitting "Fife, you know a damn sight more about this game than I do."

MRS. FIFE (*mooning at him with adoring eyes—simply*). You know more than anyone, Ramsay.

FIFE (*pleased, but amused—teasing her as he would a big child*). Oho, I do, do I ? How the hell do you know? (*Then complacently.*) Well, I do know more than most. There isn't a damn job in the game I haven't had a hand at some time or another.

(*He looks at her and sees she is not listening any more.*) Look at her! . . . in a dope dream again . . . I might as well be married to a cow . . . (*Then amusedly.*) Well, she's a damn funny woman . . . I've never seen her equal anywhere . . .

(*He sees the newspaper on the table and reaches for it. He glances at the headlines and settles down to reading with a grunt of awakened interest.*)

MRS. FIFE (*has again fallen to dreaming sentimentally of the past*). When I first met Ramsay he was a linesman . . . I loved him at first sight . . . he was so romantic looking with those steel climbing things on his legs . . . and he wore a coloured handkerchief round his neck just like a cowboy . . . Pa and Ma warned me linesmen were no good . . . they just ruined you and went their way . . . they were wrong about Ramsay . . . except he did ruin me . . . I said, why is it wrong when I love him? . . . Pa yelled to get out, I'd disgraced the family . . . I never expected Ramsay'd marry me . . . he was the roving kind . . . but as soon as he knew he'd got me into trouble he spoke right up . . . "Oh, hell, then I guess I've got to marry you" . . . and I said yes, and I was awful happy . . . and five months after Ada was born and he was crazy about her from the first . . . and we've all been happy ever since . . . (*She sighs contentedly.*)

ADA (*in the bedroom above, finishes making up and inspects herself critically in the mirror—approvingly*). I got to hand it to you, baby, you're there! . . . Gosh, how long is it since I put on that record? . . . Rube'll be waiting . . . he's as bashful as a kid . . . but that's what I like about him . . . I'm sick of these fresh guys that think all they have to do is wink and you fall! . . . Rube has got honest-to-God feelings . . . but of course, I'd never love him . . . he's too big a Mamma's boy for me . . . (*She goes to the door and puts her hand on the switch.*) Well, let's go . . . I'm dying to see if he'll have nerve enough to kiss me . . . (*She turns out the light.*)

REUBEN (*crouched by the hedge, gives a start as a flash of lightning flickers over the sky*). Gosh, I wish Ada'd hurry up . . . this isn't much fun . . . I'm losing all my nerve waiting . . .

MRS. LIGHT (*bending out of the window in Reuben's bedroom—in suspense between suspicion and hope*). She doesn't seem to be coming . . . maybe it's only some game he's playing . . . waiting to scare some friend of his . . .

FIFE (*looking up from his paper with a snort of rage and disgust just as Ada enters the room*). The bloody swinepot!

ADA (*comes and puts an arm around his shoulder teasingly*). What's the bad news, Pop? Has another Fundamentalist been denying Darwin?

FIFE (*boiling over with indignation, thrusting the paper on her, his finger pointing out the article*). Read this and you won't joke about it! (*As Ada begins to read, he speaks to his wife.*) Of all the yellow tricks!

MRS. FIFE (*coming out of her dream with a start*). What, Ramsay?

FIFE. This story in the paper! There was a man in Ohio many years back killed another fellow in a fight about a girl. He got twenty years for it, but the girl helped him to escape and they both got clean away to the Coast, where he settled down under another name and they were married and had a daughter. He became one of the town's best citizens, and damned if his daughter didn't get engaged to the minister's son! Then, just before the wedding, the old man feels he's honour bound to tell his future son-in-law the secret of his past; so the damned idiot blathers the whole story of his killing the man and breaking jail! And what do you suppose that young skunk does? Breaks off with the girl and goes to the police with the story, saying he's bound by his conscience to squeal on him!

ADA (*who has finished reading the story*). Phew! Some louse, that boy!

FIFE. Arrh! They're all the same, the Bible-punching breed! (*Then with a touch of severity.*) And mind you bear that in mind, young lady, when you're fooling with that young ass next door!

ADA. Hey listen, Pop! Honestly, I think you've got a nerve to— Why, it was you said to start up an acquaintance with him, when I told you I'd caught him staring at me, because you knew how it'd get his old man's goat!

FIFE (*his sense of humour returning—with a malicious grin*). Aye, it will that! I gave him a strong hint on the street to-day that upset him. Oh, if you'd only make a prize jackass of that yellow Nancy son of his !

ADA. Say, why have you got it in for Rube so ? He's not to blame for his father. (*Then hastily.*) Not that it's anything in my young life. I'm simply having fun kidding him along. (*Then defensively again.*) But Rube's a good scout—in his way. He isn't yellow.

MRS. FIFE (*suddenly—with a placid certainty*). You're falling in love, Ada.

ADA (*confused*). Aw, Mom, where d'you get that stuff ?

FIFE (*has glanced at her with suspicion*). So you don't believe that lad's yellow, don't you ? What'll you bet he isn't ? (*Then as she doesn't answer.*) I dare you to bring him in to-night, and let me talk to him and you listen, and if I don't show him up yellow then I'll buy you the best dress you can find in the town ! (*As she hesitates—tauntingly.*) Are you afraid to take me up ?

ADA (*with defensive flippancy, turns to go*). I'll think about it. There's a dress in Steele's I've had my eye on. (*She goes out the door on left.*)

FIFE (*looks after her—frowning*). She acts queer about him . . . it's time I took a hand in this . . . I've got to fix up a scheme on him quick . . . she'll bring him back if she has to drag him . . .

ADA (*has come out of the house by the front door, off left, and enters from the left, then hesitates for a moment, debating with herself*). Shall I make him come in ? . . . he'll be scared stiff ! . . . but Pop was only bluffing . . . well, I'll just call his bluff ! . . . He can't get away with that stuff with me ! . . . (*She walks toward the gap in the hedge.*)

MRS. LIGHT (*has caught a glimpse of her from the window*). There she comes now ! . . .

ADA (*calling*). Rube.

REUBEN (*comes through the hedge to her—sheepishly*). Hello, Ada. (*Then, as he stands beside her, looking down into her face, a sudden thrill of desire almost overcomes his timidity.*) Gosh, Ada—you're pretty in the moonlight. I—I wish— (*His courage fails him—lamely.*) It's certainly grand to-night, isn't it ?

ADA. Yeah. It's great. (*She takes one of his hands.*) Come on in my house and meet Pop. I want you to see he isn't the devil out of hell your old man makes him out to be.

REUBEN (*immediately terrified*). I can't, Ada ! You know I can't ! Why don't we walk the same as——

ADA. I'm sick of walking. (*As he still holds back—tauntingly.*) Are you scared Pop will eat you ? You make me sick, Rube !

REUBEN. It's not because I'm scared of your father ; it's because——

ADA. Afraid your Mamma would spank you if she found out ? (*Then as he still hesitates.*) Oh, very well, you know what you can do, don't you ? (*She turns her back on him and walks away.*)

REUBEN. Ada ! Wait a minute ! Please don't get sore ! I'll come !

ADA. Good boy ! (*She suddenly raises herself on tiptoe and kisses him—with a little laugh.*) There ! That's to help keep your nerve up !

REUBEN (*a wave of passion coming over him, grabs her by the shoulders and bends his face close to hers*). Ada !

ADA. Ouch ! That hurts, Rube !

REUBEN. I don't care if it does ! I love you, Ada ! (*He tries to kiss her.*)

ADA (*struggling away from him*). Hey, cut it out ! What do you think I am ? (*Then, as, brought back to himself, he releases her in shamefaced confusion, she adds tartly, her confidence restored and her temper a bit ruffled.*) Listen here, Rube, just because I kissed you in fun, don't get too fresh !

REUBEN. I—I didn't mean nothing bad—honest I didn't !

ADA. All right, only don't get rough again. (*Taking his hand—in a bullying tone.*) Come on ! Let's go in !

(*Reuben follows her off left mechanically, a look of growing dread on his face.*)

MRS. LIGHT. She kissed him ! . . . the brazen little harlot ! . . . where is she taking him ? . . . I've got to stop her ! . . .

(*She draws back quickly from the window.*)

FIFE (*irritably*). May the devil kill me if I can think up a good scheme . . .

(He turns his exasperation on his wife.) How can I think in the same room with you? It's like trying to swim in glue! For God's sake, get out of here!

MRS. FIFE *(raises herself to her feet placidly, without a trace of resentment).* I'll go upstairs and read the paper.

FIFE *(starts to thrust the paper on her).* Here you are then! *(But as he does so his eye lights on the same headline that had attracted his attention before and suddenly he has an inspiration and grins elatedly.)* By God, I've got it, May! I'll try that on him! All the pious folks in this town think I've a bad record behind me— *(He pushes the paper into her hands.)* Get out of here quick! I don't want you around to give me away!

(She goes out. He waits, looking at the door, a grin of malicious expectancy on his face. At this moment Mrs. Light, who has come out by her kitchen door, appears around the corner of her house and slinks hurriedly across the patch of lawn to the shadow of the lilacs at the extreme edge of the hedge, front.)

MRS. LIGHT *(peers stealthily around the corner of the hedge down the street—in an extreme state of agitation).* I can't see them . . . they're hiding somewhere . . . she'll be kissing him . . . oh, just wait till I tell her what I think of her! . . . *(She starts out of the shadow of the lilacs as if to go down the street, but the brightness of the moonlight frightens her and she moves quickly back into the shadow.)* Supposing anyone should see me! . . . oh, I don't know what to do! . . . that nasty wicked boy! . . . he'll be punished good for this! . . .

(There is darkness again for a moment, to mark the end of SCENE TWO. *No time elapses between* SCENES TWO *and* THREE.*)*

SCENE THREE

SCENE. *When the light comes on again, the wall of the Fife bedroom has been replaced. Their sitting-room is revealed as before with Fife still sitting looking expectantly at the door. And now the interior of the Light sitting-room is again shown with Light sitting as at the end of* SCENE ONE. *He holds the open Bible but he is staring moodily over it. Mrs. Light, as before, is hiding in the shadow of the lilac hedge, peering down the road, ashamed of her position and afraid she will be discovered.*

LIGHT *(thinking gloomily).* I must be honest with myself . . . who am I to cast the first stone at Reuben if he desires a woman? . . . hasn't my love for Amelia been one long desire of the senses? . . . I should understand Reuben's weakness and forgive him . . . *(Then his resentment smouldering up.)* But to betray me to Fife! . . . that would go deeper! . . . it would be treachery to God! . . .

MRS. FIFE *(leans out of the front window of the bedroom upstairs).* I don't want to read the paper . . . I'd rather look at the moon . . . *(Mooning up at the moon.)* Ada loves that Light boy . . . he must be nice . . . he isn't to blame because his father believes in religion . . . maybe his father is nice too if you got to know him off the job . . . Ramsay is always so cranky when he's at the plant . . . I love the plant . . . I love the dynamos . . . I could sit for ever and listen to them sing . . . they're always singing about everything in the world . . .

(She hums to herself for a moment—an imitation of the metallic purr of a dynamo.)

MRS. LIGHT *(hearing this noise, looks up around the corner of the hedge and sees her and immediately dissolves into abject shame and fright).* Oh, my God! . . . did she see me? . . . she'll tell the whole town I was spying! . . . Oh, this is terrible! . . . I ought to get Hutchins! . . . but I can't move while she's watching! . . .

FIFE *(standing up and looking at the door).* Ada's a long time bringing him . . . there's a lot of whispering in the hall . . . he's afraid, I'm thinking . . . about to enter the presence of Satan . . . I'll have to start in making him think that I'm the devil himself! . . .

(Ada comes in the doorway of the sitting-room, left, followed by Reuben, whose face wears an expression of mingled apprehension and bravado.)

FIFE *(without waiting for an introduction, goes up and shakes Reuben's hand with an exaggerated cordiality*). So you're young Mr. Light, are you? I'm damned glad to make your acquaintance. Sit down and make yourself at home.

(*All the time he is talking, he stares at Reuben's flustered face, keenly sizing him up. He forces him to sit in the chair across the table from him. Ada sits down at right, watching her father with a challenging smile.*)

REUBEN (*stammers*). Pleased to meet you. Thank you. Thanks.

FIFE (*with a sudden change to severity*). I want a damned serious talk with you, young man! That's why I had Ada invite you in! (*As Reuben stares at him bewilderedly.*) But before we start that, let me ask you, is your reverend father ever going to take up my challenge to debate with me?

REUBEN (*shamefacedly*). I—I don't think so.

FIFE (*jeeringly*). He's afraid I'd beat him.

REUBEN (*defensively*). No, he isn't! He can answer all your arguments easy—with things right out of the Bible! He's only scared that folks'd think he was wrong to argue with you! (*Then raising his voice defiantly.*) But I'd argue with you if I was in his place!

MRS. LIGHT (*from her hiding-place by the hedge has caught Reuben's raised voice—with horrified stupefaction*). That was Reuben's voice! . . . he's actually in there talking to that atheist! . . . Oh, I wish I could get closer the window! . . . but she'd see me! . . .

(*But she comes around the end of the hedge as far as she can get and strains her ears.*)

FIFE (*smiling mockingly at Reuben*). Well, maybe after you're a minister you and me'll argue it out some time.

REUBEN (*glad to make a show of his independence before Fife*). I'm not going to be a minister! Father wants me to, but Mother doesn't—and I don't want to be. Besides, I've never felt the call. You have to feel God calling you to His service.

FIFE (*with a leer*). And how does God call you, tell me? I'm thinkin' He wouldn't use the telegraph or telephone or radio, for they're contraptions that belong to His arch-enemy, Lucifer, the God of Electricity.

(*Reuben's face has flushed with mingled indignation and fear. He looks up at the ceiling apprehensively, then opens his mouth to make some retort to Fife when there is a vivid flash of lightning. He gives a start and half rises from his chair, controlling an impulse to run from the room. Fife's keen eyes are watching him and he grins with satisfaction.*)

REUBEN (*stammers*). You better not—talk like that, or—you better look out!

FIFE. What's the trouble, young fellow? Are you afraid of a bit of lightning? Don't worry about me. The devil looks after his own! But a minister's son has reason to worry, maybe, when he's in a den of atheism, holding intimate converse with a damned man! I'm thinking your Jehovah might aim a thunderbolt at me but Lucifer would deflect it on to you—and he's the better electrical expert of the two, being more modern in his methods than your God!

REUBEN (*in a turmoil of guilt and fright*). I wish I'd never come here! . . . God may strike him! . . . He certainly ought to! . . . if I was God, I'd kill him for blaspheming like that! . . .

ADA (*observing Reuben—worriedly*). Why did the poor boob let Pop get wise he was scared of lightning. (*Then indignantly.*) Pop has no right to pick on religion! . . . that's hitting below the belt! . . .

(*Protestingly.*) Aw, Pop, lay off religion, can't you!

FIFE (*glances at her irritably—then with a calculating tone to Reuben*). Ada's right, Mr. Light. I didn't have you in to convert you to atheism. This is a free country and you're free to believe any God-forsaken lie you like—even the book of Genesis! (*Then solemnly.*) But here's what I did have you in for, and I'll come right to the point. As a father, I want to know what your intentions are regarding my daughter!

(*Reuben stares at him in open-mouthed amazement.*)

ADA (*embarrassed but cannot help a giggle of amusement when she looks at Reuben*). Aw, Pop, what——

FIFE. Keep your tongue out of this! (*Sternly, to Reuben.*) I trust you mean honourably by her, young fellow, or it'll be the worse for you! I'll have no young spark seducing my daughter—getting her with child, maybe, and then deserting her with no marriage lines to save her from disgrace!

(*Ada begins to see this as a huge joke, and she has to bury her face in her hands to choke back her laughter as she looks at Reuben's face, on which is at first a shocked look of stupefaction. But this gives way to a fit of indignation that anyone could think him so low.*)

REUBEN. What do you think I am? You have no right to say that about me! I'm not that kind of— (*Then his voice booming like his father's with moral self-righteousness.*) I respect Ada just as much as I do my mother! I'm going to marry her!

ADA (*genuinely flustered—trying to laugh it off*). Gee, Rube, did I say you had no nerve? I take it all back!

(*Reuben's nerve immediately deserts him. He hangs his head in acute embarrassment, his eyes on the floor.*)

MRS. LIGHT (*by the end of the hedge*). Marry her! . . . I heard it clear as day! . . . respect her like he does me! . . . damn her! . . . Oh, I didn't mean to swear! . . . I don't know what I'm doing! . . . (*Then weeping hysterically and trying to stifle it.*) Oh, I'll get Hutchins to beat him within an inch of his life! . . . (*She sinks down on the ground, her hands over her face.*) I've got to stop! . . . she'll hear me up there! . . . she'll tell how I was crying! . . .

MRS. FIFE (*has noticed the noise of Mrs. Light's movements and looks down vaguely*). Some animal's in the garden . . . maybe it's a skunk . . . I'd love to have a skunk-skin coat next winter . . . maybe Ramsay'll give me one for Christmas . . . Ramsay calls the minister a skunk . . . poor Mr. Light! . . . Ramsay says awful mean things sometimes . . . but it's only because he loves to make jokes . . . he's the kindest man in the world! . . .

FIFE (*pretending to be sunk in thought, has been staring calculatingly at Reuben—solemnly*). Young man, I'll be honest with you. In view of your honourable intentions I feel bound by my conscience to let you know the secret of the family you're wanting to marry into. But you must give me your word of honour, as man to man—I don't ask you to swear on the Bible—that you'll never repeat what I'm saying to anyone, no matter how dreadful it seems to you! Will you give me your word?

REUBEN (*made visibly uneasy, but forcing a manly tone*). Sure. I wouldn't ever say anything.

ADA (*leaning forward in her chair and watching her father worriedly*). What's Pop going to spring? . . . Rube's looking pale behind the gills, poor guy! . . . aw, poor nothing! . . . he ought to have more guts! . . .

FIFE (*with a tragic sigh*). There's not a living soul knows it, barring my wife and Ada. It's like putting my life in your hands. You know, don't you, that no one knows what I done before I came to this town, nor where I came from. I've good reason for keeping it dark. Listen now. Twenty years ago there was a man by the name of Andrew Clark lived in the town of Arming, Ohio— (*He pauses significantly, giving a quick side glance at Ada to see if she's caught the joke.*)

ADA (*a light breaking on her*). Gee, it's that newspaper story! . . . he's going to pretend he's . . . (*Then indignantly.*) Does he think Rube'd ever do what that skunk did? . . .

FIFE (*goes on with a guilty furtiveness—lowering his voice*). Now Clark was in love with a girl whose family had got her engaged to another fellow, but she loved Clark and used to meet him in the woods. But this fellow who was engaged to her got suspicious and one night he sneaked up on them lying in each other's arms—in sin, as you'd call it—and he rushed out with a knife at them both, but Clark picked up an axe and split his skull! (*He finishes up with well-feigned savagery.*) And serve him right, the bloody sneak!

REUBEN (*stares at Fife with horror—stammers weakly*). You mean—Clark murdered him?

FIFE (*with a great pretence of guilt-stricken protest*). Oh, don't say that! Not murder! He killed him in self-defence—when he was crazy with rage and love. Wouldn't you do the same if Ada was the girl and you was Clark?

REUBEN. What is he asking? . . . Ada? . . . would I? . . . (*Then his horror turning to a confused rage.*) I'd kill Ada if I caught her! . . . but it was the other man who caught! . . . and they were engaged, too! . . . she belonged to him! . . .

(*Harshly and condemningly—in his father's tone.*) That other fellow should have killed them, that's what I think! That girl was engaged to the other fellow! She had no right to love Clark! That wasn't love, it was lust! She was an adulteress! It would have been only her just punishment if that fellow had killed her! I would have!

FIFE. For the love of God, don't be so hard—for what I was coming to tell you was that I was Clark!

(*As if to punctuate this dramatic confession, there is a flash of lightning, brighter than any that has gone before.*)

REUBEN (*clutches the arms of his chair in superstitious terror, all the passion drained out of him instantly, leaving him weak and penitent*). Oh, God, please forgive me! . . . I didn't mean it! . . . I wouldn't ever kill her! . . . (*Then glancing at Fife with fear.*) He's a murderer! . . . he said himself he was damned . . .

FIFE (*eyeing Reuben keenly*). After I'd killed him I gave myself up. The jury said it was murder in the second degree and gave me twenty years—but I fooled 'em with the help of the girl and escaped and we both ran off to the far west and settled down in Niclum, California, and I married her under the name of Fife and we had a daughter. That's Ada.

REUBEN (*keeping his eyes averted from Ada*). Then that's her mother! . . . she's the daughter of an adulteress! . . . and a murderer! . . . how can I ever trust her? . . . she's gone around with lots of fellows . . . how do I know she never—? . . . (*Then torturedly.*) Oh, God, why did I ever come here to-night? . . .

FIFE (*with a great pretence of uneasiness*). You don't say a word. Well, maybe I shouldn't have told you, because now I've made you an accessory in the murder, for you'll be shielding me unlawfully by keeping silence! And the devil knows what sin you'll think it in the sight of God!

(*The clap of thunder from the preceding flash comes with a great rumble.*)

REUBEN (*filled with fear*). Accessory! . . . the police can arrest me! . . . (*Then summoning his manhood.*) But I won't tell them! . . . ever! . . . I gave my word! . . . (*Then conscience-stricken.*) But God! . . . I'll be guilty before God! . . . but He knows I gave my word! . . . but does that count with Him? . . . when I didn't swear on the Bible? . . . (*Then frantically.*) But He knows I love Ada! . . . He wouldn't want me to tell on her father . . .

(*He suddenly jumps up and mumbles to Fife.*) I won't tell the police, you needn't worry.

ADA (*with a triumphant glance at her father*). Good for you, Rube!

REUBEN (*avoiding her eyes*). I've got to go home now.

FIFE (*searching Reuben's face—insistently*). I'm sorry to put such a load on your conscience, Mr. Light, but I felt it was only right of me.

REUBEN. Why does he rub it in? . . . God, I hate him! . . . I wish they'd hanged him! . . .

(*Angrily—his voice booming denouncingly like his father's.*) You needn't be afraid I'll tell—but you ought to go and tell yourself! You know you're guilty in the sight of God! Do you want to burn for ever in hell?

FIFE (*tauntingly*). Your hell and God mean no more to me than old women's nonsense when they're scared of the dark!

REUBEN (*threateningly*). Don't you dare talk like that! I won't stand for it—not now! If you don't stop your blaspheming, I'll—I mean, it'd serve you right if I— (*Hurrying toward the door as if in flight.*) I got to get home. (*He stops at the door and turns to Ada, but keeps his eyes averted.*) Good night, Ada. (*He goes out.*)

ADA. He was threatening Pop already he'd tell on him! . . . Gee, he is yellow all right! . . . (*Tears of mortification and genuine hurt come to her eyes—she brushes them back.*) Aw, what do I care about him? . . .

FIFE (*with a chuckle*). He'll be blabbin' my dreadful secret to his old man yet, wait and see!

ADA (*to his surprise, turns on him angrily*). It wasn't fair! He never had a chance!

(*She flings herself on the chaise longue and begins to cry.*)

FIFE (*stares at her in astonishment*). Are you turning against me—for that lump! (*Then he comes and pats her on the shoulder.*) I was only doing it for your sake, Ada. You ought to see him in his true colours so you'd not be thinking too much about him.

ADA (*forces back her tears and jumps up*). I didn't think anything! Leave me alone about him, can't you? (*With a great pretence of indifference she gets a book from the table and sits down again.*) I should worry about that poor fish! I've got to study my algebra.

(*Her father stares at her puzzledly. There is a bright flash of lightning and Light, sitting as before in the sitting-room of the other house reading the Bible, jumps nervously to his feet.*)

LIGHT. I ought to conquer that silly fear in myself . . . the lightning is God's will . . . what on earth can Amelia be doing with Reuben all this time? . . . (*He listens for a moment—uneasily.*) I'll go upstairs to them . . . she should be more considerate than to leave me alone when . . .

(*He walks toward the door on right.*)

(*There is a pause of darkness here to mark the end of* SCENE THREE. *In this darkness the clap of thunder from the preceding flash comes. No time elapses between Scenes Three and Four.*)

SCENE FOUR

SCENE. *When the light comes on again—but this time very dimly, as if the moon were behind clouds—the walls of the Fife and Light sitting-rooms have been replaced, while the interior of Reuben's bedroom is now revealed.*

Mrs. Fife still leans out of her bedroom window and Mrs. Light sits crouching by the hedge.

MRS. LIGHT (*suddenly jumping to her feet and peering up through the leaves at Mrs. Fife*). Oh God, isn't she ever going in? . . . I'll scream in a minute! . . .

MRS. FIFE. I love to watch lightning . . . the thunder clouds are getting nearer the moon . . . I'd like to be a cloud . . . it must be nice to float in the wind . . . but it must be getting bed-time . . .

(*She slowly backs herself into her room.*)

MRS. LIGHT (*as Mrs. Fife disappears*). Now I can get Hutchins . . .

(*She slinks back along the hedge and then quickly across the lawn around the corner of her house just as Reuben enters from the left by the Fife house.*)

REUBEN (*stands hesitating—uneasily*). I thought I'd walk around and think up some lie . . . Mother'll guess something's wrong as soon as she looks at me . . . but I'm not going to stay out in the storm . . . (*He walks slowly over to where he had stood with Ada—dully.*) Here's where she kissed me . . . why couldn't we have gone for a walk? . . . she'd have let me kiss her, . . . I'd have had her in my arms . . . like her mother was with Clark? . . . no, I didn't mean that! . . . I didn't mean sin! . . . (*Then with desperate bravado.*) Aw, what is sin, anyway? . . . maybe that's just old women's nonsense, like Fife says! . . . why should I have a guilty conscience? . . . it's God's fault! . . . why hasn't He done something to Fife? . . . I should think He'd have to punish adultery and murder . . . if there is any God . . . (*There is a great flash of lightning and he stands paralysed with superstitious terror.*) It comes every time! . . . when I deny! . . . (*More and more obsessed by a feeling of guilt, of being a condemned sinner alone in the threatening night.*) Fife's damned me with him! . . . there's no use praying! . . . it's getting black! . . . I'm afraid of God! . . .

(*There is a crash of thunder. He cowers, trembling—then cries like a frightened little boy.*) Mother! Mother!

(*He runs off right, forgetting that he has sneaked out by the back, making for the front door. At the same moment Light can be dimly made out as he enters Reuben's bedroom, and Fife sticks his head out of his sitting-room window and looks toward the Light home.*)

FIFE. That was him I heard passing . . . I'll wait here and watch the fun . . . (*He chuckles to himself.*)

LIGHT (*pauses just inside the door in alarm at finding the room dark and empty—calls uneasily*). Amelia! Reuben!

(*He lights a match with trembling fingers and hurries over to the lamp and lights it. His wife's voice comes excitedly from the hall-way, calling.*)

MRS. LIGHT. Hutchins!

LIGHT (*hurries to the door, meeting her as she comes in*). Amelia! Thank God!

MRS. LIGHT (*excitedly, her words pouring out*). Oh, Hutchins, something awful has happened—that Fife girl—I heard Reuben asking Fife if he could marry her!

(*Light, completely stunned, stares at her blankly. There is the noise of the front door being slammed and Reuben's voice calling desperately.*)

REUBEN. Mother! Where are you?

MRS. LIGHT. Sshh! Let him come up here. (*Pushing him toward the closet in rear.*) You hide in that closet and listen! I'll make him acknowledge everything! He'd only lie to you! (*Vindictively.*) I promise I won't stand between him and punishment this time! (*She gives him a final shove inside the door and closes it.*)

REUBEN (*his voice comes from the hall as he rushes upstairs*). Mother! (*A second later he runs in and, too distracted to notice her expression, throws his arms around her.*) Mother! (*He breaks down and sobs.*)

MRS. LIGHT (*alarmed by the state he is in, puts her arms around him, her immediate reaction one of maternal tenderness. She leads him front and sits on the side of the bed*). There, there! It's all right, Reuben! Mother's here! (*Then indignantly.*) What have those awful people been doing to my boy to get him in such a state? (*As he gives a start—sharply.*) Now don't deny you were there! Don't make matters worse by lying! What happened between you and that man? Tell Mother!

REUBEN (*brokenly*). I can't! I promised him I wouldn't. I can't tell anyone!

MRS. LIGHT (*changing to a tone of wheedling affection*). Yes, you can, Reuben. You can always tell Mother everything. You always have.

REUBEN (*clinging to her*). I love Mother better'n anything in the world . . . she always forgives me . . . I wish I could tell her . . . she'd know what was right . . .

(*There is a bright flash of lightning. He shrinks closer to her and blurts out.*) I'm scared, Mother! I'm guilty! I'm damned.

MRS. LIGHT (*startled*). Guilty? . . . does he mean he? . . . (*With sudden strong revulsion.*) And to think he's had those same arms hugging that little filthpot this very evening! . . .

(*She pushes him away, but, holding his shoulders, stares down into his face.*) Do you mean to say you refuse to tell your own mother, just because you were forced into promising not to by that atheist? Then all I can say is that my boy I thought I could trust has turned into a liar and a sneak, and I don't wonder you feel guilty in God's sight!

(*As she finishes speaking, the roll of the thunder from the preceding flash comes crashing and rumbling. Reuben sinks down on his knees beside her, hiding his face in her lap.*)

REUBEN (*stammers*). I'll tell you, Mother—if you promise to keep it a secret—just between me and you—and never tell Father.

MRS. LIGHT. All right. I'll promise I won't tell your father.

REUBEN (*made uneasy by something in her tone—insistently*). You'll swear it on the Bible?

MRS. LIGHT. Yes, I'll swear on the Bible I won't tell him.

REUBEN (*in a passion of eagerness to get the guilty tale off his conscience*). His name isn't even Fife, it's Clark! He changed it because he'd murdered a man out in Ohio where he used to live. He got twenty years but he escaped and ran away to California! Fife's a murderer, that's what he really is!

(*While he has been telling this story, the closet door has opened and Light stands there, listening greedily. In his hand is a belt of Reuben's.*)

LIGHT (*thinking with a fierce, revengeful joy*). Lord God of Righteous Vengeance, I thank Thee! . . . at last Thou strikest! . . .

MRS. LIGHT (*dumbfounded, not knowing what to make of this strange tale—and disappointed that it is not a confession about Ada*). Wherever did you get hold of this story?

REUBEN. He told me himself!

MRS. LIGHT. Do you expect me to believe Fife's such an idiot as to confess such things to you?

REUBEN. He had a good reason to tell me! I asked him if I could marry Ada and he thought he was honour bound to tell me ! He knew it'd be safe with me when I gave him my word——

(*Then thinking with guilty shame.*) But I've told ! . . . I've just told ! . . . why did I ? . . . Oh, how Ada would hate me if she knew ! . . .

(*Pleadingly.*) Remember you swore on the Bible you'd never tell ! Remember, Mother !

MRS. LIGHT (*still gripping him, glaring into his face vindictively*). So you want to marry that little harlot, do you ?

REUBEN (*shakes her hands off his shoulders—shrinking back from her, still on his knees*). Don't you say that, Mother ? I love Ada, Mother ! I love her with all my heart !

MRS. LIGHT (*calls over her shoulder*). Do you hear that, Hutchins ?

LIGHT (*grimly*). Yes, I hear. (*He takes a threatening step forward.*)

REUBEN. Father !

(*Then his eyes turn to his mother's vindictive face and he thinks in a tortured agony of spirit.*) He was hiding in the closet ! . . . she knew it ! . . . she cheated me ! . . . when I trusted her ! . . . when I loved her better than anyone in the world ! . . .

(*He cries out in a passion of reproach.*) Oh Mother ! Mother !

MRS. LIGHT (*misunderstanding this as a plea*). No, you needn't think I'm going to get you off this time ! You punish him good, Hutchins ! The very idea—kissing that dirty little ——!

REUBEN. Don't you say that !

LIGHT (*walks toward him*). Hold your tongue ! How dare you address your mother——! (*Reuben cowers into the left corner front, his eyes fixed on the belt his father has in his hand.*) Get down on your knees !

REUBEN (*obeys mechanically, his thoughts whirling in his head*). Belt . . . Mother's face . . . she looks terrible . . . she wants him to beat me . . . she wants to hear me yell . . . (*Then with a defiant determination as if some hidden strength in him had suddenly been tapped.*) But I won't give her the satisfaction ! . . . no matter how it hurts ! . . .

LIGHT. Let this put back the fear of God into your sinful heart, Reuben !

(*He brings the belt down heavily across Reuben's back. Reuben quivers, but not a sound comes from his lips. At the same moment there is a glaring flash of lightning and Light cringes back with a frightened exclamation.*)

MRS. LIGHT (*has winced when Reuben was hit—conscience-strickenly*). That must have hurt dreadfully ! . . . poor Reuben ! . . . (*Then with an exasperated sense of frustration, gazing at Reuben's set face.*) Why doesn't he cry ? . . . if he'd cry I'd stop Hutchins . . . that girl has changed him ! . . .

REUBEN (*expecting the next blow, thinking with a grim elation*). Come on ! . . . hit again ! . . . hit a million times ! . . . you can't make me show her you hurt me ! . . . (*Then stealing a glance up at his father's face.*) He looks scared ! . . . it was that lightning ! . . . I'll never be scared of lightning again ! . . . (*Then resolutely.*) I'll be damned if I'm going to let him beat me ! . . .

(*He jumps to his feet and faces his father defiantly, with hatred in his eyes.*)

LIGHT (*guiltily*). I can't bear him looking at me like that ! . . . I really ought to feel grateful to him . . . his folly has delivered Fife into my hands . . .

(*He throws the belt on the bed—to his wife.*) Reuben's punishment can wait. I have my duty of denouncing that murderer to the proper authorities. (*Triumphantly.*) Haven't I always said, if the truth were known, that man was a criminal ! (*Turning toward the door.*) Keep Reuben here. He might warn Fife. I'll lock this door after me. (*Then hurriedly, as a crash of thunder comes.*) I must hurry. I want to get to the police station before the rain. (*He shuts the door behind him and locks it.*)

REUBEN (*staring after him with the same fixed look of hate—calls jeeringly*). Look out for the lightning ! (*Then he turns to his mother with a sneer—contemptuously.*) Picture my being scared of that boob all my life ! What did you ever see in him, to marry him ? He's yellow !

MRS. LIGHT (*frightened by the change in him, but attempting a bullying tone*). How dare you talk so disrespectfully——!

REUBEN. But you're yellow, too. And I'm yellow. How could I help being ? It's in my blood. (*Harshly.*) But I'll get him out of my blood, by God! And I'll get you out, too!

MRS. LIGHT (*pitiably now*). What have I done, Reuben?

REUBEN (*bitterly*). You knew he was in that closet! You led me on to tell! I thought you loved me better'n anyone, and you'd never squeal on me to him! (*He starts to break down miserably.*)

MRS. LIGHT (*goes to him as if to take him in her arms*). I do love you better than anyone, Reuben! I didn't mean——

REUBEN (*steps back from her—accusingly*). And you called Ada a harlot—after I told you I loved her with all my heart. (*Then a note of pleading in his voice.*) Do you mean you didn't mean that part of it—about her?

MRS. LIGHT (*immediately furious again*). Yes, I did mean it about her! I meant it and a lot more!

REUBEN. Then I'm through with you! And as for him——!

(*He suddenly is reminded of something—thinking wildly.*) He went! . . . police station! . . . that'll finish me with Ada! . . . (*There is the noise of the front door slamming.*) There's the front door! . . . he's leaving! . . .

(*He rushes to the door but finds it locked—pushes and pulls at it, trying to force it open.*)

MRS. LIGHT. I suppose you want to run over and warn your fine friends! Fife'll be in a cell before long, please God, and if there was any real justice his girl'd be put in along with him, for she's no better than a street-walker!

REUBEN (*glares at her now*). I'm glad you're talking like that! It shows you up and I can hate you now!

MRS. LIGHT (*breaking down*). Reuben! For God's sake, don't say that—to your mother!

REUBEN. You're not my mother any more! I'll do without a mother rather than have your kind!

(*He turns from her to the window and looks out. As he does so, his father appears from right, coming from the front door. He is buttoned up to the neck in an old raincoat and carries an umbrella.*)

FIFE (*still leaning out of his sitting-room window, catches sight of Light—calls excitedly over his shoulder*). Here's the old man now! Come quick, Ada! (*A moment later, just as Light comes up, she appears at the window next to her father. Her face is set in an ugly, sneering expression. Fife calls to Light in a mocking tone.*) Good evening, Your Holiness.

LIGHT (*stops short and stares at Fife with a rage that chokes him so that for a moment his lips move, forming words, but he can't utter them—finally finding his voice, he stammers*). You—you murderer!

FIFE (*nudging Ada—with a great pretence of guilt*). Murderer? In the name of God, has your son?—after he'd sworn his word of honour——!

LIGHT (*triumphantly*). You thought you had him caught in your snares, did you?—but God was simply using Reuben to bring retribution on your head. (*In a booming triumph.*) "Vengeance is mine, saith the Lord!"

REUBEN (*watching from his window*). He's talking to Fife! . . . he's telling! . . .

(*Then cursing his father aloud.*) God damn him! I'll show him! (*He drives back at the door with the weight of his whole body, and it crashes open and he stumbles over it and disappears in the hall.*)

MRS. LIGHT (*starts after him, calling frightenedly*). Reuben! Don't! Reuben!

FIFE (*enjoying himself hugely*). You wouldn't give me up to the police, would you?—a kind-hearted Shepherd of the Lord like you!

ADA (*suddenly flares up into a temper*). Aw, cut it out, Pop! This has gone far enough! (*To Light with sneering contempt.*) No wonder your son is a sap! Can't you see this is only a joke on you? Why, you poor fish, that murder story is in to-day's *Star*—the name Clark and everything! Pop simply copied that story—and if you go to the police you'll only be making a boob of yourself—but go ahead if you like!

(*As she speaks Reuben runs in from the right. He advances threateningly on his father, who is staring at Ada stupidly, overwhelmed by the conviction that what she has told him is true.*)

REUBEN. Did you tell——?

ADA. Look who's here! I was just telling

your old man it was only a murder story out of the paper Pop told you to prove you were yellow! And you are, all right! Don't you ever dare speak to me again! You're a yellow rat! (*She breaks down, weeping, and rushes back into the room.*)

FIFE (*following her*). Ada! Don't waste crying over——

REUBEN. Ada! Listen! I didn't mean—I didn't know——!

(*He takes a few steps toward the window, then stops, thinking bitterly.*) So it was all a lie . . . a joke she played on me! . . . that's why she made me meet her old man! . . . so she could make a fool of me! . . .

(*He yells at the window.*) It's you who're the rat, Ada! You can go to hell!

MRS. LIGHT (*hurrying in from the right. She runs to him and tries to put her arms around him*). Reuben!

REUBEN (*pushing her away from him—furiously*). Leave me alone! You're to blame for this! You cheated me! I hate you!

MRS. LIGHT. For God's sake, Reuben!

LIGHT (*comes out of the state of humiliated stupefaction into which the knowledge of the joke has thrown him—bursting into a fatuous rage—to his wife*). As if I have not had enough to bear of humiliation! (*He points a shaking finger at Reuben.*) This dunce—this stupid dolt—now I shall be the butt of all their sneers! And to think I stayed my hand—! But wait! I'll show him what a real whipping is!

REUBEN (*fiercely*). You lie! You'll never dare touch me again, you old fool! I'm not scared of you any more!

(*There is a blinding flash of lightning. Light, his nerves already at the breaking point, gives a gasp of superstitious fright and backs away from his son.*)

LIGHT. God have mercy!

REUBEN (*with a sneer*). What God? Fife's God? Electricity? Are you praying to It for mercy? It can't hear you! It doesn't give a damn about you! (*There is a tremendous crash of thunder. Reuben looks up and gives a wild laugh as though the thunder elated him. His mother and father shrink back from him in abject terror as he shouts up at the sky.*) Shoot away, Old Bozo! I'm not scared of You!

MRS. LIGHT. Reuben! You don't know what you're saying!

REUBEN (*with a hard mocking laugh—to his mother*). What's the matter? Do you still believe in his fool God? I'll show you. (*He jumps to his father's side and grabs his raincoat by the lapel—addressing the sky with insulting insolence.*) If there is his God let Him strike me dead this second! I dare Him! (*His father squeals with terror and tries to break away from his hold. His mother screams. He laughs triumphantly.*) There! Didn't I tell you! (*Light finally tears his coat from Reuben's grip and runs panic-stricken off right, dragging his moaning wife by the arm. Reuben turns his back on his home determinedly and starts walking off left—with bitter defiance.*) There is no God! No God but Electricity! I'll never be scared again! I'm through with the lot of you!

(*As he disappears off left, the sound of wind and rain sweeping down on the town from the hills is heard.*)

CURTAIN

ACT TWO SCENE ONE

SCENE. *The same act as Act One. The interior of the Light sitting-room is revealed.*

It is an early morning of a hot day in August. Fifteen months have elapsed.

Mrs. Fife is leaning out of one of the windows of their sitting-room, basking contentedly in the sun. She wears a faded blue wrapper.

MRS. FIFE (*thinking with a sleepy content*). The sun is hot . . . I feel so dozy . . . I know why dogs love to lie in the sun . . . and cats and chickens . . . they forget to think they're living . . . they're just alive . . . (*She looks toward the Light house—with drowsy melancholy.*) Alive . . . poor Mrs. Light is dead . . . what is death like, I wonder? . . . I suppose I'll have to die some time . . . I don't want to die before Ramsay . . . he wouldn't know how to take care of himself. . . .

(At a noise in the room behind her she half turns her head—then Ada leans out of the window next to her mother. Her face has a peaked look. Her manner is touchy and irritable and she has lost her former air of self-assured flippancy. There is no rouge on her face and she is dressed as if she had grown indifferent about her personal appearance.)

ADA. For heaven's sake, what're you dope-dreaming about now, Mom?

MRS. FIFE. I was thinking of poor Mrs. Light——

ADA. Poor nothing! She hated us worse than poison! She'd have sung hymns of joy if any of us had cashed in! And why feel sorry for her, anyway? She's lucky, if you ask me! Life is the bunk!

MRS. FIFE *(looks at her worriedly—with a sigh)*. I wish that Light boy would come back.

ADA *(immediately flying into a temper)*. For God's sake, shut up! I've told you a million times how dumb that talk is and yet you keep on harping——!

MRS. FIFE. All right, Ada. I won't say anything.

ADA. What do I care about that poor fish! He can be dead for all I care! *(Then, as Fife's voice is heard calling from somewhere in the house.)* There's Pop howling his head off about something. You go in and smooth him down, Mom. I'm sick of his grouches.

MRS. FIFE *(as she turns to go)*. I wish you'd make it up with your Pop, Ada. He feels so bad about it. You've kept a grudge against him ever since the night that Light boy——

ADA. There you go again! For Pete's sake, leave me alone!

(Mrs. Fife disappears meekly without another word. Ada stares before her, thinking resentfully.) I've got a good right to have a grudge against him . . . what he did that night wasn't on the level . . . it isn't a question of Rube . . . I don't give a darn about him . . . then why are you all the time thinking about him? . . . I'm not! . . . I liked him but that was all . . . and he was yellow, wasn't he? . . . well, maybe you'd be worse if everything was framed against you the way Pop got him! . . . poor Rube! . . . what's he been doing all this time, I wonder? . . . *(With a sad smile of scorn for herself.)* You poor boob! . . . it must be love! . . .

(In the sitting-room of the Light home, Hutchins Light enters from the rear, right. The grief over his wife's death has made him an old man. His hair has turned almost white, his mouth droops forlornly, his eyes are dull, his whole face is a mask of stricken loneliness. He comes and sits in his old chair and mechanically picks up his Bible from the table but lets it drop again and stares before him.)

LIGHT *(thinking dully)*. Another day . . . empty . . . all days are empty now . . . how long, O Lord? . . . *(He sighs heavily.)* No sleep again last night except for a few minutes . . . and then nightmare . . . I dreamed Amelia was in my arms . . . and Reuben came and beckoned her and she went away with him . . . *(He shudders, flinging off the memory—then wondering bitterly.)* Does that dream mean Reuben is dead, too? . . . what does it matter? . . . ever since that night he has been dead for me . . . but he never gave Amelia a chance to forget him . . . a postal card every month or so . . . each with the same blasphemy . . . "We have electrocuted your God. Don't be a fool!" . . . her last words! . . . "don't be a fool," she kept saying to me . . . she couldn't have known what she was saying . . .

(He breaks down, sobbing, and buries his head in his arms on the table.)

MRS. FIFE *(reappears in the window beside Ada. She is smiling with a doting good-nature)*. Your Pop told me to get out of the room and stop looking at him or he'd start breaking plates. My, but he's in a breakfast temper, though! The men at the plant'll catch it—but they don't mind him. They know, like I do, that he's really the kindest man in the world.

ADA *(resentfully)*. Oh, is he? I suppose that's why he acted the way he did to Rube!

MRS. FIFE. He couldn't help being mean then. He'd be mean at first to any man he thought you cared for—especially a minister's son. But he'd get over it, you'd see. He'd like to see you happy, before everything. I'm sure he's been wishing for a long time that Light boy'd come home so he could make friends with him.

ADA. Aw, you're crazy, Mom! (*Suddenly she leans over and kisses her mother affectionately.*) It's you who are the kindest in the world. (*Then embarrassed—irritably.*) Gosh, this sun's hot! I don't see how you stand it. (*She retreats into the house.*)

MRS. FIFE (*blinking placidly in the sun*). It was awful nice the way Ada kissed me . . . I wish she'd get to kissing her Pop again that way . . . she does it now as if she wished she was a mosquito with a stinger . . . the screen up in her room has a hole rusted in it . . . I must remember to get it fixed or they'll be flying in keeping her awake . . .

(*A pause—then Reuben Light comes slowly in from the left and stands there, his eyes fixed for a while on his home, taking in every detail. He does not for a moment notice Mrs. Fife, nor she him. A great change has come over him; he is hardly recognizable as the Reuben of Act One. Nearly nineteen now, his body has filled out, his skin is tanned and weather-beaten. In contrast to his diffident timid attitude of before, his manner is now consciously hard-boiled. The look on his face emphasizes the change in him. It is much older than his years, and it is apparent that he has not grown its defensive callousness without a desperate struggle to kill the shrinking boy in him. But it is in his eyes that the greatest change has come. Their soft grey-blue has become chilled and frozen, and yet they burn in their depths with a queer devouring intensity. He is dressed roughly in battered shoes, dungaree trousers faded by many washings, a blue flannel shirt open at the neck, with a dirty coloured handkerchief knotted about his throat, and wears the coat of his old suit. Under his arm he carries six books, bound together with a strap.*)

REUBEN (*thinking jeeringly*). Home, Sweet Home! . . . the Prodigal returns! . . . what for? . . . I felt a sudden hunch I had to come . . . to have a talk with mother, anyway . . . well, I'll soon know what it's all about . . . and won't the old man be glad to see me! . . . yes! . . . he'll poison the fatted calf! . . .

(*He laughs aloud. Mrs. Fife turns and gives a startled exclamation as she recognizes him. He turns and looks at her for a moment—then with a swaggering impudence.*) Fine day, isn't it?

MRS. FIFE (*her eyes mooning at him, with a simple pleased smile*). I'm glad you've come home. Ada'll be glad. (*She stirs as if to go into the house.*) I'll tell her you're here.

REUBEN (*frowning*). No. I've got no time for her now. (*Then with a peculiar air of indifferent curiosity.*) Are you dead sure Ada'll be glad I'm back? I shouldn't think she would after what happened.

MRS. FIFE. That wasn't her doing. She's been sorry about it ever since.

REUBEN (*with the same detached interest*). She called me a yellow rat—and she had the right dope. I sure was dumb when it came to guessing what she really wanted or I would have—(*With a cold smile.*) Well, never mind what—but you can tell her I've changed. I've lived a lot and read a lot to find out for myself what's really what—and I've found out all right! You can tell her I've read up on love in biology, and I know what it is now, and I've proved it with more than one female.

MRS. FIFE (*preoccupied with her own thoughts*). It was just one of Ramsay's jokes.

REUBEN. He's a great little joker! And I certainly fell for it. Well, there's no hard feelings. He did me a favour. He woke me up. (*With a laugh, a queer expression coming into his eyes.*) You can tell him I've joined his church. The only God I believe in now is electricity.

MRS. FIFE (*simply*). Ramsay'll be glad.

REUBEN (*indicating the books he carries*). I'm studying a lot of science. Sometimes I've gone without eating to buy books—and often I've read all night—books on astronomy and biology and physics and chemistry and evolution. It all comes down to electricity in the end. What the fool preachers call God is in electricity somewhere. (*He breaks off—then strangely.*) Did you ever watch dynamos? What I mean is in them—somehow.

MRS. FIFE (*dreamily*). I love dynamos. I could watch them for ever. I love to hear them sing. They're singing all the time about everything in the world!

(*She hums her imitation of a dynamo's metallic purr.*)

REUBEN (*startled—looks at her with growing interest*). "Singing all the time about everything in the world" . . . listen to her . . . she's caught the sound . . . she really makes you think of a dynamo, somehow . . . she's big and warm like . . . like what? . . . damned if she doesn't remind me of mother the way she used to be . . . way back when I was a little kid and didn't know what she was really like . . . (*With a bitter grin.*) Wouldn't mother go wild if I told her that! . . . maybe I will just to get her goat! . . .

(*Abruptly he puts down his books and walks up to Mrs. Fife.*) Say, you're all right!

(*He takes one of her hands in his clumsily—then lets go of it, grinning awkwardly.*)

MRS. FIFE (*sentimentally touched—beaming on him*). I always knew you must be a nice boy. (*With a coquettish, incongruously girlish air.*) But you save your holding hands for Ada! (*Then she half turns around at some sound in the room behind her—in a hurried whisper to Reuben.*) She's coming! You hide behind those bushes and we'll surprise her!

(*Mechanically, reacting instinctively for a moment as the timid boy of formerly, he runs to the gap in the lilac bushes and hides in the old place. Ada appears in the window beside her mother. Her face wears an expression of eager expectation. Her eyes glance quickly on all sides as if searching for some one.*)

ADA (*flusteredly*). I'm sure I heard some one . . . it sounded like . . .

REUBEN (*almost as soon as he reaches his old hiding-place is overcome by shame*). What'd I do that for? . . . hide! . . . the old stuff! . . . (*Savagely.*) No, by God! . . . her mother put it in my head . . . but I'll soon show Ada! . . . She'll find out if I'm yellow now! . . .

(*With a swagger and the cold smile of his lips he walks through the gap just as Mrs. Fife speaks to Ada.*)

MRS. FIFE (*with a teasing smile*). Ada, I've got a big surprise for you. Guess—— (*But Ada has already seen him.*)

ADA. Rube!

REUBEN (*walks toward her, the smile frozen on his lips, his eyes fixed on hers*). Go right up and kiss her! . . . look at the way she's looking at you! . . . she's easy now! . . .

ADA (*staring at him, stammers his name again in a tone in which there is now a note of panic*). Rube!

REUBEN (*pulls her head down and kisses her, keeping his lips on hers while she struggles instinctively for a moment, until she gives up and returns his kiss—then he pushes her a little away from him and laughs quietly, his confidence in himself completely restored*). Well, this prodigal gets the fatted kiss even if "there ain't no calf." Hello, Ada! How's every little thing?

MRS. FIFE (*sentimentally*). That's right. You two kiss and make up. I'll leave you alone. (*She goes back into the room.*)

ADA (*is staring at him with eyes that search his face apprehensively*). Rube! You—you've changed. I—I hardly know you! I shouldn't have kissed you—like that. I don't know why I——

REUBEN. Well, I know. (*He takes her face between his hands again and brings his close to it.*) Because you love me. Isn't that right? (*As she hesitates—insistently, giving her head a little shake.*) Isn't it?

ADA (*helplessly*). I guess it is, Rube.

REUBEN. Guess, nothing! You loved me before I went away—even when you were bawling me out for a yellow rat. That was what made you so mad, wasn't it? You were ashamed of loving me when I was so dumb and didn't get what you wanted and was so damned scared to touch you. (*He laughs—a self-assured insinuating laugh that for her has something at once fascinating and frightening about it.*) But you needn't worry any more, Ada. I've learned a lot about love since I left—and I get you now, all right! (*Then with a sudden burst of threatening assertiveness.*) You're damned right, I've changed! I'm not yellow about you or God or anything else! Don't forget that, Ada! (*Then as suddenly changing to a passionate tone of desire.*) Gosh, you're pretty! I'd forgotten how pretty you were! You make all the girls I've been playing around with look like mistakes! Your eyes are grand—and your hair—and your mouth—! (*He kisses them hungrily as he speaks—then controls himself and breaks away from her, forcing a laugh.*) Continued in our next! Let's take a walk to-night.

ADA (*staring at him helplessly*). Yes—no—I don't think——

REUBEN. Sure you will. We'll walk out to the top of Long Hill. That's where I was all during the storm that night after I left here. I made myself stand there and watch the lightning. After that storm was over I'd changed, believe me! I knew nothing could ever scare me again—and a whole lot of me was dead and a new lot started living. And that's the right place for us to love—on top of that hill—close to the sky—driven to love by what makes the earth go round—by what drives the stars through space! Did you ever think that all life comes down to electricity in the end, Ada? Did you ever watch dynamos? (*She stares at him, frightened and fascinated, and shakes her head.*) I've watched them for hours. Sometimes I'd go in a plant and get talking to the guys just to hang around, and I tried everywhere to get a job in a plant but never had any luck. But every job I've had—I never stuck to one long, I wanted to keep moving and see everything—every job was connected with electricity some way. I've worked for electricians, I've gone out helping linesmen, I shovelled sand on a big water-power job out West. (*Then with sudden eagerness.*) Say, Ada, I've just had a hunch! I know now what drove me back here, all right! You've got to get your old man to give me a job in his plant—any job, I don't care what!

ADA. Sure—I'll try, Rube.

REUBEN (*with a cold assurance*). You've got to, Ada. Because I can't stay on here without a job. I'm broke and I won't live home—even if the old gent would let me. And that reminds me, I better go and pay my little visit. I don't want to see him, but I want to have a talk with Mother. I've got over my hard feelings about her. She was so crazy jealous of you she didn't care what she did. I can make allowances for her—now. So I'll be friends again if she wants to—and then you watch me convert her over from that old God stuff of his! (*He grins with resentful anticipation.*)

ADA (*has listened with blank astonishment—pityingly*). Then you don't—? Why, I thought—Didn't they send for you?

REUBEN (*unsuspectingly—with a grin*). Send for me to come home and be good? I never gave them my address, kid. I didn't want them bothering me. I never wrote, except some post-cards to mother I sent to get her goat—and his. (*Then picking up his books and turning toward his home.*) Guess I'll go round by the back. I don't want to run into him unless I have to. So long, Ada. Tell your old man I'd sure like that job!

(*He walks to the hedge and then, stealthily, across the lawn and disappears behind the house.*)

ADA (*looking after him*). He doesn't know she's dead . . . ought I to have told him? . . . oh, I couldn't! . . . poor Rube! . . . (*Then admiringly.*) How strong he's got! . . . but it makes me afraid too . . . his eyes seemed to take all the clothes off me . . . and I didn't feel ashamed . . . I felt glad! . . . (*Defiantly.*) I love him! . . . I want him as much as he wants me! . . . what of it? . . . (*Then with a shudder she cannot repress.*) But his eyes are so queer . . . like lumps of ice with fire inside them . . . and he never said he loved me . . . aw, of course he does! . . . he was nuts about me before he went away, wasn't he? . . . (*Determinedly.*) I've got to make Pop give him that job or he might beat it again . . . he owes it to Rube to do something for him . . . I'll talk to him right now . . .

(*She disappears inside the house just as Reuben slowly opens the door of the Light sitting-room. There is an expression of puzzled uneasiness on his face as he peers around the half-opened door, then slinks in as if he were a burglar. Light is still sitting, his face hidden in his arms on the table, in an attitude of exhausted grief. Reuben does not at first see him.*)

REUBEN. Something's all wrong here . . . where the hell is every one? . . . where's mother? . . . (*He has stepped on tiptoe into the room and now suddenly he sees his father and a sneering smile immediately comes to his lips.*) There he is, anyway . . . praying as usual . . . the poor boob . . . there isn't a damn prayer ever got him a thing . . . Mother used to make him pray for electric lights in the house . . . (*Suddenly with a pleased grin.*) That's a good hunch . . . I'll get them put in the first money I save . . . it'll be like bringing my gospel to the heathen . . . let there be electric light ! . . . (*He chuckles, then bends closer to look at his father.*) He must be asleep . . . that's one on him to catch him . . .

(*He speaks with mocking geniality.*) Hello ! (*His father gives a frightened start, as if dodging a blow, and stares at his son's face with stupefied bewilderment.*) Sorry to disturb your little snooze. (*His father continues to look at him, as if he can't believe his eyes.*) Oh, this is me, all right. (*Then the fact of his father's changed appearance strikes him for the first time, and he blurts out in a tone that is almost kindly.*) Say, you look all in. What's the trouble ? Been sick ?

LIGHT (*thinking gropingly*). It's Reuben . . . Reuben . . . but he doesn't seem like Reuben . . .

REUBEN (*misunderstanding his father's silence as intentional, immediately becomes resentful*). What's the matter ? Don't you want to talk to me ? Well, I'm not here to talk to you either. I was just passing this way and thought I'd drop in to say hello to Mother. Where is she ?

LIGHT (*thinking more clearly now—an unstrung fury rising within him*). Oh, yes, it's Reuben ! . . . I recognize him now ! . . . the same as that night . . . cruel and evil ! . . . and now he's asking for the mother he . . . my poor Amelia ! . . . he killed her ! . . .

(*He lurches to his feet and leans against the back of his chair weakly, glaring at his son. Violently—in a voice that is like a croak.*) Murderer ! You killed her !

REUBEN (*stares at him with a stunned look*). What the hell do you mean ? (*Then harshly, taking a threatening step forward.*) Where's Mother, I'm asking you !

LIGHT (*his strength failing him—in a faltering tone hardly above a whisper*). She's dead—Reuben.

REUBEN (*terribly shaken*). You're a liar ! You're just saying that to get my goat !

LIGHT (*going on as if he hadn't heard—in a tone of monotonous grief*). You can't see her—I can't—never—never see her again !

(*He breaks down abjectly, sinking on his chair and sobbing, his face in his hands.*)

REUBEN (*stands looking at him stupidly, convinced now of the truth and trying to make himself realize it and accept it*). Then it's straight goods . . . she is dead . . . gone . . . no use making a fuss . . . let him cry . . . why can't his religion buck him up now ? . . . he ought to feel sure he's going to see her again soon . . . in heaven . . . I'd like to see her again . . . tell her I'm sorry for acting so rough to her that night . . . (*He gulps and his lips twitch.*) I wish he'd stop crying . . .

(*He goes forward and pats his father on the back gingerly.*) Buck up.

(*His father doesn't seem to hear him. He turns and slumps into the chair at the far side of the table.*) Why couldn't I have seen her just once again . . . this is a rotten break . . .

(*He asks mechanically.*) How long ago did she die ?

LIGHT (*mechanically in his turn—without lifting his head*). Two weeks ago yesterday.

REUBEN. Two weeks . . . it was about then I first felt that hunch to come home and see her . . . that's damn queer ! . . . (*He stares at his father—uneasily.*) He said I killed her . . . what the hell did he mean ? . . .

(*Forcing a casual tone.*) What did she die of ?

LIGHT (*dully*). Pneumonia.

REUBEN (*heaving a sigh of relief*). Sure . . . I knew he was only saying that to get my goat . . .

(*He speaks to his father in a defensive, accusing tone.*) Pneumonia, eh ? Well, it's a damn wonder we didn't all die of it years ago, living in this dump ! Ever since I can remember the cellar's leaked like a sieve. You never could afford to get it fixed right. Mother was always after you about it. And I can remember the ceiling in my room. Every storm the water'd begin to drip down and Mother'd put the wash basin on the floor to catch it. It was always damp in this house. Mother was always after you to make them put in a decent furnace instead of——

LIGHT (*has lifted his head and is glaring at his son*). Are you trying to say I killed her ? It was you ! She'd been pining away for almost a year. Her heart was broken because you'd gone ! She hoped for a time you'd come back but finally she gave up hoping—and gave up wanting to live! And your horrible blasphemous postcards kept coming! She blamed herself for your ruin and she wrote long letters begging your forgiveness, and asking you to come home! But you'd never given her an address! She couldn't mail them, she knew you'd never read them, and that broke her heart most of all! You killed her as surely as if you'd given her poison, you unnatural accursed son!

REUBEN (*deeply disturbed but trying desperately to conceal it*). I never gave her my address because I thought she'd only write bawling me out. (*Then harshly.*) Where are those letters she wrote? They're mine!

LIGHT (*with a mean satisfaction*). I destroyed them! I burnt them to the last scrap!

REUBEN (*starts for his father threateningly, his fists clenched*). You rotten son of a — (*He chokes it back—then helplessly, with a wounded look.*) Say, that was a dirty trick! I'd like to have read——

(*Light averts his eyes and suddenly hides his face in his hands.*)

LIGHT (*remorsefully now*). He's right . . . I had no right . . . no right even to read them . . . how I wish I'd never read them! . . .

(*Lifting his head.*) I destroyed them in a fit of anger. When I read them I realized that Amelia had been thinking of you all the time. And I felt betrayed! I hated her and you! I was insane with hatred! God forgive me!

REUBEN (*after a pause—dully*). Did she ever talk about me?

LIGHT (*immediately jealous again*). She never mentioned your name! (*Then forcing himself to say it.*) I—I had forbidden her to.

REUBEN (*his face lights up with anger again, but he controls it*). Sure, you had to, didn't you?—so what the hell? (*Then insistently.*) But—didn't she?—at the last?—when she was dying?—say anything?

LIGHT (*fighting a furious battle with himself*). Have I got to tell him? . . . that she'd even forgotten God! . . . that her last words were his words! . . . even her soul lost to me! . . . must I tell this? . . . (*Savagely.*) No! . . . I don't owe him the truth! . . . I must make him feel he is accursed! . . .

(*He springs from his chair and leaning across the table, points his finger at Reuben denouncingly.*) Yes, with her last breath she cursed you for all the ruin and suffering you had brought on her—and on me! (*Then as he sees Reuben shrinking back in his chair, a haunted look of horror on his face, the consciousness of the evil of the lie he is telling overwhelms him with guilty remorse. He stammers.*) No!—that's a lie, Reuben!—a terrible lie!—don't listen—don't believe me! (*He stumbles hastily around the table to the dazed Reuben and with a pitiful gesture puts a trembling hand on his head—pleadingly.*) Forgive me, Reuben! You are my son as well as hers, remember. I haven't the strength to resist evil. I wanted to punish you. She didn't curse you. Her last words were the very words you had written her. "Don't be a fool!" she kept saying to me! (*He shudders.*)

REUBEN (*springs from his chair in extreme agitation and grabbing his father by both shoulders, stares hungrily in his face*). What? What's that? Mother said that?

LIGHT (*seeming to shrivel up in his son's grip—trying unconvincingly to reassure himself*). She was delirious. She must have been delirious.

REUBEN (*lets go of his father. The old man turns and stumbles back to his chair. Reuben stares before him, thinking excitedly*). "We have electrocuted your God. Don't be a fool" . . . that's what I kept writing her . . . her last words! . . . then I'd converted her away from his God! . . . the dying see things beyond . . . she saw I'd found the right path to the truth! . . . (*His eyes shine with a new elation.*) By God, I'll go on now all right! . . . (*He laughs aloud to himself exultantly.*)

LIGHT. For the love of God!

REUBEN (*immediately ashamed of himself*). I wasn't laughing at you, honest! (*Then suddenly.*) Say, I think I'll go and visit Mother's grave. There's some things I'd like to get off my chest—even if she can't hear me. (*Turning to the door.*) Well, so long.

LIGHT (*dully*). Shall I have your room put in order for you?

REUBEN (*frowning*). No. It isn't my room now. That me is dead.

(*Then an idea comes to him—thinking.*) But

maybe Mother'd want me to . . . maybe I'd get some message from her if I stayed here . . .

(*Then casually to his father.*) Oh, all right. I'll stay for a couple of days. After that I'm going to get a room out near the plant. Say, I might as well break the bad news to you. I'm getting a job in Fife's power house. (*Then quickly.*) I suppose you think I'm doing it to spite you, but I'm not.

LIGHT (*dully*). You have sold your soul to Satan, Reuben.

REUBEN (*immediately resentful—with his cold smile*). Your Satan is dead. We electrocuted him along with your God. Electricity is God now. And we've got to learn to know God, haven't we? Well, that's what I'm after! (*In a lighter tone—mockingly.*) Did you ever watch dynamos? Come down to the plant and I'll convert you! (*He cannot restrain a parting shot.*) I converted Mother, didn't I? Well, so long.

(*He goes out and a moment later walks past the front of the house from the right. He is off guard and the callousness has gone from his face, which is now very like that of the boy of* ACT ONE.) I wish she hadn't died! . . . but she forgave me . . .

ADA (*sticks her head out of their sitting-room window as he passes the lilac hedge. Her face is flushed with excitement, happy and pretty now. She calls*). It's all right, Rube. Pop's got a job for you. A floor man is leaving Saturday.

REUBEN (*startled out of his thoughts, at first frowns then forces the cold smile to his lips*). That's great.

ADA (*coquettishly*). Well, don't I get anything?

REUBEN (*with his cold smile*). Sure!

(*He goes to her and reaches up as if to kiss her—then checks himself, thinking remorsefully*). What the hell am I doing? . . . I'm going out to Mother's grave . . . she hated her . . .

(*He steps back, frowning.*) Wait till later, Ada. Well, so long. See you to-night. (*He turns his back on her abruptly and walks off left.*)

CURTAIN

SCENE TWO

SCENE. *The same except that Reuben's bedroom is now revealed while the wall of the sitting-room has been replaced. It is about half-past eleven on the same night—a sultry, hazy sky with few stars visible. There is no light in either house.*

Reuben and Ada come in from the left. She is hanging on his arm, pressing close to him as if she were afraid of his leaving her, glancing up into his face with a timid look of mingled happiness and apprehension.

Reuben's face shows that he also is struggling with conflicting emotions. There is a fixed smile of triumph and gratified vanity on his lips, but his eyes are restless and there is a nervous uneasiness apparent in his whole manner.

ADA. You're sure you don't hate me now—because I let you—maybe I shouldn't have—but, oh, Rube, I do love you so much! Say you love me just as much—that you always will!

REUBEN (*preoccupiedly*). Sure I will.

ADA (*pleadingly*). Put your arms around me tight and kiss me again. Then I won't be scared—or sorry.

REUBEN (*mechanically puts his arms around her and kisses her at first perfunctorily, then with reawakening passion*). Gee, you're pretty, Ada! You've certainly got me going!

ADA (*happily now*). Oh Rube, when you kiss me like that nothing in the world matters but you! Up on the hill when we—oh, I felt I was just you, a part of you and you were part of me! I forgot everything!

REUBEN (*suddenly moves away from her and stares around him nervously—in a strange voice*). Sure. You forget everything for a minute. You're happy. Then something has to wake you up—and start you thinking again.

ADA. What is it you're thinking about? Tell me, and maybe I can help you forget it.

REUBEN (*shaking his head*). I can't forget. (*Then determinedly.*) And I don't want to. I want to face things. I won't ever be satisfied now until I've found the truth about everything.

ADA (*trying to force a joking tone*). And where do I come in?

REUBEN (*coldly*). You don't come in.

ADA. Rube! Don't say that—not after—You scare me!

REUBEN (*irritably*). Cut out that talk of being scared! What are you scared about? Scared what we did was a sin? You're the hell of an atheist! (*Then jeeringly.*) And you're the one that used to be always kidding me about being a goody boy! There's nothing to be scared about or sorry for. What we did was just plain sex—an act of nature—and that's all there is to it!

ADA (*pitifully—her voice trembling*). Is that all—it means to you?

REUBEN. That's all it means to anyone! What people call love is just sex—and there's no sin about it!

ADA. I wasn't saying there was, was I? I've proved to you I don't—only— (*Then frightenedly.*) It's you, Rube. I can't get used to you, talking like that. You've changed so.

REUBEN (*with a coarse grin*). Well, you've got no kick coming. If I'd stayed the same poor boob I used to be you might have died an old maid.

ADA. But—you wanted to marry me then, Rube.

REUBEN (*roughly*). And a lot that got me, didn't it?

ADA (*faintly*). Don't you want to—any more?

REUBEN. Don't I what? Talk sense, Ada! We're married by Nature now. We don't need any old fool of a minister saying prayers over us! (*Then after a moment's pause—with a forced laugh.*) Say, here's one on me, Ada—speaking of praying. It was out at Mother's grave. Before I thought, I started to do a prayer act—and then suddenly it hit me that there was nothing to pray to. (*He forces another laugh.*) It just goes to show you what a hold that bunk gets on you when you've had it crammed down your throat from the time you were born! You can't pray to electricity unless you're foolish in the head, can you? (*Then strangely.*) But maybe you could, at that—if you knew how!

ADA. Is that where you went this afternoon—out to her grave?

REUBEN (*with affected indifference*). Sure. What of it?

ADA (*pityingly*). Poor Rube!

REUBEN (*frowning*). Poor nothing! She's dead, and that's all there is about it! You've got to face death as well as life.

ADA. I'm sorry she hated me so. I hope now she forgives us—for loving each other.

REUBEN (*with his cold smile*). You mean forgives us for what we did to-night? You don't know her! She never would! But what's the use of talking about it? Who gives a damn? Good night, Ada. I'm tired. I'm going to bed. See you to-morrow. (*He turns his back on her abruptly and walks off right toward the front door of his house.*)

ADA (*stands looking after him with bewildered hurt for a moment, then turns back toward her own front door and begins to cry softly, at the same time trying to reassure herself*). I mustn't . . . feel bad . . . he doesn't mean to hurt me . . . he's changed, that's all . . .

(*She disappears off left. A moment later, Reuben appears in his bedroom and lights the lamp. He sits down on the bed and stares before him.*)

REUBEN (*looking about the room now, thinking bitterly*). The last time I was here . . . there's the closet where she hid him . . . here's where she sat lying to me . . . watching him beat me . . . (*He springs to his feet—viciously.*) I'm glad she's dead! . . . (*Then immediately remorseful.*) No . . . I don't mean that, Mother . . . I was thinking of how you acted that night . . . I wish I could have seen you after you'd changed . . . after you'd come back to my side . . . (*He goes to the window on the left and looks out.*) Here's where I was looking out, waiting for Ada to signal on the Victrola . . . gosh, that seems a million years ago! . . . how scared I was of even kissing her! . . . and to-night she was dead easy . . . like rolling off a log! . . . (*He comes back to the bed and sits down.*) Mother said she was no better than a street-walker . . . she certainly didn't put up a fight . . . marry her! . . . what does she think I am, a boob? . . . she put one over on me and now I've put one over on her! . . . we're square . . . and whatever's going to happen, will happen, but it won't be a wedding! . . . (*Then with coarse sensuality.*) But it's grand to have her around handy whenever I want . . . the flesh, as the old man would call it! . . . and she's all right other ways, too . . . I like her . . . she got me the job . . . she'll be useful . . . and I'll treat her decent . . . maybe it's love . . . whatever the hell love is! . . . did Mother really love the old man? . . . she must have or how could she stand him? . . . and she made me with him . . . act of Nature . . . like me and Ada . . . (*He jumps to his feet distractedly.*) God, that seems lousy somehow! . . . I don't want to think of it! . . . (*He paces up and down—then pauses and appears to be listening for something.*) There's something queer about this dump now! . . . as if no one was living here . . . I suppose that's because Mother's gone . . . I'd like to reach her somehow . . . no one knows what happens after death . . . even science doesn't . . . there may be some kind of hereafter . . . I used to kneel down here and say my prayers . . . she taught them to me . . . then she'd tuck me in, even after I'd grown up . . . and kiss me good-night . . . (*As if automatically he slips to his knees by the bed.*) I'm sorry, Mother . . . sorry you're dead . . . I wish I could talk to you . . . (*He scrambles to his feet—angry at himself.*) You damn fool! . . . what's come over you anyway? . . . what are you praying to? . . . when there's nothing . . . (*Then strangely.*) Funny, that hunch I got when I was talking to Ada . . . about praying to electricity, if you knew how . . . it was like a message . . . Mother believed what I believed when she died . . . maybe it came from her . . . (*Then suspicious of himself again.*) Aw, that's just superstitious junk . . . but why is it? . . . look at how mysterious all this electrical wave stuff is in radio and everything . . . that's scientific fact . . . and why couldn't something like that that no one understands yet? . . . between the dead and the living? . . . (*He walks around nervously.*) No use trying to go to sleep . . . and I want to keep on thinking . . . but not in here . . . I'll go for a walk . . . why not go down to the plant? . . . take a look in at the dynamos . . . watching them always helps me somehow . . . sure, that's the stuff! . . .

(*He turns down the light and blows it out and can be seen going through the door in rear.*)

CURTAIN

SCENE THREE

SCENE. *A half-hour later. Exterior of the Light and Power Company's hydro-electric plant about two miles from the town. The building is red brick. The section on the left, the dynamo room, is much wider than the right section, but is a story less in height. An immense window and a big sliding door are in the lower part of the dynamo room wall, and there is a similar window in the upper part of the section on right. Through the window and the open door of the dynamo room, which is brilliantly lighted by a row of powerful bulbs in white globes set in brackets along both walls, there is a clear view of a dynamo, huge and black, with something of a massive female idol about it, the exciter set on the main structure like a head with blank oblong eyes above a gross rounded torso.*

Through the upper window of the right section of the building, in the switch galleries, by a dim light, one gets a glimpse of the mathematically-ordered web of the disconnecting switches, double busses, and other equipment stretching up through the roof to the outgoing feeders leading to the transmission towers.

The air is full of sound, a soft overtone of rushing water from the dam and the river bed below, penetrated dominatingly by the harsh, throaty, metallic purr of the dynamo.

Reuben comes in from the right and approaches until he is opposite the open doorway. He stands there staring at the dynamo and listening to it.

REUBEN (*after a pause—fascinatedly*). It's so mysterious . . . and grand . . . God, I love dynamos! . . . they make you feel things . . . you don't need to think . . . you almost get the secret . . . what electricity is . . . what life is . . . what God is . . . it's all the same thing . . . (*A pause—then he goes on in the same fascinated tone.*) It's like a great dark idol . . . like the old stone statues of gods people prayed to . . . only it's living and they were dead . . . that part on top is like a head . . . with eyes that see you without seeing you . . . and below it is like a body . . . not a man's . . . round like a woman's . . . as if it had breasts . . . but not like a girl . . . not like Ada . . . no, like a woman . . . like her mother . . . or mine . . . a great, dark mother! . . . that's what the dynamo is! . . . that's what life is! . . . (*He stares at it raptly now.*) Listen to her singing

. . . that beats all organs in church . . . it's the hymn of electricity . . . " always singing about everything in the world " . . . if you could only get back into that . . . know what it means . . . then you'd know the real God ! . . . (*Then longingly.*) There must be some way ! . . . there must be something in her song that'd tell you if you had ears to hear ! . . . some way that she'd teach you to know . . . (*He begins to hum, swaying his body—then stops when he can't catch the right tone.*) No, you can't get it ! . . . it's as far off as the sky and yet it's all around you ! . . . in you ! . . . (*Excitedly.*) I feel like praying now ! . . . I feel there is something in her to pray to ! . . . something that'll answer me ! . . . (*He looks around him and moves to the right out of the square of light from the open doorway.*) Supposing anyone saw me . . . they'd think I was nutty . . . that old prayer stuff . . . (*Then arguing tormentedly with himself.*) But I feel it's right . . . I feel Mother wants me to . . . it's the least I can do for her . . . to say a prayer . . . (*He gets down on his knees and prays aloud to the dynamo.*) Oh Mother of Life, my mother is dead, she has passed back into you, tell her to forgive me, and to help me find your truth ! (*He pauses on his knees for a moment, then gets slowly to his feet. There is a look of calm and relief on his face now. He thinks reverentially.*) Yes, that did it . . . I feel I'm forgiven . . . Mother will help . . . I can sleep . . . I'll go home . . . (*He walks slowly off right.*)

CURTAIN

ACT THREE
SCENE ONE

SCENE. *Same as* ACT TWO, SCENE THREE—*Exterior of the power house four months later. It is a little after sunset and the equipment on the roof is outlined blackly against a darkening crimson sky.*

The door of the dynamo room is shut but the interior is brilliantly lighted and the dynamo can be partly seen through the window. There is a dim light above in the switch galleries as in the previous scene. The overtone of rushing water from the dam sounds louder because of the closed door which muffles the noise of the dynamo to a minor strain.

Reuben enters from the left accompanied by Mrs. Fife. He has grown very thin, his dungarees sag about his angular frame. His face is gaunt and pale. His eyes are deeply sunken. He is talking with unnatural excitement as they come in. Mrs. Fife is unchanged. If anything, her moony dreaminess is more pronounced. She listens to Reuben with a fascinated far-away look, as if the sound of his voice hypnotized her rather than the meaning of the words.

REUBEN (*insistently*) You understood all I explained to you up on the dam, didn't you ?—about how life first came out of the sea ?

MRS. FIFE (*nods dreamily*). Yes, Reuben. It sounds like poetry—" life out of the sea."

REUBEN. It is like poetry. Her song in there—Dynamo's—isn't that the greatest poem of all—the poem of eternal life ? And listen to the water rushing over the dam ! Like music ! It's as if that sound was cool water washing over my hot body ! Like some one singing me to sleep—my mother—when I was a kid—calling me back to somewhere far off where I'd been once long ago and known peace ! (*He sighs with longing, his body suddenly gone limp and weary.*)

MRS. FIFE (*dreamily*). That's awful pretty, Reuben. (*She puts her arm around him—sentimentally.*) I'll be your mother—yours and Ada's. I've always wanted a boy.

REUBEN (*leans against her gratefully, his head almost on her shoulder, his eyes half closed*). Yes. You're like her—Dynamo—the Great Mother—big and warm— (*With a sudden renewal of his unnatural excitement, breaks away from her.*) But I've got to finish telling you all I've come to know about her—how all things end up in her ! Did I tell you that our blood-plasm is the same right now as the sea was when life came out of it ? We've got the sea in our blood still ! It's what makes our hearts live ! And it's the sea rising up in clouds, falling on the earth in rain, made that river that drives the turbines that drive Dynamo ! The sea makes her heart beat too !—but the sea is only hydrogen and oxygen and minerals, and they're only atoms, and atoms are only protons and electrons—even our blood and the sea are only electricity in the end ! And think of the stars ! Driving through space, round and round, just like the electrons in the atom! But there must be a centre around which all this moves, mustn't there? There is in everything else! And that centre must be the Great Mother of Eternal Life, Electricity, and Dynamo is her Divine Image on earth! Her power houses are the new churches! She wants us to realize the secret dwells in her! She wants some one man to love her purely and when she finds him worthy she will love him and tell him the secret of truth and he will become the new saviour who will bring happiness and peace to men! And I'm going to be that saviour—the miracle will happen to-night—that's why I asked you to come—I want you to be a witness! I know it will be to-night because I had a message from my mother last night. I woke up and saw her standing beside my bed—just as she used to when she came in to kiss me good-night—and she smiled and held out her arms to me. She came from the spirit of the Great Mother to tell me she had at last found me worthy of her love.

MRS. FIFE (*sentimentally*). Most people don't believe in ghosts. Ramsay doesn't. But I see them all the time. Sometimes I don't hardly know which are ghosts and which are real. Has she come many times, Reuben?

REUBEN (*strangely*). Not lately—not since I gave up seeing Ada. Before that she used to come almost every night to warn me.

MRS. FIFE. Warn you about what, Reuben?

REUBEN. That I was living in sin—that Dynamo would never find me worthy of her secret until I'd given up the flesh and purified myself! (*Then proudly.*) And I found the strength to do it. It was hard! I was beginning to really love Ada.

MRS. FIFE (*simply*). Of course, you love Ada—and you shouldn't act so mean to her, Reuben. You haven't been around in a month or more. She's making herself sick worrying.

REUBEN (*intensely*). I'd like to see her! I'd love to! But I can't! Don't you understand I can't—that my finding the secret is more important than—but when I come back bringing peace and happiness to the world it will mean peace and happiness for Ada and me too! Everything will be all right then!

(*Then thinking with sudden fear and doubt.*) But supposing the miracle doesn't happen to-night? . . . have I got to go on and on like this? . . . Ada keeps coming to me every night in dreams . . . the temptation of her body . . . I've beaten myself with my belt till the pain drove it off . . . but I can't keep on much longer . . .

(*He sways dizzily on his feet, passing his hand over his eyes—then straightens himself and turns to Mrs. Fife.*) I've got to go in. They'll be missing me. You'll stay around, won't you? (*He goes to the door.*) You wait until your husband's gone home. Then you come in.

MRS. FIFE. All right, Reuben.

(*Reuben slides back the dynamo room door and enters, closing it behind him. Mrs. Fife stares after him mooningly. A moment later the door from the dynamo room is opened again and Fife comes out, closing it behind him. He hasn't changed since his last appearance. He starts to walk hesitatingly off right—then stops without looking around him and does not notice his wife.*)

FIFE (*thinking exasperatedly*). That damned Rube! . . . there's a queer look in those cold eyes of his lately! . . . by God, I'd fire him to-night if Ada wouldn't make my life a hell for it! . . . but he does his work good . . . too damned good! . . . he's always pawing around a dynamo when he's no business . . .

MRS. FIFE. Hello, Ramsay. You better get home to supper. I had mine early. I had to go out.

FIFE (*turns on her with an irritated start*). Oh, you did, did you? You're always having to go out these days, it seems! (*Mrs. Fife stares at him as if she didn't hear him. This drives Fife into a shrill scolding.*) I won't have you gallivanting down here at all hours and staring at the dynamos and humming like a half-wit! What the hell's come over you anyway? (*He finishes up lamely, the wind taken out of his sails by her indifference.*)

MRS. FIFE. Nothing's come over me, Ramsay. I was talking to Reuben. He took me up on the dam and told me about how we all used to live in the ocean once. (*Then in her tone of childish mooning.*) D'you suppose I ever was a fish, Ramsay?

FIFE. Aye, a jellyfish, I'm thinking! You've the brains for that! (*Then angrily.*) You do too much gabbing with that Rube! He'll addle the little sense you've left! But if you've got to talk to him, make him talk turkey and say when is he planning to marry Ada! Aren't you her mother, and don't you see she's worrying her heart out? (*Lowering his voice.*) D'you think it's happened between them—you know what I mean?

MRS. FIFE (*with naïve simplicity*). Yes, of course it has, Ramsay. She loves him the same as I did you when we——

FIFE. Don't be comparing him to me! I was more of a decent man than he ever will be! (*In a passion.*) I'll have a talk with that lad and if he don't do the decent thing by her, I'll beat decency into him! (*He turns from her in a tantrum.*) To hell with you! I'm hungry! I'm going home! (*He goes off right.*)

(*Mrs. Fife looks after him with a placid smile—then she gives the big door a push that slides it open to its full width and steps inside and, as she sees Reuben, stops as she is about to pull the door closed again. He is kneeling just inside the doorway before the dynamo in the foreground, his arms stretched out to it supplicatingly.*)

REUBEN (*suddenly cries out with a note of despair*). Mother! Don't you hear me? Can't you give me some sign? O Dynamo, who gives life to all things, hear my prayer! Grant me the miracle of your love!

(*He waits, his body strained with suspense, listening as if he expected the dynamo to answer him. Ada comes from around the corner of the building at the left. Her manner is furtive as if she were doing something she is ashamed of. She looks worried and run down, although she has made a defiant effort with rouge and mascara to hide this.*)

ADA. He must be around some place . . . (*She moves cautiously to the window and peeks in, but cannot see him. Then with bitter self-contempt.*) Here I am chasing after him! . . . but I couldn't stand it any more, waiting . . . oh, what a damn fool I was to give in so easy! . . . no wonder he's sick of me! . . . but he can't throw me over this way! . . .

REUBEN (*his tense, supplicating attitude suddenly relaxing dejectedly*). She won't answer me . . . there must still be something I've got to do. (*Then guiltily.*) Maybe she feels I haven't killed all desire for Ada yet . . . that I ought to face her and conquer the flesh once for all . . .

(*He jumps to his feet and turns to Mrs. Fife pleadingly.*) Can't you tell me? You know what she means sometimes. (*He lowers his voice cautiously as if he didn't want the dynamo to overhear.*) Do you think it's something I've got to do about Ada?

MRS. FIFE (*simply*). Yes, you've got to do the right thing by Ada, Reuben.

REUBEN (*thinking with unnatural excitement*). Then that is it! . . . well, I'll go and face Ada right now!

(*Turning to Mrs. Fife.*) You stay here! I'll be back. (*He comes out, sliding the door closed after him.*)

ADA (*calls to him uncertainly*). Rube!

REUBEN (*whirls around and stands staring at her with strange fixity for a moment, his thoughts jumping at conclusions*). It's Ada! . . . Dynamo knew Ada was here! . . . she wanted me to come out and prove! . . .

ADA (*frightenedly*). What's the matter? Don't look at me like that, Rube!

REUBEN (*moved in spite of himself, instinctively takes a step toward her—in a queer detached tone*). I didn't mean to scare you, Ada. You gave me a start, seeing you all of a sudden.

ADA (*looking at him hopefully*). You're not sore at me for coming, are you?

REUBEN. No. It's as if you'd been sent. Didn't you feel something driving you to come here right now?

ADA (*quickly*). Yes, I just had to come!

REUBEN (*strangely*). It was she who made you come.

ADA. She? Who's she?

REUBEN (*a lightning change comes over his face. He takes a threatening step toward her—denouncingly, his voice booming like his father's*). You blasphemous fool, you ! Do you dare to deny her ! " The fool saith in his heart—" (*He suddenly checks himself and forces a strange, shamefaced laugh.*) Say, did you get me quoting from the Bible, Ada ? That's one on me ! That comes from arguing with the old man lately. He's got some fool notion that Dynamo is the devil ! (*Then his expression abruptly changing again—fiercely.*) But I'll make the old fool get down on his knees to her yet before I'm through with him ! And I'll make you, too, Ada !

(*This puts a sudden idea into his head—thinking excitedly.*) What made me say that ? . . . you, Mother ? . . . make her pray to you ? . . . not only conquer her flesh, but convert her ? . . .

Listen to me, Ada ! To-night the miracle will happen !—and then there will be only the kingdom of happiness on earth—my kingdom !—for us, Ada ! (*Then suddenly grabbing her by the arm.*) Only you've got to help me !

ADA (*thinking frightenedly*). For God's sake, what's come over him ! . . . the damned dynamo ! . . . it's driving him crazy ! . . .

(*She puts her arms around him pityingly and tries to hug him to her.*) I'll do anything, Rube ! Don't you know how much I love you ?

REUBEN (*pushing her away from him—in a stammering panic*). Don't do that ! (*Then pleadingly.*) Why can't you understand ? You've got to believe in Dynamo, and bow down to her will ?

ADA (*soothingly*). All right, Rube.

REUBEN (*taking her hand—insistently*). Come with me ! I want to explain everything to you —all this plant means about her—you've got to believe, Ada ! (*She follows him off left, frightened but pitying and resolved to humour him. His voice is heard explaining excitedly as they climb the path to the dam. It recedes and then grows louder as they cross from the dam to the dynamo-room roof. A moment later he is seen there. He comes forward until he stands by the coping, front. He still has Ada by the hand. She follows him, holding back as much as she dares, a nervous look on her face. His unnatural excitement has increased, he looks around him with the rapt expression of one in a trance, his eyes burning feverishly.*) Oh, Ada, you simply can't help believing in her ! You only have to listen to her ! Her song is the hymn of eternal generation, the song of eternal life !

ADA (*uneasily*). Rube ! I'm scared up here !

REUBEN (*turns and looks at her like a sleep-walker for a second—then with a sudden hungry passion*). You're so damned pretty ! God, how I wish the miracle was over and we could—— !

ADA (*persuasively*). I'm scared on this roof, Rube. Let's go down !

REUBEN (*excitedly*). Yes, down to her ! I was forgetting her ! She's waiting for me !

(*Then as she starts to go back the way they have come, he takes her hand again and pulls her through the door from the roof to the galleries.*)

ADA (*frightenedly*). Rube ! I don't want to go——

(*He slams the door behind them.*)

(*There is a pause of darkness here to indicate the end of* SCENE ONE. *No time elapses between* SCENES ONE *and* TWO.)

SCENE TWO

SCENE. *When the light comes on again the interiors of the upper and lower switch galleries are revealed. The lower gallery of the oil switches is a deep but narrow compartment with red brick walls. The oil switches, with their spindly steel legs, their square criss-crossed steel bodies (the containers inside looking like bellies), their six cupped arms stretching upward, remind one of Hindu idols tortured into scientific supplications. These switches extend in a straight row backward down the middle of the gallery, but in the dim light of one bulb in a bracket in the left wall only the front one in the foreground can be made out. Against the wall on the right is a stairway that extends backwards half-way up this wall, then turns and ascends diagonally upwards to the left to the upper gallery, and from thence up to the door to the roof of the dynamo room.*

The upper gallery contains the disconnecting

switches and the double busses. It is of double width and extends over the switchboard room also. This second gallery, dimly lighted like the one below, is a fretwork of wires, steel work, insulators, busses, switches, etc., stretching upward to the roof. Below the disconnecting switches is a raised platform.

Reuben and Ada are discovered by the dim light of this upper gallery standing just inside the door to the dynamo-room roof at the top of the stairway.

ADA (*looking around her frightenedly at the weird-shaped shadows of the equipment writhing upward in the dimly lighted gallery—shrinking close to Reuben, who is staring at all this with a rapt, questioning, listening look*). All this stuff scares me. I've only seen it in daylight before. It looks so weird—as if it was alive!

REUBEN (*strangely*). You're beginning to see, Ada! It is alive! Alive with the mighty spirit of her eternal life! (*Then with a start, he pushes her away from him roughly.*) What the hell are you doing? Don't press against me, I tell you! I'm wise to your dirty game—and I won't stand for it! Don't you realize we're in her temple now!

ADA (*pityfully*). Rube! Please don't talk like that—when you know how I love you!

REUBEN (*clutching her arm fiercely*). You mustn't say you love me in here, you fool, you! Don't you know all this is watching—listening—that she knows everything! Sssh! I want to hear if she's angry at me! (*He stands in a strained attitude of attention, listening to the dynamo's hum sounding from below—then evidently satisfied, turns to Ada with a relieved air.*) No, she isn't angry on account of you being here because she knows you're beginning to believe in her! It's all right for you to come close to me, Ada. (*He puts an arm around her and pulls her to him.*)

ADA (*persuasively*). Please let's go down, Rube.

REUBEN (*gently*). All right, Ada. (*They go down the first flight of steps. He stops as they get to the bottom and glances up and around him.*) You know, Ada, there used to be times when I was scared here too—when all these switches and busses and wires seemed like the arms of a devil fish—stretching out to suck me in—— (*He gives a shudder and presses her to him.*)

ADA (*soothingly*). You mustn't be afraid. I'm here with you.

REUBEN (*pleadingly—pointing to the platform beneath the disconnecting switches*). Listen, Ada! I want you to pray to her—up there where I pray sometimes—under her arms—with your arms like her arms, stretching out for me! (*He suddenly bends his face to her face, his eyes devouring it desirously.*) God, you're pretty! (*He controls himself with a violent effort and pushes her away from him, keeping his face averted from hers—in a voice that is almost supplicating.*) You must pray that she may find me worthy. You must pray for me, if you love me!

ADA (*soothingly—humouring him*). All right, Rube. (*She goes up the stairs to the platform and stands directly under the switches.*)

REUBEN (*remains standing below—thinking confusedly*). Mother would warn me if I was doing wrong . . . Dynamo means all this to happen to me . . . it's the great temptation . . . perhaps she wants me even to kiss Ada . . .

(*He ascends to the platform and stands holding on to the rail, afraid to look at Ada.*)

ADA (*stretching her arms up, in the same position as the switch arms—tenderly and soothingly*). Why did you say a minute ago, if I loved you? Don't you know I do? Why have you stayed away from me so long, Rube? I've almost died, longing for you!

REUBEN (*without looking at her—dazedly*). You believe in her now, don't you? You wouldn't do anything to make me unworthy in her sight, would you?—when it means happiness for me—and for all mankind? You couldn't, could you?

ADA (*humouring him—gently*). Of course not.

REUBEN (*mechanically*). You swear to her?

ADA (*in the same tone*). Yes, I swear.

REUBEN (*mechanically*). Then I'm going to kiss you, Ada—just once—only kiss you—she wants me to—as a final test—to prove I'm purified— (*He looks up at her now and lurches forward with a groan of passion and takes her in his arms.*) Ada!

(He kisses her frantically, bending her backward and down toward the floor of the platform. She cries out frightenedly.)

(There is a pause of darkness to indicate the end of SCENE TWO. *A short time is supposed to elapse between* SCENES TWO *and* THREE.*)*

SCENE THREE

SCENE. *As the light slowly comes on again, Reuben is heard sobbing brokenly from the gallery. The interiors of the dynamo and switchboard rooms are now also revealed.*

The dynamo room is high and wide with red brick walls and a row of great windows in the left wall. The floor and an observation balcony which projects into the dynamo room from the switchboard room on the right (one story up), are of concrete. The nearest dynamo, which we have seen previously through the doorway, occupies most of the floor space in the foreground. A steel ladder runs up its side on the right to a platform around the exciter.

The switchboard room is a small compartment to the right of the dynamo room, one story up in the other section of the building. In it are the switchboard and a couple of chairs. It is lighted by a shaded drop light over the desk. Jennings, the operator on duty, a man of thirty or so, is seated at the desk.

Mrs. Fife is sitting in the dynamo room just under and to the left of the observation balcony. She is staring dreamily at the front dynamo, humming to herself, her big body relaxed as if she had given herself up completely to the spell of its hypnotic, metallic purr which flows insistently through the ears, numbing the brain, charging the nerves with electricity, making the heart strain with the desire to beat in its rhythm of unbroken, eternal continuity.

In the gallery, Ada and Reuben are still on the platform beneath the disconnecting switches. Reuben is on his knees, his back bowed, his face covered by his hands. Ada is standing before him, directly beneath the switches as before. She is bending over him in a tender attitude, one hand reaching down, the fingers touching his hair.

REUBEN *(thinking torturedly)*. Mother! . . . I've betrayed you . . . you will never bless me with the miracle now! . . . you have shut me from your heart for ever! . . .

(He groans and beats his head against the floor.)

ADA *(puts her hand down and pats him on the back consolingly)*. Poor Rube! Why do you think about things so much? I love you. Why don't you be happy?

REUBEN *(shrinking away)*. Don't touch me—ever again!

(He springs to his feet, and shielding his face with one hand from the sight of her, runs down the stairs to the lower oil switch gallery. He stops there, looking around him distractedly as if he didn't know where to hide, his thoughts hounded by remorse.) Mother! . . . have mercy on me! . . . I hate her now! . . . as much as you hate her! . . . give me one more chance! . . . what can I do to get you to forgive me? . . . tell me! . . . yes! . . . I hear you, Mother! . . . and then you'll forgive me? . . . and I can come to you? . . . *(A terrible look of murder comes on his face. He starts for the stairs, his hands outstretched as if he were already strangling her—then stops.)* No . . . not with my hands . . . never touch her flesh again . . . how? . . . I see . . . switchboard room . . . in the desk. . . .

(He dashes over into the switchboard room through the door at left of the gallery. He has the startled and terrified Jennings by the throat before the latter knows it and flings him away from the desk, tears out a drawer and gets the revolver and with it motions him to the door to the office in the rear.) Get in there! Quick!

(Jennings obeys hastily. Reuben turns the key in the lock after him. In contrast to his furious haste of a moment before, he now walks deliberately back through the door to the oil switch gallery. His face is as drained of all human feeling as a plaster mask.) I won't be a murderer . . . I'm your executioner, Mother . . . that's why I'm so calm . . .

(He glides stealthily across toward the foot of the stairs.)

ADA *(worried about him, has come down from the*

platform and is beginning to descend the stairs to the lower switch gallery—she calls uneasily). Rube! Where are you?

REUBEN. Harlot! . . . that's what Mother called her!

(*He springs up the stairs, shouting fiercely.*) Harlot!

ADA (*she suddenly sees his face and the revolver aimed at her breast as he stops directly beneath her—in a terrified whisper*). Rube!

(*Reuben fires, and she jerks back and pitches sideways on the stairs, dead.*)

REUBEN (*stares down at her body for a moment and lets the gun fall from his hand and begins to tremble all over. He calls pitifully*). Ada! I didn't mean to hurt you!

(*Then thinking with an anguished appeal.*) Mother! . . . where are you? . . . I did it for your sake! . . . why don't you call to me? . . . don't leave me alone! . . .

(*He turns and runs headlong through the switchboard room, and down the stairs to the dynamo-room floor, where he lunges for the rungs on the dynamo's side and clambers-up frenziedly. Up on the platform, he stops for a moment, gasping for breath, stretching out his arms to the exciter-head of his Dynamo-Mother with its whirling metal brain and its blank oblong eyes.*)

MRS. FIFE (*dimly aware of him—dreamily*). What was that noise up there, Reuben? It sounded like a shot.

REUBEN (*pleading like a little boy*). I don't want any miracle, Mother! I don't want to know the truth! I only want you to hide me, Mother! Never let me go from you again! Please, Mother!

(*He throws his arms out over the exciter, his hands grasp the carbon brushes. There is a flash of bluish light about him and all the lights in the plant dim down until they are almost out and the noise of the dynamo dies until it is the faintest purring hum. Simultaneously Reuben's voice rises in a moan that is a mingling of pain and loving consummation, and this cry dies into a sound that is like the crooning of a baby and merges and is lost in the dynamo's hum. Then his body crumples to the steel platform and from there falls heavily to the floor. There is a startled cry from Mrs. Fife as she runs to the body. The dynamo's throaty metallic purr rises slowly in volume and the lights begin to come up again in the plant.*)

MRS. FIFE (*kneeling beside Reuben, one hand on the forehead of his upturned face*). Poor Reuben! She wouldn't tell you the secret after all, would she? (*She gets to her feet and stares with childish resentment and hurt at the dynamo.*) What are you singing for? I should think you'd be ashamed! And I thought you was nice and loved us! (*The dynamo's purr has regained its accustomed pitch now. The lights in the plant are again at their full brightness. Everything is as before. Mrs. Fife goes over and pounds the steel body of the dynamo in a fit of childish anger.*) You hateful old thing, you! (*Then she leaves off, having hurt her hands, and begins to cry softly.*)

CURTAIN

MOURNING BECOMES ELECTRA

A Trilogy

TO CARLOTTA
MY WIFE

General Scene of the Trilogy

The action of the trilogy, with the exception of an act of the second play, takes place in or immediately outside the Mannon residence, on the outskirts of one of the smaller New England seaport towns.

A special curtain shows the house as seen from the street. From this, in each play, one comes to the exterior of the house in the opening act and enters it in the following act.

This curtain reveals the extensive grounds – about thirty acres – which surround the house, a heavily wooded ridge in the background, orchards on the right and in the immediate rear, a large flower garden and a greenhouse on the left.

In the foreground, along the street, is a line of locust and elm trees. The property is enclosed by a white picket fence and a tall hedge. A drive curves up towards the house from two entrances with white gates. Between the house and the street is a lawn. By the right corner of the house is a grove of pine trees. Farther forward, along the drive, maples and locusts. By the left corner of the house is a big clump of lilacs and syringas.

The house is placed back on a slight rise of ground about three hundred feet from the street. It is a large building of the Greek temple style that was the vogue in the first half of the nineteenth century. A white wooden portico with six tall columns contrasts with the wall of the house proper which is of grey cut stone. There are five windows on the upper floor and four on the ground floor, with the main entrance in the middle, a doorway with squared transom and sidelights flanked by intermediate columns. The window shutters are painted a dark green. Before the doorway a flight of four steps leads from the ground to the portico.

The three plays take place in either spring or summer of the years 1865–1866.

PART ONE: Homecoming
PART TWO: The Hunted
PART THREE: The Haunted

HOMECOMING

A Play in Four Acts

Part One of the Trilogy
MOURNING BECOMES ELECTRA

Characters

BRIGADIER-GENERAL EZRA MANNON
CHRISTINE, *his wife*
LAVINIA, *their daughter*
CAPTAIN ADAM BRANT, *of the clipper "Flying Trades"*
CAPTAIN PETER NILES, *U.S. Artillery*
HAZEL NILES, *his sister*
SETH BECKWITH
AMOS AMES
LOUISA, *his wife*
MINNIE, *her cousin*

Scenes

ACT ONE

Exterior of the Mannon house in New England. April 1865.

ACT TWO

Ezra Mannon's study in the house. No time has elapsed.

ACT THREE

The same as Act One – exterior of the house. A night a week later.

ACT FOUR

A bedroom in the house. Later the same night.

ACT ONE

SCENE. *Exterior of the Mannon house on a late afternoon in April, 1865. In front is the drive which leads up to the house from the two entrances on the street. Behind the drive the white Grecian temple portico with its six tall columns extends across the stage. A big pine tree is on the lawn at the edge of the drive before the right corner of the house. Its trunk is a black column in striking contrast with the white columns of the portico. By the edge of the drive, left front, is a dense clump of lilacs and syringas. A bench is placed on the lawn in front of this shrubbery which partly screens anyone sitting on it from being seen from the front of the house.*

It is shortly before sunset and the soft light of the declining sun shines directly on the front of the house, shimmering in a luminous mist on the white portico and the grey stone wall behind, intensifying the whiteness of the columns, the sombre greyness of the wall, the green of the open shutters, the green of the lawn and shrubbery, the black and green of the pine tree. The white columns cast black bars of shadow on the grey wall behind them. The windows of the lower storey reflect the sun's rays in a resentful glare. The temple portico is like an incongruous white mask fixed on the house to hide its sombre grey ugliness.

In the distance, from the town, a band is heard playing "John Brown's Body." Borne on the light puffs of wind this music is at times quite loud, then sinks into faintness as the wind dies.

From the left rear, a man's voice is heard singing the chanty "Shenandoah"—a song that more than any other holds in it the brooding rhythm of the sea. The voice soon sounds nearer. It is thin and aged, the wraith of what must once have been a good baritone.

"*Oh, Shenandoah, I long to hear you*
A-way, my rolling river.
Oh, Shenandoah, I can't get near you
Way—ay, I'm bound away
Across the wide Missouri."

The singer, Seth Beckwith, finishes the last line as he enters from around the corner of the house. Closely following him are Amos Ames, his wife Louisa, and her cousin Minnie.

Seth Beckwith, the Mannons' gardener and man of all work, is an old man of seventy-five with white hair and beard, tall, raw-boned and bent-shouldered, his joints stiffened by rheumatism, but still sound and hale. He has a gaunt face that in repose gives one the strange impression of a life-like mask. It is set in a grim expression, but his small, sharp eyes still peer at life with a shrewd prying avidity and his loose mouth has a strong suggestion of ribald humour. He wears his earth-stained working clothes.

Amos Ames, carpenter by trade but now taking a holiday and dressed in his Sunday best, as are his wife and her cousin, is a fat man in his fifties. In character he is the townsfolk type of garrulous gossip-monger who is at the same time devoid of evil intent, scandal being for him merely the subject most popular with his audience.

His wife, Louisa, is taller and stouter than he and about the same age. Of a similar scandal-bearing type, her tongue is sharpened by malice.

Her cousin, Minnie, is a plump little woman of forty, of the meek, eager-listener type, with a small round face, round stupid eyes, and a round mouth pursed out to drink in gossip.

These last three are types of townsfolk rather than individuals, a chorus representing the town come to look and listen and spy on the rich and exclusive Mannons.

Led by Seth, they come forward as far as the lilac clump and stand staring at the house. Seth, in a mood of aged playfulness, is trying to make an impression on Minnie. His singing has been for her benefit. He nudges her with his elbow, grinning.

SETH. How's that fur singin' fur an old feller? I used to be noted fur my chanties. (*Seeing she is paying no attention to him but is staring with open-mouthed awe at the house, he turns to Ames—jubilantly.*) By jingo, Amos, if that news is true, there won't be a sober man in town to-night! It's our patriotic duty to celebrate!

AMES (*with a grin*). We'd ought to, that's sartin!

LOUISA. You ain't goin' to git Amos drunk to-night, surrender or no surrender! An old reprobate, that's what you be!

SETH (*pleased*). Old nothin'! On'y seventy-five! My old man lived to be ninety! Licker can't kill the Beckwiths! (*He and Ames laugh. Louisa smiles in spite of herself. Minnie is oblivious, still staring at the house.*)

MINNIE. My sakes! What a purty house!

SETH. Wal, I promised Amos I'd help show ye the sights when you came to visit him. 'Taint everyone can git to see the Mannon place close to. They're strict about trespassin'.

MINNIE. My! They must be rich! How'd they make their money?

SETH. Ezra's made a pile, and before him, his father, Abe Mannon, he inherited some and made a pile more in shippin'. Started one of the fust Western Ocean packet lines.

MINNIE. Ezra's the General, ain't he?

SETH (*proudly*). Ayeh. The best fighter in the hull of Grant's army!

MINNIE. What kind is he?

SETH (*boastfully expanding*). He's able, Ezra is! Folks think he's cold-blooded and uppish, 'cause he's never got much to say to 'em. But that's only the Mannons' way. They've been top dog around here for near on two hundred years and don't let folks fergit it.

MINNIE. How'd he come to jine the army if he's so rich?

SETH. Oh, he'd been a soldier afore this war. His paw made him go to West P'int. He went to the Mexican war and come out a major. Abe died that same year and Ezra give up the army and took hold of the shippin' business here. But he didn't stop there. He learned law in addition and got made a judge. Went in fur politics and got 'lected mayor. He was mayor when this war broke out but he resigned at once and jined the army again. And now he's riz to be General. Oh, he's able enough, Ezra is !

AMES. Ayeh. This town's real proud of Ezra.

LOUISA. Which is more'n you kin say fur his wife. Folks all hates her ! She ain't the Mannon kind. French and Dutch descended, she is. Furrin lookin' and queer. Her father's a doctor in New York, but he can't be much of a one 'cause she didn't bring no money when Ezra married her.

SETH (*his face growing grim—sharply*). Never mind her. We ain't talkin' 'bout her. (*Then abruptly changing the subject.*) Wal, I've got to see Vinnie. I'm goin' round by the kitchen. You wait here. And if Ezra's wife starts to run you off fur trespassin', you tell her I got permission from Vinnie to show you round.

(*He goes off around the corner of the house, left. The three stare about them gawkily, awed and uncomfortable. They talk in low voices.*)

LOUISA. Seth is so proud of his durned old Mannons ! I couldn't help givin' him a dig about Ezra's wife.

AMES. Wal, don't matter much. He's allus hated her.

LOUISA. Ssshh ! Someone's comin' out. Let's get back here ! (*They crowd to the rear of the bench by the lilac clump and peer through the leaves as the front door is opened and Christine Mannon comes out to the edge of the portico at the top of the steps. Louisa prods her cousin and whispers excitedly.*) That's her !

(*Christine Mannon is a tall striking-looking woman of forty but she appears younger. She has a fine, voluptuous figure and she moves with a flowing animal grace. She wears a green satin dress, smartly cut and expensive, which brings out the peculiar colour of her thick curly hair, partly a copper brown, partly a bronze gold, each shade distinct and yet blending with the other. Her face is unusual, handsome rather than beautiful. One is struck at once by the strange impression it gives in repose of being not living flesh but a wonderfully life-like pale mask, in which only the deep-set eyes, of a dark violet blue, are alive. Her black eyebrows meet in a pronounced straight line above her strong nose. Her chin is heavy, her mouth large and sensual, the lower lip full, the upper a thin bow, shadowed by a line of hair. She stands and listens defensively, as if the music held some meaning that threatened her. But at once she shrugs her shoulders with disdain and comes down the steps and walks off towards the flower garden, passing behind the lilac clump without having noticed Ames and the women.*)

MINNIE (*in an awed whisper*). My ! She's awful handsome, ain't she ?

LOUISA. Too furrin lookin' fur my taste.

MINNIE. Ayeh. There's somethin' queer-lookin' about her face.

AMES. Secret lookin'—'s if it was a mask she'd put on. That's the Mannon look. They all has it. They grow it on their wives. Seth's growed it on too, didn't you notice—from bein' with 'em all his life. They don't want folks to guess their secrets.

MINNIE (*breathlessly eager*). Secrets ?

LOUISA. The Mannons got skeletons in their closets same as others ! Worse ones. (*Lowering her voice almost to a whisper—to her husband.*) Tell Minnie about old Abe Mannon's brother David marryin' that French Canuck nurse girl he'd got into trouble.

AMES. Ssshh ! Shut up, can't you ? Here's Seth comin'. (*But he whispers quickly to Minnie.*) That happened way back when I was a youngster. I'll tell you later. (*Seth has appeared from around the left corner of the house and now joins them.*)

SETH. That durned nigger cook is allus askin' me to fetch wood fur her ! You'd think I was her slave ! That's what we get fur freein' 'em ! (*Then briskly.*) Wal, come along, folks. I'll show you the peach orchard and then we'll go to my greenhouse. I couldn't find Vinnie.

(*They are about to start when the front door of the house is opened and Lavinia comes out to the top of the steps where her mother *had stood. She is twenty-three but looks considerably older. Tall like her mother, her body is thin, flat-breasted and angular, and its unattractiveness is accentuated by her plain black dress. Her movements are stiff and she carries herself with a wooden, square-shouldered, military bearing. She has a flat dry voice and a habit of snapping out her words like an officer giving orders. But in spite of these dissimilarities, one is immediately struck by her facial resemblance to her mother. She has the same peculiar shade of copper-gold hair, the same pallor and dark violet-blue eyes, the black eyebrows meeting in a straight line above her nose, the same sensual mouth, the same heavy jaw. Above all, one is struck by the same strange, life-like mask impression her face gives in repose. But it is evident Lavinia does all in her power to emphasize the dissimilarity rather than the resemblance to her parent. She wears her hair pulled tightly back, as if to conceal its natural curliness, and there is not a touch of feminine allurement in her severely plain get-up. Her head is the same size as her mother's, but on her thin body it looks too large and heavy.*

SETH (*seeing her*). There she be now.

(*He starts for the steps—then sees she has not noticed their presence: he stops and stands waiting, struck by something in her manner. She is looking off right, watching her mother who strolls through the garden to the greenhouse. Her eyes are bleak and hard with an intense, bitter enmity. Then her mother evidently disappears in the greenhouse, for Lavinia turns her head, still oblivious of Seth and his friends, and looks off left, her attention caught by the band, the music of which, borne on a freshening breeze, has suddenly become louder. It is still playing "John Brown's Body." Lavinia listens, as her mother had a moment before, but her reaction is the direct opposite to what her mother's had been. Her eyes light up with a grim satisfaction, and an expression of strange vindictive triumph comes into her face.*)

LOUISA (*in a quick whisper to Minnie*). That's Lavinia!

MINNIE. She looks like her mother in face—queer-lookin'—but she ain't purty like her.

SETH. You git along to the orchard, folks. I'll jine you there. (*They walk back around the left of the house and disappear. He goes to Lavinia eagerly.*) Say, I got fine news fur you, Vinnie. The telegraph feller says Lee is a goner sure this time! They're only waitin' now fur the news to be made official. You can count on your paw comin' home!

LAVINIA (*grimly*). I hope so. It's time.

SETH (*with a keen glance at her—slowly*). Ayeh.

LAVINIA (*turning on him sharply*). What do you mean, Seth?

SETH (*avoiding her eyes—evasively*). Nothin'—'cept what you mean. (*Lavinia stares at him. He avoids her eyes—then heavily casual.*) Where was you gallivantin' night afore last and all yesterday?

LAVINIA (*starts*). Over at Hazel and Peter's house.

SETH. Ayeh. There's where Hannah said you'd told her you was goin'. That's funny now—'cause I seen Peter out yesterday and he asked me where you was keepin' yourself.

LAVINIA (*again starts—then slowly as if admitting a secret understanding between them*). I went to New York, Seth.

SETH. Ayeh. That's where I thought you'd gone, mebbe. (*Then with deep sympathy.*) It's durned hard on you, Vinnie. It's a durned shame.

LAVINIA (*stiffening—curtly*). I don't know what you're talking about.

SETH (*nods comprehendingly*). All right, Vinnie. Just as you say. (*He pauses—then after hesitating frowningly for a moment, blurts out.*) There's somethin' been on my mind lately I want to warn you about. It's got to do with what's worryin' you—that is, if there's anythin' in it.

LAVINIA (*stiffly*). There's nothing worrying me. (*Then sharply.*) Warn me? About what?

SETH. Mebbe it's nothin'—and then again mebbe I'm right, and if I'm right, then you'd ought t'be warned. It's to do with that Captain Brant.

LAVINIA (*starts again but keeps her tone cold and collected*). What about him?

SETH. Somethin' I calc'late no one'd notice 'specially 'ceptin' me, because—— (*Then hastily as he sees someone coming up the drive.*) Here's

Peter and Hazel comin'. I'll tell you later, Vinnie. I ain't got time now anyways. Those folks are waitin' for me.

LAVINIA. I'll be sitting here. You come back afterwards. (*Then her cold disciplined mask breaking for a moment—tensely.*) Oh, why do Peter and Hazel have to come now? I don't want to see anyone! (*She starts as if to go into the house.*)

SETH. You run in. I'll git rid of 'em fur you.

LAVINIA (*recovering herself—curtly*). No. I'll see them.

(*Seth goes back around the corner of the house, left. A moment later Hazel and Peter Niles enter along the drive from left, front. Hazel is a pretty, healthy girl of nineteen, with dark hair and eyes. Her features are small but clearly modelled. She has a strong chin and a capable, smiling mouth. One gets a sure impression of her character at a glance—frank, innocent, amiable and good—not in a negative but in a positive, self-possessed way. Her brother, Peter, is very like her in character—straightforward, guileless and good-natured. He is a heavily-built young fellow of twenty-two, awkward in movement and hesitating in speech. His face is broad, plain, with a snubby nose, curly brown hair, fine grey eyes and a big mouth. He wears the uniform of an artillery captain in the Union Army.*)

LAVINIA (*with forced cordiality*). Good afternoon. How are you? (*She and Hazel kiss and she shakes hands with Peter.*)

HAZEL. Oh, we're all right. But how are you, Vinnie, that's the question? Seems as if we hadn't seen you for ages! You haven't been ill, I hope!

LAVINIA. Well—if you call a pesky cold ill.

PETER. Gosh, that's too bad! All over now?

LAVINIA. Yes—almost. Do sit down, won't you?

(*Hazel sits at left of bench, Lavinia beside her in the middle. Peter sits gingerly on the right edge so that there is an open space between him and Lavinia.*)

HAZEL. Peter can stay a while if you want him to, but I just dropped in for a second to find out if you'd had any more news from Orin.

LAVINIA. Not since the letter I showed you.

HAZEL. But that was ages ago! And I haven't had a letter for months. I guess he must have met another girl somewhere and given me the go-by. (*She forces a smile but her tone is really hurt.*)

PETER. Orin not writing doesn't mean anything. He never was much of a hand for letters.

HAZEL. I know that, but—you don't think he's been wounded, do you, Vinnie?

LAVINIA. Of course not. Father would have let us know.

PETER. Sure he would. Don't be foolish, Hazel! (*Then after a little pause.*) Orin ought to be home before long now. You've heard the good news, of course, Vinnie?

HAZEL. Peter won't have to go back. Isn't that fine?

PETER. My wound is healed and I've got orders to leave to-morrow, but they'll be cancelled, I guess. (*Grinning.*) I won't pretend I'm the sort of hero that wants to go back, either! I've had enough!

HAZEL (*impulsively*). Oh, it will be so good to see Orin again. (*Then, embarrassed, forces a self-conscious laugh and gets up and kisses Lavinia.*) Well, I must run. I've got to meet Emily. Good-bye, Vinnie. Do take care of yourself and come to see us soon. (*With a teasing glance at her brother.*) And be kind to Peter. He's nice—when he's asleep. And he has something he's just dying to ask you!

PETER (*horribly embarrassed*). Darn you! (*Hazel laughs and goes off down the drive, left front. Peter fidgets, his eyes on the ground. Lavinia watches him. Since Hazel's teasing statement, she has visibly withdrawn into herself and is on the defensive. Finally Peter looks up and blurts out awkardly.*) Hazel feels bad about Orin not writing. Do you think he really—loves her?

LAVINIA (*stiffening—brusquely*). I don't know anything about love! I don't want to know anything! (*Intensely.*) I hate love!

PETER (*crushed by this but trying bravely to joke*). Gosh, then, if that's the mood you're in, I guess I better not ask—something I'd made up my mind to ask you to-day.

LAVINIA. It's what you asked me a year ago when you were home on leave, isn't it?

PETER. And you said wait till the war was over. Well, it's over now.

LAVINIA (*slowly*). I can't marry anyone, Peter. I've got to stay at home. Father needs me.

PETER. He's got your mother.

LAVINIA (*sharply*). He needs me more! (*A pause. Then she turns pityingly and puts her hand on his shoulder.*) I'm sorry, Peter.

PETER (*gruffly*). Oh, that's all right.

LAVINIA. I know it's what girls always say in books, but I do love you as a brother, Peter. I wouldn't lose you as a brother for anything. We've been like that ever since we were little and started playing together—you and Orin and Hazel and I. So please don't let this come between us.

PETER. 'Course it won't. What do you think I am? (*Doggedly.*) Besides, I'm not giving up hope but what you'll change your mind in time. That is, unless it's because you love someone else——

LAVINIA (*snatching her hand back*). Don't be stupid, Peter!

PETER. But how about this mysterious clipper captain that's been calling?

LAVINIA (*angrily*). Do you think I care anything about that—that——!

PETER. Don't get mad. I only meant, folks say he's courting you.

LAVINIA. Folks say more than their prayers!

PETER. Then you don't—care for him?

LAVINIA (*intensely*). I hate the sight of him!

PETER. Gosh! I'm glad to hear you say that, Vinnie. I was afraid—I imagined girls all liked him. He's such a darned romantic-looking cuss. Looks more like a gambler or a poet than a ship's captain. I got a look as he was coming out of your gate—I guess it was the last time he was here. Funny, too. He reminded me of someone. But I couldn't place who it was.

LAVINIA (*startled, glances at him uneasily*). No one around here, that's sure. He comes from out West. Grandfather Hamel happened to meet him in New York and took a fancy to him, and Mother met him at Grandfather's house.

PETER. Who is he, anyway, Vinnie?

LAVINIA. I don't know much about him in spite of what you think. Oh, he did tell me the story of his life to make himself out romantic, but I didn't pay much attention. He went to sea when he was young and was in California for the Gold Rush. He's sailed all over the world—he lived on a South Sea island once, so he says.

PETER (*grumpily*). He seems to have had plenty of romantic experience, if you can believe him!

LAVINIA (*bitterly*). That's his trade—being romantic! (*Then agitatedly.*) But I don't want to talk any more about him. (*She gets up and walks towards right to conceal her agitation, keeping her back turned to Peter.*)

PETER (*with a grin*). Well, I don't either. I can think of more interesting subjects.

(*Christine Mannon appears from left, between the clump of lilacs and the house. She is carrying a big bunch of flowers. Lavinia senses her presence and whirls around. For a moment, mother and daughter stare into each other's eyes. In their whole tense attitudes is clearly revealed the bitter antagonism between them. But Christine quickly recovers herself and her air resumes its disdainful aloofness.*)

CHRISTINE. Ah, here you are at last! (*Then she sees Peter, who is visibly embarrassed by her presence.*) Why, good afternoon, Peter, I didn't see you at first.

PETER. Good afternoon, Mrs. Mannon. I was just passing and dropped in for a second. I guess I better run along now, Vinnie.

LAVINIA (*with an obvious eagerness to get him off—quickly*). All right. Good-bye, Peter.

PETER. Good-bye. Good-bye, Mrs. Mannon.

CHRISTINE. Good-bye, Peter. (*He disappears from the drive, left. Christine comes forward.*) I must say you treat your one devoted swain pretty rudely. (*Lavinia doesn't reply. Christine goes on coolly.*) I was wondering when I was going to see you. When I returned from New York last night you seemed to have gone to bed.

LAVINIA. I had gone to bed.

CHRISTINE. You usually read long after that. I tried your door—but you had locked yourself in. When you kept yourself locked in all day I was sure you were intentionally avoiding me. But Annie said you had a headache. (*While she has been speaking she has come towards Lavinia until she is now within arm's reach of her. The facial resemblance, as they stand there, is extraordinary. Christine stares at her coolly, but one senses an uneasy wariness beneath her pose.*) Did you have a headache?

LAVINIA. No. I wanted to be alone—to think over things.

CHRISTINE. What things, if I may ask? (*Then, as if she were afraid of an answer to this question, she abruptly changes the subject.*) Who are those people I saw wandering about the grounds?

LAVINIA. Some friends of Seth's.

CHRISTINE. Because they know that lazy old sot, does it give them the privilege of trespassing?

LAVINIA. I gave Seth permission to show them round.

CHRISTINE. And since when have you the right without consulting me?

LAVINIA. I couldn't very well consult you when Seth asked me. You had gone to New York—(*she pauses a second—then adds slowly, staring fixedly at her mother*) to see Grandfather. Is he feeling any better? He seems to have been ill so much this past year.

CHRISTINE (*casually, avoiding her eyes*). Yes. He's much better now. He'll soon be going the rounds to his patients again, he hopes. (*As if anxious to change the subject, looking at the flowers she carries.*) I've been to the greenhouse to pick these. I felt our tomb needed a little brightening. (*She nods scornfully towards the house.*) Each time I come back after being away it appears more like a sepulchre! The "whited" one of the Bible—pagan temple front stuck like a mask on Puritan grey ugliness! It was just like old Abe Mannon to build such a monstrosity—as a temple for his hatred. (*Then with a little mocking laugh.*) Forgive me, Vinnie. I forgot you liked it. And you ought to. It suits your temperament. (*Lavinia stares at her but remains silent. Christine glances at her flowers again and turns towards the house.*) I must put these in water. (*She moves a few steps towards the house—then turns again—with a studied casualness.*) By the way, before I forget, I happened to run into Captain Brant on the street in New York. He said he was coming up here to-day to take over his ship and asked me if he might drop in to see you. I told him he could—and stay to supper with us. (*Without looking at Lavinia, who is staring at her with a face grown grim and hard.*) Doesn't that please you, Vinnie? Or do you remain true to your one and only beau, Peter?

LAVINIA. Is that why you picked the flowers—because he is coming? (*Her mother does not answer. She goes on with a threatening undercurrent in her voice.*) You have heard the news, I suppose? It means Father will be home soon!

CHRISTINE (*without looking at her—coolly*). We've had so many rumours lately. This report hasn't been confirmed yet, has it? I haven't heard the fort firing a salute.

LAVINIA. You will before long!

CHRISTINE. I'm sure I hope so as much as you.

LAVINIA. You can say that!

CHRISTINE (*concealing her alarm—coldly*). What do you mean? You will kindly not take that tone with me, please! (*Cuttingly.*) If you are determined to quarrel, let us go into the house. We might be overheard out here. (*She turns and sees Seth who has just come to the corner of the house, left, and is standing there watching them.*) See. There is your old crony doing his best to listen now! (*Moving to the steps.*) I am going in to rest a while. (*She walks up the steps.*)

LAVINIA (*harshly*). I've got to have a talk with you, Mother—before long!

CHRISTINE (*turning defiantly*). Whenever you wish. To-night after the Captain leaves you, if you like. But what is it you want to talk about?

LAVINIA. You'll know soon enough!

CHRISTINE (*staring at her with a questioning dread—forcing a scornful smile*). You always make such a mystery of things, Vinnie.

(*She goes into the house and closes the door behind her. Seth comes forward from where he had withdrawn beyond the corner of the house. Lavinia makes a motion for him to follow her, and goes and sits on the bench at left. A pause. She stares straight ahead, her face frozen, her eyes hard. He regards her understandingly.*)

LAVINIA (*abruptly*). Well? What is it about Captain Brant you want to warn me against? (*Then as if she felt she must defend her question from some suspicion that she knows is in his mind.*) I want to know all I can about him because—he seems to be calling to court me.

SETH (*managing to convey his entire disbelief of this statement in one word*). Ayeh.

LAVINIA (*sharply*). You say that as if you didn't believe me.

SETH. I believe anything you tell me to believe.

I ain't been with the Mannons for sixty years without learning that. (*A pause. Then he asks slowly.*) Ain't you noticed this Brant reminds you of someone in looks?

LAVINIA (*struck by this*). Yes. I have—ever since I first saw him—but I've never been able to place who—— Who do you mean?

SETH. Your Paw, ain't it, Vinnie?

LAVINIA (*startled—agitated*). Father? No! It can't be! (*Then as if the conviction were forcing itself on her in spite of herself.*) Yes! He does—something about his face—that must be why I've had the strange feeling I've known him before—why I've felt—— (*Then tensely as if she were about to break down.*) Oh! I won't believe it! You must be mistaken, Seth! That would be too——!

SETH. He ain't only like your Paw. He's like Orin, too—and all the Mannons I've known.

LAVINIA (*frightenedly*). But why—why should he——?

SETH. More speshully he calls to my mind your Grandpaw's brother, David. How much do you know about David Mannon, Vinnie? I know his name's never been allowed to be spoke among Mannons since the day he left—but you've likely heard gossip, ain't you—even if it all happened before you was born?

LAVINIA. I've heard that he loved the Canuck nurse girl who was taking care of Father's little sister who died, and had to marry her because she was going to have a baby; and that Grandfather put them both out of the house and then afterwards tore it down and built this one because he wouldn't live where his brother had disgraced the family. But what has that old scandal got to do with——

SETH. Wait. Right after they was throwed out they married and went away. There was talk they'd gone out West, but no one knew nothin' about 'em afterwards—'ceptin' your Grandpaw let out to me one time she'd had the baby—a boy. He was cussin' it. (*Then impressively.*) It's about her baby I've been thinkin', Vinnie.

LAVINIA (*a look of appalled comprehension growing on her face*). Oh!

SETH. How old is that Brant, Vinnie?

LAVINIA. Thirty-six, I think.

SETH. Ayeh! That'd make it right. And here's another funny thing—his name. Brant's sort of queer fur a name. I ain't never heard tell of it before. Sounds made up to me—like short fur somethin' else. Remember what that Canuck girl's name was, do you, Vinnie? Marie Brantôme! See what I'm drivin' at?

LAVINIA (*agitated, and fighting against a growing conviction*). But—don't be stupid, Seth—his name would be Mannon and he'd be only too proud of it.

SETH. He'd have good reason not to use the name of Mannon when he came callin' here, wouldn't he? If your Paw ever guessed——!

LAVINIA (*breaking out violently*). No! It can't be! God wouldn't let it! It would be too horrible—on top of——! I won't even think of it, do you hear? Why did you have to tell me?

SETH (*calmingly*). There now! Don't take on, Vinnie. No need gettin' riled at me. (*He waits—then goes on insistently.*) All I'm drivin' at is that it's durned funny—his looks and the name—and you'd ought fur your Paw's sake to make sartin.

LAVINIA. How can I make certain?

SETH. Catch him off guard sometime and put it up to him strong—as if you knowed it—and see if mebbe he don't give himself away. (*He starts to go—looks down the drive at left.*) Looks like him comin' up the drive now, Vinnie. There's somethin' about his walk calls back David Mannon, too. If I didn't know it was him I'd think it was David's ghost comin' home. (*He turns away abruptly.*) Wal, calc'late I better git back to work.

(*He walks around the left corner of the house. A pause. Then Captain Adam Brant enters from the drive, left, front. He starts on seeing Lavinia but immediately puts on his most polite, winning air. One is struck at a glance by the peculiar quality his face in repose has of being a life-like mask rather than living flesh. He has a broad, low forehead, framed by coal-black straight hair which he wears noticeably long, pushed back carelessly from his forehead as a poet's might be. He has a big aquiline nose, bushy eyebrows, swarthy complexion, hazel eyes. His wide mouth is sensual and moody—a mouth that can be strong and weak by turns. He wears a moustache, but his heavy cleft chin is clean-shaven. In figure he is tall, broad-shouldered and powerful. He gives the impression of being always on the offensive or defensive, always fighting life. He is dressed with an almost foppish extravagance, with touches of studied carelessness, as if a romantic Byronic appearance were the ideal in mind. There is little of the obvious sea captain about him, except his big, strong hands and his deep voice.*)

BRANT (*bowing with an exaggerated politeness*). Good afternoon. (*Coming and taking her hand which she forces herself to hold out to him.*) Hope you don't mind my walking in on you without ceremony. Your mother told me——

LAVINIA. I know. She had to go out for a while and she said I was to keep you company until she returned.

BRANT (*gallantly*). Well, I'm in good luck, then. I hope she doesn't hurry back to stand watch over us. I haven't had a chance to be alone with you since—that night we went walking in the moonlight, do you remember ?

(*He has kept her hand and he drops his voice to a low, lover-like tone. Lavinia cannot repress a start, agitatedly snatching her hand from his and turning away from him.*)

LAVINIA (*regaining command of herself—slowly*). What do you think of the news of Lee surrendering, Captain ? We expect my father home very soon now. (*At something in her tone he stares at her suspiciously, but she is looking straight before her.*) Why don't you sit down ?

BRANT. Thank you. (*He sits on the bench at her right. He has become wary now, feeling something strange in her attitude but not able to make her out—casually.*) Yes, you must be very happy at the prospect of seeing your father again. Your mother has told me how close you've always been to him.

LAVINIA. Did she ? (*Then with intensity.*) I love Father better than anyone in the world. There is nothing I wouldn't do—to protect him from hurt !

BRANT (*watching her carefully—keeping his casual tone*). You care more for him than for your mother ?

LAVINIA. Yes.

BRANT. Well, I suppose that's the usual way of it. A daughter feels closer to her father and a son to his mother. But I should think you ought to be a born exception to that rule.

LAVINIA. Why ?

BRANT. You're so like your mother in some ways. Your face is the very image of hers. And look at your hair. You won't meet hair like yours and hers again in a month of Sundays. I only know of one other woman who had it. You'll think it strange when I tell you. It was my mother.

LAVINIA (*with a start*). Ah !

BRANT (*dropping his voice to a reverent, hushed tone*). Yes, she had beautiful hair like your mother's, that hung down to her knees, and big, deep, sad eyes that were blue as the Caribbean sea !

LAVINIA (*harshly*). What do looks amount to ? I'm not a bit like her ! Everybody knows I take after Father !

BRANT (*brought back with a shock, astonished at her tone*). But—you're not angry at me for saying that, are you ? (*Then filled with uneasiness and resolving he must establish himself on an intimate footing with her again—with engaging bluntness.*) You're puzzling to-day, Miss Lavinia. You'll excuse me if I come out with it bluntly. I've lived most of my life at sea and in camps and I'm used to straight speaking. What are you holding against me ? If I've done anything to offend you, I swear it wasn't meant. (*She is silent, rigidly upright, staring before her with hard eyes. He appraises her with a calculating look, then goes on.*) I wouldn't have bad feeling come between us for the world. I may only be flattering myself, but I thought you liked me. Have you forgotten that night walking along the shore ?

LAVINIA (*in a cold, hard voice*). I haven't forgotten. Did Mother tell you you could kiss me ?

BRANT. What—what do you mean ? (*But he at once attributes the question to her naïveté—laughingly.*) Oh ! I see ! But, come now, Lavinia, you can't mean, can you, I should have asked her permission ?

LAVINIA. Shouldn't you ?

BRANT (*again uneasy—trying to joke it off*). Well, I wasn't brought up that strictly and, should or shouldn't, at any rate, I didn't—and it wasn't the less sweet for that ! (*Then at something in her face he hurriedly goes off on another tack.*) I'm afraid I gabbed too much that night. Maybe I bored you with my talk of clipper ships and my love for them?

LAVINIA (*dryly*). "Tall, white clippers," you called them. You said they were like beautiful, pale women to you. You said you loved them more than you'd ever loved a woman. Is that true, Captain?

BRANT (*with forced gallantry*). Aye. But I meant, before I met you. (*Then thinking he has at last hit on the cause of her changed attitude towards him—with a laugh.*) So that's what you're holding against me, is it? Well, I might have guessed. Women are jealous of ships. They always suspect the sea. They know they're three of a kind when it comes to a man! (*He laughs again but less certainly this time, as he regards her grim, set expression.*) Yes, I might have seen you didn't appear much taken by my sea talk that night. I suppose clippers are too old a story to the daughter of a shipbuilder. But unless I'm much mistaken, you were interested when I told you of the islands in the South Seas where I was shipwrecked my first voyage at sea.

LAVINIA (*in a dry, brittle tone*). I remember your admiration for the naked native women. You said they had found the secret of happiness because they had never heard that love can be a sin.

BRANT (*surprised—sizing her up and puzzled*). So you remember that, do you? (*Then romantically.*) Aye! And they live in as near the Garden of Paradise before sin was discovered as you'll find on this earth! Unless you've seen it, you can't picture the green beauty of their land set in the blue of the sea! The clouds like down on the mountain tops, the sun drowsing in your blood, and always the surf on the barrier reef singing a croon in your ears like a lullaby! The Blessed Isles, I'd call them! You can there forget all men's dirty dreams of greed and power!

LAVINIA. And their dirty dreams—of love?

BRANT (*startled again—staring at her uneasily*). Why do you say that? What do you mean, Lavinia?

LAVINIA. Nothing. I was only thinking—of your Blessed Isles.

BRANT (*uncertainly*). Oh! But you said—— (*Then with a confused, stupid persistence he comes closer to her, dropping his voice again to his love-making tone.*) Whenever I remember those islands now, I will always think of you, as you walked beside me that night with your hair blowing in the sea wind and the moonlight in your eyes! (*He tries to take her hand, but at his touch she pulls away and springs to her feet.*)

LAVINIA (*with cold fury*). Don't you touch me! Don't you dare——! You liar! You——! (*Then as he starts back in confusion, she seizes this opportunity to follow Seth's advice—staring at him with deliberately insulting scorn.*) But I suppose it would be foolish to expect anything but cheap romantic lies from the son of a low Canuck nurse girl!

BRANT (*stunned*). What's that? (*Then rage at the insult to his mother overcoming all prudence—springs to his feet threateningly.*) Stop, damn you!—or I'll forget you're a woman—no Mannon can insult her while I——

LAVINIA (*appalled now she knows the truth*). So—it is true—— You are her son! Oh!

BRANT (*fighting to control himself—with harsh defiance*). And what if I am? I'm proud to be! My only shame is my dirty Mannon blood! So that's why you couldn't stand my touching you just now, is it? You're too good for the son of a servant, eh? By God, you were glad enough before——!

LAVINIA (*fiercely*). It's not true! I was only leading you on to find out things!

BRANT. Oh, no! It's only since you suspected who I was! I suppose your father has stuffed you with his lies about my mother! But, by God, you'll hear the truth of it, now you know who I am—— And you'll see if you or any Mannon has the right to look down on her!

LAVINIA. I don't want to hear—— (*She starts to go towards the house.*)

BRANT (*grabbing her by the arm—tauntingly*). You're a coward, are you, like all Mannons, when it comes to facing the truth about themselves? (*She turns on him defiantly. He drops her arm and goes on harshly.*) I'll bet he never told you your grandfather, Abe Mannon, as well as his brother, loved my mother!

LAVINIA. It's a lie!

BRANT. It's the truth. It was his jealous revenge made him disown my father and cheat him out of his share of the business they'd inherited!

LAVINIA. He didn't cheat him! He bought him out!

BRANT. Forced him to sell for one-tenth its worth, you mean! He knew my father and mother were starving! But the money didn't last my father long! He'd taken to drink. He was a coward—like all Mannons—once he felt the world looked down on him. He skulked and avoided people. He grew ashamed of my mother—and me. He sank down and down and my mother worked and supported him. I can remember when men from the corner saloon would drag him home and he'd fall in the door, a sodden carcass. One night when I was seven he came home crazy drunk and hit my mother in the face. It was the first time he'd ever struck her. It made me blind mad. I hit at him with the poker and cut his head. My mother pulled me back and gave me a hiding. Then she cried over him. She'd never stopped loving him.

LAVINIA. Why do you tell me this? I told you once I don't want to hear——

BRANT (*grimly*). You'll see the point of it damned soon! (*Unheeding—as if the scene were still before his eyes.*) For days after, he sat and stared at nothing. One time when we were alone he asked me to forgive him hitting her. But I hated him and I wouldn't forgive him. Then one night he went out and he didn't come back. The next morning they found him hanging in a barn!

LAVINIA (*with a shudder*). Oh!

BRANT (*savagely*). The only decent thing he ever did!

LAVINIA. You're lying! No Mannon would ever——

BRANT. Oh, wouldn't they? They are all fine, honourable gentlemen, you think! Then listen a bit and you'll hear something about another of them! (*Then going on bitterly with his story.*) My mother sewed for a living and sent me to school. She was very strict with me. She blamed me for his killing himself. But she was bound she'd make a gentleman of me—like he was!—if it took her last cent and her last strap! (*With a grim smile.*) She didn't succeed, as you notice! At seventeen I ran away to sea—and forgot I had a mother, except I took part of her name—Brant was short and easy on ships—and I wouldn't wear the name of Mannon. I forgot her until two years ago when I came back from the East. Oh, I'd written to her now and then and sent her money when I happened to have any. But I'd forgotten her just the same—and when I got to New York I found her dying—of sickness and starvation! And I found out that when she'd been laid up, not able to work, not knowing where to reach me, she'd sunk her last shred of pride and written to your father asking for a loan. He never answered her. And I came too late. She died in my arms. (*With vindictive passion.*) He could have saved her—and he deliberately let her die! He's as guilty of murder as anyone he ever sent to the rope when he was a judge!

LAVINIA (*springing to her feet—furiously*). You dare say that about Father! If he were here——

BRANT. I wish to God he was! I'd tell him what I tell you now—that I swore on my mother's body I'd revenge her death on him.

LAVINIA (*with cold deadly intensity*). And I suppose you boast that now you've done so, don't you?—in the vilest, most cowardly way—like the son of a servant you are!

BRANT (*again thrown off guard—furiously*). Stop, I told you, that kind of talk!

LAVINIA. She is your only means of revenge on Father, is that it?

BRANT (*stunned—stammers in guilty confusion*). What?—She?—Who?—I don't know what you're talking about!

LAVINIA. Then you soon will know! And so will she! I've found out all I wanted to from you. I'm going in to talk to her now. You wait here until I call you!

BRANT (*furious at her tone*). No! Be damned if you can order me about as if I was your servant!

LAVINIA (*icily*). If you have any consideration for her, you'll do as I say and not force me to write to my father. (*She turns her back on him and walks to the steps woodenly erect and square-shouldered.*)

BRANT (*desperately now—with a grotesque catching at his lover's manner*). I don't know what you mean, Lavinia. I swear before God it is only you I——

(*She turns at the top of the steps at this and stares at him with such a passion of hatred that he is silenced. Her lips move as if she were going to speak, but she fights back the words, turns stiffly and goes into the house and closes the door behind her.*)

Curtain

ACT TWO

SCENE. *In the house—Ezra Mannon's study. No time has elapsed.*

The study is a large room with a stiff, austere atmosphere. The furniture is old colonial. The walls are plain plastered surfaces tinted a dull grey with a flat white dado. At rear, right, is a door leading to the hall. On the right wall is a painting of George Washington in a gilt frame, flanked by smaller portraits of Alexander Hamilton and John Marshall. At rear, centre, is an open fireplace. At left of fireplace, a bookcase filled with law books. Above the fireplace, in a plain frame, is a large portrait of Ezra Mannon himself, painted ten years previously. One is at once struck by the startling likeness between him and Adam Brant. He is a tall man in his early forties, with a spare, wiry frame, seated stiffly in an armchair, his hands on the arms, wearing his black judge's robe. His face is handsome in a stern, aloof fashion. It is cold and emotionless and has the same strange semblance of a life-like mask that we have already seen in the faces of his wife and daughter and Brant.

On the left are two windows. Between them a desk. A large table with an armchair on either side, right and left, stands at left centre, front. At right centre is another chair. There are rugs on the floor.

Outside the sun is beginning to set and its glow fills the room with a golden mist. As the action progresses this becomes brighter, then turns to crimson, which darkens to sombreness at the end.

Lavinia is discovered standing by the table. She is fighting to control herself, but her face is torn by a look of stricken anguish. She turns slowly to her father's portrait and for a moment stares at it fixedly. Then she goes to it and puts her hand over one of his hands with a loving, protecting gesture.

LAVINIA. Poor Father!

(*She hears a noise in the hall and moves hastily away. The door from the hall is opened and Christine enters. She is inwardly uneasy, but affects a scornful indignation.*)

CHRISTINE. Really, this unconfirmed report must have turned your head—otherwise I'd find it difficult to understand your sending Annie to disturb me when you knew I was resting.

LAVINIA. I told you I had to talk to you.

CHRISTINE (*looking around the room with aversion*). But why in this musty room, of all places?

LAVINIA (*indicating the portrait—quietly*). Because it's Father's room.

CHRISTINE (*starts, looks at the portrait and quickly drops her eyes. Lavinia goes to the door and closes it. Christine says with forced scorn*). More mystery?

LAVINIA. You better sit down. (*Christine sits in the chair at rear centre. Lavinia goes back to her father's chair at left of table.*)

CHRISTINE. Well—if you're quite ready, perhaps you will explain.

LAVINIA. I suppose Annie told you I'd been to visit Hazel and Peter while you were away?

CHRISTINE. Yes. I thought it peculiar. You never visit anyone overnight. Why did you suddenly take that notion?

LAVINIA. I didn't.

CHRISTINE. You didn't visit them?

LAVINIA. No.

CHRISTINE. Then where did you go?

LAVINIA (*accusingly*). To New York! (*Christine starts. Lavinia hurries on a bit incoherently.*) I've suspected something—lately—the excuse you've made for all your trips there the past year, that Grandfather was ill—— (*As Christine is about to protest indignantly.*) Oh! I know he has been —and you've stayed at his house—but I've suspected lately that wasn't the real reason—and now I can prove it isn't! Because I waited outside Grandfather's house and followed you. I saw you meet Brant!

CHRISTINE (*alarmed but concealing it—coolly*). Well, what if you did? I told you myself I ran into him by accident——

LAVINIA. You went to his room!

CHRISTINE (*shaken*). He asked me to meet a friend of his—a lady. It was her house we went to.

LAVINIA. I asked the woman in the basement. He had hired the room under another name, but she recognized his description. And yours too.

She said you had come there often in the past year.

CHRISTINE (*desperately*). It was the first time I had ever been there. He insisted on my going. He said he had to talk to me about you. He wanted my help to approach your father——

LAVINIA (*furiously*). How can you lie like that? How can you be so vile as to try to use me to hide your adultery?

CHRISTINE (*springing up—with weak indignation*). Vinnie!

LAVINIA. Your adultery, I said!

CHRISTINE. No!

LAVINIA. Stop lying, I tell you! I went upstairs! I heard you telling him—"I love you, Adam"—and kissing him! (*With a cold bitter fury.*) You vile——! You're shameless and evil! Even if you are my mother, I say it!

(*Christine stares at her, overwhelmed by this onslaught, her poise shattered for the moment. She tries to keep her voice indifferent but it trembles a little.*)

CHRISTINE. I—I knew you hated me, Vinnie—but not as bitterly as that! (*Then with a return of her defiant coolness.*) Very well! I love Adam Brant. What are you going to do?

LAVINIA. How you say that—without any shame! You don't give one thought to Father—who is so good—who trusts you! Oh, how could you do this to Father? How could you?

CHRISTINE (*with strident intensity*). You would understand if you were the wife of a man you hated!

LAVINIA (*horrified—with a glance at the portrait*). Don't! Don't say that—before him! I won't listen!

CHRISTINE (*grabbing her by the arm*). You will listen! I'm talking to you as a woman now, not as mother to daughter! That relationship has no meaning between us! You've called me vile and shameless! Well, I want you to know that's what I've felt about myself for over twenty years, giving my body to a man I——

LAVINIA (*trying to break away from her, half putting her hands up to her ears*). Stop telling me such things! Let me go! (*She breaks away, shrinking from her mother with a look of sick repulsion. A pause. She stammers.*) You—then you've always hated Father?

CHRISTINE (*bitterly*). No. I loved him once—before I married him—incredible as that seems now! He was handsome in his lieutenant's uniform! He was silent and mysterious and romantic! But marriage soon turned his romance into—disgust!

LAVINIA (*wincing again—stammers harshly*). So I was born of your disgust! I've always guessed that, Mother—ever since I was little—when I used to come to you—with love—but you would always push me away! I've felt it ever since I can remember—your disgust! (*Then with a flare-up of bitter hatred.*) Oh, I hate you! It's only right I should hate you!

CHRISTINE (*shaken—defensively*). I tried to love you. I told myself it wasn't human not to love my own child, born of my body. But I never could make myself feel you were born of any body but his! You were always my wedding night to me—and my honeymoon!

LAVINIA. Stop saying that! How can you be so——! (*Then suddenly—with a strange jealous bitterness.*) You've loved Orin! Why didn't you hate him too?

CHRISTINE. Because by then I had forced myself to become resigned in order to live! And most of the time I was carrying him, your father was with the army in Mexico. I had forgotten him. And when Orin was born he seemed my child, only mine, and I loved him for that! (*Bitterly.*) I loved him until he let you and your father nag him into the war, in spite of my begging him not to leave me alone. (*Staring at Lavinia with hatred.*) I know his leaving me was your doing principally, Vinnie!

LAVINIA (*sternly*). It was his duty as a Mannon to go! He'd have been sorry the rest of his life if he hadn't! I love him better than you! I was thinking of him!

CHRISTINE. Well, I hope you realize I never would have fallen in love with Adam if I'd had Orin with me. When he had gone there was nothing left—but hate and a desire to be revenged—and a longing for love! And it was then I met Adam. I saw he loved me——

LAVINIA (*with taunting scorn*). He doesn't love you! You're only his revenge on Father! Do you know who he really is? He's the son of that low nurse girl Grandfather put out of our house!

CHRISTINE (*concealing a start—coolly*). So you've found that out? Were you hoping it would be a crushing surprise to me? I've known it all along. He told me when he said he loved me.

LAVINIA. Oh! And I suppose knowing who he was gave you all the more satisfaction—to add that disgrace!

CHRISTINE (*cuttingly*). Will you kindly come to the point and tell me what you intend doing? I suppose you'll hardly let your father get in the door before you tell him!

LAVINIA (*suddenly becoming rigid and cold again—slowly*). No. Not unless you force me to. (*Then as she sees her mother's astonishment—grimly.*) I don't wonder you're surprised! You know you deserve the worst punishment you could get. And Father would disown you publicly, no matter how much the scandal cost him!

CHRISTINE. I realize that. I know him even better than you do!

LAVINIA. And I'd like to see you punished for your wickedness! So please understand this isn't for your sake. It's for Father's. He hasn't been well lately. I'm not going to have him hurt! It's my first duty to protect him from you!

CHRISTINE. I know better than to expect any generosity on my account.

LAVINIA. I won't tell him, provided you give up Brant and never see him again—and promise to be a dutiful wife to Father and make up for the wrong you've done him!

CHRISTINE (*stares at her daughter—a pause—then she laughs dryly*). What a fraud you are, with your talk of your father and your duty! Oh, I'm not denying you want to save his pride—and I know how anxious you are to keep the family from more scandal! But all the same, that's not your real reason for sparing me!

LAVINIA (*confused—guiltily*). It is!

CHRISTINE. You wanted Adam Brant yourself!

LAVINIA. That's a lie!

CHRISTINE. And now you know you can't have him, you're determined that at least you'll take him from me!

LAVINIA. No!

CHRISTINE. But if you told your father, I'd have to go away with Adam. He'd be mine still. You can't bear that thought, even at the price of my disgrace, can you?

LAVINIA. It's your evil mind!

CHRISTINE. I know you, Vinnie! I've watched you ever since you were little, trying to do exactly what you're doing now! You've tried to become the wife of your father and the mother of Orin! You've always schemed to steal my place!

LAVINIA (*wildly*). No! It's you who have stolen all love from me since the time I was born! (*Then, her manner becoming threatening.*) But I don't want to listen to any more of your lies and excuses! I want to know right now whether you're going to do what I told you or not!

CHRISTINE. Suppose I refuse! Suppose I go off openly with Adam! Where will you and your father and the family name be after that scandal? And what if I were disgraced myself? I'd have the man I love, at least!

LAVINIA (*grimly*). Not for long! Father would use all his influence and get Brant blacklisted so he'd lose his command and never get another! You know how much the "Flying Trades" means to him. And Father would never divorce you. You could never marry. You'd be an anchor around his neck. Don't forget you're five years older than he is! He'll still be in his prime when you're an old woman with all your looks gone! He'd grow to hate the sight of you!

CHRISTINE (*stung beyond bearing—makes a threatening move as if to strike her daughter's face*). You devil! You mean little—— ! (*But Lavinia stares back coldly into her eyes and she controls herself and drops her hand.*)

LAVINIA. I wouldn't call names if I were you! There is one you deserve!

CHRISTINE (*turning away—her voice still trembling*). I'm a fool to let you make me lose my temper—over your jealous spite! (*A pause. Lavinia stares at her. Christine seems considering something. A sinister expression comes to her face. Then she turns back to Lavinia—coldly*). But you wanted my answer, didn't you? Well, I agree to do as you said. I promise you I'll never see Adam again after he calls this evening. Are you satisfied?

LAVINIA (*stares at her with cold suspicion*). You seem to take giving him up pretty easily!

CHRISTINE (*hastily*). Do you think I'll ever give you the satisfaction of seeing me grieve? Oh, no, Vinnie! You'll never have a chance to gloat!

LAVINIA (*still suspiciously—with a touch of scorn*). If I loved anyone—— !

CHRISTINE (*tauntingly*). If? I think you do love him—as much as you can love! (*With a sudden flurry of jealousy.*) You little fool! Don't you know I made him flirt with you, so you wouldn't be suspicious?

LAVINIA (*gives a little shudder—then fiercely*). He didn't fool me! I saw what a liar he was! I just led him on—to find out things! I always hated him! (*Christine smiles mockingly and turns away, as if to go out of the room. Lavinia's manner becomes threatening again.*) Wait! I don't trust you! I know you're thinking already how you can fool me and break the promise you've just made! But you better not try it! I'll be watching you every minute! And I won't be the only one! I wrote to Father and Orin as soon as I got back from New York!

CHRISTINE (*startled*). About Adam?

LAVINIA. Only enough so they'd be suspicious and watch you too. I said a Captain Brant had been calling and folks had begun to gossip.

CHRISTINE. Ah! I see what it's going to mean—that you'll always have this to hold over me and I'll be under your thumb for the rest of my life! (*She cannot restrain her rage—threateningly.*) Take care, Vinnie! You'll be responsible if——! (*She checks herself abruptly.*)

LAVINIA (*suspiciously*). If what?

CHRISTINE (*quickly*). Nothing. I only meant if I went off with Adam. But of course you know I won't do that. You know there's nothing I can do now—but obey your orders!

LAVINIA (*continues to stare at her suspiciously—grimly*). You ought to see it's your duty to Father, not my orders—if you had any honour or decency! (*Then brusquely.*) Brant is waiting outside. You can tell him what you've got to do—and tell him if he ever dares come here again——! (*Forcing back her anger.*) And see that you get rid of him right now! I'm going upstreet to get the latest news. I won't be gone more than half-an-hour and I want him out of the house by the time I get back, do you hear? If he isn't, I'll write to Father again. I won't even wait for him to come home!

(*She turns her back on her mother and marches out the door, square-shouldered and stiff, without a backward glance. Christine looks after her, waiting until she hears the side door of the house close after her. Then she turns and stands in tense calculating thought. Her face has become like a sinister evil mask. Finally, as if making up her mind irrevocably, she comes to the table, tears off a slip of paper and writes two words on it. She tucks this paper in the sleeve of her dress and goes to the open window and calls.*)

CHRISTINE. Adam! (*She moves towards the door to wait for him. Her eyes are caught by the eyes of her husband in the portrait over the fireplace. She stares at him with hatred and addresses him vindictively, half under her breath.*) You can thank Vinnie, Ezra!

(*She goes to the door and reaches it just as Brant appears from the hall. She takes his hand and draws him into the room, closing the door behind him. One is immediately struck by the resemblance between his face and that of the portrait of Ezra Mannon.*)

BRANT (*glancing uneasily at her, as they come to the centre of the room*). She knows——?

CHRISTINE. Yes. She followed me to New York. And she's found out who you are too, Adam.

BRANT (*with a grim smile*). I know. She got that out of me—the proof of it, at any rate. Before I knew what was up I'd given myself away.

CHRISTINE. She must have noticed your resemblance to Orin. I was afraid that might start her thinking.

BRANT (*sees the portrait for the first time. Instantly his body shifts to a fighting tenseness. It is as if he were going to spring at the figure in the painting. He says slowly:*). That, I take it, is General Mannon?

CHRISTINE. Judge Mannon then. Don't forget he used to be a judge. He won't forget it.

BRANT (*his eyes still fixed on the portrait—comes and sits in Mannon's chair on the left of table. Unconsciously he takes the same attitude as Mannon, sitting erect, his hands on the arms of the chair—slowly:*). Does Orin by any chance resemble his father?

CHRISTINE (*stares at him—agitatedly*). No! Of course not! What put such a stupid idea in your head?

BRANT. It would be damned queer if you fell in love with me because I recalled Ezra Mannon to you!

CHRISTINE (*going to him and putting an arm around his shoulder*). No, no, I tell you! It was Orin you made me think of! It was Orin!

BRANT. I remember that night we were introduced and I heard the name Mrs. Ezra Mannon! By God, how I hated you then for being his! I thought, by God, I'll take her from him and that'll be part of my revenge! And out of that hatred my love came! It's damned queer, isn't it?

CHRISTINE (*hugging him to her*). Are you going to let him take me from you now, Adam?

BRANT (*passionately*). You ask that!

CHRISTINE. You swear you won't—no matter what you must do?

BRANT. By God, I swear it!

CHRISTINE (*kisses him*). Remember that oath! (*She glances at the portrait—then turns back to Brant with a little shiver—nervously.*) What made you sit there? It's his chair. I've so often seen him sitting there—— (*Forcing a little laugh.*) Your silly talk about resemblances—— Don't sit there. Come. Bring that chair over here. (*She moves to the chair at right centre. He brings the chair at right of table close to hers.*)

BRANT. We've got to decide what we must do. The time for skulking and lying is over—and by God I'm glad of it! It's a coward's game I have no stomach for! (*He has placed the chair beside hers. She is staring at the portrait.*) Why don't you sit down, Christine?

CHRISTINE (*slowly*). I was thinking—perhaps we had better go to the sitting-room. (*Then defiantly.*) No! I've been afraid of you long enough, Ezra! (*She sits down.*)

BRANT. I felt there was something wrong the moment I saw her. I tried my damndest to put her off the course by giving her some soft-soap—as you'd told me to do to blind her. (*Frowning.*) That was a mistake, Christine. It made her pay too much attention to me—and opened her eyes!

CHRISTINE. Oh, I know I've made one blunder after another. It's as if love drove me on to do everything I shouldn't. I never should have brought you to this house. Seeing you in New York should have been enough for me. But I loved you too much. I wanted you every possible moment we could steal! And I simply couldn't believe that he ever would come home. I prayed that he should be killed in the war so intensely that I finally believed it would surely happen! (*With savage intensity.*) Oh, if only he were dead!

BRANT. That chance is over now.

CHRISTINE (*slowly—without looking at him*). Yes—in that way.

BRANT (*stares at her*). What do you mean? (*She remains silent. He changes the subject uneasily.*) There's only one thing to do! When he comes home I'll wait for him and not give Vinnie the satisfaction of telling him. I'll tell him myself. (*Vindictively.*) By God! I'd give my soul to see his face when he knows you love Marie Brantôme's son! And then I'll take you away openly and laugh at him! And if he tries to stop me——! (*He stops and glances with savage hatred at the portrait.*)

CHRISTINE. What would you do then?

BRANT. If ever I laid hands on him, I'd kill him!

CHRISTINE. And then? You would be hanged for murder! And where would I be? There would be nothing left for me but to kill myself!

BRANT. If I could catch him alone, where no one would interfere, and let the best man come out alive—as I've often seen it done in the West!

CHRISTINE. This isn't the West.

BRANT. I could insult him on the street before everyone and make him fight me! I could let him shoot first and then kill him in self-defence.

CHRISTINE (*scornfully*). Do you imagine you could force him to fight a duel with you? Don't you know duelling is illegal? Oh, no! He'd simply feel bound to do his duty as a former judge and have you arrested! (*She adds calculatingly, seeing he is boiling with rage.*) It would be a poor revenge for your mother's death to let him make you a laughing-stock!

BRANT. But when I take you off, the laugh will be on him! You can come on the "Flying Trades."

CHRISTINE (*calculatingly reproachful*). I don't think you'd propose that, Adam, if you stopped thinking of your revenge for a moment and thought of me! Don't you realize he would never divorce me, out of spite? What would I be in the world's eyes? My life would be ruined and I would ruin yours! You'd grow to hate me!

BRANT (*passionately*). Don't talk like that! It's a lie and you know it!

CHRISTINE (*with bitter yearning*). If I could only believe that, Adam! But I'll grow old so soon! And I'm afraid of time! (*Then abruptly changing tone.*) As for my sailing on your ship, you'll find you won't have a ship! He'll see to it you lose this command and get you blacklisted so you'll have no chance of getting another.

BRANT (*angrily*). Aye! He can do that if he sets about it. There are twice as many skippers as ships these days.

CHRISTINE (*calculatingly—without looking at him*). If he had only been killed, we could be married now and I would bring you my share of the Mannon estate. That would only be justice. It's yours by right. It's what his father stole from yours.

BRANT. That's true enough, damn him!

CHRISTINE. You wouldn't have to worry about commands or owners' favours then. You could buy your own ship and be your own master!

BRANT (*yearningly*). That's always been my dream—some day to own my own clipper! And Clark and Dawson would be willing to sell the "Flying Trades." (*Then forgetting everything in his enthusiasm.*) You've seen her, Christine. She's as beautiful a ship as you're a woman. Aye, the two of you are like sisters. If she was mine, I'd take you on a honeymoon then! To China—and on the voyage back, we'd stop at the South Pacific Islands I've told you about. By God, there's the right place for love and a honeymoon!

CHRISTINE (*slowly*). Yes—but Ezra is alive!

BRANT (*brought back to earth—gloomily*). I know it's only a dream.

CHRISTINE (*turning to stare at him—slowly*). You can have your dream—and I can have mine. There is a way. (*Then turning away again.*) You remember my telling you he had written complaining of pains about his heart?

BRANT. You're surely not hoping——

CHRISTINE. No. He said it was nothing serious. But I've let it be known that he has heart trouble. I went to see our old family doctor and told him about Ezra's letter. I pretended to be dreadfully worried, until I got him worried too. He's the town's worst old gossip. I'm sure everyone knows about Ezra's weak heart by this time.

BRANT. What are you driving at, Christine?

CHRISTINE. Something I've been thinking of ever since I realized he might soon come home. And now that Vinnie—but even if we didn't have to consider her, it'd be the only way! I couldn't fool him long. He's a strange, hidden man. His silence always creeps into my thoughts. Even if he never spoke, I would feel what was in his mind and some night, lying beside him, it would drive me mad and I'd have to kill his silence by screaming out the truth! (*She has been staring before her—now she suddenly turns on Brant—slowly.*) If he died suddenly now, no one would think it was anything but heart failure. I've been reading a book in Father's medical library. I saw it there one day a few weeks ago—it was as if some fate in me forced me to see it! (*She reaches in the sleeve of her dress and takes out the slip of paper she had written on.*) I've written something here. I want you to get it for me. (*His fingers close on it mechanically. He stares at it with a strange stupid dread. She hurries on so as not to give him time for reflection.*) The work on the "Flying Trades" is all finished, isn't it? You sail to Boston to-morrow, to wait for cargo?

BRANT (*dully*). Aye.

CHRISTINE. Get this at some druggist's down by the waterfront the minute you reach there. You can make up some story about a sick dog on your ship. As soon as you get it, send it to me here. I'll be on the look out, so Vinnie will never know it came. Then you must wait on the "Flying Trades" until you hear from me or I come to you —afterwards!

BRANT (*dully*). But how can you do it—so no one will suspect?

CHRISTINE. He's taking medicine. I'll give him his medicine. Oh, I've planned it carefully.

BRANT. But—if he dies suddenly, won't Vinnie——

CHRISTINE. There'll be no reason for her to suspect. She's worried already about his heart. Besides, she may hate me, but she would never think——

BRANT. Orin will be coming home, too.

CHRISTINE. Orin will believe anything I want him to. As for the people here, they'd never dream of such a thing in the Mannon house! And the sooner I do it, the less suspicion there'll be! They will think the excitement of coming home and the reaction were too much for his weak heart! Doctor Blake will think so. I'll see that's what he thinks.

BRANT (*harshly*). Poison! It's a coward's trick!

CHRISTINE (*with fierce scorn now, seeing the necessity of goading him*). Do you think you would be braver to give me up to him and let him take away your ship ?

BRANT. No !

CHRISTINE. Didn't you say you wanted to kill him ?

BRANT. Aye ! But I'd give him his chance !

CHRISTINE. Did he give your mother her chance ?

BRANT (*aroused*). No, damn him !

CHRISTINE. Then what makes you suddenly so scrupulous about his death ? (*With a sneer.*) It must be the Mannon in you coming out ! Are you going to prove, the first time your love is put to a real test, that you're a weak coward like your father ?

BRANT. Christine ! If it was any man said that to me—— !

CHRISTINE (*passionately*). Have you thought of this side of his homecoming—that he's coming back to my bed ? If you love me as much as you claim, I should think that would rid you of any scruples ! If it was a question of some woman taking you from me, I wouldn't have qualms about which was or wasn't the way to kill her ! (*More tauntingly.*) But perhaps your love has been only a lie you told me—to take the sneaking revenge on him of being a backstairs lover ! Perhaps——

BRANT (*stung, grabbing her by the shoulders—fiercely*). Stop it ! I'll do anything you want ! You know it ! (*Then with a change to sombre grimness—putting the paper in his pocket.*) And you're right. I'm a damn fool to have any feeling about how Ezra Mannon dies !

CHRISTINE (*a look of exultant satisfaction comes to her face as she sees he is definitely won over now. She throws her arms around him and kisses him passionately*). Ah ! Now you're the man I love again, not a hypocritical Mannon ! Promise me, no more cowardly romantic scruples ! Promise me !

BRANT. I promise.

(*The boom of a cannon sounds from the fort that guards the harbour. He and Christine start frightenedly and stand staring at each other. Another boom comes, reverberating, rattling the windows. Christine recovers herself.*)

CHRISTINE. You hear ? That's the salute to his homecoming ! (*She kisses him—with fierce insistence.*) Remember your mother's death ! Remember your dream of your own ship ! Above all, remember you'll have me !—all your own—your wife ! (*Then urgently.*) And now you must go ! She'll be coming back—and you're not good at hiding your thoughts. (*Urging him towards the door.*) Hurry ! I don't want you to meet her ! (*The cannon at the fort keep booming at regular intervals until the end of the scene. Brant goes out in the hall and a moment later the front door is heard closing after him. Christine hurries from the door to the window and watches him from behind the curtains as he goes down the drive. She is in a state of tense, exultant excitement. Then, as if an idea had suddenly come to her, she speaks to his retreating figure with a strange sinister air of elation.*) You'll never dare leave me now, Adam—for your ships or your sea or your naked Island girls—when I grow old and ugly !

(*She turns back from the window. Her eyes are caught by the eyes of her husband in the portrait and for a moment she stares back into them, as if fascinated. Then she jerks her glance away and, with a little shudder she cannot repress, turns and walks quickly from the room and closes the door behind her.*)

Curtain

ACT THREE

SCENE. *The same as Act One, Scene One—exterior of the Mannon house. It is about nine o'clock at night a week later. The light of a half-moon falls on the house, giving it an unreal, detached, eerie quality. The pure white temple front seems more than ever like an incongruous mask fixed on the sombre, stone house. All the shutters are closed. The white columns of the portico cast black bars of shadow on the grey wall behind them. The trunk of the pine at right is an ebony pillar, its branches a mass of shade.*

Lavinia is sitting on the top of the steps to the portico. She is dressed, as before, severely in black. Her thin figure, seated stiffly upright, arms against her sides, the knees close together, the shoulders square, the head upright, is like that of an Egyptian statue. She is staring straight before her. The sound of Seth's thin, aged baritone mournfully singing the chanty "Shenandoah" is heard from down the drive, off right front. He is approaching the house and the song draws quickly nearer:

"Oh, Shenandoah, I long to hear you
A-way, my rolling river.
Oh, Shenandoah, I can't get near you
Way-ay, I'm bound away
Across the wide Missouri.
"Oh, Shenandoah, I love your daughter
A-way, my rolling river."

He enters right front. He is a bit drunk but holding his liquor well. He walks up by the lilacs starting the next line "Oh, Shenandoah"—then suddenly sees Lavinia on the steps and stops abruptly, a bit sheepish.

LAVINIA (*disapprovingly*). This is the second time this week I've caught you coming home like this.

SETH (*unabashed, approaches the steps—with a grin*). I'm aimin' to do my patriotic duty, Vinnie. The first time was celebratin' Lee's surrender and this time is drownin' my sorrow for the President gittin' shot! And the third'll be when your Paw gits home!

LAVINIA. Father might arrive to-night.

SETH. Gosh, Vinnie, I never calc'lated he could git here so soon!

LAVINIA. Evidently you didn't. He'd give you fits if he caught you drunk. Oh, I don't believe he'll come, but it's possible he might.

SETH (*is evidently trying to pull himself together. He suddenly leans over towards her and, lowering his voice, asks soberly*). Did you find out anything about that Brant?

LAVINIA (*sharply*). Yes. There's no connection. It was just a silly idea of yours.

SETH (*stares at her—then understandingly*). Wal, if you want it left that way, I'll leave it that way. (*A pause. He continues to stand looking at her, while she stares in front of her.*)

LAVINIA (*in a low voice*). What was that Marie Brantôme like, Seth?

SETH. Marie? She was always laughin' and singin'—frisky and full of life—with something free and wild about her like an animile. Purty she was, too! (*Then he adds:*) Hair just the colour of your Maw's and yourn she had.

LAVINIA. I know.

SETH. Oh, everyone took to Marie—couldn't help it. Even your Paw. He was only a boy then, but he was crazy about her, too, like a youngster would be. His mother was stern with him, while Marie, she made a fuss over him and petted him.

LAVINIA. Father, too!

SETH. Ayeh—but he hated her worse than anyone when it got found out she was his Uncle David's fancy woman.

LAVINIA (*in a low voice, as if to herself, staring at the house*). It's all so strange! It frightens me! (*She checks herself abruptly—turns to Seth, curtly.*) I don't believe that about Father. You've had too much whisky. Go to bed and sleep it off. (*She walks up the steps again.*)

SETH (*gazes at her with understanding*). Ayeh. (*Then warningly, making a surreptitious signal as he sees the front door opening behind her.*) Ssstt! (*Christine appears outlined in the light from the hall. She is dressed in a gown of green velvet that sets off her hair. The light behind her glows along the edges of the dress and in the colour of her hair. She closes the door and comes into the moonlight at the edge of the steps, standing above and a little to the right of Lavinia. The moonlight, falling full on them, accentuates strangely the resemblance between their faces and at the same time the hostile dissimilarity in body and dress. Lavinia does not turn or give any sign of knowing her mother is behind her. There is a second's uncomfortable silence. Seth moves off left.*) Wal, I'll trot along!

(*He disappears around the corner of the house. There is a pause. Then Christine speaks in a dry mocking tone.*)

CHRISTINE. What are you moon-gazing at? Puritan maidens shouldn't peer too inquisitively into spring! Isn't beauty an abomination and love a vile thing? (*She laughs with bitter mockery—then tauntingly.*) Why don't you marry Peter? You don't want to be left an old maid, do you?

LAVINIA (*quietly*). You needn't hope to get rid of me that way. I'm not marrying anyone. I've got my duty to Father.

CHRISTINE. Duty! How often I've heard that

word in this house ! Well, you can't say I didn't do mine all these years. But there comes an end.

LAVINIA (*grimly*). And there comes another end —and you must do your duty again !

CHRISTINE (*starts as if to retort defiantly—then says calmly*). Yes, I realize that.

LAVINIA (*after a pause—suspiciously*). What's going on at the bottom of your mind ? I know you're plotting something !

CHRISTINE (*controlling a start*). Don't be stupid, please !

LAVINIA. Are you planning how you can see Adam again ? You better not !

CHRISTINE (*calmly*). I'm not so foolish. I said good-bye once. Do you think I want to make it harder for myself ?

LAVINIA. Has it been hard for you ? I'd never guess it—and I've been watching you.

CHRISTINE. I warned you you would have no chance to gloat ! (*After a pause.*) When do you expect your father home ? You want me to play my part well when he comes, don't you ?—for his sake. I'd like to be forewarned.

LAVINIA. His letter said he wouldn't wait until his brigade was disbanded but would try to get leave at once. He might arrive to-night—or to-morrow—or the next day I don't know.

CHRISTINE. You think he might come to-night ? (*Then with a mocking smile.*) So he's the beau you're waiting for in the spring moonlight ! (*Then after a pause.*) But the night train got in long ago.

LAVINIA (*glances down the drive, left front—then starts to her feet excitedly*). Here's someone !

(*Christine slowly rises. There is the sound of footsteps. A moment later Ezra Mannon enters from left front. He stops short in the shadow for a second and stands, erect and stiff, as if at attention, staring at his house, his wife and daughter. He is a tall, spare, big-boned man of fifty, dressed in the uniform of a Brigadier-General. One is immediately struck by the mask-like look of his face in repose, more pronounced in him than in the others. He is exactly like the portrait in his study, which we have seen in Act Two, except that his face is more lined and lean and the hair and beard are grizzled. His movements are exact and wooden and he has a mannerism of standing and sitting in stiff, posed attitudes that suggest the statues of military heroes. When he speaks, his deep voice has a hollow repressed quality, as if he were continually withholding emotion from it. His air is brusque and authoritative.*)

LAVINIA (*seeing the man's figure stop in the shadow—calls excitedly*). Who's that ?

MANNON (*stepping forward into the moonlight*). It's I.

LAVINIA (*with a cry of joy*). Father ! (*She runs to him and throws her arms around him and kisses him.*) Oh, Father ! (*She bursts into tears and hides her face against his shoulder.*)

MANNON (*embarrassed—patting her head—gruffly*). Come ! I thought I'd taught you never to cry.

LAVINIA (*obediently forcing back her tears*). I'm sorry, Father—but I'm so happy !

MANNON (*awkwardly moved*). Tears are queer tokens of happiness ! But I appreciate your—your feeling.

CHRISTINE (*has slowly descended the steps, her eyes fixed on him—tensely*). Is it really you, Ezra ? We had just given up hope of your coming to-night.

MANNON (*going stiffly to meet her*). Train was late. The railroad is jammed up. Everybody has got leave. (*He meets her at the foot of the steps and kisses her with a chill dignity—formally.*) I am glad to see you, Christine. You are looking well. (*He steps back and stares at her—then in a voice that betrays a deep undercurrent of suppressed feeling.*) You have changed, somehow. You are prettier than ever—— But you always were pretty.

CHRISTINE (*forcing a light tone*). Compliments from one's husband ! How gallant you've become, Ezra ! (*Then solicitously.*) You must be terribly tired. Wouldn't you like to sit here on the steps for a while ? The moonlight is so beautiful.

LAVINIA (*who has been hovering about jealously, now manages to worm herself between them—sharply*). No. It's too damp out here. And Father must be hungry. (*Taking his arm.*) Come inside with me and I'll get you something to eat. You poor dear ! You must be starved.

MANNON (*really revelling in his daughter's coddling but embarrassed before his wife—pulling his arm back—brusquely*). No, thanks! I would rather rest here for a bit. Sit down, Vinnie. (*Christine sits on the top step at centre; he sits on the middle step at right; Lavinia on the lowest step at left. While they are doing this he keeps on talking in his abrupt sentences, as if he were trying to cover up some hidden uneasiness.*) I've got leave for a few days. Then I must go back and disband my brigade. Peace ought to be signed soon. The President's assassination is a frightful calamity. But it can't change the course of events.

LAVINIA. Poor man! It's dreadful he should die just at his moment of victory.

MANNON. Yes! (*Then after a pause—sombrely.*) All victory ends in the defeat of death. That's sure. But does defeat end in the victory of death? That's what I wonder! (*They both stare at him, Lavinia in surprise, Christine in uneasy wonder. A pause.*)

CHRISTINE. Where is Orin? Couldn't you get leave for him too?

MANNON (*hesitates—then brusquely*). I've been keeping it from you. Orin was wounded.

LAVINIA. Wounded! You don't mean—badly hurt?

CHRISTINE (*half starting to her feet, impulsively—with more of angry bitterness than grief*). I knew it! I knew when you forced him into your horrible war——! (*Then sinking back—tensely.*) You needn't trouble to break the news gradually, Ezra. Orin is dead, isn't he?

LAVINIA. Don't say that! It isn't true, is it, Father?

MANNON (*curtly—a trace of jealousy in his tone*). Of course it isn't! If your mother would permit me to finish instead of jumping at conclusions about her baby——! (*With a grim, proud satisfaction.*) He's no baby now. I've made a man of him. He did one of the bravest things I've seen in the war. He was wounded in the head—a close shave but it turned out only a scratch. But he got brain fever from the shock. He's all right now. He was in a rundown condition, they say at the hospital. I never guessed it. Nerves. I wouldn't notice nerves. He's always been restless. (*Half turning to Christine.*) He gets that from you.

CHRISTINE. When will he be well enough to come home?

MANNON. Soon. The doctor advised a few more days' rest. He's still weak. He was out of his head for a long time. Acted as if he were a little boy again. Seemed to think you were with him. That is, he kept talking to "Mother."

CHRISTINE (*with a tense intake of breath*). Ah!

LAVINIA (*pityingly—with a tinge of scorn in her voice*). Poor Orin!

MANNON. I don't want you to baby him when he comes home, Christine. It would be bad for him to get tied to your apron-strings again.

CHRISTINE. You needn't worry. That passed—when he left me. (*Another pause. Then Lavinia speaks.*)

LAVINIA. How is the trouble with your heart, Father? I've been so afraid you might be making it out less serious than it really was to keep us from worrying.

MANNON (*gruffly*). If it was serious, I'd tell you, so you'd be prepared. If you'd seen as much of death as I have in the past four years, you wouldn't be afraid of it. (*Suddenly jumping to his feet—brusquely.*) Let's change the subject! I've had my fill of death. What I want now is to forget it. (*He turns and paces up and down to the right of steps. Lavinia watches him worriedly.*) All I know is the pain is like a knife. It puts me out of commission while it lasts. The doctor gave me orders to avoid worry or any over-exertion or excitement.

CHRISTINE (*staring at him*). You don't look well. But probably that's because you're so tired. You must go to bed soon, Ezra.

MANNON (*comes to a stop in his pacing directly before her and looks into her eyes—a pause—then he says in a voice that he tries to make ordinary*). Yes, I want to—soon.

LAVINIA (*who has been watching him jealously—suddenly pulling him by the arm—with a childish volubility*). No! Not yet! Please, Father! You've only just come! We've hardly talked at all! (*Defiantly to her mother.*) How can you tell him he looks tired? He looks as well as I've ever seen him. (*Then to her father, with a vindictive look at Christine.*) We've so much to tell you. All about Captain Brant. (*If she had expected her mother to flinch at this, she is disappointed. Christine is prepared and remains unmoved beneath the searching, suspicious glance Mannon now directs at her.*)

MANNON. Vinnie wrote me you'd had company. I never heard of him. What business had he here?

CHRISTINE (*with an easy smile*). You had better ask Vinnie! He's her latest beau! She even went walking in the moonlight with him!

LAVINIA (*with a gasp at being defied so brazenly*). Oh!

MANNON (*now jealous and suspicious of his daughter*). I notice you didn't mention that in your letter, young lady!

LAVINIA. I only went walking once with him—and that was before—— (*She checks herself abruptly.*)

MANNON. Before what?

LAVINIA. Before I knew he's the kind who chases after every woman he sees.

MANNON (*angrily to Christine*). A fine guest to receive in my absence!

LAVINIA. I believe he even thought Mother was flirting with him. That's why I felt it my duty to write to you. You know how folks in town gossip, Father. I thought you ought to warn Mother she was foolish to allow him to come here.

MANNON. Foolish! It was downright——!

CHRISTINE (*coldly*). I would prefer not to discuss this until we are alone, Ezra—if you don't mind! And I think Vinnie is extremely inconsiderate the moment you're home—to annoy you with such ridiculous nonsense! (*She turns to Lavinia.*) I think you've done enough mischief. Will you kindly leave us?

LAVINIA. No.

MANNON (*sharply*). Stop your squabbling, both of you! I hoped you had grown out of that nonsense! I won't have it in my house!

LAVINIA (*obediently*). Yes, Father.

MANNON. It must be your bedtime, Vinnie.

LAVINIA. Yes, Father. (*She comes and kisses him—excitedly.*) Oh, I'm so happy you're here! Don't let Mother make you believe I—— You're the only man I'll ever love! I'm going to stay with you!

MANNON (*patting her hair—with gruff tenderness*). I hope so. I want you to remain my little girl—for a while longer, at least. (*Then suddenly catching Christine's scornful glance—pushes Lavinia away—brusquely.*) March, now!

LAVINIA. Yes, Father. (*She goes up the steps past her mother without a look. Behind her mother, in the portico, she stops and turns.*) Don't let anything worry you, Father. I'll always take care of you.

(*She goes in. Mannon looks at his wife who stares before her. He clears his throat as if about to say something—then starts pacing self-consciously up and down at the right of steps.*)

CHRISTINE (*forcing a gentle tone*). Sit down, Ezra. You will only make yourself more tired, keeping on your feet. (*He sits awkwardly two steps below her, on her left, turned sideways to face her. She asks with disarming simplicity:*) Now please tell me just what it is you suspect me of?

MANNON (*taken aback*). What makes you think I suspect you?

CHRISTINE. Everything! I've felt your distrust from the moment you came. Your eyes have been probing me, as if you were a judge again and I were the prisoner.

MANNON (*guiltily*). I——?

CHRISTINE. And all on account of a stupid letter Vinnie had no business to write. It seems to me a late day, when I am an old woman with grown-up children, to accuse me of flirting with a stupid ship's captain!

MANNON (*impressed and relieved—placatingly*). There's no question of accusing you of that. I only think you've been foolish to give the gossips a chance to be malicious.

CHRISTINE. Are you sure that's all you have in your heart against me?

MANNON. Yes! Of course! What else? (*Patting her hand embarrassedly.*) We'll say no more about it. (*Then he adds gruffly:*) But I'd like you to explain how this Brant happened——

CHRISTINE. I'm only too glad to! I met him at Father's. Father has taken a fancy to him for some reason. So when he called here I couldn't be rude, could I? I hinted that his visits weren't welcome, but men of his type don't understand hints. But he's only been here four times in all, I think. And as for there having been gossip, that's nonsense! The only talk has been that he came to court Vinnie! You can ask anyone in town.

MANNON. Damn his impudence! It was your duty to tell him flatly he wasn't wanted!

CHRISTINE (*forcing a contrite air*). Well, I must confess I didn't mind his coming as much as I might have—for one reason. He always brought me news of Father. Father's been ill for the past year, as I wrote you. (*Then with a twitch of the lips, as if she were restraining a derisive smile.*) You can't realize what a strain I've been under—worrying about Father and Orin and—you.

MANNON (*deeply moved, turns to her and takes her hand in both of his—awkwardly*). Christine—I deeply regret—having been unjust. (*He kisses her hand impulsively—then embarrassed by this show of emotion, adds in a gruff, joking tone.*) Afraid old Johnny Reb would pick me off, were you?

CHRISTINE (*controlling a wild impulse to burst into derisive laughter*). Do you need to ask that? (*A pause. He stares at her, fascinated and stirred.*)

MANNON (*finally blurts out*). I've dreamed of coming home to you, Christine! (*Leans towards her, his voice trembling with desire and a feeling of strangeness and awe—touching her hair with an awkward caress.*) You're beautiful! You look more beautiful than ever—and strange to me. I don't know you. You're younger. I feel like an old man beside you. Only your hair is the same—your strange beautiful hair I always——

CHRISTINE (*with a start of repulsion, shrinking from his hand*). Don't! (*Then as he turns away, hurt and resentful at this rebuff—hastily.*) I'm sorry, Ezra. I didn't mean—I—I'm nervous to-night.

(*Mannon paces to the right and stands looking at the trees. Christine stares at his back with hatred. She sighs with affected weariness and leans back and closes her eyes.*)

CHRISTINE. I'm tired, Ezra.

MANNON (*blurts out*). I shouldn't have bothered you with that foolishness about Brant to-night. (*He forces a strained smile.*) But I was jealous a bit, to tell you the truth.

(*He forces himself to turn and, seeing her eyes are shut, suddenly comes and leans over her awkwardly, as if to kiss her, then is stopped by some strangeness he feels about her still face.*)

CHRISTINE (*feeling his desire and instinctively shrinking—without opening her eyes*). Why do you look at me like that?

MANNON (*turns away guiltily*). Like what? (*Uneasily.*) How do you know? Your eyes are shut. (*Then, as if some burden of depression were on him that he had to throw off, he blurts out heavily:*) I can't get used to home yet. It's so lonely. I've got used to the feel of camps with thousands of men around me at night—a sense of protection, maybe! (*Suddenly uneasy again.*) Don't keep your eyes shut like that! Don't be so still! (*Then, as she opens her eyes—with an explosive appeal.*) God, I want to talk to you, Christine! I've got to explain some things—inside me—to my wife—try to, anyway! (*He sits down beside her.*) Shut your eyes again! I can talk better. It has always been hard for me to talk—about feelings. I never could when you looked at me. Your eyes were always so—so full of silence! That is, since we've been married. Not before, when I was courting you. They used to speak then. They made me talk—because they answered.

CHRISTINE (*her eyes closed—tensely*). Don't talk, Ezra.

MANNON (*as if he had determined, once started, to go on doggedly without heeding any interruption*). It was seeing death all the time in this war got me to thinking these things. Death was so common, it didn't mean anything. That freed me to think of life. Queer, isn't it? Death made me think of life. Before that life had only made me think of death!

CHRISTINE (*without opening her eyes*). Why are you talking of death?

MANNON. That's always been the Mannons' way of thinking. They went to the white meeting-house on Sabbaths and meditated on death. Life was a dying. Being born was starting to die. Death was being born. (*Shaking his head with a dogged bewilderment.*) How in hell people ever got such notions! That white meeting-house. It stuck in my mind—clean-scrubbed and white-washed—a temple of death! But in this war I've seen too many white walls splattered with blood that counted no more than dirty water. I've seen dead men scattered about, no more important than rubbish to be got rid of. That made the white meeting-house seem meaningless—making so much solemn fuss over death!

CHRISTINE (*opens her eyes and stares at him with a strange terror*). What has this talk of death to do with me?

MANNON (*avoiding her glance—insistently*). Shut your eyes again. Listen and you'll know. (*She *shuts her eyes. He plods on with a note of desperation in his voice.*) I thought about my life—lying awake nights—and about your life. In the middle of battle I'd think maybe in a minute I'll be dead. But my life as just me ending, that didn't appear worth a thought one way or another. But listen, me as your husband being killed, that seemed queer and wrong—like something dying that had never lived. Then all the years we've been man and wife would rise up in my mind and I would try to look at them. But nothing was clear except that there'd always been some barrier between us—a wall hiding us from each other! I would try to make up my mind exactly what that wall was but I never could discover. (*With a clumsy appealing gesture.*) Do you know?

CHRISTINE (*tensely*). I don't know what you're talking about.

MANNON. But you've known it was there! Don't lie, Christine! (*He looks at her still face and closed eyes, imploring her to reassure him—then blunders on doggedly.*) Maybe you've always known you didn't love me. I call to mind the Mexican War. I could see you wanted me to go. I had a feeling you'd grown to hate me. Did you? (*She doesn't answer.*) That was why I went. I was hoping I might get killed. Maybe you were hoping that too. Were you?

CHRISTINE (*stammers*). No, no, I—— What makes you say such things?

MANNON. When I came back you had turned to your new baby, Orin. I was hardly alive for you any more. I saw that. I tried not to hate Orin. I turned to Vinnie, but a daughter's not a wife. Then I made up my mind I'd do my work in the world and leave you alone in your life and not care. That's why the shipping wasn't enough—why I became a judge and a mayor and such vain truck, and why folks in town look on me as so able! Ha! Able for what? Not for what I wanted most in life! Not for your love! No! Able only to keep my mind from thinking of what I'd lost! (*He stares at her—then asks pleadingly:*) For you did love me before we were married. You won't deny that, will you?

CHRISTINE (*desperately*). I don't deny anything!

MANNON (*drawing himself up with a stern pride and dignity and surrendering himself like a commander against hopeless odds*). All right, then. I came home to surrender to you—what's inside me. I love you. I loved you then, and all the years between, and I love you now.

CHRISTINE (*distractedly*). Ezra! Please!

MANNON. I want that said! Maybe you have forgotten it. I wouldn't blame you. I guess I haven't said it or showed it much—ever. Something queer in me keeps me mum about the things I'd like most to say—keeps me hiding the things I'd like to show. Something keeps me sitting numb in my own heart—like a statue of a dead man in a town square. (*Suddenly he reaches over and takes her hand.*) I want to find what that wall is that marriage put between us! You've got to help me smash it down! We have twenty good years still before us! I've been thinking of what we could do to get back to each other. I've a notion if we'd leave the children and go off on a voyage together—to the other side of the world—find some island where we could be alone a while. You'll find I have changed, Christine. I'm sick of death! I want life! Maybe you could love me now! (*In a note of final desperate pleading.*) I've got to make you love me!

CHRISTINE (*pulls her hand away from him and springs to her feet wildly*). For God's sake, stop talking. I don't know what you're saying. Leave me alone! What must be, must be! You make me weak! (*Then abruptly.*) It's getting late.

MANNON (*terribly wounded, withdrawn into his stiff soldier armour—takes out his watch mechanically*). Yes—six past eleven. Time to turn in. (*He ascends two steps, his face towards the door. He says bitterly:*) You tell me to stop talking! By God, that's funny!

CHRISTINE (*collected now and calculating—takes hold of his arm, seductively*). I meant—what is the good of words? There is no wall between us. I love you.

MANNON (*grabs her by the shoulders and stares into her face*). Christine! I'd give my soul to believe that—but—I'm afraid! (*She kisses him. He presses her fiercely in his arms—passionately.*) Christine! (*The door behind him is opened and Lavinia appears at the edge of the portico behind and above him. She wears slippers over her bare feet and has a dark dressing-gown over her night-dress. She shrinks from their embrace with aversion. They separate, startled.*)

MANNON (*embarrassed—irritably*). Thought you'd gone to bed, young lady!

LAVINIA (*woodenly*). I didn't feel sleepy. I thought I'd walk a little. It's such a fine night.

CHRISTINE. We are just going to bed. Your father is tired. (*She moves up, past her daughter, taking Mannon's hand, leading him after her to the door.*)

MANNON. No time for a walk, if you ask me. See you turn in soon.

LAVINIA. Yes, Father.

MANNON. Good night.

(*The door closes behind them. Lavinia stands staring before her—then walks stiffly down the steps and stands again. Light appears between the chinks of the shutters in the bedroom on the second floor to the left. She looks up.*)

LAVINIA (*in an anguish of jealous hatred*). I hate you! You steal even Father's love from me again! You stole all love from me when I was born! (*Then almost with a sob, hiding her face in her hands.*) Oh, Mother! Why have you done this to me? What harm had I done you? (*Then looking up at the window again—with passionate disgust.*) Father, how can you love that shameless harlot? (*Then frenziedly.*) I can't bear it! I won't! It's my duty to tell him about her! I will! (*She calls desperately:*) Father! Father! (*The shutter of the bedroom is pushed open and Mannon leans out.*)

MANNON (*sharply*). What is it? Don't shout like that!

LAVINIA (*stammers lamely*). I—I remembered I forgot to say good night, Father.

MANNON (*exasperated*). Good heavens! What —— (*Then gently.*) Oh—all right—good night, Vinnie. Get to bed soon, like a good girl.

LAVINIA. Yes, Father. Good night.

(*He goes back in the bedroom and pulls the shutter closed. She stands staring, fascinated, up at the window, wringing her hands in a piteous desperation.*)

Curtain

ACT FOUR

SCENE. *Ezra Mannon's bedroom. A big four-poster bed is at rear, centre, the foot front, the head against the rear wall. A small stand, with a candle on it, is by the head of the bed on the left. To the left of the stand is a door leading into Christine's room. The door is open. In the left wall are two windows. At left front is a table with a lamp on it and a chair beside it. In the right wall, front, is a door leading to the hall. Farther back, against the wall, is a bureau.*

None of these details can be discerned at first because the room is in darkness, except for what moonlight filters feebly through the shutters. It is about dawn of the following morning.

Christine's form can be made out, a pale ghost in the darkness, as she slips slowly and stealthily from the bed. She tiptoes to the table, left front, and picks up a light-coloured dressing-gown that is flung over the chair and puts it on. She stands listening for some sound from the bed. A pause. Then Mannon's voice comes suddenly from the bed, dull and lifeless.

MANNON. Christine.

CHRISTINE (*starts violently—in a strained voice*). Yes.

MANNON. Must be near daybreak, isn't it?

CHRISTINE. Yes. It is beginning to get grey.

MANNON. What made you jump when I spoke? Is my voice so strange to you?

CHRISTINE. I thought you were asleep.

MANNON. I haven't been able to sleep. I've been lying here thinking. What makes you so uneasy?

CHRISTINE. I haven't been able to sleep either.

MANNON. You crept out of bed so quietly.

CHRISTINE. I didn't want to wake you.

MANNON (*bitterly*). Couldn't you bear it—lying close to me?

CHRISTINE. I didn't want to disturb you by tossing.

MANNON. We'd better light the light and talk a while.

CHRISTINE (*with dread*). I don't want to talk! I prefer the dark.

MANNON. I want to see you. (*He takes matches from the stand by the bed and lights the candle on it. Christine hastily sits down in the chair by the table, pushing it so she sits facing left front, with her face turned three-quarters away from him. He pushes his back up against the head of the bed in a half-sitting position. His face, with the flickering candle-light on its side, has a grim, bitter expression*). You like the dark where you can't see your old man of a husband, is that it?

CHRISTINE. I wish you wouldn't talk like that, Ezra. If you are going to say stupid things, I'll go in my own room. (*She gets to her feet but keeps her face turned away from him.*)

MANNON. Wait! (*Then a note of pleading in his voice.*) Don't go. I don't want to be alone. (*She sits again in the same position as before. He goes on humbly.*) I didn't mean to say those things. I guess there's bitterness inside me—my own cussedness, maybe—and sometimes it gets out before I can stop it.

CHRISTINE. You have always been bitter.

MANNON. Before we married?

CHRISTINE. I don't remember.

MANNON. You don't want to remember you ever loved me!

CHRISTINE (*tensely*). I don't want to talk of the past! (*Abruptly changing the subject.*) Did you hear Vinnie the first part of the night? She was pacing up and down before the house like a sentry guarding you. She didn't go to bed until two. I heard the clock strike.

MANNON. There is one who loves me, at least! (*Then after a pause.*) I feel strange, Christine.

CHRISTINE. You mean—your heart? You don't think you are going to be—taken ill, do you?

MANNON (*harshly*). No! (*A pause—then accusingly.*) Is that what you're waiting for? Is that why you were so willing to give yourself to-night? Were you hoping——?

CHRISTINE (*springing up*). Ezra! Stop talking like that! I can't stand it! (*She moves as if to go into her own room.*)

MANNON. Wait! I'm sorry I said that. (*Then, as she sits down again, he goes on gloomily.*) It isn't my heart. It's something uneasy troubling my mind—as if something in me was listening, watching, waiting for something to happen.

CHRISTINE. Waiting for what to happen?

MANNON. I don't know. (*A pause—then he goes on sombrely.*) This house is not my house. This is not my room nor my bed. They are empty—waiting for someone to move in! And you are not my wife! You are waiting for something!

CHRISTINE (*beginning to snap under the strain—jumps to her feet again*). What would I be waiting for?

MANNON. For death—to set you free!

CHRISTINE. Leave me alone! Stop nagging at me with your crazy suspicions! (*Then anger and hatred come into her voice.*) Not your wife! You acted as if I were your wife—your property—not so long ago!

MANNON (*with bitter scorn*). Your body? What are bodies to me? I've seen too many rotting in the sun to make grass greener! Ashes to ashes, dirt to dirt! Is that your notion of love? Do you think I married a body? (*Then, as if all the bitterness and hurt in him had suddenly burst its dam.*) You were lying to me to-night as you've always lied! You were only pretending love! You let me take you as if you were a nigger slave I'd bought at auction! You made me appear a lustful beast in my own eyes!—as you've always done since our first marriage night! I would feel cleaner now if I had gone to a brothel! I would feel more honour between myself and life!

CHRISTINE (*in a stifled voice*). Look out, Ezra! I won't stand——

MANNON (*with a harsh laugh*). And I had hoped my homecoming would mark a new beginning—new love between us! I told you my secret feelings. I tore my insides out for you—thinking you'd understand! By God, I'm an old fool!

CHRISTINE (*her voice grown strident*). Did you think you could make me weak—make me forget all the years? Oh no, Ezra! It's too late! (*Then her voice changes, as if she had suddenly resolved on a course of action, and becomes deliberately taunting.*) You want the truth? You've guessed it! You've used me, you've given me children, but I've never once been yours! I never could be! And whose fault is it? I loved you when I married you! I wanted to give myself! But you made me so I couldn't give! You filled me with disgust!

MANNON (*furiously*). You say that to me! (*Then trying to calm himself—stammers.*) No! Be quiet! We mustn't fight! I mustn't lose my temper! It will bring on——!

CHRISTINE (*goading him with calculating cruelty*). Oh, no! You needn't adopt that pitiful tone! You wanted the truth and you're going to hear it now!

MANNON (*frightened—almost pleading*). Be quiet, Christine!

CHRISTINE. I've lied about everything! I lied about Captain Brant! He is Marie Brantôme's son! And it was I he came to see, not Vinnie! I made him come!

MANNON (*seized with fury*). You dared——! You——! The son of that——!

CHRISTINE. Yes, I dared! And all my trips to New York weren't to visit Father but to be with Adam! He's gentle and tender, he's everything you've never been. He's what I've longed for all these years with you—a lover! I love him! So now you know the truth!

MANNON (*in a frenzy—struggling to get out of bed*). You—you whore—I'll kill you! (*Suddenly he falls back, groaning, doubled up on his left side, with intense pain.*)

CHRISTINE (*with savage satisfaction*). Ah!

(*She hurries through the doorway into her room and immediately returns with a small box in her hand. He is facing away from her door, and, even if the intense pain left him any perception, he could not notice her departure and return, she moves so silently.*)

MANNON (*gaspingly*). Quick—medicine!

CHRISTINE (*turned away from him, takes a pellet from the box, asking tensely as she does so*). Where is your medicine?

MANNON. On the stand! Hurry!

CHRISTINE. Wait. I have it now. (*She pretends to take something from the stand by the head of the bed—then holds out the pellet and a glass of water which is on the stand.*) Here. (*He turns to her, groaning, and opens his mouth. She puts the pellet on his tongue and presses the glass of water to his lips.*) Now drink.

MANNON (*takes a mouthful of water—then suddenly a wild look of terror comes over his face. He gasps.*) That's not—my medicine! (*She shrinks back to the table, the hand with the box held out behind her, as if seeking a hiding-place. Her fingers release the box on the table-top and she brings her hand in front of her as if instinctively impelled to prove to him she has nothing. His eyes are fixed on her in a terrible accusing glare. He tries to call for help but his voice fades to a wheezy whisper.*) Help! Vinnie!

(*He falls back in a coma, breathing stertorously. Christine stares at him, fascinated—then starts with terror as she hears a noise from the hall and frantically snatches up the box from the table and holds it behind her back, turning to face the door as it opens and Lavinia appears in the doorway. She is dressed as at the end of Act Three, in nightgown, wrapper and slippers. She stands, dazed and frightened and hesitating, as if she had just awakened.*)

LAVINIA. I had a horrible dream—I thought I heard Father calling me—it woke me up——

CHRISTINE (*trembling with guilty terror—stammers*). He just had—an attack.

LAVINIA (*hurries to the bed*). Father! (*She puts her arms around him.*) He's fainted!

CHRISTINE. No. He's all right now. Let him sleep.

(*At this moment Mannon, with a last dying effort, straightens up in a sitting position in Lavinia's arms, his eyes glaring at his wife, and manages to raise his arm and point an accusing finger at her.*)

MANNON (*gasps*). She's guilty—not medicine! (*He falls back limply.*)

LAVINIA. Father! (*Frightened, she feels for his pulse, puts her ear against his chest to listen for a heartbeat.*)

CHRISTINE. Let him alone. He's asleep.

LAVINIA. He's dead!

CHRISTINE (*repeats mechanically*). Dead? (*Then in a strange flat tone.*) I hope—he rests in peace.

LAVINIA (*turning on her with hatred*). Don't you dare pretend——! You wanted him to die! You—— (*She stops and stares at her mother with a horrified suspicion—then harshly accusing.*) Why did he point at you like that? Why did he say you were guilty? Answer me!

CHRISTINE (*stammers*). I told him—Adam was my lover.

LAVINIA (*aghast*). You told him that—when you knew his heart—— ! Oh ! You did it on purpose ! You murdered him !

CHRISTINE. No—it was your fault—you made him suspicious—he kept talking of love and death—he forced me to tell him ! (*Her voice becomes thick, as if she were drowsy and fighting off sleep. Her eyes half close.*)

LAVINIA (*grabbing her by the shoulders—fiercely*). Listen ! Look at me ! He said " not medicine " ! What did he mean ?

CHRISTINE (*keeping the hand with the poison pressed against her back*). I—I don't know.

LAVINIA. You do know ! What was it ? Tell me !

CHRISTINE (*with a last effort of will manages to draw herself up and speak with a simulation of outraged feeling*). Are you accusing your mother of——

LAVINIA. Yes ! I—— ! (*Then distractedly.*) No—you can't be that evil !

CHRISTINE (*her strength gone—swaying weakly*). I don't know what—you're talking about. (*She edges away from Lavinia towards her bedroom door, the hand with the poison stretched out behind her—weakly.*) I—feel faint. I must go—and lie down. I—— (*She turns as if to run into the room, takes a tottering step—then her knees suddenly buckle under her and she falls in a dead faint at the foot of the bed. As her hand strikes the floor the fingers relax and the box slips out on to one of the knotted rugs. Lavinia does not notice this. Startled by Christine's collapse, she automatically bends on one knee beside her and hastily feels for her pulse. Then satisfied she has only fainted, her anguished hatred immediately returns and she speaks with strident denunciation.*) You murdered him just the same—by telling him ! I suppose you think you'll be free to marry Adam now ! But you won't ! Not while I'm alive ! I'll make you pay for your crime ! I'll find a way to punish you !

(*She is starting to her feet when her eyes fall on the little box on the rug. Immediately she snatches it up and stares at it, the look of suspicion changing to a dreadful, horrified certainty. Then with a shuddering cry she shrinks back along the side of the bed, the box clutched in her hand, and sinks on her knees by the head of the bed, and flings her arms around the dead man.*)

LAVINIA (*with anguished beseeching*). Father ! Don't leave me alone ! Come back to me ! Tell me what to do !

Curtain

THE HUNTED

A Play in Five Acts

Part Two of the Trilogy
MOURNING BECOMES ELECTRA

Characters

CHRISTINE, *Ezra Mannon's widow*
LAVINIA (VINNIE), *her daughter*
ORIN, *her son, First Lieutenant of Infantry*
CAPTAIN ADAM BRANT
HAZEL NILES
PETER, *her brother, Captain of Artillery*
JOSIAH BORDEN, *manager of the shipping company*
EMMA, *his wife*
EVERETT HILLS, D.D., *of the First Congregational Church*
HIS WIFE
DOCTOR JOSEPH BLAKE
THE CHANTYMAN

Scenes

ACT ONE

Exterior of the Mannon house. A moonlight night two days after the murder of Ezra Mannon.

ACT TWO

Sitting-room in the house (immediately follows Act One).

ACT THREE

Ezra Mannon's study (immediately follows Act Two).

ACT FOUR

The stern of the clipper ship 'Flying Trades', at a wharf in East Boston. A night two days later.

ACT FIVE

Same as Act One. Exterior of the Mannon house the night of the following day.

ACT ONE

SCENE. *The same as Acts One and Three of "Homecoming"—Exterior of the Mannon House.*

It is a moonlight night two days after the murder of Ezra Mannon. The house has the same strange eerie appearance, its white portico like a mask in the moonlight, as it had on that night. All the shutters are closed. A funeral wreath is fixed to the column at the right of steps. Another wreath is on the door.

There is a sound of voices from inside the house, the front door is opened and Josiah Borden and his wife, Everett Hills, the Congregational min-

ister, and his wife, and Doctor Joseph Blake, the Mannons' family physician, come out. Christine can be seen in the hall just inside the door. There is a chorus of "Good night, Mrs. Mannon," and they turn to the steps and the door is closed.

These people—the Bordens, Hills and his wife and Doctor Blake—are, as were the Ames of Act One of "Homecoming," types of townsfolk, a chorus representing as those others had, but in a different stratum of society, the town as a human background for the drama of the Mannons.

Josiah Borden, the manager of the Mannon shipping company, is shrewd and competent. He is about sixty, small and wizened, white hair and beard, rasping nasal voice, and little sharp eyes. His wife, about ten years his junior, is a typical New England woman of pure English ancestry, with a horse face, buck teeth and big feet, her manner defensively sharp and assertive. Hills is the type of well-fed minister of a prosperous small-town congregation—stout and unctuous, snobbish and ingratiating, conscious of godliness, but timid and always feeling his way. He is in the fifties, as is his wife, a sallow, flabby, self-effacing minister's wife. Doctor Blake is the old kindly best-family physician—a stout, self-important old man with a stubborn opinionated expression.

They come down the steps to the drive. Mrs. Borden and Mrs. Hills walk together towards left front until they are by the bench. There they stop to wait for the men who stand at the foot of the steps while Borden and Blake light cigars.

MRS. BORDEN (*tartly*). I can't abide that woman!

MRS. HILLS. No. There's something queer about her.

MRS. BORDEN (*grudgingly honest*). Still and all, I come nearer to liking her now than I ever did before when I see how broken down she is over her husband's death.

MRS. HILLS. Yes. She looks terrible, doesn't she? Doctor Blake says she will have herself in bed sick if she doesn't look out.

MRS. BORDEN. I'd never have suspected she had that much feeling in her. Not but what she hasn't always been a dutiful wife, as far as anyone knows.

MRS. HILLS. Yes. She's seemed to be.

MRS. BORDEN. Well, it only goes to show how you can misjudge a person without meaning to—especially when that person is a Mannon. They're not easy to make head or tail of. Queer, the difference in her and Lavinia—the way they take his death. Lavinia is cold and calm as an icicle.

MRS. HILLS. Yes. She doesn't seem to feel as much sorrow as she ought.

MRS. BORDEN. That's where you're wrong. She feels it as much as her mother. Only she's too Mannon to let anyone see what she feels. But did you notice the look in her eyes?

MRS. HILLS. I noticed she never said a word to anyone. Where did she disappear to all of a sudden?

MRS. BORDEN. Went to the train with Peter Niles to meet Orin. I overheard her mother talking to Lavinia in the hall. She was insisting Peter should escort her to meet the train. Lavinia must have been starting to go alone. Her mother seemed really angry about it. (*Then glancing towards the men who have moved a little away from the steps and are standing talking in low tones.*) Whatever are those men gossiping about? (*She calls.*) Josiah! It's time we were getting home.

BORDEN. I'm coming, Emma. (*The three men join the women by the bench, Borden talking as they come.*) It isn't for me to question the arrangements she's made, Joe, but it does seem as if Ezra should have been laid out in the town hall where the whole town could have paid their respects to him, and had a big public funeral to-morrow.

HILLS. That's my opinion. He was mayor of the town and a national war hero——

BLAKE. She says it was Ezra's wish he'd often expressed that everything should be private and quiet. That's just like Ezra. He never was one for show. He did the work and let others do the showing-off.

HILLS (*unctuously*). He was a great man. His death is a real loss to everyone in this community. He was a power for good.

BORDEN. Yes. He got things done.

HILLS. What a tragedy to be taken his first night home after passing unharmed through the whole war!

BORDEN. I couldn't believe the news. Who'd ever suspect—— It's queer. It's like fate.

MRS. HILLS (*breaks in tactlessly*). Maybe it is fate. You remember, Everett, you've always said about the Mannons that pride goeth before a fall and that some day God would humble them in their sinful pride. (*Everyone stares at her, shocked and irritated.*)

HILLS (*flustered*). I don't remember ever saying——

BLAKE (*huffily*). If you'll excuse me, that's darn nonsense! I've known Ezra Mannon all my life, and to those he wanted to know he was as plain and simple——

HILLS (*hastily*). Of course, Doctor. My wife entirely misunderstood me. I was, perhaps wrongly, referring to Mrs. Mannon.

BLAKE. She's all right too—when you get to know her.

HILLS (*dryly*). I have no doubt.

BLAKE. And it's a poor time, when this household is afflicted by sudden death, to be——

HILLS. You are quite right, Doctor. My wife should have remembered——

MRS. HILLS (*crushed*). I didn't mean anything wrong, Doctor.

BLAKE (*mollified*). Let's forget it, then. (*Turning to Borden—with a self-satisfied, knowing air.*) As for your saying who'd ever expect it—well, you and Emma know I expected Ezra wouldn't last long.

BORDEN. Yes. I remember you said you were afraid his heart was bad.

MRS. BORDEN. I remember you did too.

BLAKE. From the symptoms Mrs. Mannon described from his letter to her, I was as certain as if I'd examined him he had angina. And I wasn't surprised neither. I'd often told Ezra he was attempting more than one man could handle and if he didn't rest he'd break down. The minute they sent for me I knew what'd happened. And what she told me about waking up to find him groaning and doubled with pain confirmed it. She'd given him his medicine—it was what I would have prescribed myself—but it was too late. And as for dying his first night home—well, the war was over, he was worn out, he'd had a long, hard trip home—and angina is no respecter of time and place. It strikes when it has a mind too.

BORDEN (*shaking his head*). Too bad. Too durned bad. The town won't find another as able as Ezra in a hurry. (*They all shake their heads and look sad. A pause.*)

MRS. BORDEN. Well, we aren't doing anyone any good standing here. We ought to get home, Josiah.

MRS. HILLS. Yes. We must, too, Everett.

(*They begin moving slowly off left, Hills going with the two women. Doctor Blake nudges Borden and motions him to stay behind. After the others disappear, he whispers with a meaning grin.*)

BLAKE. I'll tell you a secret, Josiah—strictly between you and me.

BORDEN (*sensing something from his manner—eagerly*). Of course. What is it, Joe?

BLAKE. I haven't asked Christine Mannon any embarrassing questions, but I have a strong suspicion it was love killed Ezra!

BORDEN. Love?

BLAKE. That's what! Leastways, love made angina kill him, if you take my meaning. She's a damned handsome woman and he'd been away a long time. Only natural between man and wife—but not the treatment I'd recommend for angina. He should have known better, but—well—he was human.

BORDEN (*with a salacious smirk*). Can't say as I blame him! She's handsome! I don't like her and never did, but I can imagine worse ways of dying! (*They both chuckle.*) Well, let's catch up with the folks.

(*They go off, left. They have hardly disappeared before the door of the house is opened and Christine Mannon comes out and stands at the head of the steps a moment, then descends to the drive. She is obviously in a terrible state of strained nerves. Beneath the mask-like veneer of her face there are deep lines about her mouth, and her eyes burn with a feverish light. Feeling herself free from observation for a moment she lets go, her mouth twitches, her eyes look desperately on all sides, as if she longed to fly from something. Hazel Niles comes out of the house to the head of the steps. She is the same as in "Homecoming." Christine at once senses her presence behind her and regains her tense control of herself.*)

HAZEL (*with a cheering, sympathetic air*). So here you are. I looked everywhere around the house and couldn't find you.

CHRISTINE (*tensely*). I couldn't stay in. I'm so nervous. It's been a little harrowing—all these people coming to stand around and stare at the dead—and at me.

HAZEL. I know. But there won't be any more now. (*Then a tone of eagerness breaking through in spite of herself.*) Peter and Vinnie ought to be back soon, if the train isn't late. Oh, I hope Orin will surely come!

CHRISTINE (*strangely*). The same train! It was late that night he came! Only two days ago! It seems a lifetime! I've grown old.

HAZEL (*gently*). Try not to think of it.

CHRISTINE (*tensely*). As if I hadn't tried! But my brain keeps on—over and over and over!

HAZEL. I'm so afraid you will make yourself ill.

CHRISTINE (*rallying herself and forcing a smile*). There, I'm all right. I mustn't appear too old and haggard when Orin comes, must I? He always liked me to be pretty.

HAZEL. It will be so good to see him again! (*Then quickly*). He ought to be such a comfort to you in your grief.

CHRISTINE. Yes. (*Then strangely.*) He used to be my baby, you know—before he left me. (*Suddenly staring at Hazel, as if struck by an idea.*) You love Orin, don't you?

HAZEL (*embarrassed—stammers shyly*). I—I——

CHRISTINE. I am glad. I want you to. I want him to marry you. (*Putting an arm around her—in a strained tone.*) We'll be secret conspirators, shall we, and I'll help you and you'll help me?

HAZEL. I don't understand.

CHRISTINE. You know how possessive Vinnie is with Orin. She's always been jealous of you. I warn you she'll do everything she can to keep him from marrying you.

HAZEL (*shocked*). Oh, Mrs. Mannon, I can't believe Vinnie——!

CHRISTINE (*unheeding*). So you must help me. We mustn't let Orin come under her influence again. Especially now in the morbid, crazy state of grief she's in! Haven't you noticed how queer she's become? She hasn't spoken a single word since her father's death! When I talk to her she won't answer me. And yet she follows me around everywhere—she hardly leaves me alone a minute. (*Forcing a nervous laugh.*) It gets on my nerves until I could scream!

HAZEL. Poor Vinnie! She was so fond of her father. I don't wonder she——

CHRISTINE (*staring at her—strangely*). You are genuinely good and pure of heart, aren't you?

HAZEL (*embarrassed*). Oh no! I'm not at all——

CHRISTINE. I was like you once—long ago—before—— (*Then with bitter longing.*) If I could only have stayed as I was then! Why can't all of us remain innocent and loving and trusting? But God won't leave us alone. He twists and wrings and tortures our lives with others' lives until—we poison each other to death! (*Seeing Hazel's look, catches herself—quickly.*) Don't mind what I said! Let's go in, shall we? I would rather wait for Orin inside. I couldn't bear to wait and watch him coming up the drive—just like—he looks so much like his father at times—and like—but what nonsense I'm talking! Let's go in. I hate moonlight. It makes everything so haunted.

(*She turns abruptly and goes into the house. Hazel follows her and shuts the door. There is a pause. Then footsteps and voices are heard from off right front and a moment later Orin Mannon enters with Peter and Lavinia. One is at once struck by his startling family resemblance to Ezra Mannon and Adam Brant (whose likeness to each other we have seen in "Homecoming"). There is the same life-like mask quality of his face in repose, the same aquiline nose, heavy eyebrows, swarthy complexion, thick straight black hair, light hazel eyes. His mouth and chin have the same general characteristics as his father's had, but the expression of his mouth gives an impression of tense oversensitiveness quite foreign to the General's, and his chin is a refined, weakened version of the dead man's. He is about the same height as Mannon and Brant, but his body is thin and his swarthy complexion sallow. He wears a bandage round his head high up on his forehead. He carries himself by turns with a marked slouchiness or with a self-conscious square-shouldered stiffness that indicates a soldierly bearing is unnatural to him. When he speaks it is jerkily, with a strange, vague, preoccupied air. But when he smiles naturally his face has a gentle boyish charm which makes women immediately want to mother him. He wears a moustache similar to Brant's which serves to increase their resemblance to each other. Although he is only twenty, he looks thirty. He is dressed in a baggy, ill-fitting uniform—that of a first lieutenant of infantry in the Union Army.)*

ORIN (*as they enter looks eagerly towards the house—then with bitter, hurt disappointment in his tone*). Where's Mother? I thought she'd surely be waiting for me. (*He stands staring at the house.*) God, how I've dreamed of coming home! I thought it would never end, that we'd go on murdering and being murdered until no one was left alive! Home at last! No, by God, I must be dreaming again! (*Then in an awed tone.*) But the house looks strange. Or is it something in me? I was off my head so long, everything has seemed queer since I came back to earth. Did the house always look so ghostly and dead?

PETER. That's only the moonlight, you chump.

ORIN. Like a tomb. That's what mother used to say it reminded her of, I remember.

LAVINIA (*reproachfully*). It is a tomb—just now, Orin.

ORIN (*hurriedly—shamefacedly*). I—I'd forgotten. I simply can't realize he's dead yet. I suppose I'd come to expect he would live for ever. (*A trace of resentment has crept into his tone.*) Or, at least outlive me. I never thought his heart was weak. He told me the trouble he had wasn't serious.

LAVINIA (*quickly*). Father told you that, too? I was hoping he had. (*Then turning to Peter.*) You go ahead in, Peter. Say we're coming a little behind. I want to speak to Orin a moment.

PETER. Sure thing, Vinnie. (*He goes in the front door, closing it behind him.*)

ORIN. I'm glad you got rid of him. Peter is all right but—I want to talk to you alone. (*With a boyish brotherly air—putting an arm around her.*) You certainly are a sight for sore eyes, Vinnie! How are you, anyway, you old bossy fuss-buzzer! Gosh, it seems natural to hear myself calling you that old nickname again. Aren't you glad to see me?

LAVINIA (*affectionately*). Of course I am!

ORIN. I'd never guess it! You've hardly spoken a word since you met me. What's happened to you? (*Then, as she looks at him reproachfully, he takes away his arm—a bit impatiently.*) I told you I can't get used to the idea of his being dead. Forgive me, Vinnie. I know what a shock it must be to you.

LAVINIA. Isn't it a shock to you, Orin?

ORIN. Certainly! What do you think I am? But—oh, I can't explain! You wouldn't understand, unless you'd been at the front. I hardened myself to expect my own death and everyone else's, and think nothing of it. I had to—to keep alive! It was part of my training as a soldier under him. He taught it to me, you might say! So when it's his turn he can hardly expect—— (*He has talked with increasing bitterness. Lavinia interrupts him sharply.*)

LAVINIA. Orin! How can you be so unfeeling?

ORIN (*again shamefaced*). I didn't mean that. My mind is still full of ghosts. I can't grasp anything but war, in which he was so alive. He was the war to me—the war that would never end until I died. I can't understand peace—his end! (*Then with exasperation.*) God damn it, Vinnie, give me a chance to get used to things!

LAVINIA. Orin!

ORIN (*resentfully*). I'm sorry! Oh, I know what you're thinking! I used to be such a nice gentlemanly cuss, didn't I?—and now—— Well, you wanted me to be a hero in blue, so you better be resigned! Murdering doesn't improve one's manners! (*Abruptly changing the subject.*) But what the devil are we talking about me for? Listen, Vinnie. There's something I want to ask you before I see Mother.

LAVINIA. Hurry, then! She'll be coming right out! I've got to tell you something too!

ORIN. What was that stuff you wrote about some Captain Brant coming to see Mother? Do you mean to tell me there's actually been gossip started about her? (*Then without waiting for a reply, bursting into jealous rage.*) By God, if he dares come here again, I'll make him damned sorry he did!

LAVINIA (*grimly*). I'm glad you feel that way about him. But there's no time to talk now. All I want to do is warn you to be on your guard. Don't let her baby you the way she used to and get you under her thumb again. Don't believe the lies she'll tell you! Wait until you've talked to me! Will you promise me?

ORIN (*staring at her bewilderedly*). You mean—Mother? (*Then angrily.*) What the hell are you talking about, anyway? Are you loony? Honestly, Vinnie, I call that carrying your everlasting squabble with Mother a bit too far! You ought to be ashamed of yourself! (*Then suspiciously.*) What are you being so mysterious about? Is it Brant——?

LAVINIA (*at a sound from inside the house*). Ssshh! (*The front door of the house is opened and Christine hurries out.*)

CHRISTINE (*angrily to Peter who is in the hall*). Why didn't you call me, Peter? You shouldn't have left him alone! (*She calls uncertainly:*) Orin.

ORIN. Mother! (*She runs down the steps and flings her arms around him.*)

CHRISTINE. My boy! My baby! (*She kisses him.*)

ORIN (*melting, all his suspicion forgotten*). Mother! God, it's good to see you! (*Then almost roughly, pushing her back and staring at her.*) But you're different! What's happened to you?

CHRISTINE (*forcing a smile*). I? Different? I don't think so, dear. Certainly I hope not—to you! (*Touching the bandage on his head—tenderly.*) Your head! Does it pain dreadfully? You poor darling, how you must have suffered! (*She kisses him.*) But it's all over now, thank God. I've got you back again! (*Keeping her arm around him, she leads him up the steps.*) Let's go in. There's someone else waiting who will be so glad to see you.

LAVINIA (*who has come to the foot of the steps—harshly*). Remember, Orin!

(*Christine turns round to look down at her. A look of hate flashes between mother and daughter. Orin glances at his mother suspiciously and draws away from her.*)

CHRISTINE (*immediately recovers her poise—to Orin, as if Lavinia hadn't spoken*). Come on in, dear. It's chilly. Your poor head—— (*She takes his hand and leads him through the door and closes it behind them. Lavinia remains by the foot of the steps, staring after them. Then the door is suddenly opened again and Christine comes out, closing it behind her, and walks to the head of the steps. For a moment mother and daughter stare into each other's eyes. Then Christine begins haltingly in a tone she vainly tries to make kindly and persuasive.*) Vinnie, I—I must speak with you a moment—now Orin is here. I appreciate your grief has made you—not quite normal—and I make allowances. But I cannot understand your attitude towards me. Why do you keep following me everywhere—and stare at me like that? I had been a good wife to him for twenty-three years—until I met Adam. I was guilty then, I admit. But I repented and put him out of my life. I would have been a good wife again as long as your father had lived. After all, Vinnie, I am your mother. I brought you into the world. You ought to have some feeling for me. (*She pauses, waiting for some response, but Lavinia simply stares at her, frozen and silent. Fear creeps into Christine's tone.*) Don't stare like that! What are you thinking? Surely you can't still have that insane suspicion—that I—— (*Then guiltily.*) What did you do that night after I fainted? I—I've missed something—some medicine I take to put me to sleep—— (*Something like a grim smile of satisfaction forms on Lavinia's lips. Christine exclaims, frightened:*) Oh, you did—you found—and I suppose you connect that—but don't you see how insane—to suspect—when Doctor Blake knows he died of——! (*Then angrily.*) I know what you've been waiting for—to tell Orin your lies and get him to go to the police! You don't dare do that on your own responsibility—but if you can make Orin—— Isn't that it? Isn't that what you've been planning the last two days? Tell me! (*Then as Lavinia remains silent, Christine gives way to fury and rushes down the steps and seizes her by the arm and shakes her.*) Answer me when I speak to you! What are you plotting? What are you going to do? Tell me! (*Lavinia keeps her body rigid, her eyes staring into her mother's. Christine lets go and steps away from her. Then Lavinia, turning her back, walks slowly and woodenly off left between the lilac clump and the house. Christine stares after her, her strength seems to leave her, she trembles with dread. From inside the house comes the sound of Orin's voice calling sharply, "Mother! Where are you?" Christine starts and immediately by an effort of will regains control over herself. She hurries up the steps and opens the door. She speaks to Orin and her voice is tensely quiet and normal.*) Here I am, dear! (*She shuts the door behind her.*)

Curtain

ACT TWO

SCENE. *The sitting-room of the Mannon house. Like the study, but much larger, it is an interior composed of straight severe lines with heavy detail. The walls are plain plastered surfaces, light grey with a white dado. It is a bleak room without intimacy, with an atmosphere of uncomfortable, stilted stateliness. The furniture is stationed about with exact precision. On the left, front, is a doorway leading to the dining-room. Further back, on the left, are a wall table and chair and a writing desk and chair. In the rear wall, centre, is the doorway giving on the main hall and the stairs. At right is a fireplace with a chimney-piece of black marble, flanked by two windows. Portraits of ancestors hang on the walls. At the rear of the fireplace, on the right, is one of a grim-visaged minister of the witch-burning era. Between fireplace and front is another of Ezra Mannon's grandfather, in the uniform of an officer in Washington's army. Directly over the fireplace is the portrait of Ezra's father, Abe Mannon, done when he was sixty. Except for the difference in ages, his face looks exactly like Ezra's in the painting in the study.*

Of the three portraits on the other walls, two are of women—Abe Mannon's wife and the wife of Washington's officer. The third has the appearance of a prosperous shipowner of Colonial days. All the faces in the portraits have the same mask quality of those of the living characters in the play.

At the left centre of the room, front, is a table with two chairs. There is another chair at centre, front, and a sofa at right, front, facing left.

The opening of this scene follows immediately the close of the preceding one. Hazel is discovered sitting on the chair at centre, front. Peter is sitting on the sofa at right. From the hall Orin is heard calling, "Mother! Where are you?" as at the close of the preceding act.

HAZEL. Where can she have gone? She's worked herself into such a state of grief I don't think she knows what she's doing.

PETER. Vinnie's completely knocked out, too.

HAZEL. And poor Orin! What a terrible homecoming this is for him! How ill and changed he looks, doesn't he, Peter?

PETER. Head wounds are no joke. He's darned lucky to have come out alive.

(*They self-consciously stop talking as Orin and Christine enter from the rear. Orin is questioning her suspiciously.*)

ORIN. Why did you sneak away like that? What were you doing?

CHRISTINE (*forcing a wan smile*). The happiness of seeing you again was a little too much for me, I'm afraid, dear. I suddenly felt as if I were going to faint, so I rushed out in the fresh air.

ORIN (*immediately ashamed of himself—tenderly, putting his arm around her*). Poor Mother! I'm sorry—— Look here, then. You sit down and rest. Or maybe you better go right to bed.

HAZEL. That's right, Orin, you make her. I've been trying to get her to but she won't listen to me.

CHRISTINE. Go to bed the minute he comes home! I should say not!

ORIN (*worried and pleased at the same time*). But you mustn't do anything to——

CHRISTINE (*patting his cheek*). Fiddlesticks! Having you again is just the medicine I need to give me strength—to bear things. (*She turns to Hazel.*) Listen to him, Hazel! You'd think I was the invalid and not he.

HAZEL. Yes. You've got to take care of yourself, too, Orin.

ORIN. Oh, forget me. I'm all right.

CHRISTINE. We'll play nurses, Hazel and I, and have you your old self again before you know it. Won't we, Hazel?

HAZEL (*smiling happily*). Of course we will.

CHRISTINE. Don't stand, dear. You must be worn out. Wait. We'll make you comfortable. Hazel, will you bring me a cushion?

(*Hazel gets a cushion and helps to place it behind his back in the chair at right of table. Orin's eyes light up and he grins boyishly, obviously revelling in being coddled.*)

ORIN. How's this for the comforts of home, Peter? The front was never like this, eh?

PETER. Not so you'd notice it!

ORIN (*with a wink at Hazel*). Peter will be

getting jealous! You better call Vinnie in to put a pillow behind him!

HAZEL (*with a smile*). I can't picture Vinnie being that soft.

ORIN (*a jealous resentment creeping into his voice.*) She can be soft—on occasion. She's always coddling Father and he likes it, although he pretends——

CHRISTINE (*turning away and restraining a shudder*). Orin! You're talking as if he were—alive!

(*There is an uncomfortable silence. Hazel goes quietly back to her chair at centre. Christine goes round the table to the chair opposite Orin and sits down.*)

ORIN (*with a wry smile*). We'd all forgotten he's dead, hadn't we? Well, I can't believe it even yet. I feel him in this house—alive!

CHRISTINE. Orin!

ORIN (*strangely*). Everything is changed—in some queer way—this house, Vinnie, you, I—everything but Father. He's the same and always will be—here—the same! Don't you feel that, Mother? (*She shivers, looking before her, but doesn't answer*).

HAZEL (*gently*). You mustn't make your mother think of it, Orin.

ORIN (*staring at her—in a queer tone of gratitude*). You're the same, Hazel—sweet and good. (*He turns to his mother accusingly.*) At least Hazel hasn't changed, thank God!

CHRISTINE (*rousing herself—turns to force a smile at him*). Hazel will never change, I hope. I am glad you appreciate her. (*Hazel looks embarrassed. Christine goes on—with motherly solicitude.*) Wasn't the long train trip terribly hard on you, dear?

ORIN. Well, it wasn't a pleasure trip exactly. My head got aching till I thought it would explode.

CHRISTINE (*leans over and puts her hand on his forehead*). Poor boy! Does it pain now?

ORIN. Not much. Not at all when your hand is there. (*Impulsively he takes her hand and kisses it—boyishly.*) Gosh, Mother, it feels so darned good to be home with you! (*Then staring at her suspiciously again.*) Let me have a good look at you. You're so different. I noticed it even outside. What is it?

CHRISTINE (*avoiding his eyes—forcing a smile*). It's just that I'm getting old, I'm afraid, dear.

ORIN. No. You're more beautiful than ever! You're younger, too, somehow. But it isn't that. (*Almost pushing her hand away—bitterly.*) Maybe I can guess!

CHRISTINE (*forces a laugh*). Younger and more beautiful! Do you hear him going on, Hazel? He has learned to be very gallant, I must say!

(*Lavinia appears in the doorway at rear. She enters but remains standing just inside the doorway and keeps her eyes fixed on her mother and Orin.*)

ORIN (*who is again looking at Hazel, breaks out harshly*). Do you remember how you waved your handkerchief, Hazel, the day I set off to become a hero? I thought you would sprain your wrist! And all the mothers and wives and sisters and girls did the same! Some time in some war they ought to make the women take the men's place for a month or so. Give them a taste of murder!

CHRISTINE. Orin!

ORIN. Let them batter each other's brains out with rifle butts and rip each other's guts with bayonets! After that, maybe they'd stop waving handkerchiefs and chattering about heroes! (*Hazel gives a shocked exclamation.*)

CHRISTINE. Please!

PETER (*gruffly*). Give it a rest, Orin! It's over. Give yourself a chance to forget it. None of us liked it any more than you did.

ORIN (*immediately shamefaced*). You're right, Peter. I'm a damned whining fool! I'm sorry, Hazel. That was rotten of me.

HAZEL. It was nothing, Orin. I understand how you feel. Really I do.

ORIN. I—I let off steam when I shouldn't. (*Then suddenly.*) Do you still sing, Hazel? I used to hear you singing—down there. It made me feel life might still be alive somewhere—that, and my dreams of Mother, and the memory of Vinnie bossing me around like a drill sergeant. I used to hear you singing at the queerest times—so sweet and clear and pure! It would rise above the screams of the dying——

CHRISTINE (*tensely*). I wish you wouldn't talk of death!

LAVINIA (*from the doorway—in a brusque command-*

ing tone like her father's). Orin! Come and see Father.

ORIN (*starts up from his chair and makes an automatic motion as if to salute—mechanically*). Yes, sir. (*Then confusedly.*) What the devil——? You sounded just like him. Don't do that again, for heaven's sake! (*He tries to force a laugh—then shamefacedly.*) I meant to look at him the first thing—but I got talking—I'll go in now.

CHRISTINE (*her voice tense and strained*). No! Wait! (*Angrily to Lavinia.*) Can't you let your brother have a minute to rest? You can see how worn out he is! (*Then to Orin.*) I've hardly had a chance to say a word to you yet—and it has been so long! Stay with me a little while, won't you?

ORIN (*touched, coming back to her*). Of course, Mother! You come before everything!

LAVINIA (*starts to make a bitter retort, glances at Peter and Hazel, then remarks evenly*). Very well. Only remember what I said, Orin. (*She turns her back and starts to go into the hall.*)

CHRISTINE (*frightened*). Vinnie! Where are you going?

LAVINIA (*does not answer her but calls back to her brother over her shoulder*). You'll come in a little while, won't you?

(*She disappears across the hall. Orin gives his mother a sidelong glance of uneasy suspicion. Christine is desperately trying to appear calm. Peter and Hazel stand up, feeling uncomfortable.*)

HAZEL. Peter, we really must be getting home.

PETER. Yes.

CHRISTINE. It was so kind of you to come.

HAZEL (*giving her hand to Orin*). You must rest all you can now, Orin—and try not to think about things.

ORIN. You're darned kind, Hazel. It's fine to see you again—the same as ever!

HAZEL (*delighted but pulling her hand away shyly*). I'm glad, too. Good night, Orin.

PETER (*shakes his hand*). Good night. Rest and take it easy.

ORIN. Good night, Peter. Thanks for meeting me.

CHRISTINE (*goes with them to the hall.*) I'm afraid this isn't a very cheerful house to visit just now—but please come soon again. You will do Orin more good than anyone, Hazel.

(*The look of suspicion again comes to Orin's eyes. He sits down in the chair at left of table and stares before him bitterly. Christine returns from the hall, closing the sliding doors behind her silently. She stands for a moment looking at Orin, visibly bracing herself for the ordeal of the coming interview, her eyes full of tense calculating fear.*)

ORIN (*without looking at her*). What's made you take such a fancy to Hazel all of a sudden? You never used to think much of her. You didn't want me going about with her.

CHRISTINE (*coming forward and sitting across the table from him—in her gentle motherly tone*). I was selfish then. I was jealous, too, I'll confess. But all I want now is your happiness, dear. I know how much you used to like Hazel——

ORIN (*blurts out*). That was only to make you jealous! (*Then bitterly.*) But now you're a widow, I'm not home an hour before you're trying to marry me off! You must be damned anxious to get rid of me again! Why?

CHRISTINE. You mustn't say that! If you knew how horribly lonely I've been without you——

ORIN. So lonely you've written me exactly two letters in the last six months!

CHRISTINE. But I wrote you many more! They must have been lost——

ORIN. I received all of Hazel's letters—and Vinnie's. It's darned funny yours should be the only ones to get lost! (*Unable to hold back any longer, he bursts forth*). Who is this Captain Brant who's been calling on you?

CHRISTINE (*prepared for this—with well-feigned astonishment*). On me? You mean on Vinnie, don't you? (*Then as Orin looks taken aback.*) Wherever did you get that silly idea? Oh, of course, I know! Vinnie must have written you the same nonsense she did to your father.

ORIN. She wrote it to him? What did he do?

CHRISTINE. Why, he laughed at it, naturally! Your father was very fond of Vinnie but he knew how jealous she's always been of me and he realized she'd tell any lie she could to——

ORIN. Oh, come on now, Mother! Just because you're always getting on each other's nerves it doesn't mean Vinnie would ever deliberately——

CHRISTINE. Oh, doesn't it though? I think you'll discover before you're much older that there isn't anything your sister will stop at—that she will even accuse me of the vilest, most horrible things!

ORIN. Mother! Honestly now! You oughtn't to say that!

CHRISTINE (*reaching out and taking his hand*). I mean it, Orin. I wouldn't say it to anyone but you. You know that. But we've always been so close, you and I. I feel you are really—my flesh and blood! She isn't! She is your father's! You're a part of me!

ORIN (*with strange eagerness*). Yes! I feel that, too, Mother!

CHRISTINE. I know I can trust you to understand now as you always used to. (*With a tender smile.*) We had a secret little world of our own in the old days, hadn't we?—which no one but us knew about.

ORIN (*happily*). You bet we did! No Mannons allowed was our password, remember!

CHRISTINE. And that's what your father and Vinnie could never forgive us! But we'll make that little world of our own again, won't we?

ORIN. Yes!

CHRISTINE. I want to make up to you for all the injustice you suffered at your father's hands. It may seem a hard thing to say about the dead, but he was jealous of you. He hated you because he knew I loved you better than anything in the world!

ORIN (*pressing her hand in both of his—intensely*). Do you, Mother? Do you honestly? (*Then he is struck by what she said about his father—painfully.*) I knew he disapproved of me. But I never thought he went as far as to—hate me.

CHRISTINE. He did, just the same!

ORIN (*with resentful bitterness*). All right then! I'll tell you the truth, Mother. I won't pretend to you I'm sorry he's dead!

CHRISTINE (*lowering her voice to a whisper*). Yes. I am glad, too!—that he has left us alone! Oh, how happy we'll be together, you and I, if you only won't let Vinnie poison your mind against me with her disgusting lies!

ORIN (*immediately uneasy again*). What lies? (*He releases her hand and stares at her, morbidly suspicious.*) You haven't told me about that Brant yet.

CHRISTINE. There's nothing to tell—except in Vinnie's morbid revengeful mind! I tell you, Orin, you can't realize how she's changed while you've been away! She's always been a moody and strange girl, you know that, but since you've gone she has worried and brooded until I really believe she went a little out of her mind. She got so she'd say the most terrible things about everyone. You simply wouldn't believe me, if I told you some of the things. And now, with the shock of your father's death on top of everything, I'm convinced she's actually insane. Haven't you noticed how queerly she acts? You must have!

ORIN. I saw she'd changed a lot. She seemed strange. But——

CHRISTINE. And her craziness all works out in hatred for me! Take this Captain Brant affair, for example——

ORIN. Ah!

CHRISTINE. A stupid ship's captain I happened to meet at your grandfather's who took it into his silly head to call here a few times without being asked. Vinnie thought he was coming to court her. I honestly believe she fell in love with him, Orin. But she soon discovered that he wasn't after her at all!

ORIN. Who was he after—you?

CHRISTINE (*sharply*). Orin! I'd be very angry with you if it weren't so ridiculous! (*She forces a laugh.*) You don't seem to realize I'm an old married woman with two grown-up children! No, all he was after was to insinuate himself as a family friend and use your father when he came home to get him a better ship! I soon saw through his little scheme and he'll never call here again, I promise you that! (*She laughs—then with a teasing air.*) And that's the whole of the great Captain Brant scandal! Are you satisfied now, you jealous goose, you?

ORIN (*penitent and happy*). I'm a fool! The war has got me silly, I guess! If you knew all the hell I've been through!

CHRISTINE. It was Vinnie's fault you ever went to war! I'll never forgive her for that! It broke my heart, Orin! (*Then quickly.*) But I was going to give you an example of her insane suspicions from the Captain Brant incident. Would you believe it that she has worked it all out that because his name is Brant, he must be the son of that nurse girl Marie Brantôme? Isn't that crazy? And to imagine for a moment, if he were, he'd ever come here to visit!

ORIN (*his face hardening*). By God, I'd like to see him! His mother brought disgrace enough on our family without——

CHRISTINE (*frightened, shrinking from him*). Orin! Don't look like that! You're so like your father! (*Then hurrying on.*) But I haven't told you the worst yet. Vinnie actually accuses me—your mother—of being in love with that fool and of having met him in New York and gone to his room! I am no better than a prostitute in your sister's eyes!

ORIN (*stunned*). I don't believe it! Vinnie couldn't!

CHRISTINE. I told you she'd gone crazy! She even followed me to New York, when I went to see your sick grandfather, to spy on me. She saw me meet a man—and immediately to her crazy brain the man was Brant. Oh, it's too revolting, Orin! You don't know what I've had to put up with from Vinnie, or you'd pity me!

ORIN. Good God! Did she tell Father that? No wonder he's dead! (*Then harshly.*) Who was this man you met in New York?

CHRISTINE. It was Mr. Lamar, your grandfather's old friend who has known me ever since I was a baby! I happened to meet him and he asked me to go with him to call on his daughter. (*Then, seeing Orin wavering, pitifully.*) Oh, Orin! You pretend to love me! And yet you question me as if you suspected me, too! And you haven't Vinnie's excuse! You aren't out of your mind! (*She weeps hysterically.*)

ORIN (*overcome at once by remorse and love*). No! I swear to you! (*He throws himself on his knees beside her and puts his arm around her.*) Mother! Please! Don't cry! I do love you! I do!

CHRISTINE. I haven't told you the most horrible thing of all! Vinnie suspects me of having poisoned your father!

ORIN (*horrified*). What! No, by God, that's too much! If that's true, she ought to be put in an asylum!

CHRISTINE. She found some medicine I take to make me sleep, but she is so crazy I know she thinks —— (*Then, with real terror, clinging to him.*) Oh, Orin, I'm so afraid of her! God knows what she might do, in her state! She might even go to the police and—— Don't let her turn you against me! Remember you're all I have to protect me! You are all I have in the world, dear!

ORIN (*tenderly soothing her*). Turn me against you? She can't be so crazy as to try that! But listen. I honestly think you—— You're a little hysterical, you know. That—about Father—is all such damned nonsense! And as for her going to the police—do you suppose I wouldn't prevent that—for a hundred reasons—the family's sake—my own sake and Vinnie's, too, as well as yours—even if I knew——

CHRISTINE (*staring at him—in a whisper*). Knew? Orin, you don't believe——?

ORIN. No! For God's sake! I only meant that no matter what you ever did, I love you better than anything in the world and——

CHRISTINE (*in an outburst of grateful joy—pressing him to her and kissing him*). Oh, Orin, you are my boy, my baby! I love you!

ORIN. Mother! (*Then seizing her by the shoulders and staring into her eyes—with sombre intensity.*) I could forgive anything—anything!—in my mother—except that other—that about Brant!

CHRISTINE. I swear to you——!

ORIN. If I thought that damned——! (*With savage vengefulness.*) By God, I'd show you then I hadn't been taught to kill for nothing!

CHRISTINE (*full of new terror now—for Brant's life—distractedly*). For God's sake, don't talk like that! You're not like my Orin! You're cruel and horrible! You frighten me!

ORIN (*immediately contrite and soothing, petting her*). There, there, Mother! We won't ever think about it again! We'll talk of something else. I want to tell you something. (*He sits on the floor at her feet and looks up into her face. A pause. Then he asks tenderly, taking her hand.*) Did you really want me to come back, Mother?

CHRISTINE (*has calmed herself, but her eyes are still terrified and her voice trembles*). What a foolish question, dear.

ORIN. But your letters got farther and farther between—and they seemed so cold! It drove me crazy! I wanted to desert and run home—or else get killed! If you only knew how I longed to be here with you—like this! (*He leans his head *against her knee. His voice becomes dreamy and low and caressing.)* I used to have the most wonderful dreams about you. Have you ever read a book called " Typee "—about the South Sea Islands ?

CHRISTINE *(with a start—strangely).* Islands ! Where there is peace ?

ORIN. Then you did read it ?

CHRISTINE. No.

ORIN. Someone lent me the book. I read it and re-read it until finally those Islands came to mean everything that wasn't war, everything that was peace and warmth and security. I used to dream I was there. And later on all the time I was out of my mind I seemed really to be there. There was no one there but you and me. And yet I never saw you, that's the funny part. I only felt you all around me. The breaking of the waves was your voice. The sky was the same colour as your eyes. The warm sand was like your skin. The whole island was you. *(He smiles with a dreamy tenderness.)* A strange notion, wasn't it ? But you needn't be provoked at being an island because this was the most beautiful island in the world—as beautiful as you, Mother !

CHRISTINE *(has been staring over his head, listening fascinatedly, more and more deeply moved. As he stops, an agonizing tenderness for him wells up in her —with tortured longing).* Oh, if only you had never gone away ! If you only hadn't let them take you from me !

ORIN *(uneasily).* But I've come back. Everything is all right now, isn't it ?

CHRISTINE *(hastily).* Yes ! I didn't mean that. It had to be.

ORIN. And I'll never leave you again now. I don't want Hazel or anyone. *(With a tender grin.)* You're my only girl !

CHRISTINE *(again with tenderness, stroking his hair —smiling).* You're a big man now, aren't you ? I can't believe it. It seems only yesterday when I used to find you in your nightshirt hiding in the hall upstairs on the chance that I'd come up and you'd get one more good-night kiss ! Do you remember ?

ORIN *(with a boyish grin).* You bet I remember ! And what a row there was when Father caught me ! And do you remember how you used to let me brush your hair and how I loved to ? He hated me doing that, too. You've still got the same beautiful hair, Mother. That hasn't changed. *(He reaches up and touches her hair caressingly. She gives a little shudder of repulsion and draws away from him but he is too happy to notice.)* Oh, Mother, it's going to be wonderful from now on ! We'll get Vinnie to marry Peter and there will be just you and I ! *(The sliding doors in rear are opened a little and Lavinia slips silently in and stands looking at them.)*

CHRISTINE *(immediately senses her presence—controlling a start, harshly).* What do you want ? *(Orin turns to look at his sister resentfully.)*

LAVINIA *(in a flat, emotionless voice).* Aren't you coming in to see Father, Orin ?

ORIN *(scrambling to his feet—irritably).* Oh, all right, I'll come now.

(He hurries out past Lavinia with the air of one with a disagreeable duty he wants to get over quickly, and closes the door with a bang behind him. Lavinia stares at her mother a moment—then about-faces stiffly to follow him.)

CHRISTINE *(springs to her feet).* Vinnie ! *(As Lavinia turns to face her—sharply.)* Come here—please. I don't want to shout across the room. *(Lavinia comes slowly forward until she is at arm's length. Her eyes grow bleak and her mouth tightens to a thin line. The resemblance between mother and daughter as they stand confronting each other is strikingly brought out. Christine begins to speak in a low voice, coolly defiant, almost triumphant.)* Well, you can go ahead now and tell Orin anything you wish ! I've already told him—so you might as well save yourself the trouble. He said you must be insane ! I told him how you lied about my trips to New York—for revenge !—because you loved Adam yourself ! *(Lavinia makes a movement like a faint shudder but is immediately stiff and frozen again. Christine smiles tauntingly.)* So hadn't you better leave Orin out of it ? You can't get him to go to the police for you. Even if you convinced him I poisoned your father, you couldn't ! He doesn't want—any more than you do, or your father, or any of the Mannon dead—such a public disgrace as a murder trial would be ! For it would all come out ! Everything ! Who Adam is and my adultery and your knowledge of it—and your love for Adam ! Oh, believe me, I'll see to it that comes out if anything ever gets to a trial ! I'll show you to the world as a daughter who desired her mother's lover and then tried to get her mother hanged out of hatred and jealousy ! *(She laughs tauntingly. Lavinia is trembling but her face remains hard and emotionless. Her lips open as if to speak but she closes them again. Christine seems drunk with her own defiant recklessness.*) Go on! Try and convince Orin of my wickedness! He loves me! He hated his father! He's glad he's dead! Even if he knew I had killed him, he'd protect me! (*Then all her defiant attitude collapses and she pleads, seized by an hysterical terror, by some fear she has kept hidden.*) For God's sake, keep Orin out of this! He's still ill! He's changed! He's grown hard and cruel! All he thinks of is death! Don't tell him about Adam! He would kill him! I couldn't live then! I would kill myself! (*Lavinia starts and her eyes light up with a cruel hatred. Again her pale lips part as if she were about to say something, but she controls the impulse and turns away abruptly and walks with jerky steps from the room like some tragic mechanical doll. Christine stares after her—then as she disappears, collapses, catching at the table for support—in terror.*) I've got to see Adam! I've got to warn him! (*She sinks in the chair at right of table.*)

Curtain

ACT THREE

SCENE. *The same as Act Two of "Homecoming"—Ezra Mannon's study. His body, dressed in full uniform, is laid out on a bier draped in black which is placed lengthwise directly below the portrait of him over the fireplace. His head is to right. His mask-like face is a startling reproduction of the face in the portrait above him, but grimly remote and austere in death, like the carven face of a statue.*

The table and chairs which had been at centre have been moved to the left. There is a lamp on this table. Two stands of three lighted candles are at each end of the black marble chimneypiece, throwing their light above on the portrait and below on the dead man. There is a chair by the dead man's head, at front of bier.

Orin is standing by the head of the bier, at the rear of it, stiffly erect like a sentinel at attention. He is not looking down at his father but is staring straight before him, deep in suspicious brooding. His face in the candlelight bears a striking resemblance to that of the portrait above him and the dead man's.

The time of the opening of this act precedes by a few moments that of the end of the previous act.

ORIN (*ashamed and guilty—bursts out angrily at himself*). Christ, I won't have such thoughts! I am a rotten swine to—— Damn Vinnie! She must be crazy! (*Then, as if to distract his mind from these reflections, he turns to gaze down at his father. At the same moment Lavinia appears silently in the doorway from the hall and stands looking at him. He does not notice her entrance. He stares at his father's mask-like face and addresses it with a strange friendly mockery.*) Who are you? Another corpse! You and I have seen fields and hillsides sown with them—and they meant nothing!—nothing but a dirty joke life plays on life! (*Then with a dry smile.*) Death sits so naturally on you! Death becomes the Mannons! You were always like the statue of an eminent dead man—sitting on a chair in a park or straddling a horse in a town square—looking over the head of life without a sign of recognition—cutting it dead for the impropriety of living! (*He chuckles to himself with a queer affectionate amusement.*) You never cared to know me in life—but I really think we might be friends now you are dead!

LAVINIA (*sternly*). Orin!

ORIN (*turns to her startledly*). Damn it, don't sneak around like that! What are you trying to do, anyway? I'm jumpy enough without—— (*Then as she turns and locks the door behind her—suspiciously.*) What are you locking the door for?

LAVINIA. I've got to talk to you—and I don't want to be interrupted. (*Then sternly.*) What made you say such things just then? I wouldn't believe you could have grown so callous to all feeling of respect——

ORIN (*guilty and resentful*). You folks at home take death so solemnly! You would have soon learned at the front that it's only a joke! You don't understand, Vinnie. You have to learn to mock or go crazy, can't you see? I didn't mean it in an unkind way. It simply struck me he looks so strangely familiar—the same familiar stranger I've never known. (*Then glancing at the dead man with a kindly amused smile.*) Do you know his nickname in the army? Old Stick—short for Stick-in-the-Mud. Grant himself started it—said Father was no good on an offensive but he'd trust him to stick in the mud and hold a position until hell froze over!

LAVINIA. Orin! Don't you realize he was your father and he is dead?

ORIN (*irritably*). What Grant said was a big compliment in a way.

LAVINIA. When I think of how proud of you he was when he came home! He boasted that you had done one of the bravest things he'd seen in the war!

ORIN (*astonished—then grins with bitter mockery*). One of the bravest things he'd seen! Oh, that's too rich! I'll tell you the joke about that heroic deed. It really began the night before when I sneaked through their lines. I was always volunteering for extra danger. I was so scared anyone would guess I was afraid! There was a thick mist and it was so still you could hear the fog seeping into the ground. I met a Reb crawling towards our lines. His face drifted out of the mist towards mine. I shortened my sword and let him have the point under the ear. He stared at me with an idiotic look as if he'd sat on a tack—and his eyes dimmed and went out—— (*His voice has sunk lower and lower, as if he were talking to himself. He pauses and stares over his father's body fascinatedly at nothing.*)

LAVINIA (*with a shudder*). Don't think of that now!

ORIN (*goes on with the same air*). Before I'd got back I had to kill another in the same way. It was like murdering the same man twice. I had a queer feeling that war meant murdering the same man over and over, and that in the end I would discover the man was myself! Their faces keep coming back in dreams—and they change to Father's face—or to mine—— What does that mean, Vinnie?

LAVINIA. I don't know! I've got to talk to you! For heaven's sake forget the war! It's over now!

ORIN. Not inside us who killed! (*Then quickly—with a bitter, joking tone.*) The rest is all a joke! The next morning I was in the trenches. This was at Petersburg. I hadn't slept. My head was queer. I thought what a joke it would be on the stupid Generals like Father if everyone on both sides suddenly saw the joke war was on them and laughed and shook hands! So I began to laugh and walked towards their lines with my hand out. Of course, the joke was on me and I got this wound in the head for my pains. I went mad, wanted to kill, and ran on, yelling. Then a lot of our fools went crazy too, and followed me, and we captured a part of their line we hadn't dared tackle before. I had acted without orders, of course—but Father decided it was better policy to overlook that and let me be a hero! So do you wonder I laugh?

LAVINIA (*soothingly, coming to him and taking his arm*). You were brave and you know it. I'm proud of you, too.

ORIN (*helplessly*). Oh, all right! Be proud, then! (*He leaves her and sprawls in the chair at left of table. She stands by the head of the bier and faces him. He says resentfully:*) Well? Fire away and let's get this over! But you're wasting your breath. I know what you're going to say. Mother warned me. (*The whole memory of what his mother had said rushes over him.*) My God, how can you think such things of Mother? What the hell's got into you? (*Then humouringly.*) But I realize you're not yourself. I know how hard his death has hit you. Don't you think it would be better to postpone our talk until——

LAVINIA. No! (*Bitterly*). Has she succeeded in convincing you I'm out of my mind? Oh, Orin, how can you be so stupid? (*She goes to him and, grasping him by his shoulders, brings her face close to him—compellingly.*) Look at me! You know in your heart I'm the same as I always was—your sister—who loves you, Orin!

ORIN (*moved*). I didn't mean—I only think the shock of his death——

LAVINIA. I've never lied to you, have I? Even when we were little you always knew I told you the truth, didn't you?

ORIN. Yes—but——

LAVINIA. Then you must believe I wouldn't lie to you now!

ORIN. No one is saying you'd deliberately lie. It's a question of——

LAVINIA. And even if she's got you so under her thumb again that you doubt my word, you can't doubt the absolute proof!

ORIN (*roughly*). Never mind what you call proofs! I know all about them already! (*Then excitedly.*) Now, listen here, if you think you're going to tell me a lot of crazy stuff about Mother,

I warn you I won't listen! So shut up before you start!

LAVINIA (*threateningly now*). If you don't, I'll go to the police!

ORIN. Don't be a damn fool!

LAVINIA. As a last resort I will—if you force me to!

ORIN. By God, you must be crazy even to talk of—— !

LAVINIA. They won't think so!

ORIN. Vinnie! Do you realize what it would mean—— ?

LAVINIA. I realize only too well! You and I, who are innocent, would suffer a worse punishment than the guilty—for we'd have to live on! It would mean that Father's memory and that of all the honourable Mannon dead would be dragged through the horror of a murder trial! But I'd rather suffer that than let the murder of our father go unpunished!

ORIN. Good God, do you actually believe—— ?

LAVINIA. Yes! I accuse her of murder! (*She takes the little box she has found in Christine's room soon after the murder* [*Act Four "Homecoming"*] *from the bosom of her dress and holds it out to him.*) You see this? I found it just after Father died!

ORIN. Don't be a damned lunatic! She told me all about that! It's only some stuff she takes to make her sleep!

LAVINIA (*goes on implacably, ignoring his interruptions*). And Father knew she'd poisoned him! He said to me, "She's guilty!"

ORIN. That's all your crazy imagination! God, how can you think—— ? Do you realize you're deliberately accusing your own mother—— It's too horrible and mad! I'll have you declared insane by Doctor Blake and put away in an asylum!

LAVINIA. I swear by our dead father I am telling you the truth! (*She puts her hand on the dead man and addresses him.*) Make Orin believe me, Father!

ORIN (*harshly*). Don't drag him in! He always sided with you against Mother and me! (*He grabs her arm and forces the box from her hand.*) Here! Give me that! (*He slips it into his coat pocket.*)

LAVINIA. Ah! So you are afraid it's true!

ORIN. No! But I'm going to stop your damned—— But I'm a fool to pay any attention to you! The whole thing is too insane! I won't talk to a crazy woman! But, by God, you look out, Vinnie! You leave Mother alone or—— !

LAVINIA (*regarding him bitterly*). Poor Father! He thought the war had made a man of you! But you're not! You're still the spoiled cry-baby that she can make a fool of whenever she pleases!

ORIN (*stung*). That's enough from you!

LAVINIA. Oh, she warned me just now what to expect! She boasted that you wouldn't believe me, and that even if you knew she'd murdered Father you would be glad because you hated him! (*Then a note of entreaty in her voice.*) Orin! For God's sake—here, before him!—tell me that isn't true, at least!

ORIN (*overcome by a sense of guilt—violently defensive*). Of course, I never said that—and I don't believe she did. But Mother means a thousand times more to me than he ever did! I say that before him now as I would if he could hear me!

LAVINIA (*with a calculated scornful contempt now*). Then if I can't make you see your duty one way, I will another! If you won't help me punish her, I hope you're not such a coward that you're willing to let her lover escape!

ORIN (*in a tone of awakening suspicion*). Lover? Who do you mean?

LAVINIA. I mean the man who plotted Father's murder with her, who must have got the poison for her! I mean the Captain Brant I wrote you about!

ORIN (*thickly, trying to fight back his jealous suspicion*). You lie! She told me your rotten lies—about him—about following her to New York. That was Mr. Lamar she met.

LAVINIA. So that's what she told you! As if I could mistake Lamar for Adam Brant! What a fool you are, Orin! She kisses you and pretends she loves you—when she'd forgotten you were ever alive, when all she's thought of is this low lover of hers—— !

ORIN (*wildly*). Stop! I won't stand—— !

LAVINIA. When all she is thinking of even now is how she can use you to keep me from doing anything, so she'll get a chance to run off and marry him!

ORIN. You lie!

LAVINIA. She pets you and plays the loving mother and you're so blind you can't see through her! I tell you she went to his room! I followed them upstairs. I heard her telling him, "I love you, Adam." She was kissing him!

ORIN (*takes her by the shoulder and shakes her, forcing her to her knees—frenziedly*). Damn you! Tell me you're lying or——!

LAVINIA (*unafraid—looking up into his eyes—coldly*). You know I'm not lying! She's been going to New York on the excuse of visiting Grandfather Hamel, but really to give herself to——!

ORIN (*in anguish*). You lie, damn you! (*Threateningly.*) You dare say that about Mother! Now you've got to prove it or else——! You're not insane! You know what you're saying! So you prove it—or by God, I'll——!

LAVINIA (*taking his hands off her shoulders and rising*). All I ask is a chance to prove it! (*Then intensely.*) But when I do, will you help me punish Father's murderers?

ORIN (*in a burst of murderous rage*). I'll kill that bastard! (*In anguished uncertainty again.*) But you haven't proved anything yet! It's only your word against hers! I don't believe you! You say Brant is her lover! If that's true, I'll hate her! I'll know she murdered Father then! I'll help you punish her! But you've got to prove it!

LAVINIA (*coldly*). I can do that very soon. She's frightened out of her wits! She'll go to see Brant the first chance she gets. We must give her that chance. Will you believe me when you find them together?

ORIN (*tortured*). Yes. (*Then in a burst of rage.*) God damn him, I'll——!

LAVINIA (*sharply*). Ssshh! Be quiet. There's someone in the hall! (*They wait, staring at the door. Then someone knocks loudly.*)

CHRISTINE (*her voice comes through the door, frightened and strained*). Orin!

ORIN (*stammers*). God! I can't face her now!

LAVINIA (*in a quick whisper*). Don't let her know you suspect her. Pretend you think I'm out of my mind, as she wanted you to.

CHRISTINE. Orin! Why don't you answer me? (*She tries the doorknob, and finding the door locked, her voice becomes terrified.*) Why have you locked me out? Let me in! (*She pounds on the door violently.*)

LAVINIA (*in a whisper*). Answer her. Let her in.

ORIN (*obeying mechanically—calls in a choked voice*). All right. I'm coming. (*He moves reluctantly towards the door.*)

LAVINIA (*struck by a sudden idea—grasps his arm*). Wait! (*Before he can prevent it, she reaches in his pocket and gets possession of the box and puts it conspicuously on the body over the dead man's heart.*) Watch her when she sees that—if you want proof!

CHRISTINE. Open the door! (*He forces himself to open the door and steps aside. Christine almost falls in. She is in a state bordering on collapse. She throws her arms around Orin as if seeking protection from him.*) Orin! I got so afraid—when I found the door locked!

ORIN (*controls a furious jealous impulse to push her violently away from him—harshly*). What made you afraid, Mother?

CHRISTINE (*stammers*). Why do you look at me—like that? You look—so like—your father!

ORIN. I am his son, too, remember that!

LAVINIA (*warningly*). Orin!

CHRISTINE (*turning on Lavinia who stands by the head of the bier*). I suppose you've been telling him your vile lies, you——

ORIN (*remembering his instructions, forces himself to blurt out*). She—she's out of her head, Mother.

CHRISTINE. Didn't I tell you! I knew you'd see that! (*Then anxiously, keeping her eyes on Lavinia.*) Did she tell you what she's going to do, Orin? I know she's plotting something—crazy! Did she threaten to go to the police? They might not believe she's crazy—— (*Pleading desperately, her eyes still on Lavinia.*) You won't let her do anything dreadful like that, will you?

ORIN (*feeling her guilt, stammers*). No, Mother.

CHRISTINE (*her eyes, which have been avoiding the corpse, now fasten on the dead man's face with fascinated horror*). No—remember your father wouldn't want—any scandal—he mustn't be worried, he said—he needs rest and peace—— (*She addresses the dead man directly in a strange tone of defiant scorn.*) You seem the same to me in death, Ezra! You were always dead to me! I hate the sight of death!

I hate the thought of it! (*Her eyes shift from his face and she sees the box of poison. She starts back with a stifled scream and stares at it with guilty fear.*)

ORIN. Mother! For God's sake, be quiet! (*The strain snaps for him and he laughs with savage irony.*) God! To think I hoped home would be an escape from death! I should never have come back to life—from my island of peace! (*Then staring at his mother strangely.*) But that's lost now! You're my lost island, aren't you, Mother?

(*He turns and stumbles blindly from the room. Lavinia reaches out stealthily and snatches up the box. This breaks the spell for Christine whose eyes have been fixed on it hypnotically. She looks wildly at Lavinia's frozen, accusing face.*)

LAVINIA (*in a cold, grim voice*). It was Brant who got you this—medicine to make you sleep—wasn't it?

CHRISTINE (*distractedly*). No! No! No!

LAVINIA. You're telling me it was. I knew it—but I wanted to make sure.

(*She puts the box back in the bosom of her dress—turns, rigid and square-shouldered, and walks woodenly from the room.*)

CHRISTINE (*stares after her wildly, then her eyes fasten again on the dead man's face. Suddenly she appeals to him distractedly*). Ezra! Don't let her harm Adam! I am the only guilty one! Don't let Orin——!

(*Then, as if she read some answer in the dead man's face, she stops in terror and, her eyes still fixed on his face, backs to the door and rushes out.*)

Curtain

ACT FOUR

SCENE. *The stern section of a clipper ship moored alongside a wharf in East Boston, with the floor of the wharf in the foreground. The vessel lies with her bow and amidships off left and only the part aft of the mizzenmast is visible with the curve of the stern at right. The ship is unloaded and her black side rises nine or ten feet above the level of the wharf. On the poop deck above, at right, is the wheel. At left is the chart-room and the entrance to the companionway stairs leading below to the cabin. At extreme left is the mizzenmast, the lowest yard just visible above, the boom of the spanker extending out above the deck to the right. Below the deck the portholes show a faint light from the interior of the cabin. On the wharf the end of a warehouse is at left front.*

It is a night two days after Act Two—the day following Ezra Mannon's funeral. The moon is rising above the horizon off left rear, its light accentuating the black outlines of the ship.

Borne on the wind the melancholy refrain of the capstan chanty "Shenandoah," sung by a chantyman with the crew coming in on the chorus, drifts over the water from a ship that is weighing anchor in the harbour. Half in and half out of the shadow of the warehouse, the Chantyman lies sprawled on his back, snoring in a drunken slumber. The sound of the singing seems to strike a responsive chord in his brain, for he stirs, grunts, and with difficulty raises himself to a sitting position in the moonlight beyond the shadow.

He is a thin, wiry man of sixty-five or so, with a tousled mop of black hair, unkempt black beard and moustache. His weatherbeaten face is dissipated, he has a weak mouth, his big round blue eyes are bloodshot, dreamy and drunken. But there is something romantic, a queer troubadour-of-the-sea quality about him.

CHANTYMAN (*listens to the singing with critical disapproval*). A hell of a chantyman that feller be! Screech owls is op'ry singers compared to him! I'll give him a taste of how "Shenandoah" ought t' be sung! (*He begins to sing in a surprisingly good tenor voice, a bit blurry with booze now and sentimentally mournful to a degree, but still managing to get full value out of the chanty.*)

"*Oh, Shenandoah, I long to hear you—*
A-way, my rolling river!
Oh, Shenandoah, I can't get near you—
Way—ay, I'm bound away
Across the wide Missouri!

"*Oh, Shenandoah, I love your daughter*
A-way, my rolling river!"

(*He stops abruptly, shaking his head—mournfully.*) No good! Too drunk to do myself jestice! Pipe down, my John! Sleep it off! (*He sprawls back on his elbows—confusedly.)* Where am I? What the hell difference is it? There's plenty o' fresh air and the moon fur a glim. Don't be so damn pertic'lar! What ye want anyways? Featherbed an' a grand piany? *(He sings with a maudlin zest.)*

> "*A bottle o' wine and a bottle o' beer*
> *And a bottle of Irish whisky oh!*
> *So early in the morning*
> *The sailor likes his bottle oh!*"

(He stops and mutters.) Who'll buy a drink fur the slickest chantyman on the Western or any other damn ocean? Go to hell, then! I kin buy it myself! *(He fumbles in his pants pocket.)* I had it in this pocket—I remember I put it there pertic'lar—ten dollars in this pocket—— *(He pulls the pocket inside out—with bewildered drunken anger.)* By Christ, it's gone! I'm plucked clean! *(He struggles to a sitting position.)* Where was I last? Aye, I remember! That yaller-haired pig with the pink dress on! Put her arm around me so lovin'! Told me how fine I could sing! *(He scrambles unsteadily to his feet.)* By Christ, I'll go back an' give her a seaboot in her fat tail that'll learn her——! *(He takes a step but lurches into the shadow and leans against the warehouse.)* Hard down! Heavy gales around Cape Stiff! All is sunk but honour, as the feller says, an' there's damn little o' that afloat!

(He stands against the warehouse, waiting for the swaying world to subside. The companionway door on the poop deck of the vessel is opened and Adam Brant comes cautiously out. He looks around him quickly with an uneasy suspicious air. He is dressed in a merchant captain's blue uniform. Satisfied that there is no one on the deck, he comes to the rail and stares expectantly up the wharf, off left. His attitude is tense and nervous and he keeps one hand in his coat pocket. The Chantyman loses his balance, lurches forward, then back against the warehouse with a thump. Brant leaps back from the rail, startled, jerking a revolver from his coat pocket—then leans over the rail again and calls threateningly.)

BRANT. Who's there? Come out and let me have a look at you or by God I'll shoot!

CHANTYMAN *(stares up, startled in his turn and momentarily sobered—hastily)*. Easy goes, shipmate. Stow that pistol! I'm doin' you no harm. *(He lurches out into the moonlight—suddenly pugnacious.)* Not that I'm skeered o' you or your shooter! Who the hell are you to be threatenin' the life of an honest chantyman? Tryin' to hold me up, air ye? I been robbed once to-night! I'll go to the police station and tell 'em there's a robber here——

BRANT *(hastily, with a placating air)*. No harm meant. I'm skipper of this vessel and there have been a lot of waterfront thieves around here lately. I'm lacking a watchman and I've got to keep my weather eye open.

CHANTYMAN *(again momentarily sobered—touching his forehead)*. Aye—aye, sir. Mind your eye. I heer'd tell robbers broke in the "Annie Lodge's" cabin two nights back. Smashed everything and stole two hundred dollars off her skipper. Murderous, too, they be! Near beat the watchman's brains out! *(Then drunken pugnaciousness comes over him again.)* Think I'm one o' that gang, do ye? Come down out o' that and I'll show ye who's a thief! I don't give a damn if ye air a skipper! Ye could be Bully Watermann himself an' I'd not let you insult me! I ain't signed on your old hooker! You've got no rights over me! I'm on dry land, by Christ, and this is a free country and——

(His voice has risen to a shout. Brant is alarmed that this uproar will attract someone. He puts the pistol back in his pocket hastily and peers anxiously down the wharf. Then he interrupts the Chantyman's tirade by a sharp command.)

BRANT. Stow your damned jaw! Or, by the Eternal, I'll come down and pound some sense in your head!

CHANTYMAN *(automatically reacts to the voice of authority—quietly)*. Aye—aye, sir. *(Then inconsequently.)* You ain't needin' a chantyman fur your next vi'ge, are ye, sir?

BRANT. I'm not sailing for a month yet. If you're still out of a job then——

CHANTYMAN *(proudly)*. You don't know me, that's plain! I'm the finest damn chantyman that ever put a tune to his lip! I ain't lookin' fur berths—they're lookin' fur me! Aye! Skippers are on'y too glad to git me! Many's a time I've seed a skipper an' mates sweatin' blood to beat work out of a crew but nary a lick could they git into 'em till I raised a tune—and then there'd be full sail on her afore ye knowed it!

BRANT (*impatiently*). I'm not doubting your ability. But I'd advise you to turn in and sleep it off.

CHANTYMAN (*not heeding this—sadly*). Aye, but it ain't fur long, steam is comin' in, the sea is full o' smoky tea-kettles, the old days is dyin', an' where'll you an' me be then? (*Lugubriously drunken again.*) Everything is dyin'! Abe Lincoln is dead. I used to ship on the Mannon packets an' I seed in the paper where Ezra Mannon was dead! (*Brant starts guiltily. The Chantyman goes on maudlinly.*) Heart failure killed him, it said, but I know better! I've sailed on Mannon hookers an' been worked t' death and gotten swill fur grub, an' I know he didn't have no heart in him! Open him up an' you'd find a dried turnip! The old skinflint must have left a pile o' money. Who gits it, I wonder? Leave a widder, did he?

BRANT (*harshly*). How would I know? (*Changing the subject calculatingly.*) What are you doing here, Chantyman? I'd expect a man with your voice would be in a saloon, singing and making merry!

CHANTYMAN. So I would! So I would! But I was robbed, sir—aye—an' I know who done it—a yaller-haired wench had her arm around me. Steer clear o' gals or they'll skin your hide off an' use it fur a carpet! I warn ye, skipper! They're not fur sailormen like you an' me, 'less we're lookin' fur sorrow! (*Then insinuatingly.*) I ain't got the price of a drink, that's why I'm here, sir.

BRANT (*reaches in his pocket and tosses him down a silver coin*). Here!

CHANTYMAN (*fumbles around and finds the dollar*). Thank ye, sir. (*Then flatteringly.*) It's a fine ship you've got there, sir. Crack sail on her and she'll beat most of 'em—an' you're the kind to crack sail on, I kin tell by your cut.

BRANT (*pleased, glancing up at his ship's lofty rig*). Aye! I'll make her go right enough!

CHANTYMAN. All you need is a good chantyman to help ye. Here's "Hanging Johnny" fur ye! (*Brant starts at this. The Chantyman suddenly begins to sing the chanty "Hanging Johnny" with sentimental mournfulness.*)

"*Oh, they call me Hanging Johnny*
Away—ay—i—oh!
They says I hangs for money
Oh, hang, boys, hang!"

BRANT (*harshly*). Stop that damned dirge! And get out of here! Look lively now!

CHANTYMAN (*starting to go*). Aye—aye, sir. (*Then resentfully.*) I see ye ain't got much ear fur music. Good night.

BRANT (*with exasperated relief*). Good night. (*The Chantyman goes unsteadily off left, between the warehouse and the ship. He bursts again into his mournful dirge, his voice receding.*)

"*They say I hanged my mother*
Away—ay—i—oh!
They say I hanged my mother
Oh, hang, boys, hang!"

(*Brant, standing by the rail looking after him, mutters a curse and starts pacing up and down the deck*). Damn that chanty! It's sad as death! I've a foreboding I'll never take this ship to sea. She doesn't want me now—a coward hiding behind a woman's skirts! The sea hates a coward! (*A woman's figure dressed in black, heavily veiled, moves stealthily out from the darkness between the ship and the warehouse, left. She sees the figure on the deck above her and shrinks back with a stifled gasp of fear. Brant hears the noise. Immediately his revolver is in his hand and he peers down into the shadows of the warehouse.*) Who's there?

CHRISTINE (*with a cry of relief*). Adam!

BRANT. Christine! (*Then quickly.*) Go back to the gangway. I'll meet you there. (*She goes back. He hurries along the deck and disappears off left to meet her. Their voices are heard and a moment later they enter on the poop deck, from left. She leans against him weakly and he supports her with his arm around her.*) I have to bring you this way. I bolted the door to the main deck.

CHRISTINE. I was so frightened! I wasn't sure which ship! Some drunken man came along singing——

BRANT. Aye. I just got rid of him. I fired the watchman this morning so I'd be alone at night. I was hoping you'd come soon. Did that drunk see you?

CHRISTINE. No. I hid behind some boxes. (*Then, frightened.*) Why have you got that pistol?

BRANT (*grimly*). I was going to give them a fight for it—if things went wrong.

CHRISTINE. Adam!

BRANT. By God, you don't think I'll ever let

them take me alive, do you?

CHRISTINE. Please, please! Don't talk of that for a moment! Only hold me close to you! Tell me you love me!

BRANT (*harshly*). It's no time! I want to know what's happened! (*Then immediately repentant he kisses her—with rough tenderness.*) Don't mind me! My nerves are gone from waiting alone here not knowing anything but what I read in the papers —that he was dead. These last days have been hell!

CHRISTINE. If you knew what they have been for me!

BRANT. There's something gone wrong! I can read that in your face! What is it, Christine?

CHRISTINE (*falteringly*). Vinnie knows——! She came into the room when he was dying! He told her——

BRANT (*harshly*). God! What is she going to do? (*Then, without giving her time to answer his question, he suddenly looks around uneasily.*) Christine! How did you get away? She'd suspect you weren't going to your father's now. She followed you once before——

CHRISTINE. No. It's all right. This morning Orin said his cousins, the Bradfords, had invited him and Vinnie to visit them overnight at Blackridge and he was taking Vinnie with him because he thought a change would bring her back to her senses. I've made him think she's out of her head with grief—so he wouldn't listen to her——

BRANT (*eagerly*). And he believes that?

CHRISTINE (*weakly*). Yes—he does—now—but I don't know how long——

BRANT. Ah!

CHRISTINE. So I told him by all means to go. It gave me the chance I wanted to come to you. They went this morning. They don't know I've gone and even after they've found out they can't prove where I went. I can only stay a little while, Adam—we've got to plan—so many things have happened I couldn't foresee—I came to warn you——

BRANT. Ssshh! Come below in the cabin! We're fools to be talking out here.

(*He guides her with his arm around her through the door to the companionway stairs and closes it quietly behind them. A pause in which the singing of the crew on the ship in the harbour comes mournfully over the water. Then Orin and Lavinia come in stealthily along the deck from the left. She is dressed in black as before. He wears a long cloak over his uniform and has a slouch hat pulled down over his eyes. Her manner is cold and grim. Orin is holding in a savage, revengeful rage. They approach the cabin skylight silently. Orin bends down by it to listen. His face, in the light from the skylight, becomes distorted with jealous fury. Lavinia puts a restraining hand on his arm.*

The scene fades out into darkness. Several minutes are supposed to elapse. When the light comes on again, a section of the ship has been removed to reveal the interior of the cabin, a small compartment, the walls newly painted a light brown. The skylight giving on the deck above is in the middle of the ceiling. Suspended in the skylight is a ship's compass. Beneath it is a pine table with three chairs, one at rear, the other two at the table ends, left and right. On the table is a bottle of whisky, half full, with a glass and a pitcher of water.

Built against the right wall of the cabin is a long narrow couch, like a bunk, with leather cushions. In the rear wall, at right, is a door leading into the captain's stateroom. A big sideboard stands against the left wall, centre. Above it, a ship's clock. Farther back is a door opening on the alleyway leading to the main deck. The companionway stairs lead down to this alleyway.

There is a lighted lamp on the sideboard and a ship's lantern, also lighted, at the right end of the table.

In the cabin, Brant is seated at the right of table, Christine to the rear of it. Her face looks haggard and ageing, the mouth pinched and drawn down at the corners, and her general appearance, the arrangement of her hair and clothes, has the dishevelled touch of the fugitive. She is just finishing her story of the murder and the events following it. He is listening tensely.

On the deck above, Orin and Lavinia are

discovered as before, with Orin bending down by the transom, listening.)

CHRISTINE. When he was dying he pointed at me and told her I was guilty! And afterwards she found the poison——

BRANT (*springing to his feet*). For God's sake, why didn't you——

CHRISTINE (*piteously*). I fainted before I could hide it! And I had planned it all so carefully. But how could I foresee that she would come in just at that moment? And how could I know he would talk to me the way he did? He drove me crazy! He kept talking of death! He was torturing me! I only wanted him to die and leave me alone!

BRANT (*his eyes lighting up with savage satisfaction*). He knew before he died whose son I was, you said? By God, I'll bet that maddened him!

CHRISTINE (*repeats piteously*). I'd planned it so carefully—but something made things happen!

BRANT (*overcome by gloomy dejection, sinks down on his chair again*). I knew it! I've had a feeling in my bones! It serves me right, what has happened and is to happen! It wasn't that kind of revenge I had sworn on my mother's body! I should have done as I wanted—fought with Ezra Mannon as two men fight for love of a woman! (*With bitter self-contempt.*) I have my father's rotten coward blood in me, I think! Aye!

CHRISTINE. Adam! You make me feel so guilty!

BRANT (*rousing himself—shamefacedly*). I didn't mean to blame you, Christine. (*Then harshly.*) It's too late for regrets now, anyway. We've got to think what to do.

CHRISTINE. Yes! I'm so terrified of Vinnie! Oh, Adam, you must promise me to be on your guard every minute! If she convinces Orin you are my lover—— Oh, why can't we go away, Adam? Once we're out of her reach, she can't do anything.

BRANT. The "Flying Trades" won't be sailing for a month or more. We can't get cargo as soon as the owners thought.

CHRISTINE. Can't we go on another ship—as passengers—to the East—we could be married out there——

BRANT (*gloomily*). But everyone in the town would know you were gone. It would start suspicion——

CHRISTINE. No. Orin and Vinnie would lie to people. They'd have to for their own sakes. They'd say I was in New York with my father. Oh, Adam, it's the only thing we can do! If we don't get out of Vinnie's reach right away I know something horrible will happen!

BRANT (*dejectedly*). Aye. I suppose it's the only way out for us now. The "Atlantis" is sailing on Friday for China. I'll arrange with her skipper to give us passage—and keep his mouth shut. She sails at daybreak Friday. You'd better meet me here Thursday night. (*Then with an effort.*) I'll write Clark and Dawson to-night they'll have to find another skipper for the "Flying Trades."

CHRISTINE (*noticing the hurt in his tone—miserably*). Poor Adam! I know how it hurts you to give up your ship.

BRANT (*rousing himself guiltily—pats her hand—with gruff tenderness*). There are plenty of ships—but there is only one you, Christine!

CHRISTINE. I feel so guilty! I've brought you nothing but misfortune!

BRANT. You've brought love—and the rest is only the price. It's worth it a million times! You're all mine now, anyway! (*He hugs her to him, staring over her head with sad blank eyes.*)

CHRISTINE (*her voice trembling*). But I'm afraid I'm not much to boast about having—now. I've grown old in the past few days. I'm ugly. But I'll make myself beautiful again—for you——! I'll make up to you for everything! Try not to regret your ship too much, Adam!

BRANT (*gruffly*). Let's not talk of her any more. (*Then forcing a wry smile.*) I'll give up the sea. I think it's done with me now, anyway! The sea hates a coward.

CHRISTINE (*trying hard to cheer him*). Don't talk like that! You have me, Adam! You have me! And we will be happy—once we're safe on your Blessed Islands! (*Then suddenly, with a little shudder.*) It's strange. Orin was telling me of an island——

(*On the deck above, Orin, who has bent closer to the transom, straightens up with a threatening movement. Lavinia grips his arm, restraining him.*)

BRANT (*with a bitter, hopeless yearning*). Aye—

the Blessed Isles—— Maybe we can still find happiness and forget! (*Then strangely, as if to himself.*) I can see them now—so close—and a million miles away! The warm earth in the moonlight, the trade winds rustling the coco-palms, the surf on the barrier reef singing a croon in your ears like a lullaby! Aye! There's peace and forgetfulness for us there—if we can ever find those islands now!

CHRISTINE (*desperately*). We will find them! We will! (*She kisses him. A pause. Suddenly she glances, in fear, at the clock.*) Look at the time! I've got to go, Adam!

BRANT. For the love of God, watch out for Vinnie. If anything happened to you now——!

CHRISTINE. Nothing will happen to me. But you must be on your guard in case Orin—— Good-bye, my lover! I must go! I must! (*She tears herself from his arms but immediately throws herself in them again—terrified.*) Oh! I feel so strange—so sad—as if I'd never see you again! (*She begins to sob hysterically.*) Oh, Adam, tell me you don't regret! Tell me we're going to be happy! I can't bear this horrible feeling of despair!

BRANT. Of course we'll be happy! Come now! It's only a couple of days. (*They start for the door.*) We'll go by the main deck. It's shorter. I'll walk to the end of the wharf with you. I won't go farther. We might be seen.

CHRISTINE. Then we don't have to say good-bye for a few minutes yet! Oh, thank God!

(*They go out to the alleyway, Brant closing the door behind him. A pause. On the deck above Orin pulls a revolver from under his cloak and makes a move, as if to rush off left down to the main deck after them. Lavinia has been dreading this and throws herself in his way, grasping his arm.*)

ORIN (*in a furious whisper*). Let me go!

LAVINIA (*struggling with him*). No! Be quiet! Ssshh! I hear them on the main deck! Quick! Come to his cabin!

(*She urges him to the companionway door, gets him inside and shuts the door behind them. A moment later the door on the left of the cabin below is opened and they enter.*)

LAVINIA. He's going to the end of the wharf. That gives us a few minutes. (*Grimly.*) You wanted proof! Well, are you satisfied now?

ORIN. Yes! God damn him! Death is too good for him! He ought to be——

LAVINIA (*sharply commanding*). Orin! Remember you promised not to lose your head. You've got to do everything exactly as we planned it, so there'll be no suspicion about us. There would be no justice if we let ourselves——

ORIN (*impatiently*). You've said all that before! Do you think I'm a fool? I'm not anxious to be hanged—for that skunk! (*Then with bitter anguish.*) I heard her asking him to kiss her! I heard her warn him against me! (*He gives a horrible chuckle.*) And my island I told her about—which was she and I—she wants to go there—with him! (*Then furiously.*) Damn you! Why did you stop me? I'd have shot his guts out in front of her!

LAVINIA (*scornfully*). Outside on deck where the shot would be sure to be heard? We'd have been arrested—and then I'd have to tell the truth to save us. She'd be hanged, and even if we managed to get off, our lives would be ruined! The only person to come off lucky would be Brant! He could die happy, knowing he'd revenged himself on us more than he ever dared hope! Is that what you want?

ORIN (*sullenly*). No.

LAVINIA. Then don't act like a fool again. (*Looks around the cabin calculatingly—then in a tone of command.*) Go and hide outside. He won't see you when he passes along the alleyway in the dark. He'll come straight in here. That's the time for you——

ORIN (*grimly*). You needn't tell me what to do. I've had a thorough training at this game—thanks to you and Father.

LAVINIA. Quick! Go out now! He won't be long!

ORIN (*goes to the door—then quickly*). I hear him coming.

(*He slips out silently. She hurriedly hides herself by the sideboard at left front. A moment later Brant appears in the doorway and stands just inside it blinking in the light. He looks around the cabin sadly.*)

BRANT (*huskily*). So it's good-bye to you, "Flying Trades"! And you're right! I wasn't man enough for you!

(*Orin steps through the door and with the pistol almost against Brant's body fires twice. Brant pitches forward to the floor by the table, rolls over, twitches a moment on his back and lies still. Orin springs forward and stands over the body, his pistol aimed down at it, ready to fire again.*)

LAVINIA (*stares, fascinated, at Brant's still face*). Is he—dead?

ORIN. Yes.

LAVINIA (*sharply*). Don't stand there! Where's the chisel you brought? Smash open everything in his stateroom. We must make it look as if thieves killed him, remember! Take anything valuable! We can sink it overboard afterwards! Hurry!

(*Orin puts his revolver on the table and takes a chisel that is stuck in his belt under his cloak and goes into the stateroom. A moment later there is the sound of splintering wood as he prizes open a drawer.*)

LAVINIA (*goes slowly to the body and stands looking down into Brant's face. Her own is frozen and expressionless. A pause. Orin can be heard in the stateroom prizing open Brant's desk and scattering the contents of drawers around. Finally Lavinia speaks to the corpse in a grim bitter tone*). How could you love that vile old woman so? (*She throws off this thought—harshly.*) But you're dead! It's ended! (*She turns away from him resolutely—then suddenly turns back and stands stiffly upright and grim beside the body and prays coldly, as if carrying out a duty.*) May God find forgiveness for your sins! May the soul of our cousin, Adam Mannon, rest in peace! (*Orin comes in from the stateroom and overhears the last of her prayer.*)

ORIN (*harshly*). Rest in hell, you mean! (*He comes to her.*) I've prized open everything I could find.

LAVINIA. Then come along. Quick. There's your pistol. Don't forget that. (*She goes to the door.*)

ORIN (*putting it in his pocket*). We've got to go through his pockets to make everything look like a burglary. (*He quickly turns Brant's pockets inside out and puts the revolver he finds, along with bills and coins, watch and chain, knife, etc., into his own.*) I'll drop these overboard from the deck, along with what was in his stateroom.

(*Having finished this, he still remains stooping over the body and stares into Brant's face, a queer fascinated expression in his own eyes.*)

LAVINIA (*uneasily*). Orin!

ORIN. By God, he does look like Father!

LAVINIA. No! Come along!

ORIN (*as if talking to himself*). This is like my dream. I've killed him before—over and over.

LAVINIA. Orin!

ORIN. Do you remember me telling you how the faces of the men I killed came back and changed to Father's face and finally became my own? (*He smiles grimly.*) He looks like me, too! Maybe I've committed suicide!

LAVINIA (*frightened—gripping his arm*). Hurry! Someone may come!

ORIN (*not heeding her, still staring at Brant—strangely*). If I had been he I would have done what he did! I would have loved her as he loved her—and killed Father, too—for her sake!

LAVINIA (*tensely—shaking him by the arm*). Orin, for God's sake, will you stop talking crazy and come along? Do you want us to be found here? (*She pulls him away forcibly.*)

ORIN (*with a last look at the dead man*). It's queer! It's a rotten dirty joke on someone! (*He lets her hurry him out to the alleyway.*)

Curtain

ACT FIVE

SCENE. *The same as Act Three of "Homecoming"—exterior of the Mannon house. It is the following night. The moon has just risen. The right half of the house is in the black shadow cast by the pine trees but the moonlight falls full on the part to the left of the doorway. The door at centre is open and there is a light in the hall behind. All the shutters of the windows are closed.*

Christine is discovered walking back and forth on the drive before the portico, passing from moonlight into the shadow of the pines and back again. She is in a frightful state of tension, unable to keep still.

She sees someone she is evidently expecting approaching the house from up the drive, off left, and she hurries down as far as the bench to meet her.

HAZEL (*enters from left—with a kindly smile*). Here I am! Seth brought your note and I hurried over at once.

CHRISTINE (*kissing her—with unnatural effusiveness*). I'm so glad you've come! I know I shouldn't have bothered you.

HAZEL. It's no bother at all, Mrs. Mannon. I'm only too happy to keep you company.

CHRISTINE. I was feeling so terribly sad—and nervous here. I had let Hannah and Annie have the night off. I'm all alone. (*She sits on the bench.*) Let's sit out here. I can't bear it in the house. (*Hazel sits beside her.*)

HAZEL (*pityingly*). I know. It must be terribly lonely for you. You must miss him so much.

CHRISTINE (*with a shudder*). Please don't talk about—— He is buried! He is gone!

HAZEL (*gently*). He is at peace, Mrs. Mannon.

CHRISTINE (*with bitter mockery*). I was like you once! I believed in heaven! Now I know there is only hell!

HAZEL. Ssshh! You mustn't say that.

CHRISTINE (*rousing herself—forcing a smile*). I'm not fit company for a young girl, I'm afraid. You should have youth and beauty and freedom around you. I'm old and ugly and haunted by death! (*Then, as if to herself—in a low desperate tone.*) I can't let myself get ugly! I can't!

HAZEL. You're only terribly worn out. You ought to try and sleep.

CHRISTINE. I don't believe there's such a thing on this earth as sleep! It's only in the earth one sleeps! One must feel so at peace—at last—with all one's fears ended! (*Then forcing a laugh.*) Good heavens, what a bore it must be for you, listening to my gloomy thoughts! I honestly didn't send for you to—— I wanted to ask if you or Peter had heard anything from Orin and Vinnie.

HAZEL (*surprised*). Why, no. We haven't seen them since the funeral.

CHRISTINE (*forcing a smile*). They seem to have deserted me. (*Then quickly.*) I mean they should have been home before this. I can't imagine what's keeping them. They went to Blackridge to stay overnight at the Bradfords'.

HAZEL. Then there's nothing to worry about. But I don't see how they could leave you alone—just now.

CHRISTINE. Oh, that part is all right. I urged them to go. They left soon after the funeral, and afterwards I thought it would be a good opportunity for me to go to New York and see my father. He's ill, you know, but I found him so much better I decided to come home again last night. I expected Vinnie and Orin back this noon, but here it's night and no sign of them. I—I must confess I'm worried—and frightened. You can't know the horror of being all night—alone in that house! (*She glances at the house behind her with a shudder.*)

HAZEL. Would it help you if I stayed with you to-night—I mean if they don't come?

CHRISTINE (*eagerly*). Oh, would you? (*Hysterical tears come to her eyes. She kisses Hazel with impulsive gratitude.*) I can't tell you how grateful I'd be! You're so good! (*Then forcing a laugh.*) But it's an imposition to ask you to face such an ordeal. I can't stay still. I'm terrified at every sound. You would have to sit up.

HAZEL. Losing a little sleep won't hurt me.

CHRISTINE. I mustn't sleep! If you see me falling asleep you must promise to wake me!

HAZEL. But it's just what you need.

CHRISTINE. Yes—afterwards—but not now. I must keep awake. (*In tense desperation.*) I wish Orin and Vinnie would come!

HAZEL (*worriedly*). Perhaps Orin got worse and he wasn't able to. Oh, I hope that isn't it! (*Then getting up.*) If I'm going to stay all night I'll have to run home and tell Mother, so she won't worry.

CHRISTINE. Yes—do. (*Then, frightened.*) You won't be long, will you? I'm afraid—to be alone.

HAZEL (*kisses her—pityingly*). I'll be as quick as I possibly can.

(*She walks down the drive, off left, waving her hand as she disappears. Christine stands by the bench—then begins to pace back and forth again.*)

CHRISTINE (*her eyes caught by something down the drive—in a tense whisper*). She's met someone by the gate! Oh, why am I so afraid! (*She turns, seized by panic, and runs to the house—then stops at the top of the steps and faces around, leaning against a column for support.*) Oh, God, I'm afraid to know!

(*A moment later Orin and Lavinia come up the drive from the left. Lavinia is stiffly square-shouldered, her eyes hard, her mouth grim and set. Orin is in a state of morbid excitement. He carries a newspaper in his hand.*)

ORIN (*speaking to Vinnie as they enter—harshly*). You let me do the talking! I want to be the one—— (*He sees his mother, and is startled.*) Mother! (*Then with vindictive mockery.*) Ah! So this time at least you are waiting to meet me when I come home!

CHRISTINE (*stammers*). Orin! What kept you——?

ORIN. We just met Hazel. She said you were terribly frightened at being alone here. That is strange—when you have the memory of Father for company!

CHRISTINE. You—you stayed all this time—at the Bradfords'?

ORIN. We didn't go to the Bradfords'!

CHRISTINE (*stupidly*). You didn't go—to Blackridge?

ORIN. We took the train there but we decided to stay right on and go to Boston instead.

CHRISTINE (*terrified*). To—Boston——?

ORIN. And in Boston we waited until the evening train got in. We met that train.

CHRISTINE. Ah!

ORIN. We had an idea you would take advantage of our being in Blackridge to be on it—and you were! And we followed you when you called on your lover in his cabin!

CHRISTINE (*with a piteous effort at indignation*). Orin! How dare you talk——! (*Then brokenly.*) Orin! Don't look at me like that! Tell me——

ORIN. Your lover! Don't lie! You've lied enough, Mother! I was on deck, listening! What would you have done if you had discovered me? Would you have got your lover to murder me, Mother? I heard you warning him against me! But your warning was no use!

CHRISTINE (*chokingly*). What——? Tell me——!

ORIN. I killed him!

CHRISTINE (*with a cry of terror*). Oh—oh! I knew! (*Then clutching at Orin.*) No—Orin! You—you're just telling me that—to punish me, aren't you? You said you loved me—you'd protect me—protect your mother—you couldn't murder——?

ORIN (*harshly, pushing her away*). You could murder Father, couldn't you? (*He thrusts the newspaper into her hands, pointing to the story.*) Here! Read that, if you don't believe me! We got it in Boston to see whom the police would suspect. It's only a few lines. Brant wasn't important—except to you!

(*She looks at the paper with fascinated horror. Then she lets it slip through her fingers, sinks down on the lowest step and begins to moan to herself, wringing her hands together in stricken anguish. Orin turns from her and starts to pace up and down by the steps. Lavinia stands at the left of the steps, rigid and erect, her face mask-like.*)

ORIN (*harshly*). They think exactly what we planned they should think—that he was killed by waterfront thieves. There's nothing to connect us with his death! (*He stops by her. She stares before her, wringing her hands and moaning. He blurts out.*) Mother! Don't moan like that! (*She gives no sign of having heard him. He starts to pace up and down again—with savage resentment.*) Why do you grieve for that servant's bastard? I know he was the one who planned Father's murder! You couldn't have done that! He got you under his influence to revenge himself! He hypnotized you! I saw you weren't yourself the minute I got home, remember. How else could you ever have imagined you loved that low swine? How else could you ever have said the things—— (*He stops before her.*) I heard you planning to go with him to the island I had told you about—our island—that was you and I!

(*He starts to pace up and down again distractedly. She remains as before except that her moaning has begun to exhaust itself. Orin stops before her again and grasps her by the shoulders, kneeling on the steps beside her—desperately pleading now.*) Mother! Don't moan like that! You're still under his influence! But you'll forget him! I'll make you forget him! I'll make you happy! We'll leave Vinnie here and go away on a long voyage—to the South Seas——

LAVINIA (*sharply*). Orin!

ORIN (*not heeding her, stares into his mother's face. She has stopped moaning, the horror in her eyes is dying into blankness, the expression of her mouth congealing to one of numbed grief. She gives no sign of having heard him. Orin shakes her—desperately*). Mother! Don't you hear me? Why won't you speak to me? Will you always love him? Do you hate me now? (*He sinks on his knees before her.*) Mother! Answer me! Say you forgive me!

LAVINIA (*with bitter scorn*). Orin! After all that's happened, are you becoming her cry-baby again? (*Orin starts and gets to his feet, staring at her confusedly, as if he had forgotten her existence. Lavinia speaks again in the curt, commanding tone that recalls her father.*) Leave her alone! Go in the house! (*As he hesitates—more sharply.*) Do you hear me? March!

ORIN (*automatically makes a confused motion of military salute—vaguely*). Yes, sir. (*He walks mechanically up the steps—gazing up at the house—strangely.*) Why are the shutters still closed? Father has gone. We ought to let in the moonlight.

(*He goes into the house. Lavinia comes and stands beside her mother. Christine continues to stare blankly in front of her. Her face has become a tragic death-mask. She gives no sign of being aware of her daughter's presence. Lavinia regards her with bleak, condemning eyes.*)

LAVINIA (*finally speaks sternly*). He paid the just penalty for his crime. You know it was justice. It was the only way true justice could be done. (*Her mother starts. The words shatter her merciful numbness and awaken her to agony again. She springs to her feet and stands glaring at her daughter with a terrible look in which a savage hatred fights with horror and fear. In spite of her frozen self-control, Lavinia recoils before this. Keeping her eyes on her, Christine shrinks backward up the steps until she stands at the top between the two columns of the portico before the front door. Lavinia suddenly makes a motion, as if to hold her back. She calls shakenly as if the words were wrung out of her against her will.*) Mother! What are you going to do? You can live!

CHRISTINE (*glares at her as if this were the last insult—with strident mockery*). Live!

(*She bursts into shrill laughter, stops it abruptly, raises her hands between her face and her daughter and pushes them out in a gesture of blotting Lavinia for ever from her sight. Then she turns and rushes into the house. Lavinia again makes a movement to follow her. But she immediately fights down this impulse and turns her back on the house determinedly, standing square-shouldered and stiff like a grim sentinel in black.*)

LAVINIA (*implacably to herself*). It is justice! (*From the street, away off right front, Seth's thin wraith of a baritone is raised in his favourite mournful "Shenandoah," as he nears the gateway to the drive, returning from his nightly visit to the saloon.*)

"*Oh, Shenandoah, I long to hear you*
A-way, my rolling river!
Oh, Shenandoah, I can't get near you
Way—ay, I'm bound away
Across the wide——"

(*There is the sharp report of a pistol from the left ground floor of the house where Ezra Mannon's study is. Lavinia gives a shuddering gasp, turns back to the steps, starts to go up them, stops again and stammers shakenly.*) It is justice! It is your justice, Father! (*Orin's voice is heard calling from the sitting-room at right, "What's that?" A door slams. Then Orin's horrified cry comes from the study as he finds his mother's body, and a moment later he rushes out frantically to Lavinia.*)

ORIN. Vinnie! (*He seizes her arm and stammers distractedly.*) Mother—shot herself—Father's pistol—get a doctor—— (*Then with hopeless anguish.*) No—it's too late—she's dead! (*Then wildly.*) Why—why did she, Vinnie? (*With tortured self-accusation.*) I drove her to it! I wanted to torture her! She couldn't forgive me! Why did I have to boast about killing him? Why——?

LAVINIA (*frightened, puts her hand over his mouth*). Be quiet!

ORIN (*tears her hand away—violently*). Why didn't I let her believe burglars killed him? She wouldn't have hated me then! She would have forgotten him! She would have turned to me! (*In a final frenzy of self-denunciation.*) I murdered her!

LAVINIA (*grasping him by the shoulders*). For God's sake, will you be quiet?

ORIN (*frantically—trying to break away from her*). Let me go! I've got to find her! I've got to make her forgive me! I——! (*He suddenly breaks down and weeps in hysterical anguish. Lavinia puts her arm around him soothingly. He sobs despairingly.*) But she's dead—— She's gone—how can I ever get her to forgive me now?

LAVINIA (*soothingly*). Ssshh! Ssshh! You have me, haven't you? I love you. I'll help you to forget.

(*He turns to go back into the house, still sobbing helplessly. Seth's voice comes from the drive, right, close at hand:*

"*She's far across the stormy water*
Way-ay, I'm bound away——"

He enters right front. Lavinia turns to face him.)

SETH (*approaching*). Say, Vinnie, did you hear a shot——?

LAVINIA (*sharply*). I want you to go for Doctor Blake. Tell him Mother has killed herself in a fit of insane grief over Father's death. (*Then as he stares, dumbfounded and wondering, but keeping his face expressionless—more sharply.*) Will you remember to tell him that?

SETH (*slowly*). Ayeh. I'll tell him, Vinnie—anything you say.

(*His face set grimly, he goes off, right front. Lavinia turns and, stiffly erect, her face stern and mask-like, follows Orin into the house.*)

Curtain

THE HAUNTED

A Play in Four Acts

Part Three of the Trilogy
MOURNING BECOMES ELECTRA

Characters

LAVINIA MANNON
ORIN, *her brother*
PETER NILES
HAZEL, *his sister*
SETH

AMOS AMES
IRA MACKEL
JOE SILVA
ABNER SMALL

Scenes

ACT ONE

SCENE ONE Exterior of the Mannon house. An evening in the summer of 1866.

SCENE TWO Sitting-room in the house (immediately follows Scene One).

ACT TWO

The study. An evening a month later.

ACT THREE

The sitting-room (immediately follows Act Two).

ACT FOUR

Same as Act One, Scene One. Exterior of the Mannon house. A late afternoon three days later.

ACT ONE SCENE ONE

Exterior of the Mannon house (as in the two preceding plays) on an evening of a clear day in summer a year later. It is shortly after sunset but the afterglow in the sky still bathes the white temple portico in a crimson light. The columns cast black bars of shadow on the wall behind them. All the shutters are closed and the front door is boarded up, showing that the house is unoccupied.

A group of five men is standing on the drive by the bench at left, front. Seth Beckwith is there and Amos Ames, who appeared in the first Act of "Homecoming." The others are Abner Small, Joe Silva and Ira Mackel.

These four—Ames, Small, Silva and Mackel—are, as were the townsfolk of the first acts of "Homecoming" and "The Hunted," a chorus of types representing the town as a human background for the drama of the Mannons.

Small is a wiry little old man of sixty-five, a

clerk in a hardware store. He has white hair and a wispy goat's beard, bright inquisitive eyes, ruddy complexion, and a shrill rasping voice. Silva is a Portuguese fishing captain—a fat, boisterous man, with a hoarse bass voice. He has matted grey hair and a big grizzled moustache. He is sixty. Mackel, who is a farmer, hobbles along with the aid of a cane. His shiny wrinkled face is oblong with square-cut white chin whiskers. He is bald. His yellowish brown eyes are sly. He talks in a drawling wheezy cackle.

All five are drunk. Seth has a stone jug in his hand. There is a grotesque atmosphere about these old men as of boys out on a forbidden lark.

SMALL. God A'mighty, Seth, be you glued to that jug?

MACKEL. Gol durn him, he's gittin' stingy in his old age!

SILVA (*bursts into song*).

"*A bottle of beer and a bottle of gin*
And a bottle of Irish whisky oh!
So early in the morning
A sailor likes his bottle oh!"

AMES (*derisively*). You like your bottle 'ceptin' when your old woman's got her eye on ye!

SILVA. She's visitin' her folks to New Bedford. What the hell I care! (*Bursts into song again.*)

"*Hurrah! Hurrah! I sing the jubilee*
Hurrah! Hurrah! Her folks has set me free!"

AMES (*slapping him on the back*). God damn you, Joe, you're gittin' to be a poet! (*They all laugh.*)

SMALL. God A'mighty, Seth, ain't ye got no heart in ye? Watch me perishin' fur lack o' whisky and ye keep froze to that jug! (*He reaches out for it.*)

SETH. No, ye don't! I'm on to your game! (*With a wink at the others.*) He's aimin' to git so full of Injun courage he wouldn't mind if a ghost sot on his lap! Purty slick you be, Abner! Swill my licker so's you kin skin me out o' my bet!

MACKEL. That's it, Seth! Don't let him play no skin games!

JOE. By God, if ghosts look like the livin', I'd let Ezra's woman's ghost set on my lap! M'm! (*He smacks his lips lasciviously.*)

AMES. Me, too! She was a beauty!

SMALL (*with an uneasy glance at the house*). It's her ghost folks is sayin' haunts the place, ain't it?

SETH (*with a wink at the others*). Oh, hers and a hull passel of others. The graveyard's full of Mannons and they all spend their nights at home here. You needn't worry but you'll have plenty o' company, Abner! (*The others laugh, their mirth a bit forced, but Small looks rather sick.*)

SMALL. It ain't in our bet for you to put sech notions in my head afore I go in, be it? (*Then forcing a perky bravado.*) Think you kin scare me? There ain't no sech thing as ghosts!

SETH. An' I'm sayin' you're scared to prove there ain't! Let's git our bet set out plain afore witnesses. I'm lettin' you in the Mannon house and I'm bettin' you ten dollars and a gallon of licker you dasn't stay there till moonrise at ten o'clock. If you come out afore then, you lose. An' you're to stay in the dark and not even strike a match! Is that agreed?

SMALL (*trying to put a brave face on it*). That's agreed—an' it's like stealin' ten dollars off you!

SETH. We'll see! (*Then with a grin.*) An' you're supposed to go in sober! But I won't make it too dead sober! I ain't that hard-hearted. I wouldn't face what you'll face with a gallon under my belt! (*Handing him the jug.*) Here! Take a good swig! You're lookin' a bit pale about the gills a'ready!

SMALL. No sech thing! (*But he puts the jug to his lips and takes an enormous gulp.*)

MACKEL. Whoa thar! Ye ain't drinkin' fur all on us!

(*Small hands the jug to him and he drinks and passes it round until it finally reaches Seth again. In the meantime Small talks to Seth.*)

SMALL. Be it all right fur me to go in afore dark? I'd like to know where I'm while I kin see.

SETH. Wal, I calc'late you kin. Don't want you runnin' into furniture an' breakin' things when them ghosts git chasin' you! Vinnie an' Orin's liable to be back from Chiny afore long an' she'd give me hell if anythin' was broke. (*The jug reaches him. He takes a drink—then sets it down on the drive.*) Come along! I've took the screws out o' that door. I kin let you right in. (*He goes towards the portico, Small following him, whistling with elaborate nonchalance.*)

SMALL (*to the others who remain where they are*). So long, fellers. We'll have a good spree on that ten dollars.

MACKEL (*with a malicious cackle*). Mebbe! Would you like me fur one o' your pallbearers, Abner?

AMES. I'll comfort your old woman—providin' she'll want comfortin', which ain't likely!

SILVA. And I'll water your grave every Sunday after church! That's the kind of man I be, by God. I don't forget my friends when they're gone!

SETH (*from the portico*). We'll all jine in, Joe! If he ain't dead, by God, we'll drown him!

(*They all roar with laughter. Small looks bitter. The jest strikes him as being unfeeling—All glow has faded from the sky and it is getting dark.*)

SMALL. To hell with ye! (*Seth prizes off the board door and unlocks the inner door.*)

SETH. Come on. I'll show you the handiest place to say your prayers. (*They go in. The group outside becomes serious.*)

AMES (*voicing the opinion of all of them*). Wal, all the same, I wouldn't be in Abner's boots. It don't do to monkey with them thin's.

MACKEL. You believe in ghosts, Amos?

AMES. Mebbe. Who knows there ain't?

MACKEL. Wal, I believe in 'em. Take the Nims' place out my way. Asa Nims killed his wife with a hatchet—she'd nagged him—then hung himself in the attic. I knew Ben Willett that bought the place. He couldn't live thar—had to move away. It's fallen to ruins now. Ben used to hear things clawin' at the walls an' winders and see the chairs move about. He wasn't a liar nor chicken-hearted neither.

SILVA. There is ghosts, by God! My cousin, Manuel, he seen one! Off on a whaler in the Injun Ocean, that was. A man got knifed and pushed overboard. After that, on moonlight nights, they'd see him a-settin' on the yards and hear him moanin' to himself. Yes, sir, my cousin Manuel, he ain't no liar neither—'ceptin' when he's drunk—and he seen him with his own eyes!

AMES (*with an uneasy glance around, reaching for the jug*). Wal, let's have a drink. (*He takes a swig just as Seth comes out of the house, shutting the door behind him.*)

MACKEL. That's Seth. He ain't anxious to stay in thar long, I notice! (*Seth hurries down to them, trying to appear to saunter.*)

SETH (*with a forced note to his joking*). God A'mighty, ye'd ought to see Abner! He's shyin' at the furniture covers an' his teeth are clickin' a'ready. He'll come runnin' out hell fur leather afore long. All I'm wonderin' is, has he got ten dollars.

MACKEL (*slyly*). You seem a bit shaky.

SETH (*with a scowl*). You're a liar. What're ye all lookin' glum as owls about?

MACKEL. Been talkin' of ghosts. Do you really believe that there house is haunted, Seth, or are ye only jokin' Abner?

SETH (*sharply*). Don't be a durned fool! I'm on'y jokin' him, of course!

MACKEL (*insistently*). Still, it'd be only natural if it was haunted. She shot herself there. Do you think she done it fur grief over Ezra's death, like the daughter let on to folks?

SETH. 'Course she did!

MACKEL. Ezra dyin' sudden his first night at home—that was durned queer!

SETH (*angrily*). It's durned queer old fools like you with one foot in the grave can't mind their own business in the little time left to 'em. That's what's queer!

MACKEL (*angry in his turn*). Wal, all I say is if they hadn't been Mannons with the town lickin' their boots, there'd have been queer doin's come out! And as fur me bein' an' old fool, you're older an' a worse fool! An' your foot's deeper in the grave than mine be!

SETH (*shaking his fist in Mackel's face*). It ain't so deep but what I kin whale the stuffin' out o' you any day in the week!

SILVA (*comes between them*). Here, you old roosters! No fightin' allowed!

MACKEL (*subsiding grumpily*). This is a free country, ain't it? I got a right to my opinions!

AMES (*suddenly looking off down left*). Ssshh! Look, Seth! There's someone comin' up the drive.

SETH (*peering*). Ayeh! Who the hell——?

It's Peter'n Hazel. Hide that jug, durn ye! (*The jug is hidden under the lilacs. A moment later Hazel and Peter enter. They stop in surprise on seeing Seth and his friends. Seth greets them self-consciously.*) Good evenin'. I was just showin' some friends around——

PETER. Hello, Seth. Just the man we're looking for. We've just had a telegram. Vinnie and Orin have landed in New York and——

(*He is interrupted by a muffled yell of terror from the house. As they all turn to look, the front door is flung open and Small comes tearing out and down the portico steps, his face chalky white and his eyes popping.*)

SMALL (*as he reaches them—terrified*). God A'mighty! I heard 'em comin' after me, and I run in the room opposite, an' I seed Ezra's ghost dressed like a judge comin' through the wall—and, by God, I run! (*He jerks a note out of his pocket and thrusts it on Seth.*) Here's your money, durn ye! I wouldn't stay in there fur a million!

(*This breaks the tension, and the old men give way to an hysterical, boisterous, drunken mirth, roaring with laughter, pounding each other on the back.*)

PETER (*sharply*). What's this all about? What was he doing in there?

SETH (*controlling his laughter, and embarrassed*). Only a joke, Peter. (*Then turning on Small—scornfully.*) That was Ezra's picture hangin' on the wall, not a ghost, ye durned idjut!

SMALL (*indignantly*). I know pictures when I see 'em, an' I knowed him. This was him! Let's get out o' here. I've had enough of this durned place!

SETH. You fellers trot along. I'll jine you later. (*They all mutter good evenings to Peter and Hazel and go off, left front. Small's excited voice can be heard receding as he begins to embroider on the horrors of his adventure. Seth turns to Peter apologetically.*) Abner Small's always braggin' how brave he is—so I bet him he dasn't stay in there——

HAZEL (*indignantly*). Seth! What would Vinnie say if she knew you did such things?

SETH. There ain't no harm done. I calc'late Abner didn't break nothin'. And Vinnie wouldn't mind when she knew why I done it. I was aimin' to stop the durned gossip that's been goin' round town about this house bein' haunted. You've heard it, ain't ye?

PETER. I heard some silly talk but didn't pay any attention——

SETH. That durned idjut female I got in to clean a month after Vinnie and Orin sailed started it. Said she'd felt ghosts around. You know how them things grow. Seemed to me Abner's braggin' gave me a good chance to stop it by turnin' it all into a joke on him folks'd laugh at. An' when I git through tellin' my story of it round town tomorrow you'll find folks'll shut up and not take it serious no more.

PETER (*appreciatively*). You're right, Seth. That was a darned slick notion! Nothing like a joke to lay a ghost!

SETH. Ayeh. But—— (*He hesitates—then decides to say it.*) Between you 'n' me 'n' the lamppost, it ain't all sech a joke as it sounds—that about the hauntin', I mean.

PETER (*incredulously*). You aren't going to tell me you think the house is haunted too!

SETH (*grimly*). Mebbe, and mebbe not. All I know is I wouldn't stay in there all night if you was to give me the town!

HAZEL (*impressed but forcing a teasing tone*). Seth! I'm ashamed of you!

PETER. First time I ever heard you say you were afraid of anything!

SETH. There's times when a man's a darn fool not to be scared! Oh, don't git it in your heads I take stock in spirits trespassin' round in windin' sheets or no sech lunatic doin's. But there is sech a thing as evil spirit. An' I've felt it, goin' in there daytimes to see to things—like somethin' rottin' in the walls!

PETER. Bosh!

SETH (*quietly*). 'Taint bosh, Peter. There's been evil in that house since it was first built in hate—and it's kept growin' there ever since, as what's happened there has proved. You understand I ain't sayin' this to no one but you two. An' I'm only tellin' you fur one reason—because you're closer to Vinnie and Orin than anyone and you'd ought to persuade them, now they're back, not to live in it. (*He adds impressively.*) Fur their own good! (*Then with a change of tone.*) An' now I've got that off my chest, tell me about 'em. When are they comin'?

PETER. To-morrow. Vinnie asked us to open the house. So let's start right in.

SETH (*with evident reluctance*). You want to do it to-night?

HAZEL. We must, Seth. We've got so little time. We can at least tidy up the rooms a little and get the furniture covers off.

SETH. Wal, I'll go to the barn and git lanterns. There's candles in the house. (*He turns abruptly and goes off left between the lilacs and the house.*)

HAZEL (*looking after him—uneasily*). I can't get over Seth acting so strangely.

PETER. Don't mind him. It's rum and old age.

HAZEL (*shaking her head—slowly*). No. There is something queer about this house. I've always felt it, even before the General's death and her suicide. (*She shudders.*) I can still see her sitting on that bench as she was that last night. She was so frightened of being alone. But I thought when Vinnie and Orin came back she would be all right. (*Then sadly.*) Poor Orin! I'll never forget to my dying day the way he looked when we saw him at the funeral. I hardly recognized him, did you?

PETER. No. He certainly was broken up.

HAZEL. And the way he acted—like someone in a trance! I don't believe when Vinnie rushed him off on this trip to the East he knew what he was doing or where he was going or anything.

PETER. A long voyage like that was the best thing to help them both forget.

HAZEL (*without conviction*). Yes. I suppose it was—but—— (*She stops and sighs—then worriedly.*) I wonder how Orin is. Vinnie's letters haven't said much about him, or herself, for that matter—only about the trip. (*She sees Seth approaching, whistling loudly, from left, rear, with two lighted lanterns.*) Here's Seth. (*She walks up the steps to the portico. Peter follows her. She hesitates and stands looking at the house—in a low tone, almost of dread.*) Seth was right. You feel something cold grip you the moment you set foot——

PETER. Oh, nonsense! He's got you going, too! (*Then with a chuckle.*) Listen to him whistling to keep his courage up! (*Seth comes in from the left. He hands one of the lanterns to Peter.*)

SETH. Here you be, Peter.

HAZEL. Well, let's go in. You better come out to the kitchen and help me first, Peter. We ought to start a fire.

(*They go in. There is a pause in which Peter can be heard opening windows behind the shutters in the downstairs rooms. Then silence. Then Lavinia enters, coming up the drive from left, front, and stands regarding the house. One is at once aware of an extraordinary change in her. Her body, formerly so thin and undeveloped, has filled out. Her movements have lost their square-shouldered stiffness. She now bears a striking resemblance to her mother in every respect, even to being dressed in the green her mother had affected. She walks to the clump of lilacs and stands there staring at the house.*)

LAVINIA (*turns back and calls coaxingly in the tone one would use to a child*). Don't stop there, Orin! What are you afraid of? Come on!

(*He comes slowly and hesitatingly in from left, front. He carries himself woodenly erect now like a soldier. His movements and attitudes have the statue-like quality that was so marked in his father. He now wears a close-cropped beard in addition to his moustache, and this accentuates his resemblance to the Judge. The Mannon semblance of his face in repose to a mask is more pronounced than ever. He has grown dreadfully thin and his black suit hangs loosely about him. His haggard swarthy face is set in a blank lifeless expression.*)

LAVINIA (*glances at him uneasily—concealing her apprehension under a coaxing motherly tone*). You must be brave! This is the test! You have got to face it! (*Then anxiously as he makes no reply.*) Do you feel you can—now we're here?

ORIN (*dully*). I'll be all right—with you.

LAVINIA (*takes his hand and pats it encouragingly*). That's all I wanted—to hear you say that. (*Turning to the house.*) Look, I see a light through the shutters of the sitting-room. That must be Peter and Hazel. (*Then as she sees he still keeps his eyes averted from the house.*) Why don't you look at the house? Are you afraid? (*Then sharply commanding.*) Orin! I want you to look now! Do you hear me?

ORIN (*dully obedient*). Yes, Vinnie. (*He jerks*

his head around and stares at the house and draws a deep shuddering breath.)

LAVINIA (*her eyes on his face—as if she were willing her strength into him*). Well? You don't see any ghosts, do you? Tell me!

ORIN (*obediently*). No.

LAVINIA. Because there are none! Tell me you know there are none, Orin!

ORIN (*as before*). Yes.

LAVINIA (*searches his face uneasily—then is apparently satisfied*). Come. Let's go in. We'll find Hazel and Peter and surprise them——

(*She takes his arm and leads him to the steps. He walks like an automaton. When they reach the spot where his mother had sat moaning, the last time he had seen her alive [Act Five of "The Hunted"], he stops with a shudder.*)

ORIN (*stammers—pointing*). It was here—she—the last time I saw her alive——

LAVINIA (*quickly, urging him on commandingly*). That is all past and finished! The dead have forgotten us! We've forgotten them! Come! (*He obeys woodenly. She gets him up the steps and they pass into the house.*)

Curtain

SCENE TWO

Same as Act Two of "The Hunted"—The sitting-room in the Mannon house. Peter has lighted two candles on the mantel and put the lantern on the table at front. In this dim, spotty light the room is full of shadows. It has the dead appearance of a room long shut up, and the covered furniture has a ghostly look. In the flickering candlelight the eyes of the Mannon portraits stare with a grim forbiddingness.

Lavinia appears in the doorway at rear. In the lighted room, the change in her is strikingly apparent. At a first glance, one would mistake her for her mother as she appeared in the First Act of "Homecoming." She seems a mature woman, sure of her feminine attractiveness. Her brown-gold hair is arranged as her mother's had been. Her green dress is like a copy of her mother's in Act One of "Homecoming." She comes forward slowly. The movements of her body now have the feminine grace her mother's had possessed. Her eyes are caught by the eyes of the Mannons in the portraits and she approaches as if compelled in spite of herself until she stands directly under them in front of the fireplace. She suddenly addresses them in a harsh resentful voice.

LAVINIA. Why do you look at me like that? I've done my duty by you! That's finished and forgotten! (*She tears her eyes from theirs and, turning away, becomes aware that Orin has not followed her into the room, and is immediately frightened and uneasy and hurries toward the door, calling:*) Orin!

ORIN (*his voice comes from the dark hall*). I'm here.

LAVINIA. What are you doing out there? Come here! (*Orin appears in the doorway. His face wears a dazed expression and his eyes have a wild, stricken look. He hurries to her as if seeking protection. She exclaims, frightened:*) Orin! What is it?

ORIN (*strangely*). I've just been in the study. I was sure she'd be waiting for me in there, where —— (*Torturedly.*) But she wasn't! She isn't anywhere. It's only they—— (*He points to the portraits.*) They're everywhere! But she's gone for ever. She'll never forgive me now!

LAVINIA (*harshly*). Orin! Will you be quiet!

ORIN (*unheeding—with a sudden turn to bitter resentful defiance*). Well, let her go! What is she to me? I'm not her son any more! I'm Father's! I'm a Mannon! And they'll welcome me home!

LAVINIA (*angrily commanding*). Stop it, do you hear me!

ORIN (*shocked back to awareness by her tone—miserably confused*). I—I didn't—don't be angry, Vinnie!

LAVINIA (*soothing him now*). I'm not angry, dear—only do get hold of yourself and be brave. (*Leading him to the sofa.*) Here. Come. Let's sit down for a moment, shall we, and get used to being home? (*They sit down. She puts an arm around him reproachfully.*) Don't you know how terribly you frighten me when you act so strangely? You don't mean to hurt me, do you?

ORIN (*deeply moved*). God knows I don't, Vinnie! You're all I have in the world! (*He takes her hand and kisses it humbly.*)

LAVINIA (*soothingly*). That's a good boy. (*Then with a cheerful matter-of-fact note.*) Hazel and Peter must be out in the kitchen. Won't you be glad to see Hazel again?

ORIN (*dully now*). You've kept talking about them all the voyage home. Why? What can they have to do with us—now?

LAVINIA. A lot. What we need most is to get back to simple normal things and begin a new life. And their friendship and love will help us more than anything to forget.

ORIN (*with sudden harshness*). Forget? I thought you'd forgotten long ago—if you ever remembered, which you never seemed to! (*Then with sombre bitterness.*) Love! What right have I—or you—to love?

LAVINIA (*defiantly*). Every right!

ORIN (*grimly*). Mother felt the same about—— (*Then with a strange, searching glance at her.*) You don't know how like Mother you've become, Vinnie. I don't mean only how pretty you've grown——

LAVINIA (*with a strange shy eagerness*). Do you really think I'm as pretty now as she was, Orin?

ORIN (*as if she hadn't interrupted*). I mean the change in your soul, too. I've watched it ever since we sailed for the East. Little by little it grew like Mother's soul—as if you were stealing hers—as if her death had set you free—to become her!

LAVINIA (*uneasily*). Now don't begin talking nonsense again, please!

ORIN (*grimly*). Don't you believe in souls any more? I think you will after we've lived in this house a while! The Mannon dead will convert you. (*He turns to the portraits mockingly.*) Ask them if I'm not right!

LAVINIA (*sharply*). Orin! What's come over you? You haven't had one of these morbid spells since we left the Islands. You swore to me you had had the last of them, or I'd never have agreed to come home.

ORIN (*with a strange malicious air*). I had to get you away from the Islands. My brotherly duty! If you'd stayed there much longer—— (*He chuckles disagreeably.*)

LAVINIA (*with a trace of confusion*). I don't know what you're talking about. I only went there for your sake.

ORIN (*with another chuckle*). Yes—but afterwards——

LAVINIA (*sharply*). You promised you weren't going to talk any more morbid nonsense. (*He subsides meekly. She goes on reproachfully.*) Remember all I've gone through on your account. For months after we sailed you didn't know what you were doing. I had to live in constant fear of what you might say. I wouldn't live through those horrible days again for anything on earth. And remember this homecoming is what you wanted. You told me that if you could come home and face your ghosts, you knew you could rid yourself for ever of your silly feeling of guilt about the past.

ORIN (*dully*). I know, Vinnie.

LAVINIA. And I believed you, you seemed so certain of yourself. But now you've suddenly become strange again. You frighten me. So much depends on how you start, now we're home. (*Then sharply commanding.*) Listen, Orin! I want you to start again—by facing all your ghosts here and now! (*He turns and his eyes remain fixed on hers from now on. She asks sternly.*) Who murdered Father?

ORIN (*falteringly*). Brant did—for revenge because——

LAVINIA (*more sternly*). Who murdered Father? Answer me!

ORIN (*with a shudder*). Mother was under his influence——

LAVINIA. That's a lie! It was he who was under hers. You know the truth!

ORIN. Yes.

LAVINIA. She was an adulteress and a murderess, wasn't she?

ORIN. Yes.

LAVINIA. If we'd done our duty under the law, she would have been hanged, wouldn't she?

ORIN. Yes.

LAVINIA. But we protected her. She could have lived, couldn't she? But she chose to kill herself as a punishment for her crime—of her own free will! It was an act of justice! You had nothing to do with it! You see that now, don't you? (*As he hesitates, trembling violently, she seizes his arm fiercely.*) Tell me!

ORIN (*hardly above a whisper*). Yes.

LAVINIA. And your feeling of being responsible for her death was only your morbid imagination! You don't feel it now! You'll never feel it again!

ORIN. No.

LAVINIA (*gratefully—and weakly because the strength she has willed into him has left her exhausted*). There! You see! You can do it when you will to! (*She kisses him. He breaks down, sobbing weakly against her breast. She soothes him.*) There! Don't cry! You ought to feel proud. You've proved you can laugh at your ghosts from now on. (*Then briskly, to distract his mind.*) Come now. Help me to take off these furniture covers. We might as well start making ourselves useful.

(*She starts to work. For a moment he helps. Then he goes to one of the windows and pushes back a shutter and stands staring out. Peter comes in the door from rear. At the sight of Lavinia he stops, startled, thinks for a second it is her mother's ghost and gives an exclamation of dread. At the same moment she sees him. She stares at him with a strange eager possessiveness. She calls softly.*)

LAVINIA. Peter! (*She goes towards him, smiling as her mother might have smiled.*) Don't you know me any more, Peter?

PETER (*stammers*). Vinnie! I—I thought you were——! I can't realize it's you! You've grown so like your—— (*Checking himself awkwardly.*) I mean you've changed so—and we weren't looking for you until—— (*He takes her hand automatically, staring at her stupidly.*)

LAVINIA. I know. We had intended to stay in New York to-night but we decided later we'd better come right home. (*Then taking him in with a smiling appreciative possessiveness.*) Let me look at you, Peter. You haven't gone and changed, have you? No, you're the same, thank goodness! I've been thinking of you all the way home and wondering—I was so afraid you might have.

PETER (*plucking up his courage—blurts out*). You—you ought to know I'd never change—with you! (*Then, alarmed by his own boldness, he hastily looks away from her.*)

LAVINIA (*teasingly*). But you haven't said yet you're glad to see me!

PETER (*has turned back and is staring, fascinated, at her. A surge of love and desire overcomes his timidity and he bursts out*). I—you know how much I——! (*Then he turns away again in confusion and takes refuge in a burst of talk.*) Gosh, Vinnie, you ought to have given us more warning. We've only just started to open the place up. I was with Hazel, in the kitchen, starting a fire——

LAVINIA (*laughing softly*). Yes. You're the same old Peter! You're still afraid of me. But you mustn't be now. I know I used to be an awful old stick, but——

PETER. Who said so? You were not! (*Then with enthusiasm.*) Gosh, you look so darned pretty—and healthy. Your trip certainly did you good! (*Staring at her again, drinking her in.*) I can't get over seeing you dressed in colour. You always used to wear black.

LAVINIA (*with a strange smile*). I was dead then.

PETER. You ought always to wear colour.

LAVINIA (*immensely pleased*). Do you think so?

PETER. Yes. It certainly is becoming. I——(*Then, embarrassed, he changes the subject:*) But where's Orin?

LAVINIA (*turning to look round*). Why, he was just here. (*She sees him at the window.*) Orin, what are you doing there? Here's Peter. (*Orin closes the shutter he has pushed open and turns back from the window. He comes forward, his eyes fixed in a strange preoccupation, as if he were unaware of their presence. Lavinia watches him uneasily and speaks sharply.*) Don't you see Peter? Why don't you speak to him? You mustn't be so rude.

PETER (*good-naturedly*). Give him a chance. Hello, Orin. Darned glad to see you back. (*They shake hands. Peter has difficulty in hiding his pained surprise at Orin's sickly appearance.*)

ORIN (*rousing himself, forces a smile and makes an effort at his old friendly manner with Peter*). Hello, Peter. You know I'm glad to see you without any polite palaver. Vinnie is the same old bossy fuss-buzzer—you remember—always trying to teach me manners!

PETER. You bet I remember! But I say, hasn't she changed, though? I didn't know her, she's grown so fat! And I was just telling her how well she looked in colour. Don't you agree?

ORIN (*in a sudden strange tone of jeering malice*). Did you ask her why she stole Mother's colours? I can't see why—yet—and I don't think she knows herself. But it will prove a strange reason, I'm certain of that, when I do discover it!

LAVINIA (*making a warning sign to Peter not to take this seriously—forcing a smile*). Don't mind him, Peter.

ORIN (*his tone becoming sly, insinuating and mocking*). And she's become romantic! Imagine that! Influence of the "dark and deep blue ocean"—and of the Islands, eh, Vinnie?

PETER (*surprised*). You stopped at the Islands?

ORIN. Yes. We took advantage of our being on a Mannon ship to make the captain touch there on the way back. We stopped a month. (*With resentful bitterness.*) But they turned out to be Vinnie's islands, not mine. They only made me sick—and the naked women disgusted me. I guess I'm too much of a Mannon, after all, to turn into a pagan. But you should have seen Vinnie with the men——!

LAVINIA (*indignantly, but with a certain guiltiness*). How can you——!

ORIN (*jeeringly*). Handsome and romantic-looking, weren't they, Vinnie?—with coloured rags around their middles and flowers stuck over their ears! Oh, she was a bit shocked at first by their dances, but afterwards she fell in love with the Islanders. If we'd stayed another month, I know I'd have found her some moonlight night dancing under the palm trees—as naked as the rest!

LAVINIA. Orin! Don't be disgusting!

ORIN (*points to the portraits mockingly*). Picture, if you can, the feelings of the God-fearing Mannon dead at that spectacle!

LAVINIA (*with an anxious glance at Peter*). How can you make up such disgusting fibs?

ORIN (*with a malicious chuckle*). Oh, I wasn't as blind as I pretended to be! Do you remember Avahanni?

LAVINIA (*angrily*). Stop talking like a fool! (*He subsides meekly again. She forces a smile and a motherly tone.*) You're a naughty boy, do you know it? What will Peter think? Of course, he knows you're only teasing me—but you shouldn't go on like that. It isn't nice. (*Then changing the subject abruptly.*) Why don't you go and find Hazel? Here. Let me look at you. I want you to look your best when she sees you. (*She arranges him as a mother would a boy, pulling down his coat, giving a touch to his shirt and tie. Orin straightens woodenly to a soldierly attention. She is vexed by this.*) Don't stand like a ramrod! You'd be so handsome if you'd only shave off that silly beard and not carry yourself like a tin soldier!

ORIN (*with a sly cunning air*). Not look so much like Father, eh? More like a romantic clipper captain, is that it? (*As she starts and stares at him, as in fear, he smiles an ugly taunting smile.*) Don't look so frightened, Vinnie!

LAVINIA (*with an apprehensive glance at Peter—pleading and at the same time warning*). Ssshh! You weren't to talk nonsense, remember! (*Giving him a final pat.*) There! Now run along to Hazel.

ORIN (*looks from her to Peter suspiciously*). You seem damned anxious to get rid of me.

(*He turns and stalks stiffly with hurt dignity from the room. Lavinia turns to Peter. The strain of Orin's conduct has told on her. She seems suddenly weak and frightened.*)

PETER (*in shocked amazement*). What's come over him?

LAVINIA (*in a strained voice*). It's the same thing—what the war did to him—and on top of that Father's death—and the shock of Mother's suicide.

PETER (*puts his arm around her impulsively—comfortingly*). It'll be all right! Don't worry, Vinnie!

LAVINIA (*nestling against him gratefully*). Thank you, Peter. You're so good. (*Then looking into his eyes.*) Do you still love me, Peter?

PETER. Don't have to ask that, do you? (*He squeezes her awkwardly—then stammers.*) But do you—think now—you maybe—can love me?

LAVINIA. Yes!

PETER. You really mean that?

LAVINIA. Yes! I do! I've thought of you so much! Things were always reminding me of you—the ship and the sea—everything that was honest and clean! And the natives on the Islands reminded me of you too. They were so simple and fine—— (*Then hastily.*) You mustn't mind what

Orin was saying about the Islands. He's become a regular bigoted Mannon.

PETER (*amazed*). But, Vinnie—— !

LAVINIA. Oh, I know it must sound funny hearing me talk like that. But remember I'm only half Mannon. (*She looks at the portraits defiantly.*) And I've done my duty by them ! They can't say I haven't !

PETER (*mystified but happy*). Gosh, you certainly have changed ! But I'm darned glad !

LAVINIA. Orin keeps teasing that I was flirting with that native he spoke about, simply because he used to smile at me and I smiled back.

PETER (*teasingly*). Now, I'm beginning to get jealous, too.

LAVINIA. You mustn't. He made me think of you. He made me dream of marrying you—and everything.

PETER. Oh, well then, I take it all back ! I owe him a vote of thanks ! (*He hugs her.*)

LAVINIA (*dreamily*). I loved those Islands. They finished setting me free. There was something there mysterious and beautiful—a good spirit—of love—coming out of the land and sea. It made me forget death. There was no hereafter. There was only this world—the warm earth in the moonlight—the trade wind in the cocoa palms—the surf on the reef—the fires at night and the drum throbbing in my heart—the natives dancing naked and innocent—without knowledge of sin ! (*She checks herself abruptly as if frightened.*) But what in the world ! I'm running on like a regular chatterbox. You must think I've become awfully scatterbrained !

PETER (*with a chuckle*). Gosh, no ! I'm glad you've grown that way ! You never used to say a word unless you had to !

LAVINIA (*suddenly filled with grateful love for him, lets herself go and throws her arms around him*). Oh, Peter, hold me close to you ! I want to feel love ! Love is all beautiful ! I never used to know that ! I was a fool ! (*She kisses him passionately. He returns it, aroused and at the same time a little shocked by her boldness. She goes on longingly.*) We'll be married soon, won't we, and settle out in the country away from folks and their evil talk ? We'll make an island for ourselves on land, and we'll have children and love them and teach them to love life so that they can never be possessed by hate and death ! (*She gives a start—in a whisper as if to herself.*) But I'm forgetting Orin !

PETER. What's Orin got to do with us marrying ?

LAVINIA. I can't leave him—until he's well again. I'd be afraid——

PETER. Let him live with us.

LAVINIA (*with sudden intensity*). No ! I want to be rid of the past ! (*Then after a quick look at him—in a confiding tone.*) I want to tell you what's wrong with Orin—so you and Hazel can help me. He feels guilty about Mother killing herself. You see, he'd had a quarrel with her that last night. He was jealous and mad and said things he was sorry for after and it preyed on his mind until he blames himself for her death.

PETER. But that's crazy !

LAVINIA. I know it is, Peter, but you can't do anything with him when he gets his morbid spells. Oh, I don't mean he's the way he is to-night most of the time. Usually he's like himself, only quiet and sad—so sad it breaks my heart to see him—like a little boy who's been punished for something he didn't do. Please tell Hazel what I've told you, so she'll make allowances for any crazy thing he might say.

PETER. I'll warn her. And now don't you worry any more about him. We'll get him all right again one way or another.

LAVINIA (*again grateful for his simple goodness—lovingly*). Bless you, Peter !

(*She kisses him. As she does so, Hazel and Orin appear in the doorway at rear. Hazel is a bit shocked, then smiles happily. Orin starts as if he'd been struck. He glares at them with jealous rage and clenches his fists as if he were going to attack them.*)

HAZEL (*with a teasing laugh*). I'm afraid we're interrupting, Orin. (*Peter and Vinnie jump apart in confusion.*)

ORIN (*threateningly*). So that's it ! By God —— !

LAVINIA (*frightened, but managing to be stern*). Orin !

ORIN (*pulls himself up sharply—confusedly, forcing*

a sickly smile). Don't be so solemn—Fuss Buzzer! I was only trying to scare you—for a joke! (*Turning to Peter and holding out his hand, his smile becoming ghastly.*) I suppose congratulations are in order. I—I'm glad.

(*Peter takes his hand awkwardly. Hazel moves towards Lavinia to greet her, her face full of an uneasy bewilderment. Lavinia stares at Orin with eyes full of dread.*)

Curtain

ACT TWO

SCENE. *Same as Act Three of "The Hunted"—Ezra Mannon's study—on an evening a month later. The shutters of the windows are closed. Candles on the mantel above the fireplace light up the portrait of Ezra Mannon in his judge's robes. Orin is sitting in his father's chair at left of table, writing by the light of a lamp. A small pile of manuscript is stacked by his right hand. He is intent on his work. He has aged in the intervening month. He looks almost as old now as his father in the portrait. He is dressed in black and the resemblance between the two is uncanny. A grim smile of satisfaction twitches his lips as he stops writing and reads over the paragraph he has just finished. Then he puts the sheet down and stares up at the portrait, sitting back in his chair.*

ORIN (*sardonically, addressing the portrait*). The truth, the whole truth and nothing but the truth! Is that what you're demanding, Father? Are you sure you want the whole truth? What will the neighbours say if this whole truth is ever known? (*He chuckles grimly.*) A ticklish decision for you, Your Honour! (*There is a knock on the door. He hastily grabs the script and puts it in the drawer of the desk.*) Who's there?

LAVINIA. It's I.

ORIN (*hastily locking the drawer and putting the key in his pocket*). What do you want?

LAVINIA (*sharply*). Please open the door!

ORIN. All right. In a minute.

(*He hurriedly straightens up the table and grabs a book at random from the bookcase and lays it open on the table as if he had been reading. Then he unlocks the door and comes back to his chair as Lavinia enters. She wears a green velvet gown similar to that worn by Christine in Act Three of "Homecoming." It sets off her hair and eyes. She is obviously concealing beneath a surface calm a sense of dread and desperation.*)

LAVINIA (*glances at him suspiciously, but forces a casual air*). Why did you lock yourself in? (*She comes over to the table.*) What are you doing?

ORIN. Reading.

LAVINIA (*picks up the book*). Father's law books?

ORIN (*mockingly*). Why not? I'm considering studying law. He wanted me to, if you remember.

LAVINIA. Do you expect me to believe that, Orin? What is it you're really doing?

ORIN. Curious, aren't you?

LAVINIA (*forcing a smile*). Good gracious, why wouldn't I be? You've acted so funnily lately, locking yourself in here with the blinds closed and the lamp burning even in the daytime. It isn't good for you staying in this stuffy room in this weather. You ought to get out in the fresh air.

ORIN (*harshly*). I hate the daylight. It's like an accusing eye! No, we've renounced the day, in which normal people live—or rather it has renounced us. Perpetual night—darkness of death in life—that's the fitting habitat for guilt! You believe you can escape that, but I'm not so foolish!

LAVINIA. Now you're being stupid again!

ORIN. And I find artificial light more appropriate for my work—man's light, not God's—man's feeble striving to understand himself, to exist for himself in the darkness! It's a symbol of his life—a lamp burning out in a room of waiting shadows!

LAVINIA (*sharply*). Your work? What work?

ORIN (*mockingly*). Studying the law of crime and punishment, as you saw.

LAVINIA (*forcing a smile again and turning away from him*). All right, if you won't tell me. Go on being mysterious, if you like. (*In a tense voice.*)

It's so close in here! It's suffocating! It's bad for you! (*She goes to the window and throws the shutters open and looks out.*) It's black as pitch to-night. There isn't a star.

ORIN (*sombrely*). Darkness without a star to guide us! Where are we going, Vinnie? (*Then with a mocking chuckle.*) Oh, I know you think you know where you're going, but there's many a slip, remember!

LAVINIA (*her voice strident, as if her will were snapping*). Be quiet! Can't you think of anything but—— (*Then controlling herself, comes to him—gently.*) I'm sorry. I'm terribly nervous to-night. It's the heat, I suppose. And you get me so worried with your incessant brooding over the past. It's the worst thing for your health. (*She pats him on the arm—soothingly.*) That's all I'm thinking about, dear.

ORIN. Thank you for your anxiety about my health! But I'm afraid there isn't much hope for you there! I happen to feel quite well!

LAVINIA (*whirling on him—distractedly*). How can you insinuate such horrible——! (*Again controlling herself with a great effort, forcing a smile.*) But you're only trying to rile me—and I'm not going to let you. I'm so glad you're feeling better. You ate a good supper to-night—for you. The long walk we took with Hazel did you good.

ORIN (*dully*). Yes. (*He slumps down in his chair at left of table.*) Why is it you never leave me alone with her more than a minute? You approved of my asking her to marry me—and now we're engaged you never leave us alone! (*Then with a bitter smile.*) But I know the reason well enough. You're afraid I'll let something slip.

LAVINIA (*sits in the chair opposite him—wearily*). Can you blame me, the way you've been acting?

ORIN (*sombrely*). No. I'm afraid myself of being too long with her alone—afraid of myself. I have no right in the same world with her. And yet I feel so drawn to her purity! Her love for me makes me appear less vile to myself! (*Then with a harsh laugh.*) And, at the same time, a million times more vile, that's the hell of it! So I'm afraid you can't hope to get rid of me through Hazel. She's another lost island! It's wiser for you to keep Hazel away from me, I warn you. Because when I see love for a murderer in her eyes my guilt crowds up in my throat like poisonous vomit and I long to spit it out—and confess!

LAVINIA (*in a low voice*). Yes, that is what I live in terror of—that in one of your fits you'll say something before someone—now after it's all past and forgotten—when there isn't the slightest suspicion——

ORIN (*harshly*). Were you hoping you could escape retribution? You can't! Confess and atone to the full extent of the law! That's the only way to wash the guilt of our mother's blood from our souls!

LAVINIA (*distractedly*). Ssshh! Will you stop!

ORIN. Ask our father, the Judge, if it isn't! He knows! He keeps telling me!

LAVINIA. Oh, God! Over and over and over! Will you never lose your stupid guilty conscience! Don't you see how you torture me? You're becoming my guilty conscience, too! (*With an instinctive flare-up of her old jealousy.*) How can you still love that vile woman so—when you know all she wanted was to leave you without a thought and marry that——

ORIN (*with fierce accusation*). Yes! Exactly as you're scheming now to leave me and marry Peter! But, by God, you won't! You'll damn soon stop your tricks when you know what I've been writing!

LAVINIA (*tensely*). What have you written?

ORIN (*his anger turned to gloating satisfaction*). Ah! That frightens you, does it? Well, you better be frightened!

LAVINIA. Tell me what you've written!

ORIN. None of your damned business.

LAVINIA. I've got to know!

ORIN. Well, as I've practically finished it—I suppose I might as well tell you. At his earnest solicitation—(*he waves a hand to the portrait mockingly*) as the last male Mannon—thank God for that, eh!—I've been writing the history of our family! (*He adds with a glance at the portrait and a malicious chuckle.*) But I don't wish to convey that he approves of all I've set down—not by a damned sight!

LAVINIA (*trying to keep calm—tensely*). What kind of history do you mean?

ORIN. A true history of all the family crimes, beginning with Grandfather Abe's—all of the crimes, including ours, do you understand?

LAVINIA (*aghast*). Do you mean to tell me you've

actually written——

ORIN. Yes! I've tried to trace to its secret hiding-place in the Mannon past the evil destiny behind our lives! I thought if I could see it clearly in the past I might be able to foretell what fate is in store for us, Vinnie—but I haven't dared predict that—not yet—although I can guess—— (*He gives a sinister chuckle.*)

LAVINIA. Orin!

ORIN. Most of what I've written is about you! I found you the most interesting criminal of us all!

LAVINIA (*breaking*). How can you say such dreadful things to me, after all I——

ORIN (*as if he hadn't heard—inexorably*). So many strange hidden things out of the Mannon past combine in you! For one example, do you remember the first mate, Wilkins, on the voyage to 'Frisco? Oh, I know you thought I was in a stupor of grief—but I wasn't blind! I saw how you wanted him!

LAVINIA (*angrily, but with a trace of guilty confusion*) I never gave him a thought! He was an officer of the ship to me, and nothing more!

ORIN (*mockingly*). Adam Brant was a ship's officer, too, wasn't he? Wilkins reminded you of Brant——

LAVINIA. No!

ORIN. And that's why you suddenly discarded mourning in 'Frisco and bought new clothes—in Mother's colours!

LAVINIA (*furiously*). Stop talking about her! You'd think, to hear you, I had no life of my own!

ORIN. You wanted Wilkins just as you'd wanted Brant!

LAVINIA. That's a lie!

ORIN. You're doing the lying! You know damned well that behind all your pretence about Mother's murder being an act of justice was your jealous hatred! She warned me of that and I see it clearly now! You wanted Brant for yourself!

LAVINIA (*fiercely*). It's a lie! I hated him!

ORIN. Yes, after you knew he was her lover! (*He chuckles with a sinister mockery.*) But we'll let that pass for the present—I know it's the last thing you could ever admit to yourself!—and come to what I've written about your adventures on my lost islands. Or should I say, Adam Brant's islands! He had been there too, if you'll remember! Probably he'd lived with one of the native women! He was that kind! Were you thinking of that when we were there?

LAVINIA (*chokingly*). Stop it! I—I warn you—I won't bear it much longer!

ORIN (*as if he hadn't heard—in the same sinister mocking tone*). What a paradise the Islands were for you, eh? All those handsome men staring at you and your strange beautiful hair! It was then you finally became pretty—like Mother! You knew they all desired you, didn't you? It filled you with pride! Especially Avahanni! You watched him stare at your body through your clothes, stripping you naked! And you wanted him!

LAVINIA. No!

ORIN. Don't lie! (*He accuses her with fierce jealousy.*) What did you do with him the night I was ill and you went to watch their shameless dance? Something happened between you! I saw your face when you came back and stood with him in front of our hut!

LAVINIA (*quietly—with simple dignity now*). I had kissed him good night, that was all—in gratitude! He was innocent and good. He had made me feel for the first time in my life that everything about love could be sweet and natural.

ORIN. So you kissed him, did you? And that was all?

LAVINIA (*with a sudden flare of deliberately evil taunting that recalls her mother in the last act of "Homecoming," when she was goading Ezra Mannon to fury just before his murder*). And what if it wasn't? I'm not your property! I have a right to love!

ORIN (*reacting as his father had—his face grown livid—with a hoarse cry of fury grabs her by the throat*). You—you whore! I'll kill you! (*Then suddenly he breaks down and becomes weak and pitiful.*) No! You're lying about him, aren't you? For God's sake, tell me you're lying, Vinnie!

LAVINIA (*strangely shaken and trembling—stammers*). Yes—it was a lie—how could you believe I—— Oh, Orin, something made me say that to you—against my will—something rose up in me—like an evil spirit!

ORIN (*laughs wildly*). Ghosts! You never seemed so much like Mother as you did just then!

LAVINIA (*pleading distractedly*). Don't talk about

it! Let's forget it ever happened! Forgive me! Please forget it!

ORIN. All right—if the ghosts will let us forget! (*He stares at her fixedly for a moment—then satisfied.*) I believe you about Avahanni. I never really suspected, or I'd have killed him—and you too! I hope you know that! (*Then with his old obsessed insistence.*) But you were guilty in your mind just the same!

LAVINIA (*in a flash of distracted anger*). Stop harping on that! Stop torturing me or I——! I've warned you! I warn you again! I can't bear any more! I won't!

ORIN (*with a mocking diabolical sneer—quietly*). Then why don't you murder me? I'll help you plan it, as we planned Brant's, so there will be no suspicion on you! And I'll be grateful! I loathe my life!

LAVINIA (*speechless with horror—can only gasp*). Oh!

ORIN (*with a quiet mad insistence*). Can't you see I'm now in Father's place and you're Mother? That's the evil destiny out of the past I haven't dared predict! I'm the Mannon you're chained to! So isn't it plain——

LAVINIA (*putting her hands over her ears*). For God's sake, won't you be quiet! (*Then suddenly her horror turning into a violent rage—unconsciously repeating the exact threat she had goaded her mother to make to her in Act Two of "Homecoming."*) Take care, Orin! You'll be responsible if——! (*She stops abruptly, terrified by her own words.*)

ORIN (*with a diabolical mockery*). If what? If I should die mysteriously of heart failure?

LAVINIA. Leave me alone! Leave me alone! Don't keep saying that! How can you be so horrible? Don't you know I'm your sister, who loves you, who would give her life to bring you peace?

ORIN (*with a change to a harsh, threatening tone*). I don't believe you! I know you're plotting something! But you look out! I'll be watching you! And I warn you I won't stand your leaving me for Peter! I'm going to put this confession I've written in safe hands—to be read in case you try to marry him—or if I should die——

LAVINIA (*frantically grabbing his arm and shaking him fiercely*). Stop having such thoughts! Stop making me have them! You're like a devil torturing me! I won't listen!

(*She breaks down and sobs brokenly. Orin, dazed, stares at her—seems half to come back to his natural self and the wild look fades from his eyes, leaving them glazed and lifeless.*)

ORIN (*strangely*). Don't cry. The damned don't cry. (*He sinks down heavily in his father's chair and stares at the floor. Suddenly he says harshly again:*) Go away, will you? I want to be alone—to finish my work.

(*Still sobbing, her hand over her eyes, Lavinia feels blindly for the door and goes out, closing it after her. Orin unlocks the table drawer, pulls out his manuscript, and takes up his pen.*)

Curtain

ACT THREE

SCENE. *Same as Act One, Scene Two—the sitting-room. The lamp on the table is lighted but turned low. Two candles are burning on the mantel over the fireplace at right, shedding their flickering light on the portrait of Abe Mannon above, and of the other Mannons on the walls on each side of him. The eyes of the portraits seem to possess an intense bitter life, with their frozen stare "looking over the head of life, cutting it dead for the impropriety of living," as Orin had said of his father in Act Two of "The Hunted."*

No time has elapsed since the preceding act. Lavinia enters from the hall in the rear, having just come from the study. She comes to the table and turns up the lamp. She is in a terrific state of tension. The corners of her mouth twitch, she twines and untwines the fingers of her clasped hands with a slow wringing movement which recalls her mother in the last act of "The Hunted."

LAVINIA (*torturedly—begins to pace up and down, muttering her thoughts aloud*). I can't bear it! Why does he keep putting his death in my head? He would be better off if—— Why hasn't he the courage—— ? (*Then in a frenzy of remorseful anguish, her eyes unconsciously seeking the Mannon portraits on the right wall, as if they were the visible symbol of her God.*) Oh, God, don't let me have such thoughts ! You know I love Orin ! Show me the way to save him ! Don't let me think of death ! I couldn't bear another death ! Please ! Please !

(*At a noise from the hall she controls herself and pretends to be glancing through a book on the table. Seth appears in the doorway.*)

SETH. Vinnie !

LAVINIA. What is it, Seth ?

SETH. That durned idjut, Hannah, is throwin' fits agin. Went down cellar and says she felt ha'nts crawlin' behind her. You'd better come and git her calmed down—or she'll be leavin'. (*Then he adds disgustedly:*) That's what we git fur freein' 'em !

LAVINIA (*wearily*). All right. I'll talk to her.

(*She goes out with Seth. A pause. Then a ring from the front door bell. A moment later Seth can be seen coming back along the hall. He opens the front door and is heard greeting Hazel and Peter and follows them in as they enter the room.*)

SETH. Vinnie's just seein' to somethin'. You set down and she'll be here soon as she kin.

PETER. All right, Seth.

(*Seth goes out again. They come forward and sit down. Peter looks hearty and good-natured, the same as ever, but Hazel's face wears a nervous, uneasy look although her air is determined.*)

PETER. I'll have to run along soon and drop in at the Council meeting. I can't get out of it. I'll be back in half an hour—maybe sooner.

HAZEL (*suddenly with a little shiver*). I hate this house now. I hate coming here. If it wasn't for Orin—— He's getting worse. Keeping him shut up here is the worst thing Vinnie could do.

PETER. He won't go out. You know very well she has to force him to walk with you.

HAZEL. And comes along herself ! Never leaves him alone, or hardly a second !

PETER (*with a grin*). Oh, that's what you've got against her, eh ?

HAZEL (*sharply*). Don't be silly, Peter ! I simply think, and I'd say it to her face, that she's a bad influence for Orin ! I feel there's something awfully wrong—somehow. He scares me at times—and Vinnie—I've watched her looking at you. She's changed so. There's something bold about her.

PETER (*getting up*). If you're going to talk like that—— ! You ought to be ashamed, Hazel !

HAZEL. Well, I'm not ! I've got some right to say something about how he's cared for ! And I'm going to from now on ! I'm going to make her let him visit us for a time. I've asked Mother and she'll be glad to have him.

PETER. Say, I think that's a darned good notion for both of them. She needs a rest from him, too.

HAZEL. Vinnie doesn't think it's a good notion ! I mentioned it yesterday and she gave me such a look ! (*Determinedly.*) But I'm going to make him promise to come over to-morrow, no matter what she says !

PETER (*soothingly, patting her shoulder*). Don't get angry now—about nothing. I'll help you persuade her to let him come. (*Then with a grin.*) I'll help you do anything to help Orin get well—if only for selfish reasons. As long as Vinnie's tied down to him we can't get married.

HAZEL (*stares at him—slowly*). Do you really want to marry her—now ?

PETER. Why do you ask such a fool question ? What do you mean, do I want to now ?

HAZEL (*her voice trembles and she seems about to burst into tears*). Oh, I don't know, Peter ! I don't know !

PETER (*sympathetic and at the same time exasperated*). What in the dickens is the matter with you ?

HAZEL (*hears a noise from the hall and collects herself—warningly*). Ssshh !

(*Orin appears in the doorway at rear. He glances at them, then quickly around the room to see if Lavinia is there. They both greet him with " Hello, Orin."*)

ORIN. Hello ! (*Then in an excited whisper, coming to them.*) Where's Vinnie ?

HAZEL. She's gone to see to something, Seth said.

PETER (*glancing at his watch*). Gosh, I've got to hurry to that darned Council meeting.

ORIN (*eagerly*). You're going?

PETER (*jokingly*). You needn't look so darned pleased about it! It isn't polite!

ORIN. I've got to see Hazel alone!

PETER. All right! You don't have to put me out!

(*He grins, slapping Orin on the back and goes out. Orin follows him with his eyes until he hears the front door close behind him.*)

ORIN (*turning to Hazel—with queer furtive excitement*). Listen, Hazel! I want you to do something! But wait! I've got to get—— (*He rushes out and can be heard going across the hall to the study. Hazel looks after him anxiously. A moment later he hurries back with a big sealed envelope in his hand which he gives to Hazel, talking breathlessly, with nervous jerks of his head, as he glances apprehensively at the door.*) Here! Take this! Quick! Don't let her see it! I want you to keep it in a safe place and never let anyone know you have it! It will be stolen if I keep it here! I know her! Will you promise?

HAZEL. But—what is it, Orin?

ORIN. I can't tell you. You mustn't ask me. And you must promise never to open it—unless something happens to me.

HAZEL (*frightened by his tone*). What do you mean?

ORIN. I mean if I should die—or—but this is the most important, if she tries to marry Peter—the day before the wedding—I want you to make Peter read what's inside.

HAZEL. You don't want her to marry Peter?

ORIN. No! She can't have happiness! She's got to be punished! (*Suddenly taking her hand—excitedly.*) And listen, Hazel! You mustn't love me any more. The only love I can know now is the love of guilt for guilt which breeds more guilt—until you get so deep at the bottom of hell there is no lower you can sink and you rest there in peace! (*He laughs harshly and turns away from her.*)

HAZEL. Orin! Don't talk like that! (*Then conquering her horror—resolutely tender and soothing.*) Ssshh! Poor boy! Come here to me. (*He comes to her. She puts an arm round him.*) Listen. I know something is worrying you—and I don't want to seem prying—but I've had such a strong feeling at times that it would relieve your mind if you could tell me what it is. Haven't you thought that, Orin?

ORIN (*longingly*). Yes! Yes! I want to confess to your purity! I want to be forgiven! (*Then checking himself abruptly as he is about to speak—dully.*) No. I can't. Don't ask me. I love her.

HAZEL. But, you silly boy, Vinnie told Peter herself what it is and told him to tell me.

ORIN (*staring at her wildly*). What did she tell?

HAZEL. About your having a quarrel with your poor mother that night before she—and how you've brooded over it until you blame yourself for her death.

ORIN (*harshly*). I see! So in case I did tell you—oh, she's cunning! But not cunning enough this time! (*Vindictively.*) You remember what I've given you, Hazel, and you do exactly what I said with it. (*Then with desperate pleading.*) For God's sake, Hazel, if you love me help me to get away from here—or something terrible will happen!

HAZEL. That's just what I want to do! You come over to-morrow and stay with us.

ORIN (*bitterly*). Do you suppose for a moment she'll ever let me go?

HAZEL. But haven't you a right to do as you want to?

ORIN (*furtively*). I could sneak out when she wasn't looking—and then you could hide me and when she came for me tell her I wasn't there.

HAZEL (*indignantly*). I won't do any such thing! I don't tell lies, Orin! (*Then scornfully.*) How can you be so scared of Vinnie?

ORIN (*hearing a noise from the hall—hastily*). Ssshh! She's coming! Don't let her see what I gave you. And go home right away and lock it up!

(*He tiptoes away as if he were afraid of being found close to her and sits on the sofa at right, adopting a suspiciously careless attitude. Hazel looks self-conscious and stiff. Lavinia appears in the doorway and gives a start as she sees Hazel and Orin are alone. She quickly senses something in the atmosphere and glances sharply from one to the other as she comes into the room.)*

LAVINIA (*to Hazel, forcing a casual air*). I'm sorry I've been so long.

HAZEL. I didn't mind waiting.

LAVINIA (*sitting down on the chair at centre*). Where's Peter?

HAZEL. He had to go to a Council meeting. He's coming back.

LAVINIA (*uneasiness creeping into her tone*). Has he been gone long?

HAZEL. Not very long.

LAVINIA (*turning to Orin—sharply*). I thought you were in the study.

ORIN (*sensing her uneasiness—mockingly*). I finished what I was working on.

LAVINIA. You finished——? (*She glances sharply at Hazel—forcing a joking tone.*) My, but you two look mysterious! What have you been up to?

HAZEL (*trying to force a laugh*). Why, Vinnie? What makes you think——?

LAVINIA. You're hiding something.

(*Hazel gives a start and instinctively moves the hand with the envelope farther behind her back. Lavinia notices this. So does Orin who uneasily comes to Hazel's rescue.*)

ORIN. We're not hiding anything. Hazel has invited me over to their house to stay for a while—and I'm going.

HAZEL (*backing him up resolutely*). Yes. Orin is coming to-morrow.

LAVINIA (*alarmed and resentful—coldly*). It's kind of you. I know you mean it for the best. But he can't go.

HAZEL (*sharply*). Why not?

LAVINIA. I don't care to discuss it, Hazel. You ought to know——

HAZEL (*angrily*). I don't know! Orin is of age and can go where he pleases!

ORIN. Let her talk as she likes, Hazel. I'll have the upper hand for a change, from now on! (*Lavinia looks at him, frightened by the triumphant satisfaction in his voice.*)

HAZEL (*anxious to score her point and keep Orin's mind on it*). I should think you'd be glad. It will be the best thing in the world for him.

LAVINIA (*turns on her—angrily*). I'll ask you to please mind your own business, Hazel!

HAZEL (*springs to her feet, in her anger forgetting to hide the envelope which she now holds openly in her hand*). It is my business! I love Orin better than you do! I don't think you love him at all, the way you've been acting!

ORIN (*sees the envelope in plain sight and calls to her warningly*). Hazel! (*She catches his eye and hastily puts her hand behind her. Lavinia sees the movement but doesn't for a moment realize the meaning of it. Orin goes on warningly.*) You said you had to go home early. I don't want to remind you but——

HAZEL (*hastily*). Yes, I really must. (*Starting to go, trying to keep the envelope hidden, aware that Lavinia is watching her suspiciously—defiantly to Orin.*) We'll expect you to-morrow, and have your room ready. (*Then to Lavinia—coldly.*) After the way you've insulted me, Vinnie, I hope you realize there's no more question of any friendship between us. (*She tries awkwardly to sidle towards the door.*)

LAVINIA (*suddenly gets between her and the door—with angry accusation*). What are you hiding behind your back? (*Hazel flushes guiltily, but refusing to lie, says nothing. Lavinia turns on Orin.*) Have you given her what you've written? (*As he hesitates—violently.*) Answer me!

ORIN. That's my business! What if I have?

LAVINIA. You—you traitor! You coward! (*Fiercely to Hazel.*) Give it to me! Do you hear?

HAZEL. Vinnie! How dare you talk in that way to me! (*She tries to go but Lavinia keeps directly between her and the door.*)

LAVINIA. You shan't leave here until——! (*Then breaking down and pleading.*) Orin! Think what you're doing! Tell her to give it to me!

ORIN. No!

LAVINIA (*goes and puts her arms around him—*

beseechingly as he avoids her eyes). Think sanely for a moment! You can't do this! You're a Mannon!

ORIN (*harshly*). It's because I'm one!

LAVINIA. For Mother's sake, you can't! You loved her!

ORIN. A lot she cared! Don't call on her!

LAVINIA (*desperately*). For my sake, then! You know I love you! Make Hazel give that up and I'll do anything—anything you want me to!

ORIN (*stares into her eyes, bending his head until his face is close to hers—with morbid intensity*). You mean that?

LAVINIA (*shrinking back from him—falteringly*). Yes.

ORIN (*laughs with a crazy triumph—checks this abruptly—and goes to Hazel who has been standing, bewildered, not understanding what is behind their talk but sensing something sinister, and terribly frightened. Orin speaks curtly, his eyes fixed on Lavinia*). Let me have it, Hazel.

HAZEL (*hands him the envelope—in a trembling voice*). I'll go home. I suppose—we can't expect you to-morrow—now.

ORIN. No. Forget me. The Orin you loved was killed in the war. (*With a twisted smile.*) Remember only that dead hero and not his rotting ghost! Good-bye! (*Then harshly.*) Please go! (*Hazel begins to sob and hurries blindly from the room. Orin comes back to Lavinia who remains kneeling by the chair. He puts the envelope in her hand—harshly.*) Here! You realize the promise you made means giving up Peter? And never seeing him again?

LAVINIA (*tensely*). Yes.

ORIN. And I suppose you think that's all it means, that I'll be content with a promise I've forced out of you, which you'll always be plotting to break? Oh, no! I'm not such a fool! I've got to be sure—— (*She doesn't reply or look at him. He stares at her and slowly a distorted look of desire comes over his face.*) You said you would do anything for me. That's a large promise, Vinnie—anything!

LAVINIA (*shrinking from him*). What do you mean? What terrible thing have you been thinking lately—behind all your crazy talk? No, I don't want to know! Orin! Why do you look at me like that?

ORIN. You don't seem to feel all you mean to me now—all you have made yourself mean—since we murdered Mother!

LAVINIA. Orin!

ORIN. I love you now with all the guilt in me—the guilt we share! Perhaps I love you too much, Vinnie!

LAVINIA. You don't know what you're saying!

ORIN. There are times now when you don't seem to be my sister, nor Mother, but some stranger with the same beautiful hair—— (*He touches her hair caressingly. She pulls violently away. He laughs wildly.*) Perhaps you're Marie Brantôme, eh? And you say there are no ghosts in this house?

LAVINIA (*staring at him with fascinated horror*). For God's sake——! No! You're insane! You can't mean——!

ORIN. How else can I be sure you won't leave me? You would never dare leave me—then! You would feel as guilty then as I do! You would be as damned as I am! (*Then with sudden anger as he sees the growing horrified repulsion on her face.*) Damn you, don't you see I must find some certainty some way or go mad? You don't want me to go mad, do you? I would talk too much! I would confess! (*Then as if the word stirred something within him his tone instantly changes to one of passionate pleading.*) Vinnie! For the love of God, let's go now and confess and pay the penalty for Mother's murder, and find peace together!

LAVINIA (*tempted and tortured, in a longing whisper*). Peace! (*Then summoning her will, springs to her feet wildly.*) No! You coward! There is nothing to confess! There was only justice!

ORIN (*turns and addresses the portraits on the wall with a crazy mockery*). You hear her? You'll find Lavinia Mannon harder to break than me! You'll have to haunt and hound her for a lifetime!

LAVINIA (*her control snapping—turning on him now in a burst of frantic hatred and rage*). I hate you! I wish you were dead! You're too vile to live! You'd kill yourself if you weren't a coward!

ORIN (*starts back as if he'd been struck, the tortured, mad look on his face changing to a stricken, terrified expression*). Vinnie!

LAVINIA. I mean it! I mean it! (*She breaks down and sobs hysterically.*)

ORIN (*in a pitiful, pleading whisper*). Vinnie! (*He stares at her with the lost, stricken expression for a moment more—then the obsessed wild look returns to his eyes—with harsh mockery.*) Another act of justice, eh? You want to drive me to suicide as I drove Mother! An eye for an eye, is that it? But—— (*He stops abruptly and stares before him, as if this idea were suddenly taking hold of his tortured imagination, and speaks as if hypnotized.*) Yes! That would be justice—now you are Mother! She is speaking now through you! (*More and more hypnotized by this train of thought.*) Yes! It's the way to peace—to find her again—my lost island—Death is an Island of Peace, too—Mother will be waiting for me there—— (*With excited eagerness now, speaking to the dead.*) Mother! Do you know what I'll do then? I'll get on my knees and ask your forgiveness—and say—— (*His mouth grows convulsed, as if he were retching up poison.*) I'll say, I'm glad you found love, Mother! I'll wish you happiness—you and Adam! (*He laughs exultantly.*) You've heard me! You're here in the house now! You're calling me! You're waiting to take me home! (*He turns and strides towards the door.*)

LAVINIA (*who has raised her head and has been staring at him with dread during the latter part of his talk—torn by remorse, runs after him and throws her arms around him*). No, Orin! No!

ORIN (*pushes her away—with a rough brotherly irritation*). Get out of my way, can't you? Mother's waiting! (*He gets to the door. Then he turns back and says sharply:*) Ssshh! Here's Peter! Shut up, now! (*He steps back in the room as Peter appears in the doorway.*)

PETER. Excuse my coming straight in. The door was open. Where's Hazel?

ORIN (*with unnatural casualness*). Gone home. (*Then with a quick, meaning, mocking glance at Lavinia.*) I'm just going in the study to clean my pistol. Darn thing's got so rusty. Glad you came now, Peter. You can keep Vinnie company. (*He turns and goes out the door. Peter stares after him, puzzled.*)

LAVINIA (*with a stifled cry*). Orin! (*There is no answer but the sound of the study door being shut. She starts to run after him, stops herself, then throws herself into Peter's arms, as if for protection against herself, and begins to talk volubly to drown her thoughts.*) Hold me close, Peter! Nothing matters but love, does it? That must come first! No price is too great, is it? Oh, for peace! One must have peace—one is too weak to forget—no one has the right to keep anyone from peace! (*She makes a motion to cover her ears with her hands.*)

PETER (*alarmed by her hectic excitement*). He's a darned fool to monkey with a pistol—in his state. Shall I get it away from him?

LAVINIA (*holding him tighter—volubly*). Oh, won't it be wonderful, Peter—once we're married and have a home with a garden and trees! We'll be so happy! I love everything that grows simply—up towards the sun—everything that's straight and strong! I hate what's warped and twists and eats into itself and dies for a lifetime in shadow. (*Then her voice rising as if it were about to break hysterically—again with the instinctive movement to cover her ears.*) I can't bear waiting—waiting and waiting and waiting——! (*There is a muffled shot from the study across the hall.*)

PETER (*breaking from her and running for the door*). Good God! What's that? (*He rushes into the hall.*)

LAVINIA (*sags weakly and supports herself against the table—in a faint, trembling voice*). Orin! Forgive me! (*She controls herself with a terrible effort of will. Her mouth congeals into a frozen line. Mechanically she hides the sealed envelope in a drawer of the table and locks the drawer.*) I've got to go in—— (*She turns to go and her eyes catch the eyes of the Mannons in the portraits fixed accusingly on her—defiantly.*) Why do you look at me like that? Wasn't it the only way to keep your secret, too? But I've finished with you for ever now, do you hear? I'm Mother's daughter—not one of you! I'll live in spite of you!

(*She squares her shoulders, with a return of the abrupt military movement copied from her father which she had of old—as if by the very act of disowning the Mannons she had returned to the fold—and marches stiffly from the room.*)

Curtain

ACT FOUR

SCENE. *Same as Act One, Scene One—exterior of the house. It is in the late afternoon of a day three days later. The Mannon house has much the same appearance as it had in the first act of "Homecoming." Soft golden sunlight shimmers in a luminous mist on the Greek temple portico, intensifying the whiteness of the columns, the deep green of the shutters, the green of the shrubbery, the black and green of the pines. The columns cast black bars of shadow on the grey stone wall behind them. The shutters are all fastened back, the windows open. On the ground floor, the upper part of the windows, raised from the bottom, reflect the sun in a smouldering stare, as of brooding, revengeful eyes.*

Seth appears walking slowly up the drive from right front. He has a pair of grass clippers and potters along pretending to trim the edge of the lawn along the drive. But in reality he is merely killing time, chewing tobacco, and singing mournfully to himself, in his aged, plaintive wraith of a once good baritone, the chanty "Shenandoah":

SETH.

"*Oh, Shenandoah, I long to hear you*
A-way, my rolling river.
Oh, Shenandoah, I can't get near you
Way—ay, I'm bound away
Across the wide Missouri.
"*Oh, Shenandoah, I love your daughter*
A-way, you rolling river."

SETH (*stops singing and stands peering off left towards the flower garden—shakes his head and mutters to himself*). There she be pickin' my flowers agin. Like her Maw used to—on'y wuss. She's got every room in the house full of 'em a'ready. Durn it, I hoped she'd stop that once the funeral was over. There won't be a one left in my garden! (*He looks away and begins pottering about again, and mutters grimly.*) A durn queer thin' fur a sodger to kill himself cleanin' his gun, folks is sayin'. They'll fight purty shy of her now. A Mannon has come to mean sudden death to 'em. (*Then with a grim pride.*) But Vinnie's able fur 'em. They'll never git her to show nothin'. Clean Mannon strain!

(*Lavinia enters from the left. The three days that have intervened have effected a remarkable change in her. Her body, dressed in deep mourning, again appears flat-chested and thin. The Mannon mask-semblance of her face appears intensified now. It is deeply lined, haggard with sleeplessness and strain, congealed into a stony, emotionless expression. Her lips are bloodless, drawn taut in a grim line. She is carrying a large bunch of flowers. She holds them out to Seth and speaks in a strange, empty voice.*)

LAVINIA. Take these, Seth, and give them to Hannah. Tell her to arrange them indoors. I want the house to be full of flowers. Peter is coming, and I want everything to be pretty and cheerful.

(*She goes and sits at the top of the steps, bolt upright, her arms held stiffly to her sides, her legs and feet pressed together, and stares back into the sun-glare with unblinking, frozen, defiant eyes.*)

SETH (*stands holding the flowers and regarding her anxiously*). I seed you settin' out here on the steps when I got up at five this mornin'—and every mornin' since Orin—— Ain't you been gittin' no sleep? (*She stares before her as if she had not heard him. He goes on coaxingly.*) How'd you like if I hauled one of them sofas out fur you to lie on, Vinnie? Mebbe you could take a couple o' winks an' it'd do you good.

LAVINIA. No, thank you, Seth. I'm waiting for Peter. (*Then after a pause, curiously.*) Why didn't you tell me to go in the house and lie down? (*Seth pretends not to hear the question, avoiding her eyes.*) You understand, don't you? You've been with us Mannons so long! You know there's no rest in this house which Grandfather built as a temple of Hate and Death!

SETH (*blurts out*). Don't you try to live here, Vinnie! You marry Peter and git clear!

LAVINIA. I'm going to marry him! And I'm going away with him and will forget this house, and all that ever happened in it!

SETH. That's talkin', Vinnie!

LAVINIA. I'll close it up and leave it in the sun and rain to die. The portraits of the Mannons will rot on the walls and the ghosts will fade back into death. And the Mannons will be forgotten. I'm the last and I won't be one long. I'll be Mrs. Peter Niles. Then they're finished! Thank God!

(*She leans back in the sunlight and closes her eyes. Seth stares at her again, shakes his head and spits. Then he hears something and peers down the drive, off left.*)

SETH. Vinnie, here's Hazel comin'.

LAVINIA (*jerks up stiffly with a look of alarm*). Hazel? What does she want? (*She springs up as if she were going to run in the house, then stands her ground on the top of the steps—her voice hardening.*) Seth, you go on with your work, please!

SETH. Ayeh. (*He moves slowly off behind the lilacs as Hazel enters from left front—calling back.*) Evenin', Hazel.

HAZEL. Good evening, Seth.

(*She stops short and stares at Lavinia. Lavinia's eyes are hard and defiant as she stares back. Hazel is dressed in mourning. Her face is sad and pale, her eyes show evidence of much weeping, but there is an air of stubborn resolution about her as she makes up her mind and walks to the foot of the steps.*)

LAVINIA. What do you want? I've got a lot to attend to.

HAZEL (*quietly*). It won't take me long to say what I've come to say, Vinnie. (*Suddenly she bursts out.*) It's a lie about Orin killing himself by accident! I know it is! He meant to!

LAVINIA. You better be careful what you say. I can prove what happened. Peter was here——

HAZEL. I don't care what anyone says!

LAVINIA. I should think you'd be the last one to accuse Orin——

HAZEL. I'm not accusing him! Don't you dare say that! I'm accusing you! You drove him to it! Oh, I know I can't prove it—any more than I can prove a lot of things Orin hinted at! But I know terrible things must have happened—and that you're to blame for them, somehow!

LAVINIA (*concealing a start of fear—changing to a forced reproachful tone*). What would Orin think of you coming here the day of his funeral to accuse me of the sorrow that's afflicted our family?

HAZEL (*feeling guilty and at the same time defiant and sure she is right*). All right, Vinnie. I won't say anything more. But I know there's something—and so do you—something that was driving Orin crazy—— (*She breaks down and sobs.*) Poor Orin!

LAVINIA (*stares straight before her. Her lips twitch. In a stifled voice between her clenched teeth*). Don't—do that!

HAZEL (*controlling herself—after a pause*). I'm sorry. I didn't come to talk about Orin.

LAVINIA (*uneasily*). What did you come for?

HAZEL. About Peter.

LAVINIA (*as if this were something she had been dreading—harshly*). You leave Peter and me alone!

HAZEL. I won't! You're not going to marry Peter and ruin his life! (*Pleading now.*) You can't! Don't you see he could never be happy with you, that you'll only drag him into this terrible thing—whatever it is—and make him share it?

LAVINIA. There is no terrible thing!

HAZEL. I know Peter can't believe evil of anyone, but living alone with you, married, you couldn't hide it, he'd get to feel what I feel. You could never be happy because it would come between you! (*Pleading again.*) Oh, Vinnie, you've got to be fair to Peter! You've got to consider his happiness—if you really love him!

LAVINIA (*hoarsely*). I do love him!

HAZEL. It has started already—his being made unhappy through you!

LAVINIA. You're lying!

HAZEL. He quarrelled with Mother last night when she tried to talk to him—the first time he ever did such a thing! It isn't like Peter. You've changed him. He left home and went to the hotel to stay. He said he'd never speak to Mother or me again. He's always been such a wonderful son before—and brother. We three have been so happy. It's broken Mother's heart. All she does is sit and cry. (*Desperately.*) Oh, Vinnie, you can't do it! You will be punished if you do! Peter would get to hate you in the end!

LAVINIA. No!

HAZEL. Do you want to take the risk of driving Peter to do what Orin did? He might—if he ever discovered the truth!

LAVINIA (*violently*). What truth, you little fool! Discover what?

HAZEL (*accusingly*). I don't know—but you know! Look in your heart and ask your conscience before God if you ought to marry Peter!

LAVINIA (*desperately—at the end of her tether*). Yes! Before God! Before anything! (*Then glaring at her—with a burst of rage.*) You leave me alone—go away—or I'll get Orin's pistol and kill you! (*Her rage passes, leaving her weak and shaken. She goes to her chair and sinks on it.*)

HAZEL (*recoiling*). Oh! You are wicked! I believe you would——! Vinnie! What's made you like this?

LAVINIA. Go away!

HAZEL. Vinnie! (*Lavinia closes her eyes. Hazel stands staring at her. After a pause—in a trembling voice.*) All right. I'll go. All I can do is trust you. I know in your heart you can't be dead to all honour and justice—you, a Mannon! (*Lavinia gives a little bitter laugh without opening her eyes.*) At least you owe it to Peter to let him read what Orin had in that envelope. Orin asked me to make him read it before he married you. I've told Peter about that, Vinnie.

LAVINIA (*without opening her eyes—strangely, as if to herself*). The dead! Why can't the dead die!

HAZEL (*stares at her, frightened, not knowing what to do—looks around her uncertainly and sees someone coming from off left front—quickly*). Here he comes now. I'll go by the back. I don't want him to meet me. (*She starts to go but stops by the clump of lilacs—pityingly.*) I know you're suffering, Vinnie—and I know your conscience will make you do what's right—and God will forgive you. (*She goes quickly behind the lilacs and around the house to the rear.*)

LAVINIA (*looks after her and calls defiantly*). I'm not asking God or anybody for forgiveness. I forgive myself! (*She leans back and closes her eyes again—bitterly.*) I hope there is a hell for the good somewhere!

(*Peter enters from the left front. He looks haggard and tormented. He walks slowly, his eyes on the ground—then sees Lavinia and immediately makes an effort to pull himself together and appear cheerful.*)

PETER. Hello, Vinnie. (*He sits on the edge of the portico beside her. She still keeps her eyes closed, as if afraid to open them. He looks at her anxiously.*) You look terribly worn out. Haven't you slept? (*He pats her hand with awkward tenderness. Her mouth twitches and draws down at the corners as she stifles a sob. He goes on comfortingly.*) You've had an awfully hard time of it, but never mind, we'll be married soon.

LAVINIA (*without opening her eyes—longingly*). You'll love me and keep me from remembering?

PETER. You bet I will! And the first thing is to get you away from this darned house! I may be a fool but I'm beginning to feel superstitious about it myself.

LAVINIA (*without opening her eyes—strangely*). Yes. Love can't live in it. We'll go away and leave it alone to die—and we'll forget the dead.

PETER (*a bitter, resentful note coming into his voice*). We can't move too far away to suit me! I hate this damned town now and everyone in it!

LAVINIA (*startled, opens her eyes and looks at him*). I never heard you talk in that way before, Peter—bitter!

PETER (*avoiding her eyes*). Some things would make anyone bitter!

LAVINIA. You've quarrelled with your mother and Hazel—on account of me—is that it?

PETER. How did you know?

LAVINIA. Hazel was here just now.

PETER. She told you? The darned fool! What did she do that for?

LAVINIA. She doesn't want me to marry you.

PETER (*angrily*). The little sneak! What right has she——? (*Then a bit uneasily—forcing a smile.*) Well, you won't pay any attention to her, I hope.

LAVINIA (*more as if she were answering some voice in herself than him—stiffening in her chair—defiantly*). No!

PETER. She and Mother suddenly got a lot of crazy notions in their heads. But they'll get over them.

LAVINIA (*staring at him searchingly—uneasily*). Supposing they don't?

PETER. They will after we are married—or I've done with them!

LAVINIA (*a pause. Then she takes his face in her hands and turns it to hers*). Peter! Let me look at you! You're suffering! Your eyes have a

AH! WILDERNESS

TO GEORGE JEAN NATHAN
Who also, once upon a time, in peg-top trousers went the pace that kills along the road to ruin

Characters

NAT MILLER, *owner of the "Evening Globe"*
ESSIE, *his wife*
ARTHUR, RICHARD, MILDRED, TOMMY — *their children*
SID DAVIS, *Essie's brother*
LILY MILLER, *Nat's sister*
DAVID MCCOMBER
MURIEL MCCOMBER, *his daughter*
WINT SELBY, *a classmate of Arthur's at Yale*
BELLE
NORAH
BARTENDER
SALESMAN

Scenes

ACT ONE

Sitting-room of the Miller home in a large small-town in Connecticut. Early morning, July 4th, 1906.

ACT TWO

Dining-room of the Miller home. Evening of the same day.

ACT THREE

SCENE ONE Back room of a bar in a small hotel. Ten o'clock the same night.

SCENE TWO Same as Act One. The sitting-room of the Miller home. A little after eleven o'clock the same night.

ACT FOUR

SCENE ONE The Miller sitting-room again. About one o'clock the following afternoon.

SCENE TWO A strip of beach along the harbour. About nine o'clock that night.

SCENE THREE Same as Scene One. The sitting-room. About ten o'clock the same night.

ACT ONE

SCENE. *Sitting-room of the Miller home in a large small-town in Connecticut—about 7.30 in the morning of July 4th, 1906.*

The room is fairly large, homely looking and cheerful in the morning sunlight, furnished with scrupulous medium-priced tastelessness of the period. Beneath the two windows at left, front, a sofa with silk and satin cushions stands against the wall. At rear of sofa, a bookcase with glass doors, filled with cheap sets, extends along the remaining length of wall. In the rear wall, left, is a double doorway with sliding doors and portières, leading into a dark, windowless, back parlour. At right of this doorway, another bookcase, this time a small, open one, crammed with boys' and girls' books and the best-selling novels of many past years—books the family really have read. To the right of this bookcase is the mate of the double doorway at its left, with sliding doors and portières, this one leading to a well-lighted front parlour. In the right wall, rear, a screen door opens on a porch. Farther forward in this wall are two windows, with a writing-desk and a chair between them. At centre is a big, round table with a green-shaded reading-lamp, the cord of the lamp running up to one of five sockets in the chandelier above. Five chairs are grouped about the table—three rockers at left, right, and right rear of it, two armchairs at rear and left rear. A medium-priced, inoffensive rug covers most of the floor. The walls are papered white with a cheerful, ugly blue design.

Voices are heard in a conversational tone from the dining-room beyond the back parlour, where the family are just finishing breakfast. Then Mrs. Miller's voice, raised commandingly, "Tommy! Come back here and finish your milk!" *At the same moment Tommy appears in the doorway from the back parlour—a chubby, sunburnt boy of eleven with dark eyes, blond hair wetted and plastered down in a parting, and a shiny, good-natured face, a rim of milk visible about his lips. Bursting with bottled-up energy and a longing to get started on the Fourth, he nevertheless has hesitated obediently at his mother's call.*

TOMMY (*calls back pleadingly*). Aw, I'm full, Ma. And I said excuse me and you said all right. (*His Father's voice is heard speaking to his mother. Then she calls:* "All right, Tommy," *and Tommy asks eagerly.*) Can I go out now?

MOTHER'S VOICE (*correctingly*). May I!

TOMMY (*fidgeting, but obediently*). May I, Ma?

MOTHER'S VOICE. Yes. (*Tommy jumps for the screen door to the porch at right like a sprinter released by the starting-shot.*)

FATHER'S VOICE (*shouts after him*). But you set off your crackers away from the house, remember! (*But Tommy is already through the screen door, which he leaves open behind him.*)

(*A moment later the family appear from the back parlour, coming from the dining-room. First are Mildred and Arthur. Mildred is fifteen, tall and slender, with big, irregular features, resembling her father to the complete effacing of any pretence at prettiness. But her big, grey eyes are beautiful; she has vivacity and a fetching smile, and everyone thinks of her as an attractive girl. She is dressed in blouse and skirt in the fashion of the period.*

Arthur, the eldest of the Miller children who are still living at home, is nineteen. He is tall, heavy, barrel-chested and muscular, the type of football linesman of that period, with a square, stolid face, small blue eyes and thick sandy hair. His manner is solemnly collegiate. He is dressed in the latest college fashion of that day, which has receded a bit from the extreme of preceding years, but still runs to padded shoulders and trousers half pegged at the top, and so small at their wide-cuffed bottoms that they cannot be taken off with shoes on.)

MILDRED (*as they appear—inquisitively*). Where are you going to-day, Art?

ARTHUR (*with superior dignity*). That's my business. (*He ostentatiously takes from his pocket a tobacco pouch with a big* "Y" *and class numerals stamped on it, and a heavy bulldog briar pipe with silver* "Y" *and numerals, and starts filling the pipe.*)

MILDRED (*teasingly*). Bet I know, just the same! Want me to tell you her initials? E.R.! (*She laughs.*)

(*Arthur, pleased by this insinuation at his lady-killing activities, yet finds it beneath his dignity to reply. He goes to the table, lights his pipe and picks up the local morning paper, and slouches back into the armchair at left rear of table, beginning to whistle* "Oh, Waltz Me Around Again, Willie" *as he scans the headlines. Mildred sits on the sofa at left, front.*

Meanwhile, their mother and their Aunt Lily, their father's sister, have appeared, following them from the back parlour. Mrs. Miller is around fifty, a short, stout woman with fading light-brown hair sprinkled with grey, who must have been decidedly pretty as a girl in a round-faced, cute, small-featured, wide-eyed fashion. She has big brown eyes, soft and maternal—a bustling, mother-of-a-family manner. She is dressed in blouse and skirt.

Lily Miller, her sister-in-law, is forty-two, tall, dark and thin. She conforms outwardly to the conventional type of old-maid school teacher, even to wearing glasses. But behind the glasses her grey eyes are gentle and tired, and her whole atmosphere is one of shy kindliness. Her voice presents the greatest contrast to her appearance—soft and full of sweetness. She, also, is dressed in a blouse and skirt.)

MRS. MILLER (*as they appear*). Getting milk down him is like—— (*Suddenly she is aware of the screen door standing half open.*) Goodness, look at that door he's left open! The house will be alive with flies! (*Rushing out to shut it.*) I've told him again and again—and that's all the good it does! It's just a waste of breath! (*She slams the door shut.*)

LILY (*smiling*). Well, you can't expect a boy to remember to shut doors—on the Fourth of July. (*She goes diffidently to the straight-backed chair before the desk at right, front, leaving the comfortable chairs to the others.*)

MRS. MILLER. That's you all over, Lily—always making excuses for him. You'll have him spoiled to death in spite of me. (*She sinks in rocker at right of table.*) Phew, I'm hot, aren't you? This is going to be a scorcher. (*She picks up a magazine from the table and begins to rock, fanning herself.*)

(*Meanwhile, her husband and her brother have appeared from the back parlour, both smoking cigars. Nat Miller is in his late fifties, a tall, dark, spare man, a little stoop-shouldered, more than a little bald, dressed with an awkward attempt at sober respectability imposed upon an innate heedlessness of clothes. His long face has large, irregular, undistinguished features, but he has fine, shrewd, humorous grey eyes.*

Sid Davis, his brother-in-law, is forty-five, short and fat, bald-headed, with the Puckish face of a Peck's Bad Boy who has never grown up. He is dressed in what had once been a very natty loud light suit but is now a shapeless and faded nondescript in cut and colour.)

SID (*as they appear*). Oh, I like the job first rate, Nat. Waterbury's a nifty old town with the lid off, when you get to know the ropes. I rang in a joke in one of my stories that tickled the folks there pink. Waterwagon—Waterbury—Waterloo!

MILLER (*grinning*). Darn good!

SID (*pleased*). I thought it was pretty fair myself. (*Goes on a bit ruefully, as if oppressed by a secret sorrow.*) Yes, you can see life in Waterbury, all right—that is, if you're looking for life in Waterbury!

MRS. MILLER. What's that about Waterbury, Sid?

SID. I was saying it's all right in its way—but there's no place like home.

(*As if to punctuate this remark, there begins a series of bangs from just beyond the porch outside, as Tommy inaugurates his celebration by setting off a package of firecrackers. The assembled family jump in their chairs.*)

MRS. MILLER. That boy! (*She rushes to the screen door and out on the porch, calling:*) Tommy! You mind what your Pa told you! You take your crackers out in the back-yard, you hear me!

ARTHUR (*frowning scornfully*). Fresh kid! He did it on purpose to scare us.

MILLER (*grinning through his annoyance*). Darned youngster! He'll have the house afire before the day's out.

SID (*grins and sings*).

"Dunno what ter call 'im
But he's mighty like a Rose—velt."

(*They all laugh.*)

LILY. Sid, you Crazy!

(*Sid beams at her. Mrs. Miller comes back from the porch, still fuming.*)

MRS. MILLER. Well, I've made him go out back at last. Now we'll have a little peace.

(*As if to contradict this, the bang of firecrackers and torpedoes begins from the rear of the house, left, and continues at intervals throughout the scene, not nearly so loud as the first explosion, but sufficiently emphatic to form a disturbing punctuation to the conversation.*)

MILLER. Well, what's on the tappee for all of you to-day? Sid, you're coming to the Sachem Club picnic with me, of course.

SID (*a bit embarrassedly*). You bet. I mean I'd like to, Nat—that is, if——

MRS. MILLER (*regarding her brother with smiling suspicion*). Hmm! I know what that Sachem Club picnics always meant!

LILY (*breaks in in a forced joking tone that conceals a deep earnestness*). No, not this time, Essie. Sid's a reformed character since he's been on the paper in Waterbury. At least, that's what he swore to me last night.

SID (*avoiding her eyes, humiliated—joking it off*). Pure as the driven snow, that's me. They're running me for president of the W.C.T.U.

(*They all laugh.*)

MRS. MILLER. Sid, you're a caution. You turn everything into a joke. But you be careful, you hear? We're going to have dinner in the evening to-night, you know—the best shore dinner you ever tasted and I don't want you coming home—well, not able to appreciate it.

LILY. Oh, I know he'll be careful to-day. Won't you, Sid?

SID (*more embarrassed than ever—joking it off melodramatically*). Lily, I swear to you if any man offers me a drink, I'll kill him—that is, if he changes his mind!

(*They all laugh except Lily, who bites her lip and stiffens.*)

MRS. MILLER. No use talking to him, Lily. You ought to know better by this time. We can only hope for the best.

MILLER. Now, you women stop picking on Sid. It's the Fourth of July and even a downtrodden newspaperman has a right to enjoy himself when he's on his holiday.

MRS. MILLER. I wasn't thinking only of Sid.

MILLER (*with a wink at the others*). What, are you insinuating I ever—— ?

MRS. MILLER. Well, to do you justice, no, not what you'd really call—— But I've known you to come back from this darned Sachem Club picnic—— Well, I didn't need any little bird to whisper that you'd been some place besides to the well! (*She smiles good-naturedly. Miller chuckles.*)

SID (*after a furtive glance at the stiff and silent Lily—changes the subject abruptly by turning to Arthur*). How are you spending the festive Fourth, Boola-Boola?

(*Arthur stiffens dignifiedly.*)

MILDRED (*teasingly*). I can tell you, if he won't.

MRS. MILLER (*smiling*). Off to the Rands', I suppose.

ARTHUR (*with dignity*). I and Bert Turner are taking Elsie and Ethel Rand canoeing. We're going to have a picnic lunch on Strawberry Island. And this evening I'm staying at the Rands' for dinner.

MILLER. You're accounted for, then. How about you, Mid?

MILDRED. I'm going to the beach to Anne Culver's.

ARTHUR (*sarcastically*). Of course, there won't be any boys present! Johnny Dodd, for example?

MILDRED (*giggles—then with a coquettish toss of her head*). Pooh! What do I care for him? He's not the only pebble on the beach.

MILLER. Stop your everlasting teasing, you two. How about you and Lily, Essie?

MRS. MILLER. I don't know. I haven't made any plans. Have you, Lily?

LILY (*quietly*). No. Anything you want to do.

MRS. MILLER. Well, I thought we'd just sit around and rest and talk.

MILLER. You can gossip any day. This is the Fourth. Now, I've got a better suggestion than that. What do you say to an automobile ride? I'll get out the Buick and we'll drive around town and out to the lighthouse and back. Then Sid and I will let you off here, or anywhere you say, and we'll go on to the picnic.

MRS. MILLER. I'd love it. Wouldn't you, Lily?

LILY. It would be nice.

MILLER. Then, that's all settled.

SID (*embarrassedly*). Lily, want to come with me to the fireworks display at the beach to-night?

MRS. MILLER. That's right, Sid. You take her out. Poor Lily never has any fun, always sitting home with me.

LILY (*flustered and grateful*). I—I'd like to, Sid, thank you. (*Then an apprehensive look comes over her face.*) Only not if you come home—you know.

SID (*again embarrassed and humiliated—again joking it off, solemnly*). Evil-minded, I'm afraid, Nat. I hate to say it of your sister.

(*They all laugh. Even Lily cannot suppress a smile.*)

ARTHUR (*with heavy jocularity*). Listen, Uncle Sid. Don't let me catch you and Aunt Lily spooning on a bench to-night—or it'll be my duty to call a cop!

(*Sid and Lily both look painfully embarrassed at this, and the joke falls flat, except for Mildred who can't restrain a giggle at the thought of these two ancients spooning.*)

MRS. MILLER (*rebukingly*). Arthur!

MILLER (*dryly*). That'll do you. Your education in kicking a football around Yale seems to have blunted your sense of humour.

MRS. MILLER (*suddenly—startledly*). But where's Richard? We're forgetting all about him. Why, where is that boy? I thought he came in with us from breakfast.

MILDRED. I'll bet he's off somewhere writing a poem to Muriel McComber, the silly! Or pretending to write one. I think he just copies——

ARTHUR (*looking back toward the dining-room*). He's still in the dining-room, reading a book. (*Turning back—scornfully.*) Gosh, he's always reading now. It's not my idea of having a good time in vacation.

MILLER (*caustically*). He read his school books, too, strange as that may seem to you. That's why he came out top of his class. I'm hoping before you leave New Haven they'll find time to teach you reading is a good habit.

MRS. MILLER (*sharply*). That reminds me, Nat. I've been meaning to speak to you about those awful books Richard is reading. You've got to give him a good talking to—— (*She gets up from her chair.*) I'll go up and get them right now. I found them where he'd hid them on the shelf in his wardrobe. You just wait till you see what——

(*She bustles off, rear right, through the front parlour.*)

MILLER (*plainly not relishing whatever is coming—to Sid, grumblingly*). Seems to me she might wait until the Fourth is over before bringing up—— (*Then with a grin.*) I know there's nothing to it, anyway. When I think of the books I used to sneak off and read when I was a kid.

SID. Me, too. I suppose Dick is deep in Nick Carter or Old Cap Collier.

MILLER. No, he passed that period long ago. Poetry's his red meat nowadays, I think—love poetry—and socialism, too, I suspect, from some dire declarations he's made. (*Then briskly.*) Well, might as well get him on the carpet. (*He calls.*) Richard. (*No answer—louder.*) Richard. (*No answer—then in a bellow.*) Richard!

ARTHUR (*shouting*). Hey, Dick, wake up! Pa's calling you.

RICHARD'S VOICE (*from the dining-room*). All right. I'm coming.

MILLER. Darn him! When he gets his nose in a book, the house could fall down and he'd never——

(*Richard appears in the doorway from the back parlour, the book he has been reading in one hand, a finger marking his place. He looks a bit startled still, reluctantly called back to earth from another world.*

He is going on seventeen, just out of high school. In appearance he is a perfect blend of father and mother, so much so that each is convinced he is the image of the other. He has his mother's light-brown hair, his father's grey eyes; his features are neither large nor small; he is of medium height, neither fat nor thin. One would not call him a handsome boy; neither is he homely. But he is definitely different from both of his parents, too. There is something of extreme sensitiveness added—a restless, apprehensive, defiant, shy, dreamy self-conscious intelligence about him. In manner he is alternately plain simple boy and a posy actor solemnly playing a rôle. He is dressed in prep. school reflection of the college style of Arthur.)

RICHARD. Did you want me, Pa?

MILLER. I'd hoped I'd made that plain. Come and sit down a while. (*He points to the rocking chair at the right of table near his.*)

RICHARD (*coming forward—seizing on the opportunity to play up his preoccupation—with apologetic superiority*). I didn't hear you, Pa. I was off in another world.

(*Mildred slyly shoves her foot out so that he trips over it, almost falling. She laughs gleefully. So does Arthur.*)

ARTHUR. Good for you, Mid! That'll wake him up!

RICHARD (*grins sheepishly—all boy now*). Darn you, Mid! I'll show you!

(*He pushes her back on the sofa and tickles her with his free hand, still holding the book in the other. She shrieks.*)

ARTHUR. Give it to her, Dick!

MILLER. That's enough, now. No more roughhouse. You sit down here, Richard.

(*Richard obediently takes the chair at right of table, opposite his father.*)

What were you planning to do with yourself to-day? Going out to the beach with Mildred?

RICHARD (*scornfully superior*). That silly skirt party! I should say not!

MILDRED. He's not coming because Muriel isn't. I'll bet he's got a date with her somewheres.

RICHARD (*flushing bashfully*). You shut up! (*Then to his father.*) I thought I'd just stay home, Pa—this morning, anyway.

MILLER. Help Tommy set off firecrackers, eh?

RICHARD (*drawing himself up—with dignity*). I should say not. (*Then frowning portentously.*) I don't believe in this silly celebrating the Fourth of July—all this lying talk about liberty—when there is no liberty!

MILLER (*a twinkle in his eye*). Hmm.

RICHARD (*getting warmed up*). The land of the free and the home of the brave! Home of the slave is what they ought to call it—the wage slave ground under the heel of the capitalist class, starving, crying for bread for his children, and all he gets is a stone! The Fourth of July is a stupid farce!

MILLER (*putting a hand to his mouth to conceal a grin*). Hmm. Them are mighty strong words. You'd better not repeat such sentiments outside the bosom of the family or they'll have you in jail.

SID. And throw away the key.

RICHARD (*darkly*). Let them put me in jail. But how about the freedom of speech in the Constitution, then? That must be a farce, too. (*Then he adds grimly.*) No, you can celebrate your Fourth of July. I'll celebrate the day the people bring out the guillotine again and I see Pierpont Morgan being driven by in a tumbril!

(*His father and Sid are greatly amused; Lily is shocked but taking her cue from them, smiles. Mildred stares at him in puzzled wonderment, never having heard this particular line before. Only Arthur betrays the outraged reaction of a patriot.*)

ARTHUR. Aw say, you fresh kid, tie that bull outside! You ought to get a punch in the nose for talking that way on the Fourth!

MILLER (*solemnly*). Son, if I didn't know it was you talking, I'd think we had Emma Goldman with us.

ARTHUR. Never mind, Pa. Wait till we get him down to Yale. We'll take that out of him!

RICHARD (*with high scorn*). Oh, Yale! You think there's nothing in the world besides Yale. After all, what is Yale?

ARTHUR. You'll find out what!

SID (*provocatively*). Don't let them scare you, Dick. Give 'em hell!

LILY (*shocked*). Sid! You shouldn't swear before——

RICHARD. What do you think I am, Aunt Lily—a baby? I've heard worse than anything Uncle Sid says.

MILDRED. And said worse himself, I bet.

MILLER (*with a comic air of resignation*). Well, Richard, I've always found I've had to listen to at least one stump speech every Fourth. I only hope getting your extra strong one right after breakfast will let me off for the rest of the day. (*They all laugh now, taking this as a cue.*)

RICHARD (*sombrely*). That's right, laugh! After you, the deluge, you think! But look out! Supposing it comes before? Why shouldn't the workers of the world unite and rise? They have nothing to lose but their chains! (*He recites threateningly.*) "The days grow hot, O Babylon! 'Tis cool beneath thy willow trees!"

MILLER. Hmm. That's good. But where's the connection, exactly? Something from that book you're reading?

RICHARD (*superior*). No. That's poetry. This is prose.

MILLER. I've heard there was a difference between 'em. What is the book?

RICHARD (*importantly*). Carlyle's "French Revolution."

MILLER. Hmm. So that's where you drove the tumbril from and piled poor old Pierpont in it. (*Then seriously.*) Glad you're reading it, Richard. It's a darn fine book.

RICHARD (*with unflattering astonishment*). What, have you read it?

MILLER. Well, you see, even a newspaper owner can't get out of reading a book every now and again.

RICHARD (*abashed*). I—I didn't mean—I know you—— (*Then enthusiastically.*) Say, isn't it a great book, though—that part about Mirabeau—and about Marat and Robespierre——

MRS. MILLER (*appears from the front parlour in a great state of flushed annoyance*). Never you mind Robespierre, young man! You tell me this minute where you've hidden those books! They were on the shelf in your wardrobe and now you've gone and hid them somewheres else. You go right up and bring them to your father!

(*Richard, for a second, looks suddenly guilty and crushed. Then he bristles defensively.*)

MILLER (*after a quick understanding glance at him*). Never mind his getting them now. We'll waste the whole morning over those darned books. And anyway, he has a right to keep his library to himself—that is, if they're not too—— What books are they, Richard?

RICHARD (*self-consciously*). Well—there's——

MRS. MILLER. I'll tell you, if he won't—and you give him a good talking to. (*Then, after a glance at Richard, mollifiedly.*) Not that I blame Richard. There must be some boy he knows who's trying to show off as advanced and wicked, and he told him about——

RICHARD. No! I read about them myself, in the papers and in other books.

MRS. MILLER. Well, no matter how, there they were on his shelf. Two by that awful Oscar Wilde they put in jail for heaven knows what wickedness.

ARTHUR (*suddenly—solemnly authoritative*). He committed bigamy. (*Then as Sid smothers a burst of ribald laughter.*) What are you laughing at? I guess I ought to know. A fellow at college told me. His father was in England when this Wilde was pinched—and he said he remembered once his mother asked his father about it and he told her he'd committed bigamy.

MILLER (*hiding a smile behind his hand*). Well then, that must be right, Arthur.

MRS. MILLER. I wouldn't put it past him, nor anything else. One book was called the Picture of something or other.

RICHARD. "The Picture of Dorian Gray." It's one of the greatest novels ever written!

MRS. MILLER. Looked to me like cheap trash. And the second book was poetry. The Ballad of I forget what.

RICHARD. "The Ballad of Reading Gaol," one of the greatest poems ever written. (*He pronounces it Reading Goal [as in goalpost].*)

MRS. MILLER. All about someone who murdered his wife and got hung, as he richly deserved, as far as I could make out. And then there were two books by that Bernard Shaw——

RICHARD. The greatest playwright alive to-day!

MRS. MILLER. To hear him tell it, maybe! You know, Nat, the one who wrote a play about—well, never mind—that was so vile they wouldn't even let it play in New York!

MILLER. Hmm. I remember.

MRS. MILLER. One was a book of his plays and the other had a long title I couldn't make head or tail of, only it wasn't a play.

RICHARD (*proudly*). "The Quintessence of Ibsenism."

MILDRED. Phew! Good gracious, what a name! What does it mean, Dick? I'll bet he doesn't know.

RICHARD (*outraged*). I do, too, know! It's about Ibsen, the greatest playwright since Shakespeare!

MRS. MILLER. Yes, there was a book of plays by that Ibsen there, too! And poems by Swin something——

RICHARD. "Poems and Ballads by Swinburne," Ma.

The greatest poet since Shelley! He tells the truth about real love!

MRS. MILLER. Love! Well, all I can say is, from reading here and there, that if he wasn't flung in jail along with Wilde, he should have been. Some of the things I simply couldn't read, they were so indecent—— All about—well, I can't tell you before Lily and Mildred.

SID (*with a wink at Richard—jokingly*). Remember, I'm next on that one, Dick. I feel the need of a little poetical education.

LILY (*scandalized, but laughing*). Sid! Aren't you ashamed?

MRS. MILLER. This is no laughing matter. And then there was Kipling—but I suppose he's not so bad. And last there was a poem—a long one—the Rubay—— What is it, Richard?

RICHARD. "The Rubaiyat of Omar Khayyám." That's the best of all!

MILLER. Oh, I've read that, Essie—got a copy down at the office.

SID (*enthusiastically*). So have I. It's a pippin!

LILY (*with shy excitement*). I—I've read it, too—at the library. I like—some parts of it.

MRS. MILLER (*scandalized*). Why, Lily!

MILLER. Everybody's reading that now, Essie—and it don't seem to do them any harm. There's fine things in it, seems to me—true things.

MRS. MILLER (*a bit bewildered and uncertain now*). Why, Nat, I don't see how you—— It looked terrible blasphemous—parts I read.

SID. Remember this one: (*he quotes rhetorically*) "Oh Thou, who didst with pitfall and gin beset the path I was to wander in——" Now, I've always noticed how beset my path was with gin—in the past, you understand!

(*He casts a joking side glance at Lily. The others laugh. But Lily is in a melancholy dream and hasn't heard him.*)

MRS. MILLER (*tartly, but evidently suppressing her usual smile where he is concerned*). You would pick out the ones with liquor in them!

LILY (*suddenly—with a sad pathos, quotes awkwardly and shyly*). I like—because it's true:

"The Moving Finger writes, and having writ,
Moves on: nor all your Piety nor Wit
Shall lure it back to cancel half a Line,
Nor all your Tears wash out a Word of it."

MRS. MILLER (*astonished, as are all the others*). Why, Lily, I never knew you to recite poetry before!

LILY (*immediately guilty and apologetic*). I—it just stuck in my memory somehow.

RICHARD (*looking at her as if he had never seen her before*). Good for you, Aunt Lily! (*Then enthusiastically.*) But that isn't the best. The best is:

"A Book of Verses underneath the Bough,
A Jug of Wine, A Loaf of Bread—and Thou
Beside me singing in the Wilderness——"

ARTHUR (*who, bored to death by all this poetry quoting, has wandered over to the window at rear of desk, right*). Hey! Look who's coming up the walk—— Old Man McComber!

MILLER (*irritably*). Dave? . Now what in thunder does that damned old—— Sid, I can see where we never are going to get to that picnic.

MRS. MILLER (*vexatiously*). He'll know we're in this early, too. No use lying. (*Then appalled by another thought.*) That Norah—she's that thick, she never can answer the front door right unless I tell her each time. Nat, you've got to talk to Dave. I'll have her show him in here. Lily, you run up the back stairs and get your things on. I'll be up in a second. Nat, you get rid of him the first second you can! Whatever can the old fool want——

(*She and Lily hurry out through the back parlour.*)

ARTHUR. I'm going to beat it—just time to catch the eight-twenty trolley.

MILDRED. I've got to catch that, too. Wait till I get my hat, Art!

(*She rushes into the back parlour.*)

ARTHUR (*shouts after her*). I can't wait. You can catch up with me if you hurry. (*He turns at the back-parlour door—with a grin.*) McComber may be coming to see if your intentions toward his daughter are dishonourable, Dick! You'd better beat it while your shoes are good!

(*He disappears through the back-parlour door, laughing.*)

RICHARD (*a bit shaken, but putting on a brave front*). Think I'm scared of him?

MILLER (*gazing at him—frowning*). Can't imagine what—— But it's to complain about something, I know that. I only wish I didn't have to be pleasant with the old buzzard—but he's about the most valuable advertiser I've got.

SID (*sympathetically*). I know. But tell him to go to hell, anyway. He needs that ad more than you.

(*The sound of the bell comes from the rear of the house, off left from back parlour.*)

MILLER. There he is. You clear out, Dick—but come right back as soon as he's gone, you hear? I'm not through with you, yet.

RICHARD. Yes, Pa.

MILLER. You better clear out, too, Sid. You know Dave doesn't approve jokes.

SID. And loves me like poison! Come on, Dick, we'll go out and help Tommy celebrate.

(*He takes Richard's arm and they also disappear through the back-parlour door. Miller glances through the front parlour toward the front door, then calls in a tone of strained heartiness.*)

MILLER. Hello, Dave. Come right in here. What good wind blows you around on this glorious Fourth?

(*A flat, brittle voice answers him:* "Good morning," *and a moment later David McComber appears in the doorway from the front parlour. He is a thin, dried-up little man with a head too large for his body perched on a scrawny neck, and a long solemn horse face with deep-set little black eyes, a blunt formless nose and a tiny slit of a mouth. He is about the same age as Miller but is entirely bald, and looks ten years older. He is dressed with a prim neatness in shiny old black clothes.*)

Here, sit down and make yourself comfortable. (*Holding out the cigar-box.*) Have a cigar?

MCCOMBER (*sitting down in the chair at the right of table—acidly*). You're forgetting. I never smoke.

MILLER (*forcing a laugh at himself*). That's so. So I was. Well, I'll smoke alone then. (*He bites off the end of the cigar viciously, as if he wished it were McComber's head, and sits down opposite him.*)

MCCOMBER. You asked me what brings me here, so I'll come to the point at once. I regret to say it's something disagreeable—disgraceful would be nearer the truth—and it concerns your son, Richard!

MILLER (*beginning to bristle—but calmly*). Oh, come now, Dave, I'm sure Richard hasn't——

MCCOMBER (*sharply*). And I'm positive he has. You're not accusing me of being a liar, I hope.

MILLER. No one said anything about liar. I only meant you're surely mistaken if you think——

MCCOMBER. I'm not mistaken. I have proof of everything in his own handwriting!

MILLER (*sharply*). Let's get down to brass tacks. Just what is it you're charging him with?

MCCOMBER. With being dissolute and blasphemous—with deliberately attempting to corrupt the morals of my young daughter Muriel.

MILLER. Then I'm afraid I will have to call you a liar, Dave!

MCCOMBER (*without taking offence—in the same flat, brittle voice*). I thought you'd get around to that, so I brought some of the proofs with me. I've a lot more of 'em at home. (*He takes a wallet from his inside coat pocket, selects five or six slips of paper, and holds them out to Miller.*) These are good samples of the rest. My wife discovered them in one of Muriel's bureau drawers hidden under the underwear. They're all in his handwriting, you can't deny it. Anyway, Muriel's confessed to me he wrote them. You read them and then say I'm a liar.

(*Miller has taken the slips and is reading them frowningly. McComber talks on.*)

Evidently you've been too busy to take the right care about Richard's bringing up or what he's allowed to read—though I can't see why his mother failed in her duty. But that's your misfortune, and none of my business. But Muriel is my business and I can't and I won't have her innocence exposed to the contamination of a young man whose mind, judging from his choice of reading matter, is as foul——

MILLER (*making a tremendous effort to control his temper*). Why, you damned old fool! Can't you see Richard's only a fool kid who's just at the stage when he's out to rebel against all authority, and so he grabs at everything radical to read and wants to pass it on to his elders and his girl and boy friends to show off what a young hellion he is! Why, at heart you'd find Richard is just as innocent and as big a kid as Muriel is! (*He pushes the slips of paper across the table contemptuously.*) This stuff doesn't mean anything to me—that is, nothing of what you think it means. If you believe this would corrupt Muriel, then you must believe she's easily corrupted! But I'll bet you'd find she knows a lot more about life than you give her credit for—and can guess a stork didn't bring her down your chimney!

MCCOMBER. Now you're insulting my daughter. I won't forget that.

MILLER. I'm not insulting her. I think Muriel is a darn nice girl. That's why I'm giving her credit for ordinary good sense. I'd say the same about my own Mildred, who's the same age.

MCCOMBER. I know nothing about your Mildred except that she's known all over as a flirt. (*Then more sharply.*) Well, I knew you'd prove obstinate, but I certainly never dreamed you'd have the impudence, after reading those papers, to claim your son was innocent of all wrongdoing!

MILLER. And what did you dream I'd do?

MCCOMBER. Do what it's your plain duty to do as a citizen to protect other people's children! Take and give him a hiding he'd remember to the last day of his life! You'd ought to do it for his sake, if you had any sense—unless you want him to end up in jail!

MILLER (*his fists clenched, leans across the table*). Dave, I've stood all I can stand from you! You get out! And get out quick, if you don't want a kick in the rear to help you!

MCCOMBER (*again in his flat, brittle voice, slowly getting to his feet*). You needn't lose your temper. I'm only demanding you do your duty by your own as I've already done by mine. I'm punishing Muriel. She's not to be allowed out of the house for a month and she's to be in bed every night by eight sharp. And yet she's blameless, compared to that——

MILLER. I said I'd had enough out of you, Dave! (*He makes a threatening movement.*)

MCCOMBER. You needn't lay hands on me. I'm going. But there's one thing more. (*He takes a letter from his wallet.*) Here's a letter from Muriel for your son. (*Puts it on the table.*) It makes clear, I think, how she's come to think about him, now that her eyes have been opened. I hope he heeds what's inside—for his own good and yours—because if I ever catch him hanging about my place again I'll have him arrested! And don't think I'm not going to make you regret the insults you've heaped on me. I'm taking the advertisement for my store out of your paper—and it won't go in again, I tell you, not unless you apologize in writing and promise to punish——

MILLER. I'll see you in hell first! As for your damned old ad, take it out and go to hell!

MCCOMBER. That's plain bluff. You know how badly you need it. So do I. (*He starts stiffly for the door.*)

MILLER. Here! Listen a minute! I'm just going to call *your* bluff and tell you that, whether you want to reconsider your decision or not, I'm going to refuse to print your damned ad after to-morrow! Put that in your pipe and smoke it! Furthermore, I'll start a campaign to encourage outside capital to open a dry-goods store in opposition to you that won't be the public swindle I can prove yours is!

MCCOMBER (*a bit shaken by this threat—but in the same flat tone*). I'll sue you for libel.

MILLER. When I get through, there won't be a person in town will buy a dish-rag in your place!

MCCOMBER (*more shaken, his eyes shifting about furtively*). That's all bluff. You wouldn't dare—— (*Then finally he says uncertainly:*) Well, good day. (*And turns and goes out.*)

(*Nat stands looking after him. Slowly the anger drains from his face and leaves him looking a bit sick and disgusted. Sid appears from the back parlour. He is nursing a burn on his right hand, but his face is one broad grin of satisfaction.*)

SID. I burned my hand with one of Tommy's damned firecrackers and came in to get some vaseline. I was listening to the last of your scrap. Good for you, Nat! You sure gave him hell!

MILLER (*dully*). Much good it'll do. He knows it was all talk.

SID. That's just what he don't know, Nat. The old skinflint has a guilty conscience.

MILLER. Well, anyone who knows me knows I wouldn't use my paper for a dirty, spiteful trick like that—no matter what he did to me.

SID. Yes, everyone knows you're an old sucker, Nat, too decent for your own good. But McComber never saw you like this before. I tell you you scared the pants off him. (*He chuckles.*)

MILLER (*still dejectedly*). I don't know what made me let go like that. The hell of skunks like McComber is that after being with them ten minutes you become as big skunks as they are.

SID (*notices the slips of paper on the table*). What's this? Something he brought? (*He picks them up and starts to read.*)

MILLER (*grimly*). Samples of the new freedom—from those books Essie found—that Richard's been passing on to Muriel to educate her. They're what started the rumpus. (*Then frowning.*) I've got to do something about that young anarchist or he'll be getting me, and himself, in a peck of trouble. (*Then pathetically helpless.*) But what can I do? Putting the curb bit on would make him worse. Then he'd have a harsh tyrant to defy. He'd love that, darn him!

SID (*has been reading the slips, a broad grin on his face—suddenly he whistles*). Phew! This is a warm lulu for fair! (*He recites with a joking intensity.*)

"My life is bitter with thy love; thine eyes
Blind me, thy tresses burn me, thy sharp sighs
Divide my flesh and spirit with soft sound——"

MILLER (*with a grim smile*). Hmm. I missed that one. That must be Mr. Swinburne's copy. I've never read him, but I've heard something like that was the matter with him.

SID. Yes, it's labelled Swinburne—"Anactoria." Whatever that is. But wait, watch and listen! The worst is yet to come! (*He recites with added comic intensity:*)

"That I could drink thy veins as wine, and eat
Thy breasts like honey, that from face to feet
Thy body were abolished and consumed,
And in my flesh thy very flesh entombed!"

MILLER (*an irrepressible boyish grin coming to his face*). Hell and hallelujah! Just picture old Dave digesting that for the first time! Gosh, I'd give a lot to have seen his face! (*Then a trace of shocked reproof showing in his voice.*) But it's no joking matter. That stuff *is* warm—too damned warm, if you ask me! I don't like this a damned bit, Sid. That's no kind of thing to be sending a decent girl. (*More worriedly.*) I thought he was really stuck on her—as one gets stuck on a decent girl at his age—all moonshine and holding hands and a kiss now and again. But this looks—I wonder if he is hanging around her to see what he can get? (*Angrily.*) By God, if that's true, he deserves that licking McComber says it's my duty to give him! I've got to draw the line somewhere!

SID. Yes, it won't do to have him getting any decent girl in trouble.

MILLER. The only thing I can do is put it up to him straight. (*With pride.*) Richard'll stand up to his guns, no matter what. I've never known him to lie to me.

SID (*at a noise from the back parlour, looks that way—in a whisper*). Then now's your chance. I'll beat it and leave you alone—see if the women folks are ready upstairs. We ought to get started soon—if we're ever going to make that picnic.

(*He is half-way to the entrance to the front parlour as Richard enters from the back parlour, very evidently nervous about McComber's call.*)

RICHARD (*adopting a forced, innocent tone*). How's your hand, Uncle Sid?

SID. All right, Dick, thanks—only hurts a little.

(*He disappears. Miller watches his son frowningly. Richard gives him a quick side glance and grows more guiltily self-conscious.*)

RICHARD (*forcing a snicker*). Gee, Pa, Uncle Sid's a bigger kid than Tommy is. He was throwing firecrackers in the air and catching them on the back of his hand and throwing 'em off again just before they went off—and one came and he wasn't quick enough, and it went off almost on top of——

MILLER. Never mind that. I've got something else to talk to you about besides firecrackers.

RICHARD (*apprehensively*). What, Pa?

MILLER (*suddenly puts both hands on his shoulders—quietly*). Look here, Son. I'm going to ask you a question, and I want an honest answer. I warn you beforehand if the answer is "yes" I'm going to punish you and punish you hard because you'll have done something no boy of mine ought to do. But you've never lied to me before, I know, and I don't believe, even to save yourself punishment, you'd lie to me now, would you?

RICHARD (*impressed—with dignity*). I won't lie, Pa.

MILLER. Have you been trying to have something to do with Muriel—something you shouldn't—you know what I mean.

RICHARD (*stares at him for a moment, as if he couldn't comprehend—then, as he does, a look of shocked indignation comes over his face*). No! What do you think I am, Pa? I never would! She's not that kind! Why, I—I love her! I'm going to marry her—after I get out of college! She's said she would! We're engaged!

MILLER (*with great relief*). All right. That's all I wanted to know. We won't talk any more about it. (*He gives him an approving pat on the back.*)

RICHARD. I don't see how you could think—— Did that old idiot McComber say that about me?

MILLER (*joking now*). Shouldn't call your future father-in-law names, should you? 'Tain't respectful. (*Then after a glance at Richard's indignant face—points to the slips of paper on the table.*) Well, you can't exactly blame old Dave, can you, when you read through that literature you wished on his innocent daughter?

RICHARD (*sees the slips for the first time and is overcome by embarrassment, which he immediately tries to cover up with a superior carelessness*). Oh, so that's why. He found those, did he? I told her to be careful—— Well, it'll do him good to read the truth about life for once and get rid of his old-fogy ideas.

MILLER. I'm afraid I've got to agree with him, though, that they're hardly fit reading for a young girl. (*Then with subtle flattery.*) They're all well enough, in their way, for you who're a man, but—— Think it over, and see if you don't agree with me.

RICHARD (*embarrassedly*). Aw, I only did it because I liked them—and I wanted her to face life as it is. She's so darned afraid of life—afraid of her Old Man—afraid of people saying this or that about her—afraid of being in love—afraid of everything. She's even afraid to let me kiss her. I thought, maybe, reading those things—they're beautiful, aren't they, Pa?—I thought they would give her the spunk to lead her own life, and not be—always thinking of being afraid.

MILLER. I see. Well, I'm afraid she's still afraid. (*He takes the letter from the table.*) Here's a letter from her he said to give you.

(*Richard takes the letter from him uncertainly, his expression changing to one of apprehension.*)

(*Miller adds with a kindly smile:*) You better be prepared for a bit of a blow. But never mind. There's lots of other fish in the sea.

(*Richard is not listening to him, but staring at the letter with a sort of fascinated dread. Miller looks into his son's face a second, then turns away, troubled and embarrassed.*)

Darn it! I better go upstairs and get rigged out or I never will get to that picnic.

(*He moves awkwardly and self-consciously off through the front parlour. Richard continues to stare at the letter for a moment—then girds up his courage and tears it open and begins to read swiftly. As he reads, his face grows more and more wounded and tragic, until at the end his mouth draws down at the corners, as if he were about to break into tears. With an effort he *forces them back and his face grows flushed with humiliation and wronged anger.*)

RICHARD (*blurts out to himself*). The little coward ! I hate her ! She can't treat me like that ! I'll show her !

(*At the sound of voices from the front parlour, he quickly shoves the letter into the inside pocket of his coat and does his best to appear calm and indifferent, even attempting to whistle "Waiting at the Church." But the whistle peters out miserably as his mother, Lily and Sid enter from the front parlour. They are dressed in all the elaborate paraphernalia of motoring at that period—linen dusters, veils, goggles, Sid in a snappy cap.*)

MRS. MILLER. Well, we're about ready to start at last, thank goodness ! Let's hope no more callers are on the way. What did that McComber want, Richard, do you know ? Sid couldn't tell us.

RICHARD. You can search me. Ask Pa.

MRS. MILLER (*immediately sensing something "down" in his manner—going to him worriedly*). Why, whatever's the matter with you, Richard ? You sound as if you'd lost your last friend ! What is it ?

RICHARD (*desperately*). I—I don't feel so well—my stomach's sick.

MRS. MILLER (*immediately all sympathy—smoothing his hair back from his forehead*). You poor boy ! What a shame—on the Fourth, too, of all days ! (*Turning to the others.*) Maybe I better stay home with him, if he's sick.

LILY. Yes, I'll stay, too.

RICHARD (*more desperately*). No ! You go, Ma ! I'm not really sick. I'll be all right. You go. I want to be alone ! (*Then, as a louder bang comes from in back as Tommy sets off a cannon cracker, he jumps to his feet.*) Darn Tommy and his darned firecrackers ! You can't get any peace in this house with that darned kid around ! Darn the Fourth of July, anyway ! I wish we still belonged to England ! (*He strides off in an indignant fury of misery through the front parlour.*)

MRS. MILLER (*stares after him worriedly—then sighs philosophically*). Well, I guess he can't be so very sick—after that. (*She shakes her head.*) He's a queer boy. Sometimes I can't make head or tail of him.

MILLER (*calls from the front door beyond the back parlour*). Come along, folks. Let's get started.

SID. We're coming, Nat.

(*He and the two women move off through the front parlour.*)

CURTAIN

ACT TWO

SCENE. *Dining-room of the Miller home—a little after six o'clock in the evening of the same day.*

The room is much too small for the medium-priced, formidable dining-room set, especially now when all the leaves of the table are in. At left, toward rear, is a double doorway with sliding doors and portières leading into the back parlour. In the rear wall, left, is the door to the pantry. At the right of door is the china closet with its display of the family cut glass and fancy china. In the right wall are two windows looking out on a side lawn. In front of the windows is a heavy, ugly sideboard with three pieces of old silver on its top. In the left wall, extreme front, is a screen door opening on a side porch. A dark rug covers most of the floor. The table, with a chair at each end, left and right, three chairs on the far side, facing front, and two on the near side, their backs to front, takes up most of the available space. The walls are papered in a sombre brown and dark-red design.

Mrs. Miller is supervising and helping the second girl, Norah, in the setting of the table. Norah is a clumsy, heavy-handed, heavy-footed, long-jawed, beamingly good-natured young Irish girl—a "greenhorn."

MRS. MILLER. I really think you better put on the lights, Norah. It's getting so cloudy out, and this pesky room is so dark, anyway.

NORAH. Yes, Mum. (*She stretches awkwardly over the table to reach the chandelier that is suspended from the middle of the ceiling and manages to turn one light on—scornfully.*) Arrah, the contraption !

MRS. MILLER (*worriedly*). Careful !

NORAH. Careful as can be, Mum. (*But in moving around to reach the next bulb she jars heavily against the table.*)

MRS. MILLER. There ! I knew it ! I do wish you'd watch—— !

NORAH (*a flustered appeal in her voice.*) Arrah, what have I done wrong now ?

MRS. MILLER (*draws a deep breath—then sighs helplessly*). Oh, nothing. Never mind the rest of the lights. You might as well go out in the kitchen and wait until I ring.

NORAH (*relieved and cheerful again*). Yes, Mum. (*She starts for the pantry.*)

MRS. MILLER. But there's one thing—— (*Norah turns apprehensively.*) No, two things—things I've told you over and over, but you always forget. Don't pass the plates on the wrong side at dinner to-night, and do be careful not to let that pantry door slam behind you. Now you will try to remember, won't you?

NORAH. Yes, Mum.

(*She goes into the pantry and shuts the door behind her with exaggerated care as Mrs. Miller watches her apprehensively. Mrs. Miller sighs and reaches up with difficulty and turns on another of the four lights in the chandelier. As she is doing so, Lily enters from the back parlour.*)

LILY. Here, let me do that, Essie. I'm taller. You'll only strain yourself. (*She quickly lights the other two bulbs.*)

MRS. MILLER (*gratefully*). Thank you, Lily. It's a stretch for me, I'm getting so fat.

LILY. But where's Norah? Why didn't she——?

MRS. MILLER (*exasperatedly*). Oh, that girl! Don't talk about her! She'll be the death of me! She's that thick, you honestly wouldn't believe it possible.

LILY (*smiling*). Why, what did she do now?

MRS. MILLER. Oh, nothing. She means all right.

LILY. Anything else I can do, Essie?

MRS. MILLER. Well, she's got the table all wrong. We'll have to reset it. But you're always helping me. It isn't fair to ask you—in your vacation. You need your rest after teaching a pack of wild Indians of kids all year.

LILY (*beginning to help with the table*). You know I love to help. It makes me feel I'm some use in this house instead of just sponging——

MRS. MILLER (*indignantly*). Sponging! You pay, don't you?

LILY. Almost nothing. And you and Nat only take that little to make me feel better about living with you. (*Forcing a smile.*) I don't see how you stand me—having a cranky old maid around all the time.

MRS. MILLER. What nonsense you talk! As if Nat and I weren't only too tickled to death to have you! Lily Miller, I've no patience with you when you go on like that. We've been over this a thousand times before, and still you go on! Crazy, that's what it is! (*She changes the subject abruptly.*) What time's it getting to be?

LILY (*looking at her watch*). Quarter past six.

MRS. MILLER. I do hope those men folks aren't going to be late for dinner. (*She sighs.*) But I suppose with that darned Sachem Club picnic it's more likely than not. (*Lily looks worried, and sighs. Mrs. Miller gives her a quick side glance.*) I see you've got your new dress on.

LILY (*embarrassedly*). Yes, I thought—if Sid's taking me to the fireworks—I ought to spruce up a little.

MRS. MILLER (*looking away*). Hmm. (*A pause—then she says with an effort to be casual:*) You mustn't mind if Sid comes home feeling a bit—gay. I expect Nat to—and we'll have to listen to all those old stories of his about when he was a boy. You know what those picnics are, and Sid'd be running into all his old friends.

LILY (*agitatedly*). I don't think he will—this time—not after his promise.

MRS. MILLER (*avoiding looking at her*). I know. But men are weak. (*Then quickly.*) That was a good notion of Nat's, getting Sid the job on the Waterbury "Standard." All he ever needed was to get away from the rut he was in here. He's the kind that's the victim of his friends. He's easily led—but there's no real harm in him, you know that. (*Lily keeps silent, her eyes downcast. Mrs. Miller goes on meaningly.*) He's making good money in Waterbury, too—thirty-five a week. He's in a better position to get married than he ever was.

LILY (*stiffly*). Well, I hope he finds a woman who's willing—though after he's through with his betting on horse-races, and dice, and playing Kelly pool, there won't be much left for a wife—even if there was nothing else he spent his money on.

MRS. MILLER. Oh, he'd give up all that—for the right woman. (*Suddenly she comes directly to the point.*) Lily, why don't you change your mind and marry Sid and reform him? You love him and always have——

LILY (*stiffly*). I can't love a man who drinks.

MRS. MILLER. You can't fool me. I know darned well you love him. And he loves you and always has.

LILY. Never enough to stop drinking for. (*Cutting off Mrs. Miller's reply.*) No, it's no good in your talking, Essie. We've been over this a thousand times before and I'll always feel the same as long as Sid's the same. If he gave me proof he'd—but even then I don't believe I could. It's sixteen years since I broke off our engagement, but what made me break it off is as clear to me to-day as it was then. It was what he'd be liable to do now to anyone who married him—his taking up with bad women.

MRS. MILLER (*protests half-heartedly*). But he's always sworn he got raked into that party and never had anything to do with those harlots.

LILY. Well, I don't believe him—didn't then and don't now. I do believe he didn't deliberately plan to, but—— Oh, it's no good talking, Essie. What's done is done. But you know how much I like Sid—in spite of everything. I know he was just born to be what he is—irresponsible, never meaning to harm but harming in spite of himself. But don't talk to me about marrying him—because I never could.

MRS. MILLER (*angrily*). He's a dumb fool—a stupid dumb fool, that's what he is!

LILY (*quietly*). No. He's just Sid.

MRS. MILLER. It's a shame for you—a measly shame—you that would have made such a wonderful wife for any man—that ought to have your own home and children!

LILY (*winces but puts her arm around her affectionately—gently*). Now don't you go feeling sorry for me. I won't have that. Here I am, thanks to your and Nat's kindness, with the best home in the world; and as for the children, I feel the same love for yours as if they were mine, and I didn't have the pain of bearing them. And then there are all the boys and girls I teach every year. I like to feel I'm a sort of second mother to them and helping them to grow up to be good men and women. So I don't feel such a useless old maid, after all.

MRS. MILLER (*kisses her impulsively—her voice husky*). You're a good woman, Lily—too good for the rest of us. (*She turns away, wiping a tear furtively—then abruptly changing the subject.*) Good gracious, if I'm not forgetting one of the most important things! I've got to warn that Tommy against giving me away to Nat about the fish. He knows, because I had to send him to market for it, and he's liable to burst out laughing——

LILY. Laughing about what?

MRS. MILLER (*guiltily*). Well, I've never told you, because it seemed sort of a sneaking trick, but you know how Nat carries on about not being able to eat bluefish.

LILY. I know he says there's a certain oil in it that poisons him.

MRS. MILLER (*chuckling*). Poisons him, nothing! He's been eating bluefish for years—only I tell him each time it's weakfish. We're having it to-night—and I've got to warn that young imp to keep his face straight.

LILY (*laughing*). Aren't you ashamed, Essie!

MRS. MILLER. Not much, I'm not! I like bluefish! (*She laughs.*) Where is Tommy? In the sitting-room?

LILY. No, Richard's there alone. I think Tommy's out on the piazza with Mildred.

(*Mrs. Miller bustles out through the back parlour. As soon as she is gone, the smile fades from Lily's lips. Her face grows sad and she again glances nervously at her watch. Richard appears from the back parlour, moving in an aimless way. His face wears a set expression of bitter gloom; he exudes tragedy. For Richard, after his first outburst of grief and humiliation, has begun to take a masochistic satisfaction in his great sorrow, especially in the concern which it arouses in the family circle. On seeing his aunt, he gives her a dark look and turns and is about to stalk back toward the sitting-room when she speaks to him pityingly.*)

Feel any better, Richard?

RICHARD (*sombrely*). I'm all right, Aunt Lily. You mustn't worry about me.

LILY (*going to him*). But I do worry about you. I hate to see you so upset.

RICHARD. It doesn't matter. Nothing matters.

LILY (*puts her arm around him sympathetically*). You really mustn't let yourself take it so seriously. You know, something happens and things like that come up, and we think there's no hope——

RICHARD. Things like what come up?

LILY. What's happened between you and Muriel.

RICHARD (*with disdain*). Oh, her! I wasn't even thinking about her. I was thinking about life.

LILY. But then—if we really, *really* love—why, then something else is bound to happen soon that changes everything again, and it's all as it was before the misunderstanding, and everything works out all right in the end. That's the way it is with life.

RICHARD (*with a tragic sneer*). Life! Life is a joke! And everything comes out all wrong in the end!

LILY (*a little shocked*). You mustn't talk that way. But I know you don't mean it.

RICHARD. I do too mean it! You can have your silly optimism, if you like, Aunt Lily. But don't ask me to be so blind. I'm a pessimist! (*Then with an air of cruel cynicism.*) As for Muriel, that's all dead and past. I was only kidding her, anyway, just to have a little fun, and she took it seriously, like a fool. (*He forces a cruel smile to his lips.*) You know what they say about women and trolley cars, Aunt Lily: there's always another one along in a minute.

LILY (*really shocked this time*). I don't like you when you say such horrible, cynical things. It isn't nice.

RICHARD. Nice! That's all you women think of! I'm proud to be a cynic. It's the only thing you can be when you really face life. I suppose you think I ought to be heart-broken about Muriel—a little coward that's afraid to say her soul's her own, and keeps tied to her father's apron strings! Well, not for mine! There's plenty of other fish in the sea! (*As he is finishing, his mother comes back through the back parlour.*)

MRS. MILLER. Why, hello. You here, Richard? Getting hungry, I suppose?

RICHARD (*indignantly*). I'm not hungry a bit! That's all you think of, Ma—food!

MRS. MILLER. Well, I must say I've never noticed you to hang back at mealtimes. (*To Lily.*) What's that he was saying about fish in the sea?

LILY (*smiling*). He says he's through with Muriel now.

MRS. MILLER (*tartly—giving her son a rebuking look*). She's through with him, he means! The idea of your sending a nice girl like her things out of those indecent books!

(*Deeply offended, Richard disdains to reply but

stalks woundedly to the screen door at left, front, and puts a hand on the knob.)

Where are you going?

RICHARD (*quotes from "Candida" in a hollow voice*). "Out, then, into the night with me!"

(*He stalks out, slamming the door behind him.*)

MRS. MILLER (*calls*). Well, don't you go far, 'cause dinner'll be ready in a minute, and I'm not coming running after you! (*She turns to Lily with a chuckle.*) Goodness, that boy! He ought to be on the stage! (*She mimics.*) "Out—into the night"—and it isn't even dark yet! He got that out of one of those books, I suppose. Do you know, I'm actually grateful to old Dave McComber for putting an end to his nonsense with Muriel. I never did approve of Richard getting so interested in girls. He's not old enough for such silliness. Why, seems to me it was only yesterday he was still a baby. (*She sighs—then matter-of-factly.*) Well, nothing to do now till those men turn up. No use standing here like gawks. We might as well go in the sitting-room and be comfortable.

LILY (*the nervous, worried note in her voice again*). Yes, we might as well. (*They go out through the back parlour. They have no sooner disappeared than the screen door is opened cautiously and Richard comes back in the room.*)

RICHARD (*stands inside the door, looking after them—quotes bitterly*). "They do not know the secret in the poet's heart." (*He comes nearer the table and surveys it, especially the cut-glass dish containing olives, with contempt and mutters disdainfully.*) Food!

(*But the dish of olives seems to fascinate him and presently he has approached nearer, and stealthily lifts a couple and crams them into his mouth. He is just reaching out for more when the pantry door is opened slightly and Norah peers in.*)

NORAH. Mister Dick, you thief, lave them olives alone, or the missus'll be swearing it was me at them!

RICHARD (*draws back his hand as if he had been stung—too flustered to be anything but guilty boy for a second*). I—I wasn't eating——

NORAH. Oho, no, of course not, divil fear you, you was only feeling their pulse! (*Then warningly.*) Mind what I'm saying now, or I'll have to tell on you to protect me good name!

(*She draws back into the pantry, closing the door. Richard stands, a prey to feelings of bitterest humiliation and seething revolt against everyone and everything. A low whistle comes from just outside the porch door. He starts. Then a masculine voice calls:* "Hey, Dick." *He goes over to the screen door grumpily—then as he recognizes the owner of the voice, his own as he answers becomes respectful and admiring.*)

RICHARD. Oh, hello, Wint. Come on in.

(*He opens the door and Wint Selby enters and stands just inside the door. Selby is nineteen, a classmate of Arthur's at Yale. He is a typical, good-looking college boy of the period, not the athletic but the hell-raising sport type. He is tall, blond, dressed in extreme collegiate cut.*)

WINT (*as he enters—warningly, in a low tone*). Keep it quiet, Kid. I don't want the folks to know I'm here. Tell Art I want to see him a second—on the Q.T.

RICHARD. Can't. He's up at the Rands'—won't be home before ten, anyway.

WINT (*irritably*). Damn! I thought he'd be here for dinner. (*More irritably.*) Hell, that gums the works for fair!

RICHARD (*ingratiatingly*). What is it, Wint? Can't I help?

WINT (*gives him an appraising glance*). I might tell you, if you can keep your face shut.

RICHARD. I can.

WINT. Well, I ran into a couple of swift babies from New Haven this after. and I dated them up for to-night, thinking I could catch Art. But now it's too late to get anyone else and I'll have to pass it up. I'm nearly broke and I can't afford to blow them both to drinks.

RICHARD (*with shy eagerness*). I've got eleven dollars saved up. I could loan you some.

WINT (*surveys him appreciatively*). Say, you're a good sport. (*Then shaking his head.*) Nix, Kid, I don't want to borrow your money. (*Then getting an idea.*) But say, have you got anything on for to-night?

RICHARD. No.

WINT. Want to come along with me? (*Then quickly.*) I'm not trying to lead you astray, understand. But it'll be a help if you would just sit around with Belle and feed her a few drinks while I'm off with Edith. (*He winks.*) See what I mean? You don't have to do anything, not even take a glass of beer—unless you want to.

RICHARD (*boastfully*). Aw, what do you think I am—a rube?

WINT. You mean you're game for anything that's doing?

RICHARD. Sure I am!

WINT. Ever been out with any girls—I mean, real swift ones that there's something doing with, not these dead Janes around here?

RICHARD (*lies boldly*). Aw, what do you think? Sure I have!

WINT. Ever drink anything besides sodas?

RICHARD. Sure. Lots of times. Beer and sloe-gin fizz and—Manhattans.

WINT (*impressed*). Hell, you know more than I

thought. (*Then considering.*) Can you fix it so your folks won't get wise? I don't want your old man coming after me. You can get back by half-past ten or eleven, though, all right. Think you can cook up some lie to cover that? (*As Richard hesitates—encouraging him.*) Ought to be easy—on the Fourth.

RICHARD. Sure. Don't worry about that.

WINT. But you've got to keep your face closed about this, you hear?—to Art and everybody else. I tell you straight, I wouldn't ask you to come if I wasn't in a hole—and if I didn't know you were coming down to Yale next year, and didn't think you're giving me the straight goods about having been around before. I don't want to lead you astray.

RICHARD (*scornfully*). Aw, I told you that was silly.

WINT. Well, you be at the Pleasant Beach Hotel at half-past nine then. Come in the back room. And don't forget to grab some cloves to take the booze off your breath.

RICHARD. Aw, I know what to do.

WINT. See you later, then. (*He starts out and is just about to close the door when he thinks of something.*) And say, I'll say you're a Harvard freshman, and you back me up. They don't know a damn thing about Harvard. I don't want them thinking I'm travelling around with any high-school kid.

RICHARD. Sure. That's easy.

WINT. So long, then. You better beat it right after your dinner while you've got a chance, and hang around until it's time. Watch your step, Kid.

RICHARD. So long. (*The door closes behind Wint. Richard stands for a moment, a look of bitter, defiant rebellion coming over his face, and mutters to himself.*) I'll show her she can't treat me the way she's done! I'll show them all!

(*Then the front door is heard slamming, and a moment later Tommy rushes in from the back parlour.*)

TOMMY. Where's Ma?

RICHARD (*surlily*). In the sitting-room. Where did you think, Bonehead?

TOMMY. Pa and Uncle Sid are coming. Mid and I saw them from the front piazza. Gee, I'm glad. I'm awful hungry, ain't you? (*He rushes out through the back parlour, calling*:) Ma! They're coming! Let's have dinner quick! (*A moment later Mrs. Miller appears from the back parlour accompanied by Tommy, who keeps insisting urgently*:) Gee, but I'm awful hungry, Ma!

MRS. MILLER. I know. You always are. You've got a tape-worm, that's what I think.

TOMMY. Have we got lobsters, Ma? Gee, I love lobsters.

MRS. MILLER. Yes, we've got lobsters. And fish. You remember what I told you about that fish. (*He snickers.*) Now, do be quiet, Tommy! (*Then with a teasing smile at Richard*:) Well, I'm glad to see you've got back out of the night, Richard.

(*He scowls and turns his back on her. Lily appears through the back parlour, nervous and apprehensive. As she does so, from the front yard Sid's voice is heard singing "Poor John!" Mrs. Miller shakes her head forebodingly—but, so great is the comic spell for her even in her brother's voice, a humorous smile hovers at the corners of her lips.*)

Mmm! Mmm! Lily, I'm afraid——

LILY (*bitterly*). Yes, I might have known.

(*Mildred runs in through the back parlour. She is laughing to herself a bit shamefacedly. She rushes to her mother.*)

MILDRED. Ma, Uncle Sid's—— (*She whispers in her ear.*)

MRS. MILLER. Never mind! You shouldn't notice such things—at your age! And don't you encourage him by laughing at his foolishness, you hear!

TOMMY. You needn't whisper, Mid. Think I don't know? Uncle Sid's soused again.

MRS. MILLER (*shakes him by the arm indignantly*). You be quiet! Did I ever! You're getting too smart! (*Gives him a push.*) Go to your place and sit right down and not another word out of you!

TOMMY (*aggrieved—rubbing his arm as he goes to his place*). Aw, Ma!

MRS. MILLER. And you sit down, Richard and Mildred. You better, too, Lily. We'll get him right in here and get some food in him. He'll be all right then.

(*Richard, preserving the pose of the bitter, disillusioned pessimist, sits down in his place in the chair at right of the two whose backs face front. Mildred takes the other chair facing back, at his left. Tommy has already slid into the end chair at right of those at the rear of table facing front. Lily sits in the one of those at left, by the head of the table, leaving the middle one [Sid's] vacant. While they are doing this, the front screen door is heard slamming and Miller and Sid's laughing voices, raised as they come in and for a moment after, then suddenly cautiously lowered. Mrs. Miller goes to the entrance to the back parlour and calls peremptorily.*)

You come right in here! Don't stop to wash up or anything. Dinner's coming right on the table.

MILLER'S VOICE (*jovially*). All right, Essie. Here we are! Here we are!

MRS. MILLER (*goes to pantry door, opens it and calls*). All right, Norah. You can bring in the soup.

(*She comes back to the back-parlour entrance just as Miller enters. He isn't drunk by any means. He is just mellow and benignly ripened. His face is one large, smiling, happy beam of utter appreciation of life. All's right with the world, so satisfyingly right that he becomes sentimentally moved even to think of it.*)

MILLER. Here we are, Essie! Right on the dot! Here we are!

(*He pulls her to him and gives her a smacking kiss on the ear as she jerks her head away. Mildred and Tommy giggle. Richard holds rigidly aloof and disdainful, his brooding gaze fixed on his plate. Lily forces a smile.*)

MRS. MILLER (*pulling away—embarrassedly, almost blushing*). Don't, you Crazy! (*Then recovering herself—tartly.*) So I see, you're here! And if I didn't, you've told me four times already!

MILLER (*beamingly*). Now, Essie, don't be critical. Don't be carpingly critical. Good news can stand repeating, can't it? 'Course it can!

(*He slaps her jovially on her fat buttocks. Tommy and Mildred roar with glee. And Norah, who has just entered from the pantry with a huge tureen of soup in her hands, almost drops it as she explodes in a merry guffaw.*)

MRS. MILLER (*scandalized*). Nat! Aren't you ashamed!

MILLER. Couldn't resist it! Just simply couldn't resist it!

(*Norah, still standing with the soup tureen held out stiffly in front of her, again guffaws.*)

MRS. MILLER (*turns on her with outraged indignation*). Norah! Bring that soup here this minute! (*She stalks with stiff dignity toward her place at the foot of the table, right.*)

NORAH (*guiltily*). Yes, Mum. (*She brings the soup around the head of the table, passing Miller.*)

MILLER (*jovially*). Why, hello, Norah!

MRS. MILLER. Nat! (*She sits down stiffly at the foot of the table.*)

NORAH (*rebuking him familiarly*). Arrah now, don't be making me laugh and getting me into trouble!

MRS. MILLER. Norah!

NORAH (*a bit resentfully*). Yes, Mum. Here I am. (*She sets the soup tureen down with a thud in front of Mrs. Miller and passes around the other side, squeezing with difficulty between the china closet and the backs of chairs at the rear of the table.*)

MRS. MILLER. Tommy! Stop spinning your napkin ring! How often have I got to tell you? Mildred! Sit up straight in your chair! Do you want to grow up a humpback? Richard! Take your elbows off the table!

MILLER (*coming to his place at the head of the table, rubbing his hands together genially*). Well, well, well. Well, well, well. It's good to be home again.

(*Norah exits into the pantry and lets the door slam with a bang behind her.*)

MRS. MILLER (*jumps*). Oh! (*Then exasperatedly.*) Nat, I do wish you wouldn't encourage that stupid girl by talking to her, when I'm doing my best to train——

MILLER (*beamingly*). All right, Essie. Your word is law! (*Then laughingly.*) We did have the darndest fun to-day! And Sid was the life of that picnic! You ought to have heard him! Honestly, he had that crowd just rolling on the ground and splitting their sides! He ought to be on the stage.

MRS. MILLER (*as Norah comes back with a dish of saltines—begins ladling soup into the stack of plates before her*). He ought to be at this table eating something to sober him up, that's what he ought to be! (*She calls.*) Sid! You come right in here! (*Then to Norah, handing her a soup plate.*) Here, Norah. (*Norah begins passing soup.*) Sit down, Nat, for goodness' sakes. Start eating, everybody. Don't wait for me. You know I've given up soup.

MILLER (*sits down but bends forward to call to his wife in a confidential tone*). Essie—Sid's sort of embarrassed about coming—I mean I'm afraid he's a little bit—not too much, you understand—but he met such a lot of friends and—well, you know, don't be hard on him. Fourth of July is like Christmas—comes but once a year. Don't pretend to notice, eh? And don't you kids, you hear! And don't you, Lily. He's scared of you.

LILY (*with stiff meekness*). Very well, Nat.

MILLER (*beaming again—calls*). All right, Sid. The coast's clear. (*He begins to absorb his soup ravenously.*) Good soup, Essie! Good soup!

(*A moment later Sid makes his entrance from the back parlour. He is in a condition that can best be described as blurry. His movements have a hazy uncertainty about them. His shiny fat face is one broad, blurred, Puckish, naughty-boy grin; his eyes have a blurred, wondering vagueness. As he enters he makes a solemnly intense effort to appear casual and dead, cold sober. He waves his hand aimlessly and speaks with a silly gravity.*)

SID. Good evening. (*They all answer* " Good evening," *their eyes on their plates. He makes his way vaguely toward his place, continuing his grave effort at conversation.*)

Beautiful evening. I never remember seeing—more beautiful sunset. (*He bumps vaguely into Lily's chair as he attempts to pass behind her—immediately he is all grave politeness.*) Sorry—sorry, Lily—deeply sorry.

LILY (*her eyes on her plate—stiffly*). It's all right.

SID (*manages to get into his chair at last—mutters to himself*). Wha' was I sayin'? Oh, sunsets. But why butt in? Hasn't sun—perfect right to set? Mind y'r own business. (*He pauses thoughtfully, considering this—then looks around from face to face, fixing each with a vague, blurred, wondering look, as if some deep puzzle were confronting him. Then suddenly he grins mistily and nods with satisfaction.*) And there you are! Am I right?

MILLER (*humouring him*). Right.

SID. Right! (*He is silent, studying his soup plate, as if it were some strange enigma. Finally he looks up and regards his sister and asks with wondering amazement.*) Soup?

MRS. MILLER. Of course, it's soup. What did you think it was? And you hurry up and eat it.

SID (*again regards his soup with astonishment*). Well! (*Then suddenly.*) Well, all right then! Soup be it! (*He picks up his spoon and begins to eat, but after two tries in which he finds it difficult to locate his mouth, he addresses the spoon plaintively*). Spoon, is this any way to treat a pal? (*Then suddenly comically angry, putting the spoon down with a bang.*) Down with spoons! (*He raises his soup plate and declaims:*) "We'll drink to the dead already, and hurrah for the next who dies." (*Bowing solemnly to right and left.*) Your good health, ladies and gents.

(*He starts drinking the soup. Miller guffaws and Mildred and Tommy giggle. Even Richard forgets his melancholy and snickers, and Mrs. Miller conceals a smile. Only Lily remains stiff and silent.*)

MRS. MILLER (*with forced severity*). Sid!

SID (*peers at her muzzily, lowering the soup plate a little from his lips*). Eh?

MRS. MILLER. Oh, nothing. Never mind.

SID (*solemnly offended*). Are you—publicly rebuking me before assembled——? Isn't soup liquid? Aren't liquids drunk? (*Then considering this to himself.*) What if they are drunk? It's a good man's failing. (*He again peers mistily about at the company.*) Am I right or wrong?

MRS. MILLER. Hurry up and finish your soup, and stop talking nonsense!

SID (*turning to her—again offendedly* . Oh, no, Essie, if I ever so far forget myself as to drink a leg of lamb, then you might have some—excuse for—— Just think of waste effort eating soup with spoons—fifty gruelling lifts per plate—billions of soup-eaters on globe—why, it's simply staggering! (*Then darkly to himself.*) No more spoons for me! If I want to develop my biceps, I'll buy Sandow Exerciser! (*He drinks the rest of his soup in a gulp and beams around at the company, suddenly all happiness again.*) Am I right, folks?

MILLER (*who has been choking with laughter*). Haw, haw! You're right, Sid.

SID (*peers at him blurredly and shakes his head sadly*). Poor old Nat! Always wrong—but heart of gold, heart of purest gold. And drunk again, I regret to note. Sister, my heart bleeds for you and your poor fatherless chicks!

MRS. MILLER (*restraining a giggle—severely*). Sid! Do shut up for a minute! Pass me your soup plates, everybody. If we wait for that girl to take them, we'll be here all night.

(*They all pass their plates, which Mrs. Miller stacks up and then puts on the sideboard. As she is doing this, Norah appears from the pantry with a platter of broiled fish. She is just about to place these before Miller when Sid catches her eye mistily and rises to his feet, making her a deep, uncertain bow.*)

SID (*rapidly*). Ah, Sight for Sore Eyes, my beautiful Macushla, my star-eyed Mavourneen——

MRS. MILLER. Sid!

NORAH (*immensely pleased—gives him an arch, flirtatious glance*). Ah sure, Mister Sid, it's you that have kissed the Blarney Stone, when you've a drop taken!

MRS. MILLER (*outraged*). Norah! Put down that fish!

NORAH (*flusteredly*). Yes, Mum. (*She attempts to put the fish down hastily before Miller, but her eyes are fixed nervously on Mrs. Miller and she gives Miller a nasty swipe on the side of the head with the edge of the dish.*)

MILLER. Ouch!

(*The children, even Richard, explode into laughter.*)

NORAH (*almost lets the dish fall*). Oh, glory be to God! Is it hurted you are?

MILLER (*rubbing his head—good-naturedly*). No, no harm done. Only careful, Norah, careful.

NORAH (*gratefully*). Yes, sorr. (*She thumps down the dish in front of him with a sigh of relief.*)

SID (*who is still standing—with drunken gravity*). Careful, Mavourneen, careful! You might have hit him some place besides the head. Always aim at his head, remember—so as not to worry us.

(*Again the children explode. Also Norah. Even Lily suddenly lets out an hysterical giggle and is furious with herself for doing so.*)

LILY. I'm so sorry, Nat. I didn't mean to laugh.

(*Turning on Sid furiously.*) Will you please sit down and stop making a fool of yourself!

(*Sid gives her a hurt, mournful look and then sinks meekly down on his chair.*)

NORAH (*grinning cheerfully, gives Lily a reassuring pat on the back*). Ah, Miss Lily, don't mind him. He's only under the influence. Sure, there's no harm in him at all.

MRS. MILLER. Norah!

(*Norah exits hastily into the pantry, letting the door slam with a crash behind her. There is silence for a moment as Miller serves the fish and it is passed around. Norah comes back with the vegetables and disappears again, and these are dished out.*)

MILLER (*is about to take his first bite—stops suddenly and asks his wife*). This isn't, by any chance, bluefish, is it, my dear?

MRS. MILLER (*with a warning glance at Tommy*). Of course not. You know we never have bluefish, on account of you.

MILLER (*addressing the table now with the gravity of a man confessing his strange peculiarities*). Yes, I regret to say, there's a certain peculiar oil in bluefish that invariably poisons me.

(*At this, Tommy cannot stand it any more but explodes into laughter. Mrs. Miller, after a helpless glance at him, follows suit; then Lily goes off into uncontrollable, hysterical laughter, and Richard and Mildred are caught in the contagion. Miller looks around at them with a weak smile, his dignity now ruffled a bit.*)

Well, I must say I don't see what's so darned funny about my being poisoned.

SID (*peers around him—then with drunken cunning*). Aha! Nat, I suspect—plot! This fish looks blue to me—very blue—in fact despondent, desperate, and—— (*He points his fork dramatically, at Mrs. Miller.*) See how guilty she looks—a ver—veritable Lucretia Georgia! Can it be this woman has been slowly poisoning you all these years? And how well—you've stood it! What iron constitution! Even now, when you are invariably at death's door, I can't believe——

(*Everyone goes off into uncontrollable laughter.*)

MILLER (*grumpily*). Oh, give us a rest, you darned fool! A joke's a joke, but—— (*He addresses his wife in a wounded tone.*) Is this true, Essie?

MRS. MILLER (*wiping the tears from her eyes—defiantly*). Yes, it is true, if you must know, and you'd never have suspected it, if it weren't for that darned Tommy, and Sid poking his nose in. You've eaten bluefish for years and thrived on it and it's all nonsense about that peculiar oil.

MILLER (*deeply offended*). Kindly allow me to know my own constitution! Now I think of it, I've felt upset afterwards every damned time we've had fish! (*He pushes his plate away from him with proud renunciation.*) I can't eat this.

MRS. MILLER (*insultingly matter-of-fact*). Well, don't then. There's lots of lobster coming and you can fill up on that.

(*Richard suddenly bursts out laughing again.*)

MILLER (*turns to him caustically*). You seem in a merry mood, Richard. I thought you were the original of the Heart Bowed Down to-day.

SID (*with mock condolence*). Never mind, Dick. Let them—scoff! What can they understand about girls whose hair sizzchels, whose lips are fireworks, whose eyes are red-hot sparks——

MILDRED (*laughing*). Is that what he wrote to Muriel? (*Turning to her brother.*) You silly goat, you!

RICHARD (*surlily*). Aw, shut up, Mid. What do I care about her? I'll show all of you how much I care!

MRS. MILLER. Pass your plates as soon as you're through, everybody. I've rung for the lobster. And that's all. You don't get any dessert or tea after lobster, you know.

(*Norah appears bearing a platter of cold boiled lobsters which she sets before Miller, and disappears.*)

TOMMY. Gee, I love lobster!

(*Miller puts one on each plate, and they are passed around and everyone starts in pulling the cracked shells apart.*)

MILLER (*feeling more cheerful after a couple of mouthfuls—determining to give the conversation another turn, says to his daughter*). Have a good time at the beach, Mildred?

MILDRED. Oh, fine, Pa, thanks. The water was wonderful and warm.

MILLER. Swim far?

MILDRED. Yes, for me. But that isn't so awful far.

MILLER. Well, you ought to be a good swimmer, if you take after me. I used to be a regular water-rat when I was a boy. I'll have to go down to the beach with you one of these days—though I'd be rusty, not having been in in all these years. (*The reminiscent look comes into his eyes of one about to embark on an oft-told tale of childhood adventure.*) You know, speaking of swimming, I never go down to that beach but what it calls to mind the day I and Red Sisk went in swimming there and I saved his life.

(*By this time the family are beginning to exchange amused, guilty glances. They all know what is coming.*)

SID (*with a sly, blurry wink around*). Ha! Now we—have it again!

MILLER (*turning on him*). Have what?

SID. Nothing—go on with your swimming—don't mind me.

MILLER (*glares at him—but immediately is overcome by the reminiscent mood again*). Red Sisk—his father kept a blacksmith shop where the Union Market is now—we kids called him Red because he had the darndest reddest crop of hair——

SID (*as if he were talking to his plate*). Remarkable! —the curious imagination—of little children.

MRS. MILLER (*as she sees Miller about to explode—interposes tactfully*). Sid! Eat your lobster and shut up! Go on, Nat.

MILLER (*gives Sid a withering look—then is off again*). Well, as I was saying, Red and I went swimming that day. Must have been—let me see—Red was fourteen, bigger and older than me, I was only twelve—forty-five years ago—wasn't a single house down there then—but there was a stake out where the whistling buoy is now, about a mile out.

(*Tommy, who has been having difficulty restraining himself, lets out a stifled giggle. Miller bends a frowning gaze on him.*)

One more sound out of you, young man, and you'll leave the table!

MRS. MILLER (*quickly interposing, trying to stave off the story*). Do eat your lobster, Nat. You didn't have any fish, you know.

MILLER (*not liking the reminder—pettishly*). Well, if I'm going to be interrupted every second anyway—— (*He turns to his lobster and chews in silence for a moment.*)

MRS. MILLER (*trying to switch the subject*). How's Anne's mother's rheumatism, Mildred?

MILDRED. Oh, she's much better, Ma. She was in wading to-day. She says salt water's the only thing that really helps her bunion.

MRS. MILLER. Mildred! Where are your manners? At the table's no place to speak of——

MILLER (*fallen into the reminiscent obsession again*). Well, as I was saying, there was I and Red, and he dared me to race him out to the stake and back. Well, I didn't let anyone dare me in those days. I was a spunky kid. So I said all right and we started out. We swam and swam and were pretty evenly matched; though, as I've said, he was bigger and older than me, but finally I drew ahead. I was going along easy, with lots in reserve, not a bit tired, when suddenly I heard a sort of gasp from behind me—like this—"help!" (*He imitates. Everyone's eyes are firmly fixed on their plates, except Sid's.*) And I turned and there was Red, his face all pinched and white, and he says weakly: "Help, Nat! I got a cramp in my leg!" Well, I don't mind telling you I got mighty scared. I didn't know what to do. Then suddenly I thought of the pile. If I could pull him to that, I could hang on to him till someone'd notice us. But the pile was still—well, I calculate it must have been two hundred feet away.

SID. Two hundred and fifty!

MILLER (*in confusion*). What's that?

SID. Two hundred *and* fifty! I've taken down the distance every time you've saved Red's life for thirty years and the mean average to that pile is two hundred and fifty feet! (*There is a burst of laughter from around the table. Sid continues complainingly.*) Why didn't you let that Red drown, anyway, Nat? I never knew him but I know I'd never have liked him.

MILLER (*really hurt, forces a feeble smile to his lips and pretends to be a good sport about it*). Well, guess you're right, Sid. Guess I have told that one too many times and bored everyone. But it's a good true story for kids because it illustrates the danger of being foolhardy in the water——

MRS. MILLER (*sensing the hurt in his tone, comes to his rescue*). Of course it's a good story—and you tell it whenever you've a mind to. And you, Sid, if you were in any responsible state, I'd give you a good piece of my mind for teasing Nat like that.

MILLER (*with a sad, self-pitying smile at his wife*). Getting old, I guess, Mother—getting to repeat myself. Someone ought to stop me.

MRS. MILLER. No such thing! You're as young as you ever were. (*She turns on Sid again angrily.*) You eat your lobster and maybe it'll keep your mouth shut!

SID (*after a few chews—irrepressibly*). Lobster! Did you know, Tommy, your Uncle Sid is the man invented lobster? Fact! One day—when I was building the Pyramids—took a day off and just dashed off lobster. He was bigger'n' older than me and he had the darndest reddest crop of hair but I dashed him off just the same! Am I right, Nat? (*Then suddenly in the tones of a side-show barker.*) Ladies *and* Gents——

MRS. MILLER. Mercy sakes! Can't you shut up?

SID. In this cage you see the lobster. You will not believe me, ladies *and* gents, but it's a fact that this interesting bivalve only makes love to his mate once in every thousand years—but, dearie me, how he does enjoy it!

(*The children roar. Lily and Mrs. Miller laugh in spite of themselves—then look embarrassed. Miller guffaws—then suddenly grows shocked.*)

MILLER. Careful, Sid, careful. Remember you're at home.

TOMMY (*suddenly in a hoarse whisper to his mother, with an awed glance of admiration at his uncle*). Ma! Look at him! He's eating that claw, shells and all!

MRS. MILLER (*horrified*). Sid, do you want to kill yourself? Take it away from him, Lily!

SID (*with great dignity*). But I prefer the shells. All famous epicures prefer the shells—to the less delicate, coarser meat. It's the same with clams. Unless I eat the shells there is a certain, peculiar oil that invariably poisons—— Am I right, Nat?

MILLER (*good-naturedly*). You seem to be getting a lot of fun kidding me. Go ahead, then. I don't mind.

MRS. MILLER. He better go right up to bed for a while, that's what he better do.

SID (*considering this owlishly*). Bed? Yes, maybe you're right. (*He gets to his feet.*) I am not at all well—in very delicate condition—we are praying for a boy. Am I right, Nat? Nat, I kept telling you all day I was in delicate condition and yet you kept forcing demon chowder on me, although you knew full well—even if you were full—that there is a certain, peculiar oil in chowder that invariably—— (*They are again all laughing—Lily, hysterically.*)

MRS. MILLER. *Will* you get to bed, you idiot!

SID (*mutters graciously*). Immediately—if not sooner. (*He turns to pass behind Lily, then stops, staring down at her.*) But wait. There is still a duty I must perform. No day is complete without it. Lily, answer once and for all, will you marry me?

LILY (*with an hysterical giggle*). No, I won't—never!

SID (*nodding his head*). Right! And perhaps it's all for the best. For how could I forget the pre—precepts taught me at mother's dying knee. "Sidney," she said, "never marry a woman who drinks! Lips that touch liquor shall never touch yours!" (*Gazing at her mournfully.*) Too bad! So fine a woman once—and now such a slave to rum! (*Turning to Miller.*) What can we do to save her, Nat? (*In a hoarse, confidential whisper.*) Better put her in institution where she'll be removed from temptation! The mere smell of it seems to drive her frantic!

MRS. MILLER (*struggling with her laughter*). You leave Lily alone, and go to bed!

SID. Right! (*He comes around behind Lily's chair and moves toward the entrance to the back parlour—then suddenly turns and says with a bow.*) Good night, ladies—*and* gents. We will meet—by and by! (*He gives an imitation of a Salvation Army drum.*) Boom! Boom! Boom! Come and be saved, Brothers! (*He starts to sing the old Army hymn.*)

"In the sweet
By and by
We will meet on that beautiful shore."

(*He turns and marches solemnly out through the back parlour, singing.*)

"Work and pray
While you may.
We will meet in the sky by and by."

(*Miller and his wife and the children are all roaring with laughter. Lily giggles hysterically.*)

MILLER (*subsiding at last*). Haw, haw. He's a case, if ever there was one! Darned if you can help laughing at him—even when he's poking fun at you!

MRS. MILLER. Goodness, but he's a caution! Oh, my sides ache, I declare! I was trying so hard not to—but you can't help it, he's so silly! But I suppose we really shouldn't. It only encourages him. But, my lands——!

LILY (*suddenly gets up from her chair and stands rigidly, her face working—jerkily*). That's just it—you shouldn't—even I laughed—it does encourage—that's been his downfall—everyone always laughing, everyone always saying what a card he is, what a case, what a caution, so funny—and he's gone on—and we're all responsible—making it easy for him—we're all to blame—and all we do is laugh!

MILLER (*worriedly*). Now, Lily, now, you mustn't take on so. It isn't as serious as all that.

LILY (*bitterly*). Maybe—it is—to me. Or was—once. (*Then contritely.*) I'm sorry, Nat. I'm sorry, Essie. I didn't mean to—I'm not feeling myself tonight. If you'll excuse me, I'll go in the front parlour and lie down on the sofa awhile.

MRS. MILLER. Of course, Lily. You do whatever you've a mind to.

(*Lily goes out.*)

MILLER (*frowning—a little shamefaced*). Hmm. I suppose she's right. Never knew Lily to come out with things that way before. Anything special happened, Essie?

MRS. MILLER. Nothing I know—except he'd promised to take her to the fireworks.

MILLER. That's so. Well, supposing I take her. I don't want her to feel disappointed.

MRS. MILLER (*shaking her head*). Wild horses couldn't drag her there now.

MILLER. Hmm. I thought she'd got completely over her foolishness about him long ago.

MRS. MILLER. She never will.

MILLER. She'd better. He's got fired out of that Waterbury job—told me at the picnic after he'd got enough Dutch courage in him.

MRS. MILLER. Oh, dear! Isn't he the fool!

MILLER. I knew something was wrong when he came home. Well, I'll find a place for him on my paper again, of course. He always was the best news-getter this town ever had. But I'll tell him he's got to stop his damn nonsense.

MRS. MILLER (*doubtfully*). Yes.

MILLER. Well, no use sitting here mourning over spilt milk.

(*He gets up, and Richard, Mildred, Tommy and Mrs. Miller follow his example, the children quiet and a bit awed.*)

You kids go out in the yard and try to keep quiet for a while, so's your Uncle Sid'll get to sleep and your Aunt Lily can rest.

TOMMY (*mournfully*). Ain't we going to set off the sky rockets and Roman candles, Pa?

MILLER. Later, Son, later. It isn't dark enough for them yet anyway.

MILDRED. Come on, Tommy. I'll see he keeps quiet, Pa.

MILLER. That's a good girl.

(*Mildred and Tommy go out through the screen door. Richard remains standing, sunk in bitter, gloomy thoughts.*)

(*Miller glances at him—then irritably.*) Well, Melancholy Dane, what are you doing?

RICHARD (*darkly*). I'm going out—for a while. (*Then suddenly.*) Do you know what I think? It's Aunt Lily's fault, Uncle Sid's going to ruin. It's all because he loves her, and she keeps him dangling after her, and eggs him on and ruins his life—like all women love to ruin men's lives! I don't blame him for drinking himself to death! What does he care if he dies, after the way she's treated him! I'd do the same thing myself if I were in his boots!

MRS. MILLER (*indignantly*). Richard! You stop that talk!

RICHARD (*quotes bitterly*).

" Drink! for you know not whence you come nor why.
Drink! for you know not why you go nor where!"

MILLER (*losing his temper—harshly*). Listen here, young man! I've had about all I can stand of your nonsense for one day! You're growing a lot too big for your size, seems to me! You keep that damn fool talk to yourself, you hear me—or you're going to regret it! Mind, now! (*He strides angrily away through the back parlour.*)

MRS. MILLER (*still indignant*). Richard, I'm ashamed of you, that's what I am.

(*She follows her husband. Richard stands for a second, bitter, humiliated, wronged, even his father turned enemy, his face growing more and more rebellious. Then he forces a scornful smile to his lips.*)

RICHARD. Aw, what the hell do I care? I'll show them! (*He turns and goes out the screen door.*)

CURTAIN

ACT THREE

SCENE ONE

SCENE. *The back room of a bar in a small hotel—a small, dingy room, dimly lighted by two fly-specked globes in a fly-specked gilt chandelier suspended from the middle of the ceiling. At left, front, is the swinging door leading to the bar. At rear of door, against the wall, is a nickel-in-the-slot player-piano. In the rear wall, right, is a door leading to the "Family Entrance" and the stairway to the upstairs rooms. In the middle of the right wall is a window with closed shutters. Three tables with stained tops, four chairs around each table, are placed at centre, front, at right, toward rear, and at rear, centre. A brass cuspidor is on the floor by each table. The floor is unswept, littered with cigarette and cigar-butts. The hideous saffron-coloured wallpaper is blotched and spotted.*

It is about 10 o'clock the same night. Richard and Belle are discovered sitting at the table at centre, Belle at left of it, Richard in the next chair at the middle of table, rear, facing front.

Belle is twenty, a rather pretty peroxide blonde, a typical college "tart" of the period, and of the cheaper variety, dressed with tawdry flashiness. But she is a fairly recent recruit to the ranks, and is still a bit remorseful behind her make-up and defiantly careless manner.

Belle has an empty gin-rickey glass before her, Richard a half-empty glass of beer. He looks horribly timid, embarrassed and guilty, but at the same time thrilled and proud of at last mingling with the pace that kills.

The player-piano is grinding out "Bedelia." The Bartender, a stocky young Irishman with a foxily cunning, stupid face and a cynically wise grin, stands just inside the bar entrance, watching them over the swinging door.

BELLE (*with an impatient glance at her escort—rattling the ice in her empty glass*). Drink up your beer, why don't you? It's getting flat.

RICHARD (*embarrassedly*). I let it get that way on purpose. I like it better when it's flat.

(*But he hastily gulps down the rest of his glass, as if it were some nasty-tasting medicine. The Bartender chuckles audibly. Belle glances at him.*)

BELLE (*nodding at the player-piano scornfully*). Say,

George, is " Bedelia " the latest to hit this hick burg? Well, it's only a couple of years old! You'll catch up in time! Why don't you get a new roll for that old box?

BARTENDER (*with a grin*). Complain to the boss, not me. We're not used to having Candy Kiddoes like you around—or maybe we'd get up to date.

BELLE (*with a professionally arch grin at him*). Don't kid me, please. I can't bear it. (*Then she sings to the music from the piano, her eyes now on Richard.*) " Bedelia, I'd like to feel yer." (*The Bartender laughs. She smirks at Richard.*) Ever hear those words to it, Kid?

RICHARD (*who has heard them but is shocked at hearing a girl say them—putting on a blasé air*). Sure, lots of times. That's old.

BELLE (*edging her chair closer and putting a hand over one of his*). Then why don't you act as if you knew what they were all about?

RICHARD (*terribly flustered*). Sure, I've heard that old parody lots of times. What do you think I am?

BELLE. I don't know, Kid. Honest to God, you've got me guessing.

BARTENDER (*with a mocking chuckle*). He's a hot sport, can't you tell it? I never seen such a spender. My head's dizzy bringing you in drinks!

BELLE (*laughs irritably—to Richard*). Don't let him kid you. You show him. Loosen up and buy another drink, what say?

RICHARD (*humiliated—manfully*). Sure. Excuse me. I was thinking of something else. Have anything you like. (*He turns to the Bartender who has entered from the bar.*) See what the lady will have—and have one on me yourself.

BARTENDER (*coming to the table—with a wink at Belle*). That's talking! Didn't I say you were a sport? I'll take a cigar on you. (*To Belle.*) What's yours, Kiddo—the same?

BELLE. Yes. And forget the house rules this time and remember a rickey is supposed to have gin in it.

BARTENDER (*grinning*). I'll try to—seeing it's you. (*Then to Richard.*) What's yours—another beer?

RICHARD (*shyly*). A small one, please. I'm not thirsty.

BELLE (*calculatedly taunting*). Say, honest, are things that slow up at Harvard? If they had you down at New Haven, they'd put you in a kindergarten! Don't be such a dead one! Filling up on beer will only make you sleepy. Have a man's drink!

RICHARD (*shamefacedly*). All right. I was going to. Bring me a sloe-gin fizz.

BELLE (*to Bartender*). And make it a real one.

BARTENDER (*with a wink*). I get you. Something that'll warm him up, eh? (*He goes into the bar, chuckling.*)

BELLE (*looks around the room—irritably*). Christ, what a dump! (*Richard is startled and shocked by this curse and looks down at the table.*) If this isn't the deadest burg I ever struck! Bet they take the side-walks in after nine o'clock! (*Then turning on him.*) Say, honestly, Kid, does your mother know you're out?

RICHARD (*defensively*). Aw, cut it out, why don't you—trying to kid me!

BELLE (*glances at him—then resolves on a new tack—patting his hand*). All right. I didn't mean to, Dearie. Please don't get sore at me.

RICHARD. I'm not sore.

BELLE (*seductively*). You see, it's this way with me. I think you're one of the sweetest kids I've ever met—and I could like you such a lot if you'd give me half a chance—instead of acting so cold and indifferent.

RICHARD. I'm not cold and indifferent. (*Then solemnly tragic.*) It's only that I've got—a weight on my mind.

BELLE (*impatiently*). Well, get it off your mind and give something else a chance to work.

(*The Bartender comes in, bringing the drinks.*)

BARTENDER (*setting them down—with a wink at Belle*). This'll warm him for you. Forty cents, that is—with the cigar.

RICHARD (*pulls out his roll and hands a dollar bill over—with exaggerated carelessness*). Keep the change.

(*Belle emits a gasp and seems about to protest, then thinks better of it. The Bartender cannot believe his luck for a moment—then pockets the bill hastily, as if afraid Richard will change his mind.*)

BARTENDER (*respect in his voice*). Thank you, sir.

RICHARD (*grandly*). Don't mention it.

BARTENDER. I hope you like the drink. I took special pains with it. (*The voice of the Salesman, who has just come in the bar, calls* " Hey! Anybody here? " *and a coin is rapped on the bar.*) I'm coming. (*The Bartender goes out.*)

BELLE (*remonstrating gently, a new appreciation for her escort's possibilities in her voice*). You shouldn't be so generous, Dearie. Gets him in bad habits. A dime would have been plenty.

RICHARD. Ah, that's all right. I'm no tightwad.

BELLE. That's the talk I like to hear. (*With a quick look toward the bar, she stealthily pulls up her dress—to Richard's shocked fascination—and takes a package of cheap cigarettes from her stocking.*) Keep an eye out for that bartender, Kid, and tell me if you see him coming. Girls are only allowed to smoke upstairs in the rooms, he said.

RICHARD (*embarrassedly*). All right. I'll watch.

BELLE (*having lighted her cigarette and inhaled deeply, holds the package out to him*). Have a Sweet? You smoke, don't you?

RICHARD (*taking one*). Sure! I've been smoking for the last two years—on the sly. But next year I'll be allowed—that is, pipes and cigars. (*He lights his cigarette with elaborate nonchalance, puffs, but does not inhale—then, watching her, with shocked concern.*) Say, you oughtn't to inhale like that! Smoking's awful bad for girls, anyway, even if they don't——

BELLE (*cynically amused*). Afraid it will stunt my growth? Gee, Kid, you are a scream! You'll grow up to be a minister yet! (*Richard looks shamefaced. She scans him impatiently—then holds up her drink.*) Well, here's how! Bottoms up, now! Show me you really know how to drink. It'll take that load off your mind.

(*Richard follows her example, and they both drink the whole contents of their glasses before setting them down.*)

There! That's something like! Feel better?

RICHARD (*proud of himself—with a shy smile*). You bet.

BELLE. Well, you'll feel still better in a minute—and then maybe you won't be so distant and unfriendly, eh?

RICHARD. I'm not.

BELLE. Yes, you are. I think you just don't like me.

RICHARD (*more manfully*). I do too like you.

BELLE. How much? A lot?

RICHARD. Yes, a lot.

BELLE. Show me how much! (*Then as he fidgets embarrassedly.*) Want me to come sit on your lap?

RICHARD. Yes—I—— (*She comes and sits on his lap. He looks desperately uncomfortable, but the gin is rising to his head and he feels proud of himself and devilish, too.*)

BELLE. Why don't you put your arm around me? (*He does so awkwardly.*) No, not that dead way. Hold me tight. You needn't be afraid of hurting me. I like to be held tight, don't you?

RICHARD. Sure I do.

BELLE. 'Specially when it's by a nice handsome kid like you. (*Ruffling his hair.*) Gee, you've got pretty hair; do you know it? Honest, I'm awfully strong for you! Why can't you be about me? I'm not so awfully ugly, am I?

RICHARD. No, you're—you're pretty.

BELLE. You don't say it as if you meant it.

RICHARD. I do mean it—honest.

BELLE. Then why don't you kiss me? (*She bends down her lips toward his. He hesitates, then kisses her and at once shrinks back.*) Call that kissing? Here. (*She holds his head and fastens her lips on his and holds them there. He starts and struggles. She laughs.*) What's the matter, Honey Boy? Haven't you ever kissed like that before?

RICHARD. Sure. Lots of times.

BELLE. Then why did you jump as if I'd bitten you? (*Squirming around on his lap.*) Gee, I'm getting just crazy about you! What shall we do about it, eh? Tell me.

RICHARD. I—don't know. (*Then boldly.*) I—I'm crazy about you, too.

BELLE (*kissing him again*). Just think of the wonderful time Edith and your friend, Wint, are having upstairs—while we sit down here like two dead ones. A room only costs two dollars. And, seeing I like you so much, I'd only take five dollars—from you. I'd do it for nothing—for you—only I've got to live and I owe my room rent in New Haven—and you know how it is. I get ten dollars from everyone else. Honest! (*She kisses him again, then gets up from his lap—briskly.*) Come on. Go out and tell the bartender you want a room. And hurry. Honest, I'm so strong for you I can hardly wait to get you upstairs!

RICHARD (*starts automatically for the door to the bar—then hesitates, a great struggle going on in his mind—timidity, disgust at the money element, shocked modesty, and the guilty thought of Muriel, fighting it out with the growing tipsiness that makes him want to be a hell of a fellow and go in for all forbidden fruit, and makes this tart a romantic, evil vampire in his eyes. Finally, he stops and mutters in confusion*). I can't.

BELLE. What, are you too bashful to ask for a room? Let me do it, then.

(*She starts for the door.*)

RICHARD (*desperately*). No—I don't want you to—I don't want to.

BELLE (*surveying him, anger coming into her eyes*). Well, if you aren't the lousiest cheap skate!

RICHARD. I'm not a cheap skate!

BELLE. Keep me around here all night fooling with you when I might be out with some real live one—if there is such a thing in this burg!—and now you quit on me! Don't be such a piker! You've got five dollars! I seen it when you paid for the drinks, so don't hand me any lies!

RICHARD. I—— Who said I hadn't? And I'm not a piker. If you need the five dollars so bad—for your room rent—you can have it without—I mean, I'll be glad to give—— (*He has been fumbling in his pocket and pulls out his nine-dollar roll and holds out the five to her.*)

BELLE (*hardly able to believe her eyes, almost snatches it from his hand—then laughs and immediately becomes senti-*

mentally grateful). Thanks, Kid. Gee—oh, thanks——Gee, forgive me for losing my temper and bawling you out, will you? Gee, you're a regular peach! You're the nicest kid I've ever met! (*She kisses him and he grins proudly, a hero to himself now on many counts.*) Gee, you're a peach! Thanks, again!

RICHARD (*grandly—and quite tipsily*). It's—nothing—only too glad. (*Then boldly.*) Here—give me another kiss, and that'll pay me back.

BELLE (*kissing him*). I'll give you a thousand, if you want 'em. Come on, let's sit down, and we'll have another drink—and this time I'll blow you just to show my appreciation. (*She calls.*) Hey, George! Bring us another round—the same!

RICHARD (*a remnant of caution coming to him*). I don't know as I ought to——

BELLE. Oh, another won't hurt you. And I want to blow you, see.

(*They sit down in their former places.*)

RICHARD (*boldly draws his chair closer and puts an arm around her—tipsily*). I like you a lot—now I'm getting to know you. You're a darned nice girl.

BELLE. Nice is good! Tell me another! Well, if I'm so nice, why didn't you want to take me upstairs? That's what I don't get.

RICHARD (*lying boldly*). I did want to—only I——(*Then he adds solemnly.*) I've sworn off.

(*The Bartender enters with the drinks.*)

BARTENDER (*setting them on the table*). Here's your pleasure. (*Then regarding Richard's arm about her waist.*) Ho-ho, we're coming on, I see.

(*Richard grins at him muzzily.*)

BELLE (*digs into her stocking and gives him a dollar*). Here. This is mine. (*He gives her change and she tips him a dime, and he goes out. She puts the five Richard had given her in her stocking and picks up her glass.*) Here's how—and thanks again. (*She sips.*)

RICHARD (*boisterously*). Bottoms up! Bottoms up! (*He drinks all of his down and sighs with exaggerated satisfaction.*) Gee, that's good stuff, all right. (*Hugging her.*) Give me another kiss, Belle.

BELLE (*kisses him*). What did you mean a minute ago when you said you'd sworn off?

RICHARD (*solemnly*). I took an oath I'd be faithful.

BELLE (*cynically*). Till death do us part, eh? Who's the girl?

RICHARD (*shortly*). Never mind.

BELLE (*bristling*). I'm not good enough to talk about her, I suppose?

RICHARD. I didn't—mean that. You're all right. (*Then with tipsy gravity.*) Only you oughtn't to lead this kind of life. It isn't right—for a nice girl like you. Why don't you reform?

BELLE (*sharply*). Nix on that line of talk! Can it, you hear! You can do a lot with me for five dollars—but you can't reform me, see. Mind your own business, Kid, and don't butt in where you're not wanted!

RICHARD. I—I didn't mean to hurt your feelings.

BELLE. I know you didn't mean. You're only like a lot of people who mean well, to hear them tell it. (*Changing the subject.*) So you're faithful to your one love, eh? (*With an ugly sneer.*) And how about her? Bet you she's out with a guy under some bush this minute, giving him all he wants. Don't be a sucker, Kid! Even the little flies do it!

RICHARD (*starting up in his chair—angrily*). Don't you say that. Don't you dare!

BELLE (*unimpressed—with a cynical shrug of her shoulders*). All right. Have it your own way and be a sucker! It cuts no ice with me.

RICHARD. You don't know her or——

BELLE. And don't want to. Shut up about her, can't you?

(*She stares before her bitterly. Richard subsides into scowling gloom. He is becoming perceptibly more intoxicated with each moment now. The Bartender and the Salesman appear just inside the swinging door. The Bartender nods toward Belle, giving the Salesman a drink. The Salesman grins and comes into the room, carrying his highball in his hand. He is a stout, jowly-faced man in his late thirties, dressed with cheap nattiness, with the professional breeziness and jocular, kid-'em-along manner of his kind. Belle looks up as he enters and he and she exchange a glance of complete recognition. She knows his type by heart and he knows hers.*)

SALESMAN (*passes by her to the table at right—grinning genially*). Good evening.

BELLE. Good evening.

SALESMAN (*sitting down*). Hope I'm not butting in on your party—but my dogs were giving out standing at that bar.

BELLE. All right with me. (*Giving Richard a rather contemptuous look.*) I've got no party on.

SALESMAN. That sounds hopeful.

RICHARD (*suddenly recites sentimentally*).

"But I wouldn't do such, 'cause I loved her too much,
But I learned about women from her."

(*Turns to scowl at the Salesman—then to Belle.*) Let's have 'nother drink!

BELLE. You've had enough.

(*Richard subsides, muttering to himself.*)

SALESMAN. What is it—a child poet or a child actor?

BELLE. Don't know. Got me guessing.

SALESMAN. Well, if you could shake the cradle-robbing act, maybe we could do a little business.

BELLE. That's easy. I just pull my freight. (*She shakes Richard by the arm.*) Listen, Kid. Here's an old friend of mine, Mr. Smith of New Haven, just come in. I'm going over and sit at his table for a while, see. And you better go home.

RICHARD (*blinking at her and scowling*). I'm never going home! I'll show them!

BELLE. Have it your own way—only let me up.

(*She takes his arm from around her and goes to sit by the Salesman. Richard stares after her offendedly.*)

RICHARD. Go on. What do I care what you do? (*He recites scornfully.*) "For a woman's only a woman, but a good cigar's a smoke."

SALESMAN (*as Belle sits beside him*). Well, what kind of beer will you have, Sister?

BELLE. Mine's a gin rickey.

SALESMAN. You've got extravagant tastes, I'm sorry to see.

RICHARD (*begins to recite sepulchrally*).

"Yet each man kills the thing he loves,
By each let this be heard."

SALESMAN (*grinning*). Say, this is rich! (*He calls encouragement.*) That's swell dope, young feller. Give us some more.

RICHARD (*ignoring him—goes on more rhetorically*).

"Some do it with a bitter look,
Some with a flattering word,
The coward does it with a kiss,
The brave man with a sword!"

(*He stares at Belle gloomily and mutters tragically.*) I did it with a kiss! I'm a coward.

SALESMAN. That's the old stuff, Kid. You've got something on the ball, all right, all right! Give us another—right over the old pan, now!

BELLE (*with a laugh*). Get the hook!

RICHARD (*glowering at her—tragically*).

"'Oho,' they cried, 'the world is wide,
But fettered limbs go lame!
And once, or twice, to throw the dice
Is a gentlemanly game,
But he does not win who plays with Sin
In the secret House of Shame!'"

BELLE (*angrily*). Aw, can it! Give us a rest from that bunk!

SALESMAN (*mockingly*). This gal of yours don't appreciate poetry. She's a lowbrow. But I'm the kid that eats it up. My middle name is Kelly and Sheets! Give us some more of the same! Do you know "The Lobster and the Wise Guy"? (*Turns to Belle seriously.*) No kidding, that's a peacherino. I heard a guy recite it at Poli's. Maybe this nut knows it. Do you, Kid? (*But Richard only glowers at him gloomily without answering.*)

BELLE (*surveying Richard contemptuously*). He's copped a fine skinful—and gee, he's hardly had anything.

RICHARD (*suddenly—with a dire emphasis*). "And then—at ten o'clock—Eilert Lovborg will come—with vine leaves in his hair!"

BELLE. And bats in his belfry, if he's you!

RICHARD (*regards her bitterly—then starts to his feet bellicosely—to the Salesman*). I don't believe you ever knew her in New Haven at all! You just picked her up now! You leave her alone, you hear! You won't do anything to her—not while I'm here to protect her!

BELLE (*laughing*). Oh, my God! Listen to it!

SALESMAN. Ssshh! This is a scream! Wait! (*He addresses Richard in tones of exaggerated melodrama.*) Curse you, Jack Dalton, if I won't unhand her, what then?

RICHARD (*threateningly*). I'll give you a good punch in the snoot, that's what! (*He moves toward their table.*)

SALESMAN (*with mock terror—screams in falsetto*). Help! Help!

(*The Bartender comes in irritably.*)

BARTENDER. Hey. Cut out the noise. What the hell's up with you?

RICHARD (*tipsily*). He's too—damn fresh!

SALESMAN (*with a wink*). He's going to murder me! (*Then gets a bright idea for eliminating Richard—seriously to the Bartender.*) It's none of my business, Brother, but if I were in your boots I'd give this young souse the gate. He's under age; any fool can see that.

BARTENDER (*guiltily*). He told me he was over eighteen.

SALESMAN. Yes, and I tell you I'm the Pope—but you don't have to believe me. If you're not looking for trouble, I'd advise you to get him started for some other gin mill and let them do the lying, if anything comes up.

BARTENDER. Hmm. (*He turns to Richard angrily and gives him a push.*) Come on, now. On your way! You'll start no trouble in here! Beat it now!

RICHARD. I will not beat it!

BARTENDER. Oho, won't you? (*He gives him another push that almost sends him sprawling.*)

BELLE (*callously*). Give him the bum's rush! I'm sick of his bull!

(*Richard turns furiously and tries to punch the Bartender.*)

BARTENDER (*avoids the punch*). Oho, you would, would you! (*He grabs Richard by the back of the neck and the seat of the pants and marches him ignominiously toward the swinging door.*)

RICHARD. Leggo of me, you dirty coward!

BARTENDER. Quiet now—or I'll pin a Mary Ann on your jaw that'll quiet you! (*He rushes him through the screen door and a moment later the outer doors are heard swinging back and forth.*)

SALESMAN (*with a chuckle*). Hand it to me, Kid. How was that for a slick way of getting rid of him?

BELLE (*suddenly sentimental*). Poor kid. I hope he makes home all right. I liked him—before he got soused.

SALESMAN. Who is he?

BELLE. The boy who's upstairs with my friend told me, but I didn't pay much attention. Name's Miller. His old man runs a paper in this one-horse burg, I think he said.

SALESMAN (*with a whistle*). Phew! He must be Nat Miller's kid, then.

BARTENDER (*coming back from the bar*). Well, he's on his way—with a good boot in the tail to help him!

SALESMAN (*with a malicious chuckle*). Yes? Well maybe that boot will cost you a job, Brother. Know Nat Miller who runs the "Globe"? That's his kid.

BARTENDER (*his face falling*). The hell he is! Who said so?

SALESMAN. This baby doll. (*Getting up.*) Say, I'll go keep cases on him—see he gets on the trolley all right, anyway. Nat Miller's a good scout. (*He hurries out.*)

BARTENDER (*viciously*). God damn the luck! If he ever finds out I served his kid, he'll run me out of town. (*He turns on Belle furiously.*) Why didn't you put me wise, you lousy tramp, you!

BELLE. Hey! I don't stand for that kind of talk—not from no hick beer-squirter like you, see!

BARTENDER (*furiously*). You don't, don't you! Who was it but you told me to hand him dynamite in that fizz? (*He gives her chair a push that almost throws her to the floor.*) Beat it, you—and beat it quick—or I'll call Sullivan from the corner and have you run in for street-walking! (*He gives her a push that lands her against the family-entrance door.*) Get the hell out of here—and no long waits!

BELLE (*opens the door and goes out—turns and calls back viciously*). I'll fix you for this, you thick Mick, if I have to go to jail for it. (*She goes out and slams the door.*)

BARTENDER (*looks after her worriedly for a second—then shrugs his shoulders*). That's only her bull. (*Then with a sigh as he returns to the bar.*) Them lousy tramps is always getting this dump in Dutch!

CURTAIN

SCENE TWO

SCENE. *Same as Act One—Sitting-room of the Miller home—about 11 o'clock the same night.*

Miller is sitting in his favourite rocking-chair at left of table, front. He has discarded collar and tie, coat and shoes, and wears an old, worn, brown dressing-gown and disreputable-looking carpet slippers. He has his reading specs on and is running over items in a newspaper. But his mind is plainly preoccupied and worried, and he is not paying much attention to what he reads.

Mrs. Miller sits by the table at right, front. She also has on her specs. A sewing-basket is on her lap and she is trying hard to keep her attention fixed on the doily she is doing. But, as in the case of her husband, but much more apparently, her mind is preoccupied, and she is obviously on tenterhooks of nervous uneasiness.

Lily is sitting in the armchair by the table at rear, facing right. She is pretending to read a novel, but her attention wanders, too, and her expression is sad, although now it has lost all its bitterness and become submissive and resigned again.

Mildred sits at the desk at right, front, writing two words over and over again, stopping each time to survey the result critically, biting her tongue, intensely concentrated on her work.

Tommy sits on the sofa at left, front. He has had a hard day and is terribly sleepy but will not acknowledge it. His eyes blink shut on him, his head begins to nod, but he isn't giving up, and every time he senses any of the family glancing in his direction, he goads himself into a bright-eyed wakefulness.

MILDRED (*finally surveys the two words she has been writing and is satisfied with them*). There. (*She takes the paper over to her mother.*) Look, Ma. I've been practising a new way of writing my name. Don't look at the others, only the last one. Don't you think it's the real goods?

MRS. MILLER (*pulled out of her preoccupation*). Don't talk that horrible slang. It's bad enough for boys, but for a young girl supposed to have manners—my goodness, when I was your age, if my mother'd ever heard me——

MILDRED. Well, don't you think it's nice, then?

MRS. MILLER (*sinks back into preoccupation—scanning the paper—vaguely*). Yes, very nice, Mildred—very nice, indeed. (*Hands the paper back mechanically.*)

MILDRED (*is a little piqued, but smiles*). Absent-minded! I don't believe you even saw it.

(*She passes around the table to show her Aunt Lily. Miller gives an uneasy glance at his wife and then, as if afraid of meeting her eye, looks quickly back at his paper again.*)

MRS. MILLER (*staring before her—sighs worriedly*). Oh, I do wish Richard would come home!

MILLER. There now, Essie. He'll be in any minute now. Don't you worry about him.

MRS. MILLER. But I do worry about him!

LILY (*surveying Mildred's handiwork—smiling*). This is fine, Mildred. Your penmanship is improving wonderfully. But don't you think that maybe you've got a little too many flourishes?

MILDRED (*disappointedly*). But, Aunt Lily, that's just what I was practising hardest on.

MRS. MILLER (*with another sigh*). What time is it now, Nat?

MILLER (*adopting a joking tone*). I'm going to buy a clock for in here. You have me reaching for my watch every couple of minutes. (*He has pulled his watch out of his vest pocket—with forced carelessness.*) Only a little past ten.

MRS. MILLER. Why, you said it was that an hour ago! Nat Miller, you're telling me a fib, so's not to worry me. You let me see that watch!

MILLER (*guiltily*). Well, it's quarter to eleven—but that's not so late—when you remember it's Fourth of July.

MRS. MILLER. If you don't stop talking Fourth of July——! To hear you go on, you'd think that was an excuse for anything from murder to picking pockets!

MILDRED (*has brought her paper around to her father and now shoves it under his nose*). Look, Pa.

MILLER (*seizes on this interruption with relief*). Let's see. Hmm. Seems to me you've been inventing a new signature every week lately. What are you in training for—writing cheques? You must be planning to catch a rich husband.

MILDRED (*with an a rchtoss of her head*). No wedding bells for me! But how do you like it, Pa?

MILLER. It's overpowering—no other word for it, overpowering! You could put it on the Declaration of Independence and not feel ashamed.

MRS. MILLER (*desolately, almost on the verge of tears*). It's all right for you to laugh and joke with Mildred! I'm the only one in this house seems to care——(*Her lips tremble.*)

MILDRED (*a bit disgustedly*). Ah, Ma, Dick only sneaked off to the fireworks at the beach, you wait and see.

MRS. MILLER. Those fireworks were over long ago. If he had, he'd be home.

LILY (*soothingly*). He probably couldn't get a seat, the trolleys are so jammed, and he had to walk home.

MILLER (*seizing on this with relief*). Yes, I never thought of that, but I'll bet that's it.

MILDRED. Ah, don't let him worry you, Ma. He just wants to show off he's heart-broken about that silly Muriel—and get everyone fussing over him and wondering if he hasn't drowned himself or something.

MRS. MILLER (*snappily*). You be quiet! The way you talk at times, I really believe you're that hard-hearted you haven't got a heart in you! (*With an accusing glance at her husband.*) One thing I know, you don't get that from me!

(*He meets her eye and avoids it guiltily. She sniffs and looks away from him around the room. Tommy, who is nodding and blinking, is afraid her eye is on him. He straightens alertly and speaks in a voice that, in spite of his effort, is dripping with drowsiness.*)

TOMMY. Let me see what you wrote, Mid.

MILDRED (*cruelly mocking*). You? You're so sleepy you couldn't see it!

TOMMY (*valiantly*). I am not sleepy!

MRS. MILLER (*has fixed her eye on him*). My gracious, I was forgetting you were still up! You run up to bed this minute! It's hours past your bedtime!

TOMMY. But it's the Fourth of July. Ain't it, Pa?

MRS. MILLER (*gives her husband an accusing stare*). There! You see what you've done? You might know he'd copy your excuses! (*Then sharply to Tommy.*) You heard what I said, Young Man!

TOMMY. Aw, Ma, can't I stay up a *little* longer?

MRS. MILLER. I said, no! You obey me and no more arguing about it!

TOMMY (*drags himself to his feet*). Aw! I should think I could stay up till Dick——

MILLER (*kindly but firmly*). You heard your ma say no more arguing. When she says git, you better git.

(*Tommy accepts his fate resignedly and starts around kissing them all good night.*)

TOMMY (*kissing her*). Good night, Aunt Lily.

LILY. Good night, dear. Sleep well.

TOMMY (*pecking at Mildred*). Good night, you.

MILDRED. Good night, you.

TOMMY (*kissing him*). Good night, Pa.

MILLER. Good night, Son. Sleep tight.

TOMMY (*kissing her*). Good night, Ma.

MRS. MILLER. Good night. Here! You look feverish. Let me feel of your head. No, you're all right. Hurry up, now. And don't forget your prayers.

(*Tommy goes slowly to the doorway—then turns suddenly, the discovery of another excuse lighting up his face.*)

TOMMY. Here's another thing, Ma. When I was up to the water-closet last——

MRS. MILLER (*sharply*). When you were *where*?

TOMMY. The bathroom.

MRS. MILLER. That's better.

TOMMY. Uncle Sid was snoring like a fog-horn—and he's right next to my room. How can I ever get to sleep while he's—— (*He is overcome by a jaw-cracking yawn.*)

MRS. MILLER. I guess you'd get to sleep all right if you were inside a fog-horn. You run along now.

(*Tommy gives up, grins sleepily, and moves off to bed. As soon as he is off her mind, all her former uneasiness comes back on Mrs. Miller tenfold. She sighs, moves restlessly, then finally asks:*)

What time is it now, Nat?

MILLER. Now, Essie, I just told you a minute ago.

MRS. MILLER (*resentfully*). I don't see how you can take it so calm! Here it's midnight, you might say, and our Richard still out, and we don't even know where he is.

MILDRED. I hear someone on the piazza. Bet that's him now, Ma.

MRS. MILLER (*her anxiety immediately turning to relieved anger*). You give him a good piece of your mind, Nat, you hear me! You're too easy with him, that's the whole trouble! The idea of him daring to stay out like this!

(*The front door is heard being opened and shut, and someone whistling "Watlz Me Around Again, Willie."*)

MILDRED. No, that isn't Dick. It's Art.

MRS. MILLER (*her face falling*). Oh.

(*A moment later Arthur enters through the front parlour, whistling softly, half under his breath, looking complacently pleased with himself.*)

MILLER (*surveys him over his glasses, not with enthusiasm—shortly*). So you're back, eh? We thought it was Richard.

ARTHUR. Is he still out? Where'd he go to?

MILLER. That's just what we'd like to know. You didn't run into him anywhere, did you?

ARTHUR. No. I've been at the Rands' ever since dinner. (*He sits down in the armchair at left of table, rear.*) I suppose he sneaked off to the beach to watch the fireworks.

MILLER (*pretending an assurance he is far from feeling*). Of course. That's what we've been trying to tell your mother, but she insists on worrying her head off.

MRS. MILLER. But if he was going to the fireworks, why wouldn't he say so? He knew we'd let him.

ARTHUR (*with calm wisdom*). That's easy, Ma. (*He grins superiorly.*) Didn't you hear him this morning showing off bawling out the Fourth like an anarchist? He wouldn't want to reneg on that to you—but he'd want to see the old fireworks just the same. (*He adds complacently.*) I know. He's at the foolish age.

MILLER (*stares at Arthur with ill-concealed astonishment, then grins*). Well, Arthur, by gosh, you make me feel as if I owed you an apology when you talk horse sense like that. (*He turns to his wife, greatly relieved.*) Arthur's hit the nail right on the head, I think, Essie. That was what I couldn't figure out—why he—but now it's clear as day.

MRS. MILLER (*with a sigh*). Well, I hope you're right. But I wish he was home.

ARTHUR (*takes out his pipe and fills and lights it with solemn gravity*). He oughtn't to be allowed out this late at his age. I wasn't, Fourth or no Fourth—if I remember.

MILLER (*a twinkle in his eyes*). Don't tax your memory trying to recall those ancient days of your youth.

(*Mildred laughs and Arthur looks sheepish. But he soon regains his aplomb.*)

ARTHUR (*importantly*). We had a corking dinner at the Rands'. We had sweetbreads on toast.

MRS. MILLER (*arising momentarily from her depression*). Just like the Rands to put on airs before you! I never could see anything to sweetbreads. Always taste like soap to me. And no real nourishment to them. I wouldn't have the pesky things on my table!

(*Arthur again feels sat upon.*)

MILDRED (*teasingly*). Did you kiss Elsie good night?

ARTHUR. Stop trying to be so darn funny all the time! You give me a pain in the ear!

MILDRED. And that's where she gives me a pain, the stuck-up thing!—thinks she's the whole cheese!

MILLER (*irritably*). And it's where your everlasting wrangling gives me a pain, you two! Give us a rest!

(*There is silence for a moment.*)

MRS. MILLER (*sighs worriedly again*). I do wish that boy would get home !

MILLER (*glances at her uneasily, peeks surreptitiously at his watch—then has an inspiration and turns to Arthur*). Arthur, what's this I hear about your having such a good singing voice ? Rand was telling me he liked nothing better than to hear you sing—said you did every night you were up there. Why don't you ever give us folks at home here a treat ?

ARTHUR (*pleased, but still nursing wounded dignity*). I thought you'd only sit on me.

MRS. MILLER (*perking up—proudly*). Arthur has a real nice voice. He practises when you're not at home. I didn't know you cared for singing, Nat.

MILLER. Well, I do—nothing better—and when I was a boy I had a fine voice myself and folks used to say I'd ought—— (*Then abruptly, mindful of his painful experience with reminiscence at dinner, looking about him guiltily.*) Hmm. But don't hide your light under a bushel, Arthur. Why not give us a song or two now ? You can play for him, can't you, Mildred ?

MILDRED (*with a toss of her head*). I can play as well as Elsie Rand, at least !

ARTHUR (*ignoring her—clearing his throat importantly*). I've been singing a lot to-night. I don't know if my voice——

MILDRED (*forgetting her grudge, grabs her brother's hand and tugs at it*). Come on. Don't play modest. You know you're just dying to show off.

(*This puts Arthur off it at once. He snatches his hand away from her angrily.*)

ARTHUR. Let go of me, you ! (*Then with surly dignity.*) I don't feel like singing to-night, Pa. I will some other time.

MILLER. You let him alone, Mildred !

(*He winks at Arthur, indicating with his eyes and a nod of his head Mrs. Miller, who has again sunk into worried brooding. He makes it plain by this pantomime that he wants him to sing to distract his mother's mind.*)

ARTHUR (*puts aside his pipe and gets up promptly*). Oh—sure, I'll do the best I can. (*He follows Mildred into the front parlour, where he switches on the lights.*)

MILLER (*to his wife*). It won't keep Tommy awake. Nothing could. And Sid, he'd sleep through an earthquake. (*Then suddenly, looking through the front parlour—grumpily.*) Darn it, speak of the devil, here he comes. Well, he's had a good sleep and he'd ought to be sobered up. (*Lily gets up from her chair and looks around her huntedly, as if for a place to hide. Miller says soothingly:*) Lily, you just sit down and read your book and don't pay any attention to him.

(*She sits down again and bends over her book tensely. From the front parlour comes the tinkling of a piano as Mildred runs over the scales. In the midst of this, Sid enters through the front parlour. All the effervescence of his jag has worn off and he is now suffering from a bad case of hangover—nervous, sick, a prey to gloomy remorse and bitter feelings of self-loathing and self-pity. His eyes are bloodshot and puffed, his face bloated, the fringe of hair around his baldness tousled and tufty. He sidles into the room guiltily, his eyes shifting about, avoiding looking at anyone.*)

SID (*forcing a sickly, twitching smile*). Hello.

MILLER (*considerately casual*). Hello, Sid. Had a good nap ?

(*Then, as Sid swallows hard and is about to break into further speech, Mildred's voice comes from the front parlour,* " I haven't played that in ever so long, but I ll try," *and she starts an accompaniment. Miller motions Sid to be quiet.*)

Ssshh ! Arthur's going to sing for us.

(*Sid flattens himself against the edge of the bookcase at centre, rear, miserably self-conscious and ill at ease there but nervously afraid to move anywhere else. Arthur begins to sing. He has a fairly decent voice but his method is untrained sentimentality to a dripping degree. He sings that old sentimental favourite, " Then You'll Remember Me." The effect on his audience is instant. Miller gazes before him with a ruminating melancholy, his face seeming to become gently sorrowful and old. Mrs. Miller stares before her, her expression becoming more and more doleful. Lily forgets to pretend to read her book but looks over it, her face growing tragically sad. As for Sid, he is moved to his remorseful, guilt-stricken depths. His mouth pulls down at the corners and he seems about to cry. The song comes to an end. Miller starts, then claps his hands enthusiastically and calls :*)

Well done, Arthur—well done ! Why, you've got a splendid voice ! Give us some more ! You liked that, didn't you, Essie ?

MRS. MILLER (*dolefully*). Yes—but it's sad—terrible sad.

SID (*after swallowing hard, suddenly blurts out*). Nat and Essie—and Lily—I—I want to apologize—for coming home—the way I did—there's no excuse—but I didn't mean——

MILLER (*sympathetically*). Of course, Sid. It's all forgotten.

MRS. MILLER (*rousing herself—affectionately pitying*).

Don't be a goose, Sid. We know how it is with picnics. You forget it.

(*His face lights up a bit but his gaze shifts to Lily with a mute appeal, hoping for a word from her which is not forthcoming. Her eyes are fixed on her book, her body tense and rigid.*)

SID (*finally blurts out desperately*). Lily—I'm sorry—about the fireworks. Can you—forgive me?

(*But Lily remains implacably silent. A stricken look comes over Sid's face. In the front parlour Mildred is heard saying* "But I only know the chorus"—*and she starts another accompaniment.*)

MILLER (*comes to Sid's rescue*). Ssshh! We're going to have another song. Sit down, Sid.

(*Sid, hanging his head, flees to the farthest corner, left, front, and sits at the end of the sofa, facing front, hunched up, elbows on knees, face in hands, his round eyes childishly wounded and woebegone. Arthur sings the popular "Dearie," playing up its sentimental values for all he is worth. The effect on his audience is that of the previous song, intensified—especially upon Sid. As he finishes, Miller again starts and applauds.*)

Mighty fine, Arthur! You sang that darned well! Didn't he, Essie?

MRS. MILLER (*dolefully*). Yes—but I wish he wouldn't sing such sad songs. (*Then, her lips trembling.*) Richard's always whistling that.

MILLER (*hastily—calls*). Give us something cheery, next one, Arthur. You know, just for variety's sake.

SID (*suddenly turns toward Lily—his voice choked with tears—in a passion of self-denunciation*). You're right, Lily!—right not to forgive me!—I'm no good and never will be!—I'm a no-good drunken bum!—you shouldn't even wipe your feet on me!—I'm a dirty, rotten drunk!—no good to myself or anybody else!—if I had any guts I'd kill myself, and good riddance!—but I haven't!—I'm yellow, too!—a yellow, drunken bum!

(*He hides his face in his hands and begins to sob like a sick little boy. This is too much for Lily. All her bitter hurt and steely resolve to ignore and punish him vanish in a flash, swamped by a pitying love for him. She runs and puts her arm around him—even kisses him tenderly and impulsively on his bald head, and soothes him as if he were a little boy. Mrs. Miller, almost equally moved, has half risen to go to her brother, too, but Miller winks and shakes his head vigorously and motions her to sit down.*)

LILY. There! Don't cry, Sid! I can't bear it! Of course, I forgive you! Haven't I always forgiven you? I know you're not to blame—— So don't, Sid!

SID (*lifts a tearful, humbly grateful, pathetic face to her—but a face that the dawn of a cleansed conscience is already beginning to restore to its natural Puckish expression*). Do you really forgive me—— I know I don't deserve it—can you really——?

LILY (*gently*). I told you I did, Sid—and I do.

SID (*kisses her hand humbly, like a big puppy licking it*). Thanks, Lily. I can't tell you——

(*In the front parlour, Arthur begins to sing rollickingly "Waiting at the Church," and after the first line or two Mildred joins in. Sid's face lights up with appreciation and, automatically, he begins to tap one foot in time, still holding fast to Lily's hand. When they come to "sent around a note, this is what she wrote," he can no longer resist, but joins in a shaky bawl.*)

"Can't get away to marry you to-day, My wife won't let me!"

(*As the song finishes, the two in the other room laugh. Miller and Sid laugh. Lily smiles at Sid's laughter. Only Mrs. Miller remains dolefully preoccupied, as if she hadn't heard.*)

MILLER. That's fine, Arthur and Mildred. That's darned good.

SID (*turning to Lily enthusiastically*). You ought to hear Vesta Victoria sing that! Gosh, she's great! I heard her at Hammerstein's Victoria—you remember, that trip I made to New York.

LILY (*her face suddenly tired and sad again—for her memory of certain aspects of that trip is the opposite from what he would like her to recall at this moment—gently disengaging her hand from his—with a hopeless sigh*). Yes, I remember, Sid.

(*He is overcome momentarily by guilty confusion. She goes quietly and sits down in her chair again. In the front parlour, from now on, Mildred keeps starting to run over popular tunes but always gets stuck and turns to another.*)

MRS. MILLER (*suddenly*). What time is it now, Nat? (*Then without giving him a chance to answer.*) Oh, I'm getting worried something dreadful, Nat! You don't know what might have happened to Richard! You read in the papers every day about boys getting run over by automobiles.

LILY. Oh, don't say that, Essie!

MILLER (*sharply, to conceal his own reawakened apprehension*). Don't get to imagining things, now!

MRS. MILLER. Well, why couldn't it happen, with everyone that owns one out to-night, and lots of those driving, drunk? Or he might have gone down to the beach dock and fallen overboard! (*On the verge of hysteria.*) Oh, I know something dreadful's happened! And you can sit there listening to songs and laughing as if—— Why don't you do something? Why don't you go out and find him? (*She bursts into tears.*)

LILY (*comes to her quickly and puts her arm around her*). Essie, you mustn't worry so! You'll make yourself sick! Richard's all right. I've got a feeling in my bones he's all right.

MILDRED (*comes hurrying in from the front parlour*). What's the trouble? (*Arthur appears in the doorway beside her. She goes to her mother and also puts an arm around her.*) Ah, don't cry, Ma! Dick'll turn up in a minute or two, wait and see!

ARTHUR. Sure, he will!

MILLER (*has gotten to his feet, frowning—soberly*). I was going out to look—if he wasn't back by twelve sharp. That'd be the time it'd take him to walk from the beach if he left after the last car. But I'll go now, if it'll ease your mind. I'll take the auto and drive out the beach road—and likely pick him up on the way. (*He has taken his collar and tie from where they hang from one corner of the bookcase at rear, centre, and is starting to put them on.*) You better come with me, Arthur.

ARTHUR. Sure thing, Pa. (*Suddenly he listens and says.*) Ssshh! There's someone on the piazza now—coming around to this door, too. That must be him. No one else would——

MRS. MILLER. Oh, thank God, thank God!

MILLER (*with a sheepish smile*). Darn him! I've a notion to give him hell for worrying us all like this.

(*The screen door is pushed violently open and Richard lurches in and stands swaying a little, blinking his eyes in the light. His face is a pasty pallor, shining with perspiration, and his eyes are glassy. The knees of his trousers are dirty, one of them torn from the sprawl on the sidewalk he had taken, following the Bartender's kick. They all gape at him, too paralysed for a moment to say anything.*)

MRS. MILLER. Oh God, what's happened to him! He's gone crazy! Richard!

SID (*the first to regain presence of mind—with a grin*). Crazy, nothing. He's only soused!

ARTHUR. He's drunk, that's what! (*Then shocked and condemning.*) You've got your nerve! You fresh kid! We'll take that out of you when we get you down to Yale!

RICHARD (*with a wild gesture of defiance—maudlinly dramatic*).

"Yesterday this Day's Madness did prepare
To-morrow's Silence, Triumph, or Despair.
Drink! for——"

MILLER (*his face grown stern and angry, takes a threatening step toward him*). Richard! How dare——!

MRS. MILLER (*hysterically*). Don't you strike him, Nat! Don't you——!

SID (*grabbing his arm*). Steady, Nat! Keep your temper! No good bawling him out now! He don't know what he's doing!

MILLER (*controlling himself and looking a bit ashamed*). All right—you're right, Sid.

RICHARD (*drunkenly glorying in the sensation he is creating—recites with dramatic emphasis*). "And then—I will come—with vine leaves in my hair!" (*He laughs with a double-dyed sardonicism.*)

MRS. MILLER (*staring at him as if she couldn't believe her eyes*). Richard! You're intoxicated!—you bad, wicked boy, you!

RICHARD (*forces a wicked leer to his lips and quotes with ponderous mockery*). "Fancy that, Hedda!" (*Then suddenly his whole expression changes, his pallor takes on a greenish, seasick tinge, his eyes seem to be turned inward uneasily—and, all pose gone, he calls to his mother appealingly, like a sick little boy.*) Ma! I feel—rotten!

(*Mrs. Miller gives a cry and starts to go to him, but Sid steps in her way.*)

SID. You let me take care of him, Essie. I know this game backwards.

MILLER (*putting his arm around his wife*). Yes, you leave him to Sid.

SID (*his arm around Richard—leading him off through the front parlour*). Come on, Old Sport! Upstairs we go! Your old Uncle Sid'll fix you up. He's the kid that wrote the book!

MRS. MILLER (*staring after them—still aghast*). Oh, it's too terrible! Imagine our Richard! And did you hear him talking about some Hedda? Oh, I know he's been with one of those bad women, I know he has—my Richard! (*She hides her face on Miller's shoulder and sobs heart-brokenly.*)

MILLER (*a tired, harassed, deeply worried look on his face—soothing her*). Now, now, you mustn't get to imagining such things! You mustn't, Essie! (*Lily and Mildred and Arthur are standing about awkwardly with awed, shocked faces.*)

CURTAIN

ACT FOUR SCENE ONE

SCENE. *The same—Sitting-room of the Miller house—about* 1 *o'clock in the afternoon of the following day.*

As the curtain rises, the family, with the exception of Richard, are discovered coming in through the back parlour from dinner in the dining-room. Miller and his wife come first. His face is set in an expression of frowning severity. Mrs. Miller's face is drawn and worried. She has evidently had no rest yet from a sleepless, tearful night. Sid is himself again, his expression as innocent as if nothing had occurred the previous day that remotely concerned him. And, outside of eyes that are bloodshot and nerves that are shaky, he shows no after-effects except that he is terribly sleepy. Lily is gently sad and depressed. Arthur is self-consciously a virtuous young man against whom nothing can be said. Mildred and Tommy are subdued, covertly watching their father.

They file into the sitting-room in silence and then stand around uncertainly, as if each were afraid to be the first to sit down. The atmosphere is as stiltedly grave as if they were attending a funeral service. Their eyes keep fixed on the head of the house, who has gone to the window at right and is staring out frowningly, savagely chewing a toothpick.

MILLER (*finally—irritably*). Damn it, I'd ought to be back at the office putting in some good licks! I've a whole pile of things that have got to be done to-day!

MRS. MILLER (*accusingly*). You don't mean to tell me you're going back without seeing him? It's your duty——!

MILLER (*exasperatedly*). 'Course I'm not! I wish you'd stop jumping to conclusions! What else did I come home for, I'd like to know? Do I usually come way back here for dinner on a busy day? I was only wishing this hadn't come up—just at this particular time. (*He ends up very lamely and is irritably conscious of the fact.*)

TOMMY (*who has been fidgeting restlessly—unable to bear the suspense a moment longer*). What is it Dick done? Why is everyone scared to tell me?

MILLER (*seizes this as an escape valve—turns and fixes his youngest son with a stern, forbidding eye*). Young man, I've never spanked you yet, but that don't mean I never will! Seems to me that you've been just itching for it lately! You keep your mouth shut till you're spoken to—or I warn you something's going to happen!

MRS. MILLER. Yes, Tommy, you keep still and don't bother your pa. (*Then warningly to her husband.*) Careful what you say, Nat. Little pitchers have big ears.

MILLER (*peremptorily*). You kids skedaddle—all of you. Why are you always hanging around the house? Go out and play in the yard, or take a walk, and get some fresh air.

(*Mildred takes Tommy's hand and leads him out through the front parlour. Arthur hangs back, as if the designation "kids" couldn't possibly apply to him. His father notices this—impatiently.*)

You, too, Arthur.

(*Arthur goes out with a stiff, wounded dignity.*)

LILY (*tactfully*). I think I'll go for a walk, too.

(*She goes out through the front parlour. Sid makes a movement as if to follow her.*)

MILLER. I'd like you to stay, Sid—for a while, anyway.

SID. Sure. (*He sits down in the rocking-chair at right, rear, of table and immediately yawns.*) Gosh, I'm dead. Don't know what's the matter with me to-day. Can't seem to keep awake.

MILLER (*with caustic sarcasm*). Maybe that demon chowder you drank at the picnic poisoned you!

(*Sid looks sheepish and forces a grin. Then Miller turns to his wife with the air of one who determinedly faces the unpleasant.*)

Where is Richard?

MRS. MILLER (*flusteredly*). He's still in bed. I made him stay in bed to punish him—and I thought he ought to, anyway, after being so sick. But he says he feels all right.

SID (*with another yawn*). 'Course he does. When you're young you can stand anything without it feazing you. Why, I remember when I could come down on the morning after, fresh as a daisy, and eat a breakfast of pork chops and fried onions and—— (*He stops guiltily.*)

MILLER (*bitingly*). I suppose that was before eating lobster shells had ruined your iron constitution!

MRS. MILLER (*regards her brother severely*). If I was in your shoes, I'd keep still! (*Then turning to her husband.*) Richard must be feeling better. He ate all the dinner I sent up, Norah says.

MILLER. I thought you weren't going to give him any dinner—to punish him.

MRS. MILLER (*guiltily*). Well—in his weakened condition—I thought it best—— (*Then defensively.*) But you needn't think I haven't punished him. I've given him pieces of my mind he won't forget in a hurry. And I've kept reminding him his real punishment was still to come—that you were coming home to dinner on purpose—and then he'd learn that you could be terrible stern when he did such awful things.

MILLER (*stirs uncomfortably*). Hmm!

MRS. MILLER. And that's just what it's your duty to

do—punish him good and hard! The idea of him daring—— (*Then hastily.*) But you be careful how you go about it, Nat. Remember he's like you inside—too sensitive for his own good. And he never would have done it, I know, if it hadn't been for that darned little dunce, Muriel, and her numbskull father—and then all of us teasing him and hurting his feelings all day—and then you lost your temper and were so sharp with him right after dinner before he went out.

MILLER (*resentfully*). I see this is going to work round to where it's all my fault!

MRS. MILLER. Now, I didn't say that, did I? Don't go losing your temper again. And here's another thing. You know as well as I, Richard would never have done such a thing alone. Why, he wouldn't know how! He must have been influenced and led by someone.

MILLER. Yes, I believe that. Did you worm out of him who it was? (*Then angrily.*) By God, I'll make whoever it was regret it!

MRS. MILLER. No, he wouldn't admit there was anyone. (*Then triumphantly.*) But there is one thing I did worm out of him—and I can tell you it relieved my mind more'n anything. You know, I was afraid he'd been with one of those bad women. Well, turns out there wasn't any Hedda. She was just out of those books he's been reading. He swears he's never known a Hedda in his life. And I believe him. Why, he seemed disgusted with me for having such a notion. (*Then lamely.*) So somehow—I can't kind of feel it's all as bad as I thought it was. (*Then quickly and indignantly.*) But it's bad enough, goodness knows—and you punish him good just the same. The idea of a boy of his age——! Shall I go up now and tell him to get dressed, you want to see him?

MILLER (*helplessly—and irritably*). Yes! I can't waste all day listening to you!

MRS. MILLER (*worriedly*). Now you keep your temper, Nat, remember!

(*She goes out through the front parlour.*)

MILLER. Darn women, anyway! They always get you mixed up. Their minds simply don't know what logic is! (*Then he notices that Sid is dozing—sharply.*) Sid!

SID (*blinking—mechanically*). I'll take the same. (*Then hurriedly.*) What'd you say, Nat?

MILLER (*caustically*). What I didn't say was what'll you have. (*Irritably.*) Do you want to be of some help, or don't you? Then keep awake and try and use your brains! This is a damned sight more serious than Essie has any idea! She thinks there weren't any girls mixed up with Richard's spree last night—but I happen to know there were! (*He takes a letter from his pocket.*) Here's a note a woman left with one of the boys downstairs at the office this morning—didn't ask to see me, just said give me this. He'd never seen her before—said she looked like a tart. (*He has opened the letter and reads:*) "Your son got the booze he drank last night at the Pleasant Beach House. The bartender there knew he was under age but served him just the same. He thought it was a good joke to get him soused. If you have any guts you will run that bastard out of town." Well, what do you think of that? It's a woman's handwriting—not signed, of course.

SID. She's one of the babies, all right—judging from her elegant language.

MILLER. See if you recognize the handwriting.

SID (*with a reproachful look*). Nat, I resent the implication that I correspond with all the tramps around this town. (*Looking at the letter.*) No, I don't know who this one could be. (*Handing the letter back.*) But I deduce that the lady had a run-in with the barkeep and wants revenge.

MILLER (*grimly*). And I deduce that before that she must have picked up Richard—or how would she know who he was?—and took him to this dive.

SID. Maybe. The Pleasant Beach House is nothing but a bed house—— (*Quickly.*) At least, so I've been told.

MILLER. That's just the sort of damned fool thing he might do to spite Muriel, in the state of mind he was in—pick up some tart. And she'd try to get him drunk so——

SID. Yes, it might have happened like that—and it might not. How're we ever going to prove it? Everyone at the Pleasant Beach will lie their heads off.

MILLER (*simply and proudly*). Richard won't lie.

SID. Well, don't blame him if he don't remember everything that happened last night. (*Then sincerely concerned.*) I hope you're wrong, Nat. That kind of baby is dangerous for a kid like Dick—in more ways than one. You know what I mean.

MILLER (*frowningly*). Yep—and that's just what's got me worried. Damn it, I've got to have a straight talk with him—about women and all those things. I ought to have long ago.

SID. Yes. You ought.

MILLER. I've tried to a couple of times. I did it all right with Wilbur and Lawrence and Arthur, when it came time—but, hell, with Richard I always get sort of ashamed of myself and can't get started right. You feel, in spite of all his bold talk out of books, that he's so darned innocent inside.

SID. I know. I wouldn't like the job. (*Then after a pause—curiously.*) How were you figuring to punish him for his sins?

MILLER (*frowning*). To be honest with you, Sid, I'm damned if I know. All depends on what I feel about what he feels when I first size him up—and then it'll be like shooting in the dark.

SID. If I didn't know you so well, I'd say don't be too hard on him. (*He smiles a little bitterly.*) If you remember, I was always getting punished—and see what a lot of good it did me!

MILLER (*kindly*). Oh, there's lots worse than you around, so don't take to boasting. (*Then, at a sound from the front parlour—with a sigh.*) Well, here comes the Bad Man, I guess.

SID (*getting up*). I'll beat it.

(*But it is Mrs. Miller who appears in the doorway, looking guilty and defensive. Sid sits down again.*)

MRS. MILLER. I'm sorry, Nat—but he was sound asleep and I didn't have the heart to wake him. I waited for him to wake up but he didn't.

MILLER (*concealing a relief of which he is ashamed—exasperatedly*). Well, I'll be double damned! If you're not the——

MRS. MILLER (*defensively aggressive*). Now don't lose your temper at me, Nat Miller! You know as well as I do he needs all the sleep he can get to-day—after last night's ructions! Do you want him to be taken down sick? And what difference does it make to you, anyway? You can see him when you come home for supper, can't you? My goodness, I never saw you so savage-tempered! You'd think you couldn't bear waiting to punish him?

MILLER (*outraged*). Well, I'll be eternally—— (*Then suddenly he laughs.*) No use talking, you certainly take the cake! But you know darned well I told you I'm not coming home to supper to-night. I've got a date with Jack Lawson that may mean a lot of new advertising and it's important.

MRS. MILLER. Then you can see him when you do come home.

MILLER (*covering his evident relief at this respite with a fuming manner*). All right! All right! I give up! I'm going back to the office. (*He starts for the front parlour.*) Bring a man all the way back here on a busy day and then you—— No consideration——

(*He disappears, and a moment later the front door is heard shutting behind him.*)

MRS. MILLER. Well! I never saw Nat so bad-tempered.

SID (*with a chuckle*). Bad temper, nothing. He's so tickled to get out of it for a while he can't see straight!

MRS. MILLER (*with a sniff*). I hope I know him better than you. (*Then fussing about the room, setting this and that in place, while Sid yawns drowsily and blinks his eyes.*) Sleeping like a baby—so innocent-looking. You'd think butter wouldn't melt in his mouth. It all goes to show you never can tell by appearances—not even when it's your own child. The idea!

SID (*drowsily*). Oh, Dick's all right, Essie. Stop worrying.

MRS. MILLER (*with a sniff*). Of course, you'd say that. I suppose you'll have him out with you painting the town red the next thing!

(*As she is talking, Richard appears in the doorway from the sitting-room. He shows no ill effects from his experience the night before. In fact, he looks surprisingly healthy. He is dressed in old clothes that look as if they had been hurriedly flung on. His expression is one of hang-dog guilt mingled with a defensive defiance.*)

RICHARD (*with self-conscious unconcern, ignoring his mother*). Hello, Sid.

MRS. MILLER (*whirls on him*). What are you doing here, Young Man? I thought you were asleep! Seems to me you woke up pretty quick—just after your pa left the house!

RICHARD (*sulkily*). I wasn't asleep. I heard you in the room.

MRS. MILLER (*outraged*). Do you mean to say you were deliberately deceiving——

RICHARD. I wasn't deceiving. You didn't ask if I was asleep.

MRS. MILLER. It amounts to the same thing and you know it! It isn't enough your wickedness last night, but now you have to take to lying!

RICHARD. I wasn't lying, Ma. If you'd asked if I was asleep I'd have said no.

MRS. MILLER. I've a good mind to send you straight back to bed and make you stay there!

RICHARD. Ah, what for, Ma? It was only giving me a headache, lying there.

MRS. MILLER. If you've got a headache, I guess you know it doesn't come from that! And imagine me standing there, and feeling sorry for you, like a fool—even having a run-in with your pa because—— But you wait till he comes back to-night! If you don't catch it!

RICHARD (*sulkily*). I don't care.

MRS. MILLER. You don't care? You talk as if you weren't sorry for what you did last night!

RICHARD (*defiantly*). I'm not sorry.

MRS. MILLER. Richard! You ought to be ashamed! I'm beginning to think you're hardened in wickedness, that's what!

RICHARD (*with bitter despondency*). I'm not sorry

because I don't care a darn what I did, or what's done to me, or anything about anything! I won't do it again——

MRS. MILLER (*seizing on this to relent a bit*). Well, I'm glad to hear you say that, anyway!

RICHARD. But that's not because I think it was wicked or any such old-fogy moral notion, but because it wasn't any fun. It didn't make me happy and funny like it does Uncle Sid——

SID (*drowsily*). What's that? Who's funny?

RICHARD (*ignoring him*). It only made me sadder—and sick—so I don't see any sense in it.

MRS. MILLER. Now you're talking sense! That's a good boy.

RICHARD. But I'm not sorry I tried it once—curing the soul by means of the senses, as Oscar Wilde says. (*Then with despairing pessimism.*) But what does it matter what I do or don't do? Life is all a stupid farce! I'm through with it! (*With a sinister smile.*) It's lucky there aren't any of General Gabler's pistols around—or you'd see if I'd stand it much longer!

MRS. MILLER (*worriedly impressed by this threat—but pretending scorn*). I don't know anything about General Gabler—I suppose that's more of those darned books—but you're a silly gabbler yourself when you talk that way!

RICHARD (*darkly*). That's how little you know about me.

MRS. MILLER (*giving in to her worry*). I wish you wouldn't say those terrible things—about life and pistols! You don't want to worry me to death, do you?

RICHARD (*reassuringly stoical now*). You needn't worry, Ma. It was only my despair talking. But I'm not a coward. I'll face—my fate.

MRS. MILLER (*stands looking at him puzzledly—then gives it up with a sigh*). Well, all I can say is you're the queerest boy I ever did hear of! (*Then solicitously, putting her hand on his forehead.*) How's your headache? Do you want me to get you some Bromo Seltzer?

RICHARD (*taken down—disgustedly*). No, I don't! Aw, Ma, you don't understand anything!

MRS. MILLER. Well, I understand this much: It's your liver, that's what! You'll take a good dose of salts to-morrow morning, and no nonsense about it! (*Then suddenly.*) My goodness, I wonder what time it's getting to be. I've got to go upstreet. (*She goes to the front-parlour doorway—then turns.*) You stay here, Richard, you hear? Remember you're not allowed out to-day—for a punishment.

(*She hurries away. Richard sits in tragic gloom. Sid, without opening his eyes, speaks to him drowsily.*)

SID. Well, how's my fellow Rum Pot, as good old Dowie calls us? Got a head?

RICHARD (*startled—sheepishly*). Aw, don't go dragging that up, Uncle Sid. I'm never going to be such a fool again, I tell you.

SID (*with drowsy cynicism—not unmixed with bitterness at the end*). Seems to me I've heard someone say that before. Who could it have been, I wonder? Why, if it wasn't Sid Davis! Yes, sir, I've heard him say that very thing a thousand times, must be. But then he's always fooling; you can't take a word he says seriously; he's a card, that Sid is!

RICHARD (*darkly*). I was desperate, Uncle—even if she wasn't worth it. I was wounded to the heart.

SID. I like to the quick better myself—more stylish. (*Then sadly.*) But you're right. Love is hell on a poor sucker. Don't I know it?

(*Richard is disgusted and disdains to reply. Sid's chin sinks on his chest and he begins to breathe noisily, fast asleep. Richard glances at him with aversion. There is a sound of someone on the porch and the screen door is opened and Mildred enters. She smiles on seeing her uncle, then gives a start on seeing Richard.*)

MILDRED. Hello! Are you allowed up?

RICHARD. Of course, I'm allowed up.

MILDRED (*comes and sits in her father's chair at right, front, of table*). How did Pa punish you?

RICHARD. He didn't. He went back to the office without seeing me.

MILDRED. Well, you'll catch it later. (*Then rebukingly.*) And you ought to. If you'd ever seen how awful you looked last night!

RICHARD. Ah, forget it, can't you?

MILDRED. Well, are you ever going to do it again, that's what I want to know.

RICHARD. What's that to you?

MILDRED (*with suppressed excitement*). Well, if you don't solemnly swear you won't—then I won't give you something I've got for you.

RICHARD. Don't try to kid me. You haven't got anything.

MILDRED. I have, too.

RICHARD. What?

MILDRED. Wouldn't you like to know! I'll give you three guesses.

RICHARD (*with disdainful dignity*). Don't bother me. I'm in no mood to play riddles with kids!

MILDRED. Oh, well, if you're going to get snippy! Anyway, you haven't promised yet.

RICHARD (*a prey to keen curiosity now*). I promise. What is it?

MILDRED. What would you like best in the world?

RICHARD. I don't know. What?

MILDRED. And you pretend to be in love! If I told Muriel that!

RICHARD (*breathlessly*). Is it—from her?

MILDRED (*laughing*). Well, I guess it's a shame to keep you guessing. Yes. It is from her. I was walking past her place just now when I saw her waving from their parlour window, and I went up and she said give this to Dick, and she didn't have a chance to say anything else because her mother called her and said she wasn't allowed to have company. So I took it—and here it is. (*She gives him a letter folded many times into a tiny square. Richard opens it with a trembling eagerness and reads. Mildred watches him curiously—then sighs affectedly.*) Gee, it must be nice to be in love like you are—all with one person.

RICHARD (*his eyes shining*). Gee, Mid, do you know what she says—that she didn't mean a word in that other letter. Her old man made her write it. And she loves me and only me and always will, no matter how they punish her!

MILDRED. My! I'd never think she had that much spunk.

RICHARD. Huh! You don't know her! Think I could fall in love with a girl that was afraid to say her soul's her own? I should say not! (*Then more gleefully still.*) And she's going to try and sneak out and meet me to-night. She says she thinks she can do it. (*Then suddenly feeling this enthusiasm before Mildred is entirely the wrong note for a cynical pessimist—with an affected bitter laugh.*) Ha! I knew darned well she couldn't hold out—that she'd ask to see me again. (*He misquotes cynically.*) "Women never know when the curtain has fallen. They always want another act."

MILDRED. Is that so, Smarty?

RICHARD (*as if he were weighing the matter*). I don't know whether I'll consent to keep this date or not.

MILDRED. Well, I know! You're not allowed out, you silly! So you can't!

RICHARD (*dropping all pretense—defiantly*). Can't I, though! You wait and see if I can't! I'll see her to-night if it's the last thing I ever do! I don't care how I'm punished after!

MILDRED (*admiringly*). Goodness! I never thought you had such nerve!

RICHARD. You promise to keep your face shut, Mid—until after I've left—then you can tell Pa and Ma where I've gone—I mean, if they're worrying I'm off like last night.

MILDRED. All right. Only you've got to do something for me when I ask.

RICHARD. 'Course I will. (*Then excitedly.*) And say, Mid! Right now's the best chance for me to get away—while everyone's out! Ma'll be coming back soon and she'll keep watching me like a cat—— (*He starts for the back parlour.*) I'm going. I'll sneak out the back.

MILDRED (*excitedly*). But what'll you do till night-time? It's ages to wait.

RICHARD. What do I care how long I wait! (*Intensely sincere now.*) I'll think of her—and dream! I'd wait a million years and never mind it—for her! (*He gives his sister a superior scornful glance.*) The trouble with you is, you don't understand what love means!

(*He disappears through the back parlour. Mildred looks after him admiringly. Sid puffs and begins to snore peacefully.*)

CURTAIN

SCENE TWO

SCENE. *A strip of beach along the harbour. At left, a bank of dark earth, running half-diagonally back along the beach, marking the line where the sand of the beach ends and fertile land begins. The top of the bank is grassy and the trailing boughs of willow trees extend out over it and over a part of the beach. At left, front, is a path leading up the bank, between the willows. On the beach, at centre, front, a white, flat-bottomed rowboat is drawn up, its bow about touching the bank, the painter trailing up the bank, evidently made fast to the trunk of a willow. Half-way down the sky, at rear, left, the crescent of the new moon casts a soft, mysterious, caressing light over everything. The sand of the beach shimmers palely. The forward half (left of centre) of the rowboat is in the deep shadow cast by the willow, the stern section is in moonlight. In the distance, the orchestra of a summer hotel can be heard very faintly at intervals.*

Richard is discovered sitting sideways on the gunwale of the rowboat near the stern. He is facing left, watching the path. He is in a great state of anxious expectancy, squirming about uncomfortably on the narrow gunwale, kicking at the sand restlessly, twirling his straw hat, with a bright-coloured band in stripes, around on his finger.

RICHARD (*thinking aloud*). Must be nearly nine. . . . I can hear the Town Hall clock strike, it's so still to-night . . . Gee, I'll bet Ma had a fit when she found out I'd sneaked out . . . I'll catch hell when I get back, but it'll be worth it . . . if only Muriel turns up . . . she didn't say for certain she could . . . gosh, I wish she'd come ! . . . am I sure she wrote nine ? . . . (*He puts the straw hat on the seat amidships and pulls the folded letter out of his pocket and peers at it in the moonlight.*) Yes, it's nine, all right. (*He starts to put the note back in his pocket, then stops and kisses it—then shoves it away hastily, sheepish, looking around him shamefacedly, as if afraid he were being observed.*) Aw, that's silly . . . no, it isn't either . . . not when you're really in love. . . . (*He jumps to his feet restlessly.*) Darn it, I wish she'd show up ! . . . think of something else . . . that'll make the time pass quicker . . . where was I this time last night ? . . . waiting outside the Pleasant Beach House . . . Belle . . . ah, forget her ! . . . now, when Muriel's coming . . . that's a fine time to think of—— ! . . . but you hugged and kissed her . . . not until I was drunk, I didn't . . . and then it was all showing off . . . darned fool ! . . . and I didn't go upstairs with her . . . even if she was pretty . . . aw, she wasn't pretty . . . she was all painted up . . . she was just a whore . . . she was everything dirty . . . Muriel's a million times prettier anyway . . . Muriel and I will go upstairs . . . when we're married . . . but that will be beautiful . . . but I oughtn't even to think of that yet . . . it's not right . . . I'd never—now . . . and she'd never . . . she's a decent girl . . . I couldn't love her if she wasn't . . . but after we're married. . . . (*He gives a little shiver of passionate longing—then resolutely turns his mind away from these improper, almost desecrating thoughts.*) That damned barkeep kicking me . . . I'll bet you if I hadn't been drunk I'd have given him one good punch in the nose, even if he could have licked me after ! . . . (*Then with a shiver of shamefaced revulsion and self-disgust.*) Aw, you deserved a kick in the pants . . . making such a darned slob of yourself . . . reciting the Ballad of Reading Gaol to those lowbrows ! . . . you must have been a fine sight when you got home ! . . . having to be put to bed and getting sick ! . . . Phaw ! . . . (*He squirms disgustedly.*) Think of something else, can't you ? . . . recite something . . . see if you remember . . .

" Nay, let us walk from fire unto fire,
From passionate pain to deadlier delight—
I am too young to live without desire,
Too young art thou to waste this summer night——"

. . . gee, that's a peach ! . . . I'll have to memorize the rest and recite it to Muriel the next time. . . . I wish I could write poetry . . . about her and me. . . . (*He sighs and stares around him at the night.*) Gee, it's beautiful to-night . . . as if it was a special night . . . for me and Muriel. . . . Gee, I love to-night. . . . I love the sand, and the trees, and the grass, and the water and the sky, and the moon . . . it's all in me and I'm in it . . . God, it's so beautiful ! (*He stands staring at the moon with a rapt face. From the distance the Town Hall clock begins to strike. This brings him back to earth with a start.*) There's nine now. . . . (*He peers at the path apprehensively.*) I don't see her . . . she must have got caught. . . . (*Almost tearfully.*) Gee, I hate to go home and catch hell . . . without having seen her ! . . . (*Then calling a manly cynicism to his aid.*) Aw, who ever heard of a woman ever being on time. . . . I ought to know enough about life by this time not to expect . . . (*Then with sudden excitement.*) There she comes now. . . . Gosh ! (*He heaves a huge sigh of relief—then recites dramatically to himself, his eyes on the approaching figure.*)

" And lo my love, mine own soul's heart, more dear
Than mine own soul, more beautiful than God,
Who hath my being between the hands of her——"

(*Then hastily.*) Mustn't let her know I'm so tickled. . . . I ought to be about that first letter, anyway . . . if women are too sure of you, they treat you like slaves . . . let her suffer, for a change. . . . (*He starts to stroll around with exaggerated carelessness, turning his back on the path, hands in pockets, whistling with insouciance " Waiting at the Church."*)

(*Muriel McComber enters from down the path, left front. She is fifteen, going on sixteen. She is a pretty girl with a plump, graceful little figure, fluffy, light-brown hair, big naïve wondering dark eyes, a round, dimpled face, a melting drawly voice. Just now she is in a great thrilled state of timid adventurousness. She hesitates in the shadow at the foot of the path, waiting for Richard to see her ; but he resolutely goes on whistling with back turned, and she has to call him.*)

MURIEL. Oh, Dick !

RICHARD (*turns around with an elaborate simulation of being disturbed in the midst of profound meditation*). Oh, hello. Is it nine already ? Gosh, time passes—when you're thinking.

MURIEL (*coming toward him as far as the edge of the shadow—disappointedly*). I thought you'd be waiting right here at the end of the path. I'll bet you'd forgotten I was even coming.

RICHARD (*strolling a little toward her but not too far—carelessly*). No, I hadn't forgotten, honest. But I got to thinking about life.

MURIEL. You might think of me for a change, after all the risk I've run to see you ! (*Hesitating timidly on the edge of the shadow.*) Dick ! You come here to me.

I'm afraid to go out in that bright moonlight where anyone might see me.

RICHARD (*coming toward her—scornfully*). Aw, there you go again—always scared of life!

MURIEL (*indignantly*). Dick Miller, I do think you've got an awful nerve to say that after all the risks I've run making this date and then sneaking out! You didn't take the trouble to sneak any letter to me, I notice!

RICHARD. No, because after your first letter, I thought everything was dead and past between us.

MURIEL. And I'll bet you didn't care one little bit! (*On the verge of humiliated tears.*) Oh, I was a fool ever to come here! I've got a good notion to go right home and never speak to you again! (*She half turns back toward the path.*)

RICHARD (*frightened—immediately becomes terribly sincere—grabbing her hand*). Aw, don't go, Muriel! Please! I didn't mean anything like that, honest I didn't! Gee, if you knew how broken-hearted I was by that first letter, and how darned happy your second letter made me——!

MURIEL (*happily relieved—but appreciates she has the upper hand now and doesn't relent at once*). I don't believe you.

RICHARD. You ask Mid how happy I was. She can prove it.

MURIEL. She'd say anything you told her to. I don't care anything about what she'd say. It's you. You've got to swear to me——

RICHARD. I swear!

MURIEL (*demurely*). Well then, all right, I'll believe you.

RICHARD (*his eyes on her face lovingly—genuine adoration in his voice*). Gosh, you're pretty to-night, Muriel! It seems ages since we've been together! If you knew how I've suffered——!

MURIEL. I did, too.

RICHARD (*unable to resist falling into his tragic literary pose for a moment*). The despair in my soul—— (*He recites dramatically:*) "Something was dead in each of us, And what was dead was Hope!" That was me! My hope of happiness was dead! (*Then with sincere boyish fervour.*) Gosh, Muriel, it sure is wonderful to be with you again! (*He puts a timid arm around her awkwardly.*)

MURIEL (*shyly*). I'm glad—it makes you happy. I'm happy, too.

RICHARD. Can't I—won't you let me kiss you—now? Please! (*He bends his face toward hers.*)

MURIEL (*ducking her head away—timidly*). No. You mustn't. Don't——

RICHARD. Aw, why can't I?

MURIEL. Because—I'm afraid.

RICHARD (*discomfited—taking his arm from around her—a bit sulky and impatient with her*). Aw, that's what you always say! You're always so afraid! Aren't you ever going to let me?

MURIEL. I will—sometime.

RICHARD. When?

MURIEL. Soon, maybe.

RICHARD. To-night, will you?

MURIEL (*coyly*). I'll see.

RICHARD. Promise?

MURIEL. I promise—maybe.

RICHARD. All right. You remember you've promised. (*Then coaxingly:*) Aw, don't let's stand here. Come on out and we can sit down in the boat.

MURIEL (*hesitantly*). It's so bright out there.

RICHARD. No one'll see. You know there's never anyone around here at night.

MURIEL (*illogically*). I know there isn't. That's why I thought it would be the best place. But there might be someone.

RICHARD (*taking her hand and tugging at it gently*). There isn't a soul. (*Muriel steps out a little and looks up and down fearfully. Richard goes on insistently.*) Aw, what's the use of a moon if you can't see it!

MURIEL. But it's only a new moon. That's not much to look at.

RICHARD. But I want to see you. I can't here in the shadow. I want to—drink in—all your beauty.

MURIEL (*can't resist this*). Well, all right—only I can't stay only a few minutes. (*She lets him lead her toward the stern of the boat.*)

RICHARD (*pleadingly*). Aw, you can stay a little while, can't you? Please! (*He helps her in and she settles herself in the stern seat of the boat, facing diagonally left front.*)

MURIEL. A little while. (*He sits beside her.*) But I've got to be home in bed again pretending to be asleep by ten o'clock. That's the time Pa and Ma come up to bed, as regular as clockwork, and Ma always looks into my room.

RICHARD. But you'll have oodles of time to do that.

MURIEL (*excitedly*). Dick, you have no idea what I went through to get here to-night! My, but it was exciting! You know Pa's punishing me by sending me to bed at eight sharp, and I had to get all undressed and into bed 'cause at half-past he sends Ma up to make sure I've obeyed, and she came up, and I pretended to be asleep, and she went down again, and I got up and dressed in such a hurry—I must look a sight, don't I?

RICHARD. You do not! You look wonderful!

MURIEL. And then I sneaked down the back stairs. And the pesky old stairs squeaked, and my heart was in my mouth, I was so scared, and then I sneaked out through the back yard, keeping in the dark under the trees, and—— My, but it was exciting! Dick, you don't realize how I've been punished for your sake. Pa's been so mean and nasty, I've almost hated him!

RICHARD. And you don't realize what I've been through for you—and what I'm in for—for sneaking out—— (*Then darkly.*) And for what I did last night —what your letter made me do!

MURIEL (*made terribly curious by his ominous tone*). What did my letter make you do?

RICHARD (*beginning to glory in this*). It's too long a story—and let the dead past bury its dead. (*Then with real feeling.*) Only it isn't past, I can tell you! What I'll catch when Pa gets hold of me!

MURIEL. Tell me, Dick! Begin at the beginning and tell me!

RICHARD (*tragically*). Well, after your old—your father left our place I caught holy hell from Pa.

MURIEL. Dick! You mustn't swear!

RICHARD (*sombrely*). Hell is the only word that can describe it. And on top of that, to torture me more, he gave me your letter. After I'd read that I didn't want to live any more. Life seemed like a tragic farce.

MURIEL. I'm so awful sorry, Dick—honest I am! But you might have known I'd never write that unless——

RICHARD. I thought your love for me was dead. I thought you'd never loved me, that you'd only been cruelly mocking me—to torture me!

MURIEL. Dick! I'd never! You know I'd never!

RICHARD. I wanted to die. I sat and brooded about death. Finally I made up my mind I'd kill myself.

MURIEL (*excitedly*). Dick! You didn't!

RICHARD. I did, too! If there'd been one of Hedda Gabler's pistols around, you'd have seen if I wouldn't have done it beautifully! I thought, when I'm dead, she'll be sorry she ruined my life!

MURIEL (*cuddling up a little to him*). If you ever had! I'd have died, too! Honest, I would!

RICHARD. But suicide is the act of a coward. That's what stopped me. (*Then with a bitter change of tone.*) And anyway, I thought to myself, she isn't worth it.

MURIEL (*huffily*). That's a nice thing to say!

RICHARD. Well, if you meant what was in that letter, you wouldn't have been worth it, would you?

MURIEL. But I've told you Pa——

RICHARD. So I said to myself, I'm through with women; they're all alike!

MURIEL. I'm not.

RICHARD. And I thought, what difference does it make what I do now? I might as well forget her and lead the pace that kills, and drown my sorrows! You know I had eleven dollars saved up to buy you something for your birthday, but I thought, she's dead to me now and why shouldn't I throw it away? (*Then hastily.*) I've still got almost five left, Muriel, and I can get you something nice with that.

MURIEL (*excitedly*). What do I care about your old presents? You tell me what you did!

RICHARD (*darkly again*). After it was dark, I sneaked out and went to a low dive I know about.

MURIEL. Dick Miller, I don't believe you ever!

RICHARD. You ask them at the Pleasant Beach House if I didn't! They won't forget me in a hurry!

MURIEL (*impressed and horrified*). You went there? Why, that's a terrible place! Pa says it ought to be closed by the police!

RICHARD (*darkly*). I said it was a dive, didn't I? It's a "secret house of shame." And they let me into a secret room behind the bar-room. There wasn't anyone there but a Princeton Senior I know—he belongs to Tiger Inn and he's full-back on the football team—and he had two chorus girls from New York with him, and they were all drinking champagne.

MURIEL (*disturbed by the entrance of the chorus girls*). Dick Miller! I hope you didn't notice——

RICHARD (*carelessly*). I had a highball by myself and then I noticed one of the girls—the one that wasn't with the full-back—looking at me. She had strange-looking eyes. And then she asked me if I wouldn't drink champagne with them and come and sit with her.

MURIEL. She must have been a nice thing! (*Then a bit falteringly.*) And did—you?

RICHARD (*with tragic bitterness*). Why shouldn't I, when you'd told me in that letter you'd never see me again?

MURIEL (*almost tearfully*). But you ought to have known Pa made me——

RICHARD. I didn't know that then. (*Then rubbing it in.*) Her name was Belle. She had yellow hair—the kind that burns and stings you!

MURIEL. I'll bet it was dyed!

RICHARD. She kept smoking one cigarette after another—but that's nothing for a chorus girl.

MURIEL (*indignantly*). She was low and bad, that's what she was or she couldn't be a chorus girl, and her smoking cigarettes proves it! (*Then falteringly again.*) And then what happened?

RICHARD (*carelessly*). Oh, we just kept drinking champagne—I bought a round—and then I had a fight with the barkeep and knocked him down because he'd insulted her. He was a great big thug but——

MURIEL (*huffily*). I don't see how he could—insult that kind! And why did you fight for her? Why didn't the Princeton full-back who'd brought them there? He must have been bigger than you.

RICHARD (*stopped for a moment—then quickly*). He was too drunk by that time.

MURIEL. And were you drunk?

RICHARD. Only a little then. I was worse later. (*Proudly.*) You ought to have seen me when I got home! I was on the verge of delirium tremens!

MURIEL. I'm glad I didn't see you. You must have been awful. I hate people who get drunk. I'd have hated you!

RICHARD. Well, it was all your fault, wasn't it? If you hadn't written that letter——

MURIEL. But I've told you I didn't mean—— (*Then faltering but fascinated.*) But what happened with that Belle—after—before you went home?

RICHARD. Oh, we kept drinking champagne and she said she'd fallen in love with me at first sight and she came and sat on my lap and kissed me.

MURIEL (*stiffening*). Oh!

RICHARD (*quickly, afraid he has gone too far*). But it was only all in fun, and then we just kept on drinking champagne, and finally I said good night and came home.

MURIEL. And did you kiss her?

RICHARD. No, I didn't.

MURIEL (*distractedly*). You did, too! You're lying and you know it. You did, too! (*Then tearfully.*) And there I was right at that time lying in bed not able to sleep, wondering how I was ever going to see you again and crying my eyes out, while you——! (*She suddenly jumps to her feet in a tearful fury.*) I hate you! I wish you were dead! I'm going home this minute! I never want to lay eyes on you again! And this time I mean it!

(*She tries to jump out of the boat, but he holds her back. All the pose has dropped from him now and he is in a frightened state of contrition.*)

RICHARD (*imploringly*). Muriel! Wait! Listen!

MURIEL. I don't want to listen! Let me go! If you don't I'll bite your hand!

RICHARD. I won't let you go! You've got to let me explain! I never——! Ouch!

(*For Muriel has bitten his hand and it hurts, and, stung by the pain, he lets go instinctively, and she jumps quickly out of the boat and starts running toward the path. Richard calls after her with bitter despair and hurt.*)

All right! Go if you want to—if you haven't the decency to let me explain! I hate you, too! I'll go and see Belle!

MURIEL (*seeing he isn't following her, stops at the foot of the path—defiantly*). Well, go and see her—if that's the kind of girl you like! What do I care? (*Then as he only stares before him broodingly, sitting dejectedly in the stern of the boat, a pathetic figure of injured grief.*) You can't explain! What can you explain? You owned up you kissed her!

RICHARD. I did not. I said she kissed me.

MURIEL (*scornfully, but drifting back a step in his direction*). And I suppose you just sat and let yourself be kissed! Tell that to the Marines!

RICHARD (*injuredly*). All right! If you're going to call me a liar every word I say——

MURIEL (*drifting back another step*). I didn't call you a liar. I only meant—it sounds fishy. Don't you know it does?

RICHARD. I don't know anything. I only know I wish I was dead!

MURIEL (*gently reproving*). You oughtn't to say that. It's wicked. (*Then after a pause.*) And I suppose you'll tell me you didn't fall in love with her?

RICHARD (*scornfully*). I should say not! Fall in love with that kind of girl! What do you take me for?

MURIEL (*practically*). How do you know what you did if you drank so much champagne?

RICHARD. I kept my head—with her. I'm not a sucker, no matter what you think!

MURIEL (*drifting nearer*). Then you didn't—love her?

RICHARD. I hated her! She wasn't even pretty! And I had a fight with her before I left, she got so fresh. I told her I loved you and never could love anyone else, and for her to leave me alone.

MURIEL. But you said just now you were going to see her——

RICHARD. That was only bluff. I wouldn't—unless you left me. Then I wouldn't care what I did—any more than I did last night. (*Then suddenly defiant.*) And what if I did kiss her once or twice? I only did it to get back at you!

MURIEL. Dick!

RICHARD. You're a fine one to blame me—when it was all your fault! Why can't you be fair? Didn't I think you were out of my life for ever? Hadn't you written me you were? Answer me that!

MURIEL. But I've told you a million times that Pa——

RICHARD. Why didn't you have more sense than to let him make you write it? Was it my fault you didn't?

MURIEL. It was your fault for being so stupid! You ought to have known he stood right over me and told me each word to write. If I'd refused, it would only have made everything worse. I had to pretend, so I'd get a chance to see you. Don't you see, Silly? And I had sand enough to sneak out to meet you to-night, didn't I? (*He doesn't answer. She moves nearer.*) Still I can see how you felt the way you did—and maybe I am to blame for that. So I'll forgive and forget, Dick—if you'll swear to me you didn't even think of loving that——

RICHARD (*eagerly*). I didn't! I swear, Muriel. I couldn't. I love you!

MURIEL. Well, then—I still love you.

RICHARD. Then come back here, why don't you?

MURIEL (*coyly*). It's getting late.

RICHARD. It's not near half-past yet.

MURIEL (*comes back and sits down by him shyly*). All right—only I'll have to go soon, Dick. (*He puts his arm around her. She cuddles up close to him.*) I'm sorry—I hurt your hand.

RICHARD. That was nothing. It felt wonderful—even to have you bite!

MURIEL (*impulsively takes his hand and kisses it*). There! That'll cure it. (*She is overcome by confusion at her boldness.*)

RICHARD. You shouldn't—waste that—on my hand. (*Then tremblingly.*) You said—you'd let me——

MURIEL. I said, maybe.

RICHARD. Please, Muriel. You know—I want it so!

MURIEL. Will it wash off—her kisses—make you forget you ever—for always?

RICHARD. I should say so! I'd never remember—anything but it—never want anything but it—ever again.

MURIEL (*shyly lifting her lips*). Then—all right—Dick. (*He kisses her tremblingly and for a moment their lips remain together. Then she lets her head sink on his shoulder and sighs softly.*) The moon *is* beautiful, isn't it?

RICHARD (*kissing her hair*). Not as beautiful as you! Nothing is! (*Then after a pause.*) Won't it be wonderful when we're married?

MURIEL. Yes—but it's so long to wait.

RICHARD. Perhaps I needn't go to Yale. Perhaps Pa will give me a job. Then I'd soon be making enough to——

MURIEL. You better do what your pa thinks best—and I'd like you to be at Yale. (*Then patting his face.*) Poor you! Do you think he'll punish you awful?

RICHARD (*intensely*). I don't know and I don't care! Nothing would have kept me from seeing you to-night—not if I'd had to crawl over red-hot coals! (*Then falling back on Swinburne—but with passionate sincerity.*) You have my being between the hands of you! You are "my love, mine own soul's heart, more dear than mine own soul, more beautiful than God!"

MURIEL (*shocked and delighted*). Ssshh! It's wrong to say that.

RICHARD (*adoringly*). Gosh, but I love you! Gosh, I love you—Darling!

MURIEL. I love you, too—Sweetheart!

(*They kiss. Then she lets her head sink on his shoulder again and they both sit in a rapt trance, staring at the moon.*)

(*After a pause—dreamily.*) Where'll we go on our honeymoon, Dick? To Niagara Falls?

RICHARD (*scornfully*). That dump where all the silly fools go? I should say not! (*With passionate romanticism.*) No, we'll go to some far-off wonderful place! (*He calls on Kipling to help him.*) Somewhere out on the Long Trail—the trail that is always new—on the road to Mandalay! We'll watch the dawn come up like thunder out of China!

MURIEL (*hazily but happily*). That'll be wonderful, won't it?

CURTAIN

SCENE THREE

SCENE. *The sitting-room of the Miller house again—about 10 o'clock the same night. Miller is sitting in his rocker at left, front, of table, his wife in the rocker at right, front, of table. Moonlight shines through the screen door at right, rear. Only the green-shaded reading lamp is lit and by its light Miller, his specs on, is reading a book while his wife, sewing basket in lap, is working industriously on a doily. Mrs. Miller's face wears an expression of unworried content. Miller's face has also lost its look of harassed preoccupation, although he still is a prey to certain misgivings, when he allows himself to think of them. Several books are piled on the table by his elbow, the books that have been confiscated from Richard.*

MILLER (*chuckles at something he reads—then closes the book and puts it on the table. Mrs. Miller looks up from her sewing*). This Shaw's a comical cuss—even if his ideas are so crazy they oughtn't to allow them to be printed. And that Swinburne's got a fine swing to his poetry—if he'd only choose some other subjects besides loose women.

MRS. MILLER (*smiling teasingly*). I can see where you're becoming corrupted by those books, too—pretending to read them out of duty to Richard, when your nose has been glued to the page!

MILLER. No, no—but I've got to be honest. There's something to them. That Rubaiyat of Omar Khayyâm, now. I read that over again and liked it even better than I had before—parts of it, that is, where it isn't all about boozing.

MRS. MILLER (*has been busy with her own thoughts during this last—with a deep sigh of relief*). My, but I'm glad Mildred told me where Richard went off to. I'd have worried my heart out if she hadn't. But now, it's all right.

MILLER (*frowning a little*). I'd hardly go so far as to say that. Just because we know he's all right to-night doesn't mean last night is wiped out. He's still got to be punished for that.

MRS. MILLER (*defensively*). Well, if you ask me, I think after the way I punished him all day, and the way I know he's punished himself, he's had about all he deserves. I've told you how sorry he was, and how he said he'd never touch liquor again. It didn't make him feel happy like Sid, but only sad and sick, so he didn't see anything in it for him.

MILLER. Well, if he's really got that view of it driven into his skull, I don't know but I'm glad it all happened. That'll protect him more than a thousand lectures—just horse sense about himself. (*Then frowning again.*) Still, I can't let him do such things and go scot-free. And then; besides, there's another side to it—— (*He stops abruptly.*)

MRS. MILLER (*uneasily*). What do you mean, another side?

MILLER (*hastily*). I mean, discipline. There's got to be some discipline in a family. I don't want him to get the idea he's got a stuffed shirt at the head of the table. No, he's got to be punished, if only to make the lesson stick in his mind, and I'm going to tell him he can't go to Yale, seeing he's so undependable.

MRS. MILLER (*up in arms at once*). Not go to Yale! I guess he can go to Yale! Every man of your means in town is sending his boys to college! What would folks think of you? You let Wilbur go, and you'd have let Lawrence, only he didn't want to, and you're letting Arthur! If our other children can get the benefit of a college education, you're not going to pick on Richard——

MILLER. Hush up, for God's sake! If you'd let me finish what I started to say! I said I'd *tell* him that now—bluff—then later on I'll change my mind, if he behaves himself.

MRS. MILLER. Oh well, if that's all—— (*Then defensively again.*) But it's your duty to give him every benefit. He's got an exceptional brain, that boy has! He's proved it by the way he likes to read all those deep plays and books and poetry.

MILLER. But I thought you—— (*He stops, grinning helplessly.*)

MRS. MILLER. You thought I what?

MILLER. Never mind.

MRS. MILLER (*sniffs, but thinks it better to let this pass*). You mark my words, that boy's going to turn out to be a great lawyer, or a great doctor, or a great writer, or——

MILLER (*grinning*). You agree he's going to be great, anyway.

MRS. MILLER. Yes, I most certainly have a lot of faith in Richard.

MILLER. Well, so have I, as far as that goes.

MRS. MILLER (*after a pause—judicially*). And as for his being in love with Muriel, I don't see but what it might work out real well. Richard could do worse.

MILLER. But I thought you had no use for her, thought she was stupid.

MRS. MILLER. Well, so I did, but if she's good for Richard and he wants her—— (*Then inconsequentially.*) Ma used to say you weren't overbright, but she changed her mind when she saw I didn't care if you were or not.

MILLER (*not exactly pleased by this*). Well, I've been bright enough to——

MRS. MILLER (*going on as if he had not spoken*). And Muriel's real cute-looking, I have to admit that. Takes after her mother. Alice Briggs was the prettiest girl before she married.

MILLER. Yes, and Muriel will get big as a house after she's married, the same as her mother did. That's the trouble. A man never can tell what he's letting himself in for—— (*He stops, feeling his wife's eyes fixed on him with indignant suspicion.*)

MRS. MILLER (*sharply*). I'm not too fat and don't you say it!

MILLER. Who was talking about you?

MRS. MILLER. And I'd rather have some flesh on my bones than be built like a string bean and bore a hole in a chair every time I sat down—like some people!

MILLER (*ignoring the insult—flatteringly*). Why, no one'd ever call you fat, Essie. You're only plump, like a good figure ought to be.

MRS. MILLER (*childishly pleased—gratefully giving tit for tat*). Well, you're not skinny, either—only slender—and I think you've been putting on weight lately, too.

(*Having thus squared matters she takes up her sewing again. A pause. Then Miller asks incredulously.*)

MILLER. You don't mean to tell me you're actually taking this Muriel crush of Richard's seriously, do you? I know it's a good thing to encourage right now but—pshaw, why, Richard'll probably forget all about her before he's away six months, and she'll have forgotten him.

MRS. MILLER. Don't be so cynical. (*Then, after a pause, thoughtfully.*) Well, anyway, he'll always have it to remember—no matter what happens after—and that's something.

MILLER. You bet that's something. (*Then with a grin.*) You surprise me at times with your deep wisdom.

MRS. MILLER. You don't give me credit for ever having common sense, that's why. (*She goes back to her sewing.*)

MILLER (*after a pause*). Where'd you say Sid and Lily had gone off to?

MRS. MILLER. To the beach to listen to the band. (*She sighs sympathetically.*) Poor Lily! Sid'll never change, and she'll never marry him. But she seems to get some queer satisfaction out of fussing over him like a hen that's hatched a duck—though Lord knows I wouldn't in her shoes!

MILLER. Arthur's up with Elsie Rand, I suppose?

MRS. MILLER. Of course.

MILLER. Where's Mildred?

MRS. MILLER. Out walking with her latest. I've forgot who it is. I can't keep track of them. (*She smiles.*)

MILLER (*smiling*). Then, from all reports, we seem to be completely surrounded by love!

MRS. MILLER. Well, we've had our share, haven't we? We don't have to begrudge it to our children. (*Then has a sudden thought.*) But I've done all this talking about Muriel and Richard and clean forgot how wild old McComber was against it. But he'll get over that, I suppose.

MILLER (*with a chuckle*). He has already. I ran into him upstreet this afternoon and he was meek as pie. He backed water and said he guessed I was right. Richard had just copied stuff out of books, and kids would be kids, and so on. So I came off my high horse a bit—but not too far—and I guess all that won't bother anyone any more. (*Then rubbing his hands together—with a boyish grin of pleasure.*) And I told you about getting that business from Lawson, didn't I? It's been a good day, Essie—a darned good day!

(*From the hall beyond the front parlour the sound of the front door being opened and shut is heard. Mrs. Miller leans forward to look, pushing her specs up.*)

MRS. MILLER (*in a whisper*). It's Richard.

MILLER (*immediately assuming an expression of becoming gravity*). Hmm.

(*He takes off his spectacles and puts them back in their case and straightens himself in his chair. Richard comes slowly in from the front parlour. He walks like one in a trance, his eyes shining with a dreamy happiness, his spirit still too exalted to be conscious of his surroundings, or to remember the threatened punishment. He carries his straw hat dangling in his hand, quite unaware of its existence.*)

RICHARD (*dreamily, like a ghost addressing fellow shades*). Hello.

MRS. MILLER (*staring at him worriedly*). Hello, Richard.

MILLER (*sizing him up shrewdly*). Hello, Son.

(*Richard moves past his mother and comes to the far corner, left front, where the light is dimmest, and sits down on the sofa, and stares before him, his hat dangling in his hand.*)

MRS. MILLER (*with frightened suspicion now*). Goodness, he acts queer! Nat, you don't suppose he's been——?

MILLER (*with a reassuring smile*). No. It's love, not liquor, this time.

MRS. MILLER (*only partly reassured—sharply*). Richard! What's the matter with you? (*He comes to himself with a start. She goes on scoldingly.*) How many times have I told you to hang up your hat in the hall when you come in! (*He looks at his hat as if he were surprised at its existence. She gets up fussily and goes to him.*) Here. Give it to me. I'll hang it up for you this once. And what are you sitting over here in the dark for? Don't forget your father's been waiting to talk to you!

(*She comes back to the table and he follows her, still half in a dream, and stands by his father's chair. Mrs. Miller starts for the hall with his hat.*)

MILLER (*quietly but firmly now*). You better leave Richard and me alone for a while, Essie.

MRS. MILLER (*turns to stare at him apprehensively*). Well—all right. I'll go sit on the piazza. Call me if you want me. (*Then a bit pleadingly.*) But you'll remember all I've said, Nat, won't you?

(*Miller nods reassuringly. She disappears through the front parlour. Richard, keenly conscious *of himself as the about-to-be-sentenced criminal by this time, looks guilty and a bit defiant, searches his father's expressionless face with uneasy side glances, and steels himself for what is coming.*)

MILLER (*casually, indicating Mrs. Miller's rocker*). Sit down, Richard.

(*Richard slumps awkwardly into the chair and sits in a self-conscious, unnatural position. Miller sizes him up keenly—then suddenly smiles and asks with quiet mockery.*)

Well, how are the vine leaves in your hair this evening?

RICHARD (*totally unprepared for this approach—shamefacedly mutters*). I don't know, Pa.

MILLER. Turned out to be poison ivy, didn't they? (*Then kindly.*) But you needn't look so alarmed. I'm not going to read you any temperance lecture. That'd bore me more than it would you. And, in spite of your damn foolishness last night, I'm still giving you credit for having brains. So I'm pretty sure anything I could say to you you've already said to yourself.

RICHARD (*his head down—humbly*). I know I was a darned fool.

MILLER (*thinking it well to rub in this aspect—disgustedly*). You sure were—not only a fool but a downright, stupid, disgusting fool!

(*Richard squirms, his head still lower.*)

It was bad enough for you to let me and Arthur see you, but to appear like that before your mother and Mildred——! And I wonder if Muriel would think you were so fine if she ever saw you as you looked and acted then. I think she'd give you your walking papers for keeps. And you couldn't blame her. No nice girl wants to give her love to a stupid drunk!

RICHARD (*writhing*). I know, Pa.

MILLER (*after a pause—quietly*). All right. Then that settles—the booze end of it. (*He sizes Richard up searchingly—then suddenly speaks sharply.*) But there is another thing that's more serious. How about that tart you went to bed with at the Pleasant Beach House?

RICHARD (*flabbergasted—stammers*). You know——? But I didn't! If they've told you about her down there, they must have told you I didn't! She wanted me to—but I wouldn't. I gave her the five dollars just so she'd let me out of it. Honest, Pa, I didn't! She made everything seem rotten and dirty—and—I didn't want to do a thing like that to Muriel—no matter how bad I thought she'd treated me—even after I felt drunk, I didn't. Honest!

MILLER. How'd you happen to meet this lady, anyway?

RICHARD. I can't tell that, Pa. I'd have to snitch on someone—and you wouldn't want me to do that.

MILLER (*a bit taken aback*). No. I suppose I wouldn't. Hmm. Well, I believe you—and I guess that settles that. (*Then, after a quick, furtive glance at Richard, he nerves himself for the ordeal and begins with a shamefaced, self-conscious solemnity.*) But listen here, Richard, it's about time you and I had a serious talk about—hmm—certain matters pertaining to—and now that the subject's come up of its own accord, it's good time—I mean, there's no use in procrastinating further—so, here goes.

(*But it doesn't go smoothly and as he goes on he becomes more and more guiltily embarrassed and self-conscious and his expressions more stilted. Richard sedulously avoids even glancing at him, his own embarrassment made tenfold more painful by his father's.*)

Richard, you have now come to the age when—— Well, you're a fully developed man, in a way, and it's only natural for you to have certain desires of the flesh, to put it that way—— I mean, pertaining to the opposite sex—certain natural feelings and temptations—that'll want to be gratified—and you'll want to gratify them. Hmm—well, human society being organized as it is, there's only one outlet for—unless you're a scoundrel and go around ruining decent girls—which you're not, of course. Well, there are a certain class of women—always have been and always will be as long as human nature is what it is—— It's wrong, maybe, but what can you do about it? I mean, girls like that one you—girls there's something doing with—and lots of 'em are pretty, and it's human nature if you—— But that doesn't mean to ever get mixed up with them seriously! You just have what you want and pay 'em and forget it. I know that sounds hard and unfeeling, but we're talking facts and—— But don't think I'm encouraging you to—— If you can stay away from 'em, all the better—but if—why—hmm—— Here's what I'm driving at, Richard. They're apt to be whited sepulchres—I mean, your whole life might be ruined if—so, darn it, you've got to know how to—— I mean, there are ways and means—— (*Suddenly he can go no farther and winds up helplessly.*) But, hell, I suppose you boys talk all this over among yourselves and you know more about it than I do. I'll admit I'm no authority. I never had anything to do with such women, and it'll be a hell of a lot better for you if you never do!

RICHARD (*without looking at him*). I'm never going to, Pa. (*Then shocked indignation coming into his voice.*) I don't see how you could think I could—now—when you know I love Muriel and am going to marry her. I'd die before I'd——!

MILLER (*immensely relieved—enthusiastically*). That's the talk! By God, I'm proud of you when you talk like that! (*Then hastily.*) And now that's all of that. There's nothing more to say and we'll forget it, eh?

RICHARD (*after a pause*). How are you going to punish me, Pa?

MILLER. I *was* sort of forgetting that, wasn't I? Well, I'd thought of telling you you couldn't go to Yale——

RICHARD (*eagerly*). Don't I have to go? Gee, that's great! Muriel thought you'd want me to. I was telling her I'd rather you gave me a job on the paper because then she and I could get married sooner. (*Then with a boyish grin.*) Gee, Pa, you picked a lemon. That isn't any punishment. You'll have to do something besides that.

MILLER (*grimly—but only half concealing an answering grin*). Then you'll go to Yale and you'll stay there till you graduate, that's the answer to that! Muriel's got good sense and you haven't! (*Richard accepts this philosophically.*) And now we're finished, you better call your mother.

(*Richard opens the screen door and calls* "Ma," *and a moment later she comes in. She glances quickly from son to husband and immediately knows that all is well and tactfully refrains from all questions.*)

MRS. MILLER. My, it's a beautiful night. The moon's way down low—almost setting.

(*She sits in her chair and sighs contentedly. Richard remains standing by the door, staring out at the moon, his face pale in the moonlight.*)

MILLER (*with a nod at Richard, winking at his wife*). Yes, I don't believe I've hardly ever seen such a beautiful night—with such a wonderful moon. Have you, Richard?

RICHARD (*turning to them—enthusiastically*). No! It was wonderful—down at the beach—— (*He stops abruptly, smiling shyly.*)

MILLER (*watching his son—after a pause—quietly*). I can only remember a few nights that were as beautiful as this—and they were long ago, when your mother and I were young and planning to get married.

RICHARD (*stares at him wonderingly for a moment, then quickly from his father to his mother and back again, strangely, as if he'd never seen them before—then he looks almost disgusted and swallows as if an acrid taste had come into his mouth—but then suddenly his face is transfigured by a smile of shy understanding and sympathy. He speaks shyly*). Yes, I'll bet those must have been wonderful nights, too. You sort of forget the moon was the same way back then—and everything.

MILLER (*huskily*). You're all right, Richard. (*He gets up and blows his nose.*)

MRS. MILLER (*fondly*). You're a good boy, Richard.

(*Richard looks dreadfully shy and embarrassed at this. His father comes to his rescue.*)

MILLER. Better get to bed early to-night, Son, hadn't you?

RICHARD. I couldn't sleep. Can't I go out on the piazza and sit for a while—until the moon sets?

MILLER. All right. Then you better say good night now. I don't know about your mother, but I'm going to bed right away. I'm dead tired.

MRS. MILLER. So am I.

RICHARD (*goes to her and kisses her*). Good night, Ma.

MRS. MILLER. Good night. Don't you stay up till all hours now.

RICHARD (*comes to his father and stands awkwardly before him*). Good night, Pa.

MILLER (*puts his arm around him and gives him a hug*). Good night, Richard.

(*Richard turns impulsively and kisses him—then hurries out the screen door. Miller stares after him—then says huskily.*)

First time he's done that in years. I don't believe in kissing between fathers and sons after a certain age—seems mushy and silly—but that meant something! And I don't think we'll ever have to worry about his being safe—from himself—again. And I guess no matter what life will do to him, he can take care of it now. (*He sighs with satisfaction and, sitting down in his chair, begins to unlace his shoes.*) My darned feet are giving me fits!

MRS. MILLER (*laughing*). Why do you bother unlacing your shoes now, you big goose—when we're going right up to bed?

MILLER (*as if he hadn't thought of that before, stops*). Guess you're right. (*Then getting to his feet—with a grin.*) Mind if I don't say my prayers to-night, Essie? I'm certain God knows I'm too darned tired.

MRS. MILLER. Don't talk that way. It's real sinful. (*She gets up—then laughing fondly.*) If that isn't you all over! Always looking for an excuse to—— You're worse than Tommy! But all right. I suppose to-night you needn't. You've had a hard day. (*She puts her hand on the reading-lamp switch.*) I'm going to turn out the light. All ready?

MILLER. Yep. Let her go, Gallagher. (*She turns out the lamp. In the ensuing darkness the faint moonlight shines full in through the screen door. Walking together toward the front parlour they stand full in it for a moment, looking out. Miller puts his arm around her. He says in a low voice.*) There he is—like a statue of Love's Young Dream. (*Then he sighs and speaks with a gentle nostalgic melancholy.*) What's it that Rubaiyat says:

"Yet Ah, that Spring should vanish with the Rose!
That Youth's sweet-scented manuscript should close!"

(*Then throwing off his melancholy, with a loving smile at her.*) Well, Spring isn't everything, is it, Essie? There's a lot to be said for Autumn. That's got beauty, too. And Winter—if you're together.

MRS. MILLER (*simply*). Yes, Nat.

(*She kisses him and they move quietly out of the moonlight, back into the darkness of the front parlour.*)

CURTAIN

DAYS WITHOUT END

A Modern Miracle Play

TO CARLOTTA

Characters

JOHN
LOVING
WILLIAM ELIOT
FATHER MATTHEW BAIRD
ELSA, *John Loving's wife*
MARGARET
LUCY HILLMAN
DR. HERBERT STILLWELL
NURSE

Scenes

ACT ONE

PLOT FOR A NOVEL

SCENE John Loving's office in the offices of Eliot and Company, New York City. An afternoon in early spring, 1932.

ACT TWO

PLOT FOR A NOVEL (*continued*)

SCENE Living-room of the Lovings' duplex apartment. Later the same afternoon.

ACT THREE

PLOT FOR A NOVEL (*continued*)

SCENE ONE The living-room again. Evening of the same day.

SCENE TWO John Loving's study. Later that night.

ACT FOUR

THE END OF THE END

SCENE ONE The study and Elsa's bedroom. A little before dawn of a day about a week later.

SCENE TWO The interior of a church. A few minutes later.

ACT ONE

PLOT FOR A NOVEL

SCENE. *John Loving's private office in the offices of Eliot and Company, New York City. On the left, a window. Before it, a chair, its back to the window, and a table. At rear of table, an armchair, facing front. A third chair is at right of table. In the rear wall, a door leading to the outer offices. At centre of the room, toward right, another chair.*

It is afternoon of a cloudy day in Spring, 1932. The light from the window is chill and grey. At the rise of the curtain, this light is concentrated around the two figures seated at the table. As the action goes on, the light imperceptibly spreads until, at the close of the opening scene between John and Loving, it has penetrated to all parts of the room.

John is seated in the chair at left of desk. He is forty, of medium height. His face is handsome, with the rather heavy, conventional American type of good looks—a straight nose and a square jaw, a wide mouth that has an incongruous feminine sensitiveness, a broad forehead, blue eyes. He is dressed in a dark suit, white shirt and collar, a dark tie, black shoes and socks.

Loving sits in the armchair at rear of table. He is the same age, of the same height and figure, is dressed in every detail exactly the same. His hair is the same—dark, streaked with grey. In contrast to this similarity between the two, there is an equally strange dissimilarity. For Loving's face is a mask whose features reproduce exactly the features of John's face—the death mask of a John who has died with a sneer of scornful mockery on his lips. And this mocking scorn is repeated in the expression of the eyes which stare bleakly from behind the mask.

John nervously writes a few words on a pad—then stops abruptly and stares before him. Loving watches him.

LOVING (*his voice singularly toneless and cold but at the same time insistent*). Surely, you don't need to make any more notes for the second part—your hero's manhood up to the time he (*a sneer comes into his voice*) at last finds love. I should think you could remember that—only too well.

JOHN (*mechanically*). Yes.

LOVING (*sneeringly*). As for the third part, I know you have the most vivid recollection of his terrible sin.

JOHN. Don't mock, damn you!

LOVING. So it's only in the last part that you will have to use your imagination. How are you going to end this interesting plot of yours? Given your hero's ridiculous conscience, what happens then?

JOHN. He has the courage to confess—and she forgives.

LOVING. The wish is father to that thought, eh? A pretty, sentimental ending—but a bit too pointed, don't you think? I'm afraid she might begin to wonder——

JOHN (*apprehensively*). Yes. That's true.

LOVING. I advise you to make the last part so obviously fictitious that it will kill any suspicion which might be aroused by what has gone before.

JOHN. How can I end it, then?

LOVING (*after a second's pause—in a voice he tries to make casual but which is indefinitely sinister*). Why not have the wife die?

JOHN (*starts—with a shudder*). Damn you! What makes you think of that?

LOVING. Why, nothing—except I thought you'd agreed that the further removed from present actuality you make your ending, the better it will be.

JOHN. Yes—but——

LOVING (*mockingly*). I hope you don't suspect some hidden, sinister purpose behind my suggestion.

JOHN. I don't know. I feel—— (*Then as if desperately trying to shake off his thoughts.*) No! I won't think of it!

LOVING. And I was thinking, too, that it would be interesting to work out your hero's answer to his problem, if his wife died, and imagine what he would do with his life then.

JOHN. No! Damn you, stop making me think——!

LOVING. Afraid to face your ghosts—even by proxy? Surely, even you can have that much courage!

JOHN. It is dangerous—to call things.

LOVING. Still superstitious? Well, I hope you realize I'm only trying to encourage you to make something of this plot of yours more significant—for your soul, shall I say?—than a cowardly trick!

JOHN. You know it's more than that. You know I'm doing it to try and explain to myself, as well as to her.

LOVING (*sneeringly*). To excuse yourself to yourself, you mean! To lie and escape admitting the obvious natural reason for——

JOHN. You lie! I want to get at the real truth and understand what was behind—what evil spirit of hate possessed me to make me—

LOVING (*contemptuously—but as he goes on a strange defiant note of exultance comes into his voice*). So it's come back to that again, eh? Your old familiar nightmare! You poor, damned superstitious fool! I tell you again what I have always told you: There is nothing—nothing to hope for, nothing to fear—neither devils nor gods—nothing at all!

(*There is a knock on the door at rear. John immediately pretends to be writing. At the same time his features automatically assume the meaninglessly affable expression which is the American business man's welcoming poker face. Loving sits motionlessly regarding him with scornful eyes.*)

JOHN (*without looking up, calls*). Come in.

(*The door in rear is half opened and William Eliot, John Loving's partner, looks in. He is about forty, stout, with a prematurely bald head, a round face, a humorous, good-natured mouth, small eyes behind horn-rimmed spectacles.*)

ELIOT. Hello, John. Busy?

JOHN. Foolish question, Bill.

ELIOT (*his eyes pass over Loving without seeing him. He does not see him now or later. He sees and hears only John, even when Loving speaks. And it will be so with all the characters. They are quite unaware of Loving's existence, although at times one or another may subtly sense his presence. Eliot comes forward. He says jokingly*). You sound downhearted, John. Don't let our little depression get you. There's always the poorhouse. Quite cosy, too, they say. Peace for the weary—

LOVING (*cuts in—mockingly*). There is much to be said for peace.

ELIOT (*as if it were John who had spoken*). Yes, John, there sure is—these damned days. (*Then giving John a glance of concern.*) Look here. I think our troubles are getting your nerve. You've seemed worn ragged lately. Why not take a few days in the country?

JOHN. Nonsense! I'm fine. (*Forcing a humorous tone.*) What, besides the poorhouse, is on your mind, Bill?

ELIOT. Nothing but lunch. Ate too much again, damn it. What were you doping out when I came in? Got some new scheme for us?

JOHN. No.

LOVING. Merely trying to work out the answer to a puzzle—a human puzzle.

JOHN (*hurriedly*). That is, I'm playing around with a plot for a novel that's come into my mind lately.

ELIOT (*with amused surprise*). What? Good God, don't tell me the literary bug is biting you again? I thought you'd got that out of your system long ago when you got engaged to Elsa and decided to come in with me and make some money.

JOHN. Well, I thought I might as well do something with all this leisure. Oh, I'll probably never write it, but it's amusing to dope out.

ELIOT. Why shouldn't you write it? You certainly showed you could write in the old days—articles, anyway. (*Then with a grin.*) Why, I can remember when I couldn't pick up an advanced-thinker organ without running into a red-hot article of yours denouncing Capitalism or religion or something.

JOHN (*smiling good-naturedly*). You always did have a mean memory, Bill.

ELIOT (*laughs*). God, John, how you've changed! What hymns of hate you used to emit against poor old Christianity! Why, I remember one article where you actually tried to prove that no such figure as Christ had ever existed.

LOVING (*his tone suddenly cold and hostile*). I still feel the same on that subject.

ELIOT (*gives John a surprised glance*). Feel? Can't understand anyone having feelings any more on such a dead issue as religion.

JOHN (*confused*). Well, to tell the truth, I haven't given it a thought in years, but—— (*Then hurriedly.*) But, for Pete's sake, let's not get started on religion.

ELIOT (*changes the subject tactfully*). Tell me about this novel of yours, John. What's it all about?

JOHN. Nothing to tell yet. I haven't got it finally worked out.

LOVING. The most important part, that is—the end.

JOHN (*in a joking tone*). But when I have, Bill, I'll be only too glad to get your esteemed criticism.

ELIOT. That's a promise, remember—— (*Then getting up.*) Well, I suppose I better get back to my office. (*He starts for the door—then turns back.*) Oh, I knew there was something I'd forgotten to tell you. Lucy Hillman called up while you were out.

JOHN (*carelessly*). Yes? What did she want?

ELIOT. Wanted you. Got my office by mistake. She'll call up later. It was important, she said to tell you.

JOHN. Her idea of important! Probably wants my advice on what to give Walter for a birthday present.

ELIOT. What the devil's got into Walter lately, anyway? Getting drunk as a pastime may have its points, but as an exclusive occupation—— Not to mention all his affairs with women. How does Lucy stand it? But I hear she's going to pieces, too.

JOHN. I don't believe it. She isn't the kind to have affairs.

ELIOT. I don't mean that. I mean booze.

JOHN. Oh! Well, if it's true, you can hardly blame her.

ELIOT. There are children, aren't there? Why hasn't she the guts to divorce him?

JOHN. Don't ask me. We haven't seen much of Lucy, either, for a long time. (*He dismisses the subject by looking down at his pad, as if he wanted to start writing.*)

ELIOT (*taking the hint*). Well, I'll move along.

JOHN. See you later, Bill.

(*Eliot goes out, rear. After the door closes behind him John speaks tensely.*)

Why did she phone? Important, she said. What can have happened?

LOVING (*coldly*). Who knows? But you know very well she can't be trusted. You'd better be prepared for any stupid folly. And better get the end of your novel decided upon, so you can tell your plot—before it's too late.

JOHN (*tensely*). Yes.

LOVING (*the hidden sinister note again creeping into his coldly casual tone*). There can be only one sensible, logical end for your hero, after he has lost his wife for ever—that is, provided he loves her as much as he boasts to himself he does—and if he has any honour or courage left!

JOHN (*gives a start—then bitterly*). Ah! I see now what you're driving at! And you talk of courage and honour! (*Defiantly.*) No! He must go on! He must find a faith—somewhere!

LOVING (*an undercurrent of anger in his sneering*). Somewhere, eh? Now I wonder what hides behind that somewhere? Is it your old secret weakness—the cowardly yearning to go back——?

JOHN (*defensively*). I don't know what you're thinking about.

LOVING. You lie! I know you! And I'll make you face it in the end of your story—face it and kill it, finally and for ever!

(*There is again a knock on the door and John's eyes go to his pad. This time Eliot comes in immediately, without waiting for an answer.*)

JOHN. Hello, Bill. What's up now?

ELIOT (*comes forward, a twinkle in his eye*). John, there's a mysterious visitor outside demanding to see you.

JOHN. You mean—Lucy?

ELIOT. Lucy? No. This is a man. He ran into me before he got to Miss Sims and asked for you. (*Grinning.*) And as it's liable to be a bitter blow, I thought I better break the news in person.

JOHN. What's the joke? Who is it?

ELIOT. It's a priest.

JOHN. A priest?

LOVING (*harshly*). I don't know any priests! Tell him to get out!

ELIOT. Now don't be disrespectful. He claims he's your uncle.

JOHN. My uncle? Did he give his name?

ELIOT. Yes. Father Baird. Said he'd just got in from the West.

JOHN (*dumbfounded—forcing a smile*). Well, I'll be damned.

ELIOT (*laughs*). My God, think of you having a priest for an uncle! That's too rich!

JOHN. I haven't seen him since I was a boy.

ELIOT. Why so scared? Afraid he's come to lecture you on your sins?

LOVING (*angrily*). He may be a joke to you. He's not to me, damn him!

ELIOT (*gives John a surprised, disapproving glance*). Oh, come, John. Not as bad as that, is it? He struck me as a nice old guy.

JOHN (*hurriedly*). He is. I didn't mean that. I always liked him. He was very kind to me when I was a kid. He acted as my guardian for a while. But I wish he'd given me warning. (*Then picking up the telephone.*) Well, it's rotten to keep him cooling his heels. Hello. Send Father Baird in.

ELIOT (*turning to the door*). I'll get out.

JOHN. No, as a favour, stay around until the ice is broken.

(*He has gotten up and is going toward the door. Loving remains in his chair, his eyes fixed before him in a hostile stare, his body tensed defensively.*)

ELIOT. Sure.

(*A knock comes on the door. John opens it and Father Matthew Baird enters. He is seventy, about John and Loving's height, erect, robust, with thick white hair, ruddy complexion. There is a clear resemblance to John and Loving in the general cast of his features and the colour of his eyes. His appearance and personality radiate health and observant kindliness—also the confident authority of one who is accustomed to obedience and deference—and one gets immediately from him the sense of an unshakable inner calm and certainty, the peace of one whose goal in life is fixed by an end beyond life.*)

JOHN (*constrained and at the same time affectionate*). Hello, Uncle! What in the world brings you——

FATHER BAIRD (*clasping John's hand in a strong grip*). Jack! (*His manner is very much what it must have been when John was a boy and he was the guardian. Deeply moved, he puts his arm around John and gives him an affectionate hug.*) My dear Jack! This is—— (*He sees Eliot and stops, a bit embarrassed.*)

JOHN (*moved and embarrassed, getting away from his arm*). I want you to meet my partner—Bill Eliot—my uncle, Father Baird.

ELIOT. It's a great pleasure, Father.

FATHER BAIRD (*shakes his hand—a formal, old-fashioned courtesy in his manner*). The pleasure is mine, Mr. Eliot. But I feel I've had the privilege of your acquaintance already through Jack's letters.

JOHN. Sit down, Uncle. (*He indicates the chair at right of desk. Father Baird sits down. John sits in his chair at left. Eliot stands by the chair at right, centre.*)

ELIOT. Well, I'll leave you two alone and pretend to be busy. That's the hardest job we have now, Father —keeping up the pretence of work.

FATHER BAIRD. You have plenty of company, if that's any consolation. I get the same tale of woe from everyone in our part of the country.

ELIOT. I'm afraid the company doesn't console a bit. They're all too darned whiny.

FATHER BAIRD (*a twinkle coming into his eye*). Ah, who can blame you for whining when your omnipotent Golden Calf explodes into sawdust before your adoring eyes right at the height of his deification? It's tragic, no other word—unless the word be comic.

LOVING (*his voice a mocking sneer*). And what salvation for us are you preaching? The Second Coming?

FATHER BAIRD (*startled, turns to stare at John. Eliot also looks at him, surprised and disapproving of this taunt. Father Baird says quietly, without any sign of taking offence*). The First Coming is enough, Jack—for those who remember it. (*Then he turns to Eliot—in a joking tone.*) If you knew how familiar that note sounds from him, Mr. Eliot. Here I've been feeling strange, looking at him and seeing what a big man of affairs he'd grown, and saying to myself, can this be my old Jack? And then he has to go and give himself away with a strain of his old bold whistling in the dark, and I see he's still only out of short pants a while, as I knew him last! (*He gives a comic sigh of relief.*) Thank you, Jack. I feel quite at home with you now.

ELIOT (*immensely amused, especially at the expression of boyish discomfiture on John's face—laughingly*). John, I begin to feel sorry for you. You've picked on some one out of your class.

FATHER BAIRD (*with a wink at Eliot*). Did you hear him throw the word preaching in my face, Mr. Eliot —with a dirty sneer in his voice? There's injustice for you. If you knew what a burden he made my life for years with his preaching. Letter upon letter—each with a soap box enclosed, so to speak. The plague began right after I'd had to go West and leave him to his own devices. He was about to pass out of my guardianship and go to college with the bit of money his parents had left for him when he reached eighteen. So I had to let him go his own way. I'd learned it was no use fighting him, anyway. I'd done that and found it was a great satisfaction to him and only made him worse. And I had faith, if let alone, he'd come back to his senses in the end.

LOVING (*sneeringly*). And how mistaken you were in that faith!

FATHER BAIRD (*without turning—quietly*). No. The end isn't yet, Jack. (*He goes on to Eliot with a renewal of his humorously complaining tone.*) You wouldn't believe what a devil's advocate he was in those days, Mr. Eliot.

ELIOT. You needn't tell me, Father. I was his classmate. He organized an Atheists' Club—or tried to— and almost got fired for it.

FATHER BAIRD. Yes, I remember his writing to boast about that. Well, you can appreciate then what I went through, even if he didn't write you letters.

ELIOT. But he delivered harangues, Father, when he could get anybody to listen!

FATHER BAIRD (*pityingly*). Ah, that must have been cruel, too. Mr. Eliot, I feel drawn to you. We've been through the same frightful trials.

JOHN (*with a boyishly discomfited air*). I hope you're having a good time, you two.

FATHER BAIRD (*ignoring him*). Not a moment's peace did he give me. I was the heathen to him and he was bound he'd convert me to something. First it was Atheism unadorned. Then it was Atheism wedded to Socialism. But Socialism proved too weak-kneed a mate, and the next I heard Atheism was living in free love with Anarchism, with a curse by Nietzsche to bless the union. And then came the Bolshevik dawn, and he greeted that with unholy howls of glee and wrote me he'd found a congenial home at last in the bosom of Karl Marx. He was particularly delighted when he thought they'd abolished love and marriage, and he couldn't contain himself when the news came they'd turned naughty schoolboys and were throwing spitballs at Almighty God and had supplanted Him with the slave-owning State—the most grotesque god that ever came out of Asia!

ELIOT (*chuckling*). I recognize all this, Father. I used to read his articles, as I was reminding him just before you came.

FATHER BAIRD. Don't I know them! Didn't he send me every one with blue pencil underlinings! But to get back to my story: Thinks I at this juncture, well, he's run away as far as he can get in that direction. Where will he hide himself next?

LOVING (*stiffening in his chair—with angry resentment*). Run away. You talk as if I were afraid of something. Hide? Hide from what?

FATHER BAIRD (*without turning—quietly*). Don't you know, Jack? Well, if you don't yet, you will some day. (*Again to Eliot.*) I knew Communism wouldn't hold him long—and it didn't. Soon his letters became full of pessimism, and disgust with all sociological nostrums. Then followed a long silence. And what do you think was his next hiding place? Religion, no less —but as far away as he could run from home—in the defeatist mysticism of the East. First it was China and Lao Tze that fascinated him, but afterwards he ran on to Buddha, and his letters for a time extolled passionless contemplation so passionately that I had a mental view of him regarding his navel frenziedly by the hour and making nothing of it!

(*Eliot laughs and John chuckles sheepishly in spite of himself. Loving stares before him with a cold, angry disdain.*)

ELIOT. Gosh, I'm sorry I missed that! When was all this, Father?

FATHER BAIRD. In what I'd call his middle hide-and-go-seek period. But the next I knew, he was through with the East. It was not for the Western soul, he decided, and he was running through Greek philosophy and found a brief shelter in Pythagoras and numerology. Then came a letter which revealed him bogged down in evolutionary scientific truth again—a dyed-in-the-wool mechanist. That was the last I heard of his perigrinations—and, thank heaven, it was long ago. I enjoyed a long interval of peace from his missionary zeal, until finally he wrote me he was married. That letter was full of more ardent hymns of praise for a mere living woman than he'd ever written before about any of his great spiritual discoveries. And ever since then I've heard nothing but the praises of Elsa—in which I know I'll be ready to join after I've met her.

JOHN (*his face lighting up*). You bet you will! We can agree on that, at least.

FATHER BAIRD (*with a wink at Eliot*). He seems to be fixed in his last religion. I hope so. The only constant faith I've found in him before was his proud belief in himself as a bold Antichrist. (*He gives John a side glance, half smiling and half reproachful.*) Ah, well, it's a rocky road full of twists and blind alleys, isn't it, Jack—this running away from truth in order to find it? I mean, until the road finally turns back toward home.

LOVING (*with harsh defiance*). You believe I—— ? (*Then sneeringly.*) But, of course, you would read that into it.

JOHN (*bursts out irritably, as if he couldn't control his nerves*). But don't you think I'm about exhausted as a subject, Uncle? I do. (*He gets up nervously and moves around and stands behind Loving's chair, his hands on the back of the chair, his face directly above Loving's masked one.*)

ELIOT (*gives the priest an amused smile*). Well, I'll get back to my office. (*Father Baird gets up and he shakes his hand heartily.*) I hope we'll meet again, Father. Are you here for long?

FATHER BAIRD. Only a few days, I'm afraid.

JOHN (*coming around to them*). I'll fix up something with Elsa for the four of us, Bill—as soon as she's feeling stronger. We won't let him run away in a few days, now we've got him here.

ELIOT. Fine! See you again, then, Father. (*He goes toward the door.*)

FATHER BAIRD. I hope so, Mr. Eliot. Good day to you.

ELIOT (*with the door open, turns back with a grin*). I feel it my duty, Father, to warn you that John's got writer's itch again. He's going to give us a novel. (*He laughs and closes the door behind him. John frowns and gives his uncle a quick uneasy glance.*)

JOHN (*indicating the chair at right, centre*). Take that chair, Uncle. It's more comfortable.

(*He sits down in the chair at right of table where Father Baird had sat, while the priest sits in the one at right, centre. Father Baird gives him a puzzled, concerned look, as if he were trying to figure something out. Then he speaks casually.*)

FATHER BAIRD. A novel? Is that right, Jack?

JOHN (*without looking at him*). Thinking of it—to pass the time.

FATHER BAIRD. Then, judging from your letters, it ought to be a love story.

JOHN. It is—a love story.

LOVING (*mockingly*). About God's love for us!

FATHER BAIRD (*quietly rebuking*). Jack! (*A pause of silence. Father Baird gives John a quick glance again—then casually.*) If you've any appointments, don't stand on ceremony; just shoo me out.

JOHN (*turns to him shamefacedly*). Don't talk that way, Uncle. You know I wouldn't—(*with a natural, boyishly affectionate smile*). You know darned well how tickled I am to have you here.

FATHER BAIRD. I hope you're half as glad as I am to see you, Jack. (*He sighs.*) It has been a long time—too long.

JOHN. Yes. (*Smiling.*) But I'm still flabbergasted. I never dreamed you—— Why didn't you wire me you were coming?

FATHER BAIRD. Oh, I thought I'd surprise you. (*He smiles.*) To tell you the truth, I confess I had a sneaking Sherlock Holmes desire to have a good look at you before you were expecting it.

JOHN (*frowning—uneasily*). Why? Why should you?

FATHER BAIRD. Well, I suppose because, not having seen you, I'm afraid that to me you were still the boy I'd known, and I was still your suspicious guardian.

JOHN (*relieved—with a boyish grin*). Oh! I see.

FATHER BAIRD. And now I have seen you, I still must admit that the grey in your hair is lost on me, and I can't get it out of my head you're the same old Jack.

JOHN (*grinning with a boyish discomfiture*). Yes, and the devil of it is you make me feel that way, too. It's an unfair advantage, Uncle.

(*Father Baird laughs and John joins in.*)

FATHER BAIRD. Well, I never took unfair advantage of you in the old days, did I?

JOHN. You certainly didn't. When I look back, I'm amazed you could have been so fair. (*Quickly—changing the subject.*) But you haven't told me yet how you happened to come East.

FATHER BAIRD (*a bit evasively*). Oh, I decided a vacation was due me. And I've had a great longing for some time to see you again.

JOHN. I only wish I could have you stay with us, but there's no room. But you must have dinner with us to-night, and every night you're here, of course.

FATHER BAIRD. Yes, I'd like to see all of you I can. But there's this, Jack. You spoke to Mr. Eliot as if Elsa were ill.

JOHN. Oh, it's nothing serious. She's just getting over the flu, and still feels a bit low.

FATHER BAIRD. Then I'd better not come to-night.

JOHN. You better had or she'll never forgive you—or me!

FATHER BAIRD. Very well. I'm only too happy.

(*A pause. He glances at John again with a curious puzzled fixity. John catches his eyes, is held by them for a moment, then looks away almost furtively.*)

JOHN (*forcing a smile*). Is that the suspicious guardian look? I've forgotten.

FATHER BAIRD (*as if to himself—slowly*). I feel—— (*Then suddenly.*) There's something I want to tell you, Jack. (*A stern note comes into his voice.*) But first give me your word of honour there will be no cheap sneering.

JOHN (*stares at him, taken aback—then quietly*). There won't be.

FATHER BAIRD. Well, it's often come to me in the past that I shouldn't have let you get so far from me, that I might be in part responsible for your continued estrangement from your Faith.

LOVING (*with mocking scorn*). My faith?

JOHN. You know that's nonsense, Uncle.

LOVING. You have always nobly done your duty. You've never let a letter pass without some pious reminder of my fall—with the calm assurance that I would again see the light. That never failed to make me laugh—your complacent assumption that like the Prodigal of His fairy tale, I——

FATHER BAIRD (*sharply*). Jack! You promised!

JOHN (*confusedly*). I know. I didn't mean—— Go on with what you started to tell me.

FATHER BAIRD. First answer me frankly one question. Have you been greatly troubled in spirit by anything lately?

JOHN (*startled*). I? Why do you ask that? Of course not. (*Then evasively.*) Oh, well—yes, maybe, if you mean business worries.

FATHER BAIRD. Nothing else?

JOHN. No. What could there be?

FATHER BAIRD (*unconvinced—looking away*). The reason I asked—— You'll see in what I'm going to tell you. It happened one night while I was praying for you in my church, as I have every day since I left you. A strange feeling of fear took possession of me—a feeling you were unhappy, in some great spiritual danger. I told myself it was foolish. I'd had a letter from you only that day, reiterating how happy you were. I tried to lose my dread in prayer—and my guilt. Yes, I felt stricken with guilt, too—that I was to blame for whatever was happening to you. Then, as I prayed, suddenly as if by some will outside me, my eyes were drawn to the Cross, to the face of Our Blessed Lord. And it was like a miracle! His face seemed alive as a living man's would be, but radiant with eternal life, too, especially the sad, pitying eyes. But there was a sternness in His eyes, too, an accusation against me—a command about you! (*He breaks off and gives John a quick glance, as if afraid of finding him sneering. Then, looking away, he adds simply:*) That's the real reason I decided to take my vacation in the East, Jack.

JOHN (*stares at him fascinatedly*). You saw——?

LOVING (*in a bitter, sneering tone*). It could hardly have been any concern for me you saw in His face—even if He did exist or ever had existed!

FATHER BAIRD (*sternly*). Jack! (*Then, after a pause, quietly.*) Do you know Francis Thompson's poem—The Hound of Heaven?

LOVING. I did once. Why?

FATHER BAIRD (*quotes in a low voice but with deep feeling*).
"Ah, fondest, blindest, weakest,
I am He Whom thou seekest!
Thou dravest love from thee, who dravest Me."

LOVING (*in what is close to a snarl of scorn*). Love!

JOHN (*defensively*). I have love!

FATHER BAIRD (*as if he hadn't heard*). Why do you run and hide from Him, as from an enemy? Take care. There comes a time in every man's life when he must have his God for friend, or he has no friend at all, not even himself. Who knows? Perhaps you are on the threshold of that time now.

JOHN (*uneasily*). What do you mean?

FATHER BAIRD. I don't know. It's for you to know that. You say you have love?

JOHN. You know I have. Or, if you don't, you soon will after you've met Elsa.

FATHER BAIRD. I'm not doubting your love for her nor hers for you. It's exactly because I do not doubt. I am thinking that such love needs the hope and promise of eternity to fulfil itself—above all, to feel itself secure. Beyond the love for each other should be the love of God, in Whose Love yours may find the triumph over death.

LOVING (*sneeringly*). Old superstition, born of fear! Beyond death there is nothing. That, at least, is certain—a certainty we should be thankful for. One life is boring enough. Do not condemn us to another. Let us rest in peace at last!

FATHER BAIRD (*quietly*). Would you talk that way if Elsa should die?

JOHN (*with a shudder*). For God's sake, don't speak about——

LOVING. Do you think I haven't imagined her death many times?

JOHN. The dread of it has haunted me ever since we were married.

FATHER BAIRD. Ah!

LOVING. You'll see that I face it—by proxy, at least—in my novel. (*A sneering taunt in his voice.*) I think you'll be interested in this novel, Uncle.

FATHER BAIRD (*staring at John, whose face is averted*). It's autobiographical, then?

JOHN (*hastily*). No. Of course not. I only meant—— Don't get that idea in your head, for Pete's sake. As I explained to Elsa, when I told her about the first part, it's really the story of a man I once knew.

LOVING. The first part will particularly interest you, Uncle. I am afraid you will be terribly shocked—especially in the light of your recent mystic vision!

FATHER BAIRD. I'm very curious to hear it, Jack. When will you tell me?

LOVING (*defiantly*). Now!

JOHN (*uneasily*). But no. I don't want to bore you.

FATHER BAIRD. You won't bore me.

JOHN. No—— I——

LOVING (*with harsh insistence*). The first part concerns my hero's boyhood here in New York, up to the age of fifteen.

JOHN (*under Loving's compulsion, he picks up the thread of the story*). He was an only child. His father was a fine man. The boy adored him. And he adored his mother even more. She was a wonderful woman, a perfect type of our old beautiful ideal of wife and mother.

LOVING (*sneeringly*). But there was one ridiculous weakness in her character, an absurd obsession with religion. In the father's, too. They were both devout Catholics.

(*The priest gives a swift, reproachful look at John, seems about to protest, thinks better of it, and drops his eyes.*)

JOHN (*quickly*). But not the ignorant, bigoted sort, please understand. No, their piety had a genuine, gentle, mystic quality to it. Their faith was the great comforting inspiration of their lives. And their God was One of Infinite Love—not a stern, self-righteous Being Who condemned sinners to torment, but a very human, lovable God Who became man for love of men and gave His life that they might be saved from themselves. And the boy had every reason to believe in such a Divinity of Love as the Creator of Life. His home atmosphere was one of love. Life *was* love for him then. And he was happy, happier than he ever afterward—— (*He checks himself abruptly.*)

FATHER BAIRD (*nods his head approvingly*). Yes.

JOHN. Later, at school, he learned of the God of Punishment, and he wondered. He couldn't reconcile Him with his parents' faith. So it didn't make much impression on him.

LOVING (*bitterly*). Then! But afterward he had good reason to——

JOHN. But then he was too sure in his faith. He grew up as devout as his parents. He even dreamed of becoming a priest. He used to love to kneel in the church before the Cross.

LOVING. Oh, he was a remarkably superstitious young fool! (*His voice suddenly changes to hard bitterness.*) And then when he was fifteen all these pious illusions of his were destroyed for ever! Both his parents were killed!

JOHN (*hurriedly*). That is, they died during a flu epidemic in which they contracted pneumonia—and he was left alone—without love. First, his father died. The boy had prayed with perfect faith that his father's life might be spared.

LOVING. But his father died! And the poor simpleton's naïve faith was a bit shaken, and a sinful doubt concerning the Divine Love assailed him!

JOHN. Then his mother, worn out by nursing his father and by her grief, was taken ill. And the horrible fear came to him that she might die, too.

LOVING. It drove the young idiot into a panic of superstitious remorse. He imagined her sickness was a terrible warning to him, a punishment for the doubt inspired in him by his father's death. (*With harsh bitterness.*) His God of Love was beginning to show Himself as a God of Vengeance, you see!

JOHN. But he still trusted in His Love. Surely He would not take his mother from him, too.

LOVING. So the poor fool prayed and prayed and

vowed his life to piety and good works! But he began to make a condition now—*if* his mother were spared to him!

JOHN. Finally he knew in his heart she was going to die. But even then he hoped and prayed for a miracle.

LOVING. He abased and humbled himself before the Cross—and, in reward for his sickening humiliation, saw that no miracle would happen.

JOHN. Something snapped in him then.

LOVING (*his voice suddenly takes on a tone of bitter hatred*). He saw his God as deaf and blind and merciless—a Deity Who returned hate for love and revenged Himself upon those who trusted Him!

JOHN. His mother died. And, in a frenzy of insane grief——

LOVING. No! In his awakened pride he cursed his God and denied Him, and, in revenge, promised his soul to the Devil—on his knees, when everyone thought he was praying! (*He laughs with malignant bitterness.*)

JOHN (*quickly—in a casual tone*). And that's the end of Part One, as I've outlined it.

FATHER BAIRD (*horrified*). Jack! I can't believe that you——

JOHN (*defensively*). I? What have I to do with it? You're forgetting I explained to you—— Oh, I admit there are certain points of resemblance between some of his boyhood experiences and mine—his parents' death, for example. But that's only coincidence.

FATHER BAIRD (*recovered now—staring at him—quietly*). I see.

JOHN (*forcing a smile*). And please don't bring up those coincidences before Elsa, Uncle. She didn't notice them because I've never bored her with boyhood reminiscences. And I don't want her to get the wrong angle on my plot.

FATHER BAIRD. I'll remember, Jack. When will you tell me the rest of it?

JOHN. Oh, some time while you're here, maybe.

FATHER BAIRD. Why not to-night at your home?

JOHN. Well, I might——

LOVING. That is, if I can decide on my end before then!

JOHN. It would give me a chance to get your and Elsa's criticisms at the same time. She's been wanting to hear the rest of it, too.

FATHER BAIRD (*regarding him—quietly*). Then, by all means. (*Abruptly changing to a brisk casualness.*) Well, I'll leave you and attend to some errand I have to do. (*He gets to his feet. He takes John's hand.*)

JOHN. Dinner is at seven-thirty. But come as long before that as you like. I'll be home early. (*Then with a genuine boyish affection.*) I want to tell you again, Uncle, how grand it is to have you here—in spite of our arguments.

FATHER BAIRD. I'm not worried by our arguments. But I am about something about you that admits of no argument—to me.

JOHN (*forcing a smile*). You're wasting worry. But what is it?

FATHER BAIRD. You've written me you were happy, and I believed you. But, now I see you, I don't believe you. You're not happy. Why? Perhaps if you had it out with me——

LOVING (*mockingly*). Confess, eh?

JOHN. Don't be foolish, Uncle. I am happy, happier than I ever dreamed I could be. And, for heaven's sake, don't go telling Elsa I'm unhappy!

FATHER BAIRD (*quietly*). Very well. We'll say no more about it. And now I'll be off. Good-bye until this evening, Jack.

JOHN. So long, Uncle.

(*Father Baird goes out. John stands by the door, looking after him—then he comes slowly back and sits down in his chair and stares before him. Loving's eyes are fastened on him with a cold contempt.*)

LOVING. Damned old fool with his bedtime tales for second childhood about the love of God! And you—you're worse—with your hypocritical lies about your great happiness!

(*The telephone on the table rings. John jumps nervously—then answers it in an apprehensive voice.*)

JOHN. Hello. Who? Tell her I'm out.

LOVING. You'd better find out what she wants.

JOHN. No, wait, I'll take it. (*Then, his voice becoming guarded and pleasantly casual.*) Hello, Lucy. Bill told me you'd called. What——? (*He listens—then anxiety creeping into his tone.*) She phoned again? What about? Oh! I'm glad you called me. Yes, she has been wondering why she hasn't heard from you in so long. Yes, by all means, go. Yes, she's sure to be in this afternoon. Good-bye. (*He hangs up mechanically.*)

LOVING (*sneeringly*). Your terrible sin begins to close in on you, eh? But then, it wasn't you, was it? It was some evil spirit that possessed you! (*He gives a mocking laugh—then stops abruptly and continues in his tone of cold, sinister insistence.*) But enough of that nonsense. Let's return to your plot. The wife dies—of influenza that turns into pneumonia, let's say.

JOHN (*starts violently—stammers*). What—God damn you—what makes you choose that?

CURTAIN

ACT TWO
PLOT FOR A NOVEL (*Continued*)

SCENE. *The living-room of the Lovings' duplex apartment. Venetian blinds soften the light from a big window at right. In front of this window is a table with a lamp. At left, front, an upholstered chair. At right of chair, a small table with a lamp. At right of table, in the centre of the room, a sofa. In front of sofa, a low stand with cigarette-box and ash-trays. Toward right, another chair. In the left wall is a door leading to the dining-room. At rear of door, a writing-desk. In the middle of the rear wall is a doorway leading to the hall.*

It is later the same afternoon.

Elsa enters from the hall at rear. She is thirty-five but looks much younger. She is beautiful with that Indian Summer renewal of physical charm which comes to a woman who loves and is loved, particularly to one who has not found that love until comparatively late in life. This beauty is a trifle dimmed now by traces of recent illness. Her face is drawn and she fights against a depressing lassitude. She wears a simple négligée.

As she comes in, she presses a button by the door and a buzzer is heard in the pantry. She comes forward and sits on the sofa. A moment later Margaret, the maid, appears from the dining-room at left. She is a middle-aged Irishwoman with a kindly face.

MARGARET. Yes, Madame ?

ELSA. Hasn't the afternoon paper come yet, Margaret ?

MARGARET. No, Madame, not yet. (*Then with kindly reproof.*) Didn't you take a nap like you promised you would ?

ELSA. I couldn't get to sleep. But I do feel rested, so don't begin to scold me. (*She smiles and Margaret smiles back, a look of devoted affection lighting up her face.*)

MARGARET. You have to take care. The flu's a bad thing the way it leaves you weak after. And you're only out of your bed two days.

ELSA. Oh, I'm really quite well again. And I was too excited to sleep. I kept thinking of Mr. Loving's uncle.

(*The telephone in the hall rings and Margaret goes toward the door in rear to answer it.*)

Heavens, I hope that isn't he now. Mr. Loving phoned me he told him to come early. But surely he wouldn't this early !

MARGARET (*disappears in the hall. Her voice comes*). Just a moment and I'll see if she's in. (*She appears again in the doorway.*) It's Mrs. Hillman calling to see you, Madame.

ELSA. Oh, I'm glad. Tell her to come right up. (*Margaret disappears and is heard relaying this instruction. Then she appears in the hall outside the doorway, waiting to answer the door. Elsa speaks to her.*) I wish I didn't look so like a sick cat. Why is it everyone decides to turn up when you look your worst ?

MARGARET. Ah, you needn't worry, Madame. You look fine.

ELSA. Well, anyway, I don't mind Lucy.

(*Nevertheless, she goes to the desk at left, rear, takes out a vanity case, powders her nose, etc. While she is doing this, Margaret moves to the entrance door in the hall and is heard admitting Mrs. Hillman and exchanging greetings with her, as she helps her off with her things. Elsa calls.*)

Hello, Stranger.

LUCY (*calls back in a voice whose breeziness rings a bit strained*). That's right, sit on me the minute I set foot in your house ! Well, I know I deserve it.

(*Elsa goes to the doorway and meets her as she comes in, kissing her affectionately. Lucy Hillman is about the same age as Elsa. She is still an extremely attractive woman but, in contrast to Elsa, her age shows, in spite of a heavy make-up. There are wrinkles about her eyes, and her small, full, rather weak mouth is drawn down by sharp lines at the corners. She is dressed expensively in clothes a bit too youthful and extreme in style. She responds to Elsa's greeting with a nervous constraint.*)

Hello, Elsa.

ELSA. You're a nice one ! How long has it been —months !—not since before I went to Boston in February. (*She sits on the sofa and draws Lucy down beside her.*)

LUCY. I know. I'm in the dust at your feet.

ELSA. I've phoned you a dozen times, but you were always out. Or did you just tell them to say that ? I've completely lost faith in you.

LUCY. But I was out, Elsa. How can you think——

ELSA (*laughing—gives her a hug*). You're not taking me seriously, are you ? I know you'd hardly do that with me, after all these years.

LUCY. Of course, I wouldn't.

ELSA. But I did wonder a little at your sudden complete ignoring of our existence. So did John.

LUCY (*hurriedly*). If you know all the stupid engagements that pile up—and all the idiotic parties Walter lets me in for. (*Then changing the subject abruptly.*) May I have a cigarette? (*She takes one from the box on the stand and lights it.*) Aren't you having one?

ELSA. Not now. (*She gives Lucy a puzzled glance. Lucy avoids her eyes, nervously flipping her cigarette over the ash-tray. Elsa asks:*) How are the kids?

LUCY. Oh, fine, thanks. At least, I think so, from the little I get to see of them nowadays. (*Bitterness has crept into this last. She again hurriedly changes the subject.*) But tell me all your news. What have you been doing with yourself?

ELSA. Oh, the same peaceful routine—going to a concert now and then, reading a lot, keeping house, taking care of John.

LUCY. The old perfect marriage that's been the wonder of us all, eh? (*Again changing the subject.*) What time does John usually get home? I don't want to run into him.

ELSA. Oh, not for an hour or so yet. (*Smiling.*) But why? What have you got against John?

LUCY (*smiling with a strange wryness*). Nothing—except myself. (*Then hurriedly.*) I mean, look at me, I look like hell. I've had the damnedest insomnia lately. And I'm vain enough not to crave any male viewing the wreckage until I've spruced up on a bath and cocktails.

ELSA. But that's silly. You look wonderful.

LUCY (*dryly*). Thanks, liar! (*With a side glance of frank envy—unable to keep resentment out of her voice.*) I especially don't care to be up for inspection beside you. The contrast is too glaring.

ELSA. But it's I who look like the devil, not you. I'm just getting over flu.

LUCY. Flu makes—no, never mind. It doesn't affect—what I mean. (*Then with a hard flippant air.*) Pardon me if I seem to indulge in the melancholy jitters. I'm becoming the damnedest whiner and self-pitier. It's really too boring.

(*She lights another cigarette. Her hands have a nervous tremor. Elsa watches her with a worried, affectionately pitying look.*)

ELSA. What is it, Lucy? Tell me.

LUCY (*stiffening defensively*). What is what?

ELSA. I want to know what's troubling you. Now, there's no use denying it. I've known you too long. I felt it the moment you came in, that you were upset about something and trying to hide it.

LUCY. I don't know where you got that idea. (*Defensively flippant.*) Oh, really now, Elsa. Don't you go psychic on us!

ELSA. All right, then. Forgive my trying to pump you. But you got me into the bad habit yourself, you know, by always coming to me with your troubles. I only thought I might be able to help.

LUCY. You! (*She gives a hard little laugh.*)

ELSA (*hurt*). You used to think I could.

LUCY. "Once, long ago——" (*Then, suddenly with repentant shamefacedness.*) Forgive me, Elsa. I'm rotten to be flip about that. You've been the most wonderful friend. And I'm such an ungrateful little slut!

ELSA. Lucy! You mustn't say that.

LUCY (*hurries on with a simulation of frankness*). But honestly, you're mistaken this time. There's nothing wrong, except what seems to be wrong with everyone, the stupid lives we lead—and, of course, the usual financial worries. So please don't bother your head about my troubles.

ELSA. All right, dear. (*Then, after a slight pause—casually*). How is Walter these days?

LUCY (*with a twisted smile*). I thought we weren't going to talk about my troubles! Oh, Walter is—Walter. You know him, Elsa. Why ask? But do you know anyone, I wonder? Darned if I think you ever see what people really are. You somehow manage to live in some lost world where human beings are still decent and honourable. I don't see how you do it. If you'd always been a little innocent, protected from all ugly contacts—— But, my God, your first marriage must have slapped your face with about every filthy thing a man can be—and that's plenty! Yet you sit here, calm and beautiful and unscarred——!

ELSA (*quietly*). I had my share of scars. But the wounds are all healed—completely healed. John's love has done that for me.

LUCY. Yes—of course. (*Then, as if she couldn't control herself, she bursts out:*) Oh, you and your John! You bring him up as the answer to everything.

ELSA (*smiling*). Well, he is for me.

LUCY. Do you mean to tell me you're as much in love with him now as when you married him?

ELSA. Oh, much more so, for he's become my child and father now, as well as being a husband and——

LUCY. Lover. Say it. How incredibly mid-Victorian you can be! Don't you know that's all we married ladies discuss nowadays? But you're lucky. Usually the men discussed aren't our husbands, and aren't even good lovers. But never say die. We keep on hoping and experimenting!

ELSA (*repelled*). Don't talk in that disgusting way. I know you don't mean a word of it.

LUCY (*stares at her resentfully for a second, then turns*

away, reaching for another cigarette—dryly). Oh, you're quite sure of that, are you?

ELSA (*gently*). Lucy, what is it has made you so bitter? I've noticed it growing on you for the past few years, but now it's completely got you. I—honestly, I hardly know you this time, you've changed so.

LUCY (*hurriedly*). Oh, it's nothing that happened lately. You mustn't get that idea. (*Then letting herself go—with increasing bitterness.*) It's simply that I've grown sick of my life, sick of all the lying and faking of it, sick of marriage and motherhood, sick of myself! Particularly sick of myself because I endure the humiliation of Walter's open affairs with every damned floosie he meets! And I'm tired of pretending I don't mind, tired of really minding underneath, tired of pretending to myself I have to go on for the children's sakes, and that they make up to me for everything, which they don't at all!

ELSA (*indignantly*). How can Walter be such a beast!

LUCY (*with a look at Elsa that is almost vindictive*). Oh, he's no worse than a lot of others. At least, he doesn't lie about it.

ELSA. But, for heaven's sake, why do you stand it? Why don't you leave him?

LUCY. Oh, don't be so superior and scornful, Elsa. I'll bet you wouldn't—— (*She checks herself abruptly.*)

ELSA. What do you mean? You know very well I left my first husband the minute I found out——

LUCY (*hurriedly*). I know. I didn't—— Why don't I leave Walter? I guess because I'm too worn out to have the guts. And then I did try it once. The first time I knew he'd been unfaithful I did the correct thing and went home. I intended to tell Father I was through as Walter's wife. Only Father was away. Mother was there, and I broke down and told her. She took it quite philosophically—said I was a fool to expect too much, men were like that, even my father had—— (*She gives a little shiver of aversion.*) That sort of squelched me. So I went back to Walter and he doesn't know to this day I ever left him.

ELSA. I'm so sorry, Lucy.

LUCY (*returning to her air of hard cynicism*). No pity, please. After all, the situation has its compensations. He has tried nobly to be fair. He said I could have equal liberty to indulge any of my sexual whims.

ELSA. What a stupid fool!

LUCY (*bitterly*). Oh, he didn't really mean it, you know. His vanity couldn't admit I'd ever feel the slightest desire outside of him. It was only a silly gesture he felt safe in making because he was so damned sure of me—because he knows, damn him, that in spite of all he's done to kill it there's still a cowardly slavish something in me, dating back to the happiness of our first married days, which still—loves him! (*She starts to break down, but fights this back and bursts out vindictively, a look of ugly satisfaction coming into her face.*) But I warned him he'd humiliate me once too often—and he did!

ELSA (*shocked*). You mean you——

LUCY (*with a return of her flippant tone*). Yes, I went in for a little fleeting adultery. And I must say, as a love substitute or even a pleasurable diversion, it's greatly overrated. (*She gives a hard little laugh.*) How horribly shocked you look! Are you going to order me from your virtuous home?

ELSA. Lucy! Don't talk like that! It's only that I can't believe—none of this is really you. That's what makes it so—— But please don't think I'm condemning you. You know how I love you, don't you?

LUCY (*stares at her with a strange panic*). Don't, for God's sake! I don't want you to love me! I'd rather you hated me!

(*But Elsa pulls her to her and she breaks down finally, sobbing, her face buried against Elsa's shoulder.*)

ELSA. There, there. You mustn't, dear. (*Then as Lucy grows calmer—quietly.*) Don't think I don't understand, because I do. I felt exactly the same when I found out about Ned Howell. Even though I'd stopped caring for him and our marriage had always been unhappy, my pride was so hurt I wanted to revenge myself and take the first man I met for a lover.

LUCY (*looks up in amazement*). You went through that? I never dreamed——

ELSA. All that saved me from doing something stupid was the faith I had that somewhere the man was waiting whom I could really love. I felt I owed it to him and to my own self-respect not to deliberately disfigure myself out of wounded pride and spite.

LUCY (*with sad bitterness*). You hit it when you say disfigure. That's how I've felt ever since. Cheap! Ugly! As if *I'd* deliberately disfigured *myself*. And not only myself—the man—and others I wouldn't hurt for anything in the world—if I was in my right mind. But I wasn't! You realize I wasn't, don't you, Elsa? You must! You above everyone!

ELSA. I do, dear. Of course I do.

LUCY. I've got to tell you just how it came to happen—so you'll see. It was one of Walter's parties. You know the would-be Bohemian gang he likes to have. They were there in all their vulgarity, their poisonous, envious tongues wise-cracking at everything with any decent human dignity and worth. Oh, there were a few others there, too—our own people—this man was one of them. Walter was drunk, pawing over his latest female, and she got him to go home with her. Everybody watched me to see how I'd take it. I wanted to kill him and her, but I only laughed and had some more to drink. But I was in hell, I can tell you, and inside I kept swearing to myself that I'd show Walter—— And I picked out this man—yes, deliberately ! It was all deliberate and crazy ! And I had to do all the seducing —because he's quite happy. I knew that, but I was crazy. His happiness filled me with rage—the thought that he made others happy. I wanted to take his happiness from him and kill it as mine had been killed !

ELSA. Lucy !

LUCY (*with a hard laugh*). I told you I was in hell, didn't I ? You can't live there without becoming like the rest of the crowd ! (*Hurrying on with her story.*) I got him in my bedroom on some excuse. But he pushed me away, as if he were disgusted with himself and me. But I wouldn't let him go. And then came the strange part of it. Suddenly, I don't know how to explain it, you'll think I'm crazy, or being funny, but it was as if he were no longer there. It was another man, a stranger whose eyes were hateful and frightening. He seemed to look through me at someone else, and I seemed for a moment to be watching some hidden place in his mind where there was something as evil and revengeful as I was. It frightened and fascinated me—and called to me too ; that's the hell of it ! (*She forces a laugh.*) I suppose all this sounds too preposterous. Well, maybe it was the booze working. I'd had a lot. (*She reaches for a cigarette—returning to her hard flippancy.*) And then followed my little dip into adultery.

ELSA (*with a little shiver of repulsion*). Oh !

LUCY. But what a hideous bore this must be to you. Why did I have to tell you, I wonder. It was the last thing I ever wanted—— (*Turns on her in a flash of resentful vindictiveness.*) It makes me out worse than you expected, eh ? But suppose John were unfaithful to you——

ELSA (*startled—frightenedly*). Don't ! (*Then indignantly.*) Lucy ! I won't have you say that, not even——

LUCY. I'm only asking you to suppose.

ELSA. I can't ! I won't ! And I won't let you ! It's too—— ! (*Then controlling herself—forcing a smile.*) But I'm a bigger fool than you are to get angry. You simply don't know John, that's all. You don't know what an old-fashioned romantic idealist he is at heart about love and marriage. And I thank God he is ! You'll laugh at me but I know he never had a single affair in his life before he met me.

LUCY. Oh, come on, Elsa. That's too much !

ELSA. Oh, please don't think I'm a naïve fool. I was as cynical about men in those days as you are now. I wouldn't have believed it of another man in the world, but with John I felt it was absolutely true to what I knew he was like inside him.

LUCY. You loved him and you wanted to believe.

ELSA. No. Even before I loved him, I felt that. It was what made me love him, more than anything else —the feeling that he would be mine, only mine, that I wouldn't have to share him even with the past. If you only could realize how much that meant to me—especially at that time, when I was still full of the disgust and hurt of my first marriage.

LUCY. Well, that's all very fine, but it's not proving to me how you can be so certain that never since then——

ELSA (*proudly*). I know he loves me. I know he knows how much I love him. He knows what that would do to me. It would kill for ever all my faith in life—all truth, all beauty, all love ! I wouldn't want to live !

LUCY. You shouldn't let yourself be so completely at the mercy of any man—not even John.

ELSA. I'm not afraid. (*She smiles.*) The trouble with you is, you old cynic, you can't admit that our marriage is a real ideal marriage. But it is—and that's entirely John's work, not mine.

LUCY. His work ?

ELSA. Yes. When I first met him I thought I was through with marriage for good. Even after I fell in love with him, I didn't want to marry. I was afraid of marriage. I proposed quite frankly that we should simply live together and each keep entire freedom of action. (*She laughs.*) Oh, I was quite ultra-modern about it ! And it shocked John terribly, poor dear—in spite of all his old radical ideas. I'm sure it almost disillusioned him with me for life ! He sternly scorned my offer. He argued with me. How he argued—like a missionary converting a heathen ! He said he loathed the ordinary marriage as much as I did, but that the ideal in back of marriage was a beautiful one, and he knew we could realize that ideal.

LUCY. Ah, yes, the ideal ! I heard a little talk about that once, too !

ELSA. He said no matter if every other marriage on earth were rotten and a lie, our love could make ours into a true sacrament—sacrament was the word he used —a sacrament of faith in which each of us would find the completest self-expression in making our union a beautiful thing. (*She smiles lovingly.*) You see, all this was what I had longed to hear the man I loved say about the spiritual depth of his love for me—what every woman dreams of hearing her lover say, I think.

LUCY (*stirring uneasily—mechanically*). Yes. I know.

ELSA. And, of course, it blew my petty modern selfishness right out the window. I couldn't believe he meant it at first, but when I saw he did, that finished me. (*She smiles—then with quiet pride.*) And I think we've lived up to that ideal ever since. I hope I have. I know he has. It was his creation, you see.

LUCY. Of course he has. Of course.

ELSA. And our marriage has meant for us, not slavery or boredom but freedom and harmony within ourselves—and happiness. So we must have both lived true to it. Happiness is proof, isn't it?

LUCY (*deeply moved—without looking at Elsa, takes her hand and squeezes it—huskily*). Of course it is. Please forget the stupid rot I've said. I was only trying to get a rise out of you. We all know how wonderfully happy you and John are. Only remember, the world is full of spiteful liars who would do anything to wreck your happiness and drag you down to their level—what I was doing. So never listen—— But of course you won't, will you? You have faith. (*She turns and kisses her impulsively.*) God bless you—and preserve your happiness!

ELSA. Thank you, Lucy. That's dear of you. (*Then puzzledly.*) But why should you be afraid that anyone——

LUCY (*jumps to her feet nervously*). Only my morbidness. I've been accused of so many rotten things I never did that I suppose I'm hipped on the subject. (*Then abruptly.*) Got to run now, Elsa—go home and get on my armour for another of Walter's parties. It's a gay life. The only hope is he'll be so broke before long no one will call on us but our forgotten friends. (*She gives a bitter little laugh and starts to go around the left of sofa—then, at a noise of a door opening in the hall—nervously.*) Isn't that someone——?

ELSA. It must be John. (*She hurries around the right of sofa and back towards the doorway.*)

JOHN (*calls from the hall*). Hello.

ELSA (*going out, meets him as he appears in the hall just beyond the doorway—kissing him*). Hello, darling. You're early. I'm so glad.

JOHN. I thought, as I'd told Uncle to come early, I better—— (*He kisses her.*) How do you feel, dear? You look much better.

ELSA. Oh, I'm fine, John.

(*Lucy has remained standing by the left corner of the sofa, in a stiff, strained attitude, the expression on her face that of one caught in a corner, steeling herself for an ordeal. Elsa and John come in, their arms around each other. As they do so, Lucy recovers her poise and calls to him.*)

LUCY. Hello, John.

JOHN (*coming to her, his face wearing its most cordial, poker-faced smile*). Why, hello, Lucy, I thought I heard a familiar voice when I came in. (*They shake hands.*) A pleasant surprise. Been a long time since we've had this pleasure.

(*Elsa has come forward behind him. The figure of the masked Loving appears in the doorway. During the next few speeches he moves silently to the corner of the long table before the window, right-front, and stands there, without looking at them, facing front, his eyes fixed in the same cold stare, the expression of his masked face seeming to be more than ever sneering and sinister.*)

LUCY. Now, don't you begin on that! Elsa has already given me hell.

ELSA (*laughing*). And she's repented and been forgiven.

JOHN. Oh, that's all right, then.

LUCY (*nervously*). I was just leaving. Sorry I've got to run, John.

ELSA. Oh, you can't, now. John will think he's driven you out.

LUCY. No, really, Elsa, I——

ELSA. You simply must keep John company for a few minutes. Because I've got to go to the kitchen. I trust Emmy on ordinary occasions, but when a long-lost uncle is coming to dinner, a little personal supervision is in order. (*She moves toward the dining-room at left.*)

LUCY (*with a note of desperation*). Well—but I can't stay more than a second.

ELSA. I'll be back right away.

(*She disappears through the dining-room door. The moment she is gone, John's cordial smile vanishes and his face takes on a tense, harried look. He is now standing behind the right end of sofa, Lucy behind the left end. In the pause while they wait for Elsa to get out of earshot, Loving moves silently over until he is standing just behind John but a step toward rear from him, facing half toward him, half toward front.*)

JOHN (*lowering his voice—hurriedly*). I hope you've been careful and not said anything that——

LUCY. Might give you away? Of course, I didn't. And even if I were rotten enough to come right out and tell her, she'd never believe me, she has such a touching faith in you.

JOHN (*wincing*). Don't!

LUCY. No. You're perfectly safe. There's only one thing I've got to warn you about. It's nothing, really, but——

JOHN. What?

LUCY. Walter has been telling people. He has to, you see, to keep up his pose of friendly understanding——

JOHN. But how does Walter know?

LUCY. Don't look so dismayed! He doesn't know

—who it was. And you'd be the last one he'd ever suspect.

JOHN. How is it he knows about you?

LUCY (*hesitates—then defiantly*). I told him.

JOHN. You told him? In God's name, why? But I know. You couldn't resist—watching him squirm!

LUCY (*stung*). Exactly, John. Why do you suppose I ever did it, except for his benefit—if you want the truth.

JOHN. Good God, don't you think I know that? Do you imagine I ever thought it was anything but revenge on your part?

LUCY. And whom were you revenging yourself on, John?—now we're being frank.

LOVING (*with sinister mockery*). Who knows? Perhaps on love. Perhaps, in my soul, I hate love!

LUCY (*stares at John with frightened bewilderment*). John! Now you're like—that night!

JOHN (*confusedly*). I? It wasn't I. (*Angrily.*) What do you mean by saying I was revenging myself? Why should I revenge myself on her?

LUCY. I don't know, John. That's a matter for your conscience. I've got enough on my own, thank you. I must say I resent your attitude, John. (*With a flippant sneer.*) Hardly the lover-like tone, is it?

JOHN (*with disgust*). Lover!

LUCY. Oh, I know. I feel the same way. But why hate me? Why not hate yourself?

JOHN. As if I didn't! Good God, if you knew! (*Then bitterly.*) And how long do you think you'll be able to resist telling Walter it was I, his old friend—so you can watch him squirm some more!

LUCY. John!

JOHN. And Walter will have to tell that to everyone, too—to live up to his pose! And then——

LUCY. John! You know I wouldn't, even if I hated you as you seem to hate me. I wouldn't for Elsa's sake. Oh, I know you think I'm a rotten liar, but I love Elsa! (*Then brokenly.*) Oh, it's such a vile mess! What fools we were!

JOHN (*dully*). Yes. (*Bitterly again.*) I'm sorry I can't trust you, Lucy. I can when you're yourself. But full of booze—— I see what it will come to. I'll have to tell her myself to save her the humiliation of hearing it through dirty gossip!

LUCY. John! Oh, please don't be such a fool! Please!

JOHN. You think she couldn't forgive?

LUCY. I'm thinking of what it would do to her. Can't you see——?

JOHN (*warningly, as he hears the pantry door opening*). Ssshh! (*Quickly, raising his voice to a conversational tone.*) Uncle is a grand old fellow. You'll have to meet him some time. You'd like him.

LUCY. I'm sure I would. (*Then, as Elsa comes in from the dining-room.*) Ah, here you are. Well, I've got to fly. (*She holds out her hand to John.*) Good-bye, John. Take care of Elsa.

JOHN. Good-bye, Lucy.

(*Elsa puts an arm around her waist and they go back to the hall doorway.*)

ELSA. I'll get your things.

(*They disappear in the hall. As soon as they have gone, John turns and, coming around the sofa, sits down on it and stares before him with hunted eyes. Loving moves until he is standing directly behind him. He bends over and whispers mockingly.*)

LOVING. I warned you it was closing in! You had better make up your mind now to tell the rest of your novel to-night—while there is still time!

JOHN (*tensely*). Yes. I must.

LOVING. But, first it still remains to decide what is to be your hero's end. (*He gives a little jeering laugh.*) Strange, isn't it, what difficult problems your little dabble in fiction has brought up which demand a final answer!

(*He laughs again—then turns to face the doorway as Elsa re-enters the room. His eyes remain fixed on her as she comes forward. She comes quietly to the right end of the sofa. John does not notice her coming. Loving remains standing at right, rear, of John.*)

ELSA. A penny for your thoughts, John. (*He starts. She sits down beside him—with a smile.*) Did I scare you?

JOHN (*forcing a smile*). Don't know what's the matter with me. I seem to have the nervous jumps lately. (*Then carelessly.*) Glad to see Lucy again, were you?

ELSA. Yes—of course. Only she's changed so. Poor Lucy.

JOHN. Why poor? Oh, you mean on account of Walter's antics?

ELSA. Then you know?

JOHN. Who doesn't? He's been making as public an ass of himself as possible. But let's not talk about Walter. What did you think of the big event to-day: Uncle dropping out of the blue?

ELSA. It must have been a surprise for you. I'm dying to meet him. I'm so glad he could come to-night.

JOHN. Yes. So am I.

(*As if his conversation had run dry, he falls into an uneasy silence. Elsa looks at him worriedly. Then she nestles up close to him.*)

ELSA (*tenderly*). Still love me, do you?

JOHN (*takes her in his arms and kisses her—with intense feeling*). You know I do! There's nothing in life I give a damn about except your love! You know that, don't you?

ELSA. Yes, dear.

JOHN (*avoiding her eyes now*). And you'll always love me—no matter what an unworthy fool I am?

ELSA. Ssshh! You mustn't say things like that. It's not true. (*Then smiling teasingly.*) Well, if you love me so much, prove it by telling me.

JOHN (*controlling a start*). Telling you what?

ELSA. Now, don't pretend. I know there's something that's been troubling you for weeks—ever since I came back from Boston.

JOHN. No, honestly, Elsa.

ELSA. Something you're keeping back because you're afraid of worrying me. So you might as well confess.

JOHN (*forcing a smile*). Confess? And will you promise—to forgive?

ELSA. Forgive you for not wanting to worry me? Foolish one!

JOHN (*hurriedly*). No, I was only joking. There's nothing.

ELSA. Now! But I think I can guess. It's about business, isn't it?

JOHN (*grasps at this*). Well—yes, if you must know.

ELSA. And you were afraid that would upset me? Oh, John, you're such a child at times you ought to be spanked. You must think I've become a poor, helpless doll!

JOHN. No, but——

ELSA. Just because you've pampered me so terribly the past few years! But remember, we had barely enough to get along on when we were married—and I didn't appear so terribly unhappy then, did I? And no matter how poor we become, do you think it would ever really matter one bit to me as long as I had you?

JOHN (*stammers miserably*). Sweetheart! You make me feel—so damned ashamed! God, I can't tell you!

ELSA (*kissing him*). But, darling, it's nothing! And now promise me you'll forget it and not worry any more?

JOHN. Yes.

ELSA. Good! Let's talk of something else. Tell me, have you been doing anything more on the rest of your idea for a novel?

JOHN. Yes, I—I've got most of it thought out.

ELSA (*encouragingly*). That's splendid. You just put your mind on that and forget your silly worries. But when am I going to hear it?

JOHN. Well, I told Uncle the first part and he was curious, too. So I threatened him I might give you both an outline of the rest to-night.

ELSA. Oh, that's fine. (*Then she laughs.*) And I'll confess it will be a great aid to me as a hostess. I'll probably feel a bit self-conscious, entertaining a strange priest-uncle for the first time.

JOHN. Oh, you won't be with him a minute before you'll feel he's an old friend.

ELSA. Well, that sounds encouraging. But you tell your story just the same. (*She gets up.*) It must be getting on. I'd better go up and start getting dressed. (*She goes around the left end of the sofa and back toward the hall door.*) Are you going up to your study for a while?

JOHN. Yes, in a minute. I want to do a little more work on my plot. The end isn't clearly worked out yet.

LOVING. That is, my hero's end!

ELSA (*smiling at John encouragingly*). Then you get busy, by all means, so you'll have no excuse!

(*She goes out. As soon as she is gone, John's expression changes and becomes tense and hunted again. Loving remains standing behind him, staring down at him with cold, scornful eyes. There is a pause of silence.*)

JOHN (*suddenly—his face full of the bitterest, tortured self-loathing—aloud to himself*). You God-damned rotten swine!

LOVING (*mockingly*). Yes, unfit to live. Quite unfit for life, I think. But there is always death to wash one's sins away—sleep, untroubled by Love's betraying dream! (*He gives a low, sinister laugh.*) Merely a consoling reminder—in case you've forgotten!

(*John listens fascinatedly, as if to an inner voice. Then a look of terror comes into his face and he shudders.*)

JOHN (*torturedly*). For God's sake! Leave me alone!

CURTAIN

ACT THREE

PLOT FOR A NOVEL (*Continued*)

SCENE ONE

SCENE. *The living-room again. It is immediately after dinner. Father Baird is sitting in the chair at left, front, Elsa on the sofa, John beside her on her left, the masked Loving at right, rear, of John, in the chair by the end of the table before the window. John and Loving are in dinner clothes of identical cut. Elsa wears a white evening gown of extremely simple lines. Father Baird is the same as in Act One.*

Margaret is serving them the after-dinner coffee. She goes out through the dining-room door.

JOHN (*puts an arm around Elsa's waist playfully*). Well, now you've got to know her, what do you think of her, Uncle? Weren't my letters right?

FATHER BAIRD (*gallantly*). They were much too feeble. You didn't do her justice by half!

ELSA. Thank you, Father. It's so kind of you to say that.

JOHN. Ah! I told you that was one subject we'd agree on! (*Then to Elsa in a tenderly chiding tone.*) But I've got a bone to pick with you, my lady. You ate hardly any dinner, do you know it?

ELSA. Oh, but I did, dear.

JOHN. No, you only went through the motions. I was watching you. That's no way to get back your strength.

FATHER BAIRD. Yes, you need all the nourishment you can take when you're getting over the flu.

JOHN (*worriedly—grasping her hand*). Sure you're warm enough? Want me to get you something to put over your shoulders?

ELSA. No, dear, thank you.

JOHN. Remember it's a rotten, chilly, rainy day out and even indoors you can't be too careful.

ELSA. Oh, but I'm quite all right now, John. Please don't worry about me.

JOHN. Well, don't let yourself get tired now, you hear? If you find yourself feeling at all worn-out, you just send Uncle and me off to my study. He'll understand. Won't you, Uncle?

FATHER BAIRD. Of course. I hope Elsa will feel I'm one of the family and treat me without ceremony.

ELSA. I do feel that, Father. (*Then teasingly.*) But do you know what I think is behind all this solicitude of John's? He's simply looking for an excuse to get out of telling us the rest of his novel. But we won't let him back out, will we?

FATHER BAIRD. Indeed we won't.

ELSA. The first part is so unusual and interesting. Don't you think so, Father?

FATHER BAIRD (*quietly*). Yes. Tragic and revealing to me.

ELSA. You see, John, it's no use. We're simply going to insist.

LOVING (*coldly mocking*). You're sure—you insist?

ELSA. Of course I do. So come on.

JOHN (*nervously*). Well—— (*He hesitates—gulps down the rest of his coffee.*)

ELSA (*smiling*). I never saw you so flustered before, John. You'd think you were going to address an audience of literary critics.

JOHN (*begins jerkily*). Well—— But before I start, there's one thing I want to impress on you both again. My plot, up to the last part, which is wholly imaginary, is taken from life. It's the story of a man I once knew.

LOVING (*mockingly*). Or thought I knew.

ELSA. May I be inquisitive? Did I ever know the man?

LOVING (*a hostile, repellent note in his voice*). No. I can swear to that. You have never known him.

ELSA (*taken aback, gives John a wondering look—then apologetically*). I'm sorry I butted in with a silly question. Go on, dear.

JOHN (*nervously—forcing a laugh*). I—— It's hard getting started. (*He turns and reaches for his coffee, forgetting he has drunk it—sets the cup down again abruptly and goes on hurriedly.*) Well, you will remember my first part ended when the boy's parents had died.

LOVING. And he had denied all his old superstitions!

JOHN. Well, as you can imagine, for a long while after their deaths, he went through a terrific inner conflict. He was seized by fits of terror, in which he felt he really had given his soul to some evil power. He would feel a tortured longing to pray and beg for forgiveness. It seemed to him that he had forsworn all love for ever—and was cursed. At these times he wanted only to die. Once he even took his father's revolver——

LOVING (*sneeringly*). But he was afraid to face death. He was still too religious-minded, you see, to accept the one beautiful, comforting truth of life: that death is final release, the warm, dark peace of annihilation.

FATHER BAIRD (*quietly*). I cannot see the beauty and comfort.

LOVING. He often regretted afterwards he had not had the courage to die then. It would have saved him so much silly romantic pursuit of meaningless illusions.

ELSA (*uneasily*). Oh, you mustn't talk that way, John. It sounds so bitter—and false—coming from you.

JOHN (*confusedly*). I—— I didn't—— You forget I'm simply following what this man told me. (*Hurrying on.*) Well, finally, he came out of this period of black despair. He taught himself to take a rationalistic attitude. He read all sorts of scientific books. He ended up by becoming an atheist. But his experience had left an indelible scar on his spirit. There always remained something in him that felt itself damned by life, damned with distrust, cursed with the inability ever to reach a lasting belief in any faith, damned by a fear of the lie hiding behind the mask of truth.

FATHER BAIRD. Ah!

LOVING (*sneeringly*). So romantic, you see—to think of himself as possessed by a damned soul!

JOHN. And in after years, even at the height of his rationalism, he never could explain away a horror of death—and a strange fascination it had for him. And coupled with this was a dread of life—as if he constantly sensed a malignant Spirit hiding behind life, waiting to catch men at its mercy, in their hour of secure happiness—— Something that hated life!—— Something that laughed with mocking scorn!

(*He stares before him with a fascinated dread, as if he saw this Something before him. Then, suddenly, as if in reply, Loving gives a little mocking laugh, barely audible. John shudders. Elsa and Father Baird start and stare at John uneasily, but he is looking straight ahead and they turn away again.*)

LOVING. A credulous, religious-minded fool, as I've pointed out! And he carried his credulity into the next period of his life, where he believed in one social or philosophical Ism after another, always on the trail of Truth! He was never courageous enough to face what he really knew was true, that there is no truth for men, that human life is unimportant and meaningless. No. He was always grasping at some absurd new faith to find an excuse for going on!

JOHN (*proudly*). And he did go on! And he found his truth at last—in love, where he least expected he ever would find it. For he had always been afraid of love. And when he met the woman who afterwards became his wife and realized he was in love with her, it threw him into a panic of fear. He wanted to run away from her—but found he couldn't.

LOVING (*scornfully*). So he weakly surrendered—and immediately began building a new superstition of love around her.

JOHN. He was happy again for the first time since his parents' death—to his bewildered joy.

LOVING (*mockingly*). And secret fear!

ELSA (*gives John a curious, uneasy glance*). Secret fear?

JOHN. Yes, he—he came to be afraid of his happiness. His love made him feel at the mercy of that mocking Something he dreaded. And the more peace and security he found in his wife's love, the more he was haunted by fits of horrible foreboding—the recurrent dread that she might die and he would be left alone again, without love. So great was the force of this obsession at times that he felt caught in a trap, desperate——

LOVING. And he often found himself regretting——

JOHN (*hastily*). Against his will——

LOVING (*inexorably*). That he had again let love put him at the mercy of life!

JOHN (*hurriedly*). But, of course, he realized this was all morbid and ridiculous—for wasn't he happier than he had ever dreamed he could be again?

LOVING (*with gloating mockery*). And so he deliberately destroyed that happiness!

ELSA (*startledly*). Destroyed his happiness? How, John?

JOHN (*turns to her, forcing a smile*). I'm afraid you will find this part of his story hard to believe, Elsa. This damned fool, who loved his wife more than anything else in life, was unfaithful to her. (*Father Baird starts and stares at him with a shocked expression.*)

ELSA (*frightenedly*). It is—hard to believe. But this part is all the story of the man you knew, isn't it?

JOHN. Yes, of course, and you mustn't condemn him entirely until you've heard how it came to happen. (*He turns away from her again—jerkily.*) His wife had gone away. It was the first time. He felt lost without her—fearful, disintegrated. His familiar dread seized him. He began imagining all sorts of catastrophes. Horrible pictures formed in his mind. She was run over by a car. Or she had caught pneumonia and lay dying. Every day these evil visions possessed him. He tried to escape them in work. He couldn't. (*He pauses for a second, nerving himself to go on. Then starts again.*) Then one night an old friend called—to drag him off to a party. He loathed such affairs usually, but this time he thought it would help him to escape himself for a while. So he went. He observed with disgust how his friend, who was drunk, was pawing over some woman right under the nose of his wife. He knew that this friend was continually having affairs of this sort and that his wife was aware of it. He had often wondered if she cared, and he was curious now to watch her reactions. And very soon he had an example of what her pride had to endure, for the husband went off openly with his lady. The man felt a great sympathy for her—and, as if she guessed his thought, she came to him, and he overdid himself in being kind. (*He gives a short bitter laugh.*) A great mistake ! For she reacted to it in a way that at first shocked him but ended up in arousing his curiosity. He had known her for years. It wasn't like her. It fascinated him, in a way, that she should have become so corrupted. He became interested to see how far she would go with it—purely as an observer, he thought—the poor idiot ! (*He laughs again. Father Baird has remained motionless, his eyes on the floor. Elsa's face is pale and set, her eyes have a bewildered, stricken look. John goes on.*) Remember, all this time he saw through her ; he laughed to himself at her crude vamping ; he felt he was only playing a game. Just as he knew she was playing a game ; that it was no desire for him but hatred for her husband that inspired her. (*He gives a short contemptuous laugh again.*) Oh, he had it all analysed quite correctly, considering the known elements. It was the unknown——

FATHER BAIRD (*without raising his head*). Yes.

(*He casts a quick glance at Elsa, then looks as quickly away. Her eyes are fastened on the floor now. Her face has frozen into a mask with the tense effort she is making not to give herself away.*)

JOHN. He had not the slightest desire for this woman. When she threw herself into his arms, he was repelled. He determined to end the game. He thought of his wife—— (*He forces a laugh.*) But, as I've said, there was the unknown to reckon with. At the thought of his wife, suddenly it was as if something outside him, a hidden spirit of evil, took possession of him.

LOVING (*coldly vindictive now*). That is, he saw clearly that this situation was the climax of a long death struggle between his wife and him. The woman with him counted only as a means. He saw that underneath all his hypocritical pretences he really hated love. He wanted to deliver himself from its power and be free again. He wanted to kill it !

ELSA (*with horrified pain*). Oh ! (*Trying to control herself.*) I—I don't understand. He hated love ? He wanted to kill it ? But that's—too horrible !

JOHN (*stammers confusedly*). No—I—— Don't you see it wasn't he ?

LOVING. But, I'm afraid, Elsa, that my hero's silly idea that he was possessed by a demon must strike you as an incredible superstitious excuse to lie out of his responsibility.

FATHER BAIRD (*without lifting his eyes—quietly*). Quite credible to me, Jack. One may not give one's soul to a devil of hate—and remain for ever scatheless.

LOVING (*sneeringly*). As for the adultery itself, the truth is that this poor fool was making a great fuss about nothing—an act as meaningless as that of one fly with another, of equal importance to life !

ELSA (*stares at John as if he had become a stranger—a look of sick repulsion coming over her face*). John ! You're disgusting ! (*She shrinks away from him to the end of the sofa near Father Baird.*)

JOHN (*stammers confusedly*). But I—I didn't mean—forgive me. I only said that—as a joke—to get a rise out of Uncle.

FATHER BAIRD (*gives a quick anxious look at Elsa—then quietly, an undercurrent of sternness in his voice*). I don't think it's a joke. But go on with your story, Jack.

JOHN (*forcing himself to go on*). Well I—I know you can imagine the hell he went through from the moment he came to himself and realized the vileness he had been guilty of. He couldn't forgive himself—and that's what his whole being now cried out for—forgiveness !

FATHER BAIRD (*quietly*). I can well believe that, Jack.

JOHN. He wanted to tell his wife and beg for forgiveness—but he was afraid of losing her love. (*He gives a quick glance at Elsa, as if to catch her reaction to this, but she is staring straight before her with a still, set face. He forces a smile and adopts a joking tone.*) And here's where I'd like to have your opinion, Elsa. The question doesn't come up in my story, as you'll see, but—— Could his wife have forgiven him, do you think ?

ELSA (*starts—then tensely*). You want me to put myself in the wife's place ?

JOHN. Yes. I want to see whether the man was a fool or not—in his fear.

ELSA (*after a second's pause—tensely*). No. She could never forgive him.

JOHN (*desperately*). But it wasn't he ! Can't you see——

ELSA. No. I'm afraid—I can't see.

JOHN (*dully now*). Yes. That's what I thought you'd say.

ELSA. But what does it matter what I think ? You said the question of her forgiving doesn't come up in your novel.

LOVING (*coldly*). Not while the wife is alive.

JOHN (*dully*). He never tells her.

LOVING. She becomes seriously ill.

ELSA (*with a start*). Oh.

LOVING (*in a cold voice, as if he were pronouncing a death sentence*). 'Flu, which turns into pneumonia. And she dies.

ELSA (*frightenedly now*). Dies?

LOVING. Yes. I need her death for my end. (*Then in a sinister, jeering tone.*) That is, to make my romantic hero come finally to a rational conclusion about his life!

ELSA (*stares before her, not seeming to have heard this last—her eyes full of a strange, horrified fascination—as if she were talking aloud to herself*). So she dies.

FATHER BAIRD (*after a worried glance at her—an undercurrent of warning in his quiet tone*). I think you've tired Elsa out with your sensational imaginings, Jack. I'd spare her, for the present, at least, the fog of gloom your novel is plunging into.

ELSA (*grasps at this—tensely*). Yes, I'm afraid it has been too exciting—— I really don't feel up to—— During dinner I began to get a headache and it's splitting now.

JOHN (*gets up—worriedly*). But why didn't you tell me? If I'd known that, I'd never have bored you with my damned plot.

ELSA. I—I think I'll lie down here on the sofa—and take some aspirin—and rest for a while. You can go with your uncle up to your study—and tell him the rest of your story there.

FATHER BAIRD (*gets up*). An excellent idea. Come on, Jack, and give your poor wife a respite from the horrors of authorship. (*He goes to the doorway in rear.*)

JOHN (*comes to Elsa. As he does so, Loving comes and stands behind her, at rear of sofa*). I'm so darned sorry, Elsa, if I've——

ELSA. Oh, please! It's only a headache.

JOHN. You—you don't feel really sick, do you, dearest? (*He puts a hand to her forehead timidly.*)

ELSA (*shrinks from his touch*). No, no, it's nothing.

LOVING (*slowly, in his cold tone with its undercurrent of sinister hidden meaning*). You must be very careful, Elsa. Remember it's cold and raining out.

ELSA (*staring before her strangely—repeats fascinatedly*). It's raining?

LOVING. Yes.

JOHN (*stammers confusedly*). Yes, you—you must be careful, dearest.

FATHER BAIRD (*from the doorway in rear—sharply*). Come along, Jack!

(*John goes back to him and Loving follows John. Father Baird goes into the hall, turning left to go upstairs to the study. John stops in the doorway and looks back for a moment at Elsa frightenedly. Loving comes to his side and also stops and looks at her, his eyes cold and remorseless in his mask of sinister mockery. They stand there for a moment side by side. Then John turns and disappears in the hall toward left, following Father Baird. Loving remains, his gaze concentrated on the back of Elsa's head with a cruel, implacable intensity. She is still staring before her with the same strange fascinated dread. Then, as if in obedience to his will, she rises slowly to her feet and walks slowly and woodenly back past him and disappears in the hall, turning right toward the entrance door to the apartment. For a second Loving remains looking after her. Then he turns and disappears in the hall toward left, following Father Baird and John to the study.*)

CURTAIN

SCENE TWO

SCENE. *John Loving's study on the upper floor of the apartment. At left, front, is a door leading into Elsa's bedroom. Bookcases extend along the rear and right walls. There is a door to the upper hall at rear, right. A long table with a lamp is at centre, front. At left of table is a chair. In front of table a similar chair. At right, front, is a chaise-longue, facing left.*

Father Baird, John and Loving are discovered. The priest is sitting on the chaise-longue, John in the chair at front of table, Loving in the chair at left of table. Father Baird sits in the same attitude as he had in the previous scene, his eyes on the floor, his expression sad and a bit stern. Loving's masked face stares at John, his eyes cold and still. John is talking in a strained tone, monotonously, insistently. It is as if he were determinedly talking to keep himself from thinking.

JOHN. I listen to people talking about this universal breakdown we are in and I marvel at their stupid cowardice. It is so obvious that they deliberately cheat themselves because their fear of change won't let them face the truth. They don't want to understand what has happened to them. All they want is to start the merry-go-round of blind greed all over again. They no longer know what they want this country to be, what they want it to become, where they want it to go. It has lost all meaning for them except as a pig-wallow. And so their lives as citizens have no beginnings, no ends. They have lost the ideal of the Land of the Free. Freedom demands initiative, courage, the need to decide what life must mean to oneself. To them, that is terror. They explain away their spiritual cowardice by whining that the time for individualism is past, when it is their courage to possess their own souls which is dead—and stinking! No, they don't want to be free. Slavery means security—of a kind, the only kind they have courage for. It means they need not think. They have only to obey orders from owners who are, in turn, their slaves!

LOVING (*breaks in—with bored scorn*). But I'm denouncing from my old soap-box again. It's all silly twaddle, of course. Freedom was merely our romantic delusion. We know better now. We know we are all the slaves of meaningless chance—electricity or something, which whirls us—on to Hercules!

JOHN (*with a proud assertiveness*). But, in spite of that, I say: Very well! On to Hercules! Let us face that! Once we have accepted it without evasion, we can begin to create new goals for ourselves, ends for our days! A new discipline for life will spring into being, a new will and power to live, a new ideal to measure the value of our lives by!

LOVING (*mockingly*). What? Am I drooling on about my old social ideals again? Sorry to bore you, Uncle.

FATHER BAIRD (*quietly, without looking up*). You are not boring me, Jack.

JOHN (*an idealistic exaltation coming into his voice*). We need a new leader who will teach us that ideal, who by his life will exemplify it and make it a living truth for us—a man who will prove that man's fleeting life in time and space can be noble. We need, above all, to learn again to believe in the possibility of nobility of spirit in ourselves! A new saviour must be born who will reveal to us how we can be saved from ourselves, so that we can be free of the past and inherit the future and not perish by it!

LOVING (*mockingly*). Must sound like my old letters to you, Uncle. It's more nonsense, of course. But there are times of stress and flight when one hides in any old empty barrel!

FATHER BAIRD (*ignoring this—quietly*). You are forgetting that men have such a Saviour, Jack. All they need is to remember Him.

JOHN (*slowly*). Yes, perhaps if we could again have faith in——

LOVING (*harshly*). No! We have passed beyond gods! There can be no going back!

FATHER BAIRD. Jack! Take care!

LOVING (*mockingly again*). But, on the other hand, I'll grant you the pseudo-Nietzschean saviour I just evoked out of my past is an equally futile ghost. Even if he came, we'd only send him to the insane asylum for teaching that we should have a nobler aim for our lives than getting all four feet in a trough of swill! (*He laughs sardonically.*) How could we consider such an unpatriotic idea as anything but insane, eh?

(*There is a pause. Father Baird looks up and studies John's face searchingly, hopefully.*)

FATHER BAIRD (*finally speaks quietly*). Jack, ever since we came upstairs, I've listened patiently while you've discussed every subject under the sun except the one I know is really on your mind.

JOHN. I don't know what you mean.

FATHER BAIRD. The end of our story.

JOHN. Oh, forget that. I'm sick of the damned thing—now, at any rate.

FATHER BAIRD. Sick of the damned thing, yes. That's why I feel it's important you tell it—now. This man's wife dies, you said. (*He stares fixedly at John now and adds slowly.*) Of influenza which turns into pneumonia.

JOHN (*uneasily*). Why do you stare like that?

FATHER BAIRD (*dropping his eyes—quietly*). Go on with your story.

JOHN (*hesitantly*). Well—I—— You can imagine the anguish he feels after his wife's death—the guilt which tortures him a thousandfold now she is dead.

FATHER BAIRD. I can well imagine it, Jack.

LOVING (*sneeringly*). And under the influence of his ridiculous guilty conscience, all the superstitions of his childhood, which he had prided himself his reason had killed, return to plague him. He feels at times an absurd impulse to pray. He fights this nonsense back. He analyses it rationally. He sees it clearly as a throwback to boyhood experiences. But, in spite of himself, that cowardly something in him he despises as superstition seduces his reason with the old pathetic life of survival after death. He begins to believe his wife is alive in some mythical hereafter!

JOHN (*strangely*). He knows she knows of his sin now. He can hear her promising to forgive if he can only believe again in his old God of Love, and seek her through Him. She will be beside him in spirit in this life, and at his death she will be waiting. Death will not be an end but a new beginning, a reunion with her in which their love will go on for ever within the eternal peace and love of God! (*His voice has taken on a note of intense longing.*)

FATHER BAIRD. Ah, then you do see, Jack! Thank God!

JOHN (*as if he hadn't heard*). One night when he is hounded beyond endurance he rushes out—in the hope that if he walks himself into exhaustion he may be able to sleep for a while and forget. (*Strangely, staring before him, as if he were visualizing the scene he is describing.*) Without his knowing how he got there, he finds he has walked in a circle and is standing before the old church, not far from where he now lives, in which he used to pray as a boy.

LOVING (*jeeringly*). And now we come to the great temptation scene, in which he finally confronts his ghosts! (*With harsh defiance.*) The church challenges him—and he accepts the challenge and goes in!

JOHN. He finds himself kneeling at the foot of the Cross. And he feels he is forgiven, and the old comforting peace and security and joy steal back into his heart! (*He hesitates, as if reluctant to go on, as if this were the end.*)

FATHER BAIRD (*deeply moved*). And that is your end? Thank God!

LOVING (*jeeringly*). I'm afraid your rejoicing is a bit premature—for this cowardly giving in to his weakness is not the end! Even while he is kneeling, there is a mocking rational something in him that laughs with scorn—and at the last moment his will and pride revive in him again! He sees clearly by the light of reason the degradation of his pitiable surrender to old ghostly comforts—and he rejects them! (*His voice with surprising suddenness takes on a savage vindictive quality.*) He curses his God again as he had when a boy! He defies Him finally! He——!

FATHER BAIRD (*sternly*). Jack! Take care!

JOHN (*protests confusedly*). No—that's not right—I——

LOVING (*strangely confused in his turn—hurriedly*). Pardon me, Uncle. Of course, that's wrong—afraid for a moment I let an author's craving for a dramatic moment run away with my sane judgment. Naturally, he could never be so stupid as to curse what he knew didn't exist!

JOHN (*despondently*). No. He realizes he can never believe in his lost faith again. He walks out of the church—without love for ever now—but daring to face his eternal loss and hopelessness, to accept it as his fate and go on with life.

LOVING (*mockingly*). A very, very heroic end, as you see! But, unfortunately, absolutely meaningless!

FATHER BAIRD. Yes. Meaningless. I'm glad you see that.

JOHN (*rousing a bit—defensively*). No—I take that back—it isn't meaningless. It is man's duty to life to go on!

LOVING (*jeeringly*). The romantic idealist again speaks! On to Hercules! What an inspiring slogan! (*Then a sinister note coming into his voice.*) But there is still another end to my story—the one sensible happy end!

FATHER BAIRD (*as if he hadn't heard this last*). Jack! Are you so blind you cannot see what your imagining his finding peace in the church reveals about the longing of your own soul—the salvation from yourself it holds out to you? Why, if you had any honesty, with yourself, you would get down on your knees now and——

LOVING. Rot! How can you believe such childish superstition!

FATHER BAIRD (*angrily*). Jack! I've endured all I can of your blasphemous insults to——

JOHN (*confused—hurriedly*). I—I didn't mean—I'm sorry, Uncle. But it's only a story. Don't take it so seriously.

FATHER BAIRD (*has immediately controlled himself—quietly*). Only a story, Jack? You're sure you still want me to believe that?

JOHN (*defensively*). Why, what else could you believe? Do you think I——? (*Then in an abrupt, angry tone.*) But that's enough about the damned story. I don't want to talk any more about it!

(*Father Baird stares at him but keeps silent. John starts to pace up and down with nervous restlessness—then stops abruptly.*)

I—if you'll excuse me—I think I'll go down and see how Elsa is. (*He goes back toward the door. Loving follows him.*) I'll be right back.

FATHER BAIRD (*quietly*). Of course, Jack. Don't bother about me. I'll take a look at your library.

(*He gets up. John goes out. Loving turns for a moment to Father Baird, his eyes full of a mocking derision. Then he turns and follows John. Father Baird goes to the bookcase at right and runs his eyes over the titles of books. But he only does this mechanically. His mind is preoccupied, his expression sad and troubled. John's voice can be heard from below calling "Elsa." Father Baird starts and listens. Then from Elsa's bedroom John's voice is heard, as he looks for her there. He calls anxiously "Elsa"—then evidently hurries out again, closing the door behind him. Father Baird's face grows more worried. He goes to the doorway in rear and stands listening to a brief conversation from below. A moment later John comes in from rear. He is making a great effort to conceal a feeling of dread. He comes forward. Loving follows silently but stops and remains standing by the bookcase at left of doorway.*)

JOHN. She's—gone out.

FATHER BAIRD. Gone out? But it's still raining, isn't it?

JOHN. Pouring. I—I can't understand. It's a crazy thing for her to do when she's just getting over——

FATHER BAIRD (*with an involuntary start*). Ah!

JOHN. What?

FATHER BAIRD. Nothing.

JOHN (*frightenedly*). I can't imagine——

FATHER BAIRD. How long has she been gone?

JOHN. I don't know. Margaret says she heard someone go out right after we came upstairs.

FATHER BAIRD (*with lowered voice to himself*). My fault, God forgive me. I had a feeling then I shouldn't leave her.

(*John sinks down in the chair by the table and waits tensely—then suddenly he bursts out.*)

JOHN. I never should have told her the story! I'm a God-damned fool.

FATHER BAIRD (*sternly*). You would be more honest with yourself if you said a self-damned fool! (*Hearing a sound from below.*) There. Isn't that someone now?

(*John stops for a second to listen, then hurries to the door in rear. Loving remains where he is, standing motionlessly by the bookcase.*)

JOHN (*calls*). Is that you, Elsa?

ELSA (*from downstairs—hurriedly*). Yes. Don't come down. I'm coming up.

(*A moment later she appears in the hallway.*)

JOHN. Darling! I've been so damned worried. (*He starts to take her in his arms.*)

ELSA. Please!

(*She wards him off and steps past him into the study. She has taken off her coat and hat downstairs, but the lower part of her skirt and her stockings and shoes are soaking wet. Her face is pinched and drawn and pale, with flushed spots over the cheek-bones, and her eyes are bright and hard. Father Baird stares at her searchingly, his face sad and pitying.*)

FATHER BAIRD (*forcing a light tone—as she comes forward*). Well! You have given us a scare, my lady.

ELSA (*tensely*). I'm sorry, Father.

FATHER BAIRD. Your husband was half out of his mind worrying what had happened to you.

(*She sits in the chair in front of table. John stands at right of her. Loving has gone up and stands by the right end of table, at right, rear, of John. His eyes are fixed on Elsa's face with an eager, sinister intentness.*)

JOHN (*with increasing uneasiness*). Elsa! You look sick. Do you feel——?

FATHER BAIRD. I'll get her some whisky. And you, make her go to bed at once. (*He goes out the door in rear.*)

JOHN (*grabbing her hands*). Your hands are like ice!

ELSA (*pulls them away from him—coldly, without looking at him*). It's chilly out.

JOHN. Look at your shoes! They're soaked!

ELSA. It doesn't matter, does it? (*A chill runs through her body.*)

JOHN. You've taken a chill. (*Then forcing a tenderly bullying tone.*) You'll go right to bed, that's what. And no nonsense about it, you hear!

ELSA. Are you trying the bossy tender husband on me, John? I'm afraid that's no longer effective.

JOHN (*guiltily*). Why do you say that?

ELSA. Are you determined to act out this farce to the end?

JOHN. I—I don't know what you mean. What makes you look at me—as if you hated me?

ELSA (*bitterly*). Hate you? No, I only hate myself for having been such a fool! (*Then with a hard, mocking tone.*) Shall I tell you where I went, and why? But perhaps I'd better put it in the form of a novel plot!

JOHN. I—I don't know what you're driving at.

ELSA. I went out because I thought I'd like to drop in on one of Lucy's parties. But it wasn't exciting—hardly any adultery going on—I had no opportunity—even if I'd been seized by any peculiar impulse of hatred and revenge on you. So I came home. (*She forces a hard, bitter laugh.*) There! Are you satisfied? It's all a lie, of course. I simply went for a walk. But so is your story about the novel a lie.

JOHN (*stunned—stammers*). Elsa, I——

ELSA. For God's sake, John, don't lie to me any more or I—I know, I tell you! Lucy told me all about it this afternoon.

JOHN. She told you? The damned——

ELSA. Oh, she didn't tell me it was you. But she gave me all the sordid details and they were the same as those in your story. So it was you who told on yourself. Rather a joke on you, isn't it? (*She laughs bitterly.*)

JOHN. I—— (*He blurts out miserably.*) Yes—it's true.

ELSA. And it was a fine joke on me, her coming here. You would appreciate it, if you had seen how I sympathized with her, how I excused her to myself and pitied her. And all the while, she was pitying me! She was gloating! She's always envied us our happiness. Our happiness!

JOHN (*writhing*). Don't!

ELSA. She must have been laughing at me for a fool, sneering to herself about my stupid faith in you. And you gave her that chance—you ! You made our love a smutty joke for her and everyone like her—you whom I loved so ! And all the time I was loving you, you were only waiting for this chance to kill that love, you were hating me underneath, hating our happiness, hating the ideal of our marriage you had given me, which had become all the beauty and truth of life to me ! (*She springs to her feet—distractedly.*) Oh, I can't—— I can't ! (*She starts as if to run from the room.*)

JOHN (*grabbing her—imploringly*). Elsa ! For God's sake ! Didn't my story explain ? Can't you believe —it wasn't I ? Can't you forgive ?

ELSA. No ! I can't forgive ! How can I forgive —when all that time I loved you so, you were wishing in your heart that I would die !

JOHN (*frantically*). Don't say that ! It's mad ! Elsa ! Good God, how can you think——

ELSA. What else can I think ? (*Then wildly.*) Oh, John, stop talking ! What's the good of talk ? I only know I hate life ! It's dirty and insulting—and evil ! I want my dream back—or I want to be dead with it ! (*She is shaken again by a wave of uncontrollable chill, her teeth chatter—pitiably.*) Oh, John, leave me alone ! I'm cold, I'm sick. I feel crazy !

FATHER BAIRD (*comes in through the doorway at rear—sharply*). Jack ! Why haven't you got her to bed ? Can't you see she's ill ? Phone for your doctor.

(*John goes out. Loving, his eyes remaining fixed on Elsa with the same strange look, backs out of the doorway after him.*)

(*Coming to Elsa—with great compassion.*) My dear child, I can't tell you how deeply——

ELSA (*tensely*). Don't ! I can't bear—— (*She is shaken again by a chill.*)

FATHER BAIRD (*worriedly, but trying to pretend to treat it lightly, reassuringly*). You've taken a bad chill. You were very foolhardy to—— But a day or two in bed and you'll be fine again.

ELSA (*strangely serious and bitterly mocking at the same time*). But that would spoil John's story, don't you think ? That would be very inconsiderate after he's worked out such a convenient end for me.

FATHER BAIRD. Elsa ! For the love of God, don't tell me you took his morbid nonsense seriously ! Is that why you—— ?

ELSA (*as if she hadn't heard him*). And when he reminded me it was raining, it all seemed to fit in so perfectly—like the will of God ! (*She laughs with hysterical mockery, her eyes shining feverishly.*)

FATHER BAIRD (*sternly—more to break her mood than because he takes her impiety seriously*). Elsa ! Stop that mockery ! It has no part in you !

ELSA (*confusedly*). I'm sorry. I forgot you were—— (*Then suddenly hectic again.*) But I've never had any God, you see—until I met John. (*She laughs hysterically—then suddenly forces control on herself and gets shakily to her feet.*) I'm sorry. I seem to be talking nonsense. My head has gone woolly. I——

(*John enters from the hall at rear. As ne comes forward, Loving appears in the doorway behind him.*)

JOHN (*coming to Elsa*). Stillwell says for you to——

ELSA (*distractedly*). No ! (*Then dully.*) I'll go—to my room. (*She sways weakly. John starts toward her.*)

JOHN. Elsa ! Sweetheart !

ELSA. No !

(*By an effort of will, she overcomes her weakness and walks woodenly into her bedroom and closes the door behind her. John makes a movement as if to follow her.*)

FATHER BAIRD (*sharply*). Leave her alone, Jack.

(*John sinks down hopelessly on the chaise-longue. Loving stands behind him, his cold eyes fixed with a sinister intensity on the door through which Elsa has just disappeared. Father Baird makes a movement as if he were going to follow Elsa into her room. Then he stops. There is an expression of sorrowful foreboding on his face. He bows his head with a simple dignity and begins to pray silently.*)

LOVING (*his eyes now on John—with a gloating mockery*). She seems to have taken her end in your story very seriously. Let's hope she doesn't carry that too far ! You have enough on your conscience already—without murder ! You couldn't live, I know, if——

JOHN (*shuddering—clutches his head in both hands as if to crush out his thoughts*). For God's sake ! (*His eyes turn to the priest. Then their gaze travels to a point in front of Father Baird, and slowly his expression changes to one of fearful, fascinated awe, as if he suddenly sensed a Presence there the priest is praying to. His lips part and words come haltingly, as if they were forced out of him, full of imploring fear.*) Thou wilt not—do that to me again—wilt Thou ? Thou wilt not—take love from me again ?

LOVING (*jeeringly*). Is it your old demon you are praying to for mercy ? Then I hope you hear his laughter ! (*Then breaking into a cold, vicious rage.*) You cowardly fool ! I tell you there is nothing—nothing !

JOHN (*starts back to himself—stammers with a confused air of relief*). Yes—of course—what's the matter with me ? There's nothing—nothing to fear !

CURTAIN

ACT FOUR

THE END OF THE END

SCENE ONE

SCENE. *The study is shown as in preceding scene, but this scene also reveals the interior of Elsa's bedroom at left of study.*

At right of bedroom, front, is the door between the two rooms. At rear of this door, in the middle of the wall, is a dressing table, mirror and chair. In the left wall, rear, is the door to the bathroom. Before this door is a screen. At left, front, is the bed, its head against the left wall. By the head of the bed is a small stand on which is a reading lamp with a piece of cloth thrown over it to dim its light. An upholstered chair is beside the foot of the bed. Another chair is by the head of the bed at rear. A chaise-longue is at right, front, of the room.

It is nearing daybreak of a day about a week later.

In the bedroom, Elsa lies in the bed, her eyes closed, her face pallid and wasted. John sits in the chair toward the foot of the bed, front. He looks on the verge of complete mental and physical collapse. His unshaven cheeks are sunken and sallow. His eyes, bloodshot from sleeplessness, stare from black hollows with a frozen anguish at Elsa's face.

Loving stands by the back of his chair, facing front. The sinister, mocking character of his mask is accentuated now, evilly intensified.

Father Baird is standing by the middle of the bed, at rear. His face also bears obvious traces of sleepless strain. He is conferring in whispers with Doctor Stillwell, who is standing at his right. Both are watching Elsa with anxious eyes. At rear of Stillwell on his right, a trained nurse is standing.

Stillwell is in his early fifties, tall, with a sharp, angular face and grey hair. The Nurse is a plump woman in her late thirties.

For a moment after the curtain rises the whispered pantomime between Stillwell and the priest continues, the Nurse watching and listening. Then Elsa stirs restlessly and moans. She speaks without opening her eyes, hardly above a whisper, in a tone of despairing bitterness.

ELSA. John! How could you? Our dream! (*She moans.*)

JOHN (*in anguish*). Elsa! Forgive!

LOVING (*in a cold, inexorable tone*). She will never forgive.

STILLWELL (*frowning, makes a motion to John to be silent*). Ssshh!

(*He whispers to Father Baird, his eyes on John. The priest nods and comes around the corner of the bed toward John. Stillwell sits in the chair by the head of the bed, rear, and feels Elsa's pulse. The Nurse moves close behind him.*)

FATHER BAIRD (*bends over John's chair and speaks in a low cautioning voice*). Jack. You must be quiet.

JOHN (*his eyes are on Stillwell's face, desperately trying to read some answer there. He calls to him frightenedly*). Doctor! What is it? Is she——?

STILLWELL. Ssshh! (*He gives John a furious look and motions Father Baird to keep him quiet.*)

FATHER BAIRD. Jack! Don't you realize you're only harming her?

JOHN (*confusedly repentant—in a low voice*). I'm sorry. I try not to, but—— I know it's crazy, but I can't help being afraid——

LOVING. That my prophecy is coming true—her end in my story.

JOHN (*with anguished appeal*). No! Elsa! Don't believe that!

(*Elsa moans.*)

FATHER BAIRD. You see! You've disturbed her again!

(*Stillwell gets up and after exchanging a whispered word with the Nurse, who nods and takes his place by the bedside, comes quickly around the end of the bed to John.*)

STILLWELL. What the devil is the matter with you? I thought you promised me if I let you stay in here you'd keep quiet.

JOHN (*dazedly now—suddenly overcome by a wave of drowsiness he tries in vain to fight back*). I won't again. (*His head nods.*)

STILLWELL (*gives him a searching look—to Father Baird*). We've got to get him out of here.

JOHN (*rousing himself—desperately fighting back his drowsiness*). I won't sleep! God, how can I sleep when——!

STILLWELL (*taking one arm and signalling Father Baird to take the other—sharply but in a voice just above a whisper*). Loving, come into your study. I want to talk with you about your wife's condition.

JOHN (*terrified*). Why? What do you mean? She isn't——?

STILLWELL (*hastily, in a forced tone of reassurance*). No, no, no! What put that nonsense in your head? (*He flashes a signal to the priest and they both lift John to his feet.*) Come along, that's a good fellow.

(*They lead John to the door to the study at right. Loving follows them silently, moving backward, his eyes fixed with sinister gloating intentness on Elsa's face. Father Baird opens the door and they pass through, Loving slipping after them. Father Baird closes the door. They lead John to the chaise-longue at right, front, of study, passing in front of the table. Loving keeps pace with them, passing to rear of table.*)

JOHN (*starts to resist feebly*). Let me go! I mustn't leave her! I'm afraid!

(*They get him seated on the chaise-longue, Loving taking up a position directly behind him on the other side of the chaise-longue.*)

I feel there's something——

LOVING (*with a gloating mockery*). A demon who laughs, hiding behind the end of my story!

(*He gives a sinister laugh. Father Baird and even Stillwell, in spite of himself, are appalled by this laughter.*)

JOHN (*starts to his feet—in anguish*). No!

FATHER BAIRD. Jack!

STILLWELL (*recovering, angry at himself and furious with John—seizes him by the arm and forces him down on the chaise-longue again*). Stop your damned nonsense! Get a grip on yourself! I've warned you you'd go to pieces like this if you kept on refusing to rest or take nourishment. But that's got to stop, do you hear me? You've got to get some sleep!

FATHER BAIRD. Yes, Jack. You must!

STILLWELL. You've been a disturbing factor from the first and I've been a fool to stand—— But I've had enough! You'll stay out of her room——

JOHN. No!

STILLWELL. Don't you want her to get well? By God, from the way you've been acting——

JOHN (*wildly*). For God's sake, don't say that!

STILLWELL. Can't you see you're no help to her in this condition? While if you'll sleep for a while——

JOHN. No! (*Imploringly.*) She's much better, isn't she? For God's sake, tell me you know she isn't going to—— Tell me that and I'll do anything you ask!

LOVING. And don't lie, please! I want the truth!

STILLWELL (*forcing an easy tone*). What's all this talk? She's resting quietly. There's no question of—— (*Then quickly.*) And now I've satisfied you on that, lie down as you promised.

(*John stares at him uncertainly for a moment—then obediently lies down.*)

Close your eyes now.

(*John closes his eyes. Loving stands by his head, staring down at his face. John almost immediately drops off into a drugged half-sleep, his breathing becomes heavy and exhausted. Stillwell nods to Father Baird with satisfaction—then moves quietly to the other side of the room, by the door to Elsa's bedroom, beckoning Father Baird to follow him.*)

(*He speaks to him in a low voice.*)

We'll have to keep an eye on him. He's headed straight for a complete collapse. But I think he'll sleep now, for a while, anyway.

(*He opens the door to the bedroom, looks in and catches the eye of the Nurse, who is still sitting in the chair by the head of the bed, watching Elsa. The Nurse shakes her head, answering his question. He softly closes the door again.*)

FATHER BAIRD. No change, Doctor?

STILLWELL. No. But I'm not giving up hope! She still has a fighting chance! (*Then in a tone of exasperated dejection.*) If she'd only fight!

FATHER BAIRD (*nods with sad understanding*). Yes. That's it.

STILLWELL. Damn it, she seems to want to die. (*Then angrily.*) And, by God, in spite of his apparent grief I've suspected at times that underneath he wants——

LOVING (*his eyes fixed on John's face, speaks in a cold, implacable tone*). She is going to die.

JOHN (*starts half-awake—mutters*). No! Elsa! Forgive! (*He sinks into drugged sleep again.*)

STILLWELL. You see. He keeps insisting to himself——

FATHER BAIRD (*defensively*). That's a horrible charge for you to make, Doctor. Why, anyone can see the poor boy is crazed with fear and grief.

STILLWELL (*a bit ashamed*). Sorry. But there have been times when I've had the strongest sense of—well, as he said, Something—— (*Then curtly, feeling this makes him appear silly.*) Afraid I've allowed this case to get on my nerves. Don't usually go in for psychic nonsense.

FATHER BAIRD. Your feeling isn't nonsense, Doctor.

STILLWELL. She won't forgive him. That's her trouble as well as his. (*He sighs, giving way for a moment to his own physical weariness.*) A strange case. Too many undercurrents. The pneumonia has been more a means than a cause. (*With a trace of condescension.*) More in your line. A little casting out of devils would have been of benefit—might still be.

FATHER BAIRD. Might still be. Yes.

STILLWELL (*exasperatedly*). Damn it, I've seen many worse cases where the patient pulled through. If I could only get her will to live functioning again! If she'd forgive him and get that off her mind, I know she'd fight. (*He abruptly gets to his feet—curtly.*) Well, talk won't help her, that's sure. I'll get back.

(*He goes into the bedroom and closes the door silently behind him. Father Baird remains for a moment staring sadly at the floor. In the bedroom, Stillwell goes to the bedside. The Nurse gets up and he speaks to her in a whisper, hears what she has to report, gives her some quick instructions. She goes to the bathroom. He sits in the chair by the bed and feels Elsa's pulse. The Nurse comes back and hands him a hypodermic needle. He administers this in Elsa's arm. She moans and her body twitches for a second. He sits, watching her face worriedly, his fingers on her wrist. In the study, Father Baird starts to pace back and forth, frowning, his face tense, feeling desperately that he is facing inevitable tragedy, that he must do something to thwart it at once. He stops at the foot of the chaise-longue and stares down at the sleeping John. Then he prays.*)

FATHER BAIRD. Dear Jesus, grant me the grace to bring Jack back to Thee. Make him see that Thou, alone, hast the words of Eternal Life, the power still to save——

LOVING (*his eyes fixed on John's face in the same stare—speaks as if in answer to Father Baird's prayer*). Nothing can save her.

JOHN (*shuddering in his sleep*). No !

LOVING. Her end in your story is coming true. It was a cunning method of murder !

FATHER BAIRD (*horrified*). Jack !

JOHN (*with a tortured cry that starts him awake*). No ! It's a lie ! (*He stares around him at the air, as if he were trying to see some presence he feels there.*) Liar ! Murderer ! (*Suddenly he seems to see Father Baird for the first time—with a cry of appeal—brokenly.*) Uncle ! For God's sake, help me ! I—I feel I'm going mad !

FATHER BAIRD (*eagerly*). If you would only let me help you, Jack ! If you would only be honest with yourself and admit the truth in your own soul now, for Elsa's sake—while there is still time.

JOHN (*frightenedly*). Still time ? What do you mean ? Is she—worse ?

FATHER BAIRD. No. You've only been sleeping a few minutes. There has been no change.

JOHN. Then why did you say—— ?

FATHER BAIRD. Because I have decided you must be told the truth now, the truth you already know in your heart.

JOHN. What—truth ?

FATHER BAIRD. It is the crisis. Human science has done all it can to save her. Her life is in the hands of God now.

LOVING. There is no God !

FATHER BAIRD (*sternly*). Do you dare say that—now !

JOHN (*frightenedly*). No—I—I don't know what I'm saying—— It isn't I——

FATHER BAIRD (*recovering himself—quietly*). No. I know you couldn't blaspheme at such a time—not your true self.

LOVING (*angrily*). It is my true self—my only self ! And I see through your stupid trick—to use the fear of death to——

FATHER BAIRD. It's the hatred you once gave your soul to which speaks, not you ! (*Pleadingly.*) I implore you to cast that evil from your soul ! If you would only pray !

LOVING (*fiercely*). No !

JOHN (*stammers torturedly*). I—I don't know—— I can't think !

FATHER BAIRD (*intensely*). Pray with me, Jack. (*He sinks to his knees.*) Pray that Elsa's life may be spared to you ! It is only God Who can open her heart to forgiveness and give her back the will to live ! Pray for His forgiveness, and He will have compassion on you ! Pray to Him Who is Love. Who is Infinite Tenderness and Pity !

JOHN (*half-slipping to his knees—longingly*). Who is Love ! If I could only believe again !

FATHER BAIRD. Pray for your lost faith and it will be given you !

LOVING (*sneeringly*). You forget I once prayed to your God and His answer was hatred and death—and a mocking laughter !

JOHN (*starts up from his half-kneeling position, under the influence of this memory*). Yes, I prayed then. No. It's no good, Uncle. I can't believe. (*Then suddenly—with eagerness.*) Let Him prove to me His Love exists ! Then I will believe in Him again !

FATHER BAIRD. You may not bargain with your God, Jack. (*He gets wearily to his feet, his shoulders bowed, looking tragically old and beaten—then with a last appeal.*) But I beseech you still ! I warn you !—before it's too late !—look into your soul and force yourself to admit the truth you find there—the truth you have yourself revealed in your story where the man, who is you, goes to the church and, at the foot of the Cross, is granted the grace of faith again !

LOVING. In a moment of stupid madness ! But remember that is not the end !

FATHER BAIRD (*ignoring this*). There is a fate in that story, Jack—the fate of the will of God made manifest to you through the secret longing of your own heart for faith! Take care! It has come true so far, and I am afraid if you persist in your mad denial of Him and your own soul, you will have willed for yourself the accursed end of that man—and for Elsa, death!

JOHN (*terrified*). Stop! Stop talking damned nonsense! (*Distractedly.*) Leave me alone! I'm sick of your damned croaking! You're lying! Stillwell said there was no danger! She's asleep! She's getting better! (*Then terrified again.*) What made you say, a fate in my story—the will of God? Good God, that's—that's nonsense! I—— (*He starts for the bedroom door.*) I'm going back to her. There's Something——

FATHER BAIRD (*tries to hold him back*). You can't go there now, Jack.

JOHN (*pushing him roughly away*). Leave me alone!

(*He opens the bedroom door and lurches in. Loving has come around behind the table and slips in after him. Father Baird, recovering from the push which has sent him back against the table, front, comes quickly to the doorway.*)

(*As John comes in, Stillwell turns from where he sits beside the bedside, a look of intense anger and exasperation on his face. John, as soon as he enters, falls under the atmosphere of the sick-room, his wildness drops from him and he looks at Stillwell with pleading eyes.*)

STILLWELL (*giving up getting him out again as hopeless, makes a gesture for him to be silent*). Ssshh!

(*The Nurse looks at John with shocked rebuke. Stillwell motions John to sit down. He does so meekly, sinking into the chair at right, centre. Loving stands behind the chair. Father Baird, after a look into the room to see if his help is needed, exchanges a helpless glance with Stillwell, and then, turning back into the study but leaving the communicating door ajar, goes back as far as the table. There, after a moment's pause, he bows his head and begins praying silently to himself. In the bedroom, Stillwell turns back to his patient. There is a pause of silent immobility in the room. John's eyes are fixed on Elsa's face with a growing terror. Loving stares over his head with cold, still eyes.*)

JOHN (*in a low, tense voice—as if he were thinking aloud*). A fate in my story—the will of God! Something—— (*He shudders.*)

LOVING (*in the same low tone, but with a cold, driving intensity*). She will soon be dead.

JOHN. No!

LOVING. What will you do then? Love will be lost to you for ever. You will be alone again. There will remain only the anguish of endless memories, endless regrets—a torturing remorse for murdered happiness!

JOHN. I know! For God's sake, don't make me think——

LOVING (*coldly remorseless—sneeringly*). Do you think you can choose your stupid end in your story now, when you have to live it?—on to Hercules? But if you love her, how can you desire to go on—with all that was Elsa rotting in her grave behind you!

JOHN (*torturedly*). No! I can't! I'll kill myself!

ELSA (*suddenly moans frightenedly*). No, John! No!

LOVING (*triumphantly*). Ah! At last you accept the true end! At last you see the empty posing of your old ideal about man's duty to go on for Life's sake, your meaningless gesture of braving fate—a childish nose-thumbing at Nothingness at which Something laughs with a weary scorn! (*He gives a low, scornful laugh.*) Shorn of your boastful words, all it means is to go on like an animal in dumb obedience to the law of the blind stupidity of life that it must live at all costs! But where will you go—except to death? And why should you wait for an end you know when it is in your power to grasp that end—now!

ELSA (*again moans frightenedly*). No, John—no!—please, John!

LOVING. Surely you cannot be afraid of death. Death is not the dying. Dying is life, its last revenge upon itself. But death is what the dead know, the warm, dark womb of Nothingness—the Dream in which you and Elsa may sleep as one for ever, beyond fear of separation!

JOHN (*longingly*). Elsa and I—for ever beyond fear!

LOVING. Dust within dust to sleep!

JOHN (*mechanically*). Dust within dust. (*Then frightenedly questioning.*) Dust? (*A shudder runs over him and he starts as if awakening from sleep.*) Fool! Can the dust love the dust? No! (*Desperately.*) Oh God, have pity! Show me the way!

LOVING (*furiously—as if he felt himself temporarily beaten*). Coward!

JOHN. If I could only pray! If I could only believe again!

LOVING. You cannot!

JOHN. A fate in my story, Uncle said—the will of God!—I went to the church—a fate in the church—— (*He suddenly gets to his feet as if impelled by some force outside him. He stares before him with obsessed eyes.*) Where I used to believe, where I used to pray!

LOVING. You insane fool! I tell you that's ended!

JOHN. If I could see the Cross again——

LOVING (*with a shudder*). No! I don't want to see! I remember too well!—when Father and Mother——!

JOHN. Why are you so afraid of Him, if——

LOVING (*shaken—then with fierce defiance*). Afraid?

I who once cursed Him, who would again if—— (*Then hurriedly catching himself.*) But what superstitious nonsense you make me remember. He doesn't exist!

JOHN (*takes a step toward the door*). I am going!

LOVING (*tries to bar his path*). No!

JOHN (*without touching him, makes a motion of pushing him aside*). I am going.

(*He goes through the door to the study, moving like one in a trance, his eyes fixed straight before him. Loving continues to try to bar his path, always without touching him. Father Baird looks up as they pass the table.*)

LOVING (*in impotent rage*). No! You coward!

(*John goes out the door in rear of study and Loving is forced out before him.*)

FATHER BAIRD (*starting after him*). Jack!

(*But he turns back in alarm as, in the bedroom, Elsa suddenly comes out of the half-coma she is in with a cry of terror and, in spite of Stillwell, springs up to a half-sitting position in bed, her staring eyes on the doorway to the study.*)

ELSA. John! (*Then to Stillwell.*) Oh, please! Look after him! He might—— John! Come back! I'll forgive!

STILLWELL (*soothingly*). There, don't be frightened. He's only gone to lie down for a while. He's very tired.

(*Father Baird has come in from the study and is approaching the bed. Stillwell, with a significant look, calls on him for confirmation.*)

Isn't that right, Father?

FATHER BAIRD. Yes, Elsa.

ELSA (*relieved*). Oh! (*She smiles faintly.*) Poor John. I'm so sorry. Tell him he mustn't worry. I understand now. I love—I forgive.

(*She sinks back and closes her eyes. Stillwell reaches for her wrist in alarm, but as he feels her pulse his expression changes to one of excited surprise.*)

FATHER BAIRD (*misreading his look—in a frightened whisper*). Merciful God! She isn't——?

STILLWELL. No. She's asleep. (*Then with suppressed excitement.*) That's done it! She'll want to live now!

FATHER BAIRD. God be praised!

(*Stillwell, his air curtly professional, again turns and whispers some orders to the Nurse.*)

CURTAIN

SCENE TWO

SCENE. *A section of the interior of an old church. A side wall runs diagonally back from left, front, two-thirds of the width of the stage, where it meets an end wall that extends back from right, front. The walls are old grey stone. In the middle of the side wall is a great cross, its base about five feet from the floor, with a life-size figure of Christ, an exceptionally fine piece of wood carving. In the middle of the end wall is an arched doorway. On either side of this door, but high up in the wall, their bases above the level of the top of the doorway, are two narrow, stained-glass windows.*

It is a few minutes after the close of the preceding scene. The church is dim and empty, and still. The only light is the reflection of the dawn, which, stained by the colour in the windows, falls on the wall on and around the Cross.

The outer doors beyond the arched doorway are suddenly pushed open with a crash and John and Loving appear in the doorway. Loving comes first, retreating backward before John whom he desperately, but always without touching him, endeavours to keep from entering the church. But John is the stronger now and, the same look of obsessed resolution in his eyes, he forces Loving back.

LOVING (*as they enter—desperately, as if he were becoming exhausted by the struggle*). You fool! There is nothing here but hatred!

JOHN. No! There was love! (*His eyes fasten themselves on the Cross and he gives a cry of hope.*) The Cross!

LOVING. The symbol of hate and derision!

JOHN. No! Of love!

(*Loving is forced back until the back of his head is against the foot of the Cross. John throws himself on his knees before it and raises his hands up to the figure of Christ in supplication.*)

Mercy! Forgive!

LOVING (*raging*). Fool! Grovel on your knees! It is useless! To pray, one must believe!

JOHN. I have come back to Thee!

LOVING. Words! There is nothing!

JOHN. Let me believe in Thy love again!

LOVING. You cannot believe!

JOHN (*imploringly*). O God of Love, hear my prayer!

LOVING. There is no God! There is only death!

JOHN (*more weakly now*). Have pity on me! Let Elsa live!

LOVING. There is no pity! There is only scorn!

JOHN. Hear me while there is still time! (*He waits, staring at the Cross with anguished eyes, his arms outstretched. There is a pause of silence.*)

LOVING (*with triumphant mockery*). Silence! But behind it I hear mocking laughter!

JOHN (*agonized*). No! (*He gives way, his head bowed, and sobs heartbrokenly—then stops suddenly, and looking up at the Cross again, speaks sobbingly in a strange humble tone of broken reproach.*) O Son of Man, I am Thou and Thou art I! Why hast Thou forsaken me? O Brother Who lived and loved and suffered and died with us, Who knoweth the tortured hearts of men, canst Thou not forgive—now—when I surrender all to Thee—when I have forgiven Thee—the love that Thou once took from me!

LOVING (*with a cry of hatred*). No! Liar! I will never forgive!

JOHN (*his eyes fixed on the face of the Crucified suddenly lighting up as if he now saw there the answer to his prayer—in a voice trembling with awakening hope and joy*). Ah! Thou hast heard me at last! Thou hast not forsaken me! Thou hast always loved me! I am forgiven! I can forgive myself—through Thee! I can believe!

LOVING (*stumbles weakly from beneath the Cross*). No! I deny! (*He turns to face the Cross with a last defiance.*) I defy Thee! Thou canst not conquer me! I hate Thee! I curse Thee!

JOHN. No! I bless! I love!

LOVING (*as if this were a mortal blow, seems to sag and collapse—with a choking cry*). No!

JOHN (*with a laugh that is half sob*). Yes! I see now! At last I see! I have always loved! O Lord of Love, forgive Thy poor blind fool!

LOVING. No! (*His legs crumple under him, he slumps to his knees beside John, as if some invisible force crushed him down.*)

JOHN (*his voice rising exultantly, his eyes on the face of the Crucified*). Thou art the Way—the Truth—the Resurrection and the Life, and he that believeth in Thy Love, his love shall never die!

LOVING (*faintly, at last surrendering, addressing the Cross not without a final touch of pride in his humility*). Thou hast conquered, Lord. Thou art—the End. Forgive—the damned soul—of John Loving!

(*He slumps forward to the floor and rolls over on his back, dead, his head beneath the foot of the Cross, his arms outflung so that his body forms another cross. John rises from his knees and stands with arms stretched up and out, so that he, too, is like a cross. While this is happening the light of the dawn on the stained-glass windows swiftly rises to a brilliant intensity of crimson and green and gold, as if the sun had risen. The grey walls of the church, particularly the wall where the Cross is, and the face of the Christ shine with this radiance.*)

John Loving—he, who had been only John—remains standing with his arms stretched up to the Cross, an expression of mystic exaltation on his face. The corpse of Loving lies at the foot of the Cross, like a cured cripple's testimonial offering in a shrine.

(*Father Baird comes in hurriedly through the arched doorway. He stops on seeing John Loving, then comes quietly up beside him and stares searchingly into his face. At what he sees there he bows his head and his lips move in grateful prayer. John Loving is oblivious to his presence.*)

FATHER BAIRD (*finally taps him gently on the shoulder*). Jack.

JOHN LOVING (*still in his ecstatic mystic vision—strangely*). I am John Loving.

FATHER BAIRD (*stares at him—gently*). It's all right now, Jack. Elsa will live.

JOHN LOVING (*exaltedly*). I know! Love lives forever! Death is dead! Ssshh! Listen! Do you hear?

FATHER BAIRD. Hear what, Jack?

JOHN LOVING. Life laughs with God's love again! Life laughs with love!

CURTAIN

A TOUCH OF THE POET

A Play in Four Acts

Characters

MICKEY MALOY
JAMIE CREGAN
SARA MELODY
NORA MELODY
CORNELIUS MELODY
DAN ROCHE
PADDY O'DOWD
PATCH RILEY
DEBORAH (MRS. HENRY HARFORD)
NICHOLAS GADSBY

Scenes

ACT ONE

Dining-room of Melody's Tavern. 9 a.m. on July 27th, 1828.

ACT TWO

The same, about a half-hour later.

ACT THREE

The same, around eight that evening.

ACT FOUR

The same, around midnight.

ACT ONE

SCENE. *The dining-room of Melody's Tavern, in a village a few miles from Boston. The tavern is over a hundred years old. It had once been prosperous, a breakfast stop for the stagecoach, but the stage line had been discontinued and for some years now the tavern has fallen upon neglected days.*

The dining-room and barroom were once a single spacious room, low-ceilinged, with heavy oak beams and panelled walls – the taproom of the tavern in its prosperous days, now divided into two rooms by a flimsy partition, the barroom being off left. The partition is painted to imitate the old panelled walls but this only makes it more of an eyesore.

At left front, two steps lead up to a closed door opening on a flight of stairs in the floor above. Farther back is the door to the bar. Between these doors hangs a large mirror. Beyond the bar door a small cabinet is fastened to the wall. At rear are four windows. Between the middle two is the street door. At right front is another door, open, giving on a hallway and the main stairway to the second floor, and leading to the kitchen. Farther front at right, there is a high schoolmaster's desk with a stool.

In the foreground are two tables. One, with four chairs, at left centre; a larger one, seating six, at right centre. At left and right rear, are two more tables, identical with the ones at right centre. All these tables are set with white tablecloths, etc., except the small ones in the foreground of left.

It is around nine in the morning of July 27, 1828. Sunlight shines in through the windows at rear.

Mickey Maloy sits at the table at left front, facing right. He is glancing through a newspaper. Maloy is twenty-six, with a sturdy physique and an amiable, cunning face, his mouth usually set in a half-leering grin.

Jamie Cregan peers around the half-open door to the bar. Seeing Maloy, he comes in. As obviously Irish as Maloy, he is middle-aged, tall, with a lantern-jawed face. There is a scar of a sabre cut over one cheekbone. He is dressed neatly but in old, worn clothes. His eyes are bloodshot, his manner sickly, but he grins as he greets Maloy sardonically.

CREGAN. God bless all here — even the barkeep.

MALOY (*with an answering grin*). Top o' the mornin'.

CREGAN. Top o' me head. (*He puts his hand to his head and groans.*) Be the saints, there's a blacksmith at work on it!

MALOY. Small wonder. You'd the divil's own load when you left at two this mornin'.

CREGAN. I must have. I don't remember leaving. (*He sits at right of table.*) Faix, you're takin' it aisy.

MALOY. There's no trade this time o' day.

CREGAN. It was a great temptation, when I saw no one in the bar, to make off with a bottle. A hair av the dog is what I need, but I've divil a penny in my pantaloons.

MALOY. Have one on the house. (*He goes to the cupboard and takes out a decanter of whiskey and a glass.*)

CREGAN. Thank you kindly. Sure, the good Samaritan was a crool haythen beside you.

MALOY (*putting the decanter and glass before him*). It's the same you was drinking last night — his private dew. He keeps it here for emergencies when he don't want to go in the bar.

CREGAN (*pours out a big drink*). Lave it to Con never to be caught dry. (*Raising his glass.*) Your health and inclinations — if they're virtuous! (*He drinks and sighs with relief.*) God bless you, Whiskey, it's you can rouse the dead! Con hasn't been down yet for his morning's morning?

MALOY. No. He won't be till later.

CREGAN. It's like a miracle, me meeting him again. I came to these parts looking for work. It's only by accident I heard talk of a Con Melody and come here to see was it him. Until last night, I'd not seen hide nor hair of him since the war with the French in Spain — after the battle of Salamanca in '12. I was a corporal in the Seventh Dragoons and he was major. (*Proudly.*) I got this cut from a sabre at Talavera, bad luck to it! — serving under him. He was a captain then.

MALOY. So you told me last night.

CREGAN (*with a quick glance at him*). Did I now? I must have said more than my prayers, with the lashings of whiskey in me.

MALOY (*with a grin*). More than your prayers is the truth.

(*Cregan glances at him uneasily. Maloy pushes the decanter towards him.*)

Take another taste.

CREGAN. I don't like sponging. Sure, my credit ought to be good in this shebeen! Ain't I his cousin?

MALOY. You're forgettin' what himself told you last night as he went up to bed. You could have all the whiskey you could pour down you, but not a penny's worth of credit. This house, he axed you to remember, only gives credit to gentlemen.

CREGAN. Divil mend him!

MALOY (*with a chuckle*). You kept thinking about his insults after he'd gone out, getting madder and madder.

CREGAN. God pity him, that's like him. He hasn't changed much. (*He pours out a drink and gulps it with a cautious look at Maloy.*) If I was mad at Con, and me blind drunk, I must have told you a power of lies.

MALOY (*winks slyly*). Maybe they wasn't lies.

CREGAN. If I said any wrong of Con Melody —

MALOY. Arrah, are you afraid I'll gab what you said to him? I won't, you can take my oath.

CREGAN (*his face clearing*). Tell me what I said and I'll tell you if it was lies.

MALOY. You said his father wasn't of the quality of Galway like he makes out, but a thievin' shebeen keeper who got rich by moneylendin' and squeezin' tenants and every manner of trick. And when he'd enough he married, and bought an estate with a pack of hounds and set up as one of the gentry. He'd hardly got settled when his wife died givin' birth to Con.

CREGAN. There's no lie there.

MALOY. You said none of the gentry would speak to auld Melody, but he had a tough hide and didn't heed them. He made up his mind he'd bring Con up a true gentleman, so he packed him off to Dublin to school, and after that to the College with sloos of money to prove himself the equal of any gentleman's son. But Con found, while there was plenty to drink on him and borrow money, there was few didn't sneer behind his back at his pretensions.

CREGAN. That's the truth, too. But Con wiped the sneer off their mugs when he called one av thim out and put a bullet in his hip. That was his first duel. It gave his pride the taste for revenge and after that he was always lookin' for an excuse to challenge someone.

MALOY. He's done a power av boastin' about his duels, but I thought he was lyin'.

CREGAN. There's no lie in it. It was that brought disgrace on him in the end, right after he'd been promoted to major. He got caught by a Spanish noble making love to his wife, just after the battle of Salamanca, and there was a duel and Con killed him. The scandal was hushed up but Con had to resign from the army. If it wasn't for his fine record for bravery in battle, they'd have court-martialled him. (*Then guiltily.*) But I'm sayin' more than my prayers again.

MALOY. It's no news about his women. You'd think, to hear him when he's drunk, there wasn't one could resist him in Portugal and Spain.

CREGAN. If you'd seen him then, you wouldn't wonder. He was as strong as an ox, and on a thoroughbred horse, in his uniform, there wasn't a handsomer man in the army. And he had the chance he wanted in Portugal and Spain where a British officer was welcome in the gentry's houses. At home, the only women he'd known was whores. (*He adds hastily.*) Except Nora, I mean. (*Lowering his voice.*) Tell me, has he done any rampagin' wid women here?

MALOY. He hasn't. The damned Yankee gentry won't let him come near them, and he considers the few Irish around here to be scum beneath his notice. But once in a while there'll be some Yankee stops overnight wid his wife or daughter and then you'd laugh to see Con, if he thinks she's gentry, sidlin' up to her, playin' the great gentleman and makin' compliments, and then boasting afterwards he could have them in bed if he'd had a chance at it, for all their modern Yankee airs.

CREGAN. And maybe he could. If you'd known him in the auld days, you'd nivir doubt any boast he makes about fightin' and women, and gamblin' or any kind av craziness. There nivir was a madder divil.

MALOY (*lowering his voice*). Speakin' av Nora, you nivir mentioned her last night, but I know all about it without you telling me. I used to have my room here, and there's nights he's madder drunk than most when he throws it in her face he had to marry her because — Mind you, I'm not saying anything against poor Nora. A sweeter woman never lived. And I know you know all about it.

CREGAN (*reluctantly*). I do. Wasn't I raised on his estate?

MALOY. He tells her it was the priests tricked him into marrying her. He hates priests.

CREGAN. He's a liar, then. He may like to blame it on them but it's little Con Melody cared what they said. Nothing ever made him do anything, except himself. He married her because he'd fallen in love with her, but he was ashamed of her in his pride at the same time because her folks were only ignorant peasants on his estate, as poor as poor. Nora was as pretty a girl as you'd find in a year's travel, and he'd come to be bitter lonely, with no woman's company but the whores was helpin' him ruin the estate. (*He shrugs his shoulders.*) Well, anyways, he married her and then went off to the war, and left her alone in the castle to have her child, and nivir saw her again till he was sent home from Spain. Then he raised what money he still was able, and took her and Sara here to America where no one would know him.

MALOY (*thinking this over for a moment*). It's hard for me to believe he ever loved her. I've seen the way he treats her now. Well, thank you for telling me, and I take my oath I'll nivir breathe a word of it — for Nora's sake, not his.

CREGAN (*grimly*). You'd better kape quiet for fear of him, too. If he's one-half the man he was, he could bate the lights out of the two av us.

MALOY. He's strong as a bull still for all the whiskey he's drunk. (*He pushes the bottle towards Cregan.*) Have another taste.

(*Cregan pours out a drink.*)

Drink hearty.

CREGAN. Long life.

(*He drinks. Maloy puts the decanter and glass back on the cupboard. A girl's voice is heard from the hall at right. Cregan jumps up — hastily.*)

That's Sara, isn't it? I'll get out. She'll likely blame me for Con getting so drunk last night. I'll be back after Con is down.

(*He goes out. Maloy starts to go in the bar, as if he too wanted to avoid Sara. Then he sits down defiantly.*)

MALOY. Be damned if I'll run from her.

(*He takes up the paper as Sara Melody comes in from the hall at right.*

Sara is twenty, an exceedingly pretty girl with a mass of black hair, fair skin with rosy cheeks and beautiful, deep-blue eyes. There is a curious blending in her of what are commonly considered aristocratic and peasant characteristics. She has a fine forehead. Her nose is thin and straight. She has small ears set close to her well-shaped head, and a slender neck. Her mouth, on the other hand, has a touch of coarseness and sensuality and her jaw is too heavy. Her figure is strong and graceful, with full, firm breasts and hips, and a slender waist. But she has large feet and broad, ugly hands with stubby fingers. Her voice is soft and musical, but her speech has at times a self-conscious, stilted quality about it, due to her restraining a tendency to lapse into brogue. Her everyday working dress is of cheap material, but she wears it in a way that gives a pleasing effect of beauty unadorned.)

SARA (*with a glance at Maloy, sarcastically*). I'm sorry to interrupt you when you're so busy, but have you your bar book ready for me to look over?

MALOY (*surlily*). I have. I put it on your desk.

SARA. Thank you. (*She turns her back on him, sits at the desk, takes a small account book from it, and begins checking figures.*)

MALOY (*watches her over his paper*). If it's profits you're looking for, you won't find them — not with all the drinks himself's been treating to.

(*She ignores this. He becomes resentful.*)

You've got your airs of a grand lady this morning, I see. There's no talkin' to you since you've been playin' nurse to the young Yankee upstairs.

(*She makes herself ignore this, too.*)

Well, you've had your cap set for him ever since he came to live by the lake, and now's your chance, when he's here sick and too weak to defend himself.

SARA (*turns on him — with quiet anger*). I warn you to mind your own business, Mickey, or I'll tell my father of your impudence. He'll teach you to keep your place, and God help you.

MALOY (*doesn't believe this threat but is frightened by the possibility*). Arrah, don't try to scare me. I know you'd never carry tales to him. (*Placatingly.*) Can't you take a bit of teasing, Sara?

SARA (*turns back to her figuring*). Leave Simon out of your teasing.

MALOY. Oho, he's Simon to you now, is he? Well, well. (*He gives her a cunning glance.*) Maybe, if you'd come down from your high horse, I could tell you some news.

SARA. You're worse than an old woman for gossip. I don't want to hear it.

MALOY. When you was upstairs at the back taking him his breakfast, there was a grand carriage with a nigger coachman stopped at the corner and a Yankee lady got out and came in here. I was sweeping and Nora was scrubbing the kitchen.

(*Sara has turned to him, all attention now.*)

She asked me what road would take her near the lake —

SARA (*starts*). Ah.

MALOY. So I told her, but she didn't go. She kept looking around, and said she'd like a cup of tea, and where was the waitress. I knew she must be connected someway with Harford or why would she want to go to the lake, where no one's ever lived but him. She didn't want tea at all, but only an excuse to stay.

SARA (*resentfully*). So she asked for the waitress, did she? I hope you told her I'm the owner's daughter, too.

MALOY. I did. I don't like Yankee airs any more than you. I was short with her. I said you was out for a walk, and the tavern wasn't open yet, anyway. So she went out and drove off.

SARA (*worriedly now*). I hope you didn't insult her with your bad manners. What did she look like, Mickey?

MALOY. Pretty, if you like that kind. A pale, delicate wisp of a thing with big eyes.

SARA. That fits what he's said of his mother. How old was she?

MALOY. It's hard to tell, but she's too young for his mother, I'd swear. Around thirty, I'd say. Maybe it's his sister.

SARA. He hasn't a sister.

MALOY (*grinning*). Then maybe she's an old sweetheart looking for you to scratch your eyes out.

SARA. He's never had a sweetheart.

MALOY (*mockingly*). Is that what he tells you, and you believe him? Faix, you must be in love!

SARA (*angrily*). Will you mind your own business? I'm not such a fool! (*Worried again.*) Maybe you ought to have told her he's here sick to save her the drive in the hot sun and the walk through the woods for nothing.

MALOY. Why would I tell her, when she never mentioned him?

SARA. Yes, it's her own fault. But — Well, there's no use thinking of it now — or bothering my head about her, anyway, whoever she was.

(*She begins checking figures again. Her mother appears in the doorway at right.*

Nora Melody is forty, but years of overwork and worry have made her look much older. She must have been as pretty as a girl as Sara is now. She still has the beautiful eyes her daughter has inherited. But she has become too worn out to take care of her appearance. Her black hair, streaked with grey, straggles in untidy wisps about her face. Her body is dumpy, with sagging breasts, and her old clothes are like a bag covering it, tied around the middle. Her red hands are knotted by rheumatism. Cracked working shoes, run down at the heel, are on her bare feet. Yet in spite of her slovenly appearance there is a spirit which shines through and makes her lovable, a simple sweetness and charm, something gentle and sad and, somehow, dauntless.)

MALOY (*jumps to his feet, his face lighting up with affection*). God bless you, Nora, you're the one I was waitin' to see. Will you keep an eye on the bar while I run to the store for a bit av 'baccy?

SARA (*sharply*). Don't do it, Mother.

NORA (*smiles — her voice is soft, with a rich brogue*). Why wouldn't I? 'Don't do it, Mother.'

MALOY. Thank you, Nora. (*He goes to the door at rear and opens it, burning for a parting shot at Sara.*) And the back o' my hand to you, your Ladyship! (*He goes out, closing the door.*)

SARA. You shouldn't encourage his laziness. He's always looking for excuses to shirk.

NORA. Ah, nivir mind, he's a good lad. (*She lowers herself painfully on the nearest chair at the rear of the table at centre front.*) Bad cess to the rheumatism. It has me destroyed this mornin'.

SARA (*still checking figures in the book — gives her mother an impatient but at the same time worried glance. Her habitual manner towards her is one of mingled love and pity and exasperation*). I've told you a hundred times to see the doctor.

NORA. We've no money for doctors. They're bad luck, anyway. They bring death with them. (*A pause. Nora sighs.*) Your father will be down soon. I've some fine fresh eggs for his breakfast.

SARA (*her face becomes hard and bitter*). He won't want them.

NORA (*defensively*). You mean he'd a drop too much taken last night? Well, small blame to him, he hasn't seen Jamie since —

SARA. *Last* night? What night hasn't he?

NORA. Ah, don't be hard on him. (*A pause — worriedly.*) Neilan sent round a note to me about his bill. He says we'll have to settle by the end of the week or we'll get no more groceries. (*With a sigh.*) I can't blame him. How we'll manage, I dunno. There's the intrist on the mortgage due the first. But that I've saved, God be thanked.

SARA (*exasperatedly*). If you'd only let me take charge of the money.

NORA (*with a flare of spirit*). I won't. It'd mean you and himself would be at each other's throats from dawn to dark. It's bad enough between you as it is.

SARA. Why didn't you pay Neilan the end of last week? You told me you had the money put aside.

NORA. So I did. But Dickinson was tormentin' your father with his feed bill for the mare.

SARA (*angrily*). I might have known! The mare comes first, if she takes the bread out of our mouths! The grand gentleman must have his thoroughbred to ride out in state!

NORA (*defensively*). Where's the harm? She's his greatest pride. He'd be heartbroken if he had to sell her.

SARA. Oh yes, I know well he cares more for a horse than for us!

NORA. Don't be saying that. He has great love for you, even if you do be provokin' him all the time.

SARA. Great love for me! Arrah, God pity you, Mother!

NORA (*sharply*). Don't put on the brogue, now. You know how he hates to hear you. And I do, too. There's no excuse not to cure yourself. Didn't he send you to school so you could talk like a gentleman's daughter?

SARA (*resentfully but more careful of her speech*). If he did, I wasn't there long.

NORA. It was you insisted on leavin'.

SARA. Because if he hadn't the pride or love for you not to live on your slaving your heart out, I had that pride and love!

NORA (*tenderly*). I know, Acushla. I know.

SARA (*with bitter scorn*). We can't afford a waitress, but he can afford to keep a thoroughbred mare to prance around on and show himself off! And he can afford a barkeep when, if he had any decency, he'd do his part and tend the bar himself.

NORA (*indignantly*). Him, a gentleman, tend bar!

SARA. A gentleman! Och, Mother, it's all right for the two of us, out of our own pride, to pretend to the world we believe that lie, but it's crazy for you to pretend to me.

NORA (*stubbornly*). It's no lie. He *is* a gentleman. Wasn't he born rich in a castle on a grand estate and educated in college, and wasn't he an officer in the Duke of Wellington's army —

SARA. All right, Mother. You can humour his craziness, but he'll never make me pretend to him I don't know the truth.

NORA. Don't talk as if you hated him. You ought to be shamed —

SARA. I do hate him for the way he treats you. I heard him again last night, raking up the past, and blaming his ruin on his having to marry you.

NORA (*protests miserably*). It was the drink talkin', not him.

SARA (*exasperated*). It's you ought to be ashamed, for not having more pride! You bear all his insults as meek as a lamb! You keep on slaving for him when it's that has made you old before your time! (*Angrily.*) You can't much longer, I tell you! He's getting worse. You'll have to leave him.

NORA (*aroused*). I'll never! Howld your prate!

SARA. You'd leave him today, if you had any pride!

NORA. I've pride in my love for him! I've loved him since the day I set eyes on him, and I'll love him till the day I die! (*With a strange superior scorn.*) It's little you know of love, and you never will, for there's the same divil of pride in you that's in him, and it'll kape you from ivir givin' all of yourself, and that's what love is.

SARA. I could give all of myself if I wanted to, but—

NORA. If! Wanted to! Faix, it proves how little of love you know when you prate about ifs and want-tos. It's when you don't give a thought for all the ifs and want-tos in the world! It's when, if all the fires of hell was between you, you'd walk in them gladly to be with him, and sing with joy at your own burnin', if only his kiss was on your mouth! That's love, and I'm proud I've known the great sorrow and joy of it!

SARA (*cannot help being impressed—looks at her mother with wondering respect*). You're a strange woman, Mother. (*She kisses her impulsively.*) And a grand woman! (*Defiant again, with an arrogant toss of her head.*) I'll love—but I'll love where it'll gain me freedom and not put me in slavery for life.

NORA. There's no slavery in it when you love! (*Suddenly her exultant expression crumbles and she breaks down.*) For the love of God, don't take the pride of my love from me, Sara, for without it what am I at all but an ugly, fat woman gettin' old and sick!

SARA (*puts her arm around her—soothingly*). Hush, Mother. Don't mind me. (*Briskly, to distract her mother's mind.*) I've got to finish the bar book. Mickey can't put two and two together without making five. (*She goes to the desk and begins checking figures again.*)

NORA (*dries her eyes—after a pause she sighs worriedly*). I'm worried about your father. Father Flynn stopped me on the road yesterday and tould me I'd better warn him not to sneer at the Irish around here and call thim scum, or he'll get in trouble. Most of thim is in a rage at him because he's come out against Jackson and the Democrats and says he'll vote with the Yankees for Quincy Adams.

SARA (*contemptuously*). Faith, they can't see a joke, then, for it's a great joke to hear him shout against mob rule, like one of the Yankee gentry, when you know what he came from. And after the way the Yanks swindled him when he came here, getting him to buy this inn by telling him a new coach line was going to stop here. (*She laughs with bitter scorn.*) Oh, he's the easiest fool ever came to America! It's that I hold against him as much as anything, that when he came here the chance was before him to make himself all his lies pretended to be. He had education above most Yanks, and he had money enough to start him, and this is a country where you can rise as high as you like, and no one but the fools who envy you care what you rose from, once you've the money and the power goes with it. (*Passionately.*) Oh, if I was a man with the chance he had, there wouldn't be a dream I'd not make come true!

(*She looks at her mother, who is staring at the floor dejectedly and hasn't been listening. She is exasperated for a second—then she smiles pityingly.*)

You're a fine one to talk to, Mother. Wake up. What's worrying you now?

NORA. Father Flynn tould me again I'd be damned in hell for lettin' your father make a haythen of me and bring you up a haythen, too.

SARA (*with an arrogant toss of her head*). Let Father Flynn mind his own business, and not frighten you with fairy tales about hell.

NORA. It's true, just the same.

SARA. True, me foot! You ought to tell the good Father we aren't the ignorant shanty scum he's used to dealing with. (*She changes the subject abruptly—closing Mickey's bar book.*) There. That's done. (*She puts the book in the desk.*) I'll take a walk to the store and have a talk with Neilan. Maybe I can blarney him to let the bill go another month.

NORA (*gratefully*). Oh, you can. Sure, you can charm a bird out of a tree when you want to. But I don't like you beggin' to a Yankee. It's all right for me but I know how you hate it.

SARA (*puts her arms around her mother—tenderly*). I don't mind at all, if I can save you a bit of the worry that's killing you. (*She kisses her.*) I'll change to my Sunday dress so I can make a good impression.

NORA (*with a teasing smile*). I'm thinkin' it isn't on Neilan alone you want to make an impression. You've changed to your Sunday best a lot lately.

SARA (*coquettishly*). Aren't you the sly one! Well, maybe you're right.

NORA. How was he when you took him his breakfast?

SARA. Hungry, and that's a good sign. He had no fever last night. Oh, he's on the road to recovery now, and it won't be long before he'll be back in his cabin by the lake.

NORA. I'll never get it clear in my head what he's been doing there the past year, living like a tramp or a tinker, and him a rich gentleman's son.

SARA (*with a tender smile*). Oh, he isn't like his kind, or like anyone else at all. He's a born dreamer with a raft of great dreams, and he's very serious about them. I've told you before he wanted to get away from his father's business, where he worked for a year after he graduated from Harvard College, because he didn't like being in trade, even if it is a great company that trades with the whole world in its own ships.

NORA (*approvingly*). That's the way a true gentleman would feel—

SARA. He wanted to prove his independence by living alone in the wilds, and build his own cabin, and do all the work, and support himself simply and feel one with Nature, and think great thoughts about what life means, and write a book about how the world can be changed so people won't be greedy to own money and land and get the best of each other but will be content with little and live in peace and freedom together, and it will be like heaven on earth. (*She laughs fondly — and a bit derisively.*) I can't remember all of it. It seems crazy to me, when I think of what people are like. He hasn't written any of it yet, anyway — only the notes for it. (*She smiles coquettishly.*) All he's written the last few months are love poems.

NORA. That's since you began to take long walks by the lake. (*She smiles.*) It's you are the sly one.

SARA (*laughing*). Well, why shouldn't I take walks on our own property? (*Her tone changes to a sneer.*) The land our great gentleman was swindled into buying when he came here with grand ideas of owning an American estate! — a bit of farm land no one would work any more, and the rest all wilderness! You couldn't give it away.

NORA (*soothingly*). Hush now. (*Changing the subject.*) Well, it's easy to tell young Master Harford has a touch av the poet in him — (*She adds before she thinks.*) The same as your father.

SARA (*scornfully*). God help you, Mother! Do you think Father's a poet because he shows off reciting Lord Byron?

NORA (*with an uneasy glance at the door at left front*). Whist, now. Himself will be down at any moment. (*Changing the subject.*) I can see the Harford lad is falling in love with you.

SARA (*her face lights up triumphantly*). Falling? He's fallen head over heels. He's so timid, he hasn't told me yet, but I'll get him to soon.

NORA. I know you're in love with him.

SARA (*simply*). I am, Mother. (*She adds quickly.*) But not too much. I'll not let love make me any man's slave. I want to love him just enough so I can marry him without cheating him, or myself. (*Determinedly.*) For I'm going to marry him, Mother. It's my chance to rise in the world and nothing will keep me from it.

NORA (*admiringly*). Musha, but you've boastful talk! What about his fine Yankee family? His father'll likely cut him off widout a penny if he marries a girl who's poor and Irish.

SARA. He may at first, but when I've proved what a good wife I'll be — He can't keep Simon from marrying me. I know that. Simon doesn't care what his father thinks. It's only his mother I'm afraid of. I can tell she's had great influence over him. She must be a queer creature, from all he's told me. She's very strange in her ways. She never goes out at all but stays home in their mansion, reading books, or in her garden. (*She pauses.*) Did you notice a carriage stop here this morning, Mother?

NORA (*preoccupied — uneasily*). Don't count your chickens before they're hatched. Young Harford seems a dacent lad. But maybe it's not marriage he's after.

SARA (*angrily*). I won't have you wronging him, Mother. He has no thought — (*Bitterly.*) I suppose you're bound to suspect — (*She bites her words back, ashamed.*) Forgive me, Mother. But it's wrong of you to think badly of Simon. (*She smiles.*) You don't know him. Faith, if it came to seducing, it'd be me that'd have to do it. He's that respectful you'd think I was a holy image. It's only in his poems, and in the diary he keeps — I had a peek in it one day I went to tidy up his cabin for him. He's terribly ashamed of his sinful inclinations and the insult they are to my purity. (*She laughs tenderly.*)

NORA (*smiling, but a bit shocked*). Don't talk so bould. I don't know if it's right, you to be in his room so much, even if he is sick. There's a power av talk about the two av you already.

SARA. Let there be, for all I care! Or all Simon cares, either. When it comes to not letting others rule him, he's got a will of his own behind his gentleness. Just as behind his poetry and dreams I feel he has it in him to do anything he wants. So even if his father cuts him off, with me to help him we'll get on in the world. For I'm no fool, either.

NORA. Glory be to God, you have the fine opinion av yourself!

SARA (*laughing*). Haven't I, though! (*Then bitterly.*) I've had need to have, to hold my head up, slaving as a waitress and chambermaid so my father can get drunk every night like a gentleman!

(*The door at left front is slowly opened and Cornelius Melody appears in the doorway above the two steps. He and Sara stare at each other. She stiffens into hostility and her mouth sets in scorn. For a second his eyes waver and he looks guilty. Then his face becomes expressionless. He descends the steps and bows — pleasantly.*)

MELODY. Good morning, Sara.

SARA (*curtly*). Good morning. (*Then, ignoring him.*) I'm going up and change my dress, Mother. (*She goes out right.*)

(*Cornelius Melody is forty-five, tall, broad-shouldered, deep-chested, and powerful, with long muscular arms, big feet, and large hairy hands. His heavy-boned body is still firm, erect, and soldierly. Beyond shaky nerves, it shows no effects of hard drinking. It has a bull-like, impervious strength, a tough peasant vitality. It is his face that reveals the ravages of dissipation — a ruined face, which was once extraordinarily hand-*

some in a reckless, arrogant fashion. It is still handsome — the face of an embittered Byronic hero, with a finely chiselled nose over a domineering sensual mouth set in disdain, pale, hollow-cheeked, framed by thick, curly iron-grey hair. There is a look of wrecked distinction about it, of brooding, humiliated pride. His bloodshot grey eyes have an insulting cold stare which anticipates insult. His manner is that of a polished gentleman. Too much so. He overdoes it and one soon feels that he is overplaying a role which has become more real than his real self to him. But in spite of this, there is something formidable and impressive about him. He is dressed with foppish elegance in old, expensive, finely tailored clothes of the style worn by English aristocracy in Peninsula War days.)

MELODY (*advancing into the room — bows formally to his wife*). Good morning, Nora. (*His tone condescends. It addresses a person of inferior station.*)

NORA (*stumbles to her feet — timidly*). Good mornin', Con. I'll get your breakfast.

MELODY. No. Thank you. I want nothing now.

NORA (*coming towards him*). You look pale. Are you sick, Con, darlin'?

MELODY. No.

NORA (*puts a timid hand on his arm*). Come and sit down.

(*He moves his arm away with instinctive revulsion and goes to the table at centre front, and sits in the chair she had occupied. Nora hovers round him.*)

I'll wet a cloth in cold water to put round your head.

MELODY. No! I desire nothing — except a little peace in which to read the news. (*He picks up the paper and holds it so it hides his face from her.*)

NORA (*meekly*). I'll lave you in peace.

(*She starts to go to the door at right but turns to stare at him worriedly again. Keeping the paper before his face with his left hand, he reaches out with his right and pours a glass of water from the carafe on the table. Although he cannot see his wife, he is nervously conscious of her. His hand trembles so violently that when he attempts to raise the glass to his lips the water sloshes over his hand and he sets the glass back on the table with a bang. He lowers the paper and explodes nervously.*)

MELODY. For God's sake, stop your staring!

NORA. I — I was only thinkin' you'd feel better if you'd a bit av food in you.

MELODY. I told you once — ! (*Controlling his temper.*) I am not hungry, Nora.

(*He raises the paper again. She sighs, her hands fiddling with her apron. A pause.*)

NORA (*dully*). Maybe it's a hair av the dog you're needin'.

MELODY (*as if this were something he had been waiting to hear, his expression loses some of its nervous strain. But he replies virtuously*). No, damn the liquor. Upon my conscience, I've about made up my mind I'll have no more of it. Besides, it's a bit early in the day.

NORA. If it'll give you an appetite —

MELODY. To tell the truth, my stomach is out of sorts. (*He licks his lips.*) Perhaps a drop wouldn't come amiss.

(*Nora gets the decanter and glass from the cupboard and sets them before him. She stands gazing at him with a resigned sadness. Melody, his eyes on the paper, is again acutely conscious of her. His nerves cannot stand it. He throws his paper down and bursts out in bitter anger.*)

Well? I know what you're thinking! Why haven't you the courage to say it for once? By God, I'd have more respect for you! I hate the damned meek of this earth! By the rock of Cashel, I sometimes believe you have always deliberately encouraged me to — It's the one point of superiority you can lay claim to, isn't it?

NORA (*bewilderedly — on the verge of tears*). I don't — It's only your comfort — I can't bear to see you —

MELODY (*his expression changes and a look of real affection comes into his eyes. He reaches out a shaking hand to pat her shoulder with an odd, guilty tenderness. He says quietly and with genuine contrition*). Forgive me, Nora. That was unpardonable.

(*Her face lights up. Abruptly he is ashamed of being ashamed. He looks away and grabs the decanter. Despite his trembling hand he manages to pour a drink and get it to his mouth and drain it. Then he sinks back in his chair and stares at the table, waiting for the liquor to take effect. After a pause he sighs with relief.*)

I confess I needed that as medicine. I begin to feel more myself. (*He pours out another big drink and this time his hand is steadier, and he downs it without much difficulty. He smacks his lips.*) By the Immortal, I may have sunk to keeping an inn but at least I've a conscience in my trade. I keep liquor a gentleman can drink. (*He starts looking over the paper again — scowls at something — disdainfully, emphasizing his misquote of the line from Byron.*) 'There shall he rot — Ambition's *dis*honoured fool!' The paper is full of the latest swindling lies of that idol of the riffraff, Andrew Jackson. Contemptible, drunken scoundrel! But he will be the next President, I predict, for all we others can do to prevent. There is a cursed destiny in these decadent times. Everywhere the scum rises to the top. (*His eyes fasten on the date and suddenly he strikes the table with his fist.*) Today is the 27th! By God, and I would have forgotten!

NORA. Forgot what?

MELODY. The anniversary of Talavera!

NORA (*hastily*). Oh, ain't I stupid not to remember.

MELODY (*bitterly*). I had forgotten myself and no wonder. It's a far cry from this dunghill on which I rot to that glorious day when the Duke of Wellington — Lord Wellesley, then — did me the honour before all the army to commend my bravery. (*He glances around the room with loathing.*) A far cry, indeed! It would be better to forget!

NORA (*rallying him*). No, no, you mustn't. You've never missed celebratin' it and you won't today. I'll have a special dinner for you like I've always had.

MELODY (*with a quick change of manner — eagerly*). Good, Nora. I'll invite Jamie Cregan. It's a stroke of fortune he is here. He served under me at Talavera, as you know. A brave soldier, if he isn't a gentleman. You can place him on my right hand. And we'll have Patch Riley to make music, and O'Dowd and Roche. If they are rabble, they're full of droll humour at times. But put them over there. (*He points to the table at left front.*) I may tolerate their presence out of charity, but I'll not sink to dining at the same table.

NORA. I'll get your uniform from the trunk, and you'll wear it for dinner like you've done each year.

MELODY. Yes, I must confess I still welcome an excuse to wear it. It makes me feel at least the ghost of the man I was then.

NORA. You're so handsome in it still, no woman could take her eyes off you.

MELODY (*with a pleased smile*). I'm afraid you've blarney on your tongue this morning, Nora. (*Then boastfully.*) But it's true, in those days in Portugal and Spain — (*He stops a little shamefacedly, but Nora gives no sign of offence. He takes her hand and pats it gently — avoiding her eyes.*) You have the kindest heart in the world, Nora. And I — (*His voice breaks.*)

NORA (*instantly on the verge of grateful tears*). Ah, who wouldn't, Con darlin', when you — (*She brushes a hand across her eyes — hastily.*) I'll go to the store and get something tasty. (*Her face drops as she remembers.*) But, God help us, where's the money?

MELODY (*stiffens — haughtily*). Money? Since when has my credit not been good?

NORA (*hurriedly*). Don't fret, now. I'll manage.

(*He returns to his newspaper, disdaining further interest in money matters.*)

MELODY. Ha. I see work on the railroad at Baltimore is progressing. (*Lowering his paper.*) By the Eternal, if I had not been a credulous gull and let the thieving Yankees swindle me of all I had when we came here, that's how I would invest my funds now. And I'd become rich. This country, with its immense territory cannot depend solely on creeping canal boats, as short-sighted fools would have us believe. We must have railroads. Then you will see how quickly America will become rich and great! (*His expression changes to one of bitter hatred.*) Great enough to crush England in the next war between them, which I know is inevitable! Would I could live to celebrate that victory! If I have one regret for the past — and there are few things in it that do not call for bitter regret — it is that I shed my blood for a country that thanked me with disgrace. But I will be avenged. This country — my country, now — will drive the English from the face of the earth their shameless perfidy has dishonoured!

NORA. Glory be to God for that! And we'll free Ireland!

MELODY (*contemptuously*). Ireland? What benefit would freedom be to her unless she could be freed from the Irish? (*Then irritably.*) But why do I discuss such things with you?

NORA (*humbly*). I know. I'm ignorant.

MELODY. Yet I tried my best to educate you, after we came to America — until I saw it was hopeless.

NORA. You did, surely. And I tried, too, but —

MELODY. You won't even cure yourself of that damned peasant's brogue. And your daughter is becoming as bad.

NORA. She only puts on the brogue to tease you. She can speak as fine as any lady in the land if she wants.

MELODY (*is not listening — sunk in bitter brooding*). But, in God's name, who am I to reproach anyone with anything? Why don't you tell me to examine my own conduct?

NORA. You know I'd never.

MELODY (*stares at her — again he is moved — quietly*). No. I know you would not, Nora. (*He looks away — after a pause.*) I owe you an apology for what happened last night.

NORA. Don't think of it.

MELODY (*with assumed casualness*). Faith, I'd a drink too many, talking over old times with Jamie Cregan.

NORA. I know.

MELODY. I am afraid I may have — The thought of old times — I become bitter. But you understand, it was the liquor talking, if I said anything to wound you.

NORA. I know it.

MELODY (*deeply moved, puts his arm around her*). You're a sweet, kind woman, Nora — too kind. (*He kisses her.*)

NORA (*with blissful happiness*). Ah, Con darlin', what do I care what you say when the black thoughts are on you? Sure, don't you know I love you?

MELODY (*a sudden revulsion of feeling convulses his face. He bursts out with disgust, pushing her away from him*). For God's sake, why don't you wash your hair? It turns my stomach with its stink of onions and stew!

(*He reaches for the decanter and shakingly pours a drink. Nora looks as if he had struck her.*)

NORA (*dully*). I do be washin' it often to plaze you. But when you're standin' over the stove all day, you can't help—

MELODY. Forgive me, Nora. Forget I said that. My nerves are on edge. You'd better leave me alone.

NORA (*her face brightening a little*). Will you ate your breakfast now? I've fine fresh eggs—

MELODY (*grasping at this chance to get rid of her—impatiently*). Yes! In a while. Fifteen minutes, say. But leave me alone now.

(*She goes out right. Melody drains his drink. Then he gets up and paces back and forth, his hands clasped behind him. The third drink begins to work and his face becomes arrogantly self-assured. He catches his reflection in the mirror on the wall at left and stops before it. He brushes a sleeve fastidiously, adjusts the set of his coat, and surveys himself.*)

Thank God, I still bear the unmistakable stamp of an officer and a gentleman. And so I will remain to the end, in spite of all fate can do to crush my spirit! (*He squares his shoulders defiantly. He stares into his eyes in the glass and recites from Byron's 'Childe Harold', as if it were an incantation by which he summons pride to justify his life to himself.*)

'I have not loved the World, nor the World me;
I have not flattered its rank breath, nor bowed
To its idolatries a patient knee,
Nor coined my cheek to smiles,—nor cried aloud
In worship of an echo: in the crowd
They could not deem me one of such—I stood
Among them, but not of them . . .'

(*He pauses, then repeats:*)

'Among them, but not of them.' By the Eternal, that expresses it! Thank God for you, Lord Byron—poet and nobleman who made of his disdain immortal music!

(*Sara appears in the doorway at right. She has changed to her Sunday dress, a becoming blue that brings out the colour of her eyes. She draws back for a moment—then stands watching him contemptuously. Melody senses her presence. He starts and turns quickly away from the mirror. For a second his expression is guilty and confused, but he immediately assumes an air of gentlemanly urbanity and bows to her.*)

Ah, it's you, my dear. Are you going for a morning stroll? You've a beautiful day for it. It will bring fresh roses to your cheeks.

SARA. I don't know about roses, but it will bring a blush of shame to my cheeks. I have to beg Neilan to give us another month's credit, because you made Mother pay the feed bill for your fine thoroughbred mare! (*He gives no sign he hears this. She adds scathingly.*) I hope you saw something in the mirror you could admire!

MELODY (*in a light tone*). Faith, I suppose I must have looked a vain peacock, preening himself, but you can blame the bad light in my room. One cannot make a decent toilet in that dingy hole in the wall.

SARA. You have the best room in the house, that we ought to rent to guests.

MELODY. Oh, I've no complaints. I was merely explaining my seeming vanity.

SARA. Seeming!

MELODY (*keeping his tone light*). Faith, Sara, you must have risen the wrong side of the bed this morning, but it takes two to make a quarrel and I don't feel quarrelsome. Quite the contrary. I was about to tell you how exceedingly charming and pretty you look, my dear.

SARA (*with a mocking, awkward, servant's curtsy—in broad brogue*). Oh, thank ye, yer Honour.

MELODY. Every day you resemble your mother more, as she looked when I first knew her.

SARA. Musha, but it's you have the blarneyin' tongue, God forgive you!

MELODY (*in spite of himself, this gets under his skin—angrily*). Be quiet! How dare you talk to me like a common, ignorant— You're my daughter, damn you. (*He controls himself and forces a laugh.*) A fair hit! You're a great tease, Sara. I shouldn't let you score so easily. Your mother warned me you only did it to provoke me. (*Unconsciously he reaches out for the decanter on the table—then pulls his hand back.*)

SARA (*contemptuously—without brogue now*). Go on and drink. Surely you're not ashamed before me, after all these years.

MELODY (*haughtily*). Ashamed? I don't understand you. A gentleman drinks as he pleases—provided he can hold his liquor as he should.

SARA. A gentleman!

MELODY (*pleasantly again*). I hesitated because I had made a good resolve to be abstemious today. But if you insist— (*He pours a drink—a small one—his hand quite steady now.*) To your happiness, my dear.

(*She stares at him scornfully. He goes on graciously.*)

Will you do me the favour to sit down? I have wanted a quiet chat with you for some time. (*He holds out a chair for her at rear of the table at centre.*)

SARA (*eyes him suspiciously — then sits down*). What is it you want?

MELODY (*with a playfully paternal manner*). Your happiness, my dear, and what I wish to discuss means happiness to you, unless I have grown blind. How is our patient, young Simon Harford, this morning?

SARA (*curtly*). He's better.

MELODY. I am delighted to hear it. (*Gallantly.*) How could he help but be with such a charming nurse?

(*She stares at him coldly. He goes on.*)

Let us be frank. Young Simon is in love with you. I can see that with half an eye — and, of course, you know it. And you return his love, I surmise.

SARA. Surmise whatever you please.

MELODY. Meaning you do love him? I am glad, Sara. (*He becomes sentimentally romantic.*) Requited love is the greatest blessing life can bestow on us poor mortals; and first love is the most blessed of all. As Lord Byron has it: (*He recites.*)

'But sweeter still than this, than these, than all,
Is first and passionate Love — it stands alone,
Like Adam's recollection of his fall . . .'

SARA (*interrupts him rudely*). Was it to listen to you recite Byron — ?

MELODY (*concealing discomfiture and resentment — pleasantly*). No. What I was leading up to is that you have my blessing, if that means anything to you. Young Harford is, I am convinced, an estimable youth. I have enjoyed my talks with him. It has been a privilege to be able to converse with a cultured gentleman again. True, he is a bit on the sober side for one so young, but by way of compensation, there is a romantic touch of the poet behind his Yankee phlegm.

SARA. It's fine you approve of him!

MELODY. In your interest I have had some enquiries made about his family.

SARA (*angered — with taunting brogue*). Have you, indade? Musha, that's cute av you! Was it auld Patch Riley, the Piper, made them? Or was it Dan Roche or Paddy O'Dowd, or some other drunken sponge —

MELODY (*as if he hadn't heard — condescendingly*). I find his people will pass muster.

SARA. Oh, do you? That's nice!

MELODY. Apparently, his father is a gentleman — that is, by Yankee standards, in so far as one in trade can lay claim to the title. But as I've become an American citizen myself, I suppose it would be downright snobbery to hold to old world standards.

SARA. Yes, wouldn't it be!

MELODY. Though it is difficult at times for my pride to remember I am no longer the master of Melody Castle and an estate of three thousand acres of as fine pasture and woodlands as you'd find in the whole United Kingdom, with my stable of hunters, an —

SARA (*bitterly*). Well, you've a beautiful thoroughbred mare now, at least — to prove you're still a gentleman!

MELODY (*stung into defiant anger*). Yes, I've the mare! And by God, I'll keep her if I have to starve myself so she may eat.

SARA. You mean, make Mother slave to keep her for you, even if she has to starve!

MELODY (*controls his anger — and ignores this*). But what was I saying? Oh, yes, young Simon's family. His father will pass muster, but it's through his mother, I believe, he comes by his really good blood. My information is, she springs from generations of well-bred gentlefolk.

SARA. It would be a great pride to her, I'm sure, to know you found her suitable.

MELODY. I suppose I may expect the young man to request an interview with me as soon as he is up and about again?

SARA. To declare his honourable intentions and ask you for my hand, is that what you mean?

MELODY. Naturally. He is a man of honour. And there are certain financial arrangements Simon's father or his legal representative will wish to discuss with me. The amount of your settlement has to be agreed upon.

SARA (*stares at him as if she could not believe her ears*). My settlement! Simon's father! God pity you — !

MELODY (*firmly*). Your settlement, certainly. You did not think, I hope, that I would give you away without a penny to your name as if you were some poverty-stricken peasant's daughter? Please remember I have my own position to maintain. Of course, it is a bit difficult at present. I am temporarily hard pressed. But perhaps a mortgage on the inn —

SARA. It's mortgaged to the hilt already, as you very well know.

MELODY. If nothing else, I can always give my note at hand for whatever amount —

SARA. You can give it, sure enough! But who'll take it?

MELODY. Between gentlemen, these matters can always be arranged.

SARA. God help you, it must be a wonderful thing to

live in a fairy tale where only dreams are real to you. (*Then sharply.*) But you needn't waste your dreams worrying about my affairs. I'll thank you not to interfere. Attend to your drinking and leave me alone. (*He gives no indication that he has heard a word she has said. She stares at him and a look almost of fear comes into her eyes. She bursts out with a bitter exasperation in which there is a strong undercurrent of entreaty.*) Father! Will you never let yourself wake up — not even now when you're sober, or nearly? Is it stark mad you've gone, so you can't tell any more what's dead and a lie, and what's the living truth?

MELODY (*his face is convulsed by a spasm of pain as if something vital had been stabbed in him — with a cry of tortured appeal*). Sara! (*But instantly his pain is transformed into rage. He half rises from his chair threateningly.*) Be quiet, damn you! How dare you —

(*She shrinks away and rises to her feet. He forces control on himself and sinks back in his chair, his hands gripping the arms.*

The street door at rear is flung open and Dan Roche, Paddy O'Dowd, and Patch Riley attempt to pile in together and get jammed for a moment in the doorway. They all have hangovers, and Roche is talking boisterously. Dan Roche is middle-aged, squat, bowlegged, with a pot belly and short arms, lumpy with muscle. His face is flat with a big mouth, protruding ears, and red-rimmed little pig's eyes. He is dressed in dirty, patched clothes. Paddy O'Dowd is thin, round-shouldered, and flat-chested, with a pimply complexion, bulgy eyes, and a droopy mouth. His manner is oily and fawning, that of a born sponger and parasite. His clothes are those of a cheap sport. Patch Riley is an old man with a thatch of dirty white hair. His washed-out blue eyes have a wandering, half-witted expression. His skinny body is clothed in rags and there is nothing under his tattered coat but his bare skin. His mouth is sunken in, toothless. He carries an Irish bagpipe under his arm.)

ROCHE (*his back is half turned as he harangues O'Dowd and Riley, and he does not see Melody and Sara*). And I says, it's Andy Jackson will put you in your place, and all the slave-drivin' Yankee skinflints like you! Take your damned job, I says, and —

O'DOWD (*warningly, his eyes on Melody*). Whist! Whist! Hold your prate!

(*Roche whirls around to face Melody, and his aggressiveness oozes from him, changing to a hangdog apprehension. For Melody has sprung to his feet, his eyes blazing with an anger which is increased by the glance of contempt Sara casts from him to the three men. O'Dowd avoids Melody's eyes, busies himself in closing the door. Patch Riley stands gazing at Sara with a dreamy, admiring look, lost in a world of his own fancy, oblivious to what is going on.*)

ROCHE (*placatingly*). Good mornin' to ye, Major.

O'DOWD (*fawning*). Good mornin', yer Honour.

MELODY. How dare you come tramping in here in that manner! Have you mistaken this inn for the sort of dirty shebeen you were used to in the old country where the pigs ran in and out the door?

O'DOWD. We ask pardon, yer Honour.

MELODY (*to Roche — an impressive menace in his tone*). You, Paddy. Didn't I forbid you ever to mention that scoundrel Jackson's name in my house or I'd horsewhip the hide off your back? (*He takes a threatening step towards him.*) Perhaps you think I cannot carry out that threat.

ROCHE (*backs away frightenedly*). No, no, Major. I forgot — Good mornin' to ye, Miss.

O'DOWD. Good mornin', Miss Sara.

(*She ignores them. Patch Riley is still gazing at her with dreamy admiration, having heard nothing, his hat still on his head. O'Dowd officiously snatches it off for him — rebukingly.*)

Where's your wits, Patch? Didn't ye hear his Honour?

RILEY (*unheeding — addresses Sara*). Sure it's you, God bless you, looks like a fairy princess as beautiful as a rose in the mornin' dew. I'll raise a tune for you. (*He starts to arrange his pipes.*)

SARA (*curtly*). I want none of your tunes. (*Then, seeing the look of wondering hurt in the old man's eyes, she adds kindly.*) That's sweet of you, Patch. I know you'd raise a beautiful tune, but I have to go out.

(*Consoled, the old man smiles at her gratefully.*)

MELODY. Into the bar, all of you, where you belong! I told you not to use this entrance! (*With disdainful tolerance.*) I suppose it's a free drink you're after. Well, no one can say of me that I turned away anyone I knew thirsty from my door.

O'DOWD. Thank ye, yer Honour. Come along, Dan. (*He takes Riley's arm.*) Come on, Patch.

(*The three go into the bar and O'Dowd closes the door behind them.*)

SARA (*in derisive brogue*). Sure, it's well trained you've got the poor retainers on your American estate to respect the master!

(*Then as he ignores her and casts a furtive glance at the door to the bar, running his tongue over his dry lips, she says acidly, with no trace of brogue.*)

Don't let me keep you from joining the gentlemen! (*She turns her back on him and goes out the street door at rear.*)

MELODY (*his face is again convulsed by a spasm of pain — pleadingly*). Sara!

(Nora enters from the hall at right, carrying a tray with toast, eggs, bacon, and tea. She arranges his breakfast on the table at front centre, bustling garrulously.)

NORA. Have I kept you waitin'? The divil was in the toast. One lot burned black as a naygur when my back was turned. But the bacon is crisp, and the eggs not too soft, the way you like them. Come and sit down now. *(Melody does not seem to hear her. She looks at him worriedly.)* What's up with you, Con? Don't you hear me?

O'DOWD *(pokes his head in the door from the bar)*. Mickey won't believe you said we could have a drink, yer Honour, unless ye tell him.

MELODY *(licking his lips)*. I'm coming. *(He goes to the bar door.)*

NORA. Con! Have this in your stomach first! It'll all get cauld.

MELODY *(without turning to her — in his condescendingly polite tone)*. I find I am not the least hungry, Nora. I regret your having gone to so much trouble.

(He goes into the bar, closing the door behind him. Nora slumps on a chair at the rear of the table and stares at the breakfast with a pitiful helplessness. She begins to sob quietly.)

CURTAIN

ACT TWO

SCENE. *Same as Act One. About half an hour has elapsed. The barroom door opens and Melody comes in. He has had two more drinks and still no breakfast, but this has had no outward effect except that his face is paler and his manner more disdainful. He turns to give orders to the spongers in the bar.*

MELODY. Remember what I say. None of your loud brawling. And you, Riley, keep your bagpipe silent, or out you go. I wish to be alone in quiet for a while with my memories. When Corporal Cregan returns, Mickey, send him in to me. He, at least, knows Talavera is not the name of a new brand of whiskey. *(He shuts the door contemptuously on Mickey's 'Yes, Major' and the obedient murmur of the others. He sits at rear of the table at left front. At first, he poses to himself, striking an attitude — a Byronic hero, noble, embittered, disdainful, defying his tragic fate, brooding over past glories. But he has no audience and he cannot keep it up. His shoulders sag and he stares at the table top, hopelessness and defeat bringing a trace of real tragedy to his ruined, handsome face.)*

(The street door is opened and Sara enters. He does not hear the click of the latch, or notice her as she comes forward. Fresh from the humiliation of cajoling the storekeeper to extend more credit, her eyes are bitter. At sight of her father they become more so. She moves towards the door at right, determined to ignore him, but something unusual in his attitude strikes her and she stops to regard him searchingly. She starts to say something bitter — stops — finally, in spite of herself, she asks with a trace of genuine pity in her voice.)

SARA. What's wrong with you, Father! Are you really sick or is it just —

(He starts guiltily, ashamed of being caught in such a weak mood.)

MELODY *(gets to his feet politely and bows)*. I beg your pardon, my dear. I did not hear you come in. *(With a deprecating smile.)* Faith, I was far away in spirit, lost in memories of a glorious battle in Spain, nineteen years ago today.

SARA *(her face hardens)*. Oh. It's the anniversary of Talavera, is it? Well, I know what that means — a great day for the spongers and a bad day for this inn!

MELODY *(coldly)*. I don't understand you. Of course I shall honour the occasion.

SARA. You needn't tell me. I remember the other celebrations — and this year, now Jamie Cregan has appeared, you've an excuse to make it worse.

MELODY. Naturally, an old comrade in arms will be doubly welcome —

SARA. Well, I'll say this much. From the little I've seen of him, I'd rather have free whiskey go down his gullet than the others'. He's a relation, too.

MELODY *(stiffly)*. Merely a distant cousin. That has no bearing. It's because Corporal Cregan fought by my side —

SARA. I suppose you've given orders to poor Mother to cook a grand feast for you, as usual, and you'll wear your beautiful uniform, and I'll have the honour of waiting on table. Well, I'll do it just this once more for Mother's sake, or she'd have to, but it'll be the last time. *(She turns her back on him and goes to the door at right.)* You'll be pleased to learn your daughter had almost to beg on her knees to Neilan before he'd let us have another month's credit. He made it plain it was to Mother he gave it because he pities her for the husband she's got. But what do you care about that, as long as you and your fine thoroughbred mare can live in style!

Melody is shaken for a second. He glances towards the bar as if he longed to return there to escape her. Then he gets hold of himself. His face becomes ex-

pressionless. He sits in the same chair and picks up the paper, ignoring her. She starts to go out just as her mother appears in the doorway. Nora is carrying a glass of milk.)

NORA. Here's the milk the doctor ordered for the young gentleman. It's time for it, and I knew you'd be going upstairs.

SARA (*takes the milk*). Thank you, Mother. (*She nods scornfully towards her father.*) I've just been telling him I begged another month's credit from Neilan, so he needn't worry.

NORA. Ah, thank God for that. Neilan's a kind man.

MELODY (*explodes*). Damn his kindness! By the Eternal, if he'd refused, I'd have — ! (*He controls himself, meeting Sara's contemptuous eyes. He goes on quietly, a bitter sneering antagonism underneath.*) Don't let me detain you, my dear. Take his milk to our Yankee guest, as your mother suggests. Don't miss any chance to play the ministering angel. (*Vindictively.*) Faith, the poor young devil hasn't a chance to escape with you two scheming peasants laying snares to trap him!

SARA. That's a lie! And leave Mother out of your insults!

MELODY. And if all other tricks fail, there's always one last trick to get him through his honour!

SARA (*tensely*). What trick do you mean?

(*Nora grabs her arm.*)

NORA. Hould your prate, now! Why can't you leave him be? It's your fault, for provoking him.

SARA (*quietly*). All right, Mother. I'll leave him to look in the mirror, like he loves to, and remember what he said, and be proud of himself.

(*Melody winces. Sara goes out right.*)

MELODY (*after a pause — shakenly*). I — She mistook my meaning — It's as you said. She goads me into losing my temper, and I say things —

NORA (*sadly*). I know what made you say it. You think maybe she's like I was, and you can't help remembering my sin with you.

MELODY (*guiltily vehement*). No! No! I tell you she mistook my meaning, and now you — (*Then exasperatedly.*) Damn your priests' prating about your sin! (*With a strange, scornful vanity.*) To hear you tell it, you'd think it was you who seduced me! That's likely, isn't it? — remembering the man I was then!

NORA. I remember well. Sure, you was that handsome, no woman could resist you. And you are still.

MELODY (*pleased*). None of your blarney, Nora. (*With Byronic gloom.*) I am but a ghost haunting a ruin. (*Then gallantly without looking at her.*) And how about you in those days? Weren't you the prettiest girl in all Ireland? (*Scornfully.*) And be damned to your lying, pious shame! You had no shame then, I remember. It was love and joy and glory in you and you were proud!

NORA (*her eyes shining*). I'm still proud and will be to the day I die!

MELODY (*gives her an approving look which turns to distaste at her appearance — looks away irritably*). Why do you bring up the past? I do not wish to discuss it.

NORA (*after a pause — timidly*). All the same, you shouldn't talk to Sara as if you thought she'd be up to anything to catch young Harford.

MELODY. I did not think that! She is my daughter —

NORA. She is surely. And he's a dacent lad. (*She smiles a bit scornfully.*) Sure, from all she's told me, he's that shy he's never dared even to kiss her hand!

MELODY (*with more than a little contempt*). I can well believe it. When it comes to making love the Yankees are clumsy, fish-blooded louts. They lack savoir-faire. They have no romantic fire! They know nothing of women. (*He snorts disdainfully.*) By the Eternal, when I was his age — (*Then quickly.*) Not that I don't approve of young Harford, mind you. He is a gentleman. When he asks me for Sara's hand I will gladly give my consent, provided his father and I can agree on the amount of her settlement.

NORA (*hastily*). Ah, there's no need to think of that yet. (*Then lapsing into her own dream.*) Yes, she'll be happy because she loves him dearly, a lot more than she admits. And it'll give her a chance to rise in the world. We'll see the day when she'll live in a grand mansion, dressed in silks and satins, and riding in a carriage with coachman and footman.

MELODY. I desire that as much as you do, Nora. I'm done — finished — no future but the past. But my daughter has the looks, the brains — ambition, youth — She can go far. (*Then sneeringly.*) That is, if she can remember she's a gentlewoman and stop acting like a bog-trotting peasant wench! (*He hears Sara returning downstairs.*) She's coming back. (*He gets up — bitterly.*) As the sight of me seems to irritate her, I'll go in the bar awhile. I've had my fill of her insults for one morning.

(*He opens the bar door. There is a chorus of eager, thirsty welcome from inside. He goes in, closing the door. Sara enters from right. Her face is flushed and her eyes full of dreamy happiness.*)

NORA (*rebukingly*). Himself went in the bar to be out of reach of your tongue. A fine thing! Aren't you ashamed you haven't enough feeling not to torment him, when you know it's the anniversary —

SARA. All right, Mother. Let him take what joy he can out of the day. I'll even help you get his uniform out of the trunk in the attic and brush and clean it for you.

NORA. Ah, God bless you, that's the way — (*Then, astonished at this unexpected docility.*) Glory be, but you've changed all of a sudden. What's happened to you.

SARA. I'm so happy now — I can't feel bitter against anyone. (*She hesitates — then shyly.*) Simon kissed me. (*Having said this, she goes on triumphantly.*) He got his courage up at last, but it was me made him. I was freshening up his pillows and leaning over him, and he couldn't help it, if he was human. (*She laughs tenderly.*) And then you'd have laughed to see him. He near sank through the bed with shame at his boldness. He began apologizing as if he was afraid I'd be so insulted I'd never speak to him again.

NORA (*teasingly*). And what did you do? I'll wager you wasn't as brazen as you pretend.

SARA (*ruefully*). It's true, Mother. He made me as bashful as he was. I felt a great fool.

NORA. And was that all? Sure, kissing is easy. Didn't he ask you if you'd marry — ?

SARA. No. (*Quickly.*) But it was my fault he didn't. He was trying to be brave enough. All he needed was a word of encouragement. But I stood there, dumb as a calf, and when I did speak it was to say I had to come and help you, and the end was I ran from the room, blushing as red as a beet —

(*She comes to her mother. Nora puts her arms around her. Sara hides her face on her shoulder, on the verge of tears.*)

Oh, Mother, ain't it crazy to be such a fool?

NORA. Well, when you're in love —

SARA (*breaking away from her — angrily*). That's just it! I'm too much in love and I don't want to be! I won't let my heart rule my head and make a slave of me! (*Suddenly she smiles confidently.*) Ah well, he loves me as much, and more, I know that, and the next time I'll keep my wits. (*She laughs happily.*) You can consider it as good as done, Mother. I'm Mrs. Simon Harford, at your pleasure. (*She makes a sweeping bow.*)

NORA (*smiling*). Arrah, none of your airs and graces with me! Help me, now, like you promised, and we'll get your father's uniform out of the trunk. It won't break your back in the attic, like it does me.

SARA (*gaily puts her arm around her mother's waist*). Come along then.

NORA (*as they go out right*). I disremember which trunk — and you'll have to help me find the key.

(*There is a pause. Then the bar door is opened and Melody enters again in the same manner as he did at the beginning of the act. There is the same sound of voices from the bar but this time Melody gives no parting orders but simply shuts the door behind him. He scowls with disgust.*)

MELODY. Cursed ignorant cattle. (*Then with a real lonely yearning.*) I wish Jamie Cregan would come. (*Bitterly.*) Driven from pillar to post in my own home! Everywhere ignorance — or the scorn of my own daughter! (*Then defiantly.*) But by the Eternal God, no power on earth, nor in hell itself, can break me! (*His eyes are drawn irresistibly to the mirror. He moves in front of it, seeking the satisfying reassurance of his reflection there. What follows is an exact repetition of his scene before the mirror in Act One. There is the same squaring of his shoulders, arrogant lifting of his head, and then the favourite quote from Byron, recited aloud to his own image.*)

'I have not loved the World, nor the World me;
I have not flattered its rank breath, nor bowed
To its idolatries a patient knee,
Nor coined my cheek to smiles, — nor cried aloud
In worship of an echo: in the crowd
They could not deem me one of such — I stood
Among them, but not of them . . .'

(*He stands staring in the mirror and does not hear the latch of the street door click. The door opens and Deborah (Mrs Henry Harford), Simon's mother, enters, closing the door quietly behind her, Melody continues to be too absorbed to notice anything. For a moment, blinded by the sudden change from the bright glare of the street, she does not see him. When she does, she stares incredulously. Then she smiles with an amused and mocking relish.*

Deborah is forty-one, but looks to be no more than thirty. She is small, a little over five feet tall, with a fragile, youthful figure. One would never suspect that she is the middle-aged mother of two grown sons. Her face is beautiful — that is, it is beautiful from the standpoint of the artist with an eye for bone structure and unusual character. It is small, with high cheekbones, wedge-shaped, narrowing from a broad forehead to a square chin, framed by thick, wavy red-brown hair. The nose is delicate and thin, a trifle aquiline. The mouth, with full lips and even white teeth, is too large for her face. So are the long-lashed, green-flecked brown eyes, under heavy angular brows. These would appear large in any face, but in hers they seem enormous and made more startling by the pallor of her complexion. She has tiny, high-arched feet and thin, tapering hands. Her slender, fragile body is dressed in white with calcu-

lated simplicity. About her whole personality is a curious atmosphere of deliberate detachment, the studied aloofness of an ironically amused spectator. Something perversely assertive about it too, as if she consciously carried her originality to the point of whimsical eccentricity.

DEBORAH. I beg your pardon.

(*Melody jumps and whirls around. For a moment his face has an absurdly startled, stupid look. He is shamed and humiliated and furious at being caught for a second time in one morning before the mirror. His revenge is to draw himself up haughtily and survey her insolently from head to toe. But at once, seeing she is attractive and a lady, his manner changes. Opportunity beckons and he is confident of himself, put upon his mettle. He bows, a gracious, gallant gentleman. There is seductive charm in his welcoming smile and in his voice.*)

MELODY. Good morning, Mademoiselle. It is an honour to welcome you to this unworthy inn. (*He draws out a chair at rear of the larger table in the foreground — bowing again.*) If I may presume. You will find it comfortable here, away from the glare of the street.

DEBORAH (*regards him for a second puzzledly. She is impressed in spite of herself by his bearing and distinguished, handsome face*). Thank you.

(*She comes forward. Melody makes a gallant show of holding her chair and helping her to be seated. He takes in all her points with sensual appreciation. It is the same sort of pleasure a lover of horseflesh would have in the appearance of a thoroughbred horse. Meanwhile he speaks with caressing courtesy.*)

MELODY. Mademoiselle — (*He sees her wedding ring.*) Pray forgive me, I see it is Madame — Permit me to say again, how great an honour I will esteem it to be of any service.

(*He manages, as he turns away, as if by accident to brush his hand against her shoulder. She is startled and caught off guard. She shrinks and looks up at him. Their eyes meet and at the naked physical appraisement she sees in his, a fascinated fear suddenly seizes her. But at once she is reassured as he shifts his gaze, satisfied by her reactions to his first attack, and hastens to apologize.*)

I beg your pardon, Madame. I am afraid my manners have grown clumsy with disuse. It is not often a lady comes here now. This inn, like myself, has fallen upon unlucky days.

DEBORAH (*curtly ignoring this*). I presume you are the innkeeper, Melody?

MELODY (*a flash of anger in his eyes — arrogantly*). I am *Major* Cornelius Melody, one time of His Majesty's Seventh Dragoons, at your service. (*He bows with chill formality.*)

DEBORAH (*is now an amused spectator again — apologetically*). Oh. Then it is I who owe you an apology, Major Melody.

MELODY (*encouraged — gallantly*). No, no, dear lady, the fault is mine. I should not have taken offence. (*With the air of one frankly admitting a praiseworthy weakness.*) Faith, I may as well confess my besetting weakness is that of all gentlemen who have known better days. I have a pride unduly sensitive to any fancied slight.

DEBORAH (*playing up to him now*). I assure you, sir, there was no intention on my part to slight you.

MELODY (*his eyes again catch hers and hold them — his tone insinuatingly caressing*). You are as gracious as you are beautiful, Madame.

(*Deborah's amusement is gone. She is again confused and, in spite of herself, frightened and fascinated. Melody proceeds with his attack, full of confidence now, the successful seducer of old. His voice takes on a calculated melancholy cadence. He becomes a romantic tragic figure, appealing for a woman's understanding and loving compassion.*)

I am a poor fool, Madame. I would be both wiser and happier if I could reconcile myself to being the proprietor of a tawdry tavern, if I could adjure pride and forget the past. Today of all days it is hard to forget, for it is the anniversary of the battle of Talavera. The most memorable day of my life, Madame. It was on that glorious field I had the honour to be commended for my bravery by the great Duke of Wellington, himself — Sir Arthur Wellesley, then. So I am sure you can find it in your heart to forgive — (*His tone more caressing.*) One so beautiful must understand the hearts of men full well, since so many must have given their hearts to you. (*A coarse passion comes into his voice.*) Yes, I'll wager my all against a penny that even among the fish-blooded Yankees there's not a man whose heart doesn't catch flame from your beauty! (*He puts his hand over one of her hands on the table and stares into her eyes ardently.*) As mine does now!

DEBORAH (*feeling herself borne down weakly by the sheer force of his physical strength, struggles to release her hand. She stammers, with an attempt at lightness*). Is this — what the Irish call blarney, sir?

MELODY (*with a fierce, lustful sincerity*). No! I take my oath by the living God, I would charge a square of Napoleon's Old Guard singlehanded for one kiss of your lips.

(*He bends lower, while his eyes hold hers. For a second it seems he will kiss her and she cannot help herself. Then abruptly the smell of whiskey on his breath brings her to herself, shaken with disgust and coldly angry. She snatches her hand from his and speaks with withering contempt.)*

DEBORAH. Pah! You reek of whiskey! You are drunk, sir! You are insolent and disgusting! I do not wonder your inn enjoys such meagre patronage, if you regale all your guests of my sex with this absurd performance!

(Melody straightens up with a jerk, taking a step back as though he had been slapped in the face. Deborah rises to her feet, ignoring him disdainfully. At this moment Sara and her mother enter through the doorway at right. They take in the scene at a glance. Melody and Deborah do not notice their entrance.)

NORA *(half under her breath)*. Oh, God help us!

SARA *(guesses at once this must be the woman Mickey had told her about. She hurries towards them quickly, trying to hide her apprehension and anger and shame at what she knows must have happened)*. What is it, Father? What does the lady wish?

(Her arrival is a further blow for Melody, seething now in a fury of humiliated pride. Deborah turns to face Sara.)

DEBORAH *(coolly self-possessed — pleasantly)*. I came here to see you, Miss Melody, hoping you might know the present whereabouts of my son, Simon.

(This is a bombshell for Melody.)

MELODY *(blurts out with no apology in his tone but angrily, as if she had intentionally made a fool of him)*. You're his mother? In God's name, Madame, why didn't you say so!

DEBORAH *(ignoring him — to Sara)*. I've been out to his hermit's cabin, only to find the hermit flown.

SARA *(stammers)*. He's here, Mrs Harford — upstairs in bed. He's been sick —

DEBORAH. Sick? You don't mean seriously?

SARA *(recovering a little from her confusion)*. Oh, he's over it now, or almost. It was only a spell of chills and fever he caught from the damp of the lake. I found him there shivering and shaking and made him come here where there's a doctor handy and someone to nurse him.

DEBORAH *(pleasantly)*. The someone being you, Miss Melody?

SARA. Yes, me and — my mother and I.

DEBORAH *(graciously)*. I am deeply grateful to you and your mother for your kindness.

NORA *(who has remained in the background, now comes forward — with her sweet, friendly smile)*. Och, don't be thankin' us, ma'am. Sure, your son is a gentle, fine lad, and we all have great fondness for him. He'd be welcome here if he never paid a penny —

(She stops embarrassedly, catching a disapproving glance from Sara. Deborah is repelled by Nora's slovenly appearance, but she feels her simple charm and gentleness, and returns her smile.)

SARA *(with embarrassed stiffness)*. This is my mother, Mrs Harford.

(Deborah inclines her head graciously. Nora instinctively bobs in a peasant's curtsy to one of the gentry. Melody, snubbed and seething, glares at her.)

NORA. I'm pleased to make your acquaintance, ma'am.

MELODY. Nora! For the love of God, stop — *(Suddenly he is able to become the polished gentleman again — considerately and even a trifle condescendingly.)* I am sure Mrs Harford is waiting to be taken to her son. Am I not right, Madame?

(Deborah is so taken aback by his effrontery that for a moment she is speechless. She replies coldly, obviously doing so only because she does not wish to create further embarrassment.)

DEBORAH. That is true, sir. *(She turns her back on him.)* If you will be so kind, Miss Melody. I've wasted so much of the morning and I have to return to the city. I have only time for a short visit —

SARA. Just come with me, Mrs Harford. *(She goes to the door at right, and steps aside to let Deborah precede her.)* What a pleasant surprise this will be for Simon. He'd have written you he was sick, but he didn't want to worry you. *(She follows Deborah into the hall.)*

MELODY. Damned fool of a woman! If I'd known — No, be damned if I regret! Cursed Yankee upstart! *(With a sneer.)* But she didn't fool me with her insulted airs! I've known too many women — *(In a rage.)* 'Absurd performance', was it? God damn her!

NORA *(timidly)*. Don't be cursing her and tormenting yourself. She seems a kind lady. She won't hold it against you, when she stops to think, knowing you didn't know who she is.

MELODY *(tensely)*. Be quiet!

NORA. Forget it now, do, for Sara's sake. Sure, you wouldn't want anything to come between her and the lad. *(He is silent. She goes on comfortingly.)* Go on up to your room now and you'll find something to take your mind off. Sara and I have your uniform brushed and laid out on the bed.

MELODY *(harshly)*. Put it back in the trunk! I don't want it to remind me — *(With humiliated rage again.)* By the Eternal, I'll wager she believed what I told her of Talavera and the Great Duke honouring me was a drunken liar's boast!

NORA. No, she'd never, Con. She couldn't.

MELODY *(seized by an idea)*. Well, seeing would be believing, eh, my fine lady? Yes, by God, that will prove to her— (*He turns to Nora, his self-confidence partly restored.*) Thank you for reminding me of my duty to Sara. You are right. I do owe it to her interests to forget my anger and make a formal apology to Simon's mother for our little misunderstanding. (*He smiles, condescendingly.*) Faith, as a gentleman, I should grant it is a pretty woman's privilege to be always right even when she is wrong. (*He goes to the door at extreme left front and opens it.*) If the lady should come back, kindly keep her here on some excuse until I return. (*This is a command. He disappears, closing the door behind him.*)

NORA (*sighs*). Ah well, it's all right. He'll be on his best behaviour now, and he'll feel proud again in his uniform.

(*She sits at the end of centre table right and relaxes wearily. A moment later Sara enters quickly from right and comes to her.*)

SARA. Where's Father?

NORA. I got him to go up and put on his uniform. It'll console him.

SARA (*bitterly*). Console *him*? It's me ought to be consoled for having such a great fool for a father!

NORA. Hush now! How could he know who—?

SARA (*with a sudden reversal of feeling — almost vindictively*). Yes, it serves her right. I suppose she thinks she's such a great lady anyone in America would pay her respect. Well, she knows better now. And she didn't act as insulted as she might. Maybe she liked it, for all her pretences. (*Again with an abrupt reversal of feeling.*) Ah, how can I talk such craziness! Him and his drunken love-making! Well, he got put in his place, and aren't I glad. He won't forget in a hurry how she snubbed him, as if he was no better than dirt under her feet!

NORA. She didn't. She had the sense to see he'd been drinking and not to mind him.

SARA (*dully*). Maybe. But isn't that bad enough? What woman would want her son to marry the daughter of a man like— (*She breaks down.*) Oh, Mother, I was feeling so happy and sure of Simon, and now— Why did she have to come today? If she'd waited till to-morrow, even, I'd have got him to ask me to marry him, and once he'd done that no power on earth could change him.

NORA. If he loves you no power can change him, anyway. (*Proudly.*) Don't I know! (*Reassuringly.*) She's his mother, and she loves him and she'll want him to be happy, and she'll see he loves you. What makes you think she'll try to change him?

SARA. Because she hates me, Mother — for one reason.

NORA. She doesn't. She couldn't.

SARA. She does. Oh, she acted as nice as nice, but she didn't fool me. She's the kind would be polite to the hangman, and her on the scaffold. (*She lowers her voice.*) It isn't just to pay Simon a visit she came. It's because Simon's father got a letter telling him about us, and he showed it to her.

NORA. Who did a dirty trick like that?

SARA. It wasn't signed, she said. I suppose someone around here that hates Father — and who doesn't?

NORA. Bad luck to the blackguard, whoever it was!

SARA. She said she'd come to warn Simon his father is wild with anger and he's gone to see his lawyer— But that doesn't worry me. It's only her influence I'm afraid of.

NORA. How do you know about the letter?

SARA (*avoiding her eyes*). I sneaked back to listen outside the door.

NORA. Shame on you! You should have more pride!

SARA. I was ashamed, Mother, after a moment or two, and I came away. (*Then defiantly.*) No, I'm not ashamed. I wanted to learn what tricks she might be up to, so I'll be able to fight them. I'm not ashamed at all. I'll do anything to keep him. (*Lowering her voice.*) She started talking the second she got in the door. She had only a few minutes because she has to be home before dinner so her husband won't suspect she came here. He's forbidden her to see Simon ever since Simon came out here to live.

NORA. Well, doesn't her coming against her husband's orders show she's on Simon's side?

SARA. Yes, but it doesn't show she wants him to marry me. (*Impatiently.*) Don't be so simple, Mother. Wouldn't she tell Simon that anyway, even if the truth was her husband sent her to do all she could to get him away from me?

NORA. Don't look for trouble before it comes. Wait and see, now. Maybe you'll find—

SARA. I'll find what I said, Mother — that she hates me. (*Bitterly.*) Even if she came here with good intentions, she wouldn't have them now, after our great gentleman has insulted her. Thank God, if he's putting on his uniform, he'll be hours before the mirror, and she'll be gone before he can make a fool of himself again.

(*Nora starts to tell her the truth — then thinks better of it. Sara goes on, changing her tone.*)

But I'd like her to see him in his uniform, at that, if he was sober. She'd find she couldn't look down on him— (*Exasperatedly.*) Och! I'm as crazy as he is. As if she hasn't the brains to see through him.

NORA (*wearily*). Leave him be, for the love of God.

SARA (*after a pause — defiantly*). Let her try whatever game she likes. I have brains too, she'll discover. (*Then uneasily.*) Only, like Simon's told me, I feel she's strange and queer behind her lady's airs, and it'll be hard to tell what she's really up to.

(*They both hear a sound from upstairs.*)

That's her, now. She didn't waste much time. Well, I'm ready for her. Go in the kitchen, will you, Mother? I want to give her the chance to have it out with me alone.

(*Nora gets up — then, remembering Melody's orders, glances towards the door at left front uneasily and hesitates. Sara says urgently.*)

Don't you hear me? Hurry, Mother!

(*Nora sighs and goes out quickly right. Sara sits at rear of the centre table and waits, drawing herself up in an unconscious imitation of her father's grand manner. Deborah appears in the doorway at right. There is nothing in her expression to betray any emotion resulting from her interview with her son. She smiles pleasantly at Sara, who rises graciously from her chair.*)

DEBORAH (*coming to her*). I am glad to find you here, Miss Melody. It gives me another opportunity to express my gratitude for your kindness to my son during his illness.

SARA. Thank you, Mrs Harford. My mother and I have been only too happy to do all we could. (*She adds defiantly.*) We are very fond of Simon.

DEBORAH (*a glint of secret amusement in her eyes*). Yes, I feel you are. And he has told me how fond he is of you. (*Her manner becomes reflective. She speaks rapidly in a remote, detached way, lowering her voice unconsciously as if she were thinking aloud to herself.*) This is the first time I have seen Simon since he left home to seek self-emancipation at the breast of Nature. I find him not so greatly changed as I had been led to expect from his letters. Of course, it is some time since he has written. I had thought his implacably honest discovery that the poetry he hoped the pure freedom of Nature would inspire him to write is, after all, but a crude imitation of Lord Byron's would have more bitterly depressed his spirit. (*She smiles.*) But evidently he has found a new romantic dream by way of recompense. As I might have known he would. Simon is an inveterate dreamer — a weakness he inherited from me, I'm afraid, although I must admit the Harfords have been great dreamers, too, in their way. Even my husband has a dream — a conservative, material dream, naturally. I have just been reminding Simon that his father is rigidly unforgiving when his dream is flouted, and very practical in his methods of defending it. (*She smiles again.*) My warning was the mechanical gesture of a mother's duty, merely. I realized it would have no effect. He did not listen to what I said. For that matter, neither did I. (*She laughs a little detached laugh, as if she were secretly amused.*)

SARA (*stares at her, unable to decide what is behind all this and how she should react — with an undercurrent of resentment*). I don't think Simon imitates Lord Byron. I hate Lord Byron's poetry. And I know there's a true poet in Simon.

DEBORAH (*vaguely surprised — speaks rapidly again*). Oh, in feeling, of course. It is natural you should admire that in him — now. But I warn you it is a quality difficult for a woman to keep on admiring in a Harford, judging from what I know of the family history. Simon's greatgrandfather, Jonathan Harford, had it. He was killed at Bunker Hill, but I suspect the War for Independence was merely a symbolic opportunity for him. His was a personal war, I am sure — for pure freedom. Simon's grandfather, Evan Harford, had the quality too. A fanatic in the cause of pure freedom, he became scornful of our Revolution. It made too many compromises with the ideal to free him. He went to France and became a rabid Jacobin, a worshipper of Robespierre. He would have liked to have gone to the guillotine with his incorruptible Redeemer, but he was too unimportant. They simply forgot to kill him. He came home and lived in a little temple of Liberty he had built in a corner of what is now my garden. It is still there. I remember him well. A dry, gentle, cruel, indomitable, futile old idealist who used frequently to wear his old uniform of the French Republican National Guard. He died wearing it. But the point is, you can have no idea what revengeful hate the Harford pursuit of freedom imposed upon the women who shared their lives. The three daughters-in-law of Jonathan, Evan's half-sisters, had to make a large, greedy fortune out of privateering and the Northwest trade, and finally were even driven to embrace the profits of the slave trade — as a triumphant climax, you understand, of their long battle to escape the enslavement of freedom by enslaving it. Evan's wife, of course, was drawn into this conflict, and became their tool and accomplice. They even attempted to own me, but I managed to escape because there was so little of me in the flesh that aged, greedy fingers could clutch. I am sorry they are dead and cannot know you. They would approve of you, I think. They would see that you are strong and ambitious and determined to take what you want. They would have smiled like senile hungry serpents and welcomed you into their coils. (*She laughs.*) Evil old witches! Detestable, but I could not help admiring them — pitying them, too — in the end. We had a bond in common. They idolized Napoleon. They used to say he was the only man they would ever have married. And I used to dream I was Josephine — even after my marriage, I'm afraid. The Sisters, as everyone called them, and all of the family accompanied my husband and me on our honeymoon — to Paris to witness the Emperor's coronation. (*She pauses, smiling at her memories.*)

SARA (*against her will, has become a bit hypnotized by Deborah's rapid, low, musical flow of words, as she strains to grasp the implication for her. She speaks in a low, confidential tone herself, smiling naturally*). I've always admired him too. It's one of the things I've held against my father, that he fought against him and not for him.

DEBORAH (*starts, as if awakening — with a pleasant smile*). Well, Miss Melody, this is tiresome of me to stand here giving you a discourse on Harford family history. I don't know what you must think of me — but doubtless Simon has told you I am a bit eccentric at times. (*She glances at Sara's face — amusedly.*) Ah, I can see he has. Then I am sure you will make allowances. I really do not know what inspired me — except perhaps, that I wish to be fair and warn you, too.

SARA (*stiffens*). Warn me about what, Mrs Harford?

DEBORAH. Why, that the Harfords never part with their dreams even when they deny them. They cannot. That is the family curse. For example, this book Simon plans to write to denounce the evil of greed and possessive ambition, and uphold the virtue of freeing oneself from the lust for power and saving our souls by being content with little. I cannot imagine you taking that seriously. (*She again flashes a glance at Sara.*) I see you do not. Neither do I. I do not even believe Simon will ever write this book on paper. But I warn you it is already written on his conscience and — (*She stops with a little disdaining laugh.*) I begin to resemble Cassandra with all my warnings. And I continue to stand here boring you with words. (*She holds out her hand graciously.*) Goodbye, Miss Melody.

SARA (*takes her hand mechanically*). Goodbye, Mrs Harford.

(*Deborah starts for the door at rear. Sara follows her, her expression confused, suspicious, and at the same time hopeful. Suddenly she blurts out impulsively.*)

Mrs Harford, I —

DEBORAH (*turns on her, pleasantly*). Yes, Miss Melody? (*But her eyes have become blank and expressionless and discourage any attempt at further contact.*)

SARA (*silenced — with stiff politeness*). Isn't there some sort of cooling drink I could get you before you go? You must be parched after walking from the road to Simon's cabin and back on this hot day.

DEBORAH. Nothing, thank you. (*Then talking rapidly again in her strange detached way.*) Yes, I did find my walk alone in the woods a strangely overpowering experience. Frightening — but intoxicating, too. Such a wild feeling of release and fresh enslavement. I have not ventured from my garden in many years. There, nature is tamed, constrained to obey and adorn. I had forgotten how compelling the brutal power of primitive, possessive nature can be — when suddenly one is attacked by it. (*She smiles.*) It has been a most confusing morning for a tired, middle-aged matron, but I flatter myself I have preserved a philosophic poise, or should I say, pose, as well as may be. Nevertheless, it will be a relief to return to my garden and books and meditations and listen indifferently again while the footsteps of life pass and recede along the street beyond the high wall. I shall never venture forth again to do my duty. It is a noble occupation, no doubt, for those who can presume they know what their duty to others is; but I — (*She laughs.*) Mercy, here I am chattering on again. (*She turns to the door.*) Cato will be provoked at me for keeping him waiting. I've already caused his beloved horses to be half-devoured by flies. Cato is our black coachman. He also is fond of Simon, although since Simon became emancipated he has embarrassed Cato acutely by shaking his hand whenever they meet. Cato was always a self-possessed free man even when he was a slave. It astonishes him that Simon has to prove that he — I mean Simon — is free. (*She smiles.*) Goodbye again, Miss Melody. This time I really am going.

(*Sara opens the door for her. She walks past Sara into the street, turns left, and passing before the two windows, disappears. Sara closes the door and comes back slowly to the head of the table at centre. She stands thinking, her expression puzzled, apprehensive, and resentful. Nora appears in the doorway at right.*)

NORA. God forgive you, Sara, why did you let her go? Your father told me —

SARA. I can't make her out, Mother. You'd think she didn't care, but she does care. And she hates me. I could feel it. But you can't tell — She's crazy, I think. She talked on and on as if she couldn't stop — queer blather about Simon's ancestors, and herself, and Napoleon, and Nature, and her garden and freedom, and God knows what — but letting me know all the time she had a meaning behind it, and was warning and threatening me. Oh, she may be daft in some ways, but she's no fool. I know she didn't let Simon guess she'd rather have him dead than married to me. Oh, no, I'm sure she told him if he was sure he loved me and I meant his happiness — But then she'd say he ought to wait and prove he's sure — anything to give her time. She'd make him promise to wait. Yes, I'll wager that's what she's done!

NORA (*who has been watching the door at left front, preoccupied by her own worry — frightenedly*). Your father'll be down any second. I'm going out in the garden. (*She grabs Sara's arm.*) Come along with me, and give him time to get over his rage.

SARA (*shakes off her hand — exasperatedly*). Leave me be, Mother. I've enough to worry me without bothering about him. I've got to plan the best way to act when I see Simon. I've got to be as big a liar as she was. I'll have to pretend I liked her and I'd respect whatever advice she gave him. I mustn't let him see — But I won't go to him again today, Mother. You can take up his meals and his milk, if you will. Tell him I'm too busy. I want to get him anxious and afraid maybe I'm mad at him for something, that maybe his mother said something. If he once has the idea maybe he's lost me — that ought to help, don't you think, Mother?

NORA (*sees the door at left front begin to open — in a whisper*). Oh, God help me! (*She turns in panicky flight and disappears through the doorway, right.*)

(*The door at left front slowly opens — slowly because Melody, hearing voices in the room and hoping Deborah is there, is deliberately making a dramatic entrance. And in spite of its obviousness, it is effective. Wearing the brilliant scarlet full-dress uniform of a major in one of Wellington's dragoon regiments, he looks extraordinarily handsome and distinguished — a startling, colourful, romantic figure, possessing now a genuine quality he has not had before, the quality of the formidably strong, disdainfully fearless cavalry officer he really had been. The uniform has been preserved with the greatest care. Each button is shining and the cloth is spotless. Being in it has notably restored his self-confident arrogance. Also, he has done everything he can to freshen up his face and hide any effect of his morning's drinks. When he discovers Deborah is not in the room, he is mildly disappointed and, as always when he first confronts Sara alone, he seems to shrink back guiltily within himself. Sara's face hardens and she gives no sign of knowing he is there. He comes slowly around the table at left front, until he stands at the end of the centre table facing her. She still refuses to notice him and he is forced to speak. He does so with the air of one who condescends to be amused by his own foibles.*)

MELODY. I happened to go to my room and found you and your mother had laid out my uniform so invitingly that I could not resist the temptation to put it on at once instead of waiting until evening.

SARA (*turns on him. In spite of herself she is so struck by his appearance that the contempt is forced back and she can only stammer a bit foolishly*). Yes, I — I see you did. (*There is a moment's pause. She stares at him fascinatedly — then blurts out with impulsive admiration.*) You look grand and handsome, Father.

MELODY (*as pleased as a child*). Why, it is most kind of you to say that, my dear Sara. (*Preening himself.*) I flatter myself I do not look too unworthy of the man I was when I wore this uniform with honour.

SARA (*an appeal forced out of her that is both pleading and a bitter reproach*). Oh, Father, why can't you ever be the thing you can seem to be? (*A sad scorn comes into her voice.*) The man you were. I'm sorry I never knew that soldier. I think he was the only man who wasn't just a dream.

MELODY (*his face becomes a blank disguise — coldly*). I don't understand you. (*A pause. He begins to talk in an arrogantly amused tone.*) I suspect you are still holding against me my unfortunate blunder with your future mother-in-law. I would not blame you if you did. (*He smiles.*) Faith, I did put my foot in it. (*He chuckles.*) The devil of it is, I can never get used to these Yankee ladies. I do them the honour of complimenting them with a bit of harmless flattery and, lo and behold, suddenly my lady acts as if I had insulted her. It must be their damned narrow Puritan background. They can't help seeing sin hiding under every bush, but this one need not have been alarmed. I never had an eye for skinny, pale snips of women — (*Hastily.*) But what I want to tell you is I am sorry it happened, Sara, and I will do my best, for the sake of your interests, to make honourable amends. I shall do the lady the honour of tendering her my humble apologies when she comes downstairs. (*With arrogant vanity.*) I flatter myself she will be graciously pleased to make peace. She was not as outraged by half as her conscience made her pretend, if I am any judge of feminine frailty.

SARA (*who has been staring at him with scorn until he says this last — impulsively, with a sneer of agreement*). I'll wager she wasn't for all her airs. (*Then furious at herself and him.*) Ah, will you stop telling me your mad dreams! (*Controlling herself — coldly.*) You'll have no chance to make bad worse by trying to fascinate her with your beautiful uniform. She's gone.

MELODY (*stunned*). Gone? (*Furiously.*) You're lying, damn you!

SARA. I'm not. She left ten minutes ago, or more.

MELODY (*before he thinks*). But I told your mother to keep her here until — (*He stops abruptly.*)

SARA. So that's why Mother is so frightened. Well, it was me let her go, so don't take out your rage on poor Mother.

MELODY. Rage? My dear Sara, all I feel is relief. Surely you can't believe I could have looked forward to humbling my pride, even though it would have furthered your interests.

SARA. Furthered my interests by giving her another reason to laugh up her sleeve at your pretences? (*With angry scorn, lapsing into broad brogue.*) Arrah, God pity you!

(*She turns her back on him and goes off, right. Melody stands gripping the back of the chair at the foot of the table in his big, powerful hands in an effort to control himself. There is a crack as the chair back snaps in half. He stares at the fragments in his hands with stupid surprise. The door to the bar is shoved open and Mickey calls in.*)

MALOY. Here's Cregan back to see you, Major.

MELODY (*startled, repeats stupidly*). Cregan? (*Then his*

face suddenly lights up with pathetic eagerness and his voice is full of welcoming warmth as he calls.) Jamie! My old comrade in arms!

(*As Cregan enters, he grips his hand.*)

By the Powers, I'm glad you're here, Jamie.

(*Cregan is surprised and pleased by the warmth of his welcome. Melody draws him into the room.*)

Come. Sit down. You'll join me in a drink, I know. (*He gets Cregan a glass from the cupboard. The decanter and Melody's glass are already on table.*)

CREGAN (*admiringly*). Be God, it's the old uniform, no less, and you look as fine a figure in it as ever you did in Spain.

(*He sits at right of table at left front as Melody sits at rear.*)

MELODY (*immensely pleased — deprecatingly*). Hardly, Jamie — but not a total ruin yet, I hope. I put it on in honour of the day. I see you've forgotten. For shame, you dog, not to remember Talavera.

CREGAN (*excitedly*). Talavera, is it? Where I got my sabre cut. Be the mortal, I remember it, and you've a right to celebrate. You was worth any ten men in the army that day!

(*Melody has shoved the decanter towards him. He pours a drink.*)

MELODY (*this compliment completely restores him to his arrogant self*). Yes, I think I may say I did acquit myself with honour. (*Patronizingly.*) So, for that matter, did you. (*He pours a drink and raises his glass.*) To the day and your good health, Corporal Cregan.

CREGAN (*enthusiastically*). To the day and yourself, God bless you, Con!

(*He tries to touch brims with Melody's glass, but Melody holds his glass away and draws himself up haughtily.*)

MELODY (*with cold rebuke*). I said, to the day and your good health, *Corporal Cregan.*

CREGAN (*for a second is angry — then he grins and mutters admiringly*). Be God, it's you can bate the world and never let it change you! (*Correcting his toast with emphasis.*) To the day and yourself, *Major Melody.*

MELODY (*touches his glass to Cregan's — graciously condescending*). Drink hearty, Corporal.

(*They drink.*)

CURTAIN

ACT THREE

SCENE. *The same. The door to the bar is closed. It is around eight that evening and there are candles on the centre table. Melody sits at the head of this table. In his brilliant uniform he presents more than ever an impressively colourful figure in the room, which appears smaller and dingier in the candlelight. Cregan is in the chair on his right. The other chairs at this table are unoccupied. Riley, O'Dowd, and Roche sit at the table at left front. Riley is at front, but his chair is turned sideways so he faces right. O'Dowd has the chair against the wall, facing right, with Roche across the table from him, his back to Melody. All five are drunk, Melody more so than any of them, but except for the glazed glitter in his eyes and his deathly pallor, his appearance does not betray him. He is holding his liquor like a gentleman.*

Cregan is the least drunk. O'Dowd and Roche are boisterous. The effect of the drink on Riley is merely to sink him deeper in dreams. He seems oblivious to his surroundings.

An empty and a half-empty bottle of port are on the table before Melody and Cregan, and their glasses are full. The three at the table have a decanter of whiskey.

Sara, wearing her working dress and an apron, is removing dishes and the remains of the dinner. Her face is set. She is determined to ignore them, but there is angry disgust in her eyes. Melody is arranging forks, knives, spoons, saltcellar, etc., in a plan of battle on the table before him. Cregan watches him. Patch Riley gives a few tuning-up quavers on his pipes.

MELODY. Here's the river Tagus. And here, Talavera. This would be the French position on a rise of ground with the plain between our lines and theirs. Here is our redoubt with the Fourth Division and the Guards. And here's our cavalry brigade in a valley towards our left, if you'll remember, Corporal Cregan.

CREGAN (*excitedly*). Remember? Sure I see it as clear as yesterday!

RILEY (*bursts into a rollicking song, accompanying himself on the pipes, his voice the quavering ghost of a tenor but still true — to the tune of 'Baltiorum'.*)

'She'd a pig and boneens,
She'd a bed and a dresser,
And a 'nate little room
For the father confessor;
With a cupboard and curtains, and something, I'm towld,
That his riv'rance liked when the weather was cowld.
And it's hurroo, hurroo! Biddy O'Rafferty!'

(*Roche and O'Dowd roar after him, beating time on the table with their glasses — 'Hurroo, hurroo! Biddy*

O'Rafferty!' — and laugh drunkenly. Cregan, too, joins in this chorus. Melody frowns angrily at the interruption, but at the end he smiles with lordly condescension, pleased by the irreverence of the song.)

O'DOWD (*after a cunning glance at Melody's face to see what his reaction is — derisively*). Och, lave it to the priests, divil mend thim! Ain't it so, Major?

MELODY. Ay, damn them all! A song in the right spirit, Piper. Faith, I'll have you repeat it for my wife's benefit when she joins us. She still has a secret fondness for priests. And now, less noise, you blackguards. Corporal Cregan and I cannot hear each other with your brawling.

O'DOWD (*smirkingly obedient*). Quiet it is, yer Honour. Be quiet, Patch.

(*He gives the old man, who is lost in dreams, a shove that almost knocks him off his chair. Riley stares at him bewilderedly. O'Dowd and Roche guffaw.*)

MELODY (*scowls at them, then turns to Cregan*). Where was I, Corporal? Oh, yes, we were waiting in the valley. We heard a trumpet from the French lines and saw them forming for the attack. An aide-de-camp galloped down the hill to us —

SARA (*who has been watching him disdainfully, reaches out to take his plate — rudely in mocking brogue*). I'll have your plate, av ye plaze, Major, before your gallant dragoons charge over it and break it.

MELODY (*holds his plate on the table with one hand so she cannot take it, and raises his glass of wine with the other — ignoring her*). Wet your lips, Corporal. Talavera was a devilish thirsty day, if you'll remember. (*He drinks.*)

CREGAN (*glances uneasily at Sara*). It was that. (*He drinks.*)

MELODY (*smacking his lips*). Good wine, Corporal. Thank God, I still have wine in my cellar fit for a gentleman.

SARA (*angrily*). Are you going to let me take your plate?

MELODY (*ignoring her*). No, I have no need to apologize for the wine. Nor for the dinner, for that matter. Nora is a good cook when she forgets her infernal parsimony and buys food that one can eat without disgust. But I do owe you an apology for the quality of the service. I have tried to teach the waitress not to snatch plates from the table as if she were feeding dogs in a kennel but she cannot learn. (*He takes his hand from the plate — to Sara.*) There. Now let me see you take it properly.

(*She stares at him for a moment, speechless with anger — then snatches the plate from in front of him.*)

CREGAN (*hastily recalls Melody to the battlefield*). You were where the aide-de-camp galloped up to us, Major. It was then the French artillery opened on us.

(*Sara goes out right, carrying a tray laden with plates.*)

MELODY. We charged the columns on our left — here — (*He marks the tablecloth.*) that were pushing back the Guards. I'll never forget the blast of death from the French squares. And then their chasseurs and lancers were on us! By God, it's a miracle any of us came through!

CREGAN. You wasn't touched except you'd a bullet through your coat, but I had this token on my cheek to remember a French sabre by.

MELODY. Brave days, those! By the Eternal, then one lived! Then one forgot! (*He stops — when he speaks again it is bitterly.*) Little did I dream then the disgrace that was to be my reward later on.

CREGAN (*consolingly*). Ah well, that's the bad luck of things. You'd have been made a colonel soon, if you'd left the Spanish woman alone and not fought that duel.

MELODY (*arrogantly threatening*). Are you presuming to question my conduct in that affair, Corporal Cregan?

CREGAN (*hastily*). Sorra a bit! Don't mind me, now.

MELODY (*stiffly*). I accept your apology.

(*He drinks the rest of his wine, pours another glass, then stares moodily before him. Cregan drains his glass and refills it.*)

O'DOWD (*peering past Roche to watch Melody, leans across to Roche — in a sneering whisper*). Ain't he the lunatic, sittin' like a play-actor in his red coat, lyin' about his battles with the French!

ROCHE (*sullenly — but careful to keep his voice low*). He'd ought to be shamed he ivir wore the bloody red av England, God's curse on him!

O'DOWD. Don't be wishin' him harm, for it's thirsty we'd be without him. Drink long life to him, and may he always be as big a fool as he is this night! (*He sloshes whiskey from the decanter into both their glasses.*)

ROCHE (*with a drunken leer*). Thrue for you! I'll toast him on that. (*He twists round to face Melody, holds up his glass and bawls.*) To the grandest gintleman ivir come from the shores av Ireland! Long life to you, Major!

O'DOWD. Hurroo! Long life, yer Honour!

RILEY (*awakened from his dream, mechanically raises his glass*). And to all that belong to ye.

MELODY (*startled from his thoughts, becomes at once the condescending squire — smiling tolerantly*). I said, less noise, you dogs. All the same, I thank you for your toast.

(*They drink. A pause. Abruptly Melody begins to recite from Byron. He reads the verse well, quietly, with a bitter eloquence.*)

'But midst the crowd, the hum, the shock of men,
To hear, to see, to feel, and to possess,
And roam along, the World's tired denizen,
With none who bless us, none whom we can bless;
Minions of Splendour shrinking from distress!
None that, with kindred consciousness endued,
If we were not, would seem to smile the less,
Of all that flattered — followed — sought, and sued;
This is to be alone — This, this is Solitude!'

(*He stops and glances from one face to another. Their expressions are all blank. He remarks with insulting derisiveness.*) What? You do not understand, my lads? Well, all the better for you. So may you go on fooling yourselves that I am fooled in you. (*Then with a quick change of mood, heartily.*) Give us a hunting song, Patch. You've not forgotten 'Modideroo', I'll be bound.

RILEY (*roused to interest immediately*). Does a duck forget wather? I'll show ye! (*He begins the preliminary quavers on his pipes.*)

O'DOWD. Modideroo!

ROCHE. Hurroo!

RILEY (*accompanying himself, sings with wailing melancholy the first verse that comes to his mind of an old hunting song*).

'And the fox set him down and looked about,
And many were feared to follow;
"Maybe I'm wrong," says he, "but I doubt
That you'll be as gay tomorrow.
For loud as you cry, and high as you ride,
And little you feel my sorrow,
I'll be free on the mountainside
While you'll lie low tomorrow.
Oh, Modideroo, aroo, aroo!"'

(*Melody, excited now, beats time on the table with his glass along with Cregan, Roche, and O'Dowd, and all bellow the refrain, 'Oh, Modideroo, aroo, aroo!'*)

MELODY (*his eyes alight, forgetting himself, a strong lilt of brogue coming into his voice*). Ah, that brings it back clear as life! Melody Castle in the days that's gone! A wind from the south, and a sky grey with clouds — good weather for the hounds. A true Irish hunter under me that knows and loves me and would raise to a jump over hell if I gave the word! To hell with men, I say! — and women, too! — with their cowardly hearts rotten and stinking with lies and greed and treachery! Give me a horse to love and I'll cry quits to men! And then away, with the hounds in full cry, and after them! Off with divil a care for your neck, over ditches and streams and stone walls and fences, the fox doubling up the mountainside through the furze and the heather — !

(*Sara has entered from right as he begins this longing invocation of old hunting days. She stands behind his chair, listening contemptuously. He suddenly feels her presence and turns his head. When he catches the sneer in her eyes, it is as if cold water were dashed in his face. He addresses her as if she were a servant.*)

Well, What is it? What are you waiting for now?

SARA (*roughly, with coarse brogue*). What would I be waitin' for but for you to get through with your blather about lovin' horses, and give me a chance to finish my work? Can't you — and the other gintlemen — finish gettin' drunk in the bar and lave me clear the tables?

(*O'Dowd conceals a grin behind his hand; Roche stifles a malicious guffaw.*)

CREGAN (*with an apprehensive glance at Melody, shakes his head at her admonishingly.*) Now, Sara, be aisy.

(*But Melody suppresses any angry reaction. He rises to his feet, a bit stiffly and carefully, and bows.*)

MELODY (*coldly*). I beg your pardon if we have interfered with your duties. (*To O'Dowd and his companions.*) Into the bar, you louts!

O'DOWD. The bar it is, sorr. Come, Dan. Wake up, Patch.

(*He pokes the piper. He and Roche go into the bar, and Riley stumbles vaguely after them. Cregan waits for Melody.*)

MELODY. Go along, Corporal. I'll join you presently. I wish to speak to my daughter.

CREGAN. All right, Major.

(*He again shakes his head at Sara, as if to say, don't provoke him. She ignores him. He goes into the bar, closing the door behind him. She stares at her father with angry disgust.*)

SARA. You're drunk. If you think I'm going to stay here and listen to —

MELODY (*his face expressionless, draws out his chair at the head of the centre table for her — politely*). Sit down, my dear.

SARA. I won't. I have no time. Poor Mother is half dead on her feet. I have to help her. There's a pile of dishes to wash after your grand anniversary feast! (*With bitter anger.*) Thank God it's over, and it's the last time you'll ever take satisfaction in having me wait on table for drunken scum like O'Dowd and —

MELODY (*quietly*). A daughter who takes satisfaction in letting even the scum see that she hates and despises her father! (*He shrugs his shoulders.*) But no matter. (*Indicating the chair again.*) Won't you sit down, my dear?

SARA. If you ever dared face the truth, you'd hate and despise yourself! (*Passionately.*) All I pray to God is that someday when you're admiring yourself in the mirror something will make you see at last what you really are! That will be revenge in full for all you've done to Mother and me!

(*She waits defiantly, as if expecting him to lose his temper and curse her. But Melody acts as if he had not heard her.*)

MELODY (*his face expressionless, his manner insistently bland and polite*). Sit down, my dear. I will not detain you long, and I think you will find what I have to tell you of great interest.

(*She searches his face, uneasy now, feeling a threat hidden behind his cold, quiet, gentlemanly tone. She sits down and he sits at rear of table, with an empty chair separating them.*)

SARA. You'd better think well before you speak, Father. I know the devil that's in you when you're quiet like this with your brain mad with drink.

MELODY. I don't understand you. All I wish is to relate something which happened this afternoon.

SARA (*giving way to bitterness at her humiliation again—sneeringly*). When you went riding on your beautiful thoroughbred mare while Mother and I were sweating and suffocating in the heat of the kitchen to prepare your Lordship's banquet? Sure, I hope you didn't show off and jump your beauty over a fence into somebody's garden, like you've done before, and then have to pay damages to keep out of jail!

MELODY (*roused by mention of his pet—disdainfully*). The damned Yankee yokels should feel flattered that she deigns to set her dainty hooves in their paltry gardens! She's a truer-born, well-bred lady than any of their women—than the one who paid us a visit this morning, for example.

SARA. Mrs Harford was enough of a lady to put you in your place and make a fool of you.

MELODY (*seemingly unmoved by this taunt—calmly*). You are very simple-minded, my dear, to let yourself be taken in by such an obvious bit of clever acting. Naturally, the lady was a bit discomposed when she heard you and your mother coming, after she had just allowed me to kiss her. She had to pretend—

SARA (*eagerly*). She let you kiss her? (*Then disgustedly.*) It's a lie, but I don't doubt you've made yourself think it's the truth by now. (*Angrily.*) I'm going. I don't want to listen to the whiskey in your boasting of what never happened—as usual! (*She puts her hands on the table and starts to rise.*)

MELODY (*with a quick movement pins her down with one of his*). Wait! (*A look of vindictive cruelty comes into his eyes—quietly.*) Why are you so jealous of the mare, I wonder? Is it because she has such slender ankles and dainty feet? (*He takes his hand away and stares at her hands—with disgust, commandingly.*) Keep your thick wrists and ugly, peasant paws off the table in my presence, if you please! They turn my stomach! I advise you never to let Simon get a good look at them—

SARA (*instinctively jerks her hands back under the table guiltily. She stammers.*) You—you cruel devil! I knew you'd—

MELODY (*for a second is ashamed and really contrite*). Forgive me, Sara. I didn't mean—the whiskey talking—as you said. (*He adds in a forced tone, a trace of mockery in it.*) An absurd taunt, when you really have such pretty hands and feet, my dear.

(*She jumps to her feet, so hurt and full of hatred her lips tremble and she cannot speak. He speaks quietly.*)

Are you going? I was about to tell you of the talk I had this afternoon with young Harford.

(*She stares at him in dismay. He goes on easily.*)

It was after I returned from my ride. I cantered the mare by the river and she pulled up lame. So I dismounted and led her back to the barn. No one noticed my return and when I went upstairs it occurred to me I would not find again such an opportunity to have a frank chat with Harford—free from interruptions. (*He pauses, as if he expects her to be furious, but she remains tensely silent, determined not to let him know her reaction.*) I did not beat about the bush. I told him he must appreciate, as a gentleman, it was my duty as your father to demand he lay his cards on the table. I said he must realize that even before you began nursing him here and going alone to his bedroom, there was a deal of gossip about your visits to his cabin, and your walks in the woods with him. I put it to him that such an intimacy could not continue without gravely compromising your reputation.

SARA (*stunned—weakly*). God forgive you! And what did he say?

MELODY. What could he say? He is a man of honour. He looked damned embarrassed and guilty for a moment, but when he found his tongue, he agreed with me most heartily. He said his mother had told him the same thing.

SARA. Oh, she did, did she? I suppose she did it to find out by watching him how far—

MELODY (*coldly*). Well, why not? Naturally, it was her duty as his mother to discover all she could about you. She is a woman of the world. She would be bound to suspect that you might be his mistress.

SARA (*tensely*). Oh, would she!

MELODY. But that's beside the point. The point is, my bashful young gentleman finally blurted out that he wanted to marry you.

SARA (*forgetting her anger—eagerly*). He told you that?

MELODY. Yes, and he said he had told his mother, and she had said all she wanted was his happiness but she felt in fairness to you and to himself — and I presume she also meant to both families concerned — he should test his love and yours by letting a decent interval of time elapse before your marriage. She mentioned a year, I believe.

SARA (*angrily*). Ah! Didn't I guess that would be her trick!

MELODY (*lifting his eyebrows — coldly*). Trick? In my opinion, the lady displayed more common sense and knowledge of the world than I thought she possessed. The reasons she gave him are sound and show a consideration for your good name which ought to inspire gratitude in you and not suspicion.

SARA. Arrah, don't tell me she's made a fool of you again! A lot of consideration she has for me!

MELODY. She pointed out to him that if you were the daughter of some family in their own little Yankee clique, there would be no question of a hasty marriage, and so he owed it to you —

SARA. I see. She's the clever one!

MELODY. Another reason was — and here your Simon stammered so embarrassedly I had trouble making him out — she warned him a sudden wedding would look damnably suspicious and start a lot of evil-minded gossip.

SARA (*tensely*). Oh, she's clever, all right! But I'll beat her.

MELODY. I told him I agreed with his mother. It is obvious that were there a sudden wedding without a suitable period of betrothal, everyone would believe —

SARA. I don't care what they believe! Tell me this! Did she get him to promise her he'd wait? (*Before he can answer — bitterly.*) But of course she did! She'd never have left till she got that out of him!

MELODY (*ignores this*). I told him I appreciated the honour he did me in asking for your hand, but he must understand that I could not commit myself until I had talked to his father and was assured the necessary financial arrangements could be concluded to our mutual satisfaction. There was the amount of settlement to be agreed upon, for instance.

SARA. That dream, again! God pity you! (*She laughs helplessly and a bit hysterically.*) And God help Simon. He must have thought you'd gone out of your mind! What did he say?

MELODY. He said nothing, naturally. He is well bred and he knows this is a matter he must leave to his father to discuss. There is also the equally important matter of how generous an allowance Henry Harford is willing to settle on his son. I did not mention this to Simon, of course, not wishing to embarrass him further with talk of money.

SARA. Thank God for that, at least! (*She giggles hysterically.*)

MELODY (*quietly*). May I ask what you find so ridiculous in an old established custom? Simon is an elder son, the heir to his father's estate. No matter what their differences in the past may have been, now that Simon has decided to marry and settle down his father will wish to do the fair thing by him. He will realize, too, that although there is no more honourable calling than that of poet and philosopher, which his son has chosen to pursue, there is no decent living to be gained by its practice. So naturally he will settle an allowance on Simon, and I shall insist it be a generous one, befitting your position as my daughter. I will tolerate no niggardly trader's haggling on his part.

SARA (*stares at him fascinatedly, on the edge of helpless, hysterical laughter*). I suppose it would never occur to you that old Harford might not think it an honour to have his son marry your daughter.

MELODY (*calmly*). No, it would never occur to me — and if it should occur to him, I would damned soon disabuse his mind. Who is he but a money-grubbing trader? I would remind him that I was born in a castle and there was a time when I possessed wealth and position, and an estate compared to which any Yankee upstart's home in this country is but a hovel stuck in a cabbage patch. I would remind him that you, my daughter, were born in a castle!

SARA (*impulsively, with a proud toss of her head*). Well, that's no more than the truth. (*Then furious with herself and him.*) Och, what crazy blather! (*She springs to her feet.*) I've had enough of your mad dreams!

MELODY. Wait! I haven't finished yet. (*He speaks quietly, but as he goes on there is an increasing vindictiveness in his tone.*) There is another reason why I told young Harford I could not make a final decision. I wished time to reflect on a further aspect of this proposed marriage. Well, I have been reflecting, watching you and examining your conduct, without prejudice, trying to be fair to you and make every possible allowance — (*He pauses.*) Well, to be brutally frank, my dear, all I can see in you is a common, greedy, scheming, cunning peasant girl, whose only thought is money and who has shamelessly thrown herself at a young man's head because his family happens to possess a little wealth and position.

SARA (*trying to control herself*). I see your game, Father. I told you when you were drunk like this — But this time, I won't give you the satisfaction — (*Then she bursts out angrily.*) It's a lie! I love Simon, or I'd never —

MELODY (*as if she hadn't spoken*). So, I have about made up my mind to decline for you Simon Harford's request for your hand in marriage.

SARA (*jeers angrily now*). Oh, you have, have you? As

if I cared a damn what you — !

MELODY. As a gentleman, I feel I have a duty, in honour, to Simon. Such a marriage would be a tragic misalliance for him — and God knows I know the sordid tragedy of such a union.

SARA. It's Mother has had the tragedy!

MELODY. I hold young Harford in too high esteem. I cannot stand by and let him commit himself irrevocably to what could only bring him disgust and bitterness, and ruin to all his dreams.

SARA. So I'm not good enough for him, you've decided now?

MELODY. That is apparent from your every act. No one, no matter how charitably inclined, could mistake you for a lady. I have tried to make you one. It was an impossible task. God Himself cannot transform a sow's ear into a silk purse!

SARA (*furiously*). Father!

MELODY. Young Harford needs to be saved from himself. I can understand his physical infatuation. You are pretty. So was your mother pretty once. But marriage is another matter. The man who would be the ideal husband for you, from a standpoint of conduct and character, is Mickey Maloy, my bartender, and I will be happy to give him my parental blessing —

SARA. Let you stop now, Father!

MELODY. You and he would be congenial. You can match tongues together. He's a healthy animal. He can give you a raft of peasant brats to squeal and fight with the pigs on the mud floor of your hovel.

SARA. It's the dirty hut in which your father was born and raised you're remembering, isn't it?

MELODY (*stung to fury, glares at her with hatred. His voice quivers but is deadly quiet*). Of course, if you trick Harford into getting you with child, I could not refuse my consent. (*Letting go, he bangs his fist on the table.*) No, by God, even then, when I remember my own experience, I'll be damned if I could with a good conscience advise him to marry you!

(*Nora comes in the doorway at right and hurries to them.*)

SARA (*glaring back at him with hatred*). You drunken devil! (*She makes a threatening move towards him, raising her hand as if she were going to slap his face — then she controls herself and speaks with quiet, biting sarcasm.*) Consent or not, I want to thank you for your kind, fatherly advice on how to trick Simon. I don't think I'll need it but if the worst comes to the worst I promise you I'll remember —

MELODY (*coldly, his face expressionless*). I believe I have said all I wished to say to you. (*He gets up and bows stiffly.*) If you will excuse me, I shall join Corporal Cregan.

(*He goes to the bar door. Sara turns and goes quietly out right, forgetting to clear the few remaining dishes on the centre table. His back turned, he does not see her go. With his hand on the knob of the bar door, he hesitates. For a second he breaks — torturedly.*)

Sara! (*Then quietly.*) There are things I said which I regret — even now. I — I trust you will overlook — As your mother knows, it's the liquor talking, not — I must admit that, due to my celebrating the anniversary, my brain is a bit addled by whiskey — as you said. (*He waits, hoping for a word of forgiveness. Finally, he glances over his shoulder. As he discovers she is not there and has not heard him, for a second he crumbles, his soldierly erectness sags and his face falls. He looks sad and hopeless and bitter and old, his eyes wandering dully. But, as in the two preceding acts, the mirror attracts him, and as he moves from the bar door to stand before it he assumes his arrogant, Byronic pose again. He repeats in each detail his pantomime before the mirror. He speaks proudly.*) Myself to the bitter end! No weakening, so help me God! (*There is a knock on the street door but he does not hear it. He starts his familiar incantation quotes from Byron.*)

'I have not loved the World, nor the World me;
I have not flattered its rank breath, nor bowed
To its idolatries a patient knee . . .'

(*The knock on the door is repeated more loudly. Melody starts guiltily and steps quickly away from the mirror. His embarrassment is transformed into resentful anger. He calls.*) Come in, damn you! Do you expect a lackey to open the door for you?

(*The door opens and Nicholas Gadsby comes in. Gadsby is in his late forties, short, stout, with a big bald head, round florid face, and small blue eyes. A rigidly conservative, best-family attorney, he is stiffly correct in dress and manner, drily portentous in speech, and extremely conscious of his professional authority and dignity. Now, however, he is venturing on unfamiliar ground and is by no means as sure of himself as his manner indicates. The unexpected vision of Melody in his uniform startles him and for a second he stands, as close to gaping as he can be, impressed by Melody's handsome distinction. Melody, in his turn, is surprised. He had not thought the intruder would be a gentleman. He unbends, although his tone is still a bit curt. He bows a bit stiffly, and Gadsby finds himself returning the bow.*)

Your pardon, sir. When I called, I thought it was one of the damned riffraff mistaking the barroom door. Pray be seated, sir.

(*Gadsby comes forward and takes the chair at the head of the centre table, glancing at the few dirty dishes on it with distaste. Melody says.*)

Your pardon again, sir. We have been feasting late, which

accounts for the disarray. I will summon a servant to inquire your pleasure.

GADSBY (*beginning to recover his aplomb — shortly*). Thank you, but I want nothing, sir. I came here to seek a private interview with the proprietor of this tavern, by name, Melody. (*He adds a bit hesitantly.*) Are you, by any chance, he?

MELODY (*stiffens arrogantly*). I am not, sir. But if you wish to see Major Cornelius Melody, one time of his Majesty's Seventh Dragoons, who served with honour under the Duke of Wellington in Spain, I am he.

GADSBY (*drily*). Very well, sir. Major Melody, then.

MELODY (*does not like his tone — insolently sarcastic*). And whom have I the *honour* of addressing?

(*As Gadsby is about to reply, Sara enters from right, having remembered the dishes. Melody ignores her as he would a servant. Gadsby examines her carefully as she gathers up the dishes. She notices him staring at her and gives him a resentful, suspicious glance. She carries the dishes out, right, to the kitchen, but a moment later she can be seen just inside the hall at right, listening. Meanwhile, as soon as he thinks she has gone, Gadsby speaks.*)

GADSBY (*with affected casualness*). A pretty young woman. Is she your daughter, sir? I seemed to detect a resemblance —

MELODY (*angrily*). No! Do I look to you, sir, like a man who would permit his daughter to work as a waitress? Resemblance to me? You must be blind, sir. (*Coldly.*) I am still waiting for you to inform me who you are and why you should wish to see me.

GADSBY (*hands him a card — extremely nettled by Melody's manner — curtly*). My card, sir.

MELODY (*glances at the card*). Nicholas Gadsby. (*He flips it aside disdainfully.*) Attorney, eh? The devil take all your tribe, say I. I have small liking for your profession, sir, and I cannot imagine what business you can have with me. The damned thieves of the law did their worst to me many years ago in Ireland. I have little left to tempt you. So I do not see — (*Suddenly an idea comes to him. He stares at Gadsby, then goes on in a more friendly tone.*) That is, unless — Do you happen by any chance to represent the father of young Simon Harford?

GADSBY (*indignant at Melody's insults to his profession — with a thinly veiled sneer*). Ah, then you were expecting — That makes things easier. We need not beat about the bush. I do represent Mr Henry Harford, sir.

MELODY (*thawing out, in his total misunderstanding of the situation*). Then accept my apologies, sir, for my animadversions against your profession. I am afraid I may be prejudiced. In the army, we used to say we suffered more casualties from your attacks at home than the French ever inflicted. (*He sits down on the chair on Gadsby's left, at rear of table — remarking with careless pride.*) A word of explanation as to why you find me in uniform. It is the anniversary of the battle of Talavera, sir, and —

GADSBY (*interrupts drily*). Indeed, sir? But I must tell you my time is short. With your permission, we will proceed at once to the matter in hand.

MELODY (*controlling his angry discomfiture — coldly*). I think I can hazard a guess as to what that matter is. You have come about the settlement?

GADSBY (*misunderstanding him, replies in a tone almost openly contemptuous*). Exactly, sir. Mr Harford was of the opinion, and I agreed with him, that a settlement would be foremost in your mind.

MELODY (*scowls at his tone, but, as he completely misunderstands Gadsby's meaning, he forces himself to bow politely*). It does me honour, sir, that Mr Harford appreciates he is dealing with a gentleman and has the breeding to know how these matters are properly arranged.

(*Gadsby stares at him, absolutely flabbergasted by what he considers a piece of the most shameless effrontery. Melody leans towards him confidentially.*)

I will be frank with you, sir. The devil of it is, this comes at a difficult time for me. Temporary, of course, but I cannot deny I am pinched at the moment — devilishly pinched. But no matter. Where my only child's happiness is at stake, I am prepared to make every possible effort. I will sign a note of hand, no matter how ruinous the interest demanded by the scoundrelly moneylenders. By the way, what amount does Mr Harford think proper? Anything in reason —

GADSBY (*listening in utter confusion, finally gets the idea Melody is making him the butt of a joke — fuming*). I do not know what you are talking about, sir, unless you think to make a fool of me! If this is what is known as Irish wit —

MELODY (*bewildered for a second — then in a threatening tone*). Take care, sir, and watch your words or I warn you you will repent them, no matter whom you represent! No damned pettifogging dog can insult me with impunity!

(*As Gadsby draws back apprehensively, he adds with insulting disdain.*)

As for making a fool of you, sir, I would be the fool if I attempted to improve on God's handiwork!

GADSBY (*ignoring the insults, forces a placating tone*). I wish no quarrel with you, sir. I cannot for the life of me see — I fear we are dealing at cross purposes. Will you tell me plainly what you mean by your talk of settlement?

MELODY. Obviously, I mean the settlement I am prepared to make on my daughter.

(*As Gadsby only looks more dumbfounded, he continues sharply.*)

Is not your purpose in coming here to arrange, on Mr Harford's behalf, for the marriage of his son with my daughter?

GADSBY. Marriage? Good God, no! Nothing of the kind!

MELODY (*dumbfounded*). Then what have you come for?

GADSBY (*feeling he has now the upper hand — sharply*). To inform you that Mr Henry Harford is unalterably opposed to any further relationship between his son and your daughter, whatever the nature of that relationship in the past.

MELODY (*leans forward threateningly*). By the Immortal, sir, if you dare insinuate — !

GADSBY (*draws back again, but he is no coward and is determined to carry out his instructions.*) I insinuate nothing, sir. I am here on Mr Harford's behalf, to make you an offer. That is what I thought you were expecting when you mentioned a settlement. Mr Harford is prepared to pay you the sum of three thousand dollars — provided, mark you, that you and your daughter sign an agreement I have drawn up which specifies that you relinquish all claims, of whatever nature. And also provided you agree to leave this part of the country at once with your family. Mr Harford suggests it would be advisable that you go West — to Ohio, say.

MELODY (*so overcome by a rising tide of savage, humiliated fury, he can only stammer hoarsely*). So Henry Harford does me the honour — to suggest that, does he?

GADSBY (*watching him uneasily, attempts a reasonable persuasive tone*). Surely you could not have spoken seriously when you talked of marriage. There is such a difference in station. The idea is preposterous. If you knew Mr Harford, you would realize he would never countenance —

MELODY (*his pent-up rage bursts out — smashing his fist on the table*). Know him? By the Immortal God, I'll know him soon! And he'll know me! (*He springs to his feet.*) But first, you Yankee scum, I'll deal with you!

(*He draws back his fist to smash Gadsby in the face, but Sara has run from the door at right and she grabs his arm. She is almost as furious as he is and there are tears of humiliated pride in her eyes.*)

SARA. Father! Don't! He's only a paid lackey. Where is your pride that you'd dirty your hands on the like of him?

(*While she is talking the door from the bar opens and Roche, O'Dowd, and Cregan crowd into the room. Mickey stands in the doorway. Nora follows Sara in from right.*)

ROCHE (*with drunken enthusiasm*). It's a fight! For the love of God, clout the damned Yankee, Major!

MELODY (*controls himself — his voice shaking*). You are right. Sara. It would be beneath me to touch such a vile lickspittle. But he won't get off scot-free. (*Sharply, a commander ordering his soldiers.*) Here you, Roche and O'Dowd! Get hold of him! (*They do so with enthusiasm and yank Gadsby from his chair.*)

GADSBY. You drunken ruffians! Take your hands off me!

MELODY (*addressing him — in his quiet threatening tone now*). You may tell the swindling trader, Harford, who employs you that he'll hear from me! (*To Roche and O'Dowd.*) Throw this thing out! Kick it down to the crossroads!

ROCHE. Hurroo!

(*He and O'Dowd run Gadsby to the door at rear. Cregan jumps ahead, grinning, and opens the door for them.*)

GADSBY (*struggling futilely as they rush him through the door*). You scoundrels! Take your hands off me! Take —

(*Melody looks after them. The two women watch him, Nora frightened, Sara with a strange look of satisfied pride.*)

CREGAN (*in the doorway, looking out — laughing*). Oh, it'd do your heart good, Con, to see the way they're kicking his butt down the street! (*He comes in and shuts the door.*)

MELODY (*his rage welling again, as his mind dwells on his humiliation — starting to pace up and down*). It's with his master I have to deal, and, by the Powers, I'll deal with him! You'll come with me, Jamie. I'll want you for a witness. He'll apologize to me — more than that, he'll come back here this very night and apologize publicly to my daughter, or else he meets me in the morning! By God, I'll face him at ten paces or across a handkerchief! I'll put a bullet through him, so help me, Christ!

NORA (*breaks into a dirgelike wail*). God forgive you, Con, is it a duel again — murtherin' or gettin' murthered?

MELODY. Be quiet, woman! Go back to your kitchen! Go, do you hear me!

(*Nora turns obediently towards the door at right, beginning to cry.*)

SARA (*puts an arm around her mother. She is staring at Melody apprehensively now*). There, Mother, don't worry. Father knows that's all foolishness. He's only talking. Go on now in the kitchen and sit down and rest, Mother.

(*Nora goes out left. Sara closes the door after her and comes back.*)

MELODY (*turns on her with bitter anger*). Only talking, am I? It's the first time in my life I ever heard anyone say

Con Melody was a coward! It remains for my own daughter — !

SARA (*placatingly*). I didn't say that, Father. But can't you see — you're not in Ireland in the old days now. The days of duels are long past and dead, in this part of America anyway. Harford will never fight you. He —

MELODY. He won't, won't he? By God, I'll make him! I'll take a whip. I'll drag him out of his house and lash him down the street for all his neighbours to see! He'll apologize, or he'll fight, or I'll brand him a craven before the world!

SARA (*frightened now*). But you'll never be let see him! His servants will keep you out! He'll have the police arrest you, and it'll be in the papers about another drunken Mick raising a crazy row! (*She appeals to Cregan.*) Tell him I'm telling the truth, Jamie. You've still got some sober sense in you. Maybe he'll listen to you.

CREGAN (*glances at Melody uneasily*). Maybe Sara's right, Major.

MELODY. When I want your opinion, I'll ask for it! (*Sneeringly.*) Of course, if you've become such a coward you're afraid to go with me —

CREGAN (*stung*). Coward, is ut? I'll go, and be damned to you!

SARA. Jamie, you fool! Oh, it's like talking to crazy men! (*She grabs her father's arm — pleadingly.*) Don't do it, Father, for the love of God! Have I ever asked you anything? Well, I ask you to heed me now! I'll beg you on my knees, if you like! Isn't it me you'd fight about, and haven't I a right to decide? You punished that lawyer for the insult. You had him thrown out of here like a tramp. Isn't that your answer to old Harford that insults him? It's for him to challenge you, if he dares, isn't it? Why can't you leave it at that and wait —

MELODY (*shaking off her hand — angrily*). You talk like a scheming peasant! It's a question of my honour!

SARA. No! It's a question of my happiness, and I won't have your mad interfering — ! (*Desperately forcing herself to reason with him again.*) Listen, Father! If you'll keep out of it, I'll show you how I'll make a fool of old Harford! Simon won't let anything his father does keep him from marrying me. His mother is the only one who might have the influence over him to come between us. She's only watching for a good excuse to turn Simon against marrying me, and if you go raising a drunken row at their house, and make a public scandal, shouting you want to murder his father, can't you see what a chance that will give her?

MELODY (*raging*). That damned, insolent Yankee bitch! She's all the more reason. Marry, did you say? You dare to think there can be any question now of your marrying the son of a man who has insulted my honour — and yours?

SARA (*defiantly*). Yes, I dare to think it! I love Simon and I'm going to marry him!

MELODY. And I say you're not! If he wasn't sick, I'd — But I'll get him out of here tomorrow! I forbid you ever to see him again! If you dare disobey me I'll — ! (*Beginning to lose all control of himself.*) If you dare defy me — for the sake of the dirty money you think you can beg from his family, if you're his wife — !

SARA (*fiercely*). You lie! (*Then with quiet intensity.*) Yes. I defy you or anyone who tries to come between us!

MELODY. You'd sell your pride as my daughter — ! (*His face convulsed by fury.*) You filthy peasant slut! You whore! I'll see you dead first — ! By the living God, I'd kill you myself! (*He makes a threatening move towards her.*)

SARA (*shrinks back frightenedly*). Father! (*Then she stands and faces him defiantly.*)

CREGAN (*steps between them*). Con! In the name of God!

(*Melody's fit of insane fury leaves him. He stands panting for breath, shuddering with the effort to regain some sort of poise. Cregan speaks, his only thought to get him away from Sara.*)

If we're going after old Harford, Major, we'd better go. That thief of a lawyer will warn him —

MELODY (*seizing on this — hoarsely*). Yes, let's go. Let's go, Jamie. Come alone, Corporal. A stirrup cup, and we'll be off. If the mare wasn't lame, I'd ride alone — but we can get a rig at the livery stable. Don't let me forget to stop at the barn for my whip. (*By the time he finishes speaking, he has himself in hand again and his ungovernable fury has gone. There is a look of cool, menacing vengefulness in his face. He turns towards the bar door.*)

SARA (*helplessly*). Father! (*Desperately, as a last, frantic threat.*) You'll force me to go to Simon — and do what you said!

(*If he hears this, he gives no sign of it. He strides into the bar. Cregan follows him, closing the door. Sara stares before her, the look of defiant desperation hardening on her face. The street door is flung open and O'Dowd and Roche pile in, laughing uproariously.*)

ROCHE. Hurroo!

O'DOWD. The army is back, Major, with the foe flying in retreat. (*He sees Melody is not there — to Sara.*) Where's himself?

(*Sara appears not to see or hear him.*)

ROCHE (*after a quick glance at her*). Lave her be. He'll be in the bar. Come on. (*He goes to the bar.*)

O'DOWD (*following him, speaks over his shoulder to Sara*). You should have seen the Yank! His coachman had to help him in his rig at the corner — and Roche gave the coachman a clout too, for good measure!

(*He disappears, laughing, slamming the door behind him. Nora opens the door at right and looks in cautiously. Seeing Sara alone, she comes in.*)

NORA. Sara. (*She comes over to her.*) Sara. (*She takes hold of her arm — whispers uneasily.*) Where's himself?

SARA (*dully*). I couldn't stop him.

NORA. I could have told you you was wastin' breath. (*With a queer pride.*) The divil himself couldn't kape Con Melody from a duel! (*Then mournfully.*) It's like the auld times come again, and the same worry and sorrow. Even in the days before ivir I'd spoke a word to him, or done more than make him a bow when he'd ride past on his hunter, I used to lie awake and pray for him when I'd hear he was fightin' a duel in the mornin'. (*She smiles a shy, gentle smile.*) I was in love with him even then.

(*Sara starts to say something bitter but what she sees in her mother's face stops her. Nora goes on, with a feeble attempt at boastful confidence.*)

But I'll not worry this time, and let you not, either. There wasn't a man in Galway was his equal with a pistol, and what chance will this auld stick av a Yankee have against him?

(*There is a noise of boisterous farewells from the bar and the noise of an outer door shutting. Nora starts.*)

That's him leavin'! (*Her mouth pulls down pitiably. She starts for the bar with a sob.*) Ah, Con darlin', don't — ! (*She stops, shaking her head helplessly.*) But what's the good? (*She sinks on a chair with a weary sigh.*)

SARA (*bitterly, aloud to herself more than to her mother*). No good. Let him go his way — and I'll go mine. (*Tensely.*) I won't let him destroy my life with his madness, after all the plans I've made and the dreams I've dreamed. I'll show him I can play at the game of gentleman's honour too!

(*Nora has not listened. She is sunk in memories of old fears and her present worry about the duel. Sara hesitates — then, keeping her face turned away from her mother, touches her shoulder.*)

I'm going upstairs to bed, Mother.

NORA (*starts — then indignantly*). To bed, is it? You can think of sleepin' when he's —

SARA. I didn't say sleep, but I can lie down and try to rest. (*Still avoiding looking at her mother.*) I'm dead tired, Mother.

NORA (*tenderly solicitous now, puts an arm around her*). You must be, darlin'. It's been the divil's own day for you, with all — (*With sudden remorse.*) God forgive me, darlin'. I was forgettin' about you and the Harford lad. (*Miserably.*) Oh, God help us! (*Suddenly with a flash of her strange, fierce pride in the power of love.*) Never mind! If there's true love between you, you'll not let a duel or anything in the world kape you from each other, whatever the cost! Don't I know!

SARA (*kisses her impulsively, then looks away again*). You're going to sit up and wait down here?

NORA. I am. I'd be destroyed with fear lying down in the dark. Here, the noise of them in the bar kapes up my spirits, in a way.

SARA. Yes, you'd better stay here. Good night, Mother.

NORA. Good night, darlin'.

(*Sara goes out at right, closing the door behind her.*)

CURTAIN

ACT FOUR

SCENE. *The same. It is around midnight. The room is in darkness except for one candle on the table, centre. From the bar comes the sound of Patch Riley's pipes playing a reel and the stamp of dancing feet.*

Nora sits at the foot of the table at centre. She is hunched up in an old shawl, her arms crossed over her breast, hugging herself as if she were cold. She looks on the verge of collapse from physical fatigue and hours of worry. She starts as the door from the bar is opened. It is Mickey. He closes the door behind him, shutting out an uproar of music and drunken voices. He has a decanter of whiskey and a glass in his hand. He has been drinking, but is not drunk.

NORA (*eagerly*). There's news of himself?

MALOY (*putting the decanter and glass on the table*). Sorra a bit. Don't be worryin' now. Sure, it's not so late yet.

NORA (*dully*). It's aisy for you to say —

MALOY. I came in to see how you was, and bring you a taste to put heart in you. (*As she shakes her head.*) Oh, I know you don't indulge, but I've known you once in a while, and you need it this night. (*As she again shakes her head — with kindly bullying.*) Come now, don't be stubborn. I'm the doctor and I highly recommend a drop to drive out black thoughts and rheumatism.

NORA. Well — maybe — a taste, only.

MALOY. That's the talkin'. (*He pours a small drink and hands it to her.*) Drink hearty, now.

NORA (*takes a sip, then puts the glass on the table and pushes it away listlessly*). I've no taste for anything. But I thank you for the thought. You're a kind lad, Mickey.

MALOY. Here's news to cheer you. The word has got round among the boys, and they've all come in to wait for Cregan and himself. (*With enthusiasm.*) There'll be more money taken over the bar than any night since this shebeen started!

NORA. That's good.

MALOY. If they do hate Con Melody, he's Irish, and they hate the Yanks worse. They're all hopin' he's bate the livin' lights out of Harford.

NORA (*with belligerent spirit*). And so he has, I know that!

MALOY (*grins*). That's the talk. I'm glad to see you roused from your worryin'. (*Turning away.*) I'd better get back. I left O'Dowd to tend bar and I'll wager he had three drinks stolen already. (*He hesitates.*) Sara's not been down?

NORA. No.

MALOY (*resentfully*). It's a wonder she wouldn't have more thought for you than to lave you sit up alone.

NORA (*stiffens defensively*). I made her go to bed. She was droppin' with tiredness and destroyed with worry. She must have fallen asleep, like the young can. None of your talk against Sara, now!

MALOY (*starts an exasperated retort*). The divil take — (*He stops and grins at her with affection.*) There's no batin' you, Nora. Sure, it'd be the joy av me life to have a mother like you to fight for me—or, better still, a wife like you.

NORA (*a sweet smile of pleased coquetry lights up her drawn face*). Arrah, save your blarney for the young girls!

MALOY. The divil take young girls. You're worth a hundred av thim.

NORA (*with a toss of her head*). Get along with you!

(*Mickey grins with satisfaction at having cheered her up and goes in the bar, closing the door. As soon as he is gone, she sinks back into apprehensive brooding.*

Sara appears silently in the doorway at right. She wears a faded old wrapper over her nightgown, slippers on her bare feet. Her hair is down over her shoulders, reaching to her waist. There is a change in her. All the bitterness and defiance have disappeared from her face. It looks gentle and calm and at the same time dreamily happy and exultant. She is much prettier than she has ever been before. She stands looking at her mother, and suddenly she becomes shy and uncertain — as if, now that she'd come this far, she had half a mind to retreat before her mother discovered her. But Nora senses her presence and looks up.)

NORA (*dully*). Ah, it's you, darlin'! (*Then gratefully.*) Praise be, you've come at last! I'm sick with worry and I've got to the place where I can't bear waitin' alone, listenin' to drunks dancin' and celebratin'.

(*Sara comes to her. Nora breaks. Tears well from her eyes.*)

It's cruel, it is! There's no heart or thought for himself in divil a one av thim.

(*She starts to sob. Sara hugs her and kisses her cheek gently. But she doesn't speak. It is as if she were afraid her voice would give her away. Nora stops sobbing. Her mood changes to resentment and she speaks as if Sara had spoken.*)

Don't tell me not to worry. You're as bad as Mickey. The Yankee didn't apologize or your father'd been back here long since. It's a duel, that's certain, and he must have taken a room in the city so he'll be near the ground. I hope he'll sleep, but I'm feared he'll stay up drinkin', and at the dawn he'll have had too much to shoot his best and maybe — (*Then defiantly, self-reassuringly.*) Arrah, I'm the fool! It's himself can keep his head clear and his eyes sharp, no matter what he's taken! (*Pushing Sara away — with nervous peevishness.*) Let go of me. You've hardened not to care. I'd rather stay alone. (*She grabs Sara's hand.*) No. Don't heed me. Sit down, darlin'.

(*Sara sits down on her left at rear of table. She pats her mother's hand, but remains silent, her expression dreamily happy, as if she heard Nora's words but they had no meaning for her. Nora goes on worriedly again.*)

But if he's staying in the city, why hasn't he sent Jamie Cregan back for his duellin' pistols? I know he'd nivir fight with any others. (*Resentful now at Melody.*) Or you'd think he'd send Jamie or someone back with a word for me. He knows well how tormented I'd be waiting. (*Bitterly.*) Arrah, don't talk like a loon! Has he ever cared for anyone except himself and his pride? Sure, he'd never stoop to think of me, the grand gentleman in his red livery av bloody England! His pride, indade! What is it but a lie? What's in his veins, God pity him, but the blood of thievin' auld Ned Melody who kept a dirty shebeen? (*Then is horrified at herself as if she had blasphemed.*) No! I won't say it! I've nivir! It would break his heart if he heard me! I'm the only one in the world he knows nivir sneers at his dreams! (*Working herself to rebellion again.*) All the same, I won't stay here the rist of the night worryin' my heart out for a man who — it isn't only fear over the duel. It's because I'm afraid it's God's punishment, all the sorrow and trouble that's come on us, and I have the black tormint in my mind that it's the fault of the mortal sin I did with him unmarried, and the promise he made me make to leave the Church that's kept me from ever confessin' to a priest. (*She pauses — dully.*) Go to a doctor, you say, to cure the rheumatism. Sure, what's rheumatism but a pain in your body? I could bear ten of it. It's the pain of guilt in my soul. Can a doctor's medicine cure that? No, only a priest of Almighty God — (*With a roused rebellion again.*) It would serve Con right if I took the chance now and broke my promise and woke up the priest to hear my confession and give me God's forgiveness that'd bring my soul peace and comfort so I wouldn't feel the three of us were damned. (*Yearningly.*) Oh, if I only had the courage! (*She rises suddenly from her chair — with brave defiance.*) I'll do it, so I will! I'm going to the priest's, Sara. (*She starts for the street door — gets halfway to it and stops.*)

SARA (*a strange, tenderly amused smile on her lips — teasingly*). Well, why don't you go, Mother?

NORA (*defiantly*). Ain't I goin'? (*She takes a few more steps towards the door — stops again — she mutters beatenly.*) God forgive me, I can't. What's the use pretendin'?

SARA (*as before*). No use at all, Mother. I've found that out.

NORA (*as if she hadn't heard, comes back slowly*). He'd feel I'd betrayed him and my word and my love for him — and for all his scorn, he knows my love is all he has in the world to comfort him. (*Then spiritedly, with a proud toss of her head.*) And it's my honour, too! It's not for his sake at all! Divil mend him, he always prates as if he had all the honour there is, but I've mine, too, as proud as his. (*She sits down in the same chair.*)

SARA (*softly*). Yes, the honour of her love to a woman. I've learned about that too, Mother.

NORA (*as if this were the first time she was really conscious of Sara speaking, and even now had not heard what she said — irritably*). So you've found your tongue, have you? Thank God. You're cold comfort, sitting silent like a statue, and me making talk to myself. (*Regarding her as if she hadn't really seen her before — resentfully.*) Musha but it's pleased and pretty you look, as if there wasn't a care in the world, while your poor father —

SARA (*dreamily amused, as if this no longer had any importance or connection with her*). I know it's no use telling you there won't be any duel, Mother, and it's crazy to give it a thought. You're living in Ireland long ago, like Father. But maybe you'll take Simon's word for it, if you won't mine. He said his father would be paralysed with indignation just at the thought he'd ever fight a duel. It's against the law.

NORA (*scornfully*). Och, who cares for the law? He must be a coward. (*She looks relieved.*) Well, if the young lad said that, maybe it's true.

SARA. Of course it's true, Mother.

NORA. Your father'd be satisfied with Harford's apology and that'd end it.

SARA (*helplessly*). Oh, Mother! (*Then quickly.*) Yes, I'm sure it ended hours ago.

NORA (*intent on her hope*). And you think what's keeping him out is he and Jamie would take a power av drinks to celebrate.

SARA. They'd drink, that's sure, whatever happened. (*She adds dreamily.*) But that doesn't matter now at all.

NORA (*stares at her — wonderingly*). You've a queer way of talking, as if you'd been asleep and was still half in a dream.

SARA. In a dream right enough, Mother, and it isn't half of me that's in it but all of me, body and soul. And it's a dream that's true, and always will be to the end of life, and I'll never wake from it.

NORA. Sure, what's come over you at all?

SARA (*gets up impulsively and comes around to the back of her mother's chair and slips to her knees and puts her arms about her — giving her a hug*). Joy. That's what's come over me. I'm happy, Mother. I'm happy because I know now Simon is mine, and no one can ever take him from me.

NORA (*at first her only reaction is pleased satisfaction*). God be thanked! It was a great sorrow tormentin' me that the duel would come between you. (*Defiantly.*) Honour or not, why should the children have their lives and their love destroyed!

SARA. I was a great fool to fear his mother could turn him against me, no matter what happened.

NORA. You've had a talk with the lad?

SARA. I have. That's where I've been.

NORA. You've been in his room ever since you went up?

SARA. Almost. After I'd got upstairs it took me a while to get up my courage.

NORA (*rebukingly*). All this time — in the dead of the night!

SARA (*teasingly*). I'm his nurse, aren't I? I've a right.

NORA. That's no excuse!

SARA (*her face hardening*). Excuse? I had the best in the world. Would you have me do nothing to save my happiness and my chance in life, when I thought there was danger they'd be ruined forever? Don't you want me to have love and be happy, Mother?

NORA (*melting*). I do, darlin'. I'd give my life — (*Then rebuking again.*) Were you the way you are, in only a nightgown and wrapper?

SARA (*gaily*). I was—and Simon liked my costume, if you don't, although he turned red as a beet when I came in.

NORA. Small wonder he did! Shame on you!

SARA. He was trying to read a book of poetry, but he

couldn't he was that worried hoping I'd come to say good night, and being frightened I wouldn't. (*She laughs tenderly.*) Oh, it was the cutest thing I've ever done, Mother, not to see him at all since his mother left. He kept waiting for me, and when I didn't come he got scared to death that his kissing me this morning had made me angry. So he was wild with joy to see me —

NORA. In your bare legs with only your nightgown and wrapper to cover your nakedness! Where's your modesty?

SARA (*gaily teasing*). I had it with me, Mother, though I'd tried hard to leave it behind. I got as red as he was. (*She laughs.*) Oh, Mother, it's a great joke on me. Here I'd gone to his room with my mind made up to be as bold as any street woman and tempt him because I knew his honour would make him marry me right away if — (*She laughs.*) And then all I could do was stand and gape at him and blush!

NORA. Oh. (*Rebukingly.*) I'm glad you had the dacency to blush.

SARA. It was Simon spoke first, and once he started, all he'd been holding back came out. The waiting for me, and the fear he'd had made him forget all his shyness, and he said he loved me and asked me to marry him the first day we could. Without knowing how it happened, there I was with his arms around me and mine around him and his lips on my lips and it was heaven, Mother.

NORA (*moved by the shining happiness on Sara's face*). God bless the two av you.

SARA. Then I was crying and telling him how afraid I'd been his mother hated me, Father's madness about the duel would give her a good chance to come between us; Simon said no one could ever come between us and his mother would never try to, now she knew he loved me, which was what she came over to find out. He said all she wanted was for him to be free to do as he pleased, and she only suggested he wait a year, she didn't make him promise. And Simon said I was foolish to think she would take the duel craziness serious. She'd only be amused at the joke it would be on his father, after he'd been so sure he could buy us off, if he had to call the police to save him.

NORA (*aroused at the mention of police*). Call the police, is it? The coward!

SARA (*goes on, unheedingly*). Simon was terribly angry at his father for that. And at Father too when I told how he threatened he'd kill me. But we didn't talk of it much. We had better things to discuss. (*She smiles tenderly.*)

NORA (*belligerently*). A lot Con Melody cares for police, and him in a rage! Not the whole dirty force av thim will dare interfere with him!

SARA (*goes on as if she hadn't heard*). And then Simon told me how scared he'd been I didn't love him and wouldn't marry him. I was so beautiful, he said, and he wasn't handsome at all. So I kissed him and told him he was the handsomest in the world, and he is. And he said he wasn't worthy because he had so little to offer, and was a failure at what he'd hoped he could be, a poet. So I kissed him and told him he was too a poet, and always would be, and it was what I loved most about him.

NORA. The police! Let one av thim lay his dirty hand on Con Melody, and he'll knock him senseless with one blow.

SARA. Then Simon said how poor he was, and he'd never accept a penny from his father, even if he offered it. And I told him never mind, that if we had to live in a hut, or sleep in the grass of a field without a roof to our heads, and work our hands to the bone, or starve itself, I'd be in heaven and sing with the joy of our love! (*She looks up at her mother.*) And I meant it, Mother! I meant every word of it from the bottom of my heart!

NORA (*answers vaguely from her preoccupation with the police — patting Sara's hair mechanically*). Av course you did, darlin'.

SARA. But he kissed me and said it wouldn't be as bad as that, he'd been thinking and he'd had an offer from an old college friend who'd inherited a cotton mill and who wants Simon to be equal partners if he'll take complete charge of it. It's only a small mill and that's what tempts Simon. He said maybe I couldn't believe it but he knows from his experience working for his father he has the ability for trade, though he hates it, and he could easily make a living for us from this mill — just enough to be comfortable, and he'd have time over to write his book, and keep his wisdom, and never let himself become a slave to the greed for more than enough that is the curse of mankind. Then he said he was afraid maybe I'd think it was weakness in him, not wisdom, and could I be happy with enough and no more. So I kissed him and said all I wanted in life was his love, and whatever meant happiness to him would be my only ambition. (*She looks up at her mother again — exultantly.*) And I meant it, Mother! With all my heart and soul!

NORA (*as before, patting her hair*). I know, darlin'.

SARA. Isn't that a joke on me, with all my crazy dreams of riches and a grand estate and me a haughty lady riding around in a carriage with coachman and footman! (*She laughs at herself.*) Wasn't I the fool to think that had any meaning at all when you're in love? You were right, Mother. I knew nothing of love, or the pride a woman can take in giving everything — the pride in her own love! I was only an ignorant, silly girl boasting, but I'm a woman now, Mother, and I know.

NORA (*as before, mechanically*). I'm sure you do, darlin'. (*She mutters fumingly to herself.*) Let the police try it! He'll whip them back to their kennels, the dirty curs!

SARA (*lost in her happiness*). And then we put out the light and talked about how soon we'd get married, and how happy we'd be the rest of our lives together, and we'd have children — and he forgot whatever shyness was left in the dark and said he meant all the bold things he'd written in the poems I'd seen. And I confessed that I was up to every scheme to get him, because I loved him so much there wasn't anything I wouldn't do to make sure he was mine. And all the time we were kissing each other, wild with happiness. And — (*She stops abruptly and looks down guiltily.*)

NORA (*as before*). Yes, darlin', I know.

SARA (*guiltily, keeping her eyes down*). You — know, Mother?

NORA (*abruptly comes out of her preoccupation, startled and uneasy*). I know what? What are you sayin'? Look up at me! (*She pulls Sara's head back so she can look down in her face — falteringly.*) I can see — You let him! You wicked, sinful girl!

SARA (*defiantly and proudly*). There was no letting about it, only love making the two of us!

NORA (*helplessly resigned already but feeling it her duty to rebuke*). Ain't you ashamed to boast — ?

SARA. No! There was no shame in it! (*Proudly.*) Ashamed? You know I'm not! Haven't you told me of the pride in your love? Were you ashamed?

NORA (*weakly*). I was. I was dead with shame.

SARA. You were not! You were proud like me!

NORA. But it's a mortal sin. God will punish you —

SARA. Let him! If He'd say to me, for every time you kiss Simon you'll have a thousand years in hell, I wouldn't care, I'd wear out my lips kissing him!

NORA (*frightenedly*). Whist, now! He might hear you.

SARA. Wouldn't you have said the same — ?

NORA (*distractedly*). Will you stop! Don't torment me with your sinful questions! I won't answer you!

SARA (*hugging her*). All right. Forgive me, Mother. (*A pause — smilingly.*) It was Simon who felt guilty and repentant. If he'd had his way, he'd be out of bed now, and the two of us would be walking around in the night, trying to wake up someone who could marry us. But I was so drunk with love, I'd lost all thought or care about marriage. I'd got to the place where all you know or care is that you belong to love, and you can't call your soul your own any more, let alone your body, and you're proud you've given them to love. (*She pauses — then teasing lovingly.*) Sure, I've always known you're the sweetest woman in the world, Mother, but I never suspected you were a wise woman too, until I knew tonight the truth of what you said this morning, that a woman can forgive whatever the man she loves could do and still love him, because it was through him she found the love in herself; that, in one way, he doesn't count at all, because it's love, your own love, your love in him, and to keep that your pride will do anything. (*She smiles with a self-mocking happiness.*) It's love's slaves we are, Mother, not men's — and wouldn't it shame their boasting and vanity if we ever let them know our secret? (*She laughs — then suddenly looks guilty.*) But I'm talking great nonsense. I'm glad Simon can't hear me. (*She pauses. Nora is worrying and hasn't listened. Sara goes on.*) Yes, I can even understand now — a little anyway — how you can still love Father and be proud of it, in spite of what he is.

NORA (*at the mention of Melody, comes out of her brooding*). Hush now! (*Miserably.*) God help us, Sara, why doesn't he come, what's happened to him?

SARA (*gets to her feet exasperatedly*). Don't be a fool, Mother. (*Bitterly.*) Nothing's happened except he's made a public disgrace of himself, for Simon's mother to sneer at. If she wanted revenge on him, I'm sure she's had her fill of it. Well, I don't care. He deserves it. I warned him and I begged him, and got called a peasant slut and a whore for my pains. All I hope now is that whatever happened wakes him from his lies and mad dreams so he'll have to face the truth of himself in that mirror. (*Sneeringly.*) But there's devil a chance he'll ever let that happen. Instead, he'll come home as drunk as two lords, boasting of his glorious victory over old Harford, whatever the truth is!

(*But Nora isn't listening. She has heard the click of the latch on the street door at rear.*)

NORA (*excitedly*). Look, Sara!

(*The door is opened slowly and Jamie Cregan sticks his head in cautiously to peer around the room. His face is battered, nose red and swollen, lips cut and puffed, and one eye so blackened it is almost closed. Nora's first reaction is a cry of relief.*)

Praise be to the Saints, you're back, Jamie!

CREGAN (*puts a finger to his lips — cautioningly*). Whist!

NORA (*frightenedly*). Jamie! Where's himself?

CREGAN (*sharply*). Whist, I'm telling you! (*In a whisper.*) I've got him in a rig outside, but I had to make sure no one was here. Lock the bar door, Sara, and I'll bring him in.

(*She goes and turns the key in the door, her expression contemptuous. Cregan then disappears, leaving the street door half open.*)

NORA. Did you see Jamie's face? They've been fightin' terrible. Oh, I'm afraid, Sara.

SARA. Afraid of what? It's only what I told you to

expect. A crazy row — and now he's paralysed drunk.

(*Cregan appears in the doorway at rear. He is half leading, half supporting Melody. The latter moves haltingly and woodenly. But his movements do not seem those of drunkenness. It is more as if a sudden shock or stroke had shattered his co-ordination and left him in a stupor. His scarlet uniform is filthy and torn and pulled awry. The pallor of his face is ghastly. He has a cut over his left eye, a blue swelling on his left cheekbone, and his lips are cut and bloody. From a big raw bruise on his forehead, near the temple, trickles of dried blood run down to his jaw. Both his hands are swollen, with skinned knuckles, as are Cregan's. His eyes are empty and lifeless. He stares at his wife and daughter as if he did not recognize them.*)

NORA (*rushes and puts her arm around him*). Con, darlin'! Are you hurted bad?

(*He pushes her away without looking at her. He walks dazedly to his chair at the head of the centre table. Nora follows him, breaking into lamentations.*)

Con, don't you know me? Oh, God help us, look at his head!

SARA. Be quiet, Mother. Do you want them in the bar to know he's come home — the way he is. (*She gives her father a look of disgust.*)

CREGAN. Ay, that's it, Sara. We've got to rouse him first. His pride'd nivir forgive us if we let thim see him dead bate like this.

(*There is a pause. They stare at him and he stares sightlessly at the table top. Nora stands close to his side, behind the table, on his right, Sara behind her on her right, Cregan at right of Sara.*)

SARA. He's drunk, isn't that all it is, Jamie?

CREGAN (*sharply*). He's not. He's not taken a drop since we left here. It's the clouts on the head he got, that's what ails him. A taste of whiskey would bring him back, if he'd only take it, but he won't.

SARA (*gives her father a puzzled, uneasy glance*). He won't?

NORA (*gets the decanter and a glass and hands them to Cregan*). Here. Try and make him.

CREGAN (*pours out a big drink and puts it before Melody — coaxingly*). Drink this now, Major, and you'll be right as rain!

(*Melody does not seem to notice. His expression remains blank and dead. Cregan scratches his head puzzledly.*)

He won't. That's the way he's been all the way back when I tried to persuade him. (*Then irritably.*) Well, if he won't, I will, be your leave. I'm needin' it bad. (*He downs the whiskey, and pours out another — to Nora and Sara.*) It's the divil's own rampage we've had.

SARA (*quietly contemptuous, but still with the look of puzzled uneasiness at her father*). From your looks it must have been.

CREGAN (*indignantly*). You're takin' it cool enough, and you seein' the marks av the batin' we got! (*He downs his second drink — boastfully.*) But if we're marked, there's others is marked worse and some av thim is police!

NORA. God be praised! The dirty cowards!

SARA. Be quiet, Mother. Tell us what happened, Jamie.

CREGAN. Faix, what didn't happen? Be the rock av Cashel, I've nivir engaged in a livelier shindy! We had no trouble findin' where Harford lived. It's a grand mansion, with a big walled garden behind it, and we wint to the front door. A flunkey in livery answered wid two others behind. A big black naygur one was. That pig av a lawyer must have warned Harford to expect us. Con spoke wid the airs av a lord. 'Kindly inform your master,' he says, 'that Major Cornelius Melody, late of His Majesty's Seventh Dragoons, respectfully requests a word with him.' Well, the flunkey put an insolent sneer on him. 'Mr Harford won't see you,' he says. I could see Con's rage risin' but he kept polite. 'Tell him,' he says, 'if he knows what's good for him he'll see me. For if he don't, I'll come in and see him.' 'Ye will, will ye?' says the flunkey, 'I'll have you know Mr Harford don't allow drunken Micks to come here disturbing him. The police have been informed,' he says, 'and you'll be arrested if you make trouble.' Then he started to shut the door. 'Anyway, you've come to the wrong door,' he says, 'the place for the loiks av you is the servants' entrance.'

NORA (*angrily*). Och, the impident divil!

SARA (*in spite of herself her temper has been rising. She looks at Melody with angry scorn*). You let Harford's servants insult you! (*Then quickly.*) But it serves you right! I knew what would happen! I warned you!

CREGAN. Let thim be damned! Kape your mouth shut, and lave me tell it, and you'll see if we let them! When he'd said that, the flunkey tried to slam the door in our faces, but Con was too quick. He pushed it back on him and lept in the hall, roarin' mad, and hit the flunkey a cut with his whip across his ugly mug that set him screaming like a stuck pig!

NORA (*enthusiastically*). Good for you, Con darlin'!

SARA (*humiliatedly*). Mother! Don't! (*To Melody with biting scorn.*) The famous duellist — in a drunken brawl with butlers and coachmen!

(*But he is staring sightlessly at the table top as if he didn't see her or know her.*)

CREGAN (*angrily, pouring himself another drink*). Shut your mouth, Sara, and don't be trying to plague him. You're wastin' breath anyway, the way he is. He doesn't know you or hear you. And don't put on lady's airs about fighting when you're the whole cause of it.

SARA (*angrily*). It's a lie! You know I tried to stop —

CREGAN (*gulps down his drink, ignoring this, and turns to Nora — enthusiastically*). Wait till you hear, Nora! (*He plunges into the midst of battle again.*) The naygur hit me a clout that had my head dizzy. He'd have had me down only Con broke the butt av the whip over his black skull and knocked him to his knees. Then the third man punched Con and I gave him a kick where it'd do him least good, and he rolled on the floor, grabbin' his guts. The naygur was in again and grabbed me, but Con came at him and knocked him down. Be the mortal, we had the three av thim licked, and we'd have dragged auld Harford from his burrow and tanned his Yankee hide if the police hadn't come!

NORA (*furiously*). Arrah, the dirthy cowards! Always takin' sides with the rich Yanks against the poor Irish!

SARA (*more and more humiliated and angry and torn by conflicting emotions — pleadingly*). Mother! Can't you keep still?

CREGAN. Four av thim wid clubs came behind us. They grabbed us before we knew it and dragged us into the street. Con broke away and hit the one that held him, and I gave one a knee in his belly. And then, glory be, there was a fight! Oh, it'd done your heart good to see himself! He was worth two men, lettin' out right and left, roarin' wid rage and cursin' like a trooper —

MELODY (*without looking up or any change in his dazed expression, suddenly speaks in a jeering mumble to himself*). Bravely done, Major Melody! The Commander of the Forces honours your exceptional gallantry! Like the glorious field of Talavera! Like the charge on the French square! Cursing like a drunken, foul-mouthed son of a thieving shebeen keeper who sprang from the filth of a peasant hovel, with pigs on the floor — with that pale Yankee bitch watching from a window, sneering with disgust!

NORA (*frightenedly*). God preserve us, it's crazed he is!

SARA (*stares at him startled and wondering. For a second there is angry pity in her eyes. She makes an impulsive move towards him*). Father! (*Then her face hardening.*) He isn't crazed, Mother. He's come to his senses for once in his life! (*To Melody.*) So she was sneering, was she? I don't blame her! I'm glad you've been taught a lesson! (*Then vindictively.*) But I've taught her one, too. She'll soon sneer from the wrong side of her mouth!

CREGAN (*angrily*). Will you shut your gab, Sara! Lave him be and don't heed him. It's the same crazy blather he's talked every once in a while since they brought him to — about the Harford woman — and speakin' av the pigs and his father one minute, and his pride and honour and his mare the next. (*He takes up the story again.*) Well, anyways, they was too much for us, the four av thim wid clubs. The last thing I saw before I was knocked senseless was three av thim clubbing Con. But, be the powers, we wint down fightin' to the last for the glory av auld Ireland!

MELODY (*in a jeering mutter to himself*). Like a rum-soaked trooper, brawling before a brothel on a Saturday night, puking in the gutter!

SARA (*strickenly*). Don't, Father!

CREGAN (*indignantly to Melody*). We wasn't in condition. If we had been — but they knocked us senseless and rode us to the station and locked us up. And we'd be there yet if Harford hadn't made thim turn us loose, for he's rich and has influence. Small thanks to him! He was afraid the row would get in the paper and put shame on him!

(*Melody laughs crazily and springs to his feet. He sways dizzily, clutching his head — then goes towards the door at left front.*)

NORA. Con! Where are you goin'?

(*She starts after him and grabs his arm. He shakes her hand off roughly as if he did not recognize her.*)

CREGAN. He don't know you. Don't cross him now, Nora. Sure, he's only goin' upstairs to bed. (*Wheedlingly.*) You know what's best for you, don't you, Major?

(*Melody feels his way gropingly through the door and disappears, leaving it open.*)

SARA (*uneasy, but consoling her mother*). Jamie's right, Mother. If he'll fall asleep, that's the best thing — (*Abruptly she is terrified.*) Oh God, maybe he'll take revenge on Simon — (*She rushes to the door and stands listening — with relief.*) No, he's gone to his room. (*She comes back — a bit ashamed.*) I'm a fool. He'd never harm a sick man, no matter — (*She takes her mother's arm — gently.*) Don't stand there, Mother. Sit down. You're tired enough —

NORA (*frightenedly*). I've never heard him talk like that in all the years — with that crazy dead look in his eyes. Oh, I'm afeered, Sara. Lave go of me. I've got to make sure he's gone to bed.

(*She goes quickly to the door and disappears. Sara makes a move to follow her.*)

CREGAN (*roughly*). Stay here, unless you're a fool, Sara. He might come to all av a sudden and give you a hell av a thrashin'. Troth, you deserve one. You're to blame for what's happened. Wasn't he fightin' to revenge the insults to you? (*He sprawls on a chair at rear of the table at centre.*)

SARA (*sitting down at rear of the small table at left front — angrily*). I'll thank you to mind your own business, Jamie Cregan. Just because you're a relation —

CREGAN (*harshly*). Och, to hell with your airs? (*He

pours out a drink and downs it. He is becoming drunk again.)

SARA. I can revenge my own insults, and I have! I've beaten the Harfords — and he's only made a fool of himself for her to sneer at. But I've beaten her and I'll sneer last! (*She pauses, a hard, triumphant smile on her lips. It fades. She gives a little bewildered laugh.*) God forgive me, what a way to think of — I must be crazy, too.

CREGAN (*drunkenly*). Ah, don't be talkin'! Didn't the two of us lick them all! And Con's all right. He's all right, I'm sayin'! It's only the club on the head makes him quare a while. I've seen it often before. Ay, and felt it meself. I remember at a fair in the auld country I was clouted with the butt av a whip and I didn't remember a thing for hours, but they told me after I never stopped gabbin' but went around tellin' every stranger all my secrets. (*He pauses. Sara hasn't listened. He goes on uneasily.*) All the same, it's no fun listening to his mad blather about the pale bitch, as he calls her, like she was a ghost, haunting and scorning him. And his gab about his beautiful thoroughbred mare is madder still, raving what a grand, beautiful lady she is, with her slender ankles and dainty feet, sobbin' and beggin' her forgiveness and talkin' of dishonour and death — (*He shrinks superstitiously — then angrily, reaching for the decanter.*) Och, be damned to this night!

(*Before he can pour a drink, Nora comes hurrying in from the door at left front.*)

NORA (*breathless and frightened*). He's come down! He pushed me away like he didn't see me. He's gone out to the barn. Go after him, Jamie.

CREGAN (*drunkenly*). I won't. He's all right. Lave him alone.

SARA (*jeeringly*). Sure, he's only gone to pay a call on his sweetheart, the mare, Mother, and hasn't he slept in her stall many a time when he was dead drunk, and she never even kicked him?

NORA (*distractedly*). Will you shut up, the two av you! I heard him opening the closet in his room where he keeps his auld set of duellin' pistols, and he was carryin' the box when he came down —

CREGAN (*scrambles hastily to his feet*). Oh, the lunatic!

NORA. He'll ride the mare back to Harford's! He'll murther someone! For the love av God, stop him, Jamie!

CREGAN (*drunkenly belligerent*). Be Christ, I'll stop him for you, Nora, pistols or no pistols! (*He walks a bit unsteadily out the door at left front.*)

SARA (*stands tensely — bursts out with a strange triumphant pride.*) Then he's not beaten! (*Suddenly she is overcome by a bitter, tortured revulsion of feeling.*) Merciful God, what am I thinking? As if he hadn't done enough to destroy — (*Distractedly.*) Oh, the mad fool! I wish he was —

(*From the yard, off right front, there is the muffled crack of a pistol shot hardly perceptible above the noise in the barroom. But Sara and Nora both hear it and stand frozen with horror. Sara babbles hysterically.*)

I didn't mean it, Mother! I didn't!

NORA (*numb with fright — mumbles stupidly*). A shot!

SARA. You know I didn't mean it, Mother!

NORA. A shot! God help us, he's kilt Jamie!

SARA (*stammers*). No—not Jamie — (*Wildly.*) Oh, I can't bear waiting! I've got to know — (*She rushes to the door at left front — then stops frightenedly.*) I'm afraid to know! I'm afraid —

NORA (*mutters stupidly*). Not Jamie? Then who else? (*She begins to tremble — in a horrified whisper.*) Sara! You think — Oh, God have mercy!

SARA. Will you hush, Mother! I'm trying to hear — (*She retreats quickly into the room and backs around the table at left front until she is beside her mother.*) Someone's at the yard door. It'll be Jamie coming to tell us —

NORA. It's a lie! He'd nivir. He'd nivir!

(*They stand paralysed by terror, clinging to each other, staring at the open door. There is a moment's pause in which the sound of drunken roistering in the bar seems louder. Then Melody appears in the doorway with Cregan behind him. Cregan has him by the shoulder and pushes him roughly into the room, like a bouncer handling a drunk. Cregan is shaken by the experience he has just been through and his reaction is to make him drunkenly angry at Melody. In his free hand is a duelling pistol. Melody's face is like grey wax. His body is limp, his feet drag, his eyes seem to have no sight. He appears completely possessed by a paralysing stupor.*)

SARA (*impulsively*). Father! Oh, thank God! (*She takes one step towards him — then her expression begins to harden.*)

NORA (*sobs with relief*). Oh, praise God you're alive! Sara and me was dead with fear — (*She goes towards them.*) Con! Con, darlin'!

CREGAN (*dumps Melody down on the nearest chair at left of the small table — roughly, his voice trembling*). Let you sit still now, Con Melody, and behave like a gintleman! (*To Nora.*) Here he is for ye, Nora, and you're welcome, bad luck to him!

(*He moves back as Nora comes and puts her arms around Melody and hugs him tenderly.*)

NORA. Oh, Con, Con, I was so afeered for you! (*He does not seem to hear or see her, but she goes on crooning to him comfortingly as if he were a sick child.)*

CREGAN. He was in the stable. He'd this pistol in his hand, with the mate to it on the floor beside the mare. (*He shudders and puts the pistol on the table shakenly.*) It's mad he's grown entirely! Let you take care av him now, his wife and daughter! I've had enough. I'm no damned keeper av lunatics! (*He turns towards the barroom.*)

SARA. Wait, Jamie. We heard a shot. What was it?

CREGAN (*angrily*). Ask him, not me! (*Then with bewildered horror.*) He kilt the poor mare, the mad fool! (*Sara stares at him in stunned amazement.*) I found him on the floor with his head in his lap, and her dead. He was sobbing like a soul in hell — (*He shudders.*) Let me get away from the sight of him where there's men in their right senses laughing and singing! (*He unlocks the barroom door.*) And don't be afraid, Sara, that I'll tell the boys a word av this. I'll talk of our fight in the city only, because it's all I want to remember.

(*He jerks open the door and goes in the bar, slamming the door quickly behind him. A roar of welcome is heard as the crowd greets his arrival. Sara locks the door again. She comes back to the centre table, staring at Melody, an hysterical, sneering grin making her lips quiver and twitch.*)

SARA. What a fool I was to be afraid! I might know you'd never do it as long as a drink of whiskey was left in the world! So it was the mare you shot?

(*She bursts into uncontrollable, hysterical laughter. It penetrates Melody's stupor and he stiffens rigidly on his chair, but his eyes remain fixed on the table top.*)

NORA. Sara! Stop! For the love av God, how can you laugh — !

SARA. I can't — help it, Mother. Didn't you hear — Jamie? It was the mare he shot! (*She gives way to laughter again.*)

NORA (*distractedly*). Stop it, I'm sayin'!

(*Sara puts her hand over her mouth to shut off the sound of her laughing, but her shoulders still shake. Nora sinks on the chair at rear of the table. She mutters dazedly.*)

Kilt his beautiful mare? He must be mad entirely.

MELODY (*suddenly speaks, without looking up, in the broadest brogue, his voice coarse and harsh*). Lave Sara laugh. Sure, who could blame her? I'm roarin' meself inside me. It's the damnedest joke a man ivir played on himself since time began.

(*They stare at him. Sara's laughter stops. She is startled and repelled by his brogue. Then she stares at him suspiciously, her face hardening.*)

SARA. What joke? Do you think murdering the poor mare a good joke?

(*Melody stiffens for a second, but that is all. He doesn't look up or reply.*)

NORA (*frightened*). Look at the dead face on him, Sara. He's like a corpse. (*She reaches out and touches one of his hands on the table top with a furtive tenderness — pleadingly.*) Con, darlin'. Don't!

MELODY (*looks up at her. His expression changes so that his face loses all its remaining distinction and appears vulgar and common, with a loose, leering grin on his swollen lips*). Let you not worry, Allanah. Sure, I'm no corpse, and with a few drinks in me, I'll soon be lively enough to suit you.

NORA (*miserably confused*). Will you listen to him, Sara — puttin' on the brogue to torment us.

SARA (*growing more uneasy but sneering*). Pay no heed to him, Mother. He's play-acting to amuse himself. If he's that cruel and shameless after what he's done —

NORA (*defensively*). No, it's the blow on the head he got fightin' the police.

MELODY (*vulgarly*). The blow, me foot! That's Jamie Cregan's blather. Sure, it'd take more than a few clubs on the head to darken my wits long. Me brains, if I have any, is clear as a bell. And I'm not puttin' on brogue to tormint you, me darlint. Nor play-actin', Sara. That was the Major's game. It's quare, surely, for the two av ye to object when I talk in me natural tongue, and yours, and don't put on airs loike the late lamented auld liar and lunatic, Major Cornelius Melody, av His Majesty's Seventh Dragoons, used to do.

NORA. God save us, Sara, will you listen!

MELODY. But he's dead now, and his last bit av lyin' pride is murthered and stinkin'. (*He pats Nora's hand with what seems to be genuine comforting affection.*) So let you be aisy, darlint. He'll nivir again hurt you with his sneers, and his pretindin' he's a gintleman, blatherin' about pride and honour, and his boastin' av duels in the days that's gone, and his showin' off before the Yankees, and thim laughin' at him, prancing around drunk on his beautiful thoroughbred mare — (*He gulps as if he were choking back a sob.*) For she's dead, too, poor baste.

SARA (*this is becoming unbearable for her — tensely*). Why — why did you kill her?

MELODY. Why did the Major, you mean! Be Christ, you're stupider than I thought you, if you can't see that. Wasn't she the livin' reminder, so to spake, av all his lyin' boasts and dreams? He meant to kill her first wid one pistol, and then himself wid the other. But faix, he saw the shot that killed her had finished him, too. There wasn't much pride left in the auld lunatic, anyway, and seeing her die made an end av him. So he didn't bother shooting himself, because it'd be a mad thing to waste a good bullet on a corpse! (*He laughs coarsely.*)

SARA (*tensely*). Father! Stop it!

MELODY. Didn't I tell you there was a great joke in it? Well, that's the joke. (*He begins to laugh again but he chokes on a stifled sob. Suddenly his face loses the coarse, leering, brutal expression and is full of anguished grief. He speaks without brogue, not to them but aloud to himself.*) Blessed Christ, the look in her eyes by the lantern light with life ebbing out of them — wondering and sad, but still trustful, not reproaching me — with no fear in them — proud, understanding pride — loving me — she saw I was dying with her. She understood! She forgave me! (*He starts to sob but wrenches himself out of it and speaks in broad, jeering brogue.*) Begorra, if that wasn't the mad Major's ghost speakin'! But be damned to him, he won't haunt me long, if I know it! I intind to live at my ease from now on and not let the dead bother me, but enjoy life in my proper station as auld Nick Melody's son. I'll bury his Major's damned red livery av bloody England deep in the ground and he can haunt its grave if he likes, and boast to the lonely night av Talavera and the ladies of Spain and fightin' the French! (*With a leer.*) Troth, I think the boys is right when they say he stole the uniform and he nivir fought under Wellington at all. He was a terrible liar, as I remember him.

NORA. Con, darlin', don't be grievin' about the mare. Sure, you can get another. I'll manage —

SARA. Mother! Hush! (*To Melody, furiously.*) Father, will you stop this mad game you're playing — ?

MELODY (*roughly*). Game, is it? You'll find it's no game. It was the Major played a game all his life, the crazy auld loon, and cheated only himself. But I'll be content to stay meself in the proper station I was born to, from this day on. (*With a cunning leer at Sara.*) And it's meself feels it me duty to give you a bit av fatherly advice, Sara darlint, while my mind is on it. I know you've great ambition, so remember it's to hell wid honour if ye want to rise in this world. Remember the blood in your veins and be your grandfather's true descendant. There was an able man for you! Be Jaysus, he nivir felt anything beneath him that could gain him something, and for lyin' tricks to swindle the bloody fools of gintry, there wasn't his match in Ireland, and he ended up wid a grand estate, and a castle, and a pile av gold in the bank.

SARA (*distractedly*). Oh, I hate you!

NORA. Sara!

MELODY (*goes on as if he hadn't heard*). I know he'd advise that to give you a first step up, darlint, you must make the young Yankee gintleman have you in his bed, and afther he's had you, weep great tears and appeal to his honour to marry you and save yours. Be God, he'll nivir resist that, if I know him, for he's a young fool, full av dacency and dreams, and looney, too, wid a touch av the poet in him. Oh, it'll be aisy for you —

SARA (*goaded beyond bearing*). I'll make you stop your dirty brogue and your play-acting! (*She leans towards him and speaks with taunting vindictiveness, in broad brogue herself.*) Thank you kindly but I've already taken your wise advice, Father. I made him have me in his bed, while you was out drunk fightin' the police!

NORA (*frightenedly*). Sara! Hault your brazen tongue!

MELODY (*his body stiffens on his chair and the coarse leer vanishes from his face. It becomes his old face. His eyes fix on her in a threatening stare. He speaks slowly, with difficulty keeping his words in brogue*). Did you now, God bless you! I might have known you'd not take any chance that the auld loon av a Major, going out to revenge an insult to you, would spoil your schemes. (*He forces a horrible grin.*) Be the living God, it's me should be proud this night that one av the Yankee gintry has stooped to be seduced by my slut av a daughter!

(*Still keeping his eyes fixed on hers, he begins to rise from his chair, his right hand groping along the table top until it clutches the duelling pistol. He aims it at Sara's heart, like an automaton, his eyes as cold, deadly, and merciless as they must have been in his duels of long ago. Sara is terrified but she stands unflinchingly.*)

NORA (*horror-stricken, lunges from her chair and grabs his arm*). Con! For the love av God! Would you be murthering Sara? (*A dazed look comes over his face. He grows limp and sinks back on his chair and lets the pistol slide from his fingers on the table. He draws a shuddering breath — then laughs hoarsely.*)

MELODY (*with a coarse leer*). Murtherin' Sara, is it? Are ye daft, Nora? Sure, all I want is to congratulate her!

SARA (*hopelessly*). Oh! (*She sinks down on her chair at rear of the centre table and covers her face with her hands.*)

NORA (*with pitifully well-meant reassurance*). It's all right, Con. The young lad wants to marry her as soon as can be, she told me, and he did before.

MELODY. Musha, but that's kind of him! Be God, we ought to be proud av our daughter, Nora. Lave it to her to get what she wants by hook or crook. And won't we be proud watchin' her rise in the world till she's a grand lady!

NORA (*simply*). We will, surely.

SARA. Mother!

MELODY. She'll have some trouble, rootin' out his dreams. He's set in his proud, noble ways, but she'll find the right trick! I'd lay a pound, if I had one, to a shilling she'll see the day when she'll wear fine silks and drive in a carriage wid a naygur coachman behind spankin' thoroughbreds, her nose in the air; and she'll live in a Yankee mansion, as big as a castle, on a grand estate av stately woodland and soft green meadows and a lake. (*With a leering chuckle.*) Be the Saints, I'll start her on her way by making her a wedding present av the Major's place where he let her young gintleman build his cabin — the land the Yankees swindled him into buyin' for his American estate, the mad fool! (*He glances at the duelling pistol — jeeringly.*) Speakin' av the departed, may his soul roast in hell, what am I doin' wid his pistol? Be God, I don't need pistols. Me fists, or a club if it's handy, is enough. Didn't me and Jamie lick a whole regiment av police this night?

NORA (*stoutly*). You did, and if there wasn't so many av thim —

MELODY (*turns to her — grinningly*). That's the talk, darlint! Sure, there's divil a more loyal wife in the whole world — (*He pauses, staring at her — then suddenly kisses her on the lips, roughly but with a strange real tenderness.*) and I love you.

NORA (*with amazed, unthinking joy*). Oh, Con!

MELODY (*grinning again*). I've meant to tell you often, only the Major, damn him, had me under his proud thumb. (*He pulls her over and kisses her hair.*)

NORA. Is it kissin' my hair — !

MELODY. I am. Why wouldn't I? You have beautiful hair, God bless you! And don't remember what the Major used to tell you. The gintleman's sneers he put on is buried with him. I'll be a real husband to you, and help ye run this shebeen, instead of being a sponge. I'll fire Mickey and tend the bar myself, like my father's son ought to.

NORA. You'll not! I'll nivir let you!

MELODY (*leering cunningly*). Well, I offered, remember. It's you refused. Sure, I'm not in love with work, I'll confess, and maybe you're right not to trust me too near the whiskey. (*He licks his lips.*) Be Jaysus, that reminds me. I've not had a taste for hours. I'm dyin' av thirst.

NORA (*starts to rise*). I'll get you —

MELODY (*pushes her back on her chair*). Ye'll not. I want company and singin' and dancin' and great laughter. I'll join the boys in the bar and help Cousin Jamie celebrate our wonderful shindy wid the police. (*He gets up. His old soldierly bearing is gone. He slouches and his movements are shambling and clumsy, his big hairy hands dangling at his sides. In his torn, dishevelled, dirt-stained uniform, he looks like a loutish grinning clown.*)

NORA. You ought to go to bed, Con darlin', with your head hurted.

MELODY. Me head? Faix, it was nivir so clear while the Major lived to tormint me, makin' me tell mad lies to excuse his divilments. (*He grins.*) And I ain't tired a bit. I'm fresh as a man new born. So I'll say good night to you, darlint.

(*He bends and kisses her. Sara has lifted her tearstained face from her hands and is staring at him with a strange, anguished look of desperation. He leers at her.*)

And you go to bed, too, Sara. Troth, you deserve a long, dreamless slape after all you've accomplished this day.

SARA. Please! Oh, Father, I can't bear — Won't you be yourself again?

MELODY (*threatening her good-humouredly*). Let you kape your mouth closed, ye slut, and not talk like you was ashamed of me, your father. I'm not the Major who was too much of a gintleman to lay hand on you. Faix, I'll give you a box on the ear that'll teach you respect, if ye kape on trying to raise the dead!

(*She stares at him, sick and desperate. He starts towards the bar door.*)

SARA (*springs to her feet*). Father! Don't go in with those drunken scum! Don't let them hear and see you! You can drink all you like here. Jamie will come and keep you company. He'll laugh and sing and help you celebrate Talavera —

MELODY (*roughly*). To hell with Talavera! (*His eyes are fastened on the mirror. He leers into it.*) Be Jaysus, if it ain't the mirror the auld loon was always admirin' his mug in while he spouted Byron to pretend himself was a lord wid a touch av the poet — (*He strikes a pose which is a vulgar burlesque of his old before-the-mirror one and recites in mocking brogue.*)

'I have not loved the World, nor the World me;
I have not flatthered uts rank breath, nor bowed
To uts idolatries a pashunt knee,
Nor coined me cheek to smiles, — nor cried aloud
In worship av an echo: in the crowd
They couldn't deem me one av such — I stood
Among thim, but not av thim . . .'

(*He guffaws contemptuously.*) Be Christ, if he wasn't the joke av the world, the Major. He should have been a clown in a circus. God rest his soul in the flames av tormint! (*Roughly.*) But to hell wid the dead.

(*The noise in the bar rises to an uproar of laughter as if Jamie had just made some climactic point in his story. Melody looks away from the mirror to the bar door.*)

Be God, *I'm* alive and in the crowd they *can* deem me one av such! I'll be among thim and av thim, too — and make up for the lonely dog's life the Major led me. (*He goes to the bar door.*)

SARA (*starts towards him — beseechingly*). Father! Don't put this final shame on yourself. You're not drunk now. There's no excuse you can give yourself. You'll be as dead to yourself after, as if you'd shot yourself along with the mare!

MELODY (*leering — with a wink at Nora*). Listen to her, Nora, reproachin' me because I'm not drunk. Troth, that's a condition soon mended. (*He puts his hand on the knob of the door.*)

SARA. Father!

NORA (*has given way to such complete physical exhaustion, she hardly hears, much less comprehends what is said — dully*). Lave him alone, Sara. It's best.

MELODY (*as another roar is heard from the bar*). I'm missin' a lot av fun. Be God, I've a bit of news to tell the boys that'll make them roar the house down. The Major's passin' to his eternal rest has set me free to jine the Democrats, and I'll vote for Andy Jackson, the friend av the common men like me, God bless him! (*He grins with anticipation.*) Wait till the boys hear that! (*He starts to turn the knob.*)

SARA (*rushes to him and grabs his arm*). No! I won't let you! It's my pride, too! (*She stammers.*) Listen! Forgive me, Father! I know it's my fault — always sneering and insulting you — but I only meant the lies in it. The truth — Talavera — the Duke praising your bravery — an officer in his army — even the ladies in Spain — deep down that's been my pride, too — that I was your daughter. So don't — I'll do anything you ask — I'll even tell Simon — that after his father's insult to you — I'm too proud to marry a Yankee coward's son!

MELODY (*has been visibly crumbling as he listens until he appears to have no character left in which to hide and defend himself. He cries wildly and despairingly, as if he saw his last hope of escape cut off*). Sara! For the love of God, stop — let me go — !

NORA (*dully*). Lave your poor father be. It's best.

(*In a flash Melody recovers and is the leering peasant again.*)

SARA (*with bitter hopelessness*). Oh, Mother! Why couldn't you be still!

MELODY (*roughly*). Why can't you, ye mean. I warned ye what ye'd get if ye kept on interferin' and tryin' to raise the dead.

(*He cuffs her on the side of the head. It is more of a playful push than a blow, but it knocks her off balance back to the end of the table at centre.*)

NORA (*aroused — bewilderedly*). God forgive you, Con! (*Angrily.*) Don't be hittin' Sara now. I've put up with a lot but I won't —

MELODY (*with rough good nature*). Shut up, darlint. I won't have to again. (*He grins lovingly at Sara.*) That'll teach you, me proud Sara! I know you won't try raisin' the dead any more. And let me hear no more gab out of you about not marryin' the young lad upstairs. Be Jaysus, haven't ye any honour? Ye seduced him and ye'll make an honest gentleman av him if I have to march ye both by the scruff av the neck to the nearest church. (*He chuckles — then leeringly.*) And now with your permission, ladies both, I'll join me good friends in the bar.

(*He opens the door and passes into the bar, closing the door behind him. There is a roar of welcoming drunken shouts, pounding of glasses on bar and tables, then quiet, as if he had raised a hand for silence, followed by his voice greeting them and ordering drinks, and other roars of acclaim mingled with the music of Riley's pipes. Sara remains standing by the side of the centre table, her shoulders bowed, her head hanging, staring at the floor.*)

NORA (*overcome by physical exhaustion again, sighs*). Don't mind his giving you a slap. He's still quare in his head. But he'll sing and laugh and drink a power av whiskey and slape sound after, and tomorrow he'll be himself again — maybe.

SARA (*dully — aloud to herself rather than to her mother*). No. He'll never be. He's beaten at last and he wants to stay beaten. Well, I did my best. Though why I did, I don't know. I must have his crazy pride in me. (*She lifts her head, her face hardening — bitterly.*) I mean, the late Major Melody's pride. I mean, I did have it. Now it's dead — thank God — and I'll make a better wife for Simon.

(*There is a sudden lull in the noise from the bar, as if someone had called for silence — then Melody's voice is plainly heard in the silence as he shouts a toast: 'Here's to our next President, Andy Jackson! Hurroo for Auld Hickory, God bless him!' There is a drunken chorus of answering 'hurroos' that shake the walls.*)

NORA. Glory be to God, cheerin' for Andy Jackson! Did you hear him, Sara?

SARA (*her face hard*). I heard someone. But it wasn't anyone I ever knew or want to know.

NORA (*as if she hadn't heard*). Ah well, that's good. They won't all be hatin' him now. (*She pauses — her tired, worn face becomes suddenly shy and tender.*) Did you hear him tellin' me he loved me, Sara? Did you see him kiss me on the mouth — and then kiss my hair? (*She gives a little, soft laugh.*) Sure, he must have gone mad altogether!

SARA (*stares at her mother. Her face softens*). No, Mother, I know he meant it. He'll keep on meaning it, too, Mother. He'll be free to, now. (*She smiles strangely.*) Maybe I deserved the slap for interfering.

NORA (*preoccupied with her own thoughts*). And if he wants to kape on makin' game of everyone, puttin' on the brogue and actin' like one av thim in there — (*She nods towards the bar.*) Well, why shouldn't he if it brings him peace and company in his loneliness? God pity him, he's had to live all his life alone in the hell av pride. (*Proudly.*) And I'll play any game he likes and give him love in it. Haven't

I always? (*She smiles.*) Sure, I have no pride at all—except that.

SARA (*stares at her—moved*). You're a strange, noble woman, Mother. I'll try and be like you. (*She comes over and hugs her—then she smiles tenderly.*) I'll wager Simon never heard the shot or anything. He was sleeping like a baby when I left him. A cannon wouldn't wake him.

(*In the bar, Riley starts playing a reel on his pipes and there is the stamp of dancing feet. For a moment Sara's face becomes hard and bitter again. She tries to be mocking.*)

Faith, Patch Riley don't know it but he's playing a requiem for the dead. (*Her voice trembles.*) May the hero of Talavera rest in peace! (*She breaks down and sobs, hiding her face on her mother's shoulder—bewilderedly.*) But why should I cry, Mother? Why do I mourn for him?

NORA (*at once forgetting her own exhaustion, is all tender loving help and comfort*). Don't, darlin', don't. You're destroyed with tiredness, that's all. Come on to bed, now, and I'll help you undress and tuck you in. (*Trying to rouse her—in a teasing tone.*) Shame on you to cry when you have love. What would the young lad think of you?

CURTAIN

MORE STATELY MANSIONS

A Play in Three Acts

Shortened from the author's partly revised script by Karl Ragnar Gierow
and edited by Donald Gallup

Characters

SIMON HARFORD
SARA HARFORD, *his wife*
DEBORAH HARFORD, *his mother*
JOEL HARFORD, *his brother*
NICHOLAS GADSBY, *the Harford family lawyer*
BENJAMIN TENARD, *a banker*

Scenes

ACT ONE

SCENE ONE A log cabin on a small lake near a Massachusetts village. An afternoon in October 1832.

SCENE TWO Deborah Harford's garden, the Henry Harford home in the city. A night in June 1836.

SCENE THREE Sitting-room of Sara Harford's home in a neighbouring textile-mill town. The following night.

ACT TWO

SCENE ONE Simon Harford's office at Simon Harford Inc. in the city. A morning in late summer 1840.

SCENE TWO Deborah Harford's garden. Late afternoon of the same day.

SCENE THREE Parlour of the Harford home. Night of the same day.

ACT THREE

SCENE ONE Simon Harford's office. A morning in mid-summer 1841.

SCENE TWO Deborah Harford's garden. The same night.

ACT ONE, SCENE ONE

SCENE. *A log cabin by a lake in the woods about two miles from a village in Massachusetts. It is just before three in the afternoon of a day in October 1832.*

The cabin is ten feet by fifteen, made of logs with a roof of warped, hand-hewn shingles. It is placed in a small clearing, overgrown with rank, matted grass. The front of the cabin, with a door at centre, and a small window at left of door, overlooks the lake. Another window is in the wall facing right. At the left-rear is a stone chimney. Close by the left and rear of the cabin is the wood—oak, pine, birch, and maple trees. The foliage is at the full of brilliant autumn colour, purple and red and gold mingled with the deep green of the conifers.

The cabin gives evidence of having been abandoned for

years. The mortar between the stones of the chimney has crumbled and fallen out in spots. The moss stuffing between the logs hangs here and there in strips. The windows have boards nailed across them. A weather-beaten bench stands against the front wall, at left of the door. It is home-made, heavily constructed, and is still sturdy.

The clearing is partly in sunlight, partly shadowed by the woods.

As the curtain rises, SARA *(Mrs Simon Harford) appears by the corner of the cabin, right. She is twenty-five, exceedingly pretty in a typically Irish fashion, with a mass of black hair, a fair skin with rosy cheeks, and beautiful deep-blue eyes. There is a curious blending in her appearance of what are commonly considered to be aristocratic and peasant characteristics. She has a fine thoughtful forehead. Her eyes are not only beautiful but intelligent. Her nose is straight and finely modelled. She has small ears set close to her head, a well-shaped head on a slender neck. Her mouth, on the other hand, has a touch of coarse sensuality about its thick, tight lips, and her jaw is a little too long and heavy for the rest of her face, with a quality of masculine obstinacy and determination about it. Her body is concealed by the loose dress of mourning black she wears but, in spite of it, her pregnancy, now six months along, is apparent. One gets the impression of a strong body, full-breasted, full of health and vitality, and retaining its grace despite her condition. Its bad points are thick ankles, large feet, and big hands, broad and strong, with thick, stubby fingers. Her voice is low and musical. She has rid her speech of brogue, except in moments of extreme emotion.*

She has evidently hurried, for she is breathless and panting. She looks around the clearing furtively. Her expression is a mixture of defiant resentment and guilt. She hastily unlocks the door of the cabin and changes the key to the inside. Leaving the door ajar, she comes stealthily to the edge of the woods at left-front, and peers up a path which leads from the clearing into the woods. She starts and darts back to the door, enters the cabin and closes the door noiselessly behind her and locks herself in. For a moment there is silence. Then DEBORAH *(Mrs Henry Harford), Simon's mother, steps into the clearing from the path.*

Deborah is forty-five but looks much younger. She is small, not over five feet tall, with the slender immature figure of a young girl. Her face is small, astonishingly youthful, with only the first tracing of wrinkles about the eyes and mouth. It is framed by a mass of wavy white hair, which by contrast with the youthfulness of her face gives her the appearance of a girl wearing a becoming wig at a costume ball. Her nose is dainty and delicate above a full-lipped mouth, too large and strong for her face, showing big, even, white teeth when she smiles. Her forehead is high and a trifle bulging, with sunken temples. Her eyes are so large they look enormous, black, deep-set, beneath pronounced brows that meet above her nose. Her hands are small with thin, strong, tapering fingers, and she has tiny feet. She is dressed with extreme care and good taste, entirely in white.

DEBORAH *(looks around the clearing—bitterly, forces a self-mocking smile)*. What can you expect, Deborah? At your age, a woman must become resigned to wait upon every man's pleasure, even her son's. *(She picks her way daintily through the grass towards the bench.)* Age? You harp on age as though I were a withered old hag! I still have years before me. *(She sits down.)* And what will you do with these years, Deborah? Dream them away as you have all the other years since Simon deserted you? Dream yourself back until you become not the respectable, if a trifle mad, wife of the well-known merchant, but a noble adventuress of Louis' Court, and your little walled garden the garden of Versailles, your pathetic summer-house a Temple of Love the King has built as an assignation place where he keeps passionate trysts with you, his mistress, greedy for lust and power! Really, Deborah, I begin to believe that truly you must be a little mad! You had better take care! One day you may lose yourself so deeply in that romantic evil, you will not find your way back. *(With defiant bravado.)* Well, let that happen! I would welcome losing myself! *(She stops abruptly—exasperatedly.)* But how stupid! These insane interminable dialogues with self! I must find someone outside myself in whom I can confide, and so escape myself—someone strong and healthy and sane, who dares to love and live life greedily instead of reading and dreaming about it! *(Derisively.)* Ah, you are thinking of the Simon that was, *your* Simon—not the husband of that vulgar Irish biddy, who evidently has found such a comfortable haven in her arms! Yes. Why did I come? Perhaps he is not coming. Perhaps she would not permit him. Am I to sit all afternoon and wait upon his pleasure? *(Springing to her feet.)* I will go! *(Controlling herself—in a forced reasonable tone)*. Nonsense! He told the servant to tell me he would come. He would never break his word to me, not even for her. *(She sits down again.)* It is I who am early. I have only to be patient, keep my mind off bitter thoughts, while away the time—with any dream, no matter how absurd—shut my eyes and forget—not open them until he comes—*(She relaxes, her head back, her eyes shut. A pause. Then she dreams aloud.)* The Palace at Versailles—I wear a gown of crimson satin and gold, embroidered in pearls—Louis gives me his arm, while all the Court watches enviously—the men, old lovers that my ambition has used and discarded, or others who desire to be my lovers but dare not hope—the women who hate me for my wit and beauty, who envy me my greater knowledge of love and of men's hearts—I walk with the King in the gardens—he whispers tenderly: 'My throne it is your heart, Beloved, and my fair kingdom your beauty.' He kisses me on the lips—as I lead him into the little Temple of Love he built for me—

(There is a sound from up the path at left-front, through the woods. Deborah starts quickly and opens her eyes

as SIMON HARFORD *comes into the clearing.*

He is twenty-six but the poise of his bearing makes him appear much more mature. He is tall and loose-jointed with a wiry strength of limb. A long Yankee face, with Indian resemblances, swarthy, with a big straight nose, a wide sensitive mouth, a fine forehead, large ears, thick brown hair, light-brown eyes, set wide apart, their expression sharply observant and shrewd, but in their depths ruminating and contemplative. He speaks quietly, in a deep voice with a slight drawl.)

SIMON. Mother! (*He strides towards her.*)

DEBORAH (*rising—in a tone of arrogant pleasure*). You have been pleased to keep me waiting, Monsieur.

SIMON (*disconcerted—then decides she is joking and laughs*). Not I, Madame! I'm on the dot. It's you who are early. (*He kisses her.*) Mother, it's so good to—

DEBORAH (*her arrogance gone—clinging to him almost hysterically*). Yes! Yes! Dear Simon! (*She begins to sob.*)

SIMON. Mother! Don't! You crying! I don't remember ever seeing you cry.

DEBORAH (*pulling away from him*). No. And it is a poor time to begin. Tears may become a woman while she's young. When she grows old they are merely disgusting. (*She dabs her eyes with her handkerchief.*)

SIMON. You're as young and pretty as ever.

DEBORAH. You are gallant, Sir. My mirror tells me a crueler story. Do you mean to say you don't see all the wrinkles?

SIMON. I can see a few. But for your age—

DEBORAH (*flashes him a resentful glance—then forcing a laugh*). It is true, I am well preserved. But how foolish of us to waste precious moments discussing an old woman's vanity. (*She puts her hands on his shoulders.*) Here. Turn about is fair play. Let me examine you. Yes, you have changed. And quite as I had expected. You are getting your father's successful-merchant look.

SIMON (*frowns and turns away from her*). I hope not! Sit down, Mother. (*She does so. He stands examining the cabin. He tries the door—searches his pocket.*) Funny, I could have sworn I had the key. But perhaps it is better. It would only make me melancholy.

DEBORAH. Yes, it is always sad to contemplate the corpse of a dream.

SIMON (*answers before he thinks*). Yes. (*Then—defensively.*) Unless you have found a finer dream.

DEBORAH. How *is* Sara?

SIMON. Well—and happy.

DEBORAH. You are as much in love as ever?

SIMON. More. I cannot imagine a marriage happier than ours.

DEBORAH. I am glad. You have protested in every letter how happy you were. And the children? Sara expects another before long?

SIMON. Yes.

DEBORAH. All this child-bearing—it must be a strain on Sara. Is she pretty still?

SIMON. More beautiful than ever.

DEBORAH. I was wondering if you would bring her with you today.

SIMON. I thought you wanted to see me alone.

DEBORAH. I did. But perhaps I see now it might have been as well—(*Quickly.*) I had begun to think perhaps Sara might not permit you to come—

SIMON. You talk as though I were a slave.

DEBORAH. Well, one is, isn't one, when one is in love? Or so I have read in the poets.

SIMON. Oh, to love I am a willing slave. But what made you think Sara—?

DEBORAH. Well, a woman's love is jealously possessive—or so I have read—and she knows how close you and I used to be in the old happy days. You were happy in those days with me, weren't you?

SIMON. Of course I was, Mother—never more happy.

DEBORAH. I am glad you still remember, dear. (*She pats his hand*).

SIMON. And I am grateful for all you did for us afterwards.

DEBORAH. It was Sara, wasn't it, who insisted on your paying back what I had meant as a gift?

SIMON. She is very sensitive and proud— (*Hurriedly.*) But she is as grateful to you as I am. She will never forget your kindness.

DEBORAH. I am grateful for her appreciation. Tell me, Simon, do you ever think now of the book you were so eager to write when you resigned in disgust from your father's business and came out here to live alone—your plan for a new society where there would be no rich nor poor. Have you abandoned the idea entirely?

SIMON. For the present. I think of it often.

DEBORAH. I see.

SIMON. What made you ask about that now, Mother?

DEBORAH. This place reminded me, I suppose. And you really should write it. The times are ripe for such a book. With four years more of Mr Jackson in power—and even your father admits he is sure of re-election—the precedent will be irrevocably set. We shall be governed by the ignorant greedy mob for all future time. Your poor father! He wishes Massachusetts would secede from the Union. One has but to mention the name of Jackson to give him violent dyspepsia.

SIMON. It's ridiculous snobbery for him to sneer at the common people. In a free society there must be no private property to tempt men's greed into enslaving one another. We must protect man from his stupid possessive instincts until he can be educated to outgrow them spiritually. In my book I will prove this can easily be done if only men—

DEBORAH. Ah, yes, if only men—and women—were not men and women!

SIMON. You're as cynical as Sara. That is her objection, too. But I'm afraid I'm boring you with my perfect society.

DEBORAH. I'm only too happy to discover the dreamer still exists in you.

SIMON. I haven't spoken of such matters in so long— You were always such a sympathetic audience.

DEBORAH. I still am. But are you, I wonder?

SIMON. I still believe with Rousseau, as firmly as ever, that at bottom human nature is good and unselfish. It is what we are pleased to call civilization that has corrupted it. We must return to Nature and simplicity and then we'll find that the People—those whom Father sneers at as greedy Mob—are as genuinely noble and honourable as the false aristocracy of our present society pretends to be!

DEBORAH. However, I would still be nauseated by their thick ankles, and ugly hands and dirty fingernails, were they ever so noble-hearted! Good Heavens, did I come here to discuss the natural rights of man—I who pray the Second Flood may come and rid the world of this stupid race of men and wash the earth clean! (*She gets to her feet.*) It is getting late, I must go.

SIMON. Go? You've just come! Come. Sit down, Mother. (*She sits down again.*) You haven't told me a word about yourself yet.

DEBORAH. I am afraid, though you might listen kindly, you could not hear me, Simon.

SIMON. I used to hear, didn't I?

DEBORAH. Once long ago. In another life. Before we had both changed.

SIMON. It hurts that you can believe that of me, Mother.

DEBORAH. Oh, I no longer know what to believe about anything or anyone!

SIMON. Not even about me?

DEBORAH. Not even about myself.

SIMON. What has happened, Mother? Is it anything Father has done?

DEBORAH. What an absurd idea! Your father is much too worried about what President Jackson will do or say next, and what effect it will have on imports and exports, to bother with me, even if I would permit him to.

SIMON. Is it anything Joel has done?

DEBORAH. Worse and worse! If you could see your brother now! He is head of the bookkeeping department, which is about as high as his ability can ever take him.

SIMON. I knew Joel had no ability.

DEBORAH. Joel has become a confirmed ledger-worm. I think he tried once to find me listed on the profit side of the ledger. Not finding me there, he concluded he must merely be imagining that I existed. I invited him to visit me in my garden not long ago—

SIMON. What could you want with him?

DEBORAH. Poor Joel! He looked as astounded as if a nun had asked him to her bedroom. And when he came—with the air, I might say, of a correct gentleman who pays a duty call on a woman of whom he disapproves—he determinedly recited impeccable platitudes, stared the flowers out of countenance for half an hour, and then—fled! You would have laughed to see him.

SIMON. Yes, he must have been out of place.

DEBORAH. He was indeed. So you need not be jealous, dear. No, I have not changed because of anything Joel has done. Hardly!

SIMON. Then what is it, Mother?

DEBORAH. Nothing has happened, except time and change.

SIMON. You seem so lonely.

DEBORAH (*patting his hand*). You know that. Now I feel less lonely.

SIMON. It's hard to believe about you. You were always so independent of others.

DEBORAH. But a time comes when, suddenly, discontent gnaws at your heart while you cast longing eyes beyond the garden wall at Life which passes by so horribly unaware that you are still alive!

SIMON. How can you say Life has passed you by? You—

DEBORAH. While you are still beautiful and Life still woos you, it is such a fine gesture of disdainful pride to jilt it. But when the change comes and an indifferent Life jilts *you*— Oh, I realize I am hardly as bad as that yet. But I will be, for I constantly sense in the seconds and minutes and hours flowing through me, the malignant hatred of life against those who have disdained it! But the body is least important. It is the soul, staring into the mirror of itself, seeing the skull of Death leer over its shoulder in the glass!

SIMON (*shrinking with repulsion*). Mother! That's too morbid!

DEBORAH. Poor Simon. Mothers should never have such thoughts, should they? Forgive me.

SIMON. Are you still as accomplished an actress as you used to be?

DEBORAH. Why, what a thing to say, Simon!

SIMON. I was remembering how you used to act out each part when you'd read me fairy stories. One moment you'd be the good fairy, or the good queen, or the poor abused little princess— That was wonderful. But the next moment you'd be the evil queen, or the bad fairy, or the wicked witch, and I'd be all goose-flesh with terror!

DEBORAH. You were extremely sensitive and imaginative—as a child.

SIMON. What role do you play nowadays, Mother?

DEBORAH (*stiffens, avoiding his eyes and forcing a laugh*). Nonsense! You forget I have no audience now.

SIMON (*teasingly*). Oh, you were always your own audience, too. So tell me—

DEBORAH. You would be horribly shocked if I should tell you the nature of the part I play in my eighteenth-century past!

SIMON. Your old wicked witches led me always to be prepared for the worst!

DEBORAH (*playfully, but with a growing undercurrent of compulsive, deadly seriousness as she goes on*). This is more wicked than any witch. This is real life, even though it be past.

SIMON. Well, out with the terrible secret, Mother. I promise not to be too horrified. Are you an evil Queen of France?

DEBORAH (*suddenly seems to loose herself—arrogantly*). No. I prefer to be the secret power behind the Throne—a greedy adventuress who has risen from the gutter to nobility by her wit and charm—who uses love but loves only herself, who is entirely ruthless and lets nothing stand in the way of the final goal of power she has set for herself—to become the favourite of the King and make him, through his passion for her, her slave! (*She ends on a note of strange, passionate exultance.*)

SIMON (*startled and repelled*). Mother! (*She starts dazedly. He goes on quickly.*) No, I am not shocked. It is too damned idiotic! (*She gives a shrinking, cowering movement as though he had struck her in the face.*) No, that's a lie. You really did shock me for a second, Mother. Stunned me, even! (*He chuckles.*) But now I have a picture in my mind of you sitting in your walled-in garden, dressed all in white, so sedulously protected and aloof from all life's sordidness, so delicate and fastidious and spiritually remote—and yet in your dreams playing make-believe with romantic iniquity out of scandalous French memoirs! (*He laughs almost derisively.*)

DEBORAH (*stung to fury, a flash of bitter hatred in her eyes, drawing herself up with fierce, threatening arrogance*). You dare to laugh at me, Monsieur! Take care—! (*Then as he stares at her in petrified amazement, she controls herself and forces an hysterical laugh.*) There! You see! I can still be a convincing actress if I wish! Poor Simon, if you could see your horrified face!

SIMON (*relieved, grins sheepishly*). You did fool me. For a moment I thought you were serious—

DEBORAH. My dear boy, I hope you don't think your poor mother has gone quite insane! But let's forget my stupid joke and return to common sense in the little time left us. How is your business progressing these days? Judging from your letters, you must be making a great success of it.

SIMON. Oh, only in a very modest way as yet, Mother.

DEBORAH. You hope to do even better? I am sure you will—with Sara to inspire you.

SIMON. Yes, it is all for her.

DEBORAH. I see.

SIMON. See what? I owe it to her—

DEBORAH. Of course you do. But I didn't mean that. My thought was fanciful—that perhaps thus you continued to hide from yourself.

SIMON. You are right to call that fanciful.

DEBORAH. Why, in one of your letters, you boasted that the town considered you the most talented of its young merchants.

SIMON. I wasn't boasting, Mother. I thought it would make you laugh.

DEBORAH. Oh, I did laugh then. Now I see there is nothing incongruous about it. After all, you are your father's son. You are so like him now, in many ways, it's astonishing.

SIMON. Oh, nonsense, Mother.

DEBORAH. One would think you were ashamed of your success.

SIMON. Why should I be ashamed?

DEBORAH. Why, indeed? Unless you regret your lost poet's dream of a perfect society.

SIMON. I haven't lost it! And it isn't just a dream. I can prove—

DEBORAH. Oh, I know. Your book. But you said you had given that up.

SIMON. I said I had had no time lately—

DEBORAH. Four years is a long 'lately'. But why should you be ashamed of that?

SIMON. I am not ashamed! Why do you keep insisting? Well, perhaps, now and then, I do feel a little guilty.

DEBORAH. Ah!

SIMON. But I remind myself that what I am doing is merely a means. The end is Sara's happiness. And that justifies any means!

DEBORAH. I've found the means always becomes the end—and the end is always oneself.

SIMON. I propose to retire as soon as we have enough. I'll write my book then.

DEBORAH. You have agreed with Sara how much is enough?

SIMON (*hesitates—then lies*). Yes, of course. (*A pause. He frowns and goes on moodily.*) I'll admit I do get deathly sick of the daily grind of the counting-house— It is not the career I would have chosen. I would have lived here in freedom with Nature, and earned just enough to support myself, and kept my dreams.

DEBORAH. Ah.

SIMON. But when I come home and see Sara's happiness and hold her in my arms, then discontent seems mean and selfish.

DEBORAH. Of course. The danger is that your discontent will grow and grow with your success until— But good Heavens, I sound like Cassandra! Forgive me! And now I really must go, Simon. (*She gets up and they come to the path at left-front. Suddenly she says, strangely.*) No, you go first.

SIMON (*bewilderedly*). But why don't we walk together as far as the road?

DEBORAH. Please obey me! You have forgotten me, I think. Can't I be whimsical, as of old, if it please me?

SIMON (*puzzled but smiling*). Of course you can.

DEBORAH (*kissing him*). Goodbye, dear. Write me frankly of your discontents. I shall be, as ever, your Mother Confessor. (*She gives him a little push.*) Now go!

SIMON (*hesitates—moved*). I— Goodbye, Mother. (*He turns reluctantly.*)

DEBORAH (*suddenly overcome by contrition*). Wait! (*She embraces him again.*) My dear son! Forgive me for trying to poison your happiness. Forget all I have said! Have no regrets! Love is worth everything! Be happy! (*She kisses him—then pushes him away down the path—sharply commanding.*) Don't speak! Go!

(*She turns away. Simon stares at her for a moment, deeply moved, then turns and disappears down the path. She turns back to look after him.*)

Bosh, Deborah! He will forget in her arms. I have dismissed that Irish biddy's husband from my life for ever. I shall never see him again.

(*As she says this last the cabin door is silently unlocked and opened and Sara comes out. She stands outside the door for a moment hesitantly. Then, her face set and determined, she advances noiselessly until she stands a few paces from the oblivious Deborah.*)

SARA (*speaks quietly in a polite, carefully considered and articulated English*). I beg your pardon, Mrs Harford.

(*Deborah gives a frightened gasp, whirling to face her.*)

I am happy to meet you again—and to know you at last. I was in the cabin all the while.

DEBORAH. You dared to listen!

SARA. I came on purpose to listen. Though after all I've heard, I know now I was a fool to be afraid of you.

DEBORAH. Well, I expected you to be low and unscrupulous, considering your origin, but I never thought you'd boast of it!

SARA (*stung—her inward anger beginning to show, and with it her brogue, but still keeping her voice quiet*). I have my honour and it's a true woman's honour that you'd give your soul to know! To have love and hold it against the world, no matter how! That's my honour! (*Gradually losing her control and lapsing more and more into brogue.*) As for what you're after saying about my origin— Don't put on your fine lady's airs and graces with me! I'm too strong for you! Life is too strong for you! But it's not too strong for me! I'll take what I want from it and make it mine! (*Mockingly.*) You to talk of honour when in your dream what are you but a greedy, contrivin' whore!

(*Deborah shrinks back. Sara goes on more quietly.*)

But it's only in a dream! You've the wish for life but you haven't the strength except to run and hide in fear of it, sittin' lonely in your garden, hearin' age creep up on you, and beyond the wall the steps of Life growin' fainter down the street, like the beat of your heart, as he strolls away forgettin' you, whistlin' a love tune to himself, dreamin' of another woman!

DEBORAH (*stammers*). That's a lie! (*She sways weakly as though she were about to faint—exhaustedly.*) I—I feel a little faint—I—(*She starts for the bench.*)

SARA (*with an abrupt change to her quiet polite manner and brogueless English, takes her arm*). Let me help you, Mrs Harford. You must rest a while.

DEBORAH (*sinks down on the bench*). Thank you.

SARA. I ask your pardon for losing my temper, Mrs Harford. But the things you said—

DEBORAH. I know. Please forgive me.

SARA. I came out of the cabin because there's a lot of things I want to say to you. And I'm going to say them! But before that I want to tell you how sorry I was when Simon laughed. I could feel it coming. I waited, praying he wouldn't. When he did, it was like a knife in me, too.

(*Deborah raises her eyes for a second to stare at her with an instinctive grateful wonder. Sara goes on.*)

I want to apologize for him. How can a man know about the truth of the lies in a woman's dreams?

DEBORAH (*with a faint smile*). I thought you were a fool. I am afraid I am beginning to like you, Sara.

SARA (*embarrassedly—forcing a joking tone*). Oh, don't try to fool me with blarney. You hate me worse than poison. And I hate you. I'm glad I listened. You wanted to put doubt and disgust for himself in his mind, and make him blame me for a greedy fool who'd made him a slave and killed his fine poet's dream. (*She laughs scornfully.*) It's little you know Simon, if you *are* his mother. Sure, what man doesn't complain of his work, and pretend he's a slave? But if ever you saw him when he comes home to me, so proud and happy because he's beat someone on a sale, laughing and boasting to me, you wouldn't hope you could use his old dream of a book that'll change the world to dissatisfy him. I know what he really likes—the world as it is.

(*She pauses. Deborah sits in silence, her eyes on the ground.*)

But what I wanted to say is, you don't know me. I may have a greed in me. I've had good reason to have. There's nothing like hunger to make you greedy. But the thing you don't know is that there's love in me too, great enough to destroy all the greed in the world. If I thought it meant his happiness, I'd live here in this hut, or in a ditch with him, and steal praties from the farmers to feed him, and beg pennies with my children, on the road, to buy pen and ink and paper for his book, and still I'd laugh with the joy of love! I heard you, when he said he'd retire to write his book when we had enough, sneer to him that we'd never have enough. All I'm dreaming of is to make him retire, a landed gentleman, the minute we've enough, and to bring my children up as gentlemen. You think in your Yankee pride and ignorance, because my father ruined himself with drink and gambling in Ireland, that the dirty inn he came down to here is all I've known. But I was born on a great estate that was my father's, in a grand mansion like a castle, with sloos of servants, and stables, and beautiful hunters. My father was a gentleman, and an officer, who served with honour in Spain under the great Duke of Wellington. (*Abruptly.*) I beg your pardon, Mrs Harford, for boring you with talk of my father. He was a drunken fool, full of lying pretensions— But what I've said is true all the same!

DEBORAH. I am beginning to know you, Sara.

SARA. I don't care what you know. Stay in your dreams and leave me and mine alone. Simon is mine now. (*Politely.*) I must go. Simon will be wondering where I have gone. I promise you I won't confess that. I'll bid you goodbye now, Mrs Harford.

DEBORAH (*looks up—coldly*). Goodbye. I promise you, in turn, I never intend to see your husband again, or even write to him. (*With arrogant disdain.*) Do you presume to think I would touch anything of yours?

SARA. No. You know I wouldn't let you. (*She smiles mockingly and goes off right-rear.*)

DEBORAH. Vulgar, common slut! If I wished—if I had the opportunity— No. It is ended—forgotten—dead. It is cheap and mean and sordid like life. I will not let it touch me. (*Gradually her tension relaxes, her eyes become dreamy, and she stares before her unseeingly.*)

The Palace at Versailles—the King and I walk in the moonlit gardens—'My throne it is your heart, Beloved, and my fair kingdom your beauty'— (*She starts awake and springs to her feet.*) No! I have done with that insane romantic vapouring! I will never dream again! Never! I will face change and ugliness, and Time and Death, and make myself resigned! (*A bitter ironical smile comes to her lips.*) After all, what else can you do now, Deborah? You would always hear his laughter!

CURTAIN

ACT ONE, SCENE TWO

SCENE. *A corner of the garden of Deborah Harford's home in the city on a warm moonlight night in June 1836.*

The corner is formed by a brick enclosing wall, eight feet high, at rear and right. At centre is an octagonal summer-house, its walls and pointed roof entirely covered by ivy. At left and right of the summer-house are shrubs, with a line of Italian cypresses behind them along the wall. The shrubs, of various sizes, are all clipped into geometrical shapes—cones, cubes, cylinders, spheres, pyramids, etc. They give the place a curious, artificial atmosphere. In the side of the summer-house facing front is a narrow arched door, painted a Chinese lacquer red. Three steps lead up to the door. Two small stone benches face right-front and left-front, on the edge of a narrow brick-paved walk which surrounds a little oval pool. From this pool two paths lead directly right and left, the left one passing behind a spherical shrub at left-front to the house. The right one leads to an arched door, painted green, in the wall at right, opening on the street. There is a wrought-iron lantern hanging from a bracket in the wall above the door, in which a little lamp burns brightly.

There is a sound of men's voices from down the path off left, and a moment later NICHOLAS GADSBY, *the Harford lawyer, appears accompanied by Deborah's younger son,* JOEL. *Gadsby is a short, tubby man of fifty-six, almost completely bald, with a round red face, and shrewd little grey eyes. Every inch the type of conservative, best-family legal adviser, he is gravely self-important and pretentious in manner and speech, extremely conscious of the respect due his professional dignity. He is dressed with a fastidious propriety in well-tailored mourning black. Joel Harford is twenty-nine, tall and thin, with a slight stoop in his carriage. His face is pale and handsome—the face of a methodical mediocrity, who within his narrow limits is not without determination and a rigid integrity, but lacks all self-confidence or ambition beyond these limits. His whole character has something aridly prim and puritanical about it. He has brown hair, cold light-blue eyes, a pointed chin, an obstinate mouth. His voice is dry—prematurely old.*

They stop as they come to the pool. Gadsby stares around him, looking for someone. His manner is shocked and indignant, and at the same time pathetically confused.

GADSBY. Well? She isn't here. I didn't think she would be.

JOEL (*dryly, indicating the summer-house*). You will find her hiding in there.

GADSBY. God bless me. I cannot believe—?

JOEL. Since Father died she has appeared—well, deliberately deranged—

GADSBY. Come, come, Joel. Naturally, the shock—her grief.

JOEL. Whatever the cause be, it is not grief.

GADSBY. You said 'deliberately'.

JOEL. You may judge for yourself.

GADSBY. Ridiculous! I have known your mother since before you were born. Eccentric, yes. Provokingly unconventional. Whimsical and fanciful. But always a well-bred gentlewoman, a charming hostess, witty and gay—and beautiful.

JOEL. You are forgetting the business which brings us here.

GADSBY. I wish I could forget. I still cannot believe that your father could—

JOEL. It would be better if you were the one to call her out. I have never been welcome here.

GADSBY (*turns to the summer-house and calls*). Deborah! (*He goes to the foot of the steps.*) Deborah! This is Nicholas! (*He pauses, then turns to Joel uneasily.*) God bless me, Joel, you don't think anything can have happened to her?

(*But even as he is speaking the door is slowly opened outwards and Deborah appears. Her back is to the door as though she had groped backwards in the darkness, her hand behind her feeling for the knob, keeping her face turned towards something from which she retreats. As the door opens, her body, pressed against it, turns as it turns until it faces towards left-front, as the door is two-thirds open. But she keeps her head turned so that she is still looking back over her shoulder into the dark interior. Suddenly a little shudder runs over her; she gives a smothered gasp, wrenches her eyes from the darkness inside, pushes the door back against the house, wide open, and faces front. As he sees her face, Gadsby cannot restrain a startled exclamation.*

Deborah now seems much older than her forty-nine years. Her olive complexion has turned a displeasing swarthy colour. The dry skin is stretched tightly over the bones and has the lifeless sheen of a shed snakeskin. Her black eyes are sunk in deep hollows beneath their heavy brows and have an unhealthy feverish glitter. They appear more enormous than ever in her small oval face. There are deep lines from her nose and the corners of her mouth. Her lips appear contracted. There are hollows under her cheekbones and in her slender neck. There is the quality of a death's head about her face, of a skull beginning to emerge from its mask of flesh. Her figure is still graceful in all its movements, and by contrast with her face, youthful. She is dressed all in white.)

DEBORAH (*staring at Gadsby—in a low voice that has lost its old musical quality and become flat and brittle*). I am glad you came, Nicholas. I must never go in there again!

GADSBY. There is something in there that frightens you, Deborah?

DEBORAH. Something? Outside me? No, nothing is there but me. My mind. My life, I suppose you might call it, since I have never lived except in mind. A very frightening prison it becomes at last, full of ghosts and corpses. Yes, in the end—and I have reached the end—the longing for a moment's unthinking peace, a second's unquestioning acceptance of oneself, becomes so terrible that I would do anything, give anything, to escape! That is what frightened me. After you called—not before. Before, I was so longingly fascinated, I had forgotten fear. The temptation to escape—open the door—step boldly across the threshold. And, after all, good God, why should I be frightened? What have I to lose except myself as I am here?

GADSBY. God bless me, Deborah, you cannot mean—

DEBORAH. Death? Oh, no. There is a better way—a way by which one still may live—as the woman one has always desired to be. One has only to concentrate one's mind enough, and one's pride to choose of one's own free will, and one can cheat life, and death, of oneself. It would be so easy for me! Like pushing open a door in the mind and then passing through with the freedom of one's lifelong desire! I tell you, before you called, I saw that door, as real as the door I have just opened, and I was reaching out my hand to— (*With a frightened shudder.*) I am glad you called. Because I am not sure that one completely forgets then. If I were, I would have gone. (*Abruptly.*) No, don't fear, Nicholas, that I will outrage your sense of propriety by suicide. I assure you Henry's dying completely disillusioned me with death.

GADSBY. It is very bad for you to come out here to brood over Henry's death.

DEBORAH. Brood? No. But I have tried to make it real to myself. I have said to myself: 'Your husband is dead. He was buried this morning. You should surely be experienced in facing facts by this time.' Yes, God knows I should. That afternoon at the cabin with Simon seems a lifetime ago, and he is more dead to me than Henry. I have kept the oath I made to myself then. Have made myself accept life as it is. Made myself a decently resigned old woman. Made myself each morning and night confront myself in the mirror and bow a well-mannered bow to Age and Ugliness—greet them as my life-end guests—as elderly suitors for my body, roués in their bored, withered hearts. Not charming company, but a hostess must honour even unwelcome guests. So all day for years I have lived with them. And every night they have lain abed with me. Oh, yes, indeed! I have disciplined my will to be possessed by facts—like a whore in a brothel!

GADSBY. Deborah!

DEBORAH. I have deliberately gone out of my way to solicit even the meanest, most sordid facts, to prove how thoroughly I was resigned to reality. Joel will remember one night at supper when I actually asked my husband: 'How is trade these days? I feel a deep interest. Has President Jackson's feud with the Bank of the United States had an adverse effect on your exports and imports?' A silence that shrank back, stamping on its own toes. In his eyes and Joel's a wondering alarm. Has this alien woman gone completely insane? No, she is merely being fantastical again. Deborah has always been fantastical.

JOEL. That is what you are being now, Mother. And we have no time to listen—

GADSBY (*he has been staring at Deborah, bewilderedly uncomprehending but disturbed because he senses her despair, and now attempts to regain a brisk, professional air, clearing his throat importantly*). Humph. Yes, Deborah.

DEBORAH (*ignoring this*). And now Henry is dead. I am free. Can't you understand that? (*She shakes her head slowly.*) No. His death will not live in me. It is meaningless. Perhaps I am too dead myself. The dutiful wife sat by his bedside. He seemed not to suffer but to be impatient and exasperated—as though he had an important appointment with God to discuss terms for the export of his soul, and Life was needlessly delaying him. And then came nothing—an expiring into nothing. Did I think death would be something in itself—a beginning, not just the end of life? Did I expect death to open the door and enter the room, visible to me, the good King of Life come at last to escort one into his palace of peace, a lover keeping a life-long promised tryst? If life had meaning, then we might properly expect its end to have as much significance as—the period at the close of a simple sentence, say. But it has no meaning, and death is no more than a muddy well into which I and a dead cat are cast aside indifferently! (*She presses both hands to her temples.*) Good God, you wonder I was tempted to open that door and escape! I tell you I am still tempted—that I will not endure being the tortured captive of my mind much longer—whatever the cost of release—

GADSBY. Deborah, compose yourself. This—this is most unsuitable conduct—

DEBORAH (*stares at him—a sudden transformation comes over her. She smiles at him—an amused, derisive smile*). Your rebuke is well taken, Nicholas. May I ask to what I owe the honour of your visit, gentlemen? It is a rare pleasure indeed to see you in my garden, Joel.

JOEL. I assure you, Mother, I would never intrude unless circumstances—

GADSBY. The circumstances are these, Deborah: In going over Henry's private papers, we made the astounding discovery— Upon my soul, I could not credit the evidence of my own eyes! I have known Henry since we were boys together.

I would have sworn he would be the last man on earth to indulge in such outrageous folly!

DEBORAH. Outrageous folly? That does not sound like Henry. I think we could discuss this mystery more calmly if we sat down.

(*She sits on the step of the summer-house, Gadsby and Joel on the stone benches by the pool, at left-front and right-front of her, respectively.*)

JOEL. We found two letters in Father's strong-box, one addressed to Mr Gadsby, the other to me.

GADSBY. These letters are confessions that Henry had been secretly gambling in Western lands.

DEBORAH. Gambling? Henry?

GADSBY. Yes, Deborah. Unbelievable!

JOEL. As a result, Mother, the Company stands on the brink of bankruptcy.

GADSBY. It appears he had overreached his resources during the past few years—sunk too much capital in new ships—borrowed too freely, and then yielded to the temptation to regain a sound position by making a quick profit in Western lands. He lost, of course. What could an honourable, conservative merchant like Henry know of such wild speculation?

DEBORAH. It would appear I have spent my life with a stranger. If I had guessed he had folly hidden in his heart and a gambler's daring— Who knows? (*She shrugs her shoulders.*) Too late, Deborah.

JOEL. I said, Mother, that the Company is faced with ruin.

GADSBY. In his letters Henry suggests certain steps should be taken which, if they can be successfully negotiated, may save the firm.

DEBORAH (*indifferently*). Then you have only to take the steps, Nicholas.

GADSBY. They can be taken only with your consent, since Henry's will bequeathes the Company jointly to you and Joel. I may add that Joel has already given his consent.

JOEL. I consider it my duty to Father's memory.

DEBORAH. If you only knew, Joel, how many times I wish to pinch you to discover if you're stuffed!

JOEL (*with cold indifference*). I have long realized I bore you, Mother. You will doubtless find Simon more congenial.

DEBORAH (*stiffens. Her face becomes as hard and cold as Joel's*). Pray, what has your brother to do with this?

GADSBY. Simon has everything to do with it.

DEBORAH. I forbid you to bring his name into this discussion. I have forgotten him.

GADSBY. Deborah, for the sake of the Company—

DEBORAH. I care nothing for the Company!

JOEL. You will have to sell this home. You will have nothing. What will you do? Go and beg Simon and his wife to let you live on charity with them?

DEBORAH. I would rather beg in the gutter—!

JOEL. Of course, you may always have a home with me. But on a bookkeeper's wage—

DEBORAH. Can you possibly imagine—?

JOEL. No. So I advise you to listen to Mr Gadsby, as he requests.

GADSBY. Your position is—er—precarious, unless— What Henry suggested is this: He realized that Joel has not had the requisite executive experience to take control under such difficult circumstances.

JOEL. Father knew I have not the ability to be head of the Company under any circumstances.

DEBORAH (*stares at him wonderingly—slowly*). There are times when I almost respect you, Joel.

GADSBY. Humm. Henry appears to have had complete confidence in Simon's ability. He seems to have carefully followed Simon's career.

JOEL. I know that because the reports were made through me. Father did not wish to appear in the matter.

DEBORAH. Poor Joel. Your father never had time to spare others' feelings.

JOEL. I dislike pity, Mother.

GADSBY. Henry's suggestion is that you and Joel approach Simon—

DEBORAH. Go begging to Simon? I did that once—

GADSBY. What Henry recommended is a straight business deal, which will be equally to Simon's advantage and yours. He knew that Simon's business is still a small local affair—nothing to compare to the Harford Company. To be its head is to be a leading figure in commerce, as Simon, who once worked under his father and knows the business, will be the first to appreciate.

DEBORAH. So I am to ask Simon to accept the leadership of the Company, is that it?

GADSBY. Yes. A controlling interest. That is only just if he saves it from ruin. And Henry believed he has the means to save it. He has been shrewd enough to anticipate conditions and foresee the panic and ruin which is gathering around us. (*He hesitates—then uncomfortably.*) Humm— Of course,

Henry foresaw that there might be difficult personal aspects. He knew that Simon still feels a resentment—

DEBORAH. If we are facing facts, let us face them. Simon hated him.

GADSBY. But Henry evidently believed that you and Simon still—

JOEL. Simon will not wish you to be ruined, Mother.

DEBORAH. So I am cast in the role of chief beggar! Henry must have lost his famous shrewdness in more ways than one. He fails to consider the one person who can laugh at his calculations, and who will take great pleasure in doing so—Simon's wife! If you think she will ever consent— Oh no, you will find she has never forgiven Henry for humiliating her pride.

GADSBY. Henry knew that. He—er—evidently relied on your tact and diplomacy, Deborah, to convince her.

DEBORAH. I? She hates me!

GADSBY. One further thing Henry suggested, to make his proposal as equitable as possible for Simon and his—er—family. He thought, as they would have to sell their present home and come to the city, and as this home is much too large for you and Joel, that—

DEBORAH. That I should invite that vulgar Irish biddy and her brats to live with me! (*With almost a gloating smile.*) Yes, that would be a greater opportunity than I had ever hoped—(*Then resisting more violently than before—furiously.*) No! How dare you make such a shameless proposal!

JOEL. It is Father who proposes it, Mother.

DEBORAH. And I hoped I had at last escaped the dunning of wifely duty! For the love of God, hasn't his death even that meaning?

JOEL. We are waiting for your consent, Mother.

DEBORAH. What an implacable bill-collector you would make, Joel. (*Violently.*) No, I will not have it! What have I to do with the Company? Let it be ruined! Do you think I fear poverty?

GADSBY. Humm! As your attorney, Deborah, I strongly advise you to consent.

DEBORAH (*rising to her feet*). No! I tell you I swore to myself years ago I would never involve myself in such a low intrigue! And I still desired life then. Do you think you can tempt me now when I am an ugly, resigned old woman whose life is only in the mind? You are wasting your time, gentlemen. (*She makes a gesture of arrogant dismissal.*)

JOEL (*with cold condemnation*). How long are you going to keep us waiting here on your perverse whims? I have always disliked this garden. (*He stares around him with dislike.*) Nothing is natural, not even Nature.

GADSBY (*staring around him in turn—as if fighting against an influence*). Yes, Deborah, the atmosphere is hardly conducive to—common sense, shall I say? (*Then haltingly, as if the influence took hold on him, staring at her.*) My dear Deborah. Why should you talk of being old? Ridiculous! You ugly? You are beautiful!

(*Instinctively her face lights up with an eager grateful smile.*)

Why, you could be the most wooed widow in the city! I myself would jump at the chance—

(*Deborah gives a soft, gratified little laugh. He goes on hastily.*)

Not that there ever was a chance—I know that. Besides, this is hardly the time to speak of— You will forgive me, Joel. Your father always permitted me a little harmless gallantry. He knew your mother could never take a short, fat man seriously. Nor could any other woman. Of course, there was Napoleon. But I admit I am no Napoleon, although at times I have dreamed— (*Abruptly wrenching his eyes from hers—grumbles irritably to himself.*) Humph! What rubbishy thoughts for a man of my years and profession! Her eyes always did make a fool of me. (*Reacts—with an extreme professional portentousness.*) I must protest against your acting so childishly, Deborah. You know there is one honourable course to take. As a woman of breeding and honour, you have no possible choice.

DEBORAH (*with an undercurrent of tense eagerness*). Yes, I suppose it is my duty to see it only in that light. And then there is no choice, is there? It is fate! (*With a strange frightened urgency.*) But you must bear witness, won't you, Nicholas, that I fought against this opportunity, that I did not desire it and did all in my power to reject it?

JOEL. You consent?

DEBORAH (*slowly—as if forcing the words out in spite of herself*). Yes, I consent. Ah! I feel tempted to live in life again—and I am afraid!

JOEL. It's settled, then. We will go and see Simon tomorrow. I shall arrange for places in the stage. (*He bows with cold courtesy to his mother.*) Good night, Mother. Are you coming, Gadsby?

GADSBY. Yes, Joel. (*He starts to go with Joel—then stops, after a glance at Deborah.*) Go on. I'll follow in a moment.

(*Joel goes. Deborah is staring before her. Gadsby coughs embarrassedly.*)

Upon my soul, Deborah, I—er—I cannot see what there is to be apprehensive about in your consenting to the one sensible course.

DEBORAH. I am afraid of myself, Nicholas.

GADSBY. Stuff and nonsense! It will distract your mind and give you a new interest in life.

DEBORAH. Ah, if it only could be a new interest, Nicholas, and not an old one risen from my dead. With what joy I would welcome it, then! With what humble gratitude would I give thankfulness to God for the undreamed-of miracle! Oh, if you knew how I have prayed for resurrection from the death in myself!

GADSBY. I—I do not understand you.

DEBORAH (*forcing a smile—contemptuous and at the same time affectionate*). No, that is why I can safely tell you all my secrets, Nicholas.

GADSBY. I remember how devoted you once were to Simon. You may even find you can like his wife, when you know her. Forgetting prejudice, you must admit she has been an estimable wife and mother. Oh, I expect you to storm at me for pleading her case—

DEBORAH. I will not storm. I understand her feeling towards me. In her place, I would feel the same. (*She smiles wryly.*) There. You see how just I am.

GADSBY (*eagerly*). I do, indeed! But I was thinking most of your grandchildren—the opportunity they present to you. You can have no feeling against them, nor blame them in any way for the past. Your blood is in them. Children in this garden—

DEBORAH. Yes, I do see, Nicholas. Like an amazing revelation—a miraculous hope that would never have occurred to me if you hadn't— It could be the chance for a new life—escape from the death within myself. Resign myself to be a grandmother! You astonish me, Nicholas. I have heard of wisdom from babes, but who could dream of it from a bachelor! I really believe you are trying to make a good woman of me, Nicholas! (*She laughs softly—then quickly, seeing he is hurt.*) No. Forgive my teasing. I am truly grateful. If you could know how grateful! And I swear to you I will try. It will not be easy. You do not know how bitterly Sara suspects me. Or how well she understands—what I was. It will be difficult to convince her of my good motives, and persuade her to trust me with her children. I shall have to be very cunning. I must be very meek and humble. (*Suddenly, angry at herself.*) No! I talk as if I were planning to pretend and play a part! But I *am* meek now! I *am* humble! I am willing to beg her on my knees to give me this chance to be reborn! I can love her for it if she does! Because if she can trust me, I can learn to trust myself again! I can make her love me and her children love me! I can love again! Oh, I may surprise myself, I think, with my undreamed-of talents as a good woman! Already at the mere prospect of escape, I feel a rebirth stirring in me! I feel free!

GADSBY. Good! Excellent! I am delighted you—

DEBORAH. And to prove my escape—as a symbol— Watch and bear witness, Nicholas! I will cast out my devil, the old Deborah—drag her from her sneering-place in my mind and heart, and push her back where she belongs—in there—in perpetual darkness. (*She advances up the steps—with a final push.*) 'Depart from me, ye cursed!' (*She grabs the doorknob, shutting the door.*) And shut the door! Lock it! (*She does so.*) There! Now question, and sneer and laugh at your dreams, and sleep with ugliness, and deny yourself, until at last you fall in love with madness, and implore it to possess you, and scream in silence, and beat on the walls until you die of starvation. That won't take long, now you no longer have me to devour, Cannibal!

GADSBY. Come, come, Deborah. This is all most unseemly!

DEBORAH (*turns to him*). It is done! She is dead to me. Sshh! Do you hear, Nicholas?

GADSBY. Hear what?

DEBORAH. The footsteps beyond the wall. They have stopped receding. I think Life remembers he had forgotten me and is turning back. (*Suddenly she is conscious of the expression on Gadsby's face and she bursts into natural teasing laughter.*) Heavens, Nicholas! What an alarmed face! Did you think it was a burglar I heard?

GADSBY. God bless me! Who could know what to think? Life, indeed! What fantastic rubbish, Deborah!

CURTAIN

ACT ONE, SCENE THREE

SCENE. *Sitting-room of Sara Harford's home in a textile-mill town about forty miles from the city. The following night. The room is small, a typical room of the period, furnished without noticeable good or bad taste. The atmosphere is one of comfort and a moderate prosperity. At front, to the left of centre, is a table with a lamp and three chairs. In the middle of the left wall is a closed door leading into Simon's study. In the left corner, rear, is a sofa. The doorway to the entrance hall—and the stairs to the first floor—is in the middle of the rear wall. At right of this doorway is a cabinet with a lamp. There are two windows in the right wall, looking out on the front garden and the street. Between the windows is a desk with a chair. At right-front is a big armchair.*

As the curtain rises, from the hall at rear the sound of small boys' arguing voices is heard coming down the stair-well from the floor above. Then Sara's voice trying to quiet them and, for the moment, succeeding. In this pause, the door at left is opened and SIMON *enters. Physically, he appears to have changed no more than one would normally expect. His spare frame has put on ten pounds or so, but it still has the same general effect of loose-jointed, big-boned leanness. His large-featured Yankee face looks his thirty-one years. But there is a noticeable change in the impression his personality projects—a quality of nervous tension, the mental strain of a man who has been working too hard and puts unrelieved pressure on himself. As he comes into the room, he is frowning, his eyes pre-occupied. He comes to the table and stands staring down at it preoccupiedly. He is startled by a hubbub from the floor above, a chorus of boys' excited voices, the sound of scuffling coming through the ceiling, followed by a resounding thump and a chorus of laughter. His face lights up. He smiles and chuckles to himself.*

Then Sara's voice is heard in a commanding tone, and the uproar subsides obediently. Simon sits in the chair at left-front of table. He picks up two folded newspapers from the table, puts one paper aside, starts to open the other, hesitates, then determinedly opens it. His eyes fix on one story. As he reads it, his face becomes hard and bitter. Finished, he lowers the paper to his lap and stares over it. He hears Sara coming down the stairs in the hall and at once represses his thoughts and looks back towards the doorway at rear smilingly.

SARA *enters at rear. She is flushed, her hair disarranged on one side, her eyes laughing and fondly maternal. She exudes an atmosphere of self-confident loving happiness and contentment. She is much better looking than she had been in her pregnancy. Her figure is buxom, but beautifully proportioned, with full breasts and a slender waist.*

SIMON (*rising as she enters—smilingly*). Well! What's been going on up there?

SARA. We had a pillow fight. (*She laughs—then suddenly shamefaced.*) But what a way for me—and you in your study trying to write! (*She kisses him impulsively.*)

SIMON. I couldn't get interested in it tonight, anyway.

(*He looks away from her. She sits in the chair at right-front, and he sits where he had been.*)

SARA (*too casually*). What paper is it you've been reading?

SIMON. Garrison's *Liberator*.

SARA (*uneasily*). Oh, I meant to hide it. I didn't want you to see—

SIMON. Why? I knew Father had died. The report of his funeral means nothing.

SARA (*resentfully*). I can't understand your Mother not inviting you to the funeral. (*Bitterly.*) Unless she thought I wouldn't let you go without me, and she didn't want her poor Irish relations shaming her before the notables!

SIMON. Now, now. She knew Father wouldn't have wished me to come and pretend grief for public opinion's sake. As for her having Joel write me he was dead instead of writing me herself, you know I've never had a letter from her since I saw her that time at my cabin.

SARA. She's a wise woman and knows it'd do no good for her to interfere—

SIMON. I'd hardly call the letters she once wrote me interfering.

SARA. She was always reminding you about your book.

SIMON (*stares at her—smilingly*). You objected to that? And for the last couple of years, who has been encouraging me to write it?

SARA. I have. But that's different. (*She grasps his hand and presses it—tenderly possessive.*) Because I love you, and you're mine, and your happiness is my happiness.

SIMON. Why, often I had forgotten all about the darned thing, but you would send me into my study to work on it like a regular slave-driver!

SARA (*laughingly*). Oh, I'm not as bad as that, darling.

SIMON. But I've had a dark suspicion for some time. I think you calculated very cunningly the best way to convince me it was nonsense was to make me attempt it and then prove to myself—

SARA (*guiltily*). No.

SIMON. There I was at night in my study trying to convince myself of the possibility of a greedless Utopia, while all day in my office I was really getting the greatest satisfaction and sense of self-fulfilment and pride out of beating my competitors in the race for power and wealth and possessions! (*He laughs, bitterly amused.*) It was too absurd.

SARA. You're giving it up forever?

SIMON. I threw all I've done in the fireplace and burned it. You don't have to look so triumphant, Sara.

SARA (*guiltily*). I'm not. I— No, I won't lie. I am glad you have found it out for yourself. You know I've never believed your dream would work, with men and women what they are.

SIMON. With us as we are, for example? But you're quite right. Rousseau was simply hiding from himself in a superior, idealistic dream—as Mother has always done, in a different way. You were right to blame her, Sara. It was really her influence that made me first conceive the idea of my book. I can see that now—her haughty disdain for Father because he was naturally absorbed in his business. And yet all the time she owed everything to his business—the comfort she loved, the protected privacy, her fanciful walled-in garden, the material security which gave her the chance to remain aloof and scornful! But why think of that now? Except I thank God I freed myself in time, and then met you, who are so simply and passionately conscious of life as it is, and love it and are healthily eager and happy to be alive and get all you can from it. (*Abruptly.*) But all I wanted to tell you was my final decision about the book.

SARA. I'll never mention it again.

SIMON. No, all you have to do is read your daily newspaper and see what man is doing with himself. There's the book that ought to be written—a frank study of the true nature of man as he really is and not as he pretends to himself to be—a courageous facing of the truth about him—and in the end, a daring assertion that what he is, no matter how it shocks our sentimental moral and religious delusions about him, is good because it is true, and should, in a world of facts, become the foundation of a new morality which would destroy all our present hypocritical pretences and virtuous lies about ourselves. By God, it's a fascinating idea. I've half a mind to try it!

SARA. If it isn't just like you to start dreaming a new dream the moment after you've woke up from the old! It's the touch of the poet in you!

SIMON. Nonsense! There never was any poet in me. I couldn't spare the time, for one thing. It's a difficult period for trade this country is in now. I've got to concentrate all my brains and energy on our business affairs. That mad fool, Jackson! His insane banking policy is ruining the country!

SARA. Well, he can't ruin us. We've got fifty thousand dollars, the most of it in gold English guineas. The hard times won't touch that.

SIMON. No. They will make it more valuable.

SARA. And you had the brains to see the hard times coming before anyone.

SIMON. But my competitors kept on expanding, and now it's too late, poor devils. And when the time comes we will be in a position to take advantage of others' lack of foresight. That will be our opportunity to expand. It won't take long for us to get the hundred thousand we have set as our goal. Or more.

SARA. No. That's enough. We promised ourselves—

SIMON. You don't realize what extraordinary opportunities there will be, Sara. In shipping, for example, there are many firms on the verge of bankruptcy already. Later on I know we could buy up one for comparatively nothing.

SARA (*uneasily*). No, stick to your own trade, Simon, whatever you do.

SIMON. Don't forget I had my first business training with my father's company. And we can't dismiss the shipping trade as something that doesn't concern us. Our cotton is brought to us in ships, isn't it? If we owned our own shipping company, managed as economically and efficiently as I know I could manage it, it would be of tremendous advantage to our mills— I tell you, Sara, the more I think of it, the more opportunities I foresee. Take banking. Banks are beginning to fail right and left already, and before long I prophesy—

SARA (*laughingly*). Stop! You have my head spinning! You'll be dreaming yourself the King of America before you know it!

SIMON. Still, if we had that two hundred thousand in specie now—

SARA (*scolding him as though he were a small boy*). Now, now, you're too greedy. And you mustn't do so much planning and scheming, when it's getting near bedtime, or you'll never settle down to sleep.

SIMON (*leans back in his chair, suddenly conscious of weariness*). Yes, I am tired. But I'll sleep soundly again now I've put that damned book out of my mind. (*He closes his eyes, and then opens them to stare before him.*) What a damned fool a man can make of himself. Keep on deliberately denying what he knows himself to be in fact, and encourage a continual conflict in his mind, so that he lives split into opposites and divided against himself! All in the name of Freedom! As if at the end of every dream of liberty one did not find the slave, oneself, to whom oneself, the Master, is enslaved! (*He chuckles bitterly.*)

SARA. Ah now, darling, don't start that black loneliness—

SIMON (*throws off his mood*). Oh, I'm not. That's finished and done with. I promise not to bewilder you with opposites ever again.

(*They are interrupted by the sound of the knocker on the front door, coming from the hall at rear.*)

Now who the devil—?

(*He gets up and goes out, rear, frowning irritably. Sara sits listening. From the hall Simon's voice is heard exclaiming with astonishment,* 'Mother!' *and Deborah's voice* 'Simon.' *Sara springs to her feet and stands tensely defensive, her expression frightened for a second, then hardening into hostility. Deborah's voice again. Then Simon's and Joel's in cold formal greeting to each other. A moment later* DEBORAH *and Simon appear in the doorway at rear with* JOEL *behind them. Deborah wears deep mourning. Her face is extremely pale. Outwardly she is all disciplined composure, the gracious, well-bred gentlewoman, with just the correct touch of quiet resignation in her bearing which goes with her widow's black. But one senses an inner tense excitement, a vital eager mental aliveness. At sight of her, Sara instantly puts on her most ladylike manners, as if responding in kind to a challenge.)*

DEBORAH (*comes forward with a gracious smile, holding out her hand*). I am glad to see you again, Sara.

SARA (*takes her hand, smiling in return—a bit stiltedly*). It is a great pleasure, Mrs Harford.

SIMON. This is my brother Joel, Sara.

(*Joel makes her a formal bow. Sara acknowledges the introduction in silence, then turns to Deborah.*)

SARA. Won't you sit down?

(*She indicates the chair in which she had been sitting. Deborah takes it.*)

You sit there by your mother Simon.

(*She goes to the armchair at right-front. Simon sits in his old place at left-front of table. Joel takes the chair at rear of table.*)

SIMON. This *is* a surprise, Mother.

DEBORAH. We arrived on the stage about an hour ago and went to the hotel to make ourselves presentable.

SIMON. You must stay with us. We have a room for you, if not for Joel—

JOEL. I should stay at the hotel in any case.

DEBORAH. No, no. I would not dream of imposing on Sara's hospitality.

SARA. We've a fine room always ready. We've had Southern planters as our guests, who are used to great mansions on their estates. (*Abruptly, she is ashamed of her bragging and adds lamely.*) We should feel very offended if you refused us, Mrs Harford.

DEBORAH. Why then, I accept your hospitality. It will give me an opportunity of knowing your children. (*For a moment she looks into Sara's eyes with a strange, almost pleading earnestness.*)

SARA. I'm sure you'll like them. No one could help— (*She smiles.*) But of course they're mine and I'd be bound to think that.

JOEL. We must obtain Simon's decision tonight, Mother, so I can return on the first stage tomorrow.

SIMON. My decision?

DEBORAH. And Sara's decision. (*To Joel.*) I suggest Simon take you to his study. You can explain your mission there, and leave me to tell Sara.

SIMON. My decision on what?

DEBORAH. Certain last wishes of your father's, and a bargain he proposes. (*She smiles.*) I need not warn you to scrutinize it closely.

JOEL. Mother!

SIMON. Thank you for the warning.

DEBORAH. It was your father's wish that you decide this matter solely on its merits as a business opportunity. That is my wish too.

JOEL. Father's proposal is immensely to your advantage.

SIMON (*getting to his feet*). We shall see.

(*He starts for the study door at the left, Joel following.*)

SARA (*warningly*). Simon, remember—

SIMON (*turns back—reassuringly*). You know that I will make no decision without your consent.

(*He turns and opens the study door and bows curtly to Joel to precede him. They go inside and shut the door. There is a pause in which Deborah and Sara stare at each other. Deborah again with the strange earnest, almost pleading look. Sara suspicious, puzzled.*)

DEBORAH. It is a long time since our meeting at the cabin. I am sure you notice how greatly I have changed.

SARA (*with a cruel revengeful satisfaction*). You look an old woman now. But I suppose you still dream you're the King of France's sweetheart!

DEBORAH. I *am* an old woman, Sara. And I have not dreamed that dream since that day. Can you believe that, Sara?

SARA. I believe you. You couldn't, remembering how he'd laughed. (*Impatiently.*) But it's no business of mine. And it isn't telling me why you're here or what you want of me.

DEBORAH. I came to beg charity from you, Sara.

SARA. You! To beg charity from me! Ah, what trick are you up to now?

DEBORAH. No. There is no trick now, Sara. I have come to beg—

SARA (*lapsing into broad brogue*). You, the great lady Harford! Glory be to God, if my father could have lived to see this day!

DEBORAH. There is only one possible chance for me to live

again, Sara, and only you can give it to me.

SARA. I'm buying no pig in a poke.

DEBORAH. I want the chance to be unselfish, to live in others' lives for their sake and not my sake. I want to make myself an unselfish mother and grandmother. I want even to become a loving mother-in-law who can rejoice in your happiness as my son's wife and his happiness as your husband.

SARA (*moved—impulsively*). Ah, that's good and kind of you, Madam. (*Abruptly hostile—contemptuously.*) If you're not lying to play me some trick!

DEBORAH. I feel now what I felt that day at the cabin that you and I in a way complement each other and each has something the other lacks and needs—

SARA. If you imagine I have any need for your great lady's airs and graces, you're badly mistaken, Mrs Harford!

DEBORAH (*continuing as if she hadn't heard*). —that if we gave each other the chance, we could be close friends and allies.

SARA. Are you begging me for—? (*With a strange derisive satisfaction.*) Indeed and you've changed entirely. (*Grudgingly.*) I know I don't hate you any more. I'm too sure of Simon now. And if I could trust you—

DEBORAH. What I'm begging for above all, Sara, is the chance to find a new life. If you knew how horribly alone I have been for so long, Sara, sitting in my garden with an empty dreamless mind, with only the hope of death for company. I need to be reminded that life is not the long dying of death by the happy greedy laughter of children! Will you give me that chance, Sara?

SARA. It's true you have nothing in life, poor woman, and how could I be so cruel and hard-hearted as to turn you away, when I'm so rich and you so poverty-stricken.

DEBORAH. Oh, thank you, Sara. It means the difference between life and death to me!

SARA (*uneasy, as if already regretting her consent*). I'm only doing it because it was through the money you loaned us when we were married we got our start. (*Then suddenly suspicious.*) Wait! What has this got to do with the business his brother is telling Simon?

DEBORAH (*smilingly evasive*). I'd rather not, Sara, if you don't mind. My only real interest is the chance for a new life, which you can give me whether you and Simon decline his father's offer or not.

SARA. But what is the offer? You can tell me that.

DEBORAH (*carelessly*). Why, all I understand about it is that my husband suggested that Joel and I should offer Simon a controlling interest if he would assume direction of the Company's affairs.

SARA. My husband to be head of the Harford Company? (*Abruptly—then frowning.*) But I don't see—

DEBORAH. The Company, I believe, is at present in need of cash—

SARA. Ah, so that's it! The gold we've slaved to save! No, thank you. Mrs Harford. My husband has his own business, and it's enough. He don't want the Harford Company.

DEBORAH (*shrugs her shoulders indifferently*). Well, that's for you and Simon to decide. My husband proposed that I make over to you, as part of the bargain, a one-half interest in my house and garden—

SARA. The Harford mansion! It's one of the finest in the city!

DEBORAH. Yes, it is really a very beautiful and valuable property, Sara. And I need not tell you how delighted I would be. In fact I want to double my husband's offer and deed the whole property over to you. All I ask in return is that you allow me to live there with you—and my grandchildren. (*She adds laughingly.*) Oh, I admit this is shameless bribery on my part, Sara, but I am so alone, and it would mean so much to me—

SARA (*touched and greedy*). I think it's very generous of you, Mrs Harford. (*Then warily.*) But, of course, it depends on what Simon—

DEBORAH. Oh, certainly. And now, let us not talk of business any more. (*Eagerly.*) Could I see my grandchildren now? Oh, I know they must be asleep. All I wish is a peek at them, so I can begin feeling myself an actual, living, breathing grandmother! (*She laughs gaily.*)

SARA. Indeed you can.

(*She runs from her chair and Deborah gets up, too.*)

Only I better go up alone first and make sure they're asleep. If one of them was awake and saw you he'd be so excited and full of questions—

DEBORAH (*smiling*). Oh, I know. I remember Simon—(*She stops abruptly, her expression suddenly bitterly resentful.*)

SARA. I'll be right back, Mrs Harford.

DEBORAH (*throws off her mood—smilingly*). I would be grateful if you could call me Deborah from now on.

SARA (*with instinctive humility*). No, that's too familiar—(*Then hating herself for this—assertively.*) All right, I will, Deborah. (*She goes out, rear.*)

DEBORAH (*stares after her—jeeringly*). At least old age has not impaired your talent for acting, Deborah! (*Then savagely.*) No! You lie! You know you lie! I meant every word sincerely! I will make myself love her! She has given me life again! I—

(*She stops abruptly and sits down again as the door from the study is opened and Simon enters with Joel. Joel's expression is one of cold, bitter humiliation. Simon is repressing a feeling of gloating satisfaction and excited calculation. He comes and puts a protecting, possessive hand on his mother's shoulder.*)

SIMON. Poor Mother. (*She gives a quick bitter look up at his face and moves her shoulder away.*) I think I can promise I'll soon win back for you all his stupid folly has lost.

JOEL. It is cowardly to insult the dead.

SIMON. He did act like a fool, as Mother will agree—

DEBORAH. I agree with Joel that the dead are, after all, the dead. (*Simon stares at her in resentful surprise.*) Am I to understand you accept your father's proposal?

SIMON. Did you think I would refuse to save you from being ruined?

DEBORAH. No, no! I told you it is my wish that there be no hypocritical family sentiment in this bargain.

SIMON. Hypocritical, Mother?

DEBORAH. You hated him. As for you and me, we have not even corresponded in years. In the meanwhile, we have both changed completely in character—

SIMON. Yes, I begin to see how completely you have changed!

DEBORAH. Anyway. I warn you frankly that I could never play the role of a slavish loving mother convincingly again.

SIMON. I am glad you admit it was just a role.

DEBORAH. So now you must consider your father's and my proposal purely and simply as a business deal. Accept, if it strikes you as a profitable opportunity. I refuse to be indebted—to you—for anything.

SIMON. Very well, Mother. (*He sits at the table—Joel behind it—curtly.*) As I have told Joel, I will accept Father's proposal only on one condition. If you cannot agree to it, there is no more to be said.

DEBORAH. And what is the condition?

JOEL. It is preposterous, Mother—an insult to Father's memory!

SIMON. There can be no question of my giving up my prosperous business here to take up his bankrupt one. Father, in his blind vanity, overestimated the prestige of his name. I have never needed that prestige. I do not need it now. My condition is that I absorb his Company in mine. There must be only my Company.

JOEL. Father would rather have faced ruin a thousand times—

DEBORAH. But unfortunately he left me to face it. I see, Simon, what an opportunity this is for you. I accept your condition.

JOEL. You have let him beat you down like a swindling horse-trader! He would accept unconditionally if you—

DEBORAH. I want your brother to drive the hardest bargain he can—

SIMON. Naturally you could expect no mercy in a strictly business deal, Mother. Then the matter is settled—provided, of course, Sara consents.

DEBORAH. Yes, I have talked with Sara and I think you will have no trouble convincing her.

SIMON. I know that, Mother. Sara does as I advise in these matters.

JOEL (*gets to his feet—stiffly to Simon*). I bid you goodnight. I shall go to the city by the morning stage and have the announcement made that you are assuming control of the Company.

SIMON. The sooner the better. Creditors may grow uneasy.

JOEL. Before I go— You will, of course, wish me to resign from my position—

SIMON. No. You are an excellent head bookkeeper, I know. Why should I? And I shall see that you are given an interest in my Company commensurate with the interest you were left in Father's Company.

JOEL. I shall engage an attorney to protect that interest.

SIMON. Attorney or no attorney, I could easily swindle you out of it, if I liked. But you are too helpless a foe. Goodnight.

JOEL. I will keep my position only because I feel it my duty to Father's memory to do all I can—for the Company will always be Father's Company in my eyes.

SIMON. I do not care a tinker's damn what it is in your eyes.

(*Joel stares at him, is about to say something more, then bows stiffly, and stalks out the door at rear. Simon frowns after him—then suddenly chuckles, with a change of manner towards Deborah.*)

God, he'll never change, will he, Mother? He isn't a man. He's a stuffed moral attitude!

DEBORAH (*unconsciously falling into the mood of their old affectionate intimacy*). Yes, haven't I always said Joel is God's most successful effort in taxidermy!

(*They laugh amusedly together—then stop abruptly and stare at each other.*)

SIMON. I must confess, Mother, I do not see why you should suddenly take such an antagonistic attitude towards me.

DEBORAH. You are wrong to think my present feeling is one of antagonism. No, my feeling is one of indifference.

SIMON. Mother!

DEBORAH. That is what Time does to us all. We forget and pass on. You have your life of a husband to live. You have your children. One must eliminate the past. Why not admit that?

SIMON. Very well. I do admit it.

DEBORAH. Good! There the past is finally buried, and we can start again and learn to become friends. I want to be the friend of Sara's husband, Simon. I want to be proud of what you are, of the great success I see before you. I am determined to live with a world that exists, Simon, and accept it as good. I have forgotten my old silly presumptuous cowardly disdain for material success. I hope to live to see you become a Napoleon of finance.

SIMON (*stares at her*). It is no lie that you have changed—incredibly. (*Sara enters from the rear.*)

SARA. I'm sorry to keep you waiting so long, Deborah, but our talking here had wakened Jonathan and I had to get him back to sleep. (*Glancing from one to the other—with a trace of suspicion.*) What are you talking about? Where's Simon's brother?

DEBORAH. Simon was talking over this business—for the last time, I hope.

SIMON. Joel has just left. I'm sending him to the city by the first stage to announce that we are taking over Father's Company. Do you understand, Sara? His Company ceases to exist. We absorb it.

SARA. Ah, if my father had only lived to see—! (*With sudden dismay.*) Then you decided it all—without waiting to ask me!

SIMON. Because I was sure of your consent and I knew Mother had talked to you.

SARA. She was begging me—

DEBORAH. Yes, I begged Sara to forget all the bitterness in the past and allow me to become her friend. And she promised she would try.

SARA. Yes, I did. But—

SIMON. It is strange to think of you two as friends.

DEBORAH. He doesn't believe we can be, Sara.

SARA. Why can't we, I'd like to know? I've always felt grateful to her for giving us our start in life.

DEBORAH. Yes, we will prove it to him. We won't let him discourage us.

SIMON. What a stupid thing to say, Mother! You know very well nothing would please me more.

DEBORAH (*laughingly*). There, Sara. Now we have your husband's blessing.

SIMON. To get back to business: I tell you, Sara, this is exactly the chance for expansion we were hoping for. And a finer bargain than I would have dreamed possible, thanks to Mother. She insisted I consider it nothing but a business deal, and I don't mind confessing, now the deal is completed, that we will be getting something for practically nothing.

DEBORAH (*laughing*). And so am I. I had nothing and I am getting Sara's friendship and a chance to make a new start in life as a good grandmother. (*She turns to Sara—eagerly*). May I go up and see my grandchildren now, Sara?

SIMON. No. You'd only wake them.

SARA. All she wants is to peek at them from the door.

DEBORAH. You can trust me not to wake them, Simon. Many a time I looked in at you and never disturbed you.

SARA. Oh, him. It's hard to get him to sleep but once he drops off you could fire a cannon and he'd never budge.

DEBORAH. Yes, that's the way he used to be when he was little. (*She laughs.*) I can see you have made him your eldest son, as well as your husband, Sara.

SARA (*laughingly*). Oh, he's been that from the day we married. Only don't let him hear you, Deborah. It'd offend his dignity. (*She takes Deborah's arm—gently.*) Come along now and see the children.

(*They start back, ignoring Simon, who has listened frowningly, feeling completely out of it.*)

SIMON. Wait! (*As they turn back—injuredly.*) You might at least wait until I have finished explaining about the bargain I drove, Sara.

SARA. Much good it will do me to listen now after you've gone ahead and agreed without consulting me at all!

SIMON. You know very well my asking your consent has never been anything but a formality. What do you really know of business? It is I alone who have the right—

SARA (*suddenly frightened and hurt.*) Simon! You've never said that before! You—

SIMON. I'm sorry, Sara. But nothing is signed yet. I can still back out, if you wish.

DEBORAH. Can't you see, Sara, all he wants is to prove to

you how clever he has been for your sake, and have you say you're proud of him.

SARA (*smiling*). I'm all the time telling him how proud I am, and making him vain and spoiling him! So go on now and tell me, darling.

SIMON (*made self-conscious and ill-at-ease*). What I wanted to say is— (*Suddenly he stares at his mother—sneeringly.*) You a doting old grandmother, Mother? You've never cared about children, except as toys to play with—unless my memory is all wrong!

DEBORAH. He doesn't want to believe that I have changed, Sara.

SIMON. Oh, I'm open to proof.

SARA. Ah now, you shouldn't sneer at your mother like that. What do you know of women?

DEBORAH. I am absolutely sure now we can become great friends.

SARA. What is it you were going to say about the bargain, Simon? Maybe you don't know or you couldn't act so unfriendly towards her, that your mother is going to deed over her fine mansion and land in the city to us? She'll only live there as our guest and I'll have the whole management and be the mistress.

SIMON. I will not consent to that.

SARA (*defiantly*). But I have consented, and it's only fair you leave me to decide about our home, if you want me to agree with what you've decided about the Company.

SIMON. I told Joel I did not want even the one-half interest in Mother's home that Father suggested she offer me. We will rent a house first, and later buy our own home. We need be under no obligation to Mother—

DEBORAH. I told you there could be no question of obligations. I made the offer to Sara as part of my bargain with her, and, to be frank, I think I am getting all the best of it. I will still have all the privileges of my home and none of the responsibilities of actual ownership. And I will have Sara and my grandchildren for company. No, if there is any obligation, I am obliged to Sara.

SARA. No, Deborah, it's a great bargain for us, too. Can't you see, Simon, that we'll be getting a fine mansion for nothing at all, with a beautiful, spacious garden for the children to play in?

DEBORAH. Really, Sara, your husband's attitude is most unflattering. You would think I was some wicked old witch, the way he dreads the thought of living in the same house with me!

SIMON. Don't be silly, Mother. I—

DEBORAH. He seems to feel so antagonistic to me because I didn't answer a few letters. But I know you appreciate my reasons for that, Sara.

SARA. I do, and I'm grateful you had the fairness and good sense not to—

SIMON. So it is I who am antagonistic, Mother? Well, perhaps I am—now—with good reason—but if I am, whose wish was it—? (*Then abruptly, with cold curtness, shrugging his shoulders.*) But, as you said, Sara, our home should be your business, and I am willing to abide by your decision. I shall have to concentrate all my attention on reorganizing my Company. (*Eagerly.*) You can't realize what an opportunity this is for me, Sara, and what a tremendous bargain I have got! Father became panic-stricken the minute he found himself out of his conservative depth. He greatly exaggerated the danger. It will be easy for me—

DEBORAH. Let's leave our Napoleon to his ambitious destiny and go up to the children, Sara.

SARA. He'll be owning the whole world in his mind before you know it.

(*They turn towards the door at rear, laughingly.*)

SIMON. Wait! Sara, I would like to utter a word of warning—in Mother's presence. I do not possess the entire confidence in this sudden friendship between you you both appear to have. It will be a difficult matter when two such opposites as you are have to live together in the same home day after day, with continual friction and conflict of character developing. And remember I have the right to expect a peaceful atmosphere in my home. I will have too many important things on my mind to be distracted by domestic dissensions. So please don't come to me—

DEBORAH (*gaily—but with a strange undercurrent*). I hereby take a solemn oath never to come to you.

SARA. What's come over you, darling? It isn't like you to act so grudging and stubborn—

DEBORAH. Yes, one would think he preferred us to be jealous enemies—

SIMON. You know very well, and Sara knows, it has always been my dearest hope that you should know and love each other. I made the objection I did only because I wanted to convince myself you were sure of each other's good faith. It needed only your reconciliation to complete my happiness and give me absolute confidence in the future.

(*He kisses them. Sara's face lights up happily. Deborah's remains teasingly mocking.*)

CURTAIN

ACT TWO, SCENE ONE

SCENE. *Simon's private office in the offices of Simon Harford Inc. It is late summer, 1840.*

The room is small, well-proportioned, panelled in dark wood. The furniture is old, heavy and conservative. A dark rug is on the floor of polished oak boards. On the walls are pictures of Washington, Hamilton, Daniel Webster, and, incongruously, John C. Calhoun. In the left wall are two windows looking out on the street. Between the windows is a chair. Before the chair, Simon's desk, with another chair on the other side of it. In the rear wall right is a door leading into the hall. At left of this door, a tall cabinet stands against the wall. At right-front is a door leading into the bookkeeper's office. Farther back against the wall is a high desk with a tall stool in front of it. At front-right is another chair.

As the curtain rises, SIMON *enters at rear and comes to his table. He has changed greatly in the four years and looks older than the thirty-five he is. His body has put on twenty pounds or more of solid flesh, mostly around his chest and shoulders and arms, which gives him a formidably powerful appearance, but there is also a suggestion of paunch. His face has become thinner, more heavily lined and gaunt and angular. There are patches of grey over his temples. His expression is that of one habitually tense. His manner is curtly dictatorial. He speaks rapidly and incisively. He is dressed conservatively in dark clothes, obviously expensive. He wears them well but indifferently, as becoming to his position and not himself.*

He sits down, picks up the morning mail stacked on his desk, and at once becomes concentrated on going through it. The manner in which he does this is characteristic. He goes from one letter to the next with astonishing rapidity, seeming to take in the contents of each at a glance and make an instant decision, setting it on the table at his right, or dropping it in the wastebasket.

The door at right is opened and JOEL HARFORD *enters, closing the door quietly behind him. He stops to glance at his brother, then comes and stands in front of his desk. Joel looks older. The stoop in his shoulders is more pronounced, with a suggestion of weariness and resignation now beneath the uncompromising rigidity of his habitual poise. He stands waiting. Simon deliberately ignores his presence—or attempts to, but it immediately gets on his nerves, and at last he exclaims exasperatedly.*

SIMON. Well? Is this another of your periodical duty-to-the-Company protests against my management? If so, I don't care to listen.

JOEL. As a stockholder, it is my right—

SIMON. Your right has no power. So you have no right. But relieve your conscience, if you must. You can have the stupid effrontery to criticize my leadership in the face of all I've accomplished in four years! I have five mills now, all running profitably, instead of one. I have transformed what was Father's bankrupt business into a marine division of my Company which is a model of its kind. I have—

JOEL (*interrupts coldly*). You pay off debts only in order to borrow more largely. You go on gambling—

SIMON. Don't be a frightened old woman! It is not gambling when I know the dice are loaded in my favour.

JOEL. I refer now to the deal for the railroad you are to conclude this morning. You know nothing of railroading.

SIMON. I *will* know all there is to know.

JOEL. Finally, I want to warn you again against the growing unscrupulousness with which you take advantage of others' misfortunes. You are making the Company feared and hated.

SIMON. I want it to be feared. As for others, I do to them as they would do to me—if they could! I ask no quarter. Why should they? What a sentimental ass you are, Joel! The only moral law here is the strong are rewarded, the weak are punished. All else is an idealistic lie—a lie that I would be stupid to permit to get in my way, or in my Company's way.

JOEL. I am thinking of Father's Company, not of you. But I am wasting words. (*He turns towards the door to right.*) I will go back to my work.

SIMON. Yes, for God's sake!

(*Then as Joel goes towards the door, he speaks in a conciliating tone.*)

Wait! Sit down a while.

(*He indicates the chair at right of his desk. As Joel stares in cold surprise without making any move, he bursts out angrily.*)

I said sit down! Either you obey me or you look for another job!

(*Joel's face betrays no emotion. He comes back and sits down stiffly in the chair.*)

I'm sorry, Joel. It has been a strain getting this affair of the railroad settled. (*He pauses, then goes on. Gradually his eyes drop from Joel to his desk, and more and more it seems he is talking to himself.*) I concentrate all my mind and energy to get a thing done. I live with it, think of nothing else, eat with it, take it to bed with me, sleep with it, dream of it—and then suddenly one day it is accomplished—finished, dead!—and I become empty, but at the same time restless and aimless, as if I had lost my meaning to myself. A vacation would be in order at such times. But where? How? A voyage to France, say—with Sara—a second honeymoon. But Sara would not leave the children, and to take the children along would mean it would be their vacation with their mother, not mine with my wife. Perhaps Sara would even insist on taking Mother with us! They have grown to be such loving friends, drawn to each other by their devotion to the children! I assure you, I am left entirely out of it now. That is Mother's doing, of course. She imagines she has been very subtle, that I have not seen. But I have promised myself that as soon as I had time, I would put a stop to her greedy scheming, and now the railroad deal is completed— (*He smiles strangely.*) That may be the change in activity I need. (*He pauses.*) If you ever fall in love, Joel, take my advice and do not marry. Keep your love your mistress, with no right of ownership except what she earns day by day, what she can make you pay for possession. Love should be a deal forever incomplete, never finally settled, with each party continually raising the bids, but neither one concluding a final role. (*He laughs mockingly at Joel's cold disapproval.*) Yes, my advice to you would be to shun marriage and keep a whore instead!

JOEL. I cannot see why you wish to discuss such matters with me.

SIMON. No, neither can I—except that I can trust you to listen without hearing much. (*With a conciliating manner.*) Why is it you never come to visit Mother?

JOEL. You know she has as little desire to see me as I have to see her.

SIMON. You would be astounded at the way she has transformed herself. It is as though she had slowly taken possession of Sara in order to make of my wife a second self through which she could live again. Or, in another aspect, trick Sara into being an accessory in the murder of that old self, which was once my mother. And so leave me motherless. But at the same time by becoming Sara, leave me wifeless, for naturally I could not regard— (*He stops abruptly—then goes on with an increasing brooding strangeness.*) Sometimes the two have appeared to lose their separate identities in my mind's eye—have seemed, through the subtle power of Mother's fantastic will, to merge and become one woman—a spirit of Woman made flesh and flesh of her made spirit, mother and wife in one—to whom I was never anything more than a necessary adjunct of a means to motherhood—a son in one case, a husband in the other—but now no longer needed since the mother by becoming the wife has my four sons to substitute for me, and the wife having them, no longer needs a husband to use in begetting— And so I am left alone, an unwanted son, a discarded lover, an outcast without meaning or function in my own home but pleasantly tolerated in memory of old service and as a domestic slave whose greed can be used to bring in money to support Woman! (*With vindictive calculation.*) Yes, that is what Mother flatters herself she has accomplished. But she doesn't realize there are fundamental weaknesses in her plan, that the past is never dead as long as we live because all we are is the past. She is going to discover, beginning today, and Sara, too, that whenever I wish, I take back what belongs to me, no matter— (*He checks himself with a sudden wary glance at Joel.*) But all these fanciful speculations are nonsense.

JOEL (*gets up from his chair*). If you have done, may I go back to my work?

SIMON. Yes. Take your idiotic conscience to hell out of here!

(*Joel turns and goes into the bookkeeper's office at right, closing the door behind him.*)

Even that dull fool realized I was really addressing myself—because I have no one but myself. Yes, Mother has left me with no life but this one which she always despised—the ambition to be a Napoleon among traders! I, who once dreamed—! Rubbish! The possession of power is the only freedom, and your pretended disgust with it is a lie. You must allow for your present state of mind—the reaction of emptiness after success—you've always felt it—but never so strongly before— There is a finality in this—as if some long patient tension had snapped—as if I no longer had the power to discipline my will to keep myself united—another self rebels—secedes—as if at last I must become two selves from now on—division and confusion—a war—a duel to the death— (*With revengeful bitterness.*) Well, let those who are responsible for the challenge beware, for I will make it their duel, too! Yes, Mother and Sara, henceforth I must demand that each of you takes upon herself her full responsibility for what I have become. Bah! What rubbishy fantasies!— As if I really desired two damned possessive women prying and interfering in my private business! All I know is that on an impulse I asked Sara to come here—some confused feeling that if I get her alone away from Mother's influence, I would desire her again. Hadn't I better think out more exactly how I shall attack?— No, wait until you feel her out and see how much of the old greedy Sara still lies behind her present self—the ambitious Sara who used to long to own an Irish-castle-in-Spain, gentleman's estate!—who was willing to use any means—even her beautiful body—to get what she wanted. I should have swindled her into giving herself by promising marriage—and then having had all I wanted of her, deserted her—it would have served her right to be beaten at her own game—I would have forgotten her and returned to Mother, waiting for me in her garden— (*Bitterly.*) But she wasn't waiting—She was just as ruthless and unscrupulous about discarding you as Sara was in taking you. Mother took pains to point it out to me by implication that day she deliberately made up the fairy tale about the exiled Prince and the magic door—

(*He sits staring before him, frowningly concentrated, and his face sets into a mask of calculating ruthlessness. The *door from the hall at rear is opened and* SARA *enters. She has not changed much in the five years. Has grown a little more matronly, perhaps, but seems no older. Is still exceedingly pretty, strong and healthy, with the same firm, pronouncedly female figure. But she is dressed much better, with discriminating taste and style now, and expensively. Her manner has taken on a lot of Deborah's well-bred, self-assured poise, and her way of speaking copies Deborah, although the rhythm of Irish speech still underlies it. She stands looking at Simon but he is oblivious of her presence. She smiles assuredly, a smile that has lost its old passionate tenderness and become entirely maternal, complacent in possessiveness—a smile that takes its proprietorship for granted. With growing amusement, she tiptoes forward until she stands by his table.)*

SARA. You might ask me to sit down, Simon. (*He jumps startledly in his chair.*)

SIMON. What do you mean by sneaking—! Oh, it's you.

SARA. That's a nice greeting, after you begged me to come.

SIMON. I apologize, Sara. For a moment, I didn't recognize who it was. (*He springs to his feet, indicating the chair across the table.*) Sit down, do.

(*She sits down and he sits down again.*)

SARA. I had no idea you'd gotten so nervous.

SIMON. You have been too occupied with family affairs to notice!

SARA (*smiling*). If that isn't like you, to put the blame on me, when it's you who come home every night with your head so full of business you might as well be on the moon. Speaking of business, tell me about the Company. You never mention it any more to us at home, but everyone tells us you're becoming the young Napoleon of trade here in the city.

SIMON. Here's a bit of news you haven't heard yet, Sara. I've got the railroad now. You remember I promised myself I would. Well, it's mine!

SARA (*with a forced enthusiasm*). Isn't that fine! I congratulate you, Simon.

SIMON. I have a final meeting with the directors this morning. Not very easy terms for them to accept, but they had no choice. They were on the verge of bankruptcy. I have learned from their mistakes. I'll make no mistakes!

SARA. I'm sure you won't.

SIMON. You're not very enthusiastic.

SARA. Oh, I am. But you used to say 'us' and 'ours'.

SIMON. Ah, you feel that?

SARA. No. God knows I've as happy a life as a woman could wish with Deborah and my children.

SIMON. Yes, one should never complain of the price one must pay for what one wants from life—or thinks one wants.

SARA. I know what I want, and I have it.

SIMON. I might complain that you used to speak of our home and our children, while now—

SARA. Ah, you feel that?

SIMON. I always have the feeling at home that, although Mother has relinquished all outward show of ownership and authority, she has managed to keep in possession.

SARA. I have the only say about everything, and she's happy to let me have it.

SIMON (*smiling*). Mother has always had a subtle talent for contriving it so that others must desire what she desires—and then generously giving them their way!

SARA. I'm not such a fool—

SIMON. Not when you're on your guard.

SARA. There's nothing to suspect! And she's been such a good grandmother to the children—even if she does spoil them.

SIMON (*gives her a sharp, calculating glance—quickly*). Yes, she is spoiling them. There's no doubt about that.

SARA. And there's no harm.

SIMON. If you're sure you haven't let it go too far.

SARA (*almost angrily*). I can take care of my children, thank you— Is that your reason for inviting me here—to try and make trouble between your mother and me?

SIMON. Don't be ridiculous! I'm delighted at the friendship which has developed between you. The more so because I never dared hope—

SARA (*almost tauntingly*). We know you didn't. Well, we fooled you!

SIMON. Do you imagine I'd prefer to have you at each other's throats?

SARA. No. That'd be crazy. But, Simon, I know you've kept a secret grudge against her in your heart. Isn't it about time you stopped being so childish, and forgave—?

SIMON. Don't be stupid. There's nothing to forgive. Am I not always pleasant with her?

SARA. Yes, as you'd be to an acquaintance in the street!

SIMON. But what's the use of pretending we have anything in common any more? Just because she happened to bear me into the world! Almost any fool of a woman can have a son, and every fool of a man has had a mother! It's no great achievement on either side, and all the hypocritical values we set on the relationship are mere stupidity.

SARA. That's not true! I've my four sons and I know the love I feel for them, and the love they feel for me!

SIMON. And don't tell me Mother minds my indifference. She has learned not to need me.

SARA (*with a trace of vindictive satisfaction*). That's true enough. She doesn't miss you now she has the children.

SIMON (*bitterly*). Yes. As you have.

SARA (*stares at him—defiantly*). As I have, yes. (*With a strange eagerness—teasingly.*) Don't tell me you're jealous of the children—with me? (*Forcing a smile—placatingly.*) But I hope you didn't ask me here just to quarrel with me. (*She gets up and comes around the table to him.*)

SIMON. Forgive me. This railroad deal has been a strain.

SARA. You haven't looked well for a long time.

SIMON. Then you do notice once in a while.

SARA. Your mother has seen it too.

SIMON. Indeed? And what was it you both noticed?

SARA. That you've been changing in some queer way inside you. Sometimes at night when you sit in the parlour with us, all of a sudden, it's like a stranger staring at me. It's a frightening feeling, Simon. I think I began to notice it around the time you started sleeping in your own room away from me—

SIMON. Ah, that's it, eh? Your body felt swindled and it made you suspicious, I suppose, that I might have found another woman's body that is more beautiful and desirable to mine than yours? You probably think I must be secretly keeping some beautiful mistress who has stolen your place in bed!

SARA (*startled and repelled*). Simon! I don't see how it could come to your mind— (*She gives him a look of frightened suspicion.*) Unless you've had the thought yourself—

SIMON (*his face lighting up with a pleased satisfaction*). No, no. I was only joking.

SARA (*forgetting her ladylike poise*). I don't believe you! You must have had the wish— (*With a sudden fierce passion she grabs his head and turns his face up to hers.*) Look at me! If I thought you wanted another woman—!

SIMON (*puts his arm around her and hugs her to him, his face triumphantly gratified—teasingly*). Well, what would you do?

SARA. I'd kill her! And you, too! Simon! You don't deny it! Tell me—!

SIMON (*still provocatively unconvincing, hugging her again*). No, no. Of course I would never—

SARA. You don't say that as if you meant it! (*Struggling to free herself.*) Let me go! I don't want you hugging me when maybe you're wishing it was another— (*Furious at the thought, she grabs his shoulders and shakes him fiercely.*) Is it to confess that you had me come here? Are you going to ask me to set you free to be hers? You can hold your prate! I'll see her in hell first! If any woman thinks she can take you from me, she'll find I'll fight to the death! (*She sits down on the arm of his chair and hugs him to her.*) You're mine till death, and beyond death, and I'll never let you go, do you hear? (*She kisses him passionately on the lips.*)

SIMON (*his face happy now with confident possession and aroused desire—but still provocatively*). So you really are jealous?

SARA. Am I flesh and blood? Don't I love you more than all the world?

SIMON. Do you? I thought the children—

SARA. Ah, the children! Not that I don't love them with all my heart. But they're not my lover and husband! You come first!

SIMON. Do I? I shouldn't say from your actions for a long time—

SARA (*indignantly*). Are you trying to say I'm to blame? Why, there's nights at home when you stare as if you were wondering what was my business there. Or you converse with us so pleasant and polite, like a gentleman guest come in to spend the evening.

SIMON. Perhaps I do feel like an intruder—

SARA. I don't know how to say it, darling, but it's as though the minute you came home I felt everything begin to change until nothing is what it seems to be, and we all get suspicious of each other.

SIMON. Even you and Mother?

SARA (*reluctantly*). Yes. (*Hastily.*) No, I meant it might if we weren't careful. It's like a spell that tries to come between us.

SIMON. That is strange. I thought that you both lived in a perfect unity of interests and desires now. Sometimes I become so intensely conscious of your unity that you appear as one woman to me. I cannot distinguish my wife from— It is a bewildering confusion.

SARA. Is that when you stare at us as though you hated us? (*Forces a smile.*) That's a queer crazy notion for you to have, Simon— But I think I know the kind of feeling you mean. I've felt myself at times—oh, only once in a while—that she'd like me to have no wish but her wish, and no life that wasn't ruled by her life.

SIMON (*watching her*). Yes, Mother has always been extremely greedy for others' lives. You have to be constantly on guard—

SARA (*defiantly*). But she knows I'm too strong— (*Abruptly shamefaced.*) Ah, what am I saying! It's mean and wrong of me to suspect her. And don't think I don't see how you've changed the subject to her so you wouldn't have to answer me about having a mistress. Tell me you haven't, Simon! I couldn't bear— (*She starts to sob.*)

SIMON (*springs up and hugs her to him—passionately*). Of course I haven't, sweetheart! Look at me! (*He lifts her face to his.*) I swear—!

SARA. Oh, darling. I know I'm foolish—but I love you so! (*She kisses him and he responds, hugging her to him with a passionate desire. She breaks away, stirred and happy, but modestly embarrassed—with a soft laugh.*) We mustn't. Supposing someone came in! It's a long time since you've kissed me—like that, darling.

SIMON. A long time since you've given me the chance!

SARA. I like that! You'll say next it was I that wanted you to sleep alone. You don't know how you hurt me when you did that, Simon. I tried to believe your excuse that you didn't want to keep me awake when you couldn't sleep because your mind kept making plans for the Company. But I couldn't help fearing the real reason was you didn't want me.

SIMON (*hugs her passionately*). You know I want you now, don't you?

SARA. Oh, here—now—yes— But at home—

SIMON. That's why I asked you to come. Because I want you to want me as you used to, but at home there is always Mother coming between us.

SARA (*frowns*). Yes, it's true you feel her always there, watching— But she doesn't mean to interfere. The trouble is you haven't noticed the change in her. You don't know the nice, kind, contented old grandmother she is now.

SIMON (*pretending to give in*). I must admit she seems sincere in her affection for your children.

SARA. Oh, she is, Simon!

SIMON. From their talk, they must spend a great deal of their time in her garden.

SARA (*a shadow of resentment shows in her face*). Yes, they do. But now they'll be away at school a lot of the day. (*Defensively.*) It's good for them to be with her. She's a great lady and her influence—

SIMON. I remember my own experience. If I hadn't got away from her before it was too late, she'd have made me dependent upon her for life. So you can understand why I am worried. After all, they are my sons, too.

SARA. I'm so happy to know you think of them.

SIMON. We want them trained to live with reality so when the time comes they will be capable of serving our Company—Ethan as manager of our marine division, Wolfe to direct the banking branch which we will own before long, Jonathan as our railroad executive, and Honey our representative in politics.

SARA. And I thought you'd forgotten— Forgive me, darling.

SIMON. And I am confident they will have the brains and ability—provided we don't permit Mother to poison their minds with nonsense.

SARA. Yes. (*Hesitantly.*) I could ask her not to— (*Guiltily.*) No. It would be like breaking my part of a bargain I'd made in honour to trust her.

SIMON. It was no part of the bargain that she should steal your children.

SARA (*defensively*). Ah, now, that's going too far. Anyway, they know who their mother is and who they love best.

SIMON. I have the idea they are becoming as confused between you as I. I mean as I am at home. Here you are yourself, my wife, my partner—my mistress, too, I hope. (*He hugs her desirously.*)

SARA (*responding passionately*). Don't ever dream of having another!

SIMON (*abruptly, with a business-like tone*). We've allowed things to get in a confused muddle at home. I've been too preoccupied with the Company's affairs, and you've been too busy housekeeping for Mother and acting as nurse girl while she's left free to play she's their mother to them.

SARA (*with a flash of resentful anger*). Ah, I'd like to see her try—! I begin to see a lot of things I've been blind to.

SIMON. The thing you must bear in mind is that she has never been quite normal. We might as well be frank, Sara.

SARA (*uneasily*). You mean she's insane? Ah no, that's crazy, Simon. I won't let you say such wicked things. The poor woman!

SIMON. I didn't say insane. I meant she has no sense of the rights to freedom of others.

SARA. And didn't she tell me herself she'd got to the point where she didn't dare go in that summer-house of hers for fear she'd never come out again. That's crazy, isn't it?

SIMON (*strangely*). Who knows? It all depends— Do you know if she ever goes in the summer-house now?

SARA. No. The children used to plague her to open the door but she never would. Why do you ask?

SIMON. The children must be forbidden to go to her garden or her rooms in future. She can see quite enough of them when you and I are present. And you stay away from her garden, too.

SARA. I hardly ever go.

SIMON. Then you'll give orders to the children?

SARA. Yes. But who will tell her?

SIMON. Why you, of course.

SARA. She's been so good—I hate hurting her.

SIMON (*avoiding her eyes—calculatingly, with feigned reluctance*). Well, I suppose I could tell her, if you want to be spared.

SARA. Would you? But promise me you won't be cruel to her, Simon.

SIMON. Don't be foolish, dear. I want peace in my home. I'll drop in at her garden on my way home this evening. (*With a strange happy satisfied air.*) There. That puts Mother in her place—back where she belongs. Let's forget her now and think only of us. (*He gives her a loving, possessive hug.*) As we did in the old days.

SARA. I'm only too glad to, darling.

SIMON. I have grown very lonely, Sara.

SARA. If you knew how unhappy and ugly I've felt since you started sleeping alone—and even before that when you'd lie beside me as if I wasn't there.

SIMON. Because I never felt we were really alone—there, in Mother's house. That's why I had you come here. I want to ask you to help me create a new life—a life in which we can be lovers again. (*He presses her to him passionately.*)

SARA (*sensually aroused—kissing his hair*). Darling! You know I'd love nothing better!

SIMON. I want the old Sara, whose beautiful body was so greedily hungry for lust and possession, whose will was as devoid of scruple, as ruthlessly determined to devour and live as the spirit of life itself! The Sara who came to my room on that night long ago, with her mind made up to use her beautiful body to keep anyone from taking what she regarded as hers.

SARA (*guiltily*). Ah, don't say— (*Reproachfully.*) You loved me for it! So you shouldn't remember it against me.

SIMON. Against you? I desired her more than anything in life! And now I desire her to come back more than anything in life! I owe her all my success. She is the cause of the Company! Now I need her again. I want her to come back to me here, as she came to me that night, willing to gamble with the highest possible stake, all she has, to sell her dearly.

SARA (*half pleased and flattered and half guiltily defensive*). Ah, don't talk of it that way—as if I was some low street girl who came that night to sell herself. I was bound I'd have you because I loved you so much.

SIMON. Well then, I know you will be willing to become your old true self again for me.

SARA. Well, look out then. I could be her, for I love you just as much now. But maybe you'd better let her sleep. She might be bolder than ever and want more! (*She kisses him—then suddenly embarrassed and shy, pushes back from him.*) But what a way for me to act! Here in your office, of all places! There's a queer thing in the air here, that makes you—and I'd stayed at home so long I'd forgotten— But I don't know what I mean— (*She hugs him passionately again.*) Except I love you now with all of me and all my strength, and there's no one else in the world, and I'm yours and you're mine, and I don't care how shameless I am!

SIMON. Sweetheart! That fits in exactly with my plans for our future here, because the Company is you. Your nature is its nature. It derived its life from your life, which you must claim for your own again.

SARA. Darling! Tell me plainly what your plan is.

SIMON (*with a brisk, business-like air now*). This: The children will be away most of the day at school from now on. You'll be free. Well, I want you to work with me here in the Company as my secretary and secret partner.

SARA. Darling! Do you really mean—?

SIMON. Then you'll do it?

SARA. Will I? It's too good to be true! (*She kisses him.*) Oh, you make me so happy, darling, when you prove you want me that much!

SIMON. Wait! There's a condition. Nothing for nothing is the rule here, you know. You'll have to pay for this opportunity.

SARA. Stop teasing now and tell me. I'll do anything you want.

SIMON. What! Do you mean to tell me a virtuous wife and mother like you will agree to become my mistress?

SARA (*shocked, embarrassed, and at the same time amused and curiously fascinated and delighted*). So— Then I'm the mistress you were wishing for! Well, God be thanked, you weren't dreaming of any other!

SIMON. I don't know of anyone else who would be more desirable. And I can make you a most favourable offer.

SARA. That's a nice way to talk to a decent wife! But let's

hear your offer. Maybe it's not enough. I value myself highly!

SIMON. I'll agree to pay with all my worldly goods. You can get the whole Company from me—that is, of course, piece by piece, as you earn it!

SARA. The whole Company to be mine! (*She kisses him suddenly with passionate gratitude.*) Oh, darling, and I was so afraid I'd become ugly to you and you were sick of me.

SIMON. Then you will take the place?

SARA. You know I will. (*She hides her face on his shoulder shamefacedly—then suddenly lifts it and bursts out.*) I'll play any game with you you like, and it will be fun playing I'm a wicked, lustful, wanton creature and making you a slave to my beauty.

SIMON. I was afraid you might raise objections.

SARA. Objections? When you want me and I want you?

SIMON. Well, Mother won't approve of my taking you away, as well as the children.

SARA (*resentfully*). It's none of her business.

SIMON (*with a strange gloating air*). Poor Mother. She will be very lonely again. I think she will welcome visits even from me.

SARA. Don't make me think of her now. (*She kisses him.*) All I want to think of now is that you want me again.

SIMON (*hugs her—passionately*). I have never wanted you so much! No, not even in the days before we were married! Your body is beautiful, sweetheart!

SARA (*kisses him passionately*). Darling! (*She breaks away—with a soft happy laugh.*) Aren't we the shameless ones!

SIMON. Yes, you will have to learn to be shameless here. You will have to deal daily with the greedy fact of life as it really lives. You will have to strip life naked, and face it. And accept it as truth. And strip yourself naked and accept yourself as you are in the greedy mind and flesh. Then you can go on—successfully—with a clear vision—without false scruple—on to demand and take what you want—as I have done! But you will discover all this for yourself. You will be successful. You have the natural talent. And I know you will find the game I play here in the Company as fascinating a gamble as I find it! (*Strangely now—as if he were talking aloud to himself.*) A fascinating game—resembling love, I think a woman will find. A game of secret, cunning strategems, in which only the fools who are fated to lose reveal their true aims or motives—even to themselves. You have to become a gambler whose face is a mask. But one grows lonely and haunted. One finally gets a sense of confusion in the meaning of the game, so that one's winnings have the semblance of losses. The adversary across the table in whose eyes one can read no betraying emotion beyond an identical lust—this familiar stranger to whom with a trustful smile one passes the cards one has marked, or the dice one has loaded, at the moment he accepts them trustfully becomes oneself. (*He frowns and shakes his head.*)

SARA. Now, darling, please don't be mixing everything up in my mind. I don't know what you mean by that queer talk of marked cards and loaded dice.

SIMON (*smilingly, but with a threat underneath*). Oh, you will some day. I promise you you will. (*Then, as she stares at him uneasily—abruptly business-like.*) Well, I think we've settled everything. (*He glances at his watch.*) The railroad directors will be here in a few minutes. You will start your work here tomorrow morning.

SARA (*has got off the arm of his chair—jokingly bobs him a curtsy*). At your service. But remember I've no experience.

SIMON. At first, all I wish you to do is sit and watch how I deal with everything. As though you were an understudy learning to play my part. As you learn, I will let you act in my stead now and then until finally you will find yourself capable of taking my place. In your spare time, when I am away, I want you to draw plans for the country estate with the great mansion you used to dream about where we are going to retire when we have enough. (*He gets up and kisses her.*) No price is too high for me to pay my mistress for her love, eh?

SARA (*pulling away*). I wish you wouldn't talk as if love—

SIMON. You shall have your estate. Of course, it wouldn't do to withdraw that much capital now. There is so much to be accomplished before the Company can be free and independent and self-sufficient. Meanwhile, if you get it actually planned to the last detail—

SARA. Yes! Oh, that will be fun! And I've got every bit of it clear in my mind—or I used to have—

SIMON. You can afford to make bigger, more ambitious plans now, in view of the Company's progress since you last dreamed of it.

SARA. Oh, I can always dream bigger dreams, and I'll be only too delighted to make plans. Well, I'd better go now. (*She kisses him—tenderly.*) Goodbye, my darling! You've made me so happy! (*She breaks from his arms and opens the door.*)

SIMON. Wait! Mother will be curious about your visit here but don't tell her anything. I can make the meaning clearer to her, I think.

SARA (*pityingly, but at the same time scornfully*). Ah, poor woman. I'm not anxious to tell her— Well, it'll do her good! She's gotten to think she owns me! (*She stops abruptly.*) Ah, I ought to be ashamed! What makes me feel like that here?

(*She looks around the office almost frightenedly—then hastily.*) I'll go now. (*She goes out and closes the door.*)

SIMON (*looks after her and smiles strangely—ironically*). Well, that half of my domestic responsibility-sharing scheme is launched successfully. (*He walks back to his desk.*) Yes, that part will work itself out according to plan. (*He suddenly frowns resentfully.*) Plan?— What plan?— You'd think this was some intricate intrigue you were starting, whereas it is very simple— You want Sara— All right, you take her back, and that's all there is to it— As for Mother, she has interfered and carried on an intrigue to isolate you— She must be taught to confine her activities to their proper sphere—to remain back where she belongs— Very well, put her in her place this afternoon—and that will settle her half of it.

(*He sits down at his desk—with a strange smile of anticipation. His expression becomes relaxed and dreamy.*)

It will be pleasant to find myself in her garden again after all these years.

(*A pause. There is a knock on the door at right. At once Simon becomes the formidable, ruthless head of the Company.*)

Come in.

(*Joel enters.*)

JOEL. The directors are in the outer office. I thought I should pay them the courtesy of announcing them myself considering their importance.

SIMON. They had it when they had power. But I took it from them. And your courtesy is meaningless and a cruel joke which mocks at their plight. If I was one of them, I would knock you down. Tell them to come in.

(*Joel stares at him—then goes out.*)

CURTAIN

ACT TWO, SCENE TWO

SCENE. *Same as Scene Two of Act One, the corner of the Harford garden with the octagonal Chinese summer-house. Late afternoon sunlight from beyond the wall at right falls on the pointed roof and the upper part of the arched lacquer-red door and ivy-covered walls of the summer-house. The shrubs, clipped as before in arbitrary geometrical designs, and the trees along the brick wall at rear glow in different shades of green. The water in the small oval pool before the summer-house is still another shade of green. The garden has the same appearance as before of everything being meticulously tended and trimmed. This effect is of nature distorted and humiliated by a deliberately mocking, petulant arrogance.*

DEBORAH *is sitting on the steps leading up to the summer-house door, dressed all in white. She appears greatly changed from the previous act. Where she had seemed a prematurely old, middle-aged woman then, she now has the look of a surprisingly youthful grandmother. Her body and face have filled out a little. There is something of repose and contentment in her expression, something of an inner security and harmony. But her beautiful dark eyes and her smile still retain their old imaginative, ironical aloofness and detachment.*

As the curtain rises, Deborah is reading from a volume of Byron's poems. Suddenly she stops, and listens to something beyond the wall at right. Her expression changes to one of alarmed surprise and she stares at the door in the wall with dread. For a moment there is a tense silence. Then there is a sharp rap of the knocker on the door. After another moment there is a louder knock and Simon's voice calls sharply: 'It's I, Mother. Open the door!' *A little smile of gloating scorn comes to Deborah's lips. She allows the book to slip from her hand and goes and opens the door, then sits down by the steps again.* SIMON *comes in, closing the door after him.*

SIMON. Good evening, Mother.

DEBORAH (*coldly pleasant*). This is an unexpected pleasure, Simon.

SIMON. Evidently. Such cooling my heels before the sacred portals. I trust I have not intruded? May I sit down?

DEBORAH. This is your property. Pray do so.

SIMON. Sara's property. (*He sits on the stone bench on her left.*)

DEBORAH (*with a trace of mockery*). But what is hers is yours.

SIMON. Yes, that is quite true. Sara has probably told you of her visit to my office this morning.

DEBORAH. She told me before she left you had asked her to come there.

SIMON (*feigning surprise*). That I had asked her?

(*She glances at him sharply. He goes on carelessly.*)

Well, it is of no importance who asked whom. You say she has not mentioned our interview in any way?

DEBORAH (*with forced indifference*). I imagine it concerned property of yours—her name and papers you wished her to sign. She knows I would not be interested in that.

SIMON. It had nothing to do with papers. Although, of course, it did concern property. You know Sara.

DEBORAH (*as if caught off guard*). Yes, you may be sure I— (*She catches herself and looks at him defensively.*)

SIMON. I was very glad she came. It gave me a chance to talk over with her a new arrangement at the office. I find it advisable to add a private secretary to my employ.

DEBORAH. And you had to have Sara's consent for that?

SIMON (*smilingly*). You will understand why when I tell you the one person who possesses the qualifications I desire is a young and very beautiful woman.

DEBORAH (*starts—her first instinctive reaction one of vindictive satisfaction and gloating pity*). Ah! Poor Sara! So this is what your great romantic love comes to in the end! I always knew— (*Abruptly and guiltily her reaction changes to one of over-stressed moral indignation.*) How dare you mention such filth to your mother! Have you become so utterly coarse that you feel no shame but actually boast you are deliberately planning to dishonour yourself and your family? But I don't know why I should be surprised. After all, this is an inevitable step in the corruption of your character that I have had to watch for years, until I could hardly recognize my son in the unscrupulous greedy trader, whose one dream was material gain!

SIMON. May I point out that you have been jumping too eagerly to conclusions, Mother? I have not said my secretary was to be anything more intimate than my secretary.

(*Deborah looks guilty and discomfited. He adds with a mocking smile.*)

I am afraid the good grandmother you have become has not entirely forgotten the French eighteenth-century memoirs in which she once lived.

DEBORAH (*stares at him strickenly—pleadingly*). Simon! It is not kind to make me remember— (*With dread.*) Oh, why did you come here? What—?

SIMON. And I don't see how you can think Sara would ever consent—unless you secretly believe her true nature is so greedy that she would sell anything if offered the right price.

DEBORAH. No! How dare you—! I will not have you put such thoughts in my mind about a woman to whom I owe an eternal debt of gratitude, who is the sweetest, kindest, most generous-hearted—

SIMON. I am sorry to have to disillusion you, Mother, but I think you will discover before our interview is over that Sara has not been as blind as you hoped, nor as unsuspectingly trustful.

(*Deborah starts and stares at him uneasily.*)

It does not do to hold one's enemy in the battle for supremacy in too much contempt—

DEBORAH. As though Sara and I were engaged in some fantastic duel! I bitterly resent your intruding here and attempting to create suspicion and jealousy between Sara and me. I trust her and I know she trusts me!

SIMON. We will deal with the facts, if you please, Mother, not with sentimental posing.

DEBORAH (*staring at him with a fascinated dread—stammers*). Simon! What are you trying to do? I know this is some insane plot to revenge yourself on me!

SIMON. Revenge for what? It was I who long ago, of my own free will, freed myself from your influence.

DEBORAH (*with a little smile—carelessly*). So you have never forgotten that old quarrel? I remember now I used to be of the opinion it was I who forced you out into your own life. So that I might be free.

SIMON. Yes, you consoled your pride with that lie.

DEBORAH. If you wish. I appreciate that a Napoleon of affairs must believe implicitly in his own star. (*She laughs softly—teasingly.*) You are still such a strange, greedy boy, do you know it?

SIMON (*glancing around the garden—with a tone of nostalgic yearning*). I had forgotten the quiet and the peace here. Nothing has changed. The past is the present. (*Suddenly he turns on her—harshly accusing.*) You are the one jarring discordant note. The garden of your old self disowns the doting old Granny you have made yourself pretend to be.

DEBORAH (*with a soft teasing laugh*). Don't tell me you are jealous of your children, too!

SIMON. Too? Beyond observing your obvious campaign to obtain control of the children, and pitying Sara for what I mistakenly thought was her blind trustfulness, I have regarded the matter as none of my business.

DEBORAH (*checks herself—quietly casual*). Speaking of business, you must be becoming richer and more powerful all the time.

SIMON. I concluded a deal today which adds a railroad to the Company's properties.

DEBORAH (*flatteringly but with underlying sarcasm*). My congratulations, dear.

SIMON. Thank you, Mother. It has significance as a link in the chain in which my ships bring cotton to my mills to be made into my cloth and shipped on my railroad. But there is a lot to be done before the chain is complete.

DEBORAH (*with a little mocking smile*). Yes, I perceive it is not enough.

SIMON (*deadly serious*). Far from it. The next step must be to acquire my own bank. Then I can manipulate all the Company's financing.

DEBORAH. And you will want your own stores here in the city to sell your goods.

SIMON. Yes. I have that in mind.

DEBORAH. And at the other end of your chain you should possess plantations in the South and own your own slaves, imported in your own slave ships.

SIMON (*staring before him, tense and concentrated*). Yes. Of course. I had not considered that but it is obviously the logical final step at that end. You are wonderfully shrewd and far-sighted, Mother, for a beautiful lady who has always affected a superior disdain for greedy traders like my father and me.

DEBORAH. You find me still a little beautiful? I fear you are merely flattering a poor ugly old woman.

SIMON. I am glad to find you changed in one respect, Mother. You now have the courage to face some of the things that have reality. Father had scruples. He disguised his greed with Sabbath potions of God-fearing unction at the First Congregationalist Church. I fear no God but myself! I will let nothing stand between me and my goal!

DEBORAH. What goal, Simon?

SIMON (*turns to her in surprise*). But I thought you saw that, Mother. To make the Company entirely self-sufficient. It must attain the all-embracing security of complete self-possession—the might which is the sole right not to be a slave! Do you see?

DEBORAH. I see, dear—that you have gone very far away from me—and become lost in yourself and very lonely.

SIMON. Lost? Oh no, don't imagine I have lost. I always win. Wait and see, Mother! I'll prove to you I can lead the Company to a glorious, final triumph—complete independence and freedom within itself! (*He pauses and looks around the garden. Then he sighs wearily.*) But sometimes lately, Mother, alone in my office, I have felt so weary of the game—of watching suspiciously each card I led to myself from across the table—even though I had marked them all—watching my winnings pile up and becoming confused with losses—feeling my swindler's victorious gloating die into boredom and discontent—the flame of ambition smoulder into a chill dismay—as though that opponent within had spat an extinguishing poison of disdain—

DEBORAH (*strangely, tenderly sympathetic*). I used to know so well. (*Tensely.*) I had once reached a point where I had grown so lost, I had not even a dream left I could dream without screaming scornful laughter at myself. I would sit locked in the summer-house here—sit there for hours in wisdom-ridiculing contemplation of myself, and spit in my mind, and my heart, like a village idiot in a country store spitting at the belly of a stove—cursing the day I was born, the day I indifferently conceived, the day I bore— (*With a terrible intensity.*) Until I swear to you I felt I could by just one tiny further wish, one little effort more of will, push open the door to madness where I could at least believe in a dream again! And how I longed for that final escape! (*She suddenly turns and stares at him with hatred.*) Ah! And you wonder why I hate you! (*Abruptly overcome by a panic of dread, starting to her feet.*) Simon! What are you trying to do? Leave me alone! Leave the past in its forgotten grave! (*Trying to control herself and be casual and indifferent.*) Frankly, I am bored with listening to your nonsense. I will go in the house now. Sara must be wondering what is keeping me, now the sun is setting.

(*She starts for the path off left. Simon, without looking at her, begins to speak again. She stops, makes herself go on, finally stops and turns to stare at him.*)

SIMON. I began to remember lately—and long for this garden—and you, as you used to be and are no longer—and I as I was then—in this safe haven, where we could repose our souls in fantasy—evade, escape, forget, rest in peace! I regret that paradise in which you were the good, kind, beloved, beautiful Queen. I have become so weary of what they call life beyond the wall, Mother.

DEBORAH (*moved and fascinated, takes a step towards him—tenderly*). I see you have, my son. Who knows?—your loss is not irrevocable. We—you and I—in partnership in a new company of the pure spirit, might reorganize your bankruptcy—if I may put it in terms you understand. (*She smiles teasingly.*)

SIMON (*with a passionate eagerness*). Yes! (*He grabs her hand.*)

DEBORAH (*as if the touch of his hand alarmed her—shrinks back, turning away from him—guiltily stammers to herself*). No! I swore to her I would never interfere. I cannot! I am content. I have all I desire. (*She turns to Simon—resentfully and derisively.*) My dear boy, your childish fancies are ridiculous. We do not really wish such nonsense. And if we did, it would be impossible, we have both changed so much. (*Carelessly taunting.*) But if you care to drop in here once in a while on your return from work, I know the children would be pleased to see you. You could boast to them of your heroic exploits.

SIMON (*stiffens, stares at her with hatred for a second—then coldly, in a curt tone*). I'm glad you mentioned the children. It reminds me of my real purpose in coming here. I must inform you that Sara and I have decided you are having a very bad influence on our children—

DEBORAH (*startled—resentful and uneasy*). That is ridiculous! I have been at pains not to influence them at all!

SIMON. Sara decided that henceforth the children must be

forbidden to see you except in the house when either she or I are present to protect them.

DEBORAH (*strickenly*). You mean they are to be taken from me? I am to be left entirely alone again—with no life but the memory of the past—? You can't be so cruel! I have made myself love them! I have created a new life— (*Abruptly—with an eager hatred.*) And you say Sara decided this? No! I won't believe it!

SIMON. I would hardly lie about something you can confirm as soon as you see her. You'll find she is giving them their orders in the house right now.

DEBORAH (*with an almost joyous vindictiveness*). Ah, if she has betrayed me and broken all her pledges! That releases me!

SIMON. You know there is nothing strange about her being jealous of your stealing her children.

DEBORAH (*with a vindictive satisfaction*). Well, perhaps she has cause to be! They can never forget me! You are right! I have never entirely trusted her! I have resented her interference and possessiveness—I have hated the intolerable debt of daily gratitude! (*Then brokenly.*) But how could she do this to me! She knows how much the children have meant to me! She knows without them I shall be lost again!

SIMON. Come now, Mother. You are not really as exercised by the loss of the children as you pretend. You were never intended for the job of Sara's unpaid nursemaid. I have seen you fall completely under Sara's influence and become merely a female, common, vulgar—a greedy home-owner, dreamless and contented!

DEBORAH (*angrily*). You are talking nonsense! It is I who have influenced her! Deliberately! As part of my scheme! (*Hastily.*) No! What made me say that?

SIMON (*with a resentful intensity*). By God, there have been times when, as I watched you together in the house at night, she would seem to steal all identity from you—until there was but one woman—she!

DEBORAH (*with an exultant satisfaction*). Ah, you felt that? That we were one, united against—? That is what I wished to do! Poor boy! But you are blind or you would have seen it was I who took possession of her in order to— (*She checks herself.*) But as you say, it is very confusing. One cannot see clearly what or why— (*Frightenedly.*) And I do not care to see. Besides, you have shown me clearly I do not need her to take back what is mine.

SIMON (*staring before him*). Yes, Mother, I rely on you to help me keep her in her rightful place hereafter.

DEBORAH (*regards him calculatingly—then with a caressingly gentle air*). And my place?

SIMON (*with queer, hesitating embarrassment*). Why, here in your garden, of course, as always in the past.

DEBORAH (*softly insinuating*). Alone? I was not always alone in the past. (*She pats his hair—with a teasing laugh.*) What? Have you no hope to offer your poor lonely mother?

SIMON (*awkwardly stiff and formal*). I do not wish you to be too lonely. I will be happy to consider any suggestion you—

DEBORAH (*with a teasing laugh, ruffling his hair playfully*). Ah! I see! Still Napoleon! Still so proud! Very well. I will play your humble slave, sire. Will you deign to visit me here and comfort my exile?

SIMON (*stiffly*). Yes, it is very restful here. (*Eagerly, under his awkward formality.*) I shall be delighted to drop in and keep you company here for a while each afternoon on my way home. A little rest here each day will restore the soul—the change I so badly need— (*He breaks off. He sees the volume of Byron on the steps. He picks it up—with a forced casual air.*) What's this? Ah, Byron— (*He examines the volume—with pleased boyish surprise.*) I thought this looked familiar. Here's the inscription 'To my beloved mother.' Here are the parts I marked, and the parts you marked, and the parts we marked together. Do you remember, Mother, we would be sitting here just as we are now, and I'd ask you to read aloud to me—?

DEBORAH (*softly*). I remember, dear, as clearly as if it were yesterday. Or, even, as though it were now.

SIMON (*turns the pages*). Here is our favourite! I don't have to look at the book. I still know it by heart. But I'll bet you can guess what it is, Mother.

DEBORAH (*smiling fondly*). Yes, I'm sure I can guess— (*She recites—with growing arrogance.*)

> 'I have not loved the World, nor the World me;
> I have not flattered its rank breath—'

SIMON (*breaks in and takes it up, taking on her tone*).

> '—nor bowed
> To its idolatries a patient knee,
> Nor coined my cheek to smiles—'

DEBORAH.

> '—nor cried aloud
> In worship of an echo:'

SIMON (*his face hardening into his office mask of the ruthless executive*).

> '—in the crowd
> They could not deem me one of such—'

DEBORAH.

> '—I stood
> Among them, but not of them—'

(*He joins in here and they both finish together.*)
'—in a shroud
Of thoughts which were not their thoughts—'

(*They stop abruptly and stare at each other—then they both burst out laughing merrily, and Deborah claps her hands.*)

SIMON. I remember so well now, Mother!

DEBORAH. Yes, that was just as it used to be.

(*From the house off left Sara's voice is heard calling in a tone of repressed uneasiness:* 'Simon, are you in the garden?' *The two start resentfully. Deborah gives him a hostile, contemptuous look.*)

She wants her husband.

SIMON (*angrily, as if aloud to himself*). God, can I never know a moment's freedom! (*He calls curtly, almost insultingly.*) I am here with Mother. What do you want now?

(*Sara's voice answers with an attempt at carelessness:* 'Nothing, darling. I simply wanted to be sure.' *A door is heard closing.*)

SIMON (*with a gloating chuckle*). She wants to be sure. I thought she sounded a little uneasy.

DEBORAH (*with a malicious smile*). Even a little frightened perhaps.

SIMON (*frowning*). I have already ordered her never to come here again. (*Eagerly insistent.*) Let's forget her existence. We were back in the past before she lived in us.

DEBORAH. Take my hand so you will not get lost.

SIMON (*kisses her hand with a shy, boyish impulsiveness*). I will never leave you again, Mother. Do you know what had come into my mind? A memory that goes back long before our Byron days, when I was still at the fairy-tale age, and you would read tales aloud to me, here. Or, what I liked better, you would make up your own. They seemed so much more real than the book ones.

DEBORAH (*uneasily, forcing a laugh*). Good Heavens, you are going far back! I had forgotten—

SIMON (*insistently, almost commandingly*). You can't have forgotten the one I just remembered. It was your favourite. And mine. I can see you sitting there, as you are now, dressed all in white, so beautiful and so unreal, more like a character in your story than a flesh-and-blood mother. One would have thought you were afraid that even your own child was a greedy interloper plotting to steal you from your dreams!

DEBORAH (*uneasily and guiltily—forcing a laugh*). Why, what a mean suspicious thought—about your poor devoted mother, dear!

SIMON. You would be sitting there before the summer-house, like a sentry guarding the door. (*He turns to her resentfully.*) Why did you make that silly rule that no one was ever allowed to go in the summer-house but you? As if it were some secret temple of which you were high priestess! No one would have cared about going in there, anyway!

DEBORAH. You used to plead and beg—

SIMON. Well, naturally, when you forbid a boy to go anywhere, without giving him any sensible reason—

DEBORAH (*a bit sharply, as if he were still the little boy.*) I explained over and over again that I felt all the rooms in the house, even my bedroom, were your father's property. And this garden I shared with you. I naturally desired one place, no matter how tiny, that would be mine alone. It's just that you stubbornly refused to believe that. You didn't want to admit I could live, even for a moment, without you. (*With a shiver—hurriedly.*) Why do you remember that so well? You were starting to remember a fairy tale.

SIMON. There is a connection with the summer-house.

DEBORAH (*startled*). Then I do not care to hear—

SIMON. Oh, not in your story. The connection was in my imagination. (*He begins to tell the story, staring before him as if he visualized it.*) There was once upon a time a young King of a happy land who, through the evil magic of a beautiful enchantress, had been dispossessed of his realm and banished to wander over the world, a homeless, unhappy outcast. Now the enchantress, it appeared, had in a last moment of remorse, when he was being sent into exile, revealed to him that there was a way in which he might regain his lost kingdom. He must search the world for a certain magic door.

DEBORAH. Ah.

SIMON. It might be any door, but if he wished to find it with all his heart, he would recognize it when he came to it, and know that on the other side was his lost kingdom. After enduring bitter trials, and numberless disappointments, he at last found himself before a door, and the wish in his heart told him his quest was ended. But just as he was about to open it and cross the threshold, he heard the voice of the enchantress speaking from the other side, for she was there awaiting his coming. 'Wait. Before you open I must warn you to remember how evil I can be and that it is probable I maliciously lied and gave you a false hope. If you dare to open the door you may discover this is no longer your old happy realm but a barren desert, where it is always night, haunted by terrible ghosts and ruled over by a hideous old witch, who wishes to destroy your claim to her realm, and the moment you cross the threshold she will tear you to pieces and devour you.'

DEBORAH (*with a little shudder—forcing a laugh*). Oh, come

now, dear. I am sure I never— I remember the story as an ironically humorous tale.

SIMON. 'So you had better be sure of your courage,' the enchantress called warningly, 'and remember that as long as you stay where you are you will run no risk of anything worse than your present unhappy exile.' Then he heard her laugh. She did not speak again, although he knew she remained there, and would always remain, waiting to see if he would dare open the door. (*With a strange bitterness.*) But he never did, you said. He felt she was lying to test his courage. Yet, at the same time, he felt she was not lying, and he was afraid. He wanted to turn his back on the door and go far away, but it held him in a spell and he could never leave it. So he remained for the rest of his life standing before the door, and became a beggar, whining for alms from all who passed by. (*He turns to stare at her—forcing a smile, resentfully.*) That, I suppose, constitutes the humorous irony you remembered?

DEBORAH (*laughingly, with an undercurrent of taunting satisfaction*). Yes, I can remember how resentful you were at the ending. You used to insist I imagine a new ending in which the wicked enchantress had become a good fairy and opened the door and welcomed him home and they were both happy ever after. (*She laughs.*)

SIMON. And you would laugh at me. (*With a strange challenging look.*) I would still like to discover if you could possibly imagine a happy ending to that tale.

DEBORAH. What silly nonsense, Simon! Fairy tales, indeed! What a preoccupation for a Napoleon of facts!

SIMON. Yes, absurd, I admit. But I was very impressionable then and your story was very real to me. The door of the tale became identified in my mind with the door there to your forbidden summer-house. I used to boast to myself that if I were that King I would gamble recklessly on the chance— (*Suddenly, moved by a strange urgency, he springs to his feet and goes past her up the steps to the door.*) Let's have done with this mystery right now! (*He seizes the knob.*)

DEBORAH (*starts to her feet in a panic of dread and grabs his other arm*). No, Simon! No! (*Her panic is transformed into an outraged fury.*) Come away! Obey me this instant! How dare you! Will your vulgar greed leave me nothing I can call my own?

SIMON (*overcome by this outburst, moves back down the steps obediently like a cowed boy*). I'm sorry, Mother. I— I didn't think you'd mind now—

DEBORAH (*suddenly calm and relieved and a bit guilty*). I can't help minding. The truth is I have become superstitious—remembering the last time I was in there—and I was afraid—

SIMON (*has recovered his poise as she has weakened—curtly*). That is damned nonsense, Mother. There's nothing there, of course.

DEBORAH (*with a little shiver*). *I* am there.

SIMON. That's insanity, Mother.

DEBORAH. Yes. I know. There is nothing in there but dark and dust and spiderwebs—and the silence of dead dreams.

SIMON (*smiling*). Well, anyway, it would not be a happy ending, would it, for me to go in alone? No, some day, I will give you the courage to open the door yourself and we will go together—

DEBORAH (*turning on him with forced scorn*). It is grotesque for a grown man to act so childishly. I forbid you ever to mention this subject again. It is only on that condition I can agree to welcome you in my garden.

SIMON (*with a mocking gallantry, kissing her hand*). Your wish my law, madame.

DEBORAH (*abruptly changing to a gay, arrogantly-pleased, seductive coquetry*). That is as should be, monsieur.

(*From the house off left comes Sara's voice:* 'Simon, are you still in the garden?')

SIMON (*exasperatedly*). Yes! What do you want of me now?

(*A pause. Then Sara's voice comes, hurt and a little forlorn:* 'Nothing, darling. It's getting near supper time, that's all.' *Her voice suddenly takes on a resentful commanding tone:* 'It's time you came in, do you hear me?')

DEBORAH (*with a bitter, jealous derisiveness*). Your slut commands you now! (*She calls, with an undertone of gloating mockery.*) Don't worry, Sara. I'll bring him back to you. (*She gets up. He also rises. She speaks with a cruel eagerness.*) Let us go in—together. I am eager to see her. I want to see how frightened she is. (*She takes his arm—tenderly.*) Oh, I am so happy—so very happy, dear!—to have my son again!

SIMON. Not half so happy as I am to have my mother again!

(*They start to go off, left. Abruptly he stops—in a tone of warning advice made more effective by a provocative hint of taunting behind it.*)

But remember she is strong, too. Take care that the moment you see her you do not surrender to her influence again. I know you do not want her laughing at you up her sleeve any more, as she has been doing.

DEBORAH (*with growing anger—blurts out*). Laughing at me! The stupid vulgar fool! If she only knew! It is I who have been laughing in my mind at her! It is singular that such a conquering Napoleon cannot recognize a complete victory and a crushing defeat when he sees them!

SIMON (*stares at her with a curious objectively appraising look—then with a satisfied nod*). Yes, make yourself believe that, Mother, and you can safely defy her. After all, there is a great deal of truth in that aspect of it, as I have suspected. Your truth, of course—not Sara's—nor mine. And not even the whole of your truth. But you and I can wait to discover what that is later on. (*He smiles with pleasant casualness.*) Just now I think we had better go in to supper.

DEBORAH (*pulling away, stares at him with a puzzled frightened dread*). Simon! What—? (*Conquering her fear and suddenly gloating, takes his arm—eagerly.*) Yes! Let us go in. I can't wait to tell her you are going to be with me each evening, that you are now my own dear son again!

SIMON (*sharply commanding*). No! Not until I give you permission to speak. You will kindly not forget, Mother, all this reorganization of my home is my affair and must be carried out exactly as I have calculated. You had better not interfere if you expect me ever to keep you company. Come. It is getting late.

(*She is again looking at him with bewildered dread, has shrunk back, taking her hand from his arm. But he ignores this and grasps her arm and makes her walk off beside him up the path to the house.*)

CURTAIN

ACT TWO, SCENE THREE

SCENE. *Parlour of the Harford mansion—a high-ceilinged, finely-proportioned room such as one finds in the Massachusetts houses designed by Bulfinch or McIntire and built in the late 1790's. The walls and ceiling are white. A rug covers most of the floor of waxed dark wood. A crystal chandelier hangs from the middle of the ceiling at centre. At extreme left-front a small table against the wall, then a door leading to the entrance hall, another chair, and, farther back, a table. In the middle of the rear wall is the door to Simon's study. On either side of it, a chair facing front. Against the right wall, towards rear, another table. Farther forward, a high window looking out on the street, then a chair, and finally at right-front, a fireplace. At left-rear of the fireplace is a long sofa with a small table and reading-lamp by its left end. Towards front, at left, is an oval table with another lamp. A chair is by right-rear of this table, facing right-front. Another chair is at left-front of this table, facing directly front. It is around nine o'clock at night of the same day.*

As the curtain rises, Sara is sitting in the chair at left-front of the table, Simon across the table from her in the chair at rear-right of it, and Deborah on the left end of the sofa by the lamp. Sara is pretending to work on a piece of needle-point. Deborah has a book in her hands, but she stares over it. Simon also holds a book and keeps his eyes fixed on it, but his eyes do not move. The two women wear semi-formal evening gowns, Deborah's all white, Sara's a blue that matches the colour of her eyes. Simon is dressed in black.

For a moment after the curtain rises there is an atmosphere of tense quiet in the room, an eavesdropping silence that waits, holding its breath and straining its ears. Then, as though the meaning of the silence were becoming audible, their thoughts are heard.

SARA (*thinking*). You'd think taking the children away meant nothing to her— No, I know she loved them—it's her great-lady pride won't give me the satisfaction to know she's hurt— And there's something more behind it—I thought they'd never come in—I heard them laughing—and when they came she looked as gay as you please—something about him, too—sly—like there was a secret between them—

DEBORAH (*thinking*). In the garden, at the end, I was so sure of him—but—he changed when he saw her— She was not half as frightened as I hoped— When he tells her he is coming to my garden every evening—that he is my son again— Why does he wait?

SARA (*reassuring herself—thinking*). Ah, I'm a fool to waste a thought on her— Even the part of him that belongs to the Company will be mine now—all of him—and my children, too, will be all mine!— This is my home!— Let her keep to her garden—let her sit and dream herself into a madhouse!

DEBORAH (*thinking*). She is only pretending to work on her needle-point— Yes, quite as frightened as Simon and I had hoped— She will become no more than the empty name of wife, a housekeeper, a mother of children, our Irish biddy nurse girl and house servant!

SIMON (*thinking*). They do not sit together on the sofa as has been their wont—I am where I belong between them—two women—opposites—whose lives have meaning only in so far as they live within my living— Henceforth this is my home and I own my own mind again!

(*He smiles to himself gloatingly and begins to read. As if their minds had partly sensed the tenor of his thought, the two women turn to stare at him, with a stirring of suspicion and resentment. They both look quickly away.*)

SARA (*thinking*). He isn't reading—just pretending to—smiling to himself—sly—

DEBORAH (*thinking*). What is he thinking, I wonder?—of the Company and this secretary-mistress he boasted of— I hate that smug, lustful, greedy trader's smile of his!

SARA (*thinking*). I know that smile—when he's managed a foxy deal for the Company— I hope he doesn't think he'll cheat me— I was a fool to let him see I wanted him so much!—

DEBORAH (*thinking*). This is stupid!—to make myself uneasy—after he's proved so conclusively— I'll be sensible now and read my book—

(*She begins to read determinedly. There is a pause in which each of the three attends to the matter in hand. It is Simon who stops first. His eyes cease reading and stare at the book preoccupiedly.*)

SIMON (*thinking—frowning*). I control the game now and can have it played as I wish— But it means I must always remain in the game myself—be as careful and watchful now outside the office as in it—never relax my vigilance— There is always the danger of alliance of conniving enemies—an unceasing duel to the death with life!

SARA (*has stopped sewing—thinking*). I feel something is staring over my shoulder— It's strange here tonight —It's not the home it's been—not like home at all—no peace— (*Unconsciously she sighs regretfully.*) She and I would be sitting together on the sofa, laughing and telling each other about the children—he sitting alone, thinking out schemes for his Company—not bothering us—

DEBORAH (*has stopped reading—thinking*). How tense the quiet is in this house tonight—as though a bomb were concealed in the room with a fuse slowly sputtering towards— And the silence waits—hands clapped over its ears— (*Unconsciously she sighs regretfully.*) So changed from what it was last night— We would laugh together, thinking of the children— I had forgotten him sitting alone there—

SIMON (*thinking—uneasily*). Perhaps I should have waited— What made their petty sentimental women's world assume such a false importance for me?

SARA (*thinking—regretfully*). He's a fool to think she could ever have taken my children—I can keep what's mine—

DEBORAH (*thinking—regretfully*). I have grown to lean upon her health and strength—as one leans against a tree, deep-rooted in the common earth—

SIMON (*thinking*). What the devil possessed me to ask Sara to come to the office? Now I won't have a separate man's life free of woman even there! (*He turns to stare at her with a vindictive hostility.*)

SARA (*thinking*). Treating his wife as if she was a whore he'd pick up on the street and ask her price!—

(*She turns to stare at him with a revengeful hostility. As they meet each other's eyes, each turns away guiltily. Forcing a casual tone, she speaks to him.*)

Yes, Simon? You were going to say something?

SIMON (*in a like casual tone*). I? No. I thought you—

SARA. No.

SIMON. I was preoccupied with my thoughts.

SARA. So was I.

SIMON. I was thinking of Mother, as it happens.

SARA. That's strange. So was I.

(*Neither of them looks at Deborah. A pause.*)

DEBORAH (*thinking—resentfully*). He lied—he said that to hurt her— Much as I ought to hate her, I pity her when I see him deliberately trying to humiliate—

SIMON (*thinking—resentfully*). By that lie I've put Mother back in my mind— Good God, I'll be playing with toys next, and begging her to tell me a fairy tale! (*He stares at her with vindictive hostility.*)

DEBORAH (*thinking*). His proposal to visit me each evening —as if he were doing me a favour—I never even wanted him to be conceived—I was glad to be rid of him when he was born— He had made my beauty grotesquely ugly by his presence, bloated and misshapen— And then the compulsion to love him after he was born—

(*She turns to stare at him with vindictive hostility. Then, as each meets the other's eyes, each turns away guiltily.*)

SIMON (*speaks—forcing a casual tone*). Yes, Mother? You wanted to say something?

DEBORAH (*echoing his tone*). No. I thought you—

SIMON. No. I was thinking of Sara.

DEBORAH. That is strange, I was thinking of her, too.

(*Neither of them looks at Sara. A pause.*)

SARA (*thinking—resentfully*). Poor woman! She can't read—she's thinking how she'll miss the children—alone all day—He'll have me at the office— Alone in the past— He'll have her in an asylum in the end!— It's a terrible thing he can hate his own mother so!—

DEBORAH (*thinking*). She had begun to look upon me as a second mother—and I was happy to regard her as my daughter—because her strength and health and acceptance of life gave me a faith in my own living—and now he dares to take that security away from me!—to offer me in exchange ghosts from the past to haunt me—

SARA (*thinking*). I'm not a thought he moves around in his mind to suit his pleasure—

DEBORAH (*thinking*). If she'd sit with me here as on other nights, we'd understand and forgive each other—

(*They both speak to each other simultaneously:* 'Sara' 'Deborah.' *They bend forward so they can see each other past him and smile at each other with a relieved understanding. Deborah speaks with a strange gentleness.*)

Yes, daughter. I ought to have known you guessed my thoughts.

SARA (*getting up—with a quiet smile*). I hope you guessed mine. May I come and sit with you?

DEBORAH. I was going to ask you to.

(*Sara goes around the table and passes behind Simon, ignoring him, and goes to the sofa. Deborah pats the sofa on her left, smiling an affectionate welcome.*)

This is your place, beside me.

SARA (*bends impulsively and gives her a daughterly kiss on the cheek*). I know. (*She sits down, close beside her, so their arms touch.*)

SIMON (*thinking—with contemptuous relief*). Ah, so they have decided to forget and forgive— This hate was becoming a living presence in the room—and in my mind— But now we will be back where we were on other nights. Meanwhile, keeping an eye on them to make sure this sentimental reunion is not too successful— But each is lying and acting, of course—playing the hypocrite in the hope of gaining some advantage— It will be amusing to watch.

SARA (*turns to Deborah with impulsive frankness*). I want to beg your forgiveness, Mother—about the children. It was mean of me not to trust you.

DEBORAH (*takes her hand—gently*). One cannot help being jealous. It is part of the curse of love.

SARA (*with a quick resentful look at Simon*). Yes, you do feel cursed by it when it's too greedy.

DEBORAH (*patting Sara's hand*). Thank goodness, we've understood each other and what might have developed into a stupid quarrel is all forgotten now, isn't it? (*Presses her hand and keeps it in hers.*) I had begun to feel so weak and at the mercy of the past.

SARA. Shame on you. And you with four handsome grandchildren to love, and everything in life to live for.

DEBORAH. Then I may have the children back?

SARA. Indeed you may! And remember I wasn't really the one who took them away from you. (*She casts a resentful look at Simon.*)

DEBORAH. You are so kind and generous. I hate myself for having permitted my mind to be tempted— (*She gives Simon a bitter hostile look—then quickly to Sara.*) But that's over.

(*A pause. The two women sit with clasped hands, their faces relieved, affectionate and contented, staring defiantly at Simon.*)

SARA. I know how unhappy you felt. I was miserable myself over there, with him between us.

DEBORAH (*glancing at Simon resentfully—lowering her voice to a whisper*). Yes. That's just it, Sara. We must never again allow him to come between—

(*They bend closer to each other until their heads are about touching, and all during the following scene talk in whispers, their eyes fixed on Simon.*)

SARA. Men are never content.

DEBORAH (*beginning to smile*). He was always a greedy, jealous boy. That's where we may have him at our mercy. His jealousy drives him to need us. But we already have four sons—

SARA (*beginning to smile, too*). And so we don't have to need him.

(*She laughs softly and jeeringly. Simon stirs uneasily and his eyes cease to follow the lines. He stares at the page.*)

DEBORAH (*laughs with Sara*). It is really he who is helpless and lost—and completely at our mercy!

SIMON (*thinking—with a tense dread*). I still feel hatred like a living presence in this room—strange—drawing close—surrounding—threatening—*me*— But that's absurd—they hate each other now— (*Frightenedly.*) But it has become dark in here and Mother and Sara have vanished— Mother took her hand and led her back—as if she opened a door into the past in whose darkness they vanished to reappear as one woman—a woman recalling Mother but a strange woman—unreal, a ghost inhumanly removed from living, beautiful and coldly remote and proud—with a smile deliberately amused by its own indifference—because she no longer wants me—has taken all she needed—I have served my purpose—she has ruthlessly got rid of me—she is free—and I am left lost in myself, with nothing! (*He has dropped the book in his lap and straightened himself tensely, gripping the arms of his chair, staring before him frightenedly. As his thoughts have progressed the expressions on the two women's faces have mirrored his description as though, subconsciously, their mood was created by his mind. They become proudly arrogant and coldly indifferent to him. He goes on thinking with increasing dread.*) But her nature has changed—she stares at me with hate—she is revengeful and evil—a cannibal witch whose greed will devour!

(*Their expressions have changed to revengeful, gloating cruelty and they stare at him with hate. He starts forward in his chair as if he were about to fly in horror from the room.*)

DEBORAH (*smiling gloatingly*). See, Sara, he is not even pretending to read now.

SARA (*smiling gloatingly*). As scared as if he saw a ghost!

DEBORAH (*her expression softens to a condescending maternal tenderness*). Perhaps we are being too hard on him. What he has tried to do has been obviously childish and futile.

SARA. It's because he's jealous, and that proves how much he loves us.

DEBORAH. Yes, I think we should merely be amused, as we would be at the mischief of a bad sulky boy.

SARA (*smilingly—complacently maternal*). And forgive him if he promises not to do it again.

DEBORAH (*speaks to Simon with an amused, teasing smile*). Wake up, dear.

(*He starts and turns to stare at them bewilderedly.*)

Why do you stare like that?

SARA. You might be more polite to your ladies, darling.

SIMON (*as if suddenly emerging from a spell—with an impulsive grateful relief*). I beg your pardon. I must have dozed off and dreamed—

DEBORAH. My poor boy! Do tell us what you dreamed.

(*He ignores her. She laughs teasingly.*)

He won't do it, Sara. But we know he is very uneasy now, not sure of himself at all, wondering what we will decide to do about him.

SARA (*with a little laugh*). Yes, he has a guilty conscience and he knows he ought to be punished.

SIMON (*as if he hadn't heard them, but confusedly apologetic and apprehensive, avoiding their eyes*). I—I am afraid I interrupted a private discussion. Pray continue. I am interested in this book—

DEBORAH (*smiles at him now, cajolingly affectionate*). We have agreed to forgive you, dear—just because you are such a silly jealous boy.

SARA. Come over here and sit with us now. You look so lost over there alone. (*She moves over and pats the sofa between her and Deborah—enticingly.*) Look, you can sit here and have love all around you. You'll be between us, as you've been trying to be.

DEBORAH (*she pats the sofa invitingly*). Come, dear.

(*He does not seem to hear.*)

Still so vain and stubborn? (*To Sara.*) Well, since the mountain is too proud to come to Mahomet—

(*She takes Sara's hand and they rise. Their arms around each other's waists, they advance on Simon with mocking, enticing smiles. They are like two mothers who, confident of their charm, take a possessive gratification in teasing a young, bashful son. But there is something more behind this—the calculating coquetry of two prostitutes trying to entice a man.*)

We must humour his manly pride, Sara. Anything to keep peace in our home! (*She laughs.*)

SARA (*laughingly*). Yes. Anything to give him his way, as long as it's our way!

(*They have come to Simon who stares as if he did not notice their approach, and yet instinctively shrinks back in his chair. They group together in back of him, Deborah at left-rear and Sara at right-rear of his chair. They bend over, each with an arm about the other, until their faces touch the side of his head. Their other arms go around him so that their hands touch on his chest.*)

DEBORAH. Why are you so afraid of us?

SARA. We're not going to eat you, darling, if you are that sweet.

(*Their arms hug him.*)

SIMON (*thinking—with a mingling of fascinated dread and an anguished yearning*). I cannot keep them separate—they are too strong here in their home—they unite against the invader—But I must remember they only seem to become one— But I feel her arms around me—and she is good now, not evil—she loves me—and so I can surrender and be hers— (*He relaxes with a dreamy smile of content in their arms and murmurs drowsily in gentle wonder.*) And I have won the deciding victory over them! (*He gives a strange chuckle of satisfaction, and closes his eyes.*)

DEBORAH. You see, Sara. There was no cause for us to be afraid. I can always, whenever I wish, make him my little boy again. (*She kisses him on the cheek.*) Can't I, dear?

SARA (*gives her a quick resentful jealous look*). I wasn't the one who was afraid. Don't I know whenever I want, I can make him my lover again, who'd give anything he has for me! (*She kisses his other cheek.*) Can't I, darling?

(*She and Deborah suddenly turn and stare at each other with defiant, jealous enmity over his head, pulling their hands away so they no longer touch on his chest, but each still holding him. Simon starts and stiffens in his chair.*)

SIMON. No! (*Jerks forward to his feet from their arms. They each give a frightened pleading cry. He turns to stare from one to the other for a moment in a dazed awakening confusion, stammering.*) Ah! You are both there. I thought— I beg your pardon

— I must have dozed off again— (*Then curtly and rudely.*) Well, now that the little farce is over, if you will permit me to sit, and return where you belong—

(*The two women's faces grow cold and hostile and defiant. But they are also full of dread.*)

DEBORAH (*takes Sara's hand*). Come, Sara.

(*They pass behind him to sit on the sofa, side by side as before, clasping each other's hand. They stare at Simon defiantly and apprehensively. He sits in his chair and stares at his book again.*)

SIMON (*suddenly looks up, but avoids their eyes*). For God's sake, why do you stare like that? (*He snaps his book shut and springs to his feet—angrily, to conceal his apprehension.*) Can I never have a moment's privacy in my own home? I work like a slave all day to stuff your insatiable maws with luxury and security for the rearing of children! Is it too much to ask in return that I be permitted a little peace of mind at night here? I will not tolerate any more of your interference! If you persist in it, I will be compelled to force either one or the other of you to leave my home—and my life!—for ever! That is my final warning! (*He turns towards the door at left, avoiding their eyes.*) I'm going to my study. Hereafter, I shall spend my evenings there alone, and you may do as you please. Tear this house apart, devour each other, if you must, until only one of you survives! After all, that would be one solution— But leave me alone! (*He strides to the study door and opens it—then turns and murmurs.*) I— I beg your pardon for being rude—I am worn out—have worked too hard on this railroad deal—and now I have it, I seem to have nothing—

(*He pauses. Suddenly he has the beaten quality of one begging for pity. But they remain staring as one at him, their eyes hard and unforgiving.*)

You—you know how much I love each of you—it is only when you unite to dispossess me that you compel me to defend my right to what is mine—all I ask is that each of you keep your proper place in my mind— (*Abruptly his tone becomes slyly taunting.*) But I am forgetting I arranged all that today. I will leave you now to inform each other of the secret you are each so cunningly concealing.

(*He smiles sneeringly, but is afraid to meet their eyes. He turns quickly, goes into his study, and locks the door. They stare at the door. There is a moment's silence.*)

DEBORAH (*slowly, hardly above a whisper, but with a taunting, threatening scorn in her tone*). I have a suspicion, Sara, that our big jealous boy has become very frightened and wishes now he hadn't been so wicked—now, when it's too late.

SARA. I have the same suspicion myself, Deborah.

DEBORAH (*hesitates uneasily—then trying desperately to be confidently matter-of-fact, and forcing a smile*). Then I think we can now safely tell each other what the arrangements he spoke of are. As far as I am concerned, I was hiding mine from you only because he said he wished to tell you and made me promise I wouldn't.

SARA. He did the same with me. (*With a sudden underlying hostility.*) I was only too eager to let you know. (*Guiltily.*) I mean—

DEBORAH (*stiffening*). I think not any more eager than I was — (*She checks herself. Then says gently.*) Tell me your secret, daughter. Whatever it is, I will remember it is his doing, and I will understand.

SARA. Thank you, Mother. And I'll understand when you tell me— (*She blurts out hastily with an undercurrent of guilty defiance.*) He got me to agree to work with him at his office from now on. I'm to start tomorrow—

DEBORAH (*startled and unable to conceal an uprush of jealous hate*). Ah! Then you are the woman he boasted he was living with as a —(*Instinctively she withdraws her hand from Sara's.*)

SARA (*bitterly*). You said you'd understand!

DEBORAH (*contritely—grabbing her hand again*). I will! I do!

SARA. I'm to be his secretary and a secret partner. He seemed so nervous and tired out and distracted, and he asked me wouldn't I please help him with his work and share—You can understand that, Deborah?

DEBORAH (*sneeringly*). I can. I know only too well how greedy— (*Fighting this back—guiltily.*) I mean, it is your right.

SARA (*defensively*). It's my right, surely. I'm glad you admit that. He said he was so lonely. He said he missed me so much and wouldn't I let him have a life just with me again. He said I was still so beautiful to him and I knew he was telling the truth.

DEBORAH. Ah! (*She again jerks her hand away.*)

SARA. I'm sorry. I didn't mean to boast. (*She reaches for Deborah's hand again.*) But wait till you hear the rest. I could feel the change in him as he is now in his office—that he's grown so greedy and unscrupulous and used to having his own way that if I refused him, he'd only buy another woman. You can understand that, can't you? You're a woman, too.

DEBORAH (*tensely*). I am making myself understand. Besides, this has nothing to do with me. It is entirely your business.

SARA. Yes, business. If you think I liked him insulting his wife and acting as if I was a street whore—

DEBORAH. Why should I think of it, Sara? But—you appealed to me as a woman, didn't you? You mean forget he is anything to me? I can. I have forgotten him several times before in my life—completely, as if he had never been born. That is what he has never forgiven. If I were in your place I would hate him, and I would revenge myself by becoming what he wished me to be! I would make him pay for me until I had taken everything he possessed! And when he had no more to pay me, I would drive him out of my life to beg outside my door!

SARA (*with a vindictive smile—strangely*). I felt exactly like that! (*Abruptly changing the subject.*) But now tell me what he made you agree to.

DEBORAH. He begged me to give him a life alone with me again away from his office and his home.

SARA (*stares at her suspiciously*). What do you mean? (*Instinctively she starts to pull her hand away.*)

DEBORAH. You promised to understand. He begged me to let him keep me company in my garden every evening from now on. And, as I knew how lonely I would be in the future without the children—

SARA. But I've told you you'll have them back.

DEBORAH. No, Sara, you are very generous, but I really will not need them, now that I have my own son again.

SARA (*gives way to a flash of jealous, uneasy anger*). Ah, and so that's what it is! I've always known if you were ever given the chance—! (*She jerks her hand from Deborah's.*)

DEBORAH (*pleading now frightenedly, grabbing Sara's hand*). Sara! You promised to remember! The truth is—I didn't want him in my garden ever again. He made himself appear like a little boy again, so forlorn and lost in himself—needing my love so terribly! So I couldn't help but consent. As a mother, you can understand that, Sara!

SARA. You've a right. And I'll have my own sons all to myself now. I'll have him all day at the office. No, you're entirely welcome. And when I think of all he's done today to make us hate each other—I tell you, as woman to woman, I'd let him go back and back into the past until he got so lost in his dreams he'd be no more a man at all, but a timid little boy hiding from life behind my skirts!

DEBORAH. I do not think we have anything to fear, Sara. In a very short time he will beg us on his knees to restore that peace and take him back into our home again.

SARA. And won't I laugh to see him beg!

DEBORAH. We will both laugh.

(*They laugh softly together.*)

But we must trust each other and never let him make us hate each other! Let us swear that again, Sara!

SARA. I swear I won't!

DEBORAH. And I swear! (*She smiles contentedly and pats Sara's hand.*) That's settled, then. Now I think we can be as we have been.

SARA. Yes, and it's a help to have him out of the room. (*With a change of tone to that of the doting mother.*) Tell me about the children when they were with you, like you always do.

DEBORAH. Of course I will. (*She pauses—trying to remember.*) I can't seem to— I'm afraid I have entirely forgotten, Sara.

SARA (*piqued—resentfully*). You've always remembered before.

DEBORAH (*reproachfully*). Now! I know I have, but— A lot of things have happened since then to disturb my mind.

SARA. Ah, don't I know. (*Uneasily.*) And they're still happening—even if he is locked in his study. I can still feel his thoughts reaching out—

DEBORAH (*with a little shiver of dread*). Yes, I, too—

(*There is a pause during which they both stare straight before them. Their clasped hands, without their being aware, let go and draw apart. Each sneaks a suspicious, probing glance at the other. Their eyes meet and at once each looks away and forces a hypocritically affectionate, disarming smile. Deborah speaks quickly and lightly.*)

How quiet we are. What are you thinking, daughter?

SARA (*quickly and lightly*). Of how foolish men can be, Mother, never content with what we give them, but always wanting more.

DEBORAH. Yes, they never grow up. They remain greedy little boys demanding the moon.

SARA (*getting up from the sofa*). I'll get my sewing, and come back to you.

DEBORAH. And I will read my book.

(*Sara goes slowly towards her old chair at left-front of table. Deborah's eyes remain fixed on her and abruptly her expression changes to one of arrogant disdainful repulsion and hatred. She thinks.*)

You vile degraded slut! As if you needed encouragement from me to become the vulgar grasping harlot you were born to be! But I am glad I encouraged you because that is the one sure way to make him loathe the sight of you— In the end he will know you for what you are and you will so disgust him that he will drive you out of his life into the gutter where you belong!

SARA (*having come to the chair, fiddles around unnecessarily gathering up her sewing things, keeping her back turned to Deborah, while she thinks*). As if he'd waste his time in her crazy garden every evening, humouring her airs and graces, if she hadn't begged him to! But let her look out, I'll keep what's mine from her if I have to drive her into the asylum itself!

(*A pause. She stands motionless. Both their expressions change to a triumphant possessive tenderness.*)

DEBORAH (*thinking*). Then my beloved son will have no one but me!

SARA (*thinking*). Then my darling will have only me!

(*She turns, making her face smilingly expressionless, and goes back towards the sofa. She sits down beside Deborah, and they smile a confidential smile at each other.*)

CURTAIN

ACT THREE, SCENE ONE

SCENE. *Same as Scene One of Act Two—Simon's private office. Changes have been made in its appearance. A sofa has been added to the furniture. Placed at front-centre, it is too large for the room, too garishly expensive and luxurious, in vulgar contrast to the sober, respectable conservatism of the old office. A mirror in an ornate gilt frame hangs over Sara's high desk at right-rear, and tacked on the right wall beside her desk is a large architect's drawing in perspective of a pretentious, nouveau-riche country estate on the shore of a small lake, with an immense mansion, a conglomerate of various styles of architecture, as if additions had been made at different times to an original structure conceived on the model of a medieval, turreted castle.*

It is early morning in mid-summer of the following year, 1841.

Sara is discovered seated on the high stool before her desk, working with a ruler and drafting instruments on a plan. Her body has grown strikingly voluptuous and provocatively female. She is dressed extravagantly in flamboyant clothes. Her face has a bloated, dissipated look, with dark shadows under her eyes. Her mouth seems larger, its full lips redder, its stubborn character become repellently sensual, ruthlessly cruel and greedy. Her eyes have hardened, grown cunning and unscrupulous. Her manner varies between an almost masculine curt abruptness and brutal frankness, plainly an imitation and distortion of Simon's professional manner, and a calculating feminine seductiveness.

The door from the bookkeeper's room at right is opened noiselessly and JOEL HARFORD *enters, closing the door behind him. He is the same in appearance, retains the cold emotionless mask of his handsome face. But there is a startling change in his manner, which now seems weak, insecure, and furtive, as though he were thrown off balance by some emotion he tries to repress, which fascinates and at the same time humiliates him. For a moment he stands glancing about the room vaguely, his gaze avoiding Sara. She is conscious of his presence but ignores him. Finally, seeing she is apparently absorbed in her work, he stares up and down the curves of her body with a sly desire.*

SARA (*suddenly explodes, slamming her rule on the desk*). Don't stand there gawking! How dare you come in here without knocking? You know your orders! You better remember, if you want to keep your job!

JOEL. Mr Tenard, the banker, is in the outer office. I thought, considering his position, I had better announce him myself.

SARA. His position? His position now is under Simon's feet, and my feet!

JOEL. He states he had a letter from you making an appointment with Simon.

SARA. What Simon wants of him I can't see. We've taken his bank from him. Well, you see Simon's not here yet.

JOEL. My brother seems to be late every day now.

SARA (*forcing a too-careless tone*). Ah, he's taken to paying your old mother a morning visit in her garden as well as in the evening. (*Abruptly.*) And what if he is late?

JOEL. As long as you don't mind his keeping *you* waiting.

SARA. Just what do you mean by that?

JOEL (*betraying an inner jealous excitability, his eyes fixed on the sofa—sneeringly*). I—I am not unaware why you are so insistent about my knocking before I—intrude.

SARA (*mockingly*). Well, that's my business.

JOEL (*his eyes fixed fascinatedly on her now*). Your business! Yes, I quite realize you are—what you are.

SARA (*plainly enjoying this, moves her body seductively—teasingly*). And what am I, Joel darlin'?

JOEL (*trying to take his eyes from her*). I—I am fully aware of the means you have used in the past year to get my brother to sign over his interests one by one to you.

SARA. You don't think my love is worth it?

JOEL. I would not use the word love—

SARA. What else is love, I'm asking you?

JOEL. You pride yourself you have cunningly swindled him? (*He laughs gratingly.*) But it's you who have been swindled!

SARA. That's a lie!

JOEL. It was bad enough before you came here, but since

he started playing Napoleon to show off his genius to you, he has abandoned all caution! If you had to pay the debts on the properties he has made over to you tomorrow—there would be nothing left! But once let his enemies see his true position—

SARA (*abruptly—frightened and shaken*). Oh, I know, Joel! Sometimes, I go mad worrying! But I can't stop him.

JOEL. It would take only a rumour—a whisper spoken in the right ear. This banker who is waiting—how he must hate Simon. If he had the slightest inkling—

SARA. I know. (*Frightenedly.*) You sound as though you'd like— You wouldn't—!

JOEL. I? Do you believe everyone is like you and Simon? Besides, you forget I still own an interest—which is not yet for sale, although I might consider—

SARA (*harshly*). Get back to your work! You're wasting my time and I'm sick of you! (*She turns back to her desk.*)

JOEL (*moves mechanically to the door at right and is about to open it when suddenly he turns—angrily*). I do protest!—against you and my brother turning this office—my father's office—into a— Everyone is getting to know—to smirk and whisper! It is becoming an open scandal!

(*He stammers to a halt—his eyes fixed on her in helpless fascination. She has turned to him.*)

SARA (*smiling—teasingly*). Now, Joel darlin', you shouldn't look at me like that, and me your brother's wife. (*She laughs.*)

JOEL (*fighting with himself*). I do not understand you. I do not see why you should laugh—like a common street woman. (*He swallows as if he were strangling and tears his eyes from hers—stammers.*) No, no! I do not mean— I do not recognize myself. I no longer recognize this as my father's office—or myself as my father's son. So please forgive and overlook—

SARA (*pitying and frightened*). Oh, don't I know! It's Simon. I've got to be what he wants. He makes me want to be what he wants! I forgive you, Joel. And please forgive me.

JOEL. I? Of course, Sara. And thank you for your kindness. (*He turns to the door but again, with his hand on the knob, his eyes fix on her body and grow greedy.*) I only wish to say—I've quite decided to sell my interest in the business—that is, to you, if you would care to consider—

(*He stops. She laughs teasingly. He wrenches open the door and flings himself into the bookkeeper's room, slamming the door behind him.*)

SARA (*looks after him and chuckles. She stares in the mirror at herself admiringly*). Who'd have dreamed it, Sara Melody—you in your beauty to have such power! By the Eternal, as my father used to swear, I think you could take what you wanted from any one of them! (*She suddenly shivers with repulsion and tears her eyes from the mirror strickenly, in a guilty whisper.*) God forgive me! Me, to have such thoughts! (*She stares around her frightenedly.*) It's being here so long, with no life except in his greed— He's made me think that life means selling yourself, and that love is lust— It's only lust he wants—and he's made me feel it's all I want and if I didn't have that hold on him, I'd lose him!—she'd take him back with her entirely— (*With angry defiance.*) She'll never! I've only to kiss him and he forgets she's alive! And what if I was having thoughts about Joel? He's a handsome man. It was only what every woman thinks at times in her heart— Was any one of us ever content with one man? (*She laughs—then suddenly tears her eyes from the mirror and shrinks into herself with horrified disgust.*) Oh, God help me! I must be going daft—as daft as that mad old witch in her garden. (*She jumps from her stool.*) Why doesn't he come? She keeps him dreaming in her garden to make him late on purpose to torment me! And he lets her do it!—Well, I won't wait, my fine Simon! Not alone!

(*She is moving towards the bookkeeper's room when the door from the rear is opened and* SIMON *comes in. He has changed greatly, grown terribly thin, his countenance is pale and haggard, his eyes deep sunken. There is, however, a strange expression of peace and relaxation on his face as he enters, a look of bemused dreaminess in his eyes. With a cry of happy relief, Sara rushes to him and hugs him passionately.*)

Oh, darling! I love you so! (*Then her tension snapping she bursts into sobs and hides her face against his shoulder.*)

SIMON (*startled and bewildered as if only half awakened from a dream—pats her shoulder mechanically—vaguely*). There, there. (*He stares around him, thinking and frowning, as though not quite realizing yet where he is or how he got there.*)

SARA (*stops crying instantly at the tone of his voice, holds him by the shoulders, and stares into his face—frightened*). Simon! You sound—! (*Forcing a joking tone.*) For the love of Heaven, don't you know who I am?

SIMON (*trying to force himself from his day dream—vaguely placating.*) Don't be silly. (*He relapses and smiles dreamily.*) Do you know, this morning, talking with Mother, I suddenly remembered something I had never remembered before. Nothing important. The astonishing thing is that she says I wasn't more than a year old at the time. Nothing important, as I've said. But it gave me a feeling of power and happiness to be able to recall the past so distinctly.

SARA (*stares at him—frightened and resentful*). Simon! Wake up! You're here with me! (*She kisses him fiercely.*) Come back to me! I love you! I'm your wife and you're mine. Tell me you love me.

SIMON (*awakes completely. His expression changes and he presses her body to his and kisses her passionately*). Sweetheart! You know I want you more than life!

SARA (*with a sudden revulsion, pushes back from him*). No! I want love— (*Then, forcing a laugh, she throws herself in his arms again.*) Oh, I don't care as long as I have you!

SIMON. My dear beautiful mistress! (*Tries to take her to the couch.*)

SARA (*breaks away from him. She laughs tantalizingly*). Oh no, you don't! You've a lot of business to attend to. You've got to earn me, you know!

SIMON. What do you want me to pay you this time? You have about all I possess already.

SARA. Well, there's the bank we've just got control of.

SIMON (*laughingly*). Oh, so that's it! I have had the papers drawn. But of course I won't sign them until after—

SARA. But how do I know you mightn't refuse to sign after—?

SIMON (*tries to draw her to him*). Darling! Haven't you learned by this time that my greatest happiness is to prove to you—and to myself—how much you are worth to me?

SARA (*coquettishly*). No, I said. Later. (*She kisses him tantalizingly.*) But here's a kiss to bind the bargain.

SIMON. But I have to run down to the mills today. There's been some discontent about our lowering wages and the hands are sending a deputation.

SARA. Fire them! There's plenty to take their place.

SIMON. I agree with you. But about our bargain. You said later, but I can't get back until late afternoon just in time for my evening visit with Mother. So—

SARA (*harshly domineering*). So you'll forget her and only remember me!

SIMON (*struggling to resist*). But I promised her—

SARA. You were late again this morning on account of seeing her. She did it on purpose! Ah, don't make excuses for her.

SIMON (*sharply matter-of-fact*). I've explained until I'm tired that I think it advisable, for our own sakes if not for hers, to humour her. And someone has to humour her and keep her from being too much alone in her fantastic mind—

SARA. I've told you before I'm willing to let her have the children for company again—

SIMON. Nonsense. I would never permit— She does not want your children now that she has— (*Abruptly changing the subject, going to his desk with his most alert authoritative executive air.*) Well, I'll make up for lost time. Tenard is here, isn't he? You can tell Joel to have him sent in.

SARA (*her manner that of an efficient, obedient secretary*). Yes, sir. (*She opens the door at right, sticks her head in and speaks to Joel, then comes back to the desk opposite Simon and waits for orders.*)

SIMON. I'll have time to dispose of him before I catch my train. You can go back to work on your plans for the estate.

(*She turns back towards the desk at right-rear. He glances at the plans—with an undercurrent of mockery.*)

Now that you'll soon possess a bank, too, you can afford to add still more. I am sure in your dreams you have already thought of more.

SARA. Oh, trust me, I can always think of more! Ah, won't it be a beautiful life, when I can sit back at my ease there, without a care in the world, watching my sons grow up handsome rich gentlemen, having my husband and my lover always by me and with no thought in his heart or brain but the great need to love me!

SIMON (*stares at her back—quietly, with a mocking irony tinged with a bitter, tragic sadness*). There is a poem by Doctor Holmes you should read some time—for added inspiration.

(*He quotes from 'The Chambered Nautilus'.*)

'Build thee more stately mansions, O my soul,
As the swift seasons roll!
Leave thy low-vaulted past!
Let each new temple, nobler than the last,
Shut thee from heaven with a dome more vast,
Till thou at length art free,
Leaving thine outgrown shell—'

(*He pauses—then his gaze turned inward, he murmurs aloud to himself, as Sara continues to stare with fascinated, dreamy longing at the plan.*)

You must have that engraved over the entrance. And Mother should put it over the magic door to her summer-house. And I, on the ceiling of this Company's offices—in letters of gold!

(*There is a knock on the door at rear.*)

SARA (*her attitude becoming again that of the efficient secretary*). That must be Tenard, sir. Shall I let him in?

SIMON (*a strange, calculating gloating comes into his face*). No. I've just had an idea, Sara. Let Tenard wait outside the door for a while like the ruined beggar he is. (*He gets up from his chair.*) Come and sit in my place. I'd like to see you prove that, no matter what happened to me, you are fully competent to direct the destiny of this Company.

SARA. What could happen to you?

SIMON. Who knows? All men are mortal.

SARA. Don't say it, darling.

SIMON. Or I might simply go away—for a long, much-needed rest.

SARA (*with frightened jealous anger*). Ah, I know who put that in your mind! And I know she'd stop at nothing now to get you away with her!

SIMON. You've bought the Company, anyway, so—

SARA (*frightenedly*). You'd leave me—? (*Coarsely self-confident.*) I'd like to see you try to want to! Don't you know I've bought you, too?

(*There is another knock on the door, but neither heeds it.*)

SIMON. Yes, I know—and it is my greatest happiness to belong to you—to escape myself and be lost in you—I'll pay anything!

SARA (*laughs softly*). That's my Simon! That's the way I like you to talk—about life and love—and not about death.

SIMON (*starts towards her*). Beloved!

(*There is another knock on the door, sharp and impatient. Simon tears his eyes from Sara.*)

I think our friend is now sufficiently fearful and humiliated. Sit here, Sara. I am confident you can soon show him his place.

SARA (*comes to the desk—smiling gloatingly. She sits down in Simon's chair*). But I don't even know why you had him come, Simon. We've ruined him. He has nothing left we want, has he?

SIMON. Yes. A few years of his life. He's a capable banker and can still be useful to us. Not as he is now, of course. He is too full of old-fashioned ethics and honour. We know that because it made him so easy to ruin. If you can, discover his weakness and then use it without scruple. You will find a couple of notes I made on the pad about his present circumstances. The rest I leave in your capable hands, my beautiful. (*He laughs, moving away from her to her desk at right-rear. There is another, banging knock on the door. He calls curtly.*) Come in!

(*The door is opened and* BENJAMIN TENARD *enters. He is a tall, full-chested man in his sixties, with a fine-looking Roman face, his clothes expensively conservative. He has the look of success, of financial prosperity still stamped on him from long habit. This façade makes all the more pityingly acute the sense one immediately gets that he is a broken man inside. His face as he enters is flushed with humiliated pride.*)

TENARD. See here, Harford! You made an appointment with me, not I with you! Yet I am allowed to cool my heels in your outer office and then stand outside your door knocking and knocking like someone—!

SARA (*breaks in—without any hint of apology*). Sorry to have kept you waiting, Mr Tenard. (*He turns to stare at her in surprised confusion, not having noticed her at first.*)

TENARD. I—I beg your pardon, Mrs Harford. I did not see—

SARA (*nodding at the chair opposite her*). Won't you sit down?

TENARD (*uncertainly, glancing at Simon*). Thank you.

SIMON (*smiling with cold pleasantness*). It's all right. Your appointment is really with my wife. So if you will pardon me—

(*He nods at the plans on Sara's desk, turns his back on Tenard, and sits down. Tenard comes and sits in the chair opposite Sara.*)

SARA (*after a quick glance at the pad*). I presume you wonder why I wished to see you, Mr Tenard. Just as I was wondering why you ever consented to come—under the circumstances.

TENARD. You mean because your husband is responsible for ruining me?

SARA. Simon does nothing without my consent, Mr Tenard. I thought that was the cheapest way to take possession of your bank.

TENARD. Yes, I have heard rumours that you advise him. I could not believe— (*Then avoiding her eye and forcing a smile.*) I bear no grudge. All is fair in war. Perhaps, I considered the methods used not quite ethical—not to say ruthless. There are some who would describe them in even stronger terms.

SARA. You owned something I desired. I was strong enough to take it. I am good because I am strong. You are evil because you are weak.

TENARD. An infamous credo, Madam! (*Then almost cringingly.*) I—I beg your pardon. You may be right. New times, new customs—and methods. (*Forcing a laugh.*) I suppose I am too old a dog to learn new tricks of a changed era.

SARA. I hope not—for your sake, Mr Tenard.

TENARD. Eh? I don't believe I understand— (*Hastily forcing a good-natured, good-loser air.*) But, as I said, I have no hard feelings. That's why I consented to come here—

SARA. I know your true reason for coming. You haven't a dollar. But you have an old mother, a wife, a widowed daughter with two children. You have applied to various banks for a position. You are too old. The evil reputation of recent failure prejudices them against you. One or two have offered you a minor clerk's job—like a penny of charity tossed to a beggar.

TENARD. Yes, damn them! But I—

SARA. Moreover, the wage would have been insufficient to support your family except in a shameful poverty. You were afraid that your mother, your wife, your daughter, would begin to blame you for your weakness.

TENARD (*staring at her fascinatedly—blurts out in anguish*). That would be the worst! To feel them hiding it—out of pity.

SARA. But there was one last desperate hope. You heard I had not yet chosen anyone to manage your old bank for me. You came here hoping against hope that the reason I had sent for you— (*She pauses—then smiles with cold pleasantry.*) I am pleased to tell you that is the reason. Mr Tenard, I do offer you that position.

TENARD (*gives way to relief and gratitude*). I—I don't know how to thank you—I apologize for having misjudged you— Of course, I accept the position gladly.

SARA. Wait! There are conditions. But before I state them, let me say that any sentiment of gratitude on your part is uncalled for. What happens to you and yours is naturally a matter of entire indifference to me. I am solely concerned with what is mine.

TENARD. You are—brutally frank, at least, Mrs Harford. What are your conditions?

SARA. I warn you your pride will probably be impelled to reject them. The conditions are that you agree to obey every order mechanically, instantly, unquestioningly, as though you were the meanest worker in my mills.

TENARD (*humiliated, but forcing a reasonable tone*). You can rely on me; I have been the head of a business myself. I know the desirability of prompt obedience.

SARA. I can offer you a salary that will enable you to provide very moderate comfort for your family, and so continue to purchase, in part at least, their former love and respect.

TENARD (*stammers confusedly*). I—I thank you—

SARA. I am saying these things because, in order to avoid all future misunderstanding, I want you to face the cost of my offer before you accept.

TENARD. I understand. But you need not— I have no choice. I accept.

SARA. I hope you appreciate from your recent experience with my methods that you will have to forget all scruples. Where it is necessary, you must faithfully do things which may appear to your old conceptions of honour like plain swindling and theft. Are you willing to become a conscious thief and swindler?

TENARD (*at last insulted beyond all prudent submission*). I— You must be mad, Madam— You dare—! But I cannot answer a woman— I know it must be your husband who— (*He springs to his feet and turns on Simon in a fury.*) Damn you, sir! Do you think I have sunk to your level? I'd rather starve in the gutter like a dog! That's my answer to your infamous offer, sir.

(*Simon has not turned, gives no sign of hearing him. Tenard grabs the handle of the door.*)

SARA (*suddenly bursts out—lapsing into broad brogue, forgetting all her office attitudes*). Arrah, God's curse on you for a man! You're pretending to love your women and children and you're willing to drag them down with you in the gutter, too!

TENARD. It's a lie! They would never wish me— (*All at once he seems to collapse inside. He nods his head in a numbed acquiescence, forcing a vacant smile.*) Yes, I suppose, entirely selfish—no time to remember self. Thank you, Madam, for reminding me of my duty. I wish to say I see your point about policy of bank—only practical viewpoint—business is business— (*He forces a choked chuckle.*) Must remember the old adage—sticks and stones—and poverty—break—but names don't hurt. Let who will cry thief! I accept the position, Madam—and thank you again—for your—charity!

(*He wrenches open the door and flings himself into the hall, slamming the door. Simon gets off his stool and comes to Sara.*)

SIMON. Well done! I'm proud of you.

SARA (*her expression is changing. There is a look of dawning horror in her eyes. She forces a smile—mechanically*). I'm glad you're proud. But it was you—what you wanted me—

SIMON. Oh, no. Don't play modest now. That last touch finished him, and that was all your own. I had calculated he would leave, but be forced to come back after he'd faced his women again. But your method was far cleverer. (*He pats her shoulder.*)

SARA. Yes, I didn't leave him one last shred of his pride, did I? (*She suddenly breaks—with a sob.*) God forgive me! (*Abruptly she turns on Simon—with rising bitter anger.*) It wasn't I! It was you! Don't I know what you're trying to do, so you can go back and sneer with her at what a low, common slut I am in my heart! (*Revengefully.*) But I won't let you! I'll go to Tenard! He'll be crazy to revenge himself now! I've only to give him a hint of the true condition of the Company, and then where would you be, you and your Company? You'd not have a penny! And I'd be free to take my children and go to the old farm and live like a decent, honest woman working in the earth! (*Sobbing, hiding her face in her hands.*) I can't go on with this! I won't!

SIMON. Come now, Sara. I know you've just been under a severe strain. (*With a strange tense excitement.*) Of course you are right in thinking there is constant danger—that a whisper, a hint of the truth, a rumour started among the many defeated enemies who have such good reason to envy and hate you—

SARA. Reason to hate *me*?

SIMON. Well, do you imagine Tenard loves you, for example?

SARA. But it was you—

SIMON. There's no question about the danger. It's like walking a tight-rope over an abyss—

SARA. Oh, I know! It's driving me crazy! I can't sleep, worrying!

SIMON. But you mustn't look down, for then you grow confused and the temptation seizes you to hurl yourself— Don't you think I know how that impulse fascinates you, to make an end of suspense and gain forgetfulness and peace at any cost—to destroy oneself and be free!

SARA. Darling! Don't think of it! Don't make me think—

SIMON. I know only too well how tempted you are to whisper and start the rumour of the truth among your enemies—to throw off the burden of responsibility and guilt—not to have to go on! To be able to be still, or to turn back to rest! (*He is staring before him with a fascinated yearning.*)

SARA (*frightened—grasping his arm*). Darling! Please don't stare like that! It makes you look so—strange and crazed—you frighten me!

SIMON. I? I was only warning you against it. You must not be weak. You must go on to more and more!

SARA. No. I don't want to. Oh, Simon darling, won't you be content now you've got the bank? Won't you let the profit add up, and pay off what you owe? And we'll pension off your mother, and give her the house to live alone in, and I'll build my estate and have a home of my own for my husband and my children— (*She presses against him.*) And best of all, for my lover.

SIMON (*ignoring this last—curtly*). The battle for this bank has strained your resources to the breaking point. A dollar in cash is worth a hundred to you now. No. You must go on.

SARA (*distractedly*). No! I can't! I've come to the end!

SIMON. You still have to have stores to retail your cotton goods— Your own plantations worked by your own slaves—Your own slave ships and your own slave dealers in Africa. That will complete the chain on that end. On this end, the stores are the last possible link— Of course, it would be the crowning achievement if I could conceive a scheme by which the public could be compelled to buy your cotton goods and only yours—so you would own your own consumer slaves, too. That would complete the circle with a vengeance! You would have life under your feet then, just as you have me! (*He laughs, his eyes glowing with desire, and hugs her.*)

SARA (*her face lighting up—laughingly*). I'd be satisfied then. So see that you find a way to do it! Haven't I always said you've the strength and the power to take anything from life your heart wished for!

SIMON. With such an insatiable mistress to inspire me, how could I dare be weak? I could not respect myself unless you were proud of me.

SARA. And I am proud! I've the grandest, strongest lover that was ever owned by a woman! (*She kisses him ardently.*) Darling!

SIMON (*abruptly, with a matter-of-fact tone*). Well, that's settled. (*He glances at his watch.*) And now I'll have to go and catch my train. (*He starts for the door. She gets in his way.*)

SARA. Leaving me without a kiss? When I'm making myself all you want me to be? Never mind! Be cruel to me! I'm dirt under your feet and proud to be! If it's a whore you love me to be, then I am it, body and soul, as long as you're mine! (*She kisses him fiercely.*) I want you! I can't bear you to leave me now! But you'll come back here. I'll be waiting and longing—

SIMON (*kisses her passionately*). Yes! I swear to you! Nothing could keep me from—

SARA. You won't forget me like you did this morning. You'll remember you promised me you'd forget her and let her wait.

SIMON. Let the cowardly old witch wait until Domesday! It will serve her right to be alone in the twilight she dreads so with her idiotic superstitious terror of the haunted summer-house! (*He stops abruptly and his expression changes to bitter resentment.*) What are you trying to do, eh? I had forgotten her! Why do you make me remember? Can't I be free of her even here in your arms? Why do you think I pay such an outlandish price to keep a mistress? Have you made a secret bargain with her to play one another's game? She never lets me forget you for long in her garden. She pretends to be jealous of you, just as you pretend— But I know you hate me more and have determined to get rid of me! But you had better not go on with your plot, because I warn you—it will be I who— (*He checks himself, his eyes gleaming with a wild threat.*)

SARA (*staring at him—in a panic of dread*). Simon! Don't look like that! What's happened to you? (*Suddenly resentful and angry herself.*) God pity you for a fool! Play her game for her? When my one wish about her is to drive her away for ever where she can never come back to steal what's mine—

SIMON (*with a cold calculating sneer*). So you boast here behind her back, but with her you're afraid of her!

SARA. I, afraid of a poor old—!

SIMON. I will believe your boasting, Sara, when you prove you want me to be yours enough that you have the courage to— (*In a burst of strange deadly hatred.*) Are you going to let her come between us for ever? Can't you rid our life of that damned greedy evil witch?

SARA (*stares at him with dread—but with a fascinated eagerness too. In a whisper*). You mean you want me to—?

SIMON (*with a change to a lover's playful teasing—pats her cheek*). I want you to do anything in life your heart desires to make me yours. God knows I have paid you enough to prove it to you! (*He laughs and kisses her.*) I must catch my train. Goodbye until this afternoon.

(*He goes out rear. She stands looking after him, the same expression of horrified eagerness on her face.*)

CURTAIN

ACT THREE, SCENE TWO

SCENE. *Same as Scene Two of Act Two—the corner of Deborah's garden with the summer-house. It is around nine o'clock the same night. There is a full moon, but clouds keep passing across it so that the light is a ghostly grey, in which all objects are indistinct and their outlines merge into one another, with intermittent brief periods of moonlight so clear the geometrical form of each shrub and its black shadow are sharply defined. Their alternating lights are like intense brooding moods of the garden itself, and it has more compellingly than ever before the atmosphere of a perversely magnified child's toy garden, distorted and artificial.*

DEBORAH *is discovered pacing back and forth along the path between the pool in front of the summer-house and the door to the street in the wall at right. One feels she is fighting back complete nervous collapse, wild hysterical tears. Yet at the same time she is a prey to a passionate anger and her eyes smoulder with a bitter, jealous hatred. A great physical change is noticeable in her. Her small, girlish figure has grown so terribly emaciated that she gives the impression of being bodiless, a little, skinny, witch-like, old woman, an evil godmother conjured to life from the pages of a fairy tale. Her small, delicate, oval face is haggard with innumerable wrinkles, and so pale it seems bloodless and corpse-like, a mask of death, the great dark eyes staring from black holes. She is dressed in white, as ever, but with pathetically obvious touches of calculating, coquettish feminine adornment. Her beautiful white hair is piled up on her head in curls so that it resembles an eighteenth-century mode. Her withered lips are rouged and there is a beauty-spot on each rouged cheek. There is an aspect about her of an old portrait of a bygone age come back to haunt the scene of long-past assignation.*

DEBORAH. God, how long have I waited like this—hours!—hours since supper even—the children watching, their prying eyes sneering—mocking, snickering—but frightened, too—She has told them to beware of me, I am a little crazy— Then after supper out here again—waiting again— Why do I?—(*She suddenly stops and listens, tensely—eagerly. She rushes over, pulls open the door in the wall at right, and looks out in the street—then closes it again—dully.*) No one—except Life, perhaps, who walks away again now— How many times now have I run to open the door, hoping each time—? How dare he humiliate me like this! You had better beware, Simon, if you think I will bear your insults without retaliating! No, no, I must not blame him— He has been detained at the mills— He loves me— He knows that his visits here are all that is left me — But if he had been detained at the mills, that does not explain why she has not returned home either— He must be with her!— He is even now lying in the arms of that slut, laughing with her to think of the pitiable spectacle I make waiting in vain! Oh why does she force me to hate her so terribly?— I know so well the scheme she has in mind to get rid of me—to drive me insane— She deliberately goads me!—but of course she hopes I would go alone— (*She laughs sneeringly.*) Oh no, my dear Sara, I would take what is mine with me! (*As she is speaking the moon comes from behind a cloud and shines clearly on the summer-house door. She stops and stares at it fascinatedly—then turns away hastily with a shiver of dread.*) No! I could not!—there is no need—I have encouraged him to make a whore of her—until now he sees her as the filthy slut she is—soon she will disgust him so he will drive her out of my house—meanwhile— (*Her face has taken on a soft, dreamy, ecstatic look—exultantly.*) My beloved son and I—one again—happily ever after. (*Her eyes fasten on the summer-house door again. Abruptly frightened, she turns away to stare about the garden uneasily.*) If he would only come! I am afraid alone in this garden at night— It becomes strange—sombre and threatening— And something in my nature responds— (*She pauses—then with increasing bitterness and suspicion.*) Why do I lie and tell myself it is I who have led Simon back into the past, when I know it is he who has forced me to carry out his evil scheme of revenge—? No!— How can I have such a mad suspicion? I should be glad— It proves how he loves me—how much he needs my love— (*Suspiciously again—sneering at herself.*) Love? You know he is incapable of love— Lust is the only passion he feels now—and the hate for me she has put in his mind—a conspiracy with her to drive me back further and further within myself—until he finally tricks me into unlocking the door, taking his hand— And at the last moment he will snatch his hand away, push me inside alone with that mad woman I locked in there— (*The moon again comes from behind a cloud and shines on the summer-house. She gives a dreadful little laugh.*) And then, of course, it would be so simple to have me locked up in an asylum— But take care, Simon! I will be the one to snatch away my hand and leave you alone in there with that old mad Deborah, who will have no scruple—and you beat the walls, screaming for escape at any cost! (*She suddenly stops and presses her hands to her head torturedly.*) Oh, God have mercy!— I must stop thinking— If I go on like this, there will be no need for anyone outside me to— I will drive myself in there! (*She paces back and forth.*) He has been detained— I must be patient—find some way to pass the time—I remember when I waited for him at the cabin that afternoon, I passed the time pleasantly in dreaming—and when I opened my eyes he was there— (*She sits on the stone bench at right-rear of the pool, closing her eyes; her face grows tense as she concentrates her will, deliberately hypnotizing herself into a trance. She relaxes slowly and murmurs dreamily.*) The gardens at Malmaison—the summer-house—the Emperor— (*Her dream becomes disturbed, but she only half awakes.*) No—I do not wish this—not Versailles and the King—the Emperor Napoleon?—I had thought I hated him— Father's silly confusing him with God —and Simon pretending he is like— (*Sinking happily into dreams.*) The Emperor kisses me—'My Throne, it is your heart, dear love, and I—'

(*While she is saying this last,* SARA *slinks in noiselessly along the path from the house at left. She looks worn out and dissipated, with dark circles under her eyes. She stands regarding Deborah with a cruel mocking leer of satisfaction. Deborah's face, in her dream, lights up.*)

At last you have come, sire. My poor heart was terrified you had forgotten I was waiting. (*Laughs softly and seductively, rising to her feet.*) Give me your hand and let us go within, sire—in our Temple of Love where there is only beauty and forgetfulness! (*She holds out her hand and clasps that of her royal dream lover, turns towards the door and slowly begins to ascend the steps.*) I have the key here, sire. I have worn it lately over my heart. (*She reaches down inside her bodice and pulls out a key on a cord around her neck—hesitates frightenedly—then unlocks, but does not open the door.*) I—I confess I am a little frightened, sire. Oh, swear to me again you would not deceive me—that it is love and forgetfulness!

SARA (*struggling with herself.*) She knows, even in her dream!

DEBORAH (*forcing a determined, exulting tone*). But even if it were hell, it will be heaven to me with your love! (*She puts her hand on the knob.*)

SARA. Yes, go to hell and be damned to you and leave Simon alone to me! (*Then, just as Deborah is turning the knob, she springs towards her.*) Stop! Let go of that door, you damned old fool!

(*Deborah starts and half-awakens with a bewildered cry, pulling her hand from the door, and stands dazed and trembling. Sara grabs her by the shoulders and shakes her roughly.*)

Wake up from your mad dreams, I'm saying!

DEBORAH (*whimpering like a child*). Let go! You are hurting me! It isn't fair! You are so much stronger! Simon! Make her let me alone!

(*Sara has let go of her. Deborah stares at her, fully awake now. She makes a shaken attempt to draw herself up with her old arrogance.*)

You! How dare you touch me!

SARA. I'm sorry if I hurt you, but I had to wake you—

DEBORAH. Oh, I'd like to have you beaten! Lashed till the blood ran down your fat white shoulders!

SARA. And that's the thanks I get for stopping you!

DEBORAH. How dare you come here!

SARA. To hell with your airs and graces! Whose property is it, I'd like to know? You're the one who has no right here!

DEBORAH. Oh!

SARA. I took pity on you, knowing you'd be kept waiting out here all night like an old fool, if I didn't tell you he'd come home with me and forgotten all about you.

DEBORAH. Then—it is true. He did go back to the office, instead of— You made him, with your filthy—!

SARA (*tauntingly*). Made him? I couldn't have kept him from me if I'd wanted!

DEBORAH. You came here to tell me—so you could gloat! You vulgar common slut!

SARA. And I've more to tell you. He's paid the last visit here he'll ever pay you. He swore to me on his honour, lying in my arms!

DEBORAH. You lie! He will come!

SARA. He'll never come here again, I'm telling you! So don't be dreaming and hoping! A filthy harlot, am I? Well, I'm what he loves me to be! What were you in your crazy dreams just now—?

DEBORAH (*shrinking back to the foot of the steps—guiltily*). No, no! Only in a silly fancy—to while away the time—

SARA. You don't fool me! It used to be King Louis of France. But now it's the Emperor Napoleon, God pity you! You've never enough! It'll be the Czar of Russia next!

DEBORAH (*shrinking back to the top step—distractedly*). Don't! Don't! Let me alone!

SARA (*following her*). Begging you to let them sleep with you! When out of your mad dreams you're only a poor little wizened old woman no common man on the street would turn to look at, and who, in the days when the men did want you, didn't have the strength to want them but ran and hid in her garden.

DEBORAH (*with a pitiful, stammering, hysterical laugh*). Yes! So ridiculous, isn't it? So pitiful and disgusting and horrible! Don't! Don't make me see! I can't endure myself! I won't! I'll be free at any cost! I— (*She turns and grabs the knob of the door.*)

SARA (*instinctively makes a grab for her and pulls her away—covering her guilty fear with a rough anger*). Come away from that!

DEBORAH. No! Let me go!

SARA. You will, will you? (*She picks Deborah up in her strong arms, as if she weighed nothing, sets her down before the bench at right and forces her down on it.*) Sit there and be quiet now! If you think you'll make me have your madness on my conscience, you're mistaken!

(*Deborah crumples up and falls sideways face down on the bench and bursts into hysterical sobbing.*)

Ah, thank God, you can cry. Maybe that will bring some sense back in your head. (*Her tone becomes more and more persuasive as Deborah's crying gradually spends itself.*) I've told you the truth. Simon swore he'd never come to you again. It was part of the price I made him pay for me when he came back from the mills. He's mine now! He's paid me everything he has. He has nothing left but me and my love. I'm mother, wife, and mistress in one. He doesn't need you, Deborah.

(*Deborah is still now and listening tensely, but she does not raise her head.*)

The real reason I came here was to have a sensible talk with you. If you'll swear to stop your mad schemes, I'll make peace with you. And I'll give the children back to you to keep you company and you'll be as contented as you were before. And I won't hate you. You know I don't like your forcing me to hate you, don't you? (*She pauses. Deborah remains still. Sara's anger rises.*) Haven't you a tongue in your head? It's you, not me, ought to beg for peace!

DEBORAH (*abruptly straightens up and stares at her—with a mocking smile*). You are even more stupid than I thought. Don't you know your begging for peace is a confession of how insecure you are in your fancied victory? You realize that any time I choose I can take Simon away with me!

SARA (*frightenedly*). You mean, into madness, with you? I swear by Almighty God I'll murder you if you try that.

DEBORAH (*coldly disdainful*). And get your children's mother hanged?

SARA. I'll do it a way no one will discover!

DEBORAH. Simon would know. Do you think your husband would love a wife who had murdered his mother?

SARA. He'd thank me for it!

DEBORAH. You lie! He loves me! It's you he hates. He loathes your foul flesh, your filthy, insatiable greeds!

SARA. Ah, it's the evil liar you are! He loves me!

DEBORAH. You stopped me from opening the door. You could really have won then but you are weakly sentimental and pitiful. You will always defeat yourself at the last.

SARA. You old lunatic, you'll see if I have any pity on you the next time!

DEBORAH (*haughtily—as if addressing a servant*). You have no business in this garden. Will you be good enough to return to the house where you belong and attend to your children? I know my son is waiting for an opportunity to see me alone.

SARA (*angrily, turning towards the path off left.*) He's waiting, hoping to hear I've found you locked inside there and we can get the asylum to take you away!

DEBORAH (*with a pitiful frightened cry*). Sara! No! (*She runs to her wildly and grabs her arm—stammering with terror.*) Don't go! Don't leave me alone, here! I—I'm afraid! Please stay! I—I'll do anything you ask! I'll promise anything you want! Only—don't leave me here! (*She throws her arms around Sara and begins to sob hysterically.*) Oh, how can you be so cruel to me?

SARA (*has stared at her at first suspiciously—then gloating triumphantly but moved in spite of herself—finally, as Deborah weeps, she is overcome by pity and soothes her as she would a child*). There, there now. Don't be frightened. I'm strong enough for the two of us. We won't destroy each other any more. You'll have the children back. You'll be happy and contented. Come in the house with me now. It's a wonder if you haven't caught your death already, chilled by the night and the dew. Come.

DEBORAH. You are so thoughtful and good.

(*Sarah begins to lead her off left. Abruptly she stops—with dread.*)

No. We're forgetting he is there, Sara. We can't face him yet. We would be too weak. We must stay here together, trusting each other, until we get back our old strength—the strength his evil jealous greed has corrupted and destroyed. Yes, it is he! He! Not us! We have been driven to this!

SARA (*resentfully*). Ah, don't I know how he's driven me!

DEBORAH. He! He! Only he! We saw that so clearly when he first started to goad us into this duel to the death! We swore to each other that we would constantly bear in mind it was he, not us.

SARA. I know! But he made us deceive each other and hate and scheme—

DEBORAH. How could we be so blind and stupid!

SARA. Because we loved him so much! And didn't he know that, and use it!

DEBORAH. We could have defeated him so easily! We would have been so much stronger!

SARA. And he'd have been happy and content.

DEBORAH. But instead we let him revive a dead hate of the past to start us clawing and tearing at each other's hearts like two mad female animals he had thrown in a pit—while he stands apart and watches and sneers and laughs with greedy pride and goads each on—!

SARA. And when only one is left living, he knows she'll never have strength to claim her body or soul her own again!

(*While she is talking, unnoticed by them both,* SIMON *appears behind them, entering from the path at left. He stands staring at them. He is in a state of terrific tension, and there is a wild look in his eyes, calculating and threatening and at the same time baffled and panic-stricken.*)

DEBORAH. It would serve him right if we turned the tables on him, Sara. We could have the strength now as we are united again as one woman.

SARA. You mean, throw him in the pit—to fight it out with himself?

DEBORAH. For our love—while we watched with gratified womanly pride and laughed and goaded him on!

SARA. Until—

DEBORAH. Yes, Sara. Until at last we'd finally be rid of him. Oh God, think of how simply contented we could be alone together with our children—grandmother and mother, mother and daughter, sister and sister, one woman and another, with the way so clear before us, the meaning of life so happily implicit, the feeling of living life so deeply sure of itself, not needing thought, beyond all torturing doubt, the passive 'yes' welcoming the peaceful procession of demanding days! (*She pauses—then a bit guiltily.*) I hope you do not think it evil of me that I can find it in myself to wish he were not here.

SARA. There have been times at the office when I—

DEBORAH. He has taught us that whatever is in oneself is good—that whatever one desires is good, that the one evil is to deny oneself. It is not us but what he has made us be! So on his head—

SIMON (*with a tense casualness*). You are mistaken, Mother.

(*They both whirl on him with startled gasps of terror and cling to one another defensively. Then as he advances, they shrink back to the edge of the bench at the right-rear of pool, keeping the pool between them and him.*)

I have merely insisted that you both be what you are—that what you are is good because it is fact and reality— What is evil is the stupid theory that man is naturally what we call virtuous and good—instead of being what he is, a hog. It is that idealistic fallacy which is responsible for all the confusion in our minds, the conflicts within the self, and for all the confusion in our relationships with one another, within the family particularly, for the blundering of our desires which are disciplined to covet what they don't want and be afraid to crave what they wish for in truth. In a nutshell, all one needs to remember is that good is evil, and evil, good.

(*As they have listened, the faces of the two women have hardened into a deadly enmity.*)

DEBORAH. Do you hear, Sara? We must not forget.

SARA. No, we owe it to him to be what he wants.

SIMON (*his tense quiet beginning to snap*). But I did not come out here to discuss my meditations on the true nature of man. (*He pauses, then blurts out in violent accusation.*) I—I was trying to concentrate my thoughts on the final solution of the problem. I have been forced to the conclusion lately that in the end, if the conflicting selves within a man are too evenly matched—if neither is strong enough to destroy the other before the man himself is in danger of being torn apart between them—then that man is forced at last, in self-defence, to choose one or the other—

DEBORAH (*starts—staring at him uneasily*). To choose?

SARA. To choose?

SIMON. That appears to me now to be the one possible way he can end the conflict and save his sanity.

DEBORAH. You hear what he's confessing, Sara? He is much nearer the end than I had thought.

SARA. Yes, we've only to wait and we'll soon be free of him. (*Scornfully resentful.*) So he'll choose, will he, the great man? Like a master picking which of two slaves he'd like to own! But suppose they don't choose to let him choose?

DEBORAH. All they have to do is to wait together and stand apart and watch while he destroys himself. (*She laughs softly and Sara laughs with her.*)

SIMON (*with an abrupt change to his matter-of-fact tone*). I don't know what you're talking about, Mother. I attempt to explain an abstract problem of the nature of man, and you and Sara begin talking as if you, personally, were directly concerned in it! (*He chuckles dryly.*) An amusing example of the insatiable ambition of female possessiveness, don't you think? (*Curtly.*) Never mind, it is my fault for being such a fool as to discuss it with you. I know the one problem that interests you. (*He becomes angrily excited.*) God knows I could hardly be unaware of it tonight! I heard you from my study quarrelling out here, clawing and tearing at each other like two drunken drabs. Do you want to create a public scandal, cursing and threatening each other?

DEBORAH. You could not possibly have heard us in your study. What you heard were the voices of your own mind.

SIMON. I heard you as clearly as if I were here! It seemed

there would never be a moment's peace in my life again—that you would go on with your horrible duel, clawing and tearing each other, until my mind would be ripped apart! Are you trying to insinuate I am going insane? Ridiculous! I heard you, I tell you. And then when you finally did become quiet, it was the stillness that follows a shriek of terror, waiting to become aware— I was afraid one of you here—

DEBORAH (*staring at him—cannot control a shudder*). We know—you have been hoping—

SARA. Ah, God forgive you!

SIMON (*wildly*). Well, I might have been hoping. Suppose I was? Do you think I can endure living with your murderous duel for ever—a defenceless object for your hatred of each other—rent in twain by your tearing greedy claws? (*He suddenly breaks and sinks on the bench at left of pool, his head clutched convulsively in his hands—brokenly.*) Why can't you stop? I will do anything you wish! Is there no love or pity left in your hearts? Can't you see you are driving me insane?

(*He begins to sob exhaustedly—the two women sit together, as one, on the other bench, staring at him, exhausted and without feeling.*)

DEBORAH (*dully*). We have won, Sara.

SARA. Yes, Deborah. He admits he's beaten.

(*They stare at him. Suddenly their faces, as one face, are convulsed by pitying, forgiving maternal love.*)

DEBORAH. Our poor boy! How could we be so cruel!

SARA. Our poor darling! How could we feel as we were feeling about you!

(*As one, they spring to their feet and go to him, separating, one coming round one side of the pool, the other round the other. They kneel at each side of him, putting an arm around him, hastening to console and comfort him.*)

DEBORAH. There, there! Our beloved son!

SARA. Our husband! Our lover!

DEBORAH. You mustn't cry, dear.

SARA. There's nothing need frighten you now. We've forgiven you.

SIMON (*raises his head, a confused, dreamy wondering peace in his face—dazedly*). Yes. It is very restful here. I am very grateful to you. (*He turns to Sara.*) I love you, my mother. (*He turns to Deborah.*) I love you, my— (*He stops guiltily—then springs from their arms to his feet, stammering distractedly.*) No, no! If you think I can be taken in by such an obvious sham—

(*The two women spring to their feet. Both cry as one:* 'Simon!' *and each grabs one of his arms and clings to it. Simon trembles with his effort to control himself. He speaks with hurried acquiescence.*)

I ask your pardon. My mind is still extremely confused. It is such an unexpected shock—to find Sara here where she never intrudes—and then to hear of your reconcilement— But it is my dearest wish—

SARA. Darling! (*She hugs his arm.*)

DEBORAH. Dear! (*She kisses his cheek.*)

SIMON. Thank you, Mother. Well, all is forgotten and forgiven, is that it?

DEBORAH. Oh yes, dear! And we will make you so happy! Won't we, Sara?

SARA. Indeed we will! He won't know himself!

SIMON. Let us sit down and rest for a moment together then, in this garden so hidden from the ugliness of reality.

(*As they are about to sit, he suddenly exclaims.*)

Ah, what a fool I am! I came to remind you, Sara, it's the children's bedtime and they are waiting for your goodnight kiss.

SARA. Ah, the poor darlings!

SIMON (*with a calculating insistence*). You'd better take a good look at Honey. It seemed to me he was a bit feverish.

SARA. Ah, the poor lamb! (*She starts off the path at left, then hesitates.*) You're coming in?

DEBORAH (*quickly*). Yes, of course—

SIMON. Yes, it's too damp and chilly. We'll go in, Mother. But you better run ahead, Sara, and see Honey.

SARA. Ah, I hope he's not going to be sick. I'll—

(*She hurries off, left. Simon turns and stares at his mother.*)

SIMON (*with a sneering chuckle*). Well, you must admit I got rid of her very successfully. She will not notice we have remained out here.

DEBORAH (*stiffening—coldly*). I am not remaining here.

SIMON (*ignoring this*). It will give us an opportunity to be alone.

DEBORAH. I am going in and help her with the children. At once!

(*She takes a step towards left, stiffly, as if by a determined effort of will, staring at him with a fascinated uneasiness. He reaches out and takes one of her hands and she stops, trembling, rooted to the spot. She stammers.*)

You—you may do as you please. If you choose to stay out here alone in the darkness—dreaming childish make-believe—you, a grown man! Will you kindly let go my hand? I wish to go in and join Sara.

SIMON (*quietly*). What has your race and fastidious, dreaming poet's soul in common with that female animal?

DEBORAH. It is despicable of you to speak like that about a woman who loves you so deeply.

SIMON. You are speaking of my mistress. She made me pay two-fold the value of every pound of flesh—All I want now is to get rid of her for ever.

DEBORAH (*struggling with herself.*) No! You do not fool me! It is she who is tired of you. Good heavens, what woman wouldn't be disgusted with the greedy, soulless trader in the slave market of life you have become—! (*Vindictively.*) We will give you the freedom you used to dream about!

SIMON (*tensely*). Oh, if you knew how desperately I long to escape her and become again only your son!

DEBORAH. Oh, how can you lie like that? —when you deliberately kept me waiting here hour after hour—while you lay in her arms— Ah, how I hated you! How I cursed the night you were conceived, the morning you were born!

SIMON. What could I do? She is so beautiful and she demanded it as part of her price. And you must remember that there, with her, my life lives in her life, and hers in mine, and I am her Simon, not yours. So how could I wish to remember you?

DEBORAH (*tensely—making a futile movement to rise*). And you think that excuses—?

SIMON. Just as here with you now, as always in the past before she intruded— (*Goes on in the same tone of tense quiet.*) You know her true nature well enough to realize it was she who made me laugh with her in her arms to think of you waiting here like an old fool—

DEBORAH (*in a deadly fury*). I could hear her! The infamous harlot! But there will be no peace as long as we both remain alive! (*She stops frightenedly.*)

SIMON. If someone stumbled and fell against her when she was starting to descend the steep front stairs, if—

DEBORAH (*in a shuddering whisper*). Simon!

SIMON. Yes, I agree that is too uncertain.

DEBORAH (*stammers in confused horror*). Agree? But I never—!

SIMON. Poison would be certain. And no one would ever suspect anything but natural illness in an eminent, wealthy family like ours.

DEBORAH. Simon! Good God in heaven, have you gone mad?

SIMON. No. Quite the contrary. I am being extremely sane. I am alive to life as it is behind our hypocritical pretences and our weak sentimental moral evasions of our natural selves. I am not frightened by the bad names we have called certain acts, which in themselves are perfectly logical—the killing of one's enemies, for example. Our whole cowardly moral code about murder is but another example of the stupid insane impulsion of man's petty vanity to believe human lives are valuable, and related to some God-inspired meaning. But the obvious fact is that their lives are without any meaning whatever—that human life is a silly disappointment, a liar's promise, a perpetual in-bankruptcy for debts we never contracted, a daily appointment with peace and happiness in which we wait day after day, hoping against hope, and when finally the bride or the bridegroom cometh, we discover we are kissing Death.

DEBORAH. No! Stop!

SIMON. Or, obsessed by a fairy tale, we spend our lives searching for a magic door and a lost kingdom of peace—

DEBORAH (*suddenly taunting*). Ah, if you are going to start harping on that childish nonsense—

SIMON. And when we find it we stand and beg before it. But the door is never opened. And at last we die and the starving scavenger hogs of life devour our carrion!

DEBORAH. Simon! Don't look like that! You frighten me!

SIMON (*quietly again*). Regarded sensibly, we should all have clauses in our wills expressing gratitude to, and suitably rewarding, anyone who should murder us. The murderer possesses the true quality of mercy. (*He chuckles sardonically.*) So, although I know how you have always, at any cost, escaped confronting facts—

DEBORAH (*with strange scorn*). You are a fool! As if I did not once think exactly as you have been thinking.

SIMON. So I cannot see why the thought should make you shudder now.

DEBORAH. But those were dreams. Now it becomes real—when you put it in my mind. It begins to live in my will. It is born. It begins to be, to direct itself towards a consummation. And one day soon I will be hating her young body and her pretty face, and I will follow her to the top of the stairs—! Or I will remember that the gardener keeps arsenic in the cellar for killing vermin—! (*Deliberately jumping to her feet.*) You are insane! I am afraid to be alone with you! (*Pulling at her hand.*) Let me go! I will call Sara! (*She calls.*) Sara! Sara!

SIMON (*keeps hold of her hand—quietly*). She cannot hear. (*He pulls her gently back—quietly.*) Come. Sit down, Mother. What have you and I to do with her—? (*Deborah weakly lets herself be pulled down beside him.*) Can't you see I am trying to make clear to you that I have chosen you?

DEBORAH (*her face lighting up with a passionate joy*). You mean—you really mean—? Oh, I knew! I knew in the end I could not fail! Oh, my son! My beloved son! (*Then frightened.*) But not murder—You must not murder—Promise me you will not—

SIMON. No. There is another way. We will leave her here. We will go together so far away from the reality that not even the memory of her can follow to haunt my mind. You have only to open that door—(*His eyes fasten on the summer-house door with a fascinated longing.*)

DEBORAH (*stares at it with dread and longing herself—forcing a belittling tone*). Now, dear, you mustn't start harping on that fantastic childish nonsense again!

SIMON. I have waited ever since I was a little boy. All my life since then I have stood outside that door in my mind, begging you to let me re-enter that lost life of peace and trustful faith and happiness! You once drove me out, and all that has happened since began. Now you must either choose to repudiate that old choice, and give me back the faith you stole from me, or I will choose her!

DEBORAH. No!

SIMON. And then there will be no choice left to you but to run and hide in there again, and dream yourself into the madhouse to escape yourself!

DEBORAH (*horrified*). Simon! For God's sake, how can you say such things to your mother who loves you more than life! As if you wished—

SIMON. I wish to be free, Mother!—free of one of my two selves, of one of the enemies within my mind, before their duel for possession destroys it. I have no longer any choice but to choose. Or would you prefer I should go insane—and so be rid of me again?

DEBORAH (*shuddering*). No! Oh, how can you say—? You must be insane already—!

SIMON (*coldly.*) You are compelling me to choose her. (*He lets go her hand.*) Very well. I shall go to her. Do not attempt to follow me. I shall lock you out as you once did me. You will stay here alone until you do what you must do to escape. I have no doubt you will find happiness in a foolish dream as a King's courtesan! And I shall be free to be Sara's, body and soul. Goodbye, Mother. (*He turns to go.*)

DEBORAH (*grabs his hand—pleading frantically*). No! For God's sake! I will do anything you ask. (*She leads him a step towards the door—then falters and begins to argue desperately as if she were trying to convince a child.*) But—you, a grown man—to make into a literal fact—an old fairy story I made up in an idle moment to make you laugh!

SIMON. You know that is a lie, Mother! To make me realize you hated your love for me because it possessed you and you wanted to be free!

DEBORAH. But to connect the door and that silly tale with the actual wooden door—that really is insane, Simon.

SIMON (*tensely*). I know very well it is a wooden door—But in the deeper reality inside us, it has the meaning our minds have given it. Your opening it will be the necessary physical act by which your mind wills to take me back into your love, and become again the mother who loved me alone, whom alone I loved! (*He smiles at her with a sudden awkward tenderness.*) So you see it is all perfectly rational and logical, and there is nothing insane about it, Mother. The kingdom of peace and happiness in your story is love. You dispossessed yourself when you dispossessed me. Since then we have both been condemned to an insatiable greed for substitutes—(*He stares obsessedly at the door again.*) But you have only to open that door, Mother—really a door in your own mind—

DEBORAH (*with a shudder*). I know!—and I know only too well the escape it leads to!

SIMON (*pats her hand—tenderly persuasive, but his eyes fixed on the door*). Forget those silly fears, Mother. We have gone back before they existed, before Sara existed in me and I in her. We are back here in your garden on the day you told me that story. (*He pauses—then turns on her with a bitter vindictive condemnation.*) I have never forgotten the anguished sense of being suddenly betrayed, of being wounded and deserted and left alone in a life in which there was no security or faith or love but only danger and suspicion and devouring greed! By God, I hated you then! I wished you dead! I wished I had never been born!

DEBORAH (*with an obviously fake air of contrition thinly masking a cruel satisfaction*). Did you, dear? I am sorry if I hurt you. It is true I hoped you would guess what I meant. You were such a stubborn greedy little boy. I could feel your grasping fingers groping towards every secret, private corner of my soul. So I had to do something to warn you, and I thought a fairy tale—(*Abruptly her expression changes to one of horror for herself—distractedly.*) No! I never meant—! You put it in my mind! It's insane of you to make me confess such horrible things! And how can you admit you hated your mother and wished her dead!

SIMON (*passionately*). All I ask is that you go back and change that—change the ending—open the door and take me back—There will be only you and I! There will be peace and happiness to the end of our days! Can't you believe me, Mother? I tell you I know.

DEBORAH (*staring at the door fascinatedly*). Oh, if I could, dear! If I only could believe! If you knew how desperately I have longed to have you back, to know you were mine alone. Yes! I believe now—believe that if the mind wills anything with enough intensity of love it can force life to its desire, create a heaven, if need be, out of hell!

SIMON. God, if the reality of dog-eat-dog and lust-devour-love is sane, then what man of honourable mind would not prefer to be considered lunatic! Come, Mother! Let us leave this vile sty of lust and hatred and the wish to murder! Let us escape back into peace—while there is still time!

DEBORAH (*with forced eagerness, mounts the first step*). Yes—before I can think— Come, dear.

SIMON. We shall have gone back beyond separations. We shall be one again. (*Suddenly in a panic.*) But hurry, Mother! Hurry! I hear someone coming!

(*Deborah moves so that she stands protectingly before Simon, her right hand on the knob of the door. Sara comes hurrying in from the left. She is in a panic of apprehensive dread. When she sees them both still outside the summer-house, this changes to rage against Deborah.*)

SARA (*to Deborah.*) You liar! You thief! You traitor! I should have known better than to leave you— But God be praised I'm back in time!

DEBORAH (*jeering quietly*). Yes. You are just in time—to bid us farewell!

SARA. Simon! Come here! Do you want to lose what little wits you've left?

(*But Simon appears not to have heard her, or to have noticed her coming. He keeps behind his mother, turned sideways to Sara, his eyes fixed fascinatedly on the door.*)

DEBORAH (*addressing him over her shoulder her eyes on Sara*). My love, you no longer remember this woman, do you?

SIMON (*turns his head to stare at Sara without recognition. His face has a strange, mad, trance-like look. He murmurs obediently*). No, Mother. (*He addresses Sara.*) How dare you trespass here? Do you think my mother's garden is a brothel?

SARA (*shrinks as if she'd been struck—strickenly*). Simon! Don't speak like that— It is mad you are!

SIMON (*disdainfully*). Begone! Before I summon the police! (*Pointing to the door in the wall at right.*) That door leads to the street. Go back and ply your trade there.

SARA. Darling! It's I! Your Sara!

DEBORAH (*gloating—haughtily*). You have my son's orders! (*To Simon.*) But I think, dear, it might be simpler for us to leave her now.

SIMON (*eagerly*). Yes, Mother. Let us go!

DEBORAH (*exultantly*). Yes! I can now! I will take what my whim desires from life, and laugh at the cost!

(*She laughs and with an abrupt movement jerks open the door behind her so it stands back against the wall. Simon gives a gasping eager cry and leans forward, staring into the darkness inside. But Deborah does not turn to it and remains confronting Sara.*)

SARA (*wildly*). No! (*Rushes up and grabs Deborah's skirt and falls on her knees before her.*) For the love of God have pity, Deborah!

DEBORAH. Pity? Would you remind me of pity now, you scheming slut?

SARA (*pleadingly*). I'm asking your pity for him, not for me! You love him! You can't do this!

DEBORAH. Love is proud, not pitiful! Let go! (*She kicks her skirt from Sara's hand and half turns to the door, grabbing Simon's arm.*) Come, dear! Quick! Let us go where we cannot hear her lies about love and pity!

SIMON (*turns his head a little from staring inside the summer-house—dazedly and uneasily*). Who are you talking to, Mother? What is she trying to make me remember? This is long before any other woman.

DEBORAH (*cruelly scornful and at the same time uneasy*). Yes, I will not listen to her pleading lies! We will go—

SARA (*wildly, grabbing Deborah's skirt again*). No! Wait! Listen, Deborah! I give up! I admit I'm beaten now! (*Throws herself forward and flings her arms around Deborah's legs—pleading.*) Deborah! You can't! You can have him back! I'll go away! I'll never trouble you again! And that's all you've wanted, isn't it?

DEBORAH (*stares at her, unable to believe her ears*). You really mean—you will give up—go away—?

SARA. I will—for love of him—to save him. I'll sign everything over to you. All I'll keep is the old farm, so I'll have a home for my children, and can make a living with them. I'll take them there tomorrow. (*She gets to her feet slowly and exhaustedly.*)

SIMON (*he has remained tense and motionless, staring into the darkness inside the summer-house. In a boyish uneasy whisper, tugging at Deborah's hand*). Why are you waiting, Mother? We mustn't wait—or it may be too late!

(*But neither woman seems to hear.*)

SARA. You know no woman could love a man more than when she gives him up to save him!

DEBORAH (*sneeringly*). How shamelessly humble you are!

SARA. If I'm humbled, it's by myself and my love, not by you. I can wish him happiness without me, and mean it! Yes, and I can even wish you to be happy so you can make him happy!

DEBORAH (*with strange repressed fury*). I begin to see your scheme—you want to make me feel contemptible—

SARA (*quietly and exhaustedly*). I've told you I'm beyond scheming. I'll leave you now, Deborah. I'll get the children up now and take them to a hotel where he can't find us. Give him a good excuse to give himself to forget me. That's all he needs to bring him peace with you alone. (*She turns to go off left—brokenly, without looking at Simon.*) God bless you, Simon, darling, for all the joy and love you gave me, and give you peace and happiness!

SIMON (*with a sort of bewildered anguish*). Mother! Someone is calling me! I cannot remain back here much longer! Hurry, Mother!

SARA. Goodbye, Deborah. (*She starts to walk away.*)

DEBORAH. Sara—wait—forgive— I want to say—my gratitude—want to tell you—you are beautiful and fine—so much more fine—than I— (*Bursting into a jealous fury, glaring at her with hatred.*) Damn you! You the noble loving woman! I the evil one who desires her son's life! As if a low lustful creature like you could even imagine the depth of the love I have for him! But I'll prove to you who is the final victor between us, who is the one who loves him most! (*She turns to face the darkness within the doorway.*)

SIMON (*with an eager cry*). Mother! At last!

SARA (*frightenedly*). Simon!

DEBORAH (*pulls her hand violently from his*). No! Alone!

SIMON (*despairingly—grabbing at her hand*). Mother!

DEBORAH (*flings his hand away—with a strange boastful arrogance*). Alone, I said! As I have always been! As my pride and disdain have always willed I be! Do not dare to touch me! Get back to the greasy arms of your wife! (*With extraordinary strength she gives him a push in the chest that drives him off balance and sends him spinning down the steps to fall heavily and lie still by the stone bench at left of pool. She turns and stops on the threshold, confronting the darkness—with a self-contemptuous laugh.*) To think you were afraid, Deborah! Why, what is waiting to welcome you is merely your last disdain! (*She goes in quietly and shuts the door.*)

SARA (*has flung herself on her knees beside Simon and raised his head, oblivious to Deborah's going*). Darling! Are you hurt bad? Simon! Merciful God! Speak to me, darling! (*In a panic she puts her hand over his heart—relieved.*) No, he's only fainted. (*She begins to chafe his wrists.*) Maybe it's best. He'd be trying to get in there. (*She stops rubbing his wrists and turns to stare at the summer-house—in an awed, horrified whisper.*) God help me, she's done it! Ah, it's a great noble lady you couldn't help proving yourself in the end, and it's you that beat me, for your pride paid a price for love my pride would never dare to pay! (*She shudders.*) I see now the part my greed and my father's crazy dreams in me had in leading Simon away from himself until he lost his way and began destroying all that was best in him! To make me proud of him! Ah, forgive me, darling! But I'll give my life now to setting you free to be again the man you were when I first met you—the man I loved best!—the dreamer with a touch of the poet in his soul, and the heart of a boy! (*With an almost masochistic satisfaction.*) Don't I know, darling, the longing in your heart that I'd smash the Company into smithereens to prove my love for you and set you free from the greed of it! Well, by the Eternal, I'll smash it so there'll be nothing left to tempt me! It's easy. It needs only a whisper of the true condition to Tenard, now he's in the Company. (*With a gloating smile.*) I can hear the revenge in his heart laughing, rushing out to tell all our enemies and combine with them to pounce down and ruin us! Well, they can't take the old farm anyway, and we'll live there, and the boys will work with me, and you can write poetry again of your love for me, and plan your book that will save the world and free men from the curse of greed in them! (*She pauses guiltily.*) God forgive me, I'm happy at the mere thought of it, and it's no price at all I'll be paying to match yours, Deborah. (*With an abrupt change to practical calculation.*) That reminds me, before I start the whisper, I'll get all the Company's cash from the banks and put it in her name, along with this house, with Joel to take care of it, so she'll have enough and plenty to keep her here, with her garden, and the comfort and riches and luxury that's due the great Princess on her grand estate she'll be in her dream till the day she dies!

(*While she has been saying this last, the door of the summer-house has slowly opened and Deborah has appeared. She now stands on the top of the steps. Her eyes have a still, fixed, sightless, trance-like look, but her face is proud, self-assured, arrogant and happy. She looks beautiful and serene, and many years younger.*)

DEBORAH (*in a tone of haughty command*). Who is talking? How dare you come here?

SARA (*starts and stares at her—in an awed whisper*). Ah, God pity her, the poor woman!

DEBORAH (*coming down the steps— As she does so, Sara gets to her feet, letting Simon's head rest back on the grass. A look of recognition comes over her face—with a regal gracious condescension*). Ah, you are the Irish kitchen maid, are you not? (*Approaching her, erect and arrogant and graceful, her head held high.*) What are you doing in the Palace grounds at this hour? Do you not know there is a terrible punishment for trespassing in my domain?

SARA (*humouring her—bobs her an awkward servant-girl curtsy and speaks humbly*). I know I have no right here, My Lady.

DEBORAH. This garden is the Emperor's gift to me. (*With a gloating little laugh. Then suddenly—sharply and suspiciously.*) Why are you silent? Do you dare to doubt me?

SARA. Indeed I don't, Your Majesty.

DEBORAH (*reassured and pleasant*). I am not Majesty, my poor woman. Of course, if it were my whim— (*Her eyes fall on Simon. She starts—then indifferently.*) Who is that lying at your feet? Your lover? Is he dead? Did you murder him for love of him? Oh, do not be afraid, I understand everything a woman's love could possibly compel her to desire. I know she can even kill herself to prove her love, so proud can she be of it.

SARA (*quietly*). I am sure you know that, My Lady. (*She stares at Deborah and suddenly her face is convulsed with horrified suspicion and she grabs her by the arm and stammers.*) For the love of God, Deborah, tell me you're not just pretending now—for the love of him, to save him and set him free! That would be too great a price—

DEBORAH (*with haughty anger—snatching Sara's hand off her arm*). Do not presume to touch me! See that you take your lover away at once and never return here!

SARA. Yes, My Lady. But— Tell me this, are you happy now, My Lady?

DEBORAH (*smiles condescendingly*). You are impertinent. But I forgive it, because I *am* happy. (*She holds out her hand arrogantly.*) You may kneel and kiss my hand.

SARA (*a flash of insulted pride comes to her eyes and for a second she seems about to retreat angrily—then impulsively she kneels and kisses her hand.*) Thank you for your great kindness, My Lady. (*Deborah turns from her to ascend the steps. Sara adds huskily.*) And God bless you.

DEBORAH (*ascending the steps, looks back, with a smile of gracious understanding amusement*). Why, thank you, good woman. I think that I may say that He has blessed me. (*She goes into the summer-house and closes the door behind her.*)

SARA (*stares after her—miserably*). I wonder—I wonder—Oh, God help me, I'll never be sure of the truth of it now!

(*Simon groans and stirs and looks up at her,*)

SIMON. Mother. Hurry! Let us go. Peace and happiness.

SARA (*at once forgetting everything but him*). Yes, darling. We'll go. Come on. Raise yourself. (*She bends and puts her arm around his shoulder to help him.*) That's it.

SIMON (*dazedly—like a little boy*). I fell and hit my head, Mother. It hurts.

SARA. I'll bathe it for you when we get in the house. Come along now. (*She turns him into the path leading off left and urges him along it.*)

SIMON (*dazedly*). Yes, Mother.

SARA (*with a fierce, passionate, possessive tenderness*). Yes, I'll be your mother, too, now, and your peace and happiness and all you'll ever need in life! Come!

CURTAIN

THE ICEMAN COMETH

Characters

HARRY HOPE, *proprietor of a saloon and rooming house**

ED MOSHER, *Hope's brother-in-law, one-time circus man**

PAT MCGLOIN, *one-time Police Lieutenant**

WILLIE OBAN, *a Harvard Law School alumnus**

JOE MOTT, *one-time proprietor of a Negro gambling house*

PIET WETJOEN ("THE GENERAL"), *one-time leader of a Boer commando**

CECIL LEWIS ("THE CAPTAIN"), *one-time Captain of British infantry**

JAMES CAMERON ("JIMMY TOMORROW"), *one-time Boer War correspondent**

HUGO KALMAR, *one-time editor of Anarchist periodicals*

LARRY SLADE, *one-time Syndicalist-Anarchist**

ROCKY PIOGGI, *night bartender**

DON PARRITT*

PEARL*, MARGIE*, CORA — *street-walkers*

CHUCK MORELLO, *day bartender**

THEODORE HICKMAN (HICKEY), *a hardware salesman*

MORAN

LIEB

* *Roomers at Harry Hope's*

Scenes

ACT ONE

Back room and a section of the bar at Harry Hope's. Early morning in summer, 1912.

ACT TWO

Back room, around midnight of the same day.

ACT THREE

Bar and a section of the back room. Morning of the following day.

ACT FOUR

Same as Act One. Back room and a section of the bar. Around 1.30 a.m. of the next day.

General Scene

Harry Hope's is a Raines-Law hotel of the period, a cheap ginmill of the five-cent whisky, last-resort variety situated on the downtown West Side of New York. The building, owned by Hope, is a narrow five-storey structure of the tenement type, the second floor a flat occupied by the proprietor. The renting of rooms on the upper floors, under the Raines-Law loopholes, makes the establishment legally a hotel and gives it the privilege of serving liquor in the back room of the bar after closing hours and on Sundays, provided a meal is served with the booze, thus making a back room legally a hotel restaurant. This food provision was generally circumvented by putting a property sandwich in the middle of each table, an old desiccated ruin of dust-laden bread and mummified ham or cheese which only the drunkest yokel from the sticks ever regarded as anything but a noisome table decoration. But at Harry Hope's, Hope being a former minor Tammanyite and still possessing friends, this food technicality is ignored as irrelevant, except during the fleeting alarms of reform agitation. Even Hope's back room is not a separate room, but simply the rear of the bar-room divided from the bar by drawing a dirty black curtain across the room.

ACT ONE

SCENE. *The back room and a section of the bar of Harry Hope's saloon on an early morning in summer,* 1912.

The right wall of the back room is a dirty black curtain which separates it from the bar. At rear, this curtain is drawn back from the wall so the bartender can get in and out. The back room is crammed with round tables and chairs placed so close together that it is a difficult squeeze to pass between them. In the middle of the rear wall is a door opening on a hallway. In the left corner, built out into the room, is the toilet with a sign "This is it" on the door. Against the middle of the left wall is a nickel-in-the-slot phonograph. Two windows, so glazed with grime one cannot see through them, are in the left wall, looking out on a backyard. The walls and ceiling once were white, but it was a long time ago, and they are now so splotched, peeled, stained and dusty that their colour can best be described as dirty. The floor, with iron spittoons placed here and there, is covered with sawdust. Lighting comes from single wall-brackets, two at left and two at rear.

There are three rows of tables, from front to back. Three are in the front line. The one at left-front has four chairs; the one at centre-front, four; the one at right-front, five. At rear of, and half between, front tables one and two is a table of the second row with five chairs. A table, similarly placed at rear of front tables two and three, also has five chairs. The third row of tables, four chairs to one and six to the other, is against the rear wall on either side of the door.

At right of this dividing curtain is a section of the bar-room, with the end of the bar seen at rear, a door to the hall at left of it. At front is a table with four chairs. Light comes from the street windows off right, the grey subdued light of early morning in a narrow street. In the back room, Larry Slade and Hugo Kalmar are at the table at left-front, Hugo in a chair facing right, Larry at rear of table facing front, with an empty chair between them. A fourth chair is at right of table, facing left. Hugo is a small man in his late fifties. He has a head much too big for his body, a high forehead, crinkly long black hair streaked with grey, a square face with a pug nose, a walrus moustache, black eyes which peer near-sightedly from behind thick-lensed spectacles, tiny hands and feet. He is dressed in threadbare black clothes and his white shirt is frayed at collar and cuffs, but everything about him is fastidiously clean. Even his flowing tie is neatly tied. There is a foreign atmosphere about him, the stamp of an alien radical, a strong resemblance to the type Anarchist as portrayed, bomb in hand, in newspaper cartoons. He is asleep now, bent forward in his chair, his arms folded on the table, his head resting sideways on his arms.

Larry Slade is sixty. He is tall, raw-boned, with coarse straight white hair, worn long and raggedly cut. He has a gaunt Irish face with a big nose, high cheek-bones, a lantern jaw with a week's stubble of beard, a mystic's meditative pale-blue eyes with a gleam of sharp sardonic humour in them. As slovenly as Hugo is neat, his clothes are dirty and much slept in. His grey flannel shirt, open at the neck, has the appearance of having never been washed. From the way he methodically scratches himself with his long-fingered, hairy hands, he is lousy and reconciled to being so. He is the only occupant of the room who is not asleep. He stares in front of him, an expression of tired tolerance giving his face the quality of a pitying but weary old priest's.

All four chairs at the middle table, front, are occupied. Joe Mott sits at left-front of the table, facing front. Behind him, facing right-front, is Piet Wetjoen ("The General"). At centre of the table, rear, James Cameron ("Jimmy Tomorrow") sits facing front. At right of table, opposite Joe, is Cecil Lewis ("The Captain").

Joe Mott is a Negro, about fifty years old, brown-skinned, stocky, wearing a light suit that had once been flashily sporty but is now about to fall apart. His pointed tan buttoned shoes, faded pink shirt and bright tie belong to the same vintage. Still, he manages to preserve an atmosphere of nattiness and there is nothing dirty about his appearance. His face is only mildly negroid in type. The nose is thin and his lips are not noticeably thick. His hair is crinkly and he is beginning to get bald. A scar from a knife slash runs from his left cheek-bone to jaw. His face would be hard and tough if it were not for its good nature and lazy humour. He is asleep, his nodding head supported by his left hand.

Piet Wetjoen, the Boer, is in his fifties, a huge man with a bald head and a long grizzled beard. He is slovenly dressed in a dirty shapeless patched suit, spotted by food. A Dutch farmer type, his once great muscular strength has been debauched into flaccid tallow. But despite his blubbery mouth and sodden bloodshot blue eyes, there is still a suggestion of old authority lurking in him like a memory of the drowned. He is hunched forward, both elbows on the table, his hand on each side of his head for support.

James Cameron ("Jimmy Tomorrow") is about the same size and age as Hugo, a small man. Like Hugo he wears threadbare black, and everything about him is clean. But the resemblance ceases there. Jimmy has a face like an old well-bred gentle bloodhound's, with folds of flesh hanging from each side of his mouth, and big brown friendly guileless eyes, more bloodshot than any bloodhound's ever were. He has mouse-coloured thinning hair, a little bulbous nose, buck teeth in a small rabbit mouth. But his forehead is fine, his eyes are intelligent and there once was a competent ability in him. His speech is educated, with the ghost of a Scotch rhythm in it. His manners are those of a gentleman. There is a quality about him of a prim, Victorian old maid, and at the same time of a likeable affectionate boy who has never grown up. He sleeps, chin on chest, hands folded in his lap.

Cecil Lewis ("The Captain") is as obviously English as Yorkshire pudding and just as obviously the former army officer. He is going on sixty. His hair and military moustache are white, his eyes bright blue, his complexion that of a turkey. His lean figure is still erect and square-shouldered. He is stripped to the waist, his coat, shirt, undershirt, collar and tie crushed up into a pillow on the table in front of him, his head sideways on this pillow, facing front, his arms dangling towards the floor. On his lower left shoulder is the big ragged scar of an old wound.

At the table at right, Harry Hope, the proprietor, sits in the middle, facing front, with Pat McGloin on his right and Ed Mosher on his left, the other two chairs being unoccupied.

Both McGloin and Mosher are big paunchy men. McGloin has his old occupation of policeman stamped all over him. He is in his fifties, sandy-haired, bullet-headed, jowly, with protruding ears and little round eyes. His face must once have been brutal and greedy, but time and whisky have melted it down into a good-humoured, parasite's characterlessness. He wears old clothes and is slovenly. He is slumped sideways on his chair, his head drooping jerkily towards one shoulder.

Ed Mosher is going on sixty. He has a round kewpie's face—a kewpie who is an unshaven habitual drunkard. He looks like an enlarged, elderly, bald edition of the village fat boy—a sly fat boy, congenitally indolent, a practical joker, a born grafter and con merchant. But amusing and essentially harmless, even in his most enterprising days, because always too lazy to carry crookedness beyond petty swindling. The influence of his old circus career is apparent in his get-up. His worn clothes are flashy; he wears phony rings and a heavy brass watch-chain (not connected to a watch). Like McGloin, he is slovenly. His head is thrown back, his big mouth open.

Harry Hope is sixty, white-haired, so thin the description "bag of bones" was made for him. He has the face of an old family horse, prone to tantrums, with balkiness always smouldering in its wall eyes, waiting for any excuse to shy and pretend to take the bit in its teeth. Hope is one of those men whom everyone likes on sight, a soft-hearted slob, without malice, feeling superior to no one, a sinner among sinners, a born easy mark for every appeal. He attempts to hide his defencelessness behind a testy truculent manner, but this has never fooled anyone. He is a little deaf, but not half as deaf as he sometimes pretends. His sight is failing but is not as bad as he complains it is. He wears five-and-ten-cent-store spectacles which are so out of alignment that one eye at times peers half over one glass while the other eye looks half under the other. He has badly fitting store teeth, which click like castanets when he begins to fume. He is dressed in an old coat from one suit and pants from another.

In a chair facing right at the table in the second line, between the first two tables, front, sits Willie Oban, his head on his left arm outstretched along the table edge. He is in his late thirties, of average height, thin. His haggard, dissipated face has a small nose, a pointed chin, blue eyes with colourless lashes and brows. His blond hair, badly in need of a cut, clings in a limp part to his skull. His eyelids flutter continually as if any light were too strong for his eyes. The clothes he wears belong on a scarecrow. They seem constructed of an inferior grade of dirty blotting paper. His shoes are even more disreputable, wrecks of imitation leather, one laced with twine, the other with a bit of wire. He has no socks, and his bare feet show through holes in the soles, with his big toes sticking out of the uppers. He keeps muttering and twitching in his sleep.

As the curtain rises, Rocky, the night bartender, comes from the bar through the curtain and stands looking over the back room. He is a Neapolitan-American in his late twenties, squat and muscular, with a flat, swarthy face and beady eyes. The sleeves of his collarless shirt are rolled up on his thick, powerful arms and he wears a soiled apron. A tough guy but sentimental, in his way, and good-natured. He signals to Larry with a cautious "Sstt" and motions him to see if Hope is asleep. Larry rises from his chair to look at Hope and nods to Rocky. Rocky goes back in the bar but immediately returns with a bottle of bar whisky and a glass. He squeezes between the tables to Larry.

ROCKY (*in a low voice out of the side of his mouth*). Make it fast.

(*Larry pours a drink and gulps it down. Rocky takes the bottle and puts it on the table where Willie Oban is.*)

Don't want de Boss to get wise when he's got one of his tightwad buns on. (*He chuckles with an amused glance at Hope.*) Jees, ain't de old bastard a riot when he starts dat bull about turnin' over a new leaf? "Not a damned drink on de house," he tells me, "and all dese bums got to pay up deir room rent. Beginnin' tomorrow," he says. Jees, yuh'd tink he meant it ! (*He sits down in the chair at Larry's left.*)

LARRY (*grinning*). I'll be glad to pay up—tomorrow. And I know my fellow inmates will promise the same. They've all a touching credulity concerning tomorrows. (*A half-drunken mockery in his eyes.*) It'll be a great day for them, tomorrow—the Feast of All Fools, with brass bands playing ! Their ships will come in, loaded to the gunwales with cancelled regrets and promises fulfilled and clean slates and new leases !

ROCKY (*cynically*). Yeah, and a ton of hop !

LARRY (*leans toward him, a comical intensity in his low voice*). Don't mock the faith ! Have you no respect for religion, you unregenerate Wop ? What's it matter if the truth is that their favouring breeze has the stink of nickel whisky on its breath, and their sea is a growler of lager and ale, and their ships are long since looted and scuttled and sunk on the bottom ? To hell with the truth ! As the history of the world proves, the truth has no bearing on anything. It's irrelevant and immaterial, as the lawyers say. The lie of a pipe dream is what gives life to the whole misbegotten mad lot of us, drunk or sober. And that's enough philosophic wisdom to give you for one drink of rot-gut.

ROCKY (*grins kiddingly*). De old Foolosopher, like Hickey calls yuh, ain't yuh ? I s'pose you don't fall for no pipe dream ?

LARRY (*a bit stiffly*). I don't, no. Mine are all dead and buried behind me. What's before me is the comforting fact that death is a fine long sleep, and I'm damned tired, and it can't come too soon for me.

ROCKY. Yeah, just hangin' around hopin' you'll croak, ain't yuh ? Well, I'm bettin' you'll have a good long wait. Jees, somebody'll have to take an axe to croak you !

LARRY (*grins*). Yes, it's my bad luck to be cursed with an iron constitution that even Harry's booze can't corrode.

ROCKY. De old anarchist wise guy dat knows all de answers ! Dat's you, huh ?

LARRY (*frowns*). Forget the anarchist part of it. I'm through with the Movement long since. I saw men didn't want to be saved from themselves, for that would mean they'd have to give up greed, and they'll never pay that price for liberty. So I said to the world, God bless all here, and may the best man win and die of gluttony ! And I took a seat in the grandstand of philosophical detachment to fall asleep observing the cannibals do their death dance. (*He chuckles at his own fancy—reaches over and shakes Hugo's shoulder.*) Ain't I telling him the truth, Comrade Hugo ?

ROCKY. Aw, fer Chris' sake, don't get dat bughouse bum started !

HUGO (*raises his head and peers at Rocky blearily through his thick spectacles—in a guttural declamatory tone*). Capitalist swine ! Bourgeois stool pigeons ! Have the slaves no right to sleep even ? (*Then he grins at Rocky and his manner changes to a giggling, wheedling playfulness, as though he were talking to a child.*) Hello, leedle Rocky ! Leedle monkey-face ! Vere is your leedle slave-girls ? (*With an abrupt change to a bullying tone.*) Don't be a fool ! Loan me a dollar ! Damned bourgeois Wop ! The great Malatesta is my good friend ! Buy me a trink ! (*He seems to run down, and is overcome by drowsiness. His head sinks to the table again and he is at once fast asleep.*)

ROCKY. He's out again. (*More exasperated than angry.*) He's lucky no one don't take his cracks serious or he'd wake up every mornin' in a hospital.

LARRY (*regarding Hugo with pity*). No. No one takes him seriously. That's his epitaph. Not even the comrades any more. If I've been through with the Movement long since, it's been through with him, and, thanks to whisky, he's the only one doesn't know it.

ROCKY. I've let him get by wid too much. He's goin' to pull dat slave-girl stuff on me once too often. (*His manner changes to defensive argument.*) Hell, yuh'd tink I wuz a pimp or somethin'. Everybody knows me knows I ain't. A pimp don't hold no job. I'm a bartender. Dem tarts, Margie and Poil, dey're just a side-line to pick up some extra dough. Strictly business like dey was fighters and I was deir manager, see ? I fix the cops fer dem so's dey can hustle widhout gettin' pinched. Hell, dey'd be on de Island most of de time if it wasn't fer me. And I don't beat dem up like a pimp would. I treat dem fine. Dey like me. We're pals, see ? What if I do take deir dough ? Dey'd on'y trow it away. Tarts can't hang on to dough. But I'm a bartender and I work hard for my livin' in dis dump. You know dat, Larry.

LARRY (*with inner sardonic amusement—flatteringly*). A shrewd business man, who doesn't miss any opportunity to get on in the world. That's what I'd call you.

ROCKY (*pleased*). Sure ting. Dat's me. Grab another ball, Larry.

(*Larry pours a drink from the bottle on Willie's table and gulps it down. Rocky glances around the room.*)

Yuh'd never tink all dese bums had a good bed upstairs to go to. Scared if dey hit the hay dey wouldn't be here when Hickey showed up, and dey'd miss a coupla drinks. Dat's what kept you up too, ain't it ?

LARRY. It is. But not so much the hope of booze, if you can believe that. I've got the blues and Hickey's a great one to make a joke of everything and cheer you up.

ROCKY. Yeah, some kidder ! Remember how he woiks up dat gag about his wife, when he's cockeyed, cryin' over her picture and den springin' it on yuh all of a sudden dat he left her in de hay wid de iceman ? (*He laughs.*) I wonder what's happened to him. Yuh could set your watch by his periodicals before dis. Always got here a coupla days before Harry's birthday party, and now he's on'y got till tonight to make it. I hope he shows soon. Dis dump is like de morgue wid all dese bums passed out.

(*Willie Oban jerks and twitches in his sleep and begins to mumble. They watch him.*)

WILLIE (*blurts from his dream*). It's a lie! (*Miserably.*) Papa! Papa!

LARRY. Poor devil. (*Then angry with himself.*) But to hell with pity! It does no good. I'm through with it!

ROCKY. Dreamin' about his old man. From what de old-timers say, de old gent sure made a pile of dough in de bucket-shop game before de cops got him. (*He considers Willie frowningly.*) Jees, I've seen him bad before but never dis bad. Look at dat get-up. Been playin' de old reliever game. Sold his suit and shoes at Solly's two days ago. Solly give him two bucks and a bum outfit. Yesterday he sells de bum one back to Solly for four bits and gets dese rags to put on. Now he's through. Dat's Solly's final edition he wouldn't take back for nuttin'. Willie sure is on de bottom. I ain't never seen no one so bad, except Hickey on de end of a coupla his bats.

LARRY (*sardonically*). It's a great game, the pursuit of happiness.

ROCKY. Harry don't know what to do about him. He called up his old lady's lawyer like he always does when Willie gets licked. Yuh remember dey used to send down a private dick to give him the rush to a cure, but de lawyer tells Harry nix, de old lady's off of Willie for keeps dis time and he can go to hell.

LARRY (*watches Willie, who is shaking in his sleep like an old dog*). There's the consolation that he hasn't far to go!

(*As if replying to this, Willie comes to a crisis of jerks and moans. Larry adds in a comically intense, crazy whisper.*)

Be God, he's knocking on the door right now!

WILLIE (*suddenly yells in his nightmare*). It's a God-damned lie! (*He begins to sob.*) Oh, Papa! Jesus!

(*All the occupants of the room stir on their chairs but none of them wakes up except Hope.*)

ROCKY (*grabs Willie's shoulder and shakes him*). Hey, you! Nix! Cut out de noise!

(*Willie opens his eyes to stare around him with a bewildered horror.*)

HOPE (*opens one eye to peer over his spectacles—drowsily*). Who's that yelling?

ROCKY. Willie, Boss. De Brooklyn boys is after him.

HOPE (*querulously*). Well, why don't you give the poor feller a drink and keep him quiet? Bejees, can't I get a wink of sleep in my own back room?

ROCKY (*indignantly to Larry*). Listen to that blind-eyed, deef old bastard, will yuh? He give me strict orders not to let Willie hang up no more drinks, no matter——

HOPE (*mechanically puts a hand to his ear in the gesture of deafness*). What's that? I can't hear you. (*Then drowsily irascible.*) You're a cockeyed liar. Never refused a drink to anyone needed it bad in my life! Told you to use your judgment. Ought to know better. You're too busy thinking up ways to cheat me. Oh, I ain't as blind as you think. I can still see a cash register, bejees!

ROCKY (*grins at him affectionately now—flatteringly*). Sure, Boss. Swell chance of foolin' you!

HOPE. I'm wise to you and your sidekick, Chuck. Bejees, you're burglars, not barkeeps! Blind-eyed, deef old bastard, am I? Oh, I heard you! Heard you often when you didn't think. You and Chuck laughing behind my back, telling people you throw the money up in the air and whatever sticks to the ceiling is my share! A fine couple of crooks! You'd steal the pennies off your dead mother's eyes!

ROCKY (*winks at Larry*). Aw, Harry, me and Chuck was on'y kiddin'.

HOPE (*more drowsily*). I'll fire both of you. Bejees, if you think you can play me for an easy mark, you've come to the wrong house. No one ever played Harry Hope for a sucker!

ROCKY (*to Larry*). No one but everybody.

HOPE (*his eyes shut again—mutters*). Least you could do—keep things quiet—— (*He falls asleep.*)

WILLIE (*pleadingly*). Give me a drink, Rocky. Harry said it was all right. God, I need a drink.

ROCKY. Den grab it. It's right under your nose.

WILLIE (*avidly*). Thanks. (*He takes the bottle with both twitching hands and tilts it to his lips and gulps down the whisky in big swallows.*)

ROCKY (*sharply*). When! When! (*He grabs the bottle.*) I didn't say, take a bath! (*Showing the bottle to Larry—indignantly.*) Jees, look! He's killed a half pint or more!

(*He turns on Willie angrily, but Willie has closed his eyes and is sitting quietly, shuddering, waiting for the effect.*)

LARRY (*with a pitying glance*). Leave him be, the poor devil. A half pint of that dynamite in one swig will fix him for a while—if it doesn't kill him.

ROCKY (*shrugs his shoulders and sits down again*). Aw right by me. It ain't my booze.

(*Behind him, in the chair at left of the middle table, Joe Mott, the Negro, has been waking up.*)

JOE (*his eyes blinking sleepily*). Whose booze? Gimme some. I don't care whose. Where's Hickey? Ain't he come yet? What time's it, Rocky?

ROCKY. Gettin' near time to open up. Time you begun to sweep up in de bar.

JOE (*lazily*). Never mind de time. If Hickey ain't come, it's time Joe goes to sleep again. I was dreamin' Hickey come in de door, crackin' one of dem drummer's jokes, wavin' a big bankroll and we was all goin' be drunk for two weeks. Wake up and no luck. (*Suddenly his eyes open wide.*) Wait a minute, dough. I got idea. Say, Larry, how 'bout dat young guy, Parritt, came to look you up last night and rented a room? Where's he at?

LARRY. Up in his room, asleep. No hope in him, anyway, Joe. He's broke.

JOE. Dat what he told you? Me and Rocky knows different. Had a roll when he paid you his room rent, didn't he, Rocky? I seen it.

ROCKY. Yeah. He flashed it like he forgot and den tried to hide it quick.

LARRY (*surprised and resentful*). He did, did he?

ROCKY. Yeah, I figgered he don't belong, but he said he was a friend of yours.

LARRY. He's a liar. I wouldn't know him if he hadn't told me who he was. His mother and I were friends years ago on the Coast. (*He hesitates—then lowering his voice.*) You've read in the papers about that bombing on the Coast when several people got killed? Well, the one woman they pinched, Rosa Parritt, is his mother. They'll be coming up for trial soon, and there's no chance for them. She'll get life, I think. I'm telling you this so you'll know why if Don acts a bit queer, and not jump on him. He must be hard hit. He's her only kid.

ROCKY (*nods—then thoughtfully*). Why ain't he out dere stickin' by her?

LARRY (*frowns*). Don't ask questions. Maybe there's a good reason.

ROCKY (*stares at him—understandingly*). Sure. I get it. (*Then wonderingly.*) But den what kind of a sap is he to hang on to his right name?

LARRY (*irritably*). I'm telling you I don't know anything and I don't want to know. To hell with the Movement and all connected with it! I'm out of it, and everything else, and damned glad to be.

ROCKY (*shrugs his shoulders—indifferently*). Well, don't tink I'm interested in dis Parritt guy. He's nuttin' to me.

JOE. Me neider. If dere's one ting more'n anudder I cares nuttin' about, it's de sucker game you and Hugo call de Movement. (*He chuckles—reminiscently.*) Reminds me of damn fool argument me and Mose Porter has de udder night. He's drunk and I'm drunker. He says, "Socialist and Anarchist, we ought to shoot dem dead. Dey's all no-good sons of bitches." I says, "Hold on, you talk 's if Anarchists and Socialists was de same." "Dey is," he says. "Dey's both no-good bastards." "No, dey ain't," I says. "I'll explain the difference. De Anarchist he never works. He drinks but he never buys, and if he do ever get a nickel, he blows it in on bombs, and he wouldn't give you nothin'. So go ahead and shoot him. But de Socialist, sometimes, he's got a job, and if he gets ten bucks, he's bound by his religion to split fifty-fifty wid you. You say—how about my cut, Comrade? And you gets de five. So you don't shoot no Socialists while I'm around. Dat is, not if they got anything. Of course, if dey's broke, den dey's no-good bastards, too." (*He laughs, immensely tickled.*)

LARRY (*grins with sardonic appreciation*). Be God, Joe, you've got all the beauty of human nature and the practical wisdom of the world in that little parable.

ROCKY (*winks at Joe*). Sure, Larry ain't de on'y wise guy in dis dump, hey, Joe?

(*At a sound from the hall he turns as Don Parritt appears in the doorway. Rocky speaks to Larry out of the side of his mouth.*)

Here's your guy.

(*Parritt comes forward. He is eighteen, tall and broad-shouldered but thin, gangling and awkward. His face is good-looking, with blond curly hair and large regular features, but his personality is unpleasant. There is a shifting defiance and ingratiation in his light-blue eyes and an irritating aggressiveness in his manner. His clothes and shoes are new, comparatively expensive, sporty in style. He looks as though he belonged in a pool room patronized by would-be sports. He glances around defensively, sees Larry and comes forward.*)

PARRITT. Hello, Larry. (*He nods to Rocky and Joe.*) Hello.

(*They nod and size him up with expressionless eyes.*)

LARRY (*without cordiality*). What's up? I thought you'd be asleep.

PARRITT. Couldn't make it. I got sick of lying awake. Thought I might as well see if you were around.

LARRY (*indicates the chair on the right of table*). Sit down and join the bums then.

(*Parritt sits down. Larry adds meaningfully.*)

The rules of the house are that drinks may be served at all hours.

PARRITT (*forcing a smile*). I get you. But, hell, I'm just about broke. (*He catches Rocky's and Joe's con-

temptuous glances—quickly.) Oh, I know you guys saw—— You think I've got a roll. Well, you're all wrong. I'll show you. *(He takes a small wad of dollar bills from his pocket.)* It's all ones. And I've got to live on it till I get a job. *(Then with defensive truculence.)* You think I fixed up a phony, don't you? Why the hell would I? Where would I get a real roll? You don't get rich doing what I've been doing. Ask Larry. You're lucky in the Movement if you have enough to eat.

(Larry regards him puzzledly.)

ROCKY *(coldly)*. What's de song and dance about? We ain't said nuttin'.

PARRITT *(lamely—placating them now)*. Why, I was just putting you right. But I don't want you to think I'm a tightwad. I'll buy a drink if you want one.

JOE *(cheering up)*. If? Man, when I don't want a drink, you call de morgue, tell dem come take Joe's body away, 'cause he's sure enuf dead. Gimme de bottle quick, Rocky, before he changes his mind!

(Rocky passes him the bottle and glass. He pours a brimful drink and tosses it down his throat, and hands the bottle and glass to Larry.)

ROCKY. I'll take a cigar when I go in de bar. What're you havin'?

PARRITT. Nothing. I'm on the wagon. What's the damage? *(He holds out a dollar bill.)*

ROCKY. Fifteen cents. *(He makes change from his pocket.)*

PARRITT. Must be some booze!

LARRY. It's cyanide cut with carbolic acid to give it a mellow flavour. Here's luck! *(He drinks.)*

ROCKY. Guess I'll get back in de bar and catch a coupla winks before opening-up time. *(He squeezes through the tables and disappears, right-rear, behind the curtain. In the section of bar at right, he comes forward and sits at the table and slumps back, closing his eyes and yawning.)*

JOE *(stares calculatingly at Parritt and then looks away—aloud to himself, philosophically)*. One-drink guy. Dat well done run dry. No hope till Harry's birthday party. 'Less Hickey shows up. *(He turns to Larry.)* If Hickey comes, Larry, you wake me up if you has to bat me wid a chair. *(He settles himself and immediately falls asleep.)*

PARRITT. Who's Hickey?

LARRY. A hardware drummer. An old friend of Harry Hope's and all the gang. He's a grand guy. He comes here twice a year regularly on a periodical drunk and blows in all his money.

PARRITT *(with a disparaging glance around)*. Must be hard up for a place to hang out.

LARRY. It has its points for him. He never runs into anyone he knows in his business here.

PARRITT *(lowering his voice)*. Yes, that's what I want, too. I've got to stay under cover, Larry, like I told you last night.

LARRY. You did a lot of hinting. You didn't tell me anything.

PARRITT. You can guess, can't you? *(He changes the subject abruptly.)* I've been in some dumps on the Coast, but this is the limit. What kind of joint is it, anyway?

LARRY *(with a sardonic grin)*. What is it? It's the No Chance Saloon. It's Bedrock Bar, The End of the Line Café, The Bottom of the Sea Rathskeller! Don't you notice the beautiful calm in the atmosphere? That's because it's the last harbour. No one here has to worry about where they're going next, because there is no farther they can go. It's a great comfort to them. Although even here they keep up the appearances of life with a few harmless pipe dreams about their yesterdays and tomorrows, as you'll see for yourself if you're here long.

PARRITT *(stares at him curiously)*. What's your pipe dream, Larry?

LARRY *(hiding resentment)*. Oh, I'm the exception. I haven't any left, thank God. *(Shortly.)* Don't complain about this place. You couldn't find a better for lying low.

PARRITT. I'm glad of that, Larry. I don't feel any too damned good. I was knocked off my base by that business on the Coast, and since then it's been no fun dodging around the country, thinking every guy you see might be a dick.

LARRY *(sympathetically now)*. No, it wouldn't be. But you're safe here. The cops ignore this dump. They think it's as harmless as a graveyard. *(He grins sardonically.)* And, be God, they're right.

PARRITT. It's been lonely as hell. *(Impulsively.)* Christ, Larry, I was glad to find you. I kept saying to myself, "If I can only find Larry. He's the one guy in the world who can understand——" *(He hesitates, staring at Larry with a strange appeal.)*

LARRY *(watching him puzzledly)*. Understand what?

PARRITT *(hastily)*. Why, all I've been through. *(Looking away.)* Oh, I know you're thinking, This guy has a hell of a nerve. I haven't seen him since he was a kid. I'd forgotten he was alive. But I've never forgotten you, Larry. You were the only friend of Mother's who ever paid attention to me, or knew I was alive. All the others were too busy with the Movement. Even Mother. And I had no Old Man. You used to take me on your knee and tell me stories and crack jokes and make me laugh. You'd ask me questions and take what

I said seriously. I guess I got to feel in the years you lived with us that you'd taken the place of my Old Man. (*Embarrassedly.*) But, hell, that sounds like a lot of mush. I suppose you don't remember a damned thing about it.

LARRY (*moved in spite of himself*). I remember well. You were a serious lonely little shaver. (*Then, resenting being moved, changes the subject.*) How is it they didn't pick you up when they got your mother and the rest?

PARRITT (*in a lowered voice but eagerly, as if he wanted this chance to tell about it*). I wasn't around, and as soon as I heard the news I went under cover. You've noticed my glad rags. I was staked to them—as a disguise, sort of. I hung around pool rooms and gambling joints and hooker shops, where they'd never look for a Wobblie, pretending I was a sport. Anyway, they'd grabbed everyone important, so I suppose they didn't think of me until afterward.

LARRY. The papers say the cops got them all dead to rights, that the Burns dicks knew every move before it was made, and someone inside the Movement must have sold out and tipped them off.

PARRITT (*turns to look Larry in the eyes—slowly*). Yes, I guess that must be true, Larry. It hasn't come out who it was. It may never come out. I suppose whoever it was made a bargain with the Burns men to keep him out of it. They won't need his evidence.

LARRY (*tensely*). By God, I hate to believe it of any of the crowd, if I am through long since with any connection with them. I know they're damned fools, most of them, as stupidly greedy for power as the worst capitalist they attack, but I'd swear there couldn't be a yellow stool pigeon among them.

PARRITT. Sure. I'd have sworn that, too, Larry.

LARRY. I hope his soul rots in hell, whoever it is!

PARRITT. Yes, so do I.

LARRY (*after a pause—shortly*). How did you locate me? I hoped I'd found a place of retirement here where no one in the Movement would ever come to disturb my peace.

PARRITT. I found out through Mother.

LARRY. I asked her not to tell anyone.

PARRITT. She didn't tell me, but she'd kept all your letters and I found where she'd hidden them in the flat. I sneaked up there one night after she was arrested.

LARRY. I'd never have thought she was a woman who'd keep letters.

PARRITT. No, I wouldn't, either. There's nothing soft or sentimental about Mother.

LARRY. I never answered her last letters. I haven't written her in a couple of years—or anyone else. I've gotten beyond the desire to communicate with the world—or, what's more to the point, let it bother me any more with its greedy madness.

PARRITT. It's funny Mother kept in touch with you so long. When she's finished with anyone, she's finished. She's always been proud of that. And you know how she feels about the Movement. Like a revivalist preacher about religion. Anyone who loses faith in it is more than dead to her; he's a Judas who ought to be boiled in oil. Yet she seemed to forgive you.

LARRY (*sardonically*). She didn't, don't worry. She wrote to denounce me and try to bring the sinner to repentance and a belief in the One True Faith again.

PARRITT. What made you leave the Movement, Larry? Was it on account of Mother?

LARRY (*starts*). Don't be a damned fool! What the hell put that in your head?

PARRITT. Why, nothing—except I remember what a fight you had with her before you left.

LARRY (*resentfully*). Well, if you do, I don't. That was eleven years ago. You were only seven. If we did quarrel, it was because I told her I'd become convinced the Movement was only a beautiful pipe dream.

PARRITT (*with a strange smile*). I don't remember it that way.

LARRY. Then you can blame your imagination—and forget it. (*He changes the subject abruptly.*) You asked me why I quit the Movement. I had a lot of good reasons. One was myself, and another was my comrades, and the last was the breed of swine called men in general. For myself, I was forced to admit, at the end of thirty years' devotion to the Cause, that I was never made for it. I was born condemned to be one of those who has to see all sides of a question. When you're damned like that, the questions multiply for you until in the end it's all question and no answer. As history proves, to be a worldly success at anything, especially revolution, you have to wear blinders like a horse and see only straight in front of you. You have to see, too, that this is all black, and that is all white. As for my comrades in the Great Cause, I felt as Horace Walpole did about England, that he could love it if it weren't for the people in it. The material the ideal free society must be constructed from is men themselves and you can't build a marble temple out of a mixture of mud and manure. When man's soul isn't a sow's ear, it will be time enough to dream of silk purses. (*He chuckles sardonically—then irritably as if suddenly provoked at himself for talking so much.*) Well, that's why I quit the Movement, if it leaves you any wiser. At any rate, you see it had nothing to do with your mother.

PARRITT (*smiles almost mockingly*). Oh, sure, I see. But I'll bet Mother has always thought it was on her account. You know her, Larry. To hear her go on sometimes, you'd think she was the Movement.

LARRY (*stares at him, puzzled and repelled—sharply*). That's a hell of a way for you to talk, after what happened to her!

PARRITT (*at once confused and guilty*). Don't get me wrong. I wasn't sneering, Larry. Only kidding. I've said the same thing to her lots of times to kid her. But you're right. I know I shouldn't now. I keep forgetting she's in jail. It doesn't seem real. I can't believe it about her. She's always been so free. I—— But I don't want to think of it. (*Larry is moved to a puzzled pity in spite of himself. Parritt changes the subject.*) What have you been doing all the years since you left—the Coast, Larry?

LARRY (*sardonically*). Nothing I could help doing. If I don't believe in the Movement, I don't believe in anything else either, especially not the State. I've refused to become a useful member of its society. I've been a philosophical drunken bum, and proud of it. (*Abruptly his tone sharpens with resentful warning.*) Listen to me. I hope you've deduced that I've my own reason for answering the impertinent questions of a stranger, for that's all you are to me. I have a strong hunch you've come here expecting something of me. I'm warning you, at the start, so there'll be no misunderstanding, that I've nothing left to give, and I want to be left alone, and I'll thank you to keep your life to yourself. I feel you're looking for some answer to something. I have no answer to give anyone, not even myself. Unless you can call what Heine wrote in his poem to morphine an answer. (*He quotes a translation of the closing couplet sardonically.*)

"Lo, sleep is good; better is death; in sooth,
The best of all were never to be born."

PARRITT (*shrinks a bit frightenedly*). That's the hell of an answer. (*Then with a forced grin of bravado.*) Still, you never know when it might come in handy. (*He looks away.*)

(*Larry stares at him puzzledly, interested in spite of himself and at the same time vaguely uneasy.*)

LARRY (*forcing a casual tone*). I don't suppose you've had much chance to hear news of your mother since she's been in jail?

PARRITT. No. No chance. (*He hesitates—then blurts out.*) Anyway, I don't think she wants to hear from me. We had a fight just before that business happened. She bawled me out because I was going around with tarts. That got my goat, coming from her. I told her, "You've always acted the free woman, you've never let anything stop you from——" (*He checks himself—goes on hurriedly.*) That made her sore. She said she wouldn't give a damn what I did except she'd begun to suspect I was too interested in outside things and losing interest in the Movement.

LARRY (*stares at him*). And were you?

PARRITT (*hesitates—then with intensity*). Sure I was! I'm no damned fool! I couldn't go on believing forever that gang was going to change the world by shooting off their loud traps on soapboxes and sneaking around blowing up a lousy building or a bridge! I got wise it was all a crazy pipe dream! (*Appealingly.*) The same as you did, Larry. That's why I came to you. I knew you'd understand. What finished me was this last business of someone selling out. How can you believe anything after a thing like that happens? It knocks you cold! You don't know what the hell is what! You're through! (*Appealingly.*) You know how I feel, don't you, Larry?

(*Larry stares at him, moved by sympathy and pity in spite of himself, disturbed, and resentful at being disturbed, and puzzled by something he feels about Parritt that isn't right. But before he can reply, Hugo suddenly raises his head from his arms in a half-awake alcoholic daze and speaks.*)

HUGO (*quotes aloud to himself in a gutteral declamatory style*). "The days grow hot, O Babylon! 'Tis cool beneath thy villow trees!"

(*Parritt turns startledly as Hugo peers muzzily without recognition at him. Hugo exclaims automatically in his tone of denunciation.*)

Gottammed stool pigeon!

PARRITT (*shrinks away—stammers*). What? Who do you mean? (*Then furiously.*) You lousy bum, you can't call me that! (*He draws back his fist.*)

HUGO (*ignores this—recognizing him now, bursts into his childish teasing giggle*). Hellow, leedle Don! Leedle monkey-face. I did not recognize you. You have grown big boy. How is your mother? Where you come from? (*He breaks into his wheedling, bullying tone.*) Don't be a fool! Loan me a dollar! Buy me a trink! (*As if this exhausted him, he abruptly forgets it and plumps his head down on his arms again and is asleep.*)

PARRITT (*with eager relief*). Sure, I'll buy you a drink Hugo. I'm broke, but I can afford one for you. I'm sorry I got sore. I ought to have remembered when you're soused you call everyone a stool pigeon. But it's no damned joke right at this time. (*He turns to Larry, who is regarding him now fixedly with an uneasy expression as if he suddenly were afraid of his own thoughts—forcing a smile.*) Gee, he's passed out again. (*He stiffens defensively.*) What are you giving me the hard look for? Oh, I know. You thought I was going to hit him? What do you think I am? I've always had a lot of respect for Hugo. I've always stood up for him when people in the Movement panned him for an old drunken has-been. He had the guts to serve ten years in the can in his own country and get his eyes ruined in solitary. I'd like to see some of them here stick that. Well, they'll get a chance now to show—— (*Hastily.*) I don't mean—— But let's forget that. Tell me some more about this dump. Who are all these tanks? Who's that guy trying to catch pneumonia? (*He indicates Lewis.*)

LARRY (*stares at him almost frightenedly—then looks away and grasps eagerly this chance to change the subject. He begins to describe the sleepers with sardonic relish but at the same time showing his affection for them*). That's Captain Lewis, a one-time hero of the British Army. He strips to display that scar on his back he got from a native spear whenever he's completely plastered. The bewhiskered bloke opposite him is General Wetjoen, who led a commando in the War. The two of them met when they came here to work in the Boer War spectacle at the St. Louis Fair and they've been bosom pals ever since. They dream the hours away in happy dispute over the brave days in South Africa when they tried to murder each other. The little guy between them was in it, too, as correspondent for some English paper. His nickname here is Jimmy Tomorrow. He's the leader of our Tomorrow Movement.

PARRITT. What do they do for a living?

LARRY. As little as possible. Once in a while one of them makes a successful touch somewhere, and some of them get a few dollars a month from connections at home, who pay it on condition they never come back. For the rest, they live on free lunch and their old friend, Harry Hope, who doesn't give a damn what anyone does or doesn't do, as long as he likes you.

PARRITT. It must be a tough life.

LARRY. It's not. Don't waste your pity. They wouldn't thank you for it. They manage to get drunk, by hook or crook, and keep their pipe dreams, and that's all they ask of life. I've never known more contented men. It isn't often that men attain the true goal of their heart's desire. The same applies to Harry himself and his two cronies at the far table. He's so satisfied with life he's never set foot out of this place since his wife died twenty years ago. He has no need of the outside world at all. This place has a fine trade from the Market people across the street and the waterfront workers, so in spite of Harry's thirst and his generous heart, he comes out even. He never worries in hard times because there's always old friends from the days when he was a jitney Tammany politician, and a friendly brewery to tide him over. Don't ask me what his two pals work at because they don't. Except at being his lifetime guests. The one facing this way is his brother-in-law, Ed Mosher, who once worked for a circus in the ticket wagon. Pat McGloin, the other one, was a police lieutenant back in the flush times of graft when everything went. But he got too greedy and when the usual reform investigation came he was caught red-handed and thrown off the Force. (*He nods at Joe.*) Joe here has a yesterday in the same flush period. He ran a coloured gambling-house then and was a hell of a sport, so they say. Well, that's our whole family circle of inmates, except the two barkeeps and their girls, three ladies of the pavement that room on the third floor.

PARRITT (*bitterly*). To hell with them! I never want to see a whore again! (*As Larry flashes him a puzzled glance, he adds confusedly.*) I mean, they always get you in dutch.

(*While he is speaking Willie Oban has opened his eyes. He leans toward them, drunk now from the effect of the huge drink he took, and speaks with a mocking suavity.*)

WILLIE. Why omit me from your Who's Who in Dypsomania, Larry? An unpardonable slight, especially as I am the only inmate of royal blood. (*To Parritt—ramblingly.*) Educated at Harvard, too. You must have noticed the atmosphere of culture here. My humble contribution. Yes, Generous Stranger—I trust you're generous—I was born in the purple, the son, but unfortunately not the heir, of the late world-famous Bill Oban, King of the Bucket Shops. A revolution deposed him, conducted by the District Attorney. He was sent into exile. In fact, not to mince matters, they locked him in the can and threw away the key. Alas, his was an adventurous spirit that pined in confinement. And so he died. Forgive these reminiscences. Undoubtedly all this is well known to you. Everyone in the world knows.

PARRITT (*uncomfortably*). Tough luck. No, I never heard of him.

WILLIE (*blinks at him incredulously*). Never heard? I thought everyone in the world—— Why, even at Harvard I discovered my father was well known by reputation, although that was some time before the District Attorney gave him so much unwelcome publicity. Yes, even as a freshman I was notorious. I was accepted socially with all the warm cordiality that Henry Wadsworth Longfellow would have shown a drunken Negress dancing the can can at high noon on Brattle Street. Harvard was my father's idea. He was an ambitious man. Dictatorial, too. Always knowing what was best for me. But I did make myself a brilliant student. A dirty trick on my classmates, inspired by revenge, I fear. (*He quotes.*) "Dear college days, with pleasure rife! The grandest gladdest days of life!" But, of course, that is a Yale hymn, and they're given to rah-rah exaggeration at New Haven. I was a brilliant student at Law School, too. My father wanted a lawyer in the family. He was a calculating man. A thorough knowledge of the law close at hand in the house to help him find fresh ways to evade it. But I discovered the loophole of whisky and escaped his jurisdiction. (*Abruptly to Parritt.*) Speaking of whisky, sir, reminds me—and, I hope, reminds you—that when meeting a Prince the customary salutation is "What'll you have?"

PARRITT (*with defensive resentment*). Nix! All you guys seem to think I'm made of dough. Where would I get the coin to blow everyone?

WILLIE (*sceptically*). Broke? You haven't the thirsty look of the impecunious. I'd judge you to be a plutocrat, your pockets stuffed with ill-gotten gains. Two or three dollars, at least. And don't think we will question how you got it. As Vespasian remarked, the smell of all whisky is sweet.

PARRITT. What do you mean, how I got it? (*To Larry, forcing a laugh.*) It's a laugh, calling me a plutocrat, isn't it, Larry, when I've been in the Movement all my life.

(*Larry gives him an uneasy suspicious glance, then looks away, as if avoiding something he does not wish to see.*)

WILLIE (*disgustedly*). Ah, one of those, eh? I believe you now, all right! Go away and blow yourself up, that's a good lad. Hugo is the only licensed preacher of that gospel here. A dangerous terrorist, Hugo! He would as soon blow the collar off a schooner of beer as look at you! (*To Larry.*) Let us ignore this useless youth, Larry. Let us join in prayer that Hickey, the Great Salesman, will soon arrive bringing the blessed bourgeois long green! Would that Hickey or Death would come! Meanwhile, I will sing a song. A beautiful old New England folk ballad which I picked up at Harvard amid the debris of education. (*He sings in a boisterous baritone, rapping on the table with his knuckles at the indicated spots in the song.*)

"Jack, oh, Jack, was a sailor lad
And he came to a tavern for gin.
He rapped and he rapped with a (*Rap, rap, rap*)
But never a soul seemed in."

(*The drunks at the tables stir. Rocky gets up from his chair in the bar and starts back for the entrance to the back room. Hope cocks one irritable eye over his specs. Joe Mott opens both of his and grins. Willie interposes some drunken whimsical exposition to Larry.*)

The origin of this beautiful ditty is veiled in mystery, Larry. There was a legend bruited about in Cambridge lavatories that Waldo Emerson composed it during his uninformative period as a minister, while he was trying to write a sermon. But my own opinion is, it goes back much further, and Jonathan Edwards was the author of both words and music. (*He sings.*)

"He rapped and rapped, and tapped and tapped
Enough to wake the dead
Till he heard a damsel (*Rap, rap, rap*)
On a window right over his head."

(*The drunks are blinking their eyes now, grumbling and cursing. Rocky appears from the bar at rear, right, yawning.*)

HOPE (*with fuming irritation*). Rocky! Bejees, can't you keep that crazy bastard quiet?

(*Rocky starts for Willie.*)

WILLIE. And now the influence of a good woman enters our mariner's life. Well, perhaps "good" isn't the word. But very, very kind. (*He sings.*)

"'Oh, come up,' she cried, 'my sailor lad,
And you and I'll agree.
And I'll show you the prettiest (*Rap, rap, rap*)
That ever you did see.'"

(*He speaks.*) You see, Larry? The lewd Puritan touch, obviously, and it grows more marked as we go on. (*He sings.*)

"Oh, he put his arm around her waist,
He gazed in her bright blue eyes
And then he——"

(*But here Rocky shakes him roughly by the shoulder.*)

ROCKY. Piano! What d'yuh tink dis dump is, a dump?

HOPE. Give him the bum's rush upstairs! Lock him in his room!

ROCKY (*yanks Willie by the arm*). Come on, Bum.

WILLIE (*dissolves into pitiable terror*). No! Please, Rocky! I'll go crazy up in that room alone! It's haunted! I—— (*He calls to Hope.*) Please, Harry! Let me stay here! I'll be quiet!

HOPE (*immediately relents—indignantly*). What the hell you doing to him, Rocky? I didn't tell you to beat up the poor guy. Leave him alone, long as he's quiet.

(*Rocky lets go of Willie disgustedly and goes back to his chair in the bar.*)

WILLIE (*huskily*). Thanks, Harry. You're a good scout. (*He closes his eyes and sinks back in his chair exhaustedly, twitching and quivering again.*)

HOPE (*addressing McGloin and Mosher, who are sleepily awake—accusingly*). Always the way. Can't trust nobody. Leave it to that Dago to keep order and it's like bedlam in a cathouse, singing and everything. And you two big barflies are a hell of a help to me, ain't you? Eat and sleep and get drunk! All you're good for, bejees! Well, you can take that "I'll-have-the-same" look off your maps! There ain't going to be no more drinks on the house till hell freezes over! (*Neither of the two is impressed either by his insults or his threats. They grin hangover grins of tolerant affection at him and wink at each other. Harry fumes.*) Yeah, grin! Wink, bejees! Fine pair of sons of bitches to have glued on me for life!

(*But he can't get a rise out of them and he subsides into a fuming mumble. Meanwhile, at the middle table, Captain Lewis and General Wetjoen are as wide awake as heavy hangovers permit. Jimmy Tomorrow nods, his *eyes blinking. Lewis is gazing across the table at Joe Mott, who is still chuckling to himself over Willie's song. The expression on Lewis's face is that of one who can't believe his eyes.)*

LEWIS (*aloud to himself, with a muzzy wonder*). Good God! Have I been drinking at the same table with a bloody Kaffir?

JOE (*grinning*). Hello, Captain. You comin' up for air? Kaffir? Who's he?

WETJOEN (*blurrily*). Kaffir, dot's a nigger, Joe.

(*Joe stiffens and his eyes narrow. Wetjoen goes on with heavy jocosity.*)

Dot's joke on him, Joe. He don't know you. He's still plind drunk, the ploody Limey chentleman! A great mistake I missed him at the pattle of Modder River. Vit mine rifle I shoot damn fool Limey officers py the dozen, but him I miss. De pity of it! (*He chuckles and slaps Lewis on his bare shoulder.*) Hey, wake up, Cecil, you ploody fool! Don't you know your old friend, Joe? He's no damned Kaffir! He's white, Joe is!

LEWIS (*light dawning—contritely*). My profound apologies, Joseph, old chum. Eyesight a trifle blurry, I'm afraid. Whitest coloured man I ever knew. Proud to call you my friend. No hard feelings, what? (*He holds out his hand.*)

JOE (*at once grins good-naturedly and shakes his hand*). No, Captain, I know it's mistake. Youse regular, if you is a Limey. (*Then his face hardening.*) But I don't stand for "nigger" from nobody. Never did. In de old days, people calls me "nigger" wakes up in de hospital. I was de leader ob de Dirty Half-Dozen Gang. All six of us coloured boys, we was tough and I was de toughest.

WETJOEN (*inspired to boastful reminiscence*). Me, in old days in Transvaal, I vas so tough and strong I grab axle of ox wagon mit full load and lift like feather.

LEWIS (*smiling amiably*). As for you, my balmy Boer that walks like a man, I say again it was a grave error in our foreign policy ever to set you free, once we nabbed you and your commando with Cronje. We should have taken you to the London zoo and incarcerated you in the baboons' cage. With a sign: "Spectators may distinguish the true baboon by his blue behind."

WETJOEN (*grins*). Gott! To dink, ten better Limey officers, at least, I shoot clean in the mittle of forehead at Spion Kopje, and you I miss! I neffer forgive myself!

(*Jimmy Tomorrow blinks benignantly from one to the other with a gentle drunken smile.*)

JIMMY (*sentimentally*). Now, come, Cecil, Piet! We must forget the War. Boer and Briton, each fought fairly and played the game till the better man won and then we shook hands. We are all brothers within the Empire united beneath the flag on which the sun never sets. (*Tears come to his eyes. He quotes with great sentiment, if with slight application.*) "Ship me somewhere east of Suez——"

LARRY (*breaks in sardonically*). Be God, you're there already, Jimmy. Worst is best here, and East is West, and tomorrow is yesterday. What more do you want?

JIMMY (*with bleary benevolence, shaking his head in mild rebuke*). No, Larry, old friend, you can't deceive me. You pretend a bitter, cynic philosophy, but in your heart you are the kindest man among us.

LARRY (*disconcerted—irritably*). The hell you say!

PARRITT (*leans toward him—confidentially*). What a bunch of cuckoos!

JIMMY (*as if reminded of something—with a pathetic attempt at a brisk, no-more-nonsense air*). Tomorrow, yes. It's high time I straightened out and got down to business again. (*He brushes his sleeve fastidiously.*) I must have this suit cleaned and pressed. I can't look like a tramp when I——

JOE (*who has been brooding—interrupts*). Yes, suh, white folks always said I was white. In de days when I was flush, Joe Mott's de only coloured man dey allows in de white gamblin' houses. "You're all right, Joe, you're white," dey says. (*He chuckles.*) Wouldn't let me play craps, dough. Dey know I could make dem dice behave. "Any odder game and any limit you like, Joe," dey says. Man, de money I lost! (*He chuckles—then with an underlying defensiveness.*) Look at de Big Chief in dem days. He knew I was white. I'd saved my dough so I could start my own gamblin' house. Folks in de know tells me, see de man at de top, den you never has trouble. You git Harry Hope give you a letter to de Chief. And Harry does. Don't you, Harry?

HOPE (*preoccupied with his own thoughts*). Eh? Sure. Big Bill was a good friend of mine. I had plenty of friends high up in those days. Still could have if I wanted to go out and see them. Sure, I gave you a letter. I said you was white. What the hell of it?

JOE (*to Captain Lewis, who has relapsed into a sleepy daze and is listening to him with an absurd strained attention without comprehending a word*). Dere. You see, Captain. I went to see de Chief, shakin' in my boots, and dere he is sittin' behind a big desk, lookin' as big as a freight train. He don't look up. He keeps me waitin' and waitin', and after 'bout an hour, seems like to me, he says slow and quiet like dere wasn't no harm in him, "You want to open a gamblin' joint, does you, Joe?" But he don't give me no time to answer. He jumps up, lookin' as big as two freight trains, and he pounds his fist like a ham on de desk, and he shouts, "You black son of a bitch, Harry says you're white and you better be white or dere's a little iron room up de river waitin' for you!" Den he sits down and says quiet again, "All right. You can open. Git de hell outa here!" So I opens, and he finds out I'se white sure 'nuff, 'cause I run wide open for years and pays my sugar on de dot, and de cops and I is friends. (*He chuckles with pride.*) Dem old days! Many's de night I come in here. Dis was a first-class hangout for sports in dem days. Good whisky, fifteen cents, two for two bits. I t'rows down a fifty-dollar bill like it was trash paper and says, "Drink it up, boys, I don't want no change." Ain't dat right, Harry?

HOPE (*caustically*). Yes, and bejees, if I ever seen you throw fifty cents on the bar now, I'd know I had delirium tremens! You've told that story ten million times and if I have to hear it again, that'll give me D.T.s anyway!

JOE (*chuckling*). Gettin' drunk every day for twenty years ain't give you de Brooklyn boys. You needn't be scared of me!

LEWIS (*suddenly turns and beams on Hope*). Thank you, Harry, old chum. I will have a drink, now you mention it, seeing it's so near your birthday.

(*The others laugh.*)

HOPE (*puts his hand to his ear—angrily*). What's that? I can't hear you.

LEWIS (*sadly*). No, I fancied you wouldn't.

HOPE. I don't have to hear, bejees! Booze is the only thing you ever talk about!

LEWIS (*sadly*). True. Yet there was a time when my conversation was more comprehensive. But as I became burdened with years, it seemed rather pointless to discuss my other subject.

HOPE. You can't joke with me! How much room rent do you owe me, tell me that?

LEWIS. Sorry. Adding has always baffled me. Subtraction is my forte.

HOPE (*snarling*). Arrh! Think you're funny! Captain, bejees! Showing off your wounds! Put on your clothes, for Christ's sake! This ain't no Turkish bath! Lousy Limey army! Took 'em years to lick a gang of Dutch hayseeds!

WETJOEN. Dot's right, Harry. Gif him hell!

HOPE. No lip out of you, neither, you Dutch spinach! General, hell! Salvation Army, that's what you'd ought t'been General in! Bragging what a shot you were, and, bejees, you missed him! And he missed you, that's just as bad! And now the two of you bum on me! (*Threateningly.*) But you've broke the camel's back this time, bejees! You pay up tomorrow or out you go!

LEWIS (*earnestly*). My dear fellow, I give you my word of honour as an officer and a gentleman, you shall be paid tomorrow.

WETJOEN. Ve swear it, Harry! Tomorrow vidout fail!

MCGLOIN (*a twinkle in his eye*). There you are, Harry. Sure, what could be fairer?

MOSHER (*with a wink at McGloin*). Yes, you can't ask more than that, Harry. A promise is a promise—as I've often discovered.

HOPE (*turns on them*). I mean the both of you, too! An old grafting flatfoot and a circus bunco steerer! Fine company for me, bejees! Couple of con men living in my flat since Christ knows when! Getting fat as hogs, too! And you ain't even got the decency to get me upstairs where I got a good bed! Let me sleep on a chair like a bum! Kept me down here waitin' for Hickey to show up, hoping I'd blow you to more drinks!

MCGLOIN. Ed and I did our damnedest to get you up, didn't we, Ed?

MOSHER. We did. But you said you couldn't bear the flat because it was one of those nights when memory brought poor old Bessie back to you.

HOPE (*his face instantly becoming long and sad and sentimental—mournfully*). Yes, that's right, boys. I remember now. I could almost see her in every room just as she used to be—and it's twenty years since she—— (*His throat and eyes fill up.*)

(*A suitable sentimental hush falls on the room.*)

LARRY (*in a sardonic whisper to Parritt*). Isn't a pipe dream of yesterday a touching thing? By all accounts, Bessie nagged the hell out of him.

JIMMY (*who has been dreaming, a look of prim resolution on his face, speaks aloud to himself*). No more of this sitting around and loafing. Time I took hold of myself. I must have my shoes soled and heeled and shined first thing tomorrow morning. A general spruce-up. I want to have a well-groomed appearance when I—— (*His voice fades out as he stares in front of him.*)

(*No one pays any attention to him except Larry and Parritt.*)

LARRY (*as before, in a sardonic aside to Parritt*). The tomorrow movement is a sad and beautiful thing, too!

MCGLOIN (*with a huge sentimental sigh—and a calculating look at Hope*). Poor old Bessie! You don't find her like in these days. A sweeter woman never drew breath.

MOSHER (*in a similar calculating mood*). Good old Bess. A man couldn't want a better sister than she was to me.

HOPE (*mournfully*). Twenty years, and I've never set foot out of this house since the day I buried her. Didn't have the heart. Once she'd gone, I didn't give a damn for anything. I lost all my ambition. Without her, nothing seemed worth the trouble. You remember, Ed, you, too, Mac—the boys was going to nominate me for Alderman. It was all fixed. Bessie wanted it and she was so proud. But when she was taken, I told them, "No, boys, I can't do it. I simply haven't the heart. I'm through." I would have won the election easy, too. (*He says this a bit defiantly.*) Oh, I know there was jealous wise guys said the boys was giving me the nomination because they knew they couldn't win that year in this ward. But that's a damned lie! I knew every man, woman and child in the ward, almost. Bessie made me make friends with everyone, helped me remember all their names. I'd have been elected easy.

MCGLOIN. You would, Harry. It was a sure thing.

MOSHER. A dead cinch, Harry. Everyone knows that.

HOPE. Sure they do. But after Bessie died, I didn't have the heart. Still, I know while she'd appreciate my grief, she wouldn't want it to keep me cooped up in here all my life. So I've made up my mind I'll go out soon. Take a walk around the ward, see all the friends I used to know, get together with the boys and maybe tell 'em I'll let 'em deal me a hand in their game again. Yes, bejees, I'll do it. My birthday, tomorrow, that'd be the right time to turn over a new leaf. Sixty. That ain't too old.

MCGLOIN (*flatteringly*). It's the prime of life, Harry.

MOSHER. Wonderful thing about you, Harry, you keep young as you ever was.

JIMMY (*dreaming aloud again*). Get my things from the laundry. They must still have them. Clean collar and shirt. If I wash the ones I've got on any more, they'll fall apart. Socks, too. I want to make a good appearance. I met Dick Trumbull on the street a year or two ago. He said, "Jimmy, the publicity department's never been the same since you got—resigned. It's dead as hell." I said, "I know. I've heard rumours the management were at their wits' end and would be only too glad to have me run it for them again. I think all I'd have to do would be go and see them and they'd offer me the position. Don't you think so, Dick?" He said, "Sure, they would, Jimmy. Only take my advice and wait a while until business conditions are better. Then you can strike them for a bigger salary than you got before, do you see?" I said, "Yes, I do see, Dick, and many thanks for the tip." Well, conditions must be better by this time. All I have to do is get fixed up with a decent front tomorrow, and it's as good as done.

HOPE (*glances at Jimmy with a condescending affectionate pity—in a hushed voice*). Poor Jimmy's off on his pipe dream again. Bejees, he takes the cake!

(*This is too much for Larry. He cannot restrain a sardonic guffaw. But no one pays any attention to him.*)

LEWIS (*opens his eyes, which are drowsing again—dreamily to Wetjoen*). I'm sorry we had to postpone our trip again this April, Piet. I hoped the blasted old estate would be settled up by then. The damned lawyers can't hold up the settlement much longer. We'll make it next year, even if we have to work and earn our passage money, eh? You'll stay with me at the old place as long as you like, then you can take the *Union Castle* from Southampton to Cape Town. (*Sentimentally, with real yearning.*) England in April, I want you to see that, Piet. The old veldt has its points, I'll admit, but it isn't home—especially home in April.

WETJOEN (*blinks drowsily at him—dreamily*). Ja, Cecil, I know how beautiful it must be, from all you tell me many times. I vill enjoy it. But I shall enjoy more ven I am home, too. The veldt, ja! You could put England on it, and it would look like a farmer's small garden. Py Gott, there is space to be free, the air like vine is, you don't need booze to be drunk! My relations vill so surprised be. They vill not know me, it is so many years. Dey vill be so glad I haf come home at last.

JOE (*dreamily*). I'll make my stake and get my new gamblin' house open before you boys leave. You got to come to de openin'. I'll treat you white. If you're broke, I'll stake you to buck any game you chooses. If you wins, dat's velvet for you. If you loses, it don't count. Can't treat you no whiter dan dat, can I?

HOPE (*again with condescending pity*). Bejees, Jimmy's started them off smoking the same hop.

(*But the three are finished, their eyes closed again in sleep or a drowse.*)

LARRY (*aloud to himself—in his comically tense, crazy whisper*). Be God, this bughouse will drive me stark, raving loony yet!

HOPE (*turns on him with fuming suspicion*). What? What d'you say?

LARRY (*placatingly*). Nothing, Harry. I had a crazy thought in my head.

HOPE (*irascibly*). Crazy is right! Yah! The old wise guy! Wise, hell! A damned old fool Anarchist I-Won't-Worker! I'm sick of you and Hugo, too. Bejees, you'll pay up tomorrow, or I'll start a Harry Hope Revolution! I'll tie a dispossess bomb to your tails that'll blow you out in the street! Bejees, I'll make your Movement move! (*The witticism delights him and he bursts into a shrill cackle.*)

(*At once McGloin and Mosher guffaw enthusiastically.*)

MOSHER (*flatteringly*). Harry, you sure say the funniest things! (*He reaches on the table as if he expected a glass to be there—then starts with well-acted surprise.*) Hell, where's my drink? That Rocky is too damned fast cleaning tables. Why, I'd only taken one sip of it.

HOPE (*his smiling face congealing*). No, you don't! (*Acidly.*) Any time you only take one sip of a drink, you'll have lockjaw and paralysis! Think you can kid me with those old circus con games?—me, that's known you since you was knee-high, and, bejees, you was a crook even then!

MCGLOIN (*grinning*). It's not like you to be so hard-hearted, Harry. Sure, it's hot, parching work laughing at your jokes so early in the morning on an empty stomach!

HOPE. Yah! You, Mac! Another crook! Who asked you to laugh? We was talking about poor old Bessie, and you and her no-good brother start to laugh! A hell of a thing! Talking mush about her, too! "Good old Bess." Bejees, she'd never forgive me if she knew I had you two bums living in her flat, throwing ashes and cigar butts on her carpet. You know her opinion of you, Mac. "That Pat McGloin is the biggest drunken grafter that ever disgraced the police force," she used to say to me. "I hope they send him to Sing Sing for life."

MCGLOIN (*unperturbed*). She didn't mean it. She was angry at me because you used to get me drunk. But Bess had a heart of gold underneath her sharpness. She knew I was innocent of all the charges.

WILLIE (*jumps to his feet drunkenly and points a finger at McGloin—imitating the manner of a cross-examiner—coldly*). One moment, please. Lieutenant McGloin! Are you aware you are under oath? Do you realize what the penalty for perjury is? (*Purringly.*) Come now, Lieutenant, isn't it a fact that you're as guilty as hell? No, don't say, "How about your old man?" I am asking the questions. The fact that he was a crooked old bucket-shop bastard has no bearing on your case. (*With a change to maudlin joviality.*) Gentlemen of the Jury, court will now recess while the D.A. sings out a little ditty he learned at Harvard. It was composed in a wanton moment by the Dean of the Divinity School on a moonlight night in July, 1776, while sobering up in a Turkish bath. (*He sings.*)

"'Oh, come up,' she cried, 'my sailor lad,
And you and I'll agree.
And I'll show you the prettiest (*Rap, rap, rap on table*)
That ever you did see.'"

(*Suddenly he catches Hope's eyes fixed on him condemningly, and sees Rocky appearing from the bar. He collapses back on his chair, pleading miserably.*)

Please, Harry! I'll be quiet! Don't make Rocky bounce me upstairs! I'll go crazy alone! (*To McGloin.*) I apologize, Mac. Don't get sore. I was only kidding you.

(*Rocky, at a relenting glance from Hope, returns to the bar.*)

MCGLOIN (*good-naturedly*). Sure, kid all you like, Willie. I'm hardened to it. (*He pauses—seriously.*) But I'm telling you some day before long I'm going to make them reopen my case. Everyone knows there was no real evidence against me, and I took the fall for the ones higher up. I'll be found innocent this time and reinstated. (*Wistfully.*) I'd like to have my old job on the Force back. The boys tell me there's fine pickings these days, and I'm not getting rich here, sitting with a parched throat waiting for Harry Hope to buy a drink. (*He glances reproachfully at Hope.*)

WILLIE. Of course, you'll be reinstated, Mac. All you need is a brilliant young attorney to handle your case. I'll be straightened out and on the wagon in a day or two. I've never practised but I was one of the most brilliant students in Law School, and your case is just the opportunity I need to start. (*Darkly.*) Don't worry about my not forcing the D.A. to reopen your case. I went through my father's papers before the cops destroyed them and I remember a lot of people, even if I can't prove—— (*Coaxingly.*) You will let me take your case, won't you, Mac?

MCGLOIN (*soothingly*). Sure I will and it'll make your reputation, Willie.

(*Mosher winks at Hope, shaking his head, and Hope answers with identical pantomime, as though to say, "Poor dopes, they're off again!"*)

LARRY (*aloud to himself more than to Parritt—with irritable wonder*). Ah, be damned! Haven't I heard their visions a thousand times? Why should they get under my skin now? I've got the blues, I guess. I wish to hell Hickey'd turn up.

MOSHER (*calculatingly solicitous—whispering to Hope*). Poor Willie needs a drink bad, Harry—and I think if we all joined him it'd make him feel he was among friends and cheer him up.

HOPE. More circus con tricks! (*Scathingly.*) You talking of your dear sister! Bessie had you sized up. She used to tell me, "I don't know what you can see in that worthless, drunken, petty-larceny brother of mine. If I had my way," she'd say, "he'd get booted out in the gutter on his fat behind." Sometimes she didn't say behind, either.

MOSHER (*grins genially*). Yes, dear old Bess had a quick temper, but there was no real harm in her. (*He chuckles reminiscently.*) Remember the time she sent me down to the bar to change a ten-dollar bill for her?

HOPE (*has to grin himself*). Bejees, do I! She coulda bit a piece out of a stove lid, after she found it out. (*He cackles appreciatively.*)

MOSHER. I was sure surprised when she gave me the ten spot. Bess usually had better sense, but she was in a hurry to go to church. I didn't really mean to do it, but you know how habit gets you. Besides, I still worked then, and the circus season was going to begin soon, and I needed a little practice to keep my hand in.

Or, you never can tell, the first rube that came to my wagon for a ticket might have left with the right change and I'd be disgraced. (*He chuckles.*) I said, "I'm sorry, Bess, but I had to take it all in dimes. Here, hold out your hands and I'll count it out for you, so you won't kick afterwards I short-changed you." (*He begins a count which grows more rapid as he goes on.*) Ten, twenty, thirty, forty, fifty, sixty, seventy, eighty, ninety, a dollar. Ten, twenty, thirty, forty, fifty, sixty—— You're counting with me, Bess, aren't you?—eighty, ninety, two dollars. Ten, twenty—— Those are pretty shoes you got on, Bess—forty, fifty, seventy, eighty, ninety, three dollars. Ten, twenty, thirty—— What's on at the church tonight, Bess?—fifty, sixty, seventy, ninety, four dollars. Ten, twenty, thirty, fifty, seventy, eighty, ninety—— That's a swell new hat, Bess, looks very becoming—six dollars. (*He chuckles.*) And so on. I'm bum at it now for lack of practice, but in those days I could have short-changed the Keeper of the Mint.

HOPE (*grinning*). Stung her for two dollars and a half, wasn't it, Ed?

MOSHER. Yes. A fine percentage, if I do say so, when you're dealing to someone who's sober and can count. I'm sorry to say she discovered my mistakes in arithmetic, just after I beat it around the corner. She counted it over herself. Bess somehow never had the confidence in me a sister should. (*He sighs tenderly.*) Dear old Bess.

HOPE (*indignant now*). You're a fine guy bragging how you short-changed your own sister! Bejees, if there was a war and you was in it, they'd have to padlock the pockets of the dead!

MOSHER (*a bit hurt at this*). That's going pretty strong, Harry. I always gave a sucker some chance. There wouldn't be no fun robbing the dead. (*He becomes reminiscently melancholy.*) Gosh, thinking of the old ticket wagon brings those days back. The greatest life on earth with the greatest show on earth! The grandest crowd of regular guys ever gathered under one tent! I'd sure like to shake their hands again!

HOPE (*acidly*). They'd have guns in theirs. They'd shoot you on sight. You've touched every damned one of them. Bejees, you've even borrowed fish from the seals and peanuts from every elephant that remembered you! (*This fancy tickles him and he gives a cackling laugh.*)

MOSHER (*overlooking this—dreamily*). You know, Harry, I've made up my mind I'll see the boss in a couple of days and ask for my old job. I can get back my magic touch with change easy, and I can throw him a line of bull that'll kid him I won't be so unreasonable about sharing the profits next time. (*With insinuating complaint.*) There's no percentage in hanging around this dive, taking care of you and shooting away your snakes, when I don't even get an eye-opener for my trouble.

HOPE (*implacably*). No!

(*Mosher sighs and gives up and closes his eyes. The others, except Larry and Parritt, are all dozing again now. Hope goes on grumbling.*)

Go to hell or the circus, for all I care. Good riddance bejees! I'm sick of you! (*Then worriedly.*) Say, Ed what the hell you think's happened to Hickey? I hope he'll turn up. Always got a million funny stories. You and the other bums have begun to give me the graveyard fantods. I'd like a good laugh with old Hickey. (*He chuckles at a memory.*) Remember that gag he always pulls about his wife and the iceman? He'd make a cat laugh!

(*Rocky appears from the bar. He comes front, behind Mosher's chair, and begins pushing the black curtain along the rod to the rear wall.*)

ROCKY. Openin' time, Boss. (*He presses a button at rear which switches off the lights. The back room becomes drabber and dingier than ever in the grey daylight that comes from the street windows, off right, and what light can penetrate the grime of the two backyard windows at left. Rocky turns back to Hope—grumpily.*) Why don't you go up to bed, Boss? Hickey'd never turn up dis time of de mornin'!

HOPE (*starts and listens*). Someone's coming now.

ROCKY (*listens*). Aw, dat's on'y my two pigs. It's about time dey showed. (*He goes back towards the door of the bar.*)

HOPE (*sourly disappointed*). You keep them dumb broads quiet. I don't want to go to bed. I'm going to catch a couple more winks here and I don't want no damn-fool laughing and screeching. (*He settles himself in his chair, grumbling.*) Never thought I'd see the day when Harry Hope's would have tarts rooming in it. What'd Bessie think? But I don't let 'em use my rooms for business. And they're good kids. Good as anyone else. They got to make a living. Pay their rent, too, which is more than I can say for—— (*He cocks an eye over his specs at Mosher and grins with satisfaction.*) Bejees, Ed, I'll bet Bessie is doing somersaults in her grave! (*He chuckles.*)

(*But Mosher's eyes are closed, his head nodding, and he doesn't reply, so Hope closes his eyes. Rocky has opened the bar-room door at rear and is standing in the hall beyond it, facing right. A girl's laugh is heard.*)

ROCKY (*warningly*). Nix! Piano!

(*He comes in, beckoning them to follow. He goes behind the bar and gets a whisky bottle and glasses and chairs. Margie and Pearl follow him, casting a glance around. Everyone except Larry and Parritt is asleep or dozing. Even Parritt has his eyes closed. The two girls, neither much over twenty, are typically dollar street-walkers, dressed in the usual *tawdry get-up. Pearl is obviously Italian with black hair and eyes. Margie has brown hair and hazel eyes, a slum New Yorker of mixed blood. Both are plump and have a certain prettiness that shows even through their blobby make-up. Each retains a vestige of youthful freshness, although the game is beginning to get them and give them hard, worn expressions. Both are sentimental, feather-brained, giggly, lazy, good-natured and reasonably contented with life. Their attitude towards Rocky is much that of two maternal affectionate sisters toward a bullying brother whom they like to tease and spoil. His attitude towards them is that of the owner of two performing pets he has trained to do a profitable act under his management. He feels a proud proprietor's affection for them, and is tolerantly lax in his discipline.)*

MARGIE (*glancing around*). Jees, Poil, it's de Morgue wid all de stiffs on deck. (*She catches Larry's eye and smiles affectionately.*) Hello, Old Wise Guy, ain't you died yet?

LARRY (*grinning*). Not yet, Margie. But I'm waiting impatiently for the end.

(*Parritt opens his eyes to look at the two girls, but a soon as they glance at him he closes them again and turns his head away.*)

MARGIE (*as she and Pearl come to the table at right, front, followed by Rocky*). Who's de new guy? Friend of yours, Larry? (*Automatically she smiles seductively and addresses him in a professional chant.*) Wanta have a good time, kid?

PEARL. Aw, he's passed out. Hell wid him!

HOPE (*cocks an eye over his specs at them—with drowsy irritation*). You dumb broads cut the loud talk. (*He shuts his eye again.*)

ROCKY (*admonishing them good-naturedly*). Sit down before I knock yuh down.

(*Margie and Pearl sit at left, and rear, of table, Rocky at right of it. The girls pour drinks. Rocky begins in a brisk, business-like manner but in a lowered voice with an eye on Hope.*)

Well, how'd you tramps do?

MARGIE. Pretty good. Didn't we, Poil?

PEARL. Sure. We nailed a coupla all-night guys.

MARGIE. On Sixth Avenoo. Boobs from de sticks.

PEARL. Stinko, de bot' of 'em.

MARGIE. We thought we was in luck. We steered dem to a real hotel. We figgered dey was too stinko to bother us much and we could cop a good sleep in beds that ain't got cobble stones in de mattress like de ones in dis dump.

PEARL. But we was outa luck. Dey didn't bother us much dat way, but dey wouldn't go to sleep either, see? Jees, I never hoid such gabby guys.

MARGIE. Dey got onta politics, drinkin' outa de bottle. Dey forgot we was around. "De Bull Moosers is de on'y reg'lar guys," one guy says. And de other guy says. "You're a God-damned liar! And I'm a Republican!" Den dey'd laugh.

PEARL. Den dey'd get mad and make a bluff dey was goin' to scrap, and den dey'd make up and cry and sing "School Days." Jees, imagine tryin' to sleep wid dat on de phonograph!

MARGIE. Maybe you tink we wasn't glad when de house dick come up and told us all to git dressed and take de air!

PEARL. We told de guys we'd wait for dem 'round de corner.

MARGIE. So here we are.

ROCKY (*sententiously*). Yeah. I see you. But I don't see no dough yet.

PEARL (*with a wink at Margie—teasingly*). Right on de job, ain't he, Margie?

MARGIE. Yeah, our little business man! Dat's him!

ROCKY. Come on! Dig!

(*They both pull up their skirts to get the money from their stockings. Rocky watches this move carefully.*)

PEARL (*amused*). Pipe him keepin' cases, Margie.

MARGIE (*amused*). Scared we're holdin' out on him.

PEARL. Way he grabs, yuh'd tink it was him done de woik. (*She holds out a little roll of bills to Rocky.*) Here y'are, Grafter!

MARGIE (*holding hers out*). We hope it chokes yuh.

(*Rocky counts the money quickly and shoves it in his pocket.*)

ROCKY (*genially*). You dumb baby dolls gimme a pain. What would you do wid money if I wasn't around? Give it all to some pimp.

PEARL (*teasingly*). Jees, what's the difference——? (*Hastily.*) Aw, I don't mean dat, Rocky.

ROCKY (*his eyes growing hard—slowly*). A lotta difference, get me?

PEARL. Don't get sore. Jees, can't yuh take a little kiddin'?

MARGIE. Sure, Rocky, Poil was on'y kiddin'. (*Soothingly.*) We know yuh got a reg'lar job. Dat's why we like yuh, see? Yuh don't live offa us. Yuh're a bartender.

ROCKY (*genially again*). Sure, I'm a bartender. Everyone knows me knows dat. And I treat you goils right, don't I? Jees, I'm wise yuh hold out on me, but I know it ain't much, so what the hell, I let yuh get away wid it. I tink yuh're a coupla good kids. Yuh're aces wid me, see?

PEARL. You're aces wid us, too. Ain't he, Margie?

MARGIE. Sure, he's aces.

(*Rocky beams complacently and takes the glasses back to the bar. Margie whispers.*)

Yuh sap, don't yuh know enough not to kid him on dat? Serve yuh right if he beat yuh up!

PEARL (*admiringly*). Jees, I'll bet he'd give yuh an awful beatin', too, once he started. Ginnies got awful tempers.

MARGIE. Anyway, we wouldn't keep no pimp, like we was reg'lar old whores. We ain't dat bad.

PEARL. No. We're tarts, but dat's all.

ROCKY (*rinsing glasses behind the bar*). Cora got back around three o'clock. She woke up Chuck and dragged him outa de hay to go to a chop suey joint. (*Disgustedly.*) Imagine him standin' for dat stuff!

MARGIE (*disgustedly*). I'll bet dey been sittin' around kiddin' demselves wid dat old pipe dream about gettin' married and settlin' down on a farm. Jees, when Chuck's on de wagon, dey never lay off dat dope! Dey give yuh an earful every time yuh talk to 'em!

PEARL. Yeah. Chuck wid a silly grin on his ugly map, de big boob, and Cora gigglin' like she was in grammar school and some tough guy'd just told her babies wasn't brung down de chimney by a boid!

MARGIE. And her on de turf long before me and you was! And bot' of 'em arguin' all de time, Cora sayin' she's scared to marry him because he'll go on drunks again. Just as dough any drunk could scare Cora!

PEARL. And him swearin', de big liar, he'll never go on no more periodicals! An' den her pretendin'—— But it gives me a pain to talk about it. We ought to phone de booby hatch to send round de wagon for 'em.

ROCKY (*comes back to the table—disgustedly*). Yeah, of all de pipe dreams in dis dump dey got de nuttiest! And nuttin' stops dem. Dey been dreamin' it for years, every time Chuck goes on de wagon. I never could figger it. What would gettin' married get dem? But de farm stuff is de sappiest part. When bot' of 'em was dragged up in dis ward and ain't never been nearer a farm dan Coney Island! Jees, dey'd tink dey'd gone deef if dey didn't hear de El rattle! Dey'd get D.T.'s if dey ever hoid a cricket choip! I hoid crickets once on my cousin's place in Joisey. I couldn't sleep a wink. Dey give me de heebie-jeebies. (*With deeper disgust.*) Jees, can yuh picture a good barkeep like Chuck diggin' spuds? And imagine a whore hustlin' de cows home! For Christ sake! Ain't dat a sweet picture!

MARGIE (*rebukingly*). Yuh oughtn't to call Cora dat, Rocky. She's a good kid. She may be a tart, but——

ROCKY (*considerately*). Sure, dat's all I meant, a tart.

PEARL (*giggling*). But he's right about de damned cows, Margie. Jees, I bet Cora don't know which end of de cow has de horns! I'm goin' to ask her.

(*There is the noise of a door opening in the hall and the sound of a man's and woman's arguing voices.*)

ROCKY. Here's your chance. Dat's dem two nuts now.

(*Cora and Chuck look in from the hallway and then come in. Cora is a thin peroxide blonde, a few years older than Pearl and Margie, dressed in similar style, her round face showing more of the wear and tear of her trade than theirs, but still with traces of a doll-like prettiness. Chuck is a tough, thick-necked, barrel-chested Italian-American, with a fat, amiable, swarthy face. He has on a straw hat with a vivid band, a loud suit, tie and shirt, and yellow shoes. His eyes are clear and he looks healthy and strong as an ox.*)

CORA (*gaily*). Hello, bums. (*She looks around.*) Jees, de Morgue on a rainy Sunday night! (*She waves to Larry—affectionately.*) Hello, Old Wise Guy! Ain't you croaked yet?

LARRY (*grins*). Not yet, Cora. It's damned tiring, this waiting for the end.

CORA. Aw, gwan, you'll never die! Yuh'll have to hire someone to croak yuh wid an axe.

HOPE (*cocks one sleepy eye at her—irritably*). You dumb hookers, cut the loud noise! This ain't a cat-house!

CORA (*teasingly*). My, Harry! Such language!

HOPE (*closes his eyes—to himself with a gratified chuckle*). Bejees, I'll bet Bessie's turning over in her grave!

(*Cora sits down between Margie and Pearl, Chuck takes an empty chair from Hope's table and puts it by hers and sits down. At Larry's table, Parritt is glaring resentfully towards the girls.*)

PARRITT. If I'd known this dump was a hooker hangout, I'd never have come here.

LARRY (*watching him*). You seem down on the ladies.

PARRITT (*vindictively*). I hate every bitch that ever lived! They're all alike! (*Catching himself guiltily.*) You can understand how I feel, can't you, when it was getting mixed up with a tart that made me have that fight with Mother? (*Then with a resentful sneer.*) But what the hell does it matter to you? You're in the grandstand. You're through with life.

LARRY (*sharply*). I'm glad you remember it. I don't want to know a damned thing about your business. (*He closes his eyes and settles on his chair as if preparing for sleep.*)

(*Parritt stares at him sneeringly. Then he looks away and his expression becomes furtive and frightened.*)

CORA. Who's de guy wid Larry?

ROCKY. A tightwad. To hell wid him.

PEARL. Say, Cora, wise me up. Which end of a cow is de horns on?

CORA (*embarrassed*). Aw, don't bring dat up. I'm sick of hearin' about dat farm.

ROCKY. You got nuttin' on us!

CORA (*ignoring this*). Me and dis overgrown tramp has been scrappin' about it. He says Joisey's de best place, and I says Long Island because we'll be near Coney. And I tells him, How do I know yuh're off of periodicals for life? I don't give a damn how drunk yuh get, the way we are, but I don't wanta be married to no soak.

CHUCK. And I tells her I'm off de stuff for life. Den she beefs we won't be married a month before I'll trow it in her face she was a tart. "Jees, Baby," I tells her. "Why should I? What de hell yuh tink I tink I'm marryin', a voigin? Why should I kick as long as yuh lay off it and don't do no cheatin' wid de iceman or nobody? (*He gives her a rough hug.*) Dat's on de level, Baby. (*He kisses her.*)

CORA (*kissing him*). Aw, yuh big tramp!

ROCKY (*shakes his head with profound disgust*). Can yuh tie it? I'll buy a drink. I'll do anything. (*He gets up.*)

CORA. No, dis round's on me. I run into luck. Dat's why I dragged Chuck outa bed to celebrate. It was a sailor. I rolled him. (*She giggles.*) Listen, it was a scream. I've run into some nutty souses, but dis guy was de nuttiest. De booze dey dish out around de Brooklyn Navy Yard must be as turrible bugjuice as Harry's. My dogs was givin' out when I seen dis guy holdin' up a lamp-post, so I hurried to get him before a cop did. I says, "Hello, Handsome, wanta have a good time?" Jees, he was paralysed! One of dem polite jags. He tries to bow to me, imagine, and I had to prop him up or he'd fell on his nose. And what d'yuh tink he said? "Lady," he says, "can yuh kindly tell me de nearest way to de Museum of Natural History?" (*They all laugh.*) Can yuh imagine! At two a.m. As if I'd know where de dump was anyway. But I says, "Sure ting, Honey Boy, I'll be only too glad." So I steered him into a side street where it was dark and propped him against a wall and give him a frisk. (*She giggles.*) And what d'yuh tink he does? Jees, I ain't lyin', he begins to laugh, de big sap! He says, "Quit ticklin' me." While I was friskin' him for his roll! I near died! Den I toined him 'round and give him a push to start him. "Just keep goin'," I told him. "It's a big white building on your right. You can't miss it." He must be swimmin' in de North River yet!

(*They all laugh.*)

CHUCK. Ain't Uncle Sam de sap to trust guys like dat wid dough!

CORA (*with a business-like air*). I picked twelve bucks offa him. Come on, Rocky. Set 'em up.

(*Rocky goes back to the bar. Cora looks around the room.*)

Say, Chuck's kiddin' about de iceman a minute ago reminds me. Where de hell's Hickey?

ROCKY. Dat's what we're all wonderin'.

CORA. He oughta be here. Me and Chuck seen him.

ROCKY (*excited, comes back from the bar, forgetting the drinks*). You seen Hickey? (*He nudges Hope.*) Hey, Boss, come to! Cora's seen Hickey.

(*Hope is instantly wide awake and everyone in the place except Hugo and Parritt, begins to rouse up hopefully, as if a mysterious wireless message had gone round.*)

HOPE. Where'd you see him, Cora?

CORA. Right on de next corner. He was standin' dere. We said, "Welcome to our city. De gang is expectin' yuh wid deir tongues hangin' out a yard long." And I kidded him, "How's de iceman, Hickey? How's he doin' at your house?" He laughs and says, "Fine." And he says, "Tell de gang I'll be along in a minute. I'm just finishin' figurin' out de best way to save dem and bring dem peace."

HOPE (*chuckles*). Bejees, he's thought up a new gag! It's a wonder he didn't borry a Salvation Army uniform and show up in that! Go out and get him, Rocky. Tell him we're waitin' to be saved!

(*Rocky goes out, grinning.*)

CORA. Yeah, Harry, he was only kiddin'. But he was funny, too, somehow. He was different, or somethin'.

CHUCK. Sure, he was sober, Baby. Dat's what made him different. We ain't never seen him when he wasn't on a drunk, or had de willies gettin' over it.

CORA. Sure! Gee, ain't I dumb?

HOPE (*with conviction*). The dumbest broad I ever seen! (*Then puzzledly.*) Sober? That's funny. He's always lapped up a good starter on his way here. Well, bejees, he won't be sober long! He'll be good and ripe for my birthday party tonight at twelve. (*He chuckles with excited anticipation—addressing all of them.)* Listen! He's fixed some new gag to pull on us. We'll pretend to let him kid us, see? And we'll kid the pants off him.

(They all say laughingly, "Sure, Harry," "Righto," "That's the stuff," "We'll fix him," *etc., etc., their faces excited with the same eager anticipation. Rocky appears in the doorway at the end of the bar with Hickey, his arm around Hickey's shoulders.)*

ROCKY *(with an affectionate grin).* Here's the old son of a bitch!

(They all stand up and greet him with affectionate acclaim, "Hello, Hickey!" *etc. Even Hugo comes out of his coma to raise his head and blink through his thick spectacles with a welcoming giggle.)*

HICKEY *(jovially).* Hello, Gang! *(He stands a moment, beaming around at all of them affectionately. He is about fifty, a little under medium height, with a stout, roly-poly figure. His face is round and smooth and big-boyish with bright blue eyes, a button nose, a small, pursed mouth. His head is bald except for a fringe of hair around his temples and the back of his head. His expression is fixed in a salesman's winning smile of self-confident affability and hearty good fellowship. His eyes have the twinkle of a humour which delights in kidding others but can also enjoy equally a joke on himself. He exudes a friendly, generous personality that makes everyone like him on sight. You get the impression, too, that he must have real ability in his line. There is an efficient, business-like approach in his manner, and his eyes can take you in shrewdly at a glance. He has the salesman's mannerisms of speech, an easy flow of glib, persuasive convincingness. His clothes are those of a successful drummer whose territory consists of minor cities and small towns—not flashy but conspicuously spic and span. He immediately puts on an entrance act, places a hand affectedly on his chest, throws back his head, and sings in a falsetto tenor.)* "It's always fair weather, when good fellows get together!" *(Changing to a comic bass and another tune.)* "And another little drink won't do us any harm!" *(They all roar with laughter at this burlesque which his personality makes really funny. He waves his hand in a lordly manner to Rocky.)* Do your duty, Brother Rocky. Bring on the rat poison!

(Rocky grins and goes behind the bar to get drinks amid an approving cheer from the crowd. Hickey comes forward to shake hands with Hope—with affectionate heartiness.)

How goes it, Governor?

HOPE *(enthusiastically).* Bejees, Hickey, you old bastard, it's good to see you!

(Hickey shakes hands with Mosher and McGloin; leans right to shake hands with Margie and Pearl; moves to the middle table to shake hands with Lewis, Joe Mott, Wetjoen and Jimmy; waves to Willie, Larry and Hugo. He greets each by name with the same affectionate heartiness and there is an interchange of "How's the kid?" "How's the old scout?" "How's the boy?" "How's everything?" *etc., etc. Rocky begins setting out drinks, whisky glasses with chasers, and a bottle for each table, starting with Larry's table. Hope says:)*

Sit down, Hickey. Sit down.

(Hickey takes the chair, facing front, at the front of the table in the second row which is half between Hope's table and the one where Jimmy Tomorrow is. Hope goes on with excited pleasure:)

Bejees, Hickey, it seems natural to see your ugly, grinning map. *(With a scornful nod to Cora.)* This dumb broad was tryin' to tell us you'd changed, but you ain't a damned bit. Tell us about yourself. How've you been doin'? Bejees, you look like a million dollars.

ROCKY *(coming to Hickey's table, puts a bottle of whisky, a glass and a chaser on it—then hands Hickey a key).* Here's your key, Hickey. Same old room.

HICKEY *(shoves the key in his pocket).* Thanks, Rocky. I'm going up in a little while and grab a snooze. Haven't been able to sleep lately and I'm tired as hell. A couple of hours good kip will fix me.

HOPE *(as Rocky puts drinks on his table).* First time I ever heard you worry about sleep. Bejees, you never would go to bed.

(He raises his glass, and all the others except Parritt do likewise.)

Get a few slugs under your belt and you'll forget sleeping. Here's mud in your eye, Hickey.

(They all join in with the usual humorous toasts.)

HICKEY *(heartily).* Drink hearty, boys and girls!

(They all drink, but Hickey drinks only his chaser.)

HOPE. Bejees, is that a new stunt, drinking your chaser first?

HICKEY. No, I forgot to tell Rocky—— You'll have to excuse me, boys and girls, but I'm off the stuff. For keeps.

(They stare at him in amazed incredulity.)

HOPE. What the hell—— *(Then with a wink at the others, kiddingly.)* Sure! Joined the Salvation Army, ain't you? Been elected President of the W.C.T.U.? Take that bottle away from him, Rocky. We don't want to tempt him into sin. *(He chuckles and the others laugh.)*

HICKEY *(earnestly).* No, honest, Harry. I know it's hard to believe but—— *(He pauses—then adds simply.)* Cora was right, Harry. I have changed. I mean, about booze. I don't need it any more.

(*They all stare, hoping it's a gag, but impressed and disappointed and made vaguely uneasy by the change they now sense in him.*)

HOPE (*his kidding a bit forced*). Yeah, go ahead, kid the pants off us! Bejees, Cora said you was coming to save us! Well, go on. Get this joke off your chest! Start the service! Sing a God-damned hymn if you like. We'll all join in the chorus. "No drunkard can enter this beautiful home." That's a good one. (*He forces a cackle.*)

HICKEY (*grinning*). Oh, hell, Governor! You don't think I'd come around here peddling some brand of temperance bunk, do you? You know me better than that! Just because I'm through with the stuff don't mean I'm going Prohibition. Hell, I'm not that ungrateful! It's given me too many good times. I feel exactly the same as I always did. If anyone wants to get drunk, if that's the only way they can be happy, and feel at peace with themselves, why the hell shouldn't they? They have my full and entire sympathy. I know all about that game from soup to nuts. I'm the guy that wrote the book. The only reason I've quit is—— Well, I finally had the guts to face myself and throw overboard the damned lying pipe dream that'd been making me miserable, and do what I had to do for the happiness of all concerned—and then all at once I found I was at peace with myself and I didn't need booze any more. That's all there was to it. (*He pauses. They are staring at him, uneasy and beginning to feel defensive. Hickey looks round and grins affectionately—apologetically.*) But what the hell! Don't let me be a wet blanket, making fool speeches about myself. Set 'em up again, Rocky. Here. (*He pulls a big roll from his pocket and peels off a ten-dollar bill. The faces of all brighten.*) Keep the balls coming until this is killed. Then ask for more.

ROCKY. Jees, a roll dat'd choke a hippopotamus! Fill up, youse guys.

(*They all pour out drinks.*)

HOPE. That sounds more like you, Hickey. That water-wagon bull—— Cut out the act and have a drink, for Christ's sake.

HICKEY. It's no act, Governor. But don't get me wrong. That don't mean I'm a teetotal grouch and can't be in the party. Hell, why d'you suppose I'm here except to have a party, same as I've always done and help celebrate your birthday tonight? You've all been good pals to me, the best friends I've ever had. I've been thinking about you ever since I left the house—all the time I was walking over here——

HOPE. Walking? Bejees, do you mean to say you walked?

HICKEY. I sure did. All the way from the wilds of darkest Astoria. Didn't mind it a bit, either. I seemed to get here before I knew it. I'm a bit tired and sleepy but otherwise I feel great. (*Kiddingly.*) That ought to encourage you, Governor—show you a little walk around the ward is nothing to be so scared about. (*He winks at the others. Hope stiffens resentfully for a second. Hickey goes on.*) I didn't make such bad time either for a fat guy, considering it's a hell of a ways, and I sat in the park a while thinking. It was going on twelve when I went in the bedroom to tell Evelyn I was leaving. Six hours, say. No, less than that. I'd been standing on the corner some time before Cora and Chuck came along, thinking about all of you. Of course, I was only kidding Cora with that stuff about saving you. (*Then seriously.*) No, I wasn't either. But I didn't mean booze. I meant save you from pipe dreams. I know now, from my experience, they're the things that really poison and ruin a guy's life and keep him from finding any peace. If you knew how free and contented I feel now. I'm like a new man. And the cure for them is so damned simple, once you have the nerve. Just the old dope of honesty is the best policy—honesty with yourself, I mean. Just stop lying about yourself and kidding yourself about tomorrows. (*He is staring ahead of him now as if he were talking aloud to himself as much as to them. Their eyes are fixed on him with uneasy resentment. His manner becomes apologetic again.*) Hell, this begins to sound like a damned sermon on the way to lead the good life. Forget that part of it. It's in my blood, I guess. My old man used to whale salvation into my heinie with a birch rod. He was a preacher in the sticks of Indiana, like I've told you. I got my knack of sales gab from him, too. He was the boy who could sell those Hoosier hayseeds building lots along the Golden Street! (*Taking on a salesman's persuasiveness.*) Now listen, boys and girls, don't look at me as if I was trying to sell you a goldbrick. Nothing up my sleeve, honest. Let's take an example. Any one of you. Take you, Governor. That walk around the ward you never take——

HOPE (*defensively sharp*). What about it?

HICKEY (*grinning affectionately*). Why, you know as well as I do, Harry. Everything about it.

HOPE (*defiantly*). Bejees, I'm going to take it!

HICKEY. Sure, you're going to—this time. Because I'm going to help you. I know it's the thing you've got to do before you'll ever know what real peace means. (*He looks at Jimmy Tomorrow.*) Same thing with you, Jimmy. You've got to try and get your old job back. And no tomorrow about it! (*As Jimmy stiffens with a pathetic attempt at dignity—placatingly.*) No, don't tell me, Jimmy. I know all about tomorrow. I'm the guy that wrote the book.

JIMMY. I don't understand you. I admit I've foolishly delayed, but as it happens, I'd just made up my mind that as soon as I could get straightened out——

HICKEY. Fine! That's the spirit! And I'm going to help you. You've been damned kind to me, Jimmy, and I want to prove how grateful I am. When it's all over and you don't have to nag at yourself any more, you'll be grateful to me, too! (*He looks around at the others.*) And all the rest of you, ladies included, are in the same boat, one way or another.

LARRY (*who has been listening with sardonic appreciation —in his comically intense, crazy whisper*). Be God, you've hit the nail on the head, Hickey! This dump is the Palace of Pipe Dreams!

HICKEY (*grins at him with affectionate kidding*). Well, well! The Old Grandstand Foolosopher speaks! You think you're the big exception, eh? Life doesn't mean a damn to you any more, does it? You're retired from the circus. You're just waiting impatiently for the end —the good old Long Sleep! (*He chuckles.*) Well, I think a lot of you, Larry, you old bastard. I'll try and make an honest man of you, too!

LARRY (*stung*). What the devil are you hinting at, anyway?

HICKEY. You don't have to ask me, do you, a wise old guy like you? Just ask yourself. I'll bet you know.

PARRITT (*is watching Larry's face with a curious sneering satisfaction*). He's got your number all right, Larry! (*He turns to Hickey.*) That's the stuff, Hickey. Show the old faker up! He's got no right to sneak out of everything.

HICKEY (*regards him with surprise at first, then with a puzzled interest*). Hello. A stranger in our midst. I didn't notice you before, Brother.

PARRITT (*embarrassed, his eyes shifting away*). My name's Parritt. I'm an old friend of Larry's. (*His eyes come back to Hickey to find him still sizing him up—defensively.*) Well? What are you staring at?

HICKEY (*continuing to stare—puzzledly*). No offence, Brother. I was trying to figure—— Haven't we met before some place?

PARRITT (*reassured*). No. First time I've ever been East.

HICKEY. No, you're right. I know that's not it. In my game, to be a shark at it, you teach yourself never to forget a name or a face. But still I know damned well I recognized something about you. We're members of the same lodge—in some way.

PARRITT (*uneasy again*). What are you talking about? You're nuts.

HICKEY (*dryly*). Don't try to kid me, Little Boy. I'm a good salesman—so damned good the firm was glad to take me back after every drunk—and what made me good was I could size up anyone. (*Frowningly puzzled again.*) But I don't see—— (*Suddenly breezily good-natured.*) Never mind. I can tell you're having trouble with yourself and I'll be glad to do anything I can to help a friend of Larry's.

LARRY. Mind your own business, Hickey. He's nothing to you—or to me, either. (*Hickey gives him a keen inquisitive glance. Larry looks away and goes on sarcastically.*) You're keeping us all in suspense. Tell us more about how you're going to save us.

HICKEY (*good-naturedly but seeming a little hurt*). Hell, don't get sore, Larry. Not at me. We've always been good pals, haven't we? I know I've always liked you a lot.

LARRY (*a bit shamefacedly*). Well, so have I liked you. Forget it, Hickey.

HICKEY (*beaming*). Fine! That's the spirit! (*Looking around at the others, who have forgotten their drinks.*) What's the matter, everybody? What is this, a funeral? Come on and drink up! A little action! (*They all drink.*) Have another. Hell, this is a celebration! Forget it, if anything I've said sounds too serious. I don't want to be a pain in the neck. Any time you think I'm talking out of turn, just tell me to go chase myself! (*He yawns with growing drowsiness and his voice grows a bit muffled.*) No, boys and girls, I'm not trying to put anything over on you. It's just that I know now from experience what a lying pipe dream can do to you—and how damned relieved and contented with yourself you feel when you're rid of it. (*He yawns again.*) God, I'm sleepy all of a sudden. That long walk is beginning to get me. I better go upstairs. Hell of a trick to go dead on you like this. (*He starts to get up but relaxes again. His eyes blink as he tries to keep them open.*) No, boys and girls, I've never known what real peace was until now. It's a grand feeling, like when you're sick and suffering like hell and the Doc gives you a shot in the arm, and the pain goes, and you drift off. (*His eyes close.*) You can let go of yourself at last. Let yourself sink down to the bottom of the sea. Rest in peace. There's no farther you have to go. Not a single damned hope or dream left to nag you. You'll all know what I mean after you—— (*He pauses—mumbles.*) Excuse—all in—got to grab forty winks—— Drink up, everybody—on me—— (*The sleep of complete exhaustion overpowers him. His chin sags to his chest.*)

(*They stare at him with puzzled uneasy fascination.*)

HOPE (*forcing a tone of irritation*). Bejees, that's a fine stunt, to go to sleep on us! (*Then fumingly to the crowd.*) Well, what the hell's the matter with you bums? Why don't you drink up? You're always crying for booze, and now you've got it under your nose, you sit like dummies! (*They start and gulp down their whiskies and pour another. Hope stares at Hickey.*) Bejees, I can't figure Hickey. I still say he's kidding us. Kid his own grandmother, Hickey would. What d'you think, Jimmy?

JIMMY (*unconvincingly*). It must be another of his jokes, Harry, although—— Well, he does appear changed. But he'll probably be his natural self again tomorrow—— (*Hastily.*) I mean, when he wakes up.

LARRY (*staring at Hickey frowningly—more aloud to himself than to them*). You'll make a mistake if you think he's only kidding.

PARRITT (*in a low confidential voice*). I don't like that guy, Larry. He's too damned nosy. I'm going to steer clear of him.

(*Larry gives him a suspicious glance, then looks hastily away.*)

JIMMY (*with an attempt at open-minded reasonableness*). Still, Harry, I have to admit there was some sense in his nonsense. It is time I got my job back—although I hardly need him to remind me.

HOPE (*with an air of frankness*). Yes, and I ought to take a walk around the ward. But I don't need no Hickey to tell me, seeing I got it all set for my birthday tomorrow.

LARRY (*sardonically*). Ha! (*Then in his comically intense, crazy whisper.*) Be God, it looks like he's going to make two sales of his peace at least! But you'd better make sure first it's the real McCoy and not poison.

HOPE (*disturbed—angrily*). You bughouse I-Won't-Work harp, who asked you to shove in an oar? What the hell d'you mean, poison? Just because he has your number—— (*He immediately feels ashamed of this taunt and adds apologetically.*) Bejees, Larry, you're always croaking about something to do with death. It gets my nanny. Come on, fellers, let's drink up. (*They drink. Hope's eyes are fixed on Hickey again.*) Stone cold sober and dead to the world! Spilling that business about pipe dreams! Bejees, I don't get it. (*He bursts out again in angry complaint.*) He ain't like the old Hickey! He'll be a fine wet blanket to have around at my birthday party! I wish to hell he'd never turned up!

MOSHER (*who has been the least impressed by Hickey's talk and is the first to recover and feel the effect of the drinks on top of his hangover—genially*). Give him time, Harry, and he'll come out of it. I've watched many cases of almost fatal teetotalism, but they all came out of it completely cured and as drunk as ever. My opinion is the poor sap is temporarily bughouse from overwork. (*Musingly.*) You can't be too careful about work. It's the deadliest habit known to science, a great physician once told me. He practised on street corners under a torchlight. He was positively the only doctor in the world who claimed that rattlesnake oil, rubbed on the prat, would cure heart failure in three days. I remember well his saying to me, "You are naturally delicate, Ed, but if you drink a pint of bad whisky before breakfast every evening, and never work if you can help it, you may live to a ripe old age. It's staying sober and working that cuts men off in their prime."

(*While he is talking, they turn to him with eager grins. They are longing to laugh, and as he finishes they roar. Even Parritt laughs. Hickey sleeps on like a dead man, but Hugo, who had passed into his customary coma again, head on table, looks up through his thick spectacles and giggles foolishly.*)

HUGO (*blinking around at them. As the laughter dies he speaks in his giggling, wheedling manner, as if he were playfully teasing children*). Laugh, leedle bourgeois monkey-faces! Laugh like fools, leedle stupid peoples! (*His tone suddenly changes to one of guttural soapbox denunciation and he pounds on the table with a small fist.*) I vill laugh, too! But I vill laugh last! I vill laugh at you! (*He declaims his favourite quotation.*) "The days grow hot, O Babylon! 'Tis cool beneath thy villow trees!"

(*They all hoot him down in a chorus of amused jeering. Hugo is not offended. This is evidently their customary reaction. He giggles good-naturedly. Hickey sleeps on. They have all forgotten their uneasiness about him now and ignore him.*)

LEWIS (*tipsily*). Well, now that our little Robespierre has got the daily bit of guillotining off his chest, tell me more about your doctor friend, Ed. He strikes me as the only bloody sensible medico I ever heard of. I think we should appoint him house physician here without a moment's delay.

(*They all laughingly assent.*)

MOSHER (*warming to his subject, shakes his head sadly*). Too late! The old Doc has passed on to his Maker. A victim of overwork, too. He didn't follow his own advice. Kept his nose to the grindstone and sold one bottle of snake oil too many. Only eighty years old when he was taken. The saddest part was that he knew he was doomed. The last time we got paralysed together he told me: "This game will get me yet, Ed. You see before you a broken man, a martyr to medical science. If I had any nerves I'd have a nervous breakdown. You won't believe me, but this last year there was actually one night I had so many patients, I didn't even have time to get drunk. The shock to my system brought on a stroke which, as a doctor, I recognized was the beginning of the end." Poor old Doc! When he said this he started crying. "I hate to go before my task is completed, Ed," he sobbed. "I'd hoped I'd live to see the day when, thanks to my miraculous cure, there wouldn't be a single vacant cemetery lot left in this glorious country." (*There is a roar of laughter. He waits for it to die and then goes on sadly.*) I miss Doc. He was a gentleman of the old school. I'll bet he's standing on a street corner in hell right now, making suckers of the damned, telling them there's nothing like snake oil for a bad burn.

(*There is another roar of laughter. This time it penetrates Hickey's exhausted slumber. He stirs on his chair, trying to wake up, managing to raise his head a little and force his eyes half open. He speaks with a drowsy, affectionately encouraging smile. At once the laughter stops *abruptly and they turn to him startledly.)*

HICKEY. That's the spirit—don't let me be a wet blanket—all I want is to see you happy—— (*He slips back into heavy sleep again.*)

(*They all stare at him, their faces again puzzled, resentful and uneasy.*)

CURTAIN

ACT TWO

SCENE. *The back room only. The black curtain dividing it from the bar is the right wall of the scene. It is getting on towards midnight of the same day.*

The back room has been prepared for a festivity. At centre, front, four of the circular tables are pushed together to form one long table with an uneven line of chairs behind it, and chairs at each end. This improvised banquet table is covered with old table-cloths, borrowed from a neighbouring beanery, and is laid with glasses, plates and cutlery before each of the seventeen chairs. Bottles of bar whisky are placed at intervals within reach of any sitter. An old upright piano and stool have been moved in and stand against the wall at left, front. At right, front, is a table without chairs. The other tables and chairs that had been in the room have been moved out, leaving a clear floor space at rear for dancing. The floor has been swept clean of sawdust and scrubbed. Even the walls show evidence of having been washed, although the result is only to heighten their splotchy leprous look. The electric light brackets are adorned with festoons of red ribbon. In the middle of the separate table at right, front, is a birthday cake with six candles. Several packages, tied with ribbon, are also on the table. There are two necktie boxes, two cigar boxes, a fifth containing a half-dozen handkerchiefs, the sixth is a square jeweller's watch box.

As the curtain rises, Cora, Chuck, Hugo, Larry, Margie, Pearl and Rocky are discovered. Chuck, Rocky and the three girls have dressed up for the occasion. Cora is arranging a bouquet of flowers in a vase, the vase being a big schooner glass from the bar, on top of the piano. Chuck sits in a chair at the foot (left) of the banquet table. He has turned it so he can watch her. Near the middle of the row of chairs behind the table, Larry sits, facing front, a drink of whisky before him. He is staring before him in frowning, disturbed meditation. Next to him, on his left, Hugo is in his habitual position, passed out, arms on table, head on arms, a full whisky glass by his head. By the separate table at right, front, Margie and Pearl are arranging the cake and presents, and Rocky stands by them. All of them, with the exception of Chuck and Rocky, have had plenty to drink and show it, but no one, except Hugo, seems to be drunk. They are trying to act up in the spirit of the occasion but there is something forced about their manner, an undercurrent of nervous irritation and preoccupation.

CORA (*standing back from the piano to regard the flower effect*). How's dat, Kid?

CHUCK (*grumpily*). What de hell do I know about flowers?

CORA. Yuh can see dey're pretty, can't yuh, yuh big dummy?

CHUCK (*mollifyingly*). Yeah, Baby, sure. If yuh like 'em, dey're aw right wid me.

(*Cora goes back to give the schooner of flowers a few more touches.*)

MARGIE (*admiring the cake*). Some cake, huh, Poil? Lookit! Six candles. Each for ten years.

PEARL. When do we light de candles, Rocky?

ROCKY (*grumpily*). Ask dat bughouse Hickey. He's elected himself boss of dis boithday racket. Just before Harry comes down, he says. Den Harry blows dem out wid one breath, for luck. Hickey was goin' to have sixty candles, but I says, Jees, if de old guy took dat big a breath, he'd croak himself.

MARGIE (*challengingly*). Well, anyways, it's some cake, ain't it?

ROCKY (*without enthusiasm*). Sure, it's aw right by me. But what de hell is Harry goin' to do wid a cake? If he ever et a hunk, it'd croak him.

PEARL. Jees, yuh're a dope! Ain't he, Margie?

MARGIE. A dope is right!

ROCKY (*stung*). You broads better watch your step or——

PEARL (*defiantly*). Or what?

MARGIE. Yeah! Or what?

(*They glare at him truculently.*)

ROCKY. Say, what de hell's got into youse? It'll be twelve o'clock and Harry's boithday before long. I ain't lookin' for no trouble.

PEARL (*ashamed*). Aw, we ain't neider, Rocky.

(*For the moment this argument subsides.*)

CORA (*over her shoulder to Chuck—acidly*). A guy what can't see flowers is pretty must be some dumb-bell.

CHUCK. Yeah? Well, if I was as dumb as you—— (*Then mollifyingly.*) Jees, yuh got your scrappin' pants on, ain't yuh? (*Grins good-naturedly.*) Hell, Baby, what's eatin' yuh ? All I'm tinkin' is, flowers is dat louse Hickey's stunt. We never had no flowers for Harry's boithday before. What de hell can Harry do wid flowers ? He don't know a cauliflower from a geranium.

ROCKY. Yeah, Chuck, it's like I'm tellin' dese broads about de cake. Dat's Hickey's wrinkle, too. (*Bitterly.*) Jees, ever since he woke up, yuh can't hold him. He's taken on de party like it was his boithday.

MARGIE. Well, he's payin' for everything, ain't he ?

ROCKY. Aw, I don't mind de boithday stuff so much. What gets my goat is de way he's tryin' to run de whole dump and everyone in it. He's buttin' in all over de place, tellin' everybody where dey get off. On'y he don't really tell yuh. He just keeps hintin' around.

PEARL. Yeah. He was hintin' to me and Margie.

MARGIE. Yeah, de lousy drummer.

ROCKY. He just gives yuh an earful of dat line of bull about yuh got to be honest wid yourself and not kid yourself, and have de guts to be what yuh are. I got sore. I told him dat's aw right for de bums in dis dump. I hope he makes dem wake up. I'm sick of listenin' to dem hop demselves up. But it don't go wid me, see ? I don't kid myself wid no pipe dream. (*Pearl and Margie exchange a derisive look. He catches it and his eyes narrow.*) What are yuh grinnin' at ?

PEARL (*her face hard—scornfully*). Nuttin'.

MARGIE. Nuttin'.

ROCKY. It better be nuttin' ! Don't let Hickey put no ideas in your nuts if you wanta stay healthy ! (*Then angrily.*) I wish de louse never showed up ! I hope he don't come back from de delicatessen. He's gettin' everyone nuts. He's ridin' someone every minute. He's got Harry and Jimmy Tomorrow run ragged, and de rest is hidin' in deir rooms so dey won't have to listen to him. Dey're all actin' cagey wid de booze, too, like dey was scared if dey get too drunk, dey might spill deir guts, or somethin'. And everybody's gettin' a prize grouch on.

CORA. Yeah, he's been hintin' round to me and Chuck, too. Yuh'd tink he suspected me and Chuck hadn't no real intention of gettin' married. Yuh'd tink he suspected Chuck wasn't goin' to lay off periodicals—or maybe even didn't want to.

CHUCK. He didn't say it right out or I'da socked him one. I told him, " I'm on de wagon for keeps and Cora knows it."

CORA. I told him, " Sure, I know it. And Chuck ain't never goin' to trow it in my face dat I was a tart, neider. And if yuh tink we're just kiddin' ourselves, we'll show yuh ! "

CHUCK. We're goin' to show him !

CORA. We got it all fixed. We've decided Joisey is where we want de farm, and we'll get married dere, too, because yuh don't need no licence. We're goin' to get married tomorrow. Ain't we, Honey ?

CHUCK. You bet, Baby.

ROCKY (*disgusted*). Christ, Chuck, are yuh lettin' dat bughouse louse Hickey kid yuh into——

CORA (*turns on him angrily*). Nobody's kiddin' him into it, nor me neider ! And Hickey's right. If dis big tramp's goin' to marry me, he ought to do it, and not just shoot off his old bazoo about it.

ROCKY (*ignoring her*). Yuh can't be dat dumb, Chuck.

CORA. You keep outa dis ! And don't start beefin' about crickets on de farm drivin' us nuts. You and your crickets ! Yuh'd tink dey was elephants !

MARGIE (*coming to Rocky's defence—sneeringly*). Don't notice dat broad, Rocky. Yuh heard her say " tomorrow," didn't yuh ? It's de same old crap.

CORA (*glares at her*). Is dat so ?

PEARL (*lines up with Margie—sneeringly*). Imagine Cora a bride ! Dat's a hot one ! Jees, Cora, if all de guys you've stayed wid was side by side, yuh could walk on 'em from here to Texas !

CORA (*starts moving toward her threateningly*). Yuh can't talk like dat to me, yuh fat Dago hooker ! I may be a tart, but I ain't a cheap old whore like you !

PEARL (*furiously*). I'll show yuh who's a whore !

(*They start to fly at each other, but Chuck and Rocky grab them from behind.*)

CHUCK (*forcing Cora on to a chair*). Sit down and cool off, Baby.

ROCKY (*doing the same to Pearl*). Nix on de rough stuff, Poil.

MARGIE (*glaring at Cora*). Why don't you leave Poil alone, Rocky ? She'll fix dat blonde's clock ! Or if she don't, I will !

ROCKY. Shut up, you ! (*Disgustedly.*) Jees, what dames ! D'yuh wanta gum Harry's party ?

PEARL (*a bit shamefaced—sulkily*). Who wants to ? But nobody can't call me a——

ROCKY (*exasperatedly*). Aw, bury it ! What are you, a voigin ?

(*Pearl stares at him, her face growing hard and bitter. So does Margie.*)

PEARL. Yuh mean you tink I'm a whore, too, huh ?

MARGIE. Yeah, and me ?

ROCKY. Now don't start nuttin' !

PEARL. I suppose it'd tickle you if me and Margie did what dat louse, Hickey, was hintin' and come right out and admitted we was whores.

ROCKY. Aw right! What of it? It's de truth, ain't it?

CORA (*lining up with Pearl and Margie—indignantly*). Jees, Rocky, dat's a fine hell of a ting to say to two goils dat's been as good to yuh as Poil and Margie! (*To Pearl.*) I didn't mean to call yuh dat, Poil. I was on'y mad.

PEARL (*accepts the apology gratefully*). Sure, I was mad, too, Cora. No hard feelin's.

ROCKY (*relieved*). Dere. Dat fixes everything, don't it?

PEARL (*turns on him—hard and bitter*). Aw right, Rocky. We're whores. You know what dat makes you, don't you?

ROCKY (*angrily*). Look out, now!

MARGIE. A lousy little pimp, dat's what!

ROCKY. I'll loin yuh! (*He gives her a slap on the side of the face.*)

PEARL. A dirty little Ginny pimp, dat's what!

ROCKY (*gives her a slap, too*). And dat'll loin you!

(*But they only stare at him with hard sneering eyes.*)

MARGIE. He's provin' it to us, Poil.

PEARL. Yeah! Hickey's convoited him. He's give up his pipe dream!

ROCKY (*furious and at the same time bewildered by their defiance*). Lay off me or I'll beat de hell——

CHUCK (*growls*). Aw, lay off dem. Harry's party ain't no time to beat up your stable.

ROCKY (*turns to him*). Whose stable? Who d'yuh tink yuh're talkin' to? I ain't never beat dem up! What d'yuh tink I am? I just give dem a slap, like any guy would his wife, if she got too gabby. Why don't yuh tell dem to lay off me? I don't want no trouble on Harry's boithday party.

MARGIE (*a victorious gleam in her eye—tauntingly*). Aw right, den, yuh poor little Ginny. I'll lay off yuh till de party's over if Poil will.

PEARL (*tauntingly*). Sure, I will. For Harry's sake, not yours, yuh little Wop!

ROCKY (*stung*). Say, listen, youse! Don't get no wrong idea——

(*But an interruption comes from Larry, who bursts into a sardonic laugh. They all jump startledly and look at him with unanimous hostility. Rocky transfers his anger to him.*)

Who de hell yuh laughin' at, yuh half-dead old stew bum?

CORA (*sneeringly*). At himself, he ought to be! Jees, Hickey's sure got his number!

LARRY (*ignoring them, turns to Hugo and shakes him by the shoulders—in his comically intense, crazy whisper*). Wake up, Comrade! Here's the Revolution starting on all sides of you and you're sleeping through it! Be God, it's not to Bakunin's ghost you ought to pray in your dreams, but to the great Nihilist, Hickey! He's started a movement that'll blow up the world!

HUGO (*blinks at him through his thick spectacles—with guttural denunciation*). You, Larry! Renegade! Traitor! I vill have you shot! (*He giggles.*) Don't be a fool! Buy me a trink! (*He sees the drink in front of him, and gulps it down. He begins to sing the Carmagnole in a guttural basso, pounding on the table with his glass.*) "Dansons la Carmagnole! Vive le son! Vive le son! Dansons la Carmagnole! Vive le son des canons!"

ROCKY. Can dat noise!

HUGO (*ignores this—to Larry, in a low tone of hatred*). That bourgeois svine, Hickey! He laughs like good fellow, he makes jokes, he dares make hints to me so I see what he dares to think. He thinks I am finish, it is too late, and so I do not vish the Day come because it vill not be my Day. Oh, I see what he thinks! He thinks lies even vorse, dat I—— (*He stops abruptly with a guilty look, as if afraid he was letting something slip—then revengefully.*) I vill have him hanged the first one of all on de first lamp-post! (*He changes his mood abruptly and peers around at Rocky and the others—giggling again.*) Vhy you so serious, leedle monkey-faces? It's all great joke, no? So ve get drunk, and ve laugh like hell, and den ve die, and de pipe dream vanish! (*A bitter mocking contempt creeps into his tone.*) But be of good cheer, leedle stupid peoples! "The days grow hot, O Babylon!" Soon, leedle proletarians, ve vill have free picnic in the cool shade, ve vill eat hot dogs and trink free beer beneath the villow trees! Like hogs, yes! Like beautiful leedle hogs! (*He stops startledly, as if confused and amazed at what he has heard himself say. He mutters with hatred.*) Dot Gottamned liar, Hickey. It is he who makes me sneer. I want to sleep. (*He lets his head fall forward on his folded arms again and closes his eyes.*)

(*Larry gives him a pitying look, then quickly drinks his drink.*)

CORA (*uneasily*). Hickey ain't overlookin' no bets, is he? He's even give Hugo de woiks.

LARRY. I warned you this morning he wasn't kidding.

MARGIE (*sneering*). De old wise guy!

PEARL. Yeah, still pretendin' he's de one exception, like Hickey told him. He don't do no pipe dreamin'! Oh, no!

LARRY (*sharply resentful*). I——! (*Then abruptly he is drunkenly good-natured, and you feel this drunken manner is an evasive exaggeration.*) All right, take it out on me, if it makes you more content. Sure, I love every hair of your heads, my great big beautiful baby dolls, and there's nothing I wouldn't do for you!

PEARL (*stiffly*). De old Irish bunk, huh? We ain't big. And we ain't your baby dolls! (*Suddenly she is mollified and smiles.*) But we admit we're beautiful. Huh, Margie?

MARGIE (*smiling*). Sure ting! But what would he do wid beautiful dolls, even if he had de price, de old goat? (*She laughs teasingly—then pats Larry on the shoulder affectionately.*) Aw, yuh're aw right at dat, Larry, if yuh are full of bull!

PEARL. Sure. Yuh're aces wid us. We're noivous, dat's all. Dat lousy drummer—why can't he be like he's always been? I never seen a guy change so. You pretend to be such a fox, Larry. What d'yuh tink's happened to him?

LARRY. I don't know. With all his gab I notice he's kept that to himself so far. Maybe he's saving the great revelation for Harry's party. (*Then irritably.*) To hell with him! I don't want to know. Let him mind his own business and I'll mind mine.

CHUCK. Yeah, dat's what I say.

CORA. Say, Larry, where's dat young friend of yours disappeared to?

LARRY. I don't care where he is, except I wish it was a thousand miles away! (*Then, as he sees they are surprised at his vehemence, he adds hastily.*) He's a pest.

ROCKY (*breaks in with his own preoccupation*). I don't give a damn what happened to Hickey, but I know what's gonna happen if he don't watch his step. I told him, "I'll take a lot from you, Hickey, like everyone else in dis dump, because yuh've always been a grand guy. But dere's tings I don't take from you nor nobody, see? Remember dat, or you'll wake up in a hospital—or maybe worse, wid your wife and de iceman walkin' slow behind yuh."

CORA. Aw, yuh shouldn't make dat iceman crack, Rocky. It's aw right for him to kid about it but—I notice Hickey ain't pulled dat old iceman gag dis time. (*Excitedly.*) D'yuh suppose dat he did catch his wife cheatin'? I don't mean wid no iceman, but wid some guy.

ROCKY. Aw, dat's de bunk. He ain't pulled dat gag or showed her photo around because he ain't drunk. And if he'd caught her cheatin' he'd be drunk, wouldn't he? He'd have beat her up and den gone on de woist drunk he'd ever staged. Like any other guy'd do.

(*The girls nod, convinced by this reasoning.*)

CHUCK. Sure! Rocky's got de right dope, Baby. He'd be paralysed.

(*While he is speaking, the Negro, Joe, comes in from the hallway. There is a noticeable change in him. He walks with a tough, truculent swagger and his good-natured face is set in sullen suspicion.*)

JOE (*to Rocky—defiantly*). I's stood tellin' people dis dump is closed for de night all I's goin' to. Let Harry hire a doorman, pay him wages, if he wants one.

ROCKY (*scowling*). Yeah? Harry's pretty damned good to you.

JOE (*shamefaced*). Sure he is. I don't mean dat. Anyways, it's all right. I told Schwartz, de cop, we's closed for de party. He'll keep folks away. (*Aggressively again.*) I want a big drink, dat's what!

CHUCK. Who's stoppin' yuh? Yuh can have all yuh want on Hickey.

JOE (*has taken a glass from the table and has his hand on a bottle when Hickey's name is mentioned. He draws his hand back as if he were going to refuse—then grabs it defiantly and pours a big drink*). All right, I'd earned all de drinks on him I could drink in a year for listenin' to his crazy bull. And here's hopin' he gets de lockjaw! (*He drinks and pours out another.*) I drinks on him but I don't drink wid him. No, suh, never no more!

ROCKY. Aw, bull! Hickey's aw right. What's he done to you?

JOE (*sullenly*). Dat's my business. I ain't buttin' in yours, is I? (*Bitterly.*) Sure, you think he's all right. He's a white man, ain't he? (*His tone becomes aggressive.*) Listen to me, you white boys! Don't you get it in your heads I's pretendin' to be what I ain't, or dat I ain't proud to be what I is, get me? Or you and me's goin' to have trouble! (*He picks up his drink and walks left as far away from them as he can get and slumps down on the piano stool.*)

MARGIE (*in a low angry tone*). What a noive! Just because we act nice to him, he gets a swelled nut! If dat ain't a coon all over!

CHUCK. Talkin' fight talk, huh? I'll moider de nigger! (*He takes a threatening step toward Joe, who is staring before him guiltily now.*)

JOE (*speaks up shamefacedly*). Listen, boys, I's sorry. I didn't mean dat. You been good friends to me. I's nuts, I guess. Dat Hickey, he gets my head all mixed up wit' craziness.

(*Their faces at once clear of resentment against him.*)

CORA. Aw, dat's aw right, Joe. De boys wasn't takin' yuh serious. (*Then to the others, forcing a laugh.*) Jees, what'd I say, Hickey ain't overlookin' no bets. Even Joe. (*She pauses—then adds puzzledly.*) De funny ting is, yuh can't stay sore at de bum when he's around. When he forgets de bughouse preachin', and quits tellin' yuh where yuh get off, he's de same old Hickey. Yuh can't help likin' de louse. And yuh got to admit he's got de right dope—— (*She adds hastily.*) I mean, on some of de bums here.

MARGIE (*with a sneering look at Rocky*). Yeah, he's coitinly got one guy I know sized up right! Huh, Poil?

PEARL. He coitinly has !

ROCKY. Cut it out, I told yuh !

LARRY (*is staring before him broodingly. He speaks more aloud to himself than to them*). It's nothing to me what happened to him. But I have a feeling he's dying to tell us, inside him, and yet he's afraid. He's like that damned kid. It's strange the queer way he seemed to recognize him. If he's afraid, it explains why he's off booze. Like that damned kid again. Afraid if he got drunk, he'd tell——

(*While he is speaking, Hickey comes in the doorway at rear. He looks the same as in the previous act, except that now his face beams with the excited expectation of a boy going to a party. His arms are piled with packages.*)

HICKEY (*booms in imitation of a familiar Polo Grounds bleacherite cry—with rising volume*). Well ! Well ! ! Well ! ! ! (*They all jump startledly. He comes forward, grinning.*) Here I am in the nick of time. Give me a hand with these bundles, somebody.

(*Margie and Pearl start taking them from his arms and putting them on the table. Now that he is present, all their attitudes show the reaction Cora has expressed. They can't help liking him and forgiving him.*)

MARGIE. Jees, Hickey, yuh scared me outa a year's growth, sneakin' in like dat.

HICKEY. Sneaking ? Why, me and the taxi man made enough noise getting my big surprise in the hall to wake the dead. You were all so busy drinking in words of wisdom from the Old Wise Guy here, you couldn't hear anything else. (*He grins at Larry.*) From what I heard, Larry, you're not so good when you start playing Sherlock Holmes. You've got me all wrong. I'm not afraid of anything now—not even myself. You better stick to the part of Old Cemetery, the Barker for the Big Sleep—that is, if you can still let yourself get away with it ! (*He chuckles and gives Larry a friendly slap on the back.*)

(*Larry gives him a bitter angry look.*)

CORA (*giggles*). Old Cemetery ! That's him, Hickey. We'll have to call him dat.

HICKEY (*watching Larry quizzically*). Beginning to do a lot of puzzling about me, aren't you, Larry ? But that won't help you. You've got to think of yourself. I couldn't give you my peace. You've got to find your own. All I can do is help you, and the rest of the gang, by showing you the way to find it. (*He has said this with a simple persuasive earnestness. He pauses, and for a second they stare at him with fascinated resentful uneasiness.*)

ROCKY (*breaks the spell*). Aw, hire a church !

HICKEY (*placatingly*). All right ! All right ! Don't get sore, boys and girls. I guess that did sound too much like a lousy preacher. Let's forget it and get busy on the party.

(*They look relieved.*)

CHUCK. Is dose bundles grub, Hickey ? You bought enough already to feed an army.

HICKEY (*with boyish excitement again*). Can't be too much ! I want this to be the biggest birthday Harry's ever had. You and Rocky go in the hall and get the big surprise. My arms are busted lugging it.

(*They catch his excitement. Chuck and Rocky go out, grinning expectantly. The three girls gather around Hickey, full of thrilled curiosity.*)

PEARL. Jees, yuh got us all het up ! What is it, Hickey ?

HICKEY. Wait and see. I got it as a treat for the three of you more than anyone. I thought to myself, I'll bet this is what will please those whores more than anything. (*They wince as if he had slapped them, but before they have a chance to be angry, he goes on affectionately.*) I said to myself, I don't care how much it costs, they're worth it. They're the best little scouts in the world, and they've been damned kind to me when I was down and out ! Nothing is too good for them. (*Earnestly.*) I mean every word of that, too—and then some ! (*Then, as if he noticed the expression on their faces for the first time.*) What's the matter ? You look sore. What——? (*Then he chuckles.*) Oh, I see. But you know how I feel about that. You know I didn't say it to offend you. So don't be silly now.

MARGIE (*lets out a tense breath*). Aw right, Hickey. Let it slide.

HICKEY (*jubilantly, as Chuck and Rocky enter carrying a big wicker basket*). Look ! There it comes ! Unveil it, boys.

(*They pull off a covering burlap bag. The basket is piled with quarts of champagne.*)

PEARL (*with childish excitement*). It's champagne ! Jees, Hickey, if you ain't a sport ! (*She gives him a hug, forgetting all animosity, as do the other girls.*)

MARGIE. I never been soused on champagne. Let's get stinko, Poil.

PEARL. You betcha my life ! De bot' of us !

(*A holiday spirit of gay festivity has seized them all. Even Joe Mott is standing up to look at the wine with an admiring grin, and Hugo raises his head to blink at it.*)

JOE. You sure is hittin' de high spots, Hickey. (*Boastfully.*) Man, when I runs my gamblin' house, I drinks dat old bubbly water in steins ! (*He stops guiltily and gives Hickey a look of defiance.*) I's goin' to drink it dat way again, too, soon's I make my stake ! And dat ain't no pipe dream, neider ! (*He sits down where he was, his back turned to them.*)

ROCKY. What'll we drink it outa, Hickey? Dere ain't no wine glasses.

HICKEY (*enthusiastically*). Joe has the right idea! Schooners! That's the spirit for Harry's birthday!

(*Rocky and Chuck carry the basket of wine into the bar. The three girls go back and stand around the entrance to the bar, chatting excitedly among themselves and to Chuck and Rocky in the bar.*)

HUGO (*with his silly giggle*). Ve vill trink vine beneath the villow trees!

HICKEY (*grins at him*). That's the spirit, Brother—and let the lousy slaves drink vinegar!

(*Hugo blinks at him startledly, then looks away.*)

HUGO (*mutters*). Gottamned liar! (*He puts his head back on his arms and closes his eyes, but this time his habitual pass-out has a quality of hiding.*)

LARRY (*gives Hugo a pitying glance—in a low tone of anger*). Leave Hugo be! He rotted ten years in prison for his faith! He's earned his dream! Have you no decency or pity?

HICKEY (*quizzically*). Hello, what's this? I thought you were in the grandstand. (*Then with a simple earnestness, taking a chair by Larry, and putting a hand on his shoulder.*) Listen, Larry, you're getting me all wrong. Hell, you ought to know me better. I've always been the best-natured slob in the world. Of course, I have pity. But now I've seen the light, it isn't my old kind of pity—the kind yours is. It isn't the kind that lets itself off easy by encouraging some poor guy to go on kidding himself with a lie—the kind that leaves the poor slob worse off because it makes him feel guiltier than ever—the kind that makes his lying hopes nag at him and reproach him until he's a rotten skunk in his own eyes. I know all about that kind of pity. I've had a bellyful of it in my time, and it's all wrong! (*With a salesman's persuasiveness.*) No, sir. The kind of pity I feel now is after final results that will really save the poor guy, and make him contented with what he is, and quit battling himself, and find peace for the rest of his life. Oh, I know how you resent the way I have to show you up to yourself. I don't blame you. I know from my own experience it's bitter medicine, facing yourself in the mirror with the old false whiskers off. But you forget that, once you're cured. You'll be grateful to me when all at once you find you're able to admit, without feeling ashamed, that all the grandstand foolosopher bunk and the waiting for the Big Sleep stuff is a pipe dream. You'll say to yourself, I'm just an old man who is scared of life, but even more scared of dying. So I'm keeping drunk and hanging on to life at any price, and what of it? Then you'll know what real peace means, Larry, because you won't be scared of either life or death any more. You simply won't give a damn! Any more than I do!

LARRY (*has been staring into his eyes with a fascinated wondering dread*). Be God, if I'm not beginning to think you've gone mad! (*With a rush of anger.*) You're a liar!

HICKEY (*injuredly*). Now, listen, that's no way to talk to an old pal who's trying to help you. Hell, if you really wanted to die, you'd just take a hop off your fire escape, wouldn't you? And if you really were in the grandstand, you wouldn't be pitying everyone. Oh, I know the truth is tough at first. It was for me. All I ask is for you to suspend judgment and give it a chance. I'll absolutely guarantee—— Hell, Larry, I'm no fool. Do you suppose I'd deliberately set out to get under everyone's skin and put myself in dutch with all my old pals, if I wasn't certain, from my own experience, that it means contentment in the end for all of you? (*Larry again is staring at him fascinatedly. Hickey grins.*) As for my being bughouse, you can't crawl out of it that way. Hell, I'm too damned sane. I can size up guys, and turn 'em inside out, better than I ever could. Even where they're strangers like that Parritt kid. He's licked, Larry. I think there is only one possible way out you can help him to take. That is, if you have the right kind of pity for him.

LARRY (*uneasily*). What do you mean? (*Attempting indifference.*) I'm not advising him, except to leave me out of his troubles. He's nothing to me.

HICKEY (*shakes his head*). You'll find he won't agree to that. He'll keep after you until he makes you help him. Because he has to be punished, so he can forgive himself. He's lost all his guts. He can't manage it alone, and you're the only one he can turn to.

LARRY. For the love of God, mind your own business! (*With forced scorn.*) A lot you know about him! He's hardly spoken to you!

HICKEY. No, that's right. But I do know a lot about him just the same. I've had hell inside me. I can spot it in others. (*Frowning.*) Maybe that's what gives me the feeling there's something familiar about him, something between us. (*He shakes his head.*) No, it's more than that. I can't figure it. Tell me about him. For instance, I don't imagine he's married, is he?

LARRY. No.

HICKEY. Hasn't he been mixed up with some woman? I don't mean trollops. I mean the old real love stuff that crucifies you.

LARRY (*with a calculating relieved look at him—encouraging him along this line*). Maybe you're right. I wouldn't be surprised.

HICKEY (*grins at him quizzically*). I see. You think I'm on the wrong track and you're glad I am. Because then I won't suspect whatever he did about the Great Cause. That's another lie you tell yourself, Larry, that the good old Cause means nothing to you any more. (*Larry is about to burst out in denial but Hickey goes on.*) But you're all wrong about Parritt. That isn't what's behind that. And it's a woman. I recognize the symptoms.

LARRY (*sneeringly*). And you're the boy who's never wrong! Don't be a damned fool. His trouble is he was brought up a devout believer in the Movement and now he's lost his faith. It's a shock, but he's young and he'll soon find another dream just as good. (*He adds sardonically.*) Or as bad.

HICKEY. All right. I'll let it go at that, Larry. He's nothing to me except I'm glad he's here because he'll help me make you wake up to yourself. I don't even like the guy, or the feeling there's anything between us. But you'll find I'm right just the same, when you get to the final showdown with him.

LARRY. There'll be no showdown! I don't give a tinker's damn——

HICKEY. Sticking to the old grandstand, eh? Well, I knew you'd be the toughest to convince of all the gang, Larry. And, along with Harry and Jimmy Tomorrow, you're the one I want most to help. (*He puts an arm around Larry's shoulder and gives him an affectionate hug.*) I've always liked you a lot, you old bastard! (*He gets up and his manner changes to his bustling party excitement—glancing at his watch.*) Well, well, not much time before twelve. Let's get busy, boys and girls. (*He looks over the table where the cake is.*) Cake all set. Good. And my presents, and yours, girls, and Chuck's, and Rocky's. Fine. Harry'll certainly be touched by your thought of him. (*He goes back to the girls.*) You go in the bar, Pearl and Margie, and get the grub ready so it can be brought right in. There'll be some drinking and toasts first, of course. My idea is to use the wine for that, so get it all set. I'll go upstairs now and root everyone out. Harry the last. I'll come back with him. Somebody light the candles on the cake when you hear us coming, and you start playing Harry's favourite tune, Cora. Hustle now, everybody. We want this to come off in style.

(*He bustles into the hall. Margie and Pearl disappear in the bar. Cora goes to the piano. Joe gets off the stool sullenly to let her sit down.*)

CORA. I got to practise. I ain't laid my mits on a box in Gawd knows when. (*With the soft pedal down, she begins gropingly to pick out "The Sunshine of Paradise Alley."*) Is dat right, Joe? I've forgotten dat has-been tune. (*She picks out a few more notes.*) Come on, Joe, hum de tune so I can follow.

(*Joe begins to hum and sing in a low voice and correct her. He forgets his sullenness and becomes his old self again.*)

LARRY (*suddenly gives a laugh—in his comically intense, crazy tone*). Be God, it's a second feast of Belshazzar, with Hickey to do the writing on the wall!

CORA. Aw, shut up, Old Cemetery! Always beefin'!

(*Willie comes in from the hall. He is in a pitiable state, his face pasty, haggard with sleeplessness and nerves, his eyes sick and haunted. He is sober. Cora greets him over her shoulder kiddingly.*)

If it ain't Prince Willie! (*Then kindly.*) Gee, kid, yuh look sick. Git a coupla shots in yuh.

WILLIE (*tensely*). No, thanks. Not now. I'm tapering off. (*He sits down weakly on Larry's right.*)

CORA (*astonished*). What d'yuh know? He means it!

WILLIE (*leaning toward Larry confidentially—in a low shaken voice*). It's been hell up in that damned room, Larry! The things I've imagined! (*He shudders.*) I thought I'd go crazy. (*With pathetic boastful pride.*) But I've got it beat now. By tomorrow morning I'll be on the wagon. I'll get back my clothes the first thing. Hickey's loaning me the money. I'm going to do what I've always said—go to the D.A.'s office. He was a good friend of my Old Man's. He was only assistant, then. He was in on the graft, but my Old Man never squealed on him. So he certainly owes it to me to give me a chance. And he knows that I really was a brilliant law student. (*Self-reassuringly.*) Oh, I know I can make good, now I'm getting off the booze for ever. (*Moved.*) I owe a lot to Hickey. He's made me wake up to myself—see what a fool—— It wasn't nice to face but—— (*With bitter resentment.*) It isn't what he says. It's what you feel behind—what he hints—— Christ, you'd think all I really wanted to do with my life was sit here and stay drunk. (*With hatred.*) I'll show him!

LARRY (*masking pity behind a sardonic tone*). If you want my advice, you'll put the nearest bottle to your mouth until you don't give a damn for Hickey!

WILLIE (*stares at a bottle greedily, tempted for a moment—then bitterly*). That's fine advice! I thought you were my friend! (*He gets up with a hurt glance at Larry, and moves away to take a chair in back of the left end of the table, where he sits in dejected, shaking misery, his chin on his chest.*)

JOE (*to Cora*). No, like dis. (*He beats time with his finger and sings in a low voice.*) "She is the sunshine of Paradise Alley." (*She plays.*) Dat's more like it. Try it again.

(*She begins to play through the chorus again. Don Parritt enters from the hall. There is a frightened look on his face. He slinks in furtively, as if he were escaping from someone. He looks relieved when he sees Larry and comes and slips into the chair on his right. Larry pretends not to notice his coming, but he instinctively shrinks with repulsion. Parritt leans toward him and speaks ingratiatingly in a low secretive tone.*)

PARRITT. Gee, I'm glad you're here, Larry. That

damned fool, Hickey, knocked on my door. I opened up because I thought it must be you, and he came busting in and made me come downstairs. I don't know what for. I don't belong in this birthday celebration. I don't know this gang and I don't want to be mixed up with them. All I came here for was to find you.

LARRY (*tensely*). I've warned you——

PARRITT (*goes on as if he hadn't heard*). Can't you make Hickey mind his own business? I don't like that guy, Larry. The way he acts, you'd think he had something on me. Why, just now he pats me on the shoulder, like he was sympathizing with me, and says, "I know how it is, Son, but you can't hide from yourself, not even here on the bottom of the sea. You've got to face the truth and then do what must be done for your own peace and the happiness of all concerned." What did he mean by that, Larry?

LARRY. How the hell would I know?

PARRITT. Then he grins and says, "Never mind, Larry's getting wise to himself. I think you can rely on his help in the end. He'll have to choose between living and dying, and he'll never choose to die while there is a breath left in the old bastard!" And then he laughs like it was a joke on you. (*He pauses. Larry is rigid on his chair, staring before him. Parritt asks him with a sudden taunt in his voice.*) Well, what do you say to that, Larry?

LARRY. I've nothing to say. Except you're a bigger fool than he is to listen to him.

PARRITT (*with a sneer*). Is that so? He's no fool where you're concerned. He's got your number, all right! (*Larry's face tightens but he keeps silent. Parritt changes to a contrite, appealing air.*) I don't mean that. But you keep acting as if you were sore at me, and that gets my goat. You know what I want most is to be friends with you, Larry. I haven't a single friend left in the world, I hoped you—— (*Bitterly.*) And you could be, too, without it hurting you. You ought to, for Mother's sake. She really loved you. You loved her, too, didn't you?

LARRY (*tensely*). Leave what's dead in its grave.

PARRITT. I suppose, because I was only a kid, you didn't think I was wise about you and her. Well, I was. I've been wise, ever since I can remember, to all the guys she's had, although she'd tried to kid me along it wasn't so. That was a silly stunt for a free Anarchist woman, wasn't it, being ashamed of being free?

LARRY. Shut your damned trap!

PARRITT (*guiltily but with a strange undertone of satisfaction*). Yes, I know I shouldn't say that now. I keep forgetting she isn't free any more. (*He pauses.*) Do you know, Larry, you're the one of them all she cared most about? Anyone else who left the Movement would have been dead to her, but she couldn't forget you. She'd always made excuses for you. I used to try and get her goat about you. I'd say, "Larry's got brains and yet he thinks the Movement is just a crazy pipe dream." She'd blame it on booze getting you. She'd kid herself that you'd give up booze and come back to the Movement—tomorrow! She'd say, "Larry can't kill in himself a faith he's given his life to, not without killing himself." (*He grins sneeringly.*) How about it, Larry? Was she right? (*Larry remains silent. He goes on insistently.*) I suppose what she really meant was, come back to her. She was always getting the Movement mixed up with herself. But I'm sure she really must have loved you, Larry. As much as she could love anyone besides herself. But she wasn't faithful to you, even at that, was she? That's why you finally walked out on her, isn't it? I remember that last fight you had with her. I was listening. I was on your side, even if she was my mother, because I liked you so much; you'd been so good to me—like a father. I remember her putting on her high-and-mighty free-woman stuff, saying you were still a slave to bourgeois morality and jealousy and you thought a woman you loved was a piece of private property you owned. I remember that you got mad and you told her, "I don't like living with a whore, if that's what you mean!"

LARRY (*bursts out*). You lie! I never called her that!

PARRITT (*goes on as if Larry hadn't spoken*). I think that's why she still respects you, because it was you who left her. You were the only one to beat her to it. She got sick of the others before they did of her. I don't think she ever cared much about them, anyway. She just had to keep on having lovers to prove to herself how free she was. (*He pauses—then with a bitter repulsion.*) It made home a lousy place. I felt like you did about it. I'd get feeling it was like living in a whorehouse—only worse, because she didn't have to make her living——

LARRY. You bastard! She's your mother! Have you no shame?

PARRITT (*bitterly*). No! She brought me up to believe that family-respect stuff is all bourgeois, property-owning crap. Why should I be ashamed?

LARRY (*making a move to get up*). I've had enough!

PARRITT (*catches his arm—pleadingly*). No! Don't leave me! Please! I promise I won't mention her again!

(*Larry sinks back in his chair.*)

I only did it to make you understand better. I know this isn't the place to—— Why didn't you come up to my room, like I asked you? I kept waiting. We could talk everything over there.

LARRY. There's nothing to talk over!

PARRITT. But I've got to talk to you. Or I'll talk to Hickey. He won't let me alone! I feel he knows, anyway! And I know he'd understand, all right—in his way. But I hate his guts! I don't want anything to do with him! I'm scared of him, honest. There's something not human behind his damned grinning and kidding.

LARRY (*starts*). Ah! You feel that, too?

PARRITT (*pleadingly*). But I can't go on like this. I've got to decide what I've got to do. I've got to tell you, Larry!

LARRY (*again starts up*). I won't listen!

PARRITT (*again holds him by the arm*). All right I won't. Don't go!

(*Larry lets himself be pulled down on his chair. Parritt examines his face and becomes insultingly scornful.*)

Who do you think you're kidding? I know damned well you've guessed——

LARRY. I've guessed nothing!

PARRITT. But I want you to guess now! I'm glad you have! I know now, since Hickey's been after me, that I meant you to guess right from the start. That's why I came to you. (*Hurrying on with an attempt at a plausible frank air that makes what he says seem doubly false.*) I want you to understand the reason. You see, I began studying American history. I got admiring Washington and Jefferson and Jackson and Lincoln. I began to feel patriotic and love this country. I saw it was the best government in the world, where everybody was equal and had a chance. I saw that all the ideas behind the Movement came from a lot of Russians like Bakunin and Kropotkin and were meant for Europe, but we didn't need them here in a democracy where we were free already. I didn't want this country to be destroyed for a damned foreign pipe dream. After all, I'm from old American pioneer stock. I began to feel I was a traitor for helping a lot of cranks and bums and free women plot to overthrow our government. And then I saw it was my duty to my country——

LARRY (*nauseated—turns on him*). You stinking rotten liar! Do you think you can fool me with such hypocrite's cant! (*Then turning away.*) I don't give a damn what you did! It's on your head—whatever it was! I don't want to know—and I won't know!

PARRITT (*as if Larry had never spoken—falteringly*). But I never thought Mother would be caught. Please believe that, Larry. You know I never would have——

LARRY (*his face haggard, drawing a deep breath and closing his eyes—as if he were trying to hammer something into his own brain*). All I know is I'm sick of life! I'm through! I've forgotten myself! I'm drowned and contented on the bottom of a bottle. Honour or dishonour, faith or treachery are nothing to me but the opposites of the same stupidity which is ruler and king of life, and in the end they rot into dust in the same grave. All things are the same meaningless joke to me, for they grin at me from the one skull of death. So go away. You're wasting breath. I've forgotten your mother.

PARRITT (*jeers angrily*). The old foolosopher, eh? (*He spits out contemptuously.*) You lousy old faker!

LARRY (*so distracted he pleads weakly*). For the love of God, leave me in peace the little time that's left to me!

PARRITT. Aw, don't pull that pitiful old-man junk on me! You old bastard, you'll never die as long as there's a free drink of whisky left!

LARRY (*stung—furiously*). Look out how you try to taunt me back into life, I warn you! I might remember the thing they call justice there, and the punishment for—— (*He checks himself with an effort—then with a real indifference that comes from exhaustion.*) I'm old and tired. To hell with you! You're as mad as Hickey, and as big a liar. I'd never let myself believe a word you told me.

PARRITT (*threateningly*). The hell you won't! Wait till Hickey gets through with you!

(*Pearl and Margie come in from the bar. At the sight of them, Parritt instantly subsides and becomes self-conscious and defensive, scowling at them and then quickly looking away.*)

MARGIE (*eyes him jeeringly*). Why, hello, Tightwad Kid. Come to join de party? Gee, don't he act bashful, Poil?

PEARL. Yeah. Especially wid his dough.

(*Parritt slinks to a chair at the left end of the table, pretending he hasn't heard them. Suddenly there is a noise of angry, cursing voices and a scuffle from the hall. Pearl yells.*)

Hey, Rocky! Fight in de hall!

(*Rocky and Chuck run from behind the bar curtain and rush into the hall. Rocky's voice is heard in irritated astonishment,* "What de hell?" *and then the scuffle stops and Rocky appears holding Captain Lewis by the arm, followed by Chuck with a similar hold on General Wetjoen. Although these two have been drinking they are both sober, for them. Their faces are sullenly angry, their clothes disarranged from the tussle.*)

ROCKY (*leading Lewis forward—astonished, amused and irritated*). Can yuh beat it? I've heard youse two call each odder every name yuh could think of but I never seen you—— (*Indignantly.*) A swell time to stage your first bout, on Harry's boithday party! What started de scrap?

LEWIS (*forcing a casual tone*). Nothing, old chap. Our business, you know. That bloody ass, Hickey, made some insinuation about me, and the boorish Boer had the impertinence to agree with him.

WETJOEN. Dot's a lie! Hickey made joke about

me, and this Limey said yes, it was true!

ROCKY. Well, sit down, de bot' of yuh, and cut out de rough stuff.

(*He and Chuck dump them down in adjoining chairs toward the left end of the table, where, like two sulky boys, they turn their backs on each other as far as possible in chairs which both face front.*)

MARGIE (*laughs*). Jees, lookit de two bums! Like a coupla kids! Kiss and make up, for Gawd's sakes!

ROCKY. Yeah. Harry's party begins in a minute and we don't want no soreheads around.

LEWIS (*stiffly*). Very well, in deference to the occasion, I apologize, General Wetjoen—provided that you do also.

WETJOEN (*sulkily*). I apologize, Captain Lewis—because Harry is my goot friend.

ROCKY. Aw, hell! If yuh can't do better'n dat——!

(*Mosher and McGloin enter together from the hall. Both have been drinking but are not drunk.*)

PEARL. Here's de star boarders.

(*They advance, their heads together, so interested in a discussion they are oblivious to everyone.*)

MCGLOIN. I'm telling you, Ed, it's serious this time. That bastard, Hickey, has got Harry on the hip.

(*As he talks, Margie, Pearl, Rocky and Chuck prick up their ears and gather round. Cora, at the piano, keeps running through the tune, with soft pedal, and singing the chorus half under her breath, with Joe still correcting her mistakes. At the table, Larry, Parritt, Willie, Wetjoen and Lewis sit motionless, staring in front of them. Hugo seems asleep in his habitual position.*)

And you know it isn't going to do us no good if he gets him to take that walk tomorrow.

MOSHER. You're damned right. Harry'll mosey around the ward, dropping in on everyone who knew him then. (*Indignantly.*) And they'll all give him a phony glad hand and a ton of good advice about what a sucker he is to stand for us.

MCGLOIN. He's sure to call on Bessie's relations to do a little cryin' over dear Bessie. And you know what that bitch and all her family thought of me.

MOSHER (*with a flash of his usual humour—rebukingly*). Remember, Lieutenant, you are speaking of my sister! Dear Bessie wasn't a bitch. She was a God-damned bitch! But if you think my loving relatives will have time to discuss you, you don't know them. They'll be too busy telling Harry what a drunken crook I am and saying he ought to have me put in Sing Sing!

MCGLOIN (*dejectedly*). Yes, once Bessie's relations get their hooks in him, it'll be as tough for us as if she wasn't gone.

MOSHER (*dejectedly*). Yes, Harry has always been weak and easily influenced, and now he's getting old he'll be an easy mark for those grafters. (*Then with forced reassurance.*) Oh, hell, Mac, we're saps to worry. We've heard Harry pull that bluff about taking a walk every birthday he's had for twenty years.

MCGLOIN (*doubtfully*). But Hickey wasn't sicking him on those times. Just the opposite. He was asking Harry what he wanted to go out for when there was plenty of whisky here.

MOSHER (*with a change to forced carelessness*). Well, after all, I don't care whether he goes out or not. I'm clearing out tomorrow morning anyway. I'm just sorry for you, Mac.

MCGLOIN (*resentfully*). You needn't be, then. Ain't I going myself? I was only feeling sorry for you.

MOSHER. Yes, my mind is made up. Hickey may be a lousy, interfering pest, now he's gone teetotal on us, but there's a lot of truth in some of his bull. Hanging around here getting plastered with you, Mac, is pleasant, I won't deny, but the old booze gets you in the end, if you keep lapping it up. It's time I quit for a while. (*With forced enthusiasm.*) Besides, I feel the call of the old carefree circus life in my blood again. I'll see the boss tomorrow. It's late in the season but he'll be glad to take me on. And won't all the old gang be tickled to death when I show up on the lot!

MCGLOIN. Maybe—if they've got a rope handy!

MOSHER (*turns on him—angrily*). Listen! I'm damned sick of that kidding!

MCGLOIN. You are, are you? Well, I'm sicker of your kidding me about getting reinstated on the Force. And whatever you'd like, I can't spend my life sitting here with you, ruining my stomach with rotgut. I'm tapering off, and in the morning I'll be fresh as a daisy. I'll go and have a private chin with the Commissioner. (*With forced enthusiasm.*) Man alive, from what the boys tell me, there's sugar galore these days, and I'll soon be ridin' around in a big red automobile——

MOSHER (*derisively—beckoning an imaginary Chinese*). Here, One Lung Hop! Put fresh peanut oil in the lamp and cook the Lieutenant another dozen pills! It's his gowed-up night!

MCGLOIN (*stung—pulls back a fist threateningly*). One more crack like that and I'll——!

MOSHER (*putting up his fists*). Yes? Just start——!

(*Chuck and Rocky jump between them.*)

ROCKY. Hey! Are you guys nuts? Jees, it's Harry's boithday party! (*They both look guilty.*) Sit down and behave.

MOSHER (*grumpily*). All right. Only tell him to lay off me.

(*He lets Rocky push him in a chair, at the right end of the table, rear.*)

MCGLOIN (*grumpily*). Tell him to lay off me.

(*He lets Chuck push him into the chair on Mosher's left. At this moment Hickey bursts in from the hall, bustling and excited.*)

HICKEY. Everything all set? Fine! (*He glances at his watch.*) Half a minute to go. Harry's starting down with Jimmy. I had a hard time getting them to move! They'd rather stay hiding up there, kidding each other along. (*He chuckles.*) Harry don't even want to remember it's his birthday now! (*He hears a noise from the stairs.*) Here they come! (*Urgently.*) Light the candles! Get ready to play, Cora! Stand up, everybody! Get that wine ready, Chuck and Rocky!

(*Margie and Pearl light the candles on the cake. Cora gets her hands set over the piano keys, watching over her shoulder. Rocky and Chuck go in the bar. Everybody at the table stands up mechanically. Hugo is the last, suddenly coming to and scrambling to his feet. Harry Hope and Jimmy Tomorrow appear in the hall outside the door. Hickey looks up from his watch.*)

On the dot! It's twelve! (*Like a cheer leader.*) Come on now, everybody, with a Happy Birthday, Harry!

(*With his voice leading they all shout* "Happy, Birthday, Harry!" *in a spiritless chorus. Hickey signals to Cora, who starts playing and singing in a whisky soprano* "*She's the Sunshine of Paradise Alley.*" *Hope and Jimmy stand in the doorway. Both have been drinking heavily. In Hope the effect is apparent only in a bristling, touchy, pugnacious attitude. It is entirely different from the usual irascible beefing he delights in and which no one takes seriously. Now he really has a chip on his shoulder. Jimmy, on the other hand, is plainly drunk, but it has not had the desired effect, for beneath a pathetic assumption of gentlemanly poise, he is obviously frightened and shrinking back within himself. Hickey grabs Hope's hand and pumps it up and down. For a moment Hope appears unconscious of this handshake. Then he jerks his hand away angrily.*)

HOPE. Cut out the glad hand, Hickey. D'you think I'm a sucker? I know you, bejees, you sneaking, lying drummer! (*With rising anger, to the others.*) And all you bums! What the hell you trying to do, yelling and raising the roof? Want the cops to close the joint and get my licence taken away? (*He yells at Cora, who has stopped singing but continues to play mechanically with many mistakes.*) Hey, you dumb tart, quit banging that box! Bejees, the least you could do is learn the tune!

CORA (*stops—deeply hurt*). Aw, Harry! Jees, ain't I—— (*Her eyes begin to fill.*)

HOPE (*glaring at the other girls*). And you two hookers, screaming at the top of your lungs! What d'you think this is, a dollar cat-house? Bejees, that's where you belong!

PEARL (*miserably*). Aw, Harry—— (*She begins to cry.*)

MARGIE. Jees, Harry, I never thought you'd say that—like yuh meant it. (*She puts her arm around Pearl—on the verge of tears herself.*) Aw, don't bawl, Poil. He don't mean it.

HICKEY (*reproachfully*). Now, Harry! Don't take it out on the gang because you're upset about yourself. Anyway, I've promised you you'll come through all right, haven't I? So quit worrying. (*He slaps Hope on the back encouragingly. Hope flashes him a glance of hate.*) Be yourself, Governor. You don't want to bawl out the old gang just when they're congratulating you on your birthday, do you? Hell, that's no way!

HOPE (*looking guilty and shamefaced now—forcing an unconvincing attempt at his natural tone*). Bejees, they ain't as dumb as you. They know I was only kidding them. They know I appreciate their congratulations. Don't you, fellers?

(*There is a listless chorus of* "Sure, Harry," "Yes," "Of course we do," *etc. He comes forward to the two girls, with Jimmy and Hickey following him, and pats them clumsily.*)

Bejees, I like you broads. You know I was only kidding. (*Instantly they forgive him and smile affectionately.*)

MARGIE. Sure we know, Harry.

PEARL. Sure.

HICKEY (*grinning*). Sure. Harry's the greatest kidder in this dump and that's saying something! Look how he's kidded himself for twenty years! (*As Hope gives him a bitter, angry glance, he digs him in the ribs with his elbow playfully.*) Unless I'm wrong, Governor, and I'm betting I'm not. We'll soon know, eh? Tomorrow morning. No, by God, it's *this* morning now!

JIMMY (*with a dazed dread*). *This* morning?

HICKEY. Yes, it's today at last, Jimmy. (*He pats him on the back.*) Don't be so scared! I've promised I'll help you.

JIMMY (*trying to hide his dread behind an offended, drunken dignity*). I don't understand you. Kindly remember I'm fully capable of settling my own affairs!

HICKEY (*earnestly*). Well, isn't that exactly what I

want you to do, settle with yourself once and for all? (*He speaks in his ear in confidential warning.*) Only watch out on the booze, Jimmy. You know, not too much from now on. You've had a lot already, and you don't want to let yourself duck out of it by being too drunk to move—not this time!

(*Jimmy gives him a guilty, stricken look and turns away and slumps into the chair on Mosher's right.*)

HOPE (*to Margie—still guiltily*). Bejees, Margie, you know I didn't mean it. It's that lousy drummer riding me that's got my goat.

MARGIE. I know. (*She puts a protecting arm around Hope and turns him to face the table with the cake and presents.*) Come on. You ain't noticed your cake yet. Ain't it grand?

HOPE (*trying to brighten up*). Say, that's pretty. Ain't ever had a cake since Bessie—— Six candles. Each for ten years, eh? Bejees, that's thoughtful of you.

PEARL. It was Hickey got it.

HOPE (*his tone forced*). Well, it was thoughtful of him. He means well, I guess. (*His eyes, fixed on the cake, harden angrily.*) To hell with his cake. (*He starts to turn away.*)

(*Pearl grabs his arm.*)

PEARL. Wait, Harry. Yuh ain't seen de presents from Margie and me and Cora and Chuck and Rocky. And dere's a watch all engraved wid your name and de date from Hickey.

HOPE. To hell with it! Bejees, he can keep it! (*This time he does turn away.*)

PEARL. Jees, he ain't even goin' to look at our presents.

MARGIE (*bitterly*). Dis is all wrong. We gotta put some life in dis party or I'll go nuts! Hey, Cora, what's de matter wid dat box? Can't yuh play for Harry? Yuh don't have to stop just because he kidded yuh!

HOPE (*rouses himself—with forced heartiness*). Yes, come on, Cora. You was playing it fine.

(*Cora begins to play half-heartedly. Hope suddenly becomes almost tearfully sentimental.*)

It was Bessie's favourite tune. She was always singing it. It brings her back. I wish—— (*He chokes up.*)

HICKEY (*grins at him—amusedly*). Yes, we've all heard you tell us you thought the world of her, Governor.

HOPE (*looks at him with frightened suspicion*). Well, so I did, bejees! Everyone knows I did! (*Threateningly.*) Bejees, if you say I didn't——

HICKEY (*soothingly*). Now, Governor. I didn't say anything. You're the only one knows the truth about that.

(*Hope stares at him confusedly. Cora continues to play. For a moment there is a pause, broken by Jimmy Tomorrow, who speaks with muzzy, self-pitying melancholy out of a sentimental dream.*)

JIMMY. Marjorie's favourite song was "Loch Lomond." She was beautiful and she played the piano beautifully and she had a beautiful voice. (*With gentle sorrow.*) You were lucky, Harry. Bessie died. But there are more bitter sorrows than losing the woman one loves by the hand of death——

HICKEY (*with an amused wink at Hope*). Now, listen, Jimmy, you needn't go on. We've all heard that story about how you came back to Cape Town and found her in the hay with a staff officer. We know you like to believe that was what started you on the booze and ruined your life.

JIMMY (*stammers*). I—I'm talking to Harry. Will you kindly keep out of—— (*With a pitiful defiance.*) My life is not ruined!

HICKEY (*ignoring this—with a kidding grin*). But I'll bet when you admit the truth to yourself, you'll confess you were pretty sick of her hating you for getting drunk. I'll bet you were really damned relieved when she gave you such a good excuse. (*Jimmy stares at him strickenly. Hickey pats him on the back again—with sincere sympathy.*) I know how it is, Jimmy. I—— (*He stops abruptly and for a second he seems to lose his self-assurance and become confused.*)

LARRY (*seizing on this with vindictive relish*). Ha! So that's what happened to you, is it? Your iceman joke finally came home to roost, did it? (*He grins tauntingly.*) You should have remembered there's truth in the old superstition that you'd better look out what you call because in the end it comes to you!

HICKEY (*himself again—grins to Larry kiddingly*). Is that a fact, Larry? Well, well! Then you'd better watch out how you keep calling for that old Big Sleep! (*Larry starts and for a second looks superstitiously frightened. Abruptly Hickey changes to his jovial, bustling, master-of-ceremonies manner.*) But what are we waiting for, boys and girls? Let's start the party rolling! (*He shouts to the bar.*) Hey, Chuck and Rocky! Bring on the big surprise! Governor, you sit at the head of the table here.

(*He makes Harry sit down on the chair at the end of the table, right.*)

(*To Margie and Pearl.*) Come on, girls, sit down.

(*They sit side by side on Jimmy's right. Hickey bustles down to the left end of table.*)

I'll sit here at the foot.

(*He sits, with Cora on his left and Joe on her left, Rocky and Chuck appear from the bar, each bearing a big tray laden with schooners of *champagne which they start shoving in front of each member of the party.*)

ROCKY (*with forced cheeriness*). Real champagne, bums ! Cheer up ! What is dis, a funeral ? Jees, mixin' champagne wid Harry's redeye will knock yuh paralysed ! Ain't yuh never satisfied ?

(*He and Chuck finish serving out the schooners, grab the last two themselves and sit down in the two vacant chairs remaining near the table. As they do so, Hickey rises, a schooner in his hand.*)

HICKEY (*rapping on the table for order when there is nothing but a dead silence*). Order ! Order, Ladies and Gents ! (*He catches Larry's eyes on the glass in his hand.*) Yes, Larry, I'm going to drink with you this time. To prove I'm not teetotal because I'm afraid booze would make me spill my secrets, as you think. (*Larry looks sheepish. Hickey chuckles and goes on.*) No, I gave you the simple truth about that. I don't need booze or anything else any more. But I want to be sociable and propose a toast in honour of our old friend, Harry, and drink it with you. (*His eyes fix on Hugo, who is out again, his head on his plate. To Chuck, who is on Hugo's left*). Wake up our demon bomb-tosser, Chuck. We don't want corpses at this feast.

CHUCK (*gives Hugo a shake*). Hey, Hugo, come up for air ! Don't yuh see de champagne ?

(*Hugo blinks around and giggles foolishly.*)

HUGO. Ve vill eat birthday cake and trink champagne beneath the villow tree ! (*He grabs his schooner and takes a greedy gulp—then sets it back on the table with a grimace of distaste—in a strange, arrogantly disdainful tone, as if he were rebuking a butler.*) Dis vine is unfit to trink. It has not properly been iced.

HICKEY (*amusedly*). Always a high-toned swell at heart, eh, Hugo ? God help us poor bums if you'd ever get to telling us where to get off ! You'd have been drinking our blood beneath those willow trees ! (*He chuckles. Hugo shrinks back in his chair, blinking at him, but Hickey is now looking up the table at Hope. He starts his toast, and as he goes on he becomes more moved and obviously sincere.*) Here's the toast, Ladies and Gents ! Here's to Harry Hope, who's been a friend in need to every one of us ! Here's to the old Governor, the best sport and the kindest, biggest-hearted guy in the world ! Here's wishing you all the luck there is, Harry, and long life and happiness ! Come on, everybody ! To Harry ! Bottoms up !

(*They have all caught his sincerity with eager relief. They raise their schooners with an enthusiastic chorus of* " Here's how, Harry ! " " Here's luck, Harry ! " *etc., and gulp half the wine down, Hickey leading them in this.*)

HOPE (*deeply moved—his voice husky*). Bejees, thanks, all of you. Bejees, Hickey, you old son of a bitch, that's white of you ! Bejees, I know you meant it, too.

HICKEY (*moved*). Of course I meant it, Harry, old friend ! And I mean it when I say I hope today will be the biggest day in your life, and in the lives of everyone here, the beginning of a new life of peace and contentment where no pipe dreams can ever nag at you again. Here's to that, Harry ! (*He drains the remainder of his drink, but this time he drinks alone. In an instant the attitude of everyone has reverted to uneasy, suspicious defensiveness.*)

ROCKY (*growls*). Aw, forget dat bughouse line of bull for a minute, can't yuh ?

HICKEY (*sitting down—good-naturedly*). You're right, Rocky, I'm talking too much. It's Harry we want to hear from. Come on, Harry ! (*He pounds his schooner on the table.*) Speech ! Speech !

(*They try to recapture their momentary enthusiasm, rap their schooners on the table, call* " Speech," *but there is a hollow ring in it. Hope gets to his feet reluctantly, with a forced smile, a smouldering resentment beginning to show in his manner.*)

HOPE (*lamely*). Bejees, I'm no good at speeches. All I can say is thanks to everybody again for remembering me on my birthday. (*Bitterness coming out.*) Only don't think because I'm sixty I'll be a bigger damned fool easy mark than ever ! No, bejees ! Like Hickey says, it's going to be a new day ! This dump has got to be run like other dumps, so I can make some money and not just split even. People has got to pay what they owe me ! I'm not running a damned orphan asylum for bums and crooks ! Nor a God-damned hooker shanty, either ! Nor an Old Men's Home for lousy Anarchist tramps that ought to be in jail ! I'm sick of being played for a sucker ! (*They stare at him with stunned, bewildered hurt. He goes on in a sort of furious desperation, as if he hated himself for every word he said, and yet couldn't stop.*) And don't think you're kidding me right now, either ! I know damned well you're giving me the laugh behind my back, thinking to yourselves, The old, lying, pipe-dreaming faker, we've heard his bull about taking a walk around the ward for years, he'll never make it ! He's yellow, he ain't got the guts, he's scared he'll find out—— (*He glares around at them almost with hatred.*) But I'll show you, bejees ! (*He glares at Hickey.*) I'll show you, too, you son of a bitch of a frying-pan-peddling bastard !

HICKEY (*heartily encouraging*). That's the stuff, Harry ! Of course you'll try to show me ! That's what I want you to do !

(*Harry glances at him with helpless dread—then drops his eyes and looks furtively around the table. All at once he becomes miserably contrite.*)

HOPE (*his voice catching*). Listen, all of you ! Bejees, forgive me. I lost my temper ! I ain't feeling well !

I got a hell of a grouch on! Bejees, you know you're all as welcome here as the flowers in May!

(*They look at him with eager forgiveness. Rocky is the first one who can voice it.*)

ROCKY. Aw, sure, Boss, you're always aces wid us, see?

HICKEY (*rises to his feet again. He addresses them now with the simple, convincing sincerity of one making a confession of which he is genuinely ashamed*). Listen, everybody! I know you are sick of my gabbing, but I think this is the spot where I owe it to you to do a little explaining and apologize for some of the rough stuff I've had to pull on you. I know how it must look to you. As if I was a damned busybody who was not only interfering in your private business, but even sicking some of you on to nag at each other. Well, I have to admit that's true, and I'm damned sorry about it. But it simply had to be done! You must believe that! You know old Hickey. I was never one to start trouble. But this time I had to—for your own good! I had to make you help me with each other. I saw I couldn't do what I was after alone. Not in the time at my disposal. I knew when I came here I wouldn't be able to stay with you long. I'm slated to leave on a trip. I saw I'd have to hustle and use every means I could. (*With a joking boastfulness.*) Why, if I had enough time, I'd get a lot of sport out of selling my line of salvation to each of you all by my lonesome. Like it was fun in the old days, when I travelled house to house, to convince some dame, who was sicking the dog on me, her house wouldn't be properly furnished unless she bought another wash boiler. And I could do it with you, all right. I know every one of you, inside and out, by heart. I may have been drunk when I've been here before, but old Hickey could never be so drunk he didn't have to see through people. I mean, everyone except himself. And, finally, he had to see through himself, too. (*He pauses. They stare at him, bitter, uneasy and fascinated. His manner changes to deep earnestness.*) But here's the point to get. I swear I'd never act like I have if I wasn't absolutely sure it will be worth it to you in the end, after you're rid of the damned guilt that makes you lie to yourselves you're something you're not, and the remorse that nags at you and makes you hide behind lousy pipe dreams about tomorrow. You'll be in a today where there is no yesterday or tomorrow to worry you. You won't give a damn what you are any more. I wouldn't say this unless I knew, Brothers and Sisters. This peace is real! It's a fact! I know! Because I've got it! Here! Now! Right in front of you! You see the difference in me! You remember how I used to be! Even when I had two quarts of rotgut under my belt and joked and sang "Sweet Adeline," I still felt like a guilty skunk. But you can all see that I don't give a damn about anything now. And I promise you, by the time this day is over, I'll have every one of you feeling the same way! (*He pauses. They stare at him fascinatedly. He adds with a grin.*) I guess that'll be about all from me, boys and girls—for the present. So let's get on with the party. (*He starts to sit down.*)

LARRY (*sharply*). Wait! (*Insistently—with a sneer.*) I think it would help us poor pipe-dreaming sinners along the sawdust trail to salvation if you told us now what it was happened to you that converted you to this great peace you've found. (*More and more with a deliberate, provocative taunting.*) I notice you didn't deny it when I asked you about the iceman. Did this great revelation of the evil habit of dreaming about tomorrow come to you after you found your wife was sick of you?

(*While he is speaking the faces of the gang have lighted up vindictively, as if all at once they saw a chance to revenge themselves. As he finishes, a chorus of sneering taunts begins, punctuated by nasty, jeering laughter.*)

HOPE. Bejees, you've hit it, Larry! I've noticed he hasn't shown her picture around this time!

MOSHER. He hasn't got it! The iceman took it away from him!

MARGIE. Jees, look at him! Who could blame her?

PEARL. She must be hard up to fall for an iceman!

CORA. Imagine a sap like him advisin' me and Chuck to git married!

CHUCK. Yeah! He done so good wid it!

JIMMY. At least I can say Marjorie chose an officer and a gentleman.

LEWIS. Come to look at you, Hickey, old chap, you've sprouted horns like a bloody antelope!

WETJOEN. Pigger, py Gott! Like a water buffalo's!

WILLIE (*sings to his Sailor Lad tune*).

"'Come up,' she cried, 'my iceman lad,
And you and I'll agree——'"

(*They all join in a jeering chorus, rapping with knuckles or glasses on the table at the indicated spot in the lyric.*)

"'And I'll show you the prettiest (*Rap, rap, rap*)
That ever you did see!'"

(*A roar of derisive, dirty laughter. But Hickey has remained unmoved by all this taunting. He grins good-naturedly, as if he enjoyed the joke at his expense, and joins in the laughter.*)

HICKEY. Well, boys and girls, I'm glad to see you getting in good spirits for Harry's party, even if the joke is on me. I admit I asked for it by always pulling that iceman gag in the old days. So laugh all you like. (*He pauses. They do not laugh now. They are again staring at him with baffled uneasiness. He goes on thoughtfully.*) Well, this forces my hand, I guess, your bringing up the subject of Evelyn. I didn't want to tell you yet. It's hardly an appropriate time. I meant to wait until the party was over. But you're getting the wrong idea about poor Evelyn, and I've got to stop that. (*He pauses again. There is a tense stillness in the room. He bows his head a little and says quietly.*) I'm sorry to tell you my dearly beloved wife is dead.

(*A gasp comes from the stunned company. They look away from him, shocked and miserably ashamed of themselves, except Larry, who continues to stare at him.*)

LARRY (*aloud to himself with a superstitious shrinking*). Be God, I felt he'd brought the touch of death on him! (*Then suddenly he is even more ashamed of himself than the others and stammers.*) Forgive me, Hickey ! I'd like to cut my dirty tongue out !

(*This releases a chorus of shamefaced mumbles from the crowd.* " Sorry, Hickey." " I'm sorry, Hickey." " We're sorry, Hickey.")

HICKEY (*looking around at them—in a kindly, reassuring tone*). Now look here, everybody. You mustn't let this be a wet blanket on Harry's party. You're still getting me all wrong. There's no reason—— You see, I don't feel any grief. (*They gaze at him startledly. He goes on with convincing sincerity.*) I've got to feel glad, for her sake. Because she's at peace. She's rid of me at last. Hell, I don't have to tell you—you all know what I was like. You can imagine what she went through, married to a no-good cheater and drunk like I was. And there was no way out of it for her. Because she loved me. But now she is at peace like she always longed to be. So why should I feel sad ? She wouldn't want me to feel sad. Why, all that Evelyn ever wanted out of life was to make me happy. (*He stops, looking around at them with a simple, gentle frankness.*)

(*They stare at him in bewildered, incredulous confusion.*)

CURTAIN

ACT THREE

SCENE. *Bar-room of Harry Hope's, including a part of what had been the back room in Acts One and Two.*

In the right wall are two big windows, with the swinging doors to the street between them. The bar itself is at rear. Behind it is a mirror, covered with white mosquito netting to keep off the flies, and a shelf on which are barrels of cheap whisky with spiggots and a small showcase of bottled goods. At left of the bar is the doorway to the hall. There is a table at left, front of bar-room proper, with four chairs. At right, front, is a small free-lunch counter, facing left, with a space between it and the window for the dealer to stand when he dishes out soup at the noon hour. Over the mirror behind the bar are framed photographs of Richard Croker and Big Tim Sullivan, flanked by framed lithographs of John L. Sullivan and Gentleman Jim Corbett in ring costume.

At left, in what had been the back room, with the dividing curtain drawn, the banquet table of Act Two has been broken up, and the tables are again in the crowded arrangement of Act One. Of these, we see one in the front row with five chairs at left of the bar-room table, another with five chairs at left-rear of it, a third back by the rear wall with five chairs, and finally, at extreme left-front, one with four chairs, partly on and partly off stage, left.

It is around the middle of the morning of Hope's birthday, a hot summer day. There is sunlight in the street outside, but it does not hit the windows and the light in the back-room section is dim.

Joe Mott is moving around, a box of sawdust under his arm, strewing it over the floor. His manner is sullen, his face set in gloom. He ignores everyone. As the scene progresses, he finishes his sawdusting job, goes behind the lunch counter and cuts loaves of bread. Rocky is behind the bar, wiping it, washing glasses, etc. He wears his working clothes, sleeves rolled up. He looks sleepy, irritable and worried. At the bar-room table, front, Larry sits in a chair, facing right-front. He has no drink in front of him. He stares ahead, deep in harried thought. On his right, in a chair facing right, Hugo sits sprawled forward, arms and head on the table as usual, a whisky glass beside his limp hand. At rear of the front table at left of them, in a chair facing left, Parritt is sitting. He is staring in front of him in a tense, strained immobility.

As the curtain rises, Rocky finishes his work behind the bar. He comes forward and drops wearily in the chair at right of Larry's table, facing left.

ROCKY. Nuttin' now till de noon rush from de Market. I'm goin' to rest my fanny. (*Irritably.*) If I ain't a sap to let Chuck kid me into workin' his time so's he can take de mornin' off. But I got sick of arguin' wid 'im. I says, " Aw right, git married ! What's it to me ? " Hickey's got de bot' of dem bugs. (*Bitterly.*) Some party last night, huh ? Jees, what a funeral ! It was jinxed from de start, but his tellin' about his wife croakin' put de K.O. on it.

LARRY. Yes, it turned out it wasn't a birthday feast but a wake !

ROCKY. Him promisin' he'd cut out de bughouse bull about peace—and den he went on talkin' and talkin' like he couldn't stop ! And all de gang sneakin' upstairs, leavin' free booze and eats like dey was poison ! It didn't do dem no good if dey thought dey'd shake him. He's been hoppin' from room to room all night. Yuh can't stop him. He's got his Reform Wave goin' strong dis mornin' ! Did yuh notice him drag Jimmy out de foist ting to get his laundry and his clothes pressed so he wouldn't have no excuse ? And he give Willie de dough to buy his stuff back from Solly's. And all de rest been brushin' and shavin' demselves wid de shakes——

LARRY (*defiantly*). He didn't come to my room ! He's afraid I might ask him a few questions.

ROCKY (*scornfully*). Yeah ? It don't look to me he's scared of yuh. I'd say you was scared of him.

LARRY (*stung*). You'd lie, then !

PARRITT (*jerks round to look at Larry—sneeringly*). Don't let him kid you, Rocky. He had his door locked. I couldn't get in, either.

ROCKY. Yeah, who d'yuh tink yuh're kiddin', Larry ? He's showed you up, aw right. Like he says, if yuh was so anxious to croak, why wouldn't yuh hop off your fire escape long ago ?

LARRY (*defiantly*). Because it'd be a coward's quitting, that's why !

PARRITT. He's all quitter, Rocky. He's a yellow old faker !

LARRY (*turns on him*). You lying punk ! Remember what I warned you——!

ROCKY (*scowls at Parritt*). Yeah, keep outta dis, you ! Where d'yuh get a licence to butt in ? Shall I give him de bum's rush, Larry ? If you don't want him around, nobody else don't.

LARRY (*forcing an indifferent tone*). No. Let him stay. I don't mind him. He's nothing to me.

(*Rocky shrugs his shoulders and yawns sleepily.*)

PARRITT. You're right, I have nowhere to go now. You're the only one in the world I can turn to.

ROCKY (*drowsily*). Yuh're a soft old sap, Larry. He's a no-good louse like Hickey. He don't belong. (*He yawns.*) I'm all in. Not a wink of sleep. Can't keep my peepers open. (*His eyes close and his head nods.*)

(*Parritt gives him a glance and then gets up and slinks over to slide into the chair on Larry's left, between him and Rocky. Larry shrinks away, but determinedly ignores him.*)

PARRITT (*bending towards him—in a low, ingratiating, apologetic voice*). I'm sorry for riding you, Larry. But you get my goat when you act as if you didn't care a damn what happened to me, and keep your door locked so I can't talk to you. (*Then hopefully.*) But that was to keep Hickey out, wasn't it ? I don't blame you. I'm getting to hate him. I'm getting more and more scared of him. Especially since he told us his wife was dead. It's that queer feeling he gives me that I'm mixed up with him some way. I don't know why, but it started me thinking about Mother—as if she was dead. (*With a strange undercurrent of something like satisfaction in his pitying tone.*) I suppose she might as well be. Inside herself, I mean. It must kill her when she thinks of me—I know she doesn't want to, but she can't help it. After all, I'm her only kid. She used to spoil me and made a pet of me. Once in a great while, I mean. When she remembered me. As if she wanted to make up for something. As if she felt guilty. So she must have loved me a little, even if she never let it interfere with her freedom. (*With a strange pathetic wistfulness.*) Do you know, Larry, I once had a sneaking suspicion that maybe, if the truth was known, you were my father.

LARRY (*violently*). You damned fool ! Who put that insane idea in your head ? You know it's a lie ! Anyone in the Coast crowd could tell you I never laid eyes on your mother till after you were born.

PARRITT. Well, I'd hardly ask them, would I ? I know you're right, though, because I asked her. She brought me up to be frank and ask her anything, and she'd always tell me the truth. (*Abruptly.*) But I was talking about how she must feel now about me. My getting through with the Movement. She'll never forgive that. The Movement is her life. And it must be the final knockout for her if she knows I was the one who sold——

LARRY. Shut up, damn you !

PARRITT. It'll kill her. And I'm sure she knows it must have been me. (*Suddenly with desperate urgency.*) But I never thought the cops would get her ! You've got to believe that ! You've got to see what my only reason was ! I'll admit what I told you last night was a lie—that bunk about getting patriotic and my duty to my country. But here's the true reason, Larry—the only reason ! It was just for money ! I got stuck on a whore and wanted dough to blow in on her and have a good time ! That's all I did it for ! Just money ! Honest ! (*He has the terrible grotesque air, in confessing his sordid baseness, of one who gives an excuse which exonerates him from any real guilt.*)

LARRY (*grabs him by the shoulder and shakes him*). God damn you, shut up ! What the hell is it to me ?

(*Rocky starts awake.*)

ROCKY. What's comin' off here ?

LARRY (*controlling himself*). Nothing. This gabby young punk was talking my ear off, that's all. He's a worse pest than Hickey.

ROCKY (*drowsily*). Yeah, Hickey—— Say, listen, what d'yuh mean about him bein' scared you'd ask him questions ? What questions ?

LARRY. Well, I feel he's hiding something. You notice he didn't say what his wife died of.

ROCKY (*rebukingly*). Aw, lay off dat. De poor guy—— What are yuh gettin' at, anyway ? Yuh don't tink it's just a gag of his ?

LARRY. I don't. I'm damned sure he's brought death here with him. I feel the cold touch of it on him.

ROCKY. Aw, bunk! You got croakin' on de brain, Old Cemetery. (*Suddenly Rocky's eyes widen.*) Say! D'yuh mean yuh tink she committed suicide, 'count of his cheatin' or someting?

LARRY (*grimly*). It wouldn't surprise me. I'd be the last to blame her.

ROCKY (*scornfully*). But dat's crazy! Jees, if she'd done dat, he wouldn't tell us he was glad about it, would he? He ain't dat big a bastard.

PARRITT (*speaks up from his own preoccupation—strangely*). You know better than that, Larry. You know she'd never commit suicide. She's like you. She'll hang on to life even when there's nothing left but——

LARRY (*stung—turns on him viciously*). And how about you? Be God, if you had any guts or decency——! (*He stops guiltily.*)

PARRITT (*sneeringly*). I'd take that hop off your fire escape you're too yellow to take, I suppose?

LARRY (*as if to himself*). No! Who am I to judge? I'm done with judging.

PARRITT (*tauntingly*). Yes, I suppose you'd like that, wouldn't you?

ROCKY (*irritably mystified*). What de hell's all dis about? (*To Parritt.*) What d'you know about Hickey's wife? How d'yuh know she didn't——?

LARRY (*with forced belittling casualness*). He doesn't. Hickey's addled the little brains he's got. Shove him back to his own table, Rocky. I'm sick of him.

ROCKY (*to Parritt, threateningly*). Yuh heard Larry? I'd like an excuse to give yuh a good punch in de snoot. So move quick!

PARRITT (*gets up—to Larry*). If you think moving to another table will get rid of me! (*He moves away—then adds with bitter reproach.*) Gee, Larry, that's a hell of a way to treat me, when I've trusted you and I need your help. (*He sits down in his old place and sinks into a wounded, self-pitying brooding.*)

ROCKY (*going back to his train of thought*). Jees, if she committed suicide, yuh got to feel sorry for Hickey, huh? Yuh can understand how he'd go bughouse and not be responsible for all de crazy stunts he's stagin' here. (*Then puzzledly.*) But how can yuh be sorry for him when he says he's glad she croaked, and yuh can tell he means it? (*With weary exasperation.*) Aw, nuts! I don't get nowhere tryin' to figger his game. (*His face hardening.*) But I know dis. He better lay off me and my stable! (*He pauses—then sighs.*) Jees, Larry, what a night dem two pigs give me! When de party went dead, dey pinched a coupla bottles and brung dem up deir room and got stinko. I don't get a wink of sleep, see? Just as I'd drop off on a chair here, dey'd come down lookin' for trouble. Or else dey'd raise hell upstairs, laughin' and singin', so I'd get scared dey'd get de joint pinched and go up to tell dem to can de noise. And every time dey'd crawl my frame wid de same old argument. Dey'd say, "So yuh agreed wid Hickey, do yuh, yuh dirty little Ginny? We're whores, are we? Well, we agree wid Hickey about you, see! Yuh're nuttin' but a lousy pimp!" Den I'd slap dem. Not beat 'em up, like a pimp would. Just slap dem. But it don't do no good. Dey'd keep at it over and over. Jees, I get de earache just thinkin' of it! "Listen," dey'd say, "if we're whores we gotta right to have a reg'lar pimp and not stand for no punk imitation! We're sick of wearin' out our dogs poundin' sidewalks for a double-crossin' bartender, when all de thanks we get is he looks down on us. We'll find a guy who really needs us to take care of him and ain't ashamed of it. Don't expect us to work tonight, 'cause we won't, see? Not if de streets was blocked wid sailors! We're goin' on strike and yuh can like it or lump it!" (*He shakes his head.*) Whores goin' on strike! Can yuh tie dat? (*Going on with his story.*) Dey says, "We're takin' a holiday. We're goin' to beat it down to Coney Island and shoot the chutes and maybe we'll come back and maybe we won't. And you can go to hell!" So dey put on deir lids and beat it, de bot' of dem stinko.

(*He sighs dejectedly. He seems grotesquely like a harried family man, henpecked and browbeaten by a nagging wife. Larry is deep in his own bitter preoccupation and hasn't listened to him. Chuck enters from the hall at rear. He has his straw hat with the gaudy band in his hand and wears a Sunday-best blue suit with a high stiff collar. He looks sleepy, hot uncomfortable and grouchy.*)

CHUCK (*glumly*). Hey, Rocky. Cora wants a sherry flip. For her noives.

ROCKY (*turns indignantly*). Sherry flip! Christ, she don't need nuttin' for her noive! What's she tink dis is, de Waldorf?

CHUCK. Yeah, I told her, what would we use for sherry, and dere wasn't no egg unless she laid one. She says, "Is dere a law yuh can't go out and buy de makings, yuh big tramp?" (*Resentfully puts his straw hat on his head at a defiant tilt.*) To hell wid her! She'll drink booze or nuttin'! (*He goes behind the bar to draw a glass of whisky from a barrel.*)

ROCKY (*sarcastically*). Jees, a guy oughta give his bride anything she wants on de weddin' day, I should tink!

(*As Chuck comes from behind the bar, Rocky surveys him derisively.*)

Pipe de bridegroom, Larry! All dolled up for de killin'!

(*Larry pays no attention.*)

CHUCK. Aw, shut up!

ROCKY. One week on dat farm in Joisey, dat's what I give yuh! Yuh'll come runnin' in here some night yellin' for a shot of booze 'cause de crickets is after yuh! (*Disgustedly.*) Jees, Chuck, dat louse Hickey's coitinly made a prize coupla suckers outa youse.

CHUCK (*unguardedly*). Yeah. I'd like to give him one sock in de puss—just one! (*Then angrily.*) Aw, can dat! What's he got to do wid it? Ain't we always said we was goin' to? So we're goin' to, see? And don't give me no argument! (*He stares at Rocky truculently. But Rocky only shrugs his shoulders with weary disgust and Chuck subsides into complaining gloom.*) If on'y Cora'd cut out de beefin'. She don't gimme a minute's rest all night. De same old stuff over and over! Do I really want to marry her? I says, "Sure, Baby, why not?" She says, "Yeah, but after a week yuh'll be tinkin' what a sap you was. Yuh'll make dat an excuse to go off on a periodical, and den I'll be tied for life to a no-good soak, and de foist ting I know yuh'll have me out hustlin' again, your own wife!" Den she'd bust out cryin', and I'd get sore. "Yuh're a liar," I'd say. "I aint never taken your dough 'cept when I was drunk and not workin'!" "Yeah," she'd say, "and how long will yuh stay sober now? Don't tink yuh can kid me wid dat water wagon bull! I've heard it too often." Dat'd make me sore and I'd say, "Don't call me a liar. But I wish I was drunk right now, because if I was, yuh wouldn't be keepin' me awake all night beefin'. If yuh opened your yap, I'd knock de stuffin' outa yuh!" Den she'd yell, "Dat's a sweet way to talk to de goil yuh're goin' to marry." (*He sighs explosively.*) Jees, she's got me hangin' on de ropes! (*He glances with vengeful yearning at the drink of whisky in his hand.*) Jees, would I like to get a quart of dis redeye under my belt!

ROCKY. Well, why de hell don't yuh?

CHUCK (*instantly suspicious and angry*). Sure! You'd like dat, wouldn't yuh? I'm wise to you! Yuh don't wanta see me get married and settle down like a reg'lar guy! Yuh'd like me to stay paralysed all de time, so's I'd be like you, a lousy pimp!

ROCKY (*springs to his feet, his face hardened viciously*). Listen! I don't take dat even from you, see!

CHUCK (*puts his drink on the bar and clenches his fists*) Yeah? Wanta make sometin' of it? (*Jeeringly.*) Don't make me laugh! I can lick ten of youse wid one mit!

ROCKY (*reaching for his hip pocket*). Not wid lead in your belly, yuh won't!

JOE (*has stopped cutting when the quarrel started—expostulating*). Hey, you, Rocky and Chuck! Cut it out! You's ole friends! Don't let dat Hickey make you crazy!

CHUCK (*turns on him*). Keep outa our business, yuh black bastard!

ROCKY (*like Chuck, turns on Joe, as if their own quarrel was forgotten and they became natural allies against an alien*). Stay where yuh belong, yuh doity nigger!

JOE (*snarling with rage, springs from behind the lunch counter with the bread knife in his hand*). You white sons of bitches! I'll rip your guts out!

(*Chuck snatches a whisky bottle from the bar and raises it above his head to hurl at Joe. Rocky jerks a short-barrelled, nickel-plated revolver from his hip pocket. At this moment Larry pounds on the table with his fist and bursts into a sardonic laugh.*)

LARRY. That's it! Murder each other, you damned loons, with Hickey's blessing! Didn't I tell you he'd brought death with him?

(*His interruption startles them. They pause to stare at him, their fighting fury suddenly dies out and they appear deflated and sheepish.*)

ROCKY (*to Joe*). Aw right, you. Leggo dat shiv and I'll put dis gat away.

(*Joe sullenly goes back behind the counter and slaps the knife on top of it. Rocky slips the revolver back in his pocket. Chuck lowers the bottle to the bar. Hugo, who has awakened and raised his head when Larry pounded on the table, now giggles foolishly.*)

HUGO. Hello, leedle peoples! Neffer mind! Soon you vill eat hot dogs beneath the villow trees and trink free vine—— (*Abruptly in a haughty fastidious tone.*) The champagne vas not properly iced. (*With guttural anger.*) Gottamned liar, Hickey! Does that prove I vant to be aristocrat? I love only the proletariat! I vill lead them! I vill be like a Gott to them! They vill be my slaves! (*He stops in bewildered self-amazement—to Larry appealingly.*) I am very trunk, no, Larry? I talk foolishness. I am so trunk, Larry, old friend, am I not, I don't know vhat I say?

LARRY (*pityingly*). You're raving drunk, Hugo. I've never seen you so paralysed. Lay your head down now and sleep it off.

HUGO (*gratefully*). Yes. I should sleep. I am too crazy trunk. (*He puts his head on his arms and closes his eyes.*)

JOE (*behind the lunch counter—brooding superstitiously*). You's right, Larry. Bad luck come in de door when Hickey come. I's an ole gamblin' man and I knows bad luck when I feels it! (*Then defiantly.*) But it's white man's bad luck. He can't jinx me! (*He comes from behind the counter and goes to the bar—addressing Rocky stiffly.*) De bread's cut and I's finished my job. Do I get de drink I's earned?

(*Rocky gives him a hostile look but shoves a bottle and

glass at him. Joe pours a brimful drink—sullenly.)

I's finished wid dis dump for keeps. (*He takes a key from his pocket and slaps it on the bar.*) Here's de key to my room. I ain't comin' back. I's goin' to my own folks where I belong. I don't stay where I's not wanted. I's sick and tired of messin' round wid white men. (*He gulps down his drink—then looking around defiantly he deliberately throws his whisky glass on the floor and smashes it.*)

ROCKY. Hey! What de hell——!

JOE (*with a sneering dignity*). I's on'y savin' you de trouble, White Boy. Now you don't have to break it, soon's my back's turned, so's no white man kick about drinkin' from de same glass. (*He walks stiffly to the street door—then turns for a parting shot—boastfully.*) I's tired of loafin' 'round wid a lot of bums. I's a gamblin' man. I's gonna get in a big crap game and win me a big bank-roll. Den I'll get de okay to open up my old gamblin' house for coloured men. Den maybe I comes back here sometime to see de bums. Maybe I throw a twenty-dollar bill on de bar and say, "Drink it up," and listen when dey all pat me on de back and say, "Joe, you sure is white." But I'll say, "No, I'm black and my dough is black man's dough, and you's proud to drink wid me or you don't get no drink!" Or maybe I just says, "You can all go to hell. I don't lower myself drinkin' wid no white trash!" (*He opens the door to go out—then turns again.*) And dat ain't no pipe dream! I'll git de money for my stake today, somehow, somewheres! If I has to borrow a gun and stick up some white man, I gets it! You wait and see! (*He swaggers out through the swinging doors.*)

CHUCK (*angrily*). Can yuh beat de noive of dat dinge! Jees, if I wasn't dressed up, I'd go out and mop up de street wid him!

ROCKY. Aw, let him go, de poor old dope! Him and his gamblin' house! He'll be back tonight askin' Harry for his room and bummin' me for a ball. (*Vengefully.*) Den I'll be de one to smash de glass. I'll loin him his place!

(*The swinging doors are pushed open and Willie Oban enters from the street. He is shaved and wears an expensive, well-cut suit, good shoes and clean linen. He is absolutely sober, but his face is sick, and his nerves in a shocking state of shakes.*)

CHUCK. Another guy all dolled up! Got your clothes from Solly's, huh, Willie? (*Derisively.*) Now yuh can sell dem back to him again tomorrow.

WILLIE (*stiffly*). No, I—I'm through with that stuff. Never again. (*He comes to the bar.*)

ROCKY (*sympathetically*). Yuh look sick, Willie. Take a ball to pick yuh up. (*He pushes a bottle toward him.*)

WILLIE (*eyes the bottle yearningly but shakes his head—determinedly*). No, thanks. The only way to stop is to stop. I'd have no chance if I went to the D.A.'s office smelling of booze.

CHUCK. Yuh're really goin' dere?

WILLIE (*stiffly*). I said I was, didn't I? I just came back here to rest a few minutes, not because I needed any booze. I'll show that cheap drummer I don't have to have any Dutch courage—— (*Guiltily.*) But he's been very kind and generous staking me. He can't help his insulting manner, I suppose. (*He turns away from the bar.*) My legs are a bit shaky yet. I better sit down a while.

(*He goes back and sits at the left of the second table, facing Parritt, who gives him a scowling, suspicious glance and then ignores him. Rocky looks at Chuck and taps his head disgustedly. Captain Lewis appears in the doorway from the hall.*)

CHUCK (*mutters*). Here's anudder one.

(*Lewis looks spruce and clean-shaven. His ancient tweed suit has been brushed and his frayed linen is clean. His manner is full of a forced, jaunty self-assurance. But he is sick and beset by katzenjammer.*)

LEWIS. Good morning, gentlemen all. (*He passes along the front of bar to look out in the street.*) A jolly fine morning, too. (*He turns back to the bar.*) An eye-opener? I think not. Not required, Rocky, old chum. Feel extremely fit, as a matter of fact. Though can't say I slept much, thanks to that interfering ass, Hickey and that stupid bounder of a Boer. (*His face hardens.*) I've had about all I can take from that fellow. It's my own fault of course, for allowing a brute of a Dutch farmer to become familiar. Well, it's come to a parting of the ways now, and good riddance. Which reminds me, here's my key. (*He puts it on the bar.*) I shan't be coming back. Sorry to be leaving good old Harry and the rest of you, of course, but I can't continue to live under the same roof with that fellow.

(*He stops, stiffening into hostility as Wetjoen enters from the hall, and pointedly turns his back on him. Wetjoen glares at him sneeringly. He, too, has made an effort to spruce up his appearance, and his bearing has a forced swagger of conscious physical strength. Behind this, he is sick and feebly holding his booze-sodden body together.*)

ROCKY (*to Lewis—disgustedly putting the key on the shelf in back of the bar*). So Hickey's kidded the pants offa you, too? Yuh tink yuh're leavin' here, huh?

WETJOEN (*jeeringly*). Ja! Dot's vhat he kids himself.

LEWIS (*ignores him—airily*). Yes, I'm leaving, Rocky. But that ass, Hickey, has nothing to do with it. Been thinking things over. Time I turned over a new leaf, and all that.

WETJOEN. He's going to get a job! Dot's what he says!

ROCKY. What at, for Chris' sake?

LEWIS (*keeping his airy manner*). Oh, anything. I mean, not manual labour, naturally, but anything that calls for a bit of brains and education. However humble. Beggars can't be choosers. I'll see a pal of mine at the Consulate. He promised any time I felt an energetic fit he'd get me a post with the Cunard—clerk in the office or something of the kind.

WETJOEN. Ja! At Limey Consulate they promise anything to get rid of him vhen he comes there tronk! They're scared to call the police and have him pinched because it vould scandal in the papers make about a Limey officer and chentleman!

LEWIS. As a matter of fact, Rocky, I only wish a post temporarily. Means to an end, you know. Save up enough for a first-class passage home, that's the bright idea.

WETJOEN. He's sailing back to home, sveet home! Dot's biggest pipe dream of all. What leetle brain the poor Limey has left, dot isn't in whisky pickled, Hickey has made crazy!

(*Lewis's fists clench, but he manages to ignore this.*)

CHUCK (*feels sorry for Lewis and turns on Wetjoen—sarcastically*). Hickey ain't made no sucker outa you, huh? You're too foxy, huh? But I'll bet you tink yuh're goin' out and land a job, too.

WETJOEN (*bristles*). I am, ja. For me, it is easy. Because I put on no airs of chentleman. I am not ashamed to vork vith my hands. I vas a farmer before the war ven ploody Limey thieves steal my country. (*Boastfully.*) Anyone I ask for job can see vith one look I have the great strength to do work of ten ordinary mens.

LEWIS (*sneeringly*). Yes, Chuck, you remember he gave a demonstration of his extraordinary muscles last night when he helped to move the piano.

CHUCK. Yuh couldn't even hold up your corner. It was your fault de damned box almost fell down de stairs.

WETJOEN. My hands vas sweaty! Could I help dot my hands slip? I could de whole veight of it lift! In old days in Transvaal, I lift loaded oxcart by the axle! So vhy shouldn't I get job? Dot longshoreman boss, Dan, he tell me any time I like, he take me on. And Benny from de Market he promise me same.

LEWIS. You remember, Rocky, it was one of those rare occasions when the Boer that walks like a man—spelled with a double o, by the way—was buying drinks and Dan and Benny were stony. They'd bloody well have promised him the moon.

ROCKY. Yeah, yuh big boob, dem boids was on'y kiddin' yuh.

WETJOEN (*angrily*). Dot's lie! You vill see dis morning I get job! I'll show dot bloody Limey chentleman, and dot liar, Hickey! And I need vork only leetle vhile to save money for my passage home. I need not much money because I am not ashamed to travel steerage. I don't put on first-cabin airs! (*Tauntingly.*) Und *I can* go home to my country! Vhen I get there, they vill let *me* come in!

LEWIS (*grows rigid—his voice trembling with repressed anger*). There was a rumour in South Africa, Rocky, that a certain Boer officer—if you call the leaders of a rabble of farmers officers—kept advising Cronje to retreat and not stand and fight——

WETJOEN. And I vas right! I vas right! He got surrounded at Poardeberg! He had to surrender!

LEWIS (*ignoring him*). Good strategy, no doubt, but a suspicion grew afterwards into a conviction among the Boers that the officer's caution was prompted by a desire to make his personal escape. His countrymen felt extremely savage about it, and his family disowned him. So I imagine there would be no welcoming committee waiting on the dock, nor delighted relatives making the veldt ring with their happy cries——

WETJOEN (*with guilty rage*). All lies! You Gottamned Limey—— (*Trying to control himself and copy Lewis's manner.*) I also haf heard rumours of a Limey officer who, after the war, lost all his money gambling vhen he vas tronk. But they found out it was regiment money, too, he lost——

LEWIS (*loses his control and starts for him*). You bloody Dutch scum!

ROCKY (*leans over the bar and stops Lewis with a straight-arm swipe on the chest*). Cut it out!

(*At the same moment Chuck grabs Wetjoen and yanks him back.*)

WETJOEN (*struggling*). Let him come! I saw them come before—at Modder River, Magersfontein, Spion Kopje—waving their silly swords, so afraid they couldn't show off how brave they vas!—and I kill them vith my rifle so easy! (*Vindictively.*) Listen to me, you Cecil! Often vhen I am tronk and kidding you I say I am sorry I missed you, but now, py Gott, I am sober, and I don't joke, and I say it!

LARRY (*gives a sardonic guffaw—with his comically crazy, intense whisper*). Be God, you can't say Hickey hasn't the miraculous touch to raise the dead, when he can start the Boer War raging again!

(*This interruption acts like a cold douche on Lewis and Wetjoen. They subside, and Rocky and Chuck let go of them. Lewis turns his back on the Boer.*)

LEWIS (*attempting a return of his jaunty manner, as if*

nothing had happened). Well, time I was on my merry way to see my chap at the Consulate. The early bird catches the job, what? Good-bye and good luck, Rocky, and everyone. (*He starts for the street door.*)

WETJOEN. Py Gott, if dot Limey can go, I can go!

(*He hurries after Lewis. But Lewis, his hand about to push the swinging doors open, hesitates, as though struck by a sudden paralysis of the will, and Wetjoen has to jerk back to avoid bumping into him. For a second they stand there, one behind the other, staring over the swinging doors into the street.*)

ROCKY. Well, why don't yuh beat it?

LEWIS (*guiltily casual*). Eh? Oh, just happened to think. Hardly the decent thing to pop off without saying good-bye to old Harry. One of the best, Harry. And good old Jimmy, too. They ought to be down any moment. (*He pretends to notice Wetjoen for the first time and steps away from the door—apologizing as to a stranger.*) Sorry. I seem to be blocking your way out.

WETJOEN (*stiffly*). No. I vait to say good-bye to Harry and Jimmy, too.

(*He goes to right of door behind the lunch counter and looks through the window, his back to the room. Lewis takes up a similar stand at the window on the left of door.*)

CHUCK. Jees, can yuh beat dem simps! (*He picks up Cora's drink at the end of the bar.*) Hell, I'd forgot Cora. She'll be trowin' a fit. (*He goes into the hall with the drink.*)

ROCKY (*looks after him disgustedly*). Dat's right, wait on her and spoil her, yuh poor sap! (*He shakes his head and begins to wipe the bar mechanically.*)

WILLIE (*is regarding Parritt across the table from him with an eager, calculating eye. He leans over and speaks in a low confidential tone*). Look here, Parritt. I'd like to have a talk with you.

PARRITT (*starts—scowling defensively*). What about?

WILLIE (*his manner becoming his idea of a crafty criminal lawyer's*). About the trouble you're in. Oh, I know. You don't admit it. You're quite right. That's my advice. Deny everything. Keep your mouth shut. Make no statements whatever without first consulting your attorney.

PARRITT. Say! What the hell——?

WILLIE. But you can trust me. I'm a lawyer, and it's just occurred to me you and I ought to co-operate. Of course I'm going to see the D.A. this morning about a job on his staff. But that may take time. There may not be an immediate opening. Meanwhile it would be a good idea for me to take a case or two, on my own, and prove my brilliant record in law school was no flash in the pan. So why not retain me as your attorney?

PARRITT. You're crazy! What do I want with a lawyer?

WILLIE. That's right. Don't admit anything. But you can trust me, so let's not beat about the bush. You got in trouble out on the Coast, eh? And now you're hiding out. Any fool can spot that. (*Lowering his voice still more.*) You feel safe here, and maybe you are, for a while. But remember, they get you in the end. I know from my father's experience. No one could have felt safer than he did. When anyone mentioned the law to him, he nearly died laughing. But——

PARRITT. You crazy mutt! (*Turning to Larry with a strained laugh.*) Did you get that, Larry? This damned fool thinks the cops are after me!

LARRY (*bursts out with his true reaction before he thinks to ignore him*). I wish to God they were! And so should you, if you had the honour of a louse!

(*Parritt stares into his eyes guiltily for a second. Then he smiles sneeringly.*)

PARRITT. And you're the guy who kids himself he's through with the Movement! You old lying faker, you're still in love with it!

(*Larry ignores him again now.*)

WILLIE (*disappointedly*). Then you're not in trouble, Parritt? I was hoping—— But never mind. No offence meant. Forget it.

PARRITT (*condescendingly—his eyes on Larry*). Sure. That's all right, Willie. I'm not sore at you. It's that damned old faker that gets my goat. (*He slips out of his chair and goes quietly over to sit in the chair beside Larry he had occupied before—in a low, insinuating, intimate tone.*) I think I understand, Larry. It's really Mother you still love—isn't it?—in spite of the dirty deal she gave you. But hell, what did you expect? She was never true to anyone but herself and the Movement. But I understand how you can't help still feeling—because I still love her, too. (*Pleading in a strained, desperate tone.*) You know I do, don't you? You must! So you see I couldn't have expected they'd catch her! You've got to believe me that I sold them out just to get a few lousy dollars to blow in on a whore. No other reason, honest! There couldn't possibly be any other reason! (*Again he has a strange air of exonerating himself from guilt by this shameless confession.*)

LARRY (*trying not to listen, has listened with increasing tension*). For the love of Christ will you leave me in peace! I've told you you can't make me judge you! But if you don't keep still, you'll be saying something soon that will make you vomit your own soul like a drink of nickel rotgut that won't stay down! (*He pushes back his chair and springs to his feet.*) To hell with you! (*He goes to the bar.*)

PARRITT (*jumps up and starts to follow him—desper-*

ately). Don't go, Larry! You've got to help me!

(*But Larry is at the bar, back turned, and Rocky is scowling at him. He stops, shrinking back into himself helplessly, and turns away. He goes to the table where he had been before, and this time he takes the chair at rear facing directly front. He puts his elbows on the table, holding his head in his hands as if he had a splitting headache.*)

LARRY. Set 'em up, Rocky. I swore I'd have no more drinks on Hickey, if I died of drought, but I've changed my mind! Be God, he owed it to me, and I'd get blind to the world now if it was the Iceman of Death himself treating! (*He stops, startledly, a superstitious awe coming into his face.*) What made me say that, I wonder. (*With a sardonic laugh.*) Well, be God, it fits, for Death was the Iceman Hickey called to his home!

ROCKY. Aw, forget dat iceman gag! De poor dame is dead. (*Pushing a bottle and glass at Larry.*) Gwan and get paralysed! I'll be glad to see one bum in dis dump act natural.

(*Larry downs a drink and pours another. Ed Mosher appears in the doorway from the hall. The same change which is apparent in the manner and appearance of the others shows in him. He is sick, his nerves are shattered, his eyes are apprehensive, but he, too, puts on an exaggeratedly self-confident bearing. He saunters to the bar between Larry and the street entrance.*)

MOSHER. Morning, Rocky. Hello, Larry. Glad to see Brother Hickey hasn't corrupted you to temperance. I wouldn't mind a shot myself. (*As Rocky shoves a bottle toward him he shakes his head.*) But I remember the only breath-killer in this dump is coffee beans. The boss would never fall for that. No man can run a circus successfully who believes guys chew coffee beans because they like them. (*He pushes the bottle away.*) No, much as I need one after the hell of a night I've had—— (*He scowls.*) That drummer son of a drummer! I had to lock him out. But I could hear him through the wall doing his spiel to someone all night long. Still at it with Jimmy and Harry when I came down just now. But the hardest to take was that flannel-mouth, flatfoot Mick trying to tell me where I got off! I had to lock him out, too.

(*As he says this, McGloin comes in the doorway from the hall. The change in his appearance and manner is identical with that of Mosher and the others.*)

MCGLOIN. He's a liar, Rocky! It was me locked him out!

(*Mosher starts to flare up—then ignores him. They turn their backs on each other. McGloin starts into the back-room section.*)

WILLIE. Come and sit here, Mac. You're just the man I want to see. If I'm to take your case, we ought to have a talk before we leave.

MCGLOIN (*contemptuously*). We'll have no talk. You damned fool, do you think I'd have your father's son for my lawyer? They'd take one look at you and bounce us both out on our necks! (*Willie winces and shrinks down in his chair. McGloin goes to the first table beyond him and sits with his back to the bar.*) I don't need a lawyer, anyway. To hell with the law! All I've got to do is see the right ones and get them to pass the word. They will, too. They know I was framed. And once they've passed the word, it's as good as done, law or no law.

MOSHER. God, I'm glad I'm leaving this madhouse! (*He pulls his key from his pocket and slaps it on the bar.*) Here's my key, Rocky.

MCGLOIN (*pulls his from his pocket*). And here's mine. (*He tosses it to Rocky.*) I'd rather sleep in the gutter than pass another night under the same roof with that loon, Hickey, and a lying circus grifter! (*He adds darkly.*) And if that hat fits anyone here, let him put it on!

(*Mosher turns toward him furiously but Rocky leans over the bar and grabs his arm.*)

ROCKY. Nix! Take it easy! (*Mosher subsides. Rocky tosses the keys on the shelf—disgustedly.*) You boids gimme a pain. It'd soive you right if I wouldn't give de keys back to yuh tonight.

(*They both turn on him resentfully, but there is an interruption as Cora appears in the doorway from the hall with Chuck behind her. She is drunk, dressed in her gaudy best, her face plastered with rouge and mascara, her hair a bit dishevelled, her hat on anyhow.*)

CORA (*comes a few steps inside the bar—with a strained bright giggle*). Hello, everybody! Here we go! Hickey just told us, ain't it time we beat it, if we're really goin'. So we're showin' de bastard, ain't we. Honey? He's comin' right down wid Harry and Jimmy. Jees, dem two look like dey was goin' to de electric chair! (*With frightened anger.*) If I had to listen to any more of Hickey's bunk, I'd brain him. (*She puts her hand on Chuck's arm.*) Come on, Honey. Let's get started before he comes down.

CHUCK (*sullenly*). Sure, anyting yuh say, Baby.

CORA (*turns on him truculently*). Yeah? Well, I say we stop at de foist reg'lar dump and yuh gotta blow me to a sherry flip—or four or five, if I want 'em!—or all bets is off!

CHUCK. Aw, yuh got a fine bun on now!

CORA. Cheap skate! I know what's eatin' you, Tightwad! Well, use my dough, den, if yuh're so stingy. Yuh'll grab it all, anyway, right after de ceremony. I know you! (*She hikes her skirt up and reaches inside the top of her stocking.*) Here, yuh big tramp!

CHUCK (*knocks her hand away—angrily*). Keep your lousy dough! And don't show off your legs to dese bums when yuh're goin' to be married, if yuh don't want a sock in de puss!

CORA (*pleased—meekly*). Aw right, Honey. (*Looking around with a foolish laugh.*) Say, why don't all you barflies come to de weddin'? (*But they are all sunk in their own apprehensions and ignore her. She hesitates, miserably uncertain.*) Well, we're goin', guys. (*There is no comment. Her eyes fasten on Rocky—desperately.*) Say, Rocky, yuh gone deef? I said me and Chuck was goin' now.

ROCKY (*wiping the bar—with elaborate indifference*). Well, good-bye. Give my love to Joisey.

CORA (*tearfully indignant*). Ain't yuh goin' to wish us happiness, yuh doity little Ginny?

ROCKY. Sure. Here's hopin' yuh don't moider each odder before next week.

CHUCK (*angrily*). Aw, Baby, what d'we care for dat pimp? (*Rocky turns on him threateningly, but Chuck hears someone upstairs in the hall and grabs Cora's arm.*) Here's Hickey comin'! Let's get outa here!

(*They hurry into the hall. The street door is heard slamming behind them.*)

ROCKY (*gloomily pronounces an obituary*). One regular guy and one all-right tart gone to hell! (*Fiercely.*) Dat louse Hickey oughta be croaked!

(*There is a muttered growl of assent from most of the gathering. Then Harry Hope enters from the hall, followed by Jimmy Tomorrow, with Hickey on his heels. Hope and Jimmy are both putting up a front of self-assurance, but Cora's description of them was apt. There is a desperate bluff in their manner as they walk in, which suggests the last march of the condemned. Hope is dressed in an old black Sunday suit, black tie, shoes, socks, which give him the appearance of being in mourning. Jimmy's clothes are pressed, his shoes shined, his white linen immaculate. He has a hangover and his gently appealing dog's eyes have a boiled look. Hickey's face is a bit drawn from lack of sleep and his voice is hoarse from continued talking, but his bustling energy appears nervously intensified, and his beaming expression is one of triumphant accomplishment.*)

HICKEY. Well, here we are! We've got this far, at least! (*He pats Jimmy on the back.*) Good work, Jimmy. I told you you weren't half as sick as you pretended. No excuse whatever for postponing——

JIMMY. I'll thank you to keep your hands off me! I merely mentioned I would feel more fit tomorrow. But it might as well be today, I suppose.

HICKEY. Finish it now, so it'll be dead for ever, and you can be free! (*He passes him to clap Hope encouragingly on the shoulder.*) Cheer up, Harry. You found your rheumatism didn't bother you coming downstairs, didn't you? I told you it wouldn't. (*He winks around at the others. With the exception of Hugo and Parritt, all their eyes are fixed on him with bitter animosity. He gives Hope a playful nudge in the ribs.*) You're the damnedest one for alibis, Governor! As bad as Jimmy!

HOPE (*putting on his deaf manner*). Eh? I can't hear—— (*Defiantly.*) You're a liar! I've had rheumatism on and off for twenty years. Ever since Bessie died. Everybody knows that.

HICKEY. Yes, we know it's the kind of rheumatism you turn on and off! We're on to you, you old faker! (*He claps him on the shoulder again, chuckling.*)

HOPE (*looks humiliated and guilty—by way of escape he glares around at the others*). Bejees, what are all you bums hanging round staring at me for? Think you was watching a circus! Why don't you get the hell out of here and 'tend to your own business, like Hickey's told you?

(*They look at him reproachfully, their eyes hurt. They fidget as if trying to move.*)

HICKEY. Yes, Harry, I certainly thought they'd have had the guts to be gone by this time. (*He grins.*) Or maybe I did have my doubts. (*Abruptly he becomes sincerely sympathetic and earnest.*) Because I know exactly what you're up against, boys. I know how damned yellow a man can be when it comes to making himself face the truth. I've been through the mill, and I had to face a worse bastard in myself than any of you will have to in yourselves. I know you become such a coward you'll grab at any lousy excuse to get out of killing your pipe dreams. And yet, as I've told you over and over, it's exactly those damned tomorrow dreams which keep you from making peace with yourself. So you've got to kill them like I did mine. (*He pauses. They glare at him with fear and hatred. They seem about to curse him, to spring at him. But they remain silent and motionless. His manner changes and he becomes kindly bullying.*) Come on, boys! Get moving! Who'll start the ball rolling? You, Captain, and you, General. You're nearest the door. And besides, you're old war heroes! You ought to lead the forlorn hope! Come on, now, show us a little of that good old battle of Modder River spirit we've heard so much about! You can't hang around all day looking as if you were scared the street outside would bite you!

LEWIS (*turns with humiliated rage—with an attempt at jaunty casualness*). Right you are, Mister Bloody Nosey Parker! Time I pushed off. Was only waiting to say good-bye to you, Harry, old chum.

HOPE (*dejectedly*). Good-bye, Captain. Hope you have luck.

LEWIS. Oh, I'm bound to, Old Chap, and the same to you.

(*He pushes the swinging doors open and makes a brave exit, turning to his right and marching off outside the window at right of door.*)

WETJOEN. Py Gott, if dot Limey can, I can!

(*He pushes the door open and lumbers through it like a bull charging an obstacle. He turns left and disappears off rear, outside the farthest window.*)

HICKEY (*exhortingly*). Next? Come on, Ed. It's a fine summer's day and the call of the old circus lot must be in your blood!

(*Mosher glares at him, then goes to the door. McGloin jumps up from his chair and starts moving towards the door. Hickey claps him on the back as he passes.*)

That's the stuff, Mac.

MOSHER. Good-bye, Harry.

(*He goes out, turning right outside.*)

MCGLOIN (*glowering after him*). If that crooked grifter has the guts——

(*He goes out, turning left outside. Hickey glances at Willie who, before he can speak, jumps from his chair.*)

WILLIE. Good-bye, Harry, and thanks for all your kindness.

HICKEY (*claps him on the back*). That's the way, Willie! The D.A.'s a busy man. He can't wait all day for you, you know.

(*Willie hurries to the door.*)

HOPE (*dully*). Good luck, Willie.

(*Willie goes out and turns right outside. While he is doing so, Jimmy, in a sick panic, sneaks to the bar and furtively reaches for Larry's glass of whisky.*)

HICKEY. And now it's your turn, Jimmy, old pal. (*He sees what Jimmy is at and grabs his arm just as he is about to down the drink.*) Now, now, Jimmy! You can't do that to yourself. One drink on top of your hangover and an empty stomach and you'll be oreyeyed. Then you'll tell yourself you wouldn't stand a chance if you went up soused to get your old job back.

JIMMY (*pleads abjectly*). Tomorrow! I will tomorrow! I'll be in good shape tomorrow! (*Abruptly getting control of himself—with shaken firmness.*) All right. I'm going. Take your hands off me.

HICKEY. That's the ticket! You'll thank me when it's all over.

JIMMY (*in a burst of futile fury*). You dirty swine!

(*He tries to throw the drink in Hickey's face, but his aim is poor and it lands on Hickey's coat. Jimmy turns and dashes through the door, disappearing outside the window at right of door.*)

HICKEY (*brushing the whisky off his coat—humorously*). All set for an alcohol rub! But no hard feelings. I know how he feels. I wrote the book. I've seen the day when if anyone forced me to face the truth about my pipe dreams, I'd have shot them dead. (*He turns to Hope—encouragingly.*) Well, Governor, Jimmy made the grade. It's up to you. If he's got the guts to go through with the test, then certainly you——

LARRY (*bursts out*). Leave Harry alone, damn you!

HICKEY (*grins at him*). I'd make up my mind about myself if I was you, Larry, and not bother over Harry. He'll come through all right. I've promised him that. He doesn't need anyone's bum pity. Do you, Governor?

HOPE (*with a pathetic attempt at his old fuming assertiveness*). No, bejees! Keep your nose out of this, Larry. What's Hickey got to do with it? I've always been going to take this walk, ain't I? Bejees, you bums want to keep me locked up in here 's if I was in jail! I've stood it long enough! I'm free, white and twenty-one, and I'll do as I damned please, bejees! You keep your nose out, too, Hickey! You'd think you was boss of this dump, not me. Sure, I'm all right! Why shouldn't I be? What the hell's to be scared of, just taking a stroll around my own ward? (*As he talks he has been moving towards the door. Now he reaches it.*) What's the weather like outside, Rocky?

ROCKY. Fine day, Boss.

HOPE. What's that? Can't hear you. Don't look fine to me. Looks 's if it'd pour down cats and dogs any minute. My rheumatism—— (*He catches himself.*) No, must be my eyes. Half blind, bejees. Makes things look black. I see now it's a fine day. Too damned hot for a walk, though, if you ask me. Well, do me good to sweat the booze out of me. But I'll have to watch out for the damned automobiles. Wasn't none of them around the last time, twenty years ago. From what I've seen of 'em through the window, they'd run over you as soon as look at you. Not that I'm scared of 'em. I can take care of myself. (*He puts a reluctant hand on the swinging door.*) Well, so long—— (*He stops and looks back—with frightened irascibility.*) Bejees, where are you, Hickey? It's time we got started.

HICKEY (*grins and shakes his head*). No, Harry. Can't be done. You've got to keep a date with yourself alone.

HOPE (*with forced fuming*). Hell of a guy, you are! Thought you'd be willing to help me across the street, knowing I'm half blind. Half deaf, too. Can't bear those damned automobiles. Hell with you! Bejees, I've never needed no one's help and I don't now!

(*Egging himself on.*) I'll take a good long walk now I've started. See all my old friends. Bejees, they must have given me up for dead. Twenty years is a long time. But they know it was grief over Bessie's death that made me—— (*He puts his hand on the door.*) Well, the sooner I get started—— (*Then he drops his hand —with sentimental melancholy.*) You know, Hickey, that's what gets me. Can't help thinking the last time I went out was to Bessie's funeral. After she'd gone, I didn't feel life was worth living. Swore I'd never go out again. (*Pathetically.*) Somehow, I can't feel it's right for me to go, Hickey, even now. It's like I was doing wrong to her memory.

HICKEY. Now, Governor, you can't let yourself get away with that one any more!

HOPE (*cupping his hand to his ear*). What's that? Can't hear you. (*Sentimentally again but with desperation.*) I remember now clear as day the last time before she—— It was a fine Sunday morning. We went out to church together. (*His voice breaks on a sob.*)

HICKEY (*amused*). It's a great act, Governor. But I know better, and so do you. You never did want to go to church or any place else with her. She was always on your neck, making you have ambition and go out and do things, when all you wanted was to get drunk in peace.

HOPE (*falteringly*). Can't hear a word you're saying. You're a God-damned liar, anyway! (*Then in a sudden fury, his voice trembling with hatred.*) Bejees, you son of a bitch, if there was a mad dog outside I'd go and shake hands with it rather than stay here with you!

(*The momentum of his fit of rage does it. He pushes the door open and strides blindly out into the street and as blindly past the window behind the free-lunch counter.*)

ROCKY (*in amazement*). Jees, he made it! I'd a give yuh fifty to one he'd never—— (*He goes to the end of the bar to look through the window—disgustedly.*) Aw, he's stopped. I'll bet yuh he's comin' back.

HICKEY. Of course, he's coming back. So are all the others. By tonight they'll all be here again. You dumbell, that's the whole point.

ROCKY (*excitedly*). No, he ain't neider! He's gone to de coib. He's lookin' up and down. Scared stiff of automobiles. Jees, dey ain't more'n two an hour comes down dis street, de old boob! (*He watches excitedly, as if it were a race he had a bet on, oblivious to what happens in the bar.*)

LARRY (*turns on Hickey with bitter defiance*). And now it's my turn, I suppose? What is it I'm to do to achieve this blessed peace of yours?

HICKEY (*grins at him*). Why, we've discussed all that, Larry. Just stop lying to yourself——

LARRY. You think when I say I'm finished with life, and tired of watching the stupid greed of the human circus, and I'll welcome closing my eyes in the long sleep of death—you think that's a coward's lie?

HICKEY (*chuckling*). Well, what do you think, Larry?

LARRY (*with increasing bitter intensity, more as if he were fighting with himself than with Hickey*). I'm afraid to live, am I?—and even more afraid to die! So I sit here, with my pride drowned on the bottom of a bottle, keeping drunk so I won't see myself shaking in my britches with fright, or hear myself whining and praying: Beloved Christ, let me live a little longer at any price! If it's only for a few days more, or a few hours even, have mercy, Almighty God, and let me still clutch greedily to my yellow heart this sweet treasure, this jewel beyond price, the dirty, stinking bit of withered old flesh which is my beautiful little life! (*He laughs with a sneering, vindictive self-loathing, staring inward at himself with contempt and hatred. Then abruptly he makes Hickey again the antagonist.*) You think you'll make me admit that to myself?

HICKEY (*chuckling*). But you just did admit it, didn't you?

PARRITT (*lifts his head from his hands to glare at Larry—jeeringly*). That's the stuff, Hickey! Show the old yellow faker up! He can't play dead on me like this! He's got to help me!

HICKEY. Yes, Larry, you've got to settle with him. I'm leaving you entirely in his hands. He'll do as good a job as I could at making you give up that old grandstand bluff.

LARRY (*angrily*). I'll see the two of you in hell first!

ROCKY (*calls excitedly from the end of the bar*). Jees, Harry's startin' across de street! He's goin' to fool yuh, Hickey, yuh bastard! (*He pauses, watching—then worriedly.*) What de hell's he stoppin' for? Right in de middle of de street! Yuh'd tink he was paralysed or somethin'! (*Disgustedly.*) Aw, he's quittin'! He's turned back! Jees, look at de old bastard travel! Here he comes!

(*Hope passes the window outside the free-lunch counter in a shambling, panic-stricken run. He comes lurching blindly through the swinging doors and stumbles to the bar at Larry's right.*)

HOPE. Bejees, give me a drink quick! Scared me out of a year's growth! Bejees, that guy ought to be pinched! Bejees, it ain't safe to walk in the streets! Bejees, that ends me! Never again! Give me that bottle! (*He slops a glass full and drains it and pours another—to Rocky, who is regarding him with scorn—appealingly.*) You seen it, didn't you, Rocky?

ROCKY. Seen what?

HOPE. That automobile, you dumb Wop! Feller

driving it must be drunk or crazy. He'd run right over me if I hadn't jumped. (*Ingratiatingly.*) Come on, Larry, have a drink. Everybody have a drink. Have a cigar, Rocky. I know you hardly ever touch it.

ROCKY (*resentfully*). Well, dis is de time I do touch it! (*Pouring a drink.*) I'm goin' to get stinko, see! And if yuh don't like it, yuh know what yuh can do! I gotta good mind to chuck my job, anyway. (*Disgustedly.*) Jees, Harry, I thought yuh had some guts! I was bettin' yuh'd make it and show dat four-flusher up. (*He nods at Hickey—then snorts.*) Automobile, hell! Who d'yuh tink yuh're kiddin'? Dey wasn' no automobile! Yuh just quit cold!

HOPE (*feebly*). Guess I ought to know! Bejees, it almost killed me!

HICKEY (*comes to the bar between him and Larry, and puts a hand on his shoulder—kindly*). Now, now, Governor. Don't be foolish. You've faced the test and come through. You're rid of all that nagging dream stuff now. You know you can't believe it any more.

HOPE (*appeals pleadingly to Larry*). Larry, you saw it, didn't you? Drink up! Have another! Have all you want! Bejees, we'll go on a grand old souse together! You saw that automobile, didn't you?

LARRY (*compassionately, avoiding his eyes*). Sure, I saw it, Harry. You had a narrow escape. Be God, I thought you were a goner!

HICKEY (*turns on him with a flash of sincere indignation*). What the hell's the matter with you, Larry? You know what I told you about the wrong kind of pity. Leave Harry alone! You'd think I was trying to harm him, the fool way you act! My oldest friend! What kind of a louse do you think I am? There isn't anything I wouldn't do for Harry, and he knows it! All I've wanted to do is fix it so he'll be finally at peace with himself for the rest of his days! And if you'll only wait until the final returns are in, you'll find that's exactly what I've accomplished! (*He turns to Hope and pats his shoulder—coaxingly.*) Come now, Governor. What's the use of being stubborn, now when it's all over and dead? Give up that ghost automobile.

HOPE (*beginning to collapse within himself—dully*). Yes, what's the use—now? All a lie! No automobile. But, bejees, something ran over me! Must have been myself, I guess. (*He forces a feeble smile—then wearily.*) Guess I'll sit down. Feel all in. Like a corpse, bejees. (*He picks a bottle and glass from the bar and walks to the first table and slumps down in the chair, facing left-front. His shaking hand misjudges the distance and he sets the bottle on the table with a jar that rouses Hugo, who lifts his head from his arms and blinks at him through his thick spectacles. Hope speaks to him in a flat, dead voice.*) Hello, Hugo. Coming up for air? Stay passed out, that's the right dope. There ain't any cool willow trees—except you grow your own in a bottle. (*He pours a drink and gulps it down.*)

HUGO (*with his silly giggle*). Hello, Harry, stupid proletarian monkey-face! I vill trink champagne beneath the villow—— (*With a change to aristocratic fastidiousness.*) But the slaves must ice it properly! (*With guttural rage.*) Gottamned Hickey! Peddler pimp for nouveau-riche capitalism! When I lead the jackass mob to the sack of Babylon, I vill make them hang him to a lamp-post the first one!

HOPE (*spiritlessly*). Good work. I'll help pull on the rope. Have a drink, Hugo.

HUGO (*frightenedly*). No, thank you. I am too trunk now. I hear myself say crazy things. Do not listen, please. Larry vill tell you I haf never been so crazy trunk. I must sleep it off. (*He starts to put his head on his arms but stops and stares at Hope with growing uneasiness.*) What's matter, Harry? You look funny. You look dead. What's happened? I don't know you. Listen, I feel I am dying, too. Because I am so crazy trunk! It is very necessary I sleep. But I can't sleep here vith you. You look dead. (*He scrambles to his feet in a confused panic, turns his back on Hope and settles into the chair at the next table which faces left. He thrusts his head down on his arms like an ostrich hiding its head in the sand. He does not notice Parritt, nor Parritt him.*)

LARRY (*to Hickey with bitter condemnation*). Another one who's begun to enjoy your peace!

HICKEY. Oh, I know it's tough on him right now, the same as it is on Harry. But that's only the first shock. I promise you they'll both come through all right.

LARRY. And you believe that! I see you do! You mad fool!

HICKEY. Of course, I believe it! I tell you I know from my own experience!

HOPE (*spiritlessly*). Close that big clam of yours, Hickey. Bejees, you're a worse gabber than that nagging bitch, Bessie, was. (*He drinks his drink mechanically and pours another.*)

ROCKY (*in amazement*). Jees, did yuh hear dat?

HOPE (*dully*). What's wrong with this booze? There's no kick in it.

ROCKY (*worriedly*). Jees, Larry, Hugo had it right. He does look like he'd croaked.

HICKEY (*annoyed*). Don't be a damned fool! Give him time. He's coming along all right. (*He calls to Hope with a first trace of underlying uneasiness.*) You're all right, aren't you, Harry?

HOPE (*dully*). I want to pass out like Hugo.

LARRY (*turns to Hickey—with bitter anger*). It's the peace of death you've brought him.

HICKEY (*for the first time loses his temper*). That's a lie! (*But he controls this instantly and grins.*) Well, well, you did manage to get a rise out of me that time. I think such a hell of a lot of Harry—— (*Impatiently.*) You know that's damned foolishness. Look at me. I've been through it. Do I look dead? Just leave Harry alone and wait until the shock wears off and you'll see. He'll be a new man. Like I am. (*He calls to Hope coaxingly.*) How's it coming, Governor? Beginning to feel free, aren't you? Relieved and not guilty any more?

HOPE (*grumbles spiritlessly*). Bejees, you must have been monkeying with the booze, too, you interfering bastard! There's no life in it now. I want to get drunk and pass out. Let's all pass out. Who the hell cares?

HICKEY (*lowering his voice—worriedly to Larry*). I admit I didn't think he'd be hit so hard. He's always been a happy-go-lucky slob. Like I was. Of course, it hit me hard, too. But only for a minute. Then I felt as if a ton of guilt had been lifted off my mind. I saw what had happened was the only possible way for the peace of all concerned.

LARRY (*sharply*). What was it happened? Tell us that! And don't try to get out of it! I want a straight answer! (*Vindictively.*) I think it was something you drove someone else to do!

HICKEY (*puzzled*). Someone else?

LARRY (*accusingly*). What did your wife die of? You've kept that a deep secret, I notice—for some reason!

HICKEY (*reproachfully*). You're not very considerate, Larry. But, if you insist on knowing now, there's no reason you shouldn't. It was a bullet through the head that killed Evelyn.

(*There is a second's tense silence.*)

HOPE (*dully*). Who the hell cares? To hell with her and that nagging old hag, Bessie.

ROCKY. Christ. You had de right dope, Larry.

LARRY (*revengefully*). You drove your poor wife to suicide? I knew it! Be God, I don't blame her! I'd almost do as much myself to be rid of you! It's what you'd like to drive us all to—— (*Abruptly he is ashamed of himself and pitying.*) I'm sorry, Hickey. I'm a rotten louse to throw that in your face.

HICKEY (*quietly*). Oh, that's all right, Larry. But don't jump at conclusions. I didn't say poor Evelyn committed suicide. It's the last thing she'd ever have done, as long as I was alive for her to take care of and forgive. If you'd known her at all, you'd never get such a crazy suspicion. (*He pauses—then slowly.*) No, I'm sorry to have to tell you my poor wife was killed.

(*Larry stares at him with growing horror and shrinks back along the bar away from him. Parritt jerks his head up from his hands and looks around frightenedly, not at Hickey, but at Larry. Rocky's round eyes are popping. Hope stares dully at the table top. Hugo, his head hidden in his arms, gives no sign of life.*)

LARRY (*shakenly*). Then she—was murdered.

PARRITT (*springs to his feet—stammers defensively*). You're a liar, Larry! You must be crazy to say that to me! You know she's still alive!

(*But no one pays any attention to him.*)

ROCKY (*blurts out*). Moidered? Who done it?

LARRY (*his eyes fixed with fascinated horror on Hickey—frightenedly*). Don't ask questions, you dumb Wop! It's none of our damned business! Leave Hickey alone!

HICKEY (*smiles at him with affectionate amusement*). Still the old grandstand bluff, Larry? Or is it some more bum pity? (*He turns to Rocky—matter-of-factly.*) The police don't know who killed her yet, Rocky. But I expect they will before very long. (*As if that finished the subject, he comes forward to Hope and sits beside him, with an arm around his shoulder—affectionately coaxing.*) Coming along fine now, aren't you, Governor? Getting over the first shock? Beginning to feel free from guilt and lying hopes and at peace with yourself?

HOPE (*with a dull callousness*). Somebody croaked your Evelyn, eh? Bejees, my bets are on the iceman! But who the hell cares? Let's get drunk and pass out. (*He tosses down his drink with a lifeless, automatic movement—complainingly.*) Bejees, what did you do to the booze, Hickey? There's no damned life left in it.

PARRITT (*stammers, his eyes on Larry, whose eyes in turn remain fixed on Hickey*). Don't look like that, Larry! You've got to believe what I told you! It had nothing to do with her! It was just to get a few lousy dollars!

HUGO (*suddenly raises his head from his arms and, looking straight in front of him, pounds on the table frightenedly with his small fists*). Don't be a fool! Buy me a trink! But no more vine! It is not properly iced! (*With guttural rage.*) Gottamned stupid proletarian slaves! Buy me a trink or I vill have you shot! (*He collapses into abject begging.*) Please, for Gott's sake! I am not trunk enough! I cannot sleep! Life is a crazy monkey-face! Always there is blood beneath the villow trees! I hate it and I am afraid! (*He hides his face on his arms, sobbing muffledly.*) Please, I am crazy trunk! I say crazy things! For Gott's sake, do not listen to me!

(*But no one pays any attention to him. Larry stands shrunk back against the bar. Rocky is leaning over it. They stare at Hickey. Parritt stands looking pleadingly at Larry.*)

HICKEY (*gazes with worried kindliness at Hope*). You're beginning to worry me, Governor. Something's holding you up somewhere. I don't see why—— You've faced the truth about yourself. You've done what you had to do to kill your nagging pipe dreams. Oh, I know it knocks you cold. But only for a minute. Then you see it was the only possible way to peace. And you feel happy. Like I did. That's what worries me about you, Governor. It's time you began to feel happy——

CURTAIN

ACT FOUR

SCENE. *Same as Act One—the back room with the curtain separating it from the section of the bar-room with its single table at right of curtain, front. It is around half-past one in the morning of the following day.*

The tables in the back room have a new arrangement. The one at left, front, before the window to the yard, is in the same position. So is the one at the right, rear, of it in the second row. But this table now has only one chair. This chair is at right of it, facing directly front. The two tables on either side of the door at rear are unchanged. But the table which was at centre, front, has been pushed towards right so that it and the table at right, rear, of it in the second row, and the last table at right in the front row, are now jammed so closely together that they form one group.

Larry, Hugo and Parritt are at the table at left, front. Larry is at left of it, beside the window, facing front. Hugo sits at rear, facing front, his head on his arms in his habitual position, but he is not asleep. On Hugo's left is Parritt, his chair facing left, front. At right of table, an empty chair, facing left. Larry's chin is on his chest, his eyes fixed on the floor. He will not look at Parritt, who keeps staring at him with a sneering, pleading challenge.

Two bottles of whisky are on each table, whisky and chaser glasses, a pitcher of water.

The one chair by the table at right, rear, of them is vacant.

At the first table at right of centre, Cora sits at left, front, of it, facing front. Around the rear of this table are four empty chairs. Opposite Cora, in a sixth chair, is Captain Lewis, also facing front. On his left, McGloin is facing front in a chair before the middle table of his group. At right, rear, of him, also at this table, General Wetjoen sits facing front. In back of this table are three empty chairs.

At right, rear, of Wetjoen, but beside the last table of the group, sits Willie. On Willie's left, at rear of table, is Hope. On Hope's left, at right, rear, of table, is Mosher. Finally, at right of table is Jimmy Tomorrow. All of the four sit facing front.

There is an atmosphere of oppressive stagnation in the room, and a quality of insensibility about all the people in this group at right. They are like wax figures, set stiffly on their chairs, carrying out mechanically the motions of getting drunk but sunk in a numb stupor which is impervious to stimulation.

In the bar section, Joe is sprawled in the chair at right of table, facing left. His head rolls forward in a sodden slumber. Rocky is standing behind his chair, regarding him with dull hostility. Rocky's face is set in an expression of tired, callous toughness. He looks now like a minor Wop gangster.

ROCKY (*shakes Joe by the shoulder*). Come on, yuh damned nigger! Beat it in de back room! It's after hours. (*But Joe remains inert. Rocky gives up.*) Aw, to hell wid it. Let de dump get pinched. I'm through wid dis lousy job, anyway! (*He hears someone at rear and calls.*) Who's dat?

(*Chuck appears from rear. He has been drinking heavily, but there is no lift to his jag; his manner is grouchy and sullen. He has evidently been brawling. His knuckles are raw and there is a mouse under one eye. He has lost his straw hat, his tie is awry, and his blue suit is dirty. Rocky eyes him indifferently.*)

Been scrappin', huh? Started off on your periodical, ain't yuh? (*For a second there is a gleam of satisfaction in his eyes.*)

CHUCK. Yeah, ain't yuh glad? (*Truculently.*) What's it to yuh?

ROCKY. Not a damn ting. But dis is someting to me. I'm out on my feet holdin' down your job. Yuh said if I'd take your day, yuh'd relieve me at six, and here it's half-past one a.m. Well, yuh're takin' over now, get me, no matter how plastered yuh are!

CHUCK. Plastered, hell! I wisht I was. I've lapped up a gallon, but it don't hit me right. And to hell wid de job. I'm goin' to tell Harry I'm quittin'.

ROCKY. Yeah? Well, I'm quittin', too.

CHUCK. I've played sucker for dat crummy blonde long enough, lettin' her kid me into woikin'. From now on I take it easy.

ROCKY. I'm glad yuh're gettin' some sense.

CHUCK. And I hope yuh're gettin' some. What a prize sap you been, tendin' bar when yuh got two good hustlers in your stable!

ROCKY. Yeah, but I ain't no sap now. I'll loin dem, when dey get back from Coney. (*Sneeringly.*) Jees, dat Cora sure played you for a dope, feedin' yuh dat marriage-on-de-farm hop!

CHUCK (*dully*). Yeah. Hickey got it right. A lousy pipe dream. It was her pulling sherry flips on me woke me up. All de way walkin' to de ferry, every ginmill we come to she'd drag me in to blow her. I got tinkin',

Christ, what won't she want when she gets de ring on her finger and I'm hooked? So I tells her at de ferry, "Kiddo, yuh can go to Joisey, or to hell, but count me out."

ROCKY. She says it was her told you to go to hell, because yuh'd started hittin' de booze.

CHUCK (*ignoring this*). I got tinkin', too, Jees, won't I look sweet wid a wife dat if yuh put all de guys she's stayed wid side by side, dey'd reach to Chicago. (*He sighs gloomily.*) Dat kind of dame, yuh can't trust 'em. De minute your back is toined, dey're cheatin' wid de iceman or someone. Hickey done me a favour, makin' me wake up. (*He pauses—then adds pathetically.*) On'y it was fun, kinda, me and Cora kiddin' ourselves—— (*Suddenly his face hardens with hatred.*) Where is dat son of a bitch, Hickey? I want one good sock at dat guy—just one!—and de next buttin' in he'll do will be in de morgue! I'll take a chance on goin' to de Chair——!

ROCKY (*starts—in a low warning voice*). Piano! Keep away from him, Chuck! He ain't here now, anyway. He went out to phone, he said. He wouldn't call from here. I got a hunch he's beat it. But if he does come back, yuh don't know him, if anyone asks yuh, get me? (*As Chuck looks at him with dull surprise he lowers his voice to a whisper.*) De Chair, maybe dat's where he's goin'. I don't know nuttin', see, but it looks like he croaked his wife.

CHUCK (*with a flash of interest*). Yuh mean she really was cheatin' on him? Den I don't blame de guy——

ROCKY. Who's blamin' him? When a dame asks for it—— But I don't know nuttin' about it, see?

CHUCK. Is any of de gang wise?

ROCKY. Larry is. And de boss ought to be. I tried to wise de rest of dem up to stay clear of him, but dey're all so licked, I don't know if dey got it. (*He pauses—vindictively.*) I don't give a damn what he done to his wife, but if he gets de Hot Seat I won't go into no mournin'!

CHUCK. Me, neider!

ROCKY. Not after his trowin' it in my face I'm a pimp. What if I am? Why de hell not? And what he's done to Harry. Jees, de poor old slob is so licked he can't even get drunk. And all de gang. Dey're all licked. I couldn't help feelin' sorry for de poor bums when dey showed up tonight, one by one, lookin' like pooches wid deir tails between deir legs, dat everyone'd been kickin' till dey was too punch-drunk to feel it no more. Jimmy Tomorrow was de last. Schwartz, de copper, brung him in. Seen him sittin' on de dock on West Street, lookin' at de water and cryin'! Schwartz thought he was drunk and I let him tink it. But he was cold sober. He was tryin' to jump in and didn't have de noive, I figgered it. Noive! Jees, dere ain't enough guts left in de whole gang to battle a mosquito!

CHUCK. Aw, to hell wid 'em! Who cares? Gimme a drink.

(*Rocky pushes the bottle toward him apathetically.*)

I see you been hittin' de redeye, too.

ROCKY. Yeah. But it don't do no good. I can't get drunk right.

(*Chuck drinks. Joe mumbles in his sleep. Chuck regards him resentfully.*)

Dis doity dinge was able to get his snootful and pass out. Jees, even Hickey can't faze a nigger! Yuh'd tink he was fazed if yuh'd seen him come in. Stinko, and he pulled a gat and said he'd plug Hickey for insultin' him. Den he dropped it and begun to cry and said he wasn't a gamblin' man or a tough guy no more; he was yellow. He'd borrowed de gat to stick up someone, and den didn't have de guts. He got drunk panhandlin' drinks in nigger joints, I s'pose. I guess dey felt sorry for him.

CHUCK. He ain't got no business in de bar after hours. Why don't yuh chuck him out?

ROCKY (*apathetically*). Aw, to hell wid it. Who cares?

CHUCK (*lapsing into the same mood*). Yeah. I don't.

JOE (*suddenly lunges to his feet dazedly—mumbles in humbled apology*). Scuse me, White Boys. Scuse me for livin'. I don't want to be where I's not wanted. (*He makes his way swayingly to the opening in the curtain at rear and tacks down to the middle table of the three at right, front. He feels his way around it to the table at its left and gets to the chair in back of Captain Lewis.*)

CHUCK (*gets up—in a callous, brutal tone*). My pig's in de back room, ain't she? I wanna collect de dough I wouldn't take dis mornin', like a sucker, before she blows it. (*He goes rear.*)

ROCKY (*getting up*). I'm comin', too. I'm trough woikin'. I ain't no lousy bartender.

(*Chuck comes through the curtain and looks for Cora as Joe flops down in the chair in back of Captain Lewis.*)

JOE (*taps Lewis on the shoulder—servilely apologetic*). If you objects to my sittin' here, Captain, just tell me and I pulls my freight.

LEWIS. No apology required, old chap. Anybody could tell you I should feel honoured a bloody Kaffir would lower himself to sit beside me.

(*Joe stares at him with sodden perplexity—then closes his eyes. Chuck comes forward to take the chair behind Cora's, as Rocky enters the back room and starts over toward Larry's table.*)

CHUCK (*his voice hard*). I'm waitin', Baby. Dig!

CORA (*with apathetic obedience*). Sure. I been expectin' yuh. I got it all ready. Here.

(*She passes a small roll of bills she has in her hand over her shoulder, without looking at him. He takes it, glances at it suspiciously, then shoves it in his pocket without a word of acknowledgment. Cora speaks with a tired wonder at herself rather than resentment toward him.*)

Jees, imagine me kiddin' myself I wanted to marry a drunken pimp.

CHUCK. Dat's nuttin', Baby. Imagine de sap I'da been, when I can get your dough just as easy widout it!

ROCKY (*takes the chair on Parritt's left, facing Larry—dully*). Hello, Old Cemetery. (*Larry doesn't seem to hear. To Parritt.*) Hello, Tightwad. You still around?

PARRITT (*keeps his eyes on Larry—in a jeeringly challenging tone*). Ask Larry! He knows I'm here, all right, although he's pretending not to! He'd like to forget I'm alive! He's trying to kid himself with that grandstand philosopher stuff! But he knows he can't get away with it now! He kept himself locked in his room until a while ago, alone with a bottle of booze, but he couldn't make it work! He couldn't even get drunk! He had to come out! There must have been something there he was even more scared to face than he is Hickey and me! I guess he got looking at the fire escape and thinking how handy it was, if he was really sick of life and only had the nerve to die! (*He pauses sneeringly.*)

(*Larry's face has tautened, but he pretends he doesn't hear. Rocky pays no attention. His head has sunk forward, and he stares at the table top, sunk in the same stupor as the other occupants of the room. Parritt goes on, his tone becoming more insistent.*)

He's been thinking of me, too, Rocky. Trying to figure a way to get out of helping me! He doesn't want to be bothered understanding. But he does understand all right! He used to love her, too. So he thinks I ought to take a hop off the fire escape! (*He pauses.*)

(*Larry's hands on the table have clinched into fists, as his nails dig into his palms, but he remains silent. Parritt breaks and starts pleading.*)

For God's sake, Larry, can't you say something? Hickey's got me all balled up. Thinking of what he must have done has got me so I don't know any more what I did or why. I can't go on like this! I've got to know what I ought to do——

LARRY (*in a stifled tone*). God damn you? Are you trying to make me your executioner?

PARRITT (*starts frightenedly*). Execution? Then you do think——?

LARRY. I don't think anything!

PARRITT (*with forced jeering*). I suppose you think I ought to die because I sold out a lot of loud-mouthed fakers, who were cheating suckers with a phony pipe dream, and put them where they ought to be, in jail? (*He forces a laugh.*) Don't make me laugh! I ought to get a medal! What a damned old sap you are! You must still believe in the Movement! (*He nudges Rocky with his elbow.*) Hickey's right about him, isn't he, Rocky? An old no-good drunken tramp, as dumb as he is, ought to take a hop off the fire escape!

ROCKY (*dully*). Sure. Why don't he? Or you? Or me? What de hell's de difference? Who cares?

(*There is a faint stir from all the crowd, as if this sentiment struck a responsive chord in their numbed minds. They mumble almost in chorus as one voice, like sleepers talking out of a dully irritating dream,* "The hell with it!" "Who cares?" *Then the sodden silence descends again on the room. Rocky looks from Parritt to Larry puzzledly. He mutters.*)

What am I doin' here wid youse two? I remember I had something on my mind to tell yuh. What——? Oh, I got it now. (*He looks from one to the other of their oblivious faces with a strange, sly, calculating look—ingratiatingly.*) I was tinking how you was bot' reg'lar guys. I tinks, ain't two guys like dem saps to be hangin' round like a coupla stew bums and wastin' demselves. Not dat I blame yuh for not woikin'. On'y suckers woik. But dere's no percentage in bein' broke when yuh can grab good jack for yourself and make someone else woik for yuh, is dere? I mean, like I do. So I tinks, Dey're my pals and I ought to wise up two good guys like dem to play my system, and not be lousy barflies, no good to demselves or nobody else. (*He addresses Parritt now—persuasively.*) What yuh tink, Parritt? Ain't I right? Sure, I am. So don't be a sucker, see? Yuh ain't a bad-lookin' guy. Yuh could easy make some gal who's a good hustler, an' start a stable. I'd help yuh and wise yuh up to de inside dope on de game. (*He pauses inquiringly. Parritt gives no sign of having heard him. Rocky asks impatiently.*) Well, what about it? What if dey do call yuh a pimp? What de hell do you care—any more'n I do.

PARRITT (*without looking at him—vindictively*). I'm through with whores. I wish they were all in jail—or dead!

ROCKY (*ignores this—disappointedly*). So yuh won't touch it, huh? Aw right, stay a bum! (*He turns to Larry.*) Jees, Larry, he's sure one dumb boob, ain't he? Dead from de neck up! He don't know a good ting when he sees it. (*Oily, even persuasive again.*) But how about you, Larry? You ain't dumb. So why not, huh? Sure, yuh're old, but dat don't matter. All de hustlers tink yuh're aces. Dey fall for yuh like yuh was deir uncle or old man or something. Dey'd like takin' care of yuh. And de cops 'round here, dey like yuh, too. It'd be a pipe for yuh, 'specially wid me to help yuh and wise yuh up. Yuh wouldn't have to worry where de next drink's comin' from, or wear doity clothes. (*Hopefully.*) Well, don't it look good to yuh?

LARRY (*glances at him—for a moment he is stirred to sardonic pity*). No, it doesn't look good, Rocky. I mean the peace Hickey's brought you. It isn't contented enough, if you have to make everyone else a pimp, too.

ROCKY (*stares at him stupidly—then pushes his chair back and gets up, grumbling*). I'm a sap to waste time on yuh. A stew bum is a stew bum and yuh can't change him. (*He turns away—then turns back for an afterthought.*) Like I was sayin' to Chuck, yuh better keep away from Hickey. If anyone asks yuh, yuh don't know nuttin', get me? Yuh never even hoid he had a wife. (*His face hardens.*) Jees, we all ought to git drunk and stage a celebration when dat bastard goes to de Chair.

LARRY (*vindictively*). Be God, I'll celebrate with you and drink long life to him in hell! (*Then guiltily and pityingly.*) No! The poor mad devil—— (*Then with angry self-contempt.*) Ah, pity again! The wrong kind! He'll welcome the Chair!

PARRITT (*contemptuously*). Yes, what are you so damned scared of death for? I don't want your lousy pity.

ROCKY. Christ, I hope he don't come back, Larry. We don't know nuttin' now. We're on'y guessin', see? But if de bastard keeps on talkin——

LARRY (*grimly*). He'll come back. He'll keep on talking. He's got to. He's lost his confidence that the peace he's sold us is the real McCoy, and it's made him uneasy about his own. He'll have to prove to us——

(*As he is speaking Hickey appears silently in the doorway at rear. He has lost his beaming salesman's grin. His manner is no longer self-assured. His expression is uneasy, baffled and resentful. It has the stubborn set of an obsessed determination. His eyes are on Larry as he comes in. As he speaks, there is a start from all the crowd, a shrinking away from him.*)

HICKEY (*angrily*). That's a damned lie, Larry! I haven't lost confidence a damned bit! Why should I? (*Boastfully.*) By God, whenever I made up my mind to sell someone something I knew they ought to want, I've sold 'em! (*He suddenly looks confused—haltingly.*) I mean—it isn't kind of you, Larry, to make that kind of crack when I've been doing my best to help——

ROCKY (*moving away from him toward right—sharply*). Keep away from me! I don't know nuttin' about yuh, see? (*His tone is threatening but his manner as he turns his back and ducks quickly across to the bar entrance is that of one in flight. In the bar he comes forward and slumps in a chair at the table, facing front.*)

HICKEY (*comes to the table at right, rear, of Larry's table and sits in the one chair there, facing front. He looks over the crowd at right, hopefully and then disappointedly. He speaks with a strained attempt at his old affectionate jollying manner*). Well, well! How are you coming along, everybody? Sorry I had to leave you for a while, but there was something I had to get finally settled. It's all fixed now.

HOPE (*in the voice of one reiterating mechanically a hopeless complaint*). When are you going to do something about this booze, Hickey? Bejees, we all know you did something to take the life out of it. It's like drinking dish-water! We can't pass out! And you promised us peace.

(*His group all join in in a dull, complaining chorus,* "We can't pass out! You promised us peace!")

HICKEY (*bursts into resentful exasperation*). For God's sake, Harry, are you still harping on that damned nonsense! You've kept it up all afternoon and night! And you've got everybody else singing the same crazy tune! I've had about all I can stand—that's why I phoned—— (*He controls himself.*) Excuse me, boys and girls. I don't mean that. I'm just worried about you, when you play dead on me like this. I was hoping by the time I got back you'd be like you ought to be! I thought you were deliberately holding back, while I was around, because you didn't want to give me the satisfaction of showing me I'd had the right dope. And I did have! I know from my own experience. (*Exasperatedly.*) But I've explained that a million times! And you've all done what you needed to do! By rights you should be contented now, without a single damned hope or lying dream left to torment you! But here you are, acting like a lot of stiffs cheating the undertaker! (*He looks around accusingly.*) I can't figure it—unless it's just your damned pigheaded stubbornness! (*He breaks—miserably.*) Hell, you oughtn't to act this way with me! You're my old pals, the only friends I've got. You know the one thing I want is to see you all happy before I go—— (*Rousing himself to his old brisk, master-of-ceremonies manner.*) And there's damned little time left now. I've made a date for two o'clock. We've got to get busy right away and find out what's wrong. (*There is a sodden silence. He goes on exasperatedly.*) Can't you appreciate what you've got, for God's sake? Don't you know you're free now to be yourselves, without having to feel remorse or guilt, or lie to yourselves about reforming tomorrow? Can't you see there is no to-morrow now? You're rid of it for ever! You've killed it! You don't have to care a damn about anything any more! You've finally got the game of life licked, don't you see that? (*Angrily exhorting.*) Then why the hell don't you get pie-eyed and celebrate? Why don't you laugh and sing "Sweet Adeline"? (*With bitterly hurt accusation.*) The only reason I can think of is, you're putting on this rotten half-dead act just to get back at me! Because you hate my guts! (*He breaks again.*) God, don't do that, gang! It makes me feel like hell to think you hate me. It makes me feel you suspect I must have hated you. But that's a lie! Oh, I know I used to hate everyone in the world who wasn't as rotten a bastard as I was! But that was when I was still living in hell—before I faced the truth and saw the one possible way to free poor Evelyn and give her the peace she'd always dreamed about. (*He pauses.*)

(*Everyone in the group stirs with awakening dread and they all begin to grow tense on their chairs.*)

CHUCK (*without looking at Hickey—with dull, resentful viciousness*). Aw, put a bag over it! To hell wid Evelyn! What if she was cheatin'? And who cares what yuh did to her? Dat's your funeral. We don't give a damn, see?

(*There is a dull, resentful chorus of assent,* "We don't give a damn," *Chuck adds dully.*)

All we want outa you is keep de hell away from us and give us a rest.

(*A muttered chorus of assent.*)

HICKEY (*as if he hadn't heard this—an obsessed look on his face*). The one possible way to make up to her for all I'd made her go through, and get her rid of me so I couldn't make her suffer any more, and she wouldn't have to forgive me again! I saw I couldn't do it by killing myself, like I wanted to for a long time. That would have been the last straw for her. She'd have died of a broken heart to think I could do that to her. She'd have blamed herself for it, too. Or I couldn't just run away from her. She'd have died of grief and humiliation if I'd done that to her. She'd have thought I'd stopped loving her. (*He adds with a strange impressive simplicity.*) You see, Evelyn loved me. And I loved her. That was the trouble. It would have been easy to find a way out if she hadn't loved me so much. Or if I hadn't loved her. But as it was, there was only one possible way. (*He pauses—then adds simply.*) I had to kill her.

(*There is a second's dead silence as he finishes—then a tense indrawn breath like a gasp from the crowd, and a general shrinking movement.*)

LARRY (*bursts out*). You mad fool, can't you keep your mouth shut! We may hate you for what you've done this time, but we remember the old times, too, when you brought kindness and laughter with you instead of death! We don't want to know things that will make us help send you to the Chair!

PARRITT (*with angry scorn*). Ah, shut up, you yellow faker! Can't you face anything? Wouldn't I deserve the Chair, too, if I'd—— It's worse if you kill someone and they have to go on living. I'd be glad of the Chair! It'd wipe it out! It'd square me with myself!

HICKEY (*disturbed—with a movement of repulsion*). I wish you'd get rid of that bastard, Larry. I can't have him pretending there's something in common between him and me. It's what's in your heart that counts. There was love in my heart, not hate.

PARRITT (*glares at him in angry terror*). You're a liar! I don't hate her! I couldn't! And it had nothing to do with her, anyway! You ask Larry!

LARRY (*grabs his shoulder and shakes him furiously*). God damn you, stop shoving your rotten soul in my lap!

(*Parritt subsides, hiding his face in his hands and shuddering.*)

HICKEY (*goes on quietly now*). Don't worry about the Chair, Larry. I know it's still hard for you not to be terrified by death, but when you've made peace with yourself, like I have, you won't give a damn. (*He addresses the group at right again—earnestly.*) Listen, everybody. I've made up my mind the only way I can clear things up for you, so you'll realize how contented and carefree you ought to feel, now I've made you get rid of your pipe dreams, is to show you what a pipe dream did to me and Evelyn. I'm certain if I tell you about it from the beginning, you'll appreciate what I've done for you and why I did it, and how damned grateful you ought to be—instead of hating me. (*He begins eagerly in a strange running narrative manner.*) You see, even when we were kids, Evelyn and me——

HOPE (*bursts out, pounding with his glass on the table*). No! Who the hell cares? We don't want to hear it. All we want is to pass out and get drunk and a little peace!

(*They are all, except Larry and Parritt, seized by the same fit and pound with their glasses, even Hugo, and Rocky in the bar, and shout in chorus,* "Who the hell cares? We want to pass out!")

HICKEY (*with an expression of wounded hurt*). All right, if that's the way you feel. I don't want to cram it down your throats. I don't need to tell anyone. I don't feel guilty. I'm only worried about you.

HOPE. What did you do to this booze? That's what we'd like to hear. Bejees, you done something. There's no life or kick in it now. (*He appeals mechanically to Jimmy Tomorrow.*) Ain't that right, Jimmy?

JIMMY (*more than any of them, his face has a wax-figure blankness that makes it look embalmed. He answers in a precise, completely lifeless voice, but his reply is not to Harry's question, and he does not look at him or anyone else*). Yes. Quite right. It was all a stupid lie—my nonsense about tomorrow. Naturally, they would never give me my position back. I would never dream of asking them. It would be hopeless. I didn't resign. I was fired for drunkenness. And that was years ago. I'm much worse now. And it was absurd of me to excuse my drunkenness by pretending it was my wife's adultery that ruined my life. As Hickey guessed, I was a drunkard before that. Long before. I discovered early in life that living frightened me when I was sober. I have forgotten why I married Marjorie. I can't even remember now if she was pretty. She was a blonde, I think, but I couldn't swear to it. I had some idea of wanting a home, perhaps. But, of course, I much preferred the nearest pub. Why Marjorie married me, God knows. It's impossible to believe she loved me. She soon found I much preferred drinking all night with my pals to being in bed with her. So, naturally, she was unfaithful. I didn't blame her. I really didn't care. I was glad to be free—even grateful to her, I think, for giving me such a good tragic excuse to drink as much as I damned well pleased. (*He stops like a mechanical doll that has run down.*)

(*No one gives any sign of having heard him. There is a heavy silence. Then Rocky, at the table in the bar, turns grouchily as he hears a noise behind him. Two men come quietly forward. One, Moran, is middle-aged. The other, Lieb, is in his twenties. They look ordinary in every way, without anything distinctive to indicate what they do for a living.*)

ROCKY (*grumpily*). In de back room if yuh wanta drink.

(*Moran makes a peremptory sign to be quiet. All of a sudden Rocky senses they are detectives and springs up to face them, his expression freezing into a wary blankness. Moran pulls back his coat to show his badge.*)

MORAN (*in a low voice*). Guy named Hickman in the back room?

ROCKY. Tink I know de names of all de guys——?

MORAN. Listen, you! This is murder. And don't be a sap. It was Hickman himself phoned in and said we'd find him here around two.

ROCKY (*dully*). So dat's who he phoned to. (*He shrugs his shoulders.*) Aw right, if he asked for it. He's de fat guy sittin' alone. (*He slumps down in his chair again.*) And if yuh want a confession all yuh got to do is listen. He'll be tellin' all about it soon. Yuh can't stop de bastard talkin'.

(*Moran gives him a curious look, then whispers to Lieb, who disappears rear and a moment later appears in the hall doorway of the back room. He spots Hickey and slides into a chair at the left of the doorway, cutting off escape by the hall. Moran goes back and stands in the opening in the curtain leading to the back room. He sees Hickey and stands watching him and listening.*)

HICKEY (*suddenly bursts out*). I've got to tell you! Your being the way you are now gets my goat! It's all wrong! It puts things in my mind—about myself. It makes me think, if I got balled up about you, how do I know I wasn't balled up about myself? And that's plain damned foolishness. When you know the story of me and Evelyn, you'll see there wasn't any other possible way out of it, for her sake. Only I've got to start way back at the beginning or you won't understand. (*He starts his story, his tone again becoming musingly reminiscent.*) You see, even as a kid I was always restless. I had to keep on the go. You've heard the old saying, "Ministers' sons are sons of guns." Well, that was me, and then some. Home was like a jail. I didn't fall for the religious bunk. Listening to my old man whooping up hell fire and scaring those Hoosier suckers into shelling out their dough only handed me a laugh, although I had to hand it to him, the way he sold them nothing for something. I guess I take after him, and that's what made me a good salesman. Well, anyway, as I said, home was like jail, and so was school, and so was that damned hick town. The only place I liked was the pool rooms, where I could smoke Sweet Caporals, and mop up a couple of beers, thinking I was a hell-on-wheels sport. We had one hooker shop in town, and, of course, I liked that, too. Not that I hardly ever had entrance money. My old man was a tight old bastard. But I liked to sit around in the parlour and joke with the girls, and they liked me because I could kid 'em along and make 'em laugh. Well, you know what a small town is. Everyone got wise to me. They all said I was a no-good tramp. I didn't give a damn what they said. I hated everybody in the place. That is, except Evelyn. I loved Evelyn. Even as a kid. And Evelyn loved me. (*He pauses.*)

(*No one moves or gives any sign except by the dread in their eyes that they have heard him. Except Parritt, who takes his hands from his face to look at Larry pleadingly.*)

PARRITT. I loved Mother, Larry! No matter what she did! I still do! Even though I know she wishes now I was dead! You believe that, don't you? Christ, why can't you say something?

HICKEY (*too absorbed in his story now to notice this—goes on in a tone of fond, sentimental reminiscence*). Yes, sir, as far back as I can remember, Evelyn and I loved each other. She always stuck up for me. She wouldn't believe the gossip—or she'd pretend she didn't. No one could convince her I was no good. Evelyn was stubborn as all hell once she'd made up her mind. Even when I'd admit things and ask her forgiveness, she'd make excuses for me and defend me against myself. She'd kiss me and say she knew I didn't mean it and I wouldn't do it again. So I'd promise I wouldn't. I'd have to promise, she was so sweet and good, though I knew darned well—— (*A touch of strange bitterness comes into his voice for a moment.*) No, sir, you couldn't stop Evelyn. Nothing on earth could shake her faith in me. Even I couldn't. She was a sucker for a pipe dream. (*Then quickly.*) Well, naturally, her family forbid her seeing me. They were one of the town's best, rich for that hick burg, owned the trolley line and lumber company. Strict Methodists, too. They hated my guts. But they couldn't stop Evelyn. She'd sneak notes to me and meet me on the sly. I was getting more restless. The town was getting more like a jail. I made up my mind to beat it. I knew exactly what I wanted to be by that time. I'd met a lot of drummers around the hotel and liked 'em. They were always telling jokes. They were sports. They kept moving. I liked their life. And I knew I could kid people and sell things. The hitch was how to get the railroad fare to the Big Town. I told Mollie Arlington my trouble. She was the madame of the cathouse. She liked me. She laughed and said, "Hell, I'll stake you, Kid! I'll bet on you. With that grin of yours and that line of bull, you ought to be able to sell skunks for good ratters!" (*He chuckles.*) Mollie was all right. She gave me confidence in myself. I paid her back, the first money I earned. Wrote her a kidding letter, I remember, saying I was peddling baby carriages and she and the girls had better take advantage of our bargain offer. (*He chuckles.*) But that's ahead of my story. The night before I left town, I had a date with Evelyn. I got all worked up, she was so pretty and sweet and good. I told her straight, "You better forget me, Evelyn, for your own sake. I'm no good and never will be. I'm not worthy to wipe your shoes." I broke down and cried. She just said, looking white and scared, "Why, Teddy? Don't you still love me?" I said, "Love you? God, Evelyn, I love you more than anything in the world. And I always will!" She said, "Then nothing else matters, Teddy, because nothing but death could stop my loving you. So I'll wait, and when you're ready you send for me and we'll be married. I know I can make you happy, Teddy, and once you're happy you won't want to do any of the bad things you've done any more." And I said, "Of course, I won't, Evelyn!" I meant it, too. I believed it. I loved her so much she could make me believe anything. (*He sighs.*)

(*There is a suspended, waiting silence. Even the two detectives are drawn into it. Then Hope breaks into dully exasperated, brutally callous protest.*)

HOPE. Get it over, you long-winded bastard! You married her, and you caught her cheating with the iceman, and you croaked her, and who the hell cares? What's she to us? All we want is to pass out in peace, bejees!

(*A chorus of dull, resentful protest from all the group. They mumble, like sleepers who curse a person who keeps awakening them,* "What's it to us? We want to pass out in peace!" *Hope drinks and they mechanically follow his example. He pours another and they do the same. He complains with a stupid, nagging insistence.*)

No life in the booze! No kick! Dishwater. Bejees, I'll never pass out!

HICKEY (*goes on as if there had been no interruption*). So I beat it to the Big Town. I got a job easy, and it was a cinch for me to make good. I had the knack. It was like a game, sizing people up quick, spotting what their pet pipe dreams were, and then kidding 'em along that line, pretending you believed what they wanted to believe about themselves. Then they liked you, they trusted you, they wanted to buy something to show their gratitude. It was fun. But still, all the while I felt guilty, as if I had no right to be having such a good time away from Evelyn. In each letter I'd tell her how I missed her, but I'd keep warning her, too. I'd tell her all my faults, how I liked my booze every once in a while, and so on. But there was no shaking Evelyn's belief in me, or her dreams about the future. After each letter of hers, I'd be as full of faith as she was. So as soon as I got enough saved to start us off, I sent for her and we got married. Christ, wasn't I happy for a while! And wasn't she happy! I don't care what anyone says, I'll bet there never was two people who loved each other more than me and Evelyn. Not only then but always after, in spite of everything I did—— (*He pauses—then sadly.*) Well, it's all there, at the start, everything that happened afterwards. I never could learn to handle temptation. I'd want to reform and mean it. I'd promise Evelyn, and I'd promise myself, and I'd believe it. I'd tell her, it's the last time. And she'd say, "I know it's the last time, Teddy. You'll never do it again." That's what made it so hard. That's what made me feel such a rotten skunk—her always forgiving me. My playing around with women, for instance. It was only a harmless good time to me. Didn't mean anything. But I'd know what it meant to Evelyn. So I'd say to myself, never again. But you know how it is, travelling around. The damned hotel rooms. I'd get seeing things in the wall paper. I'd get bored as hell. Lonely and homesick. But at the same time sick of home. I'd feel free and I'd want to celebrate a little. I never drank on the job, so it had to be dames. Any tart. What I'd want was some tramp I could be myself with without being ashamed—someone I could tell a dirty joke to and she'd laugh.

CORA (*with a dull, weary bitterness*). Jees, all de lousy jokes I've had to listen to and pretend was funny!

HICKEY (*goes on obliviously*). Sometimes I'd try some joke I thought was a corker on Evelyn. She'd always make herself laugh. But I could tell she thought it was dirty, not funny. And Evelyn always knew about the tarts I'd been with when I came home from a trip. She'd kiss me and look in my eyes, and she'd know. I'd see in her eyes how she was trying not to know, and then telling herself even if it was true, he couldn't help it, they tempt him, and he's lonely, he hasn't got me, it's only his body, anyway, he doesn't love them, I'm the only one he loves. She was right, too. I never loved anyone else. Couldn't if I wanted to. (*He pauses.*) She forgave me even when it all had to come out in the open. You know how it is when you keep taking chances. You may be lucky for a long time, but you get nicked in the end. I picked up a nail from some tart in Altoona.

CORA (*dully, without resentment*). Yeah. And she picked it up from some guy. It's all in de game. What de hell of it?

HICKEY. I had to do a lot of lying and stalling when I got home. It didn't do any good. The quack I went to got all my dough and then told me I was cured and I took his word. But I wasn't, and poor Evelyn—— But she did her best to make me believe she fell for my lie about how travelling men get things from drinking-cups on trains. Anyway, she forgave me. The same way she forgave me every time I'd turn up after a periodical drunk. You all know what I'd be like at the end of one. You've seen me. Like something lying in the gutter that no alley cat would lower itself to drag in—something they threw out of the D.T. ward in Bellevue along with the garbage, something that ought to be dead and isn't! (*His face is convulsed with self-loathing.*) Evelyn wouldn't have heard from me in a month or more. She'd have been waiting there alone, with the neighbours shaking their heads and feeling sorry for her out loud. That was before she got me to move to the outskirts, where there weren't any next-door neighbours. And then the door would open and in I'd stumble—looking like what I've said—into her home, where she kept everything so spotless and clean. And I'd sworn it would never happen again, and now I'd have to start swearing again this was the last time. I could see disgust having a battle in her eyes with love. Love always won. She'd make herself kiss me, as if nothing had happened, as if I'd just come home from a business trip. She'd never complain or bawl me out. (*He bursts out in a tone of anguish that has anger and hatred beneath it.*) Christ, can you imagine what a guilty skunk she made me feel! If she'd only admitted once she didn't believe any more in her pipe dream that some day I'd behave! But she never would. Evelyn was stubborn as hell. Once she'd set her heart on anything, you couldn't shake her faith that it had to come true—tomorrow! It was the same old story, over and over, for years and years. It kept piling up, inside her and inside me. God, can you picture all I made her suffer, and all the guilt she made me feel, and how I hated myself! If she only hadn't been so damned good—if she'd been the same kind of wife I was a husband. God, I used to pray sometimes she'd—I'd even say to her, "Go on, why don't you, Evelyn? It'd serve me right. I wouldn't mind. I'd forgive you." Of course, I'd pretend I was kidding—the same way I used to joke here about her being in the hay with the iceman. She'd have been so hurt if I'd said it seriously. She'd have thought I'd stopped loving her. (*He pauses—then looking around at them.*) I suppose you think I'm a liar, that no woman could have stood all she stood and still loved me so much—that it isn't human for any woman to be so pitying and forgiving. Well, I'm not lying, and if you'd ever seen her, you'd realize I wasn't. It was written all over her face, sweetness and love and pity and forgiveness. (*He reaches mechanically for the inside pocket of his coat.*) Wait! I'll show you. I always carry her picture. (*Suddenly he looks startled. He stares before him, his hand falling back—quietly.*) No, I'm forgetting I tore it up—afterwards. I didn't need it any more. (*He pauses.*)

(*The silence is like that in the room of a dying man where people hold their breath, waiting for him to die.*)

CORA (*with a muffled sob*). Jees, Hickey! Jees! (*She shivers and puts her hands over her face.*)

PARRITT (*to Larry in a low insistent tone*). I burnt up Mother's picture, Larry. Her eyes followed me all the time. They seemed to be wishing I was dead!

HICKEY. It kept piling up, like I've said. I got so I thought of it all the time. I hated myself more and more, thinking of all the wrong I'd done to the sweetest woman in the world who loved me so much. I got so I'd curse myself for a lousy bastard every time I saw myself in the mirror. I felt such pity for her it drove me crazy. You wouldn't believe a guy like me, that's knocked around so much, could feel such pity. It got so every night I'd wind up hiding my face in her lap, bawling and begging her forgiveness. And, of course, she'd always comfort me and say, "Never mind, Teddy, I know you won't ever again." Christ, I loved her so, but I began to hate that pipe dream! I began to be afraid I was going bughouse, because sometimes I couldn't forgive her for forgiving me. I even caught myself hating her for making me hate myself so much. There's a limit to the guilt you can feel and the forgiveness and the pity you can take! You have to begin blaming someone else, too. I got so sometimes when she'd kiss me it was like she did it on purpose to humiliate me, as if she'd spit in my face! But all the time I saw how crazy and rotten of me that was and it made me hate myself all the more. You'd never believe I could hate so much, a good-natured, happy-go-lucky slob like me. And as the time got nearer to when I was due to come here for my drunk around Harry's birthday, I got nearly crazy. I kept swearing to her every night that this time I really wouldn't, until I'd made it a real final test to myself—and to her. And she kept encouraging me and saying, "I can see you really mean it now, Teddy. I know you'll conquer it this time, and we'll be so happy, dear." When she'd say that and kiss me, I'd believe it, too. Then she'd go to bed, and I'd stay up alone because I couldn't sleep and I didn't want to disturb her, tossing and rolling around. I'd get so damned lonely. I'd get thinking how peaceful it was here, sitting around with the old gang, getting drunk and forgetting love, joking and laughing and singing and swapping lies. And finally I knew I'd have to come. And I knew if I came this time, it was the finish. I'd never have the guts to go back and be forgiven again, and that would break Evelyn's heart because to her it would mean I didn't love her any more. (*He pauses.*) That last night, I'd driven myself crazy trying to figure some way out for her. I went in the bedroom. I was going to tell her it was the end. But I couldn't do that to her. She was sound asleep. I thought, God, if she'd only never wake up, she'd never know! And then it came to me—the only possible way out, for her sake. I remembered I'd given her a gun for protection while I was away and it was in the bureau drawer. She'd never feel any pain, never wake up from her dream. So I——

HOPE (*tries to ward this off by pounding with his glass on the table—with brutal, callous exasperation*). Give us a rest, for the love of Christ! Who the hell cares? We want to pass out in peace!

(*They all, except Parritt and Larry, pound with their glasses and grumble in chorus:* "Who the hell cares? We want to pass out in peace!" *Moran, the detective, moves quietly from the entrance in the curtain across the back of the room to the table where his companion, Lieb, is sitting. Rocky notices his leaving and gets up from the table in the rear and goes back to stand and watch in the entrance. Moran exchanges a glance with Lieb, motioning him to get up. The latter does so. No one notices them. The clamour of banging glasses dies out as abruptly as it started. Hickey hasn't appeared to hear it.*)

HICKEY (*simply*). So I killed her.

(*There is a moment of dead silence. Even the detectives are caught in it and stand motionless.*)

PARRITT (*suddenly gives up and relaxes limply in his chair—in a low voice in which there is a strange exhausted relief*). I may as well confess, Larry. There's no use lying any more. You know, anyway. I didn't give a damn about the money. It was because I hated her.

HICKEY (*obliviously*). And then I saw I'd always known that was the only possible way to give her peace and free her from the misery of loving me. I saw it meant peace for me, too, knowing she was at peace. I felt as though a ton of guilt was lifted off my mind. I remember I stood by the bed and suddenly I had to laugh. I couldn't help it, and I knew Evelyn would forgive me. I remember I heard myself speaking to her, as if it was something I'd always wanted to say: "Well, you know what you can do with your pipe dream now, you damned bitch!" (*He stops with a horrified start, as if shocked out of a nightmare, as if he couldn't believe he heard what he had just said. He stammers.*) No! I never——!

PARRITT (*to Larry—sneeringly*). Yes, that's it! Her and the damned old Movement pipe dream! Eh, Larry?

HICKEY (*bursts into frantic denial*). No! That's a lie! I never said——! Good God, I couldn't have said that! If I did, I'd gone insane! Why, I loved Evelyn better than anything in life! (*He appeals brokenly to the crowd.*) Boys, you're all my old pals! You've known old Hickey for years! You know I'd never—— (*His eyes fix on Hope.*) You've known me longer than anyone, Harry. You know I must have been insane, don't you, Governor?

HOPE (*at first with the same defensive callousness—without looking at him*). Who the hell cares? (*Then suddenly he looks at Hickey and there is an extraordinary change in his expression. His face lights up, as if he were grasping at some dawning hope in his mind. He speaks with a groping eagerness.*) Insane? You mean—you went really insane?

(*At the tone of his voice, all the group at the tables by him start and stare at him as if they caught his thought. Then they all look at Hickey eagerly, too.*)

HICKEY. Yes! Or I couldn't have laughed! I couldn't have said that to her!

(*Moran walks up behind him on one side, while the second detective, Lieb, closes in on him from the other.*)

MORAN (*taps Hickey on the shoulder*). That's enough, Hickman. You know who we are. You're under arrest.

(*He nods to Lieb, who slips a pair of handcuffs on Hickey's wrists. Hickey stares at them with stupid incomprehension. Moran takes his arm.*)

Come along and spill your guts where we can get it on paper.

HICKEY. No, wait Officer! You owe me a break! I phoned and made it easy for you, didn't I? Just a few minutes! (*To Hope—pleadingly.*) You know I couldn't say that to Evelyn, don't you, Harry—unless——

HOPE (*eagerly*). And you've been crazy ever since? Everything you've said and done here——

HICKEY (*for a moment forgets his own obsession and his face takes on its familiar expression of affectionate amusement and he chuckles*). Now, Governor! Up to your old tricks, eh? I see what you're driving at, but I can't let you get away with—— (*Then, as Hope's expression turns to resentful callousness again and he looks away, he adds hastily with pleading desperation.*) Yes, Harry, of course, I've been out of my mind ever since! All the time I've been here! You saw I was insane, didn't you?

MORAN (*with cynical disgust*). Can it! I've had enough of your act. Save it for the jury. (*Addressing the crowd sharply.*) Listen, you guys. Don't fall for his lies. He's starting to get foxy now and thinks he'll plead insanity. But he can't get away with it.

(*The crowd at the grouped tables are grasping at hope now. They glare at him resentfully.*)

HOPE (*begins to bristle in his old-time manner*). Bejees, you dumb dick, you've got a crust trying to tell us about Hickey! We've known him for years, and every one of us noticed he was nutty the minute he showed up here! Bejees, if you'd heard all the crazy bull he was pulling about bringing us peace—like a bughouse preacher escaped from an asylum! If you'd seen all the damned-fool things he made us do! We only did them because—— (*He hesitates—then defiantly.*) Because we hoped he'd come out of it if we kidded him along and humoured him. (*He looks around at the others.*) Ain't that right, fellers ?

(*They burst into a chorus of eager assent :* " Yes, Harry ! " " That's it, Harry ! " " That's why ! " " We knew he was crazy ! " " Just to humour him ! ")

MORAN. A fine bunch of rats ! Covering up for a dirty, cold-blooded murderer.

HOPE (*stung into recovering all his old fuming truculence*). Is that so ? Bejees, you know the old story, when Saint Patrick drove the snakes out of Ireland they swam to New York and joined the police force ! Ha ! (*He cackles insultingly.*) Bejees, we can believe it now when we look at you, can't we, fellers ?

(*They all growl assent, glowering defiantly at Moran. Moran glares at them, looking as if he'd like to forget his prisoner and start cleaning out the place. Hope goes on pugnaciously.*)

You stand up for your rights, bejees, Hickey ! Don't let this smart-aleck dick get funny with you. If he pulls any rubber-hose tricks, you let me know ! I've still got friends at the Hall ! Bejees, I'll have him back in uniform pounding a beat where the only graft he'll get will be stealing tin cans from the goats !

MORAN (*furiously*). Listen, you cockeyed old bum, for a plugged nickel I'd—— (*Controlling himself, turns to Hickey, who is oblivious to all this, and yanks his arm.*) Come on, you !

HICKEY (*with a strange mad earnestness*). Oh, I want to go, Officer. I can hardly wait now. I should have phoned you from the house right afterwards. It was a waste of time coming here. I've got to explain to Evelyn. But I know she's forgiven me. She knows I was insane. You've got me all wrong, Officer. I want to go to the Chair.

MORAN. Crap !

HICKEY (*exasperatedly*). God, you're a dumb dick ! Do you suppose I give a damn about life now ? Why, you bonehead, I haven't got a single damned lying hope or pipe dream left !

MORAN (*jerks him around to face the door to the hall*). Get a move on !

HICKEY (*as they start walking toward rear—insistently*). All I want you to see is I was out of my mind afterwards, when I laughed at her ! I was a raving rotten lunatic or I couldn't have said—— Why, Evelyn was the only thing on God's earth I ever loved ! I'd have killed myself before I'd ever have hurt her !

(*They disappear in the hall. Hickey's voice keeps on protesting.*)

HOPE (*calls after him*). Don't worry, Hickey ! They can't give you the Chair ! We'll testify you was crazy ! Won't we, fellers ?

(*They all assent. Two or three echo Hope's* " Don't worry, Hickey." *Then from the hall comes the slam of the street door. Hope's face falls —with genuine sorrow.*)

He's gone. Poor crazy son of a bitch ! (*All the group around him are sad and sympathetic, too. Hope reaches for his drink.*) Bejees, I need a drink. (*They grab their glasses. Hope says hopefully.*) Bejees, maybe it'll have the old kick, now he's gone.

(*He drinks and they follow suit.*)

ROCKY (*comes forward from where he has stood in the bar entrance—hopefully*). Yeah, Boss, maybe we can get drunk now. (*He sits in the chair by Chuck and pours a drink and tosses it down.*)

(*Then they all sit still, waiting for the effect, as if this drink were a crucial test, so absorbed in hopeful expectancy that they remain oblivious to what happens at Larry's table.*)

LARRY (*his eyes full of pain and pity—in a whisper, aloud to himself*). May the Chair bring him peace at last, the poor tortured bastard !

PARRITT (*leans toward him—in a strange low insistent voice*). Yes, but he isn't the only one who needs peace, Larry. I can't feel sorry for him. He's lucky. He's through, now. It's all decided for him. I wish it was decided for me. I've never been any good at deciding things. Even about selling out, it was the tart the detective agency got after me who put it in my mind. You remember what Mother's like, Larry. She makes all the decisions. She's always decided what I must do. She doesn't like anyone to be free but herself. (*He pauses, as if waiting for comment, but Larry ignores him.*) I suppose you think I ought to have made those dicks take me away with Hickey. But how could I prove it, Larry ! They'd think I was nutty. Because she's still alive. You're the only one who can understand how guilty I am. Because you know her and what I've done to her. You know I'm really much guiltier than he is. You know what I did is a much worse murder. Because she is dead and yet she has to live. For a while. But she can't live long in jail. She loves freedom too much. And I can't kid myself like Hickey, that she's at peace. As long as she lives, she'll never be able to forget what I've done to her even in her sleep. She'll never have a second's peace. (*He pauses—then bursts out.*) Jesus, Larry, can't you say something ? (*Larry is at the breaking point. Parritt goes on.*) And I'm not putting up any bluff, either, that I was crazy afterwards when I laughed to myself and thought, " You know what you can do with your freedom pipe dream now, don't you, you damned old bitch ! "

LARRY (*snaps and turns on him, his face convulsed with detestation. His quivering voice has a condemning command in it*). Go ! Get the hell out of life, God damn you, before I choke it out of you ! Go up——!

PARRITT (*his manner is at once transformed. He seems suddenly at peace with himself. He speaks simply and gratefully*). Thanks, Larry. I just wanted to be sure. I can see now it's the only possible way I can ever get free from her. I guess I've really known that all my life. (*He pauses—then with a derisive smile.*) It ought to comfort Mother a little, too. It'll give her the chance to play the great incorruptible Mother of the Revolution, whose only child is the Proletariat. She'll be able to say : " Justice is done ! So may all traitors die ! " She'll be able to say : " I am glad he's dead ! Long live the Revolution ! " (*He adds with a final implacable jeer.*) You know her, Larry ! Always a ham !

LARRY (*pleads distractedly*). Go, for the love of Christ, you mad tortured bastard, for your own sake !

(*Hugo is roused by this. He lifts his head and peers uncomprehendingly at Larry. Neither Larry nor Parritt notices him.*)

PARRITT (*stares at Larry. His face begins to crumble as if he were going to break down and sob. He turns his head away, but reaches out fumblingly and pats Larry's arm and stammers*). Jesus, Larry, thanks. That's kind. I knew you were the only one who could understand my side of it. (*He gets to his feet and turns towards the door.*)

HUGO (*looks at Parritt and bursts into his silly giggle*). Hello, leedle Don, leedle monkey-face ! Don't be a fool ! Buy me a trink !

PARRITT (*puts on an act of dramatic bravado—forcing a grin*). Sure, I will, Hugo ! Tomorrow ! Beneath the willow trees !

(*He walks to the door with a careless swagger and disappears in the hall. From now on, Larry waits, listening for the sound he knows is coming from the backyard outside the window, but trying not to listen, in an agony of horror and cracking nerve.*)

HUGO (*stares after Parritt stupidly*). Stupid fool ! Hickey make you crazy, too. (*He turns to the oblivious Larry—with a timid eagerness.*) I'm glad, Larry, they take that crazy Hickey avay to asylum. He makes me have bad dreams. He makes me tell lies about myself. He makes me want to spit on all I have ever dreamed. Yes, I am glad they take him to asylum. I don't feel I am dying now. He vas selling death to me, that crazy salesman. I think I have a trink now, Larry. (*He pours a drink and gulps it down.*)

HOPE (*jubilantly*). Bejees, fellers, I'm feeling the old kick, or I'm a liar ! It's putting life back in me ! Bejees, if all I've lapped up begins to hit me, I'll be paralysed before I know it ! It was Hickey kept it from—— Bejees, I know that sounds crazy, but he was crazy, and he'd got all of us as bughouse as he was. Bejees, it does queer things to you, having to listen day and night to a lunatic's pipe dreams—pretending you believe them, to kid him along and doing any crazy thing he wants to humour him. It's dangerous, too. Look at me pretending to start fer a walk just to keep him quiet. I knew damned well it wasn't the right day for it. The sun was broiling and the streets full of automobiles. Bejees, I could feel myself getting sunstroke, and an automobile damn near ran over me. (*He appeals to Rocky, afraid of the result, but daring it.*) Ask Rocky. He was watching. Didn't it, Rocky ?

ROCKY (*a bit tipsily*). What's dat, Boss ? Jees, all de booze I've mopped up is beginning to get to me. (*Earnestly.*) De automobile, Boss ? Sure, I seen it ! Just missed yuh ! I thought yuh was a goner. (*He pauses—then looks around at the others, and assumes the old kidding tone of the inmates, but hesitantly, as if still a little afraid.*) On de woid of a honest bartender ! (*He tries a wink at the others.*)

(*They all respond with smiles that are still a little forced and uneasy.*)

HOPE (*flashes him a suspicious glance. Then he understands—with his natural testy manner*). You're a bartender, all right. No one can say different. (*Rocky looks grateful.*) But, bejees, don't pull that honest junk ! You and Chuck ought to have cards in the Burglars' Union ! (*This time there is an eager laugh from the group. Hope is delighted.*) Bejees, it's good to hear someone laugh again ! All the time that bas—poor old Hickey was here, I didn't have the heart—— Bejees, I'm getting drunk and glad of it ! (*He cackles and reaches for the bottle.*) Come on, fellers. It's on the house. (*They pour drinks. They begin rapidly to get drunk now. Hope becomes sentimental.*) Poor old Hickey ! We musn't hold him responsible for anything he's done. We'll forget that and only remember him the way we've always known him before—the kindest, biggest-hearted guy ever wore shoe leather.

(*They all chorus hearty sentimental assent :* " That's right, Harry ! " " That's all ! " " *Finest fellow !* " " Best scout ! " *etc. Hope goes on.*)

Good luck to him in Matteawan ! Come on, bottoms up !

(*They all drink. At the table by the window Larry's hands grip the edge of the table. Unconsciously his head is inclined toward the window as he listens.*)

LARRY (*cannot hold back an anguished exclamation*). Christ ! Why don't he——!

HUGO (*beginning to be drunk again—peers at him*). Vhy don't he what ? Don't be a fool ! Hickey's gone. He vas crazy. Have a trink. (*Then as he receives no reply—with vague uneasiness.*) What's matter vith you, Larry ? You look funny. What you listen to out in backyard, Larry ?

(*Cora begins to talk in the group at right.*)

CORA (*tipsily*). Well, I thank Gawd now me and

Chuck did all we could to humour de poor nut. Jees, imagine us goin' off like we really meant to git married, when we ain't even picked out a farm yet!

CHUCK (*eagerly*). Sure ting, Baby. We kidded him we was serious.

JIMMY (*confidently—with a gentle, drunken unction*). I may as well say I detected his condition almost at once. All that talk of his about tomorrow, for example. He had the fixed idea of the insane. It only makes them worse to cross them.

WILLIE (*eagerly*). Same with me, Jimmy. Only I spent the day in the park. I wasn't such a damned fool as to——

LEWIS (*getting jauntily drunk*). Picture my predicament if I *had* gone to the Consulate. The pal of mine ıere is a humorous blighter. He would have got me a job out of pure spite. So I strolled about and finally came to roost in the park. (*He grins with affectionate kidding at Wetjoen.*) And lo and behold, who was on the neighbouring bench but my old battlefield companion, the Boer that walks like a man—who, if the British Government had taken my advice, would have been removed from his fetid kraal on the veldt straight to the baboon's cage at the London Zoo, and little children would now be asking their nurses: "Tell me, Nana, is that the Boer General, the one with the blue behind?" (*They all laugh uproariously. Lewis leans over and slaps Wetjoen affectionately on the knee.*) No offence meant, Piet, old chap.

WETJOEN (*beaming at him*). No offence taken, you tamned Limey! (*Wetjoen goes on—grinningly.*) About a job, I felt the same as you, Cecil.

(*At the table by the window Hugo speaks to Larry again.*)

HUGO (*with uneasy insistence*). What's matter, Larry? You look scared. What you listen for out there?

(*But Larry doesn't hear, and Joe begins talking in the group at right.*)

JOE (*with drunken self-assurance*). No, suh, I wasn't fool enough to git in no crap game. Not while Hickey's around. Crazy people puts a jinx on you.

(*McGloin is now heard. He is leaning across in front of Wetjoen to talk to Ed Mosher on Hope's left.*)

MCGLOIN (*with drunken earnestness*). I know you saw how it was, Ed. There was no good trying to explain to a crazy guy, but it ain't the right time. You know how getting reinstated is.

MOSHER (*decidedly*). Sure, Mac. The same way with the circus. The boys tell me the rubes are wasting all their money buying food and times never was so hard. And I never was one to cheat for chicken feed.

HOPE (*looks around him in an ecstasy of bleary sentimental content*). Bejees, I'm cockeyed! Bejees, you're all cockeyed! Bejees, we're all all right! Let's have another!

(*They pour out drinks. At the table by the window Larry has unconsciously shut his eyes as he listens. Hugo is peering at him frightenedly now.*)

HUGO (*reiterates stupidly*). What's matter, Larry? Why you keep eyes shut? You look dead. What you listen for in backyard? (*Then, as Larry doesn't open his eyes or answer, he gets up hastily and moves away from the table, mumbling with frightened anger.*) Crazy fool! You vas crazy like Hickey! You give me bad dreams too. (*He shrinks quickly past the table where Hickey had sat to the rear of the group at right.*)

ROCKY (*greets him with boisterous affection*). Hello, dere, Hugo! Welcome to de party!

HOPE. Yes, bejees, Hugo! Sit down! Have a drink! Have ten drinks, bejees!

HUGO (*forgetting Larry and bad dreams, gives his familiar giggle*). Hello, leedle Harry! Hello, nice, leedle, funny monkey-faces! (*Warming up, changes abruptly to his usual declamatory denunciation.*) Gottamned stupid bourgeois! Soon comes the Day of Judgment! (*They make derisive noises and tell him to sit down. He changes again, giggling good-naturedly, and sits at rear of the middle table.*) Give me ten trinks, Harry. Don't be a fool.

(*They laugh. Rocky shoves a glass and bottle at him. The sound of Margie's and Pearl's voices is heard from the hall, drunkenly shrill. All of the group turn toward the door as the two appear. They are drunk and look blowsy and dishevelled. Their manner as they enter hardens into a brazen defensive truculence.*)

MARGIE (*stridently*). Gangway for two good whores!

PEARL. Yeah! And we want a drink quick!

MARGIE (*glaring at Rocky*). Shake de lead outa your pants, Pimp! A little soivice!

ROCKY (*his black bullet eyes sentimental, his round Wop face grinning welcome*). Well, look who's here! (*He goes to them unsteadily, opening his arms.*) Hello, dere, Sweethearts! Jees, I was beginnin' to worry about yuh, honest! (*He tries to embrace them.*)

(*They push his arms away, regarding him with amazed suspicion.*)

PEARL. What kind of a gag is dis?

HOPE (*calls to them effusively*). Come on and join the party, you broads! Bejees, I'm glad to see you!

(*The girls exchange a bewildered glance, taking in the party and the changed atmosphere.*)

MARGIE. Jees, what's come off here?

PEARL. Where's dat louse, Hickey ?

ROCKY. De cops got him. He'd gone crazy and croaked his wife. (*The girls exclaim,* "Jees !" *But there is more relief than horror in it. Rocky goes on.*) He'll get Matteawan. He ain't responsible. What he's pulled don't mean nuttin'. So forget dat whore stuff. I'll knock de block off anyone calls you whores ! I'll fill de bastard full of lead ! Yuh're tarts, and what de hell of it ? Yuh're as good as anyone ! So forget it, see ?

(*They let him get his arms around them now. He gives them a hug. All the truculence leaves their faces. They smile and exchange maternally amused glances.*)

MARGIE (*with a wink*). Our little bartender, ain't he, Poil ?

PEARL. Yeah, and a cute little Ginny at dat !

(*They laugh.*)

MARGIE. And is he stinko !

PEARL. Stinko is right. But he ain't got nuttin' on us. Jees, Rocky, did we have a big time at Coney !

HOPE. Bejees, sit down, you dumb broads ! Welcome home ! Have a drink ! Have ten drinks, bejees !

(*They take the empty chairs on Chuck's left, warmly welcomed by all. Rocky stands in back of them, a hand on each of their shoulders, grinning with proud proprietorship. Hope beams over and under his crooked spectacles with the air of a host whose party is a huge success, and rambles on happily.*)

Bejees, this is all right ! We'll make this my birthday party, and forget the other. We'll get paralysed ! But who's missing ? Where's the Old Wise Guy ? Where's Larry ?

ROCKY. Over by de window, Boss. Jees, he's got his eyes shut. De old bastard's asleep. (*They turn to look. Rocky dismisses him.*) Aw, to hell wid him. Let's have a drink.

(*They turn away and forget him.*)

LARRY (*torturedly arguing to himself in a shaken whisper*). It's the only way out for him ! For the peace of all concerned, as Hickey said ! (*Snapping.*) God damn his yellow soul, if he doesn't soon, I'll go up and throw him off !—like a dog with its guts ripped out you'd put out of misery !

(*He half rises from his chair just as from outside the window comes the sound of something hurtling down, followed by a muffled, crunching thud. Larry gasps and drops back on his chair, shuddering, hiding his face in his hands. The group at right hear it but are too preoccupied with drinks to pay much attention.*)

HOPE (*wonderingly*). What the hell was that ?

ROCKY. Aw, nuttin'. Something fell off de fire escape. A mattress, I'll bet. Some of dese bums been sleepin' on de fire escapes.

HOPE (*his interest diverted by this excuse to beef—testily*). They've got to cut it out ! Bejees, this ain't a fresh-air cure. Mattresses cost money.

MOSHER. Now don't start crabbing at the party, Harry. Let's drink up.

(*Hope forgets it and grabs his glass, and they all drink.*)

LARRY (*in a whisper of horrified pity*). Poor devil ! (*A long-forgotten faith returns to him for a moment and he mumbles.*) God rest his soul in peace. (*He opens his eyes—with a bitter self-derision.*) Ah, the damned pity—the wrong kind, as Hickey said ! Be God, there's no hope ! I'll never be a success in the grandstand—or anywhere else ! Life is too much for me ! I'll be a weak fool looking with pity at the two sides of everything till the day I die ! (*With an intense bitter sincerity.*) May that day come soon ! (*He pauses startledly, surprised at himself—then with a sardonic grin.*) Be God, I'm the only real convert to death Hickey made here. From the bottom of my coward's heart I mean that now !

HOPE (*calls effusively*). Hey there, Larry ! Come over and get paralysed ! What the hell you doing, sitting there ? (*Then as Larry doesn't reply he immediately forgets him and turns to the party. They are all very drunk now, just a few drinks ahead of the passing-out stage, and hilariously happy about it.*) Bejees, let's sing ! Let's celebrate ! It's my birthday party ! Bejees, I'm oreyeyed ! I want to sing !

(*He starts the chorus* " *She's the Sunshine of Paradise Alley,*" *and instantly they all burst into song. But not the same song. Each starts the chorus of his or her choice. Jimmy Tomorrow's is* " *A Wee Dock and Doris* " ; *Ed Mosher's,* " *Break the News to Mother* " ; *Willie Oban's, the Sailor Lad ditty he sang in Act One ; General Wetjoen's,* " *Waiting at the Church* " ; *McGloin's,* " *Tammany* " ; *Captain Lewis's,* " *The Old Kent Road* " ; *Joe's,* " *All I Got Was Sympathy* " ; *Pearl's and Margie's,* " *Everybody's Doing It* " ; *Rocky's,* " *You Great Big Beautiful Doll* " ; *Chuck's,* " *The Curse of an Aching Heart* " ; *Cora's,* " *The Oceana Roll* " ; *while Hugo jumps to his feet and, pounding on the table with his fist, bellows in his guttural basso the French Revolutionary* " *Carmagnole.*" *A weird cacophony results from this mixture and they stop singing to roar with laughter. All but Hugo, who keeps on with drunken fervour.*)

HUGO. " Dansons la Carmagnole !
Vive le son ! Vive le son !
Dansons la Carmagnole !
Vive le son des canons ! "

(*They all turn on him and howl him down with amused derision. He stops singing to denounce them in his most fiery style.*)

Capitalist svine ! Stupid bourgeois monkeys ! (*He declaims.*) " The days grow hot, O Babylon ! "

(*They all take it up and shout in enthusiastic ieering chorus.*)

" 'Tis cool beneath thy willow trees ! "

(*They pound their glasses on the table, roaring with laughter, and Hugo giggles with them. In his chair by the window, Larry stares in front of him, oblivious to their racket.*)

CURTAIN

LONG DAY'S JOURNEY INTO NIGHT

FOR CARLOTTA, ON OUR 12TH WEDDING ANNIVERSARY

DEAREST: *I give you the original script of this play of old sorrow, written in tears and blood. A sadly inappropriate gift, it would seem, for a day celebrating happiness. But you will understand. I mean it as a tribute to your love and tenderness which gave me the faith in love that enabled me to face my dead at last and write this play – write it with deep pity and understanding and forgiveness for all the four haunted Tyrones.*

These twelve years, Beloved One, have been a Journey into Light – into love. You know my gratitude. And my love!

GENE

Tao House
July 22nd, 1941

Characters

JAMES TYRONE
MARY CAVAN TYRONE, *his wife*
JAMES TYRONE, JR., *their elder son*
EDMUND TYRONE, *their younger son*
CATHLEEN, *second girl*

Scenes

ACT ONE

Living-room of the Tyrones' summer home. 8.30 a.m. on a day in August 1912.

ACT TWO

SCENE ONE The same. Around 12.45.
SCENE TWO The same. About a half-hour later.

ACT THREE

The same. Around 6.30 that evening.

ACT FOUR

The same. Around midnight.

ACT ONE

SCENE. *Living-room of James Tyrone's summer home on a morning in August, 1912.*

At rear are two double doorways with portières. The one at right leads into a front parlour with the formally arranged, set appearance of a room rarely occupied. The other opens on a dark, windowless back parlour, never used except as a passage from living-room to dining-room. Against the wall between the doorways is a small bookcase, with a picture of Shakespeare above it, containing novels by Balzac, Zola, Stendhal, philosophical and sociological works by Schopen-

hauer, Nietzsche, Marx, Engels, Kropotkin, Max Sterner, plays by Ibsen, Shaw, Strindberg, poetry by Swinburne, Rossetti, Wilde, Ernest Dowson, Kipling, etc.

In the right wall, rear, is a screen door leading out on the porch which extends halfway around the house. Farther forward, a series of three windows looks over the front lawn to the harbour and the avenue that runs along the water front. A small wicker table and an ordinary oak desk are against the wall, flanking the windows.

In the left wall, a similar series of windows looks out on the grounds behind the house. Beneath them is a wicker couch with cushions, its head toward rear. Farther back is a large, glassed-in bookcase with sets of Dumas, Victor Hugo, Charles Lever, three sets of Shakespeare, The World's Best Literature in fifty large volumes, Hume's History of England, Thiers' History of the Consulate and Empire, Smollett's History of England, Gibbon's Roman Empire and miscellaneous volumes of old plays, poetry, and several histories of Ireland. The astonishing thing about these sets is that all the volumes have the look of having been read and reread.

The hardwood floor is nearly covered by a rug, inoffensive in design and colour. At centre is a round table with a green-shaded reading lamp, the cord plugged in one of the four sockets in the chandelier above. Around the table within reading-light range are four chairs, three of them wicker armchairs, the fourth (at right front of table) a varnished oak rocker with leather bottom.

It is about 8.30. Sunshine comes through the windows at right.

As the curtain rises, the family have just finished breakfast. Mary Tyrone and her husband enter together from the back parlour, coming from the dining-room.

Mary is fifty-four, about medium height. She still has a young, graceful figure, a trifle plump, but showing little evidence of middle-aged waist and hips, although she is not tightly corseted. Her face is distinctly Irish in type. It must once have been extremely pretty, and is still striking. It does not match her healthy figure but is thin and pale with the bone structure prominent. Her nose is long and straight, her mouth wide with full, sensitive lips. She uses no rouge or any sort of make-up. Her high forehead is framed by thick, pure white hair. Accentuated by her pallor and white hair, her dark brown eyes appear black. They are unusually large and beautiful, with black brows and long curling lashes.

What strikes one immediately is her extreme nervousness. Her hands are never still. They were once beautiful hands, with long, tapering fingers, but rheumatism has knotted the joints and warped the fingers, so that now they have an ugly crippled look. One avoids looking at them, the more so because one is conscious she is sensitive about their appearance and humiliated by her inability to control the nervousness which draws attention to them.

She is dressed simply but with a sure sense of what becomes her. Her hair is arranged with fastidious care. Her voice is soft and attractive. When she is merry, there is a touch of Irish lilt in it.

Her most appealing quality is the simple, unaffected charm of a shy convent-girl youthfulness she has never lost — an innate unworldly innocence.

James Tyrone is sixty-five but looks ten years younger. About five feet eight, broad-shouldered and deep-chested, he seems taller and slenderer because of his bearing, which has a soldierly quality of head up, chest out, stomach in, shoulders squared. His face has begun to break down but he is still remarkably good-looking — a big, finely shaped head, a handsome profile, deep-set light-brown eyes. His grey hair is thin with a bald spot like a monk's tonsure.

The stamp of his profession is unmistakably on him. Not that he indulges in any of the deliberate temperamental posturings of the stage star. He is by nature and preference a simple, unpretentious man, whose inclinations are still close to his humble beginnings and his Irish farmer forebears. But the actor shows in all his unconscious habits of speech, movement and gesture. These have the quality of belonging to a studied technique. His voice is remarkably fine, resonant and flexible, and he takes great pride in it.

His clothes, assuredly, do not costume any romantic part. He wears a threadbare, ready-made, grey sack suit and shineless black shoes, a collar-less shirt with a thick white handkerchief knotted loosely around his throat. There is nothing picturesquely careless about this get-up. It is commonplace shabby. He believes in wearing his clothes to the limit of usefulness, is dressed now for gardening, and doesn't give a damn how he looks.

He has never been really sick a day in his life. He has no nerves. There is a lot of stolid, earthy peasant in him, mixed with streaks of sentimental melancholy and rare flashes of intuitive sensibility.

Tyrone's arm is around his wife's waist as they appear from the back parlour. Entering the living-room he gives her a playful hug.

TYRONE. You're a fine armful now, Mary, with those twenty pounds you've gained.

MARY (*smiles affectionately*). I've gotten too fat, you mean, dear. I really ought to reduce.

TYRONE. None of that, my lady! You're just right. We'll have no talk of reducing. Is that why you ate so little breakfast?

MARY. So little? I thought I ate a lot.

TYRONE. You didn't. Not as much as I'd like to see, anyway.

MARY (*teasingly*). Oh you! You expect everyone to eat the enormous breakfast you do. No one else in the world could without dying of indigestion. (*She comes forward to stand by the right of table.*)

TYRONE (*following her*). I hope I'm not as big a glutton as that sounds. (*With hearty satisfaction.*) But thank God, I've kept my appetite and I've the digestion of a young man of twenty, if I am sixty-five.

MARY. You surely have, James. No one could deny that.

(*She laughs and sits in the wicker armchair at right rear of table. He comes around behind her and selects a cigar from a box on the table and cuts off the end with a little clipper. From the dining-room Jamie's and Edmund's voices are heard. Mary turns her head that way.*)

Why did the boys stay in the dining-room, I wonder? Cathleen must be waiting to clear the table.

TYRONE (*jokingly but with an undercurrent of resentment*). It's a secret confab they don't want me to hear, I suppose. I'll bet they're cooking up some new scheme to touch the Old Man.

(*She is silent on this, keeping her head turned toward their voices. Her hands appear on the table top, moving restlessly. He lights his cigar and sits down in the rocker at right of table, which is his chair, and puffs contentedly.*)

There's nothing like the first after-breakfast cigar, if it's a good one, and this new lot have the right mellow flavour. They're a great bargain, too. I got them dead cheap. It was McGuire put me on to them.

MARY (*a trifle acidly*). I hope he didn't put you on to any new piece of property at the same time. His real-estate bargains don't work out so well.

TYRONE (*defensively*). I wouldn't say that, Mary. After all, he was the one who advised me to buy that place on Chestnut Street and I made a quick turnover on it for a fine profit.

MARY (*smiles now with teasing affection*). I know. The famous one stroke of good luck. I'm sure McGuire never dreamed — (*Then she pats his hand.*) Never mind, James. I know it's a waste of breath trying to convince you you're not a cunning real-estate speculator.

TYRONE (*huffily*). I've no such idea. But land is land, and it's safer than the stocks and bonds of Wall Street swindlers. (*Then placatingly.*) But let's not argue about business this early in the morning.

(*A pause. The boys' voices are again heard and one of them has a fit of coughing. Mary listens worriedly. Her fingers play nervously on the table top.*)

MARY. James, it's Edmund you ought to scold for not eating enough. He hardly touched anything except coffee. He needs to eat to keep up his strength. I keep telling him that but he says he simply has no appetite. Of course, there's nothing takes away your appetite like a bad summer cold.

TYRONE. Yes, it's only natural. So don't let yourself get worried —

MARY (*quickly*). Oh, I'm not. I know he'll be all right in a few days if he takes care of himself. (*As if she wanted to dismiss the subject but can't.*) But it does seem a shame he should have to be sick right now.

TYRONE. Yes, it is bad luck. (*He gives her a quick, worried look.*) But you mustn't let it upset you, Mary. Remember, you've got to take care of yourself, too.

MARY (*quickly*). I'm not upset. There's nothing to be upset about. What makes you think I'm upset?

TYRONE. Why, nothing, except you've seemed a bit high-strung the past few days.

MARY (*forcing a smile*). I have? Nonsense, dear. It's your imagination. (*With sudden tenseness.*) You really must not watch me all the time, James. I mean, it makes me self-conscious.

TYRONE (*putting a hand over one of her nervously playing ones*). Now, now, Mary. That's your imagination. If I've watched you it was to admire how fat and beautiful you looked. (*His voice is suddenly moved by deep feeling.*) I can't tell you the deep happiness it gives me, darling, to see you as you've been since you came back to us, your dear old self again. (*He leans over and kisses her cheek impulsively — then turning back adds with a constrained air.*) So keep up the good work, Mary.

MARY (*has turned her head away*). I will, dear. (*She gets up restlessly and goes to the windows at right.*) Thank heavens, the fog is gone. (*She turns back.*) I do feel out of sorts this morning. I wasn't able to get much sleep with that awful foghorn going all night long.

TYRONE. Yes, it's like having a sick whale in the back yard. It kept me awake, too.

MARY (*affectionately amused*). Did it? You had a strange way of showing your restlessness. You were snoring so hard I couldn't tell which was the foghorn! (*She comes to him, laughing, and pats his cheek playfully.*) Ten foghorns couldn't disturb you. You haven't a nerve in you. You've never had.

TYRONE (*his vanity piqued — testily*). Nonsense. You always exaggerate about my snoring.

MARY. I couldn't. If you could only hear yourself once —

(*A burst of laughter comes from the dining-room. She turns her head, smiling.*)

What's the joke, I wonder?

TYRONE (*grumpily*). It's on me. I'll bet that much. It's always on the Old Man.

MARY (*teasingly*). Yes, it's terrible the way we all pick on you, isn't it? You're so abused! (*She laughs — then with a pleased, relieved air.*) Well, no matter what the joke is about, it's a relief to hear Edmund laugh. He's been so down in the mouth lately.

TYRONE (*ignoring this — resentfully*). Some joke of Jamie's,

I'll wager. He's for ever making sneering fun of somebody, that one.

MARY. Now don't start in on poor Jamie, dear. (*Without conviction.*) He'll turn out all right in the end, you wait and see.

TYRONE. He'd better start soon, then. He's nearly thirty-four.

MARY (*ignoring this*). Good heavens, are they going to stay in the dining-room all day? (*She goes to the back parlour doorway and calls.*) Jamie! Edmund! Come in the living-room and give Cathleen a chance to clear the table.

(*Edmund calls back, "We're coming, Mama." She goes back to the table.*)

TYRONE (*grumbling*). You'd find excuses for him no matter what he did.

MARY (*sitting down beside him, pats his hand*). Shush.

(*Their sons James, Jr., and Edmund enter together from the back parlour. They are both grinning, still chuckling over what had caused their laughter, and as they come forward they glance at their father and their grins grow broader.*

Jamie, the elder, is thirty-three. He has his father's broad-shouldered, deep-chested physique, is an inch taller and weighs less, but appears shorter and stouter because he lacks Tyrone's bearing and graceful carriage. He also lacks his father's vitality. The signs of premature disintegration are on him. His face is still good-looking, despite marks of dissipation, but it has never been handsome like Tyrone's, although Jamie resembles him rather than his mother. He has fine brown eyes, their colour midway between his father's lighter and his mother's darker ones. His hair is thinning and already there is indication of a bald spot like Tyrone's. His nose is unlike that of any other member of the family, pronouncedly aquiline. Combined with his habitual expression of cynicism it gives his countenance a Mephistophelian cast. But on the rare occasions when he smiles without sneering, his personality possesses the remnant of a humorous, romantic, irresponsible Irish charm — that of the beguiling ne'er-do-well, with a strain of the sentimentally poetic, attractive to women and popular with men.

He is dressed in an old sack suit, not as shabby as Tyrone's, and wears a collar and tie. His fair skin is sunburned a reddish, freckled tan.

Edmund is ten years younger than his brother, a couple of inches taller, thin and wiry. Where Jamie takes after his father, with little resemblance to his mother, Edmund looks like both his parents, but is more like his mother. Her big, dark eyes are the dominant feature in his long, narrow Irish face. His mouth has the same quality of hypersensitiveness hers possesses. His high forehead is hers, accentuated, with dark brown hair, sunbleached to red at the ends, brushed straight back from it. But his nose is his father's, and his face in profile recalls Tyrone's. Edmund's hands are noticeably like his mother's, with the same exceptionally long fingers. They even have to a minor degree the same nervousness. It is in the quality of extreme nervous sensibility that the likeness of Edmund to his mother is most marked.

He is plainly in bad health. Much thinner than he should be, his eyes appear feverish and his cheeks are sunken. His skin, in spite of being sunburned a deep brown, has a parched sallowness. He wears a shirt, collar and tie, no coat, old flannel trousers, brown sneakers.)

MARY (*turns smilingly to them, in a merry tone that is a bit forced*). I've been teasing your father about his snoring. (*To Tyrone.*) I'll leave it to the boys, James. They must have heard you. No, not you, Jamie. I could hear you down the hall almost as bad as your father. You're like him. As soon as your head touches the pillow you're off and ten foghorns couldn't wake you. (*She stops abruptly, catching Jamie's eyes regarding her with an uneasy, probing look. Her smile vanishes and her manner becomes self-conscious.*) Why are you staring, Jamie? (*Her hands flutter up to her hair.*) Is my hair coming down? It's hard for me to do it up properly now. My eyes are getting so bad and I never can find my glasses.

JAMIE (*looks away guiltily*). Your hair's all right, Mama. I was only thinking how well you look.

TYRONE (*heartily*). Just what I've been telling her, Jamie. She's so fat and sassy, there'll soon be no holding her.

EDMUND. Yes, you certainly look grand, Mama.

(*She is reassured and smiles at him lovingly. He winks with a kidding grin.*)

I'll back you up about Papa's snoring. Gosh, what a racket!

JAMIE. I heard him, too. (*He quotes, putting on a ham-actor manner.*) "The Moor, I know his trumpet."

(*His mother and brother laugh.*)

TYRONE (*scathingly*). If it takes my snoring to make you remember Shakespeare instead of the dope sheet on the ponies, I hope I'll keep on with it.

MARY. Now, James! You mustn't be so touchy.

(*Jamie shrugs his shoulders and sits down in the chair on her right.*)

EDMUND (*irritably*). Yes, for Pete's sake, Papa! The first thing after breakfast! Give it a rest, can't you?

(*He slumps down in the chair at left of table next to his

brother. His father ignores him.)

MARY (*reprovingly*). Your father wasn't finding fault with you. You don't have to always take Jamie's part. You'd think you were the one ten years older.

JAMIE (*boredly*). What's all the fuss about? Let's forget it.

TYRONE (*contemptuously*). Yes, forget! Forget everything and face nothing! It's a convenient philosophy if you've no ambition in life except to —

MARY. James, do be quiet. (*She puts an arm around his shoulder — coaxingly.*) You must have gotten out of the wrong side of the bed this morning. (*To the boys, changing the subject.*) What were you two grinning about like Cheshire cats when you came in? What was the joke?

TYRONE (*with a painful effort to be a good sport*). Yes, let us in on it, lads. I told your mother I knew damned well it would be one on me, but never mind that, I'm used to it.

JAMIE (*dryly*). Don't look at me. This is the Kid's story.

EDMUND (*grins*). I meant to tell you last night, Papa, and forgot it. Yesterday when I went for a walk I dropped in at the Inn —

MARY (*worriedly*). You shouldn't drink now, Edmund.

EDMUND (*ignoring this*). And who do you think I met there, with a beautiful bun on, but Shaughnessy, the tenant on that farm of yours.

MARY (*smiling*). That dreadful man! But he is funny.

TYRONE (*scowling*). He's not so funny when you're his landlord. He's a wily Shanty Mick, that one. He could hide behind a corkscrew. What's he complaining about now, Edmund — for I'm damned sure he's complaining. I suppose he wants his rent lowered. I let him have the place for almost nothing, just to keep someone on it, and he never pays that till I threaten to evict him.

EDMUND. No, he didn't beef about anything. He was so pleased with life he even bought a drink, and that's practically unheard of. He was delighted because he'd had a fight with your friend, Harker, the Standard Oil millionaire, and won a glorious victory.

MARY (*with amused dismay*). Oh, Lord! James, you'll really have to do something —

TYRONE. Bad luck to Shaughnessy, anyway!

JAMIE (*maliciously*). I'll bet the next time you see Harker at the Club and give him the old respectful bow, he won't see you.

EDMUND. Yes. Harker will think you're no gentleman for harbouring a tenant who isn't humble in the presence of a king of America.

TYRONE. Never mind the Socialist gabble. I don't care to listen —

MARY (*tactfully*). Go on with your story, Edmund.

EDMUND (*grins at his father provocatively*). Well, you remember, Papa, the ice pond on Harker's estate is right next to the farm, and you remember Shaughnessy keeps pigs. Well, it seems there's a break in the fence and the pigs have been bathing in the millionaire's ice pond, and Harker's foreman told him he was sure Shaughnessy had broken the fence on purpose to give his pigs a free wallow.

MARY (*shocked and amused*). Good heavens!

TYRONE (*sourly, but with a trace of admiration*). I'm sure he did, too, the dirty scallywag. It's like him.

EDMUND. So Harker came in person to rebuke Shaughnessy. (*He chuckles.*) A very bonehead play! If I needed any further proof that our ruling plutocrats, especially the ones who inherited their boodle, are not mental giants, that would clinch it.

TYRONE (*with appreciation, before he thinks*). Yes, he'd be no match for Shaughnessy. (*Then he growls.*) Keep your damned anarchist remarks to yourself. I won't have them in my house. (*But he is full of eager anticipation.*) What happened?

EDMUND. Harker had as much chance as I would with Jack Johnson. Shaughnessy got a few drinks under his belt and was waiting at the gate to welcome him. He told me he never gave Harker a chance to open his mouth. He began by shouting that he was no slave Standard Oil could trample on. He was a King of Ireland, if he had his rights, and scum was scum to him, no matter how much money it had stolen from the poor.

MARY. Oh, Lord! (*But she can't help laughing.*)

EDMUND. Then he accused Harker of making his foreman break down the fence to entice the pigs into the ice pond in order to destroy them. The poor pigs, Shaughnessy yelled, had caught their death of cold. Many of them were dying of pneumonia, and several others had been taken down with cholera from drinking the poisoned water. He told Harker he was hiring a lawyer to sue him for damages. And he wound up by saying that he had to put up with poison ivy, ticks, potato bugs, snakes and skunks on his farm, but he was an honest man who drew the line somewhere, and he'd be damned if he'd stand for a Standard Oil thief trespassing. So would Harker kindly remove his dirty feet from the premises before he sicked the dog on him. And Harker did!

(*He and Jamie laugh.*)

MARY (*shocked but giggling*). Heavens, what a terrible tongue that man has!

TYRONE (*admiringly before he thinks*). The damned old scoundrel! By God, you can't beat him! (*He laughs — then stops abruptly and scowls.*) The dirty blackguard! He'll get me in serious trouble yet. I hope you told him I'd be mad as hell —

EDMUND. I told him you'd be tickled to death over the great Irish victory, and so you are. Stop faking, Papa.

TYRONE. Well, I'm not tickled to death.

MARY (*teasingly*). You are, too, James. You're simply delighted!

TYRONE. No, Mary, a joke is a joke, but —

EDMUND. I told Shaughnessy he should have reminded Harker that a Standard Oil millionaire ought to welcome the flavour of hog in his ice water as an appropriate touch.

TYRONE. The devil you did! (*Frowning.*) Keep your damned Socialist anarchist sentiments out of my affairs!

EDMUND. Shaughnessy almost wept because he hadn't thought of that one, but he said he'd include it in a letter he's writing to Harker, along with a few other insults he'd overlooked.

(*He and Jamie laugh.*)

TYRONE. What are you laughing at? There's nothing funny — A fine son you are to help that blackguard get me into a lawsuit!

MARY. Now, James, don't lose your temper.

TYRONE (*turns on Jamie*). And you're worse than he is, encouraging him. I suppose you're regretting you weren't there to prompt Shaughnessy with a few nastier insults. You've a fine talent for that, if for nothing else.

MARY. James! There's no reason to scold Jamie.

(*Jamie is about to make some sneering remark to his father, but he shrugs his shoulders.*)

EDMUND (*with sudden nervous exasperation*). Oh, for God's sake, Papa! If you're starting that stuff again, I'll beat it. (*He jumps up.*) I left my book upstairs, anyway. (*He goes to the front parlour, saying disgustedly:*) God, Papa, I should think you'd get sick of hearing yourself —

(*He disappears. Tyrone looks after him angrily.*)

MARY. You mustn't mind Edmund, James. Remember he isn't well.

(*Edmund can be heard coughing as he goes upstairs.*)

(*She adds nervously.*) A summer cold makes anyone irritable.

JAMIE (*genuinely concerned*). It's not just a cold he's got. The Kid is damned sick.

(*His father gives him a sharp warning look but he doesn't see it.*)

MARY (*turns on him resentfully*). Why do you say that? It *is* just a cold! Anyone can tell that! You always imagine things!

TYRONE (*with another warning glance at Jamie — easily*). All Jamie meant was Edmund might have a touch of something else, too, which makes his cold worse.

JAMIE. Sure, Mama. That's all I meant.

TYRONE. Doctor Hardy thinks it might be a bit of malarial fever he caught when he was in the tropics. If it is, quinine will soon cure it.

MARY (*a look of contemptuous hostility flashes across her face*). Doctor Hardy! I wouldn't believe a thing he said, if he swore on a stack of Bibles! I know what doctors are. They're all alike. Anything, they don't care what, to keep you coming to them. (*She stops short, overcome by a fit of acute self-consciousness as she catches their eyes fixed on her. Her hands jerk nervously to her hair. She forces a smile.*) What is it? What are you looking at? Is my hair —?

TYRONE (*puts his arm around her — with guilty heartiness, giving her a playful hug*). There's nothing wrong with your hair. The healthier and fatter you get, the vainer you become. You'll soon spend half the day primping before the mirror.

MARY (*half reassured*). I really should have new glasses. My eyes are so bad now.

TYRONE (*with Irish blarney*). Your eyes are beautiful, and well you know it.

(*He gives her a kiss. Her face lights up with a charming, shy embarrassment. Suddenly and startlingly one sees in her face the girl she had once been, not a ghost of the dead, but still a living part of her.*)

MARY. You mustn't be so silly, James. Right in front of Jamie!

TYRONE. Oh, he's on to you, too. He knows this fuss about eyes and hair is only fishing for compliments. Eh, Jamie?

JAMIE (*his face has cleared, too, and there is an old boyish charm in his loving smile at his mother*). Yes. You can't kid us, Mama.

MARY (*laughs and an Irish lilt comes into her voice*). Go along with both of you! (*Then she speaks with a girlish gravity.*) But I did truly have beautiful hair once, didn't I, James?

TYRONE. The most beautiful in the world!

MARY. It was a rare shade of reddish brown and so long it came down below my knees. You ought to remember it, too, Jamie. It wasn't until after Edmund was born that I had a single grey hair. Then it began to turn white. (*The girlishness fades from her face.*)

TYRONE (*quickly*). And that made it prettier than ever.

MARY (*again embarrassed and pleased*). Will you listen to your father, Jamie — after thirty-five years of marriage! He isn't a great actor for nothing, is he? What's come over you, James? Are you pouring coals of fire on my head for teasing you about snoring? Well then, I take it all back. It must have been only the foghorn I heard. (*She laughs, and they laugh with her. Then she changes to a brisk businesslike air.*) But I can't stay with you any longer, even to hear compliments. I must see the cook about dinner and the day's marketing. (*She gets up and sighs with humorous exaggeration.*) Bridget is so lazy. And so sly. She begins telling me about her relatives so I can't get a word in edgeways and scold her. Well, I might as well get it over. (*She goes to the back-parlour doorway, then turns, her face worried again.*) You mustn't make Edmund work on the grounds with you, James, remember. (*Again with the strange obstinate set to her face.*) Not that he isn't strong enough, but he'd perspire and he might catch more cold.

(*She disappears through the back parlour. Tyrone turns on Jamie condemningly.*)

TYRONE. You're a fine lunkhead! Haven't you any sense? The one thing to avoid is saying anything that would get her more upset over Edmund.

JAMIE (*shrugging his shoulders*). All right. Have it your way. I think it's the wrong idea to let Mama go on kidding herself. It will only make the shock worse when she has to face it. Anyway, you can see she's deliberately fooling herself with that summer-cold talk. She knows better.

TYRONE. Knows? Nobody knows yet.

JAMIE. Well, I do. I was with Edmund when he went to Doc Hardy on Monday. I heard him pull that touch of malaria stuff. He was stalling. That isn't what he thinks any more. You know it as well as I do. You talked to him when you went uptown yesterday, didn't you?

TYRONE. He couldn't say anything for sure yet. He's to phone me today before Edmund goes to him.

JAMIE (*slowly*). He thinks it's consumption, doesn't he, Papa?

TYRONE (*reluctantly*). He said it might be.

JAMIE (*moved, his love for his brother coming out*). Poor kid! God damn it! (*He turns on his father accusingly.*) It might never have happened if you'd sent him to a real doctor when he first got sick.

TYRONE. What's the matter with Hardy? He's always been our doctor up here.

JAMIE. Everything's the matter with him! Even in this hick burg he's rated third class! He's a cheap old quack!

TYRONE. That's right! Run him down! Run down everybody! Everyone is a fake to you!

JAMIE (*contemptuously*). Hardy only charges a dollar. That's what makes you think he's a fine doctor!

TYRONE (*stung*). That's enough! You're not drunk now! There's no excuse — (*He controls himself — a bit defensively.*) If you mean I can't afford one of the fine society doctors who prey on the rich summer people —

JAMIE. Can't afford? You're one of the biggest property owners around here.

TYRONE. That doesn't mean I'm rich. It's all mortgaged —

JAMIE. Because you always buy more instead of paying off mortgages. If Edmund was a lousy acre of land you wanted, the sky would be the limit!

TYRONE. That's a lie! And your sneers against Doctor Hardy are lies! He doesn't put on frills, or have an office in a fashionable location, or drive around in an expensive automobile. That's what you pay for with those other five-dollars-to-look-at-your-tongue fellows, not their skill.

JAMIE (*with a scornful shrug of his shoulders*). Oh, all right. I'm a fool to argue. You can't change the leopard's spots.

TYRONE (*with rising anger*). No, you can't. You've taught me that lesson only too well. I've lost all hope you will ever change yours. You dare tell me what I can afford? You've never known the value of a dollar and never will! You've never saved a dollar in your life! At the end of each season you're penniless! You've thrown your salary away every week on whores and whiskey!

JAMIE. My salary! Christ!

TYRONE. It's more than you're worth, and you couldn't get that if it wasn't for me. If you weren't my son, there isn't a manager in the business who would give you a part, your reputation stinks so. As it is, I have to humble my pride and beg for you, saying you've turned over a new leaf, although I know it's a lie!

JAMIE. I never wanted to be an actor. You forced me on the stage.

TYRONE. That's a lie! You made no effort to find anything else to do. You left it to me to get you a job and I have no influence except in the theatre. Forced you! You never wanted to do anything except loaf in barrooms! You'd have been content to sit back like a lazy lunk and sponge on me for the rest of your life! After all the money I'd wasted on your education, and all you did was get fired in disgrace from every college you went to!

JAMIE. Oh, for God's sake, don't drag up that ancient history!

TYRONE. It's not ancient history that you have to come home every summer to live on me.

JAMIE. I earn my board and lodging working on the grounds. It saves you hiring a man.

TYRONE. Bah! You have to be driven to do even that much! (*His anger ebbs into a weary complaint.*) I wouldn't give a damn if you ever displayed the slightest sign of gratitude. The only thanks is to have you sneer at me for a dirty miser, sneer at my profession, sneer at every damned thing in the world — except yourself.

JAMIE (*wryly*). That's not true, Papa. You can't hear me talking to myself, that's all.

TYRONE (*stares at him puzzledly, then quotes mechanically*).

"Ingratitude, the vilest weed that grows"!

JAMIE. I could see that line coming! God, how many thousand times —! (*He stops, bored with their quarrel, an shrugs his shoulders.*) All right, Papa, I'm a bum. Anything you like, so long as it stops the argument.

TYRONE (*with indignant appeal now*). If you'd get ambition in your head instead of folly! You're young yet. You could still make your mark. You had the talent to become a fine actor! You have it still. You're my son —!

JAMIE (*boredly*). Let's forget me. I'm not interested in the subject. Neither are you.

(*Tyrone gives up. Jamie goes on casually.*)

What started us on this? Oh, Doc Hardy. When is he going to call you up about Edmund?

TYRONE. Around lunch time. (*He pauses — then defensively.*) I couldn't have sent Edmund to a better doctor. Hardy's treated him whenever he was sick up here, since he was knee-high. He knows his constitution as no other doctor could. It's not a question of my being miserly, as you'd like to make out. (*Bitterly.*) And what could the finest specialist in America do for Edmund, after he's deliberately ruined his health by the mad life he's led ever since he was fired from college? Even before that, when he was in prep school, he began dissipating and playing the Broadway sport to imitate you, when he's never had your constitution to stand it. You're a healthy hulk like me — or you were at his age — but he's always been a bundle of nerves like his mother. I've warned him for years his body couldn't stand it, but he wouldn't heed me, and now it's too late.

JAMIE (*sharply*). What do you mean, too late? You talk as if you thought —

TYRONE (*guiltily explosive*). Don't be a damned fool! I meant nothing but what's plain to anyone! His health has broken down and he may be an invalid for a long time.

JAMIE (*stares at his father, ignoring his explanation*). I know it's an Irish peasant idea consumption is fatal. It probably is when you live in a hovel on a bog, but over here, with modern treatment —

TYRONE. Don't I know that! What are you gabbing about, anyway? And keep your dirty tongue off Ireland, with your sneers about peasants and bogs and hovels! (*Accusingly.*) The less you say about Edmund's sickness, the better for your conscience! You're more responsible than anyone!

JAMIE (*stung*). That's a lie! I won't stand for that, Papa!

TYRONE. It's the truth! You've been the worst influence for him. He grew up admiring you as a hero! A fine example you set him! If you ever gave him advice except in the ways of rottenness, I've never heard of it! You made him old before his time, pumping him full of what you consider worldly wisdom, when he was too young to see that your mind was so poisoned by your own failure in life, you wanted to believe every man was a knave with his soul for sale, and every woman who wasn't a whore was a fool!

JAMIE (*with a defensive air of weary indifference again*). All right. I did put Edmund wise to things, but not until I saw he'd started to raise hell, and knew he'd laugh at me if I tried the good advice, older brother stuff. All I did was make a pal of him and be absolutely frank so he'd learn from my mistakes that — (*He shrugs his shoulders — cynically.*) Well, that if you can't be good you can at least be careful.

(*His father snorts contemptuously. Suddenly Jamie becomes really moved.*)

That's a rotten accusation, Papa. You know how much the Kid means to me, and how close we've always been — not like the usual brothers! I'd do anything for him.

TYRONE (*impressed — mollifyingly*). I know you may have thought it was for the best, Jamie. I didn't say you did it deliberately to harm him.

JAMIE. Besides, it's damned rot! I'd like to see anyone influence Edmund more than he wants to be. His quietness fools people into thinking they can do what they like with him. But he's stubborn as hell inside and what he does is what he wants to do, and to hell with anyone else! What had I to do with all the crazy stunts he's pulled in the last few years — working his way all over the map as a sailor and all that stuff. I thought that was a damned fool idea, and I told him so. You can't imagine me getting fun out of being on the beach in South America or living in filthy dives, drinking rotgut, can you? No, thanks! I'll stick to Broadway, and a room with a bath, and bars that serve bonded Bourbon.

TYRONE. You and Broadway! It's made you what you are! (*With a touch of pride.*) Whatever Edmund's done, he's had the guts to go off on his own, where he couldn't come whining to me the minute he was broke.

JAMIE (*stung into sneering jealousy*). He's always come home broke finally, hasn't he? And what did his going away get him? Look at him now! (*He is suddenly shamefaced.*) Christ! That's a lousy thing to say. I don't mean that.

TYRONE (*decides to ignore this*). He's been doing well on the paper. I was hoping he'd found the work he wants to do at last.

JAMIE (*sneering jealously again*). A hick town rag! Whatever bull they hand you, they tell me he's a pretty bum reporter. If he weren't your son — (*Ashamed again.*) No, that's not true! They're glad to have him, but it's the special stuff that gets him by. Some of the poems and parodies he's written are damned good. (*Grudgingly again.*) Not that they'd ever get him anywhere on the big time.

(*Hastily.*) But he's certainly made a damned good start.

TYRONE. Yes. He's made a start. You used to talk about wanting to become a newspaper man but you were never willing to start at the bottom. You expected —

JAMIE. Oh, for Christ's sake, Papa! Can't you lay off me!

TYRONE (*stares at him — then looks away — after a pause*). It's damnable luck Edmund should be sick right now. It couldn't have come at a worse time for him. (*He adds, unable to conceal an almost furtive uneasiness.*) Or for your mother. It's damnable she should have this to upset her, just when she needs peace and freedom from worry. She's been so well in the two months since she came home. (*His voice grows husky and trembles a little.*) It's been heaven to me. This home has been a home again. But I needn't tell you, Jamie.

(*His son looks at him, for the first time with an understanding sympathy. It is as if suddenly a deep bond of common feeling existed between them in which their antagonisms could be forgotten.*)

JAMIE (*almost gently*). I've felt the same way, Papa.

TYRONE. Yes, this time you can see how strong and sure of herself she is. She's a different woman entirely from the other times. She has control of her nerves — or she had until Edmund got sick. Now you can feel her growing tense and frightened underneath. I wish to God we could keep the truth from her, but we can't if he has to be sent to a sanatorium. What makes it worse is her father died of consumption. She worshipped him and she's never forgotten. Yes, it will be hard for her. But she can do it! She has the will-power now! We must help her, Jamie, in every way we can!

JAMIE (*moved*). Of course, Papa. (*Hesitantly.*) Outside of nerves, she seems perfectly all right this morning.

TYRONE (*with hearty confidence now*). Never better. She's full of fun and mischief. (*Suddenly he frowns at Jamie suspiciously.*) Why do you say, seems? Why shouldn't she be all right? What the hell do you mean?

JAMIE. Don't start jumping down my throat! God, Papa, this ought to be one thing we can talk over frankly without a battle.

TYRONE. I'm sorry, Jamie. (*Tensely.*) But go on and tell me —

JAMIE. There's nothing to tell. I was all wrong. It's just that last night — Well, you know how it is, I can't forget the past. I can't help being suspicious. Any more than you can. (*Bitterly.*) That's the hell of it. And it makes it hell for Mama! She watches us watching her —

TYRONE (*sadly*). I know. (*Tensely.*) Well, what was it? Can't you speak out?

JAMIE. Nothing, I tell you. Just my damned foolishness. Around three o'clock this morning, I woke up and heard her moving around in the spare room. Then she went to the bathroom. I pretended to be asleep. She stopped in the hall to listen, as if she wanted to make sure I was.

TYRONE (*with forced scorn*). For God's sake, is that all? She told me herself the foghorn kept her awake all night, and every night since Edmund's been sick she's been up and down, going to his room to see how he was.

JAMIE (*eagerly*). Yes, that's right, she did stop to listen outside his room. (*Hesitantly again.*) It was her being in the spare room that scared me. I couldn't help remembering that when she starts sleeping alone in there, it has always been a sign —

TYRONE. It isn't this time! It's easily explained. Where else could she go last night to get away from my snoring? (*He gives way to a burst of resentful anger.*) By God, how you can live with a mind that sees nothing but the worst motives behind everything is beyond me!

JAMIE (*stung*). Don't pull that! I've just said I was all wrong. Don't you suppose I'm as glad of that as you are!

TYRONE (*mollifyingly*). I'm sure you are, Jamie. (*A pause. His expression becomes sombre. He speaks slowly with a superstitious dread.*) It would be like a curse she can't escape if worry over Edmund — It was in her long sickness after bringing him into the world that she first —

JAMIE. She didn't have anything to do with it!

TYRONE. I'm not blaming her.

JAMIE (*bitingly*). Then who are you blaming? Edmund, for being born?

TYRONE. You damned fool! No one was to blame.

JAMIE. The bastard of a doctor was! From what Mama's said, he was another cheap quack like Hardy! You wouldn't pay for a first-rate —

TYRONE. That's a lie! (*Furiously.*) So I'm to blame! That's what you're driving at, is it? You evil-minded loafer!

JAMIE (*warningly as he hears his mother in the dining-room*). Ssh!

(*Tyrone gets hastily to his feet and goes to look out of the windows at right. Jamie speaks with a complete change of tone.*)

Well, if we're going to cut the front hedge today, we'd better go to work.

(*Mary comes in from the back parlour. She gives a quick, suspicious glance from one to the other, her manner nervously self-conscious.*)

TYRONE (*turns from the window — with an actor's heartiness*).

Yes, it's too fine a morning to waste indoors arguing. Take a look out the window, Mary. There's no fog in the harbour. I'm sure the spell of it we've had is over now.

MARY (*going to him*). I hope so, dear. (*To Jamie, forcing a smile.*) Did I actually hear you suggesting work on the front hedge, Jamie? Wonders will never cease! You must want pocket money badly.

JAMIE (*kiddingly*). When don't I? (*He winks at her, with a derisive glance at his father.*) I expect a salary of at least one large iron man at the end of the week — to carouse on!

MARY (*does not respond to his humour — her hands fluttering over the front of her dress*). What were you two arguing about?

JAMIE (*shrugs his shoulders*). The same old stuff.

MARY. I heard you say something about a doctor, and your father accusing you of being evil-minded.

JAMIE (*quickly*). Oh, that. I was saying again Doc Hardy isn't my idea of the world's greatest physician.

MARY (*knows he is lying — vaguely*). Oh. No, I wouldn't say he was, either. (*Changing the subject — forcing a smile.*) That Bridget! I thought I'd never get away. She told me all about her second cousin on the police force in St. Louis. (*Then with nervous irritation.*) Well, if you're going to work on the hedge why don't you go? (*Hastily.*) I mean, take advantage of the sunshine before the fog comes back. (*Strangely, as if talking aloud to herself.*) Because I know it will. (*Suddenly she is self-consciously aware that they are both staring fixedly at her — flurriedly, raising her hands.*) Or I should say, the rheumatism in my hands knows. It's a better weather prophet than you are, James. (*She stares at her hands with fascinated repulsion.*) Ugh! How ugly they are! Who'd ever believe they were once beautiful?

(*They stare at her with a growing dread.*)

TYRONE (*takes her hands and gently pushes them down*). Now, now, Mary. None of that foolishness. They're the sweetest hands in the world.

(*She smiles, her face lighting up, and kisses him gratefully. He turns to his son.*)

Come on, Jamie. Your mother's right to scold us. The way to start work is to start work. The hot sun will sweat some of that booze fat off your middle.

(*He opens the screen door and goes out on the porch and disappears down a flight of steps leading to the ground. Jamie rises from his chair and, taking off his coat, goes to the door. At the door he turns back but avoids looking at her, and she does not look at him.*)

JAMIE (*with an awkward, uneasy tenderness*). We're all so proud of you, Mama, so darned happy.

(*She stiffens and stares at him with a frightened defiance. He flounders on.*)

But you've still got to be careful. You mustn't worry so much about Edmund. He'll be all right.

MARY (*with a stubborn, bitterly resentful look*). Of course, he'll be all right. And I don't know what you mean, warning me to be careful.

JAMIE (*rebuffed and hurt, shrugs his shoulders*). All right, Mama. I'm sorry I spoke.

(*He goes out on the porch. She waits rigidly until he disappears down the steps. Then she sinks down in the chair he had occupied, her face betraying a frightened, furtive desperation, her hands roving over the table top, aimlessly moving objects around. She hears Edmund descending the stairs in the front hall. As he nears the bottom he has a fit of coughing. She springs to her feet, as if she wanted to run away from the sound, and goes quickly to the windows at right. She is looking out, apparently calm, as he enters from the front parlour, a book in one hand. She turns to him, her lips set in a welcoming, motherly smile.*)

MARY. Here you are. I was just going upstairs to look for you.

EDMUND. I waited until they went out. I don't want to mix up in any arguments. I feel too rotten.

MARY (*almost resentfully*). Oh, I'm sure you don't feel half as badly as you make out. You're such a baby. You like to get us worried so we'll make a fuss over you. (*Hastily.*) I'm only teasing, dear. I know how miserably uncomfortable you must be. But you feel better today, don't you? (*Worriedly, taking his arm.*) All the same, you've grown much too thin. You need to rest all you can. Sit down and I'll make you comfortable.

(*He sits down in the rocking-chair and she puts a pillow behind his back.*)

There. How's that?

EDMUND. Grand. Thanks, Mama.

MARY (*kisses him — tenderly*). All you need is your mother to nurse you. Big as you are, you're still the baby of the family to me, you know.

EDMUND (*takes her hand — with deep seriousness*). Never mind me. You take care of yourself. That's all that counts.

MARY (*evading his eyes*). But I am, dear. (*Forcing a laugh.*) Heavens, don't you see how fat I've grown! I'll have to have all my dresses let out. (*She turns away and goes to the windows at right. She attempts a light, amused tone.*) They've started clipping the hedge. Poor Jamie! How he hates working in front where everyone passing can see him. There go the Chatfields in their new Mercedes. It's a beautiful car, isn't it? Not like our secondhand Packard. Poor Jamie! He bent almost under the hedge so they wouldn't notice him. They bowed to your father and he bowed back as if he were taking a curtain call. In that filthy old suit I've tried to make him throw away. (*Her voice has grown bitter.*) Really, he ought to have more pride than to make such a show of himself.

EDMUND. He's right not to give a damn what anyone thinks. Jamie's a fool to care about the Chatfields. For Pete's sake, who ever heard of them outside this hick burg?

MARY (*with satisfaction*). No one. You're quite right, Edmund. Big frogs in a small puddle. It is stupid of Jamie. (*She pauses, looking out of the window — then with an undercurrent of lonely yearning.*) Still, the Chatfields and people like them stand for something. I mean they have decent, presentable homes they don't have to be ashamed of. They have friends who entertain them and whom they entertain. They're not cut off from everyone. (*She turns back from the window.*) Not that I want anything to do with them. I've always hated this town and everyone in it. You know that. I never wanted to live here in the first place, but your father liked it and insisted on building this house, and I've had to come here every summer.

EDMUND. Well, it's better than spending the summer in a New York hotel, isn't it? And this town's not so bad. I like it well enough. I suppose because it's the only home we've had.

MARY. I've never felt it was my home. It was wrong from the start. Everything was done in the cheapest way. Your father would never spend the money to make it right. It's just as well we haven't any friends here. I'd be ashamed to have them step in the door. But he's never wanted family friends. He hates calling on people, or receiving them. All he likes is to hobnob with men at the Club or in a bar-room. Jamie and you are the same way, but you're not to blame. You've never had a chance to meet decent people here. I know you both would have been so different if you'd been able to associate with nice girls instead of — You'd never have disgraced yourselves as you have, so that now no respectable parents will let their daughters be seen with you.

EDMUND (*irritably*). Oh, Mama, forget it! Who cares? Jamie and I would be bored stiff. And about the Old Man, what's the use of talking? You can't change him.

MARY (*mechanically rebuking*). Don't call your father the Old Man. You should have more respect. (*Then dully.*) I know it's useless to talk. But sometimes I feel so lonely. (*Her lips quiver and she keeps her head turned away.*)

EDMUND. Anyway, you've got to be fair, Mama. It may have been all his fault in the beginning, but you know that later on, even if he'd wanted to, we couldn't have had people here — (*He flounders guiltily.*) I mean, you wouldn't have wanted them.

MARY (*wincing — her lips quivering pitifully*). Don't. I can't bear having you remind me.

EDMUND. Don't take it that way! Please, Mama! I'm trying to help. Because it's bad for you to forget. The right way is to remember. So you'll always be on your guard. You know what's happened before. (*Miserably.*) God, Mama, you know I hate to remind you. I'm doing it because it's been so wonderful having you home the way you've been, and it would be terrible —

MARY (*strickenly*). Please, dear. I know you mean it for the best, but — (*A defensive uneasiness comes into her voice again.*) I don't understand why you should suddenly say such things. What put it in your mind this morning?

EDMUND (*evasively*). Nothing. Just because I feel rotten and blue, I suppose.

MARY. Tell me the truth. Why are you so suspicious all of a sudden?

EDMUND. I'm not!

MARY. Oh, yes you are. I can feel it. Your father and Jamie, too — particularly Jamie.

EDMUND. Now don't start imagining things, Mama.

MARY (*her hands fluttering*). It makes it so much harder, living in this atmosphere of constant suspicion, knowing everyone is spying on me, and none of you believe in me, or trust me.

EDMUND. That's crazy, Mama. We do trust you.

MARY. If there was only some place I could go to get away for a day, or even an afternoon, some woman friend I could talk to — not about anything serious, simply laugh and gossip and forget for a while — someone besides the servants — that stupid Cathleen!

EDMUND (*gets up worriedly and puts his arm around her*). Stop it, Mama. You're getting yourself worked up over nothing.

MARY. Your father goes out. He meets his friends in bar-rooms or at the Club. You and Jamie have the boys you know. You go out. But I am alone. I've always been alone.

EDMUND (*soothingly*). Come now! You know that's a fib. One of us always stays around to keep you company, or goes with you in the automobile when you take a drive.

MARY (*bitterly*). Because you're afraid to trust me alone! (*She turns on him — sharply.*) I insist you tell me why you act so differently this morning — why you felt you had to remind me —

EDMUND (*hesitates — then blurts out guiltily*). It's stupid. It's just that I wasn't asleep when you came in my room last night. You didn't go back to your and Papa's room. You went in the spare room for the rest of the night.

MARY. Because your father's snoring was driving me

crazy! For heaven's sake, haven't I often used the spare room as my bedroom? (*Bitterly.*) But I see what you thought. That was when —

EDMUND (*too vehemently*). I didn't think anything!

MARY. So you pretended to be asleep in order to spy on me!

EDMUND. No! I did it because I knew if you found out I was feverish and couldn't sleep, it would upset you.

MARY. Jamie was pretending to be asleep, too, I'm sure, and I suppose your father —

EDMUND. Stop it, Mama!

MARY. Oh, I can't bear it, Edmund, when even you —! (*Her hands flutter up to pat her hair in their aimless, distracted way. Suddenly a strange undercurrent of revengefulness comes into her voice.*) It would serve all of you right if it was true!

EDMUND. Mama! Don't say that! That's the way you talk when —

MARY. Stop suspecting me! Please, dear! You hurt me! I couldn't sleep because I was thinking about you. That's the real reason! I've been so worried ever since you've been sick. (*She puts her arms around him and hugs him with a frightened, protective tenderness.*)

EDMUND (*soothingly*). That's foolishness. You know it's only a bad cold.

MARY. Yes, of course, I know that!

EDMUND. But listen, Mama. I want you to promise me that even if it should turn out to be something worse, you'll know I'll soon be all right again, anyway, and you won't worry yourself sick, and you'll keep on taking care of yourself —

MARY (*frightenedly*). I won't listen when you're so silly! There's absolutely no reason to talk as if you expected something dreadful! Of course, I promise you. I give you my sacred word of honour! (*Then with a sad bitterness.*) But I suppose you're remembering I've promised before on my word of honour.

EDMUND. No!

MARY (*her bitterness receding into a resigned helplessness*). I'm not blaming you, dear. How can you help it? How can any one of us forget? (*Strangely.*) That's what makes it so hard — for all of us. We can't forget.

EDMUND (*grabs her shoulder*). Mama! Stop it!

MARY (*forcing a smile*). All right, dear. I didn't mean to be so gloomy. Don't mind me. Here. Let me feel your head. Why, it's nice and cool. You certainly haven't any fever now.

EDMUND. Forget! It's you —

MARY. But I'm quite all right, dear. (*With a quick, strange, calculating, almost sly glance at him.*) Except I naturally feel tired and nervous this morning, after such a bad night. I really ought to go upstairs and lie down until lunch-time and take a nap. (*He gives her an instinctive look of suspicion — then, ashamed of himself, looks quickly away. She hurries on nervously.*) What are you going to do? Read here? It would be much better for you to go out in the fresh air and sunshine. But don't get overheated, remember. Be sure and wear a hat. (*She stops, looking straight at him now. He avoids her eyes. There is a tense pause. Then she speaks jeeringly.*) Or are you afraid to trust me alone?

EDMUND (*tormentedly*). No! Can't you stop talking like that? I think you ought to take a nap. (*He goes to the screen door — forcing a joking tone.*) I'll go down and help Jamie bear up. I love to lie in the shade and watch him work.

(*He forces a laugh in which she makes herself join. Then he goes out on the porch and disappears down the steps. Her first reaction is one of relief. She appears to relax. She sinks down in one of the wicker armchairs at rear of table and leans her head back, closing her eyes. But suddenly she grows terribly tense again. Her eyes open and she strains forward, seized by a fit of nervous panic. She begins a desperate battle with herself. Her long fingers, warped and knotted by rheumatism, drum on the arms of the chair, driven by an insistent life of their own, without her consent.*)

CURTAIN

ACT TWO, SCENE ONE

SCENE. *The same. It is around quarter to one. No sunlight comes into the room now through the windows at right. Outside the day is still fine but increasingly sultry, with a faint haziness in the air which softens the glare of the sun.*

Edmund sits in the armchair at left of table, reading a book. Or rather he is trying to concentrate on it but cannot. He seems to be listening for some sound from upstairs. His manner is nervously apprehensive and he looks more sickly than in the previous act.

The second girl, Cathleen, enters from the back parlour. She carries a tray on which is a bottle of bonded Bourbon, several whiskey glasses, and a pitcher of ice water. She is a buxom Irish peasant, in her early twenties, with a red-cheeked comely face, black hair and blue eyes — amiable, ignorant, clumsy, and possessed by a dense, well-meaning stupidity. She puts the tray on the table. Edmund pretends to be so absorbed in his book he does not notice her, but she ignores this.

CATHLEEN (*with garrulous familiarity*). Here's the whiskey. It'll be lunch-time soon. Will I call your father and Mister Jamie, or will you?

EDMUND (*without looking up from his book*). You do it.

CATHLEEN. It's a wonder your father wouldn't look at his watch once in a while. He's a divil for making the meals late, and then Bridget curses me as if I was to blame. But he's a grand handsome man, if he is old. You'll never see the day you're as good-looking – nor Mister Jamie, either. (*She chuckles.*) I'll wager Mister Jamie wouldn't miss the time to stop work and have his drop of whiskey if he had a watch to his name!

EDMUND (*gives up trying to ignore her and grins*). You win that one.

CATHLEEN. And here's another I'd win, that you're making me call them so you can sneak a drink before they come.

EDMUND. Well, I hadn't thought of that –

CATHLEEN. Oh no, not you! Butter wouldn't melt in your mouth, I suppose.

EDMUND. But now you suggest it –

CATHLEEN (*suddenly primly virtuous*). I'd never suggest a man or a woman touch drink, Mister Edmund. Sure didn't it kill an uncle of mine in the old country. (*Relenting.*) Still, a drop now and then is no harm when you're in low spirits, or have a bad cold.

EDMUND. Thanks for handing me a good excuse. (*Then with forced casualness.*) You'd better call my mother, too.

CATHLEEN. What for? She's always on time without any calling. God bless her, she has some consideration for the help.

EDMUND. She's been taking a nap.

CATHLEEN. She wasn't asleep when I finished my work upstairs a while back. She was lying down in the spare room with her eyes wide open. She'd a terrible headache, she said.

EDMUND (*his casualness more forced*). Oh well then, just call my father.

CATHLEEN (*goes to the screen door, grumbling good-naturedly*). No wonder my feet kill me each night. I won't walk out in this heat and get sunstroke. I'll call from the porch.

(*She goes out on the side porch, letting the screen door slam behind her, and disappears on her way to the front porch. A moment later she is heard shouting.*)

Mister Tyrone! Mister Jamie! It's time!

(*Edmund, who has been staring frightenedly before him, forgetting his book, springs to his feet nervously.*)

EDMUND. God, what a wench!

(*He grabs the bottle and pours a drink, adds ice water and drinks. As he does so, he hears someone coming in the front door. He puts the glass hastily on the tray and sits down again, opening his book. Jamie comes in from the front parlour, his coat over his arm. He has taken off collar and tie and carries them in his hand. He is wiping sweat from his forehead with a handkerchief. Edmund looks up as if his reading was interrupted. Jamie takes one look at the bottle and glasses and smiles cynically.*)

JAMIE. Sneaking one, eh? Cut out the bluff, Kid. You're a rottener actor than I am.

EDMUND (*grins*). Yes, I grabbed one while the going was good.

JAMIE (*puts a hand affectionately on his shoulder*). That's better. Why kid me? We're pals, aren't we?

EDMUND. I wasn't sure it was you coming.

JAMIE. I made the Old Man look at his watch. I was halfway up the walk when Cathleen burst into song. Our wild Irish lark! She ought to be a train announcer.

EDMUND. That's what drove me to drink. Why don't you sneak one while you've got a chance?

JAMIE. I was thinking of that little thing. (*He goes quickly to the window at right.*) The Old Man was talking to old Captain Turner. Yes, he's still at it. (*He comes back and takes a drink.*) And now to cover up from his eagle eye. (*He memorizes the level in the bottle after every drink. He measures two drinks of water and pours them in the whiskey bottle and shakes it up.*) There. That fixes it. (*He pours water in the glass and sets it on the table by Edmund.*) And here's the water you've been drinking.

EDMUND. Fine! You don't think it will fool him, do you?

JAMIE. Maybe not, but he can't prove it. (*Putting on his collar and tie.*) I hope he doesn't forget lunch listening to himself talk. I'm hungry. (*He sits across the table from Edmund – irritably.*) That's what I hate about working down in front. He puts on an act for every damned fool that comes along.

EDMUND (*gloomily*). You're in luck to be hungry. The way I feel I don't care if I ever eat again.

JAMIE (*gives him a glance of concern*). Listen, Kid. You know me. I've never lectured you, but Doctor Hardy was right when he told you to cut out the redeye.

EDMUND. Oh, I'm going to after he hands me the bad news this afternoon. A few before then won't make any difference.

JAMIE (*hesitates – then slowly*). I'm glad you've got your mind prepared for bad news. It won't be such a jolt. (*He catches Edmund staring at him.*) I mean, it's a cinch you're really sick, and it would be wrong dope to kid yourself.

EDMUND (*disturbed*). I'm not. I know how rotten I feel, and the fever and chills I get at night are no joke. I think Doctor Hardy's last guess was right. It must be the damned malaria come back on me.

JAMIE. Maybe, but don't be too sure.

EDMUND. Why? What do you think it is?

JAMIE. Hell, how would I know? I'm no Doc. (*Abruptly.*) Where's Mama?

EDMUND. Upstairs.

JAMES (*looks at him sharply*). When did she go up?

EDMUND. Oh, about the time I came down to the hedge, I guess. She said she was going to take a nap.

JAMIE. You didn't tell me —

EDMUND (*defensively*). Why should I? What about it? She was tired out. She didn't get much sleep last night.

JAMIE. I know she didn't.

(*A pause. The brothers avoid looking at each other.*)

EDMUND. That damned foghorn kept me awake, too.

(*Another pause.*)

JAMIE. She's been upstairs alone all morning, eh? You haven't seen her?

EDMUND. No. I've been reading here. I wanted to give her a chance to sleep.

JAMIE. Is she coming down to lunch?

EDMUND. Of course.

JAMIE (*dryly*). No of course about it. She might not want any lunch. Or she might start having most of her meals alone upstairs. That's happened, hasn't it?

EDMUND (*with frightened resentment*). Cut it out, Jamie! Can't you think anything but —? (*Persuasively.*) You're all wrong to suspect anything. Cathleen saw her not long ago. Mama didn't tell her she wouldn't be down to lunch.

JAMIE. Then she wasn't taking a nap?

EDMUND. Not right then, but she was lying down, Cathleen said.

JAMIE. In the spare room?

EDMUND. Yes. For Pete's sake, what of it?

JAMIE (*bursts out*). You damned fool! Why did you leave her alone so long? Why didn't you stick around?

EDMUND. Because she accused me — and you and Papa — of spying on her all the time and not trusting her. She made me feel ashamed. I know how rotten it must be for her. And she promised on her sacred word of honour —

JAMIE (*with a bitter weariness*). You ought to know that doesn't mean anything.

EDMUND. It does this time!

JAMIE. That's what we thought the other times. (*He leans over the table to give his brother's arm an affectionate grasp.*) Listen, Kid, I know you think I'm a cynical bastard, but remember I've seen a lot more of this game than you have. You never knew what was really wrong until you were in prep school. Papa and I kept it from you. But I was wise ten years or more before we had to tell you. I know the game backwards and I've been thinking all morning of the way she acted last night when she thought we were asleep. I haven't been able to think of anything else. And now you tell me she got you to leave her alone upstairs all morning.

EDMUND. She didn't! You're crazy!

JAMIE (*placatingly*). All right, Kid. Don't start a battle with me. I hope as much as you do I'm crazy. I've been as happy as hell because I'd really begun to believe that this time — (*He stops — looking through the front parlour toward the hall — lowering his voice, hurriedly.*) She's coming downstairs. You win on that. I guess I'm a damned suspicious louse.

(*They grow tense with a hopeful, fearful expectancy. Jamie mutters.*)

Damn! I wish I'd grabbed another drink.

EDMUND. Me, too.

(*He coughs nervously and this brings on a real fit of coughing. Jamie glances at him with worried pity. Mary enters from the front parlour. At first one notices no change except that she appears to be less nervous, to be more as she was when we first saw her after breakfast, but then one becomes aware that her eyes are brighter, and there is a peculiar detachment in her voice and manner, as if she were a little withdrawn from her words and actions.*)

MARY (*goes worriedly to Edmund and puts her arm around him*). You mustn't cough like that. It's bad for your throat. You don't want to get a sore throat on top of your cold.

(*She kisses him. He stops coughing and gives her a quick apprehensive glance, but if his suspicions are aroused her tenderness makes him renounce them and he believes what he wants to believe for the moment. On the other hand, Jamie knows after one probing look at her that his suspicions are justified. His eyes fall to stare at the floor, his face sets in an expression of embittered, defensive cynicism. Mary goes on, half sitting on the arm of Edmund's chair, her arm around him, so her face is above and behind his and he cannot look into her eyes.*)

But I seem to be always picking on you, telling you don't do this and don't do that. Forgive me, dear. It's just that

I want to take care of you.

EDMUND. I know, Mama. How about you? Do you feel rested?

MARY. Yes, ever so much better. I've been lying down ever since you went out. It's what I needed after such a restless night. I don't feel nervous now.

EDMUND. That's fine.

(*He pats her hand on his shoulder. Jamie gives him a strange, almost contemptuous glance, wondering if his brother can really mean this. Edmund does not notice but his mother does.*)

MARY (*in a forced teasing tone*). Good heavens, how down in the mouth you look, Jamie! What's the matter now?

JAMIE (*without looking at her*). Nothing.

MARY. Oh, I'd forgotten you've been working on the front hedge. That accounts for your sinking into the dumps, doesn't it?

JAMIE. If you want to think so, Mama.

MARY (*keeping her tone*). Well, that's the effect it always has, isn't it? What a big baby you are! Isn't he, Edmund?

EDMUND. He's certainly a fool to care what anyone thinks.

MARY (*strangely*). Yes, the only way is to make yourself not care. (*She catches Jamie giving her a bitter glance and changes the subject.*) Where is your father? I heard Cathleen call him.

EDMUND. Gabbing with old Captain Turner, Jamie says. He'll be late, as usual.

(*Jamie gets up and goes to the windows at right, glad of an excuse to turn his back.*)

MARY. I've told Cathleen time and again she must go wherever he is and tell him. The idea of screaming as if this were a cheap boardinghouse!

JAMIE (*looking out of the window*). She's down there now. (*Sneeringly.*) Interrupting the famous Beautiful Voice! She should have more respect.

MARY (*sharply — letting her resentment toward him come out*). It's you who should have more respect! Stop sneering at your father! I won't have it! You ought to be proud you're his son! He may have his faults. Who hasn't? But he's worked hard all his life. He made his way up from ignorance and poverty to the top of his profession! Everyone else admires him and you should be the last one to sneer — you, who, thanks to him, have never had to work hard in your life!

(*Stung, Jamie has turned to stare at her with accusing antagonism. Her eyes waver guiltily and she adds in a tone which begins to placate.*)

Remember your father is getting old, Jamie. You really ought to show more consideration.

JAMIE. *I* ought to?

EDMUND (*uneasily*). Oh, dry up, Jamie!

(*Jamie looks out of the window again.*)

And, for Pete's sake, Mama, why jump on Jamie all of a sudden?

MARY (*bitterly*). Because he's always sneering at someone else, always looking for the worst weakness in everyone. (*Then with a strange, abrupt change to a detached, impersonal tone.*) But I suppose life has made him like that, and he can't help it. None of us can help the things life has done to us. They're done before you realize it, and once they're done they make you do other things until at last everything comes between you and what you'd like to be, and you've lost your true self for ever.

(*Edmund is made apprehensive by her strangeness. He tries to look up in her eyes but she keeps them averted. Jamie turns to her — then looks quickly out of the window again.*)

JAMIE (*dully*). I'm hungry. I wish the Old Man would get a move on. It's a rotten trick the way he keeps meals waiting, and then beefs because they're spoiled.

MARY (*with a resentment that has a quality of being automatic and on the surface while inwardly she is indifferent*). Yes, it's very trying, Jamie. You don't know how trying. You don't have to keep house with summer servants who don't care because they know it isn't a permanent position. The really good servants are all with people who have homes and not merely summer places. And your father won't even pay the wages the best summer help ask. So every year I have stupid, lazy greenhorns to deal with. But you've heard me say this a thousand times. So has he, but it goes in one ear and out the other. He thinks money spent on a home is money wasted. He's lived too much in hotels. Never the best hotels, of course. Second-rate hotels. He doesn't understand a home. He doesn't feel at home in it. And yet, he wants a home. He's even proud of having this shabby place. He loves it here. (*She laughs — a hopeless and yet amused laugh.*) It's really funny, when you come to think of it. He's a peculiar man.

EDMUND (*again attempting uneasily to look up in her eyes*). What makes you ramble on like that, Mama?

MARY (*quickly casual — patting his cheek*). Why, nothing in particular, dear. It *is* foolish.

(*As she speaks, Cathleen enters from the back parlour.*)

CATHLEEN (*volubly*). Lunch is ready, Ma'am. I went down to Mister Tyrone, like you ordered, and he said he'd come right away, but he kept on talking to that man, telling him of the time when —

MARY (*indifferently*). All right, Cathleen. Tell Bridget I'm sorry but she'll have to wait a few minutes until Mister Tyrone is here.

(*Cathleen mutters,* "Yes, Ma'am," *and goes off through the back parlour, grumbling to herself.*)

JAMIE. Damn it! Why don't you go ahead without him? He's told us to.

MARY (*with a remote, amused smile*). He doesn't mean it. Don't you know your father yet? He'd be so terribly hurt.

EDMUND (*jumps up — as if he was glad of an excuse to leave*). I'll make him get a move on. (*He goes out on the side porch. A moment later he is heard calling from the porch exasperatedly.*) Hey! Papa! Come on! We can't wait all day!

(*Mary has risen from the arm of the chair. Her hands play restlessly over the table top. She does not look at Jamie but she feels the cynically appraising glance he gives her face and hands.*)

MARY (*tensely*). Why do you stare like that?

JAMIE. You know. (*He turns back to the window.*)

MARY. I don't know.

JAMIE. Oh, for God's sake, do you think you can fool me, Mama? I'm not blind.

MARY (*looks directly at him now, her face set again in an expression of blank, stubborn denial*). I don't know what you're talking about.

JAMIE. No? Take a look at your eyes in the mirror!

EDMUND (*coming in from the porch*). I got Papa moving. He'll be here in a minute. (*With a glance from one to the other, which his mother avoids — uneasily.*) What's happened? What's the matter, Mama?

MARY (*disturbed by his coming, gives way to a flurry of guilty, nervous excitement*). Your brother ought to be ashamed of himself. He's been insinuating I don't know what.

EDMUND (*turns on Jamie*). God damn you!

(*He takes a threatening step toward him. Jamie turns his back with a shrug and looks out of the window.*)

MARY (*more upset, grabs Edmund's arm — excitedly*). Stop this at once, do you hear me? How dare you use such language before me! (*Abruptly her tone and manner change to the strange detachment she has shown before.*) It's wrong to blame your brother. He can't help being what the past has made him. Any more than your father can. Or you. Or I.

EDMUND (*frightenedly — with a desperate hoping against hope*). He's a liar! It's a lie, isn't it, Mama?

MARY (*keeping her eyes averted*). What is a lie? Now you're talking in riddles like Jamie. (*Then her eyes meet his stricken, accusing look. She stammers.*) Edmund! Don't! (*She looks away and her manner instantly regains the quality of strange detachment — calmly.*) There's your father coming up the steps now. I must tell Bridget.

(*She goes through the back parlour. Edmund moves slowly to his chair. He looks sick and hopeless.*)

JAMIE (*from the window, without looking around*). Well?

EDMUND (*refusing to admit anything to his brother yet — weakly defiant*). Well, what? You're a liar.

(*Jamie again shrugs his shoulders. The screen door on the front porch is heard closing. Edmund says dully.*)

Here's Papa. I hope he loosens up with the old bottle.

(*Tyrone comes in through the front parlour. He is putting on his coat.*)

TYRONE. Sorry I'm late. Captain Turner stopped to talk and once he starts gabbing you can't get away from him.

JAMIE (*without turning — dryly*). You mean once he starts listening.

(*His father regards him with dislike. He comes to the table with a quick measuring look at the bottle of whiskey. Without turning, Jamie senses this.*)

It's all right. The level in the bottle hasn't changed.

TYRONE. I wasn't noticing that. (*He adds caustically.*) As if it proved anything with you around. I'm on to your tricks.

EDMUND (*dully*). Did I hear you say, let's all have a drink?

TYRONE (*frowns at him*). Jamie is welcome after his hard morning's work, but I won't invite you. Doctor Hardy —

EDMUND. To hell with Doctor Hardy! One isn't going to kill me. I feel — all in, Papa.

TYRONE (*with a worried look at him — putting on a false heartiness*). Come along, then. It's before a meal and I've always found that good whiskey, taken in moderation as an appetizer, is the best of tonics.

(*Edmund gets up as his father passes the bottle to him. He pours a big drink. Tyrone frowns admonishingly.*)

I said, in moderation. (*He pours his own drink and passes the bottle to Jamie, grumbling.*) It'd be a waste of breath mentioning moderation to you.

(*Ignoring the hint, Jamie pours a big drink. His father scowls — then, giving it up, resumes his hearty air, raising his glass.*)

Well, here's health and happiness!

(*Edmund gives a bitter laugh.*)

EDMUND. That's a joke!

TYRONE. What is?

EDMUND. Nothing. Here's how.

(*They drink.*)

TYRONE (*becoming aware of the atmosphere*). What's the matter here? There's gloom in the air you could cut with a knife. (*Turns on Jamie resentfully.*) You got the drink you were after, didn't you? Why are you wearing that gloomy look on your mug?

JAMIE (*shrugging his shoulders*). You won't be singing a song yourself soon.

EDMUND. Shut up, Jamie.

TYRONE (*uneasy now — changing the subject*). I thought lunch was ready. I'm hungry as a hunter. Where is your mother?

MARY (*returning through the back parlour, calls*). Here I am. (*She comes in. She is excited and self-conscious. As she talks, she glances everywhere except at any of their faces.*) I've had to calm down Bridget. She's in a tantrum over your being late again, and I don't blame her. If your lunch is dried up from waiting in the oven, she said it served you right, you could like it or leave it for all she cared. (*With increasing excitement.*) Oh, I'm so sick and tired of pretending this is a home! You won't help me! You won't put yourself out the least bit! You don't know how to act in a home! You don't really want one! You never have wanted one — never since the day we were married! You should have remained a bachelor and lived in second-rate hotels and entertained your friends in bar-rooms! (*She adds strangely, as if she were now talking aloud to herself rather than to Tyrone.*) Then nothing would ever have happened.

(*They stare at her. Tyrone knows now. He suddenly looks a tired, bitterly sad old man. Edmund glances at his father and sees that he knows, but he still cannot help trying to warn his mother.*)

EDMUND. Mama! Stop talking. Why don't we go in to lunch.

MARY (*starts and at once the quality of unnatural detachment settles on her face again. She even smiles with an ironical amusement to herself*). Yes, it is inconsiderate of me to dig up the past, when I know your father and Jamie must be hungry. (*Putting her arm around Edmund's shoulder — with a fond solicitude which is at the same time remote.*) I do hope you have an appetite, dear. You really must eat more. (*Her eyes become fixed on the whiskey glass on the table beside him — sharply.*) Why is that glass there? Did you take a drink? Oh, how can you be such a fool? Don't you know it's the worst thing? (*She turns on Tyrone.*) You're to blame, James. How could you let him? Do you want to kill him? Don't you remember my father? He wouldn't stop after he was stricken. He said doctors were fools! He thought, like you, that whiskey is a good tonic! (*A look of terror comes into her eyes and she stammers.*) But, of course, there's no comparison at all. I don't know why I — Forgive me for scolding you, James. One small drink won't hurt Edmund. It might be good for him, if it gives him an appetite.

(*She pats Edmund's cheek playfully, the strange detachment again in her manner. He jerks his head away. She seems not to notice, but she moves instinctively away.*)

JAMIE (*roughly, to hide his tense nerves*). For God's sake, let's eat. I've been working in the damned dirt under the hedge all morning. I've earned my grub. (*He comes around behind his father, not looking at his mother, and grabs Edmund's shoulder.*) Come on, Kid. Let's put on the feed bag.

(*Edmund gets up, keeping his eyes averted from his mother. They pass her, heading for the back parlour.*)

TYRONE (*dully*). Yes, you go in with your mother, lads. I'll join you in a second.

(*But they keep on without waiting for her. She looks at their backs with a helpless hurt and, as they enter the back parlour, starts to follow them. Tyrone's eyes are on her, sad and condemning. She feels them and turns sharply without meeting his stare.*)

MARY. Why do you look at me like that? (*Her hands flutter up to pat her hair.*) Is it my hair coming down? I was so worn out from last night. I thought I'd better lie down this morning. I drowsed off and had a nice refreshing nap. But I'm sure I fixed my hair again when I woke up. (*Forcing a laugh.*) Although, as usual, I couldn't find my glasses. (*Sharply.*) Please stop staring! One would think you were accusing me — (*Then pleadingly.*) James! You don't understand!

TYRONE (*with dull anger*). I understand that I've been a God-damned fool to believe in you! (*He walks away from her to pour himself a big drink.*)

MARY (*her face again sets in stubborn defiance*). I don't know what you mean by "believing in me". All I've felt was distrust and spying and suspicion. (*Then accusingly.*) Why are you having another drink? You never have more than one before lunch. (*Bitterly.*) I know what to expect. You will be drunk tonight. Well, it won't be the first time, will it — or the thousandth? (*Again she bursts out pleadingly.*) Oh, James, please! You don't understand! I'm so worried about Edmund! I'm so afraid he —

TYRONE. I don't want to listen to your excuses, Mary.

MARY (*strickenly*). Excuses? You mean —? Oh, you can't believe that of me! You mustn't believe that, James! (*Then slipping away into her strange detachment — quite casually.*) Shall we not go in to lunch, dear? I don't want anything but I know you're hungry.

(*He walks slowly to where she stands in the doorway. He

walks like an old man. As he reaches her she bursts out piteously.)

James! I tried so hard! I tried so hard! Please believe —!

TYRONE (*moved in spite of himself — helplessly*). I suppose you did, Mary. (*Then grief-strickenly.*) For the love of God, why couldn't you have the strength to keep on?

MARY (*her face setting into that stubborn denial again*). I don't know what you're talking about. Have the strength to keep on what?

TYRONE (*hopelessly*). Never mind. It's no use now.

(*He moves on and she keeps beside him as they disappear in the back parlour.*)

CURTAIN

ACT TWO, SCENE TWO

SCENE. *The same, about half an hour later. The tray with the bottle of whiskey has been removed from the table. The family are returning from lunch as the curtain rises. Mary is the first to enter from the back parlour. Her husband follows. He is not with her as he was in the similar entrance after breakfast at the opening of Act One. He avoids touching her or looking at her. There is condemnation in his face, mingled now with the beginning of an old weary, helpless resignation. Jamie and Edmund follow their father. Jamie's face is hard with defensive cynicism. Edmund tries to copy this defence but without success. He plainly shows he is heartsick as well as physically ill.*

Mary is terribly nervous again, as if the strain of sitting through lunch with them had been too much for her. Yet at the same time, in contrast to this, her expression shows more of that strange aloofness which seems to stand apart from her nerves and the anxieties which harry them.

She is talking as she enters — a stream of words that issues casually, in a routine of family conversation, from her mouth. She appears indifferent to the fact that their thoughts are not on what she is saying any more than her own are. As she talks, she comes to the left of the table and stands, facing front, one hand fumbling with the bosom of her dress, the other playing over the table top. Tyrone lights a cigar and goes to the screen door, staring out. Jamie fills a pipe from a jar on top of the bookcase at rear. He lights it as he goes to look out of the window at right. Edmund sits in a chair by the table, turned half away from his mother so he does not have to watch her.

MARY. It's no use finding fault with Bridget. She doesn't listen. I can't threaten her, or she'd threaten she'd leave. And she does do her best at times. It's too bad they seem to be just the times you're sure to be late, James. Well, there's this consolation: it's difficult to tell from her cooking whether she's doing her best or her worst. (*She gives a little laugh of detached amusement — indifferently.*) Never mind. The summer will soon be over, thank goodness. Your season will open again and we can go back to second-rate hotels and trains. I hate them, too, but at least I don't expect them to be like a home, and there's no housekeeping to worry about. It's unreasonable to expect Bridget or Cathleen to act as if this was a home. They know it isn't as well as we know it. It never has been and it never will be.

TYRONE (*bitterly without turning around*). No, it never can be now. But it was once, before you —

MARY (*her face instantly set in blank denial*). Before I what? (*There is a dead silence. She goes on with a return of her detached air.*) No, no. Whatever you mean, it isn't true, dear. It was never a home. You've always preferred the Club or a bar-room. And for me it's always been as lonely as a dirty room in a one-night stand hotel. In a real home one is never lonely. You forget I know from experience what a home is like. I gave up one to marry you — my father's home. (*At once, through an association of ideas she turns to Edmund. Her manner becomes tenderly solicitous, but there is the strange quality of detachment in it.*) I'm worried about you, Edmund. You hardly touched a thing at lunch. That's no way to take care of yourself. It's all right for me not to have an appetite. I've been growing too fat. But you must eat. (*Coaxingly maternal.*) Promise me you will, dear, for my sake.

EDMUND (*dully*). Yes, Mama.

MARY (*pats his cheek as he tries not to shrink away*). That's a good boy.

(*There is another pause of dead silence. Then the telephone in the front hall rings and all of them stiffen startledly.*)

TYRONE (*hastily*). I'll answer. McGuire said he'd call me. (*He goes out through the front parlour.*)

MARY (*indifferently*). McGuire. He must have another piece of property on his list that no one would think of buying except your father. It doesn't matter any more, but it's always seemed to me your father could afford to keep on buying property but never to give me a home. (*She stops to listen as Tyrone's voice is heard from the hall.*)

TYRONE. Hello. (*With forced heartiness.*) Oh, how are you, Doctor?

(*Jamie turns from the window. Mary's fingers play more rapidly on the table top. Tyrone's voice, trying to conceal, reveals that he is hearing bad news.*)

I see — (*Hurriedly.*) Well, you'll explain all about it when you see him this afternoon. Yes, he'll be in without fail. Four o'clock. I'll drop in myself and have a talk with you before that. I have to go uptown on business, anyway. Goodbye, Doctor.

EDMUND (*dully*). That didn't sound like glad tidings.

(*Jamie gives him a pitying glance — then looks out of the window again. Mary's face is terrified and her hands flutter distractedly. Tyrone comes in. The strain is obvious in his casualness as he addresses Edmund.*)

TYRONE. It was Doctor Hardy. He wants you to be sure and see him at four.

EDMUND (*dully*). What did he say? Not that I give a damn now.

MARY (*bursts out excitedly*). I wouldn't believe him if he swore on a stack of Bibles. You mustn't pay attention to a word he says, Edmund.

TYRONE (*sharply*). Mary!

MARY (*more excitedly*). Oh, we all realize why you like him, James! Because he's cheap! But please don't try to tell me! I know all about Doctor Hardy. Heaven knows I ought to after all these years. He's an ignorant fool! There should be a law to keep men like him from practising. He hasn't the slightest idea — When you're in agony and half insane, he sits and holds your hand and delivers sermons on will-power! (*Her face is drawn in an expression of intense suffering by the memory. For the moment, she loses all caution. With bitter hatred.*) He deliberately humiliates you! He makes you beg and plead! He treats you like a criminal! He understands nothing! And yet it was exactly the same type of cheap quack who first gave you the medicine — and you never knew what it was until too late! (*Passionately.*) I hate doctors! They'll do anything — anything to keep you coming to them. They'll sell their souls! What's more, they'll sell yours, and you never know it till one day you find yourself in hell!

EDMUND. Mama! For God's sake, stop talking.

TYRONE (*shakenly*). Yes, Mary, it's no time —

MARY (*suddenly is overcome by guilty confusion — stammers*). I — Forgive me, dear. You're right. It's useless to be angry now. (*There is again a pause of dead silence. When she speaks again, her face has cleared and is calm, and the quality of uncanny detachment is in her voice and manner.*) I'm going upstairs for a moment, if you'll excuse me. I have to fix my hair. (*She adds smilingly.*) That is if I can find my glasses. I'll be right down.

TYRONE (*as she starts through the doorway — pleading and rebuking*). Mary!

MARY (*turns to stare at him calmly*). Yes, dear? What is it?

TYRONE (*helplessly*). Nothing.

MARY (*with a strange derisive smile*). You're welcome to come up and watch me if you're so suspicious.

TYRONE. As if that could do any good! You'd only postpone it. And I'm not your jailor. This isn't a prison.

MARY. No. I know you can't help thinking it's a home. (*She adds quickly with a detached contrition.*) I'm sorry, dear. I don't mean to be bitter. It's not your fault.

(*She turns and disappears through the back parlour. The three in the room remain silent. It is as if they were waiting until she got upstairs before speaking.*)

JAMIE (*cynically brutal*). Another shot in the arm!

EDMUND (*angrily*). Cut out that kind of talk!

TYRONE. Yes! Hold your foul tongue and your rotten Broadway loafer's lingo! Have you no pity or decency? (*Losing his temper.*) You ought to be kicked out in the gutter! But if I did it, you know damned well who'd weep and plead for you, and excuse you and complain till I let you come back.

JAMIE (*a spasm of pain crosses his face*). Christ, don't I know that? No pity? I have all the pity in the world for her. I understand what a hard game to beat she's up against — which is more than you ever have! My lingo didn't mean I had no feeling. I was merely putting bluntly what we all know, and have to live with now, again. (*Bitterly.*) The cures are no damned good except for a while. The truth is there is no cure and we've been saps to hope — (*Cynically.*) They never come back!

EDMUND (*scornfully parodying his brother's cynicism*). They never come back! Everything is in the bag! It's all a frame-up! We're all fall guys and suckers and we can't beat the game! (*Disdainfully.*) Christ, if I felt the way you do —!

JAMIE (*stung for a moment — then shrugging his shoulders, dryly*). I thought you did. Your poetry isn't very cheery. Nor the stuff you read and claim you admire. (*He indicates the smart bookcase at rear.*) Your pet with the unpronounceable name, for example.

EDMUND. Nietzsche. You don't know what you're talking about. You haven't read him.

JAMIE. Enough to know it's a lot of bunk!

TYRONE. Shut up, both of you! There's little choice between the philosophy you learned from Broadway loafers, and the one Edmund got from his books. They're both rotten to the core. You've both flouted the faith you were born and brought up in — the one true faith of the Catholic Church — and your denial has brought nothing but self-destruction!

(*His two sons stare at him contemptuously. They forget their quarrel and are as one against him on this issue.*)

EDMUND. That's the bunk, Papa!

JAMIE. We don't pretend, at any rate. (*Caustically.*) I don't notice you've worn any holes in the knees of your pants going to Mass.

TYRONE. It's true I'm a bad Catholic in the observance, God forgive me. But I believe! (*Angrily.*) And you're a liar! I may not go to church but every night and morning of my life I get on my knees and pray!

EDMUND (*bitingly*). Did you pray for Mama?

TYRONE. I did. I've prayed to God these many years for her.

EDMUND. Then Nietzsche must be right. (*He quotes from Thus Spake Zarathustra.*) "God is dead: of His pity for man hath God died."

TYRONE (*ignores this*). If your mother had prayed, too — She hasn't denied her faith, but she's forgotten it, until now there's no strength of the spirit left in her to fight against her curse. (*Then dully resigned.*) But what's the good of talk? We've lived with this before and now we must again. There's no help for it. (*Bitterly.*) Only I wish she hadn't led me to hope this time. By God, I never will again!

EDMUND. That's a rotten thing to say, Papa! (*Defiantly.*) Well, I'll hope! She's just started. It can't have got a hold on her yet. She can still stop. I'm going to talk to her.

JAMIE (*shrugs his shoulders*). You can't talk to her now. She'll listen but she won't listen. She'll be here but she won't be here. You know the way she gets.

TYRONE. Yes, that's the way the poison acts on her always. Every day from now on, there'll be the same drifting away from us until by the end of each night —

EDMUND (*miserably*). Cut it out, Papa! (*He jumps up from his chair.*) I'm going to get dressed. (*Bitterly, as he goes.*) I'll make so much noise she can't suspect I've come to spy on her. (*He disappears through the front parlour and can be heard stamping noisily upstairs.*)

JAMIE (*after a pause*). What did Doc Hardy say about the Kid?

TYRONE (*dully*). It's what you thought. He's got consumption.

JAMIE. God damn it!

TYRONE. There is no possible doubt, he said.

JAMIE. He'll have to go to a sanatorium.

TYRONE. Yes, and the sooner the better, Hardy said, for him and everyone around him. He claims that in six months to a year Edmund will be cured, if he obeys orders. (*He sighs — gloomily and resentfully.*) I never thought a child of mine — It doesn't come from my side of the family. There wasn't one of us that didn't have lungs as strong as an ox.

JAMIE. Who gives a damn about that part of it! Where does Hardy want to send him?

TYRONE. That's what I'm to see him about.

JAMIE. Well, for God's sake, pick out a good place and not some cheap dump!

TYRONE (*stung*). I'll send him wherever Hardy thinks best!

JAMIE. Well, don't give Hardy your old over-the-hills-to-the-poorhouse song about taxes and mortgages.

TYRONE. I'm no millionaire who can throw money away! Why shouldn't I tell Hardy the truth?

JAMIE. Because he'll think you want him to pick a cheap dump, and because he'll know it isn't the truth — especially if he hears afterwards you've seen McGuire and let that flannel-mouth, gold-brick merchant sting you with another piece of bum property!

TYRONE (*furiously*). Keep your nose out of my business!

JAMIE. This is Edmund's business. What I'm afraid of is, with your Irish bog-trotter idea that consumption is fatal, you'll figure it would be a waste of money to spend any more than you can help.

TYRONE. You liar!

JAMIE. All right. Prove I'm a liar. That's what I want. That's why I brought it up.

TYRONE (*his rage still smouldering*). I have every hope Edmund will be cured. And keep your dirty tongue off Ireland! You're a fine one to sneer, with the map of it on your face!

JAMIE. Not after I wash my face. (*Then before his father can react to this insult to the Old Sod, he adds dryly, shrugging his shoulders.*) Well, I've said all I have to say. It's up to you. (*Abruptly.*) What do you want me to do this afternoon, now you're going uptown? I've done all I can do on the hedge until you cut more of it. You don't want me to go ahead with your clipping, I know that.

TYRONE. No. You'd get it crooked, as you get everything else.

JAMIE. Then I'd better go uptown with Edmund. The bad news coming on top of what's happened to Mama may hit him hard.

TYRONE (*forgetting his quarrel*). Yes, go with him, Jamie. Keep up his spirits, if you can. (*He adds caustically.*) If you can without making it an excuse to get drunk!

JAMIE. What would I use for money? The last I heard they were still selling booze, not giving it away. (*He starts for the front-parlour doorway.*) I'll get dressed.

(*He stops in the doorway as he sees his mother approaching from the hall, and moves aside to let her come in. Her eyes look brighter, and her manner is more detached. This change becomes more marked as the scene goes on.*)

MARY (*vaguely*). You haven't seen my glasses anywhere, have you, Jamie?

(*She doesn't look at him. He glances away, ignoring her question but she doesn't seem to expect an answer. She comes forward, addressing her husband without looking at him.*)

You haven't seen them, have you, James?

(*Behind her Jamie disappears through the front parlour.*)

TYRONE (*turns to look out of the screen door*). No, Mary.

MARY. What's the matter with Jamie? Have you been nagging at him again? You shouldn't treat him with such contempt all the time. He's not to blame. If he'd been brought up in a real home, I'm sure he would have been different. (*She comes to the windows at right — lightly.*) You're not much of a weather prophet, dear. See how hazy it's getting. I can hardly see the other shore.

TYRONE (*trying to speak naturally*). Yes, I spoke too soon. We're in for another night of fog, I'm afraid.

MARY. Oh, well, I won't mind it tonight.

TYRONE. No, I don't imagine you will, Mary.

MARY (*flashes a glance at him — after a pause*). I don't see Jamie going down to the hedge. Where did he go?

TYRONE. He's going with Edmund to the Doctor's. He went up to change his clothes. (*Then, glad of an excuse to leave her.*) I'd better do the same or I'll be late for my appointment at the Club.

(*He makes a move toward the front-parlour doorway, but with a swift impulsive movement she reaches out and clasps his arm.*)

MARY (*a note of pleading in her voice*). Don't go yet, dear. I don't want to be alone. (*Hastily.*) I mean, you have plenty of time. You know you boast you can dress in one-tenth the time it takes the boys. (*Vaguely.*) There is something I wanted to say. What is it? I've forgotten. I'm glad Jamie is going uptown. You didn't give him any money, I hope.

TYRONE. I did not.

MARY. He'd only spend it on drink and you know what a vile, poisonous tongue he has when he's drunk. Not that I would mind anything he said tonight, but he always manages to drive you into a rage, especially if you're drunk, too, as you will be.

TYRONE (*resentfully*). I won't. I never get drunk.

MARY (*teasing indifferently*). Oh, I'm sure you'll hold it well. You always have. It's hard for a stranger to tell, but after thirty-five years of marriage —

TYRONE. I've never missed a performance in my life. That's the proof! (*Then bitterly.*) If I did get drunk it is not you who should blame me. No man has ever had a better reason.

MARY. Reason? What reason? You always drink too much when you go to the Club, don't you? Particularly when you meet McGuire. He sees to that. Don't think I'm finding fault, dear. You must do as you please. I won't mind.

TYRONE. I know you won't. (*He turns toward the front parlour, anxious to escape.*) I've got to get dressed.

MARY (*again she reaches out and grasps his arm — pleadingly*). No, please wait a little while, dear. At least, until one of the boys comes down. You will all be leaving me so soon.

TYRONE (*with bitter sadness*). It's you who are leaving us, Mary.

MARY. I? That's a silly thing to say, James. How could I leave? There is nowhere I could go. Who would I go to see? I have no friends.

TYRONE. It's your own fault — (*He stops and sighs helplessly — persuasively.*) There's surely one thing you can do this afternoon that will be good for you, Mary. Take a drive in the automobile. Get away from the house. Get a little sun and fresh air. (*Injuredly.*) I bought the automobile for you. You know I don't like the damned things. I'd rather walk any day, or take a trolley. (*With growing resentment.*) I had it here waiting for you when you came back from the sanatorium. I hoped it would give you pleasure and distract your mind. You used to ride in it every day, but you've hardly used it at all lately. I paid a lot of money I couldn't afford, and there's the chauffeur I have to board and lodge and pay high wages whether he drives you or not. (*Bitterly.*) Waste! The same old waste that will land me in the poorhouse in my old age! What good did it do you? I might as well have thrown the money out of the window.

MARY (*with detached calm*). Yes, it was a waste of money, James. You shouldn't have bought a secondhand automobile. You were swindled again as you always are, because you insist on secondhand bargains in everything.

TYRONE. It's one of the best makes! Everyone says it's better than any of the new ones!

MARY (*ignoring this*). It was another waste to hire Smythe, who was only a helper in a garage and had never been a chauffeur. Oh, I realize his wages are less than a real chauffeur's, but he more than makes up for that, I'm sure, by the graft he gets from the garage on repair bills. Something is always wrong. Smythe sees to that, I'm afraid

TYRONE. I don't believe it! He may not be a fancy millionaire's flunkey but he's honest! You're as bad as Jamie, suspecting everyone!

MARY. You mustn't be offended, dear. I wasn't offended when you gave me the automobile. I knew you didn't mean to humiliate me. I knew that was the way you had to do everything. I was grateful and touched. I knew buying the car was a hard thing for you to do, and it proved how much you loved me, in your way, especially when you couldn't really believe it would do me any good.

TYRONE. Mary! (*He suddenly hugs her to him — brokenly.*) Dear Mary! For the love of God, for my sake and the boys' sake and your own, won't you stop now?

MARY (*stammers in guilty confusion for a second*). I — James! Please! (*Her strange, stubborn defence comes back instantly.*) Stop what? What are you talking about?

(*He lets his arm fall to his side brokenly. She impulsively puts her arm around him.*)

James! We've loved each other! We always will! Let's remember only that, and not try to understand what we cannot understand, or help things that cannot be helped — the things life has done to us we cannot excuse or explain.

TYRONE (*as if he hadn't heard — bitterly*). You won't even try?

MARY (*her arms drop hopelessly and she turns away — with detachment*). Try to go for a drive this afternoon, you mean? Why, yes, if you wish me to, although it makes me feel lonelier than if I stayed here. There is no one I can invite to drive with me, and I never know where to tell Smythe to go. If there was a friend's house where I could drop in and laugh and gossip awhile. But, of course, there isn't. There never has been. (*Her manner becoming more and more remote.*) At the Convent I had so many friends. Girls whose families lived in lovely homes. I used to visit them and they'd visit me in my father's home. But, naturally, after I married an actor — you know how actors were considered in those days — a lot of them gave me the cold shoulder. And then, right after we were married, there was the scandal of that woman who had been your mistress, suing you. From then on, all my old friends either pitied me or cut me dead. I hated the ones who cut me much less than the pitiers.

TYRONE (*with guilty resentment*). For God's sake, don't dig up what's long forgotten. If you're that far gone in the past already, when it's only the beginning of the afternoon, what will you be tonight?

MARY (*stares at him defiantly now*). Come to think of it, I do have to drive uptown. There's something I must get at the drugstore.

TYRONE (*bitterly scornful*). Leave it to you to have some of the stuff hidden, and prescriptions for more! I hope you'll lay in a good stock ahead so we'll never have another night like the one when you screamed for it, and ran out of the house in your nightdress half crazy, to try and throw yourself off the dock!

MARY (*tries to ignore this*). I have to get tooth powder and toilet soap and cold cream — (*She breaks down pitiably.*) James! You mustn't remember! You mustn't humiliate me so!

TYRONE (*ashamed*). I'm sorry. Forgive me, Mary!

MARY (*defensively detached again*). It doesn't matter. Nothing like that ever happened. You must have dreamed it.

(*He stares at her hopelessly. Her voice seems to drift farther and farther away.*)

I was so healthy before Edmund was born. You remember, James. There wasn't a nerve in my body. Even travelling with you season after season, with week after week of one-night stands, in trains without Pullmans, in dirty rooms of filthy hotels, eating bad food, bearing children in hotel rooms, I still kept healthy. But bearing Edmund was the last straw. I was so sick afterwards, and that ignorant quack of a cheap hotel doctor — All he knew was I was in pain. It was easy for him to stop the pain.

TYRONE. Mary! For God's sake, forget the past!

MARY (*with strange objective calm*). Why? How can I? The past is the present, isn't it? It's the future, too. We all try to lie out of that but life won't let us. (*Going on.*) I blame only myself. I swore after Eugene died I would never have another baby. I was to blame for his death. If I hadn't left him with my mother to join you on the road, because you wrote telling me you missed me and were so lonely, Jamie would never have been allowed, when he still had measles, to go in the baby's room. (*Her face hardening.*) I've always believed Jamie did it on purpose. He was jealous of the baby. He hated him. (*As Tyrone starts to protest.*) Oh, I know Jamie was only seven, but he was never stupid. He'd been warned it might kill the baby. He knew. I've never been able to forgive him for that.

TYRONE (*with bitter sadness*). Are you back with Eugene now? Can't you let our dead baby rest in peace?

MARY (*as if she hadn't heard him*). It was my fault. I should have insisted on staying with Eugene and not have let you persuade me to join you, just because I loved you. Above all, I shouldn't have let you insist I have another baby to take Eugene's place, because you thought that would make me forget his death. I knew from experience by then that children should have homes to be born in, if they are to be good children, and women need homes, if they are to be good mothers. I was afraid all the time I carried Edmund. I knew something terrible would happen. I knew I'd proved by the way I'd left Eugene that I wasn't worthy to have another baby, and that God would punish me if I did. I never should have borne Edmund.

TYRONE (*with an uneasy glance through the front parlour*). Mary! Be careful with your talk. If he heard you he might think you never wanted him. He's feeling bad enough already without —

MARY (*violently*). It's a lie! I did want him! More than anything in the world! You don't understand! I meant, for his sake. He has never been happy. He never will be. Nor healthy. He was born nervous and too sensitive, and that's my fault. And now, ever since he's been so sick I've kept remembering Eugene and my father and I've been so frightened and guilty — (*Then, catching herself, with an instant change to stubborn denial.*) Oh, I know it's foolish to imagine dreadful things when there's no reason for it. After all, everyone has colds and gets over them.

(*Tyrone stares at her and sighs helplessly. He turns away toward the front parlour and sees Edmund coming down the stairs in the hall.*)

TYRONE (*sharply, in a low voice*). Here's Edmund. For God's sake try and be yourself — at least until he goes! You can do that much for him!

(*He waits, forcing his face into a pleasantly paternal expression. She waits frightenedly, seized again by a nervous panic, her hands fluttering over the bosom of her dress, up to her throat and hair, with a distracted aimlessness. Then, as Edmund approaches the doorway, she cannot face him. She goes swiftly away to the windows at left and stares out with her back to the front parlour. Edmund enters. He has changed to a ready-made blue serge suit, high stiff collar and tie, black shoes.*)

(*With an actor's heartiness.*) Well! You look spick and span. I'm on my way up to change, too. (*He starts to pass him.*)

EDMUND (*dryly*). Wait a minute, Papa. I hate to bring up disagreeable topics, but there's the matter of carfare. I'm broke.

TYRONE (*starts automatically on a customary lecture*). You'll always be broke until you learn the value — (*Checks himself guiltily, looking at his son's sick face with worried pity.*) But you've been learning, lad. You worked hard before you took ill. You've done splendidly. I'm proud of you.

(*He pulls out a small roll of bills from his pants pocket and carefully selects one. Edmund takes it. He glances at it and his face expresses astonishment. His father again reacts customarily — sarcastically.*)

Thank you. (*He quotes.*) "How sharper than a serpent's tooth it is —"

EDMUND. "To have a thankless child." I know. Give me a chance, Papa. I'm knocked speechless. This isn't a dollar. It's a ten spot.

TYRONE (*embarrassed by his generosity*). Put it in your pocket. You'll probably meet some of your friends uptown and you can't hold your end up and be sociable with nothing in your jeans.

EDMUND. You meant it? Gosh, thank you, Papa. (*He is genuinely pleased and grateful for a moment — then he stares at his father's face with uneasy suspicion.*) But why all of a sudden —? (*Cynically.*) Did Doc Hardy tell you I was going to die? (*Then he sees his father is bitterly hurt.*) No! That's a rotten crack. I was only kidding, Papa. (*He puts an arm around his father impulsively and gives him an affectionate hug.*) I'm very grateful. Honest, Papa.

TYRONE (*touched, returns his hug*). You're welcome, lad.

MARY (*suddenly turns to them in a confused panic of frightened anger*). I won't have it! (*She stamps her foot.*) Do you hear, Edmund! Such morbid nonsense! Saying you're going to die! It's the books you read! Nothing but sadness and death! Your father shouldn't allow you to have them. And some of the poems you've written yourself are even worse! You'd think you didn't want to live! A boy of your age with everything before him! It's just a pose you get out of books! You're not really sick at all!

TYRONE. Mary! Hold your tongue!

MARY (*instantly changing to a detached tone*). But, James, it's absurd of Edmund to be so gloomy and make such a great to-do about nothing. (*Turning to Edmund but avoiding his eyes — teasingly affectionate.*) Never mind, dear. I'm on to you. (*She comes to him.*) You want to be petted and spoiled and made a fuss over, isn't that it? You're still such a baby.

(*She puts her arm around him and hugs him. He remains rigid and unyielding. Her voice begins to tremble.*)

But please don't carry it too far, dear. Don't say horrible things. I know it's foolish to take them seriously, but I can't help it. You've got me — so frightened.

(*She breaks and hides her face on his shoulder, sobbing. Edmund is moved in spite of himself. He pats her shoulder with an awkward tenderness.*)

EDMUND. Don't, mother. (*His eyes meet his father's.*)

TYRONE (*huskily — clutching at hopeless hope*). Maybe if you asked your mother now what you said you were going to — (*He fumbles with his watch.*) By God, look at the time! I'll have to shake a leg.

(*He hurries away through the front parlour. Mary lifts her head. Her manner is again one of detached motherly solicitude. She seems to have forgotten the tears which are still in her eyes.*)

MARY. How do you feel, dear? (*She feels his forehead.*) Your head is a little hot, but that's just from going out in the sun. You look ever so much better than you did this morning. (*Taking his hand.*) Come and sit down. You mustn't stand on your feet so much. You must learn to husband your strength. (*She gets him to sit and she sits sideways on the arm of his chair, an arm around his shoulder, so he cannot meet her eyes.*)

EDMUND (*starts to blurt out the appeal he now feels is quite hopeless*). Listen, Mama—

MARY (*interrupting quickly*). Now, now! Don't talk. Lean back and rest. (*Persuasively.*) You know, I think it would be much better for you if you stayed home this afternoon and let me take care of you. It's such a tiring trip uptown in the dirty old trolley on a hot day like this. I'm sure you'd be much better off here with me.

EDMUND (*dully*). You forget I have an appointment with Hardy. (*Trying again to get his appeal started.*) Listen, Mama—

MARY (*quickly*). You can telephone and say you don't feel well enough. (*Excitedly.*) It's simply a waste of time and money seeing him. He'll only tell you some lie. He'll pretend he's found something serious the matter because that's his bread and butter. (*She gives a hard sneering little laugh.*) The old idiot! All he knows about medicine is to look solemn and preach will-power!

EDMUND (*trying to catch her eyes*). Mama! Please listen! I want to ask you something! You—you're only just started. You can still stop. You've got the will-power! We'll all help you. I'll do anything! Won't you, Mama?

MARY (*stammers pleadingly*). Please don't—talk about things you don't understand!

EDMUND (*dully*). All right, I give up. I knew it was no use.

MARY (*in blank denial now*). Anyway, I don't know what you're referring to. But I do know you should be the last one— Right after I returned from the sanatorium, you began to be ill. The doctor there had warned me I must have peace at home with nothing to upset me, and all I've done is worry about you. (*Then distractedly.*) But that's no excuse! I'm only trying to explain. It's not an excuse! (*She hugs him to her—pleadingly.*) Promise me, dear, you won't believe I made you an excuse.

EDMUND (*bitterly*). What else can I believe?

MARY (*slowly takes her arm away—her manner remote and objective again*). Yes, I suppose you can't help suspecting that.

EDMUND (*ashamed but still bitter*). What do you expect?

MARY. Nothing, I don't blame you. How could you believe me—when I can't believe myself? I've become such a liar. I never lied about anything once upon a time. Now I have to lie, especially to myself. But how can you understand, when I don't myself. I've never understood anything about it, except that one day long ago I found I could no longer call my soul my own. (*She pauses—then lowering her voice to a strange tone of whispered confidence.*) But some day, dear, I will find it again—some day when you're all well, and I see you healthy and happy and successful, and I don't have to feel guilty any more—some day when the Blessed Virgin Mary forgives me and gives me back the faith in Her love and pity I used to have in my convent days, and I can pray to Her again—when She sees no one in the world can believe in me even for a moment any more, then She will believe in me, and with Her help it will be so easy. I will hear myself scream with agony, and at the same time I will laugh because I will be so sure of myself. (*Then as Edmund remains hopelessly silent, she adds sadly.*) Of course, you can't believe that, either. (*She rises from the arm of his chair and goes to stare out of the windows at right with her back to him—casually.*) Now I think of it, you might as well go uptown. I forgot I'm taking a drive. I have to go to the drugstore. You would hardly want to go there with me. You'd be so ashamed.

EDMUND (*brokenly*). Mama! Don't!

MARY. I suppose you'll divide that ten dollars your father gave you with Jamie. You always divide with each other, don't you? Like good sports. Well, I know what he'll do with his share. Get drunk someplace where he can be with the only kind of woman he understands or likes. (*She turns to him, pleading frightenedly.*) Edmund! Promise me you won't drink! It's so dangerous! You know Doctor Hardy told you—

EDMUND (*bitterly*). I thought he was an old idiot.

MARY (*pitifully*). Edmund!

(*Jamie's voice is heard from the front hall,* Come on, Kid, let's beat it. *Mary's manner at once becomes detached again.*)

Go on, Edmund. Jamie's waiting. (*She goes to the front-parlour doorway.*) There comes your father downstairs, too.

(*Tyrone's voice calls,* Come on, Edmund.)

MARY (*kisses him with detached affection*). Goodbye, dear. If you're coming home for dinner, try not to be late. And tell your father. You know what Bridget is.

(*He turns and hurries away. Tyrone calls from the hall,* Goodbye, Mary, *and then Jamie,* Goodbye, Mama. *She calls back.*)

Goodbye.

(*The front screen door is heard closing after them. She comes and stands by the table, one hand drumming on it, the other fluttering up to pat her hair. She stares about the room with frightened, forsaken eyes and whispers to herself.*)

It's so lonely here. (*Then her face hardens into bitter self-contempt.*) You're lying to yourself again. You wanted to get rid of them. Their contempt and disgust aren't pleasant company. You're glad they're gone. (*She gives a little despairing laugh.*) Then Mother of God, why do I feel so lonely?

CURTAIN

ACT THREE

SCENE. *The same. It is around half-past six in the evening. Dusk is gathering in the living-room, an early dusk due to the fog which has rolled in from the Sound and is like a white curtain drawn down outside the windows. From a lighthouse beyond the harbour's mouth, a foghorn is heard at regular intervals, moaning like a mournful whale in labour, and from the harbour itself, intermittently, comes the warning ringing of bells on yachts at anchor.*

The tray with the bottle of whiskey, glasses, and pitcher of ice water is on the table, as it was in the pre-luncheon scene of the previous act.

Mary and the second girl, Cathleen, are discovered. The latter is standing at left of table. She holds an empty whiskey glass in her hand as if she'd forgotten she had it. She shows the effects of drink. Her stupid, good-humoured face wears a pleased and flattered simper.

Mary is paler than before and her eyes shine with unnatural brilliance. The strange detachment in her manner has intensified. She has hidden deeper within herself and found refuge and release in a dream where present reality is but an appearance to be accepted and dismissed unfeelingly — even with a hard cynicism — or entirely ignored. There is at times an uncanny gay, free youthfulness in her manner, as if in spirit she were released to become again, simply and without self-consciousness, the naïve, happy, chattering schoolgirl of her convent days. She wears the dress into which she had changed for her drive to town, a simple, fairly expensive affair, which would be extremely becoming if it were not for the careless, almost slovenly way she wears it. Her hair is no longer fastidiously in place. It has a slightly dishevelled, lopsided look. She talks to Cathleen with a confiding familiarity, as if the second girl were an old, intimate friend. As the curtain rises, she is standing by the screen door looking out. A moan of the foghorn is heard.

MARY (*amused — girlishly*). That foghorn! Isn't it awful, Cathleen?

CATHLEEN (*talks more familiarly than usual but never with intentional impertinence because she sincerely likes her mistress*). It is indeed, Ma'am. It's like a banshee.

MARY (*goes on as if she hadn't heard. In nearly all the following dialogue there is the feeling that she has Cathleen with her merely as an excuse to keep talking*). I don't mind it tonight. Last night it drove me crazy. I lay awake worrying until I couldn't stand it any more.

CATHLEEN. Bad cess to it. I was scared out of my wits riding back from town. I thought that ugly monkey, Smythe, would drive us in a ditch or against a tree. You couldn't see your hand in front of you. I'm glad you had me sit in back with you, Ma'am. If I'd been in front with that monkey — He can't keep his dirty hands to himself. Give him half a chance and he's pinching me on the leg or you-know-where — asking your pardon, Ma'am, but it's true.

MARY (*dreamily*). It wasn't the fog I minded, Cathleen. I really love fog.

CATHLEEN. They say it's good for the complexion.

MARY. It hides you from the world and the world from you. You feel that everything has changed, and nothing is what it seemed to be. No one can find or touch you any more.

CATHLEEN. I wouldn't care so much if Smythe was a fine, handsome man like some chauffeurs I've seen — I mean, if it was all in fun, for I'm a decent girl. But for a shrivelled runt like Smythe —! I've told him, you must think I'm hard up that I'd notice a monkey like you. I've warned him, one day I'll give him a clout that'll knock him into next week. And so I will!

MARY. It's the foghorn I hate. It won't let you alone. It keeps reminding you, and warning you, and calling you back. (*She smiles strangely.*) But it can't tonight. It's just an ugly sound. It doesn't remind me of anything. (*She gives a teasing, girlish laugh.*) Except, perhaps, Mr. Tyrone's snores. I've always had such fun teasing him about it. He has snored ever since I can remember, especially when he's had too much to drink, and yet he's like a child, he hates to admit it. (*She laughs, coming to the table.*) Well, I suppose I snore at times, too, and I don't like to admit it. So I have no right to make fun of him, have I? (*She sits in the rocker at right of table.*)

CATHLEEN. Ah, sure, everybody healthy snores. It's a sign of sanity, they say. (*Then, worriedly.*) What time is it, Ma'am? I ought to go back in the kitchen. The damp is in Bridget's rheumatism and she's like a raging divil. She'll bite my head off. (*She puts her glass on the table and makes a movement toward the back parlour.*)

MARY (*with a flash of apprehension*). No, don't go, Cathleen. I don't want to be alone, yet.

CATHLEEN. You won't be for long. The Master and the boys will be home soon.

MARY. I doubt if they'll come back for dinner. They have too good an excuse to remain in the bar-rooms where they feel at home.

(*Cathleen stared at her, stupidly puzzled. Mary goes on smilingly.*)

Don't worry about Bridget. I'll tell her I kept you with me, and you can take a big drink of whiskey to her when you go. She won't mind then.

CATHLEEN (*grins — at her ease again*). No, Ma'am. That's

the one thing can make her cheerful. She loves her drop.

MARY. Have another drink yourself, if you wish, Cathleen.

CATHLEEN. I don't know if I'd better, Ma'am. I can feel what I've had already. (*Reaching for the bottle.*) Well, maybe one more won't harm. (*She pours a drink.*) Here's your good health, Ma'am. (*She drinks without bothering about a chaser.*)

MARY (*dreamily*). I really did have good health once, Cathleen. But that was long ago.

CATHLEEN (*worried again*). The Master's sure to notice what's gone from the bottle. He has the eye of a hawk for that.

MARY (*amusedly*). Oh, we'll play Jamie's trick on him. Just measure a few drinks of water and pour them in.

CATHLEEN (*does this — with a silly giggle*). God save me, it'll be half water. He'll know by the taste.

MARY (*indifferently*). No, by the time he comes home he'll be too drunk to tell the difference. He has such a good excuse, he believes, to drown his sorrows.

CATHLEEN (*philosophically*). Well, it's a good man's failing. I wouldn't give a trauneen for a teetotaller. They've no high spirits. (*Then, stupidly puzzled.*) Good excuse? You mean Master Edmund, Ma'am? I can tell the Master is worried about him.

MARY (*stiffens defensively — but in a strange way the reaction has a mechanical quality, as if it did not penetrate to real emotion*). Don't be silly, Cathleen. Why should he be? A touch of grippe is nothing. And Mr. Tyrone never is worried about anything, except money and property and the fear he'll end his days in poverty. I mean, deeply worried. Because he cannot really understand anything else. (*She gives a little laugh of detached, affectionate amusement.*) My husband is a very peculiar man, Cathleen.

CATHLEEN (*vaguely resentful*). Well, he's a fine, handsome, kind gentleman just the same, Ma'am. Never mind his weakness.

MARY. Oh, I don't mind. I've loved him dearly for thirty-six years. That proves I know he's lovable at heart and can't help being what he is, doesn't it?

CATHLEEN (*hazily reassured*). That's right, Ma'am. Love him dearly, for any fool can see he worships the ground you walk on. (*Fighting the effect of her last drink and trying to be soberly conversational.*) Speaking of acting, Ma'am, how is it you never went on the stage?

MARY (*resentfully*). I? What put that absurd notion in your head? I was brought up in a respectable home and educated in the best convent in the Middle West. Before I met Mr. Tyrone I hardly knew there was such a thing as a theatre. I was a very pious girl. I even dreamed of becoming a nun. I've never had the slightest desire to be an actress.

CATHLEEN (*bluntly*). Well, I can't imagine you a holy nun, Ma'am. Sure, you never darken the door of a church, God forgive you.

MARY (*ignores this*). I've never felt at home in the theatre. Even though Mr. Tyrone has made me go with him on all his tours, I've had little to do with the people in his company, or with anyone on the stage. Not that I have anything against them. They have always been kind to me, and I to them. But I've never felt at home with them. Their life is not my life. It has always stood between me and — (*She gets up — abruptly.*) But let's not talk of old things that couldn't be helped. (*She goes to the porch door and stares out.*) How thick the fog is. I can't see the road. All the people in the world could pass by and I would never know. I wish it was always that way. It's getting dark already. It will soon be night, thank goodness. (*She turns back — vaguely.*) It was kind of you to keep me company this afternoon, Cathleen. I would have been lonely driving uptown alone.

CATHLEEN. Sure, wouldn't I rather ride in a fine automobile than stay here and listen to Bridget's lies about her relations? It was like a vacation, Ma'am. (*She pauses — then stupidly.*) There was only one thing I didn't like.

MARY (*vaguely*). What was that, Cathleen?

CATHLEEN. The way the man in the drugstore acted when I took in the prescription for you. (*Indignantly.*) The impidence of him!

MARY (*with stubborn blankness*). What are you talking about? What drugstore? What prescription? (*Then hastily, as Cathleen stares in stupid amazement.*) Oh, of course, I'd forgotten. The medicine for the rheumatism in my hands. What did the man say? (*Then with indifference.*) Not that it matters, as long as he filled the prescription.

CATHLEEN. It mattered to me, then! I'm not used to being treated like a thief. He gave me a long look and says insultingly, "Where did you get hold of this?" and I says, "It's none of your damned business, but if you must know, it's for the lady I work for, Mrs. Tyrone, who's sitting out in the automobile." That shut him up quick. He gave a look out at you and said, "Oh," and went to get the medicine.

MARY (*vaguely*). Yes, he knows me. (*She sits in the armchair at right rear of table. She adds in a calm, detached voice.*) I have to take it because there is no other that can stop the pain — *all* the pain — I mean, in my hands. (*She raises her hands and regards them with melancholy sympathy. There is no tremor in them now.*) Poor hands! You'd never believe it, but they were once one of my good points, along with my hair and eyes, and I had a fine figure, too. (*Her tone has become more and more far-off and dreamy.*) They were a musician's hands. I used to love the piano. I worked so hard at my music in the Convent — if you can call it work when you do something you love. Mother Elizabeth and my music teacher both said I had more talent than any student they remembered. My father paid for special lessons. He spoiled me. He would do anything I asked. He would have sent me to Europe to study after I graduated from the Convent. I might have gone — if I hadn't fallen in love with Mr. Tyrone. Or I might have become a nun. I had two dreams. To be a nun, that was the more beautiful one. To become a concert pianist, that was the other.

(*She pauses, regarding her hands fixedly. Cathleen blinks her eyes to fight off drowsiness and a tipsy feeling.*)

I haven't touched a piano in so many years. I couldn't play with such crippled fingers, even if I wanted to. For a time after my marriage I tried to keep up my music. But it was hopeless. One-night stands, cheap hotels, dirty trains, bearing children, never having a home — (*She stares at her hands with fascinated disgust.*) See, Cathleen, how ugly they are! So maimed and crippled! You would think they'd been through some horrible accident! (*She gives a strange little laugh.*) So they have, come to think of it. (*She suddenly thrusts her hands behind her back.*) I won't look at them. They're worse than the foghorn for reminding me — (*Then with defiant self-assurance.*) But even they can't touch me now. (*She brings her hands from behind her back and deliberately stares at them — calmly.*) They're far away. I see them, but the pain has gone.

CATHLEEN (*stupidly puzzled*). You've taken some of the medicine? It made you act funny, Ma'am. If I didn't know better, I'd think you'd a drop taken.

MARY (*dreamily*). It kills the pain. You go back until at last you are beyond its reach. Only the past when you were happy is real. (*She pauses — then as if her words had been an evocation which called back happiness she changes in her whole manner and facial expression. She looks younger. There is a quality of an innocent convent girl about her, and she smiles shyly.*) If you think Mr. Tyrone is handsome now, Cathleen, you should have seen him when I first met him. He had the reputation of being one of the best-looking men in the country. The girls in the Convent who had seen him act, or seen his photographs, used to rave about him. He was a great matinée idol then, you know. Women used to wait at the stage door just to see him come out. You can imagine how excited I was, when my father wrote me he and James Tyrone had become friends, and that I was to meet him when I came home for Easter vacation. I showed the letter to all the girls, and how envious they were! My father took me to see him at first. It was a play about the French Revolution and the leading part was a nobleman. I couldn't take my eyes off him. I wept when he was thrown in prison — and then was so mad at myself because I was afraid my eyes and nose would be red. My father had said we'd go backstage to his dressing-room right after the play, and so we did. (*She gives a little excited, shy laugh.*) I was so bashful all I could do was stammer and blush like a little fool. But he didn't seem to think I was a fool. I know he liked me the first moment we were introduced. (*Coquettishly.*) I guess my eyes and nose couldn't have been red, after all. I was really very pretty then, Cathleen. And he was handsomer than my wildest dream, in his make-up and his nobleman's costume that was so becoming to him. He was different from all ordinary men, like someone from another world. At the same time he was simple, and kind, and unassuming, not a bit stuck-up or vain. I fell in love right then. So did he, he told me afterwards. I forgot all about becoming a nun or a concert pianist. All I wanted was to be his wife. (*She pauses, staring before her with unnaturally bright, dreamy eyes, and a rapt, tender, girlish smile.*) Thirty-six years ago, but I can see it as clearly as if it were tonight! We've loved each other ever since. And in all those thirty-six years, there has never been a breath of scandal about him. I mean, with any other woman. Never since he met me. That has made me very happy, Cathleen. It has made me forgive so many other things.

CATHLEEN (*fighting tipsy drowsiness — sentimentally*). He's a fine gentleman and you're a lucky woman. (*Then, fidgeting.*) Can I take the drink to Bridget, Ma'am? It must be near dinner-time and I ought to be in the kitchen helping her. If she don't get something to quiet her temper, she'll be after me with the cleaver.

MARY (*with a vague exasperation at being brought back from her dream*). Yes, yes, go. I don't need you now.

CATHLEEN (*with relief*). Thank you, Ma'am. (*She pours out a big drink and starts for the back parlour with it.*) You won't be alone long. The Master and the boys —

MARY (*impatiently*). No, no, they won't come. Tell Bridget I won't wait. You can serve dinner promptly at half-past six. I'm not hungry but I'll sit at the table and we'll get it over with.

CATHLEEN. You ought to eat something, Ma'am. It's a queer medicine if it takes away your appetite.

MARY (*has begun to drift into dreams again — reacts mechanically*). What medicine? I don't know what you mean. (*In dismissal.*) You better take the drink to Bridget.

CATHLEEN. Yes, Ma'am.

(*She disappears through the back parlour. Mary waits until she hears the pantry door close behind her. Then she settles back in relaxed dreaminess, staring fixedly at nothing. Her arms rest limply along the arms of the chair, her hands with long, warped, swollen-knuckled, sensitive fingers drooping in complete calm. It is growing dark in the room. There is a pause of dead quiet. Then from the world outside comes the melancholy moan of the foghorn, followed by a chorus of bells, muffled by the fog, from the anchored craft in the harbour. Mary's face gives no sign she has *heard, but her hands jerk and the fingers automatically play for a moment on the air. She frowns and shakes her head mechanically as if a fly had walked across her mind. She suddenly loses all the girlish quality and is an ageing, cynically sad, embittered woman.)*

MARY (*bitterly*). You're a sentimental fool. What is so wonderful about that first meeting between a silly romantic schoolgirl and a matinée idol? You were much happier before you knew he existed, in the Convent when you used to pray to the Blessed Virgin. (*Longingly.*) If I could only find the faith I lost, so I could pray again! (*She pauses — then begins to recite the Hail Mary in a flat, empty tone.*) "Hail, Mary, full of grace! the Lord is with Thee; blessed art Thou among women." (*Sneeringly.*) You expect the Blessed Virgin to be fooled by a lying dope fiend reciting words! You can't hide from Her! (*She springs to her feet. Her hands fly up to pat her hair distractedly.*) I must go upstairs. I haven't taken enough. When you start again you never know exactly how much you need. (*She goes toward the front parlour — then stops in the doorway as she hears the sound of voices from the front path. She starts guiltily.*) That must be them — (*She hurries back to sit down. Her face sets in stubborn defensiveness — resentfully.*) Why are they coming back? They don't want to. And I'd much rather be alone. (*Suddenly her whole manner changes. She becomes pathetically relieved and eager.*) Oh, I'm so glad they've come! I've been so horribly lonely!

(*The front door is heard closing and Tyrone calls uneasily from the hall.*)

TYRONE. Are you there, Mary?

(*The light in the hall is turned on and shines through the front parlour to fall on Mary.*)

MARY (*rises from her chair, her face lighting up lovingly — with excited eagerness*). I'm here, dear. In the living-room. I've been waiting for you.

(*Tyrone comes in through the front parlour. Edmund is behind him. Tyrone has had a lot to drink but beyond a slightly glazed look in his eyes and a trace of blur in his speech, he does not show it. Edmund has also had more than a few drinks without much apparent effect, except that his sunken cheeks are flushed and his eyes look bright and feverish. They stop in the doorway to stare appraisingly at her. What they see fulfils their worst expectations. But for the moment Mary is unconscious of their condemning eyes. She kisses her husband and then Edmund. Her manner is unnaturally effusive. They submit shrinkingly. She talks excitedly.*)

I'm so happy you've come. I had given up hope. I was afraid you wouldn't come home. It's such a dismal, foggy evening. It must be much more cheerful in the bar-rooms uptown, where there are people you can talk and joke with. No, don't deny it. I know how you feel. I don't blame you a bit. I'm all the more grateful to you for coming home. I was sitting here so lonely and blue. Come and sit down.

(*She sits at left rear of table, Edmund at left of table, and Tyrone in the rocker at right of it.*)

Dinner won't be ready for a minute. You're actually a little early. Will wonders never cease? Here's the whiskey, dear. Shall I pour a drink for you? (*Without waiting for a reply she does so.*) And you, Edmund? I don't want to encourage you, but one before dinner, as an appetizer, can't do any harm.

(*She pours a drink for him. They make no move to take the drinks. She talks on as if unaware of their silence.*)

Where's Jamie? But, of course, he'll never come home so long as he has the price of a drink left. (*She reaches out and clasps her husband's hand — sadly.*) I'm afraid Jamie has been lost to us for a long time, dear. (*Her face hardens.*) But we mustn't allow him to drag Edmund down with him, as he's like to do. He's jealous because Edmund has always been the baby — just as he used to be of Eugene. He'll never be content until he makes Edmund as hopeless a failure as he is.

EDMUND (*miserably*). Stop talking, Mama.

TYRONE (*dully*). Yes, Mary, the less you say now — (*Then to Edmund, a bit tipsily.*) All the same there's truth in your mother's warning. Beware of that brother of yours, or he'll poison life for you with his damned sneering serpent's tongue!

EDMUND (*as before*). Oh, cut it out, Papa.

MARY (*goes on as if nothing had been said*). It's hard to believe, seeing Jamie as he is now, that he was ever my baby. Do you remember what a healthy, happy baby he was, James? The one-night stands and filthy trains and cheap hotels and bad food never made him cross or sick. He was always smiling or laughing. He hardly ever cried. Eugene was the same, too, happy and healthy, during the two years he lived before I let him die through my neglect.

TYRONE. Oh, for the love of God! I'm a fool for coming home!

EDMUND. Papa! Shut up!

MARY (*smiles with detached tenderness at Edmund*). It was Edmund who was the crosspatch when he was little, always getting upset and frightened about nothing at all. (*She pats his hand — teasingly.*) Everyone used to say, dear, you'd cry at the drop of a hat.

EDMUND (*cannot control his bitterness*). Maybe I guessed there was a good reason not to laugh.

TYRONE (*reproving and pitying*). Now, now, lad. You know better than to pay attention —

MARY (*as if she hadn't heard — sadly again*). Who would have thought Jamie would grow up to disgrace us. You remember, James, for years after he went to boarding school, we received such glowing reports. Everyone liked him. All his teachers told us what a fine brain he had, and how easily he learned his lessons. Even after he began to drink and they had to expel him, they wrote us how sorry they were, because he was so likeable and such a brilliant student. They predicted a wonderful future for him if he would only learn to take life seriously. (*She pauses — then adds with a strange, sad detachment.*) It's such a pity. Poor Jamie! It's hard to understand — (*Abruptly a change comes over her. Her face hardens and she stares at her husband with accusing hostility.*) No, it isn't at all. You brought him up to be a boozer. Since he first opened his eyes, he's seen you drinking. Always a bottle on the bureau in the cheap hotel rooms! And if he had a nightmare when he was little, or a stomach-ache, your remedy was to give him a teaspoonful of whiskey to quiet him.

TYRONE (*stung*). So I'm to blame because that lazy hulk has made a drunken loafer of himself? Is that what I came home to listen to? I might have known! When you have the poison in you, you want to blame everyone but yourself!

EDMUND. Papa! You told me not to pay attention. (*Then, resentfully.*) Anyway it's true. You did the same thing with me. I can remember that teaspoonful of booze every time I woke up with a nightmare.

MARY (*in a detached reminiscent tone*). Yes, you were continually having nightmares as a child. You were born afraid. Because I was so afraid to bring you into the world. (*She pauses — then goes on with the same detachment.*) Please don't think I blame your father, Edmund. He didn't know any better. He never went to school after he was ten. His people were the most ignorant kind of poverty-stricken Irish. I'm sure they honestly believed whiskey is the healthiest medicine for a child who is sick or frightened.

(*Tyrone is about to burst out in angry defence of his family but Edmund intervenes.*)

EDMUND (*sharply*). Papa! (*Changing the subject.*) Are we going to have this drink, or aren't we?

TYRONE (*controlling himself — dully*). You're right. I'm a fool to take notice. (*He picks up his glass listlessly.*) Drink hearty, lad.

(*Edmund drinks but Tyrone remains staring at the glass in his hand. Edmund at once realizes how much the whiskey has been watered. He frowns, glancing from the bottle to his mother — starts to say something but stops.*)

MARY (*in a changed tone — repentantly*). I'm sorry if I sounded bitter, James. I'm not. It's all so far away. But I did feel a little hurt when you wished you hadn't come home. I was so relieved and happy when you came, and grateful to you. It's very dreary and sad to be here alone in the fog with night falling.

TYRONE (*moved*). I'm glad I came, Mary, when you act like your real self.

MARY. I was so lonesome I kept Cathleen with me just to have someone to talk to. (*Her manner and quality drift back to the shy convent girl again.*) Do you know what I was telling her, dear? About the night my father took me to your dressing-room and I first fell in love with you. Do you remember?

TYRONE (*deeply moved — his voice husky*). Can you think I'd ever forget, Mary?

(*Edmund looks away from them, sad and embarrassed.*)

MARY (*tenderly*). No. I know you still love me, James, in spite of everything.

TYRONE (*his face works and he blinks back tears — with quiet intensity*). Yes! As God is my judge! Always and for ever, Mary!

MARY. And I love you, dear, in spite of everything.

(*There is a pause in which Edmund moves embarrassedly. The strange detachment comes over her manner again as if she were speaking impersonally of people seen from a distance.*)

But I must confess, James, although I couldn't help loving you, I would never have married you if I'd known you drank so much. I remember the first night your bar-room friends had to help you up to the door of our hotel room, and knocked and then ran away before I came to the door. We were still on our honeymoon, do you remember?

TYRONE (*with guilty vehemence*). I don't remember! It wasn't on our honeymoon! And I never in my life had to be helped to bed, or missed a performance!

MARY (*as though he hadn't spoken*). I had waited in that ugly hotel room hour after hour. I kept making excuses for you. I told myself it must be some business connected with the theatre. I knew so little about the theatre. Then I became terrified. I imagined all sorts of horrible accidents. I got on my knees and prayed that nothing had happened to you — and then they brought you up and left you outside the door. (*She gives a little, sad sigh.*) I didn't know how often that was to happen in the years to come, how many times I was to wait in ugly hotel rooms. I became quite used to it.

EDMUND (*bursts out with a look of accusing hate at his father*). Christ! No wonder —! (*He controls himself — gruffly.*) When is dinner, Mama? It must be time.

TYRONE (*overwhelmed by shame which he tries to hide, fumbles with his watch*). Yes. It must be. Let's see. (*He stares at his watch without seeing it. Pleadingly.*) Mary! Can't you forget —?

MARY (*with detached pity*). No, dear. But I forgive. I always forgive you. So don't look so guilty. I'm sorry I remembered out loud. I don't want to be sad, or to make you sad. I want to remember only the happy part of the past. (*Her manner drifts back to the shy, gay convent girl.*) Do you remember our wedding, dear? I'm sure you've completely forgotten what my wedding gown looked like. Men don't notice such things. They don't think they're important. But it was important to me, I can tell you! How I fussed and worried! I was so excited and happy! My father told me to buy anything I wanted and never mind what it cost. The best is none too good, he said. I'm afraid he spoiled me dreadfully. My mother didn't. She was very pious and strict. I think she was a little jealous. She didn't approve of my marrying — especially an actor. I think she hoped I would become a nun. She used to scold my father. She'd grumble, "You never tell me, never mind what it costs, when I buy anything! You've spoiled that girl so, I pity her husband if she ever marries. She'll expect him to give her the moon. She'll never make a good wife." (*She laughs affectionately.*) Poor mother! (*She smiles at Tyrone with a strange, incongruous coquetry.*) But she was mistaken, wasn't she, James? I haven't been such a bad wife, have I?

TYRONE (*huskily, trying to force a smile*). I'm not complaining, Mary.

MARY (*a shadow of vague guilt crosses her face*). At least, I've loved you dearly, and done the best I could — under the circumstances. (*The shadow vanishes and her shy, girlish expression returns.*) That wedding gown was nearly the death of me and the dressmaker, too! (*She laughs.*) I was so particular. It was never quite good enough. At last she said she refused to touch it any more or she might spoil it, and I made her leave so I could be alone to examine myself in the mirror. I was so pleased and vain. I thought to myself, "Even if your nose and mouth and ears are a trifle too large, your eyes and hair and figure, and your hands, make up for it. You're just as pretty as any actress he's ever met, and you don't have to use paint." (*She pauses, wrinkling her brow in an effort of memory.*) Where is my wedding gown now, I wonder? I kept it wrapped up in tissue paper in my trunk. I used to hope I would have a daughter and when it came time for her to marry — She couldn't have bought a lovelier gown, and I knew, James, you'd never tell her, never mind the cost. You'd want her to pick up something at a bargain. It was made of soft, shimmering satin, trimmed with wonderful old duchesse lace, in tiny ruffles around the neck and sleeves, and worked in with the folds that were draped round in a bustle effect at the back. The basque was boned and very tight. I remember I held my breath when it was fitted, so my waist would be as small as possible. My father even let me have duchesse lace on my white satin slippers, and lace with the orange blossoms in my veil. Oh, how I loved that gown! It was so beautiful! Where is it now, I wonder? I used to take it out from time to time when I was lonely, but it always made me cry, so finally a long while ago — (*She wrinkles her forehead again.*) I wonder where I hid it? Probably in one of the old trunks in the attic. Some day I'll have to look.

(*She stops, staring before her. Tyrone sighs, shaking his head hopelessly, and attempts to catch his son's eye, looking for sympathy, but Edmund is staring at the floor.*)

TYRONE (*forces a casual tone*). Isn't it dinner time, dear? (*With a feeble attempt at teasing.*) You're for ever scolding me for being late, but now I'm on time for once, it's dinner that's late. (*She doesn't appear to hear him. He adds, still pleasantly.*) Well, if I can't eat yet, I can drink. I'd forgotten I had this.

(*He drinks his drink. Edmund watches him. Tyrone scowls and looks at his wife with sharp suspicion — roughly.*)

Who's been tampering with my whiskey? The damned stuff is half water! Jamie's been away and he wouldn't overdo his trick like this, anyway. Any fool could tell — Mary, answer me! (*With angry disgust.*) I hope to God you haven't taken to drink on top of —

EDMUND. Shut up, Papa! (*To his mother, without looking at her.*) You treated Cathleen and Bridget, isn't that it, Mama?

MARY (*with indifferent casualness*). Yes, of course. They work hard for poor wages. And I'm the housekeeper, I have to keep them from leaving. Besides, I wanted to treat Cathleen because I had her drive uptown with me, and sent her to get my prescription filled.

EDMUND. For God's sake, Mama! You can't trust her! Do you want everyone on earth to know?

MARY (*her face hardening stubbornly*). Know what? That I suffer from rheumatism in my hands and have to take medicine to kill the pain? Why should I be ashamed of that? (*Turns on Edmund with a hard, accusing antagonism — almost a revengeful enmity.*) I never knew what rheumatism was before you were born! Ask your father!

(*Edmund looks away, shrinking into himself.*)

TYRONE. Don't mind her, lad. It doesn't mean anything. When she gets to the stage where she gives the old crazy excuse about her hands she's gone far away from us.

MARY (*turns on him — with a strangely triumphant, taunting smile*). I'm glad you realize that, James! Now perhaps you'll give up trying to remind me, you and Edmund! (*Abruptly, in a detached, matter-of-fact tone.*) Why don't you light the light, James? It's getting dark. I know you hate to, but Edmund has proved to you that one bulb burning doesn't cost much. There's no sense letting your fear of the poorhouse make you too stingy.

TYRONE (*reacts mechanically*). I never claimed one bulb cost much! It's having them on, one here and one there, that makes the Electric Light Company rich. (*He gets up and turns on the reading lamp — roughly.*) But I'm a fool to talk reason to you. (*To Edmund.*) I'll get a fresh bottle of whiskey, lad, and we'll have a real drink. (*He goes through the back parlour.*)

MARY (*with detached amusement*). He'll sneak around to the outside cellar door so the servants won't see him. He's really ashamed of keeping his whiskey padlocked in the cellar. Your father is a strange man, Edmund. It took many years before I understood him. You must try to understand and forgive him, too, and not feel contempt because he's close-fisted. His father deserted his mother and their six children a year or so after they came to America. He told them he had a premonition he would die soon, and he was homesick for Ireland, and wanted to go back there to die. So he went and he did die. He must have been a peculiar man, too. Your father had to go to work in a machine shop when he was only ten years old.

EDMUND (*protests dully*). Oh, for Pete's sake, Mama. I've heard Papa tell that machine-shop story ten thousand times.

MARY. Yes, dear, you've had to listen, but I don't think you've ever tried to understand.

EDMUND (*ignoring this — miserably*). Listen, Mama! You're not so far gone yet you've forgotten everything. You haven't asked me what I found out this afternoon. Don't you care a damn?

MARY (*shakenly*). Don't say that! You hurt me, dear!

EDMUND. What I've got is serious, Mama. Doc Hardy knows for sure now.

MARY (*stiffens into scornful, defensive stubbornness*). That lying old quack! I warned you he'd invent —!

EDMUND (*miserably dogged*). He called in a specialist to examine me, so he'd be absolutely sure.

MARY (*ignoring this*). Don't tell me about Hardy! If you heard what the doctor at the sanatorium, who really knows something, said about how he'd treated me! He said he ought to be locked up! He said it was a wonder I hadn't gone mad! I told him I had once, that time I ran down in my nightdress to throw myself off the dock. You remember that, don't you? And yet you want me to pay attention to what Doctor Hardy says. Oh, no!

EDMUND (*bitterly*). I remember, all right. It was right after that Papa and Jamie decided they couldn't hide it from me any more. Jamie told me. I called him a liar, I tried to punch him in the nose. But I knew he wasn't! lying. (*His voice trembles, his eyes begin to fill with tears.*) God' it made everything in life seem rotten!

MARY (*pitiably*). Oh, don't. My baby! You hurt me so dreadfully!

EDMUND (*dully*). I'm sorry, Mama. It was you who brought it up. (*Then with a bitter, stubborn persistence.*) Listen, Mama. I'm going to tell you whether you want to hear or not. I've got to go to a sanatorium.

MARY (*dazedly, as if this was something that had never occurred to her*). Go away? (*Violently.*) No! I won't have it! How dare Doctor Hardy advise such a thing without consulting me! How dare your father allow him! What right has he? You are my baby! Let him attend to Jamie! (*More and more excited and bitter.*) I know why he wants you sent to a sanatorium. To take you from me! He's always tried to do that. He's been jealous of every one of my babies! He kept finding ways to make me leave them. That's what caused Eugene's death. He's been jealous of you most of all. He knew I loved you most because —

EDMUND (*miserably*). Oh, stop talking crazy, can't you, Mama! Stop trying to blame him. And why are you so against my going away now? I've been away a lot, and I've never noticed it broke your heart!

MARY (*bitterly*). I'm afraid you're not very sensitive, after all. (*Sadly.*) You might have guessed, dear, that after I knew you knew — about me — I had to be glad whenever you were where you couldn't see me.

EDMUND (*brokenly*). Mama! Don't! (*He reaches out blindly and takes her hand — but he drops it immediately, overcome by bitterness again.*) All this talk about loving me — and you won't even listen when I try to tell you how sick —

MARY (*with an abrupt transformation into a detached bullying motherliness*). Now, now. That's enough! I don't care to hear because I know it's nothing but Hardy's ignorant lies.

(*He shrinks back into himself. She keeps on in a forced, teasing tone but with an increasing undercurrent of resentment.*)

You're so like your father, dear. You love to make a scene out of nothing so you can be dramatic and tragic. (*With a belittling laugh.*) If I gave you the slightest encouragement, you'd tell me next you were going to die —

EDMUND. People do die of it. Your own father —

MARY (*sharply*). Why do you mention him? There's no comparison at all with you. He had consumption. (*Angrily.*) I hate you when you become gloomy and morbid! I forbid you to remind me of my father's death, do you hear me?

EDMUND (*his face hard — grimly*). Yes, I hear you, Mama. I wish to God I didn't! (*He gets up from his chair *and stands staring condemningly at her — bitterly.)* It's pretty hard to take at times, having a dope fiend for a mother!

(She winces — all life seeming to drain from her face, leaving it with the appearance of a plaster cast. Instantly Edmund wishes he could take back what he has said. He stammers miserably.)

Forgive me, Mama. I was angry. You hurt me.

(There is a pause in which the foghorn and the ships' bells are heard.)

MARY *(goes slowly to the windows at right like an automaton — looking out, a blank, far-off quality in her voice)*. Just listen to that awful foghorn. And the bells. Why is it fog makes everything sound so sad and lost, I wonder?

EDMUND *(brokenly)*. I — I can't stay here. I don't want any dinner.

(He hurries away through the front parlour. She keeps staring out of the window until she hears the front door close behind him. Then she comes back and sits in her chair, the same blank look on her face.)

MARY *(vaguely)*. I must go upstairs. I haven't taken enough. *(She pauses — then longingly.)* I hope, sometime, without meaning it, I will take an overdose. I never could do it deliberately. The Blessed Virgin would never forgive me, then.

(She hears Tyrone returning and turns as he comes in, through the back parlour, with a bottle of whiskey he has just uncorked. He is fuming.)

TYRONE *(wrathfully)*. The padlock is all scratched. That drunken loafer has tried to pick the lock with a piece of wire, the way he's done before. *(With satisfaction, as if this was a perpetual battle of wits with his elder son.)* But I've fooled him this time. It's a special padlock a professional burglar couldn't pick. *(He puts the bottle on the tray and suddenly is aware of Edmund's absence.)* Where's Edmund?

MARY *(with a vague far-away air)*. He went out. Perhaps he's going uptown again to find Jamie. He still has some money left, I suppose, and it's burning a hole in his pocket. He said he didn't want any dinner. He doesn't seem to have any appetite these days. *(Then stubbornly.)* But it's just a summer cold.

(Tyrone stares at her and shakes his head helplessly and pours himself a big drink and drinks it. Suddenly it is too much for her and she breaks out and sobs.)

Oh, James, I'm so frightened! *(She gets up and throws her arms around him and hides her face on his shoulder — sobbingly.)* I know he's going to die!

TYRONE. Don't say that! It's not true! They promised me in six months he'd be cured.

MARY. You don't believe that! I can tell when you're acting! And it will be my fault. I should never have borne him. It would have been better for his sake. I could never hurt him then. He wouldn't have had to know his mother was a dope fiend — and hate her!

TYRONE *(his voice quivering)*. Hush, Mary, for the love of God! He loves you. He knows it was a curse put on you without your knowing or willing it. He's proud you're his mother! *(Abruptly as he hears the pantry door opening.)* Hush, now! Here comes Cathleen. You don't want her to see you crying.

(She turns quickly away from him to the windows at right, hastily wiping her eyes. A moment later Cathleen appears in the back-parlour doorway. She is uncertain in her walk and grinning woozily.)

CATHLEEN *(starts guiltily when she sees Tyrone — with dignity)*, Dinner is served, Sir. *(Raising her voice unnecessarily.)* Dinner is served, Ma'am. *(She forgets her dignity and addresses Tyrone with good-natured familiarity.)* So you're here, are you? Well, well. Won't Bridget be in a rage! I told her the Madame said you wouldn't be home. *(Then reading accusation in his eye.)* Don't be looking at me that way. If I've a drop taken, I didn't steal it. I was invited. *(She turns with huffy dignity and disappears through the back parlour.)*

TYRONE *(sighs — then summoning his actor's heartiness)*. Come along, dear. Let's have our dinner. I'm hungry as a hunter.

MARY *(comes to him — her face is composed in plaster again and her tone is remote)*. I'm afraid you'll have to excuse me, James. I couldn't possibly eat anything. My hands pain me dreadfully. I think the best thing for me is to go to bed and rest. Good night, dear. *(She kisses him mechanically and turns toward the front parlour.)*

TYRONE *(harshly)*. Up to take more of that God-damned poison, is that it? You'll be like a mad ghost before the night's over!

MARY *(starts to walk away — blankly)*. I don't know what you're talking about, James. You say such mean, bitter things when you've drunk too much. You're as bad as Jamie or Edmund.

(She moves off through the front parlour. He stands a second as if not knowing what to do. He is a sad, bewildered, broken old man. He walks wearily off through the back parlour toward the dining-room.)

CURTAIN

ACT FOUR

SCENE. *The same. It is around midnight. The lamp in the front hall has been turned out, so that now no light shines through the front parlour. In the living-room only the reading-lamp on the table is lighted. Outside the windows the wall of fog appears denser than ever. As the curtain rises, the foghorn is heard, followed by the ships' bells from the harbour.*

Tyrone is seated at the table. He wears his pince-nez, and is playing solitaire. He has taken off his coat and has on an old brown dressing-gown. The whiskey bottle on the tray is three-quarters empty. There is a fresh full bottle on the table, which he has brought from the cellar so there will be an ample reserve at hand. He is drunk and shows it by the owlish, deliberate manner in which he peers at each card to make certain of its identity, and then plays it as if he wasn't certain of his aim. His eyes have a misted, oily look and his mouth is slack. But despite all the whiskey in him, he has not escaped, and he looks as he appeared at the close of the preceding act, a sad, defeated old man, possessed by hopeless resignation.

As the curtain rises, he finishes a game and sweeps the cards together. He shuffles them clumsily, dropping a couple on the floor. He retrieves them with difficulty, and starts to shuffle again, when he hears someone entering the front door. He peers over his pince-nez through the front parlour.

TYRONE (*his voice thick*). Who's that? Is it you, Edmund?

(*Edmund's voice answers curtly,* Yes. *Then he evidently collides with something in the dark hall and can be heard cursing. A moment later the hall lamp is turned on. Tyrone frowns and calls.*)

Turn that light out before you come in.

(*But Edmund doesn't. He comes in through the front parlour. He is drunk now, too, but like his father he carries it well, and gives little physical sign of it except in his eyes and a chip-on-the-shoulder aggressiveness in his manner. Tyrone speaks, at first with a warm, relieved welcome.*)

I'm glad you've come, lad. I've been damned lonely. (*Then resentfully.*) You're a fine one to run away and leave me to sit alone here all night when you know — (*With sharp irritation.*) I told you to turn out that light! We're not giving a ball. There's no reason to have the house ablaze with electricity at this time of night, burning up money!

EDMUND (*angrily*). Ablaze with electricity! One bulb! Hell, everyone keeps a light on in the front hall until they go to bed. (*He rubs his knee.*) I damned near busted my knee on the hat stand.

TYRONE. The light from here shows in the hall. You could see your way well enough if you were sober.

EDMUND. If *I* was sober? I like that!

TYRONE. I don't give a damn what other people do. If they want to be wasteful fools, for the sake of show, let them be!

EDMUND. One bulb! Christ, don't be such a cheap skate! I've proved by figures if you left the light bulb on all night it wouldn't be as much as one drink!

TYRONE. To hell with your figures! The proof is in the bills I have to pay!

EDMUND (*sits down opposite his father — contemptuously*). Yes, facts don't mean a thing, do they? What you want to believe, that's the only truth! (*Derisively.*) Shakespeare was an Irish Catholic, for example.

TYRONE (*stubbornly*). So he was. The proof is in his plays.

EDMUND. Well he wasn't, and there's no proof of it in his plays, except to you! (*Jeeringly.*) The Duke of Wellington, there was another good Irish Catholic!

TYRONE. I never said he was a good one. He was a renegade, but a Catholic just the same.

EDMUND. Well, he wasn't. You just want to believe no one but an Irish Catholic general could beat Napoleon.

TYRONE. I'm not going to argue with you. I asked you to turn out that light in the hall.

EDMUND. I heard you, and as far as I'm concerned it stays on.

TYRONE. None of your damned insolence! Are you going to obey me or not?

EDMUND. Not! If you want to be a crazy miser put it out yourself!

TYRONE (*with threatening anger*). Listen to me! I've put up with a lot from you because from the mad things you've done at times I've thought you weren't quite right in your head. I've excused you and never lifted my hand to you. But there's a straw that breaks the camel's back. You'll obey me and put out that light or, big as you are, I'll give you a thrashing that'll teach you —! (*Suddenly he remembers Edmund's illness and instantly becomes guilty and shamefaced.*) Forgive me, lad. I forgot — You shouldn't goad me into losing my temper.

EDMUND (*ashamed himself now*). Forget it, Papa. I apologize, too. I had no right being nasty about nothing. I am a bit soused, I guess. I'll put out the damned light.

(*He starts to get up.*)

TYRONE. No, stay where you are. Let it burn. (*He stands up abruptly — and a bit drunkenly — and begins turning on the three bulbs in the chandelier, with a childish, bitterly dramatic self-pity.*) We'll have them all on! Let them burn! To hell with them! The poorhouse is the end of the road, and it might as well be sooner as later! (*He finishes turning on the lights.*)

EDMUND (*has watched this proceeding with an awakened sense of humour — now he grins, teasing affectionately*). That's a grand curtain. (*He laughs.*) You're a wonder, Papa.

TYRONE (*sits down sheepishly — grumbles pathetically*). That's right, laugh at the old fool! The poor old ham! But the final curtain will be in the poorhouse just the same, and that's not comedy! (*Then as Edmund is still grinning, he changes the subject.*) Well, well, let's not argue. You've got brains in that head of yours, though you do your best to deny them. You'll live to learn the value of a dollar. You're not like your damned tramp of a brother. I've given up hope he'll ever get sense. Where is he, by the way?

EDMUND. How would I know?

TYRONE. I thought you'd gone back uptown to meet him.

EDMUND. No. I walked out to the beach. I haven't seen him since this afternoon.

TYRONE. Well, if you split the money I gave you with him, like a fool —

EDMUND. Sure I did. He's always staked me when he had anything.

TYRONE. Then it doesn't take a soothsayer to tell he's probably in the whorehouse.

EDMUND. What of it if he is? Why not?

TYRONE (*contemptuously*). Why not, indeed. It's the fit place for him. If he's ever had a loftier dream than whores and whiskey, he's never shown it.

EDMUND. Oh, for Pete's sake, Papa! If you're going to start that stuff, I'll beat it. (*He starts to get up.*)

TYRONE (*placatingly*). All right, all right, I'll stop. God knows, I don't like the subject either. Will you join me in a drink?

EDMUND. Ah! Now you're talking!

TYRONE (*passes the bottle to him — mechanically*). I'm wrong to treat you. You've had enough already.

EDMUND (*pouring a big drink — a bit drunkenly*). Enough is *not* as good as a feast. (*He hands back the bottle.*)

TYRONE. It's too much in your condition.

EDMUND. Forget my condition! (*He raises his glass.*) Here's how.

TYRONE. Drink hearty.

(*They drink.*)

If you walked all the way to the beach you must be damp and chilled.

EDMUND. Oh, I dropped in at the Inn on the way out and back.

TYRONE. It's not a night I'd pick for a long walk.

EDMUND. I loved the fog. It was what I needed. (*He sounds more tipsy and looks it.*)

TYRONE. You should have more sense than to risk —

EDMUND. To hell with sense! We're all crazy. What do we want with sense? (*He quotes from Dowson sardonically.*)

"They are not long, the weeping and the laughter,
Love and desire and hate:
I think they have no portion in us after
We pass the gate.

They are not long, the days of wine and roses:
Out of a misty dream
Our path emerges for a while, then closes
Within a dream."

(*Staring before him.*) The fog was where I wanted to be. Halfway down the path you can't see this house. You'd never know it was here. Or any of the other places down the avenue. I couldn't see but a few feet ahead. I didn't meet a soul. Everything looked and sounded unreal. Nothing was what it is. That's what I wanted — to be alone with myself in another world where truth is untrue and life can hide from itself. Out beyond the harbour, where the road runs along the beach, I even lost the feeling of being on land. The fog and the sea seemed part of each other. It was like walking on the bottom of the sea. As if I had drowned long ago. As if I was a ghost belonging to the fog, and the fog was the ghost of the sea. It felt damned peaceful to be nothing more than a ghost within a ghost. (*He sees his father staring at him with mingled worry and irritated disapproval. He grins mockingly.*) Don't look at me as if I'd gone nutty. I'm talking sense. Who wants to see life as it is, if they can help it? It's the three Gorgons in one. You look in their faces and turn to stone. Or it's Pan. You see him and you die — that is, inside you — and have to go on living as a ghost.

TYRONE (*impressed and at the same time revolted*). You have a poet in you but it's a damned morbid one! (*Forcing a smile.*) Devil take your pessimism. I feel low-spirited enough. (*He sighs.*) Why can't you remember your Shakespeare and forget the third-raters? You'll find what you're trying to say in him — as you'll find everything else worth saying. (*He quotes, using his fine voice.*) "We are such stuff as dreams are made on, and our little life is rounded with a sleep."

EDMUND (*ironical*). Fine! That's beautiful. But I wasn't trying to say that. We are such stuff as manure is made on, so let's drink up and forget it. That's more my idea.

TYRONE (*disgustedly*). Ach! Keep such sentiments to yourself. I shouldn't have given you that drink.

EDMUND. It did pack a wallop, all right. On you, too. (*He grins with affectionate teasing.*) Even if you've never missed a performance! (*Aggressively.*) Well, what's wrong with being drunk? It's what we're after, isn't it? Let's not kid each other, Papa. Not tonight. We know what we're trying to forget. (*Hurriedly.*) But let's not talk about it. It's no use now.

TYRONE (*dully*). No. All we can do is try to be resigned — again.

EDMUND. Or be so drunk you can forget. (*He recites, and recites well, with bitter, ironical passion, the Symons' translation of Baudelaire's prose poem.*) "Be always drunken. Nothing else matters: that is the only question. If you would not feel the horrible burden of Time weighing on your shoulders and crushing you to the earth, be drunken continually.

Drunken with what? With wine, with poetry, or with virtue, as you will. But be drunken.

And if sometimes, on the stairs of a palace, or on the green side of a ditch, or in the dreary solitude of your own room, you should awaken and the drunkenness be half or wholly slipped away from you, ask of the wind, or of the wave, or of the star, or of the bird, or of the clock, of whatever flies, or sighs, or rocks, or sings, or speaks, ask what hour it is; and the wind, wave, star, bird, clock, will answer you: 'It is the hour to be drunken! Be drunken, if you would not be martyred slaves of Time; be drunken continually! With wine, with poetry, or with virtue, as you will.' " (*He grins at his father provocatively.*)

TYRONE (*thickly humorous*). I wouldn't worry about the virtue part of it, if I were you. (*Then disgustedly.*) Pah! It's morbid nonsense! What little truth is in it you'll find nobly said in Shakespeare. (*Then appreciatively.*) But you recited it well, lad. Who wrote it?

EDMUND. Baudelaire.

TYRONE. Never heard of him.

EDMUND (*grins provocatively*). He also wrote a poem about Jamie and the Great White Way —

TYRONE. That loafer! I hope to God he misses the last car and has to stay uptown!

EDMUND (*goes on, ignoring this*). Although he was French and never saw Broadway and died before Jamie was born. He knew him and Little Old New York just the same. (*He recites the Symons' translation of Baudelaire's "Epilogue".*)

"With heart at rest I climbed the citadel's
Steep height, and saw the city as from a tower,
Hospital, brothel, prison, and such hells.

Where evil comes up softly like a flower.
Thou knowest, O Satan, patron of my pain,
Not for vain tears I went up at that hour;

But like an old sad faithful lecher, fain
To drink delight of that enormous trull
Whose hellish beauty makes me young again.

Whether thou sleep, with heavy vapours full,
Sodden with day, or, new apparelled, stand
In gold-laced veils of evening beautiful,

I love thee, infamous city! Harlots and
Hunted have pleasures of their own to give,
The vulgar herd can never understand."

TYRONE (*with irritable disgust*). Morbid filth! Where the hell do you get your taste in literature? Filth and despair and pessimism! Another atheist, I suppose. When you deny God, you deny hope. That's the trouble with you. If you'd get down on your knees —

EDMUND (*as if he hadn't heard — sardonically*). It's a good likeness of Jamie, don't you think, hunted by himself and whiskey, hiding in a Broadway hotel room with some fat tart — he likes them fat — reciting Dowson's Cynara to her. (*He recites derisively, but with deep feeling.*)

"All night upon mine heart I felt her warm heart beat,
Night-long within mine arms in love and sleep she lay;
Surely the kisses of her bought red mouth were sweet;
But I was desolate and sick of an old passion,
When I awoke and found the dawn was gray:
I have been faithful to thee, Cynara! in my fashion."

(*Jeeringly.*) And the poor fat burlesque queen doesn't get a word of it, but suspects she's being insulted! And Jamie never loved any Cynara, and was never faithful to a woman in his life, even in his fashion! But he lies there, kidding himself he is superior and enjoys pleasures "the vulgar herd can never understand"! (*He laughs.*) It's nuts — completely nuts!

TYRONE (*vaguely — his voice thick*). It's madness, yes. If you'd get on your knees and pray. When you deny God, you deny sanity.

EDMUND (*ignoring this*). But who am I to feel superior? I've done the same damned thing. And it's no more crazy than Dowson himself, inspired by an absinthe hangover, writing it to a dumb barmaid, who thought he was a poor crazy souse, and gave him the gate to marry a waiter! (*He laughs — then soberly, with genuine sympathy.*) Poor Dowson.

Booze and consumption got him. (*He starts and for a second looks miserable and frightened. Then with defensive irony.*) Perhaps it would be tactful of me to change the subject.

TYRONE (*thickly*). Where you get your taste in authors — That damned library of yours! (*He indicates the small bookcase at rear.*) Voltaire, Rousseau, Schopenhauer, Nietzsche, Ibsen! Atheists, fools, and madmen! And your poets! This Dowson, and this Baudelaire, and Swinburne and Oscar Wilde, and Whitman and Poe! Whoremongers and degenerates! Pah! When I've three good sets of Shakespeare there (*he nods at the large bookcase*) you could read.

EDMUND (*provocatively*). They say he was a souse, too.

TYRONE. They lie! I don't doubt he liked his glass — it's a good man's failing — but he knew how to drink so it didn't poison his brain with morbidness and filth. Don't compare him with the pack you've got in there. (*He indicates the small bookcase again.*) Your dirty Zola! And your Dante Gabriel Rossetti who was a dope fiend! (*He starts and looks guilty.*)

EDMUND (*with defensive dryness*). Perhaps it would be wise to change the subject. (*A pause.*) You can't accuse me of not knowing Shakespeare. Didn't I win five dollars from you once when you bet me I couldn't learn a leading part of his in a week, as you used to do in stock in the old days. I learned Macbeth and recited it letter-perfect, with you giving me the cues.

TYRONE (*approvingly*). That's true. So you did. (*He smiles teasingly and sighs.*) It was a terrible ordeal, I remember, hearing you murder the lines. I kept wishing I'd paid over the bet without making you prove it. (*He chuckles and Edmund grins. Then he starts as he hears a sound from upstairs — with dread.*) Did you hear? She's moving around. I was hoping she'd gone to sleep.

EDMUND. Forget it! How about another drink? (*He reaches out and gets the bottle, pours a drink and hands it back. Then with a strained casualness, as his father pours a drink.*) When did Mama go to bed?

TYRONE. Right after you left. She wouldn't eat any dinner. What made you run away?

EDMUND. Nothing. (*Abruptly raising his glass.*) Well, here's how.

TYRONE (*mechanically*). Drink hearty, lad.

(*They drink. Tyrone again listens to sounds upstairs — with dread.*)

She's moving around a lot. I hope to God she doesn't come down.

EDMUND (*dully*). Yes. She'll be nothing but a ghost haunting the past by this time. (*He pauses — then miserably.*) Back before I was born —

TYRONE. Doesn't she do the same with me? Back before she ever knew me. You'd think the only happy days she's ever known were in her father's home, or at the Convent, praying and playing the piano. (*Jealous resentment in his bitterness.*) As I've told you before, you must take her memories with a grain of salt. Her wonderful home was ordinary enough. Her father wasn't the great, generous, noble Irish gentleman she makes out. He was a nice enough man, good company and a good talker. I liked him and he liked me. He was prosperous enough, too, in his wholesale grocery business, an able man. But he had his weakness. She condemns my drinking but she forgets his. It's true he never touched a drop till he was forty, but after that he made up for lost time. He became a steady champagne drinker, the worst kind. That was his grand pose, to drink only champagne. Well, it finished him quick — that and the consumption — (*He stops with a guilty glance at his son.*)

EDMUND (*sardonically*). We don't seem able to avoid unpleasant topics, do we?

TYRONE (*sighs sadly*). No. (*Then with a pathetic attempt at heartiness.*) What do you say to a game or two of Casino, lad?

EDMUND. All right.

TYRONE (*shuffling the cards clumsily*). We can't lock up and go to bed till Jamie comes on the last trolley — which I hope he won't — and I don't want to go upstairs, anyway, till she's asleep.

EDMUND. Neither do I.

TYRONE (*keeps shuffling the cards fumblingly, forgetting to deal them*). As I was saying, you must take her tales of the past with a grain of salt. The piano playing and her dream of becoming a concert pianist. That was put in her head by the nuns flattering her. She was their pet. They loved her for being so devout. They're innocent women, anyway, when it comes to the world. They don't know that not one in a million who shows promise ever rises to concert playing. Not that your mother didn't play well for a schoolgirl, but that's no reason to take it for granted she could have —

EDMUND (*sharply*). Why don't you deal, if we're going to play.

TYRONE. Eh? I am. (*Dealing with very uncertain judgment of distance.*) And the idea she might have become a nun. That's the worst. Your mother was one of the most beautiful girls you could ever see. She knew it, too. She was a bit of a rogue and a coquette, God bless her, behind all her shyness and blushes. She was never made to renounce the world. She was bursting with health and high spirits and the love of loving.

EDMUND. For God's sake, Papa! Why don't you pick up your hand?

TYRONE (*picks it up — dully*). Yes, let's see what I have here.

(*They both stare at their cards unseeingly. Then they both start. Tyrone whispers.*)

Listen!

EDMUND. She's coming downstairs.

TYRONE (*hurriedly*). We'll play our game. Pretend not to notice and she'll soon go up again.

EDMUND (*staring through the front parlour — with relief*). I don't see her. She must have started down and then turned back.

TYRONE. Thank God.

EDMUND. Yes. It's pretty horrible to see her the way she must be now. (*With bitter misery.*) The hardest thing to take is the blank wall she builds around her. Or it's more like a bank of fog in which she hides and loses herself. Deliberately, that's the hell of it! You know something in her does it deliberately — to get beyond our reach, to be rid of us, to forget we're alive! It's as if, in spite of loving us, she hated us!

TYRONE (*remonstrates gently*). Now, now, lad. It's not her. It's the damned poison.

EDMUND (*bitterly*). She takes it to get that effect. At least, I know she did this time! (*Abruptly.*) My play, isn't it? Here. (*He plays a card.*)

TYRONE (*plays mechanically — gently reproachful*). She's been terribly frightened about your illness, for all her pretending. Don't be too hard on her, lad. Remember she's not responsible. Once that cursed poison gets a hold on anyone —

EDMUND (*his face grows hard and he stares at his father with bitter accusation*). It never should have gotten a hold on her! I know damned well she's not to blame! And I know who is! You are! Your damned stinginess! If you'd spent money for a decent doctor when she was so sick after I was born, she'd never have known morphine existed! Instead you put her in the hands of a hotel quack who wouldn't admit his ignorance and took the easiest way out, not giving a damn what happened to her afterwards! All because his fee was cheap! Another one of your bargains!

TYRONE (*stung — angrily*). Be quiet! How dare you talk of something you know nothing about! (*Trying to control his temper.*) You must try to see my side of it, too, lad. How was I to know he was that kind of a doctor? He had a good reputation —

EDMUND. Among the souses in the hotel bar, I suppose!

TYRONE. That's a lie! I asked the hotel proprietor to recommend the best —

EDMUND. Yes! At the same time crying poorhouse and making it plain you wanted a cheap one! I know your system! By God, I ought to after this afternoon!

TYRONE (*guiltily defensive*). What about this afternoon?

EDMUND. Never mind now. We're talking about Mama! I'm saying no matter how you excuse yourself you know damned well your stinginess is to blame —

TYRONE. And I say you're a liar! Shut your mouth right now, or —

EDMUND (*ignoring this*). After you found out she'd been made a morphine addict, why didn't you send her to a cure then, at the start, while she still had a chance? No, that would have meant spending some money! I'll bet you told her all she had to do was use a little will-power! That's what you still believe in your heart, in spite of what doctors, who really know something about it, have told you!

TYRONE. You lie again! I know better than that now! But how was I to know then? What did I know of morphine? It was years before I discovered what was wrong. I thought she'd never got over her sickness, that's all. Why didn't I send her to a cure, you say? (*Bitterly.*) Haven't I? I've spent thousands upon thousands in cures! A waste. What good have they done her? She always started again.

EDMUND. Because you've never given her anything that would help her want to stay off it! No home except this summer dump in a place she hates and you've refused even to spend money to make this look decent, while you keep buying more property, and playing sucker for every con man with a gold mine, or a silver mine, or any kind of get-rich-quick swindle! You've dragged her around on the road, season after season, on one-night stands, with no one she could talk to, waiting night after night in dirty hotel rooms for you to come back with a bun on after the bars closed! Christ, is it any wonder she didn't want to be cured. Jesus, when I think of it I hate your guts!

TYRONE (*strickenly*). Edmund! (*Then in a rage.*) How dare you talk to your father like that, you insolent young cub! After all I've done for you.

EDMUND. We'll come to that, what you're doing for me!

TYRONE (*looking guilty again — ignores this*). Will you stop repeating your mother's crazy accusations, which she never makes unless it's the poison talking? I never dragged her on the road against her will. Naturally, I wanted her with me. I loved her. And she came because she loved me and wanted to be with me. That's the truth, no matter what she says when she's not herself. And she needn't have been lonely. There was always the members of my company to talk to, if she'd wanted. She had her children, too, and I insisted, in spite of the expense, on having a nurse to travel with her.

EDMUND (*bitterly*). Yes, your one generosity, and that because you were jealous of her paying too much attention to us, and wanted us out of your way! It was another mistake, too! If she'd had to take care of me all by herself, and had that to occupy her mind, maybe she'd have been able —

TYRONE (*goaded into vindictiveness*). Or for that matter, if you insist on judging things by what she says when she's not in her right mind, if you hadn't been born she'd never — (*He stops ashamed.*)

EDMUND (*suddenly spent and miserably*). Sure. I know that's what she feels, Papa.

TYRONE (*protests penitently*). She doesn't! She loves you as dearly as ever mother loved a son! I only said that because you put me in such a God-damned rage, raking up the past, and saying you hate me —

EDMUND (*dully*). I didn't mean it, Papa. (*He suddenly smiles — kidding a bit drunkenly.*) I'm like Mama, I can't help liking you, in spite of everything.

TYRONE (*grins a bit drunkenly in return*). I might say the same of you. You're no great shakes as a son. It's a case of "A poor thing but mine own."

(*They both chuckle with real, if alcoholic, affection. Tyrone changes the subject.*)

What's happened to our game? Whose play is it?

EDMUND. Yours, I guess.

(*Tyrone plays a card which Edmund takes and the game gets forgotten again.*)

TYRONE. You mustn't let yourself be too downhearted, lad, by the bad news you had today. Both the doctors promised me, if you obey orders at this place you're going, you'll be cured in six months, or a year at most.

EDMUND (*his face hard again*). Don't kid me. You don't believe that.

TYRONE (*too vehemently*). Of course I believe it! Why shouldn't I believe it when both Hardy and the specialist —?

EDMUND. You think I'm going to die.

TYRONE. That's a lie! You're crazy!

EDMUND (*more bitterly*). So why waste money? That's why you're sending me to a state farm —

TYRONE (*in guilty confusion*). What state farm? It's the Hilltown Sanatorium, that's all I know, and both doctors said it was the best place for you.

EDMUND (*scathingly*). For the money! That is, for nothing, or practically nothing. Don't lie, Papa! You know damned well Hilltown Sanatorium is a state institution! Jamie suspected you'd cry poorhouse to Hardy and he wormed the truth out of him.

TYRONE (*furiously*). That drunken loafer! I'll kick him out in the gutter! He's poisoned your mind against me ever since you were old enough to listen!

EDMUND. You can't deny it's the truth about the state farm, can you?

TYRONE. It's not true the way you look at it! What if it is run by the state? That's nothing against it. The state has the money to make a better place than any private sanatorium. And why shouldn't I take advantage of it? It's my right — and yours. We're residents. I'm a property owner. I help to support it. I'm taxed to death —

EDMUND (*with bitter irony*). Yes, on property valued at a quarter of a million.

TYRONE. Lies! It's all mortgaged!

EDMUND. Hardy and the specialist know what you're worth. I wonder what they thought of you when they heard you moaning poorhouse and showing you wanted to wish me on charity!

TYRONE. It's a lie! All I told them was I couldn't afford any millionaire's sanatorium because I was land poor. That's the truth!

EDMUND. And then you went to the Club to meet McGuire and let him stick you with another bum piece of property! (*As Tyrone starts to deny.*) Don't lie about it! We met McGuire in the hotel bar after he left you. Jamie kidded him about hooking you, and he winked and laughed!

TYRONE (*lying feebly*). He's a liar if he said —

EDMUND. Don't lie about it! (*With gathering intensity.*) God, Papa, ever since I went to sea and was on my own, and found out what hard work for little pay was, and what it felt like to be broke, and starve, and camp on park benches because I had no place to sleep, I've tried to be fair to you because I knew what you'd been up against as a kid. I've tried to make allowances. Christ, you have to make allowances in this damned family or go nuts! I have tried to make allowances for myself when I remember all the rotten stuff I've pulled! I've tried to feel like Mama that you can't help being what you are where money is concerned. But God Almighty, this last stunt of yours is too much! It makes me want to puke! Not because of the rotten way you're treating me. To hell with that! I've treated you rottenly, in my way, more than once. But to think when it's a question of your son having consumption, you can show yourself up before the whole town as such a stinking old tightwad! Don't you know Hardy will talk and the whole damned town will know? Jesus, Papa, haven't you any pride or shame? (*Bursting with rage.*) And don't think I'll let you get away with it! I won't go to any damned state farm just to save you a few lousy dollars to buy more bum property with! You stinking old miser —! (*He chokes huskily, his voice trembling with rage, and then is shaken by a fit of coughing.*

TYRONE (*has shunk back in his chair under this attack, his guilty contrition greater than his anger. He stammers*). Be quiet! Don't say that to me! You're drunk! I won't mind you. Stop coughing, lad. You've got yourself worked up over nothing. Who said you had to go to this Hilltown place? You can go anywhere you like. I don't give a damn what it costs. All I care about is to have you get well. Don't call me a stinking miser, just because I don't want doctors to think I'm a millionaire they can swindle.

(*Edmund has stopped coughing. He looks sick and weak. His father stares at him frightenedly.*)

You look weak, lad. You'd better take a bracer.

EDMUND (*grabs the bottle and pours his glass brimful — weakly*). Thanks. (*He gulps down the whiskey.*)

TYRONE (*pours himself a big drink, which empties the bottle, and drinks it. His head bows and he stares dully at the cards on the table — vaguely*). Whose play is it? (*He goes on dully, without resentment.*) A stinking old miser. Well, maybe you're right. Maybe I can't help being, although all my life since I had anything I've thrown money over the bar to buy drinks for everyone in the house, or loaned money to sponges I knew would never pay it back — (*With a loose-mouthed sneer of self-contempt.*) But, of course, that was in bar-rooms, when I was full of whiskey. I can't feel that way about it when I'm sober in my home. It was at home I first learned the value of a dollar and the fear of the poor-house. I've never been able to believe in my luck since. I've always feared it would change and everything I had would be taken away. But still, the more property you own, the safer you think you are. That may not be logical, but it's the way I have to feel. Banks fail, and your money's gone, but you think you can keep land beneath your feet. (*Abruptly his tone becomes scornfully superior.*) You said you realized what I'd been up against as a boy. The hell you do! How could you? You've had everything — nurses, schools, college, though you didn't stay there. You've had food, clothing. Oh, I know you had a fling of hard work with your back and hands, a bit of being homeless and penniless in a foreign land, and I respect you for it. But it was a game of romance and adventure to you. It was play.

EDMUND (*dully sarcastic*). Yes, particularly the time I tried to commit suicide at Jimmie the Priest's, and almost did.

TYRONE. You weren't in your right mind. No son of mine would ever — You were drunk.

EDMUND. I was stone cold sober. That was the trouble. I'd stopped to think too long.

TYRONE (*with drunken peevishness*). Don't start your damned atheist morbidness again! I don't care to listen. I was trying to make plain to you — (*Scornfully.*) What do you know of the value of a dollar? When I was ten my father deserted my mother and went back to Ireland to die. Which he did soon enough, and deserved to, and I hope he's roasting in hell. He mistook rat poison for flour, or sugar, or something. There was gossip it wasn't by mistake but that's a lie. No one in my family ever —

EDMUND. My bet is, it wasn't by mistake.

TYRONE. More morbidness! Your brother put that in your head. The worst he can suspect is the only truth for him. But never mind. My mother was left, a stranger in a strange land, with four small children, me and a sister a little older and two younger than me. My two older brothers had moved to other parts. They couldn't help. They were hard put to it to keep themselves alive. There was no damned romance in our poverty. Twice we were evicted from the miserable hovel we called home, with my mother's few sticks of furniture thrown out in the street, and my mother and sisters crying. I cried, too, though I tried hard not to, because I was the man of the family. At ten years old! There was no more school for me. I worked twelve hours a day in a machine shop, learning to make files. A dirty barn of a place where rain dripped through the roof, where you roasted in summer, and there was no stove in winter, and your hands got numb with cold, where the only light came through two small filthy windows, so on grey days I'd have to sit bent over with my eyes almost touching the files in order to see! You talk of work! And what do you think I got for it? Fifty cents a week! It's the truth! Fifty cents a week! And my poor mother washed and scrubbed for the Yanks by the day, and my older sister sewed, and my two younger stayed at home to keep the house. We never had clothes enough to wear, nor enough food to eat. Well I remember one Thanksgiving, or maybe it was Christmas, when some Yank in whose house mother had been scrubbing gave her a dollar extra for a present, and on the way home she spent it all on food. I can remember her hugging and kissing us and saying with tears of joy running down her tired face: "Glory be to God, for once in our lives we'll have enough for each of us!" (*He wipes tears from his eyes.*) A fine, brave, sweet woman. There never was a braver or finer.

EDMUND (*moved*). Yes, she must have been.

TYRONE. Her one fear was she'd get old and sick and have to die in the poorhouse. (*He pauses — then adds with grim humour.*) It was in those days I learned to be a miser. A dollar was worth so much then. And once you've learned a lesson, it's hard to unlearn it. You have to look for bargains. If I took this state farm sanatorium for a good bargain, you'll have to forgive me. The doctors did tell me it's a good place. You must believe that, Edmund. And I swear I never meant you to go there if you didn't want to. (*Vehemently.*) You can choose any place you like! Never mind what it costs! Any place I can afford. Any place you like — within reason.

(*At this qualification, a grin twitches Edmund's lips. His resentment has gone. His father goes on with an elaborately offhand, casual air.*)

There was another sanatorium the specialist recommended. He said it had a record as good as any place in the country. It's endowed by a group of millionaire factory owners, for the benefit of their workers principally, but you're eligible to go there because you're a resident. There's such a pile of money behind it, they don't have to charge much. It's only seven dollars a week but you get ten times that value. (*Hastily.*) I don't want to persuade you to anything, understand. I'm simply repeating what I was told.

EDMUND (*concealing his smile — casually*). Oh, I know that. It sounds like a good bargain to me. I'd like to go there. So that settles that. (*Abruptly he is miserably desperate again — dully.*) It doesn't matter a damn now, anyway. Let's forget it! (*Changing the subject.*) How about our game? Whose play is it?

TYRONE (*mechanically*). I don't know. Mine, I guess. No, it's yours.

(*Edmund plays a card. His father takes it. Then about to play from his hand, he again forgets the game.*)

Yes, maybe life overdid the lesson for me, and made a dollar worth too much, and the time came when that mistake ruined my career as a fine actor. (*Sadly.*) I've never admitted this to anyone before, lad, but tonight I'm so heartsick I feel at the end of everything, and what's the use of fake pride and pretence. That God-damned play I bought for a song and made such a great success in — a great money success — it ruined me with its promise of an easy fortune. I didn't want to do anything else, and by the time I woke up to the fact I'd become a slave to the damned thing and did try other plays, it was too late. They had identified me with that one part, and didn't want me in anything else. They were right, too. I'd lost the great talent I once had through years of easy repetition, never learning a new part, never really working hard. Thirty-five to forty thousand dollars net profit a season like snapping your fingers! It was too great a temptation. Yet before I bought the damned thing I was considered one of the three or four young actors with the greatest artistic promise in America. I'd worked like hell. I'd left a good job as a machinist to take supers' parts because I loved the theatre. I was wild with ambition. I read all the plays ever written. I studied Shakespeare as you'd study the Bible. I educated myself. I got rid of an Irish brogue you could cut with a knife. I loved Shakespeare. I would have acted in any of his plays for nothing, for the joy of being alive in his great poetry. And I acted well in him. I felt inspired by him. I could have been a great Shakespearean actor, if I'd kept on. I know that! In 1874 when Edwin Booth came to the theatre in Chicago where I was leading man, I played Cassius to his Brutus one night, Brutus to his Cassius the next, Othello to his Iago, and so on. The first night I played Othello, he said to our manager, "That young man is playing Othello better than I ever did!" (*Proudly.*) That from Booth, the greatest actor of his day or any other! And it was true! And I was only twenty-seven years old! As I look back on it now, that night was the high spot in my career. I had life where I wanted it! And for a time after that I kept on upward with ambition high. Married your mother. Ask her what I was like in those days. Her love was an added incentive to ambition. But a few years later my good bad luck made me find the big money-maker. It wasn't that in my eyes at first. It was a great romantic part I knew I could play better than anyone. But it was a great box-office success from the start — and then life had me where it wanted me — at from thirty-five to forty thousand net profit a season! A fortune in those days — or even in these. (*Bitterly.*) What the hell was it I wanted to buy, I wonder, that was worth — Well, no matter. It's a late day for regrets. (*He glances vaguely at his cards.*) My play, isn't it?

EDMUND (*moved, stares at his father with understanding — slowly*). I'm glad you've told me this, Papa. I know you a lot better now.

TYRONE (*with a loose, twisted smile*). Maybe I shouldn't have told you. Maybe you'll only feel more contempt for me. And it's a poor way to convince you of the value of a dollar. (*Then as if this phrase automatically aroused an habitual association in his mind, he glances up at the chandelier disapprovingly.*) The glare from those extra lights hurts my eyes. You don't mind if I turn them out, do you? We don't need them, and there's no use making the Electric Company rich.

EDMUND (*controlling a wild impulse to laugh — agreeably*). No, sure not. Turn them out.

TYRONE (*gets heavily and a bit waveringly to his feet and gropes uncertainly for the lights — his mind going back to its line of thought*). No, I don't know what the hell it was I wanted to buy. (*He clicks out one bulb.*) On my solemn oath, Edmund, I'd gladly face not having an acre of land to call my own, nor a penny in the bank — (*He clicks out another bulb.*) I'd be willing to have no home but the poorhouse in my old age if I could look back now on having been the fine artist I might have been.

(*He turns out the third bulb, so only the reading lamp is on, and sits down again heavily. Edmund suddenly cannot hold back a burst of strained, ironical laughter. Tyrone is hurt.*)

What the devil are you laughing at?

EDMUND. Not at you, Papa. At life. It's so damned crazy.

TYRONE (*growls*). More of your morbidness! There's

nothing wrong with life. It's we who — (*He quotes.*) "The fault, dear Brutus, is not in our stars, but in ourselves that we are underlings." (*He pauses — then sadly.*) The praise Edwin Booth gave my Othello. I made the manager put down his exact words in writing. I kept it in my wallet for years. I used to read it every once in a while until finally it made me feel so bad I didn't want to face it any more. Where is it now, I wonder? Somewhere in this house. I remember I put it away carefully —

EDMUND (*with a wry ironical sadness*). It might be in an old trunk in the attic, along with Mama's wedding dress. (*Then as his father stares at him, he adds quickly.*) For Pete's sake, if we're going to play cards, let's play.

(*He takes the card his father had played and leads. For a moment, they play the game, like mechanical chess players. Then Tyrone stops, listening to a sound upstairs.*)

TYRONE. She's still moving around. God knows when she'll go to sleep.

EDMUND (*pleads tensely*). For Christ's sake, Papa, forget it!

(*He reaches out and pours a drink. Tyrone starts to protest, then gives it up. Edmund drinks. He puts down the glass. His expression changes. When he speaks it is as if he were deliberately giving way to drunkenness and seeking to hide behind a maudlin manner.*)

Yes, she moves above and beyond us, a ghost haunting the past, and here we sit pretending to forget, but straining our ears listening for the slightest sound, hearing the fog drip from the eaves like the uneven tick of a rundown, crazy clock — or like the dreary tears of a trollop spattering in a puddle of stale beer on a honky-tonk table top! (*He laughs with maudlin appreciation.*) Not so bad, that last, eh? Original, not Baudelaire. Give me credit! (*Then with alcoholic talkativeness.*) You've just told me some high spots in your memories. Want to hear mine? They're all connected with the sea. Here's one. When I was on the Squarehead square rigger, bound for Buenos Aires. Full moon in the Trades. The old hooker driving fourteen knots. I lay on the bowsprit, facing astern, with the water foaming into spume under me, the masts with every sail white in the moonlight, towering high above me. I became drunk with the beauty and singing rhythm of it, and for a moment I lost myself — actually lost my life. I was set free! I dissolved in the sea, became white sails and flying spray, became beauty and rhythm, became moonlight and the ship and the high dim-starred sky! I belonged, without past or future, within peace and unity and a wild joy, within something greater than my own life, or the life of Man, to Life itself! To God, if you want to put it that way. Then another time, on the American Line, when I was lookout on the crow's nest in the dawn watch. A calm sea, that time. Only a lazy ground swell and a slow drowsy roll of the ship. The passengers asleep and none of the crew in sight. No sound of man. Black smoke pouring from the funnels behind and beneath me. Dreaming, not keeping lookout, feeling alone, and above, and apart, watching the dawn creep like a painted dream over the sky and sea which slept together. Then the moment of ecstatic freedom came. The peace, the end of the quest, the last harbour, the joy of belonging to a fulfilment beyond men's lousy, pitiful, greedy fears and hopes and dreams! And several other times in my life, when I was swimming far out, or lying alone on a beach, I have had the same experience. Became the sun, the hot sand, green seaweed anchored to a rock, swaying in the tide. Like a saint's vision of beatitude. Like the veil of things as they seem drawn back by an unseen hand. For a second you see — and seeing the secret, are the secret. For a second there is meaning! Then the hand lets the veil fall and you are alone, lost in the fog again, and you stumble on toward nowhere, for no good reason! (*He grins wryly.*) It was a great mistake, my being born a man, I would have been much more successful as a sea-gull or a fish. As it is, I will always be a stranger who never feels at home, who does not really want and is not really wanted, who can never belong, who must always be a little in love with death!

TYRONE (*stares at him — impressed*). Yes, there's the makings of a poet in you all right. (*Then protesting uneasily.*) But that's morbid craziness about not being wanted and loving death.

EDMUND (*sardonically*). The *makings* of a poet. No, I'm afraid I'm like the guy who is always panhandling for a smoke. He hasn't even got the makings. He's got only the habit. I couldn't touch what I tried to tell you just now. I just stammered. That's the best I'll ever do. I mean, if I live. Well, it will be faithful realism, at least. Stammering is the native eloquence of us fog people.

(*A pause. Then they both jump startledly as there is a noise from outside the house, as if someone had stumbled and fallen on the front steps. Edmund grins.*)

Well, that sounds like the absent brother. He must have a peach of a bun on.

TYRONE (*scowling*). That loafer! He caught the last car, bad luck to it. (*He gets to his feet.*) Get him to bed, Edmund. I'll go out on the porch. He has a tongue like an adder when he's drunk. I'd only lose my temper.

(*He goes out of the door to the side porch as the front door in the hall bangs shut behind Jamie. Edmund watches with amusement Jamie's wavering progress through the front parlour. Jamie comes in. He is very drunk and woozy on his legs. His eyes are glassy, his face bloated, his speech blurred, his mouth slack like his father's, a leer on his lips.*)

JAMIE (*swaying and blinking in the doorway — in a loud voice*).

What ho! What ho!

EDMUND (*sharply*). Nix on the loud noise!

JAMIE (*blinks at him*). Oh, hello, Kid. (*With great seriousness.*) I'm as drunk as a fiddler's bitch.

EDMUND (*dryly*). Thanks for telling me your great secret.

JAMIE (*grins foolishly*). Yes. Unnecessary information Number One, eh? (*He bends and slaps at the knees of his trousers.*) Had serious accident. The fron' steps tried to trample on me. Took advantage of fog to waylay me. Ought to be a lighthouse out there. Dark in here, too. (*Scowling.*) What the hell is this, the morgue? Lesh have some light on sibject. (*He sways forward to the table, reciting Kipling.*)

"Ford, ford, ford o' Kabul river,
Ford o' Kabul river in the dark!
Keep the crossing-stakes beside you, an' they will surely guide you
'Cross the ford o' Kabul river in the dark."

(*He fumbles at the chandelier and manages to turn on the three bulbs.*) Thash more like it. To hell with old Gaspard. Where is the old tightwad?

EDMUND. Out on the porch.

JAMIE. Can't expect us to live in the Black Hole of Calcutta. (*His eyes fix on the full bottle of whiskey.*) Say! Have I got the d.t.'s? (*He reaches out fumblingly and grabs it.*) By God, it's real. What's matter with the Old Man tonight? Must be ossified to forget he left this out. Grab opportunity by the forelock. Key to my success. (*He slops a big drink into a glass.*)

EDMUND. You're stinking now. That will knock you stiff.

JAMIE. Wisdom from the mouth of babes. Can the wise stuff, Kid. You're still wet behind the ears. (*He lowers himself into a chair, holding the drink carefully aloft.*)

EDMUND. All right. Pass out if you want to.

JAMIE. Can't, that's trouble. Had enough to sink a ship, but can't sink. Well, here's hoping. (*He drinks.*)

EDMUND. Shove over the bottle. I'll have one, too.

JAMIE (*with sudden, big-brotherly solicitude, grabbing the bottle*). No, you don't. Not while I'm around. Remember doctor's orders. Maybe no one else gives a damn if you die, but I do. My kid brother. I love your guts, Kid. Everything else is gone. You're all I've got left. (*Pulling bottle closer to him.*) So no booze for you, if I can help it. (*Beneath his drunken sentimentality there is a genuine sincerity.*)

EDMUND (*irritably*). Oh, lay off it.

JAMIE (*is hurt and his face hardens*). You don't believe I care, eh? Just drunken bull. (*He shoves the bottle over.*) All right. Go ahead and kill yourself.

EDMUND (*seeing he is hurt — affectionately*). Sure I know you care, Jamie, and I'm going on the wagon. But tonight doesn't count. Too many damned things have happened today. (*He pours a drink.*) Here's how. (*He drinks.*)

JAMIE (*sobers up momentarily and with a pitying look*). I know, Kid. It's been a lousy day for you. (*Then with sneering cynicism.*) I'll bet old Gaspard hasn't tried to keep you off booze. Probably give you a case to take with you to the state farm for pauper patients. The sooner you kick the bucket, the less expense. (*With contemptuous hatred.*) What a bastard to have for a father! Christ, if you put him in a book, no one would believe it!

EDMUND (*defensively*). Oh, Papa's all right, if you try to understand him — and keep your sense of humour.

JAMIE (*cynically*). He's been putting on the old sob act for you, eh? He can always kid you. But not me. Never again. (*Then slowly.*) Although, in a way, I do feel sorry for him about one thing. But he has even that coming to him. He's to blame. (*Hurriedly.*) But to hell with that. (*He grabs the bottle and pours another drink, appearing very drunk again.*) That lash drink's getting me. This one ought to put the lights out. Did you tell Gaspard I got it out of Doc Hardy this sanatorium is a charity dump?

EDMUND (*reluctantly*). Yes. I told him I wouldn't go there. It's all settled now. He said I can go anywhere I want. (*He adds, smiling without resentment.*) Within reason, of course.

JAMIE (*drunkenly imitating his father*). Of course, lad. Anything within reason. (*Sneering.*) That means another cheap dump. Old Gaspard, the miser in "The Bells", that's a part he can play without make-up.

EDMUND (*irritably*). Oh, shut up, will you. I've heard that Gaspard stuff a million times.

JAMIE (*shrugs his shoulders — thickly*). Aw right, if you're shatisfied — let him get away with it. It's your funeral — I mean, I hope it won't be.

EDMUND (*changing the subject*). What did you do uptown tonight? Go to Mamie Burns?

JAMIE (*very drunk, his head nodding*). Sure thing. Where else could I find suitable feminine companionship? And love. Don't forget love. What is a man without a good woman's love? A God-damned hollow shell.

EDMUND (*chuckles tipsily, letting himself go now and be drunk*). You're a nut.

JAMIE (*quotes with gusto from Oscar Wilde's "The Harlot's House"*).

"Then, turning to my love, I said,
'The dead are dancing with the dead,
The dust is whirling with the dust.'

But she — she heard the violin,
And left my side and entered in:
Love passed into the house of lust.

Then suddenly the tune went false,
The dancers wearied of the waltz . . ."

(*He breaks off, thickly.*) Not strictly accurate. If my love was with me, I didn't notice it. She must have been a ghost. (*He pauses.*) Guess which one of Mamie's charmers I picked to bless me with her woman's love. It'll hand you a laugh, Kid. I picked Fat Violet.

EDMUND (*laughs drunkenly*). No, honest? Some pick! God, she weighs a ton. What the hell for, a joke?

JAMIE. No joke. Very serious. By the time I hit Mamie's dump I felt very sad about myself and all the other poor bums in the world. Ready for a weep on any old womanly bosom. You know how you get when John Barleycorn turns on the soft music inside you. Then, soon as I got in the door, Mamie began telling me all her troubles. Beefed how rotten business was, and she was going to give Fat Violet the gate. Customers didn't fall for Vi. Only reason she'd kept her was she could play the piano. Lately Vi's gone on drunks and been too boiled to play, and was eating her out of house and home, and although Vi was a goodhearted dumbbell, and she felt sorry for her because she didn't know how the hell she'd make a living, still business was business, and she couldn't afford to run a home for fat tarts. Well, that made me feel sorry for Fat Violet, so I squandered two bucks of your dough to escort her upstairs. With no dishonourable intentions whatever. I like them fat, but not that fat. All I wanted was a little heart-to-heart talk concerning the infinite sorrow of life.

EDMUND (*chuckles drunkenly*). Poor Vi! I'll bet you recited Kipling and Swinburne and Dowson and gave her "I have been faithful to thee, Cynara, in my fashion."

JAMIE (*grins loosely*). Sure — with the Old Master, John Barleycorn, playing soft music. She stood it for a while. Then she got good and sore. Got the idea I took her upstairs for a joke. Gave me a grand bawling out. Said she was better than a drunken bum who recited poetry. Then she began to cry. So I had to say I loved her because she was fat, and she wanted to believe that, and I stayed with her to prove it, and that cheered her up, and she kissed me when I left, and said she'd fallen hard for me, and we both cried a little more in the hallway, and everything was fine, except Mamie Burns thought I'd gone bughouse.

EDMUND (*quotes derisively*).

"Harlots and
Hunted have pleasures of their own to give,
The vulgar herd can never understand."

JAMIE (*nods his head drunkenly*). Egzactly! Hell of a good time, at that. You should have stuck around with me, Kid. Mamie Burns inquired after you. Sorry to hear you were sick. She meant it, too. (*He pauses — then with a maudlin humour, in a ham-actor tone.*) This night has opened my eyes to a great career in store for me, my boy! I shall give the art of acting back to the performing seals, which are its most perfect expression. By applying my natural God-given talents in their proper sphere, I shall attain the pinnacle of success! I'll be the lover of the fat woman in Barnum and Bailey's circus!

(*Edmund laughs. Jamie's mood changes to arrogant disdain.*)

Pah! Imagine me sunk to the fat girl in a hick town hooker shop! Me! Who have made some of the best-lookers on Broadway sit up and beg! (*He quotes from Kipling's "Sestina of the Tramp-Royal".*)

"Speakin' in general, I 'ave tried 'em all,
The 'appy roads that take you o'er the world."

(*With sodden melancholy.*) Not so apt. Happy roads is bunk. Weary roads is right. Get you nowhere fast. That's where I've got — nowhere. Where everyone lands in the end, even if most of the suckers won't admit it.

EDMUND (*derisively*). Can it! You'll be crying in a minute.

JAMIE (*starts and stares at his brother for a second with bitter hostility — thickly*). Don't get — too damned fresh. (*Then abruptly.*) But you're right. To hell with repining! Fat Violet's a good kid. Glad I stayed with her. Christian act. Cured her blues. Hell of a good time. You should have stuck with me, Kid. Taken your mind off your troubles. What's the use coming home to get the blues over what can't be helped. All over — finished now — not a hope! (*He stops, his head nodding drunkenly, his eyes closing — then suddenly he looks up, his face hard, and quotes jeeringly.*)

"If I were hanged on the highest hill,
Mother o' mine, O mother o' mine!
I know whose love would follow me still . . ."

EDMUND (*violently*). Shut up!

JAMIE (*in a cruel, sneering tone with hatred in it*). Where's the hophead? Gone to sleep?

(*Edmund jerks as if he'd been struck. There is a tense silence. Edmund's face looks stricken and sick. Then in a burst of rage he springs from his chair.*)

EDMUND. You dirty bastard!

(*He punches his brother in the face, a blow that glances off the cheekbone. For a second Jamie reacts pugnaciously and half rises from his chair to do battle, but suddenly he seems to sober up to a shocked realization of what he has said and he sinks back limply.*)

JAMIE (*miserably*). Thanks, Kid. I certainly had that coming. Don't know what made me — booze talking — You know me, Kid.

EDMUND (*his anger ebbing*). I know you'd never say that unless — But God, Jamie, no matter how drunk you are, it's no excuse! (*He pauses — miserably.*) I'm sorry I hit you. You and I never scrap — that bad. (*He sinks back on his chair.*)

JAMIE (*huskily*). It's all right. Glad you did. My dirty tongue. Like to cut it out. (*He hides his face in his hands — dully.*) I suppose it's because I feel so damned sunk. Because this time Mama had me fooled. I really believed she had it licked. She thinks I always believe the worst, but this time I believed the best. (*His voice flutters.*) I suppose I can't forgive her — yet. It meant so much. I'd begun to hope, if she'd beaten the game, I could, too. (*He begins to sob, and the horrible part of his weeping is that it appears sober, not the maudlin tears of drunkenness.*)

EDMUND (*blinking back tears himself*). God, don't I know how you feel! Stop it, Jamie!

JAMIE (*trying to control his sobs*). I've known about Mama so much longer than you. Never forget the first time I got wise. Caught her in the act with a hypo. Christ, I'd never dreamed before that any women but whores took dope! (*He pauses.*) And then this stuff of you getting consumption. It's got me licked. We've been more than brothers. You're the only pal I've ever had. I love your guts. I'd do anything for you.

EDMUND (*reaches out and pats his arm*). I know that, Jamie.

JAMIE (*his crying over — drops his hands from his face — with a strange bitterness*). Yet I'll bet you've heard Mama and old Gaspard spill so much bunk about my hoping for the worst, you suspect right now I'm thinking to myself that Papa is old and can't last much longer, and if you were to die, Mama and I would get all he's got, and so I'm probably hoping —

EDMUND (*indignantly*). Shut up, you damned fool! What the hell put that in your nut? (*He stares at his brother accusingly.*) Yes, that's what I'd like to know. What put that in your mind?

JAMIE (*confusedly — appearing drunk again*). Don't be a dumbbell! What I said! Always suspected of hoping for the worst. I've got so I can't help — (*Then drunkenly resentful.*) What are you trying to do, accuse me? Don't play the wise guy with me! I've learned more of life than you'll ever know! Just because you've read a lot of highbrow junk, don't think you can fool me! You're only an overgrown kid! Mama's baby and Papa's pet! The family White Hope! You've been getting a swelled head lately. About nothing! About a few poems in a hick town newspaper! Hell, I used to write better stuff for the Lit magazine in college! You better wake up! You're setting no rivers on fire! You let hick town boobs flatter you with bunk about your future —

(*Abruptly his tone changes to disgusted contrition. Edmund has looked away from him, trying to ignore this tirade.*)

Hell, Kid, forget it. That goes for Sweeny. You know I don't mean it. No one is prouder you've started to make good. (*Drunkenly assertive.*) Why shouldn't I be proud? Hell, it's purely selfish. You reflect credit on me. I've had more to do with bringing you up than anyone. I wised you up about women, so you'd never be a fall guy, or make any mistakes you didn't want to make! And who steered you on to reading poetry first? Swinburne, for example? I did! And because I once wanted to write, I planted it in your mind that someday you'd write! Hell, you're more than my brother. I made you! You're my Frankenstein!

(*He has risen to a note of drunken arrogance. Edmund is grinning with amusement now.*)

EDMUND. All right, I'm your Frankenstein. So let's have a drink. (*He laughs.*) You crazy nut!

JAMIE (*thickly*). I'll have a drink. Not you. Got to take care of you. (*He reaches out with a foolish grin of doting affection and grabs his brother's hand.*) Don't be scared of this sanatorium business. Hell, you can beat that standing on your head. Six months and you'll be in the pink. Probably haven't got consumption at all. Doctors lot of fakers. Told me years ago to cut out booze or I'd soon be dead — and here I am. They're all con men. Anything to grab your dough. I'll bet this state farm stuff is political graft game. Doctors get a cut for every patient they send.

EDMUND (*disgustedly amused*). You're the limit! At the Last Judgment, you'll be around telling everyone it's in the bag.

JAMIE. And I'll be right. Slip a piece of change to the Judge and be saved, but if you're broke you can go to hell!

(*He grins at this blasphemy and Edmund has to laugh. Jamie goes on.*)

"Therefore put money in thy purse." That's the only dope. (*Mockingly.*) The secret of my success! Look, what it's got me!

(*He lets Edmund's hand go to pour a big drink, and gulps it down. He stares at his brother with bleary affection — takes his hand again and begins to talk thickly but with a strange, convincing sincerity.*)

Listen, Kid, you'll be going away. May not get another chance to talk. Or might not be drunk enough to tell you truth. So got to tell you now. Something I ought to have told you long ago — for your own good.

(*He pauses — struggling with himself. Edmund stares, impressed and uneasy. Jamie blurts out.*)

Not drunken bull, but "in vino veritas" stuff. You better take it seriously. Want to warn you — against me. Mama and Papa are right. I've been rotten bad influence. And worst of it is, I did it on purpose.

EDMUND (*uneasily*). Shut up! I don't want to hear —

JAMIE. Nix, Kid! You listen! Did it on purpose to make a bum of you. Or part of me did. A big part. That part that's been dead so long. That hates life. My putting you wise so you'd learn from my mistakes. Believed that myself at times, but it's a fake. Made my mistakes look good. Made getting drunk romantic. Made whores fascinating vampires instead of poor, stupid, diseased slobs they really are. Made fun of work as sucker's game. Never wanted you succeed and make me look even worse by comparison. Wanted you to fail. Always jealous of you. Mama's baby, Papa's pet! (*He stares at Edmund with increasing enmity.*) And it was your being born that started Mama on dope. I know that's not your fault, but all the same, God damn you, I can't help hating your guts —!

EDMUND (*almost frightenedly*). Jamie! Cut it out! You're crazy!

JAMIE. But don't get wrong idea, Kid. I love you more than I hate you. My saying what I'm telling you now proves it. I run the risk you'll hate me — and you're all I've got left. But I didn't mean to tell you that last stuff — go that far back. Don't know what made me. What I wanted to say is, I'd like to see you become the greatest success in the world. But you'd better be on your guard. Because I'll do my damnedest to make you fail. Can't help it. I hate myself. Got to take revenge. On everyone else. Especially you. Oscar Wilde's "Reading Gaol" has the dope twisted. The man was dead, and so he had to kill the thing he loved. That's what it ought to be. The dead part of me hopes you won't get well. Maybe he's even glad the game has got Mama again! He wants company, he doesn't want to be the only corpse around the house! (*He gives a hard, tortured laugh.*)

EDMUND. Jesus, Jamie! You really have gone crazy!

JAMIE. Think it over and you'll see I'm right. Think it over when you're away from me in the sanatorium. Make up your mind you've got to tie a can to me — get me out of your life — think of me as dead — tell people, "I had a brother, but he's dead." And when you come back, look out for me. I'll be waiting to welcome you with that "my old pal" stuff, and give you the glad hand, and at the first good chance I get stab you in the back.

EDMUND. Shut up! I'll be God-damned if I'll listen to you any more —!

JAMIE (*as if he hadn't heard*). Only don't forget me. Remember I warned you — for your sake. Give me credit. Greater love hath no man than this, that he saveth his brother from himself. (*Very drunkenly, his head bobbing.*) That's all. Feel better now. Gone to confession. Know you absolve me, don't you, Kid? You understand. You're a damned fine kid. Ought to be. I made you. So go and get well. Don't die on me. You're all I've got left. God bless you, K.O.

(*He falls into a drunken doze, not completely asleep. Edmund buries his face in his hands miserably. Tyrone comes in quietly through the screen door from the porch, his dressing gown wet with fog, the collar turned up around his throat. His face is stern and disgusted but at the same time pitying. Edmund does not notice his entrance.*)

TYRONE (*in a low voice*). Thank God he's asleep.

(*Edmund looks up with a start.*)

I thought he'd never stop talking. (*He turns down the collar of his dressing gown.*) We'd better let him stay where he is and sleep it off.

(*Edmund remains silent. Tyrone regards him — then goes on.*)

I heard the last part of his talk. It's what I've warned you. I hope you'll heed the warning, now it comes from his own mouth.

(*Edmund gives no sign of having heard. Tyrone adds pityingly.*)

But don't take it too much to heart, lad. He loves to exaggerate the worst of himself when he's drunk. He's devoted to you. It's the one good thing left in him. (*He looks down on Jamie with a bitter sadness.*) A sweet spectacle for me! My first-born, who I hoped would bear my name in honour and dignity, who showed such brilliant promise!

EDMUND (*miserably*). Keep quiet, can't you, Papa?

TYRONE (*pours a drink*). A waste! A wreck, a drunken hulk, done with and finished!

(*He drinks. Jamie has become restless, sensing his father's presence, struggling up from his stupor. Now he gets his eyes open to blink up at Tyrone. The latter moves back a step defensively, his face growing hard.*)

JAMIE (*suddenly points a finger at him and recites with dramatic emphasis*).

"Clarence is come, false, fleeting, perjured Clarence,
That stabbed me in the field by Tewksbury.
Seize on him, Furies, take him into torment."

(*Then resentfully.*) What the hell are you staring at? (*He recites sardonically from Rossetti.*)

"Look in my face. My name is Might-Have-Been;
I am also called No More, Too Late, Farewell."

TYRONE. I'm well aware of that, and God knows I don't want to look at it.

EDMUND. Papa! Quit it!

JAMIE (*derisively*). Got a great idea for you, Papa. Put on revival of "The Bells" this season. Great part in it you can play without make-up. Old Gaspard, the miser!

(*Tyrone turns away, trying to control his temper.*)

EDMUND. Shut up, Jamie!

JAMIE (*jeeringly*). I claim Edwin Booth never saw the day when he could give as good a performance as a trained seal. Seals are intelligent and honest. They don't put up any bluffs about the Art of Acting. They admit they're just hams earning their daily fish.

TYRONE (*stung, turns on him in a rage*). You loafer!

EDMUND. Papa! Do you want to start a row that will bring Mama down? Jamie, go back to sleep! You've shot off your mouth too much already.

(*Tyrone turns away.*)

JAMIE (*thickly*). All right, Kid. Not looking for argument. Too damned sleepy.

(*He closes his eyes, his head nodding. Tyrone comes to the table and sits down, turning his chair so he won't look at Jamie. At once he becomes sleepy, too.*)

TYRONE (*heavily*). I wish to God she'd go to bed so that I could, too. (*Drowsily.*) I'm dog tired. I can't stay up all night like I used to. Getting old — old and finished. (*With a bone-cracking yawn.*) Can't keep my eyes open. I think I'll catch a few winks. Why don't you do the same, Edmund? It'll pass the time until she —

(*His voice trails off. His eyes close, his chin sags, and he begins to breathe heavily through his mouth. Edmund sits tensely. He hears something and jerks nervously forward in his chair, staring through the front parlour into the hall. He jumps up with a hunted, distracted expression. It seems for a second he is going to hide in the back parlour. Then he sits down again and waits, his eyes averted, his hands gripping the arms of his chair. Suddenly all five bulbs of the chandelier in the front parlour are turned on from a wall switch, and a moment later someone starts playing the piano in there — the opening of one of Chopin's simpler waltzes, done with a forgetful, stiff-fingered groping, as if an awkward schoolgirl were practising it for the first time. Tyrone starts to wide-awakeness and sober dread, and Jamie's head jerks back and his eyes open. For a moment they listen frozenly. The playing stops as abruptly as it began, and Mary appears in the doorway. She wears a sky-blue dressing gown over her nightdress, dainty slippers with pompons on her bare feet. Her face is paler than ever. Her eyes look enormous. They glisten like polished black jewels. The uncanny thing is that her face now appears so youthful. Experience seems ironed out of it. It is a marble mask of girlish innocence, the mouth caught in a shy smile. Her white hair is braided in two pigtails which hang over her breast. Over one arm, carried neglectfully, trailing on the floor, as if she had forgotten she held it, is an old-fashioned white satin wedding gown, trimmed with duchesse lace. She hesitates in the doorway, glancing round the room, her forehead puckered puzzledly, like someone who has come to a room to get something but has become absent-minded on the way and forgotten what it was. They stare at her. She seems aware of them merely as she is aware of other objects in the room, the furniture, the windows, familiar things she accepts automatically as naturally belonging there but which she is too preoccupied to notice.*)

JAMIE (*breaks the cracking silence — bitterly, self-defensively sardonic*). The Mad Scene. Enter Ophelia!

(*His father and brother both turn on him fiercely. Edmund is quicker. He slaps Jamie across the mouth with the back of his hand.*)

TYRONE (*his voice trembling with suppressed fury*). Good boy, Edmund. The dirty blackguard! His own mother!

JAMIE (*mumbles guiltily, without resentment*). All right, Kid. Had it coming. But I told you how much I'd hoped — (*He puts his hands over his face and begins to sob.*)

TYRONE. I'll kick you out in the gutter tomorrow, so help me God. (*But Jamie's sobbing breaks his anger, and he turns and shakes his shoulder, pleading.*) Jamie, for the love of God, stop it!

(*Then Mary speaks, and they freeze into silence again, staring at her. She has paid no attention whatever to the incident. It is simply a part of the familiar atmosphere of the room, a background which does not touch her preoccupation; and she speaks aloud to herself, not to them.*)

MARY. I play so badly now. I'm all out of practice. Sister Theresa will give me a dreadful scolding. She'll tell me it isn't fair to my father when he spends so much money for extra lessons. She's quite right, it isn't fair, when he's so good and generous, and so proud of me. I'll practise every day from now on. But something horrible has happened to my hands. The fingers have gotten so stiff — (*She lifts her hands to examine them with a frightened puzzlement.*) The knuckles are all swollen. They're so ugly. I'll have to go to the Infirmary and show Sister Martha. (*With a sweet smile of affectionate trust.*) She's old and a little cranky, but I love her just the same, and she has things in her medicine chest that'll cure anything. She'll give me something to rub on my hands, and tell me to pray to the Blessed Virgin, and they'll be well again in no time. (*She *forgets her hands and comes into the room, the wedding gown trailing on the floor. She glances around vaguely, her forehead puckered again.*) Let me see. What did I come here to find? It's terrible, how absent-minded I've become. I'm always dreaming and forgetting.

TYRONE (*in a stifled voice*). What's that she's carrying, Edmund?

EDMUND (*dully*). Her wedding gown, I suppose.

TYRONE. Christ! (*He gets to his feet and stands directly in her path — in anguish.*) Mary! Isn't it bad enough —? (*Controlling himself — gently persuasive.*) Here, let me take it, dear. You'll only step on it and tear it and get it dirty dragging it on the floor. Then you'd be sorry afterwards.

(*She lets him take it, regarding him from somewhere far away within herself, without recognition, without either affection or animosity.*)

MARY (*with the shy politeness of a well-bred young girl toward an elderly gentleman who relieves her of a bundle*). Thank you. You are very kind. (*She regards the wedding gown with a puzzled interest.*) It's a wedding gown. It's very lovely, isn't it? (*A shadow crosses her face and she looks vaguely uneasy.*) I remember now. I found it in the attic hidden in a trunk. But I don't know what I wanted it for. I'm going to be a nun — that is, if I can only find — (*She looks around the room, her forehead puckered again.*) What is it I'm looking for? I know it's something I lost. (*She moves back from Tyrone, aware of him now only as some obstacle in her path.*)

TYRONE (*in hopeless appeal*). Mary!

(*But it cannot penetrate her preoccupation. She doesn't seem to hear him. He gives up helplessly, shrinking into himself, even his defensive drunkenness taken from him, leaving him sick and sober. He sinks back on his chair, holding the wedding gown in his arms with an unconscious clumsy, protective gentleness.*)

JAMIE (*drops his hand from his face, his eyes on the table top. He has suddenly sobered up, too — dully*). It's no good, Papa. (*He recites from Swinburne's "A Leave-taking" and does it well, simply but with a bitter sadness.*)

"Let us rise up and part; she will not know.
Let us go seaward as the great winds go,
Full of blown sand and foam; what help is here?
There is no help, for all these things are so,
And all the world is bitter as a tear.
And how these things are, though ye strove to show,
She would not know."

MARY (*looking around her*). Something I miss terribly. It can't be altogether lost. (*She starts to move around behind Jamie's chair.*)

JAMIE (*turns to look up into her face — and cannot help appealing pleadingly in his turn*). Mama! (*She does not seem to hear. He looks away hopelessly.*) Hell! What's the use? It's no good. (*He recites from "A Leave-taking" again with increased bitterness.*)

"Let us go hence, my songs; she will not hear.
Let us go hence together without fear;
Keep silence now, for singing-time is over,
And over all old things and all things dear.
She loves not you nor me as all we love her.
Yea, though we sang as angels in her ear,
She would not hear."

MARY (*looking around her*). Something I need terribly. I remember when I had it I was never lonely nor afraid. I can't have lost it for ever. I would die if I thought that. Because then there would be no hope. (*She moves like a sleepwalker, around the back of Jamie's chair, then forward toward left front, passing behind Edmund.*)

EDMUND (*turns impulsively and grabs her arm. As he pleads he has the quality of a bewilderedly hurt little boy*). Mama! It isn't a summer cold! I've got consumption!

MARY (*for a second he seems to have broken through to her. She trembles and her expression becomes terrified. She calls distractedly, as if giving a command to herself*). No! (*And instantly she is far away again. She murmurs gently but impersonally.*) You must not try to touch me. You must not try to hold me. It isn't right, when I am hoping to be a nun.

(*He lets his hand drop from her arm. She moves left to the front end of the sofa beneath the windows and sits down, facing front, her hands folded in her lap, in a demure schoolgirlish pose.*)

JAMIE (*gives Edmund a strange look of mingled pity and jealous gloating*). You damned fool. It's no good. (*He recites again from the Swinburne poem.*)

"Let us go hence, go hence; she will not see.
Sing all once more together; surely she,
She too, remembering days and words that were,
Will turn a little toward us, sighing; but we,
We are hence, we are gone, as though we had not been there.
Nay, and though all men seeing had pity on me,
She would not see."

TYRONE (*trying to shake off his hopeless stupor*). Oh, we're fools to pay any attention. It's the damned poison. But I've never known her to drown herself in it as deep as this. (*Gruffly.*) Pass me that bottle, Jamie. And stop reciting that damned morbid poetry. I won't have it in my house!

(*Jamie pushes the bottle toward him. He pours a drink without disarranging the wedding gown he holds carefully over his other arm and on his lap, and shoves the bottle back. Jamie pours his and passes the bottle to Edmund, who, in turn, pours one. Tyrone lifts his glass and his sons follow suit mechanically, but before they can drink Mary speaks and they slowly lower their drinks to the table, forgetting them.*)

MARY (*staring dreamily before her. Her face looks extraordinarily youthful and innocent. The shyly eager, trusting smile is on her lips as she talks aloud to herself*). I had a talk with Mother Elizabeth. She is so sweet and good. A saint on earth. I love her dearly. It may be sinful of me but I love her better than my own mother. Because she always understands, even before you say a word. Her kind blue eyes look right into your heart. You can't keep any secrets from her. You couldn't deceive her, even if you were mean enough to want to. (*She gives a little rebellious toss of her head — with girlish pique.*) All the same, I don't think she was so understanding this time. I told her I wanted to be a nun. I explained how sure I was of my vocation, that I had prayed to the Blessed Virgin to make me sure, and to find me worthy. I told Mother I had had a true vision when I was praying in the shrine of Our Lady of Lourdes, on the little island in the lake. I said I knew, as surely as I knew I was kneeling there, that the Blessed Virgin had smiled and blessed me with her consent. But Mother Elizabeth told me I must be more sure than that, even, that I must prove it wasn't simply my imagination. She said, if I was so sure, then I wouldn't mind putting myself to a test by going home after I graduated and living as other girls lived, going out to parties and dances and enjoying myself; and then if after a year or two I still felt sure, I could come back to see her and we would talk it over again. (*She tosses her head — indignantly.*) I never dreamed Holy Mother would give me such advice! I was really shocked. I said, of course, I would do anything she suggested, but I knew it was simply a waste of time. After I left her, I felt all mixed up, so I went to the shrine and prayed to the Blessed Virgin and found peace again because I knew she heard my prayer and would always love me and see no harm ever came to me so long as I never lost my faith in her. (*She pauses and a look of growing uneasiness comes over her face. She passes a hand over her forehead as if brushing cobwebs from her brain — vaguely.*) That was in the winter of senior year. Then in the spring something happened to me. Yes, I remember. I fell in love with James Tyrone and was so happy for a time.

(*She stares before her in a sad dream. Tyrone stirs in his chair. Edmund and Jamie remain motionless.*)

CURTAIN

Tao House
December 20, 1940

HUGHIE

Characters

"ERIE" SMITH, *a Teller of Tales*

A NIGHT CLERK

SCENE. *The desk and a section of lobby of a small hotel on a West Side street in midtown New York. It is between 3 and 4 a.m. of a day in the summer of 1928.*

It is one of those hotels, built in the decade 1900–10 on the side streets of the Great White Way sector, which began as respectable second class but soon were forced to deteriorate in order to survive. Following the First World War and Prohibition, it had given up all pretence of respectability, and now is anything a paying guest wants it to be, a third-class dump, catering to the catch-as-catch-can trade. But still it does not prosper. It has not shared in the Great Hollow Boom of the 'twenties. The Everlasting Opulence of the New Economic Law has overlooked it. It manages to keep running by cutting the overhead for service, repairs, and cleanliness to a minimum.

The desk faces left along a section of seedy lobby with shabby chairs. The street entrance is off-stage, left. Behind the desk are a telephone switchboard and the operator's stool. At right, the usual numbered tiers of mailboxes, and above them a clock.

The Night Clerk sits on the stool, facing front, his back to the switchboard. There is nothing to do. He is not thinking. He is not sleepy. He simply droops and stares acquiescently at nothing. It would be discouraging to glance at the clock. He knows there are several hours to go before his shift is over. Anyway, he does not need to look at clocks. He has been a night clerk in New York hotels so long he can tell time by sounds in the street.

He is in his early forties: tall, thin, with a scrawny neck and jutting Adam's apple. His face is long and narrow, greasy with perspiration, sallow, studded with pimples from ingrowing hairs. His nose is large and without character. So is his mouth. So are his ears. So is his thinning brown hair, powdered with dandruff. Behind hornrimmed spectacles, his blank brown eyes contain no discernible expression. One would say they had even forgotten how it feels to be bored. He wears an ill-fitting blue serge suit, white shirt and collar, a blue tie. The suit is old and shines at the elbows as if it had been waxed and polished.

Footsteps echo in the deserted lobby as someone comes in from the street. The Night Clerk rises wearily. His eyes remain empty but his gummy lips part automatically in a welcoming The-Patron-Is-Always-Right grimace, intended as a smile. His big uneven teeth are in bad condition.

Erie Smith enters and approaches the desk. He is about the same age as the Night Clerk and has the same pasty, perspiry, night-life complexion. There the resemblance ends. Erie is around medium height but appears shorter because he is stout and his fat legs are too short for his body. So are his fat arms. His big head squats on a neck which seems part of his beefy shoulders. His face is round, his snub nose flattened at the tip. His blue eyes have drooping lids and puffy pouches under them. His sandy hair is falling out, and the top of his head is bald. He walks to the desk with a breezy, familiar air, his gait a bit waddling because of his short legs. He carries a Panama hat and mops his face with a red-and-blue silk handkerchief. He wears a light grey suit cut in the extreme, tight-

waisted, Broadway mode, the coat open to reveal an old and faded but expensive silk shirt in a shade of blue that sets teeth on edge, and a gay red and blue foulard tie, its knot stained by perspiration. His trousers are held up by a braided brown leather belt with a brass buckle. His shoes are tan and white, his socks white silk.

In manner, he is consciously a Broadway sport and a Wise Guy—the type of small-fry gambler and horse-player, living hand-to-mouth on the fringe of the rackets. Infesting corners, doorways, cheap restaurants, the bars of minor speakeasies, he and his kind imagine they are in the Real Know, cynical oracles of the One True Grapevine.

Erie usually speaks in a low, guarded tone, his droop-lidded eyes suspiciously wary of non-existent eavesdroppers. His face is set in the prescribed pattern of gambler's dead-pan. His small, pursy mouth is always crooked in the cynical leer of one who possesses superior, inside information, and his shifty once-over glances never miss the price tags he detects on everything and everybody. Yet there is something phoney about his characterization of himself, some sentimental softness behind it which doesn't belong in the hard-boiled picture.

Erie avoids looking at the Night Clerk, as if he resented him.

ERIE (*peremptorily*). Key. (*Then as the Night Clerk gropes with his memory—grudgingly.*) Forgot you ain't seen me before. Erie Smith's the name. I'm an old timer in this fleabag. 492.

NIGHT CLERK (*in a tone of one who is wearily relieved when he does not have to remember anything—he plucks out the key*). 492. Yes, sir.

ERIE (*taking the key, gives the Clerk the once-over. He appears not unfavourably impressed but his tone still holds resentment*). How long you been on the job? Four, five days, huh? I been off on a drunk. Come to now, though. Tapering off. Well, I'm glad they fired that young squirt they took on when Hughie got sick. One of them fresh wise punks. Couldn't tell him nothing. Pleased to meet you, pal. Hope you stick around.

(*He shoves out his hand. The Night Clerk takes it obediently*).

NIGHT CLERK (*with a compliant, uninterested smile*). Glad to know you, Mr. Smith.

ERIE. What's your name?

NIGHT CLERK (*as if he had half forgotten, because what did it matter, anyway?*). Hughes. Charlie Hughes.

ERIE (*starts*). Huh? Hughes? Say, is that on the level?

NIGHT CLERK. Charlie Hughes.

ERIE. Well, I be damned! What the hell d'you know about that! (*Warming towards the Clerk.*) Say, now I notice, you don't look like Hughie, but you remind me of him somehow. You ain't by any chance related?

NIGHT CLERK. You mean to the Hughes who had this job so long and died recently? No, sir. No relation.

ERIE (*gloomily*). No, that's right. Hughie told me he didn't have no relations left—except his wife and kids, of course. (*He pauses—more gloomily.*) Yeah. The poor guy croaked last week. His funeral was what started me off on a bat. (*Then boastfully, as if defending himself against gloom.*) Some drunk! I don't go on one often. It's bum dope in my book. A guy gets careless and gabs about things he knows and when he comes to he's liable to find there's guys who'd feel easier if he wasn't around no more. That's the trouble with knowing things. Take my tip, pal. Don't never know nothin'. Be a sap and stay healthy.

(*His manner has become secretive, with sinister undertones. But the Night Clerk doesn't notice this. Long experience with guests who stop at his desk in the small hours to talk about themselves has given him a foolproof technique of self-defence. He appears to listen with agreeable submissiveness and be impressed, but his mind is blank and he doesn't hear, unless a direct question is put to him, and sometimes not even then. Erie thinks he is impressed.*)

But hell, I always keep my noggin working, booze or no booze. I'm no sucker. What was I sayin'? Oh, some drunk. I sure hit the high spots. You shoulda seen the doll I made night before last. And did she take me to the cleaners! I'm a sucker for blondes. (*He pauses—giving the Night Clerk a cynical, contemptuous glance.*) You're married, ain't you?

NIGHT CLERK (*long ago he gave up caring whether*

questions were personal or not). Yes, sir.

ERIE. Yeah, I'd'a laid ten to one on it. You got that old look. Like Hughie had. Maybe that's the resemblance. (*He chuckles contemptuously.*) Kids, too, I bet?

NIGHT CLERK. Yes, sir. Three.

ERIE. You're worse off than Hughie was. He only had two. Three, huh? Well, that's what comes of being careless!

(*He laughs. The Night Clerk smiles at a guest. He had been a little offended when a guest first made that crack—must have been ten years ago—yes, Eddie, the oldest, is eleven now—or is it twelve? Erie goes on with good-natured tolerance.*)

Well, I suppose marriage ain't such a bum racket, if you're made for it. Hughie didn't seem to mind it much, although if you want my low-down, his wife is a bum—in spades! Oh, I don't mean cheatin'. With her puss and figure, she'd never make no one except she raided a blind asylum.

(*The Night Clerk feels that he has been standing a long time, his feet are beginning to ache, and he wishes 492 would stop talking and go to bed so that he can sit down again and listen to the noises in the street and think about nothing. Erie gives him an amused, condescending glance.*)

How old are you? Wait! Let me guess. You look fifty or over, but I'll lay ten to one you're forty-three or maybe forty-four.

NIGHT CLERK. I'm forty-three. (*He adds, vaguely.*) Or maybe it is forty-four.

ERIE (*elated*). I win, huh? I sure can call the turn on ages, buddy. You ought to see the dolls get sored up when I work it on them! You're like Hughie. He looked like he'd never see fifty again and he was only forty-three. Me, I'm forty-five. Never think it, would you? Most of the dames don't think I've hit forty yet.

(*The Night Clerk shifts his position so that he can lean more on the desk. Maybe those shoes he sees advertised for fallen arches—but they cost eight dollars, so that's out—Get a pair when he goes to Heaven. Erie is sizing him up with another cynical, friendly glance.*)

I make another bet about you. Born and raised in the sticks, wasn't you?

NIGHT CLERK (*faintly aroused and defensive*). I come originally from Saginaw, Michigan, but I've lived here in the Big Town so long I consider myself a New Yorker now. (*This is a long speech for him, and he wonders sadly why he took the trouble to make it.*)

ERIE. I don't deserve no medal for picking that one. Nearly every guy I know on the Big Stem—and I know most of 'em—hails from the sticks. Take me. You'd never guess it but I was dragged up in Erie, P-a. Ain't that a knock-out! Erie, P-a! That's how I got my moniker. No one calls me nothing but Erie. You better call me Erie, too, pal, or I won't know when you're talkin' to me.

NIGHT CLERK. All right, Erie.

ERIE. Atta boy. (*He chuckles.*) Here's another knock-out. Smith is my real name. A Broadway guy like me named Smith and it's my real name! Ain't that a knock-out! (*He explains carefully so there will be no misunderstanding.*) I don't remember nothing much about Erie, P-a, you understand—or want to. Some punk burg! After grammar school, my Old Man put me to work in his store, dealing out groceries. Some punk job! I stuck it till I was eighteen before I took a run-out powder.

(*The Night Clerk seems turned into a drooping wax-work, draped along the desk. This is what he used to dread before he perfected his technique of not listening: The Guest's Story of His Life. He fixes his mind on his aching feet. Erie chuckles.*)

Speaking of marriage, that was the big reason I ducked. A doll nearly had me hooked for the old shotgun ceremony. Closest I ever come to being played for a sucker. This doll in Erie—Daisy's her name—was one of them dumb wide-open dolls. All the guys give her a play. Then one day she wakes up and finds she's going to have a kid. I never figured she meant to frame me in particular. Way I always figured, she didn't have no idea who, so she holds a lottery all by herself. Put about a thousand guys' names in a hat—all she could remember—and drew one out and I was it. Then she told her Ma, and her Ma told her Pa, and her Pa come round looking for me. But I was no fall guy even in them days. I took it on the lam. For Saratoga, to look the bangtails over. I'd started to be a horse-player in Erie, though I'd never seen a track. I been one ever since. (*With a touch of bravado.*) And I ain't done so bad, pal. I've made some killings in my time the gang still gab about. I've been in the big bucks. More'n once, and I will be again. I've had tough breaks too, but what the hell, I always get by. When the horses won't run for me, there's draw or stud. When they're bad, there's a crap game. And when they're all bad, there's always bucks to pick up for little errands I ain't talkin' about, which they give a guy who can keep his clam shut. Oh, I get along, buddy. I get along fine.

(*He waits for approving assent from the Night Clerk, but the latter is not hearing—so intently, that he misses his cue until the expectant silence crashes his ears.*)

NIGHT CLERK (*hastily, gambling on "yes"*). Yes, sir.

ERIE (*bitingly*). Sorry if I'm keeping you up, sport. (*With an aggrieved air.*) Hughie was a wide-awake guy. He was always waiting for me to roll in. He'd say, "Hello, Erie, how'd the bangtails treat you?" Or, "How's luck?" Or, "Did you make the old bones behave?" Then I'd tell him how I'd done. He'd ask, "What's new along the Big Stem?" and I'd tell him the latest off the grapevine. (*He grins with affectionate condescension.*) It used to hand me a laugh to hear old Hughie crackin' like a sport. In all the years I knew him, he never bet a buck on nothin'. (*Excusingly.*) But it ain't his fault. He'd have took a chance, but how could he with his wife keepin' cases on every nickel of his salary? I showed him lots of ways he could cross her up, but he was too scared. (*He chuckles.*) The biggest knock-out was when he'd kid me about dames. He'd crack, "What? No blonde tonight, Erie? You must be slippin'." Jeez, you never see a guy more bashful with a doll around than Hughie was. I used to introduce him to the tramps I'd drag home with me. I'd wise them up to kid him along and pretend they'd fell for him. In two minutes, they'd have him hanging on the ropes. His face'd be red and he'd look like he wanted to crawl under the desk and hide. Some of them dolls was raw babies. They'd make him pretty raw propositions. He'd stutter like he was paralysed. But he ate it up, just the same. He was tickled pink. I used to hope maybe I could nerve him up to do a little cheatin'. I'd offer to fix it for him with one of my dolls. Hell, I got plenty, I wouldn't have minded. I'd tell him, "Just let that wife of yours know you're cheatin', and she'll have some respect for you." But he was too scared. (*He pauses—boastfully.*) Some queens I've brought here in my time, brother—frails from the Follies, or the Scandals, or the Frolics, that'd knock your eye out! And I still can make 'em. You watch. I ain't slippin'.

(*He looks at the Night Clerk expecting reassurance, but the Clerk's mind has slipped away to the clanging bounce of garbage-cans in the outer night. He is thinking: "A job I'd like. I'd bang those cans louder than they do! I'd wake up the whole damned city!" Erie mutters disgustedly to himself.*)

Jesus, what a dummy! (*He makes a move in the direction of the elevator, off right front—gloomily.*) Might as well hit the hay, I guess.

NIGHT CLERK (*Comes to—with the nearest approach to feeling he has shown in many a long night—approvingly*). Good night, Mr. Smith. I hope you have a good rest.

(*But Erie stops, glancing around the deserted lobby with forlorn distaste, jiggling the room key in his hand.*)

ERIE. What a crummy dump! What did I come back for? I shoulda stayed on a drunk. You'd never guess it, buddy, but when I first come here this was a classy hotel—and clean, can you believe it? (*He scowls.*) I've been campin' here, off and on, fifteen years, but I've got a good notion to move out. It ain't the same place since Hughie was took to the hospital. (*Gloomily.*) Hell with going to bed! I'll just lie there worrying—

(*He turns back to the desk. The Clerk's face would express despair, but the last time he was able to feel despair was back around World War days when the cost of living got so high and he *was out of a job for three months. Erie leans on the desk—in a dejected, confidential tone.)*

Believe me, brother, I never been a guy to worry, but this time I'm on a spot where I got to, if I ain't a sap.

NIGHT CLERK *(in the vague tone of a corpse which admits it once overheard a favourable rumour about life)*. That's too bad, Mr. Smith. But they say most of the things we worry about never happen. *(His mind escapes to the street again, to play bouncing cans with the garbage men.)*

ERIE *(grimly)*. This thing happens, pal. I ain't won a bet at nothin' since Hughie was took to the hospital. I'm jinxed. And that ain't all— But to hell with it! You're right, at that. Something always turns up for me. I was born lucky. I ain't worried. Just moaning low. Hell, who don't when they're getting over a drunk? You know how it is. The Brooklyn Boys march over the bridge with bloodhounds to hunt you down. And I'm still carrying the torch for Hughie. His checking out was a real K. O. for me. Damn if I know why. Lots of guys I've been pals with, in a way, croaked from booze or something, or got rubbed out, but I always took it as part of the game. Hell, we all gotta croak. Here today, gone tomorrow, so what's the good of beefin'? When a guy's dead, he's dead. He don't give a damn, so why should anybody else? *(But this fatalistic philosophy is no comfort, and Erie sighs.)* I miss Hughie, I guess. I guess I'd got to like him a lot. *(Again he explains carefully, so there will be no misunderstanding.)* Not that I was ever real pals with him, you understand. He didn't run in my class. He didn't know none of the answers. He was just a sucker. *(He sighs again.)* But I sure am sorry he's gone. You missed a lot not knowing Hughie, pal. He sure was one grand little guy.

(He stares at the lobby floor. The Night Clerk regards him with vacant, bulging eyes—full of a vague envy for the blind. The garbage men have gone their predestined way. Time is that much older. The Clerk's mind remains in the street, to greet the noise of a far-off El train. Its approach is pleasantly like a memory of hope; then it roars and rocks and rattles past the near-by corner, and the noise pleasantly deafens memory; then it recedes and dies, and there is something melancholy about that. But there is hope. Only so many El trains pass in one night, and each one passing leaves one less to pass, so the night recedes, too, until at last it must die and join all the other long nights in Nirvana, the Big Night of Nights. And that's life. "What I always tell Jess when she nags me to worry about something: 'That's life, isn't it? What can you do about it?'" Erie sighs again—then turns to the Clerk, his foolishly wary, wise-guy eyes defenceless, his poker-face as self-betraying as a hurt dog's—appealingly.)

Say, you do remind me of Hughie somehow, pal. You got the same look on your map.

(But the Clerk's mind is far away attending the obsequies of night, and it takes it some time to get back. Erie is hurt—contemptuously.)

But I guess it's only that old night-clerk look! There's one of 'em born every minute!

NIGHT CLERK *(his mind arrives just in time to catch this last—with a bright grimace)*. Yes, Mr. Smith. That's what Barnum said, and it's certainly true, isn't it?

ERIE *(grateful even for this sign of companionship; growls)*. Nix on the Mr. Smith stuff, Charlie. There's ten of *them* born every minute. Call me Erie, like I told you.

NIGHT CLERK *(automatically, as his mind tiptoes into the night again)*. All right, Erie.

ERIE *(encouraged, leans on the desk, clacking his room key like a castanet)*. Yeah. Hughie was one grand little guy. All the same, like I said, he wasn't the kind of guy you'd ever figure a guy like me would take to. Because he was a sucker, see—the kind of sap you'd take to the cleaners a million times and he'd never wise up he was took. Why, night after night, just for a gag, I'd get him to shoot crap with me here on the desk. With *my* dice. And he'd never ask to give 'em the once-over. Can you beat that! *(He chuckles—then earnestly—)* Not that I'd ever ring in no phoneys on a pal. I'm no heel. *(He chuckles again.)* And anyway, I didn't need none to take Hughie because he never even made me knock 'em against nothing. Just a roll on the desk here. Boy, if they'd ever let me throw 'em that way in a real game, I'd be worth ten million dollars. *(He laughs.)*

You'da thought Hughie woulda got wise something was out of order when, no matter how much he'd win on a run of luck like suckers have sometimes, I'd always take him to the cleaners in the end. But he never suspicioned nothing. All he'd say was "Gosh, Erie, no wonder you took up gambling. You sure were born lucky." (*He chuckles.*) Can you beat that? (*He hastens to explain, earnestly.*) Of course, like I said, it was only a gag. We'd play with real jack, just to make it look real, but it was all my jack. He never had no jack. His wife dealt him four bits a day for spending money. So I'd stake him at the start to half of what I got—in chicken-feed, I mean. We'd pretend a cent was a buck, and a nickel was a fin and so on. Some big game! He got a big kick out of it. He'd get all het up. It give me a kick, too—especially when he'd say, "Gosh, Erie, I don't wonder you never worry about money, with your luck." (*He laughs.*) That guy would believe anything! Of course, I'd stall him off when he'd want to shoot nights when I didn't have a goddamned nickel. (*He chuckles.*) What laughs he used to hand me! He'd always call horses "the bangtails," like he'd known 'em all his life— and he'd never seen a race-horse, not till I kidnapped him one day and took him down to Belmont. What a kick he got out of that! I got scared he'd pass out with excitement. And he wasn't doing no betting either. All he had was four bits. It was just the track, and the crowd, and the horses got him. Mostly the horses. (*With a surprised, reflective air.*) Y'know, it's funny how a dumb, simple guy like Hughie will all of a sudden get something right. He says, "They're the most beautiful things in the world, I think." And he wins! I tell you, pal, I'd rather sleep in the same stall with old Man o' War than make the whole damn Follies. What do you think?

NIGHT CLERK (*his mind darts back from a cruising taxi and blinks bewilderedly in the light: "Say yes"*). Yes, I agree with you, mister—I mean, Erie.

ERIE (*with good-natured contempt*). Yeah? I bet you never seen one, except back at the old fairgrounds in the sticks. I don't mean them kind of turtles. I mean a real horse.

(*The Clerk wonders what horses have to do with anything—or for that matter, what anything has to do with anything—then gives it up. Erie takes up his tale.*)

And what d'you think happened the next night? Damned if Hughie didn't dig two bucks out of his pants and try to slip 'em to me. "Let this ride on the nose of whatever horse you're betting on tomorrow," he told me. I got sore. "Nix," I told him, "if you're going to start playin' sucker and bettin' on horse-races, you don't get no assist from me." (*He grins wryly.*) Was that a laugh! Me advising a sucker not to bet when I've spent a lot of my life tellin' saps a story to make 'em bet! I said, "Where'd you grab this dough? Outa the Little Woman's purse, huh? What tale you going to give her when you lose it? She'll start breaking up the furniture with you!" "No," he says, "she'll just cry." "That's worse," I said, "no guy can beat that racket. I had a doll cry on me once in a restaurant full of people till I had to promise her a diamond engagement-ring to sober her up." Well, anyway, Hughie sneaked the two bucks back in the Little Woman's purse when he went home that morning, and that was the end of that. (*Cynically.*) Boy Scouts got nothin' on me, pal, when it comes to good deeds. That was one I done. It's too bad I can't remember no others. (*He is well wound up now, and goes on without noticing that the Night Clerk's mind has left the premises in his sole custody.*) Y'know I had Hughie sized up for a sap the first time I see him. I'd just rolled in from Tia Juana. I'd made a big killing down there and I was lousy with jack. Came all the way in a drawing-room, and I wasn't lonely in it neither. There was a blonde movie doll on the train – and I was lucky in them days. Used to follow the horses South every winter. I don't no more. Sick of travelling. And I ain't as lucky as I was— (*Hastily.*) Anyway, this time I'm talkin' about, soon as I hit this lobby I see there's a new night clerk, and while I'm signing up for the bridal suite I make a bet with myself he's never been nothin' but a night clerk. And I win. At first, he wouldn't open up. Not that he was cagey about gabbin' too much. But like he couldn't think of nothin' about himself worth saying. But after he'd seen me roll in here the last one every night, and I'd stop to kid him along and tell him the tale of what I'd win that day, he got friendly and talked. He'd come from a hick burg upstate. Graduated from high school, and had a shot at different jobs in the old home-town but couldn't make the grade until he was took on as night clerk in the hotel there. Then he made good. But he wasn't satisfied. Didn't like being only a night clerk where everybody knew him. He'd read somewhere—in the Suckers' Almanac, I guess—that all a guy had to do was come to the Big Town and Old Man Success would be waitin' at the Grand Central to give him the key to the city. What a gag that is! Even I believed that once, and no one could ever call me a sap. Well, anyway, he made the break and come here and the only job he could get was night clerk. Then he fell in love—or kidded himself he was — and got married. Met her on a subway train. It stopped sudden and she was jerked into him, and he put his arms around her, and they started talking, and the poor boob never stood a chance. She was a salesgirl in some punk department store, and she was sick of standing on her dogs all day, and all the way home to Brooklyn, too. So, the way I figure it, knowing Hughie and dames, she proposed and said "yes" for him, and married him, and after that, of course, he never dared stop being a night clerk, even if he could. (*He pauses.*) Maybe you think I ain't giving her a square shake. Well, maybe I ain't. She never give me one. She put me down as a bad influence, and let her chips ride. And maybe Hughie couldn't have done no better. Dolls didn't call him no riot. Hughie and her seemed happy enough the time he had me out to dinner in their flat. Well, not happy. Maybe contented. No, that's boosting it, too. Resigned comes nearer, as if each was givin' the other a break by thinking, "Well, what more could I expect?" (*Abruptly he addresses the Night Clerk with contemptuous good nature.*) How d'you and your Little Woman hit it off, brother?

NIGHT CLERK (*his mind has been counting the footfalls of the cop on the beat as they recede, sauntering longingly towards the dawn's release. "If he'd only shoot it out with a gunman some night! Nothing exciting has happened in any night I've ever lived through!" He stammers gropingly among the echoes of Erie's last words*). Oh—you mean *my* wife? Why, we get along all right, I guess.

ERIE (*disgustedly*). Better lay off them headache pills, pal. First thing you know, some guy is going to call you a dope.

(*But the Night Clerk cannot take this seriously. It is years since he cared what anyone called him. So many guests have called him so many things. The "Little Woman" has, too. And, of course, he has, himself. But that's all past. Is daybreak coming now? No, too early yet. He can tell by the sound of that surface car. It is still lost in the night. Flat-wheeled and tired. Distant the carbarn, and far away the sleep. Erie, having soothed resentment with his wisecrack, goes on with a friendly grin.*)

Well, keep hoping, pal. Hughie was as big a dope as you until I give him some interest in life. (*Slipping back into narrative.*) That time he took me home to dinner. Was that a knock-out! It took him a hell of a while to get up nerve to ask me. "Sure, Hughie," I told him, "I'll be tickled to death." I was thinking, I'd rather be shot. For one thing, he lived in Brooklyn, and I'd sooner take a trip to China. Another thing, I'm a guy that likes to eat what I order and not what somebody deals me. And he had kids and a wife, and the family racket is out of my line. But Hughie looked so tickled I couldn't welsh on him. And it didn't work out so bad. Of course, what he called home was only a dump of a cheap flat. Still, it wasn't so bad for a change. His wife had done a lot of stuff to doll it up. Nothin' with no class, you understand. Just cheap stuff to make it comfortable. And his kids wasn't the gorillas I'd expected, neither. No throwin' spitballs in my soup or them kind of gags. They was quiet like Hughie. I kinda liked 'em. After dinner I started tellin' 'em a story about a race-horse a guy I know owned once. I thought it was up to me to put out something, and kids like animal stories, and this one was true, at that. This old turtle never wins a race, but he was as foxy as ten guys, a natural born crook, the goddamnedest thief, he'd steal anything in reach that wasn't nailed down—well, I didn't get far. Hughie's wife butt in and stopped me cold. Told the kids it was bedtime and hustled 'em off like I was giving 'em measles. It got my goat, kinda. I coulda liked her—a little—if she'd give me a chance. Not that she was nothin' Ziegfeld would want to glorify. When you call her plain, you give her all the breaks. (*Resentfully.*) Well, to hell with it. She had me tagged for a bum, and seein' me made her sure she was right. You can bet she told Hughie never invite me again, and he never did. He tried to apologize, but I shut him up quick. He says, "Irma was brought up strict. She can't help being narrow-minded about gamblers." I said, "What's it to me? I don't want to hear your dame troubles. I got plenty of my own. Remember that doll I brung home night before last? She gives me an argument I promised her ten bucks. I told her, 'Listen, baby, I got an impediment in my speech. Maybe it sounded like ten, but it was two, and that's all you get. Hell, I don't want to buy your soul! What would I do with it?' Now she's peddling the news along Broadway I'm a rat and a chiseller, and of course all the rats and chisellers believe her. Before she's through, I won't have a friend left." (*He pauses—confidentially.*) I switched the subject on Hughie, see, on purpose. He never did beef to me about his wife again. (*He gives a forced chuckle.*) Believe me, pal, I can stop guys that start telling me their family troubles!

NIGHT CLERK (*his mind has hopped an ambulance clanging down Sixth Avenue, and is asking without curiosity: "Will he die, Doctor, or isn't he lucky?" "I'm afraid not, but he'll have to be absolutely quiet for months and months." "With a pretty nurse taking care of him?" "Probably not pretty." "Well, anyway, I claim he's lucky. And now I must get back to the hotel. 492 won't go to bed and insists on telling me jokes. It must have been a joke because he's chuckling." He laughs with a heartiness which has forgotten that heart is more than a word used in "Have a heart," an old slang expression*). Ha—Ha! That's a good one, Erie. That's the best I've heard in a long time!

ERIE (*for a moment is so hurt and depressed he hasn't the spirit to make a sarcastic crack. He stares at the floor, twirling his room key—to himself*). Jesus, this sure is a dead dump. About as homy as the Morgue. (*He glances up at the clock.*) Gettin' late. Better beat it up to my cell and grab some shut-eye. (*He makes a move to detach himself from the desk, but fails, and remains wearily glued to it. His eyes prowl the lobby and finally come to rest on the Clerk's glistening, sallow face. He summons up strength for a withering crack.*) Why didn't you tell me you was deef, buddy? I know guys is sensitive about them little afflictions, but I'll keep it confidential.

(*But the Clerk's mind has rushed out to follow the siren-wail of a fire-engine. "A fireman's life must be exciting." His mind rides the engine, and asks a fireman with disinterested eagerness: "Where's the fire? Is it a real good one this time? Has it a good start? Will it be big enough, do you think?" Erie examines his face—bitingly.*)

Take my tip, pal, and don't never try to buy from a dope-pedlar. He'll tell you you had enough already.

(*The Clerk's mind continues its dialogue with the fireman. "I mean, big enough to burn down the whole damn city?" "Sorry, brother, but there's no chance. There's too much stone and steel. There'd always be something left." "Yes, I guess you're right. There's too much stone and steel. I wasn't really hoping, anyway. It really doesn't matter to me." Erie gives him up and again attempts to pry himself from the desk, twirling his key frantically as if it were a fetish which might set him free.*)

Well, me for the hay. (*But he can't dislodge himself—then dully—*) Christ, it's lonely. I wish Hughie was here. By God, if he was, I'd tell him a tale that'd make his eyes pop! The bigger the story the harder he'd fall. He was that kind of sap. He thought gambling was romantic. I guess he saw me like a sort of dream guy, the sort of guy he'd like to be if he could take a chance. I guess he lived a sort of double life listening to me gabbin' about hittin' the high-spots. Come to figure it, I'll bet he even cheated on his wife that way, using me and my dolls. (*He chuckles.*) No wonder he liked me, huh? And the bigger I made myself, the more he lapped it up. I went easy on him at first. I didn't lie—not any more'n a guy naturally does when he gabs about the bets he wins and the dolls he's made. But I soon see he was cryin' for more, and when a sucker cries for more, you're a dope if you don't let him have it. Every tramp I made got to be a Follies' doll. Hughie liked 'em to be Follies' dolls. Or in the Scandals or Frolics. He wanted me to be the Sheik of Araby, or something that any blonde'd go round-heeled about. Well, I give him plenty of that. And I give him plenty of gambling tales. I explained my campin' in this dump was because I don't want to waste jack on nothin' but gambling. It was like dope to me, I told him. I couldn't quit. He lapped that up. He liked to kid himself I'm mixed up in the racket. He thought gangsters was romantic. So I fed him some boloney about highjacking I'd done once. I told him I knew all the big-shots. Well, so I do, most of 'em, to say hello, and sometimes they hello back. Who wouldn't know 'em that hangs around Broadway and the joints? I run errands for 'em sometimes, because there's dough in it, but I'm cagey about gettin' in where it ain't healthy. Hughie wanted to think me and Legs Diamond was old pals. So I give him that too. I give him anything he cried for. (*Earnestly.*) Don't get the wrong idea, pal. What I fed Hughie wasn't all lies. The tales about gambling wasn't. They was stories of big games and killings that really happened since I've been hangin' round. Only I wasn't in on 'em like I made out—except one or two from way back when I had a run of big luck and was in the bucks for a while until I was took to the cleaners. (*He stops to pay tribute of a sigh to the memory of brave days that were and that never were—then meditatively—*) Yeah, Hughie lapped up my stories like they was duck soup, or a beakful of heroin. I sure took him around with me in tales and showed him one hell of a time. (*He chuckles—then seriously—*) And, d'you know, it done me good, too, in a way. Sure. I'd get to seein' myself like he seen me. Some nights I'd come back here without a buck, feeling lower than a snake's belly, and first thing you know I'd be lousy with jack, bettin' a grand a race. Oh, I was wise I was kiddin' myself. I ain't a sap. But what the hell, Hughie loved it, and it didn't cost nobody nothin', and if every guy along Broadway who kids himself was to drop dead there wouldn't be nobody left. Ain't it the truth, Charlie?

(*He again stares at the Night Clerk appealingly, forgetting past rebuffs. The Clerk's face is taut with vacancy: his mind has been trying to fasten itself to some noise in the night, but a rare and threatening pause of silence has fallen on the city, and here he is, chained behind a hotel desk for ever, awake when everyone else in the world is asleep, except Room 492, and he won't go to bed, he's still talking, and there is no escape.*)

NIGHT CLERK (*his glassy eyes stare through Erie's face. He stammers deferentially*). Truth? I'm afraid I didn't get— What's the truth?

ERIE (*hopelessly*). Nothing, pal. Not a thing.

(*His eyes fall to the floor. For a while he is too defeated even to twirl his room key. The Clerk's mind still cannot make a getaway, because the city remains silent, and the night vaguely reminds him of death, and he is vaguely frightened, and now that he remembers, his feet are giving him hell, but that's no excuse not to act as if the guest is always right: "I should have paid 492 more attention. After all, he is company. He is awake and alive. I should use him to help me live through the night. What's he been talking about? I must have caught some of it without meaning to." The Night Clerk's forehead puckers perspiringly as he tries to remember. Erie begins talking again, but this time it is obviously aloud to himself, without hope of a listener.*)

I could tell by Hughie's face before he went to the hospital, he was through. I've seen the same look on guys' faces when they knew they was on the spot, just before guys caught up with them. I went to see him twice in the hospital. The first time, his wife was there and give me a dirty look, but he cooked up a smile and said, "Hello, Erie, how're the bangtails treating you?" I see he wants a big story to cheer him, but his wife butts in and says he's weak and he mustn't get excited. I felt like crackin', "Well, the docs in this dump got the right dope. Just leave you with him and he'll never get excited." The second time I went, they wouldn't let me see him. That was near the end. I went to his funeral, too. There wasn't nobody but a coupla his wife's relations. I had to feel sorry for her. She looked like she ought to be parked in a coffin, too. The kids was bawlin'. There wasn't no flowers but a coupla lousy wreaths. It woulda been a punk showing for poor old Hughie, if it hadn't been for my flower piece. (*He swells with pride.*) That was some display, pal. It'd knock your eye out! Set me back a hundred bucks, and no kiddin'! A big horseshoe of red roses! I knew Hughie'd want a horseshoe because that made it look like he'd been a horse-player. And around the top printed in forget-me-nots was "Goodbye, Old Pal."

Hughie liked to kid himself he was my pal. (*He adds, sadly—*) And so he was, at that—even if he was a sucker.

(*He pauses, his false poker-face as nakedly forlorn as an organ-grinder's monkey's. Outside, the spell of abnormal quiet presses suffocatingly upon the street, enters the deserted, dirty lobby. The Night Clerk's mind cowers away from it. He cringes behind the desk, his feet aching like hell. There is only one possible escape. If his mind could only fasten on to something 492 has said. "What's he been talking about? A clerk should always be attentive. You even are duty bound to laugh at a guest's smutty jokes, no matter how often you've heard them. That's the policy of the hotel. 492 has been gassing for hours. What's he been telling me? I must be slipping. Always before this I've been able to hear without bothering to listen, but now when I need company—Ah! I've got it! Gambling! He said a lot about gambling. That's something I've always wanted to know more about, too. Maybe he's a professional gambler. Like Arnold Rothstein."*)

NIGHT CLERK (*blurts out with an uncanny, almost life-like eagerness*). I beg your pardon, mister—Erie—but did I understand you to say you are a gambler by profession? Do you, by any chance, know the big-shot, Arnold Rothstein?

(*But this time it is Erie who doesn't hear him. And the Clerk's mind is now suddenly impervious to the threat of night and silence as it pursues an ideal of fame and glory within itself, called Arnold Rothstein.*)

ERIE (*with mournful longing*). Christ, I wish Hughie was alive and kickin'. I'd tell him I win ten grand from the bookies, and ten grand at stud, and ten grand in a crap game! I'd tell him I bought one of those Mercedes sports roadsters with nickel pipes sticking out of the hood! I'd tell him I lay three babes from the Follies—two blondes and one brunette!

(*The Night Clerk dreams, a rapt hero-worship transfiguring his pimply face: "Arnold Rothstein! He must be some guy! I read a story about him. He'll gamble for any limit on anything, and always wins. The story said he wouldn't bother playing in a poker game unless the smallest bet you could make—one white chip—was a hundred dollars. Christ, that's going some! I'd like to have the dough to get in a game with him once! The last pot, everyone would drop out but him and me. I'd say, 'O.K., Arnold, the sky's the limit,' and I'd raise him five grand, and he'd call, and I'd have a royal flush to his four aces. Then I'd say, 'O.K., Arnold, I'm a good sport, I'll give you a break. I'll cut you double or nothing. Just one cut. I want quick action for my dough.' And I'd cut the ace of spades and win again." Beatific vision swoons on the empty pools of the Night Clerk's eyes. He resembles a holy saint, recently elected to Paradise. Erie breaks the silence—bitterly resigned.*)

But Hughie's better off, at that, being dead. He's got all the luck. He needn't do no worryin' now. He's out of the racket. I mean, the whole goddamned racket. I mean life.

NIGHT CLERK (*kicked out of his dream—with detached, pleasant acquiescence*). Yes, it is a goddamned racket when you stop to think, isn't it, 492? But we might as well make the best of it, because— Well, you can't burn it all down, can you? There's too much steel and stone. There'd always be something left to start it going again.

ERIE (*scowls bewilderedly*). Say, what is this? What the hell you talkin' about?

NIGHT CLERK (*at a loss—in much confusion*). Why, to be frank, I really don't— Just something that came into my head.

ERIE (*bitingly, but showing he is comforted at having made some sort of contact*). Get it out of your head quick, Charlie, or some guys in uniform will walk in here with a butterfly-net and catch you. (*He changes the subject—earnestly.*) Listen, pal, maybe you guess I was kiddin' about that flower piece for Hughie costing a hundred bucks? Well, I ain't! I didn't give a damn what it cost. It was up to me to give Hughie a big-time send-off, because I knew nobody else would.

NIGHT CLERK. Oh, I'm not doubting your word, Erie. You won the money gambling, I suppose—I mean, I beg your pardon if I'm mistaken, but you are a gambler, aren't you?

ERIE (*preoccupied*). Yeah, sure, when I got scratch to put up. What of it? But I don't win that hundred bucks. I don't win a bet since Hughie was took to the hospital. I had to get down on my knees and beg every guy I know for a sawbuck here and a sawbuck there until I raised it.

NIGHT CLERK (*his mind concentrated on the Big Ideal—insistently*). Do you by any chance know—Arnold Rothstein?

ERIE (*his train of thought interrupted—irritably*). Arnold? What's he got to do with it? He wouldn't loan a guy like me a nickel to save my grandmother from streetwalking.

NIGHT CLERK (*with humble awe*). Then you do know him!

ERIE. Sure I know the bastard. Who don't on Broadway? And he knows me—when he wants to. He uses me to run errands when there ain't no one else handy. But he ain't my trouble, pal. My trouble is, some of these guys I put the bite on is dead wrong G's, and they expect to be paid back next Tuesday, or else I'm outa luck and have to take it on the lam, or I'll get beat up and maybe sent to a hospital. (*He suddenly rouses himself and there is something pathetically but genuinely gallant about him.*) But what the hell. I was wise I was takin' a chance. I've always took a chance, and if I lose I pay, and no welshing! It sure was worth it to give Hughie the big send-off.

(*He pauses. The Night Clerk hasn't paid any attention except to his own dream. A question is trembling on his parted lips, but before he can get it out, Erie goes on gloomily.*)

But even that ain't my big worry, Charlie. My big worry is the run of bad luck I've had since Hughie got took to the hospital. Not a win. That ain't natural. I've always been a lucky guy—lucky enough to get by and pay up, I mean. I wouldn't never worry about owing guys, like I owe them guys. I'd always know I'd make a win that'd fix it. But now I got a lousy hunch when I lost Hughie I lost my luck—I mean, I've lost the old confidence. He used to give me confidence. (*He turns away from the desk.*) No use gabbin' here all night. You can't do me no good. (*He starts towards the elevator.*)

NIGHT CLERK (*pleadingly*). Just a minute, Erie, if you don't mind. (*With awe.*) So you're an old friend of Arnold Rothstein! Would you mind telling me if it's really true when Arnold Rothstein plays poker, one white chip is—a hundred dollars?

ERIE (*dully exasperated*). Say, for Christ's sake, what's it to you—?

(*He stops abruptly, staring probingly at the Clerk. There is a pause. Suddenly his face lights up with a saving revelation. He grins warmly, and saunters confidently back to the desk.*)

Say, Charlie, why didn't you put me wise before, you was interested in gambling? Hell, I got you all wrong, pal. I been tellin' myself, this guy ain't like old Hughie. He ain't got no sportin' blood. He's just a dope. (*Generously.*) Now I see you're a right guy. Shake.

(*He shoves out his hand, which the Clerk clasps with a limp pleasure. Erie goes on with gathering warmth and self-assurance.*)

That's the stuff. You and me'll get along. I'll give you all the breaks, like I give Hughie.

NIGHT CLERK (*gratefully*). Thank you, Erie. (*Then insistently.*) Is it true when Arnold Rothstein plays poker, one white chip—

ERIE (*with magnificent carelessness*). Sets you back a hundred bucks? Sure. Why not? Arnold's in the bucks, ain't he? And when you're in the bucks, a C note is chicken-feed. I ought to know, pal. I was in the bucks when Arnold was a piker. Why, one time down in New Orleans I lit a cigar with a C note, just for a gag, y'understand. I was with a bunch of high-class dolls and I wanted to see their eyes pop out—and believe me, they sure popped! After that, I coulda made 'em one at a time or all together! Hell, I once win twenty grand on a single race. That's action! A good crap game is action, too. Hell, I've been in games where there was a hundred grand in real folding money lying around the floor. That's travellin'!

(*He darts a quick glance at the Clerk's face and begins to hedge warily. But he needn't. The Clerk sees him now as the gambler in 492, the *friend of Arnold Rothstein—and nothing is incredible. Erie goes on.)*

Of course, I wouldn't kid you. I'm not in the bucks now—not right this moment. You know how it is, Charlie. Down today and up tomorrow. I got some dough ridin' on the nose of a turtle in the 4th at Saratoga. I hear a story he'll be so full of hop, if the joc can keep him from jumpin' over the grandstand, he'll win by a mile. So if I roll in here with a blonde that'll knock your eyes out, don't be surprised. (*He winks and chuckles.*)

NIGHT CLERK (*ingratiatingly pally, smiling*). Oh, you can't surprise me that way. I've been a night clerk in New York all my life, almost. (*He tries out a wink himself.*) I'll forget the house rules, Erie.

ERIE (*drily*). Yeah. The manager wouldn't like you to remember something he ain't heard of yet. (*Then, slyly feeling his way.*) How about shootin' a little crap, Charlie? I mean just in fun, like I used to with Hughie. I know you can't afford takin' no chances. I'll stake you, see? I got a coupla bucks. We gotta use real jack or it don't look real. It's all my jack, get it? You can't lose. I just want to show you how I'll take you to the cleaners. It'll give me confidence. (*He has taken two one-dollar bills and some change from his pocket. He pushes most of it across to the Clerk.*) Here y'are. (*He produces a pair of dice—carelessly.*) Want to give these dice the once-over before we start?

NIGHT CLERK (*earnestly*). What do you think I am? I know I can trust you.

ERIE (*smiles*). You remind me a lot of Hughie, pal. He always trusted me. Well, don't blame me if I'm lucky. (*He clicks the dice in his hand—thoughtfully.*) Y'know, it's time I quit carryin' the torch for Hughie. Hell, what's the use? It don't do him no good. He's gone. Like we all gotta go. Him yesterday, me or you tomorrow, and who cares, and what's the difference? It's all in the racket, huh? (*His soul is purged of grief, his confidence restored.*) I shoot two bits.

NIGHT CLERK (*manfully, with an excited dead-pan expression he hopes resembles Arnold Rothstein's*). I fade you.

ERIE (*throws the dice*). Four's my point. (*Gathers them up swiftly and throws them again.*) Four it is. (*He takes the money.*) Easy when you got my luck—and know how. Huh, Charlie? (*He chuckles, giving the Night Clerk the slyly amused, contemptuous, affectionate wink with which a wise guy regales a sucker.*)

CURTAIN

A MOON FOR THE MISBEGOTTEN

A Play in Four Acts

Characters

JOSIE HOGAN
PHIL HOGAN, *her father*
MIKE HOGAN, *her brother*
JAMES TYRONE, JR.
T. STEDMAN HARDER

Scenes

ACT ONE

The farmhouse. Around noon. Early September 1923.

ACT TWO

The same, but with the interior of sitting-room revealed. Eleven o'clock that night.

ACT THREE

The same as Act One. No time elapses between Acts Two and Three.

ACT FOUR

The same. Dawn of the following morning.

General Scene

The play takes place in Connecticut at the home of tenant farmer Phil Hogan, between the hours of noon on a day in early September, 1923, and sunrise of the following day.

The house is not, to speak mildly, a fine example of New England architecture, placed so perfectly in its setting that it appears a harmonious part of the landscape, rooted in the earth. It has been moved to its present site, and looks it. An old box-like, clapboarded affair, with a shingled roof and brick chimney, it is propped up about two feet above ground by layers of timber blocks. There are two windows on the lower floor of this side of the house which faces front, and one window on the floor above. These windows have no shutters, curtains or shades. Each has at least one pane missing, a square of cardboard taking its place. The house had once been painted a repulsive yellow with brown trim, but the walls now are a blackened and weathered grey, flaked with streaks and splotches of dim lemon. Just around the left corner of the house, a flight of steps leads to the front door.

To make matters worse, a one-storey, one-room addition has been tacked on at right. About twelve feet long by six high, this room, which is Josie Hogan's bedroom, is evidently home made. Its walls and sloping roof are covered with tar paper, faded to dark grey. Close to where it joins the house, there is a door with a flight of three unpainted steps leading to the ground. At right of door is a small window.

From these steps there is a footpath going around an old pear tree, at right-rear, through a field of hay stubble to a patch of woods. The same path also extends left to join a dirt road which leads up from the county highway (about a hundred yards off left) to the front door of the house, and thence back through a scraggly orchard of apple trees to the barn. Close to the house, under the window next to Josie's bedroom, there is a big boulder with a flat top.

ACT ONE

SCENE. *As described. It is just before noon. The day is clear and hot.*

The door of Josie's bedroom opens and she comes out on the steps, bending to avoid bumping her head.

Josie is twenty-eight. She is so oversize for a woman that she is almost a freak — five feet eleven in her stockings and weighs around one hundred and eighty. Her sloping shoulders are broad, her chest deep with large, firm breasts, her waist wide but slender by contrast with her hips and thighs. She has long smooth arms, immensely strong, although no muscles show. The same is true of her legs.

She is more powerful than any but an exceptionally strong man, able to do the manual labour of two ordinary men. But there is no mannish quality about her. She is all woman.

The map of Ireland is stamped on her face, with its long upper lip and small nose, thick black eyebrows, black hair as coarse as a horse's mane, freckled, sunburned fair skin, high cheekbones and heavy jaw. It is not a pretty face, but her large dark-blue eyes give it a note of beauty, and her smile, revealing even white teeth, gives it charm.

She wears a cheap, sleeveless, blue cotton dress. Her feet are bare, the soles earth-stained and tough as leather.

She comes down the steps and goes left to the corner of the house and peers round it toward the barn. Then she moves swiftly to the right of the house and looks back.

JOSIE. Ah, thank God. (*She goes back toward the steps as her brother, Mike, appears hurrying up from right-rear.*)

(*Mike Hogan is twenty, about four inches shorter than his sister. He is sturdily built, but seems almost puny compared to her. He has a common Irish face, its expression sullen, or slyly cunning, or primly self-righteous. He never forgets that he is a good Catholic, faithful to all the observances, and so is one of the élite of Almighty God in a world of damned sinners composed of Protestants and bad Catholics. In brief, Mike is a New England Irish Catholic Puritan, Grade B, and an extremely irritating youth to have around.*)

(*Mike wears dirty overalls, a sweat-stained brown shirt. He carries a pitchfork.*)

JOSIE. Bad luck to you for a slowpoke. Didn't I tell you half-past eleven?

MIKE. How could I sneak here sooner with him peeking round the corner of the barn to catch me if I took a minute's rest, the way he always does? I had to wait till he went to the pig pen. (*He adds viciously.*) Where he belongs, the old hog!

(*Josie's right arm strikes with surprising swiftness and her big hand lands on the side of his jaw. She means it to be only a slap, but his head jerks back and he stumbles, dropping the pitchfork, and pleads cringingly.*)

Don't hit me, Josie! Don't, now!

JOSIE (*quietly*). Then keep your tongue off him. He's my father, too, and I like him, if you don't.

MIKE (*out of her reach — sullenly*). You're two of a kind, and a bad kind.

JOSIE (*good-naturedly*). I'm proud of it. And I didn't hit you, or you'd be flat on the ground. It was only a love tap to waken your wits, so you'll use them. If he catches you running away, he'll beat you half to death. Get your bag now. I've packed it. It's inside the door of my room with your coat laid over it. Hurry now, while I see what he's doing.

(*She moves quickly to peer around the corner of the house at left. He goes up the steps into her room and returns carrying an old coat and a cheap bulging satchel. She comes back.*)

There's no sight of him.

(*Mike drops the satchel on the ground while he puts on the coat.*)

I put everything in the bag. You can change to your Sunday suit in the can at the station or in the train, and don't forget to wash your face. I know you want to look your best when our brother, Thomas, sees you on his doorstep. (*Her tone becomes derisively amused.*) And him way up in the world, a noble sergeant of the Bridgeport police. Maybe he'll get you on the force. It'd suit you. I can see you leading drunks to the lockup while you give them a lecture on temperance. Or if Thomas can't get you a job, he'll pass you along to our brother, John, the noble bar-keep in Meriden. He'll teach you the trade. You'll make a nice one, who'll never steal from the till, or drink, and who'll tell customers they've had enough and better go home just when they're beginning to feel happy. (*She sighs regretfully.*) Ah, well, Mike, you was born a priest's pet, and there's no help for it.

MIKE. That's right! Make fun of me again, because I want to be decent.

JOSIE. You're worse than decent. You're virtuous.

MIKE. Well, that's a thing nobody can say about — (*He stops, a bit ashamed, but mostly afraid to finish.*)

JOSIE (*amused*). About me? No, and what's more, they don't. (*She smiles mockingly.*) I know what a trial it's been to you, Mike, having a sister who's the scandal of the neighbourhood.

MIKE. It's you that's saying it, not me. I don't want to part with hard feelings. And I'll keep on praying for you.

JOSIE (*roughly*). Och! To hell with your prayers!

MIKE (*stiffly*). I'm going. (*He picks up his bag.*)

JOSIE (*her manner softening*). Wait. (*She comes to him.*) Don't mind my rough tongue, Mike. I'm sorry to see you go, but it's the best thing for you. That's why I'm helping you, the same as I helped Thomas and John. You can't stand up to the Old Man any more than Thomas or John could, and the old divil would always keep you a slave. I wish you all the luck in the world, Mike. I know you'll get on — and God bless you. (*Her voice has softened, and she blinks back tears. She kisses him — then fumbling in the pocket of her dress, pulls out a little roll of one-dollar bills and presses it in his hand.*) Here's a little present over your fare. I took it from his little green bag, and won't he be wild when he finds out! But I can handle him.

MIKE (*enviously*). You can. You're the only one. (*Gratefully moved for a second.*) Thank you, Josie. You've a kind heart. (*Then virtuously.*) But I don't like taking stolen money.

JOSIE. Don't be a bigger jackass than you are already. Tell your conscience it's a bit of the wages he's never given you.

MIKE. That's true, Josie. It's rightfully mine. (*He shoves the money into his pocket.*)

JOSIE. Get along now, so you won't miss the trolley. And don't forget to get off the train at Bridgeport. Give my love to Thomas and John. No, never mind. They've not written me in years. Give them a boot in the tail for me.

MIKE. That's nice talk for a woman. You've a tongue as dirty as the Old Man's.

JOSIE (*impatiently*). Don't start preaching, like you love to, or you'll never go.

MIKE. You're as bad as he is, almost. It's his influence made you what you are, and him always scheming how he'll cheat people, selling them a broken-down nag or a sick cow or pig that he's doctored up to look good for a day or two. It's no better than stealing, and you help him.

JOSIE. I do. Sure, it's grand fun.

MIKE. You ought to marry and have a home of your own away from this shanty and stop your shameless ways with men. (*He adds, not without moral satisfaction.*) Though it'd be hard to find a decent man who'd have you now.

JOSIE. I don't want a decent man, thank you. They're no fun. They're all sticks like you. And I wouldn't marry the best man on earth and be tied down to him alone.

MIKE (*with a cunning leer*). Not even Jim Tyrone, I suppose? (*She stares at him.*) You'd like being tied to money, I know that, and he'll be rich when his mother's estate is settled. (*Sarcastically.*) I suppose you've never thought of that ? Don't tell me! I've watched you making sheep's eyes at him.

JOSIE (*contemptuously*). So I'm leading Jim on to propose, am I?

MIKE. I know it's crazy, but maybe you're hoping if you got hold of him alone when he's mad drunk — Anyway, talk all you please to put me off, I'll bet my last penny you've cooked up some scheme to hook him, and the Old Man put you up to it. Maybe he thinks if he caught you with Jim and had witnesses to prove it, and his shotgun to scare him —

JOSIE (*controlling her anger*). You're full of bright thoughts. I wouldn't strain my brains any more, if I was you.

MIKE. Well, I wouldn't put it past the Old Man to try any trick. And I wouldn't put it past you, God forgive you. You've never cared about your virtue, or what man you went out with. You've always been brazen as brass and proud of your disgrace. You can't deny that, Josie.

JOSIE. I don't. (*Then ominously.*) You'd better shut up now. I've been holding my temper, because we're saying good-bye. (*She stands up.*) But I'm losing patience.

MIKE (*hastily*). Wait till I finish and you won't be mad at me. I was going to say I wish you luck with your scheming, for once. I hate Jim Tyrone's guts, with his quotin' Latin and his high-toned Jesuit College education, putting on airs as if he was too good to wipe his shoes on me, when he's nothing but a drunken bum who never done a tap of work in his life, except acting on the stage while his father was alive to get him the jobs. (*Vindictively.*) I'll pray you'll find a way to nab him, Josie, and skin him out of his last nickel!

JOSIE (*makes a threatening move toward him*). One more word out of you — (*Then contemptuously.*) You're a dirty tick and it'd serve you right if I let you stay gabbing until Father came and beat you to a jelly, but I won't. I'm too anxious to be rid of you. (*Roughly.*) Get out of here, now! Do you think he'll stay all day with the pigs, you gabbing fool? (*She goes left to peer around the corner of the house — with real alarm.*) There he is, coming up to the barn.

(*Mike grabs the satchel, terrified. He slinks swiftly around the corner and disappears along the path to the woods, right-rear. She keeps watching her father and does not notice Mike's departure.*)

He's looking toward the meadow. He sees you're not working. He's running down there. He'll come here next. You'd better run for your life! (*She turns and sees he's gone — contemptuously.*) I might have known. I'll bet you're a mile away by now, you rabbit! (*She peeks around the corner again — with amused admiration.*) Look at my poor old father pelt. He's as spry on his stumpy legs as a yearling — and as full of rage as a nest of wasps! (*She laughs and comes back to look along the path to the woods.*) Well, that's the last of you, Mike, and good riddance. It was the little boy you used to be that I had to mother, and not you, I stole the money for. (*This dismisses him. She sighs.*) Well, himself will be here in a minute. I'd better be ready. (*She reaches in her bedroom corner by the door and takes out a sawed-off broom handle.*) Not that I need it, but it saves his pride. (*She sits on the steps with the broom handle propped against the steps near her right hand.*)

(*A moment later, her father, Phil Hogan, comes running up from left-rear and charges around the corner of the house, his arms pumping up and down, his fists clenched, his face full of fighting fury.*

(*Hogan is fifty-five, about five feet six. He has a thick neck, lumpy, sloping shoulders, a barrel-like trunk, stumpy legs, and big feet. His arms are short and muscular, with large hairy hands. His head is round with thinning sandy hair. His face is fat with a snub nose, long upper lip, big mouth, and little blue eyes with bleached lashes and eyebrows that remind one of a white pig's. He wears heavy brogans, filthy overalls, and a dirty short-sleeved undershirt. Arms and face are sunburned and freckled. On his head is an old wide-brimmed hat of coarse straw that would look more becoming on a horse. His voice is high-pitched with a pronounced brogue.*)

HOGAN (*stops as he turns the corner and sees her — furiously*). Where is he? Is he hiding in the house? I'll wipe the floors with him, the lazy bastard! (*Turning his anger against her.*) Haven't you a tongue in your head, you great slut you?

JOSIE (*with provoking calm*). Don't be calling me names, you bad-tempered old hornet, or maybe I'll lose my temper, too.

HOGAN. To hell with your temper, you overgrown cow!

JOSIE. I'd rather be a cow than an ugly little buck goat. You'd better sit down and cool off. Old men shouldn't run around raging in the noon sun. You'll get sunstroke.

HOGAN. To hell with sunstroke! Have you seen him?

JOSIE. Have I seen who?

HOGAN. Mike! Who else would I be after, the Pope? He was in the meadow, but the minute I turned my back he sneaked off. (*He sees the pitchfork.*) There's his pitchfork! Will you stop your lying!

JOSIE. I haven't said I didn't see him.

HOGAN. Then don't try to help him hide from me, or — Where is he?

JOSIE. Where you'll never find him.

HOGAN. We'll soon see! I'll bet he's in your room under the bed, the cowardly lump! (*He moves toward the steps.*)

JOSIE. He's not. He's gone like Thomas and John before him to escape your slave-driving.

HOGAN (*stares at her incredulously*). You mean he's run off to make his own way in the world?

JOSIE. He has. So make up your mind to it, and sit down.

HOGAN (*baffled, sits on the boulder and takes off his hat to scratch his head — with a faint trace of grudging respect*). I'd never dream he had that much spunk. (*His temper rising again.*) And I know damned well he hadn't, not without you to give him the guts and help him, like the great soft fool you are!

JOSIE. Now don't start raging again, Father.

HOGAN (*seething*). You've stolen my satchel to give him, I suppose, like you did before for Thomas and John?

JOSIE. It was my satchel, too. Didn't I help you in the trade for the horse, when you got the Crowleys to throw in the satchel for good measure? I was up all night fixing that nag's forelegs so his knees wouldn't buckle together till after the Crowleys had him a day or two.

HOGAN (*forgets his anger to grin reminiscently*). You've a wonderful way with animals, God bless you. And do you remember the two Crowleys came back to give me a beating, and I licked them both?

JOSIE (*with calculating flattery*). You did. You're a wonderful fighter. Sure, you could give Jack Dempsey himself a run for his money.

HOGAN (*with sharp suspicion*). I could, but don't try to

change the subject and fill me with blarney.

JOSIE. All right. I'll tell the truth then. They were getting the best of you till I ran out and knocked one of them tail over tin cup against the pigpen.

HOGAN (*outraged*). You're a liar! They was begging for mercy before you came. (*Furiously.*) You thief, you! You stole my fine satchel for that lump! And I'll bet that's not all. I'll bet, like when Thomas and John sneaked off, you — (*He rises from the boulder threateningly.*) Listen, Josie, if you found where I hid my little green bag, and stole my money to give to that lousy altar boy, I'll —

JOSIE (*rises from the steps with the broom handle in her right hand*). Well, I did. So now what'll you do? Don't be threatening me. You know I'll beat better sense in your skull if you lay a finger on me.

HOGAN. I never yet laid hands on a woman — not when I was sober — but if it wasn't for that club — (*Bitterly.*) A fine curse God put on me when he gave me a daughter as big and strong as a bull, and as vicious and disrespectful. (*Suddenly his eyes twinkle and he grins admiringly.*) Be God, look at you standing there with the club! If you ain't the damnedest daughter in Connecticut, who is? (*He chuckles and sits on the boulder again.*)

JOSIE (*laughs and sits on the steps, putting the club away*). And if you ain't the damnedest father in Connecticut, who is?

HOGAN (*takes a clay pipe and plug of tobacco and knife from his pocket. He cuts the plug and stuffs his pipe — without rancour*). How much did you steal, Josie?

JOSIE. Six dollars only.

HOGAN. *Only!* Well, God grant someone with wits will see that dopey gander at the depot and sell him the railroad for the six. (*Grumbling.*) It isn't the money I mind, Josie —

JOSIE. I know. Sure, what do you care for money? You'd give your last penny to the first beggar you met — if he had a shotgun pointed at your heart!

HOGAN. Don't be teasing. You know what I mean. It's the thought of that pious lump having my money that maddens me. I wouldn't put it past him to drop it in the collection plate next Sunday, he's that big a jackass.

JOSIE. I knew when you'd calmed down you'd think it worth six dollars to see the last of him.

HOGAN (*finishes filling his pipe*). Well, maybe I do. To tell the truth, I never liked him. (*He strikes a match on the seat of his overalls and lights his pipe.*) And I never liked Thomas and John, either.

JOSIE (*amused*). You've the same bad luck in sons I have in brothers.

HOGAN (*puffs ruminatively*). They all take after your mother's family. She was the only one in it had spirit, God rest her soul. The rest of them was a pious lot. They wouldn't dare put food in their mouths before they said grace for it. They was too busy preaching temperance to have time for a drink. They spent so much time confessing their sins, they had no chance to do any sinning. (*He spits disgustedly.*) The scum of the earth! Thank God, you're like me and your mother.

JOSIE. I don't know if I should thank God for being like you. Sure, everyone says you're a wicked old tick, as crooked as a corkscrew.

HOGAN. I know. They're an envious lot, God forgive them. (*They both chuckle. He pulls on his pipe reflectively.*) You didn't get much thanks from Mike, I'll wager, for your help.

JOSIE. Oh, he thanked me kindly. And then he started to preach about my sins — and yours.

HOGAN. Oho, did he? (*Exploding.*) For the love of God, why didn't you hold him till I could give him one good kick for a father's parting blessing!

JOSIE. I near gave him one myself.

HOGAN. When I think your poor mother was killed bringing that crummy calf into life! (*Vindictively.*) I've never set foot in a church since, and never will. (*A pause. He speaks with a surprising sad gentleness.*) A sweet woman. Do you remember her, Josie? You were only a little thing when she died.

JOSIE. I remember her well. (*With a teasing smile which is half sad.*) She was the one could put you in your place when you'd come home drunk and want to tear down the house for the fun of it.

HOGAN (*with admiring appreciation*). Yes, she could do it, God bless her. I only raised my hand to her once — just a slap because she told me to stop singing, it was after daylight. The next moment I was on the floor thinking a mule had kicked me. (*He chuckles.*) Since you've grown up, I've had the same trouble. There's no liberty in my own home.

JOSIE. That's lucky — or there wouldn't be any home.

HOGAN (*after a pause of puffing on his pipe*). What did that donkey, Mike, preach to you about?

JOSIE. Oh, the same as ever — that I'm the scandal of the countryside, carrying on with men without a marriage licence.

HOGAN (*gives her a strange, embarrassed glance and then looks away. He does not look at her during the following dia-*

logue. His manner is casual). Hell roast his soul for saying it. But it's true enough.

JOSIE (*defiantly*). It is, and what of it? I don't care a damn for the scandal.

HOGAN. No. You do as you please and to hell with everyone.

JOSIE. Yes, and that goes for you, too, if you are my father. So don't you start preaching too.

HOGAN. Me, preach? Sure, the divil would die laughing. Don't bring me into it. I learned long since to let you go your own way because there's no controlling you.

JOSIE. I do my work and I earn my keep and I've a right to be free.

HOGAN. You have. I've never denied it.

JOSIE. No. You've never. I've often wondered why a man that likes fights as much as you didn't grab at the excuse of my disgrace to beat the lights out of the men.

HOGAN. Wouldn't I look a great fool, when everyone knows any man who tried to make free with you, and you not willing, would be carried off to the hospital? Anyway, I wouldn't want to fight an army. You've had too many sweethearts.

JOSIE (*with a proud toss of her head — boastfully*). That's because I soon get tired of any man and give him his walking papers.

HOGAN. I'm afraid you were born to be a terrible wanton woman. But to tell the truth, I'm well satisfied you're what you are, though I shouldn't say it, because if you was the decent kind you'd have married some fool long ago, and I'd have lost your company and your help on the farm.

JOSIE (*with a trace of bitterness*). Leave it to you to think of your own interest.

HOGAN (*puffs on his pipe*). What else did my beautiful son, Mike, say to you?

JOSIE. Oh, he was full of stupid gab, as usual. He gave me good advice —

HOGAN (*grimly*). That was kind of him. It must have been good —

JOSIE. I ought to marry and settle down — if I could find a decent man who'd have me, which he was sure I couldn't.

HOGAN (*beginning to boil*). I tell you, Josie, it's going to be the saddest memory of my life I didn't get one last swipe at him!

JOSIE. So the only hope, he thought, was for me to catch some indecent man, who'd have money coming to him I could steal.

HOGAN (*gives her a quick, probing side glance — casually*). He meant Jim Tyrone?

JOSIE. He did. And the dirty tick accused you and me of making up a foxy scheme to trap Jim. I'm to get him alone when he's crazy drunk and lead him on to marry me. (*She adds in a hard, scornful tone.*) As if that would ever work. Sure, all the pretty little tarts on Broadway, New York, must have had a try at that, and much good it did them.

HOGAN (*again with a quick side glance — casually*). They must have, surely. But that's in the city where he's suspicious. You can never tell what he mightn't do here in the country, where he's innocent, with a moon in the sky to fill him with poetry and a quart of bad hooch inside of him.

JOSIE (*turns on him angrily*). Are you taking Mike's scheme seriously, you old goat?

HOGAN. I'm not. I only thought you wanted my opinion. (*She regards him suspiciously, but his face is blank, as if he hadn't a thought beyond enjoying his pipe.*)

JOSIE (*turning away*). And if that didn't work, Mike said maybe we had a scheme that I'd get Jim in bed with me and you'd come with witnesses and a shotgun, and catch him there.

HOGAN. Faith, me darlin' son never learnt that from his prayer book! He must have improved his mind on the sly.

JOSIE. The dirty tick!

HOGAN. Don't call him a tick. I don't like ticks but I'll say this for them, I never picked one off me yet was a hypocrite.

JOSIE. Him daring to accuse us of planning a rotten trick like that on Jim!

HOGAN (*as if he misunderstood her meaning*). Yes, it's as old as the hills. Everyone's heard of it. But it still works now and again, I'm told, and sometimes an old trick is best because it's so ancient no one would suspect you'd try it.

JOSIE (*staring at him resentfully*). That's enough out of you, Father. I never can tell to this day, when you put that dead mug on you, whether you're joking or not, but I don't want to hear any more —

HOGAN (*mildly*). I thought you wanted my honest opinion on the merits of Mike's suggestion.

JOSIE. Och, shut up, will you? I know you're only trying to make game of me. You like Jim and you'd never play a dirty trick on him, not even if I was willing.

HOGAN. No — not unless I found he was playing one on me.

JOSIE. Which he'd never.

HOGAN. No, I wouldn't think it, but my motto in life is never trust anyone too far, not even myself.

JOSIE. You've reason for the last. I've often suspected you sneak out of bed in the night and pick your own pockets.

HOGAN. I wouldn't call it a dirty trick on him to get you for a wife.

JOSIE (*exasperatedly*). God save us, are you off on that again?

HOGAN. Well, you've put marriage in my head and I can't help considering the merits of the case, as they say. Sure, you're two of a kind, both great disgraces. That would help make a happy marriage because neither of you could look down on the other.

JOSIE. Jim mightn't think so.

HOGAN. You mean he'd think he was marrying beneath his station? He'd be a damned fool if he had that notion, for his Old Man who'd worked up from nothing to be rich and famous didn't give a damn about station. Didn't I often see him working on his grounds in clothes I wouldn't put on a scarecrow, not caring who saw him? (*With admiring affection.*) God rest him, he was a true Irish gentleman.

JOSIE. He was, and didn't you swindle him, and make me help you at it? I remember when I was a slip of a girl, and you'd get a letter saying his agent told him you were a year behind in the rent, and he'd be damned if he'd stand for it, and he was coming here to settle the matter. You'd make me dress up, with my hair brushed and a ribbon in it, and leave me to soften his heart before he saw you. So I'd skip down the path to meet him, and make him a courtesy, and hold on to his hand, and bat my eyes at him and lead him in the house, and offer him a drink of the good whiskey you didn't keep for company, and gape at him and tell him he was the handsomest man in the world, and the fierce expression he'd put on for you would go away.

HOGAN (*chuckles*). You did it wonderful. You should have gone on the stage.

JOSIE (*dryly*). Yes, that's what he'd tell me, and he'd reach in his pocket and take out a half dollar, and ask me if you hadn't put me up to it. So I'd say yes, you had.

HOGAN (*sadly*). I never knew you were such a black traitor, and you only a child.

JOSIE. And then you'd come and before he could get a word out of him, you'd tell him you'd vacate the premises unless he lowered the rent and painted the house.

HOGAN. Be God, that used to stop him in his tracks.

JOSIE. It didn't stop him from saying you were the damnedest crook ever came out of Ireland.

HOGAN. He said it with admiration. And we'd start drinking and telling stories, and singing songs, and by the time he left we were both too busy cursing England to worry over the rent. (*He grins affectionately.*) Oh, he was a great man entirely.

JOSIE. He was. He always saw through your tricks.

HOGAN. Didn't I know he would? Sure, all I wanted was to give him the fun of seeing through them so he couldn't be hard-hearted. That was the real trick.

JOSIE (*stares at him*). You old divil, you've always a trick hidden behind your tricks, so no one can tell at times what you're after.

HOGAN. Don't be so suspicious. Sure, I'd never try to fool you. You know me too well. But we've gone off the track. It's Jim we're discussing, not his father. I was telling you I could see the merit in your marrying him.

JOSIE (*exasperatedly*). Och, a cow must have kicked you in the head this morning.

HOGAN. I'd never give it a thought if I didn't know you had a soft spot in your heart for him.

JOSIE (*resentfully*). Well, I haven't! I like him, if that's what you mean, but it's only to talk to, because he's educated and quiet-spoken and has politeness even when he's drunkest, and doesn't roar around cursing and singing like some I could name.

HOGAN. If you could see the light in your eyes when he blarneys you —

JOSIE (*roughly*). The light in me foot! (*Scornfully.*) I'm in love with him, you'll be saying next!

HOGAN (*ignores this*). And another merit of the case is, he likes you.

JOSIE. Because he keeps dropping in here lately? Sure, it's only when he gets sick of the drunks at the Inn, and it's more to joke with you than see me.

HOGAN. It's your happiness I'm considering when I recommend your using your wits to catch him, if you can.

JOSIE (*jeeringly*). If!

HOGAN. Who knows? With all the sweethearts you've had, you must have a catching way with men.

JOSIE (*boastfully*). Maybe I have. But that doesn't mean —

HOGAN. If you got him alone tonight — there'll be a beautiful moon to fill him with poetry and loneliness, and —

JOSIE. That's one of Mike's dirty schemes.

HOGAN. Mike be damned! Sure, that's every woman's scheme since the world was created. Without it there'd be no population. (*Persuasively.*) There'd be no harm trying it, anyway.

JOSIE. And no use, either. (*Bitterly.*) Och, Father, don't play the jackass with me. You know, and I know, I'm an ugly overgrown lump of a woman, and the men that want me are no better than stupid bulls. Jim can have all the pretty, painted little Broadway girls he wants — and dancers on the stage, too — when he comes into his estate. That's the kind he likes.

HOGAN. I notice he's never married one. Maybe he'd like a fine strong handsome figure of a woman for a change, with beautiful eyes and hair and teeth and a smile.

JOSIE (*pleased, but jeering*). Thank you kindly for your compliments. Now I know a cow kicked you in the head.

HOGAN. If you think Jim hasn't been taking in your fine points, you're a fool.

JOSIE. You mean you've noticed him? (*Suddenly furious.*) Stop your lying!

HOGAN. Don't fly in a temper. All I'm saying is, there may be a chance in it to better yourself.

JOSIE (*scornfully*). Better myself by being tied down to a man who's drunk every night of his life? No, thank you!

HOGAN. Sure, you're strong enough to reform him. A taste of that club you've got, when he came home to you paralysed, and in a few weeks you'd have him a dirty prohibitionist.

JOSIE (*seriously*). It's true, if I was his wife, I'd cure him of drinking himself to death, if I had to kill him. (*Then angrily.*) Och, I'm sick of your crazy gab, Father! Leave me alone!

HOGAN. Well, let's put it another way. Don't tell me you couldn't learn to love the estate he'll come into.

JOSIE (*resentfully*). Ah, I've been waiting for that. That's what Mike said, again. Now we've come to the truth behind all your blather of my liking him or him liking me. (*Her manner changing — defiantly.*) All right, then. Of course I'd love the money. Who wouldn't? And why shouldn't I get my hands on it, if I could? He's bound to be swindled out of it, anyway. He'll go back to the Broadway he thinks is heaven, and by the time the pretty little tarts, and the bar-room sponges and race-track touts and gamblers are through with him he'll be picked clean. I'm no saint, God knows, but I'm decent and deserving compared to those scum.

HOGAN (*eagerly*). Be God, now you're using your wits. And where there's a will there's a way. You and me have never been beat when we put our brains together. I'll keep thinking it over, and you do the same.

JOSIE (*with illogical anger*). Well, I won't! And you keep your mad scheming to yourself. I won't listen to it.

HOGAN (*as if he were angry, too*). All right. The divil take you. It's all you'll hear from me. (*He pauses — then with great seriousness, turning toward her.*) Except one thing — (*As she starts to shut him up — sharply.*) I'm serious, and you'd better listen, because it's about this farm, which is home to us.

JOSIE (*surprised, stares at him*). What about the farm?

HOGAN. Don't forget, if we have lived on it twenty years, we're only tenants and we could be thrown out on our necks any-time. (*Quickly.*) Mind you, I don't say Jim would ever do it, rent or no rent, or let the executors do it, even if they wanted, which they don't, knowing they'd never find another tenant.

JOSIE. What's worrying you, then?

HOGAN. This. I've been afraid lately the minute the estate is out of probate, Jim will sell the farm.

JOSIE (*exasperatedly*). Of course he will! Hasn't he told us and promised you can buy it on easy time payments at the small price you offered?

HOGAN. Jim promises whatever you like when he's full of whiskey. He might forget a promise as easy when he's drunk enough.

JOSIE (*indignantly*). He'd never! And who'd want it except us? No one ever has in all the years —

HOGAN. Someone has lately. The agent got an offer last month, Jim told me, bigger than mine.

JOSIE. Och, Jim loves to try and get your goat. He was kidding you.

HOGAN. He wasn't. I can tell. He said he told the agent to tell whoever it was the place wasn't for sale.

JOSIE. Of course he did. Did he say who'd made the offer?

HOGAN. He didn't know. It came through a real-estate man who wouldn't tell who his client was. I've been trying to guess, but I can't think of anyone crazy enough unless it'd be some damn fool of a millionaire buying up land to make a great estate for himself, like our beautiful neighbour, Harder, the Standard Oil thief, did years ago. (*He adds with bitter fervency.*) May he roast in hell and his Limey superintendent with him!

JOSIE. Amen to that. (*Then scornfully.*) This land for an estate? And if there was an offer, Jim's refused it, and that ends it. He wouldn't listen to any offer, after he's given his word to us.

HOGAN. Did I say he would — when he's in his right mind? What I'm afraid of is, he might be led into it sometime when he has one of his sneering bitter drunks on and talks like a Broadway crook himself, saying money is the only thing in the world, and everything and anyone can be bought if the price is big enough. You've heard him.

JOSIE. I have. But he doesn't fool me at all. He only acts like he's hard and shameless to get back at life when it's tormenting him — and who doesn't?

(*He gives her a quick, curious side glance which she doesn't notice.*)

HOGAN. Or take the other kind of queer drunk he gets on sometimes when, without any reason you can see, he'll suddenly turn strange, and look sad, and stare at nothing as if he was mourning over some ghost inside him, and —

JOSIE. I think I know what comes over him when he's like that. It's the memory of his poor mother comes back and his grief for her death. (*Pityingly.*) Poor Jim.

HOGAN (*ignoring this*). And whiskey seems to have no effect on him, like water off a duck's back. He'll keep acting natural enough, and you'd swear he wasn't bad at all, but the next day you find his brain was so paralysed he don't remember a thing until you remind him. He's done a lot of mad things, when he was that way, he was sorry for after.

JOSIE (*scornfully*). What drunk hasn't? But he'd never — (*Resentfully.*) I won't have you suspecting Jim without any cause, d'you hear me!

HOGAN. I don't suspect him. All I've said is, when a man gets as queer drunk as Jim, he doesn't know himself what he mightn't do, and we'd be damned fools if we didn't fear the possibility, however small it is, and do all we can to guard against it.

JOSIE. There's no possibility! And how could we guard against it, if there was?

HOGAN. Well, you can put yourself out to be extra nice to him, for one thing.

JOSIE. How nice is extra nice?

HOGAN. You ought to know. But here's one tip. I've noticed when you talk rough and brazen like you do to other men, he may grin like they do, as if he enjoyed it, but he don't. So watch your tongue.

JOSIE (*with a defiant toss of her head*). I'll talk as I please, and if he don't like it he can lump it! (*Scornfully.*) I'm to pretend I'm a pure virgin, I suppose? That would fool him, wouldn't it, and him hearing all about me from the men at the Inn? (*She gets to her feet, abruptly changing the subject.*) We're wasting the day, blathering. (*Then her face hardening.*) If ever he went back on his word, no matter how drunk he was, I'd be with you in any scheme you made against him, no matter how dirty. (*Hastily.*) But it's all your nonsense. I'd never believe it. (*She comes and picks up the pitchfork.*) I'll go to the meadow and finish Mike's work. You needn't fear you'll miss his help on the farm.

HOGAN. A hell of a help! A weak lazy back and the appetite of a drove of starving pigs! (*As she turns to go — suddenly bellicose.*) Leaving me, are you? When it's dinner-time? Where's my dinner, you lazy cow?

JOSIE. There's stew on the stove, you bad-tempered runt. Go in and help yourself. I'm not hungry. Your gab has bothered my mind. I need hard work in the sun to clear it. (*She starts to go off toward rear-right.*)

HOGAN (*glancing down the road, off left-front*). You'd better wait. There's a caller coming to the gate — and if I'm not mistaken, it's the light of your eyes himself.

JOSIE (*angrily*). Shut up! (*She stares off — her face softens and grows pitying.*) Look at him when he thinks no one is watching, with his eyes on the ground. Like a dead man walking slow behind his own coffin. (*Then roughly.*) Faith, he must have a hangover. He sees us now. Look at the bluff he puts up, straightening himself and grinning. (*Resentfully.*) I don't want to meet him. Let him make jokes with you and play the old game about a drink you both think is such fun. That's all he comes for, anyway. (*She starts off again.*)

HOGAN. Are you running away from him? Sure, you must be afraid you're in love.

(*Josie halts instantly and turns back defiantly.*)

(*He goes on.*) Go in the house now and wash your face, and tidy your dress, and give a touch to your hair. You want to look decent for him.

JOSIE (*angrily*). I'll go in the house, but only to see the stew ain't burned, for I suppose you'll have the foxiness to ask him to have a bite to eat to keep in his good graces.

HOGAN. Why shouldn't I ask him? I know damned well he has no appetite this early in the day, but only a thirst.

JOSIE. Och, you make me sick, you sly miser! (*She goes in through her bedroom, slamming the door behind her.*)

(*Hogan refills his pipe, pretending he doesn't notice Tyrone approaching, his eyes bright with droll expectation. Jim Tyrone enters along the road from the highway, left.*)

(*Tyrone is in his early forties, around five feet nine, broad-shouldered and deep-chested. His naturally fine physique has become soft and soggy from dissipation, but his face is still good-looking despite its unhealthy puffiness and the bags under the eyes. He has thinning dark hair, parted and brushed back to cover a bald spot. His eyes are brown, the whites congested and yellowish. His nose, big and aquiline, gives his face a certain Mephistophelian quality which is accentuated by his habitually cynical expression. But when he smiles without sneering, he still has the ghost of a former youthful, irresponsible Irish charm — that of the beguiling ne'er-do-well, sentimental and romantic. It is his humour and charm which have kept him attractive to women, and popular with men as a drinking companion. He is dressed in an expensive dark-brown suit, tight-fitting and drawn in at the waist, dark brown made-to-order shoes and silk socks, a white silk shirt, silk handkerchief in breast pocket, a dark tie. This get-up suggests that he follows a style set by well-groomed Broadway gamblers who would like to be mistaken for Wall Street brokers.*)

(*He has had enough pick-me-ups to recover from morning-after nausea and steady his nerves. During the following dialogue, he and Hogan are like players at an old familiar game where each knows the other's moves, but which still amuses them.*)

TYRONE (*approaches and stands regarding Hogan with sardonic relish. Hogan scratches a match on the seat of his overalls and lights his pipe, pretending not to see him. Tyrone recites with feeling.*)

"Fortunate senex, ergo tua rura manebunt,
et tibi magna satis, quamvis lapis omnia nudus."

HOGAN (*mutters*). It's the landlord again, and my shotgun not handy. (*He looks up at Tyrone.*) Is it Mass you're saying, Jim? That was Latin. I know it by ear. What the hell — insult does it mean?

TYRONE. Translated very freely into Irish English, something like this. (*He imitates Hogan's brogue.*) "Ain't you the lucky old bastard to have this beautiful farm, if it is full of nude rocks."

HOGAN. I like that part about the rocks. If cows could eat them this place would make a grand dairy farm. (*He spits.*) It's easy to see you've a fine college education. It must be a big help to you, conversing with whores and bar-keeps.

TYRONE. Yes, a very worldly asset. I was once offered a job as office boy — until they discovered I wasn't qualified because I had no Bachelor of Arts diploma. There had been a slight misunderstanding just before I was to graduate.

HOGAN. Between you and the Fathers? I'll wager!

TYRONE. I made a bet with another Senior I could get a tart from Haymarket to visit me, introduce her to the Jebs as my sister — and get away with it.

HOGAN. But you didn't?

TYRONE. Almost. It was a memorable day in the halls of learning. All the students were wise and I had them rolling in the aisles as I showed Sister around the grounds, accompanied by one of the Jebs. He was a bit suspicious at first, but Dutch Maisie — her professional name — had no make-up on, and was dressed in black, and had eaten a pound of Sen-Sen to kill the gin on her breath, and seemed such a devout girl that he forgot his suspicions. (*He pauses.*) Yes, all would have been well, but she was a mischievous minx, and had her own ideas of improving on my joke. When she was saying good-bye to Father Fuller, she added innocently: "Christ, Father, it's nice and quiet out here away from the damned Sixth Avenue El. I wish to hell I could stay here!" (*Dryly.*) But she didn't, and neither did I.

HOGAN (*chuckles delightedly*). I'll bet you didn't! God bless Dutch Maisie! I'd like to have known her.

TYRONE (*sits down on the steps — with a change of manner*). Well, how's the Duke of Donegal this fine day?

HOGAN. Never better.

TYRONE. Slaving and toiling as usual, I see.

HOGAN. Hasn't a poor man a right to his noon rest without being sneered at by his rich landlord?

TYRONE. "Rich" is good. I would be, if you'd pay up your back rent.

HOGAN. You ought to pay me, instead, for occupying this rockpile, miscalled a farm. (*His eyes twinkling.*) But I have fine reports to give you of a promising harvest. The milkweed and the thistles is in thriving condition, and I never saw the poison ivy so bounteous and beautiful.

(*Tyrone laughs. Without their noticing, Josie appears in the doorway behind Tyrone. She has tidied up and arranged her hair. She smiles down at Jim, her face softening, pleased to hear him laugh.*)

TYRONE. You win. Where did Josie go, Phil? I saw her here —

HOGAN. She ran in the house to make herself beautiful for you.

JOSIE (*breaks in roughly*). You're a liar. (*To Tyrone, her manner one of bold, free-and-easy familiarity.*) Hello, Jim.

TYRONE (*starts to stand up*). Hello, Josie.

JOSIE (*puts a hand on his shoulder and pushes him down*). Don't get up. Sure you know I'm no lady. (*She sits on the top step — banteringly.*) How's my fine Jim this beautiful day? You don't look so bad. You must have stopped at the Inn for an eye-opener — or ten of them.

TYRONE. I've felt worse. (*He looks up at her sardonically.*) And how's my virgin Queen of Ireland?

JOSIE. Yours, is it? Since when? And don't be miscalling me a virgin. You'll ruin my reputation, if you spread that lie about me. (*She laughs. Tyrone is staring at her. She goes on quickly.*) How is it you're around so early? I thought you never got up till afternoon.

TYRONE. Couldn't sleep. One of those heebie-jeebie nights when the booze keeps you awake instead of — (*He catches her giving him a pitying look — irritably.*) But what of it!

JOSIE. Maybe you had no woman in bed with you, for a change. It's a terrible thing to break the habit of years.

TYRONE (*shrugs his shoulders*). Maybe.

JOSIE. What's the matter with the tarts in town, they let you do it? I'll bet the ones you know on Broadway, New York, wouldn't neglect their business.

TYRONE (*pretends to yawn boredly*). Maybe not. (*Then irritably.*) Cut out the kidding, Josie. It's too early.

HOGAN (*who has been taking everything in without seeming to*). I told you not to annoy the gentleman with your rough tongue.

JOSIE. Sure I thought I was doing my duty as hostess making him feel at home.

TYRONE (*stares at her again*). Why all the interest lately in the ladies of the profession, Josie?

JOSIE. Oh, I've been considering joining their union. It's easier living than farming, I'm sure. (*Then resentfully.*) You think I'd starve at it, don't you, because your fancy is for dainty dolls of women? But other men like —

TYRONE (*with sudden revulsion*). For God's sake, cut out that kind of talk, Josie! It sounds like hell.

JOSIE (*stares at him startledly — then resentfully*). Oh, it does, does it? (*Forcing a scornful smile.*) I'm shocking you, I suppose?

(*Hogan is watching them both, not missing anything in their faces, while he seems intent on his pipe.*)

TYRONE (*looking a bit sheepish and annoyed at himself for his interest — shrugs his shoulders*). No. Hardly. Forget it. (*He smiles kiddingly.*) Anyway, who told you I fall for the dainty dolls? That's all a thing of the past. I like them tall and strong and voluptuous, now, with beautiful big breasts.

(*She blushes and looks confused and is furious with herself for doing so.*)

HOGAN. There you are, Josie, darlin'. Sure he couldn't speak fairer than that.

JOSIE (*recovers herself*). He couldn't, indeed. (*She pats Tyrone's head — playfully.*) You're a terrible blarneying liar, Jim, but thank you just the same.

(*Tyrone turns his attention to Hogan. He winks at Josie and begins in an exaggeratedly casual manner.*)

TYRONE. I don't blame you, Mr. Hogan, for taking it easy on such a blazing hot day.

HOGAN (*doesn't look at him. His eyes twinkle.*) Hot, did you say? I find it cool, meself. Take off your coat if you're hot, Mister Tyrone.

TYRONE. One of the most stifling days I've ever known. Isn't it, Josie?

JOSIE (*smiling*). Terrible. I know you must be perishing.

HOGAN. I wouldn't call it a damned bit stifling.

TYRONE. It parches the membranes in your throat.

HOGAN. The what? Never mind. I can't have them, for my throat isn't parched at all. If yours is, Mister Tyrone, there's a well full of water at the back.

TYRONE. Water? That's something people wash with, isn't it? I mean, some people.

HOGAN. So I've heard. But, like you, I find it hard to believe. It's a dirty habit. They must be foreigners.

TYRONE. As I was saying, my throat is parched after the long dusty walk I took just for the pleasure of being your guest.

HOGAN. I don't remember inviting you, and the road is hard macadam with divil a speck of dust, and it's less than a quarter mile from the Inn here.

TYRONE. I didn't have a drink at the Inn. I was waiting until I arrived here, knowing that you —

HOGAN. Knowing I'd what?

TYRONE. Your reputation as a generous host —

HOGAN. The world must be full of liars. So you didn't have a drink at the Inn? Then it must be the air itself smells of whiskey today, although I didn't notice it before you came. You've gone on the water-wagon, I suppose? Well, that's fine, and I ask pardon for misjudging you.

TYRONE. I've wanted to go on the wagon for the past twenty-five years, but the doctors have strictly forbidden it. It would be fatal — with my weak heart.

HOGAN. So you've a weak heart? Well, well, and me thinking all along it was your head. I'm glad you told me. I was just going to offer you a drink, but whiskey is the worst thing —

TYRONE. The docs say it's a matter of life and death. I must have a stimulant — one big drink at least, whenever I strain my heart walking in the hot sun.

HOGAN. Walk back to the Inn, then, and give it a good strain, so you can buy yourself two big drinks.

JOSIE (*laughing*). Ain't you the fools, playing that old game between you, and both of you pleased as punch!

TYRONE (*gives up with a laugh*). Hasn't he ever been known to loosen up, Josie?

JOSIE. You ought to know. If you need a drink you'll have to buy it from him or die of thirst.

TYRONE. Well, I'll bet this is one time he's going to treat.

HOGAN. Be God, I'll take that bet!

TYRONE. After you've heard the news I've got for you, you'll be so delighted you won't be able to drag out the old bottle quick enough.

HOGAN. I'll have to be insanely delighted.

JOSIE (*full of curiosity*). Shut up, Father. What news, Jim?

TYRONE. I have it off the grapevine that a certain exalted personage will drop in on you before long.

HOGAN. It's the sheriff again. I know by the pleased look on your mug.

TYRONE. Not this time. (*He pauses tantalizingly.*)

JOSIE. Bad luck to you, can't you tell us who?

TYRONE. A more eminent grafter than the sheriff — (*Sneeringly.*) A leading aristocrat in our Land of the Free and Get-Rich-Quick, whose boots are licked by one and all — one of the Kings of our Republic by Divine Right of Inherited Swag. In short, I refer to your good neighbour, T. Stedman Harder, Standard Oil's sappiest child, whom I know you both love so dearly.

(*There is a pause after this announcement. Hogan and Josie stiffen, and their eyes begin to glitter. But they can't believe their luck at first.*)

HOGAN (*in an ominous whisper*). Did you say Harder is coming to call on us, Jim?

JOSIE. It's too good to be true.

TYRONE (*watching them with amusement*). No kidding. The great Mr. Harder intends to stop here on his way back to lunch from a horseback ride.

JOSIE. How do you know?

TYRONE. Simpson told me. I ran into him at the Inn.

HOGAN. That English scum of a superintendent!

TYRONE. He was laughing himself sick. He said he suggested the idea to Harder — told him you'd be overwhelmed with awe if he deigned to interview you in person.

HOGAN. Overwhelmed isn't the word. Is it, Josie?

JOSIE. It isn't indeed, Father.

TYRONE. For once in his life, Simpson is cheering for you. He doesn't like his boss. In fact, he asked me to tell you he hopes you kill him.

HOGAN (*disdainfully*). To hell with the Limey's good wishes. I'd like both of them to call together.

JOSIE. Ah, well, we can't have everything. (*To Tyrone.*) What's the reason Mr. Harder decided to notice poor, humble scum the like of us?

TYRONE (*grinning*). That's right, Josie. Be humble. He'll expect you to know your place.

HOGAN. Will he now? Well, well. (*With a great happy sigh.*) This is going to be a beautiful day entirely.

JOSIE. But what's Harder's reason, Jim?

TYRONE. Well, it seems he has an ice pond on his estate.

HOGAN. Oho! So that's it!

TYRONE. Yes. That's it. Harder likes to keep up the good old manorial customs. He clings to his ice pond. And your pigpen isn't far from his ice pond.

HOGAN. A nice little stroll for the pigs, that's all.

TYRONE. And somehow Harder's fence in that vicinity has a habit of breaking down.

HOGAN. Fences are queer things. You can't depend on them.

TYRONE. Simpson says he's had it repaired a dozen times, but each time on the following night it gets broken down again.

JOSIE. What a strange thing! It must be the bad fairies. I can't imagine who else could have done it. Can you, Father?

HOGAN. I can't, surely.

TYRONE. Well, Simpson can. He knows you did it and he told his master so.

HOGAN (*disdainfully*). Master is the word. Sure, the English can't live unless they have a lord's backside to kiss, the dirty slaves.

TYRONE. The result of those breaks in the fence is that your pigs stroll — as you so gracefully put it — stroll through to wallow happily along the shores of the ice pond.

HOGAN. Well, why not? Sure, they're fine ambitious American-born pigs and they don't miss any opportunities. They're like Harder's father who made the money for him.

TYRONE. I agree, but for some strange reason Harder doesn't look forward to the taste of pig in next summer's ice water.

HOGAN. He must be delicate. Remember he's delicate, Josie, and leave your club in the house. (*He bursts into joyful menacing laughter.*) Oh, be God and be Christ in the mountains! I've pined to have a quiet word with Mr. Harder for years, watching him ride past in his big shiny automobile with his snoot in the air, and being tormented always by the complaints of his Limey superintendent. Oh, won't I welcome him!

JOSIE. Won't *we*, you mean. Sure, I love him as much as you.

HOGAN. I'd kiss you, Jim, for this beautiful news, if you wasn't so damned ugly. Maybe Josie'll do it for me. She has a stronger stomach.

JOSIE. I will! He's earned it. (*She pulls Tyrone's head back and laughingly kisses him on the lips. Her expression changes. She looks startled and confused, stirred and at the same time frightened. She forces a scornful laugh.*) Och, there's no spirit in you! It's like kissing a corpse.

TYRONE (*gives her a strange surprised look — mockingly*). Yes? (*Turning to Hogan.*) Well, how about that drink, Phil? I'll leave it to Josie if drinks aren't on the house.

HOGAN. *I* won't leave it to Josie. She's prejudiced, being in love.

JOSIE (*angrily*). Shut up, you old liar! (*Then guiltily, forcing a laugh.*) Don't talk nonsense to sneak out of treating Jim.

HOGAN (*sighing*). All right, Josie. Go get the bottle and one small glass, or he'll never stop nagging me. I can turn my back, so the sight of him drinking free won't break my heart.

(*Josie gets up, laughing, and goes in the house. Hogan peers at the road off left.*)

On his way back to lunch, you said? Then it's time — (*Fervently.*) O Holy Joseph, don't let the bastard change his mind.

TYRONE (*beginning to have qualms*). Listen, Phil. Don't get too enthusiastic. He has a big draw around here, and he'll have you pinched, sure as hell, if you beat him up.

HOGAN. Och, I'm no fool.

(*Josie comes out with a bottle and a tumbler.*)

Will you listen to this, Josie. He's warning me not to give Harder a beating — as if I'd dirty my hands on the scum.

JOSIE. As if we'd need to. Sure, all we want is a quiet chat with him.

HOGAN. That's all. As neighbour to neighbour.

JOSIE (*hands Tyrone the bottle and tumbler*). Here you are, Jim. Don't stint yourself.

HOGAN (*mournfully*). A fine daughter! I tell you a small glass and you give him a bucket! (*As Tyrone pours a big drink, grinning at him, he turns away with a comic shudder.*) That's a fifty-dollar drink, at least.

TYRONE. Here's luck, Phil.

HOGAN. I hope you drown.

(*Tyrone drinks and makes a wry face.*)

TYRONE. The best chicken medicine I've ever tasted.

HOGAN. That's gratitude for you! Here, pass me the bottle. A drink will warm up my welcome for His Majesty. (*He takes an enormous swig from the bottle.*)

JOSIE (*looking off left*). There's two horseback riders on the county road now.

HOGAN. Praise be to God! It's him and a groom. (*He sets the bottle on top of the boulder.*)

JOSIE. That's McCabe. An old sweetheart of mine. (*She glances at Tyrone provokingly—then suddenly worried and protective.*) You get in the house, Jim. If Harder sees you here, he'll lay the whole blame on you.

TYRONE. Nix, Josie. You don't think I'm going to miss this, do you?

JOSIE. You can sit inside by my window and take in everything. Come on, now, don't be stubborn with me. (*She puts her hands under his arms and lifts him to his feet as easily as if he was a child—banteringly.*) Go into my beautiful bedroom. It's a nice place for you.

TYRONE (*kiddingly*). Just what I've been thinking for some time, Josie.

JOSIE (*boldly*). Sure, you've never given me a sign of it. Come up tonight and we'll spoon in the moonlight and you can tell me your thoughts.

TYRONE. That's a date. Remember, now.

JOSIE. It's you who'll forget. Get inside now, before it's too late. (*She gives him a shove inside and closes the door.*)

HOGAN (*has been watching the visitor approach*). He's dismounting — as graceful as a scarecrow, and his poor horse longing to give him a kick. Look at Mac grinning at us. Sit down, Josie. (*She sits on the steps, he on the boulder.*) Pretend you don't notice him.

(*T. Stedman Harder appears at left. They act as if they didn't see him. Hogan knocks out his pipe on the palm of his hand.*)

(*Harder is in his late thirties but looks younger because his face is unmarked by worry, ambition, or any of the common hazards of life. No matter how long he lives, his four undergraduate years will always be for him the most significant in his life, and the moment of his highest achievement the time he was tapped for an exclusive Senior Society at the Ivy university to which his father had given millions. Since that day he has felt no need for further aspiring, no urge to do anything except settle down on his estate and live the life of a country gentleman, mildly interested in saddle horses and sport models of foreign automobiles. He is not the blatantly silly, playboy heir to millions whose antics make newspaper headlines. He doesn't drink much except when he attends his class reunion every spring — the most exciting episode of each year for him. He doesn't give wild parties, doesn't chase after musical-comedy cuties, is a mildly contented husband and father of three children. A not unpleasant man, affable, good-looking in an ordinary way, sunburnt and healthy, beginning to take on fat, he is simply immature, naturally lethargic, a bit stupid. Coddled from birth, everything arranged and made easy for him, deferred to because of his wealth, he usually has the self-confident attitude of acknowledged superiority, but assumes a supercilious, insecure air when dealing with people beyond his ken. He is dressed in a beautifully tailored English tweed coat and whipcord riding breeches, immaculately polished English riding boots with spurs, and carries a riding crop in his hand.*)

(*It would be hard to find anyone more ill-equipped for combat with the Hogans. He has never come in contact with anyone like them. To make matters easier for them he is deliberate in his speech, slow on the uptake, and has no sense of humour. The experienced strategy of the Hogans in verbal battle is to take the offensive at once and never let an opponent get set to hit back. Also, they use a beautifully co-ordinated, bewildering change of pace, switching suddenly from jarring shouts to low, confidential vituperation. And they exaggerate their Irish brogues to confuse an enemy still further.*)

HARDER (*walks toward Hogan — stiffly*). Good morning. I want to see the man who runs this farm.

HOGAN (*surveys him deliberately, his little pig eyes gleaming with malice*). You do, do you? Well, you've seen him. So now run along and play with your horse, and don't bother me. (*He turns to Josie, who is staring at Harder, much to his discomfiture, as if she had discovered a cockroach in her soup.*) D'you see what I see, Josie? Be God, you'll have to give that damned cat of yours a spanking for bringing it to our doorstep.

HARDER (*determined to be authoritative and command respect — curtly*). Are you Hogan?

HOGAN (*insultingly*). I am *Mister* Philip Hogan — to a gentleman.

JOSIE (*glares at Harder*). Where's your manners, you spindle-shanked jockey? Were you brought up in a stable?

HARDER (*does not fight with ladies, and especially not with this lady — ignoring her*). My name is Harder. (*He obviously expects them to be immediately impressed and apologetic.*)

HOGAN (*contemptuously*). Who asked you your name, me little man?

JOSIE. Sure, who in the world cares who the hell you are?

HOGAN. But if you want to play politeness, we'll play with you. Let me introduce you to my daughter, Harder — Miss Josephine Hogan.

JOSIE (*petulantly*). I don't want to meet him, Father. I don't like his silly sheep's face, and I've no use for jockeys, anyway. I'll wager he's no damned good to a woman.

(*From inside her bedroom comes a burst of laughter. This revelation of an unseen audience startles Harder. He begins to look extremely unsure of himself.*)

HOGAN. I don't think he's a jockey. It's only the funny pants he's wearing. I'll bet if you asked his horse, you'd find he's no cowboy either. (*To Harder, jeeringly.*) Come, tell us the truth, me honey. Don't you kiss your horse each time you mount and beg him, please don't throw me today, darlin', and I'll give you an extra bucket of oats. (*He bursts into an extravagant roar of laughter, slapping his thigh, and Josie guffaws with him, while they watch the disconcerting effect of this theatrical mirth on Harder.*)

HARDER (*beginning to lose his temper*). Listen to me, Hogan! I didn't come here — (*He is going to add "to listen to your damned jokes" or something like that, but Hogan silences him.*)

HOGAN (*shouts*). What! What's that you said? (*He stares at the dumbfounded Harder with droll amazement, as if he couldn't believe his ears*). You didn't come here? (*He turns to Josie — in a whisper.*) Did you hear that, Josie? (*He takes off his hat and scratches his head in comic bewilderment.*) Well, that's a puzzle, surely. How d'you suppose he got here?

JOSIE. Maybe the stork brought him, bad luck to it for a dirty bird.

(*Again Tyrone's laughter is heard from the bedroom.*)

HARDER (*so off balance now he can only repeat angrily*). I said I didn't come here —

HOGAN (*shouts*). Wait! Wait, now! (*Threateningly.*) We've had enough of that. Say it a third time and I'll send my daughter to telephone the asylum.

HARDER (*forgetting he's a gentleman*). Damn you, I'm the one who's had enough — !

JOSIE (*shouts*). Hold your dirty tongue! I'll have no foul language in my presence.

HOGAN. Och, don't mind him, Josie. He's said he isn't here, anyway, so we won't talk to him behind his back. (*He regards Harder with pitying contempt.*) Sure, ain't you the poor crazy creature? Do you want us to believe you're your own ghost?

HARDER (*notices the bottle on the boulder for the first time — tries to be contemptuously tolerant and even to smile with condescending disdain*). Ah! I understand now. You're drunk. I'll come back sometime when you're sober — or send Simpson — (*He turns away, glad of an excuse to escape.*)

JOSIE (*jumps up and advances on him menacingly*). No, you don't! You'll apologize first for insulting a lady — insinuating I'm drunk this early in the day — or I'll knock some good breeding in you!

HARDER (*actually frightened now*). I — I said nothing about you —

HOGAN (*gets up to come between them*). Aisy now, Josie. He didn't mean it. He don't know what he means, the poor loon. (*To Harder — pityingly.*) Run home, that's a good lad, before your keeper misses you.

HARDER (*hastily*). Good day.

(*He turns eagerly toward left but suddenly Hogan grabs his shoulder and spins him around — then shifts his grip to the lapel of Harder's coat.*)

HOGAN (*grimly*). Wait now, me Honey Boy. I'll have a word with you, if you plaze. I'm beginning to read some sense into this. You mentioned that English bastard, Simpson. I know who you are now.

HARDER (*outraged*). Take your hands off me, you drunken fool. (*He raises his riding crop.*)

JOSIE (*grabs it and tears it from his hand with one powerful twist — fiercely*). Would you strike my poor infirm old father, you coward, you!

HARDER (*calling for help*). McCabe!

HOGAN. Don't think McCabe will hear you, if you blew Gabriel's horn. He knows I or Josie can lick him with one hand. (*Sharply.*) Josie! Stand between us and the gate.

(*Josie takes her stand where the path meets the road. She turns her back for a moment, shaking with suppressed laughter, and waves her hand at McCabe and turns back. Hogan releases his hold on Harder's coat.*)

There now. Don't try running away or my daughter will knock you senseless. (*He goes on grimly before Harder can speak.*) You're the blackguard of a millionaire that owns the estate next to ours, ain't you? I've been meaning to call on you, for I've a bone to pick with you, you bloody tyrant! But I couldn't bring myself to set foot on land bought with Standard Oil money that was stolen from the poor it ground in the dust beneath its dirty heel — land that's watered with the tears of starving widows and orphans — (*He abruptly switches from this eloquence to a matter-of-fact tone.*) But never mind that, now. I won't waste words trying to reform a born crook. (*Fiercely, shoving his dirty unshaven face almost into Harder's.*) What I want to know is, what the hell d'you mean by your contemptible trick of breaking down your fence to entice my poor pigs to take their death in your ice pond?

(*There is a shout of laughter from Josie's bedroom, and Josie doubles up and holds her sides. Harder is so flabbergasted by this mad accusation he cannot even sputter. But Hogan acts as if he'd denied it — savagely.*)

Don't lie, now! None of your damned Standard Oil excuses, or be Jaysus, I'll break you in half! Haven't I mended that fence morning after morning, and seen the footprints where you had sneaked up in the night to pull it down again. How many times have I mended that fence, Josie?

JOSIE. If it's once, it's a hundred, Father.

HOGAN. Listen, me little millionaire! I'm a peaceful, mild man that believes in live and let live, and as long as the neighbouring scum leave me alone, I'll let them alone, but when it comes to standing by and seeing my poor pigs murthered one by one — ! Josie! How many pigs is it caught their death of cold in his damned ice pond and died of pneumonia?

JOSIE. Ten of them, Father. And ten more died of cholera after drinking the dirty water in it.

HOGAN. All prize pigs, too! I was offered two hundred dollars apiece for them. Twenty pigs at two hundred, that's four thousand. And a thousand to cure the sick and cover funeral expenses for the dead. Call it four thousand you owe me. (*Furiously.*) And you'll pay it, or I'll sue you, so help me Christ! I'll drag you in every court in the land! I'll paste your ugly mug on the front page of every newspaper as a pig-murdering tyrant! Before I'm through with you, you'll think you're the King of England at an Irish wake! (*With a quick change of pace to a wheedling confidential tone.*) Tell me now, if it isn't a secret, whatever made you take such a savage grudge against pigs? Sure, it isn't reasonable for a Standard Oil man to hate hogs.

HARDER (*manages to get in three sputtering words*). I've had enough — !

HOGAN (*with a grin*). Be God, I believe you! (*Switching to fierceness and grabbing his lapel again.*) Look out, now! Keep your place and be soft-spoken to your betters! You're not in your shiny automobile now with your funny nose cocked so you won't smell the poor people. (*He gives him a shake.*) And let me warn you! I have to put up with a lot of pests on this heap of boulders some joker once called a farm. There's a cruel skinflint of a landlord who swindles me out of my last drop of whiskey, and there's poison ivy, and ticks and potato bugs, and there's snakes and skunks! But, be God, I draw the line somewhere, and I'll be damned if I'll stand for a Standard Oil man trespassing! So will you kindly get the hell out of here before I plant a kick on your backside that'll land you in the Atlantic Ocean! (*He gives Harder a shove.*) Beat it now!

(*Harder tries to make some sort of disdainfully dignified exit. But he has to get by Josie.*)

JOSIE (*leers at him idiotically*). Sure, you wouldn't go without a word of good-bye to me, would you, darlin'? Don't scorn me just because you have on your jockey's pants. (*In a hoarse whisper.*) Meet me tonight, as usual, down by the pigpen.

(*Harder's retreat becomes a rout. He disappears on left, but a second later his voice, trembling with anger, is heard calling back threateningly.*)

HARDER. If you dare touch that fence again, I'll put this matter in the hands of the police!

HOGAN (*shouts derisively*). And I'll put it in my lawyer's hands and in the newspapers! (*He doubles up with glee.*) Look at him fling himself on his nag and spur the poor beast! And look at McCabe behind him! He can hardly stay in the saddle for laughing! (*He slaps his thigh.*) O Jaysus, this is a great day for the poor and oppressed! I'll do no more work! I'll go down to the Inn and spend money and get as drunk as Moses!

JOSIE. Small blame to you. You deserve it. But you'll have your dinner first, to give you a foundation. Come on, now.

(*They turn back toward the house. From inside another burst of laughter from Tyrone is heard. Josie smiles.*)

Listen to Jim still in stitches. It's good to hear him laugh as if he meant it.

(*Tyrone appears in the doorway of her bedroom.*)

TYRONE. O God, my sides are sore.

(*They all laugh together. He joins them at the left corner of the house.*)

JOSIE. It's dinner time. Will you have a bite to eat with us, Jim? I'll boil you some eggs.

HOGAN. Och, why do you have to mention eggs? Don't you know it's the one thing he might eat? Well, no matter. Anything goes today. (*He gets the bottle of whiskey.*) Come in, Jim. We'll have a drink while Josie's fixing the grub.

(*They start to go in the front door, Hogan in the lead.*)

TYRONE (*suddenly — with sardonic amusement*). Wait a minute. Let us pause to take a look at this very valuable property. Don't you notice the change, Phil? Every boulder on the place has turned to solid gold.

HOGAN. What the hell —? You didn't get the D.T.'s from my whiskey, I know that.

TYRONE. No D.T.'s about it. This farm has suddenly become a goldmine. You know that offer I told you about? Well, the agent did a little detective work and he discovered it came from Harder. He doesn't want the damned place but he dislikes you as a neighbour and he thinks the best way to get rid of you would be to become your landlord.

HOGAN. The sneaking skunk! I'm sorry I didn't give him that kick.

TYRONE. Yes. So am I. That would have made the place even more valuable. But as it is, you did nobly. I expect him to double or triple his first offer. In fact, I'll bet the sky is the limit now.

HOGAN (*gives Josie a meaningful look*). I see your point! But we're not worrying you'd ever forget your promise to us for any price.

TYRONE. Promise? What promise? You know what Kipling wrote. (*Paraphrasing the "Rhyme of the Three Sealers".*) There's never a promise of God or man goes north of ten thousand bucks.

HOGAN. D'you hear him, Josie? We can't trust him.

JOSIE. Och, you know he's kidding.

HOGAN. I don't. I'm becoming suspicious.

TYRONE (*a trace of bitterness beneath his amused tone*). That's wise dope, Phil. Trust and be a sucker. If I were you, I'd be seriously worried. I've always wanted to own a goldmine — so I could sell it.

JOSIE (*bursts out*). Will you shut up your rotten Broadway blather!

TYRONE (*stares at her in surprise*). Why so serious and indignant, Josie? You just told your unworthy Old Man I was kidding. (*To Hogan.*) At last, I've got you by the ears, Phil. We must have a serious chat about when you're going to pay that back rent.

HOGAN (*groans*). A landlord who's a blackmailer! Holy God, what next!

(*Josie is smiling with relief now.*)

TYRONE. And you, Josie, please remember when I keep that moonlight date tonight I expect you to be very sweet to me.

JOSIE (*with a bold air*). Sure, you don't have to blackmail me. I'd be that to you, anyway.

HOGAN. Are you laying plots in my presence to seduce my only daughter? (*Then philosophically.*) Well, what can I do? I'll be drunk at the Inn, so how could I prevent it? (*He goes up the steps.*) Let's eat, for the love of God. I'm starving. (*He disappears inside the house.*)

JOSIE (*with an awkward playful gesture, takes Tyrone by the hand*). Come along, Jim.

TYRONE (*smiles kiddingly*). Afraid you'll lose me? Swell chance! (*His eyes fix on her breasts — with genuine feeling.*) You have the most beautiful breasts in the world, do you know it, Josie?

JOSIE (*pleased — shyly*). I don't — but I'm happy if you think — (*Then quickly.*) But I've no time now to listen to your kidding, with my mad old father waiting for his dinner. So come on. (*She tugs at his hand and he follows her up the steps. Her manner changes to worried solicitude.*) Promise me you'll eat something, Jim. You've got to eat. You can't go on the way you are, drinking and never eating, hardly. You're killing yourself.

TYRONE (*sardonically*). That's right. Mother me, Josie, I love it.

JOSIE (*bullyingly*). I will, then. You need one to take care of you.

(*They disappear inside the house.*)

CURTAIN

ACT TWO

SCENE. *The same, with the wall of the living room removed. It is a clear warm moonlight night, around eleven o'clock. Josie is sitting on the steps before the front door. She has changed to her Sunday best, a cheap dark blue dress, black stockings and shoes. Her hair is carefully arranged, and by way of adornment a white flower is pinned on her bosom. She is hunched up, elbows on knees, her chin in her hands. There is an expression on her face we have not seen before, a look of sadness and loneliness and humiliation.*

She sighs and gets slowly to her feet, her body stiff from sitting long in the same position. She goes into the living room, fumbles around for a box of matches, and lights a kerosene lamp on the table.

The living room is small, low-ceilinged, with faded, fly-specked wallpaper, a floor of bare boards. It is cluttered up with furniture that looks as if it had been picked up at a fire sale. There is a table at centre, a disreputable old Morris chair beside it; two ugly sideboards, one at left, the other at right-rear; a porch rocking-chair, painted green, with a hole in its cane bottom; a bureau against the rear wall, with two chairs on either side of a door to the kitchen. On the bureau is an alarm clock which shows the time to be five past eleven. At right-front is the door to Josie's bedroom.

JOSIE (*looks at the clock — dully*). Five past eleven, and he said he'd be here around nine. (*Suddenly in a burst of humiliated anger, she tears off the flower pinned to her bosom and throws it in the corner.*) To hell with you, Jim Tyrone!

(*From down the road, the quiet of the night is shattered by a burst of melancholy song. It is unmistakably Hogan's voice wailing an old Irish lament at the top of his lungs. Josie starts — then frowns irritably.*)

What's bringing him home an hour before the Inn closes? He must be more paralysed than ever I've known him. (*She listens to the singing — grimly.*) Ah, here you come, do you, as full as a tick! I'll give you a welcome, if you start cutting up! I'm in no mood to put up with you.

(*She goes into her bedroom and returns with her broomstick club. Outside the singing grows louder as Hogan approaches the house. He only remembers one verse of the song and he has been repeating it.*)

HOGAN.

"Oh, the praties they grow small
Over here, over here,
Oh, the praties they grow small
Over here.
Oh, the praties they grow small
And we dig them in the fall
And we eat them skins and all
Over here, over here."

(*He enters left-front, weaving and lurching a bit. But he is not as drunk as he appears. Or rather, he is one of those people who can drink an enormous amount and be absolutely plastered when they want to be for their own pleasure, but at the same time are able to pull themselves together when they wish and be cunningly clear-headed. Just now, he is letting himself go and getting great satisfaction from it. He pauses and bellows belligerently at the house.*)

Hurroo! Down with all tyrants, male and female! To hell with England, and God damn Standard Oil!

JOSIE (*shouts back*). Shut up your noise, you crazy old billy goat!

HOGAN (*hurt and mournful*). A sweet daughter and a sweet welcome home in the dead of night. (*Beginning to boil.*) Old goat! There's respect for you! (*Angrily — starting for the front door.*) Crazy billy goat, is it? Be God, I'll learn you manners! (*He pounds on the door with his fist.*) Open the door! Open this door, I'm saying, before I drive a fist through it, or kick it into flinders! (*He gives it a kick.*)

JOSIE. It's not locked, you drunken old loon! Open it yourself!

HOGAN (*turns the knob and stamps in*). Drunken old loon, am I? Is that the way to address your father?

JOSIE. No. It's too damned good for him.

HOGAN. It's time I taught you a lesson. Be Jaysus, I'll take you over my knee and spank your tail, if you are as big as a cow! (*He makes a lunge to grab her.*)

JOSIE. Would you, though! Take that, then! (*She raps him smartly, but lightly, on his bald spot with the end of her broom handle.*)

HOGAN (*with an exaggerated howl of pain*). Ow! (*His anger evaporates and he rubs the top of his head ruefully — with bitter complaint.*) God forgive you, it's a great shame to me I've raised a daughter so cowardly she has to use a club.

JOSIE (*puts her club on the table – grimly*). Now I've no club.

HOGAN (*evades the challenge*). I never thought I'd see the day when a daughter of mine would be such a coward as to threaten her old father when he's helpless drunk and can't hit back. (*He slumps down on the Morris chair.*)

JOSIE. Ah, that's better. Now that little game is over. (*Then angrily.*) Listen to me, Father. I have no patience left, so get up from that chair, and go in your room, and go to bed, or I'll take you by the scruff of your neck and the seat of your pants and throw you in and lock the door on you! I mean it, now! (*On the verge of angry tears.*) I've had all I can bear this night, and I want some peace and sleep, and not to listen to an old lush!

HOGAN (*appears drunker, his head wagging, his voice thick, his talk rambling*). That's right. Fight with me. My own daughter has no feelings or sympathy. As if I hadn't enough after what's happened tonight.

JOSIE (*with angry disgust*). Och, don't try — (*Then curiously.*) What's happened? I thought something must be queer, you coming home before the Inn closed, but then I thought maybe for once you'd drunk all you could hold. (*Scathingly.*) And, God pity you, if you ain't that full, you're damned close to it.

HOGAN. Go on. Make fun of me. Old lush! You wouldn't feel so comical, if — (*He stops, mumbling to himself.*)

JOSIE. If what?

HOGAN. Never mind. Never mind. I didn't come home to fight, but seek comfort in your company. And if I was singing coming along the road, it was only because there's times you have to sing to keep from crying.

JOSIE. I can see you crying!

HOGAN. You will. And you'll see yourself crying, too,

when — (*He stops again and mumbles to himself.*)

JOSIE. When what? (*Exasperatedly.*) Will you stop your whiskey drooling and talk plain?

HOGAN (*thickly*). No matter. No matter. Leave me alone.

JOSIE (*angrily*). That's good advice. To hell with you! I know your game. Nothing at all has happened. All you want is to keep me up listening to your guff. Go to your room, I'm saying, before —

HOGAN. I won't. I couldn't sleep with my thoughts tormented the way they are. I'll stay here in this chair, and you go to your room and let me be.

JOSIE (*snorts*). And have you singing again in a minute and smashing the furniture —

HOGAN. Sing, is it? Are you making fun again? I'd give a keen of sorrow or howl at the moon like an old mangy hound in his sadness if I knew how, but I don't. So rest aisy. You won't hear a sound from me. Go on and snore like a pig to your heart's content. (*He mourns drunkenly.*) A fine daughter! I'd get more comfort from strangers.

JOSIE. Och, for God's sake, dry up! You'll sit in the dark then. I won't leave the lamp lit for you to turn over and burn down the house. (*She reaches out to turn down the lamp.*)

HOGAN (*thickly*). Let it burn to the ground. A hell of a lot I care if it burns.

JOSIE (*in the act of turning down the lamp, stops and stares at him, puzzled and uneasy*). I never heard you talk that way before, no matter how drunk you were. (*He mumbles. Her tone becomes persuasive.*) What's happened to you, Father?

HOGAN (*bitterly*). Ah, it's "Father" now, is it, not old billy goat? Well, thank God for small favours. (*With heavy sarcasm.*) Oh, nothing's happened to me at all, at all. A trifle, only. I wouldn't waste your time mentioning it, or keep you up when you want sleep so bad.

JOSIE (*angrily*). Och, you old loon, I'm sick of you. Sleep it off till you get some sense. (*She reaches for the lamp again.*)

HOGAN. Sleep it off? We'll see if you sleep it off when you know — (*He lapses into drunken mumbling.*)

JOSIE (*again stares at him*). Know what, Father?

HOGAN (*mumbles*). The son of a bitch!

JOSIE (*trying a lighter tone*). Sure, there's a lot of those in the neighbourhood. Which one do you mean? Is Harder on your mind again?

HOGAN (*thickly*). He's one and a prize one, but I don't mean him. I'll say this for Harder, you know what to expect from him. He's no wolf in sheep's clothing, nor a treacherous snake in the grass who stabs you in the back with a knife —

JOSIE (*apprehensive now — forces a joke*). Sure, if you've found a snake who can stab you with a knife, you'd better join the circus with him and make a pile of money.

HOGAN (*bitterly*). Make jokes, God forgive you! You'll soon laugh from the wrong end of your mouth! (*He mumbles.*) Pretending he's our friend! The lying bastard!

JOSIE (*bristles resentfully*). Is it Jim Tyrone you're calling hard names?

HOGAN. That's right. Defend him, you big soft fool! Faith, you're a prize dunce! You've had a good taste of believing his word, waiting hours for him dressed up in your best like a poor sheep without pride or spirit —

JOSIE (*stung*). Shut up! I was calling him a lying bastard myself before you came, and saying I'd never speak to him again. And I knew all along he'd never remember to keep his date after he got drunk.

HOGAN. He's not so drunk he forgot to attend to business.

JOSIE (*as if she hadn't heard — defiantly*). I'd have stayed up anyway a beautiful night like this to enjoy the moonlight, if there wasn't a Jim Tyrone in the world.

HOGAN (*with heavy sarcasm*). In your best shoes and stockings? Well, well. Sure, the moon must feel flattered by your attentions.

JOSIE (*furiously*). You won't feel flattered if I knock you tail over tincup out of that chair! And stop your whiskey gabble about Jim. I see what you're driving at with your dark hints and curses, and if you think I'll believe — (*With forced assurance.*) Sure, I know what's happened as well as if I'd been there. Jim saw you'd got drunker than usual and you were an easy mark for a joke, and he's made a goat of you!

HOGAN (*bitterly*). Goat, again! (*He struggles from his chair and stands swaying unsteadily — with offended dignity.*) All right, I won't say another word. There's no use telling the truth to a bad-tempered woman in love.

JOSIE. Love be damned! I hate him now!

HOGAN. Be Christ, you have me stumped. A great proud slut who's played games with half the men around here, and now you act like a numbskull virgin that can't believe a man would tell her a lie!

JOSIE (*threateningly*). If you're going to your room, you'd better go quick!

HOGAN (*fixes his eyes on the door at rear — with dignity*). That's where I'm going, yes — to talk to meself so I'll know someone with brains is listening. Good night to you, Miss Hogan. (*He starts — swerves left — tries to correct this and lurches right and bumps against her, clutching the supporting arm she stretches out.*)

JOSIE. God help you, if you try to go upstairs now, you'll end up in the cellar.

HOGAN (*hanging on to her arm and shoulder — maudlinly affectionate now*). You're right. Don't listen to me. I'm wrong to bother you. You've had sorrow enough this night. Have a good sleep, while you can, Josie, darlin' — and good night and God bless you. (*He tries to kiss her, but she wards him off and steers him back to the chair.*)

JOSIE. Sit down before you split in pieces on the floor and I have to get the wheelbarrow to collect you. (*She dumps him in the chair where he sprawls limply, his chin on his chest.*)

HOGAN (*mumbles dully*). It's too late. It's all settled. We're helpless, entirely.

JOSIE (*really worried now*). How is it all settled? If you're helpless, I'm not. (*Then as he doesn't reply — scornfully.*) It's the first time I ever heard you admit you were licked. And it's the first time I ever saw you so paralysed you couldn't shake the whiskey from your brains and get your head clear when you wanted. Sure, that's always been your pride — and now look at you, the stupid object you are, mumbling and drooling!

HOGAN (*struggles up in his chair — angrily*). Shut up your insults! Be God, I can get my head clear if I like! (*He shakes his head violently.*) There! It's clear. I can tell you each thing that happened tonight as clear as if I'd not taken a drop, if you'll listen and not keep calling me a liar.

JOSIE. I'll listen, now I see you have hold of your wits.

HOGAN. All right, then. I'll begin at the beginning when him and me left here, and you gave him a sweet smile, and rolled your big beautiful cow's eyes at him, and wiggled your backside, and stuck out your beautiful breasts you know he admires, and said in a sick sheep's voice, "Don't forget our moonlight date, Jim."

JOSIE (*with suppressed fury*). You're a —! I never —! You old —!

HOGAN. And he said: "You bet I won't forget, Josie."

JOSIE. The lying crook!

HOGAN (*his voice begins to sink into a dejected monotone*). We went to the Inn and started drinking whiskey. And I got drunk.

JOSIE (*exasperatedly*). I guessed that! And Jim got drunk, too. And then what?

HOGAN (*dully*). Who knows how drunk he got? He had one of his queer fits when you can't tell. He's the way I told you about this morning, when he talks like a Broadway crook, who'd sell his soul for a price, and there's a sneering divil in him, and he loves to pick out the weakness in people and say cruel, funny things that flay the hide off them, or play cruel jokes on them. (*With sudden rage.*) God's curse on him, I'll wager he's laughing to himself this minute, thinking it's the cutest joke in the world, the fools he's made of us. You in particular. Be God, I had my suspicions, at least, but your head was stuffed with mush and love, and you wouldn't —

JOSIE (*furiously*). You'll tell that lie about my love once too often! And I'll play a joke on him yet that'll make him sorry he —

HOGAN (*sunk in drunken defeatism again*). It's too late. You shouldn't have let him get away from you to the Inn. You should have kept him here. Then maybe, if you'd got him drunk enough you could have — (*His head nodding, his eyes blinking — thickly.*) But it's no good talking now — no good at all — no good —

JOSIE (*gives him a shake*). Keep hold of your wits or I'll give you a cuff on both ears! Will you stop blathering like an old woman and tell me plainly what he's done!

HOGAN. He's agreed to sell the farm, that's what! Simpson came to the Inn to see him with a new offer from Harder. Ten thousand, cash.

JOSIE (*overwhelmed*). Ten thousand! Sure, three is all it's worth at most. And two was what you offered that Jim promised —

HOGAN. What's money to Harder? After what we did to him, all he wants is revenge. And here's where he's foxy. Simpson must have put him up to it knowing how Jim hates it here living on a small allowance, and he longs to go back to Broadway and his whores. Jim won't have to wait for his half of the cash till the estate's settled. Harder offers to give him five thousand cash as a loan against the estate the second the sale is made. Jim can take the next train to New York.

JOSIE (*tensely, on the verge of tears*). And Jim accepted? I don't believe it!

HOGAN. Don't then. Be God, you'll believe it tomorrow! Harder proposed that he meet with Jim and the executors in the morning and settle it, and Jim promised Simpson he would.

JOSIE (*desperately*). Maybe he'll get so drunk he'll never remember —

HOGAN. He won't. Harder's coming in his automobile to pick him up and make sure of him. Anyway don't think because he forgot you were waiting — in the moonlight, eating your heart out, that he'd ever miss a date with five thousand dollars, and all the pretty whores of Broadway he can buy with it.

JOSIE (*distractedly*). Will you shut up! (*Angrily.*) And where were you when all this happened? Couldn't you do anything to stop it, you old loon?

HOGAN. I couldn't. Simpson came and sat at the table with us —

JOSIE. And you let him!

HOGAN. Jim invited him. Anyway, I wanted to find out what trick he had up his sleeve, and what Jim would do. When it was all over, I got up and took a swipe at Simpson, but I missed him. (*With drunken sadness.*) I was too drunk — too drunk — too drunk — I missed him, God forgive me! (*His chin sinks on his chest and his eyes shut.*)

JOSIE (*shakes him*). If you don't keep awake, be God, I won't miss you!

HOGAN. I was going to take a swipe at Jim, too, but I couldn't do it. My heart was too broken with sorrow. I'd come to love him like a son — a real son of my heart! — to take the place of that jackass, Mike, and me two other jackasses.

JOSIE (*her face hard and bitter*). I think now Mike was the only one in this house with sense.

HOGAN. I was too drowned in sorrow by his betraying me — and you he'd pretended to like so much. So I only called him a dirty lying skunk of a treacherous bastard, and I turned my back on him and left the Inn, and I made myself sing on the road so he'd hear, and they'd all hear in the Inn, to show them I didn't care a damn.

JOSIE (*scathingly*). Sure, wasn't you the hero! A hell of a lot of good —

HOGAN. Ah, well, I suppose the temptation was too great. He's weak, with one foot in the grave from whiskey. Maybe we shouldn't blame him.

JOSIE (*her eyes flashing*). Not blame him? Well, I blame him, God damn him! Are you making excuses for him, you old fool?

HOGAN. I'm not. He's a dirty snake! But I was thinking how do I know what I wouldn't do for five thousand cash, and how do you know what you wouldn't do?

JOSIE. Nothing could make me betray him! (*Her face grows hard and bitter.*) Or it couldn't before. There's nothing I wouldn't do now.

(*Hogan suddenly begins to chuckle.*)

Do you think I'm lying? Just give me a chance —

HOGAN. I remembered something. (*He laughs drunkenly.*) Be Christ, Josie, for all his Broadway wisdom about women, you've made a prize damned fool of him and that's some satisfaction!

JOSIE (*bewildered*). How'd you mean?

HOGAN. You'll never believe it. Neither did I, but he kept on until, be God, I saw he really meant it.

JOSIE. Meant what?

HOGAN. It was after he'd turned queer — early in the night before Simpson came. He started talking about you, as if you was on his mind, worrying him — and before he finished I take my oath I began to hope you could really work Mike's first scheme on him, if you got him alone in the moonlight, because all his gab was about his great admiration for you.

JOSIE. Och! The liar!

HOGAN. He said you had great beauty in you that no one appreciated but him.

JOSIE (*shakenly*). You're lying.

HOGAN. Great strength you had, and great pride, he said — and great goodness, no less! But here's where you've made a prize jackass of him, like I said. (*With a drunken leer.*) Listen now, darlin', and don't drop dead with amazement. (*He leans toward her and whispers.*) He believes you're a virgin!

(*Josie stiffens as if she'd been insulted. Hogan goes on.*)

He does, so help me! He means it, the poor dunce! He thinks you're a poor innocent virgin! He thinks it's all boasting and pretending you've done about being a slut. (*He chuckles.*) A virgin, no less! You!

JOSIE (*furiously*). Stop saying it! Boasting and pretending, am I? The dirty liar!

HOGAN. Faith, you don't have to tell me. (*Then he looks at her in drunken surprise — thickly.*) Are you taking it as an insult? Why the hell don't you laugh? Be God, you ought to see what a stupid sheep that makes him.

JOSIE (*forces a laugh*). I do see it.

HOGAN (*chuckling drunkenly*). Oh, be God, I've just remembered another thing, Josie. I know why he didn't keep his date with you. It wasn't that he'd forgot. He remembered well enough, for he talked about it —

JOSIE. You mean he deliberately, knowing I'd be

waiting — (*Fiercely.*) God damn him!

HOGAN. He as much as told me his reason, though he wouldn't come out with it plain, me being your father. His conscience was tormenting him. He's going to leave you alone and not see you again — for your sake, because he loves you! (*He chuckles.*)

JOSIE (*looks stricken and bewildered — her voice trembling*). Loves me? You're making it up.

HOGAN. I'm not. I know it sounds crazy but —

JOSIE. What did he mean, for my sake?

HOGAN. Can't you see? You're a pure virgin to him, but all the same there's things besides your beautiful soul he feels drawn to, like your beautiful hair and eyes, and —

JOSIE (*strickenly*). Och, don't, Father! You know I'm only a big —

HOGAN (*as if she hadn't spoken*). So he'll keep away from temptation because he can't trust himself, and it'd be a sin on his conscience if he was to seduce you. (*He laughs drunkenly.*) Oh, be God! If that ain't rich!

JOSIE (*her voice trembles*). So that was his reason — (*Then angrily.*) So he thinks all he has to do is crook a finger and I'll fall for him, does he, the vain Broadway crook!

HOGAN (*chuckling*). Be Jaysus, it was the maddest thing in the world, him gabbing like a soft loon about you — and there at the bar in plain sight was two of the men you've been out with, the gardener at Smith's and Regan, the chauffeur for Driggs, having a drink together!

JOSIE (*with a twitching smile*). It must have been mad, surely. I wish I'd been there to laugh up my sleeve. (*Angry.*) But what's all his crazy lying blather got to do with him betraying us and selling the place?

HOGAN (*at once hopelessly dejected again*). Nothing at all. I only thought you'd like to know you'd had that much revenge.

JOSIE. A hell of a revenge! I'll have a better one than that on him — or I'll try to! I'm not like you, owning up I'm beaten and crying wurra-wurra like a coward and getting hopeless drunk! (*She gives him a shake.*) Get your wits about you and answer me this: Did Simpson get him to sign a paper?

HOGAN. No, but what good is that? In the morning he'll sign all they shove in front of him.

JOSIE. It's this good. It means we still have a chance. Or I have.

HOGAN. What chance? Are you going to beg him to take pity on us?

JOSIE. I'll see him in hell first! There's another chance, and a good one. But I'll need your help — (*Angrily.*) And look at you, your brains drowned in whiskey, so I can't depend on you!

HOGAN (*rousing himself*). You can, if there's any chance. Be God, I'll make myself as sober as a judge for you in the wink of an eye! (*Then dejectedly.*) But what can you do now, darlin'? You haven't even got him here. He's down at the Inn sitting alone, drinking and dreaming of the little whores he'll be with tomorrow night on Broadway.

JOSIE. I'll get him here! I'll humble my pride and go down to the Inn for him! And if he doesn't want to come I've a way to make him. I'll raise a scene and pretend I'm in a rage because he forgot his date. I'll disgrace him till he'll be glad to come with me to shut me up. I know his weakness, and it's his vanity about his women. If I was a dainty, pretty tart he'd be proud I'd raise a rumpus about him. But when it's a big, ugly hulk like me — (*She falters and forces herself to go on.*) If he ever was tempted to want me, he'd be ashamed of it. That's the truth behind the lies he told you of his conscience and his fear he might ruin me, God damn him!

HOGAN. No, he meant it, Josie. But never mind that now. Let's say you've got him here. Then what will you do?

JOSIE. I told you this morning if he ever broke his promise to us I'd do anything and not mind how crooked it was. And I will! Your part in it is to come at sunrise with witnesses and catch us in — (*She falters.*)

HOGAN. In bed, is it? Then it's Mike's second scheme you're thinking about?

JOSIE. I told you I didn't care how dirty a trick — (*With a hard bitter laugh.*) The dirtier the better now!

HOGAN. But how'll you get him in bed, with all his honourable scruples, thinking you're a virgin? But I'm forgetting he stayed away because he was afraid he'd be tempted. So maybe —

JOSIE (*tensely*). For the love of God, don't harp on his lies. He won't be tempted at all. But I'll get him so drunk he'll fall asleep and I'll carry him in and put him in bed —

HOGAN. Be God, that's the way! But you'll have to get a pile of whiskey down him. You'll never do it unless you're more sociable and stop looking at him, the way you do, whenever he takes a drink, as if you was praying Almighty God to forgive a poor drunkard. You've got to encourage him. The best way would be for you to drink with him. It would put him at his ease and unsuspecting, and it'd give you courage, too, so you'd act bold for a change instead of giving him brazen talk he's tired of hearing, while you act shy as a mouse.

JOSIE (*gives her father a bitter, resentful look*). You're full of sly advice all of a sudden, ain't you? You dirty little tick!

HOGAN (*angrily*). Didn't you tell me to get hold of my wits? Be God, if you want me drunk, I've only to let go. That'd suit me. I want to forget my sorrow, and I've no faith in your scheme because you'll be too full of scruples. Like the drinking. You're such a virtuous teetotaller —

JOSIE. I've told you I'd do anything now! (*Then confusedly.*) All I meant was, it's not right, a father to tell his daughter how to — (*Then angrily.*) I don't need your advice. Haven't I had every man I want around here?

HOGAN. Ah, thank God, that sounds natural! Be God, I thought you'd started playing virgin with me just because that Broadway sucker thinks you're one.

JOSIE (*furiously*). Shut up! I'm not playing anything. And don't worry I can't do my part of the trick.

HOGAN. That's the talk! But let me get it all clear. I come at sunrise with my witnesses, and you've forgot to lock your door, and we walk in, and there's the two of you in bed, and I raise the roof and threaten him if he don't marry you —

JOSIE. Marry him? After what he's done to us? I wouldn't marry him now if he was the last man on earth! All we want is a paper signed by him with witnesses that he'll sell the farm to you for the price you offered, and not to Harder.

HOGAN. Well, that's justice, but that's all it is. I thought you wanted to make him pay for his black treachery against us, the dirty bastard!

JOSIE. I do want! (*She again gives him a bitter resentful glance.*) It's the estate money you're thinking of, isn't it? Leave it to you! (*Hastily.*) Well, so am I! I'd like to get my hooks on it! (*With a hard, brazen air.*) Be God, if I'm to play whore, I deserve my pay! We'll make him sign a paper he owes me ten thousand dollars the minute the estate is settled. (*She laughs.*) How's that? I'll bet none of his tarts on Broadway ever got a thousandth part of that out of him, no matter how dainty and pretty! (*Laughing again.*) And here's what'll be the greatest joke to teach him a lesson. He'll pay it for nothing! I'll get him in bed but I'll never let him —

HOGAN (*with delighted admiration*). Och, by Jaysus, Josie, that's the best yet! (*He slaps his thigh enthusiastically.*) Oh, that'll teach him to double-cross his friends! That'll show him two can play at tricks! And him believing you so innocent! Be God, you'll make him the prize sucker of the world! Won't I roar inside me when I see his face in the morning! (*He bursts into coarse laughter.*)

JOSIE (*again with illogical resentment*). Stop laughing! You're letting yourself be drunk again. (*Then with a hard, business-like air.*) We've done enough talking. Let's start —

HOGAN. Wait, now. There's another thing. Just what do you want me to threaten him with when I catch you? That we'll sue him for outraging your virtue? Sure, his lawyer would have all your old flames in the witness box, till the jury would think you'd been faithful to the male inhabitants of America. So what threat — I can't think of any he wouldn't laugh at.

JOSIE (*tensely*). Well, I can! Do I have to tell you his weakness again? It's his vanity about women, and his Broadway pride he's so wise no woman could fool him. It's the disgrace to his vanity — being caught with the likes of me — (*Falteringly, but forcing herself to go on.*) My mug beside his in all the newspapers — the New York papers, too — he'll see the whole of Broadway splitting their sides laughing at him — and he'll give anything to keep us quiet, I tell you. He will! I know him! So don't worry — (*She ends up on the verge of bitter humiliated tears.*)

HOGAN (*without looking at her — enthusiastic again*). Be God, you're right!

JOSIE (*gives him a bitter glance — fiercely*). Then get the hell out of that chair and let's start it! (*He gets up. She surveys him resentfully.*) You're steady on your pins, ain't you, you scheming old thief, now there's the smell of money around! (*Quickly.*) Well, I'm glad. I know I can depend on you now. You'll walk down to the Inn with me and hide outside until you see me come out with him. Then you can sneak in the Inn yourself and pick the witnesses to stay up with you. But mind you don't get drunk again, and let them get too drunk.

HOGAN. I won't, I take my oath! (*He pats her on the shoulder approvingly.*) Be God, you've got the proud, fighting spirit in you that never says die, and you make me ashamed of my weakness. You're that eager now, be damned if I don't almost think you're glad of the excuse!

JOSIE (*stiffens*). Excuse for what, you old —

HOGAN. To show him no man can get the best of you — what else? — like you showed all the others.

JOSIE. I'll show him to his sorrow! (*Then abruptly, starting for the screen door at left.*) Come on. We've no time to waste. (*But when she gets to the door, she appears suddenly hesitant and timid — hurriedly.*) Wait. I'd better give a look at myself in the mirror. (*In a brazen tone.*) Sure, those in my trade have to look their best! (*She *hurries back across the room into her bedroom and closes the door.*)

(*Hogan stares after her. Abruptly he ceases to look like a drunk who, by an effort, is keeping himself half-sober. He is a man who has been drinking a lot but is still clear-headed and has complete control of himself.*)

HOGAN (*watches the crack under Josie's door and speaks half-aloud to himself, shaking his head pityingly*). A look in the mirror and she's forgot to light her lamp! (*Remorsefully.*) God forgive me, it's bitter medicine. But it's the only way I can see that has a chance now.

(*Josie's door opens. At once he is as he was. She comes out, a fixed smile on her lips, her head high, her face set defiantly. But she has evidently been crying.*)

JOSIE (*brazenly*). There, now. Don't I look ten thousand dollars' worth to any drunk?

HOGAN. You look a million, darlin'!

JOSIE (*goes to the screen door and pushes it open with the manner of one who has burned all bridges*). Come along, then. (*She goes out. He follows close on her heels. She stops abruptly on the first step — startledly.*) Look! There's someone on the road —

HOGAN (*pushes past her down the steps — peering off left-front — as if aloud to himself, in dismay*). Be God, it's him! I never thought —

JOSIE (*as if aloud to herself*). So he didn't forget —

HOGAN (*quickly*). Well, it proves he can't keep away from you, and that'll make it easier for you — (*Then furiously.*) Oh, the dirty, double-crossing bastard! The nerve of him! Coming to call on you, after making you wait for hours, thinking you don't know what he's done to us this night, and it'll be a fine cruel joke to blarney you in the moonlight, and you trusting him like a poor sheep, and never suspecting —

JOSIE (*stung*). Shut up! I'll teach him who's the joker! I'll let him go on as if you hadn't told me what he's done —

HOGAN. Yes, don't let him suspect it, or you wouldn't fool him. He'd know you were after revenge. But he can see me here now. I can't sneak away or he'd be suspicious. We've got to think of a new scheme quick to get me away —

JOSIE (*quickly*). I know how. Pretend you're as drunk as when you came. Make him believe you're so drunk you don't remember what he's done, so he can't suspect you told me.

HOGAN. I will. Be God, Josie, damned if I don't think he's so queer drunk himself he don't remember, or he'd never come here.

JOSIE. The drunker he is the better! (*Lowering her voice — quickly.*) He's turned in the gate where he can hear us. Pretend we're fighting and I'm driving you off till you're sober. Say you won't be back tonight. It'll make him sure he'll have the night alone with me. You start the fight.

HOGAN (*becomes at once very drunk. He shouts*). Put me out of my own home, will you, you undutiful slut!

JOSIE. Celebration or not, I'll have no drunks cursing and singing all night. Go back to the Inn.

HOGAN. I will! I'll get a room and two bottles and stay drunk as long as I please!

JOSIE. Don't come back till you've slept it off, or I'll wipe the floor with you!

(*Tyrone enters, left-front. He does not appear to be drunk — that is, he shows none of the usual symptoms. He seems much the same as in Act One. The only perceptible change is that his eyes have a peculiar fixed, glazed look, and there is a certain vague quality in his manner and speech, as if he were a bit hazy and absent-minded.*)

TYRONE (*dryly*). Just in time for the Big Bout. Or is this the final round?

HOGAN (*whirls on him unsteadily*). Who the hell — (*Peering at him.*) Oh, it's you, is it?

TYRONE. What was the big idea, Phil, leaving me flat?

HOGAN. Leave you flat? Be Jaysus, that reminds me I owe you a swipe on the jaw for something. What was it? Be God, I'm too drunk to remember. But here it is, anyway.

(*He turns loose a round-house swing that misses Tyrone by a couple of feet, and reels away. Tyrone regards him with vague surprise.*)

JOSIE. Stop it, you damned old fool, and get out of here!

HOGAN. Taking his side against your poor old father, are you? A hell of a daughter! (*He draws himself up with drunken dignity.*) Don't expect me home tonight, Miss Hogan, or tomorrow either, maybe. You can take your bad temper out on your sweetheart, here. (*He starts off down the road, left-front, with a last word over his shoulder.*) Bad luck to you both. (*He disappears. A moment later he begins to bawl his mournful Irish song.*) "Oh, the praties they grow small, Over here, over here," etc.

(*During a part of the following scene the song continues to be heard at intervals, receding as he gets farther off on his way to the Inn.*)

JOSIE. Well, thank God. That's good riddance. (*She comes to Tyrone, who stands staring after Hogan with a puzzled look.*)

TYRONE. I've never seen him that stinko before. Must have got him all of a sudden. He didn't seem so lit up at the Inn, but I guess I wasn't paying much attention.

JOSIE (*forcing a playful air*). I should think, if you were a real gentleman, you'd be apologizing to me, not thinking of him. Don't you know you're two hours and a half late? I oughtn't to speak to you, if I had any pride.

TYRONE (*stares at her curiously*). You've got too damn much pride, Josie. That's the trouble.

JOSIE. And just what do you mean by that, Jim?

TYRONE (*shrugs his shoulders*). Nothing. Forget it. I do apologize, Josie. I'm damned sorry. Haven't any excuse. Can't think up a lie. (*Staring at her curiously again.*) Or, now I think of it, I had a damned good honourable excuse, but — (*He shrugs.*) Nuts. Forget it.

JOSIE. Holy Joseph, you're full of riddles tonight. Well, I don't need excuses. I forgive you, anyway, now you're here. (*She takes his hand — playfully.*) Come on now, and we'll sit on my bedroom steps and be romantic in the moonlight, like we planned to. (*She leads him there. He goes along in an automatic way, as if only half-conscious of what he is doing. She sits on the top step and pulls him down on the step beneath her. A pause. He stares vaguely at nothing. She bends to give him an uneasy appraising glance.*)

TYRONE (*suddenly, begins to talk mechanically*). Had to get out of the damned Inn. I was going batty alone there. The old heebie-jeebies. So I came to you. (*He pauses — then adds with strange, wondering sincerity.*) I've really begun to love you a lot, Josie.

JOSIE (*blurts out bitterly*). Yes, you've proved that tonight, haven't you? (*Hurriedly regaining her playful tone.*) But never mind. I said I'd forgive you for being so late. So go on about love. I'm all ears.

TYRONE (*as if he hadn't listened*). I thought you'd have given me up and gone to bed. I remember I had some nutty idea I'd get in bed with you — just to lie with my head on your breast.

JOSIE (*moved in spite of herself — but keeps her bold, playful tone*). Well, maybe I'll let you — (*Hurriedly.*) Later on, I mean. The night's young yet, and we'll have it all to ourselves. (*Boldly again.*) But here's for a starter. (*She puts her arms around him and draws him back till his head is on her breast.*) There, now.

TYRONE (*relaxes — simply and gratefully.*) Thanks, Josie. (*He closes his eyes.*)

(*For a moment, she forgets everything and stares down at his face with a passionate, possessive tenderness. A pause. From far-off on the road to the Inn, Hogan's mournful song drifts back through the moonlight quiet: "Oh, the praties they grow small, Over here, over here." Tyrone rouses himself and straightens up. He acts embarrassed, as if he felt he'd been making a fool of himself — mockingly.*)

Hark, Hark, the Donegal lark! "Thou wast not born for death, immortal bird." Can't Phil sing anything but that damned dirge, Josie? (*She doesn't reply. He goes on hazily.*) Still, it seems to belong tonight — in the moonlight — or in my mind — (*He quotes.*)

"Now more than ever seems it rich to die,
To cease upon the midnight with no pain,
In such an ecstasy!"

(*He has recited this with deep feeling. Now he sneers.*) Good God! Ode to Phil the Irish Nightingale! I must have the D.T.'s.

JOSIE (*her face grown bitter*). Maybe it's only your bad conscience.

TYRONE (*starts guiltily and turns to stare into her face — suspiciously*). What put that in your head? Conscience about what?

JOSIE (*quickly*). How would I know, if you don't? (*Forcing a playful tone.*) For the sin of wanting to be in bed with me. Maybe that's it.

TYRONE (*with strange relief*). Oh. (*A bit shamefacedly.*) Forget that stuff, Josie. I was half nutty.

JOSIE (*bitterly*). Och, for the love of God, don't apologize as if you was ashamed of — (*She catches herself.*)

TYRONE (*with a quick glance at her face*). All right. I certainly won't apologize — if you're not kicking. I was afraid I might have shocked your modesty.

JOSIE (*roughly*). *My* modesty? Be God, I didn't know I had any left.

TYRONE (*draws away from her — irritably*). Nix, Josie. Lay off that line, for tonight at least. (*He adds slowly.*) I'd like tonight to be different.

JOSIE. Different from what? (*He doesn't answer. She forces a light tone.*) All right. I'll be as different as you please.

TYRONE (*simply*). Thanks, Josie. Just be yourself. (*Again as if he were ashamed, or afraid he had revealed some weakness — off-handedly.*) This being out in the moonlight instead of the lousy Inn isn't a bad bet, at that.

I don't know why I hang out in that dump, except I'm even more bored in the so-called good hotels in this hick town.

JOSIE (*trying to examine his face without his knowing*). Well, you'll be back on Broadway soon now, won't you?

TYRONE. I hope so.

JOSIE. Then you'll have all the pretty little tarts to comfort you when you get your sorrowful spell on.

TYRONE. Oh, to hell with the rough stuff, Josie! You promised you'd can it tonight.

JOSIE (*tensely*). You're a fine one to talk of promises!

TYRONE (*vaguely surprised by her tone*). What's the matter? Still sore at me for being late?

JOSIE (*quickly*). I'm not. I was teasing you. To prove there's no hard feelings, how would you like a drink? But I needn't ask. (*She gets up.*) I'll get a bottle of his best.

TYRONE (*mechanically*). Fine. Maybe that will have some kick. The booze at the Inn didn't work tonight.

JOSIE. Well, this'll work. (*She starts to go into her bedroom.*)

(*He sits hunched up on the step, staring at nothing. She pauses in the doorway to glance back. The hard, calculating expression on her face softens. For a second she stares at him, bewildered by her conflicting feelings. Then she goes inside, leaving the door open. She opens the door from her room to the lighted living room, and is seen going to the kitchen on the way to the cellar. She has left the door from the living room to her bedroom open and the light reveals a section of the bedroom framed in the doorway behind Tyrone. The foot of the bed which occupies most of the room can be seen, and that is all except that the walls are unpainted pine boards. Tyrone continues to stare at nothing, but becomes restless. His hands and mouth twitch.*)

TYRONE (*suddenly, with intense hatred*). You rotten bastard! (*He springs to his feet—fumbles in his pockets for cigarettes—strikes a match which lights up his face, on which there is now an expression of miserable guilt. His hand is trembling so violently he cannot light the cigarette.*)

CURTAIN

ACT THREE

SCENE. *The living-room wall has been replaced and all we see now of its lighted interior is through the two windows. Otherwise, everything is the same, and this Act follows the preceding without any lapse of time.*

Tyrone is still trying with shaking hands to get his cigarette lighted. Finally he succeeds, and takes a deep inhale, and starts pacing back and forth a few steps, as if in a cell of his own thought. He swears defensively.

TYRONE. God damn it. You'll be crying in your beer in a minute. (*He begins to sing sneeringly half under his breath a snatch from an old sob song, popular in the Nineties.*)

"And baby's cries can't waken her
In the baggage coach ahead."

(*His sneer changes to a look of stricken guilt and grief.*) Christ! (*He seems about to break down and sob but he fights this back.*) Cut it out, you drunken fool!

(*Josie can be seen through the windows, returning from the kitchen. He turns with a look of relief and escape.*)

Thank God!

(*He sits on the boulder and waits. Josie stops by the table in the living room to turn down the lamp until only a dim light remains. She has a quart of whiskey under her arm, two tumblers, and a pitcher of water. She goes through her bedroom and appears in the outer doorway. Tyrone gets up.*)

Ah! At last the old booze! (*He relieves her of the pitcher and tumblers as she comes down the steps.*)

JOSIE (*with a fixed smile*). You'd think I'd been gone years. You didn't seem so perishing for a drink.

TYRONE (*in his usual, easy, kidding way*). It's you I was perishing for. I've been dying of loneliness—

JOSIE. You'll die of lying some day. But I'm glad you're alive again. I thought when I left you really were dying on me.

TYRONE. No such luck.

JOSIE. Och, don't talk like that. Come and have a drink. We'll use the boulder for a table and I'll be barkeep. (*He puts the pitcher and tumblers on the boulder and she uncorks the bottle. She takes a quick glance at his face—startledly.*) What's come over you, Jim? You look as if you've seen a ghost.

TYRONE (*looks away — dryly*). I have. My own. He's punk company.

JOSIE. Yes, it's the worst ghost of all, your own. Don't I know? But this will keep it in its place. (*She pours a tumbler half full of whiskey and hands it to him.*) Here. But wait till I join you. (*She pours the other tumbler half full.*)

TYRONE (*surprised*). Hello! I thought you never touched it.

JOSIE (*glibly*). I have on occasion. And this is one. I don't want to be left out altogether from celebrating our victory over Harder. (*She gives him a sharp bitter glance. Meeting his eyes, which are regarding her with puzzled wonder, she forces a laugh.*) Don't look at me as if I was up to some game. A drink or two will make me better company, and help me enjoy the moon and the night with you. Here's luck. (*She touches his glass with hers.*)

TYRONE (*shrugs his shoulders*). All right. Here's luck.

(*They drink. She gags and sputters. He pours water in her glass. She drinks it. He puts his glass and the pitcher back on the boulder. He keeps staring at her with a puzzled frown.*)

JOSIE. Some of it went down the wrong way.

TYRONE. So I see. That'll teach you to pour out baths instead of drinks.

JOSIE. It's the first time I ever heard you complain a drink was too big.

TYRONE. Yours was too big.

JOSIE. I'm my father's daughter. I've a strong head. So don't worry I'll pass out and you'll have to put me to bed. (*She gives a little bold laugh.*) Sure, that's a beautiful notion. I'll have to pretend I'm —

TYRONE (*irritably*). Nix on the raw stuff, Josie. Remember you said —

JOSIE (*resentment in her kidding*). I'd be different? That's right. I'm forgetting it's your pleasure to have me pretend I'm an innocent virgin tonight.

TYRONE (*in a strange tone that is almost threatening*). If you don't look out, I'll call you on that bluff, Josie. (*He stares at her with a deliberate sensualist's look that undresses her.*) I'd like to. You know that, don't you?

JOSIE (*boldly*). I don't at all. You're the one who's bluffing.

TYRONE (*grabs her in his arms — with genuine passion*). Josie! (*Then as suddenly he lets her go.*) Nix. Let's cut it out. (*He turns away. Her face betrays the confused conflict within her of fright, passion, happiness, and bitter resentment. He goes on with an abrupt change of tone.*) How about another drink? That's honest-to-God old bonded Bourbon. How the devil did Phil get hold of it?

JOSIE. Tom Lombardo, the bootlegger, gave him a case for letting him hide a truckload in our barn when the agents were after him. He stole it from a warehouse on faked permits. (*She pours out drinks as she speaks, a half tumblerful for him, a small one for herself.*) Here you are. (*She gives him his drink — smiles at him coquettishly, beginning to show the effect of her big drink by her increasingly bold manner.*) Let's sit down where the moon will be in our eyes and we'll see romance. (*She takes his arm and leads him to her bedroom steps. She sits on the top step, pulling him down beside her but on the one below. She raises her glass.*) Here's hoping before the night's out you'll have more courage and kiss me at least.

TYRONE (*frowns — then kiddingly*). That's a promise. Here's how. (*He drains his tumbler. She drinks half of hers. He puts his glass on the ground beside him. A pause. She tries to read his face without his noticing. He seems to be lapsing again into vague preoccupation.*)

JOSIE. Now don't sink back half-dead-and-alive in dreams the way you were before.

TYRONE (*quickly*). I'm not. I had a good final dose of heebie-jeebies when you were in the house. That's all for tonight. (*He adds a bit maudlinly, his two big drinks beginning to affect him.*) Let the dead past bury its dead.

JOSIE. That's the talk. There's only tonight, and the moon, and us — and the bonded Bourbon. Have another drink, and don't wait for me.

TYRONE. Not now, thanks. They're coming too fast. (*He gives her a curious, cynically amused look.*) Trying to get me soused, Josie?

JOSIE (*starts — quickly*). I'm not. Only to get you feeling happy, so you'll forget all sadness.

TYRONE (*kiddingly*). I might forget all my honourable intentions too. So look out.

JOSIE. I'll look forward to it — and I hope that's another promise, like the kiss you owe me. If you're suspicious I'm trying to get you soused — well, here goes. (*She drinks what is left in her glass.*) There, now. I must be scheming to get myself soused, too.

TYRONE. Maybe you are.

JOSIE (*resentfully*). If I was, it'd be to make you feel at home. Don't all the pretty little Broadway tarts get soused with you?

TYRONE (*irritably*). There you go again with that old line!

JOSIE. All right, I won't! (*Forcing a laugh.*) I must be

eaten up with jealousy for them, that's it.

TYRONE. You needn't be. They don't belong.

JOSIE. And I do?

TYRONE. Yes. You do.

JOSIE. For tonight only, you mean?

TYRONE. We've agreed there is only tonight — and it's to be different from any past night — for both of us.

JOSIE (*in a forced, kidding tone*). I hope it will be. I'll try to control my envy for your Broadway flames. I suppose it's because I have a picture of them in my mind as small and dainty and pretty —

TYRONE. They're just gold-digging tramps.

JOSIE (*as if he hadn't spoken*). While I'm only a big, rough, ugly cow of a woman.

TYRONE. Shut up! You're beautiful.

JOSIE (*jeeringly, but her voice trembles*). God pity the blind!

TYRONE. You're beautiful to me.

JOSIE. It must be the Bourbon —

TYRONE. You're real and healthy and clean and fine and warm and strong and kind —

JOSIE. I have a beautiful soul, you mean?

TYRONE. Well, I don't know much about ladies' souls — (*He takes her hand.*) But I do know you're beautiful. (*He kisses her hand.*) And I love you a lot — in my fashion.

JOSIE (*stammers*). Jim — (*Hastily forcing her playful tone.*) Sure, you're full of fine compliments all of a sudden, and I ought to show you how pleased I am. (*She pulls his head back and kisses him on the lips — a quick, shy kiss.*) That's for my beautiful soul.

TYRONE (*the kiss arouses his physical desire. He pulls her head down and stares into her eyes.*) You have a beautiful strong body, too, Josie — and beautiful eyes and hair, and a beautiful smile and beautiful warm breasts. (*He kisses her on the lips. She pulls back frightenedly for a second — then returns his kiss. Suddenly he breaks away — in a tone of guilty irritation.*) Nix! Nix! Don't be a fool, Josie. Don't let me pull that stuff.

JOSIE (*triumphant for a second*). You meant it! I know you meant it! (*Then with resentful bitterness — roughly.*) Be God, you're right I'm a damned fool to let you make me forget you're the greatest liar in the world! (*Quickly.*) I mean, the greatest kidder. And now, how about another drink?

TYRONE (*staring at nothing vaguely*). You don't get me, Josie. You don't know — and I hope you never will know —

JOSIE (*blurts out bitterly*). Maybe I know more than you think.

TYRONE (*as if she hadn't spoken*). There's always the aftermath that poisons you. I don't want you to be poisoned —

JOSIE. Maybe you know what you're talking about —

TYRONE. And I don't want to be poisoned myself — not again — not with you. (*He pauses — slowly.*) There have been too many nights — and dawns. This must be different. I want — (*His voice trails off into silence.*)

JOSIE (*trying to read his face — uneasily*). Don't get in one of your queer spells, now. (*She gives his shoulder a shake — forcing a light tone.*) Sure, I don't think you know what you want. Except another drink. I'm sure you want that. And I want one, too.

TYRONE (*recovering himself*). Fine! Grand idea. (*He gets up and brings the bottle from the boulder. He picks up his tumbler and pours a big drink. She is holding out her tumbler but he ignores it.*)

JOSIE. You're not polite, pouring your own first.

TYRONE. I said a drink was a grand idea — for me. Not for you. You skip this one.

JOSIE (*resentfully*). Oh, I do, do I? Are you giving me orders?

TYRONE. Yes. Take a big drink of moonlight instead.

JOSIE (*angrily*). You'll pour me a drink, if you please, Jim Tyrone, or —

TYRONE (*stares at her — then shrugs his shoulders*). All right, if you want to take it that way, Josie. It's your funeral. (*He pours a drink into her tumbler.*)

JOSIE (*ashamed but defiant — stiffly*). Thank you kindly. (*She raises her glass — mockingly.*) Here's to tonight.

(*Tyrone is staring at her, a strange bitter disgust in his eyes. Suddenly he slaps at her hand, knocking the glass to the ground.*)

TYRONE (*his voice hard with repulsion*). I've slept with drunken tramps on too many nights!

JOSIE (*stares at him, too startled and bewildered to be angry. Her voice trembles with surprising meekness*). All right, Jim, if you don't want me to —

TYRONE (*now looks as bewildered by his action as she does*). I'm sorry, Josie. Don't know what the drink got into me. (*He picks up her glass.*) Here. I'll pour you another.

JOSIE (*still meek*). No, thank you. I'll skip this one. (*She puts her glass on the ground.*) But you drink up.

TYRONE. Thanks. (*He gulps down his drink. Mechanically, as if he didn't know what he was doing, he pours another. Suddenly he blurts out with guilty loathing.*) That fat blonde pig on the train — I got her drunk! That's why — (*He stops guiltily.*)

JOSIE (*uneasily*). What are you talking about? What train?

TYRONE. No train. Don't mind me. (*He gulps down the drink and pours another with the same strange air of acting unconsciously.*) Maybe I'll tell you — later, when I'm — That'll cure you — for all time! (*Abruptly he realizes what he is saying. He gives the characteristic shrug of shoulders — cynically.*) Nuts! The Brooklyn boys are talking again. I guess I'm more stewed than I thought — in the centre of the old bean, at least. (*Dully.*) I better beat it back to the Inn and go to bed and stop bothering you, Josie.

JOSIE (*bullyingly — and pityingly*). Well, you won't, not if I have to hold you. Come on now, bring your drink and sit down like you were before. (*He does so. She pats his cheek — forcing a playful air.*) That's a good boy. And I won't take any more whiskey. I've all the effect from it I want already. Everything is far away and doesn't matter — except the moon and its dreams, and I'm part of the dreams — and you are, too. (*She adds with a rueful little laugh.*) I keep forgetting the thing I've got to remember. I keep hoping it's a lie, even though I know I'm a damned fool.

TYRONE (*hazily*). Damned fool about what?

JOSIE. Never mind. (*Forcing a laugh.*) I've just had a thought. If my poor old father had seen you knocking his prize whiskey on the ground — Holy Joseph, he'd have had three paralytic strokes!

TYRONE (*grins*). Yes, I can picture him. (*He pauses — with amused affection.*) But that's all a fake. He loves to play tightwad, but the people he likes know better. He'd give them his shirt. He's a grand old scout, Josie. (*A bit maudlin.*) The only real friend I've got left — except you. I love his guts.

JOSIE (*tensely — sickened by his hypocrisy*). Och, for the love of God —!

TYRONE (*shrugs his shoulders*). Yes, I suppose that does sound like moaning-at-the-bar stuff. But I mean it.

JOSIE. Do you? Well, I know my father's virtues without you telling me.

TYRONE. You ought to appreciate him because he worships the ground you walk on — and he knows you a lot better than you think. (*He turns to smile at her teasingly.*) As well as I do — almost.

JOSIE (*defensively*). That's not saying much. Maybe I can guess what you think you know — (*Forcing a contemptuous laugh.*) If it's that, God pity you, you're a terrible fool.

TYRONE (*teasingly*). If it's what? I haven't said anything.

JOSIE. You'd better not, or I'll die laughing at you. (*She changes the subject abruptly.*) Why don't you drink up? It makes me nervous watching you hold it as if you didn't know it was there.

TYRONE. I didn't, at that. (*He drinks.*)

JOSIE. And have another.

TYRONE (*a bit drunkenly*). Will a whore go to a picnic? Real bonded Bourbon. That's my dish. (*He goes to the boulder for the bottle. He is as steady on his feet as if he were completely sober.*)

JOSIE (*in a light tone*). Bring the bottle back so it'll be handy and you won't have to leave me. I miss you.

TYRONE (*comes back with the bottle. He smiles at her cynically*). Still trying to get me soused, Josie?

JOSIE. I'm not such a fool — with your capacity.

TYRONE. You better watch your step. It might work — and then think of how disgusted you'd feel, with me lying beside you, probably snoring, as you watched the dawn come. You don't know —

JOSIE (*defiantly*). The hell I don't! Isn't that the way I've felt with every one of them, after?

TYRONE (*as if he hadn't heard — bitterly*). But take it from me, I know. I've seen too God-damned many dawns creeping greyly over too many dirty windows.

JOSIE (*ignores this — boldly*). But it might be different with you. Love could make it different. And I've been head over heels in love ever since you said you loved my beautiful soul. (*Again he doesn't seem to have heard — resentfully.*) Don't stand there like a loon, mourning over the past. Why don't you pour yourself a drink and sit down?

TYRONE (*looks at the bottle and tumbler in his hands, as if he'd forgotten them — mechanically*). Sure thing. Real bonded Bourbon. I ought to know. If I had a dollar for every drink of it I had before Prohibition, I'd hire our dear bully, Harder, for a valet.

(*Josie stiffens and her face hardens. Tyrone pours a drink and sets the bottle on the ground. He looks up suddenly into her eyes — warningly.*)

You'd better remember I said you had beautiful eyes and hair — and breasts.

JOSIE. I remember you did. (*She tries to be calculatingly enticing.*) So sit down and I'll let you lay your head —

TYRONE. No. If you won't watch your step, I've got to. (*He sits down but doesn't lean back.*) And don't let me get away with pretending I'm so soused I don't know what I'm doing. I always know. Or part of me does. That's the trouble. (*He pauses — then bursts out in a strange threatening tone.*) You better look out, Josie. She was tickled to death to get me pie-eyed. Had an idea she could roll me, I guess. She wasn't so tickled about it — later on.

JOSIE. What she? (*He doesn't reply. She forces a light tone.*) I hope you don't think I'm scheming to roll you.

TYRONE (*vaguely*). What? (*Coming to — indignantly.*) Of course not. What are you talking about? For God's sake, you're not a tart.

JOSIE (*roughly*). No, I'm a fool. I'm always giving it away.

TYRONE (*angrily*). That lousy bluff again, eh? You're a liar! For Christ sake, quit the smut stuff, can't you!

JOSIE (*stung*). Listen to me, Jim! Drunk or not, don't you talk that way to me or —

TYRONE. How about your not talking the old smut stuff to me? You promised you'd be yourself. (*Pauses — vaguely.*) You don't get it, Josie. You see, she was one of the smuttiest talking pigs I've ever listened to.

JOSIE. What she? Do you mean the blonde on the train?

TYRONE (*starts — sharply*). Train? Who told you —? (*Quickly.*) Oh — that's right — I did say — (*Vaguely.*) What blonde? What's the difference? Coming back from the Coast. It was long ago. But it seems like tonight. There is no present or future — only the past happening over and over again — now. You can't get away from it. (*Abruptly.*) Nuts! To hell with that crap.

JOSIE. You came back from the Coast about a year ago after — (*She checks herself.*)

TYRONE (*dully*). Yes. After Mama's death. (*Quickly.*) But I've been to the Coast a lot of times during my career as a third-rate ham. I don't remember which time — or anything much — except I was pie-eyed in a drawing room the whole four days. (*Abruptly.*) What were we talking about before? What a grand guy Phil is. You ought to be glad you've got him for a father. Mine was an old bastard.

JOSIE. He wasn't! He was one of the finest, kindest gentlemen ever lived.

TYRONE (*sneeringly*). Outside the family, sure. Inside, he was a lousy tightwad bastard.

JOSIE (*repelled*). You ought to be ashamed!

TYRONE. To speak ill of the dead? Nuts! He can't hear, and he knows I hated him, anyway — as much as he hated me. I'm glad he's dead. So is he. Or he ought to be. Everyone ought to be, if they have any sense. Out of a bum racket. At peace. (*He shrugs his shoulders.*) Nuts! What of it?

JOSIE (*tensely*). Don't, Jim. I hate you when you talk like that. (*Forcing a light tone.*) Do you want to spoil our beautiful moonlight night? And don't be telling me of your old flames, on trains or not. I'm too jealous.

TYRONE (*with a shudder of disgust*). Of that pig? (*He drinks his whiskey as if to wash a bad taste from his mouth — then takes one of her hands in both of his — simply.*) You're a fool to be jealous of anyone. You're the only woman I care a damn about.

JOSIE (*deeply stirred, in spite of herself — her voice trembling*). Jim, don't — (*Forcing a tense little laugh.*) All right, I'll try and believe that — for tonight.

TYRONE (*simply*). Thanks, Josie. (*A pause. He speaks in a tone of random curiosity.*) Why did you say a while ago I'd be leaving for New York soon?

JOSIE (*stiffens — her face hardening*). Well, I was right, wasn't I? (*Unconsciously she tries to pull her hand away.*)

TYRONE. Why are you pulling your hand away?

JOSIE (*stops*). Was I? (*Forcing a smile.*) I suppose because it seems crazy for you to hold my big ugly paw so tenderly. But you're welcome to it, if you like.

TYRONE. I do like. It's strong and kind and warm — like you. (*He kisses it.*)

JOSIE (*tensely*). Och, for the love of God —! (*She jerks her hand away — then hastily forces a joking tone.*) Wasting kisses on my hand! Sure, even the moon is laughing at us.

TYRONE. Nuts for the moon! I'd rather have one light on Broadway than all the moons since Rameses was a pup. (*He takes cigarettes from his pocket and lights one.*)

JOSIE (*her eyes searching his face, lighted up by the match*). You'll be taking a train back to your dear old Broadway tomorrow night, won't you?

TYRONE (*still holding the burning match, stares at her in surprise*). Tomorrow night? Where did you get that?

JOSIE. A little bird told me.

TYRONE (*blows out the match in a cloud of smoke*). You'd better give that bird the bird. By the end of the week, is the right dope. Phil got his dates mixed.

JOSIE (*quickly*). He didn't tell me. He was too drunk to remember anything.

TYRONE. He was sober when I told him. I called up the executors when we reached the Inn after leaving here. They said the estate would be out of probate within a few days. I told Phil the glad tidings and bought drinks for all and sundry. There was quite a celebration. Funny, Phil wouldn't remember that.

JOSIE (*bewildered — not knowing what to believe*). It is — funny.

TYRONE (*shrugs his shoulders*). Well, he's stewed to the ears. That always explains anything. (*Then strangely.*) Only sometimes it doesn't.

JOSIE. No — sometimes it doesn't.

TYRONE (*goes on without real interest, talking to keep from thinking*). Phil certainly has a prize bun on tonight. He never took a punch at me before. And that drivel he talked about owing me one — What got into his head, I wonder.

JOSIE (*tensely*). How would I know, if you don't?

TYRONE. Well, I don't. Not unless — I remember I did try to get his goat. Simpson sat down with us. Harder sent him to see me. You remember after Harder left here I said the joke was on you, that you'd made this place a goldmine. I was kidding, but I had the right dope. What do you think he told Simpson to offer? Ten grand! On the level, Josie.

JOSIE (*tense*). So you accepted?

TYRONE. I told Simpson to tell Harder I did. I decided the best way to fix him was to let him think he'd got away with it, and then when he comes tomorrow morning to drive me to the executors' office, I'll tell him what he can do with himself, his bankroll, and tin oil tanks.

JOSIE (*knows he is telling the truth — so relieved she can only stammer stupidly*). So that's — the truth of it.

TYRONE (*smiles*). Of course, I did it to kid Phil, too. He was right there, listening. But I know I didn't fool him.

JOSIE (*weakly*). Maybe you did fool him, for once. But I don't know.

TYRONE. And that's why he took a swing at me? (*He laughs, but there is a forced note to it.*) Well, if so, it's one hell of a joke on him. (*His tone becomes hurt and bitter.*) All the same, I'll be good and sore, Josie. I promised this place wouldn't be sold except to him. What the hell does he think I am? He ought to know I wouldn't double-cross you and him for ten million!

JOSIE (*giving way at last to her relief and joy*). Don't I know! Oh, Jim, darling! (*She hugs him passionately and kisses him on the lips.*) I knew you'd never — I told him — (*She kisses him again.*) Oh, Jim, I love you.

TYRONE (*again with a strange, simple gratitude*). Thanks, Josie. I mean, for not believing I'm a rotten louse. Everyone else believes it — including myself — for a damned good reason. (*Abruptly changing the subject.*) I'm a fool to let this stuff about Phil get under my skin, but — Why, I remember telling him tonight I'd even written my brother and got his okay on selling the farm to him. And Phil thanked me. He seemed touched and grateful. You wouldn't think he'd forget that.

JOSIE (*her face hard and bitter*). I wouldn't, indeed. There's a lot of things he'll have to explain when he comes at sun — (*Hastily.*) When he comes back. (*She pauses — then bursts out.*) The damned old schemer, I'll teach him to — (*again checking herself*) to act like a fool.

TYRONE (*smiles*). You'll get out the old club, eh? What a bluff you are, Josie. (*Teasingly.*) You and your lovers, Messalina — when you've never —

JOSIE (*with a faint spark of her old defiance*). You're a liar.

TYRONE. "Pride is the sin by which the angels fell." Are you going to keep that up — with me?

JOSIE (*feebly*). You think I've never because no one would — because I'm a great ugly cow —

TYRONE (*gently*). Nuts! You could have had any one of them. You kidded them till you were sure they wanted you. That was all you wanted. And then you slapped them groggy when they tried for more. But you had to keep convincing yourself —

JOSIE (*tormentedly*). Don't, Jim.

TYRONE. You can take the truth, Josie — from me. Because you and I belong to the same club. We can kid the world but we can't fool ourselves, like most people, no matter what we do — nor escape ourselves no matter where we run away. Whether it's the bottom of a bottle, or a South Sea Island, we'd find our own ghosts there waiting to greet us — "sleepless with pale commemorative eyes," as Rossetti wrote. (*He sneers to himself.*) The old poetic bull, eh? Crap! (*Reverting to a teasing tone.*) You don't ask how I saw through your bluff, Josie. You pretend too much. And so do the guys. I've listened to them at the Inn. They all lie to each other. No one wants to admit all he got was a slap in the puss, when he thinks a lot of other guys made it. You can't blame them. And they know you don't give a damn how they lie. So —

JOSIE. For the love of God, Jim! Don't!

TYRONE. Phil is wise to you, of course, but although he knew I knew, he would never admit it until tonight.

JOSIE (*startled — vindictively*). So he admitted it, did he? Wait till I get hold of him!

TYRONE. He'll never admit it to you. He's afraid of hurting you.

JOSIE. He is, is he? Well — (*Almost hysterically.*) For the love of God, can't you shut up about him!

TYRONE (*glances up at her, surprised — then shrugs his shoulders*). Oh, all right. I wanted to clear things up, that's all — for Phil's sake as well as yours. You have a hell of a licence to be sore. He's the one who ought to be. Don't you realize what a lousy position you've put him in with your brazen-trollop act?

JOSIE (*tensely*). No. He doesn't care, except to use me in his scheming. He —

TYRONE. Don't be a damned fool. Of course he cares. And so do I. (*He turns and pulls her head down and kisses her on the lips.*) I care, Josie. I love you.

JOSIE (*with pitiful longing*). Do you, Jim? Do you? (*She forces a trembling smile — faintly.*) Then I'll confess the truth to you. I've been a crazy fool. I am a virgin. (*She begins to sob with a strange forlorn shame and humiliation.*) And now you'll never — and I want you to — now more than ever — because I love you more than ever, after what's happened — (*Suddenly she kisses him with fierce passion.*) But you will! I'll make you! To hell with your honourable scruples! I know you want me! I couldn't believe that until tonight — but now I know. It's in your kisses! (*She kisses him again — with passionate tenderness.*) Oh, you great fool! As if I gave a damn what happened after! I'll have had tonight and your love to remember for the rest of my days! (*She kisses him again.*) Oh, Jim, darling, haven't you said yourself there's only tonight? (*She whispers tenderly.*) Come. Come with me. (*She gets to her feet, pulling at his arm — with a little self-mocking laugh.*) But I'll have to make you leave before sunrise. I mustn't forget that.

TYRONE (*a strange change has come over his face. He looks her over now with a sneering cynical lust. He speaks thickly as if he was suddenly very drunk*). Sure thing, Kiddo. What the hell else do you suppose I came for? I've been kidding myself. (*He steps up beside her and puts his arm round her and presses his body to hers.*) You're the goods, Kid. I've wanted you all along. Love, nuts! I'll show you what love is. I know what you want, Bright Eyes. (*She is staring at him now with a look of frightened horror. He kisses her roughly.*) Come on, Baby Doll, let's hit the hay. (*He pushes her back in the doorway.*)

JOSIE (*strickenly*). Jim! Don't! (*She pulls his arms away so violently that he staggers back and would fall down the steps if she didn't grab his arm in time. As it is he goes down on one knee. She is on the verge of collapse herself — brokenly.*) Jim! I'm not a whore.

TYRONE (*remains on one knee — confusedly, as if he didn't know what had happened*). What the hell? Was I trying to rape you, Josie? Forget it. I'm drunk — not responsible. (*He gets to his feet, staggering a bit, and steps down to the ground.*)

JOSIE (*covering her face with her hands*). Oh, Jim! (*She sobs.*)

TYRONE (*with vague pity*). Don't cry. No harm done. You stopped me, didn't you? (*She continues to sob. He mutters vaguely, as if talking to himself.*) Must have drawn a blank for a while. Nuts! Cut out the faking. I knew what I was doing. (*Slowly, staring before him.*) But it's funny. I *was* seeing things. That's the truth, Josie. For a moment I thought you were that blonde pig — (*Hastily.*) The old heebie-jeebies. Hair of the dog. (*He gropes around for the bottle and his glass.*) I'll have another shot —

JOSIE (*takes her hands from her face — fiercely*). Pour the whole bottle down your throat, if you like! Only stop talking! (*She covers her face with her hands and sobs again.*)

TYRONE (*stares at her with a hurt and sad expression — dully*). Can't forgive me, eh? You ought to. You ought to thank me for letting you see — (*He pauses, as if waiting for her to say something, but she remains silent. He shrugs his shoulders, pours out a big drink mechanically.*) Well, here's how. (*He drinks and puts the bottle and glass on the ground — dully.*) That was a nightcap. Our moonlight romance seems to be a flop, Josie. I guess I'd better go.

JOSIE (*dully*). Yes. You'd better go. Good night.

TYRONE. Not good night. Good-bye.

JOSIE (*lifts her head*). Good-bye?

TYRONE. Yes. I won't see you again before I leave for New York. I was a damned fool to come tonight. I hoped — But you don't get it. How could you? So what's the good — (*He shrugs his shoulders hopelessly and turns toward the road.*)

JOSIE. Jim!

TYRONE (*turning back — bitter accusation in his tone now*). Whore? Who said you were a whore? But I warned you, didn't I, if you kept on — Why did you have to act like one, asking me to come to bed? That wasn't what I came here for. And you promised tonight would be different. Why the hell did you promise that, if all you wanted was what all the others want, if that's all love means to you? (*Then guiltily.*) Oh, Christ, I don't mean that, Josie. I know how you feel, and if I could give you happiness —

But it wouldn't work. You don't know me. I'd poison it for myself and for you. I've poisoned it already, haven't I, but it would be a million times worse after— No matter how I tried not to, I'd make it like all the other nights—for you, too. You'd lie awake and watch the dawn come with disgust, with nausea retching your memory, and the wine of passion poets blab about, a sour aftertaste in your mouth of Dago red ink! (*He gives a sneering laugh.*)

JOSIE (*distractedly*). Oh, Jim, don't! Please don't!

TYRONE. You'd hate me and yourself—not for a day or two but for the rest of your life. (*With a perverse, jeering note of vindictive boastfulness in his tone.*) Believe me, Kid, when I poison them, they stay poisoned!

JOSIE (*with dull bitterness*). Good-bye, Jim.

TYRONE (*miserably hurt and sad for a second—appealingly*). Josie— (*Gives the characteristic shrug of his shoulders—simply.*) Good-bye. (*He turns toward the road—bitterly.*) I'll find it hard to forgive, too. I came here asking for love—just for this one night, because I thought you loved me. (*Dully.*) Nuts. To hell with it. (*He starts away.*)

JOSIE (*watches him for a second, fighting the love that, in spite of her, responds to his appeal—then she springs up and runs to him—with fierce, possessive, maternal tenderness*). Come here to me, you great fool, and stop your silly blather. There's nothing to hate you for. There's nothing to forgive. Sure, I was only trying to give you happiness, because I love you. I'm sorry I was so stupid and didn't see— But I see now, and you'll find I have all the love you need. (*She gives him a hug and kisses him. There is passion in her kiss but it is a tender, protective maternal passion, which he responds to with an instant grateful yielding.*)

TYRONE (*simply*). Thanks, Josie. You're beautiful. I love you. I knew you'd understand.

JOSIE. Of course I do. Come, now. (*She leads him back, her arm around his waist.*)

TYRONE. I didn't want to leave you. You know that.

JOSIE. Indeed I know it. Come now. We'll sit down. (*She sits on the top step and pulls him down on the step below her.*) That's it—with my arm around you. Now lay your head on my breast—the way you said you wanted to do— (*He lets his head fall back on her breast. She hugs him—gently.*) There, now. Forget all about my being a fool and forgive— (*Her voice trembles—but she goes on determinedly.*) Forgive my selfishness, thinking only of myself. Sure, if there's one thing I owe you tonight, after all my lying and scheming, it's to give you the love you need, and it'll be my pride and my joy— (*Forcing a trembling echo of her playful tone.*) It's easy enough, too, for I have all kinds of love for you—and maybe this is the greatest of all—because it costs so much. (*She pauses, looking down at his face. He has closed his eyes and his haggard, dissipated face looks like a pale mask in the moonlight—at peace as a death mask is at peace. She becomes frightened.*) Jim! Don't look like that!

TYRONE (*opens his eyes—vaguely*). Like what?

JOSIE (*quickly*). It's the moonlight. It makes you look so pale, and with your eyes closed—

TYRONE (*simply*). You mean I looked dead?

JOSIE. No! As if you'd fallen asleep.

TYRONE (*speaks in a tired, empty tone, as if he felt he ought to explain something to her—something which no longer interests him*). Listen, and I'll tell you a little story, Josie. All my life I had just one dream. From the time I was a kid, I loved racehorses. I thought they were the most beautiful things in the world. I liked to gamble, too. So the big dream was that some day I'd have enough dough to play a cagey system of betting on favourites, and follow the horses south in the winter, and come back north with them in the spring, and be at the track every day. It seemed that would be the ideal life—for me. (*He pauses.*)

JOSIE. Well, you'll be able to do it.

TYRONE. No. I won't be able to do it, Josie. That's the joke. I gave it a try-out before I came up here. I borrowed some money on my share of the estate and started going to tracks. But it didn't work. I played my system, but I found I didn't care if I won or lost. The horses were beautiful, but I found myself saying to myself, what of it? Their beauty didn't mean anything. I found that every day I was glad when the last race was over, and I could go back to the hotel—and the bottle in my room. (*He pauses, staring into the moonlight with vacant eyes.*)

JOSIE (*uneasily*). Why did you tell me this?

TYRONE (*in the same listless monotone*). You said I looked dead. Well, I am.

JOSIE. You're not! (*She hugs him protectively.*) Don't talk like that!

TYRONE. Ever since Mama died.

JOSIE (*deeply moved—pityingly*). I know. I've felt all along it was that sorrow was making you— (*She pauses—gently.*) Maybe if you talked about your grief for her, it would help you. I think it must be all choked up inside you, killing you.

TYRONE (*in a strange warning tone*). You'd better look out, Josie.

JOSIE. Why?

TYRONE (*quickly, forcing his cynical smile*). I might develop a crying jag, and sob on your beautiful breast.

JOSIE (*gently*). You can sob all you like.

TYRONE. Don't encourage me. You'd be sorry. (*A deep

conflict shows in his expression and tone. He is driven to go on in spite of himself.) But if you're such a glutton for punishment — After all, I said I'd tell you later, didn't I?

JOSIE (*puzzled*). You said you'd tell me about the blonde on the train.

TYRONE. She's part of it. I lied about that. (*He pauses — then blurts out sneeringly.*) You won't believe it could have happened. Or if you did believe, you couldn't understand or forgive — (*Quickly.*) But you might. You're the one person who might. Because you really love me. And because you're the only woman I've ever met who understands the lousy rotten things a man can do when he's crazy drunk, and draws a blank — especially when he's nutty with grief to start with.

JOSIE (*hugging him tenderly*). Of course I'll understand, Jim, darling.

TYRONE (*stares into the moonlight — hauntedly*). But I didn't draw a blank. I tried to. I drank enough to knock out ten men. But it didn't work. I knew what I was doing. (*He pauses — dully.*) No, I can't tell you, Josie. You'd loathe my guts, and I couldn't blame you.

JOSIE. No! I'll love you no matter what —

TYRONE (*with strange triumphant harshness*). All right! Remember that's a promise! (*He pauses — starts to speak — pauses again.*)

JOSIE (*pityingly*). Maybe you'd better not — if it will make you suffer.

TYRONE. Trying to welch now, eh? It's too late. You've got me started. Suffer? Christ, I ought to suffer! (*He pauses. Then he closes his eyes. It is as if he had to hide from sight before he can begin. He makes his face expressionless. His voice becomes impersonal and objective, as though what he told concerned some man he had known, but had nothing to do with him. This is the only way he can start telling the story.*) When Mama died, I'd been on the wagon for nearly two years. Not even a glass of beer. Honestly. And I know I would have stayed on. For her sake. She had no one but me. The Old Man was dead. My brother had married — had a kid — had his own life to live. She'd lost him. She had only me to attend to things for her and take care of her. She'd always hated my drinking. So I quit. It made me happy to do it. For her. Because she was all I had, all I cared about. Because I loved her. (*He pauses.*) No one would believe that now, who knew — But I did.

JOSIE (*gently*). I know how much you loved her.

TYRONE. We went out to the Coast to see about selling a piece of property the Old Man had bought there years ago. And one day she suddenly became ill. Got rapidly worse. Went into a coma. Brain tumour. The docs said, no hope. Might never come out of coma. I went crazy. Couldn't face losing her. The old booze yen got me. I got drunk and stayed drunk. And I began hoping she'd never come out of the coma, and see I was drinking again. That was my excuse, too — that she'd never know. And she never did. (*He pauses — then sneeringly.*) Nix! Kidding myself again. I know damned well just before she died she recognized me. She saw I was drunk. Then she closed her eyes so she couldn't see, and was glad to die! (*He opens his eyes and stares into the moonlight as if he saw this deathbed scene before him.*)

JOSIE (*soothingly*). Ssshh. You only imagine that because you feel guilty about drinking.

TYRONE (*as if he hadn't heard, closes his eyes again*). After that, I kept so drunk I did draw a blank most of the time, but I went through the necessary motions and no one guessed how drunk — (*He pauses.*) But there are things I can never forget — the undertakers, and her body in a coffin with her face made up. I couldn't hardly recognize her. She looked young and pretty like someone I remembered meeting long ago. Practically a stranger. To whom I was a stranger. Cold and indifferent. Not worried about me any more. Free at last. Free from worry. From pain. From me. I stood looking down at her, and something happened to me. I found I couldn't feel anything. I knew I ought to be heartbroken but I couldn't feel anything. I seemed dead, too. I knew I ought to cry. Even a crying jag would look better than just standing there. But I couldn't cry. I cursed to myself, "You dirty bastard, it's Mama. You loved her, and now she's dead. She's gone away from you for ever. Never, never again —" But it had no effect. All I did was to try to explain to myself, "She's dead. What does she care now if I cry or not, or what I do? It doesn't matter a damn to her. She's happy to be where I can't hurt her ever again. She's rid of me at last. For God's sake, can't you leave her alone even now? For God's sake, can't you let her rest in peace?" (*He pauses — then sneeringly.*) But there were several people around and I knew they expected me to show something. Once a ham, always a ham! So I put on an act. I flopped on my knees and hid my face in my hands and faked some sobs and cried, "Mama! Mama! My dear mother!" But all the time I kept saying to myself, "You lousy ham! You God-damned lousy ham! Christ, in a minute you'll start singing 'Mother Machree'!" (*He opens his eyes and gives a tortured, sneering laugh, staring into the moonlight.*)

JOSIE (*horrified, but still deeply pitying*). Jim! Don't! It's past. You've punished yourself. And you were drunk. You didn't mean —

TYRONE (*again closes his eyes*). I had to bring her body East to be buried beside the Old Man. I took a drawing room and hid in it with a case of booze. She was in her coffin in the baggage car. No matter how drunk I got, I couldn't forget that for a minute. I found I couldn't stay alone in the drawing room. It became haunted. I was going crazy. I had to go out and wander up and down the train looking for company. I made such a public nuisance of myself that the conductor threatened if I didn't quit, he'd keep me locked in the drawing room. But I'd spotted one passenger who was used to drunks and could pretend to like them, if there was enough dough in it. She had parlour house written all over her — a blonde pig who looked more like a whore than twenty-five whores, with a face like an overgrown doll's and a come-on smile as cold as a polar bear's feet. I bribed the porter to take a message to her and that night she sneaked into my drawing room. She was bound for New York, too. So every night — for fifty bucks a night — (*He opens his eyes and now he stares torturedly through the moonlight into the drawing room.*)

JOSIE (*her face full of revulsion — stammers*). Oh, how could you! (*Instinctively she draws away, taking her arms from around him.*)

TYRONE. How could I? I don't know. But I did. I suppose I had some mad idea she could make me forget — what was in the baggage car ahead.

JOSIE. Don't. (*She draws back again so he has to raise his head from her breast. He doesn't seem to notice this.*)

TYRONE. No, it couldn't have been that. Because I didn't seem to want to forget. It was like some plot I had to carry out. The blonde — she didn't matter. She was only something that belonged in the plot. It was as if I wanted revenge — because I'd been left alone — because I knew I was lost, without any hope left — that all I could do would be drink myself to death, because no one was left who could help me. (*His face hardens and a look of cruel vindictiveness comes into it — with a strange horrible satisfaction in his tone.*) No, I didn't forget even in that pig's arms! I remembered the last two lines of a lousy tear-jerker song I'd heard when I was a kid kept singing over and over in my brain.

"And baby's cries can't waken her
In the baggage coach ahead."

JOSIE (*distractedly*). Jim!

TYRONE. I couldn't stop it singing. I didn't want to stop it!

JOSIE. Jim! For the love of God. I don't want to hear!

TYRONE (*after a pause — dully*). Well, that's all — except I was too drunk to go to her funeral.

JOSIE. Oh! (*She has drawn away from him as far as she can without getting up. He becomes aware of this for the first time and turns slowly to stare at her.*)

TYRONE (*dully*). Don't want to touch me now, eh? (*He shrugs his shoulders mechanically.*) Sorry. I'm a damned fool. I shouldn't have told you.

JOSIE (*her horror ebbing as her love and protective compassion returns — moves nearer him — haltingly*). Don't, Jim. Don't say — I don't want to touch you. It's — a lie. (*She puts a hand on his shoulder.*)

TYRONE (*as if she hadn't spoken — with hopeless longing*). Wish I could believe in the spiritualists' bunk. If I could tell her it was because I missed her so much and couldn't forgive her for leaving me —

JOSIE. Jim! For the love of God — !

TYRONE (*unheeding*). She'd understand and forgive me, don't you think? She always did. She was simple and kind and pure of heart. She was beautiful. You're like her deep in your heart. That's why I told you. I thought — (*Abruptly his expression becomes sneering and cynical — harshly.*) My mistake. Nuts! Forget it. Time I got a move on. I don't like your damned moon, Josie. It's an ad for the past. (*He recites mockingly.*)

"It is the very error of the moon:
She comes more nearer earth than she was wont,
And makes men mad."

(*He moves.*) I'll grab the last trolley for town. There'll be a speak open, and some drunk laughing. I need a laugh. (*He starts to get up.*)

JOSIE (*throws her arms around him and pulls him back — tensely*). No! You won't go! I won't let you! (*She hugs him close — gently.*) I understand now, Jim, darling, and I'm proud you came to me as the one in the world you know loves you enough to understand and forgive — and I do forgive!

TYRONE (*lets his head fall back on her breast — simply*). Thanks, Josie. I knew you —

JOSIE. And *she* forgives, do you hear me! As *she* loves and understands and forgives!

TYRONE (*simply*). Yes, I know she — (*His voice breaks.*)

JOSIE (*bends over him with a brooding maternal tenderness*). That's right. Do what you came for, my darling. It isn't drunken laughter in a speakeasy you want to hear at all, but the sound of yourself crying your heart's repentance against her breast. (*His face is convulsed. He hides it on her breast and sobs rackingly. She hugs him more tightly and speaks softly, staring into the moonlight.*) She hears. I feel her in the moonlight, her soul wrapped in it like a silver mantle, and I know she understands and forgives me, too, and her blessing lies on me. (*A pause. His sobs begin to stop exhaustedly. She looks down at him again and speaks soothingly as she would to a child.*) There. There, now. (*He stops. She goes on in a gentle, bullying tone.*) You're a fine one, wanting to leave me when the night I promised I'd give you has just begun, our night that'll be different from all the others, with a dawn that won't creep over dirty window-panes but will wake in the sky like a promise of God's peace in the soul's dark sadness. (*She smiles a little amused smile.*) Will you listen to me, Jim! I must be a poet. Who would have guessed it? Sure, love is a wonderful mad inspiration! (*A pause. She looks down. His eyes are closed. His face against her breast looks pale and haggard in the moonlight. Calm with the drained, exhausted peace of death. For a second she is frightened. Then she realizes and whispers softly.*) Asleep. (*In a tender crooning tone like a lullaby.*) That's right. Sleep in peace, my darling. (*Then with sudden anguished longing.*) Oh, Jim, Jim, maybe my love could still save you, if you could want it enough! (*She shakes her head.*) No. That can never be. (*Her eyes leave his face to stare up at the sky. She looks weary and stricken and sad. She forces a defensive, self-derisive smile.*) God forgive me, it's a fine end to all my scheming, to sit here with the dead hugged to my breast, and the silly mug of the moon grinning down, enjoying the joke!

CURTAIN

ACT FOUR

SCENE. *Same as Act Three. It is dawn. The first faint streaks of colour, heralding the sunrise, appear in the eastern sky at left.*

Josie sits in the same position on the steps, as if she had not moved, her arms around Tyrone. He is still asleep, his head on her breast. His face has the same exhausted, death-like repose. Josie's face is set in an expression of numbed, resigned sadness. Her body sags tiredly. In spite of her strength, holding herself like this for hours, for fear of waking him, is becoming too much for her.

The two make a strangely tragic picture in the wan dawn light — this big sorrowful woman hugging a haggard-faced, middle-aged drunkard against her breast, as if he were a sick child.

Hogan appears at left-rear, coming from the barn. He approaches the corner of the house stealthily on tiptoe. Wisps of hay stick to his clothes and his face is swollen and sleepy, but his little pig's eyes are sharply wide awake and sober. He peeks around the corner, and takes in the two on the steps. His eyes fix on Josie's face in a long, probing stare.

JOSIE (*speaks in a low grim tone*). Stop hiding, Father. I heard you sneak up.

(*He comes guiltily around the corner. She keeps her voice low, but her tone is commanding.*)

Come here, and be quiet about it.

(*He obeys meekly, coming as far as the boulder silently, his eyes searching her face, his expression becoming guilty and miserable at what he sees. She goes on in the same tone, without looking at him.*)

Talk low, now. I don't want him wakened — (*She adds strangely.*) Not until the dawn has beauty in it.

HOGAN (*worriedly*). What? (*He decides it's better for the present to ask no questions. His eyes fall on Tyrone's face. In spite of himself, he is startled — in an awed, almost frightened whisper.*) Be God, he looks dead!

JOSIE (*strangely*). Why wouldn't he? He is.

HOGAN. Is?

JOSIE. Don't be a fool. Can't you see him breathing? Dead asleep, I mean. Don't stand there gawking. Sit down.

(*He sits meekly on the boulder. His face betrays a guilty dread of what is coming. There is a pause in which she doesn't look at him but he keeps glancing at her, growing visibly more uneasy. She speaks bitterly.*)

Where's your witnesses?

HOGAN (*guiltily*). Witnesses? (*Then forcing an amused grin.*) Oh, be God, if that ain't a joke on me! Sure, I got so blind drunk at the Inn I forgot all about our scheme and came home and went to sleep in the hayloft.

JOSIE (*her expression harder and more bitter*). You're a liar.

HOGAN. I'm not. I just woke up. Look at the hay sticking to me. That's proof.

JOSIE. I'm not thinking of that, and well you know it. (*With bitter voice.*) So you just woke up — did you? — and then came sneaking here to see if the scheme behind your scheme had worked!

HOGAN (*guiltily*). I don't know what you mean.

JOSIE. Don't lie any more, Father. This time, you've told one too many.

(*He starts to defend himself but the look on her face makes him think better of it and he remains uneasily silent. A pause.*)

HOGAN (*finally has to blurt out*). Sure, if I'd brought the witnesses, there's nothing for them to witness that —

JOSIE. No. You're right, there. There's nothing. Nothing at all. (*She smiles strangely.*) Except a great miracle they'd never believe, or you either.

HOGAN. What miracle?

JOSIE. A virgin who bears a dead child in the night, and the dawn finds her still a virgin. If that isn't a miracle, what is?

HOGAN (*uneasily*). Stop talking so queer. You give me the shivers. (*He attempts a joking tone.*) Is it you who's the virgin? Faith, that *would* be a miracle, no less! (*He forces a chuckle.*)

JOSIE. I told you to stop lying, Father.

HOGAN. What lie? (*He stops and watches her face worriedly. She is silent, as if she were not aware of him now. Her eyes are fixed on the wanton sky.*)

JOSIE (*as if to herself*). It'll be beautiful soon, and I can wake him.

HOGAN (*can't retain his anxiety any longer*). Josie, darlin'! For the love of God, can't you tell me what happened to you?

JOSIE (*her face hard and bitter again*). I've told you once. Nothing.

HOGAN. Nothing? If you could see the sadness in your face —

JOSIE. What woman doesn't sorrow for the man she loved who has died? But there's pride in my heart, too.

HOGAN (*tormentedly*). Will you stop talking as if you'd gone mad in the night! (*Raising his voice — with revengeful anger.*) Listen to me! If Jim Tyrone has done anything to bring you sorrow —

(*Tyrone stirs in his sleep and moans, pressing his face against her breast as if for protection. She looks down at him and hugs him close.*)

JOSIE (*croons softly*). There, there, my darling. Rest in peace a while longer. (*Turns on her father angrily and whispers.*) Didn't I tell you to speak low and not wake him! (*She pauses — then quietly.*) He did nothing to bring me sorrow. It was my mistake. I thought there was still hope. I didn't know he'd died already — that it was a damned soul coming to me in the moonlight, to confess and be forgiven and find peace for a night —

HOGAN. Josie! Will you stop!

JOSIE (*after a pause — dully*). He'd never do anything to hurt me. You know it. (*Self-mockingly.*) Sure, hasn't he told me I'm beautiful to him and he loves me — in his fashion. (*Then matter-of-factly.*) All that happened was that he got drunk and he had one of his crazy notions he wanted to sleep the way he is, and I let him sleep. (*With forced roughness.*) And, be God, the night's over. I'm half dead with tiredness and sleepiness. It's that you see in my face, not sorrow.

HOGAN. Don't try to fool me, Josie. I —

JOSIE (*her face hard and bitter — grimly*). Fool you, is it? It's you who made a fool of me with your lies, thinking you'd use me to get your dirty greasy paws on the money he'll have!

HOGAN. No! I swear by all the saints —

JOSIE. You'd swear on a Bible while you were stealing it! (*Grimly.*) Listen to me, Father. I didn't call you here to answer questions about what's none of your business. I called you here to tell you I've seen through all the lies you told last night to get me to — (*As he starts to speak.*) Shut up! I'll do the talking now. You weren't drunk. You were only putting it on as part of your scheme —

HOGAN (*quietly*). I wasn't drunk, no. I admit that, Josie. But I'd had slews of drinks and they were in my head or I'd never have the crazy dreams —

JOSIE (*with biting scorn*). Dreams, is it? The only dream you've ever had, or will have, is of yourself counting a fistful of dirty money, and divil a care how you got it, or who you robbed or made suffer!

HOGAN (*winces — pleadingly*). Josie!

JOSIE. Shut up. (*Scathingly.*) I'm sure you've made up a whole new set of lies and excuses. You're that cunning and clever, but you can save your breath. They wouldn't fool me now. I've been fooled once too often. (*He gives her a frightened look, as if something he had dreaded has happened. She goes on, grimly accusing.*) You lied about Jim selling the farm. You knew he was kidding. You knew the estate would be out of probate in a few days, and he'd go back to Broadway, and you had to do something quick or you'd lose the last chance of getting your greedy hooks on his money.

HOGAN (*miserably*). No. It wasn't that, Josie.

JOSIE. You saw how hurt and angry I was because he'd kept me waiting here, and you used that. You knew I loved him and wanted him and you used that. You used all you knew about me — Oh, you did it clever! You ought to be proud! You worked it so it was me who did all the dirty scheming — You knew I'd find out from Jim you'd lied about the farm, but not before your lie had done its work — made me go after him, get him drunk, get drunk myself so I could be shameless — and when the truth did come out, wouldn't it make me love him all the more and be more shameless and willing? Don't tell me you didn't count on that, and you such a clever schemer! And if he once had me, knowing I was a virgin, didn't you count on his honour and remorse, and his loving me in his fashion, to make him offer to marry me? Sure, why wouldn't he, you thought. It wouldn't hold him. He'd go back to Broadway just the same and never see me again. But there'd be money in it, and when he'd finished killing himself, I'd be his legal widow and get what's left.

HOGAN (*miserably*). No! It wasn't that.

JOSIE. But what's the good of talking? It's all over. I've only one more word for you, Father, and it's this: I'm leaving you today, like my brothers left. You can live alone and work alone your cunning schemes on yourself.

HOGAN (*after a pause — slowly*). I knew you'd be bitter against me, Josie, but I took the chance you'd be so happy you wouldn't care how —

JOSIE (*as if she hadn't heard, looking at the eastern sky which is now glowing with colour*). Thank God, it's beautiful. It's time. (*To Hogan.*) Go in the house and stay there till he's gone. I don't want you around to start some new scheme.

(*He looks miserable, starts to speak, thinks better of it, and meekly tiptoes past her up the steps and goes in, closing the door quietly after him. She looks down at Tyrone. Her face softens with a maternal tenderness — sadly.*)

I hate to bring you back to life, Jim, darling. If you could have died in your sleep, that's what you would have liked, isn't it? (*She gives him a gentle shake.*) Wake up, Jim. (*He moans in his sleep and presses more closely against her. She stares at his face.*) Dear God, let him remember that one thing and forget the rest. That will be enough for me. (*She gives him a more vigorous shake.*) Jim! Wake up, do you hear? It's time.

TYRONE (*half wakens without opening his eyes — mutters*). What the hell? (*Dimly conscious of a woman's body — cynically.*) Again, eh? Same old stuff. Who the hell are you, sweetheart? (*Irritably.*) What's the big idea, waking me up? What time is it?

JOSIE. It's dawn.

TYRONE (*still without opening his eyes*). Dawn? (*He quotes drowsily.*)

"But I was desolate and sick of an old passion,
When I awoke and found the dawn was grey."

(*Then with a sneer.*) They're all grey. Go to sleep, Kid — and let me sleep. (*He falls asleep again.*)

JOSIE (*tensely*). This one isn't grey, Jim. It's different from all the others — (*She sees he is asleep — bitterly.*) He'll have forgotten. He'll never notice. And I'm the whore on the train to him now, not — (*Suddenly she pushes him away from her and shakes him roughly.*) Will you wake up, for God's sake! I've had all I can bear —

TYRONE (*still half asleep*). Hey! Cut out the rough stuff, Kid. What? (*Awake now, blinking his eyes — with dazed surprise.*) Josie.

JOSIE (*still bitter*). That's who, and none of your damned tarts! (*She pushes him.*) Get up now, so you won't fall asleep again. (*He does so with difficulty, still in a sleepy daze, his body stiff and cramped. She conquers her bitter resentment and puts on her old free-and-easy kidding tone with him, but all the time waiting to see how much he will remember.*) You're stiff and cramped, and no wonder. I'm worse from holding you, if that's any comfort. (*She stretches and rubs her numbed arms, groaning comically.*) Holy Joseph, I'm a wreck entirely. I'll never be the same. (*Giving him a quick glance.*) You look as if you'd drawn a blank and were wondering how you got here. I'll bet you don't remember a thing.

TYRONE (*moving his arms and legs gingerly — sleepily*). I don't know. Wait till I'm sure I'm still alive.

JOSIE. You need an eye-opener. (*She picks up the bottle and glass and pours him a drink.*) Here you are.

TYRONE (*takes the glass mechanically*). Thanks, Josie. (*He goes and sits on the boulder, holding the drink as if he had no interest in it.*)

JOSIE (*watching him*). Drink up or you'll be asleep again.

TYRONE. No, I'm awake now, Josie. Funny. Don't seem to want a drink. Oh, I've got a head all right. But no heebie-jeebies — yet.

JOSIE. That's fine. It must be a pleasant change —

TYRONE. It is. I've got a nice, dreamy peaceful hangover for once — as if I'd had a sound sleep without nightmares.

JOSIE. So you did. Divil a nightmare. I ought to know. Wasn't I holding you and keeping them away?

TYRONE. You mean you — (*Suddenly.*) Wait a minute. I remember now I was sitting alone at a table in the Inn, and I suddenly had a crazy notion I'd come up here and sleep with my head on your — So that's why I woke up in your arms. (*Shamefacedly.*) And you let me get away with it. You're a nut, Josie.

JOSIE. Oh, I didn't mind.

TYRONE. You must have seen how blotto I was, didn't you?

JOSIE. I did. You were as full as a tick.

TYRONE. Then why didn't you give me the bum's rush?

JOSIE. Why would I? I was glad to humour you.

TYRONE. For God's sake, how long was I cramped on you like that?

JOSIE. Oh, a few hours, only.

TYRONE. God, I'm sorry, Josie, but it's your own fault for letting me —

JOSIE. Och, don't be apologizing. I was glad of the excuse to stay awake and enjoy the beauty of the moon.

TYRONE. Yes, I can remember what a beautiful night it was.

JOSIE. Can you? I'm glad of that, Jim. You seemed to enjoy it the while we were sitting here together before you fell asleep.

TYRONE. How long a while was that?

JOSIE. Not long. Less than an hour, anyway.

TYRONE. I suppose I bored the hell out of you with a lot of drunken drivel.

JOSIE. Not a lot, no. But some. You were full of blarney, saying how beautiful I was to you.

TYRONE (*earnestly*). That wasn't drivel, Josie. You were. You are. You always will be.

JOSIE. You're a wonder, Jim. Nothing can stop you, can it? Even me in the light of dawn, looking like something you'd put in the field to scare the crows from the corn. You'll kid at the Day of Judgment.

TYRONE (*impatiently*). You know damned well it isn't kidding. You're not a fool. You can tell.

JOSIE (*kiddingly*). All right, then, I'm beautiful and you love me — in your fashion.

TYRONE. "In my fashion," eh? Was I reciting poetry to you? That must have been hard to take.

JOSIE. It wasn't. I liked it. It was all about beautiful nights and the romance of the moon.

TYRONE. Well, there was some excuse for that, anyway. It sure was a beautiful night. I'll never forget it.

JOSIE. I'm glad, Jim.

TYRONE. What other bunk did I pull on you — or I mean, did old John Barleycorn pull?

JOSIE. Not much. You were mostly quiet and sad — in a kind of daze, as if the moon was in your wits as well as whiskey.

TYRONE. I remember I was having a grand time at the Inn, celebrating with Phil, and then suddenly, for no reason, all the fun went out of it, and I was more melancholy than ten Hamlets. (*He pauses.*) Hope I didn't tell you the sad story of my life and weep on your bosom, Josie.

JOSIE. You didn't. The one thing you talked a lot about was that you wanted the night with me to be different from all the other nights you'd spent with women.

TYRONE (*with revulsion*). God, don't make me think of those tramps now! (*Then with deep, grateful feeling.*) It sure was different, Josie. I may not remember much, but I know how different it was from the way I feel now. None of my usual morning-after stuff — the damned sick remorse that makes you wish you'd died in your sleep so you wouldn't have to face the rotten things you're afraid you said and did the night before, when you were so drunk you didn't know what you were doing.

JOSIE. There's nothing you said or did last night for you to regret. You can take my word for that.

TYRONE (*as if he hadn't heard — slowly*). It's hard to describe how I feel. It's a new one on me. Sort of at peace with myself and this lousy life — as if all my sins had been forgiven — (*He becomes self-conscious — cynically.*) Nuts with that sin bunk, but you know what I mean.

JOSIE (*tensely*). I do, and I'm happy you feel that way, Jim. (*A pause. She goes on.*) You talked about how you'd watched too many dawns come creeping greyly over dirty window-panes, with some tart snoring beside you —

TYRONE (*winces*). Have a heart. Don't remind me of that now, Josie. Don't spoil this dawn!

(*A pause. She watches him tensely. He turns slowly to face the east, where the sky is now glowing with all the colours of an exceptionally beautiful sunrise. He stares, drawing a deep breath. He is profoundly moved but immediately becomes self-conscious and tries to sneer it off — cynically.*)

God seems to be putting on quite a display. I like Belasco better. Rise of curtain, Act-Four stuff. (*Her face has fallen into lines of bitter hurt, but he adds quickly and angrily.*) God damn it! Why do I have to pull that lousy stuff? (*With genuine deep feeling.*) God, it's beautiful, Josie! I — I'll never forget it — here with you.

JOSIE (*her face clearing — simply*). I'm glad, Jim. I was hoping you'd feel beauty in it — by way of a token.

TYRONE (*watching the sunrise — mechanically*). Token of what?

JOSIE. Oh, I don't know. Token to me that — never mind. I forget what I meant. (*Abruptly changing the subject.*) Don't think I woke you just to admire the sunrise. You're on a farm, not Broadway, and it's time for me to start work, not go to bed. (*She gets to her feet and stretches. There is a growing strain behind her free-and-easy manner.*) And that's a hint, Jim. I can't stay entertaining you. So go back to the Inn, that's a good boy. I know you'll understand the reason, and not think I'm tired of your company. (*She forces a smile.*)

TYRONE (*gets up*). Of course I understand. (*He pauses — then blurts out guiltily.*) One more question. You're sure I didn't get out of order last night — and try to make you, or anything like that.

JOSIE. You didn't. You kidded back when I kidded you, the way we always do. That's all.

TYRONE. Thank God for that. I'd never forgive myself if — I wouldn't have asked you except I've pulled some pretty rotten stuff when I was drawing a blank. (*He becomes conscious of the forgotten drink he has in his hand.*) Well, I might as well drink this. The bar at the Inn won't be open for hours. (*He drinks — then looks pleasantly surprised.*) I'll be damned! That isn't Phil's rotgut. That's real honest-to-God bonded Bourbon. Where —

(*This clicks in his mind and suddenly he remembers everything and Josie sees that he does. The look of guilt and shame and anguish settles over his face. Instinctively he throws the glass away, his first reaction one of loathing for the drink which brought back memory. He feels Josie staring at him and fights desperately to control his voice and expression.*)

Real Bourbon. I remember now you said a bootlegger gave it to Phil. Well, I'll run along and let you do your work. See you later, Josie. (*He turns toward the road.*)

JOSIE (*strickenly*). No! Don't, Jim! Don't go like that! You won't see me later. You'll never see me again now, and I know that's best for us both, but I can't bear to have you ashamed you wanted my love to comfort your sorrow — when I'm so proud I could give it. (*Pleadingly.*) I hoped, for your sake, you wouldn't remember, but now you do, I want you to remember my love for you gave you peace for a while.

TYRONE (*stares at her, fighting with himself. He stammers defensively*). I don't know what you're talking about. I don't remember —

JOSIE (*sadly*). All right, Jim. Neither do I then. Good-bye, and God bless you. (*She turns as if to go up the steps into the house.*)

TYRONE (*stammers*). Wait, Josie! (*Coming to her.*) I'm a liar! I'm a louse! Forgive me, Josie. I do remember! I'm glad I remember! I'll never forget your love! (*He kisses her on the lips.*) Never! (*Kissing her again.*) Never, do you hear! I'll always love you, Josie. (*He kisses her again.*) Good-bye — and God bless you!

(*He turns away and walks quickly down the road off left without looking back. She stands, watching him go, for a moment, then she puts her hands over her face, her head bent, and sobs. Hogan comes out of her room and stands on top of the steps. He looks after Tyrone and his face is hard with bitter anger.*)

JOSIE (*sensing his presence, stops crying and lifts her head — dully.*) I'll get your breakfast in a minute, Father.

HOGAN. To hell with my breakfast! I'm not a pig that has no other thought but eating! (*Then pleadingly.*) Listen, darlin'. All you said about my lying and scheming, and what I hoped would happen, is true. But it wasn't his money, Josie. I did see it was the last chance — the only one left to bring the two of you to stop your damned pretending, and face the truth that you loved each other. I wanted you to find happiness — by hook or crook, one way or another, what did I care how? I wanted to save him, and I hoped he'd see that only your love could — It was his talk of the beauty he saw in you that made me hope — And I knew he'd never go to bed with you even if you'd let him unless he married you. And if I gave a thought to his money at all, that was the least of it, and why shouldn't I want to have you live in ease and comfort for a change, like you deserve, instead of in this shanty on a lousy farm, slaving for me? (*He pauses — miserably.*) Can't you believe that's the truth, Josie, and not feel so bitter against me?

JOSIE (*her eyes still following Tyrone — gently*). I know it's the truth, Father. I'm not bitter now. Don't be afraid I'm going to leave you. I only said it to punish you for a while.

HOGAN (*with humble gratitude*). Thank God for that, darlin'.

JOSIE (*forces a teasing smile and a little of her old manner*). A ginger-haired, crooked old goat like you to be playing Cupid!

HOGAN (*his face lights up joyfully. He is almost himself again — ruefully*). You had me punished, that's sure. I was thinking after you'd gone I'd drown myself in Harder's ice pond. There was this consolation in it, I knew that the bastard would never look at a piece of ice again without remembering me.

(*She doesn't hear this. Her thoughts are on the receding figure of Tyrone again. Hogan looks at her sad face worriedly — gently.*)

Don't, darlin'. Don't be hurting yourself. (*Then as she still doesn't hear, he puts on his old, fuming irascible tone.*) Are you going to moon at the sunrise for ever, and me with the sides of my stomach knocking together?

JOSIE (*gently*). Don't worry about me, Father. It's over now. I'm not hurt. I'm only sad for him.

HOGAN. For him? (*He bursts out in a fit of smouldering rage.*) May the blackest curse from the pit of hell —

JOSIE (*with an anguished cry*). Don't, Father! I love him!

HOGAN (*subsides, but his face looks sorrowful and old — dully*). I didn't mean it. I know whatever happened he meant no harm to you. It was life I was cursing — (*With a trace of his natural manner.*) And, be God, that's a waste of breath, if it does deserve it. (*Then as she remains silent — miserably.*) Or maybe I was cursing myself for a damned old scheming fool, like I ought to.

JOSIE (*turns to him, forcing a teasing smile*). Look out. I might say Amen to that. (*Gently.*) Don't be sad, Father. I'm all right — and I'm well content here with you. (*Forcing her teasing manner again.*) Sure, living with you has spoilt me for any other man, anyway. There'd never be the same fun or excitement.

HOGAN (*plays up to this — in his fuming manner*). There'll be excitement if I don't get my breakfast soon, but it won't be fun, I'm warning you!

JOSIE (*forcing her usual reaction to his threats*). Och, don't be threatening me, you bad-tempered old tick. Let's go in the house and I'll get your damned breakfast.

HOGAN. Now you're talking.

(*He goes in the house through her room. She follows him as far as the door — then turns for a last look down the road.*)

JOSIE (*her face sad, tender and pitying — gently*). May you have your wish and die in your sleep soon, Jim, darling. May you rest for ever in forgiveness and peace. (*She turns slowly and goes into the house.*)

CURTAIN

Chronological List of O'Neill's Published Plays

Title	Year Written*	Date and Place of First Production
A Wife For A Life	1913	Unproduced
Thirst	1913–14	Wharf Theater, Provincetown, Mass., summer, 1916
The Web	1913–14	39th Street Theater, New York, March 17, 1924
Warnings	1913–14	Unproduced
Fog	1913–14	The Playwrights' Theater, New York, Jan. 5, 1917
Recklessness	1913–14	Unproduced
Bound East For Cardiff	1913–14	Wharf Theater, Provincetown, Mass., summer, 1916
Servitude	1913–14	Skylark Theater, New York International Airport, April 22, 1960
Abortion	1913–14	Key Theater, New York, Oct. 27, 1959
The Movie Man	1914	Key Theater, New York, Oct. 27, 1959
The Sniper	1915	The Playwrights' Theater, New York, Feb. 16, 1917
Before Breakfast	1916	The Playwrights' Theater, New York, Dec. 1, 1916
Ile	1916–17	The Playwrights' Theater, New York, Nov. 30, 1917
In the Zone	1916–17	Comedy Theater, New York, Oct. 31, 1917
The Long Voyage Home	1916–17	The Playwrights' Theater, New York, Nov. 2, 1917
The Moon Of The Caribbees	1916–17	The Playwrights' Theater, New York, Dec. 20, 1918
The Rope	1918	The Playwrights' Theater, New York, April 26, 1918
The Dreamy Kid	1918	The Playwrights' Theater, New York, Oct. 31, 1919
Beyond The Horizon	1918	Morosco Theater, New York, Feb. 2, 1920
Where The Cross Is Made	1918	The Playwrights' Theater, New York, Nov. 22, 1918
The Straw	1918–19	Greenwich Village Theater, New York, Nov. 10, 1921
Gold	1920	Frazee Theater, New York, June 1, 1921
Anna Christie	1920	Vanderbilt Theater, New York, Nov. 10, 1921
The Emperor Jones	1920	The Playwrights' Theater, New York, Nov. 3, 1920
Diff'rent	1920	The Playwrights' Theater, New York, Dec. 27, 1920

* It is impossible to give a precise date of composition for every play; O'Neill often made major revisions to earlier drafts of his plays and was deliberately vague about the details of his writing to protect his personal privacy. For the purposes of this Collection, the chronology established in Arthur and Barbara Gelb's biography, *O'Neill* (Cape, 1962), has been followed.

The First Man	1921	Neighborhood Playhouse, New York, March 4, 1922
The Hairy Ape	1921	The Playwrights' Theater, New York, March 9, 1922
The Fountain	1921–22	Greenwich Village Theater, New York, Dec. 10, 1925
Welded	1922–23	39th Street Theater, New York, March 17, 1924
All God's Chillun Got Wings	1923	Provincetown Playhouse, New York, May 15, 1924
Desire Under The Elms	1924	Greenwich Village Theater, New York, Nov. 11, 1924
Marco Millions	1923–25	Guild Theater, New York, Jan. 9, 1928
The Great God Brown	1925	Greenwich Village Theater, New York, Jan. 23, 1926
Lazarus Laughed	1925–26	Pasadena Community Playhouse, Cal., April 9, 1928
Strange Interlude	1926–27	John Golden Theater, New York, Jan. 30, 1928
Dynamo	1928	Martin Beck Theater, New York, Feb. 11, 1929
Mourning Becomes Electra	1929–31	Guild Theater, New York, Oct. 26, 1931
Ah! Wilderness	1932	Nixon Theater, Pittsburgh, Pa., Sept. 25, 1933
Days Without End	1932–33	Plymouth Theater, Boston, Mass., Dec. 27, 1933
A Touch Of The Poet	1935–42	Royal Dramatic Theatre, Stockholm, Mar. 29, 1957 (First produced in English at Helen Hayes Theater, New York, Oct. 2, 1958)
More Stately Mansions	1936–42	Royal Dramatic Theatre, Stockholm, Sept. 11, 1962 (First produced in English at Ahmanson Theater, Los Angeles, Cal., Nov. 12, 1967)
The Iceman Cometh	1939	Martin Beck Theater, New York, Oct. 9, 1946
Long Day's Journey Into Night	1939–41	Royal Dramatic Theatre, Stockholm, Feb. 10, 1956 (First produced in English at Helen Hayes Theater, New York, Nov. 7, 1956)
Hughie	1941–42	Royal Dramatic Theatre, Stockholm, Sept. 18, 1958
A Moon For The Misbegotten	1943	Hartman Theater, Columbus, Ohio, Feb. 20, 1947